Koren Talmud Bavli
THE NOÉ EDITION

SOTA

Steinsaltz Center

KOREN

תלמוד בבלי

KOREN TALMUD BAVLI

THE NOÉ EDITION

סוטה

SOTA

COMMENTARY BY

Rabbi Adin Even-Israel Steinsaltz

EDITOR-IN-CHIEF

Rabbi Dr Tzvi Hersh Weinreb

EXECUTIVE EDITOR

Rabbi Joshua Schreier

•

STEINSALTZ CENTER

KOREN PUBLISHERS JERUSALEM

Supported by the Matanel Foundation

The Noé Edition Koren Talmud Bavli
Volume 20: Tractate Sota

Daf Yomi Size B&W edition, ISBN 978 965 301 626 2

First Hebrew/English Edition, 2015

Koren Publishers Jerusalem Ltd.
PO Box 4044, Jerusalem 9104001, ISRAEL
PO Box 8531, New Milford, CT 06776, USA
www.korenpub.com

Steinsaltz Center

Steinsaltz Center is the parent organization of institutions established by Rabbi Adin Even-Israel Steinsaltz

PO Box 45187, Jerusalem 91450 ISRAEL
Telephone: +972 2 646 0900, Fax +972 2 624 9454
www.steinsaltz-center.org

Hardcover design by Ben Gasner

This book was published in cooperation with the Israel Institute for Talmudic Publications.

The publication of this work was made possible through the generous support of British Friends of ATID.

Second printing, 2020

Printed in PRC

הִנֵּה יָמִים בָּאִים, נְאֻם אֲדֹנָי יֱהוִה, וְהִשְׁלַחְתִּי רָעָב בָּאָרֶץ,
לֹא־רָעָב לַלֶּחֶם וְלֹא־צָמָא לַמַּיִם, כִּי אִם־לִשְׁמֹעַ אֵת דִּבְרֵי יהוה.

Behold, days are coming – says the Lord God –
I will send a hunger to the land, not a hunger for bread
nor a thirst for water, but to hear the words of the Lord.

(AMOS 8:11)

The Noé edition of the Koren Talmud Bavli
with the commentary of Rabbi Adin Even-Israel Steinsaltz
is dedicated to all those who open its cover
to quench their thirst for Jewish knowledge,
in our generation of Torah renaissance.

This beautiful edition is for the young, the aged,
the novice and the savant alike,
as it unites the depth of Torah knowledge
with the best of academic scholarship.

Within its exquisite and vibrant pages,
words become worlds.

It will claim its place in the library of classics,
in the bookcases of the Beit Midrash,
the classrooms of our schools,
and in the offices of professionals and businesspeople
who carve out precious time to grapple with its timeless wisdom.

For the Student and the Scholar

DEDICATED BY LEO AND SUE NOÉ

Steinsaltz Center

Executive Director, Steinsaltz Center

Rabbi Meni Even-Israel

Managing Editor

Rabbi Jason Rappoport

Senior Content Editor

Rabbi Dr. Shalom Z. Berger

Editors

Rabbi Dr. Joshua Amaru, *Coordinating Editor*
Rabbi Avishai Magence, *Content Curator*
Menucha Chwat
Rabbi Yehoshua Duker
Betzalel Philip Edwards
Rabbi Yonatan Shai Freedman
Rabbi Ayal Geffon
Nechama Greenberg
Rabbi Yonatan Kohn
Rabbi Jason Leib
Elie Leshem
Elisha Loewenstern
Yedidya Naveh
Jay Shapiro
Ami Silver
Ami Vick
Rabbi Binyamin Zimmerman

Copy Editors

Aliza Israel, *Coordinator*
Bracha Hermon
Ita Olesker
Debbie Ismailoff
Shira Finson
Ilana Sobel
Deena Nataf
Eliana Kurlantzick Yorav
Erica Hirsch Edvi
Nava Wieder

Language Consultants

Dr. Stephanie E. Binder, *Greek & Latin*
Rabbi Yaakov Hoffman, *Arabic*
Dr. Shai Secunda, *Persian*
Shira Shmidman, *Aramaic*

KOREN

Design & Typesetting

Dena Landowne Bailey, *Typesetting*
Tani Bayer, *Jacket Design*
Raphaël Freeman, *Design & Typography*

Images

Eliahu Misgav, *Illustration & Image Acquisition*
Daniel Gdalevich, *Illustration & Image Acquisition*

This volume is dedicated by

Barbara (Malka Rosa) Hines

In honor of her beloved grandchildren

May they grow to know and love their heritage

Contents

For the vocalized Vilna Shas layout, please open as a Hebrew book.

Haskama
Rabbi Moshe Feinstein

RABBI MOSES FEINSTEIN
455 F. D. R. DRIVE
New York, N. Y. 10002
ORegon 7-1222

משה פיינשטיין
ר"ם תפארת ירושלים
בנוא יארק

בע"ה

בי זהו ראיתי הפירוש החשוב של הרב הגאון מוהר"ר עדין שטיינזלץ
שליט"א מעיה"ק ירושלים, על מסכתות ביצה ור"ה. באמת כבר ידוע
לי פירושו של הרה"ג הנ"ל על מסכתות מתלמוד בבלי, וכבר כתבתי
מכתב הסכמה עליהם. ובאתי בזה רק להדגיש מחוש איך שהפירושים
של הרה"ג הנ"ל, שכולל פירוש חדש על הגמרא עצמו וגם פירוש שיש
בו סיכום להלכה מהנידונים שבגמרא, נוסף לעוד כמה חלקים, הם
באמת עבודה גדולה, שיכולים להיות לתועלת לא רק לאלו שכבר
מורגלים בלמוד הגמרא, ורוצים להעמק יותר, אלא גם לאלו שמתחילים
ללמוד, להדריכם בדרכי התורה איך להבין ולהעמיק בים התלמוד.

והריני מברך להרה"ג הנ"ל שיצליחהו השי"ת בספריו אלו ושיזכה
לחבר עוד ספרים, להגדיל תורה ולהאדירה, לתפארת השם ותורתו.

ועל זה באתי על החתום לכבוד התורה ביום ז' לחודש אייר תשמ"ג.

משה פיינשטיין

משה פיינשטיין

…These new commentaries – which include a new interpretation of the Talmud, a halakhic summary of the debated issues, and various other sections – are a truly outstanding work; they can be of great benefit not only to those familiar with talmudic study who seek to deepen their understanding, but also to those who are just beginning to learn, guiding them through the pathways of the Torah and teaching them how to delve into the sea of the Talmud.

I would like to offer my blessing to this learned scholar. May the Holy One grant him success with these volumes and may he merit to write many more, to enhance the greatness of Torah, and bring glory to God and His word…

Rabbi Moshe Feinstein
New York, 7 Adar 5743

ר׳ משה פיינשטיין שליט״א
הנה ראיתי את מסכת אחת מהש״ס שנקד אותה וגם צייר צורות הצמחים וכדומה מדברים שלא ידוע לכמה אנשים הרה״ג ר׳ עדין שטיינזלץ מירושלים שליט״א וגם הוסיף שם בגליון פירושים וחידושים וניכר שהוא ת״ח וראויין לעיין בהם ת״ח ובני הישיבה וטוב גם לקנותם בבתי כנסיות ובבתי מדרשות שיש שיהיו להם לתועלת. — ועל זה באתי עה״ח ג׳ אדר ב׳ תש״ל.
נאם משה פיינשטיין
ר״מ תפארת ירושלים, ניו־יורק, ארה״ב

I have seen one tractate from the Talmud to which the great scholar Rabbi Adin Steinsaltz שליט״א has added *nikkud* (vowels) and illustrations to explain that which is unknown to many people; he has also added interpretations and innovations, and is evidently a *talmid ḥakham*. *Talmidei ḥakhamim* and yeshiva students ought to study these volumes, and synagogues and *batei midrash* would do well to purchase them, as they may find them useful.

Rabbi Moshe Feinstein
New York, Adar 5730

Haskama

Rabbi Menachem Mendel Schneerson

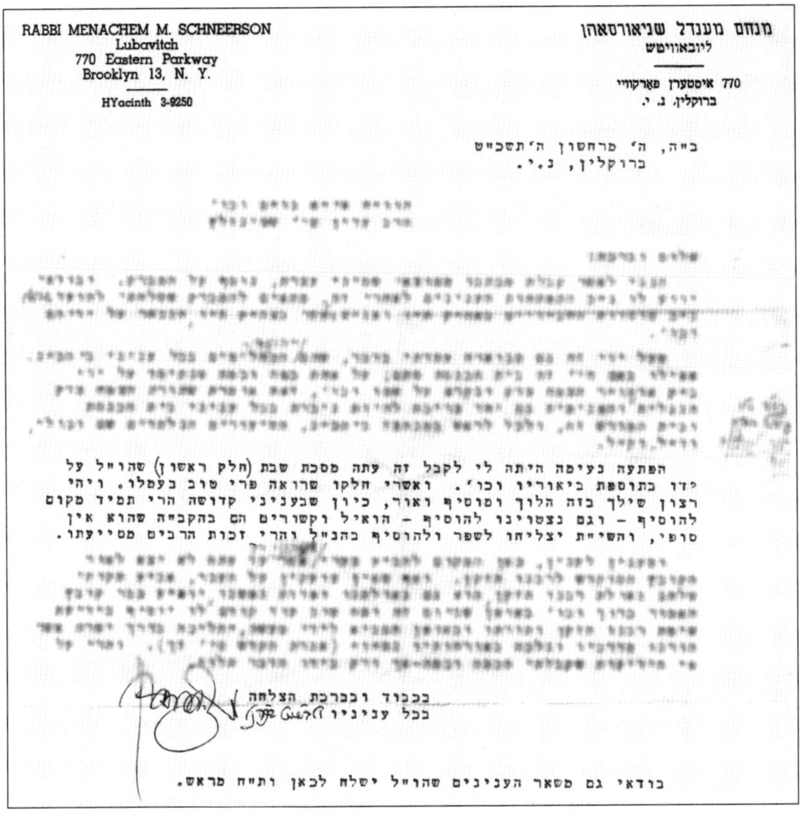

RABBI MENACHEM M. SCHNEERSON
Lubavitch
770 Eastern Parkway
Brooklyn 13, N. Y.
HYacinth 3-9250

מנחם מענדל שניאורסאהן
ליובאוויטש
770 איסטערן פארקוויי
ברוקלין, נ. י.

ב"ה, ה' מרחשון ה'תשכ"ט
ברוקלין, נ.י.

הפתעה נעימה היתה לי לקבל זה עתה מסכת שבת (חלק ראשון) שהו"ל על ידו בתוספת ביאוריו וכו'. ואשרי חלקו שרואה פרי טוב בעמלו. ויהי רצון שילך בזה הלוך ומוסיף ואור, כיון שבעניני קדושה הרי תמיד מקום להוסיף – וגם נצטוינו להוסיף – הואיל וקשורים הם בהקב"ה שהוא אין סופי, והשי"ת יצליחו לשפר ולהוסיף בהנ"ל והרי זכות הרבים מסייעתו.

בכבוד ובברכת הצלחה
בכל עניניו

בודאי גם משאר הענינים שהו"ל ישלח לכאן ות"ח מראש.

… I have just had the pleasant surprise of receiving tractate *Shabbat* (part one), which has been published by [Rabbi Steinsaltz] along with his explanations, etc. Happy is the man who sees good fruits from his labors. May he continue in this path and increase light, for in the matters of holiness there is always room to add – and we have been commanded to add – for they are linked to the Holy One, Blessed be He, Who is infinite. And may the Holy One grant him success to improve and enhance this work, since the greater good strengthens his hand …

Rabbi Menachem Mendel Schneerson
The Lubavitcher Rebbe
Brooklyn, 5 Marḥeshvan 5729

Haskama

Rabbi Moshe Zvi Neria

מכתבו של הרב משה צבי נריה

ב"ה

"ושמעו ביום ההוא החרשים דברי ספר"
(ישעי' כט' יח')

תרגום ספרי קדמונים לשפת דורות אחרונים – היא משימתם של חכמי
דור ודור. ובישראל שמצוות "ושננתם לבניך" מקיפה את כל חלקי
האומה, ודאי שהיתה זאת המשימה בכל עידן ועידן.
בכל דור כך, ובדורנו אשר רבים בו הקרובים שנתרחקו וחוזרים
ומתקרבים – לא כל שכן. כי רבים היום האומרים "מי ישקנו מים
מבאר" התלמוד, ומועטים הם הדולים ומשקים.
ראוי אפוא להערכה מיוחדת נסיונו המבורך של הצעיר המופלא,
הרב עדין שטיינזלץ, לפרש פרקי-תלמוד בהסברה מורחבת-תמציתית,
אשר נוסף על הפרוש המלולי והעניני היא מעלה גם את ההגיון של
הדברים ומתרגמת אותם לשפת-המושגים של בן-דורנו.
דומה שכל הנגשים אל חומר למודי מתוך רצון להבינו – התלמיד
החרוץ והמבוגר המשכיל – לא יתקלו בשום קושי בבואם ללמוד
סוגיא תלמודית לפי פרוש זה. ולא עוד אלא שיש לקוות כי ההסברה
ההגיונית תעמידם מיד על טוב-הטעם של דף-הגמרא, והם ימשכו
יותר ויותר אל הלמוד העיוני הזה אשר טובי המוחות בישראל לנו
בעומקו, ואשר ממנו פינה, ממנו יתד לבנין חיינו.
נועם ד' על המפרש הנמרץ להמשיך במפעלו, וברוכים כל העוזרים
להוצאתו לאור-עולם.

ביקר אורייתא

(חתימה)

The translation of the books of our past into the language of the present – this was the task of the sages of every generation. And in Israel, where the command to "teach them repeatedly to your children" applies to all parts of the nation, it was certainly the task of every era. This is true for every generation, and in our time – when many of those who have strayed far are once again drawing near – all the more so. For many today say, "Who will let us drink from the well" of Talmud, and few are those who offer up the waters to drink.

We must, therefore, particularly commend the blessed endeavor of Rabbi Adin Steinsaltz to explain the chapters of the Talmud in this extensive yet succinct commentary, which, in addition to its literal interpretation of the text, also explicates the latter's underlying logic and translates it into the language of our generation.

It appears that all those who seek to study Talmud – the diligent student and the learned adult – will have no difficulty understanding when using this commentary. Moreover, we may hope that the logical explanation will reveal to them the beauty of the talmudic page, and they will be drawn deeper and deeper into the intellectual pursuit which has engaged the best Jewish minds, and which serves as the cornerstone of our very lives…

Rabbi Moshe Zvi Neria

Haskama

Rabbi Mordechai Eliyahu

ב"ה

MORDECHAI ELIAHU | **מרדכי אליהו**

FORMER CHIEF RABBI OF ISRAEL & RICHON LEZION | ראשון לציון והרב הראשי לישראל לשעבר

ז' בתשרי תשנ"ד
5-137.נד

מכתב ברכה

הגמרא בעירובין כ"א: אומרת: דרש רבא מאי דכתיב ויותר שהיה קהלת חכם, עוד לימד דעת את העם - ואזן וחקר תקן משלים הרבה". לימד דעת את העם - קבע כיצד לקרוא פסוק וסימנים בין תיבות המקרא וממשיכה הגמרא ואומרת: אמר עולא אמר ר' אליעזר בתחילה היתה תורה דומה לכפיפה שאין לה אזנים עד שבא שלמה ועשה לה אזנים". וכדברי רש"י שם: "וע"י כך אוחזין ישראל במצוות שנתרחקו מן העבירה כדרך שנוח לאחוז בכלי שיש לו בית יד וכו' (עירובין כ"א, י').

דברים מעין אלו אפשר לאמר על האי גברא יקירא, על איש מורם מעם, משכמו ומעלה בתורה ובמידות. ויותר ממה שעשה בתורה שבע"פ עושה בתורה שבכתב - מלמד דעת את העם. ולא זו בלבד אלא גם עושה אזנים לתורה, היא תורת התלמוד שהוא חתום וסתום בפני רבים. ורק מעט מזער מבני עליה שהם מועטים ומי שלומד בישיבה יכל כיום ללמוד בש"ס ולהבין מה שלפניו, ואף שיש לנו פירוש רש"י, עדין לא הכל ממשמשין בו. עד שקם הרב הגדול מעוז ומגדול הרה"ג ר' **עדין שטיינזלץ** שליט"א ועשה אזנים לתורה, שאפשר לאחוז גמרא ביד וללמוד, ואפי' לפשוטי העם ועשה פרושים ושם אותם בצד הארון, פרושים נאים בשפה ברורה ונעימה דבר דבור על אופניו. ועם הסברים וציורים להבין ולהשכיל, כדי שמי שרוצה לקרבה אל מלאכת ה' ללמוד יכל לעשות זאת.

ועיני ראו ולא זר שבשיעורי תורה בגמרא הרבה באים עם גמרות בידם ואלה שבאים עם "פירוש הרב שטיינזלץ לתלמוד הבבלי" הם מוכנים ומבינים טוב יותר. כי כבר יש להם הקדמה מפרושיו ומבאוריו.
ואמינא לפועלו יישר ומן שמיא זכו ליה ללמד דעת את העם .

ויהי רצון שחפץ בידו יצלח, וכל אשר יפנה ישכיל ויצליח, ויזכה להגדיל תורה ולהאדירה, ויוסיף לנו עוד גמרות מבוארות כהנה וכהנה עד לסיומו , "וישראל עושה חיל".

ובזכות לימוד תורה ואני זאת בריתי וכו', ובא לציון גואל, בב"א.

מרדכי אליהו
ראשון לציון הרב הראשי לישראל לשעבר

The Talmud in *Eruvin* 21b states: Rava continued to interpret verses homiletically. What is the meaning of the verse: "And besides being wise, Kohelet also taught the people knowledge; and he weighed, and sought out, and set in order many proverbs" (Ecclesiastes 12:9)? He explains: He taught the people knowledge; he taught it with the accentuation marks in the Torah, and explained each matter by means of another matter similar to it. And he weighed [*izen*], and sought out, and set in order many proverbs; Ulla said that Rabbi Eliezer said: At first the Torah was like a basket without handles [*oznayim*] until Solomon came and made handles for it. And as Rashi there explains: And thus were Israel able to grasp the mitzvot and distance themselves from transgressions – just as a vessel with handles is easily held, etc.

Such things may be said of this beloved and eminent man, a great sage of Torah and of virtue. And far more than he has done with the Oral Torah, he does with the Written Torah – teaching the people knowledge. And beyond that, he also affixes handles to the Torah, i.e., to the Talmud, which is obscure and difficult for many. Only the intellectual elite, which are a precious few, and those who study in yeshiva, can today learn the Talmud and understand what it says – and even though we have Rashi, still not everyone uses him. But now the great scholar Rabbi Adin Steinsaltz שליט״א has come and affixed handles to the Torah, allowing the Talmud to be held and studied, even by simple men. And he has composed a commentary alongside the text, a fine commentary in clear, comprehensible language, "a word fitly spoken" with explanations and illustrations, so that all those who seek to study the work of God can do so.

Rabbi Mordechai Eliyahu
Former Chief Rabbi of Israel, 7 Tishrei 5754

Message from Rabbi Adin Even-Israel Steinsaltz

The Talmud is the cornerstone of Jewish culture. True, our culture originated in the Bible and has branched out in directions besides the Talmud, yet the latter's influence on Jewish culture is fundamental. Perhaps because it was composed not by a single individual, but rather by hundreds and thousands of Sages in *batei midrash* in an ongoing, millennium-long process, the Talmud expresses the deepest themes and values not only of the Jewish people, but also of the Jewish spirit. As the basic study text for young and old, laymen and learned, the Talmud may be said to embody the historical trajectory of the Jewish soul. It is, therefore, best studied interactively, its subject matter coming together with the student's questions, perplexities, and innovations to form a single intricate weave. In the entire scope of Jewish culture, there is not one area that does not draw from or converse with the Talmud. The study of Talmud is thus the gate through which a Jew enters his life's path.

The *Koren Talmud Bavli* seeks to render the Talmud accessible to the millions of Jews whose mother tongue is English, allowing them to study it, approach it, and perhaps even become one with it.

This project has been carried out and assisted by several people, all of whom have worked tirelessly to turn this vision into an actual set of books to be studied. It is a joyful duty to thank the many partners in this enterprise for their various contributions. Thanks to Koren Publishers Jerusalem, both for the publication of this set and for the design of its very complex graphic layout. Thanks of a different sort are owed to the Steinsaltz Center and its director, Rabbi Menachem Even-Israel, for their determination and persistence in setting this goal and reaching it. Many thanks to the translators, editors, and proofreaders for their hard and meticulous work. Thanks to the individuals and organizations that supported this project, chief among them the Matanel Foundation and the Noé family of London. And thanks in advance to all those who will invest their time, hearts, and minds in studying these volumes – to learn, to teach, and to practice.

Rabbi Adin Even-Israel Steinsaltz
Jerusalem 5773

Acknowledgments

We are indeed privileged to dedicate this edition of the *Koren Talmud Bavli* in honor of the generous support of Leo and Sue Noé of London.

The name Noé is synonymous with philanthropy. The family's charitable endeavors span a vast range of educational projects, welfare institutions, and outreach organizations across the globe, with a particular emphasis on the "nurturing of each individual." Among so many other charitable activities, the Noés have been deeply involved with Kisharon, which provides the British Jewish community with vital support for hundreds of people with learning difficulties and their families; they provide steadfast support of SEED, which stands at the forefront of adult Jewish education in the UK, and Kemach, an organization in Israel that "helps Haredi students sustain themselves in dignity," providing both professional and vocational training for the Haredi community in Israel.

The Noés are not simply donors to institutions. They are partners. Donors think of a sum. Partners think of a cause, becoming rigorously and keenly involved, and giving of their time and energy. We are honored that they have chosen to partner with our two organizations, the Steinsaltz Center and Koren Publishers Jerusalem, enabling us to further and deepen learning among all Jews.

Leo and Sue are the proud parents and grandparents of five children and their families. The next generation has been taught by example that with life's gifts come the responsibilities to be active within and contribute to society – both Jewish and non-Jewish – as is consistent with the noblest of Jewish values.

Rabbi Adin Even-Israel Steinsaltz
Matthew Miller, Publisher
Jerusalem 5773

Introduction by the Editor-in-Chief

The vastly expanded audience of Talmud study in our generation is a phenomenon of historical proportions. The reasons for this phenomenon are many, and include the availability of a wide array of translations, commentaries, and study aids.

One outstanding example of such a work is the translation of the Talmud into modern Hebrew by Rabbi Adin Even-Israel Steinsaltz. The product of a lifetime of intense intellectual labor, this translation stands out in its uniqueness.

But what can the interested student do if he or she does not comprehend the Hebrew, even in its modern form? Where is the English speaker who wishes to access this instructive material to turn? The *Koren Talmud Bavli* that you hold in your hand is designed to be the answer to those questions.

This work is the joint effort of Rabbi Steinsaltz himself, his closest advisory staff, and Koren Publishers Jerusalem. It is my privilege to have been designated editor-in-chief of this important project, and to have worked in close collaboration with a team of translators and copy editors, artists and graphic designers, scholars and editors.

Together we are presenting to the English-speaking world a translation that possesses all the merits of the original Hebrew work by Rabbi Steinsaltz and provides assistance for the beginner of any age who seeks to obtain the necessary skills to become an adept talmudist.

To date we have completed the orders of *Zera'im* and *Moed*. Our work has been enthusiastically received by a broad and diverse audience. Particularly gratifying is the fact that many have chosen to use our text as the basis for the group study of Talmud. We appreciate the comments and suggestions from our readers the world over and are committed to improving future editions of the *Koren Talmud Bavli* on the basis of that input. Indeed, a second edition of our first volume, *Berakhot*, has already been released, incorporating much of the advice brought to our attention by our readers. We encourage you to continue to advise us of your experience with our work.

Sota is the twentieth volume of this project. It includes the entire original text, in the traditional configuration and pagination of the famed Vilna edition of the Talmud. This enables the student to follow the core text with the commentaries of Rashi, *Tosafot*, and the customary marginalia. It also provides a clear English translation in contemporary idiom, faithfully based upon the modern Hebrew edition.

At least equal to the linguistic virtues of this edition are the qualities of its graphic design. Rather than intimidate students by confronting them with a page-size block of text, we have divided the page into smaller thematic units. Thus, readers can focus their attention and absorb each discrete discussion before proceeding to the next unit. The design of each page allows for sufficient white space to ease the visual task of reading. The illustrations, one of the most innovative features of the Hebrew edition, have been substantially enhanced and reproduced in color.

The end result is a literary and artistic masterpiece. This has been achieved through the dedicated work of a large team of translators, headed by Rabbi Joshua Schreier, and through the unparalleled creative efforts of Raphaël Freeman and the gifted staff at Koren.

The group of individuals who surround Rabbi Steinsaltz and support his work deserve our thanks as well. I have come to appreciate their energy, initiative, and persistence. And I thank the indefatigable Rabbi Menachem Even-Israel, whom I cannot praise highly enough. The quality of his guidance and good counsel is surpassed only by his commitment to the dissemination and perpetuation of his father's precious teachings.

Finally, in humility, awe, and great respect, I acknowledge Rabbi Adin Even-Israel Steinsaltz. I thank him for the inspirational opportunity he has granted me to work with one of the outstanding sages of our time.

Rabbi Tzvi Hersh Weinreb
Jerusalem 5775

Preface by the Executive Editor

Toward the beginning of tractate *Pesaḥim* (3a), the Gemara questions the Mishna's use of the term *or* rather than the standard term *leil* when referring to the evening of the fourteenth of Nisan. The Gemara introduces a discussion of the value of euphemism and refraining from the use of crude language. It concludes that despite the importance of euphemism, if the euphemism comes at the expense of clarity and requires a less succinct formulation, it is preferable to speak concisely. Only when the choice is between equally concise phrases is the euphemism preferred.

In his *peirush*, Rabbi Steinsaltz's language is both concise and aesthetic. While explaining often difficult passages, he avoids the temptation to over-explain, inviting the reader to study the Talmud with him rather than doing all the thinking in the reader's place. We have attempted to follow his path in translating and editing the *Koren Talmud Bavli*.

My involvement in the production of the *Koren Talmud Bavli* has been both a privilege and a pleasure. The Steinsaltz Center, headed by Rabbi Menachem Even-Israel and devoted to the dissemination of the wide-ranging, monumental works of Rabbi Adin Even-Israel Steinsaltz, constitutes the Steinsaltz side of this partnership; Koren Publishers Jerusalem, headed by Matthew Miller, with the day-to-day management of the project in the able hands of Dena Landowne Bailey, constitutes the publishing side of this partnership. The combination of the inspiration, which is the hallmark of the Steinsaltz Center, with the creativity and professionalism for which Koren is renowned and which I experience on a daily basis, has lent the *Koren Talmud Bavli* its outstanding quality in terms of both content and form.

I would like to express my appreciation for Rabbi Dr. Tzvi Hersh Weinreb, the editor-in-chief, whose insight and guidance have been invaluable. The contribution of my friend and colleague, Rabbi Dr. Shalom Z. Berger, the senior content editor, cannot be overstated; his title does not begin to convey the excellent direction he has provided in all aspects of this project. In addition, I would like to thank Rabbi Jason Rappoport, managing editor; Rabbi Joshua Amaru, coordinating editor; and Rabbi Avishai Magence, content curator, whose tireless devotion to this project has been and continues to be crucial to the continued success of this project. The erudite and articulate men and women who serve as translators, editors, and copy editors have ensured that this project adheres to the highest standards.

There are several others whose contributions to this project cannot be overlooked. On the Steinsaltz side: Meir HaNegbi, Yacov Elbert, and Tsipora Ifrah. On the Koren side: Rabbi David Fuchs, Rabbi Hanan Benayahu, Efrat Gross, Rachel Hanstater Meghnagi, Rabbi Eliahu Misgav, and Rabbi Yinon Chen. Their assistance in all matters, large and small, is appreciated.

At the risk of being repetitious, I would like to thank Rabbi Dr. Berger for introducing me to the world of Steinsaltz. Finally, I would like to thank Rabbi Menachem Even-Israel, with whom it continues to be a pleasure to move forward in this great enterprise.

Rabbi Joshua Schreier
Jerusalem 5773

Introduction by the Publisher

The Talmud has sustained and inspired Jews for thousands of years. Throughout Jewish history, an elite cadre of scholars has absorbed its learning and passed it on to succeeding generations. The Talmud has been the fundamental text of our people.

Beginning in the 1960s, Rabbi Adin Even-Israel Steinsaltz שליט״א created a revolution in the history of Talmud study. His translation of the Talmud, first into modern Hebrew and then into other languages, as well the practical learning aids he added to the text, have enabled millions of people around the world to access and master the complexity and context of the world of Talmud.

It is thus a privilege to present the *Koren Talmud Bavli*, an English translation of the talmudic text with the brilliant elucidation of Rabbi Steinsaltz. The depth and breadth of his knowledge are unique in our time. His rootedness in the tradition and his reach into the world beyond it are inspirational.

Working with Rabbi Steinsaltz on this remarkable project has been not only an honor, but a great pleasure. Never shy to express an opinion, with wisdom and humor, Rabbi Steinsaltz sparkles in conversation, demonstrating his knowledge (both sacred and worldly), sharing his wide-ranging interests, and, above all, radiating his passion. I am grateful for the unique opportunity to work closely with him, and I wish him many more years of writing and teaching.

Our intentions in publishing this new edition of the Talmud are threefold. First, we seek to fully clarify the talmudic page to the reader – textually, intellectually, and graphically. Second, we seek to utilize today's most sophisticated technologies, both in print and electronic formats, to provide the reader with a comprehensive set of study tools. And third, we seek to help readers advance in their process of Talmud study.

To achieve these goals, the *Koren Talmud Bavli* is unique in a number of ways:

- The classic *tzurat hadaf* of Vilna, used by scholars since the 1800s, has been reset for greater clarity, and opens from the Hebrew "front" of the book. Full *nikkud* has been added to both the talmudic text and Rashi's commentary, allowing for a more fluent reading with the correct pronunciation; the commentaries of *Tosafot* have been punctuated. Upon the advice of many English-speaking teachers of Talmud, we have separated these core pages from the translation, thereby enabling the advanced student to approach the text without the distraction of the translation. This also reduces the number of volumes in the set. At the bottom of each *daf*, there is a reference to the corresponding English pages. In addition, the Vilna edition was read against other manuscripts and older print editions, so that texts which had been removed by non-Jewish censors have been restored to their rightful place.

- The English translation, which starts on the English "front" of the book, reproduces the *menukad* Talmud text alongside the English translation (in bold) and commentary and explanation (in a lighter font). The Hebrew and Aramaic text is presented in logical paragraphs. This allows for a fluent reading of the text for the non-Hebrew or non-Aramaic reader. It also allows for the Hebrew reader to refer easily to the text alongside. Where the original text features dialogue or poetry, the English text is laid out in a manner appropriate to the genre. Each page refers to the relevant *daf*.
- Critical contextual tools surround the text and translation: personality notes, providing short biographies of the Sages; language notes, explaining foreign terms borrowed from Greek, Latin, Persian, or Arabic; and background notes, giving information essential to the understanding of the text, including history, geography, botany, archaeology, zoology, astronomy, and aspects of daily life in the talmudic era.
- Halakhic summaries provide references to the authoritative legal decisions made over the centuries by the rabbis. They explain the reasons behind each halakhic decision as well as the ruling's close connection to the Talmud and its various interpreters.
- Photographs, drawings, and other illustrations have been added throughout the text – in full color in the Standard and Electronic editions, and in black and white in the Daf Yomi edition – to visually elucidate the text.

This is not an exhaustive list of features of this edition; it merely presents an overview for the English-speaking reader who may not be familiar with the "total approach" to Talmud pioneered by Rabbi Steinsaltz.

Several professionals have helped bring this vast collaborative project to fruition. My many colleagues are noted on the Acknowledgments page, and the leadership of this project has been exceptional.

RABBI MENACHEM EVEN-ISRAEL, DIRECTOR OF THE STEINSALTZ CENTER, was the driving force behind this enterprise. With enthusiasm and energy, he formed the happy alliance with Koren and established close relationships among all involved in the work.

RABBI DR. TZVI HERSH WEINREB שליט״א, EDITOR-IN-CHIEF, brought to this project his profound knowledge of Torah, intellectual literacy of Talmud, and erudition of Western literature. It is to him that the text owes its very high standard, both in form and content, and the logical manner in which the beauty of the Talmud is presented.

RABBI JOSHUA SCHREIER, EXECUTIVE EDITOR, assembled an outstanding group of scholars, translators, editors, and copy editors, whose standards and discipline enabled this project to proceed in a timely and highly professional manner.

RABBI MEIR HANEGBI, EDITOR OF THE HEBREW EDITION OF THE STEINSALTZ TALMUD, lent his invaluable assistance throughout the work process, supervising the reproduction of the Vilna pages.

RAPHAËL FREEMAN created this Talmud's unique typographic design which, true to the Koren approach, is both elegant and user friendly.

It has been an enriching experience for all of us at Koren Publishers Jerusalem to work with the Steinsaltz Center to develop and produce the *Koren Talmud Bavli*. We pray that this publication will be a source of great learning and, ultimately, greater *avodat Hashem* for all Jews.

Matthew Miller, Publisher
Koren Publishers Jerusalem
Jerusalem 5773

Introduction to **Sota**

Tractate *Sota* deals primarily with the *halakhot* associated with a *sota*, a woman whose husband suspects that she is unfaithful, and warns her not to seclude herself with a specific man. In the event that she secludes herself with that man, she is considered a *sota*, and it is prohibited for her to remain married to her husband unless she is taken to the Temple and undergoes an evaluation rite in order to determine whether she was in fact unfaithful. This rite includes the offering of a special meal-offering, the taking of an oath, and the drinking of the bitter water of a *sota*. However, the tractate also discusses the *halakhot* of those who go out to battle, the blessing given by the priests, and other topics.

The process by which a woman is given the status of a *sota* and the subsequent evaluation of her fidelity comprises two separate stages: First, seclusion with another man, the means by which a woman becomes a *sota*. Second, the evaluation rite by which it is determined miraculously whether the woman is guilty of infidelity. Although the evaluation rite might bring about the death of a guilty woman, nevertheless, the purpose of such a procedure is to return peace and harmony to the marriage (see *Shabbat* 116a). This rite is not practiced in every instance when the husband suspects his wife of infidelity. Rather, it is performed when the level of suspicion is sufficient to suggest that the woman was unfaithful. The *sota* process involves a warning, which is likely the result of suspected promiscuous behavior on the part of the wife. If the woman is subsequently seen by two witnesses secluding herself for a sufficient amount of time to engage in sexual intercourse with the man about whom she was warned, then she must undergo the evaluation rite. Even if she didn't actually commit adultery, the woman's behavior is referred to by the Torah as an act of betrayal, both to her husband and to God, Who commanded the couple with regard to the sanctity of marriage (*Midrash Tanḥuma*, Numbers 5).

Under these circumstances, the husband is permitted to divorce his wife due to her immodest behavior, and therefore, if he opts to evaluate whether she is permitted to him by means of the *sota* rite, it is indicative of the fact that he is interested in removing his doubts about her fidelity and rebuilding the relationship. Additionally, the wife has the prerogative to refuse to undergo the rite, and to be divorced without any payment of her marriage contract. If she opts to undergo the demeaning rite to prove her innocence, it is indicative of her remorse for her suspicious behavior and of her desire to put an end to their marital distrust and strife. In such a situation, where logic would call for dissolution of the marriage, the Torah provides a miraculous means of evaluating the woman's fidelity, which is ordinarily not verifiable by means of witnesses. The purpose of this rite is to bring peace to a marriage where the woman is, in fact, innocent, and the various elements of the rite would seem not only to evaluate whether she was faithful but also to contribute to rebuilding the necessary trust of the husband in his wife if she did not engage in adulterous sexual intercourse.

In a number of places (see 8b, 9a, 14a) the Gemara explains that the actions of the *sota* are like the actions of an animal. This description of her actions is clearly true if she actually engaged in adulterous sexual intercourse, a transgression punished by capital punishment or excision, but the description of her actions as animal-like is accurate even if she merely secluded herself with the man after the warning. Since she has degraded herself by engaging in such behavior, the evaluation rite in the Temple calls for certain acts that serve to degrade the woman and remind her of her behavior: The priest publicly tears her upper garment and then ties it up with a thick rope; he removes her hair covering and unbraids her hair; the woman drinks the bitter water from a plain, earthenware vessel; and the meal-offering of the *sota* is brought from barley, which is animal food, unlike virtually all other meal-offerings, which are brought from wheat, a human staple. Additionally, no oil or frankincense is added to the meal-offering, to ensure that it is very plain.

One of the unique elements of the *sota* evaluation rite is that it is the only mitzva in the Torah whose entire essence is rooted in a miraculous process. The evaluation of the woman through the drinking of the bitter water is not a natural act, as the ingredients alone are not responsible for the death of an adulterous woman. Rather, it is a supernatural test, which results in guilty women meeting a unique death, while women who were not adulterous receive an extra blessing concerning their childbearing abilities. Additionally, the woman's drinking of the water evaluates not only her fidelity; if she is guilty, her paramour, wherever he may be, will die the same terrible death.

Another unique aspect of this mitzva is that the preparation of the bitter water involves the erasing of God's name, an act that is prohibited under all other circumstances due to a negative mitzva. Because of these exceptional aspects of the mitzva of the *sota* rite, both the miraculous nature of the evaluation as well as the need to erase God's name, the court would try to discourage a woman from drinking the bitter water unless she was entirely convinced of her innocence. They would try to dissuade her through either explanation, invoking fear, or attempting to weaken her resolve if she was in fact guilty.

In order for the evaluation rite to be effective, the husband himself had to be free of any iniquity, which is understood to mean either that he never committed any act of illicit sexual activity in his adult life, or that he did not have relations with his wife after her seclusion with the paramour. The Gemara also discusses a dispute initially recorded in the mishna as to whether a woman's punishment can be delayed due to her observing the mitzvot, learning Torah, or enabling her husband's or children's Torah study.

Due to the miraculous nature of the evaluation rite and the fact that not every generation is worthy of having such open miracles performed in its midst, the Sages no longer allowed the rite to be performed from the time of the generation prior to the destruction of the Second Temple.

Although the *halakhot* involving a *sota* comprise an independent unit of *halakhot*, they also overlap with a number of more general aspects of *halakhot* involving marriage. A woman who was warned by her husband and secluded herself with the suspected man essentially puts into question her fidelity to her husband, and her halakhic status with regard to certain marital issues is altered. Until she is able to prove her innocence through the evaluation rite, it is prohibited for her to engage in sexual intercourse with her husband. And even in the event of divorce from her husband, it is forbidden for her to marry her paramour. Additionally, if she is married to a priest it is prohibited for her to partake of *teruma*. Furthermore, due to the strong basis of suspicion that her seclusion has raised, she almost always loses the right to payment of her marriage contract, unless she proves her innocence. Finally, even one witness testifying to her engaging in sexual intercourse with her paramour suffices to render it prohibited for her to attempt to prove her innocence through the *sota* rite.

In connection with the discussions of the *sota* process and the evaluation rite, a number of other issues are discussed in the tractate. Some of these issues are discussed at length, particularly matters that aren't directly related to any particular tractate in the Talmud. For example, ceremonial mitzvot that involve a lengthy process and are also associated with the Temple and performed by priests are discussed here. Also discussed are the *halakhot* involved in going out to battle, which involve a speech by the priest appointed to prepare the soldiers for battle. The blessings and the curses that were said by the people upon their arrival to Eretz Yisrael in the days of Joshua; the mitzva of assembly, consisting of a public reading of the Torah in the Temple area; as well as the *halakhot* of the heifer whose neck is broken at the scene of an unsolved murder are all discussed at great length.

Tractate *Sota* also contains a large amount of aggadic material, much of it stemming from the unique nature of the punishments discussed in the tractate. The miraculous nature of the evaluation rite, and its purpose in identifying whether or not adultery occurred, is also the source for a larger discussion about the nature of sin in general, and the nature of particular transgressions of famous biblical figures. This also leads to discussion with regard to divine retribution in general, and the aspects of measure for measure, which are used to define the means of God's system of reward and punishment.

The statement at the end of the tractate discussing the need to discontinue the use of the evaluation rite when the nation was no longer worthy of such a miraculous occurrence in their midst leads to the discussion of other, similar procedures that were discontinued for the same reason. This opens the text for a discussion of the unfortunate downfall of the Jewish people from their glorious spiritual levels to the depths of disgrace, which camouflaged the inner, spiritual beauty of the nation.

The tractate contains nine chapters, the majority of which deal primarily with clearly defined topics:

Chapter One deals with the *halakhot* of the husband's warning to his wife, the definition of seclusion, and the initial process of the husband's bringing his wife to the Temple for the evaluation rite. It also contains a lengthy description of the measure-for-measure nature of divine retribution.

Chapter Two describes bringing the meal-offering of the *sota*, writing the scroll of the *sota*, the oath of the *sota*, and the preparation of the bitter water.

Chapter Three deals with the meal-offering of the *sota*, the instances in which the meal-offering may not be brought, the punishment of the *sota*, and the merits that can delay divine execution of these punishments.

Chapter Four discusses which women are permitted to take part in the *sota* evaluation rite, and lists and discusses those who may not.

Chapter Five records a number of statements that were taught in the study hall on the day that Rabbi Elazar ben Azarya was appointed to lead the Sanhedrin.

Chapter Six deals with the type of testimony that can be used to determine that the accused woman has indeed committed adultery.

Chapter Seven lists several mitzvot that may be recited in any language alongside those mitzvot that may be recited only in Hebrew.

Chapter Eight deals with the *halakhot* of going out to battle.

Chapter Nine addresses the *halakhot* of the heifer whose neck is broken, and discusses matters that were discontinued due to the diminishing spiritual commitment of certain generations.

Introduction to **Perek I**

Speak to the children of Israel, and say to them: If any man's wife goes aside, and acts unfaithfully against him; and a man lie with her carnally, and it was hidden from the eyes of her husband, and she was defiled secretly, and there is no witness against her, and she was not taken in the act. And the spirit of jealousy came upon him, and he warned his wife, and she had become defiled; or if the spirit of jealousy came upon him, and he warned his wife, and she was not defiled. Then shall the man bring his wife to the priest, and shall bring her offering for her, the tenth part of an ephah of barley meal; he shall pour no oil upon it, nor put frankincense thereon; for it is a meal-offering of jealousy, a meal-offering of memorial, bringing iniquity to remembrance.

(Numbers 5:11–15)

And the priest shall stand the woman before the Lord and uncover the hair of the woman's head, and put the meal-offering of memorial in her hands, which is the meal-offering of jealousy; and the priest shall have in his hand the bitter water that causes the curse.

(Numbers 5:18)

The above verses describe the formal process by which a husband issues a warning to his wife whom he suspects of unfaithful behavior and the result of the woman's violations of his warning by secluding herself with the man that aroused her husband's suspicion. A woman who secludes herself with such a man after being warned by her husband is a *sota*, and her questionable faithfulness to her husband must be evaluated by the *sota* rite, discussed in the rest of chapter 5 of Numbers and in this tractate, to determine if it is permitted for her to remain married to her husband.

In this chapter, the nature and details of this warning will be discussed. For instance, is the husband obligated to warn his wife if he suspects her of engaging in promiscuous behavior? Is it sufficient to warn one's wife privately, or must it be done in the presence of one or more witnesses?

Additionally, it is unclear from the verses what degree of knowledge is necessary to determine that the woman has, in fact, secluded herself after the warning, and how it is to be known if the woman actually defiled herself through adulterous sexual intercourse. In this chapter there will be discussions concerning whether the husband's word suffices in these matters or whether it is necessary to hear testimony from one or more witnesses.

The husband's bringing his wife to the priest is discussed as well (see Numbers 5:15), including at what point the husband must bring his wife, and how it is done.

The chapter also discusses the evaluation rite, the miraculous procedure for determining the woman's guilt or innocence, where, as the verse states: "The priest shall set the woman before the Lord" (Numbers 5:18). The discussion includes the question of where this is done, and what exactly is done to the woman at the outset of the rite.

Also addressed is the issue of why the woman is subjected to such a miraculous yet demeaning procedure in order to evaluate her faithfulness, as well as other aggadic issues relating to the nature of divine retribution and additional matters.

מתני׳ הַמְקַנֵּא לְאִשְׁתּוֹ, רַבִּי אֱלִיעֶזֶר אוֹמֵר: מְקַנֵּא לָהּ עַל פִּי שְׁנַיִם, וּמַשְׁקָה עַל פִּי עֵד אֶחָד אוֹ עַל פִּי עַצְמוֹ; רַבִּי יְהוֹשֻׁעַ אוֹמֵר: מְקַנֵּא לָהּ עַל פִּי שְׁנַיִם וּמַשְׁקָה עַל פִּי שְׁנַיִם.

MISHNA With regard to **one who issues a warning**[N] **to his wife** not to seclude herself with a particular man, so that if she does not heed his warning she will assume the status of a woman suspected by her husband of having been unfaithful [*sota*], **Rabbi Eliezer says:** He **issues a warning to her based on,** i.e., in the presence of, **two**[H] witnesses for the warning to be effective. If two witnesses were not present for the warning, she is not a *sota* even if two witnesses saw her seclusion with another man. **And** the husband **gives** the bitter water to her **to drink based on** the testimony of **one witness** who saw the seclusion, **or** even **based on his own** testimony that he himself saw them secluded together, as Rabbi Eliezer holds that only the warning requires witnesses, not the seclusion. **Rabbi Yehoshua says:** He both **issues a warning to her based on two** witnesses **and gives** the bitter water to her **to drink based on** the testimony of **two**[H] witnesses.

כֵּיצַד מְקַנֵּא לָהּ? אוֹמֵר לָהּ בִּפְנֵי שְׁנַיִם ״אַל תְּדַבְּרִי עִם אִישׁ פְּלוֹנִי״, וְדִבְּרָה עִמּוֹ – עֲדַיִין הִיא מוּתֶּרֶת לְבֵיתָהּ וּמוּתֶּרֶת לֶאֱכוֹל בִּתְרוּמָה.

The mishna asks: **How does he issue a warning to her** in an effective manner? If he **says to her in the presence of two** witnesses: **Do not speak with** the **man** called **so-and-so,**[H] **and she** nevertheless **spoke with him, she is still permitted to her home,** i.e., she is permitted to engage in sexual intercourse with her husband, **and** if she is the wife of a priest **she is** still **permitted to partake of *teruma*.**[B]

נִכְנְסָה עִמּוֹ לְבֵית הַסֵּתֶר וְשָׁהֲתָה עִמּוֹ כְּדֵי טוּמְאָה – אֲסוּרָה לְבֵיתָהּ וַאֲסוּרָה לֶאֱכוֹל בִּתְרוּמָה. וְאִם מֵת – חוֹלֶצֶת וְלֹא מִתְיַיבֶּמֶת.

However, if after he told her not to speak with so-and-so, **she entered into a secluded place and remained with** that man[H] long **enough to** become **defiled,** i.e., sufficient time to engage in sexual intercourse, **she is forbidden to her home** from that moment until she undergoes the *sota* rite. **And** likewise, if she was the wife of a priest **she is prohibited from partaking of *teruma*,**[H] as she was possibly disqualified by her infidelity, so long as her innocence is not proven by means of the bitter water. **And if** her husband **dies** childless before she drinks the bitter water, **she perform *ḥalitza*** with her late husband's brother **and may not enter into levirate marriage,**[H] as, if she had been unfaithful, levirate marriage is forbidden.

גמ׳ מִכְּדִי תַּנָּא מִנָּזִיר סְלֵיק, מַאי תְּנָא דְּקָא תָנֵי סוֹטָה?

GEMARA The Gemara questions the placement of this tractate within the mishnaic order of *Nashim*. **Now, the *tanna* arose from** tractate ***Nazir*,** which is the tractate preceding *Sota* in the order of the Mishna. **What** did he **teach** in *Nazir* **that** required that he **teach** tractate ***Sota*** immediately afterward, as at first glance there seems to be no connection between this tractate and *Nazir*?

כְּדְרַבִּי; דְּתַנְיָא, רַבִּי אוֹמֵר: לָמָּה נִסְמְכָה פָּרָשַׁת נָזִיר לְפָרָשַׁת סוֹטָה? לוֹמַר לָךְ, שֶׁכָּל הָרוֹאֶה סוֹטָה בְּקִלְקוּלָהּ יַזִּיר עַצְמוֹ מִן הַיַּיִן.

The Gemara answers: This was done **in accordance with** the statement **of Rabbi** Yehuda HaNasi with regard to the sequence of passages in the Torah, **as it is taught** in a *baraita* that **Rabbi** Yehuda HaNasi **says: Why is the portion of a nazirite** (Numbers, chapter 6) **placed adjacent to the portion of a *sota*** (Numbers, chapter 5)? This was done **to tell you that anyone who sees a *sota* in her disgrace** as she undergoes the rite of the bitter water **should renounce**[N] **wine,** as wine is one of the causes of sexual transgression, as it loosens inhibitions. For the same reason that the Torah teaches these passages one after the other, Rabbi Yehuda HaNasi arranged these tractates one after the other.

BACKGROUND

To partake of *teruma* – לֶאֱכוֹל בִּתְרוּמָה: The Torah bestows twenty-four different awards on priests, who serve the entire community in the Temple and do not receive a portion in Eretz Yisrael. One of these awards is *teruma*, which must be eaten or used in a state of ritual purity by the priests, who confer that right on other members of their household, including their wives, children, slaves, and animals.

NOTES

One who issues a warning [*hamekanneh*] – הַמְקַנֵּא: As Rashi and other commentaries note, this term is used based on the language in the verse in this context: "And he warned [*vekinneh*] his wife" (Numbers 5:14). The commentaries, however, differ as to the precise implications of this term, *hamekanneh*, as well as the meaning of the term *vekinneh* used in the verse. Some explain that it is referring to a warning (Rambam's Commentary on the Mishna; *Tosefot HaRosh*). Others explain that it is a term indicating anger and annoyance (see *Tosefot Yom Tov*). In truth, the interpretation of this term is dependent upon the dispute (see 3a) as to whether it is proper for a suspicious husband to issue a warning to his wife.

Should renounce, etc. – יַזִּיר עַצְמוֹ וכו׳: Some understand that the Gemara is not advising one to actually become a nazirite, as the Gemara in tractate *Nazir* (19a) states that the acceptance of a vow of naziriteship is a sin. Rather, the Gemara means that those who see a *sota* in her disgrace should reduce their consumption of wine (*Be'er Sheva*; see *Tosafot* on *Nazir* 2a).

HALAKHA

He issues a warning to her based on two – מְקַנֵּא לָהּ עַל פִּי שְׁנַיִם: A man issues a warning to his wife by stating in the presence of two witnesses: Do not seclude yourself with so-and-so (Rambam *Sefer Nashim, Hilkhot Sota* 1:1; *Shulḥan Arukh, Even HaEzer* 178:2).

And gives to her to drink based on two – וּמַשְׁקָה עַל פִּי שְׁנַיִם: The seclusion described in the verse is where a woman is secluded with the specific man about whom she was warned and there are two witnesses attesting to this seclusion, in accordance with Rabbi Yehoshua's opinion, based on the principle that his opinion is accepted in his disputes with Rabbi Eliezer (Rambam *Sefer Nashim, Hilkhot Sota* 1:2; *Shulḥan Arukh, Even HaEzer* 178:4).

Do not speak with the man called so-and-so – אַל תְּדַבְּרִי עִם אִישׁ פְּלוֹנִי: If one says to his wife in the presence of two witnesses: Do not speak with so-and-so, it is not a warning, and she remains permitted to her husband even if she secludes herself with that man (Rambam *Sefer Nashim, Hilkhot Sota* 1:4; *Shulḥan Arukh, Even HaEzer* 178:6).

She entered into a secluded place and remained with that man, etc. – נִכְנְסָה עִמּוֹ לְבֵית הַסֵּתֶר וְשָׁהֲתָה עִמּוֹ וכו׳: If one issued a warning to his wife about secluding herself with a specific man and she secluded herself with him for a sufficient amount of time to engage in sexual intercourse, she is forbidden to her husband unless she is found innocent through the *sota* rite (Rambam *Sefer Nashim, Hilkhot Sota* 1:2; *Shulḥan Arukh, Even HaEzer* 178:4).

And she is prohibited from partaking of *teruma* – וַאֲסוּרָה לֶאֱכוֹל תְּרוּמָה: If two valid witnesses testify that a woman married to a priest was properly warned by her husband, and she subsequently secluded herself with the man about whom she was warned, it is prohibited for her to partake of *teruma* until she drinks the bitter water. If her husband dies before she is able to drink the bitter water, or if she is unable to drink the water for some other reason, she is permanently prohibited from partaking of *teruma*, as she may have committed adultery (Rambam *Sefer Zera'im, Hilkhot Terumot* 8:15).

She performs *ḥalitza* and may not enter into levirate marriage – חוֹלֶצֶת וְלֹא מִתְיַיבֶּמֶת: If a married woman secludes herself with another man after having been warned by her husband, and her husband dies without children before she drinks the bitter water, she performs *ḥalitza* with her husband's brother and may not enter into levirate marriage (Rambam *Sefer Nashim, Hilkhot Yibbum* 6:19; *Shulḥan Arukh, Even HaEzer* 173:11).

וְלִיתְנֵי סוֹטָה וַהֲדַר לִיתְנֵי נָזִיר! אַיְּידֵי דִּתְנָא כְּתוּבּוֹת וּתְנָא "הַמַּדִּיר" תְּנָא נְדָרִים, וְאַיְּידֵי דִּתְנָא נְדָרִים תְּנָא נָזִיר דְּדָמֵי לִנְדָרִים, וְקָתָנֵי סוֹטָה כְּדְרַבִּי.

The Gemara asks: **But** if so, **let** him **teach** tractate ***Sota* first and then let** him **teach** tractate ***Nazir*,** which is the way these topics are ordered in the Torah, and also accords better with the statement of Rabbi Yehuda HaNasi. The Gemara answers: **Since the** *tanna* **taught** tractate ***Ketubot*, and** in that tractate he **taught** a chapter that begins: **One who vows,** in which there are several *mishnayot* concerning vows between husbands and wives, he then **taught** tractate ***Nedarim*,** whose subject is the *halakhot* of vows. **And since** he **taught** tractate ***Nedarim*,** he then **taught** tractate ***Nazir*, which is similar to** tractate ***Nedarim*** in that one becomes a nazirite by taking a vow. **And** he then **teaches** tractate ***Sota*, in accordance with** the statement **of Rabbi** Yehuda HaNasi.

"הַמְקַנֵּא" – דִּיעֲבַד אִין, לְכַתְּחִילָּה לָא. קָסָבַר תַּנָּא דִּידַן: אָסוּר לְקַנְּאוֹת.

§ The Gemara begins clarifying the mishna. The mishna states: **One who issues a warning** to his wife. By employing the descriptive phrase: One who issues a warning, and not the prescriptive phrase: One issues a warning, the *tanna* indicates that **after the fact, yes,** it is effective if he issues a warning in this manner, but ideally, **no,** one should not issue a warning to his wife at all ***ab initio*.** Apparently, **the *tanna* of our** mishna **holds** that it **is prohibited to issue a warning** to one's wife *ab initio* in a manner that can cause her to become a *sota*, and all the *halakhot* concerning a *sota* are for one who issued a warning when not obligated to do so.

אָמַר רַב שְׁמוּאֵל בַּר רַב יִצְחָק: כִּי הֲוָה פָּתַח רֵישׁ לָקִישׁ בְּסוֹטָה, אָמַר הָכִי: אֵין מְזַוְּוגִין לוֹ לְאָדָם אִשָּׁה אֶלָּא לְפִי מַעֲשָׂיו, שֶׁנֶּאֱמַר: "כִּי לֹא יָנוּחַ שֵׁבֶט הָרֶשַׁע עַל גּוֹרַל הַצַּדִּיקִים". אָמַר רַבָּה בַּר בַּר חָנָה אָמַר רַבִּי יוֹחָנָן: וְקָשִׁין לְזַוְּוגָן כִּקְרִיעַת יַם סוּף, שֶׁנֶּאֱמַר: "אֱלֹהִים מוֹשִׁיב יְחִידִים בַּיְתָה מוֹצִיא אֲסִירִים בַּכּוֹשָׁרוֹת".

Rav Shmuel bar Rav Yitzḥak says: When Reish Lakish would introduce[N] his discussion of the Torah passage **of *sota*** he would **say this:** Heaven **matches a woman to a man only according to his actions, as it is stated: "For the rod of wickedness shall not rest upon the lot of the righteous"** (Psalms 125:3), indicating that if one has a wicked wife it is due to his own evil conduct. **Rabba bar bar Ḥana says** that **Rabbi Yoḥanan says: And it is as difficult to match** a couple together **as was the splitting of the Red Sea,**[N] **as it is stated** in a verse that speaks of the exodus from Egypt: **"God makes the solitary individuals dwell in a house; He brings out prisoners into prosperity [*bakosharot*]"** (Psalms 68:7). God takes single individuals and causes them to dwell in a house by properly matching a man to a woman. This is similar to the exodus from Egypt, which culminated in the splitting of the Red Sea, where He released prisoners into prosperity.

אִינִי? וְהָא אָמַר רַב יְהוּדָה אָמַר רַב: אַרְבָּעִים יוֹם קוֹדֶם יְצִירַת הַוָּלָד, בַּת קוֹל יוֹצֵאת וְאוֹמֶרֶת: בַּת פְּלוֹנִי לִפְלוֹנִי, בֵּית פְּלוֹנִי לִפְלוֹנִי, שְׂדֵה פְּלוֹנִי לִפְלוֹנִי! לָא קַשְׁיָא: הָא בְּזִוּוּג רִאשׁוֹן, הָא בְּזִוּוּג שֵׁנִי.

The Gemara asks: **Is that so** that a man is matched to a woman according to his actions? **But Rav Yehuda says** that **Rav says: Forty days before an embryo is formed a Divine Voice issues forth and says: The daughter of so-and-so**[N] is destined **to** marry **so-and-so; such and such a house is** destined **to** be inhabited by **so-and-so; such and such a field is** destined **to** be farmed by **so-and-so.** This clearly states that these matters, including marriage, are decreed for a person even before he is formed. The Gemara answers: This is **not difficult. This** statement that Rav Yehuda says in the name of Rav is **with regard to a first match [*zivug*],**[NL] while **this** statement of Rabba bar bar Ḥana in the name of Rabbi Yoḥanan is **with regard to a second match.** A first match is decreed in heaven; a second match is according to one's actions.

"רַבִּי אֱלִיעֶזֶר אוֹמֵר: מְקַנֵּא לָהּ עַל פִּי שְׁנַיִם" וכו׳. עַד כָּאן לָא פְּלִיגִי אֶלָּא בְּקִינּוּי וּסְתִירָה, אֲבָל בְּטוּמְאָה – עֵד אֶחָד מְהֵימַן.

§ The Gemara now clarifies the dispute in the mishna. **Rabbi Eliezer says:** The husband must **issue a warning to her based on,** i.e., in the presence of, **two** witnesses, and he gives the bitter water to her to drink based on the testimony of one witness. Rabbi Yehoshua says: He both issues a warning to her based on two witnesses and gives the bitter water to her to drink based on the testimony of two witnesses who saw them secluded together. The Gemara notes: Rabbi Eliezer and Rabbi Yehoshua **disagree only with regard to** the requisite number of witnesses for the **warning and** the **seclusion,** whether one or two witnesses are required, **but with regard to** the testimony concerning **defilement** after the warning was issued and seclusion had occurred, they agree that even the testimony of **one witness is deemed credible**[H] to establish that the woman actually engaged in sexual intercourse with the man while secluded.

NOTES

When Reish Lakish would introduce – כִּי הֲוָה פָּתַח רֵישׁ לָקִישׁ: The phrase: Would introduce, is often found in aggadic midrash, and it was regularly used to introduce a lecture on a specific topic by use of an aggadic interpretation of a verse that would facilitate a novel approach to that topic. Some explain that Reish Lakish would teach this statement to explain why, as the Gemara will note is the opinion of some *tanna'im*, it is prohibited for a husband to issue a warning to his wife. As the aggadic interpretation explains, a spouse is designated in accordance with one's own behavior, and since the Gemara (28a) notes that the bitter water is ineffective if her husband is guilty of adultery, before issuing a warning to one's wife one should examine one's own behavior. According to this understanding, the conclusion of the Gemara noting a distinction between a first and second match also relates to this issue, as it indicates that there are still occasions when a warning is appropriate (*Yagel Ya'akov*).

As the splitting of the Red Sea – כִּקְרִיעַת יַם סוּף: The early commentaries discuss why it is that the Gemara compares matchmaking to the splitting of the sea, rather than the actual exodus from Egypt, which is the subject of the verse quoted in the Gemara. Some explain that the term *bakosharot* in the verse alludes to the splitting of the sea, as it is a contraction of *bebekhi uveshirot*, with crying and singing, referring to the crying of the Egyptians and the singing of the Jews (*Tosefot HaRosh*).

The daughter of so-and-so, etc. – בַּת פְּלוֹנִי וכו׳: *Tosafot* infer from this formulation that a Divine Voice issues forth at the time that the man is formed, at which time his future mate might not be born yet, and therefore she is referred to only by her father's name (see Maharsha). Other early commentaries explain that the Divine Voice issues forth when the first of the couple is born, regardless of whether it is the male or the female.

This is with regard to a first match, etc. – הָא בְּזִוּוּג רִאשׁוֹן וכו׳: *Tosefot HaRash* explains that the term second match is applicable only if it is a second marriage for both the man and the woman. If either spouse has not yet been married, it is still referred to as a first match. The *Be'er Sheva*, based on the esoterica, explains that the term first match refers to the divinely ordained mate of an individual, whereas the phrase second match refers to one matched with a person based on their actions, and it may be that one will marry only the second match. There is a certain similarity between this explanation and that of the Meiri, who explains that a first match refers to one who marries at a young age, when one is too young to be matched based on his actions, and therefore the mate is ordained by a Divine Voice, while a second match refers to one who marries at an older age, since his conduct can be evaluated to ordain a fitting match.

LANGUAGE

Match [*zivug*] – זוּג: Although this word as well as several others derived from it are found in ancient Hebrew and in other Semitic languages, it is believed that the original source is the Greek ζυγόν, *zugon*, which refers to a team of two oxen, or yoke. It was extended to include any grouping together of two entities, and is used by the Sages with specific emphasis on the joining of a couple in marriage.

HALAKHA

With regard to defilement one witness is deemed credible – בְּטוּמְאָה עֵד אֶחָד מְהֵימַן: If a woman had been warned by her husband, and witnesses testify with regard to the seclusion, then even if only one witness testifies that she engaged in sexual intercourse with the man, she is permanently forbidden to her husband and does not drink the bitter water, but she is divorced without receiving payment of her marriage contract (Rambam *Sefer Nashim*, *Hilkhot Sota* 1:14; *Shulḥan Arukh*, *Even HaEzer* 178:14).

וְתַנְיָא נַמִי: עֵד אֶחָד אוֹמֵר אֲנִי רָאִיתִי שֶׁנִּטְמֵאת – לֹא הָיְתָה שׁוֹתָה.

The Gemara comments: **And we learned also** in another mishna (31a) that if **a single witness says: I saw that she was defiled,** then **she would not drink** the bitter water, as the testimony is accepted, and her husband must divorce her and she forfeits payment of her marriage contract. Therefore, there is no need to perform the *sota* rite.

מִדְּאוֹרַיְיתָא מְנָלַן דִּמְהֵימַן עֵד אֶחָד? דְּתָנוּ רַבָּנַן: ״וְעֵד אֵין בָּהּ״ – בִּשְׁנַיִם הַכָּתוּב מְדַבֵּר.

The Gemara asks: **By Torah law, from where do we** derive **that one witness is deemed credible** with regard to testifying that a *sota* engaged in sexual intercourse? The Gemara answers: **As the Sages taught** in reference to the verse describing the circumstances in which a woman defiled through an act of adultery becomes forbidden to her husband, which states: "And a man lie with her carnally and it be hid from the eyes of her husband, she being defiled secretly, **and there is no witness** [*ed*] **against her**" (Numbers 5:13), **the verse is speaking of** a lack of **two** witnesses. When the verse refers to the lack of an *ed*, written in the singular, it actually indicates that there are not two witnesses against her, but only one, as the *baraita* will now explain.

אוֹ אֵינוֹ אֶלָּא אֲפִילּוּ בְּאֶחָד? תַּלְמוּד לוֹמַר: ״לֹא יָקוּם עֵד אֶחָד בְּאִישׁ״.

The *baraita* continues and asks: **Or** perhaps the verse is referring **only** to a case where there was not **even one** witness to the act of sexual intercourse, as the singular usage of the word *ed* would seem to indicate? The *baraita* now proves that elsewhere the word *ed* is used to indicate two witnesses, as **the verse states: "One witness** [*ed*] **shall not rise up against a man** for any iniquity or any sin that he sins; by the mouth of two witnesses or by the mouth of three witnesses shall a matter be established" (Deuteronomy 19:15).

Perek **I**
Daf **2** Amud **b**

מִמַּשְׁמַע שֶׁנֶּאֱמַר: ״לֹא יָקוּם עֵד בְּאִישׁ״, אֵינִי יוֹדֵעַ שֶׁהוּא אֶחָד? מַה תַּלְמוּד לוֹמַר ״אֶחָד״? זֶה בָּנָה אָב: כׇּל מָקוֹם שֶׁנֶּאֱמַר ״עֵד״, הֲרֵי כָּאן שְׁנַיִם, עַד שֶׁיִּפְרוֹט לְךָ הַכָּתוּב ״אֶחָד״.

The *baraita* infers a general principle from this verse by asking: **By inference from that** which **is stated** in the verse, even with the omission of the word "one": **"A witness shall not rise up against a man"** (Deuteronomy 19:15), **do I not know that it is** referring to **one** witness, as the term "rise up [*yakum*]" is written in the singular form? **What** is the meaning when **the verse states** explicitly: **"One** witness," since it is obviously referring to only one witness? The *baraita* answers: **This established a paradigm** that **every place** where the word **"witness** [*ed*]**" is stated** in the Torah without specifying a number, **there are two** witnesses **here, unless the verse specifies** that it is referring to only one witness by writing the word **"one."**

וְאָמַר רַחֲמָנָא: תְּרֵי לֵית בָּהּ אֶלָּא חַד, ״וְהִיא לֹא נִתְפָּשָׂה״ – אֲסוּרָה.

The *baraita* returns to discuss the verse concerning a *sota*. **And the Merciful One states:** "There is no witness [*ed*] against her" (Numbers 5:13), which therefore means that **there are not two** witnesses to the sexual intercourse that could testify **with regard to her; rather,** there is only **one** witness. The *baraita* completes its interpretation: Further in the verse it states: **"And she was not taken,"** indicating that the verse is referring to a case in which it is known that the woman had not been raped. This knowledge is based on the testimony of only one witness, as the verse had already stated that there were not two witnesses, and since one witness saw her willingly engage in sexual intercourse with another man, **she is forbidden.**

אלא טעמא דכתיב: "לא יקום עד אחד באיש", הא לאו הכי, הוה אמינא עד דסוטה חד הוא. ואי אפילו חד ליכא, אלא במאי מיתסרא?

The Gemara questions this reasoning: **But** this would seem to indicate that **the** only **reason** to interpret the verse concerning a *sota* as referring to a case where there is only one witness is **that it is written** in the other verse: **"One witness shall not rise up against a man"** (Deuteronomy 19:15), indicating that any unspecified usage of the word *ed* in the Torah refers to two witnesses, **but** were it **not** for **this** inference, **I would say** that when the term **witness** is employed in the verse **concerning a** ***sota*** it **is** referring to **one** witness. However, this would mean that the woman is forbidden to her husband even if there is not even one witness who saw the alleged sexual intercourse, **and if there is not even one** witness to testify, **then with what** testimony **does she become forbidden** to her husband? Obviously, even without another verse, it must be understood that the verse is indicating that there are not two witnesses but there is one, or else there would be no testimony to her actions.

איצטריך, סלקא דעתך אמינא: "עד אין בה" – אין נאמן בה.

The Gemara answers: It **was necessary** to infer the interpretation of the verse concerning the *sota* from the other verse mentioning one witness. Otherwise it might **enter your mind to say** that the verse here that states: **"There is no witness against her,"** means that a single witness testifying about the sexual intercourse **is not deemed credible with regard to her** under any circumstances, and the testimony of one witness is not accepted in the case of a *sota*.

אין נאמן בה? ואלא מאי בעי?

The Gemara questions this analysis: What would be the logic in interpreting the verse as indicating that a single witness **is not deemed credible with regard to her? But** if that is the interpretation, **what** does the verse **require** in order for a *sota* to be rendered forbidden?

עד דאיכא תרי, לישתוק קרא מיניה, דאתיא "דבר" "דבר" מממון, ואנא ידענא, מידי דהוה אכל עדיות שבתורה!

The Gemara explains its question: If the verse is understood as indicating that a woman isn't forbidden **until there are two witnesses** to testify to her infidelity, then **let the verse be silent from** any mention of witnesses, **as** the requirement for two witnesses in matters of sexual impropriety **is derived** by means of a verbal analogy **from** the word **"matter"** written with regard to forbidden relations, and the word **"matter"** written with regard to **monetary matters.** The verbal analogy by which it is learned that two witnesses are required is as follows: A verse concerning forbidden relations states: "Because he has found some unseemly matter about her" (Deuteronomy 24:1), and a verse concerning monetary matters states: "By the mouth of two witnesses or by the mouth of three witnesses shall a matter be established" (Deuteronomy 19:15). **And I** would **know** that the requirement that two witnesses testify applies in the case of a *sota*, **just as it does in all** other matters of **testimony in the Torah.**

איצטריך, סלקא דעתך אמינא: סוטה שאני, דרגלים לדבר, שהרי קינא לה ונסתרה, ליתהימן בה עד אחד.

The Gemara answers: It **was necessary** that the verse be stated in the case of a *sota* as well, for it might **enter your mind to say** that testimony concerning **a** ***sota*** **is different** from other testimony, and even testimony of one witness would be sufficient **because** there is **a basis for** anticipating **the matter. Since** the husband **issued a warning to her** about this particular man **and she** then **secluded** herself with him, perhaps even **one witness should be deemed credible with regard to her.** Therefore, the verse informs us that one witness is not deemed credible to render her forbidden to her husband.

ומי מצית אמרת דאין נאמן בה ושריא? והא מדכתיב "והיא לא נתפשה", מכלל דאסורה!

The Gemara asks another question concerning its earlier analysis: **But how can you** think to **say** that the verse would be stating that one witness **is not deemed credible with regard to her** having engaged in sexual intercourse **and she** would remain **permitted** to her husband? **But from** the continuation of the same verse, from the fact **that it is written: "And she was not taken,"** which indicates that the verse is referring to a case where she was not raped, one concludes **by inference** that the verse is referring to a woman **who** becomes **forbidden** to her husband for engaging in consensual adulterous sexual intercourse.

אִיצְטְרִיךְ, סָלְקָא דַּעְתָּךְ אָמֵינָא: אֵין נֶאֱמָן בָּהּ עַד דְּאִיכָּא תְּרֵי, וּבִתְרֵי נָמֵי הִיא דְּלֹא נִתְפְּשָׂה. קָא מַשְׁמַע לַן.

The Gemara answers: Nevertheless, it still **was necessary** to teach the principle derived from the other verse that the term "*ed*" is referring to two witnesses even in the context of a *sota*, as it might **enter your mind to say** that the verse should be understood to mean that one witness **is not deemed credible with regard to her,** and she remains permitted **until there are two** witnesses who testify to the sexual intercourse, **and with** the testimony of **two witnesses as well, it is** only **when she was not seized** and forced to cohabit with the man. Therefore, to refute this possible interpretation, the *baraita* **teaches us** that "*ed*" always refers to two witnesses unless stated otherwise. Therefore, the phrase in the verse concerning a *sota* that says: "There is no witness [*ed*] against her," means that there were not two witnesses, but if there was only one witness he is deemed credible.

"רַבִּי יְהוֹשֻׁעַ אוֹמֵר: מְקַנֵּא לָהּ עַל פִּי שְׁנַיִם" וכו׳. מַאי טַעְמָא דְּרַבִּי יְהוֹשֻׁעַ? אָמַר קְרָא: "בָּהּ", בָּהּ – וְלֹא בְּקִינּוּי, בָּהּ – וְלֹא בִּסְתִירָה.

The mishna teaches that **Rabbi Yehoshua says:** He both **issues a warning to her based on two** witnesses, and he gives the bitter water to her to drink based on the testimony of two witnesses who saw her secluded. The Gemara asks: **What is the reasoning of Rabbi Yehoshua?** The Gemara answers: The **verse states:** "And there is no witness [*ed*] **against her** [*bah*]" (Numbers 5:13), which was explained to mean there were not two witnesses, but only one, who testified concerning her defilement. Rabbi Yehoshua derives from the term *bah*, which could also be understood as: **With regard to it,** that in this matter of defilement one witness suffices, **but not with regard to** the **warning.** Additionally, he derives: **With regard to it, but not with regard to** the **seclusion.** Therefore, there must be two witnesses to testify about both the warning and the seclusion.

וְרַבִּי אֱלִיעֶזֶר אוֹמֵר: בָּהּ – וְלֹא בְּקִינּוּי.

The Gemara now explains Rabbi Eliezer's opinion. **And Rabbi Eliezer says** that the only derivation to be learned is: **With regard to it, but not with regard to** the **warning.**[N] Therefore, the warning, unlike the defilement, requires two witnesses. The seclusion is not contrasted with the defilement, and, like the defilement, requires only one.

וְאֵימָא: בָּהּ – וְלֹא בִּסְתִירָה! סְתִירָה אִיתַּקַּשׁ לְטוּמְאָה, דִּכְתִיב: "וְנִסְתְּרָה וְהִיא נִטְמָאָה".

The Gemara questions Rabbi Eliezer's opinion: **But** why not **say** that one should also derive: **With regard to it, but not with regard to** the **seclusion,**[N] as does Rabbi Yehoshua? The Gemara answers: Rabbi Eliezer does not accept that derivation, as **seclusion is juxtaposed to defilement** by the verse, **as it is written: "And she was defiled secretly"** (Numbers 5:13), and the term "secretly" is referring to seclusion. Therefore, the same *halakha* should apply to both.

קִינּוּי נָמֵי אִיתַּקַּשׁ לְטוּמְאָה, דִּכְתִיב: "וְקִנֵּא אֶת אִשְׁתּוֹ וְהִיא נִטְמָאָה"! הָא מִיעֵט רַחֲמָנָא "בָּהּ".

The Gemara asks: But the **warning is also juxtaposed to defilement, as it is written: "And he warned his wife, and she had become defiled"** (Numbers 5:14) and the same *halakha* should apply to both. The Gemara answers: **The Merciful One excluded** at least one of the two by use of the expression ***bah***, which teaches that in one matter other than defilement, two witnesses are required.

וּמָה רָאִיתָ? מִסְתַּבְּרָא סְתִירָה עֲדִיפָא, שֶׁכֵּן אוֹסַרְתָּהּ כְּטוּמְאָה.

The Gemara asks: **And what did you see** to determine that the exclusion from the *halakha* of one witness sufficing is with regard to the warning? Perhaps the exclusion from the *halakha* of one witness sufficing is with regard to the seclusion. The Gemara answers: It **stands to reason** that it is **preferable** to compare **seclusion** to defilement, **as** testimony with regard to seclusion **forbids her** to her husband **just as** testimony with regard to **defilement** does.

אַדְּרַבָּה, קִינּוּי עָדִיף, שֶׁכֵּן עִיקַּר גָּרַם לָהּ!

The Gemara rejects this reasoning: **On the contrary,** it is **preferable** to compare the **warning** to the defilement, **as** it is the **main cause** of **her** becoming forbidden. Seclusion alone, absent a warning, would not cause her to be forbidden to her husband.

אִי לָאו סְתִירָה, קִינּוּי מִי אִיכָּא? וְאִי לָאו קִינּוּי, סְתִירָה מַאי אַהֲנֵי?

The Gemara counters: If there is **no seclusion, is there** any significance to the **warning?** The warning results in a prohibition only after the warned woman secludes herself with the man. The Gemara counters: **And if** there is **no warning, what effectiveness does seclusion have?** Both the warning and the seclusion are required for her to be forbidden.

NOTES

With regard to it but not with regard to the warning – בָּהּ וְלֹא בְּקִינּוּי: In the Jerusalem Talmud it is explained that this dispute is related to another dispute. Rabbi Eliezer's opinion is in accordance with the opinion of Beit Shammai (*Gittin* 90a) that one may not divorce his wife unless she committed adultery. As such, it must be that he can have her drink the bitter water to clarify her status even if there is only one witness with regard to the seclusion. Otherwise, the husband would remain without any options, as he may neither divorce her nor continue living with her. By contrast, Rabbi Yehoshua's opinion is in accordance with the opinion of Beit Hillel (*Gittin* 90a) that one can divorce his wife if he finds any fault in her. Therefore, if there is testimony of one witness that she secluded herself, he has the option to divorce her, and it is not necessary to perform the *sota* rite.

With regard to it but not with regard to the seclusion, etc. – בָּהּ וְלֹא בִּסְתִירָה וכו׳: In the Jerusalem Talmud it is explained that the dispute with regard to the number of witnesses is predicated upon alternative interpretations of the verse: "He has found some unseemly matter [*davar*] about her" (Deuteronomy 24:1). Everyone agrees that the expression "he has found" refers to having found out by means of the testimony of witnesses. The dispute concerns the meaning of the expression "an unseemly matter." According to Rabbi Yehoshua, it refers to having found out through witnesses about the unseemly matter of his wife secluding herself with another man. By contrast, Rabbi Eliezer interprets the word "matter [*davar*]" as related to the similar word *dibbur*, meaning speech. Consequently, he interprets that the actual speaking involved in the *sota* process must be found through witness testimony. Therefore, only the warning, not the seclusion, must be testified about by two witnesses.

NOTES

There is no end to the matter – אֵין לַדָּבָר סוֹף: The commentaries differ as to the nature of this claim. Some explain that enabling the performance of the *sota* rite based on the husband's word alone will call into question the efficacy of the rite, as it will be performed many times when the woman has not in fact committed adultery (*Tosefot HaRash*). Others explain that the Rabbis wish to avoid the needless erasure of the name of God, as erasing a scroll containing the name of God is a stage of the rite (*Torat HaKenaot*).

In the Jerusalem Talmud it is explained that the dispute between Rabbi Yosei, son of Rabbi Yehuda, and the Rabbis with regard to whether she is given to drink the bitter waters based on the husband's word alone is dependent upon a different dispute, i.e., whether a husband can issue a warning to his wife not to seclude herself with those with whom she is ordinarily permitted to be secluded, such as her father or brother. Rabbi Yosei, son of Rabbi Yehuda, holds that one may not issue a warning to his wife with regard to these men. Therefore, even if the husband can issue a warning based on his own word, the *sota* rite will be performed only rarely, as it is not common for a woman to seclude herself in a prohibited manner. By contrast, the Rabbis hold that one can issue a warning to his wife with regard to these men. Since it is likely that she will then seclude herself with them, as they are her close relatives, they are concerned that the *sota* rite will be performed frequently when she has not committed adultery, as above.

אֲפִילּוּ הָכִי סְתִירָה עֲדִיפָא, דְּאַתְחַלְתָּא דְּטוּמְאָה הִיא.

The Gemara concludes: **Even so,** it is **preferable** to compare the **seclusion** to the defilement, **as** the seclusion **is the beginning of defilement.** Therefore, just as the testimony of one witness suffices with regard to the defilement, the testimony of one witness suffices with regard to the seclusion.

מַתְנִיתִין דְּלָא כִּי הַאי תַּנָּא; דְּתַנְיָא, רַבִּי יוֹסֵי בְּרַבִּי יְהוּדָה אוֹמֵר מִשּׁוּם רַבִּי אֱלִיעֶזֶר: הַמְקַנֵּא לְאִשְׁתּוֹ, מְקַנֵּא עַל פִּי עֵד אֶחָד אוֹ עַל פִּי עַצְמוֹ, וּמַשְׁקָה לָהּ עַל פִּי שְׁנַיִם. הֵשִׁיבוּ חֲכָמִים: לְדִבְרֵי רַבִּי יוֹסֵי בְּרַבִּי יְהוּדָה, אֵין לַדָּבָר סוֹף.

The Gemara comments: **The mishna is not in accordance with** the opinion of **this** ***tanna***, who presents a different version of Rabbi Eliezer's opinion, **as it is taught** in a *baraita* (*Tosefta* 1:1) that **Rabbi Yosei, son of Rabbi Yehuda, says in the name of Rabbi Eliezer: One who issues a warning to his wife issues a warning based on one witness or based on his own** testimony, **and** he **gives** the bitter water to her **to drink based on** the testimony of **two** witnesses who saw her secluded. The *baraita* further states that **the Rabbis responded: According to the statement of Rabbi Yosei, son of Rabbi Yehuda,** as to Rabbi Eliezer's opinion that one need not issue a warning in the presence of two witnesses, **there is no end to the matter,**[N] as the Gemara will explain.

מַאי טַעֲמָא דְּרַבִּי יוֹסֵי בְּרַבִּי יְהוּדָה? אָמַר קְרָא: "בָּהּ", בָּהּ – וְלֹא בִּסְתִירָה.

The Gemara explains: **What is the reasoning of Rabbi Yosei, son of Rabbi Yehuda? The verse states: "*Bah*,"** from which he infers that one witness suffices to testify **with regard to it,** i.e., the defilement, **but not with regard to seclusion,** as above.

וְאֵימָא: בָּהּ – וְלֹא בְּקִינּוּי! קִינּוּי אִיתַּקַּשׁ לְטוּמְאָה, דִּכְתִיב: "וְקִנֵּא אֶת אִשְׁתּוֹ וְהִיא נִטְמָאָה".

The Gemara asks: **But** why not **say** that one should also derive: **With regard to it, but not with regard to** the **warning?** The Gemara answers: The **warning is juxtaposed to defilement, as it is written: "And he warned his wife, and she had become defiled"** (Numbers 5:14), and the same *halakha* should apply to both.

סְתִירָה נַמִּי אִיתַּקַּשׁ לְטוּמְאָה, דִּכְתִיב: "וְנִסְתְּרָה וְהִיא נִטְמָאָה"! הַהוּא, לְכַמָּה שִׁיעוּר סְתִירָה – כְּדֵי טוּמְאָה, הוּא דְּאָתָא.

The Gemara counters this argument: **Seclusion is also juxtaposed** in the verse **to defilement, as it is written: "And she was defiled secretly"** (Numbers 5:13). Therefore, the same *halakha* should apply to both. The Gemara responds: **That** verse **is coming to** teach **how much** is the **measure of seclusion,** i.e., the amount of time that the man and woman must be secluded together for it to be defined as seclusion, which, as the comparison indicates, is the amount of time **sufficient for defilement.**

"הֵשִׁיבוּ חֲכָמִים: לְדִבְרֵי רַבִּי יוֹסֵי בְּרַבִּי יְהוּדָה, אֵין לַדָּבָר סוֹף". מַאי נִיהוּ? דִּזְמְנִין דְּלָא קַנֵּי וְאָמַר "קַנֵּאי".

The Gemara continues to clarify the *baraita*. **The Rabbis responded: According to the statement of Rabbi Yosei, son of Rabbi Yehuda,** as to Rabbi Eliezer's opinion, **there is no end to the matter.** The Gemara asks: **What is** the meaning of: There is no end to the matter? The Gemara answers: It is **that** there may be **times when** the husband **did not warn** his wife **but** after hearing of her seclusion with another man **says: I warned her,** which will be sufficient to render her forbidden to him until she drinks.

הָא לְמִשְׁנָתֵינוּ יֵשׁ לַדָּבָר סוֹף? זִמְנִין דְּלָא אִיסְתַּתַּר וְאָמַר "אִיסְתַּתַּר"!

The Gemara is puzzled by this logic: **But according to our mishna, does the matter** in fact **have an end?** Rabbi Eliezer states in the mishna that a woman must drink the bitter water based upon her husband's own statement that she secluded herself with the man about whom he had warned her. There too, one could ask whether there may be **times when she did not seclude herself** with the other man **and** where **her husband says: She secluded herself,** thereby rendering her forbidden to him until she drinks the bitter water. If so, why do the Rabbis take issue only with the version of Rabbi Eliezer's opinion as presented by Rabbi Yosei, son of Rabbi Yehuda, and not with the version recorded in the mishna?

אָמַר רַב יִצְחָק בַּר יוֹסֵף אָמַר רַבִּי יוֹחָנָן: אַף לְדִבְרֵי רַבִּי יוֹסֵי בְּרַבִּי יְהוּדָה, אֵין לַדָּבָר סוֹף.

Rav Yitzḥak bar Yosef says that **Rabbi Yoḥanan says:** The Rabbis in the *baraita* meant to state that **even according to the statement of Rabbi Yosei, son of Rabbi Yehuda, there is no end to the matter.** The Rabbis wished to say that even according to his version of Rabbi Eliezer's opinion, the husband can cause her to drink if he were to lie. The same is obviously true for the mishna.

אַף לְדִבְרֵי רַבִּי יוֹסֵי בְּרַבִּי יְהוּדָה, וְלָא מִיבַּעְיָא לְמִשְׁנָתֵינוּ? אַדְּרַבָּה, לְמִשְׁנָתֵינוּ אִיכָּא עִיקָּר, הָתָם לֵיכָּא עִיקָּר!

The Gemara notes: The phrase **even according to the statement of Rabbi Yosei, son of Rabbi Yehuda,** indicates it is a lesser novelty to say that there is no end to the matter according to him, **and it is not necessary** to say that the same would be true **according to** the opinion of Rabbi Eliezer cited in **our mishna.** The Gemara asks: **On the contrary, according to** the opinion of Rabbi Eliezer cited in **our mishna,** there **is** a legitimate **basis** of suspicion with regard to the woman, as there are witnesses who saw the husband issue a warning to her, and therefore, it is understandable that the testimony of the husband may be relied upon when he testifies that she secluded herself with another man. By contrast, **there,** according to the opinion of Rabbi Yosei, son of Rabbi Yehuda, **there is no** legitimate **basis** to prohibit her to him, since there are no witnesses that she had been warned by her husband at all. Therefore, it may be that the Rabbis took issue only with the version of Rabbi Eliezer's opinion presented by Rabbi Yosei, son of Rabbi Yehuda.

אֶלָּא אִי אִיתְּמַר הָכִי אִיתְּמַר, אָמַר רַב יִצְחָק בַּר יוֹסֵף אָמַר רַבִּי יוֹחָנָן: לְדִבְרֵי רַבִּי יוֹסֵי בְּרַבִּי יְהוּדָה, אַף לְמִשְׁנָתֵינוּ אֵין לַדָּבָר סוֹף.

The Gemara clarifies the statement of Rabbi Yoḥanan: **Rather, if it was stated, it was stated like this: Rav Yitzḥak bar Yosef says** that **Rabbi Yoḥanan says** that the Rabbis said: **According to the statement of Rabbi Yosei, son of Rabbi Yehuda,** who is not concerned that accepting the testimony of one person with regard to the warning will enable false claims by the husband, **even according to** the opinion of Rabbi Eliezer cited in **our mishna there is no end to the matter,** since the concern there is less severe, as there is no legitimate basis to render her forbidden to her husband.

אָמַר רַב חֲנִינָא מִסּוּרָא: לָא לֵימָא אִינִישׁ לְאִיתְּתֵיהּ בִּזְמַן הַזֶּה לָא תִּיסַּתְרִי בַּהֲדֵי פְּלוֹנִי. דִּילְמָא קַיְימָא לָן כְּרַבִּי יוֹסֵי בְּרַבִּי יְהוּדָה, דְּאָמַר: קִינּוּי עַל פִּי עַצְמוֹ, וּמִיסְתַּתְרָא, וְלֵיכָּא הָאִידָּנָא מֵי סוֹטָה לְמִיבְדְּקַהּ, וְקָאָסַר לַהּ עִילָּוֵיהּ אִיסּוּרָא דִּלְעוֹלָם.

Rav Ḥanina of Sura says: In the present[N] **a man should not say to his wife:**[H] **Do not seclude yourself with so-and-so.** The reason is that **perhaps we maintain**[N] that the *halakha* is **in accordance with** the opinion of **Rabbi Yosei, son of Rabbi Yehuda, who says** that **a warning** is effective even **based on his own** testimony, **and** if she were then to **seclude herself** with that man she would be required to drink the bitter water to render herself permitted to her husband, **and** since **today** the bitter **water of a** ***sota*** is **not** used **to evaluate her** fidelity and permit her to her husband, **he will** end up **forbidding her to himself** with **an irrevocable prohibition.**

אָמַר רֵישׁ לָקִישׁ: מַה לְּשׁוֹן קִינּוּי? דָּבָר הַמַּטִּיל קִנְאָה בֵּינָהּ לְבֵין אֲחֵרִים. אַלְמָא קָסָבַר: קִינּוּי עַל פִּי עַצְמוֹ, וְכוּלֵּי עָלְמָא לָא יָדְעִי דְּקַנֵּי לַהּ, וְאָמְרִי: מַאי דְּקַמָּא דְּקָא בָּדְלָה? וְאָתוּ לְמֶיעֱבַד קִנְאָה בַּהֲדַהּ.

§ **Reish Lakish says: What** is the meaning of the **term: Warning** [*kinnui*]?[L] It means **a matter that causes anger** [*kina*] **between her and others,** as other men will not understand why she does not wish to be friendly with them any longer. The Gemara comments: **Apparently, he holds** that **a warning** is effective **based on** the husband's **own** testimony, **and** therefore **everyone else will not know that her husband issued a warning to her, and they will say: What is this** matter happening **before us that she separates herself** from us, **and they will come to act in anger with her.**

וְרַב יֵימָר בַּר רַבִּי שֶׁלֶמְיָא מִשְּׁמֵיהּ דְּאַבַּיֵי אָמַר: דָּבָר הַמַּטִּיל קִנְאָה בֵּינוֹ לְבֵינָהּ. אַלְמָא קָסָבַר: קִינּוּי עַל פִּי שְׁנַיִם עֵדִים, וְכוּלֵּי עָלְמָא יָדְעִי דְּקַנֵּי לַהּ, וְאִיהוּ הוּא דְּאָתֵי לְמֶיעֱבַד קִנְאָה בַּהֲדַהּ.

And Rav Yeimar bar Rabbi Shelemya says in the name of Abaye: The term *kinnui* means **a matter that causes anger between him and her,** i.e., between husband and wife. The Gemara comments: **Apparently, he holds** that **a warning** is effective **based on** the testimony of **two witnesses.** And since there are two witnesses, **everyone knows that he issued a warning to her.** Therefore, the warning does not cause anger between her and others. **And the husband is he who will come to act in anger with her,** as they will have mutual antagonism toward each other.

NOTES

In the present – בִּזְמַן הַזֶּה: Seemingly, this concern should have applied even in the time when the Temple was standing, as the *sota* rite would not have been performed to satisfy an individual opinion. Some explain that during the time of the Temple, the uncertainty can be resolved in the event that the husband repeats his warning before witnesses, thereby enabling the *sota* rite to be performed. Once it is performed, it will also clarify whether she committed adultery the first time (*Tosefot Yom Tov*). Others explain that the expression should be read: Even in the present, indicating that in Temple times one should certainly not tell his wife not to seclude herself with a particular man, as it may lead to an improper performance of the *sota* rite. And even in the present, when this concern is not in effect, one should not warn his wife, as it may cause her to become forbidden to him (*Maharit*).

Perhaps we maintain, etc. – דִּילְמָא קַיְימָא לָן וכו׳: The commentaries differ as to whether or not the Gemara is asserting definitively that the *halakha* is in accordance with the opinion of Rabbi Yosei, son of Rabbi Yehuda, even though his opinion is cited only in a *baraita* that contradicts a mishna, and additionally, the *halakha* usually is in accordance with the opinion of Rabbi Yehoshua in his disputes with Rabbi Eliezer (see *Tosefot HaRosh*; *Maharik*; *Rashash*).

HALAKHA

A man should not say to his wife, etc. – לָא לֵימָא אִינִישׁ לְאִיתְּתֵיהּ וכו׳: A man should not say to his wife, even in private: Do not seclude yourself with so-and-so, as the *halakha* may be in accordance with the opinion of Rabbi Yosei, son of Rabbi Yehuda, that if the woman would then seclude herself with that man, she would become forbidden to her husband forever, since the *sota* rite cannot be performed. Some say that this prohibition is not by Torah law (Rashba), and others say that it is a prohibition only for those who want to fulfill their moral obligation to Heaven (*Arukh HaShulḥan*). The *Rema* holds that if a husband does issue such a warning he should immediately retract it.

If, after warning her, the husband himself sees his wife in seclusion with that man, she is forbidden to her husband and he must divorce her. However, he is obligated to pay the value of her marriage contract (Rambam *Sefer Nashim, Hilkhot Ishut* 24:25; *Shulḥan Arukh, Even HaEzer* 115:9, 178:7).

LANGUAGE

Warning [*kinnui*] – קִינּוּי: The root of this word has several different meanings. It is generally followed by the preposition: Of [*beh*], and generally means a strong desire for an item or some character trait belonging to another, i.e., jealousy. At other times, it is followed by the preposition: For [*le*]. In those contexts, it indicates a positive expression of love and suggests anger over another's causing injury or loss to someone or something one holds dear. It is possible that both meanings are related in that they both indicate an arousal of strong feelings and anger caused by others. As used with regard to *sota*, *kinnui* carries the second meaning. Yet, as explained in the Gemara, the word also indicates a warning and threat to one's wife, as he cautions her to stay away from another man. This idea is also reflected in the verse: "He will stir up jealousy [*kina*] as a man of war" (Isaiah 42:13).

אַלְמָא קָסָבְרִי, דְּאָסוּר לְקַנְּאוֹת.

Apparently, both Reish Lakish and Rav Yeimar bar Rabbi Shelemya **hold that** it is **prohibited to issue a warning.** Both are of the opinion that the word *kinnui* is a term for anger. Since causing anger is a negative trait, it follows that it is prohibited to issue a warning.

וּמַאן דְּאָמַר: מוּתָּר לְקַנְּאוֹת, מַהוּ לְשׁוֹן קִינּוּי? אָמַר רַב נַחְמָן בַּר יִצְחָק: אֵין קִינּוּי אֶלָּא לְשׁוֹן הַתְרָאָה, וְכֵן הוּא אוֹמֵר: ״וַיְקַנֵּא ה׳ לְאַרְצוֹ״.

The Gemara asks: **And** according to **the one who says** that it is **permitted** for him **to issue a warning, what is** the meaning of the **term** ***kinnui?*** **Rav Naḥman bar Yitzḥak says:** The term ***kinnui*** means **nothing other** than **a term of forewarning, and so it says: "Then the Lord warned [*vayekanneh*] concerning His land**[N] and had pity for His people" (Joel 2:18). As detailed in that passage, the Lord ordered the locusts to stop destroying Eretz Yisrael.

תַּנְיָא, הָיָה רַבִּי מֵאִיר אוֹמֵר: אָדָם עוֹבֵר עֲבֵירָה בַּסֵּתֶר וְהַקָּדוֹשׁ בָּרוּךְ הוּא מַכְרִיז עָלָיו בְּגָלוּי, שֶׁנֶּאֱמַר: ״וְעָבַר עָלָיו רוּחַ קִנְאָה״, וְאֵין עֲבִירָה אֶלָּא לְשׁוֹן הַכְרָזָה, שֶׁנֶּאֱמַר: ״וַיְצַו מֹשֶׁה וַיַּעֲבִירוּ קוֹל בַּמַּחֲנֶה״.

It is **taught** in a *baraita* that **Rabbi Meir would say: A person commits a transgression in private and the Holy One, Blessed be He, proclaims about him openly,** i.e., in public, that he transgressed, **as it is stated** concerning a *sota*, who transgressed in private: **"The spirit of jealousy came [*avar*] upon him"** (Numbers 5:14); **and** the term ***avira*** means **nothing other** than **a term of proclamation, as it is stated: "And Moses gave the commandment, and they caused it to be proclaimed [*vaya'aviru*] throughout the camp"** (Exodus 36:6).

רֵישׁ לָקִישׁ אָמַר: אֵין אָדָם עוֹבֵר עֲבֵירָה אֶלָּא אִם כֵּן נִכְנַס בּוֹ רוּחַ שְׁטוּת, שֶׁנֶּאֱמַר: ״אִישׁ אִישׁ כִּי תִשְׂטֶה אִשְׁתּוֹ״, ״תִּשְׁטֶה״ כְּתִיב.

Reish Lakish says: A man commits a transgression only if a spirit of folly [*shetut*][N] **enters him, as it is stated: "If any man's wife goes aside [*tisteh*]"** (Numbers 5:12). The word *tisteh* is **written** with the Hebrew letter *shin*, affording an alternative reading of ***tishteh,*** which is related to the term for folly, the word *shetut*.

תַּנְיָא דְּבֵי רַבִּי יִשְׁמָעֵאל: מִפְּנֵי מָה הֶאֱמִינָה תּוֹרָה עֵד אֶחָד בְּסוֹטָה? שֶׁרַגְלַיִם לַדָּבָר, שֶׁהֲרֵי קִינֵּא לָהּ וְנִסְתְּרָה, וְעֵד אֶחָד מְעִידָהּ שֶׁהִיא טְמֵאָה.

§ The Gemara discusses why the testimony of one witness suffices with regard to defilement. **The school of Rabbi Yishmael taught** a *baraita*: **For what** reason **did the Torah deem credible a single witness with regard to** the defilement of **a** ***sota?*** It is **because there is a basis for** anticipating **the matter,** as there is strong circumstantial evidence that she committed adultery. What is the basis for anticipating the matter? **As he warned her** not to seclude herself with a specific man, **and she** nevertheless **secluded herself** with him, **and one witness testifies that she is defiled,** then the combination of her behavior and the testimony renders it reasonable to assume that she has in fact committed adultery.

אֲמַר לֵיהּ רַב פַּפָּא לְאַבַּיֵי: וְהָא כִּי כְּתִיבָה קִינּוּי – בָּתַר סְתִירָה וְטוּמְאָה הוּא דִּכְתִיבָה!

Rav Pappa said to Abaye: But when the warning is written in the Torah, **it is written** in the verse **after seclusion and defilement** are mentioned, indicating that the circumstance in which one witness is deemed credible with regard to defilement is even when there was no previous warning. The order in which the Torah describes the *sota* process seems to indicate that the husband's warning is issued only after the wife already secluded herself with the other man and was defiled, as the verses state: "And a man lie with her carnally, and it was hidden from the eyes of her husband, and she was defiled secretly, and there is no witness against her, and she was not taken. And the spirit of jealousy came [*ve'avar*] upon him, and he warned his wife, and she had become defiled" (Numbers 5:13–14).

אֲמַר לֵיהּ: ״וְעָבַר״, וּכְבָר עָבַר.

Abaye **said to him** in response: That which the verse states: **"And** the spirit of jealousy **came [*ve'avar*]** upon him," means: **And** it had **already come** upon him, that the husband warned his wife not to seclude herself with a specific man prior to her seclusion and defilement.

אֶלָּא מֵעַתָּה, ״וְעָבַר לָכֶם כׇּל חָלוּץ״, הָכִי נַמִי!

The Gemara asks: **If that is so,** that *"ve'avar"* is referring to a matter that already occurred, then in the case of the agreement between Moses and the tribes of Gad and Reuben before they entered Eretz Yisrael, where he stated: **"And every armed man of you will pass over [*ve'avar*]** the Jordan" (Numbers 32:21), **so too** did he mean that they had already crossed? Moses was stipulating a condition with regard to the future; they had yet to cross the Jordan.

NOTES

Then the Lord warned concerning His land, etc. – **וַיְקַנֵּא ה׳ לְאַרְצוֹ וכו׳**: Rashi interprets this verse to mean that God, as it were, orders the locusts, mentioned previously in the verses as consuming the produce, to leave the land. The *Devar Shaul* adds that since this order concerns locusts, it clearly doesn't have any implications of anger, as it is not possible that God was angry with locusts. Rather, it clearly indicates an admonition without any antagonistic connotation. The Meiri explains that the presence of the locusts had been a warning given to the land, indicating that if repentance was not forthcoming, an even harsher punishment would be imposed.

A spirit of folly – **רוּחַ שְׁטוּת**: The *Iyyun Ya'akov* explains that this refers to the ability of one to convince himself that his actions are not being observed by God, and therefore he can sin. Alternatively, in the *Tanya* it is explained that this spirit of folly is a mechanism employed to allow one to avoid the cognitive dissonance engendered by believing that he is not a sinner while simultaneously committing a transgression.

הָתָם, מִדִּכְתִיב: ״וְנִכְבְּשָׁה הָאָרֶץ לִפְנֵי ה׳ וְאַחַר תָּשֻׁבוּ״, מַשְׁמַע דִּלְהַבָּא. אֶלָּא הָכָא אִי סָלְקָא דַּעְתָּךְ כִּדְכְתִיבִי, ״וְעָבַר״ בָּתַר טוּמְאָה וּסְתִירָה, קִינּוּי לָמָּה לִי?

The Gemara answers: **There, from** the fact **that it is written: "And the land be subdued before the Lord, and you return afterward"** (Numbers 32:22), it is clear that it **teaches concerning the future. But here, if it enters your mind** that the verses should be understood **as they are written** in the Torah, that "*ve'avar*" (Numbers 5:14) is **after** the **defilement and seclusion,** then **why do I need a warning?** If the woman had already secluded herself with the man and become defiled, the husband's warning would be irrelevant, as she had already become forbidden to him. Therefore, the word *ve'avar* in this context must be referring to a past event, i.e., the husband issuing a warning to his wife prior to the seclusion.

תָּנָא דְּבֵי רַבִּי יִשְׁמָעֵאל: אֵין אָדָם מְקַנֵּא לְאִשְׁתּוֹ אֶלָּא אִם כֵּן נִכְנְסָה בּוֹ רוּחַ, שֶׁנֶּאֱמַר: ״וְעָבַר עָלָיו רוּחַ קִנְאָה וְקִנֵּא אֶת אִשְׁתּוֹ״. מַאי רוּחַ?

The school of Rabbi Yishmael taught: A man issues a warning to his wife only if a spirit entered him, as it is stated: "And the spirit of jealousy came upon him, and he warned his wife" (Numbers 5:14). The Gemara asks: Of **what spirit** does Rabbi Yishmael speak?

רַבָּנַן אָמְרִי: רוּחַ טוּמְאָה. רַב אַשִׁי אָמַר: רוּחַ טָהֳרָה.

The Rabbis say: A spirit of impurity,[N] as one should not issue a warning to one's wife. **Rav Ashi says: A spirit of purity,** as issuing a warning indicates that he will not tolerate promiscuous behavior.

וּמִסְתַּבְּרָא כְּמַאן דְּאָמַר רוּחַ טָהֳרָה, דְּתַנְיָא: ״וְקִנֵּא אֶת אִשְׁתּוֹ״ – רְשׁוּת, דִּבְרֵי רַבִּי יִשְׁמָעֵאל, רַבִּי עֲקִיבָא אוֹמֵר: חוֹבָה. אִי אָמְרַתְּ בִּשְׁלָמָא רוּחַ טָהֳרָה – שַׁפִּיר, אֶלָּא אִי אָמְרַתְּ רוּחַ טוּמְאָה, רְשׁוּת וְחוֹבָה לְעַיּוֹלֵי לְאִינִישׁ רוּחַ טוּמְאָה בְּנַפְשֵׁיהּ?

The Gemara comments: **And** it **stands to reason like the one who says** that Rabbi Yishmael was speaking of **a spirit of purity, as it is taught** in a *baraita*: **"And he warned his wife,"** i.e., the issuing of the warning, is **optional,** that the husband is neither enjoined to nor prohibited from issuing a warning; this is **the statement of Rabbi Yishmael. Rabbi Akiva says:** It is **mandatory,**[H] as one who sees his wife behaving in an inappropriate manner with another man is obligated to warn her. The Gemara explains: **Granted, if you say** that Rabbi Yishmael was speaking of **a spirit of purity,** then it is **well,** as it may be optional, or even mandatory, to issue a warning. **But if you say** that he was speaking of **a spirit of impurity,** can it be **optional or mandatory for a person to introduce a spirit of impurity into himself?** The Torah would not require a husband to act in a manner that results from having a spirit of impurity enter him.

גּוּפָא: ״וְקִנֵּא אֶת אִשְׁתּוֹ״ – רְשׁוּת, דִּבְרֵי רַבִּי יִשְׁמָעֵאל, וְרַבִּי עֲקִיבָא אוֹמֵר חוֹבָה. ״לָהּ יִטַּמָּא״ – רְשׁוּת, דִּבְרֵי רַבִּי יִשְׁמָעֵאל, וְרַבִּי עֲקִיבָא אוֹמֵר: חוֹבָה.

§ The Gemara discusses **the** matter **itself. "And he warned his wife,"** i.e., the warning, is **optional;** this is **the statement of Rabbi Yishmael. And Rabbi Akiva says:** It is **mandatory.** The Gemara notes that Rabbi Yishmael and Rabbi Akiva engage in a similar dispute with regard to several other verses. Although under normal circumstances it is prohibited for a priest to become ritually impure through contact with a corpse, the verse states that he may do so for the sake of burying his relatives. The *baraita* teaches: **"For her may he become impure"** (Leviticus 21:3), i.e., for a priest to participate in the burial of his sister, despite the fact that he will contract ritual impurity, is **optional;** this is **the statement of Rabbi Yishmael.** A priest is not obligated to participate, but he may. **And Rabbi Akiva says:** It is **mandatory**[H] for him to do so.

״לְעֹלָם בָּהֶם תַּעֲבֹדוּ״ – רְשׁוּת, דִּבְרֵי רַבִּי יִשְׁמָעֵאל, רַבִּי עֲקִיבָא אוֹמֵר: חוֹבָה.

The verse states: **"Of them may you take your bondmen forever"** (Leviticus 25:46), i.e., keeping one's Canaanite slave forever, is **optional, this is the statement of Rabbi Yishmael.** One is not enjoined against emancipating a Canaanite slave, but one is permitted to keep his Canaanite slaves forever. **Rabbi Akiva says:** It is **mandatory,**[H] and it is prohibited for one to free his Canaanite slave.

אֲמַר לֵיהּ רַב פַּפָּא לְאַבָּיֵי, וְאָמְרִי לָהּ רַב מְשַׁרְשִׁיָּא לְרָבָא: לֵימָא, רַבִּי יִשְׁמָעֵאל וְרַבִּי עֲקִיבָא בְּכָל הַתּוֹרָה כּוּלָּהּ הָכִי פְּלִיגִי, דְּמָר אָמַר: רְשׁוּת, וּמָר אָמַר: חוֹבָה? אֲמַר לֵיהּ: הָכָא בִּקְרָאֵי פְּלִיגִי.

Rav Pappa said to Abaye, and some say that **Rav Mesharshiyya** said **to Rava: Shall we say** that **Rabbi Yishmael and Rabbi Akiva disagree** in **this** manner **with regard to the entire Torah?**[N] In other words, is it so that whenever there is a statement where it is unclear whether it is referring to an optional or mandatory act, **that** one **master,** Rabbi Yishmael, **says** that it is **optional, and** the other **master,** Rabbi Akiva, **says** that it is **mandatory.** Abaye **said to** Rav Pappa in response: **Here,** in these particular cases, **they disagree with regard to** the meaning of these specific **verses,** but it is not a general dispute.

NOTES

A spirit of impurity, etc. – רוּחַ טוּמְאָה וכו׳: Some commentaries have suggested that both opinions cited in the Gemara are correct, and refer to two situations. If the woman will in fact commit adultery, then a spirit of purity caused him to warn her, enabling him to end his marriage, while if his wife will not commit adultery, then a spirit of impurity had caused him to issue a warning to his wife unnecessarily, causing the name of God to be erased and his wife to be shamed (*Or HaYashar*; *Iyyun Ya'akov*).

With regard to the entire Torah, etc. – בְּכָל הַתּוֹרָה כּוּלָּהּ וכו׳: *Tosefot HaRosh* and the Meiri explain that the questioner was referring only to the mitzvot in the Torah where the wording employed in the verse is ambiguous as to whether it is mandatory or not, as Rabbi Yishmael certainly cannot hold that there are no mandatory mitzvot in the entire Torah. *Tosafot* note that while according to this Gemara, Rabbi Akiva would count three mitzvot not counted by Rabbi Yishmael, this does not mean that Rabbi Yishmael disagrees with the well-known statement (see *Makkot* 23b) that there are 613 mitzvot in the Torah. Rather, there must be three other mitzvot that are counted as mitzvot by Rabbi Yishmael but not by Rabbi Akiva.

HALAKHA

"And he warned his wife"…is mandatory – וְקִנֵּא אֶת אִשְׁתּוֹ...חוֹבָה: It is a mitzva by rabbinic law for a man who sees his wife engaging in promiscuous behavior (*Arukh HaShulḥan*) to issue a warning to her. The Sages say that a man issues a warning to his wife only if a spirit of purity enters him.

The *Kesef Mishne* questions why the Rambam does not rule in accordance with the opinion of Rabbi Akiva, i.e., that it is a mitzva by Torah law, as his rulings are generally accepted as *halakha* over those of his disputants. He explains that the Rambam may have based his ruling on the Jerusalem Talmud, or he may have held that Rabbi Yehoshua agrees with Rabbi Yishmael that it is optional (Rambam *Sefer Nashim, Hilkhot Ishut* 15:17 and *Hilkhot Sota* 4:18; *Shulḥan Arukh, Even HaEzer* 178:21).

"For her may he become impure"…is mandatory – לָהּ יִטַּמָּא...חוֹבָה: A priest is obligated to participate in the burial of any of the relatives for whom the Torah permits him to do so, including his wife, even though his participation renders him impure, and he may even be coerced into doing so. This is in accordance with the opinion of Rabbi Akiva (Rambam *Sefer Shofetim, Hilkhot Evel* 2:6; *Shulḥan Arukh, Yoreh De'a* 373:3).

"Of them may you take your bondmen forever"…is mandatory – לְעֹלָם בָּהֶם תַּעֲבֹדוּ...חוֹבָה: It is prohibited to emancipate a Canaanite slave, in accordance with the opinion of Rabbi Akiva. One who does so transgresses a positive mitzva. However, under certain exigent circumstances one is permitted to emancipate a slave, e.g., in order to facilitate the performance of a significant mitzva, even one by rabbinic law. Similarly, one is obligated to emancipate his female slave if by doing so he will enable her to marry, thereby preventing her from engaging in promiscuous behavior with others (Rambam *Sefer Kinyan, Hilkhot Avadim* 9:6; *Shulḥan Arukh, Yoreh De'a* 267:79).

NOTES

What is the reason of Rabbi Yishmael – מַאי טַעֲמָא דְּרַבִּי יִשְׁמָעֵאל: The Gemara here is questioning why Rabbi Yishmael would interpret specifically this verse in the Torah as being optional rather than mandatory, and explains that since there is reason to prohibit a husband from issuing a warning to his wife, it was necessary for the verse to state that he may in fact do so (*Tosefot HaRosh*).

״וְקִנֵּא אֶת אִשְׁתּוֹ״ – רְשׁוּת, דִּבְרֵי רַבִּי יִשְׁמָעֵאל. רַבִּי עֲקִיבָא אוֹמֵר: חוֹבָה.

The Gemara explains their dispute in these specific contexts, beginning with the dispute concerning a man's warning to his wife: **"And he warned his wife,"** the warning is **optional;** this is **the statement of Rabbi Yishmael. Rabbi Akiva says:** It is **mandatory.**

מַאי טַעֲמָא דְּרַבִּי יִשְׁמָעֵאל? סָבַר לָהּ כִּי הַאי תַּנָּא; דְּתַנְיָא: רַבִּי אֱלִיעֶזֶר בֶּן יַעֲקֹב אוֹמֵר, כְּלַפֵּי שֶׁאָמְרָה תּוֹרָה: ״לֹא תִשְׂנָא אֶת אָחִיךָ בִּלְבָבֶךָ״, יָכוֹל כְּגוֹן זוֹ? תַּלְמוּד לוֹמַר: ״וְעָבַר עָלָיו רוּחַ קִנְאָה וְקִנֵּא אֶת אִשְׁתּוֹ״.

What is the reason of Rabbi Yishmael?[N] He **holds in accordance with** the statement of **this *tanna*, as it is taught** in a *baraita*: **Rabbi Eliezer ben Ya'akov says: With regard to** that **which the Torah said: "You shall not hate your brother in your heart"** (Leviticus 19:17), one **might** have thought that this prohibition applies in a case **such as this** one, when one sees his wife behaving improperly with another man, and the verse would instruct the husband to avoid conflict and strife. Therefore, **the verse states: "And the spirit of jealousy came upon him, and he warned his wife"** (Numbers 5:14), teaching that it is permitted for one to issue a warning to his wife in such a case.

וְרַבִּי עֲקִיבָא? קִינּוּי אַחֲרִינָא כְּתִיב.

The Gemara asks: **And** how does **Rabbi Akiva** derive that it is mandatory? The Gemara answers: There **is another warning written** in the same verse, as the entire verse reads: "And the spirit of jealousy came upon him, and he warned his wife, and she be defiled; or if the spirit of jealousy came upon him, and he warned his wife, and she be not defiled." Therefore, the first half of the verse teaches that it is permitted to issue a warning, and the second half teaches that it is in fact mandatory.

וְרַבִּי יִשְׁמָעֵאל? אַיְּידֵי דְּבָעֵי לְמִיכְתַּב ״וְהִיא נִטְמָאָה״, ״וְהִיא לֹא נִטְמָאָה״, כְּתִיב נַמִי ״וְקִנֵּא אֶת אִשְׁתּוֹ״.

The Gemara asks: **And** how does **Rabbi Yishmael** explain the repetition? The Gemara answers: **Since it needed to write** in this verse both possibilities as to whether the woman was unfaithful: **"And she be defiled,"** and also: **"And she be not defiled,"** to teach that although it is uncertain whether she had become defiled, she is still forbidden to her husband, therefore, **it is also written: "And he warned his wife,"** a second time. This repetition should not be interpreted as rendering the issuance of the warning as mandatory.

לְכִדְתָנָא דְּבֵי רַבִּי יִשְׁמָעֵאל, דְּתָנָא דְּבֵי רַבִּי יִשְׁמָעֵאל: כָּל פָּרָשָׁה שֶׁנֶּאֶמְרָה וְנִישְׁנֵית, לֹא נִישְׁנֵית אֶלָּא בִּשְׁבִיל דָּבָר שֶׁנִּתְחַדֵּשׁ בָּהּ.

This manner of interpreting verses is **as taught by the school of Rabbi Yishmael, as the school of Rabbi Yishmael taught: Every passage** in the Torah **that was stated and repeated was repeated only for the novel element introduced therein.** Although the Torah could have merely mentioned the element necessary to teach an additional *halakha*, one should not interpret the repetition of a previously mentioned matter as teaching a second additional *halakha*, as the style of the Torah is to repeat a passage even to teach only one additional *halakha*. In the case of the passage concerning a *sota* as well, the repetition of the warning does not teach a new *halakha*.

״לָהּ יִטַּמָּא״ – רְשׁוּת, דִּבְרֵי רַבִּי יִשְׁמָעֵאל. רַבִּי עֲקִיבָא אוֹמֵר: חוֹבָה.

The Gemara discusses the second dispute between Rabbi Yishmael and Rabbi Akiva. The *baraita* teaches: "And for his sister a virgin, that is near to him, that has had no husband, **for her may he become impure"** (Leviticus 21:3), i.e., for a priest to participate in the burial of his sister despite the fact that he will contract ritual impurity is **optional;** this is **the statement of Rabbi Yishmael.** A priest is not obligated to participate, but he may do so. **Rabbi Akiva says:** It is **mandatory** for him to do so.

מַאי טַעֲמָא דְּרַבִּי יִשְׁמָעֵאל? אַיְּידֵי דִּכְתִיב: ״אֱמֹר אֶל הַכֹּהֲנִים בְּנֵי אַהֲרֹן וְאָמַרְתָּ אֲלֵיהֶם לְנֶפֶשׁ לֹא יִטַּמָּא בְּעַמָּיו״, אִיצְטְרִיכָא לְמִיכְתַּב ״לָהּ יִטַּמָּא״.

What is the reason of Rabbi Yishmael? Since it is written: "Speak to the priests, the sons of Aaron, and say to them: There shall none become impure for the dead among his people" (Leviticus 21:1), indicating that a priest is enjoined from contact with the dead, it **was necessary to be written: "For her may he become impure,"** which teaches that a priest may become impure at the burial of a relative.

וְרַבִּי עֲקִיבָא? מִ״כִּי אִם לִשְׁאֵרוֹ״ נָפְקָא. ״לָהּ יִטַּמָּא״ לָמָּה לִי? לְחוֹבָה.

The Gemara asks: **And** how does **Rabbi Akiva** derive that it is mandatory? The Gemara answers: He **derives** that it is permissible **from** the previous verse, which states: **"Except for his kin,** that is near to him" (Leviticus 21:2). Since it is derived that it is permitted from that verse, **why do I** need the additional verse: **"For her may he become impure"? To** teach that it is **mandatory.**

וְרַבִּי יִשְׁמָעֵאל? לָהּ מִיטַּמֵּא, וְאֵין מִיטַּמֵּא לְאֵיבָרֶיהָ.

The Gemara asks: **And** how does **Rabbi Yishmael** explain the repetition? The Gemara answers: He explains that the verse teaches that **he may become impure for her, but he may not become impure to** bury only one of **her limbs.**[NH] This additional verse teaches that a priest may become ritually impure to bury a relative only in the case of burying a complete body.

NOTES

But he may not become impure to bury one of her limbs – וְאֵין מִיטַּמֵּא לְאֵיבָרֶיהָ: Rashi interprets this to mean that it is prohibited for a priest to become ritually impure in order to bury a limb detached from a living person, e.g., as a result of illness, amputation, or accident, as a detached limb from a living individual imparts impurity just as does a limb from a corpse. The *Tosefot HaRosh* notes that the same would be the case with regard to a limb from a corpse.

HALAKHA

He may not become impure to bury one of her limbs – אֵין מִיטַּמֵּא לְאֵיבָרֶיהָ: It is prohibited for a priest to contract ritual impurity as a result of burying a limb from a living relative, and it is also prohibited for him to bury any of his relatives' bones. A priest is also prohibited from becoming ritually impure to bury the corpse of a relative if one of the deceased's limbs is missing, as it is permitted for a priest to become ritually impure only to bury a complete corpse.

There are those who say that the prohibition against becoming ritually impure to bury the corpse of a relative that is missing a limb applies only if the limb was detached after death. If, however, the deceased was missing a limb while alive, then the priest may become ritually impure to bury the corpse. The Rema records an opinion that a priest may not become ritually impure to bury the corpse of a relative who was decapitated, as the corpse is missing a limb, and he rules that it is proper to be stringent in this matter. All these limitations refer to instances where there are others to tend to the corpse. However, for a corpse with no one available to bury it, a priest may become ritually impure in all cases, even in the case of one who is not a relative (Rambam *Sefer Shofetim*, *Hilkhot Evel* 2:14–15; *Shulḥan Arukh*, *Yoreh De'a* 373:9).

Perek **I**
Daf **3** Amud **b**

וְרַבִּי עֲקִיבָא? אִם כֵּן, לִיכְתּוֹב רַחֲמָנָא ״לָהּ״ וְלִישְׁתּוֹק, ״יִטַּמָּא״ לָמָּה לִי? שְׁמַע מִינָּהּ.

And what does **Rabbi Akiva** respond to this claim? The Gemara answers: **If so,** that the verse serves to render it prohibited for a priest to become impure to bury a limb, then **let the Merciful One write:** "And for his sister a virgin, that is near to him, that has had no husband, **for her,"** **and** then **be silent. Why do I** need the verse to write: **"May he become impure"? Learn from** the additional phrase that making himself impure is mandatory.

וְרַבִּי יִשְׁמָעֵאל? אַיְּידֵי דִּכְתַב ״לָהּ״, כְּתַב נַמִּי ״יִטַּמָּא״; לִכְדְתָנֵי דְּבֵי רַבִּי יִשְׁמָעֵאל, דְּתָנָא דְּבֵי רַבִּי יִשְׁמָעֵאל: כׇּל פָּרָשָׁה שֶׁנֶּאֶמְרָה וְנִשְׁנֵית, לֹא נִשְׁנֵית אֶלָּא בִּשְׁבִיל דָּבָר שֶׁנִּתְחַדֵּשׁ בָּהּ.

And how does **Rabbi Yishmael** explain the additional phrase? **Since** the verse **wrote: "For her,"** it **also wrote: "May he become impure," for** the same reason **as was taught by the school of Rabbi Yishmael. As the school of Rabbi Yishmael taught: Every passage** in the Torah **that was stated and repeated, was repeated only for the novel element introduced therein.** Therefore, it is possible that the verse serves to teach the *halakha* that a priest may not become impure in order to bury a limb, and that would account for the repetition of the phrase "may he become impure" as well.

״לְעֹלָם בָּהֶם תַּעֲבֹדוּ״ – רְשׁוּת דִּבְרֵי רַבִּי יִשְׁמָעֵאל, רַבִּי עֲקִיבָא אוֹמֵר: חוֹבָה.

The Gemara discusses the third dispute between Rabbi Yishmael and Rabbi Akiva. The verse states: **"Of them may you take your bondmen forever"** (Leviticus 25:46), i.e., the *halakha* that one keeps his Canaanite slave forever, is **optional;** this is **the statement of Rabbi Yishmael.** One is not enjoined against emancipating a Canaanite slave, but one is permitted to keep a Canaanite slave forever. **Rabbi Akiva says:** It is **mandatory,** and one is prohibited from freeing his Canaanite slave.

מַאי טַעְמָא דְּרַבִּי יִשְׁמָעֵאל? אַיְּידֵי דִּכְתִיב: ״לֹא תְחַיֶּה כׇּל נְשָׁמָה״, אִיצְטְרִיךְ נַמִּי לְמִיכְתַּב ״לְעֹלָם בָּהֶם תַּעֲבֹדוּ״, לְמִישְׁרֵי אֶחָד מִכׇּל הָאוּמּוֹת שֶׁבָּא עַל הַכְּנַעֲנִית וְהוֹלִיד מִמֶּנָּה בֵּן, שֶׁאַתָּה רַשַּׁאי לִקְנוֹתוֹ.

What is the reason of Rabbi Yishmael? Since it is written with regard to Canaanites: **"You shall save alive nothing that breathes"** (Deuteronomy 20:16), **it was necessary to write: "Of them may you take your bondmen forever"** (Leviticus 25:46), **as well,** in order **to permit one from any of the** other, non-Canaanite **nations who engaged in sexual intercourse with a Canaanite woman and she bore him a child.** This verse teaches **that you are permitted to purchase** the child as a slave, as he is not included in the mitzva "You shall save alive nothing that breathes" that was stated with regard to full-fledged Canaanites. Therefore, this verse cannot be teaching that it is mandatory.

דְּתַנְיָא: מִנַּיִן לְאֶחָד מִן הָאוּמּוֹת שֶׁבָּא עַל הַכְּנַעֲנִית וְהוֹלִיד מִמֶּנָּה בֵּן, שֶׁאַתָּה רַשַּׁאי לִקְנוֹתוֹ בְּעֶבֶד? תַּלְמוּד לוֹמַר: "וְגַם מִבְּנֵי הַתּוֹשָׁבִים הַגָּרִים עִמָּכֶם מֵהֶם תִּקְנוּ".

This is **as it is taught** in a *baraita*: **From where** is it derived **that** in the case of **one from** any of **the** other, non-Canaanite **nations**[H] **who engaged in sexual intercourse with a Canaanite woman, and she bore him a child, that you are permitted to purchase** the child **as a slave? The verse states: "Moreover, of the children of the strangers that do sojourn among you, of them may you buy"** (Leviticus 25:45). This verse permits the purchase of slaves from among those individuals who are not members of the Canaanite nations, even if they settle in Eretz Yisrael.

יָכוֹל אַף הַכְּנַעֲנִי שֶׁבָּא עַל אַחַת מִן הָאוּמּוֹת וְהוֹלִיד מִמֶּנָּה בֵּן, שֶׁאַתָּה רַשַּׁאי לִקְנוֹתוֹ בְּעֶבֶד? תַּלְמוּד לוֹמַר: "אֲשֶׁר הוֹלִידוּ בְּאַרְצְכֶם", מִן הַנּוֹלָדִים בְּאַרְצְכֶם וְלֹא מִן הַגָּרִים בְּאַרְצְכֶם.

The *baraita* continues: One **might** have thought that **even** in the case of **a Canaanite** man **who engaged in sexual intercourse with a woman from** one of **the** other **nations and she bore him a child, that you are permitted to purchase** the child **as a slave,** despite the fact that his father is a Canaanite. Therefore, **the** same **verse states: "Which they have given birth to in your land,"** teaching that one is permitted to purchase slaves only **from the** ones who are **born in your land** but whose paternal origins are from other lands, **but not from the** ones who already **reside**[N] **in your land,** i.e., ones who have a Canaanite father.

וְרַבִּי עֲקִיבָא? מִ"מֵּהֶם תִּקְנוּ" נָפְקָא. "לְעֹלָם בָּהֶם תַּעֲבֹדוּ" לָמָּה לִי? לְחוֹבָה.

The Gemara asks: **And** how does **Rabbi Akiva** derive this *halakha*? The Gemara answers: He **derives** it **from** the words in the same verse: **"Of them may you buy."** Once the *halakha* is already taught that one may purchase as a slave the child of a Canaanite woman and a man from another nation, **why do I** need the verse to state: **"Of them may you take your bondmen forever"** (Leviticus 25:46)? It is stated **to** teach that it is **mandatory** to enslave a Canaanite slave forever.

וְרַבִּי יִשְׁמָעֵאל? "בָּהֶם" – וְלֹא בַּאֲחֵיכֶם.

The Gemara asks: **And** what does **Rabbi Yishmael** derive from this verse? The Gemara answers: "Of them may you take your bondmen forever," teaches that you can enslave **"of them," but not of your brethren,** i.e., it is prohibited to enslave a fellow Jew, even a slave, forever.

וְרַבִּי עֲקִיבָא? בַּאֲחֵיכֶם מִסֵּיפָא דִּקְרָא נָפְקָא: "וּבְאַחֵיכֶם בְּנֵי יִשְׂרָאֵל אִישׁ בְּאָחִיו לֹא תִרְדֶּה בוֹ בְּפָרֶךְ".

The Gemara asks: **And** how does **Rabbi Akiva** derive this *halakha*? The Gemara answers: The prohibition against enslaving **your brethren is derived from the latter** phrase **of the verse,** where it is explicitly stated: **"But over your brethren the children of Israel you shall not rule, one over another, with rigor"** (Leviticus 25:46).

וְרַבִּי יִשְׁמָעֵאל? אַיְּידֵי דִּכְתִיב "וּבְאַחֵיכֶם", כְּתִיב נַמִי "בָּהֶם"; לְכִדְתָנֵי דְּבֵי רַבִּי יִשְׁמָעֵאל, דְּתָנָא דְּבֵי רַבִּי יִשְׁמָעֵאל: כָּל פָּרָשָׁה שֶׁנֶּאֶמְרָה וְנִישְׁנֵית, לֹא נִישְׁנֵית אֶלָּא בִּשְׁבִיל דָּבָר שֶׁנִּתְחַדֵּשׁ בָּהּ.

The Gemara asks: **And** what does **Rabbi Yishmael** derive from this verse? The Gemara answers: He holds that **since it is written: "But over your brethren,"** which explicitly states that it is prohibited to subjugate a Jew forever, **it also writes** with regard to Canaanites **"of them,"** but that phrase does not teach any novel *halakha*, **because of** the reason **that was taught by the school of Rabbi Yishmael. As the school of Rabbi Yishmael taught: Every passage** in the Torah **that was stated and repeated, was repeated only for the novel element introduced therein.** Therefore, it is possible that the verse serves to teach the *halakha* that one may enslave a Canaanite forever, and that would account for the ostensibly superfluous phrase "of them."

HALAKHA

One from the nations, etc. – אֶחָד מִן הָאוּמּוֹת וכו׳: The Rambam writes that when a man from another nation engages in sexual intercourse with the female Canaanite slave of a Jew, their child is a Canaanite slave. By contrast, if a male Canaanite slave of a Jew engages in sexual intercourse with a gentile woman, their child is not a Canaanite slave. The Ra'avad, in agreement with Rashi, disagrees with this interpretation, based on the Gemara here. Apparently, the Rambam interpreted this passage as discussing the principles of determining lineage, rather than discussing the *halakhot* of whom one may own as a slave. The *Kesef Mishne* explains that the Rambam had a different text of the Gemara. The *Leḥem Mishne* holds that the Rambam agrees that the *baraita* is primarily addressing the issue of whether one is allowed to let different Canaanite children live as slaves, and his conclusions with regard to lineage are not connected to this Gemara (Rambam *Sefer Kinyan*, *Hilkhot Avadim* 9:3).

NOTES

Not from the ones who already reside, etc. – לֹא מִן הַגָּרִים וכו׳: The distinction is between those who were born in Eretz Yisrael to fathers from other nations and those children of Canaanite males who had resided in Eretz Yisrael. The Meiri explains that it was common for a husband to reside in his wife's homeland. As such, it was common for there to be children born of Canaanite women whose fathers were not Canaanites, and conversely, it was common for there to be children of Canaanite men who married non-Canaanite women. *Tosafot* explain that this is the source of the principle that the genealogy of the father is the deciding factor in determining the lineage of gentile children.

אָמַר רַב חִסְדָּא: זְנוּתָא בְּבֵיתָא – כִּי קַרְיָא לְשׁוּמְשְׁמָא. וְאָמַר רַב חִסְדָּא: תּוּקְפָּא בְּבֵיתָא – כִּי קַרְיָא לְשׁוּמְשְׁמָא. אִידִי וְאִידִי בְּאִיתְּתָא, אֲבָל בְּגַבְרָא לֵית לַן בָּהּ.

§ The Gemara discusses matters related to sin and sexual impropriety. **Rav Ḥisda says: Licentious** behavior **in a home** causes damage **like a worm** [*karya*][L] causes damage **to sesame** [***shumeshema***].[N] **And Rav Ḥisda says: Anger in a home**[N] causes damage **like a worm** causes damage **to sesame.** The Gemara comments: Both **this and that,** i.e., that licentious behavior and anger destroy a home, were said **with regard to the woman** of the house, **but with regard to the man,** although these behaviors are improper, **we do not have** the same extreme consequences **with regard to it,** as the woman's role in the home is more significant, resulting in a more detrimental result if she acts improperly.

וְאָמַר רַב חִסְדָּא: בַּתְּחִילָּה קוֹדֶם שֶׁחָטְאוּ יִשְׂרָאֵל, הָיְתָה שְׁכִינָה שׁוֹרָה עִם כָּל אֶחָד וְאֶחָד, שֶׁנֶּאֱמַר: "כִּי ה׳ אֱלֹהֶיךָ מִתְהַלֵּךְ בְּקֶרֶב מַחֲנֶךָ". כֵּיוָן שֶׁחָטְאוּ נִסְתַּלְּקָה שְׁכִינָה מֵהֶם, שֶׁנֶּאֱמַר: "וְלֹא יִרְאֶה בְךָ עֶרְוַת דָּבָר וְשָׁב מֵאַחֲרֶיךָ".

And Rav Ḥisda says: Initially, before the Jewish people sinned, the Divine Presence resided with each and every one[N] of them, **as it is stated: "For the Lord your God walks in the midst of your camp"** (Deuteronomy 23:15). **Once they sinned, the Divine Presence withdrew from them, as it is stated** in that same verse: **"That He see no unseemly matter in you, and turn away from you"** (Deuteronomy 23:15), teaching that when there is an "unseemly matter" among the Jewish people, the Divine Presence no longer resides among them.

אָמַר רַבִּי שְׁמוּאֵל בַּר נַחְמָנִי אָמַר רַבִּי יוֹנָתָן: כָּל הָעוֹשֶׂה מִצְוָה אַחַת בָּעוֹלָם הַזֶּה – מְקַדַּמְתּוֹ וְהוֹלֶכֶת לְפָנָיו לָעוֹלָם הַבָּא, שֶׁנֶּאֱמַר: "וְהָלַךְ לְפָנֶיךָ צִדְקֶךָ", וְכָל הָעוֹבֵר עֲבֵירָה אַחַת בָּעוֹלָם הַזֶּה – מְלַפַּפְתּוֹ וְהוֹלֶכֶת לְפָנָיו לְיוֹם הַדִּין, שֶׁנֶּאֱמַר: "יִלָּפְתוּ אָרְחוֹת דַּרְכָּם יַעֲלוּ בַתֹּהוּ וְיֹאבֵדוּ".

Rabbi Shmuel bar Naḥmani says that **Rabbi Yonatan says: Anyone who fulfills one mitzva in this world,** that mitzva **precedes him and goes before him to the World-to-Come, as it is stated: "And your righteousness shall go before you,** the glory of the Lord shall be your reward" (Isaiah 58:8). **And anyone who commits one transgression in this world, it shrouds him and goes before him to the Day of Judgment, as it is stated: "The paths of their way do wind, they go up into the waste, and are lost"** (Job 6:18).

רַבִּי אֶלְעָזָר אוֹמֵר: קְשׁוּרָה בּוֹ כְּכֶלֶב, שֶׁנֶּאֱמַר: "וְלֹא שָׁמַע אֵלֶיהָ לִשְׁכַּב אֶצְלָהּ לִהְיוֹת עִמָּהּ", "לִשְׁכַּב אֶצְלָהּ" – בָּעוֹלָם הַזֶּה, "לִהְיוֹת עִמָּהּ" – לָעוֹלָם הַבָּא.

Rabbi Elazar says: The transgression **is chained to him** and accompanies him **like a dog, as it is stated** concerning Joseph's refusal to commit adultery with the wife of Potiphar: **"That he listened not to her, to lie by her, or to be with her"** (Genesis 39:10), which is understood to mean: If he would agree **"to lie by her" in this world,** the result would be that he would have **"to be with her"** forever, as the transgression would accompany him **to the World-to-Come.**

תְּנַן הָתָם: שֶׁהָיָה בַּדִּין:

§ The Gemara returns to its discussion of the number of witnesses necessary for different elements of the process of a woman becoming a *sota*. **We learned** in a mishna **elsewhere** (31a) with regard to the credibility of one witness who testifies concerning a woman's infidelity: The *halakha* that one witness is deemed credible concerning defilement needs to be stated, **as, by right,** it **should** not **have been** deemed credible based on the following *a fortiori* inference:

LANGUAGE

Worm [*karya*] – קַרְיָא: The root of this word and its meaning are not clear. It has been suggested that it is based on the Latin caries, meaning lack, rot, or decay.

NOTES

Like a worm [*karya*] to sesame [*shumeshema*] – כִּי קַרְיָא לְשׁוּמְשְׁמָא: Rashi explains this to mean: Like a worm consuming sesame. The *Arukh* explains similarly, though he may understand *karya* as referring to decay or spoilage. Others hold that the word *shumeshema* refers to the worm itself and *karya* means the heat or cold that kills the worm (*Tosefot HaRash*).

Anger in a home – תּוּקְפָּא בְּבֵיתָא: Rashi translates this as anger, and the *Arukh* similarly defines it as strife. According to Rashi this means that the woman is easily angered and quarrelsome. The Meiri explains that a woman who is constantly angered by her husband may neglect her household chores.

The Divine Presence resided with each and every one, etc. – הָיְתָה שְׁכִינָה שׁוֹרָה עִם כָּל אֶחָד וְאֶחָד וכו׳: The Meiri explains this passage in a general sense, that divine providence is granted to those who act properly. One who transgresses loses this divine providence, and this, in and of itself, is a punishment for the transgression. In addition, one who transgresses will be judged in the World-to-Come.

וּמָה עֵדוּת הָרִאשׁוֹנָה שֶׁאֵין אוֹסַרְתָּהּ אִיסּוּר עוֹלָם – אֵינָהּ מִתְקַיֶּימֶת בְּפָחוּת מִשְּׁנַיִם; עֵדוּת הָאַחֲרוֹנָה שֶׁאוֹסַרְתָּהּ אִיסּוּר עוֹלָם – אֵינוֹ דִּין שֶׁלֹּא תִּתְקַיֵּים בְּפָחוּת מִשְּׁנַיִם?

And just as with regard to **the first testimony** concerning seclusion, **which does not forbid her** to her husband with **an irrevocable prohibition,** as the woman can be found innocent, permitting her again to her husband by drinking the bitter water, it **is not established with fewer than two** witnesses, as that mishna is written in accordance with the opinion of Rabbi Yehoshua, who stated (2a) that testimony of two witnesses must be provided by two witnesses, then with regard to **the final testimony** concerning defilement, **which forbids her** with **an irrevocable prohibition, is it not logical that it not be established with fewer than two** witnesses?

תַּלְמוּד לוֹמַר: "וְעֵד אֵין בָּהּ", כָּל שֶׁיֵּשׁ בָּהּ.

Therefore, to counter this derivation, **the verse states: "And there is no witness against her"** (Numbers 5:13), teaching that **any** testimony **that there is against her** with regard to her defilement is sufficient, and two witnesses are not required.

וְקַל וָחוֹמֶר לְעֵדוּת הָרִאשׁוֹנָה מֵעַתָּה: וּמָה עֵדוּת הָאַחֲרוֹנָה שֶׁאוֹסַרְתָּהּ אִיסּוּר עוֹלָם – מִתְקַיֶּימֶת בְּעֵד אֶחָד; עֵדוּת הָרִאשׁוֹנָה שֶׁאֵין אוֹסַרְתָּהּ אִיסּוּר עוֹלָם – אֵינוֹ דִּין שֶׁתִּתְקַיֵּים בְּעֵד אֶחָד?

The mishna asks: **And now** that it is established that one witness suffices to testify with regard to defilement, **an *a fortiori*** inference can be made **with regard to the first testimony** of seclusion: **And just as** with regard to **the final testimony** concerning defilement, **which forbids her** with **an irrevocable prohibition,** yet it **is established with one witness,** then with regard to **the first testimony, which does not forbid her** with **an irrevocable prohibition, is it not logical that it should be established with** only **one witness?**

תַּלְמוּד לוֹמַר: "כִּי מָצָא בָהּ עֶרְוַת דָּבָר", וּלְהַלָּן הוּא אוֹמֵר: "עַל פִּי שְׁנֵי עֵדִים אוֹ עַל פִּי שְׁלֹשָׁה עֵדִים יָקוּם דָּבָר". מַה דָּבָר הָאָמוּר לְהַלָּן עַל פִּי שְׁנַיִם עֵדִים, אַף כָּאן עַל פִּי שְׁנַיִם.

Therefore, to counter this derivation, **the verse states:** "If a man marries a woman and lives with her and it will be that she not find favor in his eyes, **because he has found some unseemly matter [*davar*] about her"** (Deuteronomy 24:1), **and there,** in the verses concerning the *halakhot* of monetary matters, **it states: "By the mouth of two witnesses or by the mouth of three witnesses shall a matter [*davar*] be established"** (Deuteronomy 19:15). This teaches that **just as** the **"matter" stated there** is established **by the mouth of two witnesses, so too here,** the "matter" of her seclusion must be established **by the mouth of two** witnesses.

הַאי מִ"כִּי מָצָא בָהּ עֶרְוַת דָּבָר" נָפְקָא? מִ"בָּהּ" נָפְקָא: "בָּהּ" – וְלֹא בְּקִינּוּי, "בָּהּ" – וְלֹא בִּסְתִירָה, מִיבָּעֵי לֵיהּ!

The Gemara asks: Is **this** need for two witnesses **derived from: "Because he has found some unseemly matter about her"** (Deuteronomy 24:1)? **It is derived from:** "And there is no witness [*ed*] **against her [*bah*]"** (Numbers 5:13), which was explained to mean there were not two witnesses, but only one, who testified concerning her defilement (2a). The Gemara above (2b) derives from the term "*bah*," which could also be understood as: **With regard to it,** that in this matter of defilement one witness suffices, **but not with regard to the warning.** And one also derives: **With regard to it, but not with regard to** the **seclusion.** Therefore, there must be two witnesses to testify about both the warning and the seclusion. The mishna **should have** given this inference as the source for requiring two witnesses for seclusion, and not the juxtaposition of "matter" and "matter."

הָכִי נַמִי קָאָמַר: תַּלְמוּד לוֹמַר: "בָּהּ", "בָּהּ" – וְלֹא בְּקִינּוּי, "בָּהּ" – וְלֹא בִּסְתִירָה.

The Gemara answers: **That is also what he is saying.** The mishna should read: **The verse states:** "And there is no witness **against her [*bah*],"** teaching that: **With regard to it [*bah*], but not with regard to the warning.** And one also derives: **With regard to it, but not with regard to** the **seclusion.**

וְטוּמְאָה בְּעָלְמָא בְּלֹא קִינּוּי וּבְלֹא סְתִירָה דְּלָא מְהֵימַן עֵד אֶחָד מְנָלַן? נֶאֱמַר כָּאן: "כִּי מָצָא בָהּ עֶרְוַת דָּבָר", וְנֶאֱמַר לְהַלָּן: "עַל פִּי שְׁנֵי עֵדִים אוֹ עַל פִּי שְׁלֹשָׁה עֵדִים יָקוּם דָּבָר". מַה "דָּבָר" הָאָמוּר לְהַלָּן עֵדִים שְׁנַיִם, אַף כָּאן עֵדִים שְׁנַיִם.

The Gemara comments: **And** with regard to **defilement in general, without** a prior **warning and without** witnesses to **seclusion, from where do we** derive **that one witness is not deemed credible? Here it is stated: "Because he has found some unseemly matter about her"** (Deuteronomy 24:1), **and there it is stated: "By the mouth of two witnesses or by the mouth of three witnesses shall a matter be established"** (Deuteronomy 19:15), teaching that **just as** the **"matter" stated there** is established by **two witnesses, so too here,** with regard to defilement it is established by **two witnesses.**

תָּנוּ רַבָּנַן: אֵי זוֹ הִיא עֵדוּת הָרִאשׁוֹנָה? זוֹ עֵדוּת סְתִירָה. עֵדוּת אַחֲרוֹנָה? זוֹ עֵדוּת טוּמְאָה.

The Sages taught (*Tosefta* 1:1): In the mishna quoted above, **which is the first testimony? This** is referring to the **testimony of seclusion.** Which is **the final testimony? This** is referring to the **testimony of defilement.**

וְכַמָּה שִׁיעוּר סְתִירָה? כְּדֵי טוּמְאָה, כְּדֵי בִּיאָה, כְּדֵי הַעֲרָאָה,

The *baraita* clarifies: **And what is the measure of seclusion,**[H] i.e., how is the seclusion of a *sota* defined? The measure of seclusion is **equivalent** to the time needed for **defilement,** which is **equivalent** to the time needed to perform **intercourse,** which is **equivalent** to the time needed to perform the **initial stage of intercourse.**[N]

כְּדֵי הַקָּפַת דֶּקֶל, דִּבְרֵי רַבִּי יִשְׁמָעֵאל; רַבִּי אֱלִיעֶזֶר אוֹמֵר: כְּדֵי מְזִיגַת הַכּוֹס; רַבִּי יְהוֹשֻׁעַ אוֹמֵר: כְּדֵי לְשָׁתוֹתוֹ;

The *baraita* quotes several practical examples of this period of time. This is **equivalent** to the time needed for **circling a palm** tree; this is **the statement of Rabbi Yishmael. Rabbi Eliezer says:** This is **equivalent** to the time needed **for mixing a cup** of wine with water, with the total volume of a quarter-*log*. **Rabbi Yehoshua says:** This is **equivalent** to the time needed **to drink** that cup of wine.

בֶּן עַזַּאי אוֹמֵר: כְּדֵי לִצְלוֹת בֵּיצָה; רַבִּי עֲקִיבָא אוֹמֵר: כְּדֵי לְגוֹמְעָהּ; רַבִּי יְהוּדָה בֶּן בְּתֵירָא אוֹמֵר: כְּדֵי לִגְמוֹעַ שָׁלֹשׁ בֵּיצִים זוֹ אַחַר זוֹ; רַבִּי אֶלְעָזָר בֶּן יִרְמְיָה אוֹמֵר: כְּדֵי לִקְשׁוֹר גַּרְדִּי נִימָא;

The *baraita* quotes several more examples. **Ben Azzai says:** This is **equivalent** to the time needed **to roast an egg.**[N] **Rabbi Akiva says:** This is **equivalent** to the time needed **to swallow it. Rabbi Yehuda ben Beteira says:** This is **equivalent** to the time needed **to swallow three eggs one after another. Rabbi Elazar ben Yirmeya says:** This is **equivalent** to the time needed for **a weaver** [*gardi*][L] **to tie a string** [*nima*].[L]

חָנִין בֶּן פִּנְחָס אוֹמֵר: כְּדֵי שֶׁתּוֹשִׁיט יָדָהּ לְתוֹךְ פִּיהָ לִיטּוֹל קֵיסָם; פְּלֵימוֹ אוֹמֵר: כְּדֵי שֶׁתּוֹשִׁיט יָדָהּ לַסַּל לִיטּוֹל כִּכָּר. אַף עַל פִּי שֶׁאֵין רְאָיָה לַדָּבָר – זֵכֶר לַדָּבָר: ״כִּי בְעַד אִשָּׁה זוֹנָה עַד כִּכַּר לָחֶם״.

Ḥanin ben Pineḥas says: This is **equivalent** to the time **that** a woman **may** need to **extend her hand into her mouth to remove a wood chip** from between her teeth. The Sage **Peleimu**[P] **says:** This is **equivalent** to the time **that she may** need to **extend her hand into a basket** in order **to take a loaf** of bread. He adds: **Although there is no** explicit **proof**[N] from a verse **for the matter,** there is **an allusion to the matter** from the verse: **"For on account of a harlot a man is brought to a loaf of bread"** (Proverbs 6:26).

וְכׇל הָנֵי לָמָּה לִי?

The *baraita* stated that the measure of seclusion is equivalent to the time needed for defilement, which is equivalent to the time needed to perform sexual intercourse, which is equivalent to the time needed to perform the initial stage of intercourse, and it added nine practical examples of that length of time. The Gemara asks: **And why do I** need **all these** times when one should have sufficed?

צְרִיכִי, דְּאִי תְּנָא כְּדֵי טוּמְאָה, הֲוָה אָמֵינָא כְּדֵי טוּמְאָתָהּ וְאַרְצוּיָתָהּ, קָא מַשְׁמַע לַן כְּדֵי בִּיאָה.

The Gemara answers: All three **are necessary, as if** the *baraita* **taught** only: **Equivalent** to the time needed for **defilement, I would say** that the measure is **equivalent** to the time for **her defilement and her appeasement,** i.e., the amount of time needed to convince her to engage in sexual intercourse. Therefore, the *baraita* **teaches us** that the measure is **equivalent** to the time needed to perform **sexual intercourse** alone.

וְאִי תְּנָא כְּדֵי בִיאָה, הֲוָה אָמֵינָא כְּדֵי גְּמַר בִּיאָה, קָא מַשְׁמַע לַן כְּדֵי הַעֲרָאָה.

And if the *baraita* **taught** only: The measure of seclusion is **equivalent** to the time needed to perform **sexual intercourse, I would say** that the measure is **equivalent** to the time needed for the **completion of** the act of **intercourse.** Therefore, the *baraita* **teaches us** that the measure is **equivalent** to the time needed to perform the **initial stage of intercourse.**

וְאִי אַשְׁמְעִינַן כְּדֵי הַעֲרָאָה, הֲוָה אָמֵינָא כְּדֵי הַעֲרָאָה וְאַרְצוּיָתָהּ, קָא מַשְׁמַע לַן כְּדֵי טוּמְאָה. וְכַמָּה כְּדֵי [הַעֲרָאָה]? כְּדֵי הַקָּפַת דֶּקֶל.

And if the *baraita* **taught** only: The measure of seclusion is **equivalent** to the time needed to perform the **initial stage of intercourse, I would say** that the measure is **equivalent** to the time needed to perform the **initial stage of intercourse and her appeasement.**[N] Therefore, the *baraita* **teaches us** that the measure is **equivalent** to the time needed for **defilement,** which does not include appeasement. The *baraita* concludes by offering a practical measure: **And what is the measure** of the **equivalent** amount of time needed to perform the **initial stage of intercourse?** It is **equivalent** to the time needed for **circling a palm** tree. Other Sages then offered their own practical examples.

HALAKHA

Measure of seclusion – שִׁיעוּר סְתִירָה: The seclusion of a *sota* is defined as when witnesses see a woman secluded with a man with whom her husband had warned her not to be secluded. The duration of the seclusion is the time needed for defilement, which is equivalent to the time required for roasting and swallowing an egg. This ruling is in accordance with the opinion of Rabbi Akiva, whose opinion is accepted when he is involved in a dispute with others (Rambam *Sefer Nashim, Hilkhot Sota* 1:2; *Shulḥan Arukh, Even HaEzer* 178:4).

NOTES

Equivalent to the time needed to perform the initial stage of intercourse – כְּדֵי הַעֲרָאָה: Rashi here defines the initial stage of intercourse as the initial contact between the male and female sexual organs. Most commentaries, however, accept the opposing opinion in tractate *Yevamot* (55b), which defines the initial stage of intercourse as the insertion of the corona.

To roast an egg – לִצְלוֹת בֵּיצָה: In the Jerusalem Talmud the expression used is: Equivalent to the time needed to roll an egg, which involves roasting an egg slightly to the point where it will roll easily. This is a more precise measurement of time than that of the time needed to roast an egg.

Although there is no explicit proof, etc. – אַף עַל פִּי שֶׁאֵין רְאָיָה וכו׳: This phrase, which is found in several places in the Talmud, indicates that the quoted verse cannot serve as a definitive proof, as it does not relate directly to the matter under discussion. However, the verse does present a verbal linkage or an association in meaning to the matter and is worth noting.

I would say the equivalent to the time needed to perform the initial stage of intercourse and her appeasement – הֲוָה אָמֵינָא כְּדֵי הַעֲרָאָה וְאַרְצוּיָתָהּ: *Tosafot* cite the Jerusalem Talmud, where it is explicitly stated that all these measures of time refer only to the time necessary for the defilement itself. As such, one must add the measure of time needed for the woman to remove her undergarments. It is discussed in the *Torat HaKenaot* whether this should be understood as disagreeing with the measures stated here in that it requires additional time, or whether it may be that the Babylonian Talmud is discussing a case where her undergarments had been removed prior to the seclusion, and therefore only the actual time needed for the act of sexual intercourse itself is listed.

LANGUAGE

Weaver [*gardi*] – גַּרְדִּי: From the Greek γέρδιός, *gerdios*, meaning weaver.

String [*nima*] – נִימָא: From the Greek νῆμα, *nēma*, meaning string.

PERSONALITIES

Peleimu – פְּלֵימוֹ: The Sage Peleimu was one of the prized students of Rabbi Yehuda HaNasi, and in several instances he is quoted as asking his teacher brilliant questions. Several of his statements are recorded in *baraitot*, where he often disagrees with Rabbi Eliezer, son of Rabbi Shimon, another student of Rabbi Yehuda HaNasi. There are also a number of narratives in the Talmud describing his great righteousness.

BACKGROUND

Shall stand [*teiku*] – תיקו: Various explanations have been offered with regard to the etymology of this term. One explanation is that the word is an abbreviated form of the word *tikom*, meaning let it stand. Another explanation is that its source is the word *tik*, meaning a case or pouch. Just as upon seeing a case or pouch one is unsure of its contents, so too, the word *teiku* is used in a situation where a resolution is unknown to us, as if the solution were hidden inside a case (*Arukh*). Although not the literal meaning, some suggest that the term *teiku* is an allusion to the acrostic for the phrase: The Tishbite, i.e., Elijah the prophet, will resolve questions and dilemmas (*Tosefot Yom Tov*). This is in reference to the tradition that when Elijah returns to the Jewish people to herald the advent of the Messiah he will also reveal the solutions to outstanding halakhic difficulties.

ורמינהי: "ונסתרה" – וכמה שיעור סתירה לא שמענו. כשהוא אומר "והיא נטמאה", הוי אומר: כדי טומאה, כדי ביאה, כדי העראה, כדי חזרת דקל, דברי רבי אליעזר;

And the Gemara **raises a contradiction** from a different *baraita* (*Tosefta* 1:2): The verse states: "**And she was** defiled **secretly**" (Numbers 5:13), **and we have not heard what is the measure** of **seclusion. When it says** in that verse: "**And she was defiled** secretly," **you must say** that the measure of seclusion is **equivalent** to the time needed for **defilement**, which is **equivalent** to the time needed to perform **sexual intercourse**, which is **equivalent** to the time needed to perform the **initial stage of intercourse**, which is **equivalent** to the time needed for the **returning of a palm** tree; this is **the statement of Rabbi Eliezer.**

רבי יהושע אומר: כדי מזיגת הכוס; בן עזאי אומר: כדי לשתותו; רבי עקיבא אומר: כדי לצלות ביצה; רבי יהודה בן בתירא אומר: כדי לגומעה;

The *baraita* continues: **Rabbi Yehoshua says:** This is **equivalent** to the time needed for **mixing a cup** of wine with water, with the total volume of a quarter-*log*. **Ben Azzai says:** This is **equivalent** to the time needed **to drink** that cup of wine. **Rabbi Akiva says:** This is **equivalent** to the time needed **to roast an egg. Rabbi Yehuda ben Beteira says:** This is **equivalent** to the time needed **to swallow it.**

קא סלקא דעתין היינו הקפת דקל היינו חזרת דקל. התם אמר רבי ישמעאל כדי הקפת דקל ופליג רבי אליעזר עליה. הכא אמר רבי אליעזר כדי חזרת דקל!

The Gemara now addresses several contradictions between this *baraita* and the one quoted earlier. The Gemara first comments: It might **enter our mind** to say that **circling a palm tree is** the same as the **returning of a palm** tree. The Gemara asks: **There,** in the first *baraita*, **Rabbi Yishmael says** it is **equivalent** to the time needed for **circling a palm tree and Rabbi Eliezer disagreed with him,** while **here,** in the second *baraita*, **Rabbi Eliezer** himself **says** it is **equivalent** to the time needed for the **returning of a palm** tree; doesn't this contradict what he stated in the previous *baraita*?

אמר אביי: הקפה ברגל, חזרה ברוח.

To resolve this contradiction, **Abaye says:** These measures are not the same, as **circling** is referring to the amount of time it takes for one to circle a palm tree **by foot,** and **returning** is referring to the amount of time it takes for a palm branch blown **by the wind** to revert to its prior position.

בעי רב אשי: חזרה ברוח כי היכי דאזיל והדר אתי, או דילמא כי היכי דאזיל ואתי והדר קאי בדוכתיה? תיקו.

Rav Ashi asks: This **returning** of the palm branch **by the wind,** is this the time only **so that it goes** forward with the wind **and returns** to its place one time, not including the time it is still moving back and forth due to the wind? **Or perhaps** it is the time **so that it goes** forward with the wind **and comes back and returns** until it **settles in its place.** The Gemara states: The question **shall stand**[B] unresolved.

התם אמר רבי אליעזר: כדי מזיגת הכוס, הכא – כדי חזרת דקל! אידי ואידי חד שיעורא הוא.

The Gemara presents another contradiction. **There,** in the first *baraita*, **Rabbi Eliezer says:** This is **equivalent** to the time needed **for pouring a cup** of wine. **Here,** in the second *baraita*, he says: This is **equivalent** to the time needed for the **returning of a palm** tree. The Gemara answers: **This and that are one,** i.e., the same, **measure.**

התם אמר רבי יהושע: כדי לשתותו, הכא אמר: כדי מזיגת הכוס! אימא: כדי למזוג ולשתות. ולימא: אידי ואידי חד שיעורא הוא! אם כן, היינו רבי אליעזר.

The Gemara presents another contradiction. **There,** in the first *baraita*, **Rabbi Yehoshua says:** This is **equivalent** to the time needed for **drinking** a cup of wine. **Here,** in the second *baraita*, **he says:** This is **equivalent** to the time needed for **mixing a cup** of wine. The Gemara answers: **Say** that he requires both together, i.e., he requires an amount of time **equivalent** to the time needed **to** both **mix and drink** a cup of wine. The Gemara asks: Instead of combining the measures, why not **let us say** that **this and that are one measure?** The Gemara answers: **If so, this is** the same as the opinion of **Rabbi Eliezer** in the first *baraita*, with whom Rabbi Yehoshua disagrees.

התם אמר בן עזאי: כדי לצלות ביצה, הכא אמר: כדי לשתותו! אידי ואידי חד שיעורא הוא.

The Gemara presents another contradiction. **There,** in the first *baraita*, **ben Azzai says:** This is **equivalent** to the time needed **to roast an egg. Here,** in the second *baraita*, **he says:** This is **equivalent** to the time needed **to drink** a cup of wine. The Gemara answers: **This and that are one measure.**

הָתָם אָמַר רַבִּי עֲקִיבָא: כְּדֵי לְגוֹמְעָהּ, הָכָא אָמַר: כְּדֵי לִצְלוֹת בֵּיצָה! אֵימָא: כְּדֵי לִצְלוֹת בֵּיצָה וּלְגוֹמְעָהּ. וְלֵימָא: אִידִי וְאִידִי חַד שִׁיעוּרָא הוּא! אִם כֵּן, הַיְינוּ בֶּן עַזַּאי.

The Gemara presents another contradiction. **There,** in the first *baraita,* **Rabbi Akiva says:** This is **equivalent** to the time needed **to swallow** an egg. **Here,** in the second *baraita,* **he says:** This is **equivalent** to the time needed **to roast an egg.** The Gemara answers: **Say** that he requires both together, i.e., he requires an amount of time **equivalent** to the time needed **to roast an egg and to swallow it.** The Gemara asks: Instead of combining the measures, why not **let us say** that **this and that are one measure?** The Gemara answers: **If so, this is** the same as the opinion of **ben Azzai** in the first *baraita,* with whom Rabbi Akiva disagrees.

הָתָם אָמַר רַבִּי יְהוּדָה בֶּן בְּתֵירָא: כְּדֵי לִגְמוֹעַ שָׁלֹשׁ בֵּיצִים זוֹ אַחַר זוֹ, הָכָא אָמַר: כְּדֵי לְגוֹמְעָהּ! לִדְבָרָיו דְּרַבִּי עֲקִיבָא קָאָמַר, דְּקָאָמַר: מְשַׁעֲרִין בִּצְלִיָּאָה וּבִגְמִיעָה – אֵימָא: שִׁיעוּר גְּמִיעָה לְחוּדָהּ, כְּדֵי לִגְמֹעַ שָׁלֹשׁ בֵּיצִים זוֹ אַחַר זוֹ, דְּהַיְינוּ צְלִיָּאָה וּגְמִיעָה.

The Gemara presents another contradiction. **There,** in the first *baraita,* **Rabbi Yehuda ben Beteira says:** This is **equivalent** to the time needed **to swallow three eggs one after another. Here,** in the second *baraita,* **he says:** This is **equivalent** to the time needed **to swallow** an egg, meaning one egg. The Gemara answers: In the first *baraita,* he did not state his own opinion, but **stated** his opinion **in accordance with the statement of Rabbi Akiva, who stated** that one **measures** according to the time needed **for roasting and swallowing.** Rabbi Yehoshua responded: **Say** instead the **measure** of the time needed for **swallowing alone,** i.e., an amount of time **equivalent** to the time needed to **swallow three eggs one after another, which is** equal to the amount of time necessary for **roasting and swallowing,** and therefore Rabbi Akiva would not need to include roasting in the measurement.

״רַבִּי אֶלְעָזָר בֶּן יִרְמְיָה אוֹמֵר: כְּדֵי שֶׁיִּקְשׁוֹר גַּרְדִּי נִימָא״. בָּעֵי רַב אַשִׁי: דְּמִרְחַק אוֹ דְּמִקְרַב? תֵּיקוּ.

The Gemara discusses an opinion cited in the first *baraita.* **Rabbi Elazar ben Yirmeya says:** This is **equivalent** to the time needed for **a weaver to tie a string. Rav Ashi asks:** Is this speaking of **where** the ends of the string to be tied **are far** apart from each other, **or** is it speaking of **where** they **are near**[NB] to each other? The Gemara states: The question **shall stand** unresolved.

״חָנִין בֶּן פִּנְחָס אוֹמֵר: כְּדֵי שֶׁתּוֹשִׁיט יָדָהּ לְתוֹךְ פִּיהָ לִיטּוֹל קֵיסָם״. בָּעֵי רַב אַשִׁי: דִּמְהַדַּק אוֹ דְּלָא מְהַדַּק? תֵּיקוּ.

The Gemara discusses another opinion cited in the first *baraita.* **Ḥanin ben Pineḥas says:** This is **equivalent** to the time **that** a woman **may** need to **extend her hand into her mouth to remove a wood chip** from between her teeth. **Rav Ashi asks:** Is this speaking of a case **where** the wood chip **is stuck** between her teeth, **or** is it speaking of a case **where** it **is not stuck?** The Gemara states: The question **shall stand** unresolved.

״פְּלֵימוֹ אוֹמֵר: כְּדֵי שֶׁתּוֹשִׁיט יָדָהּ לַסַּל לִיטּוֹל כִּכָּר״. בָּעֵי רַב אַשִׁי: דִּמְהַדַּק אוֹ דְּלָא מְהַדַּק? בְּחַדְתָּא אוֹ בְּעַתִּיקָא? בַּחֲמִימָא אוֹ בִּקְרִירָא?

The Gemara discusses another opinion cited in the first *baraita.* **Peleimu says:** This is **equivalent** to the time **that** a woman **may** need to **extend her hand into a basket** in order **to take a loaf** of bread. **Rav Ashi asks:** Is this speaking of an occasion **where** the loaf **adheres** to the basket, **or** is it speaking of a case **where** it **does not adhere?** Is this speaking of a case **where** the basket is **new,** whereby the tips of the shoots forming the basket might restrain the loaf, **or** this speaking of **where** the basket is **old** and smooth, enabling easy removal? Is this speaking of a case **where** the loaf is **hot** and therefore softer and may adhere to the basket, **or** is this speaking of a case **where** the loaf is **cold** and easily removed?

Perek **I**
Daf **4** Amud **b**

בִּדְחִטֵּי אוֹ בִּדְשַׂעֲרֵי? בְּרַכִּיכָא אוֹ בְּאַקּוּשָׁא? תֵּיקוּ.

Is this speaking of a case **where** the loaf is made **of wheat,** which is slippery and takes longer to remove, **or** is this speaking of a case **where** the loaf is made **of barley,** which is easily removed? Is this speaking of a case **where** the loaf is **soft,** so that it may catch upon the side of the basket, **or** a case **where** the loaf is **hard,** where this is not a concern? The Gemara states: These questions **shall stand** unresolved.

NOTES

Where the ends are far or where they are near – דְּמִרְחַק אוֹ דְּמִקְרַב: *Tosafot* explain that Rav Ashi does not ask about the thickness of the palm tree to be circled or the size of the egg to be roasted, as they were already compared to other measures in the *baraita*. *Tosefot HaRash* explains that in all cases it refers to an average-sized item. The Ya'avetz notes that since the word used here to describe the palm tree, *dekel*, refers specifically to a large palm, as a small palm tree is called by another name, there was no need to clarify further. Others explain that there was no need to clarify further because the palm is thick enough that it must be circled by foot (*Meromei Sadeh*).

BACKGROUND

Where the ends are far or where they are near – דְּמִרְחַק אוֹ דְּמִקְרַב: Since all the estimates of time for defilement are extremely short, the difference between them can be a matter of seconds. Therefore, it was necessary to attempt to give as precise a measure as possible, leading to these very specific questions.

אָמַר רַב יִצְחָק בַּר רַב יוֹסֵף אָמַר רַבִּי יוֹחָנָן: כׇּל אֶחָד וְאֶחָד בְּעַצְמוֹ שִׁיעֵר. וְהָאִיכָּא בֶּן עַזַּאי דְּלָא נְסֵיב!

The Gemara notes: **Rav Yitzḥak bar Rav Yosef says that Rabbi Yoḥanan says: Each and every one** of these Sages who presented an opinion with regard to the time needed for the initial stage of intercourse **estimated based on himself,** i.e., based on his own experience. The Gemara asks: **But there is ben Azzai,**[P] **who did not marry,** so how could he estimate based on his own experience?

אִיבָּעֵית אֵימָא: נְסֵיב וּפֵירֵשׁ הֲוָה; וְאִיבָּעֵית אֵימָא: מֵרַבֵּיהּ שְׁמִיעַ לֵיהּ; וְאִיבָּעֵית אֵימָא: ״סוֹד ה׳ לִירֵאָיו״.

The Gemara answers: **If you wish, say** that **he was married and separated** from his wife. **And if you wish, say** that **he heard from his teacher. And if you wish, say** his knowledge can be understood based on the verse: **"The counsel of the Lord is with them that fear Him"** (Psalms 25:14), teaching that those who fear God are privy to knowledge beyond their personal experience.

דָּרַשׁ רַב עֲוִירָא, זִמְנִין אֲמַר לָהּ מִשְּׁמֵיהּ דְּרַבִּי אַמִי, וְזִמְנִין אֲמַר לָהּ מִשְּׁמֵיהּ דְּרַבִּי אַסִי: כׇּל הָאוֹכֵל לֶחֶם בְּלֹא נְטִילַת יָדַיִם – כְּאִילּוּ בָּא עַל אִשָּׁה זוֹנָה, שֶׁנֶּאֱמַר: ״כִּי בְעַד אִשָּׁה זוֹנָה עַד כִּכַּר לָחֶם״.

§ Having quoted an allusion from the verse: "For on account of a harlot a man is brought to a loaf of bread" (Proverbs 6:26), the Gemara offers another interpretation of that verse. **Rav Avira interpreted** a verse **homiletically;** there were **times he said** this interpretation **in the name of Rabbi Ami and** there were **times he said it in the name of Rabbi Asi:** Concerning **anyone who eats bread without washing** his **hands,** it is as if he **engaged in sexual intercourse with a prostitute,**[N] **as it is stated: "For on account of a harlot a man is brought to a loaf of bread."**

אֲמַר רָבָא: הַאי ״בְּעַד אִשָּׁה זוֹנָה עַד כִּכַּר לָחֶם״, ״בְּעַד כִּכַּר לֶחֶם עַד אִשָּׁה זוֹנָה״ מִיבָּעֵי לֵיהּ! אֶלָּא אֲמַר רָבָא: כׇּל הַבָּא עַל אִשָּׁה זוֹנָה – לְסוֹף מְבַקֵּשׁ כִּכַּר לֶחֶם.

Rava said: This phrase: **"For on account of a harlot a man is brought to a loaf of bread,"** is not how the verse would present this idea. **It should have** stated: **"On account of a loaf a man is brought to a harlot." Rather, Rava says** the verse should be interpreted as follows: **Anyone who engages in sexual intercourse with a harlot** will **eventually** be reduced to poverty and **beg** people for **a loaf of bread.**

אָמַר רַבִּי זְרִיקָא אָמַר רַבִּי אֶלְעָזָר: כׇּל הַמְזַלְזֵל בִּנְטִילַת יָדַיִם נֶעֱקָר מִן הָעוֹלָם. אָמַר רַב חִיָּיא בַּר אַשִׁי אָמַר רַב: מַיִם רִאשׁוֹנִים – צָרִיךְ שֶׁיַּגְבִּיהַּ יָדָיו לְמַעְלָה, מַיִם אַחֲרוֹנִים – צָרִיךְ שֶׁיַּשְׁפִּיל יָדָיו לְמַטָּה. תַּנְיָא נַמִי הָכִי: הַנּוֹטֵל יָדָיו צָרִיךְ שֶׁיַּגְבִּיהַּ יָדָיו לְמַעְלָה, שֶׁמָּא יֵצְאוּ הַמַּיִם חוּץ לַפֶּרֶק וְיַחְזְרוּ וִיטַמְּאוּ אֶת הַיָּדַיִם.

The Gemara continues its discussion of washing hands. **Rabbi Zerika says** that **Rabbi Elazar says: Anyone who treats** the ritual of **washing hands with contempt**[NH] **is uprooted from the world. Rav Ḥiyya bar Ashi says** that **Rav says:** With regard to the **first water,** i.e., the water used when washing one's hands before a meal, one **must raise**[H] **his hands upward** after washing. With regard to the **last water,** i.e., the water used when washing one's hands at the conclusion of the meal before reciting Grace after Meals, one **must lower**[H] **his hands downward. This** distinction **is also taught** in a *baraita* (*Tosefta, Yadayim* 2:2): **One who washes his hands** before a meal **must raise his hands upward** after washing, **lest the water advance**[N] **past the joint** onto the part of the hands that he was not required to wash, becoming impure, **and** then **return** to the area he had washed, **rendering** his **hands ritually impure.**

PERSONALITIES

Ben Azzai – בֶּן עַזַּאי: This is Shimon ben Azzai, one of the *tanna'im* in Yavne. Shimon ben Azzai was never ordained, which is why he is called by his name alone, without a title. He is usually referred to simply as ben Azzai. He was considered one of the outstanding Sages and his wisdom was celebrated for many generations. Apparently, he did not study Torah in his youth until he met Rabbi Akiva's daughter. She promised to marry him if he studied Torah. Consequently, he went to study with Rabbi Yehoshua and Rabbi Yishmael and was the primary student and even a disciple-colleague of Rabbi Akiva, whom he considered to be the preeminent Sage of his generation. It is unclear whether he never married or whether he married Rabbi Akiva's daughter and left her a short time later due to his overwhelming desire to study Torah. He completely devoted himself to the study of Torah, as can be seen in the mishna (49a), which says: Since ben Azzai died, there are no more diligent people. His statements can be found in the Mishna and in the Gemara. Apparently, he had several disciples in Tiberias, his city of residence. Ben Azzai engaged in the study of esoterica and is one of the four who entered the mystical orchard, as recorded in tractate *Ḥagiga* (14b), where it states that upon doing so, ben Azzai glimpsed at the Divine Presence and died. The verse: "Precious in the sight of the Lord is the death of His pious ones" (Psalms 116:15), was quoted in reference to his death.

NOTES

As if he engaged in sexual intercourse with a prostitute, etc. – כְּאִילּוּ בָּא עַל אִשָּׁה זוֹנָה וכו׳: *Tosefot HaRash* explains this analogy by noting that one who eats without washing his hands fulfills his desire without forethought, as does one who engages in sexual intercourse with a prostitute. The Maharal offers another connection between the two by noting that both eating without washing one's hands and engaging in forbidden sexual relations are forms of benefiting from the world without first sanctifying oneself, by washing one's hands in the one case and by betrothal in the other.

Anyone who treats the ritual of washing hands with contempt – כׇּל הַמְזַלְזֵל בִּנְטִילַת יָדַיִם: Rashi explains this to refer to someone who never washes his hands before eating. This is also indicated in the Gemara in tractate *Shabbat* (62a), which refers to one who does not wash his hands at all. By contrast, the *She'iltot deRav Aḥai Gaon* presents an alternative text of that Gemara that indicates that it refers even to one who only occasionally washes his hands before eating.

Lest the water advance, etc. – שֶׁמָּא יֵצְאוּ הַמַּיִם וכו׳: Rashi explains that this *baraita* is based on a mishna in tractate *Yadayim* (2:3) that states that one must wash his hands twice: One washes the first time in order to remove the impurity from his hands, as the Sages decreed that one's hands up to the wrist are ritually impure. Afterward one washes his hands again to wash away the impure water remaining on the hands from the initial washing. The mishna there continues that if one did not wash his hands a second time, or if he washed a second time but the water did not reach all the parts of his hand that remained wet from the initial water, then if the water remaining from the first washing were to touch his hand beneath the wrist, his hands would once again become impure. Accordingly, Rashi explains the *baraita* quoted here that one must lift up his hands so that the initial waters do not again touch his hands. *Tosefot HaRosh* and Rabbi Shimshon of Saens note that the water of the second washing will not purify the water beyond the wrist even if it reaches to there.

The Ra'avad, in his commentary on tractate *Yadayim*, notes that the *halakhot* of washing the hands are based not only on impurity but also on cleanliness. One must wash twice because the first washing cleans the hands and the second clears away any dirt remaining from the first washing. Raising the hands thereby ensures that the dirt beneath the wrist will not dirty the hands a second time.

HALAKHA

Anyone who treats the ritual of washing hands with contempt – כׇּל הַמְזַלְזֵל בִּנְטִילַת יָדַיִם: One must be careful with washing hands, as one who treats this ritual with contempt is uprooted from this world. The Sages also said that such a person should be punished by excommunication, and he will eventually become impoverished (*Shulḥan Arukh, Oraḥ Ḥayyim* 158:9).

With regard to the first water one must raise, etc. – מַיִם רִאשׁוֹנִים צָרִיךְ לְהַגְבִּיהַּ וכו׳: After washing with the first water, one must raise his hands so that the water does not run past the wrist and return to render the hands impure. This applies only to one who does not wash the entire hand up to the wrist. The Rema notes that some hold that this applies even if one washes his entire hand up to the wrist. He also writes that if one keeps his hands directed downward while washing and does not raise them, or if one washes his hands three times, then there is no concern, and one need not raise his hands. Other later authorities question the efficacy of directing the hands downward. The *Shulḥan Arukh* writes that if the amount of the initial water poured on his hands was a quarter-*log*, there is no need to raise one's hands. There is also no need to raise one's hands in the event that one washed his hands in a ritual bath or a river. Since there are many circumstances in which one need not raise his hands, many were not meticulous to observe this custom. However, because raising one's hands has a basis in a verse, it is proper that one observe this ritual *ab initio*. This is the custom in Sephardic communities. However, those who do not do so but rather wash with a quantity equal to a full quarter-*log* should be considered as acting properly (Rambam *Sefer Ahava, Hilkhot Berakhot* 6:16; *Shulḥan Arukh, Oraḥ Ḥayyim* 162:1).

With regard to the last water one must lower, etc. – מַיִם אַחֲרוֹנִים צָרִיךְ שֶׁיַּשְׁפִּיל וכו׳: After washing following a meal, one's fingertips must be directed downward (Rambam *Sefer Ahava, Hilkhot Berakhot* 6:16; *Shulḥan Arukh, Oraḥ Ḥayyim* 181:5).

אָמַר רַבִּי אַבָּהוּ: כָּל הָאוֹכֵל פַּת בְּלֹא נִיגּוּב יָדַיִם – כְּאִילּוּ אוֹכֵל לֶחֶם טָמֵא, שֶׁנֶּאֱמַר: ״וַיֹּאמֶר ה׳ כָּכָה יֹאכְלוּ בְנֵי יִשְׂרָאֵל אֶת לַחְמָם טָמֵא״ וגו׳.

Rabbi Abbahu says: **Anyone who eats bread without wiping his hands**[HN] dry after washing them causes the bread to become repulsive and is considered **as if he were eating impure bread,** since the verse refers to repulsive bread as impure bread, **as it is stated: "And the Lord said: Even thus shall the children of Israel eat their bread unclean** among the nations where I will drive them" (Ezekiel 4:13). Eating bread with wet hands causes the bread to become repulsive. The verse deems eating in an uncouth manner, as did the gentiles among whom the Jewish people were exiled, as akin to eating ritually impure bread.

וּמַאי ״וְאֵשֶׁת אִישׁ נֶפֶשׁ יְקָרָה תָצוּד״? אָמַר רַבִּי חִיָּיא בַּר אַבָּא אָמַר רַבִּי יוֹחָנָן: כָּל אָדָם שֶׁיֵּשׁ בּוֹ גַּסּוּת הָרוּחַ – לְבַסּוֹף נִכְשָׁל בְּאֵשֶׁת אִישׁ, שֶׁנֶּאֱמַר: ״וְאֵשֶׁת אִישׁ נֶפֶשׁ יְקָרָה תָצוּד״.

§ The Gemara now continues the interpretation of the above quoted verse: "For on account of a harlot a man is brought to a loaf of bread" (Proverbs 6:26). The Gemara asks: **And what** is the meaning of the continuation of the verse: **"But the adulteress hunts for the precious life"? Rabbi Ḥiyya bar Abba says** that **Rabbi Yoḥanan says: Any person who has arrogance within him will eventually stumble** by sinning **with an adulteress, as it is stated: "But the adulteress hunts for the precious life,"** i.e., she sins with one who considers himself precious.

אֲמַר רָבָא: הַאי ״נֶפֶשׁ יְקָרָה״. ״נֶפֶשׁ גְּבוֹהָה״ מִיבָּעֵי לֵיהּ! וְעוֹד, ״הִיא תָצוּד״ מִיבָּעֵי לֵיהּ! אֶלָּא אָמַר רָבָא: כָּל הַבָּא עַל אֵשֶׁת אִישׁ, אֲפִילּוּ לָמַד תּוֹרָה, דִּכְתִיב בָּהּ: ״יְקָרָה הִיא מִפְּנִינִים״ – מִכֹּהֵן גָּדוֹל שֶׁנִּכְנָס לִפְנַי וְלִפְנִים, הִיא תְּצוּדֶנּוּ לְדִינָהּ שֶׁל גֵּיהִנָּם.

Rava said: This phrase: **"The precious life,"** is not how the verse would present this idea. **It should have** stated: **An arrogant life.**[N] **And further, it should have** stated: A precious life, **she hunts** for the adulteress, indicating that the precious soul will entrap the adulteress, and not vice versa, as the verse indicates as written. **Rather, Rava says** that the verse should be interpreted as follows: **Anyone who engages in sexual intercourse with an adulteress, even** if that man **studied Torah, about which it is written: "She is more precious than rubies [*peninim*]"** (Proverbs 3:15), which, based on its etymological connection with the Hebrew term for the Holy of Holies, *lifnai velifnim*, is interpreted by the Sages to mean that one who studies Torah is more precious **than a High Priest, who enters the innermost sanctum,** still, **this** transgression of adultery **will entrap him into the judgment of Gehenna,** and the Torah he studied will not be able to save him.

אָמַר רַבִּי יוֹחָנָן מִשּׁוּם רַבִּי שִׁמְעוֹן בֶּן יוֹחַי: כָּל אָדָם שֶׁיֵּשׁ בּוֹ גַּסּוּת הָרוּחַ – כְּאִילּוּ עוֹבֵד עֲבוֹדָה זָרָה; כְּתִיב הָכָא: ״תּוֹעֲבַת ה׳ כָּל גְּבַהּ לֵב״, וּכְתִיב הָתָם: ״וְלֹא תָבִיא תוֹעֵבָה אֶל בֵּיתֶךָ״.

Rabbi Yoḥanan says in the name of Rabbi Shimon ben Yoḥai: Any person who has arrogance within him is considered **as if he were an idol worshipper,**[N] as **it is written here: "Everyone that is proud in heart is an abomination to the Lord"** (Proverbs 16:5), **and it is written there** concerning the destruction of idols: **"And you shall not bring an abomination into your house"** (Deuteronomy 7:26).

וְרַבִּי יוֹחָנָן דִּידֵיהּ אָמַר: כְּאִילּוּ כָּפַר בָּעִיקָּר, שֶׁנֶּאֱמַר: ״וְרָם לְבָבֶךָ וְשָׁכַחְתָּ אֶת ה׳ אֱלֹהֶיךָ״ וגו׳.

And Rabbi Yoḥanan said his own statement: Any person who has arrogance within him is considered **as if he has denied the core** belief in God's existence, **as it is stated: "Then your heart be lifted up, and you forget the Lord your God"** (Deuteronomy 8:14).

רַבִּי חָמָא בַּר חֲנִינָא אָמַר: כְּאִילּוּ בָּא עַל כָּל הָעֲרָיוֹת; כְּתִיב הָכָא: ״תּוֹעֲבַת ה׳ כָּל גְּבַהּ לֵב״, וּכְתִיב הָתָם: ״כִּי אֶת כָּל הַתּוֹעֵבוֹת הָאֵל״ וגו׳.

Rabbi Ḥama bar Ḥanina says: Any person who has arrogance within him is considered **as if he engaged in sexual intercourse with all of those with whom relations are forbidden,** as **it is written here: "Everyone who is proud in heart is an abomination to the Lord"** (Proverbs 16:5), **and it is written there,** at the end of the passage concerning forbidden sexual relationships: **"For all these abominations** have the men of the land done" (Leviticus 18:27).

עוּלָּא אָמַר: כְּאִילּוּ בָּנָה בָּמָה, שֶׁנֶּאֱמַר: ״חִדְלוּ לָכֶם מִן הָאָדָם אֲשֶׁר נְשָׁמָה בְּאַפּוֹ כִּי בַמֶּה נֶחְשָׁב הוּא״, אַל תִּיקְרֵי ״בַּמֶּה״ אֶלָּא ״בָּמָה״.

Ulla says: Any person who has arrogance within him is considered **as if he built** a personal **altar**[NB] for idol worship, **as it is stated: "Cease you from man, in whose nostrils there is breath, for how little [*bammeh*] is he to be accounted"** (Isaiah 2:22), referring to an arrogant person. **Do not read** the verse **as** it is written, *bammeh*, how little. **Rather,** read it as ***bama*, altar.**

HALAKHA

Anyone who eats bread without wiping his hands – כָּל הָאוֹכֵל פַּת בְּלֹא נִיגּוּב יָדַיִם: After washing one's hands for bread, one must dry them before eating. One who eats without drying his hands is considered as if he were eating impure bread, as noted in the Gemara. In the *Shulḥan Arukh* it states that if one would wash his hands in a manner where there is no possibility of his hands becoming impure, e.g., if he dipped them in a ritual bath or poured on them a large amount of water, equal to or greater than a quarter-*log*, then there is no need to dry one's hands afterward. The Maharshal, however, disagrees, explaining that the primary reason one must dry his hands is not due to concerns of impurity but to the repulsiveness of eating wet bread. Therefore, the requirement to dry one's hands applies even when there is no possibility of the hands becoming impure. See the discussion of this issue in the *Mishna Berura* (Rambam *Sefer Ahava, Hilkhot Berakhot* 6:20; *Shulḥan Arukh, Oraḥ Ḥayyim* 158:12–13).

NOTES

Anyone who eats bread without wiping his hands – כָּל הָאוֹכֵל פַּת בְּלֹא נִיגּוּב יָדַיִם: Rashi explains that touching bread with wet hands causes the food to become repulsive, which is akin to impurity. Rabbeinu Ḥananel adds that wet hands moisten the food and consequently make it susceptible to contracting ritual impurity, as food does not contract impurity unless first moistened by one of the seven liquids, one of which is water.

It should have stated: An arrogant life – נֶפֶשׁ גְּבוֹהָה מִיבָּעֵי לֵיהּ: The Maharsha explains that an arrogant person is one who is excessively concerned with his appearance, who dresses in fancy clothing, and who adorns himself with jewelry. This type of person eventually entraps women, as exemplified by the biblical narrative about Joseph (see Rashi on Genesis 39:6).

As if he were an idol worshipper – כְּאִילּוּ עוֹבֵד עֲבוֹדָה זָרָה: The *Tanya* explains at length that idolatry is essentially the attribution of independent significance to an entity, separating it from its place within God's world. Similarly, an arrogant individual essentially turns his own personality into a form of idolatry by attributing significance to his successes.

As if he built a personal altar – כְּאִילּוּ בָּנָה בָּמָה: The Maharal explains that the arrogant individual separates himself from others, as he places himself on a pedestal, and he is therefore likened to one who has built an altar to himself. The Maharsha notes that the word used here for altar, *bama*, is used in the Bible in reference to a high place, and therefore is used here as a metaphor for one who views himself as higher than others.

BACKGROUND

As if he built a personal altar – כְּאִילּוּ בָּנָה בָּמָה: While some early commentaries interpret this to refer to an altar for idol worship, Rashi in tractate *Yevamot* (109b) understands it to mean building an altar to worship God at a time when such altars are forbidden.

Reconstruction of a Jewish altar found in Tel Be'er Sheva, Israel

NOTES

Just as Abraham our forefather, etc. – כְּאַבְרָהָם אָבִינוּ וכו׳: The reference to Abraham is interpreted by the Meiri as referring to one who does great deeds and publicly spreads the message of God's greatness, as was done by Abraham.

מַאי ״יָד לְיָד לֹא יִנָּקֶה״? אָמַר רַב: כָּל הַבָּא עַל אֵשֶׁת אִישׁ, אֲפִילּוּ הִקְנָהוּ לְהַקָּדוֹשׁ בָּרוּךְ הוּא שָׁמַיִם וָאָרֶץ כְּאַבְרָהָם אָבִינוּ, דִּכְתִיב בֵּיהּ: ״הֲרִימֹתִי יָדִי אֶל ה׳ אֵל עֶלְיוֹן קֹנֵה שָׁמַיִם וָאָרֶץ״, לֹא יִנָּקֶה מִדִּינָהּ שֶׁל גֵּיהִנָּם.

Having interpreted the phrase: "Everyone who is proud in heart is an abomination to the Lord" (Proverbs 16:5), the Gemara interprets the continuation of the verse. **What** is the meaning of: **"Hand to hand, he shall not be unpunished"** (Proverbs 16:5)? **Rav says: Anyone who engages in sexual intercourse with an adulteress, even if he** were to have **attributed possession of heaven and earth to the Holy One, Blessed be He, just as Abraham our forefather**[N] did, **that it is written with regard to him: "I have lifted up my hand to the Lord, God Most High, Maker of heaven and earth"** (Genesis 14:22), **he will not be unpunished from the judgment of Gehenna.** Abraham is described as one whose hands were lifted to declare the glory of God, yet this verse declares that even if one who engaged in forbidden sexual intercourse were to use his hands in the same way, still, due to his sin, the verse says: "He shall not be unpunished."

קַשְׁיָא לְהוּ לִדְבֵי רַבִּי שֵׁילָא: הַאי ״יָד לְיָד לֹא יִנָּקֶה״, ״יָדִי״ מִיבָּעֵי לֵיהּ!

This interpretation **poses a difficulty to** the Sages of **the school of Rabbi Sheila: This** phrase: **"Hand to hand, he shall not be unpunished,"** is not how the verse would present this idea. **It should have** stated: **My hand,** as that is the term employed in the verse with regard to Abraham.

אֶלָּא אָמְרִי דְּבֵי רַבִּי שֵׁילָא: אֲפִילּוּ קִיבֵּל תּוֹרָה כְּמֹשֶׁה רַבֵּינוּ, דִּכְתִיב בֵּיהּ: ״מִימִינוֹ אֵשְׁ דָּת לָמוֹ״, לֹא יִנָּקֶה מִדִּינָהּ שֶׁל גֵּיהִנָּם.

Rather, the Sages **of the school of Rabbi Sheila say:** This teaches that **even** if one who engages in sexual intercourse with an adulteress had **received the Torah** from the hand of God **like Moses our teacher** did, **that it is written with regard to him: "At His right hand was a fiery law unto them"** (Deuteronomy 33:2), i.e., God gave the Torah from His right hand into the hand of Moses in order to give to the Jewish people, the sinner **will not be unpunished from the judgment of Gehenna.**

קַשְׁיָא לֵיהּ לְרַבִּי יוֹחָנָן: הַאי ״יָד לְיָד״, ״יָד מִיָּד״ מִיבַּעְיָא לֵיהּ!

This interpretation also **poses a difficulty to Rabbi Yoḥanan: This** phrase **"hand to hand"** is not how the verse would present this idea. **It should have** stated: **Hand from hand,** as that is the term employed in the verse with regard to Moses.

אֶלָּא אָמַר רַבִּי יוֹחָנָן:

Rather Rabbi Yoḥanan says:

Perek **I**
Daf **5** Amud **a**

HALAKHA

The warning of the arrogant – אַזְהָרָה לְגַסֵּי הָרוּחַ: The proper path is that one not only be modest, but one should conduct himself with great humility. An arrogant person is like one who denies the very existence of God. One who is even a little bit arrogant should be excommunicated (Rambam *Sefer HaMadda*, *Hilkhot Deot* 2:3).

NOTES

Then your heart be lifted up and you forget – וְרָם לְבָבֶךָ וְשָׁכַחְתָּ: The *Smag* counts this verse as an independent prohibition, prohibiting one from being arrogant due to his wealth, as this will lead to forgetting God. By contrast, the Ramban holds that this is not an independent prohibition, but it is rather a detail within the general prohibition against forgetting God, as arrogance is a trait that results in forgetting God.

אֲפִילּוּ עוֹשֶׂה צְדָקָה בַּסֵּתֶר, דִּכְתִיב: ״מַתָּן בַּסֵּתֶר יִכְפֶּה אָף״ וגו׳, לֹא יִנָּקֶה מִדִּינָהּ שֶׁל גֵּיהִנָּם.

Even if the one who committed adultery **performs charitable** deeds **secretly,** as alluded to in the phrase "hand to hand," and even if one might think that one who does so will go unpunished, **as it is written** with regard to charity of this kind: **"A gift in secret pacifies wrath"** (Proverbs 21:14), nevertheless, **he will not be unpunished from the judgment of Gehenna.**

אַזְהָרָה לְגַסֵּי הָרוּחַ מִנַּיִן? אָמַר רָבָא אָמַר זְעֵירִי: ״שִׁמְעוּ וְהַאֲזִינוּ אַל תִּגְבָּהוּ״. רַב נַחְמָן בַּר יִצְחָק אָמַר, מֵהָכָא: ״וְרָם לְבָבֶךָ וְשָׁכַחְתָּ״, וּכְתִיב: ״הִשָּׁמֶר לְךָ פֶּן תִּשְׁכַּח אֶת ה׳ אֱלֹהֶיךָ״.

§ The Gemara previously discussed the impropriety of the trait of arrogance. Now the Gemara discusses the source of its prohibition. **From where is the warning** derived, i.e., what is the source prohibiting the behavior **of the arrogant?**[H] **Rava says** that **Ze'eiri says:** The source is from the verse: **"Hear, you, and give ear, be not proud,** for the Lord has spoken" (Jeremiah 13:15). **Rav Naḥman bar Yitzḥak said** the warning is **from here: "Then your heart be lifted up, and you forget**[N] the Lord your God" (Deuteronomy 8:14), **and it is** also **written** in that same passage: **"Beware lest you forget the Lord your God"** (Deuteronomy 8:11).

וְכִדְרַבִּי אָבִין אָמַר רַבִּי אֶילְעָא, דְּאָמַר רַבִּי אָבִין אָמַר רַבִּי אֶילְעָא: כָּל מָקוֹם שֶׁנֶּאֱמַר ״הִשָּׁמֵר״ ״פֶּן״ וְ״אַל״, אֵינוֹ אֶלָּא בְּלֹא תַעֲשֶׂה.

The Gemara explains: **And** these sources are **in accordance with** a statement **that Rabbi Avin** says that **Rabbi Ile'a says, as Rabbi Avin says** that **Rabbi Ile'a says: Wherever it is stated** in a verse **"beware," "lest," or "not,"** this is **nothing other** than **a prohibition.** Since these verses employ these terms in the context of one who is arrogant, they serve as sources for the prohibition.

דָּרַשׁ רַב עֲוִירָא, זִמְנִין אָמַר לָהּ מִשְּׁמֵיהּ דְּרַב אַסִי, וְזִמְנִין אָמַר לָהּ מִשְּׁמֵיהּ דְּרַב אַמִי: כָּל אָדָם שֶׁיֵּשׁ בּוֹ גַּסּוּת הָרוּחַ – לְסוֹף מִתְמַעֵט, שֶׁנֶּאֱמַר: ״רוֹמּוּ מְעַט״. וְשֶׁמָּא תֹּאמַר: יֶשְׁנוֹ בָּעוֹלָם? תַּלְמוּד לוֹמַר: ״וְאֵינֶנּוּ״.

Rav Avira interpreted the following verse **homiletically:** "They are exalted for a little while, and they are gone; yes, they are brought low, they are gathered in as all others, and wither as the tops of the husks" (Job 24:24). There were **times** when **he said this** interpretation **in the name of Rav Asi and** there were **times** when **he said it in the name of Rav Ami: Any person who has arrogance within him will ultimately be diminished** in standing, **as it is stated** in the phrase: **"They are exalted for a little while,"** indicating that one who raises himself above others will be exalted only briefly. **And lest you say that** even if he is diminished **he** will still **exist in this world** and live a full life, **the verse states: "And they are gone,"** indicating that they die before their time.

וְאִם חוֹזֵר בּוֹ – נֶאֱסָף בִּזְמַנּוֹ כְּאַבְרָהָם אָבִינוּ, שֶׁנֶּאֱמַר: ״וְהֻמְּכוּ כַּכֹּל יִקָּפְצוּן״, כְּאַבְרָהָם יִצְחָק וְיַעֲקֹב דִּכְתִיב בְּהוּ ״בַּכֹּל״, ״מִכֹּל״, ״כֹּל״. וְאִם לָאו – ״וּכְרֹאשׁ שִׁבֹּלֶת יִמָּלוּ״.

He continues the interpretation: **But if he repents from** his arrogance, **he is gathered** in death **at his proper time like Abraham our forefather, as it is stated: "Yes, they are brought low, they are gathered in as all [*kakkol*] others"** (Job 24:24), indicating that when he repents from his arrogance he will die **like Abraham, Isaac, and Jacob, as it is written about them** that they were blessed with the term "all," as in the verse above. With regard to Abraham, the verse states: "And the Lord had blessed Abraham **in all** things [***bakkol***]" (Genesis 24:1). With regard to Isaac, the verse states: "And I have eaten **of all** [***mikkol***]" (Genesis 27:33). With regard to Jacob, the verse states: "And because I have **all** [***khol***]" (Genesis 33:11). **And if** one does **not** repent, then, the verse in Job continues: **"And wither like the tops of the husk."**

מַאי ״וּכְרֹאשׁ שִׁבֹּלֶת״? רַב הוּנָא וְרַב חִסְדָּא, חַד אָמַר: כִּי סָאסָא דְּשִׁיבָּלְתָּא, וְחַד אָמַר: כְּשִׁיבּוֹלֶת עַצְמָהּ. בִּשְׁלָמָא לְמַאן דְּאָמַר כִּי סָאסָא דְּשִׁיבָּלְתָּא, הַיְינוּ דִּכְתִיב: ״וּכְרֹאשׁ שִׁבֹּלֶת״, אֶלָּא לְמַאן דְּאָמַר כִּי שׁוּבַּלְתָּא עַצְמָהּ, מַאי ״וּכְרֹאשׁ שִׁבֹּלֶת״? אָמַר רַב אַסִי, וְכֵן תָּנָא דְּבֵי רַבִּי יִשְׁמָעֵאל: מָשָׁל לְאָדָם שֶׁנִּכְנָס לְתוֹךְ שָׂדֵהוּ, גְּבוֹהָה גְּבוֹהָה הוּא מְלַקֵּט.

The Gemara asks: **What** is the meaning of the phrase **"and** wither **like the tops of the husks"? Rav Huna and Rav Ḥisda** offered differing interpretations. **One says** that it means: **Like the awn**[B] of bristle-like growth on the top **of the husk, and one says** that it means: **Like the husk itself.** The Gemara comments: **Granted, according to the one who says: Like the awn** of bristle-like growth on the top **of the husk,**[N] **that is that which is written** in the verse: **"And** wither **like the tops of the husks,"** since this awn is on the top of the husk. **But according to the one who says: Like the husk itself, what** is the meaning of the expression **"and** wither **like the tops of the husks"? Rav Asi says, and similarly the school of Rabbi Yishmael taught:** This can be explained by way of **an analogy to a person who enters into his field,** as **he gathers the taller** stalks before the shorter ones. The verse is therefore referring to the tallest stalks, not the tops of the stalks.

״וְאֶת דַּכָּא וּשְׁפַל רוּחַ״ – רַב הוּנָא וְרַב חִסְדָּא, חַד אָמַר: אִתִּי דַּכָּא, וְחַד אָמַר: אֲנִי אֶת דַּכָּא.

The Gemara continues the discussion of arrogance, and its converse, humility. The verse states: "For thus says the High and Lofty One that inhabits eternity, whose name is Holy: I dwell in the high and holy place, **also with him that is of a contrite and humble spirit,** to revive the spirit of the humble, and to revive the heart of the contrite ones" (Isaiah 57:15). **Rav Huna and Rav Ḥisda** offered differing interpretations of this verse. **One says** that the verse means: Together **with Me** is the person who is **contrite** and humble. In other words, God elevates the humble. **And one says** that the verse means: **I,** God, descend, and am found together **with** the person who is **contrite**[N] and humble.

וּמִסְתַּבְּרָא כְּמַאן דְּאָמַר אֲנִי אֶת דַּכָּא, שֶׁהֲרֵי הַקָּדוֹשׁ בָּרוּךְ הוּא הֵנִיחַ כָּל הָרִים וּגְבָעוֹת וְהִשְׁרָה שְׁכִינָתוֹ עַל הַר סִינַי, וְלֹא גָּבַהּ הַר סִינַי לְמַעְלָה.

The Gemara comments on this: **And** it **stands to reason** that the meaning of the verse is **like the one who says:** I am **with** the **contrite** person, **as the Holy One, Blessed be He, disregarded all** of the **mountains and hills, and rested His Divine Presence on** the lowly **Mount Sinai, and** He **did not** choose to **raise Mount Sinai up** toward Him. God chose to give the Torah on Mount Sinai, as it was a symbol of humility due to its lack of height, and He lowered His Divine Presence, as it were, to the mountain.

אָמַר רַב יוֹסֵף: לְעוֹלָם יִלְמַד אָדָם מִדַּעַת קוֹנוֹ, שֶׁהֲרֵי הַקָּדוֹשׁ בָּרוּךְ הוּא הֵנִיחַ כָּל הָרִים וּגְבָעוֹת וְהִשְׁרָה שְׁכִינָתוֹ עַל הַר סִינַי, וְהֵנִיחַ כָּל אִילָנוֹת טוֹבוֹת וְהִשְׁרָה שְׁכִינָתוֹ בַּסְּנֶה.

Rav Yosef says: A person should always learn proper behavior **from the wisdom of his Creator, as the Holy One, Blessed be He, disregarded all** of the **mountains and hills and rested His Divine Presence on the** lowly **Mount Sinai. And** similarly, when appearing to Moses, **He disregarded all** of the **beautiful trees and rested His Divine Presence on the bush** (Exodus 3:2).

BACKGROUND

Awn – סָאסָא:

Awn at top of wheat stalk

NOTES

Like the awn on the top of the husk – כִּי סָאסָא דְּשִׁיבָּלְתָּא: The Maharal explains that just as the awn on the top of the husk appears to be primarily decorative and does not contribute to the nutritive value of the stalk, so too, an arrogant person has no real internal substance but merely presents himself as one worthy of esteem.

I am with the contrite – אֲנִי אֶת דַּכָּא: This verse also serves as a directive to people that they should emulate God and associate themselves with the contrite and humble (Maharsha). One who does so finds himself in the company of God (Meiri).

NOTES

To hew him down as a tree designated for idolatry – לְגַדְּעוֹ כַּאֲשֵׁירָה: The Maharsha explains that this specific simile is used because a tree designated for idolatry must not only be hewn down, but it also must be uprooted and totally destroyed.

The elevated sees the elevated – גָּבוֹהַּ רוֹאֶה אֶת הַגָּבוֹהַּ: Beyond the straightforward explanation that one who is tall looks opposite himself and sees those of the same height, Rashi and others explain that customarily, one who is part of high society interacts only with those of similar stature, and he does not show honor to those considered less respected than he.

A slight wind disturbs him – רוּחַ קִימְעָא עוֹכַרְתּוֹ: The *Ben Yehoyada* explains that the verse also alludes to the fact that an arrogant person is disturbed by even the slightest of insults.

אָמַר רַבִּי אֶלְעָזָר: כׇּל אָדָם שֶׁיֵּשׁ בּוֹ גַּסּוּת הָרוּחַ – רָאוּי לְגַדְּעוֹ כַּאֲשֵׁירָה. כְּתִיב הָכָא: ״וְרָמֵי הַקּוֹמָה גְּדוּעִים״, וּכְתִיב הָתָם: ״וַאֲשֵׁירֵיהֶם תְּגַדֵּעוּן״.

Rabbi Elazar says: Concerning **any person who has arrogance within him,** it is **fitting to hew him down, as a tree designated for idolatry** [*asheira*][N] is hewn down, as **it is written here** with regard to the arrogant: **"And the high ones of stature shall be hewn down** [*gedu'im*]**"** (Isaiah 10:33), **and it is written there** with regard to trees designated for idolatry: **"And hew down** [*teggade'un*] **their trees worshipped as part of idolatrous rites** [*asheireihem*]**"** (Deuteronomy 7:5).

וְאָמַר רַבִּי אֶלְעָזָר: כׇּל אָדָם שֶׁיֵּשׁ בּוֹ גַּסּוּת הָרוּחַ – אֵין עֲפָרוֹ נִנְעָר שֶׁנֶּאֱמַר: ״הָקִיצוּ וְרַנְּנוּ שֹׁכְנֵי עָפָר״; ״שֹׁכְבֵי בְּעָפָר״ לֹא נֶאֱמַר, אֶלָּא ״שֹׁכְנֵי עָפָר״, מִי שֶׁנַּעֲשָׂה שָׁכֵן לְעָפָר בְּחַיָּיו.

And Rabbi Elazar also **says:** Concerning **any person who has arrogance within him, his dust,** i.e., his remains in his grave, **will not stir** at the time of the resurrection of the dead, **as it is stated: "Awake and sing for joy, you who dwell in the dust"** (Isaiah 26:19). **It is not stated: You who lie in the dust,** which would indicate that all the dead will be awakened in the future, **but rather: "You who dwell in the dust,"** indicating that only **one who became a neighbor to the dust in his lifetime** by living with extreme humility will stir at the time of the resurrection.

וְאָמַר רַבִּי אֶלְעָזָר: כׇּל אָדָם שֶׁיֵּשׁ בּוֹ גַּסּוּת הָרוּחַ – שְׁכִינָה מְיַלֶּלֶת עָלָיו, שֶׁנֶּאֱמַר: ״וְגָבֹהַּ מִמֶּרְחָק יְיֵדָע״.

And Rabbi Elazar says: Concerning **any person who has arrogance within him, the Divine Presence wails over him. As it is stated:** "For though the Lord is high, yet regards He the lowly, **and from the haughty He is pained from afar"** (Psalms 138:6).

דָּרַשׁ רַב עֲוִירָא, וְאִיתֵּימָא רַבִּי אֶלְעָזָר: בֹּא וּרְאֵה שֶׁלֹּא כְּמִדַּת הַקָּדוֹשׁ בָּרוּךְ הוּא מִדַּת בָּשָׂר וָדָם. מִדַּת בָּשָׂר וָדָם – גָּבוֹהַּ רוֹאֶה אֶת הַגָּבוֹהַּ וְאֵין גָּבוֹהַּ רוֹאֶה אֶת הַשָּׁפָל, אֲבָל מִדַּת הַקָּדוֹשׁ בָּרוּךְ הוּא אֵינוֹ כֵּן, הוּא גָּבוֹהַּ וְרוֹאֶה אֶת הַשָּׁפָל, שֶׁנֶּאֱמַר: ״כִּי רָם ה׳ וְשָׁפָל יִרְאֶה״.

Rav Avira interpreted a verse **homiletically, and some say** that **Rabbi Elazar** interpreted as follows: **Come and see that the attribute of the Holy One, Blessed be He, is not like the attribute of flesh and blood. The attribute of flesh and blood** is that the **elevated sees the elevated,**[N] **but the elevated does not see the lowly. But the attribute of the Holy One, Blessed be He, is not** like **that. He is elevated but sees** specifically **the lowly, as it is stated: "For though the Lord is high, yet regards He the lowly"** (Psalms 138:6).

אָמַר רַב חִסְדָּא, וְאִיתֵּימָא מָר עוּקְבָא: כׇּל אָדָם שֶׁיֵּשׁ בּוֹ גַּסּוּת הָרוּחַ – אָמַר הַקָּדוֹשׁ בָּרוּךְ הוּא: אֵין אֲנִי וְהוּא יְכוֹלִין לָדוּר בָּעוֹלָם, שֶׁנֶּאֱמַר: ״מְלָשְׁנִי בַסֵּתֶר רֵעֵהוּ אוֹתוֹ אַצְמִית גְּבַהּ עֵינַיִם וּרְחַב לֵבָב אֹתוֹ לֹא אוּכָל״, אַל תִּקְרֵי ״אֹתוֹ״ אֶלָּא ״אִתּוֹ לֹא אוּכָל״. אִיכָּא דְּמַתְנֵי לָהּ אַמְסַפְּרֵי לָשׁוֹן הָרָע, שֶׁנֶּאֱמַר: ״מְלָשְׁנִי בַסֵּתֶר רֵעֵהוּ אוֹתוֹ אַצְמִית״.

Rav Ḥisda says, and some say that **Mar Ukva** says: Concerning **any person who has arrogance within him, the Holy One, Blessed be He, said: He and I cannot dwell** together **in the world, as it is stated: "He who slanders his neighbor in secret, him will I destroy; he who is haughty of eye and proud of heart, him will I not suffer** [*oto lo ukhal*]**"** (Psalms 101:5–6). These verses should be understood as follows: **Do not read** the verse as: **"*Oto lo ukhal*"; rather,** read it as: ***Itto lo ukhal*,** meaning, **with him, I cannot** bear to dwell. **There are** those **who teach** that **this** was stated **with regard to those who speak slander** because the beginning of the verse states: **"He who slanders his neighbor in secret, him will I destroy."**

אָמַר רַבִּי אֲלֶכְּסַנְדְּרִי: כׇּל אָדָם שֶׁיֵּשׁ בּוֹ גַּסּוּת הָרוּחַ – אֲפִילּוּ רוּחַ קִימְעָא עוֹכַרְתּוֹ, שֶׁנֶּאֱמַר: ״וְהָרְשָׁעִים כַּיָּם נִגְרָשׁ״. וּמָה יָם שֶׁיֵּשׁ בּוֹ כַּמָּה רְבִיעִיּוֹת – רוּחַ קִימְעָא עוֹכַרְתּוֹ, אָדָם שֶׁאֵין בּוֹ אֶלָּא רְבִיעִית אַחַת – עַל אַחַת כַּמָּה וְכַמָּה.

Rabbi Alexandri says: Concerning **any person who has arrogance within him, even a slight wind disturbs him,**[N] **as it is stated: "But the wicked are like the troubled sea,** for it cannot rest" (Isaiah 57:20). **And if** with regard to the **sea,** which **contains many** quantities of **quarters** of a *log* of water, yet **a slight wind disturbs it,** certainly with regard to **a person, who has** in his body **only one quarter-*log*** of essential lifeblood,[B] **all the more so** will a slight wind disturb him.

BACKGROUND

One quarter-*log* of lifeblood – רְבִיעִית אַחַת דָּם: It is readily apparent that the human body contains more than a quarter-*log* of blood. As such, some explain that the Gemara is referring to the blood supply of an infant; although he has a larger quantity of blood in his body, the loss of a quarter-*log* of blood will endanger his life. Another explanation offered is that this amount refers to the quantity of blood contained in the heart. Every beat of the heart propels approximately 80 cc of blood, approximately a quarter-*log*, through the circulatory system.

אָמַר רַב חִיָּיא בַּר אַשִׁי אָמַר רַב: תַּלְמִיד חָכָם צָרִיךְ שֶׁיְּהֵא בּוֹ אֶחָד מִשְּׁמוֹנֶה בִּשְׁמִינִית. אֲמַר רַב הוּנָא בְּרֵיהּ דְּרַב יְהוֹשֻׁעַ: וּמְעַטַּרְתָּא לֵיהּ כִּי סָאסָא לְשִׁבּוֹלְתָּא. אֲמַר רָבָא: בְּשַׁמְתָּא דְּאִית בֵּיהּ, וּבְשַׁמְתָּא דְּלֵית בֵּיהּ.

Rav Ḥiyya bar Ashi says that **Rav says:** Despite the opprobrium assigned to one who exhibits the trait of arrogance, **a Torah scholar must have one-eighth of one-eighth**[N] of arrogance. **Rav Huna, son of Rav Yehoshua, said: And** this minute measure of arrogance **crowns him as the awn** of bristle-like growth on the top **of the husk.**[N] **Rava said:** A Torah scholar **who has** arrogance **should be excommunicated, and one who does not have** arrogance at all **should be excommunicated** as well. As such, he must have only a minute measure of arrogance.

אֲמַר רַב נַחְמָן בַּר יִצְחָק: לָא מִינָּהּ וְלָא מִקְצָתָהּ. מִי זוּטַר דִּכְתִיב בֵּיהּ: ״תּוֹעֲבַת ה׳ כָּל גְּבַהּ לֵב״?

Rav Naḥman bar Yitzḥak said: Even a Torah scholar **should not have any** arrogance **or any part of** arrogance, i.e., not even one-eighth of one-eighth. He explains why arrogance should be avoided entirely by asking: **Is it a small** matter **that it is written with regard to** arrogance: **"Everyone that is proud of heart is an abomination to the Lord"** (Proverbs 16:5)?

אָמַר חִזְקִיָּה: אֵין תְּפִלָּתוֹ שֶׁל אָדָם נִשְׁמַעַת אֶלָּא אִם כֵּן מֵשִׂים לִבּוֹ כְּבָשָׂר, שֶׁנֶּאֱמַר: ״וְהָיָה מִדֵּי חֹדֶשׁ בְּחָדְשׁוֹ [וגו׳] יָבֹא כָל בָּשָׂר לְהִשְׁתַּחֲווֹת״ וגו׳.

Ḥizkiyya says: The prayers of a person are heard only if he casts his heart to be **like flesh,** by being free of arrogance. **As it is stated: "And it shall come to pass, that from one New Moon to another,** and from one Sabbath to another, **shall all flesh come to worship** before Me, says the Lord" (Isaiah 66:23).

אֲמַר רַבִּי זֵירָא: בָּשָׂר כְּתִיב בֵּיהּ ״וְנִרְפָּא״, אָדָם לָא כְּתִיב בֵּיהּ ״וְנִרְפָּא״.

Rabbi Zeira said: Concerning leprosy of the **flesh, it is written** in the verse **with regard to it:** "And when the flesh has in the skin thereof a boil, **and it is healed"** (Leviticus 13:18), but concerning the leprosy of **a person, it is not written** in the verse **with regard to it: And it is healed.** Both verses discussing leprosy of a person make no mention of healing (Leviticus 13:2, 13:9). This indicates that one who sees himself as flesh will be cured, but one who holds himself in high regard will not be cured.

אָמַר רַבִּי יוֹחָנָן: אָדָ״ם – אֵפֶר, דָּם, מָרָה; בָּשָׂ״ר – בּוּשָׁה, סְרוּחָה, רִמָּה; אִיכָּא דְּאָמְרִי: שְׁאוֹל, דִּכְתִיב בְּשִׁין.

Rabbi Yoḥanan said: The Hebrew word for person, *adam,* written: *Alef, dalet, mem,* is an acronym for *efer,* dust; *dam,* blood; and *mara,* bile,[N] alluding to man's insignificance. Similarly, the Hebrew word for flesh, *basar,* written: *Beit, sin, reish,* is an acronym for ***busha,*** shame; ***seruḥa,*** putrid; and ***rimma,*** worm, also alluding to his insignificance. **There are** those **who say** that the letter *sin* of the word *basar* actually is referring to a different word, ***sheol,* the netherworld, as it is written with** the Hebrew letter ***shin.*** The letter *sin* is phonetically similar to the letter *samekh,* the first letter of the word *seruḥa,* but is orthographically similar to the letter *shin,* the first letter of the word *sheol.* The dispute is whether the acronym should be based upon the pronunciation or upon the way it is written.

אָמַר רַב אַשִׁי: כָּל אָדָם שֶׁיֵּשׁ בּוֹ גַּסּוּת הָרוּחַ – לְסוֹף נִפְחַת, שֶׁנֶּאֱמַר:

Rav Ashi says: Any person who has arrogance within him will ultimately be diminished in stature, **as it is stated** with regard to different types of leprosy:

NOTES

One-eighth of one-eighth – אֶחָד מִשְּׁמוֹנָה בִּשְׁמִינִית: The straightforward interpretation is that of Rashi, who notes that one-eighth of one-eighth is the smallest unit of measure that has a name in the Talmud, the *ukhla* (see *Bava Batra* 89b). As such, it means one should have a negligibly small measure of arrogance.

The Maharsha explains that this indicates that a Torah scholar must at times act with a modicum of arrogance in order to preserve the honor of the Torah he represents. This is alluded to by the measure of one-eighth of one-eighth, as the praises of the Torah are enumerated at length in Psalm 119, which is composed of eight verses for each letter of the alphabet, comprising 176 verses in all. Therefore, one-eighth of one-eighth alludes to incorporating at least one of the eight praises for the Torah included in every letter.

And crowns him as the awn on the top of the husk – וּמְעַטַּרְתָּא לֵיהּ כִּי סָאסָא לְשִׁבּוֹלְתָּא: The Meiri writes that a small measure of arrogance protects a Torah scholar against being belittled by others, in the same way that the awn protects the husk.

Dust, blood, bile – אֵפֶר, דָּם, מָרָה: This indicates that if one would give consideration to the matter from which his body is composed, and if one would contemplate from what substance he was formed, and that he will eventually die and become wormy, he will not be arrogant (see Maharsha and Maharal).

BACKGROUND

Burnt-offering – עוֹלָה: A burnt-offering is an offering whose meat is totally consumed on the altar in the Temple, and no part other than the animal's hide is given to the priests. A burnt-offering must be male, and it may be brought from cattle, sheep, goats, or doves. Private individuals generally bring this offering as a voluntary offering. However, there are times when one makes a sacrifice to atone for the willful non-fulfillment of a positive mitzva or for immoral or idolatrous thoughts. Additionally, there are certain situations where individuals are required to bring a burnt-offering together with other offerings.

Burnt-offerings are considered offerings of the most sacred order. They must be slaughtered in the northern portion of the Temple courtyard and their blood is sprinkled at two opposite corners of the altar, the northeastern and southwestern corners. Therefore, although the blood is sprinkled only twice, it reaches all four sides of the altar. Afterward, the animal's hide is removed and given to the priests, and its limbs are separated. The remainder of the blood is then poured out at the base of the altar and the limbs are burned on the altar.

Meal-offering – מִנְחָה: There are a variety of offerings of flour or bread that were brought in the Temple. The Gemara is discussing a voluntary meal-offering, which could be prepared in one of four ways: Mixed with oil, baked in an oven, fried on a griddle, or fried in a pan (Leviticus 2:1–13). All of these offerings were made of fine wheat flour.

HALAKHA

Whoever appraises his ways – כָּל הַשָּׁם אוֹרְחוֹתָיו: The correct path to follow is the middle path, where all actions are performed in proper proportion. Therefore, the Sages commanded that one organize his opinions and thoughts, evaluate his character traits, and direct them along the middle path (Rambam *Sefer HaMadda*, *Hilkhot Deot* 1:4).

״וְלַשְׂאֵת וְלַסַּפַּחַת״, וְאֵין שְׂאֵת אֶלָּא לְשׁוֹן גָּבוֹהַּ, שֶׁנֶּאֱמַר: ״וְעַל [כָּל] הֶהָרִים הָרָמִים וְעַל [כָּל] הַגְּבָעוֹת הַנִּשָּׂאוֹת״, וְאֵין סַפַּחַת אֶלָּא טְפֵילָה, שֶׁנֶּאֱמַר: ״סְפָחֵנִי נָא אֶל אַחַת הַכְּהֻנּוֹת לֶאֱכֹל פַּת לָחֶם״.

"And for a sore [*se'et*] and for a scab [*sappaḥat*]" (Leviticus 14:56), **and** ***se'et*** **means nothing other** than **elevated, as it is stated: "And upon all the high mountains, and upon all the hills that are lifted up [*nissaot*]"** (Isaiah 2:14). **And** ***sappaḥat*** **means nothing other** than **an appendage, as it is stated** in the context of the curse given to the descendants of Eli: **"Put me [*sefaḥeni*], I pray of you, into one of the priests' offices, that I may eat a morsel of bread"** (1 Samuel 2:36). They will have to be joined with another priestly family to receive their priestly gifts. One can therefore interpret the verses discussing leprosy as teaching that one who initially is arrogant, *se'et*, will eventually become a *sappaḥat*, diminished in stature.

אָמַר רַבִּי יְהוֹשֻׁעַ בֶּן לֵוִי: בֹּא וּרְאֵה כַּמָּה גְּדוֹלִים נְמוּכֵי הָרוּחַ לִפְנֵי הַקָּדוֹשׁ בָּרוּךְ הוּא, שֶׁבְּשָׁעָה שֶׁבֵּית הַמִּקְדָּשׁ קַיָּים, אָדָם מַקְרִיב עוֹלָה – שְׂכַר עוֹלָה בְּיָדוֹ, מִנְחָה – שְׂכַר מִנְחָה בְּיָדוֹ, אֲבָל מִי שֶׁדַּעְתּוֹ שְׁפָלָה, מַעֲלֶה עָלָיו הַכָּתוּב כְּאִילּוּ הִקְרִיב כָּל הַקָּרְבָּנוֹת כּוּלָּם, שֶׁנֶּאֱמַר: ״זִבְחֵי אֱלֹהִים רוּחַ נִשְׁבָּרָה״; וְלֹא עוֹד, אֶלָּא שֶׁאֵין תְּפִלָּתוֹ נִמְאֶסֶת, שֶׁנֶּאֱמַר: ״לֵב נִשְׁבָּר וְנִדְכֶּה אֱלֹהִים לֹא תִבְזֶה״.

Rabbi Yehoshua ben Levi says: Come and see how great the lowly in spirit are before the Holy One, Blessed be He. For when the Temple was **standing, a person** would **sacrifice a burnt-offering**[B] **and the merit of a burnt-offering would be his;** he would sacrifice **a meal-offering**[B] **and the merit of a meal-offering would be his. But** with regard to **one whose spirit is lowly, the verse ascribes him** credit **as if he had sacrificed all the sacrificial offerings, as it is stated: "The sacrifices of God are a broken spirit"** (Psalms 51:19), indicating that one who is humble of spirit is regarded as if he offered all the "sacrifices of God." **And not only** that, **but his prayer is not despised** by God, **as it is stated** at the end of that verse: **"A broken and contrite heart, O God, You will not despise."**

וְאָמַר רַבִּי יְהוֹשֻׁעַ בֶּן לֵוִי: כָּל הַשָּׁם אוֹרְחוֹתָיו בָּעוֹלָם הַזֶּה – זוֹכֶה וְרוֹאֶה בִּישׁוּעָתוֹ שֶׁל הַקָּדוֹשׁ בָּרוּךְ הוּא, שֶׁנֶּאֱמַר: ״וְשָׂם דֶּרֶךְ אַרְאֶנּוּ בְּיֵשַׁע אֱלֹהִים״, אַל תִּקְרֵי ״וְשָׂם״ אֶלָּא ״וְשָׁם דֶּרֶךְ״.

And Rabbi Yehoshua ben Levi also **says: Whoever appraises his ways**[HN] **in this world,** i.e., whoever carefully considers all his actions before deciding on the proper mode of conduct, **merits and sees the salvation of the Holy One, Blessed be He, as it is stated: "And to him that orders his way aright [*vesam derekh*] will I show the salvation of God"** (Psalms 50:23). **Do not read** it as ***"vesam,"*** "that orders"; **rather,** read it as ***vesham derekh,*** that appraises his way.

[״כֵּיצַד מְקַנֵּא לָהּ״ כו׳.] הָא גּוּפָא קַשְׁיָא: אָמְרַתְּ: אָמַר לָהּ בִּפְנֵי שְׁנַיִם ״אַל תְּדַבְּרִי עִם אִישׁ פְּלוֹנִי זֶה״, אַלְמָא דִּבּוּר סְתִירָה הוּא,

§ The mishna teaches: **How** does he **issue a warning to her** in an effective manner? If he says to her in the presence of two witnesses: Do not speak with the man called so-and-so, and she nevertheless spoke with him, she is still permitted to engage in sexual intercourse with her husband. However, if after he told her not to speak with so-and-so, she entered into a secluded place and remained with that man for sufficient time to engage in sexual intercourse, she is forbidden to her home, i.e., to engage in sexual intercourse with her husband, from that moment until she undergoes the *sota* rite. The Gemara notes the apparent contradiction in the mishna: **This** matter **itself is difficult: You said** in detailing the wording of the warning that **he said to her in the presence of two** witnesses: **Do not speak with the man** called **so-and-so, apparently** indicating that **speaking is** tantamount to **seclusion.**[N] Therefore, speaking with that man should result in the woman becoming forbidden to her husband.

NOTES

Whoever appraises his ways – כָּל הַשָּׁם אוֹרְחוֹתָיו: Rashi explains that this is referring to one who weighs the reward for the performance of a mitzva against the loss incurred by doing so. The *Sefat Emet* adds that not only should one contemplate the importance of performing mitzvot, but one must also take into consideration the possible negative results caused by the performance of certain mitzvot at the wrong time, or in the wrong setting. Therefore, the Gemara indicates that one should weigh his actions, and one should be careful of how and when he performs mitzvot. In the *Ben Yehoyada* it is explained that this Gemara teaches that one should contemplate all the events in his life and realize that they are not by chance. Rather, there is divine providence that directs what occurs to him. Through this realization, one merits salvation.

Apparently speaking is tantamount to seclusion, etc. – אַלְמָא דִּבּוּר סְתִירָה הוּא וכו׳: This apparent contradiction is discussed in the Jerusalem Talmud. There it is explained that the term: Speak, as used in the mishna, is a euphemism that in fact refers to seclusion. Therefore, the husband's warning to his wife: Don't speak with so-and-so, is a more polite way of saying: Don't seclude yourself with so-and-so.

Tosafot note that even according to the Jerusalem Talmud, the term speak is used in the mishna as a euphemism referring to seclusion only the first time. When mentioned a second time, it is referring to her actually speaking with the other man, which is why she remains permitted to her husband. The *Keren Ora* explains that there is an actual dispute between the Babylonian Talmud and the Jerusalem Talmud with regard to this matter, as the Babylonian Talmud holds that if he uses the expression: Do not speak, then even if he actually meant: Do not seclude yourself, it is not considered to be an effective warning.

וַהֲדַר תָּנֵי: דִּיבְּרָה עִמּוֹ, עֲדַיִין מוּתֶּרֶת לְבֵיתָהּ וּמוּתֶּרֶת לֶאֱכוֹל בִּתְרוּמָה, אַלְמָא דִּבּוּר לָא כְּלוּם הוּא!

But then the mishna **teaches:** If **she** nevertheless **spoke with him, she is still permitted to her home,** i.e., to engage in sexual intercourse with her husband, **and** if she is the wife of a priest **she is** still **permitted to partake of *teruma*, apparently** indicating that **speaking is nothing.** Therefore, issuing a warning to her not to speak with a particular man should not qualify as an effective warning.

אָמַר אַבָּיֵי, הָכִי קָאָמַר: "אַל תְּדַבְּרִי" וְדִבְּרָה, "אַל תְּדַבְּרִי" וְנִסְתְּרָה – וְלֹא כְּלוּם. "אַל תִּסָּתְרִי" וְדִבְּרָה עִמּוֹ – עֲדַיִין מוּתֶּרֶת לְבֵיתָהּ וּמוּתֶּרֶת לֶאֱכוֹל בִּתְרוּמָה. נִכְנְסָה עִמּוֹ לְבֵית הַסֵּתֶר וְשָׁהֲתָה כְּדֵי טוּמְאָה – אֲסוּרָה לְבֵיתָהּ וַאֲסוּרָה לֶאֱכוֹל בִּתְרוּמָה.

Abaye said an explanation: **This is what** the mishna **is saying:** If he said to her: **Do not speak** with so-and-so, **and she** later **spoke**[H] with him; or if the husband said to her: **Do not speak** with so-and-so, **and she** later **secluded herself** with him, **it is nothing,** as this was not an effective warning. Similarly, if he said to her: **Do not seclude yourself** with so-and-so, **and** then **she spoke with him** without secluding herself with him, **she is still permitted to her home,** i.e., her husband, **and she is** still **permitted to partake of *teruma*.** However, **if** after he issued a warning to her not to seclude herself with someone, **she entered with** that man **into a secluded place and remained** there with him for a period of time **sufficient for defilement,** then **she is forbidden to her home,** i.e., her husband, **and forbidden to partake of *teruma*.**

וְאִם מֵת – חוֹלֶצֶת. אַמַּאי? תִּתְיַיבֵּם נַמִּי יַבּוּמֵי!

§ The mishna teaches that after a woman who was warned by her husband not to seclude herself with another man, nevertheless secludes herself with another man, she becomes forbidden to her husband, **and** if her husband **dies** childless before she drank the bitter water, **she performs *ḥalitza*** with her late husband's brother and does not enter into levirate marriage. The Gemara asks: **Why** must she perform *ḥalitza*? **Let her enter into levirate marriage.**[B] After all, although she secluded herself with the other man after the warning, there is only an unverified suspicion of adultery. Why should it be prohibited for her to enter into levirate marriage with her deceased husband's brother, the *yavam*?

אָמַר רַב יוֹסֵף, אָמַר קְרָא: "וְיָצְאָה מִבֵּיתוֹ וְהָלְכָה וְהָיְתָה לְאִישׁ אַחֵר", לְאִישׁ אַחֵר – וְלֹא לְיָבָם.

Rav Yosef said: With regard to a man who divorces his wife because: "He has found some unseemly matter about her" (Deuteronomy 24:1), i.e., he suspects her of sexual impropriety, **the verse states: "And she departs out of his house, and goes and becomes another man's wife"** (Deuteronomy 24:2). It is inferred from this that she is free **to** marry **another man, but** she is **not** permitted **to** marry **the *yavam*.** The *yavam* is not considered "another man," as he takes the place of his brother.

אָמַר לֵיהּ אַבָּיֵי: אֶלָּא מֵעַתָּה, חֲלִיצָה נַמִּי לָא תִּיבְּעֵי! אָמַר לֵיהּ: אִילּוּ אִיתֵיהּ לְבַעַל, מִי לָא בָּעֲיָא גֵּט? הַשְׁתָּא נַמִּי תִּיבְּעֵי חֲלִיצָה.

Abaye said to him: If that is so, that the Torah explicitly prohibits levirate marriage in this case, then **she should not require *ḥalitza* as well,** as the verse explicitly permitted her to marry another man, seemingly abrogating the need for *ḥalitza* to free her from the bond to the *yavam*. Rav Yosef **said to him** in response: **If the husband were** alive, **would she not require a bill of divorce** to permit her to remarry, even though she was forbidden to him? **Now, as well, she should require *ḥalitza*** in order to release her bond with the *yavam*, even though, as the verse indicates, it remains prohibited for them to enter into levirate marriage.

BACKGROUND

Levirate marriage and *ḥalitza* – יִבּוּם וַחֲלִיצָה: The *halakhot* of levirate marriage and *ḥalitza* appear in the Torah (Deuteronomy 28:5–10) and are articulated at length in tractate *Yevamot*, which is devoted primarily to this topic. The basic concept is that if a man dies with no living descendants, his wife is bound to her husband's brother. The brother must either take her as a wife through levirate marriage, or sever the bond through the ceremony of *ḥalitza*. As long as the levirate bond is intact, it is prohibited for her to marry a different man.

HALAKHA

Do not speak, and she spoke, etc. – אַל תְּדַבְּרִי וְדִיבְּרָה וכו׳: If one says to his wife in the presence of two people: Do not speak with so-and-so, it is not considered a warning, and she remains permitted to her husband even if she secluded herself with that man afterward. Additionally, if he said to her: Do not seclude yourself with so-and-so, and she spoke with him in the presence of witnesses, she is permitted to her husband (Rambam *Sefer Nashim*, *Hilkhot Sota* 1:4–5; *Shulḥan Arukh*, *Even HaEzer* 178:6).

וְאִית דְּאָמְרִי: אֲמַר רַב יוֹסֵף, רַחֲמָנָא אָמַר: ״וְיָצְאָה מִבֵּיתוֹ וְהָלְכָה וְהָיְתָה לְאִישׁ אַחֵר״, דְּלָא לִיסַתְּרֵיהּ לְבֵיתֵיהּ, וְאַתְּ אָמְרַתְּ: תִּתְיַיבֵּם נַמִּי יַבּוּמֵי?

And there are those **who say** that say that in answer to Abaye's question **Rav Yosef said: The Merciful One said** with regard to a man who divorces his wife because he has found some unseemly matter about her: **"And she departs out of his house, and goes and becomes another man's wife,"** indicating that the man should divorce her **so that his house not be destroyed** by his continuing to dwell with her, **and you** want to **say that she should enter into levirate marriage?** How can it be that the same verse instructing the husband to divorce her would also instruct the *yavam* to marry her? However, there is no reason to exempt her from performing *ḥalitza*.

אֲמַר לֵיהּ אַבַּיֵי: אֶלָּא מֵעַתָּה, לְאַחֵר לֹא תִּינָּשֵׂא, דְּלָא תִּיסַתְּרֵיהּ לְבֵיתֵיהּ!

Abaye said to him: If that is so, that the verse would not tell the *yavam* to marry her, **she should not marry another** man either, **so that** the second husband's **house not be destroyed.** How can it be that the same verse instructing the husband to divorce her would also instruct another man to marry her?

אֲמַר לֵיהּ:

Rav Yosef **said to him:**

Perek **I**
Daf **6** Amud **a**

מִי קָא רָמֵינַן לָהּ עֲלֵיהּ בְּעַל כָּרְחֵיהּ?

Do we impose on him an obligation to marry **her against his will?** Unlike levirate marriage, there is no obligation for another man to marry her. Therefore, the verse is not instructing him to do so.

וְאִיכָּא דְּאָמְרִי, אָמַר רַב יוֹסֵף: הַכָּתוּב קְרָאוֹ ״אַחֵר״, שֶׁאֵין בֶּן זוּגוֹ שֶׁל רִאשׁוֹן, שֶׁזֶּה הוֹצִיא רְשָׁעָה מִבֵּיתוֹ וְזֶה הִכְנִיס רְשָׁעָה לְתוֹךְ בֵּיתוֹ, וְאַתְּ אָמְרַתְּ: תִּתְיַיבֵּם נַמִּי יַבּוּמֵי?

And there are those **who say** that **Rav Yosef said** differently: **The verse calls** a man who marries a woman after she was divorced from her first husband due to suspicion of adultery **"another** man,"[N] as the verse states: "And she departs out of his house and goes and becomes another man's wife" (Deuteronomy 24:2). This indicates that one who subsequently marries her **is not a peer of** her **first** husband **because this** one, the first husband, **removed an evil woman**[H] **from his house, and that** one **brought an evil woman into his house.** There is an implied criticism of the second husband in the verse; **and** yet **you say** that the verse instructs that **she should also enter into levirate marriage.**[N]

אֲמַר לֵיהּ אַבַּיֵי: אֶלָּא מֵעַתָּה, נִשֵּׂאת לְאַחֵר וּמֵת בְּלֹא בָּנִים, לֹא תִּתְיַיבֵּם, דְּהַכָּתוּב קְרָאוֹ ״אַחֵר״! גַּבֵּיהּ דְּהַאי מִיהָא בְּשֵׁם טוֹב הֲוָה קָיְימָא.

Abaye said to him: If that is so, then **if she married another** man **and he died without children,** then **she should not enter into levirate marriage** with the brother of her second husband even if she did not commit adultery during the second marriage, since **the verse calls** the second husband **"another** man," which excluded the possibility of levirate marriage. Rav Yosef answered Abaye: **With regard to that one,** i.e., this second husband, **at least she remained with a good name.** Since she did not engage in illicit behavior during her second marriage, she can enter into levirate marriage with the brother of her second husband.

רָבָא אָמַר: קַל וָחוֹמֶר, אִם נֶאֶסְרָה בַּמּוּתָּר לָהּ, בָּאָסוּר לָהּ לֹא כָּל שֶׁכֵּן!

Rava says a different reason why a *sota* cannot enter into levirate marriage: This prohibition can be deduced through **an *a fortiori*** inference: **If,** due to the suspicion of adultery, **she becomes forbidden to the one who was** previously **permitted to her,** i.e., her first husband, then **with regard to one who was forbidden to her,** i.e., the husband's brother, is it **not all the more so** that she remains forbidden to him?

NOTES

The verse calls him another man – הַכָּתוּב קְרָאוֹ אַחֵר: This inference is from the use of the term "another [*aḥer*]," which almost always carries a negative connotation. The verse could have described him as the second husband, mirroring the reference there to "the first husband" (Deuteronomy 24:4). By choosing to refer to him as "another," the verse portrays the second marriage in a negative light (Maharsha on *Gittin* 90a).

And you say that she should also enter into levirate marriage – וְאַתְּ אָמְרַתְּ תִּתְיַיבֵּם נַמִּי יַבּוּמֵי: The Meiri explains that although this logic dictates only that the *yavam* cannot be required to enter into levirate marriage with a suspected adulterous, this would not mean that he is prohibited from doing so. However, he is in fact prohibited from entering into levirate marriage with her, as allowing him to do so may result in a *yavam* in such a situation believing that he has a mitzva to do so. Others explain that once it is determined that there is no mitzva for him to enter into levirate marriage with her, it is by default prohibited, as one is not permitted to marry his brother's former wife unless it is in performance of the mitzva of levirate marriage (Rashi; Rosh).

HALAKHA

This one removed an evil woman, etc. – שֶׁזֶּה הוֹצִיא רְשָׁעָה וכו׳: One should not marry a woman who was divorced on grounds of immorality. After her prior husband divorced her to remove her wickedness from his home, it is improper for another man to bring her into his home (Rambam *Sefer Nashim, Hilkhot Geirushin* 10:22; *Shulḥan Arukh, Even HaEzer* 119:5).

אָמַר לֵיהּ אַבַּיֵי: אֶלָּא מֵעַתָּה, כֹּהֵן גָּדוֹל שֶׁקִּידֵּשׁ אֶת הָאַלְמָנָה וּמֵת, וְיֵשׁ לוֹ אָח כֹּהֵן הֶדְיוֹט – לֹא תִּתְיַבֵּם, אִם נֶאֶסְרָה בְּמוּתָּר לָהּ, בְּאָסוּר לָהּ לֹא כׇּל שֶׁכֵּן!

Abaye said to him: If that is so, if this *a fortiori* reasoning is the basis of the prohibition against her entering into levirate marriage, then in the case of **a High Priest who betrothed a widow,** which he is prohibited from doing, **and he died** before the marriage took place, **and he has a brother** who is **a common priest,** who is permitted to marry a widow, **she should** still **not** be permitted to **enter into levirate marriage** with him, since the same inference can be stated: **If she becomes forbidden to the one who was permitted to her,** i.e., her husband the High Priest, who was prohibited from marrying a widow, then **with regard to one who was forbidden to her,** i.e., his brother, the common priest who wishes to enter into levirate marriage with her, is it **not all the more so** that she should be forbidden?

נֶאֶסְרָה? הָא אֲסִירָא וְקָיְימָא! מוּתָּר לָהּ? אָסוּר לָהּ הוּא!

The Gemara refutes this inference. In the case of the High Priest, can one say: **She becomes forbidden? But** she **was forbidden** to him **and remains** forbidden to him. She did not become forbidden to her husband, the High Priest, due to the marriage. Furthermore, in the case of the High Priest, can one say: **Permitted to her? But** the High Priest **is forbidden to her** always. Therefore, the case of the High Priest does not serve as a refutation of the *a fortiori* inference.

אֶלָּא, אֵשֶׁת כֹּהֵן שֶׁנֶּאֶנְסָה וּמֵת, וְיֵשׁ לוֹ אָח חָלָל, לֹא תִּתְיַבֵּם, אִם נֶאֶסְרָה בְּמוּתָּר לָהּ, בְּאָסוּר לָהּ לֹא כׇּל שֶׁכֵּן!

Rather, the refutation is as follows: In the case of **a priest's wife who was raped,**[B] who becomes forbidden to her husband, **and** then her husband **dies; and he has a brother who is a priest disqualified due to flawed lineage** [***halal***],[B] who is not bound by the restrictions on marriage given to a priest, then **she should not** be permitted to **enter into levirate marriage** with him. **If she becomes forbidden to the one who was permitted to her,** i.e., her husband the priest, then **with regard to one who was forbidden to her,** i.e., her brother-in-law, is it **not all the more so** that she remains forbidden to him?

אוֹנֶס בְּיִשְׂרָאֵל מִישְׁרָא שָׁרֵי, וְגַבֵּי דְּהַאי מִיהָא לֵיכָּא אִיסּוּרָא.

The Gemara answers: Nevertheless, this *a fortiori* inference is not applicable here because **a raped** woman **is completely permitted to an Israelite.**[H] Therefore, a married woman raped by another man may remain with her Israelite husband. **And with regard to this** person, i.e., the brother of the deceased, who is a *ḥalal*, **in any event there is no prohibition.** The fact that the woman was forbidden to her *ḥalal* brother-in-law while she was married to her husband is immaterial. This is because, had she been raped while she was married to the *ḥalal*, it would not render her forbidden to him, as he has the status of an Israelite with regard to marriage. Consequently, this case cannot be compared to the case of the mishna, as a woman who commits adultery is forbidden to any husband, not only a priest.

מתני׳ וְאֵלּוּ אֲסוּרוֹת מִלֶּאֱכוֹל בִּתְרוּמָה: הָאוֹמֶרֶת טְמֵאָה אֲנִי לָךְ, וְשֶׁבָּאוּ עֵדִים שֶׁהִיא טְמֵאָה, וְהָאוֹמֶרֶת אֵינִי שׁוֹתָה, וְשֶׁבַּעְלָהּ אֵינוֹ רוֹצֶה לְהַשְׁקוֹתָהּ, וְשֶׁבַּעְלָהּ בָּא עָלֶיהָ בַּדֶּרֶךְ.

MISHNA And these are women who, despite being married to priests, **are prohibited from partaking of *teruma***[HN] due to suspicion of adultery: A woman **who says** to her husband: **I am defiled to you,** i.e., she admitted to having committed adultery with another man; **and** in a case **where witnesses came**[N] forth and testified **that she is defiled;** **and** a woman **who says** after a warning and seclusion: **I will not drink** the bitter water of a *sota;* **and** in a case **where her husband does not want to force her to drink** the water even after she secluded herself with another man after his warning; **and** in a case **where her husband engaged in sexual intercourse with her on the way**[N] to bringing her to the Temple to drink the bitter water, as in such a case the water will not be effective in evaluating whether she was unfaithful, due to the husband's own prohibited act.

NOTES

Where her husband engaged in sexual intercourse with her on the way – שֶׁבַּעְלָהּ בָּא עָלֶיהָ בַּדֶּרֶךְ: Although the mishna specifically mentions a case where the husband and wife engaged in sexual intercourse while on the way to the Temple, that is merely one possible scenario, and the *halakha* would be the same in any instance where they engaged in sexual intercourse after the warning and seclusion (Meiri).

BACKGROUND

A priest's wife who was raped – אֵשֶׁת כֹּהֵן שֶׁנֶּאֶנְסָה: The Torah places restrictions on the women a priest may marry. For example, a priest may not marry a woman who was divorced or a woman who has engaged in sexual intercourse with someone who is forbidden to her by Torah law (Leviticus 21:7). If the wife of an Israelite or Levite is raped, she is permitted to continue living with her husband, since the intercourse took place against her will. However, if the wife of a priest is raped, she has had sexual intercourse with someone who is forbidden to her, albeit against her will. For this reason, she is now forbidden to her husband and he is obligated to divorce her.

Ḥalal – חָלָל: A *ḥalal* is a male disqualified from priesthood. Usually, it refers to the child of a priest and a woman who was prohibited in marriage to a priest, e.g., a divorcée, a *zona*, or a woman disqualified from marrying a priest [*ḥalala*]. Although the *ḥalal* is born to a priestly father, he does not have the legal status of a priest but rather that of an Israelite.

HALAKHA

A raped woman is completely permitted to an Israelite – אוֹנֶס בְּיִשְׂרָאֵל מִישְׁרָא שָׁרֵי: If the wife of a priest engages in sexual intercourse outside of her marriage, even if she was raped, she becomes forbidden to her husband. However, the wife of a Levite or Israelite who was raped remains permitted to her husband, although if she is later widowed it will be prohibited for her to marry a priest (Rambam *Sefer Nashim, Hilkhot Ishut* 4:18 and *Sefer Kedusha, Hilkhot Issurei Bia* 18:7–8; *Shulḥan Arukh, Even HaEzer* 6:10–11).

Prohibited from partaking of *teruma* – אֲסוּרוֹת מִלֶּאֱכוֹל בִּתְרוּמָה: The women listed in the mishna who do not drink the bitter water but are not entitled to receive payment of their marriage contracts are forever prohibited from partaking of *teruma*. Similarly, the wife of a priest who states: I was defiled, is forbidden to partake of *teruma* (Rambam *Sefer Zera'im, Hilkhot Teruma* 8:15).

NOTES

And these are prohibited from partaking of *teruma*, etc. – וְאֵלּוּ אֲסוּרוֹת מִלֶּאֱכוֹל בִּתְרוּמָה וכו׳: Some explain the common factor unifying the various women listed here is that there is an issue other than their warning and seclusion that causes the prohibition against them partaking of *teruma* (*Devar Shaul*). Although there are differing opinions on the details, it seems that all these women are prohibited from partaking of *teruma* immediately and are no longer afforded the opportunity to prove their innocence by drinking the bitter water (see *Ḥeshek Shlomo* and *Ḥiddushei HaGriz*).

The commentaries discuss what the novelty of this ruling is, being that the earlier mishna (2a) already stated that it becomes prohibited for a woman to partake of *teruma* from the moment she secludes herself with the man about whom she has been warned. Some explain that unlike a regular *sota*, who can prove her innocence through the testing of the bitter water, the women listed here cannot drink it and therefore have no recourse (*Mishne LaMelekh*). It seems that a woman will become prohibited from partaking of *teruma* even if she were to make such a claim after having drunk the bitter water and been proven faithful (*Ḥeshek Shlomo*).

Where witnesses came, etc. – שֶׁבָּאוּ עֵדִים וכו׳: Although the language of the mishna and Gemara seem to indicate that two witnesses testified to her infidelity, *Tosafot* conclude that testimony of even one witness would be sufficient, even if he were to testify after she already drank the bitter water.

גמ׳ אמר רב עמרם: הא מילתא אמר לן רב ששת, ואנהר לן עינין ממתניתין: סוטה שיש לה עדים במדינת הים – אין המים בודקין אותה. מאי טעמא? דאמר קרא: ״ונסתרה והיא נטמאה ועד אין בה״, דליכא דידע בה, לאפוקי הא, דהא איכא דידע בה.

GEMARA **Rav Amram says: Rav Sheshet told us this matter, and he enlightened our eyes for us** by citing support for his statement **from the mishna:** In the case of **a *sota*** for **whom there are witnesses concerning her in a country overseas,**[H] who can testify that she engaged in sexual intercourse, **the** bitter **water** of a *sota* **does not evaluate** whether or not **she** was unfaithful. Although she committed adultery, the water evaluates her fidelity only when there is no possibility of proving her guilt in court. **What is the reason** for this? It is **as the verse states:** "And a man lie with her carnally, and it was hidden from the eyes of her husband, **and she was defiled secretly,**[N] **and there was no witness against her"** (Numbers 5:13). This indicates that the bitter water is given only **when there is no** one **who knows about her** action, **to the exclusion** of the case **of this** woman who is not given the bitter water, **as there are** those **who know about her.**

ואנהר לן עינין ממתניתין, דקתני: ושבאו לה עדים שהיא טמאה. דאתו עדים אימת? אי נימא מקמי דתשתי, זונה היא!

And Rav Sheshet **enlightened our eyes for us** by adducing support for his ruling **from the mishna, as it teaches: And where witnesses came** forth and testified **that she is defiled,** this is one of the women who can no longer partake of *teruma*: Rav Sheshet asks: This is a case **where** the **witnesses came when? If we say** that they came **before she drank,** then what is novel about the fact that it is prohibited for her to partake of *teruma*? **She is a woman who had sexual relations with a man forbidden to her by the Torah [*zona*],** as she is a confirmed adulteress, and it is obviously prohibited for her to partake of *teruma*.

אלא לבתר דשתאי. אי אמרת בשלמא אין המים בודקין אותה – שפיר, אלא אי אמרת מים בודקין אותה, תיגלי מילתא למפרע דסהדי שקרי נינהו!

Rav Sheshet answers: **Rather,** it must be referring to a case where the witnesses testified **after she** already **drank. Granted, if you say** that **the** bitter **water** of a *sota* **does not evaluate her** in a case where there are witnesses elsewhere who can testify with regard to her infidelity, **it is well. But if you say** that **the water evaluates her** in a case where there are witnesses elsewhere who can testify with regard to her infidelity, then **it should be revealed retroactively that they are false witnesses,**[N] as the fact that she survived the drinking of the bitter water would indicate that she never committed adultery.

אמר ליה רב יוסף, לעולם אימא לך: מים בודקין אותה, והא אימור זכות תולה לה.

Rav Yosef said to Rav Sheshet: **Actually, I will say to you** that the bitter **water evaluates her** in a case where there are witnesses elsewhere who can testify with regard to her infidelity. Nevertheless, the fact that the woman survived the drinking of the water does not prove her innocence, **and** one can **say** that **this** woman who already drank had **merit** that **delayed** the punishment **for her.** According to some opinions, if an unfaithful woman has certain merits, she will not die immediately upon drinking the water. Therefore, if witnesses were to testify to her infidelity after she drank the water without dying, it is not clear that their testimony is false.

במאי קמיפלגי? במתנוונה דרבי, דתנן, רבי אומר: זכות תולה במים המרים, ואינה יולדת ואינה משבחת אלא מתנוונה והולכת, לסוף שהיא מתה באותה מיתה.

The Gemara explains: **With regard to what** principle **do** Rav Sheshet and Rav Yosef **disagree? With regard to** whether she **deteriorates [*mitnavvena*],**[L] **as** explained by **Rabbi** Yehuda HaNasi, **as we learned** in a mishna (22a): **Rabbi** Yehuda HaNasi **says: Merit delays** punishment **with regard to the bitter water** of a *sota*. Even if a woman actually committed adultery, she will not die immediately due to the merit that she has. **But she will not give birth, and she will not improve** in terms of her physical condition after having drunk the bitter water. **Rather, she will progressively deteriorate** until **she ultimately dies in the same** manner of **death** as suffered by a *sota* who drank the bitter water without having merit.

HALAKHA

There are witnesses concerning her in a country overseas – יש לה עדים במדינת הים: If two witnesses testify with regard to the infidelity of a *sota* who exhibited none of the effects of guilt from drinking the bitter water, she becomes forbidden to her husband and is divorced without receiving payment of her marriage contract, as the water tests only a woman for whom there are no witnesses at all to her infidelity. If, after drinking the bitter water, one witness testifies with regard to her infidelity, she is not required to leave her husband (Rambam *Sefer Nashim*, *Hilkhot Sota* 3:23, and see *Mishne LaMelekh* there).

NOTES

As the verse states: And she was defiled secretly – דאמר קרא: ונסתרה: Rashi explains that Rav Sheshet's inference from the verse is based on the words: "And there was no witness against her," which indicates that the *sota* rite is performed only when there are no witnesses to her infidelity. The Rosh questions this explanation for two reasons: First, as Rashi himself notes, these words are already the source of other *halakhot* and cannot be used to teach this *halakha* as well. Second, there are alternate versions of the text that do not quote that part of the verse, but only "and she was defiled secretly." Therefore, the Rosh explains that Rav Sheshet derives his *halakha* from the word "secretly," which he interprets to mean that the *halakhot* of a *sota* apply to a woman who was secluded entirely, meaning that no witnesses saw her.

That they are false witnesses – דסהדי שקרי נינהו: *Tosefot HaRash* presents the question: Isn't there another possibility, that the witnesses are testifying truthfully, but the bitter water did not examine the woman due to her engaging in sexual intercourse with her husband prior to drinking? He cites Rabbeinu Tam, who explains that according to the opinion of the Rabbis quoted in the mishna (7a), two Torah scholars accompany the husband and wife, and therefore there is no reason to suspect that the husband and wife engaged in sexual intercourse. He adds that even according to the opinion of Rabbi Yehuda cited there, that the couple does not require an escort, it is unreasonable to assume that if the husband engaged in sexual intercourse with his wife while on the journey he would still insist that she drink the bitter water. Therefore, the court assumes that the testing of the water was foolproof, and therefore the witnesses must be false.

There is room, however, to ask a more fundamental question: The testimony of two witnesses is deemed credible even with regard to capital crimes, so how can the fact that she did not die as a result of drinking the bitter water call the credibility of their testimony into question? One answer cited is that testimony concerning sexual intercourse is deemed credible even when witnesses testify only that the man and woman were acting in the manner of those engaging in sexual intercourse, even if they cannot testify that the act was completed. Therefore, if the bitter water seems to verify the woman's innocence, the court will assume that although the witnesses are not testifying falsely, there was in fact no actual sexual intercourse (*Torat HaKenaot*).

LANGUAGE

Deteriorates [*mitnavvena*] – מתנוונה: This word indicates a continuous decrease in bodily strength through sickness or weakness. In the words of the Rambam: Sickness comes upon her until she rots.

רַב שֵׁשֶׁת סָבַר: בֵּין לְרַבִּי וּבֵין לְרַבָּנַן הָוְיָא מִתְנַוְּונָה, וְרַב יוֹסֵף סָבַר: לְרַבִּי הָוְיָא מִתְנַוְּונָה, לְרַבָּנַן לָא הָוְיָא מִתְנַוְּונָה.

Rav Sheshet holds: Both according to the opinion of **Rabbi** Yehuda HaNasi **and according to** the opinion of **the Rabbis,** who disagree with him, **she** begins to **deteriorate** despite her merit. Therefore, if she doesn't begin to deteriorate immediately, the witnesses who testified subsequent to her drinking must be false witnesses. **And Rav Yosef holds:** Only **according to** the opinion of **Rabbi** Yehuda HaNasi is it so that **she** begins to **deteriorate** when she has merit. **According to** the opinion of **the Rabbis, she does not** begins to **deteriorate.** Therefore, Rav Yosef explains that the mere fact that she survived the drinking of the bitter water and didn't begin deteriorating does not prove that the testimony was false.

מְתִיב רַב שִׁימִי בַּר אַשִׁי, רַבִּי שִׁמְעוֹן אוֹמֵר: אֵין זְכוּת תּוֹלָה בַּמַּיִם הַמָּרִים, וְאִם אַתָּה אוֹמֵר: זְכוּת תּוֹלָה בַּמַּיִם הַמָּרִים, מְדַחֶה אַתָּה אֶת הַמַּיִם בִּפְנֵי כָּל הַנָּשִׁים הַשּׁוֹתוֹת, וְאַתָּה מוֹצִיא שֵׁם רַע עַל הַטְּהוֹרוֹת שֶׁשָּׁתוּ, וְהֵן אוֹמְרִים: טְמֵאוֹת הָיוּ, אֶלָּא שֶׁתָּלְתָה לָהֶן זְכוּת.

Rav Shimi bar Ashi raises an objection from the aforementioned mishna (22a), which also teaches that **Rabbi Shimon says: Merit does not delay** punishment **with regard to the bitter water** of a *sota*, **and if you say** that **merit delays** punishment **with regard to the bitter water,** then **you push aside** the deterrent force of **the** bitter **water before all the women who** must **drink** it, as guilty women will rely on their merit to protect them from the immediate consequences. **And** furthermore, **you defame the untainted women who drank** and survived. People will not view this as proof of their innocence, **and they** will **say: They are defiled, but** their **merit delayed** the punishment **for them.**

וְאִם אִיתָא, יֵשׁ לָהּ עֵדִים בִּמְדִינַת הַיָּם נָמֵי, אַתָּה מוֹצִיא שֵׁם רַע עַל הַטְּהוֹרוֹת שֶׁשָּׁתוּ, וְהֵן אוֹמְרִים: טְמֵאוֹת הָיוּ, אֶלָּא שֶׁיֵּשׁ לָהֶן עֵדִים בִּמְדִינַת הַיָּם!

After quoting the statement of Rabbi Shimon, Rav Shimi bar Ashi now explains his objection: **And if it is so** that the bitter water of a *sota* does not evaluate the faithfulness of a women **about whom there are witnesses in a country overseas,** then the same claim can be made **as well: You defame the untainted women who drank** and survived. People will not view this as proof of their innocence, **and they** will **say: They are defiled, but there are witnesses about them in a country overseas.**

לְרַבִּי שִׁמְעוֹן קָאָמְרַתְּ? לְרַבִּי שִׁמְעוֹן, מִדִּזְכוּת לָא תַּלְיָא, עֵדִים נָמֵי לָא תָּלוּ.

The Gemara responds: Do **you say** this **according to** the opinion of **Rabbi Shimon?** Indeed, **according to Rabbi Shimon, from** the same logic that **merit does not delay** punishment, **witnesses** in a country overseas **do not delay** it **either,** and Rav Sheshet would concede that his statement would not be accepted by Rabbi Shimon.

מְתִיב רַב – וְאֵלּוּ שֶׁמִּנְחוֹתֵיהֶן נִשְׂרָפוֹת:

Rav raises an objection from the latter clause of the mishna there (22a), which teaches: **And these are** the *sota* women **whose meal-offerings are burned** and not offered on the altar:[B]

BACKGROUND

Meal-offering of a ***sota*** **– מִנְחַת סוֹטָה:** This is the meal-offering brought by a suspected adulteress that is mentioned in the *sota* passage in the Torah. A *sota* is brought by her husband to the Temple to undergo the rite necessary to evaluate her faithfulness to him. There she is required to bring a meal-offering of barley flour, unlike most meal-offerings, which are brought from wheat flour. No oil or incense is added to the offering. A handful of flour is removed from this offering, and the remainder of it is eaten by the priests (see Numbers, chapter 5).

Perek **I**
Daf **6** Amud **b**

הָאוֹמֶרֶת טְמֵאָה אֲנִי, וְשֶׁבָּאוּ לָהּ עֵדִים שֶׁהִיא טְמֵאָה.

One who says: I am defiled,[H] **and witnesses came** forth and testified **with regard to her that she is defiled.**

דְּאָתוּ עֵדִים אֵימַת? אִילֵימָא מִקַּמֵּי דְּתִקְדּוֹשׁ, תֵּיפּוֹק לְחוּלִּין!

Rav clarifies: In the case **where witnesses came** forth, **when** did they come forth? **If we say** that they came forth **before** the meal-offering **was sanctified,** as all meal-offerings become sanctified only when placed in the service vessels used in the Temple service, then the testimony should obviate the need for the *sota* rite, and the meal-offering **should be transferred to non-sacred** status, as any meal-offering that was found to be consecrated in error before it was sanctified in a service vessel reverts to non-sacred status. Therefore, Rav infers that the witnesses could not have testified before the offering's sanctification, or the meal-offering would not be burned.

HALAKHA

One who says, I am defiled – הָאוֹמֶרֶת טְמֵאָה אֲנִי: If, after the meal-offering has been sanctified in a service vessel but before the handful was taken, a woman says: I am defiled to you, or if at that point witnesses testify that the woman had been defiled, the meal-offering is burned in its entirety. This is in accordance with the opinion of Rav Pappa (Rambam *Sefer Nashim*, *Hilkhot Sota* 4:14).

אֶלָּא לְבָתַר דְּקַדּוּשׁ. אִי אָמְרַתְּ בִּשְׁלָמָא מַיִם בּוֹדְקִין אוֹתָהּ, אַלְמָא בַּת מִקְדַּשׁ וּמִקְרַב הִיא, וְכִי קַדּוּשׁ מֵעִיקָּרָא שַׁפִּיר קַדּוּשׁ, וּמִשּׁוּם הָכִי מִנְחָתָהּ נִשְׂרֶפֶת.

Rav states his objection: **Rather,** the witnesses must have come forth **after** the meal-offering **was sanctified. Granted, if you say** the bitter **water** of a *sota* **evaluates** whether **she** was unfaithful in a case where there are witnesses to her infidelity, even if they have not testified, **evidently** the meal-offering **is suitable to be sanctified and sacrificed; and when it was sanctified at the outset,** although there were witnesses who could have testified, it **was properly sanctified, and due to that** reason **her meal-offering is burned,**[N] because once an offering has been properly sanctified it cannot be transferred to non-sacred status.

אֶלָּא אִי אָמְרַתְּ אֵין הַמַּיִם בּוֹדְקִין אוֹתָהּ, תִּיגְלֵי מִילְּתָא לְמַפְרֵעַ דְּכִי קַדּוּשׁ מֵעִיקָּרָא בְּטָעוּת קַדּוּשׁ, וְתֵיפּוּק לְחוּלִּין!

But if you say that **the** bitter **water does not evaluate** whether **she** was unfaithful so long as there are witnesses to her infidelity, **then** once the witnesses come forth, **the matter should be revealed retroactively that when** the meal-offering was **sanctified at the outset, it was sanctified in error. And** the meal-offering should therefore be **transferred to non-sacred** status, not burned.

אֲמַר רַב יְהוּדָה מִדִּיסְקַרְתָּא: כְּגוֹן שֶׁזִּינְּתָה בָּעֲזָרָה, דְּכִי קַדּוּשׁ מֵעִיקָּרָא שַׁפִּיר קַדּוּשׁ.

Rav Yehuda from Diskarta said, in response, that the mishna concerning meal-offerings is referring to a case **where** the woman **committed adultery in the** Temple **courtyard** after the meal-offering had been sanctified in a service vessel, **as at the outset, when** the meal-offering **was sanctified** due to the previous seclusion, it **was properly sanctified,** as the witnesses were to the infidelity that occurred in the Temple courtyard, not to infidelity during the seclusion.

מַתְקִיף לָהּ רַב מְשָׁרְשִׁיָּא: וַהֲלֹא פִּירְחֵי כְהוּנָּה מְלַוִּין אוֹתָהּ! שֶׁזִּינְּתָה מִפִּירְחֵי כְהוּנָּה עַצְמָן.

Rav Mesharshiyya objects to this explanation: **But** how can she commit adultery in the Temple courtyard? **Don't young priests** [***pirḥei kehunna***][L] **accompany her** to the place where she drinks? The Gemara answers: This is a case **where she committed adultery with the young priests themselves.**

רַב אַשִׁי אֲמַר: כְּגוֹן שֶׁנִּצְרְכָה לִנְקָבֶיהָ, דְּאַטּוּ פִּירְחֵי כְהוּנָּה בְּכִיפָּה תָּלֵי לָהּ?

Rav Ashi said differently: It is a case **where she needed to relieve herself** and the accompanying young priest allowed her to go relieve herself in private, and she committed adultery there, **for is that to say** that **the young priests hold her in a cell?**[N] Since there are times when she is out of their sight, there remains a possibility that she will commit adultery with others even when accompanied by the young priests.

רַב פַּפָּא אֲמַר: לְעוֹלָם כִּדְאָמְרִינַן מֵעִיקָּרָא. וּדְקָאָמְרַתְּ: תֵּיפּוּק לְחוּלִּין! מִדְּרַבָּנַן, גְּזֵירָה שֶׁמָּא יֹאמְרוּ: מוֹצִיאִין מִכְּלֵי שָׁרֵת לְחוֹל.

Rav Pappa said differently: **Actually,** the explanation is **as we initially said,** that the witnesses testify that she had been defiled during the initial seclusion for which she must drink, and not for adultery committed in the Temple courtyard. **And that which you say,** that if the bitter water does not evaluate a woman about whom there are witnesses concerning her infidelity, and therefore the offering was sanctified in error and it should be **transferred to non-sacred** status, you are correct that by Torah law it is non-sacred. However, it is considered sacred **by rabbinic law,** due to a rabbinic **decree, lest** people who do not know that the sanctification was done in error **will** mistakenly **say: One can transfer** a meal-offering **to non-sacred** status without it being redeemed even after it had been sanctified in **a service vessel.**

מְתִיב רַב מָרִי: נִטְמֵאת מִנְחָתָהּ, עַד שֶׁלֹּא קָדְשָׁה בִּכְלִי – הֲרֵי הִיא כְּכָל הַמְּנָחוֹת וְתִפָּדֶה. מִשֶּׁקָּדְשָׁה בִּכְלִי – הֲרֵי הִיא כְּכָל הַמְּנָחוֹת וְתִשָּׂרֵף;

Rav Mari raises an objection to Rav Pappa's interpretation from a *baraita* in the *Tosefta* (2:4–6) that states: If **the meal-offering** of a *sota* **became ritually impure,** its status is determined by when it became impure. If it became impure **before it was sanctified** by being placed **in** a service **vessel, it is like all** other **meal-offerings** that became impure prior to sanctification, **and it should be redeemed** by a replacement offering brought in its stead. **If it** became impure **after it had been sanctified** by being placed **in a** service **vessel, it is like all** other **meal-offerings** that became impure after sanctification **and must be burned.**

קָדַשׁ הַקּוֹמֶץ וְלֹא הִסְפִּיק לְהַקְרִיבוֹ עַד שֶׁמֵּת הוּא אוֹ עַד שֶׁמֵּתָה הִיא – הֲרֵי הִיא כְּכָל הַמְּנָחוֹת וְתִשָּׂרֵף.

The *baraita* continues: If, after the meal-offering was sanctified by being placed in a service vessel, the priest removed a handful from it to be sacrificed on the altar, and **the handful was sanctified**[H] by being placed in its own service vessel, **but the priest did not manage to sacrifice it before he,** the husband, **died,**[N] **or before she,** the wife, **died,** rendering the offering irrelevant, then **it is like all** other **meal-offerings** that are invalidated between the removal of the handful and its being sacrificed, **and it must be burned.**

NOTES

Her meal-offering is burned – מִנְחָתָהּ נִשְׂרֶפֶת: Generally, a handful is removed from the meal-offering mixture and sacrificed on the altar, with the remainder consumed by the priests. In the cases specified here, her meal-offering is burned in its entirety in the place where the ashes from the altar were put, without the handful being removed by the priest. *Tosafot* discuss whether there would be an option of asking a halakhic authority to retroactively dissolve the consecration, as it was done in error (see *Ḥiddushei HaGriz*).

Hold her in a cell – בְּכִיפָּה תָּלֵי לָהּ: According to the *Arukh*, the text states: Do they hold the woman by her shoulders at all times so that she cannot escape from their custody?

He died, etc. – מֵת הוּא וכו׳: Rashi explains that the death of the husband obviates the need for the evaluation, as the bitter water will no longer serve the function of permitting the wife to her husband. The Rashash questions this interpretation and maintains that the drinking of the water would still serve an additional function, as it can permit her to partake of *teruma* and will enable her to marry her putative paramour. Therefore, the Rashash explains as Rashi himself does (24a), that once the husband dies the woman may no longer drink, as the verse states: "Then shall the man bring his wife" (Numbers 5:15), requiring that the husband bring her for the evaluation to take place.

The *Minḥa Ḥareva*, however, explains that in the case where a husband dies after already having initiated the *sota* process, there is no proof from the verse quoted in the previous paragraph that she does not drink. Therefore, Rashi explains that this evaluation, which includes erasing the name of God, is primarily for the purpose of bringing peace between a man and his wife. If this result is not obtainable, e.g., the husband has died, the evaluation is not performed merely to determine the *halakha* with regard to secondary matters.

LANGUAGE

Young priests [*pirḥei kehunna*] – פִּרְחֵי כְהוּנָּה: The word *pirḥei* refers to something young and small that is still in the process of maturation and blooming, as in *peraḥ*, a flower. For the same reason, a chick is referred to as a *pirḥata* in Aramaic. Accordingly, *pirḥei kehunna* means young priests.

HALAKHA

The handful was sanctified, etc. – קָדַשׁ הַקּוֹמֶץ וכו׳: If the meal-offering of a *sota* becomes ritually impure before it is sanctified in a service vessel, it can be redeemed and transferred to non-sacred status. If it became impure after being sanctified in a service vessel, it must be burned in its entirety. If any of the following occurs after the handful is sacrificed, the remainder of the meal-offering is not eaten by the priests: If she says: I am defiled; or if she says: I will not drink; or if her husband does not want her to drink; or if witnesses arrive and testify that she was defiled; or if the husband or wife dies. Alternate versions of the text of the Rambam state that the remainder is eaten (Rambam *Sefer Nashim*, *Hilkhot Sota* 4:14).

קָרַב הַקּוֹמֶץ וְלֹא הִסְפִּיק לֶאֱכוֹל שִׁירַיִם עַד שֶׁמֵּת הוּא אוֹ עַד שֶׁמֵּתָה הִיא – הֲרֵי הִיא כְּכָל הַמְּנָחוֹת וְתֵאָכֵל, שֶׁעַל הַסָּפֵק בָּאת מִתְּחִילָּה, כִּיפְּרָה סְפֵיקָהּ וְהָלְכָה לָהּ.

The *baraita* continues: If **the handful was sacrificed but** the priest **did not manage to eat the remainder** of the meal-offering **before** the husband **died, or before** the wife **died, it is like all** other **meal-offerings** that become invalidated after the handful has been sacrificed, **and it must be eaten** by the priests. The *baraita* explains why, despite the death of the husband or wife, which renders this meal-offering irrelevant as the woman will not drink the bitter water, the meal-offering still is eaten: **Because** this meal-offering **initially came due to an uncertainty** as to whether the woman had been unfaithful, and **it atoned** for **its uncertainty and left,** i.e., it fulfilled its purpose of being sacrificed at the time when the husband and wife were still alive, it remains valid afterward as well.

בָּאוּ לָהּ עֵדִים שֶׁהִיא טְמֵאָה – מִנְחָתָהּ נִשְׂרֶפֶת. נִמְצְאוּ עֵדֶיהָ זוֹמְמִין – מִנְחָתָהּ חוּלִּין!

The *baraita* continues: **If witnesses came** forth before the handful was offered and testified **with regard to her that she is defiled, her meal-offering is burned.** If the **witnesses** who testified about **her** infidelity **are** later **found** to be **conspiring,**[HB] **her meal-offering is** transferred to **non-sacred** status. This final clause teaches that if the witnesses to the wife's infidelity are found to be conspiring witnesses, then the meal-offering is transferred to non-sacred status even after it was already sanctified in a service vessel. This is difficult for Rav Pappa, for he said that in a similar case, where witnesses testified about her infidelity after the offering was sanctified, the Sages decreed that the offering should be burned, in order to prevent people from saying that a meal-offering that has been sanctified in a service vessel may be transferred afterward to non-sacred status.

עֵדִים זוֹמְמִין קָאָמְרַתְּ? עֵדִים זוֹמְמִין קָלָא אִית לְהוּ.

The Gemara refutes this objection: Do **you say** that one can question Rav Pappa's statement from a ruling concerning **conspiring witnesses?** The cases are not comparable, as **conspiring witnesses generate publicity.**[N] Since the circumstances of these cases are well publicized, everyone knows that the offering was sanctified in error.

תַּנְיָא כְּוָותֵיהּ דְּרַב שֵׁשֶׁת, וְלָאו מִטַּעְמֵיהּ.

After attempting to question Rav Sheshet's novel ruling, that in the case of a *sota* with regard to whom there are witnesses in a country overseas who can testify that she engaged in sexual intercourse, the bitter water does not evaluate whether she was unfaithful, the Gemara attempts to adduce support for his ruling: **It is taught** in a *baraita* **in accordance with** the opinion of **Rav Sheshet, but not due to his reasoning,** rather based upon the explication of a verse.

״טְהוֹרָה״ – וְלֹא שֶׁיֵּשׁ לָהּ עֵדִים בִּמְדִינַת הַיָּם.

The *baraita* expounds several words in the verse concerning a *sota* who survives the drinking of the bitter water and is found to have been faithful: "And if the woman be not defiled, but be clean [*utehora hee*], then she shall be cleared and shall conceive seed" (Numbers 5:28). Noting that the phrase "but be clean," is apparently redundant, the *baraita* explains: The usage of the word **"clean [*tehora*]"** in the verse indicates that only one who survived the drinking of the bitter water due to her fidelity will conceive a child, **but** this will **not** happen in a case **where** she did not die because **there are witnesses for her in a country overseas** who can testify that she engaged in sexual intercourse.

״וּטְהוֹרָה״ – וְלֹא שֶׁתָּלְתָה לָהּ זְכוּת.

Additionally, from the additional letter *vav* in the word **"*utehora*,"** meaning "but be clean," another case is excluded. Only one who survived the drinking of the bitter water due to her fidelity will conceive a child, **but** this will **not** happen in a case **where merit delays** punishment **for her,** and she consequently doesn't die immediately after drinking the bitter water.

״הִיא״ – וְלֹא שֶׁיִּשְׂאוּ וְיִתְּנוּ בָּהּ מוֹזְרוֹת בַּלְּבָנָה.

The *baraita* continues: The next word in the verse, **"she [*hee*],"** excludes a third case: **But not where she,** i.e., her infidelity, **is discussed by weavers [*mozerot*]**[L] **in the moonlight.** Women would sit in groups while spinning thread in the moonlight and gossip about the goings-on in the city. If they discuss her having committed adultery, then it is considered public knowledge, and the bitter water would not evaluate her in that case, as evaluation is not needed.

HALAKHA

Witnesses who testified about her are found to be conspiring – נִמְצְאוּ עֵדֶיהָ זוֹמְמִים: The meal-offering of the *sota* is transferred to non-sacred status if the witnesses who testify about her are found to be conspiring witnesses (Rambam *Sefer Nashim, Hilkhot Sota* 4:15).

BACKGROUND

Conspiring witnesses [*edim zomemin*] – עֵדִים זוֹמְמִין: This term refers specifically to witnesses who are proven to have perjured themselves through the arrival of a second pair of witnesses. The second pair testifies to the first pair's inability to have testified in the case, based on not having been present at the time of the event in question. In general, there are several ways by which the testimony of a second set of witnesses can invalidate the testimony of a previous pair of witnesses.

First, the second pair contradicts the testimony of the first pair by testifying that the matter did not occur as described by the first pair. In this situation, the testimony of neither pair is accepted, and the matter remains unresolved.

Second, the second pair testifies that the first set of witnesses are not capable of testifying on the matter, either because they are disqualified from bearing witness or because they are relatives of the party about whom they testified. Neither of these first two cases are included in the term: Conspiring witnesses.

Third, the second pair testifies that the first pair, whose testimony resulted in an assessment of liability, was actually elsewhere with the second pair of witnesses when the alleged incident transpired, and they therefore they could not have witnessed the events about which they testified. In such a case, the first pair is determined to be conspiring witnesses. In such a case, the testimony of the second pair is accepted, and the testimony of the first pair is rejected. Furthermore, the first pair is punished with the penalty they sought to inflict through their testimony (see Deuteronomy 19:16–19). Consequently, if their testimony would have resulted in court-imposed capital punishment, they are both put to death. If their testimony would have resulted in a monetary judgment, these witnesses are themselves required to compensate their victim the sum they sought to have him pay.

The specifics of these *halakhot* are analyzed in great detail in tractate *Makkot*.

NOTES

Generate publicity – קָלָא אִית לְהוּ: Since the determination that witnesses are conspiring occurs in court and requires the testimony of other witnesses, the matter would become known, especially when the conspiring witnesses are punished by being flogged. By contrast, when the offering was consecrated in error, the matter will not generate publicity, and there is concern that people will understand that items that have already been sanctified in service vessels can be transferred to non-sanctified status.

LANGUAGE

Weavers [*mozerot*] – מוֹזְרוֹת: This word is similar to the word for people who twist or splice. It refers to women who sat and wove ropes of flax by the moonlight while discussing local news and gossip. The text in the Jerusalem Talmud refers to both *motezrot*, women who comb wool, and *mozerot*, women who weave flax.

NOTES

He does not interpret the letter *vav* – **וי״ו לָא דָּרֵישׁ**: *Tosafot* on *Sanhedrin* 14a explain that Rabbi Shimon generally does expound the letter *vav*, but he derives a different *halakha* from the letter *vav* in this case.

וְרַבִּי שִׁמְעוֹן, נְהִי דְּוי״ו לָא דָּרֵישׁ, וְהָא אִיכָּא

After citing this *baraita* as proof for the ruling of Rav Sheshet, albeit from a different source, the Gemara questions how Rabbi Shimon could deny the ability of the woman's merit to delay the *sota* punishment due to fear that it will discredit the whole *sota* rite, being that there is another case that prevents the bitter water from evaluating a woman, i.e., where witnesses in a country overseas are able to testify. **And Rabbi Shimon, granted that he does not interpret** the letter ***vav***,[N] as he holds that its addition is not significant, and therefore he holds that her merit does not delay her punishment, **but there is**

Perek **I**
Daf **7** Amud **a**

HALAKHA

What does he do with her – **כֵּיצַד עוֹשֶׂה לָהּ**: The husband states before his local court: I warned my wife not to seclude herself with so-and-so, and she then secluded herself with him, and these are the witnesses. She claims that she is undefiled, and I want her to be evaluated by drinking the bitter water. The court then hears the testimony of the witnesses. If their testimony is accepted, the court provides two Torah scholars to accompany the husband and wife on their journey to the Temple, in order to prevent them from engaging in sexual intercourse on the way (Rambam *Sefer Nashim*, *Hilkhot Sota* 3:1).

NOTES

But on the way, unless there are three – **אֲבָל בַּדֶּרֶךְ עַד דְּאִיכָּא שְׁלֹשָׁה**: The commentaries offer several reasons for the requirement that there be an additional man during travel. First, on a long journey it is inevitable that one of them will need to relieve himself and will probably distance himself from the man and woman, so as to have privacy. Second, while in the city, if one man needs to leave for some time, the second man can leave as well, thereby avoiding seclusion with the woman; but on the road there is nowhere for the other man to go. Even if there were a way for the second man to distance himself from the woman, he would not do so out of fear for the woman's safety (*Devar Shaul*).

יֵשׁ לָהּ עֵדִים בִּמְדִינַת הַיָּם!

the case where **there are witnesses for her in a country overseas** who can testify that she engaged in sexual intercourse, when the bitter water will not evaluate her faithfulness. Therefore, Rabbi Shimon should be concerned that such a dispensation will result in the defamation of the untainted women who drank and were unaffected, as people will view them as guilty women who were not affected because there were witnesses overseas.

לָא שְׁכִיחָא.

The Gemara answers: The case of witnesses in a country overseas is **not common,** and therefore no one will assume that that is the reason why the woman was not affected. By contrast, a woman having merit is common.

מתני׳ כֵּיצַד עוֹשֶׂה לָהּ? מוֹלִיכָהּ לְבֵית דִּין שֶׁבְּאוֹתוֹ מָקוֹם, וּמוֹסְרִין לוֹ שְׁנֵי תַלְמִידֵי חֲכָמִים, שֶׁמָּא יָבֹא עָלֶיהָ בַּדֶּרֶךְ. רַבִּי יְהוּדָה אוֹמֵר: בַּעְלָהּ נֶאֱמָן עָלֶיהָ.

MISHNA The mishna details the procedure for administering the drinking of the bitter water of a *sota*. **What does** her husband **do with her**[H] after she secluded herself with the man about whom she had been warned? **He brings her to the court that is** found **in that location, and** the court **provides him** with **two Torah scholars** to accompany him, **lest he engage in sexual intercourse with her on the way** to the Temple, which is not only prohibited but will also prevent the bitter water from evaluating her. **Rabbi Yehuda says: Her husband is trusted with regard to her,** so there is no need to provide scholars to accompany him.

גמ׳ תְּרֵי וְאִיהוּ – הָא תְּלָתָא. לֵימָא מְסַיֵּיע לֵיהּ לְרַב, דְּאָמַר רַב יְהוּדָה אָמַר רַב: לֹא שָׁנוּ אֶלָּא בָּעִיר, אֲבָל בַּדֶּרֶךְ – עַד דְּאִיכָּא שְׁלֹשָׁה, שֶׁמָּא יִצְטָרֵךְ אֶחָד מֵהֶן לִנְקָבָיו, וְנִמְצָא אֶחָד מֵהֶן מִתְיַיחֵד עִם הָעֶרְוָה!

GEMARA The Gemara assumes that the requirement for there to be two Torah scholars is to avoid the prohibition against a woman being alone with a man. The Gemara notes: **Two** additional men **and he,** the husband, **are three** people altogether. **Let us say** that **this** mishna **supports** the opinion of **Rav, as Rav Yehuda says** that **Rav says:** When they taught that it is permitted for a woman to be secluded with two men, **they taught** that this is permitted **only in the town** (see *Kiddushin* 80b). **But on the way,** when traveling, this is not permitted **unless there are three**[N] men with the woman. The reason for this stringency is that if there are only two men with her, **perhaps one will need to relieve himself** and will seek privacy, **and it will be found that one of them is in seclusion with a woman forbidden to him.**

לָא, הָכָא הַיְינוּ טַעְמָא, כִּי הֵיכִי דְּלֶיהֱווּ עֲלַהּ סָהֲדֵי.

The Gemara refutes this assumption: **No, here,** in the case of a *sota*, **this is the reason** why there is a requirement for two scholars, **so that there are two witnesses with regard to her,** i.e., there will be two witnesses to testify in the event that the husband engages in sexual intercourse with her on the way to the Temple. The reason is not to avoid the prohibition against her being alone with a man, as one scholar would suffice for that.

תַּלְמִידֵי חֲכָמִים אִין, כּוּלֵּי עָלְמָא לָא. לֵימָא מְסַיַּיע לֵיהּ לְאִידָּךְ דְּרַב, דְּאָמַר רַב יְהוּדָה אָמַר רַב: לֹא שָׁנוּ אֶלָּא כְּשֵׁירִין, אֲבָל פְּרוּצִין – אֲפִילּוּ עֲשָׂרָה נַמִּי לָא. מַעֲשֶׂה הָיָה וְהוֹצִיאוּהָ עֲשָׂרָה בְּמִטָּה!

The mishna teaches that the husband is provided with Torah scholars. The Gemara further comments: **Torah scholars, yes; anyone** else, **no.** It is specifically Torah scholars who are provided to accompany the husband and wife. **Let us say** that this mishna **supports another** statement **of Rav, as Rav Yehuda says** that **Rav says:** When they taught that it is permitted for a woman to be secluded with two men, **they taught** that this is permitted **only** with regard **to** men of fit morals.[H] **But** with regard to **those of loose morals,** she may **not** be secluded **even with ten** men. The Gemara adds: **There was an incident and ten** men **carried out** a woman **on a bier,** as if she were dead, and engaged in sexual intercourse with her.

לָא. הָכָא הַיְינוּ טַעְמָא, דְּיָדְעִי לְאַתְרוּיֵי בֵּיהּ.

The Gemara refutes this assumption: **No, here,** in the case of a *sota,* **this is the reason** why there is a requirement for two scholars, **that they know** how **to** properly **warn him**[N] not to engage in sexual intercourse with her. Therefore, this mishna does not support the opinion of Rav.

״רַבִּי יְהוּדָה אוֹמֵר: בַּעְלָהּ״ וכו׳. תַּנְיָא, רַבִּי יְהוּדָה אוֹמֵר: בַּעְלָהּ נֶאֱמָן מִקַּל וָחוֹמֶר, וּמַה נִּדָּה שֶׁהִיא בְּכָרֵת – בַּעְלָהּ נֶאֱמָן עָלֶיהָ, סוֹטָה שֶׁהִיא בְּלָאו – לֹא כׇּל שֶׁכֵּן!

§ The Gemara now discusses Rabbi Yehuda's statement in the mishna. **Rabbi Yehuda says: Her husband** is trusted with regard to her. **It is taught** in a *baraita* in the *Tosefta* (1:2): **Rabbi Yehuda says: Her husband is trusted due to an *a fortiori*** inference: **And just as** in the case of **a menstruating woman, who is** prohibited from engaging in sexual intercourse with her husband **by** penalty of ***karet,* her husband is** nevertheless **trusted with regard to her,** as he is permitted to seclude himself with her, so too, with regard to **a *sota,* who is** prohibited from engaging in sexual intercourse with her husband only **by** penalty of **a prohibition,** is it **not all the more so** that he should be trusted?

וְרַבָּנַן? הִיא הַנּוֹתֶנֶת: נִדָּה דְּכָרֵת – חֲמִירָא לֵיהּ וּמְהֵימַן, סוֹטָה דְּלָאו – לָא חֲמִירָא לֵיהּ וְלָא מְהֵימַן.

And the Rabbis say: **That provides** support for the contrary opinion, as these considerations lead to the opposite conclusion. **A menstruating woman** is forbidden **by** penalty of ***karet.*** This is **a stringent** prohibition **for him, and** this is why **he is trusted** not to engage in sexual intercourse with her. By contrast, **a *sota*** is forbidden to him only **by a prohibition.** This is **not a stringent** prohibition **to him, and he is** therefore **not trusted** with her.

וְרַבִּי יְהוּדָה מִקַּל וָחוֹמֶר מַיְיתֵי לַהּ? וְהָא רַבִּי יְהוּדָה מִקְּרָאֵי מַיְיתֵי לַהּ! דְּתַנְיָא: ״וְהֵבִיא הָאִישׁ אֶת אִשְׁתּוֹ אֶל הַכֹּהֵן״ – מִן הַתּוֹרָה הָאִישׁ מֵבִיא אֶת אִשְׁתּוֹ, אֲבָל אָמְרוּ חֲכָמִים: מוֹסְרִין לוֹ שְׁנֵי תַּלְמִידֵי חֲכָמִים, שֶׁמָּא יָבֹא עָלֶיהָ בַּדֶּרֶךְ.

The Gemara asks: **And does Rabbi Yehuda** in fact **derive this** *halakha* **from an *a fortiori*** inference? **But Rabbi Yehuda derives it from a verse, as it is taught** in a *baraita*: The verse: **"Then shall the man bring his wife to the priest"** (Numbers 5:15), teaches that **by Torah** law **the man** alone **brings his wife** to the Temple, **but the Sages said:** The court **provides him** with **two Torah scholars** to accompany him, **lest he engage in sexual intercourse with her on the way** to the Temple.

רַבִּי יוֹסֵי אוֹמֵר: בַּעְלָהּ נֶאֱמָן עָלֶיהָ מִקַּל וָחוֹמֶר, וּמַה נִּדָּה שֶׁהִיא בְּכָרֵת – בַּעְלָהּ נֶאֱמָן עָלֶיהָ, סוֹטָה שֶׁהִיא בְּלָאו – לֹא כׇּל שֶׁכֵּן!

The *baraita* records a second opinion. **Rabbi Yosei says: Her husband is trusted with regard to her** based on **an *a fortiori*** inference: **And just as a menstruating woman, who is** prohibited from engaging in sexual intercourse with her husband **by** penalty of ***karet,*** and **her husband is** nevertheless **trusted with regard to her,** then with regard to **a *sota,* who is** prohibited from engaging in sexual intercourse with her husband **by** penalty of only **a prohibition,** should he **not all the more so** be trusted?

אָמְרוּ לוֹ: לֹא, אִם אָמַרְתָּ בְּנִדָּה – שֶׁכֵּן יֵשׁ לָהּ הֶיתֵּר, תֹּאמַר בְּסוֹטָה שֶׁאֵין לָהּ הֶיתֵּר? וְאוֹמֵר: ״מַיִם גְּנוּבִים יִמְתָּקוּ״ וגו׳.

The Sages **said to him: No, if you say** that this is true **with regard to a menstruating woman,** the reason he is trusted is not due to the severity of the prohibition. Rather, he is trusted **because she has** the ability to become **permitted** to her husband after her menstrual flow has ceased and she has immersed in a ritual bath. **Shall you** also **say** that this is the case **with regard to a *sota,* who** potentially **does not have** the ability to become **permitted** to her husband due to her suspected adultery? **And** proof to the notion that people will more readily commit illicit acts that are permanently prohibited comes from the verse that **states: "Stolen waters are sweet** and bread eaten in secret is pleasing" (Proverbs 9:17). Consequently, there is a concern that the husband will engage in sexual intercourse with his *sota* wife if not accompanied by scholars.

HALAKHA

They taught only with regard to men of fit morals – לֹא שָׁנוּ אֶלָּא כְּשֵׁירִין: A woman should not seclude herself with several men, unless the wife of one of the men is present. The Rema notes that there are those (Rosh) who hold that while in a town, one woman can seclude herself with two men of fit morals during the day, and he adds that most men meet this standard for purposes of this *halakha.* If they are in a field any time of the day or in a town at night, there needs to be a minimum of three men of fit morals. Some authorities permit one man to seclude himself with several women, provided that his profession is one that doesn't bring him into constant contact with women (Rambam *Sefer Kedusha, Hilkhot Issurei Bia* 22:8; *Shulḥan Arukh, Even HaEzer* 22:5).

NOTES

That they know how to warn him – דְּיָדְעִי לְאַתְרוּיֵי בֵּיהּ: A warning must include the specification of the prohibition that will be transgressed and its punishment, and therefore not all have the knowledge to give a proper warning (see *Tosafot*).

HALAKHA

They would bring her up to the Sanhedrin, etc. – **מַעֲלִין אוֹתָהּ לְבֵית דִּין הַגָּדוֹל וכו׳**: When the husband and wife arrive at the Sanhedrin in Jerusalem, the court threatens her without her husband present, to encourage her to admit her sin. They also offer words of encouragement, such as: My daughter, wine and frivolity cause much immoral behavior. If she admits her sin or says: I will not drink, she is divorced and forfeits her rights to payment of her marriage contract (Rambam *Sefer Nashim, Hilkhot Sota* 3:2).

רַבִּי יְהוּדָה אוֹמֵר: מִן הַתּוֹרָה הָאִישׁ מֵבִיא אֶת אִשְׁתּוֹ אֶל הַכֹּהֵן, שֶׁנֶּאֱמַר: ״וְהֵבִיא הָאִישׁ אֶת אִשְׁתּוֹ״!

The *baraita* quotes a third opinion. **Rabbi Yehuda says: By Torah** law,[N] **the man** alone **brings his wife** to the Temple, **as is stated: "Then shall the man bring his wife to the priest."** This *baraita* states explicitly that Rabbi Yehuda derives this *halakha* from the verse itself, not from an *a fortiori* inference.

אֲמַר לְהוּ קַל וָחוֹמֶר בְּרֵישָׁא וּפִרְכוּהּ, וַהֲדַר אֲמַר לְהוּ קְרָא.

The Gemara answers: Rabbi Yehuda **first said to them** the ***a fortiori*** inference, **and they refuted it** as mentioned above, **and** he **then said to them** the derivation from the **verse.**

רַבִּי יְהוּדָה הַיְינוּ תַּנָּא קַמָּא! אִיכָּא בֵּינַיְיהוּ: ״אֲבָל אָמְרוּ״.

The Gemara clarifies: Apparently, the opinion of **Rabbi Yehuda is** the same as that of **the first *tanna*** in the *baraita*, who also cites the verse as proof that by Torah law the husband alone brings his wife to the priest. The Gemara explains: The difference **between them** concerns the following clause: **But the Sages said** that the court provides him with two Torah scholars to accompany him. The first *tanna* holds that the Sages require two scholars to accompany the husband and wife, while Rabbi Yehuda holds that they do not.

מתני׳ הָיוּ מַעֲלִין אוֹתָהּ לְבֵית דִּין הַגָּדוֹל שֶׁבִּירוּשָׁלַיִם, וּמְאַיְּימִין עָלֶיהָ כְּדֶרֶךְ שֶׁמְּאַיְּימִין עַל עֵדֵי נְפָשׁוֹת,

MISHNA The mishna details the next stage of the process. **They would bring her up to the Sanhedrin**[H] **that was in Jerusalem, and** the judges would **threaten her** in order that she admit her sin. **And** this was done **in the manner that they** would **threaten witnesses** testifying **in** cases of **capital** law.[N] In those cases, the judges would explain to the witnesses the gravity of their testimony by stressing the value of human life. Here too, the judges would attempt to convince the woman to admit her sin, to avoid the loss of her life.

וְאוֹמֵר לָהּ: בִּתִּי, הַרְבֵּה יַיִן עוֹשֶׂה, הַרְבֵּה שְׂחוֹק עוֹשֶׂה, הַרְבֵּה יַלְדוּת עוֹשָׂה, הַרְבֵּה שְׁכֵנִים הָרָעִים עוֹשִׂין.

And additionally, the judge would **say to her: My daughter, wine causes a great deal** of immoral behavior, **levity causes a great deal** of immoral behavior, **immaturity causes a great deal** of immoral behavior, and **bad neighbors cause a great deal** of immoral behavior. The judge encouraged her to admit her sin by explaining to her that he understands that there may have been mitigating factors.

עֲשִׂי לִשְׁמוֹ הַגָּדוֹל שֶׁנִּכְתַּב בִּקְדוּשָּׁה שֶׁלֹּא יִמָּחֶה עַל הַמַּיִם. וְאוֹמֵר לְפָנֶיהָ דְּבָרִים שֶׁאֵינָם כְּדַי לְשׁוֹמְעָן הִיא וְכׇל מִשְׁפַּחַת בֵּית אָבִיהָ.

The judge then continues: **Act for the sake of His great name, so that** God's name, **which is written in sanctity, shall not be erased on the water.** If the woman admits to having committed adultery, the scroll upon which the name of God is written will not be erased. **And** additionally, the judge **says in her presence matters that are not worthy of being heard** by **her and all her father's family,**[N] in order to encourage her to admit her sin, as the Gemara will explain.

NOTES

Rabbi Yehuda says: By Torah law – **רַבִּי יְהוּדָה אוֹמֵר מִן הַתּוֹרָה**: The *Tosefot HaRosh* does not include the phrase: By Torah law, in the statement of the leniency stated by Rabbi Yehuda (see *Yagel Ya'akov*). This omission seems to be correct, as Rabbi Yehuda holds that this is the *halakha* also by rabbinic law, not only by Torah law. The version of the text here, which does include this phrase, can be explained according to what is written in the Jerusalem Talmud: Rabbi Yehuda says that despite the logical reasons to the contrary, there is a verse in the Torah teaching that a man is trusted to bring his *sota* wife to the Temple. Others explain that Rabbi Yehuda's rationale is based on the principle, propounded by the *Taz* among others, that the Sages did not have the ability to prohibit that which is explicitly permitted in the Torah. Therefore, due to the verse cited by Rabbi Yehuda, the Sages could not prohibit the husband alone to bring her despite the compelling reason for the prohibition.

And this was done in the manner that they would threaten witnesses testifying in cases of capital law – **וּמְאַיְּימִין עָלֶיהָ כְּדֶרֶךְ שֶׁמְּאַיְּימִין עַל עֵדֵי נְפָשׁוֹת**: *Tosefot Yom Tov* explains that this should not be understood to mean that they threaten her with the same threats used in cases of capital law. Rather, just as the court threatens witnesses testifying in cases of capital law in more explicit terms than they do to those testifying in monetary cases, the *sota* is also extensively threatened. Others explain that since her drinking the bitter water involves possible death for her and her paramour, she is warned exactly as she would be in a case of capital law (*Minḥat Kenaot*).

Her and all her father's family – **הִיא וְכׇל מִשְׁפַּחַת בֵּית אָבִיהָ**: The Meiri explains that this is a figure of speech, indicating that what is said to her would be difficult for her to hear even if her entire family were present to support her. Rambam, in his Commentary on the Mishna, explains simply that her family is presumably with her and they also hear what is being said.

אִם אָמְרָה טְמֵאָה אֲנִי, שׁוֹבֶרֶת כְּתוּבָּתָהּ וְיוֹצֵאת.

If after the judge's warning **she says: I am defiled,** she writes a **receipt** for **her marriage contract.** That is, she writes a receipt indicating that she has no claims on her husband with regard to the sum written in her marriage contract, as a woman who admits to adultery forfeits her right to this payment. **And she is** then **divorced** from her husband.

וְאִם אָמְרָה טְהוֹרָה אֲנִי, מַעֲלִין אוֹתָהּ לְשַׁעַר הַמִּזְרָח שֶׁעַל פֶּתַח שַׁעַר נִקָּנוֹר, שֶׁשָּׁם מַשְׁקִין אֶת הַסּוֹטוֹת וּמְטַהֲרִין אֶת הַיּוֹלְדוֹת וּמְטַהֲרִין אֶת הַמְּצוֹרָעִין.

But if after the warning **she** maintains her innocence and **says: I am pure, they bring her up to the Eastern Gate,**[NH] **which is at the opening of** the **Gate of Nicanor,**[B] **because** three rites were performed **there: They give the *sota* women** the bitter water **to drink,**[N] **and they purify women who have given birth** (see Leviticus 12:6–8), **and they purify the lepers**[H] (see Leviticus 14:10–20).

וְכֹהֵן אוֹחֵז בִּבְגָדֶיהָ, אִם נִקְרְעוּ נִקְרָעוּ, וְאִם נִפְרְמוּ נִפְרָמוּ, עַד שֶׁהוּא מְגַלֶּה אֶת לִבָּהּ, וְסוֹתֵר אֶת שְׂעָרָהּ. רַבִּי יְהוּדָה אוֹמֵר: אִם הָיָה לִבָּהּ נָאֶה לֹא הָיָה מְגַלֵּהוּ, וְאִם הָיָה שְׂעָרָהּ נָאֶה לֹא הָיָה סוֹתֵר.

The mishna continues describing the *sota* rite. **And the priest grabs hold**[N] **of her clothing**[H] and pulls them, unconcerned about what happens to the clothing. **If** the clothes **are torn,**[N] so **they are torn; if the stitches come apart,** so **they come apart.** And he pulls her clothing **until he reveals her heart,** i.e., her chest. **And** then **he unbraids her hair. Rabbi Yehuda says: If her heart was attractive he would not reveal it, and if her hair was attractive he would not unbraid** it.

הָיְתָה מִתְכַּסָּה בִּלְבָנִים, מְכַסָּהּ בִּשְׁחוֹרִים. הָיָה עָלֶיהָ כְּלֵי זָהָב

If **she was dressed in white**[H] garments, **he** would now **cover her with black** garments. If **she was wearing gold adornments,**

BACKGROUND

Gate of Nicanor – שַׁעַר נִיקָנוֹר: The Gate of Nicanor is well known for the beauty of its copper doors, as well as for the miracles that occurred while the doors were being transported by ship from Egypt. This gate stood at the main entrance to the Temple, and it was the site of rituals that had to be performed as close to the Temple as possible without being inside the Temple.

Gate of Nicanor

NOTES

To the Eastern Gate, etc. – לְשַׁעַר הַמִּזְרָח וכו׳: This language is somewhat difficult as two different gates are mentioned, and there are several versions of the text of the mishna. According to Rashi, she is first brought up to the Eastern Gate, which is the outer gate of the women's courtyard, and then she is lead to Gate of Nicanor, which is the gate to the Israelite courtyard. Alternatively, the *Kaftor VaFeraḥ* explains that the Eastern Gate is the Gate of Nicanor.

Because there they give the *sota* women to drink – שֶׁשָּׁם מַשְׁקִין אֶת הַסּוֹטוֹת: The reason lepers and women who have given birth are purified at the Eastern Gate is obvious, as they are still impure and cannot enter further into the Temple. However, the reason the *sota* drinks there is not clear. It has been proposed that because her hair is uncovered and her clothes torn, it would be disgraceful and improper to bring her into the Temple itself (*Minḥa Ḥareva*).

And the priest grabs hold – וְכֹהֵן אוֹחֵז: The *Tosefta* (1:7) states that this priest was chosen by drawing lots, and any priest who is chosen, even the High Priest, is obligated to perform the task.

If the clothes are torn, etc. – אִם נִקְרְעוּ וכו׳: The Gemara uses two terms to describe the ripping of the clothing, *keria* and *ferima*, which are translated in the text as tearing and the forcing apart of stitches respectively, in line with Rabbeinu Ḥananel's explanation of the Gemara. In the context of this Gemara, however, a number of other explanations are given in the commentaries. Rashi explains that *keria* is ripping one large tear, while *ferima* means tearing into small pieces. The Meiri and Rambam's Commentary on the Mishna explain that *keria* is ripping one large tear in the front of the garment and *ferima* is causing several small tears on the side of the garment. Others explain that *keria* is a vertical tear and *ferima* is a lateral tear (*Tosefot Yom Tov*).

HALAKHA

They bring her up to the Eastern Gate – מַעֲלִין אוֹתָהּ לְשַׁעַר הַמִּזְרָח: If the woman insists that she was faithful, she is brought to the Eastern Gate of the Temple courtyard, where she is led to and fro in order to fatigue her, so that she will admit her sin. If she continues to maintain her innocence, she is led to the outside of the Eastern Gate, where she remains standing until the next stage of the process (Rambam *Sefer Nashim*, *Hilkhot Sota* 3:3–4).

And they purify the lepers – וּמְטַהֲרִין אֶת הַמְּצוֹרָעִין: During the purification process of a leper, he stands outside the Israelite courtyard, in front of the eastern entrance, at the lintel of the Gate of Nicanor, facing west. This is where all those who have not yet brought an atonement offering to complete the purification process stand at the time they are being purified, and there a *sota* drinks the bitter water (Rambam *Sefer Korbanot*, *Hilkhot Meḥusrei Kappara* 4:2).

The priest grabs hold of her clothing – כֹּהֵן אוֹחֵז בִּבְגָדֶיהָ: After God's name is erased into the water, the priest, chosen by lot (*Mishne LaMelekh*), grabs hold of the clothing of the *sota* and pulls them off until he exposes her chest, and he uncovers and unbraids her hair (Rambam *Sefer Nashim*, *Hilkhot Sota* 3:11).

If she was dressed in white – הָיְתָה מִתְכַּסָּה בִּלְבָנִים: If she was dressed in white garments, she would put on black garments. If the black clothing enhances her appearance, she is clothed in garments that cause her to appear unattractive (Rambam *Sefer Nashim*, *Hilkhot Sota* 3:4).

LANGUAGE

Chokers [*katliyot*] – קַטְלִיאוֹת: The source of this word is the Latin catella, referring to a chain that is hung around the neck.

BACKGROUND

Egyptian rope – חֶבֶל מִצְרִי: This is a coarse rope that is generally fashioned of peels of willow leaves or palm fibers. Some explain that it is a rope that is brought from Egypt (*Tosefot Yom Tov*).

Dry poison – סַם יָבֵשׁ: Most medicines and poisons that are put on the skin do not act until they penetrate into the blood stream. If the skin is unbroken and free from wounds they will remain on the surface and have no effect. In a similar manner, the bitter water will have no effect on a woman who is free from sin.

NOTES

And the Gemara raises a contradiction – וּרְמִינְהוּ: The commentaries note that this is not the standard usage of this term, as there is no contradiction between the mishna and the *Tosefta*, as the *Tosefta* merely adds that the *sota* is also encouraged to drink (*Keren Ora*). Others add one could even infer this *halakha* from the wording of the mishna, as it says that the court warns the *sota* as witnesses are warned in cases of capital law, where the witnesses are warned that they must testify if they know the truth (*Torat HaKenaot*).

וְקַטְלִיאוֹת נְזָמִים וְטַבָּעוֹת, מַעֲבִירִין מִמֶּנָּה כְּדֵי לְנַוְּולָהּ. וְאַחַר כָּךְ מֵבִיא חֶבֶל מִצְרִי וְקוֹשְׁרוֹ לְמַעְלָה מִדַּדֶּיהָ.

or chokers [*katliyot*],[L] or nose rings, or finger rings,[H] **they removed them from her in order to render her unattractive. And afterward** the priest **would bring an Egyptian rope**[BH] fashioned from palm fibers, **and he would tie it above her breasts.**

וְכׇל הָרוֹצֶה לִרְאוֹת בָּא לִרְאוֹת, חוּץ מֵעֲבָדֶיהָ וְשִׁפְחוֹתֶיהָ, מִפְּנֵי שֶׁלִּבָּהּ גַּס בָּהֶן. וְכׇל הַנָּשִׁים מוּתָּרוֹת לִרְאוֹתָהּ, שֶׁנֶּאֱמַר: ״וְנִוַּסְּרוּ כׇּל הַנָּשִׁים וְלֹא תַעֲשֶׂינָה כְּזִמַּתְכֶנָה״.

And anyone who desires to watch[H] **her may come to watch, except for her slaves and maidservants,**[H] who are not permitted to watch **because her heart is emboldened by them,** as seeing one's slaves reinforces one's feeling of pride, and their presence may cause her to maintain her innocence. **And all of the women**[H] **are permitted to watch her, as it is stated:** "Thus will I cause lewdness to cease out of the land, **that all women may be taught not to do after your lewdness**" (Ezekiel 23:48).

גמ׳ מְנָהָנֵי מִילֵּי? אָמַר רַבִּי חִיָּיא בַּר גַּמְדָּא אָמַר רַבִּי יוֹסֵי בְּרַבִּי חֲנִינָא: אָתְיָא ״תּוֹרָה״, ״תּוֹרָה״. כְּתִיב הָכָא: ״וְעָשָׂה לָהּ הַכֹּהֵן אֵת כׇּל הַתּוֹרָה״, וּכְתִיב הָתָם: ״עַל פִּי הַתּוֹרָה אֲשֶׁר יוֹרוּךָ״, מָה לְהַלָּן בְּשִׁבְעִים וְאֶחָד, אַף כָּאן בְּשִׁבְעִים וְאֶחָד.

GEMARA The Gemara asks concerning the *halakha* that the *sota* is brought before the Sanhedrin: **From where are these matters** derived? **Rabbi Ḥiyya bar Gamda says that Rabbi Yosei, son of Rabbi Ḥanina, says:** This **is derived** by means of a verbal analogy between the words **"*tora*"** and **"*tora*."** It **is written here,** with regard to a *sota*: **"And the priest shall execute upon her all this law [*tora*]"** (Numbers 5:30), **and** it **is written there,** with regard to a rebellious Elder, who must go to the place chosen by God and follow the ruling of the Sanhedrin: **"According to the law [*tora*] that they shall teach you"** (Deuteronomy 17:11). **Just as there** the verse is referring to what occurs **in** the presence of the Sanhedrin of **seventy-one** judges, **so too here,** with regard to a *sota*, the verse is referring to what occurs **in** the presence of the Sanhedrin of **seventy-one** judges.

״וּמְאַיְּימִין עָלֶיהָ״ וכו׳. וּרְמִינְהוּ: כְּדֶרֶךְ שֶׁמְּאַיְּימִין עָלֶיהָ שֶׁלֹּא תִּשְׁתֶּה כָּךְ מְאַיְּימִין עָלֶיהָ שֶׁתִּשְׁתֶּה. אוֹמְרִים לָהּ: בִּתִּי, אִם בָּרוּר לָךְ הַדָּבָר שֶׁטְּהוֹרָה אַתְּ, עִמְדִי עַל בּוּרְיֵיךְ וּשְׁתִי, לְפִי שֶׁאֵין מַיִם הַמָּרִים דּוֹמִין אֶלָּא לְסַם יָבֵשׁ שֶׁמּוּנָּח עַל בָּשָׂר חַי, אִם יֵשׁ שָׁם מַכָּה מְחַלְחֵל וְיוֹרֵד. אֵין שָׁם מַכָּה אֵינוֹ מוֹעִיל כְּלוּם!

§ The mishna teaches: **And they threaten her** in order that she admit her sin, to obviate the need to erase God's name. **And** the Gemara **raises a contradiction**[N] from that which was taught in a *baraita* in the *Tosefta* (1:6): **In the same manner that they threaten her so that she will not drink, so too, they threaten her so that she will drink,**[H] as **they say to her: My daughter, if the matter is clear to you that you are pure, arise for** the sake of **your clear** position **and drink.** If you are innocent you have nothing to fear, **because the bitter water is similar only to a dry poison**[B] **placed on the flesh. If there is a wound** there, the poison will **penetrate and enter** the blood stream, but if **there is no wound there, it does not have any effect.** This teaches that the woman is warned not to drink if she is guilty, but if she is not guilty she is encouraged to drink. There is no mention of the latter in the mishna.

לָא קַשְׁיָא: כָּאן קוֹדֶם שֶׁנִּמְחֲקָה מְגִילָּה, כָּאן לְאַחַר שֶׁנִּמְחֲקָה מְגִילָּה.

The Gemara answers: This is **not difficult. Here** the mishna is referring to **before the scroll was erased,** and at that point the woman is warned only not to drink if she is guilty, so that the name of God will not be erased. **There** the *baraita* is referring to **after the scroll was erased.** Then she is warned that if she is innocent she should drink because if she now refuses to drink, it will turn out that the scroll was erased for no purpose.

HALAKHA

Nose rings or finger rings, etc. – נְזָמִים וְטַבָּעוֹת וכו׳: All the jewelry of the *sota* is removed in preparation for her drinking (Rambam *Sefer Nashim, Hilkhot Sota* 3:4).

Would bring an Egyptian rope – מֵבִיא חֶבֶל מִצְרִי: The priest brings an Egyptian rope after he has uncovered her hair and torn her clothes. If an Egyptian rope is not available, he brings a rope of any kind and ties it above her chest so that her clothes won't fall off (Rambam *Sefer Nashim, Hilkhot Sota* 3:11).

Anyone who desires to watch – כׇּל הָרוֹצֶה לִרְאוֹת: Anyone who desires to watch the *sota* rite may do so (Rambam *Sefer Nashim, Hilkhot Sota* 3:5).

Except for her slaves and maidservants – חוּץ מֵעֲבָדֶיהָ וְשִׁפְחוֹתֶיהָ: The slaves and maidservants of a *sota* are not permitted to be present during the *sota* rite, as their presence may embolden her to falsely maintain her innocence (Rambam *Sefer Nashim, Hilkhot Sota* 3:6).

And all of the women, etc. – וְכׇל הַנָּשִׁים וכו׳: All the women present in the Temple when a *sota* is given to drink are obligated to watch (Rambam *Sefer Nashim, Hilkhot Sota* 3:5).

They threaten her so that she will drink – מְאַיְּימִין עָלֶיהָ שֶׁתִּשְׁתֶּה: A *sota* is encouraged to drink. The judges tell her that if she is innocent she need not worry because the bitter water harms only those who sinned (Rambam *Sefer Nashim, Hilkhot Sota* 4:5).

״וְאוֹמֵר לְפָנֶיהָ״ וכו׳. תָּנוּ רַבָּנַן: אוֹמֵר לְפָנֶיהָ דְּבָרִים שֶׁל הַגָּדָה וּמַעֲשִׂים שֶׁאֵירְעוּ בַּכְּתוּבִים הָרִאשׁוֹנִים, כְּגוֹן: ״אֲשֶׁר חֲכָמִים יַגִּידוּ וְלֹא כִחֲדוּ מֵאֲבוֹתָם״.

§ The mishna teaches: **And** the judge **says in her presence**[H] matters that are not worthy of being heard by her and all her father's family in order to encourage her to admit her sin. The Gemara cites a *baraita* that details what was said. **The Sages taught** in a *baraita*: The judge **says in her presence words of homiletical** interpretation **and** mentions **incidents that happened** to previous generations that are recorded **in the early** prophetic **writings.**[N] **For example,** they expound the following verse: **"That wise men told and did not hide from their fathers"** (Job 15:18); this teaches that even during the time of the forefathers, there were people who admitted their sins despite the shame they incurred.

יְהוּדָה הוֹדָה וְלֹא בּוֹשׁ, מֶה הָיָה סוֹפוֹ? נָחַל חַיֵּי הָעוֹלָם הַבָּא. רְאוּבֵן הוֹדָה וְלֹא בּוֹשׁ, מֶה הָיָה סוֹפוֹ? נָחַל חַיֵּי הָעוֹלָם הַבָּא. וּמַה שְּׂכָרָן? מַה שְּׂכָרָן? כִּדְקָא אָמְרִינַן! אֶלָּא מַה שְּׂכָרָן בָּעוֹלָם הַזֶּה? ״לָהֶם לְבַדָּם נִתְּנָה הָאָרֶץ וְלֹא עָבַר זָר בְּתוֹכָם״.

For example, **Judah admitted** that he sinned with Tamar **and was not embarrassed** to do so, and **what was his end? He inherited the life of the World-to-Come. Reuben admitted** that he lay with his father's concubine Bilhah **and was not embarrassed,** and **what was his end? He** too **inherited the life of the World-to-Come.** The Gemara asks: **And what is their reward?** The Gemara interjects: **What is their reward?** Their reward was clearly **as we say,** that they inherited the life of the World-to-Come. The Gemara clarifies: **Rather,** the second question was: **What is their reward in this world?** The Gemara answers by citing the next verse in the book of Job: **"To them alone the land was given, and no stranger passed among them"** (Job 15:19). Judah was given the kingship, and Reuben inherited a portion of land in the Transjordan before the other tribes.

בִּשְׁלָמָא בִּיהוּדָה אַשְׁכְּחַן דְּאוֹדִי, דִּכְתִיב: ״וַיַּכֵּר יְהוּדָה וַיֹּאמֶר צָדְקָה מִמֶּנִּי״. אֶלָּא רְאוּבֵן מְנָלַן דְּאוֹדִי?

The Gemara questions the source for Reuben's admission. **Granted, with regard to Judah we have found** a source **that he admitted** his sin with Tamar, **as it is written: "And Judah acknowledged them and said: She is more righteous than I"** (Genesis 38:26). Judah admitted that he was the one who had impregnated Tamar. **But from where do we** derive **that Reuben admitted** his sin?

דְּאָמַר רַבִּי שְׁמוּאֵל בַּר נַחְמָנִי אָמַר רַבִּי יוֹחָנָן, מַאי דִּכְתִיב: ״יְחִי רְאוּבֵן וְאַל יָמֹת. וְזֹאת לִיהוּדָה״?

The Gemara answers: It is **as Rabbi Shmuel bar Naḥmani says** that **Rabbi Yoḥanan says: What is** the meaning of that **which is written** concerning Reuben and Judah in Moses' blessing of the tribes at the end of his life: **"Let Reuben live and not die in that his men become few"** (Deuteronomy 33:6), and immediately afterward, in the following verse, it is stated: **"And this for Judah,** and he said: Hear, Lord, the voice of Judah, and bring him in unto his people; his hands shall contend for him, and You shall be a help against his adversaries" (Deuteronomy 33:7). What is the connection between the blessing of Reuben and that of Judah, juxtaposed with the conjunction "and"?

כָּל אוֹתָן שָׁנִים שֶׁהָיוּ יִשְׂרָאֵל בַּמִּדְבָּר, הָיוּ עַצְמוֹתָיו שֶׁל יְהוּדָה מְגוּלְגָּלִין בָּאָרוֹן, עַד שֶׁעָמַד מֹשֶׁה וּבִקֵּשׁ עָלָיו רַחֲמִים. אָמַר לְפָנָיו: רִבּוֹנוֹ שֶׁל עוֹלָם, מִי גָּרַם לִרְאוּבֵן שֶׁהוֹדָה – יְהוּדָה, ״וְזֹאת לִיהוּדָה״?

Rabbi Yoḥanan says: **All those years that the Jewish people were in the desert, the bones of Judah,** which the Jewish people took with them from Egypt along with the bones of his brothers, **were rolling** around **in the coffin, until Moses arose and asked for compassion on** Judah's behalf. Moses **said before** God: **Master of the Universe, who served as the impetus for Reuben that he admit** his sin, through which he merited a blessing and was not excluded from the count of the twelve sons of Jacob (see Genesis 35:22)? It was **Judah,**[N] as Reuben saw him confess his sin, and thereby did the same. Moses continues in the next verse: **"And this for Judah,"** as if to say: Is this Judah's reward for serving as an example of confessing to one's sins, that his bones roll around?

HALAKHA

And the judge says in her presence, etc. – וְאוֹמֵר לְפָנֶיהָ וכו׳: When the *sota* is brought before the court, they tell her: Great and important people were overcome by their desires and transgressed. They recount to her the episodes of Judah and Tamar, Reuben and Bilhah, and Amnon and Tamar, as written in the Bible, without interpretation. This is in order to encourage her to admit her sin (Rambam *Sefer Nashim*, *Hilkhot Sota* 3:2).

NOTES

And incidents that happened that are in the early writings, etc. – וּמַעֲשִׂים שֶׁאֵירְעוּ בַּכְּתוּבִים הָרִאשׁוֹנִים וכו׳: Rashi and the Meiri explain this phrase to mean that the priests cite examples of people who admitted their sins. However, the Rambam explains that the priests cite instances where great people sinned in sexual matters, e.g., Judah and Tamar, Reuben and Bilhah, David and Bathsheba, and Amnon and Tamar. This is to encourage the *sota* to come to terms with her actions if she is guilty so that she will confess.

The Rambam adds that at least some of these stories are told as they are written in the Torah, without the exposition of the Sages, whose interpretations often minimized the severity of the sins, e.g., the priests explain that Reuben only moved his father's bed out of the tent of Bilhah. Apparently, the Rambam understood the mishna's statement: They say matters that she is not worthy of hearing, as meaning that they tell her stories from the Bible in a way in which it is not proper to be heard, i.e., without the rabbinic interpretation. This is especially notable when one takes into consideration that some of these episodes were not translated into Aramaic, the vernacular, when they were publicly taught, as were all other verses (see *Megilla* 25a).

Who served as the impetus for Reuben that he admit his sin, Judah – מִי גָּרַם לִרְאוּבֵן שֶׁהוֹדָה, יְהוּדָה: Although the Sages teach that Reuben fasted and repented to atone for his sin even before the incident with Judah and Tamar, he did not admit his sin in public until he saw Judah do so.

LANGUAGE

Sockets [*shafa*] – שָׁפָא: There are those who hold that the source of this word is the Greek σιπύη, *sipuē*, meaning a jar, bin, or box.

מִיָּד "שְׁמַע ה׳ קוֹל יְהוּדָה"! עַל אֵיבְרֵיהּ לְשָׁפָא. וְלָא הֲוָה קָא מְעַיְּילִין לֵיהּ לִמְתִיבְתָּא דִרְקִיעָא – "וְאֶל עַמּוֹ תְּבִיאֶנּוּ". וְלָא הֲוָה קָא יָדַע מִשְׁקַל וּמִטְרַח בִּשְׁמַעְתָּא בַּהֲדֵי רַבָּנַן – "יָדָיו רָב לוֹ". לָא הֲוָה קָא סָלְקָא לֵיהּ שְׁמַעְתָּא אַלִּיבָּא דְהִילְכְתָא – "וְעֵזֶר מִצָּרָיו תִּהְיֶה".

Immediately after Moses prayed, the verse states: **"Hear, Lord, the voice of Judah"** (Deuteronomy 33:7). **His bones** then **entered** their **sockets** [*shafa*],[L] and his skeleton was reassembled. **But** the angels still **did not elevate** him **into the heavenly study hall.** Moses then prayed: **"And bring him in unto his people"** (Deuteronomy 33:7), i.e., those in the heavenly study hall. This prayer was accepted, **but he** still **did not know** how **to deliberate** in Torah matters **with the** heavenly **sages.** Moses then prayed: **"His hands shall contend for him"** (Deuteronomy 33:7), meaning that he should have the ability to contend with them in study. But still **he was unable to draw** conclusions from **his discussion in accordance with the** ***halakha.*** Moses then prayed: **"And You shall be a help against his adversaries"** (Genesis 33:7).

בִּשְׁלָמָא יְהוּדָה דְּאוֹדֵי, כִּי הֵיכִי דְּלָא תִּישָּׂרֵף תָּמָר. אֶלָּא רְאוּבֵן לָמָּה לֵיהּ דְּאוֹדֵי? וְהָאָמַר רַב שֵׁשֶׁת: חֲצִיף עָלַי דִּמְפָרֵיט חֲטָאֵיהּ! כִּי הֵיכִי דְּלָא לִיחַשְׁדוּ אֲחוּהִי.

The Gemara discusses the propriety of admitting one's sins in public. **Granted,** with regard to **Judah,** it was proper **that he admitted** his sin in public, as he did so **in order that Tamar not be burned** innocently. **But why did Reuben admit** his sin in public? **But didn't Rav Sheshet say: I** consider one **who specifies his sins** in public to be **brazen,**[NH] as one who does so indicates that he is not embarrassed by his actions? The Gemara answers: The reason he admitted his sin in public was **in order that his brothers should not be suspected** of having committed the deed.

"אִם אָמְרָה טְמֵאָה אֲנִי" וכו׳. שָׁמְעַתְּ מִינָּהּ: כּוֹתְבִין שׁוֹבֵר!

§ The mishna teaches: **If** after the judge's warning **she says: I am defiled,** she writes a receipt for her marriage contract. The Gemara comments: **You can learn from this** mishna **that one writes a receipt** to serve as proof that a debt has been paid rather than tearing the promissory note. This matter is the subject of a dispute between the *tanna'im* in tractate *Bava Batra* (170b).

אֲמַר אַבַּיֵי, תְּנֵי: מְקָרַעַת. אֲמַר לֵיהּ רָבָא: וְהָא שׁוֹבֶרֶת קָתָנֵי! אֶלָּא אֲמַר רָבָא: בְּמָקוֹם שֶׁאֵין כּוֹתְבִין כְּתוּבָּה עָסְקִינַן.

Abaye said: Teach in the mishna differently. Rather than understanding that she writes a receipt, explain it to mean: **She tears**[N] her marriage contract. **Rava said to him: But** the mishna **teaches** explicitly that **she writes a receipt. Rather,** to explain the mishna, **Rava said: We are dealing with a place in** which **they do not write a marriage contract,** as they rely on the rabbinical ordinance that all wives are entitled to the sum of a standard marriage contract upon divorce or being widowed, even if no marriage contract has been written. Because there is no marriage contract to tear, a receipt is written so that the man can prove that he no longer has a monetary obligation. However, generally, it is possible that the document would be torn, and no proof can be adduced from this mishna.

"וְאִם אָמְרָה טְהוֹרָה אֲנִי, מַעֲלִין אוֹתָהּ לְשַׁעֲרֵי מִזְרָח". מַעֲלִין אוֹתָהּ?

§ The mishna teaches: **But if** after the warning **she** maintains her innocence and **says: I am pure, they** would **bring her up to the Eastern Gate.** The Gemara asks: Would **they bring her up?**

NOTES

I consider one who specifies his sins in public to be brazen – חֲצִיף עָלַי דִּמְפָרֵיט חֲטָאֵיהּ: The *Tosefot HaRosh* (*Berakhot* 34b) explains that there is a distinction between a transgression done in public, for which one should confess in public in order to add shame as an element of one's repentance, and a transgression done in private, for which a public admission could be interpreted as a brazen statement that one is not embarrassed by his actions. The *Iyyun Ya'akov* notes that based on the same principle, those condemned to death are told to publicly admit to their sins, for once one has been judged and their sins are now a matter of public record, it is proper to atone publicly.

Teach she tears – תְּנֵי מְקָרַעַת: While the term *shoveret*, in the context of documents of monetary obligations, means to write a receipt, Abaye suggests that it should be understood here in line with its more global meaning of breaking. According to this explanation, the mishna would mean that the marriage contract itself is broken, i.e., physically torn (*Shita Mekubbetzet*).

HALAKHA

I consider one who specifies his sins in public to be brazen – חֲצִיף עָלַי דִּמְפָרֵיט חֲטָאֵיהּ: It is proper that one who repents should admit the details of his sin not only before God, but in public. When is this principle applicable? Only with regard to transgressions against one's fellow man; but with regard to transgressions against God it is an act of brazenness to publicly divulge one's transgressions. According to the Ra'avad and others, if his transgression against God was public knowledge, it is proper that he admit to it in public so as to publicize his repentance. Public confessions that are said by a congregation in unison are not subject to this principle, and may be said in any case (Rambam *Sefer HaMadda*, *Hilkhot Teshuva* 2:5; *Shulḥan Arukh*, *Oraḥ Ḥayyim* 607:2, and in the comment of Rema; see *Magen Avraham* and *Taz* there).

הָתָם קָיְימָא! דִּמַסְקִינַן לַהּ וּמַחְתִּינַן לַהּ כְּדֵי לְיַיגְּעָהּ. דְּתַנְיָא, רַבִּי שִׁמְעוֹן בֶּן אֶלְעָזָר אוֹמֵר: בֵּית דִּין מַסִּיעִין אֶת הָעֵדִים מִמָּקוֹם לְמָקוֹם, כְּדֵי שֶׁתִּטָּרֵף דַּעְתָּן עֲלֵיהֶן וְיַחְזְרוּ בָּהֶן.

She is already **standing there** in the Temple courtyard, as that is where the Sanhedrin sits. The Gemara answers: This teaches **that** they would **bring her up**[H] **and** would **bring her down** repeatedly **in order to fatigue her,** with the hope that her worn-down mental state will lead to her confession. This was also done with witnesses testifying in cases of capital law, **as it is taught** in the *Tosefta* (*Sanhedrin* 9:1): **Rabbi Shimon ben Elazar says:** In cases of capital law, the **court brings the witnesses**[H] **from** one **place to** another **place in order to confuse them so that they will retract** their testimony if they are lying.

"שֶׁשָּׁם מַשְׁקִין אֶת הַסּוֹטוֹת" וכו׳. בִּשְׁלָמָא סוֹטוֹת, דִּכְתִיב: "וְהֶעֱמִיד הַכֹּהֵן אֶת הָאִשָּׁה לִפְנֵי ה׳". מְצוֹרָעִין נָמֵי, דִּכְתִיב: "וְהֶעֱמִיד הַכֹּהֵן הַמְטַהֵר" וגו׳, אֶלָּא יוֹלֶדֶת מַאי טַעְמָא?

§ The mishna teaches: **Because there,** at the Eastern Gate, **they give the** *sota* **women** the bitter water **to drink,** and there the lepers and women who have given birth are purified. The Gemara asks: **Granted, the** *sota* **women** are given the bitter water to drink there, **as it is written: "And the priest shall stand the woman before the Lord"** (Numbers 5:18),[N] and the Eastern Gate is directly opposite the Sanctuary, which is the area referred to as "before the Lord." Similarly, with regard to **lepers as well,** this is **as it is written: "And the priest that cleans** him shall set the man that is to be cleansed, and those things, before the Lord" (Leviticus 14:11). **But what is the reason that** a woman **who has given birth** must also be purified there?

אִילֵימָא מִשּׁוּם דְּאָתְיָין וְקָיְימִין אַקּוּרְבְּנַיְיהוּ, דְּתַנְיָא: אֵין קׇרְבָּנוֹ שֶׁל אָדָם קָרֵב אֶלָּא אִם כֵּן עוֹמֵד עַל גַּבָּיו? אִי הָכִי, זָבִין וְזָבוֹת נָמֵי! אִין הָכִי נָמֵי, וְתָנָא חֲדָא מִינַּיְיהוּ נָקַט.

The Gemara suggests: **If we say** it is **because** of the requirement **for** the women who have given birth to **come and stand over their offerings, as it is taught** in a *baraita*: **The offering of a person is brought only**[H] **if he stands over it** while it is being sacrificed, and that is why they stand at this gate, which is as close to the sacrifice as they are permitted to be while they are ritually impure. **If that is so,** then the same *halakha* should apply to **men who experience a gonorrhea-like discharge** [*zavim*] **and women who experience a discharge of uterine blood after their menstrual period** [*zavot*][H] **as well.** They are also ritually impure while their offerings are sacrificed. Why would the mishna then specify women who have given birth? The Gemara answers: **Yes, it is indeed so, and the** *tanna* **cited one of them,** and the same *halakha* applies to all others in that category.

תָּנוּ רַבָּנַן: אֵין מַשְׁקִין שְׁתֵּי סוֹטוֹת כְּאַחַת, כְּדֵי שֶׁלֹּא יְהֵא לִבָּהּ גַּס בַּחֲבֶירְתָּהּ. רַבִּי יְהוּדָה אוֹמֵר: לֹא מִן הַשֵּׁם הוּא זֶה, אֶלָּא אָמַר קְרָא: "אֹתָהּ", לְבַדָּהּ.

§ **The Sages taught** in a *baraita* in the *Tosefta* (1:6): **Two** *sota* **women are not given to drink simultaneously,**[H] **in order that the heart** of each one **not be emboldened by the other,** as there is a concern that when one sees that the other woman is not confessing, she will maintain her innocence even if she is guilty. **Rabbi Yehuda says: This is not for** that **reason. Rather,** it is because **the verse states:** "And the priest shall bring **her** [*ota*] near and stand her before the Lord" (Numbers 5:16). Rabbi Yehuda explains his inference: The word "*ota*" indicates her **alone,** and therefore there is a Torah edict not to have two women drink the bitter water simultaneously.

וְתַנָּא קַמָּא, הָכְתִיב: "אֹתָהּ"! תַּנָּא קַמָּא רַבִּי שִׁמְעוֹן הִיא, דְּדָרֵישׁ טַעְמָא דִּקְרָא. וּמָה טַעַם קָאָמַר? מָה טַעַם אוֹתָהּ לְבַדָּהּ? כְּדֵי שֶׁלֹּא יְהֵא לִבָּהּ גַּס בַּחֲבֶירְתָּהּ.

The Gemara asks: **And** as for **the first** *tanna*, **isn't it written "*ota*"?** The Gemara answers: **The first** *tanna* **is** actually **Rabbi Shimon, who interprets the reasons of** *halakhot* **written in verses, and he is saying: What is the reason? What is the reason** the Torah requires **her alone,** that each *sota* drink individually? **In order that the heart** of each woman **not be emboldened by the other.**

מַאי בֵּינַיְיהוּ? אִיכָּא בֵּינַיְיהוּ רוֹתֶתֶת.

The Gemara asks: **What is** the difference **between them?** Why should it matter if this *halakha* is due to a logical reasoning or due to a Torah edict? The Gemara answers: The difference **between them** is in a case where one of the women is **trembling**[N] from fear. Since she has obviously not been emboldened by the presence of the other, Rabbi Shimon would allow her to be given to drink at the same time as the other.

HALAKHA

They would bring her up – מַסְקִינַן לַהּ: If the *sota* maintains her innocence before the court, she is brought up to the Eastern Gate, and she is then brought from place to place in order to fatigue her so that she will admit to her sin (Rambam *Sefer Nashim, Hilkhot Sota* 3:3).

Brings the witnesses, etc. – מַסִּיעִין אֶת הָעֵדִים וכו׳: When investigating the testimony of witnesses in cases of capital law, the judges should abruptly shift the topic of their questions in an attempt to confuse the witnesses and catch them in an inconsistency or falsehood. The *Kesef Mishne* notes that this is the Rambam's interpretation of: The witnesses are brought from place to place (Rambam *Sefer Shofetim, Hilkhot Edut* 1:4).

The offering of a person is brought only, etc. – אֵין קׇרְבָּנוֹ שֶׁל אָדָם קָרֵב אֶלָּא וכו׳: A person's offering cannot be sacrificed if he is not standing over it. Therefore, non-priestly watches were instituted so that Israelite representatives would be present on behalf of the entire people during the offering of communal sacrifices (Rambam *Sefer Avoda, Hilkhot Kelei HaMikdash* 6:1).

Zavim and *zavot*, etc. – זָבִין וְזָבוֹת וכו׳: A leper, and all others lacking atonement, such as *zavim*, *zavot*, and women who have given birth, stand outside the Israelite courtyard, at the opening of the Gate of Nicanor (Rambam *Sefer Korbanot, Hilkhot Meḥusrei Kappara* 4:2).

Two *sota* women are not given to drink simultaneously – אֵין מַשְׁקִין שְׁתֵּי סוֹטוֹת כְּאַחַת: It is a Torah edict that two *sota* women are not given to drink simultaneously, even if one is trembling, as the *halakha* is not in accordance with the opinion of Rabbi Shimon (Rambam *Sefer Nashim, Hilkhot Sota* 4:2).

NOTES

Before the Lord – לִפְנֵי ה׳: Rashi explains that although there were a total of seven gates to the courtyard, the Gate of Nicanor was considered "before the Lord," as it was the main gate through which people entered. Others explain that the Gate of Nicanor most resembled the placement of the solitary gate found in the Tabernacle, which was likewise located on the east side. It appears that the Rambam understands that the Eastern Gate and the Gate of Nicanor were considered "before the Lord" because they stood directly opposite the Holy of Holies.

The difference between them is in a case where one of the women is trembling [*rotetet*] – אִיכָּא בֵּינַיְיהוּ רוֹתֶתֶת: Rashi explains that in such a case, the woman who is trembling is clearly not emboldened by the presence of the other woman, and therefore she is able to drink along with another woman. However, *Tosefot HaRosh* asks: In such a case, what would allow for the woman who is not trembling to drink in the presence of a trembling woman, as one should be concerned that she will be emboldened to persist in her denial due to the presence of another woman? *Tosefot HaRosh* explains that the text of the Gemara should be emended to read *rotetot*, in the plural, indicating that only in a case where both women are trembling may they be given to drink simultaneously. The *Devar Shaul* answers in support of Rashi's explanation that in an instance where one woman is trembling, the other woman will certainly not be emboldened to remain defiant, and in fact it may influence her to admit to her guilt.

וְרוֹתַתֶת מִי מַשְׁקִין? וְהָא אֵין עוֹשִׂין מִצְוֹת חֲבִילוֹת חֲבִילוֹת!

The Gemara asks: **And** if she is **trembling,** can the court **give her to drink** at the same time as the other? **But** there is a general principle that **one does not perform mitzvot in bundles,**[N] as one who does so appears as if the mitzvot are a burden upon him, and he is trying to finish with them as soon as possible.

דִּתְנַן: אֵין מַשְׁקִין שְׁתֵּי סוֹטוֹת כְּאַחַת, וְאֵין מְטַהֲרִין שְׁנֵי מְצוֹרָעִין כְּאַחַת, וְאֵין רוֹצְעִין שְׁנֵי עֲבָדִים כְּאַחַת, וְאֵין עוֹרְפִין שְׁתֵּי עֶגְלוֹת כְּאַחַת, לְפִי שֶׁאֵין עוֹשִׂין מִצְוֹת חֲבִילוֹת חֲבִילוֹת!

As we learned in a *baraita*: **Two *sota* women are not given to drink simultaneously, and two lepers are not purified simultaneously,**[H] **and two slaves are not pierced simultaneously,**[H] **and two heifers do not have their necks broken simultaneously,**[H] **because one does not perform mitzvot in bundles.** Accordingly, even Rabbi Shimon would agree that under no circumstances can a priest give two *sota* women to drink simultaneously. How, then, can the Gemara say that a trembling woman can be given to drink together with another *sota*?

אֲמַר אַבַּיֵי, וְאִיתֵּימָא רַב כָּהֲנָא, לָא קַשְׁיָא: כָּאן בְּכֹהֵן אֶחָד, כָּאן בִּשְׁנֵי כֹהֲנִים.

Abaye said, and some say it was **Rav Kahana** who said: This is **not difficult. Here,** the second *baraita,* which says that it is prohibited to give two *sota* women to drink simultaneously because one does not perform mitzvot in bundles, is speaking **with regard to one priest. There,** Rabbi Shimon in the first *baraita,* who permits a trembling *sota* to be given to drink together with another *sota,* is speaking **with regard to two priests.** Since no individual priest is giving two women to drink simultaneously, mitzvot are not being performed in bundles.

״וְהַכֹּהֵן אוֹחֵז בִּבְגָדֶיהָ״. תָּנוּ רַבָּנַן: ״וּפָרַע אֶת רֹאשׁ הָאִשָּׁה״ – אֵין לִי אֶלָּא רֹאשָׁהּ, גּוּפָהּ מִנַּיִן? תַּלְמוּד לוֹמַר: ״הָאִשָּׁה״. אִם כֵּן, מַה תַּלְמוּד לוֹמַר ״וּפָרַע אֶת רֹאשָׁהּ״? מְלַמֵּד, שֶׁהַכֹּהֵן סוֹתֵר אֶת שְׂעָרָהּ.

§ The mishna teaches: **And the priest grabs hold of her clothing** and pulls them until he reveals her heart, and he unbraids her hair. The Gemara cites the source for these acts. **The Sages taught:** The verse states: "And the priest shall stand the woman before the Lord **and uncover**[N] **the woman's head**" (Numbers 5:18). From this verse **I have** derived **only** that he uncovers **her head; from where** do I derive that he uncovers **her body? The verse states: "The woman,"** rather than just stating: And uncovers her head. This indicates that the woman's body should be uncovered as well. **If so, what** is the meaning when **the verse states** specifically: **"And uncover her head"?** Once it has stated that he uncovers the woman, it is already apparent that she, including her hair, is uncovered. It **teaches that the priest** not only uncovers her hair but also **unbraids her hair.**

״רַבִּי יְהוּדָה אוֹמֵר: אִם הָיָה לִבָּהּ״ וכו׳. לְמֵימְרָא, דְּרַבִּי יְהוּדָה חָיֵישׁ לְהִרְהוּרָא, וְרַבָּנַן לָא חָיְישִׁי?

The mishna continues by citing that **Rabbi Yehuda says: If her heart was** attractive he would not reveal it, and if her hair was attractive he would not unbraid it. The Gemara asks: **Is this to say that Rabbi Yehuda,** who maintains that it is prohibited to uncover an attractive woman, **is concerned about** onlookers having sexual **thoughts, and the Rabbis,** who permit it, **are not concerned** about this?

וְהָא אִיפְּכָא שָׁמְעִינַן לְהוּ! דְּתַנְיָא: הָאִישׁ מְכַסִּין אוֹתוֹ פֶּרֶק אֶחָד מִלְּפָנָיו, וְהָאִשָּׁה – שְׁנֵי פְרָקִים, אֶחָד מִלְּפָנֶיהָ וְאֶחָד מִלְּאַחֲרֶיהָ, מִפְּנֵי שֶׁכּוּלָּהּ עֶרְוָה, דִּבְרֵי רַבִּי יְהוּדָה. וַחֲכָמִים אוֹמְרִים: הָאִישׁ נִסְקָל עָרוֹם, וְאֵין הָאִשָּׁה נִסְקֶלֶת עֲרוּמָּה!

But we have heard the opposite from them, as it is taught in the *Tosefta* (*Sanhedrin* 9:6): Although **a man** condemned to stoning is stoned unclothed, the court **covers him** with **one** small **piece** of material **in front of him,** to obscure his genitals, and they cover **a woman with two** small **pieces** of material, **one in front of her and one behind her, because all of her** loins are **nakedness,** as her genitals are visible both from the front and from the back. This is **the statement of Rabbi Yehuda. And the Rabbis say: A man is stoned** while **naked,**[H] **but a woman is not stoned** while **naked,** but fully clothed. Apparently, Rabbi Yehuda is not concerned that the onlookers seeing the woman unclothed will lead to sexual thoughts, but the Rabbis are concerned about this.

אֲמַר רַבָּה: הָכָא טַעְמָא מַאי? שֶׁמָּא תֵּצֵא מִבֵּית דִּין זַכָּאִית וְיִתְגָּרוּ בָּהּ פִּרְחֵי כְהוּנָּה. הָתָם הָא מִסְתַּלְּקָא. וְכִי תֵּימָא, אָתֵי לְאִיגָּרוּיֵי בְּאַחֲרָנְיָיתָא – הָאָמַר רָבָא: גְּמִירִי, דְּאֵין יֵצֶר הָרַע שׁוֹלֵט אֶלָּא בְּמַה שֶּׁעֵינָיו רוֹאוֹת.

Rabba said: What is the reason here, with regard to a *sota,* that Rabbi Yehuda is concerned? **Perhaps** the *sota* **will leave the court** having been proven **innocent, and the young priests** in the Temple who saw her partially naked **will become provoked by** the sight of **her. There,** in the case of a woman who is stoned, **she departs** from this world by being stoned and there is no concern for sexual thoughts. The Gemara comments: **And if you would say** that the fact that she is killed is irrelevant to their sexual thoughts, as the onlookers **will be provoked with regard to other** women, this is not a concern. As **didn't Rava say:** It **is learned** as a tradition **that the evil inclination controls only that which** a person's **eyes see.**

NOTES

One does not perform mitzvot in bundles – אֵין עוֹשִׂין מִצְוֹת חֲבִילוֹת חֲבִילוֹת: Rashi explains that in doing so, one appears as if he considered mitzvot to be a burden that he hastens to unload. Alternatively, the *Mitzpe Eitan* here cites *Tosafot* on *Moed Katan* 8b: The reason one should not perform mitzvot in bundles is because performing more than one mitzva at a time will prevent one from having the proper focus.

And uncover [*para*] – וּפָרַע: The Hebrew term *para* has two meanings. It can mean to uncover or it can mean to disarrange that which was orderly. Both of these meanings apply to the *sota*. Her hair is uncovered by removing the covering on her head, and her body is uncovered by the tearing of some of her clothes. Also, her hair is disarranged by untying her braids and making her hair disheveled.

HALAKHA

Two lepers are not purified simultaneously – אֵין מְטַהֲרִין שְׁנֵי מְצוֹרָעִין כְּאַחַת: Two lepers are not purified simultaneously because one does not perform mitzvot in bundles (Rambam *Sefer Tahara, Hilkhot Tumat Tzara'at* 11:6).

Two slaves are not pierced simultaneously – אֵין רוֹצְעִין שְׁנֵי עֲבָדִים כְּאַחַת: The ears of two slaves are not pierced simultaneously because one does not perform mitzvot in bundles (Rambam *Sefer Kinyan, Hilkhot Avadim* 3:9).

Two heifers do not have their necks broken simultaneously – אֵין עוֹרְפִין שְׁתֵּי עֶגְלוֹת כְּאַחַת: Two heifers do not have their necks broken simultaneously because one does not perform mitzvot in bundles (Rambam *Sefer Nezikin, Hilkhot Rotze'aḥ UShmirat HaNefesh* 10:5).

A man is stoned while naked, etc. – הָאִישׁ נִסְקָל עָרוֹם וכו׳: Before the stoning of a condemned man, his clothes are removed and his genitals are covered in front. Condemned women are stoned while enrobed in a cloak (Rambam *Sefer Shofetim, Hilkhot Sanhedrin* 15:1).

אֲמַר רָבָא: דְּרַבִּי יְהוּדָה אַדְּרַבִּי יְהוּדָה קַשְׁיָא, דְּרַבָּנַן אַדְּרַבָּנַן לָא קַשְׁיָא? אֶלָּא אֲמַר רָבָא: דְּרַבִּי יְהוּדָה אַדְּרַבִּי יְהוּדָה לָא קַשְׁיָא, כִּדְשַׁנִּין;

Rava said: Is the contradiction between one statement **of Rabbi Yehuda** and the other statement **of Rabbi Yehuda difficult,** while the contradiction between one statement **of the Rabbis** and the other statement **of the Rabbis** is **not difficult?** There is also an apparent contradiction between the two rulings of the Rabbis, as with regard to a *sota*, they are not concerned about sexual thoughts, but with regard to a woman who is stoned they are. **Rather, Rava said:** The contradiction between one statement **of Rabbi Yehuda** and the other statement **of Rabbi Yehuda** is **not difficult, as we answered** above.

Perek **I**
Daf **8** Amud **b**

דְּרַבָּנַן אַדְּרַבָּנַן נַמִי לָא קַשְׁיָא. הָכָא טַעְמָא מַאי? מִשּׁוּם ״וְנִוַּסְּרוּ כָּל הַנָּשִׁים״, הָתָם אֵין לָךְ יִיסּוּר גָּדוֹל מִזֶּה.

The contradiction between one ruling **of the Rabbis and** the other ruling **of the Rabbis** is **not difficult as well. Here,** with regard to a *sota*, **what is the reason** that her hair and body are uncovered? **Because** of what is stated in the verse, that other women should be warned: "Thus will I cause lewdness to cease out of the land, **that all women may be chastened** not to do after your lewdness" (Ezekiel 23:48). **There,** with regard to stoning, **you have no greater chastening than** seeing **this** stoning itself.

וְכִי תֵּימָא, לַעֲבֵיד בָּהּ תַּרְתֵּי – אֲמַר רַב נַחְמָן אָמַר רַבָּה בַּר אֲבוּהּ, אָמַר קְרָא: ״וְאָהַבְתָּ לְרֵעֲךָ כָּמוֹךָ״, בְּרוֹר לוֹ מִיתָה יָפָה.

And if you would say that two forms of chastening, both stoning and humiliation, **should be done with her, Rav Naḥman said** that **Rabba bar Avuh said:** The **verse states: "You shall love your neighbor as yourself"** (Leviticus 19:18), teaching that even with regard to a condemned prisoner, **select a good,** i.e., a compassionate, **death for him.** Therefore, when putting a woman to death by stoning, she should not be humiliated in the process.

לֵימָא, דְּרַב נַחְמָן תַּנָּאֵי הִיא? לָא, דְּכוּלֵּי עָלְמָא אִית לְהוּ דְּרַב נַחְמָן, וְהָכָא בְּהָא קָמִיפַּלְגִי, מָר סָבַר: בִּזְיוֹנֵיהּ עָדִיף לֵיהּ טְפֵי מִצַּעֲרָא דְגוּפֵיהּ, וּמָר סָבַר: צַעֲרָא דְגוּפֵיהּ עָדִיף לֵיהּ טְפֵי מִבִּזְיוֹנֵיהּ.

The Gemara suggests: **Let us say that** the statement **of Rav Naḥman is** a dispute between ***tanna'im*,** and according to Rabbi Yehuda there is no mitzva to select a compassionate death. The Gemara refutes this: **No,** it may be **that everyone agrees with** the opinion of **Rav Naḥman, and here they disagree about this:** One **Sage,** i.e., the Rabbis, **holds:** Minimizing **one's degradation is preferable to him than** minimizing **his physical pain.** Therefore, the Rabbis view the more compassionate death as one without degradation, even if wearing clothes will increase the pain of the one being executed, as the clothes will absorb the blow and prolong death. **And one Sage,** Rabbi Yehuda, **holds that** minimizing **physical pain is preferable to a person than** minimizing **his degradation,** and therefore the one being executed prefers to be stoned unclothed, without any chance of the clothing prolonging the death, although this adds to the degradation.

״הָיְתָה מְכוּסָּה לְבָנִים״ וכו׳. תָּנָא: אִם הָיוּ שְׁחוֹרִים נָאִים לָהּ, מְכַסִּין אוֹתָהּ בְּגָדִים מְכוֹעָרִים.

§ The mishna teaches: If **she was dressed in white** garments, he would cover her with black garments. A Sage **taught: If black** garments **are becoming to her,**[H] then **she is covered in unsightly garments.**

״הָיוּ עָלֶיהָ כְּלֵי זָהָב״ וכו׳. פְּשִׁיטָא, הַשְׁתָּא נוֹוּלֵי מְנַוֵּיל לָהּ, הָנֵי מִיבַּעְיָא? מַהוּ דְּתֵימָא: בְּהָנֵי אִית לָהּ בִּזָּיוֹן טְפֵי, כִּדְאָמְרִי אִינָשֵׁי: שְׁלִיחַ עַרְטִיל וְסָיֵים מְסָאנֵי. קָא מַשְׁמַע לַן.

The mishna teaches: If **she was wearing gold adornments** or other jewelry, they are removed from her. The Gemara asks: **Isn't** this **obvious? Now** that the priest **renders her unattractive** by uncovering her and dressing her in unsightly garments, **is it necessary** to teach that they remove **these** adornments from her? The Gemara answers: **Lest you say** that **with these** adornments on her, **she has more degradation, as people say** in a known aphorism: **Undressed, naked, and wearing shoes.** This means that a naked person who wears shoes emphasizes the fact that he is naked. Perhaps one would think that by a *sota* wearing jewelry, her nakedness is emphasized and her degradation is amplified. Therefore, the mishna **teaches us** that this is not so.

HALAKHA

If black garments are becoming to her – הָיוּ שְׁחוֹרִים נָאִים לָהּ: A *sota* who was accustomed to wearing white garments is dressed in black. If the black garments enhance her appearance, she is dressed in in a manner that renders her unattractive (Rambam *Sefer Nashim, Hilkhot Sota* 3:4).

״וְאַחַר כָּךְ מֵבִיא חֶבֶל״ וכו׳. בְּעָא מִינֵּיהּ רַבִּי אַבָּא מֵרַב הוּנָא: חֶבֶל הַמִּצְרִי מַהוּ שֶׁיְּעַכֵּב בְּסוֹטָה? מִשּׁוּם שֶׁלֹּא יִשָּׁמְטוּ בְּגָדֶיהָ מֵעָלֶיהָ הוּא, וּבִצְלְצוּל קָטָן נַמִּי סַגִּי, אוֹ דִילְמָא מִשּׁוּם דְּאָמַר מָר: הִיא חָגְרָה לוֹ בִּצְלְצוּל לְפִיכָךְ כֹּהֵן מֵבִיא חֶבֶל הַמִּצְרִי וְקוֹשֵׁר לָהּ לְמַעְלָה מִדַּדֶּיהָ, מְעַכֵּב?

The mishna continues: **And afterward** the priest **would bring** an Egyptian **rope,** and he would tie it above her breasts. **Rabbi Abba raised a dilemma before Rav Huna: What is** the *halakha* as to whether the lack of **an Egyptian rope**[N] **will preclude**[N] the performance of the rite **with regard to a** ***sota*****?** Does any means of tying suffice? Perhaps the primary function of the rope **is so that her clothes will not fall off her, and** therefore even **a small ribbon** [***tziltzul***][LH] **would also suffice. Or, perhaps** the rope is used **because** of what **the Master said: She girded** herself **with** a comely **ribbon** when she committed her transgression, and **therefore the priest brings** specifically **an Egyptian rope,** which is coarse, **and ties it above her breasts.** If that is the case, then the Egyptian rope should be **indispensable.**

אֲמַר לֵיהּ, תְּנֵיתוּהָ: וְאַחַר כָּךְ מֵבִיא חֶבֶל הַמִּצְרִי וְקוֹשְׁרוֹ לָהּ לְמַעְלָה מִדַּדֶּיהָ, כְּדֵי שֶׁלֹּא יִשָּׁמְטוּ בְּגָדֶיהָ מֵעָלֶיהָ.

Rav Huna **said to him: You learned** the answer to this dilemma in a *baraita* that teaches: **And afterward** the priest **would bring an Egyptian rope** and he would tie it above her breasts, **so that her clothes would not fall off her.** The *baraita* states that the use of an Egyptian rope is primarily for holding up her clothing, and therefore use of specifically Egyptian rope is not essential.

״וְכָל הָרוֹצֶה לִרְאוֹת בָּהּ יִרְאֶה״ וכו׳. הָא גּוּפָא קַשְׁיָא, אָמְרַתְּ: כָּל הָרוֹצֶה לִרְאוֹת בָּהּ רוֹאֶה. אַלְמָא לָא שְׁנָא גַּבְרֵי וְלָא שְׁנָא נָשֵׁי. וַהֲדַר תָּנֵי: כָּל הַנָּשִׁים מוּתָּרוֹת לִרְאוֹתָהּ – נָשִׁים אִין, אֲנָשִׁים לָא!

§ The mishna teaches: **And anyone who desires to watch her may watch,** except for her slaves and maidservants, who are not permitted to watch because her heart is emboldened by them. And all of the women are permitted to watch her. The Gemara comments: **This** matter **is itself difficult,** as there is an internal contradiction in the mishna. First **you say: And anyone who desires to watch her may watch. Apparently,** there **is no difference** whether the onlookers are **men and** there **is no difference** whether they are **women;** all are permitted to observe the rite. **And then** the mishna **teaches: And all of the women are permitted to watch her,** which indicates **women, yes,** they may watch her, but **men, no,** they may not.

אֲמַר אַבַּיֵי: תַּרְגְּמָהּ אַנָּשִׁים. אֲמַר לֵיהּ רָבָא: וְהָא כָּל הָרוֹצֶה לִרְאוֹת בָּהּ רוֹאֶה קָתָנֵי!

Abaye said: Interpret the first statement, which permits all people to observe the *sota,* as pertaining **to women,** but men may not be onlookers. **Rava said to him: But** it **teaches** in that first statement that **anyone who desires to watch her may watch,** and one cannot limit this to women.

אֶלָּא אֲמַר רָבָא: כָּל הָרוֹצֶה לִרְאוֹת בָּהּ רוֹאֶה – לָא שְׁנָא גַּבְרֵי וְלָא שְׁנָא נָשֵׁי. וְנָשִׁים חַיָּיבוֹת לִרְאוֹתָהּ, שֶׁנֶּאֱמַר: ״וְנִוַּסְּרוּ כָּל הַנָּשִׁים וְלֹא תַעֲשֶׂינָה כְּזִמַּתְכֶנָה״.

Rather, Rava said: Anyone who desires to watch her may watch, there **is no difference** whether the onlookers are **men** and there **is no difference** whether they are **women. And** the next clause of the mishna teaches that **women are obligated to watch her,**[NH] **as is stated:** "Thus will I cause lewdness to cease out of the land, **that all women may be chastened not to do after your lewdness"** (Ezekiel 23:48).

מתני׳ בְּמִדָּה שֶׁאָדָם מוֹדֵד – בָּהּ מוֹדְדִין לוֹ: הִיא קִשְּׁטָה אֶת עַצְמָהּ לַעֲבֵירָה, הַמָּקוֹם נִוְּולָהּ. הִיא גִּלְּתָה אֶת עַצְמָהּ לַעֲבֵירָה, הַמָּקוֹם גִּלָּה עָלֶיהָ. בַּיָּרֵךְ הִתְחִילָה בַּעֲבֵירָה תְּחִילָּה וְאַחַר כָּךְ הַבֶּטֶן, לְפִיכָךְ תִּלְקֶה הַיָּרֵךְ תְּחִילָּה וְאַחַר כָּךְ הַבֶּטֶן, וּשְׁאָר כָּל הַגּוּף לֹא פָּלֵט.

MISHNA The mishna teaches lessons that can be derived from the actions and treatment of a *sota.* **With the measure that a person measures, he is measured with it.** For example, **she,** the *sota,* **adorned herself to** violate **a transgression, the Omnipresent** therefore decreed that **she** be **rendered unattractive; she exposed herself for** the purpose of violating **a transgression,** as she stood in places where she would be noticed by potential adulterers, so **the Omnipresent** therefore decreed that **her** body be **exposed** publicly; **she began her transgression with** her **thigh and afterward with** her **stomach, therefore the thigh is smitten first and then the stomach, and the rest of all** her **body** does **not escape** punishment.

גמ׳ אָמַר רַב יוֹסֵף: אַף עַל גַּב דְּמִדָּה בְּטֵילָה, בְּמִדָּה לָא בָּטֵיל.

GEMARA **Rav Yosef says: Although the measure** with regard to court-imposed capital punishment **has ceased,** as there is no court today empowered to adjudicate and apply corporal punishment, punishment that is suitable to be applied **with a measure** by God **has not ceased,**[N] as a person is punished by Heaven in accordance with his sin.

NOTES

Egyptian rope – חֶבֶל הַמִּצְרִי: The Jerusalem Talmud notes that an Egyptian rope and an Egyptian basket (see 14a) are significant in that they were selected to allude to the fact that the *sota* engaged in immoral sexual behavior, which, in the Bible, is described as a characteristic of the Egyptian people (see Leviticus, chapter 18).

Will preclude [*ye'akkev*] – שֶׁיְּעַכֵּב: *Tosafot* and *Tosefot HaRosh* question why there would be any reason to think that a *sota* rite lacking an Egyptian rope should be invalid. After all, the absence of uncovering of the *sota,* which is mentioned in the verse, does not preclude the ritual from being valid. *Tosefot HaRosh* explains that the word *ye'akkev,* in this context, is not to be understood according to its standard meaning, that not using it will preclude the rite from being valid. Rather, it should be understood according to the standard meaning of the related word *ikkuv,* meaning delay, and the question of the Gemara is whether the priest should delay the performance of the rite in order to bring an Egyptian rope.

And women are obligated to watch her – וְנָשִׁים חַיָּיבוֹת לִרְאוֹתָהּ: The Gemara's conclusion that there is an obligation incumbent upon women to watch the rite seems to contradict the expression in the mishna: And women are permitted to watch. Accordingly one must understand that the statement of the mishna is either as a contrast to the slaves, who are not permitted to watch, or should be understood as: Once they are permitted to watch, they must do so (*Melekhet Shlomo*; *Tiferet Yisrael*).

With a measure by God has not ceased – בְּמִדָּה לָא בָּטֵיל: The *Iyyun Ya'akov* explains that this principle: With a measure, is applicable to a *sota* in present times as well. Although the bitter water is no longer given, adulterers and those who exhibit immodest behavior will eventually be punished in a manner similar to their actions.

LANGUAGE

Ribbon [*tziltzul*] – צִלְצוּל: The sources indicate that the *tziltzul* is an ornamental belt or ribbon that is worn like a belt. Some explain that the word resembles the word *shalshelet,* meaning chain, with the letter *tzadi* replacing the letter *shin,* and it refers to a thin chain or braided belt.

HALAKHA

A small ribbon, etc. – צִלְצוּל קָטָן וכו׳: She is tied *ab initio* using an Egyptian rope. However, if one is not available, any type of rope can be used. The rope is tied above her breasts so that her clothes do not fall off, in accordance with the conclusion of the Gemara (Rambam *Sefer Nashim, Hilkhot Sota* 3:11).

Women are obligated to watch her – נָשִׁים חַיָּיבוֹת לִרְאוֹתָהּ: All the women who are in the Temple are obligated to watch the humiliation of the *sota* in order to be cautioned (Rambam *Sefer Nashim, Hilkhot Sota* 3:5).

דְּאָמַר רַב יוֹסֵף, וְכֵן תָּנֵי רַבִּי חִיָּיא: מִיּוֹם שֶׁחָרַב בֵּית הַמִּקְדָּשׁ, אַף עַל פִּי שֶׁבָּטְלָה סַנְהֶדְרִי, אַרְבַּע מִיתוֹת לֹא בָּטְלוּ. וְהָא בָּטְלוּ! אֶלָּא דִּין אַרְבַּע מִיתוֹת לֹא בָּטְלוּ.

As Rav Yosef says, and Rabbi Ḥiyya similarly teaches: **From the day that the Temple was destroyed, although the Sanhedrin ceased,** the **four** types of court-imposed **capital punishment**[B] **have not ceased.** The Gemara asks: **But they have ceased;** court-imposed capital punishment is no longer given. **Rather,** the intention is: **The law of** the **four** types of court-imposed **capital punishment has not ceased.**

מִי שֶׁנִּתְחַיֵּיב סְקִילָה – אוֹ נוֹפֵל מִן הַגַּג אוֹ חַיָּה דּוֹרַסְתּוֹ. מִי שֶׁנִּתְחַיֵּיב שְׂרֵיפָה – אוֹ נוֹפֵל בִּדְלֵיקָה אוֹ נָחָשׁ מַכִּישׁוֹ. מִי שֶׁנִּתְחַיֵּיב הֲרִיגָה – אוֹ נִמְסָר לַמַּלְכוּת אוֹ לִיסְטִין בָּאִין עָלָיו. מִי שֶׁנִּתְחַיֵּיב חֲנִיקָה – אוֹ טוֹבֵעַ בְּנָהָר אוֹ מֵת בִּסְרוֹנְכִי.

The Gemara explains: How so? **One who is liable** to be executed by **stoning either falls from a roof or an animal mauls him** and breaks his bones. This death is similar to the experience of stoning, in which the one liable to be executed is pushed from a platform and his bones break from the impact of the fall. **One who is liable** to be executed by **burning either falls into a fire** and is burned **or a snake bites him,**[B] as a snakebite causes a burning sensation. **One who is liable to** be executed by **slaying** of the sword **either is turned over to the authorities** and they execute him with a sword, **or robbers come upon him** and murder him. **One who is liable** to be executed by **strangling either drowns in a river** and is choked by the water **or dies of diphtheria [*seronekhi*],**[L] which causes his throat to become clogged, and he dies.

תַּנְיָא, הָיָה רַבִּי אוֹמֵר: מִנַּיִן שֶׁבְּמִדָּה שֶׁאָדָם מוֹדֵד בָּהּ מוֹדְדִין לוֹ? שֶׁנֶּאֱמַר: "בְּסַאסְּאָה בְּשַׁלְּחָהּ תְּרִיבֶנָּה".

It is taught in a baraita in the *Tosefta* (3:1–5) that **Rabbi** Yehuda HaNasi **would say: From where** is it derived **that with the measure that a person measures, he is measured with it? As it is stated: "In full measure [*besase'a*], when you send her away, you contend with her"** (Isaiah 27:8). In other words, in the measure, *bese'a*, that one used in one's sin, God will contend with, i.e., punish, him.

אֵין לִי אֶלָּא סְאָה. מִנַּיִן לְרַבּוֹת תַּרְקַב וַחֲצִי תַּרְקַב, קַב וַחֲצִי קַב, רוֹבַע וַחֲצִי רוֹבַע, תּוֹמֶן וְעוּכְלָא מִנַּיִן? תַּלְמוּד לוֹמַר: "כִּי כָל סְאוֹן סֹאֵן בְּרַעַשׁ".

The *baraita* continues: **I have** derived **only** the relatively large measurement of **a *se'a*,** which alludes to a significant sin. **From where** do I know **to include** even lesser sins that are comparable to smaller measurements, e.g., **a half-*se'a* [*tarkav*]**[L] **and a half-*tarkav*; a *kav* and a half-*kav*; a quarter-*kav* and half of a quarter-*kav*; an eighth-*kav* [*toman*] and an *ukla*,**[B] which is one-thirty-second of a *kav*. **From where** is it derived that all these lesser sins are also dealt with in accordance with the measure of the sin? **The verse states: "For every boot [*sa'on*] stamped with fierceness,** and every cloak rolled in blood, shall even be for burning, for fuel of fire" (Isaiah 9:4), indicating that every *sa'on*, which **Rabbi** Yehuda HaNasi interprets as a small *se'a*, is "stamped with fierceness" and doesn't go unpunished.

וּמִנַּיִן שֶׁכָּל פְּרוּטָה וּפְרוּטָה מִצְטָרֶפֶת לְחֶשְׁבּוֹן גָּדוֹל? תַּלְמוּד לוֹמַר: "אַחַת לְאַחַת לִמְצֹא חֶשְׁבּוֹן".

And from where is it derived **that each and every *peruta* combine** to add up **to a great sum,** alluding to the notion that even if one is not immediately punished for a small transgression, in the final accounting all misdeeds will combine together and be addressed by the imposition of a large punishment? **The verse states:** "Behold, this have I found, says Koheleth, **adding one thing to another,**[N] **to find out the account"** (Ecclesiastes 7:27).

וְכֵן מָצִינוּ בְּסוֹטָה, שֶׁבְּמִדָּה שֶׁמָּדְדָה – בָּהּ מָדְדוּ לָהּ: הִיא עָמְדָה עַל פֶּתַח בֵּיתָהּ לֵירָאוֹת לוֹ, לְפִיכָךְ כֹּהֵן מַעֲמִידָהּ עַל שַׁעַר נִקָּנוֹר וּמַרְאֶה קְלוֹנָהּ לַכֹּל. הִיא פָּרְסָה לוֹ סוּדָרִין נָאִין עַל רֹאשָׁהּ, לְפִיכָךְ כֹּהֵן נוֹטֵל כִּפָּה מֵעַל רֹאשָׁהּ וּמַנִּיחוֹ תַּחַת רַגְלֶיהָ. הִיא קִשְּׁטָה לוֹ פָּנֶיהָ, לְפִיכָךְ

The *baraita* continues: **And we found this with regard to a *sota*, that with the measure with which she measured, she is measured with it: She stood by the opening of her house to exhibit herself** to her paramour, **therefore a priest has her stand at the Gate of Nicanor and exhibits her disgrace to all; she spread beautiful shawls [*sudarin*]**[L] **on her head for** her paramour, **therefore a priest removes** her **kerchief from her head and places it under her feet; she adorned her face for** her paramour, **therefore**

BACKGROUND

Four types of court-imposed capital punishment – אַרְבַּע מִיתוֹת בֵּית דִּין: These four forms of court-imposed capital punishment are prescribed by the Torah for different transgressions. They are administered by a court of twenty-three members. They are, in diminishing order of severity: Stoning, burning, decapitation, and strangulation.

A snake bites him – נָחָשׁ מַכִּישׁוֹ: There are a number of different types of poisonous snakes that inject their venom into an individual upon biting them. The majority of snakes in Eretz Yisrael are vipers, and their bites can cause an internal burning sensation. Therefore, there is reason to compare one burned to death with one who dies by snakebite.

Ukla – עוּכְלָא: This is the Aramaic term for a small measurement. There are conflicting opinions as to its exact size. Some identify it as a measurement of one-twentieth of a *kav*.

LANGUAGE

Diphtheria [*seronekhi*] – סְרוֹנְכִי: According to some, this word is from a Semitic language. Others explain that it is derived from the Greek συνάγχη, *sunnankhē*, referring to a form of strangulation that results from complications of diphtheria due to the trachea being blocked by pus.

Half-*se'a* [*tarkav*] – תַּרְקַב: *Tarkav* is a measuring vessel for the measurement of a half-*se'a*. Early commentaries explain that the word *tarkav* is a composite of the word for two and the word *kav*, which together indicates three *kav*, which equals a half-*se'a*. It is also possible that the source of the word is the Greek τρίκαβος, *trikabos*, meaning three *kav*.

Shawls [*sudarin*] – סוּדָרִין: From the Greek σουδάριον, *soudarion*, or the Latin sudarium, meaning a towel or napkin. In the Talmud, this usually refers to a woven piece of cloth that was used for various purposes, e.g., a wrap for one's neck or a covering for one's hair. It was often worn as a head covering for married scholars, as a sign of distinction.

NOTES

Adding one thing to another, etc. – אַחַת לְאַחַת וכו׳: In the Jerusalem Talmud, there are two interpretations of this verse. One is identical to the one found here, that at times a number of smaller unpunished transgressions are punished through one severe punishment. By contrast, at times one major transgression is not punished all at once, but rather through small punishments over a longer period of time, and these small punishments combine to atone for the one severe transgression.

פָּנֶיהָ מוֹרִיקוֹת. הִיא כָּחֲלָה לוֹ עֵינֶיהָ, לְפִיכָךְ עֵינֶיהָ בּוֹלְטוֹת. הִיא קָלְעָה לוֹ אֶת שְׂעָרָהּ, לְפִיכָךְ כֹּהֵן סוֹתֵר אֶת שְׂעָרָהּ. הִיא הֶרְאֲתָה לוֹ בְּאֶצְבַּע, לְפִיכָךְ צִיפּוֹרְנֶיהָ נוֹשְׁרוֹת. הִיא חָגְרָה לוֹ בְּצִילְצוֹל, לְפִיכָךְ כֹּהֵן מֵבִיא חֶבֶל הַמִּצְרִי וְקוֹשֵׁר לָהּ לְמַעְלָה מִדַּדֶּיהָ. הִיא פָּשְׁטָה לוֹ אֶת יְרֵיכָהּ, לְפִיכָךְ יְרֵיכָהּ נוֹפֶלֶת.

her face becomes sallow after drinking the bitter water; **she painted her eyes**[B] **for** her paramour, **therefore her eyes bulge** after she drinks; **she braided her hair for** her paramour, **therefore a priest unbraids her hair** and makes it disheveled; **she indicated to** her paramour **with a finger**[N] that he should come to her, **therefore her fingernails fall off; she girded herself for** her paramour **with a ribbon** as a belt, **therefore a priest brings an Egyptian rope and ties it for her above her breasts; she extended her thigh for** her paramour, **therefore her thigh falls away** after drinking.

הִיא קִיבְּלַתּוּ עַל כְּרֵיסָהּ, לְפִיכָךְ בִּטְנָהּ צָבָה. הִיא הֶאֱכִילַתּוּ מַעֲדַנֵּי עוֹלָם, לְפִיכָךְ קָרְבָּנָהּ מַאֲכַל בְּהֵמָה. הִיא הִשְׁקַתְהוּ יַיִן מְשׁוּבָּח בְּכוֹסוֹת מְשׁוּבָּחִים, לְפִיכָךְ כֹּהֵן מַשְׁקָהּ מַיִם הַמָּרִים בִּמְקֵידָה שֶׁל חֶרֶשׂ.

She received her paramour **upon her stomach, therefore her stomach swells; she fed him delicacies of the world, therefore her offering** is **animal food,** as it is from oats; **she gave him fine wine to drink in fine cups, therefore a priest gives her bitter water in an earthenware** ***mekeida***,[B] a simple clay vessel, **to drink.**

הִיא עָשְׂתָה בַּסֵּתֶר, יוֹשֵׁב בְּסֵתֶר עֶלְיוֹן שָׂם בָּהּ פָּנִים, שֶׁנֶּאֱמַר: "וְעֵין נֹאֵף שָׁמְרָה נֶשֶׁף לֵאמֹר לֹא תְשׁוּרֵנִי עָיִן" וגו'.

She acted in secret; therefore, God, referred to in the verse **"Who dwell in secret, with the Most High"** (Psalms 91:1), **turns** His **face to her, as it is stated: "The eye of the adulterer waits for the twilight, saying: No eye shall see me;** and the Hidden Face will turn" (Job 24:15). The adulterer acts in the twilight of the night to act in secrecy, and therefore God, Who is concealed, arranges that the matter is revealed in public.

דָּבָר אַחֵר: הִיא עָשְׂתָה בַּסֵּתֶר, הַמָּקוֹם פִּירְסְמָהּ בְּגָלוּי, שֶׁנֶּאֱמַר: "תִּכַּסֶּה שִׂנְאָה בְּמַשָּׁאוֹן תִּגָּלֶה רָעָתוֹ בְקָהָל" (וגו').

Alternatively, she acted in secret, and therefore **the Omnipresent revealed it in the open, as it is stated: "Though his hatred be concealed with deceit, his wickedness shall be revealed before the congregation"** (Proverbs 26:26), i.e., concealed acts of sin are ultimately revealed in public.

וּמֵאַחַר דְּנָפְקָא לֵיהּ מֵ"אַחַת לְאַחַת לִמְצֹא חֶשְׁבּוֹן", "כִּי כָל סְאוֹן סֹאֵן בְּרַעַשׁ" לָמָּה לִי? לְכַמְּדָּה.

§ The Gemara questions the need for two verses to indicate that small transgressions are addressed through one significant punishment. **And since Rabbi** Yehuda HaNasi **derives** that small transgressions are combined and punished together **from:** "Behold, this have I found, says Koheleth, **adding one thing to another, to find out the account"** (Ecclesiastes 7:27), **why do I** need the verse: **"For every boot stamped with fierceness"** (Isaiah 9:4)? The Gemara answers: This verse serves **to** teach that even small transgressions are punished **by the measure,** i.e., with a punishment appropriate to the transgression.

וּמֵאַחַר דְּנָפְקָא לֵיהּ מִ"כִּי כָל סְאוֹן סֹאֵן בְּרַעַשׁ", "בְּסַאסְּאָה בְּשַׁלְּחָהּ תְּרִיבֶנָּה" לָמָּה לִי?

The Gemara asks: **And since he derives it from "for every boot stamped with fierceness," why do I** need **"in full measure, when you send her away, you contend with her"** (Isaiah 27:8)?

לִכְדְרַב חִינָּנָא בַּר פַּפָּא, דְּאָמַר רַב חִינָּנָא בַּר פַּפָּא: אֵין הַקָּדוֹשׁ בָּרוּךְ הוּא נִפְרָע מִן הָאוּמָּה עַד שְׁעַת שִׁילּוּחָהּ, שֶׁנֶּאֱמַר: "בְּסַאסְּאָה בְּשַׁלְּחָהּ" וגו'.

The Gemara answers: This verse serves **to** teach the statement as taught **by Rav Ḥinnana bar Pappa, for Rav Ḥinnana bar Pappa says: The Holy One, Blessed be He, does not punish a nation**[N] deserving of punishment **until its time to be banished,** i.e., until the time of its final eradication from the world, **as it is stated: "In full measure, when you send her away,** you contend with her" (Isaiah 27:8).

BACKGROUND

Eye paint – כְּחָל: This was a black-blue color whose source is the mineral stibnite, Sb_2S_3. Ground stibnite crystals were used by women to color the area around their eyes in order to emphasize them and make them appear larger. Apparently, it was also used for medicinal purposes.

Mekeida **– מְקֵידָה:** This type of vessel was generally made of clay. According to the *ge'onim*, it is identical to a vessel known as a *kod*, which is made of either clay or wood. It was used primarily for drinking, and some say that it was made in such a manner that it could easily be disassembled into two parts, so that each one could be used separately.

NOTES

She indicated to him with a finger – הִיא הֶרְאֲתָה לוֹ בְּאֶצְבַּע: Rashi explains that she indicated with her finger that he should come to her. Others interpret this to mean that she painted her fingernails to beautify herself for him (*Eshel Avraham*). Others explain this metaphorically, meaning that she selected her paramour, as if she pointed to him when he was in a group of men (*Tosefta KiFshuta*).

The Holy One, Blessed be He, does not punish a nation, etc. – אֵין הַקָּדוֹשׁ בָּרוּךְ הוּא נִפְרָע מִן הָאוּמָּה: The Maharal explains that as a collective entity, partial punishment cannot be given to a whole nation as it is given to an individual. A nation is either deserving of existence or not, and therefore its punishment, when it is deserving, is extinction.

אִינִי? וְהָאָמַר רָבָא: שְׁלֹשָׁה כּוֹסוֹת הָאֲמוּרוֹת בְּמִצְרַיִם לָמָּה? אַחַת שֶׁשָּׁתַת בִּימֵי מֹשֶׁה, וְאַחַת שֶׁשָּׁתַת בִּימֵי פַּרְעֹה נְכֹה, וְאַחַת שֶׁעֲתִידָה לִשְׁתּוֹת עִם חַבְרוֹתֶיהָ!

Is that so? But didn't Rava say: Why are there specifically **three cups** of misfortune **that are stated**[N] **with regard to Egypt** in the dream of its chief butler (see Genesis 40:11–13)? They are an allusion to three cups of misfortune that would later befall Egypt: **One that it drank in the days of Moses** during the ten plagues and the Exodus; **one that it drank in the days of Pharaoh Neco,** the king of Egypt who was defeated by Nebuchadnezzar; **and one that it will drink in the future with its companions,** i.e., the other nations, when they are punished during the days of the Messiah. This indicates that nations can be punished several times, not only when they are eradicated.

וְכִי תֵּימָא, הָנָךְ אֲזַדוּ וְהָנֵי אַחֲרִינֵי נִינְהוּ, וְהָתַנְיָא, אָמַר רַבִּי יְהוּדָה: מִנְיָמִין גֵּר הַמִּצְרִי הָיָה לִי חָבֵר מִתַּלְמִידֵי רַבִּי עֲקִיבָא. אָמַר מִנְיָמִין גֵּר הַמִּצְרִי: אֲנִי מִצְרִי רִאשׁוֹן וְנָשָׂאתִי מִצְרִית רִאשׁוֹנָה. אַשִּׂיא לִבְנִי מִצְרִית שְׁנִיָּה כְּדֵי שֶׁיְּהֵא בֶּן בְּנִי מוּתָּר לָבֹא בַּקָּהָל!

And if you would say that **those** ancient Egyptians, **have gone, and these** later Egyptians **are different ones, but isn't it taught** in a *baraita* in the *Tosefta* (*Kiddushin* 4:3): **Rabbi Yehuda said: Minyamin,**[L] **an Egyptian convert, was a friend of mine from among the students of Rabbi Akiva,** and **Minyamin the Egyptian convert said:** After I converted **I** was **a first**-generation **Egyptian** convert, **and** so **I married** another **first**-generation **Egyptian** convert. **I will marry off my son,** who is **a second**-generation Egyptian convert, **to** another **second**-generation **Egyptian** convert, **in order that my son's son will be permitted to enter into the congregation.** The Torah prohibits Egyptian converts before the third generation to enter into the congregation (see Deuteronomy 23:8–9). By Minyamin's observance of this prohibition even during the time of Rabbi Akiva, it indicates that Egypt during the tannaitic period was still viewed as biblical Egypt.

אֶלָּא אִי אִיתְּמַר הָכִי אִיתְּמַר, אָמַר רַב חִינָּנָא בַּר פַּפָּא: אֵין הַקָּדוֹשׁ בָּרוּךְ הוּא נִפְרָע מִן הַמֶּלֶךְ עַד שְׁעַת שִׁילּוּחוֹ, שֶׁנֶּאֱמַר: ״בְּסַאסְּאָה בְּשַׁלְחָהּ תְּרִיבֶנָּה״ וגו׳.

Rather, if anything **was stated** with regard to the delay of punishment, it **was stated like this: Rav Ḥinnana bar Pappa says: The Holy One, Blessed be He, does not punish** a sinful **king until his time to be banished, as it is stated: "In full measure, when you send her away, you contend with her"** (Isaiah 27:8).

אַמֵימָר מַתְנֵי לְהָא דְּרַב חִינָּנָא בַּר פַּפָּא אַהָא – מַאי דִּכְתִיב: ״כִּי אֲנִי ה׳ לֹא שָׁנִיתִי וְאַתֶּם בְּנֵי יַעֲקֹב לֹא כְלִיתֶם״? ״אֲנִי ה׳ לֹא שָׁנִיתִי״ – לֹא הִכֵּיתִי לְאוּמָּה וְשָׁנִיתִי לָהּ, ״וְאַתֶּם בְּנֵי יַעֲקֹב לֹא כְלִיתֶם״ – הַיְינוּ דִּכְתִיב: ״חִצַּי אֲכַלֶּה בָּם״, חִצַּי כָּלִין וְהֵן אֵינָן כָּלִין.

Ameimar teaches that statement **of Rav Ḥinnana bar Pappa with regard to this: What is** the meaning of that **which is written: "For I the Lord change not; and you, sons of Jacob, are not consumed"** (Malachi 3:6)? **"For I the Lord change** [*shaniti*] **not"** is interpreted to mean: **I did not strike a nation and repeat** [*shaniti*][N] striking **it,** as a stricken nation never recovers from the initial strike. **"And you, sons of Jacob, are not consumed,"** is interpreted to mean: Despite the fact that I strike you many times for your sins, I do not let you perish. **This is** the same **as that which is written:** "I will heap evils upon them; **I will consume My arrows upon them"** (Deuteronomy 32:23), which is interpreted to mean: **My arrows are consumed** and used up, **and they,** the Jewish people, **are not consumed** but will continue to endure despite the many calamities that will befall them.

אָמַר רַב הַמְנוּנָא: אֵין הַקָּדוֹשׁ בָּרוּךְ הוּא נִפְרָע מִן הָאָדָם עַד שֶׁתִּתְמַלֵּא סְאָתוֹ, שֶׁנֶּאֱמַר: ״בִּמְלֹאות שִׂפְקוֹ יֵצֶר לוֹ״ וגו׳.

Rav Hamnuna says: The Holy One, Blessed be He, does not punish a person until his *se'a,* the measure that is suitable for him, **is filled, as it is stated: "In the fullness of his sufficiency he shall be in straits;** the hand of every one that is in misery shall come upon him" (Job 20:22). In other words, when the sufficient measure of sin has been reached, then the trouble will overtake him.

דָּרַשׁ רַב חִינָּנָא בַּר פַּפָּא, מַאי דִּכְתִיב: ״רַנְּנוּ צַדִּיקִים בַּה׳ לַיְשָׁרִים נָאוָה תְהִלָּה״? אַל תִּקְרֵי ״נָאוָה תְהִלָּה״ אֶלָּא ״נְוֵה תְהִלָּה״, זֶה מֹשֶׁה וְדָוִד שֶׁלֹּא שָׁלְטוּ שׂוֹנְאֵיהֶם בְּמַעֲשֵׂיהֶם.

Having mentioned Rav Ḥinnana bar Pappa, the Gemara quotes another of his interpretations. **Rav Ḥinnana bar Pappa interpreted** a verse **homiletically: What is** the meaning of that **which is written: "Rejoice in the Lord, you righteous, praise is comely for the upright** [*nava tehilla*]" (Psalms 33:1)? **Do not read** the conclusion of the verse as: **Praise is comely** [*nava*]; **rather,** read it as: **A house** [*naveh*] **of praise. This** is referring to **Moses and David, whose enemies did not rule over their achievements,** as they each built a *naveh,* a house for the Lord, and this house remained in existence.

NOTES

Three cups that are stated, etc. – שְׁלֹשָׁה כּוֹסוֹת הָאֲמוּרוֹת וכו׳: Although the vision of these three cups appeared in the private dream of Pharaoh's chief butler, it also served as an indication of positive developments for the Jewish people while alluding to the punishment of Egypt.

In truth, Pharaoh's cup is mentioned four times in that passage of the Torah, corresponding to the four cups that are drunk at the Passover seder. However, only three are counted here, as only three cups are mentioned in the dream itself, while the fourth appears in Joseph's interpretation of the dream (Maharsha).

I did not strike a nation and repeat, etc. – לֹא הִכֵּיתִי לְאוּמָּה וְשָׁנִיתִי וכו׳: *Tosafot* ask: Doesn't this statement contradict the Torah's description of the plagues in Egypt, as the Egyptians were struck more than once? The Maharsha explains that the intention of the Gemara's statement is that God does not strike an entire nation with identical punishments, and the ten plagues in Egypt were each of a different nature. By contrast, the same punishment is meted out to the Jewish people repeatedly, yet they are not destroyed.

LANGUAGE

Minyamin – מִנְיָמִין: Although the name Minyamin is already mentioned as a name in the Bible (II Chronicles 31:15), it would appear by comparison with other sources that the name Minyamin that appears here, and similarly the amoraic name Minyumi, is actually a variation in pronunciation of the name Binyamin. This change in pronunciation is related to the interchangeability of the letters *mem* and *bet,* both bilabials, which appears in other contexts as well.

דָּוִד – דִּכְתִיב: "טָבְעוּ בָאָרֶץ שְׁעָרֶיהָ". מֹשֶׁה – דְּאָמַר מָר: מִשֶּׁנִּבְנָה מִקְדָּשׁ רִאשׁוֹן, נִגְנַז אֹהֶל מוֹעֵד, קְרָשָׁיו, קְרָסָיו וּבְרִיחָיו וְעַמּוּדָיו וַאֲדָנָיו. הֵיכָא? אָמַר רַב חִסְדָּא אָמַר אֲבִימִי: תַּחַת מְחִילּוֹת שֶׁל הֵיכָל.

With regard to **David**,[N] the citadel that housed his home and city, was not destroyed, **as it is written: "Her gates are sunk into the ground"** (Lamentations 2:9), as the gates of Jerusalem built by David were not destroyed by enemies, but sunk into the ground and were buried there. This is also so with regard to **Moses, as the Master said: When the first Temple was built, the Tent of Meeting was sequestered,** including **its boards, its clasps, and its bars, and its pillars, and its sockets.** The Gemara asks: **Where is it** sequestered? **Rav Ḥisda says that Avimi says: Beneath the tunnels of the Sanctuary.**[B]

תָּנוּ רַבָּנַן: סוֹטָה נָתְנָה עֵינֶיהָ בְּמִי שֶׁאֵינוֹ רָאוּי לָהּ, מַה שֶּׁבִּיקְּשָׁה לֹא נִיתַּן לָהּ, וּמַה שֶּׁבְּיָדָהּ נְטָלוּהוּ מִמֶּנָּה. שֶׁכָּל הַנּוֹתֵן עֵינָיו בְּמַה שֶּׁאֵינוֹ שֶׁלּוֹ, מַה שֶּׁמְּבַקֵּשׁ אֵין נוֹתְנִין לוֹ, וּמַה שֶּׁבְּיָדוֹ נוֹטְלִין הֵימֶנּוּ.

§ **The Sages taught** in a *baraita* in the *Tosefta* (4:16–19): **The** ***sota*** **placed her eyes,** fixed her gaze, **on one who is unfit for her,** i.e., another man, so this is her punishment: **That which she desired,** i.e., to be with her paramour, **is not given to her,** as she becomes forbidden to him forever. **And that which she had,** i.e., her husband, **was taken away from her,** as she is now forbidden to him as well. This teaches **that anyone who places his eyes on that which is not his is not given what he desires, and that which he had is taken from him.**

NOTES

David – דָּוִד: The Gemara applies this interpretation to David before it applies it to Moses, although Moses preceded David chronologically. This is because the Gemara cites a verse in David's context, whereas the application to Moses is known only through tradition (*Iyyun Ya'akov*).

BACKGROUND

The tunnels of the Sanctuary – מְחִילּוֹת שֶׁל הַהֵיכָל: There are many tunnels, caves, and hidden rooms under the Temple Mount. A number of these tunnels were used during the Second Temple period, such as one that was used as a passage down from the Temple courtyard for the priests to immerse and be purified in the waters of the Siloam pool. There were also many hidden doors around the Temple Mount that were unknown to the general public. The tunnels under the Sanctuary were even less known, since there were generally fewer people in the Sanctuary than elsewhere in the Temple. The location of the tunnels in which the Tabernacle and its vessels were hidden was not known even during the Temple period. There was a tradition that an opening in the Chamber of the Wood led to these tunnels.

Perek I
Daf 9 Amud b

וְכֵן מָצִינוּ בְּנָחָשׁ הַקַּדְמוֹנִי, שֶׁנָּתַן עֵינָיו בְּמַה שֶּׁאֵינוֹ רָאוּי לוֹ, מַה שֶּׁבִּיקֵּשׁ לֹא נְתָנוּ לוֹ, וּמַה שֶּׁבְּיָדוֹ נְטָלוּהוּ מִמֶּנּוּ. אָמַר הַקָּדוֹשׁ בָּרוּךְ הוּא: אֲנִי אָמַרְתִּי יְהֵא מֶלֶךְ עַל כָּל בְּהֵמָה וְחַיָּה, וְעַכְשָׁיו אָרוּר הוּא מִכָּל הַבְּהֵמָה וּמִכָּל חַיַּת הַשָּׂדֶה.

And, so too, we found with regard to the primeval snake[N] who seduced Eve, **for he placed his eyes on that which was unfit for him,** as he wanted to marry Eve. Consequently, **that which he desired was not given to him, and that which was in his possession was taken from him. The Holy One, Blessed be He, said:** I initially **said** that the snake **will be king over every domesticated animal and non-domesticated animal, but now he is cursed more than all the domesticated animals and all the non-domesticated animals of the field,** as it is stated: "And the Lord God said unto the serpent: Because you have done this, you are cursed from among all cattle, and from among all beasts of the field; upon your belly shall you go, and dust shall you eat all the days of your life" (Genesis 3:14).

אֲנִי אָמַרְתִּי יְהַלֵּךְ בְּקוֹמָה זְקוּפָה, עַכְשָׁיו עַל גְּחוֹנוֹ יֵלֵךְ. אֲנִי אָמַרְתִּי יְהֵא מַאֲכָלוֹ מַאֲכַל אָדָם, עַכְשָׁיו עָפָר יֹאכַל. הוּא אָמַר אֶהֱרוֹג אֶת אָדָם וְאֶשָּׂא אֶת חַוָּה, עַכְשָׁיו אֵיבָה אָשִׁית בֵּינְךָ וּבֵין הָאִשָּׁה וּבֵין זַרְעֲךָ וּבֵין זַרְעָהּ.

The *baraita* explains the elements of this curse. **I said** that the snake **will walk upright,** but **now he shall go on his belly; I said** that **his food will be** the same as the **food** eaten by **a person,** but **now he shall eat dust.** The snake **said: I will kill Adam**[N] **and marry Eve,** but **now: "I will put enmity between you and the woman and between your seed and her seed"** (Genesis 3:15).

וְכֵן מָצִינוּ בְּקַיִן, וְקֹרַח, וּבִלְעָם, וְדוֹאֵג, וַאֲחִיתוֹפֶל, וְגֵיחֲזִי, וְאַבְשָׁלוֹם, וַאֲדוֹנִיָּהוּ, וְעוּזִּיָּהוּ, וְהָמָן, שֶׁנָּתְנוּ עֵינֵיהֶם בְּמַה שֶּׁאֵינוֹ רָאוּי לָהֶם, מַה שֶּׁבִּיקְּשׁוּ לֹא נִיתַּן לָהֶם, וּמַה שֶּׁבְּיָדָם נְטָלוּהוּ מֵהֶם.

The *baraita* continues: **And so we found with regard to Cain,**[N] who desired to inherit the whole world alone (see Genesis 4); **and Korah,** who desired the priesthood (see Numbers 16); **and Balaam,** who desired Balak's money (see Numbers 22); **and Doeg,** who was jealous of David (see I Samuel 21–22); **and Ahithophel,** who was also jealous of David (see II Samuel 16); **and Gehazi,** who took Naaman's money (see II Kings 5); **and Absalom,**[N] who wanted the kingdom (see II Samuel 15); **and Adonijah,** who also wanted the kingdom (see I Kings 1); **and Uzziah,** who wanted to be the High Priest (see II Chronicles 26); **and Haman,** who wanted to kill all the Jews (see Esther 3:13). All of these were people **who placed their eyes on that which is unfit for them, and** consequently **what they desired was not given to them, and what they had was taken from them.**

NOTES

And so too we found with regard to the primeval snake – וְכֵן מָצִינוּ בְּנָחָשׁ הַקַּדְמוֹנִי: The episode involving Adam, Eve, and the primeval snake is one of the more mysterious in the Bible, and much of what is taught concerning this is found in the esoterica. Apparently, this snake was a representation of the forces of evil and served to cause Adam and Eve to sin and to introduce evil into humanity. This may be the meaning of the passage in tractate *Shabbat* (146a) that teaches that the snake engaged in sexual intercourse with Eve and infected her with moral contamination. As punishment, all of the characteristics of the snake that had been similar to humans, by which the snake was elevated above all the other animals, were taken away from it (see *Otzar HaKavod*).

I will kill Adam, etc. – אֶהֱרוֹג אֶת אָדָם וכו׳: Many question why the snake thought that only Adam would die, as both Adam and Eve ate from the Tree of Knowledge and would therefore be deserving of punishment. One explanation is that since the initial instruction from God was stated directly to Adam, the snake thought that only he would be punished by death for eating from the tree, not Eve (*Iyyun Ya'akov*; see Maharsha).

Cain – קַיִן: Rashi and *Tosefot HaRash* explain, based upon a midrash, that a twin sister was born together with Cain, and two sisters were born with Abel. Cain desired to marry the additional woman, and therefore he killed Abel to prevent Abel form marrying her. Others explain that the verses indicate that Cain was a farmer and Abel was a shepherd, and Cain desired Abel's portion of the pasture land. Another possibility is that Cain wanted the whole world for himself and his progeny, but in the end they were all wiped out in the flood (Maharsha).

And Gehazi and Absalom – וְגֵיחֲזִי וְאַבְשָׁלוֹם: Although chronologically Gehazi should be mentioned after Adonijah, the reason why Gehazi is listed immediately following Balaam, Doeg, and Ahithophel is that they are all included among the individuals listed in tractate *Sanhedrin* (107b) who have no share in the World-to-Come (*Ben Yehoyada*).

״בְּיָרֵךְ הִתְחִילָה בַּעֲבֵירָה״ וכו׳. מְנָא הָנֵי מִילֵּי? אִילֵימָא מִשּׁוּם דִּכְתִיב: ״בְּתֵת ה׳ אֶת יְרֵכֵךְ נוֹפֶלֶת וְאֶת בִּטְנֵךְ צָבָה״? וְהָכְתִיב: ״וְצָבְתָה בִטְנָהּ וְנָפְלָה יְרֵכָהּ״!

§ The mishna teaches: **She began her transgression with** her **thigh**[N] and afterward with her stomach, therefore the thigh is smitten first and then the stomach. The Gemara asks: **From where are these matters** derived, i.e., that this is the order of her punishment? **If we say** it is **because it is written** in the verse detailing the priest's curse: "Then the priest shall cause the woman to swear with the oath of cursing, and the priest shall say unto the woman: The Lord make you a curse and an oath among your people, **when the Lord does make your thigh to fall away, and your belly to swell"** (Numbers 5:21), which indicates the sequence of her punishment; **but isn't** the opposite **written** in the verse describing what actually occurs to a guilty *sota*: **"And her belly shall swell, and her thigh shall fall away"** (Numbers 5:27), indicating that the punishment begins with her stomach and then her thigh?

אֲמַר אַבַּיֵי: כִּי לָיֵיט – לָיֵיט תְּחִילָּה יָרֵךְ וַהֲדַר בֶּטֶן לָיֵיט, וּמַיָּא כִּי בָּדְקִי – כִּי אוֹרְחַיְיהוּ בָּדְקִי, בֶּטֶן בְּרֵישָׁא וַהֲדַר יָרֵךְ. בִּקְלָלָה נַמִי כְּתִיב: ״לַצְבּוֹת בֶּטֶן וְלַנְפִּל יָרֵךְ״! הַהוּא דְּמוֹדַע לָהּ כֹּהֵן דְּבֶטֶן בְּרֵישָׁא וַהֲדַר יָרֵךְ, שֶׁלֹּא לְהוֹצִיא לַעַז עַל מַיִם הַמָּרִים.

Abaye said in explanation: **When** the priest **curses** the woman, **he first curses the thigh and then he curses the stomach, but when the** bitter **water evaluates** her, **it evaluates** her **along its way**[H] through the body. The water **first** enters the **stomach and then** reaches the **thigh.** The Gemara asks: But **in** the verse detailing the **curse it is also written:** "And this water that causes the curse shall go into your bowels, **and will cause your belly to swell, and your thigh to fall away"** (Numbers 5:22). The Gemara answers: **That** verse teaches **that the priest notifies her that** the **stomach** will be affected **first and then** the **thigh, so that** one **not cast aspersions on the bitter water.**

מתני׳ שִׁמְשׁוֹן הָלַךְ אַחַר עֵינָיו, לְפִיכָךְ נִקְּרוּ פְלִשְׁתִּים אֶת עֵינָיו, שֶׁנֶּאֱמַר: ״וַיֹּאחֲזוּהוּ פְלִשְׁתִּים וַיְנַקְּרוּ אֶת עֵינָיו״.

MISHNA The mishna provides additional examples of people who were treated by Heaven commensurate with their actions. **Samson followed his eyes,**[N] **therefore** he was punished measure for measure, as **the Philistines gouged out his eyes, as it is stated: "And the Philistines laid hold on him, and put out his eyes"** (Judges 16:21).

אַבְשָׁלוֹם נִתְגָּאָה בִּשְׂעָרוֹ, לְפִיכָךְ נִתְלָה בִּשְׂעָרוֹ. וּלְפִי שֶׁבָּא עַל עֶשֶׂר פִּלַגְשֵׁי אָבִיו, לְפִיכָךְ נִתְּנוּ בּוֹ עֶשֶׂר לוֹנְבִיּוֹת, שֶׁנֶּאֱמַר: ״וַיָּסֹבּוּ עֲשָׂרָה אֲנָשִׁים נוֹשְׂאֵי כְּלֵי יוֹאָב״. וּלְפִי שֶׁגָּנַב שְׁלֹשָׁה גְּנֵבוֹת, לֵב אָבִיו וְלֵב בֵּית דִּין וְלֵב יִשְׂרָאֵל, שֶׁנֶּאֱמַר: ״וַיְגַנֵּב אַבְשָׁלוֹם אֶת לֵב אַנְשֵׁי יִשְׂרָאֵל״, לְפִיכָךְ נִתְקְעוּ בּוֹ שְׁלֹשָׁה שְׁבָטִים, שֶׁנֶּאֱמַר: ״וַיִּקַּח שְׁלֹשָׁה שְׁבָטִים בְּכַפּוֹ וַיִּתְקָעֵם בְּלֵב אַבְשָׁלוֹם״.

Absalom was excessively **proud of his hair,** and **therefore he was hanged by his hair. And** furthermore, **because he engaged in sexual intercourse with ten of his father's concubines** (see II Samuel 15:16 and 16:22), **therefore ten spears** [*loneviyyot*][L] **were put,** i.e., thrust, **into him, as it is stated: "And ten young men that bore Joab's armor compassed about** and smote Absalom, and slew him" (II Samuel 18:15). **And because he stole** three times, committing **three thefts** of people's hearts: **The heart of his father,** as he tricked him by saying that he was going to sacrifice offerings; **the heart of the court,** as he tricked them into following him; **and the heart of the Jewish people, as it is stated: "So Absalom stole the hearts of the men of Israel"** (II Samuel 15:6), **therefore three spears were embedded into** his heart, **as it is stated:** "Then said Joab: I may not tarry like this with you. **And he took three spears in his hand, and thrust them through the heart of Absalom,** while he was yet alive" (II Samuel 18:14).

וְכֵן לְעִנְיַן הַטּוֹבָה. מִרְיָם הִמְתִּינָה לְמֹשֶׁה שָׁעָה אַחַת, שֶׁנֶּאֱמַר: ״וַתֵּתַצַּב אֲחוֹתוֹ מֵרָחוֹק״, לְפִיכָךְ נִתְעַכְּבוּ לָהּ יִשְׂרָאֵל שִׁבְעָה יָמִים, שֶׁנֶּאֱמַר: ״וְהָעָם לֹא נָסַע עַד הֵאָסֵף מִרְיָם״.

The mishna continues: **And the same** is so **with regard to the** reward of **good** deeds; a person is rewarded measure for measure. **Miriam waited for** the baby **Moses** for **one hour** at the shore of the Nile, **as it is stated: "And his sister stood afar off,** to know what would be done to him" (Exodus 2:4). **Therefore the Jewish people delayed** their travels in the desert for **seven days** to wait **for her** when she was smitten with leprosy, **as it is stated:** "And Miriam was confined outside of the camp seven days; **and the people journeyed not until Miriam was brought in again"** (Numbers 12:15).

יוֹסֵף זָכָה לִקְבּוֹר אֶת אָבִיו וְאֵין בְּאֶחָיו גָּדוֹל מִמֶּנּוּ, שֶׁנֶּאֱמַר: ״וַיַּעַל יוֹסֵף לִקְבֹּר אֶת אָבִיו...וַיַּעַל עִמּוֹ גַּם רֶכֶב גַּם פָּרָשִׁים״. מִי לָנוּ גָּדוֹל מִיּוֹסֵף שֶׁלֹּא נִתְעַסֵּק בּוֹ אֶלָּא מֹשֶׁה.

Joseph merited to bury his father, resulting in a display of great honor to his father, **and there was none among his brothers greater than he** in importance, for he was viceroy of Egypt, **as it is stated: "And Joseph went up to bury his father;** and with him went up all the servants of Pharaoh, the Elders of his house, and all the Elders of the land of Egypt, and all the house of Joseph, and his brethren, and his father's house; only their little ones, and their flocks, and their herds, they left in the land of Goshen. **And there went up with him both chariots and horsemen;** and it was a very great company" (Genesis 50:7–9). **Who, to us,** had **a greater** burial **than Joseph, as it was none** other than **Moses who involved** himself in transporting **his** coffin.

NOTES

Thigh, etc. – יָרֵךְ וכו׳: In the Jerusalem Talmud, there are other solutions presented to resolve this contradiction. One explanation found there is that the punishment of the woman drinking the bitter water begins in the stomach, while the punishment of her paramour begins in his thigh (*Ḥeshek Shlomo*).

Samson followed his eyes – שִׁמְשׁוֹן הָלַךְ אַחַר עֵינָיו: The Riaf explains that Samson's act of transgression was sexual intercourse. However, since these unions were part of God's plan for the Jewish people at the time, it was not the act of intercourse per se that was problematic. Rather, the problem was that Samson acted out of his desire to follow his eyes rather than to execute the plan of Heaven. He was punished accordingly, not as one who transgresses with regard to sexual intercourse but as one who sinned with his eyes.

HALAKHA

When the bitter water evaluates her it evaluates her along its way – מַיָּא כִּי בָּדְקִי כִּי אוֹרְחַיְיהוּ בָּדְקִי: If the *sota* was guilty of adultery, her face immediately turned sallow and her eyes bulged out, then her stomach distended, and finally her thighs fell away, until ultimately she died (Rambam *Sefer Nashim, Hilkhot Sota* 3:16).

LANGUAGE

Spears [*loneviyyot*] – לוֹנְבִיּוֹת: This word appears in other versions of the text as *lonekiyyot*, which appears to be the proper text. The source of the word is the Greek λόγχη, *lonkhē*, meaning a lance or javelin.

מֹשֶׁה זָכָה בְּעַצְמוֹת יוֹסֵף וְאֵין בְּיִשְׂרָאֵל גָּדוֹל מִמֶּנּוּ, שֶׁנֶּאֱמַר: ״וַיִּקַּח מֹשֶׁה אֶת עַצְמוֹת יוֹסֵף עִמּוֹ״. מִי גָּדוֹל מִמֹּשֶׁה שֶׁלֹּא נִתְעַסֵּק בּוֹ אֶלָּא הַמָּקוֹם, שֶׁנֶּאֱמַר: ״וַיִּקְבֹּר אוֹתוֹ בַגַּי״. לֹא עַל מֹשֶׁה בִּלְבַד אָמְרוּ, אֶלָּא עַל כׇּל הַצַּדִּיקִים, שֶׁנֶּאֱמַר: ״וְהָלַךְ לְפָנֶיךָ צִדְקֶךָ כְּבוֹד ה׳ יַאַסְפֶךָ״.

Moses merited to be the only person involved **in** the transportation of **Joseph's bones** to be buried in Eretz Yisrael, **and there was none among the Jewish people greater than he, as it is stated: "And Moses took the bones of Joseph with him"** (Exodus 13:19). **Who** had **a greater** burial **than Moses, as no one involved himself in his** burial **other than the Omnipresent** Himself, **as it is stated: "And He buried him in the valley** in the land of Moab over against Beth Peor; and no man knows of his sepulcher unto this day" (Deuteronomy 34:6). The mishna comments: **Not only with regard to Moses did** the Sages **say** that God takes part in his burial, **but** also **with regard to all the righteous individuals, as it is stated: "Your righteousness shall go before you and the glory of the Lord shall gather you in"** (Isaiah 58:8).

גמ׳ תָּנוּ רַבָּנַן: שִׁמְשׁוֹן בְּעֵינָיו מָרַד, שֶׁנֶּאֱמַר: ״וַיֹּאמֶר שִׁמְשׁוֹן אֶל אָבִיו אוֹתָהּ קַח לִי כִּי הִיא יָשְׁרָה בְעֵינָי״, לְפִיכָךְ נִקְּרוּ פְּלִשְׁתִּים אֶת עֵינָיו, שֶׁנֶּאֱמַר: ״וַיֹּאחֲזוּהוּ פְלִשְׁתִּים וַיְנַקְּרוּ אֶת עֵינָיו״.

GEMARA **The Sages taught** (*Tosefta* 3:15): **Samson rebelled with his eyes, as it is stated:** "Then his father and his mother said to him: Is there never a woman among the daughters of your brethren, or among all my people, that you go out to take a wife of the uncircumcised Philistines? **And Samson said to his father: Get her for me; for she is pleasant in my eyes"** (Judges 14:3). **Therefore, the Philistines gouged out his eyes, as it is stated: "And the Philistines laid hold on him, and put out his eyes"** (Judges 16:21).

אִינִי? וְהָכְתִיב: ״וְאָבִיו וְאִמּוֹ לֹא יָדְעוּ כִּי מֵה׳ הִיא״! כִּי אֲזַל מִיהָא בָּתַר יַשְׁרוּתֵיהּ אֲזַל.

The Gemara asks: **Is that so? But isn't it written: "But his father and his mother knew not that it was from the Lord;** as he sought a subterfuge against the Philistines" (Judges 14:4), indicating that Samson's searching for a Philistine wife was due to a Divine mission? The Gemara answers: Although God did plan the punishment of the Philistines, **in any event when he went, he followed his inclination** and did not act for the sake of Heaven.

תַּנְיָא, רַבִּי אוֹמֵר: תְּחִילַּת קִלְקוּלוֹ בְּעַזָּה, לְפִיכָךְ לָקָה בְּעַזָּה. תְּחִילַּת קִלְקוּלוֹ בְּעַזָּה, דִּכְתִיב: ״וַיֵּלֶךְ שִׁמְשׁוֹן עַזָּתָה וַיַּרְא שָׁם אִשָּׁה זוֹנָה״ וגו׳, לְפִיכָךְ לָקָה בְּעַזָּה, דִּכְתִיב: ״וַיּוֹרִידוּ אוֹתוֹ עַזָּתָה״.

It is taught in a *baraita* in the *Tosefta* (3:15): **Rabbi** Yehuda HaNasi **says: His initial wrongdoing was in Gaza,** and **therefore he was smitten in Gaza.** The Gemara explains: **His initial wrongdoing was in Gaza, as it is written: "And Samson went to Gaza, and saw there a harlot,** and went in unto her" (Judges 16:1). **Therefore, he was smitten in Gaza, as it is written:** "And the Philistines laid hold on him, and put out his eyes; **and they brought him down to Gaza,** and bound him with fetters of brass; and he did grind in the prison-house" (Judges 16:21).

וְהָכְתִיב: ״וַיֵּרֶד שִׁמְשׁוֹן תִּמְנָתָה״! תְּחִלַּת קִלְקוּלוֹ מִיהָא בְּעַזָּה הָיָה.

The Gemara asks: **But isn't it written** earlier: **"And Samson went down to Timnah,** and saw a woman in Timnah of the daughters of the Philistines" (Judges 14:1), indicating that his initial wrongdoing was in Timnah? The **Gemara answers: In any event, his initial wrongdoing**[N] **was in Gaza,** for at least he had married the woman in Timnah; in Gaza, Samson never wed the woman but only engaged in sexual intercourse with her.

״וַיְהִי אַחֲרֵי כֵן וַיֶּאֱהַב אִשָּׁה בְּנַחַל שֹׂרֵק וּשְׁמָהּ דְּלִילָה״. תַּנְיָא, רַבִּי אוֹמֵר: אִילְמָלֵא לֹא נִקְרָא שְׁמָהּ דְּלִילָה, רְאוּיָה הָיְתָה שֶׁתִּקָּרֵא דְּלִילָה – דִּילְדְּלָה אֶת כֹּחוֹ, דִּילְדְּלָה אֶת לִבּוֹ, דִּילְדְּלָה אֶת מַעֲשָׂיו.

The Gemara continues its discussion of Samson. The verse states: **"And it came to pass afterward, that he loved a woman in the valley of Sorek, whose name was Delilah"** (Judges 16:4). **It is taught** in a *baraita* that **Rabbi** Yehuda HaNasi **says:** Even **if she had not been called** by the **name Delilah, it would have been fitting that she be called Delilah,** for **she weakened** [*dildela*] **his strength, she weakened his heart,** and **she weakened his deeds,** thereby decreasing his merits.

NOTES

His initial wrongdoing – תְּחִילַּת קִלְקוּלוֹ: It is difficult to understand why Samson's engaging in sexual intercourse with a prostitute is viewed as more incriminating than his marrying the Philistine woman from Timnah, as the verse explicitly states: "Neither shall you make marriages with them" (Deuteronomy 7:3). The Maharsha answers that Samson presumably had the woman whom he married convert, and therefore did not violate this transgression. The Rambam also explains that Samson converted all the women he wed (see *Mishne Torah Sefer Kedusha, Hilkhot Issurei Bia* 3:14–16).

דִּילְדְּלָה אֶת כֹּחוֹ, דִּכְתִיב: ״וַיָּסַר כֹּחוֹ מֵעָלָיו״. דִּילְדְּלָה אֶת לִבּוֹ, דִּכְתִיב: ״וַתֵּרֶא דְּלִילָה כִּי הִגִּיד לָהּ אֶת כָּל לִבּוֹ״. דִּילְדְּלָה אֶת מַעֲשָׂיו, דְּאִיסְתַּלַּק שְׁכִינָה מִינֵּיהּ, דִּכְתִיב: ״וְהוּא לֹא יָדַע כִּי ה׳ סָר מֵעָלָיו״.

The Gemara explains: **She weakened his strength, as it is written:** "And she made him sleep upon her knees; and she called for a man and had the seven locks of his head shaved off; and she began to afflict him, **and his strength went from him**" (Judges 16:19). **She weakened his heart, as it is written: "And when Delilah saw that he had told her all his heart,** she sent and called for the lords of the Philistines, saying: Come up this once, for he has told me all his heart" (Judges 16:18). **She weakened his deeds,** thereby decreasing his merits, **as the Divine Presence left him, as it is written:** "And she said: The Philistines are upon you, Samson. And he awoke out of his sleep, and said: I will go out as at other times, and shake myself. **But he knew not that the Lord was departed from him**" (Judges 16:20).

״וַתֵּרֶא דְּלִילָה כִּי הִגִּיד לָהּ אֶת כָּל לִבּוֹ״ – מְנָא יָדְעָה? אָמַר רַבִּי חָנִין אָמַר רַב: נִיכָּרִין דִּבְרֵי אֱמֶת. אַבַּיֵּי אָמַר: יָדְעָה בּוֹ בְּאוֹתוֹ צַדִּיק דְּלָא מַפֵּיק שֵׁם שָׁמַיִם לְבַטָּלָה. כֵּיוָן דַּאֲמַר: נְזִיר אֱלֹהִים אֲנִי, אָמְרָה: הָשְׁתָּא וַדַּאי קוּשְׁטָא קָאָמַר.

The verse states: "**And when Delilah saw that he had told her all his heart**" (Judges 16:18). The Gemara asks: **From where did she know** that this time he had told her the truth about the source of his strength, as he had lied about it previously? **Rabbi Ḥanin says** that **Rav says: Words of truth are recognizable,**[N] and she felt that this time he was telling the truth. **Abaye says** differently: **She knew about** Samson being **a righteous individual, that he would not express the name of Heaven in vain. Once he said:** "And he told her all his heart, and said to her: There has not come a razor upon my head; for **I have been a nazirite unto God** from my mother's womb" (Judges 16:17), **she said: Now he is certainly saying the truth.**

״וַיְהִי כִּי הֵצִיקָה לּוֹ בִּדְבָרֶיהָ כָּל הַיָּמִים וַתְּאַלְצֵהוּ״. מַאי ״וַתְּאַלְצֵהוּ״? אָמַר רַבִּי יִצְחָק דְּבֵי רַבִּי אַמִּי: בִּשְׁעַת גְּמַר בִּיאָה נִשְׁמְטָה מִתַּחְתָּיו.

The verse states: "**And it came to pass, when she pressed him daily with her words, and urged him,** that his soul was vexed unto death" (Judges 16:16). The Gemara asks: **What** is the meaning of "**and urged him**"? How did she do so? **Rabbi Yitzḥak of the school of Rabbi Ami says: At the moment** immediately before his **completion of** the act of **intercourse, she slipped away from beneath him.** By doing this, she urged him to reveal his secret.

״וְעַתָּה הִשָּׁמְרִי נָא וְאַל תִּשְׁתִּי יַיִן וְשֵׁכָר וְאַל תֹּאכְלִי כָּל טָמֵא״. מַאי ״כָּל טָמֵא״? וְתוּ, עַד הָשְׁתָּא דְּבָרִים טְמֵאִים קָאָכְלָה? אָמַר רַבִּי יִצְחָק דְּבֵי רַבִּי אַמִּי: דְּבָרִים הָאֲסוּרִים בְּנָזִיר.

When the angel spoke to Samson's mother, he said: "**Now therefore beware, I pray of you, and drink no wine nor strong drink, and eat not any unclean thing**" (Judges 13:4). The Gemara asks, **what** is the meaning of "**any unclean thing**"? That term usually means non-kosher foods, but obviously she would not eat them anyway. **And** what's **more, until now was she eating unclean things,** that she should have to be warned not to continue doing so? **Rabbi Yitzḥak of the school of Rabbi Ami says:** The angel was not referring to foods that are actually unclean, but rather **items that are forbidden to a nazirite.**

״וַיִּבְקַע אֱלֹהִים אֶת הַמַּכְתֵּשׁ אֲשֶׁר בַּלֶּחִי״. אָמַר רַבִּי יִצְחָק דְּבֵי רַבִּי אַמִּי: הוּא אִיוָּה לְדָבָר טָמֵא, לְפִיכָךְ נִתְלוּ חַיָּיו בְּדָבָר טָמֵא.

After Samson smote one thousand Philistines with the jawbone of a donkey, he called the place Lehi, and God miraculously granted him to drink, as he was dying of thirst. The verse states: "**But God cleaved the hollow place that is in Lehi,** and out of there came water; and when he had drunk, his spirit came back, and he revived" (Judges 15:19). **Rabbi Yitzḥak of the school of Rabbi Ami says: He desired something unclean,** as he was driven by lust to Philistine women. **Therefore,** the saving of **his life was dependent on something unclean,** the jawbone of a donkey.

״וַתָּחֶל רוּחַ ה׳״ וגו׳ – אָמַר רַבִּי חָמָא בְּרַבִּי חֲנִינָא: חָלְתָה נְבוּאָתוֹ שֶׁל יַעֲקֹב אָבִינוּ, דִּכְתִיב: ״יְהִי דָן נָחָשׁ עֲלֵי דֶרֶךְ״.

The verse states with regard to Samson: "**And the spirit of the Lord began** [*vataḥel*] to move him in Mahaneh Dan, between Zorah and Eshtaol" (Judges 13:25). **Rabbi Ḥama, son of Rabbi Ḥanina, says: The prophecy of Jacob our forefather** concerning the tribe of Dan **took effect** [*ḥaleta*] through Samson, a member of the tribe of Dan, **as it is written: "Dan shall be a serpent in the way,** a horned snake in the path, that bites the horse's heels, so that his rider falls backward" (Genesis 49:17).

NOTES

Words of truth are recognizable – נִיכָּרִין דִּבְרֵי אֱמֶת: Delilah recognized that Samson's statement that he was a nazirite was true because she had seen that he conducted himself like a nazirite by allowing his hair to grow long and by not drinking wine (Rashi).

LANGUAGE

Bell [*zog*] – זוֹג: Apparently related to the Persian word zang, meaning bell.

״לְפַעֲמוֹ בְּמַחֲנֵה דָן״. אָמַר רַבִּי יִצְחָק דְּבֵי רַבִּי אַמִי: מְלַמֵּד, שֶׁהָיְתָה שְׁכִינָה מְקַשְׁקֶשֶׁת לְפָנָיו כְּזוֹג, כְּתִיב הָכָא: ״לְפַעֲמוֹ בְּמַחֲנֵה דָן״, וּכְתִיב הָתָם: ״פַּעֲמֹן וְרִמּוֹן״.

The verse continues: **"To move him [*lefa'amo*] in Mahaneh Dan." Rabbi Yitzḥak of the school of Rabbi Ami says:** This **teaches that the Divine Presence jangled before him,** inspiring him, **like a bell [*zog*],**[L] as **it is written here: "To move him [*lefa'amo*] in Mahaneh Dan," and it is written there** with regard to the clothing of the High Priest: **"A bell [*pa'amon*] and a pomegranate"** (Exodus 39:26).

״בֵּין צָרְעָה וּבֵין אֶשְׁתָּאוֹל״ – אָמַר רַבִּי אַסִי: צָרְעָה וְאֶשְׁתָּאוֹל שְׁנֵי הָרִים גְּדוֹלִים הָיוּ, וַעֲקָרָן שִׁמְשׁוֹן וּטְחָנָן זֶה בָּזֶה.

The verse concludes: **"Between Zorah and Eshtaol." Rabbi Asi says: Zorah and Eshtaol were two large mountains, and Samson uprooted them and ground them one against the other.**

״וְהוּא יָחֵל לְהוֹשִׁיעַ אֶת יִשְׂרָאֵל״ – אָמַר רַבִּי חָמָא בְּרַבִּי חֲנִינָא:

Samson's parents were told: "For behold, you shall conceive, and bear a son; and no razor shall come upon his head; for the child shall be a nazirite unto God from the womb; **and he shall begin to save Israel** out of the hand of the Philistines" (Judges 13:5). **Rabbi Ḥama, son of Rabbi Ḥanina, says:**

NOTES

The oath of Abimelech was negated – הוּחַל שְׁבוּעָתוֹ שֶׁל אֲבִימֶלֶךְ: Rashi explains that since the Philistines subjected the Jewish people to their rule, they violated the oath and therefore Abraham's obligation to Abimelech and his descendants was negated. Although the Philistines had previously tormented the Jewish people, it was only at this point that they attempted to rule over them. *Tosefot HaRash* writes that this does not agree with the interpretation of Rashi that King David did not attempt to conquer Jerusalem until the oath of Abimelech was negated, as King David lived many years later. *Tosefot HaRosh* explains that the general oath to Abimelech was negated, but there was an additional promise made by Abraham to the Jebusites with regard to Jerusalem because he purchased the Cave of Machpelah from them (see Genesis, chapter 23).

With what did He bless him – בַּמֶּה בֵּרְכוֹ: The commentaries explain that since the term blessing generally refers to riches, a long life, or children, none of which Samson had, the Gemara offers an explanation specific to his life (see Rashi; Riaf).

Twenty-two years – עֶשְׂרִים וּשְׁתַּיִם שָׁנָה: This appears to be in direct opposition to the verse stating that Samson judged the Jewish people for twenty years (see Judges 16:31). Rav Hai Gaon explains that the Gemara here includes the two years that Samson spent in prison, as he was imprisoned due to his actions on behalf of the Jewish people (see Maharsha).

BACKGROUND

That goes in reverse – שֶׁחוֹזֵר לַאֲחוֹרָיו: The fox is considered to be a clever animal, and there are many stories told by hunters of various methods used by the fox to conceal its tracks. One of the strategies it employs to escape the tracking of a hunter is that it does not always run in a straight path. A fox changes direction frequently and often runs backward in the direction from which it came while the pursuers continue to chase it forward.

הוּחַל שְׁבוּעָתוֹ שֶׁל אֲבִימֶלֶךְ, דִּכְתִיב: ״אִם תִּשְׁקֹר לִי וּלְנִינִי וּלְנֶכְדִּי״.

Samson's parents were being told that **the oath of Abimelech,** king of the Philistines, **was negated,**[N] **as it is written** that Abimelech said to our forefather Abraham: "Now therefore swear unto me here by God **that you will not deal falsely with me, nor with my son, nor with my son's son;** but according to the kindness that I have done unto you, you shall do to me, and to the land wherein you have sojourned" (Genesis 21:23). The oath of the descendants of Abraham was no longer binding since the Philistines broke their oath by subjugating the Jewish people.

״וַיִּגְדַּל הַנַּעַר וַיְבָרְכֵהוּ ה׳״. בַּמֶּה בֵּרְכוֹ? אָמַר רַב יְהוּדָה אָמַר רַב: שֶׁבֵּרְכוֹ בְּאַמָּתוֹ. אַמָּתוֹ כִּבְנֵי אָדָם, וְזַרְעוֹ כְּנַחַל שׁוֹטֵף.

The verse states: "And the woman bore a son, and called his name Samson; **and the child grew, and the Lord blessed him"** (Judges 13:24). The Gemara asks: **With what did He bless him?**[N] **Rav Yehuda says** that **Rav says:** It means **that He blessed him with regard to his penis,** that despite his youth **his penis** should function **like** that of physically mature **men, and** that **his seed** should be **like an overflowing river.**

״וַיִּקְרָא שִׁמְשׁוֹן אֶל ה׳ וַיֹּאמַר ה׳ אֱלֹהִים זָכְרֵנִי נָא וְחַזְּקֵנִי נָא אַךְ הַפַּעַם הַזֶּה...וְאִנָּקְמָה נְקַם אַחַת מִשְּׁתֵי עֵינַי מִפְּלִשְׁתִּים״ – אָמַר רַב, אָמַר שִׁמְשׁוֹן לִפְנֵי הַקָּדוֹשׁ בָּרוּךְ הוּא: רִבּוֹנוֹ שֶׁל עוֹלָם, זְכוֹר לִי עֶשְׂרִים וּשְׁתַּיִם שָׁנָה שֶׁשָּׁפַטְתִּי אֶת יִשְׂרָאֵל, וְלֹא אָמַרְתִּי לְאֶחָד מֵהֶם ״הַעֲבֵר לִי מַקֵּל מִמָּקוֹם לְמָקוֹם״.

Prior to Samson's death, the verse states: **"And Samson called unto the Lord, and said: Lord God, remember me, I pray to You, and strengthen me, I pray to You, only this once,** O God, **that I may be this once avenged of the Philistines for my two eyes"** (Judges 16:28). **Rav said** that **Samson said before the Holy One, Blessed be He: Master of the Universe, remember** on **my** behalf the **twenty-two years**[N] **that I judged the Jewish people** without receiving any reward, **and I did not** even say **to any one of them: Move a stick for me from** one **place to** another **place.**

״וַיֵּלֶךְ שִׁמְשׁוֹן וַיִּלְכֹּד שְׁלֹשׁ מֵאוֹת שׁוּעָלִים״. מַאי שְׁנָא שׁוּעָלִים? אָמַר רַבִּי אַיְבוּ בַּר נַגְּדִי אָמַר רַבִּי חִיָּיא בַּר אַבָּא: אָמַר שִׁמְשׁוֹן: יָבֹא מִי שֶׁחוֹזֵר לַאֲחוֹרָיו, וְיִפָּרַע מִפְּלִשְׁתִּים שֶׁחָזְרוּ בִּשְׁבוּעָתָן.

The verse states earlier: **"And Samson went and caught three hundred foxes,** and took torches, and turned tail to tail, and put a torch in the midst between every two tails" (Judges 15:4). The Gemara asks: **What is different** about **foxes** than any other animal, that he chose them for this purpose? **Rabbi Aivu bar Nagdi says** that **Rabbi Ḥiyya bar Abba says: Samson said: Let** the animal **that goes in reverse**[B] when it tries to escape, i.e., the fox, **come and exact punishment from the Philistines, who reneged on their oath** that Abimelech swore to Abraham.

תַּנְיָא, אָמַר רַבִּי שִׁמְעוֹן הֶחָסִיד: בֵּין כְּתֵיפָיו שֶׁל שִׁמְשׁוֹן שִׁשִּׁים אַמָּה הָיָה, שֶׁנֶּאֱמַר: ״וַיִּשְׁכַּב שִׁמְשׁוֹן עַד חֲצִי הַלַּיְלָה וַיָּקָם בַּחֲצִי הַלַּיְלָה וַיֶּאֱחֹז בְּדַלְתוֹת שַׁעַר הָעִיר וּבִשְׁתֵּי הַמְּזֻזוֹת וַיִּסָּעֵם עִם הַבְּרִיחַ וַיָּשֶׂם עַל כְּתֵיפָיו״, וּגְמִירִי, דְּאֵין דַּלְתוֹת עַזָּה פְּחוּתוֹת מִשִּׁשִּׁים אַמָּה.

It is taught in a *baraita* that **Rabbi Shimon the Pious said:** The width **between the shoulders of Samson was sixty cubits, as it is stated: "And Samson lay till midnight, and arose at midnight, and grabbed hold of the doors of the gate of the city, and the two posts, and plucked them up, bar and all, and put them upon his shoulders,** and carried them up to the top of the mountain that is before Hebron" (Judges 16:3). The verse indicates that the width of the gate of the city of Gaza was equal to the width of Samson's shoulders, **and it is learned** as a tradition **that doors** of the gate **of Gaza were no less than sixty cubits** wide.

״וַיְהִי טוֹחֵן בְּבֵית הָאֲסוּרִים״ – אָמַר רַבִּי יוֹחָנָן: אֵין טְחִינָה אֶלָּא לְשׁוֹן עֲבֵירָה, וְכֵן הוּא אוֹמֵר: ״תִּטְחַן לְאַחֵר אִשְׁתִּי״, מְלַמֵּד, שֶׁכָּל אֶחָד וְאֶחָד הֵבִיא לוֹ אֶת אִשְׁתּוֹ לְבֵית הָאֲסוּרִים כְּדֵי שֶׁתִּתְעַבֵּר הֵימֶנּוּ. אֲמַר רַב פַּפָּא, הַיְינוּ דְּאָמְרִי אֱינָשֵׁי: קַמֵּי דְּשָׁתֵי חַמְרָא – חַמְרָא, קַמֵּי רְפוֹקָא גְרִידַיָא – דּוּבְלָא.

With regard to Samson's capture, the verse states: "And the Philistines laid hold on him, and put out his eyes; and they brought him down to Gaza, and bound him with fetters of brass; **and he did grind in the prison-house"** (Judges 16:21). **Rabbi Yoḥanan says: Grinding is nothing other** than **a language of a transgression**[N] of sexual intercourse, **and so the verse says: "Then let my wife grind unto another man"** (Job 31:10). This **teaches that each and every** Philistine man **brought his wife to the prison in order that she should be impregnated by** Samson. **Rav Pappa said: This** is an example of the folk saying **that people say: Before a wine drinker,** bring **wine; before one who digs in the ground,** bring **figs.**[B] So too, Samson, who married Philistine women, was brought more Philistine women while in prison.

וְאָמַר רַבִּי יוֹחָנָן: כָּל הַמְזַנֶּה – אִשְׁתּוֹ מְזַנֶּנֶת עָלָיו, שֶׁנֶּאֱמַר: ״אִם נִפְתָּה לִבִּי עַל אִשָּׁה וְעַל פֶּתַח רֵעִי אָרַבְתִּי״, וּכְתִיב: ״תִּטְחַן לְאַחֵר אִשְׁתִּי וְעָלֶיהָ יִכְרְעוּן אֲחֵרִין״. וְהַיְינוּ דְּאָמְרִי אֱינָשֵׁי: אִיהוּ בֵּי קָארֵי, וְאִיתְּתֵיה בֵּי בּוּצִינֵי.

And Rabbi Yoḥanan says: With regard to **anyone who commits adultery, his wife commits adultery against him,**[N] **as it is stated: "If my heart has been enticed unto a woman, and I have lain in wait at my neighbor's door"** (Job 31:9), **and it is written: "Then let my wife grind unto another man and may strangers kneel over her"** (Job 31:10). **And this** explains the folk saying **that people say: He is** found **among the pumpkins** [*karei*][L] **and his wife among the zucchinis** [*butzinei*],[N] which are similar types of vegetables. In other words, she acts the same way that he does.

NOTES

Grinding is nothing other than a language of a transgression – אֵין טְחִינָה אֶלָּא לְשׁוֹן עֲבֵירָה: The commentaries question why the Gemara provides a homiletical interpretation for Samson's grinding in the prison. The verse can easily be understood to mean that the blinded Samson ground with a millstone, as this was a common punishment for prisoners. Some explain that the interpretation here is based on what the Gemara will soon state, that Samson was lame in both legs, and therefore would not have been able to turn a millstone (*Iyyun Ya'akov*). Others suggest that since the verse indicates that Samson was chained, he would not have been able to turn a millstone (Riaf).

There are those who ask how Samson permitted himself to engage in sexual intercourse with married women, as intercourse with the wife of a gentile is considered an act of adultery. One answer suggested is that adultery with a married gentile is viewed as a form of theft from the husband. Here there was no theft, as the husbands themselves brought their wives to Samson, and therefore there would be no prohibition of adultery (*Eshel Avraham*).

Anyone who commits adultery, his wife commits adultery against him – כָּל הַמְזַנֶּה אִשְׁתּוֹ מְזַנֶּנֶת: The Maharal explains that spouses are suitable to each other, and the shortcomings of one can be found in the other.

Others ask: If this statement in the Gemara is in fact accurate, then what is the purpose of a *sota* drinking the bitter water, as the water is ineffective if the woman's husband was also unfaithful? An answer given is that the Gemara means to say that it is likely that if one spouse is unfaithful the other spouse will be so as well, but there are still spouses that remain faithful and avoid transgression even when their partner does not.

He is found among the pumpkins and his wife among the zucchinis – אִיהוּ בֵּי קָארֵי וְאִיתְּתֵיה בֵּי בּוּצִינֵי: The straightforward understanding of this phrase is that a wife's behavior is just like that of her husband. The *Arukh* also offers a literal explanation, that they masturbate using these vegetables.

BACKGROUND

Before one who digs in the ground bring figs – קַמֵּי רְפוֹקָא גְרִידַיָא דּוּבְלָא: The meaning of these words is unclear. The difficulty is compounded due to the fact that there are several versions of the text. The *Arukh* cites a different version of the text that reads: Before the hoe that weeds the fields, bring a *se'a* of grass.

LANGUAGE

Pumpkins [*karei*] – קָארֵי: This refers to the calabash, also known as bottle gourd, *Lagenaria siceraria*. It is a summer vegetable from the squash family grown either on the ground or trellised over a frame. It is quite large, approximately 45 cm long and 25 cm wide, and shaped like a bottle. The vegetable itself is eaten cooked, and its seeds are eaten as a snack. Calabash is harvested young for consumption and late for use as a bottle or other utensil.

Traditional African musical instrument made out of a dried bottle gourd

Bottle gourd

וְאָמַר רַבִּי יוֹחָנָן: שִׁמְשׁוֹן דָּן אֶת יִשְׂרָאֵל כַּאֲבִיהֶם שֶׁבַּשָּׁמַיִם, שֶׁנֶּאֱמַר: ״דָּן יָדִין עַמּוֹ כְּאַחַד״ וגו׳. וְאָמַר רַבִּי יוֹחָנָן: שִׁמְשׁוֹן עַל שְׁמוֹ שֶׁל הַקָּדוֹשׁ בָּרוּךְ הוּא נִקְרָא, שֶׁנֶּאֱמַר: ״כִּי שֶׁמֶשׁ וּמָגֵן ה׳ אֱלֹהִים״ וגו׳. אֶלָּא מֵעַתָּה, לֹא יִמָּחֶה! אֶלָּא מֵעֵין שְׁמוֹ שֶׁל הַקָּדוֹשׁ בָּרוּךְ הוּא. מַה הַקָּדוֹשׁ בָּרוּךְ הוּא מָגֵין עַל כָּל הָעוֹלָם כּוּלּוֹ, אַף שִׁמְשׁוֹן מָגֵין בְּדוֹרוֹ עַל יִשְׂרָאֵל.

And Rabbi Yoḥanan says: Samson judged the Jewish people as their Father in Heaven[N] does, with complete justice, **as it is stated: "Dan shall judge his people, as one** of the tribes of Israel" (Genesis 49:16), which is interpreted to mean that Samson, from the tribe of Dan, judges his people just as God, Who is "One." **And Rabbi Yoḥanan says: Samson [*Shimshon*] is called by the name of the Holy One, Blessed be He, as it is stated: "For the Lord God is a sun [*shemesh*] and a shield"** (Psalms 84:12). The Gemara comments: **If that is so,** then his name **should not be erased** just like other sanctified names are not erased. **Rather,** he is not called by the name of God but his name **is akin to the name of the Holy One, Blessed be He,** for **just as the Holy One, Blessed be He, protects the entire world, so too Samson, in his generation, protected all the Jewish people.**

וְאָמַר רַבִּי יוֹחָנָן: בִּלְעָם חִיגֵּר בְּרַגְלוֹ אַחַת הָיָה, שֶׁנֶּאֱמַר: ״וַיֵּלֶךְ שֶׁפִי״, שִׁמְשׁוֹן חִיגֵּר בִּשְׁתֵּי רַגְלָיו הָיָה, שֶׁנֶּאֱמַר: ״שְׁפִיפֹן עֲלֵי אֹרַח״.

And Rabbi Yoḥanan says: Balaam was lame in one of his legs, as it is stated with regard to him: **"And he went, limping [*shefi*]"** (Numbers 23:3). **Samson was lame in** both of **his two legs, as it is stated** that when Jacob mentioned the tribe of Dan in the prophecy that pertained to Samson, he referred to him as: "Dan shall be a serpent in the way, **a horned snake [*shefifon*] in the path"** (Genesis 49:17),[B] which is double *shefi*, i.e., doubly lame.

תָּנוּ רַבָּנַן: חֲמִשָּׁה נִבְרְאוּ מֵעֵין דּוּגְמָא שֶׁל מַעְלָה, וְכוּלָּן לָקוּ בָּהֶן: שִׁמְשׁוֹן בְּכֹחוֹ, שָׁאוּל בְּצַוָּארוֹ, אַבְשָׁלוֹם בִּשְׂעָרוֹ, צִדְקִיָּה בְּעֵינָיו, אָסָא בְּרַגְלָיו.

§ **The Sages taught** in a *baraita*: **Five** individuals **were created** with a characteristic that is **akin to a representation of the** One on **High, and they were all stricken by that** characteristic. **Samson** was glorified **in his strength, Saul in his neck** (see I Samuel 9:2), **Absalom in his hair, Zedekiah in his eyes,**[N] and **Asa in his feet.**

שִׁמְשׁוֹן בְּכֹחוֹ, דִּכְתִיב: ״וַיָּסַר כֹּחוֹ מֵעָלָיו״.

The Gemara clarifies: **Samson** was stricken **by his strength,** which led to his demise, **as it is written:** "And she made him sleep upon her knees; and she called for a man and had the seven locks of his head shaved off; and she began to afflict him, **and his strength went from him"** (Judges 16:19).

שָׁאוּל בְּצַוָּארוֹ, דִּכְתִיב: ״וַיִּקַּח שָׁאוּל אֶת הַחֶרֶב וַיִּפֹּל עָלֶיהָ״.

Saul was smitten **in his neck, as it is written:** "Then said Saul to his armor-bearer: Draw your sword, and thrust me through with it; lest these uncircumcised come and thrust me through, and make a mock of me. But his armor-bearer would not; for he was sore afraid. **Therefore, Saul took his sword and fell upon it"** (I Samuel 31:4); he fell with his neck upon the sword.

אַבְשָׁלוֹם בִּשְׂעָרוֹ, כִּדְבָעֵינַן לְמֵימַר קַמָּן. צִדְקִיָּה בְּעֵינָיו, דִּכְתִיב: ״וְאֶת עֵינֵי צִדְקִיָּהוּ עִוֵּר״.

Absalom was stricken **in his hair, as we will state later. Zedekiah** was stricken **in his eyes, as it is written:** "And they slew the sons of Zedekiah before his eyes, **and put out the eyes of Zedekiah,** and bound him in fetters, and carried him to Babylon" (II Kings 25:7).

אָסָא בְּרַגְלָיו, דִּכְתִיב: ״רַק לְעֵת זִקְנָתוֹ חָלָה אֶת רַגְלָיו״ – וְאָמַר רַב יְהוּדָה אָמַר רַב: שֶׁאֲחָזַתּוּ פָּדַגְרָא. אֲמַר לֵיהּ מָר זוּטְרָא בְּרֵיהּ דְּרַב נַחְמָן לְרַב נַחְמָן: הֵיכִי דָּמֵי פָּדַגְרָא? אֲמַר לֵיהּ: כְּמַחַט בְּבָשָׂר הַחַי. מְנָא יָדַע? אִיכָּא דְּאָמְרִי: מֵיחַשׁ הֲוָה חָשׁ בֵּיהּ. וְאִיכָּא דְּאָמְרִי: מֵרַבֵּיהּ שְׁמַע לֵיהּ. וְאִיכָּא דְּאָמְרִי: ״סוֹד ה׳ לִירֵאָיו וּבְרִיתוֹ לְהוֹדִיעָם״.

Asa was stricken **in his feet, as it is written:** "Now the rest of all the acts of Asa, and all his might, and all that he did, and the cities that he built, are they not written in the book of the chronicles of the kings of Judah? **But in the time of his old age he was diseased in his feet"** (I Kings 15:23). **And Rav Yehuda says** that **Rav says:** This indicates **that gout [*padagra*]**[LB] **grabbed hold of him. Mar Zutra, son of Rav Naḥman, said to Rav Naḥman: What are the circumstances** of gout? What pain does it involve? **He said to him:** It feels **like a needle** inserted **into living flesh.** The Gemara asks: **From where did he know this?** The Gemara answers: **Some say** that he himself **suffered from this** condition, **and some say** that **he heard it from his teacher, and some say** that he knew it through divine inspiration, as it stated: **"The secret of the Lord is with them that fear Him; and His covenant, to make them know it"** (Psalms 25:14).

NOTES

As their Father in Heaven – כַּאֲבִיהֶם שֶׁבַּשָּׁמַיִם: The *Iyyun Ya'akov* explains this to mean that he judged through divine inspiration, without hearing testimony or evidence.

Zedekiah in his eyes, etc. – צִדְקִיָּה בְּעֵינָיו וכו׳: Rashi writes that he cannot find a source that Zedekiah and Asa were blessed with special eyes and feet, respectively. Some explain that the fact that they were blessed in this regard is derived from the nature of their punishment, as they were certainly stricken in a way that was connected to their outstanding characteristics (see Maharsha). With regard to Asa, perhaps it is based on the verses in II Chronicles, chapter 14, which detail how Asa pursued the army of Zerah HaKushi, intimating that he was particularly fleet of foot.

BACKGROUND

A horned snake in the path – שְׁפִיפֹן עֲלֵי אֹרַח: This blessing, bestowed by Jacob to his son Dan, is viewed by the Talmud as a reference to Samson, who was from the tribe of Dan. As is clear from the stories that appear in Judges (chapters 13–16), the ongoing tension between the tribe of Dan and the Philistines was carried out at that time largely in a snakelike manner, by means of guerrilla warfare rather than direct warfare.

LANGUAGE

Gout [*padagra*] – פָּדַגְרָא: From the Greek ποδάγρα, *podagra*, whose literal meaning is a trap for the foot. It is used to refer to gout, which is a sickness of the foot.

BACKGROUND

Gout – פָּדַגְרָא: Gout results from disturbances in the secretion of uric acid from the body. Crystals of the acid accumulate in various joints in the body, particularly in the toes, causing the severe pain that Rav Naḥman described as being like a needle inserted into living flesh.

דָּרַשׁ רָבָא: מִפְּנֵי מָה נֶעֱנַשׁ אָסָא? מִפְּנֵי שֶׁעָשָׂה אַנְגַּרְיָא בְּתַלְמִידֵי חֲכָמִים, שֶׁנֶּאֱמַר: ״וְהַמֶּלֶךְ אָסָא הִשְׁמִיעַ אֶת כׇּל יְהוּדָה אֵין נָקִי״. מַאי ״אֵין נָקִי״? אָמַר רַב יְהוּדָה אָמַר רַב: אֲפִילּוּ חָתָן מֵחַדְרוֹ וְכַלָּה מֵחוּפָּתָהּ.

Rava taught: For what reason was **Asa punished** in his feet? **Because he made Torah scholars perform forced labor** [*angarya*],[L] **as it is stated: "Then King Asa made a proclamation unto all Judah; none was exempted;** and they carried away the stones of Ramah and the timber thereof, with which Baasa had built, and King Asa built with them Geba of Benjamin and Mizpah" (I Kings 15:22). The superfluous expression "unto all" indicates that the proclamation was issued to **everyone, including** Torah scholars. The Gemara asks: **What** is the meaning of the next phrase in the verse: **"None was exempted** [*ein naki*]"? **Rav Yehuda says** that **Rav says:** This includes **even a bridegroom from his chamber and a bride from her canopy,** as the verse states with regard to a bridegroom: "He shall be free [*naki*] for his house one year" (Deuteronomy 24:5).

כְּתִיב: ״וַיֵּרֶד שִׁמְשׁוֹן תִּמְנָתָה״, וּכְתִיב: ״הִנֵּה חָמִיךָ עֹלֶה תִמְנָתָה״! אָמַר רַבִּי אֶלְעָזָר: שִׁמְשׁוֹן שֶׁנִּתְגַּנָּה בָּהּ – כְּתִיב בֵּיהּ יְרִידָה. יְהוּדָה שֶׁנִּתְעַלָּה בָּהּ – כְּתִיב בֵּיהּ עֲלִיָּה.

§ **It is written** with regard to Samson: **"And Samson went down to Timnah,** and saw a woman in Timnah of the daughters of the Philistines" (Judges 14:1), **and it is written** in the Torah passage concerning the incident of Judah and Tamar: "And it was told to Tamar, saying: **Behold, your father-in-law is going up to Timnah** to sheer his sheep" (Genesis 38:13). The verses contain an apparent contradiction as to whether Timnah was a place to which one must descend or a place to which one must ascend. **Rabbi Elazar says:** These terms do not refer to the manner of traveling to Timnah but are used figuratively. Concerning **Samson, who was disgraced there** in Timnah, the term indicating **descent is written with regard to his** journey. Concerning **Judah, who was elevated there,** the term indicating **ascent is written with regard to his** journey.

רַבִּי שְׁמוּאֵל בַּר נַחְמָנִי אָמַר: שְׁתֵּי תִמְנָאוֹת הָיוּ, חֲדָא בִּירִידָה וַחֲדָא בַּעֲלִיָּה.

Rabbi Shmuel bar Naḥmani says differently: **There were two** cities named **Timnah, one** was reached **by descent** into a valley, **and one** was reached **by ascent.**

רַב פָּפָּא אָמַר: חֲדָא תִּמְנָה הֲוַאי, דְּאָתֵי מֵהַאי גִּיסָא – יְרִידָה, וּדְאָתֵי מֵהַאי גִּיסָא – עֲלִיָּה, כְּגוֹן וַרְדּוֹנְיָא וּבֵי בָארֵי וְשׁוּקָא דְּנֶרֶשׁ.

Rav Pappa said differently: **There was one Timnah,** and it was located on the slope of a mountain. One **who came from this side** reached it by **descent, and** one **who came from that side** reached it by **ascent.** The Gemara presents examples of such cities: **For example: Vardonia, and Bei Varei, and the market of Neresh.**[B]

״וַתֵּשֶׁב בְּפֶתַח עֵינַיִם״ – אָמַר רַבִּי אֲלֶכְּסַנְדְּרִי: מְלַמֵּד, שֶׁהָלְכָה וְיָשְׁבָה לָהּ בְּפִתְחוֹ שֶׁל אַבְרָהָם אָבִינוּ, מָקוֹם שֶׁכׇּל עֵינַיִם צוֹפוֹת לִרְאוֹתוֹ. רַבִּי חָנִין אָמַר רַב: מָקוֹם הוּא שֶׁשְּׁמוֹ ״עֵינַיִם״. וְכֵן הוּא אוֹמֵר: ״תַּפּוּחַ וְהָעֵינָם״.

The verse states with regard to Tamar: "And she put off from her the garments of her widowhood, and covered herself with her veil, and wrapped herself, **and sat in the entrance of Enaim** [*befetaḥ einayim*],[N] which is by the way to Timnah; for she saw that Shelah was grown up, and she was not given unto him to wife" (Genesis 38:14). The *amora'im* dispute the meaning of the word *einayim*. **Rabbi Alexandri says:** This **teaches that she went and she sat at the entrance** of the home **of Abraham our forefather, a place that all eyes hope to see it,** as she was certain that Judah would pass there. **Rabbi Ḥanin** says that **Rav says:** It is **a place called Enaim, and similarly** the verse **states** in the list of cities in Eretz Yisrael in the portion of Judah: **"Tappuah and Enam"** (Joshua 15:34).

רַבִּי שְׁמוּאֵל בַּר נַחְמָנִי אָמַר: שֶׁנָּתְנָה עֵינַיִם לִדְבָרֶיהָ; כְּשֶׁתְּבָעָהּ, אָמַר לָהּ: שֶׁמָּא נׇכְרִית אַתְּ? אָמְרָה לֵיהּ: גִּיּוֹרֶת אֲנִי; שֶׁמָּא אֵשֶׁת אִישׁ אַתְּ? אָמְרָה לֵיהּ: פְּנוּיָה אֲנִי; שֶׁמָּא קִיבֵּל בָּךְ אָבִיךְ קִידּוּשִׁין? אָמְרָה לֵיהּ: יְתוֹמָה אֲנִי; שֶׁמָּא טְמֵאָה אַתְּ? אָמְרָה לֵיהּ: טְהוֹרָה אֲנִי.

Rabbi Shmuel bar Naḥmani says: She provided eyes [*einayim*] **for her statements,** i.e., with her words she provided an opening [*petaḥ*] for Judah to solicit her. **When** Judah **solicited her** to engage in sexual intercourse with him, **he** first attempted to verify her status and **said to her:** Are **you perhaps are a gentile? She said to him: I am a convert.** He asked: **Perhaps you are a married woman? She said to him: I am an unmarried woman.** He asked: **Perhaps your father accepted betrothal for you** and you are unaware of it? **She said to him: I am an orphan.** He asked: **Maybe you are impure? She said to him: I am pure.**

״וַיִּטַּע אֶשֶׁל בִּבְאֵר שָׁבַע״ – אָמַר רֵישׁ לָקִישׁ: מְלַמֵּד, שֶׁעָשָׂה פַּרְדֵּס וְנָטַע בּוֹ כׇּל מִינֵי מְגָדִים.

The Gemara discusses Abraham's house: It is written: **"And he planted an *eshel* in Beersheba,** and called there on the name of the Lord, the Everlasting God" (Genesis 21:33). **Reish Lakish says:** This **teaches that** Abraham **made an orchard and planted in it all kinds of sweet things.**

LANGUAGE

Forced labor [*angarya*] – אַנְגַּרְיָא: From the Greek ἀγγαρεία, *angareya*, which means forced labor performed for the authorities.

BACKGROUND

Neresh – נֶרֶשׁ: A Babylonian city near the Neresh River, south of Sura, this was an important agricultural and commercial center. It was home to a large number of date palm farmers and producers of alcoholic beverages. Their community straddled the desert and was cut off from culture. Despite its isolation, it was home to a Jewish community for many generations, producing no small number of Sages. At one point, the prominent Sage Rav Pappa was the head of the yeshiva in Neresh.

NOTES

Entrance of Enaim [*petaḥ einayim*] – פֶּתַח עֵינַיִם: The midrash explains that the reason for all the expositions is because there is no explicit mention in the Bible of a place called Enaim or Petaḥ Enaim. Therefore, it was assumed that it is not the name of a place.

LANGUAGE

Orchard [*pardes*] – פַּרְדֵּס: This word is found in the Bible as an appellation for a pomegranate orchard (see Song of Songs 4:13). In the language of the Sages, it means an orchard of fruit trees of any kind. At times the word is used to refer to a garden enjoyed as a place of rest and relaxation.

Inn [*pundak*] – פּוּנְדָּק: From the Greek πανδοκεῖα, *pandokeya*, which means a guesthouse or hotel.

רַבִּי יְהוּדָה וְרַבִּי נְחֶמְיָה – חַד אָמַר: פַּרְדֵּס, וְחַד אָמַר: פּוּנְדָּק. בִּשְׁלָמָא לְמַאן דְּאָמַר פַּרְדֵּס, הַיְינוּ דִּכְתִיב: ״וַיִּטַּע״; אֶלָּא לְמַאן דְּאָמַר פּוּנְדָּק, מַאי ״וַיִּטַּע״? כִּדְכְתִיב: ״וַיִּטַּע אָהֳלֵי אַפַּדְנוֹ״ וגו׳.

The tanna'im **Rabbi Yehuda and Rabbi Neḥemya** disagree as to the meaning of the word "*eshel*." **One said** that it means **an orchard** [***pardes***],[L] **and one said** that it means **an inn** [***pundak***].[L] The Gemara continues: **Granted, according to the one who said** that it means **an orchard, this is what is written: "And he planted,"** and this is suitable language for an orchard. **But according to the one who said** that he opened **an inn, what is** the meaning of the phrase **"and he planted"?** The Gemara answers: **As it is written: "And he shall plant** [***vayitta***] **the tents of his palace** between the seas and the beauteous holy mountain; and he shall come to his end, and none shall help him" (Daniel 11:45), indicating that the word vayitta, and he planted, is also used to indicate pitching tents.

״וַיִּקְרָא שָׁם בְּשֵׁם ה׳ אֵל עוֹלָם״ – אָמַר רֵישׁ לָקִישׁ: אַל תִּיקְרֵי ״וַיִּקְרָא״

The verse there states: "And he planted an *eshel* in Beersheba, **and called there** [***vayyikra***] **on the name of the Lord, the Everlasting God"** (Genesis 21:33). **Reish Lakish said: Do not read** this word literally as **"*vayyikra*,"** and he called,

Perek **I**
Daf **10** Amud **b**

NOTES

Rather as *vayyakri* – אֶלָּא וַיַּקְרִיא: Some explain that since the verse is stated in the context of building an inn or planting an orchard, which is generally not a means by which one typically proclaims in the name of God, Reish Lakish therefore understands that its purpose was to cause others to recognize God (*Maharsha*).

Modest in the house of her father-in-law – צְנוּעָה בְּבֵית חָמִיהָ: Generally, when a married woman is in close quarters with her husband, there will be times when her modesty is compromised. Therefore, a woman who conducts herself with modesty while living in close quarters with her husband in the house of her father-in-law is indicative of an extremely modest woman (*Iyyun Ya'akov*).

אֶלָּא ״וַיַּקְרִיא״ – מְלַמֵּד, שֶׁהִקְרִיא אַבְרָהָם אָבִינוּ לִשְׁמוֹ שֶׁל הַקָּדוֹשׁ בָּרוּךְ הוּא בְּפֶה כׇּל עוֹבֵר וָשָׁב. כֵּיצַד? לְאַחַר שֶׁאָכְלוּ וְשָׁתוּ עָמְדוּ לְבָרְכוֹ. אָמַר לָהֶם: וְכִי מִשֶּׁלִּי אֲכַלְתֶּם? מִשֶּׁל אֱלֹהֵי עוֹלָם אֲכַלְתֶּם! הוֹדוּ וְשַׁבְּחוּ וּבָרְכוּ לְמִי שֶׁאָמַר וְהָיָה הָעוֹלָם!

but **rather as *vayyakri*,**[N] **and he caused** others **to call.** This **teaches that Abraham our forefather caused the name of the Holy One, Blessed be He, to be called** out **in the mouth of all passersby. How so? After** the guests of Abraham **ate and drank, they arose to bless him. He said to them: But did you eat from** what is **mine?** Rather, **you ate from** the food of **the God of the world.** Therefore, you should **thank and praise and bless the One Who spoke and the world was** created. In this way, Abraham caused everyone to call out to God.

״וַיִּרְאֶהָ יְהוּדָה וַיַּחְשְׁבֶהָ לְזוֹנָה כִּי כִסְּתָה פָּנֶיהָ״. מִשּׁוּם דְּכִסְּתָה פָּנֶיהָ חֲשָׁבָהּ לְזוֹנָה?

The Gemara continues its discussion of the incident of Judah and Tamar. It is written: **"When Judah saw her, he thought her to be a prostitute, for she had covered her face"** (Genesis 38:15). The Gemara asks: **Because she had covered her face he thought her to be a prostitute?** Prostitutes usually uncover their faces in order to attract men.

אָמַר רַבִּי אֶלְעָזָר: שֶׁכִּסְּתָה פָּנֶיהָ בְּבֵית חָמִיהָ. דְּאָמַר רַבִּי שְׁמוּאֵל בַּר נַחְמָנִי אָמַר רַבִּי יוֹנָתָן: כׇּל כַּלָּה שֶׁהִיא צְנוּעָה בְּבֵית חָמִיהָ – זוֹכָה וְיוֹצְאִין מִמֶּנָּה מְלָכִים וּנְבִיאִים. מְנָלַן? מִתָּמָר. נְבִיאִים, דִּכְתִיב: ״חֲזוֹן יְשַׁעְיָהוּ בֶן אָמוֹץ״; מְלָכִים, מִדָּוִד. וְאָמַר רַבִּי לֵוִי: דָּבָר זֶה מָסוֹרֶת בְּיָדֵינוּ מֵאֲבוֹתֵינוּ, אָמוֹץ וַאֲמַצְיָה אַחִים הֲווּ.

Rabbi Elazar says: The verse means **that** Tamar **covered her face in the home of her father-in-law,** Judah. Therefore, he did not recognize her when her face was uncovered. **As Rabbi Shmuel bar Naḥmani says** that **Rabbi Yonatan says: Any daughter-in-law who is modest in the house of her father-in-law**[N] **merits that kings and prophets emerge from her. From where do we** derive this? **From Tamar. Prophets** emerged from her, **as it is written: "The vision of Isaiah, the son of Amoz"** (Isaiah 1:1). **Kings** emerged from her, as seen **from David. And Rabbi Levi says: This matter is a tradition** that we received **from our ancestors: Amoz,** father of Isaiah, **and Amaziah,** king of Judea, **were brothers.** This indicates that Isaiah was also from the house of David and therefore a descendant of Tamar.

״הִיא מוּצֵאת״ – ״הִיא מִיתּוֹצֵאת״ מִיבְּעֵי לֵיהּ! אָמַר רַבִּי אֶלְעָזָר: לְאַחַר שֶׁנִּמְצְאוּ סִימָנֶיהָ בָּא סַמָּאֵל וְרִיחֲקָן, בָּא גַּבְרִיאֵל וְקֵירְבָן.

The verse describes Tamar's court hearing: **"When she was brought forth** [***mutzet***], she sent to her father-in-law, saying: By the man whose these are, am I with child" (Genesis 38:25). The Gemara comments: **It should have** stated: **When she was *mitutzet*.** The word *mutzet* also carries the implication of being found. What then, is taught by the use of that term? **Rabbi Elazar says: After her signs,** which she was using to prove that she was impregnated by Judah, **were brought out,** the evil angel **Samael came and distanced them** from each other in an attempt to prevent Judah's admission and Tamar's survival, which would enable the birth of King David. The angel **Gabriel** then **came and moved** the signs **closer** again. Therefore, the word *mutzet* is used, as it alludes to the signs being found again.

הַיְינוּ דִּכְתִיב: "לַמְנַצֵּחַ עַל יוֹנַת אֵלֶם רְחוֹקִים לְדָוִד מִכְתָּם" – אָמַר רַבִּי יוֹחָנָן: מִשָּׁעָה שֶׁנִּתְרַחֲקוּ סִימָנֶיהָ נַעֲשֵׂית כְּיוֹנָה אִילֶּמֶת; "לְדָוִד מִכְתָּם" – שֶׁיָּצָא מִמֶּנָּה דָּוִד שֶׁהָיָה מָךְ וְתַם לַכֹּל. דָּבָר אַחֵר: "מִכְתָּם" – שֶׁהָיְתָה מַכָּתוֹ תַּמָּה, שֶׁנּוֹלַד כְּשֶׁהוּא מָהוּל. דָּבָר אַחֵר: "מִכְתָּם" – כְּשֵׁם שֶׁבְּקַטְנוּתוֹ הִקְטִין עַצְמוֹ אֵצֶל מִי שֶׁגָּדוֹל מִמֶּנּוּ לִלְמוֹד תּוֹרָה, כָּךְ בִּגְדוּלָּתוֹ.

The Gemara comments: **This is as it is written: "For the leader, upon *yonat eilem reḥokim*, a psalm [*mikhtam*] of David"** (Psalms 56:1). **Rabbi Yoḥanan says** the verse means: **From the moment that her signs were distanced [*reḥokim*], she became like a mute dove [*yona illemet*].** And the phrase **"a psalm [*mikhtam*] of David"** means: The one **from whom David emerged, as he was modest [*makh*] and flawless [*tam*] with everyone. Alternatively, *mikhtam*** indicates **that *makkato*,** the place on his body that would have required wounding [*makka*], **was complete [*tama*],** i.e., **that** David **was born circumcised. Alternatively, *mikhtam*** indicates that **just as in his youth** David **made himself small in front of one who was greater than him** in order **to learn Torah** from that person, **so too, when he became great** and was crowned king, he still behaved in this manner, so that his modesty, *makh*, was complete, *tam*, all of his life.

"וְהִיא שָׁלְחָה אֶל חָמִיהָ לֵאמֹר לְאִישׁ אֲשֶׁר אֵלֶּה לּוֹ אָנֹכִי הָרָה". וְתֵימָא לֵיהּ מֵימַר! אָמַר רַב זוּטְרָא בַּר טוֹבִיָּה אָמַר רַב, וְאָמְרִי לָהּ אָמַר רַב חָנָא בַּר בִּיזְנָא אָמַר רַבִּי שִׁמְעוֹן חֲסִידָא, וְאָמְרִי לָהּ אָמַר רַבִּי יוֹחָנָן מִשּׁוּם רַבִּי שִׁמְעוֹן בֶּן יוֹחַי: נוֹחַ לוֹ לְאָדָם שֶׁיַּפִּיל עַצְמוֹ לְתוֹךְ כִּבְשַׁן הָאֵשׁ וְאַל יַלְבִּין פְּנֵי חֲבֵירוֹ בָּרַבִּים. מְנָלַן? מִתָּמָר.

The verse concerning Tamar then states: **"She sent to her father-in-law, saying: By the man whose these are, am I with child"** (Genesis 38:25). The Gemara comments: **And let her say to him** explicitly that she was impregnated by him. **Rav Zutra bar Tuviyya says** that **Rav says, and some say Rav Ḥana bar Bizna says** that **Rabbi Shimon Ḥasida says, and some say** that **Rabbi Yoḥanan says in the name of Rabbi Shimon ben Yoḥai: It is more amenable for a person**[NH] **to throw himself into a fiery furnace** if faced with the choice of publicly embarrassing another or remaining silent even if it leads to being burned, **and not humiliate another in public. From where do we** derive this? **From Tamar,** as she was prepared to be burned if Judah did not confess, rather than humiliate him in public.

"הַכֶּר נָא" – אָמַר רַבִּי חָמָא בְּרַבִּי חֲנִינָא: בְּ"הַכֶּר" בִּישֵּׂר לְאָבִיו, בְּ"הַכֶּר" בִּישְּׂרוּהוּ; בְּ"הַכֶּר" בִּישֵּׂר – "הַכֶּר נָא הַכְּתֹנֶת בִּנְךָ הִיא"; בְּ"הַכֶּר" בִּישְּׂרוּהוּ – "הַכֶּר נָא לְמִי".

The verse continues: "And she said: **Discern, please,** whose are these, the signet, and the cords, and the staff" (Genesis 38:25). **Rabbi Ḥama, son of Rabbi Ḥanina, says: With** use of the word **discern** Judah **informed his father** that Joseph was lost, and also **with** use of the word **discern they informed** Judah about the signs. The Gemara explains: **With** the word **discern he informed** Jacob his father when he brought him the coat of Joseph and said to his father: "And they sent the coat of many colors, and they brought it to their father; and said: This have we found. **Discern now whether it is your son's coat** or not" (Genesis 37:32). **With** the word **discern they informed him:** "And she said: **Discern, please, whose are** these."

"נָא" – אֵין "נָא" אֶלָּא לְשׁוֹן בַּקָּשָׁה. אָמְרָה לֵיהּ: בְּבַקָּשָׁה מִמְּךָ, הַכֵּר פְּנֵי בוֹרַאֲךָ וְאַל תַּעֲלִים עֵינֶיךָ מִמֶּנִּי.

It states: "Discern, **please** [*na*]." The word ***na*** is **nothing other** than **a language of request.** The Gemara explains: **She said to him: I request of you: Discern the image of your Creator** in every person, **and do not avert your eyes from me.**

"וַיַּכֵּר יְהוּדָה וַיֹּאמֶר צָדְקָה מִמֶּנִּי" – הַיְינוּ דְּאָמַר רַב חָנִין בַּר בִּיזְנָא אָמַר רַבִּי שִׁמְעוֹן חֲסִידָא: יוֹסֵף שֶׁקִּידֵּשׁ שֵׁם שָׁמַיִם בַּסֵּתֶר – זָכָה וְהוֹסִיפוּ לוֹ אוֹת אַחַת מִשְּׁמוֹ שֶׁל הַקָּדוֹשׁ בָּרוּךְ הוּא, דִּכְתִיב: "עֵדוּת בִּיהוֹסֵף שָׂמוֹ".

The verse states: **"And Judah acknowledged them, and said: She is more righteous than I;** forasmuch as I gave her not to Shelah my son" (Genesis 38:26). **This is** the same **as Rav Ḥanin bar Bizna says** that **Rabbi Shimon Ḥasida says: Joseph, who sanctified the name of Heaven in private** by not committing adultery with the wife of Potiphar, **merited that one letter from the name of the Holy One, Blessed be He, was added to his** name, **as it is written: "He appointed it in Joseph [*bihosef*] for a testimony in his name,** when He went forth against the land of Egypt" (Psalms 81:6). In this verse the name Joseph is written with an additional letter *heh*, found in the ineffable name of God.

יְהוּדָה שֶׁקִּידֵּשׁ שֵׁם שָׁמַיִם בְּפַרְהֶסְיָא – זָכָה וְנִקְרָא כּוּלּוֹ עַל שְׁמוֹ שֶׁל הַקָּדוֹשׁ בָּרוּךְ הוּא. כֵּיוָן שֶׁהוֹדָה וְאָמַר "צָדְקָה מִמֶּנִּי", יָצְתָה בַּת קוֹל וְאָמְרָה: אַתָּה הִצַּלְתָּ תָּמָר וּשְׁנֵי בָנֶיהָ מִן הָאוּר, חַיֶּיךָ שֶׁאֲנִי מַצִּיל בִּזְכוּתְךָ שְׁלֹשָׁה מִבָּנֶיךָ מִן הָאוּר; מַאן נִינְהוּ? חֲנַנְיָה מִישָׁאֵל וַעֲזַרְיָה.

He continues: **Judah, who sanctified the name of Heaven in public, merited that his entire** name **is called**[N] **by the name of the Holy One, Blessed be He,** for all the letters of the ineffable name of God are included within the name of Judah, with the addition of the letter *dalet*. **When he confessed and said: "She is more righteous than I," a Divine Voice went forth and said: You saved Tamar and her two children** in her womb **from** being burned by **the fire.** By **your life,** i.e., **in your merit, I will save three of your children from the fire.** And **who are they? Hananiah, Mishael, and Azariah** (see Daniel, chapter 3).

NOTES

It is more amenable for a person, etc. – נוֹחַ לוֹ לְאָדָם וכו׳: *Tosafot* explain that this statement should be taken literally, that one is halakhically required to allow himself to be killed if the alternative is the public humiliation of another. The Rashbatz maintains that the rationale for this is that humiliating another is included in the general prohibition against murder, as when one humiliates another to the extent that he causes the blood to drain from his face, it is akin to spilling his blood. He adds that the severity of humiliating others is stressed because generally people don't realize how deleterious it is and therefore do not properly atone for this transgression, thereby losing their place in the World-to-Come. The Maharal explains that humiliating someone lessens his human dignity. As human dignity stems from one's having been formed in the image of God, this can be viewed as a more severe transgression than causing bodily injury.

However, many early and later commentaries (see Meiri) explain that this statement is not meant to be a practical halakhic ruling, as the wording of the Gemara: It is more amenable, indicates that it is not an actual *halakha* but a description of pious behavior.

His entire name is called, etc. – נִקְרָא כּוּלּוֹ וכו׳: Some commentaries note that Judah did not have any letters added to his name, as this was his name from birth, even before he sanctified the name of God in public. One answer suggested is that Judah was given his name as a result of the divine inspiration of his mother, Leah, who chose the name as a foreshadowing of his future actions. Additionally, she could have named him Odeh, which would also carry her intended meaning of thanking God. The fact that the name she gave him contains the letters of the name of God is a result of this divine influence.

HALAKHA

It is more amenable for a person, etc. – נוֹחַ לוֹ לְאָדָם וכו׳: One who embarrasses another in public has no share in the World-to-Come (Rambam *Sefer HaMadda*, *Hilkhot Deot* 6:8).

"צָדְקָה מִמֶּנִּי" – מְנָא יָדַע? יָצְתָה בַּת קוֹל וְאָמְרָה: מִמֶּנִּי יָצְאוּ כְּבוּשִׁים.

Judah said: **"She is more righteous than I** [*mimmenni*]." The word "*mimmenni*" can also be understood as "from me," with Judah thereby admitting that he is the father. The Gemara asks: **From where did he know** that it was in fact from him that Tamar was pregnant? The Gemara answers: **A Divine Voice went forth and said: From Me these hidden** matters **emerged,**[N] and this woman will be the mother of royalty, which requires that Judah be the father.

"וְלֹא יָסַף עוֹד לְדַעְתָּהּ" – אָמַר שְׁמוּאֵל סָבָא חֲמוּהּ דְּרַב שְׁמוּאֵל בַּר אַמִּי מִשְּׁמֵיהּ דְּרַב שְׁמוּאֵל בַּר אַמִּי: כֵּיוָן שֶׁיְּדָעָהּ שׁוּב לֹא פָּסַק מִמֶּנָּה, כְּתִיב הָכָא: "וְלֹא יָסַף עוֹד לְדַעְתָּהּ", וּכְתִיב הָתָם: "קוֹל גָּדוֹל וְלֹא יָסָף".

The same verse continues: **"And he knew her** [*leda'atah*] **again no more** [*velo yasaf*]," seemingly indicating that Judah did not engage in sexual intercourse with Tamar again. **Shmuel the Elder, father-in-law of Rav Shmuel bar Ami, says in the name of Rav Shmuel bar Ami:** The verse actually means that **once he knew of her**[N] that her intentions were for the sake of Heaven, **he did not desist from** engaging in sexual intercourse with **her again, as it is written here: "*Velo yasaf od leda'atah,*" and it is written there** at the giving of the Torah: "These words the Lord spoke unto all your assembly in the mount out of the midst of the fire, of the cloud, and of the thick darkness, **with a great voice and it went on no more** [*velo yasaf*]" (Deuteronomy 5:18), which is interpreted to mean: A great voice that did not cease.

"אַבְשָׁלוֹם נִתְגָּאָה בִּשְׂעָרוֹ" וכו'. תָּנוּ רַבָּנַן: אַבְשָׁלוֹם בִּשְׂעָרוֹ מָרַד, שֶׁנֶּאֱמַר: "וּכְאַבְשָׁלוֹם לֹא הָיָה אִישׁ יָפֶה וגו' וּבְגַלְּחוֹ אֶת רֹאשׁוֹ וְהָיָה מִקֵּץ יָמִים לַיָּמִים אֲשֶׁר יְגַלֵּחַ כִּי כָבֵד עָלָיו וְגִלְּחוֹ וְשָׁקַל אֶת שְׂעַר רֹאשׁוֹ מָאתַיִם שְׁקָלִים בְּאֶבֶן הַמֶּלֶךְ". תָּנָא: אֶבֶן שֶׁאַנְשֵׁי טִבֶרְיָא וְאַנְשֵׁי צִיפּוֹרִי שׁוֹקְלִים בָּהּ –

§ The mishna teaches: **Absalom was** excessively **proud of his hair,**[N] and therefore he was hung by his hair. **The Sages taught** (*Tosefta* 3:16): **Absalom rebelled** and sinned **due to his hair, as it is stated:** "Now in all Israel **there was none** to be so much praised **as Absalom for his beauty;** from the sole of his foot even to the crown of his head there was no blemish in him. **And when he shaved his head, as it was at every year's end that he shaved it; because the hair was heavy on him, therefore he shaved it, and he weighed the hair of his head at two hundred shekels, by the king's stone"** (II Samuel 14:25–26). What is the king's stone? The Sages **taught: A stone with which the people of Tiberias and the people of Tzippori weigh**[B] items.

לְפִיכָךְ נִתְלָה בִּשְׂעָרוֹ, שֶׁנֶּאֱמַר: "וַיִּקָּרֵא אַבְשָׁלוֹם לִפְנֵי עַבְדֵי דָוִד וְאַבְשָׁלוֹם רֹכֵב עַל הַפֶּרֶד וַיָּבֹא הַפֶּרֶד תַּחַת שׂוֹבֶךְ הָאֵלָה הַגְּדוֹלָה וַיֶּחֱזַק רֹאשׁוֹ בָאֵלָה וַיֻּתַּן בֵּין הַשָּׁמַיִם וּבֵין הָאָרֶץ וְהַפֶּרֶד אֲשֶׁר תַּחְתָּיו עָבָר". שָׁקַל סַפְסֵירָא בָּעָא לְמִיפְסְקֵיהּ. תָּנָא דְּבֵי רַבִּי יִשְׁמָעֵאל: בְּאוֹתָהּ שָׁעָה נִבְקַע שְׁאוֹל מִתַּחְתָּיו.

The *baraita* continues: And since he was proud of his hair, **therefore, he was hung by his hair, as it is stated** in the verse describing the battle between the forces of David and Absalom: **"And Absalom chanced to meet the servants of David. And Absalom was riding upon his mule, and the mule went under the thick boughs of a great terebinth, and his head caught hold of the terebinth, and he was taken up between the heaven and the earth; and the mule that was under him went on"** (II Samuel 18:9). After he was spotted by the opposing troops, Absalom **took a sword** [*safseira*][L] **and wanted to cut his hair** to save himself. **The school of Rabbi Yishmael taught: At that moment,** the gates of **the netherworld opened beneath him**[N] and he was afraid to fall into it, so he did not cut his hair, and he was killed by the opposing troops.

"וַיִּרְגַּז הַמֶּלֶךְ וַיַּעַל עַל עֲלִיַּת הַשַּׁעַר וַיֵּבְךְּ וְכֹה אָמַר בְּלֶכְתּוֹ בְּנִי אַבְשָׁלוֹם בְּנִי בְנִי אַבְשָׁלוֹם מִי יִתֵּן מוּתִי אֲנִי תַחְתֶּיךָ אַבְשָׁלוֹם בְּנִי בְנִי...וְהַמֶּלֶךְ לָאַט אֶת פָּנָיו וַיִּזְעַק הַמֶּלֶךְ קוֹל גָּדוֹל בְּנִי אַבְשָׁלוֹם אַבְשָׁלוֹם בְּנִי בְנִי". הָנֵי תְּמָנְיָא "בְּנִי" לְמָּה? שִׁבְעָה, דְּאַסְּקֵיהּ מִשִּׁבְעָה מְדוֹרֵי גֵיהִנָּם; וְאִידָּךְ, אִיכָּא דְּאָמְרִי: דְּקָרֵיב רֵישֵׁיהּ לְגַבֵּי גּוּפֵיהּ, וְאִיכָּא דְּאָמְרִי: דְּאַיְיתֵיהּ לְעָלְמָא דְאָתֵי.

It is written with regard to David's reaction after he learns of the death of Absalom: **"And the king was much moved, and went up to the chamber over the gate, and wept; and as he went about he said: O my son Absalom, my son, my son Absalom! Would I had died in your place, O Absalom, my son, my son"** (II Samuel 19:1), and a few verses later it adds: **"And the king covered his face, and the king cried with a loud voice: O my son Absalom, O Absalom, my son, my son"** (II Samuel 19:5). The Gemara asks: **Why** are there **these eight** mentions of **"my son"** by David, i.e., to what do they correspond? The Gemara answers: **Seven** times he said "my son," by **which he raised him up from the seven chambers of Gehenna. And** as for **the other,** eighth, time, **some say that** David **brought** the **head** of Absalom **close to** Absalom's **body, and some say that** with this eighth mention David **brought** Absalom **to the World-to-Come.**

NOTES

From Me these hidden matters [*kevushim*] emerged – מִמֶּנִּי יָצְאוּ כְּבוּשִׁים: According to the standard version of the Gemara, this means that God declared that the hidden matters emerged from Him. Similarly, the Midrash adds that this entire episode occurred in a manner that was clearly divinely orchestrated so as to eventually bring about the monarchy of David and the Messiah. This matter is discussed at length by the kabbalists (see *Sefer HaGilgulim*). The *ge'onim* had a different version of the text that read: From you came out two pressed ones [*kevushim*]. This would mean that Judah was told that the two twin boys who were, so to speak, pressed together in Tamar's womb, were his children. Another version reads: From you conquerors [*kovshim*] emerged, indicating that from these children conquerors would go forth in the future to conquer Eretz Yisrael.

Once he knew of her, etc. – כֵּיוָן שֶׁיְּדָעָהּ וכו': The term: He knew, is often a euphemism connoting sexual intimacy, similar to "And the man knew Eve his wife" (Genesis 4:1), and the phrase thereby means that Judah no longer separated himself from Tamar. However, Rashi interprets the phrase as a term indicating actual knowledge, as once Judah realized that she had righteous intentions, he no longer separated himself from her.

The Ramban in his commentary on the Torah writes that the actions of Judah were a fulfillment of the mitzva of levirate marriage as performed in his day. He elaborates that before the giving of the Torah, levirate marriage was a mitzva not specifically incumbent upon the brother of the deceased but for all relatives. Therefore, Tamar was permitted to remain married to Judah, as he had actually entered into levirate marriage with her.

Absalom was proud of his hair – אַבְשָׁלוֹם נִתְגָּאָה בִּשְׂעָרוֹ: The length of his hair does not indicate anything negative, as Absalom was a nazirite and obviously had long hair. However, the manner in which he weighed his hair is indicative of the pride he placed in it (*Iyyei HaYam*).

The netherworld opened beneath him – נִבְקַע שְׁאוֹל מִתַּחְתָּיו: Rashi explains that this statement explains why Absalom did not cut his hair, as he was afraid to fall into Gehenna. In *Pirkei DeRabbi Eliezer* (50:3) it says that Absalom was aware of his sin and was afraid that he would be punished there. He therefore preferred to be killed by humans so that his gruesome death would atone for some of his sins. This might also be the allegorical meaning of the statement in the Gemara that Absalom allowed himself to be killed by people (*Iyyei HaYam*).

BACKGROUND

A stone with which the people of Tiberias…weigh – אֶבֶן שֶׁאַנְשֵׁי טִבֶרְיָא...שׁוֹקְלִים בָּהּ: The idea of a stone being used as a weighing device is mentioned in the Torah (Deuteronomy 25:13). The king's stone recorded here is a formal royal weight. Apparently, here the expression king's stone refers simply to a large weight, and indicates that the measures of weight that the people of Tiberias and Tzippori used were larger than those previously used in Jerusalem or in the desert.

LANGUAGE

Sword [*safseira*] – סַפְסֵירָא: Related to the Persian šafšēr, also known as shamshir, and meaning sword.

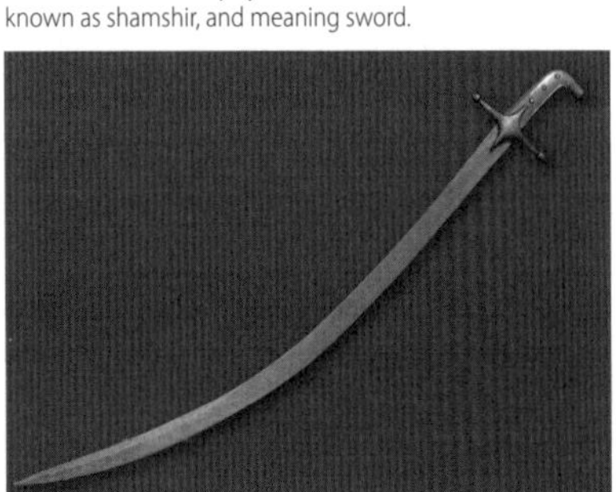

Shamshir

"וְאַבְשָׁלוֹם לָקַח וַיַּצֶּב לוֹ בְחַיָּיו". מַאי לָקַח? אָמַר רֵישׁ לָקִישׁ: שֶׁלָּקַח מִקָּח רַע לְעַצְמוֹ. "אֶת מַצֶּבֶת אֲשֶׁר בְּעֵמֶק הַמֶּלֶךְ" וגו' – אָמַר רַבִּי חֲנִינָא בַּר פָּפָּא: בְּעֵצָה עֲמוּקָּה שֶׁל מַלְכּוֹ שֶׁל עוֹלָם,

It is written there: "**Now Absalom in his lifetime had taken and reared up for himself** the pillar, which is in the king's valley; for he said: I have no son to keep my name in remembrance" (II Samuel 18:18). The Gemara asks: **What did** Absalom **take? Reish Lakish says: He engaged in a bad transaction for himself** by accepting bad advice for which he was punished. The verse continues: "**The pillar, which is in the king's valley** [*be'emek hammelekh*]." **Rabbi Ḥanina bar Pappa says:** This alludes to the pillar that is **in the deep** [*amukka*] **counsel of the King** [*melekh*] **of the universe,** as God had already decreed in the aftermath of the incident with Bathsheba that this would occur.

דִּכְתִיב: "הִנְנִי מֵקִים עָלֶיךָ רָעָה מִבֵּיתֶךָ". כַּיּוֹצֵא בַּדָּבָר אַתָּה אוֹמֵר: "וַיִּשְׁלָחֵהוּ מֵעֵמֶק חֶבְרוֹן" – אָמַר רַבִּי חֲנִינָא בַּר פָּפָּא: בְּעֵצָה עֲמוּקָּה שֶׁל אוֹתוֹ צַדִּיק שֶׁקָּבוּר בְּחֶבְרוֹן, דִּכְתִיב: "יָדֹעַ תֵּדַע כִּי גֵר יִהְיֶה זַרְעֲךָ".

This is **as it is written** there: "Thus said the Lord: **Behold, I will raise up evil against you out of your own house**" (II Samuel 12:11), and this prophecy was fulfilled through Absalom. **Similarly, you can say** about Joseph, who was sent by his father to inquire as to the well-being of his brothers, where the verse states: "**And he sent him from the valley** [*emek*] **of Hebron**" (Genesis 37:14). **Rabbi Ḥanina bar Pappa says: From the deep** [*amukka*] **counsel of that righteous individual who is interred in Hebron,** i.e., Abraham, **as it is written:** "And He said unto Abram: **Know that your seed shall be a stranger** in a land that is not theirs, and shall serve them; and they shall afflict them four hundred years" (Genesis 15:13). The journey Joseph took to his brothers set in motion the descent of the Jewish people to Egypt.

"כִּי אָמַר אֵין לִי בֵן". וְלָא הֲווּ לֵיהּ בְּנֵי? וְהָכְתִיב: "וַיִּוָּלְדוּ לְאַבְשָׁלוֹם שְׁלוֹשָׁה בָנִים וּבַת אַחַת"! אָמַר רַב יִצְחָק בַּר אַבְדִּימִי: שֶׁלֹּא הָיָה לוֹ בֵּן הָגוּן לְמַלְכוּת. רַב חִסְדָּא אָמַר, גְּמִירִי: כׇּל הַשּׂוֹרֵף תְּבוּאָתוֹ שֶׁל חֲבֵירוֹ – אֵינוֹ מַנִּיחַ בֵּן לְיוֹרְשׁוֹ, וְאִיהוּ קַלְיֵיהּ לְדְיוֹאָב, דִּכְתִיב: "וַיֹּאמֶר אֶל עֲבָדָיו רְאוּ חֶלְקַת יוֹאָב אֶל יָדִי וְלוֹ שָׁם שְׂעֹרִים לְכוּ וְהַצִּיתוּהָ בָאֵשׁ וַיַּצִּיתוּ עַבְדֵי אַבְשָׁלוֹם אֶת הַחֶלְקָה בָּאֵשׁ".

The Gemara continues its discussion of Absalom. The verse states concerning Absalom: "**For he said: I have no son** to keep my name in remembrance; and he called the pillar after his own name; and it is called Absalom's monument to this day" (II Samuel 18:18). The Gemara asks: **And did** Absalom **not have sons? But isn't it written: "And to Absalom there were born three sons, and one daughter"** (II Samuel 14:27)? **Rav Yitzḥak bar Avdimi says:** He meant **that he did not have a son worthy for royalty. Rav Ḥisda said: It is learned** as a tradition: **Anyone who burns the produce**[N] **of another does not leave a son to inherit** from **him, and he,** Absalom, **burned** the produce **of Joab, as it is written: "Therefore he said to his servants: See, Joab's field is near mine, and he has barley there; go and set it on fire. And Absalom's servants set the field on fire"** (II Samuel 14:30).

"וְכֵן לְעִנְיַן הַטּוֹבָה, מִרְיָם" וכו'. מִי דָּמֵי? הָתָם חֲדָא שַׁעְתָּא, הָכָא שִׁבְעָה יוֹמֵי! אָמַר אַבָּיֵי – אֵימָא: וּלְעִנְיַן הַטּוֹבָה אֵינוֹ כֵּן.

§ The mishna teaches: **And the same** is so **with regard to the** reward for **good** deeds. **Miriam** waited for the baby Moses for one hour at the shore of the Nile; therefore, the Jewish people delayed their travels in the desert for seven days to wait for her when she was smitten with leprosy. The Gemara asks: **Are** these matters **comparable? There,** Miriam waited **one hour,**[N] while **here,** the Jewish people waited for her for **seven days. Abaye said: Say** this with a slight change: **And with regard to** the repaying of **good it is not so,** as a person is not rewarded precisely measure for measure, as the reward may be greater than the good deed.

אָמַר לֵיהּ רָבָא: הָא "וְכֵן לְעִנְיַן הַטּוֹבָה" קָתָנֵי! אֶלָּא אָמַר רָבָא, הָכִי קָתָנֵי: וְכֵן לְעִנְיַן הַטּוֹבָה – דִּבְאוֹתָהּ מִדָּה, וּלְעוֹלָם מִדָּה טוֹבָה מְרוּבָּה מִמִּדַּת פּוּרְעָנוּת.

Rava said to him: But the *tanna* **taught** in the mishna: **And the same** is so **with regard to the** reward of **good** deeds. **Rather, Rava said: This is what** the mishna **is teaching: And the same** is so **with regard to the** reward of **good** deeds. It is rewarded **with the same measure,** i.e., a person is rewarded in the same manner as the good deed, **but the measure of good is always greater**[N] **than the measure of punishment.** Therefore, Miriam was rewarded in the same manner as, but in a greater measure than, her deed.

NOTES

Anyone who burns the produce, etc. – כׇּל הַשּׂוֹרֵף תְּבוּאָתוֹ וכו': This punishment is measure for measure. Just as one destroyed the produce of another, he is also punished by not having produce, i.e., progeny (*Iyyun Ya'akov*).

One hour – חֲדָא שַׁעְתָּא: *Tosafot* write that one hour is not be taken literally, but indicates a short amount of time.

But the measure of good is always greater – וּלְעוֹלָם מִדָּה טוֹבָה מְרוּבָּה: *Tosafot* ask: Why doesn't the punishment for the sin of the spies, which included the Jewish people wandering in the wilderness for one year for each day the spies surveyed Eretz Yisrael, prove that the measure of punishment can be greater than the measure of good? In the *Yefe Toar* it is explained that the wandering in the wilderness should not be viewed as a punishment. This is because the punishment actually was that all the males of that generation would die in the wilderness. Therefore, the extended time they wandered was to their benefit, because their lives were thereby prolonged.

NOTES

Say to wisdom: You are my sister – אֱמֹר לַחָכְמָה אֲחֹתִי אָתְּ: Rav Sherira Gaon explains that the Divine Presence is the manifestation of God's glory in the world. This glory reveals itself in various ways, and wisdom is one of them.

For behold the Lord will come in fire – כִּי הִנֵּה ה׳ בָּאֵשׁ יָבֹא: The *Ben Yehoyada* points out that it is clear that here, as well as in other similar passages in the Gemara, the Gemara doesn't mean to say that the Egyptians cited this verse from Isaiah, as he prophesied hundreds of years later. Rather, the verse is cited by the Sages, and the Egyptians believed that God punishes with fire, as the verse writes with regard to Sodom: "Then the Lord caused to rain upon Sodom and upon Gomorrah brimstone and fire" (Genesis 19:24).

"וַתֵּתַצַּב אֲחוֹתוֹ מֵרָחוֹק" – אָמַר רַבִּי יִצְחָק: פָּסוּק זֶה כּוּלּוֹ עַל שֵׁם שְׁכִינָה נֶאֱמַר; "וַתֵּתַצַּב" – דִּכְתִיב: "וַיָּבֹא ה׳ וַיִּתְיַצַּב" וגו׳; "אֲחוֹתוֹ" – דִּכְתִיב: "אֱמֹר לַחָכְמָה אֲחוֹתִי אָתְּ"; "מֵרָחוֹק" – דִּכְתִיב: "מֵרָחוֹק ה׳ נִרְאָה לִי"; "לָדַעַת" – דִּכְתִיב: "כִּי אֵל דֵּעוֹת ה׳"; "מַה" – דִּכְתִיב: "מָה ה׳ אֱלֹהֶיךָ שֹׁאֵל מֵעִמָּךְ"; "יֵעָשֶׂה" – דִּכְתִיב: "כִּי לֹא יַעֲשֶׂה ה׳ אֱלֹהִים דָּבָר"; "לוֹ" – דִּכְתִיב: "וַיֹּאמֶר לוֹ ה׳ שָׁלוֹם".

With regard to Miriam's deed the verse states: **"And his sister stood afar off,** to know what would be done to him" (Exodus 2:4). **Rabbi Yitzḥak says: This entire verse is stated in reference to the Divine Presence,** i.e., each phrase alludes to the Divine Presence watching over Moses. **"And** his sister **stood"; as it is written: "And the Lord came, and stood"** (I Samuel 3:10). **"His sister"; as it is written: "Say to wisdom: You are my sister"** (Proverbs 7:4).[N] **"Afar off"; as it is written: "From afar the Lord appeared to me"** (Jeremiah 31:2). **"To know"; as it is written: "For the Lord is a God of knowledge"** (I Samuel 2:3). **"What"; as it is written: "What does the Lord God require of you"** (Deuteronomy 10:12). **"Would be done"; as it is written: "For the Lord God will do nothing"** (Amos 3:7). **"To him"; as it is written: "And the Lord said to him: Peace** be with you" (Judges 6:23).

"וַיָּקָם מֶלֶךְ חָדָשׁ" וגו׳ – רַב וּשְׁמוּאֵל: חַד אָמַר: חָדָשׁ מַמָּשׁ, וְחַד אָמַר: שֶׁנִּתְחַדְּשׁוּ גְּזֵירוֹתָיו. מַאן דְּאָמַר חָדָשׁ מַמָּשׁ, דִּכְתִיב: "חָדָשׁ"; וּמַאן דְּאָמַר שֶׁנִּתְחַדְּשׁוּ גְּזֵירוֹתָיו, דְּלָא כְּתִיב "וַיָּמָת וַיִּמְלוֹךְ". "אֲשֶׁר לֹא יָדַע אֶת יוֹסֵף" – דַּהֲוָה דָּמֵי כְּמַאן דְּלָא יָדַע לֵיהּ כְּלָל.

§ The Gemara proceeds to discuss the sojourn of the Jewish people in Egypt. The verse states: **"And there arose a new king** over Egypt, who knew not Joseph" (Exodus 1:8). **Rav and Shmuel** disagree about the interpretation of this verse. **One says** that this means he was **actually a new** king, **and one says** that this means **that his decrees were transformed** as if he were a new king. **The one who says** that he was **actually a new** king holds that it is **because it is written "new." And the one who says that his decrees were transformed** holds that it is **because it is not written: "And** the previous king of Egypt **died and** a new king **reigned."** This indicates that the same king remained. According to this interpretation, the words: **"Who knew not Joseph"** (Exodus 1:8), mean **that he was like someone who did not know him at all.** Although he certainly knew Joseph and his accomplishments, he acted as if he didn't.

"וַיֹּאמֶר אֶל עַמּוֹ הִנֵּה עַם בְּנֵי יִשְׂרָאֵל" – תָּנָא: הוּא הִתְחִיל בְּעֵצָה תְּחִילָּה, לְפִיכָךְ לָקָה תְּחִילָּה; הוּא הִתְחִיל בְּעֵצָה תְּחִילָּה, דִּכְתִיב: "וַיֹּאמֶר אֶל עַמּוֹ"; לְפִיכָךְ לָקָה תְּחִילָּה, כְּדִכְתִיב: "וּבְכָה וּבְעַמְּךָ וּבְכָל עֲבָדֶיךָ".

The next verse states: **"And he said to his people: Behold, the people of the children of Israel** are too many and too mighty for us" (Exodus 1:9). It was **taught** (*Tosefta* 4:11): **He,** Pharaoh, **initiated the proposal. Therefore,** of his people, **he was stricken first. He initiated the proposal, as it is written: "And he said to his people." Therefore, he was stricken first, as it is written:** "And the frogs shall come up **both upon you, and upon your people, and upon all your servants"** (Exodus 7:29).

"הָבָה נִתְחַכְּמָה לוֹ" – "לָהֶם" מִיבְּעֵי לֵיהּ! אָמַר רַבִּי חָמָא בְּרַבִּי חֲנִינָא: בֹּאוּ וְנֶחְכַּם לְמוֹשִׁיעָן שֶׁל יִשְׂרָאֵל.

The next verse states that Pharaoh said: **"Come, let us deal wisely with him** [*lo*], lest he multiply, and it come to pass that when there befalls us any war, he will also join our enemies, and fight against us" (Exodus 1:10). The Gemara comments: **He should have** said in plural: **With them** [*lahem*], rather than the singular: "With him." **Rabbi Ḥama, son of Rabbi Ḥanina, says** that Pharaoh was saying: **Come, let us deal wisely with regard to the savior of Israel,** referring to God.

בַּמֶּה נְדוּנֵם? נְדוּנֵם בָּאֵשׁ – כְּתִיב: "כִּי הִנֵּה ה׳ בָּאֵשׁ יָבֹא", וּכְתִיב: "כִּי בָאֵשׁ ה׳ נִשְׁפָּט" וגו׳! בַּחֶרֶב – כְּתִיב: ["וּבְחַרְבּוֹ אֶת כָּל בָּשָׂר"]!

His advisors asked: **With what** form of death **shall we judge** and decree upon **them?** If **we shall judge them with fire,** perhaps we will be punished measure for measure by fire, as **it is written: "For behold, the Lord will come in fire"** (Isaiah 66:15),[N] and **it is written** in the verse that follows it: **"For by fire will the Lord contend"** (Isaiah 66:16). Similarly, we cannot judge them **with the sword,** as **it is written** in the continuation of that verse: **"And by His sword with all flesh"** (Isaiah 66:16).

אֶלָּא בּוֹאוּ וּנְדוּנֵם בַּמַּיִם, שֶׁכְּבָר נִשְׁבַּע הַקָּדוֹשׁ בָּרוּךְ הוּא שֶׁאֵינוֹ מֵבִיא מַבּוּל לָעוֹלָם, שֶׁנֶּאֱמַר: "כִּי מֵי נֹחַ זֹאת לִי" וגו׳. וְהֵן אֵינָן יוֹדְעִין שֶׁעַל כָּל הָעוֹלָם כּוּלּוֹ אֵינוֹ מֵבִיא, אֲבָל עַל אוּמָּה אַחַת הוּא מֵבִיא;

Rather, let us come and judge them with water, by drowning the Jewish babies. God will not punish us with water, **for the Holy One, Blessed be He, already took an oath that He will not bring a flood upon the world, as it is stated: "For this is as the waters of Noah unto Me;** for as I have sworn that the waters of Noah should no more go over the earth" (Isaiah 54:9). The Gemara comments: **And** Pharaoh's advisors **did not know that He will not bring a flood upon all the world, but He** may bring destruction by water **upon one nation.**

אי נמי, הוא אינו מביא, אבל הן באין ונופלין בתוכו, וכן הוא אומר: "ומצרים נסים לקראתו". והיינו דאמר רבי אלעזר, מאי דכתיב: "כי בדבר אשר זדו עליהם"? בקדירה שבישלו בה נתבשלו. מאי משמע דהאי "זדו" לישנא דקדירה הוא? דכתיב: "ויזד יעקב נזיד".

Alternatively, there is an additional way to punish the Egyptians with water: **He does not bring** a flood upon them, **but they** may **come and fall into** water, **and so it says:** "And the sea returned to its strength when the morning appeared; **and the Egyptians fled toward it;** and the Lord overthrew the Egyptians in the midst of the sea" (Exodus 14:27), indicating that the Egyptians fell into the water. **And this is what Rabbi Elazar says: What is the** meaning of that **which is written:** "Now I know that the Lord is greater than all gods, **for in that which they conspired** [*zadu*] **against them**" (Exodus 18:11)? The phrase means: **In the pot in which they cooked, they** themselves **were cooked,** as they were punished through drowning, measure for measure, for drowning the Jewish babies. The Gemara asks: **From where may** it **be inferred that this** word **"*zadu*" is a term** meaning **a pot?** The Gemara answers: **As it is written: "And Jacob simmered a pot** [*vayyazed Ya'akov nazid*]" (Genesis 25:29).

אמר רבי חייא בר אבא אמר רבי סימאי, שלשה היו באותה עצה: בלעם, ואיוב, ויתרו.

Rabbi Ḥiyya bar Abba says that **Rabbi Simai says: Three** noteworthy people **were** consulted by Pharaoh **in that counsel** where Pharaoh questioned what should be done with the Jewish people. They were **Balaam, and Job, and Yitro.**

בלעם שיעץ – נהרג; איוב ששתק – נידון ביסורין; יתרו שברח – זכו מבני בניו שישבו בלשכת הגזית, שנאמר: "ומשפחות סופרים יושבי יעבץ תרעתים שמעתים שוכתים המה הקנים הבאים מחמת אבי בית רכב", וכתיב: "ובני קיני חתן משה" וגו'.

Rabbi Ḥiyya bar Abba teaches what occurred to each of them: **Balaam, who advised** Pharaoh to kill all sons born to the Jewish people, **was** punished by being **killed** in the war with Midian (see Numbers 31:8). **Job, who was silent**[N] and neither advised nor protested, **was punished by suffering,** as detailed in the eponymous book in the Bible. **Yitro, who ran away** as a sign of protest, **merited that** some **of his children's children sat** in the Sanhedrin **in the Chamber of Hewn Stone, as it is stated: "And the families of scribes**[N] **who dwelt at Jabez, Tirathites, Shimeathites, and Sucathites, these were the Kenites who descended from Hammath, the father of the house of Rechab"** (1 Chronicles 2:55). **And it is written: "The children of the Kenite, Moses' father-in-law"** (Judges 1:16). This teaches that the Kenites, descendants of Yitro, the father-in-law of Moses, dwelt at Jabez [Yabetz], referring to the place where the Jewish people go for advice [*eitza*], i.e., the Chamber of Hewn Stone.

"ונלחם בנו ועלה מן הארץ" – "ועלינו" מיבעי ליה! אמר רבי אבא בר כהנא: כאדם שמקלל את עצמו ותולה קללתו בחבירו.

The verse states: "Come, let us deal wisely with him, lest he multiply, and it come to pass that when there befalls us any war, he will also join our enemies, **and fight against us, and get him up out of the land**" (Exodus 1:10). The Gemara comments: **He should have** said: **And get us up,** as Pharaoh's fear was that the Jewish people would join the enemies of Egypt and drive Pharaoh and the Egyptians out of Egypt. **Rabbi Abba bar Kahana says:** By stating this, Pharaoh **is like a person who curses himself** but **applies his curse to another.**

"וישימו עליו שרי מסים" – "עליהם" מיבעי ליה! תנא דבי רבי אלעזר ברבי שמעון: מלמד, שהביאו מלבן ותלו לו לפרעה בצוארו, וכל אחד ואחד מישראל שאמר להם איסטניס אני, אמרו לו: כלום איסטניס אתה יותר מפרעה?

The next verse states: **"Therefore they did set over him taskmasters** in order to afflict him with their burdens" (Exodus 1:11). The Gemara comments: **It should have** stated: **Over them,** in the plural. **The school of Rabbi Elazar, son of Rabbi Shimon, taught:** This **teaches** that at first **they brought a brick mold**[B] **and they hung it on the neck of Pharaoh** to create the appearance that he was also participating in the labor. **And** with regard to **each and every Jew who said to** the Egyptians: **I am a delicate person** [*istenis*][L] and I cannot participate in the labor, **they said to him: Are you at all more of a delicate person than Pharaoh,** and he is participating. Therefore, the verse states: "They did set over him," as they first placed the burden on Pharaoh as an artifice to enslave the Jewish people.

"שרי מסים" – דבר שמשים (לבנים).

The term **"Taskmasters** [*sarei missim*]**"** is formed from the term: **A matter that compels** [*shemesim*] the manufacture of **bricks,** as the Jewish people were forced into labor when these taskmasters were assigned to them.

NOTES

Job, who was silent – **איוב ששתק**: The commentaries discuss why Job's silence was punished so severely. Where, they ask, is the measure for measure in his harsh punishment? Some explain that his silence indicated that he agreed with Balaam, which caused the advice of Balaam to be accepted. Therefore, Job was punished with suffering that he had to accept in silence. Others, citing the *Zohar*, state that Job was not completely silent. Rather, he suggested that the Jewish people not be killed but rather should be made to suffer financial loss and physical affliction. Therefore, Job was punished in a similar manner.

And the families of scribes, etc. – **ומשפחות סופרים וכו'**: See Rashi, who interprets all the names mentioned there in terms of their Torah knowledge and as alluding to the fact that they were judges.

BACKGROUND

A brick mold – **מלבן**: This is a form in which bricks are produced. In antiquity, bricks were produced by hand. However, molds were soon developed to enable the production of bricks of uniform size. These molds were box shaped, generally rectangular, but other shapes were used according to the type of brick needed. Clay was first mixed with cut straw to reinforce it, and then the mixture was pressed into the mold and subsequently removed to dry in the sun or in an oven. In ancient times, bricks were generally small. Even the fairly large ones used at the time of the Talmud were square with sides of 3 handbreadths, 24 × 24 cm. Consequently, it was possible to hang a brick of that size on a person's neck.

Brick mold

LANGUAGE

Delicate person [*istenis*] – **איסטניס**: From the Greek ἀσθενής, *astenēs*, which means weak, without power, without energy. The Sages use it to refer to an individual who is extremely refined, either physically or spiritually.

NOTES

Pithom and Raamses – פִּיתוֹם וְרַעְמְסֵס: The Maharsha writes that the Sages had a tradition that Pithom and Raamses were actually the same place, and therefore the separate names were clearly meant to teach another matter. Others explain that there would be no reason to state the names of these cities in the verse, as it would have been sufficient to simply say: "Storage cities." Therefore, the fact that the names are given is grounds for exegesis (*Iyyun Ya'akov*).

"לְמַעַן עַנֹּתוֹ בְּסִבְלוֹתָם" – ["עַנּוֹתָם" מִיבָּעֵי לֵיהּ]! לְמַעַן עַנּוֹתוֹ לְפַרְעֹה בְּסִבְלוֹתָם דְּיִשְׂרָאֵל.

The verse continues: **"In order to afflict him with their burdens"** (Exodus1:11). The Gemara comments: **It should have** stated: **"In order to afflict them,"** in the plural. Rather, the intention is, as mentioned previously, **in order to afflict Pharaoh, with** the result of causing **the burdens of the Jewish people.**

"וַיִּבֶן עָרֵי מִסְכְּנוֹת לְפַרְעֹה" – רַב וּשְׁמוּאֵל, חַד אָמַר: שֶׁמְּסַכְּנוֹת אֶת בַּעֲלֵיהֶן, וְחַד אָמַר: שֶׁמְּמַסְכְּנוֹת אֶת בַּעֲלֵיהֶן, דְּאָמַר מָר: כָּל הָעוֹסֵק בְּבִנְיָן מִתְמַסְכֵּן.

The verse concludes: **"And they built for Pharaoh storage cities** [***miskenot***], Pithom and Raamses" (Exodus 1:11). **Rav and Shmuel** disagree as to the precise interpretation of the word miskanot. **One says** that they are called this because they were the type of structures **that endanger [*mesakenot*] their owners,** as it is dangerous to work in cities with tall buildings. **And one says** that they are called this because this is the type of property **that impoverishes [*memaskenot*] their owners, as the Master said: All who engage in construction become poor.**

"אֶת פִּיתוֹם וְאֶת רַעְמְסֵס" – רַב וּשְׁמוּאֵל. חַד אָמַר: פִּיתוֹם שְׁמָהּ, וְלָמָּה נִקְרָא שְׁמָהּ רַעְמְסֵס? שֶׁרִאשׁוֹן רִאשׁוֹן מִתְרוֹסֵס; וְחַד אָמַר: רַעְמְסֵס שְׁמָהּ, וְלָמָּה נִקְרָא שְׁמָהּ פִּיתוֹם? שֶׁרִאשׁוֹן רִאשׁוֹן פִּי תְהוֹם בּוֹלְעוֹ.

The verse states that the names of the cities they built were **"Pithom and Raamses"** (Exodus 1:11).[N] **Rav and Shmuel** disagree as to the precise interpretation of this verse, both assuming that only one city was built, which had primary and secondary names. **One says** that **Pithom** was **its** real **name, and why was it called Raamses?** It is an appellation indicating **that** as the buildings were constructed **they collapsed [*mitroses*] one by one** and needed to be rebuilt. **And one says** that **Raamses** was **its** real **name, and why was it called Pithom?** Because **the opening of the abyss [*pi tehom*] swallowed** each building they constructed **one by one, and it sunk into the ground.**

"וְכַאֲשֶׁר יְעַנּוּ אוֹתוֹ כֵּן יִרְבֶּה וְכֵן יִפְרוֹץ" – "כֵּן רָבוּ וְכֵן פָּרְצוּ" מִיבָּעֵי לֵיהּ! אָמַר רֵישׁ לָקִישׁ, רוּחַ הַקֹּדֶשׁ מְבַשַּׂרְתָּן: "כֵּן יִרְבֶּה וְכֵן יִפְרוֹץ". "וַיָּקֻצוּ מִפְּנֵי בְּנֵי יִשְׂרָאֵל" – מְלַמֵּד שֶׁהָיוּ דּוֹמִין בְּעֵינֵיהֶם כְּקוֹצִים.

The next verse states: **"But the more they afflicted him, the more he would multiply and the more he would spread about"** (Exodus 1:12). The Gemara comments: **It should have** stated: **The more they multiplied and the more they spread about,** in the past tense. **Reish Lakish says: Divine inspiration proclaimed to** the Egyptians: As long as this nation is afflicted, **the more he will multiply and the more he will spread about.** As the verse states: **"And they became disgusted [*vayyakutzu*] due to the children of Israel."** The Gemara explains: This **teaches that** the Jewish people **appeared in their eyes like thorns [*kotzim*].**

"וַיַּעֲבִדוּ מִצְרַיִם אֶת בְּנֵי יִשְׂרָאֵל

The next verse states: **"And the Egyptians made the children of Israel work**

Perek **I**
Daf **11** Amud **b**

NOTES

Initially with mortar and bricks, etc. – בַּתְּחִילָּה בְּחוֹמֶר וּבִלְבֵנִים וכו׳: Initially the Egyptians instructed the Jews to work with mortar and bricks to fortify the cities, which is labor incumbent on all citizens of a country. Afterward, they forced them to work in the fields as well, and then they commanded them to perform all the work that had to be done to provide for the needs of the Egyptians (Maharsha).

בְּפָרֶךְ" – רַבִּי אֶלְעָזָר אָמַר: בְּפֶה רַךְ, רַבִּי שְׁמוּאֵל בַּר נַחְמָנִי אָמַר: בִּפְרִיכָה.

with rigor [*befarekh*]" (Exodus 1:13). **Rabbi Elazar says:** The word *befarekh* is a conjugation of the words: **With a soft mouth [*bifeh rakh*],** as the Egyptians enticed the Jewish people into slavery, gradually subjugating them until they had lost their freedom completely. **Rabbi Shmuel bar Naḥmani says:** The word *befarekh* should be understood as: **With crushing [*bifrikha*],** as the Egyptians subjugated Israel with backbreaking labor.

"וַיְמָרְרוּ אֶת חַיֵּיהֶם בַּעֲבֹדָה קָשָׁה בְּחֹמֶר וּבִלְבֵנִים" וגו׳ – אָמַר רָבָא: בַּתְּחִילָּה בְּחוֹמֶר וּבִלְבֵנִים, וּלְבַסּוֹף "וּבְכָל עֲבוֹדָה בַּשָּׂדֶה".

The next verse states: **"And they made their lives bitter through hard service, with mortar and brick,** and with every laborious service in the field" (Exodus 1:14). **Rava says:** The verse mentions specifically mortar and brick and then all forms of labor, as **initially** the Egyptians had them work **with mortar and bricks,[N] and ultimately** they subjugated them **"and with every laborious service in the field."**

״אֵת כָּל עֲבֹדָתָם אֲשֶׁר עָבְדוּ בָהֶם בְּפָרֶךְ״ – אָמַר רַבִּי שְׁמוּאֵל בַּר נַחְמָנִי אָמַר רַבִּי יוֹנָתָן: שֶׁהָיוּ מַחֲלִיפִין מְלֶאכֶת אֲנָשִׁים לְנָשִׁים וּמְלֶאכֶת נָשִׁים לַאֲנָשִׁים. וּלְמַאן דְּאָמַר נַמִּי הָתָם בְּפֶה רַךְ, הָכָא וַדַּאי בִּפְרִיכָה.

The verse concludes: **"In all their service, wherein they made them serve with rigor"** (Exodus 1:14). **Rabbi Shmuel bar Naḥmani says** that **Rabbi Yonatan says:** The meaning of *befarekh* is that the Egyptians **would exchange** the responsibilities of men and women, giving **men's work to women**[N] **and women's work to men,** requiring everyone to do work to which they were unaccustomed. **And even according to the one who says** that **there,** in the previous verse, *bifarekh* indicates that the Egyptians enslaved the Jews **with a soft mouth, here,** in this verse, which describes the physical hardship of the labor, the word befarekh **certainly** means **with crushing** labor.

דָּרַשׁ רַב עֲוִירָא: בִּשְׂכַר נָשִׁים צִדְקָנִיּוֹת שֶׁהָיוּ בְּאוֹתוֹ הַדּוֹר – נִגְאֲלוּ יִשְׂרָאֵל מִמִּצְרַיִם. בְּשָׁעָה שֶׁהוֹלְכוֹת לִשְׁאוֹב מַיִם, הַקָּדוֹשׁ בָּרוּךְ הוּא מְזַמֵּן לָהֶם דָּגִים קְטַנִּים בְּכַדֵּיהֶן וְשׁוֹאֲבוֹת מֶחֱצָה מַיִם וּמֶחֱצָה דָּגִים. וּבָאוֹת וְשׁוֹפְתוֹת שְׁתֵּי קְדֵירוֹת אַחַת שֶׁל חַמִּין וְאַחַת שֶׁל דָּגִים,

§ **Rav Avira taught: In the merit of** the **righteous women**[N] **that were in that generation, the Jewish people were redeemed from Egypt.** He tells of their righteous actions: **At the time** when these women **would go** to the river **to draw water, the Holy One, Blessed be He, would materialize for them small fish**[B] that would enter **into their pitchers, and they would** therefore **draw** pitchers that were **half** filled with **water and half** filled with **fish. And they would** then **come and place two pots on the fire, one** pot **of hot** water for washing their husbands **and one** pot **of fish** with which to feed them.

וּמוֹלִיכוֹת אֵצֶל בַּעֲלֵיהֶן לַשָּׂדֶה, וּמַרְחִיצוֹת אוֹתָן וְסָכוֹת אוֹתָן וּמַאֲכִילוֹת אוֹתָן וּמַשְׁקוֹת אוֹתָן וְנִזְקָקוֹת לָהֶן בֵּין שְׁפַתַּיִם, שֶׁנֶּאֱמַר: ״אִם תִּשְׁכְּבוּן בֵּין שְׁפַתָּיִם״ וגו׳. בִּשְׂכַר ״תִּשְׁכְּבוּן בֵּין שְׁפַתַּיִם״ זָכוּ יִשְׂרָאֵל לְבִיזַּת מִצְרַיִם, שֶׁנֶּאֱמַר: ״כַּנְפֵי יוֹנָה נֶחְפָּה בַכֶּסֶף וְאֶבְרוֹתֶיהָ בִּירַקְרַק חָרוּץ״.

And they would then **take** what they prepared **to their husbands, to the field, and would bathe** their husbands **and anoint them** with oil **and feed them** the fish **and give them to drink and bond with them** in sexual intercourse **between the sheepfolds,** i.e., between the borders and fences of the fields, **as it is stated: "When you lie among the sheepfolds,** the wings of the dove are covered with silver, and her pinions with the shimmer of gold" (Psalms 68:14), which is interpreted to mean that **as a reward** for "when you **lie among the sheepfolds," the Jewish people merited to** receive **the plunder of Egypt, as it is stated** in the continuation of the verse, as a reference to the Jewish people: **"The wings of the dove are covered with silver, and her pinions with the shimmer of gold"** (Psalms 68:14).

וְכֵיוָן שֶׁמִּתְעַבְּרוֹת בָּאוֹת לְבָתֵּיהֶם; וְכֵיוָן שֶׁמַּגִּיעַ זְמַן מוֹלְדֵיהֶן, הוֹלְכוֹת וְיוֹלְדוֹת בַּשָּׂדֶה תַּחַת הַתַּפּוּחַ, שֶׁנֶּאֱמַר: ״תַּחַת הַתַּפּוּחַ עוֹרַרְתִּיךָ״ וגו׳.

And when these women would **become pregnant, they would come** back **to their homes, and when the time for them to give birth** would arrive **they would go and give birth in the field under the apple tree, as it is stated: "Under the apple tree I awakened you;** there your mother was in travail with you; there was she in travail and brought you forth" (Song of Songs 8:5).

וְהַקָּדוֹשׁ בָּרוּךְ הוּא שׁוֹלֵחַ מִשְּׁמֵי מָרוֹם מִי שֶׁמְּנַקֵּיר וּמְשַׁפֵּיר אוֹתָן, כְּחַיָּה זוֹ שֶׁמְּשַׁפֶּרֶת אֶת הַוָּלָד, שֶׁנֶּאֱמַר: ״וּמוֹלְדוֹתַיִךְ בְּיוֹם הוּלֶּדֶת אוֹתָךְ לֹא כָרַּת שָׁרֵּךְ וּבְמַיִם לֹא רֻחַצְתְּ לְמִשְׁעִי״ וגו׳. וּמְלַקֵּט לָהֶן שְׁנֵי עִגּוּלִין אֶחָד שֶׁל שֶׁמֶן וְאֶחָד שֶׁל דְּבַשׁ, שֶׁנֶּאֱמַר: ״וַיֵּנִקֵהוּ דְבַשׁ מִסֶּלַע וְשֶׁמֶן״ וגו׳.

And the Holy One, Blessed be He, would send from the heavens above an angel **who would clean and prepare** the newborns, **just as a midwife prepares the newborn, as it is stated: "And as for your birth, on the day you were born, your navel was not cut nor were you washed with water for cleansing;** you were not salted at all, nor swaddled at all" (Ezekiel 16:4). This indicates that there were no midwives to take care of the Jews born in Egypt. **And** then, the angel **would gather for them two round** stones from the field and the babies would nurse from that which would flow out of them. **One of** the stones flowed with **oil and one of** the stones flowed with **honey, as it is stated: "And He would suckle them with honey from a crag and oil** from a flinty rock" (Deuteronomy 32:13).

וְכֵיוָן שֶׁמַּכִּירִין בָּהֶן מִצְרִים בָּאִין לְהוֹרְגָן, וְנַעֲשֶׂה לָהֶם נֵס וְנִבְלָעִין בַּקַּרְקַע. וּמְבִיאִין שְׁוָורִים וְחוֹרְשִׁין עַל גַּבָּן, שֶׁנֶּאֱמַר: ״עַל גַּבִּי חָרְשׁוּ חֹרְשִׁים״ וגו׳. לְאַחַר שֶׁהוֹלְכִין הָיוּ מְבַצְבְּצִין וְיוֹצְאִין כְּעֵשֶׂב הַשָּׂדֶה, שֶׁנֶּאֱמַר: ״רְבָבָה כְּצֶמַח הַשָּׂדֶה נְתַתִּיךְ״.

And once the Egyptians would notice them, realizing that they were Jewish babies, **they would come to kill them. But a miracle would occur for them and they would be absorbed by the earth. And** the Egyptians **would** then **bring oxen and would plow upon them, as it is stated: "The plowers plowed upon my back;** they made long their furrows" (Psalms 129:3). **After** the Egyptians **would leave,** the babies **would emerge and exit** the ground **like grass of the field, as it is stated: "I caused you to increase even as the growth of the field"** (Ezekiel 16:7).

NOTES

Men's work to women, etc. – מְלֶאכֶת אֲנָשִׁים לְנָשִׁים וכו׳: Even though men's work generally requires more physical effort, women's work requires other character traits such as patience and the ability to pay greater attention to detail. This causes suffering for one not accustomed to this kind of work (*Ben Yehoyada*).

In the merit of the righteous women – בִּשְׂכַר נָשִׁים צִדְקָנִיּוֹת: The Maharsha explains that the primary meaning of this statement relates to the fact that the women remained faithful to their husbands and even encouraged them to engage in sexual intercourse, despite their dire circumstances. In this way they helped keep the Jewish people alive.

BACKGROUND

Small fish – דָּגִים קְטַנִּים: Due to its size and slow flow, which leave deposits of organic silt, the Nile River serves as a fertile environment for fish. Moreover, in some seasons the abundance of food in the river attracts large numbers of fish from the sea. During these seasons it is not necessary to use sophisticated equipment to catch fish, as even simple vessels suffice.

וְכֵיוָן שֶׁמִּתְגַּדְּלִין בָּאִין עֲדָרִים עֲדָרִים לְבָתֵּיהֶן, שֶׁנֶּאֱמַר: "וַתִּרְבִּי וַתִּגְדְּלִי וַתָּבֹאִי בַּעֲדִי עֲדָיִים". אַל תִּקְרֵי "בַּעֲדִי עֲדָיִים" אֶלָּא "בְּעֶדְרֵי עֲדָרִים".

And once the babies **would grow, they would come like many flocks** of sheep **to their homes, as it is stated** in the continuation of the verse: **"And you did increase and grow up and you came with excellent beauty** [*ba'adi adayim*]**"** (Ezekiel 16:7). **Do not read** the verse as: **"*Ba'adi adayim*,"** "with excellent beauty." **Rather,** read it as: ***Be'edrei adarim*,** meaning: As many flocks.

וּכְשֶׁנִּגְלָה הַקָּדוֹשׁ בָּרוּךְ הוּא עַל הַיָּם, הֵם הִכִּירוּהוּ תְּחִלָּה, שֶׁנֶּאֱמַר: "זֶה אֵלִי וְאַנְוֵהוּ".

And when the Holy One, Blessed be He, revealed Himself at the Red **Sea,** these children **recognized Him first, as it is stated: "This is my God, and I will glorify Him"** (Exodus 15:2). They recognized Him from the previous time that He revealed Himself to them in their infancy, enabling them to say: "This is my God."

"וַיֹּאמֶר מֶלֶךְ מִצְרַיִם לַמְיַלְּדֹת הָעִבְרִיֹּת" וגו׳ – רַב וּשְׁמוּאֵל. חַד אָמַר: אִשָּׁה וּבִתָּהּ, וְחַד אָמַר: כַּלָּה וַחֲמוֹתָהּ. מַאן דְּאָמַר אִשָּׁה וּבִתָּהּ, יוֹכֶבֶד וּמִרְיָם; וּמַאן דְּאָמַר כַּלָּה וַחֲמוֹתָהּ, יוֹכֶבֶד וֶאֱלִישֶׁבַע.

§ The verse states: **"And the king of Egypt spoke to the Hebrew midwives,** of whom the name of the one was Shiphrah, and the name of the other Puah" (Exodus 1:15). **Rav and Shmuel** disagree as to the proper interpretation of this verse. **One says** that these midwives were **a woman and her daughter, and one says** that they were **a daughter-in-law and her mother-in-law.** According to the **one who says** that they were **a woman and her daughter,** the women were **Jochebed,** the mother of Moses and Aaron, **and** her daughter, **Miriam. And** according to the **one who says** that they were **a daughter-in-law and her mother-in-law,** the verse is referring to **Jochebed and** her daughter-in-law **Elisheba,** the wife of Aaron.

תַּנְיָא כְּמַאן דְּאָמַר אִשָּׁה וּבִתָּהּ, דְּתַנְיָא: "שִׁפְרָה" – זוֹ יוֹכֶבֶד. וְלָמָּה נִקְרָא שְׁמָהּ שִׁפְרָה? שֶׁמְּשַׁפֶּרֶת אֶת הַוָּלָד; דָּבָר אַחֵר: "שִׁפְרָה" – שֶׁפָּרוּ וְרַבּוּ יִשְׂרָאֵל בְּיָמֶיהָ.

It **is taught** in a *baraita* **according to the one who says** that they were **a woman and her daughter, because it** is **taught** in a *baraita*: With regard to **Shiphrah,** who is referred to in the verse, **this** is really a reference to **Jochebed. And why was she called Shiphrah? Because she would prepare** [*mishapperet*] **the newborn. Alternatively,** she is referred to as **Shiphrah because the Jewish people increased and multiplied** [*shepparu verabbu*] **in her days,** due to her assistance.

"פּוּעָה" – זוֹ מִרְיָם. וְלָמָּה נִקְרָא שְׁמָהּ פּוּעָה? שֶׁהָיְתָה פּוֹעָה וּמוֹצִיאָה אֶת הַוָּלָד; דָּבָר אַחֵר: "פּוּעָה" – שֶׁהָיְתָה פּוֹעָה בְּרוּחַ הַקּוֹדֶשׁ, וְאוֹמֶרֶת: עֲתִידָה אִמִּי שֶׁתֵּלֵד בֵּן שֶׁמּוֹשִׁיעַ אֶת יִשְׂרָאֵל.

The *baraita* continues: With regard to **Puah,** who is referred to in the verse, **this** is really a reference to **Miriam. And why was she called Puah? Because she would make a comforting sound** [*po'a*] **as she would remove the child** from the womb of the mother. **Alternatively,** the word **Puah** is related to one of the verbs that describe speaking, **as she would speak** [*po'a*] **through divine inspiration and say: In the future, my mother will give birth to a son who will save the Jewish people.**

"וַיֹּאמֶר בְּיַלֶּדְכֶן אֶת הָעִבְרִיּוֹת" וגו׳. מַאי "אָבְנָיִם"? אָמַר רַבִּי חָנָן: סִימָן גָּדוֹל מָסַר לָהֶן. אָמַר לָהֶן: בְּשָׁעָה שֶׁכּוֹרַעַת לֵילֵד, יַרְכוֹתֶיהָ מִצְטַנְּנוֹת כָּאֲבָנִים.

The next verse relates the instructions of Pharaoh to the midwives: **"And he said: When you deliver the Hebrew women,** and you look upon the stones [*ovnayim*], if it be a son, then you shall kill him; but if it be a daughter, then she shall live" (Exodus 1:16). The Gemara asks: **What** is the meaning of **"stones"? Rabbi Ḥanan says:** Pharaoh **transmitted a great sign to them. He said to them: At the time** when a woman **crouches to give birth, her thighs become as cold as stones,**[B] and, therefore, this shall be for you a sign that the woman is about to give birth.

וְאִית דְּאָמַר, כִּדְכְתִיב: "וָאֵרֵד בֵּית הַיּוֹצֵר וְהִנֵּה הוּא עוֹשֶׂה מְלָאכָה עַל הָאָבְנָיִם", מַה יּוֹצֵר זֶה – יָרֵךְ מִכָּאן וְיָרֵךְ מִכָּאן וְסַדָּן בְּאֶמְצַע; אַף אִשָּׁה – יָרֵךְ מִכָּאן וְיָרֵךְ מִכָּאן וְהַוָּלָד בְּאֶמְצַע.

And there are those who say an alternative explanation for *ovnayim*: **As it is written: "So I went down to the potter's shop, and behold, he was at his work on the wheels** [*ovnayim*]**"** (Jeremiah 18:3). **Just as this potter** sits so that one **thigh** is **here**[B] **and** one **thigh** is **there and the block** upon which he works **is in the middle, so too, a woman** giving birth also has one **thigh here and** one **thigh there and the newborn is in the middle.**

"אִם בֵּן הוּא וַהֲמִתֶּן אוֹתוֹ" – אָמַר רַבִּי חֲנִינָא, סִימָן גָּדוֹל מָסַר לָהֶן: בֵּן – פָּנָיו לְמַטָּה; בַּת – פָּנֶיהָ לְמַעְלָה.

The verse continues: **"If it be a son, then you shall kill him;** but if it be a daughter, then she shall live" (Exodus 1:16). **Rabbi Ḥanina says:** Pharaoh **transmitted to them a great sign** to enable them to know the gender of the infant from the beginning of the birth process: **A boy** is born with **his face downward; a girl** is born with **her face upward.** Pharaoh provided them with this sign so that they could kill the boys secretly even before the mother realized what was happening.

BACKGROUND

Her thighs become as cold as stones – יַרְכוֹתֶיהָ מִצְטַנְּנוֹת כָּאֲבָנִים: It is possible that this expression refers to the contraction and hardening of the stomach muscles and the muscles near them during the birth process, which cause these muscles to become like stone. It could be that this contraction and hardening results in a feeling of coldness in other parts of the body as well.

One thigh here – יָרֵךְ מִכָּאן: The way in which a potter sits while at his potter's wheel resembles the birth process in that his feet are spread out on both sides of the wheel, where the lump of clay usually sits. This is done both to enable him to rotate the wheel and easily reach every side of the instrument with his hand.

Potter creating a vessel with a pottery wheel

״וַתִּירֶאןָ הַמְיַלְּדוֹת אֶת הָאֱלֹהִים וְלֹא עָשׂוּ כַּאֲשֶׁר דִּבֶּר אֲלֵיהֶן״ וגו׳ – ״לָהֶן״ מִיבָּעֵי לֵיהּ! אָמַר רַבִּי יוֹסֵי בְּרַבִּי חֲנִינָא: מְלַמֵּד, שֶׁתְּבָעָן לִדְבַר עֲבֵירָה וְלֹא נִתְבְּעוּ.

The next verse states: **"But the midwives feared God, and did not as the king of Egypt spoke about them** [*aleihen*], but they kept the male children alive" (Exodus 1:17). The Gemara comments: **It should have** stated: "Spoke **to them** [*lahen*]." **Rabbi Yosei, son of Rabbi Ḥanina, says:** This **teaches that** Pharaoh **proposed to them to** engage in **a sinful act,** i.e., sexual intercourse, with him, **but they did not accept** his overtures. The word *aleihen* is often used in reference to sexual intercourse, for example: "And brought her to him; and he consorted with her [*eileha*]" (Genesis 29:23), and that is its connotation here as well.

״וַתְּחַיֶּיןָ אֶת הַיְלָדִים״ – תָּנָא: לֹא דַּיָּין שֶׁלֹּא הֵמִיתוּ אוֹתָן, אֶלָּא שֶׁהָיוּ מְסַפְּקוֹת לָהֶם מַיִם וּמָזוֹן.

The verse concludes: **"But they kept the male children alive"** (Exodus 1:17). A Sage **teaches:** It is **not only that they did not kill** the children as Pharaoh had commanded them, **but that they would** even **provide for them water and food,** as the phrase "But they kept the male children alive" indicates.

״וַתֹּאמַרְןָ הַמְיַלְּדוֹת אֶל פַּרְעֹה כִּי לֹא כַנָּשִׁים״ וגו׳. מַאי ״חָיוֹת״? אִילֵימָא חַיּוֹת מַמָּשׁ, אַטּוּ חַיָּה מִי לָא צְרִיכָה חַיָּה אַחֲרִיתִי לְאוֹלוּדָהּ?

After being questioned by Pharaoh concerning their failure to obey his command, the midwives responded, as it is written: **"And the midwives said to Pharaoh: Because** the Hebrew women **are not as the** Egyptian **women,** for they are lively [*ḥayot*], and are delivered before the midwife comes to them" (Exodus 1:19). The Gemara asks: **What** is the meaning of **"*ḥayot*"? If we say** that the Hebrew women are like *ḥayot*, meaning **actual midwives** for themselves, and therefore they do not need assistance from others, **is that to say** that **a midwife does not need** the assistance of **another midwife** in order **to help her give birth?**

אֶלָּא, אָמְרוּ לוֹ: אוּמָּה זוֹ כְּחַיָּה נִמְשְׁלָה, יְהוּדָה – גּוּר אַרְיֵה; דָּן – ״יְהִי דָן נָחָשׁ״; נַפְתָּלִי – ״אַיָּלָה שְׁלֻחָה״; יִשָּׂשכָר – ״חֲמוֹר גָּרֶם״; יוֹסֵף – ״בְּכוֹר שׁוֹר״; בִּנְיָמִין – ״זְאֵב יִטְרָף״.

Rather, the midwives **said to** Pharaoh: **This nation is compared to an animal** [*ḥayya*], and animals give birth without a midwife. For example, with regard to **Judah** it is written: "Judah is **a lion's whelp**" (Genesis 49:9); with regard to **Dan** it is written: **"Dan shall be a serpent** in the way" (Genesis 49:17); with regard to **Naphtali** it is written: **"A hind let loose"** (Genesis 49:21); with regard to **Issachar** it is written: **"A large-boned donkey"** (Genesis 49:14); with regard to **Joseph** it is written: "His **first bullock**" (Deuteronomy 33:17); with regard to **Benjamin** it is written: **"A ravenous wolf"** (Genesis 49:27).

דִּכְתִיב בֵּיהּ – כְּתִיב בֵּיהּ, וּדְלָא כְּתִיב בֵּיהּ – כְּתִיב בֵּיהּ: ״מָה אִמְּךָ לְבִיָּא בֵּין אֲרָיוֹת רָבָצָה״ וגו׳.

The Gemara comments: Concerning those individuals **where** a comparison to an animal **is written with regard to him,** it is already **written with regard to him. And** concerning those **where no** specific metaphor comparing them to an animal is **written with regard to him** explicitly, in any case a general comparison **is written about** the Jewish people: **"How your mother was a lioness; among lions she crouched,** in the midst of the young lions she reared her whelps" (Ezekiel 19:2), indicating that all the Jewish people are compared to animals.

״וַיְהִי כִּי יָרְאוּ הַמְיַלְּדוֹת אֶת הָאֱלֹהִים וַיַּעַשׂ לָהֶם בָּתִּים״ – רַב וּשְׁמוּאֵל, חַד אָמַר: בָּתֵּי כְהוּנָּה וּלְוִיָּה, וְחַד אָמַר: בָּתֵּי מַלְכוּת. מַאן דְּאָמַר בָּתֵּי כְהוּנָּה וּלְוִיָּה, אַהֲרֹן וּמֹשֶׁה; וּמַאן דְּאָמַר בָּתֵּי מַלְכוּת, דָּוִד נַמִי מִמִּרְיָם קָאָתֵי, דִּכְתִיב: ״וַתָּמָת עֲזוּבָה״, אֵשֶׁת כָּלֵב, ״וַיִּקַּח לוֹ כָלֵב אֶת אֶפְרָת וַתֵּלֶד לוֹ אֶת חוּר״, וּכְתִיב: ״וְדָוִד בֶּן אִישׁ אֶפְרָתִי״ וגו׳.

The verse relates the midwives' reward: **"And it came to pass, because the midwives feared God, that He made them houses"** (Exodus 1:21). **Rav and Shmuel** disagree as to the precise interpretation of these houses: **One says** that God made **the houses of** the **priesthood and** the **Levites** descend from the midwives, **and one says** that God made the **houses of royalty** descend from them. **The one who says** that it is referring to the **houses of** the **priesthood and** the **Levites** is referring to **Aaron and Moses,** who were sons of Jochebed. **And the one who says** that it is referring to **houses of royalty** is referring to **David,** who **also comes from Miriam, as it is written: "And Azubah,"** the wife **of Caleb, "died, and Caleb took to him Ephrath, who bore him Hur"** (I Chronicles 2:19) and, as will be explained further, Ephrath is Miriam. **And it is written: "David was the son of that Ephrathite** of Bethlehem in Judah" (I Samuel 17:12). Therefore, he was a descendant of Miriam.

"וְכָלֵב בֶּן חֶצְרוֹן הוֹלִיד אֶת עֲזוּבָה אִשָּׁה וְאֶת יְרִיעוֹת. וְאֵלֶּה בָנֶיהָ יֵשֶׁר וְשׁוֹבָב וְאַרְדּוֹן". בֶּן חֶצְרוֹן? בֶּן יְפֻנֶּה הוּא! בֵּן שֶׁפָּנָה מֵעֲצַת מְרַגְּלִים.

The Gemara discusses the family of Caleb: In Chronicles it says: **"And Caleb, the son of Hezron, begot children of Azubah his wife, and of Jerioth, and these were her sons: Jesher, and Shobab, and Ardon"** (1 Chronicles 2:18). The Gemara asks: Was Caleb actually the **son of Hezron? Wasn't he** the **son of Jephunneh,** as the verse states in Numbers 13:6? The Gemara answers: He was the son of Hezron, but he is called "son of Jephunneh" as an appellation indicating that he was **a son who turned away** [*sheppana*] **from the counsel of the spies.**

וְאַכַּתִּי בֶּן קְנַז הוּא, דִּכְתִיב: "וַיִּלְכְּדָהּ עָתְנִיאֵל בֶּן קְנַז אֲחִי כָלֵב"! אָמַר רָבָא: חוֹרְגוֹ דִּקְנַז הֲוָה.

The Gemara asks: **But** it is **still** difficult. Hezron could not be his father, as Caleb **was the son of Kenaz, as it is written: "And Othniel, the son of Kenaz, Caleb's** younger **brother, took it"** (Judges 1:13). This would mean that Caleb was also a son of Kenaz. **Rava said:** Caleb **was the stepson of Kenaz,** as he and Othniel shared a mother but had different fathers.

Perek **I**
Daf **12** Amud **a**

NOTES

Anyone who marries, etc. – כָּל הַנּוֹשֵׂא וכו׳: The Maharsha explains that this principle is derived from the case of Miriam herself, as before she was married she was sickly, and her rejuvenation after her marriage is viewed as a second birth.

As he set himself straight – שֶׁיִּשֵּׁר אֶת עַצְמוֹ: Rashi explains that he set himself straight in that he did not join the other spies in their claims against traveling to Eretz Yisrael. The Maharsha interprets this otherwise, explaining that this refers to his act of marrying Miriam for the sake of Heaven.

LANGUAGE

Rose [*vered*] – וֶרֶד: Apparently from the Persian vard, meaning a red rose. This loanword, and similarly its Greek counterpart ῥόδον, *rhodon*, was also used as a general term for the color red.

דַּיְקָא נַמִי, דִּכְתִיב: "הַקְּנִזִּי". שְׁמַע מִינַּהּ.

The Gemara comments: The language of another verse **is also precise** based on this explanation, **as it is written:** "And Caleb the son of Jephunneh **the Kenizzite** said unto him" (Joshua 14:6). Although his father was Jephunneh, he is known as "the Kenizzite," although he was not actually a son of Kenaz. The Gemara accepts this proof and states: **Conclude from it** that Rava's explanation is correct.

"עֲזוּבָה" – זוֹ מִרְיָם, וְלָמָּה נִקְרָא שְׁמָהּ עֲזוּבָה? שֶׁהַכֹּל עֲזָבוּהָ מִתְּחִילָּתָהּ. "הוֹלִיד"? וַהֲלֹא מִינְסַב הֲוָה נְסֵיב לַהּ! אָמַר רַבִּי יוֹחָנָן: כָּל הַנּוֹשֵׂא אִשָּׁה לְשֵׁם שָׁמַיִם, מַעֲלֶה עָלָיו הַכָּתוּב כְּאִילּוּ יְלָדָהּ.

The verse states: "And Caleb, the son of Hezron, begot children of Azubah his wife, and of Jerioth, and these were her sons: Jesher, and Shobab, and Ardon" (1 Chronicles 2:18). The Gemara analyzes the verse: The verse refers to the wife of Caleb by the name **Azubah.** The Sages teach that **this is Miriam. And why is she called Azubah? As everyone initially abandoned her** [*azavuha*] and did not want to marry her because she was sickly and unattractive. The verse additionally states: "And Caleb, the son of Hezron, **begot children** [*holid*] of Azubah his wife" (1 Chronicles 2:18). The Gemara asks: Why use the term "*holid*," begot children? **But** doesn't this verse state that **he married her? Rabbi Yoḥanan says:** This teaches us that with regard to **anyone who marries**[N] **a woman for the sake of Heaven,** as he married her due to her righteousness without concern for her appearance, **the verse ascribes him** credit **as if he gave birth to her.**

"יְרִיעוֹת" – שֶׁהָיוּ פָּנֶיהָ דּוֹמִין לִירִיעוֹת.

The same verse refers to Miriam additionally as **Jerioth,** which the Gemara explains was appropriate, **for her face was like** extremely pallid **curtains** [*yeriot*].

"וְאֵלֶּה בָנֶיהָ" – אַל תִּקְרֵי "בָּנֶיהָ" אֶלָּא "בּוֹנֶיהָ". "יֵשֶׁר" – שֶׁיִּשֵּׁר אֶת עַצְמוֹ. "שׁוֹבָב" – שֶׁשִּׁיבֵּב אֶת יִצְרוֹ. "וְאַרְדּוֹן" – שֶׁרָדָה אֶת יִצְרוֹ. וְאִיכָּא דְּאָמְרִי: עַל שֶׁהָיוּ פָּנֶיהָ דּוֹמִין לְוֶרֶד.

The verse continues: **"And these were her sons** [*vaneha*]." The Gemara explains: **Do not read** it as ***vaneha*, her sons; rather,** read it as ***boneha*, her builders.** In other words, the rest of the names in the verse are not the names of her children, but rather appellations for her husband, whose marriage to her built her, as it were. The first appellation for Caleb, **"Jesher,"** is referring to his actions, **as he set himself straight** [*yisher*][N] and did not join in the counsel of the spies. The second appellation, **"Shobab,"** is referring to the fact **that he broke** [*sibbev*] **his** evil **inclination** by rebelling against the other spies. The third appellation, **"and Ardon** [*veArdon*]," is referring to the fact **that he ruled** [*rada*] over **his** evil **inclination. And some say: Because the face** of his wife Miriam became beautiful **like a rose** [*vered*][L] after they were married, she was also called Vardon, due to her rose-like complexion.

"וּלְאַשְׁחוּר אֲבִי תְקוֹעַ הָיוּ שְׁתֵּי נָשִׁים חֶלְאָה וְנַעֲרָה". "אַשְׁחוּר" – זֶה כָּלֵב. וְלָמָּה נִקְרָא שְׁמוֹ אַשְׁחוּר? שֶׁהוּשְׁחֲרוּ פָּנָיו בְּתַעֲנִיּוֹת. "אֲבִי" – שֶׁנַּעֲשָׂה לָהּ כְּאָב. "תְּקוֹעַ" – שֶׁתָּקַע אֶת לִבּוֹ לְאָבִיו שֶׁבַּשָּׁמַיִם.

The Gemara interprets an additional verse as referring to Caleb. It is stated: **"And Ashhur the father of Tekoa had two wives, Helah and Naarah"** (1 Chronicles 4:5). **Ashhur is Caleb. And why was he called Ashhur? Because his face became blackened** [*husheharu*] **from** the extensive **fasts** that he accepted upon himself so that he would not be entrapped by the counsel of the spies. **"The father of"** is also referring to Caleb, **as he became like a father to** his wife. The next word in the verse, **"Tekoa,"** is an additional reference to Caleb, **as he attached** [*taka*] **his heart to his Father in Heaven.**

"הָיוּ שְׁתֵּי נָשִׁים" – נַעֲשָׂה מִרְיָם כִּשְׁתֵּי נָשִׁים. "חֶלְאָה וְנַעֲרָה" – לֹא חֶלְאָה וְנַעֲרָה הֲוַאי, אֶלָּא בַּתְּחִילָּה חֶלְאָה וּלְבַסּוֹף נַעֲרָה.

The phrase in the verse **"had two wives"** actually means it is as if **Miriam became like two wives,** because she changed over the course of time. And therefore the two names written in the verse: **"Helah and Naarah," were not** two separate women, **Helah and Naarah. Rather, initially** Miriam was **sickly** [*ḥela*] and forlorn, **and ultimately** she was healthy and beautiful like **a young woman** [*na'ara*].

"וּבְנֵי חֶלְאָה צֶרֶת וְצֹחַר וְאֶתְנָן". "צֶרֶת" – שֶׁנַּעֲשֵׂית צָרָה לַחֲבְרוֹתֶיהָ; "צֹחַר" – שֶׁהָיוּ פָּנֶיהָ דּוֹמִין כְּצָהֳרַיִם; "אֶתְנָן" – שֶׁכׇּל הָרוֹאֶה אוֹתָהּ מוֹלִיךְ אֶתְנָן לְאִשְׁתּוֹ.

The Gemara expounds the following verse as referring to Miriam: **"And the children of Helah were Zereth** [*Tzeret*] **and Zohar and Ethnan"** (1 Chronicles 4:7). She was now called *"Tzeret,"* **for she became** so beautiful that she was like **a rival** [*tzara*] **to other** women, as they were jealous of her beauty. She is called **"Zohar," as her face** shined **like** the sun does at **noon** [*tzohorayim*]. She is called **"Ethnan," as any** man **that saw her** would be aroused so much that he **would bring a gift** [*etnan*] **to his wife** to entice her.

"וַיְצַו פַּרְעֹה לְכׇל עַמּוֹ" – אָמַר רַבִּי יוֹסֵי בְּרַבִּי חֲנִינָא: אַף עַל עַמּוֹ גָּזַר. וְאָמַר רַבִּי יוֹסֵי בְּרַבִּי חֲנִינָא, שָׁלֹשׁ גְּזֵירוֹת גָּזַר: בַּתְּחִילָּה – "אִם בֵּן הוּא וַהֲמִתֶּן אוֹתוֹ"; וּלְבַסּוֹף – "כׇּל הַבֵּן הַיִּלּוֹד הַיְאֹרָה תַּשְׁלִיכֻהוּ"; וּלְבַסּוֹף – אַף עַל עַמּוֹ גָּזַר.

§ The Gemara returns to the discussion of the bondage in Egypt. **"And Pharaoh charged all his people,** saying: Every son that is born you shall cast into the river, and every daughter you shall save alive" (Exodus 1:22). **Rabbi Yosei, son of Rabbi Ḥanina, says:** The use of the phrase "every son that is born" indicates that **he decreed even on his own nation**[N] that all their male babies must be killed. **And Rabbi Yosei, son of Rabbi Ḥanina, says** further: **He decreed three decrees. Initially,** he commanded the midwives only with regard to Jewish infants: "You shall look upon the stones. **If it be a son, then you shall kill him;** but if it be a daughter, then she shall live" (Exodus 1:16). **And afterward,** he decreed with regard to the Jewish infants: **"Every son that is born you shall cast into the river"** (Exodus 1:22). **And ultimately, he decreed even on his own nation** that Egyptian infant boys should be cast into the river as well.

"וַיֵּלֶךְ אִישׁ מִבֵּית לֵוִי" – לְהֵיכָן הָלַךְ? אָמַר רַב יְהוּדָה בַּר זְבִינָא: שֶׁהָלַךְ בַּעֲצַת בִּתּוֹ.

The verse states: **"And there went a man of the house of Levi,** and took for a wife a daughter of Levi" (Exodus 2:1). The Gemara asks: **To where did he go? Rav Yehuda bar Zevina says: He went according to the advice of his daughter** Miriam, as the Gemara will proceed to explain.

תָּנָא: עַמְרָם גְּדוֹל הַדּוֹר הָיָה. כֵּיוָן שֶׁרָאָה שֶׁאָמַר פַּרְעֹה הָרָשָׁע: "כׇּל הַבֵּן הַיִּלּוֹד הַיְאֹרָה תַּשְׁלִיכֻהוּ", אָמַר: לַשָּׁוְא אָנוּ עֲמֵלִין! עָמַד וְגֵירֵשׁ אֶת אִשְׁתּוֹ. עָמְדוּ כּוּלָּן וְגֵירְשׁוּ אֶת נְשׁוֹתֵיהֶן.

A Sage **teaches: Amram,** the father of Moses, **was the great man of his generation. Once he saw that the wicked Pharaoh said: "Every son that is born you shall cast into the river,** and every daughter you shall save alive" (Exodus 1:22), **he said: We are laboring for nothing** by bringing children into the world to be killed. Therefore, **he arose and divorced his wife. All** others who saw this followed his example and **arose and divorced their wives.**

אָמְרָה לוֹ בִּתּוֹ: אַבָּא, קָשָׁה גְּזֵירָתְךָ יוֹתֵר מִשֶּׁל פַּרְעֹה, שֶׁפַּרְעֹה לֹא גָּזַר אֶלָּא עַל הַזְּכָרִים, וְאַתָּה גָּזַרְתָּ עַל הַזְּכָרִים וְעַל הַנְּקֵיבוֹת! פַּרְעֹה לֹא גָּזַר אֶלָּא בָּעוֹלָם הַזֶּה, וְאַתָּה בָּעוֹלָם הַזֶּה וְלָעוֹלָם הַבָּא!

His daughter, Miriam, **said to him: Father, your decree is more harsh** for the Jewish people **than that of Pharaoh, as Pharaoh decreed only with regard to the males, but you decreed** both **on the males and on the females.** And now no children will be born. Additionally, **Pharaoh decreed** to kill them **only in this world, but you** decreed **in this world and in the World-to-Come,**[N] as those not born will not enter the World-to-Come.

NOTES

He decreed even on his own nation – אַף עַל עַמּוֹ גָּזַר: The source for this statement is the fact that there is no mention in this verse that the decree was only upon the Jewish infants. *Iyyun Ya'akov* suggests that upon finding Moses in the water, the daughter of Pharaoh remarked: "This is one of the Hebrews' children" (Exodus 2:6), indicating that children other than those of the Jews were also thrown into the Nile.

You decreed in this world and in the World-to-Come – וְאַתָּה בָּעוֹלָם הַזֶּה וְלָעוֹלָם הַבָּא: Rashi explains that children who are killed in this world still have a portion in the World-to-Come, and therefore, failing to have children at all means not affording one's potential children this possibility. Some explain this as referring to the parents: By divorcing and purposely not having children, they are neglecting the mitzva to procreate, thereby denying themselves reward for this in the World-to-Come (*Iyyun Ya'akov*; *Ahavat Eitan*).

פַּרְעֹה הָרָשָׁע, סָפֵק מִתְקַיֶּימֶת גְּזֵירָתוֹ סָפֵק אֵינָהּ מִתְקַיֶּימֶת, אַתָּה צַדִּיק, בְּוַדַּאי שֶׁגְּזֵירָתְךָ מִתְקַיֶּימֶת, שֶׁנֶּאֱמַר: ״וְתִגְזַר אוֹמֶר וְיָקָם לָךְ״! עָמַד וְהֶחֱזִיר אֶת אִשְׁתּוֹ. עָמְדוּ כּוּלָּן וְהֶחֱזִירוּ אֶת נְשׁוֹתֵיהֶן.

Miriam continued: Additionally, concerning **Pharaoh the wicked,** it is **uncertain** whether **his decree** will be **fulfilled,** and it is **uncertain** if his decree will **not** be **fulfilled. You are a righteous person,** and as such, **your decrees** will **certainly** be **fulfilled, as it is stated** with regard to the righteous: **"You shall also decree a thing, and it shall be established unto you"** (Job 22:28). Amram accepted his daughter's words and **arose and brought back,** i.e., remarried, **his wife,** and **all** others who saw this followed his example and **arose and brought back their wives.**

״וַיִּקַּח״ – ״וַיַּחֲזוֹר״ מִיבָּעֵי לֵיהּ! אָמַר רַב יְהוּדָה בַּר זְבִינָא: שֶׁעָשָׂה לוֹ מַעֲשֵׂה לִיקּוּחִין. הוֹשִׁיבָהּ בְּאַפִּרְיוֹן, וְאַהֲרֹן וּמִרְיָם מְרַקְּדִין לְפָנֶיהָ, וּמַלְאֲכֵי הַשָּׁרֵת אָמְרוּ: אֵם הַבָּנִים שְׂמֵחָה.

The Gemara asks: If Amram remarried Jochebed, rather than say: **"And took** for a wife a daughter of Levi" (Exodus 2:1), **it should have** stated: **"And returned** for a wife the daughter of Levi." **Rav Yehuda bar Zevina says: He performed an act of marriage** just as one would do for a first marriage. **He sat her on a palanquin** [***appiryon***],[BL] **and Aaron and Miriam danced before her, and the ministering angels said: "A joyful mother of children"** (Psalms 113:9).

״אֶת בַּת לֵוִי״ – אֶפְשָׁר, בַּת מֵאָה וּשְׁלֹשִׁים שָׁנָה הָוְיָא וְקָרֵי לָהּ בַּת? דְּאָמַר רַבִּי חָמָא בְּרַבִּי חֲנִינָא: זוֹ יוֹכֶבֶד, שֶׁהוֹרָתָהּ בַּדֶּרֶךְ וְלֵידָתָהּ בֵּין הַחוֹמוֹת, שֶׁנֶּאֱמַר: ״אֲשֶׁר יָלְדָה אוֹתָהּ לְלֵוִי בְּמִצְרָיִם״,

The verse is referring to Jochebed as **"a daughter of Levi"** (Exodus 2:1). The Gemara asks: Is it **possible** that this is Jochebed? Jochebed **was** then **130 years old and** the verse still **calls her a daughter?** Jochebed's age is established based on a tradition concerning the number of the descendants of Jacob who came to Egypt, as follows: While the verse states that Leah had thirty-three descendants (Genesis 46:15), only thirty-two were enumerated. This was explained **as Rabbi Ḥama, son of Rabbi Ḥanina, says:** The "daughter of Levi" **is Jochebed, whose conception was on the road,** as the family of Jacob descended to Egypt, **and she was born between the walls,** i.e., in Egypt, **as it is stated:** "And the name of Amram's wife was Jochebed, the daughter of Levi, **who was born to Levi in Egypt"** (Numbers 26:59).

לֵידָתָהּ בְּמִצְרַיִם וְאֵין הוֹרָתָהּ בְּמִצְרַיִם! אָמַר רַבִּי יְהוּדָה: שֶׁנּוֹלְדוּ בָּהּ סִימָנֵי נַעֲרוּת.

This interpolation concerning her birth is interpreted: **Her birth** was **in Egypt, but her conception was not in Egypt.** Since the Jewish people were in Egypt for two hundred ten years and Moses was eighty years old at the time of the exodus, Jochebed was one hundred thirty years old when Moses was born. In light of this, the Gemara is asking how the verse can refer to her as a daughter. **Rabbi Yehuda says: The signs of a young woman were born in her**[N] when her husband remarried her, and she became like a young girl again.

״וַתַּהַר הָאִשָּׁה וַתֵּלֶד בֵּן״ – וְהָא הֲוַת מִיעַבְּרָא בֵּיהּ תְּלָתָא יַרְחֵי מֵעִיקָּרָא! אָמַר רַב יְהוּדָה בַּר זְבִינָא: מַקִּישׁ לֵידָתָהּ לְהוֹרָתָהּ. מָה הוֹרָתָהּ שֶׁלֹּא בְּצַעַר, אַף לֵידָתָהּ שֶׁלֹּא בְּצַעַר, מִכָּאן לְנָשִׁים צִדְקָנִיּוֹת שֶׁלֹּא הָיוּ בְּפִיתְקָהּ שֶׁל חַוָּה.

§ The verse states concerning Moses: **"And the woman conceived, and bore a son;** and when she saw him that he was a goodly child, she hid him three months" (Exodus 2:2). The Gemara asks: **But** Jochebed **was pregnant with** Moses **for three months at the outset,** before Amram remarried her, as will be explained further. **Rav Yehuda bar Zevina said:** The intention of the verse is to **juxtapose** her giving **birth to her becoming pregnant. Just as her becoming pregnant was without pain, so too, her** giving **birth was without pain. From here** it is derived **concerning righteous women**[N] **that they were not included in the verdict** [***pitkah***][L] **of Eve** that a woman will suffer pain during childbirth (see Genesis 3:16).

״וַתֵּרֶא אוֹתוֹ כִּי טוֹב הוּא״ – תַּנְיָא, רַבִּי מֵאִיר אוֹמֵר: טוֹב שְׁמוֹ; רַבִּי יְהוּדָה אוֹמֵר: טוֹבִיָּה שְׁמוֹ; רַבִּי נְחֶמְיָה אוֹמֵר: הָגוּן לִנְבִיאוּת; אֲחֵרִים אוֹמְרִים: נוֹלַד כְּשֶׁהוּא מָהוּל; וַחֲכָמִים אוֹמְרִים: בְּשָׁעָה שֶׁנּוֹלַד מֹשֶׁה – נִתְמַלֵּא הַבַּיִת כּוּלּוֹ אוֹר. כְּתִיב הָכָא: ״וַתֵּרֶא אוֹתוֹ כִּי טוֹב הוּא״, וּכְתִיב הָתָם: ״וַיַּרְא אֱלֹהִים אֶת הָאוֹר כִּי טוֹב״.

The verse states with regard to the birth of Moses: "And the woman conceived, and bore a son; **and when she saw him that he was a goodly** [***tov***] **child,** she hid him three months" (Exodus 2:2). **It is taught** in a *baraita* that **Rabbi Meir says: "Tov" is his,** Moses', real **name,**[N] as it was given to him by his parents when he was born. **Rabbi Yehuda says: His name was Toviya. Rabbi Neḥemya says:** They said he was good because they saw that he was **fit for prophecy. Others say:** They said he was good because he was **born when he was** already **circumcised. And the Rabbis say: At the time when Moses was born, the entire house was filled with light,** as **it is written here: "And when she saw him that he was a goodly** [***tov***] **child," and it is written there: "And God saw the light, that it was good** [***tov***]" (Genesis 1:4).

BACKGROUND

Palanquin – אַפִּרְיוֹן:

Egyptian palanquins

LANGUAGE

Palanquin [*appiryon*] – **אַפִּרְיוֹן:** From the Greek φορεῖον, *phoreyon*, referring to a chair used to transport people.

Verdict [*pitkah*] – **פִּתְקָה:** From the Greek πιττάκιον, *pitakion*, which means a bill, a formal document, or a material upon which to write. Among other meanings of the word is list, such as a list of persons belonging to a specific group. Here it is used in the sense of a document detailing a court verdict.

NOTES

The signs of a young woman were born in her – שֶׁנּוֹלְדוּ בָּהּ סִימָנֵי נַעֲרוּת: As noted further in the Gemara, Jochebed was already pregnant when Amram remarried her. As such, her rejuvenation was not needed so that she would conceive. Rather, it was so that people should not say that Amram remarried her only because he was not concerned that she would bear children (*Iyyun Ya'akov*; *Anaf Yosef*).

From here it is derived concerning righteous women, etc. – מִכָּאן לְנָשִׁים צִדְקָנִיּוֹת וכו׳: The Maharal writes that pain during childbirth and difficulty in earning one's livelihood are as a result of the sin of Adam and Eve. Therefore, completely righteous women, who are free of sin, may not suffer pain in childbirth.

Tov is his name – טוֹב שְׁמוֹ: Although he is generally referred to as Moses, that name was given to him by the daughter of Pharaoh. The discussion here, as well as in tractate *Megilla* and elsewhere in the midrash, relates to the question of what was the name given to him by his family.

״וַתִּצְפְּנֵהוּ שְׁלֹשָׁה יְרָחִים״ – דְּלָא מָנוּ מִצְרִים אֶלָּא מִשָּׁעָה דְּאַהַדְרָהּ, וְהִיא הֲוַת מִיעַבְּרָא בֵּיהּ תְּלָתָא יַרְחֵי מֵעִיקָּרָא.

The verse continues: **"And she hid him three months"** (Exodus 2:2). The Gemara explains that she was able to hide him for three months **because the Egyptians counted** the nine months of her pregnancy **only from the time** her husband **took her back, but she was pregnant with** Moses **for three months from the outset** of her remarriage.

״וְלֹא יָכְלָה עוֹד הַצְּפִינוֹ״ – אַמַּאי? תִּצְפְּנֵיהּ וְתֵיזִיל! אֶלָּא כָּל הֵיכָא דַּהֲווּ שָׁמְעִי מִצְרָאֵי דְּמִתְיְלִיד יָנוֹקָא, מַמְטוּ יָנוֹקָא הָתָם כִּי הֵיכִי דְּלִישְׁמְעִינְהוּ וּמַעֲוֵי בַּהֲדֵיהּ, דִּכְתִיב: ״אֶחֱזוּ לָנוּ שׁוּעָלִים שׁוּעָלִים קְטַנִּים״ וגו׳.

The next verse states: **"And when she could no longer hide him"** (Exodus 2:3). The Gemara asks: **Why** couldn't she hide him any longer? **Let her continue to hide him. Rather, anywhere that the Egyptians heard that a baby was born** and they wanted to locate the baby, **they would bring** another **baby there in order that it could be heard** crying, **and** the two babies **would cry together, as it is written: "Take us the foxes, the little foxes,** that spoil the vineyards; for our vineyards are in blossom" (Song of Songs 2:15). The infants who were used to uncover the hidden babies are referred to as little foxes.

״וַתִּקַּח לוֹ תֵּבַת גֹּמֶא״ – מַאי שְׁנָא גּוֹמֶא? אָמַר רַבִּי אֶלְעָזָר: מִיכָּן לַצַּדִּיקִים שֶׁמָּמוֹנָם חָבִיב עֲלֵיהֶן יוֹתֵר מִגּוּפָן. וְכָל כָּךְ לָמָּה? לְפִי שֶׁאֵין פּוֹשְׁטִין יְדֵיהֶן בְּגָזֵל.

The verse states: "And when she could no longer hide him, **she took for him an ark of bulrushes,** and daubed it with bitumen and with pitch; and she put the child therein, and laid it in the willows by the river's bank" (Exodus 2:3). The Gemara asks: **What is different** about **bulrushes** that she decided to use them? **Rabbi Elazar says: From here** it is derived **concerning righteous people that their money is more precious to them**[N] **than their bodies,** as she took an inexpensive material to build the ark. **And why** do they care **so much** about their money? **Because they do not stretch out their hands to** partake of **stolen property.** Therefore, their own property is very precious to them.

רַבִּי שְׁמוּאֵל בַּר נַחְמָנִי אָמַר: דָּבָר רַךְ, שֶׁיָּכוֹל לַעֲמוֹד בִּפְנֵי דָּבָר רַךְ וּבִפְנֵי דָּבָר קָשֶׁה.

Rabbi Shmuel bar Naḥmani says an alternative reason for her taking bulrushes for the ark: She took **a soft material** like bulrush, **which is able to withstand** an impact both **before a soft item and before a hard item.** She feared that if she would have made the box from a hard material like wood, if it were to collide with a hard item in the water it might break.

״וַתַּחְמְרָה בַחֵמָר וּבַזָּפֶת״ – תָּנָא: חֵמָר מִבִּפְנִים וְזֶפֶת מִבַּחוּץ, כְּדֵי שֶׁלֹּא יָרִיחַ אוֹתוֹ צַדִּיק רֵיחַ רַע.

The verse continues: **"And daubed it with bitumen and with pitch"** (Exodus 2:3). A Sage **teaches:** She daubed **bitumen on the interior**[N] **and pitch**[B] **on the exterior, so that righteous person,** i.e., Moses, **would not smell a foul odor,** such as that of pitch.

״וַתָּשֶׂם בָּהּ אֶת הַיֶּלֶד וַתָּשֶׂם בַּסּוּף״ – רַבִּי אֶלְעָזָר אוֹמֵר: יַם סוּף. רַבִּי שְׁמוּאֵל בַּר נַחְמָנִי אָמַר:

The verse continues: **"And she put the child therein, and laid it in the willows** [*bassuf*]" (Exodus 2:3). **Rabbi Elazar says:** This means she placed him **in the Suf Sea,** i.e., the Red Sea. **Rabbi Shmuel bar Naḥmani says:**

NOTES

That their money is more precious to them, etc. – שֶׁמָּמוֹנָם חָבִיב עֲלֵיהֶן יוֹתֵר וכו׳: Righteous people are willing to undergo physical pain in order to retain their money, as they work exceptionally hard to ensure that all of their wealth is obtained honestly (*Ben Yehoyada*). See also the discussion concerning Abba Ḥilkiya in tractate *Ta'anit* (23b).

Bitumen on the interior – חֵמָר מִבִּפְנִים: The Maharsha explains that there was no need to state that the bitumen was on the interior, as if it were on the exterior it would be dissolved by the water. Therefore, the additional mention that it was smeared inside is to teach that it was placed there not only to protect the ark, but also to prevent Moses from smelling the foul odor of the pitch. *Tosafot* explain the Gemara differently. They claim that the bitumen and pitch were both smeared on the interior of the ark, and that the bitumen was covering the pitch. The term: On the interior, would then mean that it was closer to Moses within the ark. The box was uncovered on the outside in order for it not to be noticeable among the reeds.

BACKGROUND

Pitch – זֶפֶת: In ancient times pitch was made by slowly burning wood, which would be transformed into charcoal. During this process, the wood emitted various fluids. Tar and pitch are made from these fluids. Pitch is the thicker substance, and its foul odor is due to additional materials found in the fluid. Pitch was sometimes made from asphalt, which also had a foul odor caused by the presence of sulfur and sulfur hydroxide.

Perek **I**
Daf **12** Amud **b**

אֲגַם, כִּדְכְתִיב: ״קָנֶה וָסוּף קָמֵלוּ״.

She placed him in a **marsh, as it is written: "The reeds and willows** [*suf*] **shall wither"** (Isaiah 19:6).

״וַתֵּרֶד בַּת פַּרְעֹה לִרְחוֹץ עַל הַיְאֹר״ – אָמַר רַבִּי יוֹחָנָן מִשּׁוּם רַבִּי שִׁמְעוֹן בֶּן יוֹחַי: מְלַמֵּד, שֶׁיָּרְדָה לִרְחוֹץ מִגִּלּוּלֵי אָבִיהָ. וְכֵן הוּא אוֹמֵר: ״אִם רָחַץ ה׳ אֵת צוֹאַת בְּנוֹת צִיּוֹן״ וגו׳.

The verse states: **"And the daughter of Pharaoh came down to bathe** [*lirḥotz*] **in the river"** (Exodus 2:5). **Rabbi Yoḥanan says in the name of Rabbi Shimon ben Yoḥai:** This **teaches that she came down** to the river **to cleanse**[N] herself **from** the impurity of **her father's idols,** as she was immersing herself as part of the conversion process. **And similarly it states: "When the Lord shall have washed** [*raḥatz*] **away the filth of the daughters of Zion,** and shall have purged the blood of Jerusalem from the midst thereof, by the spirit of judgment, and by the spirit of destruction" (Isaiah 4:4). This washing clearly refers to the purging of spiritual sins, rather than bathing for the sake of cleanliness.

NOTES

This teaches that she came down to cleanse, etc. – מְלַמֵּד שֶׁיָּרְדָה לִרְחוֹץ וכו׳: The strongest proof that Pharaoh's daughter converted is from the verse that refers to: "Bithiah the daughter of Pharaoh" (I Chronicles 4:18), who eventually married a Jew.

NOTES

Walking is nothing other than, etc. – אֵין הֲלִיכָה זוֹ אֶלָּא וכו׳: This is a reference to their imminent death, as the Gemara will soon discuss (Riaf).

The one who says that it means her arm – מַאן דְּאָמַר יָדָהּ: The fact that the verse first refers to the women as her maidens [*na'aroteha*] and then uses the term *amata* indicates that the latter expression is not a reference to one of her maidens. Additionally, the word *amata* is written without a *dagesh* in the letter *mem*; therefore, it means a maidservant. See the commentary of *Ibn Ezra* on the verse.

The verse calls him a child [*yeled*], etc. – קָרֵי לֵיהּ יֶלֶד וכו׳: The discussion here is based on the use of two alternative terms for the boy in the same verse, although either term could have been appropriate independently (Maharsha).

You made Moses our teacher blemished – עֲשִׂיתוֹ לְמֹשֶׁה רַבֵּינוּ בַּעַל מוּם: Rashi explains that since Moses was a Levite, if he had an unusual voice he would not have been permitted to sing in the Tabernacle. The Maharsha and others explain that having an unusual voice is considered a blemish, and since prophecy rests upon those who are complete in every manner, it is not reasonable to say that Moses had this blemish.

"וְנַעֲרֹתֶיהָ הוֹלְכוֹת" וגו׳ – אָמַר רַבִּי יוֹחָנָן: אֵין הֲלִיכָה זוֹ אֶלָּא לְשׁוֹן מִיתָה. וְכֵן הוּא אוֹמֵר: "הִנֵּה אָנֹכִי הוֹלֵךְ לָמוּת".

The verse continues: **"And her maidens walked** along [*holekhot*] by the riverside" (Exodus 2:5). **Rabbi Yoḥanan says: This walking is nothing other** than[N] the **terminology of** going toward **death, and similarly it states: "Behold, I am going [*holekh*] to die"** (Genesis 25:32).

"וַתֵּרֶא אֶת הַתֵּבָה בְּתוֹךְ הַסּוּף" – כֵּיוָן דַּחֲזוּ דְּקָא בָּעוּ לְאַצּוֹלֵי לְמֹשֶׁה, אָמְרוּ לָהּ: גְּבִירְתֵּנוּ! מִנְהָגוֹ שֶׁל עוֹלָם, מֶלֶךְ בָּשָׂר וָדָם גּוֹזֵר גְּזֵירָה, אִם כָּל הָעוֹלָם כּוּלּוֹ אֵין מְקַיְּימִין אוֹתָהּ – בָּנָיו וּבְנֵי בֵיתוֹ מְקַיְּימִין אוֹתָהּ, וְאַתְּ עוֹבֶרֶת עַל גְּזֵירַת אָבִיךְ! בָּא גַּבְרִיאֵל וַחֲבָטָן בַּקַּרְקַע.

The verse continues: **"And she saw the ark among the willows"** (Exodus 2:5). **Once** her maidens **saw that** the daughter of Pharaoh **was intending to save Moses, they said to her: Our mistress, the custom of the world** is that when **a king of flesh and blood decrees a decree,** even **if all the world does not fulfill it,** at least **his children and members of his household fulfill it, and** yet **you are violating the decree of your father.** After the maidens tried to convince her not to save Moses, the angel **Gabriel came and beat them to the ground** and they died.

"וַתִּשְׁלַח אֶת אֲמָתָהּ וַתִּקָּחֶהָ" – רַבִּי יְהוּדָה וְרַבִּי נְחֶמְיָה, חַד אָמַר: יָדָהּ, וְחַד אָמַר: שִׁפְחָתָהּ. מַאן דְּאָמַר יָדָהּ, דִּכְתִיב: "אֲמָתָהּ"; וּמַאן דְּאָמַר שִׁפְחָתָהּ, מִדְּלָא כְּתִיב "יָדָהּ".

The verse concludes: **"And she sent *amatah* to take it"** (Exodus 2:5). **Rabbi Yehuda and Rabbi Neḥemya** disagree as to the definition of the word "*amatah*." **One says** that it means **her arm, and one says** that it means **her maidservant.** The Gemara explains: **The one who says** that it means **her arm**[N] explained it in this manner, **as it is written "*amatah*,"** which denotes her forearm. **And the one who says** that it means **her maidservant** explained it in this manner **because it does not** explicitly **write** the more common term: **Her hand [*yadah*].** Therefore, he understands that this is the alternative term for a maidservant, *ama*.

וּלְמַאן דְּאָמַר שִׁפְחָתָהּ, הָא אָמְרַתְּ: בָּא גַּבְרִיאֵל וַחֲבָטָן בַּקַּרְקַע! דְּשַׁיֵּיר לָהּ חֲדָא, דְּלָאו אוֹרְחָא דְּבַת מַלְכָּא לְמֵיקַם לְחוּדָהּ.

The Gemara asks: **And according to the one who says** that it means **her maidservant, didn't you say** earlier: **Gabriel came and beat them to the ground** and the maidservants died, so how could Pharaoh's daughter send her? The Gemara answers: It must be **that** Gabriel **left her one** maidservant, **as it is not proper that a princess should stand alone.**

וּלְמַאן דְּאָמַר יָדָהּ, לִיכְתּוֹב "יָדָהּ"! הָא קָא מַשְׁמַע לָן, דְּאִישְׁתַּרְבַּב אִישְׁתַּרְבּוּבֵי, דְּאָמַר מָר: וְכֵן אַתָּה מוֹצֵא בְּאַמָּתָהּ שֶׁל בַּת פַּרְעֹה; וְכֵן אַתָּה מוֹצֵא בְּשִׁינֵּי רְשָׁעִים, דִּכְתִיב: "שִׁנֵּי רְשָׁעִים שִׁבַּרְתָּ", וְאָמַר רֵישׁ לָקִישׁ: אַל תִּיקְרֵי "שִׁבַּרְתָּ", אֶלָּא "שִׁרִיבַּבְתָּה".

The Gemara asks: **And according to the one who says** that it means **her hand, let** the Torah **write** explicitly: **Her hand [*yadah*].** Why use the more unusual term *amatah*? The Gemara answers: **This** verse **teaches us that her arm extended [*ishtarbav*]** many cubits. **As the Master said** in another context: **And similarly you find with regard to the hand of Pharaoh's daughter** that it extended, **and similarly you find with regard to the teeth of evildoers, as it is written: "You have broken [*shibbarta*] the teeth of the wicked"** (Psalms 3:8), **and Reish Lakish said: Do not read** the word as ***shibbarta*, rather** read it as ***sheribbavta***, you have extended.

"וַתִּפְתַּח וַתִּרְאֵהוּ אֶת הַיֶּלֶד" – "וַתֵּרֶא" מִיבָּעֵי לֵיהּ! אָמַר רַבִּי יוֹסֵי בְּרַבִּי חֲנִינָא: שֶׁרָאֲתָה שְׁכִינָה עִמּוֹ.

The next verse states: **"And she opened it and saw it [*vatirehu*], even the child"** (Exodus 2:6). The Gemara comments: The verse states: "And she saw it"; **it should have** stated: **And she saw. Rabbi Yosei, son of Rabbi Ḥanina, says:** In addition to Moses, **she saw the Divine Presence with him.** This is indicated by the usage of "saw it."

"וְהִנֵּה נַעַר בֹּכֶה" – קָרֵי לֵיהּ "יֶלֶד" וְקָרֵי לֵיהּ "נַעַר"! תָּנָא: הוּא יֶלֶד וְקוֹלוֹ כְּנַעַר, דִּבְרֵי רַבִּי יְהוּדָה; אָמַר לוֹ רַבִּי נְחֶמְיָה: אִם כֵּן, עֲשִׂיתוֹ לְמֹשֶׁה רַבֵּינוּ בַּעַל מוּם! אֶלָּא, מְלַמֵּד שֶׁעָשְׂתָה לוֹ אִמּוֹ חוּפַּת נְעוּרִים בַּתֵּיבָה, אָמְרָה: שֶׁמָּא לֹא אֶזְכֶּה לְחוּפָּתוֹ.

The verse states: "And saw it, even the child [*yeled*]; **and behold a lad [*na'ar*] that wept"** (Exodus 2:6). The verse **calls him "a child [*yeled*],"**[N] **and** the same verse **calls him "a lad [*na'ar*]."** A Sage **teaches: He is** the age of **a child but his voice** is as loud and deep **as a lad;** this is **the statement of Rabbi Yehuda. Rabbi Neḥemya said to him: If** that is **so, you made Moses our teacher blemished,**[N] since his voice was unusually deep. **Rather,** this **teaches that his mother made a canopy of youth,** i.e., a small canopy, **for him in the ark,** as **she said: Perhaps I will not merit to** see **his** wedding **canopy.**

"וַתַּחְמֹל עָלָיו וַתֹּאמֶר מִיַּלְדֵי הָעִבְרִים זֶה" – מְנָא יָדְעָה? אָמַר רַבִּי יוֹסֵי בְּרַבִּי חֲנִינָא: שֶׁרָאֲתָה אוֹתוֹ מָהוּל.

The verse concludes: **"And she had compassion on him, and said: This [*zeh*] is one of the Hebrews' children"** (Exodus 2:6). The Gemara asks: **From where did she know** that he was a Hebrew child? **Rabbi Yosei, son of Rabbi Ḥanina, says: As she saw** that **he was circumcised.**

״זֶה״ – אָמַר רַבִּי יוֹחָנָן: מְלַמֵּד, שֶׁנִּתְנַבְּאָה שֶׁלֹּא מִדַּעְתָּהּ, זֶה נוֹפֵל וְאֵין אַחֵר נוֹפֵל.

The Gemara comments: The Pharaoh's daughter said: "**This** [*zeh*] is one of the Hebrews' children" (Exodus 2:6). **Rabbi Yoḥanan says:** This **teaches that she prophesied unknowingly,** as the intention of the word "*zeh*" was: **This** one **falls,** i.e., is cast, into the water, **but no other** will **fall** by means of water, for on that day Pharaoh's decree was canceled.

וְהַיְינוּ דְּאָמַר רַבִּי אֶלְעָזָר, מַאי דִּכְתִיב: ״וְכִי יֹאמְרוּ אֲלֵיכֶם דִּרְשׁוּ אֶל הָאֹבוֹת וְאֶל הַיִּדְּעֹנִים הַמְצַפְצְפִים וְהַמַּהְגִּים״? צוֹפִין וְאֵינָם יוֹדְעִין מַה צוֹפִין, מַהְגִּים וְאֵינָן יוֹדְעִים מַה מַּהְגִּים.

The Gemara explains: **And this is what Rabbi Elazar said: What is** the meaning of that **which is written: "And when they shall say to you: Seek unto the necromancers and the diviners, that chirp** [*metzaftzefim*] **and that mutter** [*mahggim*]" (Isaiah 8:19)? The explanation of their chirping and muttering is: **They see** [*tzofin*], **but they do not know what they are seeing; they enunciate** [*mahggim*], **but they do not know what they are enunciating.** Although necromancers and diviners do have some insight into the future, they do not see clearly enough to understand what they are actually seeing.

רָאוּ שֶׁמּוֹשִׁיעָן שֶׁל יִשְׂרָאֵל בַּמַּיִם הוּא לוֹקֶה, עָמְדוּ וְגָזְרוּ ״כָּל הַבֵּן הַיִּלּוֹד הַיְאֹרָה תַּשְׁלִיכֻהוּ״. כֵּיוָן דְּשַׁדְיוּהּ לְמֹשֶׁה, אָמְרוּ: תּוּ לָא חָזֵינַן כִּי הַהוּא סִימָנָא. בִּטְּלוּ לִגְזֵירְתַיְיהוּ, וְהֵם אֵינָן יוֹדְעִין שֶׁעַל מֵי מְרִיבָה הוּא לוֹקֶה.

The Gemara applies this to Pharaoh: Pharaoh's astrologers **saw that the savior of the Jewish people would be stricken by water.** Therefore, **they arose and decreed: "Every son that is born you shall cast into the river"** (Exodus 1:22); they thought that their vision indicated that Moses would be killed in the water. **Once** Jochebed **cast Moses** into the water, although he was protected in an ark, the astrologers **said: We no longer see** in the stars anything **like that sign** we saw as to the downfall of the leader of the Jews by water, and therefore at that moment **they canceled their decree. But they did not know that** what they saw foretold that Moses **would be stricken on account of the waters of Meribah.** They envisioned a downfall for Moses by water but didn't fully comprehend their vision.

וְהַיְינוּ דְּאָמַר רַבִּי חָמָא בְּרַבִּי חֲנִינָא, מַאי דִּכְתִיב: ״הֵמָּה מֵי מְרִיבָה אֲשֶׁר רָבוּ״? הֵמָּה שֶׁרָאוּ אִיצְטַגְנִינֵי פַּרְעֹה וְטָעוּ. וְהַיְינוּ דְּקָאָמַר מֹשֶׁה: ״שֵׁשׁ מֵאוֹת אֶלֶף רַגְלִי״ וגו׳. אָמַר לָהֶן מֹשֶׁה לְיִשְׂרָאֵל: בִּשְׁבִילִי נִצַּלְתֶּם כּוּלְּכֶם.

And this is what Rabbi Ḥama, son of Rabbi Ḥanina, says: What is the meaning of that **which is written: "These** [*hemma*] **are the waters of Meribah,**[N] **where** the children of Israel **strove** with the Lord, and He was sanctified in them" (Numbers 20:13)? The verse indicates that **these are** the waters **that the astrologers of Pharaoh saw and** on account of which they **erred. And this is what Moses said:** "The people, among whom I am, **are six hundred thousand men on foot** [*ragli*]; and yet You have said: I will give them flesh, that they may eat a whole month" (Numbers 11:21). **Moses said to the Jewish people: On account of me,** which is an alternative meaning of the word ragli, **all of you were saved,** as the decree to throw all males into the river was canceled on my account.

רַבִּי חֲנִינָא בַּר פַּפָּא אָמַר: אוֹתוֹ הַיּוֹם עֶשְׂרִים וְאֶחָד בְּנִיסָן הָיָה. אָמְרוּ מַלְאֲכֵי הַשָּׁרֵת לִפְנֵי הַקָּדוֹשׁ בָּרוּךְ הוּא: רִבּוֹנוֹ שֶׁל עוֹלָם, מִי שֶׁעָתִיד לוֹמַר שִׁירָה עַל הַיָּם בְּיוֹם זֶה, יִלְקֶה בְּיוֹם זֶה?

Rabbi Ḥanina bar Pappa says: That day that Moses was placed in the river **was the twenty-first** day of the month **of Nisan. The ministering angels said before the Holy One, Blessed be He: Master of the Universe,** should the **one who in the future will say**[N] the **Song at the** Red **Sea on this day be stricken on this day?** As this was also the date on which the Red Sea would be parted during the salvation of the Exodus.

רַבִּי אַחָא בַּר חֲנִינָא אָמַר: אוֹתוֹ הַיּוֹם שִׁשָּׁה בְּסִיוָן הָיָה. אָמְרוּ מַלְאֲכֵי הַשָּׁרֵת לִפְנֵי הַקָּדוֹשׁ בָּרוּךְ הוּא: רִבּוֹנוֹ שֶׁל עוֹלָם! מִי שֶׁעָתִיד לְקַבֵּל תּוֹרָה מֵהַר סִינַי בְּיוֹם זֶה, יִלְקֶה בְּיוֹם זֶה?

Rabbi Aḥa bar Ḥanina says: That day was actually **the sixth** day of the month **of Sivan. The ministering angels said before the Holy One, Blessed be He: Master of the Universe,** should the **one who in the future will receive** the **Torah on Mount Sinai on this day be stricken on this day?** As this was also the date on which the Torah was received.

בִּשְׁלָמָא לְמַאן דְּאָמַר בְּשִׁשָּׁה בְּסִיוָן, מַשְׁכַּחַתְּ לָהּ שְׁלֹשָׁה יַרְחֵי, דְּאָמַר מָר: בְּשִׁבְעָה בַּאֲדָר מֵת וּבְשִׁבְעָה בַּאֲדָר נוֹלַד מֹשֶׁה, וּמִשִּׁבְעָה בַּאֲדָר וְעַד שִׁשָּׁה בְּסִיוָן תְּלָתָא יַרְחֵי; אֶלָּא לְמַאן דְּאָמַר בְּעֶשְׂרִים וְאֶחָד בְּנִיסָן, הֵיכִי מַשְׁכַּחַתְּ לָהּ?

The Gemara asks: **Granted, according to the one who says** that Moses was placed in the water **on the sixth of Sivan, you find** that there can be **three months** during which Moses was hidden after his birth; **as the Master said** (*Tosefta* 11:7): Moses **died on the seventh of Adar, and Moses was born on the seventh of Adar. And** based on this, **from the seventh of Adar until the sixth of Sivan** there are **three months,** which correspond to the three months Moses was hidden before being placed in the water. **But according to the one who says** that it was **on the twenty-first of Nisan, how can you find** that he was hidden for three months?

NOTES

These [*hemma*] **are the waters of Meribah – הֵמָּה מֵי מְרִיבָה:** The word *hemma*, these, indicates a reference to a matter previously mentioned. Since this event was not explicitly noted before, the Sages understood it to mean that these are the waters that the Egyptian astrologers had already envisioned.

One who in the future will say, etc. – מִי שֶׁעָתִיד לוֹמַר וכו׳: This statement is difficult. If the angels are stating that Moses would sing and accept the Torah in the future, then why were they concerned that he would die? Some explain that the intention is that although there could be other means of saving Moses, the angels prayed that God would show mercy to him and save him immediately in a way that did not involve hardship (see *Ben Yehoyada*).

אוֹתָהּ שָׁנָה מְעוּבֶּרֶת הָיְתָה; רוּבּוֹ שֶׁל רִאשׁוֹן, וְרוּבּוֹ שֶׁל אַחֲרוֹן, וְאֶמְצָעִי שָׁלֵם.

The Gemara answers: **That year was a leap year** in which there were two months of Adar. Moses was hidden **most of the first** month of the three, from the seventh day of the first Adar when he was born, **and most of the last** month of the three, i.e., all of Nisan until the twenty-first, **and the entire middle one.** All of this together is considered as three months.

״וַתֹּאמֶר אֲחוֹתוֹ אֶל בַּת פַּרְעֹה הַאֵלֵךְ וְקָרָאתִי לָךְ אִשָּׁה מֵינֶקֶת מִן הָעִבְרִיּוֹת״. וּמַאי שְׁנָא מֵעִבְרִיּוֹת?

The Gemara now discusses the next verse in Exodus: **"Then said his sister to Pharaoh's daughter: Shall I go and call you a nurse of the Hebrew women,** that she may nurse the child for you?" (Exodus 2:7). The Gemara asks: **And what is different** that Pharaoh's daughter would specifically want a nurse **of the Hebrew women?**

מְלַמֵּד, שֶׁהֶחֱזִירוּהוּ לְמֹשֶׁה עַל כָּל הַמִּצְרִיּוֹת כּוּלָּן וְלֹא יָנַק. אָמַר: פֶּה שֶׁעָתִיד לְדַבֵּר עִם הַשְּׁכִינָה יִינַק דָּבָר טָמֵא? וְהַיְינוּ דִּכְתִיב: ״אֶת מִי יוֹרֶה דֵעָה״ וגו׳, לְמִי יוֹרֶה דֵעָה וּלְמִי יָבִין שְׁמוּעָה? ״לִגְמוּלֵי מֵחָלָב וּלְעַתִּיקֵי מִשָּׁדָיִם״.

The Gemara answers: This **teaches that** prior to this, **they took Moses around**[N] **to all the Egyptian** wet nurses **and he did not** agree to **nurse** from any of them, as **he said:** Shall **a mouth that in the future** will **speak with the Divine Presence** actually **nurse something impure?**[N] **And this is as it is written: "Whom shall one teach knowledge?** And whom shall one make understand the message?" (Isaiah 28:9). The prophet is asking: **To whom shall** God **teach** the **knowledge** of the Torah, **and to whom shall** God **make to understand the message** of the Torah? The answer is as the verse continues: **"Them that are weaned from the milk, them that are drawn from the breasts"** (Isaiah 28:9). The conclusion of the verse indicates that the Torah should be taught to the one who did not want to nurse from the milk of a gentile woman, i.e., Moses.

״וַתֹּאמֶר לָהּ בַּת פַּרְעֹה לֵכִי״ וגו׳ – אָמַר רַבִּי אֶלְעָזָר: מְלַמֵּד, שֶׁהָלְכָה בִּזְרִיזוּת כְּעַלְמָה. רַבִּי שְׁמוּאֵל בַּר נַחְמָנִי אָמַר: ״הָעַלְמָה״ – שֶׁהֶעֱלִימָה אֶת דְּבָרֶיהָ.

The next verse states: **"And Pharaoh's daughter said to her: Go.** And the maiden [*ha'alma*] went and called the child's mother" (Exodus 2:8). **Rabbi Elazar says:** This **teaches that she went quickly like a maiden,** i.e., with the strength of one of marriageable age, and not as the young child that she was. **Rabbi Shmuel bar Naḥmani says:** The word *ha'alma* is related to the word meaning to hide [*le'alem*], **for she hid her words** and didn't tell Pharaoh's daughter that she was bringing the baby's mother.

״וַתֹּאמֶר לָהּ בַּת פַּרְעֹה הֵילִיכִי אֶת הַיֶּלֶד הַזֶּה״ – אָמַר רַבִּי חָמָא בְּרַבִּי חֲנִינָא: מִתְנַבְּאָה וְאֵינָהּ יוֹדַעַת מַה מִּתְנַבְּאָה, ״הֵילִיכִי״ – הָא שֶׁלִּיכִי. ״וַאֲנִי אֶתֵּן אֶת שְׂכָרֵךְ״ – אָמַר רַבִּי חָמָא בְּרַבִּי חֲנִינָא: לֹא דַּיָּין לַצַּדִּיקִים שֶׁמַּחֲזִירִין לָהֶן אֲבֵידָתָן, אֶלָּא שֶׁנּוֹתְנִין לָהֶן שְׂכָרָן.

The next verse states what Pharaoh's daughter said to Jochebed: **"And Pharaoh's daughter said to her: Take this [*heilikhi*] child away,** and nurse it for me, and I will give you your wages. And the woman took the child, and nursed it" (Exodus 2:9). **Rabbi Ḥama, son of Rabbi Ḥanina, says:** Pharaoh's daughter **is prophesying and she does not know what she is prophesying,** as the word ***heilikhi*** means: **This is yours [*ha shellikhi*],** i.e., this is your child. The next part of the verse states: **"And I will give you your wages." Rabbi Ḥama, son of Rabbi Ḥanina, says:** This teaches that **with regard to righteous people, not only** is it so **that** God arranges **that their lost items are returned to them, but** He **also** arranges **that they get their wages,** as the son of Jochebed was returned to her and she also received payment for nursing him.

״וַתִּקַּח מִרְיָם הַנְּבִיאָה אֲחוֹת אַהֲרֹן״ וגו׳ – אֲחוֹת אַהֲרֹן וְלֹא אֲחוֹת מֹשֶׁה? אָמַר רַב עַמְרָם אָמַר רַב, וְאָמְרִי לָהּ אָמַר רַב נַחְמָן אָמַר רַב: מְלַמֵּד, שֶׁהָיְתָה מִתְנַבְּאָה כְּשֶׁהִיא אֲחוֹת אַהֲרֹן,

Elsewhere, the verse states with regard to Miriam: **"And Miriam the prophetess, the sister of Aaron, took** a timbrel in her hand; and all the women went out after her with timbrels and with dances" (Exodus 15:20). The Gemara asks: Why is Miriam referred to as **"the sister of Aaron," and not the sister of Moses? Rav Amram says** that **Rav says, and some say** that **Rav Naḥman says** that **Rav says:** This **teaches that** Miriam already **prophesied when she was** still **the sister of** only **Aaron,** i.e., before Moses was born.

NOTES

This teaches that they took Moses around, etc. – מְלַמֵּד שֶׁהֶחֱזִירוּהוּ לְמֹשֶׁה וכו׳: It is apparent that they must have brought Moses to Egyptian wet nurses, otherwise Miriam would not have dared to suggest to the daughter of Pharaoh that she employ a Hebrew woman as a nursemaid. She would have feared that the ruse would be uncovered.

Nurse something impure – יִינַק דָּבָר טָמֵא: The Maharsha writes that although there is no halakhic prohibition against a Jewish baby nursing from a gentile woman, Moses refused to do so because of the additional sanctity he possessed (see *Shulḥan Arukh, Yoreh De'a* 81:7, and in the comment of Rema).

וְאוֹמֶרֶת: עֲתִידָה אִמִּי שֶׁתֵּלֵד בֵּן שֶׁמּוֹשִׁיעַ אֶת יִשְׂרָאֵל. וְכֵיוָן שֶׁנּוֹלַד מֹשֶׁה, נִתְמַלֵּא כׇּל הַבַּיִת כּוּלּוֹ אוֹר. עָמַד אָבִיהָ וּנְשָׁקָהּ עַל רֹאשָׁהּ, אָמַר לָהּ: בִּתִּי, נִתְקַיְּימָה נְבוּאָתֵיךְ! וְכֵיוָן שֶׁהִטִּילוּהוּ לַיְאוֹר, עָמַד אָבִיהָ וּטְפָחָהּ עַל רֹאשָׁהּ, אָמַר לָהּ: בִּתִּי, הֵיכָן נְבוּאָתֵיךְ! וְהַיְינוּ דִּכְתִיב: ״וַתֵּתַצַּב אֲחֹתוֹ מֵרָחֹק לְדֵעָה מַה יֵּעָשֶׂה לוֹ״, לֵידַע מַה יְּהֵא בְּסוֹף נְבוּאָתָהּ.

And as a child Miriam **would say: In the future, my mother will give birth to a son who will save the Jewish people. And once Moses was born, the entire house was filled with light. Her father arose and kissed her on her head. He said to her: My daughter, your prophecy has been fulfilled. And once they put him into the river, her father arose and hit her on her head. He said to her: My daughter, where is your prophecy? And this is as it is written: "And his sister stood**[N] **afar off, to know what would be done to him"** (Exodus 2:4), i.e., **to know what will be the ultimate** resolution **of her prophecy.**

״יוֹסֵף זָכָה״ וכו׳. מַאי שְׁנָא מֵעִיקָּרָא, דִּכְתִיב: ״וַיַּעַל יוֹסֵף לִקְבֹּר אֶת אָבִיו וַיַּעֲלוּ אִתּוֹ כׇּל עַבְדֵי פַרְעֹה״ וגו׳ וַהֲדַר: ״וְכֹל בֵּית יוֹסֵף וְאֶחָיו וּבֵית אָבִיו״, וּמַאי שְׁנָא לְבַסּוֹף דִּכְתִיב: ״וַיָּשָׁב יוֹסֵף מִצְרַיְמָה הוּא וְאֶחָיו״, וַהֲדַר ״וְכׇל הָעֹלִים אִתּוֹ לִקְבֹּר אֶת אָבִיו״?

§ The mishna teaches: **Joseph merited** to bury his father, resulting in a display of great honor to his father. The Gemara begins its discussion of the burial of Jacob by asking: **What is different initially that it is written: "And Joseph went up to bury his father; and with him went up all the servants of Pharaoh,** the elders of his house, and all the elders of the land of Egypt" (Genesis 50:7), **and afterward** it says in the following verse: **"And all the house of Joseph, and his brethren, and his father's house;** only their little ones, and their flocks, and their herds, they left in the land of Goshen" (Genesis 50:8), indicating that the brothers of Joseph were second in importance to the Egyptians? **And what is different at the end that it is written: "And Joseph returned into Egypt, he, and his brethren," and afterward** it states: **"And all that went up with him to bury his father,** after he had buried his father" (Genesis 50:14), placing the brothers before the Egyptians?

אָמַר רַבִּי יוֹחָנָן: בַּתְּחִילָּה עַד שֶׁלֹּא רָאוּ בִּכְבוֹדָן שֶׁל יִשְׂרָאֵל לֹא נָהֲגוּ בָּהֶן כָּבוֹד, וּלְבַסּוֹף שֶׁרָאוּ בִּכְבוֹדָן נָהֲגוּ בָּהֶן כָּבוֹד,

Rabbi Yoḥanan says: Initially, before the Egyptians **saw the honor of the Jewish people,** as the Gemara will soon explain, **they did not treat them** with **honor,** so the brothers were behind the servants of Pharaoh. **And in the end, when they saw their honor, they treated** the brothers with **honor.**

דִּכְתִיב: ״וַיָּבֹאוּ עַד גֹּרֶן הָאָטָד״. וְכִי גּוֹרֶן יֵשׁ לוֹ לְאָטָד? אָמַר רַבִּי אַבָּהוּ: מְלַמֵּד, שֶׁהִקִּיפוּהוּ כְּתָרִים לַאֲרוֹנוֹ שֶׁל יַעֲקֹב כְּגוֹרֶן זֶה שֶׁמַּקִּיפִים לוֹ אָטָד, שֶׁבָּאוּ בְּנֵי עֵשָׂו וּבְנֵי יִשְׁמָעֵאל וּבְנֵי קְטוּרָה.

The Gemara explains what honor was accorded to the family of Jacob: **As it is written: "And they came to the threshing floor of Atad,**[N] which is beyond the Jordan, and there they wailed with a very great and sore wailing; and he made a mourning for his father seven days" (Genesis 50:10). The word atad is the name of the boxthorn bush. **And does a boxthorn**[B] bush **have a threshing floor?** Thorns are not collected and eaten. **Rabbi Abbahu says:** This **teaches that they surrounded the casket of Jacob with crowns, like this threshing floor that is surrounded with boxthorns, because the children of Esau and the children of Ishmael and the children of Keturah** all **came** to the burial of Jacob.

תָּנָא: כּוּלָּם לְמִלְחָמָה בָּאוּ. כֵּיוָן שֶׁרָאוּ כִּתְרוֹ שֶׁל יוֹסֵף תָּלוּי בַּאֲרוֹנוֹ שֶׁל יַעֲקֹב, נָטְלוּ כּוּלָּן כִּתְרֵיהֶן וּתְלָאוּם בַּאֲרוֹנוֹ שֶׁל יַעֲקֹב. תָּנָא: שְׁלֹשִׁים וְשִׁשָּׁה כְּתָרִים נִתְלוּ בַּאֲרוֹנוֹ שֶׁל יַעֲקֹב.

A Sage **taught:** Initially, **they all came to** wage **war** with the family of Jacob, but **once they saw the crown of Joseph,** the viceroy of Egypt, **hanging on the casket of Jacob, they all took their crowns and hung them on the casket of Jacob.** A Sage **taught: Thirty-six crowns**[N] **were hung on the casket of Jacob.** This was the great honor accorded to the family of Jacob.

״וַיִּסְפְּדוּ שָׁם מִסְפֵּד גָּדוֹל וְכָבֵד מְאֹד״ – תָּנָא: אֲפִילּוּ סוּסִים וַאֲפִילּוּ חֲמוֹרִים.

The Gemara continues its discussion of Jacob's burial. The verse states: **"And there they wailed with a very great and sore wailing"** (Genesis 50:10). It is **taught: Even horses**[N] **and even donkeys** participated in the mourning.

NOTES

And this is as it is written, and his sister stood, etc. – וְהַיְינוּ דִּכְתִיב וַתֵּתַצַּב אֲחֹתוֹ וכו׳: This verse serves as proof that Miriam went alone, indicating that there was a special reason for her to do so (*Iyyun Ya'akov*).

The threshing floor of Atad – גֹּרֶן הָאָטָד: In the Jerusalem Talmud it is noted that there is no place in the Bible referred to as Atad. Therefore, it can be assumed that the name here is an allusion to some matter. According to the discussion in the Gemara here, the reason why the term "threshing floor" is used is that when grain grows it is surrounded by thorns, similar to the image of Jacob's casket surrounded by crowns.

Thirty-six crowns – שְׁלֹשִׁים וְשִׁשָּׁה כְּתָרִים: Rashi explains the calculation as follows: There were twelve crowns belonging to the princes of Ishmael, another twenty-three of the chiefs of Esau, and the crown of Joseph. The Maharsha, similar to *Tosefot HaRash* before him, explains otherwise: According to him there were twelve crowns of the princes of Ishmael, ten of the kings of Keturah, and fourteen of the princes of Edom. *Tosefot HaRosh* makes a similar calculation with one difference: He counts only nine crowns of the kings of Keturah, but includes the crown of Joseph in the final count.

Even horses, etc. – אֲפִילּוּ סוּסִים וכו׳: The simple explanation of this phrase is that the noise and the trumpet calls of the funeral caused the animals to neigh and bray, appearing as if they were participating in the crying (*Pardes Rimmonim*). Another interpretation is that due to the sorrow and mourning, the animals were not fed that day, and they cried out (Riaf). Alternatively, the horses and donkeys were enrobed in black as a sign of mourning, as is customary at the funerals of kings (Maharsha).

BACKGROUND

Boxthorn – אָטָד: The *atad*, or boxthorn, of the genus *Lycium*, is a thorny plant of the Solanaceae family. It has long, arched branches that form a bush that can reach a height of up to 3 m. It grows red fruits, some of which are edible and some of which are poisonous. Species of the *atad* grow in all parts of Eretz Yisrael and are sometimes used as hedges. In the proverb of the orphan in the book of Judges, chapter 9, the insignificant value of the *atad* is mentioned.

Boxthorn

(מאילו מאילו) כֵּיוָן שֶׁהִגִּיעוּ לִמְעָרַת הַמַּכְפֵּלָה, אֲתָא עֵשָׂו קָא מְעַכֵּב. אָמַר לָהֶן: ״מַמְרֵא קִרְיַת הָאַרְבַּע הִיא חֶבְרוֹן״, וְאָמַר רַבִּי יִצְחָק: קִרְיַת אַרְבַּע – אַרְבַּע זוּגוֹת הָיוּ: אָדָם וְחַוָּה, אַבְרָהָם וְשָׂרָה, יִצְחָק וְרִבְקָה, יַעֲקֹב וְלֵאָה. אִיהוּ קְבָרָהּ לְלֵאָה בְּדִידֵיהּ, וְהַאי דְּפָיֵישׁ דִּידִי הוּא.

Once they reached the Cave of Machpelah, Esau came and was preventing them from burying Jacob there. **He said to them:** It says: "And Jacob came unto Isaac his father to **Mamre, to Kiryat Arba, the same is Hebron,** where Abraham and Isaac sojourned" (Genesis 35:27). **And Rabbi Yitzḥak says:** It is called **Kiryat Arba** because there **were four couples** buried there: **Adam and Eve, Abraham and Sarah, Isaac and Rebecca, Jacob and Leah.** Esau said: Jacob **buried Leah in his spot, and** the spot **that is remaining is mine.**

אֲמַרוּ לֵיהּ: זְבִינְתָּהּ. אֲמַר לְהוּ: נְהִי דִּזְבִינִי בְּכֵירוּתָא, פְּשִׁיטוּתָא מִי זְבִינִי? אֲמַרוּ לֵיהּ: אִין, דִּכְתִיב: ״בְּקִבְרִי אֲשֶׁר כָּרִיתִי לִי״, וְאָמַר רַבִּי יוֹחָנָן מִשּׁוּם רַבִּי שִׁמְעוֹן בֶּן יְהוֹצָדָק: אֵין כִּירָה אֶלָּא לְשׁוֹן מְכִירָה, שֶׁכֵּן בִּכְרַכֵּי הַיָּם קוֹרִין לִמְכִירָה כִּירָה.

The children of Jacob **said to** Esau: **You sold** your rights **to** Jacob. Esau **said to them: Though I sold the birthright, did I** also **sell** my rights to the burial site as **an ordinary** brother? The brothers **said to him: Yes,** you also sold to Jacob those rights, **as it is written** that Joseph stated: "My father made me swear, saying: Behold, I die; **in my grave that I have dug** [*kariti*] **for me** in the land of Canaan, there shall you bury me" (Genesis 50:5). **And Rabbi Yoḥanan says in the name of Rabbi Shimon ben Yehotzadak:** The word ***kira*** in the verse **is nothing other** than **a term of a sale** [***mekhira***] sharing a similar root, **because in the cities overseas**[B] **they call a sale *kira*.**

אֲמַר לְהוּ: הֲבוּ לִי אִיגַּרְתָּא. אֲמַרוּ לֵיהּ: אִיגַּרְתָּא בְּאַרְעָא דְּמִצְרַיִם הִיא. וּמַאן נֵיזִיל? נֵיזִיל נַפְתָּלִי, דְּקַלִּיל כִּי אַיַּילְתָּא, דִּכְתִיב: ״נַפְתָּלִי אַיָּלָה שְׁלוּחָה הַנּוֹתֵן אִמְרֵי שָׁפֶר״ – אָמַר רַבִּי אַבָּהוּ: אַל תִּקְרֵי ״אִמְרֵי שָׁפֶר״, אֶלָּא ״אִמְרֵי סֵפֶר״.

Esau **said to them: Bring the bill** of sale **to me,** i.e., you can't prove your claims. **They said to him: The bill** of sale **is in the land of Egypt.** They said: **And who will go** to bring it? **Naphtali will go, for he is as fast as a doe, as it is written: "Naphtali is a doe let loose, he gives goodly words"** (Genesis 49:21). **Rabbi Abbahu says: Do not read** it as **"goodly words** [***imrei shafer***]**"; rather,** read it as ***imrei sefer***, i.e., the words of the book, as he returned to Egypt to retrieve the bill of sale.

חוּשִׁים בְּרֵיהּ דְּדָן תַּמָּן הֲוָה וְיַקִּירָן לֵיהּ אוּדְנֵיהּ, אֲמַר לְהוּ: מַאי הַאי? וַאֲמַרוּ לֵיהּ: קָא מְעַכֵּב הַאי עַד דְּאָתֵי נַפְתָּלִי מֵאַרְעָא דְּמִצְרַיִם. אֲמַר לְהוּ: וְעַד דְּאָתֵי נַפְתָּלִי מֵאַרְעָא דְּמִצְרַיִם יְהֵא אֲבִי אַבָּא מוּטָל בְּבִזָּיוֹן? שְׁקַל קוּלְפָּא מַחְיֵיהּ אַרֵישֵׁיהּ, נָתְרָן עֵינֵיהּ וְנָפְלוּ אַכַּרְעָא דְּיַעֲקֹב. פַּתְחִינְהוּ יַעֲקֹב לְעֵינֵיהּ וְאַחֵיךְ. וְהַיְינוּ דִּכְתִיב: ״יִשְׂמַח צַדִּיק כִּי חָזָה נָקָם פְּעָמָיו יִרְחַץ בְּדַם הָרָשָׁע״.

The Gemara relates: **Hushim, the son of Dan,**[N] **was there and his ears were heavy,** i.e., he was hard of hearing. **He said to them: What is this** that is delaying the burial? **And they said to him: This one,** Esau, **is preventing** us from burying Jacob **until Naphtali comes** back **from the land of Egypt** with the bill of sale. **He said to them: And until Naphtali comes** back **from the land of Egypt will** our **father's father lie in degradation? He took a club** [***kulepa***][L] **and hit** Esau **on the head,** and Esau's **eyes fell out and they fell on the legs of Jacob. Jacob opened his eyes**[N] **and smiled. And this is that which is written: "The righteous shall rejoice when he sees the vengeance; he shall wash his feet in the blood of the wicked"** (Psalms 58:11).

בְּאוֹתָהּ שָׁעָה נִתְקַיְּימָה נְבוּאָתָהּ שֶׁל רִבְקָה, דִּכְתִיב: ״לָמָּה אֶשְׁכַּל גַּם שְׁנֵיכֶם יוֹם אֶחָד״. וְאַף עַל גַּב דְּמִיתָתָן לָא בְּיוֹם אֶחָד הֲוַאי, קְבוּרָתָן מִיהָא בְּיוֹם אֶחָד הֲוַאי.

At that moment the prophecy of Rebecca was fulfilled, as it is written that Rebecca said of Jacob and Esau: **"Why should I be bereaved of you both in one day?"** (Genesis 27:45), as Rebecca foresaw that the future bereavement for both her sons would be on the same day. The Gemara comments: **And although their deaths were not on the same day, in any event their burials were on the same day,** as Esau was killed and buried on the same day that Jacob was buried.

וְאִי לָא עֲסַק בֵּיהּ יוֹסֵף, אֶחָיו לָא הָווּ מִעַסְּקִי בֵּיהּ? וְהָכְתִיב: ״וַיִּשְׂאוּ אוֹתוֹ בָנָיו אַרְצָה כְּנַעַן״! אָמְרוּ: הַנִּיחוּ לוֹ, כְּבוֹדוֹ בִּמְלָכִים יוֹתֵר מִבְּהֶדְיוֹטוֹת.

The Gemara returns to discuss the involvement of Joseph and his brothers in the burial of their father: **And if Joseph would not have dealt with** the burial of Jacob, **would his brothers not have dealt with it? But isn't it written: "For his sons carried him into the land of Canaan,** and buried him in the cave of the field of Machpelah" (Genesis 50:13)? Since it is evident that the brothers were involved in the burial, why did they not deal with Jacob's burial needs from the outset? The Gemara answers: **They said: Allow** Joseph to take care of it, because there is **more honor** for our father to be prepared for burial **by royalty than by common** people [***hedyotot***].[L]

BACKGROUND

The cities overseas – בְּרַכֵּי הַיָּם: This expression is understood by some scholars as a reference to Caesarea or Cyprus. In fact, the stories in the Talmud that involve the towns on the coast usually are invoked in order to answer a linguistic question, since in these towns a certain word was often used with a specific meaning, or to describe an unusual occurrence, oftentimes one of sin or of an atypical practice. For this reason it is likely that when the Sages used this term their purpose was not to refer to a specific geographic place but more to create a setting for pedagogic purposes.

NOTES

Hushim, the son of Dan, etc. – חוּשִׁים בְּרֵיהּ דְּדָן וכו׳: The Maharsha writes that there are many allusions to the details of this narrative in Psalm 58, from which the verse quoted here: "The righteous shall rejoice" (Psalms 58:11), is taken.

The Maharal explains that the brothers witnessed the unfolding of the discussion with Esau gradually. Therefore, they became desensitized to the degradation of Jacob. Hushim, by contrast, was informed of the discussion suddenly, and reacted accordingly. *Tosefot HaRash*, citing the Jerusalem Talmud, says that there is a tradition that Judah killed Esau, and suggests that Hushim struck Esau first and then Judah killed him.

Jacob opened his eyes – פַּתְחִינְהוּ יַעֲקֹב לְעֵינֵיהּ: *Pardes Rimmonim* writes that this is not meant to be interpreted literally, but merely means that if Jacob were alive he would have opened his eyes and smiled.

LANGUAGE

Club [*kulepa*] – קוּלְפָּא: Related to the Persian kūpāl, meaning a thick stick.

Ancient Egyptian relief depicting an Egyptian king holding a club

Common people [*hedyotot*] – הֶדְיוֹטוֹת: From the Greek ἰδιώτης, *idiotēs*, whose basic meaning is a simple person who does not hold any office. The word generally appears in the Talmud with another word as a compound noun, such as *kohen hedyot*, a common priest, in contrast to the High Priest, or as a term referring to the property of a common person, often in contrast to the Temple treasury of consecrated property.

"מִי לָנוּ גָּדוֹל מִיּוֹסֵף" כו׳. תָּנוּ רַבָּנַן: בֹּא וּרְאֵה כַּמָּה חֲבִיבוֹת מִצְוֹת עַל מֹשֶׁה רַבֵּינוּ, שֶׁכָּל יִשְׂרָאֵל כּוּלָּן נִתְעַסְּקוּ בַּבִּיזָּה, וְהוּא נִתְעַסֵּק בְּמִצְוֹת, שֶׁנֶּאֱמַר: "חֲכַם לֵב יִקַּח מִצְוֹת" וגו׳.

§ It states further in the mishna: **Who, to us,** had **a greater** burial **than Joseph,** as it was none other than Moses who involved himself in transporting his coffin. **The Sages taught** in the *Tosefta* (4:6–7): **Come and see how beloved mitzvot are**[N] **to Moses our teacher. As,** at the time of the Exodus, **all the Jewish people were involved in** taking **the plunder** from Egypt, **and he was involved in** the performance of **mitzvot, as it is stated: "The wise in heart will take mitzvot"** (Proverbs 10:8).

וּמִנַּיִן הָיָה יוֹדֵעַ מֹשֶׁה רַבֵּינוּ הֵיכָן יוֹסֵף קָבוּר? אָמְרוּ: סֶרַח בַּת אָשֵׁר נִשְׁתַּיְּירָה מֵאוֹתוֹ הַדּוֹר. הָלַךְ מֹשֶׁה אֶצְלָהּ, אָמַר לָהּ: כְּלוּם אַתְּ יוֹדַעַת הֵיכָן יוֹסֵף קָבוּר? אָמְרָה לוֹ: אָרוֹן שֶׁל מַתֶּכֶת עָשׂוּ לוֹ מִצְרִים וּקְבָעוּהוּ בְּנִילוּס הַנָּהָר, כְּדֵי שֶׁיִּתְבָּרְכוּ מֵימָיו. הָלַךְ מֹשֶׁה וְעָמַד עַל שְׂפַת נִילוּס, אָמַר לוֹ: יוֹסֵף, יוֹסֵף, הִגִּיעַ הָעֵת שֶׁנִּשְׁבַּע הַקָּדוֹשׁ בָּרוּךְ הוּא שֶׁאֲנִי גּוֹאֵל אֶתְכֶם, וְהִגִּיעָה הַשְּׁבוּעָה שֶׁהִשְׁבַּעְתָּ אֶת יִשְׂרָאֵל. אִם אַתָּה מַרְאֶה עַצְמְךָ – מוּטָב; אִם לָאו – הֲרֵי אָנוּ מְנוּקִּין מִשְּׁבוּעָתְךָ. מִיָּד צָף אֲרוֹנוֹ שֶׁל יוֹסֵף.

The Gemara asks: **And from where did Moses our teacher know**[N] **where Joseph was buried?** The Sages **said: Serah, the daughter of Asher, remained from that generation** that initially descended to Egypt with Jacob. **Moses went to her** and **said to her: Do you know anything** about **where Joseph is buried? She said to him: The Egyptians fashioned a metal casket for him and set it in the Nile** [*Nilus*][L] **River**[N] as an augury **so that its water would be blessed. Moses went and stood on the bank of the Nile.** He **said to** Joseph: **Joseph, Joseph, the time has arrived** about **which the Holy One, Blessed be He, took an oath** saying **that I,** i.e., God, **will redeem you. And** the time for fulfillment **of the oath that you administered to the Jewish people** that they will bury you in Eretz Yisrael **has arrived. If you show yourself,** it is **good,** but **if not, we are clear from your oath. Immediately, the casket of Joseph floated** to the top of the water.

וְאַל תִּתְמַהּ הֵיאַךְ בַּרְזֶל צָף, שֶׁהֲרֵי כְּתִיב: "וַיְהִי הָאֶחָד מַפִּיל הַקּוֹרָה וְאֶת הַבַּרְזֶל נָפַל אֶל הַמָּיִם וגו׳ אֲהָהּ אֲדוֹנִי וְהוּא שָׁאוּל. וַיֹּאמֶר אִישׁ הָאֱלֹהִים אָנָה נָפָל וַיַּרְאֵהוּ אֶת הַמָּקוֹם וַיִּקְצָב עֵץ וַיַּשְׁלֶךְ שָׁמָּה וַיָּצֶף הַבַּרְזֶל". וַהֲלֹא דְּבָרִים קַל וָחוֹמֶר: וּמָה אֱלִישָׁע תַּלְמִידוֹ שֶׁל אֵלִיָּהוּ וְאֵלִיָּהוּ תַּלְמִידוֹ שֶׁל מֹשֶׁה – צָף בַּרְזֶל מִפָּנָיו, מִפְּנֵי מֹשֶׁה רַבֵּינוּ – עַל אַחַת כַּמָּה וְכַמָּה.

And do not wonder how iron can **float,**[N] **as it is written** in the verses describing how Elisha was able to cause iron to float: **"But as one was felling a beam, the ax head fell into the water;** and he cried, and said: **Alas, my master! For it was borrowed. And the man of God said: Where did it fall? And he showed him the place. And he cut down a stick, and cast it in there, and the iron floated up"** (II Kings 6:5–6). **And are** these **matters not** inferred ***a fortiori*: And just as Elisha,** who was a mere **student of Elijah, and Elijah** was a mere **student of Moses,**[N] as Elijah studied the Torah of Moses, was able to cause the **iron** to **float before him, all the more so** would it float **before Moses our teacher** himself.

רַבִּי נָתָן אוֹמֵר: בְּקַבַּרְנִיט שֶׁל מְלָכִים הָיָה קָבוּר. הָלַךְ מֹשֶׁה וְעָמַד עַל קַבַּרְנִיט שֶׁל מְלָכִים, אָמַר: יוֹסֵף, הִגִּיעַ עֵת שֶׁנִּשְׁבַּע הַקָּדוֹשׁ בָּרוּךְ הוּא שֶׁאֲנִי גּוֹאֵל אֶתְכֶם, וְהִגִּיעָה שְׁבוּעָה שֶׁהִשְׁבַּעְתָּ אֶת יִשְׂרָאֵל. אִם אַתָּה מַרְאֶה עַצְמְךָ – מוּטָב, וְאִם לָאו – הֲרֵי אָנוּ מְנוּקִּין מִשְּׁבוּעָתְךָ. בְּאוֹתָהּ שָׁעָה נִזְדַּעְזַע אֲרוֹנוֹ שֶׁל יוֹסֵף. נְטָלוֹ מֹשֶׁה וֶהֱבִיאוֹ אֶצְלוֹ.

The Gemara now presents a different version of where Joseph was buried. **Rabbi Natan says:** Joseph **was buried in the crypt** [*kabbarnit*][L] **of kings. Moses went and stood by the crypt of kings** and **said: Joseph, the time has arrived** about **which the Holy One, Blessed be He, took an oath** saying **that: I will redeem you. And** the time for fulfillment of **the oath that you administered to the Jewish people** that they will bury you in Eretz Yisrael **has arrived. If you show yourself,** it is **good, but if not, we are clear from your oath. At that moment, the casket of Joseph shook** among the caskets. **Moses took it and brought it** over **to himself.**

וְכָל אוֹתָן שָׁנִים שֶׁהָיוּ יִשְׂרָאֵל בַּמִּדְבָּר, הָיוּ שְׁנֵי אֲרוֹנוֹת הַלָּלוּ, אֶחָד שֶׁל מֵת וְאֶחָד שֶׁל שְׁכִינָה, מְהַלְּכִין זֶה עִם זֶה, וְהָיוּ עוֹבְרִין וְשָׁבִין אוֹמְרִים: מַה טִּיבָן שֶׁל שְׁנֵי אֲרוֹנוֹת הַלָּלוּ? אָמְרוּ: אֶחָד שֶׁל מֵת וְאֶחָד שֶׁל שְׁכִינָה. וְכִי מַה דַּרְכּוֹ שֶׁל מֵת לְהַלֵּךְ עִם שְׁכִינָה? אָמְרוּ:

And all those years that the Jewish people were in the wilderness, these two arks, one a casket **of a dead man,** Joseph, **and one** the Ark **of the Divine Presence,** i.e., the Ark of the Covenant, **were traveling together, and passersby would say: What is the nature of these two arks? They said** to them: **One is of a dead person and one** is **of the Divine Presence.** The passersby would ask: **And** in **what** way is it **the manner of a dead person to travel with the Divine Presence? They said** in response:

LANGUAGE

Nile [*Nilus*] – נִילוּס: This is the Greek name, Νεῖλος, *Neilos*, for the main river in Egypt, called Shihor in the Bible (Joshua 13:3).

Crypt [*kabbarnit*] – קַבַּרְנִיט: The source and exact meaning of this word are unclear, but some suggest it is based on the morphemically similar word labyrinth. Others suggest it is based on the Latin caverna, meaning burial cave.

NOTES

How beloved mitzvot are, etc. – כַּמָּה חֲבִיבוֹת מִצְוֹת וכו׳: Although many people claim that mitzvot are more precious to them than gold and silver, Moses was in a position where he could actually seize whatever he wanted from the plunder, but he occupied himself with mitzvot instead (*Ben Yehoyada*).

And from where did Moses our teacher know – וּמִנַּיִן הָיָה יוֹדֵעַ מֹשֶׁה רַבֵּינוּ: Although, as the Gemara notes, the caskets of the other sons of Jacob were taken along by the tribes, the locations of those caskets were known to the Jews, as the other brothers were buried by their children. The burial of Joseph was performed by the Egyptians. Therefore, the Jewish people did not know the location of his resting place. Furthermore, there is no indication in the verse that prophecy was employed to locate the casket of Joseph (Maharsha).

And set it in the Nile River, etc. – וּקְבָעוּהוּ בְּנִילוּס הַנָּהָר וכו׳: The midrash provides another reason for the Egyptians' burying Joseph's casket in the river: They knew that the brothers had taken an oath to transport it to Eretz Yisrael when they would depart from Egypt. By preventing them from finding the casket, the Egyptians thought that they could prevent the Jewish people from leaving (*Tosefot HaRash*).

How iron can float – הֵיאַךְ בַּרְזֶל צָף: The Gemara questions the ability of iron to float under these circumstances. Although far greater miracles were performed by Moses, miracles are generally done at the command of God, while a miracle that occurs only at the wish of a person is unusual and requires explanation. Therefore, the Gemara provides proof from a similar act of Elisha, who performed a miracle to enable the seemingly trivial return of a borrowed ax.

Elijah was a student of Moses – אֵלִיָּהוּ תַּלְמִידוֹ שֶׁל מֹשֶׁה: Rashi explains that this does not mean that Elijah was actually a student of Moses, but rather that he was taught the Torah of Moses and transmitted it to others. In the introduction to his *Mishne Torah*, the Rambam notes that Elijah was a student of Ahijah the Shilonite, who was in turn a student of Moses. Alternatively, according to the opinion that Pinehas is also Elijah, then Elijah was actually a student of Moses, as Pinehas studied under him (*Iyyun Ya'akov*).

NOTES

His brothers kidnapped him from Shechem – מִשְּׁכֶם גְּנָבוּהוּ: Rashi comments that he was actually kidnapped from Dothan and not from Shechem (see Genesis 37:17). Rashi here explains that Dothan was not actually the name of a place, but was a description of the brothers' plan to find a legal means [*dat*] to kill Joseph. In tractate *Sanhedrin* (102a) Rashi explains differently, that Dothan was a small village close to Shechem, so it can be said that he was kidnapped from the vicinity of Shechem. The Maharsha notes that according to Rashi's commentary on the Torah (Genesis 48:22), Shechem was the special portion of the land that Jacob promised to give to Joseph.

Anyone who performs a matter but does not complete it – כָּל הָעוֹשֶׂה דָּבָר וְלֹא גְּמָרוֹ: One who does not complete a mitzva is lowered from the elevated state he was in while actually performing the mitzva, and therefore he is treated measure for measure and is demoted from his position of prominence (Maharal). One could explain in a similar manner that he is not given the ability to complete the building of his family, and therefore his wife and children die (*Iyyun Ya'akov*).

קִיֵּים זֶה כָּל מַה שֶּׁכָּתוּב בָּזֶה.

This one, i.e., the deceased Joseph, **fulfilled all that is written in this.** Therefore, it is fitting that the two arks should lie side by side.

וְאִי לָא עָסֵיק בֵּיהּ מֹשֶׁה, יִשְׂרָאֵל לָא הָווּ מִיעַסְקִי בֵּיהּ? וְהָכְתִיב: ״וְאֶת עַצְמוֹת יוֹסֵף אֲשֶׁר הֶעֱלוּ בְנֵי יִשְׂרָאֵל מִמִּצְרַיִם קָבְרוּ בִשְׁכֶם״! וְתוּ, אִי לָא אִיעַסְקוּ בֵּיהּ יִשְׂרָאֵל, בָּנָיו לָא הָווּ מִיעַסְקִי בֵּיהּ? וְהָכְתִיב: ״וַיִּהְיוּ לִבְנֵי יוֹסֵף לְנַחֲלָה״!

The Gemara asks: **And if Moses had not dealt with** the burial of Joseph, **would the Jewish people not have dealt with it? But isn't it written** that after Moses died: **"And the bones of Joseph, which the children of Israel brought up out of Egypt, they buried in Shechem"** (Joshua 24:32), which indicates that the Jewish people completed the burial of Joseph? **And furthermore, if the Jewish people had not dealt with** Joseph's burial, **would his children not have dealt with it? But isn't it written** in that same verse: **"And they became the inheritance of the children of Joseph,"** as Joseph was buried in Shechem, which was then given to his descendants? Therefore, the question arises: Why did Joseph's descendants initially leave the task of his burial to the Jewish people and Moses?

אָמְרוּ: הַנִּיחוּ לוֹ, כְּבוֹדוֹ בִּמְרוּבִּים יוֹתֵר מִבִּמְמוּעָטִין. וְתוּ אָמְרוּ: הַנִּיחוּ לוֹ, כְּבוֹדוֹ בִּגְדוֹלִים יוֹתֵר מִבִּקְטַנִּים.

The Gemara answers: **They said: Leave** Joseph for others. **It is more of an honor for** Joseph to be buried **by the many than by the few,** and therefore it is better that the Jewish people be involved in the burial. **And furthermore, they said: Leave** Joseph for others. **It is more of an honor for** Joseph to be buried **by** one of **the great** men like Moses **than by lesser ones** like us.

״קָבְרוּ בִשְׁכֶם״ – מַאי שְׁנָא בִּשְׁכֶם? אָמַר רַבִּי חָמָא בְּרַבִּי חֲנִינָא: מִשְּׁכֶם גְּנָבוּהוּ, וְלִשְׁכֶם נַחֲזִיר אֲבֵידָתוֹ.

In the aforementioned verse it states: "And the bones of Joseph, which the children of Israel brought up out of Egypt, **they buried in Shechem,** in the parcel of ground that Jacob bought from the sons of Hamor the father of Shechem for a hundred pieces of money" (Joshua 24:32). The Gemara asks: **What is different about Shechem** that they specifically chose to bury Joseph there? **Rabbi Ḥama, son of Rabbi Ḥanina, says** that the Jewish people said: His brothers **kidnapped him from Shechem**[N] (see Genesis 37:12–28), **and to Shechem we should return his lost** body.

קָשׁוּ קְרָאֵי אַהֲדָדֵי. כְּתִיב: ״וַיִּקַּח מֹשֶׁה אֶת עַצְמוֹת יוֹסֵף עִמּוֹ״, וּכְתִיב: ״וְאֶת עַצְמוֹת יוֹסֵף אֲשֶׁר הֶעֱלוּ בְנֵי יִשְׂרָאֵל״ וגו׳!

The Gemara comments: **The verses contradict each other,** as **it is written: "And Moses took the bones of Joseph with him"** (Exodus 13:19), **and it is written** elsewhere: **"And the bones of Joseph, which the children of Israel brought up** out of Egypt" (Joshua 24:32). Who in fact took Joseph's bones?

אָמַר רַבִּי חָמָא בְּרַבִּי חֲנִינָא: כָּל הָעוֹשֶׂה דָּבָר וְלֹא גְּמָרוֹ וּבָא אַחֵר וּגְמָרוֹ, מַעֲלֶה עָלָיו הַכָּתוּב עַל שֶׁגְּמָרוֹ כְּאִילּוּ עֲשָׂאוֹ.

Rabbi Ḥama, son of Rabbi Ḥanina, says: Anyone who performs a matter but does not complete it,[N] **and then another comes and completes it, the verse ascribes credit to the one who completed it as if he had** actually **performed** the entire act. Due to the fact that the children of Israel completed Joseph's burial, the Torah ascribes them credit as if they had performed the entire act.

רַבִּי אֶלְעָזָר אוֹמֵר: אַף מוֹרִידִין אוֹתוֹ מִגְּדוּלָּתוֹ, דִּכְתִיב: ״וַיְהִי בָּעֵת הַהִיא וַיֵּרֶד יְהוּדָה״.

Rabbi Elazar says with regard to one who initiates performance of a mitzva but does not complete it when capable of doing so: **He is also demoted** [*moridin*] **from his** position of **greatness, as it is written: "And it came to pass at that time, that Judah went down** [*vayyered*] from his brethren, and turned in to a certain Adullamite, whose name was Hirah" (Genesis 38:1). Usage of the term "went down" indicates that the rest of Judah's brothers had demoted him from his position of greatness because he began the process of saving Joseph, but he did not complete it.

רַבִּי שְׁמוּאֵל בַּר נַחְמָנִי אָמַר: אַף קוֹבֵר אִשְׁתּוֹ וּבָנָיו, דִּכְתִיב: ״וַתָּמָת בַּת שׁוּעַ אֵשֶׁת יְהוּדָה״ וגו׳. וּכְתִיב: ״וַיָּמָת עֵר וְאוֹנָן״.

Rabbi Shmuel bar Naḥmani says: The episode with regard to Judah also indicates that one who initiates performance of a mitzva but does not complete it will **also bury his wife and children** as Judah did, **as it is written: "And** in process of time **Shua's daughter, the wife of Judah, died"** (Genesis 38:12), **and it is written** further: "And the sons of Judah: Er, and Onan, and Shelah, and Perez, and Zerah; **but Er and Onan died** in the land of Canaan" (Genesis 46:12).

אָמַר רַב יְהוּדָה אָמַר רַב: מִפְּנֵי מָה נִקְרָא יוֹסֵף עֲצָמוֹת בְּחַיָּיו? מִפְּנֵי שֶׁלֹּא מִיחָה בִּכְבוֹד אָבִיו, דְּקָאָמְרִי לֵיהּ ״עַבְדְּךָ אָבִינוּ״, וְלָא אֲמַר לְהוּ וְלָא מִידֵּי.

Rav Yehuda says that **Rav says: For what** reason **was Joseph called: Bones,** even **during his lifetime,** as he had his brothers take an oath that "God will surely remember you, and you shall carry up my bones from here" (Genesis 50:25)? **Because he did not protest for the honor of his father, as** the brothers **said to** Joseph while unaware of his true identity: **"Your servant our father"** (Genesis 43:28, 44:31), **and** Joseph **said nothing to them** in protest that they referred to his father Jacob as Joseph's servant.

וְאָמַר רַב יְהוּדָה אָמַר רַב, וְאִיתֵּימָא רַבִּי חָמָא בְּרַבִּי חֲנִינָא: מִפְּנֵי מָה מֵת יוֹסֵף קוֹדֶם לְאֶחָיו? מִפְּנֵי שֶׁהִנְהִיג עַצְמוֹ בְּרַבָּנוּת.

And Rav Yehuda says that **Rav says, and some say** that this was said by **Rabbi Ḥama, son of Rabbi Ḥanina: For what** reason **did Joseph predecease his brothers,** as is indicated from his requesting of them to take care of his burial needs? **Because** Joseph **acted authoritatively,** and such behavior can reduce one's life span.

״וְיוֹסֵף הוּרַד מִצְרַיְמָה״ – אָמַר רַבִּי אֶלְעָזָר: אַל תִּיקְרֵי ״הוּרַד״, אֶלָּא ״הוֹרִיד״, שֶׁהוֹרִיד אִיצְטַגְנִינֵי פַּרְעֹה מִגְּדוּלָּתָן.

After describing that Judah "went down" from his greatness, the Gemara discusses a similar term employed with regard to Joseph, as the verse states: **"And Joseph was brought down** [*hurad*] **to Egypt"** (Genesis 39:1). **Rabbi Elazar says: Do not read** the word as **"*hurad*,"**[N] meaning that he was passively brought down, **but** rather read it as ***horid***, meaning: He, Joseph, brought down others, as Joseph **brought down the astrologers** [*itztagninei*][L] **of Pharaoh from their** position of **eminence** because he knew the interpretation of Pharaoh's dreams when they did not.

״וַיִּקְנֵהוּ פּוֹטִיפַר סְרִיס פַּרְעֹה״ – אָמַר רַב: שֶׁקְּנָאוֹ לְעַצְמוֹ. בָּא גַּבְרִיאֵל וְסֵירְסוֹ בָּא גַּבְרִיאֵל וּפֵירְעוֹ. מֵעִיקָּרָא כְּתִיב ״פּוֹטִיפַר״, וּלְבַסּוֹף ״פּוֹטִיפֶרַע״.

The continuation of that verse states: **"And Potiphar, an officer** [*seris*] **of Pharaoh's,** the captain of the guard, an Egyptian, **bought him** from the hand of the Ishmaelites, who had brought him down there" (Genesis 39:1). **Rav says: He purchased** the handsome Joseph **for himself,** for the intended purpose of homosexual intercourse, but was unable to fulfill his desires, as the angel **Gabriel came and castrated** Potiphar [*seireso*]. Then **Gabriel came** again **and** further **mutilated** him [*fero*] in the same part of his body. This is alluded to in the verses that write Potiphar's name differently: **Initially, it is written "Potiphar"** (Genesis 39:1) **and in the end it is written "Poti-phera"** (Genesis 41:45). The change in his name indicates that a part of himself was mutilated.

״מִי לָנוּ גָּדוֹל מִמֹּשֶׁה״ וכו׳. ״וַיֹּאמֶר ה׳ אֵלַי רַב לָךְ״ – אָמַר רַבִּי לֵוִי: בְּ״רַב״ בִּישֵּׂר, בְּ״רַב״ בִּישְּׂרוּהוּ; בְּ״רַב״ בִּישֵּׂר – ״רַב לָכֶם״, בְּ״רַב״ בִּישְּׂרוּהוּ – ״רַב לָךְ״.

§ The mishna teaches: **Who, to us,** had **a greater** burial **than Moses,** as no one involved himself in his burial other than the Omnipresent Himself. The Gemara teaches: When Moses relates how God responded to him when denying his request to enter Eretz Yisrael, he states: **"And the Lord said to me: Let it suffice for you** [*rav lakh*]; speak no more to Me of this matter" (Deuteronomy 3:26). **Rabbi Levi says:** Moses **proclaimed** to the Jewish people when rebuking them **with** the term **"*rav*,"** and therefore **it was proclaimed to him with** the term **"*rav*"** that he would not enter Eretz Yisrael. The Gemara explains: **He proclaimed with** the term **"*rav*"**[N] when speaking with the congregation of Korah: **"You take too much upon you** [*rav lakhem*], you sons of Levi" (Numbers 16:7), and **it was proclaimed to him with** the term **"*rav*,"** as God denied his request and said: **"Let it suffice for you** [*rav lakh*]."

דָּבָר אַחֵר: ״רַב לָךְ״ – רַב יֵשׁ לָךְ, וּמַנּוּ? יְהוֹשֻׁעַ.

Alternatively: God's telling Moses **"*rav lakh*"** was intended to mean: **You** now **have a *rav***, a master, **and who is it?** It is **Joshua,** who has been chosen to lead the Jewish people.

דָּבָר אַחֵר: ״רַב לָךְ״ – שֶׁלֹּא יֹאמְרוּ הָרַב כַּמָּה קָשֶׁה וְתַלְמִיד כַּמָּה סַרְבָן. וְכָל כָּךְ לָמָּה? תָּנָא דְּבֵי רַבִּי יִשְׁמָעֵאל: לְפוּם גַּמְלָא שִׁיחֲנָא.

Alternatively: God's telling Moses **"*rav lakh*"** was intended to mean: You have a *rav*, i.e., God, Who says that you may not enter Eretz Yisrael. You must not importune Me anymore, **so that** people **should not say: How difficult is the Master and how obstinate is the student.** The Gemara asks: **And why** was Moses punished **so much** in that he was not allowed to enter Eretz Yisrael, despite being so righteous? **The school of Rabbi Yishmael taught** that the reason is based on the common aphorism: **Based on the camel is the burden.** In other words, a person is judged in accordance with his stature, and therefore a righteous individual will be punished greatly due to any sins he committed.

NOTES

Do not read *hurad* – אַל תִּיקְרֵי הוּרַד: The Maharsha writes that the exposition is based on the fact that the phrase is unnecessary, as it is already stated that Joseph had been taken down to Egypt. Moreover, the midrash notes that the word "*hurad*" generally is used to refer to authority and ruling, as in the verse: "And have dominion [*urdu*] over the fish of the sea" (Genesis 1:28).

He proclaimed with *rav*, etc. – בְּרַב בִּישֵּׂר וכו׳: The word "*rav*" appears in reference to evildoers (see Genesis 33:9), and since Moses used this language when addressing Korah and his congregation, he was informed of his fate with the same word (Maharsha). *Ben Yehoyada* derives from here that even when rebuking evildoers, such as Korah and his congregation, one should be very careful to speak in a respectful manner.

Others explain that the term used in addressing Moses reflected the actual content of what he had said to the congregation of Korah. He had told them that they should be satisfied with their role as Levites, and not request the elevated position of becoming priests. God similarly informs Moses that he should be satisfied with having lived outside of Eretz Yisrael, and should not request the elevated status of living within its borders (*Iyyun Ya'akov*).

LANGUAGE

Astrologer [*itztagnini*] – אִיצְטַגְנִינִי: This refers to one who looks at the stars; an astronomer, but primarily an astrologer. The word is apparently based on a Greek root. Some believe it is related to ἀστήρ, *astēr*, meaning star, but a precise root has not been found.

LANGUAGE

Two pairs [*deyo zugei*] – דְּיוֹ זוּגֵי: From the Greek διζυγία, *dizugya*, meaning a double yoke that harnesses two animals together. From this it is extended to mean anything that is doubled, where two serve together.

״וַיֹּאמֶר אֲלֵיהֶם בֶּן מֵאָה וְעֶשְׂרִים שָׁנָה אָנֹכִי הַיּוֹם״ – שֶׁאֵין תַּלְמוּד לוֹמַר ״הַיּוֹם״, הַיּוֹם מָלְאוּ יָמַי וּשְׁנוֹתַי, לְלַמֶּדְךָ, שֶׁהַקָּדוֹשׁ בָּרוּךְ הוּא מַשְׁלִים שְׁנוֹתֵיהֶם שֶׁל צַדִּיקִים מִיּוֹם לְיוֹם וּמֵחֹדֶשׁ לְחֹדֶשׁ, דִּכְתִיב: ״אֶת מִסְפַּר יָמֶיךָ אֲמַלֵּא״.

The verse relates what Moses said to the Jewish people at the end of his life: **"And he said to them: I am a hundred and twenty years old this day;** I can no longer go out and come in; and the Lord has said to me: You shall not go over this Jordan" (Deuteronomy 31:2). The wording is problematic, as there is **no** need for **the verse to state** the term **"this day."** Moses said it in order to indicate: On **this day, my days and years have been completed** to be precisely one hundred and twenty, in order **to teach you that the Holy One, Blessed be He, completes the years of the righteous from day to day and from month to month, as it is written: "The number of your days I will fill"** (Exodus 23:26), indicating that the righteous will live out their years fully.

״לֹא אוּכַל עוֹד לָצֵאת וְלָבוֹא״ – מַאי ״לָצֵאת וְלָבוֹא״? אִילֵימָא ״לָצֵאת וְלָבֹא״ מַמָּשׁ – וְהָכְתִיב: ״וּמֹשֶׁה בֶּן מֵאָה וְעֶשְׂרִים שָׁנָה בְּמוֹתוֹ...לֹא נָס לֵחֹה״, וּכְתִיב: ״וַיַּעַל מֹשֶׁה מֵעַרְבֹת מוֹאָב אֶל הַר נְבוֹ״, וְתַנְיָא: שְׁתֵּים עֶשְׂרֵה מַעֲלוֹת הָיוּ שָׁם, וּפְסָעָן מֹשֶׁה בִּפְסִיעָה אַחַת!

The verse continues: **"I can no longer go out and come in"** (Deuteronomy 31:2). The Gemara asks: **What** is the meaning of **"go out and come in"? If we say** it means literally that Moses was **actually** physically restricted from **going out and coming in, but isn't it written: "And Moses was a hundred and twenty years old when he died,** his eye was not dim, **nor his natural force abated"** (Deuteronomy 34:7), indicating that he was at full physical strength? **And it is written** further: **"And Moses went up from the plains of Moab to Mount Nebo"** (Deuteronomy 34:1). **And it is taught** in a *baraita*: **There were twelve steps**[N] **there** to ascend the mountain, **and Moses stepped over them** all in **one step,** also indicating that he was at full physical strength.

אָמַר רַבִּי שְׁמוּאֵל בַּר נַחְמָנִי אָמַר רַבִּי יוֹנָתָן: לָצֵאת וְלָבוֹא בְּדִבְרֵי תוֹרָה. מְלַמֵּד, שֶׁנִּסְתַּתְּמוּ מִמֶּנּוּ שַׁעֲרֵי חָכְמָה.

Rabbi Shmuel bar Naḥmani says that **Rabbi Yonatan says:** The verse means that he could no longer **go out and come in with words of Torah.** This **teaches that the gates of wisdom were closed off to him.**

״וַיֵּלֶךְ מֹשֶׁה וִיהוֹשֻׁעַ וַיִּתְיַצְּבוּ בְּאֹהֶל מוֹעֵד״ – תָּנָא: אוֹתָהּ שַׁבָּת שֶׁל דְּיוֹ זוּגֵי הָיְתָה, נִיטְּלָה רְשׁוּת מִזֶּה וְנִיתְּנָה לָזֶה.

The verse discussing when Joshua was appointed to be the successor of Moses states: **"And Moses and Joshua went, and presented themselves in the Tent of Meeting"** (Deuteronomy 31:14). A Sage **taught: That Sabbath** when Moses died **was** a day **of two pairs** [*deyo zugei*],[L] i.e., two wise men, Moses and Joshua, serving together in one place. **Authority was taken from one and given to the other.**

וְתַנְיָא אָמַר רַבִּי יְהוּדָה: אִילְמָלֵא מִקְרָא כָּתוּב אִי אֶפְשָׁר לְאוֹמְרוֹ. הֵיכָן מֹשֶׁה מֵת? בְּחֶלְקוֹ שֶׁל רְאוּבֵן, דִּכְתִיב: ״וַיַּעַל מֹשֶׁה מֵעַרְבֹת מוֹאָב אֶל הַר נְבוֹ״, וּנְבוֹ בְּחֶלְקוֹ שֶׁל רְאוּבֵן קָיְימָא, דִּכְתִיב: ״וּבְנֵי רְאוּבֵן בָּנוּ וגו׳ וְאֶת נְבוֹ״ וגו׳.

And it is taught in a *baraita* that **Rabbi Yehuda said: If not for** an explicitly **written verse, one could not say** what is written with regard to the death and burial of Moses. **Where did Moses die? In the portion of Reuben, as it is written: "And Moses went up from the plains of Moab to Mount Nebo"** (Deuteronomy 34:1), **and** it is known from elsewhere that **Nebo is situated in the portion of Reuben, as it is written: "And the children of Reuben built** Heshbon, and Elealeh, and Kiriathaim, **and Nebo"** (Numbers 32:37–38).

״נְבוֹ״ – שֶׁשָּׁם מֵתוּ שְׁלֹשָׁה נְבִיאִים: מֹשֶׁה וְאַהֲרֹן וּמִרְיָם.

The name is also expounded: It is called **"Nebo [*Nevo*],"**[N] **for three prophets [*nevi'im*] died there: Moses, and Aaron, and Miriam.**

וְהֵיכָן מֹשֶׁה קָבוּר? בְּחֶלְקוֹ שֶׁל גָּד, דִּכְתִיב: ״וַיַּרְא רֵאשִׁית לוֹ״ וגו׳. וּמֵחֶלְקוֹ שֶׁל רְאוּבֵן עַד חֶלְקוֹ שֶׁל גָּד כַּמָּה הָוֵי? אַרְבָּעָה מִילִין. אוֹתָן אַרְבָּעָה מִילִין מִי הוֹלִיכוֹ?

Rabbi Yehuda continues: **And where is Moses buried? In the portion of Gad, as it is written** in the blessing of Moses to the tribe of Gad: **"And he chose a first part for himself,** for there a portion of a ruler was reserved" (Deuteronomy 33:21), indicating that Moses, the ruler, is buried in the portion of Gad. **And how much is** the distance **from the portion of Reuben to the portion of Gad? Four *mil*.** Rabbi Yehuda asks: For **those four *mil*** from Mount Nebo in the portion of Reuben to the burial place of Moses in the portion of Gad, **who transported him?**

NOTES

Twelve steps, etc. – שְׁתֵּים עֶשְׂרֵה מַעֲלוֹת וכו׳: These twelve steps are understood to allude to the twelve tribes, who together equaled Moses in stature (Maharsha). Alternatively, according to an esoteric understanding, it alludes to the twelve steps that one ascends to reach the higher worlds, and teaches that Moses ascended immediately to the highest level (*Otzar HaKavod*).

Nebo – נְבוֹ: This does not mean that all three died at Nebo, but rather that they all died in the portion of Reuben.

מלמד, שהיה משה מוטל בכנפי שכינה, ומלאכי השרת אומרים: "צדקת ה' עשה ומשפטיו עם ישראל", והקדוש ברוך הוא אומר: "מי יקום לי עם מרעים מי יתיצב לי עם פועלי און".

He answers: The contradiction between the two verses **teaches that Moses was lying in the wings of the Divine Presence,** as Moses was carried out by God Himself, **and the ministering angels were saying: "He executed the righteousness of the Lord, and His ordinances with Israel"** (Deuteronomy 33:21). **And the Holy One, Blessed be He, was saying: "Who will rise up for Me against the evildoers? Who will stand up for Me against the workers of iniquity?"** (Psalms 94:16). In other words, God asked: Who will now defend the Jewish people against its accusers? The idea that God Himself transported Moses to his burial could not have been said if not for the proof from the resolution between the contradictory verses.

ושמואל אמר: "מי כהחכם ומי יודע פשר דבר". ורבי יוחנן אמר: "החכמה מאין תמצא". ורב נחמן אמר: "וימת שם משה" וגו'. סמליון אמר: "וימת שם משה ספרא רבה דישראל".

And Shmuel says that God was saying the verse: **"Who is as the wise man and who knows the interpretation** [*pesher*] **of a matter?"** (Ecclesiastes 8:1), referring to the greatness of Moses, who was able to forge compromises, *pesharim*, between God and the Jewish people. **And Rabbi Yoḥanan says** that God was saying the verse: **"Wisdom, where can it be found?"** (Job 28:12). **And Rav Naḥman says** that God was saying the verse: **"And Moses,** the servant of God, **died there"** (Deuteronomy 34:5). **Semalyon**[N] **says** that God was saying: **And Moses, the great scribe of Israel, died there.**

תניא, רבי אליעזר הגדול אומר: שנים עשר מיל על שנים עשר מיל, כנגד מחנה ישראל, בת קול משמיע ואומר: וימת משה ספרא רבה דישראל. ויש אומרים: לא מת משה, כתיב הכא: "וימת שם", וכתיב התם: "ויהי שם עם ה'", מה להלן עומד ומשמש, אף כאן עומד ומשמש.

It is taught in a *baraita* that **Rabbi Eliezer the Great says:** Over an area of **twelve *mil* by twelve *mil*, equivalent to the** size of the **camp of Israel, a Divine Voice proclaimed and said: And Moses, the great scribe of Israel, died. And some say: Moses did not** actually **die,** as **it is written here: "And** Moses, the servant of the Lord, **died there"** (Deuteronomy 34:5), **and it is written there: "And he was there with the Lord** forty days and forty nights" (Exodus 34:28). **Just as there,** where it says: "And he was there with the Lord," it means that **he was standing and serving** before God; **so too, here,** when it says: "And Moses, the servant of the Lord, died there," it means that **he was standing and serving** before God.

"ויקבר אותו בגי בארץ מואב מול בית פעור" – אמר רבי ברכיה: סימן בתוך סימן, ואפילו הכי – "ולא ידע איש את קברתו".

The verse describing the burial of Moses states: **"And He buried him in the valley in the land of Moab over against Beth Peor;** and no man knows of his grave to this day" (Deuteronomy 34:6). **Rabbi Berekhya says:** This verse provides **a sign within a sign,** i.e., a very precise description of the location of his burial, **and even with this** the verse concludes: **"And no man knows of his grave** to this day" (Deuteronomy 34:6).

וכבר שלחה מלכות הרשעה אצל

The Gemara relates: **And the evil monarchy** of the Roman Empire **already sent** messengers **to**

NOTES

Semalyon – סמליון: *Tosafot* mention that two opinions are quoted in the name of Rabbeinu Ḥananel as to whether Semalyon is the name of an angel or a scholar.

Perek **I**
Daf **14** Amud **a**

גסטרא של בית פעור: הראנו היכן משה קבור. עמדו למעלה – נדמה להם למטה; למטה – נדמה להם למעלה. נחלקו לשתי כיתות, אותן שעומדים למעלה – נדמה להן למטה, למטה – נדמה להן למעלה. לקיים מה שנאמר: "ולא ידע איש את קברתו".

the garrison [*gastera*][L] **of Beth Peor** and said to them: **Show us where Moses is buried.** As the men **stood above** on the upper section of the mountain, **it appeared to them** as if the grave was **below** in the lower section. As they stood **below, it appeared to them** to be **above. They divided into two groups,** one above and one below. To **those who were standing above,** the grave **appeared to them** to be **below;** to those who were standing **below,** the grave **appeared to them to be above, to fulfill that which is stated: "And no man knows of his grave** to this day" (Deuteronomy 34:6).

LANGUAGE

Garrison [*gastera*] – גסטרא: A form of the Latin castra, which means military camp. In the broader sense it is used to refer to military personnel, or soldiers that are assigned to a particular stronghold.

רַבִּי חָמָא בְּרַבִּי חֲנִינָא אָמַר: אַף מֹשֶׁה רַבֵּינוּ אֵינוֹ יוֹדֵעַ הֵיכָן קָבוּר. כְּתִיב הָכָא: ״וְלֹא יָדַע אִישׁ אֶת קְבֻרָתוֹ״, וּכְתִיב הָתָם: ״וְזֹאת הַבְּרָכָה אֲשֶׁר בֵּרַךְ מֹשֶׁה אִישׁ הָאֱלֹהִים״. וְאָמַר רַבִּי חָמָא בְּרַבִּי חֲנִינָא: מִפְּנֵי מָה נִקְבַּר מֹשֶׁה אֵצֶל בֵּית פְּעוֹר? כְּדֵי לְכַפֵּר עַל מַעֲשֵׂה פְעוֹר.

Rabbi Ḥama, son of Rabbi Ḥanina, says: Even Moses our teacher himself **does not know where he is buried. It is written here: "And no man knows of his grave," and it is written there: "And this is the blessing wherewith Moses the man of God blessed** the children of Israel before his death" (Deuteronomy 33:1). In other words, even Moses, as he is referred to by the term "man," does not know his burial place. **And Rabbi Ḥama, son of Rabbi Ḥanina, says: For what** reason **was Moses buried near Beth Peor?**[N] **In order to atone for the incident** that transpired at Beth **Peor** (Numbers, chapter 25).

וְאָמַר רַבִּי חָמָא בְּרַבִּי חֲנִינָא, מַאי דִּכְתִיב: ״אַחֲרֵי ה׳ אֱלֹהֵיכֶם תֵּלֵכוּ״? וְכִי אֶפְשָׁר לוֹ לְאָדָם לְהַלֵּךְ אַחַר שְׁכִינָה? וַהֲלֹא כְּבָר נֶאֱמַר: ״כִּי ה׳ אֱלֹהֶיךָ אֵשׁ אוֹכְלָה הוּא״!

And Rabbi Ḥama, son of Rabbi Ḥanina, says: What is the meaning of that **which is written: "After the Lord your God shall you walk,** and Him shall you fear, and His commandments shall you keep, and unto His voice shall you hearken, and Him shall you serve, and unto Him shall you cleave" (Deuteronomy 13:5)? **But is it** actually **possible for a person to follow the Divine Presence?**[N] **But hasn't it already been stated: "For the Lord your God is a devouring fire,** a jealous God" (Deuteronomy 4:24), and one cannot approach fire.

אֶלָּא, לְהַלֵּךְ אַחַר מִדּוֹתָיו שֶׁל הַקָּדוֹשׁ בָּרוּךְ הוּא: מָה הוּא מַלְבִּישׁ עֲרוּמִּים, דִּכְתִיב: ״וַיַּעַשׂ ה׳ אֱלֹהִים לְאָדָם וּלְאִשְׁתּוֹ כָּתְנוֹת עוֹר וַיַּלְבִּשֵׁם״, אַף אַתָּה הַלְבֵּשׁ עֲרוּמִּים; הַקָּדוֹשׁ בָּרוּךְ הוּא בִּיקֵּר חוֹלִים, דִּכְתִיב: ״וַיֵּרָא אֵלָיו ה׳ בְּאֵלֹנֵי מַמְרֵא״, אַף אַתָּה בַּקֵּר חוֹלִים; הַקָּדוֹשׁ בָּרוּךְ הוּא נִיחֵם אֲבֵלִים, דִּכְתִיב: ״וַיְהִי אַחֲרֵי מוֹת אַבְרָהָם וַיְבָרֶךְ אֱלֹהִים אֶת יִצְחָק בְּנוֹ״, אַף אַתָּה נַחֵם אֲבֵלִים; הַקָּדוֹשׁ בָּרוּךְ הוּא קָבַר מֵתִים, דִּכְתִיב: ״וַיִּקְבֹּר אוֹתוֹ בַּגַּי״, אַף אַתָּה קְבֹר מֵתִים.

He explains: **Rather,** the meaning is **that one should follow the attributes of the Holy One, Blessed be He.**[H] He provides several examples. **Just as He clothes the naked, as it is written: "And the Lord God made for Adam and for his wife garments of skin, and clothed them"** (Genesis 3:21), **so too,** should **you clothe the naked.** Just as **the Holy One, Blessed be He, visits the sick, as it is written** with regard to God's appearing to Abraham following his circumcision: **"And the Lord appeared unto him by the terebinths of Mamre"** (Genesis 18:1), **so too,** should **you visit the sick.** Just as **the Holy One, Blessed be He, consoles mourners, as it is written: "And it came to pass after the death of Abraham, that God blessed Isaac his son"** (Genesis 25:11), **so too,** should **you console mourners.** Just as **the Holy One, Blessed be He, buried the dead, as it is written: "And he was buried in the valley** in the land of Moab" (Deuteronomy 34:6), **so too,** should **you bury the dead.**

״כָּתְנוֹת עוֹר״ – רַב וּשְׁמוּאֵל, חַד אָמַר: דָּבָר הַבָּא מִן הָעוֹר, וְחַד אָמַר: דָּבָר שֶׁהָעוֹר נֶהֱנֶה מִמֶּנּוּ.

The Gemara discusses the verse: "And the Lord God made for Adam and for his wife **garments of skin,**[N] and clothed them" (Genesis 3:21). **Rav and Shmuel** disagree as to the meaning of the term "garments of skin." **One says** that these garments were made of **something that comes from the skin, and one says** that these garments were **something from which the skin benefits.**

דָּרַשׁ רַבִּי שַׂמְלַאי: תּוֹרָה – תְּחִלָּתָהּ גְּמִילוּת חֲסָדִים וְסוֹפָהּ גְּמִילוּת חֲסָדִים; תְּחִילָּתָהּ גְּמִילוּת חֲסָדִים, דִּכְתִיב: ״וַיַּעַשׂ ה׳ אֱלֹהִים לְאָדָם וּלְאִשְׁתּוֹ כָּתְנוֹת עוֹר וַיַּלְבִּשֵׁם״; וְסוֹפָהּ גְּמִילוּת חֲסָדִים, דִּכְתִיב: ״וַיִּקְבֹּר אוֹתוֹ בַּגַּי״.

Rabbi Samlai taught: With regard to the **Torah, its beginning is an act of kindness and its end is an act of kindness. Its beginning is an act of kindness, as it is written: "And the Lord God made for Adam and for his wife garments of skin, and clothed them"** (Genesis 3:21). **And its end is an act of kindness, as it is written: "And he was buried in the valley** in the land of Moab" (Deuteronomy 34:6).

דָּרַשׁ רַבִּי שַׂמְלַאי: מִפְּנֵי מָה נִתְאַוָּה מֹשֶׁה רַבֵּינוּ לִיכָּנֵס לְאֶרֶץ יִשְׂרָאֵל? וְכִי לֶאֱכוֹל מִפִּרְיָהּ הוּא צָרִיךְ, אוֹ לִשְׂבּוֹעַ מִטּוּבָהּ הוּא צָרִיךְ? אֶלָּא כָּךְ אָמַר מֹשֶׁה: הַרְבֵּה מִצְוֹת נִצְטַוּוּ יִשְׂרָאֵל וְאֵין מִתְקַיְּימִין אֶלָּא בְּאֶרֶץ יִשְׂרָאֵל, אֶכָּנֵס אֲנִי לָאָרֶץ כְּדֵי שֶׁיִּתְקַיְּימוּ כּוּלָּן עַל יָדִי.

Rabbi Samlai taught: For what reason **did Moses our teacher** greatly **desire to enter Eretz Yisrael? Did he need to eat of its produce, or did he need to satisfy himself from its goodness? Rather, this** is what **Moses said: Many mitzvot were commanded** to the **Jewish people, and** some of **them can be fulfilled only in Eretz Yisrael, so I will enter the land in order that they can all be fulfilled by me.**

NOTES

Moses buried near Beth Peor – נִקְבַּר מֹשֶׁה אֵצֶל בֵּית פְּעוֹר: The Maharsha explains that the question is why the bones of Moses were not taken to Eretz Yisrael just as were those of Joseph and his brothers. Moreover, his bones were buried in a location that recalls a sin of the Jewish people. The Gemara answers that the reason Moses was specifically buried near Beth Peor was in order to atone for the transgressions that were performed there. *Tosafot* cite a midrash that every year on the anniversary of the transgressions at Beth Peor, an angel attempts to arise and castigate the Jewish people for their actions there, yet the presence of Moses' grave there prevents this. The Maharal explains that because the sin of Peor was the most shameful transgression of idol worship committed by the people, therefore Moses, who achieved the highest level of holiness, is specifically the one who can counter the enormity of this sin.

To follow the Divine Presence, etc. – לְהַלֵּךְ אַחַר שְׁכִינָה וכו׳: The intention of the phrase: To follow, as used here, is that one should bind himself to God by emulating His holy attributes. The Maharal notes that the specific Godly acts chosen here are all primarily associated with His attribute of benevolence and kindness, and people should emulate them, while they should not emulate God's attribute of strict justice. The *Iyyun Ya'akov* explains that these acts of kindness were emphasized because one might think that performing them is beneath his dignity. Therefore, it is necessary to teach that even God involves Himself in these acts.

HALAKHA

That one should follow His attributes – לְהַלֵּךְ אַחַר מִדּוֹתָיו: One is commanded to emulate the good and honest ways by which God is known. These specific attributes are mentioned only in order to teach us that these are the ones one must emulate (Rambam *Sefer HaMadda*, *Hilkhot Deot* 1:6).

NOTES

Garments of skin, etc. – כָּתְנוֹת עוֹר וכו׳: Rashi explains that this refers to garments of wool, which grows upon the skin of an animal.

The Maharsha, citing the Ḥizkuni, notes that Adam had not been granted permission to kill animals, and therefore no animal at that time would have been skinned. This is why the Sages offer other interpretations of the verse. However, the *Minḥa Ḥareva* quotes other commentaries who explain that although it was prohibited for Adam to kill animals, he was permitted to make use of those that died of natural causes. Therefore, the verse can actually refer to clothes made of animal skins. The Maharal writes that the dispute between Rav and Shmuel is concerned essentially with whether the reason for wearing garments is to cover one's nakedness or to provide pleasure to the wearer.

אָמַר לוֹ הַקָּדוֹשׁ בָּרוּךְ הוּא: כְּלוּם אַתָּה מְבַקֵּשׁ אֶלָּא לְקַבֵּל שָׂכָר, מַעֲלֶה אֲנִי עָלֶיךָ כְּאִילּוּ עֲשִׂיתָם, שֶׁנֶּאֱמַר: ״לָכֵן אֲחַלֶּק לוֹ בָרַבִּים וְאֶת עֲצוּמִים יְחַלֵּק שָׁלָל תַּחַת אֲשֶׁר הֶעֱרָה לַמָּוֶת נַפְשׁוֹ וְאֶת פּוֹשְׁעִים נִמְנָה וְהוּא חֵטְא רַבִּים נָשָׂא וְלַפּוֹשְׁעִים יַפְגִּיעַ״.

The Holy One, Blessed be He, said to him: Do you seek to enter the land to perform these mitzvot **for any** reason **other than to receive a reward?**[N] **I will ascribe you** credit **as if you had performed them** and you will receive your reward, **as it is stated: "Therefore will I divide him a portion among the great, and he shall divide the spoil with the mighty; because he bared his soul unto death, and was numbered with the transgressors; yet he bore the sin of many, and made intercession for the transgressors"** (Isaiah 53:12).

״לָכֵן אֲחַלֶּק לוֹ בָרַבִּים״ – יָכוֹל כָּאַחֲרוֹנִים וְלֹא כָּרִאשׁוֹנִים? תַּלְמוּד לוֹמַר: ״וְאֶת עֲצוּמִים יְחַלֵּק שָׁלָל״, כְּאַבְרָהָם יִצְחָק וְיַעֲקֹב שֶׁהֵן עֲצוּמִים בְּתוֹרָה וּבְמִצְוֹת; ״תַּחַת אֲשֶׁר הֶעֱרָה לַמָּוֶת נַפְשׁוֹ״ – שֶׁמָּסַר עַצְמוֹ לְמִיתָה, שֶׁנֶּאֱמַר: ״וְאִם אַיִן מְחֵנִי נָא״ וגו׳;

Rabbi Samlai proceeds to expound the verse **"Therefore will I divide him a portion among the great"** to mean that he will receive reward. One **might** have thought that he will receive reward **like the later ones and not like the earlier ones,** so **the verse states: "And he shall divide the spoil with the mighty,"** meaning **like Abraham, Isaac, and Jacob, who were mighty in Torah and in mitzvot. "Because he bared his soul unto death,"** meaning **he gave himself over to death** on behalf of the Jewish people, **as it is stated:** "Yet now, if You will forgive their sin; **and if not, blot me, I pray** You, out of Your book that You have written" (Exodus 32:32).

״וְאֶת פּוֹשְׁעִים נִמְנָה״ – שֶׁנִּמְנָה עִם מֵתֵי מִדְבָּר; ״וְהוּא חֵטְא רַבִּים נָשָׂא״ – שֶׁכִּיפֵּר עַל מַעֲשֵׂה הָעֵגֶל; ״וְלַפּוֹשְׁעִים יַפְגִּיעַ״ – שֶׁבִּיקֵּשׁ רַחֲמִים עַל פּוֹשְׁעֵי יִשְׂרָאֵל שֶׁיַּחְזְרוּ בִּתְשׁוּבָה, וְאֵין פְּגִיעָה אֶלָּא תְּפִלָּה, שֶׁנֶּאֱמַר: ״וְאַתָּה אַל תִּתְפַּלֵּל בְּעַד הָעָם הַזֶּה וְאַל תִּשָּׂא בַעֲדָם רִנָּה וּתְפִלָּה וְאַל תִּפְגַּע בִּי״.

"And was numbered with the transgressors," meaning **that he was counted among those who died in the desert,** for, just like them, he did not enter Eretz Yisrael. **"Yet he bore the sin of many,"** as **he atoned for the incident of the Golden Calf. "And made intercession** [*yafgia*] **for the transgressors,"** as **he requested mercy for the sinners of Israel** so **that they should engage in repentance. And** the word ***pegia*** means **nothing other** than **prayer, as it is stated: "Therefore pray not you for this people, neither lift up cry nor prayer for them, neither make intercession** [*tifga*] **to Me;** for I will not hear you" (Jeremiah 7:16).

הדרן עלך המקנא לאשתו

NOTES

Other than to receive a reward – אֶלָּא לְקַבֵּל שָׂכָר: The Maharsha writes that although generally it is improper for one to perform mitzvot for the sake of a reward, if he expends effort to perform a mitzva that he was not commanded to do it is acceptable to request a reward.

Summary of **Perek I**

The chapter began with a discussion of the three initial stages of the *sota* process: The warning issued by the husband, the woman's seclusion with the man about whom she was warned, and the defilement of the woman through adulterous sexual intercourse. There is a dispute as to whether the warning need be issued in the presence of witnesses, as well as a dispute as to whether the woman's seclusion needs to be known through the testimony of two witnesses. The halakhic conclusion is that the warning must be issued in the presence of two witnesses and the seclusion must be known through the testimony of two witnesses. Once these conditions are met, the wife and husband may not engage in sexual intercourse until and unless it has been proven through the *sota* evaluation (see Numbers, chapter 5) that she is innocent of any wrongdoing. However, it is sufficient for one witness to testify to the woman's actual defilement in order to render her forbidden to her husband and deny her the possibility of proving her innocence through the drinking of the bitter water.

The wording to be employed when issuing a warning was also discussed, specifically, that the warning must state that the woman should not seclude herself with a particular man. A man who suspects his wife of adultery is enjoined to issue a warning to her. In order for the woman to assume the status of a *sota*, her seclusion with the man must be for a specific duration, as recorded in the Gemara.

After the woman secludes herself with the man, the husband does not immediately bring his wife to the Temple. First he goes to his local court, which decides whether the evidence requires that the wife be brought to the Temple for the *sota* evaluation rite. If the court decides in the affirmative, it appoints two Torah scholars to escort the couple to the Temple. After arriving at the Temple the woman is taken to the Sanhedrin, where its members attempt to persuade her not to drink the water if she is guilty. Only if the woman is adamant in her desire to drink and be evaluated is she then brought before a priest, who has her stand at the eastern gate of the Temple in the presence of the public. He then tears part of her outer garment and removes her head covering.

A fair amount of *aggada* was taught in this chapter, including a discussion of some devastating character traits that can bring about one's downfall, as well as the power of repentance. The nature of divine retribution in the case of an unfaithful *sota* also generated a discussion of divine retribution in general. God's administration of punishments and rewards measure for measure for sins or good deeds was also discussed at length.

Introduction to **Perek II**

And the priest shall bring her near, and set her before the Lord.

And the priest shall take holy water in an earthen vessel; and of the dust that is on the floor of the Tabernacle the priest shall take, and put it into the water.

And the priest shall set the woman before the Lord, and let the hair of the woman's head go loose, and put the meal-offering of memorial in her hands, which is the meal-offering of jealousy; and the priest shall have in his hand the water of bitterness that causes the curse.

And the priest shall cause her to swear, and shall say to the woman: If no man has lain with you, and if you have not gone astray to defilement while under your husband, you shall be free from this water of bitterness that causes the curse;

But if you have gone astray while under your husband, and if you are defiled, and some man has lain with you besides your husband;

Then the priest shall cause the woman to swear with the oath of cursing, and the priest shall say to the woman: The Lord shall make you a curse and an oath among your people, when the Lord will cause your thigh to fall away, and your belly to swell;

And this water that causes the curse shall go into your bowels, and cause your belly to swell, and your thigh to fall away; and the woman shall say: Amen, amen.

And the priest shall write these curses in a scroll, and he shall blot them out into the water of bitterness.

(Numbers 5:16–23)

This chapter clarifies many of the *halakhot* recorded in these verses. It enumerates the sacrifice of the meal-offering of the *sota*, the drinking of the bitter water of a *sota*, and the oath administered to the *sota*, and describes the acts of the priest administering the ritual. Furthermore, it discusses the source of the water to be drunk and the proper amount of water to use, as well as the source of the dust described in the verses and the amount that must be placed in the water. The Gemara also elaborates on the order in which the water and dust are applied and the type of drinking utensil used.

Also addressed are various questions concerning the scroll of the *sota*: Which curses must be written in the scroll? Must the entire passage of the Torah be written? What ink should be used, and on what surface are the words to be written?

Finally, the chapter addresses the range of cases that are to be included in the oath of the *sota*.

מתני׳ הָיָה מֵבִיא אֶת מִנְחָתָהּ בְּתוֹךְ כְּפִיפָה מִצְרִית, וְנוֹתְנָהּ עַל יָדֶיהָ כְּדֵי לְיַגְּעָהּ.

MISHNA The husband of the *sota* **would bring**[N] his wife's **meal-offering** to the priest **in an Egyptian wicker basket**[HB] made of palm branches, **and he would place**[N] the meal-offering **in her hands** for her to hold throughout the ritual **in order to fatigue her.** This might lead her to confess her guilt and not drink the water of a *sota* unnecessarily.

כָּל הַמְּנָחוֹת תְּחִילָּתָן וְסוֹפָן בִּכְלִי שָׁרֵת, וְזוֹ תְּחִלָּתָהּ בִּכְפִיפָה מִצְרִית וְסוֹפָהּ בִּכְלִי שָׁרֵת.

The mishna lists differences between this meal-offering and other meal-offerings. Generally, **all meal-offerings,** from **their beginnings,** i.e., the moment they are consecrated, **and** until **their ends,** i.e., the moment they are sacrificed, must be **in a service vessel. But** in the case of **this one, its beginning is in a wicker basket and** only at **its end,** immediately before it is offered, is it placed **in a service vessel.**

כָּל הַמְּנָחוֹת טְעוּנוֹת שֶׁמֶן וּלְבוֹנָה, וְזוֹ אֵינָהּ טְעוּנָה לֹא שֶׁמֶן וְלֹא לְבוֹנָה. כָּל הַמְּנָחוֹת בָּאוֹת מִן הַחִטִּין, וְזוֹ בָּאָה מִן הַשְּׂעוֹרִין. מִנְחַת הָעוֹמֶר אַף עַל פִּי שֶׁבָּאָה מִן הַשְּׂעוֹרִין, הִיא הָיְתָה בָּאָה גֶּרֶשׂ, וְזוֹ בָּאָה קֶמַח. רַבָּן גַּמְלִיאֵל אוֹמֵר: כְּשֵׁם שֶׁמַּעֲשֶׂיהָ מַעֲשֵׂה בְהֵמָה, כָּךְ קׇרְבָּנָהּ מַאֲכַל בְּהֵמָה.

All other **meal-offerings require oil**[H] **and frankincense, and this one requires neither oil nor frankincense.** Furthermore, **all** other **meal-offerings are brought from wheat,**[H] **and this one is brought from barley. Although** in fact **the *omer* meal-offering**[HB] is also **brought from barley,** it is still different in that **it was brought as groats,** i.e., high-quality meal. The meal-offering of the *sota,* however, **is brought as** unsifted barley **flour. Rabban Gamliel says:** This hints that **just as her actions** of seclusion with another man **were the actions of an animal, so too her offering is animal food,** i.e., barley and not wheat.

גמ׳ תַּנְיָא, אַבָּא חָנִין אוֹמֵר מִשּׁוּם רַבִּי אֱלִיעֶזֶר: [וְכׇל כָּךְ לָמָּה?] כְּדֵי לְיַגְּעָהּ, כְּדֵי שֶׁתַּחֲזוֹר בָּהּ. אִם כָּכָה חָסָה תּוֹרָה עַל עוֹבְרֵי רְצוֹנוֹ, קַל וָחוֹמֶר עַל עוֹשֵׂי רְצוֹנוֹ.

GEMARA It is taught in a *baraita* that **Abba Ḥanin says in the name of Rabbi Eliezer: And why** is **so much** done to her? It is **in order to fatigue her, so that she will retract** and confess her guilt and be spared death. **And if the Torah is so protective of those who transgress His will,** i.e., the *sota,* who secluded herself with the man she was warned against, then by ***a fortiori*** inference He is protective **of those who do His will.**

וּמְמַּאי מִשּׁוּם דְּחָסָה הוּא? דִּילְמָא כִּי הֵיכִי דְּלָא תִּימָּחֵק מְגִילָּה! קָסָבַר

The Gemara asks: **And from where** is it derived that they attempt to induce her to confess **because** the Torah **is protective** of the *sota*? **Perhaps** it is **in order that the scroll** of the *sota,* containing the name of God, **will not be erased.** The Gemara responds: Rabbi Eliezer **holds**

NOTES

The husband would bring – הָיָה מֵבִיא: The Jerusalem Talmud states explicitly that the husband must bring this meal-offering from his own funds. The reason is that the husband has a personal need for this offering, as he must clarify for himself the innocence or guilt of his wife (*Kerem Nata*).

Would bring…and he would place – הָיָה מֵבִיא...וְנוֹתְנָהּ: *Tosafot* point out that the order of the *sota* procedure recorded in the mishna does not match the order as recorded in the Torah (see Numbers 5:11–31). In a comment on 17b, *Tosafot* conclude that the order in the Torah is authoritative, rather than the order in the mishna. However, the Rambam in the *Mishne Torah* appears to present a different order than the one presented by *Tosafot.*

HALAKHA

In an Egyptian wicker basket – בְּתוֹךְ כְּפִיפָה מִצְרִית: The priest brings a tenth of an ephah of barley flour belonging to the husband, puts it in a basket made of palm branches, and then puts this basket in the hands of the *sota* in order to exhaust her (Rambam *Sefer Nashim, Hilkhot Sota* 3:12).

All meal-offerings require oil, etc. – כָּל הַמְּנָחוֹת טְעוּנוֹת שֶׁמֶן וכו׳: All meal-offerings placed on the altar require oil and frankincense: A *log* of oil for each tenth of an ephah of flour and a handful of frankincense for every meal-offering. The exceptions are the meal-offerings of a sinner and a *sota* (Rambam *Sefer Nashim, Hilkhot Sota* 3:13 and *Sefer Avoda, Hilkhot Ma'aseh HaKorbanot* 12:7).

All meal-offerings are brought from wheat – כָּל הַמְּנָחוֹת בָּאוֹת מִן הַחִטִּין: All meal-offerings are brought from fine wheat flour except for the *omer* meal-offering and the meal-offering of the *sota,* which are brought from barley (Rambam *Sefer Avoda, Hilkhot Ma'aseh HaKorbanot* 12:2).

The *omer* meal-offering – מִנְחַת הָעוֹמֶר: The *omer* meal-offering brought from the choicest barley flour, sifted thirteen times, while the meal-offering of the *sota* is brought from ordinary barley flour (Rambam *Sefer Nashim, Hilkhot Sota* 3:13 and *Sefer Avoda, Hilkhot Temidin UMusafin* 7:11–12).

BACKGROUND

Egyptian wicker basket – כְּפִיפָה מִצְרִית: These baskets are made by bending thin willow branches into a bowl shape.

The *omer* meal-offering – מִנְחַת הָעוֹמֶר: The *omer* meal-offering, which consisted of one tenth of an ephah of barley flour, was sacrificed in the Temple on the sixteenth of Nisan, the second day of the festival of Passover. The *omer* was harvested from newly ripe barley on the second night of Passover and was prepared as roasted flour. A handful was burned on the altar, while the rest was eaten by the priests. In addition to the *omer* offering, a male sheep was sacrificed as a burnt-offering, together with a wine libation and two-tenths of an ephah of wheat flour as a meal-offering. Once the *omer* offering was sacrificed, the general populace was permitted to eat grain from the new harvest. It is a mitzva by Torah law to count the days from the sixteenth of Nisan, the day the *omer* meal-offering was brought, until the festival of *Shavuot.* This mitzva is known as *sefirat haomer,* the counting of the *omer.*

מַשְׁקֶה וְאַחַר כָּךְ מַקְרִיב אֶת מִנְחָתָהּ, דְּאִי מִשּׁוּם מְגִילָּה, הָא אִימְחִיקָא לָהּ.

that the priest would first **give** her the water of the *sota* **to drink, and** only **afterward** would he **sacrifice her meal-offering.** Therefore, **if** the concern were **due to the scroll,** it would no longer be applicable, as **it was** already **erased**[N] in the water of the *sota* before the meal-offering was brought. The efforts to fatigue her by making her hold the meal-offering must indicate that the Torah is protective of her.

״כָּל הַמְּנָחוֹת״ וכו׳. וּרְמִינְהוּ: סֵדֶר מְנָחוֹת כֵּיצַד? אָדָם מֵבִיא מִנְחָה מִתּוֹךְ בֵּיתוֹ בִּקְלָתוֹת שֶׁל כֶּסֶף וְשֶׁל זָהָב, וְנוֹתְנָהּ לְתוֹךְ כְּלִי שָׁרֵת וּמְקַדְּשָׁהּ בִּכְלִי שָׁרֵת, וְנוֹתֵן עָלֶיהָ שַׁמְנָהּ וּלְבוֹנָתָהּ וּמוֹלִיכָהּ אֵצֶל כֹּהֵן, וְכֹהֵן מוֹלִיכָהּ אֵצֶל מִזְבֵּחַ וּמַגִּישָׁהּ בְּקֶרֶן דְּרוֹמִית מַעֲרָבִית כְּנֶגֶד חוּדָּהּ שֶׁל קֶרֶן וְדַיּוֹ.

It was taught in the mishna: **All meal-offerings,** from their beginning until their end, are placed in service vessels and remain there. The Gemara **raises a contradiction** from the *Tosefta* (*Menaḥot* 1:16): **What is the procedure for meal-offerings?**[H] **A person brings his meal-offering from his property in baskets** [*kelatot*][L] **of silver and of gold, and** when he reaches the Temple **he places it in a service vessel and sanctifies it in** the **service vessel, and he puts its oil and frankincense on it, and he carries it to the priest. And the priest** then **carries it to the altar and brings it near to the southwest horn** of the altar, **opposite the corner of the horn** of the altar. **And this is sufficient.**

וּמְסַלֵּק אֶת הַלְּבוֹנָה לְצַד אֶחָד, וְקוֹמֵץ מִמָּקוֹם שֶׁנִּתְרַבָּה שַׁמְנָהּ, וְנוֹתְנוֹ לְתוֹךְ כְּלִי שָׁרֵת וּמְקַדְּשׁוֹ בִּכְלִי שָׁרֵת. וּמְלַקֵּט אֶת לְבוֹנָתָהּ וְנוֹתְנָהּ עַל גַּבָּיו וּמַעֲלֶה אוֹתוֹ לְגַבֵּי מִזְבֵּחַ, וּמַעֲלֵהוּ וּמַקְטִירוֹ בִּכְלִי שָׁרֵת, וּמוֹלְחוֹ וְנוֹתְנוֹ עַל גַּבֵּי הָאִישִּׁים.

The *baraita* continues: **And** the priest then **removes the frankincense to one side, and he removes a handful from the place where its oil has accumulated** and mixed with the flour, **and he puts** the handful **into a service vessel and consecrates it in** the **service vessel. And he** then **gathers its frankincense and puts it on top of** the handful **and brings it up onto the altar. And he brings it up and burns it in** the **service vessel; and he salts it and places it upon the fires.**

קָרַב הַקּוֹמֶץ – שְׁיָרֶיהָ נֶאֱכָלִין, וְרַשָּׁאִין הַכֹּהֲנִים לִיתֵּן לְתוֹכָהּ יַיִן וְשֶׁמֶן וּדְבַשׁ, וְאֵין אֲסוּרִין אֶלָּא מִלְּחַמֵּץ.

The *baraita* continues: After **the handful is sacrificed,**[H] **the remainders of** the meal-offering **are eaten. And the priests are permitted**[H] **to put wine and oil and honey in it,** even though it is prohibited to offer honey on the altar. **And they are prohibited only from allowing** the meal-offering **to become leavened.**

קָתָנֵי מִיהָא: בִּקְלָתוֹת שֶׁל כֶּסֶף וּבִקְלָתוֹת שֶׁל זָהָב! אָמַר רַב פַּפָּא, אֵימָא: בְּכֵלִים הָרְאוּיִין לִכְלֵי שָׁרֵת.

The Gemara asks: **In any event,** the *baraita* **teaches** that the meal-offering is first placed **in baskets of silver and baskets of gold** brought from one's home. This seems to contradict the mishna's statement that all other meal-offerings are initially in service vessels. **Rav Pappa said:** The mishna means to **say** that meal-offerings are placed **in vessels** of silver and gold, as **these are suitable to be service vessels** if consecrated.

מִכְּלָל דִּכְפִיפָה מִצְרִית לָא חַזְיָא, כְּמַאן? דְּלָא כְּרַבִּי יוֹסֵי בְּרַבִּי יְהוּדָה! דְּתַנְיָא: כְּלֵי שָׁרֵת שֶׁעֲשָׂאָן שֶׁל עֵץ – רַבִּי פּוֹסֵל, וְרַבִּי יוֹסֵי בְּרַבִּי יְהוּדָה מַכְשִׁיר!

The Gemara notes: Since the mishna distinguishes in this regard between the meal-offering of the *sota* and all other meal-offerings, one may learn **by inference that an Egyptian wicker basket is not suitable** to be a service vessel even if it is consecrated. **In accordance with whose** opinion is this the case? It is **not in accordance with** the opinion of **Rabbi Yosei, son of Rabbi Yehuda, as it is taught** in a *baraita*: With regard to **service vessels that were made of wood,**[H] **Rabbi** Yehuda HaNasi **deems them unfit, and Rabbi Yosei, son of Rabbi Yehuda, deems them fit.**

אֲפִילּוּ תֵּימָא רַבִּי יוֹסֵי בְּרַבִּי יְהוּדָה, אֵימַר דְּאָמַר רַבִּי יוֹסֵי בְּרַבִּי יְהוּדָה – בַּחֲשׁוּבִין, בִּפְחוּתִין מִי אֲמַר? לֵית לֵיהּ לְרַבִּי יוֹסֵי בְּרַבִּי יְהוּדָה ״הַקְרִיבֵהוּ נָא לְפֶחָתֶךָ״?!

The Gemara responds: **You** can **even say that** the mishna is in accordance with the opinion of **Rabbi Yosei, son of Rabbi Yehuda. Say that Rabbi Yosei, son of Rabbi Yehuda, says** that wooden vessels are deemed fit **with regard to** those of **superior** quality; but **does he say** likewise **with regard to** vessels of **lesser** quality, e.g., a basket made of palm branches? **Doesn't Rabbi Yosei, son of Rabbi Yehuda, hold** to the principle articulated in the verse: "And when you offer the blind for a sacrifice, is it not evil! …If you would **present it now unto your governor,** will he be pleased with you or show you favor?" (Malachi 1:8)? Nothing that is unfit for presentation to a ruler may be brought to the Temple. Therefore, even Rabbi Yosei, son of Rabbi Yehuda, must agree that a basket made of palm branches cannot be a service vessel.

NOTES

It was already erased – הָא אִימְחִיקָא לָהּ: *Tosafot* note that the Gemara previously stated (7a) that after the scroll is erased the *sota* is encouraged to drink the water of the *sota* . However, according to the Gemara here she is encouraged to confess even after the scroll has been erased. The *Sefat Emet* explains that prior to the erasing of the scroll, the woman is discouraged from drinking even if she is innocent, so that the scroll with the name of God need not be erased. After the scroll has been erased, she is encouraged to drink if she is innocent, but if she is guilty she should confess her guilt instead (see *Minḥat Kenaot*).

HALAKHA

What is the procedure for meal-offerings – סֵדֶר מְנָחוֹת כֵּיצַד: The procedure for the sacrifice of meal-offerings is as follows: One who brings a meal-offering brings fine flour from his home in a vessel of silver or gold, suitable to be a service vessel. If it is a meal-offering of fine flour, he places it in a service vessel and sanctifies it in the Temple. Baked meal-offerings are baked in the Temple and broken into pieces. Oil and frankincense are placed upon the flour, and it is brought to the priest, who carries it to the altar. The priest brings it opposite the corner of the horn of the altar. He removes the frankincense to one side, removes a handful of the meal-offering from the place where the oil has accumulated, puts it into a service vessel, and sanctifies it there. He then gathers all the frankincense and places it on top of the handful in the vessel, brings the handful up to the altar, salts it, and places it on the fire (Rambam *Sefer Avoda, Hilkhot Ma'aseh HaKorbanot* 13:12).

After the handful is sacrificed – קָרַב הַקּוֹמֶץ: After the priest places the handful on the fire of the altar and most of it has ignited, the remainder of the meal-offering may be eaten by the priests. However, the meal-offering brought by a priest is not eaten at all (Rambam *Sefer Avoda, Hilkhot Ma'aseh HaKorbanot* 12:9, 13).

The priests are permitted, etc. – וְרַשָּׁאִין הַכֹּהֲנִים וכו׳: The priests are permitted to eat meal-offerings together with other foods and are even permitted to place honey on them. However, they are prohibited by Torah law from eating them in leavened form (Rambam *Sefer Avoda, Hilkhot Ma'aseh HaKorbanot* 12:14).

Service vessels that were made of wood – כְּלֵי שָׁרֵת שֶׁעֲשָׂאָן שֶׁל עֵץ: Service vessels may be fashioned only of metallic substances; if they are made of wood or glass they are invalid. This ruling is in accordance with Rabbi Yehuda HaNasi's opinion, as the *halakha* is generally ruled in his favor in disputes with his colleagues (Rambam *Sefer Avoda, Hilkhot Beit HaBeḥira* 1:18).

LANGUAGE

Baskets [*kelatot*] – קְלָתוֹת: From the Greek κάλαθος, *kalathos*, a basket with a narrow base used primarily by women for holding wool and work utensils.

״וְנוֹתְנָהּ לִכְלִי שָׁרֵת וּמְקַדְּשָׁהּ בִּכְלִי שָׁרֵת״. שָׁמְעַתְּ מִינָּהּ: כְּלֵי שָׁרֵת אֵין מְקַדְּשִׁין אֶלָּא מִדַּעַת! אֵימָא: נוֹתְנָהּ בִּכְלִי שָׁרֵת לְקַדְּשָׁהּ בִּכְלִי שָׁרֵת.

§ The *baraita* states: **He places it in a service vessel and sanctifies it in the service vessel.** The Gemara asks: Can one **learn from** the unnecessary repetition of the term service vessel, that **service vessels can sanctify** their contents **only with intention?**[NH] Must one place the meal-offering in the service vessel with express intent to sanctify it? The Gemara answers: **Say: He** simply **places it in the service vessel** in order **to sanctify it in the service vessel.** He need not to intend to sanctify it.

״וְנוֹתֵן עָלֶיהָ שַׁמְנָהּ וּלְבוֹנָתָהּ״, שֶׁנֶּאֱמַר: ״וְיָצַק עָלֶיהָ שֶׁמֶן וְנָתַן עָלֶיהָ לְבֹנָה״.

§ The *baraita* teaches: The owner of the meal-offering **puts its oil and frankincense on it.** The Gemara cites the source of this *halakha*: **As it is stated:** "And when anyone brings a meal-offering unto the Lord, his offering shall be of fine flour; **and he shall pour oil upon it, and put frankincense thereon**" (Leviticus 2:1).

״וּמוֹלִיכָהּ אֵצֶל כֹּהֵן״, דִּכְתִיב: ״וֶהֱבִיאָהּ אֶל בְּנֵי אַהֲרֹן״ וגו׳.

The *baraita* states: **And he carries it to the priest.** The Gemara cites the source: **As it is written: "And he shall bring it to Aaron's sons,** the priests" (Leviticus 2:2).

״וְכֹהֵן מוֹלִיכָהּ אֵצֶל מִזְבֵּחַ״, דִּכְתִיב: ״וְהִגִּישָׁהּ אֵצֶל הַמִּזְבֵּחַ״.

The *baraita* states: **And the priest** then **carries it to the altar.** The Gemara cites the source: **As it is written:** "And you shall bring the meal-offering that is made of these things unto the Lord; and it shall be presented unto the priest, **and he shall bring it unto the altar**" (Leviticus 2:8).

״מַגִּישָׁהּ בְּקֶרֶן דְּרוֹמִית מַעֲרָבִית כְּנֶגֶד חוּדָּהּ שֶׁל קֶרֶן וְדַיּוֹ״. מְנָלַן?

The *baraita* states: The priest **brings it near to the southwest horn** of the altar, **opposite the corner of the horn. And** this **is sufficient.** The Gemara asks: **From where do we** derive this?

דִּכְתִיב: ״וְזֹאת תּוֹרַת הַמִּנְחָה הַקְרֵב אוֹתָהּ בְּנֵי אַהֲרֹן לִפְנֵי ה׳ אֶל פְּנֵי הַמִּזְבֵּחַ״. וְתַנְיָא: ״לִפְנֵי ה׳״, יָכוֹל בַּמַּעֲרָב? תַּלְמוּד לוֹמַר: ״אֶל פְּנֵי הַמִּזְבֵּחַ״, אִי ״אֶל פְּנֵי הַמִּזְבֵּחַ״ יָכוֹל בַּדָּרוֹם? תַּלְמוּד לוֹמַר: ״לִפְנֵי ה׳״. הָא כֵּיצַד? מַגִּישָׁהּ בְּקֶרֶן דְּרוֹמִית מַעֲרָבִית כְּנֶגֶד חוּדָּהּ שֶׁל קֶרֶן וְדַיּוֹ.

The Gemara responds: **As it is written: "And this is the law of the meal-offering: The sons of Aaron shall offer it before the Lord in front of the altar"** (Leviticus 6:7). **And it is taught** in a *baraita*: When the verse states: **"Before the Lord,"** one **might** have understood this to mean **on the western side** of the altar, opposite the Holy of Holies. Therefore, **the verse states: "In front of the altar."** This must be the south of the altar, where the ramp is located. **If** the verse had stated only: **In front of the altar,** one **might** have understood it to mean specifically **on the southern side.** Therefore, **the verse states: "Before the Lord,"** indicating the western side. **How** can **these** texts be reconciled? The priest **brings it near to the southwest corner** of the altar, **opposite the corner of the horn. And** this **is sufficient.**

רַבִּי אֶלְעָזָר אוֹמֵר: יָכוֹל יַגִּישֶׁנָּה בְּמַעֲרָבָהּ שֶׁל קֶרֶן אוֹ לִדְרוֹמָהּ שֶׁל קֶרֶן? אָמַרְתָּ: כָּל מָקוֹם שֶׁאַתָּה מוֹצֵא שְׁנֵי מִקְרָאוֹת, אֶחָד מְקַיֵּים עַצְמוֹ וּמְקַיֵּים דִּבְרֵי חֲבֵירוֹ, וְאֶחָד מְקַיֵּים עַצְמוֹ וּמְבַטֵּל דִּבְרֵי חֲבֵירוֹ, מַנִּיחִין אֶת שֶׁמְּקַיֵּים עַצְמוֹ וּמְבַטֵּל חֲבֵירוֹ וְתוֹפְסִין אֶת שֶׁמְּקַיֵּים עַצְמוֹ וּמְקַיֵּים חֲבֵירוֹ. כְּשֶׁאַתָּה אוֹמֵר ״לִפְנֵי ה׳״ בַּמַּעֲרָב – בִּטַּלְתָּה ״אֶל פְּנֵי הַמִּזְבֵּחַ״ בַּדָּרוֹם, וּכְשֶׁאַתָּה אוֹמֵר ״אֶל פְּנֵי הַמִּזְבֵּחַ״ בַּדָּרוֹם – קִיַּימְתָּה ״לִפְנֵי ה׳״ בַּמַּעֲרָב. הָא כֵּיצַד? מַגִּישָׁהּ לִדְרוֹמָהּ שֶׁל קֶרֶן.

Rabbi Elazar says another interpretation: One **might** have thought that **he offers it up on the western side of the corner or on the southern side of the corner. Say: Anywhere you find two verses, one** of which **fulfills itself and fulfills the statement of the other, and one** of which **fulfills itself and nullifies the statement of the other, leave** the verse **that fulfills itself and nullifies the other, and seize the one that fulfills itself and fulfills the other.** The principle is applied as follows: **When you say: "Before the Lord," on the western side, you have nullified** the other part of the verse: **"In front of the altar," on the southern side. But when you say: "In front of the altar," on the southern side, you have** also **fulfilled: "Before the Lord," on the western side. How so? He brings it near to the southern side of the corner.**

וְהֵיכָן קִיַּימְתָּהּ? אֲמַר רַב אַשִׁי, קָסָבַר הַאי תַּנָּא: כּוּלֵּיהּ מִזְבֵּחַ בַּצָּפוֹן קָאֵי.

The Gemara asks: **But where have you fulfilled** the phrase "before the Lord"? **Rav Ashi said: This** ***tanna*** **holds** that **the entire altar stands in the north** of the Temple courtyard. Therefore, the entire southern side of the altar stood opposite the Holy of Holies in the west, and it can therefore be called: Before the Lord.

מַאי ״וְדַיּוֹ״? אֲמַר רַב אַשִׁי: אִיצְטְרִיךְ, סָלְקָא דַּעְתָּךְ אָמִינָא תִּיבָּעֵי הַגָּשַׁת מִנְחָה גּוּפָהּ. קָמַשְׁמַע לַן.

The Gemara asks: **What** is taught by the phrase: **And** this **is sufficient? Rav Ashi said:** This phrase **was necessary,** as otherwise it might **enter your mind to say: Require** the priest **to bring the meal-offering itself near** to the corner of the altar without the use of a vessel. The *baraita* **teaches us** that this is not so, and one can bring it to the altar in its service vessel.

NOTES

Service vessels can sanctify only with intention – **כְּלֵי שָׁרֵת אֵין מְקַדְּשִׁין אֶלָּא מִדַּעַת:** *Tosefot HaRosh* cites a textual variant entertaining the possibility that placing an item in a service vessel can render it sanctified even without intention. Although the Rambam rules that intention is necessary for a service vessel to sanctify that which is placed in it, the Meiri disagrees.

HALAKHA

Service vessels can sanctify only with intention – **אֵין מְקַדְּשִׁין אֶלָּא מִדַּעַת:** Service vessels sanctify items placed in them only if one placed the items there with that intention (Rambam *Sefer Avoda, Hilkhot Pesulei HaMukdashin* 3:20).

The Gemara asks: **And** why not **say** that this is **indeed** so? The Gemara responds: **The verse states:** "And you shall bring the meal-offering that is made of these things unto the Lord; **and it shall be presented unto the priest, and he shall bring it unto the altar**" (Leviticus 2:8); **just as presentation to the priest is in a vessel, so too bringing** it **to the altar** must be **in a vessel.**

וְאֵימָא הָכִי נַמִי! אָמַר קְרָא: "וְהִקְרִיבָהּ אֶל הַכֹּהֵן וגו׳ וְהִגִּישָׁהּ אֶל הַמִּזְבֵּחַ", מָה הַקְרָבָה אֵצֶל כֹּהֵן בִּכְלִי, אַף הַגָּשָׁה אֵצֶל מִזְבֵּחַ בִּכְלִי.

The *baraita* states: **And he removes its frankincense to one side.** The Gemara explains: This is done **in order that** the frankincense **not be removed along with the meal-offering**[N] when the priest removes a handful. **As we learned** in a mishna (*Menaḥot* 6a): If he **removed** the **handful and a pebble, or a grain of salt, or a crumb** [*koret*][L] **of frankincense came out in his hand,**[H] **it is invalid.** The handful must be entirely fine flour.

"וּמְסַלֵּק אֶת לְבוֹנָתָהּ לְצַד אֶחָד", כִּי הֵיכִי דְּלָא תִּקְמוֹץ בַּהֲדֵי מִנְחָה, כִּדְתְנַן: קָמַץ, וְעָלָה בְּיָדוֹ צְרוֹר אוֹ גַּרְגִּר מֶלַח אוֹ קוֹרֶט לְבוֹנָה – פָּסוּל.

The *baraita* continues: **And he removes a handful from the place where its oil has accumulated.** The Gemara asks: **From where do we** derive this? **As it is written:** "And he shall take from there his handful **of the fine flour thereof, and of the oil thereof**" (Leviticus 2:2). The Torah also states: "And the priest shall make the memorial part of it smoke, even **of the groats thereof, and of the oil thereof**" (Leviticus 2:16). The handful should be taken from the area where there is an abundance of oil.

"וְקוֹמֵץ מִמָּקוֹם שֶׁנִּתְרַבָּה שַׁמְנָהּ". מְנָלַן? דִּכְתִיב: "מִסָּלְתָּהּ וּמִשַּׁמְנָהּ...מִגִּרְשָׂהּ וּמִשַּׁמְנָהּ".

The *baraita* continues: **And he puts** the handful **into a service vessel and sanctifies it in** the **service vessel.** The Gemara asks: **Why do I** need this sanctification? **He has** already **sanctified it once,** when he initially brought it to the Temple. The Gemara responds: The sanctification here is **just as with** the **blood** of the offerings. **Although the knife sanctifies blood**[N] by contact with **the neck of the animal,** since the knife itself is a service vessel, the priest **sanctifies it again** when he collects it **in the service vessel. Here too, it is not different;**[N] the meal-offering must be sanctified twice.

"וְנוֹתְנוֹ לְתוֹךְ כְּלִי שָׁרֵת וּמְקַדְּשׁוֹ בִּכְלִי שָׁרֵת". לָמָּה לִי? הָא קַדְּשֵׁהּ חֲדָא זִימְנָא! מִידֵי דְּהָוֵה אַדָּם, דָּם אַף עַל גַּב דְּקַדְּשִׁתֵּיהּ סַכִּין בְּצַוַּאר בְּהֵמָה, הֲדַר מַקְדִּישׁ לֵיהּ בִּכְלִי שָׁרֵת, הָכָא נַמִי לָא שְׁנָא.

The *baraita* continues: **And he gathers its frankincense and puts it on top of** the handful. The Gemara cites the source: **As it is written:** "And he shall take up from his handful, of the fine flour of the meal-offering, and of the oil thereof, **and all the frankincense which is upon the meal-offering**" (Leviticus 6:8).

"וּמְלַקֵּט אֶת לְבוֹנָתָהּ וְנוֹתְנָהּ עַל גַּבָּיו", דִּכְתִיב: "וְאֵת כׇּל הַלְּבוֹנָה אֲשֶׁר עַל הַמִּנְחָה".

The *baraita* continues: **And he** then **brings it up**

"וּמַעֲלֵהוּ

NOTES

In order that it not be removed along with the meal-offering – דְּלָא תִּקְמוֹץ בַּהֲדֵי מִנְחָה: The verse states: "He shall take from there his handful" (Leviticus 2:2). If anything else is in his hand when he removes the handful, the handful will not be whole (Rashi; *Tosefot HaRash*).

Although the knife sanctifies blood – אַף עַל גַּב דְּקַדְּשִׁתֵּיהּ סַכִּין: The Gemara apparently indicates that the slaughtering knives in the Temple must be consecrated as service vessels. According to Rabbeinu Efrayim, however, other statements in the Gemara prove that the knife need not be a service vessel. The *Tosefot HaRash* and the *Tosefot HaRosh* discuss this issue, and both note that there is no conclusive proof for either opinion. It is possible that the knife must be consecrated as a service vessel *ab initio*, but if one slaughtered with an unconsecrated knife the offering would be valid after the fact.

Here too it is not different – הָכָא נַמִי לָא שְׁנָא: Animal offerings and meal-offerings are comparable in many ways. There are four sacrificial rites involved in animal offerings: Slaughter, receiving the blood, carrying it to the altar, and sprinkling it on the altar. There are likewise four sacrificial rites involved in the meal-offering: Removing the handful from the vessel, placing it in a service vessel, carrying it to the altar, and burning it on the altar. The initial placement of the entire meal-offering in a service vessel is not considered a true part of its service. The structure of tractate *Menaḥot*, which deals with meal-offerings, is parallel to that of tractate *Zevaḥim*, which deals with animal offerings.

LANGUAGE

Crumb [*koret*] – קוֹרֶט: This word refers to a small item or fraction, similar to the Greek κεράτιον, *keration*. The word carat, a measurement used for the weight of diamonds, may be derived from this Greek word. However, both may derive originally from older Semitic words. Some sources assert that *koret* is a variation of the word *keretz*, meaning slice or small piece.

HALAKHA

Came out in his hand – עָלָה בְּיָדוֹ: If the priest removed the handful, and a pebble, a grain of salt, or a crumb of frankincense came up with it, it is invalid (Rambam *Sefer Avoda, Hilkhot Pesulei HaMukdashin* 11:3).

Perek **II**
Daf **15** Amud **a**

and burns it in the **service vessel.** The Gemara asks: **Does he** really **burn it in a service vessel? Rather, say: He brings it up** to the altar **in a service vessel** in order **to burn it.**

וּמַקְטִירוֹ בִּכְלִי שָׁרֵת". בִּכְלִי שָׁרֵת מַקְטִיר לֵיהּ? אֶלָּא אֵימָא: מַעֲלֵהוּ בִּכְלִי שָׁרֵת לְהַקְטִירוֹ.

The *baraita* continues: **And he salts it and places it on the fires.** The Gemara cites the source: **As it is written: "And every meal-offering of yours you shall season with salt"** (Leviticus 2:13).

"וּמוֹלְחוֹ וְנוֹתְנוֹ עַל גַּבֵּי הָאִישִּׁים" – דִּכְתִיב: "וְכׇל קׇרְבַּן מִנְחָתְךָ בַּמֶּלַח תִּמְלָח" וגו׳.

The *baraita* continues: After **the handful is sacrificed, the remainders of** the meal-offering **are eaten.** The Gemara asks: **From where do we** derive this? **As it is written:** "And he shall bring it to Aaron's sons, the priests… **and the priest shall make the memorial part thereof smoke** upon the altar" (Leviticus 2:2). The memorial part is the handful. **And it is written** afterward: **"But that which is left of the meal-offering shall be for Aaron and his sons"** (Leviticus 2:3).

"קָרַב הַקּוֹמֶץ – שְׁיָרֶיהָ נֶאֱכָלִין". מְנָלַן? דִּכְתִיב: "וְהִקְטִיר הַכֹּהֵן אֶת אַזְכָּרָתָהּ" וגו׳, וּכְתִיב: "וְהַנּוֹתֶרֶת מִן הַמִּנְחָה לְאַהֲרֹן וּלְבָנָיו".

״קָרַב הַקּוֹמֶץ״ – לְמָר כִּדְאִית לֵיהּ וּלְמָר כִּדְאִית לֵיהּ, דְּאִיתְּמַר: הַקּוֹמֶץ מֵאֵימָתַי מַתִּיר שִׁירַיִים בַּאֲכִילָה? רַבִּי חֲנִינָא אָמַר: מִשֶּׁתִּשְׁלוֹט בּוֹ הָאוּר, רַבִּי יוֹחָנָן אָמַר: מִשֶּׁתַּצִּית הָאוּר בְּרוּבּוֹ.

The *baraita* uses the phrase: After **the handful is sacrificed.** This phrase can be understood **according to** one **Sage as he holds, and according to** another **Sage as he holds. As it is stated** that there is a dispute between the Sages: **From when does the** sacrifice of the **handful render the remainder** of the meal-offering **permitted**[H] **for consumption** by the priests? **Rabbi Ḥanina says:** It is **when the fire takes hold of it,** i.e., when it ignites. **Rabbi Yoḥanan says:** It is **when the fire consumes most of** the handful. Each of these *amora'im* understands the *baraita* in accordance with his opinion.

״וְרַשָּׁאִין הַכֹּהֲנִים לִיתֵּן לְתוֹכוֹ יַיִן וְשֶׁמֶן וּדְבַשׁ״. מַאי טַעְמָא? אָמַר קְרָא: ״לְמָשְׁחָה״ – לִגְדוּלָּה, כְּדֶרֶךְ שֶׁהַמְּלָכִים אוֹכְלִין.

The *baraita* continues: **And the priests are permitted**[N] **to put wine and oil and honey in** the remainder of the meal-offering. **What is the reason? The verse states** with regard to the gifts given to the priests: "And I, behold, I have given you the charge of My *terumot*… **for a consecrated portion**" (Numbers 18:8). The phrase "for a consecrated portion" indicates that the gifts are given as a mark of **greatness** and should be eaten **in the manner that the kings eat.**

״וְאֵין אֲסוּרִין אֶלָּא מִלְּחַמֵּץ״, דִּכְתִיב: ״לֹא תֵאָפֶה חָמֵץ חֶלְקָם״, אָמַר רַבִּי שִׁמְעוֹן בֶּן לָקִישׁ: אֲפִילּוּ חֶלְקָם לֹא תֵאָפֶה חָמֵץ.

The *baraita* concludes: **And they are prohibited only from allowing** the meal-offering **to become leavened.** The Gemara cites the source: **As it is written** with regard to meal-offerings: **"It shall not be baked with leaven. Their portion** I have given it of My offerings made by fire" (Leviticus 6:10). **Rabbi Shimon ben Lakish says:** One should read the verse as if the phrase "their portion" is part of the same phrase as the prohibition of baking with leaven. This teaches that **even their portion,**[N] i.e., the portion given to the priests, **shall not be baked with leaven.**[H]

״כׇּל הַמְּנָחוֹת״ כו׳. וְכׇל הַמְּנָחוֹת טְעוּנוֹת שֶׁמֶן וּלְבוֹנָה? וְהָאִיכָּא מִנְחַת חוֹטֵא, דְּרַחֲמָנָא אָמַר: ״לֹא יָשִׂים עָלֶיהָ שֶׁמֶן וְלֹא יִתֵּן עָלֶיהָ לְבֹנָה״!

§ The mishna states: **All** other **meal-offerings** require oil and frankincense. The Gemara asks: **But** do **all** other **meal-offerings** actually **require oil and frankincense? But isn't there the meal-offering of a sinner,**[HN] with regard to **which the Merciful One states: "He shall put no oil upon it, neither shall he put any frankincense thereon;** for it is a sin-offering" (Leviticus 5:11).

הָכִי קָאָמַר: כׇּל הַמְּנָחוֹת טְעוּנוֹת שֶׁמֶן וּלְבוֹנָה, וּבָאוֹת מִן הַחִיטִּין, וּבָאוֹת סֹלֶת; מִנְחַת חוֹטֵא, אַף עַל פִּי שֶׁאֵינָהּ טְעוּנָה שֶׁמֶן וּלְבוֹנָה – בָּאָה מִן הַחִטִּין וּבָאָה סֹלֶת; מִנְחַת הָעוֹמֶר אַף עַל פִּי שֶׁהִיא בָּאָה מִן הַשְּׂעוֹרִין – טְעוּנָה שֶׁמֶן וּלְבוֹנָה, וּבָאָה גֶּרֶשׂ; וְזוֹ אֵינָהּ טְעוּנָה לֹא שֶׁמֶן וְלֹא לְבוֹנָה, וּבָאָה מִן הַשְּׂעוֹרִין, וּבָאָה קֶמַח.

The Gemara responds: **This is what** the mishna **is saying: All meal-offerings** other than that of the *sota* **require oil and frankincense, and they are brought from wheat; and** they **are** also **brought from fine flour.** However, **the meal-offering of a sinner, even though it does not require oil and frankincense,** must still be **brought from wheat and brought from fine flour.** Similarly, **the** *omer* **meal-offering, even though it is brought from barley, requires oil and frankincense, and it is brought** as **groats.**[B] **But this one,** the *sota* meal-offering, **requires neither**[N] **oil nor frankincense, and it is brought from barley and brought** as unsifted **flour.** While the meal-offering of a sinner and the *omer* meal-offering are similar to other meal-offerings in one of these respects, the *sota* meal-offering is different in both respects.

תַּנְיָא, אָמַר רַבִּי שִׁמְעוֹן: בְּדִין הוּא שֶׁתְּהֵא מִנְחַת חוֹטֵא טְעוּנָה שֶׁמֶן וּלְבוֹנָה, שֶׁלֹּא יְהֵא חוֹטֵא נִשְׂכָּר. וּמִפְּנֵי מָה אֵינָהּ טְעוּנָה? שֶׁלֹּא יְהֵא קׇרְבָּנוֹ מְהוּדָּר.

It is taught in a *baraita* (*Tosefta* 1:10) that **Rabbi Shimon said: By right,** it should have been the *halakha* **that the meal-offering of a sinner requires oil and frankincense, so that a sinner should not** stand to **gain** by not having to pay for them. **For what** reason **does** the verse **not require** them? It is **so that his offering will not be of superior** quality.

BACKGROUND

Groats – גֶּרֶשׂ: Wheat and barley were ground in the following manner: First, one would grind the grains crudely with some becoming finely ground flour and the rest remaining coarse. After the contents were ground, they were sifted to separate the finely ground flour from the coarser meal. The finely ground flour was considered of lower quality, while the coarser meal was considered more desirable. This coarse meal is called *solet* when made from wheat and *geres* when made from barley.

HALAKHA

From when does the sacrifice of the handful render the remainder permitted – הַקּוֹמֶץ מֵאֵימָתַי מַתִּיר שִׁירַיִים: The remainder of the offering is permitted for consumption once the fire has consumed most of the handful. The Rambam rules in accordance with the opinion of Rabbi Yoḥanan and his understanding of tractate *Menaḥot* (Rambam *Sefer Avoda, Hilkhot Ma'aseh HaKorbanot* 12:13 and *Kesef Mishne* there).

Even their portion shall not be baked with leaven – אֲפִילּוּ חֶלְקָם לֹא תֵאָפֶה חָמֵץ: It is prohibited to allow any part of the meal-offering to become leavened, even the portion eaten by the priests. One who causes the offering to become leavened is liable to be flogged (Rambam *Sefer Avoda, Hilkhot Ma'aseh HaKorbanot* 12:14).

Meal-offering of a sinner – מִנְחַת חוֹטֵא: No oil or frankincense is placed on the meal-offering of a sinner (Rambam *Sefer Avoda, Hilkhot Ma'aseh HaKorbanot* 12:7).

NOTES

The priests are permitted, etc. – וְרַשָּׁאִין הַכֹּהֲנִים וכו׳: The Torah (Leviticus 2:11) prohibits leavening or adding honey to the portion of a meal-offering burned on the altar. As the prohibition against leavening applies the remainder of the offering as well, one might assume that the same is true with regard to honey. Therefore, the *baraita* states that honey may in fact be placed on the remainder (*Minḥa Ḥareva*).

Even their portion – אֲפִילּוּ חֶלְקָם: This interpretation does fit the straightforward meaning of the verse, which states literally: "It shall not be baked with leaven. Their portion I have given it of My offerings made by fire" (Leviticus 6:10). According to Rashi, Reish Lakish places the period after the word "portion," indicating that it is the object of the first sentence. Others explain that according to Reish Lakish, the clear intention of the entire verse is that no part of the meal-offering may be allowed to leaven. His reading of the phrase "their portion" as connected to "not baked with leaven" is meant only as an allusion to the straightforward meaning of the verse.

Meal-offering of a sinner – מִנְחַת חוֹטֵא: The meal-offering of a sinner is a poor man's sin-offering. Generally, those obligated to bring a sliding-scale sin-offering must bring a lamb or a goat or, if they cannot afford one, two birds. One who cannot afford even this brings the meal-offering of a sinner.

This one requires neither, etc. – וְזוֹ אֵינָהּ טְעוּנָה וכו׳: The Ramban notes that the Hebrew word for barley, *seora*, is similar to the word for an angry storm [*se'ara*]. The verse (Numbers 5:25) refers to this meal-offering as a *minḥat kenaot*, a meal-offering of jealousy. For this reason, the *sota* drinks out of an earthenware cup, a symbol of breaking and destruction, and dust is placed in the water of the *sota*, symbolizing death. The *Sefer HaḤinnukh* explains that since oil is used for anointing kings, it is not proper to use oil for offerings related to sin.

וּבְדִין הוּא שֶׁתְּהֵא חַטַּאת חֵלֶב טְעוּנָה נְסָכִים, שֶׁלֹּא יְהֵא חוֹטֵא נִשְׂכָּר. וּמִפְּנֵי מָה אֵינָהּ טְעוּנָה? שֶׁלֹּא יְהֵא קׇרְבָּנוֹ מְהוּדָּר.

And by right, it should have been the *halakha* **that a sin-offering** brought for transgression of a prohibition punishable by *karet*, e.g., consumption **of forbidden fat,**[NH] **requires** fine flour and **libations** of oil, and wine. Just as burnt-offerings and peace-offerings require these, a sin-offering should require them as well **so that a sinner should not** stand to **gain** by not having to pay for them. **For what** reason **does it not require** them? It is **so that his offering will not be** of **superior** quality.

אֲבָל חַטָּאתוֹ שֶׁל מְצוֹרָע וַאֲשָׁמוֹ טְעוּנִין נְסָכִים, לְפִי שֶׁאֵין בָּאִין עַל חֵטְא. אִינִי? וְהָאָמַר רַבִּי שְׁמוּאֵל בַּר נַחְמָנִי אָמַר רַבִּי יוֹנָתָן: עַל שִׁבְעָה דְּבָרִים נְגָעִים בָּאִין וכו'! הָתָם מִנִּגְעֵיהּ הוּא דְּאִיכַּפַּר לֵיהּ, כִּי מַיְיתֵי קׇרְבָּן – לְאִשְׁתְּרוּיֵי בְּקָדָשִׁים הוּא דְּקָא מַיְיתֵי.

But the sin-offering of a leper[B] **and his guilt-offering require libations, as they are not brought on account of a sin.** The Gemara asks: **Is that so? But didn't Rabbi Shmuel bar Naḥmani say** that **Rabbi Yonatan says: Leprosy comes on account of seven matters.**[N] Leprosy develops on account of sin, so by extension the leper's offerings are also brought on account of sin. The Gemara answers: **There, from** the time he contracts **his leprosy** he **gains atonement for** his sin through the plague of leprosy itself. Consequently, **when he brings the offering, he brings it** only **in order to permit him** to eat **sacrificial** food.

אֶלָּא מֵעַתָּה, חַטַּאת נָזִיר תְּהֵא טְעוּנָה נְסָכִים, לְפִי שֶׁאֵינָהּ בָּאָה עַל חֵטְא! סָבַר לַהּ כְּרַבִּי אֶלְעָזָר הַקַּפָּר, דְּאָמַר: נָזִיר נַמִי חוֹטֵא הוּא.

The Gemara asks: **If that is so, then the sin-offering of a nazirite**[B] **should require libations, because it is not brought on account of a sin.** The Gemara answers: Rabbi Shimon **holds in accordance with** the opinion of **Rabbi Elazar HaKappar, who says: The nazirite is also a sinner,** since he denies himself wine unnecessarily.

״רַבָּן גַּמְלִיאֵל אוֹמֵר: כְּשֵׁם״ כו׳. תַּנְיָא, אָמַר לָהֶן רַבָּן גַּמְלִיאֵל לַחֲכָמִים: סוֹפְרִים, הַנִּיחוּ לִי וְאֶדְרְשֶׁנָּה כְּמִין חוֹמֶר,

The mishna states that **Rabban Gamliel says: Just as** her actions were the actions of an animal, so too, her offering is animal food. **It is taught** in a *baraita* that **Rabban Gamliel said to the Sages: Scribes, permit me, and I will explain it as a type of decorative wreath** [*ḥomer*],[L] i.e., an allegory.

NOTES

Sin-offering of forbidden fat – חַטַּאת חֵלֶב: Certain sin-offerings are brought for unintentional transgression of prohibitions that are punishable by *karet* when violated intentionally. All such sin-offerings are referred to as a sin-offering of forbidden fat, as distinguished from communal sin-offerings or the sin-offering of a nazirite. Rashi explains that this name is used as a general term because the prohibition: "You shall eat neither fat nor blood" (Leviticus 3:17), immediately precedes the *halakhot* of sin-offerings in the Torah. The Rosh suggests an alternative explanation, that this sin is particularly common. It could easily happen that a butcher would fail to remove all of the forbidden fats from the animal, resulting in the consumer unintentionally violating the prohibition. Furthermore, once the fat has been removed from the animal it is difficult to distinguish between permitted and forbidden fats, and a person is therefore likely to eat the forbidden fat unwittingly, requiring him to bring a sin-offering.

On account of seven matters, etc. – עַל שִׁבְעָה דְּבָרִים וכו׳: In tractate *Arakhin* these seven matters are enumerated and derived from verses. They are: Evil speech, murder, an oath taken in vain, forbidden sexual relations, arrogance, robbery, and envy.

HALAKHA

Sin-offering of forbidden fat – חַטַּאת חֵלֶב: Libations are not brought to accompany guilt-offerings and sin-offerings, with the exception of the sin-offering and guilt-offering of a leper. The Torah expressly instructs that these be accompanied by libations (Rambam *Sefer Avoda, Hilkhot Ma'aseh HaKorbanot* 2:2–3).

LANGUAGE

Decorative wreath [*ḥomer*] – חוֹמֶר: The text here reads: *Ḥomer*, which is understood to mean a ring on which spices are hung. This indicates that the explanation provided is homiletical, adding additional ideas like a spice adds flavor. Some understood the word to be related to the term *ḥumra*, meaning stringency. Rav Se'adya Gaon's text reads: *Homer*, which he explains is derived from Aramaic and denotes a story.

BACKGROUND

The sin-offering of a leper – חַטַּאת מְצוֹרָע: The illness referred to in the Torah as *tzara'at* is traditionally translated as leprosy, although it is not identical medically to that disease. The *halakhot* of leprosy are recorded in the book of Leviticus in the portions of *Tazria* and *Metzora* (see Leviticus chapters 13–14). In the Mishna, tractate *Nega'im* deals exclusively with different types of leprosy. After a leper has been healed, he must follow a procedure established by the Torah (Leviticus 14:1–32), part of which, e.g., shaving his hair and cutting his fingernails, is performed outside the Temple. Afterward, the leper comes to the Temple with a lamb for a guilt-offering and a *log* of oil for waving by the priest. After the sacrifice of the guilt-offering, the priest applies some of the animal's blood to the leper's right earlobe, right thumb, and right big toe. Next, the priest takes some of the oil in his hand and sprinkles it seven times opposite the Holy of Holies. Some of the remaining oil is placed on the earlobe of the leper, his thumb, and his big toe. Finally, some of the remaining oil is placed on the head of the leper. When all this has been done, the leper sacrifices a lamb as a sin-offering and a second lamb as a burnt-offering. If he is poor he sacrifices a bird instead of a lamb for both offerings.

The sin-offering of a nazirite – חַטַּאת נָזִיר: When a nazirite completes his term of naziriteship, he must bring one female lamb as a sin-offering, one male lamb as a burnt-offering, and a ram as a peace-offering (Numbers 6:13–21). He must shave his hair and burn it beneath the pot in which the meat of the peace-offering is cooked. After these offerings have been sacrificed, his period as a nazirite ends, and he is no different from anyone else. The *halakhot* of the nazirite are discussed in the Talmud in tractate *Nazir*.

דִּשְׁמָעֵיהּ לְרַבִּי מֵאִיר דְּקָאָמַר: הִיא הֶאֱכִילַתּוּ מַעֲדַנֵּי עוֹלָם לְפִיכָךְ קׇרְבָּנָהּ מַאֲכַל בְּהֵמָה, אָמַר לוֹ: הָתִינַח עֲשִׁירָה, עֲנִיָּה מַאי אִיכָּא לְמֵימַר? אֶלָּא, כְּשֵׁם שֶׁמַּעֲשֶׂיהָ מַעֲשֵׂה בְּהֵמָה, כָּךְ קׇרְבָּנָהּ מַאֲכַל בְּהֵמָה.

And why did Rabban Gamliel speak up? It was **because he heard Rabbi Meir saying** an alternative explanation: **She fed him,** i.e., her paramour, **delicacies from around the world; therefore, her offering is animal food.** Rabban Gamliel **said to him:** Your explanation **works out well** in the case of **a rich** *sota*, but with regard to **a poor** *sota*, who cannot afford such delicacies, **what is there to say? Rather,** the reason she brings an offering of animal food is: **Just as her actions were the actions of an animal, so too her offering is animal food.**

מתני׳ הָיָה מֵבִיא פַּיָלִי שֶׁל חֶרֶס, וְנוֹתֵן לְתוֹכָהּ חֲצִי לוֹג מַיִם מִן הַכִּיּוֹר; רַבִּי יְהוּדָה אוֹמֵר: רְבִיעִית. כְּשֵׁם שֶׁמְּמַעֵט בַּכְּתָב כָּךְ מְמַעֵט בַּמַּיִם.

MISHNA The priest **would bring an earthenware drinking vessel** [*peyalei*][HL] **and he would pour into it half a** ***log***[N] **of water from the basin** in the Temple. **Rabbi Yehuda says:** The priest would pour only **a quarter**-*log* of water. **Just as** Rabbi Yehuda **minimizes the writing,** as he requires that less be written on the scroll of the *sota* than do the Rabbis, **so too he minimizes the** amount of **water** to be taken from the basin for the erasing of the text.

נִכְנַס לַהֵיכָל וּפָנָה לִימִינוֹ. וּמָקוֹם הָיָה שָׁם אַמָּה עַל אַמָּה, וְטַבְלָא שֶׁל שַׁיִשׁ וְטַבַּעַת הָיְתָה קְבוּעָה בָּהּ, כְּשֶׁהוּא מַגְבִּיהָהּ, וְנוֹטֵל עָפָר מִתַּחְתֶּיהָ וְנוֹתֵן כְּדֵי שֶׁיֵּרָאֶה עַל הַמַּיִם, שֶׁנֶּאֱמַר: ״וּמִן הֶעָפָר אֲשֶׁר יִהְיֶה בְּקַרְקַע הַמִּשְׁכָּן יִקַּח הַכֹּהֵן וְנָתַן אֶל הַמָּיִם״.

The priest **would enter the Sanctuary and turn to his right.**[H] **And there was a place there,**[N] on the Sanctuary floor, with an area of **a cubit by a cubit, and a marble tablet** [*tavla*][L] was there, **and a ring was fastened to** the tablet to assist the priest **when** he **would raise** it. **And** the priest **would take** loose **dust from underneath it and place** the dust into the vessel with the water, **so that** the dust **would be visible upon the water, as it is stated:** "And the priest shall take holy water in an earthen vessel; **and of the dust that is on the floor of the Tabernacle the priest shall take, and put it into the water**" (Numbers 5:17).

גמ׳ תָּנָא: פַּיָלִי שֶׁל חֶרֶס חֲדָשָׁה, דִּבְרֵי רַבִּי יִשְׁמָעֵאל. מַאי טַעְמָא דְּרַבִּי יִשְׁמָעֵאל? גָּמַר ״כְּלִי״ ״כְּלִי״ מִמְּצוֹרָע, מָה לְהַלָּן חֶרֶס חֲדָשָׁה, אַף כָּאן חֶרֶס חֲדָשָׁה.

GEMARA The Sages **taught:** It must be **a new earthenware vessel;**[H] this is **the statement of Rabbi Yishmael.** The Gemara asks: **What is the reasoning of Rabbi Yishmael?** The Gemara answers: Rabbi Yishmael **derives** this by means of a verbal analogy between **"vessel"** in the case of the *sota* (Numbers 5:17) and **"vessel" from** the case of **a leper** (Leviticus 14:5). **Just as there,** with regard to the leper, **a new**[H] **earthenware** vessel is required, **so too here,** a **new earthenware** vessel is required.

וְהָתָם מְנָלַן? דִּכְתִיב: ״וְשָׁחַט אֶת הַצִּפּוֹר הָאֶחָת אֶל כְּלִי חֶרֶשׂ עַל מַיִם חַיִּים״, מָה מַיִם חַיִּים שֶׁלֹּא נַעֲשְׂתָה בָּהֶן מְלָאכָה, אַף כְּלִי שֶׁלֹּא נַעֲשְׂתָה בּוֹ מְלָאכָה.

And there, with regard to the leper, **from where do we** derive that a new vessel is required? The Gemara answers: **As it is written: "And he shall slaughter one of the birds in an earthen vessel over running water"** (Leviticus 14:5). **Just as running water has not been used** beforehand **for work,** i.e., once used it is no longer considered to be running, **so too** the **vessel** must **not have been used for work.**

אִי מָה לְהַלָּן מַיִם חַיִּים, אַף כָּאן מַיִם חַיִּים!

The Gemara asks: **If** this verbal analogy is extended, then **just as there, running water** from a flowing spring is required, **so too here,** with regard the *sota*, **running water** from a spring should be required for the water of a *sota*.

לְרַבִּי יִשְׁמָעֵאל הָכִי נָמֵי, דְּאָמַר רַבִּי יוֹחָנָן: מֵי כִּיּוֹר – רַבִּי יִשְׁמָעֵאל אוֹמֵר: מֵי מַעְיָן הֵן, וַחֲכָמִים אוֹמְרִים: מִשְּׁאָר מֵימוֹת הֵן.

The Gemara answers: **According to Rabbi Yishmael** it is **indeed** so, **as Rabbi Yoḥanan says:** With regard to **the water of the basin** in the Temple **Rabbi Yishmael says: It is** collected from **spring water. And the Rabbis say: It** may also be **from** any **other** type **of water**[H] and need not be collected from spring water.

אִיכָּא לְמִיפְרַךְ: מָה לִמְצוֹרָע שֶׁכֵּן טָעוּן עֵץ אֶרֶז וְאֵזוֹב וּשְׁנִי תוֹלַעַת!

The Gemara asks: The verbal analogy **can be refuted:** One cannot apply *halakhot* stated with regard to a leper to a *sota*, as **what is** unique **about a leper** is **that he requires cedar wood, and the hyssop, and the scarlet** wool for the performance of his purification ritual, and these are not required of the *sota*. Why, then, should a new vessel be required by the *sota*?

HALAKHA

Would bring an earthenware vessel – הָיָה מֵבִיא פַּיָלִי שֶׁל חֶרֶס: An earthenware vessel is brought and a half a *log* of water is poured into it for the *sota* to drink, in accordance with the opinion of the first *tanna* (Rambam *Sefer Nashim, Hilkhot Sota* 3:9).

He would enter the Sanctuary and turn to his right, etc. – נִכְנַס לַהֵיכָל וּפָנָה לִימִינוֹ וכו׳: The priest would take the vessel and enter the Sanctuary. There was an area of one square cubit to the right of where he entered where there was a tablet and a ring affixed to it. The priest would raise the tablet and take dust from underneath it (Rambam *Sefer Nashim, Hilkhot Sota* 3:9–10).

A new earthenware vessel – פַּיָלִי שֶׁל חֶרֶס חֲדָשָׁה: The *sota* drinks from an earthenware cup that has never been used, in accordance with the statement of Rabbi Yishmael (Rambam *Sefer Nashim, Hilkhot Sota* 3:9).

New – חֲדָשָׁה: A new vessel must be used for the process of purifying the leper (Rambam *Sefer Tahara, Hilkhot Tumat Tzara'at* 11:1).

From any other type of water – מִשְּׁאָר מֵימוֹת: The water of the basin, which the priests use to purify their hands and feet, need not be spring water. It may be any water fit for use in a ritual bath, in accordance with the opinion of the Rabbis (Rambam *Sefer Avoda, Hilkhot Biat HaMikdash* 5:12).

LANGUAGE

Drinking vessel [*peyalei*] – פַּיָלִי: This refers to a phiale, from the Greek φιάλη, *fialē*, and the Latin phiala, meaning a vessel used for cooking and drinking. The *peyalei* was made from clay, metal, or other materials, and was apparently shaped like a shallow pan. This is the Aramaic translation of the Hebrew *ke'arot* (Exodus 25:29), which are among the vessels of the Temple.

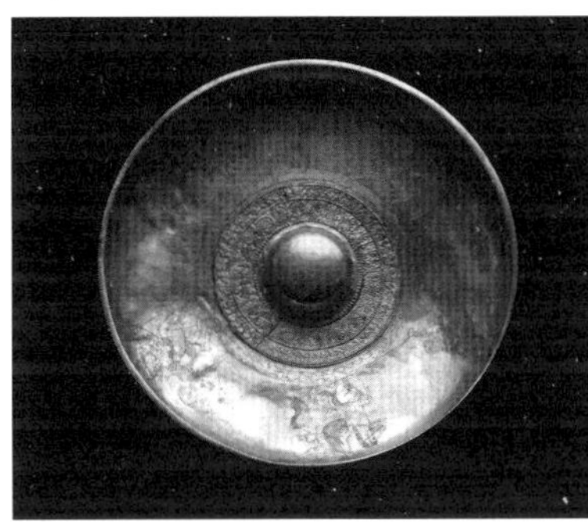

Phiale

Tablet [*tavla*] – טַבְלָא: From the Latin tabula, probably via the Greek loanword τάβλα, *tabla*, meaning a flat table-like surface.

NOTES

Half a *log* – חֲצִי לוֹג: Rashi on *Menaḥot* 86a explains that this amount is known by oral tradition (see Griz there). However, *Tosefot Yom Tov* asserts that the tradition does not indicate a specific amount of water but rather demands that there be enough water to ensure that the scroll can be erased easily. Since Rabbi Yehuda requires less to be written on the scroll, he infers from the same tradition that less water is necessary (see *Tosafot* on *Menaḥot* 86a).

And there was a place there – וּמָקוֹם הָיָה שָׁם: This spot was noticeably different from the rest of the floor of the Sanctuary (Rabbi Ovadya Bartenura). Although there were other tablets on the floor of the Sanctuary that could be raised, there was still a need for a designated tablet, as the Temple was built on rocky terrain, and not all of its tablets had dust beneath them.

אֲמַר רַבָּה, אָמַר קְרָא: ״בִּכְלִי חֶרֶס״, כְּלִי שֶׁאָמַרְתִּי לְךָ כְּבָר.

Rabba said: The verse cited in the mishna **states:** "And the priest shall take holy water **in an earthen vessel"** (Numbers 5:17). The Torah makes no prior mention of the need for the priest to bring with him an earthenware vessel. Therefore, the verse must mean that the water should be placed in **the vessel that I have already told you** about, i.e., the vessel used for the leper.

אָמַר רָבָא: לֹא שָׁנוּ אֶלָּא שֶׁלֹּא נִתְאַכְּמוּ פָּנָיו, אֲבָל נִתְאַכְּמוּ פָּנָיו – פְּסוּלִין. מַאי טַעְמָא? דּוּמְיָא דְּמַיִם, מָה מַיִם שֶׁלֹּא נִשְׁתַּנּוּ, אַף כְּלִי שֶׁלֹּא נִשְׁתַּנָּה.

Rava says: Even according to the opinion that a new vessel is not required, **they taught** that the earthenware vessel is taken **only when its exterior was not blackened** from usage. **But if its exterior was blackened,**[NH] **then it is unfit** for use by the *sota*. **What is the reason** for this? Its requirements are **similar** to those **of water: Just as** the **water** must be clear and **unchanged** in **appearance, so too** the **vessel** must **be unchanged** in appearance.

בָּעֵי רָבָא: נִתְאַכְּמוּ, וְהֶחֱזִירָן לְתוֹךְ כִּבְשַׁן הָאֵשׁ וְנִתְלַבְּנוּ, מַהוּ? מִי אָמְרִינַן כֵּיוָן דְּאִידְּחוּ – אִידְּחוּ, אוֹ דִילְמָא כֵּיוָן דַּהֲדוּר – הֲדוּר?

Rava raised a dilemma: If the vessel's exterior **was blackened, and it was returned to the furnace**[H] **and became white** again, **what is the** *halakha*? **Do we say** that **once it has been disqualified, it is disqualified** forever and can never be rendered fit for use? **Or perhaps since it has returned** to a white appearance **it has returned** to a state of fitness.

תָּא שְׁמַע, רַבִּי אֶלְעָזָר אוֹמֵר: עֵץ אֶרֶז וְאֵזוֹב וּשְׁנִי תוֹלַעַת שֶׁהִפְשִׁיל בָּהֶן קוּפָּתוֹ לַאֲחוֹרָיו – פְּסוּלִין. וְהָא הָתָם הָדְרִי וּמִפְשְׁטִי!

Come and **hear** evidence from that which **Rabbi Elazar says: If** the leper **tied** the **cedar wood, and** the **hyssop, and** the **scarlet** wool for his purification **to his basket**[B] **behind him,** so as to carry it on his back, they are **disqualified,** since their form has changed. **But there,** after those items have been tied, they can be **smoothed out again** as if they had never been used, and still they are unfit. Evidently, after being disqualified an item cannot become fit again.

הָתָם דְּאִיקְלוּף אִיקְלוּפֵי.

The Gemara answers: **There,** the items are permanently unfit **because they are peeled**[H] due to tying and can never truly return to their original appearance. That case does not provide proof.

״נִכְנַס לַהֵיכָל וּפָנָה לִימִינוֹ״ וכו׳. מַאי טַעְמָא? דְּאָמַר מָר: כׇּל פִּינּוֹת שֶׁאַתָּה פּוֹנֶה, לֹא יְהוּ אֶלָּא דֶּרֶךְ יָמִין.

The mishna states: The priest **would enter the Sanctuary and turn to his right.**[N] The Gemara asks: **What is the reason** that he should do so? The Gemara responds: **As the Master said: All turns**[N] that **you turn should be only to the right.**

״מָקוֹם הָיָה שָׁם אַמָּה״ כו׳. תָּנוּ רַבָּנַן: ״וּמִן הֶעָפָר אֲשֶׁר יִהְיֶה״ – יָכוֹל יְתַקֵּן מִבַּחוּץ וְיַכְנִיס,

The mishna continues: **There was a place there,** on the Sanctuary floor, with an area of **a cubit** by a cubit, and a marble tablet was there and a ring was fastened to the tablet so that it could be raised. When the priest would raise the tablet, he would take loose dust from underneath it and place the dust into the vessel with the water, so that the dust would be visible upon the water, as it is stated: "And the priest shall take holy water in an earthen vessel; and of the dust that is on the floor of the Tabernacle the priest shall take, and put it into the water" (Numbers 5:17). **The Sages taught** in a *baraita*: If the verse had stated only: **"And of the dust that is** on the floor," one **might** have thought that the priest could **prepare** the concoction from dust **from outside** the Sanctuary **and bring it in** afterward.

NOTES

Its exterior was blackened, etc. – נִתְאַכְּמוּ פָּנָיו וכו׳: Many commentaries discuss whether this *halakha* is only according to the opinion of Rabbi Yishmael, who requires the water of a *sota* to come from the spring water in the basin, or whether it is true even according to the opinion of the Rabbis (see Jerusalem Talmud). Although the Rambam does not rule in accordance with the opinion of Rabbi Yishmael requiring the water of a *sota* to be taken from the basin, he nevertheless rules that it is necessary to use a new earthenware vessel. Some explain that this is due to a textual variant in the mishna (see *Melekhet Shlomo*). According to others, the Rambam maintains that only *halakhot* concerning the vessel itself can be derived from the *halakhot* of the leper, but not *halakhot* concerning its contents.

The commentaries also discuss whether blackening caused by age, even in the absence of use, is sufficient to disqualify the vessel.

Turn to his right, etc. – פָּנָה לִימִינוֹ וכו׳: Certain commentaries question the import of this requirement, as the tablet was located to the priest's right in any event (*Be'er Sheva*). According to some, the reason that the tablet was deliberately placed in that spot was in order to require the priest to turn to his right (*Yad HaMelekh*; see *Ḥiddushei Batra*).

All turns, etc. – כׇּל פִּינּוֹת וכו׳: According to Rashi, the source for this principle is a midrash concerning the twelve oxen under Solomon's Sea in the First Temple, which teaches that they faced right. Others explain that this statement of the Gemara is not a binding *halakha* but a praiseworthy suggestion.

BACKGROUND

Tied…to his basket – הִפְשִׁיל בָּהֶן קוּפָּתוֹ: This type of basket was normally woven from willow or date branches and was formed into various shapes. Often there were handles attached to these baskets to aid in carrying them when heavy. The baskets were sometimes carried on one's back, in which case one could stabilize the basket by tying items to the handles or hanging the basket over a wooden rod.

HALAKHA

Was blackened – נִתְאַכְּמוּ: The *sota* may not drink from an earthenware vessel that appears aged, in accordance with the opinion of Rava (Rambam *Sefer Nashim*, *Hilkhot Sota* 3:9).

Returned to the furnace – הֶחֱזִירָן לְתוֹךְ כִּבְשַׁן הָאֵשׁ: A blackened earthenware vessel is considered new after emerging from a furnace. The *Kesef Mishne* questions why the Rambam rules leniently on this matter, given that the matter is not decided in the Gemara and the principle in cases of uncertainty with regard to Torah law is to be stringent. The *Mishne LaMelekh* suggests that the Rambam agrees with *Tosafot*, who claim that a blackened vessel is prohibited by rabbinic law. Therefore, one may be lenient in cases of uncertainty (Rambam *Sefer Nashim*, *Hilkhot Sota* 3:9).

Are peeled – אִיקְלוּף אִיקְלוּפֵי: The cedar, hyssop, and scarlet wool used to purify a leper are disqualified if peeled, in accordance with the Gemara here (Rambam *Sefer Tahara*, *Hilkhot Tumat Tzara'at* 11:1).

תַּלְמוּד לוֹמַר: ״בְּקַרְקַע הַמִּשְׁכָּן״. אִי ״בְּקַרְקַע הַמִּשְׁכָּן״, יָכוֹל יַחְפּוֹר בְּקַרְדּוּמוֹת? תַּלְמוּד לוֹמַר: ״אֲשֶׁר יִהְיֶה״. הָא כֵּיצַד? יֵשׁ שָׁם – הָבֵא; אֵין שָׁם – תֵּן שָׁם.

Therefore, **the verse states:** "The dust that is **on the floor of the Tabernacle,**" indicating that the dust must be from inside the Sanctuary. **If** the verse had stated only: **"On the floor of the Tabernacle,"** one **might** have thought that the priest may **dig with axes**[B] to loosen the dust there. Therefore, **the verse states:** "And of the dust **that is** on the floor of the Tabernacle," indicating that the dust must be lying there loosely. **How so? If there is** already loose earth **there** on the Sanctuary floor, **bring** it; if **there is none there,** then **place** loose dust **there** from elsewhere, and then pick it up and use it.

תַּנְיָא אִידָךְ: ״וּמִן הֶעָפָר אֲשֶׁר יִהְיֶה״ וגו׳ – מְלַמֵּד, שֶׁהָיָה מְתַקֵּן מִבַּחוּץ וּמַכְנִיס. ״בְּקַרְקַע הַמִּשְׁכָּן״ – אִיסִי בֶּן יְהוּדָה אוֹמֵר: לְהָבִיא קַרְקַע

It is taught in **another** *baraita*: The verse states: **"And of the dust that is** on the floor of the Tabernacle"; the fact that the verse does not explicitly state to take the dust from the floor of the Tabernacle **teaches that** the priest **would prepare** dust **from outside**[N] **and bring it into** the Sanctuary. When the verse states: "The dust that is **on the floor of the Tabernacle," Isi ben Yehuda says** that this phrase serves **to include the floor of** the Tabernacle when it stood in

BACKGROUND

Ax [*kardom*] – קַרְדּוֹם: Based on the description here and elsewhere, a *kardom* is the Roman dolabra, a two-sided implement. Its broader end was used for chopping, while its narrower side was used for hoeing or breaking. The narrow end was either bent, as depicted here, or straight.

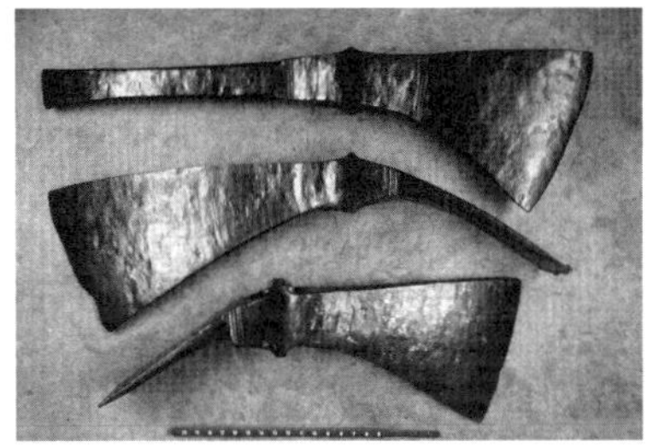

Roman dolabrae

NOTES

That he would prepare dust from outside – שֶׁהָיָה מְתַקֵּן מִבַּחוּץ: Rashi notes that since the verse does not state that the dust is from the floor of the Tabernacle, this teaches that the dust can be from elsewhere. The *Tosefot HaRosh* objects, as the verse clearly refers to the dust of the floor of the Tabernacle. He explains that the dust may originate elsewhere, and need not be taken initially from the floor of the Tabernacle, but it must be placed on the floor there and raised before being mixed with the water.

Perek **II**
Daf **16** Amud **a**

שִׁילֹה, נוֹב וְגִבְעוֹן, וּבֵית עוֹלָמִים.

Shiloh, Nob, and Gibeon,[NB] **and** also **the Eternal House,** i.e., the Temple in Jerusalem. The dust for the *sota* is still brought from the ground of the Sanctuary wherever it is located, even after the Jewish people are no longer in the wilderness.

אִיסִי בֶּן מְנַחֵם אוֹמֵר: אֵינוֹ צָרִיךְ. וּמַה בְּטוּמְאָה קַלָּה לֹא חָלַק הַכָּתוּב, בְּטוּמְאַת אֵשֶׁת אִישׁ חֲמוּרָה לֹא כׇּל שֶׁכֵּן! אִם כֵּן, מַה תַּלְמוּד לוֹמַר ״בְּקַרְקַע הַמִּשְׁכָּן״? שֶׁלֹּא יָבִיא מִתּוֹךְ קוּפָּתוֹ.

Isi ben Menaḥem says: There is no need to derive this *halakha* from the verse. It may be learned by an *a fortiori* inference: **With regard to** the prohibition against entering the Sanctuary in a state of **impurity, a lenient** matter for which there is no court-imposed capital punishment, **the Torah does not differentiate.** It is prohibited for an impure person to enter the Tabernacle no matter where it stands. Therefore, **with regard to the impurity of a married woman,** which is **stringent** and carries the penalty of strangulation, **all the more so** is it **not** clear that the Torah does not differentiate? The dust must be brought from the Sanctuary no matter where it stands. **If so, what** is the meaning when **the verse states:** "And of the dust that is **on the floor of the Tabernacle"? It** teaches **that one should not bring** dust **from his** own **basket** and place it directly into the water; he must first place it on the floor.

אִיבַּעְיָא לְהוּ: אֵין שָׁם עָפָר, מַהוּ שֶׁיִּתֵּן אֵפֶר? אַלִּיבָּא דְּבֵית שַׁמַּאי לָא תִּיבָּעֵי לָךְ, דְּאָמְרִי: לֹא מָצִינוּ אֵפֶר שֶׁקְּרוּי ״עָפָר״.

A dilemma was raised before the Sages: If **there is no dust there, what is** the *halakha*? May one **place ashes** in the vessel instead? The Gemara responds: There is **no** need to **raise the dilemma** if one holds **in accordance with** the opinion of **Beit Shammai, as they say: We never find ashes referred to as dust** in the Torah.

NOTES

Shiloh, Nob, and Gibeon – שִׁילֹה נוֹב וְגִבְעוֹן: Rashi possessed a textual variant that refers only to the Temple in Jerusalem. He explains that Shiloh need not be included, as it was the home of the Tabernacle itself. Nob and Gibeon need not be included because they contained only the great altar, on which primarily communal offerings were brought. Since the meal-offering of a *sota* could not be brought there, they were not used for the *sota* ritual at all. However, according to *Tosafot* Nob and Gibeon should be included, as Isi ben Yehuda might hold that the *sota* ritual could be performed there (see also Meiri). According to *Tosefot HaRosh*, Shiloh should be included as well. Although the Tabernacle there was built on the basis of Tabernacle in the wilderness, there were also stone additions, and it was therefore distinct from the Tabernacle of the wilderness and needed to be included separately.

BACKGROUND

Shiloh, Nob, and Gibeon – שִׁילֹה נוֹב וְגִבְעוֹן: Prior to the establishment of the Temple in Jerusalem, the Jewish people erected the Tabernacle from the wilderness in Shiloh, located in the land of the tribe of Ephraim (see Judges 21:19). Shiloh is located about thirty-five km north of Jerusalem on the ancient mountain ridge road that crosses the country from north to south. The remaining foundations of the Tabernacle have been found, and a modern synagogue has been built commemorating it. After Shiloh was destroyed (see I Samuel, chapter 4), the Tabernacle was moved to Nob and then to Gibeon.

כִּי תִּיבָּעֵי לָךְ – אַלִּיבָּא דְּבֵית הִלֵּל, דְּאָמְרִי: מָצִינוּ אֵפֶר שֶׁקָּרוּי "עָפָר", מַאי? אַף עַל גַּב דְּאִיקְּרִי עָפָר – הָכָא "בְּקַרְקַע הַמִּשְׁכָּן" כְּתִיב, אוֹ דִּילְמָא הַאי "בְּקַרְקַע הַמִּשְׁכָּן" – לְכִדְאִיסִי בֶּן יְהוּדָה וּלְכִדְאִיסִי בֶּן מְנַחֵם הוּא דְּאָתֵי?

When you raise the dilemma, it is **in accordance with** the opinion of **Beit Hillel, who say: We do find ashes referred to as dust**[N] in the context of the red heifer (Numbers 19:17). They likewise hold that ashes may also be used instead of dust to cover the blood of a slaughtered bird or undomesticated animal (see Leviticus 17:13). **What** is the *halakha* here, with regard to the water of a *sota*? May ashes replace dust? **Although** elsewhere ashes may be **referred to as dust, here it is written: "On the floor of the Tabernacle,"** indicating that dust in particular is required, since dust comes from the ground. **Or perhaps** the phrase **"on the floor of the Tabernacle" comes** only to teach that the *halakha* is **in accordance with** the teaching of **Isi ben Yehuda or in accordance with** the teaching of **Isi ben Menaḥem.** If so, perhaps ashes are acceptable as well.

תָּא שְׁמַע: דְּאָמַר רַבִּי יוֹחָנָן מִשּׁוּם רַבִּי יִשְׁמָעֵאל: בִּשְׁלֹשָׁה מְקוֹמוֹת הֲלָכָה עוֹקֶבֶת מִקְרָא.

Come and **hear** evidence from **that** which **Rabbi Yoḥanan says in the name of Rabbi Yishmael: In three instances the *halakha* supersedes the verse,**[N] i.e., the tradition alters the straightforward meaning of the verse.

הַתּוֹרָה אָמְרָה בְּעָפָר, וַהֲלָכָה בְּכׇל דָּבָר; הַתּוֹרָה אָמְרָה בְּתַעַר, וַהֲלָכָה בְּכׇל דָּבָר; הַתּוֹרָה אָמְרָה סֵפֶר, וַהֲלָכָה בְּכׇל דָּבָר;

The Torah states: "And whatsoever man … that takes in hunting any beast or fowl that may be eaten, he shall pour out the blood thereof, and cover it **in dust**" (Leviticus 17:13), **but the *halakha* is** that the blood may be covered **in anything**[H] similar to dust. **The Torah states** with regard to the nazirite: "All the days of his vow of naziriteship there shall be no **razor**[N] come upon his head" (Numbers 6:5), **but the *halakha* is** that the nazirite may not remove his hair **with anything.**[H] **The Torah states:** "That he writes her a **bill** [*sefer*] of divorce" (Deuteronomy 24:1). The word *sefer* denotes a scroll, **but the *halakha* is** that the husband may inscribe the bill of divorce **on anything**[H] that is detached from the ground and suitable to be written upon, not only on a scroll.

וְאִם אִיתָא, לִיחְשׁוֹב נַמִי הַאי!

And if it is so that ashes may be placed in the water of a *sota* despite the verse's stipulation of dust, **consider this** fourth case **as well**[N] to be a *halakha* that supersedes the verse. Since it is omitted from Rabbi Yishmael's statement, it seems that ashes may not be used.

תָּנָא וְשַׁיֵּיר. וּמַאי שַׁיֵּיר דְּהַאי שַׁיֵּיר? שַׁיֵּיר מְצוֹרָע; דְּתַנְיָא: "וְהָיָה בַיּוֹם הַשְּׁבִיעִי יְגַלַּח אֶת כׇּל שְׂעָרוֹ" – כְּלָל; "אֶת רֹאשׁוֹ וְאֶת זְקָנוֹ וְאֶת גַּבֹּת עֵינָיו" – פְּרָט; "וְאֶת כׇּל שְׂעָרוֹ יְגַלֵּחַ" – חָזַר וְכָלַל. כְּלָל וּפְרָט וּכְלָל – אִי אַתָּה דָּן אֶלָּא כְּעֵין הַפְּרָט: מַה פְּרָט מְפוֹרָשׁ מְקוֹם כִּינּוּס שֵׂעָר וְנִרְאֶה, אַף כׇּל מְקוֹם כִּינּוּס שֵׂעָר וְנִרְאֶה;

The Gemara responds: Rabbi Yishmael **taught** some cases **and omitted** others; his list is not exhaustive. The Gemara asks: **What** else **did he omit that he omitted this?** It is not reasonable that he would provide a list lacking only one item. The Gemara answers: **He omitted the leper, as it is taught** in a *baraita* (*Tosefta, Nega'im* 1:9): In the verse: **"And it shall be on the seventh day, that he shall shave off all his hair"** (Leviticus 14:9), the phrase "all his hair" is **a generalization.** The phrase that follows: **"His head and his beard and his eyebrows,"** is **a detail.** And with the following phrase: **"Even all his hair he shall shave off,"** the verse **then generalized** again. In any case of **a generalization, and a detail, and a generalization, you may deduce** that the verse is referring **only** to items **similar to the detail. Just as the detail is explicitly** referring to **areas** where there is **a collection of hair which is visible, so too all areas** on the leper that have **a collection of hair which is visible** must be shaven.

מָה רִבָּה? רִבָּה שְׂעַר הָרַגְלַיִם. מַאי מִיעֵט? מִיעֵט דְּבֵית הַשֶּׁחִי וּדְכוּלֵּיהּ גּוּפֵיהּ.

To **what** otherwise excluded case does this *baraita* **extend** the *halakha*? It **extends** the *halakha* of hair to include **pubic hair. What** does the *baraita* **exclude? It excludes armpit hair,** which is not visible, **and body hair** that is not collected. This is the straightforward meaning of the verse.

NOTES

We do find ashes referred to as dust – מָצִינוּ אֵפֶר שֶׁקָּרוּי עָפָר: Some commentaries mention that according to Rabbeinu Tam, even Beit Shammai hold that ashes from burnt wood are considered dust. They disagree with regard to other kinds of ashes. Others dispute this opinion (see *Tosefot HaRash*).

***Halakha* supersedes [*okevet*] the verse** – הֲלָכָה עוֹקֶבֶת מִקְרָא: Rashi explains that *okevet* is derived from *ekev*, meaning heel, and connotes the dislodging of a heel from its grounding. According to the *Arukh*, *okevet* is related to the biblical word *vayakeveini*, meaning to supplant (Genesis 27:36). The most fitting definition appears to be that of the Meiri, who interprets *okevet* as being related to *okefet*, meaning to bypass. In this sense, the *halakha* bypasses the straightforward meaning of the verse and settles on a different meaning.

The Torah states, razor, etc. – הַתּוֹרָה אָמְרָה בְּתַעַר וכו׳: Rashi and other commentaries find the inclusion of this example difficult to understand. The *halakha* does not countermand the verse but merely adds ways in which a nazirite may not remove his hair. Rashi answers that according to the *halakha*, if the nazirite were to shave his hair without a razor he would be liable to receive lashes. However, as it is prohibited to administer lashes unlawfully, that *halakha* is therefore viewed as countermanding the Torah. The *Ḥiddushei Batra* challenges this explanation, as there are numerous recorded cases in which the Sages sentenced a person to lashes due even to infractions of rabbinic law. Because of the difficulty with the case of the nazirite, it is understandable that Rashi prefers a textual variant of the Jerusalem Talmud that lists another case instead: According to the Torah, a Hebrew slave who foregoes his emancipation must have his ear pierced with an awl; the *halakha* is that the ear may be pierced with anything.

Consider this as well – לִיחְשׁוֹב נַמִי הַאי: The early commentaries disagree as to whether one might answer simply that Rabbi Yishmael agrees with the opinion of Beit Shammai that ashes are not considered dust (see *Tosafot* and *Tosefot HaRosh*).

HALAKHA

In dust, but the *halakha* is in anything – בְּעָפָר, וַהֲלָכָה בְּכׇל דָּבָר: Although the verse states that one must cover the blood of a slaughtered animal with dust, it may be covered with any substance used for growing seeds, or with any substance called dust, including eroded gold and ashes (Rambam *Sefer Kedusha, Hilkhot Sheḥita* 14:11–13; *Shulḥan Arukh, Yoreh De'a* 28:23).

Razor, but the *halakha* is with anything – בְּתַעַר, וַהֲלָכָה בְּכׇל דָּבָר: A nazirite is liable to receive lashes if he cuts even one of his hairs, with a razor or with scissors, (Rambam *Sefer Hafla'a, Hilkhot Nezirut* 5:11).

A bill of divorce, but the *halakha* is on anything – סֵפֶר, וַהֲלָכָה בְּכׇל דָּבָר: It is permitted to write a bill of divorce on any item detached from the ground that is suitable to be written upon (Rambam *Sefer Nashim, Hilkhot Geirushin* 4:2–3; *Shulḥan Arukh, Even HaEzer* 124:1–2).

וְהִלְכְתָא: מְגַלֵּחַ כְּדַלַעַת, דִּתְנַן: בָּא לוֹ לְהַקִּיף אֶת הַמְּצוֹרָע – מַעֲבִיר תַּעַר עַל כׇּל בְּשָׂרוֹ. וְקָתָנֵי סֵיפָא: וּבַיּוֹם הַשְּׁבִיעִי מְגַלְּחוֹ, תִּגְלַחַת שְׁנִיָּה כְּתִגְלַחַת רִאשׁוֹנָה.

And yet **the *halakha* is:** The leper **shaves like a gourd,**[H] i.e., his entire body must be shaved. **As we learned** in a mishna (*Nega'im* 14:2): When the priest **comes to shave the leper, he passes a razor over all of his flesh. And** in **the latter clause,** the mishna **teaches: On the seventh day he shaves** the leper again. **The second shaving is** just **like the first shaving.**[H] The verse previously analyzed is referring to the second shaving, and its straightforward meaning is that not all of the leper's flesh needs to be shaved. However, the mishna states that the leper must shave all of his flesh in the second shaving as well. This is another instance where the *halakha* supersedes the straightforward meaning of the verse, yet it is omitted from Rabbi Yishmael's list.

אָמַר רַב נַחְמָן בַּר יִצְחָק: כִּי קָא חָשֵׁיב – הֲלָכָה עוֹקֶבֶת מִקְרָא, הָא – עוֹקֶבֶת מִדְּרַבָּנַן הִיא.

Rabbi Naḥman bar Yitzḥak said: Rabbi Yishmael consciously omitted the *halakha* of the leper because he **counted** only instances where the ***halakha* supersedes** the straightforward meaning of the **verse. This** *halakha* of the leper, however, **is** an instance where the *halakha* **supersedes** only an exegetical interpretation **of the Sages.**

רַב פָּפָּא אָמַר: כִּי קָא חָשֵׁיב – הֲלָכָה עוֹקֶבֶת וְעוֹקֶרֶת, הָא – עוֹקֶבֶת וּמוֹסֶפֶת הִיא.

Rav Pappa said: Rabbi Yishmael **counted** only cases where the ***halakha*** both **supersedes and uproots** the straightforward meaning of the verse. **This,** however, is an instance where the *halakha* **supersedes and adds.** The *halakha* does not overrule the verse but rather adds an additional requirement, i.e., that the whole body must be shaved.

רַב אַשִׁי אָמַר: הָא מַתְנִיתָא מַנִּי – רַבִּי יִשְׁמָעֵאל הִיא, דְּדָרֵישׁ כְּלָלֵי וּפְרָטֵי;

Rav Ashi said: This *baraita*, which teaches that only certain parts of the body must be shaved, **is** in accordance with **whose** opinion? **It is** in accordance with the opinion of **Rabbi Yishmael, who interprets** verses by means of the principle of **generalizations and details.** According to this interpretation, only collected areas of hair that are visible must be shaven.

HALAKHA

Shaves like a gourd – מְגַלֵּחַ כְּדַלַעַת: After the leper has been purified by the ritual of the two birds, the priest shaves off all his body hair, including his pubic and armpit hair, leaving him smooth as a gourd (Rambam *Sefer Tahara, Hilkhot Tumat Tzara'at* 11:1).

The second shaving is like the first shaving – תִּגְלַחַת שְׁנִיָּה כְּתִגְלַחַת רִאשׁוֹנָה: Seven days after the initial purification of the leper, the priest shaves him again (Rambam *Sefer Tahara, Hilkhot Tumat Tzara'at* 11:2).

Perek **II**
Daf **16** Amud **b**

כְּדַלַעַת, מַנִּי? רַבִּי עֲקִיבָא הִיא, דְּדָרֵישׁ רִיבּוּיֵי וּמִיעוּטֵי; דְּתַנְיָא: ״וְהָיָה בַיּוֹם הַשְּׁבִיעִי יְגַלַּח אֶת כׇּל שְׂעָרוֹ״ – רִיבָּה; ״אֶת רֹאשׁוֹ וְאֶת זְקָנוֹ וְאֵת גַּבֹּת עֵינָיו״ – מִיעֵט; ״וְאֶת כׇּל שְׂעָרוֹ יְגַלֵּחַ״ – חָזַר וְרִיבָּה, רִיבָּה וּמִיעֵט וְרִיבָּה – רִיבָּה הַכֹּל.

By contrast, the mishna states that the leper must be shaven **like a gourd.** In accordance with **whose** opinion is this? **It is** in accordance with the opinion of **Rabbi Akiva, who interprets** verses by means of the principle of **amplifications and restrictions.**[N] **As it is taught** in a *baraita*: In the verse: **"And it shall be on the seventh day, that he shall shave off all his hair,"** the phrase "all his hair" is an **amplification.** The phrase that follows: **"His head and his beard and his eyebrows,"** is a **restriction.** In the final phrase: **"Even all his hair he shall shave off,"** the verse **then amplified** again. The verse is therefore an instance of **amplification and restriction and amplification,** which **includes everything.**

מַאי רִיבָּה? רִיבָּה דְּכוּלֵּיהּ גּוּפֵיהּ, וּמַאי מִיעֵט? מִיעֵט שֵׂעָר שֶׁבְּתוֹךְ הַחוֹטֶם.

What does it include? It includes the hair **of all of the body. What does it** nevertheless **exclude? It excludes nose hairs,**[H] which do not need to be shaved. Since the mishna presents only the opinion of Rabbi Akiva, it poses no challenge to Rabbi Yishmael's list.

מַאי הֲוֵי עֲלַהּ? תָּא שְׁמַע, דְּאָמַר רַב הוּנָא בַּר אַשִׁי אָמַר רַב: אֵין שָׁם עָפָר, מֵבִיא רַקְבּוּבִית יָרָק וּמְקַדֵּשׁ.

The Gemara asks: **What** conclusion **was** reached **about it,**[N] i.e., whether ashes may be used instead of dust for the water of the *sota*? **Come and hear** evidence from that **which Rav Huna bar Ashi says that Rav says: If there is no dust** available for the *sota* water, the priest **brings decomposed vegetable** matter,[H] **and he consecrates**[N] the water with it. This indicates that it is permitted to substitute other substances for dust.

HALAKHA

It excludes nose hairs – מִיעֵט שֵׂעָר שֶׁבְּתוֹךְ הַחוֹטֶם: When the priest shaves the leper's hairs he does not shave the hair in his nostrils, since it is not visible (Rambam *Sefer Tahara, Hilkhot Tumat Tzara'at* 11:1).

Brings decomposed vegetable matter – מֵבִיא רַקְבּוּבִית יָרָק: If no dust is available, one may place decomposed vegetables in the water of a *sota* because they are like dust, in accordance with the statement of Rav (Rambam *Sefer Nashim, Hilkhot Sota* 4:12).

NOTES

Amplifications and restrictions – רִיבּוּיֵי וּמִיעוּטֵי: The hermeneutic principle of amplifications and restrictions and that of generalizations and details are similar in their applications. Both methods are applied to biblical verses in which there is a general statement followed by specific examples of the same *halakha*. They differ, however, in the hermeneutic weight afforded to the specific detail or restrictive phrase. The principle of generalizations and details interprets the detail mentioned in the verse as limiting the entire application of the rule to like cases. In this instance, the detail indicates that only visible collections of hair need to be shaved. The method of amplification and restriction, however, treats the restrictive phrase only as an indication that certain extreme cases should be excluded. In this case, the restrictive phrase comes only to exclude nose hair.

What conclusion was reached about it – מַאי הֲוֵי עֲלַהּ: This phrase is used when the discussion has addressed comparable cases to the issue at hand but has not yet offered a definitive answer to the original query (see *Tosafot*).

And he consecrates – וּמְקַדֵּשׁ: The water of a *sota* is not truly consecrated. Rashi explains that the decomposed vegetables may be placed in the water only after having been placed on the Temple floor. According to this explanation, the word consecrates means to connect the mixture to the Temple by means of its dust.

HALAKHA

Ashes will not become dust – **אֵפֶר לָא הֲוֵאי עָפָר**: One may not place ashes in the water of a *sota*, in accordance with the conclusion of the Gemara (Rambam *Sefer Nashim, Hilkhot Sota* 4:12).

The dust of the *sota* – **עֲפַר סוֹטָה**: Enough dust must be placed in the water of a *sota* for the dust to be visible in it (Rambam *Sefer Nashim, Hilkhot Sota* 3:10).

The ashes of the red heifer – **אֵפֶר פָּרָה**: Enough ashes must be placed in the waters of purification for them to be visible in the mixture (Rambam *Sefer Tahara, Hilkhot Para Aduma* 9:1).

The spittle of a *yevama* – **רוֹק יְבָמָה**: The spittle of a *yevama* must be visible to the judges who oversee the *ḥalitza* ritual (Rambam *Sefer Nashim, Hilkhot Yibbum* 4:7; *Shulḥan Arukh, Even HaEzer* 169:38).

That the blood of the bird will be recognizable within it – **שֶׁדַּם צִיפּוֹר נִיכָּר בָּהֶן**: For the purification process of the leper, a quarter-*log* of water is brought, and the blood of the bird must be recognizable in it (Rambam *Sefer Tahara, Hilkhot Tumat Tzara'at* 11:1).

וְלָא הִיא, רַקְבּוּבִית יָרָק הוּא דַּהֲוַאי עָפָר, אֵפֶר לָא הֲוַאי עָפָר.

The Gemara responds: **But that is not so. Decomposed vegetable** matter **is** permitted because it will **become dust,** but **ashes will not become dust.**[H]

״כְּדֵי שֶׁיֵּרָאֶה עַל הַמַּיִם״. תָּנוּ רַבָּנַן – שְׁלֹשָׁה צְרִיכִין שֶׁיֵּרָאוּ: עֲפַר סוֹטָה, וְאֵפֶר פָּרָה, וְרוֹק יְבָמָה; מִשּׁוּם רַבִּי יִשְׁמָעֵאל אָמְרוּ: אַף דַּם צִפּוֹר.

§ The mishna states: He would take loose dust from underneath the tablet and place it into the vessel with the water, **so that** the dust **would be visible upon the water. The Sages taught** (*Tosefta* 1:8): **Three** items **are required to be seen:**[N] **The dust of the *sota***[H] must be visible in the water, **the ashes of the** red **heifer**[H] must be visible when placed in the waters of purification, **and the spittle of a woman whose husband, who has a brother, died childless** [***yevama***][H] must be visible. The *yavam*, brother-in-law of the *yevama*, is bound by Torah law to marry her, and this bond is dissolved through the ritual of *ḥalitza*, in which she spits before him in the presence of judges. **In the name of Rabbi Yishmael they said: Even the blood of the bird** used in a leper's purification ritual is required to be visible in the vessel.

מַאי טַעֲמָא דְּרַבִּי יִשְׁמָעֵאל? דִּכְתִיב: ״וְטָבַל אוֹתָם בְּדַם הַצִּפּוֹר״ וגו׳, וְתַנְיָא: ״בְּדַם״ – יָכוֹל בְּדָם וְלֹא בְּמַיִם, תַּלְמוּד לוֹמַר: ״בַּמַּיִם״. אִי מַיִם, יָכוֹל בְּמַיִם וְלֹא בְּדָם? תַּלְמוּד לוֹמַר: ״בְּדַם״. הָא כֵּיצַד? מֵבִיא מַיִם שֶׁדַּם צִיפּוֹר נִיכָּר בָּהֶן. וְכַמָּה? רְבִיעִית.

The Gemara asks: **What is the reasoning of Rabbi Yishmael? As it is written** with regard to the process of the purification of a leper: "And he shall take the cedar wood, and the hyssop, and the scarlet, and the living bird, **and dip them in the blood of the slain bird,** and in the running water" (Leviticus 14:51). **And it is taught** in a *baraita*: Had the verse stated only the phrase **"in the blood,"** one **might** have thought that these items must be dipped only **in the blood and** should **not** be dipped **in the water** at all. Therefore, **the verse** also **states: "In the** running **water."** If the verse had stated only the phrase "in the running **water,"** one **might** have thought they should be dipped only **in the water and not** be dipped in **the blood** at all. Therefore, **the verse** also **states: "In the blood." How** can **these** texts be reconciled? One must **bring** little enough **water** so **that the blood of the bird** will still **be recognizable**[N] **within it.**[H] **And how much** water is this? It is **a quarter-*log*.**

וְרַבָּנַן? הַהוּא לְגוּפֵיהּ, דְּהָכִי קָאָמַר רַחֲמָנָא: אַטְבֵּיל בְּדָם וּבְמַיִם.

And the Rabbis, who do not require that the blood of the bird be visible in the water, how do they understand the verse? **That** verse is necessary **for its own** sake, **as this is what the Merciful One is saying: Dip** the objects both **in blood and in water** together. The blood need not be visible.

וְרַבִּי יִשְׁמָעֵאל? אִם כֵּן, לִכְתּוֹב רַחֲמָנָא ״וְטָבַל בָּהֶם״; ״בְּדַם...וּבַמַּיִם״ לָמָּה לִי? לְנִיכָּר.

And why does **Rabbi Yishmael** reject this straightforward understanding of the verse? It is because **if** this understanding were **so,** then **the Merciful One should have written** simply: **And dip in them,** i.e., dip the cedar wood, hyssop, scarlet wool, and live bird in the blood and water, as the blood and water have already been mentioned beforehand. **Why do I** need the verse to list explicitly: "And dip them **in the blood** of the slain bird, **and in the** running **water"?** This is **to** teach that the blood must be **recognizable** in the water.

וְרַבָּנַן? אִי כָּתַב רַחֲמָנָא ״וְטָבַל בָּהֶם״, הֲוָה אָמִינָא הַאי לְחוּדֵיהּ וְהַאי לְחוּדֵיהּ. כָּתַב רַחֲמָנָא ״בְּדַם...וּבַמַּיִם״ לְעָרְבָן.

And what would **the Rabbis** respond to this? **If the Merciful One had written** simply: **And dip in them,** then **I would say** the items should be dipped in **this** liquid **separately and** in **that** liquid **separately.** Therefore, **the Merciful One writes:** "And dip them **in the blood** of the slain bird, **and in the** running **water,"** to teach that one must **mix them** together.

וְרַבִּי יִשְׁמָעֵאל? לְעָרְבָן – קְרָא אַחֲרִינָא כְּתִיב: ״וְשָׁחַט אֶת הַצִּפּוֹר הָאֶחָת״ וגו׳.

And from where does **Rabbi Yishmael** derive that one must **mix them** together? **Another verse is written: "And he shall slaughter one of the birds** in an earthen vessel over running water" (Leviticus 14:50). This indicates that the blood of the bird must fall directly into the water below, and the blood and the water will become mixed together.

NOTES

Are required to be seen – **צְרִיכִין שֶׁיֵּרָאוּ**: Apparently, a sufficient measure of dust or ashes must be added so that they will not immediately disappear in the water. Although the dust will inevitably settle, it should initially be visible. With regard to the spittle of the *yevama*, the term refers not to a requisite amount of spittle; rather, it means that it must be spat visibly. The blood of the leper's bird must merely be recognizable in the water; there is no requirement of a specific measure of blood (*Devar Shaul*).

So that the blood of the bird will still be recognizable – **שֶׁדַּם צִיפּוֹר נִיכָּר**: This does not mean merely that a red color should be recognizable in the water; that would occur even in a large amount of water. Rather, the blood should be recognizable as blood (*Devar Shaul*; see *Tosafot*).

וְרַבָּנַן? אִי מֵהַהוּא, הֲוָה אָמֵינָא לִישְׁחֲטֵיהּ סָמוּךְ לְמָנָא, וְנִינְקְטִינְהוּ לְוְורִידִין וְלִקַבְּלֵיהּ לַדָּם בְּמָנָא אַחֲרִינָא. קָא מַשְׁמַע לַן.

And why do **the Rabbis** not learn it from that verse? **If** one were to learn it **from that** verse, **I would say** that one should **slaughter** the bird **adjacent to the vessel** holding the water, **and** one should **grasp the** opened **veins**[N] to ensure that no blood escapes immediately **and** then **collect the blood in a different vessel.** The blood and water would therefore be in separate vessels. Therefore, **this** first verse **teaches us** that the blood and water must be mixed together.

בְּעָא מִינֵּיהּ רַבִּי יִרְמְיָה מֵרַבִּי זֵירָא: גְּדוֹלָה וּמְדַחַת אֶת הַמַּיִם, קְטַנָּה וְנִדְחֵית מִפְּנֵי הַמַּיִם, מַהוּ?

Rabbi Yirmeya raised a dilemma before Rabbi Zeira: If the bird is **big and** contains such a large amount of blood that it **effaces the water,** rendering it indistinguishable, or if the bird is **small and** contains so little blood that its blood **is effaced due to the water** and indistinguishable, **what is** the *halakha*?

אֲמַר לֵיהּ, לָאו אָמֵינָא לָךְ: לָא תַּפֵּיק נַפְשָׁךְ לְבַר מֵהִילְכְתָא? בְּצִפּוֹר דְּרוֹר שִׁיעֲרוּ רַבָּנַן: אֵין לְךָ גְּדוֹלָה שֶׁמְּדַחַת אֶת הַמַּיִם, וְאֵין לְךָ קְטַנָּה שֶׁנִּדְחֵית מִפְּנֵי הַמַּיִם.

Rabbi Zeira **said to him: Haven't I told you not to take yourself**[N] **out** of the bounds **of the** practical ***halakha***? Do not ask questions about impossible eventualities. **The Sages measured** the ratio of blood to water specifically **with regard to a sparrow.**[B] **There is no** sparrow **big enough to efface the water, nor is there one small enough to be effaced due to the water.**

תָּנוּ רַבָּנַן: הִקְדִּים עָפָר לַמַּיִם פָּסוּל, וְרַבִּי שִׁמְעוֹן מַכְשִׁיר. מַאי טַעְמָא דְּרַבִּי שִׁמְעוֹן?

§ **The Rabbis taught** (*Tosefta, Para* 6:6): If one **places the dust** in the vessel **before the water,**[H] the mixture is **unfit; but Rabbi Shimon deems it fit.** The Gemara asks: **What is the reasoning of Rabbi Shimon?**

דִּכְתִיב: ״וְלָקְחוּ לַטָּמֵא מֵעֲפַר שְׂרֵפַת הַחַטָּאת״; וְתַנְיָא, אָמַר רַבִּי שִׁמְעוֹן: וְכִי עָפָר הוּא? וַהֲלֹא אֵפֶר הוּא! שִׁינָּה הַכָּתוּב בְּמַשְׁמָעוֹ לָדוּן הֵימֶנּוּ גְּזֵירָה שָׁוָה: נֶאֱמַר כָּאן ״עָפָר״, וְנֶאֱמַר לְהַלָּן ״עָפָר״, מָה לְהַלָּן עָפָר עַל גַּבֵּי מַיִם, אַף כָּאן עָפָר עַל גַּבֵּי מַיִם.

It is **as it is written** with regard to the red heifer: **"And for the unclean they shall take of the dust of the burning of the purification from sin,** and running water shall be put thereto in a vessel" (Numbers 19:17). **And it is taught** in a *baraita* that **Rabbi Shimon said: Is it dust** [*afar*] that is taken? **But isn't it** really **ashes** [*efer*]? Evidently **the Torah altered its usage**[N] and referred to ashes as dust **in order to derive a verbal analogy from it. Dust is stated** in the verse **here, and dust is stated there,** with regard to the *sota*. **Just as there,** with regard to the *sota*, the verse teaches that the **dust** must be placed **on top of water, so too here,** with regard to the red heifer, one learns that the **dust,** i.e., ashes, must be placed **on top of the water.**

וּמָה כָּאן, הִקְדִּים עָפָר לַמַּיִם – כָּשֵׁר, אַף לְהַלָּן, הִקְדִּים עָפָר לַמַּיִם – כָּשֵׁר.

And likewise, **just as here,** with regard to the red heifer, if one **places the dust** in the vessel **before the water, it is fit** after the fact, **so too there,** with regard to the *sota*, if one **places the dust** in the vessel **before the water, it is fit.**

וְהָתָם מְנָלַן? תְּרֵי קְרָאֵי כְּתִיבִי. כְּתִיב: ״עָלָיו״, אַלְמָא אֵפֶר בְּרֵישָׁא, וּכְתִיב: ״מַיִם חַיִּים אֶל כֶּלִי״, אַלְמָא מַיִם בְּרֵישָׁא. הָא כֵּיצַד? רָצָה – זֶה נוֹתֵן, רָצָה – זֶה נוֹתֵן.

The Gemara asks: **And there,** with regard to the red heifer, **from where do we** derive that the mixture is fit even if the dust is placed first? **Two phrases are written** in the verse. **It is written** that the water must be put: **"Thereto."** Therefore, **apparently,** the **ashes** should be placed **first. And it is written** that the **running water** must be placed: **"In a vessel." Apparently,** the **water** should be placed in the vessel **first,** while it is still empty. **How** can **these** texts be reconciled? If **he desires**[N] to place the water first **he places it,** and if **he desires** to place the ash first **he places it.**

וְרַבָּנַן? ״אֶל כֶּלִי״ – דַּוְקָא; ״עָלָיו״ – לְעָרְבָן.

And how do **the Rabbis,** who deem the mixture unfit, interpret the verse? The verse states: **"In a vessel,"**[H] **specifically.** The water must be placed first. When the verse states: **"Thereto,"** it teaches only that it is required **to mix** the ashes with the water.

NOTES

Grasp the veins – נִינְקְטִינְהוּ לְוְורִידִין: In slaughtering birds it is sufficient to cut either the windpipe or the gullet. It is therefore possible to leave the veins intact, even though it is proper *ab initio* to cut them as well (see, e.g., Rabbi David Luria and *Minḥa Ḥareva*). This explains the case described in the Gemara here, where the bird is slaughtered next to one vessel and bleeds into a different vessel.

Not to take yourself – לָא תַּפֵּיק נַפְשָׁךְ: This is a reference to Rabbi Yirmeya's frequent practice of raising questions about borderline issues in *halakha*, particularly with regard to the limits of legal measurements. See *Bava Batra* 23b, which relates that on one occasion he was evicted from the study hall for raising a question of this type. According to the Ritva, Rabbi Zeira holds that although measures must be clearly defined, one should not raise objections from borderline cases, since there is no end to such questions.

The Torah altered its usage – שִׁינָּה הַכָּתוּב בְּמַשְׁמָעוֹ: Beit Hillel conclude from this verse that ashes may be used in place of dust for the mitzva of covering blood. Still, the terminology of the verse is unique and teaches this verbal analogy as well (*Tosefot HaRash*).

If he desires, etc. – רָצָה וכו׳: *Tosefot HaRosh* assert that this is not a halakhic prescription. It means that had there been only two phrases, then one could decide based on personal preference. However, in fact the verbal analogy cited earlier teaches the proper order.

BACKGROUND

Sparrow – צִיפּוֹר דְּרוֹר: The sparrow, *Passer domesticus*, is one of the most common birds and can be found in almost every place where people live. It is brown-gray in color, and the males have a black spot on their necks. Sparrows can grow up to 14 cm long. Although they live alongside humans, they cannot be tamed. The Gemara (*Beitza* 24a) itself says that sparrows do not accept human authority and evade capture even in a house. In a temperate climate they lay eggs a few times a year. Although the chicks mature quickly, reaching full size after two to three weeks, the parents continue to care for them for some time.

Male house sparrow

Female house sparrow

HALAKHA

Places the dust before the water – הִקְדִּים עָפָר לַמַּיִם: If the dust is placed in the vessel before the water, the mixture is disqualified for the *sota* ritual, in accordance with the opinion of the Rabbis (Rambam *Sefer Nashim, Hilkhot Sota* 4:12).

In a vessel – אֶל כֶּלִי: When preparing the purifying waters of the red heifer, one must first place the water in a vessel and then place ashes upon it, in accordance with the opinion of the Rabbis. If one reversed the order the mixture is unfit. The verse, which states: "In a vessel," is understood to mean that one must mix the ashes in the water (Rambam *Sefer Tahara, Hilkhot Para Aduma* 9:1).

וְאֵימָא: ״עָלָיו״ דַּוְקָא, ״אֶל כֶּלִי״ – שֶׁתְּהֵא חִיּוּתָן בִּכְלִי!

The Gemara asks: **But** one could just as easily **say** the opposite: **"Thereto"** should be understood **specifically,** and the ashes must be placed first. The phrase "running water shall be put… **in a vessel,"** should indicate only **that** the water **must run** directly **into the vessel** and that it may not be brought from the spring by means of another vessel.

מַה מָּצִינוּ בְּכָל מָקוֹם מַכְשִׁיר לְמַעְלָה, אַף כָּאן מַכְשִׁיר לְמַעְלָה.

The Gemara answers: **Just as we find in every instance** that the **facilitating item** goes **above** the primary item, e.g., in the case of a *sota* the dust goes on top of the water, **so too here,** in the case of the red heifer, the **facilitating item** must go **above** the primary item. The water must be placed first, and only then the ashes.

NOTES

Comes to write, etc. – בָּא לוֹ לִכְתּוֹב וכו׳: The mishna is not explicit as to the language in which the scroll is written. Although another mishna (32a) states that the oath of the *sota* may be taken in any language that the wife understands, apparently the scroll itself was to be written specifically in Hebrew. This is true especially according to the opinion that the scroll of a *sota* may be taken from a Torah scroll (see 20b), and this is the ruling of the Rambam (*Minḥa Ḥareva*).

מתני׳ בָּא לוֹ לִכְתּוֹב אֶת הַמְּגִילָּה, מֵאֵיזֶה מָקוֹם הוּא כּוֹתֵב?

MISHNA When the priest **comes to write**[N] **the scroll** of the *sota* that is to be placed in the water, **from what place** in the Torah passage concerning the *sota* (Numbers 5:11–31) **does he write?**[H]

מֵ״וְאִם לֹא שָׁכַב אִישׁ״ וגו׳, ״וְאַתְּ כִּי שָׂטִית תַּחַת אִישֵׁךְ״.

He starts **from** the verse: **"If no man has lain** with you, and if you have not gone astray to defilement while under your husband, you shall be free from this water of bitterness that causes the curse" (Numbers 5:19); and continues: **"But if you have gone astray while under your husband,** and if you are defiled, and some man has lain with you besides your husband" (Numbers 5:20).

וְאֵינוֹ כּוֹתֵב: ״וְהִשְׁבִּיעַ הַכֹּהֵן אֶת הָאִשָּׁה״. וְכוֹתֵב: ״יִתֵּן ה׳ אוֹתָךְ לְאָלָה וְלִשְׁבֻעָה...וּבָאוּ הַמַּיִם הַמְאָרְרִים הָאֵלֶּה בְּמֵעַיִךְ לַצְבּוֹת בֶּטֶן וְלַנְפִּל יָרֵךְ״, וְאֵינוֹ כּוֹתֵב: ״וְאָמְרָה הָאִשָּׁה אָמֵן אָמֵן״.

And then **he does not write** the beginning of the following verse, which states: **"Then the priest shall cause the woman to swear** with the oath of cursing, and the priest shall say to the woman" (Numbers 5:21), **but he does write** the oath recorded in the continuation of the verse: **"The Lord shall make you a curse and an oath** among your people when the Lord will cause your thigh to fall away, and your belly to swell. **And this water that causes the curse shall go into your bowels, and cause your belly to swell, and your thigh to fall away"** (Numbers 5:21–22); **but he does not write** the conclusion of the verse: **"And the woman shall say: Amen, amen"** (Numbers 5:22).

רַבִּי יוֹסֵי אוֹמֵר: לֹא הָיָה מַפְסִיק.

Rabbi Yosei says: He does not interrupt the verses but rather writes the entire passage without any omissions.

רַבִּי יְהוּדָה אוֹמֵר: כָּל עַצְמוֹ אֵינוֹ כּוֹתֵב אֶלָּא: ״יִתֵּן ה׳ אוֹתָךְ לְאָלָה וְלִשְׁבֻעָה וגו׳ וּבָאוּ הַמַּיִם הַמְאָרְרִים הָאֵלֶּה בְּמֵעַיִךְ״ וגו׳, וְאֵינוֹ כּוֹתֵב: ״וְאָמְרָה הָאִשָּׁה אָמֵן אָמֵן״.

Rabbi Yehuda says: He writes nothing other than curses recorded in the final verses cited above: **"The Lord shall make you a curse and an oath** among your people when the Lord will cause your thigh to fall away, and your belly to swell. **And this water that causes the curse shall go into your bowels,** and cause your belly to swell, and your thigh to fall away." **And he does not write** the conclusion of the verse: **"And the woman shall say: Amen, amen."**

גמ׳ בְּמַאי קָא מִיפַּלְגִי? בְּהַאי קְרָא קָמִיפַּלְגִי: ״וְכָתַב אֶת הָאָלֹת הָאֵלֶּה הַכֹּהֵן בַּסֵּפֶר״,

GEMARA **With regard to what** issue **do** the Sages in the mishna **disagree?** What is the source of their disagreement? **They disagree concerning the** proper interpretation of the **verse: "And the priest shall write these** [*ha'eleh*] **curses** [*et ha'alot*] **in a scroll"** (Numbers 5:23).

HALAKHA

From what place does he write – מֵאֵיזֶה מָקוֹם הוּא כּוֹתֵב: The priest writes the scroll of the *sota* from the verse: "If no man has lain with you, and if you have not gone astray to defilement while under your husband, you shall be free from this water of bitterness that causes the curse" (Numbers 5:19); and continues: "But if you have gone astray while under your husband, and if you are defiled, and some man has lain with you besides your husband" (Numbers 5:20). And then he skips the beginning of the verse that follows: "Then the priest shall cause the woman to swear with the oath of cursing, and the priest shall say to the woman" (Numbers 5:21). But he does write the oath recorded in the continuation: "The Lord shall make you a curse and an oath among your people, when the Lord will cause your thigh to fall away, and your belly to swell. And this water that causes the curse shall go into your bowels, and cause your belly to swell, and your thigh to fall away" (Numbers 5:21–22). But he does not write the conclusion of the verse: "And the woman shall say: Amen, amen" (Numbers 5:22), in accordance with the first *tanna* of the mishna (Rambam *Sefer Nashim*, *Hilkhot Sota* 3:8).

רַבִּי מֵאִיר סָבַר: "אָלוֹת" - אָלוֹת מַמָּשׁ, "הָאָלוֹת" - לְרַבּוֹת קְלָלוֹת הַבָּאוֹת מֵחֲמַת בְּרָכוֹת, "אֵלֶּה" - לְמַעוֹטֵי קְלָלוֹת שֶׁבְּמִשְׁנֵה תוֹרָה, "הָאֵלֶּה" - לְמַעוֹטֵי צַוָּואוֹת וְקַבָּלוֹת אָמֵן.

Rabbi Meir, the first *tanna* of the mishna, **reasons:** The word "*alot*," curses, is referring to **actual curses.** The prefix *ha*, meaning: The, in the word **"*ha'alot*"** serves **to include curses that come on account of** the **blessings,** i.e., the curses that are inferred from the phrase: "You shall be free from this water of bitterness that causes the curse" (5:19). The word **"*eleh*,"** meaning these, is a limiting term that serves **to exclude the** long list of **curses that are** recorded **in *Mishne Torah*,**[N] the book of Deuteronomy (chapter 28). Although these curses are also referred to as "*alot*," the priest does not write them. The addition of the definite article in the word **"*ha'eleh*"** serves **to exclude the commands** recorded in the *sota* passage **and the acceptances** by the word **"amen"** recorded there as well. The priest need not write these sections of the passage.

וְרַבִּי יוֹסֵי: כּוּלְּהוּ כְּדְקָאָמְרַתְּ, "אֶת" - לְרַבּוֹת צַוָּואוֹת וְקַבָּלוֹת.

And Rabbi Yosei interprets it: **It** would **all** be **as you,** Rabbi Meir, **said;** however, the additional word **"*et*"** in the verse amplifies its scope. It serves **to include** both **commands and acceptances,** as they must be written in the scroll as well.

וְרַבִּי מֵאִיר, אֶתִּים לָא דָּרֵישׁ.

And why does **Rabbi Meir** disagree? As a rule, he **does not interpret** the additional word ***et*** as amplifying a verse's scope.

וְרַבִּי יְהוּדָה, כּוּלְּהוּ בְּמִיעוּטֵי דָּרֵישׁ לְהוּ: "אָלוֹת" - אָלוֹת מַמָּשׁ, "הָאָלוֹת" - לְמַעוֹטֵי קְלָלוֹת הַבָּאוֹת מֵחֲמַת בְּרָכוֹת, "אֵלֶּה" - לְמַעוֹטֵי קְלָלוֹת שֶׁבְּמִשְׁנֵה תוֹרָה, "הָאֵלֶּה" - לְמַעוֹטֵי צַוָּואוֹת וְקַבָּלוֹת.

And as for **Rabbi Yehuda, he interprets all of** the terms in the verse **as exclusionary:** The word **"*alot*"** is referring specifically to the **actual curses** recorded in the verses. The definite article in the word **"*ha'alot*"** serves **to exclude curses that come on account of blessings.** The word **"*eleh*"** serves **to exclude the curses** recorded **in the *Mishne Torah*.** And the definite article in the word **"*ha'eleh*"** serves **to exclude** the **commands and acceptances** recorded in the verses.

וְרַבִּי מֵאִיר, מַאי שְׁנָא הַאי הֵ"י דְּמַרְבֵּי בֵּיהּ, וּמַאי שְׁנָא הַאי הֵ"י דְּמַעֵיט בֵּיהּ?

The Gemara asks: **But** according to **Rabbi Meir, what is different** about **this** letter ***heh*** at the beginning of the word "*ha'alot*" such **that it amplifies** the *halakha* to include curses that come on account of the blessings, **and what is different** about **that** letter ***heh*** in the word "*ha'eleh*" such **that it excludes** the commands and acceptances by the word "amen"? Why should one amplify while the other excludes?

הֵ"י דְּגַבֵּיהּ דְּרִיבּוּיָא - רִיבּוּיָא הִיא; הֵ"י דְּגַבֵּיהּ דְּמִיעוּטָא - מִיעוּטָא.

The Gemara answers: The letter ***heh*** **when** written **near an amplifier is an amplifier.** The word "*alot*" itself amplifies the *halakha*, and the definite article extends that amplification; and a ***heh*** **when** written **near** a **restrictor is a restrictor.** The word "*eleh*" itself restricts the *halakha*, and the definite article before it extends that restriction.

וְהָא לֵית לֵיהּ לְרַבִּי מֵאִיר מִכְּלָל לָאו אַתָּה שׁוֹמֵעַ הֵן!

The Gemara asks: **But Rabbi Meir does not** accept the principle that **from a negative** statement **you** can **infer a positive** statement. What is to be gained by writing the blessings if one cannot infer the curses from them?

אָמַר רַבִּי תַּנְחוּם: "הִנָּקִי" כְּתִיב.

Rabbi Tanḥum says: It is written: "If no man has lain with you... **you shall be free** [*hinnaki*]" (Numbers 5:19).[N] The word "*hinnaki*" should be interpreted as if it were in fact *ḥinnaki*, meaning: You shall choke. When read with the beginning of the next verse, it then forms the sentence: You shall choke... if you have gone astray while under your husband. Therefore, Rabbi Meir understands the blessings themselves to have a dimension of a curse.

דָּרֵישׁ רַבִּי עֲקִיבָא: אִישׁ וְאִשָּׁה, זָכוּ - שְׁכִינָה בֵּינֵיהֶן, לֹא זָכוּ - אֵשׁ אוֹכַלְתָּן.

§ **Rabbi Akiva taught:** If **a man** [*ish*] **and woman** [*isha*] **merit** reward through a faithful marriage, **the Divine Presence** rests **between them.** The words *ish* and *isha* are almost identical; the difference between them is the middle letter *yod* in *ish*, and the final letter *heh* in *isha*. These two letters can be joined to form the name of God spelled *yod, heh*. But if due to licentiousness **they do not merit** reward, the Divine Presence departs, leaving in each word only the letters *alef* and *shin*, which spell *esh*, fire. Therefore, **fire consumes them.**[N]

NOTES

Curses in *Mishne Torah* – קְלָלוֹת שֶׁבְּמִשְׁנֵה תוֹרָה: There is also a long list of curses recorded in Leviticus. However, no verse is needed to exclude it, since the curses there are written in the plural and directed to the people as a whole, whereas the ones in Deuteronomy are written in the singular (*Tosefot HaRash*; *Tosefot HaRosh*). From the commentaries of Rashi and the Meiri, however, it seems that they had an alternate text that reads: To exclude all the curses in the Torah, including those in Leviticus.

You shall be free [*hinnaki*] – הִנָּקִי: A number of explanations have been given for the significance of this phrase. Most understand that the word *hinnaki* resembles *ḥinnaki*, taken to mean: You shall choke. The word is therefore a hint that if she is in fact guilty she will die a terrible death. The *Sefat Emet* adds that the phrase: You shall be free, indicates that there are additional curses not explicit in the verse from which the *sota* will be saved only if she is innocent.

Fire consumes them – אֵשׁ אוֹכַלְתָּן: A number of commentaries explain that this refers to the fire of discord, which appears as a result of the departure of the Divine Presence and leads to disputes between the couple (see, e.g., *Iyyun Ya'akov*). According to the *Halakhot Gedolot*, however, the consuming fire is the evil inclinations of the couple.

אָמַר רָבָא: וּדְאִשָּׁה עֲדִיפָא מִדְּאִישׁ. מַאי טַעְמָא? הַאי מִצָּרֵף, וְהַאי לָא מִצָּרֵף.

Rava said: And the fire **that** consumes **the woman is stronger**[N] and more immediate **than that** which consumes **the man. What is the reason** for this? The letters *alef* and *shin* in the word *isha* **are** adjacent, **joined** together, **but** in the word *ish* **they are not joined,** as the letter *yod* is written between them.

אָמַר רָבָא, מִפְּנֵי מָה אָמְרָה תּוֹרָה: הָבֵא עָפָר לַסּוֹטָה? זָכְתָה – יוֹצֵא מִמֶּנָּה בֵּן כְּאַבְרָהָם אָבִינוּ, דִּכְתִיב בֵּיהּ ״עָפָר וָאֵפֶר״, לֹא זָכְתָה – תַּחֲזוֹר לַעֲפָרָהּ.

Additionally, **Rava says: For what** reason **did the Torah say: Bring dust for the** ***sota*****?**[N] It is because if **she merits** to be proven faithful after drinking the water of the *sota*, **a child like our Patriarch Abraham will emerge from her, as it is written with regard to** Abraham that he said: "I am but **dust and ashes**" (Genesis 18:27). But **if she does not merit** to be proven faithful after drinking the water of the *sota*, **she shall** die and **return to her dust,** the soil from which mankind was formed.

דָּרֵישׁ רָבָא: בִּשְׂכַר שֶׁאָמַר אַבְרָהָם אָבִינוּ: ״וְאָנֹכִי עָפָר וָאֵפֶר״, זָכוּ בָּנָיו לִשְׁתֵּי מִצְוֹת: אֵפֶר פָּרָה וַעֲפַר סוֹטָה.

And **Rava** further **taught: As reward** for that **which our Patriarch Abraham said:**[N] **"And I am but dust and ashes"** (Genesis 18:27), **his children merited two mitzvot: The ashes of the** red **heifer** (see Numbers, chapter 19) **and the dust of the** ***sota*****.**

וְהָאִיכָּא נַמִי עֲפַר כִּיסּוּי הַדָּם!

The Gemara asks: **But there is also** another mitzva involving dust: **The dust** used for **covering the blood** of a slaughtered undomesticated animal or fowl (see Leviticus 17:13).

הָתָם הֶכְשֵׁר מִצְוָה אִיכָּא, הֲנָאָה לֵיכָּא.

The Gemara answers: **There,** the dust **does** serve as an **accessory to the mitzva** of covering the blood, but **there is no benefit** imparted by it. It occurs after the animal has been slaughtered and does not itself render the meat fit for consumption.

דָּרַשׁ רָבָא: בִּשְׂכַר שֶׁאָמַר אַבְרָהָם אָבִינוּ: ״אִם מִחוּט וְעַד שְׂרוֹךְ נַעַל״, זָכוּ בָּנָיו לִשְׁתֵּי מִצְוֹת: חוּט שֶׁל תְּכֵלֶת וּרְצוּעָה שֶׁל תְּפִלִּין.

Rava further **taught: As reward** for that **which our Patriarch Abraham said** to the king of Sodom: **"That** I will not take **a thread nor a shoe strap** nor anything that is yours" (Genesis 14:23), distancing himself from anything not rightfully his, **his children merited two mitzvot: The thread of sky-blue** wool[B] worn on ritual fringes **and the strap of phylacteries.**

בִּשְׁלָמָא רְצוּעָה שֶׁל תְּפִלִּין, דִּכְתִיב: ״וְרָאוּ כָּל עַמֵּי הָאָרֶץ כִּי שֵׁם ה׳ נִקְרָא עָלֶיךָ״, וְתַנְיָא, רַבִּי אֱלִיעֶזֶר הַגָּדוֹל אוֹמֵר: אֵלּוּ תְּפִלִּין שֶׁבָּרֹאשׁ.

The Gemara asks: **Granted, the strap of** the **phylacteries** impart benefit, **as it is written: "And all the peoples of the earth shall see that the name of the Lord is called upon you;** and they shall be afraid of you" (Deuteronomy 28:10). **And it is taught** in a *baraita* that **Rabbi Eliezer the Great says: This is** a reference to **the phylacteries of the head,** upon which the name of God is written. Phylacteries therefore impart the splendor and grandeur of God and are a fit reward.

NOTES

And the fire that consumes the woman is stronger – וּדְאִשָּׁה עֲדִיפָא: According to the *Iyyun Ya'akov*, this means that the fire that consumes the woman expiates her sins more than that of the man. This is because from the time of Eve's curse, a woman undergoes much physical suffering through menstruation, pregnancy, and childbirth. This suffering serves as an additional expiating force.

Dust for the *sota* – עָפָר לַסּוֹטָה: In the Jerusalem Talmud the symbolism of the scroll of the *sota*, the dust, and the water is explained. The dust alludes to death, while the water alludes to the beginning of one's formation. The scroll represents the accounting one must provide before God. These are the three elements that one must contemplate so as to avoid sin, as stated in the mishna in tractate *Avot* (3:1): Know from where you come, and to where you are going, and before Whom you will have to give an accounting.

As reward for that which our Patriarch Abraham said, etc. – בִּשְׂכַר שֶׁאָמַר אַבְרָהָם אָבִינוּ וכו׳: Abraham's statement displayed his modesty; the Divine Presence rests with those who are modest. God provided mitzvot that ensure that the Divine Presence rests among the Jewish people. These mitzvot help eradicate impurity and adultery, both of which banish the Divine Presence (*Iyyun Ya'akov*).

BACKGROUND

Sky-blue wool [*tekhelet*] – תְּכֵלֶת: The Torah mentions the color *tekhelet* in many situations, and the word refers specifically to the dye from which the color is made. Various discussions in the Gemara make it clear that the blue dye of the *tekhelet* was extracted from a living creature called a *ḥilazon*. Because of the many passages that describe the *ḥilazon*, it is difficult to identify one particular animal that meets all of the criteria, and there are many different opinions with regard to its classification. Already during talmudic times the use of *tekhelet* became a rarity, and soon its true source was forgotten. In recent generations there have been efforts to identify the *ḥilazon* and to resume use of the dye. Various suggestions have been made as to the identity of the *ḥilazon*, including the common cuttlefish and the raft snail. Today, many are of the opinion that the *ḥilazon* is the snail *Murex trunculus*, which is found on the shores of the Mediterranean Sea in the north of Israel. This creature has a unique liquid dye, which, when mixed with other materials, produces the blue *tekhelet* color described in the Torah.

The Torah (Numbers 15:38) delineates a positive mitzva to use wool that is dyed with this color for ritual fringes. One of the four threads of the fringes must be dyed with this blue dye, and it is wound around the other threads. However, one can fulfill the mitzva to wear fringes even if the threads are not dyed, and today most ritual fringes are made without the dyed thread.

Murex

Common cuttlefish

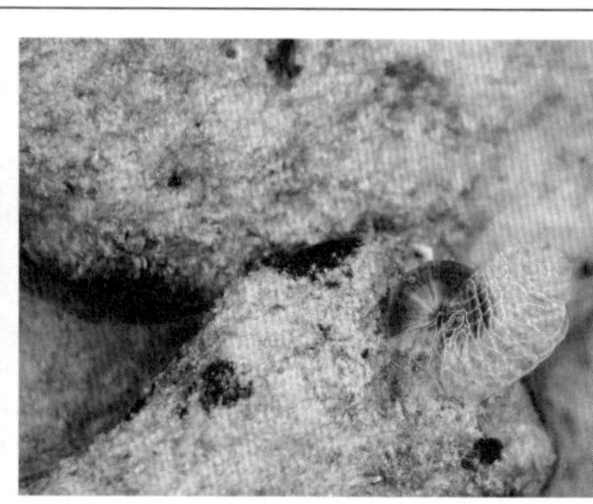

Raft snail

אֶלָּא חוּט שֶׁל תְּכֵלֶת מַאי הִיא? דְּתַנְיָא, הָיָה רַבִּי מֵאִיר אוֹמֵר: מָה נִשְׁתַּנָּה תְּכֵלֶת מִכׇּל מִינֵי צִבְעוֹנִין?

But what is the benefit imparted by **the thread of sky-blue** wool? The Gemara answers: **As it is taught** in a *baraita* that **Rabbi Meir would say: What is different about sky-blue from all other colors** such that it was specified for the mitzva of ritual fringes?

מִפְּנֵי שֶׁהַתְּכֵלֶת דּוֹמָה לַיָּם, וְיָם דּוֹמֶה לָרָקִיעַ, וְרָקִיעַ דּוֹמֶה לְכִסֵּא הַכָּבוֹד, שֶׁנֶּאֱמַר: "וַיִּרְאוּ אֵת אֱלֹהֵי יִשְׂרָאֵל וְתַחַת רַגְלָיו כְּמַעֲשֵׂה לִבְנַת הַסַּפִּיר וּכְעֶצֶם הַשָּׁמַיִם לָטֹהַר", וּכְתִיב: "כְּמַרְאֵה אֶבֶן סַפִּיר דְּמוּת כִּסֵּא".

It is **because sky-blue** dye **is similar** in its color **to the sea, and the sea is similar to the sky, and the sky is similar to the Throne of Glory, as it is stated: "And they saw the God of Israel; and there was under His feet the like of a paved work of sapphire stone, and the like of the very heaven for clearness"** (Exodus 24:10). This verse shows that the heavens are similar to sapphire, **and it is written:** "And above the firmament that was over their heads was **the likeness of a throne, as the appearance of a sapphire stone**" (Ezekiel 1:26). Therefore, the throne is similar to the heavens. The color of sky blue dye acts as an indication of the bond between the Jewish people and the Divine Presence.

מתני׳ אֵינוֹ כּוֹתֵב לֹא עַל הַלּוּחַ וְלֹא עַל הַנְּיָיר וְלֹא עַל

MISHNA The priest **does not write** the scroll of the *sota* **upon** a wooden **tablet**,[H] **and not upon paper** made from grass, **and not upon**

HALAKHA

The priest does not write upon a wooden tablet, etc. – אֵינוֹ כּוֹתֵב לֹא עַל הַלּוּחַ וכו׳: The curses of the *sota* are not written upon a wooden tablet, nor on unprocessed parchment, nor on paper. They must be written on a parchment scroll. If they are written on paper or unprocessed parchment, the scroll is unfit (Rambam *Sefer Nashim*, *Hilkhot Sota* 4:8).

Perek **II**
Daf **17** Amud **b**

הַדִּיפְתְּרָא – אֶלָּא עַל הַמְּגִילָּה, שֶׁנֶּאֱמַר: "בַּסֵּפֶר".

diftera,[L] a hide that is only partially processed, as it is salted and treated with flour but not gallnuts; **rather,** it must be written only **on a scroll** of parchment, **as it is stated:** "And the priest shall write these curses **in a scroll**" (Numbers 5:23).[N]

וְאֵינוֹ כּוֹתֵב לֹא בְּקוֹמוֹס וְלֹא בְּקַנְקַנְתּוֹם וְלֹא בְּכׇל דָּבָר שֶׁרוֹשֵׁם – אֶלָּא בִּדְיוֹ, שֶׁנֶּאֱמַר: "וּמָחָה", כְּתָב שֶׁיָּכוֹל לִמָּחוֹת.

And the scribe **may not write with gum** [*komos*],[LH] **and not with copper sulfate** [*kankantom*],[L] **nor with any substance that makes a mark** and cannot be completely erased, **but** only **with ink**[NB] made from soot, **as it is stated** in the continuation of the same verse: **"And he shall blot** them out into the water of bitterness" (Numbers 5:23). This indicates that the scroll must be written with **a writing that can be erased** in water.

גמ׳ אָמַר רָבָא: מְגִילַּת סוֹטָה שֶׁכְּתָבָהּ בַּלַּיְלָה – פְּסוּלָה. מַאי טַעְמָא? אָתְיָא "תּוֹרָה" "תּוֹרָה". כְּתִיב הָכָא: "וְעָשָׂה לָהּ הַכֹּהֵן אֵת כׇּל הַתּוֹרָה הַזֹּאת", וּכְתִיב הָתָם: "עַל פִּי הַתּוֹרָה אֲשֶׁר יוֹרוּךָ וְעַל הַמִּשְׁפָּט". מָה מִשְׁפָּט בַּיּוֹם, אַף מְגִילַּת סוֹטָה בַּיּוֹם.

GEMARA **Rava says: A scroll of a *sota* that one wrote at night**[H] **is unfit. What is the reason** for this? It is **derived** by verbal analogy between one instance of the word **"law"** and another instance of the word **"law." It is written here,** with regard to a *sota*: **"And the priest shall execute upon her all this law"** (Numbers 5:30), **and it is written there,** with regard to judgment: **"According to the law, which they shall teach you, and according to the judgment,** which they shall tell you" (Deuteronomy 17:11). **Just as judgment** may be done only **by day, so too the scroll of a *sota*** may be written only **by day.**

NOTES

On a scroll [*megilla*]…in a scroll [*sefer*] – עַל הַמְּגִילָּה...בַּסֵּפֶר: Rashi explains elsewhere (*Eiruvin* 15b) that whenever the Torah refers to a written object as a *sefer* it means a scroll [*megilla*]. This can be seen in Jeremiah (36:18–20), where the *sefer* written is later referred to as a *megilla*. The same verse in Jeremiah also indicates that one must write with ink.

But only with ink – אֶלָּא בִּדְיוֹ: Some question whether the scroll of a *sota* must be written specifically with ink, or whether it may be written with other writing substances that can be erased (see *Sefat Emet* and *Devar Shaul*). According to Rabbi David Luria, the verses in Jeremiah 36:18–20 indicate that all scrolls must be written with ink. Although it appears from the Gemara that ink must be made specifically of soot and oils, the consensus is that one may use other inks with similar stabilizing materials.

LANGUAGE

Diftera – דִּיפְתְּרָא: From the Greek διφθέρα, *difthera*, meaning a hide prepared for writing.

Gum [*komos*] – קוֹמוֹס: From the Greek κόμμι, *kommi*, meaning tree sap. It specifically refers to gum arabic from the acacia tree known as *Acacia arabica*. This sap has a variety of uses, including the production of strong inks.

Copper sulfate [*kankantom*] – קַנְקַנְתּוֹם: This word appears in other sources as *kalkantom* or *kalkantos*. It derives from the Greek χάλκανθος, *khalkanthos*, meaning copper sulfate ($CuSO_4$). This substance was used as a base for the ancient dye and ink industry and is still used nowadays to make ink and shoe polish.

HALAKHA

And the scribe may not write with gum, etc. – וְאֵינוֹ כּוֹתֵב לֹא בְּקוֹמוֹס וכו׳: The scroll of the *sota* may not be written with ink containing copper sulfate, nor may it be written with gum or any substance which makes a permanent mark (Rambam *Sefer Nashim*, *Hilkhot Sota* 3:8, 4:9).

Wrote at night – כְּתָבָהּ בַּלַּיְלָה: A scroll of a *sota* written at night is unfit, in accordance with the statement of Rava (Rambam *Sefer Nashim*, *Hilkhot Sota* 4:7).

BACKGROUND

Ink – דְּיוֹ: In talmudic times, various writing utensils and colored inks were used for writing on parchment and paper. Black was the most common color of ink. This ink was similar to India ink, a thick ink made from the soot of burnt wood or oil. The soot was collected and mixed with the appropriate quantity of oil. Sometimes sap was also added to the ink so that it would better adhere to the writing surface.

כְּתָבָהּ לְמַפְרֵעַ – פְּסוּלָה, דִּכְתִיב: "וְכָתַב אֶת הָאָלוֹת הָאֵלֶּה", כִּי דִּכְתִיבָא.

If one wrote the scroll **out of sequence,**[NH] **it is unfit, as it is written: "And** the priest **shall write these** curses in a scroll" (Numbers 5:23). They must be written in the scroll just **as they are written** in the Torah.

כְּתָבָהּ קוֹדֶם שֶׁתְּקַבֵּל עָלֶיהָ שְׁבוּעָה – פְּסוּלָה, שֶׁנֶּאֱמַר "וְהִשְׁבִּיעַ" וְאַחַר כָּךְ "וְכָתַב".

If one wrote the scroll **before** the *sota* **accepted the oath upon herself,**[NH] the scroll **is unfit, as it is stated: "Then** the priest **shall cause** the woman **to swear** with the oath of cursing" (Numbers 5:21), **and afterward** it states: **"And** the priest **shall write** these curses in a scroll" (Numbers 5:23).

כְּתָבָהּ אִיגֶּרֶת – פְּסוּלָה, "בַּסֵּפֶר" אָמַר רַחֲמָנָא.

If one wrote the scroll **as a letter,**[H] i.e., without first scoring the lines onto the parchment, **it is unfit,** as **the Merciful One states** in the Torah: **"In a scroll,"** indicating that it must be written like a Torah scroll, in which the parchment must be scored.

NOTES

If one wrote the scroll out of sequence – כְּתָבָהּ לְמַפְרֵעַ: The word "these," which is the biblical source for this *halakha*, is used in an exegetical interpretation for other purposes as well. Still, as a rule, a verse retains its straightforward meaning even when interpreted otherwise. The *halakha* here is taught based on the word's straightforward meaning.

Before she accepted the oath upon herself – קוֹדֶם שֶׁתְּקַבֵּל עָלֶיהָ שְׁבוּעָה: Although the Gemara here explicitly states that the scroll must be written after the oath is administered, the *amora'im* disagree concerning this issue. See *Tosafot* for a discussion of the source of this dispute.

HALAKHA

Wrote the scroll out of sequence – כְּתָבָהּ לְמַפְרֵעַ: A scroll of a *sota* written out of sequence is unfit (Rambam *Sefer Nashim, Hilkhot Sota* 4:7).

Before she accepted the oath upon herself – קוֹדֶם שֶׁתְּקַבֵּל עָלֶיהָ שְׁבוּעָה: If the scroll was written before the *sota* accepted the oath upon herself, it is unfit (Rambam *Sefer Nashim, Hilkhot Sota* 4:7).

Wrote the scroll as a letter – כְּתָבָהּ אִיגֶּרֶת: A scroll written in the form of a letter is unfit (Rambam *Sefer Nashim, Hilkhot Sota* 4:8).

Perek **II**
Daf **18** Amud **a**

כְּתָבָהּ עַל שְׁנֵי דַּפִּין – פְּסוּלָה, "סֵפֶר" אֶחָד אָמַר רַחֲמָנָא, וְלֹא שְׁנַיִם וּשְׁלֹשָׁה סְפָרִים.

If one wrote the scroll **on two** unattached **pages,**[HN] **it is unfit,** as **the Merciful One states** in the Torah: "Scroll," in the singular. It must be written on **one scroll and not** on **two or three scrolls.**

כָּתַב אוֹת אַחַת וּמָחַק אוֹת אַחַת, וְכָתַב אוֹת אַחַת וּמָחַק אוֹת אַחַת – פְּסוּלָה, דִּכְתִיב: "וְעָשָׂה לָהּ הַכֹּהֵן אֵת כָּל הַתּוֹרָה הַזֹּאת".

If one wrote one letter[HN] **and erased** that **one letter** in water, **and** he then **wrote one** more **letter and erased** that **one letter, it is unfit, as it is written: "And the priest shall execute upon her all this law"** (Numbers 5:30). The entire passage must be written completely and only then erased, all at once.

בָּעֵי רָבָא: כָּתַב שְׁתֵּי מְגִילּוֹת לִשְׁתֵּי סוֹטוֹת, וּמְחָקָן לְתוֹךְ כּוֹס אֶחָד, מַהוּ? כְּתִיבָה לִשְׁמָהּ בָּעֵינַן – וְהָאִיכָּא, אוֹ דִּילְמָא בָּעֵינַן נַמִי מְחִיקָה לִשְׁמָהּ?

§ **Rava raised a dilemma: If one wrote two scrolls for two** separate *sota* **women but** then **erased** both of the scrolls **in one cup, what is** the *halakha*? Do **we require** that only the **writing** be performed **for the sake of** a specific woman, in which case **that is** accomplished here? **Or perhaps we require** that **also** the **erasure** be performed **for the sake of** a specific woman,[H] which is not accomplished here, since both scrolls are erased together?

וְאִם תִּמְצָא לוֹמַר: בָּעֵינַן נַמִי מְחִיקָה לִשְׁמָהּ, מְחָקָן בִּשְׁתֵּי כוֹסוֹת וְחָזַר וְעֵירְבָן, מַהוּ? מְחִיקָה לִשְׁמָהּ בָּעֵינַן – וְהָאִיכָּא, אוֹ דִּילְמָא: הָא לָאו דִּידַהּ קָא שָׁתְיָא, וְהָא לָאו דִּידַהּ קָא שָׁתְיָא?

And if you say that **we require** that **also** the **erasure** be **for the sake of** each specific woman, then if the priest **erased them in two** different **cups**[H] and afterward **mixed** the water from both together **again, what is** the *halakha*? **Do we require** that only the **erasure** be **for the sake of** a specific woman, in which case **that is** accomplished here? **Or perhaps** since **this** *sota* **does not drink** from only **her own** water **and that** *sota* **does not drink** from only **her own** water, the water is disqualified?

HALAKHA

If one wrote the scroll on two unattached pages – כְּתָבָהּ עַל שְׁנֵי דַּפִּין: If the scroll of a *sota* is written on two pages, it is unfit (Rambam *Sefer Nashim, Hilkhot Sota* 4:8).

If one wrote one letter, etc. – כָּתַב אוֹת אַחַת וכו׳: If the priest wrote one letter and erased it, and then wrote another letter and erased it, the scroll is unfit (Rambam *Sefer Nashim, Hilkhot Sota* 4:10).

Erasure for the sake of a specific woman – מְחִיקָה לִשְׁמָהּ: If the priest erased the scroll not for the sake of a specific *sota*, the water of the *sota* is unfit. Whenever the Gemara states: If you say, this is an indication that what follows that introduction is the accepted *halakha* (Rambam *Sefer Nashim, Hilkhot Sota* 4:11).

Erased them in two different cups, etc. – מְחָקָן בִּשְׁתֵּי כוֹסוֹת וכו׳: If the priest wrote two scrolls for two *sota* women and erased them in one cup, or if he erased them in separate cups and mixed the water in one cup, the water of the *sota* is unfit (Rambam *Sefer Nashim, Hilkhot Sota* 4:11).

NOTES

If one wrote the scroll on two unattached pages – כְּתָבָהּ עַל שְׁנֵי דַּפִּין: Most commentaries, including *Tosafot*, *Tosefot HaRosh*, and the Meiri, explain this as referring to a case where the contents of the scroll were written over two unattached pages of parchment. However, if they were attached, it is fit, just as a Torah scroll is written over many attached pages of parchment. By contrast, Rashi holds that the scroll is unfit even when written on two columns of attached parchment. Some explain Rashi's reasoning as follows: Since a Torah scroll is very long, it must, of necessity, be written on many pages of parchment. Therefore, it is still considered as one item. However, a scroll of a *sota* is short, and if written on separate pages of parchment, it appears to be two separate documents (*Meromei Sadeh*).

If one wrote one letter, etc. – כָּתַב אוֹת אַחַת וכו׳: According to the Meiri, the same *halakha* applies if one wrote a complete word and then erased it, or if one wrote part of the scroll properly and erased it. The scroll must be erased only after being completely written.

ואם תמצא לומר: הא לאו דידה קא שתיא והא לאו דידה קא שתיא, חזר וחלקן מהו? יש ברירה או אין ברירה? תיקו.

And furthermore, **if you say** that the water is disqualified because **this one does not drink** from only **her own** water **and that one does not drink** from only **her own** water, what if after mixing the two cups of water together the priest **divided them again**[H] into two cups and gave one to each? **What is the** *halakha* then? **Is there** retroactive **clarification,**[N] in which case one may claim that each woman drank her own water, **or is there no** retroactive **clarification?** The Gemara responds: The dilemma **shall stand** unresolved.

בעי רבא: השקה בסיב, מהו? בשפופרת, מהו? דרך שתיה בכך, או אין דרך שתיה בכך? תיקו.

Rava raised a dilemma: If the priest **administered** the bitter water to the *sota* **to drink through** a palm **fiber,**[N] **what is** the *halakha*? Or if he administered it **through a tube, what is** the *halakha*? **Is this** considered **a normal manner of drinking, or is it not** considered **a normal manner of drinking,** in which case the act is invalid? The Gemara responds: The dilemma **shall stand** unresolved.

בעי רב אשי: נשפכו מהן ונשתיירו מהן, מהו? תיקו.

Rav Ashi raised a dilemma: If some **of the** water of the *sota* **spilled** out **and some of it remained**[HN] in the cup, **what is** the *halakha*? Is it sufficient for the woman to drink some of the water in which the scroll has been erased or must she drink all of it? The Gemara responds: The dilemma **shall stand** unresolved.

אמר רבי זירא אמר רב: שתי שבועות האמורות בסוטה למה? אחת קודם שנמחקה מגילה, ואחת לאחר שנמחקה.

§ **Rabbi Zeira says** that **Rav says:** With regard to **the two oaths**[N] **that are stated with regard to the** ***sota***: "And the priest shall cause her to swear" (Numbers 5:19), and: "Then the priest shall cause the woman to swear with the oath of cursing" (Numbers 5:21), **why** are they both necessary? **One** must be administered **before the scroll is erased and one** must be administered **after it is erased.**

מתקיף לה רבא: תרוייהו קודם שנמחקה מגילה כתיבן! אלא אמר רבא: אחת שבועה שיש עמה אלה, ואחת שבועה שאין עמה אלה.

Rava objects to this: Both of the oaths **are written** in the Torah **before** any mention of **the scroll** being **erased.** What is the basis to claim that one oath was administered afterward? **Rather, Rava said:** While both oaths are administered before the *sota* drinks, the two oaths are different: **One is an oath that has a curse with it, and one is an oath that does not have a curse with it.**

היכי דמי שבועה שיש עמה אלה? אמר רב עמרם אמר רב: "משביעני עליך שלא נטמאת, שאם נטמאת יבואו ביך".

The Gemara asks: **What are the circumstances** of **an oath that has a curse with it?** What is the language of this oath? **Rav Amram says** that **Rav says:** The priest says: **I administer an oath to you** that you are honest in your claim **that you were not defiled, as, if you were defiled,** all these curses **will come upon you.**

אמר רבא: אלה לחודה קיימא, ושבועה לחודא קיימא! אלא אמר רבא: "משביעני עליך שאם נטמאת יבואו ביך".

Rava said: This is insufficient, as **the curse stands by itself and the oath stands by itself.** They are said in separate statements, and it cannot be considered to be an oath with a curse. **Rather, Rava said:** The priest says: **I administer an oath to you that if you were defiled,** all these curses **will come upon you.**

אמר רב אשי: אלה איכא, שבועה ליכא! אלא אמר רב אשי: "משביעני עליך שלא נטמאת, ואם נטמאת יבואו ביך".

Rav Ashi said: Even this is insufficient, as **there is a curse** but **there is no oath** that she was not defiled. **Rather, Rav Ashi said:** The priest must say: **I administer an oath to you that you were not defiled and** that **if you were defiled** all these curses **will come upon you.** Here the oath itself includes the curse.

מתני׳ על מה היא אומרת אמן אמן? אמן על האלה, אמן על השבועה. אמן מאיש זה, אמן מאיש אחר. אמן שלא שטיתי ארוסה ונשואה,

MISHNA **With regard to what does she say: "Amen, amen"** (Number 5:22),[H] twice, as recorded in the verse? The mishna explains that it includes of the following: **Amen on the curse,** as she accepts the curse upon herself if she is guilty, and **amen on the oath,** as she declares that she is not defiled. She states: **Amen** if I committed adultery **with this man** about whom I was warned, **amen** if I committed adultery **with another man. Amen that I did not stray** when I was **betrothed nor** after I was **married,**

HALAKHA

If he divided them again – חזר וחילקן: If the priest wrote two scrolls for two *sota* women, erased them in separate cups, and then mixed the water together in one cup, he should not administer this water of a *sota* to the *sota* women to drink *ab initio*. However, after the fact, if he separated the water again into two separate cups and they drank, the drinking is valid. The *Kesef Mishne* explains that the Rambam rules leniently on this question since no answer is provided to the Gemara's query, and such an uncertainty does not justify erasing the Divine Name again (Rambam *Sefer Nashim, Hilkhot Sota* 4:11).

If some of the water spilled out and some of it remained – נשפכו מהן ונשתיירו מהן: If some of the water spilled out and some remained, one should not administer it to the *sota* to drink *ab initio*. However, the drinking is valid after the fact. The Rambam rules leniently on this question since no answer is provided to the Gemara's query, and such an uncertainty does not justify erasing the Divine Name again (Rambam *Sefer Nashim, Hilkhot Sota* 4:11).

NOTES

Retroactive clarification – ברירה: This principle is a matter of controversy throughout the Talmud. It posits that a case of uncertainty at a given time may be decided retroactively based on a later event. In this case, when each woman drinks the water, it will be clarified that this was the water intended for her. The consensus among the halakhic authorities is that concerning matters of Torah law one may not claim retroactive clarification, but with regard to matters of rabbinic law one may do so.

Administered the bitter water to her to drink through a palm fiber – השקה בסיב: Rashi explains that the fiber here is similar to a straw, whereas the *Arukh* asserts that it is a spongy material from which the *sota* sucks water that has been absorbed in it. According to this understanding, this question is distinct from the following question of whether the *sota* may drink the water from a tube. *Tosafot* say that the question is whether, if the water of the *sota* was absorbed by a fiber and the *sota* swallowed the fiber, this is considered valid drinking after the fact.

If some of the water spilled out and some of it remained – נשפכו מהן ונשתיירו מהן: Rashi explains that this is describing one case, in which some of the water spilled out while the rest remained. According to the *Tosefot HaRosh*, however, these are two separate cases: In one, some of the water spilled out but a majority remains. In the other, more serious case, most of the water spilled out and only a small amount remains. Some hold that at least a quarter-*log* must remain in any event, because as a rule, consumption of less than this amount is not considered drinking (*Minḥat Kenaot*).

Two oaths, etc. – שתי שבועות וכו׳: In his commentary on the Torah, Ibn Ezra explains that the priest does administer the oath to the woman twice, as the Gemara indicates here. However, the Ramban explains in his commentary on the Torah that there is only one oath. This is the ruling of the Rambam as well. The *Sefat Emet* challenges this understanding as Rabbi Zeira explicitly states that there are two oaths. The *Ḥazon Yeḥezkel* explains that Rav Ashi's opinion is that there is only one oath, and this is the source of the opinion of the Rambam and Ramban. Still, this is not the straightforward understanding of Rav Ashi's statement, which seems concerned only with the wording of the oath, while accepting that there are in fact two oaths.

HALAKHA

With regard to what does she say amen, amen – על מה היא אומרת אמן אמן: Through the principle of extension of an oath, the husband may have his wife include in her oath other cases as well. Not only did she not commit adultery with the man about whom she was warned, but neither did she do so with any other man, nor did she commit adultery even during the period of her betrothal (Rambam *Sefer Nashim, Hilkhot Sota* 4:17).

BACKGROUND

A widow waiting for her *yavam* – שׁוֹמֶרֶת יָבָם: If a married man dies childless and is survived by one or more brothers, his widow is prohibited from marrying anyone else until one of the brothers, preferably the eldest, either performs levirate marriage or releases her by performing the *ḥalitza* ceremony. Until one of these procedures is done, the widow is bound to her late husband's brothers by a bond known as a levirate bond. A woman subject to such a bond is known as a widow waiting for her *yavam*. The *amora'im* and *tanna'im* discuss the nature and strength of the levirate bond.

HALAKHA

Amen that I will not become defiled – אָמֵן שֶׁלֹּא אֶטָּמֵא: The husband may stipulate that the woman include in her oath that she will not commit adultery in the future even if he divorces and remarries her. If she will commit adultery in the future after such an oath, the water of the *sota* will then evaluate her, in accordance with the opinion of Rabbi Meir (Rambam *Sefer Nashim, Hilkhot Sota* 4:17).

With regard to what she did before becoming betrothed, etc. – עַל קוֹדֶם שֶׁתִּתְאָרֵס וכו׳: The husband may not have the *sota* include in her oath that she did not engage in sexual intercourse with another man before she was betrothed or during a period of divorce from him (Rambam *Sefer Nashim, Hilkhot Sota* 4:17).

This is the principle, etc. – זֶה הַכְּלָל וכו׳: This is the principle: A husband may stipulate that his wife include in her oath any case of adultery that would render her forbidden to him if she were guilty of it. He may not stipulate that she include in her oath any case that would not (Rambam *Sefer Nashim, Hilkhot Sota* 4:17).

A widow awaiting her *yavam* – שׁוֹמֶרֶת יָבָם: If a widow waiting for her *yavam* to perform levirate marriage commits adultery, she is permitted to the *yavam*, in accordance with the conclusion of the Gemara and contrary to the opinion of Rav Hamnuna (Rambam *Sefer Nashim, Hilkhot Yibbum VaḤalitza* 2:20; *Shulḥan Arukh, Even HaEzer* 159:3).

וְשׁוֹמֶרֶת יָבָם וּכְנוּסָה. אָמֵן שֶׁלֹּא נִטְמֵאתִי, וְאִם נִטְמֵאתִי – יָבוֹאוּ בִּי.

nor as a widow waiting for my *yavam*[B] to perform levirate marriage, since a woman at that stage is prohibited from engaging in sexual intercourse with any men, **nor** when **married** through levirate marriage to the *yavam*; **amen that I did not become defiled, and if I did become defiled, may** all these curses **come upon me.**

רַבִּי מֵאִיר אוֹמֵר: אָמֵן שֶׁלֹּא נִטְמֵאתִי, אָמֵן שֶׁלֹּא אֶטָּמֵא.

Rabbi Meir says that "amen, amen" means: **Amen that I did not become defiled** in the past, **amen that I will not become defiled**[H] in the future.

הַכֹּל שָׁוִין שֶׁאֵין מַתְנֶה עִמָּהּ לֹא עַל קוֹדֶם שֶׁתִּתְאָרֵס וְלֹא עַל אַחַר שֶׁתִּתְגָּרֵשׁ.

All agree that he may stipulate with her through this oath **neither with regard to** what she did **before becoming betrothed**[H] to him, **nor with regard to** what she will do **after she becomes divorced** from him.

נִסְתְּרָה לְאֶחָד וְנִטְמֵאת וְאַחַר כָּךְ הֶחֱזִירָהּ – לֹא הָיָה מַתְנֶה עִמָּהּ.

Similarly, if a husband divorced his wife, and while divorced **she secluded herself** with another man **and became defiled, and afterward** her husband **took her back** and remarried her, and he then warned her about a specific man, and she secluded herself, and she is now about to drink the water of the *sota*, **he cannot stipulate with her** that she take an oath that she did not become defiled during the period in which she was divorced. This is because her husband would become forbidden to her only if she had married another man after being divorced, not if she merely committed an act of promiscuity.

זֶה הַכְּלָל: כֹּל שֶׁתִּבָּעֵל וְלֹא הָיְתָה אֲסוּרָה לוֹ – לֹא הָיָה מַתְנֶה עִמָּהּ.

This is the principle:[H] In **every** case **where** if **she would engage in sexual intercourse** with someone else **she would not become forbidden to** her husband due to this act, **he may not stipulate with her** that her oath include that act. The oath can include only cases in which she would be rendered forbidden to him.

גמ׳ אָמַר רַב הַמְנוּנָא: שׁוֹמֶרֶת יָבָם שֶׁזִּינְּתָה – אֲסוּרָה לִיבָמָהּ. מְמַאי? מִדְּקָתָנֵי: שׁוֹמֶרֶת יָבָם וּכְנוּסָה.

GEMARA **Rav Hamnuna says:** In the case of **a widow awaiting her *yavam***[H] **who committed adultery,**[N] **she** becomes **forbidden to her *yavam*. From where** is this derived? It is **from** the fact **that** the mishna **teaches: Nor as a widow waiting for my *yavam*** to perform levirate marriage, **nor** when **married** through levirate marriage.

אִי אָמְרַתְּ בִּשְׁלָמָא אֲסִירָה, מִשּׁוּם הָכִי מַתְנֶה בַּהֲדָהּ. אֶלָּא אִי אָמְרַתְּ לָא אֲסִירָה, הֵיכִי מַתְנֶה בַּהֲדָהּ? וְהָתְנַן – זֶה הַכְּלָל: כֹּל שֶׁאִילּוּ תִּיבָּעֵל וְלֹא תְּהֵא אֲסוּרָה לוֹ – לֹא הָיָה מַתְנֶה עִמָּהּ!

The Gemara explains: **Granted, if you say** that a woman awaiting levirate marriage who committed adultery **is forbidden** to the *yavam*, **due to that** reason a husband **may stipulate with** a *sota* that she take an oath that she did not commit adultery while she was awaiting levirate marriage with him. **But if you say that** such a woman **does not become forbidden, how can** a husband **stipulate** this **with her? But didn't we learn** in the mishna that **this is the principle:** In **every** case **where** if **she would engage in sexual intercourse** with someone else **she would not become forbidden to** her husband due to this act, **he may not stipulate with her** that her oath include that act? Clearly she must become forbidden to the *yavam* if she commits adultery.

אָמְרִי בְּמַעְרְבָא: לֵית הִילְכְתָא כְּרַב הַמְנוּנָא.

They say in the West, Eretz Yisrael: **The *halakha* is not in accordance with** the opinion of **Rav Hamnuna.** A woman awaiting levirate marriage who commits adultery does not become forbidden to the *yavam*.

NOTES

A widow awaiting her *yavam* who committed adultery – שׁוֹמֶרֶת יָבָם שֶׁזִּינְּתָה: The status of such a woman is discussed in the Jerusalem Talmud as well. Although the Gemara here attributes a specific opinion to the inhabitants of Eretz Yisrael, this refers only to a particular Sage there.

אֶלָּא הָא דְּקָתָנֵי: שׁוֹמֶרֶת יָבָם וּכְנוּסָה, הָא מַנִּי? רַבִּי עֲקִיבָא הִיא, דְּאָמַר: אֵין קִידּוּשִׁין תּוֹפְסִין בְּחַיָּיבֵי לָאוִין, וּמְשַׁוֵּי לָהּ כִּי עֶרְוָה.

The Gemara asks: **But** with regard to **that which is taught** in the mishna: **Nor as a widow waiting for my *yavam*** to perform levirate marriage, **nor** when **married** through levirate marriage, in accordance with **whose** opinion **is this? It is** in accordance with the opinion of **Rabbi Akiva, who says: Betrothal does not take effect** even **for** those who would be merely **liable for** violating ordinary **prohibitions** were they to be married. All agree that betrothal does not take effect for forbidden unions that carry the punishment of *karet*, e.g., unions between siblings. However, according to Rabbi Akiva, in matters of personal status an ordinary Torah prohibition is equivalent to prohibitions that carry the punishment of *karet*. **And** he therefore holds that just as a wife who commits adultery, rendering her liable to receive *karet*, is forbidden to her husband and must be divorced, so too, a widow awaiting her *yavam* who commits adultery, violating an ordinary Torah prohibition, **is considered to be a woman forbidden to** her *yavam*.[N]

בָּעֵי רַבִּי יִרְמְיָה: מַהוּ שֶׁיַּתְנֶה אָדָם עַל נִישּׂוּאִין הָרִאשׁוֹנִים? עַל נִישּׂוּאֵי אָחִיו, מַהוּ?

Rabbi Yirmeya raised a dilemma: If a man divorced his wife and then remarried her, and she then secluded herself and came to drink the water of a *sota*, **what is** the *halakha* as to **whether a man** in that situation **may stipulate** with her **concerning** their **first marriage?**[H] May he compel her to include in her oath that she did not commit adultery then either? Similarly, may a *yavam* stipulate with his *yevama* **concerning the marriage of his brother,** requiring her to attest that she did not commit adultery prior to the brother's death? **What is** the *halakha*?

תָּא שְׁמַע, זֶה הַכְּלָל: כָּל שֶׁתִּיבָּעֵל וְלֹא תְּהֵא אֲסוּרָה לוֹ – לֹא הָיָה מַתְנֶה עִמָּהּ, הָא אֲסִירָה – הָכִי נַמִי דְּמַתְנֶה. שְׁמַע מִינַּהּ.

The Gemara proposes: **Come** and **hear** evidence from the conclusion of the mishna: **This is the principle:** In **every** case **where** if **she would engage in sexual intercourse** with someone else **she would not become forbidden to** her husband due to this act, **he may not stipulate with her** that her oath include that act. One may **therefore** infer **that he may indeed stipulate** with her concerning any case in which **she** would become **forbidden.** In both of the cases in question the woman would have become forbidden to her husband if she had been guilty. Therefore, the Gemara concludes: Indeed, **conclude from** the mishna that he is entitled to stipulate in these cases.

"רַבִּי מֵאִיר אוֹמֵר: אָמֵן שֶׁלֹּא נִטְמֵאתִי" וכו׳. תַּנְיָא, לֹא כְּשֶׁאָמַר רַבִּי מֵאִיר: אָמֵן שֶׁלֹּא אֶטָּמֵא, שֶׁאִם תִּטָּמֵא – מַיִם בּוֹדְקִין אוֹתָהּ מֵעַכְשָׁיו. אֶלָּא, לִכְשֶׁתִּטָּמֵא מַיִם מְעַרְעֲרִין אוֹתָהּ וּבוֹדְקִין אוֹתָהּ.

§ The mishna states: **Rabbi Meir says** that "amen, amen" means: **Amen that I did not become defiled** in the past, amen that I will not become defiled in the future. With regard to this **it is taught** in a *baraita* (*Tosefta* 2:2): **When Rabbi Meir said: Amen that I will not become defiled** in the future, he did **not** mean to say **that if** God knows that **she will become defiled** in the future, the **water** that she drinks now **evaluates** whether **she** will be unfaithful and passes judgment on her **from now. Rather,** he meant **that** in the event **that she becomes defiled** in the future, the **water** that she drinks now will **destabilize her and evaluate** then whether **she** was unfaithful.

בָּעֵי רַב אַשִׁי: מַהוּ שֶׁיַּתְנֶה אָדָם עַל נִישּׂוּאִין הָאַחֲרוֹנִים? הַשְׁתָּא מִיהָא לָא אֲסִירָה לֵיהּ, אוֹ דִּילְמָא זִימְנִין דִּמְגָרֵשׁ לָהּ וַהֲדַר מַהְדַר לָהּ?

Rav Ashi raised a dilemma: What is the *halakha* as to **whether a man may stipulate** with his wife **concerning a later marriage,**[H] in the event that he would divorce her and then remarry her? Do we say: **Now, at least,** if she remains faithful during this marriage, **she is not forbidden to him? Or perhaps** this includes a later marriage, as **sometimes** a man **divorces** his wife **and remarries her,** and if she then commits adultery she will become forbidden to him.

NOTES

And therefore she is considered to be a woman forbidden to her *yavam* – וּמְשַׁוֵּי לָהּ כִּי עֶרְוָה: The Jerusalem Talmud suggests other reasons that a man may stipulate with his wife with regard to her time as a widow awaiting levirate marriage to him. Some derive this from the stringent wording of the verse concerning the *yevama*: "The wife of the dead man shall not be married outside of the family to one not of his kin" (Deuteronomy 25:5), and explain that a widow awaiting levirate marriage who commits adultery is forbidden to her *yavam*. Others derive from the verse concerning the *sota*, which states twice: "And is jealous of his wife" (Numbers 5:14), that a man may warn even a woman who is only partially his wife, i.e., a *yevama* awaiting levirate marriage to him, who has a quasi-matrimonial relationship with him.

HALAKHA

Concerning their first marriage, etc. – עַל נִישּׂוּאִין הָרִאשׁוֹנִים וכו׳: A man who divorced his wife and remarried her may compel her to include in her oath that she did not commit adultery during the first marriage. One who performed levirate marriage may compel the *yevama* to include in her oath that she did not commit adultery when married to his brother (Rambam *Sefer Nashim, Hilkhot Sota* 4:17).

Concerning a later marriage – עַל נִישּׂוּאִין הָאַחֲרוֹנִים: The husband may stipulate that the *sota* include in her oath that the waters of a *sota* should evaluate even adultery she would commit after he divorces and remarries her, in accordance with the conclusion of the Gemara (Rambam *Sefer Nashim, Hilkhot Sota* 4:17).

תָּא שְׁמַע: הַכֹּל שָׁוִין שֶׁלֹּא הָיָה מַתְנֶה עִמָּהּ לֹא עַל קוֹדֶם שֶׁתִּתְאָרֵס וְלֹא עַל אַחַר שֶׁתִּתְגָּרֵשׁ. נִסְתְּרָה לְאֶחָד וְנִטְמֵאת וְאַחַר כָּךְ יַחֲזִירֶנָּה – לֹא הָיָה מַתְנֶה. הָא יַחֲזִירֶנָּה וְתִיטָּמֵא הָכִי נַמִי דְּמַתְנֵי. שְׁמַע מִינָּהּ.

The Gemara answers: **Come** and **hear** evidence from the mishna: **All agree that he may stipulate with her** through this oath **neither with regard to** what she did **before becoming betrothed** to him, **nor with regard to** what she will do **after she becomes divorced** from him. And if while divorced she **secluded herself** with another man **and became defiled, and afterward** her husband **took her back** and remarried her, **he may not stipulate** with her with regard to the period in which she was divorced, since that act does not render her forbidden to him. The Gemara infers: But if **he remarries her and she** then **becomes defiled,** she would be forbidden to him. Therefore, **he may indeed stipulate** with her in advance with regard to this. The Gemara states: Indeed, **conclude from** the mishna that this is so.

תָּנוּ רַבָּנַן: "זֹאת תּוֹרַת הַקְּנָאֹת" – מְלַמֵּד, שֶׁהָאִשָּׁה שׁוֹתָה וְשׁוֹנָה.

§ **The Sages taught:** The verse states: **"This is the law of jealousy"** (Numbers 5:29), indicating that the same law is to be carried out in all cases of jealousy. This **teaches that the woman drinks and repeats,**[NH] i.e., she must drink a second time if she becomes a *sota* again.

רַבִּי יְהוּדָה אוֹמֵר: "זֹאת" – שֶׁאֵין הָאִשָּׁה שׁוֹתָה וְשׁוֹנָה. אָמַר רַבִּי יְהוּדָה: מַעֲשֶׂה וְהֵעִיד לְפָנֵינוּ נְחוּנְיָא חוֹפֵר שִׁיחִין, שֶׁהָאִשָּׁה שׁוֹתָה וְשׁוֹנָה, וְקִיבַּלְנוּ עֵדוּתוֹ בִּשְׁנֵי אֲנָשִׁים, אֲבָל לֹא בְּאִישׁ אֶחָד.

The *baraita* continues: **Rabbi Yehuda says:** The word **"this"** in the verse is a restricting term, indicating **that the woman does not drink and repeat. Rabbi Yehuda said:** There was **an incident** in which **Neḥunya the ditch digger**[P] **testified before us** in the name of his teachers **that the woman drinks and repeats, and we accepted his testimony with regard to two men, but not with regard to one man.** Even if she drinks the water of a *sota* while married to her first husband, she must drink again after violating a warning by her second husband. However, one husband cannot have his wife drink twice.

וַחֲכָמִים אוֹמְרִים: אֵין הָאִשָּׁה שׁוֹתָה וְשׁוֹנָה, בֵּין בְּאִישׁ אֶחָד בֵּין בִּשְׁנֵי אֲנָשִׁים.

The *baraita* concludes: **And the Rabbis say: The woman does not drink and repeat, whether with regard to one man or with regard to two men.**

וְתַנָּא קַמָּא נַמִי הָכְתִיב: "זֹאת"! וְרַבָּנַן בַּתְרָאֵי נַמִי הָא כְּתִיב: "תּוֹרַת"!

The Gemara asks: **But** according to **the first *tanna*** of the *baraita* **as well, isn't it written** in the verse: **"This,"** restricting the number of times a woman must drink? **And** according to **the Rabbis** mentioned **later** in the *baraita* **as well, isn't it written: "The law of** jealousy," amplifying the number of times a woman must drink to include all cases of jealousy?

אֲמַר רָבָא: בְּאִישׁ אֶחָד וּבוֹעֵל אֶחָד – דְּכוּלֵּי עָלְמָא לָא פְּלִיגִי דְּאֵין הָאִשָּׁה שׁוֹתָה וְשׁוֹנָה,

Rava said: Different *halakhot* apply to different cases: **With regard to one husband** who accused his wife twice about **one paramour, everyone agrees that the woman does not drink and repeat,** having been proven innocent once,

Perek **II**
Daf **19** Amud **a**

דִּכְתִיב: "זֹאת". בִּשְׁנֵי אֲנָשִׁים וּשְׁנֵי בוֹעֲלִין – דְּכוּלֵּי עָלְמָא לָא פְּלִיגִי דְּהָאִשָּׁה שׁוֹתָה וְשׁוֹנָה, דִּכְתִיב: "תּוֹרַת".

as it is written: "This is the law of jealousy." The word "this" is a restricting term and excludes that possibility. **With regard to two** different **husbands and two** different **paramours,** where her first husband suspected her with regard to one paramour during her first marriage and the second husband suspected her with regard to a different man during the second marriage, **everyone agrees that the woman drinks and repeats, as it is written:** "This is **the law of** jealousy," in all cases of jealousy.

כִּי פְּלִיגִי – בְּאִישׁ אֶחָד וּשְׁנֵי בוֹעֲלִין, בִּשְׁנֵי אֲנָשִׁים וּבוֹעֵל אֶחָד.

They disagree when there is **one husband and two paramours,** i.e., where one husband warned her with regard to a second paramour after she survived her first ordeal. They also disagree **in** a case of **two husbands and one paramour,** i.e., if her second husband accused her with regard to the same paramour on account of whom she was compelled to drink by her first husband.

NOTES

Drinks and repeats – שׁוֹתָה וְשׁוֹנָה: The *Maharit* asks: Given that the *halakha* is in accordance with the opinion of Rabbi Meir that a man may stipulate with his wife with regard to adultery in the future, why would one ever need to have his wife drink a second time? Her initial drinking should be proof of her future fidelity. Some answer that this would be necessary if the husband himself committed adultery before she did, which would prevent the water of the *sota* from examining his wife, and after he repents, he wants her to drink again (see *Keren Ora* and *Meromei Sadeh*). Others explain that it would be necessary in the case of a woman whose punishment was initially delayed due to her merit, and whose husband therefore wished that she drink a second time (see *Sefat Emet*). Yet others say that the stipulation with regard to the fidelity of the *sota* in the future is not mandatory; in the event that the husband does not include it initially, he may have her drink again in the future (*Minḥat Ḥinnukh*).

HALAKHA

Drinks and repeats – שׁוֹתָה וְשׁוֹנָה: If a man warned his wife concerning another man, and after secluding herself with him she drank the waters of a *sota* and was found innocent, the husband may not compel her to drink a second time due to suspicion with regard to the same man. However, he may compel her to drink a second time if he suspects her with regard to another man. If a *sota* who drank waters of a *sota* and was found innocent was widowed or divorced and remarried another man, and her new husband suspects her with regard to the same man that the first husband suspected, he may compel her to drink a second time on that man's account (Rambam *Sefer Nashim, Hilkhot Sota* 1:12–13).

PERSONALITIES

Neḥunya the ditch digger – נְחוּנְיָא חוֹפֵר שִׁיחִין: This Sage lived at the time of the Second Temple and was an officer of the Temple. He was responsible for digging pits and wells for the benefit of the pilgrims and residents of Jerusalem. The Talmud relates a miracle that happened to his daughter when she fell into a large pit in Jerusalem and was saved. The Gemara also mentions elsewhere that God judges great people like him very exactingly.

תַּנָּא קַמָּא סָבַר: "תּוֹרַת" – לְרַבּוּיֵי כּוּלְּהִי, "זֹאת" – לְמַעוּטֵי אִישׁ אֶחָד וּבוֹעֵל אֶחָד.

The opinions are justified as follows: **The first *tanna* holds** that the phrase **"the law of** jealousy" serves **to include all of these** cases. In almost all cases the woman drinks and repeats. The word **"this"** serves **to exclude** only the case of **one husband and one paramour,** in which she does not drink and repeat.

וְרַבָּנַן בַּתְרָאֵי סָבְרִי: "זֹאת" – לְמַעוּטֵי כּוּלְּהִי, "תּוֹרַת" – לְרַבּוּיֵי שְׁנֵי אֲנָשִׁים וּשְׁנֵי בוֹעֲלִין.

And the Rabbis mentioned **later** in the *baraita* **hold** that the word **"this"** serves **to exclude all of these** cases. The woman almost never drinks and repeats. The phrase **"the law of** jealousy" serves **to include** only the case of **two husbands and two paramours,** in which she does drink and repeat.

וְרַבִּי יְהוּדָה: "זֹאת" – לְמַעוּטֵי תַּרְתֵּי, "תּוֹרַת" – לְרַבּוֹת תַּרְתֵּי. "זֹאת" לְמַעוּטֵי תַּרְתֵּי – אִישׁ אֶחָד וּבוֹעֵל אֶחָד, אִישׁ אֶחָד וּשְׁנֵי בוֹעֲלִין. "תּוֹרַת" לְרַבּוּיֵי תַּרְתֵּי – שְׁנֵי אֲנָשִׁים וּבוֹעֵל אֶחָד, שְׁנֵי אֲנָשִׁים וּשְׁנֵי בוֹעֲלִין.

And Rabbi Yehuda holds: The word **"this"** serves **to exclude two**[N] of the cases, and the phrase **"the law of** jealousy" serves **to include two.** The word **"this"** serves **to exclude** the **two** cases of **one husband and one paramour** and **one husband and two paramours.** In neither of these cases does the woman drink and repeat. The phrase **"the law of** jealousy" serves **to include two** cases, i.e., **two husbands and one paramour,** and all the more so **two husbands and two paramours.** In both of these cases, the woman must drink and repeat.

הדרן עלך היה מביא

NOTES

This serves to exclude two – זֹאת לְמַעוּטֵי תַּרְתֵּי: Rashi explains the logic behind the opinion of Rabbi Yehuda. If one man warns his wife a second time after she was already found to be innocent, no matter whether he suspects a different paramour or the same one, it appears that his suspicions are unfounded and he is simply a quarrelsome person.

Summary of
Perek II

The chapter began by enumerating the differences between the meal-offering of a *sota* and other meal-offerings. The meal-offering of a *sota* consists of barley, while most other meal-offerings contain wheat. Additionally, the meal-offering of a *sota* is not accompanied by oil and frankincense. The reason for these distinctions is that since the *sota* performed an animalistic and degrading act, her meal-offering must reflect this, with a grain that is usually used as animal fodder.

The chapter also discussed the procedure for drinking the bitter water. The woman drinks from a new earthenware drinking utensil, to which half a *log* of water from the Temple basin is added. Enough dust is added to be visible in the water. Ideally, the dust should be taken from a special place on the Temple floor; however, other dust is acceptable if this proves too difficult.

The scroll of the *sota* is written with the same ink and parchment as Torah scrolls, but the ink must be prepared in a way that makes it erasable in the water. The scroll must be written by a priest for the sake of the specific *sota*, and it is unfit for use by any other *sota*.

The Sages disagree as to which verses must appear on the scroll of the *sota*. The Gemara concluded that the priest must write all of the conditions and curses recorded in verses concerning the *sota* (Numbers 5:19–22), excluding the descriptions of the ritual itself.

The Gemara also addressed the oath of the *sota*. She must include in her oath that she never engaged in sexual intercourse that would render her forbidden to her husband, regardless of the identity of the paramour.

Introduction to **Perek III**

And he shall make the woman drink the water of bitterness that causes the curse; and the water that causes the curse shall enter into her and become bitter.

And the priest shall take the meal-offering of jealousy out of the woman's hand, and shall wave the meal-offering before the Lord, and bring it unto the altar.

And the priest shall take a handful of the meal-offering, as the memorial part of it, and burn it upon the altar, and afterward he shall make the woman drink the water.

And he shall make her drink the water, and then it shall come to pass, if she is defiled, and acted unfaithfully against her husband, that the water that causes the curse shall enter into her and become bitter, and her belly shall swell, and her thigh shall fall away; and the woman shall be a curse among her people.

And if the woman were not defiled, but she is untainted; then she shall be cleared, and shall conceive seed.

(Numbers 5:24–28)

The order in which the ritual of the *sota* should be performed is not clear from the above verses. It appears from the order of the description that the woman drinks the bitter water of a *sota* before the meal-offering is sacrificed. However, verse 26 states: "And afterward he shall make the woman drink the water," indicating that the meal-offering is sacrificed before the *sota* drinks the bitter water. This difficulty is one of the subjects discussed in this chapter.

Other issues related to the drinking ritual and the meal-offering of the *sota* are also discussed, including how the order is affected when certain aspects of the ritual cannot be performed. Also addressed are questions such as what should be done if the woman admits her guilt during the process or if she refuses to drink the bitter water, what happens if witnesses come forward during the ritual and testify as to her infidelity, and what is to be done if the meal-offering of the *sota* becomes ritually impure.

The chapter also enumerates the punishment of the *sota*, and what happens to a *sota* who is not affected by drinking the bitter water. The Sages discuss the possibility that if a woman drinks the water and survives, it is not always indicative of her innocence, as it is possible that her punishment is merely delayed due to her merits. This leads to a discussion concerning whether women are required or even permitted to study Torah. The chapter continues with the *halakhot* concerning the meal-offering of a *sota* who is married to a priest, and concludes with discussions about the halakhic differences between men and women.

מתני׳ הָיָה נוֹטֵל אֶת מִנְחָתָהּ מִתּוֹךְ כְּפִיפָה מִצְרִית וְנוֹתְנָהּ לְתוֹךְ כְּלִי שָׁרֵת וְנוֹתְנָהּ עַל יָדָהּ. וְכֹהֵן מֵנִיחַ יָדוֹ מִתַּחְתֶּיהָ וּמְנִיפָהּ. הֵנִיף וְהִגִּישׁ קָמַץ וְהִקְטִיר, וְהַשְּׁאָר נֶאֱכָל לַכֹּהֲנִים.

MISHNA **He would take**[N] **her meal-offering out of** the **Egyptian wicker basket** made of palm leaves in which it was lying **and would put it into a service vessel and** then **place it on her hand.**[H] **And the priest** would then **place his hand underneath hers**[N] **and wave it** together with her. The priest **waved** it **and brought** it **near** to the southwest corner of the altar, **removed a handful**[B] from it, **and burned** the handful; **and the remainder was eaten by the priests.**

הָיָה מַשְׁקָהּ וְאַחַר כָּךְ מַקְרִיב אֶת מִנְחָתָהּ. רַבִּי שִׁמְעוֹן אוֹמֵר: מַקְרִיב אֶת מִנְחָתָהּ וְאַחַר כָּךְ הָיָה מַשְׁקָהּ, שֶׁנֶּאֱמַר: ״וְאַחַר יַשְׁקֶה אֶת הָאִשָּׁה אֶת הַמָּיִם״. אִם הִשְׁקָהּ וְאַחַר כָּךְ הִקְרִיב אֶת מִנְחָתָהּ – כְּשֵׁרָה.

The priest **would force** the woman **to drink** the bitter water of a *sota*, **and afterward he would sacrifice her meal-offering.**[H] **Rabbi Shimon says:** The priest would **sacrifice her meal-offering and afterward he would force her to drink, as it is stated:** "And the priest shall take a handful of the meal-offering, as the memorial part of it, and burn it upon the altar, **and afterward he shall make the woman drink the water**" (Numbers 5:26). But Rabbi Shimon concedes that **if** the priest first **forced her to drink and afterward**[N] **sacrificed her meal-offering,** it is still **valid.**

גמ׳ אֲמַר לֵיהּ רַבִּי אֶלְעָזָר לְרַבִּי יֹאשִׁיָּה דְּדָרֵיהּ: לָא תֵּיתַב אַכַּרְעָךְ עַד דִּמְפָרְשַׁתְּ לָהּ לְהָא מִילְּתָא: מִנַּיִן לְמִנְחַת סוֹטָה שֶׁטְּעוּנָה תְּנוּפָה? מְנָא לָן? ״וְהֵנִיף״ כְּתִיב בָּהּ! בִּבְעָלִים מְנָלַן?

GEMARA **Rabbi Elazar said to Rabbi Yoshiya of his generation,**[P] i.e., his contemporary: **You shall not sit on your feet**[N] **until you explain this matter** to me: **From where** is it derived that **the meal-offering of a** ***sota*** **requires waving?** The Gemara expresses surprise at the question: **From where do we** derive this? It is explicitly **written with regard to** the meal-offering of a *sota*: "And the priest shall take the meal-offering of jealousy out of the woman's hand, **and shall wave** the meal-offering before the Lord, and bring it unto the altar" (Numbers 5:25). Rather, the question is as follows: **From where do we** derive that the waving is performed **by the owner,** i.e., the woman, and not only by the priest?

אָתְיָא ״יָד״ ״יָד״ מִשְּׁלָמִים. כְּתִיב הָכָא: ״וְלָקַח הַכֹּהֵן מִיַּד הָאִשָּׁה״, וּכְתִיב הָתָם: ״יָדָיו תְּבִיאֶינָה״,

Rabbi Yoshiya answered: This is **derived** by means of a verbal analogy between the term **"hand"** written here and **"hand" from** the **peace-offering: It is written here,** with regard to the meal-offering of a *sota*: **"And the priest shall take** the meal-offering of jealousy **out of the woman's hand"** (Numbers 5:25), **and it is written there,** with regard to the peace-offering: "He that offers his peace-offerings unto the Lord… **His own hands shall bring** the offerings…that the breast may be waved before the Lord" (Leviticus 7:29–30).

מַה כָּאן כֹּהֵן – אַף לְהַלָּן כֹּהֵן, וּמָה לְהַלָּן בְּעָלִים – אַף כָּאן בְּעָלִים. הָא כֵּיצַד? מֵנִיחַ יָדוֹ תַּחַת יְדֵי הַבְּעָלִים וּמֵנִיף.

Just as here, in the case of the *sota*, the **priest** waves the offering, **so too there,** in the case of the peace-offering, the **priest** waves the offering. **And just as there,** in the case of the peace-offering, the **owner** waves the offering, **so too here,** in the case of the *sota*, the **owner** waves the offering. **How is this** accomplished? The priest **places his hand beneath the hands of the owner and** then **waves** the offering with the owner.

״הֵנִיף וְהִגִּישׁ קָמַץ וכו׳ הָיָה מַשְׁקָהּ וְאַחַר כָּךְ מַקְרִיב אֶת מִנְחָתָהּ״. הָא אַקְרְבַהּ!

§ The mishna states: The priest **waved** it **and brought** it **near** to the southwest corner of the altar, **removed a handful** from it, and burned the handful. Yet the continuation of the mishna states: The priest **would force** the woman **to drink, and afterward he would sacrifice her meal-offering.** The Gemara asks: **Didn't** the mishna state in the previous phrase that the offering **was** already **sacrificed?**

BACKGROUND

Removed a handful – קָמַץ: Most meal-offerings require that a handful be removed by a priest and burnt on the altar. This rite parallels the rite of slaughtering performed in the case of an animal offering. However, the slaughtering of an offering may be performed by a non-priest, whereas removing the handful from a meal-offering may be performed only by a priest. According to many authorities, the priest would remove the flour with only the three middle fingers of his right hand, using his thumb and little finger to remove any surplus flour from his closed fingers. He would then place the flour in a sacred service vessel in order to consecrate it. Since the priest had to scoop out a precise amount of flour, this was one of the more difficult services in the Temple.

NOTES

He would take, etc. – הָיָה נוֹטֵל וכו׳: The subject of this sentence is not explicit in the mishna. Rashi and Rabbi Ovadya Bartenura explain that the husband takes the meal-offering, as the mishna continues: And the priest would then place his hand, indicating that the priest was not involved beforehand. However, *Tosafot* and the Meiri explain that ideally, the priest was the one who would take the meal-offering. The reference to the priest in the continuation of the mishna merely means that from that point onward the priest must perform the actions, and a non-priest is not permitted to do so. This explanation is based on the Jerusalem Talmud (see *Melekhet Shlomo*).

The priest would then place his hand underneath hers – וְכֹהֵן מֵנִיחַ יָדוֹ מִתַּחְתֶּיהָ: In the Jerusalem Talmud it is asked: Why is it not improper for the priest to touch the woman's hand? The conclusion is that since this was only for a short time, there is no reason for concern lest the priest's desire be stimulated. Some explain that the priest did not actually touch her; his hands held the vessel, lower down than her hands, and did not touch her hands directly (*Tosefot HaRash*).

If the priest first forced her to drink and afterward, etc. – אִם הִשְׁקָהּ וְאַחַר כָּךְ וכו׳: It is stated in the Jerusalem Talmud that the Rabbis concede that if the priest sacrificed the meal-offering before giving the *sota* the water to drink, the offering is valid.

You shall not sit on your feet – לָא תֵּיתַב אַכַּרְעָךְ: One understanding of this expression is based on the principle that difficult subjects are learned while one is seated, while simpler subject matter is learned while standing (see *Megilla* 21a). Rabbi Elazar intended to indicate that due to Rabbi Yoshiya's extensive knowledge, this was a simple matter for him and he would not need to sit down and consider the matter much in order to provide a correct answer (*Minḥa Ḥareva*).

HALAKHA

And then place it on her hand, etc. – וְנוֹתְנָהּ עַל יָדָהּ וכו׳: After the woman drinks the water, the service vessel with the meal-offering is placed on the woman's hands. The priest places his hand under hers and waves it to the east of the altar in the same manner as all other wavings; he waves it to and fro to each side, and also up and down. After the waving, the priest brings the meal-offering near to the southwest corner of the altar, removes a handful, and burns it. The remainder is eaten by the priests in the same manner as other meal-offerings (Rambam *Sefer Nashim*, *Hilkhot Sota* 3:15).

The priest would force the woman to drink the water and afterward he would sacrifice her meal-offering – הָיָה מַשְׁקָהּ וְאַחַר כָּךְ מַקְרִיב אֶת מִנְחָתָהּ: The priest first forces the woman to drink the bitter water and afterward he sacrifices the meal-offering, in accordance with the unattributed opinion in the mishna. If the priest sacrificed the meal-offering first and afterward forced her to drink, the offering is valid, as indicated later in the Gemara and as stated explicitly in the Jerusalem Talmud (Rambam *Sefer Nashim*, *Hilkhot Sota* 4:14).

PERSONALITIES

Rabbi Yoshiya of his generation – רַבִּי יֹאשִׁיָּה דְּדָרֵיהּ: This title is used to distinguish this Rabbi Yoshiya, who was an *amora* and a contemporary of Rabbi Elazar, from the *tanna* of the same name. Rabbi Yoshiya was an *amora* of the third generation of *amora'im*. He lived in Eretz Yisrael and apparently was one of the older students of Rabbi Yoḥanan, as was Rabbi Elazar. His statements are recorded in the Jerusalem Talmud.

NOTES

Rabbi Shimon and the Rabbis disagree, etc. – פְּלִיגִי רַבִּי שִׁמְעוֹן וְרַבָּנַן וכו׳: It is explained in the Jerusalem Talmud that in addition to the dispute between them with regard to the proper understanding of the verses, Rabbi Shimon and the Rabbis also disagree with regard to which rite is central to the evaluation of whether the *sota* was unfaithful. Rabbi Shimon holds that the essential part of the evaluation is accomplished by the water, and the meal-offering is only a supplementary offering, whereas the Rabbis hold that the evaluation is accomplished primarily by the meal-offering, although the drinking of the bitter water is necessary in order to allow the curse to enter the women's body.

הָכִי קָאָמַר: סֵדֶר מְנָחוֹת כֵּיצַד? הֵנִיף וְהִגִּישׁ קָמַץ וְהִקְטִיר, וְהַשְּׁאָר נֶאֱכָל לַכֹּהֲנִים.

The Gemara answers: **This is what** the mishna **is saying: What was the** sacrificial **order of meal-offerings** in general? The priest **waved** the meal-offering **and brought** it **near** to the southwest corner of the altar, **removed a handful** from it, **and burned** the handful, **and the remainder was eaten by the priests.**

וּבְהַשְׁקָאָה גּוּפָהּ פְּלִיגִי רַבִּי שִׁמְעוֹן וְרַבָּנַן, דְּרַבָּנַן סָבְרִי: מַשְׁקֶה וְאַחַר כָּךְ מַקְרִיב אֶת מִנְחָתָהּ, וְרַבִּי שִׁמְעוֹן סָבַר: מַקְרִיב אֶת מִנְחָתָהּ וְאַחַר כָּךְ מַשְׁקֶה, שֶׁנֶּאֱמַר: ״וְאַחַר יַשְׁקֶה״.

And as **for** the correct order for sacrificing the meal-offering of the *sota* and **forcing** her **to drink, this itself** is a matter about which **Rabbi Shimon and the Rabbis disagree,**[N] **as the Rabbis hold** that the priest would **force** the woman **to drink and afterward he** would **sacrifice her meal-offering; and Rabbi Shimon holds** that the priest would **sacrifice her meal-offering and afterward he** would **force her to drink, as** it **is stated:** "And the priest shall take a handful of the meal-offering, as the memorial part of it, and burn it upon the altar, **and afterward he shall make** the woman **drink** the water" (Numbers 5:26).

״וְאִם הִשְׁקָה וְאַחַר כָּךְ הִקְרִיב אֶת מִנְחָתָהּ – כְּשֵׁרָה״.

§ The mishna states: **But** Rabbi Shimon concedes that **if** the priest first **forced her to drink and afterward sacrificed her meal-offering,** the offering is still **valid.**

Perek **III**
Daf **19** Amud **b**

HALAKHA

If the scroll was already erased and then the woman says I will not drink – נִמְחֲקָה מְגִילָּה וְאוֹמֶרֶת אֵינִי שׁוֹתָה: Once the scroll is erased, if the woman says: I will not drink, she is forcibly compelled to drink (Rambam *Sefer Nashim, Hilkhot Sota* 4:4).

Where the impression of the ink is still discernible – לְשֶׁרִישׁוּמוֹ נִיכָּר: The scroll must be thoroughly erased so that the impression of the writing is not discernible. If the text is still discernible, it is invalid (Rambam *Sefer Nashim, Hilkhot Sota* 4:10).

LANGUAGE

Forced [*me'arerin*] – מְעַרְעֲרִין: Some explain that this term is derived from the word *irur*, which means breaking and is used here to denote the opening of her mouth by force. Others explain that the term means to place liquid in one's mouth without swallowing. It is similar to the talmudic Hebrew terms *me'arer* and *megarger*. According to this explanation, here the term means that the water is poured down her throat.

NOTES

The statement of Rabbi Akiva – דִּבְרֵי רַבִּי עֲקִיבָא: According to Rashi, Rabbi Akiva agrees with Rabbi Shimon that first the meal-offering is sacrificed and only afterward is she given to drink; however, Rabbi Akiva takes a more extreme position than Rabbi Shimon on this matter, asserting that if she were to drink first, it is considered as if nothing was done. By contrast, Rabbeinu Ḥananel asserts that Rabbi Akiva holds in accordance with the opinion of the Rabbis, who state that the woman should drink first. This explanation is based on an alternative version of the text. *Tosafot* note that later (20b) the Gemara apparently understands Rabbi Akiva's opinion as explained by Rashi; however, *Tosafot* explain that the *tanna'im* themselves disagree with regard to the opinion of Rabbi Akiva.

תָּנוּ רַבָּנַן: ״וְהִשְׁקָהּ״ – מַה תַּלְמוּד לוֹמַר? וַהֲלֹא כְּבָר נֶאֱמַר ״וְהִשְׁקָה״! שֶׁאִם נִמְחֲקָה מְגִילָּה וְאוֹמֶרֶת אֵינִי שׁוֹתָה, מְעַרְעֲרִין אוֹתָהּ וּמַשְׁקִין אוֹתָהּ בְּעַל כָּרְחָהּ, דִּבְרֵי רַבִּי עֲקִיבָא;

The Sages taught: What is the meaning when **the verse states** after the sacrifice of the meal-offering: **"And he shall make her drink** the water" (Numbers 5:27)? **But isn't it already stated: "And he shall make** the woman **drink** the water of bitterness that causes the curse" (Numbers 5:24)? The *baraita* answers: The repetition teaches **that if the scroll was** already **erased and** then the woman **says: I will not drink,**[H] **she is forced** [*me'arerin*][L] **to drink against her will.** This is **the statement of Rabbi Akiva.**[N]

רַבִּי שִׁמְעוֹן אוֹמֵר: ״וְאַחַר יַשְׁקֶה״ – מַה תַּלְמוּד לוֹמַר? וַהֲלֹא כְּבָר נֶאֱמַר ״וְהִשְׁקָה״! אֶלָּא לְאַחַר כָּל מַעֲשִׂים כּוּלָּן הָאֲמוּרִין לְמַעְלָה. מַגִּיד, שְׁלֹשָׁה דְּבָרִים מְעַכְּבִין בָּהּ: עַד שֶׁלֹּא קָרַב הַקּוֹמֶץ, וְעַד שֶׁלֹּא נִמְחֲקָה מְגִילָּה, וְעַד שֶׁלֹּא תְּקַבֵּל עָלֶיהָ שְׁבוּעָה.

Rabbi Shimon says: What is the meaning when **the verse states:** "And the priest shall take a handful of the meal-offering, as the memorial part of it, and burn it upon the altar, **and afterward he shall make** the woman **drink** the water" (Numbers 5:26)? **But isn't it already stated** previously: **"And he shall make** the woman **drink"** (Numbers 5:24)? **Rather,** this verse indicates that the *sota* is given the bitter water to drink only **after all the actions that are stated above** are performed, i.e., erasing the scroll, sacrificing the meal-offering, and administering the oath. Therefore, this verse **teaches** that **three matters preclude her** from drinking: She does not drink **until the handful is sacrificed, and until the scroll is erased, and until she accepts the oath upon herself.**

עַד שֶׁלֹּא קָרַב הַקּוֹמֶץ – רַבִּי שִׁמְעוֹן לְטַעְמֵיהּ, דְּאָמַר: מַקְרִיב אֶת מִנְחָתָהּ וְאַחַר כָּךְ מַשְׁקֶה.

The Gemara elaborates: She does not drink **until the handful is sacrificed. Rabbi Shimon** conforms **to his** line of **reasoning** stated earlier, **as he says** that the priest **sacrifices her meal-offering and afterward forces her to drink.**

עַד שֶׁלֹּא נִמְחֲקָה מְגִילָּה, אֶלָּא מַאי מַשְׁקֶה לָהּ? אָמַר רַב אַשִׁי: לֹא נִצְרְכָה לְשֶׁרִישׁוּמוֹ נִיכָּר.

The Gemara questions the second condition: She does not drink **until the scroll is erased.** Why does the *baraita* need to state this? **But what** could **he give her to drink** if the scroll was not yet erased into the water? **Rav Ashi says: No,** this *halakha* **is necessary for** an instance **where** the scroll was erased, but **the impression** of the ink **is** still **discernible**[H] on the parchment. The woman does not drink until the scroll is totally erased.

עַד שֶׁלֹּא תְּקַבֵּל עָלֶיהָ שְׁבוּעָה. מִשְׁתָּא הוּא דְּלָא שָׁתְיָא, הָא מִיכְתַּב כָּתְבֵי לַהּ? וְהָאָמַר רָבָא: מְגִילַּת סוֹטָה שֶׁכְּתָבָהּ קוֹדֶם שֶׁתְּקַבֵּל עָלֶיהָ שְׁבוּעָה – לֹא עָשָׂה וְלֹא כְלוּם! כְּדִי נַסְבַהּ.

The Gemara discusses the third condition: She does not drink **until she accepts the oath upon herself.** One might infer from this statement that **it is** only **that** she **does not drink** before she accepts the oath; **however,** the scroll **is written for her** before she accepts the oath. **But didn't Rava say:** With regard to **a scroll of a *sota* that was written before she accepted the oath upon herself,** whoever wrote it **did nothing,** and the scroll is rendered invalid. The Gemara responds: **This was cited for no reason,** as in fact the scroll is not even written before she accepts the oath upon herself, and nothing should be inferred.

בְּמַאי קָמִיפַּלְגִי? תְּלָתָא קְרָאֵי כְּתִיבִי: "וְהִשְׁקָהּ" קַמָּא, "וְאַחַר יַשְׁקֶה", "וְהִשְׁקָהּ" בַּתְרָא.

The Gemara asks: **With regard to what do** the Rabbis and Rabbi Shimon **disagree** in the mishna? The Gemara answers: **Three verses are written** which pertain to drinking the bitter water: **The first** occurrence of the term is in the verse: **"And he shall make** the woman **drink"** (Numbers 5:24); the second: **"And afterward he shall make** the woman **drink** the water" (Numbers 5:26); and **the last** occurrence of the term is in the verse: **"And he shall make her drink"** (Numbers 5:27).

רַבָּנַן סָבְרִי: "וְהִשְׁקָהּ" קַמָּא – לְגוּפוֹ, שֶׁמַּשְׁקָהּ וְאַחַר כָּךְ מַקְרִיב אֶת מִנְחָתָהּ. "וְאַחַר יַשְׁקֶה" – מִיבָּעֵי לֵיהּ לְשֶׁרִישּׁוּמוֹ נִיכָּר. "וְהִשְׁקָהּ" בַּתְרָא – שֶׁאִם נִמְחֲקָה מְגִילָּה וְאוֹמֶרֶת "אֵינִי שׁוֹתָה", מְעַרְעֲרִין אוֹתָהּ וּמַשְׁקִין אוֹתָהּ בְּעַל כָּרְחָהּ.

The Rabbis hold that **the first** occurrence of the term: "**And he shall make** the woman **drink,"** is written **to** teach the *halakha* **itself,** i.e., **that** the priest first **forces her to drink and** afterward **sacrifices her meal-offering.** The second instance: **"And afterward he shall make** the woman **drink,"** **is necessary** to teach **that** as long as **the impression** of the writing **is** still **discernible,** the *sota* is not given the bitter water to drink. The third verse, **the last** occurrence of the term: **"And he shall make her drink,"** teaches **that if the scroll was erased and** then the woman **says: I will not drink, she is forced to drink against her will.**

וְרַבִּי שִׁמְעוֹן סָבַר: "וְאַחַר יַשְׁקֶה" – לְגוּפוֹ, שֶׁמַּקְרִיב אֶת מִנְחָתָהּ וְאַחַר כָּךְ מַשְׁקָהּ. "וְהִשְׁקָהּ" קַמָּא – שֶׁאִם הִשְׁקָהּ וְאַחַר כָּךְ הִקְרִיב אֶת מִנְחָתָהּ כְּשֵׁרָה. "וְהִשְׁקָהּ" בַּתְרָא – שֶׁאִם נִמְחֲקָה מְגִילָּה וְאָמְרָה "אֵינִי שׁוֹתָה", מְעַרְעֲרִין אוֹתָהּ וּמַשְׁקִין אוֹתָהּ בְּעַל כָּרְחָהּ.

And Rabbi Shimon holds that the second verse: **"And afterward he shall make** the woman **drink** the water" (Numbers 5:26), is written **to** teach the *halakha* **itself,** i.e., **that** the priest first **sacrifices her meal-offering and afterward forces her to drink. The first** occurrence of the term: **"And he shall make** the woman **drink,"** teaches **that if he forced her to drink and** only **afterward sacrificed her meal-offering,** the offering **is** nevertheless **valid. The last** occurrence of the term: **"And he shall make her drink,"** teaches **that if** the **scroll was erased and** then **she said: I will not drink, she is forced to drink against her will.**

וְרַבָּנַן – בְּדִיעֲבַד לָא פָּתַח קְרָא.

The Gemara explains the Rabbis' opinion: **And the Rabbis** would respond to Rabbi Shimon that the **verse does not begin** the discussion **with** a *halakha* that is applicable only **after the fact,** and therefore the initial mention of the drinking is referring to the proper time for the ritual.

וְסָבַר רַבִּי עֲקִיבָא מַשְׁקִין אוֹתָהּ בְּעַל כָּרְחָהּ? וְהָתַנְיָא, רַבִּי יְהוּדָה אוֹמֵר: כְּלַבּוּס שֶׁל בַּרְזֶל מַטִּילִין לְתוֹךְ פִּיהָ, שֶׁאִם נִמְחֲקָה מְגִילָּה וְאָמְרָה "אֵינִי שׁוֹתָה", מְעַרְעֲרִין אוֹתָהּ וּמַשְׁקִין אוֹתָהּ בְּעַל כָּרְחָהּ. אָמַר רַבִּי עֲקִיבָא: כְּלוּם אָנוּ צְרִיכִין אֶלָּא לְבוֹדְקָהּ, וַהֲלֹא בְּדוּקָה וְעוֹמֶדֶת! אֶלָּא, עַד שֶׁלֹּא קָרֵב הַקּוֹמֶץ יְכוֹלָה לַחֲזוֹר בָּהּ; מִשֶּׁקָּרֵב הַקּוֹמֶץ אֵינָהּ יְכוֹלָה לַחֲזוֹר בָּהּ.

The Gemara asks: **But does Rabbi Akiva** in fact **hold** that the woman is **forced to drink against her will? But isn't it taught** in a *baraita* (*Tosefta* 2:3) that **Rabbi Yehuda says: A hook [*kelabus*]**[L] made **of iron**[N] **is** forcibly **placed into her mouth,** so **that if the scroll was erased and she said: I will not drink, she is forced to drink against her will. Rabbi Akiva said:** It is not necessary to force her to drink. **Don't we need** to force her to drink the water **only** in order **to evaluate her** fidelity? **And isn't she established as** having been **evaluated** when she refuses to drink, as she is essentially admitting her guilt? **Rather,** Rabbi Akiva's statement should be understood as follows: **Until the handful is sacrificed she can retract** her decision to drink the bitter water; however, **once the handful is sacrificed she cannot retract** her decision to drink.

וְלִיטַעֲמִיךְ, תִּיקְשֵׁי לָךְ הִיא גּוּפָהּ: מִשֶּׁקָּרֵב הַקּוֹמֶץ אֵינָהּ יְכוֹלָה לַחֲזוֹר בָּהּ – וַהֲלֹא בְּדוּקָה וְעוֹמֶדֶת!

The Gemara asks: **But according to your reasoning** in explanation of Rabbi Akiva's statement, **this** explanation **itself should pose a difficulty for you.** Why **can't she retract** her decision **once the handful is sacrificed? And isn't she established as** having been **evaluated** when she refuses to drink?

LANGUAGE

Hook [*kelabus*] – כְּלַבּוּס: Apparently from the Latin clavus, which means a nail. From the description of the *ge'onim* it appears the *kelabus* was an object similar to large tongs in which bent nails were inserted in order to grasp metal articles during forging.

NOTES

A hook [*kelabus*] made of iron – כְּלַבּוּס שֶׁל בַּרְזֶל: Although the commentaries disagree with regard to the exact meaning of the term *kelabus*, it appears that its purpose was not to open her mouth; rather, it was placed in her open mouth to ensure that her mouth remained open so that she could be forced to drink (see *Tosafot*). The *Tosefta* (2:3) cites the opinion of Rabbi Yehuda, who disagrees and holds that they opened her mouth with tongs.

NOTES

In a state of good health – **מֵחֲמַת בְּרִיוּתָא**: The Gemara explains later that if the woman admits that she is defiled, she is never given the water to drink. The discussion here refers to a woman who does not explicitly admit her guilt, yet refuses to drink. In this case, if she retracts her decision to drink while she is in good health and of clear mind, and she does not appear frightened, it is assumed that her refusal to drink is akin to a confession that she is defiled. However, if she appears frightened, it is possible that her refusal is due to fear that she will be harmed by the water even if she is innocent. In this case, if the scroll was already erased and the handful sacrificed, she is forced to drink so that the erasure will not be for nothing, as it is possible that she will be found innocent.

לָא קַשְׁיָא: הָא דְּקָהָדְרָא בָּהּ מֵחֲמַת רְתִיתָא, וְהָא דְּקָהָדְרָא בָּהּ מֵחֲמַת בְּרִיוּתָא.

The Gemara answers: This is **not difficult; this** case, where she is forced to drink, is referring to a situation **where she retracts** her decision to drink **due to fear,** as her refusal is not viewed as an admission of guilt, and it is possible that if she drinks she will be found undefiled. **And that** case, where she does not drink, is referring to a situation **where she retracts** her decision **in a state of** good **health.**[N] Since she does not appear to be afraid, her refusal is viewed as an admission of guilt.

וְהָכִי קָאָמַר: כׇּל מֵחֲמַת בְּרִיוּתָא – כְּלָל כְּלָל לָא שָׁתְיָא. מֵחֲמַת רְתִיתָא – עַד שֶׁלֹּא קָרֵב הַקּוֹמֶץ, דְּאַכַּתִּי לָא אִמְחוּק מְגִילָּה, אִי נַמִי אִמְחוּק מְגִילָּה, דְּשֶׁלֹּא כַּדִּין עֲבִיד כֹּהֲנִים דְּמָחֲקִי – מָצֵי הָדְרָא בָּהּ. מִשֶּׁקָּרֵב הַקּוֹמֶץ, דְּבְדִין עֲבִיד כֹּהֲנִים דְּמָחֲקִי – לָא מָצֵי הָדְרָא בָּהּ.

And this is what Rabbi Akiva **is saying:** In **any** case where she retracts her decision to drink **in a state of** good **health, she does not drink at all.** With regard to a *sota* who retracts her decision **due to fear,** if she retracts her decision **before the handful is sacrificed, when the scroll has not yet been erased; or** even if the **scroll was** already **erased,** since **the priests acted incorrectly when they erased** it beforehand; **she can retract** her decision. **Once the handful is sacrificed, in which** case the **priests acted correctly when they erased** the scroll, **she cannot retract** her decision, and she is forced to drink against her will.

Perek **III**
Daf **20** Amud **a**

NOTES

And then she retracted her statement and said I will drink, etc. – **וְחָזְרָה וְאָמְרָה שׁוֹתָה אֲנִי וכו׳**: If the woman said explicitly that she was defiled, she cannot retract her statement. The discussion here pertains to a woman who did not state explicitly that she was defiled; however, her refusal to drink is interpreted in this manner, and the Gemara questions whether she can claim that her refusal to drink was only due to fear. Some commentaries write that were she to claim explicitly that her initial refusal was due to fear, she would certainly be believed. This case is comparable to that of a woman who informed her husband that she was menstruating and afterward retracted her statement and claimed that she was ritually pure, in which case the *halakha* is that if she provided a pretext for her initial statement, she is believed. The Gemara raises this question only in a case where she did not explain her reasons for initially refusing to drink but merely claimed that she is now willing to drink the water (*Minḥat Ḥinnukh*).

It is necessary to put a bitter substance into the water, etc. – **צָרִיךְ שֶׁיִּתֵּן מַר לְתוֹךְ הַמַּיִם וכו׳**: The water is called "the water of bitterness" (Numbers 5:23) even before it is drunk, although it might not cause any harm. This indicates that it is not so named because it causes death, but because it is already bitter (Rashi). Others add that the additional phrase "the water of bitterness that causes the curse" (Numbers 5:18) indicates that the water's bitterness is unrelated to its causing a curse. The ink and dust added to the water do not cause it to be bitter, and therefore something bitter must be added.

קַשְׁיָא דְּרַבִּי עֲקִיבָא אַדְּרַבִּי עֲקִיבָא. הָתָם אֲמַר מְחִיקָה מְעַכְּבָא, וְהָכָא אֲמַר קוֹמֶץ מְעַכֵּב!

The Gemara asks: The statement **of Rabbi Akiva** is **difficult,** as it is contradicted **by** another statement **of Rabbi Akiva: There,** in the first *baraita*, **he said** that **erasure prevents** the authorities from compelling the woman to drink the water if she retracted her decision to drink, **and here he says** that the sacrifice of the **handful prevents** the authorities from compelling the woman to drink the water. In other words, according to the first *baraita* the woman can retract her decision to drink until the scroll is erased, whereas according to the second *baraita* she can retract her decision until the handful is sacrificed.

תְּרֵי תַּנָּאֵי וְאַלִּיבָּא דְּרַבִּי עֲקִיבָא.

The Gemara responds: There is a dispute between **two** ***tanna'im*****, and** they disagree **with regard to** the opinion **of Rabbi Akiva.** They disagree with regard to what point in time, according to Rabbi Akiva, is the final moment at which a woman can refuse to drink the bitter water without being forced to do so.

אִיבַּעְיָא לְהוּ: אָמְרָה "אֵינִי שׁוֹתָה" מֵחֲמַת בְּרִיוּתָא, וְחָזְרָה וְאָמְרָה "שׁוֹתָה אֲנִי", מַהוּ? כֵּיוָן דְּאָמְרָה "אֵינִי שׁוֹתָה" – טְמֵאָה אֲנִי קָאָמְרָה, וְכֵיוָן דְּאַחֲזִיק נַפְשָׁהּ בְּטוּמְאָה – לָא מָצְיָא הָדְרָה בָּהּ. אוֹ דִּילְמָא כֵּיוָן דְּאָמְרָה "שׁוֹתָה אֲנִי", גָּלְיָא דַּעְתָּהּ דְּמֵחֲמַת בִּיעֲתוּתָא הוּא דְּאָמְרָה? תֵּיקוּ.

A dilemma was raised before the Sages: If **she** initially **said: I will not drink, while in a state of** good **health, and** then **she retracted** her statement **and said: I will drink,**[N] **what is** the *halakha*? Does one say that **when she said: I will not drink,** it is as if **she** confessed and **said: I am defiled, and since she established herself as defiled she cannot retract** her statement?[H] **Or perhaps when she said: I will drink, she revealed her thoughts that it** was only **due to fear that she said** she will not drink? The Gemara concludes that the dilemma **shall stand** unresolved.

אָמַר אֲבוּהּ דִּשְׁמוּאֵל: צָרִיךְ שֶׁיִּתֵּן מַר לְתוֹךְ הַמַּיִם. מַאי טַעְמָא? דְּאָמַר קְרָא: "מֵי הַמָּרִים", שֶׁמָּרִים כְּבָר.

Shmuel's father says: It is **necessary** for one **to put a bitter** substance **into the water**[NH] that the *sota* drinks. **What is the reason** for this? It is **as the verse states:** "And he shall blot them out into **the water of bitterness**" (Numbers 5:23), indicating **that** they **are already bitter** before the scroll is erased.

HALAKHA

She cannot retract her statement – **לָא מָצְיָא הָדְרָה בָּהּ**: A *sota* who, due to fear, says: I will not drink, may later retract her statement and say: I will drink. However, if she said: I will not drink, when she is in good health and unafraid, she may not later recant and say: I will drink (Rambam *Sefer Nashim*, *Hilkhot Sota* 4:3).

It is necessary to put a bitter substance into the water, etc. – **צָרִיךְ שֶׁיִּתֵּן מַר לְתוֹךְ הַמַּיִם וכו׳**: A bitter substance, e.g., wormwood, must be placed into the water that the *sota* drinks, as the verse (Number 5:23) describes that water as "the water of bitterness" (Rambam *Sefer Nashim*, *Hilkhot Sota* 3:10).

מתני׳ עַד שֶׁלֹּא נִמְחֲקָה הַמְּגִילָּה אָמְרָה "אֵינִי שׁוֹתָה" – מְגִילָּתָהּ נִגְנֶזֶת, וּמִנְחָתָהּ מִתְפַּזֶּרֶת עַל הַדֶּשֶׁן, וְאֵין מְגִילָּתָהּ כְּשֵׁרָה לְהַשְׁקוֹת בָּהּ סוֹטָה אַחֶרֶת. נִמְחֲקָה הַמְּגִילָּה וְאָמְרָה "טְמֵאָה אֲנִי" – הַמַּיִם נִשְׁפָּכִין, וּמִנְחָתָהּ מִתְפַּזֶּרֶת עַל בֵּית הַדֶּשֶׁן. נִמְחֲקָה הַמְּגִילָּה וְאָמְרָה "אֵינִי שׁוֹתָה" – מְעַרְעֲרִין אוֹתָהּ וּמַשְׁקִין אוֹתָהּ בְּעַל כׇּרְחָהּ.

MISHNA **If before the scroll was erased she said: I will not drink,**[H] **the scroll** that was written for **her is sequestered, and her meal-offering is** burned and **scattered over** the place of **the ashes, and her scroll is not fit to give to another *sota* to drink. If the scroll was erased** and afterward **she said: I am defiled,**[H] **the water is poured out, and her meal-offering is scattered**[N] **in the place of the ashes.** If **the scroll was** already **erased and she said: I will not drink, she is forced to drink against her will.**

אֵינָהּ מַסְפֶּקֶת לִשְׁתּוֹת עַד שֶׁפָּנֶיהָ מוֹרִיקוֹת וְעֵינֶיהָ בּוֹלְטוֹת וְהִיא מִתְמַלֵּאת גִּידִין, וְהֵם אוֹמְרִים: הוֹצִיאוּהָ, שֶׁלֹּא תְּטַמֵּא הָעֲזָרָה.

When a guilty woman drinks **she does not manage to** finish **drinking**[N] **before her face turns green**[H] **and her eyes bulge, and her** skin becomes **full of** protruding **veins, and** the people standing in the Temple **say: Remove her,** so **that she does not render the Temple courtyard impure** by dying there.

אִם יֵשׁ לָהּ זְכוּת הָיְתָה תּוֹלָה לָהּ. יֵשׁ זְכוּת תּוֹלָה שָׁנָה אַחַת, יֵשׁ זְכוּת תּוֹלָה שְׁתֵּי שָׁנִים, יֵשׁ זְכוּת תּוֹלָה שָׁלֹשׁ שָׁנִים. מִכָּאן אוֹמֵר בֶּן עַזַּאי: חַיָּיב אָדָם לְלַמֵּד אֶת בִּתּוֹ תּוֹרָה, שֶׁאִם תִּשְׁתֶּה תֵּדַע שֶׁהַזְּכוּת תּוֹלָה לָהּ. רַבִּי אֱלִיעֶזֶר אוֹמֵר: כׇּל הַמְלַמֵּד בִּתּוֹ תּוֹרָה – (כְּאִילּוּ) לוֹמְדָהּ תִּפְלוּת.

The mishna limits the scope of the previous statement: **If she has merit, it delays** punishment **for her** and she does not die immediately. **There is a merit** that **delays** punishment for **one year, there is** a larger **merit** that **delays** punishment for **two years,** and **there is a merit** that delays punishment for **three years. From here Ben Azzai states: A person is obligated to teach**[N] **his daughter Torah,** so **that if she drinks** and does not die immediately, **she will know that** some **merit** she has **delayed** punishment **for her. Rabbi Eliezer says: Anyone who teaches his daughter Torah**[H] **is teaching her promiscuity** [*tiflut*].[NL]

רַבִּי יְהוֹשֻׁעַ אוֹמֵר: רוֹצָה אִשָּׁה בְּקַב וְתִפְלוּת מִתִּשְׁעָה קַבִּין וּפְרִישׁוּת. הוּא הָיָה אוֹמֵר: חָסִיד שׁוֹטֶה, וְרָשָׁע עָרוּם, וְאִשָּׁה פְּרוּשָׁה, וּמַכּוֹת פְּרוּשִׁין – הֲרֵי אֵלּוּ מְבַלֵּי עוֹלָם.

Rabbi Yehoshua says: A woman desires to receive the amount of **a *kav*** of food **and a sexual relationship** [*tiflut*] rather **than** to receive **nine *kav*** of food **and abstinence. He would say: A foolish man of piety, and a conniving wicked person, and an abstinent woman** [*perusha*],[B] **and those who injure** themselves out of false **abstinence;** all **these are** people **who erode the world.**[H]

HALAKHA

If before the scroll was erased she said I will not drink, etc. – עַד שֶׁלֹּא נִמְחֲקָה הַמְּגִילָּה אָמְרָה אֵינִי שׁוֹתָה וכו׳: If the woman says: I will not drink, before the scroll is erased, then the scroll is sequestered, and it is not fit to give to another *sota* to drink. Her meal-offering is scattered over the place of the ashes. If she says: I will not drink, once the scroll has been erased, she is forced to drink against her will, and it is explained to her that if she is not defiled she will not be harmed by the water (Rambam *Sefer Nashim*, *Hilkhot Sota* 4:4–5).

She said: I am defiled – אָמְרָה "טְמֵאָה אֲנִי": If she says: I am defiled, even if the scroll has been erased, the water is poured out and her meal-offering is scattered in the place of the ashes (Rambam *Sefer Nashim*, *Hilkhot Sota* 4:6).

Her face turns green, etc. – פָּנֶיהָ מוֹרִיקוֹת וכו׳: If she is defiled, her face immediately turns green, her eyes bulge out, and her veins protrude, and the people standing in the Temple say: Remove her from the Temple courtyard, lest she begin menstruating and render the Temple courtyard impure (see 20b). She is then removed from the women's courtyard where she is standing (Rambam *Sefer Nashim*, *Hilkhot Sota* 3:16).

Anyone who teaches his daughter Torah – כׇּל הַמְלַמֵּד בִּתּוֹ תּוֹרָה: A woman who studies Torah receives a reward, but her reward is not equal to that of a man because, unlike men, she is not commanded to learn. Despite the fact that women receive a reward if they study Torah, the Sages ruled that a man should not teach Torah to his daughter, since most women's minds are not attuned to learning and they render the words of the Torah into nonsense. Therefore, the Sages stated: Anyone who teaches his daughter Torah is considered as though he taught her foolishness.

This applies only with regard to the Oral Torah; however, with regard to the Written Torah, although one should not teach the Written Torah to one's daughter, it is not considered as though he taught her foolishness. The distinction between the Oral and Written Torah stems from the statement of Rabbi Elazar ben Azarya in tractate *Ḥagiga* (3a) that women are also required to participate in the mitzva of assembly, i.e., the obligation to assemble in the Temple on *Sukkot* in the year following the Sabbatical Year in order to hear the Written Torah being read publicly (*Baḥ*).

Some of the later authorities state that the above ruling does not apply to a woman who decides to study Torah on her own initiative, as by doing so she proves that she does not belong in the category of women who turn the Torah into nonsense (*Perisha*).

The Rema writes that women are certainly obligated to learn the *halakhot* that are applicable to them. The later authorities write that nowadays, when women study secular subjects, it is incumbent upon them to study Torah as well, and girls should be taught at least the entire Written Torah and the ethical teachings of tractate *Avot* (*Likkutei Halakhot*). Furthermore, some authorities state that women are required to study those parts of the Torah that deal with matters of faith, as women are obligated to believe in God and to love and fear Him (Rambam *Sefer HaMadda*, *Hilkhot Talmud Torah* 1:13; *Shulḥan Arukh*, *Yoreh De'a* 246:6).

People who erode the world – מְבַלֵּי עוֹלָם: If one gives all his money to charity or spends all his money on other mitzvot, he is not pious but foolish, and he is considered one of those who erode the world (Rambam *Sefer Hafla'a*, *Hilkhot Arakhin VaḤaramim* 8:13).

NOTES

And her meal-offering is scattered – וּמִנְחָתָהּ מִתְפַּזֶּרֶת: The commentaries explain that if the woman refuses to drink without admitting infidelity, her meal-offering is burned in the place of the ashes, located in the Temple courtyard, and its ashes are scattered (see 22b). The reason for this is that since the meal-offering was consecrated in a service vessel, it must be burned. In the second case in the mishna, where the woman admits her infidelity, the meal-offering is scattered without being burned, as, although the meal-offering was consecrated in a service vessel, her admission clarifies that the consecration was in error, and therefore it need not be burned (Meiri).

She does not manage to finish drinking – אֵינָהּ מַסְפֶּקֶת לִשְׁתּוֹת: This is an exaggeration, as the water does not affect her until she drinks the entire amount. This phrase is used to emphasize that the effect of the water occurs immediately afterward (Jerusalem Talmud).

A person is obligated to teach, etc. – חַיָּיב אָדָם לְלַמֵּד וכו׳: If a woman learns Torah and is later accused of being a *sota*, she will know that even if she survives the evaluation of the water despite her infidelity, it is not because the water is powerless but because of her merit. Although the knowledge that it is possible to survive the evaluation of the water could cause a woman to commit adultery, it is nevertheless preferable that they become aware of this possibility, as the lack of this knowledge is more likely to cause a lack of fear of the water, as rumors will be spread that the water is powerless (*Etz Yosef*).

Is teaching her promiscuity [*tiflut*] – לוֹמְדָהּ תִּפְלוּת: Rashi interprets the term *tiflut* as referring to promiscuous behavior, while the Rambam interprets the term as referring to idle nonsense (Rambam's Commentary on the Mishna). According to some versions of the text, the mishna reads: Anyone who teaches his daughter Torah is considered as though he taught her promiscuity. However, it is evident from the Gemara (21b) that this is not the actual text of the mishna; rather it is the Gemara's interpretation of the mishna (Meiri).

LANGUAGE

Promiscuity [*tiflut*] – תִּפְלוּת: The root *tav*, *peh*, *lamed* refers to that which is meaningless or worthless. This literal definition fits well according to the Rambam's interpretation that the term here is referring to idle nonsense. Alternatively, the term can be understood as a euphemism for words or acts of a sexual nature, whether adulterous, as in the statement of Rabbi Eliezer, or of a permitted nature, as in the statement of Rabbi Yehoshua. This interpretation is indicated by the fact that the term is contrasted with abstinence, both here and elsewhere, and might have been influenced by the similar root *tet*, *peh*, *lamed*, which denotes attachment and bonding, as in the attachment of a man and a woman.

BACKGROUND

An abstinent woman [*perusha*] – אִשָּׁה פְּרוּשָׁה: The mishna refers critically to women who are unwilling to accept a life of abstinence, yet at the same time it declares that an abstinent woman, as well those who injure themselves out of false abstinence, are among those who erode the world. The Gemara (22a–b) explains that the mishna's criticism pertains to individuals who are self-righteous, sanctimonious, and hypocritical. The terms *perusha* and *perushin* can be translated as those who engage in self-restraint, but they can also carry the negative connotation of separatists who reject community norms. The term *perushim*, sometimes rendered *perushin*, i.e., Pharisees, was also used by the opponents of rabbinic Judaism in reference to the rabbinic Sages, often in a derogatory sense. Its usage here appears to be an example of self-criticism on the part of the Sages with regard to the activities of some members of their community.

גמ׳ אָמַר רַב יְהוּדָה אָמַר שְׁמוּאֵל מִשּׁוּם רַבִּי מֵאִיר: כְּשֶׁהָיִיתִי לָמֵד תּוֹרָה אֵצֶל רַבִּי עֲקִיבָא, הָיִיתִי מַטִּיל קַנְקַנְתּוֹם לְתוֹךְ הַדְּיוֹ, וְלֹא אָמַר לִי דָּבָר. כְּשֶׁבָּאתִי אֵצֶל רַבִּי יִשְׁמָעֵאל, אָמַר לִי: בְּנִי, מַה מְּלַאכְתְּךָ? אָמַרְתִּי לוֹ: לַבְלָר אֲנִי. אָמַר לִי: בְּנִי, הֱוֵי זָהִיר, שֶׁמְּלַאכְתְּךָ מְלֶאכֶת שָׁמַיִם הִיא. שֶׁמָּא תַּחְסִיר אוֹת אַחַת אוֹ תַּתִּיר אוֹת אַחַת, נִמְצֵאתָ אַתָּה מַחֲרִיב אֶת כָּל הָעוֹלָם כּוּלּוֹ.

GEMARA **Rav Yehuda says** that **Shmuel says in the name of Rabbi Meir: When I was studying Torah before Rabbi Akiva,** as his disciple, **I used to put copper sulfate into the ink** with which I wrote Torah scrolls, **and he did not say anything to me** in protest. Afterward, **when I came** to learn Torah **before Rabbi Yishmael, he said to me: My son, what is your vocation? I said to him: I am a scribe** [***lavlar***][L] who writes Torah scrolls. **He said to me: My son, be careful** in your work, **as your work is the work of Heaven, lest you omit a single letter**[N] from the Torah scroll **or add a single letter,** and in this **you are found to be destroying the entire world** if the mistake alters the meaning of the verse and results in blasphemy.

אָמַרְתִּי לוֹ: דָּבָר אֶחָד יֵשׁ לִי שֶׁאֲנִי מַטִּיל לְתוֹךְ הַדְּיוֹ, וְקַנְקַנְתּוֹם שְׁמוֹ. אָמַר לִי: וְכִי מַטִּילִין קַנְקַנְתּוֹם לְתוֹךְ הַדְּיוֹ? הַתּוֹרָה אָמְרָה: ״וּמָחָה״, כְּתָב שֶׁיּוּכַל לִמָּחוֹת.

Rabbi Meir continues: **I said to** Rabbi Yishmael: **I have one substance that I put into the ink, and it is called copper sulfate,** which prevents the writing from being erased. **He said to me: And may copper sulfate be put into the ink?**[H] **The Torah** clearly **said** with regard to the scroll of the *sota*: "And the priest shall write these curses in a scroll, **and he shall blot** them out into the water of bitterness" (Numbers 5:23). This indicates that the Torah requires **writing that can be blotted out.**

מַאי קָאָמַר לֵיהּ וּמַאי קָא מַהֲדַר לֵיהּ?

Since Rabbi Meir's remark about copper sulfate seems unrelated to Rabbi Yishmael's previous statement, the Gemara asks: **What is** Rabbi Yishmael **saying to** Rabbi Meir, **and what is** Rabbi Meir **replying to** Rabbi Yishmael?

הָכִי קָאָמַר לֵיהּ: לָא מִבַּעְיָא בַּחֲסֵירוֹת וִיתֵירוֹת דְּבָקִי אֲנָא, אֶלָּא אֲפִילּוּ לְמֵיחַשׁ לִזְבוּב, דְּדִילְמָא אָתֵי וְיָתֵיב אַתָּגֵיהּ דְּדָלֵי״ת וּמָחֵיק לֵיהּ וּמְשַׁוֵּי לֵיהּ רֵי״שׁ – דָּבָר אֶחָד יֵשׁ לִי שֶׁאֲנִי מַטִּיל לְתוֹךְ הַדְּיוֹ וְקַנְקַנְתּוֹם שְׁמוֹ.

The Gemara explains: **This is what** Rabbi Meir **is saying to him: It is not necessary** to say that I do not err **in omissions and additions, as I am an expert. Rather,** there is not **even** any reason **for concern with regard to a fly lest** it **come and sit on the protrusion of** the letter ***dalet* and erase it,** thereby **rendering it** the letter ***reish*,** which could be a critical error.[N] There is no concern of this erasure occurring, since **I have a certain substance that I put into the ink** and that prevents the writing from being erased, **and it is called copper sulfate.**

אִינִי?! וְהָא תַּנְיָא, אָמַר רַבִּי מֵאִיר: כְּשֶׁהָיִיתִי לָמֵד תּוֹרָה אֵצֶל רַבִּי יִשְׁמָעֵאל, הָיִיתִי מַטִּיל קַנְקַנְתּוֹם לְתוֹךְ הַדְּיוֹ, וְלֹא אָמַר לִי דָּבָר. כְּשֶׁבָּאתִי אֵצֶל רַבִּי עֲקִיבָא אֲסָרָהּ עָלַי.

The Gemara questions the initial part of Rabbi Meir's statement: **Is that so? But isn't it taught** in a *baraita* that **Rabbi Meir said: When I was studying Torah before Rabbi Yishmael, I used to put copper sulfate into the ink** with which I wrote Torah scrolls, **and he did not say anything to me.** Afterward, **when I came** to learn Torah **with Rabbi Akiva, he prohibited me** from doing **so.**

קַשְׁיָא שִׁמּוּשׁ אַשִּׁמּוּשׁ, קַשְׁיָא אֲסָרָהּ אַאֲסָרָהּ!

The Gemara points out that there are two separate contradictions between the two statements: Rav Yehuda's statement with regard to Rabbi Meir first **serving** Rabbi Akiva as a disciple is **difficult,** as it is contradicted **by** the statement of the *baraita* with regard to his first **serving** Rabbi Yishmael. Furthermore, Rav Yehuda's statement is **difficult,** since he states that it was Rabbi Yishmael **who prohibited** the addition of copper sulfate, and this is contradicted **by** the statement of the *baraita* that it was Rabbi Akiva **who prohibited it.**

בִּשְׁלָמָא שִׁמּוּשׁ אַשִּׁמּוּשׁ לָא קַשְׁיָא. מֵעִיקָּרָא אֲתָא לְקַמֵּיהּ דְּרַבִּי עֲקִיבָא. כֵּיוָן דְּלָא מָצֵי קָם אַלִּיבֵּיהּ, אֲתָא לְקַמֵּיהּ דְּרַבִּי יִשְׁמָעֵאל וְגָמַר גְּמָרָא. הֲדַר אֲתָא לְקַמֵּיהּ דְּרַבִּי עֲקִיבָא סָבַר סְבָרָא.

The Gemara answers: **Granted,** the apparent contradiction between Rav Yehuda's statement with regard to Rabbi Meir's **serving** Rabbi Akiva first, and the statement of the *baraita* with regard to **serving** Rabbi Yishmael first, poses **no difficulty. Initially, he came before Rabbi Akiva** to study, but **since he could not comprehend his** extremely complicated **method** of learning, **he came before Rabbi Yishmael and learned** the oral **tradition** from him. Afterward, **he returned** and **came before Rabbi Akiva** and **studied** his method of logical **reasoning** in order to understand the reasons behind the *halakhot* he had already learned.

LANGUAGE

Scribe [*lavlar*] – לַבְלָר: This word is derived from the Latin librarius, which means scribe or writer, and refers to one whose profession is to write promissory notes or other documents.

NOTES

Lest you omit a single letter – שֶׁמָּא תַּחְסִיר אוֹת אַחַת: According to the Ritva, Rabbi Yishmael means that any letter omitted or added to the text of a Torah scroll invalidates it, even if it does not alter the meaning of the verse. However, most of the commentaries explain that the Gemara is referring to additional or missing letters that change the meaning of the text and transform the text into a blasphemous statement. Rashi provides some examples of this. For instance, with regard to the verse: "But the Lord God is the true God [*emet*]" (Jeremiah 10:10), if one omitted the first letter of the word *emet*, the word would become *met*, which means: He is dead.

Rendering it the letter *reish* which could be a critical error – וּמְשַׁוֵּי לֵיהּ רֵי״שׁ: For example, if when writing: "The Lord is one [*eḥad*]" (Deuteronomy 6:4), the *dalet* at the end of *eḥad* became a *reish*, it would read: The Lord is another [*aḥer*].

HALAKHA

Copper sulfate put into the ink – קַנְקַנְתּוֹם לְתוֹךְ הַדְּיוֹ: A Torah scroll, as well as phylacteries and *mezuzot*, must be written with ink prepared from the soot produced by burning oils and soaked in gallnut juice, as this ink is both durable and erasable. If one wrote with ink containing copper sulfate or similar substances that prevent the writing from being erased, the Torah scroll is valid, in accordance with the opinion of Rabbi Meir, provided that the ink is black (Rambam *Sefer Ahava, Hilkhot Tefillin UMezuza VeSefer Torah* 1:4; *Shulḥan Arukh Yoreh De'a* 271:6).

אֶלָּא אֲסָרָהּ אַאֲסָרָהּ קַשְׁיָא! קַשְׁיָא.

However, the contradiction between Rav Yehuda's statement that it was Rabbi Yishmael **who prohibited** the addition of copper sulfate and the statement of the *baraita* that it was Rabbi Akiva **who prohibited it** still poses a **difficulty.** The Gemara concludes: Indeed, the matter is **difficult.**

תַּנְיָא: רַבִּי יְהוּדָה אוֹמֵר, אוֹמֵר הָיָה רַבִּי מֵאִיר: לַכֹּל מַטִּילִין קַנְקַנְתּוֹם לְתוֹךְ הַדְּיוֹ,

It is taught in a *baraita*: **Rabbi Yehuda says** that **Rabbi Meir would say: Copper sulfate may be put into the ink** that is used **for all** sacred writings, i.e., Torah scrolls, phylacteries, and *mezuzot*,

חוּץ מִפָּרָשַׁת סוֹטָה בִּלְבַד. רַבִּי יַעֲקֹב אוֹמֵר מִשְּׁמוֹ: חוּץ מִפָּרָשַׁת סוֹטָה שֶׁל מִקְדָּשׁ. מַאי בֵּינַיְיהוּ? אָמַר רַבִּי יִרְמְיָה: לִמְחוֹק לָהּ מִן הַתּוֹרָה אִיכָּא בֵּינַיְיהוּ.

except for the ink used to write the Torah **passage about the *sota*,** even when written in a Torah scroll. **Rabbi Ya'akov says in the name of** Rabbi Meir: It is **except for** the ink used to write the scroll with the ***sota* passage** used **in the Temple.**[H] The Gemara asks: **What is** the difference **between these** two opinions? The Gemara replies: **Rabbi Yirmeya says** that there is a difference **between them** with regard to whether it is permitted **to erase** the passage **for** the *sota* **from a Torah** scroll. According to Rabbi Yehuda, Rabbi Meir holds that this is permitted, and therefore the passage in the Torah scroll must be written with ink that does not contain copper sulfate, so that it can be erased. By contrast, according to Rabbi Ya'akov, Rabbi Meir holds that it is prohibited to erase the passage from a Torah scroll, and therefore the passage may be written with ink containing copper sulfate.

וְהָנֵי תַּנָּאֵי כִּי הָנֵי תַּנָּאֵי; דְּתַנְיָא: אֵין מְגִילָּתָהּ כְּשֵׁירָה לְהַשְׁקוֹת בָּהּ סוֹטָה אַחֶרֶת. רַבִּי אַחַי בַּר יֹאשִׁיָּה אוֹמֵר: מְגִילָּתָהּ כְּשֵׁירָה לְהַשְׁקוֹת בָּהּ סוֹטָה אַחֶרֶת.

The Gemara assumes that according to Rabbi Ya'akov it is prohibited to erase the passage from a Torah scroll, since he holds that the scroll must be written for the sake of the *sota*, whereas Rabbi Yehuda, who permits this, holds that the scroll need not be written for the sake of the *sota*. **And** therefore, the opinions of **these *tanna'im* are parallel** to the opinions of **those *tanna'im*, as it is taught** in a *baraita*: **The scroll** of one *sota* **is not fit**[H] to be used in the preparation of the water **to give** to **another *sota* to drink,** as it was not written for the sake of the other *sota*. **Rabbi Aḥai bar Yoshiya says: Her scroll is fit** to be used in the preparation of the water **to give** to **another *sota* to drink,** since it does not need to be written for the sake of the *sota*.

אָמַר רַב פַּפָּא: דִּילְמָא לָא הִיא. עַד כָּאן לָא קָאָמַר תַּנָּא קַמָּא הָתָם, אֶלָּא כֵּיוָן דְּאִינְתִּיק לְשׁוּם רָחֵל – לָא הָדְרָא מִינְתְּקָא לְשׁוּם לֵאָה, אֲבָל תּוֹרָה דִּסְתָמָא כְּתִיבָה, הָכִי נַמִּי דְּמָחֲקִינַן.

Rav Pappa said: Perhaps that **is not so,** and the two disputes are not comparable. It is possible that **the first *tanna*** of the *baraita* **states** that the scroll may not be used for another *sota* **only there,** in the case if a scroll written for a specific woman; **since it was** originally **designated in the name of** one woman, e.g., **Rachel, it cannot again be designated in the name of** another woman, e.g., **Leah. However,** in the case of **a Torah** scroll, **which is written without specifying** anyone, **indeed we may erase** the passage to prepare the water for a *sota* even though it was not written for her sake.

אָמַר רַב נַחְמָן בַּר יִצְחָק: דִּילְמָא לָא הִיא. עַד כָּאן לָא קָאָמַר רַבִּי אַחַי בַּר יֹאשִׁיָּה הָתָם, אֶלָּא בִּמְגִילָּה דְּאִיכְּתוּב לְשׁוּם אָלוֹת בָּעוֹלָם, אֲבָל תּוֹרָה דִּלְהִתְלַמֵּד כְּתִיבָה, הָכִי נַמִּי דְּלָא מָחֲקִינַן.

Rav Naḥman bar Yitzḥak said that the comparison between the two disputes can be refuted for a different reason: **Perhaps** that **is not so.** It is possible that **Rabbi Aḥai bar Yoshiya states** that the scroll may be used for another *sota* **only there, with regard to the scroll** written for a specific *sota*, **as it was written for the purpose of** the **curses** of a *sota* **in general. However,** in the case of **a Torah** scroll, **which is written to be learned** from, **indeed we may not erase** it for a *sota*, as it was not written for the sake of a *sota* at all.

HALAKHA

Except for the ink used to write the scroll with the *sota* passage used in the Temple – חוּץ מִפָּרָשַׁת סוֹטָה שֶׁל מִקְדָּשׁ: The *sota* scroll is written with ink that does not contain copper sulfate and therefore can be erased (Rambam *Sefer Nashim, Hilkhot Sota* 3:8).

The scroll of one *sota* is not fit, etc. – אֵין מְגִילָּתָהּ כְּשֵׁירָה וכו׳: The *sota* scroll must be written for the sake of a specific *sota*. If it was not written for her sake, it is unfit for use. A scroll written for the sake of one woman is not fit for use in the evaluation of any other woman (Rambam *Sefer Nashim, Hilkhot Sota* 4:4).

HALAKHA

One who wrote a bill of divorce with which to divorce his wife, etc. – **כָּתַב לְגָרֵשׁ אֶת אִשְׁתּוֹ וכו׳**: If a bill of divorce was not written for the sake of the specific man and woman using the bill of divorce, it is not valid. Therefore, if one wrote a bill of divorce and then decided not to use it, then even if he later found a person from his city with the same name who is married to a woman of the same name, the second individual cannot use the bill of divorce (Rambam *Sefer Nashim, Hilkhot Geirushin* 3:1–2; *Shulḥan Arukh, Even HaEzer* 131:1–2).

NOTES

It is referring to the erasure – **מְחִיקָה**: The Rosh explains that although the *sota* passage need not be written for the sake of a specific woman, it does need to be written for the purpose of cursing, as the verse states: "And he shall write the curses" (Numbers 5:23). Therefore, the *sota* passage in the Torah scroll, which is written for study purposes, may not be used for a *sota* (*Tosefot HaRosh*).

וְרַבִּי אַחַי בַּר יֹאשִׁיָּה לֵית לֵיהּ: כָּתַב לְגָרֵשׁ אֶת אִשְׁתּוֹ וְנִמְלַךְ. מְצָאוֹ בֶּן עִירוֹ וְאָמַר לוֹ: שְׁמִי כְּשִׁמְךָ וְשֵׁם אִשְׁתִּי כְּשֵׁם אִשְׁתְּךָ – פָּסוּל לְגָרֵשׁ בּוֹ?

The Gemara asks: **And doesn't Rabbi Aḥai bar Yoshiya hold** in accordance with that which is taught in a mishna (*Gittin* 24a): With regard to one who **wrote** a bill of divorce with which **to divorce his wife**[H] **but** later **reconsidered** and did not divorce her, if **a resident of his city found him and said to him: My name** is the same **as your name, and my wife's name** is the same **as your wife's name;** give me the bill of divorce, and I will use it to divorce my wife, it **is unfit to divorce** the other woman **with it.** The reason for this is that it was written for the sake of another woman. Seemingly, the same principle should apply with regard to the scroll of a *sota*.

אָמְרִי: הָתָם "וְכָתַב לָהּ" אָמַר רַחֲמָנָא, בָּעֵינַן כְּתִיבָה לִשְׁמָהּ. הָכָא נַמִי "וְעָשָׂה לָהּ"! מַאי עֲשִׂיָּיה? מְחִיקָה.

The Sages **say** in response: **There,** with regard to a bill of divorce, **the Merciful One states: "And he shall write for her** a bill of divorce" (Deuteronomy 24:1). This teaches that **we require the writing** to be performed **for the sake of** the specific woman. However, no similar requirement is mentioned with regard to a *sota*. The Gemara asks: **Here, too,** with regard to the *sota*, the verse states: "**And** the priest shall **perform with her** all of this law" (Numbers 5:30), indicating that the ritual must be performed for the sake of the specific woman. The Gemara answers: **What** is the **performance** referred to in the verse? It is referring to the **erasure,**[N] whereas the writing need not be done for the sake of a specific woman.

"אֵינָהּ מַסְפֶּקֶת לִשְׁתּוֹת עַד שֶׁפָּנֶיהָ [כו׳]". מַנִּי? רַבִּי שִׁמְעוֹן הִיא, דְּאָמַר: מַקְרִיב אֶת מִנְחָתָהּ וְאַחַר כָּךְ מַשְׁקָהּ, דְּכַמָּה דְּלָא קָרְבָה מִנְחָתָהּ לָא בָּדְקִי לָהּ מַיָּא, דִּכְתִיב: "מִנְחַת זִכָּרוֹן מַזְכֶּרֶת עָוֹן".

§ The mishna states: When a guilty woman drinks **she does not manage to** finish **drinking before her face** turns green and her eyes bulge, and her skin becomes full of protruding veins. The Gemara asks: In accordance with **whose** opinion is this mishna, which indicates that the water evaluates her while she is still drinking? **It is** in accordance with the opinion of **Rabbi Shimon, who says:** The priest **sacrifices her meal-offering and afterward forces her to drink, because** according to the opinion of the Rabbis the meal-offering is sacrificed only after she drinks, and **as long as her meal-offering has not been sacrificed the water does not evaluate her, as it is written:** "And he shall bring her offering for her… for it is a meal-offering of jealousy, **a meal-offering of remembrance, a reminder of iniquity**" (Numbers 5:15).

אֵימָא סֵיפָא: יֵשׁ לָהּ זְכוּת הָיְתָה תּוֹלָה לָהּ. אֲתָאן לְרַבָּנַן, דְּאִי רַבִּי שִׁמְעוֹן, הָאָמַר: אֵין זְכוּת תּוֹלָה בַּמַּיִם הַמָּרִים!

The Gemara asks: **Say the latter clause** of the mishna: If **she has merit, it delays** her punishment **for her. We arrive at** the opinion of **the Rabbis, as, if** this statement were in accordance with the opinion of **Rabbi Shimon, didn't he say: Merit does not delay** punishment **in** the case of **the bitter water** of a *sota*?

אֲמַר רַב חִסְדָּא: הָא מַנִּי? רַבִּי עֲקִיבָא הִיא, דְּאָמַר: מַקְרִיב אֶת מִנְחָתָהּ וְאַחַר כָּךְ מַשְׁקָהּ. וּבִזְכוּת – סָבַר לָהּ כְּרַבָּנַן.

Rav Ḥisda said: In accordance with **whose** opinion **is this** mishna? **It is** in accordance with the opinion of **Rabbi Akiva, who says:** The priest **sacrifices her meal-offering and afterward forces her to drink.** With regard to the order of the ritual he holds in accordance with Rabbi Shimon, **and with regard to** the matter of **merit** delaying punishment, **he holds in accordance with** the opinion of **the Rabbis.**

"וְהֵם אוֹמְרִים: הוֹצִיאוּהָ" וכו׳. מַאי טַעְמָא? דְּדִילְמָא מֵתָה. לְמֵימְרָא, דְּמֵת אָסוּר בְּמַחֲנֵה לְוִיָּה?

§ The mishna states: **And** the people standing in the Temple **say: Remove her,** so that she does not render the Temple courtyard impure. The Gemara explains: **What is the reason** for this? It is **lest she die** there immediately and render the women's courtyard, where she drinks the water, impure. The Gemara asks: **Is this to say that a corpse is prohibited** from being **in** the women's courtyard, which has the same status as the **Levite camp**[B] in the desert?

BACKGROUND

In the Levite camp – **בְּמַחֲנֵה לְוִיָּה**: When the Jewish people were in the wilderness, the camp was arranged around the Tabernacle and divided into three areas. The first camp was that of the Divine Presence, which included the Tabernacle and its courtyard. The second camp was the Levite camp, whose tents surrounded the Tabernacle. Surrounding this was the Israelite camp, where the rest of the nation pitched their tents. Those who were impure were required to remain outside the first, the second, or the third camp, depending on the type of ritual impurity involved.

When the Temple was built in Jerusalem, a corresponding division was instituted. The Temple and its courtyard were equivalent to the camp of the Divine Presence, the Temple Mount was equivalent to the Levite camp, and the city of Jerusalem was equivalent to the Israelite camp. The women's courtyard was situated immediately outside the entrance to the Temple courtyard, and by Torah law its sanctity was equivalent to that of the Temple Mount. However, the Sages ordained that the sanctity of the women's courtyard would be greater than that of the Temple Mount.

וְהָתַנְיָא: טְמֵא מֵת מוּתָּר לִיכָּנֵס לְמַחֲנֵה לְוִיָּה. וְלֹא טְמֵא מֵת בִּלְבַד אָמְרוּ – אֶלָּא אֲפִילּוּ מֵת עַצְמוֹ, שֶׁנֶּאֱמַר: ״וַיִּקַּח מֹשֶׁה אֶת עַצְמוֹת יוֹסֵף עִמּוֹ״, עִמּוֹ בִּמְחִיצָתוֹ!

But isn't it taught in a *baraita*: **One who is ritually impure** with impurity imparted by **a corpse is permitted to enter**[N] **the Levite camp.**[H] **And the Sages said** this **not only** with regard to **one who is ritually impure** with impurity imparted by **a corpse; rather, even a corpse itself** may be brought into the Levite camp, **as it is stated: "And Moses took the bones of Joseph with him"** (Exodus 13:19), which is interpreted to mean: **With him, in his vicinity,** even though Moses was in the Levite camp.

אָמַר אַבָּיֵי: שֶׁמָּא תִּפְרוֹס נִדָּה. לְמֵימְרָא, דִּבְעִיתוּתָא מְרַפְיָא? אִין, דִּכְתִיב: ״וַתִּתְחַלְחַל הַמַּלְכָּה מְאֹד״, וְאָמַר רַב: שֶׁפֵּירְסָה נִדָּה. וְהָא אֲנַן תְּנַן: חֲרָדָה מְסַלֶּקֶת דָּמִים! פַּחְדָּא צָמֵית, בִּיעֲתוּתָא מְרַפְיָא.

Abaye said: The woman is removed not due to a concern that she will die there but **lest** the fear of the water cause her to **begin to menstruate,** and it is prohibited for a menstruating woman to enter the Levite camp. The Gemara asks: **Is this to say that fear causes** muscular **relaxation** and menstrual bleeding?[B] The Gemara responds: **Yes, as it is written: "And the Queen was exceedingly pained"** (Esther 4:4), and **Rav says:** This means that **she began to menstruate.** The Gemara asks: **But didn't we learn** in a mishna (*Nidda* 39a) that **trepidation eliminates** the flow of menstrual **blood?** Presumably, the *sota* experiences trepidation. The Gemara answers: **Trepidation** generated by extended worry **contracts** the muscles and prevents the blood from flowing, but sudden **fear relaxes** the muscles and causes the blood to flow.

״יֵשׁ לָהּ זְכוּת הָיְתָה״ וכו׳. מַנִּי מַתְנִיתִין? לָא אַבָּא יוֹסֵי בֶּן חָנָן, וְלָא רַבִּי אֶלְעָזָר בֶּן יִצְחָק אִישׁ כְּפַר דָּרוֹם, וְלָא רַבִּי יִשְׁמָעֵאל!

§ The mishna states: **If she has merit, it** delays punishment…for one year…for two years…for three years. The Gemara asks: **Whose** opinion is expressed in **the mishna?** It is **not** the opinion of **Abba Yosei ben Ḥanan, and not** the opinion of **Rabbi Elazar ben Yitzḥak of Kefar Darom, and not** the opinion of **Rabbi Yishmael.**

דְּתַנְיָא: אִם יֵשׁ לָהּ זְכוּת תּוֹלָה לָהּ שְׁלֹשָׁה חֳדָשִׁים, כְּדֵי הַכָּרַת הָעוּבָּר, דִּבְרֵי אַבָּא יוֹסֵי בֶּן חָנָן. רַבִּי אֶלְעָזָר בֶּן יִצְחָק אִישׁ כְּפַר דָּרוֹם אוֹמֵר: תִּשְׁעָה חֳדָשִׁים, שֶׁנֶּאֱמַר: ״וְנִקְּתָה וְנִזְרְעָה זָרַע״, וּלְהַלָּן הוּא אוֹמֵר: ״זֶרַע יַעַבְדֶנּוּ יְסֻפַּר״, זֶרַע הָרָאוּי לְסַפֵּר.

This is **as it is taught** in a *baraita*: **If she has merit, it delays** punishment **for her** for **three months, equivalent** to the time necessary **to recognize the fetus;** this is **the statement of Abba Yosei ben Ḥanan.**[N] **Rabbi Elazar ben Yitzḥak of Kefar Darom says:** Merit delays punishment for **nine months, as it is stated: "Then she shall be cleared, and shall conceive seed"** (Numbers 5:28). It is possible to infer from this that if she has merit she will be cleared temporarily, for the length of time required to conceive a child, **and there,** in Psalms, **it says: "A seed shall serve him; it shall be told** of the Lord unto the next generation" (Psalms 22:31). This indicates that the **seed** must **be fit to tell** of the Lord once it matures, and a child can live only if it is born after the culmination of nine months in the womb.

רַבִּי יִשְׁמָעֵאל אוֹמֵר: שְׁנֵים עָשָׂר חֹדֶשׁ. וְאַף עַל פִּי שֶׁאֵין רְאָיָה לַדָּבָר – זֵכֶר לַדָּבָר, דִּכְתִיב: ״לָהֵן מַלְכָּא מִלְכִּי יִשְׁפַּר עֲלָיךְ וַחֲטָיָךְ בְּצִדְקָה פְרֻק וַעֲוָיָתָךְ בְּמִחַן עֲנָיִן

Rabbi Yishmael says: Merit delays punishment for **twelve months. And although there is no** explicit **proof for the concept** of merit delaying punishment for twelve months, there is **an allusion to the concept, as it is written** that Daniel said to Nebuchadnezzar after interpreting Nebuchadnezzar's dream concerning the evil which would befall him: **"Therefore, O king, let my counsel be acceptable to you, and redeem your sins with charity, and your iniquities by showing mercy to the poor;**

HALAKHA

One who is ritually impure with impurity imparted by a corpse is permitted to enter the Levite camp – טְמֵא מֵת מוּתָּר לִיכָּנֵס לְמַחֲנֵה לְוִיָּה: The Temple Mount has a status equivalent to the Levite camp in the desert, and entry to it is prohibited for anyone who is ritually impure due to a bodily secretion, e.g., a *zav* or a *zava*. However, a corpse may be brought onto the Temple Mount, and certainly one who is ritually impure due to contact with a corpse may enter (Rambam *Sefer Avoda*, *Hilkhot Beit HaBeḥira* 7:15).

BACKGROUND

Fear causes muscular relaxation and menstrual bleeding – חֲרָדָה מְסַלֶּקֶת דָּמִים: The menstrual cycle is dependent on hormonal activity, which is heavily impacted by one's mind-set. Extreme emotional stress, e.g., a continuous state of fear, can prevent a woman from menstruating for a lengthy period of time. On the other hand, sudden fear and other strong emotions can lead to a flow of menstrual blood, even at an abnormal time in the menstrual cycle.

NOTES

One who is ritually impure with impurity imparted by a corpse is permitted to enter, etc. – טְמֵא מֵת מוּתָּר לְהִכָּנֵס וכו׳: The early commentaries raise a difficulty: A mishna (*Kelim* 1:8) states that one who contracted impurity imparted by a corpse may not enter even the rampart, which was situated beyond the women's courtyard. This contradicts the Gemara's statement here that even a corpse may reside in the women's courtyard. They answer that the prohibition cited in tractate *Kelim* is a rabbinic prohibition, whereas the Gemara here is referring to Torah law.

The commentaries ask: Why does the Gemara conclude that the *sota* is removed lest she begin to menstruate? Perhaps she is removed due to the rabbinic prohibition against a corpse being present in the women's courtyard. Some explain that the rabbinic prohibition prohibits an impure person only from entering the sanctified areas, but if one is rendered impure with impurity imparted by a corpse within the rampart, he is not obligated to leave (*Tosefot HaRash*). Similarly, the Meiri cites *Tosafot*, who explain that the Sages prohibited one from entering the rampart and the women's courtyard while impure lest one continue beyond the permitted area. However, the *sota* clearly has no intention of entering further, as she likely wishes to leave as quickly as possible, and therefore the rabbinic prohibition does not apply to her. The Meiri also cites an alternative answer in the name of *Tosafot*: If the *sota* were removed due to this rabbinic prohibition, she would not be removed until she showed signs of dying.

Equivalent to the time necessary to recognize the fetus; this is the statement of Abba Yosei ben Ḥanan – כְּדֵי הַכָּרַת הָעוּבָּר, דִּבְרֵי אַבָּא יוֹסֵי בֶּן חָנָן: Rashi explains that Abba Yosei also bases his opinion on the verse cited below by Rabbi Elazar ben Yitzḥak: "Then she shall be cleared, and shall conceive seed" (Numbers 5:28). Abba Yosei infers from the verse that if she has merit she will be cleared temporarily, for the length of time required to visibly conceive seed.

HALAKHA

One who is not commanded to do so and performs a mitzva – אינה מצווה ועושה: A woman is not commanded to learn Torah. However, if she does learn Torah, she is rewarded as one who performs a mitzva in which one is not obligated (Rambam *Sefer HaMadda, Hilkhot Talmud Torah* 1:1, 13; *Shulḥan Arukh, Yoreh De'a* 246:6).

NOTES

This is referring to the time of death – זו מיתה: Some commentaries explain that the Torah one learns protects one from a painful death. Others explain that it protects one from punishment in the grave. The Meiri explains that the Torah watches over one's soul in heaven between death and the time to come after the resurrection of the dead.

Of the thorns and of the pits, etc. – מן הקוצים ומן הפחתים וכו׳: These represent three types of spiritual dangers that one encounters during one's lifetime. Thorns, pits, and thistles are obstacles one encounters while walking; they allude to worldly temptations that do not entice one unless one engages in them of his own accord. Thieves and wild animals represent dangers that creep up on a person; they allude to wicked individuals who might persuade one to follow evil paths. The third danger, losing one's way, alludes to the fundamental question of whether one is following the right path in life (Rabbi David Luria).

הן תהוי ארכא לשלותך״, וכתיב: ״כלא מטא על נבוכדנצר מלכא״, וכתיב: ״לקצת ירחין תרי עשר״!

and then there shall be an extension to your tranquility" (Daniel 4:24). **And it is written: "All this came upon King Nebuchadnezzar"** (Daniel 4:25), **and it is written** in the following verse that this occurred: **"At the end of twelve months"** (Daniel 4:26). None of the opinions in the *baraita* are in accordance with the mishna's statement that merit can delay punishment for up to three years.

לעולם רבי ישמעאל, ואשכח קרא דאמר ותני, דכתיב: ״כה אמר ה׳ על שלשה פשעי אדום״.

The Gemara answers: **Actually,** the mishna is in accordance with the opinion of **Rabbi Yishmael,** who states that merit delays punishment for one year, **and he found a verse which states and repeats** the possibility that punishment can be delayed, indicating that merit can delay punishment up to three times, **as it is written: "Thus says the Lord: For three transgressions of Edom,** yes, but for four, I will not reverse it" (Amos 1:11). Punishment can therefore be delayed for three consecutive periods of one year.

ומאי אף על פי שאין ראיה לדבר זכר לדבר? דלמא שאני גוים, דלא מפקיד דינא עלייהו.

The Gemara asks: **And what** does Rabbi Yishmael mean by stating: **Although there is no** explicit **proof for the concept** of merit delaying punishment for twelve months, there is **an allusion to the concept?** The verses he cites state explicitly that punishment can be delayed for twelve months. The Gemara answers: The proof is not explicit, as **perhaps gentiles are different,** as swift **judgment is not administered upon them** as readily as it is upon the Jewish people, with whom God is more precise in executing judgment.

״ויש זכות תולה שלש שנים״ כו׳. זכות דמאי? אילימא זכות דתורה – הא אינה מצווה ועושה היא! אלא זכות דמצוה,

§ The mishna states: **And there is a merit** that **delays** punishment for **three years.** The Gemara asks: **Which merit** can delay the punishment of a *sota*? **If we say** it is the **merit of** the **Torah** that she has studied; **but** a woman who studies Torah **is** one who is **not commanded** to do so **and performs** a mitzva,[H] whose reward is less than that of one who is obligated? Therefore, it would be insufficient to suspend her punishment. **Rather,** perhaps it is the **merit of a mitzva** that she performed.

זכות דמצוה מי מגנא כולי האי? והתניא, את זו דרש רבי מנחם בר יוסי: ״כי נר מצוה ותורה אור״ – תלה הכתוב את המצוה בנר ואת התורה באור. את המצוה בנר, לומר לך: מה נר אינה מגינה אלא לפי שעה, אף מצוה אינה מגינה אלא לפי שעה.

The Gemara asks: **Does** the **merit of a mitzva protect** one **so much** as to delay her punishment? **But isn't it taught** in a *baraita*: **Rabbi Menaḥem bar Yosei interpreted this** verse **homiletically: "For the mitzva is a lamp and the Torah is light"** (Proverbs 6:23). **The verse associates the mitzva with a lamp and the Torah with** the **light** of the sun. **The mitzva** is associated **with a lamp** in order **to say to you: Just as a lamp does not protect** one by its light extensively but **only temporarily,** while the lamp is in one's hand, **so too, a mitzva protects** one **only temporarily,** i.e., while one is performing the mitzva.

ואת התורה באור, לומר לך: מה אור מגין לעולם, אף תורה מגינה לעולם. ואומר: ״בהתהלכך תנחה אתך״ וגו׳. ״בהתהלכך תנחה אתך״ – זה העולם הזה; ״בשכבך תשמור עליך״ – זו מיתה; ״והקיצות היא תשיחך״ – לעתיד לבא.

And the Torah is associated **with light** in order **to say to you: Just as the light** of the sun **protects** one **forever, so too,** the **Torah** one studies **protects** one **forever; and it states** in the previous verse with regard to the Torah: **"When you walk, it shall lead you;** when you lie down, it shall watch over you; and when you awake, it shall talk with you" (Proverbs 6:22). The Gemara explains: **"When you walk, it shall lead you"; this is** referring to when one is in **this world. "When you lie down, it shall watch over you"; this is** referring to the time of **death,**[N] when one lies in his grave. **"And when you awake, it shall talk with you";** this is referring **to the time to come** after the resurrection of the dead. The Torah that one studies protects and guides him both in this world and in the next world.

משל לאדם שהיה מהלך באישון לילה ואפילה, ומתיירא מן הקוצים ומן הפחתים ומן הברקנים ומחיה רעה ומן הלסטין, ואינו יודע באיזה דרך מהלך.

This can be illustrated by **a parable,** as it is comparable **to a man who is walking in the blackness of night and the darkness, and he is afraid of the thorns, and of the pits,**[N] **and of the thistles,** which he cannot see due to the darkness. **And** he is also afraid **of** the **wild animals and of the bandits** that lurk at night, **and he does not know which way he is walking.**

נִזְדַּמְּנָה לוֹ אֲבוּקָה שֶׁל אוּר, נִיצַּל מִן הַקּוֹצִים וּמִן הַפְּחָתִים וּמִן הַבַּרְקָנִים, וַעֲדַיִין מִתְיָירֵא מֵחַיָּה רָעָה וּמִן הַלִּיסְטִין וְאֵינוֹ יוֹדֵעַ בְּאֵיזֶה דֶּרֶךְ מְהַלֵּךְ. כֵּיוָן שֶׁעָלָה עַמּוּד הַשַּׁחַר נִיצַּל מֵחַיָּה רָעָה וּמִן הַלִּיסְטִין, וַעֲדַיִין אֵינוֹ יוֹדֵעַ בְּאֵיזֶה דֶּרֶךְ מְהַלֵּךְ. הִגִּיעַ לְפָרָשַׁת דְּרָכִים נִיצַּל מִכּוּלָּם.

If **a torch of fire comes his way,** which is analogous to a mitzva, **he is safe from the thorns and from the pits and from the thistles, but he is still afraid of** the **wild animals and of the bandits,** and still **does not know which way he is walking. Once the light of dawn rises,** which is analogous to Torah study, **he is safe from** the **wild animals and from the bandits,** which no longer roam the roads, **but he still does not know which way he is walking.** If **he arrives at a crossroads** and recognizes the way, **he is saved from all of them.**

דָּבָר אַחֵר: עֲבֵירָה מְכַבָּה מִצְוָה, וְאֵין עֲבֵירָה מְכַבָּה תּוֹרָה, שֶׁנֶּאֱמַר: "מַיִם רַבִּים לֹא יוּכְלוּ לְכַבּוֹת אֶת הָאַהֲבָה"!

Alternatively, the verse associates the mitzva with a lamp and the Torah with the light of the sun in order to teach that **a transgression extinguishes** the merit of **a mitzva**[N] one performed, **but a transgression does not extinguish** the merit of the **Torah** one studied, **as it is stated: "Many waters cannot extinguish the love,** neither can the floods drown it" (Song of Songs 8:7). The Torah is compared to love several times in the Song of Songs. One can conclude from the *baraita* that the merit of performing a mitzva is insufficient to suspend punishment.

אָמַר רַב יוֹסֵף: מִצְוָה, בְּעִידָּנָא דְּעָסֵיק בַּהּ – מַגְנָא וּמַצְּלָא; בְּעִידָּנָא דְּלָא עָסֵיק בַּהּ – אַגּוֹנֵי מַגְנָא, אַצּוֹלֵי לָא מַצְּלָא. תּוֹרָה, בֵּין בְּעִידָּנָא דְּעָסֵיק בַּהּ וּבֵין בְּעִידָּנָא דְּלָא עָסֵיק בַּהּ – מַגְנָא וּמַצְּלָא.

Rav Yosef **said** that with regard to **a mitzva, at the time when one is engaged in its** performance it **protects** one from misfortune **and saves** one from the evil inclination; **at the time when one is not engaged in its** performance, it **protects** one from misfortune but it **does not save** one from the evil inclination. With regard to **Torah** study, **both at the time when one is engaged in it and at the time when one is not engaged in it,** it **protects** one from misfortune **and saves** one from the evil inclination. Therefore, the merit of the woman's mitzvot does protect her from misfortune and delay her punishment.

מַתְקִיף לַהּ רַבָּה: אֶלָּא מֵעַתָּה, דּוֹאֵג וַאֲחִיתוֹפֶל מִי לָא עֲסַקֵי בַּתּוֹרָה? אַמַּאי לָא הֲגִינָּה עֲלַיְיהוּ? אֶלָּא אָמַר רָבָא: תּוֹרָה, בְּעִידָּנָא דְּעָסֵיק בַּהּ – מַגְנָא וּמַצְּלָא, בְּעִידָּנָא דְּלָא עָסֵיק בַּהּ – אַגּוֹנֵי מַגְנָא, אַצּוֹלֵי לָא מַצְּלָא. מִצְוָה, בֵּין בְּעִידָּנָא דְּעָסֵיק בַּהּ בֵּין בְּעִידָּנָא דְּלָא עָסֵיק בַּהּ – אַגּוֹנֵי מַגְנָא, אַצּוֹלֵי לָא מַצְּלָא.

Rabba objects to this explanation: **If that is so,** then with regard to **Doeg** (see I Samuel, chapters 21–22) **and Ahithophel** (see II Samuel, chapter 16), who were both wise scholars despite their wickedness, **did they not engage in the** study of **Torah?**[N] **Why did** it **not protect them** from sinning? **Rather, Rava said:** With regard to **Torah** study, **at the time when one is engaged in it, it protects and saves; at the time when one is not engaged in it, it protects** one from misfortune but **it does not save** one from the evil inclination. With regard to **a mitzva, both at the time when one is engaged in its** performance **and at the time when one is not engaged in its** performance, **it protects** one from misfortune but it **does not save** one from the evil inclination.

רָבִינָא אָמַר: לְעוֹלָם זְכוּת תּוֹרָה, וּדְקָאָמְרַתְּ אֵינָהּ מְצוּוָּה וְעוֹשָׂה, נְהִי דִּפְקוּדֵי לָא מִפַּקְדָא, בַּאֲגָרָא דְּמַקְרְיָין וּמַתְנְיָין בְּנַיְיהוּ וְנָטְרָן לְהוּ לְגַבְרַיְיהוּ עַד דְּאָתוּ מִבֵּי מִדְרְשָׁא, מִי לָא פַּלְגָאן בַּהֲדַיְיהוּ?

Ravina said: Actually, the merit that delays the punishment of the *sota* is the **merit of Torah** study, **and** with regard to that **which you say,** i.e., that **she is not commanded** to do so **and performs** a mitzva, the mishna is not referring to the merit of her own Torah study. **Granted, she is not commanded** to study Torah herself;[H] however, **in reward for causing their sons to read** the Written Torah **and to learn** the Mishna,[N] **and for waiting for their husbands until they come** home **from the study hall, don't they share** the reward **with their** sons and husbands? Therefore, if the *sota* enabled her sons and husband to study Torah, the merit of their Torah study can protect her and delay her punishment.

מַאי פָּרָשַׁת דְּרָכִים? אָמַר רַב חִסְדָּא: זֶה תַּלְמִיד חָכָם וְיוֹם מִיתָה. רַב נַחְמָן בַּר יִצְחָק אָמַר: זֶה תַּלְמִיד חָכָם וְיִרְאַת חֵטְא. מָר זוּטְרָא אָמַר: זֶה תַּלְמִיד חָכָם דְּסַלְקָא לֵיהּ שְׁמַעְתְּתָא אַלִּיבָּא דְּהִלְכְתָא.

With regard to the aforementioned parable, the Gemara asks: **What** is the meaning of the **crossroads,** which provide clarity? **Rav Ḥisda says: This** is referring to **a Torah scholar and** his **day of death.** Due to his continued commitment to the Torah, when the time comes for him to die, it is clear to him that he will go to the place of his eternal reward. **Rav Naḥman bar Yitzḥak says: This is a Torah scholar** who has also acquired **fear of sin,** as his fear of sin guides him to the correct understanding of the Torah. **Mar Zutra says: This is a Torah scholar who reaches** conclusions from **his discussion in accordance with the *halakha*,** as that is an indication that he is following the right path.

NOTES

A transgression extinguishes the merit of a mitzva – עֲבֵירָה מְכַבָּה מִצְוָה: This does not mean that one's mitzvot are offset by one's transgressions, as the reward for one's mitzvot always remains. Rather, it means that one's mitzvot will not be sufficient to protect one from punishment, due to the punishment one deserves for his transgressions (Meiri).

Doeg and Ahithophel, did they not engage in the study of Torah – דּוֹאֵג וַאֲחִיתוֹפֶל מִי לָא עֲסַקֵי בַּתּוֹרָה: Ahithophel's wisdom is mentioned explicitly in the Bible, while the description of Doeg as: "The chief of the herdsman of Saul" (I Samuel 21:8), is interpreted by the Sages as referring to the fact that he was head of the Sanhedrin. The Gemara (*Sanhedrin* 106b) describes his vast wisdom and Torah knowledge. Although the Gemara concludes that Torah study protects one from misfortune even when one is not engaged in it, the Maharsha explains that Doeg and Ahithophel were not saved from an untimely death, as the Torah protects one only from suffering but not from death. Some commentaries add that the merit of their Torah study did not extend their life, as an early death is beneficial to the wicked because it saves them from further sin (*Torat HaKenaot*).

Causing their sons to read the Written Torah and to learn the Mishna – דְּמַקְרְיָין וּמַתְנְיָין בְּנַיְיהוּ: The Gemara refers to the mothers causing their sons to study Torah and Mishna, but not to studying Talmud. The reason for this is that when the children are young, it is the mother who persuades and entices them to go and study even when they are reluctant to go. However, once they are older and reach the age of studying Talmud, it is the father who generally uses his authority to ensure that they continue learning (*Iyyun Ya'akov*).

HALAKHA

Granted, she is not commanded to study Torah herself, etc. – נְהִי דִּפְקוּדֵי לָא מִפַּקְדָא וכו׳: If a *sota* has the merit of Torah study, even though she is not commanded to study, this merit delays her punishment and she does not die immediately. The *Arukh HaShulḥan* explains that the Rambam is referring to the merit of Torah that she acquired by assisting her sons and her husband to study, as explained by Ravina (Rambam *Sefer Nashim, Hilkhot Sota* 3:20; *Arukh HaShulḥan, Even HaEzer* 178:66).

דָּבָר אַחֵר: עֲבֵירָה מְכַבָּה מִצְוָה, וְאֵין עֲבֵירָה מְכַבָּה תּוֹרָה. אָמַר רַב יוֹסֵף: דְּרָשֵׁיהּ רַבִּי מְנַחֵם בַּר יוֹסֵי לְהַאי קְרָא כִּי סִינַי, וְאִילְמָלֵא דְּרָשׁוּהָ דּוֹאֵג וַאֲחִיתוֹפֶל הָכִי, לָא רָדְפוּ בָּתַר דָּוִד, דִּכְתִיב: ״לֵאמֹר אֱלֹהִים עֲזָבוֹ״ וגו׳.

The *baraita* states: **Alternatively: A transgression extinguishes** the merit of **a mitzva, but a transgression does not extinguish** the merit of the **Torah. Rav Yosef says: Rabbi Menaḥem bar Yosei interpreted this verse as** it was given on Mount **Sinai, and had Doeg and Ahithophel only interpreted it in this way they would not have pursued David,**[N] **as it is written:** "For my enemies speak concerning **me…saying, God has forsaken him;** pursue and take him, for there is none to deliver" (Psalms 71:10–11). Doeg and Ahithophel incorrectly thought that since David had sinned, his sins had extinguished his merits and God had forsaken him.

מַאי דְּרוּשׁ? ״וְלֹא יִרְאֶה בְךָ עֶרְוַת דָּבָר״ וגו׳, וְהֵן אֵינָן יוֹדְעִין, שֶׁעֲבֵירָה מְכַבָּה מִצְוָה וְאֵין עֲבֵירָה מְכַבָּה תּוֹרָה.

The Gemara asks: **What** verse **did** Doeg and Ahithophel **interpret** incorrectly, causing them to err? They interpreted this verse: "For the Lord your God walks in the midst of your camp…to give up your enemies before you…**that He see no licentious matter in you,** and turn away from you" (Deuteronomy 23:15), to indicate that God turns away from one who engaged in forbidden relations, and since David had sinned with Bathsheba God must have turned away from him. **But they did not know that a transgression extinguishes** the merit of **a mitzva, but a transgression does not extinguish** the merit of the **Torah.**

מַאי ״בּוֹז יָבוּזוּ לוֹ״? אָמַר עוּלָּא: לֹא כְּשִׁמְעוֹן אֲחִי עֲזַרְיָה, וְלֹא כְּרַבִּי יוֹחָנָן דְּבֵי נְשִׂיאָה,

The Gemara interprets the continuation of the verse cited by the *baraita* with regard to Torah study: **What** is the meaning of: "Many waters cannot extinguish the love…if a man would give all the fortune of his house for love, **he would utterly be condemned"** (Song of Songs 8:7)? The Torah is compared to love several times in the Song of Songs. Therefore, the verse indicates that one cannot acquire a share in the reward for Torah study with money. **Ulla says:** The verse is **not** speaking of individuals **like Shimon, brother of Azarya,**[P] whose brother Azarya supported him and enabled him to study Torah. **And** it is **not** speaking of individuals **like Rabbi Yoḥanan of the house of the *Nasi*,**[P] whom the *Nasi* supported so that he could study Torah.

אֶלָּא כְּהִלֵּל וְשֶׁבְנָא. דְּכִי אֲתָא רַב דִּימִי אֲמַר: הִלֵּל וְשֶׁבְנָא אַחֵי הָווּ. הִלֵּל עָסַק בַּתּוֹרָה, שֶׁבְנָא עֲבַד עִיסְקָא. לְסוֹף אֲמַר לֵיהּ: תָּא נַעֲרוֹב וְלִיפְלוֹג. יָצְתָה בַּת קוֹל וְאָמְרָה: ״אִם יִתֵּן אִישׁ אֶת כָּל הוֹן בֵּיתוֹ״ וגו׳.

Rather, it is speaking of individuals **like Hillel and Shevna,**[N] **as when Rav Dimi came**[B] to Babylonia **he said: Hillel and Shevna were brothers; Hillel engaged in Torah** study and remained impoverished, whereas **Shevna entered into** a business **venture** and became wealthy. **In the end,** Shevna **said to** Hillel: **Come, let us join** our wealth **together and divide** it between us; I will give you half of my money and you will give me half of the reward for your Torah study. In response to this request **a Divine Voice issued forth and said: "If a man would give all the fortune of his house**[N] for love, he would utterly be condemned" (Song of Songs 8:7).

Perek **III**
Daf **21** Amud **b**

״אוֹמֵר בֶּן עַזַּאי: חַיָּיב אָדָם לְלַמֵּד אֶת וכו׳. רַבִּי אֱלִיעֶזֶר אוֹמֵר: כָּל הַמְלַמֵּד אֶת בִּתּוֹ תּוֹרָה מְלַמְּדָהּ תִּיפְלוּת״. תִּיפְלוּת סָלְקָא דַּעְתָּךְ? אֶלָּא אֵימָא: כְּאִילּוּ לִמְּדָהּ תִּיפְלוּת.

§ The mishna states: From here **ben Azzai states: A person is obligated to teach** his daughter Torah, so that if she drinks and does not die immediately, she will know that some merit of hers has delayed her punishment. **Rabbi Eliezer says: Anyone who teaches his daughter Torah is teaching her promiscuity.** The Gemara asks: Could it **enter your mind** to say that teaching one's daughter Torah is actually teaching her **promiscuity? Rather, say:** It is considered **as if he taught her promiscuity.**

NOTES

They would not have pursued David – לָא רָדְפוּ בָּתַר דָּוִד: The Rosh notes that actually, the Gemara's statement applies only to Ahithophel. Doeg's name should not appear here, since according to the Gemara elsewhere, Doeg was no longer alive at the time that the incident involving David and Bathsheba occurred. Ahithophel was still alive at the time, and in fact Bathsheba was his granddaughter (*Tosefot HaRosh*).

Shevna – שֶׁבְנָא: *Tosefot HaRash* cites Rabbeinu Tam, who says that the name here should actually read: Shekhna, as the Shevna mentioned in the Bible was wicked, and it is improper to name one's child after a wicked person. Others disagree, noting that there were two individuals by the name of Shevna, and one of them was not wicked. Therefore, the name may be used in naming the child after the other Shevna.

If a man would give all the fortune of his house – אִם יִתֵּן אִישׁ אֶת כָּל הוֹן בֵּיתוֹ: The Gemara distinguishes between one who financially assists another to learn Torah, and one who wishes to acquire the reward for the Torah that another already studied under difficult financial conditions. One who assists another to learn does share in the merit of his Torah study; by contrast, after one has already learned Torah without assistance, his merit cannot be bought, and even entertaining the thought that it could be bought is worthy of condemnation (*Iyyun Ya'akov*).

PERSONALITIES

Shimon brother of Azarya – שִׁמְעוֹן אֲחִי עֲזַרְיָה: Shimon, brother of Azarya, was a *tanna* who lived at the time of the destruction of the Temple, and he is mentioned several times in the Mishna. According to the Rambam, the Azariah mentioned here was the father of Rabbi Elazar ben Azarya. Azarya was a Torah scholar, but he was also very wealthy, and he supported his brother Shimon, who was a greater Torah scholar. Despite the fact that Shimon was a greater scholar, he is known as the brother of Azarya because Azarya supported him (see *Vayikra Rabba* 25:1).

Rabbi Yoḥanan of the house of the *Nasi* – רַבִּי יוֹחָנָן דְּבֵי נְשִׂיאָה: Apparently, this is referring to a poverty-stricken scholar unknown to us, who was known by this appellation because the house of the *Nasi* supported him and enabled him to learn Torah. It is unlikely that this is referring to the great *amora* Rabbi Yoḥanan, as he sold all his vast possessions in order to devote himself to Torah study. In fact, the *Pesikta DeRav Kahana* (27:1) cites the verse mentioned here: "If a man would give all the fortune of his house for love" (Song of Songs 8:7), in reference to Rabbi Yoḥanan.

BACKGROUND

When Rav Dimi came – כִּי אֲתָא רַב דִּימִי: Rav Dimi was one of the Sages of Eretz Yisrael who would often travel to Babylonia, primarily in order to transmit the Torah learned in the study halls of Eretz Yisrael to the Torah centers of the Diaspora, although occasionally he traveled on business as well. Many questions, particularly those concerning the opinions of the Sages of Eretz Yisrael, remained unresolved in Babylonia until one of these messengers from Eretz Yisrael arrived and elucidated the *halakha*, explained a novel expression, or clarified the unique circumstances pertaining to a particular statement.

אָמַר רַבִּי אַבָּהוּ: מַאי טַעְמָא דְּרַבִּי אֱלִיעֶזֶר? דִּכְתִיב: ״אֲנִי חָכְמָה שָׁכַנְתִּי עָרְמָה״ – כֵּיוָן שֶׁנִּכְנְסָה חָכְמָה בְּאָדָם, נִכְנְסָה עִמּוֹ עַרְמוּמִית.

Rabbi Abbahu says: What is the reason for Rabbi Eliezer's statement? It is **as it is written: "I, wisdom, dwell with cunning"** (Proverbs 8:12), which indicates that **once wisdom enters into a person, cunning enters with it.**[N] Rabbi Eliezer fears that the woman will use the cunning she achieves by learning the wisdom of the Torah to engage in promiscuous behavior.

וְרַבָּנַן, הַאי ״אֲנִי חָכְמָה״ מַאי עָבְדֵי לֵיהּ? מִיבָּעֵי לֵיהּ לְכִדְרַבִּי יוֹסֵי בְּרַבִּי חֲנִינָא, דְּאָמַר רַבִּי יוֹסֵי בְּרַבִּי חֲנִינָא: אֵין דִּבְרֵי תוֹרָה מִתְקַיְּימִין אֶלָּא בְּמִי שֶׁמַּעֲמִיד עַצְמוֹ עָרוֹם עֲלֵיהֶן, שֶׁנֶּאֱמַר: ״אֲנִי חָכְמָה שָׁכַנְתִּי עָרְמָה״. אָמַר רַבִּי יוֹחָנָן: אֵין דִּבְרֵי תוֹרָה מִתְקַיְּימִין אֶלָּא בְּמִי שֶׁמֵּשִׂים עַצְמוֹ כְּמִי שֶׁאֵינוֹ, שֶׁנֶּאֱמַר: ״וְהַחָכְמָה מֵאַיִן תִּמָּצֵא״.

The Gemara asks: **And the Rabbis** who disagree with him, **what do they do with this** verse: **"I, wisdom,** dwell with cunning [*orma*]"; how do they interpret it? The Gemara responds: **He requires that** verse **for that which Rabbi Yosei, son of Rabbi Ḥanina,** states, interpreting the word *"orma"* as nakedness rather than cunningness, **as Rabbi Yosei, son of Rabbi Ḥanina, says: The matters of Torah do not endure except in one who stands naked for them,**[N] **as it is stated: "I, wisdom, dwell with nakedness [*orma*]"** (Proverbs 8:12). This means that wisdom dwells only in one who is prepared to give away all of his possessions for the sake of Torah study. **Rabbi Yoḥanan says: The matters of Torah do not endure except in one who considers himself as one who does not** exist, **as it is stated: "But wisdom, it can be found in nothingness"** (Job 28:12).

״רַבִּי יְהוֹשֻׁעַ אוֹמֵר: רוֹצָה אִשָּׁה״ וכו׳. מַאי קָאָמַר? הָכִי קָאָמַר: רוֹצָה אִשָּׁה בְּקַב וְתִיפְלוּת עִמּוֹ, מִתִּשְׁעַת קַבִּין וּפְרִישׁוּת.

§ The mishna states that **Rabbi Yehoshua says: A woman desires** to receive the amount of a *kav* of food and a sexual relationship rather than to receive nine *kav* of food and abstinence. The Gemara asks: **What is he saying? This is what** Rabbi Yehoshua **is saying: A woman desires to** receive the amount of **a *kav*** of food **and with it a sexual relationship,**[N] i.e., her husband's availability to fulfill her sexual desires, rather **than nine *kav*** of food **and** with it **abstinence,** and since her desires are of a sexual nature, it is undesirable for her to study Torah.

״הוּא הָיָה אוֹמֵר: חָסִיד שׁוֹטֶה״ כו׳. הֵיכִי דָּמֵי חָסִיד שׁוֹטֶה? כְּגוֹן דְּקָא טָבְעָה אִיתְּתָא בְּנַהֲרָא, וְאָמַר: לָאו אוֹרַח אַרְעָא לְאִיסְתַּכּוֹלֵי בָּהּ וְאַצּוֹלָהּ.

§ The mishna continues: **He,** Rabbi Yehoshua, **would say: A foolish man of piety,**[N] and a conniving wicked person, and an abstinent woman, and those who injure themselves out of false abstinence; all these are people who erode the world. The Gemara asks: **Who is considered a foolish man of piety? For example,** it is one who sees **that a woman is drowning**[N] **in a river, and he says:** It is **not proper conduct to look at her** while she is undressed **and save her.**

NOTES

Cunning enters with it – נִכְנְסָה עִמּוֹ עַרְמוּמִית: According to Rashi, who explains the term *tiflut* as referring to licentious behavior, the connection between cunning and *tiflut* is that a woman might use the ingenuity she achieves by learning Torah in order to hide her immorality. The Meiri, who explains *tiflut* as meaning worthless matters, interprets the connection differently. Although she attains a little wisdom by learning Torah, she comprehends her studies only partially. Yet she believes herself to have understood fully, and attempts to show off her wisdom to all.

One who stands naked for them – מִי שֶׁמַּעֲמִיד עַצְמוֹ עָרוֹם עֲלֵיהֶן: Rashi, in his first interpretation, explains that this statement refers to one who relinquishes all his possessions in order to acquire wisdom. The Meiri adds that only when one does not care at all about physical possessions can he be sure that nothing will prevent him from learning. In his second interpretation, Rashi explains that in order to attain the wisdom of the Torah, one must view himself as bare and devoid of all knowledge, as this enables him to learn from everyone, even from those of lesser stature. The Meiri offers an alternative explanation as well, suggesting that Rabbi Yosei, son of Rabbi Ḥanina, also interprets *orma* in the sense of cunning and states that the matters of Torah do not endure except in one who renders himself cunning for them. One must use cunning in order to discover the methods and techniques of learning that best suit him. For example, some memorize their learning through repetition, but there are others who find other methods more efficient.

The amount of a *kav* of food and with it a sexual relationship, etc. – בְּקַב וְתִיפְלוּת עִמּוֹ וכו׳: Women generally prefer a less luxurious lifestyle that involves more sexual intercourse to a life of greater luxury that involves a lack of sexual intercourse, possibly due to a husband's extended absences from home for work. *Tosafot* cite Rabbeinu Ḥananel, who illustrates this concept by means of a halakhic ruling. The Gemara states elsewhere that a donkey driver may not become a camel driver without his wife's consent, since although a camel driver earns more than a donkey driver, he arrives home less frequently. Alternatively, the Meiri explains that a woman generally prefers that her husband attain only minimal knowledge of Torah and be at home with her, rather than attain great wisdom but be distant from her.

A foolish man of piety – חָסִיד שׁוֹטֶה: Also included in this category are those whose concepts of piety cause them to neglect mitzvot that are incumbent upon them, and those who behave with exaggerated piety, e.g., one who fasts every single day (Rambam; Meiri).

One who sees that a woman is drowning, etc. – דְּקָא טָבְעָה אִיתְּתָא וכו׳: Some of the commentaries raise the question that this behavior is not merely foolish but wicked, as the Torah explicitly obligates one to save those whose lives are in danger, as stated in the verse: "You shall not stand idly by the blood of your neighbor" (Leviticus 19:16). The commentaries therefore explain that the Gemara is referring to a case where there are others present who can perform the rescue but he, due to his misplaced piety, does not hasten to perform this mitzva (*Minḥa Ḥareva*; see *Eshel Avraham*).

הֵיכִי דָּמֵי רָשָׁע עָרוּם? אָמַר רַבִּי יוֹחָנָן: זֶה הַמַּטְעִים דְּבָרָיו לַדַּיָּין קוֹדֶם שֶׁיָּבֹא בַּעַל דִּין חֲבֵירוֹ. רַבִּי אַבָּהוּ אוֹמֵר: זֶה הַנּוֹתֵן דִּינָר לְעָנִי לְהַשְׁלִים לוֹ מָאתַיִם זוּז, דִּתְנַן: מִי שֶׁיֵּשׁ לוֹ מָאתַיִם זוּז – לֹא יִטּוֹל לֶקֶט שִׁכְחָה וּפֵאָה וּמַעֲשַׂר עָנִי. הָיָה לוֹ מָאתַיִם חָסֵר דִּינָר – אֲפִילּוּ אֶלֶף נוֹתְנִין לוֹ כְּאַחַת הֲרֵי זֶה יִטּוֹל.

The Gemara asks: **Who is considered a conniving wicked person? Rabbi Yoḥanan says: This is one who presents his statement to the judge**[NH] **before the other litigant comes** and thereby prejudices the judge in his favor. **Rabbi Abbahu says: This** is referring to **one who gives a dinar to a poor man** in order **to complete** the sum of **two hundred dinars for him,** so that he will no longer be entitled to receive charity, **as we learned** in a mishna (*Pe'a* 8:8): **One who has two hundred**[H] **dinars may not collect gleanings,**[B] **forgotten** sheaves,[B] ***pe'a,***[B] **and the poor man's tithe,**[B] since he is not defined as poor. However, if **he has two hundred less** one **dinar, even** if **he is given one thousand** dinars **at once, he may collect.**

רַבִּי אַסִי אָמַר רַבִּי יוֹחָנָן: זֶה הַמַּשִּׂיא עֵצָה לִמְכּוֹר בִּנְכָסִים מוּעָטִין, דְּאָמַר רַבִּי אַסִי אָמַר רַבִּי יוֹחָנָן: יְתוֹמִים שֶׁקָּדְמוּ וּמָכְרוּ בִּנְכָסִים מוּעָטִין, מַה שֶּׁמָּכְרוּ מָכְרוּ.

Rabbi Asi says that **Rabbi Yoḥanan says:** A conniving wicked person is **one who provides advice** to male orphans **to sell from the small quantity of property** left to them by their father, before it is appropriated by the court for the purpose of providing for the daughters, who do not inherit property. This causes the daughters to lose their right to sustenance, because although it is improper to do so, the sale is valid, **as Rabbi Asi says** that **Rabbi Yoḥanan says:** With regard to male **orphans who preemptively sold**[H] the property **from a small estate, that which they sold, they sold,** and the sons retain the money.

אַבָּיֵי אָמַר: זֶה הַמַּשִּׂיא עֵצָה לִמְכּוֹר בִּנְכָסִים כְּרַבָּן שִׁמְעוֹן בֶּן גַּמְלִיאֵל, דְּתַנְיָא: ״נְכָסַי לְךָ וְאַחֲרֶיךָ לִפְלוֹנִי״, וְיָרַד הָרִאשׁוֹן וּמָכַר וְאָכַל – הַשֵּׁנִי מוֹצִיא מִיַּד הַלָּקוֹחוֹת, דִּבְרֵי רַבִּי. רַבָּן שִׁמְעוֹן בֶּן גַּמְלִיאֵל אוֹמֵר: אֵין לַשֵּׁנִי אֶלָּא מַה שֶּׁשִּׁיֵּיר רִאשׁוֹן.

Abaye says: A conniving wicked person **is one who provides advice to sell property**[H] **in accordance with** the ruling of **Rabban Shimon ben Gamliel, as it is taught** in a *baraita*: With regard to one who said: **My property** is given **to you, and after you** die, **to so-and-so, and the first** beneficiary **entered** the property **and sold** it **and consumed** the profits, **the second** beneficiary **repossesses** the property **from the purchasers,** as the property belongs to him after the death of the first beneficiary; **this is the statement of Rabbi** Yehuda HaNasi. **Rabban Shimon ben Gamliel says: The second** beneficiary receives **only that which the first** beneficiary **left,** since his sale is valid. However, it is not permitted to sell the property *ab initio*, since the giver intended for the second beneficiary to receive the property.

רַב יוֹסֵף בַּר חָמָא אָמַר רַב שֵׁשֶׁת: זֶה הַמַּכְרִיעַ אֲחֵרִים בְּאוֹרְחוֹתָיו. רַבִּי זְרִיקָא אָמַר רַב הוּנָא: זֶה הַמֵּיקֵל לְעַצְמוֹ וּמַחֲמִיר לַאֲחֵרִים. עוּלָּא אָמַר: זֶה

Rav Yosef bar Ḥama says that **Rav Sheshet says:** A conniving wicked person is **one who persuades others with his ways,**[N] convincing others to mimic his seemingly righteous behavior, in order to hide his faults. **Rabbi Zerika** says that **Rav Huna says:** A conniving wicked person is **one who is lenient** in the *halakha* **for himself and strict for others. Ulla says: This**

NOTES

One who presents his statement to the judge, etc. – הַמַּטְעִים דְּבָרָיו לַדַּיָּין וכו׳: A judge who hears one litigant when the other litigant is not present transgresses the prohibition: "Do not accept a false report" (Exodus 23:1). The Sages expound this verse to apply to the litigant as well, prohibiting him from presenting his case when the other litigant is not present. The rationale behind this prohibition is that once a judge has heard the argument of one side while the other side is not present, the impression created is likely to remain fixed in his mind, making it difficult for him to accept the arguments of the other side (Rashi). *Ben Yehoyada* adds that the Gemara is not referring to an individual who openly states his case before the judge in this manner, as the judge will not be prepared to listen to him; rather, it refers to one who discusses the particulars of his case with the judge incidentally, or in the course of a Torah discussion.

One who persuades others with his ways – הַמַּכְרִיעַ אֲחֵרִים בְּאוֹרְחוֹתָיו: The Maharsha explains that this refers to one who gives advice to others, surreptitiously advising them to perform actions that benefit him and cause loss to others.

BACKGROUND

Gleanings – לֶקֶט: The Torah prohibits the owner of a field from gathering individual stalks that fell during the harvest (Leviticus 19:9). Less than three stalks that fell in one place are considered gleanings and belong to the poor.

Forgotten sheaves – שִׁכְחָה: If one forgot a sheaf in the field while harvesting, he may not return to collect it, as it must be left for the poor (Deuteronomy 24:19).

***Pe'a* – פֵּאָה:** The Torah states that one is prohibited from harvesting the produce in the corner of his field; rather, one must allow the poor to collect this produce themselves. The Sages decreed that the area of the corner must be at least one-sixtieth of the field. This mitzva is stated in the Torah (Leviticus 19:9, 23:22), and the details of the mitzva are explained in tractate *Pe'a*.

The poor man's tithe – מַעֲשַׂר עָנִי: During the third and sixth years of the Sabbatical cycle, after one separates *teruma* from his produce, which is given to the priests, and first tithe, which is given to the Levites, one-tenth of the remaining produce is distributed to the poor. During the other years of the Sabbatical cycle, second tithe is separated instead of the poor man's tithe.

HALAKHA

One who presents his statement to the judge, etc. – הַמַּטְעִים דְּבָרָיו לַדַּיָּין וכו׳: It is prohibited for a judge to hear the arguments of one litigant when the other litigant is not present. The litigants are also prohibited from presenting their claims in this manner (Rambam *Sefer Shofetim*, *Hilkhot Sanhedrin* 21:7; *Shulḥan Arukh*, *Ḥoshen Mishpat* 17:5).

One who has two hundred, etc. – מִי שֶׁיֵּשׁ לוֹ מָאתַיִם וכו׳: One who has two hundred dinars may not collect gleanings, forgotten sheaves, *pe'a*, or the poor man's tithe. If he has two hundred dinars less one, even if he is given one thousand dinars at once, he may collect. The same applies with regard to receiving charity. Some authorities say that these specific amounts applied only in the past; nowadays one may collect charity if one does not have sufficient funds to be able to earn a living from the profits thereof (Rambam *Sefer Zera'im*, *Hilkhot Mattenot Aniyyim* 9:13; *Shulḥan Arukh*, *Yoreh De'a* 253:1–2).

Orphans who preemptively sold, etc. – יְתוֹמִים שֶׁקָּדְמוּ וּמָכְרוּ וכו׳: If one dies and leaves insufficient property for his children to sustain themselves until his daughters reach the age of majority, the court first appropriates funds to provide for the daughters and then gives the remainder to the sons. If the estate is sufficient only to provide for the daughters, the entire estate is given to the daughters. However, if the sons preemptively sold the property from a small estate, the sale is valid, in accordance with the opinion of Rabbi Yoḥanan. The Rema, citing the Rosh, holds that the sale is valid only if it took place prior to the court's appropriating the daughters' sustenance from the estate (Rambam *Sefer Nashim*, *Hilkhot Ishut* 19:19; *Shulḥan Arukh*, *Even HaEzer* 112:11, 14).

One who provides advice to sell property – הַמַּשִּׂיא עֵצָה לִמְכּוֹר בִּנְכָסִים: If one says: My property is given to you, and after you die, to so-and-so, the second beneficiary receives only that which the first beneficiary left. Although it is prohibited for the first beneficiary to sell or give away the property, if he does so, the second beneficiary does not repossess the property from the purchasers, in accordance with the ruling of Rabban Shimon ben Gamliel. One who advises the first beneficiary to sell the property is considered wicked (Rambam *Sefer Kinyan*, *Hilkhot Zekhiya UMattana* 12:8–9; *Shulḥan Arukh*, *Ḥoshen Mishpat* 248:3).

שֶׁקָּרָא וְשָׁנָה וְלֹא שִׁימֵּשׁ תַּלְמִידֵי חֲכָמִים.

is one **who read** the Written Torah **and learned** the Mishna **but did not serve Torah scholars**[N] in order to learn the reasoning behind the *halakhot*. Since he believes himself knowledgeable, he issues halakhic rulings, but due to his lack of understanding he rules erroneously and is therefore considered wicked. His cunning is in his public display of knowledge, which misleads others into considering him a true Torah scholar.

אִתְּמַר: קָרָא וְשָׁנָה וְלֹא שִׁימֵּשׁ תַּלְמִידֵי חֲכָמִים – רַבִּי אֶלְעָזָר אוֹמֵר: הֲרֵי זֶה עַם הָאָרֶץ. רַבִּי שְׁמוּאֵל בַּר נַחְמָנִי אָמַר: הֲרֵי זֶה בּוּר. רַבִּי יַנַּאי אוֹמֵר: הֲרֵי זֶה כּוּתִי.

It was stated: With regard to one who **read** the Written Torah **and learned** the Mishna **but did not serve Torah scholars, Rabbi Elazar says: This** person **is an ignoramus. Rabbi Shmuel bar Naḥmani said: This** person **is a boor. Rabbi Yannai says: This** person **is** comparable to **a Samaritan,** who follows the Written Torah but not the traditions of the Sages.

רַב אַחָא בַּר יַעֲקֹב אוֹמֵר: הֲרֵי זֶה מָגוֹשׁ. אֲמַר רַב נַחְמָן בַּר יִצְחָק: מִסְתַּבְּרָא כְּרַב אַחָא בַּר יַעֲקֹב, דְּאָמְרִי אֱינָשֵׁי: רָטֵין מָגוֹשָׁא וְלָא יָדַע מַאי אָמַר, תָּנֵי תַּנָּא וְלָא יָדַע מַאי אָמַר.

Rav Aḥa bar Ya'akov says: This person **is** comparable to **a sorcerer** [*magosh*],[NB] who uses his knowledge to mislead people. **Rav Naḥman bar Yitzḥak said: It is reasonable to** accept the opinion **of Rav Aḥa bar Ya'akov, as people say** proverbially: **The sorcerer chants**[N] **and does not know what he is saying;** so too, **the** ***tanna*** **teaches** the Mishna **and does not know what he is saying.**

תָּנוּ רַבָּנַן: אֵיזֶהוּ עַם הָאָרֶץ? כָּל שֶׁאֵינוֹ קוֹרֵא קְרִיאַת שְׁמַע שַׁחֲרִית וְעַרְבִית בְּבִרְכוֹתֶיהָ, דִּבְרֵי רַבִּי מֵאִיר. וַחֲכָמִים אוֹמְרִים: כָּל שֶׁאֵינוֹ מַנִּיחַ תְּפִילִּין. בֶּן עַזַּאי אוֹמֵר: כָּל שֶׁאֵין לוֹ צִיצִית בְּבִגְדוֹ. רַבִּי יוֹנָתָן בֶּן יוֹסֵף אָמַר: כָּל שֶׁיֵּשׁ לוֹ בָּנִים וְאֵינוֹ מְגַדְּלָן לְלִמּוּד תּוֹרָה. אֲחֵרִים אוֹמְרִים: אֲפִילּוּ קוֹרֵא וְשׁוֹנֶה וְלֹא שִׁימֵּשׁ תַּלְמִידֵי חֲכָמִים – זֶהוּ עַם הָאָרֶץ;

§ **The Sages taught: Who is an ignoramus** [*am ha'aretz*]?[NB] It is **anyone who does not recite** ***Shema***[N] in the **morning and evening with its blessings;** this is **the statement of Rabbi Meir. And the Rabbis say:** It is **anyone who does not don phylacteries. Ben Azzai says:** It is **anyone who does not have ritual fringes on his garment. Rabbi Yonatan ben Yosef said:** It is **anyone who has sons and does not raise them to study Torah.** ***Aḥerim*** **say:**[N] **Even if one reads** the Written Torah **and learns** the Mishna **but does not serve Torah scholars, he is an ignoramus.**

NOTES

Did not serve Torah scholars – לֹא שִׁימֵּשׁ תַּלְמִידֵי חֲכָמִים: Rashi explains that this refers to one who did not study the Gemara, which teaches the proper analysis of the Mishna and the systematic reasoning underlying *halakha*. Others explain that serving Torah scholars literally means one who visits and serves Torah scholars in order to learn from their ways. One who does not do so shows that his Torah study is insincere, and he is therefore considered a conniving, wicked person (*Tosefot HaRash*; Meiri).

He is comparable to a sorcerer – הֲרֵי זֶה מָגוֹשׁ: Each of the opinions presented here voices stronger criticism than the preceding one. An ignoramus is one who has positive traits but is insufficiently educated, whereas a boor is one devoid of anything positive. A Samaritan does not even accept the Torah and therefore separates himself from the Jewish people. The comparison to a sorcerer, who was considered an apostate, is the most derogatory.

The sorcerer chants, etc. – רָטֵין מָגוֹשָׁא וכו׳: A sorcerer whispers all kinds of incantations without understanding their meaning, yet he relies upon the efficacy of his actions. So too, one who does not understand the depths of the Torah simply repeats statements that he heard, believing that by merely reciting the words he does something important (Rashi).

Who is an ignoramus [*am ha'aretz*] – אֵיזֶהוּ עַם הָאָרֶץ: *Tosafot* note that the Gemara provides varying definitions of an ignoramus, depending on the context. One definition applies when defining those who are unfit to testify, another with regard to those suspect of not tithing their produce, and yet another with regard to matters of ritual purity. *Tosefot HaRash* writes that the discussion in this *baraita* might be with regard to joining in a *zimmun*, the introductory blessing recited by three or more adults before Grace after Meals.

Who does not recite ***Shema*** – שֶׁאֵינוֹ קוֹרֵא קְרִיאַת שְׁמַע: The Gemara states elsewhere that if one is incapable of learning more, he can fulfill the obligation to study Torah by at least reciting the *Shema* with intent and understanding in the morning and the evening. Consequently, one who does so is not defined as an ignoramus (*Maharsha*; *Etz Yosef*).

Aḥerim **say** – אֲחֵרִים אוֹמְרִים: The term *aḥerim* literally means others. *Tosefot HaRash* notes that although this term generally refers to Rabbi Meir, here it obviously does not refer to Rabbi Meir, as Rabbi Meir states a different opinion in the *baraita*. *Tosafot* elsewhere suggest that perhaps the term *aḥerim* is used in cases where Rabbi Meir cited the opinion of his teacher, Elisha ben Avuya, who was referred to as *Aḥer*.

BACKGROUND

Sorcerer [*magosh*] – מָגוֹשׁ: The term *magosh* refers to Zoroastrian priests, also known in the Talmud as *ḥabbarim*. The biblical term "*rab-mag*" (Jeremiah 39:3) is apparently derived from the same Persian term. It later became an accepted term for sorcerers in Greek and Latin, as well as other languages.

These sorcerers would perform ritual ceremonies in the ancient Avestan language, an Eastern Iranian language that derives its name from the language of Zoroastrian scripture, the Avesta. The sorcerers did not understand this language, and from this stems the aphorism: The sorcerer chants and does not know what he is saying.

Relief of Zoroastrian priest, referred to in the Gemara as a *magosh*

Ignoramus [*am ha'aretz*] – עַם הָאָרֶץ: The term *am ha'aretz*, which literally means: People of the land, appears in the books of Ezra and Nehemiah, but there it refers only to gentiles. The term later evolved into a derogatory epithet referring to a Jew who behaves in the manner of a gentile.

The concept of an *am ha'aretz* was not clearly defined, and therefore there were many opinions among the *tanna'im* with regard to who should be characterized as an *am ha'aretz*. They ranged from the opinion that the term refers to one who does not serve Torah scholars and learn from them, to the opinion that the term refers to one with no Torah, no Mishna, and no manners. According to the first opinion, many learned people were included in this category. According to the second opinion, an *am ha'aretz* was the basest of individuals, to whom the most derogatory epithets were generally applied. The common application of the term was to one devoid of spirituality, with no profession or occupation, no education, and no connection to Torah and mitzvot.

In the talmudic era, and even more so in later times, the situation changed in two respects. First, while there remained many who were uneducated, the most extreme form of an *am ha'aretz* disappeared, as even simple Jews upheld Torah and mitzvot to the best of their ability. Secondly, to avoid causing rifts within the nation in exile, the *halakhot* restricting interactions with an *am ha'aretz* were repealed.

BACKGROUND

The *tanna'im* – הַתַּנָּאִים: This does not refer to the Sages of the Mishna. In the amoraic period, the term *tanna* sometimes took on another meaning, referring to those who had broad knowledge of tannaitic statements and *mishnayot*. Despite this knowledge, they were not considered among the Sages because they were unable to resolve the difficult issues that arose in the texts that they recited. The *tanna* would recite the material in the presence of one of the Sages, who would assess its accuracy and either confirm it or, if need be, correct it.

קָרָא וְלֹא שָׁנָה – הֲרֵי זֶה בּוּר; לֹא קָרָא וְלֹא שָׁנָה – עָלָיו הַכָּתוּב אוֹמֵר: ״וְזָרַעְתִּי אֶת בֵּית יִשְׂרָאֵל וְאֶת בֵּית יְהוּדָה זֶרַע אָדָם וְזֶרַע בְּהֵמָה״.

If one **read** the Written Torah **but did not learn** the Mishna, **he is a boor. With regard to** one who **did not read and did not learn** at all, **the verse states:** "Behold, the days come, says the Lord, **and I will sow the house of Israel and the house of Judah with the seed of man, and with the seed of beast"** (Jeremiah 31:26). One who has not studied at all is comparable to a beast.

״יְרָא אֶת ה׳ בְּנִי וָמֶלֶךְ עִם שׁוֹנִים אַל תִּתְעָרָב״ – אָמַר רַבִּי יִצְחָק: אֵלּוּ שֶׁשּׁוֹנִים הֲלָכוֹת. פְּשִׁיטָא! מַהוּ דְּתֵימָא שׁוֹנִין בְּחֵטְא, וְכִדְרַב הוּנָא, דְּאָמַר רַב הוּנָא: כֵּיוָן שֶׁעָבַר אָדָם עֲבֵירָה וְשָׁנָה בָּהּ הוּתְּרָה לוֹ, קָא מַשְׁמַע לַן.

The verse states: **"My son, fear the Lord and the king; and meddle not with those who are repeating"** (Proverbs 24:21). **Rabbi Yitzḥak says: These are** individuals **who repeatedly learn** the *halakhot* but do not know the reasons behind them. The Gemara asks: **Isn't** that **obvious?** How else could the verse be understood? The Gemara answers: He states this **lest you say** that the verse is referring to individuals who **repeatedly** commit **sins, and** this is **in accordance with** the words of **Rav Huna, as Rav Huna says: Once a person committed a transgression and repeated it,** in his eyes **it became permitted for him.** Since the verse could be interpreted in this manner, Rabbi Yitzḥak **teaches us** that the verse is referring to those who learn without understanding.

תָּנָא: הַתַּנָּאִים מְבַלֵּי עוֹלָם. מְבַלֵּי עוֹלָם סָלְקָא דַּעְתָּךְ? אָמַר רָבִינָא: שֶׁמּוֹרִין הֲלָכָה מִתּוֹךְ מִשְׁנָתָן. תַּנְיָא נַמִי הָכִי, אָמַר רַבִּי יְהוֹשֻׁעַ: וְכִי מְבַלֵּי עוֹלָם הֵן? וַהֲלֹא מְיַישְּׁבֵי עוֹלָם הֵן, שֶׁנֶּאֱמַר: ״הֲלִיכוֹת עוֹלָם לוֹ״! אֶלָּא, שֶׁמּוֹרִין הֲלָכָה מִתּוֹךְ מִשְׁנָתָן.

It was taught in a *baraita*: **The *tanna'im*,**[B] who recite the tannaitic sources by rote, **are** individuals **who erode the world.** The Gemara is puzzled by this statement: **Could it enter your mind** that they are individuals **who erode the world? Ravina says:** This statement is referring to those **who issue halakhic rulings based** on **their** knowledge of ***mishnayot*. This is also taught** in a *baraita*: **Rabbi Yehoshua said: Are they** individuals **who erode the world? Aren't they settling the world, as it is stated: "His ways [*halikhot*] are eternal"** (Habakkuk 3:6)? The Sages read the term *halikhot* as *halakhot*, inferring that one who learns *halakhot* attains eternal life. **Rather,** this is referring to those **who issue halakhic rulings based** on **their** knowledge of ***mishnayot*.**

״אִשָּׁה פְּרוּשָׁה״ וכו׳. תָּנוּ רַבָּנַן: בְּתוּלָה צַלְיָינִית, וְאַלְמָנָה שׁוֹבָבִית, וְקָטָן שֶׁלֹּא כָּלוּ לוֹ חֳדָשָׁיו – הֲרֵי אֵלּוּ מְבַלֵּי עוֹלָם.

§ The mishna states that **an abstinent woman** is among those who erode the world. **The Sages taught: A maiden who prays** constantly,[N] **and a neighborly [*shovavit*] widow**[N] who constantly visits her neighbors, **and a child whose months** of gestation **were not completed,** all **these are** people **who erode the world.**

אִינִי? וְהָאָמַר רַבִּי יוֹחָנָן: לָמַדְנוּ יִרְאַת חֵטְא מִבְּתוּלָה, וְקִיבּוּל שָׂכָר מֵאַלְמָנָה. יִרְאַת חֵטְא מִבְּתוּלָה, דְּרַבִּי יוֹחָנָן שַׁמְעָהּ לְהַהִיא בְּתוּלָה דְּנָפְלָה אַאַפָּהּ, וְקָאָמְרָה: רִבּוֹנוֹ שֶׁל עוֹלָם, בָּרָאתָ גַּן עֵדֶן וּבָרָאתָ גֵּיהִנָּם, בָּרָאתָ צַדִּיקִים וּבָרָאתָ רְשָׁעִים. יְהִי רָצוֹן מִלְּפָנֶיךָ שֶׁלֹּא יִכָּשְׁלוּ בִּי בְּנֵי אָדָם.

The Gemara asks: **Is that so? But didn't Rabbi Yoḥanan say: We learned** the meaning of **fear of sin from a maiden,**[N] **and** the significance of **receiving** divine **reward from a widow.** The meaning of **fear of sin** can be learned **from a maiden, as Rabbi Yoḥanan heard a certain maiden who fell on her face** in prayer, **and she was saying: Master of the Universe, You created the Garden of Eden and You created Gehenna, You created** the **righteous and You created** the **wicked. May it be Your will that men shall not stumble because of me** and consequently go to Gehenna.

NOTES

A maiden who prays constantly – בְּתוּלָה צַלְיָינִית: The *Arukh* explains that this refers to a woman who spends all day in prayer while ignoring her other obligations. According to a variation of the text found in the Jerusalem Talmud, the phrase means: A maiden who fasts constantly and loses her virginity. Some commentaries explain that literally, due to her self-mortifying behavior, her hymen is eroded. *Tosafot* suggest that this refers to a woman who fasts outwardly in order to appear righteous and hide her licentiousness.

A neighborly [*shovavit*] widow – אַלְמָנָה שׁוֹבָבִית: Various interpretations have been offered for this term. Rashi explains that it is derived from the Aramaic *shivava*, which means neighbor, referring to a widow who often visits her neighbors. The Meiri explains that Rashi is referring to one who attempts to appear God-fearing and visits her neighbors in order to show off her piety. Some early commentaries render the term as *sovavit*, which is derived from the Hebrew root *samekh*, *beit*, *beit*, meaning to circuit, to go around, and refers to a widow who constantly frequents the markets and alleys in an immodest manner (*Arukh*). This would also appear to be the understanding of the Jerusalem Talmud, in which it is explained that her behavior causes her name to become tarnished, as she is accused of immoral behavior due to the length of time she spends in the houses of others.

Others explain that the term *shovavit* means penitent, and refers to a widow who publicly acts as one who is repenting. She claims that she desires only to serve God and does not intend to remarry; however, she is unable to maintain this way of life and in the end falls into sin (Rabbeinu Nissim Gaon; *Arukh*).

The meaning of fear of sin from a maiden, etc. – יִרְאַת חֵטְא מִבְּתוּלָה וכו׳: It was not merely the maiden's fear of sin or the widow's efforts to receive reward that impressed Rabbi Yoḥanan; rather, it was the unique manner in which they expressed these traits. The maiden's fear of sin caused her to ensure not only that she did not sin herself, but also that she would not cause others to sin. Similarly, the widow concerned herself with finding new ways to increase the value of the mitzvot she performed and their reward.

קִיבּוּל שָׂכָר מֵאַלְמָנָה, דְּהַהִיא אַלְמָנָה דַּהֲוַאי בֵּי כְנִישְׁתָּא בְּשִׁיבָבוּתָהּ, כָּל יוֹמָא הֲוַת אָתְיָא וּמַצְלָה בֵּי מִדְרָשֵׁיהּ דְּרַבִּי יוֹחָנָן. אָמַר לָהּ: בִּתִּי, לֹא בֵּית הַכְּנֶסֶת בְּשִׁיבָבוּתֵךְ? אָמְרָה לֵיהּ: רַבִּי, וְלֹא שְׂכַר פְּסִיעוֹת יֵשׁ לִי?

The significance of **receiving** divine **reward** can be learned **from a widow, as** there was **a certain widow in whose neighborhood there was a synagogue,** and despite this **every day she went and prayed in the study hall of Rabbi Yoḥanan.** Rabbi Yoḥanan **said to her: My daughter,** is there **not a synagogue in your neighborhood? She said to him: My teacher, don't I attain a reward** for all **the steps** I take while walking to pray in the distant study hall?

כִּי קָאָמַר – כְּגוֹן יוֹחֲנִי בַּת רְטִיבִי.

The Gemara answers: **When it is stated** in the *baraita* that a maiden who prays constantly is one who erodes the world, it is referring, **for example,** to **Yoḥani bat Retivi,** who constantly prayed and pretended to be saintly but actually engaged in sorcery.

מַאי קָטָן שֶׁלֹּא כָּלוּ לוֹ חֳדָשָׁיו? הָכָא תַּרְגִּימוּ: זֶה תַּלְמִיד חָכָם הַמְבַעֵט בְּרַבּוֹתָיו.

The Gemara asks: **What** is the meaning of **a child whose months** of gestation **were not completed?**[N] **Here,** in Babylonia, **they interpreted this** as alluding to an imperfect, incomplete **Torah scholar who scorns his teachers.**[N]

רַבִּי אַבָּא אָמַר: זֶה תַּלְמִיד שֶׁלֹּא הִגִּיעַ לְהוֹרָאָה וּמוֹרֶה. דְּאָמַר רַבִּי אַבָּהוּ אָמַר רַב הוּנָא אָמַר רַב, מַאי דִּכְתִיב: ״כִּי רַבִּים חֲלָלִים הִפִּילָה וַעֲצוּמִים כָּל הֲרוּגֶיהָ״? ״כִּי רַבִּים חֲלָלִים הִפִּילָה״ – זֶה תַּלְמִיד חָכָם שֶׁלֹּא הִגִּיעַ לְהוֹרָאָה וּמוֹרֶה. ״וַעֲצוּמִים כָּל הֲרוּגֶיהָ״ – זֶה תַּלְמִיד חָכָם שֶׁהִגִּיעַ לְהוֹרָאָה וְאֵינוֹ מוֹרֶה.

Rabbi Abba says: This is a student who has not yet **attained** the ability **to issue** halakhic **rulings, and** yet **he issues rulings** and is therefore compared to a prematurely born child. This is **as Rabbi Abbahu says** that **Rav Huna says** that **Rav says: What is** the meaning of that **which is written: "For she has cast down many wounded; and a mighty host are all her slain"** (Proverbs 7:26)? **"For she has cast down** [*hippila*] **many wounded";**[N] **this** is referring to **a Torah scholar who has not** yet **attained** the ability **to issue rulings, and** yet **he issues rulings.**[H] **"And a mighty host** [*ve'atzumim*] **are all her slain";**[N] **this** is referring to **a Torah scholar who has attained** the ability **to issue rulings, but does not issue rulings**[NH] and prevents the masses from learning Torah properly.

NOTES

A child whose months of gestation were not completed – קָטָן שֶׁלֹּא כָּלוּ לוֹ חֳדָשָׁיו: It is explained in the Jerusalem Talmud that this refers to an extremely young but successful Torah scholar, who uses his knowledge to embarrass his elders. An alternative opinion, also found in the Jerusalem Talmud, explains that this refers literally to a child, who is only nine years old but appears much older. If he involves himself in forbidden sexual intercourse, the woman is punished, while he is exempt from punishment.

Who scorns his teachers – הַמְבַעֵט בְּרַבּוֹתָיו: Rashi explains that according to this understanding, the expression: A child whose months were not completed, refers to the fact that his actions cause his life to be shortened. Others explain that this refers to a student who is so convinced of his greatness that he feels he should already be recognized as the leader of his generation, and therefore he prays that his teachers die so that he can take their place. Consequently, he is punished measure for measure by having his own life shortened (*Iyyun Ya'akov*).

For she has cast down [*hippila*] many wounded – כִּי רַבִּים חֲלָלִים הִפִּילָה: The term *hippila* is derived from the same root as the word *nefel*, which means a stillborn child. This alludes to the aforementioned comparison of a prematurely born child to a student who issues rulings while his abilities are still premature (Rashi). The term "many wounded" referred to in the verse alludes to the many people who stumble in matters of *halakha* due to his incorrect rulings.

And a mighty host [*ve'atzumim*] are all her slain – וַעֲצוּמִים כָּל הֲרוּגֶיהָ: The term *ve'atzumim* is derived from the root *ayin, tzadi, mem*, which also denotes shutting, closing. This alludes to one who is able to issue rulings but keeps his mouth closed.

Who has attained the ability to issue rulings but does not issue rulings – שֶׁהִגִּיעַ לְהוֹרָאָה וְאֵינוֹ מוֹרֶה: The Rambam explains that the severity of this statement is not only due to the fact that such a person prevents others from learning Torah, but also because if he does not issue rulings, others issue rulings even though they are not capable of doing so, and their rulings are incorrect.

HALAKHA

Who has not yet attained the ability to issue rulings and yet he issues rulings – שֶׁלֹּא הִגִּיעַ לְהוֹרָאָה וּמוֹרֶה: A student who has not yet attained the ability to issue halakhic rulings, and yet he issues rulings, is a fool and a wicked and haughty person. It is stated with regard to these individuals: "For she has cast down many wounded" (Proverbs 7:26).

The *Kesef Mishne* discusses why the Rambam does not mention the distinction stated later in the Gemara (22b) between one who has reached the age of forty and one who has not yet reached that age (Rambam *Sefer HaMadda, Hilkhot Talmud Torah* 5:4; *Shulḥan Arukh, Yoreh De'a* 242:13).

Who has attained the ability to issue rulings but does not issue rulings – שֶׁהִגִּיעַ לְהוֹרָאָה וְאֵינוֹ מוֹרֶה: A scholar who has reached the level where he is capable of rendering halakhic decisions but does not do so withholds Torah from the people and places stumbling blocks in front of others, and the verse (Proverbs 7:26) states with regard to him: "And a mighty host are all her slain" (Rambam *Sefer HaMadda, Hilkhot Talmud Torah* 5:4; *Shulḥan Arukh, Yoreh De'a* 242:14).

וְעַד כַּמָּה? עַד אַרְבְּעִין שְׁנִין. אִינִי? וְהָא רַבָּה אוֹרִי! בְּשָׁוִין.

And until when is it considered too premature for a scholar to issue halakhic rulings? It is **until forty years.**[N] The Gemara asks: **Is that so? But didn't Rabba**[P] **issue rulings,** even though he lived for only forty years? The Gemara answers: It is permitted for a scholar who has not studied for so long to issue rulings **when** his knowledge reaches the level of the foremost scholar in his city and **they are equals.**

"וּמַכּוֹת פְּרוּשִׁין" וכו׳. תָּנוּ רַבָּנַן – שִׁבְעָה פְּרוּשִׁין הֵן: פָּרוּשׁ שִׁיכְמִי, פָּרוּשׁ נִקְפִּי, פָּרוּשׁ קִיזָאִי, פָּרוּשׁ מְדוּכְיָא, פָּרוּשׁ "מָה חוֹבָתִי וְאֶעֱשֶׂנָּה", פָּרוּשׁ מֵאַהֲבָה, פָּרוּשׁ מִיִּרְאָה.

§ It states in the mishna: **And those who injure** themselves out of false **abstinence** [*perushin*] are people who erode the world. **The Sages taught: There are seven** pseudo-**righteous** people[N] who erode the world: The **righteous of Shechem,** the self-**flagellating righteous,** the **bloodletting righteous,** the **pestle**-like **righteous,** the **righteous** who say: Tell me **what my obligation** is **and I will perform it,** those who are **righteous due to love,** and those who are **righteous due to fear.**

פָּרוּשׁ שִׁיכְמִי – זֶה הָעוֹשֶׂה מַעֲשֵׂה שְׁכֶם. פָּרוּשׁ נִקְפִּי – זֶה הַמְנַקֵּיף אֶת רַגְלָיו. פָּרוּשׁ קִיזָאִי – אָמַר רַב נַחְמָן בַּר יִצְחָק: זֶה הַמַּקִּיז דָּם לַכְּתָלִים. פָּרוּשׁ מְדוּכְיָא – אָמַר רַבָּה בַּר שֵׁילָא: דִּמְשַׁפַּע כִּי מְדוּכְיָא.

The Gemara explains: The **righteous of Shechem** [*shikhmi*];[N] **this is** one **who performs** actions comparable to the **action** of the people of **Shechem,** who agreed to circumcise themselves for personal gain (see Genesis, chapter 34); so too, he behaves righteously only in order to be honored. The self-**flagellating righteous;**[N] **this is** one **who injures his feet,** as he walks slowly, dragging his feet on the ground in an attempt to appear humble, and injures his feet in the process. The **bloodletting righteous;**[N] **Rav Naḥman bar Yitzḥak says** that **this is** one **who lets blood** by banging his head **against the walls** because he walks with his eyes shut, ostensibly out of modesty. The **pestle**-like **righteous; Rabba bar Sheila says** that this is one **who** walks **bent over like** the **pestle** of a mortar.[N]

PERSONALITIES

Rabba – רַבָּה: Rav Abba bar Naḥmani, commonly referred to as Rabba throughout the Babylonian Talmud, was a third-generation Babylonian *amora*. He was a disciple of Rav Huna, who was a disciple of Rav, and his approach to *halakha* was consistent with Rav's teachings. Rabba was considered the sharpest among his peers; he was described as one who uproots mountains, in contrast to his colleague, Rav Yosef, whose was referred to as Sinai, due to his broad knowledge (*Berakhot* 64a). In virtually every dispute between them, the *halakha* is ruled in accordance with the opinion of Rabba. Rabba had many disciples, and virtually all of the Sages of the following generation studied with him. His personal life was tragic; his children apparently died during his lifetime. He was poverty stricken throughout his life, barely subsisting on agricultural work. When his nephew Abaye was orphaned at a young age, Rabba took him into his home and raised him.

NOTES

Until forty years – עַד אַרְבְּעִין שְׁנִין: *Tosafot* explain that this means forty years from the time one commenced learning, whereas the Maharsha writes that this means until one reaches the age of forty, as the mishna states: One must reach the age of forty in order to attain understanding (*Avot* 4:21). The *Kesef Mishne* suggests a different interpretation: The Gemara's question refers to a scholar who has already attained the ability to issue rulings, and discusses the question of how long he may refrain from issuing rulings without incurring the aforementioned criticism.

There are seven pseudo-righteous people – שִׁבְעָה פְּרוּשִׁין הֵן: According to some versions of the text, the *baraita* explicitly states that all those listed here are insincere individuals who erode the world. However, in the Jerusalem Talmud (*Berakhot* 9:5) it is explained that the last two are sincerely righteous, citing Abraham as an example of the righteous due to love, and Job as an example of the righteous due to fear.

The righteous of Shechem [*shikhmi*] – פָּרוּשׁ שִׁיכְמִי: Most commentaries explain that this refers to one who acts in the manner of the people of Shechem, who circumcised themselves not for the sake of Heaven but rather for their own benefit (see Meiri). The commentaries ask how this individual differs from an individual who performs the mitzvot not for their own sake, who is referred to below in a positive context. The Maharsha, apparently understanding that the Gemara is referring to Shechem, the son of the leader of the city of that name, answers that since Shechem had already transgressed, he evidently circumcised himself only in order to appear repentant, and therefore his actions were disgraceful. Alternatively, *Ben Yehoyada* explains that performing one's obligations is worthy behavior, even if one does not do so for the sake of Heaven. However, it is disgraceful to adopt pious behavior beyond one's obligations only in order to appear righteous, in the manner of Shechem, who was not obligated to circumcise himself. In the Jerusalem Talmud this phrase is interpreted differently, and it is explained that the term *shikhmi* is derived from the word *shekhem*, which means shoulder. This refers to one who overtly carries on his shoulders items required to perform a mitzva, intending to advertise the fact that he is on his way to perform a mitzva.

The self-flagellating [*nikfi*] righteous – פָּרוּשׁ נִקְפִּי: Some explain that this refers to one who claims that his feet are bruised because he walks great distances in order to perform mitzvot (Rabbeinu Nissim Gaon). Others explain that this is one who walks slowly, his eyes upturned to heaven, attempting to appear God-fearing (Meiri). In the Jerusalem Talmud this phrase is interpreted differently, and it is explained that the term *nikfi* is derived from the term *hakafa*, which means payment on credit. This refers to one who demands to receive credit, claiming that he requires the money in order to perform mitzvot.

The bloodletting [*kiza'i*] righteous – פָּרוּשׁ קִיזָאִי: The Ran explains that this refers to one who walks close to the walls and knocks into them, as he attempts to avoid contact with other people, feeling that everyone is impure in comparison to him. In the Jerusalem Talmud this phrase is interpreted differently, and it is explained that the term *kiza'i* means one who cancels out. This refers to one who performs a mitzva for each sin he performs, believing that he can cancel out his sins in this manner.

Who walks bent over like the pestle of a mortar – דִּמְשַׁפַּע כִּי מְדוּכְיָא: According to one interpretation, this refers to an individual who bends over excessively, seemingly due to his fear of sin (Ran). Others explain that it refers to one who covers himself with clothes in order to avoid becoming impure through contact with others. Alternatively, this refers to one who cloaks himself with a large garment that covers him like an upturned mortar, in a demonstration of arrogance (*Arukh*).

פְּרוּשׁ "מָה חוֹבָתִי וְאֶעֱשֶׂנָּה" – הָא מַעֲלְיוּתָא הִיא! אֶלָּא דְּאָמַר: "מָה חוֹבָתִי תּוּ וְאֶעֱשֶׂנָּה".

With regard to the **righteous** one who says: Tell me **what my obligation is**[N] **and I will perform it,** the Gemara asks: **Isn't this virtuous** behavior, as he desires to be aware of his obligations? **Rather,** this is referring to one **who says:** Tell me **what further obligations** are incumbent **upon me and I will perform them,** indicating that he fulfills all of his mitzvot perfectly and therefore seeks additional obligations.

פְּרוּשׁ מֵאַהֲבָה, פָּרוּשׁ מִיִּרְאָה – אָמְרוּ לֵיהּ אַבָּיֵי וְרָבָא לְתַנָּא: לָא תִּיתְנֵי פָּרוּשׁ מֵאַהֲבָה פָּרוּשׁ מִיִּרְאָה, דְּאָמַר רַב יְהוּדָה אָמַר רַב: לְעוֹלָם יַעֲסוֹק אָדָם בַּתּוֹרָה וּבַמִּצְוֹת אֲפִילּוּ שֶׁלֹּא לִשְׁמָהּ, שֶׁמִּתּוֹךְ שֶׁלֹּא לִשְׁמָהּ בָּא לִשְׁמָהּ.

The *baraita* also includes in the list of pseudo-righteous people those who are **righteous due to love**[N] and those who are **righteous due to fear,** i.e., one who performs mitzvot due to love of their reward or due to fear of punishment. **Abaye and Rava said to the** ***tanna*** who transmitted this *baraita*: **Do not teach** in the *baraita*: Those who are **righteous due to love** and those who are **righteous due to fear, as Rav Yehuda says** that **Rav says: A person should always engage**[H] **in** Torah study **and in** performance of **the mitzvot even if** he does **not** do so **for their own sake,**[N] **as through** performing them **not for their own sake,** one **comes** to perform them **for their own sake.**

אָמַר רַב נַחְמָן בַּר יִצְחָק: דְּמִטַּמְּרָא מִטַּמְּרָא, וּדְמִגַּלְיָא מִגַּלְיָא, בֵּי דִינָא רַבָּה לִיתְפָּרַע מֵהָנֵי דְּחָפוּ גּוּנְדֵי. אָמַר לָהּ יַנַּאי מַלְכָּא לִדְבֵיתְהּ: אַל תִּתְיָרְאִי מִן הַפְּרוּשִׁין וְלֹא מִמִּי שֶׁאֵינָן פְּרוּשִׁין, אֶלָּא מִן הַצְּבוּעִין שֶׁדּוֹמִין לִפְרוּשִׁין, שֶׁמַּעֲשֵׂיהֶן כְּמַעֲשֵׂה זִמְרִי וּמְבַקְשִׁין שָׂכָר כְּפִנְחָס.

Rav Naḥman bar Yitzḥak said: That **which is hidden is hidden, and** that **which is revealed is revealed,** but in Heaven everything is known, and **the great court** in Heaven **will exact payment from those who wear the cloak** of the righteous[N] but are in fact unworthy. The Gemara relates: **King Yannai said to his wife**[B] before he died: **Do not be afraid of the Pharisees** [*perushin*],[B] **and neither** should you fear **from those who are not Pharisees,** i.e., the Sadducees; **rather,** beware **of the hypocrites who appear like Pharisees, as their actions are like the act of** the wicked **Zimri**[N] **and they request** a **reward like** that of the righteous **Pinehas** (see Numbers, chapter 25).

HALAKHA

A person should always engage, etc. – לְעוֹלָם יַעֲסוֹק אָדָם וכו׳: Ideally, one should engage in Torah study and in performance of the mitzvot out of love for and fear of God. Nevertheless, one should always engage in Torah study and in the performance of mitzvot, even if one does not do so for their own sake, as through performing them not for their own sake one comes to perform them for their own sake (Rambam *Sefer HaMadda, Hilkhot Talmud Torah* 3:5 and *Hilkhot Teshuva* 10:5; *Shulḥan Arukh, Yoreh De'a* 246:20).

BACKGROUND

King Yannai said to his wife – אָמַר לָהּ יַנַּאי מַלְכָּא לִדְבֵיתְהּ: Josephus (*Antiquities of the Jews* XIII) gives an account of the final will of King Yannai to his wife, which primarily involved his counsel to her to accept the authority of the Pharisees in every matter, as she did in fact do during the remaining years of her rule. According to the Gemara here, he apparently also advised her that she need not fear the Pharisees, even though they were his bitter enemies during most of his reign. Rather, she should fear the hypocrites who use the crown of Torah to further their personal objectives.

The Pharisees [*perushin*] – הַפְּרוּשִׁין: The name Pharisees is usually understood as referring to the rabbinic Sages, particularly during the late Second Temple period. Nevertheless, the Sages rarely referred to themselves by this term, and it was used more often by their opponents. Although some suggest that the term means: Those who interpret or expound, i.e., those who expound the Written Torah, many explain that the term means separatists. The reference to the Sages as separatists who reject community norms could be either a positive or a negative appellation, depending on one's perspective on general society at the time. The term *perushin* is also used by the mishna and Gemara earlier in reference to those who injure themselves as a sign of false abstinence and the pseudo-righteous. The choice of this term may be an example of self-criticism on the part of the Sages with regard to the activities of some members of their community.

NOTES

Tell me what my obligation is, etc. – מָה חוֹבָתִי וכו׳: In the Jerusalem Talmud this phrase is rendered as: Tell me what my transgression is, and I will perform a mitzva in order to cancel it out.

Those who are righteous due to love – פָּרוּשׁ מֵאַהֲבָה וכו׳: The Ran explains that this refers to one who acts righteously out of love for or fear of another person.

Engage in Torah study…even if he does not do so for their own sake – יַעֲסוֹק...בַּתּוֹרָה...אֲפִילּוּ שֶׁלֹּא לִשְׁמָהּ: *Tosafot* cite a number of sources which maintain that if one studies Torah not for its own sake, it would have been preferable for him had he not been created. This apparently contradicts Rav's statement. *Tosafot* resolve this difficulty by distinguishing between different types of impure intentions: If one studies Torah with the intention of ridiculing the Torah or Torah scholars, it would be better for him not to study at all. If, however, one studies Torah out of external motives, e.g., in order to attain honor, this is acceptable, if not ideal, behavior, as it will lead one to engage in Torah study and mitzvot for the sake of Heaven. The Rambam explains that performing mitzvot due to external motivation is a necessary educational method; children are taught to behave correctly by receiving small rewards, and as they grow older their interest shifts to more substantial rewards, until ultimately they attain the understanding that one should perform the mitzvot for no reason other than the sake of Heaven.

Who wear the cloak [*gundei*] of the righteous, etc. – דְּחָפוּ גּוּנְדֵי וכו׳: Some of the early commentaries explain that the term *gundei* refers to black garments (*Arukh*). The Maharsha explains that this might refer to individuals who wore black clothes in order to appear in mourning for the destruction of the Temple.

Their actions are like the act of the wicked Zimri, etc. – שֶׁמַּעֲשֵׂיהֶן כְּמַעֲשֵׂה זִמְרִי וכו׳: The Maharsha notes that the comparison of the pseudo-righteous to Zimri is difficult, as Zimri transgressed publicly and did not hide his actions. He explains that Pinehas received a reward because of his zeal in stopping the behavior of Zimri. The essence of this aphorism is that the pseudo-righteous behave sinfully and yet present themselves as deserving of reward for those very matters in which they secretly transgress. Others explain that Zimri claimed that his behavior was permitted, and so too, the hypocrites find justification for their actions (*Ben Yehoyada*).

Alternatively, some explain that the main emphasis of this aphorism is in the concluding statement that they request a reward like that of Pinehas. This refers to those who intend to appear zealous for the sake of Heaven like Pinehas, while their intent is not in the least for the sake of Heaven but only to attain a reward for their demonstration of zealotry. King Yannai advised his wife not to fear the actions of the Pharisees, which stemmed from true fear of God, but rather to fear the zealots whose zealotry stemmed from false motives (*Iyyun Ya'akov*; *Ben Yehoyada*).

מתני׳ רבי שמעון אומר: אין זכות תולה במים המרים. ואם אתה אומר הזכות תולה במים המאררין – מדהה אתה את המים בפני כל הנשים השותות, ומוציא אתה שם רע על הטהורות ששתו, שאומרים: טמאות הן, אלא שתלתה להן זכות. רבי אומר: הזכות תולה במים המאררים, ואינה יולדת ואינה משבחת, אלא מתנוונה והולכת, לסוף היא מתה באותה מיתה.

MISHNA **Rabbi Shimon says: Merit does not delay** the punishment **of the bitter water** of a *sota*, **and if you say** that **merit does delay** the punishment **of the water that causes the curse,** as stated earlier by the Rabbis (20a), **you weaken** [*madhe*][L] the power of **the** bitter **water before all the women who drink** the water, who will no longer be afraid of it, as they will rely on their merit to save them. **And you defame the untainted women who drank** the water and survived, **as** people **say: They are defiled but** it is their **merit that delayed** the punishment **for them. Rabbi** Yehuda HaNasi **says: Merit delays**[H] the punishment **of the water that causes the curse, but** a woman whose punishment is delayed **does not give birth and does not flourish; rather, she progressively deteriorates. Ultimately she dies by the same death** as a *sota* who dies immediately.

נטמאת מנחתה עד שלא קדשה בכלי – הרי היא ככל המנחות ותפדה. ואם משקדשה בכלי – הרי היא ככל המנחות ותשרף. ואלו שמנחותיהן נשרפות:

§ **If the meal-offering** of the *sota* **is rendered impure**[H] **before it has been sanctified in the** service **vessel, its** status **is like** that of **all the** other **meal-offerings** that are rendered impure before being sanctified in a service vessel, **and it is redeemed. But if** it is rendered impure **after it has been sanctified in the** service **vessel, its** status **is like** that of **all the** other **meal-offerings** that are rendered impure after being sanctified in a service vessel, **and it is burned. And these are** the *sota* women **whose meal-offerings are burned** if they have already been sanctified in a service vessel:

LANGUAGE

Weaken [*madhe*] – מדהה: The term *madhe* literally means to cause a color to become dull and weak. Here it is used in the borrowed sense of causing power to weaken. The root of the word is *dalet, heh, heh*, which is similar in meaning to the root *dalet, ḥet, heh*, which denotes removing an item from its place or from its previous status.

HALAKHA

Merit delays, etc. – הזכות תולה וכו׳: If a woman has the merit of Torah study, it delays the punishment of the bitter water, and she does not die immediately. Rather, she becomes sick and continually deteriorates until she finally dies the death described for a *sota* (Rambam *Sefer Nashim, Hilkhot Sota* 3:20).

If the meal-offering of the *sota* is rendered impure – נטמאת מנחתה: If the meal-offering of a *sota* is rendered impure before it has been sanctified in a service vessel, it is redeemed and another meal-offering is brought in its place. If it is rendered impure after it has been sanctified in a service vessel, it is burned (Rambam *Sefer Nashim, Hilkhot Sota* 4:14).

Perek **III**
Daf **23** Amud **a**

האומרת "טמאה אני לך"; ושבאו לה עדים שהיא טמאה; והאומרת "איני שותה"; ושבעלה אינו רוצה להשקותה, ושבעלה בא עליה בדרך.

A woman **who** confesses and **says: I am defiled,** and therefore prohibited **to you;**[H] **and** a woman **with regard to whom witnesses came** and testified **that she is defiled; and** a woman **who says: I will not drink** the bitter water of a *sota*, even if she does not confess her guilt; **and** a woman **whose husband** changed his mind and **does not want to force her to drink; and** a woman **whose husband engaged in sexual intercourse with her on the way** to the Temple.

וכל הנשואות לכהנים – מנחותיהן נשרפות. בת ישראל שנשאת לכהן – מנחתה נשרפת, וכהנת שנשאת לישראל – מנחתה נאכלת.

And all the women **who are married to priests,**[N] **their meal-offerings are** always **burned,** as the verse states: "And every meal-offering of a priest shall be completely burned; it shall not be eaten" (Leviticus 6:16). **An Israelite woman who is married to a priest, her meal-offering is burned;** and **the daughter of a priest who is married to an Israelite, her meal-offering is eaten.**

מה בין כהן לכהנת? מנחת כהנת נאכלת ומנחת כהן אינה נאכלת, כהנת מתחללת וכהן אין מתחלל,

The mishna asks a general question: **What** are the differences **between a priest and the daughter of a priest? The meal-offering of the daughter of a priest is eaten** by the priests, **but the meal-offering of a priest is not eaten.**[H] The **daughter of a priest can become disqualified**[HN] from marrying a priest and from partaking of *teruma* by engaging in sexual intercourse with someone forbidden to her, **but a priest does not become desacralized**[N] by engaging in sexual intercourse with a woman forbidden to him.

HALAKHA

A woman who confesses and says, I am defiled to you, etc. – האומרת טמאה אני לך וכו׳: If, before the handful is removed from the meal-offering, the woman confesses that she is defiled; or if she says: I will not drink; or if her husband does not want to force her to drink; or if witnesses come and say that she is defiled; or if either the man or the woman dies; then the entire meal-offering is burned. If any of these events occur after the handful is removed, then the remainder of the meal-offering is eaten (Rambam *Sefer Nashim, Hilkhot Sota* 4:14).

The meal-offering of a priest is not eaten – מנחת כהן אינה נאכלת: The handful is not removed from any of the meal-offerings brought by priests, neither from voluntary meal-offerings or from obligatory meal-offerings. Their meal-offerings are burned on the altar in their entirety (Rambam *Sefer Avoda, Hilkhot Ma'aseh HaKorbanot* 2:9).

The daughter of a priest can become disqualified, etc. – כהנת מתחללת וכו׳: If the daughter of a priest engaged in sexual intercourse with someone forbidden to her, she is disqualified from marrying a priest and from partaking of *teruma*. If a priest engaged in sexual intercourse with a woman forbidden to him, he does not become desacralized (Rambam *Sefer Zera'im, Hilkhot Terumot* 6:7 and *Sefer Kedusha, Hilkhot Issurei Bia* 19:1; *Shulḥan Arukh, Even HaEzer* 7:13).

NOTES

And all the women who are married to priests, etc. – וכל הנשואות לכהנים וכו׳: According to Rashi this principle applies to any meal-offering, both obligatory and voluntary, brought by the wife of a priest. The commentaries find this explanation difficult; if she brings a meal-offering from her own money, why should it be considered the meal-offering of a priest? Although generally anything acquired by a woman belongs to her husband, there are instances where a woman might own possessions to which her husband has no rights. Some suggest that in a case where the meal-offering belongs entirely to the woman, Rashi would agree that it is not burned (*Devar Shaul*). However, in the Jerusalem Talmud it is explained that this principle applies only to the meal-offering of a *sota*, in which the husband certainly has a share (see *Keren Ora*).

The daughter of a priest can become disqualified – כהנת מתחללת: This *halakha* applies to any woman who engages in forbidden sexual intercourse, not only to the daughter of a priest. Nevertheless, since a priest does not become desacralized in this manner, this *halakha* is listed among the differences between a priest and the daughter of a priest (*Tosefot HaRosh*).

A priest does not become desacralized – כהן אין מתחלל: Although a priest does not become desacralized by engaging in forbidden sexual intercourse, as long as he remains married to a woman forbidden to him he is unfit to serve in the Temple (Rambam's Commentary on the Mishna).

כֹּהֶנֶת מִטַּמְּאָה לַמֵּתִים וְאֵין כֹּהֵן מִטַּמֵּא לַמֵּתִים, כֹּהֵן אוֹכֵל בְּקָדְשֵׁי קָדָשִׁים וְאֵין כֹּהֶנֶת אוֹכֶלֶת בְּקָדְשֵׁי קָדָשִׁים.

The **daughter of a priest may become impure**[H] with impurity imparted **by a corpse, but a priest may not become impure** with impurity imparted **by a corpse** except for the burial of his seven closest relatives. **A priest may eat from offerings of the most sacred order,**[H] **but** the **daughter of a priest may not eat from offerings of the most sacred order.**

מַה בֵּין אִישׁ לְאִשָּׁה? הָאִישׁ פּוֹרֵעַ וּפוֹרֵם וְאֵין הָאִשָּׁה פּוֹרַעַת וּפוֹרֶמֶת, הָאִישׁ מַדִּיר אֶת בְּנוֹ בְּנָזִיר וְאֵין הָאִשָּׁה מַדֶּרֶת בְּנָהּ בְּנָזִיר, הָאִישׁ מְגַלֵּחַ עַל נְזִירוּת אָבִיו וְאֵין הָאִשָּׁה מְגַלַּחַת עַל נְזִירוּת אָבִיהָ,

What are the halakhic differences **between a man and a woman?**[N] **A man lets** his hair **grow and rends** his garments[H] when he is a leper, **but a woman does not let** her hair **grow or rend** her garments when she is a leper. **A man can vow** that **his** minor **son** shall **be a nazirite,**[HN] obligating the son to remain a nazirite even during his adulthood, **but a woman cannot vow**[N] that **her son** shall **be a nazirite. A man can shave**[H] at the culmination of his naziriteship **by** using offerings originally designated for **his father's naziriteship,** i.e., if one's father was also a nazirite and he died having already designated offerings for the culmination of his naziriteship; **but a woman cannot shave** at the culmination of her naziriteship **by** using offerings designated for **her father's naziriteship.**

הָאִישׁ מְקַדֵּשׁ אֶת בִּתּוֹ וְאֵין הָאִשָּׁה מְקַדֶּשֶׁת אֶת בִּתָּהּ, הָאִישׁ מוֹכֵר אֶת בִּתּוֹ וְאֵין הָאִשָּׁה מוֹכֶרֶת אֶת בִּתָּהּ, הָאִישׁ נִסְקָל עָרוֹם וְאֵין הָאִשָּׁה נִסְקֶלֶת עֲרוּמָּה, הָאִישׁ נִתְלֶה וְאֵין הָאִשָּׁה נִתְלֵית, הָאִישׁ נִמְכָּר בִּגְנֵיבָתוֹ וְאֵין הָאִשָּׁה נִמְכֶּרֶת בִּגְנֵיבָתָהּ.

A man can betroth his daughter[H] to another man while she is a minor, **but a woman cannot betroth her daughter** even while she is a minor. **A man can sell his daughter**[H] as a maidservant while she is a minor, **but a woman cannot sell her daughter** as a maidservant even while she is a minor. **A man is stoned naked, but a woman is not stoned naked. A man is hanged** after he is stoned for certain transgressions, **but a woman is not hanged. A man is sold for his** committing an act of **theft** in order to pay his debt, **but a woman is not sold for her** committing an act of **theft.**

גמ׳ תָּנוּ רַבָּנַן: כָּל הַנְּשׂוּאוֹת לִכְהוּנָּה – מִנְחוֹתֵיהֶן נִשְׂרָפוֹת. כֵּיצַד? כֹּהֶנֶת, לְוִיָּה וְיִשְׂרְאֵלִית שֶׁנִּשֵּׂאת לְכֹהֵן – אֵין מִנְחָתָהּ נֶאֱכֶלֶת מִפְּנֵי שֶׁיֵּשׁ לוֹ חֵלֶק בָּהּ; וְאֵינָהּ עוֹלָה כָּלִיל מִפְּנֵי שֶׁיֵּשׁ לָהּ חֵלֶק בָּהּ. אֶלָּא הַקּוֹמֶץ קָרֵב בְּעַצְמוֹ וְהַשִּׁירַיִם קְרֵיבִין בְּעַצְמָן.

GEMARA The Sages taught (*Tosefta* 2:6): **All** the **women who are married into the priesthood, their meal-offerings are burned. How so?** With regard to **the daughter of a priest,** or **the daughter of a Levite or an Israelite woman who is married to a priest, her meal-offering is not eaten due to** the fact **that** her father or husband, respectively, **has a share in** the meal-offering, and it is therefore treated as the meal-offering of a priest, which is not eaten. **But it is not completely burned** without removing a handful from it, as the Torah states with regard to the meal-offering of a priest, **due to** the fact **that she** also **has a share in it. Rather, the handful is sacrificed by itself,** and **the remainder** of the meal-offering **is sacrificed by itself.**

NOTES

What are the halakhic differences between a man and a woman – מַה בֵּין אִישׁ לְאִשָּׁה: *Tosafot* note that this list is not comprehensive, and many additional differences are listed in the *Tosefta*.

A man can vow that his minor son shall be a nazirite – הָאִישׁ מַדִּיר אֶת בְּנוֹ בְּנָזִיר: According to Rashi, the father's vow continues to obligate the son even after the son reaches the age of majority. Conversely, *Tosafot* (*Nazir* 30a) and the Rambam hold that once the son reaches the age of majority, his father ceases to have authority over him, and therefore the father's vow cannot obligate him against his will.

But a woman cannot vow, etc. – וְאֵין הָאִשָּׁה מַדֶּרֶת וכו׳: The Radak asks how Hannah could vow that if she gave birth to a son, he would be a nazirite all his life (see I Samuel, chapter 1), as a woman cannot vow that her son shall be a nazirite. Some commentaries answer that her declaration did not effect the vow; her intention was that she would entreat her husband until he imposed the vow on their son (*Tiferet Yisrael*). In any event, Hannah's vow certainly falls outside the general *halakhot* of naziriteship, as she took the vow before her son was even conceived, and a vow taken with regard to an entity that is not yet in the world does not take effect.

HALAKHA

The daughter of a priest may become impure, etc. – כֹּהֶנֶת מִטַּמְּאָה וכו׳: A priest is prohibited from becoming impure with impurity imparted by a corpse, except in the case of the burial of his seven closest relatives or of a corpse with no one to bury it. This prohibition does not apply to the daughter of a priest (Rambam *Sefer Shofetim, Hilkhot Evel* 3:1, 11; *Shulḥan Arukh, Even HaEzer* 369:1).

A priest may eat from offerings of the most sacred order, etc. – כֹּהֵן אוֹכֵל בְּקָדְשֵׁי קָדָשִׁים וכו׳: The sin-offering, the guilt-offering, and the remainder of the meal-offering are offerings of the most sacred order. They are eaten only by the males of the priesthood (Rambam *Sefer Avoda, Hilkhot Ma'aseh HaKorbanot* 10:3).

A man lets his hair grow and rends his garments, etc. – הָאִישׁ פּוֹרֵעַ וּפוֹרֵם וכו׳: It is a positive mitzva for the leper to cover his head and upper lip in the manner of a mourner throughout the period of his confirmed leprosy. He must also rend his garments. A female leper does not let her hair grow or rend her garments, and she does not cover her upper lip (Rambam *Sefer Tahara, Hilkhot Tumat Tzara'at* 10:6, 8).

A man can vow that his minor son shall be a nazirite – הָאִישׁ מַדִּיר אֶת בְּנוֹ בְּנָזִיר: A man can vow that his minor son shall be a nazirite, even before the son reaches the age at which his own vows are valid. A woman cannot vow that her son shall be a nazirite (Rambam *Sefer Hafla'a, Hilkhot Nezirut* 2:13).

A man can shave, etc. – הָאִישׁ מְגַלֵּחַ וכו׳: If a man vowed to be a nazirite, and his father was also a nazirite but died before he finished his naziriteship, then at the culmination of the son's naziriteship he can sacrifice the offerings that his father designated for his own naziriteship, and he can shave on account of them. However, a woman cannot shave at the culmination of her naziriteship by using offerings designated for her father's naziriteship (Rambam *Sefer Hafla'a, Hilkhot Nezirut* 8:15).

A man can betroth his daughter, etc. – הָאִישׁ מְקַדֵּשׁ אֶת בִּתּוֹ וכו׳: A father can betroth his daughter to another man even without her knowledge, as long as she is a minor or a young woman. However, a mother does not have the authority to betroth her daughter even while she is a minor. In the case of a minor girl who has no father, if her mother or her brothers marry her off with her consent, the marriage is valid by rabbinic ordinance. In that case, if upon reaching majority she does not wish to remain with her husband she does not require a bill of divorce, and her refusal to remain married to him is sufficient in order to annul the marriage (Rambam *Sefer Nashim, Hilkhot Ishut* 3:11 and *Hilkhot Geirushin* 11:1; *Shulḥan Arukh, Even HaEzer* 37:1, 155:1).

A man can sell his daughter – הָאִישׁ מוֹכֵר אֶת בִּתּוֹ: A minor girl who was sold by her father is considered a Hebrew maidservant (Rambam *Sefer Kinyan, Hilkhot Avadim* 4:1).

אִיקְרֵי כָּאן: כׇּל שֶׁהוּא מִמֶּנּוּ לָאִשִּׁים – הֲרֵי הוּא בְּבַל תַּקְטִירוּ! אָמַר יְהוּדָה בְּרֵיהּ דְּרַבִּי שִׁמְעוֹן בֶּן פָּזִי: דְּמַסִּיק לְהוּ לְשׁוּם עֵצִים, כְּרַבִּי אֱלִיעֶזֶר. דְּתַנְיָא, רַבִּי אֱלִיעֶזֶר אוֹמֵר: לְרֵיחַ נִיחוֹחַ אִי אַתָּה מַעֲלֶה, אֲבָל אַתָּה מַעֲלֵיהוּ לְשׁוּם עֵצִים.

The Gemara asks: One should **apply here** the principle that in the case of **any** offering **that is** meant to be **partly** burned **on the flames** of the altar,[H] one who burns the remainder of the offering **is** subject **to** the prohibition: **Do not burn.** This prohibition is derived from the verse: "You shall not burn of it as an offering made by fire unto the Lord" (Leviticus 2:11). **Yehuda, son of Rabbi Shimon ben Pazi, said that** the priest **burns** the remainder not as an offering but **for the purpose of firewood.** This is permitted, **in accordance with** the opinion of **Rabbi Eliezer, as it is taught** in a *baraita* that **Rabbi Eliezer says:** With regard to those parts of an offering which may not be burned, **for a pleasing aroma you may not burn** them; **however, you may burn them** on the altar **for the purpose of firewood.**[H]

הָנִיחָא לְרַבִּי אֱלִיעֶזֶר, דְּאִית לֵיהּ הַאי סְבָרָא, אֶלָּא לְרַבָּנַן דְּלֵית לְהוּ הַאי סְבָרָא, מַאי אִיכָּא לְמֵימַר? דְּעָבְדִי לְהוּ כְּרַבִּי אֶלְעָזָר בְּרַבִּי שִׁמְעוֹן. דְּתַנְיָא, רַבִּי אֶלְעָזָר בְּרַבִּי שִׁמְעוֹן אוֹמֵר: הַקּוֹמֶץ קָרֵב בְּעַצְמוֹ, וְהַשִּׁירַיִם מִתְפַּזְּרִים עַל בֵּית הַדֶּשֶׁן.

The Gemara continues: **This works out well according to** the opinion of **Rabbi Eliezer, who holds** in accordance with **this reasoning** and permits burning the remainder of an offering as firewood; **however,** according **to the Rabbis, who do not hold** in accordance with **this reasoning, what can be said?** How is the remainder burned on the altar? The Gemara answers: **With regard to** the remainder, **they act in accordance with** the opinion of **Rabbi Elazar, son of Rabbi Shimon, as it is taught** in a *baraita*: **Rabbi Elazar, son of Rabbi Shimon, says** with regard to the meal-offering of a sinner who is a priest: **The handful is** removed from the meal-offering and **sacrificed by itself, and the remainder** is neither eaten nor burned on the altar; rather, it **is scattered on the place of the ashes.**

HALAKHA

Any offering which is meant to be partly burned on the flames of the altar – כׇּל שֶׁהוּא מִמֶּנּוּ לָאִשִּׁים: It is prohibited to burn on the altar anything that is not fit for burning on the altar, e.g., the flesh of sin-offerings and guilt-offerings or the remainder of meal-offerings, as there is a *halakha* transmitted by tradition that prohibits burning the remainder of any offering that is meant to be partly burned on the altar (Rambam *Sefer Avoda, Hilkhot Issurei Mizbe'aḥ* 5:5).

You may burn them for the purpose of firewood – אַתָּה מַעֲלֵיהוּ לְשׁוּם עֵצִים: In a case where one burned leaven or honey by itself on the altar, if one burned it only as firewood, he is exempt from punishment, as although it is prohibited to burn these as an offering to God, it is permitted to burn them as firewood (Rambam *Sefer Avoda, Hilkhot Issurei Mizbe'aḥ* 5:3).

Perek **III**
Daf **23** Amud **b**

וַאֲפִילּוּ רַבָּנַן לָא פְּלִיגִי עֲלֵיהּ דְּרַבִּי אֶלְעָזָר בְּרַבִּי שִׁמְעוֹן אֶלָּא בְּמִנְחַת חוֹטֵא שֶׁל כֹּהֲנִים דְּבַת הַקְרָבָה הִיא, אֲבָל בְּהָא – אֲפִילּוּ רַבָּנַן מוֹדוּ.

And even the Rabbis do not disagree with Rabbi Elazar, son of Rabbi Shimon, except with regard to the meal-offering of a sinner who is **a priest, as** they hold that **it is fit to be sacrificed** in its entirety without removing a handful. **However, in this** case, i.e., in the case of the meal-offering of a *sota* who is married to a priest, **even the Rabbis agree**[H] that its remainder is scattered on the place of the ashes, since the handful is removed from the offering.

״בַּת יִשְׂרָאֵל הַנְּשׂוּאָה״ וכו׳. מַאי טַעְמָא? דְּאָמַר קְרָא: ״וְכׇל מִנְחַת כֹּהֵן כָּלִיל תִּהְיֶה, לֹא תֵאָכֵל״ – כֹּהֵן וְלֹא כֹּהֶנֶת.

§ The mishna states: In the case of **an Israelite woman who is married** to a priest, her meal-offering is burned; and in the case of the daughter of a priest who is married to an Israelite, her meal-offering is eaten. The Gemara asks: **What is the reason** for this? This is **as the verse states: "And every meal-offering of a priest shall be completely burned; it shall not be eaten"** (Leviticus 6:16). One can infer that this applies to **a priest, but not** to **the daughter of a priest.**[H]

״כֹּהֶנֶת מִתְחַלֶּלֶת, כֹּהֵן אֵין מִתְחַלֵּל״. מְנָלַן? דְּאָמַר קְרָא: ״וְלֹא יְחַלֵּל זַרְעוֹ בְּעַמָּיו״ – זַרְעוֹ מִתְחַלֵּל וְהוּא אֵינוֹ מִתְחַלֵּל.

The mishna states: The **daughter of a priest can become disqualified** from marrying a priest and from partaking of *teruma* by engaging in sexual intercourse with someone forbidden to her, but **a priest does not become desacralized** by engaging in sexual intercourse with a woman forbidden to him. The Gemara asks: **From where do we** derive this? It is **as the verse states** with regard to a priest who marries a woman forbidden to him: **"And he shall not disqualify**[N] **his offspring among his people"** (Leviticus 21:15), indicating that **his offspring** from forbidden intercourse **are desacralized, but he is not** personally **desacralized** through his actions.

״כֹּהֶנֶת מִטַּמְּאָה״ כו׳. מַאי טַעְמָא? אָמַר קְרָא: ״אֱמֹר אֶל הַכֹּהֲנִים בְּנֵי אַהֲרֹן״ – ״בְּנֵי אַהֲרֹן״ וְלֹא בְּנוֹת אַהֲרֹן.

The mishna states: **A daughter of a priest may become impure** with impurity imparted by a corpse, but a priest may not. The Gemara asks: **What is the reason** for this? The Gemara answers: **The verse states: "Speak to the priests, the sons of Aaron,** and say to them: None shall become impure for the dead among his people" (Leviticus 21:1). The verse indicates that this applies to **the sons of Aaron and not to the daughters of Aaron.**

HALAKHA

In this case even the Rabbis agree, etc. – בְּהָא אֲפִילּוּ רַבָּנַן מוֹדוּ: In the case of a woman who is married to a priest, whether she is the daughter of a priest or an Israelite, the remainder of her meal-offering is not eaten on account of the share of her husband, who is a priest; neither is it burned, on account of her share. Rather, the handful is sacrificed by itself, and the remainder is scattered on the place of the ashes, in accordance with the conclusion of the Gemara. This applies both to the meal-offering of a *sota* and to any other meal-offering brought by the wife of a priest (Rambam *Sefer Avoda, Hilkhot Ma'aseh HaKorbanot* 12:12 and *Sefer Nashim, Hilkhot Sota* 4:15).

A priest but not to the daughter of a priest – כֹּהֵן וְלֹא כֹּהֶנֶת: The meal-offering of the daughter of a priest is sacrificed in the manner of all other meal-offerings; the handful is sacrificed on the altar and the remainder is eaten (Rambam *Sefer Avoda, Hilkhot Ma'aseh HaKorbanot* 2:10).

NOTES

And he shall not disqualify etc. – וְלֹא יְחַלֵּל וכו׳: The Gemara here presents the interpretation of these verses in an abbreviated form. Elsewhere (*Kiddushin* 77a) the Gemara explains fully why a priest who engages in sexual intercourse with a woman forbidden to him does not become desacralized, yet the woman with whom he engages in intercourse is disqualified from marrying a priest.

"כֹּהֵן אוֹכֵל בְּקָדְשֵׁי קָדָשִׁים", דִּכְתִיב: "כׇּל זָכָר בִּבְנֵי אַהֲרֹן יֹאכְלֶנָּה".

The mishna states: **A priest may eat from offerings of the most sacred order,** but a daughter of a priest may not eat from offerings of the most sacred order. The Gemara explains: This is derived **as it is written** with regard to the meal-offering, which is an offering of the most sacred order: **"Every male among the children of Aaron may eat of it"** (Leviticus 6:11).

"וּמָה בֵּין אִישׁ" כו'. תָּנוּ רַבָּנַן: "אִישׁ" – אֵין לִי אֶלָּא אִישׁ, אִשָּׁה מִנַּיִן? כְּשֶׁהוּא אוֹמֵר: "וְהַצָּרוּעַ אֲשֶׁר בּוֹ" – הֲרֵי כָּאן שְׁנַיִם.

§ The mishna states: **And what** are the halakhic differences **between a man** and a woman? A man lets his hair grow and rends his garments when he is a leper, but a woman does not. **The Sages taught:** The verse states: "He is a leprous **man,** he is impure" (Leviticus 13:44). **I have** derived **only** that the *halakhot* of a confirmed leper apply to **a man; from where** do I derive that they apply to **a woman? When it says** in the subsequent verse: **"And the leper**[N] **in whom** the plague is, his clothes shall be rent, and the hair of his head shall grow wild and he shall cover his upper lip; and he shall cry: Impure, impure" (Leviticus 13:45), **there are two** individuals indicated **here,**[H] as this verse did not need to restate "and the leper," as the subject of the verse was clear from the previous verse.

אִם כֵּן מַה תַּלְמוּד לוֹמַר "אִישׁ"? לְעִנְיַן שֶׁלְּמַטָּה: "אִישׁ פּוֹרֵעַ" וכו'.

If so, what is the meaning when **the verse states:** A leprous **"man"?** This is referring **to the matter** of rending one's clothes and letting one's hair grow wild, **which** is stated in the verse **below,** and teaches that **a man lets** the hair of his head **grow** and rends his garments, but a woman does not.

"הָאִישׁ מַדִּיר אֶת בְּנוֹ בְּנָזִיר, וְאֵין הָאִשָּׁה מַדֶּרֶת בְּנָהּ בְּנָזִיר". אָמַר רַבִּי יוֹחָנָן: הֲלָכָה הִיא בְּנָזִיר. "הָאִישׁ מְגַלֵּחַ עַל נְזִירוּת אָבִיו, וְאֵין הָאִשָּׁה מְגַלַּחַת עַל נְזִירוּת אָבִיהָ". אָמַר רַבִּי יוֹחָנָן: הֲלָכָה הִיא בְּנָזִיר.

The mishna states: **A man can vow** that **his** minor **son** shall **be a nazirite, but a woman cannot vow** that **her son** shall **be a nazirite. Rabbi Yoḥanan says: This is a *halakha*** transmitted orally to Moses from Sinai **with regard to** the **nazirite,** and it is not derived from the Bible. The mishna states: **A man can shave** at the culmination of his naziriteship **by** using offerings designated for **his father's naziriteship, but a woman cannot shave by** using offerings designated for **her father's naziriteship. Rabbi Yoḥanan says: This is a *halakha*** transmitted orally to Moses from Sinai **with regard to** the **nazirite,** and it is not derived from the Bible.

"הָאִישׁ מְקַדֵּשׁ אֶת בִּתּוֹ, וְאֵין הָאִשָּׁה מְקַדֶּשֶׁת אֶת בִּתָּהּ", דִּכְתִיב: "אֶת בִּתִּי נָתַתִּי לָאִישׁ הַזֶּה". "הָאִישׁ מוֹכֵר אֶת בִּתּוֹ, וְאֵין הָאִשָּׁה מוֹכֶרֶת אֶת בִּתָּהּ", דִּכְתִיב: "וְכִי יִמְכּוֹר אִישׁ אֶת בִּתּוֹ".

The mishna states: **A man can betroth his daughter** to another man while she is a minor, **but a woman cannot betroth her daughter.** The Gemara explains: This is **as it is written:** "And the father of the maiden shall say to the elders: **I gave my daughter to this man** as a wife" (Deuteronomy 22:16), indicating that it is only the father who has the power to betroth his daughter. The mishna states: **A man can sell his daughter** as a maidservant **but a woman cannot sell her daughter.** The Gemara explains: This is derived **as it is written: "And if a man sells his daughter** to be a maidservant" (Exodus 21:7), indicating that only a man can sell his daughter, while a woman cannot.

"הָאִישׁ נִסְקָל עָרוֹם" כו'. מַאי טַעְמָא? "וְרָגְמוּ אוֹתוֹ". מַאי "אוֹתוֹ"? אִילֵימָא "אוֹתוֹ" – וְלֹא אוֹתָהּ, וְהָכְתִיב: "וְהוֹצֵאתָ אֶת הָאִישׁ הַהוּא אוֹ אֶת הָאִשָּׁה הַהִיא"! אֶלָּא אוֹתוֹ בְּלֹא כְּסוּתוֹ, וְלֹא אוֹתָהּ בְּלֹא כְּסוּתָהּ.

§ The mishna states: **A man is stoned naked,** but a woman is not stoned naked. The Gemara asks: **What is the reason** for this? The Gemara answers: The verse states: **"And let the entire congregation stone him"** (Leviticus 24:14). **What** does the term **"him"** come to exclude? **If we say** this means that they stone **him but not her,** i.e., that a woman is not stoned at all, **but isn't it written: "And you shall take out that man or that woman,** who did this evil thing, to your gates, that man or that woman; and you shall stone them with stones, and they shall die" (Deuteronomy 17:5). **Rather,** the term **"him"** excludes his garment, indicating that he is stoned **without his garment.**[H] **And** a woman is excluded from this *halakha*, as one may infer from the term "him" that they do **not** stone **her without her garment.**

"הָאִישׁ נִתְלֶה וְאֵין" כו'. מַאי טַעְמָא? אָמַר קְרָא: "וְתָלִיתָ אוֹתוֹ עַל עֵץ", "אוֹתוֹ" – וְלֹא אוֹתָהּ.

The mishna states: **A man is hanged, but** a woman is **not** hanged. The Gemara asks: **What is the reason** for this? **The verse states:** "And if a man has committed a sin worthy of death, and he is put to death, **and you shall hang him on a tree**" (Deuteronomy 21:22). The verse indicates that one should hang **"him,"** a man, **but not her,**[H] a woman.

NOTES

When it says, and the leper, etc. – כְּשֶׁהוּא אוֹמֵר "וְהַצָּרוּעַ" וכו': The later commentaries write that the *baraita* derives this from the term: And the, which is apparently superfluous and comes to include women in these *halakhot* (see *Minḥa Ḥareva*).

HALAKHA

There are two individuals indicated here – הֲרֵי כָּאן שְׁנַיִם: Even if a woman or a eunuch grows a beard, it can become impure with leprosy of the beard (Rambam *Sefer Tahara, Hilkhot Tumat Tzara'at* 8:1).

The term him, without his garment, etc. – אוֹתוֹ בְּלֹא כְּסוּתוֹ וכו': When one is taken to be stoned, he is first stripped of his clothes, and his nakedness is covered on his front. A woman is not stoned naked; rather, she wears a single robe (Rambam *Sefer Shofetim, Hilkhot Sanhedrin* 15:1).

Hang him…but not her – וְתָלִיתָ אוֹתוֹ...וְלֹא אוֹתָהּ: It is a positive mitzva to hang the body of a blasphemer or an idol worshipper after he is stoned. Only a man is hanged, but a woman is not (Rambam *Sefer Shofetim, Hilkhot Sanhedrin* 15:6).

"הָאִישׁ נִמְכָּר בִּגְנֵיבָתוֹ, וְאֵין הָאִשָּׁה נִמְכֶּרֶת בִּגְנֵיבָתָהּ". מַאי טַעְמָא? אָמַר קְרָא: "וְנִמְכַּר בִּגְנֵבָתוֹ", "בִּגְנֵיבָתוֹ" – וְלֹא בִּגְנֵיבָתָהּ.

הדרן עלך היה נוטל

The mishna states: **A man is sold for his** committing an act of **theft, but a woman is not sold for her** committing an act of **theft.** The Gemara asks: **What is the reason** for this? **The verse states:** "If the sun rose upon him, there is blood-guilt for him; he shall make restitution; if he has nothing, **then he shall be sold for his theft**" (Exodus 22:2). The verse indicates that he is sold **for his theft,**[H] **but** she is **not** sold **for her theft.**

HALAKHA

He is sold for his theft, etc. – **בִּגְנֵיבָתוֹ וכו׳**: A man is sold for committing an act of theft, but a woman is not sold for committing an act of theft (Rambam *Sefer Nezikim*, *Hilkhot Geneiva* 3:12).

Summary of **Perek III**

The chapter commenced with a discussion concerning the correct order of the Temple ritual for a *sota*. The Gemara concluded that first the woman drinks the bitter water of a *sota,* and afterward her meal-offering is sacrificed.

The chapter then proceeded to discuss the *halakha* in the case of a woman who refuses to drink the water or admits that she is defiled. If she recants before the scroll is erased she is not forced to drink the bitter water, but if she recants once the scroll is erased she is forced to drink unless she admits that she is defiled. With regard to the meal-offering of the *sota,* if the woman refuses to drink the water or admits to being defiled, her offering is scattered and burnt in the place of the ashes. The same *halakha* applies to a meal-offering that was rendered impure, and to a meal-offering that was invalidated because witnesses came and testified that the woman was unfaithful.

The Torah describes the death of a *sota* who is found to be unfaithful: Her belly swells, and her thigh falls away. The Talmud teaches that sometimes her death is delayed due to her merits, and she suffers while she slowly deteriorates until her death.

Also discussed in this chapter was whether it is proper to teach women Torah. Although the Talmud cites different opinions on this matter, the Gemara's conclusion is that women should not be taught those parts of the Torah that they are not required to learn, even though a woman who studies Torah attains reward.

This chapter also listed and discussed a number of halakhic distinctions between men and women.

Introduction to **Perek IV**

Speak to the children of Israel, and say unto them: If the wife of any man goes astray, and acts unfaithfully against him.

(Numbers 5:12)

But if you have gone astray while under your husband, and if you are defiled, and some man has lain with you besides your husband.

(Numbers 5:20)

And the man shall be clear from iniquity, and that woman shall bear her iniquity.

(Numbers 5:31)

The previous chapters detailed the manner in which a husband issues a warning to his wife not to seclude herself with another man, and explained under what circumstances the woman becomes a *sota* if she disregards the warning. The particulars of the ritual in which the *sota* drinks the bitter water were also discussed.

This chapter discusses situations in which certain aspects of the *sota* ritual do not apply. The cases discussed here fall primarily into two categories. The first consists of cases where the marriage has not yet been completed, such as the case of a betrothed woman or a *yevama*, a widow waiting for her brother-in-law to perform levirate marriage. The second concerns cases where the marriage was prohibited in the first place. The chapter also explores whether the woman collects payment of her marriage contract in cases where the *sota* ritual cannot be performed.

Additionally, the limits of the husband's ability to issue a warning to his wife are discussed. For example, can a husband warn his wife against secluding herself with another man, even if he does not suspect that she will engage in sexual intercourse with that man?

The chapter also deals with whether issuing a warning is exclusively the husband's prerogative or whether the court can issue a warning if a woman acts promiscuously during her husband's absence. In situations where the court is entitled to issue a warning, the parameters of that warning are enumerated.

מתני׳ אֲרוּסָה וְשׁוֹמֶרֶת יָבָם לֹא שׁוֹתוֹת וְלֹא נוֹטְלוֹת כְּתוּבָּה, שֶׁנֶּאֱמַר: ״אֲשֶׁר תִּשְׂטֶה אִשָּׁה תַּחַת אִישָׁהּ״, פְּרָט לַאֲרוּסָה וְשׁוֹמֶרֶת יָבָם.

MISHNA With regard to **a betrothed woman**[B] who secluded herself with another man after being warned by her betrothed, **and a widow waiting for her brother-in-law** [***yavam***] to perform levirate marriage who secluded herself with another man after being warned by her *yavam*,[N] **they neither drink** the bitter water **nor collect** payment of their **marriage contracts.**[NH] The reason they are not entitled to payment of their marriage contracts is that the betrothed woman became forbidden to her betrothed or the widow became forbidden to her *yavam* due to her own actions of entering into seclusion with the paramour. And the fact that they do not drink the bitter water is **as it is stated:** "This is the law of jealousy, **when a wife, while under her husband, goes astray,** and is defiled" (Numbers 5:29). The verse **excludes a betrothed woman and a widow awaiting her *yavam*;** since they are not yet married, neither is considered as "under her husband."

אַלְמָנָה לְכֹהֵן גָּדוֹל, גְּרוּשָׁה וַחֲלוּצָה לְכֹהֵן הֶדְיוֹט, מַמְזֶרֶת

The mishna delineates cases where the woman's marriage was prohibited in the first place: With regard to **a widow** who was married **to a High Priest,**[H] or **a divorcée or *ḥalutza***[B] who was married **to a common priest,**[B] or **a *mamzeret***

NOTES

And a widow waiting for her brother-in-law who secluded herself after being warned by her *yavam* – וְשׁוֹמֶרֶת יָבָם: The commentaries raise a difficulty: The Gemara (18b) concludes that if a widow awaiting her *yavam* engaged in sexual intercourse with another man, she is not forbidden to the *yavam*. If so, why does she forfeit payment of her marriage contract? Rashi explains that although the *yavam* is permitted to marry her, he can refuse to marry her due to her promiscuous behavior, and since his refusal is prompted by her actions, she forfeits payment of her marriage contract.

Many commentaries question Rashi's understanding and offer alternative explanations. *Tosafot* note that according to the Gemara (24b), the mishna is referring to a case where the *yavam* already engaged in sexual intercourse with the widow. In this case, by engaging in sexual intercourse with another man, the widow becomes prohibited to the *yavam*, and therefore she forfeits payment of her marriage contract.

Other early commentaries explain that this mishna is not in accordance with the *halakha*. Rather, it is in accordance with the opinion of Rabbi Akiva, who equates women who are forbidden by a standard Torah prohibition to women who are forbidden on penalty of *karet*. Since a widow awaiting her *yavam* is prohibited to everyone else, Rabbi Akiva holds that if she engages in sexual intercourse with another man she becomes prohibited to the *yavam* (*Tosefot HaRash*; *Tosefot HaRosh*).

A betrothed woman…nor collect payment of their marriage contracts – אֲרוּסָה...וְלֹא נוֹטְלוֹת כְּתוּבָּה: Although there is an amoraic dispute as to whether a betrothed woman is entitled to a marriage contract, all agree that under normal circumstances, if her betrothed wrote her a marriage contract, she is entitled to collect at least the main sum, which is one hundred dinars for a widow or a divorcée and two hundred dinars for a virgin. This is what she stands to lose if she secludes herself with another man after being warned by her betrothed.

The phrase "while under her husband" (Numbers 5:29) excludes these women only from drinking the bitter water, but not from the *halakha* that prohibits a *sota* to her husband until the bitter water evaluates her fidelity, and since she cannot drink the bitter water, divorce is the only alternative. Since the woman put herself in this position, she loses her right to collect payment of her marriage contract, even though there is no certainty that she was defiled. For this reason, even Beit Shammai, who hold that a woman who cannot drink the bitter water due to her husband's death collects payment of her marriage contract, concede that in this case she does not collect payment of her marriage contract.

BACKGROUND

A betrothed woman – אֲרוּסָה: A Jewish wedding is divided into two distinct parts: Betrothal and marriage. The betrothal is the first stage and is usually effected with money or a monetary equivalent, such as a ring, which the man gives the bride. After the betrothal, the woman is considered a married woman who does not yet reside with her husband. She therefore cannot marry another man without first receiving a bill of divorce. Although they are legally married, the couple may not yet live together as man and wife, and most of their mutual obligations do not yet apply. If a betrothed woman engages in sexual intercourse with another man, both have violated the prohibition against adultery and are liable to be executed.

The second stage of the marriage process is the marriage ceremony. Marriage is effected by having the bride and groom come under the bridal canopy, and it confers upon the couple both the rights and the responsibilities associated with marriage.

In talmudic times it was not unusual for a year to elapse between betrothal and marriage, allowing the bride and groom to prepare for the wedding. However, later it became the accepted practice to perform both the betrothal ceremony and the marriage ceremony at the same time, in order to prevent many halakhic and practical difficulties.

Ḥalutza – חֲלוּצָה: A *yevama* who performed the *ḥalitza* ritual, releasing her from her levirate bond, is known as a *ḥalutza*. The term *ḥalitza* is derived from the central element of this ritual, in which the widow removes a special sandal from the foot of one of her deceased husband's brothers, as when the verse states the mitzva for her to remove his sandal, it uses the term "*vaḥaletza*" (Deuteronomy 25:9).

A widow who was married to a High Priest or a divorcée or *ḥalutza* who was married to a common priest – אַלְמָנָה לְכֹהֵן גָּדוֹל גְּרוּשָׁה וַחֲלוּצָה לְכֹהֵן הֶדְיוֹט: By Torah law, it is prohibited for a priest to marry a divorcée and it is prohibited for a High Priest to marry a widow (Leviticus 21:7, 14). By rabbinic law, it is also prohibited for a priest to marry a *ḥalutza*. Since these prohibitions are not punishable by *karet*, if a priest betroths one of these women, the betrothal takes effect; however, it is still prohibited for them to live together, and the offspring of this union are *ḥalalim*, priests disqualified due to flawed lineage.

HALAKHA

A betrothed woman and a widow waiting for her brother-in-law…nor collect payment of their marriage contracts – אֲרוּסָה וְשׁוֹמֶרֶת יָבָם...וְלֹא נוֹטְלוֹת כְּתוּבָּה: With regard to a betrothed woman or a widow awaiting her *yavam*, whose betrothed or *yavam* issued a warning to her and who was then observed by witnesses to seclude herself with the other man, even if she wishes to drink the bitter water and the betrothed or the *yavam* wants her to drink it, she cannot drink it. Rather, she is divorced without receiving payment of her marriage contract (Rambam *Sefer Nashim*, *Hilkhot Sota* 2:2).

A widow who was married to a High Priest – אַלְמָנָה לְכֹהֵן גָּדוֹל: With regard to a man whose wife was forbidden to him, such as a High Priest who was married to a widow, if he issued a warning to her and she then secluded herself with the other man, she does not drink the bitter water. Rather, she is divorced without receiving payment of her marriage contract. This *halakha* applies whether his wife was forbidden to him by an explicit prohibition, by a prohibition stated as a positive mitzva, or even by rabbinic law, e.g., the husband and wife were secondary relatives (Rambam *Sefer Nashim*, *Hilkhot Sota* 2:9).

ונתינה לישראל, ובת ישראל לממזר ולנתין – לא שותות ולא נוטלות כתובה.

or Gibeonite woman who was married **to a Jew** of unflawed lineage, **or a Jewish woman** of unflawed lineage who was married **to a** ***mamzer*** **or a Gibeonite,** all of these women **neither drink** the bitter water **nor collect** payment of their **marriage contracts,** as the *sota* ritual applies only to permitted marriages.

ואלו לא שותות ולא נוטלות כתובה: האומרת "טמאה אני", ושבאו לה עדים שהיא טמאה, והאומרת "איני שותה".

And the following women **neither drink** the bitter water **nor collect** payment of their **marriage contracts:** A woman **who** confesses and **says: I am defiled,**[H] **and** a woman **with regard to whom witnesses came**[H] and testified **that she is defiled, and** a woman **who says: I will not drink** the bitter water,[H] even if she does not confess her guilt.

אמר בעלה "איני משקה", ושבעלה בא עליה בדרך – נוטלות כתובה ולא שותות.

However, a woman whose **husband said: I will not have** her **drink,**[H] **and** a woman **whose husband engaged in sexual intercourse with her on the way** to the Temple, **collect** payment of their **marriage contracts** even though **they do not drink** the bitter water, as it is due to the husbands that they do not drink.

מתו בעליהן עד שלא שתו – בית שמאי אומרים: נוטלות כתובה ולא שותות, ובית הלל אומרים: או שותות או לא נוטלות כתובתן.

If **the husbands** of *sota* women **died before** their wives **drank**[H] the bitter water, **Beit Shammai say: They collect** payment of their **marriage contracts and they do not drink** the bitter water. **And Beit Hillel say: They either drink** the bitter water **or they do not collect** payment of **their marriage contracts.**[N]

מעוברת חבירו ומניקת חבירו – לא שותות ולא נוטלות כתובה, דברי רבי מאיר; וחכמים אומרים: יכול הוא להפרישה ולהחזירה לאחר זמן.

A woman who was pregnant with the child **of another**[N] man[H] at the time of her marriage **and a woman who was nursing** the child **of another** man at the time of her marriage **neither drink** the bitter water **nor collect** payment of their **marriage contracts.** This is because by rabbinic law they may not marry for twenty-four months after the baby's birth, and therefore these also constitute prohibited marriages. This is **the statement of Rabbi Meir. And the Rabbis say: He can separate** from **her,**[N] **and remarry her after** the **time** of twenty-four months has elapsed, and therefore these are considered permitted marriages, and the women can drink the bitter water.

NOTES

They either drink the bitter water or they do not collect payment of their marriage contracts – או שותות או לא נוטלות כתובתן: The Gemara explains elsewhere (*Ketubot* 81a) that only the husband can bring the *sota* to the Temple to drink. The mishna's intention here is that since the *sota* women must drink the bitter water in order to collect payment of their marriage contracts, and they cannot do so once their husbands have died, they consequently do not collect payment of their marriage contracts.

A woman who was pregnant with the child of another, etc. – מעוברת חבירו וכו׳: The Sages prohibited one from marrying a pregnant or nursing woman until the child is born and weaned, as the woman is liable to become pregnant and cease lactating. This could endanger the child's life, since his sustenance must be claimed from the former husband or from his estate, and the second husband might be lax in his efforts to ensure proper care of a child who is not his own. The *tanna'im* elsewhere disagree with regard to the length of time required until the woman may remarry; however, the *halakha* is in accordance with the opinion that states that this stricture is in effect until a child is twenty-four months old.

He can separate from her, etc. – יכול הוא להפרישה וכו׳: According to the Rabbis, even if one married a pregnant or nursing woman when it was prohibited to marry her, he is permitted to separate from her and remarry her after the requisite time has elapsed. Rabbi Meir, however, disagrees with the Rabbis, and holds that since the man married the pregnant or nursing woman when he was prohibited from doing so, he is required to divorce her and may never remarry her, and therefore, this constitutes a prohibited marriage with regard to the *halakha* of a *sota* (Rambam's Commentary on the Mishna).

HALAKHA

A woman who confesses and says, I am defiled – האומרת טמאה אני: A woman who secluded herself with another man after being warned is not forced to drink the bitter water. Therefore, if she confesses and says: I am defiled, she does not drink. Her husband is required to divorce her, she forfeits payment of her marriage contract, and she is forbidden to him forever (Rambam *Sefer Nashim, Hilkhot Sota* 2:1).

And a woman with regard to whom witnesses came, etc. – ושבאו לה עדים וכו׳: If witnesses testified that a *sota* was defiled, she does not drink the bitter water. Her husband is required to divorce her, she forfeits payment of her marriage contract, and she is forbidden to him forever (Rambam *Sefer Nashim, Hilkhot Sota* 1:14).

And a woman who says, I will not drink the bitter water, etc. – והאומרת איני שותה וכו׳: A woman who does not want to drink the bitter water is not forced to drink, even if she maintains that she is innocent of adultery. However, her husband must divorce her, and she does not collect payment of her marriage contract, and she is forbidden to him forever (Rambam *Sefer Nashim, Hilkhot Sota* 2:1).

A woman whose husband said, I will not have her drink, etc. – אמר בעלה איני משקה וכו׳: If a woman secluded herself with another man after she was warned but her husband does not want to have her drink, or if her husband engaged in sexual intercourse with her after the seclusion, she does not drink the bitter water. Her husband is required to divorce her and pay her the sum of her marriage contract, and she is forbidden to him forever (Rambam *Sefer Nashim, Hilkhot Sota* 2:1).

If the husbands of *sota* women died before their wives drank – מתו בעליהן עד שלא שתו: A *sota* whose husband died before she drank the bitter water does not drink it. She also does not collect payment of her marriage contract, in accordance with the opinion of Beit Hillel (Rambam *Sefer Nashim, Hilkhot Sota* 2:7).

A woman who was pregnant with the child of another man, etc. – מעוברת חבירו וכו׳: In this case, either a man married a woman who was pregnant with the child of another man, or he married a woman who was nursing the child of another man, in violation of the rabbinic prohibition against such a marriage. Subsequently, the woman secluded herself with a different man, after being warned. The woman is required to drink the bitter water, as her marriage, though prohibited, could be rectified, in accordance with the opinion of the Rabbis (Rambam *Sefer Nashim, Hilkhot Sota* 2:9).

אַיְילוֹנִית, וּזְקֵינָה, וְשֶׁאֵינָהּ רְאוּיָה לֵילֵד – לֹא נוֹטְלוֹת כְּתוּבָּה וְלֹא שׁוֹתוֹת; רַבִּי אֶלְעָזָר אוֹמֵר: יָכוֹל הוּא לִישָּׂא אִשָּׁה אַחֶרֶת וְלִפְרוֹת וְלִרְבּוֹת הֵימֶנָּה.

A sexually underdeveloped woman who is incapable of bearing children [*ailonit*],[B] **and an elderly woman,**[H] **and** a woman **who is incapable of giving birth** for other reasons, **neither collect** payment of their **marriage contracts nor drink** the bitter water, as marrying a woman who cannot give birth constitutes a violation of the mitzva to be fruitful and multiply. **Rabbi Elazar says: He can marry another woman and procreate through her;** therefore, these are considered permitted marriages, and women in these categories can drink the bitter water.

וּשְׁאָר כָּל הַנָּשִׁים – אוֹ שׁוֹתוֹת אוֹ לֹא נוֹטְלוֹת כְּתוּבָּה. אֵשֶׁת כֹּהֵן שׁוֹתָה וּמוּתֶּרֶת לְבַעְלָהּ. אֵשֶׁת סָרִיס שׁוֹתָה.

And all other women either drink the bitter water **or do not collect** payment of their **marriage contracts. The wife of a priest drinks,**[H] **and** if she is found to be innocent of adultery, she **is permitted to her husband. The wife of a eunuch** also **drinks.**[H]

עַל יְדֵי כָּל עֲרָיוֹת מְקַנִּין, חוּץ מִן הַקָּטָן וּמִמִּי שֶׁאֵינוֹ אִישׁ.

A husband **can issue a warning** to his wife forbidding her to seclude herself with any man, even **with regard to all those** men **with whom relations are forbidden,**[H] e.g., her father or brother, with the **exception of a minor and of one who is not a man,** i.e., in a situation where a man suspects his wife of bestiality.

וְאֵלּוּ שֶׁבֵּית דִּין מְקַנִּין לָהֶן: מִי שֶׁנִּתְחָרֵשׁ בַּעְלָהּ, אוֹ נִשְׁתַּטָּה, אוֹ שֶׁהָיָה חָבוּשׁ בְּבֵית הָאֲסוּרִין. לֹא לְהַשְׁקוֹתָהּ אָמְרוּ, אֶלָּא לְפוֹסְלָהּ מִכְּתוּבָּתָהּ. רַבִּי יוֹסֵי אוֹמֵר: אַף לְהַשְׁקוֹתָהּ, לִכְשֶׁיֵּצֵא בַּעְלָהּ מִבֵּית הָאֲסוּרִין יַשְׁקֶנָּה.

And these are the women **to whom the court issues a warning**[H] in place of their husbands: **One whose husband became a deaf-mute or became an imbecile,**[B] **or was incarcerated in prison.** The Sages **said** that the court warns her **not** in order **to have her drink** the bitter water if she disobeys the warning, **but** in order **to disqualify her from** receiving payment of **her marriage contract. Rabbi Yosei says:** The court's warning **also** serves **to have her drink,** and **when her husband is released from prison he has her drink.**

BACKGROUND

A sexually underdeveloped woman who is incapable of bearing children [*ailonit*] – אַיְילוֹנִית: The Talmud discusses the *halakhot* of an *ailonit* in great detail, primarily in tractate *Yevamot*. It appears from these discussions that an *ailonit* is a woman with a genetic disorder that renders her incapable of bearing children. This condition is viewed as being distinct from that of other women, who have suffered from medical complications or defects that subsequently rendered them infertile, although their physical and sexual development was normal. By contrast, the *ailonit* can be recognized by certain abnormal physical traits, including a lack of secondary sex characteristics such as pubic hair. There appear to be several types of medical situations in which a woman is considered to be an *ailonit*, including women who suffer from a surplus of male hormones and those who suffer from Turner syndrome.

The halakhic literature contains many discussions with regard to the status of the *ailonit*, primarily due to the fact that her secondary sex characteristics are either entirely absent or appear only at an older age. One of the discussions concerns the age at which the *ailonit* reaches her majority.

One whose husband became a deaf-mute or became an imbecile – מִי שֶׁנִּתְחָרֵשׁ בַּעְלָהּ אוֹ נִשְׁתַּטָּה: In the past, individuals who were deaf and mute were generally unable to communicate with their surroundings, and as a result, their intellectual development was extremely limited. The categories of a deaf-mute, an imbecile, and a minor are frequently grouped together in the Talmud, as they were viewed as sharing the characteristics of limited intellectual capacity and the lack of ability to act responsibly. As a result, they are exempt from the obligation to perform mitzvot, and are not held responsible for any damage they may cause. They also lack the legal capacity to act as agents. Although these categories are often mentioned together, there are many differences between the *halakhot* governing each of them. The later authorities discuss the legal status of a deaf-mute who acquires the ability to communicate and is therefore not considered to be comparable to an imbecile.

HALAKHA

A sexually underdeveloped woman and an elderly woman, etc. – אַיְילוֹנִית וּזְקֵינָה וכו׳: With regard to one who married a woman who is unable to conceive, including a woman who is sexually underdeveloped or elderly; if he has not yet fulfilled the mitzva of procreation and does not have another wife who is fertile, and he issues a warning to his wife and she nevertheless secludes herself with another man, she does not drink the bitter water and she does not collect payment of her marriage contract. However, if the husband has already fulfilled the mitzva of procreation or if he has another wife who is fertile, and he issues a warning to his wife who is unable to conceive, she may drink the bitter water. This ruling is in accordance with the unattributed mishna, as explained in the Gemara (Rambam *Sefer Nashim*, *Hilkhot Sota* 2:9).

The wife of a priest drinks – אֵשֶׁת כֹּהֵן שׁוֹתָה: A *sota* who drank the bitter water and did not die immediately is permitted to her husband, even if he is a priest. She is permitted to her husband even if her health begins to deteriorate, as long as she is not afflicted in her belly and thighs in the manner described in the Torah (see Numbers 5:27) with regard to a *sota* who was defiled (Rambam *Sefer Nashim*, *Hilkhot Sota* 3:21).

The wife of a eunuch drinks – אֵשֶׁת סָרִיס שׁוֹתָה: The wife of a eunuch drinks the bitter water. This *halakha* applies both with regard to someone who was born a eunuch and to someone who was castrated, provided that the woman was permitted to marry him (Rambam *Sefer Nashim*, *Hilkhot Sota* 2:6).

A husband can issue a warning with regard to all those with whom relations are forbidden, etc. – עַל יְדֵי כָּל עֲרָיוֹת מְקַנִּין וכו׳: A husband issues a warning to his wife by cautioning her before two witnesses not to seclude herself with a particular man. He may issue a warning to his wife with regard to any man who has reached majority, even with regard to forbidden relatives, e.g., her father or brother, or with regard to a gentile. One may even warn her with regard to a man who is incapable of completing sexual intercourse. However, if one issues a warning to his wife with regard to a minor or with regard to an animal, this is not considered a valid warning (Rambam *Sefer Nashim*, *Hilkhot Sota* 1:1, 6; *Shulḥan Arukh*, *Even HaEzer* 178:2).

And these are the women to whom the court issues a warning, etc. – וְאֵלּוּ שֶׁבֵּית דִּין מְקַנִּין לָהֶן וכו׳: If a husband becomes a deaf-mute or an imbecile, or if he is in another country or incarcerated in prison, and the court hears rumors concerning the promiscuous behavior of his wife, the court summons her and warns her not to seclude herself with a particular man. If she then secludes herself with that individual, the court forbids her to her husband and tears up her marriage contract. If the husband is capable of divorcing her, he must do so; he cannot make her drink the bitter water, as he did not issue the warning himself, in accordance with the opinion of the unattributed mishna (Rambam *Sefer Nashim*, *Hilkhot Sota* 1:10–11; *Shulḥan Arukh*, *Even HaEzer* 178:13).

PERSONALITIES

Rabbi Yoshiya – רַבִּי יֹאשִׁיָּה: A fourth-generation *tanna*, Rabbi Yoshiya was one of the younger students of Rabbi Yishmael, and the colleague and regular disputant of Rabbi Yonatan. It appears that he lived a long life, as he also appears in disputes with Rabbi Yehuda HaNasi.

גמ׳ מִישְׁתָּא הוּא דְּלָא שָׁתְיָא, הָא קַנּוֹיֵי מְקַנֵּי לַהּ. מְנָא הָנֵי מִילֵּי? דְּתָנוּ רַבָּנַן: ״דַּבֵּר אֶל בְּנֵי יִשְׂרָאֵל וְאָמַרְתָּ״ – לְרַבּוֹת אֲרוּסָה וְשׁוֹמֶרֶת יָבָם לְקִינּוּי;

GEMARA The mishna states that a betrothed woman and a widow awaiting her *yavam* do not drink the bitter water. The Gemara infers: **She does not drink, but** the husband or *yavam* **can warn her** against secluding herself with another man, and if she violates his warning, she is forbidden to him. The Gemara asks: **From where are these matters** derived? The Gemara answers: This is derived **as the Sages taught** with regard to the verse: **"Speak to the children of Israel and say** unto them: If the wife of any man goes astray, and acts unfaithfully against him" (Numbers 5:12). The superfluous phrase "and say unto them" is an amplification, and serves **to include a betrothed woman and a widow awaiting her *yavam*** in the *halakhot* of **warning.**

וּמַתְנִיתִין מַנִּי? רַבִּי יוֹנָתָן הִיא, דְּתַנְיָא: ״תַּחַת אִישֵׁךְ״ – פְּרָט לַאֲרוּסָה. יָכוֹל שֶׁאֲנִי מוֹצִיא אַף שׁוֹמֶרֶת יָבָם? תַּלְמוּד לוֹמַר: ״אִישׁ אִישׁ״, דִּבְרֵי רַבִּי יֹאשִׁיָּה;

And whose opinion is expressed in the **mishna? It is** the opinion of **Rabbi Yonatan, as it is taught** in a *baraita* with regard to the verse: "And the priest shall cause her to swear, and shall say to the woman: If no man has lain with you, and if you have not gone aside to defilement **while under your husband"** (Numbers 5:19). This **excludes a betrothed woman,** who does not yet live with her betrothed, from the ritual of the bitter water. One **might** have thought **that I exclude even a widow awaiting her *yavam*;** therefore, **the verse states:** "If the wife of **any man** goes astray" (Numbers 5:12). The term "any man" serves to include a widow awaiting her *yavam* in the ritual of the bitter water. This is **the statement of Rabbi Yoshiya.**[P]

רַבִּי יוֹנָתָן אוֹמֵר: ״תַּחַת אִישֵׁךְ״ – פְּרָט לְשׁוֹמֶרֶת יָבָם. אוֹצִיא שׁוֹמֶרֶת יָבָם וְלֹא אוֹצִיא אֶת אֲרוּסָה? תַּלְמוּד לוֹמַר: ״אֲשֶׁר תִּשְׂטֶה אִשָּׁה תַּחַת אִישָׁהּ״ – פְּרָט לַאֲרוּסָה.

Rabbi Yonatan says: The phrase **"while under your husband" excludes a widow awaiting her *yavam*** from drinking the bitter water. Lest one would say that **I will exclude a widow awaiting her *yavam* but I will not exclude a betrothed woman, the verse** therefore **states:** "This is the law of jealousy, **when a wife, while under her husband, goes astray,** and is defiled" (Numbers 5:29). The term "while under her husband" **excludes a betrothed woman** from drinking the bitter water.

מָר אַלִּימָא לֵיהּ אֲרוּסָה, דְּקִידּוּשֵׁי דִּידֵיהּ וְסוֹקְלִין עַל יָדוֹ;

The Gemara explains the dispute: One **Sage,** Rabbi Yonatan, holds that the bond with the **betrothed woman is stronger, as** it is **his** own **betrothal,** whereas in the case of a widow awaiting her *yavam*, the bond stems from his brother's betrothal. **And** furthermore, if the betrothed woman commits adultery, she **is stoned due to** her bond with **him,** whereas a widow awaiting her *yavam* who engages in sexual intercourse with another man is liable only to receive lashes. Since the bond with the betrothed woman is stronger, Rabbi Yonatan derives from the phrase "while under your husband" that a widow awaiting her *yavam* is excluded with respect to the bitter water, whereas a betrothed woman is excluded only because of the phrase "and say unto them."

וּמָר אַלִּימָא לֵיהּ שׁוֹמֶרֶת יָבָם, דְּלָא מִיחַסְּרָא מְסִירָה לַחוּפָּה.

And one **Sage,** Rabbi Yoshiya, holds that the bond with the **widow awaiting her *yavam* is stronger, as she is not lacking entry into the wedding canopy,** as her marriage to the *yavam* is completed through sexual intercourse alone. Rabbi Yoshiya therefore excludes only a betrothed woman from drinking the bitter water.

וְרַבִּי יוֹנָתָן, הַאי ״אִישׁ אִישׁ״ מַאי עָבֵיד לֵיהּ? מִיבְּעֵי לֵיהּ: לְרַבּוֹת אֵשֶׁת חֵרֵשׁ, וְאֵשֶׁת שׁוֹטֶה, וְאֵשֶׁת

The Gemara asks: **And Rabbi Yonatan,** who excludes both a betrothed woman and a widow awaiting her *yavam* from drinking the bitter water, **what does he do with this** term **"any man"?** What does it serve to include? The Gemara answers: Rabbi Yonatan **requires it** in order **to include the wife of a deaf-mute and the wife of an imbecile, and the wife of**

Perek **IV**
Daf **24** Amud **b**

NOTES

A mentally ill person [*shiamum*] – שַׁעֲמוּם: The term *shiamum* refers to a form of mental illness in which one might cease functioning due to severe depression or melancholy. It is used to refer both to the illness and to the sick individual.

שַׁעֲמוּם. וְרַבִּי יֹאשִׁיָּה, הַאי ״תַּחַת אִישָׁהּ״ מַאי עָבֵיד לֵיהּ? מִיבְּעֵי לֵיהּ: לְהַקִּישׁ אִישׁ לְאִשָּׁה וְאִשָּׁה לְאִישׁ.

a mentally ill person [*shiamum*],[N] whom the court warns on behalf of the husband. The Gemara asks: **And** according to **Rabbi Yoshiya, what does he do with this** term **"while under her husband"?** The Gemara answers: Rabbi Yoshiya **requires it** in order **to compare a man to a woman and a woman to a man,** as explained later (27a).

אֶלָּא טַעְמָא דִּכְתִיבִי הָנֵי קְרָאֵי, הָא לָאו הָכִי, הֲוָה אָמֵינָא אֲרוּסָה שָׁתְיָא, וְהָא כִּי אֲתָא רַבִּי אַחָא בַּר חֲנִינָא מִדָּרוֹמָא, אֲתָא וְאַיְיתֵי מַתְנִיתָא בִּידֵיהּ: ״מִבַּלְעֲדֵי אִישֵׁךְ״ – מִשֶּׁקָּדְמָה שְׁכִיבַת בַּעַל לְבוֹעֵל, וְלֹא שֶׁקָּדְמָה שְׁכִיבַת בּוֹעֵל לְבַעַל!

The Gemara asks: **But** according to both opinions, **the reason** for the exclusion of a betrothed woman is **that these verses are written; if** it **were not so, I would say** that **a betrothed woman drinks. But when Rabbi Aḥa bar Ḥanina came from the South,**[B] **he came and brought** the following ***baraita* with him:** The verse states: "But if you have gone astray while under your husband, and if you are defiled, and some man has lain with you **besides your husband**" (Numbers 5:20). This indicates that the *halakhot* of a *sota* apply only **when sexual intercourse with the husband preceded**[H] sexual intercourse with **the paramour, and not** in a case **when sexual intercourse with the paramour preceded** intercourse with **the husband.** In the case of a betrothed woman who committed adultery, intercourse with the paramour preceded intercourse with the betrothed, and this verse excludes her from drinking the bitter water of the *sota*.

אָמַר רָמִי בַּר חָמָא: מַשְׁכַּחַתְּ לָהּ, כְּגוֹן שֶׁבָּא עָלֶיהָ אָרוּס בְּבֵית אָבִיהָ.

Rami bar Ḥama said: You find the necessity for an additional exclusion in a case **where** her **betrothed engaged in sexual intercourse with her in her father's house,** i.e., before they were married, and before the sexual intercourse with the paramour.

דִּכְווֹתַהּ גַּבֵּי שׁוֹמֶרֶת יָבָם, כְּגוֹן שֶׁבָּא עָלֶיהָ יָבָם בְּבֵית חָמִיהָ. הָא שׁוֹמֶרֶת יָבָם קָרֵית לַהּ? אִשְׁתּוֹ מְעַלַּיְיתָא הִיא. דְּהָאָמַר רַב: קָנָה לַכֹּל!

The Gemara questions this explanation: **In the corresponding** situation **with regard to a widow awaiting her *yavam*,** whom Rabbi Yonatan excludes from the *sota* ritual due to the exclusion from the phrase "while under your husband," is the necessity for this exclusion due to a case **where** the ***yavam* engaged in sexual intercourse with her in her father-in-law's house** before the levirate marriage took place? **But do you call that** woman **a widow awaiting her *yavam*? She is his full-fledged wife, as didn't Rav say:** If a widow awaiting her *yavam* engaged in sexual intercourse with her *yavam*, even without the intention of implementing a levirate marriage, he **has acquired** her as his wife with respect **to all** aspects of marriage,[H] including the *halakhot* of a *sota*.

כִּשְׁמוּאֵל, דְּאָמַר: לֹא קָנָה אֶלָּא לִדְבָרִים הָאֲמוּרִים בַּפָּרָשָׁה.

The Gemara answers: Rabbi Yonatan's opinion is **in accordance with** the opinion of **Shmuel, as Shmuel says:** A *yavam* who engages in sexual intercourse with his *yevama* without intending to consummate the levirate marriage **does not acquire** her as his wife **except with regard to** those **matters that are stated in the passage** in the Torah that deals with levirate marriage, i.e., that he inherits his brother's estate, and he can free the widow with a bill of divorce without *ḥalitza* (see *Yevamot* 56a). He is not considered fully married to the woman, and, according to Rabbi Yonatan, the *halakhot* of a *sota* do not apply to her.

אִי הָכִי, לֵימָא, רַב דְּאָמַר כְּרַבִּי יֹאשִׁיָּה, וּשְׁמוּאֵל דְּאָמַר כְּרַבִּי יוֹנָתָן! אָמַר לָךְ רַב: אֲנָא דַּאֲמַרִי אֲפִילּוּ לְרַבִּי יוֹנָתָן. מִדְּאִיצְטְרִיךְ קְרָא לְמַעוּטַהּ, מִכְּלָל דְּאִשְׁתּוֹ מְעַלַּיְיתָא הִיא.

The Gemara asks: **If so, let us say** that **Rav stated** his opinion **in accordance with** the opinion of **Rabbi Yoshiya, and Shmuel stated** his opinion **in accordance with** the opinion of **Rabbi Yonatan.** The Gemara rejects this interpretation: **Rav** could have **said to you: I state** my opinion **even according to** the opinion of **Rabbi Yonatan. Since** it **was necessary** for **the verse to exclude** a *yevama* who engaged in sexual intercourse with her *yavam* from the *sota* ritual, **by inference** one may derive **that she is his full-fledged wife** with regard to all other matters.

HALAKHA

When sexual intercourse with the husband preceded, etc. – מִשֶּׁקָּדְמָה שְׁכִיבַת בַּעַל וכו׳: With regard to a married woman who secluded herself with another man after being warned, if the seclusion occurred before her husband engaged in sexual intercourse with her, she does not drink the bitter water. Her husband is required to divorce her, she forfeits payment of her marriage contract, and she is forbidden to him forever (Rambam *Sefer Nashim, Hilkhot Sota* 2:5).

He has acquired her as his wife for all aspects of marriage – קָנָה לַכֹּל: A *yavam* who engages in sexual intercourse with his *yevama* acquires her as his wife with regard to all aspects of marriage, as the *halakha* is in accordance with Rav in his disputes with Shmuel, with the exception of disputes concerning monetary matters. He acquires her as his wife irrespective of whether he engaged in sexual intercourse with her intentionally, unwittingly, or even under duress, and irrespective of whether the intercourse was complete or partial.

However, this ruling applies only with regard to a *yevama* who had been married to the brother of the *yavam*. In the case of a *yevama* who had only been betrothed to the brother of the *yavam*, if the *yavam* engages in sexual intercourse with her unwittingly or under duress, he does not acquire her as his full-fledged wife; furthermore, if the *yavam* is a priest, he does not enable her to partake of *teruma*. In addition, some say that if the *yavam* engaged in intercourse with her unwittingly or under duress, he does not acquire her as his wife with regard to inheriting from her, becoming ritually impure for her when she dies if he is a priest, or nullifying her vows. Some authorities add that the same is true with regard to a *yavam* who performed only the initial stage of intercourse (Rambam *Sefer Zera'im, Hilkhot Terumot* 8:6 and *Sefer Nashim, Hilkhot Yibbum VaḤalitza* 2:3; *Shulḥan Arukh, Even HaEzer* 166:7, 9).

BACKGROUND

Came from the South – אֲתָא...מִדָּרוֹמָא: This refers to Judea, which is south of the Galilee. After the bar Kokheva revolt, the land of Judea was almost completely devastated and the center of Jewish life in Eretz Yisrael shifted to the Galilee. Despite this, there remained some important centers of learning in Judea, including Lod, and further south, in the vicinity of Beit Guvrin. These centers preserved many ancient traditions that were unknown in the Galilee, and at times Sages from there traveled to the Galilee and reported these traditions to the Sages in the Galilee.

Ruins of ancient synagogue in Susya, southeast of Beit Guvrin

וּשְׁמוּאֵל אָמַר: אֲנָא דַּאֲמַרִי אֲפִילּוּ לְרַבִּי יֹאשִׁיָּה. מִדְּאִיצְטְרִיךְ קְרָא לְרַבּוּיָהּ, מִכְּלָל דְּלָאו אִשְׁתּוֹ הִיא כְּלָל.

And Shmuel could have **said: I state** my opinion **even according to** the opinion of **Rabbi Yoshiya. Since it was necessary** for **the verse to** specifically **include** in the *sota* ritual a *yevama* who engaged in sexual intercourse with her *yavam*, **by inference** one may conclude **that she is not his wife at all** with regard to any matters other than those explicit in the verse.

אִיבַּעְיָא לְהוּ: עוֹבֶרֶת עַל דָּת, צְרִיכָה הַתְרָאָה לְהַפְסִידָהּ כְּתוּבָּתָהּ אוֹ אֵינָהּ צְרִיכָה? מִי אָמְרִינַן, כֵּיוָן דְּעוֹבֶרֶת עַל דָּת הִיא לָא בָּעֲיָא הַתְרָאָה? אוֹ דִּלְמָא תִּיבָּעֵי הַתְרָאָה, דְּאִי הָדְרָה בָּהּ תִּיהֲדַר בָּהּ?

§ **A dilemma was raised before** the Sages: With regard to **a woman who violates** the **precepts** of *halakha* or Jewish custom[N] with regard to modesty, who may be divorced without payment of her marriage contract, is **forewarning** from her husband **required** in order to cause **her to forfeit** her right to collect payment of **her marriage contract or is** forewarning **not required? Do we say** that **since she is a woman who violates** the **precepts, forewarning is not required,** as she is aware that her actions are prohibited? **Or perhaps forewarning is required,** so **that if she** desires to **repent, she will** be reminded to **repent?**

תָּא שְׁמַע: אֲרוּסָה וְשׁוֹמֶרֶת יָבָם לֹא שׁוֹתוֹת וְלֹא נוֹטְלוֹת כְּתוּבָּה; מִישְׁתָּא הוּא דְּלָא שָׁתְיָא, הָא קַנּוּיֵי מְקַנֵּי לָהּ. לְמַאי? לָאו לְהַפְסִידָהּ כְּתוּבָּתָהּ?

The Gemara suggests: **Come** and **hear** a proof from the mishna: **A betrothed woman and a widow awaiting her** *yavam* **neither drink** the bitter water **nor collect** payment of their **marriage contracts.** It is possible to infer that **she does not drink, but** the husband or *yavam* **can warn her** against secluding herself with another man. **For what** *halakha* is his warning relevant? **Is it not** relevant **to cause her to forfeit** her right to collect payment of **her marriage contract?** Accordingly, a woman forfeits payment of her marriage contract due to immodest behavior only if she is warned.

אֲמַר אַבַּיֵי: לָא, לְאוֹסְרָהּ עָלָיו. רַב פַּפָּא אֲמַר: לְהַשְׁקוֹתָהּ כְּשֶׁהִיא נְשׂוּאָה, כִּדְתַנְיָא: אֵין מְקַנִּין לַאֲרוּסָה לְהַשְׁקוֹתָהּ כְּשֶׁהִיא אֲרוּסָה, אֲבָל מְקַנִּין לַאֲרוּסָה לְהַשְׁקוֹתָהּ כְּשֶׁהִיא נְשׂוּאָה.

Abaye said: No, the relevance of the warning of the husband or *yavam* is **to render her forbidden to him** in the event that she secludes herself with another man. **Rav Pappa said:** The relevance of the warning is **to have her drink** if she secludes herself with another man **when she is married, as it is taught** in a *baraita*: **One does not issue a warning to a betrothed woman** in order **to have her drink while she is betrothed. However, one can issue a warning to a betrothed woman** in order **to have her drink when she is married.**[H]

אֲמַר רָבָא, תָּא שְׁמַע: אַלְמָנָה לְכֹהֵן גָּדוֹל, גְּרוּשָׁה וַחֲלוּצָה לְכֹהֵן הֶדְיוֹט, מַמְזֶרֶת וּנְתִינָה לְיִשְׂרָאֵל, בַּת יִשְׂרָאֵל לְמַמְזֵר וּלְנָתִין – לֹא שׁוֹתוֹת וְלֹא נוֹטְלוֹת כְּתוּבָּה;

Rava said: Come and **hear** a proof from the continuation of the mishna: **A widow** who was married **to a High Priest,** or **a** ***ḥalutza*** who was married **to a common priest,** or **a** ***mamzeret*** **or Gibeonite woman** who was married **to a Jew** of unflawed lineage, **or a Jewish woman** of unflawed lineage who was married **to a** ***mamzer*** **or a Gibeonite;** all of these women **neither drink** the bitter water **nor collect** payment of their **marriage contracts.**

מִישְׁתָּא הוּא דְּלָא שָׁתְיָא, הָא קַנּוּיֵי מְקַנֵּי לְהוּ, וּלְמַאי? אִי לְאוֹסְרָן עָלָיו – הָא אֲסִירָן וְקַיְימָן! אֶלָּא לָאו לְהַפְסִידָן כְּתוּבָּתָן?

The Gemara infers: **She does not drink, but** the husband or *yavam* **can warn her** against secluding herself with another man. **But for what** *halakha* is his warning relevant? **If** it is in order **to prohibit** these women **to him, aren't they currently prohibited** to him? **Rather, is it not** relevant **to cause them to forfeit** their rights to collect payment of **their marriage contracts?** This indicates that only when a woman is warned in advance does her immodest behavior cause her to forfeit her right to collect payment of her marriage contract.

אֲמַר רַב יְהוּדָה מִדִּיסְקַרְתָּא: לָא, לְאוֹסְרָהּ לַבּוֹעֵל כְּבַעַל, דִּתְנַן: כְּשֵׁם שֶׁאֲסוּרָה לַבַּעַל כָּךְ אֲסוּרָה לַבּוֹעֵל.

Rav Yehuda of Diskarta said: No, the relevance of the warning is **to render her** permanently **forbidden to** her **paramour,** should she seclude herself with him, just **as** she would become forbidden **to** her **husband, as we learned** in a mishna (27b): **Just as she is forbidden to** her **husband, so is she forbidden to** her **paramour.**

NOTES

A woman who violates the precepts of *halakha* or Jewish custom – **עוֹבֶרֶת עַל דָּת:** The mishna in tractate *Ketubot* (72a) discusses two types of women who may be divorced without payment of their marriage contracts: A woman who violates the precepts of Moses, and a woman who violates the precepts of Jewish women, i.e., custom. A woman who violates the precepts of Moses is one who violates Torah law. The early commentaries explain that this applies specifically to a woman who violates Torah law in a manner that causes her husband to transgress as well, e.g., a woman who serves him untithed food or engages in sexual intercourse with him without immersing in a ritual bath after menstruating (see Meiri). A woman who violates the precepts of Jewish women is one who conducts herself immodestly, in a manner unbefitting a Jewish woman.

HALAKHA

One can issue a warning to a betrothed woman to have her drink when she is married – **מְקַנִּין לַאֲרוּסָה לְהַשְׁקוֹתָהּ כְּשֶׁהִיא נְשׂוּאָה:** In the case of one who issues a warning to his betrothed or to his *yevama* while she is awaiting levirate marriage, and she secludes herself with the other man after they are married, the woman drinks the bitter water (Rambam *Sefer Nashim*, *Hilkhot Sota* 2:5).

אָמַר רַב חֲנִינָא מִסּוּרָא: תָּא שְׁמַע – וְאֵלּוּ שֶׁבֵּית דִּין מְקַנִּין לָהֶן: מִי שֶׁנִּתְחָרֵשׁ בַּעְלָהּ, אוֹ נִשְׁתַּטָּה, אוֹ שֶׁהָיָה חָבוּשׁ בְּבֵית הָאֲסוּרִין. וְלֹא לְהַשְׁקוֹתָהּ אָמְרוּ אֶלָּא לְפוֹסְלָהּ מִכְּתוּבָּתָהּ; שְׁמַע מִינַּהּ בָּעֵי הַתְרָאָה. שְׁמַע מִינַּהּ.

Rav Ḥanina of Sura said: Come and **hear** a proof from the continuation of the mishna: **And these** are the women **to whom the court issues a warning** in place of their husbands: **One whose husband became a deaf-mute or became an imbecile, or was incarcerated in prison. And** the Sages **said** that the court warns her **not** in order **to have her drink** the bitter water if she disobeys the warning; **rather** in order **to disqualify her from** receiving payment of **her marriage contract.** Since the sole purpose of the warning issued by the court is to disqualify her from receiving payment of her marriage contract in the event she secludes herself with the man, one can **learn from** the mishna that similarly, a woman who violates the precepts **requires forewarning.**[H] The Gemara concludes: Indeed, one can **learn from** the mishna that a warning is required.

וְכוּלְּהוּ מַאי טַעְמָא לָא אָמְרִי מֵהָא? דִּלְמָא שָׁאנֵי הָתָם, דְּלֵית לַהּ אֵימְתָא דְּבַעַל כְּלָל.

The Gemara asks: With regard to **all of** the other Sages, who proposed inconclusive proofs from other clauses of the mishna, **what is the reason they did not say** that proof can be adduced **from this** explicit statement? The Gemara answers: They reasoned that **perhaps** it **is different there, as** the wife **has no fear of** her **husband at all,** since he is either incapacitated or incarcerated, and therefore she must be warned first. In other cases, an explicit warning is unnecessary.

אִיבַּעְיָא לְהוּ: עוֹבֶרֶת עַל דָּת וְרָצָה בַּעַל לְקַיְּימָהּ, מְקַיְּימָהּ אוֹ אֵינוֹ מְקַיְּימָהּ? מִי אָמְרִינַן בִּקְפִידָה דְּבַעַל תְּלָא רַחֲמָנָא, וְהָא לָא קָפֵיד, אוֹ דִּלְמָא כֵּיוָן דְּקָפֵיד – קָפֵיד?

A dilemma was raised before the Sages: If a woman **violates the precepts and** her **husband desires to maintain her**[H] as his wife, **may he maintain her** as his wife **or may he not maintain her** as his wife? **Do we say** that **the Merciful One made** the requirement to divorce her **dependent on the husband's objection** to her behavior, **and** as **this** husband **does not raise an objection** he may maintain her as his wife? **Or perhaps, since** the Torah **objects** to this behavior, it is considered as though **he objected,** as the requirement to divorce her is due to the Torah's objection to this behavior, irrespective of the husband's wishes.

תָּא שְׁמַע, וְאֵלּוּ שֶׁבֵּית דִּין מְקַנִּין לָהֶן: מִי שֶׁנִּתְחָרֵשׁ בַּעְלָהּ, אוֹ נִשְׁתַּטָּה, אוֹ שֶׁהָיָה חָבוּשׁ בְּבֵית הָאֲסוּרִין. וְאִי אָמְרַתְּ רָצָה בַּעַל לְקַיְּימָהּ מְקַיְּימָהּ, עָבְדִי בֵּית דִּין מִידֵּי דְּדִלְמָא לָא נִיחָא לֵיהּ לַבַּעַל? סְתָמָא דְּמִילְּתָא כֵּיוָן דְּעוֹבֶרֶת עַל דָּת הִיא, מֵינָח נִיחָא לֵיהּ.

The Gemara cites poof: **Come** and **hear** the mishna: **And these** are the women **to whom the court issues a warning** in place of their husbands: **One whose husband became a deaf-mute or became an imbecile, or was incarcerated in prison. And if you say** that should the **husband desire to maintain her** as his wife **he may maintain her** as his wife, perhaps he may not want the court to warn her. Would **the court perform a matter that is perhaps not amenable to the husband?** The Gemara replies: **The ordinary situation** is that **since she is violating the precepts, it is amenable to** the husband to divorce her, and the court acts under this assumption.

אִיבַּעְיָא לְהוּ: בַּעַל שֶׁמָּחַל עַל קִינּוּיוֹ, קִינּוּיוֹ מָחוּל אוֹ אֵינוֹ מָחוּל? מִי אָמְרִינַן בְּקִינּוּי דְּבַעַל תְּלָא רַחֲמָנָא. וּבַעַל הָא מְחֵיל לֵיהּ לְקִינּוּיוֹ? אוֹ דִּלְמָא כֵּיוָן דְּקַנֵּי לֵיהּ מֵעִיקָּרָא – לָא מָצֵי מָחֵיל לֵיהּ?

§ **A dilemma was raised before** the Sages: With regard to **a husband who** issued a warning to his wife and later **retracted his warning,** as he did not wish his wife to acquire the status of a *sota*, **is his warning retracted, or is it not retracted? Do we say** that **the Merciful One made** acquiring the status of a *sota* **dependent on** the **husband's warning,**[N] **and the husband retracted his warning? Or perhaps, since he warned** her **at the outset, he can no** longer **retract** his warning?

תָּא שְׁמַע, וְאֵלּוּ שֶׁבֵּית דִּין מְקַנִּין לָהֶן: מִי שֶׁנִּתְחָרֵשׁ בַּעְלָהּ, אוֹ נִשְׁתַּטָּה, אוֹ שֶׁהָיָה חָבוּשׁ בְּבֵית הָאֲסוּרִין; וְאִי אָמְרַתְּ בַּעַל שֶׁמָּחַל עַל קִינּוּיוֹ קִינּוּיוֹ מָחוּל, עָבְדִינַן מִידֵּי דְּאָתֵי בַּעַל מָחֵיל לֵיהּ? סְתָמָא דְּמִילְּתָא אָדָם מַסְכִּים עַל דַּעַת בֵּית דִּין.

The Gemara cites proof that the husband cannot retract his warning: **Come** and **hear** the mishna: **And these** are the women **to whom the court issues a warning** in place of their husbands: **One whose husband became a deaf-mute or became an imbecile, or was incarcerated in prison. And if you say** that in the case of a **husband who retracted his warning, his warning is retracted,** would **we,** i.e., the court, **do something that** the **husband** can **come** and **retract?** This would cause a diminution of the esteem of the court. The Gemara replies: **The ordinary situation** is that **a person concurs with the opinion of the court** and would not retract a warning issued by the court, so this is not a concern. Therefore, no proof can be brought from the mishna.

HALAKHA

Learn from the mishna that a woman who violates the precepts requires forewarning – **שְׁמַע מִינַּהּ בָּעֵי הַתְרָאָה**: A woman who violates the precepts of Moses, i.e., Torah law, or the precepts of Jewish women, i.e., custom, must be warned in the presence of witnesses in order to cause her to forfeit her right to collect payment of her marriage contract. Some authorities (Maharam of Rothenberg) hold that the husband must explicitly state that if she does not repent she will forfeit payment of her marriage contract, whereas others hold that it is unnecessary to state this explicitly (see *Beit Shmuel*). If there are no witnesses and she claims that she did not violate the precepts, she may collect payment of her marriage contract only after taking an oath to that effect (Rambam *Sefer Nashim, Hilkhot Ishut* 24:16; *Shulḥan Arukh, Even HaEzer* 115:4).

A woman violates the precepts and her husband desires to maintain her – **עוֹבֶרֶת עַל דָּת וְרָצָה בַּעַל לְקַיְּימָהּ**: In the case of a woman who violates the precepts of Moses or the precepts of Jewish women, her husband is not forced to divorce her. If he wishes to maintain her as his wife, he may do so, although it is a mitzva for him to divorce her. However, even if he does not divorce her, she still forfeits her right to collect payment of her marriage contract. The *Ḥelkat Meḥokek* holds that if her husband did not divorce her and she then repented, he must write her a new marriage contract, as the old one lost its validity (Rambam *Sefer Nashim, Hilkhot Sota* 2:16; *Shulḥan Arukh, Even HaEzer* 115:4).

NOTES

The Merciful One made acquiring the status of a *sota* dependent on the husband's warning – **בְּקִינּוּי דְּבַעַל תְּלָא רַחֲמָנָא**: An alternate version of the text renders this phrase: The Merciful One made acquiring the status of a *sota* dependent on the husband's objection (*She'iltot deRav Aḥai Gaon*). This clarifies the rationale for the possibility that a husband can retract his warning: Since he issued a warning only because he objected to his wife's behavior, he can claim that he no longer objects.

תָּא שְׁמַע: וּמוֹסְרִין לוֹ שְׁנֵי תַלְמִידֵי חֲכָמִים, שֶׁמָּא יָבֹא עָלֶיהָ בַּדֶּרֶךְ; וְאִי אָמְרַתְּ בַּעַל שֶׁמָּחַל עַל קִינּוּיוֹ קִינּוּיוֹ מָחוּל, לְחַלְיֵהּ לְקִינּוּיֵהּ וְלִבְעוֹל!

The Gemara cites proof: **Come** and **hear** another mishna (7a): When the husband takes the *sota* to the Temple, he first takes her to the local court, **and** the court **provides him** with **two Torah scholars** who accompany them, **lest he engage in sexual intercourse with her on the way** to the Temple, which is prohibited due to her status as a *sota*. **And if you say** that with regard to **a husband who retracted his warning, his warning is retracted, let him retract his warning and engage in sexual intercourse** with her.

מַאי שְׁנָא תַּלְמִידֵי חֲכָמִים? דִּגְמִירִי, דְּאִי בָּעֵי לְמִיבְעַל, אָמְרִי לֵיהּ: אַחְלֵיהּ לְקִינּוּיָיךְ וּבְעָלָהּ.

The Gemara replies that perhaps the husband can retract his warning: **What is different** about **Torah scholars** that they are chosen to accompany the husband? They differ from other people **as they are learned, and if** they see that the husband **desires to engage in sexual intercourse** with his wife, **they say to him: Retract your warning and** then you **may engage in sexual intercourse with her** in a permitted manner.

תָּא שְׁמַע: דְּאָמַר רַבִּי יֹאשִׁיָּה, שְׁלֹשָׁה דְּבָרִים סָח לִי זְעֵירָא מֵאַנְשֵׁי יְרוּשָׁלַיִם: בַּעַל שֶׁמָּחַל עַל קִינּוּיוֹ – קִינּוּיוֹ מָחוּל; וְזָקֵן מַמְרֵא שֶׁרָצוּ בֵּית דִּין לִמְחוֹל לוֹ – מוֹחֲלִין לוֹ; וּבֵן סוֹרֵר וּמוֹרֶה שֶׁרָצוּ אָבִיו וְאִמּוֹ לִמְחוֹל לוֹ – מוֹחֲלִין לוֹ.

The Gemara cites proof: **Come** and **hear that** which **Rabbi Yoshiya says: Ze'eira,** who was one **of the men of Jerusalem,**[P] **told me three matters: A husband who retracted his warning, his warning is retracted; and** in the case of **a rebellious Elder**[B] **whom the court wishes to forgive,** the court **may forgive him; and** in the case of **a stubborn and rebellious son**[BH] **whose father and mother wish to forgive him** for his sins, they **may forgive him.**

וּכְשֶׁבָּאתִי אֵצֶל חֲבֵירַי שֶׁבַּדָּרוֹם, עַל שְׁנַיִם הוֹדוּ לִי, וְעַל זָקֵן מַמְרֵא לֹא הוֹדוּ לִי, שֶׁלֹּא יִרְבּוּ מַחֲלוֹקֶת בְּיִשְׂרָאֵל; שְׁמַע מִינַּהּ: בַּעַל שֶׁמָּחַל עַל קִינּוּיוֹ – קִינּוּיוֹ מָחוּל. שְׁמַע מִינַּהּ.

And when I came to my colleagues in the South and told them these rulings, **they agreed with me with regard to two** of them, **but with regard to** forgiving **a rebellious Elder they did not agree with me.**[H] They held that a rebellious Elder cannot be forgiven, in order **that discord not proliferate among the Jewish people.** The Gemara comments: One **can conclude from** Rabbi Yoshiya's statement that with regard to **a husband who retracted his warning,**[H] **his warning is retracted.** The Gemara concludes: Indeed, one **can conclude from** Rabbi Yoshiya's statement that the husband can retract his warning.

פְּלִיגִי בָּהּ רַב אַחָא וְרָבִינָא – חַד אָמַר: קוֹדֶם סְתִירָה מָחוּל, לְאַחַר סְתִירָה אֵינוֹ מָחוּל. וְחַד אָמַר: לְאַחַר סְתִירָה נַמִּי מָחוּל. וּמִסְתַּבְּרָא כְּמַאן דְּאָמַר אֵינוֹ מָחוּל.

Rav Aḥa and Ravina disagree with regard to the limits of **this** *halakha* permitting a husband to retract his warning. **One says** that if he retracts his warning **before** her **seclusion** with another man, his warning **is retracted,** but if he retracts his warning **after** her **seclusion** with another man, it **is not retracted. And one says** that if he retracts his warning **after** her **seclusion** with another man, it **is also retracted. And it is reasonable** to hold **according to the one who says** that the husband's warning **is not retracted** after her seclusion with another man.

מִמַּאי? מִדְּקָא מַהַדְרִי רַבָּנַן לְרַבִּי יוֹסֵי; דְּתַנְיָא, רַבִּי יוֹסֵי אוֹמֵר: בַּעְלָהּ נֶאֱמָן עָלֶיהָ, מִקַּל וָחוֹמֶר: וּמָה נִדָּה שֶׁהִיא בְּכָרֵת – בַּעְלָהּ נֶאֱמָן עָלֶיהָ, סוֹטָה שֶׁהִיא בְּלָאו – לֹא כׇּל שֶׁכֵּן!

The Gemara asks: **From where** can one derive that after the wife's seclusion with another man, the warning cannot be retracted? It can be derived **from** the answer **that the Rabbis gave in reply to Rabbi Yosei, as it is taught** in a *baraita*: **Rabbi Yosei says:** It is unnecessary to provide an escort to accompany the *sota* and her husband, as the **husband** of a *sota* **is trusted** not to engage in sexual intercourse **with her, on** the basis of an *a fortiori* inference: **And just as** in the case of **a menstruating woman, who is** prohibited from engaging in sexual intercourse with her husband **by** penalty of *karet*, **her husband is** nevertheless **trusted with regard to her,** as he is permitted to seclude himself with her, so too, with regard to **a** *sota*, **who is** prohibited from engaging in sexual intercourse with her husband only **by an** ordinary **prohibition,** is it **not all the more so** that he should be trusted?

אָמְרוּ לוֹ: לֹא, אִם אָמַרְתָּ בְּנִדָּה שֶׁכֵּן יֵשׁ לָהּ הֵיתֵּר, תֹּאמַר בְּסוֹטָה שֶׁאֵין לָהּ הֵיתֵּר?

The Rabbis **said to** Rabbi Yosei: **No, if you say** that he is trusted **with regard to a menstruating woman,** the reason is not due to the severity of the prohibition. Rather, he is trusted **because she has** the ability to become **permitted** to her husband after her menstrual flow has ceased and she has immersed in a ritual bath. **Shall you** also **say** that he is trusted **with regard to a** *sota*, **who** potentially **does not have** the ability to become **permitted** to her husband, due to her suspected adultery?

PERSONALITIES

Ze'eira, of the men of Jerusalem – זְעֵירָא מֵאַנְשֵׁי יְרוּשָׁלַיִם: This scholar is mentioned in a few sources, and it appears from the names of his colleagues that he lived toward the end of the tannaitic period. He cites statements of the people of Jerusalem, referring to a small community that devotedly remained in the holy city of Jerusalem even after the destruction of the city and the subsequent period of persecution.

BACKGROUND

A rebellious Elder – זָקֵן מַמְרֵא: Whenever there was a major dispute among the Sages as to how a halakhic practice should be performed, the matter was brought before the Great Sanhedrin for clarification and resolution. If the Sanhedrin did not reach a unanimous conclusion, the matter was decided according to the majority, and the decision was binding upon the entire nation. A Sage could disagree with that decision, but he was obliged to follow the opinion of the majority and to instruct others to do so. If a Sage who was ordained and fit to serve in the Great Sanhedrin instructed others to follow his opinion in contradiction of the opinion of the majority, he was deemed a rebellious Elder and liable to be executed by strangulation, provided that the question in dispute was of a significant degree of importance.

A stubborn and rebellious son – בֵּן סוֹרֵר וּמוֹרֶה: The Torah (Deuteronomy 21:18–21) states that a stubborn and rebellious son, who does not obey his parents, is liable to receive the death penalty. The Sages explain that this refers to a child between the ages of thirteen and thirteen and three months who steals money from his parents in order to eat a gluttonous meal of meat and wine in the company of worthless men. If his parents bring him to court because of this act, he is exhorted to desist and is liable to receive lashes. If he repeats the same misdeed and is again brought to court within this three-month period, he is liable to receive the death penalty. The Gemara (*Sanhedrin* 72a) explains that the severe punishment in this case stems from the fact that this individual will inevitably continue down a path of moral deterioration, eventually becoming a robber and a murderer. Therefore, it is better that he should die innocent rather than guilty. The halakhic details limiting the application of this case are so restrictive that according to some of the Sages, this *halakha* was never put into practice. The details of this *halakha* are discussed in the eighth chapter of tractate *Sanhedrin*.

HALAKHA

And a stubborn and rebellious son, etc. – וּבֵן סוֹרֵר וּמוֹרֶה וכו׳: A stubborn and rebellious son whose parents forgave him before the court issued a verdict is exempt from being punished (Rambam *Sefer Shofetim*, *Hilkhot Mamrim* 7:8).

But with regard to forgiving a rebellious Elder they did not agree with me – וְעַל זָקֵן מַמְרֵא לֹא הוֹדוּ לִי: The court may not relinquish its honor and forgive a rebellious Elder. This is so that discord will not proliferate among the Jewish people (Rambam *Sefer Shofetim*, *Hilkhot Mamrim* 3:4).

A husband who retracted his warning, etc. – בַּעַל שֶׁמָּחַל עַל קִינּוּיוֹ וכו׳: The husband can retract his warning before his wife secludes herself with the other man; however, once the seclusion occurs, he cannot retract his warning. If one divorces his wife, the divorce effects a retraction of the warning; in a case where a husband issues a warning and later divorces his wife and subsequently remarries her, then if he wants to warn her he must issue a new warning (Rambam *Sefer Nashim*, *Hilkhot Sota* 1:7; *Shulḥan Arukh*, *Even HaEzer* 178:12).

וְאִי אָמְרַתְּ לְאַחַר סְתִירָה מָחוּל לָהּ, מַשְׁכַּחַתְּ לָהּ דְּיֵשׁ לָהּ הֶיתֵּר, דְּאִי בָּעֵי מָחֵיל לֵיהּ לְקִינּוּיֵהּ וּבָעֵיל! אֶלָּא שְׁמַע מִינָּהּ: לְאַחַר סְתִירָה אֵינוֹ מָחוּל. שְׁמַע מִינָּהּ.

The Gemara explains the proof: **And if you say** that **after** her **seclusion** with another man the warning can be **retracted for her, you** therefore **find** an instance in **which** the *sota* **has** the ability to become **permitted** to her husband, **as, if** the husband **desires** he **can retract his warning and engage in sexual intercourse** with her. **Rather, conclude from** the Rabbis' statement that if he retracts his warning **after** her **seclusion** with another man, the warning **is not retracted.** The Gemara concludes: Indeed, one can **conclude from** the Rabbis' statement that the warning cannot be retracted.

"מֵתוּ בַּעְלֵיהֶן עַד שֶׁלֹּא שָׁתוּ – בֵּית שַׁמַּאי" כו׳. בְּמַאי קָמִיפַּלְגִי? בֵּית שַׁמַּאי סָבְרִי: שְׁטָר הָעוֹמֵד לִגְבּוֹת כְּגָבוּי דָּמֵי,

§ The mishna states: **If the husbands** of the *sota* women **died before** their wives **drank** the bitter water, **Beit Shammai** say: They collect payment of their marriage contracts and they do not drink the bitter water. And Beit Hillel say: They either drink the bitter water or they do not collect payment of their marriage contracts. The Gemara asks: **With regard to what do** Beit Shammai and Beit Hillel **disagree?** The Gemara answers: **Beit Shammai hold** that a promissory **note that stands to be collected is considered** to be **as** though it was already **collected,** and since the woman possesses the marriage contract, the payment of the marriage contract is considered as though it is already in her possession. Since the burden of proof rests upon the claimant, she does not lose her rights to the money unless the inheritors prove that she committed adultery.

Perek **IV**
Daf **25** Amud **b**

וּבֵית הִלֵּל סָבְרִי: שְׁטָר הָעוֹמֵד לִגְבּוֹת לָאו כְּגָבוּי דָּמֵי.

And Beit Hillel hold that a promissory **note that stands to be collected is not considered as** though it was already **collected.** Therefore, the payment of the marriage contract is not considered to be in the wife's possession, and as this means that she is the claimant, she is not entitled to the money unless she proves that she did not commit adultery.

"מְעוּבֶּרֶת חֲבֵירוֹ" כו׳. אָמַר רַב נַחְמָן אָמַר רַבָּה בַּר אֲבוּהּ: מַחְלוֹקֶת – בַּעֲקָרָה וּזְקֵינָה,

§ The mishna states (24a): **A woman who was pregnant** with the child **of another** man at the time of her marriage… A sexually underdeveloped woman, who is incapable of bearing children [*ailonit*], and an elderly woman, and a woman who is incapable of giving birth for other reasons, neither collect payment of their marriage contracts nor drink the bitter water. Rabbi Elazar says: He can marry another woman and procreate through her; therefore these are considered permitted marriages, and the women can drink the bitter water. **Rav Naḥman says** that **Rabba bar Avuh says:** The **dispute** between the first *tanna* and Rabbi Elazar is only **in** the case of **a barren woman and an elderly woman.**

אֲבָל אַיְילוֹנִית – דִּבְרֵי הַכֹּל לֹא שׁוֹתָה וְלֹא נוֹטֶלֶת כְּתוּבָּתָהּ, שֶׁנֶּאֱמַר: "וְנִקְּתָה וְנִזְרְעָה זָרַע", מִי שֶׁדַּרְכָּהּ לְהַזְרִיעַ, יָצְאָה זוֹ שֶׁאֵין דַּרְכָּהּ לְהַזְרִיעַ.

However, with regard to **a sexually underdeveloped woman, all agree** that **she neither drinks** the bitter water **nor collects** payment of **her marriage contract.** This is **as it is stated** with regard to a *sota* who is found to be innocent of adultery: **"And she shall be cleared, and shall conceive seed"** (Numbers 5:28), indicating that the *sota* ritual pertains only to **one whose way is to bear seed** and give birth, **excluding this** sexually underdeveloped woman, **whose way is not to bear seed.**[N]

מֵיתִיבִי: הַמְקַנֵּא לַאֲרוּסָתוֹ וּלְשׁוֹמֶרֶת יָבָם שֶׁלּוֹ, אִם עַד שֶׁלֹּא כְּנָסָהּ נִסְתְּרָה – לֹא שׁוֹתָה וְלֹא נוֹטֶלֶת כְּתוּבָּתָהּ;

The Gemara **raises an objection** to Rav Naḥman's statement from a *baraita* in the *Tosefta* (5:4): With regard to **one who issues a warning to his betrothed, or to his** *yevama* while she is a **widow awaiting her** *yavam*,[H] **if she secluded herself** with the other man **before** her husband **consummated** the marriage, **she neither drinks** the bitter water **nor collects** payment of **her marriage contract.**

NOTES

Whose way is not to bear seed – שֶׁאֵין דַּרְכָּהּ לְהַזְרִיעַ: According to Rav Naḥman, it is necessary to differentiate between a sexually underdeveloped woman, who is essentially unable to bear children, and barren or elderly women, who do not usually give birth but are not essentially unable to do so (*Mishne LaMelekh*).

HALAKHA

One who issues a warning to his betrothed, or to his *yevama* while she is a widow awaiting her *yavam*, etc. – הַמְקַנֵּא לַאֲרוּסָתוֹ וּלְשׁוֹמֶרֶת יָבָם שֶׁלּוֹ וכו׳: If one issues a warning to his betrothed or to his *yevama* while she is awaiting levirate marriage and she secludes herself with the other man before the marriage is consummated, she neither drinks the bitter water nor collects payment of her marriage contract (Rambam *Sefer Nashim*, *Hilkhot Sota* 2:2).

מְעוּבֶּרֶת חֲבֵירוֹ וּמֵינֶקֶת חֲבֵירוֹ – לֹא שׁוֹתוֹת וְלֹא נוֹטְלוֹת כְּתוּבָּה, דִּבְרֵי רַבִּי מֵאִיר,

The *baraita* continues: **A woman who was pregnant** with the child **of another** man at the time of her marriage **and a woman who was nursing** the child **of another** man at the time of her marriage **neither drink** the bitter water **nor collect** payment of their **marriage contracts,** as their marriages were prohibited by rabbinic law. This is **the statement of Rabbi Meir.**

שֶׁהָיָה רַבִּי מֵאִיר אוֹמֵר: לֹא יִשָּׂא אָדָם מְעוּבֶּרֶת חֲבֵירוֹ וּמֵינֶקֶת חֲבֵירוֹ; וְאִם נָשָׂא – יוֹצִיא וְלֹא יַחֲזִיר עוֹלָמִית. וַחֲכָמִים אוֹמְרִים: יוֹצִיא, וּכְשֶׁיַּגִּיעַ זְמַנּוֹ לִכְנוֹס – יִכְנוֹס.

The *baraita* continues: The reason for this is **as Rabbi Meir would say: A man may not marry a woman who is pregnant**[H] with the child **of another** man **or a woman who is nursing** the child **of another** man, until twenty-four months pass after the baby's birth, so as to ensure that the woman will not become pregnant while the child needs to nurse. **And if he married** her, **he must divorce** her **and may never remarry** her, as the Sages penalized him for transgressing the prohibition. **And the Rabbis say: He must divorce** her, **and when his time to marry** her **arrives,**[H] i.e., twenty-four months after the baby's birth, **he can marry** her again.

וְהָרוֹבָא שֶׁנָּשָׂא עֲקָרָה וּזְקֵינָה, וְאֵין לוֹ אִשָּׁה וּבָנִים מֵעִיקָּרָא – לֹא שׁוֹתָה וְלֹא נוֹטֶלֶת כְּתוּבָּה. רַבִּי אֶלְעָזָר אוֹמֵר: יָכוֹל הוּא לִישָּׂא אַחֶרֶת וְלִפְרוֹת וְלִרְבּוֹת הֵימֶנָּה.

The *baraita* continues: In **the** case of a **young man who married a barren woman**[H] **or an elderly woman, and he did not have a wife and children beforehand,** the woman **neither drinks nor collects** payment of her **marriage contract,** as it is prohibited for him to marry a woman with whom he cannot procreate. **Rabbi Elazar says:** This marriage is not forbidden, as **he can marry another** woman **and procreate through her,** and therefore she can drink the bitter water.

אֲבָל הַמְקַנֵּא לַאֲרוּסָתוֹ וּלְשׁוֹמֶרֶת יָבָם שֶׁלּוֹ וּמִשֶּׁכְּנָסָהּ נִסְתְּרָה – אוֹ שׁוֹתָה אוֹ לֹא נוֹטֶלֶת כְּתוּבָּה. מְעוּבֶּרֶת וּמֵינֶקֶת עַצְמוֹ – אוֹ שׁוֹתָה אוֹ לֹא נוֹטֶלֶת כְּתוּבָּתָהּ. הָרוֹבָא שֶׁנָּשָׂא עֲקָרָה וּזְקֵינָה וְיֵשׁ לוֹ אִשָּׁה וּבָנִים – אוֹ שׁוֹתָה אוֹ לֹא נוֹטֶלֶת כְּתוּבָּה.

The *baraita* continues: **However,** in the case of **one who issued a warning to his betrothed,**[H] **or to his** *yevama* while she was a **widow awaiting her** *yavam*, **and she secluded herself** with the other man **after he consummated** the marriage, **she either drinks** the bitter water **or does not collect** payment of her **marriage contract.** If **his own pregnant or nursing** wife[NH] becomes a *sota*, then despite the concern that the bitter water may harm the fetus, she **either drinks** the bitter water **or does not collect** payment of **her marriage contract.** In **the** case of a **young man who married a barren woman or an elderly woman, and he** already **had a wife and children**[H] and was therefore permitted to marry his barren or elderly wife, the woman **either drinks** the bitter water **or does not collect** payment of her **marriage contract.**

NOTES

His own pregnant or nursing wife – מְעוּבֶּרֶת וּמֵינֶקֶת עַצְמוֹ: Rashi and the Rambam hold that a pregnant woman drinks the bitter water immediately, even though it might cause her death and, consequently, the death of the fetus. *Tosafot*, however, explain that she does not drink immediately. Rather, the ritual is delayed until she gives birth. This opinion is supported by the statement of Rabban Gamliel in the *Sifrei Zuta* that a *sota* does not drink the bitter water while she is pregnant.

HALAKHA

A man may not marry a woman who is pregnant, etc. – לֹא יִשָּׂא אָדָם מְעוּבֶּרֶת וכו׳: The Sages decreed that a man may not marry or betroth a woman who is pregnant with the child of another man or nursing the child of another man until twenty-four months elapse after the baby's birth. This prohibition applies both with regard to a widow and with regard to a divorcée. She may not marry even if she already entrusted her child to a wet nurse or weaned the child. However, if the child died she is permitted to remarry immediately. If the mother weaned the child during her husband's lifetime, or entrusted the child to a wet nurse three months before her husband's death, or if she is a woman who does not nurse her children at all, she is required to wait only three months from the time of her husband's death in order to remarry. These three months are required in order to differentiate between a child born from the first husband and a child born from the second husband (Rambam *Sefer Nashim, Hilkhot Geirushin* 11:25; *Shulḥan Arukh, Even HaEzer* 13:11).

He must divorce her and when his time to marry her arrives, etc. – יוֹצִיא וּכְשֶׁיַּגִּיעַ זְמַנּוֹ לִכְנוֹס וכו׳: If one marries a woman who is pregnant with the child of another man or nursing the child of another man, in violation of the rabbinic decree prohibiting this marriage, he is ostracized until he divorces her. This applies even if he is a priest and he will not be permitted to remarry her. If he is an Israelite, then after the period of twenty-four months elapses he is permitted to remarry her. If he married her and fled to a distant land from which he will not return until the twenty-four months elapse, then when he returns he may maintain her as his wife.

If one betrothed a pregnant or nursing woman, he is not forced to divorce her; however, he may not consummate the marriage until after the twenty-four months elapse. The Rema, however, writes that there is no distinction between marriage and betrothal, and he must divorce her. See the *Be'er Heitev* and the *Beit Shmuel*, who discuss whether it is possible to rely on the more lenient opinion in the case of a priest who betrothed a pregnant or nursing woman, since if he divorces her, he will not be permitted to remarry her (Rambam *Sefer Nashim, Hilkhot Geirushin* 11:28; *Shulḥan Arukh, Even HaEzer* 13:12).

A young man who married a barren woman, etc. – הָרוֹבָא שֶׁנָּשָׂא עֲקָרָה וכו׳: In the case of a man young enough to father a child who has not yet fulfilled the mitzva to procreate and who married a barren or elderly woman, if the woman secluded herself with another man after being warned, she does not drink the bitter water. She must be divorced and she does not collect payment of her marriage contract (Rambam *Sefer Nashim, Hilkhot Sota* 2:10).

One who issued a warning to his betrothed, etc. – הַמְקַנֵּא לַאֲרוּסָתוֹ וכו׳: In the case of one who issued a warning to his betrothed, or to his *yevama* while she was awaiting levirate marriage, and she secluded herself with the other man after the marriage was consummated, she may drink the bitter water (Rambam *Sefer Nashim, Hilkhot Sota* 2:5).

His own pregnant or nursing wife, etc. – מְעוּבֶּרֶת וּמֵינֶקֶת עַצְמוֹ וכו׳: A husband may have his pregnant or nursing wife drink the bitter water, even while she is pregnant or nursing. The *Arukh HaShulḥan*, citing *Tosafot*, rules that in the case of a pregnant woman the ritual is delayed until she gives birth (Rambam *Sefer Nashim, Hilkhot Sota* 2:7).

The case of a young man who married a barren woman… and he already had a wife and children, etc. – הָרוֹבָא שֶׁנָּשָׂא עֲקָרָה...וְיֵשׁ לוֹ אִשָּׁה וּבָנִים וכו׳: A barren, elderly, or sexually underdeveloped woman may drink the bitter water if her husband has already fulfilled the mitzva to procreate or if he was already married to a fertile woman. This is despite the fact that the Torah states with regard to a *sota* who is found to be innocent of adultery: "And she shall be cleared, and shall conceive seed" (Numbers 5:28). This verse does not exclude a woman who cannot give birth. Rather, the verse teaches that a fertile woman who is found by the *sota* ritual to be innocent of adultery is blessed by giving birth with ease, and by giving birth to male offspring (Rambam *Sefer Nashim, Hilkhot Sota* 2:10).

אֵשֶׁת מַמְזֵר לְמַמְזֵר, וְאֵשֶׁת נָתִין לְנָתִין, וְאֵשֶׁת גֵּר, וְעֶבֶד מְשׁוּחְרָר, וְאַיְילוֹנִית – אוֹ שׁוֹתָה אוֹ לֹא נוֹטֶלֶת כְּתוּבָּה. קָתָנֵי מִיהָא אַיְילוֹנִית. תְּיוּבְתֵּיהּ דְּרַב נַחְמָן!

The *baraita* concludes: With regard to **the wife of a *mamzer***[B] who is married **to a *mamzer***[H] in a permitted marriage, **and the wife of a Gibeonite** who is married **to a Gibeonite** in a permitted marriage, **and the wife of a convert or an emancipated slave, and a sexually underdeveloped woman,** if any of these women becomes a *sota* she **either drinks** the bitter water **or does not collect** payment of her **marriage contract,** as the marriage is permitted. After citing the entire *baraita,* the Gemara explains the difficulty: **In any event,** the *baraita* **teaches** that **a sexually underdeveloped woman** can drink the bitter water if the marriage is permitted, and this is **a conclusive refutation** of the opinion **of Rav Naḥman.**

אָמַר לָךְ רַב נַחְמָן: תַּנָּאֵי הִיא, וַאֲנָא דַּאֲמַרִי כִּי הַאי תַּנָּא; דְּתַנְיָא, רַבִּי שִׁמְעוֹן בֶּן אֶלְעָזָר אוֹמֵר: אַיְילוֹנִית לֹא שׁוֹתָה וְלֹא נוֹטֶלֶת כְּתוּבָּה, שֶׁנֶּאֱמַר: ״וְנִקְּתָה וְנִזְרְעָה זָרַע״, מִי שֶׁדַּרְכָּהּ לְהַזְרִיעַ, יָצְאתָה זוֹ שֶׁאֵין דַּרְכָּהּ לְהַזְרִיעַ.

The Gemara answers: **Rav Naḥman** could have **said to you:** There **is** a dispute between ***tanna'im*** with regard to this matter, **and I state** my opinion **in accordance with** the opinion of **this *tanna*, as it is taught** in a *baraita*: **Rabbi Shimon Ben Elazar says: A sexually underdeveloped woman neither drinks nor collects** payment of her **marriage contract, as it is stated: "And she shall be cleared, and shall conceive seed"** (Numbers 5:28), indicating that the *sota* ritual pertains only to **one whose way is to bear seed** and give birth, **excluding this** sexually underdeveloped woman, **whose way is not to bear seed.**

וְרַבָּנַן, הַאי ״וְנִקְּתָה וְנִזְרְעָה זָרַע״ מַאי עָבְדִי לֵיהּ? מִיבְּעֵי לְהוּ לְכִדְתַנְיָא: ״וְנִקְּתָה וְנִזְרְעָה [זָרַע]״ – שֶׁאִם הָיְתָה עֲקָרָה נִפְקֶדֶת, דִּבְרֵי רַבִּי עֲקִיבָא. אָמַר לוֹ רַבִּי יִשְׁמָעֵאל: אִם כֵּן, יִסָּתְרוּ כׇּל הָעֲקָרוֹת וְיִפָּקְדוּ, וְזוֹ הוֹאִיל וְלֹא נִסְתְּרָה הִפְסִידָה!

The Gemara asks: **And** as for **the Rabbis, what do they do with this** verse: **"And she shall be cleared, and shall conceive seed"?** Since they hold that a sexually underdeveloped woman drinks the bitter water, what do they derive from the verse? The Gemara answers: **They require** it **for that which is taught** in a *baraita*: The verse: **"And she shall be cleared, and shall conceive seed"** (Numbers 5:28), indicates **that if she was barren, she will be remembered** and conceive a child; this is **the statement of Rabbi Akiva. Rabbi Yishmael said to him: If so, all the barren women will seclude themselves** with other men, **and they will be remembered** and conceive after drinking the bitter water and being found innocent; **but that** virtuous barren woman, who does not transgress the prohibition of seclusion, **since she does not seclude herself** with other men, **she loses** the opportunity to receive this blessing.

אִם כֵּן, מָה תַּלְמוּד לוֹמַר: ״וְנִקְּתָה וְנִזְרְעָה זָרַע״? שֶׁאִם הָיְתָה יוֹלֶדֶת בְּצַעַר – יוֹלֶדֶת בְּרֶיוַח, נְקֵבוֹת – יוֹלֶדֶת זְכָרִים, קְצָרִים – יוֹלֶדֶת אֲרוּכִּים, שְׁחוֹרִים – יוֹלֶדֶת לְבָנִים.

Rabbi Yishmael continues: **If so, what** is the meaning when **the verse states: "And she shall be cleared, and shall conceive seed"** (Numbers 5:28)? This means **that if** in the past she **would give birth in pain,** from then on **she will give birth with ease;** if she gave birth to **females, she will** now **give birth to males;** if her children were **short, she will** now **give birth to tall** children; if her children were **black, she will give birth to white** children.

״אֵשֶׁת מַמְזֵר לְמַמְזֵר״. פְּשִׁיטָא! מַהוּ דְּתֵימָא: אַפּוּשֵׁי פְּסוּלִין לָא לֵיפוּשׁ. קָא מַשְׁמַע לָן.

§ The *baraita* in the *Tosefta* cited above states: **The wife of a *mamzer*** who is married **to a *mamzer*** in a permitted marriage… either drinks the bitter water or does not collect payment of her marriage contract. The Gemara asks: **Isn't** that **obvious?** Since their marriage is permitted, why should the *sota* ritual not apply? The Gemara answers: It is necessary **lest you say** that she should not drink, since if she drinks and is found to be innocent of adultery, she is permitted to her husband. This is undesirable since their offspring are also *mamzerim,* and **we do not cause** the number of individuals **of flawed lineage to proliferate.** The *baraita* in the *Tosefta* therefore **teaches us** that this is not a concern, and the wife of a *mamzer* is permitted to drink.

״אֵשֶׁת גֵּר וְעֶבֶד מְשׁוּחְרָר וְאַיְילוֹנִית״. פְּשִׁיטָא!

The aforementioned *baraita* in the *Tosefta* states: **The wife of a convert or an emancipated slave, and a sexually underdeveloped woman** can drink the bitter water. The Gemara asks with regard to the wife of a convert or an emancipated slave, who also has the status of a convert: **Isn't** that **obvious?** Since their marriage is permitted, why should the *sota* ritual not apply?

BACKGROUND

Mamzer – מַמְזֵר: A *mamzer* or *mamzeret* is the male or female offspring, respectively, of an adulterous or incestuous relationship, i.e., a child born from relations between a married woman and a man other than her husband, or between relatives who are prohibited from marrying by a prohibition punishable by *karet*. The case of a child conceived through relations with a menstruating woman is an exception to this principle, as, although engaging in sexual relations with a menstruating woman is punishable by *karet*, the child is not a *mamzer* or *mamzeret*. Similarly, a child conceived out of wedlock by a man and woman who are permitted to marry is not a *mamzer* or *mamzeret*. A *mamzer* is prohibited from marrying a Jewish woman of unflawed lineage. However, he may marry a convert or a *mamzeret*. Similarly, a *mamzeret* can marry only a convert or a *mamzer*. The offspring of these unions are also *mamzerim*. A *mamzer* inherits from his father and is considered his father's son in all respects.

HALAKHA

The wife of a *mamzer* who is married to a *mamzer*, etc. – אֵשֶׁת מַמְזֵר לְמַמְזֵר וכו׳: If a woman is a convert, or an emancipated maidservant, or the wife of a convert or emancipated slave, or a *mamzeret*, or the wife of a *mamzer*, if she was permitted to her husband, she may drink the bitter water (Rambam *Sefer Nashim*, *Hilkhot Sota* 2:6).

מַהוּ דְּתֵימָא? ״דַּבֵּר אֶל בְּנֵי יִשְׂרָאֵל״ – וְלֹא גֵּרִים. קָא מַשְׁמַע לַן. וְאֵימָא הָכִי נַמִי! ״וְאָמַרְתָּ״ – רִבּוּיָא הוּא.

The Gemara answers: It is necessary **lest you say** that she does not drink, as the verse states: **"Speak to the children of Israel,** and say unto them: If the wife of any man goes astray, and acts unfaithfully against him" (Numbers 5:12). One might have inferred from this verse that the *sota* ritual applies only to those born as Jews **and not** to **converts;** the *baraita* in the *Tosefta* therefore **teaches us** that this is not so. The Gemara asks: Why not **say** that **indeed** the verse excludes converts? The Gemara answers: The subsequent term: **"And say** unto them" (Numbers 5:12) **is an amplification,** which serves to include converts.

״אֵשֶׁת כֹּהֵן שׁוֹתָה״ כו׳. ״אֵשֶׁת כֹּהֵן שׁוֹתָה״ פְּשִׁיטָא! מַהוּ דְּתֵימָא? ״וְהִיא לֹא נִתְפָּשָׂה״ אֲסוּרָה, הָא נִתְפְּשָׂה מוּתֶּרֶת, וְזוֹ הוֹאִיל וְנִתְפְּשָׂה אֲסוּרָה – אֵימָא לֹא תִּשְׁתֶּה. קָא מַשְׁמַע לַן.

§ The mishna states: **The wife of a priest drinks** the bitter water, and if she is found to be innocent of adultery she is permitted to her husband. The Gemara asks: Why does the mishna state: **The wife of a priest drinks? Isn't** that **obvious?** The Gemara answers: It is necessary **lest you say** that she does not drink, as the verse states: "And a man lay with **her… neither was she seized"** (Numbers 5:13). This indicates that if the *sota* was not seized **she is forbidden; however,** if she was **seized,** i.e., raped, she is **permitted** to her husband. **And** with regard to **this** woman, the wife of a priest, **since** even if she was **seized** she is **forbidden** to her husband, as a priest may not remain married to his wife if she was raped while they were married, one might **say** that the *sota* ritual does not apply to her, and she **does not drink.** Therefore, the mishna **teaches us** that she does drink.

״וּמוּתֶּרֶת לְבַעְלָהּ״. פְּשִׁיטָא! אָמַר רַב הוּנָא: בְּמִתְנַוְּונָה. מִתְנַוְּונָה, הָא בְּדָקוּהָ מַיָּא!

§ The mishna states: The wife of a priest drinks, **and** if she is found to be innocent of adultery, **she is permitted to her husband.** The Gemara asks: **Isn't** that **obvious? Rav Huna says:** The mishna is referring to a case **where** the woman's health **deteriorates** after she drinks the bitter water, and one might have thought that she is defiled. The Gemara asks: In the case of a woman whose health **deteriorates, hasn't the** bitter **water** already **evaluated** that **she** was unfaithful? The fact that her health deteriorates indicates that she is defiled and forbidden to her husband, and her death is delayed due to her merit in other matters.

בְּמִתְנַוְּונָה דֶּרֶךְ אֵבָרִים. מַהוּ דְּתֵימָא? הָא זַנּוֹיֵי זַנַּאי, וְהָא דְּלָא בְּדָקוּהָ מַיָּא כִּי אוֹרְחֵיהּ – מִשּׁוּם דְּבְאוֹנֶס זַנַּאי, וּלְגַבֵּי כֹּהֵן אֲסִירָא. קָא מַשְׁמַע לַן.

The Gemara answers: The mishna is referring to a case **where her** health **deteriorates,** but not in the manner of a *sota*, who is afflicted in her belly and thighs (see Numbers 5:27). Rather, she is afflicted **by way of** other **limbs.**[H] **Lest you say: This** woman **engaged in licentious intercourse, and** the fact **that the** bitter **water did not evaluate her in** the **usual manner is because she engaged in licentious intercourse under duress, and with regard to a priest,** even rape **renders her forbidden to her** to her husband, the mishna therefore **teaches us** that the woman's deteriorating health does not indicate anything.

״אֵשֶׁת סָרִיס שׁוֹתָה״. פְּשִׁיטָא! מַהוּ דְּתֵימָא: ״מִבַּלְעֲדֵי אִישֵׁךְ״ אָמַר רַחֲמָנָא, וְהַאי לָאו בַּר הָכִי הוּא. קָא מַשְׁמַע לַן.

§ The mishna states: **The wife of a eunuch drinks.** The Gemara asks: **Isn't** that **obvious?** Since their marriage is permitted, why should the *sota* ritual not apply? The Gemara replies: It is necessary **lest you say** that she does not drink, since **the Merciful One states** with regard to the *sota*: "But if you have gone astray while under your husband, and if you are defiled, and some man has lain with you **besides your husband"** (Numbers 5:20). This indicates that her husband had lain with her, **and this** husband, the eunuch, **is not capable of that.** The mishna therefore **teaches us** that the wife of a eunuch does drink the bitter water.

״עַל יְדֵי כׇּל עֲרָיוֹת מְקַנִּין״. פְּשִׁיטָא!

§ The mishna states: A husband **can issue a warning** to his wife **with regard to all those with whom relations are forbidden,** e.g., her father or brother. The Gemara asks: **Isn't** that **obvious?**

HALAKHA

Where her health deteriorates by way of other limbs – בְּמִתְנַוְּונָה דֶּרֶךְ אֵבָרִים: A *sota* who drinks the bitter water and does not die immediately is permitted to her husband, even if he is a priest. She is permitted to him even if she is afflicted by sickness, as long as her belly does not swell and her thigh does not fall (see Numbers 5:27). However, if her belly begins to swell and her thigh begins to fall, she is certainly forbidden to her husband, in accordance with the statement of Rav Huna (Rambam *Sefer Nashim*, *Hilkhot Sota* 3:21).

מַהוּ דְּתֵימָא: "וְנִטְמְאָה", "נִטְמָאָה" שְׁנֵי פְּעָמִים – אֶחָד לַבַּעַל וְאֶחָד לַבּוֹעֵל, הֵיכָא דְּקָא מִיתַּסְרָא בְּהָא זְנוּת, אֲבָל הָא הוֹאִיל וַאֲסוּרָה וְקַיְימָא – אֵימָא לָא. קָא מַשְׁמַע לַן.

The Gemara answers: It is necessary, **lest you say** that the *sota* ritual does not apply with regard to forbidden relatives, as the Torah states: "And she **was defiled**" (Numbers 5:13), "And she **was defiled**" (Numbers 5:14), **two times. One** verse teaches that she is defiled and forbidden **to** her **husband, and one** verse teaches that she is forbidden **to** her **paramour.** One might understand that the *sota* ritual applies only **where she is forbidden** to the paramour **due to this licentious intercourse; however,** with regard to **that** woman, who secluded herself with a forbidden relative, **since** the woman already **stands prohibited** to him due to the prohibition of incest, one might **say** that the *sota* ritual **does not** apply. The mishna therefore **teaches us** that one can issue a warning even with regard to forbidden relatives.

"חוּץ מִן הַקָּטָן" וכו'. "אִישׁ" אָמַר רַחֲמָנָא – וְלֹא קָטָן. "וְשֶׁאֵינוֹ אִישׁ" לְמַעוּטֵי מַאי? אִילֵימָא לְמַעוּטֵי שָׁחוּף – וְהָאָמַר שְׁמוּאֵל: שָׁחוּף מְקַנִּין עַל יָדוֹ וּפוֹסֵל בִּתְרוּמָה.

§ The mishna states: A husband can issue a warning to his wife with regard to all those with whom relations are forbidden, **with the exception of a minor** and of one who is not a man. The Gemara cites the source for this *halakha*: **The Merciful One states** in the Torah: "And **a man** lay with her" (Numbers 5:13), indicating that one can warn his wife with regard to a man **but not** with regard to **a minor.**[N] The Gemara asks: The phrase: **And** of one **who is not a man,** serves **to exclude what? If we say** that it serves **to exclude a sick man who lacks the ability to complete intercourse** [***shaḥuf***],[NB] **but didn't Shmuel say: One can issue a warning with regard to a *shaḥuf*,**[H] **and** if a *shaḥuf* engages in sexual intercourse with the daughter of a priest, he **disqualifies** her **from** partaking of ***teruma***.[H]

"מְקַנִּין עַל יָדוֹ", פְּשִׁיטָא! מַהוּ דְּתֵימָא: "וְשָׁכַב אִישׁ אֹתָהּ שִׁכְבַת זֶרַע" אָמַר רַחֲמָנָא, וְהָא לָאו בַּר הָכִי הוּא. קָא מַשְׁמַע לַן.

With regard to Shmuel's statement that **one can issue a warning with regard to** a *shaḥuf*, the Gemara asks: **Isn't** that **obvious?** The Gemara answers: It is necessary, **lest you say** that one cannot issue a warning with regard to a *shaḥuf*, as **the Merciful One states** in the Torah: **"And a man lay with her carnally** [***shikhvat zera***]" (Numbers 5:13), literally, a lying of seed, **and this** man **is not capable of that,** as he cannot ejaculate. Shmuel therefore **teaches us** that one can issue a warning with regard to a *shaḥuf*.

"וּפוֹסֵל בִּתְרוּמָה", פְּשִׁיטָא! מַהוּ דְּתֵימָא: "לֹא יְחַלֵּל זַרְעוֹ" אָמַר רַחֲמָנָא – דְּאִית לֵיהּ זֶרַע לִיחַלֵּל, דְּלֵית לֵיהּ זֶרַע לָא לִיחַלֵּל. קָא מַשְׁמַע לַן.

The Gemara asks with regard to Shmuel's statement that a *shaḥuf* who engages in sexual intercourse with the daughter of a priest **disqualifies** her **from** partaking of ***teruma***: **Isn't** that **obvious?** The Gemara answers: It is necessary **lest you say** that a *shaḥuf* does not disqualify the daughter of a priest from partaking of *teruma*, as **the Merciful One states** in the Torah with regard to a priest: "And **he shall not disqualify his offspring** among his people" (Leviticus 21:15). One might infer from this verse that one **who** can **have offspring disqualifies** a woman from partaking of *teruma*, through forbidden sexual intercourse, and that one **who cannot have offspring does not disqualify** a woman from partaking of *teruma*. Shmuel therefore **teaches us** that this is not so. In any event, Shmuel states that one can issue a warning on account of a *shaḥuf*, unlike the initial interpretation of the mishna.

HALAKHA

One can issue a warning with regard to a *shaḥuf* – שָׁחוּף מְקַנִּין עַל יָדוֹ: A man can issue a warning to his wife even on account of a *shaḥuf*, who is unable to maintain an erection and cannot ejaculate. If she subsequently secludes herself with the *shaḥuf* she is forbidden to her husband (Rambam *Sefer Nashim, Hilkhot Sota* 1:1; *Shulḥan Arukh, Even HaEzer* 178:2).

If a *shaḥuf* engages in intercourse with the daughter of a priest he disqualifies her from partaking of *teruma* – ...שָׁחוּף וּפוֹסֵל בִּתְרוּמָה: A woman who engaged in prohibited intercourse, even with a *shaḥuf*, is disqualified from partaking of *teruma* (Rambam *Sefer Zera'im, Hilkhot Terumot* 8:11).

NOTES

A man but not a minor – אִישׁ...וְלֹא קָטָן: The Rambam explains that this excludes a minor under the age of nine, whose sexual act does not have the legal status of a sexual act. Although a minor's sexual act does not render a woman forbidden to her husband, a verse is required in order to exclude a minor, as one might have thought that due to the husband's objection to this contact, he may issue a warning. An alternative approach is provided by *Tosafot*, who explain that the verse excludes all minors, i.e., anyone under the age of thirteen. Despite the fact that the sexual act of a minor above the age of nine renders a woman forbidden to her husband, the verse nevertheless states that one may issue a warning only on account of a man, i.e., one who has reached majority (see *Ḥeshek Shlomo*).

A sick man who lacks the ability to complete intercourse [*shaḥuf*] – שָׁחוּף: There are various opinions with regard to the exact definition of a *shaḥuf*. For the purposes of this discussion, a *shaḥuf* is an individual who suffers from impotency and is unable to properly engage in sexual intercourse. He can engage in intercourse with a flaccid penis, but this is not considered intercourse, except with regard to disqualifying a woman from partaking of *teruma*. The Meiri explains that one may issue a warning on account of a *shaḥuf* because, unlike a eunuch, a *shaḥuf* is sometimes able to maintain a partial erection.

BACKGROUND

A sick man who lacks the ability to complete intercourse [*shaḥuf*] – שָׁחוּף: The term *shaḥuf* refers to a sick individual whose illness prevents him from properly absorbing and digesting food. This causes excessive weight loss due to the body exhausting its supply of fatty tissue, and also causes impotency and a lack of sexual desire. These symptoms can appear, for example, in severe cases of diabetes mellitus.

HALAKHA

One can issue a warning with regard to a gentile – נׇכְרִי מְקַנֵּין עַל יָדוֹ: If one issued a warning to his wife on account of a gentile, and she then secluded herself with that gentile, she is forbidden to her husband (Rambam *Sefer Nashim, Hilkhot Sota* 1:1; *Shulḥan Arukh, Even HaEzer* 178:2).

If a gentile engages in intercourse with the daughter of a priest he disqualifies her from partaking of *teruma* – נׇכְרִי...וּפוֹסֵל בִּתְרוּמָה: A woman who engages in sexual intercourse with a gentile acquires the legal status of a *zona* and is disqualified from marrying a priest. If she is the daughter of a priest she is also disqualified from partaking of *teruma* (Rambam *Sefer Kedusha, Hilkhot Issurei Bia* 18:2).

The concept of licentiousness does not apply with regard to an animal – אֵין זְנוּת בִּבְהֵמָה: A woman who engages in intercourse with an animal does not acquire the legal status of a *zona*, i.e., a woman who has engaged in sexual intercourse with a man forbidden to her, and is not disqualified from marrying a priest. This is so despite the fact that this act is punishable by stoning (Rambam *Sefer Kedusha, Hilkhot Issurei Bia* 18:1; *Shulḥan Arukh, Even HaEzer* 6:8).

וְאֶלָּא לְמַעוּטֵי נׇכְרִי? וְהָאָמַר רַב הַמְנוּנָא: נׇכְרִי מְקַנֵּין עַל יָדוֹ וּפוֹסֵל בִּתְרוּמָה.

Since Shmuel's statement contradicts the suggestion that the mishna excludes a *shaḥuf*, the Gemara suggests another explanation: **Rather,** the mishna serves **to exclude a gentile,** and teaches that one cannot issue a warning with regard to him. The Gemara asks: **But didn't Rav Hamnuna say: One can issue a warning with regard to a gentile,**[H] **and** if a gentile engages in sexual intercourse with the daughter of a priest, he **disqualifies** her **from** partaking of ***teruma***.[H]

״מְקַנֵּין עַל יָדוֹ״, פְּשִׁיטָא! מַהוּ דְּתֵימָא: ״נִטְמְאָה״, ״נִטְמָאָה״ שְׁתֵּי פְּעָמִים – אֶחָד לַבַּעַל וְאֶחָד לַבּוֹעֵל הֵיכָא דְּקָמִיתַּסְרָא בְּהָא זְנוּת, אֲבָל הָא הוֹאִיל וַאֲסוּרָה וְקָיְימָא – אֵימָא לָא. קָמַשְׁמַע לָן.

The Gemara asks with regard to Rav Hamnuna's statement that **one can issue a warning with regard to** a gentile: **Isn't** that **obvious?** The Gemara answers: It is necessary **lest you say** that one cannot issue a warning in this case, as the verse states: "And she **was defiled**" (Numbers 5:13), "And she **was defiled**" (Numbers 5:14), **twice. One** verse teaches that she is defiled and forbidden **to** her **husband, and one** verse teaches that she is forbidden **to** her **paramour.** One might understand that the *sota* ritual applies only **where she is forbidden** to the paramour **due to this licentious intercourse; however,** with regard to **that** woman, who engaged in sexual intercourse with a gentile, **since** she already **stands prohibited** to him, one might **say** that the *sota* ritual **does not** apply. Rav Hamnuna therefore **teaches us** that one can issue a warning even with regard to a gentile.

״וּפוֹסֵל בִּתְרוּמָה״, פְּשִׁיטָא! מַהוּ דְּתֵימָא? ״וּבַת כֹּהֵן כִּי תִהְיֶה לְאִישׁ זָר״ אָמַר רַחֲמָנָא – דְּבַר הֲוָיָה אִין, דְּלָאו בַּר הֲוָיָה לָא. קָמַשְׁמַע לָן דְּפָסֵיל מִדְּרַבִּי יוֹחָנָן,

The Gemara asks with regard to Rav Hamnuna's statement that a gentile who engages in sexual intercourse with the daughter of a priest **disqualifies** her **from** partaking of ***teruma*: Isn't** that **obvious?** The Gemara answers: It is necessary **lest you say** that he does not disqualify her, as **the Merciful One states** in the Torah: **"And if a priest's daughter should be unto a strange man,** she shall not eat of that which is set apart from the holy things" (Leviticus 22:12), indicating that if a woman engages in sexual intercourse with one who is unfit for her, he disqualifies her from partaking of *teruma*. Since the term "should be unto" denotes marriage, one might say **that one who is eligible for betrothal, yes,** he disqualifies the woman; but a gentile, **who is not eligible for betrothal, does not** disqualify her. Rav Hamnuna therefore **teaches us that** a gentile **disqualifies** the woman from partaking of *teruma*, as one can learn **from** the ruling **of Rabbi Yoḥanan.**

דְּאָמַר רַבִּי יוֹחָנָן מִשּׁוּם רַבִּי יִשְׁמָעֵאל: מִנַּיִן לְנׇכְרִי וְעֶבֶד שֶׁבָּאוּ עַל הַכֹּהֶנֶת וְעַל הַלְּוִיָּיה וְעַל בַּת יִשְׂרָאֵל שֶׁפְּסָלוּהָ? שֶׁנֶּאֱמַר: ״וּבַת כֹּהֵן כִּי תִהְיֶה אַלְמָנָה וּגְרוּשָׁה״ – מִי שֶׁיֵּשׁ לוֹ אַלְמָנוּת וְגֵירוּשִׁין בָּהּ, יָצְאוּ נׇכְרִי וְעֶבֶד שֶׁאֵין לוֹ אַלְמָנוּת וְגֵירוּשִׁין בָּהּ!

This is **as Rabbi Yoḥanan says in the name of Rabbi Yishmael: From where** is it derived **that a gentile or a slave who engaged in sexual intercourse with the daughter of a priest or with the daughter of a Levite or with** the **daughter of an Israelite, disqualified her** from marrying a priest and from partaking of *teruma*? This is derived **as it is stated: "But if a priest's daughter should be a widow or a divorcée…** she returns to her father's house… she may eat of her father's bread" (Leviticus 22:13). This indicates that the daughter of a priest returns to eat of her father's bread, i.e., *teruma*, if she engaged in sexual intercourse with **one whose** marriage **to her has** the potential to end in **widowhood or divorce,** i.e., a Jew whom she is permitted to marry. This **excludes a gentile and a slave, whose** marriage **to her does not have** the potential to end in **widowhood or divorce,** as their betrothal is invalid.

וְאֶלָּא לְמַעוּטֵי מַאי? אָמַר רַב פַּפָּא: לְמַעוּטֵי בְּהֵמָה, דְּאֵין זְנוּת בִּבְהֵמָה.

Since Rav Hamnuna's statement contradicts the suggestion that the mishna excludes a gentile, the Gemara asks: **Rather, what** does the term: And of one who is not a man, serve **to exclude? Rav Pappa says:** This serves **to exclude an animal, as** the concept of **licentiousness does not** apply **with regard to an animal.**[H] Therefore, the *halakhot* of a *sota* do not apply in this case.

אֲמַר לֵיהּ רָבָא מִפַּרְזַקְיָא לְרַב אַשִׁי: מְנָא הָא מִילְּתָא דַּאֲמוּר רַבָּנַן אֵין זְנוּת בִּבְהֵמָה? דִּכְתִיב: ״לֹא תָבִיא אֶתְנַן זוֹנָה וּמְחִיר כֶּלֶב״ וגו׳,

Rava of Parzakya said to Rav Ashi: From where is this matter that the Sages stated derived, that **licentiousness does not** apply **with regard to an animal?** Rav Ashi replied that it is **as it is written: "You shall not bring the hire of a harlot, or the price of a dog,** into the house of the Lord your God for any vow; for both of them are an abomination to the Lord your God" (Deuteronomy 23:19). This verse prohibits one from sacrificing an animal that served as payment to a prostitute or as payment for the purchase of a dog.

וְתַנְיָא: אֶתְנַן כֶּלֶב וּמְחִיר זוֹנָה – מוּתָּרִין, שֶׁנֶּאֱמַר: "גַּם שְׁנֵיהֶם", שְׁנַיִם וְלֹא אַרְבָּעָה.

And it is taught in a mishna (*Temura* 30a): In the converse cases, **the hire of a dog,** i.e., a kosher animal that was given to the owner of a dog as payment for engaging in intercourse with it, **and the price of a prostitute,**[H] i.e., a kosher animal which served as payment in the purchase of a maidservant acquired for prostitution, **are permitted** to be sacrificed, **as it is stated** in the aforementioned verse: **For both of them.** This term indicates that only those **two** animals may not be sacrificed, i.e., those which served as the hire of a harlot and as the price of a dog; **and not four** animals, as the reverse cases are excluded from this *halakha*. This indicates that the concept of licentiousness does not apply with regard to animals, as the payment for intercourse with a dog is not considered payment for prostitution.

וְאֶלָּא "שִׁכְבַת זֶרַע" לָמָּה לִי? מִיבָּעֵי לֵיהּ לְכִדְתַנְיָא: "שִׁכְבַת זֶרַע" – פְּרָט לְדָבָר אַחֵר.

The Gemara asks: Shmuel states that one can issue a warning with regard to a *shaḥuf* even though he is unable to discharge semen. **But rather, why do I** need the verse to state: "And a man lay with her **carnally** [***shikhvat zera***]" (Numbers 5:13)? The Gemara answers: It is **necessary for that which is taught** in a *baraita*: The term **"*shikhvat zera*" excludes something else.**

מַאי "דָּבָר אַחֵר"? אָמַר רַב שֵׁשֶׁת: פְּרָט לְשֶׁקִּינֵּא לָהּ שֶׁלֹּא כְּדַרְכָּהּ. אֲמַר לֵיהּ רָבָא: שֶׁלֹּא כְּדַרְכָּהּ, "מִשְׁכְּבֵי אִשָּׁה" כְּתִיב!

The Gemara asks: **What is** meant by the term: **Something else? Rav Sheshet said:** This **excludes** a case **where** the husband **issued a warning to** his wife not to engage in sexual intercourse **in an atypical manner,** i.e., anal intercourse, with another man, and teaches that this is not considered a valid warning. **Rava said to** Rav Sheshet: Intercourse **in an atypical manner** is considered sexual intercourse, as **it is written: "The cohabitations of a woman"** (Leviticus 18:22), indicating that there are two forms of sexual intercourse with a woman, vaginal and anal, and there is no halakhic differentiation between them.

אֶלָּא אָמַר רָבָא: פְּרָט לְשֶׁקִּינֵּא לָהּ דֶּרֶךְ אֵבָרִים. אֲמַר לֵיהּ אַבַּיֵי: פְּרִיצוּתָא בְּעָלְמָא הִיא, וּפְרִיצוּתָא מִי אָסַר רַחֲמָנָא?

Rather, Rava said: It **excludes** a case **where** the husband **issued a warning to** his wife not to engage in intimate contact with another man **by way of** other **limbs,**[HN] as this is not considered sexual intercourse. **Abaye said to** Rava: That **is merely licentious** behavior, **and does the Merciful One render** a woman **forbidden** to her husband on account of merely **licentious** behavior, without sexual intercourse? Since this does not render her forbidden to her husband, it is obvious that if the husband issues a warning in this manner, violating the warning does not cause her to become a *sota*. The verse is therefore not required to exclude this case.

אֶלָּא אָמַר אַבַּיֵי: פְּרָט לְשֶׁקִּינֵּא לָהּ בִּנְשִׁיקָה. הָנִיחָא לְמַאן דְּאָמַר: הַעֲרָאָה זוֹ הַכְנָסַת עֲטָרָה, אֲבָל נְשִׁיקָה וְלָא כְּלוּם הִיא, הַיְינוּ דְּאָתֵי קְרָא לְמַעוּטֵי נְשִׁיקָה. אֶלָּא לְמַאן דְּאָמַר: הַעֲרָאָה זוֹ נְשִׁיקָה, מַאי אִיכָּא לְמֵימַר?

Rather, Abaye said: The verse **excludes** a case **where** the husband **issued a warning to** his wife **with regard to** engaging in genital **contact** without actual penetration. The Gemara asks: **This works out well according to the one who says** that the definition of the **initial stage of intercourse is the insertion of the corona**[H] **but** that genital **contact is nothing; this is** the reason **that the verse came to exclude** genital **contact. However, according to the one who says** that the definition of the **initial stage of intercourse is** genital **contact, what is there to say?** Why should this case be excluded from the *halakhot* of a *sota*?

לְעוֹלָם לְשֶׁקִּינֵּא לָהּ דֶּרֶךְ אֵבָרִים, וּמַהוּ דְּתֵימָא? בִּקְפֵידָא דְּבַעַל תַּלְיָא רַחֲמָנָא, וּבַעַל הָא קָא קָפֵיד. קָמַשְׁמַע לָן.

The Gemara answers: **Actually,** the verse serves **to** exclude a case **where** the husband **issued a warning to** his wife not to engage in intimate contact with another man **by way of** other **limbs. And** the verse explicitly excludes this case from the *halakhot* of a *sota*, **lest you say that** the woman is rendered a *sota* due to this warning, as **the Merciful One made** this *halakha* **dependent on** the **husband's objection, and** the **husband objects** to contact of this nature. The verse therefore **teaches us** that this is not considered a warning, as it does not involve sexual intercourse.

אָמַר שְׁמוּאֵל: יִשָּׂא אָדָם

§ **Shmuel says:** It is better that **a man marry**

HALAKHA

The hire of a dog and the price of a prostitute – אֶתְנַן כֶּלֶב וּמְחִיר זוֹנָה: The hire of a dog, i.e., an animal given as payment for engaging in intercourse with a dog, and the price of a prostitute, i.e., an animal which served as payment in the purchase of a prostitute, are permitted to be sacrificed on the altar (Rambam *Sefer Avoda, Hilkhot Issurei Mizbe'aḥ* 4:18).

Excludes a case where he issued a warning to her not to engage in intimate contact by way of other limbs – פְּרָט לְשֶׁקִּינֵּא לָהּ דֶּרֶךְ אֵבָרִים: The Rambam rules that if a woman's husband issued a warning to her, and she then secluded herself with another man and is given the bitter water to drink, if she engaged only in intimate contact with the paramour by way of other limbs, she is not evaluated by the bitter water. The *Arukh HaShulhan*, citing Rashi, rules that if the husband specified in his warning that she should not engage in intimate conduct with another man by way of other limbs, the warning is not a valid warning (Rambam *Sefer Nashim, Hilkhot Sota* 3:24).

The initial stage of intercourse is the insertion of the corona – הַעֲרָאָה זוֹ הַכְנָסַת עֲטָרָה: The initial stage of intercourse is the insertion of the corona into the vagina, and the final stage is the complete penetration of the penis. With regard to prohibited sexual intercourse, there is no difference between the initial stage of intercourse and complete intercourse (Rambam *Sefer Kedusha, Hilkhot Issurei Bia* 1:10; *Shulḥan Arukh, Even HaEzer* 20:1).

NOTES

Where he issued a warning to her not to engage in intimate contact by way of other limbs – לְשֶׁקִּינֵּא לָהּ דֶּרֶךְ אֵבָרִים: According to Rashi and *Tosafot* (*Yevamot* 55b), the Gemara is referring to a case where the husband issued a warning to his wife not to seclude herself with another man and engage in intimate contact by way of other limbs, without suspecting her of engaging in actual sexual intercourse with another man. Although a husband may issue a warning merely by saying: Do not seclude yourself with so-and-so, and he does not need to state the nature of his suspicions, that is because a general warning clearly expresses the husband's concern that his wife will engage in sexual intercourse with her paramour. However, if the husband explicitly states that he does not suspect her of engaging in sexual intercourse but only in other forms of sexual misconduct, since these actions would not render her forbidden to her husband, the warning is not considered a valid warning (Rosh). According to the Rambam and the Meiri, the discussion here does not pertain to the nature of the warning issued by the husband. Rather, the Gemara is discussing a case where the woman disobeyed her husband's warning and engaged in intimate contact with another man by way of other limbs. The Gemara states that since this is not considered to be sexual intercourse, the bitter water would not evaluate whether she was defiled.

דּוּמָה וְאַל יִשָּׂא בַּת דּוּמָה, שֶׁזּוֹ בָּאָה מִטִּיפָּה כְּשֵׁרָה, וְזוֹ בָּאָה מִטִּיפָּה פְּסוּלָה;

a woman whose suspected promiscuity is publicly spoken of [***duma***],[L] **and not marry the daughter of a woman suspected of promiscuity, as this** woman, who is herself suspected of promiscuity, **comes from seed** of **unflawed** lineage; **but that** woman, the daughter of a woman suspected of promiscuity, **comes from seed** of **flawed** lineage, as she might be a *mamzeret*.

וְרַבִּי יוֹחָנָן אָמַר: יִשָּׂא אָדָם בַּת דּוּמָה וְאַל יִשָּׂא דּוּמָה, שֶׁזּוֹ עוֹמֶדֶת בְּחֶזְקַת כַּשְׁרוּת, וְזוֹ אֵינָהּ עוֹמֶדֶת בְּחֶזְקַת כַּשְׁרוּת.

And Rabbi Yoḥanan says: It is better that **a man marry the daughter of a woman suspected of promiscuity, and not marry a woman suspected of promiscuity, as this** daughter **maintains** the **presumptive status of virtuousness, but that** woman suspected of promiscuity **does not maintain** the **presumptive status of virtuousness.**

מֵיתִיבֵי: נוֹשֵׂא אָדָם דּוּמָה! אֲמַר רָבָא: וְתִסְבְּרָא נוֹשֵׂא לְכַתְּחִלָּה? אֶלָּא אִם נָשָׂא; תְּנֵי נַמִּי בַּת דּוּמָה.

The Gemara **raises an objection** to Rabbi Yoḥanan's statement from a *baraita*: **A man** may **marry a woman suspected of promiscuity. Rava said** in response: **And** how can **you understand** the *baraita* at face value? The *baraita* states that a man **may marry** her ***ab initio***, yet clearly it is undesirable to do so. **Rather,** the wording of the *baraita* is imprecise, and one must render it: **If one married** a woman suspected of promiscuity, she is permitted to him. Since the *baraita* is imprecise, one should **also** correct it and **teach: The daughter of a woman suspected of promiscuity.**

וְהִלְכְתָא: יִשָּׂא אָדָם בַּת דּוּמָה וְאַל יִשָּׂא דּוּמָה, דְּתָנֵי רַב תַּחֲלִיפָא בַּר מַעַרְבָא קַמֵּיהּ דְּרַבִּי אַבָּהוּ: אִשָּׁה מְזַנָּה – בָּנֶיהָ כְּשֵׁרִין, רוֹב בְּעִילוֹת אַחַר הַבַּעַל.

The Gemara concludes: **And the *halakha*** is that it is better that **a man marry the daughter of a woman suspected of promiscuity, and not marry a woman suspected of promiscuity.** This is **as Rav Taḥalifa, from the West,** i.e., Eretz Yisrael, **taught before Rabbi Abbahu:** If a married **woman engages in adulterous sexual intercourse, her children are** considered of **unflawed** lineage,[H] as **most** instances of **sexual intercourse are attributed to the husband,** and consequently it is presumed that the children were conceived by the husband and not by the paramour. Therefore, the daughter of a woman suspected of promiscuity is not suspected of being a *mamzeret*.

בָּעֵי רַב עַמְרָם: הָיְתָה פְּרוּצָה בְּיוֹתֵר, מַהוּ? אַלִּיבָּא דְּמַאן דְּאָמַר אֵין אִשָּׁה מִתְעַבֶּרֶת אֶלָּא סָמוּךְ לְווֹסְתָּהּ, לָא תִּיבָּעֵי לָךְ, דְּלָא יָדְעִי בָּהּ וְלָא מַנְטַר לָהּ.

Rav Amram raises a dilemma: What is the *halakha* if the woman **was extremely promiscuous** and one cannot reasonably attribute most instances of intercourse to the husband? Are her children considered of unflawed lineage, or is their lineage uncertain? **According to** the opinion of **the one who says** that **a woman becomes pregnant**[B] **only close to** the time of the onset of **her menstruation, you do not** need to **raise this dilemma, as** the husband **does not know** the time of **this,** i.e., the time of her menstruation, in advance, **and** he **does not watch her** actions in order to prevent her from conceiving from another man. Her children are therefore of uncertain lineage.

כִּי תִּיבָּעֵי לָךְ – אַלִּיבָּא דְּמַאן דְּאָמַר אֵין אִשָּׁה מִתְעַבֶּרֶת אֶלָּא סָמוּךְ לִטְבִילָתָהּ. מַאי? כֵּיוָן דְּיָדַע בָּהּ – נָטוֹרֵי מַנְטַר לָהּ, אוֹ דִּלְמָא כֵּיוָן דִּפְרוּצָה בְּיוֹתֵר – לָא? תֵּיקוּ.

When do you need to **raise this dilemma?** It is necessary **according to** the opinion of **the one who says** that **a woman becomes pregnant only close to** the time of **her immersion. What** is the *halakha*? Can it be assumed that **since he knows** the time of **this,** i.e., of her immersion, **he watches her** actions on that day in order to prevent her from conceiving from another man; **or perhaps, since** she **is extremely promiscuous,** her husband **cannot** adequately watch her and her children are considered of uncertain lineage? The Gemara concludes: The dilemma **shall stand** unresolved.

LANGUAGE

A woman whose suspected promiscuity is publicly spoken of [*duma*] – דּוּמָה: The Sages use this term with regard to anything that serves as the subject of gossip and rumors. It is usually, though not always, used in a negative sense.

HALAKHA

If a married woman engages in adulterous sexual intercourse her children are considered of unflawed lineage – אִשָּׁה מְזַנָּה בָּנֶיהָ כְּשֵׁרִין: If a woman is rumored to have committed adultery, one need not be concerned that perhaps her children are *mamzerim*, even if she is the subject of communal gossip, in accordance with the ruling of Rav Taḥalifa. However, there is reason for concern that perhaps she has acquired the status of a *zona*, i.e., a woman who has engaged in sexual intercourse with a man forbidden to her, and if her husband is a priest he is forbidden by Torah law to remain married to her. Furthermore, even an Israelite should refrain from marrying her in order to distance himself from alleged impropriety. If she is extremely promiscuous, her children's lineage is also considered uncertain, as the Gemara's dilemma concerning whether the husband will ensure she does not become impregnated by another man stands unresolved. The Rema writes that even so, if she states that her children are of unflawed lineage, her testimony is accepted. If she behaved extremely licentiously before her marriage but not afterward, then even if she was once seen committing adultery, her children are considered of unflawed lineage (Rambam *Sefer Kedusha, Hilkhot Issurei Bia* 15:20; *Shulḥan Arukh, Even HaEzer* 4:15).

BACKGROUND

A woman becomes pregnant – אִשָּׁה מִתְעַבֶּרֶת: A woman can become pregnant only at the time of ovulation, which usually occurs around fourteen days before she menstruates. The time of a woman's immersion is seven days after she ceases to menstruate. Consequently, the duration of the time between ovulation and the time of menstruation or the time of immersion depends on the length of a woman's menstrual cycle. A woman with a regular menstrual cycle of approximately a month will ovulate around two weeks after the beginning of menstruation, close to the time of her immersion, while a woman with a much shorter menstrual cycle will ovulate closer to the time she ceased menstruating.

"וְאֵלּוּ שֶׁבֵּית דִּין" כו׳. תָּנוּ רַבָּנַן: "אִישׁ" – מַה תַּלְמוּד לוֹמַר: "אִישׁ אִישׁ"? לְרַבּוֹת אֵשֶׁת חֵרֵשׁ, וְאֵשֶׁת שׁוֹטֶה, וְאֵשֶׁת שִׁעֲמוּם, וְשֶׁהָלַךְ בַּעְלָהּ לִמְדִינַת הַיָּם, וְשֶׁהָיָה חָבוּשׁ בְּבֵית הָאֲסוּרִין – שֶׁבֵּית דִּין מְקַנִּין לָהֶן לְפוֹסְלָן מִכְּתוּבָּתָן.

§ The mishna states (24a): **And these** are the women **to whom the court issues a warning** in place of their husbands: One whose husband became a deaf-mute or became an imbecile, or if he were incarcerated in prison. **The Sages taught:** The verse states: "If the wife of any man goes astray" (Numbers 5:12). As the verse could have said: The wife of **a man, what** is the meaning when **the verse states:** "The wife of **any man**"? It serves **to include the wife of a deaf-mute, and the wife of an imbecile, and the wife of an insane person, and** one **whose husband went overseas, and** one **whose** husband **was incarcerated in prison;** and it teaches **that the court issues a warning to** these women in order **to disqualify them from** receiving payment of **their marriage contract.**

יָכוֹל אַף לְהַשְׁקוֹתָן – תַּלְמוּד לוֹמַר: "וְהֵבִיא הָאִישׁ אֶת אִשְׁתּוֹ". רַבִּי יוֹסֵי אוֹמֵר: אַף לְהַשְׁקוֹתָהּ, וְלִכְשֶׁיֵּצֵא בַּעְלָהּ מִבֵּית הָאֲסוּרִין יַשְׁקֶנָּה.

One **might** have thought that the court's warning is effective **even to have** the women **drink** the bitter water; therefore, **the verse states: "Then the man shall bring his wife** to the priest" (Numbers 5:15), indicating that only the warning issued by the husband causes his wife to drink. **Rabbi Yosei says:** The court's warning is effective **even to have her drink, and when her husband is released from prison he has her drink.**

בְּמַאי קָא מִיפַּלְגִי? רַבָּנַן סָבְרִי: בָּעֵינַן "וְקִנֵּא...וְהֵבִיא". וְרַבִּי יוֹסֵי סָבַר: לָא בָּעֵינַן "וְקִנֵּא...וְהֵבִיא".

The Gemara asks: **With regard to what do they disagree?** The Gemara answers: **The Rabbis hold** that **we require** the same person who issues the warning to bring the woman to the Temple, as the verse states: **"And he warned** his wife… **then** the man **shall bring** his wife to the priest" (Numbers 5:14–15). **And Rabbi Yosei holds** that **we do not require** that the actions stated in the verse, i.e., **"And he warned… then** the man **shall bring,"** be performed by the same person; and although only the husband may bring the woman to the priest to drink the bitter water, the warning may be issued by the court.

תָּנוּ רַבָּנַן: "אֲשֶׁר תִּשְׂטֶה אִשָּׁה תַּחַת אִישָׁהּ" – לְהַקִּישׁ אִישׁ לְאִשָּׁה וְאִשָּׁה לְאִישׁ. לְמַאי הִלְכְתָא? אָמַר רַב שֵׁשֶׁת: כְּשֵׁם שֶׁאִם הוּא סוּמָא לֹא הָיָה מַשְׁקֶה, דִּכְתִיב: "וְנֶעְלַם מֵעֵינֵי אִישָׁהּ", כָּךְ הִיא אִם הָיְתָה סוּמָא לֹא הָיְתָה שׁוֹתָה. רַב אַשִׁי אָמַר: כְּשֵׁם שֶׁחִיגֶּרֶת וְגִידֶּמֶת לֹא הָיְתָה שׁוֹתָה, דִּכְתִיב:

§ **The Sages taught** that the verse: "This is the law of jealousy, **when a wife, while under her husband, goes astray** and is defiled" (Numbers 5:29), is superfluous, and serves **to compare a man to a woman and a woman to a man.**[H] The Gemara asks: **With regard to what *halakha*** is this comparison necessary? **Rav Sheshet says:** This teaches that **just as if** the husband **was blind he would not have her drink, as it is written: "And it was hidden from the eyes of her husband"** (Numbers 5:13), indicating that the *sota* ritual applies only if the husband was capable of seeing her infidelity but did not do so; **so too,** with regard to the woman, **if she were blind, she would not drink. Rav Ashi** also **says: Just as a lame woman and a woman without hands would not drink, as it is written:**

Perek **IV**
Daf **27** Amud **b**

"וְהֶעֱמִיד הַכֹּהֵן אֶת הָאִשָּׁה לִפְנֵי ה׳... וְנָתַן עַל כַּפֶּיהָ", כָּךְ הוּא אִם הָיָה חִיגֵּר אוֹ גִּידֵּם לֹא הָיָה מַשְׁקֶה. מָר בַּר רַב אַשִׁי אָמַר: כְּשֵׁם שֶׁאִילֶּמֶת לֹא הָיְתָה שׁוֹתָה, דִּכְתִיב: "וְאָמְרָה הָאִשָּׁה אָמֵן אָמֵן", כָּךְ הוּא אִם הָיָה אִילֵּם לֹא הָיָה מַשְׁקֶה.

הדרן עלך ארוסה

"And the priest shall stand the woman before the Lord… and place the meal-offering of memorial **in her hands"** (Numbers 5:18), indicating that if she is unable to stand up straight or if she does not have hands with which to accept the offering, then she does not drink; **so too, if** the husband **were lame or without hands, he would not cause** his wife **to drink. Mar Bar Rav Ashi says: Just as a mute woman would not drink, as it is written: "And the woman shall say: Amen, Amen"** (Numbers 5:22), indicating that she must be able to speak; **so too, if** the husband **were mute,** he **would not cause** his wife **to drink.**

HALAKHA

To compare a man to a woman and a woman to a man – לְהַקִּישׁ אִישׁ לְאִשָּׁה וְאִשָּׁה לְאִישׁ: If the husband or the wife has a physical defect that prevents either of them from fulfilling the literal details stated in the verses, the woman does not drink the bitter water. Furthermore, because the Torah compares a man to a woman and a woman to a man, the woman does not drink the bitter water if one of them has a physical defect that would have prevented the other from fulfilling the details stated in the verses had he or she had that same defect. Consequently, the wife of a man who is blind, deaf, lame, missing a hand, or mute, does not drink the bitter water. Likewise, a woman who is blind, deaf, lame, missing a hand, or mute does not drink the bitter water (Rambam *Sefer Nashim*, *Hilkhot Sota* 2:2–3).

Summary of **Perek IV**

In this chapter the Talmud taught that there are cases where the *sota* ritual is not performed, despite the fact that the woman secluded herself with another man after being warned by her husband. There are a several restrictions that define who may undergo the entire *sota* ritual and drink the bitter water.

A woman may drink the bitter water only if the marriage bond between the couple is complete. This excludes a couple who are only betrothed, or a woman who has only a levirate bond with her *yavam* and is waiting for him to perform levirate marriage. Even after a marriage has been consummated, if the marriage is prohibited the woman cannot drink the bitter water.

The Torah states that if a *sota* drinks the bitter water and it is evaluated that she is innocent of adultery, she will conceive. It is understood, based on this, that women who cannot conceive are excluded from the *sota* ritual.

A *sota* drinks the bitter water only if her husband engaged in sexual intercourse with her at least once before she secluded herself with her paramour. If the husband or wife is blind, deaf, mute, lame, or missing a hand, then the woman does not drink the bitter water, as certain aspects of the *sota* ceremony cannot be properly fulfilled.

The chapter also discussed in which cases a *sota* who does not drink the bitter water is entitled to collect payment of her marriage contract, and when she forfeits that right. The Gemara concludes that whenever she secludes herself with another man after being warned she forfeits her right to collect payment of her marriage contract, unless she drinks the bitter water and is found to be innocent of adultery. The only exception is in a case where the husband prevented her from drinking the bitter water, either because he did not want her to drink it or because he engaged in sexual intercourse with her after she became forbidden to him.

The chapter also explained in which cases a husband can issue a warning to his wife. He can issue a warning with regard to any man, including the wife's close relatives, such as her father or son, and a gentile. However, he cannot issue a warning with regard to a minor, or with regard to animals.

In a case where a woman is acting promiscuously and her husband is unable to issue a warning to her, either because he is not present or because he is mentally ill, the court issues a warning to the woman on the husband's behalf. This warning is sufficient to cause the woman to forfeit her right to collect payment of her marriage contract; however, a woman may drink the bitter water only when warned by her husband.

Introduction to **Perek V**

And the spirit of jealousy comes upon him, and he warns his wife, and she is defiled; or if the spirit of jealousy comes upon him, and he warns his wife, and she is not defiled.

(Numbers 5:14)

And he shall make the woman drink the water of bitterness that causes the curse; and the water that causes the curse shall enter into her and become bitter.

(Numbers 5:24)

And he shall make her drink the water, and then it shall come to pass, if she is defiled, and acted unfaithfully against her husband, that the water that causes the curse shall enter into her and become bitter, and her belly shall swell, and her thigh shall fall away; and the woman shall be a curse among her people.

(Numbers 5:27)

This is the law of jealousy, when a wife, being under her husband, goes astray and is defiled.

(Numbers 5:29)

And the open land about the cities, which you shall give to the Levites, shall be from the wall of the city and outward one thousand cubits round about. And you shall measure outside the city for the east side two thousand cubits, and for the south side two thousand cubits, and for the west side two thousand cubits, and for the north side two thousand cubits, the city being in the middle. This shall be for them the open land outside the cities.

(Numbers 35:4–5)

This chapter begins with a homiletical interpretation of a verse concerning the *halakhot* of *sota* that was apparently taught on the day that Rabbi Elazar ben Azarya was appointed *Nasi* of the Sanhedrin in place of Rabban Gamliel. On that day the manner of discussion in the study hall of the Sanhedrin changed, as permission was granted to various Sages to present traditions with which they were familiar, as well as their own interpretations of biblical verses. Therefore, many new *halakhot* were revealed on that day; they serve as the basis for tractate *Eduyyot*.

As the first mishna of this chapter cites a *halakha* concerning a *sota* that was taught on that day, a number of other interpretations of verses that were taught on the same day are cited in this chapter, although they bear no relation to the *halakhot* of *sota*. The homiletical interpretations found in this chapter comprise statements of both *halakha* and *aggada*.

מתני׳ כְּשֵׁם שֶׁהַמַּיִם בּוֹדְקִין אוֹתָהּ כָּךְ הַמַּיִם בּוֹדְקִין אוֹתוֹ, שֶׁנֶּאֱמַר: "וּבָאוּ", "וּבָאוּ".

MISHNA **Just as the water evaluates her** fidelity,[NH] **so too, the water evaluates his,** i.e., her alleged paramour's, involvement in the sin, **as it is stated: "And** the water that causes the curse **shall enter** into her" (Numbers 5:24), and it is stated again: **"And** the water that causes the curse **shall enter** into her and become bitter" (Numbers 5:27). It is derived from the double mention of the phrase "and… shall enter" that both the woman and her paramour are evaluated by the water.

כְּשֵׁם שֶׁאֲסוּרָה לַבַּעַל כָּךְ אֲסוּרָה לַבּוֹעֵל, שֶׁנֶּאֱמַר: "נִטְמָאָה", "וְנִטְמָאָה", דִּבְרֵי רַבִּי עֲקִיבָא.

Furthermore, prior to her drinking the water, **just as she is forbidden to** her **husband, so too is she forbidden to** her **paramour,**[H] **because** in contrast to the verse stating: **"Is defiled [*nitma'a*]"** (Numbers 5:14), a superfluous conjoining prefix *vav* is added to a later verse, rendering the phrase: **"And is defiled [*venitma'a*]"** (Numbers 5:29). The addition indicates another prohibition, that of the woman to her paramour. This is **the statement of Rabbi Akiva.**

אָמַר רַבִּי יְהוֹשֻׁעַ: כָּךְ הָיָה דּוֹרֵשׁ זְכַרְיָה בֶּן הַקַּצָּב. רַבִּי אוֹמֵר: שְׁנֵי פְעָמִים הָאֲמוּרִים בַּפָּרָשָׁה "נִטְמָאָה", "וְנִטְמָאָה", אֶחָד לַבַּעַל וְאֶחָד לַבּוֹעֵל.

Rabbi Yehoshua said: That was how Zekharya ben HaKatzav would interpret it, i.e., he also derived from the superfluous *vav* that the woman is forbidden to her paramour. **Rabbi** Yehuda HaNasi **says** an alternate source: The **two times that** the defilement of the wife **is stated in the passage,** namely: "And he warns his wife, and **she is defiled"** (Numbers 5:14),[N] and the later verse: "When a wife, being under her husband, goes astray **and is defiled"** (Numbers 5:29), indicate that her defilement results in two prohibitions. **One** is that she is forbidden **to** her **husband and one** is that she is forbidden **to** her **paramour.**

בּוֹ בַּיּוֹם דָּרַשׁ רַבִּי עֲקִיבָא: "וְכָל כְּלִי חֶרֶשׂ אֲשֶׁר יִפֹּל מֵהֶם אֶל תּוֹכוֹ כֹּל אֲשֶׁר בְּתוֹכוֹ יִטְמָא". אֵינוֹ אוֹמֵר "טָמֵא" אֶלָּא "יִטְמָא" – לְטַמֵּא אֲחֵרִים. לִמֵּד עַל כִּכָּר שֵׁנִי שֶׁמְּטַמֵּא אֶת הַשְּׁלִישִׁי.

§ **On that same day**[N] that Rabbi Elazar ben Azarya was appointed head of the Sanhedrin, **Rabbi Akiva interpreted** the verse: **"And every earthen vessel into which any of them falls, whatever is in it shall be impure [*yitma*],** and you shall break it" (Leviticus 11:33), as follows: The verse **does not state: Is impure [*tamei*],** but **rather: "Shall be impure,"** in order **to** indicate that not only does the vessel itself become ritually impure, but it can now **render other** items **ritually impure.** This **teaches with regard to a loaf** that has **second**-degree ritual impurity status due to its being placed inside an earthenware vessel that had first-degree impurity, **that it can render** other food with which it comes into contact **impure** with **third**-degree impurity[N] status.

NOTES

Just as the water evaluates her fidelity, etc. – כְּשֵׁם שֶׁהַמַּיִם בּוֹדְקִין אוֹתָהּ וכו׳: The Jerusalem Talmud cites a number of additional derivations, most of which are quoted in *Tosafot*, for the *halakha* that the water evaluates not only the wife but the paramour as well. Among the sources is the fact that the numerical value of the word used to describe the ability of the water to cause the curse, *hame'arerim* (Numbers 5:18), is 496. This is twice the number 248, which corresponds to the number of limbs in a person's body. It indicates that the water evaluates not only the 248 limbs of the woman, but the 248 limbs of the alleged paramour as well.

The two times that it is stated in the passage: She is defiled – שְׁנֵי פְעָמִים הָאֲמוּרִים בַּפָּרָשָׁה נִטְמָאָה: In fact, this phrase is stated more than twice in the passage, and therefore the early commentaries discuss which verses are being discussed here and why the others are not counted here, as they are later. Rashi explains that only two mentions of the phrase are expounded here because the other mentions are interpreted elsewhere as teaching other *halakhot*.

On that same day – בּוֹ בַּיּוֹם: Rashi comments, based on the Gemara (*Berakhot* 28a), that whenever the Mishna uses this description it is referring to the day that Rabban Gamliel was removed from his position as *Nasi* of the Sanhedrin and was replaced by Rabbi Elazar ben Azarya. On that day many halakhic matters were discussed, elucidated, and clarified, many of which are cited in tractate *Eduyyot*. It appears that this day marked a change in the method of study in the study hall, as rather than having the discussion centered only around the Nasi, other Sages were able to express their opinions with greater freedom. Some commentaries explain that apparently the initial statement of Rabbi Akiva in this mishna was also stated on that day, and that is why the mishna continues to mention other seemingly unconnected matters that were taught on that day.

A loaf that has second-degree impurity…can render other food impure with third-degree impurity – כִּכָּר שֵׁנִי שֶׁמְּטַמֵּא אֶת הַשְּׁלִישִׁי: A loaf that has second-degree impurity refers to one that is rendered impure by being placed in an earthenware vessel, such as an oven, which itself has first-degree impurity. Rabbi Akiva states that this loaf, which has second-degree impurity, can impart third-degree impurity to another loaf, even if the other loaf is non-sacred. Rabban Yoḥanan ben Zakkai seems to take the opposite extreme opinion, that a loaf with second-degree impurity cannot transmit impurity even to a loaf of *teruma*. However, the *halakha* is not in accordance with either of these extreme opinions; an item that has second-degree impurity can transmit impurity to *teruma* and consecrated food, thereby disqualifying them from being eaten, but it cannot transmit impurity to non-sacred food.

HALAKHA

Just as the water evaluates her fidelity, etc. – כְּשֵׁם שֶׁהַמַּיִם בּוֹדְקִין אוֹתָהּ וכו׳: At the very same time that the *sota* dies, her paramour with whom she committed the act of adultery dies as well, in the same manner as she did, no matter where he may be at the time (Rambam *Sefer Nashim*, *Hilkhot Sota* 3:17).

Just as she is forbidden to her husband so too is she forbidden to her paramour – כְּשֵׁם שֶׁאֲסוּרָה לַבַּעַל כָּךְ אֲסוּרָה לַבּוֹעֵל: If a woman who was warned by her husband subsequently secludes herself with the man she was warned about, she is forbidden to her husband as well as to her paramour. If the paramour transgresses the *halakha* and marries her, he is obligated to give her a bill of divorce. However, if a man engages in sexual intercourse with a married woman in such a manner that she remains permitted to her husband, e.g., if he rapes her, she is not rendered forbidden to him in the event she is either widowed or divorced (*Beit Shmuel*). For a summary of some of the many discussions surrounding this *halakha* see *Arukh HaShulḥan* (Rambam *Sefer Nashim*, *Hilkhot Sota* 2:12; *Shulḥan Arukh*, *Even HaEzer* 11:1, 178:17).

אָמַר רַבִּי יְהוֹשֻׁעַ: מִי יְגַלֶּה עָפָר מֵעֵינֶיךָ רַבָּן יוֹחָנָן בֶּן זַכַּאי, שֶׁהָיִיתָ אוֹמֵר: עָתִיד דּוֹר אַחֵר לְטַהֵר כִּכָּר שְׁלִישִׁי, שֶׁאֵין לוֹ מִקְרָא מִן הַתּוֹרָה שֶׁהוּא טָמֵא. וַהֲלֹא רַבִּי עֲקִיבָא תַּלְמִידְךָ מֵבִיא לוֹ מִקְרָא מִן הַתּוֹרָה שֶׁהוּא טָמֵא, שֶׁנֶּאֱמַר: "כֹּל אֲשֶׁר בְּתוֹכוֹ יִטְמָא".

After hearing Rabbi Akiva's statement, **Rabbi Yehoshua said: Who will remove the dirt from your eyes,**[N] **Rabban Yoḥanan ben Zakkai,**[P] so that you could live and see this? **As you would say:** In the **future, another generation** is destined **to deem pure a loaf** that contracted **third**-degree impurity, **as there is no** explicit **verse from the Torah** stating **that it is impure. But** now **Rabbi Akiva, your disciple, brings a verse from the Torah** indicating **that it is impure, as it is stated: "Whatever is in it shall be impure."**

בּוֹ בַּיּוֹם דָּרַשׁ רַבִּי עֲקִיבָא: "וּמַדֹּתֶם מִחוּץ לָעִיר אֶת פְּאַת קֵדְמָה אַלְפַּיִם בָּאַמָּה" וגו', וּמִקְרָא אַחֵר אוֹמֵר: "מִקִּיר הָעִיר וָחוּצָה אֶלֶף אַמָּה סָבִיב".

Furthermore, **on that same day Rabbi Akiva interpreted** the verses with regard to the Levite cities as follows: One verse states: **"And you shall measure outside the city for the east side two thousand cubits…** this shall be for them the open land outside the cities" (Numbers 35:5), **and another verse states:** "And the open land around the cities, which you shall give to the Levites, shall be **from the wall of the city and outward one thousand cubits round about"** (Numbers 35:4).

אִי אֶפְשָׁר לוֹמַר "אֶלֶף אַמָּה" שֶׁכְּבָר נֶאֱמַר "אַלְפַּיִם אַמָּה", וְאִי אֶפְשָׁר לוֹמַר "אַלְפַּיִם אַמָּה" שֶׁכְּבָר נֶאֱמַר "אֶלֶף אַמָּה". הָא כֵּיצַד? אֶלֶף אַמָּה מִגְרָשׁ, וְאַלְפַּיִם אַמָּה תְּחוּם הַשַּׁבָּת.

It is impossible to say that the area around the cities given to the Levites was only **one thousand cubits, as it is already stated: "Two thousand cubits." And it is impossible to say** that **two thousand cubits** were left for them, **as it is already stated: "One thousand cubits." How can these** texts be reconciled? **One thousand cubits** are to be set aside as **a tract**[H] of open land surrounding the city, **and** the **two thousand cubits** are mentioned not in order to be given to the Levites, but to indicate the boundary of **the Shabbat limit,** beyond which it is forbidden to travel on Shabbat. This verse thereby serves as the source for the two-thousand-cubit Shabbat limit.

רַבִּי אֱלִיעֶזֶר בְּנוֹ שֶׁל רַבִּי יוֹסֵי הַגְּלִילִי אוֹמֵר: אֶלֶף אַמָּה מִגְרָשׁ, וְאַלְפַּיִם אַמָּה שָׂדוֹת וּכְרָמִים.

Rabbi Eliezer, son of Rabbi Yosei HaGelili, says otherwise: **One thousand cubits** were given to the Levites as an open **tract** of land, that could not be planted or built upon, **and two thousand cubits** of additional land were given to the Levites for planting **fields and vineyards.**[N]

בּוֹ בַּיּוֹם דָּרַשׁ רַבִּי עֲקִיבָא: "אָז יָשִׁיר מֹשֶׁה וּבְנֵי יִשְׂרָאֵל אֶת הַשִּׁירָה הַזֹּאת לַה' וַיֹּאמְרוּ לֵאמֹר" – שֶׁאֵין תַּלְמוּד לוֹמַר "לֵאמֹר", וּמָה תַּלְמוּד לוֹמַר "לֵאמֹר"? מְלַמֵּד, שֶׁהָיוּ יִשְׂרָאֵל עוֹנִין שִׁירָה אַחֲרָיו שֶׁל מֹשֶׁה עַל כׇּל דָּבָר וְדָבָר כְּקוֹרְאִין אֶת הַלֵּל ("אָשִׁירָה לַה' כִּי גָאֹה גָּאָה"). לְכָךְ נֶאֱמַר "לֵאמֹר".

Additionally, **on that same day Rabbi Akiva interpreted** the verse: **"Then Moses and the children of Israel sang this song to the Lord, and said, saying"** (Exodus 15:1), as follows: **As** there is **no** need for **the verse to state** the word **"saying,"** because it states the word "said" immediately prior to it, **why** must **the verse state** the word **"saying"? It teaches that the Jewish people would repeat in song after Moses every single statement** he said, **as** is done when **reciting *hallel*.** After Moses would recite a verse, they would say as a refrain: **"I will sing to the Lord, for He is highly exalted"** (Exodus 15:1). It is **for this** reason that the word **"saying" is stated,** in addition to the word "said."

NOTES

Who will remove the dirt from your eyes – מִי יְגַלֶּה עָפָר מֵעֵינֶיךָ: This phrase is understood to mean: How I wish that you were resurrected from death. This is because during burial the eyes of the deceased are covered with dirt, and this expression alludes to the time when the deceased will remove the dirt as he opens his eyes and sees again (*Mitzpe Eitan*).

Two thousand cubits for fields and vineyards – וְאַלְפַּיִם אַמָּה שָׂדוֹת וּכְרָמִים: Rashi explains this to mean that every Levite city was surrounded by a two-thousand-cubit area on all sides; the inner one thousand cubits were set aside as the city's tract of open space and the outer one thousand cubits were designated for fields and vineyards. The Rambam, however, rules in accordance with the straightforward meaning of the mishna (see *Kesef Mishne*), that beyond the one thousand cubits of the city's tract of open space was an additional two thousand cubits of fields and vineyards. Accordingly, the limits of the Levite cities stretched three thousand cubits outward in every direction.

HALAKHA

One thousand cubits as a tract, etc. – אֶלֶף אַמָּה מִגְרָשׁ וכו׳: The Levite cities are provided with a surrounding area spanning a radius of three thousand cubits; the first thousand cubits constitute the tract and the remaining two thousand are used for fields and vineyards. This ruling is in accordance with the Rambam's understanding of the statement of Rabbi Eliezer, son of Rabbi Yosei HaGelili. This is not in accordance with Rabbi Akiva's ruling, as most authorities agree that by Torah law the Shabbat limit is not two thousand cubits as Rabbi Akiva maintains (Rambam *Sefer Zera'im, Hilkhot Shemitta VeYovel* 13:2 and *Kesef Mishne* there).

PERSONALITIES

Rabban Yoḥanan ben Zakkai – רַבָּן יוֹחָנָן בֶּן זַכַּאי: Rabban Yoḥanan ben Zakkai was the youngest of Hillel the Elder's students. He headed the Sanhedrin after the destruction of the Second Temple and was one of the greatest leaders in the history of the Jewish people. He lived to an old age and served as the leader of the Jewish people for many years. The Sages said of him that there was not a single area of Torah that he neglected. Despite his prominence, he was a modest individual who greeted every person he met, including gentiles in the marketplace.

Even while the Temple stood Rabban Yoḥanan was acknowledged as a leading Torah scholar, and most of the Sages of that generation were his students. He strongly opposed the Jewish Great Revolt against the Romans and instead attempted to resolve issues with Rome peacefully. As one of the leaders of the besieged Jerusalem, he was aware that the city would soon fall. He succeeded in escaping with the help of several of his students in order to appear before the Roman general Vespasian, who received him warmly. When his prediction that Vespasian would be appointed emperor was fulfilled, Vespasian rewarded him by allowing him to establish a new center of Torah study and Jewish leadership in Yavne and by saving the life of the Nasi, Rabban Gamliel.

In Yavne Rabban Yoḥanan instituted a wide range of ordinances that offered hope for Jewish continuity in the absence of the Temple, even as they served to commemorate the Temple and promised the possibility of its ultimate rebuilding. The results of his efforts are integral to the modern practice of halakhic Judaism. His students taught Torah throughout Eretz Yisrael following the destruction of the Temple, and he served as a mentor for Rabban Gamliel of Yavne, who succeeded him in the leadership capacity as the acting *Nasi*.

רַבִּי נְחֶמְיָה אוֹמֵר: כְּקוֹרִין אֶת שְׁמַע וְלֹא כְּקוֹרִין אֶת הַלֵּל.

Rabbi Neḥemya says: The people sang the song together with Moses **as** is done when **reciting *Shema*,** which is recited in unison after the prayer leader begins, **and not as** is done when **reciting *hallel*.**

בּוֹ בַּיּוֹם דָּרַשׁ רַבִּי יְהוֹשֻׁעַ בֶּן הוּרְקָנוֹס: לֹא עָבַד אִיּוֹב אֶת הַקָּדוֹשׁ בָּרוּךְ הוּא אֶלָּא מֵאַהֲבָה, שֶׁנֶּאֱמַר: ״הֵן יִקְטְלֵנִי לוֹ אֲיַחֵל״. וַעֲדַיִין הַדָּבָר שָׁקוּל, לוֹ אֲנִי מְצַפֶּה אוֹ אֵינִי מְצַפֶּה? תַּלְמוּד לוֹמַר: ״עַד אֶגְוָע לֹא אָסִיר תֻּמָּתִי מִמֶּנִּי״, מְלַמֵּד שֶׁמֵּאַהֲבָה עָשָׂה.

On that same day Rabbi Yehoshua ben Hyrcanus[P] **taught: Job served the Holy One, Blessed be He, only out of love, as it is stated: "Though He will slay me, still I will trust in Him"** (Job 13:15). **And still, the matter is even,**[N] i.e., the verse is ambiguous, as there are two possible interpretations of the verse. Was Job saying: **I will await Him,** expressing his yearning for God; **or** should the verse be interpreted as saying **I will not await** Him. As the word "lo" can mean either "to him" or "not," it is unclear which meaning is intended here. This dilemma is resolved elsewhere, where **the verse states** a clearer indication of Job's intent: **"Till I die I will not put away my integrity from me"** (Job 27:5). This **teaches that he acted out of love.**

אָמַר רַבִּי יְהוֹשֻׁעַ: מִי יְגַלֶּה עָפָר מֵעֵינֶיךָ רַבָּן יוֹחָנָן בֶּן זַכַּאי, שֶׁהָיִיתָ דּוֹרֵשׁ כָּל יָמֶיךָ שֶׁלֹּא עָבַד אִיּוֹב אֶת הַמָּקוֹם אֶלָּא מִיִּרְאָה, שֶׁנֶּאֱמַר: ״אִישׁ תָּם וְיָשָׁר יְרֵא אֱלֹהִים וְסָר מֵרָע״, וַהֲלֹא יְהוֹשֻׁעַ תַּלְמִיד תַּלְמִידְךָ לִמֵּד שֶׁמֵּאַהֲבָה עָשָׂה.

Rabbi Yehoshua said: Who will remove the dirt from your eyes, Rabban Yoḥanan ben Zakkai, so that you could live and see this? **As you taught all your life that Job worshipped the Omnipresent only out of fear, as it is stated:** "And that **man** was **wholehearted and upright, and God-fearing, and shunned evil"** (Job 1:1); **but** now **Yehoshua** ben Hyrcanus, **the disciple of your disciple,**[N] **has taught that** Job **acted out of love.**

גמ׳ ״אוֹתוֹ״. לְמַאן? אִילֵימָא לְבַעַל, בַּעַל מַאי עֲבִיד? וְכִי תֵּימָא,

GEMARA It is stated in the mishna that just as the water evaluates whether the woman was unfaithful, so too, the water evaluates whether **he** committed this sin. The Gemara asks: **To whom** does this refer? **If we say** that it is referring **to the husband, what did the husband do** that he should be evaluated? **And if you would say**

PERSONALITIES

Rabbi Yehoshua ben Hyrcanus – רַבִּי יְהוֹשֻׁעַ בֶּן הוּרְקָנוֹס: This Sage is mentioned only in this mishna, and it is unknown who he was. It would appear from the context that he was a disciple of Rabbi Akiva. Some scholars maintain that he was the younger brother of Rabbi Eliezer ben Hyrcanus, but there is no evidence of this.

NOTES

And still the matter is even – וַעֲדַיִין הַדָּבָר שָׁקוּל: According to the simple interpretation of the mishna, the reason for the ambiguity is the discrepancy between the two ways in which the word *"lo"* can be understood. However, Rabbi David Luria questions this interpretation, as the word *"lo,"* written with the letter *vav*, is generally understood as meaning: To him. He therefore suggests that the ambiguity exists even assuming the meaning of: To him, as the verse can be read either as a declarative sentence: "Though He will slay me, still I will trust in Him"; or it can be read as a rhetorical question: "Shall I still trust in Him even if He slays me?" Therefore, further evidence is necessary to resolve the ambiguity, as the problem cannot be resolved through the verse itself.

The disciple of your disciple – תַּלְמִיד תַּלְמִידְךָ: Earlier in the mishna Rabbi Yehoshua refers to Rabbi Akiva as the disciple of Rabban Yoḥanan ben Zakkai, although Rabbi Akiva, like Rabbi Yehoshua ben Hyrcanus, was only a disciple of his disciples, as he studied under Rabban Yoḥanan's students Rabbi Eliezer and Rabbi Yehoshua. The Rambam (Commentary on the Mishna) explains that Rabbi Yehoshua refers to Rabbi Akiva as Rabban Yoḥanan's disciple in order to emphasize that due to the spectacular degree of Rabbi Akiva's scholarship, he could be considered worthy of being a disciple of Rabban Yoḥanan himself, while Rabbi Yehoshua ben Hyrcanus, whose greatness was of a smaller magnitude, did not deserve as lofty a description. Alternatively, since Rabbi Yehoshua ben Hyrcanus was a student of Rabbi Akiva, he was therefore referred to as a disciple of Rabban Yoḥanan ben Zakkai's disciple (*Torat Ḥayyim*).

Perek **V**
Daf **28** Amud **a**

דְּאִי אִית בֵּיהּ עָוֹן בָּדְקִי לֵיהּ מַיָּא, כִּי אִית בֵּיהּ עָוֹן בִּדְידֵיהּ מִי בָּדְקִי לַהּ מַיָּא לְדִידַהּ? וְהָא תַּנְיָא: ״וְנִקָּה הָאִישׁ מֵעָוֹן וְהָאִשָּׁה הַהִיא תִּשָּׂא אֶת עֲוֹנָהּ״ – בִּזְמַן שֶׁהָאִישׁ מְנוּקֶּה מֵעָוֹן, הַמַּיִם בּוֹדְקִין אֶת אִשְׁתּוֹ; אֵין הָאִישׁ מְנוּקֶּה מֵעָוֹן, אֵין הַמַּיִם בּוֹדְקִין אֶת אִשְׁתּוֹ!

that if he has committed a similar **iniquity**[N] **the water evaluates his** actions, this is difficult, as in a case **where he has** committed a similar **iniquity does the water** even **evaluate her** fidelity? **But isn't it taught** in a *baraita* that the verse: **"And the man shall be clear from iniquity, and that woman shall bear her iniquity"** (Numbers 5:31), indicates that only **when the man is clear of iniquity**[H] **does the water evaluate** the fidelity of **his wife,** but if **the man is not clear of iniquity**[N] **the water does not evaluate** the fidelity of **his wife?**

וְאֶלָּא לְבוֹעֵל – לִיתְנֵי כִּדְקָתָנֵי סֵיפָא: כְּשֵׁם שֶׁאֲסוּרָה לַבַּעַל, כָּךְ אֲסוּרָה לַבּוֹעֵל!

And if the mishna is **rather** referring **to the** alleged **paramour,** who is also evaluated by the water that the woman drinks, then **let** the mishna **teach as is taught** in its **latter clause: Just as she is forbidden to** her **husband, so too is she forbidden to** her **paramour.** Just as there the paramour is mentioned explicitly, so too here, the mishna should have stated: Just as the water evaluates whether she was unfaithful, so too, it evaluates whether the paramour committed this iniquity.

HALAKHA

When the man is clear of iniquity, etc. – בִּזְמַן שֶׁהָאִישׁ מְנוּקֶּה מֵעָוֹן וכו׳: The Rambam maintains that the water does not evaluate the wife of any man who has engaged in any illicit sexual intercourse during his adulthood. However, many of the early commentaries disagree; in their opinion, this fact applies only to one who engaged in sexual intercourse with his wife after she was rendered a *sota* by secluding herself with the alleged paramour after her husband's warning (Rambam *Sefer Nashim, Hilkhot Sota* 2:8).

NOTES

If he has committed a similar iniquity – אִי אִית בֵּיהּ עָוֹן בָּדְקִי לֵיהּ מַיָּא: Rashi explains that this is referring to the husband having engaged in sexual intercourse with his wife after her seclusion with the other man. However, later commentaries question the notion that this transgression should be punishable by death. One explanation is that the husband may have caused his wife to sin through his own sinful behavior, and is therefore liable to receive the same punishment (*Eshel Avraham*). Others explain that the Gemara does not entertain the possibility that the husband should die, but rather that if he is guilty of forbidden intercourse with his wife he is punished with suffering similar to hers, albeit on a smaller scale (*Torat HaKenaot; Devar Shaul*).

If the man is not clear of iniquity – אֵין הָאִישׁ מְנוּקֶּה מֵעָוֹן: The Rambam understands this principle in a very broad sense, stating that any man who has engaged in illicit sexual intercourse at any point in his adult lifetime cannot be considered clear of iniquity, and the water will not evaluate his wife. Others disagree, maintaining that this principle applies only to one who transgressed the prohibition against engaging in sexual intercourse with his wife after she was rendered a *sota*. The Ramban, in his Commentary on the Torah, rules based on the Gemara below (47b) that not only is the water ineffective in evaluating the wife when the husband is not clear of iniquity, but this is the case even if any members of their household are not clear of such a transgression. See *Mishne LaMelekh*, where there is a discussion as to why the Rambam does not cite that Gemara.

לְעוֹלָם לְבוֹעֵל, וְרֵישָׁא אַיְּידֵי דְּתָנָא "אוֹתָהּ" תָּנֵי "אוֹתוֹ"; סֵיפָא אַיְּידֵי דְּתָנָא בַּעַל תָּנָא בּוֹעֵל.

The Gemara answers: The entire mishna **actually** does refer **to the paramour, and** the reason he is not mentioned explicitly in **the first clause** of the mishna is because **since** it **teaches** that the water evaluates whether the wife was unfaithful by using the direct object **her,** it also **teaches** that the water evaluates whether the paramour committed the by act using the direct object **him,** without mentioning the paramour explicitly. In **the latter clause** of the mishna, on the other hand, **since** it **teaches** explicitly that the woman is forbidden to her **husband,** it also **teaches** explicitly that she is forbidden to her **paramour.**

"שֶׁנֶּאֱמַר: וּבָאוּ, וּבָאוּ". אִיבַּעְיָא לְהוּ: "בָּאוּ" "וּבָאוּ" קָאָמַר, אוֹ "וּבָאוּ" "וּבָאוּ" קָאָמַר?

§ In the mishna Rabbi Akiva proves that the water evaluates the paramour as well, **as it is stated: "And** the water that causes the curse **shall enter** into her" (Numbers 5:24), and: **"And** the water that causes the curse **shall enter** into her and become bitter" (Numbers 5:27). **A dilemma was raised before** the Sages concerning the precise wording of the mishna: **Does** the mishna **state: "Shall enter** [*ba'u*]," **"and shall enter** [*uva'u*]"? According to this version of the mishna, it is derived from the superfluous conjoining prefix *vav* that the paramour is also evaluated by the water. **Or,** alternatively, **does** the mishna **state: "And shall enter," "and shall enter,"** indicating that this *halakha* is derived from the repetition of the phrase in two separate verses?

תָּא שְׁמַע: כְּשֵׁם שֶׁאֲסוּרָה לַבַּעַל כָּךְ אֲסוּרָה לַבּוֹעֵל, שֶׁנֶּאֱמַר: "נִטְמָאָה", "וְנִטְמָאָה".

Come and **hear** a proof from Rabbi Akiva's second statement in the mishna, where he says: **Just as she is forbidden to** her **husband, so** too **is she forbidden to** her **paramour, as it is stated: "Is defiled** [***nitma'a***]," **"And is defiled** [***venitma'a***]" (Numbers 5:29). Here it seems that Rabbi Akiva derives his interpretation from the superfluous prefix *vav* rather than from the repetition of the phrase. Therefore, the first derivation should be understood in the same manner.

וַעֲדַיִין תִּיבְּעֵי: "נִטְמְאָה" "נִטְמָאָה" קָאָמַר, אוֹ "נִטְמָאָה" "וְנִטְמָאָה" קָאָמַר?

The Gemara asks: **But still, let the dilemma be raised** with regard to this *halakha* too: **Does** Rabbi Akiva **state** that the source for the *halakha* is the mention of the phrase **"is defiled," "is defiled,"** in two different verses (Numbers 5:14, 29), **or does he state** that the *halakha* is derived from the superfluous *vav* in the phrase **"is defiled,"** rendering it **"and is defiled"** (Numbers 5:29)?

תָּא שְׁמַע: מִדְּקָתָנֵי סֵיפָא, רַבִּי אוֹמֵר: שְׁנֵי פְּעָמִים הָאֲמוּרִין בַּפָּרָשָׁה "וְנִטְמָאָה", "וְנִטְמָאָה" – אֶחָד לַבַּעַל וְאֶחָד לַבּוֹעֵל; מִכְּלָל דְּרַבִּי עֲקִיבָא וָו"י קָדָרֵישׁ.

Come and **hear** a proof **from** the fact **that** the mishna **teaches** in **the latter clause** that **Rabbi** Yehuda HaNasi **says:** The **two times that** the wife's defilement **is stated in the passage,** namely: "And he warns his wife, **and she is defiled"** (Numbers 5:14), and the later verse: "When a wife, being under her husband, goes astray **and is defiled"** (Numbers 5:29), indicate that there are two prohibitions due to her defilement. **One is** to forbid her **to** her **husband and one is** to forbid her **to** her **paramour. By inference** from the fact that the dissenting derivation of Rabbi Yehuda HaNasi is from the repetition of the entire phrase, evidently **Rabbi Akiva derives** this *halakha* from the superfluous ***vav.***

הִלְכָּךְ לְרַבִּי עֲקִיבָא שִׁיתָּא קְרָאֵי כְּתִיבִי:

Therefore, according to the opinion of **Rabbi Akiva,** since the phrase "and the water... shall enter" is mentioned three times in the passage, and the prefix *vav,* written each time, is expounded as though the phrase were mentioned twice, the phrase is treated as though it were **written** in **six verses,** as follows.

חַד לְצַוָּאָה דִּידָהּ, וְחַד לְצַוָּאָה דִּידֵיהּ;

One of the mentions (Numbers 5:27) is interpreted **for the command concerning her,** the woman, meaning that God empowered the waters to punish the woman; **and one,** the prefix *vav* in that same verse, is expounded **for** the **command concerning him,** the paramour, i.e., that he too shall be punished by the water if he is guilty.

חַד לַעֲשִׂיָּיה דִּידָהּ, וְחַד לַעֲשִׂיָּיה דִּידֵיהּ;

One mention of the phrase, in the description of the drinking of the bitter water of a *sota* (Numbers 5:24), is interpreted **for the execution of her** punishment, as the punishment will go into effect so long as the process was performed properly; **and one,** the prefix *vav* in that verse, is expounded **for the execution of his** punishment.

חַד לִידִיעָה דִּידַהּ, וְחַד לִידִיעָה דִּידֵיהּ.

One mention (Numbers 5:22) is **for her knowledge,** i.e., the priest informs her that this punishment will be the result; **and one,** the prefix *vav*, is **for his knowledge.**

וְרַבִּי תְּלָתָא קְרָאֵי כְּתִיבִי: חַד לְצַוָּאָה, וְחַד לַעֲשִׂיָּיה, וְחַד לִידִיעָה.

But Rabbi Yehuda HaNasi maintains that only **three verses** worthy of exposition **are written** with regard to the water entering the woman; he does not derive anything additional from the prefix *vav* that introduces the various mentions of this matter. He therefore interprets **one for** the **command, and one for the execution, and one for** the **knowledge,** all with regard to the woman herself.

וְרַבִּי, כְּשֵׁם שֶׁהַמַּיִם בּוֹדְקִין אוֹתָהּ כָּךְ בּוֹדְקִין אוֹתוֹ מְנָא לֵיהּ?

The Gemara asks: **And from where does Rabbi** Yehuda HaNasi derive the principle in the mishna that **just as the water evaluates** whether **she** was unfaithful, **so** too, **it evaluates** whether **he** committed the sin?

נָפְקָא לֵיהּ מִדְּתַנְיָא: ״לַצְבּוֹת בֶּטֶן וְלַנְפִּל יָרֵךְ״ – בִּטְנוֹ וִירֵיכוֹ שֶׁל בּוֹעֵל; אַתָּה אוֹמֵר: בִּטְנוֹ וִירֵיכוֹ שֶׁל בּוֹעֵל, אוֹ אֵינוֹ אֶלָּא בִּטְנָהּ וִירֵיכָהּ שֶׁל נִבְעֶלֶת? כְּשֶׁהוּא אוֹמֵר: ״וְצָבְתָה בִטְנָהּ וְנָפְלָה יְרֵכָהּ״, הֲרֵי בִּטְנָהּ וִירֵיכָהּ שֶׁל נִבְעֶלֶת אָמוּר. וּמָה אֲנִי מְקַיֵּים ״לַצְבּוֹת בֶּטֶן וְלַנְפִּל יָרֵךְ״? בִּטְנוֹ וִירֵיכוֹ שֶׁל בּוֹעֵל.

The Gemara answers: **He derives it from that which is taught** in a *baraita*, that the verse: **"And cause the belly to swell and the thigh to fall away"** (Numbers 5:22), is referring to **the belly and thigh of the paramour.** Do **you say** that the intention is **the belly and the thigh of the paramour, or is it only the belly and the thigh of the adulteress? When it says** later: **"And her belly shall swell, and her thigh shall fall away"** (Numbers 5:27), **the belly and thigh of the adulteress are** explicitly **stated. And** therefore, **how do I realize** the meaning of the former verse: **"And cause the belly to swell, and the thigh to fall away"?** Clearly, it is referring to **the belly and thigh of the paramour.**

וְאִידָךְ? הַהוּא, דְּמוֹדַע לַהּ כֹּהֵן דְּבֶטֶן בְּרֵישָׁא וַהֲדַר יָרֵךְ, שֶׁלֹּא לְהוֹצִיא לַעַז עַל הַמַּיִם הַמָּרִים.

And how does **the other** *tanna*, Rabbi Akiva, interpret the repetition of verses? The former verse indicates **that** the **priest informs her that** her **belly** will be afflicted **first and then** her **thigh,**[H] so **as not to cast aspersions on the bitter water** of a *sota*, i.e., to prevent people from claiming that the guilty woman's death was not due to the bitter water but rather to some other cause. The reason people might claim this is that the priest says to the woman: "The Lord will make you a curse and an oath among your people, when the Lord makes your thigh fall away, and your belly swell" (Numbers 5:21). This seems to imply that her thigh is supposed to be afflicted before her belly. Therefore, when her belly swells first, people might conclude that it is not due to the water. It is for this reason that the priest needs to inform her that her belly will swell first.

וְאִידָךְ? אִם כֵּן, לִכְתּוֹב קְרָא ״בִּטְנָהּ וִירֵכָהּ״. מַאי ״בֶּטֶן וְיָרֵךְ״? שְׁמַע מִינַּהּ לַבּוֹעֵל.

And why does **the other** *tanna*, Rabbi Yehuda HaNasi, disagree with Rabbi Akiva? The Gemara answers: **If** it is **so** that the verse: "And cause the belly to swell, and the thigh to fall away" (Numbers 5:22), is referring to the woman, **the verse should have written: Her belly…and her thigh. What** is meant by the phraseology of **"the belly…and the thigh"? Conclude from it** that it is referring **to** the belly and thigh of **the paramour.**

וְאֵימָא: כּוּלֵּיהּ לְהָכִי הוּא דְּאָתָא! אִם כֵּן, לִכְתּוֹב ״בִּטְנוֹ וִירֵכוֹ״. מַאי ״בֶּטֶן וְיָרֵךְ״? שְׁמַע מִינַּהּ תַּרְתֵּי.

The Gemara asks: **And say that the entire** verse **comes for this,** to indicate that the water evaluates the paramour as well, and does not teach the order of the punishment? The Gemara answers: **If so,** the Torah **should have written: His belly…and his thigh. What** is the meaning of the general wording: **"The belly…and the thigh"? Conclude from it two** conclusions: That the paramour is punished and that the priest informs the woman with regard to the order of the punishment.

״אָמַר רַבִּי יְהוֹשֻׁעַ: כָּךְ הָיָה דּוֹרֵשׁ זְכַרְיָה״ כּוּ׳.

§ It is stated in the mishna that **Rabbi Yehoshua said: That was how Zekharya** ben HaKatzav **would interpret** it. Rabbi Yehuda HaNasi says: The two times that the defilement of the wife is stated in the passage indicate that there are two prohibitions due to her defilement; one is to forbid her to her husband and one is to forbid her to her paramour.

HALAKHA

The priest informs her that her belly will be afflicted first and then her thigh – דְּמוֹדַע לַהּ כֹּהֵן דְּבֶטֶן בְּרֵישָׁא וַהֲדַר יָרֵךְ: The priest informs the woman that her belly will be afflicted first, and then her thigh, so that people will not cast aspersions on the effectiveness of the water (Rambam *Sefer Nashim, Hilkhot Sota* 3:7).

תָּנוּ רַבָּנַן: שָׁלֹשׁ פְּעָמִים הָאֲמוּרִין בְּפָרָשָׁה "אִם נִטְמְאָה", "נִטְמָאָה", "וְנִטְמָאָה" לָמָּה? אֶחָד לַבַּעַל, וְאֶחָד לַבּוֹעֵל, וְאֶחָד לִתְרוּמָה, דִּבְרֵי רַבִּי עֲקִיבָא.

The Sages taught in a *baraita*: With regard to the **three times that** the defilement of the wife **is stated in the passage,** namely: **"If she is defiled"** (Numbers 5:27), "and he warns his wife, and **she is defiled"** (Numbers 5:14), and "when a wife being under her husband goes astray **and is defiled"** (Numbers 5:29), **why** are all three necessary? **One** is to prohibit her **to** her **husband, and one** is to prohibit her **to** her **paramour, and one** is **to** prohibit her from partaking of ***teruma,*** even if she is the wife or daughter of a priest. This is **the statement of Rabbi Akiva.**

אָמַר רַבִּי יִשְׁמָעֵאל, קַל וָחוֹמֶר: וּמָה גְּרוּשָׁה שֶׁמּוּתֶּרֶת לִתְרוּמָה – אֲסוּרָה לִכְהוּנָּה, זוֹ שֶׁאֲסוּרָה בִּתְרוּמָה – אֵינוֹ דִּין שֶׁאֲסוּרָה לִכְהוּנָּה.

Rabbi Yishmael said: It is unnecessary to derive from a verse that it would also be prohibited for this woman to marry a priest, as it can be derived ***a fortiori*: If a divorced** daughter of a priest, **who is permitted to** partake of ***teruma,*** is nevertheless **forbidden to** marry into the **priesthood,** then with regard to **this** *sota,* **who is forbidden** to partake **of *teruma,* is it not logical that it is** also **prohibited** for her **to** marry into the **priesthood?**

מָה תַּלְמוּד לוֹמַר: "וְהִיא נִטְמָאָה", "וְהִיא לֹא נִטְמָאָה"? אִם נִטְמְאָה לָמָּה שׁוֹתָה? אִם לֹא נִטְמְאָה לָמָּה מַשְׁקֶה? מַגִּיד לָךְ הַכָּתוּב, שֶׁהַסָּפֵק אֲסוּרָה;

The *baraita* continues by citing additional expositions involving the verse: "And she is defiled" (Numbers 5:14): **What** is the meaning when **the verse states** with regard to the cases in which a husband can compel his wife to drink the bitter water of a *sota*: "And he warns his wife, **and she is defiled;** or if the spirit of jealousy comes upon him, and he warns his wife, **and she is not defiled"** (Numbers 5:14)? **If she is defiled, why does she** need to **drink?** And **if she is not defiled, why does he make her drink?** The *baraita* answers: **The verse tells you that** it is discussing a case when there is **uncertainty** as to whether the woman was faithful to her husband, yet **it is prohibited** for her to engage in sexual intercourse with her husband until the matter is clarified.

מִכָּאן אַתָּה דָּן לְשֶׁרֶץ: וּמָה סוֹטָה שֶׁלֹּא עָשָׂה בָּהּ שׁוֹגֵג כְּמֵזִיד וְאוֹנֶס כְּרָצוֹן – עָשָׂה בָּהּ סָפֵק כְּוַדַּאי, שֶׁרֶץ שֶׁעָשָׂה בּוֹ שׁוֹגֵג כְּמֵזִיד וְאוֹנֶס כְּרָצוֹן – אֵינוֹ דִּין שֶׁיֵּעָשֶׂה בּוֹ סָפֵק

From here you can derive the *halakha* in a case of uncertainty **with regard to** whether the carcass of **a creeping animal**[NH] has imparted ritual impurity: **Just as** in the case of **a *sota,* where** the Torah **does not consider unwitting** adultery **like intentional** adultery,[H] **and rape** is not treated **like a willing** transgression, because if a married woman committed adultery unwittingly or was raped she is not punished, yet still the Torah **considers an uncertain** case of adultery **like a certain** violation inasmuch as the woman is forbidden to her husband until the truth is clarified; so too, with regard to **a creeping animal** or other agents of ritual impurity, **where** the Torah **does consider unwitting** contact with impure items **like intentional** contact, as one contracts impurity whether or not his contact was intentional **and an accident** is treated **like willing** contact, **is it not logical that** the Torah must also **consider an uncertain** case of transmission of ritual impurity

NOTES

From here you can derive the *halakha* with regard to a creeping animal – מִכָּאן אַתָּה דָּן לְשֶׁרֶץ: *Tosafot* note that logically one might refute this *a fortiori* argument: With regard to a *sota* there is circumstantial evidence that she is guilty, as her husband had warned her to stay away from a specific man and she subsequently secluded herself with him, and one witness testified that they engaged in sexual intercourse. With regard to uncertain ritual impurity, however, that is not the case.

Other early commentaries point out additional refutations for this *a fortiori* argument. Consequently, several of them concur with the understanding of Rabbeinu Tam (*Sefer HaYashar*), who states based on the Gemara in tractate *Ḥullin* (9b) that the real source for this *halakha* is an oral tradition from Sinai, and the *a fortiori* inference is cited only as an additional corroboration for the *halakha*. Therefore, the Gemara does not deal with the numerous possible ways of refuting the argument.

HALAKHA

From here you can derive the *halakha* with regard to a creeping animal – מִכָּאן אַתָּה דָּן לְשֶׁרֶץ: The Sages derive various *halakhot* with regard to ritual impurity from the *halakhot* of *sota*, e.g., cases of uncertain impurity that arise in the private domain are to be treated as impure, just as a *sota* is treated stringently and is forbidden to her husband in a case where she secluded herself with another man in the private domain (Rambam *Sefer Tahara, Hilkhot She'ar Avot HaTumot* 16:1–2).

In the case of a *sota* where the Torah does not consider unwitting adultery like intentional adultery, etc. – סוֹטָה שֶׁלֹּא עָשָׂה בָּהּ שׁוֹגֵג כְּמֵזִיד וכו׳: If a woman committed adultery unwittingly, or if she was raped, the water does not evaluate her (Rambam *Sefer Nashim, Hilkhot Avot HaTuma* 3:24).

כְּוַדַּאי.

like a case of **certain** contact with an impure item? Accordingly, any cases of uncertain ritual impurity should be treated like certain impurity.

וּמִמָּקוֹם שֶׁבָּאתָ: מַה סוֹטָה רְשׁוּת הַיָּחִיד, אַף שֶׁרֶץ רְשׁוּת הַיָּחִיד,

The *baraita* continues: **And** since the case of *sota* is the source for the *halakha* with regard to uncertain ritual impurity, the details of the *halakha* are also derived from the case of *sota*. Therefore, **from the place that you came** from, i.e., from the source, it is derived that **just as** the prohibition with regard to **a *sota*** applies only when the uncertainty arises in **the private domain,** i.e., when she has secluded herself with the alleged paramour, **so too,** uncertain contact with the carcass of **a creeping animal** renders an item impure only if the contact was in **the private domain.**[H]

וּמַה סוֹטָה דָּבָר שֶׁיֵּשׁ בּוֹ דַּעַת לִישָּׁאֵל, אַף שֶׁרֶץ דָּבָר שֶׁיֵּשׁ בּוֹ דַּעַת לִישָּׁאֵל.

And furthermore, **just as a *sota* is an entity that has awareness** in order for her **to be asked** whether she actually committed adultery, **so too,** contact with **a creeping animal** renders an item impure only if it is **an entity that has awareness** in order for it **to be asked,**[H] i.e., a person, or an item that may have contracted impurity in a place where a person was present and could have known.

וּמִכָּאן אָמְרוּ: דָּבָר שֶׁיֵּשׁ בּוֹ דַּעַת לִישָּׁאֵל, בִּרְשׁוּת הַיָּחִיד – סְפֵיקוֹ טָמֵא, בִּרְשׁוּת הָרַבִּים – סְפֵיקוֹ טָהוֹר; וְשֶׁאֵין בּוֹ דַּעַת לִישָּׁאֵל, בֵּין בִּרְשׁוּת הַיָּחִיד בֵּין בִּרְשׁוּת הָרַבִּים – סְפֵיקוֹ טָהוֹר.

The *baraita* concludes: **And from here** the Sages **stated** that if **an entity that has awareness** in order for it **to be asked** may have contracted impurity **in the private domain, its uncertain** impurity renders it **impure;** but if it may have contracted impurity **in the public domain, its uncertain** impurity leaves it **pure.**[N] **And** with regard to an entity **that lacks awareness** in order for it **to be asked, whether** the uncertainty arose **in the private domain or in the public domain, its uncertain** impurity is deemed **pure,** as it is not similar to a *sota*.

וְרַבִּי יִשְׁמָעֵאל, אָמַר רַבִּי עֲקִיבָא תְּרוּמָה, וּמַהֲדַר לֵיהּ אִיהוּ כְּהוּנָּה!

The Gemara begins its discussion of the *baraita* by inquiring about the exchange between Rabbi Yishmael and Rabbi Akiva: **And** what was the intention of **Rabbi Yishmael?** Apparently, he commented on a statement of **Rabbi Akiva,** who **said** that it is prohibited for a *sota* to partake of ***teruma*, and he answered him** concerning the matter of the woman's being prohibited to marry into the **priesthood,** which was not mentioned by Rabbi Akiva at all.

וְתוּ, לְרַבִּי עֲקִיבָא כְּהוּנָּה מְנָא לֵיהּ? וְכִי תֵּימָא, כְּהוּנָּה לָא צְרִיכָא קְרָא,

And furthermore, from where does Rabbi Akiva derive that it is prohibited for a *sota* to marry into the **priesthood? And if you would say** that with regard to her prohibition against marrying into the **priesthood a verse is not necessary,**

HALAKHA

So too a creeping animal in the private domain – אַף שֶׁרֶץ רְשׁוּת הַיָּחִיד: The *halakha* of *sota* is the source for the *halakha* that any case of uncertain ritual impurity that arises in the private domain is deemed impure. However, if the uncertainty arises in the public domain, which is defined as a place where three or more people are present, the uncertainty is deemed pure (Rambam *Sefer Tahara, Hilkhot She'ar Avot HaTumot* 15:8; 16:2).

An entity that has awareness for it to be asked – דָּבָר שֶׁיֵּשׁ בּוֹ דַּעַת לִישָּׁאֵל: Just as a *sota* has awareness that allows her to be asked whether she committed adultery, so too, with regard to all cases of uncertain contraction of ritual impurity, an item is deemed impure only in instances where it has the awareness to be asked whether or not it touched an impure item. Therefore, uncertain contraction of ritual impurity by a deaf-mute, an imbecile, or a minor is deemed pure, even if the uncertainty arises in a private domain (Rambam *Sefer Tahara, Hilkhot She'ar Avot HaTumot* 15:8; 16:2).

NOTES

In the public domain its uncertain impurity leaves it pure – בִּרְשׁוּת הָרַבִּים סְפֵיקוֹ טָהוֹר: The Gemara here would seem to indicate that the principle that uncertainty with regard to the contraction of ritual impurity that arises in the public domain is deemed pure is derived from the *halakhot* of *sota*. However, elsewhere, other sources are cited as the basis for this principle. In the Jerusalem Talmud and the *Tosefta*, later codified by the Rambam, it is derived from the *halakha* that a Paschal offering can be sacrificed in impurity.

One reason not to derive this principle from the case of a *sota* is that the whole concept of *sota* refers to a woman who secluded herself with another man, which is not at all applicable in a public domain. Therefore, nothing can be inferred from *sota* with regard to impurity in the public domain (*Aḥiezer*). In tractates *Ḥullin* (9b) and *Avoda Zara* (37b) the Gemara writes that this principle is a tradition transmitted to Moses from Sinai, and is not inferred by logic.

Tosafot in *Avoda Zara* (37b) explain that in fact, the case of a *sota* serves as the source only for the principle that uncertain impurity in the private domain is considered impure. By inference, one can say that any uncertainty with regard to ritual impurity that arises in the public domain is not rendered impure. However, in tractate *Ḥullin* (9b), *Tosafot* write that it is derived from *sota* that uncertainty with regard to impurity in the public domain is considered pure even if the item in question did not have a presumptive status of purity, and uncertainty with regard to impurity in the private domain is deemed impure even if the item had a presumptive status of purity. They explain that a *sota* herself has lost her presumptive status of innocence by secluding herself with the alleged paramour.

NOTES

One to priesthood and one to *teruma* – וְחַד לִכְהוּנָּה וְחַד לִתְרוּמָה: *Tosafot* ask: Why doesn't the Gemara suggest that once the verse deems a sota defiled with regard to her husband, it should follow that she is disqualified from ever marrying a priest or form partaking of *teruma* if her husband is a priest, as she is assumed to have committed adultery? They answer, somewhat cryptically, that absent the additional verses one could have said that a *sota* is considered defiled only with regard to her husband, as there could be court-imposed capital punishment because of him. The *Eshel Avraham* explains that *Tosafot* mean that even if the wife had not in fact committed adultery, her improper behavior will eventually lead to her doing so, which will render her liable to receive court-imposed capital punishment, in the event that she is caught in the act in the presence of witnesses. Therefore, it is preferable that she become forbidden to her husband until she drinks the bitter water, and she is forbidden to her husband in order that he will be more likely to make her drink the bitter water. However, this should not be taken as an indication that the verse regards her as having been defiled, and as such, one cannot assume that she will become forbidden to a priest or to partake of *teruma*.

Keren Ora suggests another explanation as to why the *halakha* that a *sota* is forbidden to her husband does not serve as proof with regard to *teruma* and marrying a priest: The reason she is forbidden to her husband could be that even if she did not actually engage in sexual intercourse, her promiscuous behavior was clearly contrary to her husband's warning and warranted his disapproval. This unique prohibition for the husband, however, does not apply to the other matters under discussion.

A matter that can be derived through an *a fortiori* inference, etc. – מִילְּתָא דְּאָתְיָא בְּקַל וָחוֹמֶר וכו׳: This principle, which is cited in many places in the Talmud, states that although the Torah will not repeat explicit *halakhot* more than once if it is not teaching a specific novelty, the Torah will state a *halakha* explicitly although it could be derived through an *a fortiori* inference. The reason why a *halakha* that could be derived through logical reasoning might be stated explicitly could be either to emphasize the *halakha*, or to provide it with the additional power that only *halakhot* stated explicitly in the Torah have, such as the ability of the court to punish one who violates such a *halakha*.

BACKGROUND

An *a fortiori* inference – קַל וָחוֹמֶר: One of the fundamental principles of rabbinic exegesis, *a fortiori* inference appears in all of the standard lists of exegetical principles. In essence, it is a principle of logical argumentation where a comparison is drawn between two cases, one more lenient and the other more stringent. The *a fortiori* inference asserts that if the *halakha* is stringent in a case where the ruling is usually lenient, then all the more so will it be stringent in a more serious case; likewise, if the *halakha* is lenient in a case where the ruling is not usually lenient, then it will certainly be lenient in a less stringent case. *A fortiori* inferences appear in the Bible, and the Sages compiled lists of verses in which they appear. For example: "If you have run with the foot soldiers, and they have wearied you, how can you contend with horses?" (Jeremiah 12:5).

שֶׁהֲרֵי עָשָׂה בָּהּ סָפֵק זוֹנָה כְּזוֹנָה, תְּרוּמָה נָמֵי לָא תִּיבְּעֵי קְרָא, שֶׁהֲרֵי עָשָׂה בָּהּ סָפֵק זוֹנָה כְּזוֹנָה!

as the Torah has already **rendered an uncertain** case of **a woman who has engaged in sexual intercourse with a man forbidden to her by the Torah** [*zona*] **as though** she is certainly **a *zona*,** since a *sota* is forbidden to her husband after seclusion even though there are no witnesses that she committed adultery, and therefore it should be prohibited for her to marry a priest just like any *zona*, then with regard to her prohibition against partaking of ***teruma* a verse should also not be necessary, as** it is prohibited for a *zona* to partake of *teruma*. Therefore, the Torah **renders an uncertain *zona* like** a certain ***zona*.**

אֶלָּא, לְרַבִּי עֲקִיבָא אַרְבְּעָה קְרָאֵי כְּתִיבִי: חַד לַבַּעַל, וְחַד לַבּוֹעֵל, וְחַד לִכְהוּנָּה וְחַד לִתְרוּמָה;

Rather, it must be explained that **according to Rabbi Akiva,** the equivalent of **four verses** worthy of exposition **are written** with regard to the defilement of a *sota*, as he maintains that an additional *halakha* should be derived from the superfluous prefix *vav* in the verse: "And is defiled [*venitma'a*]" (Numbers 5:29). Therefore, **one** verse is written to forbid her **to** her **husband, and one** is to forbid her **to** her **paramour, and one** is to forbid her **to** marry into the **priesthood, and one** is to forbid her **to** partake of ***teruma*.**[N]

וְרַבִּי יִשְׁמָעֵאל תְּלָתָא קְרָאֵי כְּתִיבִי: חַד לַבַּעַל, וְחַד לַבּוֹעֵל וְחַד לִתְרוּמָה, וּכְהוּנָּה אָתְיָא בְּקַל וָחוֹמֶר.

And Rabbi Yishmael disagrees with Rabbi Akiva, as he does not expound on the superfluous *vav*, and therefore maintains that only **three verses are written: One** is to forbid her **to** her **husband, and one** is to forbid her **to** her **paramour, and one** is to forbid her **to** partake of ***teruma*. And** her being prohibited to marry into the **priesthood is derived through an *a fortiori*** inference,[B] as described in the *baraita*.

וְרַבִּי יִשְׁמָעֵאל, מִמַּאי דְּאִיצְטְרִיךְ קְרָא לִתְרוּמָה, וּכְהוּנָּה אָתְיָא בְּקַל וָחוֹמֶר? דִּילְמָא כִּי אִיצְטְרִיךְ לִכְהוּנָּה, וּתְרוּמָה שְׁרֵיָא!

The Gemara asks: **And from where does Rabbi Yishmael** derive **that the verse was necessary** to teach the prohibition of a *sota* **to** partake of ***teruma*, and** her prohibition against marrying into the **priesthood is derived through an *a fortiori*** inference? **Perhaps** the verse **was necessary** in order to teach that it is prohibited for the woman to marry **into the priesthood, but *teruma* is permitted** for her?

אָמַר לָךְ: מִסְתַּבְּרָא דּוּמְיָא דְּבַעַל וּבוֹעֵל, מָה בַּעַל וּבוֹעֵל מֵחַיִּים, אַף תְּרוּמָה נָמֵי מֵחַיִּים, לְאַפּוֹקֵי כְּהוּנָּה דִּלְאַחַר מִיתָה.

The Gemara answers: Rabbi Yishmael could have **said to you: It is reasonable** to derive from this verse a prohibition that is **similar to** the prohibitions derived from the other verses, i.e., that she is forbidden **to** her **husband and** her **paramour. Just as** she is forbidden to her **husband and** her **paramour** even **during** the **lifetime** of her husband, **so too,** the prohibition against partaking of ***teruma*** applies **also during** the **lifetime** of her husband, **to the exclusion of** her prohibition against marrying into the **priesthood, which** is relevant only **after** the **death** of her husband. The reason is that if her husband would divorce her it would be prohibited for her to marry a priest anyway.

וְרַבִּי עֲקִיבָא – דּוּמְיָא דְּבַעַל וּבוֹעֵל לֵית לֵיהּ;

And how would **Rabbi Akiva** respond? The Gemara answers: **He is not** of the opinion that it is more reasonable to derive a prohibition from the phrase "and is defiled" that is **similar to** the prohibitions involving her **husband and** her **paramour,** and therefore he requires two separate derivations; one for *teruma* and one for the priesthood.

וְאִי נָמֵי אִית לֵיהּ, מִילְּתָא דְּאָתְיָא בְּקַל וָחוֹמֶר טָרַח וְכָתַב לַהּ קְרָא.

Or alternatively, perhaps **he accepts** the opinion that the *halakha* derived from "and is defiled" should be similar to the prohibitions involving the husband and paramour, but nevertheless, in certain instances with regard to **a matter that can be derived through an *a fortiori*** inference,[N] the **verse** nevertheless **takes the trouble and writes** explicitly. Therefore, although unnecessary, two verses are stated, one for *teruma* and one for the priesthood.

אֲמַר רַב גִּידֵּל אֲמַר רַב: דָּבָר שֶׁיֵּשׁ בּוֹ דַּעַת לִישָּׁאֵל וְאֵין בּוֹ דַּעַת לִישָּׁאֵל – מֵהַאי קְרָא נָפְקָא: ״וְהַבָּשָׂר אֲשֶׁר יִגַּע בְּכָל טָמֵא לֹא יֵאָכֵל״ – וַדַּאי טָמֵא הוּא דְּלָא יֵאָכֵל, הָא סָפֵק טָמֵא וְסָפֵק טָהוֹר – יֵאָכֵל.

The Gemara continues discussing the *baraita*. **Rav Giddel said** that **Rav said:** The *halakha* with regard to **an entity that has awareness** in order for it **to be asked and** an entity that **lacks awareness** in order for it **to be asked** in cases of uncertain ritual impurity **is derived from this verse: "And the flesh that touches any impure thing shall not be eaten"** (Leviticus 7:19). This would seem to indicate that specifically food that is **impure** for **certain is** that **which shall not be eaten, but** food for which it is **uncertain** whether it is **impure and uncertain** whether it is **pure can be eaten.**

אֵימָא סֵיפָא: ״וְהַבָּשָׂר כׇּל טָהוֹר יֹאכַל בָּשָׂר״ – וַדַּאי טָהוֹר הוּא דְּיֹאכַל בָּשָׂר, הָא סָפֵק טָמֵא וְסָפֵק טָהוֹר – לֹא יֹאכַל!

However, **say the latter clause** of the verse: **"And as for the flesh, every one that is pure may eat the flesh"** (Leviticus 7:19), which would seem to indicate that specifically one who is **pure** for **certain is** one **who shall eat meat, but** one for whom it is **uncertain** whether he is **impure and uncertain** whether he is **pure shall not eat.** The two clauses in the verse seem to contradict one another with regard to the status of uncertain purity.

אֶלָּא לָאו שְׁמַע מִינָּהּ: כָּאן שֶׁיֵּשׁ בּוֹ דַּעַת לִישָּׁאֵל, כָּאן שֶׁאֵין בּוֹ דַּעַת לִישָּׁאֵל.

Rather, must one **not conclude from it** that the Torah differentiates between two different types of uncertainty? **Here,** the latter clause, which discusses "every one that is pure," is referring to an entity **that has awareness** in order for it **to be asked,** e.g., a person, who is considered impure if he is uncertain whether he contracted ritual impurity. **There,** the former clause which discusses impure meat presents the principle of an entity **that lacks awareness** in order for it **to be asked,** where an uncertain case of ritual impurity is deemed pure.

וְאִיצְטְרִיךְ דְּרַב גִּידֵּל אֲמַר רַב וְאִיצְטְרִיךְ לְמִיגְמַר מִסּוֹטָה; דְּאִי מִדְּרַב, הֲוָה אָמִינָא בֵּין בִּרְשׁוּת הַיָּחִיד וּבֵין בִּרְשׁוּת הָרַבִּים, אִיצְטְרִיךְ לְמִיגְמַר מִסּוֹטָה;

The Gemara explains the need for two separate derivations concerning uncertain contractions of ritual impurity: **And** the derivation **that Rav Giddel** said that **Rav said was necessary, and** it **was** also **necessary to derive** the principle of uncertain ritual impurity **from *sota*; since if** it were derived only **through** the derivation **of Rav, I would say** that it makes no difference **whether** the uncertain contraction of impurity occurred **in the private domain or whether** it occurred **in the public domain.** Therefore, it **was necessary to derive from *sota*** that uncertain impurity is considered impure only in the private domain.

וְאִי מִסּוֹטָה, הֲוָה אָמִינָא עַד דְּאִיכָּא דַּעַת נוֹגֵעַ וּמַגִּיעַ, צְרִיכָא.

And if it is derived only **from *sota*, I would say** that similar to *sota*, where both the woman and the paramour possess awareness in order to be asked if they committed the act, so too, items with uncertain impurity should not be deemed impure **unless there is awareness** on the part of both **the one who touches** the impure item **and the one who causes him to touch,**[N] i.e., the agent of impurity and the recipient of impurity are both competent people. Therefore, the derivation of Rav was **necessary,** as it teaches that in an uncertain case of impurity in the private domain, one is deemed impure even if only the contractor of impurity possesses the awareness to be asked.

NOTES

Awareness of both the one who touches the impure item and the one who causes him to touch – דַּעַת נוֹגֵעַ וּמַגִּיעַ: The Gemara assumes that the awareness of both parties is not necessary with regard to uncertain ritual impurity. However, the Gemara does not specify which side needs awareness. The Meiri writes that it does not matter; if either the agent of impurity or the recipient of impurity is a human being the uncertainty is treated stringently. However, Rashi and the Rambam maintain that specifically the recipient must be a person.

BACKGROUND

Third-degree impurity – **שְׁלִישִׁי**: The further removed an item is from contact with the initial source of ritual impurity, the lower its own level of impurity. An item that comes into contact with the initial source will contract first-degree ritual impurity, and any food that the item touches thereafter will in turn have second-degree ritual impurity, and so on.

HALAKHA

An item of second-degree impurity status can impart third-degree impurity upon *teruma* – שֵׁנִי עוֹשֶׂה שְׁלִישִׁי בִּתְרוּמָה: *Teruma* that becomes impure with first- or second-degree ritual impurity can transmit ritual impurity to other *teruma*. *Teruma* that has third-degree impurity is disqualified, but it cannot transmit impurity to other *teruma*, as there is no fourth degree of impurity that applies to *teruma* (Rambam *Sefer Tahara, Hilkhot She'ar Avot HaTumot* 11:3).

״בּוֹ בַּיּוֹם דָּרַשׁ רַבִּי עֲקִיבָא: וְכׇל כְּלִי חֶרֶשׂ״ כו׳.

§ It is stated in the mishna: **On that same day Rabbi Akiva interpreted** the phrase "shall be impure" in the verse: **"And every earthen vessel** into which any of them falls, whatever is in it shall be impure [*yitma*], and you shall break it" (Leviticus 11:33), as indicating that a loaf that has second-degree ritual impurity can render other food with which it comes into contact impure with third-degree impurity. Rabbi Yehoshua related that Rabban Yoḥanan ben Zakkai had predicted that a future generation would purify a loaf that contracted third-degree impurity, as there is no explicit verse in the Torah stating that this degree of impurity exists.

וּמֵאַחַר דְּאֵין לוֹ, לָמָּה טָמֵא?

The Gemara asks: **But since** the loaf **does not have** an explicit verse stating that it is impure, **why** did Rabban Yoḥanan ben Zakkai himself maintain that it is **impure?**

אָמַר רַב יְהוּדָה אָמַר רַב: מִן הַתּוֹרָה אֵין לוֹ, מִדִּין קַל וָחוֹמֶר יֵשׁ לוֹ: וּמָה טְבוּל יוֹם שֶׁמּוּתָּר בְּחוּלִּין – פּוֹסֵל בִּתְרוּמָה, כִּכָּר שֵׁנִי שֶׁפָּסוּל בְּחוּלִּין – אֵינוֹ דִּין שֶׁיַּעֲשֶׂה שְׁלִישִׁי בִּתְרוּמָה.

Rav Yehuda says that **Rav says:** Rabban Yoḥanan ben Zakkai maintained that although **it has no** explicit basis **from** a verse in **the Torah, it has** proof for its impurity **through an *a fortiori* inference: If** even **one who immersed** in a ritual bath **that day** and will become completely purified after nightfall, **who is** therefore **permitted to** touch **non-sacred** articles, i.e., he does not transmit impurity to them, **disqualifies *teruma*** that he touches, then with regard to **a loaf** that has **second**-degree impurity as result of contact with an impure item of the first degree, **which is disqualified,** i.e., it is rendered impure, even if it is **non-sacred, isn't it logical that it should impart third**-degree impurity[B] **upon *teruma*?**[H]

אִיכָּא לְמִיפְרַךְ: מָה לִטְבוּל יוֹם שֶׁכֵּן אַב הַטּוּמְאָה!

The Gemara challenges: This *a fortiori* inference **can be refuted. What** is unique **about one** who was ritually impure **who immersed that day** and is waiting for nightfall for the purification process to be completed **is that** prior to his immersion, he was **a primary source of impurity.** He therefore retains his stringent status even after immersion with regard to his capability of disqualifying *teruma*. The loaf, by contrast, has second-degree impurity from the outset, and should therefore be treated more lightly.

תֵּיתֵי

The Gemara answers: **Derive** this *halakha*

מִטְּבוּל יוֹם דְּשֶׁרֶץ.

from one who immersed that day who was never a primary source of impurity, as he was rendered impure only **through** contact with **a creeping animal,** and nevertheless he disqualifies *teruma* upon contact.

מָה לִטְבוּל יוֹם דְּשֶׁרֶץ שֶׁכֵּן בְּמִינוֹ אַב הַטּוּמְאָה!

The Gemara continues to challenge the inference: **What** is unique **about** the impurity of **one who immersed that day** who was rendered impure **through** contact with **a creeping animal is that** this impurity can apply to either a person or a utensil, as people and utensils are capable of achieving purity through immersion, and **within its type** there can be **a primary source of impurity.** A loaf, however, is food, which can never be a primary source of impurity. It can only be rendered impure as a secondary source of impurity.

כְּלִי חֶרֶשׂ יוֹכִיחַ.

The Gemara answers: The *halakhot* of **an earthenware vessel can prove** that the fact that there are primary sources of impurity within its type is not a relevant factor. An earthenware vessel can never become a primary source of impurity, and nevertheless, if it is impure it disqualifies *teruma* upon contact.

מָה לִכְלִי חֶרֶשׂ שֶׁכֵּן מְטַמֵּא מֵאֲוִירוֹ!

The Gemara challenges: **What** is unique **about an earthenware vessel is that** unlike a loaf, it **can render** items **impure** or it can itself become impure **from its airspace.** An earthenware vessel is the only vessel that does not require direct contact with another item in order to contract or transfer impurity, but can effect or contract impurity through its airspace.

טבול יום יוכיח.

The Gemara answers: **One who immersed that day can prove** that being able to render items impure through airspace is not a relevant factor. Such an item disqualifies *teruma*, but imparts impurity only through direct contact and not through its airspace.

וחוזר הדין, לא ראי זה כראי זה ולא ראי זה כראי זה. הצד השוה שבהן – שמותרין בחולין ופוסלין בתרומה, כל שכן ככר שני שפוסל בחולין דפוסל בתרומה.

And the derivation has reverted to its starting point. **The aspect of this** case **is not like the aspect of that** case **and the aspect of that** case **is not like the aspect of this** case, as each case has its own unique stringencies. However, **their common denominator is that non-sacred** food they come into contact with **is permitted,**[N] i.e., is not rendered impure, **but they disqualify *teruma*.** Therefore, Rabban Yoḥanan ben Zakkai infers *a fortiori* that **all the more so, a loaf** that contracted **second**-degree impurity, **which is disqualified,** i.e., rendered impure, even if it is **non-sacred,** should also **disqualify *teruma*** with which it comes into contact. This was Rabban Yoḥanan ben Zakkai's logical *a fortiori* inference that led him to rule that a loaf of second-degree impurity status disqualifies *teruma*.

ודור אחר פריך: מה להצד השוה שבהן שכן יש בהן צד חמור.

And another generation, i.e., the later generation that Rabban Yoḥanan ben Zakkai predicted would deem *teruma* that came into contact with second-degree impurity pure, would **refute** this inference as follows: **What** is unique **about their common denominator is that** both cases **have a stringent aspect** that does not exist in other impure items.

ורבן יוחנן בן זכאי, צד חמור לא פריך.

And Rabban Yoḥanan ben Zakkai maintained that *teruma* that came into contact with second-degree impurity is pure, as he **would not refute** an inference that is based on two sources due to the fact that both sources have **a stringent aspect,** since each source's stringency is not shared by the other.

תניא, אמר רבי יוסי: מנין לרביעי בקודש שפסול?

§ **It is taught** in a *baraita* (*Tosefta*, *Ḥagiga* 3:18) that **Rabbi Yosei said: From where** is it derived with regard **to sacrificial** food with **fourth**-degree ritual impurity **that it is disqualified** although it is not capable of imparting impurity to other items?

ודין הוא: מה מחוסר כיפורים שמותר בתרומה – פסול בקודש, שלישי שפסול בתרומה – אינו דין הוא שיעשה רביעי בקודש;

It is derived through **logical** inference: **Just as one who is lacking atonement,** e.g., a *zav* or leper who immersed at the conclusion of his period of impurity but has not yet brought an offering for his atonement, **who is permitted** to partake **of *teruma*,** nevertheless **disqualifies sacrificial** food if he comes into contact with it, so too, with regard to an item of **third**-degree impurity status, **which disqualifies *teruma*** and is therefore more severe than one who is lacking atonement, **is it not logical that it should render sacrificial** food with which it comes into contact as having **fourth**-degree impurity?

ולמדנו שלישי לקודש מן התורה, ורביעי מקל וחומר.

The *baraita* concludes: **And we have** therefore **derived** that **third**-degree impurity applies **to sacrificial** food **from** an explicit verse in **the Torah, and** we have derived that **fourth**-degree impurity applies to sacrificial food **by** means of the above ***a fortiori*** inference.

שלישי לקודש מן התורה מנלן? דכתיב: "והבשר אשר יגע בכל טמא לא יאכל" – מי לא עסקינן דנגע בשני, ואמר רחמנא: "לא יאכל". רביעי מקל וחומר, כדאמרן.

The Gemara asks: **From where in the Torah do we** derive that third-degree impurity applies **to sacrificial** food?[H] The Gemara answers: **As it is written: "And the flesh that touches any impure thing shall not be eaten"** (Leviticus 7:19). **Are we not dealing** in the verse with meat **that touches** even an item of **second**-degree impurity? **And the Merciful One states** that it **"shall not be eaten,"** indicating that it assumes third-degree impurity. Therefore, **fourth**-degree impurity can be derived **by** means of the ***a fortiori*** inference of Rabbi Yosei, **as we stated** above.

אמר רבי יוחנן: טעם בריבי איני יודע מה הוא, שהרי תשובתו בצדו: אוכל הבא מחמת טבול יום יוכיח, שפסול בתרומה ואינו עושה רביעי בקודש!

Rabbi Yoḥanan says: With regard to **the reasoning** behind **the Distinguished** Rabbi Yosei's *a fortiori* inference, **I do not know what it is, as the response to his** inference is right **by its side: Food whose** impurity **came from** contact with **one who immersed that day can prove** that a degree of impurity that disqualifies *teruma* does not necessarily impart fourth-degree impurity to sacrificial food, **as** this food **disqualifies *teruma*** upon contact, **but it does not impart fourth**-degree impurity **upon sacrificial** food.

NOTES

That non-sacred food they come into contact with is permitted – שמותרין בחולין: Rashi rejects this version of the text, as an earthenware vessel can have only first-degree impurity and therefore will always render impure any non-sacred food that comes into contact with it. Rabbeinu Meshullam suggests that the Gemara is referring to an earthenware vessel that was purified by means of breaking the vessel, but was not broken entirely. In this case, although there is still a minor degree of impurity in the vessel, the degree is not enough to transmit impurity to non-sacred food. Rabbeinu Tam rejects the opinion of Rabbeinu Meshullam, claiming that there is no source that indicates that any level of impurity remains in the broken shards of an earthenware vessel. Other commentaries present alternative explanations of the text.

HALAKHA

From where…do we derive that third-degree impurity applies to sacrificial food – שלישי לקודש...מנלן: Sacrificial food that contracts impurity of the first, second, or third degree is considered impure, and can impart impurity to other sacrificial food. However, sacrificial food that contracts fourth-degree impurity is merely disqualified, and cannot impart impurity to other sacrificial food, as there is no fifth degree of impurity, even with regard to sacrificial food (Rambam *Sefer Tahara, Hilkhot She'ar Avot HaTumot* 11:4).

HALAKHA

Just as he disqualifies *teruma* foods, etc. – כְּשֵׁם שֶׁפּוֹסֵל אוֹכְלֵי תְרוּמָה וכו׳: One who immersed that day is considered to have second-degree impurity status. Consequently, he disqualifies *teruma* foods and liquids by touching them. Even if he touches sacrificial food, it is merely disqualified, assuming fourth-degree impurity status, but it cannot impart impurity to other sacrificial food. This is in accordance with the opinion of the Rabbis (Rambam *Sefer Tahara, Hilkhot She'ar Avot HaTumot* 10:3).

דְּתַנְיָא, אַבָּא שָׁאוּל אוֹמֵר: טְבוּל יוֹם תְּחִילָּה לְקוֹדֶשׁ, לְטַמֵּא שְׁנַיִם וְלִפְסוֹל אֶחָד;

As it is taught in a *baraita* (*Tosefta, Teharot* 1:4) that **Abba Shaul says:** With regard to **one who immersed that day,** until sunset he is treated as one who is impure with **first**-degree impurity **vis-à-vis sacrificial** food, in that he is able **to render two** items of sacrificial food **impure and to disqualify one** additional item. In other words, the first item of sacrificial food that he touches assumes the status of a second-degree impurity. A second item that comes into contact with the first one assumes third-degree impurity. A third item that comes into contact with the second assumes fourth-degree impurity and is therefore disqualified from being eaten, though it cannot impart impurity to other items.

רַבִּי מֵאִיר אוֹמֵר: מְטַמֵּא אֶחָד וּפוֹסֵל אֶחָד; וַחֲכָמִים אוֹמְרִים: כְּשֵׁם שֶׁפּוֹסֵל אוֹכְלֵי תְרוּמָה וּמַשְׁקֵי תְרוּמָה, כָּךְ פּוֹסֵל אוֹכְלֵי קוֹדֶשׁ וּמַשְׁקֵי קוֹדֶשׁ.

Rabbi Meir says: One who immersed that day is considered impure with second-degree impurity, even vis-à-vis sacrificial food, and as such **renders** only **one** item **impure and disqualifies one** additional item. **And the Rabbis say: Just as he** merely **disqualifies *teruma* foods**[H] **and *teruma* liquids,** without transferring to them impurity that can then be transferred further, **so too, he** merely **disqualifies sacrificial foods and sacrificial liquids.** In other words, the impurity imparted by one who immersed that day can reach only third-degree impurity and not fourth-degree impurity, contrary to the opinion of Rabbi Yosei.

מַתְקִיף לַהּ רַב פַּפָּא: מִמַּאי דְּרַבִּי יוֹסֵי כְּרַבָּנַן סְבִירָא לֵיהּ? דִּילְמָא כְּאַבָּא שָׁאוּל סְבִירָא לֵיהּ, דְּאָמַר: לְטַמֵּא שְׁנַיִם וְלִפְסוֹל אֶחָד!

Rav Pappa objects to Rabbi Yoḥanan's argument: **From where** is the presumption derived **that Rabbi Yosei holds in accordance with** the opinion of **the Rabbis? Perhaps he holds in accordance with** the opinion of **Abba Shaul, who says** that one who immersed that day is able **to render two** items of sacrificial food **impure, and to disqualify one** additional item.

אִי סָלְקָא דַּעְתָּךְ כְּאַבָּא שָׁאוּל סְבִירָא לֵיהּ, לֵיתֵיהּ לִרְבִיעִי בְּקוֹדֶשׁ מֵאוֹכֶל שֶׁבָּא מֵחֲמַת טְבוּל יוֹם:

The Gemara answers: **If it enters your mind** that Rabbi Yosei **holds in accordance with** the opinion of **Abba Shaul, he should have brought** proof **for** the existence of a **fourth** degree of ritual impurity **with regard to sacrificial** food **from** the case of **food whose** impurity **came from one who immersed that day,** as follows:

וּמָה אוֹכֶל הַבָּא מֵחֲמַת טְבוּל יוֹם, דִּטְבוּל יוֹם גּוּפֵיהּ מוּתָּר בְּחוּלִּין – אָמַרְתָּ עוֹשֶׂה רְבִיעִי בַּקּוֹדֶשׁ, אוֹכֶל

Just as with regard to **food whose** impurity **came from one who immersed that day, while the one who immersed that day is himself permitted to** consume **non-sacred** food, nevertheless **you say** that the food **imparts fourth**-degree impurity status **upon sacrificial** food, then with regard to **food**

Perek **V**
Daf **30** Amud **a**

שְׁלִישִׁי הַבָּא מֵחֲמַת שֵׁנִי, דְּשֵׁנִי גּוּפֵיהּ אָסוּר בְּחוּלִּין – אֵינוֹ דִּין שֶׁעוֹשֶׂה רְבִיעִי בַּקּוֹדֶשׁ.

whose third-degree impurity **came from** contact with an item of **second**-degree impurity, in **which** case the item with the **second**-degree impurity **is itself forbidden,** i.e. impure, even if it is **non-sacred** food, **isn't it logical** to infer **that it should** be able to **impart fourth**-degree impurity **upon sacrificial** food?

וְכִי תֵּימָא, מִשּׁוּם דְּאִיכָּא לְמִיפְרַךְ: מָה לִטְבוּל יוֹם שֶׁכֵּן אַב הַטּוּמְאָה! הָא אַיְיתִינָהּ מִמְּחוּסַּר כִּיפּוּרִים וְלָא פַּרְכֵיהּ.

And if you would say that the reason Rabbi Yosei did not employ this *a fortiori* inference is **because it can be refuted** as follows: **What** is unique **about one who immersed that day is that** prior to his immersion he was **a primary source of impurity,** this cannot be, as Rabbi Yosei **brought** proof for the existence of a fourth degree of impurity **from** the case of **one who has not yet** brought an **atonement** offering, who was also a primary source of impurity prior to his immersion, **and** Rabbi Yosei clearly **did not refute** the proof due to this factor. Therefore, the reason Rabbi Yosei did not employ an *a fortiori* inference from the case of food that contracted impurity from one who immersed that day is clearly that he disagrees with the opinion of Abba Shaul. Consequently, Rabbi Yoḥanan concluded that he cannot understand Rabbi Yosei's reasoning.

אָמַר רַב אַסִי אָמַר רַב, וְאָמְרִי לַהּ אָמַר רַבָּה בֶּן אִיסִי אָמַר רַב: רַבִּי מֵאִיר וְרַבִּי יוֹסֵי וְרַבִּי יְהוֹשֻׁעַ וְרַבִּי אֶלְעָזָר וְרַבִּי אֱלִיעֶזֶר, כּוּלְּהוּ סְבִירָא לְהוּ דְּאֵין שֵׁנִי עוֹשֶׂה שְׁלִישִׁי בְּחוּלִּין.

§ **Rabbi Asi said** that **Rav said, and some say Rabba ben Isi said** that **Rav said: Rabbi Meir, and Rabbi Yosei, and Rabbi Yehoshua, and Rabbi Elazar, and Rabbi Eliezer all hold that** an item of second-degree ritual impurity status **cannot impart** third-degree ritual impurity status **to non-sacred items.**[H] Rav proceeds to prove this by attributing support from the rulings of each of these *tanna'im*.

רַבִּי מֵאִיר, דִּתְנַן: כָּל הַטָּעוּן בִּיאַת מַיִם מִדִּבְרֵי סוֹפְרִים – מְטַמֵּא אֶת הַקּוֹדֶשׁ וּפוֹסֵל אֶת הַתְּרוּמָה, וּמוּתָּר בְּחוּלִּין וּבְמַעֲשֵׂר, דִּבְרֵי רַבִּי מֵאִיר; וַחֲכָמִים אוֹסְרִין בְּמַעֲשֵׂר.

Rabbi Meir is of this opinion, **as we learned** in a mishna (*Para* 11:5): **Anything that requires immersion in water**[H] **by rabbinic law renders sacrificial** food **impure** upon contact, with second-degree impurity, **and disqualifies *teruma*,** meaning that it renders the *teruma* itself impure, but not to the extent that the *teruma* can render other *teruma* impure. **And** anything that requires immersion in water by rabbinic law **is permitted for non-sacred** food **and for** the second **tithe,** i.e., it does not render these items impure. This is **the statement of Rabbi Meir. But the Rabbis prohibit** one who has this degree of impurity from partaking of the second **tithe.**[H] From the fact that Rabbi Meir permits him to partake of the second tithe, it is inferred that he maintains that an item of second-degree impurity cannot impart third-degree impurity upon non-sacred items.

רַבִּי יוֹסֵי, הָא דַּאֲמַרַן, דְּאִם אִיתֵיהּ, לֵייתֵיהּ לִרְבִיעִי בִּתְרוּמָה וַחֲמִישִׁי בְּקוֹדֶשׁ.

It is evident that **Rabbi Yosei** is of this opinion from **that which we have stated** above, that he derives that sacrificial food can contract fourth-degree impurity, **because if he holds** that non-sacred items can contract third-degree impurity, **he should have derived** through his *a fortiori* inference that there is **fourth**-degree impurity **vis-à-vis *teruma* and fifth**-degree impurity **vis-à-vis sacrificial** food, since each of these categories has a unique level of impurity.

רַבִּי יְהוֹשֻׁעַ, דִּתְנַן, רַבִּי אֱלִיעֶזֶר אוֹמֵר: הָאוֹכֵל אוֹכֶל רִאשׁוֹן – רִאשׁוֹן; שֵׁנִי – שֵׁנִי; שְׁלִישִׁי – שְׁלִישִׁי; רַבִּי יְהוֹשֻׁעַ אוֹמֵר: הָאוֹכֵל אוֹכֶל רִאשׁוֹן וְאוֹכֶל שֵׁנִי – שֵׁנִי; שְׁלִישִׁי – שֵׁנִי בַּקּוֹדֶשׁ וְאֵין שֵׁנִי בִּתְרוּמָה,

Rabbi Yehoshua is of this opinion, **as we learned** in a mishna (*Teharot* 2:2): **Rabbi Eliezer says: One who eats food** with **first**-degree impurity[H] assumes **first**-degree impurity. One who eats food with **second**-degree impurity assumes **second**-degree impurity. One who eats food with **third**-degree impurity assumes **third**-degree impurity. **Rabbi Yehoshua says: One who eats food** with **first**-degree impurity **or** food with **second**-degree impurity assumes **second**-degree impurity. One who eats food with **third**-degree impurity assumes **second**-degree impurity **vis-à-vis sacrificial** food,[H] **and** he does **not** assume **second**-degree impurity **vis-à-vis *teruma*.**

HALAKHA

An item of second-degree impurity status cannot impart third-degree impurity status to non-sacred items – אֵין שֵׁנִי עוֹשֶׂה שְׁלִישִׁי בְּחוּלִּין: A non-sacred food item with first-degree ritual impurity status imparts impurity upon other items with which it comes into contact. A non-sacred item with second-degree impurity status cannot impart impurity to another non-sacred item, as non-sacred food cannot contract third-degree impurity status (Rambam *Sefer Tahara*, *Hilkhot She'ar Avot HaTumot* 11:2).

Anything that requires immersion in water, etc. – כָּל הַטָּעוּן בִּיאַת מַיִם וכו׳: The Sages decreed that if one's head and most of his body are immersed in drawn water, he assumes second-degree impurity status until he immerses himself in a ritual bath. If this individual, or any other person who is impure due to a similar rabbinic decree, touches *teruma*, he imparts upon the *teruma* third-degree impurity status. If he touches sacrificial food, he imparts upon it fourth-degree impurity status (Rambam *Sefer Tahara*, *Hilkhot She'ar Avot HaTumot* 10:2–3).

But the Rabbis prohibit the second tithe – וַחֲכָמִים אוֹסְרִין בְּמַעֲשֵׂר: It is prohibited to partake of the second tithe if one is ritually impure. Even if he is rendered impure merely due to rabbinically enacted ritual impurity, it is still prohibited for him to partake of the second tithe (Rambam *Sefer Tahara*, *Hilkhot Tumat Okhalin* 16:8).

One who eats food with first-degree impurity – הָאוֹכֵל אוֹכֶל רִאשׁוֹן: The Sages decreed that one who eats food of first- or second-degree impurity status assumes second-degree impurity status, in accordance with the opinion of Rabbi Yehoshua (Rambam *Sefer Tahara*, *Hilkhot She'ar Avot HaTumot* 8:10).

One who eats food with third-degree impurity assumes second-degree impurity vis-à-vis sacrificial food, etc. – שְׁלִישִׁי שֵׁנִי בַּקּוֹדֶשׁ וכו׳: One who eats food with third-degree impurity status, which can be either *teruma* or non-sacred food that has been kept to the standards of *teruma*, although he remains ritually pure in that he does not render *teruma* he touches impure, nevertheless he is considered as one who has second-degree impurity status vis-à-vis sacrificial food. One who eats non-sacred food that has been kept to the standards of sacrificial food and has contracted third-degree impurity status cannot impart impurity to sacrificial food (Rambam *Sefer Tahara*, *Hilkhot She'ar Avot HaTumot* 11:12).

בְּחוּלִּין שֶׁנַּעֲשׂוּ עַל טׇהֳרַת תְּרוּמָה;

Eating an item with third-degree impurity is possible only in the case of non-sacred items, as eating impure *teruma* or sacrificial food is prohibited. However, generic non-sacred food cannot contract third-degree impurity at all. Therefore, the case of one who eats food with third-degree impurity refers specifically **to non-sacred** food items **that were prepared** as if their level of purity were **on the** level of the **purity of *teruma*.** By means of a vow, one can establish the purity status of non-sacred food items to be treated on the level of purity necessary for *teruma*.

עַל טׇהֳרַת הַתְּרוּמָה – אִין, עַל טׇהֳרַת הַקּוֹדֶשׁ – לָא.

The Gemara infers from Rabbi Yehoshua's statement that **yes,** one is able to prepare items as if their level of purity were **on the** level of the **purity of *teruma*;** but one is **not** able to prepare items as if their level of purity were **on the** level of the **purity of sacrificial** food, and such items would not contract third-degree impurity.

אַלְמָא קָסָבַר: אֵין שֵׁנִי עוֹשֶׂה שְׁלִישִׁי בְּחוּלִּין.

The Gemara concludes: **Apparently,** Rabbi Yehoshua **holds** that an item of second-degree impurity **cannot impart** third-degree impurity **upon** ordinary **non-sacred items** that were not prepared on the level of the purity of *teruma*.

רַבִּי אֶלְעָזָר, דְּתַנְיָא, רַבִּי אֶלְעָזָר אוֹמֵר: שְׁלׇשְׁתָּן שָׁוִין, הָרִאשׁוֹן שֶׁבַּקּוֹדֶשׁ וְשֶׁבַּחוּלִּין וְשֶׁבַּתְּרוּמָה –

Rabbi Elazar is of this opinion, **as it is taught** in a mishna (*Teharot* 2:7): **Rabbi Elazar says:** The **three of these** are **equal** in their ability to impart ritual impurity to other items: An item of **first**-degree impurity, whether it is an item **of sacrificial** food, **or of non-sacred** food, **or of *teruma*.**

מְטַמֵּא שְׁנַיִם וּפוֹסֵל אֶחָד בַּקּוֹדֶשׁ,

With regard to sacrificial food, such an item **renders impure two** additional levels of contact, enabling the items that contracted ritual impurity from it to transfer that impurity to items that they in turn touch afterward. **And** it **disqualifies one** level afterward, imparting upon the food fourth-degree impurity, which cannot impart impurity to a fifth item.

מְטַמֵּא אֶחָד וּפוֹסֵל אֶחָד בִּתְרוּמָה,

With regard to *teruma*, an item of first-degree impurity **renders impure one** additional level of contact, i.e., it imparts second-level impurity to *teruma* food with which it comes into contact, **and** that item in turn **disqualifies one** additional level afterward, as that *teruma* food imparts third-degree impurity upon *teruma*.

וּפוֹסֵל אֶחָד בְּחוּלִּין.

And with regard to non-sacred food, an item of first-degree impurity merely **disqualifies one** additional level of non-sacred food. Evidently, non-sacred items cannot go beyond a second-degree impurity.

רַבִּי אֱלִיעֶזֶר, דִּתְנַן, רַבִּי אֱלִיעֶזֶר אוֹמֵר: חַלָּה נִיטֶּלֶת מִן הַטְּהוֹרָה עַל הַטְּמֵאָה. כֵּיצַד? שְׁתֵּי עִיסּוֹת אַחַת טְהוֹרָה וְאַחַת טְמֵאָה, נוֹטֵל כְּדֵי חַלָּה מֵעִיסָּה שֶׁלֹּא הוּרְמָה חַלָּתָהּ, וְנוֹתֵן פָּחוֹת מִכְּבֵיצָה בָּאֶמְצַע כְּדֵי לִיטּוֹל מִן הַמּוּקָּף.

Rabbi Eliezer also agrees with this principle, **as we learned** in a mishna (*Ḥalla* 2:8): **Rabbi Eliezer says: *Ḥalla*[B] can be taken from ritually pure** dough **on** behalf of **ritually impure** dough.[N] **How so?** If there are **two batches of dough,**[H] **one** of which is **pure and one** of which is **impure,** one **takes** the required **amount of** dough for separating ***ḥalla*** for both of the batches **from the** pure **dough when its *ḥalla* has not** yet **been separated** for itself, **and** then **places less than an egg-bulk**[N] of dough, which is not susceptible becoming ritually impure due to its size, **in the middle,** between the impure dough and the pure dough set aside for being used as the separated *ḥalla*. This joins all of the dough together, **so that** one can fulfill the requirement **to take** dough for separating *ḥalla* **from** dough **that is situated near** the dough it comes to exempt.

BACKGROUND

Ḥalla – חַלָּה: The Torah commands the separation of a portion of one's dough, which is declared as *ḥalla* and is later given to the priests (see Numbers 15:20). This portion of *ḥalla* is governed by all the *halakhot* pertaining to *teruma*, the portion of produce set aside for the priests. *Ḥalla* must be taken from all dough made from any of the five types of grain, provided that the quantity of flour of the batch is at least a tenth of an ephah in volume. If *ḥalla* is not taken, the dough has the status of untithed produce and may not be eaten.

The Torah does not specify a measure for *ḥalla*. However, the Sages required an individual baking for personal use to give one twenty-fourth of his dough as *ḥalla*, and a commercial baker to give one forty-eighth. Nowadays, as all Jews are assumed to be ritually impure, *ḥalla* is governed by *halakhot* similar to impure *teruma*; it cannot be eaten and therefore must be burned. Accordingly, the measures mentioned above no longer apply; only a small portion is separated from the dough and burned, and the rest of the dough may then be used. A blessing is recited for the separation of *ḥalla*. The *halakhot* of this mitzva, which is one of the mitzvot performed particularly by women, are discussed comprehensively in tractate *Ḥalla*.

NOTES

Ḥalla can be taken from ritually pure dough on behalf of ritually impure dough – חַלָּה נִיטֶּלֶת מִן הַטְּהוֹרָה עַל הַטְּמֵאָה: Why is it necessary to separate *ḥalla* from ritually pure dough on behalf of ritually impure dough? Rashi explains that according to Rabbi Eliezer one must do so only if he purposely rendered the dough impure, as a fine. In *Tosefot HaRosh*, however, it is argued that one who has impure dough must always separate *ḥalla* from pure dough on its behalf, in order to provide the priest with ritually pure dough from which he can eat.

And places less than an egg-bulk, etc. – וְנוֹתֵן פָּחוֹת מִכְּבֵיצָה וכו׳: The way in which this process is performed would seem to indicate that it is not considered as if two batches of dough are situated near each other unless they are actually touching, and it would not be sufficient to just place the two batches in the same basket to group them together, as otherwise this whole process would be unnecessary. The Maharam of Rothenburg, however, states that this procedure needs to be done only in such a situation where one of the batches of dough is pure and the other impure; since one clearly does not want to combine the two batches, in order to separate *ḥalla* for both of them together it is necessary that they actually touch. Otherwise, placing different batches of dough in the same basket would suffice.

HALAKHA

Two batches of dough – שְׁתֵּי עִיסּוֹת: If one has two batches of dough, one of which is ritually pure and the other of which is ritually impure, he must take the entire required amount of dough for separating *ḥalla* from the pure dough, and then place less than an egg-bulk of impure dough between the pure batch and the impure batch, in order to separate *ḥalla* from dough that is situated near the dough it comes to exempt (Rambam *Sefer Zera'im*, *Hilkhot Bikkurim* 7:12).

וַחֲכָמִים אוֹסְרִין.

And the Rabbis prohibit separating *ḥalla* in this manner.

וְתַנְיָא: כַּבֵּיצָה;

And it is taught in a *baraita* that Rabbi Eliezer even allows the ritually pure dough placed in the middle to be as large as **an egg-bulk,**[N] even though dough of that size is susceptible to the *halakhot* of ritual impurity.

סַבְרוּהָ אִידִי וְאִידִי בְּעִיסָּה רִאשׁוֹנָה, וְחוּלִּין הַטְּבוּלִין לְחַלָּה לָא כְּחַלָּה דָּמוּ.

The Gemara now explains the reasoning of those who tried to prove from here that Rabbi Eliezer is of the opinion that second-degree ritual impurity cannot impart third-degree ritual impurity upon non-sacred items: **They assumed**[N] that both **this** mishna **and this** *baraita* are referring to cases **where the dough** is of **first**-degree impurity. **And** furthermore, they assumed that all the *tanna'im* agree that **non-sacred** food **that is untithed with regard to** the obligation to separate ***ḥalla***, as its *ḥalla* has not yet been separated, **is not** treated **like *ḥalla*** as far as its ability to contract third-degree ritual impurity. Rather, it is regarded as generic non-sacred food, which is susceptible only to second-degree impurity.

מַאי לָאו בְּהָא קָמִיפַּלְגִי, דְּמָר סָבַר: אֵין שֵׁנִי עוֹשֶׂה שְׁלִישִׁי בְּחוּלִּין,

Based on these assumptions the Gemara explains how these authorities understood the tannaitic dispute: **What, is it not** clear that Rabbi Eliezer and the Rabbis **disagree with regard to** the following matter:[N] One **Sage,** Rabbi Eliezer, **holds** that an item of second-degree impurity **cannot impart** third-degree impurity **to non-sacred items.** Therefore, there is no problem placing an egg-bulk of pure dough in the middle, as although it will touch the impure dough and will thereby contract second-degree impurity, nevertheless it is unable to transmit impurity to the pure dough.

וּמָר סָבַר: שֵׁנִי עוֹשֶׂה שְׁלִישִׁי בְּחוּלִּין.

And one **Sage,** i.e., the Rabbis, **holds** that an item of second-degree impurity **can impart** third-degree ritual impurity **to non-sacred items.** They therefore prohibit placing an egg-bulk of dough in the middle, as it will assume second-degree impurity status, which, in their opinion, can impart third-degree impurity status upon the pure dough.

אֲמַר רַב מָרִי בְּרֵיהּ דְּרַב כָּהֲנָא: דְּכוּלֵּי עָלְמָא אֵין שֵׁנִי עוֹשֶׂה שְׁלִישִׁי בְּחוּלִּין. וְהָכָא בְּחוּלִּין הַטְּבוּלִין לְחַלָּה קָמִיפַּלְגִי, מָר סָבַר: כְּחַלָּה דָּמוּ, וּמָר סָבַר: לָא כְּחַלָּה דָּמוּ.

Rav Mari, son of Rav Kahana, said that the dispute can be understood differently: **Everyone** agrees that an item of second-degree ritual impurity **cannot impart** third-degree ritual impurity **to non-sacred items. But here,** the dispute concerns another matter, as **they disagree with regard to** the status of **non-sacred** food that is **untithed vis-à-vis *ḥalla***, as its *ḥalla* has not yet been separated. One **Sage,** i.e., the Rabbis, **holds** that **it is** treated **like *ḥalla*** with regard to its ability to contract third-degree impurity, **and** one **Sage,** Rabbi Eliezer, **holds** that **it is not** treated **like *ḥalla*** and cannot contract third-degree impurity. Therefore, he permits separating *ḥalla* in this manner.

וְאִיבָּעֵית אֵימָא: דְּכוּלֵּי עָלְמָא – חוּלִּין הַטְּבוּלִין לְחַלָּה לָא כְּחַלָּה דָּמוּ, וְאֵין שֵׁנִי עוֹשֶׂה שְׁלִישִׁי בְּחוּלִּין. וְהָכָא בְּמוּתָּר לִגְרוֹם טוּמְאָה לְחוּלִּין שֶׁבְּאֶרֶץ יִשְׂרָאֵל קָמִיפַּלְגִי,

And if you wish, say instead that they disagree with regard to a different issue: **Everyone** agrees that **non-sacred** food that is **untithed with regard to *ḥalla* is not** treated **like *ḥalla*** and cannot contract third-degree impurity, **and** that an item of second-degree ritual impurity **cannot impart** third-degree ritual impurity **to non-sacred items. But here, they disagree with regard to** whether or not **it is permitted to cause ritual impurity to non-sacred** food **that is in Eretz Yisrael.**[HN]

NOTES

An egg-bulk – כַּבֵּיצָה: Although it is agreed upon that an egg-bulk is the minimum measurement necessary for food to contract ritual impurity, there is a dispute between Rashi and *Tosafot* with regard to the details of this requirement. Rashi understands that at least an egg-bulk of food is necessary in order for it to be capable of imparting impurity upon other food items with which it comes into contact. However, according to *Tosafot* (*Pesaḥim* 33b), less than an egg-bulk of food cannot contract ritual impurity either. This disagreement leads to conflicting interpretations of the Gemara here.

They assumed – סַבְרוּהָ: Usually when a statement is introduced by the expression: They assumed, it is an indication that this opinion was expressed in the study hall but was eventually rejected. The Meiri points out that in this case, only part of the opinion presented is rejected in the continuation of the Gemara, as there is no rejection of the assumption that the reference is to dough of first-degree impurity status.

Disagree with regard to the following matter – בְּהָא קָמִיפַּלְגִי: Does this refer to the mishna or to the *baraita*? Rashi maintains that the Gemara is explaining the dispute in the mishna. Although Rabbi Eliezer's opinion, as quoted in the mishna, is that one should use a piece of dough small enough that it is not susceptible to the *halakhot* of ritual impurity, nevertheless, the Gemara assumes that he is not concerned about it transferring impurity to the *ḥalla*. Otherwise, he would prohibit this procedure lest one accidently use an egg-bulk of dough, thereby imparting impurity upon the pure dough. Accordingly, the *baraita* is mentioned tangentially, as it is not necessary for the discussion.

According to this explanation, later commentaries ask why the Gemara does not suggest that the core dispute between Rabbi Eliezer and the Rabbis is whether or not the concern that use of a smaller piece of dough will lead to use of an egg-bulk should be taken into account. *Torat HaKenaot* answers that this concern is obviously valid, as it is difficult for people to discern between these measurements.

In the Commentary of Rabbi Shimshon of Saens on tractate *Terumot*, the Gemara here is explained as discussing the dispute between the mishna and the *baraita* with regard to the opinion of Rabbi Eliezer.

It is permitted to cause ritual impurity to non-sacred food that is in Eretz Yisrael – מוּתָּר לִגְרוֹם טוּמְאָה לְחוּלִּין שֶׁבְּאֶרֶץ יִשְׂרָאֵל: The reason why this issue applies only in Eretz Yisrael is that non-sacred food outside of Eretz Yisrael is automatically impure due to the inherent impurity of what is called the land of the nations, i.e., any territory outside of Eretz Yisrael.

The opinion that it is prohibited to cause impurity in Eretz Yisrael is perhaps related to the fact that although eating impure non-sacred food is halakhically permitted, many individuals who were devoted to the meticulous observance of mitzvot would make sure to keep their food ritually pure. Furthermore, it can be reasoned that if people are not careful to avoid causing food to become impure, they may accidently impart impurity to items that are prohibited to become impure, e.g., *teruma* and sacrificial food.

HALAKHA

It is permitted to cause ritual impurity to non-sacred food that is in Eretz Yisrael – מוּתָּר לִגְרוֹם טוּמְאָה לְחוּלִּין שֶׁבְּאֶרֶץ יִשְׂרָאֵל: Just as it is permitted to eat non-sacred food while in a state of ritual impurity, so too, it is permitted to cause impurity to non-sacred food that is in Eretz Yisrael (Rambam *Sefer Tahara*, *Hilkhot Tumat Okhalin* 16:9).

BACKGROUND

Shabbat boundary – **תְּחוּם שַׁבָּת**: By rabbinic decree, and some say by Torah law, a person is not permitted to travel more than a certain distance away from the place where he established his residence at the onset of Shabbat. That distance is known as the Shabbat boundary. Even animals and inanimate objects have a boundary, determined by that of the person to whose care they are entrusted, beyond which they may not be taken. Generally, the Shabbat boundary is defined as two thousand cubits outside of the person's city, in any direction.

NOTES

One Sage holds that the *halakha* of Shabbat boundaries is mandated by Torah law, etc. – **מָר סָבַר תְּחוּמִין דְּאוֹרָיְיתָא וכו׳**: It is explained in the Jerusalem Talmud that both *tanna'im* agree that the Shabbat limit is by Torah law and the dispute is with regard to its extent. Rabbi Akiva holds that it is two thousand cubits, and Rabbi Eliezer, son of Rabbi Yosei HaGelili, holds that by Torah law it is larger than that, and the two-thousand-cubit measure is by rabbinic law.

HALAKHA

The *halakha* of Shabbat boundaries is mandated by rabbinic law – **תְּחוּמִין...דְּרַבָּנַן**: One who goes beyond the Shabbat limit is liable to receive lashes. The extent of this limit is not explicitly defined in the Torah, but there is a tradition that by Torah law it is twelve *mil*, which is approximately twelve kilometers, whereas the Sages limited it to two thousand cubits, approximately one kilometer. The Ramban and the Rashba, cited in *Maggid Mishne*, are of the opinion that by Torah law there is no Shabbat limit at all. They claim that it is only the opinion of Rabbi Akiva that the Shabbat limit is mandated by Torah law, whereas the other Sages maintain that it is by rabbinic law (Rambam *Sefer Zemanim*, *Hilkhot Shabbat* 27:1).

מָר סָבַר: מוּתָּר לִגְרוֹם טוּמְאָה לְחוּלִּין שֶׁבְּאֶרֶץ יִשְׂרָאֵל, וּמָר סָבַר: אָסוּר לִגְרוֹם טוּמְאָה לְחוּלִּין שֶׁבְּאֶרֶץ יִשְׂרָאֵל.

One Sage, Rabbi Eliezer, **holds** that **it is permitted to cause impurity to non-sacred** food **that is in Eretz Yisrael.** Therefore, since the dough placed in the middle cannot impart third-degree ritual impurity status upon the dough designated for *ḥalla*, there is no reason to prohibit doing so. **And one Sage,** i.e., the Rabbis, **holds** that **it is prohibited to cause impurity to non-sacred** food **that is in Eretz Yisrael.** Therefore, although the dough of the ritually pure batch will not become impure, nevertheless the Rabbis prohibit separating *ḥalla* in this manner, as causing the dough in the middle to become impure is prohibited.

״בּוֹ בַּיּוֹם דָּרַשׁ רַבִּי עֲקִיבָא״ וכו׳.

§ It is stated in the mishna: **On that same day Rabbi Akiva interpreted** one of the contradictory verses with regard to the amount of land surrounding the Levite cities as teaching that one may not travel beyond a two-thousand-cubit radius around his city limits on Shabbat. Rabbi Eliezer, son of Rabbi Yosei HaGelili, on the other hand, interprets the contradictory verses as referring to different types of land left for the Levites around their cities.

בְּמַאי קָא מִיפַּלְגִי? מָר סָבַר: תְּחוּמִין דְּאוֹרָיְיתָא, וּמָר סָבַר: דְּרַבָּנַן.

The Gemara asks: **With regard to what** halakhic matter **do they disagree?** The Gemara answers: One **Sage,** Rabbi Akiva, **holds** that the *halakha* of Shabbat **boundaries**[B] is mandated **by Torah law,**[N] as he bases it on a verse; **and** one **Sage,** Rabbi Eliezer, son of Rabbi Yosei HaGelili, **holds** that the *halakha* of Shabbat boundaries is mandated **by rabbinic law,**[H] and he therefore derives other matters from the verse.

תָּנוּ רַבָּנַן, בּוֹ בַּיּוֹם דָּרַשׁ רַבִּי עֲקִיבָא: בְּשָׁעָה שֶׁעָלוּ יִשְׂרָאֵל מִן הַיָּם נָתְנוּ עֵינֵיהֶם לוֹמַר שִׁירָה. וְכֵיצַד אָמְרוּ שִׁירָה? כְּגָדוֹל הַמַּקְרֵא אֶת הַלֵּל וְהֵן עוֹנִין אַחֲרָיו רָאשֵׁי פְרָקִים. מֹשֶׁה אָמַר ״אָשִׁירָה לַה׳״ וְהֵן אוֹמְרִים ״אָשִׁירָה לַה׳״; מֹשֶׁה אָמַר ״כִּי גָאֹה גָּאָה״ וְהֵן אוֹמְרִים ״אָשִׁירָה לַה׳״.

§ **The Sages taught: On that same day Rabbi Akiva taught** that **at the time that the Jewish people ascended from the** split **sea they set their eyes on reciting a song** of gratitude to God. **And how did they recite** the **song?** In the same manner **as an adult man reciting *hallel*** on behalf of a congregation, as his reading enables all who hear to fulfill their obligation, **and** the congregation listening merely **recite after him the chapter headings** of *hallel*. So too, by the sea, **Moses said: "I will sing unto the Lord"** (Exodus 15:1), **and** the people **said** after Moses: **"I will sing unto the Lord." Moses** continued and **said: "For He is highly exalted"** (Exodus 15:1), **and they said** once again the chapter heading: **"I will sing unto the Lord."**

רַבִּי אֱלִיעֶזֶר בְּנוֹ שֶׁל רַבִּי יוֹסֵי הַגְּלִילִי אוֹמֵר: כְּקָטָן הַמַּקְרֵא אֶת הַלֵּל וְהֵן עוֹנִין אַחֲרָיו כׇּל מַה שֶּׁהוּא אוֹמֵר, מֹשֶׁה אָמַר ״אָשִׁירָה לַה׳״ וְהֵן אוֹמְרִים ״אָשִׁירָה לַה׳״; מֹשֶׁה אָמַר ״כִּי גָאֹה גָּאָה״ וְהֵן אוֹמְרִים ״כִּי גָאֹה גָּאָה״.

Rabbi Eliezer, son of Rabbi Yosei HaGelili, says: The Jewish people sang just **like a minor boy reciting *hallel* and** the congregation who hear him **repeat after him all that he says,** word for word, as hearing the recital of a minor is insufficient for fulfilling one's obligation. So too, by the sea, **Moses said: "I will sing unto the Lord"** (Exodus 15:1), **and** the people **said** after Moses: **"I will sing to the Lord." Moses said: "For He is highly exalted," and they said** after him the same words: **"For He is highly exalted."**

רַבִּי נְחֶמְיָה אוֹמֵר: כְּסוֹפֵר הַפּוֹרֵס עַל שְׁמַע בְּבֵית הַכְּנֶסֶת, שֶׁהוּא פּוֹתֵחַ תְּחִילָּה וְהֵן עוֹנִין אַחֲרָיו.

Rabbi Neḥemya says: They sang the song of the sea **like a scribe,** a cantor, **who recites** aloud **the** introductory prayers and blessings before ***Shema* in the synagogue; as he begins** by saying the **first** words of the blessing, **and they repeat after him** the initial words and continue reciting the rest of *Shema* together with him in unison. So too, in the song of the sea, Moses began and then everyone recited the entire song together with him.

בְּמַאי קָמִיפַּלְגִי? רַבִּי עֲקִיבָא סָבַר: ״לֵאמֹר״ – אַמִּילְּתָא קַמַּיְיתָא,

The Gemara asks: **With regard to what do they disagree?** The Gemara answers that they disagree with regard to the interpretation of the verse: "Then Moses and the children of Israel sang this song unto the Lord, and said, saying" (Exodus 15:1). **Rabbi Akiva holds** that the word **"saying,"** which indicates that the people sang after Moses, is referring only **to the first words** of the song, which the people continually repeated: "I will sing unto the Lord" (Exodus 15:1).

וְרַבִּי אֱלִיעֶזֶר בְּנוֹ שֶׁל רַבִּי יוֹסֵי הַגְּלִילִי סָבַר: ״לֵאמֹר״ – אַכׇּל מִילְּתָא וּמִילְּתָא, וְרַבִּי נְחֶמְיָה סָבַר: ״וַיֹּאמְרוּ״ – דְּאָמְרוּ כּוּלְּהוּ בַּהֲדֵי הֲדָדֵי; ״לֵאמֹר״ – דְּפָתַח מֹשֶׁה בְּרֵישָׁא.

And Rabbi Eliezer, son of Rabbi Yosei HaGelili, holds that the word **"saying"** is referring **to every single word,** as they would repeat after Moses every word. **And Rabbi Neḥemya holds** that the phrase **"and they said"** (Exodus 15:1) indicates **that everyone recited** the song of the sea **together,** and the word **"saying"** means **that Moses began** singing the song **first;** and then the rest of the people sang the beginning after him and they all continued in unison.

תָּנוּ רַבָּנַן, דָּרַשׁ רַבִּי יוֹסֵי הַגְּלִילִי: בְּשָׁעָה שֶׁעָלוּ יִשְׂרָאֵל מִן הַיָּם נָתְנוּ עֵינֵיהֶם לוֹמַר שִׁירָה. וְכֵיצַד אָמְרוּ שִׁירָה? עוֹלָל מוּטָל עַל בִּרְכֵּי אִמּוֹ וְתִינוֹק יוֹנֵק מִשְּׁדֵי אִמּוֹ. כֵּיוָן שֶׁרָאוּ אֶת הַשְּׁכִינָה, עוֹלָל הִגְבִּיהַּ צַוָּארוֹ וְתִינוֹק שָׁמַט דַּד מִפִּיו, וְאָמְרוּ: "זֶה אֵלִי וְאַנְוֵהוּ", שֶׁנֶּאֱמַר: "מִפִּי עוֹלְלִים וְיֹנְקִים יִסַּדְתָּ עֹז".

§ **The Sages taught** in a *baraita* that **Rabbi Yosei HaGelili taught: At the time that the Jewish people ascended from the sea they resolved to sing** a song of gratitude to God. **And how did they recite** this song? If a **baby** was **lying on his mother's lap or an infant** was **nursing from his mother's breasts, once they saw the Divine Presence, the baby straightened his neck and the infant dropped the breast from his mouth, and they recited: "This is my God and I will glorify Him"** (Exodus 15:2). **As it is stated: "Out of the mouths of babies and sucklings You have founded strength"** (Psalms 8:3).

הָיָה רַבִּי מֵאִיר אוֹמֵר: מִנַּיִן שֶׁאֲפִילּוּ עוּבָּרִים שֶׁבִּמְעֵי אִמָּן אָמְרוּ שִׁירָה? שֶׁנֶּאֱמַר:

Rabbi Meir would say: From where is it derived **that even fetuses**[N] **in their mother's womb recited** the **song** at the sea? **As it is stated:**

NOTES

Babies…fetuses – עוֹלָלִים...עוּבָּרִים: The Maharsha writes that it is possible that according to Rabbi Yosei HaGelili the infants sang but the fetuses did not, as it is stated in the Midrash that in Egypt, Jewish babies were born in the fields and God raised them miraculously. Therefore, these infants recognized God at the sea and could say: "This is my God and I will glorify Him" (Exodus 15:2). In *Iyyun Ya'akov*, however, it is claimed that both opinions agree that the fetuses sang, as the Gemara (*Nidda* 31b) writes that while in its mother's womb a fetus is taught the entire Torah by an angel, and therefore it is in a position to recognize God.

Perek **V**
Daf **31** Amud **a**

"בְּמַקְהֵלוֹת בָּרְכוּ אֱלֹהִים ה׳ מִמְּקוֹר יִשְׂרָאֵל".

"In full assemblies, bless God, the Lord, you that are from the source of Israel" (Psalms 68:27), indicating that even children that are in the "source," i.e., their mother's womb, blessed God when they gathered at the sea.

וְהָא לָא חָזוּ! אָמַר רַבִּי תַּנְחוּם: כָּרֵס נַעֲשָׂה לָהֶן כְּאַסְפַּקְלַרְיָא הַמְּאִירָה, וְרָאוּ.

The Gemara asks: **But** the fetuses **could not see,**[N] so how could they have honestly said: "This is my God and I will glorify him"? **Rabbi Tanḥum says:** Their mother's **stomach was transformed for them like luminous crystal** [*aspaklarya*],[L] **and they saw** through it.

"בּוֹ בַּיּוֹם דָּרַשׁ רַבִּי יְהוֹשֻׁעַ בֶּן הוּרְקְנוֹס, שֶׁלֹּא עָבַד אִיּוֹב" כּוּ׳. וְלֶיחֱזֵי הַאי "לֹא", אִי בְּלָמֶ"ד אָלֶ"ף כְּתִיב – "לֹא" הוּא, אִי בְּלָמֶ"ד וָי"ו כְּתִיב – "לוֹ" הוּא!

§ **On that same day Rabbi Yehoshua ben Hyrcanus taught that Job served** the Holy One, Blessed be He, **only** out of love, as it is stated: "Though He will slay me, still I will trust in Him [*lo*]" (Job 13:15). The mishna continues that the word *lo* in the verse is ambiguous as to whether it is indicative of Job expressing his yearning for God or his lack thereof. The Gemara asks: **Let us see whether this** word ***lo* is written *lamed alef*,** and therefore its meaning **is:** I will **not** trust, or **whether it is written *lamed vav*,** according to which its meaning **is:** I trust **in Him.** Why is there room for doubt with regard to the meaning of the verse?

וְכָל הֵיכָא דִּכְתִיב בְּלָמֶ"ד אָלֶ"ף – "לֹא" הוּא? אֶלָּא מֵעַתָּה "בְּכָל צָרָתָם לֹא צָר", דִּכְתִיב בְּלָמֶ"ד אָלֶ"ף, הָכִי נָמֵי דְּ"לֹא" הוּא?

The Gemara counters: **But** is it true that **anywhere that** the word *lo* **is written *lamed alef*,** its meaning **is: Not? If that is so,** then in the verse: **"In all their affliction He was [*lo*] afflicted"** (Isaiah 63:9), **where** the word *lo* **is written *lamed alef*, so too, does it** mean: **Not,** i.e., God was not afflicted in the afflictions of the Jewish people?

וְכִי תֵּימָא הָכִי נָמֵי, וְהָכְתִיב: "וּמַלְאַךְ פָּנָיו הוֹשִׁיעָם"! אֶלָּא לָאו מַשְׁמַע הָכִי וּמַשְׁמַע הָכִי.

And if you would say that **indeed** that is the meaning of the verse, **but isn't it written** in the continuation of that same verse: **"And the angel of His Presence saved them,"** which clearly indicates that God was concerned with their afflictions? Evidently, the word *lo* in that verse means: "In all their affliction He was afflicted." **Rather, is it not** clear that *lamed alef* sometimes **indicates this and** sometimes **indicates that?** Therefore, the mishna had to derive the proper meaning of the word from another verse.

תַּנְיָא, רַבִּי מֵאִיר אוֹמֵר: נֶאֱמַר "יְרֵא אֱלֹהִים" בְּאִיּוֹב וְנֶאֱמַר "יְרֵא אֱלֹהִים" בְּאַבְרָהָם, מָה "יְרֵא אֱלֹהִים" הָאָמוּר בְּאַבְרָהָם – מֵאַהֲבָה, אַף "יְרֵא אֱלֹהִים" הָאָמוּר בְּאִיּוֹב – מֵאַהֲבָה.

It is taught in a *baraita* (*Tosefta* 6:1) that **Rabbi Meir says: It is stated with regard to Job** that he was **"God-fearing"** (Job 1:1), **and it is stated with regard to Abraham** that he was **"God-fearing"** (Genesis 22:12).[N] **Just as** the description **"God-fearing," which is stated with regard to Abraham,** is referring to Abraham's fearing God **out of love, so too,** the description **"God-fearing" that is stated with regard to Job** indicates that Job feared God **out of love.**

NOTES

But the fetuses could not see – וְהָא לָא חָזוּ: The commentaries point out that the Gemara is bothered by the question of how the fetuses could see, when it is seemingly secondary to the problem of how they could sing. If their singing is not a problem, as it was miraculous, why is Gemara troubled by their inability to see? The *Torat HaKenaot* answers that the Gemara asks its question only to introduce the description of the miracle that allowed them to see.

With regard to Abraham, he was God-fearing – יְרֵא אֱלֹהִים בְּאַבְרָהָם: The fear of God mentioned with regard to Abraham is not a reference to his fear of divine retribution, but rather to his awe of God's exaltedness, an attribute that derives from one's recognition and intense love of God (see *Sefer Tanya*; *Kerem Natua*; *Ḥazon Yeḥezkel*).

LANGUAGE

Crystal [*aspaklarya*] – אַסְפַּקְלַרְיָא: From the Latin specularis, of a mirror, or speculare, to examine, which possibly derives from Greek. It refers to a transparent item, pane, or optical instrument. Sometimes it means a mirror.

Ancient lens, possibly used as part of a telescope

NOTES

One who performs mitzvot out of love and one who performs mitzvot out of fear – עוֹשֶׂה מֵאַהֲבָה לְעוֹשֶׂה מִיִּרְאָה: Rashi emphasizes that these two categories are not the same as those of a person who is righteous out of love and a person who is righteous out of fear mentioned above (22b). Here the Gemara is discussing individuals who worship God out of feelings of love and awe of God Himself, while there the Gemara discusses individuals who worship God out of love of the reward and fear of retribution. In the Jerusalem Talmud there is a description of the spiritual benefits of both love and fear of God, as both are necessary in certain situations.

HALAKHA

Greater is the one who performs mitzvot out of love – גָּדוֹל הָעוֹשֶׂה מֵאַהֲבָה: One who worships God out of love is one who is involved in Torah and mitzvot and follows the path of wisdom, not due to desire for worldly benefit or out of fear of retribution or the desire to be rewarded. But rather, he performs that which is true because it is true, and ultimately the reward will come about. This is a very lofty level of worship (Rambam *Sefer HaMadda, Hilkhot Teshuva* 10:2).

וְאַבְרָהָם גּוּפֵיהּ מְנָלַן? דִּכְתִיב: ״זֶרַע אַבְרָהָם אֹהֲבִי״.

The Gemara asks: **And** with regard to **Abraham himself, from where do we** derive that he acted out of a sense of love? **As it is written: "The offspring of Abraham who loved Me"** (Isaiah 41:8).

מַאי אִיכָּא בֵּין עוֹשֶׂה מֵאַהֲבָה לְעוֹשֶׂה מִיִּרְאָה? אִיכָּא הָא דְּתַנְיָא, רַבִּי שִׁמְעוֹן בֶּן אֶלְעָזָר אוֹמֵר: גָּדוֹל הָעוֹשֶׂה מֵאַהֲבָה יוֹתֵר מִן הָעוֹשֶׂה מִיִּרְאָה, שֶׁזֶּה תָּלוּי לְאֶלֶף דּוֹר, וְזֶה תָּלוּי לְאַלְפַּיִם דּוֹר.

The Gemara asks: **What** difference **is there between one who performs** mitzvot **out of love and one who performs** mitzvot **out of fear?**[N] The Gemara answers: **There is that which is taught** in a *baraita* that **Rabbi Shimon ben Elazar says: Greater is the one who performs** mitzvot **out of love**[H] **than the one who performs** mitzvot **out of fear, as** with regard to **this** one who acts out of fear, his merits **endure for one thousand generations, and** with regard to **that** one who serves God out of love, his merits **endure for two thousand generations.**

הָכָא כְּתִיב: ״לַאֲלָפִים לְאֹהֲבַי וּלְשֹׁמְרֵי מִצְוֹתָי״, וְהָתָם כְּתִיב: ״וּלְשֹׁמְרֵי מִצְוֹתָו לְאֶלֶף דּוֹר״.

Proof of this assertion is that **here it is written: "And showing mercy unto thousands of generations of those who love Me and keep My commandments"** (Exodus 20:5), indicating that merits can last for thousands of generations for those who act out of love, **and there it is written:** "Know therefore that the Lord your God, He is God; the faithful God, Who keeps the covenant and mercy with those who love Him **and keep His commandments for a thousand generations"** (Deuteronomy 7:9). The first verse indicates that those who act out of love retain their merits for thousands of generations, whereas the second verse, which mentions only one thousand generations of merit, is referring to the merits of those who keep God's mitzvot out of fear.

הָתָם נַמִי כְּתִיב: ״לְאֹהֲבָיו וּלְשֹׁמְרֵי מִצְוֹתָו לְאֶלֶף דּוֹר״!

The Gemara asks: But **there also,** in the second verse, **it is written:** "The faithful God, Who keeps the covenant and mercy **with those who love Him and keep His commandments for a thousand generations"** (Deuteronomy 7:9). Why is the verse interpreted specifically with regard to those who worship God out of fear, yet it is written that they keep His mitzvot out of love? Both types of people seem to be indicated in both verses.

הַאי לְדִסְמִיךְ לֵיהּ, וְהַאי לְדִסְמִיךְ לֵיהּ.

The Gemara answers: **That** verse, which mentions one thousand generations, is understood as referring **to that which is adjacent to it.** The phrase "for a thousand generations" is understood as referring those who perform mitzvot out of fear, as it is written immediately preceding the phrase "and keep His commandments," which does not mention love. **And this** verse, which mentions thousands of generations, is understood as referring **to that which is adjacent to it:** "Unto thousands of generations of those who love Me."

הָנְהוּ תְּרֵי תַּלְמִידֵי דַּהֲווּ יָתְבִי קַמֵּיהּ דְּרָבָא. חַד אֲמַר לֵיהּ: אַקְרְיוּן בְּחֶלְמַאי ״מָה רַב טוּבְךָ אֲשֶׁר צָפַנְתָּ לִּירֵאֶיךָ״, וְחַד אֲמַר לֵיהּ: אַקְרְיוּן בְּחֶלְמַאי ״וְיִשְׂמְחוּ כָל חוֹסֵי בָךְ לְעוֹלָם יְרַנֵּנוּ...וְיַעְלְצוּ בְךָ אֹהֲבֵי שְׁמֶךָ״. אֲמַר לְהוּ: תַּרְוַיְיכוּ רַבָּנַן צַדִּיקֵי גְּמוּרֵי אַתּוּן, מָר מֵאַהֲבָה, וּמָר מִיִּרְאָה.

It happened that there were **these two students who were sitting before Rava,** and **one said to him: It was read to me in my dream: "How abundant is Your goodness, which You have laid up for those who fear You"** (Psalms 31:20). **And one said to** Rava: **It was read to me in my dream: "So shall all those who take refuge in You rejoice; they will forever shout for joy,** and You will shelter them; **let them also who love Your name exult in You"** (Psalms 5:12). Rava **said to them: You are both completely righteous Sages.** One **Sage,** the second dreamer, serves God **out of love, and** one **Sage,** the first dreamer, serves God **out of fear.** Each Sage's dream corresponded to his manner of serving God.

הדרן עלך כשם שהמים

Summary of **Perek V**

The *halakhot* mentioned in this chapter are primarily derived from interpretations of biblical verses. The first *halakha* mentioned is that just as the bitter water of a *sota* evaluates the fidelity of the *sota* and causes her death if she was unfaithful to her husband, so too, her drinking evaluates the behavior of her alleged paramour; he too dies if he was a party to her adultery, even though he does not drink the bitter water.

Additionally, there was a discussion of the prohibition of the woman to her paramour after she secluded herself with him in the wake of her husband's warning. In the same way that she is forbidden to her husband unless she proves her fidelity by drinking the bitter water, likewise she is forbidden to her paramour. She may not marry him even if her husband dies or divorces her without her having been evaluated by the bitter water.

A number of statements concerning ritual impurity were cited as well in this chapter. Among them is Rabbi Akiva's exposition that even non-sacred food can contract a third-degree ritual impurity. However, his opinion is not the accepted *halakha*, even though Rabbi Yehoshua praised the opinion.

The chapter also mentioned Rabbi Akiva's opinion that the Shabbat limit is two thousand cubits by Torah law. Here too, his opinion is not the accepted *halakha*; all halakhic authorities maintain that this limit is by rabbinic law. While some of them recognize a wider limit by Torah law, others claim there is no Shabbat limit at all by Torah law.

Introduction to **Perek VI**

Speak to the children of Israel, and say to them: If any man's wife goes astray, and acts unfaithfully against him; and a man lie with her carnally, and it was hidden from the eyes of her husband, she was defiled secretly, and there was no witness against her, and she was not taken in the act.

(Numbers 5:12–13)

The *halakhot* of *sota* described in the fifth chapter of the book of Numbers refer to a woman whose husband warned her not to seclude herself with a certain man and she subsequently did so, raising the suspicion of her infidelity. This chapter will discuss the *halakhot* that apply to a woman suspected of infidelity, where there is some form of corroboration of the suspicion. Generally only the testimony of two valid witnesses can be accepted as proof that a woman has committed adultery. However, this chapter discusses cases in which a woman had previously been warned, and in such cases even corroboration by one disqualified from bearing witness may suffice.

The discussion here centers on what degree of outside corroboration is sufficient to establish the infidelity of a *sota*. Also discussed is the question of which specific suspicions can be corroborated by one disqualified from bearing witness, as well as what should be done in the event of conflicting testimony.

Although some aspects of the issues addressed here were touched upon briefly in earlier chapters, they are discussed in this chapter in more detail.

מתני׳ מִי שֶׁקִּינֵּא לְאִשְׁתּוֹ וְנִסְתְּרָה, אֲפִילּוּ שָׁמַע מֵעוֹף הַפּוֹרֵחַ – יוֹצִיא וְיִתֵּן כְּתוּבָּה, דִּבְרֵי רַבִּי אֱלִיעֶזֶר;

MISHNA In the case of **one who warned his wife** not to seclude herself with a particular man **and she** subsequently **secluded herself**[N] with the man she was warned about, **even if he heard** about it **from a flying bird,**[N] or any other source whatsoever, **he must divorce** his wife. However, he must still **grant her** the money accorded to her by her **marriage contract** because there is no actual proof of her seclusion with the man in question. This is **the statement of Rabbi Eliezer,** who, as quoted in the first mishna of the tractate (2a), holds that there is no necessity for witnesses to testify with regard to the seclusion, and the woman becomes forbidden to her husband even in the absence of witnesses, by the husband's word alone.

רַבִּי יְהוֹשֻׁעַ אוֹמֵר: עַד שֶׁיִּשְׂאוּ וְיִתְּנוּ בָּהּ מוֹזְרוֹת בַּלְּבָנָה.

Rabbi Yehoshua disagrees, as he did in the mishna (2a), and **says:** He does not divorce his wife in the absence of witnesses **until** the gossiping women who sit and **spin** thread **by the light of the moon** begin to **discuss her**[H] behavior, as they share the gossip of the town. The Gemara earlier (6b) taught that a woman whose infidelity became subject to this public discussion can no longer be tested by the bitter water of a *sota*. Consequently, she must get divorced.

אָמַר עֵד אֶחָד: אֲנִי רְאִיתִיהָ שֶׁנִּטְמֵאת – לֹא הָיְתָה שׁוֹתָה; וְלֹא עוֹד, אֶלָּא אֲפִילּוּ עֶבֶד אֲפִילּוּ שִׁפְחָה – הֲרֵי אֵלּוּ נֶאֱמָנִין אַף לְפוֹסְלָהּ מִכְּתוּבָּתָהּ.

The mishna continues to list various possible testimonies concerning of such acts of seclusion. If **one witness said: I saw that she became defiled** during her seclusion by engaging in sexual intercourse with that other man, **she does not drink** the bitter water, but rather, he divorces her immediately. **And furthermore, even** if the one who testified was **a slave or a maidservant,**[H] neither of whom is generally regarded as a valid witness, **they are deemed credible** to testify to the wife's adultery **even to** the extent that their testimony **disqualifies her from** receiving **her marriage contract**[N] and prevents her from drinking the bitter water.

חֲמוֹתָהּ, וּבַת חֲמוֹתָהּ, וְצָרָתָהּ, וִיבִמְתָּהּ, וּבַת בַּעְלָהּ – הֲרֵי אֵלּוּ נֶאֱמָנוֹת, וְלֹא לְפוֹסְלָהּ מִכְּתוּבָּתָהּ אֶלָּא שֶׁלֹּא תִּשְׁתֶּה;

The mishna continues by listing women whose testimony is only partially accepted concerning this matter: **Her mother-in-law, and her mother in-law's daughter,**[NH] **and her rival wife,** i.e., a second wife of the husband, **and her *yevama*,** i.e., her husband's brother's wife, **and her husband's daughter,** all of whom are generally not deemed credible if they say anything incriminating pertaining to this woman due to the tumultuous relationships these women often have. **They are** all **deemed credible** to testify concerning the woman's defilement while in seclusion, **but** are **not** deemed credible **to** the extent that their testimony will **disqualify her from** receiving **her marriage contract; rather,** it is deemed credible to the extent that she will **not drink** of the bitter water of a *sota*.

HALAKHA

Until the gossiping women…discuss her – עַד שֶׁיִּשְׂאוּ וְיִתְּנוּ בָּהּ: If after warning his wife not to seclude herself with a specific man the husband hears people gossiping that she had committed adultery with that man, she becomes forbidden to him. He must divorce her, although she still receives the money for her marriage contract. The *Kesef Mishne* notes that this is the *halakha* even if there were not two witnesses to her seclusion (Rambam *Sefer Nashim, Hilkhot Sota* 1:8; *Shulḥan Arukh, Even HaEzer* 178:11).

Even a slave or a maidservant – אֲפִילּוּ עֶבֶד אֲפִילּוּ שִׁפְחָה: If a woman, slave, maidservant, or any heretofore valid witness who became disqualified from bearing witness due to having violated a rabbinic prohibition testifies that a woman had committed adultery, this testimony is deemed credible so long as valid witnesses had previously testified that the wife had secluded herself with another man after being warned by her husband. In this case, the woman becomes forbidden to her husband forever, and she does not drink the bitter water, and is divorced without receiving the money stipulated in her marriage contract (Rambam *Sefer Nashim, Hilkhot Sota* 1:15; *Shulḥan Arukh, Even HaEzer* 178:14).

Her mother-in-law and her mother-in-law's daughter, etc. – חֲמוֹתָהּ וּבַת חֲמוֹתָהּ וכו׳: Even the five women listed in the mishna who are generally assumed to hate each other are nevertheless deemed credible to testify that a woman committed adultery after she was warned by her husband. Their testimony is accepted to the degree that the woman is rendered forbidden to her husband and does not have the option to drink the bitter water. However, the testimony of any of these women is not considered credible in order to deprive her of the money entitled to her by her marriage contract (Rambam *Sefer Nashim, Hilkhot Sota* 1:15; *Shulḥan Arukh, Even HaEzer* 178:15).

NOTES

One who warned his wife and she secluded herself – מִי שֶׁקִּינֵּא לְאִשְׁתּוֹ וְנִסְתְּרָה: The early commentaries provide two primary opposing explanations for this mishna. Rashi and *Tosafot* understand this mishna as referring to a person who warned his wife not to seclude herself with a specific man and later discovered, by means other than testimony of two witnesses, that his wife had subsequently secluded herself with that man. These commentaries discuss the particular details of the mishna, and whether the mishna requires the husband to divorce his wife even though he cannot compel her to drink the bitter water of a *sota* because there are no actual witnesses to testify about the seclusion, or whether the mishna merely says that the husband has the option to divorce her based on the proof that he has.

However, according to Rabbeinu Ḥananel (*Tosefot HaRash*) and the Rambam's Commentary on the Mishna, this mishna is discussing a case in which there are witnesses attesting both to the husband's warning as well as to the woman's subsequent seclusion, and afterward the man hears, through means other than eyewitness testimony, that the woman actually engaged in sexual intercourse with another man. Based on this explanation, the mishna rules that the wife cannot drink the bitter water due to the outside knowledge that she is in fact guilty. However, because there is no valid testimony, the husband cannot divorce her without paying her the money stipulated in her marriage contract. The Rosh (*Tosefot HaRosh*) writes that this dispute among the early commentaries as to the proper understanding of the mishna seems to mirror a much earlier dispute found in the Jerusalem Talmud between Rabbi Yoḥanan and Reish Lakish. Rabbi Yoḥanan maintains that the entire chapter is discussing a woman after she has secluded herself, whereas Reish Lakish holds that the mishna is referring to testimony with regard to her seclusion itself.

Even if he heard from a flying bird – אֲפִילּוּ שָׁמַע מֵעוֹף הַפּוֹרֵחַ: This refers to a rumor that has spread about the woman, the source of which cannot be verified. Consequently, there is no way to determine whether or not it is true (Jerusalem Talmud; Rashbam). Rashi explains that this case is referring to a situation where there is testimony of a slave or a maidservant, both of whom are disqualified from bearing witness. Rambam's Commentary on the Mishna explains this statement literally, that even if a bird chirps in a certain way that convinces the husband that his wife was unfaithful, it is sufficient grounds for him to divorce her (see Meiri).

Even to the extent that their testimony disqualifies her from receiving her marriage contract – אַף לְפוֹסְלָהּ מִכְּתוּבָּתָהּ: In the Jerusalem Talmud, a dispute between Rabbi Akiva and Rabbi Tarfon is cited over the question of whether testimony from a single witness testifying to a wife's infidelity is sufficient to cause her to lose the rights to her marriage contract. Rabbi Akiva states, in accordance with the mishna here, that it is sufficient, while Rabbi Tarfon disagrees and says that even though a single witness is sufficient to forbid a *sota* to her husband, it is not sufficient to cause her to forfeit the money of her marriage contract. The conclusion offered in the Jerusalem Talmud is that Rabbi Akiva changed his mind and later accepted Rabbi Tarfon's opinion.

Her mother-in-law and her mother-in-law's daughter, etc. – חֲמוֹתָהּ וּבַת חֲמוֹתָהּ וכו׳: The mishna in tractate *Yevamot* (117a) states that these five women are not allowed to testify concerning this woman, because it is suspected that they may hate her and have ill intentions toward her that will lead them to lie if it will be to her detriment. The Gemara there provides reasons why each one of these women would hate her, perhaps due to competitiveness or feelings that she is causing the family to lose money.

שֶׁהָיָה בַּדִּין: וּמָה אִם עֵדוּת רִאשׁוֹנָה שֶׁאֵין אוֹסַרְתָּהּ אִיסּוּר עוֹלָם – אֵינָהּ מִתְקַיֶּימֶת בְּפָחוֹת מִשְּׁנַיִם, עֵדוּת אַחֲרוֹנָה שֶׁאוֹסַרְתָּהּ אִיסּוּר עוֹלָם – אֵינוֹ דִּין שֶׁלֹּא תִּתְקַיֵּים בְּפָחוֹת מִשְּׁנַיִם!

This ruling allowing one witness's testimony with regard to defilement needs to be stated, **as, by right,** it **should** not **have been** deemed credible based on the following *a fortiori* inference: **And just as if** with regard to **the first testimony** concerning seclusion, **which does not forbid her** with **an irrevocable prohibition,** as the woman can be found innocent permitting her again to her husband by drinking the bitter water, **is not established with fewer than two** witnesses, since according to the mishna the testimony of seclusion requires two witnesses, then with regard to **the final testimony** concerning defilement, **which forbids her** to her husband with **an irrevocable prohibition, is it not logical that it** should also **not be established with fewer than two** witnesses?

תַּלְמוּד לוֹמַר: "וְעֵד אֵין בָּהּ", כׇּל עֵדוּת שֶׁיֵּשׁ בָּהּ.

Therefore, to counter this derivation, **the verse states: "And there be no witness against her"** (Numbers 5:13), teaching that **any** testimony with regard to defilement **that there is against her** is sufficient, and two witnesses are not required.

וְקַל וָחוֹמֶר לְעֵדוּת הָרִאשׁוֹנָה מֵעַתָּה: וּמָה אִם

The Gemara asks: **And from now** that it is established that one witness suffices to testify with regard to defilement, **an *a fortiori*** inference can be made **with regard to the first testimony** of seclusion: **And just as if**

עֵדוּת אַחֲרוֹנָה שֶׁאוֹסַרְתָּהּ אִיסּוּר עוֹלָם – הֲרֵי הִיא מִתְקַיֶּימֶת בְּעֵד אֶחָד, עֵדוּת הָרִאשׁוֹנָה שֶׁאֵין אוֹסַרְתָּהּ אִיסּוּר עוֹלָם – אֵינוֹ דִּין שֶׁתִּתְקַיֵּים בְּעֵד אֶחָד!

concerning **the final testimony** of defilement, **which forbids her** with **an irrevocable prohibition,** yet it **is established by one witness,** then with regard to **the first testimony, which does not forbid her** with **an irrevocable prohibition, is it not logical that it should be established with** only **one witness?**

תַּלְמוּד לוֹמַר: "כִּי מָצָא בָהּ עֶרְוַת דָּבָר", וּלְהַלָּן הוּא אוֹמֵר: "עַל פִּי שְׁנֵי עֵדִים יָקוּם דָּבָר", מָה לְהַלָּן עַל פִּי שְׁנַיִם, אַף כָּאן פִּי שְׁנַיִם.

Therefore, to counter this derivation, **the verse states:** "When a man takes a wife, and marries her, and it comes to pass, if she finds no favor in his eyes, **because he has found some unseemly matter [*davar*] in her"** (Deuteronomy 24:1), **and there,** in the laws concerning monetary matters, **it states: "At the mouth of two witnesses,** or at the mouth of three witnesses, **shall a matter [*davar*] be established"** (Deuteronomy 19:15), teaching that **just as** the "matter" stated **there** is established **"at the mouth of two witnesses," so too, here** the "matter" of her seclusion must be established **"at the mouth of two** witnesses."

עֵד אוֹמֵר "נִטְמֵאת" וְעֵד אוֹמֵר "לֹא נִטְמֵאת", אִשָּׁה אוֹמֶרֶת "נִטְמֵאת" וְאִשָּׁה אוֹמֶרֶת "לֹא נִטְמֵאת" – הָיְתָה שׁוֹתָה.

The mishna discusses the *halakha* in a case where two single witnesses contradict each other concerning her defilement. If one **witness says: She was defiled, and** another **witness says: She was not defiled,** or similarly in the case of those normally disqualified from bearing witness, if one **woman says: She was defiled, and** another **woman says: She was not defiled, she would drink** the bitter water of a *sota,* due to the uncertainty engendered by the contradictory testimonies.

אֶחָד אוֹמֵר "נִטְמֵאת" וּשְׁנַיִם אוֹמְרִים "לֹא נִטְמֵאת" – הָיְתָה שׁוֹתָה. שְׁנַיִם אוֹמְרִים "נִטְמֵאת" וְאֶחָד אוֹמֵר "לֹא נִטְמֵאת" – לֹא הָיְתָה שׁוֹתָה.

Similarly, if **one** witness **says: She was defiled, and two** witnesses **say: She was not defiled, she would drink** the bitter water. However, if **two** would **say: She was defiled, and one says: She was not defiled,** the testimony of the two witnesses is accepted and **she would not drink** the bitter water, and the husband must divorce her.

גמ׳ הַאי "תַּלְמוּד לוֹמַר: כִּי מָצָא בָהּ עֶרְוַת דָּבָר",

GEMARA The Gemara questions why the mishna proves the need for two witnesses to testify about the seclusion based upon the verbal analogy of "matter" and "matter," if there is an explicit source in the Torah stating that two witnesses are required. **This** reason is given by the mishna: **The verse states:** "When a man takes a wife, and marries her, and it comes to pass, if she finds no favor in his eyes, **because he has found some unseemly matter [*davar*] in her"** (Deuteronomy 24:1), which through a verbal analogy based on the word "*davar*" teaches the need for two witnesses, seems to be superfluous.

תַּלְמוּד לוֹמַר: "בָּהּ", "בָּהּ" – וְלֹא בְּקִינּוּי, "בָּהּ" – וְלֹא בִּסְתִירָה, מִיבְּעֵי לֵיהּ!

As, the mishna **should have** said in its place: The **verse states:** "She was defiled secretly and there was no witness [*ed*] **against her** [***bah***]" (Numbers 5:13), which is explained to mean there were not two witnesses, but only one, who testified concerning her defilement. One can infer from the term "*bah*," which could also be understood as: **With regard to it,** that in this matter of defilement one witness suffices, **but not with regard to** the **warning.** Additionally, one can infer: **With regard to it, but not with regard to** the **seclusion.** Therefore, there must be two witnesses to testify about both the warning and seclusion.

הָכִי נַמִּי קָאָמַר, תַּלְמוּד לוֹמַר: "בָּהּ", "בָּהּ" – וְלֹא בְּקִינּוּי, "בָּהּ" – וְלֹא בִּסְתִירָה.

The Gemara answers: **That is also what** the *tanna* of the mishna **is saying.** The source for the *halakha* that there is a requirement for two witnesses to testify about the seclusion is that **the verse states: With regard to it,** that in this matter of defilement one witness suffices, **but not with regard to** the **warning. With regard to it, but not with regard to** the **seclusion.**

וְטוּמְאָה בְּעָלְמָא בְּלֹא קִינּוּי וּבְלֹא סְתִירָה דְּלָא מְהֵימַן עֵד אֶחָד מְנָלַן? נֶאֱמַר כָּאן "דָּבָר" וְנֶאֱמַר לְהַלָּן "דָּבָר", מָה לְהַלָּן בִּשְׁנֵי עֵדִים, אַף כָּאן בִּשְׁנֵי עֵדִים.

The Gemara continues to explain the mishna: **And** concerning **an ordinary** accusation of **defilement without** a previous **warning and without** an act of **seclusion** with another man, **from where do we** derive that **a single witness is not deemed credible?** It is for this *halakha* that the mishna cites the verbal analogy: **It is stated here:** "Because he has found some unseemly **matter** [***davar***] in her" (Deuteronomy 24:1), **and it is stated there** concerning monetary matters: "At the mouth of two witnesses, or at the mouth of three witnesses, shall **a matter** [***davar***] be established" (Deuteronomy 19:15). **Just as** the "matter" stated **there** with regard to monetary matters is clarified specifically **by** the testimony of **two witnesses, so too, here** with regard to adultery the "matter" of her defilement must be established **by** the testimony of at least **two witnesses.**

"עֵד אוֹמֵר נִטְמֵאת". טַעְמָא דְּקָא מַכְחִישׁ לֵיהּ, הָא לָא קָא מַכְחִישׁ לֵיהּ – עֵד אֶחָד מְהֵימַן.

§ The mishna taught: If one **witness says: She was defiled,** and another witness says: She was not defiled, she drinks the bitter water of a *sota*. The Gemara infers from this statement in the mishna that **the reason** the woman would drink the bitter water in this case is specifically **because** the second witness **refutes his** testimony, **but if** a second witness **did not refute his testimony,** then **a single witness** would be **relied upon** in this case and the woman would be forbidden to her husband forever.

מְנָהָנֵי מִילֵּי? דְּתָנוּ רַבָּנַן: "וְעֵד אֵין בָּהּ" – בִּשְׁנַיִם הַכָּתוּב מְדַבֵּר.

From where are these matters derived? **As the Sages taught** in reference to the verse describing the circumstances in which a woman defiled through an act of adultery becomes prohibited to her husband, which states: "And a man lie with her carnally… **and there be no witness** [***ed***] **against her**" (Numbers 5:13); **the verse is speaking of** a lack of **two** witnesses. When the verse refers to the lack of an *ed*, written in the singular, it actually indicates that there are not two witnesses against her, but only one, as the *baraita* will now explain.

אַתָּה אוֹמֵר: בִּשְׁנַיִם, אוֹ אֵינוֹ אֶלָּא בְּאֶחָד? תַּלְמוּד לוֹמַר: "לֹא יָקוּם עֵד אֶחָד בְּאִישׁ" וגו׳.

The *baraita* continues and asks: Do **you say** that the verse refers **only** to a case where there was not **even one** witness to the act of sexual intercourse, as the singular usage of the word *ed* would seem to indicate? The *baraita* now proves that the singular usage notwithstanding, elsewhere the word *ed* is used to indicate two witnesses, as **the verse states: "One witness** [***ed***] **shall not rise up against a man** for any iniquity or any sin that he sins; at the mouth of two witnesses, or at the mouth of three witnesses, shall a matter be established" (Deuteronomy 19:15).

מִמַּשְׁמַע שֶׁנֶּאֱמַר "לֹא יָקוּם עֵד", אֵינִי יוֹדֵעַ שֶׁהוּא אֶחָד? מָה תַּלְמוּד לוֹמַר "אֶחָד"? זֶה בָּנָה אָב: כׇּל מָקוֹם שֶׁנֶּאֱמַר "עֵד" הֲרֵי כָּאן שְׁנַיִם, עַד שֶׁיִּפְרוֹט לְךָ הַכָּתוּב "אֶחָד".

The *baraita* infers a general principle from this verse by asking: **By inference from that** which **is stated** in the verse, even with the omission of the word "one": **"A witness shall not rise up** against a man" (Deuteronomy 19:15), **do I not know that it is** referring to **one** witness, as the verse is written in the singular form? **What** is the meaning when **the verse states** explicitly: **"One** witness," being that it is obviously referring to only one witness? The *baraita* answers: **This established a paradigm** for the principle that **every place** where the word **"witness** [***ed***]**" is stated** in the Torah without specifying a number, **there are two** witnesses **here, until the verse specifies** that it is referring to only one witness, by writing the word **"one."**

וְאָמַר רַחֲמָנָא: תְּרֵי לֵית בָּהּ אֶלָּא חַד, "וְהִיא לֹא נִתְפָּשָׂה" – אֲסוּרָה.

The *baraita* returns to discuss the verse concerning a *sota*. **And the Merciful One states:** "There was no witness [*ed*] against her," which therefore means that: **There are not two** witnesses to the sexual intercourse that could testify **with regard to her, rather** there is only **one** witness. The *baraita* completes its interpretation: Further in the verse it states: **"And she was not taken in the act"** (Numbers 5:13), indicating that the verse is referring to a case in which it is known that the woman had not been raped. This knowledge is based on the testimony of only one witness, as the verse had already stated that there were not two witnesses, and since one witness saw her willingly engage in sexual intercourse with another man, **she is forbidden** to her husband.

וְכֵיוָן דְּמִדְּאוֹרַיְיתָא עֵד אֶחָד מְהֵימַן, אִידָּךְ הֵיכִי מָצֵי מַכְחִישׁ לֵיהּ? וְהָא אָמַר עוּלָּא: כׇּל מָקוֹם שֶׁהֶאֱמִינָה תּוֹרָה עֵד אֶחָד הֲרֵי כָּאן שְׁנַיִם, וְאֵין דְּבָרָיו שֶׁל אֶחָד בִּמְקוֹם שְׁנַיִם!

The Gemara asks: **But since** the *baraita* taught **that by Torah law one witness is deemed credible** to state that the woman is defiled, **how can the other** witness who denies the wife's infidelity **refute him** with his conflicting testimony and enable the woman to drink the bitter water instead of becoming forbidden outright to her husband? **But doesn't Ulla say: Wherever the Torah relies on one witness,**[NH] **there is** the equivalent of the testimony of **two** witnesses **here.** Consequently, the testimony of the contradicting witness should be insignificant, as **the statement of one** witness **has no** standing **in a place where** it is contradicted by **two** witnesses, for the witness testifying about her infidelity is deemed credible as if two witnesses had testified.

אֶלָּא אֲמַר עוּלָּא, תְּנֵי: לֹא הָיְתָה שׁוֹתָה. וְכֵן אֲמַר רַבִּי יִצְחָק: לֹא הָיְתָה שׁוֹתָה. וְרַבִּי חִיָּיא אָמַר: הָיְתָה שׁוֹתָה.

Rather, Ulla said: Teach the mishna in the following way: If one witness says: She was defiled, and another witness says: She was not defiled, **she would not drink** the bitter water. **And likewise, Rabbi Yitzḥak said: She would not drink. But Rabbi Ḥiyya says** in line with the standard text of the mishna: **She would drink** the bitter water even in the case of a contradiction between two single witnesses with regard to her infidelity.

לְרַבִּי חִיָּיא קַשְׁיָא דְּעוּלָּא! לָא קַשְׁיָא: כָּאן בְּבַת אַחַת, כָּאן בְּזֶה אַחַר זֶה.

The Gemara asks: But **for Rabbi Ḥiyya,** how will he respond to the same **difficulty** due to the teaching **of Ulla,** who explained that when a single witness is deemed credible he is considered as two and cannot be contradicted by a single witness to the contrary? The Gemara answers: This is **not difficult: Here,** the mishna is discussing a case where both witnesses arrived in court and testified **simultaneously,** thereby canceling each other out. But **there,** Ulla's principle, that whenever a single witness's testimony is accepted it is considered as two and cannot be contradicted by a single witness testifying to the contrary, is referring to a case **in which** the two conflicting witnesses came to court and testified **one after the other.**

תְּנַן: עֵד אוֹמֵר "נִטְמֵאת" וּשְׁנַיִם אוֹמְרִים "לֹא נִטְמֵאת" – הָיְתָה שׁוֹתָה; הָא חַד וְחַד – לֹא הָיְתָה שׁוֹתָה. תְּיוּבְתָּא דְּרַבִּי חִיָּיא!

But **we learned** in the mishna above that if **one witness says: She was defiled, and two say: She was not defiled, she would drink** the bitter water. The Gemara deduces from here: The implications of this statement are that the woman drinks only because the testimony of the incriminating witness was contradicted by two witnesses, **but** if there was **one** witness saying she was defiled **and** only **one** witness saying the opposite, **she would not drink;** this is **a conclusive refutation**[B] of the opinion **of Rabbi Ḥiyya.**[N]

אָמַר לָךְ רַבִּי חִיָּיא: וְלִיטַעֲמִיךְ, אֵימָא סֵיפָא: שְׁנַיִם אוֹמְרִים "נִטְמֵאת" וְאֶחָד אוֹמֵר "לֹא נִטְמֵאת" – לֹא הָיְתָה שׁוֹתָה; הָא חַד וְחַד – הָיְתָה שׁוֹתָה!

The Gemara answers: **Rabbi Ḥiyya** could have **said to you: And according to your reasoning** that she would not drink, **say the latter clause** of the mishna, which states: If **two** witnesses **say: She was defiled, and one says: She was not defiled,** the testimony of the two witnesses is accepted and **she would not drink** the bitter water. **But** you should deduce from here that if there was **one** witness testifying to her defilement **and one** witness stating the opposite, **she would drink** the bitter water. This inference is in line with Rabbi Ḥiyya's explanation, and contradicts the inference from the previous clause.

NOTES

Wherever the Torah relies on one witness – כׇּל מָקוֹם שֶׁהֶאֱמִינָה תּוֹרָה עֵד אֶחָד: There is a dispute between the commentaries, cited in the *Nimmukei Yosef*, as to how far this principle should be taken. One opinion maintains that this principle is a general *halakha* that is applicable in all situations where the testimony of one witness is relied upon, which would include situations where the testimony of one witness is accepted with regard to matters of prohibitions. Others, however, maintain that this principle applies only to situations in which there is a corresponding biblical source that a single witness is accepted, as is the case when one witness testifies to the defilement of the *sota* and the explicit source indicates that one witness in that case should be accepted as two. With regard to the reliance on one witness in matters of prohibitions, however, since there is no explicit source, the witness is not accepted with the weight of two witnesses and may be contradicted by an opposing witness.

A conclusive refutation of the opinion of Rabbi Ḥiyya – תְּיוּבְתָּא דְּרַבִּי חִיָּיא: Rashi explains that although it would be possible to explain that the middle case in the mishna is dealing with a situation where the witnesses came to testify one after another, the Gemara does not understand the case in this manner, as the language of the mishna seems to clearly indicate that all of the witnesses testified simultaneously.

HALAKHA

Wherever the Torah relies on one witness – כׇּל מָקוֹם שֶׁהֶאֱמִינָה תּוֹרָה עֵד אֶחָד: If one valid witness testifies that a woman committed adultery, she does not drink the bitter water of a *sota*. Even if a second witness testifies and refutes the first witness's testimony, his refutation is not accepted because in the case of a *sota*, the testimony of a single witness is considered equivalent to that of two witnesses in other matters. Consequently, the second witness cannot nullify the testimony of the first, who is treated like two witnesses. However, if two contradictory witnesses come at the same time, one testifying that she committed adultery and the other testifying that she did not, then she drinks the bitter water (Rambam *Sefer Nashim*, *Hilkhot Sota* 1:16–17).

BACKGROUND

Conclusive refutation [*teyuvta*] – תְּיוּבְתָּא: An amoraic statement can be refuted on the basis of a tannaitic source that contradicts the statement of the *amora*. This word, *teyuvta*, is one of several terms based on the same Aramaic root. For example, where one *amora* raises an objection to the opinion of another *amora* by citing a tannaitic source, the expression used is *meitivei*, meaning Rabbi X raised an objection to Rabbi Y's opinion. Where an *amora* raises an objection to an unattributed amoraic opinion by citing a tannaitic source, the expression employed is *mativ*, i.e., Rabbi X raised an objection. In the case cited above, where the Gemara itself raises the objection by citing a tannaitic source, the expression used is *meitivi*. When there is no response to the objection, it is deemed a conclusive refutation and the term *teyuvta* is used.

אֶלָּא כּוּלָּהּ בִּפְסוּלֵי עֵדוּת, וְרַבִּי נְחֶמְיָה הִיא; דְּתַנְיָא, רַבִּי נְחֶמְיָה אוֹמֵר: כׇּל מָקוֹם שֶׁהֶאֱמִינָה תּוֹרָה עֵד אֶחָד – הַלֵּךְ אַחַר רוֹב דֵּעוֹת, וְעָשׂוּ שְׁתֵּי נָשִׁים בְּאִישׁ אֶחָד כִּשְׁנֵי אֲנָשִׁים בְּאִישׁ אֶחָד.

The Gemara explains: **Rather,** the correct understanding is that **the entire** mishna is not dealing with valid witnesses, and stating an obvious *halakha* in order to enable an inference, but **with** people who are **disqualified** from giving **testimony,** and is teaching us a novel ruling. **And** the mishna **is** in accordance with the opinion **of Rabbi Neḥemya. As it is taught** in a *baraita* (*Tosefta Yevamot* 14:1) that **Rabbi Neḥemya says: Wherever the Torah relies on one witness, follow the majority of opinions.** In other words, if the testimonies of two disqualified witnesses conflict, the court rules in accordance with the version supported by more witnesses, whether or not they are qualified to testify. **And the Sages established** that the testimony of **two women,** who are usually disqualified from testifying, when they testify in opposition to **one man,** should be **like** that of **two men against one man,** and the court will rule in accordance with the testimony of the two women.

וְאִיכָּא דְּאָמְרִי: כׇּל הֵיכָא דַּאֲתָא עֵד אֶחָד כָּשֵׁר מֵעִיקָּרָא, אֲפִילּוּ מֵאָה נָשִׁים נָמֵי כְּעֵד אֶחָד דָּמְיָין,

And some say that Rabbi Neḥemya actually stated something different: **And there are** those **who say** a different version of Rabbi Neḥemya's approach: **Anywhere that one valid witness came initially,**[H] **even one hundred women** who later contradict him **are considered like one** witness, and do not override his testimony.

HALAKHA

Anywhere that one valid witness came initially – כׇּל הֵיכָא דַּאֲתָא עֵד אֶחָד כָּשֵׁר מֵעִיקָּרָא: If one valid witness testifies that the woman committed adultery, and simultaneously several women or other individuals who are disqualified from bearing witness testify that the woman did not commit adultery, the matter is viewed as uncertain and the woman drinks the bitter water. This ruling, which appears second in the Gemara, is cited using the phrase: Some say.

If, however, all of the testimony is provided by those disqualified from bearing witness, then the majority is followed. For example, if two women say that she committed adultery and three say that she did not, she drinks the water. If three say that she did not and four say that she did, she does not drink it. If there were equal numbers of invalid witnesses on both sides, then she drinks due to the uncertainty. This follows the Gemara's conclusion that with regard to testimonies from invalid witnesses, the ruling follows the majority regardless if it is stringent or lenient (Rambam *Sefer Nashim, Hilkhot Sota* 1:18; *Shulḥan Arukh, Even HaEzer* 17:40).

Perek **VI**
Daf **32** Amud **a**

וְהָכָא בְּמַאי עָסְקִינַן – כְּגוֹן דַּאֲתַאי אִשָּׁה מֵעִיקָּרָא.

And with what are we dealing here in the mishna? A case **where a woman,** who is generally disqualified from bearing witness, **came initially,**[N] and testified that the woman committed adultery, and two witnesses say that she did not.

וְתַרְצָה לְדְרַבִּי נְחֶמְיָה הָכִי – רַבִּי נְחֶמְיָה אוֹמֵר: כׇּל מָקוֹם שֶׁהֶאֱמִינָה תּוֹרָה עֵד אֶחָד, הַלֵּךְ אַחַר רוֹב דֵּיעוֹת. וְעָשׂוּ שְׁתֵּי נָשִׁים בְּאִשָּׁה אַחַת כִּשְׁנֵי אֲנָשִׁים בְּאִישׁ אֶחָד, אֲבָל שְׁתֵּי נָשִׁים בְּאִישׁ אֶחָד – כִּי פַּלְגָא וּפַלְגָא דָּמֵי.

And according to this interpretation you must **amend the** statement **of Rabbi Neḥemya** so that it reads **like this: Rabbi Neḥemya says: Wherever the Torah relies on one witness, follow the majority of opinions. And** the Sages **established** that **two women against one woman** are **like two men against one man. But two women** in opposition **to one man** that is a valid witness, **is like half** of a pair of witnesses **and a half** of a pair of witnesses, and the mishna did not address that case.

וְתַרְתֵּי בִּפְסוּלֵי עֵדוּת לָמָּה לִי? מַהוּ דְּתֵימָא, כִּי אָזְלִינַן בָּתַר רוֹב דֵּיעוֹת – לְחוּמְרָא, אֲבָל לְקוּלָּא לָא אָזְלִינַן. קָא מַשְׁמַע לַן.

The Gemara poses a question on these two interpretations of the mishna: **And why do I need two** cases in the mishna to teach the *halakha* that the majority opinion of **those disqualified from** bearing **witness** is followed? The Gemara explains: It is necessary, **lest you say** that **when we follow the majority opinion** in the case of invalid witnesses, this is **to be stringent** to force the woman to drink the bitter water, e.g., if one witness said that she committed adultery and two said that she did not, **but to be lenient**[N] and absolve her from having to drink the water we do **not** follow the majority opinion, and she would still drink the water even if there is one witness saying that she did not commit adultery, therefore the mishna **teaches us** that there is no difference in this regard, and the majority opinion is followed in any case.

הדרן עלך מי שקינא

NOTES

Where a woman came initially – דַּאֲתַאי אִשָּׁה מֵעִיקָּרָא: The Gemara does not explicitly rule in an instance where a woman or any other invalid witness testified and afterward a single valid witness refuted her testimony. Consequently, the *halakha* in that case is a matter of dispute. According to the Rambam and Rashi, the testimony of a single valid witness, and likewise any number of invalid witnesses, are all considered to be equal. However, according to the Ra'avad a single valid witness is deemed credible only if the valid witness testifies initially, before others arrive.

To be stringent…but to be lenient – לְחוּמְרָא...לְקוּלָּא: Rashi explains that the lenient ruling refers to a case where the majority claims that she committed adultery, and as their testimony is accepted, she does not drink the bitter water. A stringent ruling refers to a case where the majority claims she did not commit adultery. Consequently, she is obligated to drink the bitter water. Others question this application of the terms lenient and stringent. Therefore, they explain the terms conversely (*Keren Ora*). Others maintain that concerning these matters, there is no actual leniency or stringency in any particular instance, but that every hypothetical scenario has a lenient aspect and a stringent aspect, whether the ruling is that she drinks or that she does not drink. The Sages therefore teach that they accept the majority testimony on either side in each case (*Torat HaKenaot*).

Summary of **Perek VI**

This chapter discussed the different types of testimony that are required in order to question a woman's fidelity and establish her status as a *sota*. In order to establish a woman as a *sota* of uncertain fidelity there is a requirement that either the warning, the act of seclusion, or both be corroborated through the testimony of two valid witnesses, as discussed in the first chapter of the tractate. Nevertheless, after it is determined that the woman is a *sota*, even lesser forms of corroboration are sufficient to impact the *halakhot* of the woman.

In order to put the woman to death two witnesses are necessary. To disqualify the woman from drinking the bitter water of a *sota*, however, one witness is sufficient. Even one generally disqualified from bearing witness can testify in this regard, and even the testimony of the five women normally suspected of hating this woman is accepted. Additionally, even an unsubstantiated public rumor that has become the widespread gossip of the city, e.g., after being discussed by the women who spin thread by the light of the moon, is sufficient to prohibit the woman from drinking the bitter water.

Although all these lesser forms of corroboration are sufficient to prevent the woman from drinking the bitter water, there are differences between them as to the degree of their acceptability. For instance, if the corroboration was based only on a public rumor or the testimony of one of the women who is known to hate the *sota*, then the *sota* will still receive payment of her marriage contract. However, if the corroboration is based on the testimony of a single witness, even if it is someone who is generally disqualified from testifying such as a woman or a slave, then the testimony is sufficient to cause the woman to lose her rights to the marriage contract.

These *halakhot* apply in situations where there is no testimony available to contradict the testimony concerning the woman's guilt. However, if others testify that the woman did not commit adultery, it is not always considered valid. In the event that one valid witness testified to her infidelity and his testimony was accepted initially, but it was later contradicted by another, then so long as only one individual contradicts the initial witness the woman remains disqualified from drinking. However, if there are two witnesses contradicting the testimony concerning her guilt then the individual witness's testimony is not accepted. If, however, all the witnesses testify at the same time, then the witness to her guilt is not accepted and the woman can drink the bitter water. If, however, all the witnesses are those who are usually disqualified from giving testimony, then the majority of witnesses are followed, either concerning guilt in order to prevent her from drinking, or concerning her innocence in order to allow her to drink.

Introduction to **Perek VII**

And it shall come to pass, when the Lord your God shall bring you into the land where you go to possess it, that you shall give the blessing on Mount Gerizim and the curse on Mount Ebal. Are they not beyond the Jordan, behind the way of the coming of the sun, in the land of the Canaanites that dwell in the Arabah, over against Gilgal, beside the oaks of Moreh?

(Deuteronomy 11:29–30)

Then his brother's wife shall draw near him in the presence of the Elders, and remove his shoe from off his foot, and spit in his face; and she shall speak and say: So shall be done to the man that does not build up his brother's house.

(Deuteronomy 25:9)

And you shall speak and say before the Lord your God: A wandering Aramean was my father, and he went down into Egypt, and sojourned there, few in number; and he became there a nation, great, mighty, and populous.

(Deuteronomy 26:5)

These shall stand on Mount Gerizim to bless the people, when you are passed over the Jordan: Simeon, and Levi, and Judah, and Issachar, and Joseph, and Benjamin; and these shall stand on Mount Ebal for the curse: Reuben, Gad, and Asher, and Zebulun, Dan, and Naphtali. And the Levites shall speak and say to all the men of Israel with a loud voice: Cursed is the man who makes a graven or molten image, an abomination unto the Lord, the work of the hands of the craftsman, and sets it up in secret. And all the people shall answer and say: Amen.

(Deuteronomy 27:12–15)

And Moses commanded them, saying: At the end of every seven years, in the Festival of the Sabbatical Year, in the festival of Sukkot, when all Israel comes to appear before the Lord your God in the place that He shall choose, you shall read this Torah before all Israel in their hearing. Assemble the people, the men and the women and the little ones, and your stranger that is within your gates, so that they may hear, and so that they may learn, and fear the Lord your God, and observe to perform all the words of this law.

(Deuteronomy 31:10–12)

This chapter, as well as the following chapters, lists a series of *halakhot* that are tangentially related to the *halakhot* of a *sota*. The chapter begins discussing whether various recitations mentioned in the Torah, including the warning and the oath administered by the priest to a *sota*, must be recited in Hebrew, or whether they may be recited in any language. Subsequently, the chapter discusses in detail several mitzvot that appear in the list of recitations that must be said in Hebrew. Despite the lack of an inherent connection between these issues and the tractate, tractate *Sota* became the primary source for their *halakhot*, since there is no tractate devoted to explaining these issues.

One such topic is the mitzvot that were incumbent upon the generation that entered Eretz Yisrael during the time of Joshua, such as setting up stones and writing the Torah upon them, and delivering the blessings and the curses on Mount Gerizim and Mount Ebal. As these *halakhot* pertain only to that generation, the discussion has no practical ramifications. However, the Gemara examines these *halakhot* as it analyzes all aspects of the Torah.

The chapter also discusses the Priestly Benediction extensively, describing the manner in which it is recited in the Temple and in synagogues.

Another topic considered in this chapter is the mitzva of assembly, where the king reads the Torah before the nation. The chapter discusses who reads from the Torah, what portions are read, and how the event takes place in practice.

מתני׳ אֵלּוּ נֶאֱמָרִין בְּכׇל לָשׁוֹן: פָּרָשַׁת סוֹטָה, וּוִידּוּי מַעֲשֵׂר, קְרִיַּת שְׁמַע וּתְפִלָּה, וּבִרְכַּת הַמָּזוֹן, וּשְׁבוּעַת הָעֵדוּת וּשְׁבוּעַת הַפִּיקָּדוֹן.

MISHNA These are recited[N] in any language,[N] not specifically Hebrew: **The portion of** the warning and the oath administered by the priest to **a woman suspected by her husband of having been unfaithful** [*sota*];[H] **and the declaration of tithes,**[HB] which occurs after the third and the sixth years of the seven-year Sabbatical cycle, when one declares that he has given his tithes appropriately; ***Shema*;**[H] **and the** *Amida* **prayer;**[H] **and Grace after Meals;**[H] **and an oath of testimony,**[H] where one takes an oath that he does not have any testimony to provide on a given issue; **and an oath on a deposit,**[H] where one takes an oath that he does not have possession of another's deposit.

וְאֵלּוּ נֶאֱמָרִין בִּלְשׁוֹן הַקּוֹדֶשׁ: מִקְרָא בִּיכּוּרִים, וַחֲלִיצָה, בְּרָכוֹת וּקְלָלוֹת, בִּרְכַּת כֹּהֲנִים, וּבִרְכַּת כֹּהֵן גָּדוֹל, וּפָרָשַׁת הַמֶּלֶךְ, וּפָרָשַׁת עֶגְלָה עֲרוּפָה, וּמְשׁוּחַ מִלְחָמָה בְּשָׁעָה שֶׁמְּדַבֵּר אֶל הָעָם.

And these are recited only **in the sacred tongue,** Hebrew: **The recitation of** the verses that one recounts when bringing the **first fruits**[HB] to the Temple; **and** the recitations which form an element of **the ritual through which a** ***yavam*** **frees a** ***yevama*** **of her levirate bonds** [***ḥalitza***];[HB] the **blessings and curses** that were spoken on Mount Gerizim and Mount Ebal; **the Priestly Benediction;**[H] **and the blessing** on the Torah recited **by the High Priest** on Yom Kippur; **and the portion of** the Torah read by **the king**[H] at the assembly on *Sukkot* at the conclusion of the Sabbatical Year; **and the portion** recited during the ritual **of a heifer whose neck is broken,**[H] when a person is found killed in an area that is between two cities, and the murderer is unknown; **and** the speech of a priest who is **anointed for war**[H] **when he addresses the nation** before going out to battle.

NOTES

These are recited – אֵלּוּ נֶאֱמָרִין: *Tosafot* ask why the *tanna* lists only some of the examples that fall under this category while leaving out other examples. They answer in accordance with their version of the mishna, that the mishna's statement is: These are recited in their own language, and explain that this refers specifically to those recitations that must be in a language the person reciting understands. This excludes other recitations that may be recited in any language, but not because of an imperative to understand the text.

In any language – בְּכׇל לָשׁוֹן: This is the version of Rashi. *Tosafot*, however, as well as the Jerusalem Talmud, have a different version of the text, which states: In their own language. *Tosafot* write that Rashi's version indicates that it does not matter what language is used, whereas the version that states: In their own language, implies that it must be a language that is understood by the one speaking it. However, Rashi apparently agrees that it must be a language that one understands; he simply holds that the novel element of this *halakha* is that there is no requirement that these statements be recited in Hebrew (see *Keren Ora*).

BACKGROUND

The declaration of tithes – וִידּוּי מַעֲשֵׂר: This declaration is stated on the last day of Passover of the fourth and seventh years of the Sabbatical cycle. It states that one's obligations with regard to *teruma* and the tithing of his produce were properly fulfilled. The text of this declaration is in Deuteronomy (26:13–15). During the Second Temple period, Yoḥanan the High Priest discontinued the practice of reciting this declaration due to a concern that since agricultural *halakhot* were not being properly observed, many of those making the declaration would not be speaking the truth.

First fruits – בִּיכּוּרִים: The first fruits of a new harvest are given to the priests (see Deuteronomy 26:1–11). During the period of the Temple, a farmer would select the first of the seven types of fruit with which Eretz Yisrael is favored (see Deuteronomy 8:8). He would bring them to the Temple in a basket, place them before the altar, and recite prayers of thanks to God. Afterward, the fruit was given to the priests and eaten under the same restrictions governing *teruma*. First fruits were brought to the Temple between the festivals of *Shavuot* and *Sukkot*. If they were not brought during that period, an extension was granted until Hanukkah. An entire tractate of the Mishna, *Bikkurim*, is devoted to the details of this mitzva.

Ḥalitza – חֲלִיצָה: *Ḥalitza* is the ceremony whereby a *yevama*, the widow of a man who died without children, is freed from the obligation to marry one of her deceased husband's brothers, referred to as a *yavam*, and is consequently allowed to remarry (see Deuteronomy 25:7–10). The term *ḥalitza* is derived from the central element of this ceremony, which involves the removal by the *yevama* of a special sandal from the foot of the *yavam*. *Ḥalitza* must be performed before a rabbinical court. The *halakhot* governing this ceremony are discussed in detail in tractate *Yevamot*.

HALAKHA

The portion of *sota* can be recited in any language – פָּרָשַׁת סוֹטָה בְּכׇל לָשׁוֹן: The priest speaks to the woman in a language she understands, explaining that she is in her current situation due to her husband's warning and her seclusion with another man. He says to her in her own language: If a man did not sleep with you, etc. (Rambam *Sefer Nashim*, *Hilkhot Sota* 3:7).

The declaration of tithes – וִידּוּי מַעֲשֵׂר: The declaration of tithes may be recited in any language (Rambam *Sefer Zera'im*, *Hilkhot Ma'aser Sheni* 11:5).

Shema – קְרִיַּת שְׁמַע: One may recite *Shema* in any language, and just as one must be careful to pronounce the words accurately in Hebrew, so too, one must be careful to recite it precisely in another language. The *Mishna Berura* notes that while it is permitted to recite *Shema* in any language, the preferable way to fulfill the mitzva is to recite it in Hebrew, even if one does not understand the words (Rambam *Sefer Ahava*, *Hilkhot Keriat Shema* 2:10; *Shulḥan Arukh*, *Oraḥ Ḥayyim* 62:2).

Amida prayer – תְּפִלָּה: If one is praying in a quorum of ten men, one may pray in any language that he desires. Otherwise, one must pray in Hebrew (Rif). Some say this is only the case when one is praying for his personal needs, but a fixed communal prayer may be recited in any language (Rabbeinu Yona). Others hold that even when praying for one's own needs one may pray in any language other than Aramaic, according to the subsequent Gemara (Rosh). Even a fixed communal prayer should preferably be recited in Hebrew. The *Mishna Berura* rules that a communal prayer should not be recited in another language on a regular basis (*Shulḥan Arukh*, *Oraḥ Ḥayyim* 101:4).

Grace after Meals – בִּרְכַּת הַמָּזוֹן: One may recite the Grace after Meals in any language. The *Mishna Berura* rules that it is preferable to recite it in Hebrew (Rambam *Sefer Ahava*, *Hilkhot Berakhot* 1:6; *Shulḥan Arukh*, *Oraḥ Ḥayyim* 185:1).

An oath of testimony – שְׁבוּעַת הָעֵדוּת: Witnesses are not liable to bring a sin-offering for falsely taking an oath of testimony unless the oath was administered to them in a language they understand (Rambam *Sefer Hafla'a*, *Hilkhot Shevuot* 9:12).

An oath on a deposit – שְׁבוּעַת הַפִּיקָּדוֹן: One is not liable to bring a sin-offering for falsely taking an oath on a deposit unless the oath was administered to him in a language he understands (Rambam *Sefer Hafla'a*, *Hilkhot Shevuot* 7:7).

The recitation of the verses of the first fruits – מִקְרָא בִּיכּוּרִים: The recitation over the first fruits must be performed in Hebrew, exactly as it is written in the Torah (Rambam *Sefer Zera'im*, *Hilkhot Bikkurim* 3:10).

Ḥalitza – חֲלִיצָה: Everything that the *yavam* and the *yevama* are required to recite during the *ḥalitza* ritual must be recited in Hebrew (Rambam *Sefer Nashim*, *Hilkhot Yibbum* 4:8; *Shulḥan Arukh*, *Even HaEzer* 169:29 and *Seder Ḥalitza* 48).

The Priestly Benediction – בִּרְכַּת כֹּהֲנִים: The Priestly Benediction may be recited only in Hebrew (Rambam *Sefer Ahava*, *Hilkhot Tefilla* 14:11; *Shulḥan Arukh*, *Oraḥ Ḥayyim* 128:14).

The portion read by the king – פָּרָשַׁת הַמֶּלֶךְ: When the king reads from the Torah during the assembly he must recite the blessings and the verses in Hebrew (Rambam *Sefer Korbanot*, *Hilkhot Ḥagiga* 3:5).

The portion of a heifer whose neck is broken – פָּרָשַׁת עֶגְלָה עֲרוּפָה: After the neck of the calf is broken, the elders of the city recite: "Our hands did not spill this blood, neither have our eyes seen it" (Deuteronomy 21:7), and the priests say: "Forgive, O Lord, your people, Israel" (Deuteronomy 21:8). All of this must be recited in Hebrew (Rambam *Sefer Nezikin*, *Hilkhot Rotze'aḥ* 9:3).

A priest who is anointed for war – מְשׁוּחַ מִלְחָמָה: A priest who is anointed for war stands on a high surface and calls out to the soldiers: Hear, O Israel, etc. The entire portion must be recited in Hebrew (Rambam *Sefer Shofetim*, *Hilkhot Melakhim* 7:3).

מִקְרָא בִּיכּוּרִים כֵּיצַד? ״וְעָנִיתָ וְאָמַרְתָּ לִפְנֵי ה׳ אֱלֹהֶיךָ״, וּלְהַלָּן הוּא אוֹמֵר: ״וְעָנוּ הַלְוִיִּם וְאָמְרוּ״, מַה לְּהַלָּן בִּלְשׁוֹן הַקּוֹדֶשׁ, אַף כָּאן בִּלְשׁוֹן הַקּוֹדֶשׁ.

How is it derived that the **recitation** when bringing the **first fruits** is recited specifically in Hebrew? When the Torah discusses this mitzva it states: **"And you shall speak and say before the Lord your God"** (Deuteronomy 26:5), **and below,** in the discussion of the blessings and curses, **it states: "And the Levites shall speak and say"** (Deuteronomy 27:14). **Just as there,** the Levites speak **in the sacred tongue, so too here,** the recitation is **in the sacred tongue.**

חֲלִיצָה כֵּיצַד? ״וְעָנְתָה וְאָמְרָה״, וּלְהַלָּן הוּא אוֹמֵר: ״וְעָנוּ הַלְוִיִּם וְאָמְרוּ״, מַה לְּהַלָּן בִּלְשׁוֹן הַקּוֹדֶשׁ, אַף כָּאן בִּלְשׁוֹן הַקּוֹדֶשׁ;

How is it derived that the recitation at **a *ḥalitza*** ceremony must be in Hebrew? The verse in the Torah portion discussing *ḥalitza* states: **"And she shall speak and say"** (Deuteronomy 25:9), **and below it states: "And the Levites shall speak and say"** (Deuteronomy 27:14). **Just as there,** the Levites speak **in the sacred tongue, so too here,** the recitation is **in the sacred tongue.**

רַבִּי יְהוּדָה אוֹמֵר: ״וְעָנְתָה וְאָמְרָה כָּכָה״, עַד שֶׁתֹּאמַר בַּלָּשׁוֹן הַזֶּה.

Rabbi Yehuda says: This can be derived from a different word in the verse: **"And she shall speak and say: So** shall it be done to the man that does not build up his brother's house" (Deuteronomy 25:9). The word "so" indicates that her statement is ineffective **unless she says** it **in these** exact **words.**

בְּרָכוֹת וּקְלָלוֹת כֵּיצַד? כֵּיוָן שֶׁעָבְרוּ יִשְׂרָאֵל אֶת הַיַּרְדֵּן, וּבָאוּ אֶל הַר גְּרִיזִים וְאֶל הַר עֵיבָל שֶׁבַּשּׁוֹמְרוֹן שֶׁבְּצַד שְׁכֶם שֶׁבְּאֵצֶל אֵלוֹנֵי מוֹרֶה, שֶׁנֶּאֱמַר: ״הֲלֹא הֵמָּה בְּעֵבֶר הַיַּרְדֵּן״ וגו׳, וּלְהַלָּן הוּא אוֹמֵר: ״וַיַּעֲבֹר אַבְרָם בָּאָרֶץ עַד מְקוֹם שְׁכֶם עַד אֵלוֹן מוֹרֶה״, מָה אֵלוֹן מוֹרֶה הָאָמוּר לְהַלָּן – שְׁכֶם, אַף אֵלוֹן מוֹרֶה הָאָמוּר כָּאן – שְׁכֶם.

How did the ceremony of the **blessings and curses** take place? **When the Jewish people crossed the Jordan River they came to Mount Gerizim and Mount Ebal, which are in Samaria alongside** the city of **Shechem, which is near the oaks of Moreh, as it is stated: "Are they not beyond the Jordan,** behind the way of the going down of the sun, in the land of the Canaanites that dwell in the Arabah, over against Gilgal, beside the oaks of Moreh?" (Deuteronomy 11:30), **and there it states: "And Abram passed through the land until the place of Shechem, until the oaks of Moreh"** (Genesis 12:6). **Just as the oaks of Moreh mentioned there** with regard to Abraham **are** close to **Shechem, so too, the oaks of Moreh mentioned here are** close to **Shechem.**

שִׁשָּׁה שְׁבָטִים עָלוּ לְרֹאשׁ הַר גְּרִיזִים וְשִׁשָּׁה שְׁבָטִים עָלוּ לְרֹאשׁ הַר עֵיבָל, וְהַכֹּהֲנִים וְהַלְוִיִּם וְהָאָרוֹן עוֹמְדִים לְמַטָּה בָּאֶמְצַע. הַכֹּהֲנִים מַקִּיפִין אֶת הָאָרוֹן וְהַלְוִיִּם אֶת הַכֹּהֲנִים וְכָל יִשְׂרָאֵל מִכָּאן וּמִכָּאן, שֶׁנֶּאֱמַר: ״וְכָל יִשְׂרָאֵל וּזְקֵנָיו וְשֹׁטְרִים וְשֹׁפְטָיו עוֹמְדִים מִזֶּה וּמִזֶּה לָאָרוֹן״ וגו׳.

Six tribes ascended to the top of Mount Gerizim and six tribes ascended to the top of Mount Ebal, and the priests and the Levites and the Ark were standing at the bottom in the middle, between the two mountains. **The priests were surrounding the Ark and the Levites** were surrounding **the priests, and all** the rest of **the Jewish people** were standing on the mountains **on this side and on that side, as it is stated: "And all Israel, and their elders and officers, and their judges, stood on this side of the Ark and on that side** before the priests the Levites that bore the Ark of the Covenant of the Lord" (Joshua 8:33).

הָפְכוּ פְּנֵיהֶם כְּלַפֵּי הַר גְּרִיזִים וּפָתְחוּ בִּבְרָכָה: ״בָּרוּךְ הָאִישׁ אֲשֶׁר לֹא יַעֲשֶׂה פֶסֶל וּמַסֵּכָה״, וְאֵלּוּ וָאֵלּוּ עוֹנִין ״אָמֵן״. הָפְכוּ פְּנֵיהֶם כְּלַפֵּי הַר עֵיבָל וּפָתְחוּ בִּקְלָלָה: ״אָרוּר הָאִישׁ אֲשֶׁר יַעֲשֶׂה פֶסֶל וּמַסֵּכָה״, וְאֵלּוּ וָאֵלּוּ עוֹנִין ״אָמֵן״, עַד שֶׁגּוֹמְרִין בְּרָכוֹת וּקְלָלוֹת.

The Levites then **turned to face Mount Gerizim and opened with** the **blessing: Blessed be the man who does not make a graven or molten image** (see Deuteronomy 27:15), **and these** people **and those** people, i.e., the two groups standing on either mountain, **answered: Amen.** Then **they turned to face Mount Ebal and opened with** the **curse: "Cursed be the man who makes a graven or molten image"** (Deuteronomy 27:15), **and these** people **and those** people **answered: Amen.** They continued in this manner **until they completed** reciting all of the **blessings and curses.**

וְאַחַר כָּךְ הֵבִיאוּ אֶת הָאֲבָנִים וּבָנוּ אֶת הַמִּזְבֵּחַ, וְסָדוּהוּ בְּסִיד, וְכָתְבוּ עָלָיו אֶת כָּל דִּבְרֵי הַתּוֹרָה בְּשִׁבְעִים לָשׁוֹן, שֶׁנֶּאֱמַר: ״בַּאֵר הֵיטֵב״, וְנָטְלוּ אֶת הָאֲבָנִים וּבָאוּ

And afterward they brought the stones as commanded in the Torah, **and they built the altar and plastered it with plaster, and they wrote on it all of the words of the Torah**[N] **in seventy languages, as it is stated:** "And you shall write on the stones all the words of this law **clearly elucidated"** (Deuteronomy 27:8), indicating that it was to be written in every language. **And they** then **took the stones** from there **and came**

NOTES

All of the words of the Torah – אֶת כָּל דִּבְרֵי הַתּוֹרָה: According to the Ramban and Rabbeinu Baḥyei, this is to be taken literally; the entire Torah was written on these stones. In *Tiferet Yisrael* it is explained that for that to be the case, a miracle must have taken place, as otherwise it would impossible to write out the entire Torah on stones and in such a short period of time. Rav Se'adya Gaon is quoted in the Meiri and in *Tosefot Yom Tov* as explaining that they did not write out the entire Torah, but rather they wrote a list of the mitzvot, similar to the various lists of mitzvot composed by the sages of his time.

וְלָנוּ בִּמְקוֹמָן.

to Gilgal **and slept in their** lodging **place.**

גמ׳ פָּרָשַׁת סוֹטָה מְנָלַן? דִּכְתִיב: ״וְאָמַר הַכֹּהֵן לָאִשָּׁה״, בְּכָל לָשׁוֹן שֶׁהוּא אוֹמֵר.

GEMARA From where do we derive that **the portion** of the warning and the oath administered by the priest to **a *sota*** can be recited in any language?[N] **As it is written: "And the priest shall say to the woman"** (Numbers 5:21), which indicates: **In any language that he speaks.**

תָּנוּ רַבָּנַן: מַשְׁמִיעִין אוֹתָהּ בְּכָל לָשׁוֹן שֶׁהִיא שׁוֹמַעַת, עַל מָה הִיא שׁוֹתָה וּבַמֶּה הִיא שׁוֹתָה, עַל מָה נִטְמֵאת וּבַמֶּה הִיא נִטְמֵאת.

The Sages taught (*Tosefta* 2:1): The priest **informs** the *sota* **in any language that she can hear** and understand **for what** reason **she must drink** the bitter water of a *sota*, **and from what** vessel **she will drink, on account of what** actions **she is** considered to be **defiled and in what** way **she defiled herself.**

עַל מָה הִיא שׁוֹתָה? עַל עִסְקֵי קִינּוּי וּסְתִירָה. וּבַמֶּה הִיא שׁוֹתָה? בִּמְקֵידָה שֶׁל חֶרֶשׂ.

For what reason **must she drink** the bitter water? She must drink it **on account of the matter of** the **warning** given to her by her husband, **and** her subsequent **seclusion. And from what** vessel **does she drink?** She drinks **from a *mekeida*,** a simple vessel, **of clay.**

עַל מָה נִטְמֵאת? עַל עִסְקֵי שְׂחוֹק וְיַלְדוּת, וּבַמֶּה הִיא נִטְמֵאת? בְּשׁוֹגֵג אוֹ בְּמֵזִיד, בְּאוֹנֶס [אוֹ] בְּרָצוֹן. וְכׇל כָּךְ לָמָּה? שֶׁלֹּא לְהוֹצִיא לַעַז עַל מַיִם הַמָּרִים.

On account of what actions **is she** considered to be **defiled?** It is **on account of matters of levity and immaturity. And in what** way **did she defile herself?** The priest must explain to her that there is a difference between whether she acted **unwittingly or intentionally, and** whether she acted **due to circumstances beyond** her **control, or** whether she acted **willingly. And why** does **all of this** need to be explained to her? In order **not to cast aspersions on the bitter water** of a *sota*, as, if she committed adultery unwittingly or due to circumstances beyond her control, the water will not affect her.

״וִידּוּי מַעֲשֵׂר״. מְנָלַן? דִּכְתִיב: ״וְאָמַרְתָּ לִפְנֵי ה׳ אֱלֹהֶיךָ בִּעַרְתִּי הַקֹּדֶשׁ מִן הַבַּיִת״, וְיָלֵיף אֲמִירָה מִסּוֹטָה, בְּכָל לָשׁוֹן שֶׁהוּא אוֹמֵר.

From where do we derive that **the declaration of tithes**[N] may be recited in any language? **As it is written: "Then you shall say before the Lord your God: I have put away the hallowed things out of my house"** (Deuteronomy 26:13). **And derive** a verbal analogy **from** the **saying** mentioned in this verse, and the saying mentioned in the verse with regard to **a *sota*** (Numbers 5:21), that one is permitted to recite the declaration of tithes **in any language that he speaks.**

אֲמַר לֵיהּ רַב זְבִיד לְאַבָּיֵי: וְלֵילַף אֲמִירָה מִלְוִיִּם, מָה לְהַלָּן בִּלְשׁוֹן הַקּוֹדֶשׁ אַף כָּאן בִּלְשׁוֹן הַקּוֹדֶשׁ!

Rav Zevid said to Abaye: But let us derive a verbal analogy **from** the **saying** mentioned in the verse: "And the **Levites** shall speak and say" (Deuteronomy 27:14). **Just as there,** the Levites recited the blessings and curses **in the sacred tongue, so too here,** one must recite the declaration of tithes **in the sacred tongue.**

דָּנִין אֲמִירָה גְּרֵידְתָּא מֵאֲמִירָה גְּרֵידְתָּא, וְאֵין דָּנִין אֲמִירָה גְּרֵידְתָּא מֵעֲנִיָּיה וַאֲמִירָה.

Abaye answered: **One derives** a verbal analogy **from** the term **saying** in a verse where the word "say" appears **alone** and another instance where the word **saying** appears **alone. And one does not derive** a verbal analogy **from** the word **saying** when it appears **alone,** as it does in the verse about the declaration of tithes, and in a verse that mentions **speaking and saying,** such as the verse concerning the Levites.

תַּנְיָא, רַבִּי שִׁמְעוֹן בֶּן יוֹחַי אוֹמֵר: אָדָם אוֹמֵר שִׁבְחוֹ בְּקוֹל נָמוּךְ, וּגְנוּתוֹ – בְּקוֹל רָם;

The distinction between merely saying, and speaking and saying, is significant, as **it is taught** in a *baraita* that **Rabbi Shimon ben Yoḥai says: A person should say his** own **praise in a soft voice, and** say that which is to **his discredit in a loud voice.**

שִׁבְחוֹ בְּקוֹל נָמוּךְ – מִן וִידּוּי הַמַּעֲשֵׂר; גְּנוּתוֹ בְּקוֹל רָם – מִמִּקְרָא בִּיכּוּרִים.

That one should say **his praise in a soft voice** is derived **from** the portion of **the declaration of tithes,** where one declares that he has acted appropriately, and the verse does not state: And you shall speak. That one should say that which is to **his discredit in a loud voice** is derived **from the recitation of the first fruits,** concerning which the verse states: "And you shall speak and say" (Deuteronomy 26:5), i.e., it should be recited loudly. The portion recited when bringing the first fruits details the hardships that the Jewish people suffered and denigrates Laban the Aramean, who is a progenitor of the Jewish people.

NOTES

From where do we derive that the portion of a *sota* can be recited in any language – פָּרָשַׁת סוֹטָה מְנָלַן: *Tosefot HaRash* point out that the discussion in the mishna and the Gemara is predicated on the question, raised later in the Gemara, of whether the Torah must be recited in Hebrew in public readings in the synagogue, or if it can be recited in any language. They therefore say that the Gemara is difficult in any event: If the discussion is predicated on the assumption that the Torah may be recited in any language, then why is there a need to provide explanations for the recitations that may be recited in any language, as they simply follow the standard *halakha*? Conversely, if the Torah must be recited in Hebrew, why is it necessary to provide proof for those recitations that one is required to recite in Hebrew, as they simply follow the standard *halakha*?

They explain that according to the *tanna* of the mishna, the entire Torah may be recited in any language; this is apparent, as the mishna offers proof only for those recitations that must be recited in Hebrew. The Gemara, however, explains the *halakhot* of the mishna even according to the opinion that the Torah must be recited in Hebrew, and offers proof that in certain cases it is permitted to recite Torah verses in any language.

According to *Tosefot HaRosh*, the Gemara's discussion is an attempt to resolve this issue according to both opinions.

However, Rashi's commentary on the mishna seems to present a different opinion, as he explains that it is necessary for the mishna to state that the portion of a *sota* may be recited in any language, lest one compare it to the *ḥalitza* ceremony, which must be recited in Hebrew. This could indicate that according to Rashi, every one of the recitations cited in the mishna has a specific reason requiring that it be taught that it can be recited in any language.

Declaration of tithes – וִידּוּי מַעֲשֵׂר: It is explained in *Be'er Sheva* that it is necessary to offer a proof that the declaration of tithes may be recited in any language, as it is juxtaposed with the verses recited when bringing the first fruits, and one might have concluded that the declaration of tithes must be said in Hebrew, just like the recitation of the first fruits.

וּגְנוּתוֹ בְּקוֹל רָם? וְהָאָמַר רַבִּי יוֹחָנָן מִשּׁוּם רַבִּי שִׁמְעוֹן בֶּן יוֹחַי: מִפְּנֵי מָה תִּקְּנוּ תְּפִלָּה בְּלַחַשׁ? כְּדֵי שֶׁלֹּא לְבַיֵּישׁ אֶת עוֹבְרֵי עֲבֵירָה, שֶׁהֲרֵי לֹא חִלֵּק הַכָּתוּב מָקוֹם בֵּין חַטָּאת לְעוֹלָה!

The Gemara asks: **But** should one really say that which is to **his discredit in a loud voice? But didn't Rabbi Yoḥanan say in the name of Rabbi Shimon bar Yoḥai** himself: **For what** reason **did** the Sages **institute** that the *Amida* **prayer** should be recited **in a whisper?**[H] **So as not to embarrass transgressors** who confess their transgressions during their prayer. There is proof that transgressors should not be embarrassed, **as the verse** detailing where different offerings are slaughtered **does not differentiate** between the **place** where **a sin-offering** is slaughtered **and** the place where **a burnt-offering** is slaughtered, so that it will not be recognized when one is bringing a sin-offering and the sinner will not be embarrassed. This shows that one should also say that which is to his discredit quietly.

לָא תֵּימָא גְּנוּתוֹ אֶלָּא אֵימָא צַעֲרוֹ, כִּדְתַנְיָא: ״וְטָמֵא טָמֵא יִקְרָא״ – צָרִיךְ לְהוֹדִיעַ צַעֲרוֹ לָרַבִּים וְרַבִּים מְבַקְּשִׁים עָלָיו רַחֲמִים. וְכׇל מִי שֶׁאֵירַע בּוֹ דָּבָר צָרִיךְ לְהוֹדִיעַ לָרַבִּים, וְרַבִּים מְבַקְּשִׁים עָלָיו רַחֲמִים.

The Gemara corrects the previous statement: **Do not say** that one should say that which is to **his discredit** in a loud voice; **rather, say** that one should publicize **his pain**[N] in a loud voice. **As it is taught** in a *baraita*: It is derived from the verse: **"And will cry: Impure, impure"** (Leviticus 13:45),[H] that a leper must publicize the fact that he is ritually impure. **He must announce his pain to the masses, and the masses will pray for mercy on his behalf. And** similarly, **anyone to whom** a painful **matter happens must announce it to the masses, and the masses will pray for mercy on his behalf.**

גּוּפָא, אָמַר רַבִּי יוֹחָנָן מִשּׁוּם רַבִּי שִׁמְעוֹן בֶּן יוֹחַי: מִפְּנֵי מָה תִּיקְּנוּ תְּפִלָּה בְּלַחַשׁ? שֶׁלֹּא לְבַיֵּישׁ אֶת עוֹבְרֵי עֲבֵירָה, שֶׁהֲרֵי לֹא חִלֵּק הַכָּתוּב מָקוֹם בֵּין חַטָּאת לְעוֹלָה.

The Gemara returns to **the** aforementioned matter **itself: Rabbi Yoḥanan said in the name of Rabbi Shimon bar Yoḥai: For what** reason **did** the Sages **institute** that **prayer** should be said **in a whisper?** It is **so as not to embarrass transgressors, as the verse does not differentiate** between the **place**[H] where **a sin-offering** is slaughtered **and** the place where **a burnt-offering** is slaughtered.

וְלָא? וְהָא אִיכָּא: דָּמִים, דַּם חַטָּאת לְמַעְלָה וְדַם עוֹלָה לְמַטָּה! הָתָם כֹּהֵן הוּא דְּיָדַע.

The Gemara asks: **But** is there really **no** differentiation between the places where a burnt-offering and a sin-offering are sacrificed? **But isn't there** a difference with regard to the place where the **blood** is sprinkled, as the **blood of a sin-offering is** sprinkled **above,**[H] on the upper half of the altar, **and** the **blood of a burnt-offering is** sprinkled **below,**[H] on its lower half? The Gemara answers: **There, the priest is the one who knows** what offering it is, but other people who are not standing there do not know.

וְהָאִיכָּא: חַטָּאת נְקֵבָה, עוֹלָה זָכָר! הָתָם מִיכַּסְיָא בְּאַלְיָה.

The Gemara asks: **But isn't there** a visibly apparent difference between the two offerings, as **a sin-offering is female** and **a burnt-offering is male?**[H] The Gemara answers: **There,** in the case of a sin-offering, its genitals are **covered by the tail**[B] and therefore the gender of the animal is not plainly obvious.

תֵּינַח כִּבְשָׂה, שְׂעִירָה מַאי אִיכָּא לְמֵימַר? הָתָם אִיהוּ דְּקָא מִיכְסִיף נַפְשֵׁיהּ, דְּאִיבָּעֵי לֵיהּ לְאֵיתוּיֵי כִּבְשָׂה וְקָא מַיְיתֵי שְׂעִירָה.

The Gemara asks: That **works out well** if one brings **a female lamb** for a sin-offering, as its long tail covers its genitals. However, if one brings **a female goat,** which does not have a tail, **what can be said?** The Gemara answers: If one brings a female goat, **there he is the one who embarrasses himself, as he should have brought a female lamb** if he wanted to hide the fact that he sinned, **and** instead **he brought a female goat.** It is therefore not necessary to be concerned about his embarrassment.

חַטָּאת דַּעֲבוֹדָה זָרָה דְּלָא סַגִּי דְּלָאו שְׂעִירָה, מַאי אִיכָּא לְמֵימַר? הָתָם נִיכְסִיף וְנֵיזִיל, כִּי הֵיכִי דְּנִכַּפֵּר לֵיהּ.

The Gemara asks: With regard to **a sin-offering** that is brought **for idol worship, for which it does not suffice** to bring any animal **that is not a female goat,** as it is explicitly stated that in that case one must bring a female goat as a sin-offering, **what can be said?** The Gemara answers: **There,** due to the severity of the sin, **let him go and be embarrassed, so that** his sin **will be atoned for** through his embarrassment as well.

״קְרִיַּת שְׁמַע״. מְנָלַן? דִּכְתִיב: ״שְׁמַע יִשְׂרָאֵל״, בְּכׇל לָשׁוֹן שֶׁאַתָּה שׁוֹמֵעַ.

§ The Gemara continues its discussion of the recitations that can be stated in any language. **From where do we** derive that *Shema* may be recited in any language? **As it is written: "Hear, O Israel"** (Deuteronomy 6:4), which is homiletically interpreted to mean that it can be recited **in any language that you** can **hear** and understand.

HALAKHA

The *Amida* prayer should be recited in a whisper – תְּפִלָּה בְּלַחַשׁ: One should recite the *Amida* prayer in a whisper, in a manner that is audible to his own ears but is inaudible to the ears of others. If one is unable to concentrate properly while praying silently, it is permitted for him to pray in a louder voice. However, this is the *halakha* only when one is praying alone; when praying with the community it is prohibited to do so because it will interrupt others. The Rema writes, based on the Jerusalem Talmud, that one is permitted to pray in a louder voice in order to teach the members of his family how to pray (Rambam *Sefer Ahava, Hilkhot Tefilla* 5:9; *Shulḥan Arukh, Oraḥ Ḥayyim* 101:2).

And will cry: Impure, impure – וְטָמֵא טָמֵא יִקְרָא: Not only lepers, but anyone who is ritually impure in a way that can be transmitted to others is obligated to publicize his impurity so that people will distance themselves from him (Rambam *Sefer Tahara, Hilkhot Tumat Tzara'at* 10:8).

The verse does not differentiate between the place, etc. – לֹא חִלֵּק הַכָּתוּב מָקוֹם וכו׳: Offerings of the most sacred order are slaughtered and their blood is collected on the northern side of the altar. There is no difference in this regard between a sin-offering, a guilt-offering, and a burnt-offering (Rambam *Sefer Avoda, Hilkhot Ma'aseh HaKorbanot* 5:2).

The blood of a sin-offering is sprinkled above – דַּם חַטָּאת לְמַעְלָה: The blood of a sin-offering that is eaten is sprinkled four times on the four corners of the upper half of the altar (Rambam *Sefer Avoda, Hilkhot Ma'aseh HaKorbanot* 5:7).

The blood of a burnt-offering is sprinkled below – דַּם עוֹלָה לְמַטָּה: The priest sprinkles the blood of a burnt-offering twice on two corners of the lower half of the altar (Rambam *Sefer Avoda, Hilkhot Ma'aseh HaKorbanot* 5:6).

A sin-offering is female and a burnt-offering is male – חַטָּאת נְקֵבָה עוֹלָה זָכָר: An animal brought for a burnt-offering must be male, whether it is a ram, a goat, or a bull. With the exception of a king or a High Priest, an individual brings as a sin-offering a female lamb or goat (Rambam *Sefer Avoda, Hilkhot Ma'aseh HaKorbanot* 1:8, 15).

NOTES

Rather say that one should publicize his pain – אֶלָּא אֵימָא צַעֲרוֹ: The Maharsha asks that if the purpose of publicizing one's pain is so that others will pray on his behalf, how does this explain the requirement to state the recitation of the first fruits loudly, as there one does not mention any personal pain, but merely notes the tribulations the Jewish people underwent in Egypt? The Maharsha gives an admittedly forced answer, that one who brings the first fruits mentions the tribulations the Jewish people underwent so that others will pray that he should not experience similar troubles in the future.

BACKGROUND

Tail – אַלְיָה: This refers to the thick, fatty tail of the breed of sheep found in Israel and in neighboring countries. The tails of these sheep cover them so that their genitals are not visible, especially when the sheep are young.

Fat-tailed sheep

תָּנוּ רַבָּנַן: קְרִיַּת שְׁמַע כִּכְתָבָהּ, דִּבְרֵי רַבִּי. וַחֲכָמִים אוֹמְרִים: בְּכׇל לָשׁוֹן.

The Sages taught (*Tosefta* 7:7): ***Shema*** must be recited in Hebrew **as it is written; this is the statement of Rabbi** Yehuda HaNasi. **And the Rabbis say:** It may be recited **in any language.**

מַאי טַעְמָא דְּרַבִּי? אָמַר קְרָא: ״וְהָיוּ״, בַּהֲוָיָיתָן יְהוּ.

The Gemara asks: **What is the reason** for the opinion **of Rabbi** Yehuda HaNasi? **The verse states: "And** these words, which I command you this day, **will be** upon your heart" (Deuteronomy 6:6). "Will be" means **as they are, so shall they be.** They should remain unchanged, in their original language.

וְרַבָּנַן? אָמַר קְרָא: ״שְׁמַע״, בְּכׇל לָשׁוֹן שֶׁאַתָּה שׁוֹמֵעַ.

The Gemara asks further: **And** what is the reason for **the** opinion of the **Rabbis?** The Gemara answers: **The verse states: "Hear,** O Israel" (Deuteronomy 6:4), which they explain to mean that *Shema* must be understood. Therefore, one may recite *Shema* **in any language that you** can **hear** and understand.

וְרַבָּנַן נַמִי הָא כְּתִיב ״וְהָיוּ״! הַהוּא, שֶׁלֹּא יִקְרָאֶנָּה לְמַפְרֵעַ.

The Gemara asks: **But** according to **the Rabbis as well, isn't it written: "And** these words **will be"?** The Gemara answers: From **that** it is derived **that one may not recite it out of order.**[H] One may not begin reciting *Shema* from the end, but only in the order in which it is written.

וְרַבִּי, שֶׁלֹּא יִקְרָאֶנָּה לְמַפְרֵעַ מְנָלֵיהּ? נָפְקָא לֵיהּ מִ״דְּבָרִים״, ״הַדְּבָרִים״. וְרַבָּנַן? ״דְּבָרִים״, ״הַדְּבָרִים״ לָא מַשְׁמַע לְהוּ.

The Gemara asks: **And from where does Rabbi** Yehuda HaNasi derive the *halakha* that **one may not recite it out of order?** The Gemara answers: Rabbi Yehuda HaNasi **derives it from** an additional emphasis in the verse "And the words [*hadevarim*], which I command you this day, will be upon your heart." The verse could have conveyed the same idea had it written: **Words,** without the definite article. However, it says **the words,** employing the definite article, teaching that it must be recited in the specific order in which it is written. **And the Rabbis do not learn anything from** the difference between **"words"** and **"the words."**

וְרַבִּי נַמִי הָכְתִיב: ״שְׁמַע״! הַהוּא מִיבְּעֵי לֵיהּ: לְהַשְׁמִיעַ לְאׇזְנֶיךָ מַה שֶּׁאַתָּה מוֹצִיא מִפִּיךָ. וְרַבָּנַן סָבְרִי לַהּ כְּמַאן דְּאָמַר: הַקּוֹרֵא אֶת שְׁמַע וְלֹא הִשְׁמִיעַ לְאׇזְנוֹ – יָצָא.

The Gemara asks: **But** according to **Rabbi** Yehuda HaNasi **as well, isn't** the word **"hear" written?** The Gemara answers: **He requires that for** the *halakha* that you must **have your ears hear**[H] **that which comes out of your mouth,** i.e., one must recite *Shema* audibly so he hears it while reciting it. **And** from where do **the Rabbis** derive that one must recite *Shema* audibly? The Rabbis do not accept this literal interpretation of the word *Shema*. Rather, they **hold according to the one who says: One who recites *Shema*** in a manner **inaudible to his** own **ears has fulfilled** his obligation. The Rabbis therefore interpret the word "hear" as referring to the language that one uses.

לֵימָא קָסָבַר רַבִּי:

The Gemara asks: **Shall we say that Rabbi** Yehuda HaNasi **holds**

HALAKHA

That one may not recite it out of order – שֶׁלֹּא יִקְרָאֶנָּה לְמַפְרֵעַ: One who recites *Shema* changing the order of the verses within a portion has not fulfilled the mitzva. However, if one recites the portions in a different order than that established by the Sages, although he has not followed the ordinance of the Sages, he has fulfilled the mitzva (Rambam *Sefer Ahava, Hilkhot Keriat Shema* 2:11; *Shulḥan Arukh, Oraḥ Ḥayyim* 64:1).

You must make your ears hear – לְהַשְׁמִיעַ לְאׇזְנֶיךָ: One is required to recite *Shema* in a manner that is audible to his own ears *ab initio*. However, if he does not recite it in this manner, he has still fulfilled the mitzva, as long as he pronounces the words orally (Rambam *Sefer Ahava, Hilkhot Keriat Shema* 2:8; *Shulḥan Arukh, Oraḥ Ḥayyim* 62:3).

HALAKHA

A person should never request in the Aramaic language that his needs be met – **לְעוֹלָם אַל יִשְׁאַל אָדָם צְרָכָיו בִּלְשׁוֹן אֲרַמִּית**: Some say that even in a situation where an individual can ask for his needs in any language, he should not do so in Aramaic (*Shulḥan Arukh, Oraḥ Ḥayyim* 101:4).

כָּל הַתּוֹרָה בְּכָל לָשׁוֹן נֶאֶמְרָה, דְּאִי סָלְקָא דַּעְתָּךְ בִּלְשׁוֹן הַקּוֹדֶשׁ נֶאֶמְרָה, ״וְהָיוּ״ דִּכְתַב רַחֲמָנָא לָמָּה לִי?

that **the entire Torah may be recited in any language,**[N] **as, if it should enter your mind** to say **that** the entire Torah **may be recited** only **in the sacred tongue** and not in any other language, **why do I** need **that which the Merciful One writes: "And** these words, which I command you this day, **will be"?** If in fact it is prohibited for one to recite any portion of the Torah in a language other than Hebrew, then prohibiting the recitation of *Shema* in a language other than Hebrew is superfluous. Since the Torah specifically requires *Shema* to be recited in Hebrew, it must be because the rest of the Torah may be recited in any language.

אִיצְטְרִיךְ, מִשּׁוּם דִּכְתִיב ״שְׁמַע״.

The Gemara rejects this suggestion: This is not unquestionably so, as the phrase "and these words, which I command you this day, will be" **is necessary** in this case **because "hear" is** also **written.** Had it not said "and these words, which I command you this day, will be," it would have been derived from the word "hear" that *Shema* may be recited in any language, in accordance with the opinion of the Rabbis. Therefore, the phrase "and these words, which I command you this day, will be" is necessary.

לֵימָא קָסָבְרִי רַבָּנַן: כָּל הַתּוֹרָה כּוּלָּהּ בִּלְשׁוֹן קוֹדֶשׁ נֶאֶמְרָה, דְּאִי סָלְקָא דַּעְתָּךְ בְּכָל לָשׁוֹן, ״שְׁמַע״ דִּכְתַב רַחֲמָנָא לָמָּה לִי?

The Gemara asks: **Shall we say** that **the Rabbis hold** that **the entire Torah may be recited** only **in the sacred tongue** and not in any other language? **As, if it should enter your mind** to say **that** the Torah **may be recited in any language, why do I** need **that which the Merciful One writes: "Hear"?** It is permitted for one to recite the entire Torah in any language, rendering a specific requirement with regard to *Shema* superfluous.

אִיצְטְרִיךְ, מִשּׁוּם דִּכְתִיב ״וְהָיוּ״.

The Gemara rejects this: The word "hear" **is necessary** in any case, **because "and** these words, which I command you this day, **will be" is** also **written.** Had it not been for the word "hear," the Rabbis would have understood that it is prohibited to recite *Shema* in any other language, in accordance with the opinion of Rabbi Yehuda HaNasi. Therefore, the word "hear" is necessary.

״תְּפִלָּה״. רַחֲמֵי הִיא, כָּל הֵיכִי דְּבָעֵי מְצַלֵּי.

§ It is stated in the mishna that the *Amida* **prayer** may be recited in any language. The reason for this is that since prayer **is** a request for divine **mercy, one may pray in any way that one desires.**

וּתְפִלָּה בְּכָל לָשׁוֹן? וְהָאָמַר רַב יְהוּדָה: לְעוֹלָם אַל יִשְׁאַל אָדָם צְרָכָיו בִּלְשׁוֹן אֲרַמִּית, דְּאָמַר רַבִּי יוֹחָנָן: כָּל הַשּׁוֹאֵל צְרָכָיו בִּלְשׁוֹן אֲרַמִּי – אֵין מַלְאֲכֵי הַשָּׁרֵת נִזְקָקִין לוֹ, לְפִי שֶׁאֵין מַלְאֲכֵי הַשָּׁרֵת מַכִּירִין בִּלְשׁוֹן אֲרַמִּי!

The Gemara asks: **But** may **prayer** really be recited **in any language? But didn't Rav Yehuda say: A person should never request in the Aramaic language** that **his needs** be met,[H] **as Rabbi Yoḥanan said** that with regard to **anyone who requests in the Aramaic language** that **his needs** be met, **the ministering angels do not attend to him, as the ministering angels are not familiar** [*makkirin*] **with the Aramaic language?**[N]

NOTES

The entire Torah may be recited in any language – **כָּל הַתּוֹרָה בְּכָל לָשׁוֹן נֶאֶמְרָה**: The commentaries interpret this statement in various ways. All agree that the Torah was originally stated and written in Hebrew. However, the Gemara (*Shabbat* 88b) says that when the Torah was given on Mount Sinai, it was also heard in all seventy languages.

Citing Rav Hai Gaon, the early commentaries state that the dispute in the Gemara is with regard to whether the Torah was given to Moses in the other languages besides Hebrew with a specific text. Rabbeinu Ḥananel explains that the issue is whether or not a Torah scroll may be written in another language and still maintain its sanctity as a Torah scroll.

Rashi explains that the question is whether or not the Torah may be read publicly in the synagogue in a language other than Hebrew. *Tosefot HaRash* object to this explanation, claiming that since the public Torah reading is a rabbinic ordinance, one cannot say that it must be performed in Hebrew. Rashi's explanation is defended in *Be'er Sheva*, where it is explained that according to Rashi, the question is whether one who reads or studies the Torah in another language fulfills the mitzva of studying Torah, which is a mitzva by Torah law.

Tosefot HaRash, as well as *Tosafot* in tractate *Berakhot* (13b), explain that the Gemara is referring not to the rabbinic mitzva of reading the Torah in synagogue, but to those specific passages of the Torah that are required to be read by Torah law. The Meiri explains that the debate concerns whether or not the Torah was given for the purpose of being studied in any language.

The ministering angels are not familiar [*makkirin*] with the Aramaic language – **אֵין מַלְאֲכֵי הַשָּׁרֵת מַכִּירִין בִּלְשׁוֹן אֲרַמִּי**: There are several interpretations of this statement. *Tosafot* (*Shabbat* 12a) ask how it could be said that the angels do not understand Aramaic, as, if the angels know people's thoughts then they must understand every language. They answer that the meaning of the word *makkirin* is not: To be familiar, but rather: To value and honor. The statement therefore means that although the ministering angels understand Aramaic, it is not regarded highly by them. Some commentaries cite Rabbeinu Tam as the source of this interpretation. Others explain that the angels' lack of regard for Aramaic is due to its similarity to Hebrew; it is consequently viewed as a distortion of the Hebrew language (*Eliya Rabba*). Several challenges are raised against this interpretation.

The *Sefat Emet* explains that according to the *Zohar*, the angels do not understand all the thoughts of people; they understand only those thoughts that are revealed to them. The Maharsha cites an opinion that the angels do not understand any language other than Hebrew, and that Rabbi Yoḥanan mentions Aramaic in particular to teach that even Aramaic, which is very similar to Hebrew, and which is the language in which parts of the Torah and the books of the Bible are written, is nevertheless incomprehensible to the angels.

לָא קַשְׁיָא: הָא בְּיָחִיד, הָא בְּצִבּוּר.

The Gemara answers: This is **not difficult,** as **that** statement of Rabbi Yoḥanan is referring **to** the prayer of **an individual,** who needs the support of the angels, whereas **this** statement of the mishna is referring **to communal** prayer.[N]

וְאֵין מַלְאֲכֵי הַשָּׁרֵת מַכִּירִין בִּלְשׁוֹן אֲרַמִּי? וְהָתַנְיָא: יוֹחָנָן כֹּהֵן גָּדוֹל שָׁמַע בַּת קוֹל מִבֵּית קֹדֶשׁ הַקֳּדָשִׁים שֶׁהוּא אוֹמֵר נִצְחוּ טַלְיָא דְּאָזְלוּ לְאַגָּחָא קְרָבָא לְאַנְטוֹכְיָא! וְשׁוּב מַעֲשֶׂה בְּשִׁמְעוֹן הַצַּדִּיק, שֶׁשָּׁמַע בַּת קוֹל מִבֵּית קֹדֶשׁ הַקֳּדָשִׁים שֶׁהוּא אוֹמֵר בְּטֵילַת עֲבִידְתָּא דַּאֲמַר שַׂנְאָה לְאַיְיתָאָה עַל הֵיכְלָא וְנֶהֱרַג גַּסְקַלְגָּס וּבָטְלוּ גְּזֵירוֹתָיו. וְכָתְבוּ אוֹתָהּ שָׁעָה וְכִיוְּונוּ. וּבִלְשׁוֹן אֲרַמִּי הָיָה אוֹמֵר!

The Gemara asks: **And are the ministering angels not familiar with the Aramaic language? But isn't it taught** in a *baraita* (*Tosefta* 13:5): **Yoḥanan the High Priest heard a Divine Voice** emerging **from the House of the Holy of Holies that was saying: The youth who went to wage war in Antokhya have been victorious.**[B] **And** there was **another incident involving Shimon HaTzaddik,**[B] **who heard a Divine Voice** emerging **from the House of the Holy of Holies that was saying: The decree that the enemy intended to bring against the Temple is annulled, and Gaskalgas,** Caligula, **has been killed**[B] **and his decrees have been voided. And** people **wrote** down **that time** that the Divine Voice was heard, **and** later found that it **matched** exactly the moment that Caligula was killed. The Gemara concludes: **And** this Divine Voice **was speaking in the Aramaic language.**

אִי בָּעֵית אֵימָא: בַּת קוֹל שָׁאנֵי, דִּלְאַשְׁמוּעֵי עֲבִידָא. וְאִי בָּעֵית אֵימָא: גַּבְרִיאֵל הֲוָה, דְּאָמַר מָר: בָּא גַּבְרִיאֵל וְלִימְּדוֹ שִׁבְעִים לָשׁוֹן.

The Gemara answers: **If you wish, say** that the **Divine Voice is different, as its purpose is to communicate** a message, and therefore it also communicates in Aramaic. **And if you wish, say** instead that **it was** the angel **Gabriel, as the Master said** with regard to Joseph: **Gabriel came and taught him seventy languages,** as he knows all of the languages, as opposed to the other angels, who do not.

"בִּרְכַּת הַמָּזוֹן". דִּכְתִיב: "וְאָכַלְתָּ וְשָׂבָעְתָּ וּבֵרַכְתָּ אֶת ה׳ אֱלֹהֶיךָ", בְּכׇל לָשׁוֹן שֶׁאַתָּה מְבָרֵךְ.

§ It is stated in the mishna that **Grace after Meals**[N] may be recited in any language. **As it is written: "And you shall eat, and be satisfied, and bless the Lord your God"** (Deuteronomy 8:10). The word "bless" is homiletically interpreted to mean: **In any language that you bless.**

"שְׁבוּעַת הָעֵדוּת". דִּכְתִיב: "וְנֶפֶשׁ כִּי תֶחֱטָא וְשָׁמְעָה קוֹל אָלָה", בְּכׇל לָשׁוֹן שֶׁהִיא שׁוֹמַעַת.

It is stated in the mishna that **an oath of testimony** may be said in any language, **as it is written: "And if anyone sins, in that he heard the voice of adjuration"** (Leviticus 5:1). The emphasis on hearing in the verse is interpreted to mean that it can be recited **in any language that a person hears,** i.e., understands.

שְׁבוּעַת הַפִּקָּדוֹן. אָתְיָא "תֶּחֱטָא", "תֶּחֱטָא" מִשְּׁבוּעַת הָעֵדוּת.

It is stated in the mishna that **an oath on a deposit** may be taken in any language. This **is derived** by means of a verbal analogy **from** the word **"sins"** (Leviticus 5:21) that appears in the portion of an oath on a deposit, and the word **"sins"** (Leviticus 5:1) that is mentioned in the portion of **an oath of testimony.**

NOTES

That is referring to the prayer of an individual whereas this is referring to communal prayer – הָא בְּיָחִיד, הָא בְּצִבּוּר: Rashi explains that the distinction between individual and communal prayer is that the Divine Presence dwells among a community in prayer. Therefore, a communal prayer does not require ministering angels to bring the prayers before God.

Grace after Meals – בִּרְכַּת הַמָּזוֹן: Rashi writes that the Gemara does not ask here: From where is it derived, because he asserts that there is no reason to say that Grace after Meals must be recited in Hebrew, and therefore there is no need to prove that it can be recited in other languages. However, *Tosafot* explain that without this proof, one could have derived from the blessings of the Levites at Mount Gerizim that here too, Grace after Meals must be recited in Hebrew.

BACKGROUND

The youth…have been victorious – נִצְחוּ טַלְיָא: This story is related at length in the writings of Josephus (*Antiquities of the Jews*, XIII:5). When Yoḥanan Hyrcanus led a siege on the city of Samaria, which he eventually conquered and destroyed, the Syrian king Antiochus Cyzicenus came to the aid of the Samaritans. Yoḥanan sent his sons to fight Antiochus, whose army was reinforced by the Egyptian military, and they eventually defeated him. Josephus also writes that Yoḥanan the High Priest heard a heavenly voice emerging from the Holy of Holies saying that his children had been victorious in battle.

Shimon HaTzaddik – שִׁמְעוֹן הַצַּדִּיק: There were two High Priests, grandfather and grandson, who were both called Shimon ben Ḥonyo. It is unclear which of them is referred to as Shimon HaTzaddik, and it is possible that both shared this sobriquet, which means Shimon the righteous. Shimon HaTzaddik was one of the last members of the Great Assembly. Many stories of his righteousness appear throughout the Talmud. A contemporary of his, Shimon ben Sira, uttered unique words in his praise: The greatest of his brothers and the splendor of his people…who is concerned for his people and strengthens them in times of trouble…How splendid he is as he looks out from the Temple, and as he emerges from the inner chamber behind the curtain, like a star of light between trees, like a full moon during a Festival (Ben Sira 49).

Gaskalgas has been killed – נֶהֱרַג גַּסְקַלְגָּס: This statement is historically problematic for several reasons. Some explain, based on alternative versions of the text, that Gaskalgas is another name for the Roman emperor Gaius, also known as Caligula, who decreed sometime before he died that a statue in his likeness would be brought into the Temple and worshipped as a god. This caused an uproar among the Jews, and the Roman commissioner delayed carrying out the decree for some time. In the meantime, Caligula was killed in Rome and his decree was annulled.

If the Gemara is indeed referring to this story, as is evident from the parallel text in *Megillat Ta'anit*, then the Shimon HaTzaddik mentioned here is not the well-known Shimon HaTzaddik. Rather, it refers to Shimon Kitros, the High Priest who served during Caligula's reign. He was appointed by King Agrippa, apparently because he was widely accepted and beloved by the Jews due to his righteousness.

Bust of Gaius, also known as Caligula

״וְאֵלּוּ נֶאֱמָרִין בִּלְשׁוֹן הַקּוֹדֶשׁ: מִקְרָא בִּיכּוּרִים וַחֲלִיצָה״ כו׳ עַד ״מִקְרָא בִּיכּוּרִים כֵּיצַד? ״וְעָנִיתָ וְאָמַרְתָּ לִפְנֵי ה׳ אֱלֹהֶיךָ״, וּלְהַלָּן הוּא אוֹמֵר: ״וְעָנוּ הַלְוִיִּם וְאָמְרוּ אֶל כָּל אִישׁ יִשְׂרָאֵל״, מָה עֲנִיָּיה הָאֲמוּרָה לְהַלָּן בִּלְשׁוֹן הַקּוֹדֶשׁ, אַף כָּאן בִּלְשׁוֹן הַקּוֹדֶשׁ.

§ It is stated in the mishna: **And these are recited** only **in the sacred tongue: The recitation of** the verses that one recounts when bringing the **first fruits** to the Temple; **and *ḥalitza*...how** is it derived that the **recitation** when bringing the **first fruits** is recited specifically in Hebrew? When the Torah discusses this mitzva it states: **"And you shall speak and say before the Lord your God"** (Deuteronomy 26:5), **and below,** in the discussion of the blessings and curses, **it states: "And the Levites shall speak and say to all the men of Israel"** (Deuteronomy 27:14). **Just as there,** in the portion of the Levites, they speak **in the sacred tongue, so too here,** in the portion of the first fruits, the recitation is **in the sacred tongue.**

וּלְוִיִּם גּוּפַיְיהוּ מְנָלַן? אָתְיָא ״קוֹל״ ״קוֹל״ מִמֹּשֶׁה. כְּתִיב הָכָא: ״קוֹל רָם״, וּכְתִיב הָתָם: ״מֹשֶׁה יְדַבֵּר וְהָאֱלֹהִים יַעֲנֶנּוּ בְקוֹל״, מַה לְּהַלָּן בִּלְשׁוֹן הַקּוֹדֶשׁ, אַף כָּאן בִּלְשׁוֹן הַקּוֹדֶשׁ.

The Gemara asks: **And from where do we** derive that **the Levites themselves** answered in Hebrew? The Gemara answers: It is **derived from** a verbal analogy between the word **"voice"** that appears here, in the portion of the blessings and curses, and the word **"voice"** in the verse that relates to **Moses. It is written here: "With a loud voice"** (Deuteronomy 27:14), **and it is written there: "Moses spoke, and God answered him by a voice"** (Exodus 19:19). **Just as there,** the Ten Commandments were stated **in the sacred tongue, so too here,** the Levites spoke **in the sacred tongue.**

״חֲלִיצָה כֵּיצַד״ וכו׳. וְרַבָּנַן, הַאי ״כָּכָה״ מַאי עָבְדִי לֵיהּ? מִיבָּעֵי לְהוּ: לְדָבָר שֶׁהוּא מַעֲשֶׂה מְעַכֵּב.

It is stated in the mishna: **How** is it derived that the recitation at a ***ḥalitza*** ceremony must be in Hebrew? The verse states: "And she shall speak and say: So shall it be done to the man that doth not build up his brother's house" (Deuteronomy 25:9). Rabbi Yehuda derives this *halakha* from the phrase: "And she shall speak and say: So" (Deuteronomy 25:9). The Gemara asks: **And what do the Rabbis do with,** i.e., how do they interpret, **this** word **"so"? They require** it **to** teach that any **matter** detailed in the portion **that is an action is indispensable** to the *ḥalitza* ceremony, as the verse states: "So shall it be done." However, the other aspects of the ritual, e.g., the recitations, are not indispensable, and in their absence the ritual is valid after the fact.

וְרַבִּי יְהוּדָה? מִ״כֹּה״ ״כָּכָה״. וְרַבָּנַן? ״כֹּה״ ״כָּכָה״ לָא מַשְׁמַע לְהוּ.

And Rabbi Yehuda derives this *halakha* **from** the fact that the verse could have used the shorter form of the word **so** [***ko***], and instead uses the longer form of the word **so** [***kakha***]. He therefore derives both *halakhot* from this word. **And the Rabbis do not learn anything from** the difference between ***ko*** and ***kakha*.**

וְרַבִּי יְהוּדָה, הַאי ״וְעָנְתָה וְאָמְרָה״ מַאי עָבֵיד לֵיהּ? מִיבָּעֵי לֵיהּ, לְאַגְמוּרֵי לַלְוִיִּם דְּבִלְשׁוֹן הַקּוֹדֶשׁ.

The Gemara asks: **And what does Rabbi Yehuda do with this** verse: **"And she shall speak and say,"** from which the Rabbis derive that the recitation at the *ḥalitza* ritual must be in Hebrew? The Gemara answers: **He requires it** in order **to teach** with regard **to the Levites that** they spoke **in the sacred tongue.** Whereas the Rabbis derive that the *ḥalitza* ritual is performed in Hebrew from a verbal analogy between the verses concerning *ḥalitza* and the verses about the Levites, Rabbi Yehuda derives that the Levites spoke in Hebrew due to this same verbal analogy, with *ḥalitza* serving as the source.

וְלֵילַף קוֹל מִמֹּשֶׁה! ״עֲנִיָּיה״, ״עֲנִיָּיה״ גָּמֵיר, ״קוֹל״, ״קוֹל״ לָא גָּמֵיר.

The Gemara asks: **But let** Rabbi Yehuda **derive** that the Levites spoke in Hebrew **from** a verbal analogy between the word **"voice"** that is written with regard to the Levites (Deuteronomy 27:14) and the word "voice" in the verse about **Moses** (Exodus 19:19). The Gemara answers: **He learned** the verbal analogy between **"speak"** and **"speak"** from his teacher, and **he did not learn** the verbal analogy between **"voice"** and **"voice"** from his teacher.

תַּנְיָא נַמִּי הָכִי, רַבִּי יְהוּדָה אוֹמֵר: כָּל מָקוֹם שֶׁנֶּאֱמַר ״כֹּה״, ״כָּכָה״, ״עֲנִיָּיה וַאֲמִירָה״ – אֵינוֹ אֶלָּא לְשׁוֹן הַקּוֹדֶשׁ; ״כֹּה״ – ״כֹּה תְבָרְכוּ״; ״כָּכָה״ – דַּחֲלִיצָה, ״עֲנִיָּיה וַאֲמִירָה״ – דִּלְוִיִּם.

That is also taught in a *baraita*: **Rabbi Yehuda says: Every place where it is stated** in the Torah: **"So [*ko*],"** or: **"So [*kakha*],"** or where the language of **speaking and saying** is used, **it is** referring **only** to **the sacred tongue.** The word *ko* appears in the context of the Priestly Benediction: **"So [*ko*] you shall bless** the children of Israel" (Numbers 6:23). ***Kakha*** appears in the context **of the** *ḥalitza* ceremony (Deuteronomy 25:9). The language of **speaking and saying** appears in relation **to the Levites.**

״בְּרָכוֹת וּקְלָלוֹת כֵּיצַד? כֵּיוָן שֶׁעָבְרוּ יִשְׂרָאֵל אֶת הַיַּרְדֵּן״ כו׳. תָּנוּ רַבָּנַן: ״הֲלֹא הֵמָּה בְּעֵבֶר הַיַּרְדֵּן״ – מֵעֵבֶר לַיַּרְדֵּן וְאֵילָךְ, דִּבְרֵי רַבִּי יְהוּדָה. ״אַחֲרֵי דֶּרֶךְ מְבוֹא הַשֶּׁמֶשׁ״ – מָקוֹם שֶׁחַמָּה זוֹרַחַת.

§ It is stated in the mishna: **How** did the ceremony of the **blessings and curses** take place? **When the Jewish people crossed the Jordan River, etc. The Sages taught:** When the Jewish people were in Transjordan, the location of Mount Gerizim and Mount Ebal was described to them as follows: "Are they not beyond the Jordan, behind the way of the coming of the sun, in the land of the Canaanites that dwell in the Arabah, over against Gilgal, beside the oaks of Moreh?" (Deuteronomy 11:30). **"Are they not beyond the Jordan"** means **farther** west, **beyond the Jordan** River; this is **the statement of Rabbi Yehuda. "Behind the way of the coming of the sun"**; this is referring to **the place where the sun rises,** i.e., the east. In other words, they are at a distance from the Jordan River, which is in the east.

״בְּאֶרֶץ הַכְּנַעֲנִי הַיּוֹשֵׁב בָּעֲרָבָה״ – אֵלּוּ הַר גְּרִיזִים וְהַר עֵיבָל שֶׁיּוֹשְׁבִין בָּהֶם כּוּתִיִּים. ״מוּל הַגִּלְגָּל״ – סָמוּךְ לַגִּלְגָּל. ״אֵצֶל אֵלוֹנֵי מֹרֶה״ – שְׁכֶם. וּלְהַלָּן הוּא אוֹמֵר: ״וַיַּעֲבֹר אַבְרָם בָּאָרֶץ עַד מְקוֹם שְׁכֶם עַד אֵלוֹן מוֹרֶה״, מָה אֵלוֹן מוֹרֶה הָאָמוּר לְהַלָּן שְׁכֶם, אַף כָּאן שְׁכֶם.

"In the land of the Canaanites that dwell in the Arabah"; this is referring to **Mount Gerizim and Mount Ebal, where the Samaritans**[B] now **live. "Over against Gilgal"**; this means **near Gilgal. "Beside the oaks of Moreh"**; this is referring to **Shechem. And** from where is it derived that this is Shechem? **There,** with regard to Abraham, the verse **states: "And Abram passed through the land until the place of Shechem, until the oaks of Moreh"** (Genesis 12:6). **Just as the oaks of Moreh stated there are** identified as **Shechem, so too here,** they are **Shechem.**

תַּנְיָא, אָמַר רַבִּי אֶלְעָזָר בְּרַבִּי יוֹסֵי: בְּדָבָר זֶה זִיַּיפְתִּי סִפְרֵי כּוּתִיִּים. אָמַרְתִּי לָהֶם: זִיַּיפְתֶּם תּוֹרַתְכֶם וְלֹא הֶעֱלֵיתֶם בְּיֶדְכֶם כְּלוּם. שֶׁאַתֶּם אוֹמְרִים אֵלוֹנֵי מוֹרֶה – שְׁכֶם. אַף אָנוּ מוֹדִים שֶׁאֵלוֹנֵי מוֹרֶה שְׁכֶם. אָנוּ לְמַדְנוּהָ בִּגְזֵרָה שָׁוָה, אַתֶּם בַּמֶּה לְמַדְתּוּם?

It is taught in a *baraita* that **Rabbi Elazar, son of Rabbi Yosei, said: In this matter, I proved the falsehood of the books of the Samaritans. I said to them: You forged your Torah**[B] by making additions to it, **and you have not gained anything** from it, **as,** you say that **the oaks of Moreh** is referring to **Shechem,** and **we too concede** that **the oaks of Moreh** is referring to **Shechem.** However, **we derived this by** means of **a verbal analogy** between verses. **You,** who do not use verbal analogies, **how did you derive it?**

רַבִּי אֶלְעָזָר אָמַר: ״הֲלֹא הֵמָּה בְּעֵבֶר הַיַּרְדֵּן״ – סָמוּךְ לַיַּרְדֵּן. דְּאִי מֵעֵבֶר הַיַּרְדֵּן וְאֵילָךְ, הֲלֹא כְּתִיב: ״וְהָיָה בְּעָבְרְכֶם אֶת הַיַּרְדֵּן״.

Rabbi Elazar disagrees with Rabbi Yehuda and **says: "Are they not beyond the Jordan"** means **near the Jordan** River, **as, if** it meant **farther** west **beyond the Jordan, isn't it written: "And it shall be when you have passed over the Jordan,** that you shall set up these stones which I command you this day, on Mount Ebal" (Deuteronomy 27:4)? This implies that Mount Ebal was near the location where the Jewish people crossed the Jordan.

״אַחֲרֵי דֶּרֶךְ מְבוֹא הַשֶּׁמֶשׁ״ – מָקוֹם שֶׁהַחַמָּה שׁוֹקַעַת. ״בְּאֶרֶץ הַכְּנַעֲנִי״ – אֶרֶץ חִוִּי הִיא.

"Behind the way of the coming of the sun," according to Rabbi Elazar, is referring to the **place where the sun sets,** in the west. This is distant from Shechem, which is in the center of Eretz Yisrael. Furthermore, the verse states: **"In the land of the Canaanites,"** and Shechem **is** located in the **land of the Hivites** (see Genesis 34:2).

״הַיּוֹשֵׁב בָּעֲרָבָה״ – וַהֲלֹא בֵּין הָרִים וּגְבָעוֹת הֵן יוֹשְׁבִין! ״מוּל הַגִּלְגָּל״ – וַהֲלֹא לֹא רָאוּ אֶת הַגִּלְגָּל!

Similarly, the phrase **"that dwell in the Arabah"** cannot be a description of the mountains known as Mount Gerizim and Mount Ebal that are next to Shechem; **aren't they situated among mountains and hills?** The description **"over against Gilgal"** is also difficult; **they could not see Gilgal** from Shechem, as it is far away. Rather, according to Rabbi Elazar, Mount Gerizim and Mount Ebal mentioned in the Torah are located closer to the Jordan River. They are not the mountains known by the same names that are located near Shechem.

BACKGROUND

Samaritans – כּוּתִים: These are the descendants of the nations displaced by Sennacherib, king of Assyria, and brought to settle in Eretz Yisrael. While initially they converted, over time they readopted their original religion, but they continued to fulfill several mitzvot (see II Kings, chapter 17). At the beginning of the Second Temple period, during the times of Ezra and Nehemiah, relations between the Samaritans and the Jews deteriorated. Later, the Samaritans established a center of worship on Mount Gerizim, as they claimed that the sanctity of that mountain was established by one of the Ten Commandments. Consequently, there was a very real possibility that their blessings and prayers, although somewhat similar to the Jewish liturgy, might include wording that is antithetical to Judaism.

Some generations of Jewish Sages recognized Samaritans as having the status of Jews. They went so far as to say: In the mitzvot that the Samaritans adopted, they are extremely exacting in their fulfillment, even more than the Jews are. Ultimately, as the Samaritans continued to distance themselves from the Jewish people in virtually every regard, they were accorded the legal status of gentiles.

You forged your Torah – זִיַּיפְתֶּם תּוֹרַתְכֶם: In addition to including many changes in the text, the scriptural scrolls of the Samaritans contain several essential differences in the narrative that all attempt to prove their claim that God's chosen place is Shechem and not Jerusalem. One of the most striking examples is the insertion of the blessings and curses of Mount Gerizim and Mount Ebal (Deuteronomy 11:29–30) as the ninth of the Ten Commandments. They also substituted for the tenth commandment the verse: "And it shall be when you have passed over the Jordan, that you shall set up these stones, which I command you this day, in mount Ebal, and you shalt plaster them with plaster. And there you shall build an altar to the Lord your God, an altar of stones" (Deuteronomy 27:4–5). However, according to their version, the altar must be built on Mount Gerizim, not on Mount Ebal. In light of this, the statement of Rabbi Elazar, son of Rabbi Yosei, can be better understood: Despite these changes to the text, they still have no basis for setting up an altar on Mount Gerizim, as it is necessary to establish the locations of these mountains based on a received tradition.

רַבִּי אֱלִיעֶזֶר בֶּן יַעֲקֹב אוֹמֵר: לֹא בָּא הַכָּתוּב אֶלָּא לְהַרְאוֹת לָהֶן דֶּרֶךְ בַּשְּׁנִיָּה כְּדֶרֶךְ שֶׁהֶרְאָה לָהֶן בָּרִאשׁוֹנָה. ״דֶּרֶךְ״ – בַּדֶּרֶךְ לְכוּ וְלֹא בְּשָׂדוֹת וּכְרָמִים. ״הַיּוֹשֵׁב״ – בַּיִּשּׁוּב לְכוּ וְלֹא בַּמִּדְבָּרוֹת. ״בָּעֲרָבָה״ – בָּעֲרָבָה לְכוּ וְלֹא בֶּהָרִים וּגְבָעוֹת.

Rabbi Eliezer ben Ya'akov says: The verse does not come to establish the location of Mount Gerizim and Mount Ebal. **Rather,** it comes **to show** the Jewish people **the way the second time,** when they were entering the land of Canaan, **like the way He showed them the first time,** when they left Egypt and a pillar of cloud went before them and made the terrain easier to transverse. The purpose of the verse is to instruct the Jewish people how to enter the land of Canaan with relative ease, despite the absence of the pillar of cloud. The word **"way"** instructs them to **go along** a pre-established **way, and not in fields and vineyards.** The phrase **"that dwell"** instructs them to **go in settled areas and not in the wilderness. "In the Arabah,"** which means plain, teaches them to **go in** the **plains and not over mountains and hills.**

תָּנוּ רַבָּנַן: כֵּיצַד עָבְרוּ יִשְׂרָאֵל אֶת הַיַּרְדֵּן? בְּכָל יוֹם אָרוֹן נוֹסֵעַ אַחַר שְׁנֵי דְּגָלִים וְהַיּוֹם נָסַע תְּחִילָּה, שֶׁנֶּאֱמַר: ״הִנֵּה אֲרוֹן הַבְּרִית אֲדוֹן כָּל הָאָרֶץ עֹבֵר לִפְנֵיכֶם״; בְּכָל יוֹם וָיוֹם לְוִיִּם נוֹשְׂאִין אֶת הָאָרוֹן וְהַיּוֹם נְשָׂאוּהוּ כֹּהֲנִים, שֶׁנֶּאֱמַר: ״וְהָיָה כְּנוֹחַ כַּפּוֹת רַגְלֵי הַכֹּהֲנִים נוֹשְׂאֵי אֲרוֹן ה׳״ וגו׳.

§ **The Sages taught** (*Tosefta* 8:1): **How did the Jewish people cross the Jordan? Every day the Ark would travel behind** the **two flags** of Judah and Reuben, **but** on **that day** the Ark **traveled in front, as it is stated: "Behold, the Ark of the Covenant of the Lord of all the earth is passing before you"** (Joshua 3:11). **On every** other **day, the Levites would carry the Ark, but on this day the priests carried it, as is stated: "And when the soles of the feet of the priests that bear the Ark of the Lord,** the Lord of all the earth, **shall rest"** (Joshua 3:13).

תַּנְיָא: רַבִּי יוֹסֵי אוֹמֵר, בִּשְׁלֹשָׁה מְקוֹמוֹת נָשְׂאוּ כֹּהֲנִים אֶת הָאָרוֹן: כְּשֶׁעָבְרוּ אֶת הַיַּרְדֵּן, וּכְשֶׁהֵסִיבּוּ אֶת יְרִיחוֹ, וּכְשֶׁהֶחֱזִירוּהוּ לִמְקוֹמוֹ.

It is taught in a *baraita* (*Tosefta* 8:2) that **Rabbi Yosei says: In three** different **places the priests carried the Ark.** They carried it **when** the Jewish people **crossed the Jordan, and when they surrounded Jericho** (Joshua 6:6), **and when they returned it to its** proper **place** in the Holy of Holies during the reign of King Solomon (1 Kings 8:6).

Perek **VII**
Daf **34** Amud **a**

וְכֵיוָן שֶׁנִּיטְבְּלוּ רַגְלֵי כֹּהֲנִים בַּמַּיִם חָזְרוּ הַמַּיִם לַאֲחוֹרֵיהֶם, שֶׁנֶּאֱמַר: ״וּכְבוֹא נוֹשְׂאֵי הָאָרוֹן עַד הַיַּרְדֵּן וגו׳ וַיַּעַמְדוּ הַמַּיִם הַיֹּרְדִים מִלְמַעְלָה קָמוּ נֵד אֶחָד״. וְכַמָּה גּוֹבְהָן שֶׁל מַיִם? שְׁנֵים עָשָׂר מִיל עַל שְׁנֵים עָשָׂר מִיל, כְּנֶגֶד מַחֲנֵה יִשְׂרָאֵל, דִּבְרֵי רַבִּי יְהוּדָה;

And once the feet of the priests were immersed in the water of the Jordan River, **the water flowed backward, as it is stated: "And when those carrying the Ark came to the Jordan** and the feet of the priests that bore the ark were dipped in the brink of the water, for the Jordan overflows all its banks all the time of harvest; **and the waters that came down from above stood, and rose up in one heap"** (Joshua 3:15–16). **And what was the height of the water?**[N] **Twelve** ***mil*** **by twelve** ***mil*****, parallel to** the size of **the camp of the Jewish people** who were passing through the Jordan. This is **the statement of Rabbi Yehuda.**

אָמַר לוֹ רַבִּי אֶלְעָזָר בְּרַבִּי שִׁמְעוֹן: לִדְבָרֶיךָ, אָדָם קַל אוֹ מַיִם קַלִּים? הֱוֵי אוֹמֵר: מַיִם קַלִּים. אִם כֵּן בָּאִין מַיִם וְשׁוֹטְפִין אוֹתָן!

Rabbi Elazar, son of Rabbi Shimon, said to him: According to your statement, does **a person** move **faster or** does **water** move faster? **You must say** that **water** moves **faster**[B] than a person. **If** that is **so,** then before the camp of Israel crossed the river **the water would come and drown them,** as, after the water rose up to a height of twelve *mil* it then began flowing normally again.

NOTES

What was the height of the water – כַּמָּה גּוֹבְהָן שֶׁל מַיִם: This is Rashi's version of the text. The Maharsha prefers a different version of the text: How wide was the water? According to this version, Rabbi Yehuda meant that the water moved back twelve *mil* and left a dry space in the middle of the river, and then it returned afterward, as it is stated: "The Jordan turned backward" (Psalms 114:3).

BACKGROUND

Water moves faster – מַיִם קַלִּים: There is obviously no predetermined speed at which water travels, and in a river its speed will depend on the length and angle of the incline at which the water is flowing. However, although the section of the Jordan River that is near Jericho is relatively flat and the water does not flow at a high speed, it still moves faster than the speed at which people walk, and it certainly moves faster than an entire encampment of people weighed down with possessions and animals.

Jordan River near Jericho

אֶלָּא מְלַמֵּד, שֶׁהָיוּ מַיִם נִגְדָּשִׁין וְעוֹלִין כֵּיפִין עַל גַּבֵּי כֵּיפִין יָתֵר מִשְּׁלֹשׁ מֵאוֹת מִיל, עַד שֶׁרָאוּ אוֹתָן כׇּל מַלְכֵי מִזְרָח וּמַעֲרָב, שֶׁנֶּאֱמַר: ״וַיְהִי כִשְׁמֹעַ כׇּל מַלְכֵי הָאֱמֹרִי אֲשֶׁר בְּעֵבֶר הַיַּרְדֵּן יָמָּה וְכׇל מַלְכֵי הַכְּנַעֲנִי אֲשֶׁר עַל הַיָּם אֵת אֲשֶׁר הוֹבִישׁ ה׳ אֶת מֵי הַיַּרְדֵּן מִפְּנֵי בְנֵי יִשְׂרָאֵל עַד עׇבְרָם וַיִּמַּס לְבָבָם וְלֹא הָיָה בָם עוֹד רוּחַ מִפְּנֵי בְּנֵי יִשְׂרָאֵל״.

Rather, this **teaches that the water gathered and rose in heaps upon heaps** to a height of **more than three hundred *mil*, until all the kings of the East and West saw it, as it is stated: "And it came to pass, when all the kings of the Amorites, that were beyond the Jordan westward, and all the kings of the Canaanites, that were by the sea, heard that the Lord had dried up the waters of the Jordan from before the children of Israel, until they were passed over, that their heart melted, neither was there spirit in them anymore, because of the children of Israel"** (Joshua 5:1).

וְאַף רָחָב הַזּוֹנָה אָמְרָה לִשְׁלוּחֵי יְהוֹשֻׁעַ: ״כִּי שָׁמַעְנוּ אֵת אֲשֶׁר הוֹבִישׁ ה׳ אֶת מֵי יַם סוּף״ וגו׳, וּכְתִיב: ״וַנִּשְׁמַע וַיִּמַּס לְבָבֵנוּ וְלֹא קָמָה עוֹד״ וגו׳.

And even Rahab the prostitute said to Joshua's messengers: "For we have heard how the Lord dried up the water of the Red Sea before you" (Joshua 2:10). **And it is written: "And as soon as we had heard it, our hearts melted, neither did there remain any more** spirit in any man, because of you" (Joshua 2:11). Evidently, the Canaanites were still terrified due to the splitting of the Red Sea, although that had taken place years earlier and in a distant location. It is understood from here how terrified they became when a similar miracle occurred close to where they lived.

עוֹדָם בַּיַּרְדֵּן, אָמַר לָהֶם יְהוֹשֻׁעַ: דְּעוּ עַל מָה אַתֶּם עוֹבְרִים אֶת הַיַּרְדֵּן, עַל מְנָת שֶׁתּוֹרִישׁוּ אֶת יוֹשְׁבֵי הָאָרֶץ מִפְּנֵיכֶם, שֶׁנֶּאֱמַר: ״וְהוֹרַשְׁתֶּם אֶת כׇּל יוֹשְׁבֵי הָאָרֶץ מִפְּנֵיכֶם״ וגו׳, אִם אַתֶּם עוֹשִׂין כֵּן – מוּטָב, וְאִם לָאו – בָּאִין מַיִם וְשׁוֹטְפִין אוֹתִיכֶם. מַאי ״אוֹתִיכֶם״? אוֹתִי וְאֶתְכֶם.

While the Jewish people **were still in the Jordan, Joshua said to them: Know for what** purpose **you are crossing the Jordan.** It is **in order to drive out the inhabitants of the land from before you, as it is stated: "And you shall drive out all the inhabitants of the land from before you"** (Numbers 33:52). **If you will do so,** then all is **well, but if not, water will come and drown *otikhem*.** The Gemara asks: **What** is the meaning of the word ***otikhem*?** The Gemara explains: It is a combination of the words **me [*oti*] and you [*etkhem*].**

עוֹדָם בַּיַּרְדֵּן, אָמַר לָהֶן יְהוֹשֻׁעַ: ״הָרִימוּ לָכֶם אִישׁ אֶבֶן אַחַת עַל שִׁכְמוֹ לְמִסְפַּר שִׁבְטֵי יִשְׂרָאֵל״ וגו׳, וּכְתִיב: ״לְמַעַן תִּהְיֶה זֹאת אוֹת בְּקִרְבְּכֶם כִּי יִשְׁאָלוּן בְּנֵיכֶם מָחָר לֵאמֹר מָה הָאֲבָנִים הָאֵלֶּה לָכֶם״ וגו׳, סִימָן לַבָּנִים שֶׁעָבְרוּ אָבוֹת אֶת הַיַּרְדֵּן.

While **they were still in the Jordan, Joshua said to them: "Pick up every man of you a stone upon his shoulder, according to the number of the tribes of the children of Israel"** (Joshua 4:5). **And it is written: "That this may be a sign among you, that when your children ask in time to come, saying: What do you mean by these stones?"** (Joshua 4:6). This will be **a sign for the children that** their **ancestors crossed the Jordan.**

עוֹדָם בַּיַּרְדֵּן, אָמַר לָהֶן יְהוֹשֻׁעַ: ״שְׂאוּ לָכֶם מִזֶּה מִתּוֹךְ הַיַּרְדֵּן מִמַּצַּב רַגְלֵי הַכֹּהֲנִים הָכִין שְׁתֵּים עֶשְׂרֵה אֲבָנִים וְהַעֲבַרְתֶּם אוֹתָם עִמָּכֶם וְהִנַּחְתֶּם אוֹתָם בַּמָּלוֹן אֲשֶׁר תָּלִינוּ בוֹ הַלַּיְלָה״ וגו׳. יָכוֹל בְּכׇל מָלוֹן וּמָלוֹן? תַּלְמוּד לוֹמַר: ״אֲשֶׁר תָּלִינוּ בוֹ הַלַּיְלָה״.

While **they were still in the Jordan, Joshua said to them: "Take out of the midst of the Jordan, out of the place where the priests' feet stood, twelve stones made ready, and carry them over with you, and lay them down in the lodging place, where you shall lodge this night"** (Joshua 4:3). One **might** have thought that they were required to place these stones **at each and every lodging place** where they stayed. Therefore, **the verse states: "Where you shall lodge this night,"** meaning only on that night.

אָמַר רַבִּי יְהוּדָה: אַבָּא חֲלַפְתָּא וְרַבִּי אֱלִיעֶזֶר בֶּן מַתְיָא וַחֲנַנְיָא בֶּן חֲכִינַאי עָמְדוּ עַל אוֹתָן אֲבָנִים, וְשִׁיעֲרוּם, כׇּל אַחַת וְאַחַת שְׁקוּלָה כְּאַרְבָּעִים סְאָה, וּגְמִירִי, דִּטְעוּנָא דְּמַדְלֵי אִינִישׁ לְכַתְפֵיהּ – תִּילְתָּא דִּטְעוּנֵיהּ הָוֵי.

Rabbi Yehuda says: Abba Ḥalafta, and Rabbi Eliezer ben Matya, and Ḥananya ben Ḥakhinai stood on those same stones that the Jewish people took from the Jordan, **and** they **measured them** and found that **each and every one weighed about forty *se'a*.**[B] **And** it **is learned** as a tradition **that a load that one can lift onto his shoulders is one-third of** the weight of the **load** that he can carry when others load it onto him.

מִכָּאן אַתָּה מְחַשֵּׁב לְאֶשְׁכּוֹל, שֶׁנֶּאֱמַר: ״וַיִּשָּׂאֻהוּ בַמּוֹט בִּשְׁנָיִם״. מִמַּשְׁמַע שֶׁנֶּאֱמַר ״בַּמּוֹט״, אֵינִי יוֹדֵעַ שֶׁבִּשְׁנַיִם? מָה תַּלְמוּד לוֹמַר ״בִּשְׁנָיִם״? בִּשְׁנֵי מוֹטוֹת.

From here you can calculate the size of **the cluster** of grapes that the spies carried together from Eretz Yisrael, **as it is stated: "And they carried it upon a pole between two"** (Numbers 13:23). **From the fact that it is stated** that they carried the cluster of grapes **"on a pole" do I not know that** it was carried **by two** people? That is the only way it can be carried on a pole. **What** is the meaning when **the verse states: "Between two"?** It means that the spies carried it **on two poles,** and four people carried the cluster of grapes together. From here it can be deduced that the weight of the cluster was 480 *se'a*.

BACKGROUND

Forty *se'a* – אַרְבָּעִים סְאָה: Even according to the smallest calculation of a *se'a*, this amounts to a volume of more than 300 ℓ, and the weight of this volume of stones would be around 400 kg.

LANGUAGE

Scales [*turtanei*] – טוּרְטָנֵי: From the Greek τρυτάνη, *trutanē*, which refers to a scale. Here the Gemara is referring to a pole that is held up by another pole, similar to the rod of a scale.

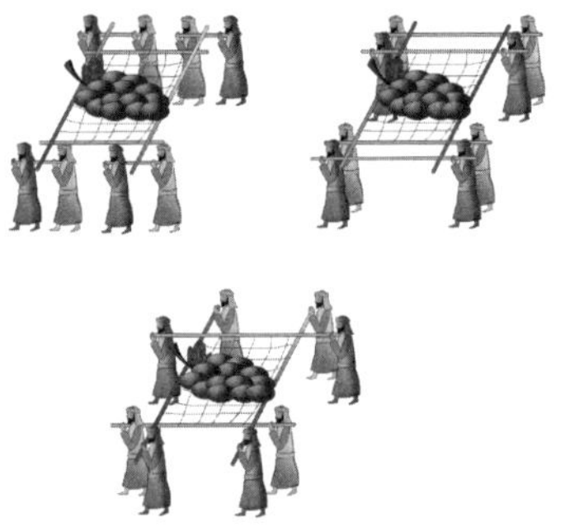

Spies carrying the poles, according to different opinions

אָמַר רַבִּי יִצְחָק: טוּרְטָנֵי וְטוּרְטָנֵי דְטוּרְטָנֵי, הָא כֵּיצַד? שְׁמֹנָה נָשְׂאוּ אֶשְׁכֹּל, אֶחָד נָשָׂא רִימּוֹן וְאֶחָד נָשָׂא תְּאֵינָה. יְהוֹשֻׁעַ וְכָלֵב לֹא נָשְׂאוּ כְּלוּם. אִי בָּעֵית אֵימָא: מִשּׁוּם דַּחֲשִׁיבִי. וְאִי בָּעֵית אֵימָא: שֶׁלֹּא הָיוּ בְּאוֹתָהּ עֵצָה.

Rabbi Yitzḥak said: They were configured like upper rods of **scales** [*turtanei*][L] that are balanced on the lower rods of **scales,** i.e., there were not two but four poles. **How so? Eight** of the spies **carried** the **cluster** of grapes,[N] **one** of them **carried a pomegranate, and one carried a fig. Joshua and Caleb did not carry anything.** Why did Joshua and Caleb not carry anything? **If you wish, say** that it is **because they were** more **prominent** than the others and it was beneath their dignity to carry such a load. **And if you wish, say** instead **that they** did **not** take part **in the** wicked **counsel** of the spies, as the cluster of grapes was brought by the spies to scare the people.

פְּלִיגִי בָּהּ רַבִּי אַמִי וְרַבִּי יִצְחָק נַפָּחָא, חַד אָמַר: לְדִבְרֵי רַבִּי יְהוּדָה,

§ **Rabbi Ami and Rabbi Yitzḥak Nappaḥa disagree with regard to** the dispute between the *tanna'im* as to the height of the water when the Jewish people crossed the Jordan. **One says: According to the statement of Rabbi Yehuda,** that the water stood at the height of twelve *mil,*

NOTES

Eight spies carried the cluster of grapes – שְׁמֹנָה נָשְׂאוּ אֶשְׁכֹּל: In contrast to the opinion of the Gemara, an entirely different description of the actions of the spies is found in *Tanna deVei Eliyahu*: Ten of the spies carried either a pomegranate or fig in their hands, and the remaining two spies carried a cluster of grapes on a pole. This description corresponds to the straightforward understanding of the verse.

NOTES

In my eyes but not in the eyes of the Omnipresent – בְּעֵינַי וְלֹא בְּעֵינָיו שֶׁל מָקוֹם: It is explained in the *Sifrei* that Moses also did not think that it was a good idea to send spies. However, he thought that if he would agree to send the spies, the Jewish people would understand that he was not hiding from them anything bad about Eretz Yisrael, and they would decide on their own that there was no need to send them.

כַּחֲנָיָיתָן עָבְרוּ, לְדִבְרֵי רַבִּי אֶלְעָזָר בְּרַבִּי שִׁמְעוֹן – בְּזֶה אַחַר זֶה עָבְרוּ.

the Jewish people **crossed** in the same formation **as they camped.** It was necessary for the water to stand only twelve *mil* high to allow for the entire encampment to pass through the Jordan. **According to the statement of Rabbi Elazar, son of Rabbi Shimon,** who said the water stood at a height of over three hundred *mil,* the water had to reach these heights to allow for enough time for everyone to cross the Jordan, as **they crossed one after the other.**

וְחַד אָמַר: בֵּין מָר וּבֵין מָר – כַּחֲנָיָיתָן עָבְרוּ. מָר סָבַר: אָדָם קַל, וּמָר סָבַר: מַיִם קַלִּים.

And one says: According to **both** this **Sage and** that **Sage, they crossed** in the same formation **as they camped.** However, one **Sage,** Rabbi Yehuda, **holds** that **a person** moves **faster** than water, **and** one **Sage,** Rabbi Elazar son of Rabbi Shimon, **holds** that **water** moves **faster** than a person does.

״שְׁלַח לְךָ אֲנָשִׁים״ – אָמַר רֵישׁ לָקִישׁ: ״שְׁלַח לְךָ״ – מִדַּעְתְּךָ, וְכִי אָדָם זֶה בּוֹרֵר חֵלֶק רַע לְעַצְמוֹ? וְהַיְינוּ דִּכְתִיב: ״וַיִּיטַב בְּעֵינַי הַדָּבָר״, אָמַר רֵישׁ לָקִישׁ: ״בְּעֵינַי״ – וְלֹא בְּעֵינָיו שֶׁל מָקוֹם.

§ Since the Gemara mentioned the cluster of grapes that the spies brought back from Eretz Yisrael, it continues discussing the story of the spies. It is stated in the Torah that God told Moses: **"Send you** men" (Numbers 13:2). **Reish Lakish says: "Send you"** means that you should send them **at your own discretion** and not as a divine command. As, if it were a divine command, **does a person choose a bad portion for himself?** Since God knew the nature of these spies and that they would ultimately slander the land, He certainly would not have sent them Himself. **And this is** the meaning of **that which is written** in the passage where Moses retold the story of the spies: **"And it was good in my eyes"** (Deuteronomy 1:23), and **Reish Lakish says:** The implication of these words is that it seemed good **"in my eyes," but not in the eyes of the Omnipresent.**[N]

״וְיַחְפְּרוּ לָנוּ אֶת הָאָרֶץ״ – אָמַר רַבִּי חִיָּיא בַּר אַבָּא: מְרַגְּלִים לֹא נִתְכַּוְּונוּ אֶלָּא לְבוֹשְׁתָּהּ שֶׁל אֶרֶץ יִשְׂרָאֵל. כְּתִיב הָכָא: ״וְיַחְפְּרוּ לָנוּ אֶת הָאָרֶץ״, וּכְתִיב הָתָם: ״וְחָפְרָה הַלְּבָנָה וּבוֹשָׁה הַחַמָּה״ וגו׳.

The Torah relates that the people asked Moses to send spies so **"that they may search the land for us"** (Deuteronomy 1:22). **Rabbi Ḥiyya bar Abba says:** When the Jewish people asked to send **spies, their intention was only to shame Eretz Yisrael. It is written here: "That they may search** [*veyaḥperu*] **the land for us," and it is written there: "Then the moon will be embarrassed** [*veḥafera*], **and the sun will be ashamed"** (Isaiah 24:23).

״וְאֵלֶּה שְׁמוֹתָם לְמַטֵּה רְאוּבֵן שַׁמּוּעַ בֶּן זַכּוּר״. אָמַר רַבִּי יִצְחָק, דָּבָר זֶה מָסוֹרֶת בְּיָדֵינוּ מֵאֲבוֹתֵינוּ: מְרַגְּלִים עַל שֵׁם מַעֲשֵׂיהֶם נִקְרְאוּ, וְאָנוּ לֹא עָלְתָה בְּיָדֵינוּ אֶלָּא אֶחָד: סְתוּר בֶּן מִיכָאֵל, סְתוּר – שֶׁסָּתַר מַעֲשָׂיו שֶׁל הַקָּדוֹשׁ בָּרוּךְ הוּא; מִיכָאֵל – שֶׁעָשָׂה עַצְמוֹ מָךְ.

The Torah states with regard to the spies: **"And these were their names: Of the tribe of Reuben, Shammua the son of Zaccur"** (Numbers 13:4). **Rabbi Yitzḥak says: This statement** that follows **is a tradition of ours** that was passed down to us **from our ancestors:** The **spies were named after their actions, but we have obtained** the interpretation of **only**[N] **one** name, the name of **"Sethur the son of Michael"** (Numbers 13:13). He is called **Sethur, as he hid** [*satar*] **the actions of the Holy One, Blessed be He.** In other words, he ignored the miracles that God performed for the Jewish people in Egypt and in the wilderness. He is called **Michael, as he made Him,** God, appear **weak** [*makh*] by saying that there was not enough food in the land for everyone.

אָמַר רַבִּי יוֹחָנָן, אַף אָנוּ נֹאמַר: נַחְבִּי בֶּן וָפְסִי, נַחְבִּי – שֶׁהֶחְבִּיא דְּבָרָיו שֶׁל הַקָּדוֹשׁ בָּרוּךְ הוּא; וָפְסִי – שֶׁפִּיסֵּעַ עַל מִדּוֹתָיו שֶׁל הַקָּדוֹשׁ בָּרוּךְ הוּא.

Rabbi Yoḥanan says: We can also say an interpretation of the name: **"Nahbi the son of Vophsi"** (Numbers 13:14): He is called **Nahbi, as he concealed** [*heḥbi*] **the statement of the Holy One, Blessed be He,** that the land is good, by delivering a distorted description of it. He is called **Vophsi, as he stomped** [*pisse'a*] **on the attributes of the Holy One, Blessed be He,** i.e., he did not believe in His promise to give Eretz Yisrael to the Jewish people.

״וַיַּעֲלוּ בַנֶּגֶב וַיָּבֹא עַד חֶבְרוֹן״ – ״וַיָּבֹאוּ״ מִבְּעֵי לֵיהּ! אָמַר רָבָא: מְלַמֵּד, שֶׁפֵּירֵשׁ כָּלֵב מֵעֲצַת מְרַגְּלִים וְהָלַךְ וְנִשְׁתַּטֵּחַ עַל קִבְרֵי אָבוֹת. אָמַר לָהֶן: אֲבוֹתַי, בַּקְּשׁוּ עָלַי רַחֲמִים שֶׁאֶנָּצֵל מֵעֲצַת מְרַגְּלִים.

It is also stated with regard to the spies: **"And they went up into the south, and he came to Hebron"** (Numbers 13:22). Why is the phrase "and he came" written in the singular form? The verse **should have** said: **And they came. Rava says:** This **teaches that Caleb separated himself**[N] **from the counsel of** the other **spies and went and prostrated himself on the graves of the forefathers** in Hebron. **He said to them: My forefathers, pray for mercy for me so that I will be saved from the counsel of the spies.**

יְהוֹשֻׁעַ כְּבָר בִּקֵּשׁ מֹשֶׁה עָלָיו רַחֲמִים, שֶׁנֶּאֱמַר: ״וַיִּקְרָא מֹשֶׁה לְהוֹשֵׁעַ בִּן נוּן יְהוֹשֻׁעַ״ – יָהּ יוֹשִׁיעֲךָ מֵעֲצַת מְרַגְּלִים. וְהַיְינוּ דִּכְתִיב: ״וְעַבְדִּי כָלֵב עֵקֶב הָיְתָה רוּחַ אַחֶרֶת עִמּוֹ״ וגו׳.

The Gemara explains: **Joshua** did not go to the graves of the forefathers because **Moses had already prayed for mercy for him, as it is stated: "And Moses called Hoshea son of Nun Joshua** [*Yehoshua*]" (Numbers 13:16), meaning: **God will save you** [*Ya yoshiakha*] **from the counsel of the spies. And this is** the meaning of **that which is written: "But My servant Caleb, because he had another spirit with him,**[N] and has followed Me fully, him will I bring into the land where into he went" (Numbers 14:24), which implies that Caleb changed his mind over time. Joshua, however, was opposed to the intentions of the other spies from the outset.

״וְשָׁם אֲחִימָן שֵׁשַׁי וְתַלְמַי״ וגו׳. אֲחִימָן – מְיוּמָּן שֶׁבְּאֶחָיו; שֵׁשַׁי – שֶׁמֵּשִׂים אֶת הָאָרֶץ כִּשְׁחָתוֹת. תַּלְמַי – שֶׁמֵּשִׂים אֶת הָאָרֶץ תְּלָמִים תְּלָמִים.

The verse continues to state about Hebron: **"And Ahiman, Sheshai, and Talmai,** the children of Anak, were there" (Numbers 13:22). **Ahiman** was called by this name because he was the most **skilled** [*meyumman*] **among his brothers. Sheshai** was called by his name **because he would turn the land** that he treaded upon **into ditches** [*sheḥatot*] due to his large dimensions. **Talmai** was called this **because he would turn the land** that he treaded upon **into furrows** upon **furrows** [*telamim*] due to his weight.

דָּבָר אַחֵר: אֲחִימָן בָּנָה עֲנָת, שֵׁשַׁי בָּנָה אָלֻשׁ, תַּלְמַי בָּנָה תַּלְבּוּשׁ. ״יְלִידֵי הָעֲנָק״ – שֶׁמַּעֲנִיקִין חַמָּה בְּקוֹמָתָן.

Alternatively, their names signify another matter: **Ahiman** is the one who **built** the city of **Anat. Sheshai built** the city of **Alush. Talmai built** the city of **Talbush.**[B] The verse describes them as **"the children of Anak"** because they were so tall and large that it appeared **as if they were wearing** [*ma'anikin*] **the sun** as a necklace **due to their height.**

״וְחֶבְרוֹן שֶׁבַע שָׁנִים נִבְנְתָה״ – מַאי נִבְנְתָה? אִילֵימָא נִבְנְתָה מַמָּשׁ, אֶפְשָׁר אָדָם בּוֹנֶה בַּיִת לִבְנוֹ קָטָן קוֹדֶם לִבְנוֹ גָּדוֹל? דִּכְתִיב: ״וּבְנֵי חָם כּוּשׁ וּמִצְרַיִם״ וגו׳!

The continuation of the verse states: **"Now Hebron was built seven years** [*shanim*] before Zoan of Egypt [*Mitzrayim*]" (Numbers 13:22). The Gemara asks: **What** is the meaning of the phrase **"was built"? If we say** that **it was actually built** seven years before Zoan, **would a person build a house for his younger son before** he builds one **for his older son?** Canaan was the youngest son of Ham, **as it is written: "And the sons of Ham: Cush, and Mizraim,** and Put, and Canaan" (Genesis 10:6). How then could Hebron, a city in the land of Canaan, have been built before Zoan, a city in the land of Egypt, occupied by the descendants of Mizraim?

NOTES

But we have obtained only, etc. – **וְאָנוּ לֹא עָלְתָה בְּיָדֵינוּ וכו׳**: In the *Midrash Tanḥuma* (*Ha'azinu* 7), similar explanations for the names of all of the spies are given, citing Rabbi Moshe HaDarshan.

This teaches that Caleb separated himself – **מְלַמֵּד שֶׁפֵּירֵשׁ כָּלֵב**: The commentaries add proofs from the verses for this assertion that Caleb separated himself from the other spies and went to Hebron. The verse states: "And I will bring him to the land to which he went" (Numbers 14:24), and in the book of Joshua it is stated that Caleb asked specifically for Mount Hebron as his inheritance: "Now therefore give me this mountain, from which the Lord spoke in that day" (Joshua 14:12).

Another spirit with him – **רוּחַ אַחֶרֶת עִמּוֹ**: The Maharsha explains that as opposed to the other spies, who followed their animalistic spirit, Caleb followed his human spirit, or soul. Others explain that "another spirit" refers to the spirit of the forefathers accompanying him to save him from the counsel of the other spies (*Iyyun Ya'akov*; Rabbi David Luria). Alternatively, the word spirit is interpreted to mean direction, meaning that Caleb went in a different direction, so to speak, than did the other spies (*Sefat Emet*).

BACKGROUND

Anat, Alush, Talbush – **עֲנָת, אָלֻשׁ, תַּלְבּוּשׁ**: The locations of these cities are unknown. They were apparently located in Eretz Yisrael or nearby. It is possible that the city of Alush that is mentioned here is the place with the same name that is mentioned among the travels of the Jewish people in the wilderness (Numbers 33:13). It would also make sense that Anat refers to Anathoth, which is in the portion of Benjamin. There were apparently large stones in these places, possibly dolmens, that looked like they had been assembled by giants.

אֶלָּא שֶׁהָיְתָה מְבוּנָּה עַל אֶחָד מִשִּׁבְעָה בְּצוֹעַן. וְאֵין לְךָ טְרָשִׁים בְּכָל אֶרֶץ יִשְׂרָאֵל יָתֵר מֵחֶבְרוֹן, מִשּׁוּם דְּקָבְרִי בָּהּ שִׁיכְבֵי. וְאֵין לְךָ מְעוּלָּה בְּכָל הָאֲרָצוֹת יָתֵר מֵאֶרֶץ מִצְרַיִם, שֶׁנֶּאֱמַר: ״כְּגַן ה׳ כְּאֶרֶץ מִצְרַיִם״, וְאֵין לְךָ מְעוּלָּה בְּכָל אֶרֶץ מִצְרַיִם יָתֵר מִצּוֹעַן, דִּכְתִיב: ״כִּי הָיוּ בְצֹעַן שָׂרָיו״, וַאֲפִילּוּ הָכִי חֶבְרוֹן מְבוּנָּה אֶחָד מִשִּׁבְעָה בְּצוֹעַן.

Rather, the meaning of the verse is **that** Hebron **was seven times more fruitful** [*mevunna*][N] **than Zoan. And there is no stonier land**[B] **in Eretz Yisrael than Hebron.** This is evident **because they would bury the dead there,** just as the forefathers were buried there. This was done only in land that was not suitable for agriculture. **And of all the lands, there is none of a higher quality than the land of Egypt, as it is stated: "Like the garden of the Lord, like the land of Egypt"** (Genesis 13:10). **And there was no higher-quality** land **in all of the land of Egypt than Zoan, as it is written** with regard to Pharaoh's ministers, who would certainly have lived on the finest land in the country: **"For his princes are in Zoan"** (Isaiah 30:4). **And even so, Hebron was seven times more fruitful than Zoan.**

וְחֶבְרוֹן טְרָשִׁים הָוֵי? וְהָא כְּתִיב: ״וַיְהִי מִקֵּץ אַרְבָּעִים שָׁנָה וַיֹּאמֶר אַבְשָׁלוֹם אֶל הַמֶּלֶךְ אֵלְכָה נָּא״ וגו׳. וְאָמַר רַב אָוְיָא, וְאִיתֵּימָא רַבָּה בַּר בַּר חָנָה: שֶׁהָלַךְ לְהָבִיא כְּבָשִׂים מֵחֶבְרוֹן. וְתַנְיָא: אֵילִים מִמּוֹאָב, כְּבָשִׂים מֵחֶבְרוֹן! מִינָּהּ! אַיְּידֵי דִּקְלִישָׁא אַרְעָא, עָבְדָה רַעְיָא וְשָׁמֵן קְנִיינָא.

The Gemara asks: **But is** the land in **Hebron** in fact **stony? But isn't it written: "And it came to pass at the end of forty years, that Absalom said to the king: I pray, let me go** and pay my vow, which I have vowed to the Lord, in Hebron" (II Samuel 15:7)? **And Rav Avya says, and some say** that it was **Rabba bar bar Ḥanan:** This means **that** Absalom **went to bring sheep** specifically **from Hebron. And it is taught** in a *baraita* (*Tosefta, Menaḥot* 9:13): One must bring the choicest animals to the Temple as offerings. **Rams** are brought **from Moab,**[H] and **sheep** are brought **from Hebron.** This indicates that Hebron has rich land where fat and healthy sheep are raised. The Gemara answers: **From this** very source it can be proven that Hebron is not suitable for agriculture. **Since the earth** there **is thin,**[B] **it produces** only grass for **grazing and fattens the livestock.**

״וַיָּשֻׁבוּ מִתּוּר הָאָרֶץ

The verse states: **"And they returned from spying out the land** at the end of forty days.

Perek **VII**
Daf **35** Amud **a**

וַיֵּלְכוּ וַיָּבֹאוּ״ – אָמַר רַבִּי יוֹחָנָן מִשּׁוּם רַבִּי שִׁמְעוֹן בֶּן יוֹחַי: מַקִּישׁ הֲלִיכָה לְבִיאָה, מַה בִּיאָה בְּעֵצָה רָעָה, אַף הֲלִיכָה בְּעֵצָה רָעָה.

And they went and they came" (Numbers 13:25–26). **Rabbi Yoḥanan says in the name of Rabbi Shimon ben Yoḥai:** This verse **likens** their **going to** their **coming. Just as** their **coming** back was **with wicked counsel, so too,** their **going** to Eretz Yisrael was **with wicked counsel.**[N]

״וַיְסַפְּרוּ לוֹ וַיֹּאמְרוּ בָּאנוּ״ וגו׳, וּכְתִיב: ״אֶפֶס כִּי עַז הָעָם״ – אָמַר רַבִּי יוֹחָנָן (סִימָן: אמ״ת לבד״ו לוי״ה) מִשּׁוּם רַבִּי מֵאִיר: כׇּל לָשׁוֹן הָרָע שֶׁאֵין בּוֹ דְּבַר אֱמֶת בִּתְחִילָּתוֹ – אֵין מִתְקַיֵּים בְּסוֹפוֹ.

The Torah states: **"And they told him, and said: We came** to the land to which you sent us, and it also flows with milk and honey" (Numbers 13:27), **and** then **it is written: "However the people** that dwell in the land **are fierce"** (Numbers 13:28). Why did the spies praise the land and then slander it? **Rabbi Yoḥanan says** three statements **in the name of Rabbi Meir,** represented by the **mnemonic** device: **Truth, alone, borrowing.**[N] The first statement answers this question: **Any slander that does not begin with a truthful statement**[N] **ultimately does not stand,** i.e., it is not accepted by others.

NOTES

That Hebron was seven times more fruitful [*mevunna*] – שֶׁהָיְתָה מְבוּנָּה עַל אֶחָד מִשִּׁבְעָה: It is not surprising that Ham gave his youngest son an inheritance superior to the inheritance of his other sons, as there are many examples in the Bible of a father favoring his youngest son over the others. However, a father would first attend to the needs of his older sons before those of the youngest (*Iyyun Ya'akov*). According to this interpretation, when the verse states: "Now Hebron was built seven *shanim* before Zoan of Egypt," the phrase "seven *shanim*" does not mean seven years, but rather sevenfold, as in the word *mishne*, which means double (*HaKetav VehaKabbala*).

BACKGROUND

Stonier land – טְרָשִׁים: This refers to very hard land that cannot be worked and used for agriculture. Generally, this kind of land is found in rocky areas where even the earth between the stones is too hard to be used for agriculture.

The earth is thin – דִּקְלִישָׁא אַרְעָא: Grain needs very deep earth in order to grow. Crops are generally grown in land that is suitable for intensive working, while sheep generally graze on the stubble that is left after the crops are harvested. Although shallow earth that rests on top of stone is not suitable for growing crops, other plants that have shorter roots can grow in this kind of earth. The nutritional value of such plants will be greater than straw and fatten the animals that graze there.

HALAKHA

Rams from Moab – אֵילִים מִמּוֹאָב: One who brings an offering must bring from the choicest selection. Therefore, animals for sacrifices were brought from the places where the livestock was superior: Rams were brought from Moab, broad-shouldered sheep from Hebron, calves from the Sharon, and chicks from Har HaMelekh (Rambam *Sefer Avoda, Hilkhot Issurei Mizbe'aḥ* 7:1–2).

NOTES

So too their going was with wicked counsel – אַף הֲלִיכָה בְּעֵצָה רָעָה: One explanation of this statement is that just as their return to the wilderness was guided by wicked counsel, so too, their departure from the Valley of Eshkol was guided by wicked counsel (*Sefat Emet*). According to this explanation, Rashi's statement (see Numbers 13:3) that when the spies left for Eretz Yisrael they were considered upright and flawless does not contradict this statement, as they were righteous until they reached Eretz Yisrael.

The mnemonic truth, alone [*levado*], borrowing – סִימָן אמ״ת לבד״ו לוי״ה: This is a mnemonic for the statements said by Rabbi Yoḥanan in the name of Rabbi Meir in this tractate. The acronym should be: Truth, ensnared [*lekhado*], borrowing, as elsewhere (42b), Rabbi Yoḥanan quotes the statement of Rabbi Meir: His own mouth ensnared that wicked one, and in another place (46b) he quotes Rabbi Meir with regard to anyone who does not lend and borrows. However, Rabbi Yoḥanan quotes Rabbi Meir in another place (36b): His bow returned to its strength, so perhaps the mnemonic should include that and be: Truth, returned, ensnared, borrowing (*Ḥeshek Shlomo*).

Slander that does not begin with a truthful statement – לָשׁוֹן הָרָע שֶׁאֵין בּוֹ דְּבַר אֱמֶת בִּתְחִילָּתוֹ: The commentaries ask: What did the spies lie about? The Maharsha explains that since the spies did not return with the basic food staples of wheat, barley, and olives, they implicitly told the people that the land did not produce sufficient food for sustenance. Furthermore, although the spies were not in Hebron, they nevertheless reported about the giants who lived there. Others explain that they lied in that they said: "The people that dwell in the land are fierce," even though the people of the land feared the Jewish people, as stated by Rahab (Joshua 2:10). Others suggest that they said Eretz Yisrael is "a land that eats its inhabitants" (Numbers 13:32), where people die frequently (see *Ir Binyamin*).

"וַיַּהַס כָּלֵב אֶת הָעָם אֶל מֹשֶׁה" – אָמַר רַבָּה: שֶׁהֱסִיתָן בִּדְבָרִים.

The verse states: **"And Caleb stilled** [*vayyahas*] **the people toward Moses"** (Numbers 13:30). **Rabba says:** This means **that he persuaded them** [*hesitan*] **with** his **words.** *Vayyahas* and *hesitan* share the same root in Hebrew.

פָּתַח יְהוֹשֻׁעַ. דְּקָא מִשְׁתָּעֵי אָמְרִי לֵיהּ: דֵּין רֹאשׁ קְטִיעָה יְמַלֵּל?

How did he do so? **Joshua began** to address the people, and **as he was speaking they said to him: Should this** person, who has **a severed head,** as he has no children, **speak** to the people about entering Eretz Yisrael?

אָמַר: אִי מִשְׁתָּעֵינָא אָמְרִי בִּי מִילְּתָא וְחָסְמִין לִי. אָמַר לְהֶן: וְכִי זוֹ בִּלְבַד עָשָׂה לָנוּ בֶּן עַמְרָם? סָבְרִי בִּגְנוּתֵיהּ קָא מִשְׁתָּעֵי, אִישְׁתִּיקוּ.

Caleb **said** to himself: **If I speak they will** also **say something about me and stop me** from speaking. He began to speak and **said to them: And** is **this** the **only** thing that **the son of Amram,** Moses, **has done to us? They thought** that he wanted **to relate** something **to the discredit of** Moses, and **they were silent.**

אֲמַר לְהוּ: הוֹצִיאָנוּ מִמִּצְרַיִם וְקָרַע לָנוּ אֶת הַיָּם וְהֶאֱכִילָנוּ אֶת הַמָּן. אִם יֹאמַר עֲשׂוּ סוּלָּמוֹת וַעֲלוּ לָרָקִיעַ, לֹא נִשְׁמַע לוֹ? "עָלֹה נַעֲלֶה וְיָרַשְׁנוּ אֹתָהּ" וגו׳.

He then **said to them: He took us out of Egypt, and split the sea for us, and fed us the manna. If he says** to us: **Build ladders and climb to the heavens, should we not listen to him? "We should go up at once,"** even to the heavens, **"and possess it"** (Numbers 13:30).

"וְהָאֲנָשִׁים אֲשֶׁר עָלוּ עִמּוֹ אָמְרוּ לֹא נוּכַל" וגו׳ – אָמַר רַבִּי חֲנִינָא בַּר פָּפָּא: דָּבָר גָּדוֹל דִּבְּרוּ מְרַגְּלִים בְּאוֹתָהּ שָׁעָה, "כִּי חָזָק הוּא מִמֶּנּוּ" – אַל תִּקְרֵי "מִמֶּנּוּ" אֶלָּא "מִמֶּנּוּ": כִּבְיָכוֹל, אֲפִילּוּ בַּעַל הַבַּיִת אֵינוֹ יָכוֹל לְהוֹצִיא כֵּלָיו מִשָּׁם.

The verses continue: **"But the men that went up with him said: We are not able** to go up against the people; as they are stronger than us" (Numbers 13:31). **Rabbi Ḥanina bar Pappa says: The spies said a serious statement at that moment.** When they said: **"They are stronger," do not read** the phrase as: Stronger **than us** [*mimmennu*],[N] but **rather** read it as: Stronger **than Him** [*mimmennu*], meaning that **even the Homeowner,** God, **is unable to remove His belongings from there, as it were.** The spies were speaking heresy and claiming that the Canaanites were stronger than God Himself.

"אֶרֶץ אֹכֶלֶת יוֹשְׁבֶיהָ הִיא" – דָּרַשׁ רָבָא, אָמַר הַקָּדוֹשׁ בָּרוּךְ הוּא: אֲנִי חֲשַׁבְתִּיהָ לְטוֹבָה וְהֵם חָשְׁבוּ לְרָעָה. אֲנִי חֲשַׁבְתִּיהָ לְטוֹבָה – דְּכׇל הֵיכָא דְּמָטוּ, מֵת חֲשִׁיבָא דִּידְהוּ, כִּי הֵיכִי דְּנִיטְרְדוּ וְלָא לִשְׁאֲלוּ אֲבַתְרַיְיהוּ. וְאִיכָּא דְּאָמְרִי: אִיּוֹב נָח נַפְשֵׁיהּ, וְאִטְרִידוּ כּוּלֵּי עָלְמָא בְּהֶסְפֵּידָא. הֵם חָשְׁבוּ לְרָעָה – "אֶרֶץ אֹכֶלֶת יוֹשְׁבֶיהָ הִיא".

The spies said: **"It is a land that consumes its inhabitants"** (Numbers 13:32). **Rava taught: The Holy One, Blessed be He, said: I intended** the land to appear to consume its inhabitants **for** their own **good, but they considered** this proof that the land was **bad. I intended** it **for** their **good** by causing many people to die there so **that anywhere that** the spies **arrived, the most important of them died, so that** the Canaanites **would be preoccupied** with mourning **and would not inquire about them. And there are** those **who say** that God caused **Job to die** at that time, **and everyone** in Canaan **was preoccupied with** his **eulogy,** and did not pay attention to the spies. However, the spies **considered** this proof that the land was **bad** and said: **"It is a land that consumes its inhabitants."**

"וַנְּהִי בְעֵינֵינוּ כַּחֲגָבִים וְכֵן הָיִינוּ" וגו׳ – אָמַר רַב מְשַׁרְשִׁיָּא: מְרַגְּלִים שַׁקָּרֵי הֲווֹ. בִּשְׁלָמָא "וַנְּהִי בְעֵינֵינוּ כַּחֲגָבִים" – לְחַיֵּי, אֶלָּא "וְכֵן הָיִינוּ בְּעֵינֵיהֶם" מְנָא הֲווֹ יָדְעִי?

The spies said: **"And we were like grasshoppers in our own eyes, and so were we** in their eyes" (Numbers 13:33). **Rav Mesharshiyya says: The spies were liars. Granted,** to say: **"We were like grasshoppers in our own eyes," is well, but** to say: **"And so were we in their eyes,"** from **where** could **they** have **known** this?

וְלָא הִיא, כִּי הֲווֹ מַבְרִי אֲבֵילֵי, תּוּתֵי אַרְזֵי הֲווֹ מַבְרֵי. וְכִי חֲזֵינְהוּ, סְלִקוּ יָתְבִי בְּאִילָנֵי. שָׁמְעִי דְּקָאָמְרִי: קָחָזֵינַן אֱינָשֵׁי דְּדָמוּ לְקַמְצֵי בְּאִילָנֵי.

The Gemara responds: **But** that **is not so,** as **when** the Canaanites **were having the mourners' meal, they had the meal beneath cedar trees, and when** the spies **saw them they climbed up** the **trees** and **sat** in them. From there **they heard** the Canaanites **saying: We see people who** look **like grasshoppers in the trees.**

"וַתִּשָּׂא כׇּל הָעֵדָה וַיִּתְּנוּ אֶת קוֹלָם וַיִּבְכּוּ" – אָמַר רַבָּה אָמַר רַבִּי יוֹחָנָן: אוֹתוֹ הַיּוֹם עֶרֶב תִּשְׁעָה בְּאָב הָיָה. אָמַר הַקָּדוֹשׁ בָּרוּךְ הוּא: הֵן בָּכוּ בְּכִיָּה שֶׁל חִנָּם, וַאֲנִי אֶקְבַּע לָהֶם בְּכִיָּה לְדוֹרוֹת.

The verse states: **"And all the congregation lifted up their voice and cried"** (Numbers 14:1). **Rabba says** that **Rabbi Yoḥanan says: That day was the eve of the Ninth of Av,** and **the Holy One, Blessed be He, said:** On that day **they wept a gratuitous weeping, so I will establish** that day **for them** as a day of **weeping for** the future **generations.**

NOTES

Do not read, than us [*mimmennu*] but rather, than Him [*mimmennu*] – אַל תִּקְרֵי מִמֶּנּוּ אֶלָּא מִמֶּנּוּ: Rashi omits this sentence, as the expression: Do not read, generally indicates that a different vocalization is being suggested. Here, however, both readings are identical. According to the *Arukh*, the Gemara is pointing out that the verse does not use the term *mennu*, meaning: Than us; rather, it says *mimmennu*, meaning: Than him. Other commentaries explain that in Babylonia, the term *mimmennu* was written with different punctuation for: Than us, and: Than him. Therefore, the Gemara, which was written in Babylonia, is teaching that it should be read not with the punctuation that would render it: Stronger than us, but with the punctuation that would render it: Stronger than him (Dunash; Rabbi Avraham Ibn Ezra; Rashba).

״וַיֹּאמְרוּ כׇּל הָעֵדָה לִרְגּוֹם אוֹתָם בָּאֲבָנִים״, וּכְתִיב: ״וּכְבוֹד ה׳ נִרְאָה בְּאֹהֶל מוֹעֵד״ – אָמַר רַבִּי חִיָּיא בַּר אַבָּא: מְלַמֵּד, שֶׁנָּטְלוּ אֲבָנִים וּזְרָקוּם כְּלַפֵּי מַעְלָה.

The verse states: **“But all the congregation bade stone them with stones”** (Numbers 14:10), **and it is written** immediately afterward: **“When the glory of the Lord appeared in the Tent of Meeting”** (Numbers 14:10). **Rabbi Ḥiyya bar Abba says:** This **teaches that they took stones and threw them upward** as if to throw them at God.

״וַיָּמֻתוּ הָאֲנָשִׁים מוֹצִאֵי דִבַּת הָאָרֶץ רָעָה בַּמַּגֵּפָה״ – אָמַר רַבִּי שִׁמְעוֹן בֶּן לָקִישׁ: שֶׁמֵּתוּ מִיתָה מְשׁוּנָּה. אָמַר רַבִּי חֲנִינָא בַּר פָּפָּא, דָּרַשׁ רַבִּי שֵׁילָא אִישׁ כְּפַר תְּמַרְתָּא: מְלַמֵּד, שֶׁנִּשְׁתַּרְבֵּב לְשׁוֹנָם וְנָפַל עַל טִיבּוּרָם, וְהָיוּ תּוֹלָעִים יוֹצְאוֹת מִלְּשׁוֹנָם וְנִכְנָסוֹת בְּטִיבּוּרָם, וּמִטִּיבּוּרָם וְנִכְנָסוֹת בִּלְשׁוֹנָם. וְרַב נַחְמָן בַּר יִצְחָק אָמַר: בְּאַסְכָּרָה מֵתוּ.

The verse states: **“And those men who brought out an evil report of the land, died by the plague before the Lord”** (Numbers 14:37). **Rabbi Shimon ben Lakish says:** This means **that they died an unusual death. Rabbi Ḥanina bar Pappa says** that **Rabbi Sheila Ish Kefar Temarta taught:** This **teaches that their tongues were stretched out** from their mouths **and fell upon their navels,**[N] **and worms were crawling out of their tongues and entering their navels, and** worms were likewise coming **out of their navels and entering their tongues.** This is the painful death that they suffered. **And Rav Naḥman bar Yitzḥak says: They died of diphtheria,**[B] which causes one to choke to death.

וְכֵיוָן שֶׁעָלָה הָאַחֲרוֹן שֶׁבְּיִשְׂרָאֵל מִן הַיַּרְדֵּן חָזְרוּ מַיִם לִמְקוֹמָן, שֶׁנֶּאֱמַר: ״וַיְהִי בַּעֲלוֹת הַכֹּהֲנִים נֹשְׂאֵי אֲרוֹן בְּרִית ה׳ מִתּוֹךְ הַיַּרְדֵּן נִתְּקוּ כַּפּוֹת רַגְלֵי הַכֹּהֲנִים אֶל הֶחָרָבָה וַיָּשֻׁבוּ מֵי הַיַּרְדֵּן לִמְקוֹמָם וַיֵּלְכוּ כִתְמוֹל שִׁלְשׁוֹם עַל כׇּל גְּדוֹתָיו״.

§ The Gemara returns to discuss the entry of the Jewish people into Eretz Yisrael. **And once the last one of the Jewish people ascended out of the Jordan, the water returned to its place, as it is stated: “And it came to pass, as the priests that bore the Ark of the Covenant of the Lord came up out of the midst of the Jordan, as soon as the soles of the priests’ feet were drawn up unto the dry ground, that the waters of the Jordan returned to their place, and went over all its banks, as it had before”** (Joshua 4:18). The Gemara understands that the priests who carried the Ark stood in the water until all of the Jewish people passed through the Jordan. Once all the Jewish people had reached the other side of the Jordan, the priests stepped back from the water and the Jordan returned to its natural state.

נִמְצָא אָרוֹן וְנוֹשְׂאָיו וְכֹהֲנִים מִצַּד אֶחָד וְיִשְׂרָאֵל מִצַּד אֶחָד. נָשָׂא אָרוֹן אֶת נוֹשְׂאָיו וְעָבַר, שֶׁנֶּאֱמַר: ״וַיְהִי כַּאֲשֶׁר תַּם כׇּל הָעָם לַעֲבוֹר וַיַּעֲבֹר אֲרוֹן ה׳ וְהַכֹּהֲנִים לִפְנֵי הָעָם״.

It follows that **the Ark and its bearers and the priests** were **on one side** of the Jordan, the east side, **and** the rest of **the Jewish people** were **on the other side,** the west side. Subsequently, **the Ark carried its bearers** in the air **and crossed** the Jordan, **as it is stated: “When all the people were completely passed over, the Ark of the Lord passed on, and the priests, before the people”** (Joshua 4:11).

וְעַל דָּבָר זֶה נֶעֱנַשׁ עוּזָּא, שֶׁנֶּאֱמַר: ״וַיָּבֹאוּ עַד גֹּרֶן כִּידֹן וַיִּשְׁלַח עֻזָּא אֶת יָדוֹ לֶאֱחֹז אֶת הָאָרוֹן״. אָמַר לוֹ הַקָּדוֹשׁ בָּרוּךְ הוּא: עוּזָּא, נוֹשְׂאָיו נָשָׂא, עַצְמוֹ לֹא כׇּל שֶׁכֵּן!

And over this matter Uzzah was punished for not taking proper care of the Ark, **as it is stated: “And when they came to the threshing floor of Chidon, Uzzah put forth his hand to hold the Ark;** for the oxen stumbled” (I Chronicles 13:9). **The Holy One, Blessed be He, said to him: Uzzah,** the Ark **carried its bearers** when it crossed the Jordan; **all the more so** is it **not** clear that it can carry **itself?**

״וַיִּחַר אַף ה׳ בְּעֻזָּה וַיַּכֵּהוּ שָׁם...עַל הַשַּׁל״ וגו׳ – רַבִּי יוֹחָנָן וְרַבִּי אֶלְעָזָר, חַד אָמַר: עַל עִסְקֵי שָׁלוּ, וְחַד אָמַר: שֶׁעָשָׂה צְרָכָיו בְּפָנָיו.

§ The verse states: **“And the anger of the Lord was kindled against Uzzah; and God smote him there for his error [*hashal*]”** (II Samuel 6:7). **Rabbi Yoḥanan and Rabbi Elazar** disagreed over the interpretation of this verse. **One says:** God smote him **for his forgetfulness [*shalo*],** because he did not remember that the Ark can carry itself. **And one says:** God smote him **because he** lifted the edges [*shulayyim*] of his garment in front of the Ark and **relieved himself in its presence.**[N]

״וַיָּמָת שָׁם עִם אֲרוֹן הָאֱלֹהִים״ – אָמַר רַבִּי יוֹחָנָן: עוּזָּא בָּא לָעוֹלָם הַבָּא, שֶׁנֶּאֱמַר: ״עִם אֲרוֹן הָאֱלֹהִים״, מָה אָרוֹן לְעוֹלָם קַיָּים, אַף עוּזָּא בָּא לָעוֹלָם הַבָּא.

The verse states: **“And he died there with the Ark of God”** (II Samuel 6:7). **Rabbi Yoḥanan says: Uzzah entered the World-to-Come, as it is stated: “With the Ark of God.” Just as the Ark exists forever, so too, Uzzah entered the World-to-Come.**

״וַיִּחַר לְדָוִד עַל אֲשֶׁר פָּרַץ ה׳ פֶּרֶץ בְּעֻזָּה״ – אָמַר רַבִּי אֶלְעָזָר: שֶׁנִּשְׁתַּנּוּ פָּנָיו כַּחֲרָרָה.

The verse states: **“And David was displeased [*vayyiḥar*] because the Lord had broken forth upon Uzzah”** (II Samuel 6:8). **Rabbi Elazar says:** *Vayyiḥar* means **that his face changed** colors and darkened **like baked bread [*ḥarara*]** from displeasure.

NOTES

Their tongues were stretched out and fell upon their navels – נִשְׁתַּרְבֵּב לְשׁוֹנָם וְנָפַל עַל טִיבּוּרָם: The *Iyyun Ya’akov* explains that they received this punishment because they spoke slander about the land with their tongues and because Eretz Yisrael is called “the navel of the earth” (Ezekiel 38:12).

Because he relieved himself [*asa tzerakhav*] in its presence – שֶׁעָשָׂה צְרָכָיו בְּפָנָיו: Many commentaries ask how such a disgraceful thing could be said about Uzzah, especially in light of the Gemara’s statement that he entered the World-to-Come. Some explain that he relieved himself far away from the Ark but was facing in its direction, which is prohibited (see *Iyyun Ya’akov*). Another explanation, based on a midrash, is that the expression *asa tzerakhav*, literally, cared for his needs, is a reference to the blessing one recites when donning his shoes in the morning: Who has provided me with all I need. In this context it refers to the fact that Uzzah put on his shoes in front of the Ark (see *Anaf Yosef*).

BACKGROUND

Diphtheria – אַסְכָּרָה: This is an infectious disease that causes the mucous membrane of the throat to swell and creates a choking feeling. It is common among young children, and until recently, with the invention of a vaccination against it, it was a fatal disease that caused its victims to die from choking. During the Second Temple period, people who served in the non-priestly watches would fast for one day each week, in the merit of which infants would not be afflicted with diphtheria.

אֶלָּא מֵעַתָּה, כָּל הֵיכָא דִּכְתִיב ״וַיִּחַר״ הָכִי נַמִי! הָתָם כְּתִיב ״אַף״, הָכָא לָא כְּתִיב ״אַף״.

The Gemara questions this statement: **If that is so, anywhere that** the word ***vayyiḥar* is written,** including when it is referring to God, should it be interpreted this way **as well?** The Gemara answers: **There, it is written:** "And **the anger** of the Lord was kindled [*vayyiḥar af*]" (II Samuel 6:7), whereas **here, the anger** [*af*] **is not written,** but only *vayyiḥar*. Therefore it is interpreted differently.

דָּרַשׁ רָבָא: מִפְּנֵי מָה נֶעֱנַשׁ דָּוִד? מִפְּנֵי שֶׁקָּרָא לְדִבְרֵי תוֹרָה זְמִירוֹת, שֶׁנֶּאֱמַר: ״זְמִרוֹת הָיוּ לִי חֻקֶּיךָ בְּבֵית מְגוּרָי״.

Rava taught: For what reason **was David punished** with Uzzah's death? He was punished **because he called matters of Torah: Songs, as it is stated: "Your statutes have been my songs in the house of my pilgrimage"** (Psalms 119:54).

אָמַר לוֹ הַקָּדוֹשׁ בָּרוּךְ הוּא: דִּבְרֵי תוֹרָה שֶׁכָּתוּב בָּהֶן ״הֲתָעִיף עֵינֶיךָ בּוֹ וְאֵינֶנּוּ״, אַתָּה קוֹרֵא אוֹתָן זְמִירוֹת? הֲרֵינִי מַכְשִׁילְךָ בְּדָבָר שֶׁאֲפִילּוּ תִּינוֹקוֹת שֶׁל בֵּית רַבָּן יוֹדְעִין אוֹתוֹ, דִּכְתִיב: ״וְלִבְנֵי קְהָת לֹא נָתָן כִּי עֲבֹדַת הַקֹּדֶשׁ״ וגו׳, וְאִיהוּ אַתְיֵיהּ בַּעֲגָלְתָא.

The Holy One, Blessed be He, said to him: Matters of Torah are so difficult and demanding **that it is written: "Will you set your eyes upon it? It is gone"** (Proverbs 23:5), i.e., one whose eyes stray from the Torah even for a moment will forget it, and **you call** them **songs?** For this reason **I will cause you to stumble in a matter that even schoolchildren know, as it is written** with regard to the wagons brought to the Tabernacle: **"And to the descendants of Kohath he did not give,**[N] **because the service of the holy things** belongs to them; they carry them upon their shoulders" (Numbers 7:9). **And** although the Ark clearly must be carried on people's shoulders, David erred and **brought it in a wagon.**[H]

״וַיַּךְ בְּאַנְשֵׁי בֵית שֶׁמֶשׁ כִּי רָאוּ בַּאֲרוֹן״ – מִשּׁוּם דְּרָאוּ וַיַּךְ אֱלֹהִים? רַבִּי אַבָּהוּ וְרַבִּי אֶלְעָזָר. חַד אָמַר: קוֹצְרִין וּמִשְׁתַּחֲוִים הָיוּ, וְחַד אָמַר: מִילֵּי נַמִי אֲמוּר.

§ When the Philistines returned the Ark during the period of Samuel, it is stated: **"And He smote of the men of Beit Shemesh because they had gazed upon the Ark of the Lord"** (I Samuel 6:19). The Gemara asks: **Because they gazed** upon it, **God smote** them? Why did their action warrant this punishment? **Rabbi Abbahu and Rabbi Elazar** disagreed with regard to the interpretation of the verse. **One says** that they were punished because **they were reaping** their crops **and prostrating themselves** at the same time; they did not stop working in reverence for the Ark. **And one says** that **they also spoke** denigrating **words:**

NOTES

And to the descendants of Kohath he did not give, etc. – וְלִבְנֵי קְהָת לֹא נָתַן וכו׳: The question arises, how could it be that David and the entire nation forgot something that was explicitly written in the Torah? One answer is that David thought that this mitzva pertained only to Israel's travels in the wilderness, when the Ark was carried on a regular basis, but it did not apply at this later time (*Keli Yakar*). Others explain, based on the tradition that Saul took the tablets during the war with the Philistines and brought them to Shiloh, that during the time of David, the Ark contained only the broken tablets. Consequently, David believed that the *halakhot* of carrying the Ark did not apply in this situation (*Zahav Sheva*). Another possibility is that because the Ark was already returned to them on a wagon by the Philistines, they believed it was permitted to transport the Ark in that manner.

HALAKHA

They carry them upon their shoulders and brought it in a wagon – בַּכָּתֵף יִשָּׂאוּ: When the Ark of the Covenant is carried from one place to another it may not be carried by an animal or on a wagon. Rather, it is a mitzva for people to carry it on their shoulders (Rambam *Sefer Avoda*, *Hilkhot Kelei HaMikdash* 2:12).

Perek **VII**
Daf **35** Amud **b**

מַאן אַמְרִיךְ (לְהָא) דְּאִימְרַיְית וּמַאן אַתָא עֲלָךְ דְּאִיפַּיְיסַתְּ.

Who angered you, i.e., the Ark, so much **that you became** so **angry** that you gave yourself into captivity? **And who came to you to appease you?**

״וַיַּךְ בָּעָם שִׁבְעִים אִישׁ חֲמִשִּׁים אֶלֶף אִישׁ״ – רַבִּי אַבָּהוּ וְרַבִּי אֶלְעָזָר, חַד אָמַר: שִׁבְעִים אִישׁ הָיוּ, וְכָל אֶחָד וְאֶחָד שָׁקוּל כַּחֲמִשִּׁים אֶלֶף; וְחַד אָמַר: חֲמִשִּׁים אֶלֶף הָיוּ, וְכָל אֶחָד וְאֶחָד שָׁקוּל כְּשִׁבְעִים סַנְהֶדְרִין.

The verse states: **"And He smote of the people seventy men, fifty thousand men"** (I Samuel 6:19).[N] **Rabbi Abbahu and Rabbi Elazar** disagree over the interpretation of the verse. **One says** that **there were seventy men, and each and every one** of them **was equivalent to fifty thousand** men. **And one says** that **there were fifty thousand men, and each and every one was equivalent to** the **seventy** men in the **Sanhedrin.**

״וַיְהִי כִּי צָעֲדוּ נֹשְׂאֵי אֲרוֹן ה׳ שִׁשָּׁה צְעָדִים וַיִּזְבַּח שׁוֹר וּמְרִיא״, וּכְתִיב: ״שִׁבְעָה פָרִים וְשִׁבְעָה אֵילִים״! אָמַר רַב פַּפָּא בַּר שְׁמוּאֵל: עַל כָּל פְּסִיעָה וּפְסִיעָה – שׁוֹר וּמְרִיא; עַל כָּל שֵׁשׁ וָשֵׁשׁ פְּסִיעוֹת – שִׁבְעָה פָּרִים וְשִׁבְעָה אֵילִים.

With regard to David's journey with the Ark to Jerusalem, the verse states: **"And when they who carried the Ark of the Lord had gone six paces, he sacrificed an ox and a fatling"** (II Samuel 6:13). **And it is written** elsewhere that he sacrificed **"seven oxen and seven rams"** (I Chronicles 15:26). **Rav Pappa bar Shmuel says: For each and every step** David took, he sacrificed **an ox and a fatling,** and **for every six steps** that he took, he sacrificed **seven oxen and seven rams.**

אֲמַר לֵיהּ רַב חִסְדָּא: אִם כֵּן, מִילֵּאתָ אֶת כָּל אֶרֶץ יִשְׂרָאֵל בָּמוֹת! אֶלָּא אֲמַר רַב חִסְדָּא: עַל כָּל שֵׁשׁ וָשֵׁשׁ פְּסִיעוֹת – שׁוֹר וּמְרִיא; עַל כָּל שִׁשָּׁה סְדָרִים שֶׁל שֵׁשׁ פְּסִיעוֹת – שִׁבְעָה פָּרִים וְשִׁבְעָה אֵילִים.

Rav Ḥisda said to him: If that is **so,** and he sacrificed an offering for every step that he took, **you have filled all of Eretz Yisrael** with **altars,** as they had to build a new altar for each offering. **Rather, Rav Ḥisda said: For every six steps** he sacrificed **an ox and a fatling,** and **for every six sets of six steps** he sacrificed **seven oxen and seven rams.**

NOTES

Seventy men, fifty thousand men – שִׁבְעִים אִישׁ חֲמִשִּׁים אֶלֶף אִישׁ: It is explained in *Targum Yonatan* that the seventy elders of the nation died, and another fifty thousand from the rest of the nation died.

The Maharsha explains that the Gemara deviates from the simple meaning that 50,070 men died, as, if this were the correct meaning, the verse should have written: Seventy men and fifty thousand men. Furthermore, the repetition of the word "men" indicates that the seventy men were actually fifty thousand men, as the Gemara explains.

כְּתִיב: "כִּידֹן", וּכְתִיב: "נָכוֹן"! אָמַר רַבִּי יוֹחָנָן: בַּתְּחִלָּה כִּידוֹן, וּלְבַסּוֹף נָכוֹן.

It is written that Uzzah died "when they came to the threshing floor of **Chidon**" (I Chronicles 13:9), **and** elsewhere **it is written** that it was "the threshing floor of **Nacon**" (II Samuel 6:6). **Rabbi Yoḥanan says: At first** the Ark was similar to **a javelin [*kidon*]**, as it caused Uzzah's death. **But ultimately,** after the people asked for forgiveness, it was **established [*nakhon*]**,[N] i.e., placed, in the house of Obed Edom, where it was a source of blessing.

נִמְצֵאתָ אַתָּה אוֹמֵר: שְׁלֹשָׁה מִינֵי אֲבָנִים הָיוּ; אֶחָד שֶׁהֵקִים מֹשֶׁה בְּאֶרֶץ מוֹאָב, שֶׁנֶּאֱמַר: "בְּעֵבֶר הַיַּרְדֵּן בְּאֶרֶץ מוֹאָב הוֹאִיל מֹשֶׁה בֵּאֵר" וגו׳, וּלְהַלָּן הוּא אוֹמֵר: "וְכָתַבְתָּ עֲלֵיהֶן אֶת כָּל דִּבְרֵי הַתּוֹרָה הַזֹּאת" וגו׳. וְאָתְיָא "בֵּאֵר", "בַּאֵר";

§ The Gemara returns to the discussion of how the Ark was brought into Eretz Yisrael. **You are found saying** that **there were three sets of stones. One** is a set **that Moses erected in the land of Moab, as it is stated: "Beyond the Jordan, in the land of Moab, Moses took upon himself to expound [*be'er*]** this law, saying" (Deuteronomy 1:5). **And it states there** with regard to the mitzva to erect the stones on Mount Ebal: **"And you shall write on the stones all the words of this law** clearly elucidated [*ba'er*]" (Deuteronomy 27:8). **It is derived** through a verbal analogy between the word ***"be'er"*** that appears with regard to Moses, and the word ***"ba'er"*** that appears with regard to the mitzva to write the Torah on the stones on Mount Ebal that Moses also wrote down the Torah on stones.

וְאֶחָד שֶׁהֵקִים יְהוֹשֻׁעַ בְּתוֹךְ הַיַּרְדֵּן, שֶׁנֶּאֱמַר: "וּשְׁתֵּים עֶשְׂרֵה אֲבָנִים הֵקִים יְהוֹשֻׁעַ בְּתוֹךְ הַיַּרְדֵּן"; וְאֶחָד שֶׁהֵקִים בַּגִּלְגָּל, שֶׁנֶּאֱמַר: "וְאֵת שְׁתֵּים עֶשְׂרֵה הָאֲבָנִים הָאֵלֶּה אֲשֶׁר לָקְחוּ" וגו׳.

And there is **one** set **that Joshua erected in the Jordan, as it is stated: "Joshua also set up twelve stones in the midst of the Jordan,** in the place where the feet of the priests that bore the Ark of the Covenant stood, and they are there to this day" (Joshua 4:9). **And** there is **one** set **that** Joshua **erected in Gilgal, as it is stated: "And these twelve stones, which they took** out of the Jordan, Joshua set up in Gilgal" (Joshua 4:20).

תָּנוּ רַבָּנַן: כֵּיצַד כָּתְבוּ יִשְׂרָאֵל אֶת הַתּוֹרָה? רַבִּי יְהוּדָה אוֹמֵר: עַל גַּבֵּי אֲבָנִים כְּתָבוּהָ, שֶׁנֶּאֱמַר: "וְכָתַבְתָּ עַל הָאֲבָנִים אֶת כָּל דִּבְרֵי הַתּוֹרָה הַזֹּאת" וגו׳, וְאַחַר כָּךְ סָדוּ אוֹתָן בְּסִיד;

The Sages taught: How did the Jewish people write the Torah? Rabbi Yehuda says: They wrote it on stones, as it is stated: "And you shall write on the stones all the words of this law" (Deuteronomy 27:8). **And afterward they plastered them** over **with plaster.**

אָמַר לוֹ רַבִּי שִׁמְעוֹן: לִדְבָרֶיךָ, הֵיאַךְ לָמְדוּ אוּמּוֹת הָעוֹלָם תּוֹרָה? אָמַר לוֹ: בִּינָה יְתֵירָה נָתַן בָּהֶם הַקָּדוֹשׁ בָּרוּךְ הוּא, וְשִׁיגְּרוּ נוֹטִירִין שֶׁלָּהֶן וְקִילְּפוּ אֶת הַסִּיד וְהִשִּׂיאוּהָ. וְעַל דָּבָר זֶה נִתְחַתֵּם גְּזַר דִּינָם לִבְאֵר שַׁחַת, שֶׁהָיָה לָהֶן לִלְמֹד וְלֹא לָמְדוּ;

Rabbi Shimon said to him: According to your statement that they plastered over the writing, **how did the nations of the world study Torah? He said to him: The Holy One, Blessed be He, granted them an extra** degree of **understanding,**[N] **and they sent their scribes [*noteirin*],**[L] **and they peeled off the plaster and copied it** down. **And on account of this matter their decree** to be sent **to the pit of destruction was sealed,** as once the Torah was in their possession **they should have studied** it, **and they did not study.**

רַבִּי שִׁמְעוֹן אוֹמֵר: עַל גַּבֵּי סִיד כְּתָבוּהָ, וְכָתְבוּ לָהֶן לְמַטָּה: "לְמַעַן אֲשֶׁר לֹא יְלַמְּדוּ אֶתְכֶם לַעֲשׂוֹת כְּכֹל" וגו׳. הָא לָמַדְתָּ, שֶׁאִם הָיוּ חוֹזְרִין בִּתְשׁוּבָה הָיוּ מְקַבְּלִין אוֹתָן.

Rabbi Shimon says: That is not what happened. Rather, the Jewish people **wrote** the text of the Torah **on top of** the **plaster, and they wrote below for** the gentiles to read that the verse commands the Jewish people to destroy the gentile inhabitants of Eretz Yisrael: **"Lest they teach you to do like all** their abominations" (Deuteronomy 20:18). **You derive** from the fact that they wrote this verse **that if** the gentiles who lived in Eretz Israel **would have repented,** the Jews **would have accepted them,** i.e., allowed them to live in Eretz Yisrael.

אָמַר רָבָא בַּר שֵׁילָא: מַאי טַעְמָא דְּרַבִּי שִׁמְעוֹן? דִּכְתִיב: "וְהָיוּ עַמִּים מִשְׂרְפוֹת סִיד", עַל עִסְקֵי סִיד.

Rava bar Sheila said: What is the reason for the opinion **of Rabbi Shimon? As it is written: "And the peoples shall be as the burnings of plaster"** (Isaiah 33:12). This is homiletically interpreted to mean that the nations were punished **on account of matters of plaster,** i.e., they did not study the Torah that was written on plaster.

וְרַבִּי יְהוּדָה? כִּי סִיד, מַה סִּיד אֵין לוֹ תַּקָּנָה אֶלָּא שְׂרֵיפָה, אַף אוּמּוֹת הָעוֹלָם אֵין לָהֶם תַּקָּנָה אֶלָּא שְׂרֵיפָה.

The Gemara asks: **And** how does **Rabbi Yehuda,** who holds that the Torah was not written on plaster, interpret this verse? The Gemara answers: He explains that the gentiles are **like plaster; just as plaster has no remedy but burning,** i.e., it is created by burning stone, **so too, the nations of the world have no remedy other than burning** in Gehenna.

NOTES

At first a javelin [*kidon*] but ultimately established [*nakhon*] – בַּתְּחִלָּה כִּידוֹן וּלְבַסּוֹף נָכוֹן: According to one interpretation in the *Arukh*, the Gemara is saying that at first there was judgment [*din*] and then there was order [*nakhon*]. According to a second interpretation, *kidon* means tragedy or brokenness. Rashi suggests a similar explanation of the phrase, based on a verse from Job.

An extra degree of understanding – בִּינָה יְתֵירָה: According to the opinion that the entire Torah was written on the stones, the extraordinary expertise of these scribes was expressed through their ability to copy the Torah within a few hours, before the stones were plastered over (see *Tosafot*). Others explain that they managed to peel off the plaster from the stones without damaging the writing (*Yagel Ya'akov*). Another explanation is that although they could see only the plaster, the scribes understood that something important was written underneath, and peeled off the plaster to copy it (*Ben Yehoyada*).

LANGUAGE

Scribes [*noteirin*] – נוֹטֵירִין: From the Latin term notarius, which is perhaps borrowed from Greek. It refers to a scribe, a writer, or someone who copies official documents.

כְּמַאן אָזְלָא הָא דְּתַנְיָא: "וְשָׁבִיתָ שִׁבְיוֹ" – לְרַבּוֹת כְּנַעֲנִים שֶׁבְּחוּצָה לָאָרֶץ שֶׁאִם חוֹזְרִין בִּתְשׁוּבָה מְקַבְּלִין אוֹתָן?

In accordance with whose opinion is **that which is taught** in a *baraita*: The verse states: "When you go forth to battle against your enemies, and the Lord your God delivers them into your hands, **and you take them captive**" (Deuteronomy 21:10), implying that there is no obligation to destroy them, **to include** not only gentiles who are not Canaanites, but even **Canaanites that are** living **outside of Eretz** Yisrael,[N] **as, if they repent, they are accepted** and allowed to live in Eretz Yisrael.

NOTES

To include Canaanites that are living outside of Eretz Yisrael – לְרַבּוֹת כְּנַעֲנִים שֶׁבְּחוּצָה לָאָרֶץ: The early commentaries have different opinions with regard to the relationship of the Jews to Canaanites living in Eretz Yisrael, Canaanites living outside of Eretz Yisrael, and other gentile nations who want to make peace with the Jews. This issue is dependent on another debate with regard to the offer that Joshua sent to the inhabitants of Eretz Yisrael to make peace with the Jewish people, as discussed in the Jerusalem Talmud: Was this offer dependent merely on their acceptance of the political rule of the Jews, or did they also have to agree to cease idol worship and to observe the seven Noahide mitzvot? See a discussion of the different opinions in *Leḥem Mishne* (Rambam *Sefer Shofetim, Hilkhot Melakhim UMilḥemoteihem* 6:1). The differing opinions with regard to that issue are dependent upon the understanding of the dispute between Rabbi Yehuda and Rabbi Shimon. Several commentaries understand that the matter under discussion is whether or not there is a distinction with regard to the possibility of accepting Canaanites under Jewish rule between the Canaanites who lived in Eretz Yisrael and those who lived outside of Eretz Yisrael; other commentaries disagree. Furthermore, the reason behind the distinction requires clarification. It is possible that the verse stating: "You shall keep alive no one who breathes" (Deuteronomy 20:16), refers only to the Canaanites living in Eretz Yisrael, and only under certain circumstances. Alternatively, it is possible that once the Jewish people entered Eretz Yisrael, the Canaanites living there could no longer be trusted to accept the mitzvot.

Perek **VII**
Daf **36** Amud **a**

כְּמַאן? כְּרַבִּי שִׁמְעוֹן.

In accordance with whose opinion is the *baraita*? It is **in accordance with** the opinion of **Rabbi Shimon,** who holds that the verse: "You shall keep alive no one who breathes" (Deuteronomy 20:16), is not referring to the gentiles living outside of Eretz Yisrael, because there is no concern that the Jewish people will learn "to do like all their abominations" (Deuteronomy 20:18), as these Canaanites are not located in Eretz Yisrael.

בֹּא וּרְאֵה כַּמָּה נִסִּים נַעֲשׂוּ בְּאוֹתוֹ הַיּוֹם: עָבְרוּ יִשְׂרָאֵל אֶת הַיַּרְדֵּן, וּבָאוּ לְהַר גְּרִיזִים וּלְהַר עֵיבָל יָתֵר מִשִּׁשִּׁים מִיל, וְאֵין כׇּל בְּרִיָּה יְכוֹלָה לַעֲמוֹד בִּפְנֵיהֶם. וְכׇל הָעוֹמֵד בִּפְנֵיהֶם מִיָּד נִתְרָז, שֶׁנֶּאֱמַר: "אֶת אֵימָתִי אֲשַׁלַּח לְפָנֶיךָ וְהַמֹּתִי אֶת כׇּל הָעָם אֲשֶׁר תָּבֹא בָּהֶם" וגו׳,

§ The Gemara continues to discuss the entrance of the Jewish people into Eretz Yisrael: **Come and see how many miracles were performed on that day:**[N] **The Jewish people crossed the Jordan, and they arrived at Mount Gerizim and Mount Ebal,** which are **more than sixty *mil*** from the river, **and** on that day **no entity was able to stand before them. And anyone who stood before them was immediately struck with diarrhea,**[N] **as it is stated: "I will send My terror before you, and will confound all the people that you encounter"** (Exodus 23:27).

וְאוֹמֵר: "תִּפֹּל עֲלֵיהֶם אֵימָתָה וָפַחַד... עַד יַעֲבֹר עַמְּךָ ה׳" – זוֹ בִּיאָה רִאשׁוֹנָה; "עַד יַעֲבֹר עַם זוּ קָנִיתָ" – זוֹ בִּיאָה שְׁנִיָּה,

And similarly, the verse **says: "Terror and dread falls upon them;** by the greatness of Your arm they are as still as a stone; **till Your people pass over, Lord"** (Exodus 15:16). **This** alludes to the **first arrival** of the Jewish people in Eretz Yisrael, during the period of Joshua. The verse continues: **"Till the people that You have gotten pass over"** (Exodus 15:16). **This** alludes to the **second arrival,** when the Jews returned to Eretz Yisrael from Babylonia after the destruction of the First Temple.

אֱמוֹר מֵעַתָּה: רְאוּיִין הָיוּ יִשְׂרָאֵל לַעֲשׂוֹת לָהֶם נֵס בְּבִיאָה שְׁנִיָּה כְּבִיאָה רִאשׁוֹנָה, אֶלָּא שֶׁגָּרַם הַחֵטְא;

Accordingly, **say from now** that **the Jewish people were worthy of having a miracle performed for them during the second arrival, just like** they were worthy of having miracles performed for them during **the first arrival, but** their **sin caused**[N] them to enter Eretz Yisrael through a natural process, with the permission of the kings of other nations.

NOTES

How many miracles were performed on that day – כַּמָּה נִסִּים נַעֲשׂוּ בְּאוֹתוֹ הַיּוֹם: This is the opinion of the mishna. However, the dissenting opinion of Rabbi Yishmael is cited in the Jerusalem Talmud, according to which the blessings and curses were recited fourteen years later, after Eretz Yisrael was conquered and divided among the tribes. See also the Maharsha, who points out that the blessings and curses appear in the book of Joshua only after the conquest of Jericho and the city of Ai.

Struck with diarrhea – מִיָּד נִתְרָז: According to Rashi, this is derived from the phrase "And I will confound." He explains that this means that their intestines were confounded and their function disrupted. In contrast, the Maharsha explains that it is derived from the phrase "I will send My terror," as diarrhea can be caused by feelings of fear.

Sin caused – שֶׁגָּרַם הַחֵטְא: Rashi explains that the sins referred to here are the sins of the Jews during the period of the First Temple. The Ya'avetz asks why a later generation would be punished for those sins, which they did not commit. He explains that the sin that the Gemara speaks of is the sin of marrying gentile women, based on the verses in the books of Ezra and Nehemiah that state that the generation that returned from Babylonia was guilty of this sin.

וְאַחַר כָּךְ הֵבִיאוּ אֶת הָאֲבָנִים וּבָנוּ אֶת הַמִּזְבֵּחַ וְסָדוּהוּ בְּסִיד, וְכָתְבוּ עֲלֵיהֶם אֶת כָּל דִּבְרֵי הַתּוֹרָה בְּשִׁבְעִים לָשׁוֹן, שֶׁנֶּאֱמַר: "בַּאֵר הֵיטֵב";

The Gemara continues its description of the entrance into Eretz Yisrael during the period of Joshua: **And afterward they brought the stones and built the altar** on Mount Ebal, **and plastered it** over **with plaster, and wrote on** the stones **all of the words of the Torah in seventy languages, as it is stated:** "And you shall write on the stones all of the words of this law **clearly elucidated**" (Deuteronomy 27:8).

וְהֶעֱלוּ עוֹלוֹת וּשְׁלָמִים וְאָכְלוּ וְשָׁתוּ וְשָׂמְחוּ, וּבֵרְכוּ וְקִלְּלוּ, וְקִיפְּלוּ אֶת הָאֲבָנִים וּבָאוּ וְלָנוּ בְּגִלְגָּל, שֶׁנֶּאֱמַר: "וְהַעֲבַרְתֶּם אוֹתָם עִמָּכֶם וְהִנַּחְתֶּם אוֹתָם בַּמָּלוֹן".

And they sacrificed burnt-offerings and peace-offerings, and they ate and drank and celebrated, and they uttered the **blessings, and they uttered** the **curses, and they took** [*kippelu*][L] **the stones with them, and they arrived and slept in Gilgal, as it is stated: "And carry them over with you, and lay them down in the lodging place,** where you shall lodge this night" (Joshua 4:3).

יָכוֹל בְּכָל מָלוֹן וּמָלוֹן? תַּלְמוּד לוֹמַר: "אֲשֶׁר תָּלִינוּ בוֹ הַלַּיְלָה", וּכְתִיב: "וְאֵת שְׁתֵּים עֶשְׂרֵה הָאֲבָנִים הָאֵלֶּה אֲשֶׁר לָקְחוּ" וגו'.

One **might** have thought that they were required to place these stones **at each and every lodging place** where they stayed. Therefore, **the verse states: "Where you shall lodge this night,"** meaning only on that night. **And it is written: "And those twelve stones, which they took** out of the Jordan, Joshua set up in Gilgal" (Joshua 4:20).

תָּנָא: צִרְעָה לֹא עָבְרָה עִמָּהֶם. וְלָא? וְהָא כְּתִיב: "וְשָׁלַחְתִּי אֶת הַצִּרְעָה לְפָנֶיךָ"!

It is **taught** in a *baraita* (*Tosefta* 11:10): The **hornet** [*tzira*][L] **did not cross** the Jordan **with them.** The Gemara asks: **And** did it **not? But isn't it written: "And I will send the hornet before you,** which shall drive out the Hivites, and the Canaanites" (Exodus 23:28)?

אָמַר רַבִּי שִׁמְעוֹן בֶּן לָקִישׁ: עַל שְׂפַת יַרְדֵּן עָמְדָה וְזָרְקָה בָּהֶן מָרָה, וְסִימְּתָה עֵינֵיהֶן מִלְמַעְלָה וְסֵירְסָתַן מִלְּמַטָּה, שֶׁנֶּאֱמַר: "וְאָנֹכִי הִשְׁמַדְתִּי אֶת הָאֱמֹרִי מִפְּנֵיהֶם אֲשֶׁר כְּגֹבַהּ אֲרָזִים גָּבְהוֹ וְחָסֹן הוּא כָּאַלּוֹנִים וָאַשְׁמִיד פִּרְיוֹ מִמַּעַל וְשָׁרָשָׁיו מִתָּחַת" וגו'.

Rabbi Shimon ben Lakish says: The hornet **stood on the banks of the Jordan and threw its venom at** the inhabitants of the land **and it blinded their eyes from above and castrated them from below, as it is stated: "Yet I destroyed the Amorites before them, whose height was like the height of the cedars, and they were strong as the oaks; yet I destroyed their fruit from above, and their roots from beneath"** (Amos 2:9).

רַב פָּפָּא אָמַר: שְׁתֵּי צִרְעוֹת הֲוַאי, חֲדָא דְּמֹשֶׁה וַחֲדָא דִּיהוֹשֻׁעַ, דְּמֹשֶׁה לָא עֲבַר, דִּיהוֹשֻׁעַ עֲבַר.

Rav Pappa said: There were two hornets. One was the hornet **of Moses,** which helped conquer the eastern side of the Jordan, **and one** was the hornet **of Joshua.** The hornet **of Moses did not cross** the Jordan, but the hornet **of Joshua did cross.**

"שִׁשָּׁה שְׁבָטִים עָלוּ לְרֹאשׁ הַר גְּרִיזִים" כו'. מַאי "וְהַחֶצְיוֹ"? אָמַר רַב כָּהֲנָא: כְּדֶרֶךְ שֶׁחֲלוּקִין כָּאן, כָּךְ חֲלוּקִין בְּאַבְנֵי אֵפוֹד.

§ It is stated in the mishna: **Six tribes ascended to the top of Mount Gerizim,** as it is stated: "Half of them in front of Mount Gerizim and the half of them in front of Mount Ebal" (Joshua 8:33). The Gemara asks: **What** is the meaning of the term **"and the half of them"?** It seems to be referring to a division that already existed. **Rav Kahana says: The same way that** the tribes **were divided up here** on the mountains, **so too were they divided on the stones of the ephod,** a garment of the High Priest.

מֵיתִיבֵי: שְׁתֵּי אֲבָנִים טוֹבוֹת הָיוּ לוֹ לְכֹהֵן גָּדוֹל עַל כְּתֵיפָיו, אַחַת מִכָּאן וְאַחַת מִכָּאן, וּשְׁמוֹת שְׁנֵים עָשָׂר שְׁבָטִים כָּתוּב עֲלֵיהֶם, שִׁשָּׁה עַל אֶבֶן זוֹ וְשִׁשָּׁה עַל אֶבֶן זוֹ, שֶׁנֶּאֱמַר: "שִׁשָּׁה מִשְּׁמוֹתָם עַל הָאֶבֶן הָאֶחָת" וגו'.

The Gemara **raises an objection** to this answer: **The High Priest had two precious stones** on the part of the ephod that rested **on his shoulders, one on this side and one on that side, and the names of the twelve tribes were written on them, six on this stone and six on that stone, as it is stated: "Six of their names on the one stone,** and the names of the six that remain on the other stone, according to their birth" (Exodus 28:10).

שְׁנִיָּה כְּתוֹלְדוֹתָם וְלֹא רִאשׁוֹנָה כְּתוֹלְדוֹתָם, מִפְּנֵי שֶׁיְּהוּדָה מוּקְדָּם. וַחֲמִשִּׁים אוֹתִיּוֹת הָיוּ, עֶשְׂרִים וְחָמֵשׁ עַל אֶבֶן זוֹ וְעֶשְׂרִים וְחָמֵשׁ עַל אֶבֶן זוֹ.

It is derived from the verse that only the names on the **second** stone were written **according to** the order of **their birth:** Gad, Asher, Issachar, Zebulun, Joseph, Benjamin. **But** the names on the **first** stone were **not** written **according to** the order of **their birth, as Judah was** written **first,** and afterward came Reuben, Simeon, Levi, Dan, and Naphtali. **And there were fifty letters** on the two stones of the ephod,[HB] **twenty-five** letters **on this stone and twenty-five on that stone.**

רַבִּי חֲנִינָא בֶּן גַּמְלִיאֵל אוֹמֵר:

Rabbi Ḥanina ben Gamliel says:

LANGUAGE

They took [*kippelu*] – קִיפְּלוּ: The root *kuf, peh, lamed* has a similar meaning to the root *khaf, peh, lamed*; its basic meaning is to fold. More broadly, the word has several meanings, among them to take or remove an object, as is the case here.

Hornet [*tzira*] – צִרְעָה: There are commentaries who maintain that this refers to a type of disease similar to leprosy (Ibn Ezra). However, most translators and commentaries explain that it is a type of flying insect. According to this interpretation, *tzira* refers to the large hornet of the species *Vespa orientalis* commonly known as the Oriental wasp. The sting of this hornet is very painful, especially if it attacks a sensitive part of the body. An attack of swarming hornets can even prove to be fatal.

Oriental wasp

HALAKHA

The stones of the ephod – אַבְנֵי הָאֵפוֹד: According to the Rambam the names on the stones of the ephod were written in the following manner: There were twenty-five letters on each stone; the stone that has Reuben's name on it was worn on the right shoulder, and the stone that has Simeon written on it was worn on the left shoulder (Rambam *Sefer Avoda, Hilkhot Kelei HaMikdash* 9:9).

BACKGROUND

The stones of the ephod – אַבְנֵי הָאֵפוֹד:

Replicas of the stones of the ephod according to the Rambam

לֹא כְּדֶרֶךְ שֶׁחֲלוּקִין בְּחוּמַּשׁ הַפְּקוּדִים חֲלוּקִין בְּאַבְנֵי אֵפוֹד, אֶלָּא כְּדֶרֶךְ שֶׁחֲלוּקִין בְּחוּמָּשׁ שֵׁנִי.

The names of the tribes were **not divided on the stones of the ephod the** same **way that they were divided in** the list found at the beginning of **the book of Numbers** (Numbers 1:1–15). **Rather** they were divided **the way that they were divided in the second book,** i.e., Exodus (Exodus 1:2–4).

כֵּיצַד? בְּנֵי לֵאָה כְּסִידְרָן, בְּנֵי רָחֵל אֶחָד מִכָּאן וְאֶחָד מִכָּאן, וּבְנֵי שְׁפָחוֹת בָּאֶמְצַע,

How were they written? On one stone, the names of **the sons of Leah** were written **in the order of their** birth: Reuben, Simeon, Levi, Judah, Issachar, and Zebulun. On the other stone **the sons of Rachel** were written. **One,** Benjamin, was written **on this side,** i.e., at the bottom of the list, **and one,** Joseph, was written **on that side,** i.e., at the top of the list. **And the children of the handmaids,** i.e., Bilhah and Zilpah, who were Dan, Naphtali, Gad, and Asher, were written on the second stone **in the middle.**

וְאֶלָּא מַאי אֲנִי מְקַיֵּים ״כְּתוֹלְדֹתָם״? כִּשְׁמוֹתָן שֶׁקָּרָא לָהֶן אֲבִיהֶן וְלֹא כַּשֵּׁמוֹת שֶׁקָּרָא לָהֶן מֹשֶׁה, רְאוּבֵן – וְלֹא רְאוּבֵנִי, שִׁמְעוֹן – וְלֹא שִׁמְעוֹנִי, דָּן – וְלֹא הַדָּנִי, גָּד – וְלֹא הַגָּדִי; תְּיוּבְתָּא דְּרַב כָּהֲנָא! תְּיוּבְתָּא.

But rather, if their names were not written in the order of their births, then **how do I establish** the meaning of the phrase: **"According to their birth"** (Exodus 28:10)? It means that their names were written **according to** the **names that their father,** Jacob, **called them, and not according to the names that Moses called them.** On the stones it said **Reuben, and not Reubenites; Simeon, and not Simeonites; Dan, and not Danites; Gad, and not Gadites.** This *baraita* contradicts Rav Kahana's opinion, as according to all of the opinions in the *baraita*, the division of the names on the ephod is not identical to the division of the tribes on Mount Gerizim and Mount Ebal. The Gemara confirms: **The refutation** of the opinion **of Rav Kahana is** in fact **a conclusive refutation.**

וְאֶלָּא מַאי ״וְהֶחֶצְיוֹ״? תָּנָא: חֶצְיוֹ שֶׁל מוּל הַר גְּרִיזִים מְרוּבֶּה מֵחֶצְיוֹ שֶׁל הַר עֵיבָל, מִפְּנֵי שֶׁלֵּוִי לְמַטָּה.

The Gemara asks: **Rather, what** is meant by the phrase: **"And the half of them** facing Mount Ebal" (Joshua 8:33)? It is **taught** in a *baraita*: The use of the definitive article in the verse indicates that the smaller half of the Jewish people was on Mount Ebal. **The half that was facing Mount Gerizim was larger than the half on Mount Ebal, because** the tribe of **Levi** was included in the group that was facing Mount Gerizim, and they remained **on the bottom** between the two mountains.

אַדְּרַבָּה, מִפְּנֵי שֶׁלֵּוִי לְמַטָּה בָּצְרִי לְהוּ! הָכִי קָאָמַר: אַף עַל פִּי שֶׁלֵּוִי לְמַטָּה בְּנֵי יוֹסֵף עִמָּהֶם, שֶׁנֶּאֱמַר: ״וַיְדַבְּרוּ בְּנֵי יוֹסֵף אֶת יְהוֹשֻׁעַ לֵאמֹר מַדּוּעַ נָתַתָּה לִּי נַחֲלָה גּוֹרָל אֶחָד וְחֶבֶל אֶחָד וַאֲנִי עַם רַב...וַיֹּאמֶר אֲלֵיהֶם יְהוֹשֻׁעַ אִם עַם רַב אַתָּה עֲלֵה לְךָ הַיַּעְרָה״.

The Gemara is puzzled by this statement: **On the contrary, because** the tribe of **Levi** remained **on the bottom they were fewer** in number. The Gemara answers: **This is what** the *baraita* **is saying: Although** the tribe of **Levi was on the bottom, the descendants of Joseph were among them,** and the tribe of Joseph was numerous, **as it is stated: "And the children of Joseph spoke to Joshua, saying: Why did you give me a single lot and one part for an inheritance, seeing I am a great people,** forasmuch as the Lord has blessed me thus, **and Joshua said to them: If you are a great people, you should go up to the forest"** (Joshua 17:14–15).

אָמַר לָהֶן: לְכוּ וְהַחְבִּאוּ עַצְמְכֶם בַּיְּעָרִים, שֶׁלֹּא תִּשְׁלוֹט בָּכֶם עַיִן הָרַע. אָמְרוּ לֵיהּ: זַרְעֵיהּ דְּיוֹסֵף לָא שָׁלְטָא בֵּיהּ עֵינָא בִּישָׁא, דִּכְתִיב: ״בֵּן פֹּרָת יוֹסֵף בֵּן פֹּרָת עֲלֵי עָיִן״, וְאָמַר רַבִּי אַבָּהוּ: אַל תְּהִי קוֹרֵא ״עֲלֵי עָיִן״ אֶלָּא ״עוֹלֵי עָיִן״.

The Gemara explains that Joshua **said to them: Go and hide yourselves in the forests, so that the evil eye will not have dominion over you,** as you are such a large number of people. The tribe of Joseph **said to him: The evil eye does not have dominion over the offspring of Joseph, as it is written: "Joseph is a fruitful vine, a fruitful vine by a fountain"** (Genesis 49:22), **and Rabbi Abbahu says: Do not read** the verse as saying: **"By a fountain** [*alei ayin*]**";**[N] **rather,** read it as: **Those who rise above** the evil **eye** [*olei ayin*], teaching that Joseph and his descendants are not susceptible to the evil eye.

רַבִּי יוֹסֵי בְּרַבִּי חֲנִינָא אָמַר, מֵהָכָא: ״וְיִדְגּוּ לָרֹב בְּקֶרֶב הָאָרֶץ״, מַה דָּגִים שֶׁבַּיָּם – מַיִם מְכַסִּין עֲלֵיהֶן וְאֵין הָעַיִן שׁוֹלֶטֶת בָּהֶן, אַף זַרְעוֹ שֶׁל יוֹסֵף אֵין הָעַיִן שׁוֹלֶטֶת בָּהֶן.

The Gemara cites an alternative source for the assertion that the evil eye holds no sway over Joseph and his descendants: **Rabbi Yosei, son of Rabbi Ḥanina, said** that it is derived **from here:** Jacob blessed Joseph's children and said: **"And let them grow** [*veyidgu*] **into a multitude in the midst of the earth"** (Genesis 48:16). **Just as** with regard to **fish** [*dagim*] **in the sea, waters cover them and the** evil **eye** therefore **has no dominion over them, so too,** with regard to **Joseph's descendants, the** evil **eye has no dominion over them.**

NOTES

By a fountain [*alei ayin*] – עֲלֵי עָיִן: Rabbeinu Ḥananel interprets this to mean: Leave [*ali*] us and go away, evil eye [*ayin*].

הָנֵי חֲמִשִּׁים אוֹתִיּוֹת – חֲמִשִּׁים נְכִי חֲדָא הָוְיָין! אָמַר רַבִּי יִצְחָק: יוֹסֵף הוֹסִיפוּ לוֹ אוֹת אַחַת, שֶׁנֶּאֱמַר: "עֵדוּת בִּיהוֹסֵף שָׂמוֹ בְּצֵאתוֹ עַל אֶרֶץ מִצְרָיִם".

The Gemara asks with regard to the *baraita* that contradicts Rav Kahana's opinion: **Are these** names of the tribes, which were written on the ephod, composed of a total of **fifty letters?** There **are** only **forty-nine. Rabbi Yitzḥak says: They added one letter to** the name of **Joseph** [*Yosef*] when it was written on the ephod, **as it is stated: "He appointed it in Joseph** [*Yehosef*] **for a testimony when He went forth against the land of Egypt"** (Psalms 81:6).

מַתְקִיף לָהּ רַב נַחְמָן בַּר יִצְחָק: "כְּתוֹלְדֹתָם" בָּעֵינַן! אֶלָּא, כָּל הַתּוֹרָה כּוּלָּהּ "בִּנְיָמִן" כְּתִיב, וְהָכָא "בִּנְיָמִין" שָׁלֵם, כְּדִכְתִיב: "וְאָבִיו קָרָא לוֹ בִנְיָמִין".

Rav Naḥman bar Yitzḥak objects to this: We require the names to be written **"according to their birth,"** and Joseph was not called *Yehosef* from birth. **Rather,** the explanation is as follows: Throughout **the entire Torah,** the name of **Benjamin is written** without a second letter *yod* between the letters *mem* and *nun*, **and here,** where he is born, **Benjamin** is written **in full,**[B] spelled with a second *yod*. **As it is written: "But his father called him Benjamin"** (Genesis 35:18). Therefore, his name was written on the ephod with a second *yod*, "according to his birth."

אָמַר רַב חָנָא בַּר בִּיזְנָא אָמַר רַבִּי שִׁמְעוֹן חֲסִידָא: יוֹסֵף שֶׁקִּידֵּשׁ שֵׁם שָׁמַיִם בְּסֵתֶר – הוֹסִיפוּ עָלָיו אוֹת אַחַת מִשְּׁמוֹ שֶׁל הַקָּדוֹשׁ בָּרוּךְ הוּא. יְהוּדָה שֶׁקִּידֵּשׁ שֵׁם שָׁמַיִם בְּפַרְהֶסְיָא – נִקְרָא כּוּלּוֹ עַל שְׁמוֹ שֶׁל הַקָּדוֹשׁ בָּרוּךְ הוּא.

§ **Rav Ḥana bar Bizna says** that **Rabbi Shimon Ḥasida says: Joseph, who sanctified the name of Heaven in private, had one letter of the name of the Holy One, Blessed be He,** the letter *heh*, **added to his** name. Whereas in the case of **Judah, who sanctified the name of Heaven in public** [*befarhesya*][L] at the Red Sea during the exodus from Egypt, merited that **his entire** name **is called by the name of the Holy One, Blessed be He,** as the entire four-letter name of God can be found within Judah's name.

יוֹסֵף מַאי הִיא? דִּכְתִיב: "וַיְהִי כְּהַיּוֹם הַזֶּה וַיָּבֹא הַבַּיְתָה לַעֲשׂוֹת מְלַאכְתּוֹ" – אָמַר רַבִּי יוֹחָנָן: מְלַמֵּד, שֶׁשְּׁנֵיהֶם לִדְבַר עֲבֵירָה נִתְכַּוְּונוּ. "וַיָּבֹא הַבַּיְתָה לַעֲשׂוֹת מְלַאכְתּוֹ" – רַב וּשְׁמוּאֵל, חַד אָמַר: לַעֲשׂוֹת מְלַאכְתּוֹ מַמָּשׁ, וְחַד אָמַר: לַעֲשׂוֹת צְרָכָיו נִכְנַס.

The Gemara explains: **What is** the situation where **Joseph** sanctified God's name in private? **As it is written: "And it came to pass on a certain day, when he went into the house to do his work"** (Genesis 39:11). **Rabbi Yoḥanan says:** This **teaches that both** Joseph and Potiphar's wife stayed in the house, as they **intended to** perform **a matter of sin.** With regard to the phrase **"when he went into the house to do his work,"**[N] **Rav and Shmuel** engage in a dispute with regard to its meaning. **One says:** It means that he went into the house **to do his work, literally. And one says: He entered** the house **in order to fulfill his** sexual **needs** with her.

"וְאֵין אִישׁ מֵאַנְשֵׁי הַבַּיִת" וגו׳ – אֶפְשָׁר בַּיִת גָּדוֹל כְּבֵיתוֹ שֶׁל אוֹתוֹ רָשָׁע לֹא הָיָה בּוֹ אִישׁ? תָּנָא דְּבֵי רַבִּי יִשְׁמָעֵאל: אוֹתוֹ הַיּוֹם יוֹם חַגָּם הָיָה, וְהָלְכוּ כּוּלָּן לְבֵית עֲבוֹדָה זָרָה שֶׁלָּהֶם, וְהִיא אָמְרָה לָהֶן חוֹלָה הִיא. אָמְרָה: אֵין לִי יוֹם שֶׁנִּיזְקָק לִי יוֹסֵף כַּיּוֹם הַזֶּה.

The verse continues: **"And there was none of the men of the house** there within" (Genesis 39:11). The Gemara asks: **Is it possible** that in such **a large** and important **house like the house of that wicked man** that **no one was in there? The school of Rabbi Yishmael taught: That day was their festival day and they all went to their house of idol worship; and she told them** that **she was sick** and could not go, as **she said** to herself: **I have no day on which Joseph will attend to me like this day.**

"וַתִּתְפְּשֵׂהוּ בְּבִגְדוֹ לֵאמֹר" וגו׳ – בְּאוֹתָהּ שָׁעָה בָּאתָה דְּיוֹקְנוֹ שֶׁל אָבִיו וְנִרְאֲתָה לוֹ בַּחַלּוֹן, אָמַר לוֹ: יוֹסֵף, עֲתִידִין אַחֶיךָ שֶׁיִּכָּתְבוּ עַל אַבְנֵי אֵפוֹד וְאַתָּה בֵּינֵיהֶם. רְצוֹנְךָ שֶׁיִּמָּחֶה שִׁמְךָ מִבֵּינֵיהֶם וְתִקָּרֵא רוֹעֵה זוֹנוֹת? דִּכְתִיב: "וְרֹעֶה זוֹנוֹת יְאַבֶּד הוֹן"!

The verse states: **"And she caught him by his garment, saying:** Lie with me" (Genesis 39:12). **At that moment his father's image** [*deyokeno*][L] **came and appeared to him in the window.** The image **said to him: Joseph,** the names of **your brothers are destined to be written on the stones of the ephod, and you** are to be included **among them. Do you desire your name to be erased from among them, and to be called an associate** [*ro'eh*] **of promiscuous women? As it is written: "But he who keeps company with harlots wastes his riches"** (Proverbs 29:3), as he loses his honor, which is more valuable than wealth.

מִיָּד: "וַתֵּשֶׁב בְּאֵיתָן קַשְׁתּוֹ" – אָמַר רַבִּי יוֹחָנָן מִשּׁוּם רַבִּי מֵאִיר: שֶׁשָּׁבָה קַשְׁתּוֹ לְאֵיתָנוֹ. "וַיָּפֹזּוּ זְרוֹעֵי יָדָיו" – נָעַץ יָדָיו בַּקַּרְקַע וְיָצְאָה שִׁכְבַת זַרְעוֹ מִבֵּין צִיפּוֹרְנֵי יָדָיו.

Immediately: "And his bow abode [*teishev*] **firm"** (Genesis 49:24). **Rabbi Yoḥanan says in the name of Rabbi Meir:** This means **that his bow,** i.e., his penis, **returned** [*shava*] **to its strength,** as he overcame his desire. The verse about Joseph continues: **"And the arms of his hands were made supple"** (Genesis 49:24), meaning that **he dug his hands into the ground and his semen was emitted between his fingernails.**[N]

BACKGROUND

Here Benjamin is written in full – הָכָא בִּנְיָמִין שָׁלֵם: The written form of the Torah as it appears in scrolls to this day lacks vowels. All Hebrew letters are consonants, but several letters occasionally serve as matres lectionis, Latin for mothers of reading, thereby contributing to the pronunciation of the words in which they appear. These letters are *alef*, *heh*, *vav*, and *yod*, which in the middle or end of a word might alter the sound and sometimes the meaning of the word. For example, the Hebrew name Benjamin can be written with two instances of the letter *yod*, or with only one. The former style is called *malei*, plene or full, and the latter is called *ḥaser*, defective.

LANGUAGE

Public [*parhesya*] **– פַּרְהֶסְיָא:** From the Greek παρρησία, *parrēsia*, meaning freedom of speech and free reign. The Sages use this word to refer to something that is done in public and is visible to all.

His image [*deyokeno*] **– דְּיוֹקְנוֹ:** This word is derived from Greek. Some explain that it comes from the word δείκανον, *deikanon*, which refers to an engraved or embroidered image. However, the *ge'onim* explain that it is a combination of two Aramaic words, *dio-ikonin*, from the Greek εἰκών, *eikon*, meaning image. The word therefore means a duplicate or copy of an image.

NOTES

His work – מְלַאכְתּוֹ: The Maharsha explains that the fact that the verse states: "His work," rather than stating work, or his master's work, implies that he went to the house for his own purposes.

From between his fingernails – מִבֵּין צִיפּוֹרְנֵי יָדָיו: Rav Hai Gaon explains that the term fingernails is not to be understood literally. Rather, it means that his semen emerged without him engaging in sexual intercourse with her (see *Ben Yehoyada*). Others have an alternative version of the text, according to which the Gemara states: His desire left him from between his fingernails. The meaning according to this version is apparently in accordance with the explanation of Rav Hai Gaon.

"מִידֵי אֲבִיר יַעֲקֹב" – מִי גָּרַם לוֹ שֶׁיֵּחָקֵק עַל אַבְנֵי אֵפוֹד? אֶלָּא אֲבִיר יַעֲקֹב, "מִשָּׁם רֹעֶה אֶבֶן יִשְׂרָאֵל" – מִשָּׁם זָכָה וְנַעֲשָׂה רוֹעֶה, שֶׁנֶּאֱמַר: "רוֹעֵה יִשְׂרָאֵל הַאֲזִינָה נֹהֵג כַּצֹּאן יוֹסֵף".

"By the hands of the Mighty One of Jacob" (Genesis 49:24): **Who caused his name to be etched onto the stones of the ephod?** It was **only the might of Jacob. "From there, from the Shepherd, the Stone of Israel"** (Genesis 49:24) means: **From there,** because of Joseph's ability to withstand this trial, **he merited to become a shepherd** [*ro'eh*] of the Jewish people, **as it is stated: "Listen, O Shepherd of Israel, who leads like the flock of Joseph"** (Psalms 80:2).

תַּנְיָא: הָיָה רָאוּי יוֹסֵף לָצֵאת מִמֶּנּוּ שְׁנֵים עָשָׂר שְׁבָטִים כְּדֶרֶךְ שֶׁיָּצְאוּ מִיַּעֲקֹב אָבִיו, שֶׁנֶּאֱמַר: "אֵלֶּה תֹּלְדוֹת יַעֲקֹב יוֹסֵף", אֶלָּא שֶׁיָּצָא שִׁכְבַת זַרְעוֹ מִבֵּין צִיפּוֹרְנֵי יָדָיו; וְאַף עַל פִּי כֵן יָצְאוּ מִבִּנְיָמִין אָחִיו, וְכוּלָּן נִקְרְאוּ עַל שְׁמוֹ, שֶׁנֶּאֱמַר: "וּבְנֵי בִנְיָמִן בֶּלַע וָבֶכֶר וְאַשְׁבֵּל" וגו׳.

It is taught in a *baraita*: **Joseph was deserving of having twelve tribes descend from him,** the same **as** twelve tribes **descended from his father Jacob, as it is stated: "These are the generations of Jacob, Joseph"** (Genesis 37:2). This implies that everything that happened to Jacob was destined to happen to Joseph. **However,** he did not merit this because **his semen was emitted from between his fingernails. And even so,** the offspring that were meant to descend from him **descended from his brother Benjamin,** who had ten sons. **And they were all named after** Joseph, **as it is stated: "And the sons of Benjamin: Bela, and Becher, and Ashbel,** Gera, and Naaman, Ehi, and Rosh, Muppim, and Huppim, and Ard" (Genesis 46:21).

"בֶּלַע" – שֶׁנִּבְלַע בֵּין הָאוּמּוֹת; "וָבֶכֶר" – בְּכוֹר לְאִמּוֹ הָיָה; "וְאַשְׁבֵּל" – שֶׁשְּׁבָאוֹ אֵל; "גֵּרָא" – שֶׁגָּר בְּאַכְסַנְיוֹת;

The Gemara explains how each name relates to Joseph: **Bela** was named after Joseph, **who was swallowed** [*nivla*] **among the nations. And Becher** received that name because Joseph **was the firstborn** [*bekhor*] **of his mother,** Rachel. **And Ashbel** received his name **because God sent** Joseph **into captivity** [*shevao El*] in Egypt. **Gera** was named after Joseph, **who dwelled** [*gar*] **in a foreign land** [*akhsaneyut*].[L]

"וְנַעֲמָן" – שֶׁנָּעִים בְּיוֹתֵר, "אֵחִי וָרֹאשׁ" – אָחִי הוּא וְרֹאשִׁי הוּא. "מֻפִּים וְחֻפִּים" – הוּא לֹא רָאָה בְּחוּפָּתִי וַאֲנִי לֹא רָאִיתִי בְּחוּפָּתוֹ. "וָאָרְדְּ" – שֶׁיָּרַד לְבֵין אוּמּוֹת הָעוֹלָם; אִיכָּא דְּאָמְרִי: "וָאָרְדְּ" – שֶׁפָּנָיו דּוֹמִין לְוֶורֶד.

And Naaman was called that **because** Joseph **was extremely pleasing** [*na'im*]. **Ehi and Rosh** received these names, as Benjamin said: Joseph **is my brother** [*aḥi*] **and my leader** [*roshi*]. Benjamin named his sons **Muppim**[N] **and Huppim,** as Benjamin said: Joseph **did not see my wedding canopy** [*ḥuppa*] **and I did not see his wedding canopy. And Ard** was named after Joseph, **who descended** [*yarad*] **to** the lands of **the nations of the world. Some say** that the name **Ard** means **that** Joseph's **face was similar** in its beauty **to a rose** [*vered*].

אָמַר רַבִּי חִיָּיא בַּר אַבָּא אָמַר רַבִּי יוֹחָנָן, בְּשָׁעָה שֶׁאָמַר לוֹ פַּרְעֹה לְיוֹסֵף: "וּבִלְעָדֶיךָ לֹא יָרִים אִישׁ אֶת יָדוֹ" וגו׳, אָמְרוּ אִיצְטַגְנִינֵי פַּרְעֹה: עֶבֶד שֶׁלְּקָחוֹ רַבּוֹ בְּעֶשְׂרִים כֶּסֶף תַּמְשִׁילֵהוּ עָלֵינוּ? אָמַר לָהֶן: גִּנּוּנֵי מַלְכוּת אֲנִי רוֹאֶה בּוֹ.

Rabbi Ḥiyya bar Abba says that **Rabbi Yoḥanan says: When Pharaoh said to Joseph: "And without you no man shall lift up his hand** or his foot in all the land of Egypt" (Genesis 41:44), **Pharaoh's astrologers said: You will appoint a slave whose master bought him for twenty silver** coins **to rule over us? He said to them: I perceive royal characteristics** [*ginnunei malkhut*][L] **in him** and see that he was not initially a slave.

אָמְרוּ לוֹ: אִם כֵּן, יְהֵא יוֹדֵעַ בְּשִׁבְעִים לָשׁוֹן! בָּא גַּבְרִיאֵל וְלִימְּדוֹ שִׁבְעִים לָשׁוֹן. לָא הֲוָה קָגָמַר, הוֹסִיף לוֹ אוֹת אַחַת מִשְּׁמוֹ שֶׁל הַקָּדוֹשׁ בָּרוּךְ הוּא וְלָמַד, שֶׁנֶּאֱמַר: "עֵדוּת בִּיהוֹסֵף שָׂמוֹ בְּצֵאתוֹ עַל אֶרֶץ מִצְרָיִם, שְׂפַת לֹא יָדַעְתִּי אֶשְׁמָע". וּלְמָחָר, כָּל לִישָּׁנָא דְּאִישְׁתָּעֵי פַּרְעֹה בַּהֲדֵיהּ אַהְדַּר לֵיהּ.

They said to him: If that is so and he is a child of royalty, **he should know** the **seventy languages**[N] that all kings' children learn. The angel **Gabriel** then **came and taught him** the **seventy languages,** but **he could not learn** all of them. Gabriel then **added one letter,** the letter *heh*, to Joseph's name **from the name of the Holy One, Blessed be He, and** then **he** was able to **learn** the languages, **as it is stated: "He appointed it in Joseph** [*Yehosef*] **for a testimony, when he went forth against the land of Egypt, the speech of one that I did not know I heard"** (Psalms 81:6). **And the next day,** when he appeared before Pharaoh, in **every language that Pharaoh spoke with him, he answered him.**

אִישְׁתָּעֵי אִיהוּ בִּלְשׁוֹן הַקֹּדֶשׁ, לָא הֲוָה קָא יָדַע מַאי הֲוָה אָמַר. אֲמַר לֵיהּ: אַגְמְרִי! אַגְמְרֵיהּ וְלָא גָּמַר. אֲמַר לֵיהּ: אִישְׁתַּבַּע לִי דְּלָא מְגַלֵּית. אִישְׁתַּבַּע לוֹ.

Joseph then **spoke in the sacred tongue,** Hebrew, and Pharaoh **did not know what he was saying.** Pharaoh **said to him: Teach me** that language. **He taught him, but he** could **not learn** it. Pharaoh **said to him: Take an oath for my** benefit **that you will not reveal** that I do not know this language. **He took an oath for his** benefit.

LANGUAGE

Foreign land [*akhsaneyut*] – אַכְסַנְיוּת: This word is used here in an unusual fashion, as a derivative of the Greek ξένια, *xenia*, which refers to an alien, or foreigner or guest status.

Royal characteristics [*ginnunei malkhut*] – גִּנּוּנֵי מַלְכוּת: According to Rashi, this word is similar to the word color [*gavan*] and it is borrowed here to refer to a behavior or a mannerism of royalty. In *Arukh* the text reads *ginisi*, which is apparently derived from the Greek γένεσις, *genesis*, meaning origin or source. In this Gemara it means that Pharaoh saw signs that Joseph came from royal lineage.

NOTES

Muppim – מֻפִּים: The meaning of this name is not explained here. Rashi quotes the *Midrash Tanḥuma*, which explains that Joseph studied from the mouth [*mippeh*] of Jacob the same way Jacob himself studied from his teachers. A similar interpretation is found in *Bereshit Rabba*, where it is also explained that the name Muppim is derived from the word beauty [*yofi*]. The explanation of *Targum Yonatan* is that Joseph was sold to Muf, another name for Egypt.

Seventy languages – שִׁבְעִים לָשׁוֹן: It appears from here that Hebrew is not counted as one of the seventy languages, and that the Jewish people are accordingly not counted as one of the seventy nations (*Tosefot HaRash*; *Tosefot HaRosh*).

כִּי אֲמַר לֵיהּ: ״אָבִי הִשְׁבִּיעַנִי לֵאמֹר״, אֲמַר לֵיהּ: זִיל אִיתַּשִׁיל אַשְׁבּוּעֲתָךְ. אֲמַר לֵיהּ: וְאִיתְשְׁלִי נַמִּי אַדִּידָךְ! וְאַף עַל גַּב דְּלָא נִיחָא לֵיהּ, אֲמַר לֵיהּ: ״עֲלֵה וּקְבֹר אֶת אָבִיךָ כַּאֲשֶׁר הִשְׁבִּיעֶךָ״.

Years later, **when** Joseph **said to** Pharaoh: **"My father made me swear, saying"** (Genesis 50:5) that I would bury him in Eretz Yisrael, Pharaoh **said to him: Go request** the dissolution **of your oath.** Joseph **said to him: And should I also request** dissolution **for** the oath that I took **for your** benefit? **And** consequently, **even though** Pharaoh **was not amenable** to letting Joseph go, he worried that Joseph would then request dissolution for the oath that he had taken for his benefit, and Pharaoh therefore **said to him: "Go up and bury your father according to what he made you swear"** (Genesis 50:6).

יְהוּדָה מַאי הִיא? דְּתַנְיָא, הָיָה רַבִּי מֵאִיר אוֹמֵר: כְּשֶׁעָמְדוּ יִשְׂרָאֵל עַל הַיָּם, הָיוּ שְׁבָטִים מְנַצְּחִים זֶה עִם זֶה, זֶה אוֹמֵר ״אֲנִי יוֹרֵד תְּחִלָּה לַיָּם״ וְזֶה אוֹמֵר ״אֲנִי יוֹרֵד תְּחִלָּה לַיָּם״. קָפַץ

§ **What** was the incident where **Judah** sanctified God's name in public? **As it is taught** in a *baraita* that **Rabbi Meir would say: When the Jewish people stood at the** Red **Sea, the tribes were arguing with one other. This one was saying: I am going into the sea first, and that one was saying: I am going into the sea first.** Then, in **jumped**

Perek **VII**
Daf **37** Amud **a**

NOTES

Tradition – קַבָּלָה: The term tradition, or the texts of tradition, refers to the Prophets and Writings sections of the Bible, as opposed to the Torah. Some explain that the term tradition is used to refer to matters whose status and sanctity are derived from oral tradition and not from the written Torah. Others explain that the statements of the Prophets are called tradition, *kabbala*, from the word *kevila*, meaning rebuke.

שִׁבְטוֹ שֶׁל בִּנְיָמִין וְיָרַד לַיָּם תְּחִילָּה, שֶׁנֶּאֱמַר: ״שָׁם בִּנְיָמִין צָעִיר רֹדֵם״. אַל תִּקְרֵי ״רֹדֵם״ אֶלָּא ״רֵד יָם״. וְהָיוּ שָׂרֵי יְהוּדָה רוֹגְמִים אוֹתָם, שֶׁנֶּאֱמַר: ״שָׂרֵי יְהוּדָה רִגְמָתָם״.

the tribe of Benjamin and descended into the sea first, as it is stated: **"There is Benjamin, the youngest, ruling them [*rodem*]"** (Psalms 68:28). **Do not read** it as: **"Ruling them [*rodem*]"; rather,** read it as: **Descending [*red*]** into the **sea [*yam*]. And the princes of** the tribe of **Judah were stoning them [*rogmim otam*]** for plunging in first and not in the proper order, **as it is stated** in the continuation of the verse: **"The princes of Judah, their council [*rigmatam*]"** (Psalms 68:28).

לְפִיכָךְ זָכָה בִּנְיָמִין הַצַּדִּיק וְנַעֲשָׂה אוּשְׁפִּיזְכָן לַגְּבוּרָה, שֶׁנֶּאֱמַר: ״וּבֵין כְּתֵפָיו שָׁכֵן״.

Therefore, Benjamin the righteous was privileged to serve as host to the Divine Presence of **the Almighty,** as the Temple was built in the territory of Benjamin, **as it is stated** in Moses' blessing for the tribe of Benjamin: "The beloved of the Lord shall dwell in safety by Him; He covers him all the day, **and He rests between his shoulders"** (Deuteronomy 33:12).

אָמַר לוֹ רַבִּי יְהוּדָה: לֹא כָּךְ הָיָה מַעֲשֶׂה, אֶלָּא זֶה אוֹמֵר ״אֵין אֲנִי יוֹרֵד תְּחִילָּה לַיָּם״ וְזֶה אוֹמֵר ״אֵין אֲנִי יוֹרֵד תְּחִילָּה לַיָּם״. קָפַץ נַחְשׁוֹן בֶּן עַמִּינָדָב וְיָרַד לַיָּם תְּחִילָּה, שֶׁנֶּאֱמַר: ״סְבָבֻנִי בְכַחַשׁ אֶפְרַיִם וּבְמִרְמָה בֵּית יִשְׂרָאֵל וִיהוּדָה עֹד רָד עִם אֵל״.

Rabbi Yehuda said to Rabbi Meir: **That is not how the incident** took place. **Rather, this tribe said: I am not going into the sea first, and that** tribe **said: I am not going into the sea first.** Then, in **jumped** the prince of Judah, **Nahshon ben Amminadab, and descended into the sea first,** accompanied by his entire tribe, **as it is stated: "Ephraim surrounds Me with lies and the house of Israel with deceit, and Judah is yet wayward toward God [*rad im El*]"** (Hosea 12:1), which is interpreted homiletically as: And Judah descended [*rad*] with God [*im El*].

וְעָלָיו מְפָרֵשׁ בַּקַּבָּלָה: ״הוֹשִׁיעֵנִי אֱלֹהִים כִּי בָאוּ מַיִם עַד נָפֶשׁ, טָבַעְתִּי בִּיוֵן מְצוּלָה וְאֵין מָעֳמָד וגו׳ אַל תִּשְׁטְפֵנִי שִׁבֹּלֶת מַיִם וְאַל תִּבְלָעֵנִי מְצוּלָה״ וגו׳.

And in this regard, the tradition,[N] i.e., the Writings, **explicates** Nahshon's prayer at that moment: **"Save me, God; for the waters are come in even unto the soul. I am sunk in deep mire, where there is no standing…let not the water flood overwhelm me, neither let the deep swallow me up"** (Psalms 69:2–3, 16).

בְּאוֹתָהּ שָׁעָה הָיָה מֹשֶׁה מַאֲרִיךְ בִּתְפִלָּה. אָמַר לוֹ הַקָּדוֹשׁ בָּרוּךְ הוּא: יְדִידַיי טוֹבְעִים בַּיָּם, וְאַתָּה מַאֲרִיךְ בִּתְפִלָּה לְפָנַי? אָמַר לְפָנָיו: רִבּוֹנוֹ שֶׁל עוֹלָם, וּמַה בְּיָדִי לַעֲשׂוֹת? אָמַר לוֹ: ״דַּבֵּר אֶל בְּנֵי יִשְׂרָאֵל וְיִסָּעוּ, וְאַתָּה הָרֵם אֶת מַטְּךָ וּנְטֵה אֶת יָדְךָ״ וגו׳.

At that time, Moses was prolonging his **prayer. The Holy One, Blessed be He, said to him: My beloved ones are drowning in the sea and you prolong your prayer to me?** Moses said **before Him: Master of the Universe, but what can I do?** God **said to him: "Speak to the children of Israel that they go forward. And you, lift up your rod and stretch out your hand"** (Exodus 14:15–16).

לְפִיכָךְ זָכָה יְהוּדָה לַעֲשׂוֹת מֶמְשָׁלָה בְּיִשְׂרָאֵל, שֶׁנֶּאֱמַר: ״הָיְתָה יְהוּדָה לְקָדְשׁוֹ יִשְׂרָאֵל מַמְשְׁלוֹתָיו״. מַה טַּעַם ״הָיְתָה יְהוּדָה לְקָדְשׁוֹ״ וְ״יִשְׂרָאֵל מַמְשְׁלוֹתָיו״? מִשּׁוּם דְּ״הַיָּם רָאָה וַיָּנֹס״.

For this reason, because Nahshon and the tribe of Judah went into the sea first, the tribe of **Judah merited to govern Israel, as it is stated: "Judah became His sanctuary, Israel His dominion.** The sea saw it and fled" (Psalms 114:2–3). The *baraita* interprets the verses in this manner: **What is the reason** that **Judah became His sanctuary** and **Israel** came under **His dominion?** It is **because "the sea saw it and fled."**

תַּנְיָא, רַבִּי אֱלִיעֶזֶר בֶּן יַעֲקֹב אוֹמֵר: אִי אֶפְשָׁר לוֹמַר לֵוִי לְמַטָּה, שֶׁכְּבָר נֶאֱמַר "לְמַעְלָה", וְאִי אֶפְשָׁר לוֹמַר "לְמַעְלָה", שֶׁכְּבָר נֶאֱמַר "לְמַטָּה".

§ The Gemara returns to discussing the blessing and curses. **It is taught** in a *baraita* (*Tosefta* 8:9) that **Rabbi Eliezer ben Ya'akov says: It is impossible to say** that the tribe of **Levi** stood **below,**[N] between the two mountains, **as it is already stated** that they were **above,** in the verse: "These shall stand on Mount Gerizim to bless the people when you have passed over the Jordan: Simeon and Levi and Judah" (Deuteronomy 27:12). **And it is impossible to say** that they stood **above** on the mountain **because it is already stated:** "And all of Israel, and their elders and officers, and their judges, stood on this side of the Ark and on that side before the priests the Levites" (Joshua 8:33). This shows that the Levites stood **below,** between the mountains, with the Ark.

הָא כֵּיצַד? זִקְנֵי כְהוּנָּה וּלְוִיָּה לְמַטָּה, וְהַשְּׁאָר לְמַעְלָה; רַבִּי יֹאשִׁיָּה אוֹמֵר: כָּל הָרָאוּי לְשָׁרֵת – לְמַטָּה, וְהַשְּׁאָר לְמַעְלָה.

How is this possible? Only **the Elders of the priesthood and the Levites** stood **below, and the rest** of the Levites stood **above** on the mountain. **Rabbi Yoshiya says: Any** Levite **who was fit to serve** in the Temple stood **below,** between the mountains, **and the rest** of the tribe, who were too young or too old to serve in the Temple, stood **above** on the mountain.

רַבִּי אוֹמֵר: אֵלּוּ וְאֵלּוּ לְמַטָּה הֵן עוֹמְדִים. הָפְכוּ פְּנֵיהֶם כְּלַפֵּי הַר גְּרִיזִים – וּפָתְחוּ בִּבְרָכָה, כְּלַפֵּי הַר עֵיבָל – וּפָתְחוּ בִּקְלָלָה. מַאי "עַל"? "עַל" – בְּסָמוּךְ,

Rabbi Yehuda HaNasi **says: Both** the Levites **and** the Israelites **were standing below. They turned to face Mount Gerizim and opened with a blessing,** and then they turned **toward Mount Ebal and opened with a curse.** Therefore, **what** is the meaning of the verse: "These shall stand **on** [*al*] Mount Gerizim to bless the people" (Deuteronomy 27:12)? **"*Al*"** means **adjacent to** the mountain but not actually on the mountain itself.

כִּדְתַנְיָא: "וְנָתַתָּ עַל הַמַּעֲרֶכֶת לְבוֹנָה זַכָּה" – רַבִּי אוֹמֵר: "עַל" – בְּסָמוּךְ. אַתָּה אוֹמֵר: "עַל" בְּסָמוּךְ, אוֹ אֵינוֹ אֶלָּא "עַל" מַמָּשׁ? כְּשֶׁהוּא אוֹמֵר: "וְסַכֹּתָ עַל הָאָרֹן", הֱוֵי אוֹמֵר: "עַל" – בְּסָמוּךְ.

As it is taught in a *baraita* that discusses the shewbread: **"And you shall put pure frankincense on** [*al*] **each row"** (Leviticus 24:7). **Rabbi** Yehuda HaNasi **says: "*Al*"** in this instance means **adjacent to.** Do **you say** that **"*al*"** means **adjacent to, or** perhaps it carries **only** its **literal** meaning of **"on"? When it says** in the verse: **"And you shall screen the Ark** [*al haAron*] with the curtain" (Exodus 40:3), the word "*al*" cannot mean on, as the curtain that separated the Sanctuary and the Holy of Holies was not placed on top of the Ark, but near it. Therefore, **you must say** that **"*al*"** means **adjacent to.**

"הָפְכוּ פְּנֵיהֶם כְּלַפֵּי הַר גְּרִיזִים וּפָתְחוּ בִּבְרָכָה" כו׳. תָּנוּ רַבָּנַן: בָּרוּךְ בִּכְלָל בָּרוּךְ בִּפְרָט, אָרוּר בִּכְלָל אָרוּר בִּפְרָט. לִלְמוֹד וּלְלַמֵּד לִשְׁמוֹר וְלַעֲשׂוֹת – הֲרֵי

§ It is stated in the mishna: **They turned to face Mount Gerizim and opened with a blessing:** Blessed be the man who does not make a graven or molten image (see Deuteronomy 27:15), and these people and those people, i.e., the two groups standing on either mountain, answered: Amen. Then they turned to face Mount Ebal and opened with the curse: "Cursed be the man who makes a graven or molten image" (Deuteronomy 27:15), and these people and those people answered: Amen. **The Sages taught** (*Tosefta* 8:10): The blessings and curses include **a general blessing** for one who fulfills the entire Torah, and **a particular blessing** for each individual statement mentioned in the blessings and curses. Likewise, there is **a general curse** for one who does not fulfill the entire Torah and **a particular curse** for each individual statement. And for each of the blessings and curses there is a mitzva **to learn and to teach,** and **to keep and to perform.**[N] **Consequently,**

NOTES

Levi stood below – לֵוִי לְמַטָּה: *Tosafot* quote an opinion found in the Jerusalem Talmud that like all the other tribes, the entire tribe of Levi stood at the top of the mountain. When the book of Joshua states that "the priests, the Levites" were standing near the Ark, it refers specifically to the priests, who are referred to in many places as the Levites.

To keep and to perform – לִשְׁמוֹר וְלַעֲשׂוֹת: Usually the term to keep means to be careful not to violate prohibitions, and to perform means to fulfill positive mitzvot. The Maharsha explains, based on the calculations stated in the continuation of the Gemara, that that cannot be the meaning here. He therefore explains the term to keep as referring to studying Mishna, in accordance with the Sages' interpretation of the term. In other words, one must strive not only to study the Torah, but also to remember it, or to keep it, through the study of Mishna. In *Iyyun Ya'akov* this expression is interpreted according to the Gemara in tractate *Eiruvin* (96a), which states concerning a similar phrase that when it is stated with regard to a positive mitzva, it is itself considered a positive mitzva, and when it is stated with regard to a prohibition, it is likewise considered a prohibition. Accordingly, to keep the mitzvot means to be extra careful and exacting in fulfilling the mitzvot, whether negative or positive.

אַרְבַּע. אַרְבַּע וְאַרְבַּע הֲרֵי שְׁמוֹנֶה. שְׁמוֹנֶה וּשְׁמוֹנֶה הֲרֵי שֵׁשׁ עֶשְׂרֵה. וְכֵן בְּסִינַי, וְכֵן בְּעַרְבוֹת מוֹאָב, שֶׁנֶּאֱמַר: ״אֵלֶּה דִבְרֵי הַבְּרִית אֲשֶׁר צִוָּה ה׳ אֶת מֹשֶׁה״ וגו׳, וּכְתִיב: ״וּשְׁמַרְתֶּם אֶת דִּבְרֵי הַבְּרִית הַזֹּאת״ וגו׳. נִמְצָא אַרְבָּעִים וּשְׁמוֹנֶה בְּרִיתוֹת עַל כָּל מִצְוָה וּמִצְוָה.

every mitzva contains **four** aspects. **Four** general aspects **and four** specific aspects add up to **eight. Eight** blessings **and eight**[N] curses add up to **sixteen. And so too at** Mount **Sinai, and so too at the plains of Moab, as it is stated: "These are the words of the covenant that the Lord commanded Moses** to make with the children of Israel in the land of Moab, besides the covenant that He made with them in Horeb" (Deuteronomy 28:69). **And it is written: "Observe therefore the words of this covenant"** (Deuteronomy 29:8). **It follows** that between the three events where sixteen covenants were made, God established **forty-eight covenants for each and every mitzva.**

רַבִּי שִׁמְעוֹן מוֹצִיא הַר גְּרִיזִים וְהַר עֵיבָל, וּמַכְנִיס אֹהֶל מוֹעֵד שֶׁבַּמִּדְבָּר.

Rabbi Shimon excludes Mount Gerizim and Mount Ebal from this list because only some of the mitzvot were mentioned there, **and he includes** instead the covenant at **the Tent of Meeting in the desert.**

וּבִפְלוּגְתָּא דְּהָנֵי תַּנָּאֵי; דְּתַנְיָא, רַבִּי יִשְׁמָעֵאל אוֹמֵר: כְּלָלוֹת נֶאֶמְרוּ בְּסִינַי וּפְרָטוֹת בְּאֹהֶל מוֹעֵד; רַבִּי עֲקִיבָא אוֹמֵר: כְּלָלוֹת וּפְרָטוֹת נֶאֶמְרוּ בְּסִינַי, וְנִשְׁנוּ בְּאֹהֶל מוֹעֵד, וְנִשְׁתַּלְּשׁוּ בְּעַרְבוֹת מוֹאָב,

The Gemara explains: **And** it is **in the dispute** between **these** ***tanna'im*** that they disagree, **as it is taught** in a *baraita* (*Tosefta* 8:11): **Rabbi Yishmael says: General statements were said at Sinai,** i.e., Moses received general mitzvot at Sinai, including the Ten Commandments. **And** the **details** of the mitzvot were explained to Moses at a later time **in the Tent of Meeting. Rabbi Akiva says:** Both **general statements and** the **details** of mitzvot **were said at Sinai, and** later **repeated in the Tent of Meeting, and** reiterated **a third time** by Moses to the Jewish people **in the plains of Moab.** Rabbi Shimon holds in accordance with his teacher, Rabbi Akiva, and counts Mount Sinai and the Tent of Meeting Tent as two distinct places where all of the mitzvot were given.

וְאֵין לְךָ כָּל דְּבַר מִצְוָה וּמִצְוָה שֶׁכְּתוּבָה בַּתּוֹרָה, שֶׁלֹּא נִכְרְתוּ עָלֶיהָ אַרְבָּעִים וּשְׁמֹנֶה בְּרִיתוֹת.

The *baraita* concludes: **And there is no mitzva written in the Torah for which forty-eight covenants were not established.**

רַבִּי שִׁמְעוֹן בֶּן יְהוּדָה אִישׁ כְּפַר עַכּוֹ אָמַר מִשּׁוּם רַבִּי שִׁמְעוֹן: אֵין לְךָ מִצְוָה וּמִצְוָה שֶׁכְּתוּבָה בַּתּוֹרָה, שֶׁלֹּא נִכְרְתוּ עָלֶיהָ אַרְבָּעִים וּשְׁמֹנֶה בְּרִיתוֹת שֶׁל שֵׁשׁ מֵאוֹת אֶלֶף וּשְׁלֹשֶׁת אֲלָפִים וַחֲמֵשׁ מֵאוֹת וַחֲמִשִּׁים.

Rabbi Shimon ben Yehuda Ish Kefar Akko said in the name of Rabbi Shimon: There is no mitzva written in the Torah for which forty-eight covenants were not established 603,550 times, corresponding to the population of the Jewish people in the desert. This is because each member of the Jewish people received the covenant both for himself and as a guarantor for the rest of the Jewish people.

אָמַר רַבִּי: לְדִבְרֵי רַבִּי שִׁמְעוֹן בֶּן יְהוּדָה אִישׁ כְּפַר עַכּוֹ, שֶׁאָמַר מִשּׁוּם רַבִּי שִׁמְעוֹן: אֵין לְךָ כָּל מִצְוָה וּמִצְוָה שֶׁבַּתּוֹרָה, שֶׁלֹּא נִכְרְתוּ עָלֶיהָ אַרְבָּעִים וּשְׁמֹנֶה בְּרִיתוֹת שֶׁל שֵׁשׁ מֵאוֹת אֶלֶף וּשְׁלֹשֶׁת אֲלָפִים וַחֲמֵשׁ מֵאוֹת וַחֲמִשִּׁים. נִמְצָא לְכָל אֶחָד וְאֶחָד מִיִּשְׂרָאֵל שֵׁשׁ מֵאוֹת אֶלֶף וּשְׁלֹשֶׁת אֲלָפִים וַחֲמֵשׁ מֵאוֹת וַחֲמִשִּׁים.

Rabbi Yehuda HaNasi **says: According to the statement of Rabbi Shimon ben Yehuda Ish Kefar Akko, who spoke in the name of Rabbi Shimon, there is no mitzva in the Torah for which forty-eight covenants were not established 603,550 times; it follows** that **for every one of the Jewish people** there were **603,550** covenants.

NOTES

Eight and eight – שְׁמוֹנֶה וּשְׁמוֹנֶה: Rashi explains that the first eight are the four aspects of the covenant, i.e., the general and particular blessings and curses, as they relate to learning and teaching the Torah; and the second eight are those four aspects as they relate to keeping and performing the Torah. The Maharsha questions why this would be a logical way to divide the total into two groups of eight, as opposed to one group of sixteen. He therefore explains that the first eight are the general and particular blessings as they relate to learning, teaching, keeping, and performing the Torah; and the second eight are the general and particular curses as they relate to the lack of fulfillment of the same (see *Iyyun Ya'akov*).

מַאי בֵּינַיְיהוּ? אֲמַר רַב מְשַׁרְשְׁיָא: עָרְבָא וְעָרְבָא דְּעָרְבָא אִיכָּא בֵּינַיְיהוּ.

The Gemara asks: **What is** the difference **between** the statements of Rabbi Shimon ben Yehuda Ish Kefar Akko and Rabbi Yehuda HaNasi? What does the statement of Rabbi Yehuda HaNasi add? **Rav Mesharshiyya said:** The matter of **a guarantor and a guarantor for a guarantor** is the difference **between them.** According to Rabbi Yehuda HaNasi, every Jew is not only rendered a guarantor for every other Jew, but he is also rendered a guarantor for every other Jew's responsibility as a guarantor. Therefore, according to his calculation, the number of covenants is multiplied again by 603,550.

דָּרַשׁ רַבִּי יְהוּדָה בֶּן נַחְמָנִי מְתוּרְגְּמָנֵיהּ דְּרַבִּי שִׁמְעוֹן בֶּן לָקִישׁ, כָּל הַפָּרָשָׁה כּוּלָּהּ לֹא נֶאֶמְרָה אֶלָּא בְּנוֹאֵף וְנוֹאֶפֶת:

§ **Rabbi Yehuda ben Naḥmani, the disseminator**[B] **of Rabbi Shimon ben Lakish, taught: The entire passage**[N] of the blessings and curses **is stated only** in reference **to an adulterer and adulteress.**

״אָרוּר הָאִישׁ אֲשֶׁר יַעֲשֶׂה פֶסֶל וּמַסֵּכָה״ וגו׳ – בְּ״אָרוּר״ סַגִּי לֵיהּ? אֶלָּא, זֶה הַבָּא עַל הָעֶרְוָה וְהוֹלִיד בֵּן, וְהָלַךְ לְבֵין אוּמּוֹת הָעוֹלָם וְעָבַד עֲבוֹדָה זָרָה, אֲרוּרִין אָבִיו וְאִמּוֹ שֶׁל זֶה שֶׁכָּךְ גָּרְמוּ לוֹ.

This is proved from the verse: **"Cursed is the man who makes a graven or molten image"** (Deuteronomy 27:15). **Is a curse a sufficient** consequence **for** the actions of an idol worshipper?[N] He has rebelled against the fundamental tenet of the Torah. **Rather, this** is referring to **one who engaged in sexual intercourse with a forbidden relative and bore** her a *mamzer* **son. And** the son, who is not allowed to marry a Jew of unflawed lineage, **went** to live **among the** other **nations of the world and engaged in idol worship. His father and mother are cursed for causing him** to worship idols. Likewise, the rest of the curses refer to sins that are the result of adultery.

תָּנוּ רַבָּנַן: ״וְנָתַתָּה אֶת הַבְּרָכָה עַל הַר גְּרִזִים וְאֶת הַקְּלָלָה״ וגו׳ – מַה תַּלְמוּד לוֹמַר? אִם לְלַמֵּד שֶׁתְּהֵא בְּרָכָה עַל הַר גְּרִזִים וּקְלָלָה עַל הַר עֵיבָל, הֲרֵי כְּבָר נֶאֱמַר: ״אֵלֶּה יַעַמְדוּ לְבָרֵךְ אֶת הָעָם עַל הַר גְּרִזִים״, וּכְתִיב: ״וְאֵלֶּה יַעַמְדוּ עַל הַקְּלָלָה בְּהַר עֵיבָל״! אֶלָּא לְהַקְדִּים בְּרָכָה לִקְלָלָה.

The Sages taught: "And you shall give the blessing on Mount Gerizim and the curse on Mount Ebal" (Deuteronomy 11:29). **Why** must **the verse state** this? **If** it is **to teach that the blessing must be** given **on Mount Gerizim and the curse on Mount Ebal, it is already stated: "These shall stand on Mount Gerizim to bless the people"** (Deuteronomy 27:12), **and it is written: "And these shall stand on Mount Ebal for the curse"** (Deuteronomy 27:13). **Rather,** the verse teaches that the proclamation of the **blessing must precede** the curse.

יָכוֹל יִהְיוּ כָּל הַבְּרָכוֹת קוֹדְמוֹת לַקְּלָלוֹת? תַּלְמוּד לוֹמַר: ״בְּרָכָה וּקְלָלָה״, בְּרָכָה אַחַת קוֹדֶמֶת לִקְלָלָה, וְאֵין כָּל הַבְּרָכוֹת קוֹדְמוֹת לַקְּלָלוֹת;

One **might** have thought that **all of the blessings** should **precede the curses.** Therefore, **the verse states "blessing" and "curse"** in the singular, to teach that **one blessing precedes** each **curse, but all of the blessings do not precede the curses.** The blessings and curses were recited alternately, first one blessing and then one curse.

וּלְהַקִּישׁ בְּרָכָה לִקְלָלָה, לוֹמַר לָךְ: מַה קְּלָלָה בַּלְוִיִּם אַף בְּרָכָה בַּלְוִיִּם, וּמַה קְּלָלָה בְּקוֹל רָם אַף בְּרָכָה בְּקוֹל רָם. וּמַה קְּלָלָה בִּלְשׁוֹן הַקּוֹדֶשׁ אַף בְּרָכָה בִּלְשׁוֹן הַקּוֹדֶשׁ. וּמַה קְּלָלָה בִּכְלָל וּפְרָט אַף בְּרָכָה בִּכְלָל וּפְרָט. וּמַה קְּלָלָה – אֵלּוּ וְאֵלּוּ עוֹנִין וְאוֹמְרִים ״אָמֵן״, אַף בְּרָכָה – אֵלּוּ וְאֵלּוּ עוֹנִין וְאוֹמְרִים ״אָמֵן״.

And furthermore, the verse comes **to juxtapose** the **blessing with the curse, to say to you** that **just as** the **curse** is recited **by** the **Levites, so too,** the **blessing** is uttered **by the Levites; and just as** the **curse** is proclaimed **loudly, so too,** the **blessing** is proclaimed **loudly; and just as** the **curse** is proclaimed **in the sacred tongue,** Hebrew, **so too,** the **blessing** is proclaimed **in the sacred tongue; and just as** the **curse** is proclaimed both **in general and in detail, so too,** the **blessing is** proclaimed **in general and in detail. And just as** after the **curse** is uttered, **both** groups of people on each mountain **respond and say amen, so too,** after the **blessing** is uttered, **both** groups **respond and say amen.**

מתני׳ בִּרְכַּת כֹּהֲנִים כֵּיצַד? בַּמְּדִינָה אוֹמֵר אוֹתָהּ שָׁלֹשׁ בְּרָכוֹת, וּבַמִּקְדָּשׁ – בְּרָכָה אַחַת; בַּמִּקְדָּשׁ אוֹמֵר אֶת הַשֵּׁם

MISHNA **How is the Priestly Benediction** recited? **In the country,** i.e., outside the Temple, the priest **recites** the verses as **three blessings,**[H] pausing between each verse while the people respond amen. **And in the Temple,** the priests recite all three verses as **one blessing,**[H] after which the people respond: Blessed be the Lord, God, the God of Israel, from eternity to eternity, as is the customary response to blessings in the Temple. **In the Temple,** the priest **utters the name of** God

BACKGROUND

The disseminator [*meturgeman*] – מְתוּרְגְּמָנֵיהּ: During talmudic times, it was common for the Sage to present his teachings quietly, oftentimes in Hebrew. The disseminator would translate [*tirgem*] and explain the teachings in Aramaic in an audible voice, so that the students would be able to listen and understand.

NOTES

The entire passage, etc. – כָּל הַפָּרָשָׁה כּוּלָּהּ וכו׳: The Maharsha asks: Is it necessary to reinterpret the entire passage of the blessings and curses just because it is difficult to explain a single verse? He suggests a different interpretation of the Gemara, according to which the word passage does not refer to all of the curses, but rather to that verse alone. Because it is separated from the other verses by a space in the Torah scroll, it is considered to be a distinct passage. However, the later commentaries point out that the Gemara's use of the expression: The entire passage, does not fit this interpretation well.

Is a curse a sufficient consequence for the actions of an idol worshipper – בְּאָרוּר סַגִּי לֵיהּ: The Maharsha explains that the Gemara is not saying that because idol worship is punishable by death, it is insufficient to say that someone who worships idols is cursed, as there are other sins mentioned in the curses that are also punishable by death, e.g., adultery.

Rather, the Gemara is saying that idol worship is the most fundamental form of heresy, and it is therefore not sufficient for one who commits this sin to be cursed in this world; he is excluded from life in the World-to-Come too. This is not true in the case of adultery or any of the other sins mentioned in the curses. Although they are grave sins that render one liable to receive the death penalty, the sinner can still have a share in the World-to-Come. This seems to be Rashi's understanding as well.

HALAKHA

In the country the priest recites the verses as three blessings – בַּמְּדִינָה אוֹמֵר אוֹתָהּ שָׁלֹשׁ בְּרָכוֹת: When the priests recite the Priestly Benediction outside of the Temple everyone present responds amen after each of the verses (Rambam *Sefer Ahava, Hilkhot Tefilla UVirkat Kohanim* 14:3; *Shulḥan Arukh, Oraḥ Ḥayyim* 128:13).

And in the Temple the priest recites one blessing – וּבַמִּקְדָּשׁ בְּרָכָה אַחַת: When the Priestly Benediction is recited in the Temple, the people do not respond amen after each verse. Rather, all of the verses are recited as a single blessing, and all of the people respond afterward: Blessed be the Lord, God, the God of Israel from eternity to eternity (Rambam *Sefer Ahava, Hilkhot Tefilla UVirkat Kohanim* 14:9).

בִּכְתָבוֹ, וּבַמְּדִינָה – בְּכִינּוּיוֹ; בַּמְּדִינָה כֹּהֲנִים נוֹשְׂאִים אֶת יְדֵיהֶן כְּנֶגֶד כִּתְפֵיהֶן, וּבַמִּקְדָּשׁ – עַל גַּבֵּי רָאשֵׁיהֶן, חוּץ מִכֹּהֵן גָּדוֹל, שֶׁאֵינוֹ מַגְבִּיהַּ אֶת יָדָיו לְמַעְלָה מִן הַצִּיץ; רַבִּי יְהוּדָה אוֹמֵר: אַף כֹּהֵן גָּדוֹל מַגְבִּיהַּ יָדָיו לְמַעְלָה מִן הַצִּיץ, שֶׁנֶּאֱמַר: ״וַיִּשָּׂא אַהֲרֹן אֶת יָדָו אֶל הָעָם וַיְבָרְכֵם״.

as it is written[H] in the Torah, i.e., the Tetragrammaton, **and in the country** they use **its substitute name** of Lordship. **In the country, the priests lift their hands** so they are **aligned with their shoulders**[H] during the benediction. **And in the Temple** they lift them **above their heads,**[H] **except for the High Priest, who does not lift his hands above the frontplate.**[B] Since the Tetragrammaton is inscribed on it, it is inappropriate for him to lift his hands above it. **Rabbi Yehuda says: Even the High Priest lifts his hands above the frontplate, as it is stated: "And Aaron lifted up his hands**[N] **toward the people and blessed them"** (Leviticus 9:22).

גמ׳ תָּנוּ רַבָּנַן: ״כֹּה תְבָרְכוּ״ – בִּלְשׁוֹן הַקּוֹדֶשׁ. אַתָּה אוֹמֵר: בִּלְשׁוֹן הַקּוֹדֶשׁ, אוֹ אֵינוֹ אֶלָּא בְּכׇל לָשׁוֹן? נֶאֱמַר כָּאן ״כֹּה תְבָרְכוּ״, וְנֶאֱמַר לְהַלָּן: ״אֵלֶּה יַעַמְדוּ לְבָרֵךְ אֶת הָעָם״, מַה לְּהַלָּן בִּלְשׁוֹן הַקּוֹדֶשׁ, אַף כָּאן בִּלְשׁוֹן הַקּוֹדֶשׁ;

GEMARA **The Sages taught:** The mitzva given to the priests: **"So you shall bless** the children of Israel" (Numbers 6:23), is that they bless them **in the sacred tongue,**[H] Hebrew. Do **you say** that the benediction must be recited **in the sacred tongue, or** perhaps it may be recited **in any language?** The *baraita* answers: **It is stated here,** with regard to the Priestly Benediction: **"So you shall bless," and it is stated there,** with regard to the blessings and curses: **"These shall stand** on Mount Gerizim **to bless the people"** (Deuteronomy 27:12). There is a verbal analogy between these two usages of the word "bless": **Just as there,** the blessings and curses were recited **in the sacred tongue,** as stated above (33a), **so too here,** the Priestly Benediction is recited **in the sacred tongue.**

רַבִּי יְהוּדָה אוֹמֵר: אֵינוֹ צָרִיךְ, הֲרֵי הוּא אוֹמֵר: ״כֹּה״, עַד שֶׁיֹּאמְרוּ בַּלָּשׁוֹן הַזֶּה.

Rabbi Yehuda says: It is not necessary to derive this from a verbal analogy, as **it says** with regard to the Priestly Benediction: **"Thus,"** which means that it is not recited correctly **unless they recite it in this** exact **language,** as it is written in the Torah.

תַּנְיָא אִידָךְ: ״כֹּה תְבָרְכוּ״ – בַּעֲמִידָה. אַתָּה אוֹמֵר: בַּעֲמִידָה, אוֹ אֵינוֹ אֶלָּא אֲפִילּוּ בִּישִׁיבָה? נֶאֱמַר כָּאן ״כֹּה תְבָרְכוּ״, וְנֶאֱמַר לְהַלָּן ״אֵלֶּה יַעַמְדוּ לְבָרֵךְ״. מַה לְּהַלָּן בַּעֲמִידָה, אַף כָּאן בַּעֲמִידָה;

It is taught in **another** *baraita*: **"So you shall bless,"** means **while standing.**[H] Do **you say** that the benediction must be recited **while standing, or** perhaps it may **even** be recited **while sitting? It is stated here: "So you shall bless," and it is stated there,** with regard to the blessings and curses: **"These shall stand** on Mount Gerizim **to bless."** **Just as there,** the blessing was recited **while standing, so too here,** the priests must recite the Priestly Benediction **while standing.**

רַבִּי נָתָן אוֹמֵר: אֵינוֹ צָרִיךְ, הֲרֵי הוּא אוֹמֵר: ״לְשָׁרְתוֹ וּלְבָרֵךְ בִּשְׁמוֹ״, מַה מְּשָׁרֵת בַּעֲמִידָה, אַף מְבָרֵךְ בַּעֲמִידָה. וּמְשָׁרֵת גּוּפֵיהּ מְנָלַן? דִּכְתִיב: ״לַעֲמֹד לְשָׁרֵת״.

Rabbi Natan says: It is not necessary to derive this from a verbal analogy, as **it says** in the verse: "At that time the Lord separated the tribe of Levi to bear the Ark of the Covenant of the Lord, to stand before the Lord **to minister to Him and to bless in His name"** (Deuteronomy 10:8). **Just as** a priest **performs the** Temple **service while standing,**[HN] **so too, he blesses while standing.** The Gemara asks: **And from where do we** derive that **he performs the service itself** while standing? **As it is written: "To stand to minister** in the name of the Lord" (Deuteronomy 18:5).

HALAKHA

In the Temple the priest utters the name of God as it is written – בַּמִּקְדָּשׁ אוֹמֵר אֶת הַשֵּׁם כִּכְתָבוֹ: When the priests bless the nation in the Temple, they utter the Tetragrammaton as it is written, i.e., *yod, heh, vav, heh*. Outside of the Temple, they use the substitute name of Lordship. After the death of Shimon HaTzaddik, the priests ceased using the Tetragrammaton when blessing the nation, even in the Temple, so that no unworthy person would be taught the name. This is in accordance with the mishna here and the Gemara in tractate *Yoma*, 39b (Rambam *Sefer Ahava, Hilkhot Tefilla UVirkat Kohanim* 14:10–11).

Lift their hands so they are aligned with their shoulders – נוֹשְׂאִים אֶת יְדֵיהֶן כְּנֶגֶד כִּתְפֵיהֶן: When the priests bless the people they must lift their hands to the level of their shoulders. According to the esoterica, the right hand should be lifted slightly higher than the left one (Rambam *Sefer Ahava, Hilkhot Tefilla UVirkat Kohanim* 14:3; *Shulḥan Arukh, Oraḥ Ḥayyim* 128:12).

And in the Temple, above their heads – וּבַמִּקְדָּשׁ עַל גַּבֵּי רָאשֵׁיהֶן: When the priests recite the blessing in the Temple, they lift their hands above their heads, except for the High Priest, who does not lift his hands higher than the frontplate (Rambam *Sefer Ahava, Hilkhot Tefilla UVirkat Kohanim* 14:9).

So you shall bless, in the sacred tongue – כֹּה תְבָרְכוּ בִּלְשׁוֹן הַקּוֹדֶשׁ: The priests may recite the Priestly Benediction only in Hebrew (Rambam *Sefer Ahava, Hilkhot Tefilla UVirkat Kohanim* 14:11; *Shulḥan Arukh, Oraḥ Ḥayyim* 128:14).

So you shall bless, while standing – כֹּה תְבָרְכוּ בַּעֲמִידָה: The priests may recite the Priestly Benediction only while standing (Rambam *Sefer Ahava, Hilkhot Tefilla UVirkat Kohanim* 14:11).

Performs the Temple service while standing – מְשָׁרֵת בַּעֲמִידָה: The Temple service must be performed while standing. Anyone who serves in the Temple while sitting has desecrated the sanctity of the Temple, and his service is invalid (Rambam *Sefer Avoda, Hilkhot Biat HaMikdash* 5:16).

BACKGROUND

Frontplate – צִיץ: The frontplate of the High Priest was a plate of gold on which the words: "Sacred to the Lord" (Exodus 28:36), were engraved. This plate was tied to the forehead of the High Priest, adjacent to where his hairline began.

The frontplate was one of the eight priestly vestments that made up the raiment of the High Priest. It is one of the four vestments that are called the golden vestments. The High Priest would wear all eight vestments the year round, except during part of the Yom Kippur service, when he would wear only the four white vestments that all priests wore.

NOTES

As it is stated: And Aaron lifted up his hands, etc. – שֶׁנֶּאֱמַר וַיִּשָּׂא אַהֲרֹן אֶת יָדָו וכו׳: The mishna seems to imply that Rabbi Yehuda presents a proof from this verse for his opinion that the High Priest does lift his hands above the frontplate, as it is stated that Aaron lifted up his hands when he recited the blessing. However, in *Tosefot Yom Tov* and other commentaries, this understanding is found to be difficult. They explain that the verse is not a continuation of Rabbi Yehuda's statement. Rather, it is a proof for the principal ruling stated in the mishna, that the Priestly Benediction must be recited with lifted hands.

Just as a priest performs the Temple service while standing – מַה מְּשָׁרֵת בַּעֲמִידָה: In *Tosefot HaRash*, *Tosefot HaRosh*, and other commentaries, other possible implications of this comparison between the service in the Temple and the Priestly Benediction are discussed. For example, they discuss whether a priest who became an apostate and then repented is again permitted to recite the benediction, or whether it is prohibited for him to do so just as he is prohibited from performing the Temple service. According to the Rambam, it is apparently prohibited. However, according to other commentaries, since the benediction is recited outside of the Temple, the priest should be allowed to recite it. Others draw a distinction between a priest who had merely become an apostate and one who engaged in idol worship.

תַּנְיָא אִידָךְ: "כֹּה תְבָרְכוּ" – בִּנְשִׂיאוּת כַּפַּיִם. אַתָּה אוֹמֵר: בִּנְשִׂיאוּת כַּפַּיִם, אוֹ אֵינוֹ אֶלָּא שֶׁלֹּא בִּנְשִׂיאוּת כַּפַּיִם? נֶאֱמַר כָּאן "כֹּה תְבָרְכוּ", וְנֶאֱמַר לְהַלָּן: "וַיִּשָּׂא אַהֲרֹן אֶת יָדָו אֶל הָעָם וַיְבָרְכֵם", מַה לְּהַלָּן בִּנְשִׂיאוּת כַּפַּיִם, אַף כָּאן בִּנְשִׂיאוּת כַּפַּיִם.

It is taught in **another** *baraita*: **"So you shall bless"** means **with lifted hands. Do you say** that the priests must recite the benediction **with lifted hands, or** perhaps they may recite it **without lifted hands? It is stated here: "So you shall bless," and it is stated there,** with regard to the dedication of the Tabernacle: **"And Aaron lifted up his hands toward the people and blessed them"** (Leviticus 9:22). **Just as there,** Aaron blessed the nation **with lifted hands, so too here,** the Priestly Benediction is recited **with lifted hands.**

קַשְׁיָא לֵיהּ לְרַבִּי יוֹנָתָן: אִי מַה לְּהַלָּן כֹּהֵן גָּדוֹל וְרֹאשׁ חוֹדֶשׁ וַעֲבוֹדַת צִבּוּר, אַף כָּאן כֹּהֵן גָּדוֹל וְרֹאשׁ חוֹדֶשׁ וַעֲבוֹדַת צִיבּוּר!

This *halakha* was **difficult for Rabbi Yonatan**[N] **to understand: If** this *halakha* is derived from the dedication of the Tabernacle, then why not also say: **Just as there,** the **High Priest** was the one who recited the blessing, **and** it was the **New Moon, and** the offerings that were brought were **a communal service, so too here,** the Priestly Benediction must be recited only by the **High Priest, and** on the **New Moon, and** when performing **a communal service?**

רַבִּי נָתָן אוֹמֵר: אֵינוֹ צָרִיךְ, הֲרֵי הוּא אוֹמֵר: "הוּא וּבָנָיו כָּל הַיָּמִים", מַקִּישׁ בָּנָיו לוֹ, מַה הוּא בִּנְשִׂיאוּת כַּפַּיִם אַף בָּנָיו בִּנְשִׂיאוּת כַּפַּיִם, וּכְתִיב: "כָּל הַיָּמִים", וְאִיתְקַשׁ בְּרָכָה לְשֵׁירוּת.

Rabbi Natan says: It is not necessary to derive from a verbal analogy that the Priestly Benediction is recited with lifted hands, as **it says** with regard to Aaron: "To stand to minister in the name of the Lord, **him and his sons forever"** (Deuteronomy 18:5). In this verse, **his sons are juxtaposed with him. Just as** Aaron recited the Priestly Benediction **with lifted hands, so too, his sons** recite the benediction **with lifted hands. And** furthermore, **it is written "forever,"** which indicates that it is referring not only to special occasions. **And** although the verse is not referring to the Priestly Benediction, the **benediction is juxtaposed to** the Temple **service** in another verse: "To minister to Him and to bless in His name" (Deuteronomy 10:8).

וְתַנְיָא אִידָךְ: "כֹּה תְבָרְכוּ אֶת בְּנֵי יִשְׂרָאֵל" – בְּשֵׁם הַמְפוֹרָשׁ. אַתָּה אוֹמֵר: בְּשֵׁם הַמְפוֹרָשׁ, אוֹ אֵינוֹ אֶלָּא בְּכִינּוּי? תַּלְמוּד לוֹמַר: "וְשָׂמוּ אֶת שְׁמִי", שְׁמִי הַמְיוּחָד לִי;

And it is taught in **another** *baraita*: **"So you shall bless the children of Israel"** means the blessing should be recited **with the ineffable name.** Do **you say** that the Priestly Benediction must be recited **with the ineffable name, or** perhaps **it is** recited **with only the substitute name,** *Adonai*? **The verse states: "So shall they put My name"** (Numbers 6:27), which means **My name that is unique to Me.**

יָכוֹל אַף בַּגְּבוּלִין כֵּן? נֶאֱמַר כָּאן: "וְשָׂמוּ אֶת שְׁמִי", וְנֶאֱמַר לְהַלָּן: "לָשׂוּם אֶת שְׁמוֹ שָׁם", מַה לְּהַלָּן בֵּית הַבְּחִירָה, אַף כָּאן בְּבֵית הַבְּחִירָה.

One **might** have thought that **even in the outlying areas,** outside the Temple, **this** ineffable name is used. **It is stated here,** with regard to the Priestly Benediction: **"So shall they put My name," and it is stated there,** with regard to the place one must sacrifice offerings: "The place that the Lord your God has chosen out of all your tribes **to put His name there"** (Deuteronomy 12:5). The verbal analogy teaches that **just as there,** the expression "to put His name there" is referring to **the Temple, so too here,** the mitzva of "so shall they put My name" applies **in the Temple** and not anywhere else.

רַבִּי יֹאשִׁיָּה אוֹמֵר: אֵינוֹ צָרִיךְ, הֲרֵי הוּא אוֹמֵר: "בְּכָל הַמָּקוֹם אֲשֶׁר אַזְכִּיר אֶת שְׁמִי אָבוֹא אֵלֶיךָ". בְּכָל מָקוֹם סָלְקָא דַּעְתָּךְ? אֶלָּא מִקְרָא זֶה מְסוֹרָס הוּא: בְּכָל מָקוֹם אֲשֶׁר אָבוֹא אֵלֶיךָ וּבֵרַכְתִּיךָ שָׁם אַזְכִּיר אֶת שְׁמִי. וְהֵיכָן אָבוֹא אֵלֶיךָ וּבֵרַכְתִּיךָ? בְּבֵית הַבְּחִירָה, שָׁם אַזְכִּיר אֶת שְׁמִי בְּבֵית הַבְּחִירָה.

Rabbi Yoshiya says: It is not necessary to derive this *halakha* from the verbal analogy, as it can be derived from a verse. **It says** in the verse: **"In every place where I cause My name to be mentioned I will come to you** and bless you" (Exodus 20:20). Does it **enter your mind** that this verse literally means that the Divine Presence will be revealed **everywhere? Rather, this verse** must be interpreted by **transposition.** It must be reordered and read as follows: **In every place where I will come to you and bless you, there I will cause My name to be mentioned.** Rabbi Yoshiya explains that God is stating: **And where will I come to you and bless you? In the Temple.** Therefore, he derives: **There, in the Temple, I will cause My name to be mentioned,** but the ineffable name is not mentioned elsewhere.

תַּנְיָא אִידָךְ: "כֹּה תְבָרְכוּ אֶת בְּנֵי יִשְׂרָאֵל" – אֵין לִי אֶלָּא בְּנֵי יִשְׂרָאֵל, גֵּרִים, נָשִׁים, וַעֲבָדִים מְשׁוּחְרָרִים מִנַּיִן? תַּלְמוּד לוֹמַר: "אָמוֹר לָהֶם", לְכוּלְּהוּ.

It is taught in **another** *baraita*: **"So you shall bless the sons of Israel"** (Numbers 6:23). **I have** derived **only** the *halakha* to bless **the sons of Israel. From where** do I derive the *halakha* of blessing **converts, women, and emancipated slaves? The verse states** immediately afterward: **"You shall say to them,"** meaning **to all** of the Jewish people.

NOTES

This *halakha* was difficult for Rabbi Yonatan – קַשְׁיָא לֵיהּ לְרַבִּי יוֹנָתָן: *Tosafot* explain that this statement is not part of the *baraita*. According to this explanation and according to the *Sifrei*, it seems that Rabbi Natan, who resolves the difficulty, is actually Rabbi Yonatan, who, after raising a difficulty with the source cited in the *baraita*, offers a different source.

HALAKHA

Face-to-face – פָּנִים כְּנֶגֶד פָּנִים: The Priestly Benediction must be delivered face-to-face, with the priests and the people facing each other (Rambam *Sefer Ahava, Hilkhot Tefilla UVirkat Kohanim* 14:11; *Shulḥan Arukh, Oraḥ Ḥayyim* 128:10, 23).

When there are two priests, he calls: Priests – לִשְׁנַיִם קוֹרֵא כֹּהֲנִים: If there are a minimum of two priests, one of the congregants calls out to them: Priests, so that they may begin reciting the Priestly Benediction. The prayer leader himself may do this, and it is not considered an interruption of the prayer. There is a custom for him to raise his voice when he says the word: Priests, in the prayer that is recited prior to the Benediction (Rambam *Sefer Ahava, Hilkhot Tefilla UVirkat Kohanim* 14:8; *Shulḥan Arukh, Oraḥ Ḥayyim* 128:10).

NOTES

Facing the back of the necks – פָּנִים כְּנֶגֶד עוֹרֶף: According to Rashi, this means that the priests face the backs of the congregation. Rabbeinu Ḥananel explains this differently: The congregation faces the backs of the priests, and the priests face the Divine Presence.

But when there is one priest he does not call: Priest – וּלְאֶחָד אֵינוֹ קוֹרֵא כֹּהֵן: An opinion is cited in *Tosefot HaRosh* that this means that when there is only a single priest in the synagogue, he does not transgress by refraining from reciting the benediction. This is dependent on a dispute among the early commentaries over whether a single priest has an obligation to recite the benediction (Rambam; Meiri), or whether the obligation exists only when two priests are present (*Tosafot* on *Menaḥot* 44a).

תַּנְיָא אִידָךְ: ״כֹּה תְבָרְכוּ״ – פָּנִים כְּנֶגֶד פָּנִים. אַתָּה אוֹמֵר: פָּנִים כְּנֶגֶד פָּנִים, אוֹ אֵינוֹ אֶלָּא פָּנִים כְּנֶגֶד עוֹרֶף? תַּלְמוּד לוֹמַר: ״אָמוֹר לָהֶם״, כְּאָדָם הָאוֹמֵר לַחֲבֵירוֹ.

It is taught in **another** ***baraita*****: "So you shall bless,"** means that the priests must recite the Priestly Benediction **face-to-face**[H] with the congregation. Do **you say** that the Benediction must be recited **face-to-face, or** perhaps **it is only** recited with the **faces** of the priests **facing the back of the necks**[N] of the congregation? **The verse states: "You shall say to them,"** face-to-face, **like a person who is talking to another.**

תַּנְיָא אִידָךְ: ״כֹּה תְבָרְכוּ״ – בְּקוֹל רָם, אוֹ אֵינוֹ אֶלָּא בְּלַחַשׁ? תַּלְמוּד לוֹמַר: ״אָמוֹר לָהֶם״, כְּאָדָם שֶׁאוֹמֵר לַחֲבֵירוֹ.

It is taught in **another** ***baraita*****: "So you shall bless"** means that the benediction must be recited **out loud. Or,** perhaps, **is it** recited **only in a whisper? The verse states: "You shall say to them," like a person who is talking to another.**

אָמַר אַבָּיֵי, נְקִטִינַן: לִשְׁנַיִם קוֹרֵא ״כֹּהֲנִים״, וּלְאֶחָד אֵינוֹ קוֹרֵא ״כֹּהֵן״, שֶׁנֶּאֱמַר: ״אָמוֹר לָהֶם״, לִשְׁנַיִם. וְאָמַר רַב חִסְדָּא, נְקִטִינַן: כֹּהֵן קוֹרֵא ״כֹּהֲנִים״, וְאֵין יִשְׂרָאֵל קוֹרֵא ״כֹּהֲנִים״, שֶׁנֶּאֱמַר: ״אָמוֹר לָהֶם״, אֲמִירָה

Abaye said: We have a tradition with regard to the prayer leader calling the priests to recite the Priestly Benediction: When there are **two** priests, **he calls: Priests,**[H] **but** when there is **one** priest **he does not call: Priest,**[N] **as it is stated: "You shall say to them,"** in plural, meaning **to** a minimum of **two** priests. **And Rav Ḥisda said: We have a tradition** that **a priest calls: Priests, but an Israelite does not call: Priests, as it is stated: "You shall say to them,"** which means that the **saying**

Perek **VII**
Daf **38** Amud **b**

NOTES

And the *halakha* is not in accordance with the opinion of Rav Ḥisda – וְלֵית הִלְכְתָא כְּווֹתֵיהּ דְּרַב חִסְדָּא: The *halakha* is in accordance with the opposite opinion stated in the Jerusalem Talmud, which cites Rav Ḥisda in the opposite manner, that it is a mitzva for an Israelite to call up the priests. This is derived from the phrase "say to them," which is interpreted to mean that someone else should call up the priests. For this reason, the Rambam rules that ideally an Israelite should call up the priests.

מִשֶּׁלָּהֶם תְּהֵא. וְהִילְכְתָא כְּווֹתֵיהּ דְּאַבָּיֵי, וְלֵית הִילְכְתָא כְּווֹתֵיהּ דְּרַב חִסְדָּא.

should be from them; one of the priests themselves should call: Priests. The Gemara concludes: **And the *halakha* is in accordance with** the opinion **of Abaye,** that when only one priest is present, the prayer leader does not call: Priest. **And the *halakha* is not in accordance with** the opinion **of Rav Ḥisda,**[NH] as an Israelite may also call: Priests.

(סִימָן: מתאו״ה לברכ״ה דוכ״ן בעבוד״ה כו״ס מכי״ר נהנ״ה בעגל״ה).

§ The Gemara cites **a mnemonic** device for the statements of Rabbi Yehoshua ben Levi: **Desires the benediction, platform, during the service, cup, recognize, derives benefit, from a heifer.**

אָמַר רַבִּי יְהוֹשֻׁעַ בֶּן לֵוִי: מִנַּיִן שֶׁהַקָּדוֹשׁ בָּרוּךְ הוּא מִתְאַוֶּה לְבִרְכַּת כֹּהֲנִים? שֶׁנֶּאֱמַר: ״וְשָׂמוּ אֶת שְׁמִי עַל בְּנֵי יִשְׂרָאֵל וַאֲנִי אֲבָרְכֵם״. וְאָמַר רַבִּי יְהוֹשֻׁעַ בֶּן לֵוִי: כׇּל כֹּהֵן שֶׁמְּבָרֵךְ מִתְבָּרֵךְ, וְשֶׁאֵינוֹ מְבָרֵךְ אֵין מִתְבָּרֵךְ, שֶׁנֶּאֱמַר: ״וַאֲבָרְכָה מְבָרְכֶיךָ״.

Rabbi Yehoshua ben Levi says: From where is it derived **that the Holy One, Blessed be He, desires the Priestly Benediction? As it is stated: "So shall they put My name upon the children of Israel, and I will bless them"** (Numbers 6:27). This shows that God waits for the priests to bless the people, and only then He Himself blesses them. **And Rabbi Yehoshua ben Levi says: Any priest who blesses**[H] the people **is blessed** from Heaven, **and one who does not bless** the people **is not blessed, as it is stated: "And I will bless those who bless you"** (Genesis 12:3).

HALAKHA

And the *halakha* is not in accordance with the opinion of Rav Ḥisda – וְלֵית הִלְכְתָא כְּווֹתֵיהּ דְּרַב חִסְדָּא: The *halakha* is in accordance with the opinion cited in the Jerusalem Talmud that the priests should be called up by an Israelite *ab initio*. If the prayer leader is a priest, then an Israelite should stand next to him and call to the priests instead (Rambam *Sefer Ahava, Hilkhot Tefilla UVirkat Kohanim* 14:8; *Shulḥan Arukh, Oraḥ Ḥayyim* 128:22).

Any priest who blesses, etc. – כׇּל כֹּהֵן שֶׁמְּבָרֵךְ וכו׳: Any priest who does not bless the people of Israel is not blessed in return, and a priest who blesses the people is in turn blessed (Rambam *Sefer Ahava, Hilkhot Tefilla UVirkat Kohanim* 15:12).

וְאָמַר רַבִּי יְהוֹשֻׁעַ בֶּן לֵוִי: כָּל כֹּהֵן שֶׁאֵינוֹ עוֹלֶה לַדּוּכָן, עוֹבֵר בִּשְׁלֹשָׁה עֲשֵׂה: ״כֹּה תְבָרְכוּ״, ״אָמוֹר לָהֶם״, ״וְשָׂמוּ אֶת שְׁמִי״.

And Rabbi Yehoshua ben Levi says: Any priest who does not ascend the platform[H] to recite the Priestly Benediction **violates three positive** mitzvot:[N] **"So you shall bless," "And you shall say to them"** (Numbers 6:23), and **"So shall they put My name"** (Numbers 6:27).

רַב אָמַר: חוֹשְׁשִׁין שֶׁמָּא בֶּן גְּרוּשָׁה אוֹ בֶּן חֲלוּצָה הוּא.

Rav says: One need be **concerned that** a priest who does not ascend to recite the Priestly Benediction **is perhaps the son of** a priest and **a divorced woman, or the son of** a priest and **a** ***yevama*** **who has performed** ***ḥalitza*** [***ḥalutza***]. Perhaps he does not ascend to recite the Priestly Benediction because he is disqualified from the priesthood.

וְלָא פְּלִיגִי: הָא דְּסָלֵיק לִפְרָקִים, הָא דְּלָא סָלֵיק לִפְרָקִים.

The Gemara comments: **And they do not disagree. This** statement of Rabbi Yehoshua ben Levi is referring to a case **where he ascends periodically.** Therefore, there is no reason to believe that he is disqualified from the priesthood, and the assumption is that he violates three positive mitzvot. Whereas **that** statement of Rav is referring to a case **where one does not ascend** to recite the Priestly Benediction even **periodically,** and therefore there is reason to suspect that he is disqualified from the priesthood.

וְאָמַר רַבִּי יְהוֹשֻׁעַ בֶּן לֵוִי: כָּל כֹּהֵן שֶׁאֵינוֹ עוֹלֶה בַּעֲבוֹדָה – שׁוּב אֵינוֹ עוֹלֶה, שֶׁנֶּאֱמַר: ״וַיִּשָּׂא אַהֲרֹן אֶת יָדָיו אֶל הָעָם וַיְבָרְכֵם וַיֵּרֶד מֵעֲשֹׂת הַחַטָּאת וְהָעֹלָה וְהַשְּׁלָמִים״. מָה לְהַלָּן בַּעֲבוֹדָה, אַף כָּאן בַּעֲבוֹדָה.

And Rabbi Yehoshua ben Levi says: Any priest who does not ascend the platform **during** the blessing of **the** Temple **service**[HN] recited in the *Amida* prayer **may no longer ascend** to recite the benediction, **as it is stated: "And Aaron lifted up his hands toward the people and blessed them; and he came down from offering the sin-offering, and the burnt-offering, and the peace-offerings"** (Leviticus 9:22). **Just as there,** in the Tabernacle, Aaron lifted up his hands **during the service,** as evident from the fact that only after he blessed them does it say that he came down from sacrificing the offerings, **so too here,** in the *Amida* prayer, the Priestly Benediction is recited **during** the blessing of Temple **service.**

אִינִי? וְהָא רַבִּי אַמִי וְרַבִּי אַסִי סָלְקִי! רַבִּי אַמִי וְרַבִּי אַסִי מֵעִיקָּרָא הֲווּ עָקְרִי כַּרְעַיְיהוּ, מִמְטָא לָא הֲוָה מָטוּ הָתָם, וּכְדְתָנֵי רַבִּי אוֹשַׁעְיָא: לֹא שָׁנוּ אֶלָּא שֶׁלֹּא עָקַר אֶת רַגְלָיו, אֲבָל עָקַר אֶת רַגְלָיו – עוֹלֶה.

The Gemara asks: **Is that so? But didn't** the priests **Rabbi Ami and Rabbi Asi ascend** after the blessing of the service? The Gemara answers: **Rabbi Ami and Rabbi Asi would begin walking** to the platform during the blessing of the service, but **they would not arrive there** until after the conclusion of this blessing. **And** this is sufficient **in accordance with what Rabbi Oshaya taught: They taught** that a priest may not recite the benediction if he did not ascend the platform during the blessing of Temple service **only** in a case **where he did not begin walking. But if he began walking** before the prayer leader finished the blessing, **he may ascend the platform** even after he has finished the blessing.

וּתְנַן נָמֵי: אִם הַבְטָחָתוֹ שֶׁנּוֹשֵׂא אֶת כַּפָּיו וְחוֹזֵר לִתְפִלָּתוֹ – רַשַּׁאי. וְהָוֵינַן בַּהּ: הָא לָא עָקַר! אֶלָּא דְּנָד פּוּרְתָּא, הָכָא נָמֵי דְּעָקַר פּוּרְתָּא.

And concerning this issue, **we also learned** in a mishna (*Berakhot* 34a): A priest who serves as prayer leader does not recite the Priestly Benediction, but **if he is certain that he can lift his hands**[H] and recite the benediction, **and** then **resume his prayer** without becoming confused, **he is permitted** to do so. **And we discussed it** and raised the following difficulty: If **he did not begin** walking to ascend the platform during the blessing of the service, how is it permitted for him to recite the benediction? **Rather,** it must be explained **that he moved slightly** to show that he also wanted to ascend the platform. **Here too,** the statement of Rabbi Oshaya is referring even to a case **where** the priest **uprooted** himself **slightly** from his place during the blessing of the service.

וְאָמַר רַבִּי יְהוֹשֻׁעַ בֶּן לֵוִי: אֵין נוֹתְנִין כּוֹס שֶׁל בְּרָכָה לְבָרֵךְ אֶלָּא לְטוֹב עַיִן, שֶׁנֶּאֱמַר: ״טוֹב עַיִן הוּא יְבֹרָךְ כִּי נָתַן מִלַּחְמוֹ לַדָּל״. אַל תִּיקְרֵי ״יְבֹרָךְ״ אֶלָּא ״יְבָרֵךְ״.

And Rabbi Yehoshua ben Levi says: One may give a cup of blessing to recite the blessing of Grace after Meals **only to** someone with **a good eye,** i.e., a generous person, **as it is stated: "One who has a good eye will be blessed** [***yevorakh***],[N] **for he gives of his bread to the poor"** (Proverbs 22:9). **Do not read** it: **"Will be blessed." Rather,** read it: **Will bless** [***yevarekh***].

HALAKHA

Any priest who does not ascend the platform – כָּל כֹּהֵן שֶׁאֵינוֹ עוֹלֶה לַדּוּכָן: If a priest is in the synagogue when they call the priests or is told to ascend the platform for the blessing, and if he does not do so when there is no reason why he may not go up to recite the blessing, it is considered as if he had violated three positive mitzvot. The *Mishna Berura* notes that in truth he actually has violated only one positive mitzva (Rambam *Sefer Ahava, Hilkhot Tefilla UVirkat Kohanim* 15:12; *Shulḥan Arukh, Oraḥ Ḥayyim* 128:2).

Any priest who does not ascend during the blessing of the Temple service – כָּל כֹּהֵן שֶׁאֵינוֹ עוֹלֶה בַּעֲבוֹדָה: Any priest who does not begin walking during the blessing of the Temple service in order to ascend to recite the Priestly Benediction may not recite the benediction during that prayer. If he did begin walking, even if he did not arrive at the platform until after the blessing of the Temple service, he may ascend and recite the benediction (Rambam *Sefer Ahava, Hilkhot Tefilla UVirkat Kohanim* 15:11; *Shulḥan Arukh, Oraḥ Ḥayyim* 128:8).

If he is certain that he can lift his hands, etc. – אִם הַבְטָחָתוֹ שֶׁנּוֹשֵׂא כַּפָּיו וכו׳: If the prayer leader is a priest, even if he is the only priest present, he may lift his hands and recite the Priestly Benediction only if he is certain that he can resume his prayer afterward without becoming confused. However, nowadays, as the prayer leader reads from a prayer book, the custom is that he recites the Priestly Benediction along with the other priests (Rambam *Sefer Ahava, Hilkhot Tefilla UVirkat Kohanim* 15:10; *Shulḥan Arukh, Oraḥ Ḥayyim* 128:20).

NOTES

Violates three positive mitzvot – עוֹבֵר בִּשְׁלֹשָׁה עֲשֵׂה: According to the Rambam, this does not mean that a priest who does not recite the Priestly Benediction actually violates three mitzvot. He violates only one mitzva, but the verse ascribes him blame tantamount to the transgression of three prohibitions.

Who does not ascend during the blessing of the Temple service – שֶׁאֵינוֹ עוֹלֶה בַּעֲבוֹדָה: In the Temple, the priests recite the benediction during the actual Temple service. However, in the *Amida* prayer, since the content of the benediction and of the blessing of Temple service are unrelated, the priests recite the benediction only after the blessings of the Temple service and thanksgiving, which are considered one and the same. Furthermore, the verse that states that Aaron blessed the people when he "came down from performing the sin-offering" indicates that the Priestly Benediction is recited after the Temple service (see Jerusalem Talmud *Berakhot* and Rabbi David Luria).

One who has a good eye will be blessed [*yevorakh*] – טוֹב עַיִן הוּא יְבֹרָךְ: This homiletic interpretation is apparently based on the identical spelling of the words *yevorakh*, will be blessed, and *yevarekh*, will bless. The Maharsha explains that one who recites the blessings is himself blessed. Therefore, it is appropriate for a generous person to recite the blessing, so that he will receive more blessing.

The Maharsha adds that the statement that one who is generous should recite the blessing applies to the Priestly Benediction as well, as the benediction should be recited with a generous attitude. For this reason, the blessing that the priests recite before the benediction includes the phrase: To bless His nation Israel with love. While the phrase: With love, is not mentioned in the Torah's description of the benediction, it is included in the blessing that the priests recite before the benediction to emphasize that the priests must deliver the blessing with a generous attitude toward the people.

וְאָמַר רַבִּי יְהוֹשֻׁעַ בֶּן לֵוִי: מִנַּיִן שֶׁאֲפִילּוּ עוֹפוֹת מַכִּירִין בְּצָרֵי הָעַיִן? שֶׁנֶּאֱמַר: ״כִּי חִנָּם מְזֹרָה הָרָשֶׁת בְּעֵינֵי כׇּל בַּעַל כָּנָף״.

And Rabbi Yehoshua ben Levi says: From where is it derived **that even birds recognize miserly** people[N] and do not eat the food they have set in bird traps? **As it is stated: "For in vain the net is spread**[N] **in the eyes of any bird"** (Proverbs 1:17).

וְאָמַר רַבִּי יְהוֹשֻׁעַ בֶּן לֵוִי: כׇּל הַנֶּהֱנֶה מִצָּרֵי הָעַיִן עוֹבֵר בְּלָאו, שֶׁנֶּאֱמַר: ״אַל תִּלְחַם אֶת לֶחֶם רַע עָיִן וגו׳, כִּי כְּמוֹ שָׁעַר בְּנַפְשׁוֹ כֵּן הוּא אֱכוֹל וּשְׁתֵה יֹאמַר לָךְ״ וגו׳. רַב נַחְמָן בַּר יִצְחָק אָמַר: עוֹבֵר בִּשְׁנֵי לָאוִין, ״אַל תִּלְחַם״ ו״אַל תִּתְאָו״.

And Rabbi Yehoshua ben Levi says: Anyone who derives benefit from miserly people transgresses a prohibition, as it is stated: "Do not eat the bread of one who has an evil eye, and do not desire his delicacies, **for as one that has reckoned within himself, so he is. He says to you: Eat and drink,** but his heart is not with you" (Proverbs 23:6–7). **Rav Naḥman bar Yitzḥak says: He transgresses two prohibitions,** as it says **"do not eat"** and also **"do not desire."**

וְאָמַר רַבִּי יְהוֹשֻׁעַ בֶּן לֵוִי: אֵין עֶגְלָה עֲרוּפָה בָּאָה אֶלָּא בִּשְׁבִיל צָרֵי הָעַיִן,

And Rabbi Yehoshua ben Levi says: When a person is found slain between two cities and it is not known who killed him, **a heifer whose neck is broken is brought.** This occurs **only because of miserly people.**

שֶׁנֶּאֱמַר: ״וְעָנוּ וְאָמְרוּ יָדֵינוּ לֹא שָׁפְכוּ אֶת הַדָּם הַזֶּה״. וְכִי עַל לִבֵּנוּ עָלְתָה שֶׁזִּקְנֵי בֵּית דִּין שׁוֹפְכֵי דָמִים הֵם? אֶלָּא, לֹא בָּא לְיָדֵינוּ וּפְטַרְנוּהוּ וְלֹא רְאִינוּהוּ וְהִנַּחְנוּהוּ. לֹא בָּא לְיָדֵינוּ וּפְטַרְנוּהוּ בְּלֹא מְזוֹנוֹת. לֹא רְאִינוּהוּ וְהִנַּחְנוּהוּ בְּלֹא לְוָיָה.

As it is stated: "And they shall speak and say: Our hands have not shed this blood" (Deuteronomy 21:7). **But did it enter our hearts** to think **that the Elders of the court are murderers?** Why it is necessary for them to publicize that they did not kill him? **Rather,** they must declare: It is **not** so that this victim **came to us and we dismissed him, and** it is **not** so that **we saw him and left him.** In other words, **he did not come to us and we** in turn **dismissed him without food,** and **we did not see him and** then **leave him without an escort.** It is miserly people who do not provide others with food and cause them to travel to places where they might be murdered.

אָמַר אַדָּא אָמַר רַבִּי שַׂמְלַאי: בֵּית הַכְּנֶסֶת שֶׁכּוּלָּהּ כֹּהֲנִים, כּוּלָּן עוֹלִין לַדּוּכָן. לְמִי מְבָרְכִין? אָמַר רַבִּי זֵירָא: לַאֲחֵיהֶם שֶׁבַּשָּׂדוֹת.

§ **Adda said** that **Rabbi Samlai says:** In **a synagogue that is** made up **entirely of priests,**[H] **everyone ascends the platform** to recite the Priestly Benediction. The Gemara asks: If the entire congregation is composed of priests, **for whom do they utter the blessing? Rabbi Zeira says:** They say the blessing **for their brethren who are in the fields.**[N]

אִינִי? וְהָתְנֵי אַבָּא בְּרֵיהּ דְּרַב מִנְיָמִין בַּר חִיָּיא: עַם שֶׁאֲחוֹרֵי כֹּהֲנִים אֵינָן בִּכְלַל בְּרָכָה! לָא קַשְׁיָא. הָא דַּאֲנִיסִי, הָא דְּלָא אֲנִיסִי.

The Gemara asks: **Is that so? But didn't Abba, son of Rav Minyamin bar Ḥiyya, teach** that the **people who are** standing **behind** the backs of **the priests**[H] **are not included in the** Priestly **Benediction?** The Gemara answers: That is **not difficult. This** is a case **where** the people **are compelled** to be in the fields because of their work, and they are therefore included in the benediction. Whereas **that** statement is referring to people **who are not compelled** to be away but still do not stand face-to-face with the priests. Consequently, they are not included in the benediction.

וְהָתְנֵי רַב שִׁימִי מִבִּירְתָא דְּשִׁיחוֹרֵי: בֵּית הַכְּנֶסֶת שֶׁכּוּלָּהּ כֹּהֲנִים, מִקְצָתָן עוֹלִין וּמִקְצָתָן עוֹנִין ״אָמֵן״!

The Gemara asks: **But didn't Rav Shimi of Birte deShiḥorei teach** the following *baraita*: In **a synagogue that is** made up **entirely of priests, some of them ascend** to recite the benediction **and some of them answer amen?**

NOTES

Even birds recognize miserly people – אֲפִילּוּ עוֹפוֹת מַכִּירִין בְּצָרֵי הָעַיִן: The Maharsha explains that even though birds do not have the capacity for this awareness, God does not allow them to be trapped in the nets of misers. In addition, he provides a rational explanation of this statement. A generous person will sometimes put out food for birds without intending to trap them. For this reason, the birds come to eat the food that they place in their nets as well. This is not the case with miserly people.

For in vain the net is spread, etc. – כִּי חִנָּם מְזֹרָה הָרָשֶׁת וכו׳: Rashi explains that in context this verse pertains to people who steal, and it is understood that they do so because of their miserly nature. It should be noted that the subsequent verse states: "So are the ways of everyone who is greedy to gain profit; it takes away the life of its owners" (Proverbs 1:19).

For their brethren who are in the fields – לַאֲחֵיהֶם שֶׁבַּשָּׂדוֹת: It is explained in the Jerusalem Talmud (*Berakhot* 5:4), that with regard to their brethren in the fields, it makes no difference whether the people are facing the priests or not. It is also explained there that it is sufficient that the women and children who are in the synagogue answer amen after the priests when there are no other Israelite men present. However, it appears from the Gemara here that if possible, ten priests must answer amen. The later commentaries explain that when there are no people present in the synagogue to be blessed, the benediction is recited only by rabbinic institution (*Peri Megadim*). The reason for this ordinance is possibly so that the mitzva of the Priestly Benediction will not be forgotten in that synagogue (*Devar Shaul*).

HALAKHA

A synagogue that is made up entirely of priests – בֵּית הַכְּנֶסֶת שֶׁכּוּלָּהּ כֹּהֲנִים: In a synagogue that is made up entirely of priests, if there are only ten priests, they all ascend to recite the Priestly Benediction, and they bless their brethren who are working in the fields. If there are women and children in the synagogue, they answer amen after the blessing. If there are more than ten priests present, ten priests remain behind to answer amen, and the rest go up and recite the benediction (Rambam *Sefer Ahava, Hilkhot Tefilla UVirkat Kohanim* 15:9; *Shulḥan Arukh, Oraḥ Ḥayyim* 128:25).

The people who are standing behind the priests – עַם שֶׁאֲחוֹרֵי כֹּהֲנִים: People standing behind the priests are not included in the benediction. However, people standing in front of the priests or at their sides are included, even if there is an iron partition between them. Those who are working in the fields and cannot make it to the synagogue are also included in the benediction (Rambam *Sefer Ahava, Hilkhot Tefilla UVirkat Kohanim* 15:8; *Shulḥan Arukh, Oraḥ Ḥayyim* 128:24).

לָא קַשְׁיָא: הָא דְּאִישְׁתַּיַּיר בֵּי עַשְׂרָה, הָא דְּלָא אִישְׁתַּיַּיר בֵּי עַשְׂרָה.

The Gemara answers: That is **not difficult. That** is a case **where,** if some of the priests recite the benediction, a quorum of **ten** priests still **remains**[N] to receive the benediction and answer amen. Therefore, only some of the priests ascend to recite the benediction. By contrast, **this** case, which Rabbi Simlai was referring to, is a case **where** a quorum of **ten does not remain** to answer amen, so it is better for all of the priests to ascend and bless the people working in the fields.

גּוּפָא, תָּנָא אַבָּא בְּרֵיהּ דְּרַב מִנְיָמִין בַּר חִיָּיא: עַם שֶׁאֲחוֹרֵי כֹהֲנִים אֵינָן בִּכְלַל בְּרָכָה.

The Gemara returns to **the** matter **itself** cited above: **Abba, son of Rav Minyamin bar Ḥiyya, taught:** The **people who are** standing **behind the priests are not included in the benediction.**

פְּשִׁיטָא, אֲרִיכֵי בְּאַפֵּי גּוּצֵי לָא מַפְסְקֵי; תֵּיבָה לָא מַפְסְקָא; מְחִיצָה מַאי? תָּא שְׁמַע, דְּאָמַר רַבִּי יְהוֹשֻׁעַ בֶּן לֵוִי: אֲפִילּוּ מְחִיצָה שֶׁל בַּרְזֶל אֵינָהּ מַפְסֶקֶת בֵּין יִשְׂרָאֵל לַאֲבִיהֶם שֶׁבַּשָּׁמַיִם.

The Gemara raises several questions with regard to this statement: It **is obvious** that **tall people** standing **in front of short people do not interpose** between the priests and the shorter people with regard to the Priestly Benediction. Similarly, **a chest** or ark containing a Torah scroll **does not interpose** between the priests and the people. However, **what** is the *halakha* with regard to **a partition? Come** and **hear** an answer from **what Rabbi Yehoshua ben Levi said: Even an iron partition**[N] **does not interpose between the Jewish people and their Father in Heaven;** the people are included in the benediction.

אִיבַּעְיָא לְהוּ: צְדָדִין, מַהוּ? אָמַר אַבָּא מָר בַּר רַב אָשֵׁי: תָּא שְׁמַע, דִּתְנַן: נִתְכַּוֵּון לְהַזּוֹת לְפָנָיו

A dilemma was raised before the Sages: **What is** the *halakha* in the case of people who are standing to **the sides** of the priests? Are they included in the blessing? **Abba Mar bar Rav Ashi said: Come** and **hear** an answer, **as we learned** in a mishna (*Para* 12:2) with regard to the *halakha* of sprinkling the waters of purification on vessels that contracted ritual impurity imparted by a corpse: If one **intended to sprinkle** the water **forward**

NOTES

Where a quorum of ten remains – דְּאִישְׁתַּיַּיר בֵּי עַשְׂרָה: It appears from here that in addition to the priests who recite the blessing, there must be another ten men present to answer amen. This is also the opinion of the *ge'onim*. However, according to the Rambam, the priests themselves count as part of the quorum of ten. The Meiri points out that according to this opinion there is no need for ten men to answer amen to the blessing (see *Bah*). The Rambam's opinion is perhaps based on the opinion found in the Jerusalem Talmud that the response of the women and children is counted in this situation.

Even an iron partition – אֲפִילּוּ מְחִיצָה שֶׁל בַּרְזֶל: According to *Tosefot HaRash*, Rabbi Yehoshua ben Levi is not addressing whether the partition precludes one from being included in the prayer quorum, as a partition certainly forms a partition in that regard. Rather, he is saying that if there is a quorum in the synagogue, a person standing outside can fulfill his obligation by hearing the benediction being recited inside.

Perek **VII**
Daf **39** Amud **a**

וְהִזָּה לְאַחֲרָיו, לְאַחֲרָיו וְהִזָּה לְפָנָיו – הַזָּאָתוֹ פְּסוּלָה; לְפָנָיו וְהִזָּה עַל צְדָדִין שֶׁבְּפָנָיו – הַזָּאָתוֹ כְּשֵׁרָה.

and instead **he sprinkled** it **backward,**[H] or if he intended to sprinkle the water **backward and** instead **he sprinkled** it **forward,** even if the water lands on vessels that require purification, **his sprinkling is invalid.** However, if one intended to sprinkle the water **forward and** instead **he sprinkled** it **forward to** the **sides,**[N] **his sprinkling is valid.** It is derived from here that one's sides are considered as though they were in front of him.

NOTES

Sides – צְדָדִין: The reason that one's sides are considered like his front is that a person naturally has peripheral vision. Furthermore, according to the principle that the Priestly Benediction must be recited face-to-face, as one would converse with another, standing to the sides of the priests is also permitted, as people sometimes speak to one another while facing each other's sides (see *Devar Shaul*).

HALAKHA

If one intended to sprinkle water forward and instead he sprinkled it backward, etc. – נִתְכַּוֵּון לְהַזּוֹת לְפָנָיו וְהִזָּה לְאַחֲרָיו וכו׳: One who sprinkles the waters of purification must intend to sprinkle it upon the person who is ritually impure in order to purify him. If one sprinkles the water without this intention, his action is invalid. The Ra'avad maintains that one's intention must be to sprinkle that particular person, but there is no requirement that one intend to purify him. If one intended to sprinkle forward and instead he sprinkled backward, or if he intended to sprinkle backward and instead sprinkled forward, his action is invalid. However, if one intended to sprinkle forward and instead he sprinkled the water to the side of where he was facing, his action is valid (Rambam *Sefer Tahara, Hilkhot Para Aduma* 10:7).

אָמַר רָבָא בַּר רַב הוּנָא: כֵּיוָן שֶׁנִּפְתָּח סֵפֶר תּוֹרָה – אָסוּר לְסַפֵּר אֲפִילּוּ בִּדְבַר הֲלָכָה, שֶׁנֶּאֱמַר: ״וּבְפִתְחוֹ עָמְדוּ כָל הָעָם״, וְאֵין עֲמִידָה אֶלָּא שְׁתִיקָה, שֶׁנֶּאֱמַר: ״וְהוֹחַלְתִּי כִּי לֹא יְדַבֵּרוּ כִּי עָמְדוּ לֹא עָנוּ עוֹד״. רַבִּי זֵירָא אֲמַר רַב חִסְדָּא, מֵהָכָא: ״וְאׇזְנֵי כׇל הָעָם אֶל סֵפֶר הַתּוֹרָה״.

§ **Rava bar Rav Huna says: Once a Torah scroll has been opened,**[H] **it is prohibited to converse, even about a matter of** ***halakha*****.**[N] **As it is stated:** "And Ezra opened the book in the sight of all the people, for he was above all the people, **and when he opened it, all the people stood up**" (Nehemiah 8:5), **and standing** is referring to **nothing other** than **silence, as it is stated: "And shall I wait, because they do not speak, because they stand still, and answer no more?"** (Job 32:16). **Rabbi Zeira** said that **Rav Ḥisda said:** The prohibition against conversing is derived **from here: "And the ears of all the people were attentive to the book of the law"** (Nehemiah 8:3). They were not listening to any other voice.

וְאָמַר רַבִּי יְהוֹשֻׁעַ בֶּן לֵוִי: כׇּל כֹּהֵן שֶׁלֹּא נָטַל יָדָיו לֹא יִשָּׂא אֶת כַּפָּיו, שֶׁנֶּאֱמַר: ״שְׂאוּ יְדֵיכֶם קֹדֶשׁ וּבָרְכוּ אֶת ה׳״.

And Rabbi Yehoshua ben Levi says: Any priest who did not first **wash his hands**[H] **may not lift his hands** to recite the Priestly Benediction; **as it is stated: "Lift up** [*se'u*] **your hands in sanctity and bless the Lord"** (Psalms 134:2), which teaches that before reciting the benediction one must sanctify his hands by washing them.

שָׁאֲלוּ תַּלְמִידָיו אֶת רַבִּי אֶלְעָזָר בֶּן שַׁמּוּעַ: בַּמֶּה הֶאֱרַכְתָּ יָמִים? אָמַר לָהֶן: מִיָּמַי לֹא עָשִׂיתִי בֵּית הַכְּנֶסֶת קַפֶּנְדַּרְיָא, וְלֹא פָּסַעְתִּי עַל רָאשֵׁי עַם קוֹדֶשׁ, וְלֹא נָשָׂאתִי כַּפַּי בְּלֹא בְּרָכָה.

§ **Rabbi Elazar ben Shammua was** once **asked by his disciples: To what** do you attribute **your longevity? He said to them: In** all **my days, I never made a shortcut** [*kappendarya*][L] through a **synagogue.**[H] **Nor did I** ever **stride over** the **heads of** the **sacred people,** i.e., I never stepped over people sitting in the study hall in order to reach my place, so as not to appear scornful of them. **And I never lifted my hands** for the Priestly Benediction **without** first reciting **a blessing.**

מַאי מְבָרֵךְ? אָמַר רַבִּי זֵירָא אָמַר רַב חִסְדָּא: ״אֲשֶׁר קִדְּשָׁנוּ בִּקְדוּשָּׁתוֹ שֶׁל אַהֲרֹן וְצִוָּנוּ לְבָרֵךְ אֶת עַמּוֹ יִשְׂרָאֵל בְּאַהֲבָה״.

The Gemara asks: **What blessing** does the priests recite[H] before the benediction? **Rabbi Zeira says that Rav Ḥisda says:** Blessed are You, Lord our God, King of the universe, **Who has sanctified us with the sanctity of Aaron and commanded us to bless His people, Israel, with love.**[N]

NOTES

It is prohibited to converse even about a matter of *halakha* – אָסוּר לְסַפֵּר אֲפִילּוּ בִּדְבַר הֲלָכָה: *Tosafot* and many other early commentaries, later commentaries, and halakhic authorities discuss the apparent contradiction between this *halakha* and the Gemara's story about Rav Sheshet, who would turn away from the Torah scroll and study. He reasoned: We are engaged in ours, the study of the Oral Torah, and they are engaged in theirs, listening to the Written Torah. The Rashbam explains that since Rav Sheshet turned away from the Torah scroll, he demonstrated that he was involved in something else and was therefore not subject to the prohibition against discussing other matters. Other commentaries explain that since Rav Sheshet was blind, he was exempt from participating in the public Torah reading and was permitted to be engaged with other matters. According to others, it is permitted to speak in a whisper (*Tosefot HaRosh*; *Sefer HaAgudda*). Alternatively, this prohibition applies only when there are not ten other men present who are listening to the reading (*Ba'al Halakhot Gedolot*). Another explanation is that this prohibition applies only where the custom is that the reader recites a blessing only at the beginning and at the end of the reading, as there is a concern that one who is talking will not hear the blessing after the reading (Meiri on *Berakhot*). However, according to most halakhic authorities, only someone who is constantly engaged in Torah study is permitted to do this, while it is prohibited for everyone else to do so.

To bless His people, Israel, with love – לְבָרֵךְ אֶת עַמּוֹ יִשְׂרָאֵל בְּאַהֲבָה: The question is raised in the *Be'er Sheva*: Where in the Torah is it taught that the benediction must be recited with love? The answer, based on the midrash, is that it is derived from the fact that the word "say" in the phrase: "Say to them" (Numbers 6:23), is written in full, including the letter *vav*. This teaches that the Priestly Benediction must not be recited haphazardly or in a rush; rather, it must be a full-hearted blessing. This is what is meant by the expression: With love.

LANGUAGE

Shortcut [*kappendarya*] – קַפֶּנְדַּרְיָא: The origin of this word appears to be the Latin term via compendaria, meaning shortcut, as in a shortcut through a courtyard or a house.

HALAKHA

Once a Torah scroll has been opened, etc. – כֵּיוָן שֶׁנִּפְתָּח סֵפֶר תּוֹרָה וכו׳: Once the reader has begun reading from a Torah scroll, it is prohibited to speak, even about matters of Torah. According to the Rema and the Vilna Gaon, this is the *halakha* from the time the scroll has been opened, although the reading has not yet begun. One is permitted to speak in order to prevent a prohibition from being violated if this cannot be accomplished in any other way. There are authorities who permit quietly studying Torah, and others who permit this only to those who engage in Torah study all the time. According to the *Eliya Rabba*, with regard to this *halakha*, nobody nowadays is considered as having this status. However, one should not reprimand people who study by themselves during the reading.

During the public Torah reading, it is permitted for one to fulfill the requirement to read the Torah text of the weekly portion twice and the translation once. Some authorities maintain that even this is prohibited, as it is prohibited to engage in any activity during the Torah reading other than listening to it (*Peri Ḥadash*), unless one reads along with the reader word for word, so that he will still hear his reading (*Mishna Berura*). It is prohibited to speak even between the different sections of the reading, though the *Baḥ* rules leniently in this regard. So long as the Torah scroll is still open, one may not speak even after the reading has been completed (Rambam *Sefer Ahava*, *Hilkhot Tefilla* 12:9; *Shulḥan Arukh*, *Oraḥ Ḥayyim* 146:1–2).

Any priest who did not wash his hands, etc. – כׇּל כֹּהֵן שֶׁלֹּא נָטַל יָדָיו וכו׳: A priest may not recite the Priestly Benediction without washing his hands, even if he already washed his hands upon getting up in the morning (*Shulḥan Arukh*). He must wash his entire hand with water up to the wrist, as is required before serving in the Temple (Rambam *Sefer Ahava*, *Hilkhot Tefilla* 15:5; *Shulḥan Arukh*, *Oraḥ Ḥayyim* 128:6).

I never made a shortcut through a synagogue – לֹא עָשִׂיתִי בֵּית הַכְּנֶסֶת קַפֶּנְדַּרְיָא: It is prohibited to use a synagogue as a shortcut for getting from one place to another. If one needs to cut through a synagogue, he should sit for a short while in the synagogue and recite a verse or a *halakha*. It is permitted to pass through the synagogue without stopping to go to its courtyard (*Arukh HaShulḥan*). It is praiseworthy for one who enters a synagogue to pray to exit through an entrance other than the one he entered (Rambam *Sefer Ahava*, *Hilkhot Tefilla* 11:8; *Shulḥan Arukh*, *Oraḥ Ḥayyim* 151:5).

What blessing does the priest recite – מַאי מְבָרֵךְ: When the priests face the congregation to bless them, they first recite the following blessing: Blessed are You, Lord our God, King of the universe, Who has sanctified us with the sanctity of Aaron and commanded us to bless His people, Israel, with love (Rambam *Sefer Ahava*, *Hilkhot Tefilla* 14:12; *Shulḥan Arukh*, *Oraḥ Ḥayyim* 128:11).

כִּי עָקַר כַּרְעֵיהּ מַאי אָמַר? "יְהִי רָצוֹן מִלְּפָנֶיךָ ה׳ אֱלֹהֵינוּ, שֶׁתְּהֵא בְּרָכָה זוֹ שֶׁצִּוִּיתָנוּ לְבָרֵךְ אֶת עַמְּךָ יִשְׂרָאֵל, לֹא יְהֵא בָּהּ מִכְשׁוֹל וְעָוֹן". וְכִי מַהֲדַר אַפֵּיהּ מִצִּיבּוּרָא מַאי אָמַר? אַדְבְּרֵיהּ רַב חִסְדָּא לְרַב עוּקְבָא וְדָרַשׁ: "רִבּוֹנוֹ שֶׁל עוֹלָם, עָשִׂינוּ מַה שֶּׁגָּזַרְתָּ עָלֵינוּ, עֲשֵׂה עִמָּנוּ

The Gemara continues: **When** the priest **begins walking**[H] to the platform to recite the benediction, **what does he say?** The Gemara answers: **May it be Your will, Lord our God, that this blessing with which You have commanded us to bless Your people, Israel, shall not contain any stumbling block or iniquity.**[N] **And** when the benediction has been completed, **when he turns his face away from the congregation,**[H] **what does he say? Rav Ḥisda instructed Rav Ukva and taught** him that this is what he would say: **Master of the Universe, we have performed that which You decreed upon us. Do unto us**

NOTES

Stumbling block or iniquity – מִכְשׁוֹל וְעָוֹן: This expression seems to be out of place, as the priest recites the benediction in the exact wording that is required and says only positive words. Some commentaries explain that since the benediction is interpreted as a blessing of wealth, a person for whom this blessing is fulfilled might find that his newfound wealth brings with it spiritual trials (*Torat HaKenaot*). Others explain, based on the *Zohar*, that if there is a person in the congregation whom the priest hates, if he blesses him he may endanger himself. For this reason, the priest must pray that his blessing will not produce any stumbling block or iniquity (*Minḥa Ḥareva*).

HALAKHA

When the priest begins walking, etc. – כִּי עָקַר כַּרְעֵיהּ וכו׳: When the priests begin walking to ascend the platform, they say: May it be Your will, Lord our God, that this blessing with which You have commanded us to bless Your people, Israel, shall be a complete blessing, and shall not contain any stumbling block or iniquity from now and forever.

They prolong their recitation until the end of the blessing of the Temple service, so that the congregation answers amen to it along with the blessing (Rambam *Sefer Ahava, Hilkhot Tefilla* 14:12; *Shulḥan Arukh, Oraḥ Ḥayyim* 128:9).

When he turns his face away from the congregation – כִּי מַהֲדַר אַפֵּיהּ מִצִּיבּוּרָא: After the priests finish reciting the Priestly Benediction, the prayer leader continues with the blessing of: Grant peace. At this point, the priests turn away from the congregation toward the ark and pray: Master of the Universe, we have performed that which You decreed upon us; do unto us as You have promised. Look down from Your sacred holy habitation, from heaven, and bless Your people, Israel.

They prolong their recitation until the prayer leader finishes the blessing of: Grant peace, so that the congregation can answer amen to their prayer along with the blessing (Rambam *Sefer Ahava, Hilkhot Tefilla* 14:12; *Shulḥan Arukh, Oraḥ Ḥayyim* 128:15, and in the comment of Rema).

Perek **VII**
Daf **39** Amud **b**

מַה שֶּׁהִבְטַחְתָּנוּ, הַשְׁקִיפָה מִמְּעוֹן קָדְשְׁךָ מִן הַשָּׁמַיִם" וגו׳.

as You have promised us, namely: "So shall they put My name upon the children of Israel, and I will bless them" (Numbers 6:27). "**Look forth from your holy habitation, from heaven,** and bless Your people, Israel" (Deuteronomy 26:15).

אָמַר רַב חִסְדָּא: אֵין הַכֹּהֲנִים רַשָּׁאִים לָכוֹף קִישְׁרֵי אֶצְבְּעוֹתֵיהֶן עַד שֶׁיַּחְזְרוּ פְּנֵיהֶם מִן הַצִּבּוּר. אָמַר רַבִּי זֵירָא אָמַר רַב חִסְדָּא: אֵין הַקּוֹרֵא רַשַּׁאי לִקְרוֹת "כֹּהֲנִים" עַד שֶׁיִּכְלֶה "אָמֵן" מִפִּי הַצִּבּוּר;

§ **Rav Ḥisda says: The priests** who spread their hands open during the benediction **are not permitted to bend the joints of their fingers**[NH] **until they turn their faces away from the congregation** once they have completed the benediction. **Rabbi Zeira says** that **Rav Ḥisda says: The one who calls** the priests forward **is not permitted**[H] **to call out: Priests, until** the response **amen** to the blessing of thanksgiving **concludes from the mouths of the congregation,** in order to ensure that everyone will hear the voices of the priests.

NOTES

To bend the joints of their fingers – לָכוֹף קִישְׁרֵי אֶצְבְּעוֹתָיו: This is the source for the *halakha* that the priests' fingers must be spread out while they are reciting the Priestly Benediction. Some of the *ge'onim* explain that the purpose is so that they appear to be shuddering in awe due to the Divine Presence that is resting upon them at this time. Another reason is that the priests would make a sign with their fingers to keep track of where they were in the blessing. The midrash and the *Pesikta deRav Kahana* teach that the priests create five spaces between their fingers, one space between the first two fingers and the second two fingers on each hand, one space between the thumb and first two fingers on each hand, and the space between the two thumbs, to allude to the revelation of the Divine Presence, as is expressed in the phrase in the verse (Song of Songs 2:9): "Peering through the lattice" (see *Tosefot HaRosh* and Abudirham).

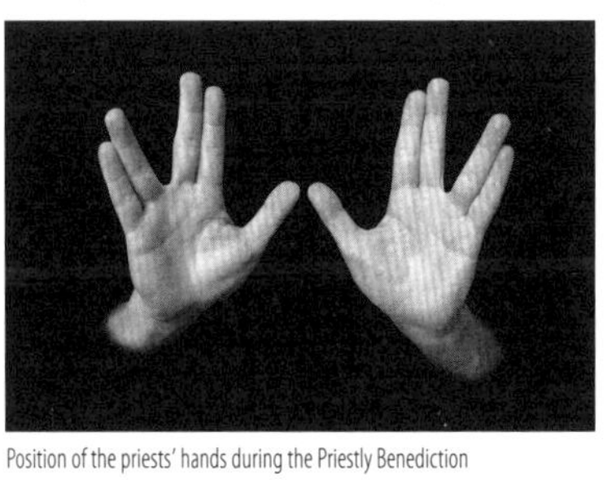

Position of the priests' hands during the Priestly Benediction

HALAKHA

The priests are not permitted to bend the joints of their fingers – אֵין הַכֹּהֲנִים רַשָּׁאִים לָכוֹף קִישְׁרֵי אֶצְבְּעוֹתֵיהֶן: It is prohibited for the priests to bend their fingers while reciting the Priestly Benediction. Their fingers must be spread until they turn around to face the ark (Rambam *Sefer Ahava, Hilkhot Tefilla UVirkat Kohanim* 14:6; *Shulḥan Arukh, Oraḥ Ḥayyim* 128:16).

The one who calls the priests is not permitted, etc. – אֵין הַקּוֹרֵא רַשַּׁאי וכו׳: The one who calls the priests forward is not permitted to call out: Priests, until the congregation finishes answering amen to the blessing of thanksgiving. The priests are not permitted to begin their blessing until the caller finishes calling out: Priests. During the blessing itself, the congregation must wait for the priests to finish each verse before answering amen, and the priests must likewise wait for the congregation to finish answering amen before beginning the next verse. There is a discussion in the *Mishna Berura* concerning whether it is necessary to wait for the entire congregation or only for the majority to finish answering amen (Rambam *Sefer Ahava, Hilkhot Tefilla UVirkat Kohanim* 14:5; *Shulḥan Arukh, Oraḥ Ḥayyim* 128:18).

וְאֵין הַכֹּהֲנִים רַשָּׁאִין לְהַתְחִיל בִּבְרָכָה עַד שֶׁיִּכְלֶה דִּיבּוּר מִפִּי הַקּוֹרֵא; וְאֵין הַצִּבּוּר רַשָּׁאִין לַעֲנוֹת ״אָמֵן״ עַד שֶׁתִּכְלֶה בְּרָכָה מִפִּי הַכֹּהֲנִים; וְאֵין הַכֹּהֲנִים רַשָּׁאִין לְהַתְחִיל בִּבְרָכָה אַחֶרֶת עַד שֶׁיִּכְלֶה ״אָמֵן״ מִפִּי הַצִּבּוּר.

And for the same reason, **the priests are not permitted to begin** reciting **the benediction until the statement of the caller,** i.e., his announcement: Priests, **concludes from his mouth.**[N] **And the congregation is not permitted to answer amen until the blessing concludes from the mouths of the priests. And the priests are not permitted to begin** reciting **another blessing until** the response **amen** to the previous blessing **concludes from the mouths of the congregation.**

וְאָמַר רַבִּי זֵירָא אָמַר רַב חִסְדָּא: אֵין הַכֹּהֲנִים רַשָּׁאִין לְהַחֲזִיר פְּנֵיהֶם מִן הַצִּבּוּר עַד שֶׁיַּתְחִיל שְׁלִיחַ צִבּוּר בְּ״שִׂים שָׁלוֹם״; וְאֵינָן רַשָּׁאִין לַעֲקוֹר רַגְלֵיהֶם וְלֵילֵךְ עַד שֶׁיִּגְמוֹר שְׁלִיחַ צִבּוּר ״שִׂים שָׁלוֹם״.

And Rabbi Zeira says that **Rav Ḥisda says: The priests are not permitted to turn away**[H] **from the congregation** after they have completed the benediction **until the prayer leader begins** saying the blessing of: **Grant peace. And they are not permitted to uproot their feet and walk** away from the platform **until the prayer leader finishes** saying the blessing of: **Grant peace.**

וְאָמַר רַבִּי זֵירָא אָמַר רַב חִסְדָּא: אֵין הַצִּבּוּר רַשָּׁאִין לַעֲנוֹת ״אָמֵן״ עַד שֶׁתִּכְלֶה בְּרָכָה מִפִּי הַקּוֹרֵא; וְאֵין הַקּוֹרֵא רַשַּׁאי לִקְרוֹת בַּתּוֹרָה עַד שֶׁיִּכְלֶה ״אָמֵן״ מִפִּי הַצִּבּוּר; וְאֵין הַמְתַרְגֵּם רַשַּׁאי לְהַתְחִיל בְּתַרְגּוּם עַד שֶׁיִּכְלֶה פָּסוּק מִפִּי הַקּוֹרֵא; וְאֵין הַקּוֹרֵא רַשַּׁאי לְהַתְחִיל בְּפָסוּק אַחֵר עַד שֶׁיִּכְלֶה תַּרְגּוּם מִפִּי הַמְתַרְגֵּם.

And in a similar vein, **Rabbi Zeira says** that **Rav Ḥisda says: The congregation is not permitted to answer amen** to the blessing recited over the Torah reading **until the blessing of the one reading** from the Torah **concludes from his mouth.**[H] **And the reader is not permitted to** begin **reading from the Torah until** the response **amen** to the preceding blessing **concludes from the mouths of the congregation. And the translator is not permitted**[H] **to begin the translation**[B] of the Torah reading **until** the reading of **the verse** from the Torah **concludes from the mouth of the reader. And the reader is not permitted to begin** reading **another verse until the translation concludes from the mouth of the translator.**

אָמַר רַבִּי תַּנְחוּם אָמַר רַבִּי יְהוֹשֻׁעַ בֶּן לֵוִי: הַמַּפְטִיר בַּנָּבִיא – צָרִיךְ שֶׁיִּקְרָא בַּתּוֹרָה תְּחִילָּה. וְאָמַר רַבִּי תַּנְחוּם אָמַר רַבִּי יְהוֹשֻׁעַ בֶּן לֵוִי: אֵין הַמַּפְטִיר רַשַּׁאי לְהַפְטִיר בַּנָּבִיא עַד שֶׁיִּגָּלֵל סֵפֶר תּוֹרָה.

Rabbi Tanḥum says that **Rabbi Yehoshua ben Levi says: The one who concludes with** a reading from **the Prophets** [*haftara*][H] **must first read** several verses **from the Torah.**[N] **And Rabbi Tanḥum says** that **Rabbi Yehoshua ben Levi says: The one who concludes is not permitted to conclude with** a reading from **the Prophets until the Torah scroll is furled.**[NH]

וְאָמַר רַבִּי תַּנְחוּם אָמַר רַבִּי יְהוֹשֻׁעַ בֶּן לֵוִי: אֵין שְׁלִיחַ צִבּוּר רַשַּׁאי לְהַפְשִׁיט אֶת הַתֵּיבָה בְּצִבּוּר, מִפְּנֵי כְּבוֹד צִבּוּר.

And Rabbi Tanḥum says that **Rabbi Yehoshua ben Levi says: The prayer leader is not permitted to uncover** the decorative covering[H] of **the ark in public, out of respect for the congregation.** It is inappropriate to have the congregation wait while doing this.

NOTES

Until the statement of the caller concludes from his mouth – **שֶׁיִּכְלֶה דִּיבּוּר מִפִּי הַקּוֹרֵא**: Rashi explains that this is referring to the prayer leader or someone else who calls out: Priests. Others explain that it is referring to the person who reads out loud the words of the Priestly Benediction for the priests to repeat. Accordingly, the Gemara states that the priests may not begin saying a word until this person finishes reading it to them (*Be'er Sheva*).

Must first read from the Torah – **צָרִיךְ שֶׁיִּקְרָא בַּתּוֹרָה תְּחִילָּה**: The Gemara in tractate *Megilla* explains that the one who concludes with a reading from the Prophets must first read several verses from the Torah out of respect for the Torah, so that is clear that there is nothing that is as important as the Torah itself.

Until the Torah scroll is furled – **עַד שֶׁיִּגָּלֵל סֵפֶר תּוֹרָה**: Rashi explains that this is so the person who is furling the scroll can also pay attention to the reading of the Prophets. An alternative explanation is that this is out of respect for the Torah, because if everyone listens immediately to the reading of the Prophets, the Torah scroll might be forgotten and left unfurled. Another reason that the Torah scroll must first be furled is so that the person reading from the Prophets does not appear to reciting a blessing over the Torah (*Be'er Sheva*).

BACKGROUND

Translation – **תַּרְגּוּם**: During the times of the Gemara and for many generations that followed, the custom was for an appointed translator to translate the Torah reading in the synagogue into Aramaic, verse by verse. The translation that was used was *Targum Onkelos*. Some early authorities insisted that this custom be continued even once most people no longer understood Aramaic. Nowadays, no congregation retains this custom, with the exception of the Yemenite Jews, who still translate the Torah reading into Aramaic.

HALAKHA

The priests are not permitted to turn away, etc. – **אֵין הַכֹּהֲנִים רַשָּׁאִין לְהַחֲזִיר פְּנֵיהֶם וכו׳**: The priests are not permitted to turn and face the ark until the prayer leader begins reciting the blessing of: Grant peace. They must stand in place without uprooting their feet until the prayer leader concludes this blessing. Some say that they must wait until the congregation has finished answering amen after this blessing. The Rema writes that this is the custom (Rambam *Sefer Ahava, Hilkhot Tefilla UVirkat Kohanim* 14:6; *Shulḥan Arukh, Oraḥ Ḥayyim* 128:16).

Until the blessing of the one reading concludes from his mouth – **עַד שֶׁתִּכְלֶה בְּרָכָה מִפִּי הַקּוֹרֵא**: The congregation may not answer amen until the person reading from the Torah finishes his blessing, and he in turn may not begin reading from the Torah until the congregation has finished answering amen (Rambam *Sefer Ahava, Hilkhot Tefilla UVirkat Kohanim* 12:6; *Shulḥan Arukh, Oraḥ Ḥayyim* 141:5).

The translator is not permitted – **אֵין הַמְתַרְגֵּם רַשַּׁאי**: The person who translates the Torah in the synagogue may not begin translating a verse until the reader finishes reading it, and the reader in turn must wait for the translator to finish before beginning the next verse (Rambam *Sefer Ahava, Hilkhot Tefilla UVirkat Kohanim* 12:11; *Shulḥan Arukh, Oraḥ Ḥayyim* 145:1).

The one who concludes with a reading from the Prophets – **הַמַּפְטִיר בַּנָּבִיא**: The person who is called up to read from the Prophets must first read from the Torah. It is enough for him to read only three verses. Usually he reads the last few verses of the Torah portion that was just read (Rambam *Sefer Ahava, Hilkhot Tefilla UVirkat Kohanim* 12:13; *Shulḥan Arukh, Oraḥ Ḥayyim* 282:4).

Until the Torah scroll is furled – **עַד שֶׁיִּגָּלֵל סֵפֶר תּוֹרָה**: The person who is called up to read from the Prophets may not begin reciting the blessing on the *haftara* until the Torah scroll has been completely furled, so that the one who is furling the Torah scroll can listen attentively to the reading of the *haftara*. The custom is to wait until the covering has been placed over the Torah scroll (Rambam *Sefer Ahava, Hilkhot Tefilla UVirkat Kohanim* 12:13; *Shulḥan Arukh, Oraḥ Ḥayyim* 147:7, 284:6; see *Peri Megadim*).

The prayer leader is not permitted to uncover the covering – **אֵין שְׁלִיחַ צִיבּוּר רַשַּׁאי לְהַפְשִׁיט**: The prayer leader may not remove the decorative covering of the ark as long as the congregation is in the synagogue (*Shulḥan Arukh, Oraḥ Ḥayyim* 148:1).

וְאָמַר רַבִּי תַּנְחוּם אָמַר רַבִּי יְהוֹשֻׁעַ בֶּן לֵוִי: אֵין הַצִּבּוּר רַשָּׁאִין לָצֵאת עַד שֶׁיִּנָּטֵל סֵפֶר תּוֹרָה וְיֻנַּח בִּמְקוֹמוֹ; וּשְׁמוּאֵל אָמַר: עַד שֶׁיֵּצֵא.

And Rabbi Tanḥum says that Rabbi Yehoshua ben Levi says: The congregation is not permitted to leave[H] the synagogue after the Torah reading **until the Torah scroll has been taken**[NB] **and** prepared to be **returned to its place,** as the Torah scroll used to be stored near the synagogue. **And Shmuel said:** They may not leave **until** the Torah scroll **is** actually **taken out** of the synagogue, out of respect for the Torah scroll.

וְלָא פְּלִיגִי: הָא דְּאִיכָּא פִּיתְחָא אַחֲרִינָא, הָא דְּלֵיכָּא פִּיתְחָא אַחֲרִינָא. אֲמַר רָבָא, בַּר אָהִינָא אַסְבְּרָהּ לִי: ״אַחֲרֵי ה׳ אֱלֹהֵיכֶם תֵּלֵכוּ״.

The Gemara comments: **And they do not disagree** about the *halakha*. Rather, they were discussing different situations. **This** statement of Rabbi Yehoshua ben Levi is referring to a case **where there is another exit.** When the Torah scroll is being taken out of one exit, people may leave through the other exit. However, **that** statement of Shmuel is referring to a case **where there is no other exit,** and therefore the congregation must wait until the Torah is carried out. **Rava said:** The Sage **bar Ahina explained to me** that this *halakha* is derived from the verse: **"After the Lord your God you shall walk"** (Deuteronomy 13:5),[N] meaning that one must walk after the Torah scroll and not in front of it.

בִּזְמַן שֶׁהַכֹּהֲנִים מְבָרְכִים אֶת הָעָם, מַה הֵן אוֹמְרִים? אָמַר רַבִּי זֵירָא אָמַר רַב חִסְדָּא: ״בָּרְכוּ ה׳ מַלְאָכָיו גִּבֹּרֵי כֹחַ וגו׳, בָּרְכוּ ה׳ כָּל צְבָאָיו מְשָׁרְתָיו עֹשֵׂי רְצוֹנוֹ, בָּרְכוּ ה׳ כָּל מַעֲשָׂיו בְּכָל מְקֹמוֹת מֶמְשַׁלְתּוֹ בָּרְכִי נַפְשִׁי אֶת ה׳״.

§ The Gemara continues to discuss the Priestly Benediction. **When the priests are blessing the people, what do** the people **say? Rabbi Zeira says** that **Rav Ḥisda says:** For each blessing that the priests recite, they respond with a blessing from Bible: **"Bless the Lord, His angels, mighty in strength** that fulfill His word, hearkening unto the voice of His word" (Psalms 103:20), **"Bless the Lord, all of His hosts, His ministers that do His pleasure"** (Psalms 103:21), and **"Bless the Lord, all of His works, in all places of His dominion, bless the Lord, O my soul"** (Psalms 103:22).

בְּמוּסָפֵי דְּשַׁבְּתָא מַה הֵן אוֹמְרִים? אָמַר רַבִּי אַסִּי: ״שִׁיר הַמַּעֲלוֹת הִנֵּה בָּרְכוּ אֶת ה׳ כָּל עַבְדֵי ה׳״ וגו׳, ״שְׂאוּ יְדֵיכֶם קֹדֶשׁ וּבָרְכוּ אֶת ה׳״, ״בָּרוּךְ ה׳ מִצִּיּוֹן שֹׁכֵן יְרוּשָׁלָם הַלְלוּיָהּ״.

When the priests ascend a second time to bless the congregation **during the additional prayer of Shabbat, what do** the people **say?** It is not appropriate for them to repeat the same verses of praise that they recited previously. **Rabbi Asi said:** They say: **"A song of ascents. Behold, bless you the Lord, all you servants of the Lord,** that stand in the house of the Lord in the night seasons" (Psalms 134:1), **"Lift up your hands in sanctity and bless the Lord"** (Psalms 134:2), and **"Blessed be the Lord out of Zion, Who dwells at Jerusalem. Hallelujah"** (Psalms 135:21).

וְלֵימָא נַמִי: ״יְבָרֶכְךָ ה׳ מִצִּיּוֹן״, דִּכְתִיב בְּהַהוּא עִנְיָנָא! אָמַר יְהוּדָה בְּרֵיהּ דְּרַבִּי שִׁמְעוֹן בֶּן פָּזִי: מִתּוֹךְ שֶׁהִתְחִיל בְּבִרְכוֹתָיו שֶׁל הַקָּדוֹשׁ בָּרוּךְ הוּא, מְסַיֵּים בְּבִרְכוֹתָיו שֶׁל הַקָּדוֹשׁ בָּרוּךְ הוּא.

The Gemara asks: **And let them also say** the third verse that appears right after the first two blessings: **"The Lord shall bless you out of Zion"** (Psalms 134:3), **as it is written in that** same **matter. Yehuda, son of Rabbi Shimon ben Pazi, says: Since** they **began with blessings of the Holy One, Blessed be He,** they must **end with a blessing of the Holy One, Blessed be He,** rather than reciting this verse, which is a blessing for the Jewish people.

בְּמִנְחָתָא דְּתַעֲנִיתָא מַאי אָמְרִי? אָמַר רַב אַחָא בַּר יַעֲקֹב: ״אִם עֲוֹנֵינוּ עָנוּ בָנוּ ה׳ עֲשֵׂה לְמַעַן שְׁמֶךָ״, ״מִקְוֵה יִשְׂרָאֵל מוֹשִׁיעוֹ בְּעֵת צָרָה לָמָּה תִהְיֶה כְּגֵר בָּאָרֶץ״ וגו׳, ״לָמָּה תִהְיֶה כְּאִישׁ נִדְהָם כְּגִבּוֹר לֹא יוּכַל לְהוֹשִׁיעַ״ וגו׳.

The Gemara asks: When the priests ascend to recite the Priestly Benediction **during the afternoon prayer of a fast day, what do** the people **say? Rav Aḥa bar Ya'akov said:** They say: **"Though our iniquities testify against us, O Lord, work for Your name's sake"** (Jeremiah 14:7), **"The Hope of Israel, its savior in times of trouble, why should You be a stranger in the land** and as a wayfaring man that turns aside to tarry for a night?" (Jeremiah 14:8), and **"Why should You be like a man overcome, as a mighty man who cannot save?** Yet You, O Lord, are in the midst of us, and Your name is called upon us; leave us not" (Jeremiah 14:9).

HALAKHA

The congregation is not permitted to leave, etc. – אֵין הַצִּבּוּר רַשָּׁאִין לָצֵאת וכו׳: The congregation may not leave the synagogue until the Torah scroll has been put away. However, an individual may leave as long as the majority of the congregation is present (Rema). When the Torah scroll is housed in another building, if the synagogue has only one exit, the congregation must wait until it is taken out and escort the Torah scroll to the place where it is kept. If there are two exits, it is permitted to leave the synagogue through the exit through which the Torah scroll will not be taken out. However, the congregation must still escort the Torah scroll to the place where it is kept. The Rema adds that when the Torah scroll is being carried to the ark, everyone in its path must escort it until it is returned to the ark (Rambam *Sefer Ahava, Hilkhot Tefilla UVirkat Kohanim* 12:24; *Shulḥan Arukh, Oraḥ Ḥayyim* 149:1).

NOTES

Until the Torah scroll has been taken – עַד שֶׁיִּנָּטֵל סֵפֶר תּוֹרָה: The Rif quotes the opinion of the *ge'onim* that this is also the *halakha* when the Torah scroll remains in the synagogue. In any event, it is not respectful to the Torah scroll to leave the synagogue before it has been returned to its proper place.

After the Lord your God you shall walk – אַחֲרֵי ה׳ אֱלֹהֵיכֶם תֵּלֵכוּ: Because of this verse, several *ge'onim* maintain that one should move a bit from one's place to escort the Torah scroll as it is being carried away from the platform and returned to its place (Meiri; *Kiryat Sefer*).

BACKGROUND

Until the Torah scroll has been taken – עַד שֶׁיִּנָּטֵל סֵפֶר תּוֹרָה: It seems from several discussions in the Gemara that oftentimes, and especially in villages, the synagogue was located at a significant distance from the city. In these cases, the Torah scroll was not kept in the synagogue's ark. Rather, for security, it was kept in a specially designated, closed room somewhat near the synagogue. Perhaps this was necessary because the synagogue was often kept open, with people coming in and out of it throughout the day, or because it was also used as a house of study or a school for children. Therefore, there was concern that someone would enter and steal the Torah scroll.

בִּנְעִילָה דְּיוֹמָא דְּכִיפּוּרֵי מַאי אָמַר? אָמַר מָר זוּטְרָא, וְאָמְרִי לָהּ בְּמַתְנִיתָא: ״הִנֵּה כִי כֵן יְבֹרַךְ גָּבֶר יְרֵא ה׳״, ״יְבָרֶכְךָ ה׳ מִצִּיּוֹן וּרְאֵה בְּטוּב יְרוּשָׁלָיִם כֹּל יְמֵי חַיֶּיךָ״, ״וּרְאֵה בָנִים לְבָנֶיךָ שָׁלוֹם עַל יִשְׂרָאֵל״.

During the closing prayer [*ne'ila*] **of Yom Kippur,** which also includes the Priestly Benediction, **what do** the people **say? Mar Zutra says, and some say** that this was taught **in a *baraita*: "Behold, surely thus shall the man who fears the Lord be blessed"** (Psalms 128:4), **"The Lord shall bless you out of Zion, and you shall see the good of Jerusalem all the days of your life"** (Psalms 128:5), and **"And see your children's children. Peace be upon Israel"** (Psalms 128:6).

הֵיכָן אוֹמְרָן? רַב יוֹסֵף אָמַר: בֵּין כׇּל בְּרָכָה וּבְרָכָה; וְרַב שֵׁשֶׁת אָמַר: בְּהַזְכָּרַת הַשֵּׁם.

The Gemara asks: **Where does** the congregation **say** these verses during the Priestly Benediction? **Rav Yosef says:** They are said **between each and every blessing. And Rav Sheshet says:** They are said **during the mention of the name** of God in each of the three blessings.

פְּלִיגִי בָּהּ רַב מָרִי וְרַב זְבִיד – חַד אָמַר: פְּסוּקָא לָקֳבֵל פְּסוּקָא, וְחַד אָמַר: אַכָּל פְּסוּקָא אָמַר לְהוּ לְכוּלְּהוּ.

Rav Mari and Rav Zevid disagree about this matter. **One says:** The congregation recites one **verse** at a time, **corresponding to** the **verse** that the priests recite. **And one says: For every** single **verse** that the priests recite, the congregation **says all** three verses.

אָמַר רַבִּי חִיָּיא בַּר אַבָּא: כׇּל הָאוֹמְרָן בַּגְּבוּלִין אֵינוֹ אֶלָּא טוֹעֶה. אָמַר רַבִּי חֲנִינָא בַּר פָּפָּא: תֵּדַע דְּבַמִּקְדָּשׁ נַמִּי לָא מִיבָּעֵי לְמֵימְרִינְהוּ, כְּלוּם יֵשׁ לְךָ עֶבֶד שֶׁמְּבָרְכִין אוֹתוֹ וְאֵינוֹ מַאֲזִין?

Rabbi Ḥiyya bar Abba says: Anyone who recites these verses **in the outlying areas,** i.e., outside the Temple, **is nothing other than mistaken** in his practice. **Rabbi Ḥanina bar Pappa said:** You should **know that in the Temple also** people **should not recite** these verses. **Do you have a servant who is being blessed and does not listen**[NH] to the blessing, but rather speaks at the same time?

אָמַר רַבִּי אַחָא בַּר חֲנִינָא: תֵּדַע דְּבַגְּבוּלִין נַמִּי מִיבָּעֵי לְמֵימְרִינְהוּ, כְּלוּם יֵשׁ עֶבֶד שֶׁמְּבָרְכִין אוֹתוֹ וְאֵין מַסְבִּיר פָּנִים? אָמַר רַבִּי אַבָּהוּ: מֵרֵישׁ הֲוָה אָמֵינָא לְהוּ. כֵּיוָן דַּחֲזֵינָא לֵיהּ לְרַבִּי אַבָּא דְּמִן עַכּוֹ דְּלָא אָמַר לְהוּ, אֲנָא נַמִּי לָא אָמֵינָא לְהוּ.

Conversely, **Rabbi Aḥa bar Ḥanina says:** You should **know that in the outlying areas one is also required to say** these verses. **Is there a servant who is being blessed and his face does not brighten?** Therefore, one must recite these verses to give thanks for receiving the Priestly Benediction. **Rabbi Abbahu**[P] **says: At first, I would recite** these verses, **but since I saw that Rabbi Abba of Akko**[P] **does not say them, I also do not recite them** anymore.

וְאָמַר רַבִּי אַבָּהוּ: מֵרֵישׁ הֲוָה אָמֵינָא עִינְוְתָנָא אֲנָא. כֵּיוָן דַּחֲזֵינָא לֵיהּ לְרַבִּי אַבָּא דְּמִן עַכּוֹ דַּאֲמַר אִיהוּ חַד טַעְמָא וַאֲמַר אָמוֹרֵיהּ חַד טַעְמָא וְלָא קָפֵיד, אָמֵינָא: לָאו עִינְוְתָנָא אֲנָא.

And Rabbi Abbahu says: At first, I would say to myself that **I was humble. Since I saw that Rabbi Abba of Akko himself stated one reason** for a matter, **and his interpreter stated one** other **reason** of his own rather than delivering the reason that Rabbi Abba stated, **and yet** Rabbi Abba **did not mind, I say** to myself that **I am not humble.**

וּמַאי עִינְוְתָנוּתֵיהּ דְּרַבִּי אַבָּהוּ? דַּאֲמַרָה לָהּ דְּבֵיתְהוּ דְּאָמוֹרֵיהּ דְּרַבִּי אַבָּהוּ לִדְבֵיתֵיהּ דְּרַבִּי אַבָּהוּ: הָא דִּידַן לָא צָרִיךְ לֵיהּ לְדִידָךְ, וְהַאי דְּגָחֵין וְזָקֵיף עֲלֵיהּ, יְקָרָא בְּעָלְמָא הוּא דְּעָבֵיד לֵיהּ. אֲזַלָא דְּבֵיתְהוּ וַאֲמַרָה לֵיהּ לְרַבִּי אַבָּהוּ. אֲמַר לָהּ: וּמַאי נָפְקָא לִיךְ מִינָּהּ? מִינִּי וּמִינֵּיהּ יִתְקַלֵּס עִילָּאָה.

The Gemara asks: **And what was the humility of Rabbi Abbahu?** The Gemara relates **that Rabbi Abbahu's interpreter's wife said to Rabbi Abbahu's wife: This one of ours,** i.e., my husband, **has no need for your** husband Rabbi Abbahu, as he could teach everything on his own. **And the fact that he bends over** to listen to Rabbi Abbahu, **and then stands up above him,** and repeats his words to the congregants **is merely to show respect for him.**[N] Rabbi Abbahu's **wife went and told** this **to Rabbi Abbahu. He said to her: And what difference does it make to you? Through me and through him the One above will be exalted,** and it does not matter which one of us is teaching.

NOTES

Do you have a servant who is being blessed and does not listen – כְּלוּם יֵשׁ לְךָ עֶבֶד שֶׁמְּבָרְכִין אוֹתוֹ וְאֵינוֹ מַאֲזִין: *Tosafot* raise a difficulty with the statement that one should not recite verses during the Priestly Benediction: The Sages created a prayer for ameliorating a bad dream, to be recited during the Priestly Benediction. They answer that reciting this prayer is permitted because the person who had a bad dream is in distress. Also, since the prayer concerning a bad dream is connected to the Priestly Benediction, as it seeks that the blessing be implemented with regard to the dream, it is not considered to be speaking about a separate matter. This is not true if one recites other verses that are not linked to the words of the blessing (*Be'er Sheva*, citing Maharil).

Is merely to show respect for him – יְקָרָא בְּעָלְמָא הוּא דְּעָבֵיד לֵיהּ: It seems that Rashi and the *Ein Ya'akov* have a different version of the text, which reads: Respect for the kingdom. Accordingly, the disseminator's wife explained that he showed respect for Rabbi Abbahu due to the latter's ties with the government and not because of his wisdom in Torah.

HALAKHA

Do you have a servant who is being blessed and does not listen – כְּלוּם יֵשׁ לְךָ עֶבֶד שֶׁמְּבָרְכִין אוֹתוֹ וְאֵינוֹ מַאֲזִין: One must remain silent and may not recite any verses while the priests are reciting their blessing, in accordance with the opinion of Rabbi Ḥiyya and Rabbi Abbahu. The Rema writes that in a place where the custom is that the priests sing during the blessing, it is customary for the congregation to recite verses during their singing, but it is still better not to recite anything. It is explained in the *Magen Avraham* and the *Taz* that if one recites verses, he should do so only while the prayer leader is calling out the words of the blessing to the priests. Others say that one should refrain from this as well, and it is the custom in many communities, including those who follow the customs of the Vilna Gaon and Chabad, not to say anything at all during the Priestly Benediction (Rambam *Sefer Ahava, Hilkhot Tefilla UVirkat Kohanim* 14:7; *Shulḥan Arukh, Oraḥ Ḥayyim* 128:26).

PERSONALITIES

Rabbi Abbahu – רַבִּי אַבָּהוּ: Rabbi Abbahu lived in the city of Caesarea and was very influential with the Roman authorities. Although he did not have an official position, he acted as the representative of the Jewish community. The house of the emperor referred to here is apparently the palace located in the city of Caesarea, where Rabbi Abbahu had an independent yeshiva.

Rabbi Abba of Akko – רַבִּי אַבָּא דְּמִן עַכּוֹ: An *amora* of Eretz Yisrael of the third generation of *amora'im*, Rabbi Abba may have been the leading Sage in the city of Akko at some point, but he then moved to the neighboring city of Caesarea. As the Gemara relates here, Rabbi Abba was impoverished and in debt, and Rabbi Abbahu's attempts to make him the head of the yeshiva were apparently not successful. He engaged in halakhic discourse with Rabbi Zeira, Rabbi Abbahu, and another Sage known as Rabbi Abba. Not many of his rulings have been preserved.

וְתוּ, רַבִּי אַבָּהוּ אִימְנוּ רַבָּנַן עֲלֵיהּ לְמַמְנְיֵיהּ בְּרֵישָׁא. כֵּיוָן דַּחֲזָיֵהּ לְרַבִּי אַבָּא דְּמִן עַכּוֹ דִּנְפִישִׁי לֵיהּ בַּעֲלֵי חוֹבוֹת, אֲמַר לְהוּ: אִיכָּא רַבָּה.

And furthermore, in another example of his humility, **the Sages were counted** and reached a decision **to appoint Rabbi Abbahu to be the head** of the yeshiva. **Since he saw that Rabbi Abba of Akko had many creditors** and was impoverished, he attempted to get him out of debt. **He said to them: There is** a man who is **greater** than me, Rabbi Abba.

רַבִּי אַבָּהוּ וְרַבִּי חִיָּיא בַּר אַבָּא אִיקְלְעוּ לְהָהוּא אַתְרָא. רַבִּי אַבָּהוּ דָּרֵשׁ בְּאַגַּדְתָּא, רַבִּי חִיָּיא בַּר אַבָּא דָּרֵשׁ בִּשְׁמַעְתָּא. שַׁבְקוּהּ כּוּלֵּי עָלְמָא לְרַבִּי חִיָּיא בַּר אַבָּא וַאֲזוּל לְגַבֵּיהּ דְּרַבִּי אַבָּהוּ. חֲלַשׁ דַּעְתֵּיהּ. אֲמַר לֵיהּ: אֶמְשׁוֹל לְךָ מָשָׁל, לְמָה הַדָּבָר דּוֹמֶה? לִשְׁנֵי בְּנֵי אָדָם, אֶחָד מוֹכֵר אֲבָנִים טוֹבוֹת וְאֶחָד מוֹכֵר מִינֵי סִידְקִית, עַל מִי קוֹפְצִין? לֹא עַל זֶה שֶׁמּוֹכֵר מִינֵי סִידְקִית?

The Gemara relates another example of his humility: **Rabbi Abbahu and Rabbi Ḥiyya bar Abba happened** to come **to a certain place. Rabbi Abbahu taught** matters of *aggada*, and at the same time **Rabbi Ḥiyya bar Abba taught** *halakha*. **Everyone left Rabbi Ḥiyya bar Abba and went to Rabbi Abbahu,** and Rabbi Ḥiyya **was offended.** Rabbi Abbahu **said to him,** to appease him: **I will tell you a parable: To what is this matter comparable?** It is comparable **to two people, one** who **sells precious stones and one** who **sells small items** [*sidkit*].[L] **Upon whom do** the customers **spring? Don't** they spring **upon the one who sells small items?** Similarly, you teach lofty and important matters that do not attract many people. Everyone comes to me because I teach minor matters.

כָּל יוֹמָא הֲוָה מְלַוֵּה רַבִּי חִיָּיא בַּר אַבָּא לְרַבִּי אַבָּהוּ עַד אוּשְׁפִּיזֵיהּ, מִשּׁוּם יְקָרָא דְּבֵי קֵיסָר. הָהוּא יוֹמָא אַלְוְיֵהּ רַבִּי אַבָּהוּ לְרַבִּי חִיָּיא בַּר אַבָּא עַד אוּשְׁפִּיזֵיהּ. וַאֲפִילּוּ הָכִי לָא אִיתּוֹתַב דַּעְתֵּיהּ מִינֵּיהּ.

The Gemara relates that **every day Rabbi Ḥiyya bar Abba would escort Rabbi Abbahu to his lodging place** [*ushpizei*][L] **out of respect for the house of the emperor,** with which Rabbi Abbahu was associated. On **that day, Rabbi Abbahu escorted Rabbi Ḥiyya bar Abba to his lodging place, and even so,** Rabbi Ḥiyya bar Abba's **mind was not at ease with** Rabbi Abbahu and he felt insulted.

בִּזְמַן שֶׁשְּׁלִיחַ צִבּוּר אוֹמֵר "מוֹדִים", הָעָם מָה הֵם אוֹמְרִים? אָמַר רַב: "מוֹדִים אֲנַחְנוּ לָךְ ה' אֱלֹהֵינוּ עַל שֶׁאָנוּ מוֹדִים לָךְ"; וּשְׁמוּאֵל אָמַר: "אֱלֹהֵי כָּל בָּשָׂר עַל שֶׁאָנוּ מוֹדִים לָךְ"; רַבִּי סִימַאי אוֹמֵר: "יוֹצְרֵנוּ יוֹצֵר בְּרֵאשִׁית עַל שֶׁאָנוּ מוֹדִים לָךְ"; נְהַרְדְּעֵי אָמְרִי מִשְּׁמֵיהּ דְּרַבִּי סִימַאי: "בְּרָכוֹת וְהוֹדָאוֹת לְשִׁמְךָ הַגָּדוֹל עַל שֶׁהֶחֱיִיתָנוּ וְקִיַּימְתָּנוּ עַל שֶׁאָנוּ מוֹדִים לָךְ"; רַב אַחָא בַּר יַעֲקֹב מְסַיֵּים בָּהּ הָכִי: "כֵּן תְּחַיֵּינוּ וּתְחָנֵּנוּ, וּתְקַבְּצֵנוּ וְתֶאֱסוֹף גָּלִיּוֹתֵינוּ לְחַצְרוֹת קׇדְשֶׁךָ, לִשְׁמוֹר חוּקֶּיךָ וְלַעֲשׂוֹת רְצוֹנְךָ בְּלֵבָב שָׁלֵם, עַל שֶׁאָנוּ מוֹדִים לָךְ".

§ The Gemara returns to discuss the response of the congregants to certain parts of the prayer service. **While the prayer leader is reciting** the blessing of: **We give thanks,**[N] **what do the people say? Rav says** that they say: **We give thanks to You, Lord our God, for the merit of giving thanks to You. And Shmuel says** that one should say: **God of all** living **flesh, for** the merit of **giving thanks to You. Rabbi Simai says** that one should say: **Our Creator, Who created** everything **in the beginning, for** the merit of **giving thanks to You.** The Sages **of Neharde'a**[B] **say in the name of Rabbi Simai** that one should say: We offer **blessings and praises to Your great name, for You have given us life and sustained us, for giving thanks to You. Rav Aḥa bar Ya'akov** would **finish** the blessing **as follows: So may You give us life, and show us favor, and collect us, and gather our exiles into Your sacred courtyards, in order to observe Your laws and to fulfill Your will wholeheartedly, for giving thanks to You.**

אָמַר רַב פָּפָּא: הִילְכָּךְ נֵימְרִינְהוּ לְכוּלְּהוּ.

Rav Pappa said: These Sages each added a different element to the prayer. **Therefore, we should** combine them together and **recite all of them.**[HN]

LANGUAGE

Small items [*sidkit*] – סִידְקִית: In this context, this term refers to small, inexpensive items, e.g., needles. There is a common term *mahat sidkit*, which refers to a small sewing needle, as opposed to larger needles that are used to sew bags and other items. It is explained in the *Arukh* that this type of needle carries that appellation because it is used to sew up holes and cracks [*sedakim*].

The origin of the term *sidkit* may come from the fact that small items such as these are sold in small stores that are like cracks or holes in the wall. However, others explain that this name is derived from the word *sarakit*, saraceni in Latin, which refers to a nomadic Arabian tribe, as during the talmudic period members of this tribe had small booths set up where they used to sell objects such as these. Another version of the word, *sitkit*, is found in the *Arukh*.

Lodging place [*ushpiza*] – אוּשְׁפִּיזָא: From the Middle Persian term aspinj, meaning hotel or hospitality.

BACKGROUND

The Sages of Neharde'a – נְהַרְדְּעֵי: The Gemara states elsewhere that anonymous statements attributed to the Sages of Neharde'a refer to statements of Rav Ḥama of Neharde'a, who served as the head of the yeshiva of Neharde'a for several years following the passing of Rav Naḥman bar Yitzḥak. Apparently, Rav Ḥama was related to the family of the Exilarch and for a time served as his official scholar. It is also possible that he is the same Rav Ḥama who met with the king of Persia and discussed Torah matters with him.

HALAKHA

Therefore we should recite all of them – הִילְכָּךְ נֵימְרִינְהוּ לְכוּלְּהוּ: While the prayer leader is reciting the blessing of thanksgiving, the congregation says: We give thanks to You, the God of all living flesh…blessed be the God of thanksgiving. This is in accordance with the opinion of Rav Pappa, that all of the versions should be incorporated (Rambam *Sefer Ahava, Hilkhot Tefilla UVirkat Kohanim* 9:4; *Shulḥan Arukh, Oraḥ Ḥayyim* 127:1).

NOTES

While the prayer leader is reciting the blessing of: We give thanks – בִּזְמַן שֶׁשְּׁלִיחַ צִיבּוּר אוֹמֵר מוֹדִים: The reason that the congregation recites a prayer at this time is to acknowledge the great merit of being able to give thanks to God (*Devar Shaul*). The *ge'onim* write that the congregation's prayer immediately follows the prayer leader's blessing and is somewhat of an addition to it. The version in the Jerusalem Talmud and in the writings of several halakhic authorities closes with a full blessing: Blessed are You, Lord, the God of thanks. According to this version, it can be understood why the congregation does not need to listen to the recitation of the prayer leader; they recite their own blessing. It is also possible that the congregation is expected to listen to the prayer leader while reciting their blessing. It is stated in the Jerusalem Talmud that this blessing is recited in an undertone, and therefore it does not obstruct one's ability to hear the blessing of the prayer leader. Furthermore, the congregants can finish their prayer before the prayer leader and then answer amen to his blessing (*Devar Shaul*).

We should recite all of them – נֵימְרִינְהוּ לְכוּלְּהוּ: In *Masoret HaShas* it is explained that this reflects Rav Pappa's approach in other discussions (see *Berakhot* 59–60), where he rules that several opinions of the early Sages should be combined. Since this prayer is a combination of statements from several Sages, it is called: The Sages' blessing of thanksgiving (*Beit Yosef*). The name can also be explained as follows: Since the uneducated people did not know how to recite the prayers on their own and had to listen closely to the words of the prayer leader, this congregation's blessing of thanksgiving could be recited only by the scholars (*Eshel Avraham*).

NOTES

Rav Naḥman said that this principle is derived from here, etc. – רַב נַחְמָן אָמַר מֵהָכָא וכו׳: According to Rashi, Rav Naḥman's proof is David's use of the term "brethren," which shows respect for the people. The Meiri as well as the Maharsha explain that the proof is from the fact that King David stood up in honor of the people. Accordingly, the subsequent interpretation of the phrase "my brethren and my people" is a separate matter that is mentioned here tangentially.

HALAKHA

The priests are not permitted to ascend the platform in their sandals – אֵין הַכֹּהֲנִים רַשָּׁאִין לַעֲלוֹת בְּסַנְדְּלֵיהֶן לַדּוּכָן: Ezra decreed that the priests must remove their shoes before ascending the platform. However, they need not remove their socks. Some rule stringently if the socks are made from leather (Rema). The custom is for the priests to remove their shoes for the Priestly Benediction, and while it would be preferable for the priests to be barefoot, the Mishna Berura notes that the custom is for the priests to leave on their socks to recite the blessing (Rambam *Sefer Ahava, Hilkhot Tefilla UVirkat Kohanim* 14:6; *Shulḥan Arukh, Oraḥ Ḥayyim* 128:5).

אָמַר רַבִּי יִצְחָק: לְעוֹלָם תְּהֵא אֵימַת צִבּוּר עָלֶיךָ, שֶׁהֲרֵי כֹּהֲנִים פְּנֵיהֶם כְּלַפֵּי הָעָם וַאֲחוֹרֵיהֶם כְּלַפֵּי שְׁכִינָה.

§ **Rabbi Yitzḥak says: The awe of the public should always be upon you,** i.e., one must always treat the public courteously. **As** when the **priests** bless the people they **face the people and their backs are toward the Divine Presence,** out of respect for the congregation.

רַב נַחְמָן אָמַר, מֵהָכָא: ״וַיָּקָם דָּוִיד הַמֶּלֶךְ עַל רַגְלָיו וַיֹּאמֶר שְׁמָעוּנִי אַחַי וְעַמִּי״. אִם ״אַחַי״ לָמָּה ״עַמִּי״, וְאִם ״עַמִּי״ לָמָּה ״אַחַי״? אָמַר רַבִּי אֶלְעָזָר, אָמַר לָהֶם דָּוִד לְיִשְׂרָאֵל: אִם אַתֶּם שׁוֹמְעִין לִי – אַחַי אַתֶּם, וְאִם לָאו – עַמִּי אַתֶּם, וַאֲנִי רוֹדֶה אֶתְכֶם בְּמַקֵּל.

Rav Naḥman said that this principle is derived **from here:**[N] **"Then King David stood up upon his feet, and said: Hear me, my brethren, and my people"** (I Chronicles 28:2). Evidently, King David stood up to address the people rather than remain seated. **If** he said **"my brethren," why** did he say **"my people"? And if** he said **"my people" why** did he say **"my brethren"? Rabbi Elazar says: David said to the Jewish people: If you listen to me, you are my brethren. And if** you do **not** listen to me willingly, **you are my people** and I am your king, **and I will rule over you** by force **with a staff.** This shows that if the nation acted properly, David would relate to them respectfully.

רַבָּנַן אָמְרִי, מֵהָכָא: דְּאֵין הַכֹּהֲנִים רַשָּׁאִין לַעֲלוֹת בְּסַנְדְּלֵיהֶן לַדּוּכָן, וְזֶהוּ אַחַת מִתֵּשַׁע תַּקָּנוֹת שֶׁהִתְקִין רַבָּן יוֹחָנָן בֶּן זַכַּאי; מַאי טַעְמָא? לָאו מִשּׁוּם כְּבוֹד צִבּוּר? אָמַר רַב אַשִׁי: לָא, הָתָם שֶׁמָּא נִפְסְקָה לוֹ רְצוּעָה בְּסַנְדָּלוֹ וַהֲדַר אָזֵיל לְמִיקְטְרֵיהּ, וְאָמְרִי: בֶּן גְּרוּשָׁה אוֹ בֶּן חֲלוּצָה הוּא.

The Sages say that the importance of showing respect for the congregation is derived **from here:** The *halakha* is **that the priests are not permitted to ascend the platform** to recite the benediction **in their sandals,**[H] as is taught in a *baraita*. **And this** *halakha* **is one of nine ordinances that Rabban Yoḥanan ben Zakkai instituted. What is the reason** for this ordinance? **Is it not out of respect for the congregation,** as it would be disrespectful for the priests to display their dirty sandals in front of the congregants? **Rav Ashi said: No,** this is not the reason. **There,** in the *baraita*, the reason is a concern **lest a strap of his sandal break, and he** will therefore **return** to his place **to go tie it** and not ascend the platform in time for the benediction, **and** people will **say** that he was removed from the platform because he is disqualified from the priesthood, as he **is the son of** a priest and **a divorced woman or the son of** a priest and **a *ḥalutza*.**

״וּבַמִּקְדָּשׁ בְּרָכָה אַחַת״ כו׳.

§ It is taught in the mishna: **And in the Temple,** the priests recite the three verses as **one blessing.**

Perek **VII**
Daf **40** Amud **b**

וְכׇל כָּךְ לָמָּה? לְפִי שֶׁאֵין עוֹנִין ״אָמֵן״ בַּמִּקְדָּשׁ.

The Gemara asks: **And why** does the practice in the Temple differ **so much** from outside the Temple? **Because one does not answer amen in the Temple,**[N] and therefore there is no pause between the blessings.

תָּנוּ רַבָּנַן: מִנַּיִן שֶׁאֵין עוֹנִין ״אָמֵן״ בַּמִּקְדָּשׁ? שֶׁנֶּאֱמַר: ״קוּמוּ בָּרְכוּ אֶת ה׳ אֱלֹהֵיכֶם מִן הָעוֹלָם עַד הָעוֹלָם״. וּמִנַּיִן שֶׁעַל כׇּל בְּרָכָה וּבְרָכָה תְּהִלָּה? שֶׁנֶּאֱמַר: ״וִיבָרְכוּ שֵׁם כְּבֹדֶךָ וּמְרוֹמַם עַל כׇּל בְּרָכָה וּתְהִלָּה״, עַל כׇּל בְּרָכָה וּבְרָכָה תֵּן לוֹ תְּהִלָּה.

The Sages taught: From where is it derived **that one does not answer amen in the Temple? As it is stated: "Stand up and bless the Lord, your God, from everlasting to everlasting"** (Nehemiah 9:5). This blessing is recited instead of amen in the Temple. **And from where** is it derived **that for each and every blessing** in the Temple the people respond with these words of **praise? As it is stated: "And let them say: Blessed be Your glorious name, which is exalted above all blessing and praise"** (Nehemiah 9:5). This verse indicates that **for each and every blessing,** you should **give Him praise.**[N] However, those present do not respond amen.

NOTES

Because one does not answer amen in the Temple – לְפִי שֶׁאֵין עוֹנִין אָמֵן בַּמִּקְדָּשׁ: The Maharsha explains that according to kabbalistic tradition one answers amen because the numerical value of its letters, 91, is equal to the sum of the numerical value of the Tetragrammaton, 26, and the name of Lordship, 65, and outside the Temple the name of Lordship is uttered instead of the Tetragrammaton. However, in the Temple, where the name of God itself is pronounced as it is written, it is not necessary to answer amen. It can also be explained that the word amen connotes acceptance and faith and is a prayer that the blessing will be accepted and come to fruition. This need not be said in the Temple, where the Divine Presence dwells.

Tosafot ask: Given that the Gemara (*Yoma* 35b) teaches that in the Temple, those hearing a blessing would say: Blessed be the name of His glorious kingdom forever and all time, how can the Gemara here state that the fact that those present did not answer amen means that there is no interruption between the blessings? They answer that since these words of praise are recited immediately upon hearing the name of God, they are recited in the middle and not at the end of the blessings. It is explained in *Tosefot Yom Tov* that although: Blessed be the name of His glorious kingdom forever and all time, is recited after most blessings in the Temple, it is not recited after the Priestly Benediction, as that is a blessing for the Jewish people and not for God.

For each and every blessing give Him praise – עַל כׇּל בְּרָכָה וּבְרָכָה תֵּן לוֹ תְּהִלָּה: It seems from Rashi's commentary and from the Rambam (*Sefer Zemanim, Hilkhot Ta'anit* 4:15) that after each blessing in the Temple, the people would answer: Blessed be the name of His glorious kingdom forever and all time. However, elsewhere the Rambam writes that after the Priestly Benediction the people would answer: Blessed be the Lord, God, God of Israel, from eternity to eternity (*Sefer Ahava, Hilkhot Tefilla* 14:9).

מתני׳ בִּרְכוֹת כֹּהֵן גָּדוֹל כֵּיצַד? חַזַּן הַכְּנֶסֶת נוֹטֵל סֵפֶר תּוֹרָה וְנוֹתְנָהּ לוֹ לְרֹאשׁ הַכְּנֶסֶת, וְרֹאשׁ הַכְּנֶסֶת נוֹתְנָהּ לַסְּגָן, וְהַסְּגָן נוֹתְנָהּ לְכֹהֵן גָּדוֹל.

MISHNA How are **the blessings of the High Priest**[NH] recited on Yom Kippur? **The synagogue attendant**[B] **takes a Torah scroll and gives it to the head of the synagogue**[B] that stands on the Temple Mount, **and the head of the synagogue gives it to the deputy** High Priest, **and the deputy** High Priest **gives it to the High Priest.**

וְכֹהֵן גָּדוֹל עוֹמֵד וּמְקַבֵּל וְקוֹרֵא ״אַחֲרֵי מוֹת״ וְ״אַךְ בֶּעָשׂוֹר״, וְגוֹלֵל אֶת הַתּוֹרָה וּמַנִּיחָהּ בְּחֵיקוֹ, וְאוֹמֵר: יָתֵר מִמַּה שֶּׁקָּרִיתִי לִפְנֵיכֶם כָּתוּב כָּאן. ״וּבֶעָשׂוֹר״ שֶׁבְּחוּמַּשׁ הַפְּקוּדִים קוֹרֵא עַל פֶּה.

And the High Priest stands; and receives the Torah scroll; **and reads** the Torah portion beginning with the verse: **"After the death"** (Leviticus 16:1–34), **and** the portion beginning with the verse: **"But on the tenth"** (Leviticus 23:26–32); **and furls the Torah** scroll; **and places it on his bosom; and says: More than what I have read before you is written here. He** then **reads by heart** the portion beginning with: **"And on the tenth,"** from the book of Numbers (see 29:7–11).

וּמְבָרֵךְ עָלֶיהָ שְׁמֹנֶה בְּרָכוֹת: עַל הַתּוֹרָה, וְעַל הָעֲבוֹדָה, וְעַל הַהוֹדָיָה, וְעַל מְחִילַת הֶעָוֹן, וְעַל הַמִּקְדָּשׁ, וְעַל יִשְׂרָאֵל, וְעַל הַכֹּהֲנִים, וְעַל יְרוּשָׁלַיִם, וְהַשְּׁאָר תְּפִלָּה.

And after the reading the High Priest **recites** the following **eight blessings:** A blessing **concerning the Torah,**[N] **and concerning the** Temple **service, and concerning thanksgiving, and concerning forgiveness for iniquity, and concerning the Temple, and concerning the Jewish people, and concerning the priests, and concerning Jerusalem, and the rest of the prayer.**

גמ׳ שָׁמְעַתְּ מִינָּהּ: חוֹלְקִין כָּבוֹד לְתַלְמִיד בִּמְקוֹם הָרַב.

GEMARA The Gemara suggests: **You can learn from** the fact that the head of the synagogue and the deputy High Priest receive the Torah scroll before the High Priest that **honor may be given to a student in the presence of the teacher.**[H] Although the High Priest is considered everyone's teacher and master, honor was nevertheless extended to other individuals in his presence without fear of impugning the High Priest's honor.

אֲמַר אַבַּיֵי: כּוּלָּהּ מִשּׁוּם כְּבוֹדוֹ דְּכֹהֵן גָּדוֹל הוּא.

Abaye said: A proof may not be adduced from here. Usually one does not show honor for a student in the presence of the teacher, but here the **entire** process **is for the honor of the High Priest.** The passing of the Torah scroll to people of increasing importance demonstrates that the High Priest is considered the most important of all those present.

״וְכֹהֵן גָּדוֹל עוֹמֵד וּמְקַבֵּל וְקוֹרֵא״ וכו׳. ״עוֹמֵד״, מִכְּלָל דְּיוֹשֵׁב הוּא? וְהָאָמַר מָר: אֵין יְשִׁיבָה בָּעֲזָרָה אֶלָּא לְמַלְכֵי בֵית דָּוִד בִּלְבַד, שֶׁנֶּאֱמַר: ״וַיָּבֹא הַמֶּלֶךְ דָּוִד וַיֵּשֶׁב לִפְנֵי ה׳ וַיֹּאמֶר מִי אָנֹכִי״ וגו׳!

It is stated in the mishna: **And the High Priest stands, and receives** the Torah scroll, **and reads** from it. The Gemara asks: From the fact that he stands, it can be understood **by inference** that until that point **he** had been **sitting. But didn't the Master say** (*Tosefta, Sanhedrin* 4:4) that **sitting in** the Temple **courtyard**[NH] is permitted **only for kings from the house of David, as it is stated: "Then King David went in, and sat before the Lord; and he said: Who am I,** O Lord God, and what is my house, that You have brought me thus far?" (II Samuel 7:18).

NOTES

The blessings of the High Priest – בִּרְכוֹת כֹּהֵן גָּדוֹל: In *Tosefot HaRosh* it is pointed out that the Gemara offers no source for the *halakha* that these blessings must be recited in Hebrew. It is explained that perhaps the blessings are recited in Hebrew due to the special sanctity of Yom Kippur. Others explain that the expression: The blessings of the High Priest, does not refer to his blessings but rather to his reading of the Torah, which must certainly be in Hebrew, as it is read from a Torah scroll (*Tosefot Yom Tov*).

A blessing concerning the Torah – עַל הַתּוֹרָה: Rashi and other commentaries ask: Since there is also the standard blessing recited before the Torah is read, there should be nine blessings in total. Rashi answers that the Gemara is referring only to the eight blessings that are recited after the Torah reading. Other commentaries explain that although the wording of the blessings that are recited before and after the Torah reading are different from one another, they are considered to be a single unit and are therefore counted as one (see Meiri).

Sitting in the Temple courtyard – יְשִׁיבָה בָּעֲזָרָה: Some explain that the reason for this *halakha* is to show respect for the Temple. In addition, the expressions used in the Bible to describe the Temple service emphasize standing, such as: "To stand to serve" (Deuteronomy 18:5), and: "Who stand in the house of the Lord" (Jeremiah 28:5). Other commentaries claim that the verses that speak of Eli the priest sitting in the Temple courtyard show that this prohibition did not always exist; rather, it was instituted to honor the kingship of the house of David (see I Samuel 1:9; *Be'er Sheva*).

BACKGROUND

The synagogue attendant [*ḥazzan hakkeneset*] – חַזַּן הַכְּנֶסֶת: The word *ḥazzan* means primarily an attendant. Some say that it is derived from the root *ḥet, zayin, heh*, meaning seeing. In other words, a *ḥazzan* is one who watches over the synagogue and attends to its needs. Similarly, there were attendants in large study halls and courthouses who fulfilled this duty. In certain synagogues, the synagogue attendant also tutored young children or supervised their independent learning. He presumably would also lead prayer services, which is why over time this title was applied to a regular prayer leader.

The head of the synagogue – רֹאשׁ הַכְּנֶסֶת: The role of head of the synagogue continued for many generations and was called ἀρχισυνάγωγος, *archisunagogos*, in Greek. The head was in charge of the synagogue and oftentimes served as the leader of the community as well. It was a position of honor, and the one who held it wielded authority over the community or at least over those who prayed in his synagogue. In some places, the head of the synagogue had an honorary chair. During the Second Temple period, there was a synagogue on the Temple Mount. The Torah scrolls were kept there, and people would pray the regular communal prayers there.

HALAKHA

The blessings of the High Priest – בִּרְכוֹת כֹּהֵן גָּדוֹל: When the High Priest comes to read from the Torah on Yom Kippur, he sits in the women's courtyard and all of the people stand before him. The synagogue attendant who serves on the Temple Mount takes a Torah scroll and gives it to the head of the synagogue, who then hands it to the deputy High Priest, who hands it to the High Priest himself. The High Priest receives the Torah scroll while standing and reads the portions beginning with the phrases "after the death of the two sons of Aaron" and "but on the tenth day of this seventh month" from the book of Leviticus. He then furls the Torah scroll and holds it in his bosom, and says: More than what I have read before you is written here. He then recites by heart the passage of "and on the tenth" from Numbers.

Before he begins reading, he recites the blessing that is recited in the synagogue before reading from the Torah. After he finishes reading, he recites the blessing recited after reading from the Torah and adds the following seven blessings: (1) the blessing of the Temple service; (2) the blessing of thanksgiving; (3) the prayer of: Forgive us, our Father, for we have sinned, concluding with: Who forgives the iniquities of His people, the house of Israel, with compassion; (4) a blessing that the Temple should remain standing and that the Divine Presence should dwell within it, concluding with: Who dwells in Zion; (5) a blessing for the Jewish people that God should redeem them and not abandon them, which closes with: Who chooses Israel; (6) a blessing that the priests' service and actions should find favor before God, which closes with: Who sanctifies the priests; (7) a standard prayer of supplication and request, concluding with: Lord, redeem Your people, Israel, for Your people, Israel, are in need of redemption. Blessed be You, Lord, Who hears prayer (Rambam *Sefer Avoda, Hilkhot Avodat Yom HaKippurim* 3:10–11).

Honor may be given to a student in the presence of the teacher – חוֹלְקִין כָּבוֹד לְתַלְמִיד בִּמְקוֹם הָרַב: One may not show honor for a student in the presence of his teacher, unless his teacher also shows him honor. The *Taz*, citing Rabbeinu Simḥa, notes that if the teacher is himself honored by his students being honored by others, then one may honor his students (Rambam *Hilkhot Talmud Torah* 5:8; *Shulḥan Arukh, Yoreh De'a* 242:21).

Sitting in the Temple courtyard – יְשִׁיבָה בָּעֲזָרָה: It is prohibited for one to sit in the Temple courtyard, with the exception of kings from the house of David (Rambam *Sefer Avoda, Hilkhot Beit HaBeḥira* 7:7).

כִּדְאָמַר רַב חִסְדָּא: בְּעֶזְרַת נָשִׁים, הָכָא נַמִי בְּעֶזְרַת נָשִׁים.

The Gemara answers: **As Rav Ḥisda said** in a similar context: This took place not in the Israelite courtyard, where the prohibition against sitting applies, but **in the women's courtyard. Here, too,** the reading was **in the women's courtyard,** where it is permitted to sit, as it does not have the sanctified status of the Temple itself.

מֵיתִיבִי: וְהֵיכָן קוֹרִין בּוֹ? בָּעֲזָרָה; רַבִּי אֱלִיעֶזֶר בֶּן יַעֲקֹב אוֹמֵר: בְּהַר הַבַּיִת, שֶׁנֶּאֱמַר:

The Gemara **raises an objection** from a *baraita* (*Tosefta* 7:13): **And where does** the High Priest **read** from the Torah scroll? He reads from it **in the** Temple **courtyard. Rabbi Eliezer ben Ya'akov says:** He reads from it **on the Temple Mount, as it is stated:**

Perek **VII**
Daf **41** Amud **a**

"וַיִּקְרָא בוֹ לִפְנֵי הָרְחוֹב אֲשֶׁר לִפְנֵי שַׁעַר הַמַּיִם"; אָמַר רַב חִסְדָּא: בְּעֶזְרַת נָשִׁים.

"And he read there before the broad place that was before the Gate of the Water" (Nehemiah 8:3). According to this opinion, the High Priest would read from the Torah in the Temple courtyard. **Rav Ḥisda says** in response: The *baraita* also means that the reading takes place **in the women's courtyard.**

"וְקוֹרֵא אַחֲרֵי מוֹת וְאַךְ בֶּעָשׂוֹר". וּרְמִינְהִי: מְדַלְּגִין בַּנָּבִיא וְאֵין מְדַלְּגִין בַּתּוֹרָה!

§ It is taught in the mishna that the High Priest receives the Torah scroll **and reads** the Torah portion beginning with the verse: **"After the death"** (Leviticus 16:1), **and** the portion beginning with the verse: **"But on the tenth"** (Leviticus 23:26). Since these two portions are not adjacent to each other, the High Priest skips the section between the two portions. The Gemara **raises a contradiction** from a mishna (*Megilla* 24a): **One may skip** sections when reading the *haftara* **in the Prophets,**[NH] **but one may not skip** sections when reading **in the Torah.**

אָמַר אַבָּיֵי, לָא קַשְׁיָא: כָּאן בִּכְדֵי שֶׁיִּפְסוֹק הַתּוּרְגְּמָן, כָּאן בִּכְדֵי שֶׁלֹּא יִפְסוֹק הַתּוּרְגְּמָן.

Abaye said: This is **not difficult. There,** in the mishna in tractate *Megilla* that teaches that one may not skip, the intention is that one should not skip if the sections are so far apart from one another that the delay caused by doing so will be **of such length that the translator** who recites the Aramaic translation **will conclude** his translation before the next section is reached. However, in the case of the mishna **here,** it is permitted to skip verses because the two passages are in close proximity to one another. The delay caused is **of such** short **length that the translator will** still **not conclude**[H] his translation.

וְהָא עֲלַהּ קָתָנֵי: מְדַלְּגִין בַּנָּבִיא וְאֵין מְדַלְּגִין בַּתּוֹרָה. וְעַד כַּמָּה מְדַלְּגִין? עַד כְּדֵי שֶׁלֹּא יִפְסוֹק הַתּוּרְגְּמָן; מִכְּלָל דְּבַתּוֹרָה כְּלָל כְּלָל לָא!

The Gemara challenges this resolution: **But isn't it taught about** this mishna in a *baraita*: **One may skip** sections when reading **in the Prophets, but one may not skip** sections when reading **in the Torah. And how much may one skip** from one passage to another **in the Prophets?** One may skip when the section skipped is **of such** short **length that** when the furling of the scroll is completed **the translator will** still **not have concluded** his translation. **By inference,** when reading **in the Torah** one may **not** skip **at all.**

אֶלָּא אָמַר אַבָּיֵי, לָא קַשְׁיָא: כָּאן בְּעִנְיָן אֶחָד, כָּאן בִּשְׁנֵי עִנְיָנִין;

Rather, Abaye said another explanation: This is **not difficult.** In the mishna **here,** it is permitted to skip because both passages pertain **to a single topic. There,** in the mishna in tractate *Megilla* that teaches that one may not skip, the *halakha* is referring to a case where the passages pertain **to two** different **topics.**

וְהָתַנְיָא: מְדַלְּגִין בַּתּוֹרָה בְּעִנְיָן אֶחָד, וּבַנָּבִיא – בִּשְׁנֵי עִנְיָנִין, וְכָאן וְכָאן בִּכְדֵי שֶׁלֹּא יִפְסוֹק הַתּוּרְגְּמָן.

And this is **as it is taught** in a *baraita*: **One may skip** sections when reading **in the Torah** when both sections pertain **to a single topic, and in the Prophets** one may skip from one section to another even if they pertain **to two** different **topics. And** both **here and there,** one may skip only **when** the section skipped is **of such** short **length that** when the furling of the scroll is completed **the translator will** still **not have concluded** his translation.

NOTES

One may skip when reading in the Prophets – מְדַלְּגִין בַּנָּבִיא: Rashi explains that it is permitted for one to skip passages in the Prophets but not in the Torah because the Torah describes the practical observance of mitzvot. It is possible that the listeners will either become distracted or confused when passages are skipped in the Torah and will not hear the relevant information.

However, if one is reading about a single topic and skips passages in a manner that does not create a recognizable interruption, the listeners will not become confused, and therefore it is permitted. It is also reasoned that the reading from the Prophets does not require the same degree of respect as the reading from the Torah, which teaches mitzvot and not only matters of prophecy and rebuke.

HALAKHA

One may skip sections in the Prophets – מְדַלְּגִין בַּנָּבִיא: One may skip sections when reading the *haftara* from the Prophets, but one may not skip sections when reading from the Torah. This is true if the two portions read from the Torah discuss two different topics, as there is a concern that the congregation will be confused. However, it is permitted to skip sections when both portions pertain to a single topic. When reading from the Prophets, it is permitted to skip even when both portions pertain to a different topic (Rambam *Sefer Ahava, Hilkhot Tefilla* 12:8; *Shulḥan Arukh, Oraḥ Ḥayyim* 144:1).

Such short length that the translator will not conclude – בִּכְדֵי שֶׁלֹּא יִפְסוֹק הַתּוּרְגְּמָן: One may skip a section during the Torah reading only if the delay caused is of such short length that the translator will still not conclude his translation (Rambam *Sefer Ahava, Hilkhot Tefilla* 12:13, citing *Ba'al Halakhot Gedolot*).

וְאֵין מְדַלְּגִין מִנָּבִיא לְנָבִיא, וּבְנָבִיא שֶׁל שְׁנֵים עָשָׂר מְדַלְּגִין, וּבִלְבַד שֶׁלֹּא יְדַלֵּג מִסּוֹף הַסֵּפֶר לִתְחִילָּתוֹ.

And one may not skip from one book of the **Prophets to** another book of the **Prophets,**[H] even if both pertain to the same topic. **But among** the books **of the Twelve Prophets**[N] **one may skip, provided that one does not skip from the end of the book to its beginning.**[H] Rather, if one wishes to read from several of the Twelve Prophets, he must read the passages in the order that they are written.

״וְגוֹלֵל אֶת הַתּוֹרָה וּמַנִּיחָהּ בְּחֵיקוֹ״ כו׳. וְכׇל כָּךְ לָמָּה? שֶׁלֹּא לְהוֹצִיא לַעַז עַל סֵפֶר תּוֹרָה.

§ It is taught in the mishna: **And he furls the Torah** scroll, **and places it on his bosom,** and says: More than what I have read before you is written here. The Gemara comments: **And why** must he say **all of this?** It is **so as to not cast aspersions on the Torah scroll,** because people might think the portion that he read by heart is not written there.

״וּבֶעָשׂוֹר שֶׁבְּחוּמַּשׁ הַפְּקוּדִים קוֹרֵא עַל פֶּה״. וְלִיכְרְכֵיהּ לְסֵפֶר וְלִיקְרֵי! אָמַר רַב הוּנָא בַּר יְהוּדָה אָמַר רַב שֵׁשֶׁת: לְפִי שֶׁאֵין גּוֹלְלִין סֵפֶר תּוֹרָה בְּצִבּוּר.

It is stated in the mishna that **he reads by heart** the portion beginning with: **"And on the tenth," from the book of Numbers** (29:7–11). The Gemara asks: **But let him furl the** Torah **scroll**[N] to that portion **and read** it from the text. **Rav Huna bar Yehuda says** that **Rav Sheshet says:** This is not done **because one may not furl**[N] **a Torah scroll in public,**[H] out of respect for the congregation.

וְלֵיתֵי סֵפֶר תּוֹרָה אַחֲרִינָא וְלִיקְרֵי! רַב הוּנָא בַּר יְהוּדָה אָמַר: מִשּׁוּם פְּגָמוֹ שֶׁל רִאשׁוֹן; רַבִּי שִׁמְעוֹן בֶּן לָקִישׁ אָמַר: לְפִי שֶׁאֵין מְבָרְכִין בְּרָכָה שֶׁאֵינָהּ צְרִיכָה.

The Gemara asks: **But** why not **let them bring another Torah scroll** that has previously been furled to that portion **and read** from it? **Rav Huna bar Yehuda says:** People might then mistakenly think that the second scroll was brought **due to a flaw** that was found **in the first** scroll.[H] **Rabbi Shimon ben Lakish says:** Another scroll is not brought **because** then the High Priest will need to recite an additional blessing over it, and **one may not recite a blessing that is unnecessary.**

וּמִי חָיְישִׁינַן לִפְגָמָא? וְהָאָמַר רַבִּי יִצְחָק נַפָּחָא: רֹאשׁ חֹדֶשׁ טֵבֵת שֶׁחָל לִהְיוֹת בְּשַׁבָּת – מֵבִיא שָׁלֹשׁ תּוֹרוֹת, וְקוֹרֵא אַחַת מֵעִנְיָינוֹ שֶׁל יוֹם, וְאַחַת שֶׁל רֹאשׁ חֹדֶשׁ, וְאַחַת בְּשֶׁל חֲנוּכָּה!

The Gemara questions Rav Huna bar Yehuda's answer: **But are we** really **concerned that** people will think that there is **a flaw** in the first scroll? **But didn't Rabbi Yitzḥak Nappaḥa say:** When **the New Moon of Tevet,** which always occurs during Hanukkah, **occurs on Shabbat, one brings three Torah** scrolls. **And he reads from one** scroll **the topic of the day,** i.e., the weekly portion; **and** from **one** scroll the portion **of the New Moon; and** from **one** scroll the portion **of Hanukkah.** It is apparent from the statement of Rabbi Yitzḥak Nappaḥa that many Torah scrolls may be used, and there is no concern that people will mistakenly think that one or more has a flaw.

תְּלָתָא גַּבְרֵי בִּתְלָתָא סִיפְרֵי לֵיכָּא פְּגָמָא; חַד גַּבְרָא בִּתְרֵי סִיפְרֵי אִיכָּא פְּגָמָא.

The Gemara answers: When **three men** read **from three scrolls, there is no** concern that people will think that one of the scrolls has **a flaw,** since people assume that it is befitting for each individual to read from his own scroll. However, when **one man** reads **from two** different Torah **scrolls, there is** a concern that people will think that the first scroll has **a flaw,** and they will not realize that this was done only to avoid forcing the community to wait while the scroll is furled.

HALAKHA

One may not skip from one book of the Prophets to another book of the Prophets – אֵין מְדַלְּגִין מִנָּבִיא לְנָבִיא: When reading from the Prophets, one may not skip from one book of Prophets to another, unless one is reading from the book of the Twelve Prophets. However, the *Mishna Berura* notes that contemporary halakhic authorities rule that since the custom in most congregations is to read without a translator, and since the readings from the Prophets are printed in their own book, nowadays it is permitted to skip from one book of Prophets to another during the reading (Rambam *Sefer Ahava, Hilkhot Tefilla* 12:13; *Shulḥan Arukh, Oraḥ Ḥayyim* 144:1).

Provided that one does not skip from the end of the book to its beginning – וּבִלְבַד שֶׁלֹּא יְדַלֵּג מִסּוֹף הַסֵּפֶר לִתְחִילָּתוֹ: In a situation where it is permitted to skip sections during the reading, this is permitted only so long as the passages are read in the proper order. It is prohibited to start at the end of a book and then return to the beginning. Nowadays, there is a dispute with regard to whether or not this prohibition is relevant. Some authorities rule that it is prohibited to skip from the end of a book to its beginning under any circumstances (*Magen Avraham*), while the *Peri Megadim* permits it when reading about a single topic within a single book of the Prophets (Rambam *Sefer Ahava, Hilkhot Tefilla* 12:13; *Shulḥan Arukh, Oraḥ Ḥayyim* 144:1).

One may not furl a Torah scroll in public – אֵין גּוֹלְלִין סֵפֶר תּוֹרָה בְּצִבּוּר: It is prohibited to furl a Torah scroll in public out of respect for the congregation, so that the congregation will not have to wait while it takes place. However, if there is only a single Torah scroll and it is necessary to read two different passages, the reading takes precedence and it is permitted to furl the scroll (Rambam *Sefer Ahava, Hilkhot Tefilla* 12:23; *Shulḥan Arukh, Oraḥ Ḥayyim* 144:3).

Due to a flaw that was found in the first scroll – מִשּׁוּם פְּגָמוֹ שֶׁל רִאשׁוֹן: It is prohibited to call up the same person to read from two different Torah scrolls, because it can cause people to mistakenly believe that a flaw was found in the first scroll. Therefore, it is prohibited to call up the same person to read the last portion in one Torah scroll and then to read the concluding verses that are read from a different Torah scroll. If someone was called up to read any portion other than the last one from the first Torah scroll, according to the *Magen Avraham* it is permitted to call him up to read the concluding verses that are read from the Torah from a different scroll. The *Baḥ* and others prohibit this. However, on Simḥat Torah, for several reasons it is permitted to call up a person to restart the Torah reading cycle from Genesis even if he was already called up to read from Deuteronomy (*Eliya Rabba*). It is permitted to call up three different people to read from three different scrolls, and there is no concern that people will mistakenly believe that a flaw was found in one of the scrolls (Rambam *Sefer Ahava, Hilkhot Tefilla* 12:23 and *Sefer Avoda, Hilkhot Avodat Yom HaKippurim* 3:10; *Shulḥan Arukh, Oraḥ Ḥayyim* 144:4).

NOTES

But among the books of the Twelve Prophets – וּבְנָבִיא שֶׁל שְׁנֵים עָשָׂר: Although each book is of a different prophet, they are considered a single book in the Jewish canon. For this reason, it is permitted to skip from one to the other.

But let him furl the Torah scroll – וְלִיכְרְכֵיהּ לְסֵפֶר: The following question is raised in *Tosefot HaRosh* and *Tosefot Yom Tov* on tractate *Yoma*: Previously, the Gemara had stated that one may not skip a section during the Torah reading. How can it now suggest furling the scroll and skipping to a distant section? In *Tosefot HaRosh*, it is explained that if the reader skips from one topic to another, even without a pause, it can create confusion among the listeners. However, if the listeners see that someone is rolling the Torah scroll, they understand that he is moving to another topic. They will remain attentive and not become distracted. For this reason, were it permitted to furl the Torah scroll in public, it would also be permitted to skip from one topic to another.

One may not furl, etc. – אֵין גּוֹלְלִין וכו׳: The *ge'onim* rule in accordance with the Jerusalem Talmud that if it is necessary to read two different topics, the scroll must be furled forward to the next passage. This can occur, for example, if the concluding verses read from the Torah pertain to the season, e.g., a festival, and are not part of the weekly portion, and there is no other Torah scroll available. However, it is preferable to do so privately and not in the presence of the congregation.

״וּמְבָרֵךְ עָלֶיהָ שְׁמוֹנֶה בְּרָכוֹת״ כו׳. תָּנוּ רַבָּנַן: [מְבָרְכִין] עַל הַתּוֹרָה כְּדֶרֶךְ שֶׁמְּבָרְכִין בְּבֵית הַכְּנֶסֶת, וְעַל הָעֲבוֹדָה וְעַל הַהוֹדָאָה וְעַל מְחִילַת עָוֹן כְּתִיקְנָן, עַל הַמִּקְדָּשׁ בִּפְנֵי עַצְמוֹ, וְעַל הַכֹּהֲנִים בִּפְנֵי עַצְמָן, עַל יִשְׂרָאֵל בִּפְנֵי עַצְמָן, וְעַל יְרוּשָׁלַיִם בִּפְנֵי עַצְמָהּ.

§ It is taught in the mishna: **And** after the reading the High Priest **recites eight blessings. The Sages taught** that these are the eight blessings: **He recites a blessing concerning the Torah in the** usual **way one recites** a blessing in **the synagogue, and** he recites the three blessings **concerning the** Temple **service, and concerning thanksgiving, and concerning forgiveness for iniquity,** and all are recited **in accordance with their established forms** in the *Amida* prayer. He recites the blessing **concerning the Temple in and of itself,** the blessing **concerning the priests in and of itself,** the blessing **concerning the Jewish people in and of itself, and** the blessing **concerning Jerusalem in and of itself.**

״וְהַשְּׁאָר תְּפִלָּה״. תָּנוּ רַבָּנַן: הַשְּׁאָר תְּפִלָּה תְּחִנָּה רִנָּה וּבַקָּשָׁה שֶׁעַמְּךָ יִשְׂרָאֵל צְרִיכִין לִיוָּשַׁע, וְחוֹתֵם בְּ״שׁוֹמֵעַ תְּפִלָּה״. מִכָּאן וְאֵילָךְ, כָּל אֶחָד וְאֶחָד מֵבִיא סֵפֶר תּוֹרָה מִתּוֹךְ בֵּיתוֹ וְקוֹרֵא בּוֹ. וְכָל כָּךְ לָמָּה? כְּדֵי לְהַרְאוֹת חֲזוּתוֹ לָרַבִּים.

With regard to the end of the mishna, which states: **And the rest of the prayer, the Sages taught: The** text of **the rest of the prayer** is as follows: **A supplication,**[N] **a song, and a request that Your people, Israel, are in need of redemption. And he concludes** the blessing **with:** Blessed are You, Lord, **the One Who hears prayer. From this** point **forward, each and every person** present **brings a Torah scroll from his home and reads from it. And why** do **all these** people bring their personal Torah scrolls? Everyone brings his own **in order to show its** beautiful **appearance to the public,** as a way of showing fondness for the mitzva.

מתני׳ פָּרָשַׁת הַמֶּלֶךְ כֵּיצַד? מוֹצָאֵי יוֹם טוֹב הָרִאשׁוֹן שֶׁל חַג בַּשְּׁמִינִי בְּמוֹצָאֵי שְׁבִיעִית, עוֹשִׂין לוֹ בִּימָה שֶׁל עֵץ בָּעֲזָרָה וְהוּא יוֹשֵׁב עָלֶיהָ, שֶׁנֶּאֱמַר: ״מִקֵּץ שֶׁבַע שָׁנִים בְּמֹעֵד״ וגו׳.

MISHNA How is **the portion of** the Torah that is read by **the king**[N] recited[H] at the assembly, when all the Jewish people would assemble? At **the conclusion of the first day of the festival** of *Sukkot*, **on the eighth,** after **the conclusion of the Sabbatical Year, they make a wooden platform for** the king[H] **in the** Temple **courtyard, and he sits on it, as it is stated: "At the end of every seven years, in the Festival** of the Sabbatical Year" (Deuteronomy 31:10).

חַזַּן הַכְּנֶסֶת נוֹטֵל סֵפֶר תּוֹרָה וְנוֹתְנָהּ לְרֹאשׁ הַכְּנֶסֶת, וְרֹאשׁ הַכְּנֶסֶת נוֹתְנָהּ לַסְּגָן, וְהַסְּגָן נוֹתְנָהּ לְכֹהֵן גָּדוֹל, וְכֹהֵן גָּדוֹל נוֹתְנָהּ לַמֶּלֶךְ, וְהַמֶּלֶךְ עוֹמֵד וּמְקַבֵּל וְקוֹרֵא יוֹשֵׁב.

The synagogue attendant takes a Torah scroll and gives it to the head of the synagogue that stands on the Temple Mount. **And the head of the synagogue gives it to the deputy** High Priest, **and the deputy** High Priest **gives it to the High Priest, and the High priest gives it to the king. And the king stands, and receives** the Torah scroll, **and reads** from it while **sitting.**

NOTES

The rest of the prayer: A supplication – הַשְּׁאָר תְּפִלָּה תְּחִנָּה: It seems from Rashi's commentary in tractate *Yoma* (70a) and other commentaries that this is the actual wording of the blessing that the priest recites. However, the Rambam holds that this is not the wording itself but rather it is describing the elements of the prayer of the High Priest, i.e., he recites a prayer of supplication, a song, and a request to the best of his abilities. Accordingly, the only part of this prayer that has a set formula is the closing blessing.

The portion of the Torah read by the king – פָּרָשַׁת הַמֶּלֶךְ: This refers to the assembly, a special mitzva for the king to read portions of the Torah before the nation. Although the Torah itself does not explicitly state that this ceremony is a mitzva that the king must perform (see Rashi), some say that this detail is deduced from the verses of the mitzva, as Moses commanded Joshua to observe this mitzva (Deuteronomy 31:7–13), speaking in the singular: "You shall read this Torah before all Israel in their hearing" (Deuteronomy 31:11). It therefore appears to be a mitzva for Joshua, who was to be the king of the Jewish people. It can therefore be extrapolated that this is a mitzva for all the kings who come afterward (see *Tosefot Yom Tov*).

It is explained in *Sefer Yere'im* that there is proof for this from the fact that King Josiah read the Torah for the nation. Others explain that it was the Sages who instituted that this mitzva is incumbent upon the king to fulfill. When there is no king, the mitzva is not negated. Rather, the nation must gather together to hear the Torah read by the greatest Sage of the generation (*Tiferet Yisrael*).

Neither the Mishna nor the Gemara cites a source for the *halakha* that the mitzva is to read these passages in Hebrew. However, in the Rambam and *Tosefot HaRosh*, it is explained that it is derived from the words: "You shall read this Torah" (Deuteronomy 31:11), that the Torah must be read as it is written, in Hebrew.

HALAKHA

How is the portion of the Torah that is read by the king recited – פָּרָשַׁת הַמֶּלֶךְ כֵּיצַד: The Rambam writes: At the conclusion of the first day of *Sukkot* and at the beginning of the intermediate days, during the first year of the new Sabbatical cycle, the king reads from the Torah before the nation in the women's courtyard of the Temple. The king is permitted to read while sitting, but if he reads standing up, it is praiseworthy. He reads from the beginning of the book of Deuteronomy until after the portion of: "Hear, O Israel" (Deuteronomy 6:4–9). He then skips and reads the portion of: "And it shall come to pass, if you shall hearken" (Deuteronomy 11:13–21). He then reads from: "You shall tithe" (Deuteronomy 14:22), until the end of the portion of the blessings and curses (Deuteronomy 28). The *Leḥem Mishne* comments that the Rambam's version of the mishna apparently did not mention the passage concerning the appointment of a king (Rambam *Sefer Korbanot*, *Hilkhot Ḥagiga* 3:3).

They make a wooden platform for the king – עוֹשִׂין לוֹ בִּימָה שֶׁל עֵץ: For the king's public reading from the Torah, a wooden platform is constructed and placed in the middle of the women's courtyard. The king sits atop it with the entire nation gathered around him. The synagogue attendant takes a Torah scroll and gives it to the head of the synagogue, the head of the synagogue gives it to the deputy High Priest, the deputy High Priest gives it to the High Priest, and the High Priest then gives it to the king. The king recites the standard blessing before reading from the Torah, and after the reading he furls it and recites the blessing recited after reading from the Torah. He then adds seven blessings: A blessing concerning the Temple service; a blessing of thanksgiving; the blessing: You have chosen us, until: Who sanctifies Israel and the Festivals, which is recited in the Festival prayer service; a prayer over the Temple that closes with: Who dwells in Zion; a prayer for the Jewish people that concludes with: Who chooses Israel; and a prayer for the priests that concludes with: Who sanctifies the priests. Finally, the king recites words of prayer and plea, and ends with: Lord, redeem Your people, Israel, for Your people are in need of redemption. Blessed are You, Lord, Who hears prayer (Rambam *Sefer Korbanot*, *Hilkhot Ḥagiga* 3:4).

אַגְרִיפָּס הַמֶּלֶךְ עָמַד וְקִבֵּל וְקָרָא עוֹמֵד, וְשִׁבְּחוּהוּ חֲכָמִים. וּכְשֶׁהִגִּיעַ לְ״לֹא תוּכַל לָתֵת עָלֶיךָ אִישׁ נׇכְרִי״, זָלְגוּ עֵינָיו דְּמָעוֹת. אָמְרוּ לוֹ: אַל תִּתְיָרֵא, אַגְרִיפָּס, אָחִינוּ אַתָּה, אָחִינוּ אַתָּה.

King Agrippa[P] **arose, and received** the Torah scroll, **and read** from it while **standing, and the Sages praised him** for this. **And when** Agrippa **arrived at** the verse in the portion read by the king that states: **"You may not appoint a foreigner over you"** (Deuteronomy 17:15), **tears flowed from his eyes,** because he was a descendant of the house of Herod and was not of Jewish origin. The entire nation **said to him: Fear not, Agrippa. You are our brother, you are our brother.**

וְקוֹרֵא מִתְּחִילַּת ״אֵלֶּה הַדְּבָרִים״ עַד ״שְׁמַע״, וּ״שְׁמַע״, ״וְהָיָה אִם שָׁמֹעַ״, ״עַשֵּׂר תְּעַשֵּׂר״, ״כִּי תְכַלֶּה לַעְשֵׂר״, וּפָרָשַׁת הַמֶּלֶךְ וּבְרָכוֹת וּקְלָלוֹת, עַד שֶׁגּוֹמֵר כׇּל הַפָּרָשָׁה.

And the king **reads from the beginning of** Deuteronomy, from the verse that states: **"And these are the words"** (Deuteronomy 1:1), **until** the words: **"Hear, O Israel"** (Deuteronomy 6:4). **And** he then reads the sections beginning with: **"Hear, O Israel"** (Deuteronomy 6:4–9), **"And it shall come to pass, if you shall hearken"** (Deuteronomy 11:13–21), **"You shall tithe"** (Deuteronomy 14:22–29),[N] **"When you have made an end of the tithing"** (Deuteronomy 26:12–15), **and the passage concerning the** appointment of a **king** (Deuteronomy 17:14–20),[N] **and the blessings and curses** (Deuteronomy 28), **until he finishes the entire portion.**

בְּרָכוֹת שֶׁכֹּהֵן גָּדוֹל מְבָרֵךְ אוֹתָן – הַמֶּלֶךְ מְבָרֵךְ אוֹתָן, אֶלָּא שֶׁנּוֹתֵן שֶׁל רְגָלִים תַּחַת מְחִילַת הֶעָוֹן.

The same **blessings that the High Priest recites** on Yom Kippur, **the king recites** at this ceremony, **but he delivers** a blessing **concerning the Festivals in place of** the blessing concerning **forgiveness for iniquity.**

גמ׳ בַּשְּׁמִינִי סָלְקָא דַּעְתָּךְ? אֵימָא: בַּשְּׁמִינִית.

GEMARA The mishna states that the assembly takes place on the eighth. The Gemara asks: Does it **enter your mind** that the assembly takes place **on the eighth** day of the festival of *Sukkot*? The mishna clearly states that the ceremony takes place at the conclusion of the first day of the Festival. Rather, **say** that it takes place **during the eighth** year of the Sabbatical cycle.

וְכׇל הָנֵי לָמָּה לִי?

The verse describes in detail when the assembly takes place: "At the end of every seven years, in the Festival of the Sabbatical Year, in the festival of *Sukkot*, when all Israel comes to appear before the Lord your God" (Deuteronomy 31:10–11). The Gemara asks: **And why do** I need **all these** details?

צְרִיכִי, דְּאִי כָּתַב רַחֲמָנָא ״מִקֵּץ״, הֲוָה אָמִינָא נִימְנוּ מֵהַשְׁתָּא וְאַף עַל גַּב דְּלָא מִתְרַמֵּי בִּשְׁמִיטָּה. כָּתַב רַחֲמָנָא ״שְׁמִטָּה״;

The Gemara answers: All of these details **are necessary, as, if the Merciful One had written** only **"at the end**[N] of every seven years" (Deuteronomy 31:10), **I would have said** that **we count from now,** i.e., from when this was said, **and** that the tally of years begins from the fortieth year in the wilderness, **even though** by this calculation the assembly **would not occur in the Sabbatical Year.** Therefore, **the Merciful One writes: "The Sabbatical Year."**

וְאִי כָּתַב רַחֲמָנָא ״שְׁמִטָּה״, הֲוָה אָמִינָא בְּסוֹף שְׁמִיטָּה, כָּתַב רַחֲמָנָא ״בְּמֹעֵד״;

And if the Merciful One had written only the phrase: At the end of every seven years of the **"Sabbatical Year," I would have said** that it takes place **at the end of the Sabbatical Year.** Therefore, **the Merciful One writes: "In the Festival,"**[N] and the first Festival following the Sabbatical Year is in the month of Tishrei.

PERSONALITIES

King Agrippa – אַגְרִיפָּס הַמֶּלֶךְ: This refers to King Agrippa I, Julius Agrippa, who was the grandson of Herod (10 BCE–44 CE). Agrippa's father was Aristoblus, the son of Herod from his Hasmonean wife, Miriam, the daughter of Hyrcanus II. His mother was Berenice, the daughter of Herod's sister. He grew up in Rome in the house of the emperor, and there he befriended the emperor's family. He was a close friend of Gaius, who, upon being designated emperor, appointed Agrippa governor over a portion of Herod's kingdom. Agrippa later became one of the driving forces behind Claudius's appointment as emperor, who in turn installed him as ruler over the rest of Herod's kingdom, including the land of Judea. Upon arriving in Eretz Yisrael as king, Agrippa developed a relationship with the Sages of the Jewish people and publicly displayed his deep connection to them through observing the mitzvot scrupulously. The Sages praised him for this. Agrippa attempted to fortify Jerusalem by building an additional wall, which included some of the city's suburbs within the city's limits.

Since the Sages regarded Herod and his household as Canaanite slaves, Agrippa's status as a member of the Jewish people was questionable. Consequently, the Sages viewed the people's words, stating that he was their brother, as mere flattery (see 41b). Agrippa himself was also considered a dubious character. He was raised and educated in Rome among friends who were wanton in every regard, and as king he continued Herod's initiatives of encouraging Greek culture, at least in the gentile cities under his reign.

Coin bearing the profile of Agrippa I

NOTES

You shall tithe – עַשֵּׂר תְּעַשֵּׂר: Rashi and the Meiri explain that since the assembly takes place during the harvest season and everyone is obligated to separate tithes from the year's harvest, the king must remind the nation of this. It is explained in the Jerusalem Talmud that since the assembly takes place immediately after the Sabbatical Year, during which there are no tithes, the king must remind the people that they are now once more obligated to separate tithes.

And the passage concerning a king – וּפָרָשַׁת הַמֶּלֶךְ: According to most commentaries, the king reads the portions that discuss the tithes first and does not read the passage concerning the appointment of a king between them, despite the fact that this breaks the order of the verses, as they discuss a single topic. He then goes back and reads the passage concerning a king. The Rambam, however, rules differently. The early commentaries address the difficulty of how it is permitted for the king to skip from one passage to another in the Torah and then go backward in the Torah scroll and read about a different topic. Rashi explains that since there is no translator present, it does not cause an interruption. Some later commentaries understand this to mean that since the people are not individually obligated to hear the reading, as the purpose of the mitzva is to publicize the Torah in general, skipping passages is not problematic (see *Eshel Avraham*). It is explained in the Meiri that the honor of the king is given precedence over that of the congregation, and since the king is honored by the reading, he is therefore permitted to roll the scroll forward and backward to read from it (see *Tosefot Yom Tov*).

If the Merciful One had written only: At the end [*mikkeitz*] – אִי כָּתַב רַחֲמָנָא מִקֵּץ: The question arises: Why doesn't the Torah simply state: At the end [*mikkeitz*] of the Sabbatical Year, and eliminate any doubt that perhaps the verse is referring to a different tally of years? It is explained in *Tosafot HaRosh* that the word *mikkeitz* does not always refer to the very end of the period in question; it can also include the time period itself. Therefore, the Torah writes both "at the end [*mikkeitz*] of every seven years" and "in the Festival of the Sabbatical Year."

In the Festival – בְּמֹעֵד: *Tosafot* suggest that the phrase "in the Festival" indicates that the assembly takes place sometime in the middle of the Festival and not at the beginning. According to this opinion, that is why the assembly does not take place on the first day of *Sukkot*. The Rambam's Commentary on the Mishna offers a similar interpretation.

וְאִי כְּתַב "בְּמֹעֵד", הֲוָה אָמֵינָא מֵרֵישׁ שַׁתָּא, כְּתַב רַחֲמָנָא "בְּחַג הַסֻּכּוֹת";

And if the Torah **had written** only: "At the end of every seven years **in the Festival** of the Sabbatical Year," **I would have said** that it takes place **on** the festival of **Rosh Hashanah,** which is on the first day of Tishrei. Therefore, **the Merciful One** also **writes: "In the festival of** ***Sukkot.***"

וְאִי כְּתַב רַחֲמָנָא "בְּחַג הַסֻּכּוֹת", הֲוָה אָמֵינָא אֲפִילּוּ יוֹם טוֹב אַחֲרוֹן. כְּתַב רַחֲמָנָא "בְּבוֹא כָל יִשְׂרָאֵל",

And if the Merciful One had written only: **"In the festival of** ***Sukkot,***" **I would have said** that it could refer **even** to **the last** day of the **Festival.** Therefore, **the Merciful One** also **writes: "When all Israel comes"** (Deuteronomy 31:11),

מֵאַתְחַלְתָּא דְּמוֹעֵד.

implying that the assembly takes place **at the beginning of the Festival,** when the entire Jewish people comes to Jerusalem.

"וְחַזַּן הַכְּנֶסֶת נוֹטֵל סֵפֶר תּוֹרָה וְנוֹתְנוֹ לְרֹאשׁ הַכְּנֶסֶת". שְׁמַעַתְּ מִינַּהּ: חוֹלְקִין כָּבוֹד לְתַלְמִיד בִּמְקוֹם הָרַב! אָמַר אַבָּיֵי: כּוּלָּהּ מִשּׁוּם כְּבוֹדוֹ דְּמֶלֶךְ.

§ It is taught in the mishna: **And the synagogue attendant takes a Torah scroll and gives it to the head of the synagogue,** until it is eventually passed to the king. The Gemara suggests: **You can learn from** the fact that all of these dignitaries receive the Torah scroll before the king that **honor may be given to a student in the presence of the teacher. Abaye said:** A proof may not be adduced from here, as the **entire** process **is for the honor of the king,**[H] to show that he is removed from ordinary people by many ranks.

"וְהַמֶּלֶךְ עוֹמֵד וּמְקַבֵּל וְקוֹרֵא יוֹשֵׁב; אַגְרִיפַּס הַמֶּלֶךְ עָמַד וְקִיבֵּל וְקָרָא עוֹמֵד". עוֹמֵד, מִכְּלָל דְּיוֹשֵׁב? וְהָאָמַר מָר: אֵין יְשִׁיבָה בָּעֲזָרָה אֶלָּא לְמַלְכֵי בֵית דָּוִד בִּלְבַד, שֶׁנֶּאֱמַר: "וַיָּבֹא הַמֶּלֶךְ דָּוִד וַיֵּשֶׁב לִפְנֵי ה' וַיֹּאמֶר" וגו'! כִּדְאָמַר רַב חִסְדָּא: בְּעֶזְרַת נָשִׁים, הָכָא נַמִי בְּעֶזְרַת נָשִׁים.

It is taught in the mishna: **And the king stands, and receives** the Torah scroll, **and reads** from it while **sitting. King Agrippa arose, and received** the Torah scroll, **and read** from it while **standing.** The Gemara asks: **By inference,** until that point he had been **sitting. But didn't the Master say** (*Tosefta, Sanhedrin* 4:4) that **sitting in the** Temple **courtyard** is permitted **only for kings from the house of David, as it is stated: "Then King David went in, and sat before the Lord; and he said:** Who am I?" (II Samuel 7:18). The Gemara answers: **As Rav Ḥisda said** in a similar context: This took place not in the Israelite courtyard, where the prohibition against sitting applies, but **in the women's courtyard. Here too,** the assembly was **in the women's courtyard.**[H]

"וְשִׁבְּחוּהוּ חֲכָמִים". "שִׁבְּחוּהוּ" מִכְּלָל דְּשַׁפִּיר עֲבַד? וְהָאָמַר רַב אָשֵׁי, אֲפִילּוּ לְמַאן דְּאָמַר: נָשִׂיא שֶׁמָּחַל עַל כְּבוֹדוֹ – כְּבוֹדוֹ מָחוּל, מֶלֶךְ שֶׁמָּחַל עַל כְּבוֹדוֹ – אֵין כְּבוֹדוֹ מָחוּל, שֶׁנֶּאֱמַר: "שׂוֹם תָּשִׂים עָלֶיךָ מֶלֶךְ", שֶׁתְּהֵא אֵימָתוֹ עָלֶיךָ!

It is stated in the mishna that King Agrippa read from the Torah while standing, **and the Sages praised him** for this. The Gemara asks: **From the fact** that **they praised him,** can it be concluded **that he acted appropriately? Didn't Rav Ashi say: Even according to the one who says** with regard to **a** ***Nasi*** **who relinquished** the **honor** due **him,**[H] **his honor is relinquished,** i.e., he may do so, with regard to **a king who relinquished** the **honor** due **him,**[H] **his honor is not relinquished, as it is stated: "You shall place a king over you"** (Deuteronomy 17:15). This is interpreted to mean **that his awe shall be upon you.** The Torah establishes that awe is an essential component of kingship, and it is not the prerogative of the king to relinquish it.

מִצְוָה שָׁאנֵי.

The Gemara answers: Since he relinquished his honor for the sake of **a mitzva,** this situation **is different** and does not dishonor him.

"וּכְשֶׁהִגִּיעַ לְלֹא תוּכַל לָתֵת". תָּנָא מִשְּׁמֵיהּ דְּרַבִּי נָתָן: בְּאוֹתָהּ שָׁעָה נִתְחַיְּיבוּ שׂוֹנְאֵי יִשְׂרָאֵל כְּלָיָה, שֶׁהֶחֱנִיפוּ לוֹ לְאַגְרִיפַּס.

The mishna continues: **And when** Agrippa **arrived at** the verse: "**You may not appoint** a foreigner over you" (Deuteronomy 17:15), tears flowed from his eyes because he was a descendant of the house of Herod and was not of Jewish origin. The entire nation said to him: You are our brother. It is **taught in the name of Rabbi Natan: At that moment the enemies of the Jewish people,** a euphemism for the Jewish people, **were sentenced to destruction for flattering Agrippa.**

HALAKHA

The entire process is for the honor of the king – כּוּלָּהּ מִשּׁוּם כְּבוֹדוֹ דְּמֶלֶךְ: One may not show honor for a student in the presence of his teacher. However, if the teacher is honored through the honor that others give his students, then one may do so (Rambam *Sefer Korbanot, Hilkhot Ḥagiga* 3:4).

In the women's courtyard – בְּעֶזְרַת נָשִׁים: The portion of the king is read in the women's courtyard in the Temple, and the king is permitted to sit while he reads from the Torah if he so desires (Rambam *Sefer Korbanot, Hilkhot Ḥagiga* 3:4).

A ***Nasi*** **who relinquished the honor due him** – נָשִׂיא שֶׁמָּחַל עַל כְּבוֹדוֹ: If a Sage, a deputy *Nasi*, or a *Nasi* relinquishes the honor due to him, his honor is relinquished. Even so, it is still a mitzva to rise slightly in his presence and to show respect for him. The Shakh, citing the Smak, rules that nowadays, the *halakhot* of a *Nasi* or the deputy *Nasi* are not applicable (Rambam *Sefer HaMadda, Hilkhot Talmud Torah* 6:12; *Shulḥan Arukh, Yoreh De'a* 244:14).

A king who relinquished the honor due him – מֶלֶךְ שֶׁמָּחַל עַל כְּבוֹדוֹ: If a king relinquishes the honor due to him, his honor is not relinquished. There is still an obligation to honor him by Torah law (Rambam *Sefer Shofetim, Hilkhot Melakhim* 2:3).

אָמַר רַבִּי שִׁמְעוֹן בֶּן חֲלַפְתָּא: מִיּוֹם שֶׁגָּבַר אֶגְרוֹפָהּ שֶׁל חֲנוּפָּה, נִתְעַוְּותוּ הַדִּינִין וְנִתְקַלְקְלוּ הַמַּעֲשִׂים, וְאֵין אָדָם יָכוֹל לוֹמַר לַחֲבֵירוֹ ״מַעֲשַׂי גְּדוֹלִים מִמַּעֲשֶׂיךָ״.

Rabbi Shimon ben Ḥalafta says: From the day that the power of flattery prevailed, the judgment has become corrupted, and people's **deeds have become corrupted, and a person cannot say to another:**[N] **My deeds are greater than your deeds,** as everyone flatters one another and people no longer know the truth.

דָּרַשׁ רַבִּי יְהוּדָה בַּר מַעַרְבָא, וְאִיתֵּימָא רַבִּי שִׁמְעוֹן בֶּן פָּזִי: מוּתָּר לְהַחֲנִיף לָרְשָׁעִים בָּעוֹלָם הַזֶּה, שֶׁנֶּאֱמַר: ״לֹא יִקָּרֵא עוֹד לְנָבָל נָדִיב וּלְכִילַי לֹא יֵאָמֵר שׁוֹעַ״, מִכְּלָל דְּבָעוֹלָם הַזֶּה שָׁרֵי.

Rabbi Yehuda of the West, Eretz Yisrael, **and some say Rabbi Shimon ben Pazi, taught: It is permitted to flatter wicked people**[N] **in this world, as it is stated** concerning the future: **"The vile person shall no longer be called generous, nor shall the churl be said to be noble"** (Isaiah 32:5). **By inference,** this indicates **that in this world it is permitted** to flatter them.

רַבִּי שִׁמְעוֹן בֶּן לָקִישׁ אָמַר, מֵהָכָא: ״כִּרְאֹת פְּנֵי אֱלֹהִים וַתִּרְצֵנִי״.

Rabbi Shimon ben Lakish said that this can be proven **from here.** Jacob said to Esau: "I have seen your face, **as one sees the face of angels, and you were pleased with me"** (Genesis 33:10). Jacob flattered him by comparing seeing him to seeing a divine vision.

וּפְלִיגָא דְּרַבִּי לֵוִי, דְּאָמַר רַבִּי לֵוִי: מָשָׁל שֶׁל יַעֲקֹב וְעֵשָׂו, לְמָה הַדָּבָר דּוֹמֶה? לְאָדָם שֶׁזִּימֵּן אֶת חֲבֵירוֹ וְהִכִּיר בּוֹ שֶׁמְּבַקֵּשׁ לְהוֹרְגוֹ, אָמַר לוֹ: טַעַם תַּבְשִׁיל זֶה שֶׁאֲנִי טוֹעֵם כְּתַבְשִׁיל שֶׁטָּעַמְתִּי בְּבֵית הַמֶּלֶךְ. אָמַר: יָדַע לֵיהּ מַלְכָּא. מִיסְתְּפֵי, וְלָא קָטֵיל לֵיהּ.

The Gemara notes: **And** Rabbi Shimon ben Lakish, in interpreting Jacob's statement, **disagrees with Rabbi Levi, as Rabbi Levi says:** With regard to the interaction between **Jacob and Esau, to what is this matter comparable? To a person who invited another** to his home **and** the guest **realized that he wants to kill him.** The guest **said to him: The flavor of this dish that I taste is like a dish that I tasted in the king's house.** The host then **said** to himself: **The king** must **know him.** Therefore, **he was afraid and did not kill him.** Similarly, when Jacob told Esau that his face is like the face of an angel, he intended to let him know that he had seen angels, in order to instill fear in him so that Esau would not seek to harm him.

אָמַר רַבִּי אֶלְעָזָר: כׇּל אָדָם שֶׁיֵּשׁ בּוֹ חֲנוּפָּה – מֵבִיא אַף לָעוֹלָם, שֶׁנֶּאֱמַר: ״וְחַנְפֵי לֵב יָשִׂימוּ אָף״; וְלֹא עוֹד, אֶלָּא שֶׁאֵין תְּפִלָּתוֹ נִשְׁמַעַת, שֶׁנֶּאֱמַר: ״לֹא יְשַׁוְּעוּ כִּי אֲסָרָם״.

Rabbi Elazar says: Any person who has flattery in him brings wrath to the world, as it is stated: "But those with flattery in their hearts bring about wrath" (Job 36:13). **And moreover, his prayer is not heard, as it is stated** in that same verse: **"They do not cry for help when He binds them."**

(סִימָן: א״ף עוב״ר גיהנ״ם ביד״ו נִד״ה גול״ה.)

(The Gemara cites a **mnemonic** device for the statements of Rabbi Elazar: **Wrath, fetus, Gehenna, in his hands, menstruating woman, exiled.**

וְאָמַר רַבִּי אֶלְעָזָר: כׇּל אָדָם שֶׁיֵּשׁ בּוֹ חֲנוּפָּה – אֲפִילּוּ עוּבָּרִין שֶׁבִּמְעֵי אִמָּן מְקַלְּלִין אוֹתוֹ, שֶׁנֶּאֱמַר: ״אֹמֵר לְרָשָׁע צַדִּיק אָתָּה יִקְּבֻהוּ עַמִּים יִזְעָמוּהוּ לְאֻמִּים״. וְאֵין קוֹב אֶלָּא קְלָלָה, שֶׁנֶּאֱמַר: ״לֹא קַבֹּה אֵל״, וְאֵין לְאוֹם אֶלָּא עוּבָּרִין, שֶׁנֶּאֱמַר: ״וּלְאֹם מִלְאֹם יֶאֱמָץ״.

And Rabbi Elazar says: Any person who has flattery in him, even fetuses in their mothers' wombs curse him, as it is stated: "He who says to the wicked: You are righteous, peoples shall curse him [*yikkevuhu*], nations [*leummim*] shall execrate him" (Proverbs 24:24); **and *kov*,** the linguistic root of the word *yikkevuhu*, means **only a curse, as it is stated:** Balaam explained that he did not curse the Jewish people, as he said: "How can I curse [*ekkov*] **whom God has not cursed [*kabbo*]?"** (Numbers 23:8). **And *le'om*** is homiletically interpreted to mean **only fetuses, as it is stated** with regard to Jacob and Esau, when they were still in Rebecca's womb: **"And one people [*le'om*] shall be stronger than the other people [*le'om*]"** (Genesis 25:23).

וְאָמַר רַבִּי אֶלְעָזָר: כׇּל אָדָם שֶׁיֵּשׁ בּוֹ חֲנוּפָּה נוֹפֵל בְּגֵיהִנָּם, שֶׁנֶּאֱמַר: ״הוֹי הָאֹמְרִים לָרַע טוֹב וְלַטּוֹב רָע״ וגו׳. מַה כְּתִיב אַחֲרָיו? ״לָכֵן כֶּאֱכֹל קַשׁ לְשׁוֹן אֵשׁ וַחֲשַׁשׁ לֶהָבָה יִרְפֶּה״ וגו׳.

And Rabbi Elazar says: Any person who has flattery in him falls into Gehenna,[N] **as it is stated: "Woe to those who call evil good, and good evil"** (Isaiah 5:20). **What is written afterward? "Therefore, as the tongue of fire devours straw, and as the chaff is consumed by the flame"** (Isaiah 5:24), meaning that the people described in the earlier verse will end up burning like straw in the fires of Gehenna.

וְאָמַר רַבִּי אֶלְעָזָר: כׇּל הַמַּחֲנִיף לַחֲבֵירוֹ – סוֹף נוֹפֵל בְּיָדוֹ. וְאִם אֵינוֹ נוֹפֵל בְּיָדוֹ – נוֹפֵל בְּיַד בָּנָיו. וְאִם אֵינוֹ נוֹפֵל בְּיַד בָּנָיו – נוֹפֵל בְּיַד בֶּן בְּנוֹ, שֶׁנֶּאֱמַר: ״וַיֹּאמֶר יִרְמְיָה הַנָּבִיא [לַחֲנַנְיָה] אָמֵן כֵּן יַעֲשֶׂה ה׳, יָקֵם ה׳ אֶת דְּבָרֶיךָ״, וּכְתִיב:

And Rabbi Elazar says: Anyone who flatters another ultimately falls into his hands. And if he does not fall into his hands, he falls into his children's hands. And if he does not fall into his children's hands, he falls into his grandchild's hands,[N] **as it is stated: "Then the prophet Jeremiah said to Hananiah... Amen, the Lord should do so, the Lord should perform your words"** (Jeremiah 28:5–6). This was a form of flattery, as Jeremiah did not explicitly say that Hananiah was a false prophet. **And it is written:**

NOTES

And a person cannot say to another, etc. – וְאֵין אָדָם יָכוֹל לוֹמַר לַחֲבֵירוֹ וכו׳: One explanation of this statement is that since people wanted to flatter one another, no one would say: My deeds are greater than yours, lest the other person be insulted (Maharatz Ḥayyut). Others explain that since everyone was flattering each other, they would even flatter a lowly person and tell him that his deeds were good. Therefore, even those lowly people would not accept that others act in a more meritorious manner than they do (see *Meromei Sadeh*).

It is permitted to flatter wicked people, etc. – מוּתָּר לְהַחֲנִיף לָרְשָׁעִים וכו׳: The *ge'onim* write that it is permitted to flatter the wicked only when such behavior is unavoidable. The Jewish people were punished for flattering Agrippa because it was not necessary for them to do so. The Meiri explains that one may do so only provided that it does not involve a desecration of God's name. It is explained in *Be'er Sheva* that it is permitted to flatter a wicked person, but it is prohibited to praise a person for his wicked deeds, unless it can prevent a life-threatening situation (see *Nedarim* 22a). In *Sha'arei Teshuva*, Rabbeinu Yona rules stringently in this matter and prohibits flattering the wicked even in a dangerous situation.

Falls into Gehenna – נוֹפֵל בְּגֵיהִנָּם: The reasoning behind this statement is that since flattery corrupts people's judgment, it causes more wickedness in the world, and the flatterer is punished for causing this (*Iyyun Ya'akov*).

He falls into his grandchild's hands – נוֹפֵל בְּיַד בֶּן בְּנוֹ: This is alluded to in the verse itself, as the official who arrested Jeremiah is not referred to by his name and his father's name alone, which is the usual custom in the Bible; rather, he is referred to by the name of his grandfather, Hananiah, as well, demonstrating that there is a connection between Jeremiah's arrest and what had happened with Hananiah, the official's grandfather.

NOTES

Repulsive as a menstruating woman – מְאוּסָה כְּנִדָּה: The ritual impurity of a menstruating woman is used throughout the Bible as a symbol for something repulsive from which everyone, including gentiles, distances himself (see Ezekiel 7:19, 36:17, and Lamentations 1:17).

Four classes of people, etc. – אַרְבַּע כִּיתּוֹת: The Maharsha explains that these classes all engage in sinful speech, and they presume that no one is aware of their actions. Additionally, it can be explained that the people in all four classes do not think that they are doing anything evil, as they are speaking the truth or they are not directly causing harm.

BACKGROUND

In the cities overseas – בִּכְרַכֵּי הַיָּם: This expression is understood by some scholars as referring to Caesarea or Cyprus. In fact, the stories in the Talmud that involve the cities overseas usually invoke them in order to solve a linguistic conundrum, since in cities overseas a certain word may be used with a specific meaning, or to describe an unusual occurrence, oftentimes a sin or an atypical halakhic practice. For this reason, it is likely that when the Sages used this term, they did so less to point to a geographic place and more to create a setting for pedagogical purposes.

LANGUAGE

Galmuda – גַּלְמוּדָה: It is not clear which cities used this term, or if it was used by Jews or gentiles. It is likely that the word *galmuda* is associated with a menstruating woman because of its Hebrew meaning of lonely and sad.

״וַיְהִי הוּא בְּשַׁעַר בִּנְיָמִן וְשָׁם בַּעַל פְּקִדֻת וּשְׁמוֹ יִרְאִיָּה בֶּן שֶׁלֶמְיָה בֶּן חֲנַנְיָה וַיִּתְפֹּשׂ אֶת יִרְמְיָהוּ הַנָּבִיא לֵאמֹר אֶל הַכַּשְׂדִּים אַתָּה נֹפֵל. וַיֹּאמֶר לוֹ יִרְמְיָהוּ שֶׁקֶר אֵינֶנִּי נֹפֵל אֶל הַכַּשְׂדִּים״ וגו׳. וּכְתִיב: ״וַיִּתְפֹּשׂ יִרְמְיָהוּ וַיְבִאֵהוּ אֶל הַשָּׂרִים״.

“And when he was in the gate of Benjamin, a captain of the ward was there, whose name was Irijah, the son of Shelemiah, the son of Hananiah; and he laid hold on Jeremiah the prophet, saying: You shall fall to the Chaldeans. Then Jeremiah said: It is false; I shall not fall to the Chaldeans” (Jeremiah 37:13–14). **And it is** then **written: “So Irijah laid hold on Jeremiah, and brought him to the princes”** (Jeremiah 37:14). Irijah was the grandson of Hananiah, and Jeremiah was punished by falling into his hands because he had flattered his grandfather.

וְאָמַר רַבִּי אֶלְעָזָר: כָּל עֵדָה שֶׁיֵּשׁ בָּהּ חֲנוּפָּה – מְאוּסָה כְּנִדָּה, שֶׁנֶּאֱמַר: ״כִּי עֲדַת חָנֵף גַּלְמוּד״, שֶׁכֵּן בִּכְרַכֵּי הַיָּם קוֹרִין לְנִדָּה גַּלְמוּדָה. מַאי גַּלְמוּדָה? גְּמוּלָה מִבַּעְלָהּ.

And Rabbi Elazar says: Any congregation in which there is flattery is as repulsive as a menstruating woman,[N] **as it is stated: “For a flattering congregation shall be desolate [*galmud*]”** (Job 15:34), **and in the cities overseas**[B] **they call a menstruating woman *galmuda*.**[L] **What is the meaning of** the word ***galmuda*?** It means **separated [*gemula*] from her husband [*mibbala*].**

וְאָמַר רַבִּי אֶלְעָזָר: כָּל עֵדָה שֶׁיֵּשׁ בָּהּ חֲנוּפָּה – לְסוֹף גּוֹלָה. כְּתִיב הָכָא: ״כִּי עֲדַת חָנֵף גַּלְמוּד״, וּכְתִיב הָתָם: ״וְאָמַרְתְּ בִּלְבָבֵךְ מִי יָלַד לִי אֶת אֵלֶּה וַאֲנִי שְׁכוּלָה וְגַלְמוּדָה גֹּלָה וְסוּרָה״ וגו׳.

And Rabbi Elazar says: Any congregation in which there is flattery is ultimately exiled. It is written here: “For a flattering congregation shall be desolate [*galmud*]” (Job 15:34), **and it is written there: “Then you will say in your heart: Who has begotten me these, seeing I have been bereaved of my children, and am solitary [*galmuda*], an exile, and wandering?”** (Isaiah 49:21). The verse states: “An exile,” as an appositive to “*galmuda*,” indicating that they are the same.

אָמַר רַבִּי יִרְמְיָה בַּר אַבָּא: אַרְבַּע כִּיתּוֹת אֵין מְקַבְּלוֹת פְּנֵי שְׁכִינָה: כַּת לֵיצִים, וְכַת חֲנֵיפִים, וְכַת שַׁקָּרִים, וְכַת מְסַפְּרֵי לָשׁוֹן הָרָע.

Rabbi Yirmeya bar Abba says: Four classes of people[N] **will not greet the Divine Presence: The class of cynics, and the class of flatterers, and the class of liars, and the class of slanderers.**

כַּת לֵיצִים, דִּכְתִיב: ״מָשַׁךְ יָדוֹ אֶת לֹצְצִים״; כַּת חֲנֵיפִים, דִּכְתִיב: ״כִּי לֹא לְפָנָיו חָנֵף יָבוֹא״; כַּת שַׁקָּרִים, דִּכְתִיב: ״דֹּבֵר שְׁקָרִים לֹא יִכּוֹן לְנֶגֶד עֵינָי״;

The proof for this statement is as follows: **The class of cynics, as it is written: “He draws His hand from cynics”** (Hosea 7:5), i.e., God does not want to be in their presence; **the class of flatterers, as it is written: “That a flatterer cannot come before Him”** (Job 13:16); **the class of liars, as it is written: “He who speaks falsehood shall not dwell before My eyes”** (Psalms 101:7).

כַּת מְסַפְּרֵי לָשׁוֹן הָרָע, דִּכְתִיב: ״כִּי לֹא אֵל חָפֵץ רֶשַׁע אָתָּה לֹא יְגֻרְךָ רָע״ – צַדִּיק אַתָּה ה׳ לֹא יָגוּר בִּמְגוּרְךָ רַע.

The class of slanderers will not greet the Divine Presence, **as it is written: “For You are not a god who has pleasure in wickedness, evil shall not sojourn with You”** (Psalms 5:5), which means: **You, the Lord, are righteous** and **evil shall not dwell** with You **in Your dwelling place.** “Evil” here is referring to slanderers, as is evident from the continuation of the chapter, which states: “For there is no sincerity in their mouth; their inward part is a yawning gulf, their throat is an open tomb, they make smooth their tongue” (Psalms 5:10).

הדרן עלך אלו נאמרין

Summary of **Perek VII**

The determination whether or not each particular recitation discussed in the chapter must be said in Hebrew is derived from verses written in the context of each of these recitations. Nevertheless, there are apparently certain general similarities among the recitations that may be recited in any language in contrast to those that must be said in Hebrew: The recitations that require either the speaker or the listener to fully understand the statement may be recited in any language, whereas those that are part of a ritual or ceremony are required to be said in Hebrew. While the Mishna establishes that certain recitations, e.g., the *Amida* prayer and *Shema*, may be stated in any language, in practice it is accepted that one should recite them in Hebrew *ab initio*.

The chapter presented different opinions with regard to the details of the mitzvot that were incumbent upon the generation that entered Eretz Yisrael in the times of Joshua. Naturally, there is no room for halakhic ruling with regard to matters that already took place; the Sages can only describe what occurred. It is concluded that the generation that entered Eretz Yisrael set up three sets of stones upon which they wrote the Torah in seventy languages: In the Jordan River, at their place of lodging, and at the place where an altar was built. With regard to the blessings and curses, the chapter described that the priests and Levites, or some of them, stood between Mount Gerizim and Mount Ebal. They recited the blessings while facing Mount Gerizim and the curses while facing Mount Ebal.

There are some differences between the manner in which the Priestly Benediction was recited in the Temple and the manner in which it is recited in the synagogue. In the Temple, the priests said all three verses as one blessing, and they uttered the Tetragrammaton. In the synagogue, the congregation answers amen after each verse, and the substitute name of Lordship is used. Furthermore, in the Temple, the priests lifted their hands above their heads when reciting the blessing, and in the synagogue they lift their hands only to the height of their shoulders. The chapter also discussed other issues with regard to the Priestly Benediction, e.g., how the priests are called up to recite the blessing, how they stand while uttering the blessing, and what the congregation recites during the blessing.

This chapter is the source for most of the *halakhot* of the mitzva of assembly. The mitzva of assembly takes place every seven years, on the first intermediate day of the festival of *Sukkot* that takes place after a Sabbatical Year. The Sages derive that the Torah is read by the king while he is sitting or standing on a special wooden platform in the Temple courtyard. The king reads from parts of the book of Deuteronomy that contain warnings about the importance of fulfilling mitzvot and from some other sections that discuss mitzvot related to that time of year.

Introduction to **Perek VIII**

When you go forth to battle against your enemies, and see horses, and chariots, and a people more than you, you shall not be afraid of them; for the Lord your God is with you, who brought you up out of the land of Egypt. And it shall be, when you draw near to battle, that the priest shall approach and speak to the people. And he shall say to them: Hear Israel, you draw near today to battle against your enemies; let not your heart faint; fear not, nor be alarmed, and do not be terrified of them; for the Lord your God is He that goes with you, to fight for you against your enemies, to save you. And the officers shall speak to the people, saying: What man is there that has built a new house, and has not dedicated it? Let him go and return to his house, lest he die in the battle, and another man dedicate it. And what man is there that has planted a vineyard, and has not used the fruit thereof? Let him go and return unto his house, lest he die in the battle and another man use the fruit thereof. And what man is there that has betrothed a wife, and has not taken her? Let him go and return to his house, lest he die in the battle, and another man take her. And the officers shall speak further to the people, and they shall say: What man is there that is fearful and fainthearted? Let him go and return unto his house, lest his brethren's heart melt as his heart.

(Deuteronomy 20:1–8)

When a man takes a new wife, he shall not go out with the army, neither shall he be charged with any business; he shall be free for his house one year, and shall cheer his wife whom he has taken.

(Deuteronomy 24:5)

On the heels of topics discussed in the previous chapter, this chapter deals primarily with the preparations for battle, and the question of who is exempt from going out to war. The addresses of the priest and the officers are stated explicitly in the Torah; however, the details still require clarification.

Among the many issues raised are: Which priest gives this address? When and where does the priest address the ranks? What exactly is said by the priest, and what is said by the officers?

In addition, the chapter will clarify and define a number of terms and circumstances mentioned in the verses, among them: What is included in the word vineyard, what is considered a house, and which wife is considered a new wife. Similarly, the Gemara explores the definition of the "fearful and fainthearted." The Torah relates directly to those who are about to dedicate their homes, or enjoy their vineyards, or marry the women whom they have betrothed. In parallel, this chapter explores the status of those who have dedicated a home, begun to benefit from a vineyard, or married over the past year.

This chapter will also address the issue of determining which kind of war is subject to these exemptions. Do these terms apply equally in every manner of military campaign and activity, or are there certain wars for which these exemptions are inapplicable?

מתני׳ משוח מלחמה בשעה שמדבר אל העם – בלשון הקודש היה מדבר, שנאמר: ״והיה כקרבכם אל המלחמה ונגש הכהן״ – זה כהן משוח מלחמה. ״ודבר אל העם״ – בלשון הקודש.

MISHNA With regard to **the** priest who was **anointed for war, at the time that he would speak to the nation,**[NH] **he would speak** to them **in the sacred tongue,** Hebrew, **as it is stated: "And it shall be, when you draw near to the battle, that the priest shall approach** and speak to the people" (Deuteronomy 20:2). **This** priest identified in the verse is **the priest anointed for war,** the priest who is inaugurated specifically to serve this function. **"And speak to the people"**; he addresses them **in the sacred tongue,** Hebrew.

״ואמר אליהם שמע ישראל״ וגו׳. ״על אויביכם״ – ולא על אחיכם, לא יהודה על שמעון ולא שמעון על בנימין, שאם תפלו בידם ירחמו עליכם, כמה שנאמר: ״ויקמו האנשים אשר נקבו בשמות ויחזיקו בשביה וכל מערמיהם הלבישו מן השלל וילבשום וינעלום ויאכלום וישקום ויסכום וינהלום בחמרים לכל כושל ויביאום ירחו עיר התמרים אצל אחיהם וישובו שמרון״ וגו׳. על אויביכם אתם הולכים, שאם תפלו בידם אין מרחמין עליכם.

The Torah dictates the priest's address: **"And** he **shall say to them: Hear Israel,** you draw near today to battle against your enemies; let not your heart faint; fear not, nor be alarmed, and do not be terrified of them" (Deuteronomy 20:3). The priest expounds: **"Against your enemies" and not against your brothers.**[N] This is **not** a war of the tribe of **Judah against Simon and not Simon against Benjamin, such that if you fall into their hands** your brothers **will have mercy on you, as it is stated** with regard to a war between Judah and Israel: **"And the men that have been mentioned by name rose up, and took the captives, and with the spoil clothed all that were naked among them, and arrayed them, and shod them, and gave them to eat and to drink, and anointed them, and carried all the feeble of them upon donkeys, and brought them to Jericho, the city of palm trees, unto their brethren; then they returned to Samaria"** (II Chronicles 28:15). Rather, **you are marching** to war **against your enemies, and if you fall into their hands, they** will **not have mercy on you.**

״אל ירך לבבכם אל תיראו ואל תחפזו״ וגו׳. ״אל ירך לבבכם״ – מפני צהלת סוסים וצחצוח חרבות; ״אל תיראו״ – מפני הגפת תריסין ושפעת הקלגסין; ״אל תחפזו״ – מקול קרנות; ״אל תערצו״ – מפני קול צווחות;

The priest continues: **"Let not your heart faint; fear not, nor be alarmed,** and do not be terrified of them" (Deuteronomy 20:3). **"Let not your heart faint" due to the neighing of horses and the sharpening of** the enemy's **swords. "Fear not" due to the knocking of shields** [***terisin***][L] **and the noise of** their **boots** [***calgassin***].[NL] **"Nor be alarmed" by the sound of trumpets.**[B] **"Do not be terrified" due to the sound of shouts.**

״כי ה׳ אלהיכם ההלך עמכם״ – הם באין בנצחונו של בשר ודם ואתם באים בנצחונו של מקום. פלשתים באו בנצחונו של גלית. מה היה סופו? לסוף נפל בחרב ונפלו עמו. בני עמון באו בנצחונו של שובך. מה היה סופו? לסוף נפל בחרב ונפלו עמו. ואתם אי אתם כן, ״כי ה׳ אלהיכם ההלך עמכם להלחם לכם״ וגו׳ – זה מחנה הארון.

The priest explains why the soldiers need not be terrified. **"For the Lord your God is He that goes with you,** to fight for you against your enemies, to save you" (Deuteronomy 20:4). Remember that **they come** to war **championed by flesh and blood, and you are coming championed by the Omnipresent. The Philistines came championed by Goliath. What was his end? In the end, he fell by the sword, and they fell with him** (see I Samuel, chapter 17). **The Ammonites came championed by Shobach. What was his end? In the end, he fell by the sword, and they fell with him** (see II Samuel, chapter 10). **But** as for **you, you are not so,** reliant upon the strength of mortals: **"For the Lord your God is He that goes with you, to fight for you** against your enemies, to save you"; **this** verse is referring to the **camp of the Ark** of the Covenant that accompanies them out to war.

NOTES

At the time that he would speak to the nation – בשעה שמדבר אל העם: According to the Meiri, a priest anointed for war would be appointed for each war, whether for wars whose mandate is a mitzva or optional wars. However, in the case of wars whose mandate is a mitzva, the priest would say only the words of encouragement, and he would not mention the other matters that do not relate to this.

And not against your brothers – ולא על אחיכם: Some commentaries discuss whether or not the mishna is spelling out the content of the priest's speech. According to one opinion, the priest recites only the words written in the Torah, and the mishna is simply interpreting and explaining those verses for didactic purposes (*Be'er Sheva*). However, some understand that the priest would elaborate and interpret the verses.

The noise of [*shifat*] their boots – שפעת הקלגסין: According to Rashi and the *Arukh*, based on the root *shin, peh, ayin*, meaning abundance, the menace identified here is the sheer volume of enemy soldiers. However, an alternative interpretation, based on the textual variant in which *shifat* is spelled *shin, yod, peh, tav*, argues it is the noise made by various weapons (Rambam's Commentary on the Mishna; Meiri).

LANGUAGE

Shields [*terisin*] – תריסין: From the Greek θυρεός, *thureos*, which means, among other things, an elongated shield.

Boots [*calgassin*] – קלגסין: From the Latin caliga, which in its linguistic declension assumes the accusative form caligas, meaning shoe, specifically the combat boot of Roman soldiers. Apparently, the word was also used as a nickname for the soldiers themselves, both by the Sages and by the Romans; the nickname of the Emperor Caligula derives from this word. In this usage, the term implicitly refers to the men who wear combat boots.

BACKGROUND

Trumpets – קרנות: The trumpets used by the Roman army were called cornua, and the soldier blowing one of the cornua was called a cornice.

Roman cornice

HALAKHA

When the priest anointed for war would speak – משוח מלחמה בשעה שמדבר: When the army is organizing and preparing to go to war, the priest anointed for war stands on a high place and says to them in Hebrew: "Hear Israel, you draw near today to battle…For the Lord your God is the one that goes with you, to fight for you against your enemies, to save you" (Deuteronomy 20:3–4). Thereafter, the priest anointed for war says: "What man is there that has built a new house, and has not dedicated it? Let him go and return to his house, lest he die in the battle, and another man dedicate it. And what man is there that has planted a vineyard, and has not used the fruit thereof? Let him go and return unto his house, lest he die in the battle and another man use the fruit thereof. And what man is there that has betrothed a wife, and has not taken her? Let him go and return to his house, lest he die in the battle, and another man take her" (Deuteronomy 20:5–7).

One commentary wonders: Why does the priest anointed for war repeat those statements that he already said at the border? He answers that no one returns from the camp upon hearing of their release at the border until they hear it a second time, at the front (*Kesef Mishne*). An alternative opinion sides with Rashi's interpretation that the release is issued only one time, at the border, although the *Tosefta* seems to support the opinion of the Rambam (Rambam *Sefer Shofetim, Hilkhot Melakhim UMilḥemoteihem* 7:3).

גמ׳ מַאי קָאָמַר? הָכִי קָאָמַר – שֶׁנֶּאֱמַר: ״וְדִבֶּר״, וּלְהַלָּן אוֹמֵר: ״מֹשֶׁה יְדַבֵּר וְהָאֱלֹהִים יַעֲנֶנּוּ בְקוֹל״, מַה לְּהַלָּן בִּלְשׁוֹן הַקּוֹדֶשׁ, אַף כָּאן בִּלְשׁוֹן הַקּוֹדֶשׁ.

GEMARA The Gemara clarifies an ambiguous point in the mishna: **What is it saying** when the mishna derives from the verse that the priest must address the people in Hebrew? The Gemara answers: **This is what** the mishna **is saying:** The ruling is derived from a verbal analogy, **as it is stated** here: **"And speak"** (Deuteronomy 20:2), **and there,** concerning the giving of the Torah, **it is stated: "Moses spoke and God answered him by a voice"** (Exodus 19:19). **Just as there,** the voice spoke **in the sacred tongue, so too here,** the priest speaks **in the sacred tongue.**

תָּנוּ רַבָּנַן: ״וְנִגַּשׁ הַכֹּהֵן וְדִבֶּר אֶל הָעָם״ – יָכוֹל כָּל כֹּהֵן שֶׁיִּרְצֶה? תַּלְמוּד לוֹמַר: ״וְדִבְּרוּ הַשֹּׁטְרִים״, מַה שּׁוֹטְרִים בִּמְמוּנֶּה, אַף כֹּהֵן בִּמְמוּנֶּה. וְאֵימָא: כֹּהֵן גָּדוֹל! דּוּמְיָא דְשׁוֹטֵר, מַה שּׁוֹטֵר שֶׁיֵּשׁ מְמוּנֶּה עַל גַּבָּיו, אַף כֹּהֵן שֶׁיֵּשׁ מְמוּנֶּה עַל גַּבָּיו.

The Sages taught: "The priest shall approach and speak to the people" (Deuteronomy 20:2). One **might** have thought that **any priest who would want** to address the people may assume this role. To counter this idea, **the verse states: "And the officers shall speak"** (Deuteronomy 20:5). **Just as the officers** described are those who have been **appointed** to discharge their responsibilities, **so too, the priest** described is one who has been **appointed** for this role. The Gemara asks: **But** if so, why not **say** that **the High Priest** should deliver this address, as he is also appointed? The Gemara replies: The appointed priest must be **similar to** an appointed **officer. Just as an officer** is one **who has** someone else, i.e., a judge, with greater authority **appointed above him, so too, the priest** described must be one **who has** someone else, i.e., the High Priest, **appointed above him.**

כֹּהֵן גָּדוֹל נַמִי, הָאִיכָּא מֶלֶךְ עַל גַּבָּיו! בַּעֲבוֹדָתוֹ קָאָמַר. וְאֵימָא: סְגָן! סְגָן לָאו מְמוּנֶּה הוּא, דְּתַנְיָא, אָמַר רַבִּי חֲנִינָא סְגַן הַכֹּהֲנִים: לָמָּה סְגָן מְמוּנֶּה? שֶׁאִם אֵירַע בּוֹ פְּסוּל בְּכֹהֵן גָּדוֹל, נִכְנָס וּמְשַׁמֵּשׁ תַּחְתָּיו.

The Gemara rejects this answer: **The High Priest also** meets this qualification, as **there is the king above him,** and therefore, the High Priest should deliver the address. The Gemara clarifies: The caveat that one must have someone appointed above him **is saying** someone above him **in his function.** That there is a king is irrelevant to the station of the High Priest, who ranks highest in the priesthood. The Gemara suggests: **Then say** it may be **the deputy** High Priest, who is second to the High Priest; he should deliver the address. The Gemara answers: **The deputy is not an appointed** office, as this position has no particular function other than being a ready substitute for the High Priest. **As it is taught** in a *baraita*: **Rabbi Ḥanina, the deputy** High **Priest, says: To what** end is **the deputy appointed?** It is merely for the possibility **that if some disqualification befalls the High Priest,** the deputy **steps in and serves in his stead.** However, the deputy has no specific role of his own.

״וְאָמַר אֲלֵיהֶם שְׁמַע יִשְׂרָאֵל״. מַאי שְׁנָא ״שְׁמַע יִשְׂרָאֵל״? אָמַר רַבִּי יוֹחָנָן מִשּׁוּם רַבִּי שִׁמְעוֹן בֶּן יוֹחַי, אָמַר לָהֶן הַקָּדוֹשׁ בָּרוּךְ הוּא לְיִשְׂרָאֵל: אֲפִילּוּ לֹא קִיַּימְתֶּם אֶלָּא קְרִיאַת שְׁמַע שַׁחֲרִית וְעַרְבִית – אִי אַתֶּם נִמְסָרִין בְּיָדָם.

§ The Torah says about the priest anointed for war: **"And he shall say to them: Hear Israel"** (Deuteronomy 20:3). The Gemara asks: **What is different** in this setting that necessitates the usage of the phrase: **"Hear Israel"? Rabbi Yoḥanan said in the name of Rabbi Shimon ben Yoḥai: The Holy One, Blessed be He, said to the Jewish people: Even if you have not fulfilled** any mitzva **except reciting *Shema* of the morning and the evening, you** will **not be delivered into the hands** of your enemies. As an allusion to this promise, the priest's address borrows the phrase "Hear Israel," a phrase most familiar from the beginning of the recitation of *Shema*.

״אַל יֵרַךְ לְבַבְכֶם אַל תִּירְאוּ״ כו׳. תָּנוּ רַבָּנַן: פַּעֲמַיִים מְדַבֵּר עִמָּם, אַחַת בַּסְּפָר וְאַחַת בַּמִּלְחָמָה. בַּסְּפָר מַה הוּא אוֹמֵר?

With respect to the mishna's comments about the verse: **"Let not your heart faint; fear not,** nor be alarmed, and do not be terrified of them" (Deuteronomy 20:3), **the Sages taught** (*Tosefta* 7:18): The priest **speaks with them twice,**[H] **one** time when they are gathered for war **at the border, and one** time when they are **on the battlefield** itself. When they are **at the border, what does he say?**

HALAKHA

The priest speaks with them twice – פַּעֲמַיִים מְדַבֵּר עִמָּם: The priest anointed for war addresses the nation twice. One time, at the border, when they are going out to war, he says to them: "And what man is there who has planted a vineyard." Another time, when they are preparing for battle, he says to them: "Hear Israel… do not be terrified" (Rambam *Sefer Shofetim*, *Hilkhot Melakhim UMilḥemoteihem* 7:2).

שִׁמְעוּ דִּבְרֵי מַעַרְכֵי הַמִּלְחָמָה, וַחֲזוֹרוּ; בַּמִּלְחָמָה מָה הוּא אוֹמֵר? ״אַל יֵרַךְ לְבַבְכֶם אַל תִּירְאוּ וְאַל תַּחְפְּזוּ וְאַל תַּעַרְצוּ״, כְּנֶגֶד אַרְבָּעָה דְּבָרִים שֶׁאוּמּוֹת הָעוֹלָם עוֹשִׂין: מַגִּיפִין וּמְרִיעִין, צוֹוְחִין וְרוֹמְסִין.

Hear my words, the regulations of war, and consider who is fit to participate in the battle. **And return** home, all of you who are exempt from combat. **What does he say on the battlefield?**[N] **"Let not your heart faint; fear not, nor be alarmed, and do not be terrified of them"** (Deuteronomy 20:3). These four cautions **correspond to four actions done by the nations of the world:** They **clash** their weapons,[N] **and** they **blast** horns, they **shout, and** they **trample** heavily with their horses to frighten their adversaries.

״פְּלִשְׁתִּים בָּאוּ בְּנִצְחוֹנוֹ שֶׁל גָּלְיָת״ כו׳. גָּלְיָת – אָמַר רַבִּי יוֹחָנָן: שֶׁעָמַד בְּגִילּוּי פָּנִים לִפְנֵי הַקָּדוֹשׁ בָּרוּךְ הוּא, שֶׁנֶּאֱמַר: ״בְּרוּ לָכֶם אִישׁ וְיֵרֵד אֵלָי״, וְאֵין ״אִישׁ״ אֶלָּא הַקָּדוֹשׁ בָּרוּךְ הוּא, שֶׁנֶּאֱמַר: ״ה׳ אִישׁ מִלְחָמָה״. אָמַר הַקָּדוֹשׁ בָּרוּךְ הוּא: הֲרֵינִי מַפִּילוֹ עַל יַד בֶּן אִישׁ, שֶׁנֶּאֱמַר: ״וְדָוִד בֶּן אִישׁ אֶפְרָתִי הַזֶּה״.

The mishna recorded the particulars of the priest's address: **The Philistines came championed by Goliath.** The Gemara describes the battle between David and Goliath. What is implied by the name **Goliath? Rabbi Yoḥanan says:** The verse indicates **that he stood before the Holy One, Blessed be He, with brazenness** [*gilui panim*],[L] **as it is stated: "Choose yourselves a man** [*ish*], **and let him come down to me"** (1 Samuel 17:8), and **man** [*ish*] is referring to **none other** than **the Holy One, Blessed be He, as it is stated: "The Lord is a man** [*ish*] **of war"** (Exodus 15:3). **The Holy One, Blessed be He, said: I will hereby fell him by the son of a man** [*ben ish*],[N] **as it is stated: "Now David was the son of that man** [*ben ish*] **of Ephrath"** (1 Samuel 17:12).

אָמַר רַבִּי יוֹחָנָן מִשּׁוּם רַבִּי מֵאִיר: בִּשְׁלֹשָׁה מְקוֹמוֹת לְכָדוֹ פִּיו לְאוֹתוֹ רָשָׁע: אֶחָד – ״בְּרוּ לָכֶם אִישׁ וְיֵרֵד אֵלָי״; וְאִידָךְ – ״אִם יוּכַל לְהִלָּחֵם אִתִּי וְהִכָּנִי״ וגו׳; וְאִידָךְ, דְּקָאָמַר לֵיהּ לְדָוִד: ״הֲכֶלֶב אָנֹכִי כִּי אַתָּה בָא אֵלַי בַּמַּקְלוֹת״. דָּוִד נַמִי אֲמַר לֵיהּ: ״אַתָּה בָּא אֵלַי בְּחֶרֶב וּבַחֲנִית וּבְכִידוֹן״! הֲדַר אֲמַר לֵיהּ: ״וְאָנֹכִי בָא אֵלֶיךָ בְּשֵׁם ה׳ צְבָאוֹת אֱלֹהֵי (יִשְׂרָאֵל) מַעַרְכוֹת יִשְׂרָאֵל אֲשֶׁר חֵרַפְתָּ״.

Rabbi Yoḥanan said in the name of Rabbi Meir: In three instances, his own **mouth ensnared that wicked one** and unwittingly foretold his own downfall. **One** time he said: **"Choose yourselves a man, and let him come down to me,"** describing himself at the bottom. **And another** time, he said: **"If he is able to fight with me and kill me** then will we be your servants; but if I prevail against him, and kill him, then shall you be our servants, and serve us" (1 Samuel 17:9). There, he supposed that his opponent would defeat him, before supposing that he, Goliath, would be victorious. Finally, **the other** time was **when he said to David** (1 Samuel 17:43): **"Am I a dog, that you come to me with staves?"** The Gemara asks: But didn't David also speak in this manner? **David also said to him: "You come to me with a sword, and with a spear, and with a javelin"** (1 Samuel 17:45). The Gemara answers: David **then said to him,** immediately afterward: **"But I come to you in the name of the Lord of hosts, the God of the armies of Israel, whom you have taunted"** (1 Samuel 17:45).

״וַיִּגַּשׁ הַפְּלִשְׁתִּי הַשְׁכֵּם וְהַעֲרֵב״ – אָמַר רַבִּי יוֹחָנָן: כְּדֵי לְבַטְּלָן מִקְּרִיאַת שְׁמַע שַׁחֲרִית וְעַרְבִית. ״וַיִּתְיַצֵּב אַרְבָּעִים יוֹם״ – אָמַר רַבִּי יוֹחָנָן: כְּנֶגֶד אַרְבָּעִים יוֹם שֶׁנִּתְּנָה בָּהֶן תּוֹרָה.

The verse says: **"And the Philistine drew near morning and evening"** (1 Samuel 17:16). **Rabbi Yoḥanan says:** He did this specifically **in order to prevent them from** completing **the recitation of *Shema*** in the required times of **morning and evening. "And** Goliath **presented himself forty days"** (1 Samuel 17:16). **Rabbi Yoḥanan says:** These days **correspond to the forty days**[N] **over which the Torah was given,** as he wanted to do away with it.

״וַיֵּצֵא אִישׁ הַבֵּינַיִם מִמַּחֲנוֹת פְּלִשְׁתִּים״ וגו׳. מַאי ״בֵּינַיִם״? אָמַר רַב: שֶׁמְּבוּנֶּה מִכׇּל מוּם; וּשְׁמוּאֵל אָמַר: בֵּינוֹנִי שֶׁבְּאֶחָיו; דְּבֵי רַבִּי שֵׁילָא אָמַר: שֶׁהוּא עָשׂוּי כְּבִנְיָן; רַבִּי יוֹחָנָן אָמַר: בַּר מְאָה פַּפֵּי וַחֲדָא נָנַאי.

The verse introduces Goliath: **"And a champion** [*ish habeinayim*] **went out from the camp of the Philistines,** named Goliath" (1 Samuel 17:4). The Gemara asks: **What** is indicated by the term ***beinayim*? Rav said:** The word is related to the root *beit, nun, heh,* meaning build, and means **that he is built** [*muvneh*] perfectly and free **of any blemish. And Shmuel said:** The word is related to the word *bein,* meaning between, and means that he was **the middle** [*beinoni*] **among his brothers.**[N] A Sage **from the school of Rabbi Sheila said:** The word is related to the root *beit, nun, heh,* meaning build, and means **that he** was **made** strong **as a building** [*binyan*]. **Rabbi Yoḥanan said:** The word is related to the word *bein,* meaning between, and means that he was born from among many, as follows: He was **the son of one hundred fathers** [***pappi***][L] **and one dog** [***nanai***],[L] as his mother engaged in sexual intercourse with one hundred men and a dog, and he was fathered from among them.

NOTES

What does he say on the battlefield – בַּמִּלְחָמָה מָה הוּא אוֹמֵר: The commentaries have pointed out that the order of events in the Gemara does not follow the order of the verses (*Devar Shaul*).

Clash their weapons – מַגִּיפִין: According to Rashi, this list omits the sharpening of swords and the marching because these serve a military purpose and are not merely forms of intimidation. Some explain that the trampling mentioned here refers to the sound of the soldiers' boots as they march.

The son of a man – בֶּן אִישׁ: Some explain that this refers to one who is still known by his father's name, as David was then still called: The son of Yishai (Riaf). Alternatively, this expression refers to one who is still young and has not yet reached the full strength of a grown man (*Iyyun Ya'akov*).

Correspond to the forty days – כְּנֶגֶד אַרְבָּעִים יוֹם: According to Rashi, the Jewish people were subject to forty days of Goliath's verbal abuse because of the forty days during which the giving of the Torah was delayed. The *Sefat Emet* writes that Goliath's intention was to prevent them from reciting *Shema* for forty days, after which they could no longer rectify their omission, in accordance with the assertion of the *Zohar* that a prayer that has been damaged for forty days can no longer be rectified.

The middle among his brothers – בֵּינוֹנִי שֶׁבְּאֶחָיו: According to the Maharal, this observation underscores that Goliath was the central and most important of his brothers.

LANGUAGE

Brazenness [*gilui panim*] – גִּילּוּי פָּנִים: This term, which literally means: Exposure of the face, denotes brazenness or impudence. Apparently, the turn of phrase derives from the fact that people often cover or hide their faces when they are embarrassed. As such, acting or speaking with a completely exposed face demonstrates a complete lack of shame.

Fathers [*pappi*] – פַּפֵּי: From the Greek πάππας, *pappas*, meaning father. The Gemara employs the term in its plural Aramaic form to mean many fathers.

Dog [*nanai*] – נָנַאי: The commentaries agree that this word means dog, but its origin is uncertain. Presuming that the first *nun* in the word *nanai* was mistakenly written in place of the letter *kaf*, which it closely resembles, one opinion suggests that the proper text should be *cani*, from the Latin word canis, which is the source of the English word canine.

"וְגָלְיָת שְׁמוֹ מִגַּת" – תָּנֵי רַב יוֹסֵף: שֶׁהַכֹּל דָּשִׁין אֶת אִמּוֹ כְּגַת. כְּתִיב: "מְעָרוֹת", וְקָרֵינַן "מַעַרְכוֹת" – תָּנֵי רַב יוֹסֵף: שֶׁהַכֹּל הֶעֱרוּ בְּאִמּוֹ.

The verse recounts that he was **"named Goliath, of Gath"** (I Samuel 17:4). **Rav Yosef taught:** This is **because everyone** would **thresh his mother** by cohabiting with her **like** people do in **a winepress** [*gat*], where everyone tramples. **It is written** that Goliath came from **"the caves** [*me'arot*] of the Philistines" (I Samuel 17:23), **but we read,** according to the Masoretic text: He came from among "the **ranks** [*ma'arkhot*] of the Philistines." What is meant by the written term *me'arot*? **Rav Yosef taught:** The word is related to the word *he'era*, meaning penetrated, and implies **that everyone penetrated** [*he'eru*], i.e., engaged in sexual intercourse **with, his mother.**

כְּתִיב: "הָרָפָה", וּכְתִיב: "עָרְפָּה" – רַב וּשְׁמוּאֵל; חַד אָמַר: הָרָפָה שְׁמָהּ, וְלָמָּה נִקְרָא שְׁמָהּ עָרְפָּה? שֶׁהַכֹּל עוֹרְפִין אוֹתָהּ מֵאַחֲרֶיהָ; וְחַד אָמַר: עָרְפָּה שְׁמָהּ, וְלָמָּה נִקְרָא שְׁמָהּ הָרָפָה? שֶׁהַכֹּל דָּשִׁין אוֹתָהּ כַּהֲרִיפוֹת, וְכֵן הוּא אוֹמֵר: "וַתִּקַּח הָאִשָּׁה וַתִּפְרֹשׂ...הַמָּסָךְ עַל פְּנֵי הַבְּאֵר וַתִּשְׁטַח עָלָיו הָרִפוֹת". וְאִי בָּעֵית אֵימָא, מֵהָכָא: "אִם תִּכְתּוֹשׁ אֶת הָאֱוִיל בַּמַּכְתֵּשׁ בְּתוֹךְ הָרִיפוֹת בַּעֱלִי".

It is written that Goliath's mother was: **"Harafa"** (II Samuel 21:16), **and** in another place **it is written: "Orpah"** (Ruth 1:4), and the Gemara will soon explain that this was the same woman. **Rav and Shmuel** engaged in a dispute concerning this matter. **One** of them **said: Her name was Harafa, and why is she called** by the **name Orpah?** It is **because everyone came at her from behind** [*orfin*] **her,** i.e., sodomized her. **And one** of them **said: Her name was Orpah, and why is she called** by the **name Harafa?** It is **because everyone threshed her like groats** [*harifot*], i.e., engaged in sexual intercourse with her, **and so it says** that this word means groats: **"And the woman took and spread the covering over the well's mouth, and strewed groats** [*harifot*] **thereon"** (II Samuel 17:19). **And if you wish,** you can **say from here: "Though you should crush a fool in a mortar with a pestle among groats** [*harifot*], yet will not his foolishness depart from him" (Proverbs 27:22).

"וְאֶת אַרְבַּעַת אֵלֶּה יֻלְּדוּ לְהָרָפָה בְּגַת וַיִּפְּלוּ בְיַד דָּוִד וּבְיַד עֲבָדָיו". מַאי נִינְהוּ? אָמַר רַב חִסְדָּא: סַף, וּמָדוֹן, גָּלְיָת, וְיִשְׁבִּי בְּנוֹב.

The Gemara continues its discussion of the battle of David and Goliath. **"These four were born to Harafa in Gath; and they fell by the hand of David, and by the hand of his servants"** (II Samuel 21:22). The Gemara asks: **What** are the names of the four siblings mentioned here? **Rav Ḥisda said:** They are **Saph, and Madon, Goliath, and Ishbi in Nob** (see II Samuel 21:16–20).

"וַיִּפְּלוּ בְיַד דָּוִד וּבְיַד עֲבָדָיו" – דִּכְתִיב: "וַתִּשַּׁק עָרְפָּה לַחֲמוֹתָהּ וְרוּת דָּבְקָה בָּהּ". אָמַר רַבִּי יִצְחָק: אָמַר הַקָּדוֹשׁ בָּרוּךְ הוּא: יָבוֹאוּ בְּנֵי הַנְּשׁוּקָה וְיִפְּלוּ בְּיַד בְּנֵי הַדְּבוּקָה. דָּרַשׁ רָבָא: בִּשְׂכַר אַרְבַּע דְּמָעוֹת שֶׁהוֹרִידָה עָרְפָּה עַל חֲמוֹתָהּ, זָכְתָה וְיָצְאוּ מִמֶּנָּה אַרְבָּעָה גִּבּוֹרִים, שֶׁנֶּאֱמַר: "וַתִּשֶּׂנָה קוֹלָן וַתִּבְכֶּינָה עוֹד".

It says: **"And they fell into the hands of David and his servants."** Why? It is because of the acts of their forebears, **as it is written: "And Orpah kissed her mother-in-law, and Ruth cleaved to her"** (Ruth 1:14). **Rabbi Yitzḥak says: The Holy One, Blessed be He, said: The children of the one who kissed,** referring to the four giants descended from Orpah, **will come and fall into the hand of the children of the one who cleaved,** referring to David, who was descended from Ruth. **Rava taught: As a reward for the four tears that Orpah shed** in sadness **over her mother-in-law, she merited four mighty warriors descended from her, as it is stated: "And they lifted up their voice**[N] **and wept again"** (Ruth 1:14).

כְּתִיב: "חֵץ חֲנִיתוֹ", וְקָרֵינַן: "עֵץ חֲנִיתוֹ" – אָמַר רַבִּי אֶלְעָזָר: עֲדַיִין לֹא הִגַּעְנוּ לַחֲצִי שִׁבְחוֹ שֶׁל אוֹתוֹ רָשָׁע. מִכָּאן שֶׁאָסוּר לְסַפֵּר בְּשִׁבְחָן שֶׁל רְשָׁעִים. וְלָא לִפְתַּח בֵּיהּ כְּלָל! לְאוֹדוּעֵי שִׁבְחֵיהּ דְּדָוִד.

It is written about Goliath: "And **the half** [*ḥetz*] **of his spear**[N] was like a weaver's beam" (I Samuel 17:7), **and we read,** according to the Masoretic tradition: "And **the shaft** [*etz*] **of his spear." Rabbi Elazar says:** The written version of the text demonstrates that **we have not yet reached half** [*ḥetzi*] **of the praise of that wicked** man. Only half of his spear was as long as a weaver's beam, but the Masoretic reading offers a less impressive description. It is learned **from here that it is prohibited to relate the praise of wicked people.** The Gemara asks: If so, **then** the verse **should not begin** by praising **him at all.** The Gemara answers: It was necessary in this case in order **to relate the praise of David,** who defeated Goliath.

"בְּנֵי עַמּוֹן בָּאוּ בְּנִצְחוֹנוֹ שֶׁל שׁוֹבַךְ" כו׳. כְּתִיב: "שׁוֹבַךְ", וּכְתִיב: "שׁוֹפַךְ" – רַב וּשְׁמוּאֵל; חַד אָמַר: שׁוֹפַךְ שְׁמוֹ. וְלָמָּה נִקְרָא שְׁמוֹ שׁוֹבַךְ? שֶׁעָשׂוּי כְּשׁוֹבַךְ; וְחַד אָמַר: שׁוֹבַךְ שְׁמוֹ. וְלָמָּה נִקְרָא שְׁמוֹ שׁוֹפַךְ? שֶׁכָּל הָרוֹאֶה אוֹתוֹ, נִשְׁפַּךְ לְפָנָיו כְּקִיתוֹן.

§ According to the mishna, the priest would say: **The Ammonites came championed by Shobach** (see II Samuel, chapter 10). In one account, his name **is written: "Shobach"** (II Samuel 10:18), **and** in another place **it is written: "Shophach"** (I Chronicles 19:18). **Rav and Shmuel** engaged in a dispute concerning this matter. **One** of them **said: His name was Shophach, and why is he called** by the **name Shobach?** It is **because he was built like a dovecote** [*shovakh*], as he was exceptionally tall. **And one** of them **said: His name was Shobach, and why is he called** by the **name Shophach?** It is **because anyone who would see him** would become terrified and his courage would be **spilled** [*nishpakh*] **before him like** water from **a jug.**

NOTES

As it is stated: And they lifted their voice, etc. – שֶׁנֶּאֱמַר: וַתִּשֶּׂנָה קוֹלָן וכו׳: Although Rava did not disclose a source for his claim that Orpah shed four tears, the commentaries suggest that the four tears are indicated in the text of the story.

According to Rashi, Orpah cried two separate times. The first time, the verse states: "And they lifted up their voice, and wept" (Ruth 1:9). The second time, after Naomi insisted that the women return to their own families, the verse states: "And they lifted up their voice, and wept again" (Ruth 1:14). Rashi learns from the term "again" that the verse is emphasizing they cried a second time. Presuming that Orpah cried from both eyes each time, Rashi concludes she shed four tears.

By contrast, the Maharsha finds evidence for four tears even without presuming that she cried from each eye, as follows: The first verse indicates one tear. In the second verse, the term "they lifted [*vatisena*]" is written in an abridged form, without an *alef*. Spelled *vav, tav, sin, nun, heh*, the word resembles the root for the word *shenayim*, meaning two, so that it implies two tears. As the second verse also states that they wept again, this implies an additional tear, which brings the total to four.

The half [*ḥetz*] of his spear – חֵץ חֲנִיתוֹ: Rashi explains that Rabbi Elazar bases his reading on the fact that the word spear [*ḥetz*] closely resembles the word half [*ḥetzi*].

"אַשְׁפָּתוֹ כְּקֶבֶר פָּתוּחַ כֻּלָּם גִּבּוֹרִים" – רַב וּשְׁמוּאֵל, וְאָמְרִי לָהּ רַבִּי אַמִי וְרַבִּי אַסִי; חַד אָמַר: בְּשָׁעָה שֶׁזּוֹרְקִין חֵץ עוֹשִׂין אַשְׁפָּתוֹת אַשְׁפָּתוֹת שֶׁל חֲלָלִים. וְשֶׁמָּא תֹּאמַר שֶׁאוּמָּנִין בִּקְרָב? תַּלְמוּד לוֹמַר: "כֻּלָּם גִּבּוֹרִים"; וְחַד אָמַר: בְּשָׁעָה שֶׁעוֹשִׂין צוֹרְכֵיהֶן עוֹשִׂין אַשְׁפָּתוֹת אַשְׁפָּתוֹת שֶׁל זֶבֶל. וְשֶׁמָּא תֹּאמַר מִפְּנֵי שֶׁחוֹלֵי מֵעַיִים הֵם? תַּלְמוּד לוֹמַר: "כֻּלָּם גִּבּוֹרִים".

The Gemara records a dispute concerning the enemy forces of Nebuchadnezzar. The prophet states: **"Their quiver [*ashpato*] is an open sepulcher, they are all mighty men"** (Jeremiah 5:16). **Rav and Shmuel, and some say Rabbi Ami and Rabbi Asi,** engaged in a dispute concerning the implication of the verse. **One** of them **said: When they shoot an arrow, they produce heaps** and **heaps [*ashpatot ashpatot*] of corpses. And lest you say that** they are **skilled in** the arts of **battle** but they are not particularly strong, **the verse states: "They are all mighty men." And one** of them **said: When they perform their needs,** i.e., relieve themselves, **they produce heaps** and **heaps [*ashpatot ashpatot*] of excrement,** which indicates they eat heartily, like mighty men. **And lest you say it is because they are ill** in their **intestines, the verse states: "They are all mighty men"** and are not ill.

אָמַר רַב מָרִי: שְׁמַע מִינַּהּ, הַאי מַאן דִּנְפִישׁ זִיבְלֵיהּ – חוֹלִי מֵעַיִים הוּא. לְמַאי נָפְקָא מִינַּהּ? לִיטְרַח בְּנַפְשֵׁיהּ.

Rav Mari said: Learn from this exchange that if there is **one whose excrement is abundant,**[B] **he is ill** in his **intestines.** The Gemara asks: **What difference is there** whether or not he is ill in his intestines? The Gemara answers: It is **so that** one who suffers these symptoms **will tend to himself** medically.

"דְּאָגָה בְלֶב אִישׁ יַשְׁחֶנָּה" – רַבִּי אַמִי וְרַבִּי אַסִי; חַד אָמַר: יַשְׁחֶנָּה מִדַּעְתּוֹ, וְחַד אָמַר: יְשִׂיחֶנָּה לַאֲחֵרִים.

In a similar vein, one is urged to relieve his distress. The verse states: **"If there is a care in the heart of a man, let him bend it [*yashḥena*]"** (Proverbs 12:25). **Rabbi Ami and Rabbi Asi** dispute the verse's meaning. **One said: He should force it [*yasḥena*] out of his mind.** He should remove his worries from his thoughts. **And one said:** It means **he should tell [*yesiḥena*]** his troubles **to others,**[N] which will relieve his anxiety.

"וְאַתֶּם אִי אַתֶּם כֵּן" כּוּ'. וְכׇל כָּךְ לָמָּה? מִפְּנֵי שֶׁהַשֵּׁם וְכׇל כִּינּוּיָו

The mishna recounts the priest's address: **But you are not like them,** because, as the verse states: "For the Lord your God is He that goes with you, to fight for you against your enemies, to save you" (Deuteronomy 20:4). **And why** does the verse elaborate **so much** in spelling out the nature of God's attendance in battle? It is **because the** ineffable **name** of God **and all of His appellations**[N] that are written on the tablets

BACKGROUND

One whose excrement is abundant – הַאי מַאן דִּנְפִישׁ זִיבְלֵיהּ: Various intestinal illnesses prevent the intestines from properly absorbing nutrition and fats from food. Symptoms of these illnesses include diarrhea or other excessive discharge. Prolonged illness of this type may result in pronounced weight loss and a general decline in health.

NOTES

He should tell his troubles to others – יְשִׂיחֶנָּה לַאֲחֵרִים: The commentaries discuss what the sufferer gains by telling his troubles to others. According to one interpretation, others will pray for him and bring about the alleviation of his suffering (*Arukh*). According to another opinion, the listeners will offer the sufferer advice for how to deal with his troubles (Rashi on *Yoma* 75a). A third explanation suggests that one experiences a measure of relief from the mere act of sharing his distress with others and hearing their responses (Riaf).

The ineffable name of God and all of His appellations – הַשֵּׁם וְכׇל כִּינּוּיָו: This matter is explored at some length in *Tosefot HaRosh*. Based on the opinion that there were two arks, the Rosh explains that each ark had a distinct function. The Ark of the Covenant, which held the second set of tablets, was left in the Holy of Holies in the Tabernacle. The other ark, a wooden ark initially fashioned by Moses for the purpose of holding the tablets, contained the shards of the original tablets that were broken at Mount Sinai. This second ark was the one carried out to war.

Once the Temple was built, the shards were transferred to the Ark of the Covenant. In their stead, the wooden ark, which was still carried out to war, held the ineffable name of God and His other appellations.

However, the Rosh notes that an opinion cited in the Jerusalem Talmud affirmed that there was only one ark. According to this opinion, the same Ark of the Covenant that normally rested in the Holy of Holies was also occasionally removed to be carried out to war.

Perek **VIII**
Daf **43** Amud **a**

מוּנָּחִין בָּאָרוֹן. וְכֵן הוּא אוֹמֵר: "וַיִּשְׁלַח אֹתָם מֹשֶׁה אֶלֶף לַמַּטֶּה לַצָּבָא אֹתָם וְאֶת פִּינְחָס". "אֹתָם" – אֵלּוּ סַנְהֶדְרִין; "פִּינְחָס" – זֶה מְשׁוּחַ מִלְחָמָה; "וּכְלֵי הַקֹּדֶשׁ" – זֶה אָרוֹן וְלוּחוֹת שֶׁבּוֹ; "וַחֲצֹצְרוֹת הַתְּרוּעָה" – אֵלּוּ הַשּׁוֹפָרוֹת.

were **resting in the Ark. And similarly, it says** in the verse with regard to the war against Midian: **"And Moses sent them, a thousand of every tribe, to the war, them and Pinehas** the son of Elazar the priest, to the war, with the holy vessels and the trumpets for the alarm in his hand" (Numbers 31:6). The verse is interpreted as follows: **"Them"; these are the Sanhedrin. "Pinehas"; he** was the priest **anointed for war. "And the holy vessels"; this is the Ark and the tablets**[N] **that were within it. "And the trumpets for the alarm"; these are** the ***shofarot.***[N]

NOTES

And the holy vessels; this is the ark and the tablets – וּכְלֵי הַקֹּדֶשׁ, זֶה אָרוֹן וְלוּחוֹת: Some sources suggest other interpretations of this verse. According to one opinion, the verse refers to the vestments of the High Priest (*Tosefta* 7:17). In a variation on this opinion, Rashi suggests that the holy vessels mentioned are the Ark and the priest's frontplate (Rashi on Numbers 31:6).

These are the *shofarot* – אֵלּוּ הַשּׁוֹפָרוֹת: The Maharsha is at a loss to explain the Gemara's interpretation that the trumpets in the verse are referring to *shofarot*. He maintains that it should be self-evident that these trumpets are those identified elsewhere (Numbers, chapter 10) as meant for use in war. The Rashash, based on the Gemara (*Shabbat* 36a), suggests that the Gemara here is referring to the trumpets, but these trumpets were called *shofarot* at that time.

תָּנָא: לֹא לְחִנָּם הָלַךְ פִּינְחָס לַמִּלְחָמָה, אֶלָּא לִיפָּרַע דִּין אֲבִי אִמּוֹ, שֶׁנֶּאֱמַר: ״וְהַמְּדָנִים מָכְרוּ אֹתוֹ אֶל מִצְרָיִם״ וגו׳. לְמֵימְרָא, דְּפִינְחָס מִיּוֹסֵף אָתֵי, וְהָא כְּתִיב: ״וְאֶלְעָזָר בֶּן אַהֲרֹן לָקַח לוֹ מִבְּנוֹת פּוּטִיאֵל לוֹ לְאִשָּׁה״. מַאי לָאו דְּאָתֵי מִיִּתְרוֹ שֶׁפִּיטֵּם עֲגָלִים לַעֲבוֹדָה זָרָה? לָא, מִיּוֹסֵף שֶׁפִּיטְפֵּט בְּיִצְרוֹ.

A *tanna* **taught:** It was **not for nothing** that specifically **Pinehas went**[N] **to war** with Midian; **rather,** it was **to exact** the rightful **judgment of his mother's father,** Joseph, **as it is stated: "And the Midianites sold him into Egypt** to Potiphar, an officer of Pharaoh's" (Genesis 37:36). The Gemara asks: **Is this to say that Pinehas came,** on his mother's side, **from** the family of **Joseph? But it is written: "And Elazar, Aaron's son, took himself a wife from the daughters of Putiel;** and she bore him Pinehas" (Exodus 6:25). **What, is it not that** Pinehas **came from** the family of **Yitro, who** was also called Putiel because he **fattened** [*pittem*] **calves for idol worship?** They answer: **No;** he was descended **from Joseph, who mocked** [*pitpet*] **his desire** by resisting the advances of Potiphar's wife.

וַהֲלֹא שְׁבָטִים מְבַזִּין אוֹתוֹ: רְאִיתֶם בֶּן פּוּטִי זֶה, בֶּן שֶׁפִּיטֵּם אֲבִי אִמּוֹ עֲגָלִים לַעֲבוֹדָה זָרָה יַהֲרוֹג נָשִׂיא מִיִּשְׂרָאֵל! אֶלָּא, אִי אֲבוּהּ דְּאִימֵּיהּ מִיּוֹסֵף – אִימֵּיהּ דְּאִימֵּיהּ מִיִּתְרוֹ, וְאִי אִימֵּיהּ דְּאִימֵּיהּ מִיּוֹסֵף – אֲבוּהּ דְּאִימֵּיהּ מִיִּתְרוֹ. דַּיְקָא נַמִי, דִּכְתִיב: ״מִבְּנוֹת פּוּטִיאֵל״, תְּרֵי מַשְׁמַע. שְׁמַע מִינָּהּ.

The Gemara asks: **But is it not** the case that, according to an oral tradition, **the tribes** were **denigrating** Pinehas after he killed Zimri, saying: Did **you see this son of Puti, the son whose mother's father fattened cows for idol worship?** Should this man **kill a prince of Israel?** Evidently, his grandfather Puti was Yitro, not Joseph. The Gemara answers: **Rather,** Pinehas was descended from both Joseph and Yitro. **If his mother's father** descended **from Joseph, his mother's mother** descended **from Yitro. And if his mother's mother** descended **from Joseph, his mother's father** descended **from Yitro.** The Gemara confirms this resolution: The language **is also precise, as it is written:** Elazar took a wife **"from the daughters of Putiel,"** which **implies** that she came from **two** daughters of men named Putiel. The Gemara concludes: You may **learn from** the verse that this is so.

מתני׳ ״וְדִבְּרוּ הַשֹּׁטְרִים אֶל הָעָם לֵאמֹר מִי הָאִישׁ אֲשֶׁר בָּנָה בַיִת חָדָשׁ וְלֹא חֲנָכוֹ יֵלֵךְ וְיָשֹׁב לְבֵיתוֹ״ וגו׳ – אֶחָד הַבּוֹנֶה בֵּית הַתֶּבֶן, בֵּית הַבָּקָר, בֵּית הָעֵצִים, בֵּית הָאוֹצָרוֹת, אֶחָד הַבּוֹנֶה וְאֶחָד הַלּוֹקֵחַ, וְאֶחָד הַיּוֹרֵשׁ וְאֶחָד שֶׁנִּתַּן לוֹ מַתָּנָה.

MISHNA The mishna continues its discussion of the speech given before battle. **"And the officers shall speak to the people, saying: What man is there that has built a new house, and has not dedicated it? Let him go and return to his house,** lest he die in the battle, and another man dedicate it" (Deuteronomy 20:5). He is sent home if he is **one who builds**[H] **a storehouse for straw, a barn for cattle, a shed for wood,** or **a warehouse.** Similarly, it applies if he is **one who builds, or** if he is **one who purchases, or** if he is **one who inherits, or** if he is **one to whom** it **is given** as **a gift.** In all these instances, the man returns from the war encampment.

״וּמִי הָאִישׁ אֲשֶׁר נָטַע כֶּרֶם וְלֹא חִלְּלוֹ״ וגו׳ – אֶחָד הַנּוֹטֵעַ כֶּרֶם, וְאֶחָד הַנּוֹטֵעַ חֲמִשָּׁה אִילָנֵי מַאֲכָל, וַאֲפִילּוּ מֵחֲמֵשֶׁת הַמִּינִין, אֶחָד הַנּוֹטֵעַ וְאֶחָד הַמַּבְרִיךְ וְאֶחָד הַמַּרְכִּיב, וְאֶחָד הַלּוֹקֵחַ וְאֶחָד הַיּוֹרֵשׁ וְאֶחָד שֶׁנִּתַּן לוֹ מַתָּנָה.

The next verse states: **"And what man is there that has planted a vineyard, and has not used the fruit** thereof? Let him go and return unto his house, lest he die in the battle and another man use the fruit thereof" (Deuteronomy 20:6). He is sent home if he is **one who plants**[H] a whole **vineyard** of many vines, **or** if he is **one who plants** as few as **five fruit trees** of another variety, **and even** if these five are **from the five species.** The produce need not be all of one species. The same applies if he is **one who plants, or** if he is **one who layers** the vine, bending a branch into the ground so that it may take root and grow as a new vine, **or** if he is **one who grafts** different trees onto one another. **And** it applies if he is **one who purchases** a vineyard, **or** if he is **one who inherits** a vineyard, **or** if he is **one to whom** the vineyard **is given** as **a gift.**

״וּמִי הָאִישׁ אֲשֶׁר אֵרַשׂ אִשָּׁה״ וגו׳ – אֶחָד הַמְאָרֵס אֶת הַבְּתוּלָה וְאֶחָד הַמְאָרֵס אֶת הָאַלְמָנָה, אֲפִילּוּ שׁוֹמֶרֶת יָבָם, וַאֲפִילּוּ שָׁמַע שֶׁמֵּת אָחִיו בַּמִּלְחָמָה – חוֹזֵר וּבָא לוֹ. כָּל אֵלּוּ וְאֵלּוּ שׁוֹמְעִין דִּבְרֵי כֹּהֵן מַעַרְכֵי מִלְחָמָה וְחוֹזְרִין, וּמְסַפְּקִין מַיִם וּמָזוֹן, וּמְתַקְּנִין אֶת הַדְּרָכִים.

The next verse states: **"And what man is there that has betrothed a wife,** and has not taken her? Let him go and return to his house, lest he die in the battle, and another man take her" (Deuteronomy 20:7). He is sent home if he is **one who betroths**[H] **a virgin, or** if he is **one who betroths a widow.** This applies **even** if his *yevama*, his late brother's wife, is a **widow waiting for** him as **her *yavam*** to perform levirate marriage; **and even if he heard that his brother died in the war** and the widow begins to wait for him only then, **he returns and goes** home. **Each of these** men, although they are exempt, still **hear the address of the priest** and **the regulations of war** at the local camp, **and** thereafter **they return** to their respective homes. However, they still support the war effort, **and** they **provide water and food** for the soldiers **and repair the roads.**

NOTES

It was not for nothing that Pinehas went, etc. – לֹא לְחִנָּם הָלַךְ פִּינְחָס וכו׳: If, as the Gemara states, Pinehas was the priest anointed for war, there need not be any other reason for him to be selected to participate in the war; he simply went out to war in this appointed role. The *Tosefot HaRash* offers two resolutions. First, it is possible that this statement contradicts the previous one, stating that Pinehas was sent for the personal reason described here and not as the anointed priest. Alternatively, Pinehas was in fact the anointed priest, and this statement is suggesting why he was singled out for this role.

The Maharal insists that the selection of Pinehas was not meant, as it would seem at first glance, to allow him to settle a personal grievance. After all, this war was waged hundreds of years after Joseph was sold into slavery, and all the relevant parties were long dead. Rather, the fact that the Midianites had sold Joseph was relevant to this war only insofar as that event demonstrated a natural opposition between Midian, a nation characterized by promiscuity, and Joseph, a man characterized by sexual self-control. Joseph's descendant, Pinehas, shared his forebear's strong personal resistance to promiscuity, and he was therefore chosen to lead this campaign, whose objective was to avenge the Midianites' luring the Jewish people into crimes of promiscuity and idolatry.

HALAKHA

One who builds – אֶחָד הַבּוֹנֶה: If one has built a home, a barn for cattle, a shed for wood, or a warehouse, if it has the potential to serve as a domicile, he returns from the military ranks. This applies not only to one who has built the house himself but also to one who has purchased or inherited a house, or was given a house as a gift.

However, if he has built a gateway, a veranda, a balcony, or a house that is smaller than four by four cubits, he does not return from the military ranks. The *Kesef Mishne* suggests that the omission of a storehouse for straw from this list may be due to a scribal error (Rambam *Sefer Shofetim, Hilkhot Melakhim UMilḥemoteihem* 7:5).

One who plants – אֶחָד הַנּוֹטֵעַ: If one planted a vineyard or five fruit trees, even from five different species, he returns home from the military ranks. This applies equally whether he planted a tree, or bent a vine into the ground, or grafted different trees together. There is no difference whether one planted the trees himself or whether he bought them, or inherited them, or if a vineyard was given to him as a gift. However, one who planted four fruit trees or five non-fruit bearing trees does not return (Rambam *Sefer Shofetim, Hilkhot Melakhim UMilḥemoteihem* 7:6).

One who betroths – אֶחָד הַמְאָרֵס: If one betrothed a woman, whether she is a virgin or a widow, or if one is in line for a levirate marriage, he returns home from the military ranks (Rambam *Sefer Shofetim, Hilkhot Melakhim UMilḥemoteihem* 7:7).

וְאֵלּוּ שֶׁאֵינָן חוֹזְרִין: הַבּוֹנֶה בֵּית שַׁעַר, אַכְסַדְרָה וּמִרְפֶּסֶת; הַנּוֹטֵעַ אַרְבַּע אִילָנֵי מַאֲכָל, וַחֲמִשָּׁה אִילָנֵי סְרָק; הַמַּחֲזִיר אֶת גְּרוּשָׁתוֹ. אַלְמָנָה לְכֹהֵן גָּדוֹל, גְּרוּשָׁה וַחֲלוּצָה לְכֹהֵן הֶדְיוֹט, מַמְזֶרֶת וּנְתִינָה לְיִשְׂרָאֵל, בַּת יִשְׂרָאֵל לְמַמְזֵר וּלְנָתִין – לֹא הָיָה חוֹזֵר. רַבִּי יְהוּדָה אוֹמֵר: אַף הַבּוֹנֶה בַּיִת עַל מְכוֹנוֹ לֹא הָיָה חוֹזֵר. רַבִּי אֱלִיעֶזֶר אוֹמֵר: אַף הַבּוֹנֶה בֵּית לְבֵינִים בַּשָּׁרוֹן לֹא הָיָה חוֹזֵר.

And these are the men **who do not return** to their homes: **One who builds a gateway,**[B] or **an enclosed veranda** [*akhsadra*],[L] **or a balcony;**[B] or **one who plants** no more than **four fruit trees or** even **five** or more **non-fruit bearing trees;** or **one who remarries his divorced** wife.[H] Nor is there an exemption for one who has betrothed a woman whom he is not permitted to marry: With regard to **a widow** betrothed **to a High Priest**[N] (see Leviticus 21:7); **a divorcée or a** ***yevama*** **who performed** ***ḥalitza*** [***ḥalutza***], in lieu of entering into a levirate marriage, betrothed **to a common priest** (see Leviticus 21:13–15); **a** ***mamzeret*** **or a Gibeonite woman** betrothed **to an Israelite;** or **an Israelite woman** betrothed **to a** ***mamzer*** **or a Gibeonite** (see Deuteronomy 23:3); such a man **does not return** to his home. **Rabbi Yehuda says: Even one who rebuilds a house** as it stood originally **would not return. Rabbi Eliezer says: Even one who builds a** new **brick house in the Sharon would not return** because these houses are not stable and are expected to collapse periodically.

אֵלּוּ שֶׁאֵין זָזִין מִמְּקוֹמָן: בָּנָה בַּיִת וַחֲנָכוֹ, נָטַע כֶּרֶם וְחִלְּלוֹ, הַנּוֹשֵׂא אֶת אֲרוּסָתוֹ, הַכּוֹנֵס אֶת יְבִמְתּוֹ, שֶׁנֶּאֱמַר: ״נָקִי יִהְיֶה לְבֵיתוֹ שָׁנָה אֶחָת״. ״לְבֵיתוֹ״ – זֶה בֵּיתוֹ; ״יִהְיֶה״ – זֶה כַּרְמוֹ; ״וְשִׂמַּח אֶת אִשְׁתּוֹ״ – זוֹ אִשְׁתּוֹ; ״אֲשֶׁר לָקָח״ – לְהָבִיא אֶת יְבִמְתּוֹ. אֵין מַסְפִּיקִין לָהֶם מַיִם וּמָזוֹן וְאֵין מְתַקְּנִין אֶת הַדְּרָכִים.

These are the men **who do not** even **move from their places**[H] because they do not even report to the camp: One who **built a house and dedicated it** within the year; one who **planted a vineyard and used its fruit** for less than a year; one **who marries his betrothed** and **one who marries his** ***yevama,*** his brother's widow who must enter into a levirate marriage or perform *ḥalitza*, **as it is stated:** "When a man takes a new wife, he shall not go out with the army… **he shall be free for his house one year,** and shall cheer his wife whom he has taken" (Deuteronomy 24:5). The mishna interprets the verse as follows: **"For his house"; this** means **his house** that he built. **"He shall be"; this** term includes **his vineyard. "And shall cheer his wife"; this is his wife. "Whom he has taken";** this phrase comes **to include his** ***yevama,*** who is considered his wife with respect to this *halakha* although he has not yet married her. Those who are exempt for these reasons **do not** even **provide water and food** to the soldiers, **and they do not repair the roads.**

גמ׳ תָּנוּ רַבָּנַן: ״וְדִבְּרוּ הַשֹּׁטְרִים״ – יָכוֹל דִּבְרֵי עַצְמָן? כְּשֶׁהוּא אוֹמֵר: ״וְיָסְפוּ הַשֹּׁטְרִים״ – הֲרֵי דְּבָרִים שֶׁל עַצְמָן אָמוּר. הָא מָה אֲנִי מְקַיֵּים ״וְדִבְּרוּ הַשֹּׁטְרִים״? בְּדִבְרֵי מְשׁוּחַ מִלְחָמָה הַכָּתוּב מְדַבֵּר. הָא כֵּיצַד? כֹּהֵן מְדַבֵּר וְשׁוֹטֵר מַשְׁמִיעַ.

GEMARA **The Sages taught: "And the officers shall speak…** What man is there that has built a new house, and has not dedicated it? Let him go and return to his house, lest he die in the battle, and another man dedicate it" (Deuteronomy 20:5). One **might** have thought that they say **their own words** and that the priest does not issue these proclamations. However, **when it says: "And the officers shall** speak **further"** (Deuteronomy 20:8), **their own words are mentioned** only in this latter verse. Evidently, then, the priest is the speaker in the earlier verse. **How** then **do I realize** the meaning of: **"And the officers shall speak"** in the first verse? **The verse is speaking of the words of the** priest **anointed for war. How so? The priest speaks**[H] in an undertone, **and an officer calls out** the priest's words so that they are audible to the assembled.

BACKGROUND

Gateway – בֵּית שַׁעַר: The gateway mentioned here is a small structure built at the entryway of a courtyard. It is meant to delay people, so that they cannot enter suddenly and directly into the courtyard. Normally, it is a very small open structure whose back wall is the gate to the courtyard. If there was a guard, he would occasionally sit in the gateway. Nevertheless, it cannot be properly defined as a living space in any way because it is so small and open on one side.

Balcony [*mirpeset*] – מִרְפֶּסֶת: The Hebrew root of this word is *reish*, *peh*, *samekh*, which means tread or trample. The term indicates a wooden board or a stone structure built as an extension at the top of a staircase to provide access to apartments located on the upper floor of a house. As such, the balcony serves as a type of open hallway alongside the house.

Some passageways of this type are roofed, and they generally have some sort of wall to prevent people from falling. Nevertheless, even when the passage is largely enclosed, it is built to be a passageway and is not truly habitable.

LANGUAGE

Veranda [*akhsadra*] – אַכְסַדְרָה: From the Greek ἐξέδρα, *exedra*, denoting a roofed entrance in front of a home.

Veranda in front of an ancient Greek house in Delos, Greece

NOTES

A widow betrothed to a High Priest – אַלְמָנָה לְכֹהֵן גָּדוֹל: Some see this as proof that the priests were also commanded to participate in wars, although they do not have their own territory in Eretz Yisrael. However, some contend that the priests are merely permitted to volunteer, but they are not obligated to fight (*Birkei Yosef*; *Minḥa Hareva*).

HALAKHA

One who remarries his divorced wife – הַמַּחֲזִיר אֶת גְּרוּשָׁתוֹ: If one remarried his ex wife or married a woman who is forbidden to him, e.g., a High Priest who married a widow or an Israelite who married a *mamzeret*, he does not return home from the ranks (Rambam *Sefer Shofetim*, *Hilkhot Melakhim UMilḥemoteihem* 7:8).

These are the men who do not even move from their places – אֵלּוּ שֶׁאֵין זָזִין מִמְּקוֹמָן: The following people do not go out to war at all and are not charged with any war-related tasks: One who built a house and dedicated it; one who married his betrothed; one who performed a levirate marriage; and one who redeemed the fruits of his vineyard. These people do not go out to war until one year after the enumerated events. Furthermore, not only do they not go out to war, but they also are not responsible for providing food and water to the soldiers, they do not guard the walls, and they do not contribute to the fortification of the city or to the military provisions (Rambam *Sefer Shofetim*, *Hilkhot Melakhim UMilḥemoteihem* 7:10–11).

The priest speaks – כֹּהֵן מְדַבֵּר: The priest who has been anointed for war says, in Hebrew: "Hear Israel…let not your heart faint… to save you," and another priest calls out his address to all the assembled. Then the priest anointed for war says: "What man is there that has built a new house, and has not dedicated it? Let him go and return to his house, lest he die in the battle, and another man dedicate it," and an officer calls out his statement to all the assembled. Thereafter, an officer arises and says: "What man is there that is fearful and fainthearted" and another officer calls out his words to all the assembled (Rambam *Sefer Shofetim*, *Hilkhot Melakhim UMilḥemoteihem* 7:3).

NOTES

What man is there that has built, etc. – מִי הָאִישׁ אֲשֶׁר בָּנָה וכו׳: The commentaries discuss precisely which term in the verse serves to include even one who has acquired a house through means other than building it himself. Rashi explains that the inclusion here is learned from the words "what man." The Rashash contends that the principle is learned from the term "that has." He adds that the word "house" has also been used elsewhere as an inclusive term. In the *Sifrei*, this derivation serves as the basis for the obligation to build a parapet even upon the roof of a structure that is not a domicile.

HALAKHA

Excludes a robber – פְּרָט לְגַזְלָן: One who has a new house or a vineyard returns home from the military ranks, whether he built it for himself or received it from someone else. However, one who stole either of these assets does not return (Rambam *Sefer Shofetim, Hilkhot Melakhim UMilḥemoteihem* 7:5–6).

תָּנֵי חֲדָא: כֹּהֵן מְדַבֵּר וְשׁוֹטֵר מַשְׁמִיעַ. וְתַנְיָא אִידָךְ: כֹּהֵן מְדַבֵּר וְכֹהֵן מַשְׁמִיעַ. וְתַנְיָא אִידָךְ: שׁוֹטֵר מְדַבֵּר וְשׁוֹטֵר מַשְׁמִיעַ! אָמַר אַבָּיֵי: הָא כֵּיצַד? מִ״וְנִגַּשׁ״ וְעַד ״וְדִבְּרוּ״ – כֹּהֵן מְדַבֵּר וְכֹהֵן מַשְׁמִיעַ; מִ״וְדִבְּרוּ״ עַד ״וְיָסְפוּ״ – כֹּהֵן מְדַבֵּר וְשׁוֹטֵר מַשְׁמִיעַ. מִ״וְיָסְפוּ״ וְאֵילָךְ – שׁוֹטֵר מְדַבֵּר וְשׁוֹטֵר מַשְׁמִיעַ.

It is taught in **one** *baraita*: **A priest speaks, and an officer calls out** his words; **and it is taught** in **another** *baraita*: **A priest speaks and a priest calls out. And it is taught** in yet **another** *baraita*: **An officer speaks and an officer calls out. Abaye said: How** can **these** texts be reconciled? **From** the words: "**That** the priest **shall approach**" (Deuteronomy 20:2), **until** the words: "**And** the officers **shall speak**" (Deuteronomy 20:5), which consist of words of encouragement and inspiration, **a priest speaks and** another **priest calls out. From** the words "**and** the officers **shall speak**" **until** the words: "**And** the officers **shall** speak **further**" (Deuteronomy 20:8), which list various people who are to return home from the battle front because of happy occasions, **a priest speaks and an officer calls out. From** the words "**and** the officers **shall** speak **further**" **and on,** which address those who are fearful and fainthearted, **an officer speaks and** another **officer calls out.**

״מִי הָאִישׁ אֲשֶׁר בָּנָה בַיִת חָדָשׁ״ כו׳. תָּנוּ רַבָּנַן: ״אֲשֶׁר בָּנָה״ – אֵין לִי אֶלָּא אֲשֶׁר בָּנָה. לָקַח וְיָרַשׁ וְנִיתַּן לוֹ בְּמַתָּנָה מִנַּיִן? תַּלְמוּד לוֹמַר: ״מִי הָאִישׁ אֲשֶׁר בָּנָה״.

§ The mishna teaches that the officers announce: "**What man is there that has built**[N] **a new house,** and has not dedicated it? Let him go and return to his house, lest he die in the battle, and another man dedicate it" (Deuteronomy 20:5). **The Sages taught:** From the phrase "**That has built,**" **I have** derived **only** that this applies to one **who has** literally **built** a house. **From where** do I derive that it includes one who **purchased, or inherited, or has been given** a house **as a gift? The verse states** broadly: "**What man is there that has built.**" By not merely stating: One that has built, but using the expanded "what man is there that has built," the verse includes any of these circumstances.

״בַּיִת״ – אֵין לִי אֶלָּא בַּיִת. מִנַּיִן לְרַבּוֹת בֵּית הַתֶּבֶן וּבֵית הַבָּקָר וּבֵית הָעֵצִים וּבֵית הָאוֹצָרוֹת? תַּלְמוּד לוֹמַר: ״אֲשֶׁר בָּנָה״, מִכׇּל מָקוֹם. יָכוֹל שֶׁאֲנִי מְרַבֶּה אַף הַבּוֹנֶה בֵּית שַׁעַר אַכְסַדְרָה וּמִרְפֶּסֶת? תַּלְמוּד לוֹמַר: ״בַּיִת״. מָה בַּיִת הָרָאוּי לְדִירָה, אַף כֹּל הָרָאוּי לְדִירָה.

From the term "**a house**" **I have** derived **only a house** in which people live. **From where** is it derived that the exemption is understood **to** also **include** one who builds **a storehouse for straw, a barn for cattle, a shed for wood, or a warehouse? The verse states:** "**That has built,**" which includes whatever one built, **in any case.** One **might** have thought that **I** should **include even one who builds a gateway,** or **an enclosed veranda, or a balcony;** however, **the verse states:** "**A house,**" which teaches that **just as a house** is, by definition, a structure that is **fit for living, so too,** this *halakha* applies to **every** structure that is potentially **fit for living,** although in practice it may be used for another purpose.

רַבִּי אֱלִיעֶזֶר בֶּן יַעֲקֹב אוֹמֵר: ״בַּיִת״ כְּמַשְׁמָעוֹ. ״לֹא חֲנָכוֹ״, ״וְלֹא חֲנָכוֹ״ – פְּרָט לְגַזְלָן. לֵימָא, דְּלָא כְּרַבִּי יוֹסֵי הַגְּלִילִי, דְּאִי רַבִּי יוֹסֵי הַגְּלִילִי, הָא אָמַר: ״וְרַךְ הַלֵּבָב״ – זֶה הַמִּתְיָירֵא

Rabbi Eliezer ben Ya'akov says: The word "**house**" is to be understood to mean, **as it indicates,** a building meant for human residence. With regard to the house for which a man may be sent back from the camp, since the verse does not state merely: "**And has not dedicated,**" but rather: "**And has not dedicated it,**" specifying the particular house to which the man is connected, the verse therefore **excludes a robber**[H] who does not own his house. The Gemara asks: **Shall we say** that this opinion is **not in accordance with** the opinion of **Rabbi Yosei HaGelili? As, if** it were in accordance with the opinion of **Rabbi Yosei HaGelili, didn't he say:** When the verse singles out the "fearful **and fainthearted**" (Deuteronomy 20:8), **this** is referring to **one who is afraid**

Perek **VIII**
Daf **43** Amud **b**

מֵעֲבֵירוֹת שֶׁבְּיָדוֹ!

because of sins that he has. According to this interpretation, one who stole another's real estate should return home from war because of his guilt, which would seem to contradict the opinion of Rabbi Eliezer ben Ya'akov.

אֲפִילּוּ תֵּימָא רַבִּי יוֹסֵי הַגְּלִילִי, כְּגוֹן דַּעֲבַד תְּשׁוּבָה וִיהַב דְּמֵי. אִי הָכִי, הֲוָה לֵיהּ לוֹקֵחַ, וְלִיהֲדַר! כֵּיוָן דְּמֵעִיקָּרָא בְּתוֹרַת גְּזֵילָה אֲתָא לִידֵיהּ – לָא.

The Gemara answers: **Even if you say** that this ruling is in accordance with the opinion of **Rabbi Yosei HaGelili,** Rabbi Eliezer ben Ya'akov still needs to exclude one in possession of a stolen house, as in a case **where one repented and gave money** to the owners of the house that he stole. Although in such a case he is not considered a criminal, the house was originally stolen, and therefore he must remain among the military ranks. The Gemara challenges this: **If so,** i.e., he repaid the owners, **he is** now a legal **purchaser** of the house **and he should return** from the military ranks. The Gemara answers: **Since initially** it **entered his possession with the status of stolen** property,[N] he does **not** return.

"וּמִי הָאִישׁ אֲשֶׁר נָטַע כֶּרֶם" כו׳. תָּנוּ רַבָּנַן: "אֲשֶׁר נָטַע" – אֵין לִי אֶלָּא נָטַע. לָקַח וְיָרַשׁ וְנִיתַּן לוֹ בְּמַתָּנָה מִנַּיִן? תַּלְמוּד לוֹמַר: "וּמִי הָאִישׁ אֲשֶׁר נָטַע".

§ The Gemara continues its discussion of those who return from the ranks. **"And what man is there that has planted a vineyard,** and has not used the fruit thereof" (Deuteronomy 20:6). **The Sages taught:** From the phrase **"that has planted," I have** derived **only** that it applies to one who actually **planted** a vineyard. **From where** is it derived that the military exemption likewise includes one who **purchased** it, one who **inherited** it, **and** one **to whom** it **was given as a gift? The verse states: "And what man is there that has planted."** By not merely stating: One that has planted, but using the expanded "what man is there that has planted," the verse includes any of these circumstances.

"כֶּרֶם" – אֵין לִי אֶלָּא כֶּרֶם. מִנַּיִן לְרַבּוֹת חֲמִשָּׁה אִילָנֵי מַאֲכָל וַאֲפִילּוּ מִשְּׁאָר מִינִין? תַּלְמוּד לוֹמַר: "אֲשֶׁר נָטַע". יָכוֹל שֶׁאֲנִי מְרַבֶּה הַנּוֹטֵעַ אַרְבָּעָה אִילָנֵי מַאֲכָל, וַחֲמִשָּׁה אִילָנֵי סְרָק? תַּלְמוּד לוֹמַר: "כֶּרֶם".

From the specific term **"vineyard," I have** derived **only a vineyard; from where** do I derive that it comes **to include five fruit trees even from other species? The verse states: "That has planted,"** to include different types of trees. **Might I** include even **one who plants** only **four fruit trees and** one who plants **five** or more **non-fruit bearing trees? The verse states: "Vineyard."** The term excludes a quantity of trees that is too few to qualify as a vineyard, as well as trees that do not yield fruit at all.

רַבִּי אֱלִיעֶזֶר בֶּן יַעֲקֹב אוֹמֵר: "כֶּרֶם" כְּמַשְׁמָעוֹ. "לֹא חִלֵּל", "וְלֹא חִלְּלוֹ" – פְּרָט לְמַבְרִיךְ וּלְמַרְכִּיב. וְהָא אֲנַן תְּנַן: אֶחָד הַנּוֹטֵעַ וְאֶחָד הַמַּבְרִיךְ וְאֶחָד הַמַּרְכִּיב! אָמַר רַבִּי זֵירָא אָמַר רַב חִסְדָּא, לָא קַשְׁיָא: כָּאן בְּהַרְכָּבַת אִיסּוּר, כָּאן בְּהַרְכָּבַת הֶיתֵּר.

Rabbi Eliezer ben Ya'akov says: The word **"vineyard"** is to be understood **as it indicates,** and it is referring only to a grape vineyard. And since the verse does not state merely: **"And has not used** the fruit," but rather: **"And has not used** the fruit **thereof,"** it **excludes one who layers**[B] the vine or branch **and one who grafts**[BN] different trees onto one another. The Gemara asks: **But didn't we learn** in the mishna: He is released if he is **one who plants, or** if he is **one who layers, or** if he is **one who grafts** trees? **Rabbi Zeira said** that **Rav Ḥisda said:** This is **not difficult. Here,** in the case where one does not return from the ranks, the man has performed **forbidden grafting;**[N] **there,** in the case where one does return from the ranks, he has performed **permitted grafting.**[H]

BACKGROUND

Layering – הַבְרָכָה: This refers to an agricultural process, particularly common in grapevines, in which a growing tree branch is inserted into the ground in such a way that it will take root. After it takes root, the branch is severed from its tree. This is similar to the method of planting a shoot, but with the added advantage that it also receives nourishment from the original tree for a period of time.

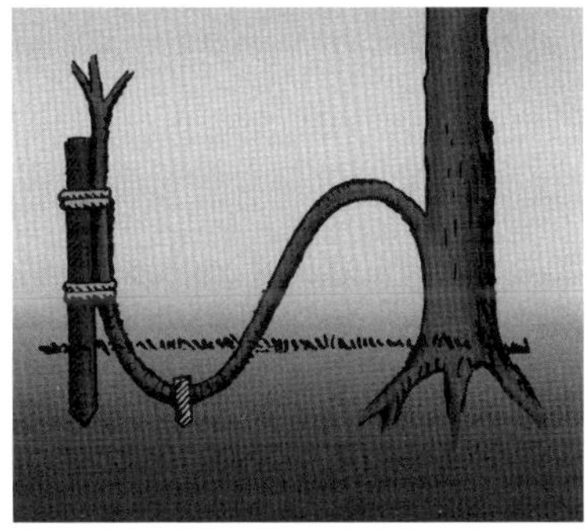

Layering

Grafting – הַרְכָּבָה: Grafting is a method for maintaining and improving trees that dates back to antiquity. While the methods of grafting have been enhanced over time, the essential principles have not changed. Grafting consists of inserting a branch from one tree into a slit made in another tree for this purpose, although the precise techniques of connecting branch to tree vary among the different species of trees. It appears from the Talmud that grafting grapevines was particularly common at that time.

In talmudic times it was also common to graft trees while the branch remained connected to the original tree. This ensured that the grafted branches would not dry out in the event that the grafting did not succeed. The Gemara refers to this method as: A young tree that was entangled with an old tree.

HALAKHA

Permitted grafting – בְּהַרְכָּבַת הֶיתֵּר: If one grafts or layers a tree in such a way that it is subject to the prohibition of *orla*, he returns home from war (Rambam *Sefer Shofetim, Hilkhot Melakhim UMilḥemoteihem* 7:6).

NOTES

It entered his possession with the status of stolen property – בְּתוֹרַת גְּזֵילָה אֲתָא לִידֵיהּ: The Torah dictates that it is inappropriate to formally dedicate an item that has entered one's possession through a sin, as this cannot be classified as an unadulterated mitzva. Therefore, although one may now have full ownership of the property in question, he does not return from the military ranks for such a house (*Minḥa Hareva*).

One who layers and one who grafts – לְמַבְרִיךְ וּלְמַרְכִּיב: The majority of the discussion here revolves around grafting. Evidently, the Gemara does not dwell on the issue of layering because it has been established that as long as the layered branch is still being nourished by its tree it is not considered to be its own tree, and the years of *orla* are counted only from the point that this nourishment ceases (Meiri).

Rav Naḥman bar Yitzḥak's statement that follows can be understood to be an example of a case of forbidden layering.

Forbidden grafting [*harkavat issur*] – בְּהַרְכָּבַת אִיסּוּר: The early commentaries ask why the Gemara does not once again contend with the opinion of Rabbi Yosei HaGelili in this context. Rabbi Yosei HaGelili maintains that an individual may be released from the ranks because of the sins he has committed. If so, that should be the *halakha* in the case of one who has grafted trees in a forbidden manner, and he should be sent back for this reason.

According to one answer, one would not return from the ranks due to the sin of grafting. Although one in possession of stolen property would be sent back, the reason is because the thief has an obligation to rectify the sin by returning the stolen property. The same is true of all similar offenses. However, that is not true of forbidden grafting, for which one is not required to destroy the grafted tree, nor is he prohibited from deriving benefit from its fruit (*Tosefot HaRosh*).

An alternative opinion is suggested by the Maharsha. He posits that this may be a case in which the owner of the vineyard does not perform the sin himself; rather, a sharecropper or someone else executes the actual forbidden grafting. In such a case, the owner would not be sent back for his sin.

Some commentaries maintain that the Rambam understands the Gemara very differently, such that it obviates any connection to Rabbi Yosei HaGelili's opinion. Accordingly, the term *harkavat issur* does not mean forbidden grafting, but rather: Grafting subject to the prohibition of *orla*. Instead of understanding that this type of grafting is insufficient to allow one to return from the military ranks, the Rambam says that this is the only manner of grafting for which a man does return. For the other type of grafting, which is called permitted grafting, insofar as it has no restrictions of *orla*, there is no particular reason for its owner to leave the military ranks (*Kesef Mishne*).

NOTES

A young tree that was entangled with an old tree – ילדה שסיבכה בזקינה: Rashi explains that this refers to removing a branch from a young tree and inserting it into an old tree. However, others maintain that the Gemara is talking about inserting the end of a branch into an old tree while it is still connected to the young tree. According to this opinion, the *halakha* of a detached branch is understood by way of an *a fortiori* inference: If a branch still attached to a young tree assumes the status of the old tree to which it is affixed, certainly a branch that is first detached assumes that status (*Tosefot HaRash*).

BACKGROUND

Orla – ערלה: It is prohibited to eat or derive benefit from fruit that grows during the first three years after a tree has been planted (see Leviticus 19:23). This prohibition applies only to the fruit and not to the other parts of the tree. In addition, the prohibition does not apply to trees planted for a purpose other than to use their fruit, e.g., trees planted to serve as a property fence or as a wind buffer.

האי הרכבת היתר היכי דמי? אילימא ילדה בילדה, תיפוק ליה דבעי מיהדר משום ילדה ראשונה! אלא ילדה בזקינה? והאמר רבי אבהו: ילדה שסיבכה בזקינה – בטלה ילדה בזקינה ואין בה דין ערלה!

The Gemara asks: With regard to **this permitted grafting, what are the circumstances? If we say** that it is **a young** tree grafted together **with** another **young** tree, then **let him derive** the *halakha* **that one must return** from the ranks **due to the first young** tree. One should be exempt because of his first tree, which is young, and the grafted tree is irrelevant. **Rather,** it is a case in which **a young** tree is grafted with **an old** tree. The Gemara objects: **But didn't Rabbi Abbahu say:** With regard to **a young** tree **that was entangled,** i.e., grafted, **with an old** tree,[NH] **the young** one **is negated by the old** one, **and the law of** ***orla***[B] does **not** apply **to it.** Therefore, the grafted tree should likewise lose its status as a young tree, and one in this situation should not return from the ranks.

אמר רבי ירמיה: לעולם ילדה בילדה, וכגון דנטע להך קמייתא לסייג ולקורות, דתנן: הנוטע לסייג ולקורות – פטור מן הערלה.

Rabbi Yirmeya said: Actually, one returns home if he grafts **a young** tree **with** another **young** tree, **and** it is a case **in which he planted this first** one **for a fence or for beams,** so that he is exempt from battle only because of the second tree, which he grafts for fruit. **As we learned** in a mishna (*Orla* 1:1): In a case of **one who plants** a tree **for a fence or** to yield wood **for beams,**[H] the tree is **exempt from the** ***halakhot*** of ***orla.***

ומאי שנא ילדה בזקינה דבטלה, ומאי שנא ילדה בילדה דלא בטלה?

The Gemara asks: **And what is different** about the case of **a young** tree paired **with an old** tree such **that** the young tree **is negated, and what is different** about the case of a **young** tree being planted for fruit paired **with a young** tree planted for wood such **that** the fruit tree **is not negated?**

התם אי מימליך עלה לאו בת מיהדר היא, הכא אי מימליך עלה בת מיהדר היא, [דהא מעיקרא לפירי קיימא], מידי דהוה אעלו מאיליהן, דתנן: עלו מאיליהן – חייבין בערלה.

The Gemara answers: **There,** in the case of an older tree, **if one changes his mind about it** and wants it to be a young tree obligated in *orla*, **it cannot return** to its previous state, as he has grafted it. Therefore, it is exempt from the *halakhot* of *orla*. **Here,** when a tree is planted for wood, **if he changes his mind** and decides to grow it for fruit, **it can return** to its default state of being planted for fruit, **because initially it stands** to be used **for fruit.** Therefore, it is not exempt from the *halakhot* of *orla*. This ruling is **just as it is concerning** trees that **grew by themselves,**[H] which are subject to *orla* although they were not consciously planted for their fruit. **As we learned** in a mishna (*Orla* 1:2): Fruit trees that **grew by themselves are obligated in** ***orla*** although the landowner did not plant them himself.

ולוקמה בכרם של שני שותפין, דהאי הדר אדידיה, והאי הדר אדידיה! אמר רב פפא, זאת אומרת: כרם של שני שותפין – אין חוזרין עליו מערכי המלחמה.

The Gemara asks: Why is there a need to establish the mishna as discussing a case where one planted the first tree for a fence or for beams? **But let** the mishna **be established** as referring **to a vineyard belonging to two partners,**[H] where the two trees involved in the grafting were co-owned by partners, and both trees were young. **As** in this case **this** one man **returns due to his** tree **and that** other man **returns due to his** tree. **Rav Pappa says:** Since the Gemara avoids the scenario of the vineyard belonging to partners in favor of discussing a case where one planted the first tree for a fence or for beams, **that is to say** if there is **a vineyard belonging to two partners,** evidently **they do not return for** the vineyard **from the ranks of** soldiers waging **war.**

HALAKHA

A young tree that was entangled with an old tree – ילדה שסיבכה בזקינה: When the branch of a young tree, which is subject to *orla*, is grafted to a tree that has completed its period of *orla*, the branch assumes the status of the older tree. In such a case, the branch's owner does not return from the ranks on account of the tree. However, if there were fruits on the young branch, those fruits are considered *orla* and remain forbidden, even if they grow significantly larger after the branch is grafted (Rambam *Sefer Zera'im*, *Hilkhot Ma'aser Sheni* 10:16; *Shulḥan Arukh*, *Yoreh De'a* 294:22).

One who plants a tree for a fence or for beams – הנוטע לסייג ולקורות: If one plants a fruit tree intending to use it as a boundary around his field or to use its wood for building or for firewood, the tree is not subject to the prohibition of *orla*. This is the case provided that it is evident from its location or the way the tree is maintained that it is not being grown for fruit. If the owner eventually decides to use the tree for its fruit, he counts the years of *orla* retroactively from the time of planting (Rambam *Sefer Zera'im*, *Hilkhot Ma'aser Sheni* 10:2; *Shulḥan Arukh*, *Yoreh De'a* 294:23).

Trees that grew by themselves – עלו מאיליהן: A tree that emerges by itself on private property is subject to the *halakhot* of *orla* (Rambam *Sefer Zera'im*, *Hilkhot Ma'aser Sheni* 10:5; *Shulḥan Arukh*, *Yoreh De'a* 294:27).

A vineyard belonging to two partners – כרם של שני שותפין: If a vineyard is jointly owned, its owners do not return from the ranks for their vineyard. There is a dispute with regard to a home that is jointly owned. According to one opinion, since each owner presumably has his own private space in the house, each partner is considered a sole owner of a domicile (*Kesef Mishne*). However, it appears from the Jerusalem Talmud that joint owners of a home have the same status as joint owners of a vineyard (Rambam *Sefer Shofetim*, *Hilkhot Melakhim UMilḥemoteihem* 7:6 and *Leḥem Mishne* there).

וּמַאי שְׁנָא מֵחֲמִשָּׁה אַחִין וּמֵת אֶחָד מֵהֶן בַּמִּלְחָמָה דְּכוּלָּן חוֹזְרִין? הָתָם כָּל חַד וְחַד קָרֵינָא בֵּיהּ "אִשְׁתּוֹ", הָכָא כָּל חַד וְחַד לָא קָרֵינָא בֵּיהּ "כַּרְמוֹ".

The Gemara asks: **And** in **what** way **is** the case of partners **different from** the following case: If there are **five brothers and one of them dies**[H] **in the war,** the *halakha* **is that they all return.** Just as each brother returns because of his shared responsibility to perform levirate marriage or *ḥalitza* for the widow, each partner should return for his share in the young tree that was grafted. The Gemara answers: **There, each and every one is considered** one who must return for **his wife,** as any of them could readily marry her. However, **here, each and every one is not considered** one who must return for **his vineyard** because it does not belong exclusively to either of them.

רַב נַחְמָן בַּר יִצְחָק אָמַר: בְּמַבְרִיךְ אִילָן בְּיָרָק. וְהַאי תַּנָּא הוּא, דְּתַנְיָא: הַמַּבְרִיךְ אִילָן בְּיָרָק – רַבָּן שִׁמְעוֹן בֶּן גַּמְלִיאֵל מַתִּיר מִשּׁוּם רַבִּי יְהוּדָה בֶּן גַּמְדָּא אִישׁ כְּפַר עַכּוֹ, וַחֲכָמִים אוֹסְרִין.

Rav Naḥman bar Yitzḥak said: In accordance with the *baraita* mentioned above, one does not normally return for a grafted or layered tree. However, the mishna states that one does return for a grafted or layered tree **in** a case where **one layers a tree** and grafts it **with a vegetable** plant.[H] **And** that ruling **is** in accordance with **this *tanna*,** Rabbi Yehuda ben Gamda, as cited in a *baraita*. **As it is taught** in a *baraita* (*Tosefta, Kilayim* 1:12): With regard to **one who layers a tree** and grafts it **with a vegetable** plant, the *tanna'im* engaged in a dispute concerning whether this kind of breeding is permitted. **Rabban Shimon ben Gamliel,** speaking **in the name of Rabbi Yehuda ben Gamda of the village of Akko, permits** one to do so, **and the Rabbis prohibit** it. Therefore, one would return from the ranks for a tree grafted to a vegetable plant, in accordance with the opinion of Rabbi Yehuda ben Gamda, although he would not return for the vegetable itself.

כִּי אֲתָא רַב דִּימִי אָמַר רַבִּי יוֹחָנָן: הָא מַנִּי? רַבִּי אֱלִיעֶזֶר בֶּן יַעֲקֹב הִיא. לָא אָמַר רַבִּי אֱלִיעֶזֶר בֶּן יַעֲקֹב הָתָם "כֶּרֶם" כְּמַשְׁמָעוֹ? הָכָא נַמִי "נָטַע" כְּמַשְׁמָעוֹ, נוֹטֵעַ – אִין, מַבְרִיךְ וּמַרְכִּיב – לָא.

The Gemara offers another alternative resolution to the contradiction over whether one returns for a grafted tree. **When Rav Dimi came** from Eretz Yisrael, **he said** that **Rabbi Yoḥanan** said: In accordance with **whose** opinion **is this** statement, which says that one does not return for a grafted tree? **It is** the opinion of **Rabbi Eliezer ben Ya'akov.** He explains: **Didn't Rabbi Eliezer ben Ya'akov say there** in the *baraita* cited earlier: The word **vineyard** is to be understood **as it indicates,** i.e., that the exemption is only for a grape vineyard? **Here too,** the word **planted** is to be understood **as it indicates;** with regard to one who **plants, yes,** he does return, but **one who grafts or layers** a tree does **not** return.

כִּי אֲתָא רַב דִּימִי אָמַר רַבִּי יוֹחָנָן מִשּׁוּם רַבִּי אֱלִיעֶזֶר בֶּן יַעֲקֹב: יַלְדָּה פְּחוּתָה מִטֶּפַח – חַיֶּיבֶת בְּעׇרְלָה כׇּל שְׁנוֹתֶיהָ, דְּמִתְחַזְיָא כְּבַת שַׁתָּא. וְהָנֵי מִילֵּי שְׁתַּיִם כְּנֶגֶד שְׁתַּיִם וְאַחַת יוֹצְאָה זָנָב, אֲבָל כּוּלֵּיהּ כֶּרֶם – קָלָא אִית לֵיהּ.

§ After citing Rabbi Yoḥanan's interpretation of the opinion of Rabbi Eliezer ben Ya'akov, the Gemara cites a string of other rulings that Rabbi Yoḥanan said in the name of Rabbi Eliezer ben Ya'akov. **When Rav Dimi came** from Eretz Yisrael, **he said** that **Rabbi Yoḥanan** said **in the name of Rabbi Eliezer ben Ya'akov:** The Sages decreed that if there is **a young** grapevine **less than** one **handbreadth** tall,[HB] it **is obligated in *orla* all its years,** even after the three years mandated by the Torah, **because it appears like** a vine of **one year.** The Sages were concerned that if they permitted one to eat from such a vine, people would also eat true *orla*. **And this** prohibition **applies** to a very small section of **two** grapevines **opposite two** grapevines **and one** more vine **emerging** and growing between them, in the formation of **a tail. But** if the **entire vineyard** grows so short, **it** generates **publicity,** and people know that the vines are old enough to no longer be subject to *orla*.

HALAKHA

If there are five brothers and one of them dies – **חֲמִשָּׁה אַחִין וּמֵת אֶחָד מֵהֶן:** If five brothers go to war, and one dies without leaving any children, all of the brothers return home. They all have the responsibility to perform levirate marriage or *ḥalitza* for the widow (Rambam *Sefer Shofetim, Hilkhot Melakhim UMilḥemoteihem* 7:7).

One layers a tree and grafts it with a vegetable plant – **הַמַּבְרִיךְ אִילָן בְּיָרָק:** If one grafts a tree with a vegetable plant, or a vegetable plant with a tree, he is liable to receive lashes (Rambam *Sefer Zera'im, Hilkhot Kilayim* 1:5; *Shulḥan Arukh, Yoreh De'a* 295:1).

A young grapevine less than one handbreadth tall – **יַלְדָּה פְּחוּתָה מִטֶּפַח:** If a tree is less than one handbreadth tall, even if it has been growing for many years, by rabbinic law the prohibition of *orla* still applies to it. This is only in the case of a single, isolated tree or a small vineyard of no more than two grapevines opposite two grapevines and one more vine growing between them. However, if there is an entire vineyard of such trees, they are exempt from *orla* after three years, because it is widely known that it is an older vineyard (Rambam *Sefer Zera'im, Hilkhot Ma'aser Sheni* 10:19; *Shulḥan Arukh, Yoreh De'a* 294:21).

BACKGROUND

A young grapevine less than one handbreadth tall – **יַלְדָּה פְּחוּתָה מִטֶּפַח:** This does not mean that the entire grapevine is shorter than one handbreadth, because such a grapevine, let alone a complete vineyard, cannot survive. The Gemara here is discussing a grapevine that, by itself or through training, has an extremely short trunk of less than a handbreadth. The leaves and clusters grow on vines stemming from this trunk, and these vines are cut and trained annually.

HALAKHA

A corpse occupies four cubits, etc. – מֵת תּוֹפֵס אַרְבַּע אַמּוֹת וכו׳: One may not recite *Shema* or other sacred matters within four cubits of a corpse. Even if one already recited *Shema* in the vicinity of a corpse, he did not fulfill the mitzva and must recite it again properly. However, with regard to prayers and blessings, the halakhic authorities hold in accordance with the Ra'avad and maintain that whatever was recited need not be repeated (Rambam *Sefer Ahava, Hilkhot Keriat Shema* 3:2; *Shulḥan Arukh, Oraḥ Ḥayyim* 71:7).

A stepdaughter who grows up among the brothers – חוֹרַגְתָּא הַגְּדֵילָה בֵּין הָאַחִין: One may marry the daughter of his stepmother, even if the daughter grew up with him and his siblings; it is not necessary to be concerned for appearances, as it is widely known that they are not siblings (*Shulḥan Arukh, Even HaEzer* 15:11).

Gleanings, forgotten sheaves, or produce in the corner, etc. – לֶקֶט שִׁכְחָה וּפֵאָה וכו׳: Gleanings, forgotten sheaves, and produce in the corner of the field are exempt from tithes and Temple contributions, even if they were bundled together in a heap. If one brings them into a threshing floor, he must separate tithes and contributions as one does for any other crop. However, if the threshing floor is in the city, this produce is exempt (Rambam *Sefer Zera'im, Hilkhot Terumot* 2:9).

A young vine less than one handbreadth, etc. – יַלְדָּה הַפְּחוּתָה מִטֶּפַח וכו׳: If a grapevine is shorter than one handbreadth, it does not render seeds that are planted near it forbidden due to the prohibition of diverse kinds. This is true for an individual, isolated vine and even for a group of five vines that are growing together like a vineyard. But in the case of a large vineyard that is comprised of vines shorter than a handbreadth, such vines do render the seeds grown near them forbidden (Rambam *Sefer Zera'im, Hilkhot Kilayim* 6:4; *Shulḥan Arukh, Yoreh De'a* 296:22).

כִּי אֲתָא רַב דִּימִי אָמַר רַבִּי יוֹחָנָן מִשּׁוּם רַבִּי אֱלִיעֶזֶר בֶּן יַעֲקֹב: מֵת תּוֹפֵס אַרְבַּע אַמּוֹת לִקְרִיאַת שְׁמַע, דִּכְתִיב: ״לֹעֵג לָרָשׁ חֵרֵף עֹשֵׂהוּ״.

When Rav Dimi came from Eretz Yisrael, **he said** that **Rabbi Yoḥanan** said **in the name of Rabbi Eliezer ben Ya'akov: A corpse occupies four cubits**[H] with regard **to** the exemption from **the recitation of *Shema*,** so that it is prohibited to recite *Shema* within this space, **as it is written** in the verse: **"Whoever mocks the poor blasphemes his Maker"** (Proverbs 17:5). Because the deceased cannot perform mitzvot, one who performs a mitzva in front of them is considered to be mocking them.

אָמַר רַבִּי יִצְחָק אָמַר רַבִּי יוֹחָנָן מִשּׁוּם רַבִּי אֱלִיעֶזֶר בֶּן יַעֲקֹב: חוֹרַגְתָּא הַגְּדֵילָה בֵּין הָאַחִין – אֲסוּרָה לִינָּשֵׂא לָאַחִין, דְּמִתְחַזְיָא כִּי אַחְתַּיְיהוּ. וְלָא הִיא, קָלָא אִית לֵיהּ לְמִילְּתָא.

Rabbi Yitzḥak says that **Rabbi Yoḥanan says in the name of Rabbi Eliezer ben Ya'akov:** With regard to a man's **stepdaughter who grows up among the brothers**[H] from a different marriage, she is eligible to be married to them in principle, because they are not actually her siblings. Nevertheless, she **is prohibited to be married to the brothers, because she appears as** though she is **their sister.** The Gemara comments: **And** that **is not so;** such a marriage is not prohibited because **the matter** generates **publicity,** and the public knows that they are not truly related.

וְאָמַר רַבִּי יִצְחָק אָמַר רַבִּי יוֹחָנָן מִשּׁוּם רַבִּי אֱלִיעֶזֶר בֶּן יַעֲקֹב: לֶקֶט שִׁכְחָה וּפֵאָה שֶׁעֲשָׂאָן בְּגוֹרֶן – הוּקְבְּעוּ לְמַעֲשֵׂר. אָמַר עוּלָּא: לֹא אָמְרָן אֶלָּא בְּשָׂדֶה, אֲבָל בָּעִיר – קָלָא אִית לֵיהּ לְמִילְּתָא.

And Rabbi Yitzḥak says that **Rabbi Yoḥanan says in the name of Rabbi Eliezer ben Ya'akov:** With regard to **gleanings** (Leviticus 19:9, 23:22), **forgotten** sheaves (Deuteronomy 24:19), **or produce in the corner**[H] **of the field which is given to the poor** [*pe'a*] (Leviticus 19:9, 23:22), three obligatory agricultural gifts that must be given to the poor, if one **gathered them into the threshing floor,** the produce **was** thereby **rendered** obligated **for tithes.** Although one does not take tithes from produce for the poor, onlookers are likely to presume that this is his own produce. **Ulla said: We stated** this *halakha* **only** when the granary is **in the field, but in the city, the matter** generates **publicity.** People see that the produce was gathered in small quantities from different places, and they know that this produce is for the poor. In that case, one need not separate tithes.

וְאָמַר רַבִּי יִצְחָק אָמַר רַבִּי יוֹחָנָן מִשּׁוּם רַבִּי אֱלִיעֶזֶר בֶּן יַעֲקֹב: יַלְדָּה הַפְּחוּתָה מִטֶּפַח – אֵינָהּ מְקַדֶּשֶׁת אֶת הַזְּרָעִים. וְהָנֵי מִילֵּי שְׁתַּיִם כְּנֶגֶד שְׁתַּיִם וְאַחַת יוֹצְאָה זָנָב, אֲבָל כּוּלֵּי כֶּרֶם – מְקַדֵּישׁ.

And Rabbi Yitzḥak says that **Rabbi Yoḥanan says in the name of Rabbi Eliezer ben Ya'akov:** If there is **a young** grapevine **less than** one **handbreadth**[H] tall, it **does not render the seeds** that are planted next to it **forbidden.**[N] Normally, diverse kinds of produce may not be planted in close proximity, but this vine is too small to qualify as a prohibited vineyard. The Gemara limits the scope of this statement: **And this statement** applies to a very small section of **two** grapevines **opposite two** grapevines **and one** more vine **emerging** and growing between them, in formation of **a tail. But** if the **entire vineyard** grows so short, a vine of this size does **render** the other seeds planted at its side **forbidden.**

וְאָמַר רַבִּי יִצְחָק אָמַר רַבִּי יוֹחָנָן מִשּׁוּם רַבִּי אֱלִיעֶזֶר בֶּן יַעֲקֹב:

And Rabbi Yitzḥak says that **Rabbi Yoḥanan says in the name of Rabbi Eliezer ben Ya'akov:**

NOTES

It does not render the seeds forbidden – אֵינָהּ מְקַדֶּשֶׁת אֶת הַזְּרָעִים: A number of commentaries address a basic question relating to the Gemara's discussion: If this kind of growth is considered a proper grapevine, why doesn't it qualify as a forbidden growth among diverse kinds? Conversely, if it is not considered a proper vine, why should there be a prohibition of diverse kinds if this kind of vine fills the whole vineyard?

Rashi explains that this Gemara presumes that by Torah law, only hemp and arum seeds are subject to the prohibition of diverse kinds. Other seeds are prohibited only by rabbinic law (see *Menaḥot* 15b). Therefore, the Sages dictated the terms of the ban and applied it in the case of short vines, only where the short vines populate a complete vineyard.

The Rambam does not differentiate between different species of seeds, and he understands this *halakha* in another manner. According to one explanation, the Rambam holds that the parameters of this prohibition are *halakhot* transmitted to Moses at Sinai, which follow their own regulations. The Radbaz suggests two other possible explanations. First, a group of five vines does not qualify as a vineyard by Torah law; and when the Sages determined that such a group should be treated like a vineyard, they did not apply this categorization to a vineyard of exceedingly short vines. Alternatively, vines this short may not constitute a proper vineyard by Torah law, but the Sages decreed that they must be treated as a vineyard with respect to the prohibition of diverse kinds when a whole vineyard grows in this manner.

מֵת תּוֹפֵס אַרְבַּע אַמּוֹת לְטוּמְאָה. וְתָנָא תּוּנָא: חֲצַר הַקֶּבֶר, הָעוֹמֵד בְּתוֹכָהּ – טָהוֹר, וְהוּא שֶׁיְּהוּ בָּהּ אַרְבַּע אַמּוֹת, דִּבְרֵי בֵּית שַׁמַּאי. בֵּית הִלֵּל אוֹמְרִים: אַרְבָּעָה טְפָחִים; בַּמֶּה דְּבָרִים אֲמוּרִים – שֶׁפִּתְחָהּ מִלְמַעְלָה, אֲבָל פִּתְחָהּ מִן הַצַּד – דִּבְרֵי הַכֹּל אַרְבַּע אַמּוֹת.

A corpse occupies four cubits[NH] **with** regard to **impurity,** as the Sages decreed that one becomes impure when he stands within four cubits of a corpse. This measure protects priests and others who are forbidden to contract ritual impurity imparted by a corpse, so that they do not inadvertently become impure. **And the** ***tanna*** of the mishna **taught** in another mishna as well (*Oholot* 15:8): With regard to **a courtyard** adjacent to **a grave,**[HB] **one who stands within it is ritually pure, provided that there are four cubits** by four cubits **within it.** A courtyard this size constitutes its own space, according to **the statement of Beit Shammai. Beit Hillel say:** A space of **four handbreadths** by four handbreadths is enough. **In what** case **is this statement said?** Four handbreadths suffice **when the entrance** to the courtyard is **from above.** In such a case there is no concern that one will cover the grave with his body, and thereby become ritually impure, when entering the courtyard. **However, if its entrance** is **from the side, everyone agrees** the courtyard must be at least **four cubits** by four cubits in size.

כְּלַפֵּי לַיָּיא? אַדְּרַבָּה, מִן הַצַּד מִידְרִיד וְנָפֵיק, מִלְמַעְלָה אִי אֶפְשָׁר דְּלָא מַאֲהִיל! אֶלָּא, בַּמֶּה דְּבָרִים אֲמוּרִים – שֶׁפִּתְחָהּ מִן הַצַּד, אֲבָל פִּתְחָהּ מִלְמַעְלָה – אַרְבַּע אַמּוֹת; וְהָנֵי מִילֵּי חֲצַר הַקֶּבֶר, דִּמְסַיְּימָא מְחִיצָתָהּ, אֲבָל מֵת בְּעָלְמָא – תָּפֵיס.

The Gemara challenges the preceding resolution: **In which direction** [***kelapei layya***][L] is there a distinction between the positions of the entrance? **On the contrary,** if one enters **from the side,** he can **slip away** and **exit** without becoming impure. However, if one enters **from above it is impossible that** he will **not overlie the grave** over the course of climbing in and out of the courtyard. **Rather,** it should say: **In what** case **is this statement** of Beit Hillel, according to which four handbreadths by four handbreadths are enough, **said?** It is **when the entrance is from the side. However, if the entrance is from above,** then the courtyard must be at least **four cubits** by four cubits according to all opinions. The Gemara further qualifies: **And this statement** applies in **a courtyard** adjacent to **a grave whose partitions** are **delineated, but** if there is **only a corpse** lying about without any enclosures, it certainly **occupies** and affects a surrounding area of four cubits.

״מִי הָאִישׁ אֲשֶׁר אֵרַשׂ אִשָּׁה״ כּוּ׳. תָּנוּ רַבָּנַן: אֲשֶׁר אֵרַס – אֶחָד הַמְאָרֵס אֶת הַבְּתוּלָה וְאֶחָד הַמְאָרֵס אֶת הָאַלְמָנָה וְאֶחָד שׁוֹמֶרֶת יָבָם. וַאֲפִילּוּ חֲמִשָּׁה אַחִין וּמֵת אֶחָד מֵהֶם בַּמִּלְחָמָה – כּוּלָּן חוֹזְרִין. ״לֹא לָקַח״, ״וְלֹא לְקָחָהּ״ – פְּרָט לְאַלְמָנָה לְכֹהֵן גָּדוֹל, גְּרוּשָׁה וַחֲלוּצָה לְכֹהֵן הֶדְיוֹט, מַמְזֶרֶת וּנְתִינָה לְיִשְׂרָאֵל, בַּת יִשְׂרָאֵל לְמַמְזֵר וּלְנָתִין.

§ The mishna teaches among the statements that were said before battle: **"What man is there that has betrothed a wife** and has not taken her? Let him go and return to his house" (Deuteronomy 20:7). **The Sages taught: "That has betrothed"** is referring to **one who betroths a virgin, and** to **one who betroths a widow, and** to **one** whose *yevama* is **a widow awaiting her** ***yavam***, i.e., this man in the military ranks, to perform levirate marriage. **And even** if there are **five brothers, and one of them dies in the war, they all return** for the widow. In addition, the verse could have singled out one who has **not taken** a wife. When the verse specifies: **"and has not taken her,"** this **excludes** men in forbidden marriages: **A widow** who is betrothed **to a High Priest;** either **a divorcée or a** ***yevama*** **who performed** ***ḥalitza*** [***ḥalutza***], who is betrothed **to a common priest;** a ***mamzeret*** **or a Gibeonite woman** who is betrothed **to an Israelite;** or **an Israelite woman** who is betrothed **to a** ***mamzer*** **or to a Gibeonite.**

לֵימָא, דְּלָא כְּרַבִּי יוֹסֵי הַגְּלִילִי, דְּאִי רַבִּי יוֹסֵי הַגְּלִילִי, הָא אָמַר: ״הַיָּרֵא וְרַךְ הַלֵּבָב״ – זֶה הַמִּתְיָירֵא מֵעֲבֵירוֹת שֶׁבְּיָדוֹ!

The Gemara asks: **Shall we say** that this opinion is **not in accordance with** the opinion of **Rabbi Yosei HaGelili? As, if** it were in accordance with the opinion of **Rabbi Yosei HaGelili, he says:** When the verse singles out **"fearful and fainthearted"** (Deuteronomy 20:8), **this** is referring to **one who is afraid because of sins that he has.** According to this interpretation, one who marries a woman forbidden to him should return home from war because of his guilt, which seems to contradict the opinion mentioned above that such a man does not return from the ranks.

NOTES

A corpse occupies four cubits – מֵת תּוֹפֵס אַרְבַּע אַמּוֹת: Rabbeinu Yehonatan of Lunel maintains that this applies only to an exposed corpse, but not to a buried one. However, a dissenting opinion is presented in *Nimmukei Yosef*. The basic concern behind this *halakha* is that one may come too near to the dead body and extend either his whole body or a limb over the corpse. As such, the concern applies to a buried body in the same way that it applies to an exposed body, so long as there is no actual barrier separating the person from the corpse.

HALAKHA

A corpse occupies four cubits – מֵת תּוֹפֵס אַרְבַּע אַמּוֹת: A corpse, as well as a grave, imparts ritual impurity within the four cubits surrounding it, and a priest who enters into this space is liable to receive lashes for rebelliousness, commensurate with violating a rabbinic prohibition. However, if the corpse or grave is surrounded by a wall ten handbreadths high or by a ditch ten handbreadths deep, a priest need not distance himself more than four handbreadths. The *Shakh* rules that when the body is clearly in a temporary position, as in when it is carried on a bed, it does not affect the four cubits surrounding it (Rambam *Sefer Shofetim, Hilkhot Evel* 3:13; *Shulḥan Arukh, Yoreh De'a* 371:5).

A courtyard adjacent to a grave – חֲצַר הַקֶּבֶר: When there is a grave within a cave and a courtyard in front of the cave, if the courtyard is uncovered, one does not contract ritual impurity merely by standing inside the courtyard. Even if the courtyard is covered, one who enters into the courtyard does not contract ritual impurity, so long as the courtyard has an area of at least of four handbreadths by four handbreadths. According to the Ra'avad, the area of four by four handbreadths must be uncovered and adjacent to the cave. However, if the covered courtyard does not have this area of four by four handbreadths, one contracts ritual impurity merely by entering into the courtyard, in accordance with the opinion of Beit Hillel (Rambam *Sefer Tahara, Hilkhot Tumat Met* 6:9).

BACKGROUND

Courtyard adjacent to a grave – חֲצַר הַקֶּבֶר:

Grave with adjacent courtyard

LANGUAGE

In which direction [*kelapei layya*] – כְּלַפֵּי לַיָּיא: This expression of puzzlement is generally understood to mean: Directed to where? That is to say: Where are you facing, or, more simply: How are you thinking about the given matter? The question implies: You are looking at the matter backward. Accordingly, some of the *ge'onim* understood the expression as: Facing the tail [*kelapei aliya*], as if to say: You are facing the direction of the tail, like a person who is riding backward on an animal. In any case, the term is understood to indicate: You are saying the opposite of what is logical.

HALAKHA

Until he engages in sexual intercourse with his wife – עַד שֶׁיִּבְעוֹל: Even if a High Priest marries a widow, or a common priest marries a divorcée, lashes will not be administered until he engages in sexual intercourse with her (Rambam *Sefer Kedusha, Hilkhot Issurei Bia* 17:4).

The Torah has taught a person the desired mode of behavior – לִימְּדָה תּוֹרָה דֶּרֶךְ אֶרֶץ: The way of sensible people is first to find an occupation to provide income; then, to buy a residence; and, finally, to marry a wife. The Ya'avetz writes that even if one does not find a sufficient income, he must still fulfill the mitzva of marrying a wife, and he should not delay to the degree that he may succumb and engage in forbidden sexual intercourse (Rambam *Sefer HaMadda, Hilkhot Deot* 5:11).

LANGUAGE

Row of stones [*dimos*] – דִּימוֹס: From the Greek δόμος, *domos*, meaning, among other definitions, a row or a layer of bricks in a building.

BACKGROUND

Brick house in the Sharon – בֵּית לְבֵנִים בַּשָּׁרוֹן: Apparently, one of the complications in building a sturdy house in the Sharon was related to the sandy earth in the plains of Eretz Yisrael, known as the *shefela*. The unstable and shifting sand, combined with a high subterranean water level, hindered the digging of deep foundations and caused the walls of the buildings to crack. Consequently, the houses needed to be practically rebuilt from time to time. The situation was so dire that it seems it was not unheard of for the houses in the Sharon to completely collapse on their inhabitants.

NOTES

Twice in seven years [*shavua*] – פַּעֲמַיִם בְּשָׁבוּעַ: The term *shavua* denotes a unit of seven. Most commentaries understand this to mean that the house is rebuilt twice in a single seven-year Sabbatical cycle, which is necessary because of the lay of the land and the type of bricks used in the construction. In a similar vein, the High Priest would pray specifically for the people of the Sharon that their houses would not become their graves.

אֲפִילּוּ תֵּימָא רַבִּי יוֹסֵי הַגְּלִילִי, כִּדְרַבָּה, דְּאָמַר רַבָּה: לְעוֹלָם אֵינוֹ חַיָּיב עַד שֶׁיִּבְעוֹל. מַה טַּעַם ״לֹא יִקָּח״? מִשּׁוּם ״לֹא יְחַלֵּל״, מִשּׁוּם הָכִי אֵינוֹ לוֹקֶה עַד שֶׁיִּבְעוֹל.

The Gemara answers: **Even if you say** that the ruling is in accordance with the opinion of **Rabbi Yosei HaGelili,** such a man does not return, **in accordance with** the opinion **of Rabba. As Rabba said:** A man is **never liable** for a forbidden marriage **until he engages in sexual intercourse** with his wife.[H] With regard to the forbidden marriages of a High Priest, the Torah states: "A widow, or a divorcée, or a profaned woman, or a harlot, these he shall not take… And he shall not profane his seed among his people" (Leviticus 21:14–15). **What is the reason** that **"he shall not take"** one of these women as a wife? It is **due to: "He shall not profane** his seed" by engaging in sexual intercourse. **Due to that** reason, **he is not flogged until he engages in sexual intercourse** with a woman who is forbidden to him. Therefore, even according to Rabbi Yosei HaGelili, one who merely betroths a forbidden wife might not return home from the ranks.

תָּנוּ רַבָּנַן: ״אֲשֶׁר בָּנָה״, ״אֲשֶׁר נָטַע״, ״אֲשֶׁר אֵרַשׂ״ – לִימְּדָה תּוֹרָה דֶּרֶךְ אֶרֶץ, שֶׁיִּבְנֶה אָדָם בַּיִת וְיִטַּע כֶּרֶם וְאַחַר כָּךְ יִשָּׂא אִשָּׁה. וְאַף שְׁלֹמֹה אָמַר בְּחָכְמָתוֹ: ״הָכֵן בַּחוּץ מְלַאכְתֶּךָ וְעַתְּדָהּ בַּשָּׂדֶה לָךְ אַחַר וּבָנִיתָ בֵיתֶךָ״. ״הָכֵן בַּחוּץ מְלַאכְתֶּךָ״ – זֶה בַּיִת; ״וְעַתְּדָהּ בַּשָּׂדֶה לָךְ״ – זֶה כֶּרֶם; ״אַחַר וּבָנִיתָ בֵיתֶךָ״ – זוֹ אִשָּׁה.

§ **The Sages taught** (*Tosefta* 7:20–21): The Torah states: "What man is there **that has built"** (Deuteronomy 20:5), and then **"that has planted"** (Deuteronomy 20:6), and finally **"that has betrothed"** (Deuteronomy 20:7). **The Torah** has **taught** a person **the desired mode of behavior:**[H] **A person should build a house,** then **plant a vineyard, and afterward marry a woman. And even** King **Solomon said in his wisdom: "Prepare your work outside, and make it fit for yourself in the field; and afterward build your house"** (Proverbs 24:27). The Sages explained: **"Prepare your work outside"; this** is **a house. "And make it fit for yourself in the field"; this is a vineyard. "And afterward you shall build your house"; this** is **a wife.**

דָּבָר אַחֵר: ״הָכֵן בַּחוּץ מְלַאכְתֶּךָ״ – זֶה מִקְרָא; ״וְעַתְּדָהּ בַּשָּׂדֶה לָךְ״ – זֶה מִשְׁנָה; ״אַחַר וּבָנִיתָ בֵיתֶךָ״ – זֶה גְּמָרָא. דָּבָר אַחֵר: ״הָכֵן בַּחוּץ מְלַאכְתֶּךָ״ – זֶה מִקְרָא וּמִשְׁנָה; ״וְעַתְּדָהּ בַּשָּׂדֶה לָךְ״ – זֶה גְּמָרָא; ״אַחַר וּבָנִיתָ בֵיתֶךָ״ – אֵלּוּ מַעֲשִׂים טוֹבִים. רַבִּי אֱלִיעֶזֶר בְּנוֹ שֶׁל רַבִּי יוֹסֵי הַגְּלִילִי אוֹמֵר: ״הָכֵן בַּחוּץ מְלַאכְתֶּךָ״ – זֶה מִקְרָא וּמִשְׁנָה וּגְמָרָא; ״וְעַתְּדָהּ בַּשָּׂדֶה לָךְ״ – אֵלּוּ מַעֲשִׂים טוֹבִים; ״אַחַר וּבָנִיתָ בֵיתֶךָ״ – דְּרוֹשׁ וְקַבֵּל שָׂכָר.

Alternatively, this verse may be understood as relating to Torah study: **"Prepare your work outside"; this** is the study of **Bible. "And make it fit for yourself in the field"; this** is the study of **Mishna. "Afterward you shall build your house"; this** is the study of **Gemara,** the analysis of and deliberation over the statements of the Sages. **Alternatively: "Prepare your work outside"; this** is the study of **Bible and Mishna. "And make it fit for yourself in the field"; this** is the study of **Gemara. "Afterward you shall build your house"; these** are **good deeds. Rabbi Eliezer, son of Rabbi Yosei HaGelili, says: "Prepare your work outside"; this** is the study of **Bible, and Mishna, and Gemara. "And make it fit for yourself in the field"; these** are **good deeds. "Afterward you shall build your house"; expound** upon new understandings of Torah **and receive reward,** which is possible only after the initial steps.

״וְאֵלּוּ שֶׁאֵינָן חוֹזְרִין: הַבּוֹנֶה בֵּית שַׁעַר״ כו׳. תָּנָא: אִם הוֹסִיף בּוֹ דִּימוֹס אֶחָד – חוֹזֵר. רַבִּי אֱלִיעֶזֶר אוֹמֵר: אַף הַבּוֹנֶה בֵּית לְבֵנִים בַּשָּׁרוֹן לֹא הָיָה חוֹזֵר. תָּנָא: מִפְּנֵי שֶׁמְּחַדְּשִׁין אוֹתוֹ פַּעֲמַיִם בְּשָׁבוּעַ.

§ The mishna teaches: **And these** are the men **who do not return** from the ranks: **One who builds a gateway,** or an enclosed veranda, or a balcony… Rabbi Yehuda says: Even one who rebuilds a house as it stood originally would not return. A Sage taught (*Tosefta* 7:18): **If** one **adds one** additional **row of stones** [*dimos*][L] **to** the original structure, **he returns** from the ranks. That is enough to render it a new building. The mishna further teaches: **Rabbi Eliezer says: Even one who builds** a new **brick house in the Sharon**[B] **would not return.** A Sage **taught:** This is **because** the owners **renew it twice in** a period of **seven years,**[N] and it is therefore not considered a permanent structure.

״וְאֵלּוּ שֶׁאֵין זָזִין מִמְּקוֹמָן: בָּנָה בַּיִת חָדָשׁ וַחֲנָכוֹ״ וכו׳. תָּנוּ רַבָּנַן: ״אִשָּׁה חֲדָשָׁה״ – אֵין לִי אֶלָּא אִשָּׁה חֲדָשָׁה; אַלְמָנָה וּגְרוּשָׁה מִנַּיִן? תַּלְמוּד לוֹמַר: ״אִשָּׁה״, מִכׇּל מָקוֹם; אִם כֵּן, מָה תַּלְמוּד לוֹמַר: ״אִשָּׁה חֲדָשָׁה״? מִי שֶׁחֲדָשָׁה לוֹ, יָצָא מַחֲזִיר גְּרוּשָׁתוֹ שֶׁאֵין חֲדָשָׁה לוֹ.

§ The mishna teaches: **These** are the men **who do not** even **move from their places:** One who **built a house and dedicated it** within the year; one who planted a vineyard and used its fruit for less than a year; one who marries his betrothed and one who marries his *yevama*, as it is stated: "When a man takes a new wife, he shall not go out with the army, neither shall he be charged with any business; he shall be free for his house one year, and shall cheer his wife whom he has taken" (Deuteronomy 24:5). With respect to a new husband's exemption, **the Sages taught** a number of *halakhot* from this verse. From the term: **"A new wife" I have** derived **only** that a man returns only for **a new** virgin **wife. From where** do I derive that it applies to **a widow or a divorcée? The verse states: "A wife," in any case. If so, what** is the meaning when **the verse states: "A new wife?"** It is referring to **one who is new for him, excluding one who remarries his divorcée, who is not new to him.**

תָּנוּ רַבָּנַן: "לֹא יֵצֵא בַּצָּבָא" – יָכוֹל בַּצָּבָא הוּא דְּלָא יָצָא, אֲבָל יְסַפֵּק מַיִם וּמָזוֹן וִיתַקֵּן הַדְּרָכִים? תַּלְמוּד לוֹמַר: "וְלֹא יַעֲבֹר עָלָיו לְכָל דָּבָר". יָכוֹל שֶׁאֲנִי מַרְבֶּה אַף הַבּוֹנֶה בַיִת וְלֹא חֲנָכוֹ, נָטַע כֶּרֶם וְלֹא חִלְּלוֹ, אֵרַס אִשָּׁה וְלֹא לְקָחָהּ? תַּלְמוּד לוֹמַר: "עָלָיו", עָלָיו אִי אַתָּה מַעֲבִיר, אֲבָל אַתָּה מַעֲבִיר עַל אֲחֵרִים. וּמֵאַחַר דִּכְתַב "לֹא יַעֲבֹר", "לֹא יֵצֵא בַּצָּבָא" לָמָּה לִי? לַעֲבוֹר עָלָיו בִּשְׁנֵי לָאוִין.

The Sages taught with regard to the verse: **"He shall not go out with the army"** (Deuteronomy 24:5); one **might** have thought it is **with the army that he does not go out, but** he does go to **supply water and food** to the army **and to repair the roads** for them. Therefore, **the verse states: "Neither shall he be charged with any business."** One **might** have thought **that I include even one who has built a house and has not dedicated it,** or **one who has planted a vineyard and has not used its fruit,** or **one who has betrothed a woman and has not taken her** as his wife? **The verse states:** "Neither shall **he** be charged with any business"; **you do not charge him with any** responsibilities, **but you do charge others.** The Gemara asks: **And since** the Torah **states: "Neither shall he be charged** with any business," **why do I** need to be taught: **"He shall not go out with the army"?** The Gemara answers: The Torah adds this clause **so that he will violate two prohibitions**[H] if he goes out to war: "He shall not go out with the army," and: "Neither shall he be charged."

מתני׳ "וְיָסְפוּ הַשֹּׁטְרִים לְדַבֵּר אֶל הָעָם" וגו׳ – רַבִּי עֲקִיבָא אוֹמֵר: "הַיָּרֵא וְרַךְ הַלֵּבָב" – כְּמַשְׁמָעוֹ, שֶׁאֵינוֹ יָכוֹל לַעֲמוֹד בְּקִשְׁרֵי הַמִּלְחָמָה וְלִרְאוֹת חֶרֶב שְׁלוּפָה. רַבִּי יוֹסֵי הַגְּלִילִי אוֹמֵר: "הַיָּרֵא וְרַךְ הַלֵּבָב" – זֶהוּ הַמִּתְיָרֵא מִן הָעֲבֵירוֹת שֶׁבְּיָדוֹ. לְפִיכָךְ תָּלְתָה לוֹ הַתּוֹרָה אֶת כׇּל אֵלּוּ שֶׁיַּחֲזוֹר בִּגְלָלָן.

MISHNA The mishna continues its discussion of the speech given before battle. **"And the officers shall speak further to the people,** and they shall say: What man is there that is fearful and fainthearted? Let him go and return unto his house" (Deuteronomy 20:8). **Rabbi Akiva says: "That is fearful and fainthearted"**[H] is to be understood **as it indicates, that** the man is **unable to stand in the battle ranks**[N] **and to see a drawn sword** because it will terrify him. **Rabbi Yosei HaGelili says: "That is fearful and fainthearted"; this is one who is afraid because of the sins that he has;** he, too, returns. **Therefore, the Torah provided him** with **all these** additional reasons for exemption from the army so he can ascribe **his leaving to** one of **them.** In this way, the sinner may leave the ranks without having to publicly acknowledge that he is a sinner.

רַבִּי יוֹסֵי אוֹמֵר: אַלְמָנָה לְכֹהֵן גָּדוֹל, גְּרוּשָׁה וַחֲלוּצָה לְכֹהֵן הֶדְיוֹט, מַמְזֶרֶת וּנְתִינָה לְיִשְׂרָאֵל, בַּת יִשְׂרָאֵל לְמַמְזֵר וּלְנָתִין – הֲרֵי הוּא "הַיָּרֵא וְרַךְ הַלֵּבָב".

Rabbi Yosei says: With regard to one who has betrothed a woman forbidden to him, including **a widow** betrothed **to a High Priest; a divorcée or a** *yevama* **who performed** ***ḥalitza*** [***ḥalutza***] betrothed **to a common priest; a** ***mamzeret*** **or a Gibeonite woman** betrothed **to an Israelite; or a daughter of an Israelite** betrothed **to a** ***mamzer*** **or a Gibeonite; this** man **is he** whom the verse calls **"fearful and fainthearted."** He fears that his sin will jeopardize his safety in the war.

"וְהָיָה כְּכַלֹּת הַשֹּׁטְרִים לְדַבֵּר אֶל הָעָם וּפָקְדוּ שָׂרֵי צְבָאוֹת בְּרֹאשׁ הָעָם" וּבַעֲקֵיבוֹ שֶׁל עָם. מַעֲמִידִין זְקִיפִין לִפְנֵיהֶם וַאֲחֵרִים מֵאֲחוֹרֵיהֶם וְכַשִּׁילִין שֶׁל בַּרְזֶל בִּידֵיהֶן. וְכׇל הַמְבַקֵּשׁ לַחֲזוֹר – הָרְשׁוּת בְּיָדוֹ לְקַפֵּחַ אֶת שׁוֹקָיו

The mishna continues its discussion. The verse states: **"And it shall be, when the officers conclude speaking to the people, that captains of legions shall be appointed at the head of the people"** (Deuteronomy 20:9). The mishna adds: **As well as at the rear of the people.** The officers **station guards** [***zekifin***][HL] **in front of them,**[N] **and other** guards **behind them, and** they have **iron rods** [***kashilin***][L] **in their hands. And** with regard to **anyone who attempts to turn back** and flee from the war, the guard **has license to beat** [***lekape'aḥ***][L] **his legs**

HALAKHA

So that he will violate two prohibitions – לַעֲבוֹר עָלָיו בִּשְׁנֵי לָאוִין: A newly married man does not go to war during the first year of marriage; he need not aid the soldiers, and he is not charged with the various obligations and taxes of the city. If he does become involved in these matters he violates two prohibitions: "He shall not go out with the army," and: "Neither shall he be charged" (Rambam *Sefer Shofetim, Hilkhot Melakhim UMilḥemoteihem* 7:11).

That is fearful and fainthearted – הַיָּרֵא וְרַךְ הַלֵּבָב: If one is deemed incapable of standing among the military ranks, he may be considered fearful and fainthearted, thereby allowing him to return from war. This is in accordance with the opinion of Rabbi Akiva, whose opinions are preferred over those of his contemporaries (Rambam *Sefer Shofetim, Hilkhot Melakhim UMilḥemoteihem* 7:15).

Station guards – מַעֲמִידִין זְקִיפִין: After all of the exempted men leave the military ranks, the leaders of the army stand at the head of the nation and position stout guards behind every platoon. These guards are armed with iron rods, and they are permitted to beat the thighs of anyone who attempts to leave the ranks from that point onward (Rambam *Sefer Shofetim, Hilkhot Melakhim UMilḥemoteihem* 7:4).

NOTES

Battle ranks [*kishrei*] – קִשְׁרֵי הַמִּלְחָמָה: Following Rashi's lead, the commentaries explain that the phalanx, or knots [*kishrei*] of the war, denotes groups of soldiers bound and tied together in battle. For Rabbi Akiva, the fearful and fainthearted soldier is the one who sees this mass of enemy soldiers and becomes terrified. According to the alternative text in the Jerusalem Talmud, the soldier fears the difficulty [*kishui*] of war.

Guards in front of them – זְקִיפִין לִפְנֵיהֶם: Both Rashi and the Meiri explain that guards are stationed in the front to support the fighters and help the fighters back to their feet in the event that they fall. Another row of guards behind the fighters serves the purpose of preventing soldiers from fleeing. According to an alternate opinion, the two rows of guards are there to ensure that no one deserts (*Arukh*).

LANGUAGE

Guards [*zekifin*] – זְקִיפִין: The root *zayin, kuf, peh* means erect or cause to stand. The job of these *zekifin* is to stand steadfast at the edge of the military ranks and keep the soldiers standing together in place so that they will not flee and cause the ranks to collapse.

Iron rods [*kashilin*] – כַּשִּׁילִין: This biblical word is also used in the Mishna, and it seems to refer to a type of heavy axe or pickaxe.

Beat [*lekape'aḥ*] – לְקַפֵּחַ: This verb seems to be borrowed from the Aramaic root whose primary meaning is hit and break.

Perek **VIII**
Daf **44** Amud **b**

שֶׁתְּחִילַּת נִיסָה נְפִילָה, שֶׁנֶּאֱמַר: "נָס יִשְׂרָאֵל לִפְנֵי פְלִשְׁתִּים וְגַם מַגֵּפָה גְדוֹלָה הָיְתָה בָעָם", וּלְהַלָּן הוּא אוֹמֵר: "וַיָּנֻסוּ אַנְשֵׁי יִשְׂרָאֵל מִפְּנֵי פְלִשְׁתִּים וַיִּפְּלוּ חֲלָלִים" וגו׳.

because the beginning of fleeing is **a downfall** on the battlefield, **as it is stated: "Israel has fled before the Philistines, and there has been also a great slaughter among the people"** (I Samuel 4:17), **and** likewise **it says further on: "And the men of Israel fled from before the Philistines, and fell down slain** in Mount Gilboa" (I Samuel 31:1).

בַּמֶּה דְּבָרִים אֲמוּרִים – בְּמִלְחֲמוֹת הָרְשׁוּת, אֲבָל בְּמִלְחֲמוֹת מִצְוָה – הַכֹּל יוֹצְאִין, אֲפִילּוּ חָתָן מֵחֶדְרוֹ וְכַלָּה מֵחוּפָּתָהּ; אָמַר רַבִּי יְהוּדָה: בַּמֶּה דְּבָרִים אֲמוּרִים – בְּמִלְחֲמוֹת מִצְוָה, אֲבָל בְּמִלְחֲמוֹת חוֹבָה – הַכֹּל יוֹצְאִין, אֲפִילּוּ חָתָן מֵחֶדְרוֹ וְכַלָּה מֵחוּפָּתָהּ.

The mishna adds: **In what** case **are** all of **these statements,** with regard to the various exemptions from war, **said?** They are said **with regard to elective wars. But in wars** whose mandate is **a mitzva, everyone goes,**[H] **even a groom from his room and a bride from her wedding canopy.**[N] **Rabbi Yehuda said: In what** case **are** all of **these statements,** with regard to the various exemptions from war, **said?** They are said **with regard to wars** whose mandate is **a mitzva. But in obligatory wars, everyone goes, even a groom from his room and a bride from her wedding canopy.**

גמ׳ מַאי אִיכָּא בֵּין רַבִּי יוֹסֵי לְרַבִּי יוֹסֵי הַגְּלִילִי? אִיכָּא בֵּינַיְיהוּ עֲבֵירָה דְּרַבָּנַן.

GEMARA The Gemara asks: With regard to their understanding that the "fearful and fainthearted" is referring to one harboring sins, **what** difference **is there between** the opinion of **Rabbi Yosei and** the opinion of **Rabbi Yosei HaGelili?** The Gemara answers: There is a practical difference **between them** with regard to **a sin** which violates a prohibition **by rabbinic law.** According to Rabbi Yosei HaGelili, one who has violated a rabbinic law returns home, whereas Rabbi Yosei maintains that one returns home only if he has violated a Torah law, as in the case of a priest who has married a divorcée.

כְּמַאן אָזְלָא הָא דְּתַנְיָא: שָׂח בֵּין תְּפִילָּה לִתְפִילָּה – עֲבֵירָה הִיא בְּיָדוֹ וְחוֹזֵר עָלֶיהָ מֵעוֹרְכֵי הַמִּלְחָמָה, כְּמַאן? כְּרַבִּי יוֹסֵי הַגְּלִילִי.

The Gemara asks: **In accordance with whose** opinion **is that which is taught** in a *baraita*: If one **spoke between** donning the **phylactery** of the arm **and** the **phylactery** of the head,[HN] he has **a sin on his hands, and due to** that sin **he returns from the ranks of** soldiers waging **war. In accordance with whose opinion** does this man return? It is **in accordance with** the opinion of **Rabbi Yosei HaGelili,** who maintains that one returns even due to a minor transgression.

מַאן תַּנָּא לְהָא דְּתָנוּ רַבָּנַן: שָׁמַע קוֹל קְרָנוֹת וְהִרְתִּיעַ, הֲגָפַת תְּרִיסִין וְהִרְתִּיעַ, צִחְצוּחַ חֲרָבוֹת וּמַיִם שׁוֹתְתִין לוֹ עַל בִּרְכָּיו – חוֹזֵר. כְּמַאן? לֵימָא, רַבִּי עֲקִיבָא הִיא וְלָא רַבִּי יוֹסֵי הַגְּלִילִי! בְּהָא אֲפִילּוּ רַבִּי יוֹסֵי הַגְּלִילִי מוֹדֶה, מִשּׁוּם דִּכְתִיב: "וְלֹא יִמַּס אֶת לְבַב אֶחָיו כִּלְבָבוֹ".

The Gemara asks: **Who** is the *tanna* who **taught this** *halakha* **that the Sages taught** in a *baraita*: If **one heard the sound of trumpets and trembled;** or he heard **the knocking of shields and** he **trembled;** or he heard **the sharpening of swords, and urine** was **trickling down his knees**[B] in fear, **he returns** from the battlefront. **In accordance with whose** opinion is this? **Shall we say** that **it is** the opinion of **Rabbi Akiva,** who interprets "fearful and fainthearted" literally, **and** it is **not** the opinion of **Rabbi Yosei HaGelili?** The Gemara answers: **In this** case **even Rabbi Yosei HaGelili** would **concede** that he should return, **because it is written:** "What man is there that is fearful and fainthearted? Let him go and return… **lest his brethren's heart melt as his heart**" (Deuteronomy 20:8). Someone so clearly frightened invariably spreads his fear to those around him.

HALAKHA

In wars whose mandate is a mitzva everyone goes – בְּמִלְחֲמוֹת מִצְוָה הַכֹּל יוֹצְאִין: Whatever is said with regard to the men who return from the ranks applies only to elective wars. However, everyone goes out to wars whose mandate is a mitzva, even a groom from his room and a bride from her wedding canopy (Rambam *Sefer Shofetim, Hilkhot Melakhim UMilḥemoteihem* 7:4).

If one spoke between donning the phylactery of the arm and the phylactery of the head – שָׂח בֵּין תְּפִילָּה לִתְפִילָּה: It is prohibited to speak between donning the phylactery of the arm and that of the head, and one who does so is required to recite the blessing: Blessed are You…about the mitzva of phylacteries. The custom of most Ashkenazim is to recite this blessing for the phylactery of the head *ab initio*, although they follow the blessing by saying: Blessed be the name of His glorious kingdom forever and all time. This utterance is commonly recited in order to avoid mentioning God's name in vain, and implicitly acknowledges that the blessing for the head phylactery may be superfluous. The Rema notes that according to this custom, if one spoke before donning the phylactery of the head, he must subsequently recite both of the blessings: Blessed are You…To don phylacteries, and: Blessed are You…about the mitzva of phylacteries (Rambam *Sefer Ahava, Hilkhot Tefillin* 4:6; *Shulḥan Arukh, Oraḥ Ḥayyim* 25:9).

BACKGROUND

Urine was trickling down his knees – מַיִם שׁוֹתְתִין לוֹ עַל בִּרְכָּיו: People may experience any of a number of common physiological responses when they enter a state of extreme fear. Aside from trembling or shaking, a common response is the loss of control over certain muscles. This may lead to the loss of control over the excretory system, causing either urination or defecation.

NOTES

A bride from her wedding canopy – כַּלָּה מֵחוּפָּתָהּ: Some commentaries find the mishna's statement surprising: Are we to understand from this singular, passing reference that women are supposed to go to war? They explain that the mishna does not say that the bride goes out to fight, but rather, that women are obligated to provide non-combat assistance in the war effort (Rashash; *Tiferet Yisrael*). Others write that the mishna does not mean to require women to participate in the war at all, asserting that the *tanna* is simply employing a turn of phrase from the Bible (see Joel 2:16).

If one spoke between donning the phylactery of the arm and the phylactery of the head – שָׂח בֵּין תְּפִילָּה לִתְפִילָּה: According to Rashi, this is a case of one who spoke between donning the phylactery of the arm and that of the head; his sin was that he did not subsequently recite a blessing for the phylactery of the head. However, many commentaries challenge Rashi's interpretation. One commentary contends that the omission of a blessing on the phylactery of the head cannot be the sin, as the mere act of speaking is a sin in that it forces one to recite an extra blessing unnecessarily (*Tosefot HaRosh*).

Early commentaries discuss this fundamental issue of whether the blessing for the phylactery of the head is always mandated. Sephardic authorities presume that the blessing is mandated only in the instance of an interruption between donning the phylactery of the arm and that of the head. By contrast, Rabbeinu Tam marshals a number of proofs to demonstrate that the blessing for the phylactery of the head is to be recited as a matter of course, even without any interruptions. Accordingly, this practice is accepted in most Ashkenazi communities. Significantly, according to this opinion, in the event of an interruption one is then required to recite two blessings over the phylactery of the head. Therefore, according to both opinions, an interruption requires an additional blessing to be said unnecessarily.

It seems that the Rambam understands, in contrast to Rashi's opinion, that the mere act of speaking between the donning of the two phylacteries is itself a sin. This is in accordance with the explanation of the Ran, which is as follows: Since the verse connects the two phylacteries: "And it shall be for a sign upon your hand, and for frontlets between your eyes" (Exodus 13:16), apparently the phylactery of the head must be donned immediately after that of the hand (*Keren Ora*).

״וְהָיָה כְּכַלֹּת הַשּׁוֹטְרִים״ כו׳. הַאי ״מִפְּנֵי שֶׁתְּחִילַּת נִיסָה נְפִילָה״, ״מִפְּנֵי שֶׁתְּחִילַּת נְפִילָה נִיסָה״ מִבָּעֵי לֵיהּ! אֵימָא: ״מִפְּנֵי שֶׁתְּחִילַּת נְפִילָה נִיסָה״.

§ The mishna teaches: **“And it shall be, when the officers conclude** speaking to the people, that captains of legions shall be appointed at the head of the people” (Deuteronomy 20:9), and that the guards have the license to beat the legs of anyone who attempts to turn back and flee from the war, because the beginning of fleeing is a downfall. The Gemara is puzzled by the language of the mishna: **This** phrase: **Because the beginning of fleeing is a downfall,** appears to be backward. The mishna **should have** said the opposite: **Because the beginning of the downfall** is the act of **fleeing.** The Gemara concedes: Indeed, **say** that the mishna means: **Because the beginning of the downfall** is the act of **fleeing.**

״בַּמֶּה דְּבָרִים אֲמוּרִים – בְּמִלְחֲמוֹת הָרְשׁוּת״ כו׳. אָמַר רַבִּי יוֹחָנָן: רְשׁוּת דְּרַבָּנַן זוֹ הִיא מִצְוָה דְּרַבִּי יְהוּדָה; מִצְוָה דְּרַבָּנַן זוֹ הִיא חוֹבָה דְּרַבִּי יְהוּדָה.

The mishna teaches: **In what** case **are these statements said?** They are said **with regard to elective wars,** as opposed to obligatory wars or wars whose mandate is a mitzva. **Rabbi Yoḥanan says** concerning the various categories of war: The **elective** war referenced **by the Rabbis is** the same as a war whose mandate is **a mitzva** referenced **by Rabbi Yehuda,** and the war that is **a mitzva** mentioned **by the Rabbis is** the same as the **obligatory** war mentioned **by Rabbi Yehuda.** Therefore, Rabbi Yehuda is merely stating that the wars which the Rabbis call elective are to be seen as mandated by a mitzva.

אָמַר רָבָא: מִלְחֲמוֹת יְהוֹשֻׁעַ לִכְבּוֹשׁ – דִּבְרֵי הַכֹּל חוֹבָה; מִלְחֲמוֹת בֵּית דָּוִד לִרְווֹחָה – דִּבְרֵי הַכֹּל רְשׁוּת. כִּי פְּלִיגִי – לְמַעוּטֵי נָכְרִים דְּלָא לֵיתֵי עֲלַיְיהוּ: מָר קָרֵי לָהּ מִצְוָה, וּמָר קָרֵי רְשׁוּת; נָפְקָא מִינָּהּ לְעוֹסֵק בְּמִצְוָה שֶׁפָּטוּר מִן הַמִּצְוָה.

Rava said: With respect to **the wars** that **Joshua** waged[H] **to conquer** Eretz Yisrael, **all agree** that they were **obligatory.** With respect to **the wars** waged by **the House of** King **David for** the sake of **territorial expansion, all agree** that they were **elective** wars. **When they disagree,** it is with regard to preventative wars that are waged **to reduce the gentiles so** that they will **not come** and wage war **against them.** One **Sage,** Rabbi Yehuda, **called this** type of war **a mitzva, and** one **Sage,** the Rabbis, **called** it **an elective** war. There is **a practical difference** between these opinions with respect **to** the principle: **One who is engaged in a mitzva is exempt from** performing another **mitzva.**[B] According to Rabbi Yehuda, one fighting in this kind of war is exempt from performing another mitzva.

הדרן עלך משוח מלחמה

HALAKHA

The wars that Joshua waged – מִלְחֲמוֹת יְהוֹשֻׁעַ: At first a king is permitted to wage only those wars that are in fulfillment of a mitzva, e.g., a war against the seven Canaanite nations, against Amalek, or to save the Jewish people from an enemy who is attacking them. Thereafter, a king may wage wars that are elective, e.g., a war against other nations with the intention of expanding the boundaries of Eretz Yisrael (Rambam *Sefer Shofetim, Hilkhot Melakhim UMilḥemoteihem* 5:1 and *Leḥem Mishne* there).

BACKGROUND

One who is engaged in a mitzva is exempt from performing another mitzva – הָעוֹסֵק בְּמִצְוָה פָּטוּר מִן הַמִּצְוָה: According to the Gemara (*Sukka* 25a), one who is actively engaged in a mitzva is exempt from performing another mitzva. For example, one who is traveling to study Torah or to greet his teacher is exempt from the obligation to dwell in a *sukka*. The principle derives from the obligation to study Torah, which applies “when you sit in your house, and when you walk by the way” (Deuteronomy 6:7). The Sages understand that the mitzva is limited to times that one is involved in personal activities, and it does not apply when one is involved in performing a mitzva. The Rambam suggests that the underlying reason for this principle is that since one cannot distinguish between the respective weight of different mitzvot (see *Avot* 2:1), an individual is obligated to complete the mitzva in which he is involved before turning his attention to another.

Summary of **Perek VIII**

It has been determined that, in preparation for war, a singular priest is appointed to address the nation. This priest, who in several respects resembles the High Priest, is termed the priest anointed for war. While the nation is still within the borders of Eretz Yisrael, the priest anointed for war announces to the assembled that men in any of three circumstances are released from combat: "What man is there that has built a new house, and has not dedicated it? Let him go and return to his house, lest he die in the battle, and another man dedicate it. And what man is there that has planted a vineyard, and has not used the fruit thereof? Let him go and return unto his house, lest he die in the battle and another man use the fruit thereof. And what man is there that has betrothed a wife, and has not taken her? Let him go and return to his house, lest he die in the battle, and another man take her" (Deuteronomy 20:5–7). The officers repeat his words more audibly, and then they add the statement: "What man is there that is fearful and fainthearted?" (Deuteronomy 20:8), also sending home any man who is afraid in the face of battle.

When the ranks come to the battle front and are preparing to engage the enemy, the priest again addresses the people. First, he recites the verses: "Hear Israel, you draw near today to battle against your enemies; let not your heart faint; fear not, nor be alarmed, and do not be terrified of them; for the Lord your God is He that goes with you, to fight for you against your enemies, to save you" (Deuteronomy 20:3–4). Thereafter, the priest and the officers repeat the announcements from the first assembly.

With respect to the terms mentioned in the verses, a vineyard is defined as any group of five fruit-bearing trees, whether they have been newly planted, layered, or grafted. A house is defined as any permanent structure that is fit for a domicile. Finally, a new wife is defined as either one whom the man has betrothed or his recently widowed *yevama*, who is waiting for him to perform levirate marriage. In addition, the vineyard and the home need not be truly new but merely new to him, e.g., purchased or inherited. Furthermore, this *halakha* applies only if the assets in question are lawfully acquired or produced; if they are forbidden to him in some way he does not return home. With respect to the term "fearful and fainthearted," it has been resolved that the phrase should be understood literally, indicating one who is terrified or is emotionally unfit to participate in the war.

All of those who are exempt from the battle for any of the aforementioned reasons must nevertheless support the troops logistically, through repairing roads and providing food. By contrast, one who in the past year has built a new house and has already dedicated it, has planted a new vineyard and has begun to enjoy its fruits, or who has married a new wife, is exempt from assisting the army altogether. Such a person is likewise exempt from all other communal work.

It has also been resolved that all these exemptions apply only to an elective war, which is a war the nation undertakes voluntarily in order to broaden its borders. However, when the Jewish people are fighting an obligatory war mandated by a mitzva for the sake of conquering Eretz Yisrael, fighting against Amalek, or fighting in self-defense against attackers, everyone is required to go to battle. In those circumstances as well, the priest anointed for war recites words of encouragement and inspiration before the battle.

Introduction to **Perek IX**

If one be found slain in the land which the Lord your God has given you to possess it, lying in the field, and it is not known who has smitten him; then your Elders and your judges shall come forth, and they shall measure unto the cities which are round about him that is slain. And it shall be, that the city that is nearest to the slain man, the Elders of that city shall take a heifer of the herd, that has not been worked with and that has not pulled a yoke. And the Elders of that city shall bring down the heifer into a hard valley, which may be neither worked nor sown, and shall break the heifer's neck there in the valley. And the priests the sons of Levi shall come near, for the Lord your God has chosen them to minister unto Him, and to bless in the name of the Lord; and every controversy and every stroke shall be according to their word. And all the Elders of that city, who are nearest unto the slain man, shall wash their hands over the heifer whose neck was broken in the valley. And they shall speak and say: Our hands did not spill this blood, nor did our eyes see. Forgive, Lord, Your people Israel, whom You have redeemed, and suffer not innocent blood to remain in the midst of Your people Israel. And the blood shall be forgiven them. So shall you put away the innocent blood from the midst of you, when you shall do that which is right in the eyes of the Lord.

(Deuteronomy 21:1–9)

This chapter covers two main topics. The first, which continues the theme of the previous chapters, is the ritual of the breaking of the heifer's neck. The chapter discusses the identity of the Elders who come to take the measurement. Who is defined as a slain victim for the purposes of this mitzva: Is it any murder victim, or could the definition be more limited? The Gemara also discusses other details of this ritual: From where the measurements are taken, and what type of city can be classified as the city closest to the victim. Furthermore, the Gemara examines the requirements in terms of the animal to be used: What is a heifer? What "work" disqualifies it? What does the Torah mean by "a hard valley"? How is the animal killed, and what *halakhot* apply to the place where it is killed?

This ritual is performed only if the identity of the murderer is unknown. This also requires clarification, e.g., what if there is conflicting testimony with regard to whether the murderer was seen, who is eligible to testify about this matter, what happens if the murderer is discovered during the performance of the ritual, and what happens if the murderer is discovered afterward.

The other main topic addressed in this chapter is the list of things that became null over the generations, due to either a deterioration in the performance of mitzvot, tragedies that happened to the Jewish people, or the death of specific Sages. Some of these changes had halakhic implications, both in the cessation of certain mitzvot and in the enactment of new decrees, while others were spiritual losses not linked to any specific mitzva.

מתני׳ עֶגְלָה עֲרוּפָה – בִּלְשׁוֹן הַקּוֹדֶשׁ, שֶׁנֶּאֱמַר: ״כִּי יִמָּצֵא חָלָל בָּאֲדָמָה...וְיָצְאוּ זְקֵנֶיךָ וְשֹׁפְטֶיךָ״. שְׁלֹשָׁה מִבֵּית דִּין הַגָּדוֹל שֶׁבִּירוּשָׁלַיִם הָיוּ יוֹצְאִין. רַבִּי יְהוּדָה אוֹמֵר: חֲמִשָּׁה, שֶׁנֶּאֱמַר: ״זְקֵנֶיךָ״ – שְׁנַיִם; ״וְשֹׁפְטֶיךָ״ – שְׁנַיִם, וְאֵין בֵּית דִּין שָׁקוּל, מוֹסִיפִין עֲלֵיהֶן עוֹד אֶחָד.

MISHNA In certain cases of unsolved murder, the Torah prescribes a ritual performed with **a heifer whose neck is broken.** During the course of this ritual, the judges say a confession **in the sacred tongue,**[H] Hebrew, **as it is stated** in the verse: **"If one be found slain in the land** which the Lord your God has given you to possess it, lying in the field, and it is not known who has smitten him; **then your Elders and your judges shall come forth"** (Deuteronomy 21:1–2). What is the procedure for this ritual? **Three members of the High Court [Sanhedrin] that is in Jerusalem**[B] **would go out** to see the corpse. **Rabbi Yehuda says: Five**[H] would go out, **as it is stated: "Your Elders,"** in the plural form, indicating at least **two;** and it is written: **"And your judges,"** in the plural form, indicating another **two** judges; **and a court may not** be comprised of **an even** number of judges because they need to be able to issue a majority ruling. Consequently, **they add to them one more** Elder.

נִמְצָא טָמוּן בְּגַל, אוֹ תָלוּי בְּאִילָן, אוֹ צָף עַל פְּנֵי הַמַּיִם – לֹא הָיוּ עוֹרְפִין, שֶׁנֶּאֱמַר: ״בָּאֲדָמָה״ – וְלֹא טָמוּן בְּגַל; ״נֹפֵל״ – וְלֹא תָלוּי בְּאִילָן; ״בַּשָּׂדֶה״ – וְלֹא צָף עַל פְּנֵי הַמַּיִם.

If the corpse **was found concealed**[H] **in a pile** of stones, **or hanging on a tree, or floating on the surface of the water,** then the judges **would not break the neck** of the heifer, **as it is stated:** "If one be found slain **in the land"** (Deuteronomy 21:1), **and not concealed in a pile** of stones;[N] **"lying"** on the ground **and not hanging on a tree; "in the field," and not floating on the surface of the water.**

נִמְצָא סָמוּךְ לַסְּפָר, אוֹ לְעִיר שֶׁרוּבָּהּ נׇכְרִים, אוֹ לְעִיר שֶׁאֵין בָּהּ בֵּית דִּין – לֹא הָיוּ עוֹרְפִין. אֵין מוֹדְדִין אֶלָּא לְעִיר שֶׁיֵּשׁ בָּהּ בֵּית דִּין.

If a corpse **was found close to the border**[H] of the country, **or** close **to a city in which the majority of its** inhabitants **are gentiles,**[N] or close **to a city that is without** a rabbinical **court** of twenty-three judges, then the judges **would not break the** heifer's **neck.** Additionally, the Elders **measure** the distance from the corpse **only to a city that has** a rabbinical **court**[H] with twenty-three judges.[B]

BACKGROUND

The High Court [Sanhedrin] that is in Jerusalem – בֵּית דִּין הַגָּדוֹל שֶׁבִּירוּשָׁלַיִם: The Sanhedrin, also referred to as the court of seventy-one, was the Jewish people's supreme legislative and religious body in antiquity. It met in the Chamber of Hewn Stone in the Temple courtyard and was vested with the power to decide all matters of national importance. Its enactments were binding on the entire nation, and it issued both permanent decrees and temporary regulations. It decided cases left undecided by the lower courts and was the final authority on *halakha*.

A lesser Sanhedrin – סַנְהֶדְרִי קְטַנָּה: A lesser Sanhedrin is a court of twenty-three judges, which has the authority to try capital cases. Such courts were established in larger Jewish communities both in Israel and in the Diaspora.

NOTES

And not concealed in a pile of stones – וְלֹא טָמוּן בְּגַל: The Meiri writes that this *halakha* excludes from the ritual not only a corpse found concealed in a pile of stones but also a corpse that had been concealed in any way, even in the earth.

In which the majority of its inhabitants are gentiles – שֶׁרוּבָּהּ גּוֹיִם: In the *Minḥat Ḥinnukh* the following objection is raised: If the majority of inhabitants of the city are gentiles, shouldn't the majority be followed, as it is in other cases? If so, the assumption should be that the victim was not killed by a Jew. Why, then, would the mishna need to teach this obvious *halakha*? The answer given there is that because of this objection, the Rambam reads the Gemara here in accordance with the text in the Jerusalem Talmud: A city in which there are gentiles. Consequently, the mishna is teaching the novelty that the ritual is not performed even in a case where there is a minority of gentiles in the nearest city.

HALAKHA

A heifer whose neck is broken, a confession in the sacred tongue – עֶגְלָה עֲרוּפָה בִּלְשׁוֹן הַקּוֹדֶשׁ: Both the confession of the city's Elders upon the broken neck of a heifer and the recitation of the priests (see Deuteronomy 21:8) may be recited only in Hebrew (Rambam *Sefer Nezikim, Hilkhot Rotze'aḥ UShmirat HaNefesh* 9:3).

Five – חֲמִשָּׁה: Five Elders from the great Sanhedrin in Jerusalem go to measure the distance from the corpse to the closest city. In the *Kesef Mishne* it is asked why the Rambam ruled in accordance with the opinion of Rabbi Yehuda and not in accordance with the unattributed opinion in the mishna that only three Elders go to measure the distance. It is answered: Since this issue is recorded as a dispute in tractate *Sanhedrin*, this is an unattributed opinion that is followed by a dispute. It therefore follows the principle that the *halakha* is in accordance with Rabbi Yehuda in his disputes with Rabbi Shimon. *Tosefot Yom Tov* explains that the Rambam based his ruling on the Jerusalem Talmud, which cites Rabbi Yehuda HaNasi as saying that the *halakha* follows Rabbi Yehuda in this case (Rambam *Sefer Nezikim, Hilkhot Rotze'aḥ UShmirat HaNefesh* 9:1).

The corpse was found concealed – נִמְצָא טָמוּן: If the corpse was found buried under a pile of stones, hanging from a tree, or floating in water, the ritual of breaking the heifer's neck is not performed (Rambam *Sefer Nezikim, Hilkhot Rotze'aḥ UShmirat HaNefesh* 9:11).

Was found close to the border – נִמְצָא סָמוּךְ לַסְּפָר: If the corpse was found close to a border or close to a city where gentiles live, measurements are not taken, and the ritual of breaking the heifer's neck is not performed (Rambam *Sefer Nezikim, Hilkhot Rotze'aḥ UShmirat HaNefesh* 9:5).

To a city that has a court – לְעִיר שֶׁיֵּשׁ בָּהּ בֵּית דִּין: The Elders measure the distance from the corpse only to a city that has a rabbinical court of twenty-three judges. Even if there is another city that is closer to the corpse, but it does not have a rabbinical court of twenty-three judges, it is not taken into consideration for the measurements (Rambam *Sefer Nezikim, Hilkhot Rotze'aḥ UShmirat HaNefesh* 9:4).

NOTES

And a court may not be composed of an even number of judges – וְאֵין בֵּית דִּין שָׁקוּל: This is to prevent a dispute among the judges from becoming deadlocked. Although here the judges are taking measurements and not issuing judgment, it is still possible for them to disagree about how to measure and about the exact point from which they should measure (*Minḥa Hareva*).

גמ׳ מַאי קָאָמַר? אֲמַר רַבִּי אַבָּהוּ: הָכִי קָאָמַר – שֶׁנֶּאֱמַר: ״וְעָנוּ וְאָמְרוּ״, וּלְהַלָּן הוּא אוֹמֵר: ״וְעָנוּ הַלְוִיִּם וְאָמְרוּ״ וגו׳, מָה עֲנִיָּיה הָאֲמוּרָה לְהַלָּן בִּלְשׁוֹן הַקּוֹדֶשׁ, אַף כָּאן בִּלְשׁוֹן הַקּוֹדֶשׁ.

GEMARA The Gemara asks: **What is** the first sentence in the mishna **saying?** The mishna is attempting to prove that the verses read during the ritual of breaking a heifer's neck are to be recited in Hebrew, yet the verse does not offer any proof of this. **Rabbi Abbahu said** that **this is what** the mishna **is saying:** The confession is recited in Hebrew, **as it is stated** with regard to the ritual of the heifer whose neck is broken: **"And they shall speak and say"** (Deuteronomy 21:7), **and later it is stated** with regard to the curses stated on Mount Ebal: **"And the Levities shall speak and say"** (Deuteronomy 27:14). **Just as** the word **"speak" that is said later** with regard to the Levites is referring to a speech that **is** recited **in the sacred tongue, so too here** the declaration is recited **in the sacred tongue.**

וְסֵדֶר עֶגְלָה עֲרוּפָה כֵּיצַד? ״כִּי יִמָּצֵא חָלָל בָּאֲדָמָה...וְיָצְאוּ זְקֵנֶיךָ וְשֹׁפְטֶיךָ״. שְׁלֹשָׁה מִבֵּית דִּין הַגָּדוֹל שֶׁבִּירוּשָׁלַיִם הָיוּ יוֹצְאִין. רַבִּי יְהוּדָה אוֹמֵר: חֲמִשָּׁה וכו׳.

The mishna continues to answer the question of: **And how** is the ritual of the **heifer whose neck is broken ordered?** The mishna states: It is written in the Torah: **"If one be found slain in the land** which the Lord your God has given you to possess it, lying in the field, and it is not known who has smitten him; **then your Elders and your judges shall come forth,** and they shall measure unto the cities which are round about him that is slain" (Deuteronomy 21:1–2). **Three members of the High Court that is in Jerusalem would go forth. Rabbi Yehuda says: Five.**

תָּנוּ רַבָּנַן: ״וְיָצְאוּ זְקֵנֶיךָ וְשֹׁפְטֶיךָ״. ״זְקֵנֶיךָ״ – שְׁנַיִם; ״וְשֹׁפְטֶיךָ״ – שְׁנַיִם, וְאֵין בֵּית דִּין שָׁקוּל, מוֹסִיפִין עֲלֵיהֶן עוֹד אֶחָד – הֲרֵי כָּאן חֲמִשָּׁה, דִּבְרֵי רַבִּי יְהוּדָה; רַבִּי שִׁמְעוֹן אוֹמֵר: ״זְקֵנֶיךָ״ – שְׁנַיִם, וְאֵין בֵּית דִּין שָׁקוּל, מוֹסִיפִין עֲלֵיהֶן עוֹד אֶחָד – הֲרֵי כָּאן שְׁלֹשָׁה.

The Sages taught: "And your Elders and judges shall come forth." "Your Elders" indicates **two; "and your judges"** also indicates **two; and a court may not** be composed of **an even** number of judges,[N] so **they add to them one more** judge. Therefore, **there are five** judges. This is **the statement of Rabbi Yehuda. Rabbi Shimon says: "Your Elders"** indicates **two, and** as **a court may not** consist of **an even** number of judges **they add to them one more.** Therefore, **there are three.**

וְרַבִּי שִׁמְעוֹן נַמִי הָא כְּתִיב: ״וְשֹׁפְטֶיךָ״! הַהוּא מִיבָּעֵי לֵיהּ: לִמְיוּחָדִין שֶׁבְּשׁוֹפְטֶיךָ. וְרַבִּי יְהוּדָה? מִ״זִּקְנֵי״, ״זְקֵנֶיךָ״ נָפְקָא.

The Gemara asks: But according to **Rabbi Shimon as well, isn't it written: "And your judges"**; why does he not agree that this indicates a need for two more judges? The Gemara answers: **He requires that** additional word "Elders" in order **to** teach that they must be **the distinguished among your judges,** i.e., judges from the Sanhedrin. **And** how does **Rabbi Yehuda,** who derives from the phrase "and your judges" that there is a need for two additional judges, know that they need to be from the Sanhedrin? **He derives it from** an extra letter. The verse could have simply stated: **The Elders.** Instead, it adds a letter and states: **"Your Elders,"** to teach that they must be the distinguished among the Elders of Israel.

וְרַבִּי שִׁמְעוֹן? אִי כָּתַב רַחֲמָנָא ״זִקְנֵי״, הֲוָה אָמִינָא אֲפִילּוּ זִקְנֵי הַשּׁוּק, כָּתַב רַחֲמָנָא ״זְקֵנֶיךָ״; וְאִי כָּתַב רַחֲמָנָא ״זְקֵנֶיךָ״, הֲוָה אָמִינָא אֲפִילּוּ סַנְהֶדְרִי קְטַנָּה, כָּתַב רַחֲמָנָא ״וְשֹׁפְטֶיךָ״ – לִמְיוּחָדִין שֶׁבְּשׁוֹפְטֶיךָ.

And Rabbi Shimon could say: **If the Merciful One had written** in the Torah: **The Elders, I would say** that it includes **even the Elders of the marketplace,** meaning any honorable people. Therefore, **the Merciful One writes** in the Torah: **"Your Elders,"** to indicate specifically Torah Sages, who are revered by all. **And if the Merciful One had written** in the Torah only: **"Your Elders," I would say** that it includes **even** Elders from **a lesser Sanhedrin.** Therefore, **the Merciful One** also **writes: "And your judges," to** teach that they must be **the distinguished among your judges,** from the Great Sanhedrin.

וְרַבִּי יְהוּדָה? גָּמַר ״זִקְנֵי״, ״זִקְנֵי״ מִזִּקְנֵי הָעֵדָה. מַה לְּהַלָּן מְיוּחָדִין שֶׁבָּעֵדָה, אַף כָּאן מְיוּחָדִין שֶׁבָּעֵדָה.

And what is the source of **Rabbi Yehuda** that the judges may not come from a lesser Sanhedrin? **He derives** this *halakha* from a verbal analogy between **"Elders,"** written here, and **"Elders,"** written with regard to the offering that the Sanhedrin brings when the nation has sinned as a result of a mistaken ruling. This offering is brought by **"the Elders of the congregation"** (Leviticus 4:15). **Just as there,** "the Elders of the congregation" are **the distinguished among the congregation,** from the Great Sanhedrin, **so too, here** the verse is referring to **the distinguished among the congregation.**

אִי גָּמַר, לִגְמְרָהּ לְכוּלָּהּ מִילְּתָא מֵהָתָם! ״זְקֵנֶיךָ וְשֹׁפְטֶיךָ״ לָמָּה לִי? אֶלָּא וי״ו ״וְשֹׁפְטֶיךָ״ לְמִנְיָנָא. וְרַבִּי שִׁמְעוֹן?

The Gemara asks: **If he derives** this *halakha* from this verbal analogy, then **he should derive the entire matter from there,** including the requirement for five judges. If so, **why do I** need the phrase **"your Elders and your judges"? Rather,** it must be that Rabbi Yehuda does not derive the *halakha* from this verbal analogy. Instead, he understands that the phrase "your Elders" indicates two, and that "your judges" indicates that they must be the distinguished among your judges, and the letter ***vav*** in the phrase **"and your judges [*veshofetekha*]" is to** add two more to **the count** of the judges. **And Rabbi Shimon** does not accept this derivation

וי״ו לָא מַשְׁמַע לֵיהּ. (מַאי קָאָמַר רַחֲמָנָא? הַמְיוּחָדִין שֶׁבְּשׁוֹפְטֶיךָ.) אֶלָּא מֵעַתָּה, ״וְיָצְאוּ״ – שְׁנַיִם; ״וּמָדְדוּ״ – שְׁנַיִם, לְרַבִּי יְהוּדָה הֲרֵי כָּאן תִּשְׁעָה, לְרַבִּי שִׁמְעוֹן הֲרֵי כָּאן שִׁבְעָה!

because **he does not learn** anything from the letter ***vav***. Rather, **what is the Merciful One saying** in the Torah with the phrase "and your judges"? He is referring to **the distinguished that are among your judges.** The Gemara raises an objection: **However, if that is so,** if every plural form in the verse adds another two judges, then when it later states: **"And they shall go out,"** this should indicate another **two.** And: **"And they shall measure"** (Deuteronomy 21:2), should indicate yet another **two.** This means that **according to** the reasoning of **Rabbi Yehuda there are nine** judges enumerated **here,** while **according to** the reasoning of **Rabbi Shimon there are seven** judges enumerated **here.**

הַהוּא מִיבָּעֵי לֵיהּ לְכִדְתַנְיָא: ״וְיָצְאוּ״ – הֵן וְלֹא שְׁלוּחֵיהֶן, ״וּמָדְדוּ״ – שֶׁאֲפִילּוּ נִמְצָא בַּעֲלִיל לָעִיר הָיוּ מוֹדְדִין, שֶׁמִּצְוָה לַעֲסוֹק בִּמְדִידָה.

The Gemara responds: **He requires that** verse: "And they shall go out… and they shall measure," **for that which is taught** in a *baraita*: **"And they shall go out,"** serves to emphasize that **they** themselves go out, **and not their agents,**[H] i.e., they may not appoint an agent to measure the distance but must do it themselves. **"And they shall measure,"** teaches **that even** if the corpse **was found clearly** near **to** a particular **city**[H] **they would** nevertheless **measure** the distance, **as** it is **a mitzva to engage in** this act of **measurement.**

מַתְנִיתִין דְּלָא כְּרַבִּי אֱלִיעֶזֶר בֶּן יַעֲקֹב, דְּתַנְיָא, רַבִּי אֱלִיעֶזֶר בֶּן יַעֲקֹב אוֹמֵר: ״זְקֵנֶיךָ״ – זוֹ סַנְהֶדְרִין; ״שֹׁפְטֶיךָ״ – זֶה מֶלֶךְ וְכֹהֵן גָּדוֹל; מֶלֶךְ, דִּכְתִיב: ״מֶלֶךְ בְּמִשְׁפָּט יַעֲמִיד אָרֶץ״; כֹּהֵן גָּדוֹל, דִּכְתִיב: ״וּבָאתָ אֶל הַכֹּהֲנִים הַלְוִיִּם וְאֶל הַשֹּׁפֵט אֲשֶׁר יִהְיֶה״ וגו׳.

§ The Gemara comments: **The mishna is not in accordance with** the opinion of **Rabbi Eliezer ben Ya'akov, as it is taught** in a *baraita*: **Rabbi Eliezer ben Ya'akov says: "Your Elders," this is the Sanhedrin; "your judges," this is the king and the High Priest.** According to Rabbi Eliezer ben Ya'akov, the king and the High Priest need to participate in the ritual of breaking the neck of the heifer. From where is it learned that they are called judges? **A king** is called a judge, **as it is written: "A king by justice establishes the land"** (Proverbs 29:4). **A High Priest** is called a judge, **as it is written:** "If there arise a matter too hard for you in judgment… **And you shall come to the priests the Levites, and to the judge who shall be** in those days" (Deuteronomy 17:8–9).

אִיבַּעְיָא לְהוּ: רַבִּי אֱלִיעֶזֶר בֶּן יַעֲקֹב – בְּמֶלֶךְ וְכֹהֵן גָּדוֹל הוּא דִּפְלִיג, אֲבָל בְּסַנְהֶדְרִי אִי כְּרַבִּי יְהוּדָה אִי כְּרַבִּי שִׁמְעוֹן סְבִירָא לֵיהּ? אוֹ דִּלְמָא בְּסַנְהֶדְרִי נַמִי פָּלֵיג עַד דְּאִיכָּא כּוּלָּהּ סַנְהֶדְרִי?

A dilemma was raised before the Sages: Is it so that **Rabbi Eliezer ben Ya'akov disagrees** only **with regard to a king and a High Priest,** contending that they too must be present at the measurement, **but** that **with regard to the Sanhedrin he holds either in accordance with** the opinion of **Rabbi Yehuda** that three Elders suffice **or in accordance with** the opinion of **Rabbi Shimon,** that five are needed? **Or, perhaps he also disagrees with regard to the Sanhedrin** and claims that the ritual is not performed **unless there is the entire Sanhedrin** participating.

HALAKHA

They and not their agents – הֵן וְלֹא שְׁלוּחֵיהֶן: The Rambam does not write this *halakha* explicitly, although he does indicate that he rules this way. The later authorities discuss whether the Elders of the Sanhedrin must actually perform the measurement themselves or whether it suffices for them to be present for the measuring (Rambam *Sefer Nezikim*, *Hilkhot Rotze'aḥ UShmirat HaNefesh* 9:1).

Even if it was found clearly near a city – אֲפִילּוּ נִמְצָא בַּעֲלִיל לָעִיר: Even if the victim is discovered adjacent to a particular city, it is nevertheless a mitzva to measure the distance from the corpse to all the surrounding cities (Rambam *Sefer Nezikim*, *Hilkhot Rotze'aḥ UShmirat HaNefesh* 9:1).

אמר רב יוסף, תא שמע: מצאן זקן ממרא אבי פגי והמרה עליהן, יכול תהא המראתו המראה? תלמוד לומר: "וקמת ועלית אל המקום", מלמד שהמקום גורם.

Rav Yosef said: Come and **hear** a proof from a *baraita*: If **a rebellious Elder**[N] **found** the Sanhedrin not in the Hewn Chamber, which was their usual place, but **in Beit Pagei,**[L] near Jerusalem, **and he rebelled against them** there, by teaching in opposition to their ruling, one **might** have thought **his rebellion should be** considered **a rebellion,** rendering him liable to punishment. **The verse** therefore **states: "And you shall arise and go up to the place"** (Deuteronomy 17:8), which **teaches that** it is **the place** where the Sanhedrin resides that **causes**[H] the *halakha* of a rebellious Elder to take effect.

דנפוק כמה? אילימא דנפוק מקצתן, דלמא הנך דאיכא גואי כוותיה סבירא להו! אלא פשיטא דנפוק כולהו.

The Gemara analyzes this statement: In this case, **how many** members of the Sanhedrin were there **who went out** to Beit Pagei? **If we say that** only **a minority of them went out,** why should he be considered a rebellious Elder? **Perhaps those** judges **who are inside** the Hewn Chamber **hold in accordance with his** opinion, which would mean that the Elder in question ruled with the majority. **Rather,** it **is obvious that they all went out.**

ולמאי? אי לדבר הרשות, מי מצו נפקי? והכתיב: "שררך אגן הסהר אל יחסר המזג", שאם נצרך אחד מהם לצאת, אם יש שם עשרים ושלשה כנגד סנהדרי קטנה – יוצא, ואם לאו – אינו יוצא!

The assumption that they all went out leads to the following question: **And for what** purpose did they all leave the Hewn Chamber? **If** it was **for an optional matter, may they leave? But isn't it written: "Your navel** [*shorerekh*] **is like a round goblet, let no mingled wine be wanting"** (Song of Songs 7:3).[NH] This verse is interpreted as referring to the Sanhedrin, the ministers [*sarei*] of Israel who sit in a semicircle, like half of a round goblet. The words "let no mingled wine be wanting" teach **that if one of** the great Sanhedrin **needed to leave,** then **if there are** still present in the Hewn Chamber **twenty-three** members, **corresponding** to the number of **a lesser Sanhedrin, he may leave; and if not, he may not leave.** This indicates that it is prohibited for the entire Sanhedrin to leave for an optional matter.

אלא פשיטא לדבר מצוה. למאי? לאו למדידת עגלה, ורבי אליעזר בן יעקב היא? אמר ליה אביי: לא, דלמא להוסיף על העיר ועל העזרות, כדתנן: אין מוסיפין על העיר ועל העזרות אלא בבית דין של שבעים ואחד.

Rather it **is obvious** that they left **for a matter of a mitzva. For what** particular mitzva did they venture out? **Is it not for the measurement** associated **with** the ritual of **the heifer, and it is** in accordance with the opinion of **Rabbi Eliezer ben Ya'akov?** This would prove that Rabbi Eliezer ben Ya'akov holds that the entire Sanhedrin goes out to measure the distance from the corpse to the nearby cities. **Abaye said to** Rav Yosef: **No,** this is not a proof, as **perhaps** they went out for a different mitzva, **to expand the city** of Jerusalem **or the courtyards** of the Temple, **as we learned** in a mishna (*Sanhedrin* 2a): **They may expand** the sanctified area of **the city** of Jerusalem **or** of **the** Temple **courtyards only**[H] **with the court of seventy-one.**

תניא כוותיה דרב יוסף: מצאן אבית פגי והמרה עליהן, כגון שיצאו למדידת עגלה או להוסיף על העיר ועל העזרות, יכול תהא המראתו המראה? תלמוד לומר: "וקמת ועלית", מלמד שהמקום גורם.

It **is taught** in a *baraita* **in accordance with** the opinion **of Rav Yosef,** that Rabbi Eliezer ben Ya'akov disagrees even with regard to the number of judges: If the rebellious Elder **found** the Sanhedrin **in Beit Pagei and rebelled against them, for example, if they went out for the measurement** of the ritual **of the heifer or to expand** the area of **the city or** that of **the courtyards,** one **might** have thought that **his rebellion should be a rebellion.** Therefore, **the verse states** with regard to the requirement to follow the rulings of the Sanhedrin: **"And you shall arise and go up to the place"** (Deuteronomy 17:8). This **teaches that the place causes** the *halakha* of a rebellious Elder to take effect, indicating that the entire Sanhedrin participates in the measurement of the distance from the corpse to the cities.

NOTES

A rebellious Elder – זקן ממרא: The rebellious Elder is a scholar who continues his dispute with the Sanhedrin even after the Sanhedrin has issued its ruling, in a matter of *halakha* that is written in the Torah and expounded by the Sages. Although he is not obligated to change his opinion, if he issues a practical ruling to others in opposition to that of the Sanhedrin, he is considered a rebellious Elder and is brought to Jerusalem, where he is executed by strangulation.

Let no mingled wine [*mazeg*] be wanting – אל יחסר המזג: A hint for this *halakha* is found in the fact that it was common for wine to be diluted [*mazug*] to a ratio of two-thirds water to one-third wine. Here too, one-third of the Sanhedrin must remain. Furthermore, the numerical value of the letters in *mazeg* is fifty, which indicates that the absence of fifty members of the Sanhedrin is prohibited, but that it is permitted for fewer than fifty to leave (*Tosefot HaRosh*; *Tosafot* on *Sanhedrin*).

LANGUAGE

Beit Pagei – בי פגי: There are several opinions as to the identity of this place. It seems that two different places were known by that name. Some say that *pagei* is related to the Greek φαγεῖν, *fagein*, meaning eat. According to this explanation, Beit Pagei means the place where one is allowed to eat the sanctified meat of offerings, as it is considered to be within the borders of Jerusalem (*Arukh*).

From other sources, it seems that this was the name of a neighborhood next to Jerusalem, perhaps called so due to the small figs that grew there, as the word *pag* means small. It was outside the borders of the city.

HALAKHA

Teaches that the place causes – מלמד שהמקום גורם: A scholar can become a rebellious Elder only if he disputes rulings of the Sanhedrin issued when they are seated in the Chamber of Hewn Stone (Rambam *Sefer Shofetim*, *Hilkhot Mamrim* 3:5).

Let no mingled wine be wanting – אל יחסר המזג: The full court of seventy-one does not have to sit in the Chamber of Hewn Stone at all times, but all must be present when the court is in session. The rest of the time, the judges may leave to attend to their business, as long as at least twenty-three remain. Before a judge leaves, he must make sure that he has left at least twenty-three others there (Rambam *Sefer Shofetim*, *Hilkhot Sanhedrin* 3:2).

They may expand the city…only, etc. – אין מוסיפין על העיר...אלא וכו׳: The size of Jerusalem and of the Temple courtyards may be increased only by means of the king, a prophet, the *Urim VeTummim*, and the Sanhedrin of seventy-one (Rambam *Sefer Avoda*, *Hilkhot Beit HaBeḥira* 6:11).

״נִמְצָא טָמוּן בְּגַל אוֹ תָּלוּי בְּאִילָן״. לֵימָא, מַתְנִיתִין רַבִּי יְהוּדָה הִיא וְלָא רַבָּנַן! דְּתַנְיָא: ״וְשָׁכַחְתָּ עֹמֶר בַּשָּׂדֶה״ – פְּרָט לְטָמוּן, דִּבְרֵי רַבִּי יְהוּדָה; וַחֲכָמִים אוֹמְרִים: ״בַּשָּׂדֶה״ – לְרַבּוֹת אֶת הַטָּמוּן!

§ The mishna teaches: If the corpse **was found concealed in a** pile of stones **or hanging on a tree,** they would not perform the ritual of the heifer. The Gemara suggests: **Let us say that the mishna is** in accordance with the opinion of **Rabbi Yehuda and not** in accordance with the opinion of **the Rabbis.** This is **as it is taught** in a *baraita* with regard to the *halakha* that sheaves of grain forgotten in the fields must be left for the poor: **"And you forget a sheaf in the field"** (Deuteronomy 24:19). This **excludes a concealed** sheaf; it is not considered forgotten and it may be collected by the owner, even if he did forget it. This is **the statement of Rabbi Yehuda. And the Rabbis say:** The phrase **"in the field"** serves **to include the concealed** sheaves, and these must be left for the poor. Rabbi Yehuda holds, like the ruling in the mishna here, that when the verse states "in the field" it excludes a concealed corpse.

אָמַר רַב: אֲפִילּוּ תֵּימָא רַבָּנַן. הָכָא מֵעִנְיָינֵיהּ דִּקְרָא, הָתָם מֵעִנְיָינֵיהּ דִּקְרָא;

Rav said: You can **even say** that the mishna is in accordance with the opinion of **the Rabbis,** as **here** they expound the *halakha* **based on the context of the verse,** and **there** too they expound the *halakha* **based on the context of the verse.**

דִּכְתִיב: ״כִּי יִמָּצֵא חָלָל״, הֵיכָא דְּמִשְׁתַּכַּח; ״בָּאֲדָמָה״ – פְּרָט לְטָמוּן; וְהָתָם מֵעִנְיָינֵיהּ דִּקְרָא, דִּכְתִיב: ״כִּי תִקְצֹר קְצִירְךָ בְשָׂדֶךָ וְשָׁכַחְתָּ עֹמֶר״, שִׁכְחָה דּוּמְיָא דְּקָצִיר: מָה קָצִיר בְּגָלוּי אַף שִׁכְחָה בְּגָלוּי. כְּתַב רַחֲמָנָא ״בַּשָּׂדֶה״ – לְרַבּוֹת אֶת הַטָּמוּן.

In this case, **as it is written: "If one be found slain"** (Deuteronomy 21:1), the default assumption is that the *halakha* applies no matter **where it is found.** When the verse then states: **"In the ground,"** it must be serving to **exclude** a matter, i.e., **a concealed** corpse. **And** similarly, **there,** in the case of forgotten sheaves, they also expound **based on the context of the verse, as it is written: "When you reap your harvest in your field, and you forget a sheaf"** (Deuteronomy 24:19). This indicates that **forgotten** sheaves **are similar to** those **of** the **harvest: Just as** the **harvest** is performed **with revealed** objects, i.e., the growing grain, **so too,** the *halakhot* of **forgetting** pertain **to revealed** sheaves. Consequently, when **the Merciful One writes** in the Torah **"in the field,"** it must be in order **to include the concealed** sheaves.[H]

לְרַבִּי יְהוּדָה נַמִי תֵּיפוֹק לֵיהּ מִשִּׁכְחָה דּוּמְיָא דְּקָצִיר! אִין הָכִי נַמִי.

In light of this explanation, the Gemara asks: **According to Rabbi Yehuda as well, let him derive** that covered sheaves are not included **from** the fact that **forgotten** sheaves **are similar to** those **of** the **harvest.** Why does he have to derive it from the words "in the field"? The Gemara answers: **Yes, it is indeed so,** he does not derive that *halakha* from the phrase "in the field."

וְאֶלָּא ״בַּשָּׂדֶה״ לָמָּה לִי? מִיבְּעֵי לֵיהּ: לְרַבּוֹת שִׁכְחַת קָמָה. וְרַבָּנַן, שִׁכְחַת קָמָה מְנָא לְהוּ? נָפְקָא לְהוּ מִ״כִּי תִקְצֹר קְצִירְךָ בְשָׂדֶךָ״.

The Gemara therefore inquires: **But** then **why do I** need the phrase **"in the field,"** which indicates either an exclusion or an inclusion? The Gemara answers: **He requires** it in order **to include the forgotten** stalks **of standing** grain.[H] Produce that one forgot to reap is considered forgotten, even if it is still attached to the ground. The Gemara asks: **And the Rabbis, from where** do they learn the *halakha* of **forgotten** stalks **of standing** grain? The Gemara answers: **They derive** it **from** the verse: **"When you reap your harvest in your field,** and you forget," which indicates that the *halakha* includes one who forgot to harvest part of his field.

וְרַבִּי יְהוּדָה – מִיבְּעֵי לֵיהּ לְכִדְרַבִּי אַבָּהוּ אָמַר רַבִּי אֶלְעָזָר, דְּאָמַר רַבִּי אַבָּהוּ אָמַר רַבִּי אֶלְעָזָר: פְּרָט לְשֶׁצָּפוּ עוֹמָרִין לְתוֹךְ שְׂדֵה חֲבֵירוֹ. וְרַבָּנַן – מִ״בַּשָּׂדֶה, בְּשָׂדְךָ״. וְרַבִּי יְהוּדָה – ״בַּשָּׂדֶה, בְּשָׂדְךָ״ לָא מַשְׁמַע לֵיהּ.

The Gemara asks: **And** what does **Rabbi Yehuda** derive from this verse? The Gemara answers: It is **necessary for him** in order **to** learn **that which Rabbi Abbahu says** that **Rabbi Elazar** says, **as Rabbi Abbahu says** that **Rabbi Elazar says:** This verse **excludes sheaves that floated**[H] through the air from his field **into another's field.** Such sheaves are not classified as forgotten and may be retrieved later by the owner. **And the Rabbis,** from where do they derive this *halakha*? They derive it **from** the fact that the verse could have stated: **In the field,** but instead states **"in your field,"** to include sheaves situated only in one's own field. The Gemara continues to ask: **And** what does **Rabbi Yehuda** learn from this phrase? The Gemara answers: **He does not learn** anything from the difference between: **In the field,** and **"in your field,"** as he holds it is not a significant difference.

HALAKHA

To include the concealed sheaves – לְרַבּוֹת אֶת הַטָּמוּן: Even a concealed sheaf is considered to be forgotten, in accordance with the opinion of the Rabbis (Rambam *Sefer Zera'im, Hilkhot Mattenot Aniyyim* 5:1).

To include the forgotten stalks of standing grain – לְרַבּוֹת שִׁכְחַת קָמָה: The *halakha* of forgetting applies to standing produce just as it does to cut produce. Therefore, if one forgot to harvest part of his field, the produce there belongs to the poor (Rambam *Sefer Zera'im, Hilkhot Mattenot Aniyyim* 1:6).

It excludes sheaves that floated – פְּרָט לְשֶׁצָּפוּ עוֹמָרִין: If sheaves were blown by the wind into the field of another and were left there by their owner, they are not considered to be forgotten, in accordance with the opinion of Rabbi Abbahu. If one forgot a sheaf after the wind dispersed his sheaves in his own field, it is classified as forgotten (Rambam *Sefer Zera'im, Hilkhot Mattenot Aniyyim* 5:5).

NOTES

Into another's field – **לתוך שדה חבירו**: The early commentaries disagree over the reason for this *halakha*. Rashi indicates that they are not considered to be forgotten because one purposely does not take them, as he cannot be sure the sheaves belong to him. The Meiri maintains that it is a Torah edict that only sheaves located in one's own field can be considered forgotten, and that sheaves in the field of another are not classified as forgotten even if one knows that they are there. The *Devar Shaul* interprets Rav Yirmeya's inquiry as based on these two possibilities.

HALAKHA

A sheaf that had been held – **עומר שהחזיק בו וכו׳**: In a case where the owner of a field picked up a sheaf to take it to the city, placed it on another sheaf, and then forgot both sheaves, if he remembered the upper one before he came across it, the lower one is not considered to be forgotten. If not, the lower sheaf is considered to be forgotten.

This ruling follows the Jerusalem Talmud in tractate *Pe'a*. The Ra'avad maintains that the distinction between one who remembers and one who fails to do so applies only according to Rabbi Shimon, and is not accepted as *halakha* (Rambam *Sefer Zera'im*, *Hilkhot Mattenot Aniyyim* 5:4).

בעי רבי ירמיה: צפו עומרין לתוך שדהו, מהו? אויר שדה כשדה דמי, או לאו כשדה דמי?

Rabbi Yirmeya raises a dilemma: If sheaves floated into his field, i.e., if one sheaf landed on another sheaf or on another item, **what is the** *halakha*? Is the **airspace of a field considered to be like** it is the **field** itself, in which case one sheaf on top of another meets the legal requirements to be deemed forgotten? **Or,** is it **not considered like** the **field,** in which case one sheaf on top of another does not meet the legal requirements to be deemed forgotten?

אמר ליה רב כהנא לרב פפי, ואמרי לה רב כהנא לרב זביד: תפשוט ליה מדרבי אבהו אמר רבי אלעזר, דאמר: פרט לשצפו עומרין לתוך שדה חבירו, דחבירו – אין, לתוך שדהו – לא!

Rav Kahana said to Rav Pappi, and some say Rav Kahana said it **to Rav Zevid: Let him resolve** the dilemma **from** the statement **of Rabbi Abbahu,** who **says that Rabbi Elazar says:** This **excludes sheaves that floated into another's field.**[N] If they floated into **another's field, yes,** Rabbi Elazar said that they are not deemed forgotten, **but** if they floated **into his** own **field,** they are **not** discussed by Rabbi Elazar, and therefore they are deemed forgotten.

וליטעמיך, לתוך שדה חבירו – צפו אין, מונחין לא, והא בעינן ״בשדך״ וליכא!

The Gemara refutes this proof: **And according to your reasoning** that the *halakha* of the *baraita* is limited to the case stated, one could infer: In a case where the sheaves drifted **into another's field,** then if **they were floating, yes,** they are not deemed to be forgotten, but if **they were resting** directly on the ground in another's field, **no,** they are deemed to be forgotten. **But** this cannot be the *halakha*, as **we require** the sheaves to be **"in your field,"** and these sheaves are **not** in his field.

אלא, לתוך שדה חבירו ואפילו מונחין, והאי דקאמר צפו? דלא משכחת לה אלא בצפו.

Rather, you must admit that the words: **Into another's field,** include not only those sheaves which are lying on other items, **but even** those **resting** directly on the ground. **And** the reason **that** Rabbi Abbahu **states: Floated,** is that **you find** a situation where sheaves end up in the field of another **only in** a case where **they floated** through the air and fell there. Since the term floated was not used to teach a *halakha*, no inference can be made from this *baraita* with regard to sheaves that floated in one's own field.

תא שמע: עומר שהחזיק בו להוליכו לעיר, והניחו על גבי חבירו ושכחו – התחתון שכחה, והעליון אינו שכחה. רבי שמעון בן יהודה אומר משום רבי שמעון: שניהם אינן שכחה, התחתון – מפני שהוא טמון, והעליון – מפני שהוא צף; עד כאן לא פליגי אלא בתחתון, אבל בעליון – דברי הכל לא הואי שכחה.

The Gemara again attempts to resolve the dilemma: **Come and hear** a proof from a *baraita* (*Tosefta, Pe'a* 3:7): In the case of **a sheaf that had been held**[H] by its owner in order **to take it to the city, and he placed it on top of another** sheaf, **and he forgot** both sheaves, **the lower** sheaf is deemed to be **a forgotten sheaf, and the upper one is not** deemed to be **a forgotten sheaf. Rabbi Shimon ben Yehuda says in the name of Rabbi Shimon: Both of them are not** deemed to be **forgotten sheaves; the lower one because it is concealed, and the upper one because it is floating** and not directly touching the field. The Gemara points out: **They disagree only with regard to** the **lower** sheaf, **but with regard to** the **upper** one **all agree** that **it is not** deemed **a forgotten sheaf.** This demonstrates that a sheaf located in the airspace of the field is not deemed to be forgotten.

שאני התם, כיון דאחזיק ביה, זכה ביה. אי הכי, מאי איריא על גבי חבירו? אפילו בשדה נמי! אין הכי נמי, והאי דקתני על גבי חבירו – משום תחתון.

The Gemara rejects this proof: **There it is different, as, since** the owner **had held it** to take it to the city, **he acquired it.** The reason it is not deemed to be a forgotten sheaf is not because it is not touching the field but because the owner had already acquired that particular sheaf before forgetting it. The Gemara raises an objection to this explanation: **If so, why specifically** state the case of a sheaf that was placed **on top of another? The same would hold true** in a case where one put the sheaf down directly **in the field as well,** as he has already acquired it. The Gemara answers: **Yes, it is indeed so, and** the reason **that** the *baraita* **teaches: On top of another,** is **due to the lower** sheaf rather than the upper one, in order to teach the dispute concerning the lower sheaf.

והא ״מפני שהוא צף״ קאמר! אימא: ״מפני שהוא כצף״.

The Gemara asks: **But** Rabbi Shimon **said: Because it is floating.** How can one then say that the reason for his ruling is because the owner of the field has acquired it? The Gemara answers: **Say** instead: **Because it is like** it is **floating.** In other words, it is as though the upper sheaf had not been put down at all, but remains in the owner's hands.

אָמַר אַבָּיֵי: הֲרֵינִי כְּבֶן עַזַּאי בְּשׁוּקֵי טְבֶרְיָא! אֲמַר לֵיהּ הַהוּא מִדְּרַבָּנַן לְאַבָּיֵי: שְׁנֵי חֲלָלִים זֶה עַל גַּבֵּי זֶה, מֵהֵיכָן הוּא מוֹדֵד?

The Gemara tells of a related incident. On one occasion **Abaye said: I am hereby** as sharp and expert **as ben Azzai,** who taught Torah **in the markets of Tiberias,** and am ready to answer any question that might be posed to me. **One of the Sages said to Abaye,** with regard to the ritual of the heifer whose neck is broken: If there were **two slain people** found **one on top of the other**[H] not precisely aligned, **from where does one measure** the distance to the surrounding cities?

מִין בְּמִינוֹ הָוֵי טָמוּן וּמִין בְּמִינוֹ לָא הָוֵי צָף, וּמֵעֶלְיוֹן מוֹדֵד? אוֹ דִּלְמָא מִין בְּמִינוֹ הָוֵי צָף וּמִין בְּמִינוֹ לָא הָוֵי טָמוּן, וּמִתַּחְתּוֹן מוֹדֵד?

The various aspects of the dilemma are as follows: **Is a substance** in contact **with** the **same** type of **substance** considered to be **concealed, and is a substance** in contact **with** the **same** type of **substance not** considered to be **floating,** which would mean that the lower, concealed corpse is ignored because one does not measure the distance from a concealed corpse, as taught in the mishna, **and one measures** the distance **from the upper one? Or perhaps a substance** in contact **with the same** type of **substance is** considered to be **floating, and a substance** in contact **with** the **same** type of **substance is not** considered to be **concealed, and he measures** the distance **from the lower one,** because it is not considered to be concealed, but not from the upper one, which is considered to be floating.

אוֹ דִּלְמָא מִין בְּמִינוֹ הָוֵי טָמוּן וּמִין בְּמִינוֹ הָוֵי צָף, וְלָא מִתַּחְתּוֹן מוֹדֵד וְלָא מֵעֶלְיוֹן מוֹדֵד?

Or perhaps a substance in contact **with** the **same** type of **substance is** considered to be **concealed, and a substance** in contact **with** the **same** type of **substance is** considered to be **floating, and he** therefore **does not measure** the distance **from the lower one nor does he measure** the distance **from the upper one.** According to this last option, in such a situation no measuring is done, and the ritual is not performed.

אֲמַר לֵיהּ:

Abaye **said to him:**

Perek **IX**
Daf **45** Amud **b**

תְּנֵיתוּהָ: עוֹמֶר שֶׁהֶחֱזִיק בּוֹ לְהוֹלִיכוֹ לָעִיר, וְהִנִּיחוֹ עַל גַּבֵּי חֲבֵירוֹ וּשְׁכָחוֹ – הַתַּחְתּוֹן שִׁכְחָה, וְהָעֶלְיוֹן אֵינוֹ שִׁכְחָה. רַבִּי שִׁמְעוֹן בֶּן יְהוּדָה אוֹמֵר מִשּׁוּם רַבִּי שִׁמְעוֹן: שְׁנֵיהֶן אֵינָן שִׁכְחָה, הַתַּחְתּוֹן – מִפְּנֵי שֶׁהוּא טָמוּן; וְהָעֶלְיוֹן – מִפְּנֵי שֶׁהוּא צָף. סְבוּרָה דְּהָנֵי תַּנָּאֵי כְּרַבִּי יְהוּדָה סְבִירָא לְהוּ, דְּאָמַר: ״בַּשָּׂדֶה״ – פְּרָט לְטָמוּן.

You learned it in the *baraita* (*Tosefta, Pe'a* 3:7): In the case of **a sheaf that had been held** by its owner in order **to take it to the city, and he placed it on top of another** sheaf, **and he forgot** both sheaves, **the lower** sheaf is deemed to be **a forgotten sheaf, and the upper one is not** deemed to be **a forgotten sheaf. Rabbi Shimon ben Yehuda says in the name of Rabbi Shimon: Both of them are not** deemed to be **forgotten sheaves; the lower one because it is concealed and the upper one because it is floating** and not directly touching the field. The Sages **assumed that these** ***tanna'im*** in the *baraita* basically **hold in accordance with** the opinion of **Rabbi Yehuda,** who **says** that the phrase **"in the field"** serves **to exclude a concealed** sheaf.

מַאי לָאו בְּהָא קָא מִיפַּלְגִי, דְּמָר סָבַר: מִין בְּמִינוֹ הָוֵי טָמוּן, וּמָר סָבַר: לָא הָוֵי טָמוּן!

The Gemara continues Abaye's statement: **What, is it not** the case **that they disagree about this, as** one **Sage,** Rabbi Shimon, **holds** that **a substance** in contact **with** the **same** type of **substance is** considered to be **concealed,** and therefore the lower sheaf is not deemed to be a forgotten sheaf, **and** one **Sage,** the Rabbis, **holds** that **it is not** considered to be **concealed,** which means it is deemed to be a forgotten sheaf. The same dispute would apply to the two corpses.

HALAKHA

Two slain people, one on top of the other – שְׁנֵי חֲלָלִים זֶה עַל גַּבֵּי זֶה: If two slain people were found on top of each other, the measurement is taken from the upper one. The Ra'avad states that this matter was left unresolved by the Gemara. The *Kesef Mishne* addresses this issue at length and concludes that the Rambam's ruling is that a substance in contact with the same type of substance is considered concealed, and only a corpse found on water is considered to be floating (Rambam *Sefer Nezikim, Hilkhot Rotze'aḥ UShmirat HaNefesh* 9:10).

NOTES

Slain but not strangled – חָלָל וְלֹא חָנוּק: The Meiri explains that if a person was found with indications that he died due to obstruction of the airways, there is always a possibility that he was not murdered but suffocated due to illness or choked to death. Based on *Tosafot* (*Nazir* 23b), some explain that the lexical meaning of "one slain [*ḥalal*]" is something cut, and that the phrase consequently refers only to one who was killed by means of cutting (see *Devar Shaul*). The Malbim claims that "*ḥalal*" means one whose blood was shed, as opposed to one who was strangled or died by other means.

HALAKHA

Slain but not strangled – חָלָל וְלֹא חָנוּק: The ritual of breaking the neck of the heifer is performed only if the victim was killed by being wounded, not if he was strangled. Likewise, the heifer is not brought if the victim was found in the throes of death, in accordance with the opinion of the Rabbis (Rambam *Sefer Nezikim*, *Hilkhot Rotze'aḥ UShmirat HaNefesh* 9:11).

לָא. אִי כְּרַבִּי יְהוּדָה סְבִירָא לְהוּ – דְּכוּלֵּי עָלְמָא מִין בְּמִינוֹ הָוֵי טָמוּן. וְהָכָא בִּפְלוּגְתָּא דְּרַבִּי יְהוּדָה וְרַבָּנַן קָמִיפַּלְגִי, דְּרַבָּנַן כְּרַבָּנַן, וְרַבִּי שִׁמְעוֹן בֶּן יְהוּדָה כְּרַבִּי יְהוּדָה.

The Gemara refutes this claim: **No, if they hold in accordance with** the opinion of **Rabbi Yehuda,** then it could be **that everyone agrees** that **a substance** in contact **with** the **same** type of **substance is** considered to be **concealed,** and they would maintain this with regard to the two corpses as well. **And here they disagree with regard to** the issue that is the subject of **the dispute of Rabbi Yehuda and the Rabbis,** in **that** the opinion of **the Rabbis** of this *baraita* is **in accordance with** the opinion of **the Rabbis** there, which claims that the *halakha* of a forgotten sheaf applies even to a concealed sheaf, **and Rabbi Shimon ben Yehuda** holds **in accordance with** the opinion of **Rabbi Yehuda,** who maintains that a concealed sheaf is exempt from the *halakha* of forgotten sheaves.

אִי הָכִי, מַאי אִירְיָא עַל גַּבֵּי חֲבֵירוֹ? אֲפִילּוּ בְּעָפָר וּבִצְרוֹר נַמִּי! אִין הָכִי נַמִּי, וּלְהוֹדִיעֲךָ כֹּחוֹ דְּרַבִּי יְהוּדָה, דְּאָמַר: אֲפִילּוּ מִין בְּמִינוֹ הָוֵי טָמוּן.

The Gemara asks: **If** that is **so,** that their dispute is with regard to the *halakha* of concealed sheaves, **why** did they **specifically** disagree in the case of a sheaf that was **on top of another** sheaf; **the same would hold true even** in a case where the sheaf was concealed **in dirt and pebbles?** The Gemara answers: **Yes, it is indeed so.** They disagree with regard to all concealed sheaves, **and** their dispute is stated with regard to a case of one sheaf on top of another in order **to convey to you the far-reaching** nature of the opinion **of Rabbi Yehuda, who says** that **even a substance** that is in contact **with** the **same** type of **substance is** considered **concealed.** Therefore, a substance concealed in a different type of matter is all the more so considered concealed.

תָּנוּ רַבָּנַן: "חָלָל" – וְלֹא חָנוּק, "חָלָל" – וְלֹא מְפַרְפֵּר, "בָּאֲדָמָה" – וְלֹא טָמוּן בְּגַל, "נֹפֵל" – וְלֹא תָּלוּי בְּאִילָן, "בַּשָּׂדֶה" – וְלֹא צָף עַל פְּנֵי הַמַּיִם. רַבִּי אֱלִיעֶזֶר אוֹמֵר: בְּכוּלָּן, אִם הָיָה חָלָל – עוֹרְפִין.

§ The Gemara returns to discuss when the ritual of breaking the neck of the heifer is performed. **The Sages taught,** expounding the verse "If one be found slain in the land which the Lord your God has given you to possess it, lying in the field" (Deuteronomy 21:1): **"Slain"** indicates one killed by a sword, **but not** one who was **strangled;**[NH] **"slain," but not** one who was found **twitching** in his death throes; **"in the land," but not concealed in a pile** of stones; **"lying," but not hanging on a tree; "in the field," but not floating on the surface of the water. Rabbi Elazar says: In all these** cases, **if** a person **was slain** by the sword, the judges **break the neck** of the heifer, and it does not matter where the corpse was found.

תַּנְיָא: אָמַר רַבִּי יוֹסֵי בַּר יְהוּדָה, אָמְרוּ לוֹ לְרַבִּי אֱלִיעֶזֶר: אִי אַתָּה מוֹדֶה שֶׁאִם הָיָה חָנוּק וּמוּטָל בָּאַשְׁפָּה שֶׁאֵין עוֹרְפִין? אַלְמָא "חָלָל" – וְלֹא חָנוּק; הָכָא נַמִּי "בָּאֲדָמָה" – וְלֹא טָמוּן בְּגַל, "נֹפֵל" – וְלֹא תָּלוּי בְּאִילָן, "בַּשָּׂדֶה" – וְלֹא צָף עַל גַּבֵּי מַיִם. וְרַבִּי אֱלִיעֶזֶר: "חָלָל" יְתֵירָא כְּתִיב.

It is taught in a *baraita*: **Rabbi Yosei bar Yehuda says** that the Sages **said to Rabbi Elazar: Do you not concede that if he was strangled and left in a garbage** heap, **that they do not break the** heifer's **neck? Apparently,** "**slain**" is a precise term that means slain **but not strangled.** If you accept that, **here too** the words **"in the land"** should indicate: In the land, **but not concealed in a pile** of stones; **"fallen"** should indicate: Fallen **but not hanging on a tree;** and **"in the field"** should indicate in the field **but not floating on the surface of the water. And Rabbi Elazar** holds that those other situations are not excluded, and that because in that first case the Torah **writes "slain" an extra** time in the next verse: "About him that is slain" (Deuteronomy 21:2), this repetition teaches that a victim of strangulation is not included in this *halakha*.

"נִמְצָא סָמוּךְ לַסְּפָר אוֹ לְעִיר שֶׁרוּבָּהּ נׇכְרִים" כו׳. דִּכְתִיב: "כִּי יִמָּצֵא" – פְּרָט לְמָצוּי.

§ The mishna taught: If a corpse **was found close to the border** of the country **or** close **to a city in which the majority** of its inhabitants **are gentiles,** the judges would not break the heifer's neck, **as it is written: "If one be found** slain" (Deuteronomy 21:1). This **excludes** places where murdered bodies **are** commonly **found,** such as the aforementioned locations.

"אוֹ לְעִיר שֶׁאֵין בָּהּ בֵּית דִּין". דִּבְעֵינָא "זִקְנֵי הָעִיר", וְלֵיכָּא. "אֵין מוֹדְדִין אֶלָּא לְעִיר" כו׳. פְּשִׁיטָא, כֵּיוָן דִּתְנָא "לְעִיר שֶׁאֵין בָּהּ בֵּית דִּין", אֲנָא יָדַעְנָא דְּאֵין מוֹדְדִין אֶלָּא לְעִיר שֶׁיֵּשׁ בָּהּ בֵּית דִּין!

The mishna taught: **Or** if the victim was discovered close **to a city that is without** a rabbinical **court** of twenty-three judges, they would not measure the distance to that city. The Gemara explains: This is **because** the verse **requires "the Elders of that city"** (Deuteronomy 21:3), **and** this is **not** the case here; therefore the rite was not performed. The mishna also taught that the Elders **measure** the distance from the corpse **only to a city** that contains a rabbinical court of twenty-three judges. The Gemara asks: This **is obvious. Since** the mishna **taught** that they do not measure the distance **to a city that does not have** a rabbinical **court** of twenty-three judges, **I know** that **they measure** the distance **only to a city that has** a rabbinical **court** of twenty-three judges.

הָא קָא מַשְׁמַע לָן, כִּדְתַנְיָא: מִנַּיִן שֶׁאִם נִמְצָא סָמוּךְ לְעִיר שֶׁאֵין בָּהּ בֵּית דִּין, שֶׁמַּנִּיחִין אוֹתָהּ וּמוֹדְדִין לְעִיר שֶׁיֵּשׁ בָּהּ בֵּית דִּין? תַּלְמוּד לוֹמַר: "וְלָקְחוּ זִקְנֵי הָעִיר הַהִיא", מִכָּל מָקוֹם.

The Gemara answers: **This *tanna* teaches us** the *halakha* **as it is taught** in a *baraita*: **From where** is it derived **that if** the corpse **was found close to a city that does not have** a rabbinical **court** of twenty-three judges, **that they leave** the city aside **and measure** the distance from the corpse **to a city that has** a rabbinical **court**[H] of twenty-three judges? **The verse states: "And the Elders of that city shall take"** (Deuteronomy 21:3), which indicates that the Elders of a city are involved **in any case,** and the measurement is taken even if it is not to the city closest to the body.

מתני׳ נִמְצָא מְכֻוָּון בֵּין שְׁתֵּי עֲיָירוֹת – שְׁתֵּיהֶן מְבִיאוֹת שְׁתֵּי עֲגָלוֹת, דִּבְרֵי רַבִּי אֱלִיעֶזֶר. וְאֵין יְרוּשָׁלַיִם מְבִיאָה עֶגְלָה עֲרוּפָה. נִמְצָא רֹאשׁוֹ בְּמָקוֹם אֶחָד וְגוּפוֹ בְּמָקוֹם אַחֵר – מוֹלִיכִין הָרֹאשׁ אֵצֶל הַגּוּף, דִּבְרֵי רַבִּי אֱלִיעֶזֶר; רַבִּי עֲקִיבָא אוֹמֵר: הַגּוּף אֵצֶל הָרֹאשׁ. מֵאַיִן הָיוּ מוֹדְדִין? רַבִּי אֱלִיעֶזֶר אוֹמֵר: מִטִּיבּוּרוֹ. רַבִּי עֲקִיבָא אוֹמֵר: מֵחוֹטְמוֹ. רַבִּי אֱלִיעֶזֶר בֶּן יַעֲקֹב אוֹמֵר: מִמָּקוֹם שֶׁנַּעֲשָׂה חָלָל, מִצַּוָּארוֹ.

MISHNA If the slain person **is found precisely between two cities,**[H] the inhabitants **of the two of them bring two heifers** total; this is **the statement of Rabbi Eliezer. And** the inhabitants of **Jerusalem do not bring a heifer**[H] **whose neck is broken,** even if Jerusalem is the city closest to the slain victim. If the **head of** the corpse **was found in one place and his body** was found **in a different place, they bring the head next to the body;** this is **the statement of Rabbi Eliezer. Rabbi Akiva says:** They bring **the body next to the head.**[H] **From where** on the body **would they measure** the distance? **Rabbi Eliezer says: From his navel. Rabbi Akiva says: From his nose.**[H] **Rabbi Eliezer ben Ya'akov says: From the place where he became a slain** person, which is **from the neck.**

גמ׳ מַאי טַעְמָא דְּרַבִּי אֱלִיעֶזֶר? קָסָבַר: אֶפְשָׁר לְצַמְצֵם, וּ"קְרוֹבָה" – וַאֲפִילּוּ קְרוֹבוֹת.

GEMARA The Gemara explains: **What is the reasoning of Rabbi Eliezer,** that when a body is found precisely between two cities, the inhabitants of each city bring a heifer? His ruling is based on two factors. First, **he holds** that **it is possible to measure precisely** and that it is a real possibility to determine that both cities are exactly the same distance from the corpse. **And** second, he interprets the term **"That is nearest"** (Deuteronomy 21:3), to be referring not only to one city. It can **even** be understood as: **That are nearest,**[N] so that the *halakhot* apply to more than one city.

"וְאֵין יְרוּשָׁלַיִם מְבִיאָה עֶגְלָה עֲרוּפָה". דְּאָמַר קְרָא: "לְרִשְׁתָּהּ", וְקָסָבַר: יְרוּשָׁלַיִם לֹא נִתְחַלְּקָה לִשְׁבָטִים.

The mishna taught: **And** the inhabitants of **Jerusalem do not bring a heifer whose neck is broken.** The Gemara explains: This is **because the verse states:** "If one be found slain in the land which the Lord your God has given **you to possess it"** (Deuteronomy 21:1), **and this *tanna* holds** that **Jerusalem was not divided among the tribes** in the division of Eretz Yisrael. It was not given as a possession to any particular person but belongs to all; therefore the *halakha* of the heifer whose neck is broken does not apply to it.

"נִמְצָא רֹאשׁוֹ בְּמָקוֹם" כּוּ׳. בְּמַאי קָמִיפַּלְגִי? אִילֵּימָא לְעִנְיַן מְדִידָה קָמִיפַּלְגִי, הָא מִדְּקָתָנֵי סֵיפָא "מֵאַיִן הָיוּ מוֹדְדִין", מִכְּלָל דְּרֵישָׁא לָא בִּמְדִידָה עָסְקִינַן! אָמַר רַבִּי יִצְחָק: בְּמֵת מִצְוָה קָנָה מְקוֹמוֹ קָמִיפַּלְגִי,

§ With regard to the *halakha* of a corpse whose **head was found** in one **place** and its body elsewhere, the Gemara asks: **With regard to what** *halakha* **do they disagree? If we say they disagree with regard to** whether the **measurement** is taken from the head or the body, **from the fact that the latter clause teaches: From where would they measure** the distance, **it may be inferred that** in **the first clause we are not dealing with measurement. Rabbi Yitzḥak said: They disagree with regard to** a different matter, the question of whether **a corpse with no one to bury it** [***met mitzva***][B] **acquires its place,**[H] meaning if an unattended corpse must be buried where it is found.

HALAKHA

Measure the distance to a city that has a rabbinical court – מוֹדְדִין לְעִיר שֶׁיֵּשׁ בָּהּ בֵּית דִּין: If the corpse was found near a city that does not have a court, the measurement is taken to a city that does have a court (Rambam *Sefer Nezikim, Hilkhot Rotze'aḥ UShmirat HaNefesh* 9:5).

Is found precisely between two cities – נִמְצָא מְכֻוָּון בֵּין שְׁתֵּי עֲיָירוֹת: If the corpse was found equidistant to two cities that contain an equal number of inhabitants, the inhabitants of the two cities bring in partnership a heifer whose neck is broken and make the following stipulation: The heifer belongs to the nearer city and the portion of the heifer owned by the farther city is given to the nearer one as a gift. They state this condition because it is impossible for any two things to be precisely equal (Rambam *Sefer Nezikim, Hilkhot Rotze'aḥ UShmirat HaNefesh* 9:8).

The inhabitants of Jerusalem do not bring a heifer – אֵין יְרוּשָׁלַיִם מְבִיאָה עֶגְלָה: Measurements are not taken from a corpse to Jerusalem because its inhabitants do not bring a heifer whose neck is broken, as Jerusalem was not given to any tribe as an inheritance (Rambam *Sefer Nezikim, Hilkhot Rotze'aḥ UShmirat HaNefesh* 9:4).

The body next to the head – הַגּוּף אֵצֶל הָרֹאשׁ: If the victim's head was found in one place and his body elsewhere, the body is brought to the head for burial there. Any *met mitzva* is treated in this manner, as the *halakha* follows Rabbi Akiva (Rambam *Sefer Nezikim, Hilkhot Rotze'aḥ UShmirat HaNefesh* 9:9).

From his nose – מֵחוֹטְמוֹ: The measurement is performed from the victim's nose, in accordance with Rabbi Akiva (Rambam *Sefer Nezikim, Hilkhot Rotze'aḥ UShmirat HaNefesh* 9:9).

A *met mitzva* acquires its place – מֵת מִצְוָה קָנָה מְקוֹמוֹ: One of the conditions Joshua stipulated with those inheriting the land was that a *met mitzva* acquires its place for the purpose of burial. However, if a corpse is found on the boundary between fields or in a city, it is removed to a cemetery. While the *halakha* of a *met mitzva* applies outside Eretz Yisrael as well, the *Shakh* notes that the common practice there is to take the corpse to a cemetery in all cases (Rambam *Sefer Nezikim, Hilkhot Nizkei Mammon* 5:3; *Shulḥan Arukh, Yoreh De'a* 364:3).

NOTES

That is nearest, even that are nearest – קְרוֹבָה וַאֲפִילּוּ קְרוֹבוֹת: Two related and conflicting *baraitot* are cited in tractate *Bekhorot*. According to one *baraita*, if the corpse is measured to be precisely between two cities, the ritual is not performed at all. The reason is that the *tanna* of that *baraita* holds that although it is possible to perform an exact measurement, the verse states: "That is nearest," and not: That are nearest, limiting the performance of the ritual to the inhabitants of one city.

The other *baraita* states that if the corpse is measured to be equidistant to the two closest cities then the inhabitants of both cities bring a single heifer in partnership and stipulate that the ritual is on behalf of whichever city is in truth nearer. The latter *baraita* holds that it is impossible to measure precisely, so the inhabitants of one city are obligated to bring the heifer, and it is uncertain which city it is. With regard to the exposition of the verse, Rashi points out that the singular form in the Torah is often used also in reference to an entire group or type.

BACKGROUND

A corpse with no one to bury it [*met mitzva*] – מֵת מִצְוָה: It is an important religious obligation to take part in the burial of the dead. If the deceased has no acquaintances or relatives to bury him, everyone is obligated to assist in his burial. The *halakha* is that a corpse with no one available to bury it acquires its place, i.e., the corpse is interred where it is found. However, if that place is not an honorable location the corpse is buried in the nearest cemetery. This religious duty is so important that even priests and nazirites, who are ordinarily prohibited from coming into contact with a corpse, may bury a *met mitzva* if there is no one else available to do so. Likewise, the obligation to bury this corpse takes precedence over nearly all other religious obligations.

וְהָכִי קָאָמַר: לְקוֹבְרוֹ קָנָה מְקוֹמוֹ. וְהֵיכָא דִּנְמְצָא רֹאשׁוֹ בְּמָקוֹם אֶחָד וְגוּפוֹ בְּמָקוֹם אַחֵר – מוֹלִיכִין הָרֹאשׁ אֵצֶל הַגּוּף, דִּבְרֵי רַבִּי אֱלִיעֶזֶר; רַבִּי עֲקִיבָא אוֹמֵר: הַגּוּף אֵצֶל הָרֹאשׁ. בְּמַאי קָמִיפַּלְגִי? מָר סָבַר: גּוּפֵיהּ בְּדוּכְתֵּיהּ נָפֵיל, רֵישָׁא דְּנָאדֵי וְנָפֵיל; וּמָר סָבַר: רֵישָׁא הֵיכָא דְּנָפֵיל נָפֵיל, גּוּפָא הוּא דְּרָהֵיט אָזֵיל.

And this is what the mishna **is saying:** With regard **to burying him,** the victim **acquires his place,** and he is buried there. The mishna continues: **And** in a case **where his head is found in one place and his body** is found **in a different place, they bring the head next to the body** and bury him there; this is **the statement of Rabbi Eliezer. Rabbi Akiva says:** They bring **the body next to the head.** The Gemara explains: **With regard to what do they disagree?** They both agree that he should be buried in the place where he was killed, but one **Sage,** Rabbi Eliezer, **holds** that **his body fell in its place,** and it was **the head that rolled away and fell. And** one **Sage,** Rabbi Akiva, **holds** that **his head fell where it fell,** and **it was the body that went and continued** onward. Therefore, the body is brought to the head.

״מֵאַיִן הָיוּ מוֹדְדִין?״ בְּמַאי קָמִיפַּלְגִי? מָר סָבַר: עִיקַּר חִיּוּתָא בְּאַפֵּיהּ, וּמָר סָבַר: עִיקַּר חִיּוּתָא בְּטִיבּוּרֵיהּ.

§ The mishna taught that there is a dispute concerning the question: **From where** on the body **would they measure** the distance? The Gemara asks: **With regard to what do they disagree?** One **Sage,** Rabbi Akiva, **holds:** A person's **life is** sustained **mainly in his nose,**[N] in his respiratory system. **And** one **Sage,** Rabbi Eliezer, **holds: His life is mainly in** the area of **his navel,** in his digestive system.

לֵימָא כִּי הָנֵי תַּנָּאֵי: מֵהֵיכָן הַוָּלָד נוֹצָר? מֵרֹאשׁוֹ. וְכֵן הוּא אוֹמֵר: ״מִמְּעֵי אִמִּי אַתָּה גוֹזִי״, וְאוֹמֵר: ״גָּזִּי נִזְרֵךְ וְהַשְׁלִיכִי״ וגו׳. אַבָּא שָׁאוּל אוֹמֵר: מִטִּיבּוּרוֹ, וּמְשַׁלֵּחַ שָׁרְשׁוֹ אֵילָךְ!

The Gemara suggests: **Shall we say that these *tanna'im* are like those *tanna'im*,** who had a dispute as it is taught in a *baraita*: **From where is an embryo formed?**[N] **From its head, and so** the verse **states: "Out of my mother's womb You pulled me [*gozi*]"** (Psalms 71:6). **And** the proof that *"gozi"* is referring to the head is from the verse that **states: "Cut off [*gozi*] your hair, and cast it away"** (Jeremiah 7:29). In this verse, the term *gozi* relates to the hair of the head. **Abba Shaul says:** An embryo is formed **from its navel, and it sends its roots forth.** This dispute concerning the initial formation of an embryo also appears to depend on where the main source of life in a person is.

אֲפִילּוּ תֵּימָא אַבָּא שָׁאוּל. עַד כָּאן לָא קָאָמַר אַבָּא שָׁאוּל אֶלָּא לְעִנְיַן יְצִירָה, דְּכִי מִיתְצַר וָלָד – מִמְּצִיעָתֵיהּ מִיתְצַר, אֲבָל לְעִנְיַן חִיּוּתָא – דְּכוּלֵּי עָלְמָא בְּאַפֵּיהּ הוּא, דִּכְתִיב: ״כֹּל אֲשֶׁר נִשְׁמַת רוּחַ חַיִּים בְּאַפָּיו״ וגו׳.

The Gemara refutes this comparison: **You** can **even say** that both *tanna'im* of the mishna agree with **Abba Shaul,** as **Abba Shaul says** his opinion **only with regard to the forming** of an embryo, **that when an embryo is formed,** it is **formed from its middle. But with regard to life, everyone,** i.e., both *tanna'im* in the *baraita*, agree that **it is in his nose, as it is written: "All in whose nostrils was the breath of the spirit of life"** (Genesis 7:22).

״רַבִּי אֱלִיעֶזֶר בֶּן יַעֲקֹב אוֹמֵר: מִמָּקוֹם שֶׁנַּעֲשֶׂה חָלָל, מִצַּוָּארוֹ״. מַאי טַעְמָא דְּרַבִּי אֱלִיעֶזֶר בֶּן יַעֲקֹב? כִּדְכְתִיב: ״לָתֵת אוֹתָךְ אֶל צַוְּארֵי חַלְלֵי רְשָׁעִים״.

The mishna taught another opinion. **Rabbi Eliezer ben Ya'akov says:** The distance should be measured **from the place where** the victim **became a slain** person,[N] **from his neck.** The Gemara poses a question: **What is the reason of Rabbi Eliezer ben Ya'akov?** The Gemara answers: **As it is written: "To lay you upon the necks of the wicked who are to be slain"** (Ezekiel 21:34), which shows that being slain occurs at the neck.

NOTES

Life is sustained mainly in his nose – עִיקַּר חִיּוּתָא בְּאַפֵּיהּ: The Jerusalem Talmud provides a different explanation of this dispute than the one offered here. The Gemara there explains that according to Rabbi Akiva the nose is the most important location on the body because facial identification is enabled by the structure of the center of the face. Conversely, Rabbi Eliezer holds that the navel is the most important location on the body because life is dependent on the internal organs, and the navel marks the center of the internal organs.

From where is an embryo formed – מֵהֵיכָן הַוָּלָד נוֹצָר: It could be explained that the dispute is how to categorize the growth of the embryo. On the one hand, when the cells begin to join and take shape, the head is the first part of the body to be recognizable. On the other hand, the fetus is sustained by means of the umbilical cord, so it could be said that its life begins there and spreads from there to the rest of the body.

From the place where he became a slain person – מִמָּקוֹם שֶׁנַּעֲשָׂה חָלָל: In other words, since the neck is mentioned in the description of a slain person, a slain victim is categorized by what occurred to his neck, even if he happened to have been fatally wounded on a different part of his body.

מתני׳ נִפְטְרוּ זִקְנֵי יְרוּשָׁלַיִם וְהָלְכוּ לָהֶן. זִקְנֵי אוֹתָהּ הָעִיר מְבִיאִין עֶגְלַת בָּקָר אֲשֶׁר לֹא מָשְׁכָה בְּעוֹל. וְאֵין הַמּוּם פּוֹסֵל בָּהּ. וּמוֹרִידִין אוֹתָהּ לְנַחַל אֵיתָן. ״אֵיתָן״ כְּמַשְׁמָעוֹ – קָשֶׁה. אַף עַל פִּי שֶׁאֵינוֹ אֵיתָן – כָּשֵׁר. וְעוֹרְפִין אוֹתָהּ בְּקוֹפִיץ מֵאֲחוֹרֶיהָ; וּמְקוֹמָהּ אָסוּר מִלִּזְרוֹעַ וּמִלַּעֲבוֹד, וּמוּתָּר לִסְרוֹק שָׁם פִּשְׁתָּן וּלְנַקֵּר שָׁם אֲבָנִים.

MISHNA The mishna continues to describe the ritual. After they would take the measurement, **the Elders of Jerusalem took their leave**[H] **and went** away. **The Elders of the city** that is closest to the corpse **bring a heifer from cattle, which has not pulled a yoke. But a blemish does not disqualify it,**[H] because, unlike the description of the red heifer, the Torah does not state that it must be without blemish. **And they bring it down to a stream** that is ***eitan*.**[HN] ***Eitan*** in this context means **as the** word generally **indicates,** powerful. The stream must have **a forceful** flow. The mishna comments: **Even if it is not forceful, it is a valid** site for the ritual. **And they break the neck of** the heifer[NH] **from behind with a cleaver.**[L] **And** with regard to **its place,** where the heifer was standing when its neck was broken, **it is prohibited** for that ground **to be sown or to be worked, but** it is **permitted to comb flax there or to cut stones there.**

זִקְנֵי אוֹתָהּ הָעִיר רוֹחֲצִין אֶת יְדֵיהֶן בְּמַיִם בִּמְקוֹם עֲרִיפָה שֶׁל עֶגְלָה, וְאוֹמְרִים: ״יָדֵינוּ לֹא שָׁפְכוּ אֶת הַדָּם הַזֶּה וְעֵינֵינוּ לֹא רָאוּ״. וְכִי עַל דַּעְתֵּינוּ עָלְתָה שֶׁזִּקְנֵי בֵּית דִּין שׁוֹפְכֵי דָמִים הֵן? אֶלָּא, שֶׁלֹּא בָא עַל יָדֵינוּ וּפְטַרְנוּהוּ (בְּלֹא מְזוֹן), וְלֹא רְאִינוּהוּ וְהִנַּחְנוּהוּ (בְּלֹא לְוָיָה).

The Elders of that city would then **wash**[H] **their hands in water in the place of the breaking of the neck of the heifer, and they would recite: "Our hands did not spill this blood, nor did our eyes see"** (Deuteronomy 21:7). The mishna explains: **But did it enter our minds that the Elders of the court are spillers of blood,** that they must make such a declaration? **Rather,** they mean to declare **that** the victim **did not come to us and** then **we let him take his leave without food, and we did not see him and** then **leave him** alone to depart **without accompaniment.** They therefore attest that they took care of all his needs and are not responsible for his death even indirectly.

LANGUAGE

Cleaver [*kofitz*] – קוֹפִיץ: From the Greek κοπίς, *kopis*, meaning a large knife with a thick blade. It was used for chopping in addition to cutting.

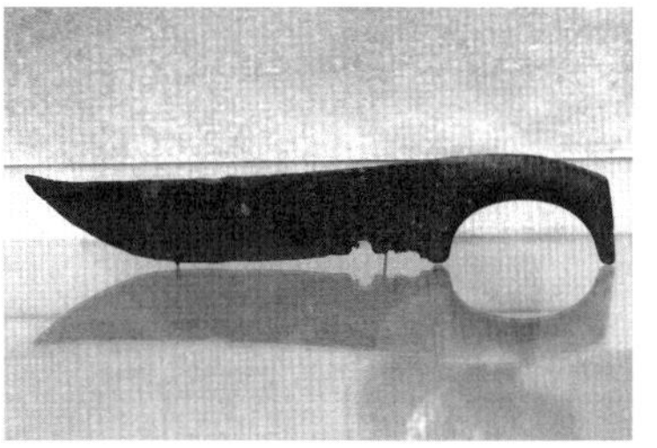

Ancient cleaver

HALAKHA

The Elders of Jerusalem took their leave, etc. – נִפְטְרוּ זִקְנֵי יְרוּשָׁלַיִם וכו׳: After the Elders measure the distances and determine the nearest city, the corpse is buried where it is, and the Elders of Jerusalem return to their place. Then, the Elders of the nearest city bring a heifer of cattle, paid for by the city's inhabitants (Rambam *Sefer Nezikim, Hilkhot Rotze'aḥ UShmirat HaNefesh* 9:2).

A blemish does not disqualify it – אֵין הַמּוּם פּוֹסֵל בָּהּ: A heifer whose neck is broken is not disqualified if it has a blemish. However, it is noted in the Jerusalem Talmud that if the animal has a condition that will cause it to die within twelve months [*tereifa*], it is disqualified (Rambam *Sefer Nezikim, Hilkhot Rotze'aḥ UShmirat HaNefesh* 10:2).

And they bring it down to a stream that is *eitan* – וּמוֹרִידִין אוֹתָהּ לְנַחַל אֵיתָן: The calf is brought down to a stream that flows forcefully (Rambam *Sefer Nezikim, Hilkhot Rotze'aḥ UShmirat HaNefesh* 9:2).

They break the neck of the heifer, etc. – עוֹרְפִין אוֹתָהּ וכו׳: The heifer's neck is broken from behind with a cleaver (Rambam *Sefer Nezikim, Hilkhot Rotze'aḥ UShmirat HaNefesh* 9:3).

The Elders of that city wash, etc. – זִקְנֵי אוֹתָהּ הָעִיר רוֹחֲצִין וכו׳: All Elders of the nearest city's court, even if there are one hundred of them, wash their hands in the place where the neck was broken. They recite there: "Our hands did not spill this blood, nor did our eyes see." The meaning of the passage is that they had not neglected to provide the victim with food and accompaniment (Rambam *Sefer Nezikim, Hilkhot Rotze'aḥ UShmirat HaNefesh* 9:3).

NOTES

Stream [*naḥal*] that is *eitan* – אֵיתָן: Most commentaries explain that *naḥal eitan* refers to a *naḥal*, a valley, that has water in the rainy season but is dry in the summer (Rashi; Rashbam; Rash; Ramban; Rosh). Accordingly, the term *eitan* means strong or firm, and is referring to land that is not able to be sown. The Rambam, however, holds that *naḥal eitan* refers to a stream that flows powerfully, with the term *eitan* referring to the strength of its current. According to this approach, the prohibition against sowing does not refer to the stream itself, which is not fit for sowing, but to its bank. The Radak accepts this interpretation, adding that the Elders would wash their hands with the water that flowed there.

And they break the neck of the heifer – וְעוֹרְפִין אוֹתָהּ: The wording of the mishna indicates that it does not matter who breaks the neck, as all are fit to do so. Rabbi Shimon in tractate *Menaḥot* states that the heifer's neck is broken by a priest, but the Rambam does not cite this minority opinion as *halakha* (Rashash).

וְהַכֹּהֲנִים אוֹמְרִים: ״כַּפֵּר לְעַמְּךָ יִשְׂרָאֵל אֲשֶׁר פָּדִיתָ ה׳ וְאַל תִּתֵּן דָּם נָקִי בְּקֶרֶב עַמְּךָ יִשְׂרָאֵל״. לֹא הָיוּ צְרִיכִין לוֹמַר ״וְנִכַּפֵּר לָהֶם הַדָּם״, אֶלָּא רוּחַ הַקּוֹדֶשׁ מְבַשַּׂרְתָּן: אֵימָתַי שֶׁתַּעֲשׂוּ כָּכָה – הַדָּם מִתְכַּפֵּר לָהֶם.

And the priests recite: "Forgive, Lord, Your people Israel, whom You have redeemed, and suffer not innocent blood to remain in the midst of Your people Israel" (Deuteronomy 21:8). **They did not have to recite**[H] the conclusion of the verse: **"And the blood shall be forgiven for them,"** as this is not part of the priests' statement, **but** rather **the Divine Spirit informs them:**[N] **When you shall do so, the blood is forgiven for you.**

גמ׳ וִיהֵא מוּם פּוֹסֵל בְּעֶגְלָה מִקַּל וָחוֹמֶר! וּמַה פָּרָה שֶׁאֵין הַשָּׁנִים פּוֹסְלוֹת בָּהּ – מוּם פּוֹסֵל בָּהּ, עֶגְלָה שֶׁשָּׁנִים פּוֹסְלוֹת בָּהּ – אֵינוֹ דִּין שֶׁיְּהֵא מוּם פּוֹסֵל בָּהּ! שָׁאנֵי הָתָם, דְּאָמַר קְרָא: ״אֲשֶׁר אֵין בָּהּ מוּם״, ״בָּהּ״ – מוּם פּוֹסֵל, וְאֵין מוּם פּוֹסֵל בְּעֶגְלָה.

GEMARA With regard to the mishna's statement that the heifer is not disqualified by a blemish, the Gemara suggests: **And a blemish should disqualify in** the case of the **heifer, by** means of **an *a fortiori*** inference: **And if** in the case of the red heifer, **which is not disqualified** by **years,**[H] as it may be of any age, and yet **a blemish disqualifies it,**[H] then **a heifer** for this ritual, **which is disqualified by years,**[NH] as it is valid only until two years of age, **is it not logical that a blemish should disqualify it?** The Gemara answers: It **is different there,** in the case of the red heifer, **as the verse states: "Wherein [*bah*] has no blemish"** (Numbers 19:2). This serves as an exclusion and teaches that it is only **with regard to it [*bah*]** that **a blemish is disqualifying, but a blemish is not disqualifying with regard to** the **heifer** of the ritual of the breaking of the neck.

אֶלָּא מֵעַתָּה, לֹא יְהוּ שְׁאָר עֲבוֹדוֹת פּוֹסְלוֹת בָּהּ!

The Gemara asks: **However, if that is so,** if the word *"bah"* precludes a derivation by an *a fortiori* inference, then any **other labor** performed with the red heifer, apart from pulling a yoke, **should not disqualify it.** While the verse disqualifies a red heifer only if it pulled a yoke, as it states: "And upon which never came a yoke" (Numbers 19:2), a similar *a fortiori* inference could be learned from the heifer whose neck is to be broken to disqualify a red heifer that has performed any labor. However, since the verse states with regard to the heifer whose neck is to be broken: "That has not been worked with [*bah*]" (Deuteronomy 21:3), this indicates that labor is disqualifying only for *"bah,"* a heifer whose neck is to be broken, but not for a red heifer.

אַלְמָה אָמַר רַב יְהוּדָה אָמַר רַב: הִנִּיחַ עָלֶיהָ עוּדָה שֶׁל שַׂקִּין – פְּסוּלָה; וּבְעֶגְלָה – עַד שֶׁתִּמְשׁוֹךְ! שָׁאנֵי פָּרָה, דְּיָלְפִינַן ״עֹל״, ״עֹל״ מֵעֶגְלָה.

Why, then, does **Rav Yehuda say** that **Rav says:** If **he placed a bundle [*uda*]**[L] **of sacks**[N] **on** a red heifer,[H] the heifer is immediately **disqualified** from being used as the red heifer; **and** as **for the heifer** whose neck is broken, it is not disqualified by such labor **until it pulls** and moves the burden, as the verse states: "That has not pulled a yoke" (Deuteronomy 21:3). Why does bearing the weight of the bundle disqualify the red heifer? The Gemara explains: The *halakha* with regard to the red **heifer is different, as we learn** by a verbal analogy between the word **"yoke"** used with regard to the red heifer and the word **"yoke"**[B] used with regard **to the heifer** whose neck is broken that any labor disqualifies the former.

NOTES

But the Divine Spirit informs them – אֶלָּא רוּחַ הַקּוֹדֶשׁ מְבַשַּׂרְתָּן: The proof that this is not part of the priests' statement is that they speak in the form of a request, saying: "Forgive, Lord, Your people Israel" (Deuteronomy 21:8), whereas the last part of the verse states: "And it shall be forgiven," as a statement of fact. The verse is stating an assurance that if the Elders and judges perform the ritual properly, they will eventually find the killer and bring him to justice, which will fully atone for the crime. The *Targum Yonatan* and several *midrashim* explain similarly (Maharsha).

Which is disqualified by years – שֶׁשָּׁנִים פּוֹסְלוֹת בָּהּ: Rashi writes that a heifer to be used in the ritual of breaking the neck must be in its first year of life. However, the *halakha* appears to be otherwise, as that is the opinion of Rabbi Eliezer (*Para* 1:1), but the Rabbis maintain that it is a heifer until it is age two. The Rambam rules in accordance with the opinion of the Rabbis (Rashash).

A bundle [*uda*] of sacks – עוּדָה שֶׁל שַׂקִּין: This translation follows Rashi. According to the Rambam, it refers to a type of sackcloth. The author of the *Arukh* asserts, citing the *ge'onim*, that *uda* is a kind of rope that is tied over sacks to prevent them from falling off an animal, as in the verse: "The Lord upholds [*me'oded*] the humble" (Psalms 147:6). He explains that Rabbi Yehuda is saying that not only does the bundle itself disqualify the animal, but the rope does as well. Rabbeinu Ḥananel similarly states that it refers to a kind of decorative belt, like the word *adi*, meaning an ornament, placed on the cow, in the manner of a donkey's girth.

BACKGROUND

Yoke [*ol*] – עוֹל: A yoke is a bar, fashioned from wood or iron, that is placed on the shoulders of oxen or cows and then connected to a cart, a plowshare, or a threshing sledge. An *ol* is for one animal, whereas a yoke for two animals is called a *tzemed*. A yoke needs to be wide enough that it will not break during the performance of labor. This is why its width is important for commercial transactions, as the Gemara notes.

Two oxen with a single yoke

LANGUAGE

Bundle [*uda*] – עוּדָה: The word seems to come from a root that means tying or the bundling of things. There is a similar word in Syriac and in Arabic, عدة, *'uddah*.

HALAKHA

They did not have to recite, etc. – לֹא הָיוּ צְרִיכִין לוֹמַר וכו׳: After the heifer's neck is broken, the priests recite: "Forgive, Lord, Your people Israel whom You have redeemed, and suffer not innocent blood to remain in the midst of Your people Israel" (Deuteronomy 21:8). They omit the conclusion of that verse: "And the blood shall be forgiven for them," as this is a promise by God that this ritual will serve to atone for them (Rambam *Sefer Nezikim, Hilkhot Rotze'aḥ UShmirat HaNefesh* 9:3).

The red heifer, which is not disqualified by years – פָּרָה שֶׁאֵין הַשָּׁנִים פּוֹסְלוֹת בָּהּ: The red heifer should be three or four years old, *ab initio*. It is valid even if it is older than this, but the priests do not wait that long to perform the ritual, in case it becomes disqualified by the growth of black hairs, as stated in tractate *Para* (Rambam *Sefer Tahara, Hilkhot Para Aduma* 1:1).

A blemish disqualifies it – מוּם פּוֹסֵל בָּהּ: All blemishes that disqualify sacred offerings disqualify the red heifer as well (Rambam *Sefer Tahara, Hilkhot Para Aduma* 1:7).

A heifer for this ritual, which is disqualified by years – עֶגְלָה שֶׁשָּׁנִים פּוֹסְלוֹת בָּהּ: The heifer whose neck is broken may be up to two years old. If it is two years and one day old it is disqualified, as stated here and in tractate *Para* (Rambam *Sefer Nezikim, Hilkhot Rotze'aḥ UShmirat HaNefesh* 10:2).

If he placed a bundle on it, etc. – הִנִּיחַ עָלֶיהָ עוּדָה וכו׳: All types of labor disqualify the red heifer. The *halakha* with regard to a yoke is even more stringent. If a yoke is merely placed on an animal it disqualifies it, even if the yoke was not pulled. However, other forms of labor must actually be performed in order to be disqualifying. If one placed a garment or sackcloth on the animal, it is disqualified (Rambam *Sefer Tahara, Hilkhot Para Aduma* 1:7).

עֶגְלָה נַמִּי תֵּיתֵי ״עֹל״, ״עֹל״ מִפָּרָה! הָא מִיעֵט רַחֲמָנָא ״בָּהּ״.

The Gemara raises an objection: If there is a verbal analogy between the red heifer and the heifer that will have its neck broken, then the *halakha* that a blemish should disqualify the heifer whose neck is broken **should also be derived** from the usage of **"yoke"** with regard to the heifer whose neck is broken and **from** the usage of **"yoke"** with regard **to** the red **heifer.** The Gemara answers: **The Merciful One has excluded** this possibility by placing in the verse the word **"*bah*,"** which indicates that disqualification due to blemish applies only to the red heifer and not to the heifer whose neck is broken.

בְּעֶגְלָה נַמִּי כְּתִיב ״בָּהּ״! הַהוּא מִיבָּעֵי לֵיהּ: לְמַעוּטֵי קָדָשִׁים דְּלָא פָּסְלָה בְּהוּ עֲבוֹדָה. סָלְקָא דַּעְתָּךְ אָמִינָא לֵיתֵי בְּקַל וָחוֹמֶר מֵעֶגְלָה: וּמָה עֶגְלָה שֶׁאֵין מוּם פּוֹסֵל בָּהּ – עֲבוֹדָה פּוֹסֶלֶת בָּהּ, קֳדָשִׁים שֶׁמּוּם פּוֹסֶלֶת בָּהֶן – אֵינוֹ דִּין שֶׁעֲבוֹדָה פּוֹסֶלֶת בָּהֶן.

The Gemara counters this claim: **In** the verse concerning **a heifer** whose neck is broken, the Torah **also writes "*bah*";** it should be the case that forms of labor other than pulling a yoke are disqualifying only with regard to it and not with regard to the red heifer. The Gemara answers: **That** word **"*bah*" is required by** Rav Yehuda in order **to exclude sacred** offerings, i.e., **which are not disqualified by labor,**[H] and one may bring an animal that has been used for labor as an offering. **It might enter your mind to say** that this **should be derived by an *a fortiori* inference from a heifer** whose neck is broken, as follows: **And if** with regard to **a heifer** whose neck is broken, **which is not disqualified by a blemish, labor** nevertheless **disqualifies it,** then with regard to **sacred** offerings, **which are disqualified by a blemish,**[H] **is it not right that labor should disqualify them?** In order to counter this argument, the word *"bah"* teaches us that a sacred offering is not disqualified by labor.

אִיכָּא לְמִיפְרַךְ: מָה לְעֶגְלָה שֶׁכֵּן שָׁנִים פּוֹסְלוֹת בָּהּ! אַטּוּ קֳדָשִׁים מִי לֵיכָּא דְּפָסְלִי בְּהוּ שָׁנִים? כִּי אִיצְטְרִיךְ קְרָא – לְהָנָךְ קֳדָשִׁים דְּפָסְלָה בְּהוּ שָׁנִים.

With regard to this suggested *a fortiori* inference, the Gemara observes that **it can be refuted** in the following manner: **What** about the fact that **a heifer** whose neck is broken **is disqualified by years,** as once it reaches two years of age it is no longer classified as a heifer? As it is clear that the heifer whose neck is to be broken carries some restrictions that do not apply to sacred offerings, perhaps being disqualified by labor is another such restriction. The Gemara refutes this argument: **Is that to say that there are no sacred** offerings **that are disqualified by years?** There are several offerings that may be brought only in their first or second year, and **where the verse is necessary** to teach that sacred offerings are not disqualified by labor, it is with regard to **those sacred** offerings **that are disqualified by years.**

וְקָדָשִׁים דְּלָא פָּסְלָה בְּהוּ עֲבוֹדָה מֵהָכָא נָפְקָא? מֵהָתָם נָפְקָא: ״עַוֶּרֶת אוֹ שָׁבוּר אוֹ חָרוּץ אוֹ יַבֶּלֶת אוֹ גָרָב אוֹ יַלֶּפֶת לֹא תַקְרִיבוּ אֵלֶּה לַה׳״ – אֵלֶּה אִי אַתָּה מַקְרִיב, אֲבָל אַתָּה מַקְרִיב קֳדָשִׁים שֶׁנֶּעֶבְדָה בָּהֶן עֲבוֹדָה! אִיצְטְרִיךְ, סָלְקָא דַּעְתָּךְ אָמִינָא הָנֵי מִילֵּי הֵיכָא דַּעֲבַד בָּהֶן עֲבוֹדַת הֶיתֵּר, אֲבָל עֲבוֹדַת אִיסּוּר – אֵימָא לִיתַּסְרוּ. צְרִיכָא.

The Gemara raises an objection: **But is** the *halakha* **that sacred** offerings **are not disqualified by labor derived from this** verse? **It is derived from elsewhere.** The verse states with regard to sacred offerings: **"Blind, or broken, or maimed, or having a wart, or scabbed, or scurvy, you shall not offer these to the Lord"** (Leviticus 22:22). This verse serves to create an exclusion, teaching that it is **these** that **you may not sacrifice, but you may sacrifice sacred** animals **that have been used for labor.** The Gemara answers: It **was necessary** to state the *halakha* twice. **It might enter your mind to say** that **this** *halakha*, that one may sacrifice animals that have been used for labor, **applies only** in a case where **they were used for permitted labor, but** if they were used for **prohibited labor,** e.g., on Shabbat, you might **say that it is prohibited** to bring **them** as offerings. In order to refute this argument, it is **necessary** to state the *halakha* again.

וְהָא נַמִּי מֵהָכָא נָפְקָא: ״וּמִיַּד בֶּן נֵכָר לֹא תַקְרִיבוּ אֶת לֶחֶם אֱלֹהֵיכֶם מִכָּל אֵלֶּה״ – ״אֵלֶּה״ אִי אַתָּה מַקְרִיב, אֲבָל אַתָּה מַקְרִיב קֳדָשִׁים שֶׁנֶּעֶבְדָה בָּהֶן עֲבוֹדָה!

The Gemara poses another question: **But this** *halakha* that prohibited labor does not disqualify offerings **is also derived from here,** a verse with regard to the sacrifice of blemished animals: **"And from the hand of a stranger you shall not offer the bread of your God from any of these, because…**there is a blemish in them" (Leviticus 22:25). This verse emphasizes that it is only **"these,"** i.e., blemished animals, that **you may not sacrifice, but you may sacrifice sacred** animals **that have been used for labor.** Since this verse is discussing the possibility of accepting offerings from a gentile, who presumably also performed prohibited labor with the animal, this demonstrates that prohibited labor does not disqualify animals from being sacrificed as offerings.

HALAKHA

Sacred offerings, which are not disqualified by labor – קָדָשִׁים דְּלָא פָּסְלָה בְּהוּ עֲבוֹדָה: Offerings are not disqualified by the performance of labor (Rambam *Sefer Tahara, Hilkhot Para Aduma* 1:7).

Sacred offerings, which are disqualified by a blemish – קָדָשִׁים שֶׁמּוּם פּוֹסֶלֶת בָּהֶן: It is a positive mitzva for all offerings to be unblemished and of good quality. A blemished animal is disqualified from being used as an offering (Rambam *Sefer Avoda, Hilkhot Issurei Mizbe'aḥ* 1:1).

אִיצְטְרִיךְ, סָלְקָא דַעְתָּךְ אָמֵינָא הָנֵי מִילֵּי הֵיכָא דַּעֲבַד בְּהֶן כְּשֶׁהֵן חוּלִּין, אֲבָל עָבַד בָּהֶן כְּשֶׁהֵן קָדָשִׁים אֵימָא לִיתַּסְרוּ. צְרִיכָא.

The Gemara answers: It **was necessary** to teach this *halakha* a third time. **It might enter your mind to say: This** *halakha*, that labor does not disqualify offerings, **applies** only where **one performed labor with them when they were non-sacred** and afterward dedicated them as offerings, **but** if **one performed labor with them when they were** already **sacred** animals, you might **say that it is prohibited** to bring **them** as offerings. In order to refute this argument, it is **necessary** to teach this *halakha* in three separate places.

גּוּפָא, אָמַר רַב יְהוּדָה אָמַר רַב: הִנִּיחַ עָלֶיהָ עוֹדֶה שֶׁל שַׂקִּין – פְּסוּלָה, וּבְעֶגְלָה – עַד שֶׁתִּמְשׁוֹךְ. מֵיתִיבִי: "עֹל" – אֵין לִי אֶלָּא עוֹל; שְׁאָר עֲבוֹדוֹת מִנַּיִן? אָמַרְתָּ קַל וָחוֹמֶר: וּמָה עֶגְלָה שֶׁאֵין מוּם פּוֹסֵל בָּהּ – שְׁאָר עֲבוֹדוֹת פּוֹסְלוֹת בָּהּ, פָּרָה שֶׁמּוּם פּוֹסֵל בָּהּ – אֵינוֹ דִּין שֶׁשְּׁאָר עֲבוֹדוֹת פּוֹסְלִין בָּהּ.

§ The Gemara returns to discuss **the** matter **itself: Rav Yehuda says** that **Rav says:** If **one placed a bundle of sacks on** a red heifer, **it is disqualified. And** as for **a heifer** whose neck is broken, it is not disqualified **until it pulls** a burden. The Gemara **raises an objection** from a *baraita*: It states with regard to the red heifer: "That upon which never came **a yoke**" (Numbers 19:2). **I have** derived **only a yoke; from where** do I derive that other types of labor also disqualify the animal? **You** can **say** the following ***a fortiori*** inference: **And if** with regard to **a heifer** whose neck is broken, **which is not disqualified by a blemish, other** types of **labor disqualify it,** then with regard to a red **heifer, which is disqualified by a blemish, is it not right that other** types of **labor should disqualify it?**

וְאִם נַפְשְׁךָ לוֹמַר – נֶאֱמַר כָּאן "עֹל" וְנֶאֱמַר לְהַלָּן "עֹל": מַה לְּהַלָּן שְׁאָר עֲבוֹדוֹת פּוֹסְלוֹת בָּהּ, אַף כָּאן שְׁאָר עֲבוֹדוֹת פּוֹסְלוֹת.

And if it is your wish to say that this *a fortiori* inference is unsound, you can learn this *halakha* by a verbal analogy: **It is stated here,** with regard to the red heifer, **"yoke"** (Numbers 19:2), **and it is stated there,** with regard to the heifer whose neck is broken, **"yoke"** (Deuteronomy 21:3). **Just as there, other** types of **labor disqualify it, so too here,** in the case of the red heifer, **other** types of **labor disqualify** it.

מַאי "אִם נַפְשְׁךָ לוֹמַר"? וְכִי תֵּימָא, אִיכָּא לְמִיפְרַךְ: מַה לְּעֶגְלָה שֶׁכֵּן שָׁנִים פּוֹסְלוֹת בָּהּ! אִי נַמִי, קָדָשִׁים יוֹכִיחוּ, שֶׁמּוּם פּוֹסֵל בָּהֶן וְאֵין עֲבוֹדָה פּוֹסֶלֶת בָּהֶן!

The Gemara asks: **What** is the meaning of: **If it is your wish to say?** What potential problem with the *a fortiori* inference necessitates the verbal analogy? The Gemara explains: **And perhaps you would say** that the *a fortiori* inference **can be refuted** in the following manner: **What** is unique **about a heifer** whose neck is broken is **that it is disqualified by years,** which is not the case for a red heifer. **Alternatively,** one could suggest that **sacred** offerings **will prove** that this inference should not be made, **as a blemish is disqualifying with regard to them, but labor is not disqualifying with regard to them.**

נֶאֱמַר כָּאן "עֹל" וְנֶאֱמַר לְהַלָּן "עֹל", מַה לְּהַלָּן שְׁאָר עֲבוֹדוֹת, אַף כָּאן שְׁאָר עֲבוֹדוֹת. וּמִמָּקוֹם שֶׁבָּאתָה: מַה לְּהַלָּן עַד שֶׁתִּמְשׁוֹךְ, אַף כָּאן עַד שֶׁתִּמְשׁוֹךְ!

As the *a fortiori* inference can be refuted in either of these ways, there is a need for the verbal analogy: **It is stated here "yoke," and it is stated there "yoke." Just as there,** in the case of **a heifer** whose neck is broken, **other** types of **labor** disqualify it, **so too, other** types of **labor** disqualify a red heifer. The Gemara raises an objection to this verbal analogy: **And from the place that you came** you can offer an alternative exposition: **Just as below,** in the case of a heifer whose neck is broken, it is not disqualified by carrying a burden **until it pulls** the yoke, **so too here,** a red heifer should not be disqualified **until it pulls** the yoke, contrary to the statement of Rav.

תַּנָּאֵי הִיא, דְּאִיכָּא דְּמַיְיתֵי לַהּ מֵעֶגְלָה, אִיכָּא דְּמַיְיתֵי לַהּ מִגּוּפַהּ דְּפָרָה.

The Gemara answers the objection to the statement of Rav from the *baraita*: It **is** a dispute among ***tanna'im*****, as there are those who cite** the source of **this** *halakha*, that labor disqualifies a red heifer, by verbal analogy **from a heifer** whose neck is broken, and therefore the red heifer is disqualified only if it pulls the burden. **There are** also **those who cite** the source of **this** *halakha* **from** a red **heifer itself,** and consequently they disqualify the red heifer even if it did not pull the yoke.

דְּתַנְיָא: "עֹל" – אֵין לִי אֶלָּא עוֹל; שְׁאָר עֲבוֹדוֹת מִנַּיִן? תַּלְמוּד לוֹמַר: "אֲשֶׁר לֹא עָלָה עָלֶיהָ עֹל", מִכׇּל מָקוֹם; אִם כֵּן, מַה תַּלְמוּד לוֹמַר "עֹל"? עוֹל פּוֹסֵל בֵּין בִּשְׁעַת עֲבוֹדָה בֵּין שֶׁלֹּא בִּשְׁעַת עֲבוֹדָה, שְׁאָר עֲבוֹדוֹת אֵין פּוֹסְלוֹת אֶלָּא בִּשְׁעַת עֲבוֹדָה.

This is **as it is taught** in a *baraita* with regard to a red heifer: From the term **"yoke" I have** derived **only** that **a yoke** disqualifies a red heifer; **from where** do I derive the **other** types of **labor? The verse states: "That upon which never came a yoke"** (Numbers 19:2). The verse could be read with a pause after the word "came," which would teach that it is disqualified **in any case,** no matter what labor was performed with it. **If so, what** is the meaning when **the verse states "yoke,"** if all forms of labor disqualify it? It teaches us that **a yoke** placed on the animal **disqualifies** it **whether** the yoke was on the animal **at the time of** performing **labor** or **whether** it was on the animal **not at the time of** performing **labor,** i.e., it was merely placed on the animal. However, **other** types of **labor** actions **disqualify** animals **only at the time of** actually performing **labor.**[N] Rav ruled in accordance with this opinion.

NOTES

At the time of performing labor – בִּשְׁעַת עֲבוֹדָה: In other words, the animal is disqualified only if the owner intended for the animal to do the action for the sake of labor, but not if it was done for any other reason. The Rambam writes, as an example, that if one brought the animal into the threshing area for a reason other than threshing, the threshing it performs incidentally while there does not disqualify the animal from being the red heifer. With regard to the carrying of a burden, however, it is disqualified even if one placed the yoke on the animal without intending it for work.

וְאֵימָא: ״אֲשֶׁר לֹא עָלָה עָלֶיהָ״ – כְּלָל; ״עֹל״ – פְּרָט; כְּלָל וּפְרָט אֵין בִּכְלָל אֶלָּא מַה שֶּׁבַּפְּרָט, עוֹל – אִין, מִידֵּי אַחֲרִינָא – לָא! ״אֲשֶׁר״ – רִבּוּיָא הוּא.

The Gemara raises an objection: **And** perhaps one can **say** a different exposition of the verse: **"That upon which never came"** is **a generalization** that disqualifies the animal after any type of labor, while **"yoke"** is **a detail.** There is **a generalization and a detail,** and the principle of halakhic exposition in that case is that **there is nothing in the generalization other** than **what is in the detail.** Therefore, with regard to **a yoke, yes,** it will disqualify an animal from being used as a red heifer; but with regard to **anything else, no,** it will not disqualify the animal. The Gemara answers: **"That** upon which never came" **is an amplification,** and the addition of this term results in this verse not belonging to the category of generalizations and details.

וְתַנְיָא נַמִי גַּבֵּי עֶגְלָה כִּי הַאי גַּוְונָא: ״עֹל״ – אֵין לִי אֶלָּא עוֹל; שְׁאָר עֲבוֹדוֹת מִנַּיִן? תַּלְמוּד לוֹמַר: ״אֲשֶׁר לֹא עֻבַּד בָּהּ״, מִכׇּל מָקוֹם. אִם כֵּן, מַה תַּלְמוּד לוֹמַר ״עֹל״? עוֹל פּוֹסֵל בֵּין בִּשְׁעַת עֲבוֹדָה בֵּין שֶׁלֹּא בִּשְׁעַת עֲבוֹדָה, שְׁאָר עֲבוֹדוֹת אֵין פּוֹסְלוֹת אֶלָּא בִּשְׁעַת עֲבוֹדָה.

The Gemara comments: **And a case like this is also taught in** a *baraita* **with regard to a heifer** whose neck is broken: From the word **"yoke" I have** derived **only** that **a yoke** disqualifies; **from where** do I derive the **other** types of **labor? The** same **verse states: "That has not been worked with"** (Deuteronomy 21:3), to teach that it is disqualified **in any case,** no matter what labor was performed with it. **If so, what** is the meaning when **the verse states "yoke"?** It serves to teach us that **a yoke** placed on the animal **disqualifies** it **whether** the yoke was on the animal **at the time of** performing **labor or whether** it was on the animal **not at the time of performing labor,** i.e., it was merely placed on the animal, whereas **other** types of **labor** actions **disqualify** animals **only at the time of** actually performing **labor.**

וְאֵימָא: ״אֲשֶׁר לֹא עֻבַּד בָּהּ״ – כְּלָל; ״עֹל״ – פְּרָט; כְּלָל וּפְרָט אֵין בִּכְלָל אֶלָּא מַה שֶּׁבַּפְּרָט, עוֹל – אִין, מִידֵּי אַחֲרִינָא – לָא! ״אֲשֶׁר״ – רִבּוּיָא הוּא.

The Gemara raises an objection: **And** perhaps one can **say** a different exposition of the verse: **"That has not been worked with"** is a **generalization** that disqualifies the animal after any type of labor, while **"yoke"** is **a detail.** There is **a generalization and a detail,** and the principle of halakhic exposition in that case is that **there is nothing in the generalization other** than **what is in the detail,** which means: With regard to **a yoke, yes,** it will disqualify an animal, but with regard to **anything else, no,** it will not disqualify it. The Gemara answers: The phrase **"that** has not been worked with" **is an amplification,** and the addition of this term results in this verse not belonging to the category of generalizations and details.

אָמַר רַבִּי אַבָּהוּ, בְּעַי מִינֵּיהּ מֵרַבִּי יוֹחָנָן: מְשִׁיכַת עוֹל בְּכַמָּה? אֲמַר לִי: כִּמְלֹא עוֹל. אִיבַּעְיָא לְהוּ: לְאׇרְכּוֹ אוֹ לְרׇחְבּוֹ? אֲמַר לְהוּ הַהוּא מֵרַבָּנַן וְרַבִּי יַעֲקֹב שְׁמֵיהּ, לְדִידִי מְפָרְשָׁא לִי מִינֵּיהּ דְּרַבִּי יוֹחָנָן: מְשִׁיכַת עוֹל לְרׇחְבּוֹ טֶפַח.

Rabbi Abbahu said: I asked of Rabbi Yoḥanan: This **pulling of a yoke** that disqualifies a heifer whose neck is broken, **with how much,** i.e., how far, must the animal pull the yoke for it to be disqualified? **He said to me: Like** the measure of the size of **a full yoke. A dilemma was raised before** the Sages: Does this mean according **to its length or** according **to its width? One of the Sages, and Rabbi Ya'akov was his name, said to them: It was explained to me personally by Rabbi Yoḥanan himself: The pulling of a yoke is** according **to its width,** which is **a handbreadth.**[HB]

וְלֵימָא טֶפַח! הָא קָא מַשְׁמַע לָן, שִׁיעוּרָא דְּעוֹל טֶפַח הָוֵי. לְמַאי נָפְקָא מִינָּהּ? לְמִקָּח וּמִמְכָּר.

The Gemara poses a question: **And** since he stated a fixed measurement, **let him** merely **state: A handbreadth.** Why was it necessary to add that this is the width of a yoke? The Gemara answers: **This teaches us** that **the measure** of **a yoke** along its width **is a handbreadth. What difference is there** in knowing this fact? This teaches that **in** the case of **commercial transactions,** a buyer may retract his purchase if the yoke he was given is less than a handbreadth wide.

HALAKHA

Pulling of a yoke – מְשִׁיכַת עוֹל: All types of labor disqualify an animal from being the heifer whose neck is broken, similar to the *halakha* concerning the red heifer. The specification of an animal "that has not pulled a yoke" teaches that a yoke is disqualifying even if no labor was performed but the yoke was merely pulled a handbreadth (Rambam *Sefer Nezikim, Hilkhot Rotze'aḥ UShmirat HaNefesh* 10:3).

BACKGROUND

Handbreadth – טֶפַח: A handbreadth is one of the measures of length frequently used in the Talmud. According to some modern halakhic opinions, the length of a handbreadth is 9.6 cm, and according to others it is 8 cm.

NOTES

That did not produce fruit – שֶׁלֹּא עָשָׂה פֵּירוֹת: The Maharsha writes, based on the Rambam, that an important aspect of the ritual of the breaking of the heifer's neck is the stimulation of public interest, as their involvement may lead to the discovery of the killer. Therefore, a young heifer is brought, in order to arouse the emotions of the observers.

אָמַר רַבִּי יוֹחָנָן בֶּן שָׁאוּל: מִפְּנֵי מָה אָמְרָה תּוֹרָה הָבֵיא עֶגְלָה בְּנַחַל? אָמַר הַקָּדוֹשׁ בָּרוּךְ הוּא: יָבֹא דָּבָר שֶׁלֹּא עָשָׂה פֵּירוֹת וְיֵעָרֵף בְּמָקוֹם שֶׁאֵין עוֹשֶׂה פֵּירוֹת, וִיכַפֵּר עַל מִי שֶׁלֹּא הִנִּיחוּ לַעֲשׂוֹת פֵּירוֹת. מַאי פֵּירוֹת? אִילֵימָא פְּרִיָּה וּרְבִיָּה, אֶלָּא מֵעַתָּה, אַזָּקֵן וְאַסָּרִיס הָכִי נַמִי דְּלָא עָרְפִינַן! אֶלָּא מִצְוֹת.

Rabbi Yoḥanan ben Shaul says: For what reason **did the Torah say to bring a heifer** whose neck is broken **to a stream? The Holy One, Blessed be He, said: Let something that did not produce fruit,**[N] i.e., a heifer that has not given birth, **come and** have its neck **be broken at** a stream that flows forcefully, which is **a place that does not produce fruit, and atone for** the murder of **one who was not given an opportunity to produce fruit.** The Gemara asks: **What** is this **fruit** that he was not given an opportunity to produce? **If we say** it refers to **being fruitful and multiplying,** i.e., that the killer prevented him from having more children, **but if that is so,** in the case **of an elderly person or a eunuch, so too** will you say **that we do not break** the heifer's neck because they could not have had any more children even had they lived? **Rather,** the fruit are **mitzvot,** as the killer deprived the victim of the opportunity to perform additional mitzvot.

״וּמוֹרִידִין אוֹתָהּ אֶל נַחַל אֵיתָן״. ״אֵיתָן״ כְּמַשְׁמָעוֹ – קָשֶׁה. תָּנוּ רַבָּנַן: מִנַּיִן לְאֵיתָן שֶׁהוּא קָשֶׁה? שֶׁנֶּאֱמַר:

The mishna taught: **And they bring it down to a stream** that is ***eitan***. ***Eitan*** in this context means **as** the word generally **indicates,** forceful. **The Sages taught: From where** is it derived **that *eitan* is forceful?** It is **as** it **is stated:**

NOTES

Eitan means old – אֵיתָן שֶׁהוּא יָשָׁן: According to Rashi, this means that they should not perform the ritual at a place whose earth has been brought from elsewhere, but at a place that has had the same soil from time immemorial. Others, perhaps the Rambam among them, explain that it means that the route in which the stream flows has been consistent over time. The Jerusalem Talmud states that the requirement of a hard stream is a halakhic preference but it is not indispensable. If the valley or stream is not hard, or even if there is no valley or stream at all, the ritual may be performed in any hard place (see Meiri).

Nor sown – וְלֹא יִזָּרֵעַ: The *Sefer HaḤinnukh* writes that the place is left unsown in order that the murder not be forgotten in the generations to come.

BACKGROUND

The bird brought as a sin-offering – חַטַּאת הָעוֹף: A bird is brought as a sin-offering in several situations. For example, it is brought by a woman who has given birth and by poor people in the case of a sliding-scale offering. When a bird is sacrificed as a sin-offering it is accompanied by a bird sacrificed as a burnt-offering. The bird sacrificed as a sin-offering is killed by the priest with his fingernail in a process called *melika*, or pinching.

״אֵיתָן מוֹשָׁבֶךָ וְשִׂים בַּסֶּלַע קִנֶּךָ״, וְאוֹמֵר: ״שִׁמְעוּ הָרִים אֶת רִיב ה׳ וְהָאֵיתָנִים מֹסְדֵי אָרֶץ״; אֲחֵרִים אוֹמְרִים: מִנַּיִן לְאֵיתָן שֶׁהוּא יָשָׁן? שֶׁנֶּאֱמַר: ״גּוֹי אֵיתָן הוּא, גּוֹי מֵעוֹלָם הוּא״.

"Firm [*eitan*] is your dwelling-place, and your nest is set in the rock" (Numbers 24:21), **and it states: "Hear, O you mountains, the Lord's controversy, and the enduring rocks [*eitanim*], the foundations of the earth"** (Micah 6:2). The use of the word in these verses indicates that "*eitan*" means something hard, like a rock or a mountain. **Others say** a different explanation of the word *eitan*: **From where** is it derived **that *eitan* means old?**[N] **As** it **is stated: "It is an ancient [*eitan*] nation, a nation from of old"** (Jeremiah 5:15).

״וְעוֹרְפִין אוֹתָהּ בְּקוֹפִיץ מֵאֲחוֹרֶיהָ״. מַאי טַעְמָא? גָּמַר ״עֲרִיפָה״, ״עֲרִיפָה״ מֵחַטַּאת הָעוֹף.

§ The mishna taught: **And they break the neck [*orfin*]** of the heifer **from behind with a cleaver.** The Gemara explains: **What is the reason** that the Sages understood that the heifer is killed in this manner? They **derive** that the term ***arifa***, which describes what is done to the heifer, refers to breaking the back of the neck, **from** the term ***arifa*** stated with regard to the **bird** brought **as a sin-offering** (see Leviticus 5:8).[B]

״וּמְקוֹמָהּ אָסוּר מִלִּזְרוֹעַ וּמִלֵּיעָבֵד״. תָּנוּ רַבָּנַן: ״אֲשֶׁר לֹא יֵעָבֵד בּוֹ וְלֹא יִזָּרֵעַ״ – לְשֶׁעָבַר, דִּבְרֵי רַבִּי יֹאשִׁיָּה; רַבִּי יוֹנָתָן אוֹמֵר: לְהַבָּא.

§ The mishna taught further: **And** with regard to **its place, it is prohibited** for that ground **to be sown or to be worked. The Sages taught:** The verse: **"Which may be neither worked nor sown"** (Deuteronomy 21:4)[N] is referring **to the past,** that is, a place which has not previously been worked or sown. This is **the statement of Rabbi Yoshiya. Rabbi Yonatan says:** It speaks **of the future,** meaning it is prohibited to sow or work the land from that point onward.

רָבָא אֲמַר: לְהַבָּא – דְּכוּלֵּי עָלְמָא לָא פְּלִיגִי, דִּכְתִיב: ״וְלֹא יִזָּרֵעַ״. כִּי פְּלִיגִי – לְשֶׁעָבַר: רַבִּי יֹאשִׁיָּה סָבַר: מִי כְּתִיב ״וְלֹא יְעוּבַּד״? וְרַבִּי יוֹנָתָן: מִי כְּתִיב ״אֲשֶׁר לֹא נֶעֱבַד״? וְרַבִּי יֹאשִׁיָּה: ״אֲשֶׁר״ – לְשֶׁעָבַר מַשְׁמַע. וְרַבִּי יוֹנָתָן: ״אֲשֶׁר״ – רִבּוּיָא הוּא.

Rava said: As **for the future, everyone agrees** that it is prohibited to sow or work the land, **as it is written** "neither worked **nor sown"** in the future tense. **When they disagree** is with regard to **the past. Rabbi Yoshiya,** who disqualifies a place that was sown beforehand, **holds: Does it state: And shall not be worked,** in the form of a future command? **And Rabbi Yonatan** responds: **Does it state: And was not worked,** in the past tense? **And Rabbi Yoshiya** answers: The term **"which" indicates the past. And** as for **Rabbi Yonatan,** in his opinion the term **"which" is** a term of **amplification,** as will be explained later in the Gemara, and it is not referring to the past.

״וּמוּתָּר לִסְרוֹק שָׁם פִּשְׁתָּן וּלְנַקֵּר שָׁם אֲבָנִים״. תָּנוּ רַבָּנַן: ״אֲשֶׁר לֹא יֵעָבֵד בּוֹ וְלֹא יִזָּרֵעַ״ – אֵין לִי אֶלָּא זְרִיעָה. שְׁאָר עֲבוֹדוֹת מִנַּיִן? תַּלְמוּד לוֹמַר: ״אֲשֶׁר לֹא יֵעָבֵד בּוֹ״, מִכׇּל מָקוֹם.

§ The mishna taught: **But it is permitted to comb flax there**[H] **or to cut stones there. The Sages taught:** From the phrase **"which may be neither worked nor sown," I have** derived **only sowing; from where** do I derive that **other** types of **labor** are also prohibited? **The verse states: "Which may be neither worked,"** indicating that it may not be worked **in any manner.**

אִם כֵּן, מַה תַּלְמוּד לוֹמַר ״וְלֹא יִזָּרֵעַ״? לוֹמַר לְךָ: מַה זְּרִיעָה מְיוּחֶדֶת שֶׁהִיא בְּגוּפָהּ שֶׁל קַרְקַע, אַף כׇּל שֶׁהוּא בְּגוּפָהּ שֶׁל קַרְקַע, יָצָא סְרִיקַת פִּשְׁתָּן וְנִיקּוּר אֲבָנִים שֶׁאֵינָן בְּגוּפָהּ שֶׁל קַרְקַע.

The *baraita* continues: **If so, why does the verse** also need to **state "nor sown"?** It is in order **to say to you: Just as sowing is unique** in **that it is** labor performed **on the land itself, so too, all** labor **that is** performed **on the land itself** is prohibited. This **excludes combing flax and cutting stones, which are not** done **on the land itself.**

וְאֵימָא: ״אֲשֶׁר לֹא יֵעָבֵד בּוֹ״ – כְּלָל; ״וְלֹא יִזָּרֵעַ״ – פְּרָט; כְּלָל וּפְרָט אֵין בַּכְּלָל אֶלָּא מַה שֶּׁבַּפְּרָט, זְרִיעָה – אִין, מִידֵּי אַחֲרִינָא – לָא! ״אֲשֶׁר״ – רִבּוּיָא הוּא.

The Gemara raises an objection: **And** perhaps one can **say** a different exposition: **"Which may be neither worked"** is **a generalization,** and **"nor sown" a detail.** When the Torah writes **a generalization and a detail, there is nothing in the generalization other** than **what is in the detail,** i.e., the detail serves to impose a limit on the generalization. Consequently, the verse is teaching that with regard to **sowing, yes,** it is prohibited, but with regard to **anything else, no,** it is not prohibited. The Gemara again answers: The term **"which" is an amplification,** and the addition of this term results in this verse not belonging to the category of generalizations and details.

״זִקְנֵי הָעִיר רוֹחֲצִין יְדֵיהֶן״ כו׳. תָּנוּ רַבָּנַן: ״וְכֹל זִקְנֵי הָעִיר הַהִיא הַקְּרֹבִים אֶל הֶחָלָל יִרְחֲצוּ אֶת יְדֵיהֶם עַל הָעֶגְלָה הָעֲרוּפָה בַנָּחַל״ – שֶׁאֵין תַּלְמוּד לוֹמַר ״הָעֲרוּפָה״. וּמַה תַּלְמוּד לוֹמַר ״הָעֲרוּפָה״? עַל מְקוֹם עֲרִיפָתָהּ שֶׁל עֶגְלָה.

§ The mishna taught that **the Elders of the city** would then **wash their hands.**[N] **The Sages taught:** With regard to the verse: **"And all the Elders of that city, who are nearest to the slain man, shall wash their hands over the heifer whose neck was broken in the valley"** (Deuteronomy 21:6), one might have thought **that** there is **no** need for **the verse to state: "Whose neck was broken,"** because there is no heifer mentioned other than the one whose neck was broken. **And what** is the meaning when **the verse states: "Whose neck was broken"?** It serves to teach us that they wash their hands **over the place where the heifer's neck was broken.**

״וְאָמְרוּ יָדֵינוּ לֹא שָׁפְכוּ אֶת הַדָּם הַזֶּה וְעֵינֵינוּ לֹא רָאוּ״ – וְכִי עַל לִבֵּנוּ עָלְתָה שֶׁבֵּית דִּין שׁוֹפְכִין דָּמִים? אֶלָּא, לֹא בָא לְיָדֵינוּ וּפְטַרְנוּהוּ בְּלֹא מְזוֹנוֹת, וְלֹא רְאִינוּהוּ וְהִנַּחְנוּהוּ בְּלֹא לְוָיָה.

The verse further states: **"And they shall say: Our hands did not spill this blood, nor did our eyes see"** (Deuteronomy 21:7). The mishna explains: **But did it enter our minds that** the Elders of **the court are spillers of blood,** that they must make such a declaration? **Rather,** they mean to declare: The victim **did not come to us and** then **we let him take his leave without food,**[N] **and we did not see him and** then **leave him** alone to depart **without accompaniment.** They therefore attest that they took care of all his needs and are not responsible for his death even indirectly.

HALAKHA

But it is permitted to comb…there, etc. – וּמוּתָּר לִסְרוֹק שָׁם וכו׳: It is permanently prohibited to sow or work the land on which the heifer's neck was broken. This ruling is accordance with Rabbi Yonatan, as the unattributed mishna follows his opinion. Anyone who works the land itself, e.g., by plowing, sowing, or planting, is liable to receive lashes. However, it is permitted to comb flax or to cut stones there, as all work that does not involve the land itself is permitted (Rambam *Sefer Nezikim, Hilkhot Rotze'aḥ UShmirat HaNefesh* 10:9).

NOTES

Wash their hands – רוֹחֲצִין יְדֵיהֶן: This is to signify that their hands are clean of any taint of the victim's blood (*Iyyun Ya'akov*).

And we let him take his leave without food – וּפְטַרְנוּהוּ בְּלֹא מְזוֹנוֹת: A different explanation of the mishna is stated in the Jerusalem Talmud, that the Sages of Eretz Yisrael hold that the Elders are referring to the killer rather than to the victim. In other words, they did not knowingly allow the killer to escape; rather, they were unaware of his identity. This explanation is supported by a variant text of the mishna that reads: And we did not let him take his leave, and did not leave him. It does not include the phrases: Without food, or: Without accompaniment. It is written in the Jerusalem Talmud that these phrases are a later addition and not part of the text of the mishna.

תַּנְיָא, הָיָה רַבִּי מֵאִיר אוֹמֵר: כּוֹפִין לִלְוָיָה, שֶׁשְּׂכַר הַלְּוָיָה אֵין לָהּ שִׁיעוּר, שֶׁנֶּאֱמַר: ״וַיִּרְאוּ הַשֹּׁמְרִים אִישׁ יוֹצֵא מִן הָעִיר וַיֹּאמְרוּ לוֹ הַרְאֵנוּ נָא אֶת מְבוֹא הָעִיר וְעָשִׂינוּ עִמְּךָ חָסֶד״, וּכְתִיב: ״וַיַּרְאֵם אֶת מְבוֹא הָעִיר״. וּמַה חֶסֶד עָשׂוּ עִמּוֹ? שֶׁכָּל אוֹתָהּ הָעִיר הָרְגוּ לְפִי חֶרֶב, וְאוֹתוֹ הָאִישׁ וּמִשְׁפַּחְתּוֹ שִׁלְּחוּ.

It is taught in a *baraita*: **Rabbi Meir would say: There is coercion with regard to accompaniment,**[H] i.e., one who does not want to accompany another is nevertheless required to do so, **as the reward for accompaniment is without measure.** The proof of the importance of accompaniment is from a verse, **as it is stated** with regard to when the Jewish people laid siege to the city of Bethel: **"And the watchers saw a man come out of the city, and they said to him: Show us, please, the entrance into the city, and we will deal kindly with you"** (Judges 1:24), **and it is written: "And he showed them the entrance to the city"** (Judges 1:25). **And what kindness did they perform with him?** It is **that they killed the entire city by the sword, but that man and his family they sent** free.

״וַיֵּלֶךְ הָאִישׁ אֶרֶץ הַחִתִּים וַיִּבֶן עִיר וַיִּקְרָא שְׁמָהּ לוּז הוּא שְׁמָהּ עַד הַיּוֹם הַזֶּה״. תַּנְיָא: הִיא לוּז שֶׁצּוֹבְעִין בָּהּ תְּכֵלֶת, הִיא לוּז שֶׁבָּא סַנְחֵרִיב וְלֹא בִּלְבְּלָהּ, נְבוּכַדְנֶצַּר וְלֹא הֶחֱרִיבָהּ, וְאַף מַלְאַךְ הַמָּוֶת אֵין לוֹ רְשׁוּת לַעֲבוֹר בָּהּ, אֶלָּא זְקֵנִים שֶׁבָּהּ בִּזְמַן שֶׁדַּעְתָּן קָצָה עֲלֵיהֶן – יוֹצְאִין חוּץ לַחוֹמָה וְהֵן מֵתִים.

The Gemara elaborates on the reward received in that story. The next verse states: **"And the man went to the land of the Hittites, and he built a city, and he called its name Luz; that is its name to this day"** (Judges 1:26). **It is taught** in a *baraita*: This **is the** city **Luz where sky blue** wool **is dyed.** It is the same city **Luz where,** although **Sennacherib came** and exiled many nations from place to place, he **did not disarrange** and exile **its** inhabitants; **Nebuchadnezzar,** who conquered many lands, **did not destroy it; and even the angel of death has no permission to pass through it. Rather, its Elders, when they have decided that they have reached the end** of life, **go outside the** city **wall and die.**

וַהֲלֹא דְּבָרִים קַל וָחוֹמֶר: וּמַה כְּנַעֲנִי זֶה, שֶׁלֹּא דִּיבֵּר בְּפִיו וְלֹא הָלַךְ בְּרַגְלָיו – גָּרַם הַצָּלָה לוֹ וּלְזַרְעוֹ עַד סוֹף כָּל הַדּוֹרוֹת, מִי שֶׁעוֹשֶׂה לְוָיָה בְּרַגְלָיו – עַל אַחַת כַּמָּה וְכַמָּה.

Are these **matters not** inferred *a fortiori*: **And if this Canaanite, who did not speak with his mouth** and explicitly tell them where the city entrance was, **and did not walk** with them **by foot,** but merely indicated the correct path to them, nevertheless **caused himself** to be **rescued and** also had the merit to provide rescue **for his descendants until the end of all generations,** then with regard to **one who accompanies** another **by foot,**[N] **all the more so** will his reward be great.

בַּמֶּה הֶרְאָה לָהֶם? חִזְקִיָּה אָמַר: בְּפִיו עִקֵּם לָהֶם, רַבִּי יוֹחָנָן אָמַר: בְּאֶצְבָּעוֹ הֶרְאָה לָהֶם. תַּנְיָא כְּוָותֵיהּ דְּרַבִּי יוֹחָנָן: בִּשְׁבִיל שֶׁכְּנַעֲנִי זֶה הֶרְאָה בְּאֶצְבָּעוֹ, גָּרַם הַצָּלָה לוֹ וּלְזַרְעוֹ עַד סוֹף כָּל הַדּוֹרוֹת.

After stating that the man did not openly guide those watching the city, the Gemara asks: **How did** that Canaanite **show them** the entrance to the city? **Ḥizkiyya says: He twisted his mouth for them,** i.e., he showed them the path to the city by moving his lips. **Rabbi Yoḥanan says: He showed them with his finger** alone. It **is taught** in a *baraita* **in accordance with** the opinion **of Rabbi Yoḥanan: Because this Canaanite showed** them **with his finger, he caused himself** to be **rescued and** merited rescue for **his descendants** as well, **until the end of all generations.**

אָמַר רַבִּי יְהוֹשֻׁעַ בֶּן לֵוִי: הַמְהַלֵּךְ בַּדֶּרֶךְ וְאֵין לוֹ לְוָיָה – יַעֲסוֹק בַּתּוֹרָה, שֶׁנֶּאֱמַר: ״כִּי לִוְיַת חֵן הֵם לְרֹאשֶׁךָ וַעֲנָקִים לְגַרְגְּרֹתֶיךָ״. וְאָמַר רַבִּי יְהוֹשֻׁעַ בֶּן לֵוִי: בִּשְׁבִיל אַרְבָּעָה פְּסִיעוֹת שֶׁלִּוָּה פַּרְעֹה לְאַבְרָהָם, שֶׁנֶּאֱמַר: ״וַיְצַו עָלָיו פַּרְעֹה אֲנָשִׁים״ וגו׳, נִשְׁתַּעְבֵּד בְּבָנָיו אַרְבַּע מֵאוֹת שָׁנָה, שֶׁנֶּאֱמַר: ״וַעֲבָדוּם וְעִנּוּ אֹתָם אַרְבַּע מֵאוֹת שָׁנָה״. אָמַר רַב יְהוּדָה אָמַר רַב: כָּל הַמְלַוֶּה אֶת חֲבֵירוֹ אַרְבַּע אַמּוֹת בָּעִיר – אֵינוֹ נִיזּוֹק. רָבִינָא אַלְוְיֵהּ לְרָבָא בַּר יִצְחָק אַרְבַּע אַמּוֹת בָּעִיר, מְטָא לִידֵיהּ הֶיזֵּיקָא וְאִיתְּצִיל.

Rabbi Yehoshua ben Levi says: One who walks along the way without having someone to **accompany** him **should occupy himself with** words of **Torah, as it is stated** with regard to words of Torah: **"For they shall be a chaplet of grace to your head, and chains around your neck"** (Proverbs 1:9). **And Rabbi Yehoshua ben Levi** further **says: Due to four steps**[N] **that Pharaoh accompanied Abraham, as it is stated: "And Pharaoh gave men charge concerning him,** and they brought him on the way, and his wife, and all that he had" (Genesis 12:20), Pharaoh **enslaved** Abraham's **descendants** for **four hundred years, as it is stated: "And shall serve them, and they shall afflict them four hundred years"** (Genesis 15:13). **Rav Yehuda says** that **Rav says: Anyone who accompanies his friend four cubits in a city will come to no harm** by accompanying him. The Gemara relates: **Ravina accompanied Rava bar Yitzḥak four cubits in a city. He came close to harm, but he was saved.**

HALAKHA

There is coercion with regard to accompaniment – כּוֹפִין לִלְוָיָה: Just as the courts would compel the giving of charity they would enforce the duty of accompaniment, by appointing messengers to accompany those traveling from place to place. If the appointed messengers neglected their duty, they are considered like spillers of blood (Rambam *Sefer Shofetim, Hilkhot Evel* 14:3).

NOTES

One who accompanies by foot, etc. – מִי שֶׁעוֹשֶׂה לְוָיָה בְּרַגְלָיו וכו׳: The Maharsha explains that although one who provides verbal directions does assist the other, this does not guarantee that he will not get lost. By contrast, one who accompanies him by foot will lead him far enough to prevent him from going astray.

NOTES

Due to four steps – בִּשְׁבִיל אַרְבָּעָה פְּסִיעוֹת: The idea is not that these four steps caused the slavery, as Abraham was not liable to punishment for being accompanied. The decree of slavery was said to Abraham at the Covenant between the Pieces because he questioned God with regard to inheriting Eretz Yisrael. It was not said then which nation would enslave Abraham's descendants. Through his actions, Pharaoh earned the right to be the one to rule over them (Maharsha).

תָּנוּ רַבָּנַן: הָרַב לְתַלְמִיד – עַד עִיבּוּרָהּ שֶׁל עִיר; חָבֵר לְחָבֵר – עַד תְּחוּם שַׁבָּת; תַּלְמִיד לְרַב – אֵין לוֹ שִׁיעוּר. וְכַמָּה? אָמַר רַב שֵׁשֶׁת: עַד פַּרְסָה. וְלָא אֲמָרַן אֶלָּא רַבּוֹ שֶׁאֵינוֹ מוּבְהָק, אֲבָל רַבּוֹ מוּבְהָק – שְׁלֹשָׁה פַּרְסָאוֹת.

The Sages taught: A teacher accompanies **a student**[H] **until the outskirts of the city; a friend** accompanies **a friend until the Shabbat boundary** of that city, which is two thousand cubits; and for **a student** who accompanies his **teacher, there is no measure** to the distance he accompanies him. The Gemara asks: **And how far?**[N] The student is certainly not required to walk with him the entire way. **Rav Sheshet says: Up to a parasang** [*parsa*],[B] which is four *mil*. The Gemara comments: **And we said** this amount **only** with regard to one who is **not his most significant teacher, but** he accompanies **his most significant teacher,** who taught him most of his knowledge, **three parasangs.**

רַב כָּהֲנָא אַלְוְיֵהּ לְרַב שִׁימִי בַּר אַשִׁי מִפּוּם נַהֲרָא עַד בֵּי צִינִיתָא דְּבָבֶל. כִּי מָטוּ הָתָם, אֲמַר לֵיהּ: וַדַּאי דְּאָמְרִיתוּ: הָנֵי צִינִיתָא דְּבָבֶל מִשְּׁנֵי אָדָם הָרִאשׁוֹן אִיתְנְהוּ?

The Gemara relates a story about accompaniment: **Rav Kahana accompanied Rav Shimi bar Ashi from** the town of **Pum Nahara to** the **palm grove in Babylonia.**[L] **When they arrived there,** Rav Kahana **said to** Rav Shimi bar Ashi: Is it **true that** you say that **these palm trees** of **Babylonia have been** in this place **since the years of Adam the first** man?

אֲמַר לֵיהּ: אַדְכַּרְתַּן מִלְּתָא, דְּאָמַר רַבִּי יוֹסֵי בְּרַבִּי חֲנִינָא, מַאי דִּכְתִיב: ״בְּאֶרֶץ לֹא עָבַר בָּהּ אִישׁ וְלֹא יָשַׁב אָדָם שָׁם״? וְכִי מֵאַחַר שֶׁלֹּא עָבַר הֵיכָן יָשַׁב? (וּמֵאַחַר שֶׁלֹּא יָשַׁב הֵיכָן עָבַר?) אֶלָּא, אֶרֶץ שֶׁגָּזַר עָלֶיהָ אָדָם הָרִאשׁוֹן לְיִשּׁוּב – נִתְיַשְּׁבָה, אֶרֶץ שֶׁלֹּא גָּזַר עָלֶיהָ אָדָם הָרִאשׁוֹן – לֹא נִתְיַשְּׁבָה.

Rav Shimi bar Ashi **said to him:** By mentioning Adam the first man **you reminded me of something that Rabbi Yosei, son of Rabbi Ḥanina, says: What is** the meaning of that **which is written: "Through a land that no man passed through, and where no person** [*adam*] **dwelt"?** (Jeremiah 2:6). This verse is difficult: **Since it** is a land **through which no** man **has passed, where would he dwell? And if he did not dwell, where did he pass?** Why does the verse add that no person has dwelled there? **Rather,** this is the meaning: Any **land** concerning **which Adam the first** man **decreed**[N] **that it would be a settled area, was settled;** but **a land** concerning **which Adam the first** man **did not decree** that it should be settled, **was not settled.**

רַב מָרְדְּכַי אַלְוְיֵהּ לְרַב אַשִׁי מֵהַגְרוֹנְיָא וְעַד בֵּי כֵּיפֵי, וְאָמְרִי לַהּ עַד בֵּי דוּרָא.

The Gemara also relates that **Rav Mordekhai accompanied Rav Ashi from** the town of **Hagronya until Bei Keifei, and some say** that he accompanied him **until Bei Dura.**

אָמַר רַבִּי יוֹחָנָן מִשּׁוּם רַבִּי מֵאִיר: כָּל שֶׁאֵינוֹ מְלַוֶּה וּמִתְלַוֶּה – כְּאִילּוּ שׁוֹפֵךְ דָּמִים, שֶׁאִילְמָלֵי לִיוּוּהוּ אַנְשֵׁי יְרִיחוֹ לֶאֱלִישָׁע לֹא גֵּירָה דּוּבִּים לַתִּינוֹקוֹת, שֶׁנֶּאֱמַר: ״וַיַּעַל מִשָּׁם בֵּית אֵל וְהוּא עֹלֶה בַדֶּרֶךְ וּנְעָרִים קְטַנִּים יָצְאוּ מִן הָעִיר וַיִּתְקַלְּסוּ בוֹ וַיֹּאמְרוּ לוֹ עֲלֵה קֵרֵחַ עֲלֵה קֵרֵחַ״.

The Gemara continues to discuss the importance of accompaniment. **Rabbi Yoḥanan says in the name of Rabbi Meir: Whoever does not accompany** another **or will not** allow himself to be **accompanied is like a spiller of blood** and is held responsible for any deaths that occur as a result of his inaction. The proof for this is **that had the inhabitants of Jericho accompanied Elisha, he would not have incited the bears to** attack **the children, as it is stated: "And he went up from there to Bethel, and as he was going up by the way, there came forth young lads out of the city and mocked him, and said to him: Go up, baldhead; go up, baldhead"** (II Kings 2:23). Had the residents of Jericho accompanied him, they would have sent away those youths and prevented what occurred next.

אָמְרוּ לוֹ: עֲלֵה שֶׁהִקְרַחְתָּ עָלֵינוּ אֶת הַמָּקוֹם. מַאי ״וּנְעָרִים קְטַנִּים״? אָמַר רַבִּי אֶלְעָזָר: שֶׁמְּנוֹעָרִים מִן הַמִּצְוֹת; ״קְטַנִּים״ – שֶׁהָיוּ מִקְטַנֵּי אֲמָנָה. תָּנָא: נְעָרִים הָיוּ, וּבִזְּבְזוּ עַצְמָן כִּקְטַנִּים.

The Gemara proceeds to discuss this episode in detail, beginning with the meaning of the youths' taunt. **They said to him: Go up,** away from here, **for you have made the place bald,** i.e., bare, **for us.** They had previously earned their living by providing the city of Jericho with water. Elisha sweetened the city's own water, rendering their services unnecessary. The Gemara asks: **What** is the meaning of: **"Young lads** [*ne'arim ketannim*]**"?** One would have expected the verse to state either "young" or "lads," but not both. **Rabbi Elazar says:** The word "lads [*ne'arim*]" means that **they were shaken** empty [*meno'arim*] **of the mitzvot;** the word **"young** [*ketannim*]**"** means **that they were of little faith** [*ketannei amana*], as they had no trust that they would be able to earn their livelihood by any other means. The Sages **taught: They were lads,** that is, already of age, **but they disgraced themselves like young** children.

HALAKHA

A teacher accompanies a student, etc. – הָרַב לְתַלְמִיד וכו׳: A teacher is obligated to accompany his student until the outskirts of the city. A friend is accompanied to the Shabbat boundary of the city. A student accompanies his teacher for the distance of a parasang, or three parasangs in the case of his most significant teacher. The *Likkutei Halakhot* comments that the custom nowadays is to accompany guests a minimum of four cubits, as the assumption is that the visitor relinquishes his right to the strict requirement of accompaniment (Rambam *Sefer Shofetim, Hilkhot Evel* 14:3).

NOTES

There is no measure, and how far – אֵין לוֹ שִׁיעוּר. וְכַמָּה: This is puzzling, as if there is no measure, how can the Gemara inquire into how much it is? One suggestion is that the phrase: No measure, means no upper limit, i.e., he may accompany him as far as he wishes; there is, however, a minimum requirement of a parasang (*Eshel Avraham*). Others explain that when the Gemara states that the student's accompaniment has no measure, this means that there is no measure within the Shabbat boundaries of the city and one accompanies his teacher out of the city. The Gemara then questions how far out of the city he accompanies him and answers that he accompanies him to the distance of a parasang beyond the city's borders (*Shevut Ya'akov*; see *Meromei Sadeh*).

Any land…decreed, etc. – אֶרֶץ שֶׁגָּזַר וכו׳: Rav Shimi bar Ashi's explanation was therefore that when Rabbi Yosei said that those dates are from the time of Adam the first man, this was not to be taken literally. Rather, it meant that the place was designated for palm trees since the days of Adam the first man.

BACKGROUND

Parasang – פַּרְסָה: One parasang is equal to four *mil*. This equals 3.86 km according to Rav Ḥayyim Na'e and 4.63 km according to the Ḥazon Ish.

LANGUAGE

Palm grove [*bei tzinita*] in Babylonia – בֵּי צִינִיתָא דְּבָבֶל: The word *tzinita*, in its various forms, can also be found in the Mishna. It is the name of a particular subspecies of palm tree. Here, it refers to a large forest of date-palms that grew near the ancient city of Babylonia.

BACKGROUND

Ne'oran – נְעוֹרָן: Also known today as Na'aran, this was a small city located near Jericho. In talmudic times, it was inhabited entirely by Jews, in contrast to Jericho, which had a mixed population. This city is now in ruins, though there are the remains of a beautiful synagogue there.

Plaited locks – בְּלוֹרִית: Many explanations have been suggested for the source of this term, mostly from Latin or Greek, yet none is entirely convincing. This hairstyle involved letting the hair on the sides and back of the head grow while tying and braiding them in different ways. The hair was later shaved in an idolatrous ritual.

NOTES

Literally saw – רָאָה מַמָּשׁ: The Maharsha explains that the problem with a literal reading of this verse is that cursing a Jew is prohibited by Torah law. For this reason, Rav stated that Elisha did not explicitly curse them but placed his eyes upon them, which was enough to cause them harm.

מַתְקִיף לָהּ רַב יוֹסֵף: וְדִלְמָא עַל שֵׁם מְקוֹמָן! מִי לָא כְּתִיב: ״וַאֲרָם יָצְאוּ גְדוּדִים וַיִּשְׁבּוּ מֵאֶרֶץ יִשְׂרָאֵל נַעֲרָה קְטַנָּה״, וְקַשְׁיָא לָן: נַעֲרָה וּקְטַנָּה! וְאָמַר רַבִּי פְּדָת: קְטַנָּה דְּמִן נְעוֹרָן! הָתָם לָא מְפָרֵשׁ מְקוֹמָהּ, הָכָא מְפוֹרָשׁ מְקוֹמָן.

Rav Yosef objects to this interpretation: **And perhaps** they were called *ne'arim* **after their place** of origin? **Isn't it written: "And** the Arameans had gone out in bands, **and had brought away captive from Eretz Yisrael a minor young woman** [*na'ara ketana*]" (II Kings 5:2), **and** this verse raised **a difficulty to us: A minor and a young woman;** how could she be both of these? **And Rabbi Pedat says** it means **a minor** girl **from** the town of **Ne'oran.**[B] This verse concerning the lads can be explained in a similar manner: They were young children from Ne'oran. The Gemara answers: These two cases are not comparable. **There** the verse **does not specify her place** of origin, so "*na'ara*" could mean from the town of Ne'oran; but **here** the verse **specifies their place** of origin, namely Jericho.

״וַיִּפֶן אַחֲרָיו וַיִּרְאֵם וַיְקַלְלֵם בְּשֵׁם ה׳״ – מָה רָאָה? אָמַר רַב: רָאָה מַמָּשׁ, כִּדְתַנְיָא, רַבָּן שִׁמְעוֹן בֶּן גַּמְלִיאֵל אוֹמֵר: כׇּל מָקוֹם שֶׁנָּתְנוּ חֲכָמִים עֵינֵיהֶם – אוֹ מִיתָה אוֹ עוֹנִי; וּשְׁמוּאֵל אָמַר: רָאָה שֶׁכּוּלָּן נִתְעַבְּרָה בָּהֶן אִמָּן בְּיוֹם הַכִּיפּוּרִים;

The verse further states with regard to the same incident: **"And he turned behind him and saw them, and he cursed them in the name of the Lord"** (II Kings 2:24). The Gemara asks: **What did he see?** There are four explanations offered. **Rav says:** He **literally saw,**[N] i.e., he stared and bored his eyes into them, **as it is taught** in a *baraita*: **Rabban Shimon ben Gamliel says: Wherever** it states **that the Sages placed their eyes** upon a certain person, they brought upon that person **either death or poverty. And Shmuel says: He saw** their essential nature, **that all their mothers became pregnant with them on Yom Kippur,** when conjugal relations are forbidden.

וְרַבִּי יִצְחָק נַפָּחָא אָמַר: בְּלוֹרִית רָאָה לָהֶן כְּגוֹיִים; וְרַבִּי יוֹחָנָן אָמַר: רָאָה שֶׁלֹּא הָיְתָה בָּהֶן לַחְלוּחִית שֶׁל מִצְוָה. וְדִלְמָא בְּזַרְעַיְיהוּ נִיהְוָה הֲוָה! אָמַר רַבִּי אֶלְעָזָר: לֹא בָּם וְלֹא בְּזַרְעָם עַד סוֹף כׇּל הַדּוֹרוֹת.

And Rabbi Yitzḥak Nappaḥa says: He saw that **they had plaited locks**[B] grown on the back of their heads **like the gentiles. And Rabbi Yoḥanan says: He saw that they did not contain** even a **smidgen of a mitzva.** The Gemara raises an objection to this last interpretation of Rabbi Yoḥanan: **But** how could he curse them just because they did not have any mitzvot? **Perhaps their descendants would have** many mitzvot. **Rabbi Elazar says:** He saw that mitzvot would be found **neither in them nor in their descendants, through all generations.**

״וַתֵּצֶאנָה שְׁתַּיִם דֻּבִּים מִן הַיַּעַר וַתְּבַקַּעְנָה מֵהֶם אַרְבָּעִים וּשְׁנֵי יְלָדִים.״

The verse states: **"And two she-bears came out of the forest and tore forty-two children from them"** (II Kings 2:24).

NOTES

Are frightened – דִּבְעִיתִי: Rashi explains that had there been no forest the bears would have been too frightened to attack the youths. The Maharsha, however, maintains that since the appearance of the bears was miraculous, ordinary animal behavior is irrelevant. Instead, he explains that if the bears would have attacked in the open, the lads would have seen them, become frightened, and ran away. The forest was therefore necessary to prevent them from observing the bears' approach.

רַב וּשְׁמוּאֵל, חַד אָמַר: נֵס, וְחַד אָמַר: נֵס בְּתוֹךְ נֵס. מַאן דְּאָמַר נֵס – יַעַר הֲוָה, דּוּבִּים לָא הֲווּ; מַאן דְּאָמַר נֵס בְּתוֹךְ נֵס – לָא יַעַר הֲוָה וְלָא דּוּבִּים הֲווּ. וְלֶיהֱוֵי דּוּבִּים וְלָא לֶיהֱוֵי יַעַר! דִּבְעִיתִי.

Rav and Shmuel had a dispute with regard to this episode. **One** says there was **a miracle, and one says** there **was a miracle within a miracle.** The Gemara explains: **The one who says** there was **a miracle** claims that **there was** already **a forest** in that place but **there were no bears,** and the miracle was the appearance of bears. **The one who says** it was **a miracle within a miracle** claims **that neither was there a forest nor were there bears** in that area. The Gemara asks with regard to the second opinion: Why was a double miracle required? **And let there be bears and no forest;** the forest served no role in the story, so why was it created? The Gemara explains: The forest was necessary, as bears **are frightened**[NB] to venture into open areas but will attack people in their natural habitat, a forest.

BACKGROUND

Are frightened – דִּבְעִיתִי: Despite the fact that bears are large, strong animals that are quite capable of killing people, it is not common for bears, especially the species that were found in Eretz Yisrael, to attack human beings. Generally, when a bear encounters a person it will turn aside and try to avoid confrontation. When a person enters the territory of the bear, especially the territory of a female bear protecting her young, the bear will overcome its fear of humans and will attack.

אָמַר רַבִּי חֲנִינָא: בִּשְׁבִיל אַרְבָּעִים וּשְׁנַיִם קָרְבָּנוֹת שֶׁהִקְרִיב בָּלָק מֶלֶךְ מוֹאָב, הוּבְקְעוּ מִיִּשְׂרָאֵל אַרְבָּעִים וּשְׁנַיִם יְלָדִים. אִינִי?

Rabbi Ḥanina says: Due to forty-two[N] **offerings that Balak, king of Moab, brought** when he tried to have Balaam curse the Jewish people, **forty-two children were broken off from Israel,** in that incident involving Elisha. The Gemara asks: **Is that so?** Was that the reward for his offerings?

וְהָאָמַר רַב יְהוּדָה אָמַר רַב: לְעוֹלָם יַעֲסוֹק אָדָם בְּתוֹרָה וּבְמִצְוֹת וְאַף עַל פִּי שֶׁלֹּא לִשְׁמָהּ, שֶׁמִּתּוֹךְ שֶׁלֹּא לִשְׁמָהּ בָּא לִשְׁמָהּ, שֶׁבִּשְׂכַר אַרְבָּעִים וּשְׁנַיִם קָרְבָּנוֹת שֶׁהִקְרִיב בָּלָק מֶלֶךְ מוֹאָב, זָכָה וְיָצְתָה מִמֶּנּוּ רוּת, שֶׁיָּצָא מִמֶּנּוּ שְׁלֹמֹה שֶׁכָּתוּב בֵּיהּ ״אֶלֶף עֹלוֹת יַעֲלֶה שְׁלֹמֹה״, וְאָמַר רַבִּי יוֹסֵי בֶּן חוֹנִי: רוּת בִּתּוֹ שֶׁל עֶגְלוֹן בְּנוֹ שֶׁל בָּלָק הָיְתָה! תַּאֲוָתוֹ מִיהָא לְקַלָּלָה הֲוַי.

But didn't Rav Yehuda say that **Rav says: A person should always engage in Torah** study **and** in performance of **mitzvot, even** if he does so **not for their own sake, as through** such acts performed **not for their own sake,** one will **come** to perform them **for their own sake.** He proves the value of a mitzva done not for its own sake: **As in reward for the forty-two offerings that Balak, king of Moab, brought, he merited that Ruth descended from him, from whom** King **Solomon descended, about whom it is written** that he brought many offerings: **"A thousand burnt-offerings did Solomon offer up"** (I Kings 3:4). **And Rabbi Yosei ben Ḥoni** similarly **says: Ruth was the daughter of Eglon, son of Balak.** These Sages state that Balak's reward was to have Ruth descend from him, not that a number of Jewish people perish. The Gemara answers: **His desire, in any event, was to curse** the Jewish people, and his reward for sacrificing his offerings was that the curse was fulfilled in the incident involving Elisha, as well.

״וַיֹּאמְרוּ אַנְשֵׁי הָעִיר אֶל אֱלִישָׁע הִנֵּה נָא מוֹשַׁב הָעִיר טוֹב כַּאֲשֶׁר אֲדֹנִי רֹאֶה״ וגו׳. וְכִי מֵאַחַר דְּמַיִם רָעִים וְאֶרֶץ מְשַׁכֶּלֶת, אֶלָּא מַה טּוֹבָתָהּ? אָמַר רַבִּי חָנִין: חֵן מָקוֹם עַל יוֹשְׁבָיו. אָמַר רַבִּי יוֹחָנָן, שְׁלֹשָׁה חִינּוֹת הֵן: חֵן מָקוֹם עַל יוֹשְׁבָיו, חֵן אִשָּׁה עַל בַּעְלָהּ, חֵן מִקָּח עַל מִקָּחוֹ.

The Gemara returns to discussing the incident involving Elisha: **"And the men of the city said to Elisha: Behold, please, the situation of this city is pleasant, as my lord sees,** but the water is bad and the land miscarries" (II Kings 2:19). The Gemara asks: **But if the water is bad and the land causes women to miscarry, what is pleasant** about **it? Rabbi Ḥanin says: The grace of a place is upon its inhabitants,** i.e., people are fond of their hometown despite its shortcomings. **Rabbi Yoḥanan says: There are three graces** that have a similar impact: **The grace of a place upon its inhabitants; the grace of a woman upon her husband,** despite her faults; and **the grace of a purchased** item **upon its buyer,** as one who has bought something views it in a positive light.

תָּנוּ רַבָּנַן, שְׁלֹשָׁה חֳלָאִין חָלָה אֱלִישָׁע: אֶחָד שֶׁגֵּירָה דּוּבִּים בְּתִינוֹקוֹת, וְאֶחָד שֶׁדְּחָפוֹ לְגֵחֲזִי בִּשְׁתֵּי יָדַיִם, וְאֶחָד שֶׁמֵּת בּוֹ, שֶׁנֶּאֱמַר: ״וֶאֱלִישָׁע חָלָה אֶת חָלְיוֹ אֲשֶׁר יָמוּת בּוֹ״.

§ **The Sages taught: Elisha fell ill three times. One** was a punishment **for inciting** the **bears to** attack **the children; and one** was a punishment **for pushing Gehazi** away **with both hands,** without leaving him the option to return; **and one** was the sickness **from which he died, as** an expression of illness **is stated** three times in the verse about Elisha: **"And Elisha became sick [*ḥala*] with his illness [*ḥolyo*] from which he would die"** (II Kings 13:14). The root *ḥet, lamed, heh,* which indicates illness, is used twice in this verse, and it is stated once that Elisha will die.

תָּנוּ רַבָּנַן: לְעוֹלָם תְּהֵא שְׂמֹאל דּוֹחָה וְיָמִין מְקָרֶבֶת, לֹא כֶּאֱלִישָׁע שֶׁדְּחָפוֹ לְגֵחֲזִי בִּשְׁתֵּי יָדָיו, וְלֹא כִּיהוֹשֻׁעַ בֶּן פְּרַחְיָה שֶׁדְּחָפוֹ לְיֵשׁוּ הַנּוֹצְרִי מִתַּלְמִידָיו בִּשְׁתֵּי יָדָיו.

The Sages taught: It should always be the left, weaker, hand that **pushes** another away **and the right,** stronger, hand that **draws** him **near.** In other words, even when a student is rebuffed, he should be given the opportunity to return. This is **not like Elisha, who pushed Gehazi** away **with both hands, and not like Yehoshua ben Peraḥya, who pushed Jesus the Nazarene,** one **of his students,** away **with both hands.**

אֱלִישָׁע מַאי הִיא? דִּכְתִיב: ״וַיֹּאמֶר נַעֲמָן הוֹאֵל קַח כִּכָּרָיִם״, וּכְתִיב: ״וַיֹּאמֶר אֵלָיו לֹא לִבִּי הָלַךְ כַּאֲשֶׁר הָפַךְ אִישׁ מֵעַל מֶרְכַּבְתּוֹ לִקְרָאתֶךָ הַעֵת לָקַחַת אֶת הַכֶּסֶף וְלָקַחַת בְּגָדִים וְזֵיתִים וּכְרָמִים וְצֹאן וּבָקָר וַעֲבָדִים וּשְׁפָחוֹת?״

The Gemara specifies: **What was** that incident with **Elisha? As it is written: "And Naaman said: Pray, take talents"** (II Kings 5:23). Naaman offered Gehazi payment for the help Elisha had given him, **and** when the verse recounts Elisha's words to Gehazi, it **is written: "And he said to him: Did not my heart go, when the man turned back from his chariot to meet you? Is it a time to take money, and to take garments, and olives, and vineyards, and sheep, and oxen, and servants, and maidservants?"** (II Kings 5:26). Here Elisha criticizes Gehazi for taking the payment.

NOTES

Due to forty-two, etc. – בִּשְׁבִיל אַרְבָּעִים וּשְׁנַיִם וכו׳: Balak's aim in bringing those offerings was to curse Israel and decrease their population, and this occurred with the death of those children (Maharsha).

וּמִי שָׁקֵיל כּוּלֵּי הַאי? כֶּסֶף וּבְגָדִים הוּא דְּשָׁקֵיל! אָמַר רַבִּי יִצְחָק: בְּאוֹתָהּ שָׁעָה הָיָה אֱלִישָׁע עוֹסֵק בִּשְׁמֹנָה שְׁרָצִים. אָמַר לוֹ: רָשָׁע! הִגִּיעַ עֵת לִיטּוֹל שְׂכַר שְׁמֹנָה שְׁרָצִים. ״וְצָרַעַת נַעֲמָן תִּדְבַּק בְּךָ וּבְזַרְעֲךָ לְעוֹלָם״. ״וְאַרְבָּעָה אֲנָשִׁים הָיוּ מְצֹרָעִים״ – אָמַר רַבִּי יוֹחָנָן: זֶה גֵּחֲזִי וּשְׁלֹשֶׁת בָּנָיו.

The Gemara clarifies the criticism: **And did he take all that?** But it was only **money and garments that he took. Rabbi Yitzḥak says: At that time, Elisha was engaged in** the study of the topic of the **eight** impure **creeping animals.**[B] **He said** to Gehazi: **Wicked one, it is time** for you **to receive** now, in this temporal world, **the reward** for studying the topic of the **eight** impure **creeping animals.** This is why the verse lists eight items. The Gemara adds parenthetically that Elisha also said to Gehazi: **"And the leprosy of Naaman shall cleave to you and to your descendants forever"** (II Kings 5:27), and that the verse later states: **"Now there were four leprous men"** (II Kings 7:3), about whom **Rabbi Yoḥanan says: This is** referring to **Gehazi and his three sons.**

״וַיָּבֹא אֱלִישָׁע דַּמֶּשֶׂק״ – לְמָה הָלַךְ? אָמַר רַבִּי יוֹחָנָן: שֶׁהָלַךְ לְהַחֲזִירוֹ לְגֵיחֲזִי בִּתְשׁוּבָה, וְלֹא חָזַר. אָמַר לוֹ: חֲזוֹר בְּךָ! אָמַר לוֹ, כָּךְ מְקוּבְּלַנִי מִמְּךָ: כׇּל מִי שֶׁחָטָא וְהֶחְטִיא אֶת הָרַבִּים – אֵין מַסְפִּיקִין בְּיָדוֹ לַעֲשׂוֹת תְּשׁוּבָה.

The verse states: **"And Elisha came to Damascus"** (II Kings 8:7). The Gemara asks: **For what** purpose did **he go** there? **Rabbi Yoḥanan says: He went to help Gehazi in repentance, but** Gehazi **would not** agree to **repent** from his evil ways. Elisha **said to him: Return from your** sins. Gehazi **said to him: This is** the tradition that **I received from you: Whoever sins and caused the masses to sin is not given the opportunity to repent.**

מַאי עֲבַד? אִיכָּא דְּאָמְרִי: אֶבֶן שׁוֹאֶבֶת תָּלָה לוֹ לְחַטַּאת יָרׇבְעָם וְהֶעֱמִידוֹ בֵּין שָׁמַיִם לָאָרֶץ. וְאִיכָּא דְּאָמְרִי: שֵׁם חָקַק לָהּ אַפּוּמַּהּ, וְהָיְתָה אוֹמֶרֶת ״אָנֹכִי״, וְ״לֹא יִהְיֶה לְךָ״.

The Gemara asks: **What did** Gehazi **do** that caused the masses to sin? **There are** those **who say** that **he hung a magnetic rock**[B] **on Jeroboam's calf,** the golden calf that Jeroboam established as an idol, and used a magnet to pull the calf off the ground so that **he suspended it between heaven and earth,** i.e., caused it to hover above the ground. This seemingly miraculous occurrence caused the people to worship it even more devoutly. **And there are** those **who say: He engraved** the sacred **name on its mouth, and it would say: "I am** the Lord your God" **and: "You shall not have** other gods" (Exodus 20:2). The idol would quote the two prohibitions from the Ten Commandments against idol worship, causing people to worship it even more devoutly.

וְאִיכָּא דְּאָמְרִי: רַבָּנַן דָּחָה מִקַּמֵּיהּ, דִּכְתִיב: ״וַיֹּאמְרוּ בְנֵי הַנְּבִיאִים אֶל אֱלִישָׁע הִנֵּה נָא הַמָּקוֹם אֲשֶׁר אֲנַחְנוּ יֹשְׁבִים שָׁם לְפָנֶיךָ צַר מִמֶּנּוּ״, מִכְּלָל דְּעַד הָאִידָּנָא לָא הֲוָה דָּחֵיק.

And there are those **who say:** Gehazi **pushed the Sages** away **from** coming **before him,** preventing them learning from Elisha, **as it is written,** after the aforementioned incident: **"And the sons of the prophets said to Elisha, behold this place where we are staying before you is too cramped for us"** (II Kings 6:1). This proves **by inference that until that time** the place **was not cramped,** as Gehazi would turn people away.

יְהוֹשֻׁעַ בֶּן פְּרַחְיָה מַאי הִיא? כִּדַהֲוָה קָא קָטֵיל יַנַּאי מַלְכָּא לְרַבָּנַן שִׁמְעוֹן בֶּן שָׁטַח אַטְמִינְהוּ אַחְתֵּיהּ. רַבִּי יְהוֹשֻׁעַ בֶּן פְּרַחְיָה אֲזַל עֲרַק לְאַלֶּכְּסַנְדְּרִיָּא שֶׁל מִצְרַיִם. כִּי הֲוָה שְׁלָמָא שְׁלַח לֵיהּ שִׁמְעוֹן בֶּן שָׁטַח: מִנִּי יְרוּשָׁלַיִם עִיר הַקּוֹדֶשׁ לָךְ אַלֶּכְּסַנְדְּרִיָּא שֶׁל מִצְרַיִם: אֲחוֹתִי, בַּעְלִי שָׁרוּי בְּתוֹכֵךְ, וַאֲנִי יוֹשֶׁבֶת שׁוֹמֵמָה! אֲמַר: שְׁמַע מִינָּהּ הֲוָה לֵיהּ שְׁלָמָא.

The Gemara returns to the incident in which **Yehoshua ben Peraḥya** turned away Jesus the Nazarene: **What is** this incident? **When King Yannai was killing the Sages,**[B] **Shimon ben Shataḥ was hidden by his sister,** Yannai's wife, while **Rabbi Yehoshua ben Peraḥya went** and **fled to Alexandria of Egypt.**[B] **When peace was made** between Yannai and the Sages, **Shimon ben Shataḥ sent him** the following letter: **From myself, Jerusalem the holy city, to you, Alexandria of Egypt. My sister, my husband dwells within you, and I am sitting desolate.** Rabbi Yehoshua ben Peraḥya **said:** I can **learn from it that there is peace,** and I can return.

כִּי אֲתָא אִקְלַע לְהַהוּא אוּשְׁפִּיזָא. קָם קַמַּיְיהוּ בִּיקָרָא שַׁפִּיר, עָבְדִי לֵיהּ יְקָרָא טוּבָא. יָתֵיב וְקָא מִשְׁתַּבַּח: כַּמָּה נָאָה אַכְסַנְיָא זוֹ! אֲמַר לֵיהּ יֵשׁוּ הַנּוֹצְרִי: רַבִּי, עֵינֶיהָ טְרוּטוֹת! אֲמַר לֵיהּ: רָשָׁע, בְּכָךְ אַתָּה עוֹסֵק! אַפֵּיק אַרְבַּע מֵאָה שִׁיפּוּרֵי, וְשַׁמְתֵּיהּ. כׇּל יוֹמָא אֲתָא לְקַמֵּיהּ, וְלָא קַבְּלֵיהּ.

When he came back to Eretz Yisrael, Rabbi Yehoshua **arrived at a certain inn.** The innkeeper **stood before him, honoring him considerably,** and overall **they accorded him great honor.** Rabbi Yehoshua ben Peraḥya then **sat and was praising** them by saying: **How beautiful is this inn. Jesus the Nazarene,**[B] one of his students, **said to him: My teacher,** but the **eyes** of the innkeeper's wife **are narrow** [*terutot*].[L] Rabbi Yehoshua ben Peraḥya **said to him: Wicked one, is this what you are engaged in,** gazing at women? **He brought out four hundred** ***shofarot*** **and excommunicated him. Every day** Jesus **would come before him, but he would not accept** his wish to return.

BACKGROUND

The eight creeping animals – שְׁמֹנָה שְׁרָצִים: These are eight creeping animals, small mammals and lizards, whose carcasses impart ritual impurity upon contact (Leviticus 11:29–30). As there is no clear oral tradition with regard to the identity of these animals, determination of their identity involves educated conjecture. Even commonly accepted identifications, such as the dab lizard [*tzav*] and the mouse [*akhbar*], are subject to debate, and the Talmud's description of these animals is insufficient to provide definitive identifications.

Magnetic rock – אֶבֶן שׁוֹאֶבֶת: People were already aware in ancient times that certain compounds, such as iron oxide, attract chunks of iron. The use of ruses such as this to purport to demonstrate the power of idols was common in that time and in the Near East, especially in Egypt.

King Yannai was killing the Sages – קָא קָטֵיל יַנַּאי מַלְכָּא לְרַבָּנַן: King Yannai, who tended, as did his father, toward the camp of the Sadducees, had an open break with the Sages after his defeat in the battle with the Nabateans. According to Josephus (Antiquities of the Jews, book 13), the split was deepened after he refused to perform the ritual of the water libation in the Temple. He was then pelted with *etrogim* from the crowd that was present there, and he had his army kill those who were in the Temple. This led to a civil war, lasting several years. After Yannai was victorious in this war, he killed many of his opponents, including many of the leaders of the Pharisees. Several of those leaders, Rabbi Yehoshua ben Peraḥya among them, escaped to outside Eretz Yisrael, while others, among them Rabbi Shimon ben Shataḥ, hid within Eretz Yisrael. Although there was a period of calm in the later years of Yannai's reign, it seems that only after his death, when control had passed into the hands of the Pharisees, did all of the Sages return to Eretz Yisrael.

Alexandria of Egypt – אַלֶּכְּסַנְדְּרִיָּא שֶׁל מִצְרַיִם: Since there were many cities in Asia and Africa that were called Alexandria, the Gemara specified that this refers to the Alexandria in Egypt. There was a large and important Jewish community in Alexandria for many generations, and its central synagogue was famous for its tremendous size. Many of the great Sages visited there and discussed many issues that arose in connection with that community. This community was apparently destroyed in the cruel crushing of the Jewish rebellion in the years 66 and 115 CE.

Jesus the Nazarene – יֵשׁוּ הַנּוֹצְרִי: Many scholars, first and foremost several of the Tosafists, have pointed out that Rabbi Yehoshua ben Peraḥya and Yannai lived, at the latest, around the year 76 BCE. This means that it is impossible that the Jesus referred to in the story was the founder of Christianity. He must have been a different person with the same name. It may be that the other talmudic references to Jesus are to this person, or it may be that some of those references are to the founder of Christianity.

LANGUAGE

Narrow [*terutot*] – טְרוּטוֹת: It may be that the source of this word is from the Greek δηρός, *dēros*, which means long or excessively long. It may also be from the Latin teretis, which means with rounded corners, smooth, or polished. In this context, it seems to mean that her eyes were extremely narrow.

יוֹמָא חַד הֲוָה קָרֵי קְרִיַּת שְׁמַע, אֲתָא לְקַמֵּיהּ. הֲוָה בְּדַעְתֵּיהּ לְקַבּוֹלֵיהּ. אַחֲוֵי לֵיהּ בִּידֵיהּ. סָבַר מִדְחָא דָּחֵי לֵיהּ. אֲזַל זְקַף לְבֵינְתָא פְּלַחָא. אֲמַר לֵיהּ: חֲזוֹר בְּךָ! אֲמַר לֵיהּ: כָּךְ מְקוּבְּלַנִי מִמְּךָ, כָּל הַחוֹטֵא וּמַחֲטִיא אֶת הָרַבִּים – אֵין מַסְפִּיקִין בְּיָדוֹ לַעֲשׂוֹת תְּשׁוּבָה. דְּאָמַר מָר: יֵשׁוּ הַנּוֹצְרִי כִּישֵּׁף וְהֵסִית וְהִדִּיחַ וְהֶחְטִיא אֶת יִשְׂרָאֵל.

One day, Rabbi Yehoshua ben Peraḥya **was reciting *Shema*** when Jesus **came before him. He intended to accept him** on this occasion, so **he signaled to him with his hand** to wait. Jesus **thought he was rejecting him** entirely. He therefore **went and stood up a brick**[B] **and worshipped it** as an idol. Rabbi Yehoshua ben Peraḥya **said to him: Return from your** sins. Jesus **said to him: This is** the tradition that **I received from you: Anyone who sins and causes the masses to sin is not given the opportunity to repent.** The Gemara explains how he caused the masses to sin: **For the Master said: Jesus the Nazarene performed sorcery, and he incited** the masses, **and subverted** the masses, **and caused the Jewish people to sin.**

תַּנְיָא, רַבִּי שִׁמְעוֹן בֶּן אֶלְעָזָר אוֹמֵר: יֵצֶר, תִּינוֹק וְאִשָּׁה, תְּהֵא שְׂמֹאל דּוֹחָה וְיָמִין מְקָרֶבֶת.

It is taught in a *baraita* that **Rabbi Shimon ben Elazar says:** With regard to the evil **inclination, to a child, and to a woman,**[N] **the left** hand **should reject**[N] **and the right** hand should **welcome.** If one pushes too forcefully, the damage might be irreversible.

מתני׳ נִמְצָא הַהוֹרֵג, עַד שֶׁלֹּא נֶעֶרְפָה הָעֶגְלָה – תֵּצֵא וְתִרְעֶה בָּעֵדֶר. מִשֶּׁנֶּעֶרְפָה הָעֶגְלָה – תִּקָּבֵר בִּמְקוֹמָהּ, שֶׁעַל סָפֵק בָּאתָה מִתְּחִילָּתָהּ, כִּיפְּרָה סְפֵיקָהּ וְהָלְכָה לָהּ. נֶעֶרְפָה הָעֶגְלָה וְאַחַר כָּךְ נִמְצָא הַהוֹרֵג – הֲרֵי זֶה יֵהָרֵג.

MISHNA **If the killer is found**[H] **before the heifer's neck was broken,** the heifer **shall go out and graze among the herd.**[N] It is not considered sacred at all, and it may rejoin the other animals. If the killer is found **from** the time **when the heifer's neck was broken,** even if the rest of the ritual has not yet been performed, it is prohibited to benefit from the animal, despite the killer having been found; it **should be buried in its place.** This is **because** the heifer **initially came for uncertainty,** as the killer was unknown, and **it atoned** for **its uncertainty and left,** i.e., it fulfilled its purpose of bringing atonement and is considered a heifer whose neck is broken in all regards. If **the heifer's neck was broken and afterward the killer was found, he is killed.** The ritual does not atone for him.

עֵד אֶחָד אוֹמֵר: "רָאִיתִי אֶת הַהוֹרֵג", וְעֵד אֶחָד אוֹמֵר: "לֹא רָאִיתָ"; אִשָּׁה אוֹמֶרֶת: "רָאִיתִי", וְאִשָּׁה אוֹמֶרֶת: "לֹא רָאִיתָ" – הָיוּ עוֹרְפִין. עֵד אֶחָד אוֹמֵר: "רָאִיתִי", וּשְׁנַיִם אוֹמְרִים: "לֹא רָאִיתָ" – הָיוּ עוֹרְפִין. שְׁנַיִם אוֹמְרִים: "רָאִינוּ", וְאֶחָד אוֹמֵר לָהֶן: "לֹא רְאִיתֶם" – לֹא הָיוּ עוֹרְפִין.

If one witness says: I saw[H] **the killer,**[N] **and one** other **witness says: You did not see** him; or if **a woman says: I saw, and** another **woman says: You did not see, they would break the neck** of the heifer, as without clear testimony about the identity of the killer the ritual is performed. Similarly, if **one witness says: I saw** the killer, **and two** witnesses **say: You did not see,**[H] **they would break the neck** of the heifer, as the pair is relied upon. If **two** witnesses **say: We saw**[H] the killer, **and one** witness **says to them: You did not see, they would not break the neck** of the heifer, as there are two witnesses to the identity of the killer.

מִשֶּׁרַבּוּ הָרוֹצְחָנִין – בָּטְלָה עֶגְלָה עֲרוּפָה. מִשֶּׁבָּא אֱלִיעֶזֶר בֶּן דִּינַאי, וּתְחִינָה בֶּן פְּרִישָׁה הָיָה נִקְרָא – חָזְרוּ לִקְרוֹתוֹ בֶּן הָרַצְחָן.

The mishna further states: **From the time when murderers proliferated,**[H] **the** ritual of the **heifer whose neck is broken was nullified.** The ritual was performed only when the identity of the murderer was completely unknown. Once there were many known murderers, the conditions for the performance of the ritual were no longer present, as the probable identity of the murderer was known. **From the time when Eliezer ben Dinai,**[P] **who was also called Teḥina ben Perisha,**[N] **came, they renamed him: Son of a murderer.** This is an example of a publicly known murderer.

BACKGROUND

Stood up a brick – זְקַף לְבֵינְתָא: It is not known if this was a common form of idol worship, or if he, in anger, simply picked up an item at hand. There are bricks that have been found with the image of idols carved into them, and perhaps in this incident he took a brick that had the image of an idol on it.

NOTES

Evil inclination, a child, and a woman – יֵצֶר, תִּינוֹק וְאִשָּׁה: Most understand the term evil inclination to be referring to sexual desire. The *ge'onim* explain that if one attempts to repress his sexual desire entirely, he will be unable to sustain this in the long term and will end up transgressing actual prohibitions. The Meiri similarly writes that a person cannot maintain the sublimation of his sexual desire, as it is an essential part of human nature. Others state that a person should not suppress sexual desire completely, as it is necessary to populate the world (see Rashi).

The left should reject, etc. – שְׂמֹאל דּוֹחָה וכו׳: The inference is that one should use the weaker hand for rejecting, indicating that it should not be done with full force (see *Iyyun Ya'akov*).

Shall go out and graze among the herd – תֵּצֵא וְתִרְעֶה בָּעֵדֶר: Rashi writes, based on *Karetot* 25a, that the *tanna* of this mishna disagrees with the opinion that it is prohibited to benefit from a heifer whose neck is broken from the time it is brought down to the valley, even before being killed, and that is why it may rejoin the flock. The Jerusalem Talmud, however, states the reverse, that this mishna offers support for the opinion that the heifer is forbidden while it is yet alive, as the term: Shall go out, indicates that it was previously sacred and now goes back to its previous, non-sacred status. The Rambam cites both rulings as *halakha*: It is prohibited to benefit from the heifer once it enters the valley and it may go out to graze.

I saw the killer – רָאִיתִי אֶת הַהוֹרֵג: The wording of the mishna indicates that the ritual is not performed if a witness merely saw the killer, even if he does not know who he is. However, it is stated in the Jerusalem Talmud that the witness must be aware of the identity of the killer, and *Tosefot HaRosh* explains similarly.

Teḥina ben Perisha, etc. – וּתְחִינָה בֶּן פְּרִישָׁה וכו׳: *Tosefot Yom Tov* expresses puzzlement at this, as it is unclear from the mishna why this man was given two names. He therefore prefers a version of the text according to which the mishna discusses two people, Eliezer ben Dinai and someone else named Teḥina ben Perisha, the latter of which was later called son of a murderer. Other commentaries explain that he was first called ben Dinai because he would sue [*mitdayen*] and fight people, and later he was given the nickname of ben Perisha, as he was separated [*parush*] and estranged from human society. When his behavior deteriorated further, they simply called him: Son of a murderer (*Tiferet Yisrael*). Alternatively, he was initially dubbed Teḥina ben Perisha because he acted for the sake of Heaven, as *teḥina* means supplication and *perishut* means asceticism, but when he became corrupt they called him son of a murderer (*Ben Yehoyada*).

PERSONALITIES

Ben Dinai – בֶּן דִּינַאי: Ben Dinai, or ben Dunai, is also mentioned as a famous murderer in tractate *Ketubot*. He is also mentioned by his contemporary, Josephus Flavius, who tells that ben Dinai led a band of armed robbers and murderers in the Galilee for twenty years, until the Romans, using subterfuge, captured him and brought him to judgment in Rome. Although it is not explicitly stated, it seems, based on the context of Josephus's writings, that ben Dinai was also active politically, a type of partisan leader who fought against the Roman rule. This would also explain why he was brought to Rome for judgment and not judged in Eretz Yisrael.

HALAKHA

If the killer is found – נִמְצָא הַהוֹרֵג: If the killer is found before the heifer's neck is broken, it goes out to graze with the rest of the herd. If he is found after the breaking of the neck, the animal is buried where it is, as it was brought only due to uncertainty in the first place. The killer is executed even if he is found after the heifer's neck was broken (Rambam *Sefer Nezikim, Hilkhot Rotze'aḥ UShmirat HaNefesh* 10:8).

One witness says: I saw, etc. – עֵד אֶחָד אוֹמֵר רָאִיתִי וכו׳: In a case where one witness said: I saw the killer, while another witness contradicts his claim, saying: You did not see him, if the two witnesses came to the court together, the ritual would be performed (Rambam *Sefer Nezikim, Hilkhot Rotze'aḥ UShmirat HaNefesh* 9:13).

And two say: You did not see – וּשְׁנַיִם אוֹמְרִים לֹא רָאִיתָ: If one witness came and said: I saw the killer, and two others said to him: You did not see him, they would break the neck of the heifer (Rambam *Sefer Nezikim, Hilkhot Rotze'aḥ UShmirat HaNefesh* 9:14).

And two say: We saw, etc. – שְׁנַיִם אוֹמְרִים רָאִינוּ וכו׳: If two witnesses said: We saw the killer, and one other witness said: You did not see him, they would not break the neck of the heifer (Rambam *Sefer Nezikim, Hilkhot Rotze'aḥ UShmirat HaNefesh* 9:14).

From the time when murderers proliferated – מִשֶּׁרַבּוּ הָרוֹצְחָנִין: Once murderers openly proliferated, the ritual of the heifer whose neck is broken was nullified, as the court would not perform the ritual if anyone saw the killer, and it is assumed that someone must have witnessed him (Rambam *Sefer Nezikim, Hilkhot Rotze'aḥ UShmirat HaNefesh* 9:12).

מִשֶּׁרַבּוּ הַמְנָאֲפִים – פָּסְקוּ הַמַּיִם הַמָּרִים, וְרַבִּי יוֹחָנָן בֶּן זַכַּאי הִפְסִיקָן, שֶׁנֶּאֱמַר: ״לֹא אֶפְקוֹד עַל בְּנוֹתֵיכֶם כִּי תִזְנֶינָה וְעַל כַּלּוֹתֵיכֶם כִּי תְנָאַפְנָה כִּי הֵם״ וגו׳.

The mishna teaches a similar occurrence: **From** the time **when adulterers proliferated,**[H] the performance of the ritual of **the bitter waters was nullified;** they would not administer the bitter waters to the *sota*. **And** it was **Rabbi Yoḥanan ben Zakkai** who **nullified it, as it is stated: "I will not punish your daughters when they commit harlotry, nor your daughters-in-law when they commit adultery; for they** consort with lewd women" (Hosea 4:14), meaning that when the husbands are adulterers, the wives are not punished for their own adultery.

מִשֶּׁמֵּת יוֹסֵי בֶּן יוֹעֶזֶר אִישׁ צְרֵידָה וְיוֹסֵי בֶּן יְהוּדָה אִישׁ יְרוּשָׁלַיִם – בָּטְלוּ הָאֶשְׁכּוֹלוֹת, שֶׁנֶּאֱמַר: ״אֵין אֶשְׁכּוֹל לֶאֱכוֹל בִּכּוּרָה אִוְּתָה נַפְשִׁי״. יוֹחָנָן כֹּהֵן גָּדוֹל הֶעֱבִיר הוֹדָיַית הַמַּעֲשֵׂר; אַף הוּא בִּטֵּל אֶת הַמְעוֹרְרִין וְאֶת הַנּוֹקְפִין.

From the time **when Yosei ben Yo'ezer of Tzereida and Yosei ben Yehuda of Jerusalem died, the clusters ceased,** i.e., they were the last of the clusters, as explained in the Gemara, **as it is stated: "There is no cluster to eat;**[N] **nor first-ripe fig that my soul desires"** (Micah 7:1). The mishna continues in the same vein: **Yoḥanan the High Priest took away the declaration of the tithe.** After his time, no one recited the passage about the elimination of tithes that had previously been said at the end of a three-year tithing cycle. **He also nullified** the actions of **the awakeners and the strikers** at the Temple.

HALAKHA

From the time when adulterers proliferated, etc. – מִשֶּׁרַבּוּ הַמְנָאֲפִים וכו׳: Once adulterous men openly proliferated, the Sanhedrin nullified the rite of the bitter waters, in reliance upon the prophet's words: "I will not punish your daughters when they commit harlotry, nor your daughters-in-law when they commit adultery." The Ramban writes that the waters would not be effective in testing a man's wife even if his son or a member of his household was an adulterer (Rambam *Sefer Nashim, Hilkhot Sota* 3:19).

NOTES

There is no cluster to eat – אֵין אֶשְׁכּוֹל לֶאֱכוֹל: In this verse, Micah laments that there are no more great people with whom he can associate, indicating that a great person is called a cluster.

Perek **IX**
Daf **47** Amud **b**

עַד יָמָיו הָיָה פַּטִּישׁ מַכֶּה בִּירוּשָׁלַיִם; וּבְיָמָיו אֵין צָרִיךְ לִשְׁאוֹל עַל הַדְּמַאי.

Until his days the hammer of smiths **would strike in Jerusalem** on the intermediate days of a Festival, but he banned the practice. **And** furthermore, **in his days there was no need to inquire about doubtfully tithed produce** [*demai*], as everyone was careful to tithe.

גמ׳ תָּנוּ רַבָּנַן: מִנַּיִן שֶׁאִם נֶעֶרְפָה הָעֶגְלָה וְאַחַר כָּךְ נִמְצָא הַהוֹרֵג, שֶׁאֵין פּוֹטֶרֶת אוֹתוֹ? תַּלְמוּד לוֹמַר: ״וְלָאָרֶץ לֹא יְכֻפַּר לַדָּם אֲשֶׁר שֻׁפַּךְ בָּהּ כִּי אִם בְּדַם שֹׁפְכוֹ״.

GEMARA **The Sages taught: From where** is it derived **that if the heifer's neck was broken and afterward the killer was found,** then the breaking of the neck **does not exempt him**[N] from punishment? **The verse states: "And the land shall not be atoned, for the blood that was spilled in it, but by the blood of he who spilled it"** (Numbers 35:33).

״עֵד אֶחָד אוֹמֵר רָאִיתִי אֶת הַהוֹרֵג״ כו׳. טַעְמָא דְּמַכְחִישׁ לֵיהּ, הָא לָא מַכְחִישׁ לֵיהּ – עֵד אֶחָד מְהֵימַן,

The mishna taught that if **one witness says: I saw the killer,** and another testifies: You did not see him, they would break the heifer's neck. The Gemara infers: **The reason** they break the neck **is** because the second witness **contradicts him, but** if **no** one **contradicts him, one witness is relied upon,** and they do not break the heifer's neck.

מְנָהָנֵי מִילֵּי? דְּתָנוּ רַבָּנַן: ״לֹא נוֹדַע מִי הִכָּהוּ״, הָא נוֹדַע מִי הִכָּהוּ – אֲפִילּוּ אֶחָד בְּסוֹף הָעוֹלָם – לֹא הָיוּ עוֹרְפִין; רַבִּי עֲקִיבָא אוֹמֵר: מִנַּיִן לְסַנְהֶדְרִין שֶׁרָאוּ אֶחָד שֶׁהָרַג אֶת הַנֶּפֶשׁ וְאֵין מַכִּירִין אוֹתוֹ, שֶׁלֹּא הָיוּ עוֹרְפִין? תַּלְמוּד לוֹמַר: ״וְעֵינֵינוּ לֹא רָאוּ״, וַהֲלֹא רָאוּ.

From where are these matters derived? The Gemara answers that it is **as the Sages taught** in a *baraita*: It states with regard to the heifer whose neck is broken: **"It is not known who has smitten him"** (Deuteronomy 21:1). **Consequently,** if **it was known**[H] **who smote him, even** if it was only **one** person **at the end of the world**[N] who knew, **they would not break the neck** of the heifer. **Rabbi Akiva says: From where** is it derived **that** if the members of the **Sanhedrin** themselves **saw one** person **kill someone, but they do not recognize him,** then **they would not break the neck** of the heifer? **The verse states: "Nor did our eyes see"** (Deuteronomy 21:7), **and** did they **not see?** Seeing the murder alone obviates the need for the performance of the ritual.

הַשְׁתָּא דְּאָמְרַתְּ עֵד אֶחָד מְהֵימַן, אִידָּךְ חַד הֵיכִי מָצֵי מַכְחִישׁ לֵיהּ? וְהָאָמַר עוּלָּא: כָּל מָקוֹם שֶׁהֶאֱמִינָה תּוֹרָה עֵד אֶחָד הֲרֵי כָּאן שְׁנַיִם, וְאֵין דְּבָרָיו שֶׁל אֶחָד בִּמְקוֹם שְׁנַיִם! אָמַר לָךְ עוּלָּא, תְּנֵי: לֹא הָיוּ עוֹרְפִין. וְכֵן אָמַר רַבִּי יִצְחָק, תְּנֵי: לֹא הָיוּ עוֹרְפִין.

The Gemara poses a question: **Now that you have said** that in this case **one witness is relied upon,** if so, **how is the other one able to contradict him? Didn't Ulla say: Wherever the Torah relies on one witness, there is** the equivalent of the testimony of **two** witnesses **here,** and **the statement of one** witness **has no** standing **in a place where** it is contradicted by **two** witnesses. The Gemara answers: **Ulla** could have **said to you** that the text of the mishna should be emended and **teach** the mishna in this way: **They would not break the neck** of the heifer. **And Rabbi Yitzḥak also said** to **teach: They would not break the neck.**

NOTES

Does not exempt him – שֶׁאֵין פּוֹטֶרֶת אוֹתוֹ: Why would one think the ritual of breaking the heifer's neck should exempt the murderer from punishment? One answer is that there are verses indicating that in the execution of a murderer there is also an element of bringing atonement for the land upon which the murder has taken place. It might be thought that the ritual of the breaking the heifer's neck could obviate this need, and as for the punishment of the murderer, that could be left to the hand of God. The mishna needs to teach that this is not the case, and the court still needs to execute him (*Devar Shaul*).

Even one at the end of the world – אֲפִילּוּ אֶחָד בְּסוֹף הָעוֹלָם: Although the murderer cannot be convicted based on the testimony of a lone witness, the ritual of the heifer whose neck is broken is performed only if the murderer's identity is not known by anyone. The later commentaries discuss the issue of how the court would know that there is one witness at the end of the world, and whether the court can rely on mere rumor in this matter (*Naḥal Eitan*).

HALAKHA

Consequently if it was known, etc. – הָא נוֹדַע וכו׳: If the identity of the murderer was known they would not break the heifer's neck (Rambam *Sefer Nezikin, Hilkhot Rotze'aḥ UShmirat HaNefesh* 9:11).

וְרַבִּי חִיָּיא אָמַר, תְּנֵי: הָיוּ עוֹרְפִין. וּלְרַבִּי חִיָּיא קַשְׁיָא דְּעוּלָּא! לָא קַשְׁיָא: כָּאן בְּבַת אַחַת, כָּאן בְּזֶה אַחַר זֶה.

And Rabbi Ḥiyya said that one should **teach: They would break the neck.** The Gemara asks: **And according to Rabbi Ḥiyya,** the above ruling **of Ulla is difficult.** The Gemara answers: This is **not difficult,** as **here,** in the mishna, the case is discussing when two witnesses came **simultaneously,**[H] and therefore both of their testimonies are rejected; whereas **there,** with regard to the statement of Ulla, it is referring to a case when they testified **one after the other.** Ulla rules that once the testimony of the first witness has been accepted the testimony of the second witness cannot nullify it.

תְּנַן: עֵד אֶחָד אוֹמֵר "רָאִיתִי אֶת הַהוֹרֵג" וּשְׁנַיִם אוֹמְרִים "לֹא רָאִיתָ" – הָיוּ עוֹרְפִין; הָא חַד וְחַד – לֹא הָיוּ עוֹרְפִין. תְּיוּבְתָּא דְּרַבִּי חִיָּיא!

We learned in the mishna: If **one witness says: I saw the killer, and two say: You did not see, they would break the neck.** This cannot be stated just to teach us this *halakha*, as the fact that two witnesses override one witness is well known. The Gemara assumes that it is stated for the following inference: **Therefore,** if **one** testified, **and** the other **one** then testified, **they would not break the neck.** This appears to be **a conclusive refutation of Rabbi Ḥiyya,** who has the text of: They would break the neck.

וְלִיטַעֲמִיךְ, אֵימָא סֵיפָא: שְׁנַיִם אוֹמְרִים "רָאִינוּ" וְעֵד אֶחָד אוֹמֵר "לֹא רְאִיתֶם" – לֹא הָיוּ עוֹרְפִין; הָא חַד וְחַד – הָיוּ עוֹרְפִין!

The Gemara answers: **And according to your reasoning** that the mishna states its cases in order to teach an inference, **say the latter clause** of the mishna: If **two** witnesses **say: We saw, and one** witness **says: You did not see, they would not break the neck.** The Gemara makes an inference from this clause: **Therefore,** if **one** came **and** then the other **one** came, i.e., they did not come simultaneously, **they would break the neck.** The two inferences from the different clauses of the mishna consequently contradict one another, and the mishna needs to be explained differently.

אֶלָּא, מַתְנִיתִין כּוּלָּהּ בִּפְסוּלֵי עֵדוּת, וּכְדְרַבִּי נְחֶמְיָה, דְּאָמַר: כָּל מָקוֹם שֶׁהֶאֱמִינָה תּוֹרָה עֵד אֶחָד – הַלֵּךְ אַחַר רוֹב דֵּעוֹת, וְעָשׂוּ שְׁתֵּי נָשִׁים בְּאִישׁ אֶחָד כִּשְׁנֵי אֲנָשִׁים בְּאִישׁ אֶחָד.

Rather, the correct understanding is that **the entire mishna** is not dealing with valid witnesses and stating an obvious *halakha* in order to enable an inference, but instead it is dealing **with** people who are **disqualified** from **bearing witness** and is also teaching us a novel ruling. **And** the mishna is **in accordance with** the opinion **of Rabbi Neḥemya, who says: Wherever the Torah relies on one witness, follow the majority of opinions.** In other words, if the testimonies of two disqualified witnesses conflict, the court rules in accordance with the testimony provided by more witnesses, whether or not they are qualified to testify. **And they established** that with regard to the testimony of **two women,** who are usually disqualified from testifying, when they testify **against one man,** it should be **like** that of **two men against one man,** and the court will rule in accordance with the testimony of the two women.

וְאִיכָּא דְּאָמְרִי: כָּל הֵיכָא דַּאֲתָא עֵד אֶחָד כָּשֵׁר מֵעִיקָּרָא – אֲפִילּוּ מֵאָה נָשִׁים כִּי אֶחָד דָּמְיָין. וְהָכָא בְּמַאי עָסְקִינַן – כְּגוֹן דַּאֲתַאי אִשָּׁה מֵעִיקָּרָא, וְתַרְצָה לִדְרַבִּי נְחֶמְיָה הָכִי, רַבִּי נְחֶמְיָה אוֹמֵר: כָּל מָקוֹם שֶׁהֶאֱמִינָה תּוֹרָה עֵד אֶחָד – הַלֵּךְ אַחַר רוֹב דֵּעוֹת, וְעָשׂוּ שְׁתֵּי נָשִׁים בְּאִשָּׁה אַחַת כִּשְׁנֵי אֲנָשִׁים בְּאִישׁ אֶחָד, אֲבָל שְׁתֵּי נָשִׁים בְּאִישׁ אֶחָד – כִּי פַּלְגָא וּפַלְגָא דָּמֵי.

And there are those **who say** a different version of Rabbi Neḥemya's opinion: **Anywhere that one valid witness came**[H] **at the outset, even one hundred women** who later contradict him **are considered like one** witness, and do not override his testimony. **And with what are we dealing here** in the mishna? A case **where a woman came at the outset,**[H] and testified that she saw the killer. Then two other women arrived to contradict her statement. **And** according to this interpretation you must **emend the** statement **of Rabbi Neḥemya** so that it reads **like this: Rabbi Neḥemya says: Wherever the Torah relies on one witness, follow the majority of opinions. And they established** that **two women**[H] **against one woman** are **like two men against one man. But two women** in opposition **to one man** who is a valid witness **is like half** of a pair of witnesses **and half** of a pair of witnesses, and the mishna did not address that case.

HALAKHA

Here, simultaneously – כָּאן בְּבַת אַחַת: If one witness came and said: I saw the murderer, and another witness, who arrived together with the first, contradicts his claim and states: You did not see him, they would break the neck. If, however, the testimony of the first witness was accepted before the second one came and contradicted his claim, the court disregards the testimony of the second witness and they do not break the heifer's neck, in accordance with the opinion of Ulla (Rambam *Sefer Nezikin, Hilkhot Rotze'aḥ UShmirat HaNefesh* 9:13).

HALAKHA

Anywhere that one valid witness came, etc. – כָּל הֵיכָא דַּאֲתָא עֵד אֶחָד כָּשֵׁר וכו׳: If one witness came and said: I saw the murderer, and two women or other disqualified witnesses came and said: You did not see him, they do not break the heifer's neck (Rambam *Sefer Nezikin, Hilkhot Rotze'aḥ UShmirat HaNefesh* 9:15).

Where a woman came at the outset – דַּאֲתַאי אִשָּׁה מֵעִיקָּרָא: If a woman says: I saw the murderer, and another woman says: You did not see him, whether they came simultaneously or one after the other they would break the heifer's neck. The Ra'avad maintains that the court follows the first witness in that case even if the others are disqualified male witnesses (Rambam *Sefer Nezikin, Hilkhot Rotze'aḥ UShmirat HaNefesh* 9:14).

They established that two women, etc. – עָשׂוּ שְׁתֵּי נָשִׁים וכו׳: If two women or two disqualified witnesses say: We saw the murderer, and one valid witness says: You did not see him, they would break the heifer's neck. Even if one hundred disqualified witnesses were contradicted by a single valid witness, they are relied upon equally. The Ra'avad states that if the valid witness came before the court after the disqualified witnesses had testified, the court follows the majority opinion (Rambam *Sefer Nezikin, Hilkhot Rotze'aḥ UShmirat HaNefesh* 9:16).

וְתַרְתֵּי פְּסוּלֵי עֵדוּת לָמָּה לִי? מַהוּ דְּתֵימָא: כִּי אָזְלִינַן בָּתַר רוֹב דֵּעוֹת – לְחוּמְרָא, אֲבָל לְקוּלָּא – לָא. קָא מַשְׁמַע לָן.

The Gemara poses a question on these two interpretations of the mishna: **And why do I** need **two** cases in the mishna to teach the *halakha* that the majority opinion of **those disqualified** from **bearing witness** is followed? The Gemara explains: It is necessary, **lest you say** that **when we follow the majority opinion**[H] in the case of invalid witnesses, this is when it results in a decision **to be stringent** and require the performance of the ritual. **But** when it results in a decision **to be lenient** and say that the ritual is not required, we do **not** follow the majority opinion, and the performance of the ritual is required even if there is one witness saying that the killer was not seen. Therefore, the mishna **teaches us** that there is no difference in this regard, and the majority opinion is followed in any case.

״מִשֶּׁרַבּוּ הָרוֹצְחִין״ כו׳. תָּנוּ רַבָּנַן: מִשֶּׁרַבּוּ הָרוֹצְחָנִין – בָּטְלָה עֶגְלָה עֲרוּפָה, לְפִי שֶׁאֵינָהּ בָּאָה אֶלָּא עַל הַסָּפֵק. מִשֶּׁרַבּוּ הָרוֹצְחָנִין בְּגָלוּי – בָּטְלָה עֶגְלָה עֲרוּפָה.

§ The mishna taught that **from** the time **when murderers proliferated,** the ritual of the heifer whose neck is broken was nullified. **The Sages taught: From** the time **when murderers proliferated,** the ritual of **the heifer whose neck is broken was nullified, because it comes only for** a case involving **uncertainty** with regard to the identity of the murderer. Therefore, **when there was an increase of murderers** acting **openly**[N] so that their identities were known, the ritual of **the heifer whose neck is broken was nullified.**

״מִשֶּׁרַבּוּ הַנּוֹאֲפִין״ כו׳. תָּנוּ רַבָּנַן: ״וְנִקָּה הָאִישׁ מֵעָוֹן״, בִּזְמַן שֶׁהָאִישׁ מְנוּקֶּה מֵעָוֹן – הַמַּיִם בּוֹדְקִין אֶת אִשְׁתּוֹ. אֵין הָאִישׁ מְנוּקֶּה מֵעָוֹן – אֵין הַמַּיִם בּוֹדְקִין אֶת אִשְׁתּוֹ. וְאוֹמֵר: ״לֹא אֶפְקוֹד עַל בְּנוֹתֵיכֶם כִּי תִזְנֶינָה״ כו׳.

The mishna also taught that **from** the time **when adulterers proliferated,**[N] the performance of the ritual of the bitter water of a *sota* was nullified. **The Sages taught:** It states: **"And the man shall be cleared of transgression,** and that woman shall bear her transgression" (Numbers 5:31), which indicates that **when the man is clear of transgression the waters evaluate** if **his wife** was unfaithful, but **if the man is not clear of transgression the waters do not evaluate** if **his wife** was unfaithful. **And it states: "I will not punish your daughters when they commit harlotry,** nor your daughters-in-law when they commit adultery; for they consort with lewd women, and they sacrifice with prostitutes; and the people that is without understanding is distraught" (Hosea 4:14).

מַאי ״וְאוֹמֵר״? וְכִי תֵּימָא, עָוֹן דִּידֵיהּ – אִין, דִּבְנֵיהּ וְדִבְנָתֵיהּ – לָא, תָּא שְׁמַע: ״לֹא אֶפְקוֹד עַל בְּנוֹתֵיכֶם כִּי תִזְנֶינָה וְעַל כַּלּוֹתֵיכֶם כִּי תְנָאַפְנָה״.

The Gemara clarifies: **What is** the purpose of the addition of: **And it states?** What is lacking in the exposition from the verse of the Torah? The Gemara explains: **And if you would say** that based on the verse: "And the man shall be cleared of transgression," the *halakha* would be that with regard to **his transgression, yes,** it will cause the waters to be ineffective, but the transgression **of his sons and daughters**[N] does **not** impact the effectiveness, **come** and **hear** the verse: **"I will not punish your daughters,"** i.e., I will not punish your wives, due to your daughters, **"when they commit harlotry, nor your daughters-in-law when they commit adultery."**

וְכִי תֵּימָא, עֲוֹן אֵשֶׁת אִישׁ – אִין, עָוֹן דִּפְנוּיָה – לָא, תָּא שְׁמַע: ״כִּי הֵם עִם הַזֹּנוֹת יְפָרֵדוּ וְעִם הַקְּדֵשׁוֹת יְזַבֵּחוּ״ וגו׳.

And if you would say: With regard to the **transgression of** adultery with **a married woman, yes,** it will cause the waters to be ineffective, but the **transgression of** one who engaged in sexual intercourse with **an unmarried woman** does **not** impact the effectiveness, **come** and **hear** the continuation of the verse: **"For they consort with lewd women, and they sacrifice with prostitutes."**

HALAKHA

We follow the majority opinion – **אָזְלִינַן בָּתַר רוֹב דֵּעוֹת**: If three invalid witnesses came and said: We saw the murderer, and four other invalid witnesses stated that the first group did not see him, they break the heifer's neck. The principle is that the court follows the majority opinion in a case of disqualified witnesses (Rambam *Sefer Nezikin, Hilkhot Rotze'aḥ UShmirat HaNefesh* 9:17).

NOTES

Murderers acting openly – **הָרוֹצְחָנִין בְּגָלוּי**: The reason for the ritual of the heifer whose neck is broken is in order to help discover the killer's identity, so that the court can then bring him to justice. The Gemara (*Avoda Zara* 8b) teaches that once murder became commonplace the courts no longer applied the death penalty. Therefore, the ritual was nullified, as it could no longer serve its purpose (Rashash).

When adulterers proliferated, etc. – **מִשֶּׁרַבּוּ הַנּוֹאֲפִין וכו׳**: The Jerusalem Talmud states that the verse "And the woman shall be a curse in the midst of her people" (Numbers 5:27) indicates that the *sota* ritual is performed only in a society where an act of adultery would be cause for the transgressor to be cursed by all. When adultery became commonplace and this objective was no longer achievable, the ritual was nullified. The Rambam follows the explanation of the Gemara here, which says that the increase of adulterers caused the bitter water of the *sota* frequently to be ineffective. Since this led people to doubt the power of the bitter water, Rabban Yoḥanan ben Zakkai relied on the words of the prophet Hosea and nullified the ritual.

Of his sons and daughters, etc. – **דִּבְנֵיהּ וְדִבְנָתֵיהּ וכו׳**: Why should the transgressions of the members of the household be reflective of whether the head of the household has transgressed? The Meiri explains that if a person sees the members of his household acting improperly and fails to reprimand them, this raises suspicion that he too is lax with regard to the same transgression. The *Tosefot HaRosh* states that if he does not object, he is considered a partner to their deeds and is therefore a sinner himself.

מַאי "וְעָם לֹא יָבִין יִלָּבֵט"? אָמַר רַבִּי אֶלְעָזָר, אָמַר לָהֶם נָבִיא לְיִשְׂרָאֵל: אִם אַתֶּם מַקְפִּידִין עַל עַצְמְכֶם – מַיִם בּוֹדְקִין נְשׁוֹתֵיכֶם, וְאִם לָאו – אֵין הַמַּיִם בּוֹדְקִין נְשׁוֹתֵיכֶם.

The Gemara turns its attention to the end of the verse. **What is** the meaning of: **"And the people that is without understanding is distraught"? Rabbi Elazar says: The prophet said to the Jewish people: If you are particular about yourselves, the water evaluates your wives; but if not, the water does not evaluate your wives.** This would make people distraught, as they would not know how to overcome their suspicion if they are concerned that their wives have been unfaithful.

מִשֶּׁרַבּוּ בַּעֲלֵי הֲנָאָה – נִתְעַוְּותוּ הַדִּינִין, וְנִתְקַלְקְלוּ הַמַּעֲשִׂים, וְאֵין נוֹחַ בָּעוֹלָם. מִשֶּׁרַבּוּ רוֹאֵי פָּנִים בַּדִּין – בָּטֵל "לֹא תָגוּרוּ", וּפָסַק "לֹא תַכִּירוּ", וּפָרְקוּ עוֹל שָׁמַיִם וְנָתְנוּ עֲלֵיהֶם עוֹל בָּשָׂר וָדָם.

§ The Gemara cites statements similar to those of the mishna. **From** the time **when those who accept benefit**[N] from others **proliferated, the laws became twisted and deeds became corrupted, and there was no comfort in the world. From** the time **when those who look at** the **faces** of the litigants **in judgment,** in order to rule based on the appearance of the litigants, **proliferated,** the fulfillment of the verse: **"You shall not fear** the face of any man" (Deuteronomy 1:17), **ceased, and** the fulfillment of the verse: **"You shall not respect** faces in judgment" (Deuteronomy 1:17), **halted, and they removed the yoke of Heaven** from themselves, **and placed upon themselves the yoke of flesh and blood.**

מִשֶּׁרַבּוּ לוֹחֲשֵׁי לְחִישׁוֹת בַּדִּין – רַבָּה חֲרוֹן אַף בְּיִשְׂרָאֵל, וְנִסְתַּלְּקָה הַשְּׁכִינָה, מִשּׁוּם שֶׁנֶּאֱמַר: "בְּקֶרֶב אֱלֹהִים יִשְׁפֹּט". מִשֶּׁרַבּוּ "אַחֲרֵי בִצְעָם לִבָּם הֹלֵךְ" – רַבּוּ "הָאוֹמְרִים לָרַע טוֹב וְלַטּוֹב רָע". מִשֶּׁרַבּוּ "הָאוֹמְרִים לָרַע טוֹב וְלַטּוֹב רָע" – רַבּוּ "הוֹי הוֹי" בָּעוֹלָם.

From the time **when those who whisper whisperings in judgment,** advising judges surreptitiously, **proliferated, fierce anger proliferated in Israel, and the Divine Presence departed, because it is stated:** "God stands in the congregation of God; **in the midst of the judges He judges"** (Psalms 82:1). The Divine Presence that dwells among judges leaves if they judge improperly. **From** the time **when** those who are referred to in the verse: **"Their heart goes after their covetousness"** (Ezekiel 33:31), **proliferated, "Those who say to evil good, and to good evil"** (Isaiah 5:20) **proliferated,** i.e., those who treat wicked people as though they were righteous proliferated as a result. **From** the time **when** the fulfillment of the verse: **"Those who say to evil good, and to good evil," proliferated,** the cry of: **Woe, woe, proliferated in the world.** There was an increase in troubles that cause people to cry out.

מִשֶּׁרַבּוּ מוֹשְׁכֵי הָרוֹק – רַבּוּ הַיְּהִירִים, וְנִתְמַעֲטוּ הַתַּלְמִידִים, וְהַתּוֹרָה חוֹזֶרֶת עַל לוֹמְדֶיהָ. מִשֶּׁרַבּוּ הַיְּהִירִים – הִתְחִילוּ בְּנוֹת יִשְׂרָאֵל לְהִנָּשֵׂא לַיְּהִירִים, שֶׁאֵין דּוֹרֵינוּ רוֹאֶה אֶלָּא לְפָנִים.

From the time **when those who** show their arrogance by **drawing** out **spittle**[N] **proliferated,** the number of **haughty people** in general **proliferated, and the** number of **students decreased,** as they would say haughtily that there was nothing left for them to learn, **and the Torah** needs to **go around to** seek **those who study it,** as people do not learn of their own initiative. Furthermore, **from** the time **when haughty people proliferated, the daughters of Israel began marrying haughty men, as our generation looks only at the face,** i.e., the external aspects of a person, and ignores the inner aspects of a person.

אִינִי? וְהָאָמַר מָר: הַאי מַאן דְּמִיהַר, אֲפִילּוּ אַאִינָשֵׁי בֵּיתֵיהּ לָא מִיקַּבַּל, שֶׁנֶּאֱמַר: "גֶּבֶר יָהִיר וְלֹא יִנְוֶה", לֹא יִנְוֶה אֲפִילּוּ בְּנָוֶה שֶׁלּוֹ! מֵעִיקָּרָא קָפְצָה עֲלֵיהּ, לְסוֹף מִיתְזִיל עֲלַיְיהוּ.

The Gemara raises a difficulty: **Is that so?** Do women wish to marry arrogant men? **But didn't the Master say: One who is haughty is not even accepted by the members of his household, as it is stated: "The haughty man abides not"** (Habakkuk 2:5)? **"Abides [*yinaveh*] not"** means that **even in his abode [*naveh*],** he is not accepted. The Gemara explains: **Initially, she jumps at** the chance to marry **him,** because he appears to be a great person to her, but **in the end,** once she gets to know him, **he is demeaned in her eyes.**

NOTES

Those who accept benefit – בַּעֲלֵי הֲנָאָה: Rashi explains that this means people who are enslaved to their pleasures, even permitted pleasures. Such a person will not have the dedication needed to render accurate judgments. The Maharsha maintains that it refers to judges who derive benefit from the money of people in their community, as this will prevent them from analyzing their cases in a fair manner. This interpretation fits in well with the other examples listed by the Gemara.

Drawing out spittle – מוֹשְׁכֵי הָרוֹק: Rashi writes that this means that they would extend their spittle. He probably means that they were excessively particular about their manners, and would even attempt to spit in a way that seemed to them to be dignified. Others explain it, based on a similar Arabic expression, to mean those who do not keep their word.

משרבו מטילי מלאי על בעלי בתים – רבה השוחד והטיית משפט, ופסקה טובה. משרבו "מקבלני טובתך" ו"מחזקני טובותיך" – רבו "איש הישר בעיניו יעשה", שפלים הוגבהו והגבוהים הושפלו, ומלכותא אזלא ונולא. משרבו צרי עין וטורפי טרף – רבו מאמצי הלב וקופצי ידים מלהלוות, ועברו על מה שכתוב בתורה: "השמר לך פן" וגו'.

The *baraita* continues: **From** the time **when there was an increase** in those who **placed upon homeowners** the obligation to designate the profits from **merchandise** for the upkeep of judges, **bribery and corruption of judgment proliferated and good ceased. From** the time **when** those judges and leaders who say: **I accept your favor, and: I hold your favor, proliferated,** the fulfillment of the verse: **"Every man did that which was right in his eyes"** (Judges 17:6), **proliferated. Lowly ones were raised and lofty ones were lowered, and the monarchy is increasingly on the decline. From** the time **when misers and those greedy for profit**[N] **proliferated, those hardened of heart and who closed their hands from lending proliferated, and they transgressed that which is written in the Torah:** "You shall not harden your heart, nor shut your hand from your needy brother… **Guard yourself in case** there is a base thought in your heart… and you do not give him" (Deuteronomy 15:7, 9).

משרבו "נטויות גרון ומשקרות עינים" – רבו מים המרים, אלא שפסקו. משרבו מקבלי מתנות – נתמעטו הימים ונתקצרו השנים, דכתיב: "ושונא מתנת יחיה". משרבו זחוחי הלב – רבו מחלוקת בישראל. משרבו תלמידי שמאי והילל שלא שימשו כל צורכן – רבו מחלוקת בישראל, ונעשית תורה כשתי תורות. משרבו מקבלי צדקה מן הנכרי – היו ישראל למעלה והם למטה, ישראל לפנים והם לאחור.

From the time **when** women with **"stretched-forth necks and wanton eyes"** (Isaiah 3:16) **proliferated, the bitter waters** of a *sota* **proliferated,** as more people were suspected of committing adultery; **but they** eventually **ceased** when licentiousness became too widespread. **From** the time **when those who accept gifts proliferated, the days decreased and the years shortened, as it is written: "And he who hates gifts lives"** (Proverbs 15:27). **From** the time **when those with boastful** [***zeḥuḥei***][L] **hearts proliferated, dispute proliferated in Israel. From** the time **when the students of Shammai and Hillel**[P] **who did not serve** their Rabbis **sufficiently**[N] **proliferated, dispute proliferated in Israel, and the Torah became like two Torahs. From** the time **when those who accept charity from gentiles**[N] **proliferated, the Jewish people were above and they below; the Jewish people ahead and they behind.** This last statement is a euphemism; it was the Jewish people that were below and behind, but the Gemara did not want to say so explicitly.

"משמת יוסי בן יועזר" כו'. מאי אשכולות? אמר רב יהודה אמר שמואל: איש שהכל בו. "יוחנן כהן גדול העביר הודיית המעשר" כו'. מאי טעמא? אמר רבי יוסי ברבי חנינא: לפי שאין נותנין אותו כתיקונו, דרחמנא אמר דיהבי ללוים,

§ The mishna taught that **from the time when Yosei ben Yo'ezer died** the clusters ceased. The Gemara poses a question: **What** is the meaning of **clusters** [***eshkolot***]?[L] **Rav Yehuda says** that **Shmuel says:** It means **a man who contains all** [***ish shehakol bo***] elements of Torah and mitzvot. The mishna further taught that **Yoḥanan the High Priest took away the declaration of the tithe.** The Gemara poses a question: **What is the reason** he did this? **Rabbi Yosei, son of Rabbi Ḥanina, says: Because they did not give** the tithe **in the proper manner**[H] as stated by the Torah. In what way is that? **As the Merciful One states** in the Torah **that they should give** the first tithe **to the Levites,**

NOTES

Those greedy for profit – טוֹרְפֵי טֶרֶף: According to the Maharsha, this refers to people who deprive others of their livelihood, including those who raise the prices of basic necessities or engage in other such practices.

Who did not serve sufficiently – שֶׁלֹּא שִׁימְּשׁוּ כָּל צוֹרְכָּן: Shammai and Hillel themselves disagreed in only three or four cases. With the increase of students who misinterpreted their Rabbi's teachings, two schools of thought were formed who disputed many issues of *halakha*.

Those who accept charity from gentiles – מְקַבְּלֵי צְדָקָה מִן הַנָּכְרִי: Accepting handouts from gentiles constitutes a desecration of the Divine Name, as it indicates that the Jewish people cannot, or will not, support their own poor, and are in need of others. When many people act in this manner, the Jewish people's image as a whole is tarnished.

LANGUAGE

Boastful [*zeḥuḥei*] – זְחוּחֵי: Other versions of the text read *zehuhei*. The root of this word is to be haughty or boastful, similar to the Arabic زهي, *zuhiya*.

Clusters [*eshkolot*] – אֶשְׁכּוֹלוֹת: The comparison of Sages to a cluster is made in other places as well (see *Ḥullin* 92a). Shmuel here added to the comparison through the exposition of *Eshkol* to mean *ish kol*, meaning a man with all. Some say that this word also alludes to the Greek σχολή, *scholē*, meaning study or logic. It is also the source of the English word scholar.

PERSONALITIES

The students of Shammai and Hillel – תַּלְמִידֵי שַׁמַּאי וְהִילֵּל: Shammai and Hillel, the last of the pairs of Sages, lived about one hundred years prior to the destruction of the Temple, at the beginning of Herod's reign. Shammai and Hillel were noted as having different personalities. Shammai took a severe approach and held others to a high standard in terms of their actions and motivation (see, e.g., *Shabbat* 31a). Nevertheless, it was Shammai who coined the phrase: One should receive all people with a pleasant countenance (*Avot*, chapter 1). Hillel, by contrast, treated himself and others in an easygoing manner, and exhibited extreme flexibility to avoid conflict. While Shammai and Hillel themselves engaged in only a handful of halakhic disputes, *tanna'im* who studied at the academies they established, known as Beit Shammai and Beit Hillel, did not attend to their masters as much attention as necessary and engaged in many more disputes (see *Sanhedrin* 88b).

HALAKHA

Because they did not give it in the proper manner – לְפִי שֶׁאֵין נוֹתְנִין אוֹתוֹ כְּתִיקּוּנוֹ: The gifts from one's produce must be separated in the proper order or else the owner cannot recite the declaration. If he gave, for instance, the second tithe before the first one, he cannot recite it. During the period when the first tithe was given to the priests instead of the Levites they would not recite the declaration, as the verse was not fulfilled in the proper manner (Rambam *Sefer Zera'im*, *Hilkhot Ma'aser Sheni* 11:13).

וַאֲנַן קָא יָהֲבִינַן לְכֹהֲנִים.

and we give it to the priests.[H] Ezra penalized the Levites for not ascending with him from Babylonia to Eretz Yisrael by taking away their right to the first tithe. Consequently, the owner of the produce can no longer recite the declaration of tithes, which includes the statement: "I have done according to all that You have commanded me" (Deuteronomy 26:14), as he did not give the tithe to the Levites.

וְלוֹדֵי אַשְּׁאָר מַעַשְׂרוֹת! אָמַר רֵישׁ לָקִישׁ: כׇּל בַּיִת שֶׁאֵין מִתְוַדֶּה עַל מַעֲשֵׂר רִאשׁוֹן, שׁוּב אֵין מִתְוַדֶּה עַל שְׁאָר מַעַשְׂרוֹת. מַאי טַעְמָא? אָמַר אַבָּיֵי: הוֹאִיל וּפָתַח בּוֹ הַכָּתוּב תְּחִילָּה.

The Gemara asks: **And let him** at least **declare** that he donated **the other tithes** in the proper manner. **Reish Lakish said: Any house that does not state the declaration**[H] **about** the **first tithe can no longer state the declaration of the other** types of **tithes.** The Gemara asks: **What is the reason** for this? **Abaye said: Because the written** verse **began** the declaration **with** the tithe given to the Levites: "And I also gave it to the Levite, and to the stranger, to the orphan, and to the widow, in accordance with all Your mitzvot that You commanded me" (Deuteronomy 26:13). If he cannot say the first part of the declaration, he cannot say the rest.

מִכְּלָל דְּאַפְרוּשֵׁי הֲווּ מַפְרְשִׁי, וְהָא תַנְיָא: אַף הוּא בִּיטֵּל אֶת הַוִּידּוּי וְגָזַר עַל הַדְּמַאי, לְפִי שֶׁשָּׁלַח בְּכׇל גְּבוּל יִשְׂרָאֵל וְרָאָה שֶׁאֵין מַפְרִישִׁין אֶלָּא תְּרוּמָה גְּדוֹלָה בִּלְבַד, וּמַעֲשֵׂר רִאשׁוֹן וּמַעֲשֵׂר שֵׁנִי מִקְצָתָן מְעַשְּׂרִין וּמִקְצָתָן אֵין מְעַשְּׂרִין.

The Gemara poses a question: The fact that Rabbi Yoḥanan canceled the declaration of tithes proves **by inference that they would separate** tithes in his days. **But isn't it taught** (*Tosefta* 13:10): **He,** Yoḥanan the High Priest, **also canceled the declaration** of tithes **and decreed with regard to doubtfully tithed produce [*demai*]?**[N] Why did he issue this decree? **Because he sent** messengers **throughout** the land, to **all the borders of** Eretz **Yisrael**[H] to investigate, **and saw that they would separate only *teruma gedola*,**[N] **and** as for **first tithe and second tithe, some** people **would tithe and some** people **would not tithe.**

אָמַר לָהֶם: בָּנַי, בּוֹאוּ וְאוֹמַר לָכֶם: כְּשֵׁם שֶׁתְּרוּמָה גְּדוֹלָה יֵשׁ בָּהּ עֲוֹן מִיתָה, כָּךְ תְּרוּמַת מַעֲשֵׂר וְטֶבֶל יֵשׁ בָּהֶן עֲוֹן מִיתָה.

He said to them: My sons, come and I will tell you something: **Just as** the *halakhot* of ***teruma gedola*** include **a transgression punishable by death** at the hand of God, as one who ate produce from which *teruma* has not been separated is punished with death from Heaven, **so too,** the ***teruma* of the tithe,** the portion the Levites must separate from their first tithe and give to priests, **and untithed produce,** these include **a transgression punishable by death** at the hand of God, if the produce is eaten without the tithes having been taken.

עָמַד וְהִתְקִין לָהֶם: הַלּוֹקֵחַ פֵּירוֹת מֵעַם הָאָרֶץ – מַפְרִישׁ מֵהֶן מַעֲשֵׂר רִאשׁוֹן וּמַעֲשֵׂר שֵׁנִי, מַעֲשֵׂר רִאשׁוֹן מַפְרִישׁ מִמֶּנָּה תְּרוּמַת מַעֲשֵׂר וְנוֹתְנָהּ לְכֹהֵן. וּמַעֲשֵׂר שֵׁנִי עוֹלֶה וְאוֹכְלוֹ בִּירוּשָׁלַיִם. מַעֲשֵׂר רִאשׁוֹן וּמַעֲשַׂר עָנִי – הַמּוֹצִיא מֵחֲבֵירוֹ עָלָיו הָרְאָיָה!

Realizing that it was uncertain with regard to whether or not people were separating tithes, **he arose and instituted an ordinance for them**[H] with regard to doubtfully tithed produce: **One who purchases produce from an *am ha'aretz*,** which may or may not have been tithed, **must separate from** the produce **first tithe and second tithe** due to the uncertainty as to whether or not the *am ha'aretz* separated them. As for **first tithe, he** then **separates *teruma* of the tithe from it and gives it to a priest, and** with regard to **second tithe, he goes up and eats it in Jerusalem.** However, with regard to the giving of **first tithe** to the Levite, **and the poor man's tithe,** which can be eaten by anyone, as the Levites and the poor only have monetary rights to the produce, **the burden of proof rests upon the claimant.** Since the Levites and the poor cannot prove that these tithes had not already been set aside by the *am ha'aretz*, they cannot force the buyer to give them those tithes.

תַּרְתֵּי תַּקֵּן, בִּיטֵּל וִידּוּי דַּחֲבֵירִים, וְגָזַר עַל דְּמַאי שֶׁל עַמֵּי הָאָרֶץ.

In any case, the Gemara proves from the *baraita* that not all people would separate tithes in the time of Yoḥanan the High Priest. The Gemara answers: **He instituted two ordinances: He canceled the declaration of tithes of those devoted to the meticulous observance of mitzvot [*ḥaverim*],** especially *halakhot* of *teruma* and tithes, **and he decreed with regard to doubtfully tithed produce** purchased **from *amei ha'aretz*,** because they may not have separated tithes at all.

HALAKHA

And we give it to the priests – **וַאֲנַן קָא יָהֲבִינַן לְכֹהֲנִים**: Ezra penalized the Levites of his time for not ascending to Jerusalem with him, decreeing that they should not receive the first tithe but that it should go to the priests instead. The Radbaz and the *Kesef Mishne* both state that the decree applied only in Ezra's time, but afterward the tithe could be given either to the Levites or the priests (Rambam *Sefer Zera'im, Hilkhot Ma'asrot* 1:4).

Any house that does not state the declaration, etc. – **כׇּל בַּיִת שֶׁאֵין מִתְוַדֶּה וכו׳**: One may recite the declaration of tithes only if none of the gifts remain in his possession, as it is stated: "I have cleared the sacred things from my house" (Deuteronomy 26:13). The Rambam indicates that not only does holding on to the first tithe preclude the recitation of the declaration, but one may not recite the declaration if he has failed to give any of the gifts in the proper manner (Rambam *Sefer Zera'im, Hilkhot Ma'aser Sheni* 11:7).

He sent throughout the land, to all the borders of Eretz Yisrael, etc. – **שָׁלַח בְּכׇל גְּבוּל יִשְׂרָאֵל וכו׳**: In the days of Yoḥanan the High Priest, the Sanhedrin conducted an investigation and found that all were careful to separate *teruma gedola*, but some *amei ha'aretz* were lax in the proper separation of both the first and second tithes and the tithe for the poor. Consequently, they decreed that only *ḥaverim* could be relied upon with regard to tithes, and the produce of *amei ha'aretz* was considered doubtfully tithed and could not be eaten until it was tithed by the new owner. Such produce is called *demai* (Rambam *Sefer Zera'im, Hilkhot Ma'asrot* 9:1).

He arose and instituted an ordinance for them, etc. – **עָמַד וְהִתְקִין לָהֶם וכו׳**: The Sages decreed that one must separate the *teruma* of the tithe from doubtfully tithed produce, as its consumption is punished by death from Heaven. One must likewise set aside the second tithe. Since it is eaten by the owner, he incurs no financial loss by doing so. However, the first tithe and the poor man's tithe are not given from doubtfully tithed produce, as it is not certain that they have not been separated by the *am ha'aretz*, and the burden of proof rests upon the claimant (Rambam *Sefer Zera'im, Hilkhot Ma'asrot* 9:2).

NOTES

And decreed with regard to doubtfully tithed produce [*demai*] – **וְגָזַר עַל הַדְּמַאי**: The standard explanation of the word *demai* is that it is an acronym of the Aramaic *da mai*, meaning: This, what is it? In other words, is this produce tithed or not? The eponymous tractate in the order of *Zera'im* is devoted to the *halakhot* of doubtfully tithed produce, which addresses issues such as which doubtfully tithed produce requires tithing, and who is believed when they claim to have separated tithes in the proper manner. The general practice with regard to doubtfully tithed produce is to assume most *amei ha'aretz* do separate tithes properly, but nevertheless a decree was instituted due to the minority who neglected to do so.

Only *teruma gedola* – **תְּרוּמָה גְּדוֹלָה בִּלְבַד**: The reason why they would separate *teruma gedola* is because they would have to give only a small amount, generally 2 percent, and according to Torah law even a single grain will exempt an entire pile. Another reason why they viewed *teruma gedola* differently is because it has special sanctity, as the *halakhot* of ritual purity apply to it from the moment it has been separated and it is prohibited to non-priests. By contrast, since tithes can be eaten like regular produce, the *amei ha'aretz* did not consider them to be sacred. They were also not concerned for the general prohibition of untithed produce, and ignored the fact that the first tithe contains within it the *teruma* of the tithe, which must be given to a priest and has the status of *teruma* in all regards.

״וְאַף הוּא בִּיטֵּל אֶת הַמְעוֹרְרִים״. מַאי מְעוֹרְרִים? אָמַר רַחֲבָה: בְּכׇל יוֹם וָיוֹם שֶׁהָיוּ עוֹמְדִים לְוִיִּם עַל דּוּכָן וְאוֹמְרִים: ״עוּרָה לָמָּה תִישַׁן ה׳״. אָמַר לָהֶן: וְכִי יֵשׁ שֵׁינָה לִפְנֵי הַמָּקוֹם? וַהֲלֹא כְּבָר נֶאֱמַר: ״הִנֵּה לֹא יָנוּם וְלֹא יִישָׁן שׁוֹמֵר יִשְׂרָאֵל״! אֶלָּא, בִּזְמַן שֶׁיִּשְׂרָאֵל שְׁרוּיִין בְּצַעַר וְאוּמּוֹת הָעוֹלָם בְּנַחַת וְשַׁלְוָה, לְכָךְ נֶאֱמַר: ״עוּרָה לָמָּה תִישַׁן ה׳״.

§ The mishna further taught: **He also nullified** the actions of **the awakeners.** The Gemara poses a question: **What are awakeners? Raḥava says: On each and every day when the Levites stood on the platform** in the Temple **they** would **say: "Awake, why do you sleep, O Lord?"** (Psalms 44:24). Therefore, they were called awakeners. Yoḥanan the High Priest **said to them: Does the Omnipresent sleep,** that you call upon Him to awaken? **But isn't it already stated: "Behold, He that keeps Israel neither slumbers nor sleeps"** (Psalms 121:4)? **Rather, when the Jewish people are in a state of suffering, and the nations of the world are in** a state of **calm and serenity,** it is **with regard to this** that **it is stated: "Awake, why do you sleep, O Lord?"** If the verse were to be recited every morning it would be interpreted in the wrong way, so Yoḥanan the High Priest therefore canceled the daily recitation of this verse.

״וְאֶת הַנּוֹקְפִים״. מַאי נוֹקְפִים? אָמַר רַב יְהוּדָה אָמַר שְׁמוּאֵל: שֶׁהָיוּ מְסָרְטִין לָעֵגֶל בֵּין קַרְנָיו כְּדֵי שֶׁיִּפּוֹל דָּם בְּעֵינָיו. אֲתָא אִיהוּ בַּטֵּיל, מִשּׁוּם דְּמִיחֲזֵי כִּי מוּמָא.

The mishna also taught that Yoḥanan the High Priest canceled **the strikers.** The Gemara asks: **What** are **strikers? Rav Yehuda says** that **Shmuel says:** They are those **who would scratch the calf** being prepared for slaughter as an offering **between its horns, in order that blood should fall in its eyes,** so that the animal would not see and resist being slaughtered. **He came** and **nullified** this practice, **because it looked like** they are causing **a blemish.**

בְּמַתְנִיתָא תָּנָא: שֶׁהָיוּ חוֹבְטִין אוֹתוֹ בְּמַקְלוֹת, כְּדֶרֶךְ שֶׁעוֹשִׂין אוֹתוֹ לִפְנֵי עֲבוֹדָה זָרָה. אָמַר לָהֶם: עַד מָתַי אַתֶּם מַאֲכִילִין נְבֵילוֹת לַמִּזְבֵּחַ! נְבֵילוֹת? הָא שָׁחֵיט לְהוּ! אֶלָּא טְרֵיפוֹת, שֶׁמָּא נִיקַּב קְרוּם שֶׁל מוֹחַ, עָמַד וְהִתְקִין לָהֶם טַבָּעוֹת בַּקַּרְקַע.

A different explanation of strikers **was taught in a *baraita*** (*Tosefta* 13:9): They are those **who would beat** the calf **with sticks,** to stun it before it was slaughtered, **in the manner that they do it before idols.** Yoḥanan the High Priest **said to them: Until when will you feed unslaughtered animal carcasses to the altar?** The Gemara asks: Are these animal carcasses actually **unslaughtered animal carcasses? They were slaughtered,** i.e., they did not die of their own accord. **Rather,** he said that the beatings would cause them to become **like animals with a wound that will cause them to die within twelve months** [*tereifot*], as **perhaps** these beatings will **perforate the membrane surrounding the brain,** which would make the calf a *tereifa*. **He** therefore **arose and instituted an ordinance for them** to put **rings**[B] **in the ground** with which they could secure the animals, thereby making it easier to slaughter the animals without having to scratch them between the horns or hit them with sticks.

״עַד יָמָיו הָיָה פַּטִּישׁ מַכֶּה בִּירוּשָׁלַיִם״. בְּחוּלּוֹ שֶׁל מוֹעֵד.

The mishna stated that **until the days** of Yoḥanan the High Priest **the hammer** of smiths **would strike in Jerusalem.** The Gemara explains: This is referring **to the intermediate days of a Festival.** Though certain types of labor are permitted on those days, the banging of a hammer was outlawed, as the noise it made would detract from the feeling of sanctity of the day.

״כׇּל יָמָיו לֹא הָיָה אָדָם צָרִיךְ לִשְׁאוֹל עַל הַדְּמַאי״ – כִּדְאָמְרַן.

They further taught that in **all of his days a person did not need to inquire with regard to doubtfully tithed produce.** The Gemara notes that this is **like that** which **we stated** above, that he instituted an ordinance with regard to the tithing of doubtfully tithed produce.

מתני׳ מִשֶּׁבָּטְלָה סַנְהֶדְרִין – בָּטֵל הַשִּׁיר מִבֵּית הַמִּשְׁתָּאוֹת, שֶׁנֶּאֱמַר: ״בַּשִּׁיר לֹא יִשְׁתּוּ יָיִן״ וגו׳.

MISHNA This mishna continues with the list of items that were nullified. **From** the time **when the Sanhedrin ceased**[N] **song was** also **nullified from the places of feasts,**[H] i.e., it was no longer permitted to sing at a feast where wine was served, **as it is stated: "With song they shall not drink wine"** (Isaiah 24:9).

מִשֶּׁמֵּתוּ נְבִיאִים הָרִאשׁוֹנִים – בָּטְלוּ אוּרִים וְתוּמִּים. מִשֶּׁחָרַב בֵּית הַמִּקְדָּשׁ – בָּטֵל הַשָּׁמִיר, וְנוֹפֶת צוּפִים, וּפָסְקוּ אַנְשֵׁי אֲמָנָה מִיִּשְׂרָאֵל, שֶׁנֶּאֱמַר: ״הוֹשִׁיעָה ה׳ כִּי גָמַר חָסִיד״ וגו׳.

From the time **when the early prophets died the *Urim VeTummim* was nullified. From** the time **when the** Second **Temple was destroyed the *shamir* worm ceased** to exist **and** also **the sweetness of the honeycomb,** as the verse says with regard to the laws of the Torah: "More to be desired are they than gold, indeed, than much fine gold; sweeter also than honey and the honeycomb" (Psalms 19:11). **And men of faith ceased from** being among **the Jewish people, as it is stated: "Help, Lord, for the pious man is finished;** for the faithful fail from among the children of men" (Psalms 12:2).

BACKGROUND

Rings – טַבָּעוֹת: These rings, described in the mishna in tractate *Middot* and elsewhere, were large, fashioned out of metal, and attached to the ground. Prior to slaughter, the animal's head would be put through the ring and the animal would be tied. This would enable the slaughtering to be done in an unhurried manner, without endangering the one doing the slaughtering and without fear of the act being disqualified. There were twenty-four rings, one for each priestly watch.

Rings in the Temple courtyard

NOTES

From the time when the Sanhedrin ceased – מִשֶּׁבָּטְלָה סַנְהֶדְרִין: The Jerusalem Talmud offers other reasons, not derived from the Bible, for this *halakha*. One explanation is that the authority of the Sanhedrin was sufficient to make sure people did not sing songs with ribald lyrics at parties with wine. After the dissolution of the Sanhedrin, the Sages saw that people were singing improper songs at these parties and consequently banned them entirely. The Gemara there also adds that in the time of the Sanhedrin, the Sages would institute additional days of rejoicing when the Jewish people were saved from trouble. Once the Sanhedrin was dissolved, these days could no longer be instituted.

HALAKHA

Song was also nullified from the places of feasts, etc. – בָּטֵל הַשִּׁיר מִבֵּית הַמִּשְׁתָּאוֹת וכו׳: The Sages decreed that one may not play musical instruments or anything that produces the sound of music intended for enjoyment. The Rema writes that some authorities hold that the prohibition applies only to people, such as kings, who habitually listen to music, in addition to the prohibition with regard to drinking houses. It is also prohibited to listen to such instruments. These prohibitions are in commemoration of the destruction of the Temple. For the same reason it is prohibited even to sing, even without instruments, while drinking wine. The Baḥ, in accordance with the Gemara, rules stringently that one may not sing even if he is not drinking wine.

The custom throughout all of Israel is to sing and recite praises over wine to express thanks for the kindness of God. If singing is performed for the sake of a mitzva, such as at a feast for a circumcision or at a wedding, then all of the above is permitted (Rema). The halakhic authorities of our generation discuss the practical applications of this *halakha* (Rambam *Sefer Zemanim*, *Hilkhot Ta'anit* 5:14; *Shulḥan Arukh*, *Oraḥ Ḥayyim* 560:3).

רַבָּן שִׁמְעוֹן בֶּן גַּמְלִיאֵל אוֹמֵר, הֵעִיד רַבִּי יְהוֹשֻׁעַ: מִיּוֹם שֶׁחָרַב בֵּית הַמִּקְדָּשׁ – אֵין יוֹם שֶׁאֵין בּוֹ קְלָלָה, וְלֹא יָרַד הַטַּל לִבְרָכָה, וְנִיטַּל טַעַם הַפֵּירוֹת. רַבִּי יוֹסֵי אוֹמֵר: אַף נִיטַּל שׁוּמַּן הַפֵּירוֹת. רַבִּי שִׁמְעוֹן בֶּן אֶלְעָזָר אוֹמֵר: הַטׇּהֳרָה – נָטְלָה אֶת הַטַּעַם וְאֶת הָרֵיחַ. הַמַּעַשְׂרוֹת – נָטְלוּ אֶת שׁוּמַּן הַדָּגָן. וַחֲכָמִים אוֹמְרִים: הַזְּנוּת וְהַכְּשָׁפִים כִּילּוּ אֶת הַכֹּל.

Rabban Shimon ben Gamliel says that **Rabbi Yehoshua testified: From the day the Temple was destroyed there is no day that does not include** some form of **curse. And** since then **the dew has not descended for blessing, and the taste has been removed from fruit. Rabbi Yosei says:** Since then, **the fat of fruit has also been removed. Rabbi Shimon ben Elazar says:** Since then, **the** lost **purity has removed the taste and the aroma** from fruit; **the tithes** that were not separated **have removed the fat of the grain. And the Sages say: Promiscuity and witchcraft** have **consumed it all.**

גמ׳ וּמִמַּאי דְּמִשֶּׁבָּטְלָה סַנְהֶדְרִי כְּתִיב? אָמַר רַב הוּנָא בְּרֵיהּ דְּרַב יְהוֹשֻׁעַ, דְּאָמַר קְרָא: ״זְקֵנִים מִשַּׁעַר שָׁבָתוּ בַּחוּרִים מִנְּגִינָתָם״!

GEMARA The Gemara poses a question with regard to the first clause of the mishna: **And from where** is it derived **that** the verse: "With song they shall not drink wine" (Isaiah 24:9) **is written** about the period **from the** time **when the Sanhedrin was nullified? Rav Huna, son of Rav Yehoshua, said:** From **that** which **the verse states: "The Elders have ceased from the gate, the young men from their music"** (Lamentations 5:14). This indicates that the dissolution of the Sanhedrin, who are the Elders from the gate, is linked to the end of the young men singing.

אָמַר רַב: אוּדְנָא דְּשָׁמְעָא זִמְרָא תִּעָקֵר. אָמַר רָבָא: זִמְרָא בְּבֵיתָא חוּרְבָּא בְּסִיפָּא, שֶׁנֶּאֱמַר: ״קוֹל יְשׁוֹרֵר בַּחַלּוֹן חֹרֶב בַּסַּף כִּי אַרְזָה עֵרָה״.

Rav said: The **ear that hears song should be uprooted,** as it is prohibited to listen to music after the destruction of the Temple. **Rava said:** If there is **song in a house** there will be **destruction on the threshold, as it is stated: "Voices shall sing in the windows; desolation shall be in the doorposts; for its cedar work shall be uncovered"** (Zephaniah 2:14).

מַאי ״כִּי אַרְזָה עֵרָה״? אָמַר רַבִּי יִצְחָק: בַּיִת הַמְסוּבָּךְ בַּאֲרָזִים עִיר הוּא? אֶלָּא אֲפִילּוּ בַּיִת הַמְסוּבָּךְ בַּאֲרָזִים מִתְרוֹעֵעַ. אָמַר רַב אָשֵׁי: שְׁמַע מִינַּהּ, כִּי מַתְחִיל חוּרְבָּא בְּסִיפָּא מַתְחִיל, שֶׁנֶּאֱמַר: ״חֹרֶב בַּסַּף״. וְאִיבָּעֵית אֵימָא, מֵהָכָא: ״וּשְׁאִיָּה יֻכַּת שָׁעַר״. אָמַר מָר בַּר רַב אָשֵׁי: לְדִידִי חֲזֵי לֵיהּ, וּמְנַגַּח כִּי תוֹרָא.

The word "uncovered" [*era*] could be read to mean: Its city [*ira*]. The Gemara asks: **What is** the meaning of: **For its cedar work shall be its city?** Furthermore, **Rabbi Yitzḥak** wondered when he **said: Is a house interlaced with cedars** not as strong as **a city,** and therefore not threatened by desolation? **Rather,** it means that **even a house interlaced with cedars will become unstable** [*mitroe'a*] if song is heard there. **Rav Ashi said: Learn from it that when the destruction starts** it **starts with the threshold, as it is stated: "Desolation shall be in the posts." And if you wish, say** instead that they derive this idea **from here:** "In the city is left desolation, **and the gate is smitten unto ruin** [***she'iyya***]"[NB] (Isaiah 24:12). The term "ruin" here is referring to the destructive demon known as *She'iyya*, who strikes the gate first. **Mar bar Rav Ashi said: I saw it,** this *She'iyya*, **and it was goring** and wreaking havoc **like an ox.**

אָמַר רַב הוּנָא: זִמְרָא דְּנַגָּדֵי וּדְבַקָּרֵי – שָׁרֵי, דְּגַרְדָּאֵי – אֲסִיר. רַב הוּנָא בַּטֵּיל זִמְרָא. קָם מְאָה אַוְוזֵי בְּזוּזָא וּמְאָה סְאָה חִיטֵּי בְּזוּזָא וְלָא אִיבְעִי. אֲתָא רַב חִסְדָּא זַלְזֵיל בֵּיהּ, אִיבַּעְאֵי אַוְּוזָא בְּזוּזָא וְלָא מִשְׁתַּכַּח.

Rav Huna said: The **song of those who pull ships**[N] **and lead the herd**[B] **is permitted,** for their singing assists them to establish a rhythm in their work. However, that **of weavers is forbidden,** as they sing only for their own enjoyment. The Gemara relates that subsequently, **Rav Huna nullified** all types of **song,** and this led to a general blessing: The price of **one hundred ducks stood at a dinar, and one hundred *se'a* of wheat at a dinar, and there was no desire** for them even at such a cheap price, due to their great abundance. Later, when **Rav Ḥisda came and belittled** this prohibition, people began to sing again. As a result, prices increased greatly, and this led to a situation whereby one **wanted** a single **duck for** one **dinar and it could not be found.**

BACKGROUND

The gate is smitten unto ruin [*she'iyya*] – שְׁאִיָּה יֻכַּת שָׁעַר: According to the *ge'onim*, who say that *she'iyya* refers to a type of woodworm, the reason why the destruction begins at the entrance to the house is that the door and its posts are generally made of wood. The destruction caused by the woodworm weakens the posts, causing the upper beams, whose weight is not properly supported, to collapse. The woodworms' burrowing can sound like a constant rapping, perhaps suggesting the comparison to the ramming of an ox.

Those who pull ships and lead the herd – נַגָּדֵי וּדְבַקָּרֵי: In inland rivers and streams, particularly when there was a need to travel against the current, there were several strategies employed to assist those directing the boat. Small boats, and some large ships, would use oars. Medium sized cargo ships would be pulled by ropes, and there was a path on the riverbank designated for those who pulled the ropes. Those who pulled the ropes, as well as those who plowed with oxen, would sing in order to set a specific pace to their walking. It was important for all those pulling the ropes to be working in unison. In tractate *Pesaḥim* (112b), there is an example of one of these rhythmic songs.

Roman relief of slaves pulling a boat containing wine barrels

NOTES

The gate is smitten unto ruin [*she'iyya*] – שְׁאִיָּה יֻכַּת שָׁעַר: In a responsum of one of the *ge'onim*, perhaps Rav Hai Gaon, it states that the *she'iyya* is a type of a worm that eats through wood, and that is what Mar bar Rav Ashi was referring to when he claimed to have seen it.

The song of those who pull ships, etc. – זִמְרָא דְנַגָּדֵי וכו׳: According to Rashi, the factor that determines the permissibility of the singing is whether the singing aids the labor. Those who pull ships or lead the herd must work in a steady rhythm, so their song is allowed. The weavers do not require singing to help them in their work, so it is prohibited. This would mean that an active reason is needed to permit singing. The *ge'onim*, however, explain that the difference lies in the content of the songs. They explain that Rav Huna listened to the songs of those pulling ships and leading the herd and found nothing inappropriate, whereas the songs of weavers and tanners included licentious verses, and that is why he banned them. According to this, the default opinion is that singing is permitted.

NOTES

With four types of instruments – בְּאַרְבָּעָה מִינֵי זֶמֶר: Despite the fact that the verse singles out four particular instruments, Rav Se'adya Gaon explained that the prohibition applies to all instruments, and the verse mentions only those that are most important.

אָמַר רַב יוֹסֵף: זָמְרֵי גַּבְרֵי וְעָנֵי נָשֵׁי – פְּרִיצוּתָא; זָמְרֵי נָשֵׁי וְעָנֵי גַּבְרֵי – כְּאֵשׁ בִּנְעוֹרֶת. לְמַאי נַפְקָא מִינָּהּ? לְבַטּוֹלֵי הָא מִקַּמֵּי הָא.

Rav Yosef said: If men sing and women respond, this is **licentiousness. If women sing and men respond,** it causes the evil inclination to burn **as if** one were setting **fire to chips** of kindling. The Gemara poses a question: **What difference is there?** Rav Yosef indicates that in any case both are prohibited. The Gemara answers: **To nullify one before the other,** i.e., if it is impossible to ban singing entirely, they should at least stop the most problematic form.

אָמַר רַבִּי יוֹחָנָן: כׇּל הַשּׁוֹתֶה בְּאַרְבָּעָה מִינֵי זֶמֶר – מֵבִיא חָמֵשׁ פּוּרְעָנִיּוֹת לָעוֹלָם, שֶׁנֶּאֱמַר: ״הוֹי מַשְׁכִּימֵי בַבֹּקֶר שֵׁכָר יִרְדֹּפוּ מְאַחֲרֵי בַנֶּשֶׁף יַיִן יַדְלִיקֵם, וְהָיָה כִנּוֹר וָנֶבֶל תֹּף וְחָלִיל וָיַיִן מִשְׁתֵּיהֶם וְאֵת פֹּעַל ה׳ לֹא יַבִּיטוּ״.

Rabbi Yoḥanan says: Anyone who drinks wine **with** the accompaniment of **four types of instruments**[N] **brings five** types of **retribution to the world, as it is stated: "Woe to them who rise early in the morning, that they may follow strong drink; who tarry late into the night, until wine inflames them. And the harp and the psaltery, the drum and the pipe and wine, are at their feasts, but they do not regard the work of the Lord"** (Isaiah 5:11–12).

מַה כְּתִיב אַחֲרָיו? ״לָכֵן גָּלָה עַמִּי מִבְּלִי דָעַת״ – שֶׁגּוֹרְמִין גָּלוּת לָעוֹלָם; ״וּכְבוֹדוֹ מְתֵי רָעָב״ – שֶׁמְּבִיאִין רָעָב לָעוֹלָם; ״וַהֲמוֹנוֹ צִחֵה צָמָא״ – שֶׁגּוֹרְמִין לַתּוֹרָה שֶׁתִּשְׁתַּכַּח מִלּוֹמְדֶיהָ; ״וַיִּשַּׁח אָדָם וַיִּשְׁפַּל אִישׁ״ – שֶׁגּוֹרְמִין שִׁפְלוּת לְשׂוֹנְאוֹ שֶׁל הַקָּדוֹשׁ בָּרוּךְ הוּא. וְאֵין ״אִישׁ״ אֶלָּא הַקָּדוֹשׁ בָּרוּךְ הוּא, שֶׁנֶּאֱמַר: ״ה׳ אִישׁ מִלְחָמָה״; ״וְעֵינֵי גְבֹהִים תִּשְׁפַּלְנָה״ – שֶׁגּוֹרְמִין שִׁפְלוּת שֶׁל יִשְׂרָאֵל.

After listing the sin of those who drink wine with musical accompaniment, the verse states their punishment: **What is written afterward? "Therefore, My people have gone into captivity, for want of knowledge"** (Isaiah 5:13), meaning **that they cause exile to the world; "and their honorable men are famished"** (Isaiah 5:13), **as they bring famine to the world; "and their multitude are parched with thirst"** (Isaiah 5:13), **that they cause the Torah,** which is compared to water, **to be forgotten by those who learn it. "And mankind is bowed down, and man is humbled"** (Isaiah 5:15), **that they cause the enemy of the Holy One, Blessed be He,** i.e., God Himself, **to be brought down,** as **"man"** in the phrase "and man is humbled" means **nothing other** than **the Holy One, Blessed be He, as it is stated: "The Lord is a man of war"** (Exodus 15:3). The verse continues: **"And the eyes of the lofty are humbled"** (Isaiah 5:15), **that they cause the Jewish people to be brought down.** These are the five retributions.

וּמַה כְּתִיב אַחֲרָיו? ״לָכֵן

And what punishment **is written afterward** for the people who drank wine with musical accompaniment? **"Therefore,**

NOTES

There were times an answer rose up, etc. – זִימְנִין סָלֵיק וכו׳: The precise description of the way the *Urim VeTummim* was constructed is unclear, and various interpretations are offered by the biblical commentaries. The standard explanation is that the ephod and the breastplate themselves were only part of the *Urim VeTummim*, and that a different part, perhaps what is called the *tummim*, consisted of a parchment inscribed with names of God, which was inserted between the folds of the breastplate. The Gemara in *Yoma* 73a–b explains that the *Urim VeTummim* were not used mechanically; rather, the priest required the help of the Divine Spirit in order to understand and interpret what he saw properly. The discussion of the Gemara indicates that the occasional inability to receive a response from the *Urim VeTummim* was a sign that this device was gradually being removed from Israel (see Maharsha).

הִרְחִיבָה שְּׁאוֹל נַפְשָׁהּ וּפָעֲרָה פִיהָ לִבְלִי חֹק וְיָרַד הֲדָרָהּ וַהֲמוֹנָהּ וּשְׁאוֹנָהּ וְעָלֵז בָּהּ״.

the netherworld has enlarged her desire, and opened her mouth without measure, and down goes their glory and their tumult and their uproar, and he who rejoices among them" (Isaiah 5:14). Their punishment is that they shall descend into the netherworld.

״מִשֶּׁמֵּתוּ נְבִיאִים הָרִאשׁוֹנִים״. מַאן ״נְבִיאִים הָרִאשׁוֹנִים״? אָמַר רַב הוּנָא: זֶה דָּוִד וּשְׁמוּאֵל וּשְׁלֹמֹה. רַב נַחְמָן אָמַר: בִּימֵי דָוִד זִימְנִין סָלֵיק וְזִימְנִין לָא סָלֵיק, שֶׁהֲרֵי שָׁאַל צָדוֹק – וְעָלְתָה לוֹ, שָׁאַל אֶבְיָתָר – וְלֹא עָלְתָה לוֹ, שֶׁנֶּאֱמַר: ״וַיַּעַל אֶבְיָתָר״.

§ The mishna taught: **From** the time **when the early prophets died,** the *Urim VeTummim* was nullified. The Gemara poses a question: **Who are the early prophets? Rav Huna says: This is** referring to **David, and Samuel, and Solomon,** and after their death the *Urim VeTummim* was no longer used. **Rav Naḥman said: In the days of David** there were **times** an answer **rose up**[N] for them from the *Urim VeTummim* **and** there were **times** an answer **did not rise up,** i.e., they did not receive an answer. The proof for this is **that Tzadok,** the High Priest in David's time, **asked** the *Urim VeTummim* **and** an answer **rose up for him,** whereas **Abiathar asked and** an answer **did not rise up for him, as it is stated: "And Abiathar went up"** (II Samuel 15:24), and he was removed from serving as the High Priest as a result.

מֵתִיב רַבָּה בַּר שְׁמוּאֵל: ״וַיְהִי לִדְרֹשׁ אֱלֹהִים בִּימֵי זְכַרְיָהוּ הַמֵּבִין בִּרְאֹת הָאֱלֹהִים״. מַאי לָאו בְּאוּרִים וְתוּמִּים! לָא, בִּנְבִיאִים.

Rabba bar Shmuel raises an objection: The verse states concerning Uzziah: **"And he set himself to seek God in the days of Zechariah, who had an understanding of the vision of God"** (II Chronicles 26:5). **What, is** the verse **not** stating that Uzziah would seek God by asking questions **of the *Urim VeTummim*,** despite the fact that he lived after the time of Solomon? The Gemara rejects this claim: **No,** he would seek God by asking questions **of the prophets,** but not of the *Urim VeTummim*.

תָּא שְׁמַע: מִשֶּׁחָרַב בֵּית הַמִּקְדָּשׁ רִאשׁוֹן בָּטְלוּ עָרֵי מִגְרָשׁ, וּפָסְקוּ אוּרִים וְתוּמִּים, וּפָסַק מֶלֶךְ מִבֵּית דָּוִד.

The Gemara suggests: **Come and hear** a proof from a *baraita* (*Tosefta* 13:2) with regard to when the *Urim VeTummim* ceased: **From** the time **when the First Temple was destroyed, the cities with fields** that were allocated to the Levites **were nullified,**[N] **and the *Urim VeTummim* ceased, and the monarchy ceased from the house of David.**

וְאִם לְחָשְׁךָ אָדָם לוֹמַר: ״וַיֹּאמֶר הַתִּרְשָׁתָא לָהֶם אֲשֶׁר לֹא יֹאכְלוּ מִקֹּדֶשׁ הַקֳּדָשִׁים עַד עֲמֹד כֹּהֵן לְאוּרִים וּלְתֻמִּים״! אֱמוֹר לוֹ: כְּאָדָם שֶׁאוֹמֵר לַחֲבֵירוֹ ״עַד שֶׁיִּחְיוּ מֵתִים וְיָבֹא מָשִׁיחַ בֶּן דָּוִד״!

And if a person would whisper to you saying that the *Urim VeTummim* was still extant, as it states with regard to when the Second Temple first stood: **"And the Tirshatha said to them that they should not eat of the most sacred things, until there stood a priest with the *Urim VeTummim*"** (Ezra 2:63), which seems to indicate that they merely had to wait until the Second Temple was built for the reappearance of the *Urim VeTummim*; you should **say to him** that this is not referring to an expectation of a short-term development, but it is **like a person who says to his friend,** with regard to something that will occur in the distant future: **Until the dead live and the Messiah,** the **son of David, comes.** In any case, the *baraita* indicates that the *Urim VeTummim* ceased only from the time when the First Temple was destroyed, and not in the time of Solomon.

אֶלָּא אָמַר רַב נַחְמָן בַּר יִצְחָק: מַאן נְבִיאִים הָרִאשׁוֹנִים? לְאַפּוֹקֵי מֵחַגַּי זְכַרְיָה וּמַלְאָכִי, דְּאַחֲרוֹנִים נִינְהוּ; דְּתָנוּ רַבָּנַן: מִשֶּׁמֵּתוּ חַגַּי זְכַרְיָה וּמַלְאָכִי נִסְתַּלְּקָה רוּחַ הַקּוֹדֶשׁ מִיִּשְׂרָאֵל, וְאַף עַל פִּי כֵן הָיוּ מִשְׁתַּמְּשִׁים בְּבַת קוֹל,

Rather, Rav Naḥman bar Yitzḥak said: Who are **the early prophets,** with regard to whom it states that use of the *Urim VeTummim* ceased immediately after their death? This term early prophets serves **to exclude Haggai, Zechariah, and Malachi,** who **are the latter prophets.** The *Urim VeTummim* was used throughout the First Temple period, up to, but not including, their time. **As the Sages taught** in a *baraita* (*Tosefta* 13:3): **From** the time **when Haggai, Zechariah, and Malachi died the Divine Spirit departed from the Jewish people,** as these three were considered to be the last prophets. **And** even after the Urim VeTummim ceased to exist, they would **nevertheless** still **make use of a Divine Voice** to receive instructions from Above, even after this time.

שֶׁפַּעַם אַחַת הָיוּ מְסוּבִּין בַּעֲלִיַּית בֵּית גּוּרְיָא בִּירִיחוֹ, נִתְּנָה עֲלֵיהֶן בַּת קוֹל מִן הַשָּׁמַיִם וְאָמְרָה: יֵשׁ בָּכֶם אָדָם אֶחָד שֶׁרָאוּי שֶׁתִּשְׁרֶה שְׁכִינָה עָלָיו, אֶלָּא שֶׁאֵין דּוֹרוֹ רָאוּי לְכָךְ. נָתְנוּ עֵינֵיהֶם בְּהִלֵּל הַזָּקֵן. וּכְשֶׁמֵּת, הִסְפִּידוּהוּ: הֵי חָסִיד, הֵי עָנָיו, תַּלְמִידוֹ שֶׁל עֶזְרָא!

For on one occasion the Sages **were reclining in the upper story**[B] **of the house of Gurya in Jericho. A Divine Voice from Heaven was issued to them, and it said: There is one person among you** for **whom it is fitting that the Divine Presence should rest upon him** as a prophet, **but his generation is not fit for it;** they do not deserve to have a prophet among them. The Sages present **directed their gaze to Hillel the Elder.**[P] **And when he died, they eulogized him** in the following manner: **Alas pious one, alas humble one, student of Ezra.**

וְשׁוּב פַּעַם אַחֶרֶת הָיוּ מְסוּבִּין בַּעֲלִיָּיה בְּיַבְנֶה, נִתְּנָה לָהֶן בַּת קוֹל מִן הַשָּׁמַיִם וְאָמְרָה לָהֶן: יֵשׁ בָּכֶם אָדָם אֶחָד שֶׁרָאוּי שֶׁתִּשְׁרֶה שְׁכִינָה עָלָיו, אֶלָּא שֶׁאֵין דּוֹרוֹ זַכָּאִין לְכָךְ. נָתְנוּ עֵינֵיהֶם בִּשְׁמוּאֵל הַקָּטָן. וּכְשֶׁמֵּת, הִסְפִּידוּהוּ: הֵי עָנָיו, הֵי חָסִיד, תַּלְמִידוֹ שֶׁל הִלֵּל.

And again, on another occasion several generations later, the Sages **were reclining in an upper story** of a house **in Yavne,** and **a Divine Voice from Heaven was issued to them, and said: There is one person among you** for **whom it is fitting that the Divine Presence should rest upon him, but his generation is not fit for it.** The Sages present **directed their gaze to Shmuel HaKatan.**[P] **And when he died, they eulogized him** in the following manner: **Alas humble one, alas pious one, student of Hillel.**

וְאַף הוּא אָמַר בִּשְׁעַת מִיתָתוֹ: שִׁמְעוֹן וְיִשְׁמָעֵאל לְחַרְבָּא, וְחַבְרוֹהִי לְקַטְלָא, וּשְׁאָר עַמָּא לְבִיזָא, וְעָקָן סַגִּיאִין עֲתִידִין לְמֵיתֵי עַל עַמָּא. וְאַף עַל רַבִּי יְהוּדָה בֶּן בָּבָא בִּקְּשׁוּ לוֹמַר ״הֵי חָסִיד, הֵי עָנָיו״, אֶלָּא שֶׁנִּטְרְפָה שָׁעָה, שֶׁאֵין מַסְפִּידִין עַל הֲרוּגֵי מַלְכוּת.

And he too, Shmuel HaKatan, **said** the following statement of divinely inspired prediction **at the time of his death: Shimon,** i.e., Rabban Shimon ben Gamliel, **and Yishmael,**[P] i.e., Rabbi Yishmael ben Elisha the High Priest, are slated **for the sword, and their colleagues for killing, and the rest of the people for plunder, and great troubles are destined to befall the people.** The Gemara relates: **And they also sought to say about Rabbi Yehuda ben Bava,**[P] when eulogizing him: **Alas pious one, alas humble one, but the moment was disturbed** and they could not do so. That is because **eulogies are not given for those killed by the monarchy,** which was Rabbi Yehuda ben Baba's fate, in order not to arouse the monarchy's wrath.

NOTES

The cities with fields that were allocated to the Levites were nullified – בָּטְלוּ עָרֵי מִגְרָשׁ: The reason for this appears to be that these cities were connected to the settlement of the tribes of Israel in their portions of Eretz Yisrael, as each tribe would set aside some cities with fields for the Levites or priests. As the destruction of the Temple led to the nullification of the division of the land between the tribes, the *halakha* of these cities was no longer kept.

BACKGROUND

In the upper story – בַּעֲלִיָּיה: Meetings held by the Sages in the attics of homes are mentioned many times in the Talmud. These meetings were held when there was a need for privacy, or even secrecy. This could be due to either limitations placed on the authority of the Sages by the gentile government, or the desire to hold discussions out of the public eye with regard to issues that were significant to the masses.

PERSONALITIES

Hillel the Elder – הִלֵּל הַזָּקֵן: Hillel the Elder and his colleague Shammai were the last of the *zugot*, the pairs of *tanna'im* who led the Sanhedrin throughout much of the Second Temple period. Hillel served as *Nasi* of the Sanhedrin and Shammai was the deputy *Nasi*, approximately one hundred years prior to the destruction of the Second Temple, at the beginning of Herod's reign. Tradition has it that Hillel began as an impoverished student who took on menial labor in order to pay to attend the lectures of Shemaya and Avtalyon. Ultimately, the Gemara compares him to Ezra the Scribe, crediting him with reestablishing Torah study at a period in history when it was being forgotten (*Sukka* 20a). His disciples were praised as well.

According to the Gemara, Hillel the Elder had eighty students. Thirty of them were worthy of having the Divine Presence rest upon them as it did for Moses, thirty were worthy of the sun standing still for them as it did for Joshua, and twenty were considered to be average, with the greatest among them Yonatan ben Uzziel and the least among them Rabban Yoḥanan ben Zakkai (*Sukka* 28a).

Shmuel HaKatan – שְׁמוּאֵל הַקָּטָן: Shmuel HaKatan was a *tanna* living at the time of the destruction of the Second Temple. Even the earlier generations were unsure why he was called *hakatan*, meaning the small one. Some say it was because he acted humbly toward others; others say it was because he was only a bit lower in his spiritual level than the prophet Samuel. Due to his humble personality, he was selected to compose the blessing against heretics in the *Amida* prayer, for no one would suspect him of harboring personal antagonism toward the subjects of that blessing.

Shimon and Yishmael – שִׁמְעוֹן וְיִשְׁמָעֵאל: Shimon is Rabban Shimon ben Gamliel the First, and Yishmael is Rabbi Yishmael, the High Priest. According to the tradition found in the Midrash, they were both executed by the Roman government, probably due to their positions of prominence within the Jewish community, which was in a state of rebellion at the time. The difference between these two and the others killed is that they were executed by the sword as an official government action, while the others were killed either during or at the end of the siege.

Rabbi Yehuda ben Bava – רַבִּי יְהוּדָה בֶּן בָּבָא: Rabbi Yehuda ben Bava was one of the *tanna'im* active during the period between the destruction of the Second Temple and the destruction of the city of Beitar. He began his studies while the Temple was still standing, but was most active during the years when the Sanhedrin was located in Yavne. His testimonies and other teachings are mentioned in many sources.

Rabbi Yehuda ben Bava was famous for his piety. In fact, there is a tradition that whenever it says: An incident occurred with a pious person, it is referring to either Rabbi Yehuda ben Bava or to Rabbi Yehuda ben Ilai. According to the Gemara in tractate *Sanhedrin*, he was cruelly executed by the Romans after ordaining five Sages to serve as judges. It was said that if not for him, the *halakhot* of fines would have disappeared from among Israel. According to calculations, he must have been over the age of ninety when he died.

״מִשֶּׁחָרַב בֵּית הַמִּקְדָּשׁ בָּטֵל הַשָּׁמִיר״ כו׳. תָּנוּ רַבָּנַן: שָׁמִיר – שֶׁבּוֹ בָּנָה שְׁלֹמֹה אֶת בֵּית הַמִּקְדָּשׁ, שֶׁנֶּאֱמַר: ״וְהַבַּיִת בְּהִבָּנֹתוֹ אֶבֶן שְׁלֵמָה מַסָּע נִבְנָה״ – הַדְּבָרִים כִּכְתָבָן, דִּבְרֵי רַבִּי יְהוּדָה.

§ The mishna taught: **From the time when the** First **Temple was destroyed the *shamir* ceased** to exist. **The Sages taught:** This ***shamir*** is the creature **with which Solomon built the Temple, as it is stated: "For the house, when it was built, was built of whole stone from the quarry"** (I Kings 6:7). Now **these words** should be understood exactly **as they are written,** that King Solomon took whole stones and shaped them by having the *shamir* do the cutting. This is **the statement of Rabbi Yehuda.**

אָמַר לוֹ רַבִּי נְחֶמְיָה: וְכִי אֶפְשָׁר לוֹמַר כֵּן? וַהֲלֹא כְּבָר נֶאֱמַר: ״כָּל אֵלֶּה אֲבָנִים יְקָרֹת וגו׳ מְגֹרָרוֹת בַּמְּגֵרָה״! אִם כֵּן, מַה תַּלְמוּד לוֹמַר: ״לֹא נִשְׁמַע בַּבַּיִת בְּהִבָּנֹתוֹ״? שֶׁהָיָה מַתְקִין מִבַּחוּץ וּמַכְנִיס מִבִּפְנִים. אָמַר רַבִּי: נִרְאִין דִּבְרֵי רַבִּי יְהוּדָה בְּאַבְנֵי מִקְדָּשׁ, וְדִבְרֵי רַבִּי נְחֶמְיָה בְּאַבְנֵי בֵיתוֹ.

Rabbi Neḥemya said to him: And is it possible to say so? But isn't it already stated: "All these were costly stones, according to the measures of hewn stones, **sawed with saws"** (II Kings 7:9), which indicates that saws, which are iron implements, were used to shape the stones? **If so, what** is the meaning when **the verse states:** "And hammer, ax, and any tool of iron **were not heard in the house when it was being built"** (I Kings 6:7)? It means **that he would prepare** the stones **outside**[H] the Temple Mount using tools, **and bring** them **inside** already cut, so that no iron tools were used inside the Temple itself. **Rabbi** Yehuda HaNasi **said: The statement of Rabbi Yehuda** that no iron tools were used **appears** to be correct **with regard to the Temple stones, and the statement of Rabbi Neḥemya** that tools were used appears to be correct **with regard to the stones of the** king's own **house.**

וְרַבִּי נְחֶמְיָה, שָׁמִיר לְמַאי אֲתָא? מִיבָּעֵי לֵיהּ לְכִדְתַנְיָא: אֲבָנִים הַלָּלוּ אֵין כּוֹתְבִין אוֹתָן בִּדְיוֹ, מִשּׁוּם שֶׁנֶּאֱמַר: ״פִּתּוּחֵי חוֹתָם״. וְאֵין מְסָרְטִין עֲלֵיהֶם בְּאִיזְמֵל, מִשּׁוּם שֶׁנֶּאֱמַר: ״בְּמִלּוּאֹתָם״,

The Gemara poses a question: **And** according to **Rabbi Neḥemya,** who maintains that they used iron tools even in the cutting of the stones for the Temple, **for what** purpose **did the *shamir* come?** The Gemara answers: It was **necessary for that which is taught** in a *baraita*: **These stones**[H] in the breastplate and ephod, upon which were inscribed the names of the tribes, **they may not be written on with ink, because it is stated: "Like the engravings of a signet"** (Exodus 28:21), which means the names must be engraved onto the stones. **And they may not be scratched on with a scalpel [*izemel*],**[L] **because it is stated: "In their full settings"** (Exodus 28:20), indicating that the stones must be complete and not missing any of their mass.

אֶלָּא כּוֹתֵב עֲלֵיהֶם בִּדְיוֹ, וּמַרְאֶה לָהֶן שָׁמִיר מִבַּחוּץ וְהֵן נִבְקָעוֹת מֵאֲלֵיהֶן, כִּתְאֵינָה זוֹ שֶׁנִּבְקַעַת בִּימוֹת הַחַמָּה וְאֵינָהּ חֲסֵירָה כְּלוּם, וּכְבִקְעָה זוֹ שֶׁנִּבְקַעַת בִּימוֹת הַגְּשָׁמִים וְאֵינָהּ חֲסֵירָה כְּלוּם.

The *baraita* continues: **Rather,** one **writes** the letters **on them in ink, and shows them,** i.e., he places the ***shamir*** close to the ink markings **from outside,** without having it touch the stones, **and they split** open along the lines of the ink **of their own accord, like this fig that splits in the summer without losing anything** of its mass, **and like this** field in **a valley that cracks in the rainy season without losing anything** of its mass. The *shamir* was used in this way for these engravings.

תָּנוּ רַבָּנַן: שָׁמִיר זֶה בְּרִיָּיתוֹ כִּשְׂעוֹרָה, וּמִשֵּׁשֶׁת יְמֵי בְרֵאשִׁית נִבְרָא, וְאֵין כָּל דָּבָר קָשֶׁה יָכוֹל לַעֲמוֹד בְּפָנָיו. בַּמֶּה מְשַׁמְּרִין אוֹתוֹ? כּוֹרְכִין אוֹתוֹ בִּסְפוֹגִין שֶׁל צֶמֶר, וּמַנִּיחִין אוֹתוֹ בְּאִיטְנֵי שֶׁל אֲבָר מְלֵיאָה סוּבֵּי שְׂעוֹרִין.

The Sages taught: This *shamir*, its size is that of a barleycorn, and it was created in the six days of creation, and nothing hard can withstand it. In what is it kept, so that it will not break everything in the vicinity? **They wrap it in tufts [*sefogin*]**[L] **of wool and place it in a leaden vessel [*itenei*],**[BL] **full of barley bran,** which is soft and will not be broken by the *shamir*.

LANGUAGE

Scalpel [*izemel*] – אִיזְמֵל: From the Greek σμίλη, *smilē*, meaning a knife used for cutting and carving, a surgeon's knife, or a knife used in pruning branches.

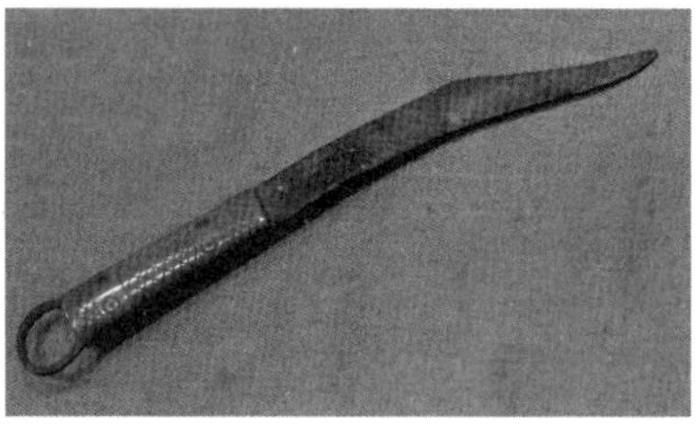

Ancient Roman scalpel

Tufts [*sefogin*] – סְפוֹגִין: From the Greek σπόγγος, *spongos*, meaning sponge. This is a type of marine organism, *Spongia officionalis*, that is taken from the ocean and used in bathing. The word was extended to mean anything soft like a sponge.

Live sponge

Skeleton of sponge

Vessel [*itenei*] – אִיטְנֵי: There are several opinions with regard to both the origin of this word and its meaning. Some say it is from the Greek, and some say it is a variant form of the Aramaic *udnei*, which is a vessel with a handle. Others say it is an Aramaic variant of the Hebrew *teneh*, small basket, which may in turn be derived from the Akkadian.

BACKGROUND

A leaden vessel – אִיטְנֵי שֶׁל אֲבָר: The assumption underlying all of the details here is that the *shamir* would break only hard substances. Therefore, it was wrapped in tufts of wool and pieces of barley bran, both of which are soft, and it was put into a container made of lead, a soft metal.

HALAKHA

He would prepare the stones outside, etc. – שֶׁהָיָה מַתְקִין מִבַּחוּץ וכו׳: The Sanctuary and the Courtyard should be constructed, if possible, with large stones. The stones may not be cut and chiseled on the Temple Mount itself, but all preparations must be performed outside of the Temple Mount. They are then brought into the building, in accordance with Rabbi Neḥemya (Rambam *Sefer Avoda*, *Hilkhot Beit HaBeḥira* 1:8; see *Kesef Mishne*).

These stones, etc. – אֲבָנִים הַלָּלוּ וכו׳: The Rambam omits this *halakha*, to the surprise of the *Mishne LaMelekh*, who cites the Ramban's opinion that this *halakha* applies to the stones of the breastplate but not to those of the ephod. Perhaps the Rambam is of the opinion that this is only a mitzva *ab initio*, but is not an indispensable requirement (Rambam *Sefer Avoda*, *Hilkhot Kelei HaMikdash* 9:7, in the *Mishne LaMelekh*).

אָמַר רַבִּי אַמִי: מִשֶּׁחָרַב מִקְדָּשׁ רִאשׁוֹן – בָּטְלָה שִׁירָא פְּרַנְדָּא, וּזְכוּכִית לְבָנָה. תַּנְיָא נַמִּי הָכִי: מִשֶּׁחָרַב מִקְדָּשׁ רִאשׁוֹן – בָּטְלָה שִׁירָא פְּרַנְדָּא, וּזְכוּכִית לְבָנָה, וְרֶכֶב בַּרְזֶל; וְיֵשׁ אוֹמְרִים: אַף יֵין קָרוּשׁ הַבָּא מִשְּׂנִיר, הַדּוֹמֶה כְּעִיגּוּלֵי דְבֵילָה.

§ **Rabbi Ami says: From** the time **when the First Temple was destroyed, shiny** [*peranda*][L] **silk** [*shira*][NL] **and white glass ceased** to exist. **This is also taught** in a *baraita*: **From** the time **when the First Temple was destroyed, shiny silk, white glass,**[B] **and iron chariots ceased; and some say** that **even congealed wine**[B] **that comes from Senir,** the Hermon, **which is similar to round fig cakes** after it congeals, ceased to exist as well.

״וְנוֹפֶת צוּפִים״. מַאי נוֹפֶת צוּפִים? אָמַר רַב: סוֹלֶת שֶׁצָּפָה עַל גַּבֵּי נָפָה, וְדוֹמָה לְעִיסָּה שֶׁנִּילּוֹשָׁה בִּדְבַשׁ וָשֶׁמֶן; וְלֵוִי אָמַר: שְׁתֵּי כִכָּרוֹת הַנִּדְבָּקוֹת בְּתַנּוּר, וְתוֹפְחוֹת וּבָאוֹת עַד שֶׁמַּגִּיעוֹת זוֹ לָזוֹ; וְרַבִּי יְהוֹשֻׁעַ בֶּן לֵוִי אָמַר: זֶה דְּבַשׁ הַבָּא מִן הַצִּיפִּיָּא. מַאי מַשְׁמַע? כִּדְמְתַרְגֵּם רַב שֵׁשֶׁת: כְּמָא דְנָתְזָן דַּבְרְיָאתָא וְשָׁיְיטָן בְּרוּמֵי עָלְמָא וּמַתְיָין דּוּבְשָׁא מֵעִישְׂבֵי טוּרָא.

The mishna taught: **And the sweetness of the honeycomb** [*nofet tzufim*] also ceased when the First Temple was destroyed. The Gemara asks: **What is *nofet tzufim*? Rav says: Fine flour that floats** up and remains **on the top of the sieve** [*nafa*]**, which is similar** in taste **to dough kneaded with honey and oil. And Levi says** that *nofet tzufim* is the term for **two loaves stuck together in an oven, which keep swelling until they reach each other. And Rabbi Yehoshua ben Levi says: This is honey that comes from elevated areas** [*tzipiyya*].[N] The Gemara explains: **From where may** it **be inferred** that this is what *nofet tzufim* is? **As Rav Sheshet would translate** the words: "As the bees do" (Deuteronomy 1:44): **Like the bees spread out and fly all over the world and bring honey from mountainous plants.** Similarly, Rabbi Yehoshua ben Levi states that honey comes from elevated areas.

תְּנַן הָתָם: כׇּל הַנִּצּוֹק טָהוֹר, חוּץ מִדְּבַשׁ זִיפִים וְהַצַּפִּיחִים. מַאי זִיפִים? אָמַר רַבִּי יוֹחָנָן: דְּבַשׁ שֶׁמְּזַיְּיפִין בּוֹ; וְרֵישׁ לָקִישׁ אָמַר: עַל שֵׁם מְקוֹמוֹ, כְּדִכְתִיב: ״זִיף וָטֶלֶם וּבְעָלוֹת״.

We learned in a mishna **there** (*Makhshirin* 5:9): **Anything that is poured** remains **ritually pure.** In other words, even if a liquid is poured into a ritually impure utensil, the stream of the liquid does not defile the contents that remain in the ritually pure utensil from which they were poured, **apart from *zifim* honey and wafer** batter. These substances are too viscous to be considered liquids. The Gemara asks: **What** is the meaning of ***zifim*? Rabbi Yoḥanan says: Honey** of such rare quality that **they** could **falsify** [***mezayyefin***] **it,**[B] by diluting it with other substances, and it would not be noticed. **And Reish Lakish says:** It is named **after its place, as it is written: "Ziph and Telem and Bealoth"** (Joshua 15:24).

כַּיּוֹצֵא בַּדָּבָר אַתָּה אוֹמֵר: ״בְּבוֹא הַזִּיפִים וַיֹּאמְרוּ לְשָׁאוּל הֲלֹא דָוִד״ וגו׳. מַאי זִיפִים? אָמַר רַבִּי יוֹחָנָן: בְּנֵי אָדָם הַמְזַיְּיפִין דִּבְרֵיהֶם; וְרַבִּי אֶלְעָזָר אוֹמֵר: עַל שֵׁם מְקוֹמָן, כְּדִכְתִיב: ״זִיף וָטֶלֶם וּבְעָלוֹת״.

Similarly, you can **say** with regard to the verse: **"When the *zifim* came and said to Saul, does not David** hide himself with us" (Psalms 54:2). **What is** the meaning of ***zifim***, mentioned in this verse? **Rabbi Yoḥanan says:** It means **people who** would **falsify** [*hamzayyefin*] **their words. And Rabbi Elazar says:** They are called **after their place, as it is written: "Ziph and Telem and Bealoth."**

״וּפָסְקוּ אַנְשֵׁי אֲמָנָה״. אָמַר רַבִּי יִצְחָק: אֵלּוּ בְּנֵי אָדָם שֶׁהֵן מַאֲמִינִין בְּהַקָּדוֹשׁ בָּרוּךְ הוּא; דְּתַנְיָא, רַבִּי אֱלִיעֶזֶר הַגָּדוֹל אוֹמֵר: כׇּל מִי שֶׁיֵּשׁ לוֹ פַּת בְּסַלּוֹ וְאוֹמֵר ״מָה אוֹכַל לְמָחָר״ – אֵינוֹ אֶלָּא מִקְּטַנֵּי אֲמָנָה.

§ The mishna states that from the time when the Second Temple was destroyed **men of faith ceased. Rabbi Yitzḥak says: These are people who believe in the Holy One, Blessed be He,** and place their trust in Him in all their ways. **As it is taught** in a *baraita*: **Rabbi Eliezer the Great says** that **whoever has bread in his basket** to eat today **and says: What shall I eat tomorrow,** meaning he does not know how he will acquire bread for tomorrow, **he is nothing other** than **from those of little faith.** One must trust in God to provide him with his sustenance.

וְהַיְינוּ דְּאָמַר רַבִּי אֶלְעָזָר, מַאי דִּכְתִיב: ״כִּי מִי בַז לְיוֹם קְטַנּוֹת״? מִי גָּרַם לַצַּדִּיקִים שֶׁיִּתְבַּזְבֵּז שׁוּלְחָנָן לֶעָתִיד לָבֹא? קַטְנוּת שֶׁהָיָה בָּהֶן, שֶׁלֹּא הֶאֱמִינוּ בְּהַקָּדוֹשׁ בָּרוּךְ הוּא. רָבָא אָמַר: אֵלּוּ קְטַנֵּי בְּנֵי רִשְׁעֵי יִשְׂרָאֵל,

And this is what Rabbi Elazar said: What is the meaning of that **which is written: "For who plunders the day of small things"**[N] (Zechariah 4:10)? **What caused the table,** i.e., the reward, **of the righteous to be plundered,** meaning wasted, **in the future?** It was **the** small-mindedness **they possessed.** And what is this small-mindedness? **That they did not believe in the Holy One, Blessed be He,** with a complete faith. **Rava said:** Who plunders the day of small things? **These are the small children of the wicked ones of the Jewish people,** who die young,

LANGUAGE

Shiny [*peranda*] – פְּרַנְדָּא: There are several theories with regard to the origin of this word, although apparently it comes from the Persian parund, a type of elaborate silk.

Silk [*shira*] – שִׁירָא: From the Greek σηρικόν, *sērikon*, meaning silk.

NOTES

Shiny silk – שִׁירָא פְּרַנְדָּא: According to Rashi this means a type of silk. Following this opinion, the *Tosefot HaRosh* states that the Gemara does not mean that this substance ceased to exist entirely, as elsewhere the Gemara mentions that it was used by *amora'im*. Rather, it became rarer than in earlier times.

Comes from elevated areas [*tzipiyya*] – הַבָּא מִן הַצִּיפִּיָּא: The *Tosefot Yom Tov*, citing Rabbi Ovadya Bartenura and others, maintains that *tzipiyya* is the name of a place. This name had been *Zofim* in biblical times, but it changed over the course of time. Many commentaries explain *tzufim* not as a name but as a general word for mountains. The Rambam in his Commentary to the Mishna indicates that *tzufim* is the name of an excellent type of honey.

Who plunders the day of small things – מִי בַז לְיוֹם קְטַנּוֹת: This exposition appears to be based on the fact that the vowel of the word *baz* is not a *kamatz*, as would be the case if it were derived from the root *beit, vav, zayin*, to despise, but a *pataḥ*, which indicates that it stems from the root *beit, zayin, zayin*, to plunder.

BACKGROUND

White glass – זְכוּכִית לְבָנָה: Apparently, this means totally transparent glass. Even though glassmaking is an ancient art, it was difficult to manufacture transparent glass due to the presence of impurities in the raw materials. White glass is mentioned throughout the ages as being an expensive type of glass.

Congealed wine – יֵין קָרוּשׁ: In the Hermon region they would congeal wine by placing it in snow. This would cause the wine to appear like a cake of pressed figs. This may have been done as a means of preservation, or to raise the alcohol content of the wine, as some of the water in the wine would freeze separately, leaving the latter more concentrated.

Honey that they could falsify it – דְּבַשׁ שֶׁמְּזַיְּיפִין בּוֹ: The higher the concentration of sugar in honey, the easier it is to add other substances, such as flour, without there being a noticeable impact on the honey's taste. After the honey absorbs the additives, it is difficult to differentiate between unadulterated honey and the inferior product.

NOTES

They say before Him – אוֹמְרִים לְפָנָיו: According to Rashi, it is the small children who will state this claim. The Maharsha maintains that the fathers, when they are brought to judgment, will argue that they were already punished in their lifetimes by the death of their children. The language of the Gemara allows for both interpretations.

Sellers of fat [*revav*] – מוֹכְרֵי רְבָב: Rashi and many other commentaries explain that *revav* means fat, and the phrase sellers of fat is referring to people who eke out their living by selling items that dirty their hands. The *Arukh* maintains that *revav* means the dregs of wax, which explains the connection between this teaching and the previous one, which spoke of the cessation of the honey. Since the honey of *nofet tzufim* has ceased, the only element left of this product is the honeycomb, used for wax.

If it were not for the prayer of Habakkuk – אִלְמָלֵא תְּפִלָּתוֹ שֶׁל חֲבַקּוּק: The Maharsha explains that David's prayer was that those who deal in trade should not have to earn their livelihood in a demeaning manner, while Habakkuk prayed for the Torah scholars.

One will die – אֶחָד מֵת: As one of the Torah scholars is presumably greater than the other, the latter must submit to his authority and is not fully responsible for the topic of their conversation while walking. Since they are not equally guilty, their respective punishments differ as well (*Iyyun Ya'akov*).

LANGUAGE

Partition [*pargod*] – פַּרְגּוֹד: From the Greek παραγαύδης, *paragaudēs*, meaning a garment with a purple border, or the Latin paragauda, a laced border on a garment. Its origin is from the Persian pargad, which refers to the screen that divides the king from his palace retinue. The king would speak from behind the screen, and this is the basis for the borrowing of this term to describe a barrier in front of the Divine Presence.

שֶׁמְּבַזְבְּזִין דִּין אֲבִיהֶם לֶעָתִיד לָבוֹא. אוֹמְרִים לְפָנָיו: רִבּוֹנוֹ שֶׁל עוֹלָם, מֵאַחַר שֶׁאַתָּה עָתִיד לִיפָּרַע מֵהֶן, לָמָּה הִקְהֵיתָה שִׁינֵּיהֶם בָּם!

who plunder, i.e., destroy, **their fathers' future judgment.** When God sits in judgment of their parents, these children **say before Him:**[N] **Master of the Universe, because You were destined to exact punishment from** our fathers in the World-to-Come for their wickedness, **why did You blunt their teeth with** the death of their children in their lifetimes? In this way, the death of their children atones for the fathers.

אָמַר רַבִּי אִילְעָא בַּר יְבֶרֶכְיָה: אִלְמָלֵא תְּפִלָּתוֹ שֶׁל דָּוִד הָיוּ כָּל יִשְׂרָאֵל מוֹכְרֵי רְבָב, שֶׁנֶּאֱמַר: ״שִׁיתָה ה׳ מוֹרָה לָהֶם״. וְאָמַר רַבִּי אִילְעָא בַּר יְבֶרֶכְיָה: אִלְמָלֵא תְּפִלָּתוֹ שֶׁל חֲבַקּוּק הָיוּ שְׁנֵי תַּלְמִידֵי חֲכָמִים מִתְכַּסִּים בְּטַלִּית אַחַת וְעוֹסְקִין בַּתּוֹרָה, שֶׁנֶּאֱמַר: ״ה׳ שָׁמַעְתִּי שִׁמְעֲךָ יָרֵאתִי ה׳ פָּעָלְךָ בְּקֶרֶב שָׁנִים חַיֵּיהוּ״. אַל תִּקְרָא ״בְּקֶרֶב שָׁנִים״ אֶלָּא ״בִּקְרוֹב שְׁנַיִם״.

§ **Rabbi Ile'a bar Yeverekhya says: If it were not for the prayer of David** for Israel to have sustenance, **all Israel would be sellers of fat [*revav*],**[N] i.e., involved in debased occupations, **as it is stated: "Place for them mastery, O Lord"** (Psalms 9:21), that is, may God grant them dignity. **And Rabbi Ile'a bar Yeverekhya** also **says: If it were not for the prayer of Habakkuk,**[N] **two Torah scholars would have to cover themselves with a single cloak** due to poverty **and engage in Torah study** dressed that way, **as it is stated: "Lord, I heard Your report and was afraid; O Lord, revive Your work in the midst of the years"** (Habakkuk 3:2). **Do not read: "In the midst [*bekerev*] of the years [*shanim*]," but in the closeness [*bikrov*] of two [*shenayim*].** In other words, Habakkuk prayed that God would nullify His decree of two Torah scholars having to share a single cloak.

וְאָמַר רַבִּי אִילְעָא בַּר יְבֶרֶכְיָה: שְׁנֵי תַלְמִידֵי חֲכָמִים הַמְהַלְּכִין בַּדֶּרֶךְ וְאֵין בֵּינֵיהֶן דִּבְרֵי תוֹרָה – רְאוּיִן לִישָּׂרֵף בָּאֵשׁ, שֶׁנֶּאֱמַר: ״וַיְהִי הֵמָּה הֹלְכִים הָלוֹךְ וְדַבֵּר וְהִנֵּה רֶכֶב אֵשׁ״ וגו׳. טַעְמָא דְּאִיכָּא דִּיבּוּר, הָא לֵיכָּא דִּיבּוּר – רְאוּיִן לִישָּׂרֵף.

And Rabbi Ile'a bar Yeverekhya says: In the case of **two Torah scholars who are walking along the way and there are no words of Torah between them,** but they are conversing about other matters, **they are deserving of being burned in fire. As it is stated** with regard to Elijah and his disciple Elisha: **"And it was as they walked along, talking, that behold, there appeared a chariot of fire** and horses of fire, which parted them both asunder" (II Kings 2:11). **The reason** they were not burned by the chariot of fire is **that there was speech** exchanged between them, which presumably was words of Torah, **but if there had been no speech, they** would have been **deserving of being burned** by the chariot.

וְאָמַר רַבִּי אִילְעָא בַּר יְבֶרֶכְיָה: שְׁנֵי תַלְמִידֵי חֲכָמִים הַדָּרִין בְּעִיר אַחַת וְאֵין נוֹחִין זֶה לָזֶה בַּהֲלָכָה – אֶחָד מֵת וְאֶחָד גּוֹלֶה, שֶׁנֶּאֱמַר: ״לָנֻס שָׁמָּה רוֹצֵחַ אֲשֶׁר יִרְצַח אֶת רֵעֵהוּ בִּבְלִי דַעַת״, וְאֵין דַּעַת אֶלָּא תּוֹרָה, שֶׁנֶּאֱמַר: ״נִדְמוּ עַמִּי מִבְּלִי הַדָּעַת״.

And Rabbi Ile'a bar Yeverekhya says: If there are **two Torah scholars who reside in the same city and they are not pleasant to each other with regard to *halakha*,** but are constantly fighting, **one** of them **will die**[N] **and the other one will be exiled. As it is stated: "That the manslayer might flee there, who slays his neighbor without knowledge"** (Deuteronomy 4:42), **and "knowledge"** means **nothing other** than **Torah, as it is stated: "My people are destroyed for lack of knowledge"** (Hosea 4:6).

אָמַר רַבִּי יְהוּדָה בְּרֵיהּ דְּרַבִּי חִיָּיא: כָּל תַּלְמִיד חָכָם הָעוֹסֵק בַּתּוֹרָה מִתּוֹךְ הַדְּחָק – תְּפִלָּתוֹ נִשְׁמַעַת, שֶׁנֶּאֱמַר: ״כִּי עַם בְּצִיּוֹן יֵשֵׁב בִּירוּשָׁלִַם בָּכוֹ לֹא תִבְכֶּה חָנוֹן יָחְנְךָ לְקוֹל זַעֲקֶךָ כְּשָׁמְעָתוֹ עָנָךְ״, וּכְתִיב בָּתְרֵיהּ: ״וְנָתַן ה׳ לָכֶם לֶחֶם צָר וּמַיִם לָחַץ״.

Rabbi Yehuda, son of Rabbi Ḥiyya, says: With regard to **any Torah scholar who engages in Torah** study **while experiencing the pressure** of poverty, **his prayer is listened to, as it is stated: "For, O people that dwells in Zion at Jerusalem, you shall weep no more; He will surely be gracious to you at the voice of your cry. When He shall hear, He will answer you"** (Isaiah 30:19), **and after it is written: "And the Lord shall give you sparse bread and scant water"** (Isaiah 30:20). This verse indicates that those who sit and study Torah, that is, the people who dwell in Zion, and eat bread sparingly, will have their prayers answered by God.

רַבִּי אַבָּהוּ אוֹמֵר: מַשְׂבִּיעִין אוֹתוֹ מִזִּיו שְׁכִינָה, שֶׁנֶּאֱמַר: ״וְהָיוּ עֵינֶיךָ רוֹאוֹת אֶת מוֹרֶיךָ״. רַבִּי אַחָא בַּר חֲנִינָא אָמַר: אַף אֵין הַפַּרְגּוֹד נִנְעָל בְּפָנָיו, שֶׁנֶּאֱמַר: ״וְלֹא יִכָּנֵף עוֹד מוֹרֶיךָ״.

Rabbi Abbahu says: A Torah scholar who engages in Torah study despite economic pressures **is satiated with the glory of the Divine Presence, as it is stated** in the same verse, above: **"And your eyes shall behold your Teacher." Rabbi Aḥa, son of Ḥanina, said: Even the** concealing **partition [*pargod*]**[L] before the Divine Presence **is not locked before him, as it is stated: "And your Teacher shall not hide Himself anymore"** (Isaiah 30:20).

״רַבָּן שִׁמְעוֹן בֶּן גַּמְלִיאֵל אוֹמֵר מִשּׁוּם רַבִּי יְהוֹשֻׁעַ: מִיּוֹם שֶׁחָרַב בֵּית הַמִּקְדָּשׁ אֵין״ וכו׳. אָמַר רָבָא: בְּכׇל יוֹם וְיוֹם מְרוּבָּה קִלְלָתוֹ מִשֶּׁל חֲבֵירוֹ, שֶׁנֶּאֱמַר: ״בַּבֹּקֶר תֹּאמַר מִי יִתֵּן עֶרֶב וּבָעֶרֶב תֹּאמַר מִי יִתֵּן בֹּקֶר״. הֵי בֹּקֶר? אִילֵימָא בֹּקֶר דִּלְמָחָר – מִי יָדַע מַאי הָוֵי? אֶלָּא דְּחָלֵיף.

§ The mishna states that **Rabban Shimon ben Gamliel says in the name of Rabbi Yehoshua: From the day that the Temple was destroyed, there is no** day that does not include some form of curse. **Rava says: Each and every day is more cursed than the previous one, as it is stated** in the chapter detailing the curses in the book of Deuteronomy: **"In the morning you will say, would that it were evening, and in the evening you will say, would that it were morning"** (Deuteronomy 28:67). It is unclear **which morning** the verse means. **If we say** that in the evening he will wish it would be **the following morning, does he know what will be** the outcome of the next morning, which would cause him to yearn for its arrival? **Rather,** it must mean the morning **that has passed;** that is, in the evening they will pine for the previous morning, because their situation is continuously worsening.

וְאֶלָּא עָלְמָא אַמַּאי קָא מְקַיֵּים? אַקְּדוּשָּׁה דְּסִידְרָא וְאַ״יְּהֵא שְׁמֵיהּ רַבָּא״ דְּאַגַּדְתָּא, שֶׁנֶּאֱמַר: ״אֶרֶץ עֵפָתָה כְּמוֹ אֹפֶל צַלְמָוֶת וְלֹא סְדָרִים״ – הָא יֵשׁ סְדָרִים, תּוֹפִיעַ מֵאוֹפֶל.

The Gemara poses a question: **But** if everything is deteriorating, **why does the world** continue to **exist?** The Gemara answers: **By the sanctification that** is said in the **order**[NB] of prayers, after the passage that begins: And a redeemer shall come to Israel, which includes the recitation and translation of the sanctification said by the angels, **and** by the response: **Let His great name** be blessed, etc., which is recited after the study **of *aggada*.**[N] **As it is stated: "A land of thick darkness, as darkness itself; a land of the shadow of death, without any order"** (Job 10:22). **Therefore,** it can be inferred from this verse that if **there are orders** of prayer and study, the land **shall appear from** amidst **the darkness.**

״וְלֹא יָרַד טַל לִבְרָכָה, וְנִיטַּל טַעַם פֵּירוֹת״ וכו׳. תַּנְיָא, רַבִּי שִׁמְעוֹן בֶּן אֶלְעָזָר אוֹמֵר: טָהֳרָה – בִּטְּלָה טַעַם וְרֵיחַ; מַעֲשֵׂר – בִּיטֵּל שׁוּמַּן דָּגָן.

§ The mishna taught that since the destruction of the Temple, **dew has not descended for a blessing, and the taste has been removed from fruit. It is taught** in a *baraita*: **Rabbi Shimon ben Elazar says:** The lost **purity has removed the taste and the aroma;**[N] the **tithes** that were not separated **have removed the fat of grain.**

רַב הוּנָא אַשְׁכַּח תּוּמַרְתָּא דְּחִינּוּנִיתָא. שְׁקָלָהּ כְּרָכָהּ בְּסוּדָרֵיהּ. אֲתָא רַבָּה בְּרֵיהּ. אֲמַר לֵיהּ: מוֹרְחִינָא רֵיחָא דְּחִינּוּנִיתָא, אֲמַר לֵיהּ: בְּנִי, טׇהֳרָה יֵשׁ בְּךָ. יְהַבָהּ נִיהֲלֵיהּ. אַדְּהָכִי אֲתָא אַבָּא בְּרֵיהּ, שְׁקָלָהּ יְהָבָהּ נִיהֲלֵיהּ. אֲמַר לֵיהּ: בְּנִי, שִׂמַּחְתָּ אֶת לִבִּי וְהִקְהִיתָה אֶת שִׁינַּי. הַיְינוּ דְּאָמְרִי אֱינָשֵׁי: רַחֲמֵי דְּאַבָּא – אַבְּנֵי, רַחֲמֵי דִּבְנֵי – אַבְּנֵי דִּהְווֹ לֵיהּ.

The Gemara relates that **Rav Huna found a fragrant date.**[N] **He took it and wrapped it in his shawl. Rabba,**[P] **his son, came** and **said to him: I smell the aroma of a fragrant** date. Rav Huna **said to him: My son, there is** clearly **purity in you,** as you were able to notice the fragrance. **He gave it to him. Meanwhile, Abba,** Rabba's **son, arrived.** Rabba **took** the date and **gave it to** him. Rav Huna **said to** Rabba: **My son, you have made my heart rejoice** with your purity, **and you have blunted my teeth,** by showing your preference for your own son. The Gemara comments: **This** explains the folk saying **that people say: The love of a father is for the sons; the love of the sons is for their own sons,** more than for their father.

רַב אַחָא בַּר יַעֲקֹב אִיטַּפַּל בֵּיהּ בְּרַב יַעֲקֹב בַּר בְּרַתֵּיהּ. כִּי גְּדַל, אֲמַר לֵיהּ: אַשְׁקְיַין מַיָּא. אֲמַר לוֹ: לָאו בְּרָיךְ אֲנָא. וְהַיְינוּ דְּאָמְרִי אֱינָשֵׁי: רְבֵי רְבֵי, בַּר בְּרַתָּךְ אֲנָא.

The Gemara relates another incident: **Rav Aḥa bar Ya'akov took care of Rav Ya'akov, the son of his daughter,** who was an orphan. **When** the grandchild **grew up,** his grandfather once **said to him: Give me water to drink. He said to him: I am not your son,**[N] and I am not obligated in your honor as a son must honor his father. The Gemara again comments: **And this** explains the folk saying **that people say: Raise, raise** your grandchild, but in the end he will retort: **I am the son of your daughter,** and I do not have to take care of you.

NOTES

By the sanctification that is said in the order, etc. – אַקְּדוּשָּׁה דְּסִידְרָא וכו׳: The Maharsha explains that these two sections of prayer are said in Aramaic and were understood even by the masses. As these passages were recited in the prayers and after the study of *aggada*, which even simple people would join in, they constituted a praise of God and the study of Torah with the participation of the entire people.

Let His great name…after the study of *aggada* – יְהֵא שְׁמֵיהּ רַבָּא דְּאַגַּדְתָּא: Many authorities infer from this passage that the *kaddish* prayer is recited only after the study of *aggada*, as it is beloved upon people and is learned with joy (*Ben Yehoyada*). This is the basis for the widespread custom of adding the short aggadic statement: Rabbi Ḥananya ben Akashya says, after Torah study before the *kaddish* prayer. The *Melekhet Shlomo* discusses this issue, and concludes that the Gemara means that the *kaddish* prayer is said even after the study of *aggada*, and certainly after the study of *halakha*. The *Be'er Sheva* addresses this topic from a slightly different angle, and he too holds that according to the Rambam in the *Mishne Torah*, the *kaddish* prayer must be recited after all Torah study, both *halakha* and *aggada*.

Lost purity has removed the taste and the aroma, etc. – טׇהֳרָה בִּטְּלָה טַעַם וְרֵיחַ וכו׳: The Maharsha writes that the cessation of purity, which is something intangible, led to the removal of tastes and aromas, which similarly are not tangible. The cancellation of the physical tithes caused the removal of the fat of grain, as both the cause and the effect are material.

A fragrant date – תּוּמַרְתָּא דְּחִינּוּנִיתָא: The *Arukh* cites three explanations of this term. The first explanation is that it means a type of date that is especially fragrant. The second explanation is that it is referring to a place where good-quality dates were cultivated. The third explanation is that this was the name given to all first fruits, and in this particular case, to a date.

I am not your son – לָאו בְּרָיךְ אֲנָא: Some authorities prove from here that a grandson, or at least the son of a daughter, is not obligated to honor his grandfather as he would honor his father. The *Yad Melekh* points out that Rav Ya'akov certainly brought the glass of water to his grandfather; he pointed out to him only that the grandfather cannot demand that he do so in the same way that a father may demand of his son. This is the intention of the comment of Rashi, who writes: I am not obligated to honor you as a son, indicating that he is obligated to honor him to some degree.

BACKGROUND

The sanctification that is said in the order – אַקְּדוּשָּׁה דְּסִידְרָא: The sanctification of the order is the text of the sanctification recited by the angels, appearing in the books of Isaiah and Ezekiel, with its Aramaic translation interspersed between the verses. This is said during the prayer of: "And a redeemer will come to Zion," after the *Amida* prayer, in the morning. The reason for its placement there is not clear. Some *ge'onim* maintain that it was moved to the end of the prayer service in response to a government decree banning its recital. Others say that it is a remnant of an ancient custom to read sections from the prophets, together with their translations, after the morning service. That custom was discontinued, but this was instituted to replace it.

PERSONALITIES

Rabba bar Rav Huna – רַבָּה בַּר רַב הוּנָא: Rabba bar Rav Huna was a third-generation *amora* in Babylonia. He merited to see Rav, and transmitted several *halakhot* in his name. He was a preeminent disciple of his father, Rav Huna, and there are several instances in the Talmud where Rav Huna gives practical halakhic guidance to his son. He was a judge in the city of Sura after the death of his father, a disciple-colleague of Rav Ḥisda, and a colleague of Rav Naḥman and Rava.

Rabba bar Rav Huna was wealthy and was close to the Exilarch, despite having several disagreements with him. He was known to be very modest. Upon his death he was brought to Eretz Yisrael for burial, and a text of a eulogy given for him is still extant.

The son mentioned here is Abba, who is the *amora* Rava, a shortened version of Rabbi Abba, son of Rabba bar Rav Huna. He was a fourth-generation *amora*, and his teachings are found throughout the Talmud.

מתני׳ בְּפוּלְמוּס שֶׁל אַסְפַּסְיָינוּס – גָּזְרוּ עַל עַטְרוֹת חֲתָנִים וְעַל הָאֵירוּס.

MISHNA In the war [*pulemus*][L] of Vespasian[B] the Sages **decreed upon the crowns of bridegrooms,**[H] i.e., that bridegrooms may no longer wear crowns, **and upon the drums,** meaning they also banned the playing of drums.

בְּפוּלְמוּס שֶׁל טִיטוּס – גָּזְרוּ עַל עַטְרוֹת כַּלּוֹת, וְשֶׁלֹּא יְלַמֵּד אָדָם אֶת בְּנוֹ יְוָונִית.

In the war of Titus[B] **they** also **decreed upon the crowns of brides, and** they decreed **that a person should not teach his son Greek.**

בְּפוּלְמוּס הָאַחֲרוֹן – גָּזְרוּ שֶׁלֹּא תֵּצֵא הַכַּלָּה בְּאַפִּרְיוֹן בְּתוֹךְ הָעִיר, וְרַבּוֹתֵינוּ הִתִּירוּ שֶׁתֵּצֵא הַכַּלָּה בְּאַפִּרְיוֹן בְּתוֹךְ הָעִיר.

In the last war,[B] meaning the bar Kokheva revolt, **they decreed that a bride may not go out in a palanquin inside the city, but our Sages permitted a bride to go out in a palanquin inside the city,** as this helps the bride maintain her modesty.

מִשֶּׁמֵּת רַבִּי מֵאִיר – בָּטְלוּ מוֹשְׁלֵי מְשָׁלִים. מִשֶּׁמֵּת בֶּן עַזַּאי – בָּטְלוּ הַשַּׁקְדָנִים. מִשֶּׁמֵּת בֶּן זוֹמָא – בָּטְלוּ הַדַּרְשָׁנִים. מִשֶּׁמֵּת רַבִּי עֲקִיבָא – בָּטֵל כְּבוֹד הַתּוֹרָה. מִשֶּׁמֵּת רַבִּי חֲנִינָא בֶּן דּוֹסָא – בָּטְלוּ אַנְשֵׁי מַעֲשֶׂה. מִשֶּׁמֵּת רַבִּי יוֹסֵי קַטְנוּתָא – פָּסְקוּ חֲסִידִים. וְלָמָּה נִקְרָא שְׁמוֹ קַטְנוּתָא? שֶׁהָיָה קַטְנוּתָא שֶׁל חֲסִידִים.

The mishna lists more things that ceased: **From the time when Rabbi Meir died, those who relate parables ceased;** from the time **when ben Azzai died, the diligent ceased;** from the time **when ben Zoma**[P] **died, the exegetists ceased; from** the time **when Rabbi Akiva died,**[N] **the honor of the Torah ceased; from** the time **when Rabbi Ḥanina ben Dosa**[P] **died, the men of** wondrous **action ceased; from** the time **when Rabbi Yosei the Small**[P] **died, the pious were no more. And why was he called the Small? Because he was the smallest of the pious,** meaning he was one of the least important of the pious men.

LANGUAGE

War [*pulemus*] – **פּוּלְמוּס**: From the Greek πόλεμος, *polemos*, meaning war or army.

HALAKHA

They decreed upon the crowns of bridegrooms – **גָּזְרוּ עַל עַטְרוֹת חֲתָנִים**: The Sages decreed that bridegrooms should not place crowns on their heads at all, as stated by Levi on 49b. They likewise prohibited brides from wearing crowns made of precious metals. This decree applied only to brides and grooms, but not to the rest of the population (Rambam *Sefer Zemanim, Hilkhot Ta'anit* 5:15; *Shulḥan Arukh, Oraḥ Ḥayyim* 560:4).

NOTES

From the time when Rabbi Akiva died, etc. – **מִשֶּׁמֵּת רַבִּי עֲקִיבָא וכו׳**: Rashi explains that the honor of the Torah here means Rabbi Akiva's technique of deriving *halakhot* from the crowns drawn above the letters in a Torah scroll. Deriving *halakhot* from the crowns increases the honor of Torah, as each small detail of the Torah is shown to be meaningful. Others add that Rabbi Akiva honored the Torah through his vast number of students (*Iyyun Ya'akov*).

BACKGROUND

The war of Vespasian – **פּוּלְמוּס שֶׁל אַסְפַּסְיָינוּס**: This refers to the great rebellion that led to the destruction of the Second Temple. The war is named after Vespasian because he was the head of the Roman army for almost the entire war, from the year 67 CE until he was crowned emperor.

The war of Titus – **פּוּלְמוּס שֶׁל טִיטוּס**: The name of this war as it appears in the standard text can be explained, albeit in a forced way, if it is assumed that the Sages made a distinction between the first part of the war, in which Jerusalem was put under siege, and the second part, in which the Temple was destroyed. In the first part, Vespasian led the Roman army. There was a brief respite in the fighting, from the time when Nero was assassinated until Vespasian became emperor. The final stage of the war, in which Jerusalem and the Temple, as well as the rest of the fortresses held by the Jews, were destroyed, was carried out with Titus leading the Roman army.

Even disregarding the forced nature of this explanation, as it is difficult to classify these as two separate wars, this also does not account for the variant version of this statement found in *Seder Olam Rabba*. Therefore, it is preferable to accept the variant text found there and in other early sources, which reads: The war of Quietus. Lusius Quietus was the general of the emperor Trajan, who slaughtered many Jews in Syria and Babylonia during his battles with the Persians, in the year 114 CE. He was also later named the ruler over Eretz Yisrael. The decrees enacted by the Sages from the time of Trajan are mentioned elsewhere in the Talmud, and, according to this modified version of the text, those decrees are ascribed in this passage to his general Quietus.

The last war – **פּוּלְמוּס הָאַחֲרוֹן**: This refers to the bar Kokheva rebellion, which was the final large-scale battle in the time of the Mishna. This hard-fought war, which ended in the destruction of the city of Beitar and the killing of bar Kokheva in the year 135 CE, was accompanied by mass killings of the Jewish people. Estimates of the total killed run up to one million Jews. Following this, the land of Judah was desolate for many years.

PERSONALITIES

Ben Zoma – **בֶּן זוֹמָא**: This is Shimon ben Zoma, one of the great Sages who lived in the generation of the destruction of the Second Temple. He was a student of Rabbi Yehoshua, and a disciple-colleague of Rabbi Akiva. Shimon ben Zoma was considered to be one of the great Torah scholars of his generation, but, perhaps due to his young age, he was never officially ordained. He therefore was not given the title of Rabbi and was called after his father's name. Many statements, in both *halakha* and *aggada*, have been said in his name. He was particularly well known for his exegeses of biblical verses, which is why it was said that when ben Zoma died, the exegetists ceased.

Rabbi Ḥanina ben Dosa – **רַבִּי חֲנִינָא בֶּן דּוֹסָא**: Rabbi Ḥanina ben Dosa was a *tanna* who lived toward the end of the Second Temple period. He was a student of Rabban Yoḥanan ben Zakkai. Even as a student he was known for his righteousness and for being a miracle worker. Very few of his statements have been recorded, and those that have are primarily in the realm of *aggada*. He is known mainly through stories about his piety and his cleaving to God, his righteousness and his willingness to make do with a minimum of earthly possessions. Rabbi Ḥanina ben Dosa served as a symbol of the righteous man in all of his behaviors.

Rabbi Yosei the Small [*Katonta*] – **רַבִּי יוֹסֵי קַטְנוּתָא**: From this mishna it seems that the appellation *Katonta* was not his name, but rather a nickname he was given. From the Jerusalem Talmud (*Bava Kamma* 3:7) it can be seen that he had several names and nicknames. He was called, on occasion, Yosei the Babylonian, or Isi ben Yehuda, or Isi ben Akiva (see *Pesaḥim* 113b). He lived in the city Huzal in Babylonia, and moved from there to Eretz Yisrael to study under the students of Rabbi Akiva. His statements are mentioned throughout the Talmud and the halakhic midrash.

מִשֶּׁמֵּת רַבָּן יוֹחָנָן בֶּן זַכַּאי – בָּטֵל זִיו הַחָכְמָה. מִשֶּׁמֵּת רַבָּן גַּמְלִיאֵל הַזָּקֵן – בָּטֵל כְּבוֹד הַתּוֹרָה, וּמֵתָה טׇהֳרָה וּפְרִישׁוּת. מִשֶּׁמֵּת רַבִּי יִשְׁמָעֵאל בֶּן פָּאבִי – בָּטְלָה זִיו הַכְּהוּנָּה. מִשֶּׁמֵּת רַבִּי – בָּטֵל עֲנָוָה וְיִרְאַת חֵטְא.	**From** the time **when Rabban Yoḥanan ben Zakkai died, the glory of wisdom ceased;**[N] **from** the time **when Rabban Gamliel the Elder died,**[N] **the honor of the Torah ceased, and purity and asceticism died. From** the time **when Rabbi Yishmael ben Pavi**[P] **died, the glory of the priesthood ceased; from** the time **when Rabbi** Yehuda HaNasi **died, humility and fear of sin ceased.**
גמ׳ תָּנוּ רַבָּנַן, רַבִּי פִּנְחָס בֶּן יָאִיר אוֹמֵר: מִשֶּׁחָרַב בֵּית הַמִּקְדָּשׁ – בּוֹשׁוּ חֲבֵרִים וּבְנֵי חוֹרִין, וְחָפוּ רֹאשָׁם. וְנִדַּלְדְּלוּ אַנְשֵׁי מַעֲשֶׂה, וְגָבְרוּ בַּעֲלֵי זְרוֹעַ וּבַעֲלֵי לָשׁוֹן, וְאֵין דּוֹרֵשׁ וְאֵין מְבַקֵּשׁ וְאֵין שׁוֹאֵל.	**GEMARA The Sages taught: Rabbi Pineḥas ben Ya'ir says: From** the time **when the** Second **Temple was destroyed, the *ḥaverim* and free men** of noble lineage **were ashamed,**[N] **and their heads were covered** in shame, **and men of action dwindled, and violent and smooth-talking men gained the upper hand, and none seek, and none ask, and none inquire** of the fear of Heaven.
עַל מִי לָנוּ לְהִשָּׁעֵן? עַל אָבִינוּ שֶׁבַּשָּׁמַיִם.	**Upon whom** is there **for us to rely?** Only **upon our Father in Heaven.**
רַבִּי אֱלִיעֶזֶר הַגָּדוֹל אוֹמֵר: מִיּוֹם שֶׁחָרַב בֵּית הַמִּקְדָּשׁ שָׁרוּ חַכִּימַיָּא לְמֶהֱוֵי כְּסָפְרַיָּא, וְסָפְרַיָּא כְּחַזָּנַיָּא, וְחַזָּנַיָּא כְּעַמָּא דְאַרְעָא, וְעַמָּא דְאַרְעָא	**Rabbi Eliezer the Great says: From the day the** Second **Temple was destroyed,** the generations have deteriorated: **Scholars have begun to become like scribes**[B] that teach children, **and scribes have become like beadles,**[B] **and beadles have become like ignoramuses, and ignoramuses**

NOTES

The glory of wisdom ceased – בָּטֵל זִיו הַחָכְמָה: Rashi comments that he does not know to what the glory of wisdom is referring. The *Penei Moshe* and the *Be'er Sheva* explain that this is referring to Rabban Yoḥanan ben Zakkai's expertise in all areas of the Torah, major and minor alike. The Maharsha states that it is referring to his knowledge of all wisdom, whether Torah knowledge or other types of wisdom.

From the time when Rabban Gamliel the Elder died, etc. – מִשֶּׁמֵּת רַבָּן גַּמְלִיאֵל הַזָּקֵן וכו׳: The honor of the Torah stated here has a different meaning from that mentioned in reference to Rabbi Akiva. Some explain that until Rabban Gamliel died, students would stand while being taught Torah by their teacher. This honors the Torah, as it replicates the giving of the Torah at Sinai, where the entire nation stood. The *Arukh* explains that after Rabban Gamliel died, people stopped according the proper respect that is due to the Torah.

The *ḥaverim* and free men were ashamed – בּוֹשׁוּ חֲבֵרִים וּבְנֵי חוֹרִין: Rashi explains that the term free men is referring to those of honored lineage. When the Temple was destroyed, they lost their high status, as lineage was relevant mostly for the priestly service in the Temple and various governmental appointments.

PERSONALITIES

Rabbi Yishmael ben Pavi – רַבִּי יִשְׁמָעֵאל בֶּן פָּאבִי: Rabbi Yishmael ben Pavi, or ben Piavi, or ben Piakhi, was appointed to the position of High Priest by King Agrippa shortly before the destruction of the Second Temple. Although the Sages were not pleased with his family in general, as they would use their power to oppress others (see *Pesaḥim* 57a), they praise his good deeds. It seems that his family was very wealthy. There are those who claim that he is the High Priest known as: The son of Kimḥit, after his pious mother. If that is so, then he had brothers who also served in the position of High Priest. Rabbi Yishmael ben Pavi served as the High Priest for ten years and is listed among the few High Priests who performed the ritual of the red heifer.

BACKGROUND

Scribes – סָפְרַיָּא: The term scribes in this instance refers to those who taught Torah to children. In smaller towns, they would also serve as local scribes who would write documents for members of the community. Although they had to possess a modicum of Torah knowledge, they were not considered to be scholars. It was rare to find a true Torah scholar who was also a scribe.

Beadles – חַזָּנַיָּא: These were the people who took care of the synagogues, and who also, on occasion, would assist those who taught Torah to the children. Due to their involvement in caring for the synagogue, they had to possess more Torah knowledge than an ignoramus, but they were certainly not numbered among the scholars.

אָזְלָא וְדַלְדְּלָה, וְאֵין שׁוֹאֵל וְאֵין מְבַקֵּשׁ. עַל מִי יֵשׁ לְהִשָּׁעֵן? עַל אָבִינוּ שֶׁבַּשָּׁמַיִם.

are increasingly diminished, and none ask[N] **and none seek. Upon whom is there to rely?** Only **upon our Father in Heaven.**

בְּעִקְבוֹת מְשִׁיחָא – חוּצְפָּא יִסְגֵּא, וְיוֹקֶר יַאֲמִיר, הַגֶּפֶן תִּתֵּן פִּרְיָהּ וְהַיַּיִן בְּיוֹקֶר, וּמַלְכוּת תֵּהָפֵךְ לְמִינוּת, וְאֵין תּוֹכֵחָה, בֵּית וַועַד יִהְיֶה לִזְנוּת. וְהַגָּלִיל יֶחֱרַב, וְהַגַּבְלָן יִשּׁוֹם, וְאַנְשֵׁי הַגְּבוּל יְסוֹבְבוּ מֵעִיר לְעִיר וְלֹא יְחוֹנָּנוּ.

He also said: **In the** times of the **approach of the Messiah,**[N] **impudence will increase and high costs will pile up.** Although **the vine shall bring forth its fruit,**[N] **wine will** nevertheless **be expensive. And the monarchy shall turn to heresy,**[B] and there will be **no** one to give **reproof** about this. **The meeting place** of the Sages **will become** a place of **promiscuity, and the Galilee shall be destroyed, and the Gavlan will be desolate,**[N] **and the men of the border shall go round from city to city** to seek charity, **but they will find no mercy.**

וְחָכְמוֹת סוֹפְרִים תִּסְרַח, וְיִרְאֵי חֵטְא יִמָּאֲסוּ, וְהָאֱמֶת תְּהֵא נֶעְדֶּרֶת. נְעָרִים פְּנֵי זְקֵנִים יַלְבִּינוּ, זְקֵנִים יַעַמְדוּ מִפְּנֵי קְטַנִּים. בֵּן מְנַוֵּול אָב, בַּת קָמָה בְּאִמָּהּ, כַּלָּה בַּחֲמוֹתָהּ. אוֹיְבֵי אִישׁ אַנְשֵׁי בֵיתוֹ. פְּנֵי הַדּוֹר כִּפְנֵי הַכֶּלֶב, הַבֵּן אֵינוֹ מִתְבַּיֵּישׁ מֵאָבִיו. וְעַל מָה יֵשׁ לָנוּ לְהִשָּׁעֵן? עַל אָבִינוּ שֶׁבַּשָּׁמַיִם.

And the wisdom of scribes will putrefy,[N] **and people who fear sin will be held in disgust, and the truth will be absent. The youth will shame the face of elders, elders will stand before minors.** Normal family relations will be ruined: **A son will disgrace a father; a daughter will rise up against her mother, a daughter-in-law against her mother-in-law. A man's enemies** will be **the members of his household. The face of the generation** will be **like the face of a dog;**[N] **a son will no longer be ashamed before his father. And upon what is there for us to rely?** Only **upon our Father in heaven.**

אָמַר רַב: לֹא שָׁנוּ אֶלָּא שֶׁל מֶלַח וְגׇפְרִית, אֲבָל שֶׁל הֲדַס וְשֶׁל וֶורֶד – מוּתָּר. וּשְׁמוּאֵל אוֹמֵר: אַף שֶׁל הֲדַס וְשֶׁל וֶורֶד – אָסוּר; שֶׁל קָנִים וְשֶׁל חִילַת – מוּתָּר. וְלֵוִי אָמַר: אַף שֶׁל קָנִים וְשֶׁל חִילַת – אָסוּר. וְכֵן תָּנֵי לֵוִי בְּמַתְנִיתֵיהּ: אַף שֶׁל קָנִים וְשֶׁל חִילַת – אָסוּר.

§ **Rav says** concerning the decree banning the wearing of crowns that **they taught** this *halakha* **only** with regard to crowns **of salt and sulfur, but** those **of myrtle and rose are permitted. And Shmuel says** that **even** crowns **of myrtle and rose are prohibited,** but those made **of reeds and bulrush are permitted. And Levi says: Even** crowns **of reeds and bulrush are prohibited. And likewise Levi teaches in his *baraita*: Even** those **of reeds and bulrush are prohibited.**

״וְעַל הָאִירוּס״. מַאי אִירוּס? אָמַר רַבִּי אֶלְעָזָר: טַבְלָא דְּחַד פּוּמָא. רַבָּה בַּר רַב הוּנָא עֲבַד לֵיהּ לִבְרֵיהּ טַנְבּוּרָא. אֲתָא אֲבוּהּ תַּבְרֵיהּ. אֲמַר לֵיהּ: מִיחֲלַף בְּטַבְלָא דְּחַד פּוּמָא. זִיל עֲבֵיד לֵיהּ אַפּוּמָא דְּחַצְבָּא אוֹ אַפּוּמָא דְּקַפִּיזָא.

The mishna taught that the Sages decreed against the wearing of crowns for bridegrooms **and upon the drums.** The Gemara poses a question: **What is this drum** [*irus*]?[L] **Rabbi Elazar says: A drum with one mouth.** The Gemara relates a story involving this instrument: **Rabba bar Rav Huna made a tambourine for his son. His father,** Rav Huna, **came and broke it. He said to him:** This instrument will be **confused for a drum with one mouth,** and people will assume that a drum with one mouth is permitted. Instead, **go and make for him** a small drum **on the mouth of an earthen jug** [*ḥatzava*],[B] **or on the mouth of** a container used for measuring **a *kefiza*,**[L] a small measurement, which did not pose the concern of being confused with a drum with one mouth.

NOTES

And none ask, etc. – **וְאֵין שׁוֹאֵל וכו׳**: The *Tosefot Yom Tov* explains that none ask and none seek the other's welfare, as people stopped caring about each other. The *Tiferet Yisrael* analyzes the differences between asking, seeking, and inquiring. He explains that the mishna is discussing the people's lack of desire for the redemption.

In the approach of the Messiah – **בְּעִקְבוֹת מְשִׁיחָא**: This passage, and the far lengthier one in the last chapter of tractate *Sanhedrin*, describes the deterioration of the world in the era just before the arrival of the Messiah, how the Jewish people will be held in the lowest esteem, and that specifically this set of circumstances will be the springboard for the redemption.

The vine shall bring forth its fruit, etc. – **הַגֶּפֶן תִּתֵּן פִּרְיָהּ וכו׳**: Rashi and many other commentaries explains that despite the fact that the vine will produce its fruit and there will be plenty of wine, it will nevertheless be expensive, as the high prevalence of drunkards will increase demand to a higher level than the supply. Some say that the excessive drinking of wine will be as a result of people attempting to drown their sorrows in wine. A variant version of the text reads: High costs will be corrupted, meaning that the prices will not be dependent on supply and demand but will be manipulated by those in the marketplace. The mishna illustrates this with the example that wine will be plentiful but will still be expensive.

And the Gavlan will be desolate, etc. – **וְהַגַּבְלָן יִשּׁוֹם וכו׳**: The Gavlan is a border region in Eretz Yisrael, identified by some as the Golan Heights in modern-day Israel, or the area of Gevel in the northwestern part of the country (Ya'avetz). This explains the connection to the subsequent teaching about the men of the border, as the border region of Eretz Yisrael will be plundered and its members will go around seeking support and charity throughout the land. The *Yad Rama* cites a version of the text that reads: The parchment will be destroyed and the men of the parchment will travel from city to city. He explains that the parchment of the Torah scroll will no longer be valued, and the men of the parchment, scribes, will have to go around seeking charity, as their services will no longer be needed.

And the wisdom of scribes will putrefy [*tissaraḥ*] – **וְחָכְמוֹת סוֹפְרִים תִּסְרַח**: This means that wisdom will no longer retain its lofty status, and its value will increasingly depreciate, like something that has spoiled. Some commentaries connect the word *tissaraḥ* to "the overhanging [*seraḥ*] part" (Exodus 26:12), meaning that wisdom will be considered superfluous. Yet others explain homiletically that the scholars will patter on to no purpose, like something unnecessary, that extends and hangs over (see *Etz Yosef*).

The face of the generation will be like the face of a dog – **פְּנֵי הַדּוֹר כִּפְנֵי הַכֶּלֶב**: Rashi in tractate *Sanhedrin* explains that this means people will have no shame in front of each other. Maharsha on tractate *Sanhedrin* explains that people will falsely present themselves as loving each other. The *Etz Yosef* explains that this passage refers to either the brazen face of the leaders or to the miserly countenances of the wealthy. According to Rabbi Elḥanan Wasserman, the leaders of the generation will be compared to dogs, who run before their masters as though they were the ones leading, when in truth the master is actually in charge. Similarly, the leaders of the people will act as if they were making the decisions, whereas they are really following the will of the masses.

BACKGROUND

The monarchy shall turn to heresy – **מַלְכוּת תֵּהָפֵךְ לְמִינוּת**: This prediction of Rabbi Eliezer the Great, who lived in the generation of the destruction of the Second Temple and immediately after, was that the pagan Roman Empire would accept as their official religion the beliefs of those groups that had separated themselves from Judaism, among them the Christians. This was fulfilled nearly two hundred years later, in the time of the emperor Constantine.

Earthen jug [*ḥatzava*] – **חַצְבָּא**: The *ḥatzava* is a very large pottery vessel that had many uses. It was sometimes used as a bucket to draw water and sometimes for the storage of liquids or for soaking objects in liquid.

LANGUAGE

Drum [*irus*] – **אִירוּס**: Some believe that the origin of this word is based in its being used at the festivities surrounding a betrothal [*eirusin*]. Most commentaries hold the *irus*, *tavla*, and *tanbora* are all different types of the same instrument, a drum with skin on only one side. However, the Meiri writes that the *irus* was a wind instrument with only one opening, and would make a sound that was a cross between a trumpeting and a hum.

Kefiza – **קְפִיזָא**: The origin of this word is Iranian. In Middle Persian, the form is kabīz, which refers to a measurement of volume.

"בְּפוּלְמוּס שֶׁל טִיטוּס גָּזְרוּ עַל עַטְרוֹת כַּלּוֹת" וכו׳. מַאי עַטְרוֹת כַּלּוֹת? אָמַר רַבָּה בַּר בַּר חָנָה אָמַר רַבִּי יוֹחָנָן: עִיר שֶׁל זָהָב. תַּנְיָא נַמִי הָכִי: אֵיזֶהוּ עַטְרוֹת כַּלּוֹת? עִיר שֶׁל זָהָב, אֲבָל עוֹשֶׂה אוֹתָהּ כִּיפָּה שֶׁל מֵילָת.

They further taught that **in the war of Titus** the Sages **decreed upon the crowns of brides.** The Gemara clarifies: **What are** the **crowns of brides?**[H] **Rabba bar bar Ḥana says** that **Rabbi Yoḥanan says: A city of gold,**[B] a gold crown engraved with the design of a city, worn by women as an ornament. **This is also taught** in a *baraita*: **Which are the crowns of brides** that were forbidden? The crown of a bride **is a city of gold. However, one may make it as a cap of fine wool** [*meilat*].[L]

תָּנָא: אַף עַל חוּפַּת חֲתָנִים גָּזְרוּ. מַאי חוּפַּת חֲתָנִים? זְהוֹרִית הַמּוּזְהָבוֹת. תַּנְיָא נַמִי הָכִי: אֵלּוּ הֵן חוּפַּת חֲתָנִים: זְהוֹרִית הַמּוּזְהָבוֹת, אֲבָל עוֹשֶׂה פַּפִּירִית וְתוֹלֶה בָּהּ כׇּל מַה שֶּׁיִּרְצֶה.

The Sage **taught:** The Sages **even decreed upon the canopy of grooms.** The Gemara asks: **What is** the type of **canopy of grooms** that was prohibited, as they certainly did not ban the marriage canopy. The Gemara answers: It means **the golden crimson** [*zehorit*][B] clothes, dyed red and crimson and decorated with gold, which they would hang on a marriage canopy. **This is also taught** in a *baraita*: **These are the canopy of grooms** the Sages banned: **The golden crimson** clothes. **But he may make a papyrus** [*papirit*][L] construction **and hang upon it whatever he wants,** even ornaments made of gold.

"וְשֶׁלֹּא יְלַמֵּד אֶת בְּנוֹ יְוָנִית". תָּנוּ רַבָּנַן: כְּשֶׁצָּרוּ מַלְכֵי בֵית חַשְׁמוֹנַאי זֶה עַל זֶה, הָיָה הוּרְקָנוֹס מִבַּחוּץ וְאַרִיסְטוֹבְלוֹס מִבִּפְנִים. בְּכׇל יוֹם וָיוֹם הָיוּ מְשַׁלְשְׁלִין דִּינָרִים בְּקוּפָּה וּמַעֲלִין לָהֶן תְּמִידִים.

§ The mishna taught that during the war of Titus the Sages decreed **that a person should not teach his son Greek. The Sages taught** that this decree came about as a result of the following incident: **When the kings of the Hasmonean monarchy besieged**[B] each **other** in their civil war, **Hyrcanus was outside of** Jerusalem, besieging it, **and Aristoblus was inside. On each and every day they would lower dinars in a box** from inside the city, **and** those on the outside **would send up** animals for them to bring the **daily offerings** in the Temple.

HALAKHA

What are crowns of brides – מַאי עַטְרוֹת כַּלּוֹת: The crowns of brides that the Sages prohibited include only those made of precious metals, such as the city of gold (Rambam *Sefer Zemanim, Hilkhot Ta'anit* 5:15; *Shulḥan Arukh, Oraḥ Ḥayyim* 560:4).

LANGUAGE

Fine wool [*meilat*] – מֵילָת: From the Greek μηλωτή, *mēlotē*, meaning wool. There are those who claim that this word is associated with the island of Malta, where high-quality wool was produced.

Papyrus [*papirit*] – פַּפִּירִית: From the Greek πάπυρος, *papuros*, papyrus sedge plant, *Cyperus papyrus* L., which was used in the manufacturing of paper. In the context of the Gemara, it means a frame-like structure made of reeds that was used for the hanging of decorative or other objects.

BACKGROUND

City of gold – עִיר שֶׁל זָהָב: This was a piece of jewelry made of gold in the shape of a crown, with the image of the walls of a city engraved upon it. It was also known as a mural crown. Only very wealthy women wore such pieces. There was also a Jerusalem of Gold, fashioned in the same way.

Greek coin depicting a woman wearing a mural crown

Golden crimson [*zehorit*] – זְהוֹרִית הַמּוּזְהָבוֹת: *Zehorit* is a woven material, made of wool or silk, and dyed crimson. Crimson is produced from the eggs of *Kermes vermilio*, a scale insect found in trees. Crimson-dyed material was used in various items in the Temple, and for decorative purposes outside of the Temple. Golden crimson is a crimson-dyed, woven material decorated with golden strands.

When the kings of the Hasmonean monarchy besieged – כְּשֶׁצָּרוּ מַלְכֵי בֵית חַשְׁמוֹנַאי: Before her death, Queen Shelomtzion appointed her son Hyrcanus the Second to serve as king. His brother, Aristoblus the Second, initiated a rebellion and took control of much of the country. Later, with the assistance and encouragement of Antipater, the father of Herod, Hyrcanus fielded an army that defeated the troops of Aristoblus and forced them to take refuge within the walls of Jerusalem. During the course of this siege, those inside Jerusalem were in need of sheep to continue the sacrificial rites in the Temple, and they paid large sums of money to those on the outside to supply them.

This story is also found in the works of Josephus (*Antiquities of the Jews* XIV:2), where he records that those in the city needed sheep for the Paschal offering, and promised the huge sum of one thousand drachma for each sheep. Josephus writes that there was an open, divine punishment for the treachery of the men of Hyrcanus in the form of a savage storm that tore through the land, damaging most of the crops. Perhaps this is what is alluded to in the expression: Eretz Yisrael shuddered, etc.

הָיָה שָׁם זָקֵן אֶחָד שֶׁהָיָה מַכִּיר בְּחׇכְמַת יְוָונִית, לָעַז לָהֶם בְּחׇכְמַת יְוָונִית, אָמַר לָהֶן: כׇּל זְמַן שֶׁעוֹסְקִים בַּעֲבוֹדָה, אֵין נִמְסָרִין בְּיֶדְכֶם. לְמָחָר שִׁלְשְׁלוּ לָהֶם דִּינָרִים בְּקוּפָּה וְהֶעֱלוּ לָהֶם חֲזִיר. כֵּיוָן שֶׁהִגִּיעַ לַחֲצִי חוֹמָה, נָעַץ צִפׇּרְנָיו נִזְדַּעְזְעָה אֶרֶץ יִשְׂרָאֵל אַרְבַּע מֵאוֹת פַּרְסָה.

A certain Elder was there, in Jerusalem, **who was familiar with Greek wisdom.**[B] **He communicated to** those on the outside **by** means of **Greek wisdom,** using words understood only by those proficient in Greek wisdom. **He said to them: As long as they are engaged in the** Temple **service, they will not be delivered into your hands.** Upon hearing this, **on the following day,** when **they lowered dinars in a box, they sent up a pig to them. Once** the pig **reached halfway** up the **wall, it inserted its hooves** into the wall and **Eretz Yisrael shuddered four hundred parasangs.**

אוֹתָהּ שָׁעָה אָמְרוּ: אָרוּר אָדָם שֶׁיְּגַדֵּל חֲזִירִים, וְאָרוּר אָדָם שֶׁיְּלַמֵּד לִבְנוֹ חׇכְמַת יְוָונִית; וְעַל אוֹתָהּ שָׁנָה שָׁנִינוּ: מַעֲשֶׂה וּבָא עוֹמֶר מִגַּגּוֹת צְרִיפִים, וּשְׁתֵּי הַלֶּחֶם מִבִּקְעַת עֵין סוֹכֵר.

When the Sages saw this, **they said at that time:**[N] **Cursed is the person who raises pigs,**[H] **and cursed is the person who teaches his son Greek wisdom. And with regard to that year** of civil war, in which the land was destroyed, **we learned** (*Menaḥot* 64b): **An incident** occurred **in which the *omer*,** the measure of barley brought as a communal offering on the sixteenth of Nisan, **came from Gaggot Tzerifim,**[B] **and the two loaves** offered on *Shavuot* came **from the valley of Ein Sokher.**[B]

אִינִי? וְהָאָמַר רַבִּי: בְּאֶרֶץ יִשְׂרָאֵל לָשׁוֹן סוּרְסִי לָמָּה? אֶלָּא אִי לְשׁוֹן הַקּוֹדֶשׁ אִי לְשׁוֹן יְוָונִית! וְאָמַר רַב יוֹסֵף: בְּבָבֶל לָשׁוֹן אֲרַמִּי לָמָּה? אֶלָּא אוֹ לְשׁוֹן הַקּוֹדֶשׁ אוֹ לְשׁוֹן פַּרְסִי!

It is understood from both the mishna and the *baraita* that it is prohibited to learn Greek. The Gemara raises a question: **Is that so? But didn't Rabbi** Yehuda HaNasi **say: In Eretz Yisrael,** why should people speak **the tongue of Syriac** [*Sursi*],[L] the Aramaic commonly spoken in Eretz Yisrael? **Rather,** they should speak **either** in **the sacred tongue,** Hebrew, **or** in **the** beautiful **tongue of Greek. And Rav Yosef** similarly **said: In Babylonia,** why should they speak in **the** vernacular **tongue of Aramaic? Rather,** they should speak **either** in **the sacred tongue,** Hebrew, **or** in **the tongue of Persian,** used by the authorities.

לָשׁוֹן יְוָונִית לְחוּד, וְחׇכְמַת יְוָונִית לְחוּד.

The Gemara answers that there is a difference: The **Greek tongue is discrete and Greek wisdom is discrete,**[N] and the Sages prohibited the latter but not the former.

וְחׇכְמַת יְוָונִית מִי אֲסִירָא? וְהָאָמַר רַב יְהוּדָה אָמַר שְׁמוּאֵל מִשּׁוּם רַבָּן שִׁמְעוֹן בֶּן גַּמְלִיאֵל, מַאי דִּכְתִיב: ״עֵינִי עוֹלְלָה לְנַפְשִׁי מִכֹּל בְּנוֹת עִירִי״? אֶלֶף יְלָדִים הָיוּ בְּבֵית אַבָּא, חֲמֵשׁ מֵאוֹת לָמְדוּ תּוֹרָה, וַחֲמֵשׁ מֵאוֹת לָמְדוּ חׇכְמַת יְוָונִית, וְלֹא נִשְׁתַּיֵּיר מֵהֶן אֶלָּא אֲנִי כָּאן וּבֶן אֲחִי אַבָּא בְּעַסְיָא!

The Gemara poses a question: **And is Greek wisdom prohibited? But didn't Rav Yehuda say** that **Shmuel said in the name of Rabban Shimon ben Gamliel: What is** the meaning of that **which is written: "My eye affected my soul, due to all the daughters of my city"** (Ecclesiastes 3:51)? **There were a thousand children in** my **father's house,** the princes' household. **Five hundred** of them **learned Torah, and** the other **five hundred learned Greek wisdom, and there only remained of them,** after the bar Kokheva revolt, **me, here** in Eretz Yisrael, **and the son of** my **father's brother,** who lives **in Asia Minor** [*Asya*].[L] The fact that Rabban Gamliel allowed half of his household to study Greek wisdom indicates that it is permitted.

BACKGROUND

Greek wisdom – **חׇכְמַת יְוָונִית**: Based on several sources, it appears that Greek wisdom refers primarily to the knowledge of Greek culture, poetry, and literature. Homer's works were to be found in Jewish homes already in the time of the Mishna. The lingua franca of the region, even among the gentiles, was Hellenistic Greek, and not many people spoke classical Greek or were familiar with Greek culture. This enabled those possessing this knowledge to hint things to each other in a way that would not be understood by most of the bystanders.

Gaggot Tzerifim – **גַּגּוֹת צְרִיפִים**: An alternate version of the text reads: Gannot Tzerifim. Either way, this place is generally identified with modern-day Tzerifin, a name preserved in Arabic as صرفند العمار, *ṣarafand al-'amār*, which is a village east of Rishon LeZion, along the road from Ramla to Jaffa.

Ein Sokher – **עֵין סוֹכֵר**: The accepted identification of Ein Sokher is the valley called in Arabic سهل عسكر, *sahl 'askar*. It is located southwest of Mount Ebal, and the main road from Shechem to Jerusalem runs through it. The name is apparently derived from a deep well [*ein*] located in a neighboring village.

HALAKHA

Cursed is the person who raises pigs – **אָרוּר אָדָם שֶׁיְּגַדֵּל חֲזִירִים**: It is prohibited to raise pigs anywhere, even if one does so only in order to sell their skin and the like. It is unnecessary to state that it is prohibited to raise them to sell (Rambam *Sefer Nezikin, Hilkhot Nizkei Mamon* 5:9; *Shulḥan Arukh, Ḥoshen Mishpat* 409:2).

LANGUAGE

Syriac [*Sursi*] – **סוּרְסִי**: This is a modified form of the Greek σύρος, *suros*, meaning Syrian or of the land of Syria.

Asia Minor [*Asya*] – **עַסְיָא**: From the Greek Ἀσία, *Asia*, which is also the appellation for the region known as Asia Minor. Part of Asia Minor was a Roman province known as Asia. It seems that when using this term, the Sages were referring to a specific district, perhaps Cilicia, located in that region.

NOTES

That time, etc. – **אוֹתָהּ שָׁעָה וכו׳**: The early commentaries note that this *baraita* indicates that the decree against the study of Greek wisdom was instituted during the Hasmonean reign, whereas the mishna states that it occurred during the war of Titus, which occurred more than one hundred years later. The *Tosefot HaRosh* explains that initially, in the Hasmonean times, they did not ban the practice entirely but simply declared that one who teaches Greek wisdom to his children would be cursed. Later, after the war with Titus, they completely prohibited the study of Greek wisdom. However, the Rosh contends that if a practice was cursed by the Sages it would not require an additional prohibition. He explains that the decree from the time of the Hasmoneans was not observed by most people, and consequently they had to institute the decree a second time.

Greek wisdom is discrete – **חׇכְמַת יְוָונִית לְחוּד**: The early commentaries explain that Greek wisdom does not include all forms of wisdom studied by the Greeks, for this would include almost all types of knowledge. Greek wisdom refers to the special way of expressing ideas through hints, or in a language that not all people can understand and use (Responsa of the Rashba; Responsa of the Rivash).

שָׁאנֵי שֶׁל בֵּית רַבָּן גַּמְלִיאֵל, דִּקְרוֹבִין לַמַּלְכוּת הָווּ; דְּתַנְיָא: מְסַפֵּר קוֹמֵי הֲרֵי זֶה מִדַּרְכֵי הָאֱמוֹרִי. אַבְטוּלוֹס בֶּן רְאוּבֵן הִתִּירוּ לְסַפֵּר קוֹמֵי, שֶׁהוּא קָרוֹב לַמַּלְכוּת; שֶׁל בֵּית רַבָּן גַּמְלִיאֵל הִתִּירוּ לָהֶן חָכְמַת יְוָנִית, מִפְּנֵי שֶׁקְּרוֹבִין לַמַּלְכוּת.

The Gemara answers: The members **of the house of Rabban Gamliel are different,** as **they were close to the monarchy,** and therefore had to learn Greek wisdom in order to converse with people of authority. **As it is taught** in a *baraita* (*Tosefta, Shabbat* 7:1): One who **cuts** his hair in the ***komi***[L] style,[H] which was the gentile fashion of cutting and wearing the hair, **is** considered to be acting in the **ways of the Amorites,** and it is prohibited to act in their way. However, **they permitted Avtolos**[L] **ben Reuven**[P] **to cut** his hair in the ***komi*** style, **as he is close to the monarchy,**[H] and similarly **they permitted the house of Rabban Gamliel** to study **Greek wisdom, because they are close to the monarchy.**

״בְּפוּלְמוּס הָאַחֲרוֹן גָּזְרוּ שֶׁלֹּא תֵּצֵא כַּלָּה בְּאַפִּרְיוֹן״ וכו׳. מַאי טַעְמָא? מִשּׁוּם צְנִיעוּתָא.

§ The mishna taught: **In the last war** the Sages **decreed that a bride may not go out in a palanquin** inside the city, but the later Sages permitted it. The Gemara explains: **What is the reason** they permitted this practice? **Due to modesty,** so that brides should not have to go out into the street and be seen by all.

״מִשֶּׁמֵּת רַבָּן יוֹחָנָן – בָּטְלָה הַחָכְמָה״. תָּנוּ רַבָּנַן: מִשֶּׁמֵּת רַבִּי אֱלִיעֶזֶר – נִגְנַז סֵפֶר תּוֹרָה. מִשֶּׁמֵּת רַבִּי יְהוֹשֻׁעַ – בָּטְלָה עֵצָה וּמַחֲשָׁבָה. מִשֶּׁמֵּת רַבִּי עֲקִיבָא – בָּטְלוּ זְרוֹעֵי תוֹרָה, וְנִסְתַּתְּמוּ מַעְיְינוֹת הַחָכְמָה.

The mishna taught that **from** the time **when Rabban Yoḥanan** ben Zakkai **died, wisdom ceased. The Sages taught: From** the time **when Rabbi Eliezer died,** it was as if **the Torah scroll had been interred,** as he had memorized many secrets of the Torah. **From** the time **when Rabbi Yehoshua died, council and** deliberate **thought ceased,** as he had the sharpest mind in Israel. **From** the time **when Rabbi Akiva died, the** powerful **arm of Torah,** meaning the exposition of all the details of Torah scripture, **ceased, and the fountains of wisdom were sealed.**

מִשֶּׁמֵּת רַבִּי אֶלְעָזָר בֶּן עֲזַרְיָה – בָּטְלוּ עֲטָרוֹת חָכְמָה, שֶׁעֲטֶרֶת חֲכָמִים עָשְׁרָם. מִשֶּׁמֵּת רַבִּי חֲנִינָא בֶּן דּוֹסָא – בָּטְלוּ אַנְשֵׁי מַעֲשֶׂה. מִשֶּׁמֵּת אַבָּא יוֹסֵי בֶּן קַטּוּנְתָּא – בָּטְלוּ חֲסִידִים. וְלָמָּה נִקְרָא שְׁמוֹ אַבָּא יוֹסֵי בֶּן קַטּוּנְתָּא? שֶׁהָיָה מִקְּטַנֵּי חֲסִידִים.

From the time **when Rabbi Elazar ben Azarya died, the crowns of wisdom ceased, as "the crown of the wise is their riches"** (Proverbs 14:24), and he was both a great Torah scholar and a very wealthy man. **From** the time **when Rabbi Ḥanina ben Dosa died, the men of** wondrous **deeds ceased. From** the time **when Abba Yosei ben Katonta died, the pious men ceased. And why was he called Abba Yosei ben Katonta? Because he was among the diminished** [*miktanei*] **of the pious people,**[N] i.e., he lived in an era when the pious had become few.

LANGUAGE

Komi – קוֹמֵי: From the Greek κόμη, *komē*, which means either hair or the tips of the hair. It is not clear what a haircut in the *komi* style looked like. It may have been a style where the hair all around the head was cut equally, without leaving any hair on the sides of the head.

Avtolos – אַבְטוּלוֹס: From the Greek εὔτολμος, *eutolmos*, meaning brave of heart.

PERSONALITIES

Avtolos ben Reuven – אַבְטוּלוֹס בֶּן רְאוּבֵן: Some identify him as Avtolomus, who was one of the teachers of Rabbi Yosei. It is not known when he lived. It may be that he had a connection with Rabbi Reuven ben Itzteroboli, about whom it is told (*Me'ila* 17a) that he would dress and style his hair like the gentiles in order to spend time in the halls of power, trying to avert decrees against the Jewish people. Avtolos ben Reuven seems to have filled a similar function.

HALAKHA

Cuts his hair in the *komi* style, etc. – מְסַפֵּר קוֹמֵי וכו׳: One is prohibited to follow gentile ways and customs. A person may not grow the locks of his hair in their fashions, nor shave off the sides and leave the hair in the middle, known in Aramaic as *belorit*, nor shave the hair above the face and leave it to grow long behind him (Rambam *Sefer HaMadda, Hilkhot Avoda Zara* 11:1; *Shulḥan Arukh, Yoreh De'a* 178:1).

As he is close to the monarchy – שֶׁהוּא קָרוֹב לַמַּלְכוּת: If one has close ties with the authorities and needs to dress and act like them, those practices that are prohibited for others as practices of the gentiles are permitted for him. The *Beit Yosef* explains that this is because the details of this prohibition are not specified in the Torah, and the Sages were granted the authority to prohibit and permit items not mentioned in the Torah, as the circumstances require (Rambam *Sefer HaMadda, Hilkhot Avoda Zara* 11:3; *Shulḥan Arukh, Yoreh De'a* 178:2).

NOTES

Among the diminished [*miktanei*] of the pious people – מִקְּטַנֵּי חֲסִידִים: This expression, as well as the corresponding phrase in the mishna, does not appear to be an expression of praise. Since the mishna and the *baraita* are listing praises of the various rabbis, several alternative explanations have been offered. The Meiri claims that Abba Yosei was the last of the pious ones, whose numbers were gradually dwindling. Conversely, the Rambam in his Commentary on the Mishna states that he was the root of the pious ones. Just as the root of a plant is relatively small in size and yet carries within it the potential for all of the growth that emerges from it, he too was the root of the pious ones in that he included all of their good traits within his character (see *Tosefot Yom Tov*).

מִשֶּׁמֵּת בֶּן עַזַּאי – בָּטְלוּ הַשַּׁקְדָנִין. מִשֶּׁמֵּת בֶּן זוֹמָא – בָּטְלוּ הַדַּרְשָׁנִין. מִשֶּׁמֵּת רַבָּן שִׁמְעוֹן בֶּן גַּמְלִיאֵל – עָלָה גּוֹבַאי וְרַבּוּ צָרוֹת. מִשֶּׁמֵּת רַבִּי – הוּכְפְּלוּ צָרוֹת.

From the time **when ben Azzai died, the diligent ceased; from** the time **when ben Zoma died, the exegetists ceased. From** the time **when Rabban Shimon ben Gamliel died, locusts ascended** upon the land **and troubles proliferated. From** the time **when Rabbi** Yehuda HaNasi **died,** the **troubles multiplied.**[B]

מִשֶּׁמֵּת רַבִּי – בָּטְלָה עֲנָוָה וְיִרְאַת חֵטְא. אֲמַר לֵיהּ רַב יוֹסֵף לְתַנָּא: לָא תִּיתְנֵי עֲנָוָה, דְּאִיכָּא אֲנָא. אֲמַר לֵיהּ רַב נַחְמָן לְתַנָּא: לָא תִּיתְנֵי יִרְאַת חֵטְא, דְּאִיכָּא אֲנָא.

The final line of the mishna states that **from** the time **when Rabbi** Yehuda HaNasi **died, humility and fear of sin ceased. Rav Yosef said to the *tanna*** who reviewed the mishna: **Do not teach** that **humility** ceased, **for there is** still one who is humble, namely **me.**[N] **Rav Naḥman** similarly **said to the *tanna*** who reviewed the mishna: **Do not teach** that **fear of sin** ceased, **for there is** still one who fears sin, namely **me.**

הדרן עלך עגלה ערופה
וסליקא לה מסכת סוטה

BACKGROUND

From the time when Rabbi Yehuda HaNasi died the troubles multiplied – מִשֶּׁמֵּת רַבִּי הוּכְפְּלוּ צָרוֹת: In the time of Rabbi Yehuda HaNasi, not only were the Roman leaders enlightened and relatively moderate, there was even a warm, personal relationship between him and the emperor Antoninus. After Rabbi Yehuda HaNasi died there was a series of emperors who were not as wealthy as previous ones, and they began many speculative wars. Consequently they imposed many taxes on the Jews to help subsidize the wars. The general attitude of the Roman leadership toward the Jewish people also took a sharp turn for the worse, particularly with the rise of Christianity.

NOTES

For there is me – דְּאִיכָּא אֲנָא: It is surprising to find a Sage praising himself for his good qualities, especially that of humility. The Maharsha states that truth always takes precedence over politeness, and the Sages did not want something inaccurate to be taught. The *Ben Yehoyada* adds that they were concerned that the masses, who viewed the Sages as humble and fearing of sin, would conclude that the *baraita* was wrong. According to the *Sefat Emet*, these Sages were of the opinion that humility and fear of sin had not in fact ceased, and there were many such people still alive. As proof they stated: For there is me, and if even I possess this attribute, it must be possessed by many others who are greater than I.

Summary of **Perek IX**

The *halakhot* of the ritual of the heifer whose neck is broken were addressed in this chapter. When a murder victim is found and the identity of the murderer is not known, five members of the Great Sanhedrin in Jerusalem come to measure the distance from the body of the victim, specifically from his nose, to the nearest city. This act of measurement is an independent mitzva, and is performed even where there is no doubt which city is closest to the victim. They would measure only to a city that had a rabbinical court with twenty-three judges, and they would not measure to Jerusalem.

After it has been determined which city is closest to the victim, the Elders of that city bring a heifer to perform the ritual. This heifer cannot be older than two years of age and cannot have performed any work for its owner. However, it is not disqualified if it has a blemish. It is preferable that the heifer be brought to a stream with a strong flow of water. A priest then breaks the neck of the animal from behind using a cleaver, and the Elders of the city state a declaration that they were not responsible for the death, directly or indirectly. The land upon which the ritual is performed may not be farmed in any way.

The Sages inferred from the wording of the verse that the performance of the ritual is required only for one killed with a sword. The victim must be found in the open, lying on the ground, and not hanging, floating on water, or covered on the ground. The ritual is only performed when there is no testimony as to the identity of the murderer. Any testimony, even that of a person ordinarily disqualified from testifying, obviates the need for the performance of the ritual. If there is conflicting testimony, then if the witnesses are qualified, the statement of two overrides the statement of a single witness. If they are witnesses that are ordinarily disqualified, whichever testimony is backed by more witnesses is followed.

There are several mitzvot that were nullified over the years due to a deterioration in the behavior of the Jewish people. Among them are the ritual of the heifer whose neck is broken, the ritual of giving the bitter water to a *sota*, and the declaration of tithes. Several decrees were enacted over the years due to changes in the circumstances of the Jewish people, e.g., decrees to separate tithes from doubtfully tithed produce, to prohibit the playing of music, and to prohibit the study of Greek wisdom.

The Gemara also tells of other effects of the regression in the spiritual level of the Jewish people. The Divine Presence was not as tangibly felt after the destruction of the First Temple, and even less so after the destruction of the Second Temple. The death of certain Sages left a vacuum, as there was no one who manifested the qualities in which each Sage particularly excelled. This deterioration will continue until the time preceding the arrival of the Messiah, upon whose arrival the decline will be ameliorated.

Common **Acronyms**

Since the publication of the first volume of the *Koren Talmud Bavli* we have employed some transliterated acronyms, such as Rambam, to give the translation a more authentic flavor. These acronyms are used throughout this volume where they are well known and where the acronym helps readers easily identify the author in question. The following chart provides the full name of each author or work alongside its common acronym.

Acronym	Full Name
HaAri	Rabbi Yitzḥak Luria
Baḥ	*Bayit Ḥadash*
Beur HaGra	Commentary of Rabbi Eliyahu of Vilna on the *Shulḥan Arukh*
Derashot Mahari Mintz	Homilies of Rabbi Yehuda Mintz
Derashot Ra'anaḥ	Homilies of Rabbi Eliyahu ben Ḥayyim
Geranat	Rabbi Naftali Trop
Gilyon Maharsha	Marginalia of Rabbi Shlomo Eiger
Gra	Rabbi Eliyahu of Vilna, the Vilna Gaon
Grib	Rabbi Yehuda Bakhrakh
Griz	Rabbi Yitzḥak Ze'ev Soloveitchik
Haggahot HaGra	Comments of Rabbi Eliyahu of Vilna on the Talmud
Haggahot Maharsha	Comments of Rabbi Shmuel Eliezer Eidels
Hassagot HaRa'avad	Comments of Rabbi Avraham ben David on the Rambam's *Mishne Torah*
Ḥida	Rabbi Ḥayyim David Azulai
Ḥiddushei Aggadot LaMaharal	*Ḥiddushei Aggadot* by Rabbi Yehuda Loew of Prague
Ḥiddushei Aggadot LaRashba	*Ḥiddushei Aggadot* by Rabbi Shlomo ben Adderet
Ḥiddushei HaGeranat	*Ḥiddushei* Rabbi Naftali Trop
Ḥiddushei HaGriz	*Ḥiddushei* Rabbi Yitzḥak Ze'ev Soloveitchik
Ḥiddushei HaRim	*Ḥiddushei* Rabbi Yitzḥak Meir of Gur
Ḥiddushei Ri Ḥaver	*Ḥiddushei* Rabbi Yitzḥak Isaac Ḥaver
Kitzur Piskei HaRosh	Abridged Halakhic Rulings of Rabbeinu Asher ben Rabbi Yeḥiel
Mabit	Rabbi Moshe ben Yosef di Trani
Maharal	Rabbi Yehuda Loew of Prague
Maharam Alashkar	Rabbi Moshe Alashkar

Acronym	Full Name
Maharam Brisk	Rabbi Mordekhai Brisk
Maharam Ḥalawa	Rabbi Moshe Ḥalawa
Maharam Lublin	Rabbi Meir of Lublin
Maharam Mintz	Rabbi Moshe Mintz
Maharam of Rothenburg	Rabbi Meir of Rothenburg
Maharam Padua	Rabbi Meir of Padua
Maharam Schick	Rabbi Moshe Schick
Maharam Schiff	Rabbi Meir Schiff
Maharatz Ḥayyut	Rabbi Tzvi Hirsch Chajes
Mahari Abuhav	Rabbi Yitzḥak Abuhav
Mahari Bassan	Rabbi Yeḥiel Bassan
Mahari Beirav	Rabbi Ya'akov Beirav
Mahari ben Lev	Rabbi Yosef ben Lev
Mahari ben Malkitzedek	Rabbi Yitzḥak ben Malkitzedek
Mahari Berona	Rabbi Yisrael Berona
Mahari Kurkus	Rabbi Yosef Kurkus
Mahari Mintz	Rabbi Yehuda Mintz
Mahari Weil	Rabbi Ya'akov Weil
Mahariḥ	Rabbi Yeḥezkia ben Ya'akov of Magdeburg
Maharik	Rabbi Yosef Colon
Maharikash	Rabbi Ya'akov Castro
Maharil	Rabbi Ya'akov HaLevi Molin
Maharit	Rabbi Yosef di Trani
Maharit Algazi	Rabbi Yom Tov Algazi
Maharsha	Rabbi Shmuel Eliezer Eidels
Maharshal	Rabbi Shlomo Luria
Malbim	Rabbi Meir Leibush ben Yeḥiel Michel Wisser
Netziv	Rabbi Naftali Tzvi Yehuda Berlin
Nimmukei HaGrib	Comments of Rabbi Yehuda Bakhrakh on the Maharsha
Piskei HaRid	Halakhic Rulings of Rabbi Yeshaya di Trani the Elder
Piskei Riaz	Halakhic Rulings of Rabbi Yeshaya di Trani the Younger
Ra'ah	Rabbi Aharon HaLevi
Ra'anaḥ	Rabbi Eliyahu ben Ḥayyim
Ra'avad	Rabbi Avraham ben David
Ra'avan	Rabbi Eliezer ben Natan
Ra'avya	Rabbi Eliezer ben Yoel HaLevi
Rabbi Avraham ben HaRambam	Rabbi Avraham, son of the Rambam
Rabbi Shlomo ben Rashbatz	Rabbi Shlomo, son of Rabbi Shimon ben Tzemaḥ Duran
Radak	Rabbi David Kimḥi

Acronym	Full Name
Radbaz	Rabbi David ben Zimra
Ralbag	Rabbi Levi ben Gershon
Ramah	Rabbi Meir HaLevi
Rambam	Rabbi Moshe ben Maimon
Ramban	Rabbi Moshe ben Naḥman
Ran	Rabbeinu Nissim ben Reuven of Gerona
Rashash	Rabbi Shmuel Strashun
Rashba	Rabbi Shlomo ben Adderet
Rashbam	Rabbi Shmuel ben Meir
Rashbatz	Rabbi Shimon ben Tzemaḥ Duran
Rashi	Rabbi Shlomo Yitzḥaki
Razah	Rabbi Zeraḥya HaLevi
Re'em Horowitz	Rabbi Elazar Moshe Horowitz
Rema	Rabbi Moshe Isserles
Ri HaLavan	Rabbeinu Yitzḥak ben Ya'akov of Prague
Ri Ḥaver	Rabbi Yitzḥak Isaac Ḥaver
Ri Migash	Rabbi Yosef Migash
Riaf	Rabbi Yoshiya Pinto
Riaz	Rabbi Yeshaya di Trani the Younger
Rid	Rabbi Yeshaya di Trani the Elder
Ridvaz	Rabbi Ya'akov David ben Ze'ev Wilovsky
Rif	Rabbi Yitzḥak Alfasi
Rim	Rabbi Yitzḥak Meir of Gur
Ritva	Rabbi Yom Tov ben Avraham Asevilli (of Seville)
Riva	Rabbeinu Yitzḥak ben Asher
Rivam	Rabbi Yitzḥak ben Meir
Rivan	Rabbi Yehuda bar Natan
Rivash	Rabbi Yitzḥak ben Sheshet
Rosh	Rabbeinu Asher ben Rabbi Yeḥiel
Shakh	*Siftei Kohen* by Rabbi Shabtai Cohen Rappaport
Shas	The Six Orders of the Mishna
She'elat Ya'avetz	Responsa of Rabbi Ya'akov Emden
Shela	*Shenei Luḥot HaBerit* by Rabbi Yeshaya HaLevi Horowitz
Siddur Rashi	Siddur compiled by Rashi's students
Sma	*Sefer Meirat Einayim* by Rabbi Yehoshua Falk
Smag	*Sefer Mitzvot Gadol* by Rabbi Moshe of Coucy
Smak	*Sefer Mitzvot Katan* by Rabbi Yitzḥak ben Yosef of Corbeil
Talmid HaRa'ah	A student of Rabbi Aharon HaLevi
Talmid HaRashba	A student of Rabbi Shlomo ben Adderet

Acronym	Full Name
Tashbetz	Responsa of Rabbi Shimon ben Tzemaḥ Duran
Taz	*Turei Zahav* by Rabbi David HaLevi
Tosefot HaRosh	*Tosefot* of Rabbeinu Asher ben Rabbi Yeḥiel
Tosefot Ri HaLavan	*Tosefot* of Rabbeinu Yitzḥak ben Ya'akov of Prague
Tosefot Rid	*Tosefot* of Rabbi Yeshaya di Trani the Elder
Tur	*Sefer HaTurim* by Rabbi Ya'akov ben Asher
Tzlaḥ	*Tziyyun LeNefesh Ḥayya* by Rabbi Yeḥezkel Landau
Ya'avetz	Rabbi Ya'akov Emden

Index of **Background**

Index of **Background**

Index of **Language**

Index of **Personalities**

Image **Credits**

תלמוד בבלי

מהדורת נאה

סוטה

Steinsaltz Center

KOREN

תלמוד בבלי

הוצאת קורן ירושלים

מהדורת נאה

סוטה

COMMENTARY BY

Rabbi Adin Even-Israel Steinsaltz

EDITOR-IN-CHIEF

Rabbi Dr Tzvi Hersh Weinreb

EXECUTIVE EDITOR

Rabbi Joshua Schreier

•

STEINSALTZ CENTER
KOREN PUBLISHERS JERUSALEM

הַמְקַנֵּא

*לְאִשְׁתּוֹ, רַבִּי אֱלִיעֶזֶר אוֹמֵר: מְקַנֵּא לָהּ עַל פִּי שְׁנַיִם, וּמַשְׁקָה עַל פִּי עֵד אֶחָד, אוֹ ע"פ עַצְמוֹ. רַבִּי יְהוֹשֻׁעַ אוֹמֵר: [א]מְקַנֵּא לָהּ עַל פִּי שְׁנַיִם, [ב]וּמַשְׁקָה ע"פ שְׁנַיִם. כֵּיצַד מְקַנֵּא לָהּ? (א) [ג]אוֹמֵר לָהּ בִּפְנֵי שְׁנַיִם: אַל תְּדַבְּרִי עִם אִישׁ פְּלוֹנִי, וְדִבְּרָה עִמּוֹ – עֲדַיִין הִיא מוּתֶּרֶת לְבֵיתָהּ, וּמוּתֶּרֶת לֶאֱכוֹל בִּתְרוּמָה. *[ד]נִכְנְסָה עִמּוֹ לְבֵית הַסֵּתֶר, וְשָׁהֲתָה עִמּוֹ כְּדֵי טוּמְאָה – אֲסוּרָה לְבֵיתָהּ [ה]וַאֲסוּרָה לֶאֱכוֹל בִּתְרוּמָה. וְאִם מֵת – [ו]חוֹלֶצֶת וְלֹא מִתְיַיבֶּמֶת.§ **גמ'** מִכְּדִי תַּנָּא מִנָּזִיר סָלֵיק, מַאי תְּנָא דְּקָא תָּנֵי סוֹטָה? כִּדְרַבִּי. *דְּתַנְיָא, רַבִּי אוֹמֵר: לָמָּה נִסְמְכָה פָּרָשַׁת נָזִיר לְפָרָשַׁת סוֹטָה – לוֹמַר לְךָ: *שֶׁכָּל הָרוֹאֶה סוֹטָה בְּקִלְקוּלָהּ יַזִּיר עַצְמוֹ מִן הַיַּיִן. וְלִיתְנֵי סוֹטָה וַהֲדַר לִיתְנֵי נָזִיר! אַיְּידֵי דִּתְנָא כְּתוּבּוֹת, וְתָנָא "הַמַּדִּיר" – תָּנָא נְדָרִים, *וְאַיְּידֵי דִּתְנָא נְדָרִים – תָּנָא נָזִיר דְּדָמֵי לִנְדָרִים, וְקָתָנֵי סוֹטָה כִּדְרַבִּי.§ "הַמְקַנֵּא" דִּיעֲבַד – אִין, לְכַתְּחִילָּה – לָא. קָסָבַר תַּנָּא דִּידָן: *אָסוּר לְקַנְּאוֹת. א"ר שְׁמוּאֵל בַּר רַב יִצְחָק, כִּי הֲוָה פָּתַח רֵישׁ לָקִישׁ בְּסוֹטָה אָמַר הָכִי: אֵין מְזַוְּוגִין לוֹ לְאָדָם אִשָּׁה אֶלָּא לְפִי מַעֲשָׂיו, שֶׁנֶּאֱ': "כִּי לֹא יָנוּחַ שֵׁבֶט הָרֶשַׁע עַל גּוֹרַל הַצַּדִּיקִים". *אָמַר רַבָּה בַּר בַּר חָנָה אָמַר ר' יוֹחָנָן: וְקָשִׁין לְזַוְּוגָן כִּקְרִיעַת יַם סוּף, שֶׁנֶּאֱמַר: "אֱלֹהִים מוֹשִׁיב יְחִידִים בַּיְתָה מוֹצִיא אֲסִירִים בַּכּוֹשָׁרוֹת". אִינִי? וְהָא *אָמַר רַב יְהוּדָה אָמַר רַב: אַרְבָּעִים יוֹם קוֹדֶם יְצִירַת הַוָּלָד בַּת קוֹל יוֹצֵאת וְאוֹמֶרֶת: בַּת פְּלוֹנִי לִפְלוֹנִי, בֵּית פְּלוֹנִי לִפְלוֹנִי, שְׂדֵה פְּלוֹנִי לִפְלוֹנִי! לָא קַשְׁיָא; הָא – בְּזוּג רִאשׁוֹן, הָא – בְּזוּג שֵׁנִי.§ "ר"א אוֹמֵר: מְקַנֵּא לָהּ עַל פִּי שְׁנַיִם" וכו'.§ עַד כָּאן לָא פְּלִיגֵי אֶלָּא בְּקִינּוּי וּסְתִירָה, אֲבָל [ז]בְּטוּמְאָה – עֵד אֶחָד מְהֵימַן, *וּתְנַן נַמִי: עֵד אֶחָד אוֹמֵר "אֲנִי רָאִיתִי שֶׁנִּיטְמֵאת" – לֹא הָיְתָה שׁוֹתָה. מִדְּאוֹרַיְיתָא מְנָלַן דִּמְהֵימַן עֵד אֶחָד? *דְּתָנוּ רַבָּנַן: "וְעֵד אֵין בָּהּ" בִּשְׁנַיִם הַכָּתוּב מְדַבֵּר, אוֹ אֵינוֹ אֶלָּא אֲפִילּוּ בְּאֶחָד? ת"ל: "לֹא יָקוּם עֵד אֶחָד בְּאִישׁ", מִמַּשְׁמַע

תהלים קכה | שם סח | במדבר ה | דברים יט

רש"י

הַמְקַנֵּא לְאִשְׁתּוֹ. לִישָּׁנָא דִּקְרָא נָקַט: "וְקִנֵּא אֶת אִשְׁתּוֹ" (במדבר ה). וּלְקַמָּן בַּגְּמָ' מְפָרֵשׁ מַאי לְשׁוֹן קִינּוּי. (ב) וּבְמַתְנִיתִין מְפָרֵשׁ: כֵּיצַד מְקַנֵּא לָהּ? אוֹמֵר לָהּ "אַל תִּסָּתְרִי עִם אִישׁ פְּלוֹנִי". **מְקַנֵּא לָהּ ע"פ** שְׁנַיִם. אִם בָּא לְהַשְׁקוֹתָהּ צָרִיךְ לְהָבִיא שְׁנֵי עֵדִים שֶׁאָמַר לָהּ בִּפְנֵיהֶם "אַל תִּסָּתְרִי עִמּוֹ". וְאִם לֹא קִינֵּא לָהּ בִּפְנֵי שְׁנַיִם, אֵינָהּ נֶאֱסֶרֶת עָלָיו בִּסְתִירָתָהּ וְאֵינוֹ מַשְׁקֶה. **וּמַשְׁקֶה ע"פ עֵד א' אוֹ ע"פ עַצְמוֹ.** וַאֲפִי' אֵין עֵדִים שֶׁנִּסְתְּרָה, אֶלָּא עֵד אֶחָד, אוֹ הוּא עַצְמוֹ אוֹמֵר "רְאִיתִיהָ שֶׁנִּסְתְּרָה אַחַר שֶׁקִּינֵּאתִי לָהּ" – נֶאֱסֶרֶת בִּסְתִירָה עַד שֶׁתִּשְׁתֶּה. וּלְקַמָּן יָלְפִינַן מִקְּרָאֵי שֶׁסְּתִירָתָהּ אוֹסַרְתָּהּ עָלָיו מִסָּפֵק. **ר' יְהוֹשֻׁעַ אוֹמֵר.** צָרִיךְ ב' עֵדִים אַף לִסְתִירָתָהּ. **וְדִבְּרָה עִמּוֹ.** שֶׁלֹּא בִּמְקוֹם סֵתֶר. **עֲדַיִין** (ג) מוּתֶּרֶת לְבֵיתָהּ. לְשַׁמֵּשׁ עִם בַּעְלָהּ. **וּמוּתֶּרֶת בִּתְרוּמָה.** אִם אֵשֶׁת כֹּהֵן הִיא. **כְּדֵי טוּמְאָה.** כְּדֵי הַעֲרָאָה. **אֲסוּרָה לְבֵיתָהּ.** מִסָּפֵק, כִּדְיָלְפִינַן לְקַמָּן (דף כח.): שְׁלֹשָׁה "וְנִטְמָאָה" אֲמוּרִים בַּפָּרָשָׁה: "וְקִנֵּא אֶת אִשְׁתּוֹ וְהִיא נִטְמָאָה", "וְנִסְתְּרָה וְהִיא נִטְמָאָה" "תַּחַת אִישָׁהּ וְנִטְמָאָה". אֶחָד – שֶׁאֲסוּרָה לַבַּעַל, וְאֶחָד – שֶׁאֲסוּרָה לַבּוֹעֵל אִם יָמוּת בַּעְלָהּ אוֹ יְגָרְשֶׁנָּה, וְאֶחָד – שֶׁאֲסוּרָה לִתְרוּמָה. **וְאִם מֵת.** קוֹדֶם שֶׁהִשְׁקָהּ וְאֵין לוֹ בָּנִים וְהִיא זְקוּקָה לְיָבָם. **חוֹלֶצֶת.** לִינָּשֵׂא לַשּׁוּק וְלֹא מִתְיַיבֶּמֶת וּבַגְּמָרָא יָלֵיף לָהּ. **גמ' מִכְּדִי תַּנָּא מִנָּזִיר קָא סָלֵיק.** כֵּן סֵדֶר הַמִּשְׁנָה, סוֹטָה אַחַר נָזִיר. **מַאי תַּנָּא דְּתָנָא סוֹטָה.** מַאי תָּנָא בִּנְזִירוּת דְּדָמֵי לְסוֹטָה, דְּתָנָא סוֹטָה בַּתְרָהּ? **בְּקִלְקוּלָהּ.** בְּנִיוּוּלָהּ וּבְבָשְׁתָּהּ. שֶׁמְּנַוְּולִין אוֹתָהּ, כִּדְקָתָנֵי מַתְנִי' (לקמן דף ז:): קוֹשֵׁר חֶבֶל לְמַעְלָה מִדַּדֶּיהָ. **יַזִּיר עַצְמוֹ מִן הַיַּיִן.** שֶׁהַיַּיִן מֵבִיא לִידֵי קַלּוּת רֹאשׁ וְהוּא גָּרַם לָהּ. **וְלִיתְנֵי סוֹטָה וַהֲדַר נָזִיר.** שֶׁכָּךְ הִיא סְמִיכַת פָּרָשָׁתַיְיהוּ. **וְתָנָא הַמַּדִּיר.** פֶּרֶק הוּא בִּכְתוּבּוֹת "הַמַּדִּיר אֶת אִשְׁתּוֹ". וְאַיְּידֵי דְּאַיְירֵי בִּנְדָרִ' – תָּנָא נְדָרִים אַחַר כְּתוּבּוֹ'. וְאַיְּידֵי דְּתָנָא נְדָרִים – תָּנָא נָזִיר בַּתְרָהּ, שֶׁאַף הַנְּזִירוּת בָּאָה עַל יְדֵי נֶדֶר. וַהֲדַר תָּנָא סוֹטָה בַּתְרָהּ. **לְכַתְּחִילָּה לָא.** מִדְּלָא תָּנֵי: רַבִּי אֱלִיעֶזֶר אוֹמֵר מְקַנֵּא אָדָם לְאִשְׁתּוֹ עַל פִּי שְׁנַיִם. **אָסוּר לְקַנְּאוֹת.** שֶׁמֵּבִיא עַצְמוֹ לִידֵי תִּגָּר, וְאֶת אִשְׁתּוֹ לִידֵי נִיוּוּל, וַאֲפִי' הִיא טְהוֹרָה. **כִּי** (ד) **פָּתַח.** כְּשֶׁהָיָה בָּא לִדְרוֹשׁ בְּפָרָשַׁת סוֹטָה. **מְזַוְּוגִין אִשָּׁה לְפִי מַעֲשָׂיו.** צְנוּעָה לַצַּדִּיק וּפְרוּצָה לָרָשָׁע. **כִּי לֹא יָנוּחַ שֵׁבֶט הָרֶשַׁע עַל גּוֹרַל הַצַּדִּיקִים.** לֹא יִזְדַּוֵּוג מֶמְשֶׁלֶת רֶשַׁע בְּגוֹרַל צַדִּיק. **וְקָשִׁין.** לִפְנֵי הַמָּקוֹם. **לְזַוְּוגָם.** הָנָךְ דִּלְפִי מַעֲשָׂיו. **כִּקְרִיעַת יַם סוּף.** שֶׁנִּשְׁתַּנּוּ סִדְרֵי בְרֵאשִׁית. **מוֹשִׁיב יְחִידִים בַּיְתָה.** אָדָם יָחִיד וְאִשָּׁה יְחִידָה, וְהוּא מְזַוְּוגָם יַחַד וּמְיַישֵּׁב מֵהֶם בַּיִת. **מוֹצִיא אֲסִירִים בַּכּוֹשָׁרוֹת.** הוֹצִיא אֶת יִשְׂרָאֵל מִמִּצְרַיִם בְּחֹדֶשׁ (ה) כָּשֵׁר, לֹא חַמָּה וְלֹא צִינָּה. מַקִּישׁ זִיוּוּג יְחִידִים לִיצִיאַת מִצְרַיִם. **אִינִי.** מִי הָוֵי זִיוּוּג לְפִי רֶשַׁע וּזְכוּת? וְהָא מִקּוֹדֶם יְצִירָתָם, שֶׁאֵין נוֹדָע רִשְׁעוֹ וּזְכוּתוֹ, מַכְרִיזִין אֶת זוּגוֹ! וְאִם תֹּאמַר: הַכֹּל גָּלוּי לְפָנָיו – הַכֹּל בִּידֵי שָׁמַיִם חוּץ מִיִּרְאַת שָׁמַיִם. כִּדְאָמַר בְּמַסֶּכֶת נִדָּה (דף טז:): מַלְאָךְ הַמְּמוּנֶּה עַל הַהֵרָיוֹן, נוֹטֵל טִיפָּה וּמְבִיאָהּ לִפְנֵי הַמָּקוֹם, וְאוֹמֵר לְפָנָיו: טִיפָּה זוֹ מַה תְּהֵא עָלֶיהָ – גִּבּוֹר אוֹ חַלָּשׁ, חָכָם אוֹ טִיפֵּשׁ, עָשִׁיר אוֹ עָנִי. אֲבָל צַדִּיק וְרָשָׁע לָא קָאָמַר לֵיהּ, דְּאֵין זֶה בִּידֵי (ו) שָׁמַיִם. **זוּג רִאשׁוֹן.** לְפִי הַמַּזָּל. **זוּג שֵׁנִי.** לְפִי מַעֲשָׂיו. וְקָשֶׁה לְזַוְּוגָן, לְפִי שֶׁאֵינָהּ בַּת זוּגוֹ. **עַד כָּאן לָא פְּלִיגֵי אֶלָּא בְּקִינּוּי וּסְתִירָה.** כְּלוֹמַר, עַד כָּאן לֹא שָׁמַעְנוּ מִפְּלוּגְתַּיְיהוּ דְּבָעֵינַן שְׁנֵי עֵדִים, אֶלָּא בְּקִינּוּי לְר"א וּבִסְתִירָה לְר' יְהוֹשֻׁעַ. **אֲבָל בְּטוּמְאָה.** אִם יֵשׁ עֵדִים בְּקִינּוּי וּסְתִירָה, וְיֵשׁ עֵד אֶחָד שֶׁקִּילְקְלָה בִּסְתִירָתָהּ – נֶאֱמָן. וְאֵינָהּ שׁוֹתָה, אֶלָּא יוֹצְאָה בְּלֹא כְּתוּבָּה, וַאֲסוּרָה לַבַּעַל וְלַבּוֹעֵל וְלִתְרוּמָה. **שֶׁנִּטְמֵאת.** בְּאוֹתָהּ סְתִירָה. **מְנָלַן דִּמְהֵימַן עֵד אֶחָד.** בְּטוּמְאָה שֶׁל סְתִירָה אַחַר קִינּוּי. **וְעֵד אֵין בָּהּ בִּשְׁנַיִם הַכָּתוּב מְדַבֵּר.** וְקָאָמַר: עֵדִים שְׁנַיִם אֵין בְּטוּמְאָה זוֹ, אֶלָּא עֵד א'. וּקְרָא בְּטוּמְאָה קָמִישְׁתָּעֵי "וְשָׁכַב אִישׁ אוֹתָהּ שִׁכְבַת זֶרַע", וְעֵדִים שְׁנַיִם אֵין בָּהּ אֶלָּא א', "וְהִיא לֹא נִתְפָּשָׂה" – לֹא נֶאֱנְסָה. וּמִמֵּילָא שָׁמְעִינַן דִּמְהֵימַן, מִדִּכְתִיב: "וְהִיא לֹא נִתְפָּשָׂה" – לְהַחְמִיר עָלֶיהָ בָּא הַכָּתוּב, לְדוּנָהּ כִּמְזִידָה. וּמֵרֵישָׁא דִּקְרָא נַמִי שָׁמְעַתְּ דִּמְהֵימַן, דְּקָאָמַר "וּמָעֲלָה בוֹ מַעַל וְשָׁכַב אִישׁ אוֹתָהּ" וְאֵין מֵעִיד בַּדָּבָר אֶלָּא זֶה. וּלְקַמָּן (דף ג.) מְפָרֵשׁ דְּהַאי קְרָא בָּתַר קִינּוּי כְּתִיב, דִּכְתִיב בַּתְרֵיהּ: "וְעָבַר עָלָיו רוּחַ קִנְאָה" וגו', וְדָרְשִׁינַן לֵיהּ לְקַמָּן: שֶׁכְּבָר עָבַר. **אוֹ אֵינוֹ אֶלָּא אֶחָד.** דְּקָאָמַר קְרָא דַּאֲפִילּוּ עֵד אֶחָד אֵין בָּהּ. וּלְקַמָּן פָּרֵיךְ: אֶלָּא בְּמַאי מִיתַּסְרָא? דְּקָאָמַר קְרָא: "וְהִיא לֹא נִתְפָּשָׂה" – אַלְמָא פְּשִׁיטָא דְּנִטְמֵאת, מִדְּמַהֲדַר בָּתַר אוֹנֶס וְרָצוֹן. **ת"ל לֹא יָקוּם עֵד א' וגו'.** מֵהַאי קְרָא שָׁמְעִינַן דְּכָל "עֵד" הָאָמוּר בַּתּוֹרָה – שְׁנַיִם הֵם, כִּדְמְפָרֵשׁ וְאָזֵיל. מִמַּשְׁמַע

סנהדרין פח. | יבמות יח. | ברכות סג. | [נזיר ב.] | [יבמות ג. וש"נ] | [לקמן ג.] | סנהדרין כב. [מו"ק יח] | [מו"ק יח: ע"ש סנהדרין כב.] | לקמן לח. | שם:

תוספות

המקנא. איידי דתנא נדרים תנא נמי נזיר דדמיא לנדרים. תימה: והא בריש מסכת נזיר (דף ב.) אמר דלא תנא ליה אלא אגב סוטה, כדרבי! וי"ל: דלא קבעה בסדר נשים אלא אגב סוטה, ומשום דדמיא לנדרים – קבעה בתר נדרים מ"ר. ותימה: אמאי (ז) לא קבעה אגב נדרים? דהא בפ"ד [דנזיר] תנא משניות טובא דמיירי בנדרי נשים ובהפרת בעל! ויש לומר: דעדיפא ליה למימר משום סוטה, דפרשיות נמי נסמכו. ובריש מסכת שבועות (ח) (דף ב:) דייק נמי בכה"ג.

המקנא דיעבד אין. וא"ת: וכי כל היכא דתני ה"א בתחילתן לשון דיעבד הוא? והא קתני בסוף "אלו עוברין" (פסחים דף מט.): ההולך לשחוט את פסחו, ובעבודה זרה פרק "השוכר" (דף סט.): המניח גוי בחנותו, דמסיק בשמעתתא קמייתא דשחיטת חולין (ט) (דף ג.) דמיירי לכתחילה. ובפרק ב' דשחיטת חולין (דף לז.): (י) השוחט את המסוכנת, ובפרק קמא דבילה (דף ו:): השוחט את התרנגולת ומצא בה ביצים גמורות! ויש לומר: דכל היכא דאיכא למיתלי (כ) בלישנא – דייק הכי, כגון הכא, ובריש פ"ב דשחיטת חולין (דף כז.), והתם נמי בפ' קמא (דף טו:): השוחט במגל יד, ובפ' קמא דבילה (דף ז:): השוחט חיה ועוף יחפור בדקר, ובפ' "חבית" (שבת דף קמז.): הרוחץ במי מערה או במי טבריא. (ל) ותימה: היכי דייק מהכא דאסור לקנאות, אמאי לא מתרץ: המקנא שבא, כדמתרץ בפ"ק דבילה (דף ז:)? ועל כרחך אית לן למימר דהכא ממשנה יתירא דייק, כדפרש"י.

הא בזוג ראשון הא בזוג שני. תימה: בפ' "ואלו מגלחין" (מו"ק דף יח:) דאמר שמואל: מותר לארס בחולו של מועד שמא יקדמנו אחר, קפריך ליה מהכא: ארבעים יום קודם יצירת הולד! אמאי לא מוקי התם מלתיה דשמואל בזוג שני?

קודם יצירת הולד. נראה לרבי: קודם יצירת הזכר, בין אם לא נולדה הנקיבה עדיין, בין אם נולדה.

אבל בטומאה עד אחד מהימן. תימה: אדרבה, איכא למימר איפכא: אבל בטומאה בעינן בי תרי, ומשום דאוסרתה איסור עולם. ואי לאו ממתני' דמייתי – מהיכא פשיטא ליה למימר הכי? וי"ל: דעדיפא ליה טומאה מקינוי וסתירה, אף על גב דאוסרתה איסור עולם – משום דרגלים לדבר. כל

עין משפט נר מצוה

א א מיי' פ"א מהל' סוטה הלכה א סמג עשין נו טוש"ע אה"ע סימן קעח סעיף ב:

ב ב מיי' שם הלכה ב טוש"ע שם סעיף ז:

ג ג מיי' שם הלכה ד טוש"ע שם סעיף ו:

ד ד מיי' שם הלכה ב סמג שם טוש"ע שם סעיף ז:

ה ה מיי' פ"ח מהלכות תרומות הלכה טו:

ו ו מיי' פ"ג מהל' יבום הל' יט סמג עשין נא טור וש"ע אה"ע סי' קעד סעיף א:

ז ז מיי' פ"א מהלכות סוטה הלכה יד סמג עשין נו טור וש"ע אה"ע סימן קעח סעיף יז:

תוספות שאנץ

אסורה לביתה פירש הקונטרס מספק כדילפינן לקמן ב' תחת אישה ונטמאה. אחד שאסורה לבעל ואחד שאסורה לבועל אם ימות בעלה או ירגשנה. ואחד שאסורה לאכול בתרומה. לשון הקו'. וה"ה דהוה מצי למימר דאסורה לבועל אלא אגב דתנא לעיל ומותרת לאכול בתרומה תנא נמי ואסורה לאכול בתרומה דלעיל לא מיירי בדין בועל כמו שהיא מותרת לביתה. ואם מת חולצת ולא מתייבמת. ובגמרא יליף מנא לן והכי נמי הוה מצי למיתני פלוגתא דב"ש וב"ה דנוטלות כתובה ולא שותות וב"ה אומר' שאינן נוטלות כתובה אלא בממונא לא מיירי הכא: גמ' מכדי תנא מנזיר סליק מאי שנא דקתני סוטה ואע"ג דאין סדר למשנה פי' בריש פ"ק דבבא מציעא: כל הרואה סוטה בקלקולה פ"ה בניוולה ובושתה שמנוולין אותה (ממקום) למקום שמטילין אותה וקושר חבל למעלה מדדיה יזיר עצמו מן היין שהיין מביא לידי קלות ראש והוא גרם לה לשון הקונ'. המקנא דיעבד אין לכתחלה לא. ותימה דהא איכא הרבה מקומות דלא פריך כי הכא כגון המביא גט לאשתו וכן השולח הדוי אפילו לכתחלה. וי"ל דלא פריך ליה אלא היכא דאיכא למטעי דהוי לשון דיעבד. אי נמי י"ל דלא פריך ליה אלא היכא דאיכא דמצי למימר ביה תירוץ: וקשה לזווגן כקריעת ים סוף שנאמר אלהים מושיב יחידים ביתה. פ"ה יחידים אדם יחיד ואשה יחידה והוא מזווגן יחד והוא קשה כמו מוציא אסירים ישראל בכושרות בחדש כשר לא חמה ולא צינה. וא"ת אמאי נקט קריעת ים סוף טפי משאר נסים של יציאת מצרים. וי"ל דמ"ד א) בכושרות דר' מדרשי' בעלמא בבכי ובשירות בכי למצרים ושירות לישראל והיינו קריעת ים סוף שבאותו נס היה כן ואמר ר"ת פי' מדמי ליה ליציאת מצרים וקריעת ים סוף שבאותו ענין שטבע הקב"ה את המצריים בים כדי להציל את ישראל כמו הורג בעלה של זה ואשתו של זה ומשיאן זה לזה דבזיווג שני קא מיירי כדמפרש בסמוך. איני והאמר רב יהודה (רב אדא) [אמר רב] ארבעים יום פ"ה איני מי הוי זווג לפי רשע וזכות והא מקודם (רשעיו וזכותיו) [יצירתו] מכריזין את זווגו וא"ת הכל גלוי לפניו והוא בידו הא אמר במסכת נדה דמלאך הממונה על ההריון נוטל הטיפה ומביאה לפני הקב"ה ואומר טפה זו מה תהא עליה גבור או חלש חכם או טפש עני או עשיר אבל צדיק ורשע לא דאין זה בידי שמים [שאין נודע רשעו וזכיותיו]. כדאמרי' הכל בידי שמים חוץ מיראת שמים כפ"ה. זוג שני כגון אלמון לאלמנה אבל בחור שנשא אלמנה או אפכא הוי כמו זוג ראשון. [illegible]

הגהות הב"ח

(א) במשנה אמר לה בפני שנים: (ב) רש"י ד"ה המקנא וכו' ובמתני' מפרש. [illegible]

[illegible]

ח א טוש"ע אה"ע סי' קעח סעיף ז:

ס"א דר"א ועי' רש"א

*מִמַּשְׁמַע שֶׁנֶּאֱמַר "לֹא יָקוּם עֵד בְּאִישׁ" אֵינִי יוֹדֵעַ שֶׁהוּא אֶחָד? מַה ת"ל "אֶחָד" — זֶה בָּנָה אָב: כָּל מָקוֹם שֶׁנֶּאֱמַר "עֵד" — הֲרֵי כָּאן שְׁנַיִם, עַד שֶׁיִּפְרוֹט לְךָ הַכָּתוּב "אֶחָד". וְאָמַר רַחֲמָנָא: תְּרֵי לֵית בַּהּ, אֶלָּא חַד °"וְהִיא לֹא נִתְפָּשָׂה" — אֲסוּרָה. אֶלָּא טַעְמָא דִּכְתִיב "לֹא יָקוּם עֵד אֶחָד בְּאִישׁ", הָא לָאו הָכִי — הֲוָה אָמִינָא "עֵד" דְּסוֹטָה חַד הוּא, וְאִי אֲפִילּוּ חַד לֵיכָּא, אֶלָּא בְּמַאי מִיתַּסְרָא? אִיצְטְרִיךְ, סד"א: "עֵד אֵין בָּהּ" — אֵין נֶאֱמָן בָּהּ. אֵין נֶאֱמָן בָּהּ?! וְאֶלָּא מַאי בָּעֵי — עַד דְּאִיכָּא תְּרֵי? לִישְׁתּוֹק קְרָא מִינֵּיהּ, דְּאָתְיָא "דָּבָר" "דָּבָר" מִמָּמוֹן, וַאֲנָא יָדַעְנָא, מִידֵּי דַּהֲוָה אַכָּל עֵדְיוֹת שֶׁבַּתּוֹרָה! אִיצְטְרִיךְ, סד"א: סוֹטָה שָׁאנֵי, *דְּרַגְלַיִם לַדָּבָר, שֶׁהֲרֵי קִינֵּא לָהּ וְנִסְתְּרָה — לִיתְהֵימַן בַּהּ עֵד אֶחָד. וּמִי מָצֵית אָמְרַתְּ דְּאֵין נֶאֱמָן בָּהּ וְשַׁרְיָא? וְהָא מִדִּכְתִיב "וְהִיא לֹא נִתְפָּשָׂה" — מִכְּלָל דַּאֲסוּרָה! אִיצְטְרִיךְ, סד"א: אֵין נֶאֱמָן בָּהּ — עַד דְּאִיכָּא תְּרֵי, וּבִתְרֵי נַמִי — הִיא דְּלֹא נִתְפָּשָׂה, קמ"ל. § "רַבִּי יְהוֹשֻׁעַ אוֹמֵר מְקַנֵּא לָהּ עַל פִּי שְׁנַיִם" וכו'. § מ"ט דְּרַבִּי יְהוֹשֻׁעַ? אָמַר קְרָא °"בָּהּ" — בָּהּ וְלֹא בְּקִינּוּי, בָּהּ וְלֹא בִּסְתִירָה. וְרַבִּי אֱלִיעֶזֶר אוֹמֵר: "בָּהּ" — וְלֹא בְּקִינּוּי. וְאֵימָא: "בָּהּ" — וְלֹא בִּסְתִירָה! סְתִירָה אִיתַּקַּשׁ לְטוּמְאָה, דִּכְתִיב: °"וְנִסְתְּרָה וְהִיא נִטְמָאָה". קִינּוּי נַמִי אִיתַּקַּשׁ לְטוּמְאָה, דִּכְתִיב: °"וְקִנֵּא אֶת אִשְׁתּוֹ וְהִיא נִטְמָאָה"! הָא מִיעֵט רַחֲמָנָא "בָּהּ". וּמָה רָאִיתָ? מִסְתַּבְּרָא סְתִירָה עֲדִיפָא, שֶׁכֵּן אוֹסַרְתָּהּ כְּטוּמְאָה. אַדְּרַבָּה, קִינּוּי עָדִיף שֶׁכֵּן עִיקָּר גָּרַם לָהּ! אִי לָאו סְתִירָה — קִינּוּי מִי אִיכָּא? וְאִי לָאו קִינּוּי — סְתִירָה מַאי אַהֲנֵי? אפ"ה סְתִירָה עֲדִיפָא, דְּאַתְחַלְתָּא דְּטוּמְאָה הִיא. מַתְנִי' דְּלָא כִּי הַאי תַּנָּא, דְּתַנְיָא, *רַבִּי יוֹסֵי בְּרַבִּי יְהוּדָה אוֹמֵר מִשּׁוּם ר' אֱלִיעֶזֶר: הַמְקַנֵּא לְאִשְׁתּוֹ — מְקַנֵּא ע"פ עֵד אֶחָד אוֹ ע"פ עַצְמוֹ, וּמַשְׁקֶה לָהּ עַל פִּי שְׁנַיִם. הֵשִׁיבוּ חֲכָמִים: לְדִבְרֵי רַבִּי יוֹסֵי בְּרַבִּי יְהוּדָה אֵין לַדָּבָר סוֹף. מ"ט דְּר' יוֹסֵי בְּרַבִּי יְהוּדָה? אָמַר קְרָא "בָּהּ" — בָּהּ וְלֹא בִּסְתִירָה. וְאֵימָא: "בָּהּ" — וְלֹא בְּקִינּוּי! קִינּוּי אִיתַּקַּשׁ לְטוּמְאָה, דִּכְתִיב: "וְקִנֵּא אֶת אִשְׁתּוֹ וְהִיא נִטְמָאָה" — סְתִירָה נַמִי אִיתַּקַּשׁ לְטוּמְאָה, דִּכְתִיב: "וְנִסְתְּרָה וְהִיא נִטְמָאָה"?! הַהוּא לְכַמָּה שִׁיעוּר סְתִירָה — כְּדֵי טוּמְאָה, הוּא דְּאָתָא. "הֵשִׁיבוּ חֲכָמִים: לְדִבְרֵי ר' יוֹסֵי בְּר' יְהוּדָה, אֵין לַדָּבָר סוֹף". מַאי נִיהוּ? דִּזְמָנִין דְּלָא קַנֵּי וְאָמַר "קַנֵּאי". הָא לְמִשְׁנָתֵינוּ יֵשׁ לַדָּבָר סוֹף? זִמְנִין דְּלָא אִיסְתַּתַּר וְאָמַר "אִיסְתַּתַּר"! אָמַר רַב יִצְחָק בַּר יוֹסֵף א"ר יוֹחָנָן: אַף לְדִבְרֵי רַבִּי יוֹסֵי בְּר' יְהוּדָה אֵין לַדָּבָר סוֹף. אַף לְדִבְרֵי רַבִּי יוֹסֵי בְּר' יְהוּדָה וְלָא מִיבַּעְיָא לְמִשְׁנָתֵינוּ?! אַדְּרַבָּה, לְמִשְׁנָתֵינוּ אִיכָּא עִיקָּר, הָתָם לֵיכָּא עִיקָּר! אֶלָּא, אִי אִיתְּמַר — הָכִי אִיתְּמַר, א"ר יִצְחָק בַּר יוֹסֵף א"ר יוֹחָנָן: לְדִבְרֵי ר' יוֹסֵי בְּר' יְהוּדָה, *אַף לְמִשְׁנָתֵינוּ אֵין לַדָּבָר סוֹף. א"ר חֲנִינָא מִסּוּרָא: אלָא לֵימָא אִינִישׁ לְאִיתְּתֵיהּ בִּזְמַן הַזֶּה "לָא תִּיסְתְּרִי בַּהֲדֵי פְּלוֹנִי", דִּילְמָא קיי"ל כְּרַבִּי יוֹסֵי בְּר' יְהוּדָה דְּאָמַר קִינּוּי עַל פִּי עַצְמוֹ, וּמִיסְתַּתְרָא, וְלֵיכָּא הָאִידָּנָא מֵי סוֹטָה לְמִיבְדְּקָהּ, וְקָאָסַר לָהּ עִילָּוֵיהּ אִיסּוּרָא דִּלְעוֹלָם. אָמַר רֵישׁ לָקִישׁ: מַה לְּשׁוֹן קִינּוּי — דָּבָר הַמַּטִּיל קִנְאָה בֵּינָהּ לְבֵין אֲחֵרִים. אַלְמָא קָסָבַר קִינּוּי עַל פִּי עַצְמוֹ, וְכוּלֵּי עָלְמָא לָא יָדְעִי דְּקַנֵּי לָהּ, וְאָמְרִי: מַאי דְּקַמָּא דְּקָא בָּדְלָה, וְאָתוּ לְמֵיעְבַד קִנְאָה בַּהֲדָהּ. וְרַב יֵימַר בַּר ר' שֶׁלֶמְיָא מִשְּׁמֵיהּ דְּאַבַּיֵּי אָמַר: דָּבָר הַמַּטִּיל קִנְאָה בֵּינוֹ לְבֵינָהּ. אַלְמָא קָסָבַר: קִינּוּי עַל פִּי שְׁנַיִם עֵדִים, וְכוּלֵּי עָלְמָא יָדְעִי דְּקַנֵּי לָהּ, וְאִיהוּ הוּא דְּאָתֵי לְמֵיעְבַד קִנְאָה בַּהֲדָהּ. אַלְמָא

מִמַּשְׁמַע שֶׁנֶּאֱמַר עֵד. וְלֹא נֶאֱמַר "עֵדִים", אֵינִי יוֹדֵעַ דְּאֶחָד קָאָמַר? אֶלָּא מִדְּאִילְטְרִיךְ לְמִיכְתַּב "אֶחָד", שְׁמַע מִינָּהּ דְּ"עֵד" – שְׁנַיִם מַשְׁמַע, דְּהַיְינוּ אֶלָּא לְשׁוֹן עֵדוּת, וּסְתָם עֵדוּת שְׁנַיִם. וְאָמַר רַחֲמָנָא תְּרֵי לֵית בַּהּ. לְעֵיל קָאֵי, לְפָרוּשֵׁי מַסְקַנָא דְּמִילְּתֵיהּ – הֵיכִי מִידְרֵישׁ "וְעֵד אֵין בָּהּ". אֶלָּא טַעְמָא כו'. קוּשְׁיָא הִיא: כְּלוֹמַר, טַעְמָא דִּכְתִיב "לֹא יָקוּם עֵד אֶחָד", דְּהַהוּא מוֹכַח לָךְ דְּהַאי "וְעֵד אֵין בָּהּ" – בִּתְרֵי קָאָמַר. הָא לָאו הָכִי – הֲוָה אָמִינָא: "עֵד" דִּכְתִיב הָכָא בְּסוֹטָה – חַד הוּא, וְקָאָמְרִינַן: אֲפִילּוּ אֶחָד אֵין בָּהּ. אִיצְטְרִיךְ. "לֹא יָקוּם עֵד אֶחָד" לְגַלּוּיֵי עֲלֵיהּ דְּהַאי, וּלְאַשְׁמְעִינַן דְּחַד מְהֵימַן. דְּאִי לָאו הָכִי הֲוָה אָמִינָא: כָּל סְתָם "עֵד" – אֶחָד הוּא, וּבְסוֹטָה לָא הֲוָה אָמִינָא דְּמִיתַּסְרָא וַאֲפִי' בְּעֵד א', וְכָל שֶׁכֵּן בְּלֹא עֵד. וְהָכִי הֲוָה דָּרְשִׁינַן לֵיהּ: "וְעֵד אֵין בָּהּ" דְּקָא אָמַר רַחֲמָנָא – הָכִי קָאָמַר: "וְעֵד אֶחָד אֵין נֶאֱמָן בָּהּ, אֶלָּא שְׁנַיִם: וּפָרְכִינַן. אֵין נֶאֱמָן בָּהּ. בִּתְמִיָּה. אֶלָּא מַאי בָּעֵי. קְרָא עַד דְּאִיכָּא תְּרֵי? בִּתְמִיָּה: אַמַּאי אֲתָא קְרָא לְהַאי? לִשְׁתּוֹק קְרָא מִינֵּיהּ כו'. דָּבָר דָּבָר מִמָּמוֹן. כְּתִיב בְּנוֹאֶפֶת: "כִּי מָצָא בָהּ עֶרְוַת דָּבָר" (דברים כד), וּכְתִיב בְּדִינֵי מָמוֹנוֹת: "ע"פ שְׁנֵי עֵדִים יָקוּם דָּבָר" (שם יט). אִיצְטְרִיךְ. "לֹא יָקוּם" לְגַלּוּיֵי עֲלֵיהּ דְּהַאי "עֵד" דִּבִשְׁנַיִם הַכָּתוּב מְדַבֵּר. דְּאִי לָא גַּלֵּי עֲלֵיהּ, הֲוָה אָמִינָא: "עֵד" – חַד מַשְׁמַע, וְאֵין נֶאֱמָן בָּהּ קָאָמַר קְרָא לְאַשְׁמוּעִינַן. וּדְקַשְׁיָא לָךְ: לָמָּה לִי קְרָא – סָלְקָא דַּעְתָּךְ אָמִינָא: סוֹטָה, שֶׁאַחַר קִינּוּי וּסְתִירָה בָּא עֵד אֶחָד וְהֵעִיד שֶׁנִּטְמְאָה בְּאוֹתָהּ סְתִירָה – שָׁאנֵי, וְרָאוּי לְהַאֲמִינוֹ כָּאן, שֶׁהֲרֵי רַגְלַיִם לַדָּבָר. וּמִי מָצֵית אָמְרַתְּ. דְּאִי לָא גַּלֵּי רַחֲמָנָא דְּכָל "עֵד" שְׁנַיִם הֵם, (א) דַּהֲוָה אָמִינָא דְּהַאי "עֵד אֵין בָּהּ" – אֵין נֶאֱמָן בָּהּ קָאָמַר, א"כ בָּא הַכָּתוּב לְהָקֵל עָלֶיהָ?. וְהָא מִדִּכְתִיב וְהִיא לֹא נִתְפָּשָׂה מִכְּלָל. דִּפְשִׁיטָא לָךְ דְּנִטְמְאָה, וְהֵיכִי קָאָמַר "וְהִיא לֹא נִתְפָּשָׂה" אַ"וְעֵד אֵין בָּהּ"? נְהִי דְּרֵישָׁא דִּקְרָא אִיכָּא לְמֵימַר ע"י שְׁנַיִם עֵדִים; "וְשָׁכַב אִישׁ אוֹתָהּ בְּעֵדִים, וְעֵד אֶחָד אֵין נֶאֱמָן בָּהּ. אֶלָּא "וְהִיא לֹא נִתְפָּשָׂה" – הֵיכִי קָאֵי אֵין נֶאֱמָן בָּהּ? הָא אָמְרַתְּ דְּלָא מַחְזְקִי לָהּ בְּנִבְעֶלֶת! בָּהּ. בְּטוּמְאָה קָאֵי, דְּהָא מִינָּהּ סָלֵיק "וְהִיא נִטְמָאָה וְעֵד אֵין בָּהּ", וְדָרְשִׁינַן: אֵין בָּהּ תְּרֵי אֶלָּא חַד. בָּהּ. עֵד אֶחָד נֶאֱמָן וְלֹא בְּקִינּוּי. סְתִירָה עֲדִיפָא. לְאַחֲמוּרֵי בָּהּ. שֶׁכֵּן אוֹסַרְתָּהּ. עַל הַבַּעַל וְעַל הַבּוֹעֵל מִסָּפֵק. כְּטוּמְאָה. וַדָּאִית, כִּדְדָרְשִׁינַן לְקַמָּן: מַגִּיד לָךְ הַכָּתוּב שֶׁעַל הַסָּפֵק אֲסוּרָה. בְּפֶרֶק "כְּשֵׁם שֶׁהַמַּיִם בּוֹדְקִין" (דף כח.). שֶׁכֵּן עִיקָּר גָּרַם לָהּ. שֶׁע"י הַקִּינּוּי סְתִירָתָהּ אוֹסַרְתָּהּ. מַתְנִי'. דְּקָתָנֵי לְר"א דְּקִינּוּי בִּשְׁנַיִם, וּסְתִירָה עַל פִּי עַצְמוֹ. דְּלָא כִּי הַאי תַּנָּא. דְּקָתָנֵי לְר"א סְתִירָה בִּשְׁנַיִם, וְקִינּוּי עַל פִּי עַצְמוֹ. לְדִבְרֵי ר"י בְּר' יְהוּדָה אֵין לְדִבְרֵי ר' אֱלִיעֶזֶר סוֹף. וּלְקַמָּן מְפָרֵשׁ לָהּ. מַאי נִיהוּ. "אֵין לַדָּבָר סוֹף" דְּקָאָמַר.

תורה אור

וְאָמַר קַנֵּאי. כְּשֶׁכּוֹעֵס עָלֶיהָ, אוֹמֵר "קִנֵּאתִי לָהּ מִפְּלוֹנִי" וּמֵבִיא עֵדִים שֶׁנִּסְתְּרָה עִמּוֹ סְתִירָה כָּל שֶׁהוּא. דְּכֵיוָן דְּלֹא קִינֵּא לָהּ – לֹא נִזְהֲרָה בּוֹ. הָא לְמִשְׁנָתֵינוּ יֵשׁ סוֹף. לְדִבְרֵי רַבִּי אֱלִיעֶזֶר? בִּתְמִיָּה. וְהָא זִמְנִין דְּלָא אִיסְתַּתַּר. וְאוֹמֵר "רְאִיתִיהָ שֶׁנִּסְתְּרָה". וְלָא מִיבַּעְיָא לְמִשְׁנָתֵינוּ. בִּתְמִיָּה. אִיכָּא עִיקָּר. שֶׁכְּבָר הִתְחִיל בְּעֵדִים שֶׁלֹּא ע"י כַּעַס. הָכָא לֵיכָּא עִיקָּר. וְלִכְשֶׁיִּכְעוֹס נָקֵל לוֹמַר "קִנֵּאתִי", וְהוּא יִמְצָא לָהּ סְתִירוֹת הַרְבֵּה. לָא לֵימָא אִינִישׁ. אֲפִילּוּ בֵּינוֹ לְבֵינָהּ. וּמִסְתַּתְרָא. וְנִסְתֶּרֶת וְנֶאֱסֶרֶת עָלָיו. קִנְאָה. כַּעַס, כְּמוֹ "הֵם קִנְאוּנִי בְלֹא אֵל" (דברים לב), "כִּי קִנְאָה חֲמַת גָּבֶר" (משלי ו). מַאי דְּקַמָּא. מַה יֵּשׁ לְפָנֵינוּ, מָה אֵירַע עַכְשָׁיו שֶׁזּוֹ בּוֹדֶלֶת מִן הָאֲנָשִׁים? וְכוּלֵּי עָלְמָא יָדְעִי דְּקַנֵּי לָהּ. שֶׁהָעֵדִים מְגַלִּין הַדָּבָר, וְאֵינָן שׂוֹנְאִין אוֹתָהּ. וְאִיהוּ דְּאָתֵי לְמֵיעְבַד קִנְאָה בַּהֲדָהּ. שֶׁזּוֹ מַקְנִיטָתוֹ עַל שֶׁחוֹשְׁדָהּ. אַלְמָא

כל מקום שנאמר עד הרי כאן שנים. ואחד דכתיב גבי "ועד אחד לא יענה בנפש" (במדבר לה), מוקי לה בפרק "אחד דיני ממונות" (סנהדרין דף לד.) בדרישה מן התלמידים. ו"לא יומת על פי עד אחד" (דברים יז) דרשינן בפרק ראשון דמכות (דף ו:) לעדות מיוחדת, לאפוקי אחד רואה מחלון זה ואחד רואה מחלון זה. אבל קשיא: דגבי שבועת העדות כתיב "והוא עד" (ויקרא ה) ומחייבין אפילו אחד, כדתנן (שבועות דף לא:) כפר אחד והודה אחד – הכופר חייב! וי"ל: דשבועת העדות לא חייבה תורה אלא בתביעה, כדילפינן התם מקראי. הילכך כל היכא דמפסידו ממון – מיחייב, דבהפסד ממון תליא מילתא.

מאי טעמא דר' יהושע. בירושלמי מפיק ליה מהני קראי; מאי טעמא (ג) *דרבי יהושע – "כי מצא בה ערות דבר" "ערוה" – זו הסתירה, "דבר" – זו הקינוי. וילפינן "דבר" "דבר", מה דבר האמור להלן – על פי שנים, אף כאן – ע"פ שנים. תני רבי יוסי בר' יהודה וכו' משקה ע"פ שנים, נאמר "כי מצא", ואין מציאה בכל מקום אלא על פי עדים. מה מקיים רבי אליעזר "דבר" – (ג) דבר שהוא מרגיל לבא לידי ערוה. עוד בירושלמי: כתיב "ועבר עליו רוח קנאה" וגו' שלא יקנא לה מתוך שחוק, ולא מתוך קלות ראש, ולא מתוך גאות, אלא מתוך דבר של אימה. עבר וקינא לה מחמת הדברים הללו, מה את אמרת, למצוה או לעיכוב? אם תאמר למצוה – קינויו קינוי, אם תאמר לעיכוב – אין קינויו קינוי. אמר רבי מנא, אתיא כהדא: כל מקום שנאמר "חוקה" "תורה" – מעכב (ד).

תוספות שאנץ

אלא טעמא דכתב רחמנא לא יקום עד אחד באיש. וא"ת לא לכתוב רחמנא ועד אין בה לא יקום עד אחד באיש וממילא שמעינן דעד אחד נאמן בסוטה משום דאיכא רגלים לדבר. וי"ל דאין זה סברא כל כך להאמין עד אחד מכח סברא אי לאו דנפיק (לך) [לן] מקרא. ואי אפי' חד ליכא אלא במאי מתסרא דאין לומר דאיתסרא משום דאיכא רגלים לדבר משום דאין לנו לאוסרה בלא עד א' לכל הפחות משום טעמא דרגלים לדבר. דאתיא דבר דבר ממון כתיב בנואפת כי מצא בה ערות דבר וכתיב בדיני ממונות על פי שנים עדים יקום דבר. ומי מצית אמרת דאין נאמן בה. פ"ה ומי מצית אמרת דאי לא גלי' רחמנא דכל עד שנים הם דאנא אמינא דהאי עד אין בה אין נאמן בה קאמר א"כ בא הכתוב להקל עליה והא מדכתיב והיא לא נתפשה א) אועד אין בה נהי דרישי' דקרא איכא למימר על ידי שנים עדים ושכב איש אותה בעדים ועד א' אין נאמן אלא והיא לא נתפשה היכא קאי אאין נאמן בה הא אמרת דלא מחזקי' לה בנבעלת. לשון הקונטרס: לדברי ר' יוסי אין לדבר סוף מאי נינהו דזימנין דלא קנאי י"מ אין לדבר סוף לפי שאין המים בודקין אותה אם לא קנא והיא אומרת שזנתה א"כ מוציא לעז על המים המאררים. אדרבה משנתינו עיקר (וי"א) [י"מ] הכי אדרבה משנתינו עיקר דכיון דקינא לה על פי שנים תהא מוזהרת אבל במילתא דר' יוסי בר' יהודה דמיירי דלא קנא לה מתחלה היא לא תזהר מליסתר: ג) שכבר קנא לה בעדים שלא על ידי כעס. הכא ליכא עיקר שהרי לא קנא לה בפני עדים ולכשיכעוס נקל לו לומר קנאתי והוא ימצא לה סתירות הרבה. ל"ה: וגם

סנהדרין ל. לקמן לא:

[לקמן ג. נדה ג.]

[תוספתא פ"א]

הגהות הב"ח

(א) רש"י ד"ה ומי מצית אמרת וכו' שנים הם דהוה אמינא: (ב) תום' ד"ה מאי וכו' מ"ט דר"א כי מצא בה. נ"ב פי' מ"ט דר"א אליבא דתנא דמתניתין דסבר מקנא ע"פ שנים ומשקה על פי עד א': (ג) בא"ד מה מקיים ר"א דבר. נ"ב פי' מה מקיים ר"א אליבא דר' יוסי בר' יהודה דמקנא ע"פ עד א' או ע"פ עצמו ומשקה ע"פ שנים והא דבר נפקא לן לקיטוי וילפינן דבר דבר ופריך דאיהו לא דריש דבר לדברי קינוי אלא דבר שהוא מרגיל לבא לידי ערוה דהיינו סתירה: (ד) בא"ד תורה מעכב ה"נ מעכב הקינוי הס"ד:

גליון הש"ס

תוס' ד"ה כל מקום כו' אבל קשיא וכו'. עיין רש"י ב"ק דף נו ע"א ד"ה אם לא יגיד וצ"ע.

א) לא נתפשה מכלל דפשיטא ליה דנטמאה והיכי קאמר והיא לא נתפשה הא ועד אין בה. ב) אולי צ"ל ובקונטרס פירש למשנתינו איכא עיקר שכבר קנא לה בעדים וכו'.

אלמא קסברי *דאסור לקנאות. ומאן דאמר מותר לקנאות, מהו לשון קינוי? אמר רב נחמן בר יצחק: אין קינוי אלא לשון התראה, וכן הוא אומר °"ויקנא ה' לארצו". תניא, היה רבי מאיר אומר: אדם עובר עבירה בסתר והקב"ה מכריז עליו בגלוי, שנאמר: °"ועבר עליו רוח קנאה", ואין עבירה אלא לשון הכרזה, שנאמר: °"ויצו משה ויעבירו קול במחנה". ריש לקיש אמר: אין אדם עובר עבירה אא"כ נכנס בו רוח שטות, א] שנא': °"איש איש כי תשטה אשתו", "תשטה" כתיב. תניא דבי רבי ישמעאל: מפני מה האמינה תורה עד אחד בסוטה — *שרגלים לדבר, שהרי קינא לה ונסתרה, ועד אחד מעידה שהיא טמאה. אמר ליה רב פפא לאביי: והא כי כתיבה קינוי — בתר סתירה וטומאה הוא דכתיבה! א"ל: "ועבר" — וכבר עבר. אלא מעתה: °"ועבר לכם כל חלוץ" ה"נ?! התם, מדכתיב: °"ונכבשה הארץ לפני ה' ואחר תשובו" משמע דלהבא. אלא הכא, אי ס"ד כדכתיבי, (א) "ועבר" בתר טומאה וסתירה — קינוי למה לי? תנא דבי רבי ישמעאל: אין אדם מקנא לאשתו אא"כ נכנסה בו רוח, שנאמר: "ועבר עליו רוח קנאה וקנא את אשתו". מאי רוח? רבנן אמרי: רוח טומאה, רב אשי אמר: רוח טהרה. אומסתברא כמאן דאמר רוח טהרה. דתניא: "וקנא את אשתו" — רשות, דברי ר' ישמעאל. ר"ע אומר: בחובה. אי אמרת בשלמא רוח טהרה — שפיר, אלא אי אמרת רוח טומאה — רשות וחובה לעיולי לאיניש רוח טומאה בנפשיה?! גופא, "וקנא את אשתו" — רשות, דברי רבי ישמעאל. ורבי עקיבא אומר: חובה. *°"לה יטמא" — רשות, דברי רבי ישמעאל. ור"ע אומר: גחובה. °"לעולם בהם תעבודו" — *רשות, דברי רבי ישמעאל. ר' עקיבא אומר: דחובה. אמר ליה רב פפא לאביי, ואמרי לה רב משרשיא לרבא: לימא ר' ישמעאל ור' עקיבא בכל התורה כולה הכי פליגי, דמר אמר רשות ומר אמר חובה? א"ל: הכא בקראי פליגי. "וקנא את אשתו" — רשות, דברי רבי ישמעאל. רבי עקיבא אומר: חובה. מ"ט דר' ישמעאל — סבר לה כי האי תנא. דתניא, רבי אליעזר בן יעקב אומר: כלפי שאמרה תורה °"לא תשנא את אחיך בלבבך", יכול כגון זו? ת"ל: "ועבר עליו רוח קנאה וקנא את אשתו". ור"ע: קינוי אחרינא כתיב. ורבי ישמעאל: *איידי דבעי למיכתב "והיא נטמאה" "והיא לא נטמאה" — כתיב נמי "וקנא את אשתו", לכדתנא דבי רבי ישמעאל. *דתנא דבי רבי ישמעאל: כל פרשה שנאמרה ונישנית — לא נישנית אלא בשביל דבר שנתחדש בה. "לה יטמא" — רשות, דברי רבי ישמעאל. ר' עקיבא אומר: חובה. מ"ט דר' ישמעאל — איידי דכתי': °"אמור אל הכהנים בני אהרן ואמרת אליהם לנפש לא יטמא בעמיו" — איצטריכא למיכתב "לה יטמא". ור' עקיבא: מ"כי °אם לשארו" נפקא, "לה יטמא" למה לי — לחובה. ורבי ישמעאל: *לה מיטמא, האין מיטמא לאיברה. ורבי

Marginal references beside the Gemara: יואל ב; במדבר ה; שמות לו; במדבר ה; שם לב; שם; ויקרא כא; שם כה; שם יט; שם כא; שם

אלמא קסברי דאסור לקנאות. כיון דאמרי לשון הטלת קנאה הוא, אלמא אסור: ולמ"ד מותר לקנאות מאי לשון קינוי. ויקנא ה' לארצו. התרה בילק וחסיל וגזם שלא ישחיתו עוד את ארצו, דבשילוח גובאי משתעי פרשה לעיל. "לארצו" — על ארצו, כמו "וישאלו אנשי המקום לאשתו" (בראשית כו) — על אשתו, "האתם תריבון לבעל" (שופטים ו). אדם עובר עבירה. כגון אשה פרוצה עוברת בסתר. והקב"ה מכריז בגלוי. שנותן בלב בעלה לקנאות לה, והדבר מתפרסם בגלוי: ואין עבירה גרסינן. לשון הכרזה. הקב"ה מתכוין להעביר קול. רגלים לדבר. שנטמאת. והא כי כתיב קינוי בתר סתירה וטומאה. דאיתהימן בה עד אחד כתיב, "ונסתרה והיא נטמאה ועד אין בה" וגו', וסמיך ליה "ועבר עליו" וגו'. אלמא בלא קינוי נמי עד אחד מהימן בטומאה!. ועבר לכם כל חלוץ. בבני גד ובבני ראובן כתיב, שהיה משה מצוה אותם לעבור עם יהושע את הירדן. תשובו. מוכיח דלהבא הוא. נכנסה בו רוח. ממרום. ולקמן מפרש רוח טהרה, או רוח טומאה, ע"י שטן הבא להחטיאו, להקניט את אשתו. רבנן. דבי רב אשי אמרי: רוח טומאה. רוח טהרה. ששונא את הפריצות. ומסתברא כמ"ד. דרוח דקאמר רבי ישמעאל — טהרה היא. דתניא. דקאמר רבי ישמעאל רשות. פלוגתא דר' ישמעאל ור' עקיבא לקמן מפרש טעמייהו. שפיר. אי רשות אי חובה. ר' עקיבא אומר חובה. שאסור לשחרר עבדו. בכל התורה. בכל עשה שבתורה, א"כ אין לך מצות עשה לרבי ישמעאל חובה!. דתניא. לא גרסינן. אלא הדר ונקיט למילתייהו, לפרושי כל חדא באפי נפשה. כלפי. כמו: אחרי שאמרה תורה שאסור להביא עצמו לידי שנאה ותגר. יכול אף זה כן. שיראה את אשתו עוברת על דת יהודית, נסתרת עם שכניה, לא יקנא לה? כלפי — לשון כנגד. תלמוד לומר וקנא. אם רצה לקנא הרשות בידו. ומשום דאי לא כתיב קרא הוה אמינא דאסור — הוא דא"ר ישמעאל הכא רשות, אבל בכל מצות עשה שבתורה לא אמר הכי. קינוי אחרינא כתיב. "ועבר עליו רוח קנאה וקנא את אשתו והיא לא נטמאה" — חד לרשות וחד לחובה. ורבי ישמעאל. אמר לך: איידי דבעי למיכתב "והיא נטמאה והיא לא נטמאה", שספק הוא בידינו, ואעפ"כ אסרה הכתוב מספק — כתב נמי "וקנא" אחרינא. ואף ע"ג דמצי למיכתב הכי: ועבר עליו רוח קנאה וקנא את אשתו והיא נטמאה או לא נטמאה — אפילו הכי אורחיה דקרא לחזור ולשנות את האמור, מפני דבר אחר המתחדש בכפילתו. איצטריך למיכתב לה יטמא. לומר שמותר ליטמא לקרובים הללו. מכי אם לשארו נפקא. "לנפש לא יטמא בעמיו כי אם לשארו הקרוב אליו לאמו ולאביו וגו' ולאחותו הבתולה", וממילא שמעינן דמיטמא לאלו. לה יטמא. אם מתה, ואינו מטמא לאיבריה. אם אחד מאלו מוכה שחין ואיבריו נופלין אין מיטמא להן, דקיימא לן ב"העור והרוטב" (חולין דף קכח:): אבר מן החי מטמא כאבר מן המת, ואיצטריך "לה" למעוטי איבריה.

Marginal references beside Rashi: [לעיל ב.]; [לעיל ב: נדה ג.]; זבחים ק.; גיטין לח:; [פסחים סז: יבמות נב: וש"נ]; ב"ק סד: שבועות יט. מנחות י.; נזיר מג:

רבי ישמעאל אומר רשות. תימה לרבי: וכי לית להו הא דאמר בשלהי מסכת מכות (דף כג:): שש מאות וי"ג מצות נאמרו למשה מסיני? וכי לרבי ישמעאל דאמר רשות בצר להו, או לר' עקיבא טפי להו? ונראה, דבשאר מצות דמפיק ר' ישמעאל מקרא — עביד ליה ר' עקיבא אסמכתא, ודריש ליה לדרשה אחריתי. בירושלמי אמרי' דר' אליעזר אמר חובה. ואין להקשות: הא אמרינן לעיל: "המקנא" — דיעבד אין. אלמא קסבר אסור לקנאות! דתנא דידן דוקא דתני כי הך לישנא סבירא ליה הכי, אבל ר' אליעזר לא סבירא ליה הכי. והכי נמי אמרי' בפ' קמא דקידושין (דף כא.): "וגאל את ממכר אחיו" ר' אליעזר אומר: חובה. ובפרק "השולח" (גיטין דף לח:) נמי *אמרינן: "לעולם בהם תעבודו" — חובה. ואין להקשות נמי מפ"ב דמכות (דף יב.), דאמר ר' עקיבא: "ורצח גואל הדם" — רשות, מי כתיב "ירצח". והכא אמרינן "וקנא" — חובה — דשאני הכא, משום דכתיב תרי קינויין. אבל קשיא מירושלמי; דרבי יהושע אמר התם רשות, ומפרש טעמא: אתיא דר' יהושע כבית הילל, דבית הילל אומרים: אפי' הקדיחה תבשילו, לפום כן הוא אמר רשות, רצה לקנא — יקנא, רצה לגרש — יגרש. והא ר' עקיבא מיקל התם טפי מבית הילל, ואמר התם: אפילו מצא אחרת נאה הימנה מגרשה, ואפי' הכי אמר חובה! והתם בירושלמי פליג רבי אליעזר עליה דר' יהושע, ואמר חובה. ואמר: אתיא דר' אליעזר כבית שמאי, דבית שמאי אומרים: לא יגרש אדם את אשתו אלא א"כ מצא בה ערות דבר. מצא בה דברים כעורים, לגרשה אינו יכול — שלא מצא בה ערוה, לקיימה אינו יכול — שמצא בה דברים כעורים, לפום כן הוא אמר חובה. והא תניא משום בית שמאי: אין לי אלא היוצאת משום ערוה, מנין היוצאת משום דראשה פרוע ולדדיה מפורמין וזרועותיה חלוצות — (ב) ת"ל: "כי מצא בה ערות דבר"! אמר רבי מנא: קיימת כאן בעדים וכאן שלא בעדים. ותימה לפי הירושלמי: כיון דתליא קינוי בגירושין — הוה ליה למיתני סוטה בתר גיטין, ובתר סוטה נזיר כסדר פרשיות, ובתר נזיר נדרים, ובתר נדרים כתובות.

לא נשנית אלא בשביל דבר שנתחדש. תימה לרבי: היכא דאיכא למדרש כי הכא, אמאי לא דרשינן לה, כדאמר *גבי קל וחומר: מילתא דאתיא מקל וחומר — טרח וכתב לה קרא, ואפילו הכי, היכא דאיכא למדרש — דרשינן. *וכן בפרק "כל שעה" (פסחים דף כד:): כל היכא דאיכא למדרש לא מוקמינן ליה בלאוי יתירי?

לה יטמא מצוה. ונ"מ לעוסק במצוה. כדאמרינן בסוף פרק "משוח מלחמה" (לקמן דף מד.), ולטמאותו בעל כרחו אם לא ירצה לטמאות, כדאמרי' בפרק "טבול יום" (זבחים ק.): מעשה ביוסף הכהן וכו'.

Marginal references beside Tosafot: נ"ל אמר; [פסחים יח: ועוד י"א פעמים בש"ס]; [פסחים עז:]

ט א ב מיי' פ"ד מהלכות סוטה הל' יח טוש"ע אה"ע סי' קעח סעיף כא:
י ג מיי' פ"ב מהלכות אבל הלכה ו סמג עשין נח ולאוין רלה טוש"ע י"ד סימן שעג סעיף ג:
יא ד מיי' פ"ט מהלכות עבדים הלכה ו טוש"ע י"ד סימן רסז סעיף עט:
יב ה מיי' פ"ב מהלכות אבל הלכה יד סמג עשין נח ולאוין רלה טור ש"ע י"ד סימן שעג סעיף ט:

הגהות מהר"ב רנשבורג

א] גמ' שנאמר איש איש כי תשטה אשתו. עי' במהרש"א בח"א שפי' דהל"ל כי תטה ומדכתיב תשטה ר"ל לשון שטות:

הגהות הב"ח

(א) גמ' אי ס"ד כדכתיבי ונסתרה והיא נטמאה ועבר בתר טומאה: (ב) תום' ד"ה ר' ישמעאל וכו' וזרועותיה חלוצות מנין ת"ל כי מצא:

גליון הש"ס

גמ' מפני מה האמינה וכו'. עיין מרדכי פרק הגוזל קמא סי' קל"ח:

יג א מיי' פ"ט מהל' עבדים הלכה ג סמג עשין רב:

ורבי עקיבא א"כ לכתוב לה. תימה: לרב חסדא, דאמר בפרק "שלשה מינין" (נזיר דף מג:): "לאביו" – בזמן שהוא שלם ולא בזמן שהוא לאיברים, לדידיה לא איצטריך "לה" לאיברים, מאי הוי דריש ב"לה יטמא"? ויש לומר: הוה דריש לחובה כדרבי עקיבא, ואיידי דכתב "יטמא" – כתב "לה".

למשרי אחד מכל האומות. מהכא נפקא לן דבאומות הלך אחר הזכר*.

כתיב נמי *(ובאחיכם) לכדתנא דבי רבי ישמעאל. וא"ת הא אצטריך, דדרשינן בפרק "איזהו נשך" (ב"מ דף עג:): מנין אם ראיתו נוהג שלא כשורה שאתה רשאי להשתעבד בו וכו'! וי"ל: אסמכתא בעלמא הוא. וקנס חכמים הוא, כדי לייסרן. **מה** עדות אחרונה שאוסרתה איסור עולם. תימה, דהוה מצי למפרך: מה לעדות האחרונה שכן רגלים לדבר, שהרי קינא לה ונסתרה!

ת"ל ועד אין בה כל שיש בה. תימה: כיון דהוא קינא לה ונסתרה, והשתא אתי עד א' דטומאה – מסתמא בעל שתיק ולא מכחיש ליה, א"כ מאי צריך קרא דעד אחד נאמן? אפילו טומאה בעלמא בלא קנוי וסתירה, בכי האי גוונא היה מהימן, כדאיתא בפרק "האומר" (קדושין דף סו.): אשתו זינתה בעד אחד וכו'. תינח לרבא דאמר התם: הוה דבר שבערוה, אלא לאביי דאמר: מהימן – מאי איכא למימר? אלא ע"כ אית לן למימר דלאביי לא איצטריך קרא אלא היכא דמכחיש, אע"ג דקינא לה.

נאמר כאן דבר ונאמר להלן דבר. תימה: למה לי ג"ש? אפילו בלא ג"ש – מהיכא תיתי ליה דליתהימן בה עד אחד, מעדות אחרונה ליכא למילף, דאיכא פירכא! כמה

וְרַבִּי עֲקִיבָא: א"כ לִיכְתּוֹב רַחֲמָנָא "לָהּ" וְלִישְׁתּוֹק,
"יִטַּמָּא" לָמָּה לִי? ש"מ. וְר' יִשְׁמָעֵאל: *אַיְּידֵי דִּכְתַב
"לָהּ" – כָּתַב נַמִי "יִטַּמָּא". •לְכִדְתָנֵי דְּבֵי ר' יִשְׁמָעֵאל,
דְּתָנָא דְּבֵי רַבִּי יִשְׁמָעֵאל: כָּל פָּרָשָׁה שֶׁנֶּאֶמְרָה
וְנִישְׁנֵית – לֹא נִשְׁנֵית אֶלָּא בִּשְׁבִיל דָּבָר
שֶׁנִּתְחַדֵּשׁ בָּהּ. °"לְעוֹלָם בָּהֶם תַּעֲבוֹדוּ" – רְשׁוּת, ויקרא כה
דִּבְרֵי ר' יִשְׁמָעֵאל. ר"ע אוֹמֵר: חוֹבָה. מַאי טַעֲמָא
דְּרַבִּי יִשְׁמָעֵאל? אַיְּידֵי דִּכְתִיב °"לֹא תְחַיֶּה כָּל דברים כ
נְשָׁמָה" – אִיצְטְרִיךְ נַמִי לְמִיכְתַּב "לְעוֹלָם בָּהֶם
תַּעֲבוֹדוּ" לְמִשְׁרֵי אֶחָד מִכָּל הָאוּמּוֹת שֶׁבָּא
עַל הַכְּנַעֲנִית וְהוֹלִיד מִמֶּנָּה בֵּן, שֶׁאַתָּה רַשַּׁאי
לִקְנוֹתוֹ. *דְּתַנְיָא: אמִנַּיִן לְאֶחָד מִן הָאוּמּוֹת שֶׁבָּא
עַל הַכְּנַעֲנִית וְהוֹלִיד מִמֶּנָּה בֵּן, שֶׁאַתָּה רַשַּׁאי
לִקְנוֹתוֹ בְּעֶבֶד – ת"ל: °"וְגַם מִבְּנֵי הַתּוֹשָׁבִים הַגָּרִים ויקרא כה
עִמָּכֶם מֵהֶם תִּקְנוּ". יָכוֹל אַף הַכְּנַעֲנִי שֶׁבָּא עַל
אַחַת מִן הָאוּמּוֹת וְהוֹלִיד מִמֶּנָּה בֵּן, שֶׁאַתָּה
רַשַּׁאי לִקְנוֹתוֹ בְּעֶבֶד – ת"ל: °"אֲשֶׁר הוֹלִידוּ שם
בְּאַרְצְכֶם", מִן הַנּוֹלָדִים בְּאַרְצְכֶם וְלֹא מִן
הַגָּרִים בְּאַרְצְכֶם. וְר"ע: מִ"מֵּהֶם תִּקְנוּ" נָפְקָא,
"לְעוֹלָם בָּהֶם תַּעֲבוֹדוּ" לָמָּה לִי – לְחוֹבָה. וְרַבִּי
יִשְׁמָעֵאל: בָּהֶם – וְלֹא בַּאֲחֵיכֶם. וְר"ע: בַּאֲחֵיכֶם
מִסֵּיפָא דִּקְרָא נָפְקָא, °"וּבַאֲחֵיכֶם בְּנֵי יִשְׂרָאֵל שם
אִישׁ בְּאָחִיו לֹא תִרְדֶּה בוֹ בְּפָרֶךְ". וְר' יִשְׁמָעֵאל:
אַיְּידֵי דִּכְתִי' "וּבַאֲחֵיכֶם" כְּתִי' נַמִי "בָּהֶם". לְכִדְתַנְ'
דְּבֵי רַבִּי יִשְׁמָעֵאל, דְּתָנָא דְּבֵי ר' יִשְׁמָעֵאל: כָּל
פָּרָשָׁה שֶׁנֶּאֶמְרָה וְנִישְׁנֵית – לֹא נִשְׁנֵית אֶלָּא
בִּשְׁבִיל דָּבָר שֶׁנִּתְחַדֵּשׁ בָּהּ. א"ר חִסְדָּא: זְנוּתָא
בְּבֵיתָא כִּי קַרְיָא לְשׁוּמְשְׁמָא. וְא"ר חִסְדָּא:
תּוּקְפָּא בְּבֵיתָא כִּי קַרְיָא לְשׁוּמְשְׁמָא. אִידִי
וְאִידִי בְּאִיתְּתָא, אֲבָל בְּגַבְרָא – לֵית לָן בָּהּ.
וְאָמַר רַב חִסְדָּא: בַּתְּחִילָּה, קוֹדֶם שֶׁחָטְאוּ יִשְׂרָאֵל, הָיְתָה שְׁכִינָה שׁוֹרָה עִם כָּל
אֶחָד וְאֶחָד, שֶׁנֶּאֱמַר: °"כִּי ה' אֱלֹהֶיךָ מִתְהַלֵּךְ בְּקֶרֶב מַחֲנֶךָ". כֵּיוָן שֶׁחָטְאוּ נִסְתַּלְּקָה דברים כג
שְׁכִינָה מֵהֶם, שֶׁנֶּאֱמַר: °"וְלֹא יִרְאֶה בְךָ עֶרְוַת דָּבָר וְשָׁב מֵאַחֲרֶיךָ". *א"ר שְׁמוּאֵל בַּר שם
נַחְמָנִי א"ר יוֹנָתָן: כָּל הָעוֹשֶׂה מִצְוָה אַחַת בָּעוה"ז – מְקַדַּמְתּוֹ וְהוֹלֶכֶת לְפָנָיו לָעוה"ב,
שֶׁנֶּאֱמַר: °"וְהָלַךְ לְפָנֶיךָ צִדְקֶךָ". וְכָל הָעוֹבֵר עֲבֵירָה אַחַת בָּעוה"ז – מְלַפַּפְתּוֹ וְהוֹלֶכֶת ישעיה נח
לְפָנָיו לְיוֹם הַדִּין, שֶׁנֶּאֱמַר: °"יִלָּפְתוּ אָרְחוֹת דַּרְכָּם יַעֲלוּ בַתֹּהוּ וְיֹאבֵדוּ". ר"א אוֹמֵר: איוב ו
קְשׁוּרָה בּוֹ כַּכֶּלֶב, שֶׁנֶּאֱמַר: °"וְלֹא שָׁמַע אֵלֶיהָ לִשְׁכַּב אֶצְלָהּ לִהְיוֹת עִמָּהּ", "לִשְׁכַּב בראשית לט
אֶצְלָהּ" – בָּעוֹלָם הַזֶּה, "לִהְיוֹת עִמָּהּ" – לָעוֹלָם הַבָּא. *תְּנַן הָתָם: שֶׁהָיָה בַּדִּין; וּמָה עֵדוּת
הָרִאשׁוֹנָה שֶׁאֵין אוֹסַרְתָּהּ אִיסּוּר עוֹלָם אֵינָהּ מִתְקַיֶּימֶת בְּפָחוֹת מִשְּׁנַיִם, עֵדוּת
הָאַחֲרוֹנָה, שֶׁאוֹסַרְתָּהּ אִיסּוּר עוֹלָם – אֵינוֹ דִין שֶׁלֹּא תִּתְקַיֵּים בְּפָחוֹת מִשְּׁנַיִם? ת"ל:
°"וְעֵד אֵין בָּהּ" – כָּל שֶׁיֵּשׁ בָּהּ. וְק"ו לְעֵדוּת הָרִאשׁוֹנָה מֵעַתָּה: וּמָה עֵדוּת הָאַחֲרוֹנָה במדבר ה
שֶׁאוֹסַרְתָּהּ אִיסּוּר עוֹלָם – מִתְקַיֶּימֶת בְּעֵד אֶחָד, עֵדוּת הָרִאשׁוֹנָה שֶׁאֵין אוֹסַרְתָּהּ
אִיסּוּר עוֹלָם – אֵינוֹ דִין שֶׁתִּתְקַיֵּים בְּעֵד אֶחָד? ת"ל: °"כִּי מָצָא בָהּ עֶרְוַת דָּבָר", וּלְהַלָּן דברים כד
הוּא אוֹמֵר: °"עַל פִּי שְׁנֵי עֵדִים אוֹ עַל פִּי שְׁלֹשָׁה עֵדִים יָקוּם דָּבָר". מַה "דָּבָר" שם יט
הָאָמוּר לְהַלָּן עַל פִּי שְׁנַיִם עֵדִים, אַף כָּאן עַל פִּי שְׁנַיִם. *הַאי מִ"כִּי מָצָא בָהּ עֶרְוַת
דָּבָר" נָפְקָא? מִ"בָּהּ" נָפְקָא: בָּהּ – וְלֹא בְקִינּוּי, בָּהּ – וְלֹא בִסְתִירָה מִיבָּעֵי לֵיהּ! הָכִי נַמִי
קָאָמַר: תַּלְמוּד לוֹמַר: "בָּהּ", בָּהּ – וְלֹא בְקִינּוּי, בָּהּ – וְלֹא בִסְתִירָה. וְטוּמְאָה בְּעָלְמָא,
בְּלֹא קִינּוּי וּבְלֹא סְתִירָה, דְּלָא מְהֵימַן עֵד אֶחָד מְנָלַן? נֶאֱמַר כָּאן "כִּי מָצָא בָהּ
עֶרְוַת דָּבָר" וְנֶאֱמַר לְהַלָּן "עַל פִּי שְׁנֵי עֵדִים אוֹ עַל פִּי שְׁלֹשָׁה עֵדִים יָקוּם דָּבָר",
מַה "דָּבָר" הָאָמוּר לְהַלָּן – עֵדִים שְׁנַיִם, אַף כָּאן – עֵדִים שְׁנַיִם. תָּנוּ רַבָּנַן: אֵי זוֹ
הִיא עֵדוּת הָרִאשׁוֹנָה – זוֹ עֵדוּת סְתִירָה, עֵדוּת אַחֲרוֹנָה – זוֹ עֵדוּת טוּמְאָה.
וְכַמָּה

אִם בֵּן. דְּלָאו לְחוֹבָה אֲתָא אֶלָּא לְהָךְ דְּרָשָׁא. לִכְתּוֹב רַחֲמָנָא לָהּ וְלִשְׁתּוֹק. דְּמַשְׁמַע "לְנֶפֶשׁ לֹא יִטַּמָּא בְּעַמָּיו כִּי אִם לִשְׁאֵרוֹ וגו' וְלַאֲחוֹתוֹ הַבְּתוּלָה לָהּ" – כְּלוֹמַר לְגוּפָהּ שָׁלֵם, וְלֹא לְאֵיבָרֶיהָ. לֹא תְחַיֶּה כָּל נְשָׁמָה. בְּשִׁבְעָה אוּמּוֹת כְּתִיב; הַחִתִּי וְהַגִּרְגָּשִׁי וְהָאֱמוֹרִי וְהַכְּנַעֲנִי וְהַפְּרִזִּי וְהַחִוִּי וְהַיְבוּסִי. לְמִשְׁרֵי אֶחָד מִן הָאוּמּוֹת. מִשְּׁאָר שִׁבְעִים אוּמּוֹת. שֶׁבָּא עַל הַכְּנַעֲנִית. כָּל ז' אוּמּוֹת נִקְרְאוּ עַל שֵׁם כְּנַעַן. וְהוֹלִיד בֵּן. דְּהָלַךְ אַחַר הָאָב, וּמוּתָּר לְהַחֲיוֹתוֹ לְךָ לְעֶבֶד. דְּתַנְיָא. דִּלְהָכִי אֲתָא קְרָא. בְּעֶבֶד. גָּרְסִי' בְּבֵי"ת. וְגַם מִבְּנֵי הַתּוֹשָׁבִים וגו'. לְעֵיל מִינֵּיהּ כְּתִיב: "מֵאֵת הַגּוֹיִם אֲשֶׁר סְבִיבוֹתֵיכֶם מֵהֶם תִּקְנוּ עֶבֶד וְאָמָה" – אֲשֶׁר סְבִיבוֹת אַרְצְכֶם, וְלֹא מִבְּנֵי אַרְצְכֶם דְּשִׁבְעָה אוּמּוֹת. "וְגַם מִבְּנֵי הַתּוֹשָׁבִים" – כָּל תּוֹשָׁב הַיְינוּ שֶׁבָּא מִמָּקוֹם אַחֵר וְנִתְיַישֵּׁב כָּאן, וְקָאָמַר קְרָא שֶׁמּוּתָּר לִקְנוֹת מִבְּנֵיהֶם אֲשֶׁר יִהְיוּ לָהֶם מִבְּנוֹת אַרְצְךָ. מִן הַנּוֹלָדִים בְּאַרְצְכֶם. בָּנִים הַנּוֹלָדִים בְּאַרְצְכֶם, וְהֵם בְּנֵי הַתּוֹשָׁבִים, דְּהַיְינוּ אֲחֵרִים שֶׁנָּשְׂאוּ בְּאַרְצְכֶם נָשִׁים – אַתָּה רַשַּׁאי לִקְנוֹת. וְלֹא מִן הַגָּרִים בְּאַרְצְכֶם. וְלֹא מִן הַבָּנִים הַנּוֹלָדִים לִבְנֵי אַרְצְכֶם בְּמָקוֹם אַחֵר מִבְּנוֹת שְׁאָר אוּמּוֹת, וֶהֱבִיאוּם לִבְנֵיהֶם לָגוּר שָׁם. וְלֹא בַּאֲחֵיכֶם. עֲבוֹדַת עֶבֶד. ה"ג: וְרַבִּי יִשְׁמָעֵאל אַיְּידֵי דִּכְתִיב "וּבַאֲחֵיכֶם" כְּתִיב נַמִי "בָּהֶם" כִּדְתַנְיָא כו'. קַרְיָא. תּוֹלַעַת שֶׁל שׁוּמְשְׁמִין הָאוֹכַלְתָּן. כָּךְ הַזְּנוּת מַחֲרֶבֶת אֶת הַבַּיִת. תּוּקְפָּא. כַּעַס. אִידִי וְאִידִי. תּוּקְפָּא וּזְנוּתָא, דְּאָמְרִינַן דְּמַחֲרֶבֶת אֶת הַבַּיִת. בְּאִיתְּתָא. כְּשֶׁהָאִשָּׁה מְזַנָּה אוֹ כַּעֲסָנִית. לְפִי שֶׁהָאִשָּׁה מִתְעַסֶּקֶת בִּזְנוּנֶיהָ וְאֵינָהּ עוֹשָׂה מְלַאכְתָּהּ, וְלֹא מְשַׁמֶּרֶת בֵּיתָהּ, וּמַפְקֶרֶת אֶת שֶׁל בַּעְלָהּ לִמְנָאֲפִים. קוֹדֶם שֶׁחָטְאוּ יִשְׂרָאֵל. בַּעֲרָיוֹת. עִם כָּל אֶחָד וְאֶחָד. בְּבֵיתוֹ. נִסְתַּלְּקָה מֵהֶם. מִלָּבֹא לְבֵיתָם, דְּאֵינוֹ יָכוֹל לִרְאוֹת בַּעֲבֵירוֹת שֶׁבְּבֵיתוֹ. מְקַדַּמְתּוֹ. לִפְנֵי מִיתָתוֹ מַכְרֶזֶת לְפָנָיו. מְלַפַּפְתּוֹ. כּוֹרַכְתּוֹ. תְּנַן הָתָם. בְּפֶ' "מִי שֶׁקִּינֵּא" (לקמן לא.) אַמַּאי דְּקָתָנֵי: אָמַר עֵד אֶחָד "רְאִיתִיהָ שֶׁנִּטְמֵאת" – לֹא הָיְתָה שׁוֹתָה. שֶׁהָיָה בַּדִּין. שֶׁלֹּא לְהַאֲמִינוֹ אִי לָאו דִּכְתִיב קְרָא. הָרִאשׁוֹנָה. סְתִירָה. אֵין אוֹסַרְתָּהּ אִיסּוּר עוֹלָם. שֶׁאִם תִּשְׁתֶּה וְתִמָּצֵא טְהוֹרָה – מוּתֶּרֶת לְבַעְלָהּ וְלִתְרוּמָה. אֵין מִתְקַיֶּימֶת בְּפָחוֹת מִשְּׁנַיִם. כִּדְבָעֵינַן לְמִיגְמַר "דָּבָר" "דָּבָר" מִמָּמוֹן. הָאַחֲרוֹנָה. טוּמְאָה שֶׁהִיא אַחַר הַסְּתִירָה. כָּל שֶׁיֵּשׁ בָּהּ. כָּל עֵדוּת שֶׁיֵּשׁ בָּהּ – נֶאֱמָן, כִּדְדָרְשִׁינַן לְעֵיל: "וְעֵד אֵין בָּהּ" – תְּרֵי אֶלָּא חַד, וְקָא אָמַר אֲסוּרָה. וְאַטּוּמְאָה קָאֵי, דְּהָא מִינָּהּ סָלֵיק "וְהִיא נִטְמָאָה וְעֵד אֵין בָּהּ". קַל וָחוֹמֶר. שֶׁתִּתְקַיֵּים בְּעֵד אֶחָד. תַּלְמוּד לוֹמַר. בְּאִשָּׁה מְקַלְקֶלֶת "כִּי מָצָא בָהּ עֶרְוַת דָּבָר" וּלְהַלָּן כו': וּפָרְכִינַן: לָמָּה לִי לְמִיכְתַּב לְמֵילְפָהּ בִּגְזֵירָה שָׁוָה. בָּהּ וְלֹא בְקִינּוּי כו' מִיבָּעֵי לֵיהּ. (א) דְּכֵיוָן דִּכְתִיב "בָּהּ" – מִיעוּטָא הוּא, וְלָא גָּמְרִי' שְׁאָר עֵדִיּוֹת דְּאִשָּׁה מִינָּהּ, וְקָמוּ לְהוּ בְּמִלְּתַיְיהוּ כְּכָל עֵדִיּוֹת שֶׁבַּתּוֹרָה. הָכִי נַמִי קָאָמַר. וּגְזֵירָה שָׁוָה לְמִילְּתָא אַחֲרִיתִי נָקֵט. וּמַתְנִיתִין חַסּוּרֵי מִיחַסְּרָא, וְהָכִי תָּנָא לֵיהּ: ת"ל "בָּהּ" וְלֹא בְקִינּוּי וּסְתִירָה. וּגְזֵירָה שָׁוָה – לְטוּמְאַת אִשָּׁה דְּעָלְמָא, שֶׁלֹּא קִינֵּא לָהּ בַּעְלָהּ, וּבָא עֵד אֶחָד וְאָמַר "אֲנִי רְאִיתִיהָ שֶׁנִּטְמְאָה" דְּלָא מְהֵימַן, וְהָכָא הוּא דִּמְהֵימַן מִשּׁוּם דְּרַגְלַיִם לַדָּבָר.
כְּדֵי

תורה אור

[פסחים סז: יבמות נג: וכס נסמן]

יבמות עח: קדושין סז:

ע"ז ה.

שם יומא לה:

לקמן לא.

לקמן לא.

[לענין יוחסין]

[נ"ל בהס]

גליון הש"ס

גמ' לכדתני דבי ר"י. ב"ק סד ע"ב שבועות יט ע"א מנחות י ע"א:

הגהות הב"ח

(א) רש"י ד"ה בה ולא בקינוי כו' מיבעי ליה. נ"ב כלומר על רש"י לומר דהכי קא קשיא ליה וקבעי ליה:

תוספות שאנץ

וגם מבני התושבים כל תושב היינו שבא ממקום אחר ונתישב כאן ואמר קרא דמותר לקנות מבניהם אשר היו להם מבנות ארצך. ולא מן הגרים בארצך בנים הנולדים במקומות אחרים מבנות שאר אומות והביאום לבניהם לגור כאן. ל"ה: הכי הוי גירסת הספרים איידי דכתיב בהם כתיב ובאחיכם לכדתנא דבי ר' ישמעאל וקשה וכי בשביל שכתוב בהם ולא באחיכם כתיב ובאחיכם וכפל את דבריו על חנם ואין חוזר ואומר כלום. והגיה רש"י איידי דכתיב ובאחיכם כתיב בהם. וכי תימא מה מועיל גרסא זו מן האחרת ואומר רבי דהועיל דהא עתה חוזר בו ממה שאמר לעיל רבי ישמעאל לעולם בהם תעבודו אתא למשרי אחד מן האומות שבא על הכנענית אלא איצטריך למדרש בהם ולא באחיכם ולרבי ישמעאל איידי דכתיב ובאחיכם כתיב נמי בהם לכדתנא [דבי ר"י] וכתיב בהם תעבודו דהוי דבר שנתחדש בה. וקשה להר"מ דאמאי לא

קאמר דאיצטריך בהם ובאחיכם לעשה ולא תעשה מדכתיב בהם ולא באחיכם [לאו] הבא מכלל עשה ובאחיכם לא תעשה דכי האי גונא בפרק איזהו נשך גבי לא תשיך. ועוד דאם נאמרה ונשנית (א) דלעולם בהם תעבודו כתיב מקמי קרא דובאחיכם ואינו כגון דאמר לעיל [איידי] דכתב לה כתב לא יטמא דלעולם כתוב הפסוק המיותר באחרונה. [ונראה] לקיים גירסת הספרים איידי דכתב בהם כתב נמי ובאחיכם לעולם כדפרקינן מהם תקנו ונפקא לן למשרי אחד מן האומות שבא על הכנענית ובהם איצטריך בהם ולא באחיכם. ואיידי דתנא בהם תנא נמי באחיכם לכדתנא דבי ר' ישמעאל דכל פרשה שנאמרה ונשנית וכו' ואיצטריך למכתב כדרשינן בב"מ בפ' איזהו נשך גבי רב שעורים באותו שאינו נוהג בשורה מנין שאתה מותר לשעבד בו ת"ל לעולם בהם תעבודו [ובאחיכם] והיינו דבר שנתחדש בה והתלמוד לא היה חושש לפרש איזהו דבר נתחדש בה:
בדקריא לשומשמא. פ"ה קריא שהוא חם וכו'. וי"א קריא לשון קרי שהוא חם ושומשמן הוי מין תולע שקורין פרמיל (דכל דבדקה ליה התולע וע"א קריא לשון קרירות דכל קרקע לו):

(א) נראה דצ"ל דאם נאמרה ונשנית בקרא דלעולם בהם תעבודו א"כ למה כתיב הך קרא מקמי קרא דבאחיכם וכו'.

וְכַמָּה שִׁיעוּר סְתִירָה — כְּדֵי טוּמְאָה, כְּדֵי בִּיאָה, כְּדֵי הַעֲרָאָה, כְּדֵי הַקָּפַת דֶּקֶל, דִּבְרֵי רַבִּי יִשְׁמָעֵאל. ר"א אוֹמֵר: כְּדֵי מְזִיגַת הַכּוֹס, רַבִּי יְהוֹשֻׁעַ אוֹמֵר: כְּדֵי לְשָׁתוֹתוֹ, בֶּן עַזַּאי אוֹמֵר: [א]כְּדֵי לִצְלוֹת בֵּיצָה, ר"ע אוֹמֵר: [ב]כְּדֵי לְגוֹמְעָהּ, רַבִּי יְהוּדָה בֶּן בְּתֵירָא אוֹמֵר: כְּדֵי לִגְמוֹעַ שָׁלֹשׁ בֵּיצִים זוֹ אַחַר זוֹ, ר"א בֶּן יִרְמְיָה אוֹמֵר: כְּדֵי לִקְשׁוֹר גַּרְדִּי נִימָא, חָנִין בֶּן פִּנְחָס אוֹמֵר: כְּדֵי שֶׁתּוֹשִׁיט יָדָהּ לְתוֹךְ פִּיהָ לִיטּוֹל קֵיסָם, פְּלֵימוֹ אוֹמֵר: כְּדֵי שֶׁתּוֹשִׁיט יָדָהּ לַסַּל לִיטּוֹל כִּכָּר, (משלי ו) אע"פ שֶׁאֵין רְאָיָה לַדָּבָר — זֵכֶר לַדָּבָר, °"כִּי בְעַד אִשָּׁה זוֹנָה עַד כִּכַּר לָחֶם". וְכָל הָנֵי לָמָּה לִי? צְרִיכִי. דְּאִי תָּנָא כְּדֵי טוּמְאָה — הֲוָה אָמִינָא כְּדֵי טוּמְאָתָהּ וְאַרְצוּתָהּ, קמ"ל כְּדֵי בִּיאָה. וְאִי תָּנָא כְּדֵי בִּיאָה — הֲוָה אָמִינָא: כְּדֵי גְּמַר בִּיאָה, קמ"ל כְּדֵי הַעֲרָאָה. וְאִי אַשְׁמַעִינַן כְּדֵי הַעֲרָאָה — ה"א כְּדֵי הַעֲרָאָה וְאַרְצוּתָהּ, קמ"ל כְּדֵי טוּמְאָה. וְכַמָּה כְּדֵי [הַעֲרָאָה] (רש"ל) — כְּדֵי הַקָּפַת דֶּקֶל. וּרְמִינְהִי:* (במדבר ה) °"וְנִסְתְּרָה" וְכַמָּה שִׁיעוּר סְתִירָה לֹא שָׁמַעְנוּ, כְּשֶׁהוּא אוֹמֵר "וְהִיא נִטְמָאָה" — הֱוֵי אוֹמֵר כְּדֵי טוּמְאָה, כְּדֵי בִּיאָה, כְּדֵי הַעֲרָאָה, כְּדֵי חֲזָרַת דֶּקֶל, דִּבְרֵי ר"א. רַבִּי יְהוֹשֻׁעַ אוֹמֵר: כְּדֵי מְזִיגַת הַכּוֹס, בֶּן עַזַּאי אוֹמֵר: כְּדֵי לְשָׁתוֹתוֹ, ר"ע אוֹמֵר: כְּדֵי לִצְלוֹת בֵּיצָה, רַבִּי יְהוּדָה בֶּן בְּתֵירָא אוֹמֵר: כְּדֵי לְגוֹמְעָהּ. קס"ד הַיְינוּ הַקָּפַת דֶּקֶל הַיְינוּ חֲזָרַת דֶּקֶל, הָתָם א"ר יִשְׁמָעֵאל כְּדֵי הַקָּפַת דֶּקֶל וּפָלֵיג ר"א עֲלֵיהּ, הָכָא אָמַר ר' אֱלִיעֶזֶר כְּדֵי חֲזָרַת דֶּקֶל! אָמַר אַבָּיֵי: הַקָּפָה — בָּרֶגֶל, חֲזָרָה — בָּרוּחַ. בָּעֵי רַב אַשִׁי: חֲזָרָה בָּרוּחַ כִּי הֵיכִי דְּאָזֵיל וַהֲדַר אָתֵי, אוֹ דִילְמָא כִּי הֵיכִי דְּאָזֵיל וְאָתֵי וַהֲדַר קָאֵי בְּדוּכְתֵיהּ? תֵּיקוּ. הָתָם אָמַר ר"א כְּדֵי מְזִיגַת הַכּוֹס, הָכָא כְּדֵי חֲזָרַת דֶּקֶל! אִידִי וְאִידִי חַד שִׁיעוּרָא הוּא. הָתָם א"ר יְהוֹשֻׁעַ כְּדֵי לְשָׁתוֹתוֹ, הָכָא אָמַר כְּדֵי מְזִיגַת הַכּוֹס! אֵימָא: כְּדֵי לִמְזוֹג וְלִשְׁתּוֹת. וְלֵימָא: אִידִי וְאִידִי חַד שִׁיעוּרָא הוּא! א"כ, הַיְינוּ ר"א. הָתָם אָמַר בֶּן עַזַּאי כְּדֵי לִצְלוֹת בֵּיצָה, הָכָא אָמַר כְּדֵי לְשָׁתוֹתוֹ! אִידִי וְאִידִי חַד שִׁיעוּרָא הוּא. הָתָם אָמַר רַבִּי עֲקִיבָא כְּדֵי לְגוֹמְעָהּ, הָכָא אָמַר כְּדֵי לִצְלוֹת בֵּיצָה! אֵימָא: כְּדֵי לִצְלוֹת בֵּיצָה וּלְגוֹמְעָהּ. וְלֵימָא: אִידִי וְאִידִי חַד שִׁיעוּרָא הוּא! אִם כֵּן הַיְינוּ בֶּן עַזַּאי. הָתָם א"ר יְהוּדָה בֶּן בְּתֵירָא כְּדֵי לִגְמוֹעַ שָׁלֹשׁ בֵּיצִים זוֹ אַחַר זוֹ, הָכָא אָמַר כְּדֵי לְגוֹמְעָהּ! לְדְבָרָיו דְּרַבִּי עֲקִיבָא קָאָמַר, דְּקָאָמַר מְשַׁעֲרִין בִּצְלִיאָה וּבִגְמִיעָה, אֵימָא שִׁיעוּר גְּמִיעָה לְחוּדָהּ — כְּדֵי לִגְמוֹעַ שָׁלֹשׁ בֵּיצִים זוֹ אַחַר זוֹ, דְּהַיְינוּ צְלִיאָה וּגְמִיעָה.§ "ר"א בֶּן יִרְמְיָה אוֹמֵר כְּדֵי שֶׁיִּקְשׁוֹר גַּרְדִּי נִימָא".§ בָּעֵי רַב אַשִׁי: דִּמְרַחֵק אוֹ דִּמְקָרֵב? תֵּיקוּ.§ "חָנִין בֶּן פִּנְחָס אוֹמֵר: כְּדֵי שֶׁתּוֹשִׁיט יָדָהּ לְתוֹךְ פִּיהָ לִיטּוֹל קֵיסָם".§ בָּעֵי רַב אַשִׁי: דִּמְהַדַּק אוֹ דְּלָא מְהַדַּק? תֵּיקוּ.§ "פְּלֵימוֹ אוֹמֵר כְּדֵי שֶׁתּוֹשִׁיט יָדָהּ לַסַּל לִיטּוֹל כִּכָּר".§ בָּעֵי רַב אַשִׁי: דִּמְהַדַּק אוֹ דְּלָא מְהַדַּק, בְּחַדְתָּא אוֹ בְּעַתִּיקָא, בַּחֲמִימָא אוֹ בְּקָרִירָא,

בִּדְחִטֵּי

רש"י

כְּדֵי טוּמְאָה. וּמַהוּ כְּדֵי טוּמְאָה – כְּדֵי בִּיאָה, וּמַהוּ כְּדֵי בִּיאָה – כְּדֵי הַעֲרָאָה, דְּהַיְינוּ נְשִׁיקַת אֵבֶר בְּאוֹתוֹ מָקוֹם. וְכַמָּה שִׁיעוּרָהּ – כְּדֵי הַקָּפַת דֶּקֶל, שֶׁיּוּכַל הָאָדָם לֵילֵךְ סְבִיבוֹת הַדֶּקֶל. וּלְקַמָּן מְפָרֵשׁ לָמָּה לִי לְמִיתְנֵי כּוּלְּהוֹן. כְּדֵי מְזִיגַת כּוֹס. לְמוֹזְגוֹ בְּמַיִם. וּסְתָם כּוֹס רְבִיעִית. וּלְקַמָּן אָמְרִי': כָּל אֶחָד וְאֶחָד מִן הַחֲכָמִים הַלָּלוּ בְּעַצְמוֹ שִׁיעֵר כַּמָּה שֶׁהוּא שׁוֹהֶה בְּהַעֲרָאָתוֹ. לִיטּוֹל קֵיסָם. מִבֵּין שִׁינֶּיהָ. וְאַף ע"פ שֶׁאֵין רְאָיָה. גְּמוּרָה לַדָּבָר, דִּקְרָא לָאו הוֹשָׁטַת יָד לַסַּל כָּתַב בֵּיהּ – יֵשׁ זֵכֶר וְרֶמֶז מִקְצָת, דְּהוּקְשָׁה אִשָּׁה זוֹנָה לְכִכַּר לֶחֶם. וְכָל הָנֵי לָמָּה לִי. לְמִיתְנֵי בְּרֵישָׁא? לִיתְנֵי: שִׁיעוּר סְתִירָה כְּדֵי טוּמְאָה, כְּדֵי הַקָּפַת דֶּקֶל!. דְּאִי תָּנָא כְּדֵי טוּמְאָה הֲוָה אָמִינָא. בְּכָל שִׁיעוּר הַצָּרִיךְ לָבֹא לִידֵי כָּךְ, דְּהַיְינוּ טוּמְאָה וְאַרְצוּתָהּ – שֶׁיְּפַתֶּה אוֹתָהּ וִידַבֵּר עַל לִבָּהּ עַד שֶׁתִּתְרַצֶּה. קמ"ל. דְּמַאי טוּמְאָה – בִּיאָה לְחוּדָהּ, דְּאִיכָּא לְמֵימַר קוֹדֶם הַסְּתִירָה נִתְרַצֵּית לוֹ. קמ"ל כְּדֵי הַעֲרָאָה. דְּקַיְ"ל בְּפֶרֶק "הַבָּא עַל יְבִמְתּוֹ" (יבמות נו.): הַעֲרָאָה כִּגְמַר בִּיאָה לְכָל הָעֲרָיוֹת. וְאִי תָּנָא כְּדֵי הַעֲרָאָה. וְלָא תָּנָא בְּרֵישָׁא כְּדֵי טוּמְאָה, הֲוָה אָמִינָא: כְּדֵי הַעֲרָאָה וְאַרְצוּתָהּ. וַאֲפִי' תָּנָא כְּדֵי בִּיאָה כְּדֵי הַעֲרָאָה – לָא הֲוָה מִימְעִיט אַרְצוּתָהּ, דַּאֲנָא אָמִינָא: הַעֲרָאָה – לְמַעוּטֵי גְּמַר בִּיאָה, וּמִיהוּ אַרְצוּתָהּ בָּעֵינַן. דְּהָכִי הָוֵי מַשְׁמַע: כַּמָּה שִׁיעוּר סְתִירָה – כְּדֵי בִּיאָה, וַאֲנָא אָמִינָא כָּל צָרְכֵי בִּיאָה, דְּהַיְינוּ אַרְצוּתָהּ וּגְמַר בִּיאָה, וַהֲדַר מְפָרֵשׁ מַה הִיא בִּיאָה – הַעֲרָאָה, אַכַּתִּי אַרְצוּתָהּ לָא אִימְעִיט. הִילְכָּךְ תָּנָא בְּרֵישָׁא כְּדֵי טוּמְאָה, דְּמַשְׁמַע טוּמְאָה וְאַרְצוּתָהּ, וַהֲדַר פָּרֵישׁ: וּמַה הִיא טוּמְאָה – כְּדֵי בִּיאָה. וְעַל כָּרְחֵיךְ אִימְעִיט אַרְצוּתָהּ, דְּהָא בִּיאָה כּוּלָּהּ גְּמַר בִּיאָה מַשְׁמַע, וְלָא מִיעֵט אֶלָּא אַרְצוּתָהּ. וַהֲדַר תָּנָא: וּמַה הִיא בִּיאָה – הַעֲרָאָה, לְמַעוּטֵי דְּלָא בָּעֵינַן גְּמַר בִּיאָה. וּמִמֵּילָא שָׁמְעִי' מִינַּהּ נַמִי (דְּאִי) לָא תָּנָא כְּדֵי בִּיאָה (ס"א ואי) אַכַּתִּי לָא הֲוָה מְמַעֲטָא אַרְצוּתָהּ, דִּכְדֵי טוּמְאָה – גְּמַר בִּיאָה וְאַרְצוּתָהּ מַשְׁמַע, וְהַעֲרָאָה דְּפָרֵישׁ בַּתְרָהּ לָא מְמַעֲטָא אֶלָּא גְּמַר בִּיאָה, הִילְכָּךְ אִיצְטְרִיכוּ כּוּלְּהוּ. וְכַמָּה. הוּא שִׁיעוּר הַעֲרָאָה לְחוּדָהּ – כְּדֵי הַקָּפַת דֶּקֶל. וְהָא לֵיכָּא לְאַקְשׁוּיֵי: הוֹאִיל וְסוֹף שִׁיעוּרָא כְּדֵי הַקָּפַת דֶּקֶל הוּא – לִיתְנֵי: כַּמָּה שִׁיעוּר סְתִירָה – כְּדֵי הַקָּפַת דֶּקֶל? דְּאִיבָּעֵי לֵיהּ לְתַנָּא לְפָרוּשֵׁי אִיסּוּר סְתִירָה מִשּׁוּם מַאי, אוֹ גְּמַר בִּיאָה אוֹ הַעֲרָאָה, מִשּׁוּם הָכִי תָּנָא: כְּדֵי טוּמְאָה כְּדֵי בִּיאָה, כִּדְפָרֵישִׁית. כְּדֵי חֲזָרַת דֶּקֶל. קס"ד הַשְׁתָּא דְּהַיְינוּ הַקָּפָה. בָּרוּחַ. שֶׁהָרוּחַ דּוֹחַפְתּוֹ לְהָעָנָף, וְהוּא חוֹזֵר לִמְקוֹמוֹ. קָאֵי בְּדוּכְתֵיהּ. נָח מִנִּיעֲנוּעוֹ. אֵימָא כְּדֵי לִמְזוֹג וְלִשְׁתּוֹת. וְהַאי כְּדֵי לְשָׁתוֹתוֹ דְּקָאָמַר לְעֵיל – אַמְּזִיגָה דְּקָאָמַר רַבִּי אֱלִיעֶזֶר קָא מוֹסִיף ר' יְהוֹשֻׁעַ, וְאָמַר: שְׁתִיָּה נַמִי בָּעֵינַן עִם הַמְּזִיגָה. וּכְדֵי מְזִיגָה דְּתָנָא הָכָא בְּבַתְרַיְיתָא – מְזִיגָה וּשְׁתִיָּה קָאָמַר. דִּסְתָם מְזִיגָה לְמִשְׁתְּיֵיהּ מִיָּד הוּא, שֶׁאַחַר שֶׁמְּזָגוֹ מִתְקַלְקֵל אִם מַשְׁהֶה אוֹתוֹ. א"כ הַיְינוּ רַבִּי אֱלִיעֶזֶר. דְּהָא ר' אֱלִיעֶזֶר בְּקַמַּיְיתָא כְּדֵי מְזִיגַת הַכּוֹס קָאָמַר, וְקָא פָּלֵיג ר' יְהוֹשֻׁעַ וְאָמַר כְּדֵי לְשָׁתוֹתוֹ. וּבְבַתְרַיְיתָא (א) (נַמִי) אָמַר רַבִּי אֱלִיעֶזֶר חֲזָרַת דֶּקֶל, וְאוֹקִימְנָא דְּהַיְינוּ כְּדֵי מְזִיגָה, וְאִי מְזִיגָה דְּקָאָמַר ר' יְהוֹשֻׁעַ בַּתְרֵיהּ, בְּלָא שְׁתִיָּה קָאָמַר – הַיְינוּ רַבִּי אֱלִיעֶזֶר. הָכָא אָמַר כְּדֵי לְשָׁתוֹתוֹ. לַכּוֹס. חַד שִׁיעוּרָא הוּא. וְלֵיכָּא לְאַקְשׁוּיֵי: א"כ הַיְינוּ ר' יְהוֹשֻׁעַ, דִּבְקַמַּיְיתָא אָמַר כְּדֵי לְשָׁתוֹתוֹ לַכּוֹס, וְאָמַר בֶּן עַזַּאי בַּתְרֵיהּ כְּדֵי לִצְלוֹת בֵּיצָה דְּהוּא כְּדֵי שְׁתִיָּה! לָאו קוּשְׁיָא הִיא, דְּהָא אוֹקִימְנָא כְּדֵי לְשָׁתוֹתוֹ דְּר' יְהוֹשֻׁעַ כְּדֵי לִמְזוֹג וְלִשְׁתּוֹת, וְקָאָמַר לֵיהּ בֶּן עַזַּאי כְּדֵי לִצְלוֹת בֵּיצָה, דְּהוּא כְּדֵי שְׁתִיָּה לְחוּדָהּ דְּכוֹס. אֵימָא כְּדֵי לִצְלוֹת וּלְגוֹמְעָהּ. גְּמִיעָה דְּקָאָמַר ר"ע בְּקַמַּיְיתָא – אַצְּלִיָּיה דְּבֶן עַזַּאי דִּלְעֵיל מִינֵּיהּ קָא מוֹסִיף לָהּ. וּבְבַתְרַיְיתָא דְּקָאָמַר כְּדֵי לִצְלוֹת – לִצְלוֹת וְלִגְמוֹעַ קָאָמַר, דִּסְתָם צְלִיָּיה – גְּמִיעָה בַּתְרָהּ, שֶׁגּוֹמְעוֹ חַם שֶׁלֹּא יִצְטַנֵּן. לְדְבָרָיו דְּר"ע קָאָמַר לָהּ. דְּאָמַר לִצְלוֹת וְלִגְמוֹעַ: לְדִידָךְ דְּקָמְשַׁעַרְתְּ בִּצְלִיָּיה וּגְמִיעָה בַּחֲדָא *(שַׁפִּיר) (ס"א שיעור) בִּגְמִיעָה דְּשָׁלֹשׁ, דְּהוּא כִּצְלִיָּיה וּגְמִיעָה בַּחֲדָא. דִּמְרַחֵק. שְׁנֵי רָאשֵׁי הַנִּימָא הַנִּפְסָקוֹת מְרוּחָקוֹת זֶה מִזֶּה, דְּאִיכָּא שְׁהִיָּיה טְפֵי. דִּמְהַדַּק. הַקֵּיסָם בְּדוֹחַק בֵּין הַשִּׁינַּיִם. בְּחַדְתָּא אוֹ בְּעַתִּיקָא. סַל יָשָׁן חָלָק הוּא, וְנוֹחַ לְהִשָּׁמֵט מִן הֶחָדָשׁ, שֶׁהֶחָדָשׁ יוֹצְאִין לְתוֹכוֹ רָאשֵׁי קִיסְמִין שֶׁל אֲרִיגָה. בְּקָרִירָא אוֹ בַּחֲמִימָא. לֶחֶם חַם נִמְעָךְ וְנִשְׁמָט מִן הַיָּד, וְצָרִיךְ לְהוֹצִיאוֹ בְּנַחַת וְשׁוֹהֶה בְּהוֹצָאָתוֹ.

בדחטי

תוספות

כמה שיעור סתירה. בירושלמי: כל אלין שיעורין אחר [התרת סינר].

בן עזאי אומר. הא דמקדים בן עזאי לרבי עקיבא, אע"ג דרבי עקיבא היה רבו, כדאמר בפרק "הרואה" (ברכות סב.): בן עזאי, עד כאן העזת פניך ברבך? משום דצלייה קודמת לגמיעה. והא דמקדים ליה באידך ברייתא – משום דמסיק שיעורין דשייכי בכוס. אבל תימה: אמאי מקדים רבי ישמעאל למילתייהו דרבי אליעזר ורבי יהושע? מיהו, י"ל: דסדר אכילה ושתיה סמיך*.

אי הכי היינו רבי אליעזר. ה"ה דהוה מצי למימר: אי הכי היינו בן עזאי, אלא (ב) ברייתא קמייתא נקט. א"נ, יתרץ בבן עזאי כדי למזוג ולשתותו.

אם כן היינו בן עזאי. ה"ה דהוה מצי למימר: היינו רבי יהודה בן בתירא, אלא (ג) ברייתא קמייתא נקט.

דמרחק או דמקרב. בחזרת דקל לא קמבעי ליה בגדול או בקטן, משום דידע שיעוריה, דהיינו כדי מזיגת הכוס וכן בצליית ביצה במדורה גדולה או קטנה, משום דפי' כבר דהיינו כדי שתיית הכוס. אבל בהקפת דקל תימה: אמאי לא קמיבעי ליה?

נעקר

תוספות שאנץ

ה"א כדי טומאה וארצותה פ"ה שיפתה אותה וידבר על לבה כדי שתתרצה קמ"ל דמאי טומאה ביאה לחוד דאיכא למימר קודם נתרצית ואי תנא כדי ביאה כו' קמ"ל כדי העראה דהעראה כגמר דביאה לכל העריות כדאיתא בפרק הבא על יבמתו. ואי תנא כדי העראה ה"א כדי העראה וארצותה ואפילו תנא כדי ביאה כדי העראה וארצותה ואפילו תנא כדי ביאה כדי העראה לא אמעוט ארצותה דהוה אמינא העראה למעוטי גמר ביאה ומיהו ארצותה בעי דהכא הוה משמע כמה שיעור סתירה כדי ביאה ואנא אמינא כל צרכי ביאה דהיינו ארצותה וגמר ביאה והדר תני העראה לומר ביאה העראה אכתי ארצותה לא ממעיט הילכך תנא ברישא כדי טומאה דמשמע טומאה וארצותה והדר מפרש ומאי היא טומאה כדי ביאה וע"כ ארצותה אימעוט דהא ביאה כולה גמר ביאה משמע ולא מיעט אלא ארצותה והדר תני העראה לומר דלא בעי גמר ביאה וממילא שמעי' דאי תנא כדי טומאה כדי העראה ולא תני כדי ביאה אכתי לא הוי ממעטינא ארצותה דכדי טומאה כדי טומאה וארצותה משמע והעראה דפריש בתריה תו לא ממעטינא אלא גמר ביאה הילכך איצטרי' כולהו ע"כ ל"ה. וכמה כדי טומאה כדי הקפת דקל וליכא לאקשויי הואיל וסוף שיעור הקפת דקל היא ליתני כמה שיעור סתירה כדי הקפת דקל דאיבעי ליה לתנא לפרושי איסור משום מאי כפ"ה ובתוס' וירושלמי גבי שיעורין הללו כמה הוא העראה כדי הקפת דקל ידו שלימה

א"ר יוסי כל השיעורין הללו חוץ מהתרת סינר. התם אמר בן עזאי כדי לצלות ביצה והכא אמר כדי לשתות ואידי ואידי חד שיעורא הוא וליכא לאקשויי א"כ היינו רבי יהושע דאמר לעיל כדי לשתותו ואמר בתריה כדי לצלות ביצה משום דר' יהושע אמר בעי מזיגה עם השתיה דסתם מזיגה למשתיה מיד הוא אבל הכא ר"ל לשתות בלא מזיגה [והיינו] כדי לצלות. בעי רב אשי במרחק או במקרב. תמה מאי לא קא בעי בהקפת דקל באלימא או בקטיפא דבשלמא גבי כוס סתם כוס הוי מרביעית. וכן ביצה סתמא דתרנגולת ובינונית אלא מדקל אמאי לא בעי באיזה דקל מיירי. ושמא ר"ל כדי הקפת דקל בינוני:

והא

עין משפט נר מצוה: יד א ב מיי' פ"א מהל' סוטה הלכה ב סמג עשין נו טוש"ע אה"ע סי' קעח סעיף ז:

[ועיין היטב תוספות ע"ז מה. ד"ה אלא עקיבא ותוספות ב"מ כד: ד"ה אתא ותוספות כתובות קה. ד"ה לחשוב]

מסורת הש"ס: [תוספתא פ"א ע"ש] | ס"א ואי | ס"א שיעור [וגי' יעב"ץ תטעה]

הגהות הב"ח: (א) רש"י ד"ה א"כ היינו וכו' ובבתרייתא דקאמר ר"א כצ"ל ותיבת נמי נמחק: (ב) תוס' ד"ה אי הכי וכו' אלא קמייתא דברייתא נקט: (ג) ד"ה אם כן וכו' אלא קמייתא דברייתא נקט:

בדחטי או בדשערי, ברכיבא או באקושא? תיקו. א"ר יצחק בר (רב) יוסף א"ר יוחנן: כל אחד ואחד בעצמו שיער. והאיכא בן עזאי *דלא נסיב! איבעית אימא: נסיב ופירש הוה, ואיבעית אימא: מרביה שמיע ליה, ואיבעית אימא: °"סוד ה' ליראיו" (תהלים כה). דרש רב עוירא, זמנין אמר לה משמיה דרבי אמי וזמנין אמר לה משמיה דרבי אסי: כל האוכל לחם בלא נטילת ידים – כאילו בא על אשה זונה, שנאמר: °"כי בעד אשה זונה עד ככר לחם" (משלי ו). אמר רבא: האי "בעד אשה זונה עד ככר לחם"?! "בעד ככר לחם עד אשה זונה" מיבעי ליה! אלא אמר רבא: כל הבא על אשה זונה – לסוף מבקש ככר לחם. א"ר זריקא אמר ר"א: [א]כל המזלזל בנטילת ידים – נעקר מן העולם. אמר רב חייא בר אשי אמר רב: [ב]מים ראשונים צריך שיגביה ידיו למעלה, [ג]מים אחרונים צריך שישפיל ידיו למטה. תניא נמי הכי: הנוטל ידיו – צריך שיגביה ידיו למעלה, [ד]שמא יצאו המים חוץ לפרק, ויחזרו ויטמאו את הידים. אמר רבי אבהו: [ה]כל האוכל פת בלא ניגוב ידים – כאילו אוכל לחם טמא, שנאמר: °"ויאמר ה' ככה יאכלו בני ישראל את לחמם טמא" וגו' (יחזקאל ד). ומאי °"ואשת איש נפש יקרה תצוד" (משלי ו)? אמר רבי חייא בר אבא א"ר יוחנן: כל אדם שיש בו גסות הרוח – לבסוף נכשל באשת איש, שנא': "ואשת איש נפש יקרה תצוד". אמר רבא: האי "נפש יקרה"? "נפש גבוהה" מיבעי ליה! ועוד: "היא תצוד" מיבעי ליה! אלא אמר רבא: כל הבא על אשת איש, אפילו למד תורה, דכתיב בה: °"יקרה היא מפנינים" (שם ג), *מכהן גדול שנכנס לפני ולפנים – היא תצודנו לדינה של גיהנם. א"ר יוחנן משום ר"ש בן יוחי: כל אדם שיש בו גסות הרוח – כאילו עובד עבודה זרה, כתי' הכא: °"תועבת ה' כל גבה לב" (שם טז), וכתיב התם: °"ולא תביא תועבה אל ביתך" (דברים ז). ורבי יוחנן דידיה אמר: [ו]כאילו כפר בעיקר, שנאמר °"ורם לבבך ושכחת את ה' אלהיך" וגו' (שם ח). ר' חמא בר חנינא אמר: כאילו בא על כל העריות, כתי' הכא: "תועבת ה' כל גבה לב", וכתי' התם: °"כי את כל התועבות האל" וגו' (ויקרא יח). עולא אמר: כאילו בנה במה, שנאמר: *°"חדלו לכם מן האדם אשר נשמה באפו כי במה נחשב הוא" (ישעיה ב). אל תיקרי "במה" אלא "במה". מאי "יד ליד לא ינקה"? אמר רב: (א) כל הבא על אשת איש, אפי' הקנהו להקב"ה שמים וארץ כאברהם אבינו, דכתיב ביה: °"הרימותי ידי אל ה' אל עליון קונה שמים וארץ" (בראשית יד) – לא ינקה מדינה של גיהנם. קשיא להו לדבי רבי שילא: האי "יד ליד לא ינקה"? "ידי" (ב) מיבעי ליה! אלא אמרי דבי רבי שילא: אפילו קיבל תורה כמשה רבינו, דכתיב ביה °"מימינו אש דת למו" (דברים לג) – לא ינקה מדינה של גיהנם. קשיא ליה לר' יוחנן: האי "יד ליד"? "יד מיד" מיבעיא ליה! אלא א"ר יוחנן: אפילו

רש"י

בדחטי או בדשערי. של חטין חלק, ונשמט יותר משל שעורים. רכיבא. נשמט יותר מאקושא. רכיבא. שנילושה העיסה רכה. כל אחד ואחד. מן המנאפים הללו. בעצמו שיער. כמה שהיה שוהה בביאתו. והאיכא בן עזאי דלא נסיב. כדאמר ביבמות (דף סג:): [תורה אור] חשק מה אעשה שנפשי חשקה בתורה, אפשר לעולם שיתקיים ע"י אחרים. בפרק "הבא על יבמתו". כי בעד אשה זונה וגו'. השתא דריש ליה מסיפיה לרישיה: בשביל ככר לחם אדם מתחייב בעונש של אשה זונה. במילתיה דרבא גרסי' בעד ככר לחם עד אשה זונה מבעי ליה. דמשמע, בשביל ככר לחם רב העונש עד כדי עונש אשה זונה. וה"ה נמי אי הוה כתיב "עד אשה זונה בעד ככר לחם" לא הוה קשיא לרבא מידי, דודאי מסיפיה לרישיה מדריש קרא. אלא "עד" ו"בעד" קא קשיא ליה, דגבי ככר לחם הוה ליה למיכתב "בעד", וגבי אשה זונה הוה ליה למיכתב "עד". המזלזל. שאוכל תמיד בלא נטילת ידים. נעקר. דעובר על דברי חכמים חייב מיתה, דכתיב: "ופורץ גדר ישכנו נחש" (קהלת י). מים ראשונים. שלפני המזון. שיגביה ידיו. ראשי אצבעותיו, שיהו המים משפעין לצד זרועותיו. ולקמן מפרש טעמא. שמא יצאו מים חוץ לפרק ויחזרו ויטמאו את הידים. כדתנן במסכת ידים (פ"ב מ"ג) שצריך ליתן המים על ידיו שני פעמים, הראשונים מטהרין את הידים והשניים מטהרין את המים הטופחים על ידיו שנטמאו בתחילה מחמת ידים. ותנן התם: הידים מטמאות ומטהרות עד הפרק, כלומר, מן הפרק ולמטה גזרו עליהן להיות שניות ופוסלות את התרומה. ומטהרות בנטילה עד הפרק, שעד הפרק צריך נטילה. נטל את הראשונים *ואת השניים (ג) עד הפרק וחזרו ליד – טהורים, שהרי טיהרו השניים את הראשונים. נטל את הראשונים חוץ לפרק ואת השניים עד הפרק, וחזרו ליד – טמאה. כלומר, יצאו הראשונים חוץ לפרק, ועל השניים לא הקפיד ליטול עד מקום שיצאו הראשונים, אלא עד הפרק כמשפטם, וחזרו הראשונים ליד – טמאה, שהרי נטמאו תחלה מחמת הידים והשניים לא טיהרו את היוצאים. הילכך צריך שיגביה ראשי אצבעותיו למעלה, שמא יצאו מים הראשונים ויחזרו ויטמאו את הידים. אחרונים. של אחר הסעודה שהוציאו חכמים מפני שמלח סדומית יש שמסמא את העינים. צריך להשפיל ידיו למטה. כדי שתרד הזוהמא של תבשיל שבידיו, שהרי להעביר הזוהמא הן. כל האוכל בלי ניגוב ידים. דבר מאוס הוא, וחשוב כטומאה. שנאמר: "ככה יאכלו בני ישראל את לחמם טמא" – אלמא, דבר מיאוס קרי טומאה. מאי ואשת איש וגו'. סיפיה דקרא דלעיל הוא: "כי בעד אשה זונה עד ככר לחם". לסוף נכשל באשת איש. והכי קאמר: בעד אשה זונה עד ככר לחם. ואשת איש זונה – נפש היקרה, הגבוהה, היא תלודנה – רודף אחריה ולד אותה, ומגיעה. היא תצוד מבעי לה. כיון דמסיפיה לרישיה קדרשת ליה, הכי איבעי ליה למכתב: ואשת איש נפש יקרה היא תצוד אותה. אבל השתא משמע שאשת איש צדה את הנפש היקרה. מכהן גדול. דאפילו ממזר תלמיד חכם קודם לכהן עם הארץ, לפתוח ראשון ולברך ראשון. ומהאי קרא ילפינן ליה בהוריות (דף יג.). ורם לבבך. מעלה אני עליך כאילו שכחתו. כי את כל התועבות. גבי עריות כתיב. במה. עבודה זרה. אשר נשמה באפו. שמחזיק עצמו כבעל נפש, דהיינו גאוה, שחשובה נפשו בעיניו. מאי יד ליד לא ינקה. סיפיה דקרא דאיירי ביה לעיל הוא: "תועבת ה' כל גבה לב יד ליד לא ינקה". ה"ג: כל שיש בו גסות הרוח אפילו הקנהו כו'. ול"ג: כל הבא על אשת איש, דלא משתעי קרא אלא בגסי הרוח. הקנהו להקב"ה כו'. השליטו בשבחו על הכל, כאברהם שקראהו "קונה שמים וארץ". והיינו "יד ליד" – אפילו דומה לאברהם שאמר "הרימותי ידי". קשיא להו לדבי רבי שילא. אהך דרשה דרב. הכי גרסינן: האי "יד ליד", ידי לא ינקה מיבעי ליה. אפילו הוא כמשה. שקבל מיד הקדוש ברוך הוא לידו תורה. יד מיד מיבעי ליה. דהא קרא במקבל מוקמינן ליה ולא בנותן. והוה ליה למיכתב: יד מיד לא ינקה, יד שקבלה מיד אף הוא לא ינקה. אפילו

תוספות

נעקר מן העולם. תימה לר"י: לפי' רש"י, דפי' דעובר על דברי חכמים חייב מיתה, (ד) מאי אריא נטילת ידים? אפי' כל דברי חכמים נמי! ועוד קשיא: דאמר הכא דעונשו מיתה, ובפ' "במה אשה יוצאה" (שבת דף סב:) אמרינן דעונשו עניות, כדאמר: שלשה דברים מביאין את האדם לידי עניות: המזלזל בנטילת ידים. ובפ' "עושין פסין" (עירובין דף כא:): מעשה ברבי עקיבא שהיה חבוש בבית האסורים וכו', עד "מה אעשה שחבירי חייבו עליה מיתה"! ונראה דזלזול שמזלזל בה תמיד – עונשו עקירה ע"י עניות, דקשה ממיתה ע"י נחש. ו"נעקר מן העולם", דאמר [בסוכה] (דף מה:) וסנהדרין (דף סג.): כל המשתף שם שמים ודבר אחר נעקר מן העולם. ובפרק "קונם יין" (נדרים דף סב.): כל המשתמש בכתרה של תורה נעקר מן העולם – לאו בהדא מחיתא נינהו דעניות, אלא מיתה חטופה או משונה. מ"ר.

היא תצודנו לדינה של גיהנם. ואמר נמי בפ"ק דחגיגה (דף ט:): כל הבא על אשת איש ואסרה על בעלה – נטרד מן העולם. וק"ק מפ' "הזהב" (ב"מ דף נט.) דאמר: הבא על אשת איש מיתתו בחנק ויש לו חלק לעוה"ב! וי"ל: דהתם מיירי כשעשה תשובה. והכי משמע בפ' (ה) ג' דיבמות (דף כב:) היכא דלא הוליד ממזר – דבר תשובה הוא. ותשובה עם יסורין דוקא, דאמר בפרק "חלק" (סנהדרין דף קז.): אמר דוד: כל הכי נטרוד ההוא גברא. א"ל: קבל עליך יסורים. ותנן נמי כיסורין, (ו) דכל המומתים מתוודין. והאי דאמר נטרד מן העולם – פי': מן העולם עם אותו עון, דכך הוא חמור אשת איש האוסרה על בעלה כמו על אחותו פנויה והוליד ממנה ממזר. ריב"א. א"נ: היכא דלא באו עליו יסורים – נטרד מן העולם.

עין משפט נר מצוה

טו א מיי' פ"ו מהלכות ברכות הלכה יט סמג עשין כז טוש"ע א"ח סימן קנח סעיף ט [וברב אלפס ברכות ספ"ח דף מו: וכהל"מ פרק כל הבשר סימן יח]:

טז ב מיי' שם הל' טז סמג שם טוש"ע א"ח סימן קסב סעיף א:

יז ג מיי' וסמג שם טור ש"ע א"ח סימן קפא סעיף ה:

יח ד מיי' וסמג שם טוש"ע א"ח סימן קסב סעיף ה:

יט ה מיי' שם הלכה כ סמג שם טוש"ע א"ח סי' קנח סעיף יב:

כ ו מיי' פ"ב מהלכות דעות הלכה ג:

תוספות שאנץ

והא איכא ב"ע דלא נסיב כדאמר ביבמות מה אעשה ונפשי חשקה בתורה אפשר לעולם להתקיים על ידי אחרים. כל האוכל לחם בלא נטילת ידים כאלו בא על אשה זונה שנאמר כי בעד אשה זונה עד ככר לחם. פי' דריש ליה מסיפיה לרישיה בשביל ככר לחם מתחייב בעונש של אשה זונה ולהכי מדמי ליה לאשה זונה משום דכשאוכל בלא נטילה הוי אכילה הפקר וזונה זו מפקרת היא. ה"ג במלתיה דרבה בעד ככר לחם עד אשה זונה מיבעיא ליה דמשמע בשביל ככר לחם רב העונש עד כדי אשה זונה. וה"ה נמי אי הוה כתיב עד אשה זונה בעד ככר לחם לא הוה קשה ליה לרבא דודאי מסיפא לרישיה מידרש קרא אלא עד ובעד קא קשיא ליה דגבי ככר לחם הוה ליה למכתב בעד ל"ה. המזלזל בנטילת ידים שאוכל תמיד בלא נטילת ידים נעקר דהעובר על דברי חכמים חייב מיתה שנאמר ופורץ גדר ישכנו נחש. מים ראשונים שלפני אכילה צריך שיגביה ידיו ראשי אצבעותיו שיהו המים משופעין לצד זרועותיו שמא יצא מים חוץ לפרק וכו' כדתנן במס' ידים שצריך לשפוך מים על ידיו ב' פעמים הראשונים מטהרין את הידים מן הטומאה והשניים מטהרין את המים הטופחין על ידיו שנטמאו תחלה מפני הידים ותנן התם הידים מטמאות עד הפרק כלומר מן הפרק ולמטה גזרו עליהם להיות שניות ופוסלות את התרומה ומטהרות בנטילה עד הפרק שעד הפרק צריך נטילה. נטל את הראשונים ואת השניים וחזרו ליד טהורות שהרי טהרו שניים את הראשונים. נטל את הראשונים חוץ לפרק ואת השניים עד לפרק וחזרו ליד טמאות כלומר על השניים לא הקפיד ליטול עד מקום שיצאו אלא עד הפרק כמשפט. וא"כ המים שניים לא טיהרו את הראשונים שיצאו חוץ לפרק הילכך צריך שיגביה ראשי אצבעותיו למעלה שלא יצאו המים הראשונים ויטמאו את הידים כן פירש הקונטרס. אחרונים של אחר הסעודה שתקנו חכמים מפני מלח סדומית שמסמא את העינים צריך שישפיל ידיו למטה כדי שתרד הזוהמא של תבשיל שבידיו שהרי להעביר את הזוהמא הן באין:

מסורת הש"ס

[עי' תוספות יבמות סג: ד"ה שיתקיים ותוספות כתובות סג. ד"ה ברתיה]

עי' בטוא"ח סי' קסב בב"י

[הוריות יג.]

[ברכות יז. ע"ש]

[ברכות סא. עירובין יח: ע"ש]

הגהות הב"ח

(א) גמ' אמר רב (כל הבא על אשת איש) תא"מ ונ"ב גי' רש"י כל שיש בו גסות הרוח: (ב) שם ידי לא ינקה מיבעי ליה: (ג) רש"י ד"ה שמא יצאו וכו' נטל את הראשונים ואת השניים חוץ לפרק וחזרו ליד טהורים. נ"ב ולפנינו במשנה היא טמאים לפי שמים שחוץ לפרק אין מטהרין השניים את הראשונים ועי' פי' הר"ש במשנה זו: (ד) תום' ד"ה נעקר וכו' חייב מיתה דכתיב ופורץ גדר ישכנו נחש מאי איריא וכו' הכא דעונשו מיתה ובפרק עושין פסין נמי קאמר מעשה בר' עקיבא וכו' עליה מיתה ובפרק במה אשה וכו' בנטילת ידים ונראה כצ"ל: (ה) ד"ה היא וכו' משמע בפ"ב ליבמות. נ"ב ע"ש בדף כ"א ע"א ובדף כ"ב ע"ב: (ו) בא"ד ותנן נמי כיסורין עם תשובה דכל המומתין:

גליון הש"ס

גמ' ואיבעית אימא מרבי' שמיע ליה. לקמן דף י ע"א:

כא א ב מיי' פ"ב מהל' דעות הלכה ג:

אֲפִילּוּ עוֹשֶׂה צְדָקָה בַּסֵּתֶר. שֶׁנּוֹתֵן מִיָּדוֹ לְיָדוֹ שֶׁל הֶעָנִי. וְהָכִי מַשְׁמַע: יָד הַנּוֹתֶנֶת לְיָד אַף הוּא לֹא יִנָּקֶה. דִּכְתִיב בֵּיהּ מַתָּן בַּסֵּתֶר כו'. לָאו דַּשַּׁיָּיךְ הַאי קְרָא בִּקְרָא דִּלְעֵיל, אֶלָּא רְבוּתָא הִיא, שֶׁאַעַ"פ שֶׁמְּכַפֶּה אַף וְחֵימָה – אֵינוֹ מְכַפֵּר עַל גַּסּוּת הָרוּחַ. אַזְהָרָה. שֶׁלֹּא יְהֵא גַּס רוּחַ. וְרָם לְבָבֶךָ וְשָׁכַחְתָּ. אַלְמָא מְגוּנֶּה לֵב בָּא לִידֵי שִׁכְחָה, שֶׁשּׁוֹכֵחַ אֶת בּוֹרְאוֹ. וּבְשִׁכְחָה הוּא מוּזְהָר: "הִשָּׁמֶר לְךָ פֶּן תִּשְׁכַּח". מִתְמַעֵט. מֵחֲשִׁיבוּתוֹ. רוֹמּוּ מְעַט. כֵּיוָן שֶׁרוֹמּוּ – מִתְמַעֵט. יֶשְׁנוֹ בָּעוֹלָם. מִתְקַיֵּים. וְהוּמְכוּ. וְאִם חָזַר וְנַעֲשָׂה עָנָיו, שֶׁמֵּמִיךְ אֶת עַצְמוֹ. כַּכֹּל. כְּאוֹתָן שֶׁנֶּאֱמַר בָּהֶן "כֹּל". יִקָּפְצוּן. מִן הָעוֹלָם, יָמוּתוּ מוֹת יְשָׁרִים. אַבְרָהָם כְּתִיב בֵּיהּ "וַה' בֵּרַךְ אֶת אַבְרָהָם בַּכֹּל", יִצְחָק כְּתִיב בֵּיהּ "וָאוֹכַל מִכֹּל", יַעֲקֹב כְּתִיב בֵּיהּ "כִּי חַנַּנִי אֱלֹהִים וְכִי יֶשׁ לִי כֹל". וְהָכִי מְפָרֵשׁ בְּהֶדְיָא בִּבְרֵאשִׁית רַבָּה. (דְּבִשְׁלָמָא "בַּכֹּל" "מִכֹּל" (ג) רְבוּתָא הוּא שֶׁנִּתְבָּרְכוּ בַּכֹּל, אֲבָל "וְכֹל אֲשֶׁר תִּתֶּן לִי" מִילְּתָא בְּעָלְמָא הוּא דְּקָאָמַר). כְּסָאסָא דְּשִׁיבָּלְתָּא. גָּבְהוֹ שֶׁל שִׁבּוֹלֶת, שֶׁקּוֹרִין זְקַן הַשִּׁבּוֹלֶת, וְהוּא נִשְׁבָּר וְנוֹפֵל מֵאֵלָיו. גְּבוֹהָה גְּבוֹהָה הוּא מְלַקֵּט. וְהַיְינוּ "וּכְרֹאשׁ שִׁבֹּלֶת", (ד) שֶׁרֹאשָׁהּ נִרְאֵית לְמַעְלָה מֵחַבְרוֹתֶיהָ. אִתִּי דַּכָּא. אֲנִי מַגְבִּיהוֹ עַד שֶׁשּׁוֹכֵן אֶצְלִי, וְהַיְינוּ "אֶשְׁכּוֹן אֶת דַּכָּא". אֲנִי אֶת דַּכָּא. אֲנִי מַרְכִּין שְׁכִינָתִי אֶצְלוֹ. יִלְמַד אָדָם מִדַּעַת קוֹנוֹ. לֶאֱהוֹב אֶת הַנְּמִיכוּת. כָּל הָרִים וּגְבָעוֹת. כְּגוֹן תָּבוֹר וְכַרְמֶל שֶׁבָּאוּ שָׁם,* כְּדִכְתִיב: "לָמָּה תְּרַצְּדוּן הָרִים גַּבְנֻנִּים" (תהלים סח). כַּאֲשֵׁירָה. יִגָּדַע וְיָשְׁרֵשׁ אַחֲרֶיהָ כַּאֲשֵׁירָה, שֶׁצָּרִיךְ גִּידּוּעַ אַחֲרֶיהָ, כִּדְכְתִיב: "וְאִבַּדְתֶּם אֶת שְׁמָם" (דברים יב). נִנְעָר. מֵקִיץ בִּתְחִיַּית הַמֵּתִים. שׁוֹכְבֵי בֶעָפָר לֹא נֶאֱמַר. דְּלִישְׁתַּמַּע עַל כָּל הַמֵּתִים. שָׁכֵן לְעָפָר. מַשְׁפִּיל עַצְמוֹ לְעָפָר. מְיַלֶּלֶת. מְקוֹנֶנֶת. וְגָבוֹהַּ מִמֶּרְחָק יְיֵדָע. רֵישֵׁיהּ דִּקְרָא "כִּי רָם ה' וְשָׁפָל יִרְאֶה וְגָבוֹהַּ". וְהַגָּבוֹהַּ "מִמֶּרְחָק" – מִקּוֹדֶם שֶׁתָּבֹא עָלָיו פּוּרְעָנוּת יָמִים רַבִּים, "יְיֵדָע" – שְׁכִינָה מִתְאוֹנֶנֶת וּמִשְׁתַּבֶּרֶת עָלָיו, כְּמוֹ "וַיֵּדַע אַלְמְנוֹתָיו" (יחזקאל יט), "וַיֹּדַע בָּהֶם אַנְשֵׁי סֻכּוֹת" (שופטים ח), "יִוָּדַע כְּמֵבִיא לְמָעְלָה" (תהלים עד) – לְשׁוֹן שֶׁבֶר. רוֹאֶה אֶת *הַגָּבוֹהַּ. לְקָרְבוֹ וּלְהִשְׁתַּדֵּל עִמּוֹ, וְחָשׁוּב בְּעֵינָיו, כְּמוֹ (הושע ט) "כְּבִיכּוּרָה בִתְאֵנָה בְּרֵאשִׁיתָהּ רָאִיתִי אֶת אֲבוֹתֵיכֶם" – נָתַתִּי עֵינַי לְקָרְבָם וּלְחַבְּבָם. וְאִיכָּא דְּמַתְנֵי לָהּ אַמְסַפְּרֵי לָשׁוֹן הָרָע. מִשּׁוּם רֵישָׁא דִּקְרָא "מְלָשְׁנִי בַסֵּתֶר רֵעֵהוּ" וגו'. רוּחַ קִימְעָא עוֹכַרְתּוֹ. פּוּרְעָנוּת קַלָּה טוֹרַפְתּוֹ וּמְאַבַּדְתּוֹ. וְהָרְשָׁעִים. גַּסֵּי הָרוּחַ. דִּקְרָאֵי דִּלְעֵיל מִשְׁתָּעֵי בִּשְׁפָלִים וְנִדְכָּאִים "לְהַחֲיוֹת רוּחַ שְׁפָלִים" וגו' "כִּי לֹא לְעוֹלָם אָרִיב" עִם אוֹתָן שְׁפָלִים, "בַּעֲוֹן בִּצְעוֹ" וגו', "דְּרָכָיו רָאִיתִי" וגו', בּוֹרֵא נִיב שְׂפָתַיִם" וגו'. אֲבָל הָרְשָׁעִים שֶׁאֵינָן שְׁפָלִים וְנִדְכָּאִים – "כַּיָּם נִגְרָשׁ" – כַּיָּם הַמְגָרֵשׁ וּמַשְׁלִיךְ רֶפֶשׁ וָטִיט לִשְׂפָתָיו סְבִיבָיו. כַּמָּה רְבִיעִיּוֹת. לוּגֵּי מַיִם, אָנוּ רוֹאִים שֶׁרוּחַ קִימְעָא עוֹכַרְתּוֹ – עוֹכֶרֶת אֶת מֵימָיו. אָדָם שֶׁאֵין בּוֹ אֶלָּא רְבִיעִית אַחַת. שֶׁבִּרְבִיעִית דָּם הוּא מִתְקַיֵּים. שִׁיעוּר זֶה הֲלָכָה לְמֹשֶׁה מִסִּינַי, שֶׁרְבִיעִית דַּם מֵת מְטַמֵּא בְּאֹהֶל, מִפְּנֵי שֶׁהִיא נֶפֶשׁ, וְקָרֵינָא בֵּיהּ "עַל כָּל נַפְשֹׁת מֵת לֹא יָבֹא".

משלי כא — אֲפִילּוּ עוֹשֶׂה צְדָקָה בַּסֵּתֶר, דִּכְתִיב (א) °"מַתָּן בַּסֵּתֶר יִכְפֶּה אַף" וגו' — לֹא יִנָּקֶה מִדִּינָהּ שֶׁל גֵּיהִנָּם. אַזְהָרָה לְגַסֵּי הָרוּחַ מִנַּיִן? אָמַר רָבָא אָמַר זְעֵירִי: °"שִׁמְעוּ וְהַאֲזִינוּ אַל תִּגְבָּהוּ" (ירמיה יג), רַב נַחְמָן בַּר יִצְחָק אָמַר, מֵהָכָא: °"וְרָם לְבָבֶךָ וְשָׁכַחְתָּ" (דברים ח), וּכְתִיב: °"הִשָּׁמֶר לְךָ פֶּן תִּשְׁכַּח אֶת ה' אֱלֹהֶיךָ" (שם), וְכִדְרַבִּי אָבִין אָמַר רַבִּי אֶילְעָא. *דְּאָמַר רַבִּי אָבִין אָמַר רַבִּי אֶילְעָא: כָּל מָקוֹם שֶׁנֶּאֱמַר "הִשָּׁמֶר" "פֶּן" וְ"אַל" — אֵינוֹ אֶלָּא בְּלֹא תַעֲשֶׂה. דָּרַשׁ רַב עֲוִירָא, זִמְנִין אֲמַר לָהּ מִשְּׁמֵיהּ דְּרַב אַסִי וְזִמְנִין אֲמַר לָהּ מִשְּׁמֵיהּ דְּרַב אַמִּי: כָּל אָדָם שֶׁיֵּשׁ בּוֹ גַּסּוּת הָרוּחַ — לְסוֹף מִתְמַעֵט, שֶׁנֶּאֱמַר: °"רוֹמּוּ מְעַט" (איוב כד), וְשֶׁמָּא תֹאמַר יֶשְׁנוֹ בָּעוֹלָם — ת"ל: "וְאֵינֶנּוּ", וְאִם חוֹזֵר בּוֹ — נֶאֱסָף בִּזְמַנּוֹ כְּאַבְרָהָם אָבִינוּ, שֶׁנֶּאֱמַר: °"וְהוּמְּכוּ כַּכֹּל יִקָּפְצוּן" (שם) — כְּאַבְרָהָם יִצְחָק וְיַעֲקֹב דִּכְתִיב בְּהוּ; °"בַּכֹּל" °"מִכֹּל" °"כֹּל" (בראשית כד, כז, לג), וְאִם לָאו — °"וּכְרֹאשׁ שִׁבֹּלֶת יִמָּלוּ" (איוב כד). מַאי "וּכְרֹאשׁ שִׁבֹּלֶת"? רַב הוּנָא וְרַב חִסְדָּא; חַד אָמַר: כִּי סָאסָא דְּשִׁיבָּלְתָּא, וְחַד אָמַר: כְּשִׁיבּוֹלֶת עַצְמָהּ. בִּשְׁלָמָא לְמַאן דְּאָמַר כִּי סָאסָא דְּשִׁיבָּלְתָּא — הַיְינוּ דִּכְתִיב "וּכְרֹאשׁ שִׁבֹּלֶת", אֶלָּא לְמַאן דְּאָמַר כִּי שׁוּבַּלְתָּא עַצְמָהּ, מַאי "וּכְרֹאשׁ שִׁבֹּלֶת"? אָמַר רַב אַסִי, וְכֵן תָּנָא דְּבֵי רַבִּי יִשְׁמָעֵאל: מָשָׁל לְאָדָם שֶׁנִּכְנָס לְתוֹךְ שָׂדֵהוּ, גְּבוֹהָה גְּבוֹהָה הוּא מְלַקֵּט.§ °"וְאֶת דַּכָּא וּשְׁפַל רוּחַ" (ישעיה נז) רַב הוּנָא וְרַב חִסְדָּא; חַד אָמַר: אִתִּי דַּכָּא, וְחַד אָמַר: אֲנִי אֶת דַּכָּא. וּמִסְתַּבְּרָא כְּמ"ד אֲנִי אֶת דַּכָּא, שֶׁהֲרֵי הקב"ה הִנִּיחַ כָּל הָרִים וּגְבָעוֹת וְהִשְׁרָה שְׁכִינָתוֹ עַל הַר סִינַי, וְלֹא גָּבַהּ הַר סִינַי לְמַעְלָה. א"ר יוֹסֵף: לְעוֹלָם יִלְמַד אָדָם מִדַּעַת קוֹנוֹ, שֶׁהֲרֵי הקב"ה הִנִּיחַ כָּל הָרִים וּגְבָעוֹת וְהִשְׁרָה שְׁכִינָתוֹ עַל הַר סִינַי, (*וְהִנִּיחַ כָּל אִילָנוֹת טוֹבוֹת וְהִשְׁרָה שְׁכִינָתוֹ בַּסְּנֶה.) א"ר אֶלְעָזָר: כָּל אָדָם שֶׁיֵּשׁ בּוֹ גַּסּוּת הָרוּחַ — רָאוּי לְגַדְּעוֹ כַּאֲשֵׁירָה, כְּתִיב הָכָא: °"וְרָמֵי הַקּוֹמָה גְּדֻעִים" (שם י), וּכְתִיב הָתָם: °"וַאֲשֵׁירֵיהֶם תְּגַדֵּעוּן" (דברים ז). וְא"ר אֶלְעָזָר: כָּל אָדָם שֶׁיֵּשׁ בּוֹ גַּסּוּת הָרוּחַ — אֵין עֲפָרוֹ נִנְעָר, שֶׁנֶּאֱ': °"הָקִיצוּ וְרַנְּנוּ שֹׁכְנֵי עָפָר" (ישעיה כו), "שֹׁכְבֵי בֶעָפָר" לֹא נֶאֱמַר, אֶלָּא "שֹׁכְנֵי עָפָר" — מִי שֶׁנַּעֲשָׂה שָׁכֵן לְעָפָר בְּחַיָּיו. וְאָמַר ר' אֶלְעָזָר: כָּל אָדָם שֶׁיֵּשׁ בּוֹ גַּסּוּת הָרוּחַ — שְׁכִינָה מְיַלֶּלֶת עָלָיו, שֶׁנֶּאֱמַר: °"וְגָבֹהַּ מִמֶּרְחָק יְיֵדָע" (תהלים קלח). דָּרַשׁ רַב עֲוִירָא, וְאִיתֵּימָא רַבִּי אֶלְעָזָר: בֹּא וּרְאֵה שֶׁלֹּא כְּמִדַּת הקב"ה מִדַּת בָּשָׂר וָדָם; מִדַּת בָּשָׂר וָדָם *גָּבוֹהַּ רוֹאֶה אֶת הַגָּבוֹהַּ, וְאֵין גָּבוֹהַּ רוֹאֶה אֶת הַשָּׁפָל. אֲבָל מִדַּת הקב"ה אֵינוֹ כֵּן, הוּא גָּבוֹהַּ וְרוֹאֶה אֶת הַשָּׁפָל, שֶׁנֶּאֱ': °"כִּי רָם ה' וְשָׁפָל יִרְאֶה" (שם). אָמַר רַב חִסְדָּא וְאִיתֵּימָא מָר עוּקְבָא: כָּל אָדָם שֶׁיֵּשׁ בּוֹ גַּסּוּת הָרוּחַ, אָמַר הקב"ה: אֵין אֲנִי וְהוּא יְכוֹלִין לָדוּר בָּעוֹלָם, שֶׁנֶּאֱ': °"מְלָשְׁנִי בַסֵּתֶר רֵעֵהוּ אוֹתוֹ אַצְמִית גְּבַהּ עֵינַיִם וּרְחַב לֵבָב אוֹתוֹ לֹא אוּכָל" (תהלים קא). אַל תִּקְרֵי "אוֹתוֹ" אֶלָּא "אִתּוֹ לֹא אוּכָל". אִיכָּא דְּמַתְנֵי לָהּ אַמְסַפְּרֵי לָשׁוֹן הָרָע: שֶׁנֶּאֱ': "מְלָשְׁנִי בַסֵּתֶר רֵעֵהוּ אוֹתוֹ אַצְמִית". א"ר אֲלֶכְּסַנְדְּרִי: כָּל אָדָם שֶׁיֵּשׁ בּוֹ גַּסּוּת הָרוּחַ — אֲפִילּוּ רוּחַ קִימְעָא עוֹכַרְתּוֹ, שֶׁנֶּאֱמַר °"וְהָרְשָׁעִים כַּיָּם נִגְרָשׁ" (ישעיה נז), וּמַה יָּם שֶׁיֵּשׁ בּוֹ כַּמָּה רְבִיעִיּוֹת — רוּחַ קִימְעָא עוֹכַרְתּוֹ, אָדָם שֶׁאֵין בּוֹ אֶלָּא *רְבִיעִית (ב) אַחַת — עאכ"ו. א"ר חִיָּיא בַּר אַשִׁי אָמַר רַב: ת"ח צָרִיךְ שֶׁיְּהֵא בּוֹ אֶחָד מִשְּׁמוֹנָה בִּשְׁמִינִית. א"ר הוּנָא בְּרֵיהּ דְּרַב יְהוֹשֻׁעַ: וּמְעַטְּרָא לֵיהּ כִּי סָאסָא לְשִׁבּוּלְתָּא. אֲמַר רָבָא: אבְּשַׁמְתָּא דְּאִית בֵּיהּ, וּבְשַׁמְתָּא דְּלֵית בֵּיהּ. א"ר נַחְמָן בַּר יִצְחָק: בלָא מִינֵּהּ וְלָא מִקְצָתָהּ, מִי זוּטָר דִּכְתִיב בֵּיהּ: °"תּוֹעֲבַת ה' כָּל גְּבַהּ לֵב" (משלי טז). אֲמַר חִזְקִיָּה: אֵין תְּפִלָּתוֹ שֶׁל אָדָם נִשְׁמַעַת אא"כ מֵשִׂים לִבּוֹ כְּבָשָׂר, שֶׁנֶּאֱ': °"וְהָיָה מִדֵּי חֹדֶשׁ בְּחָדְשׁוֹ" [וגו'] "יָבוֹא כָל בָּשָׂר לְהִשְׁתַּחֲוֹת" וגו' (ישעיה סו). א"ר זֵירָא: בָּשָׂר כְּתִיב בֵּיהּ °"וְנִרְפָּא" (ויקרא יג), אָדָם לָא כְּתִיב בֵּיהּ "וְנִרְפָּא". א"ר יוֹחָנָן: אָדָ"ם — אֵ'פֶר דָּ"ם מָ'רָה, בָּשָׂ"ר — בּ'וּשָׁה סְ'רוּחָה רִ'מָּה. אִיכָּא דְּאָמְרִי: שְׁאוֹל, דִּכְתִיב בְּשִׁין. א"ר אַשִׁי: כָּל אָדָם שֶׁיֵּשׁ בּוֹ גַּסּוּת הָרוּחַ — לְסוֹף נִפְחָת, שֶׁנֶּאֱמַר

וְלַשְׂאֵת

כל אדם שיש בו גסות הרוח אין עפרו נגער. תימה: אמאי לא חשיב האי במשנת "חלק", והא דאמר פרק בתרא דכתובות (דף קיא.): מתים שבחו"ל אינן חיים, ותו גרסינן התם: ע"ה אינן חיים אא"כ יהנו תלמידי חכמים, ומלוי (ז) רביות מלינו באגדה *שאינן חיים לעולם הבא? תוס' ר"י.

אדם שאין בו אלא רביעית דם. *פר"ח: הוא דם הגלול שממנו משתית הלב, אין בו אלא משקל כ"ה סלעים, שהיא רביעית הלוג*.

הא

[ועיין תוספות ב"מ נט: ד"ה תשיך]
[וכ"כ הערוך ערך רבע א]

מֵת לֹא יָבֹא". אֶחָד מִשְּׁמוֹנֶה בִּשְׁמִינִית. מִשְׁקָל קָטָן הוּא, וְהַיְינוּ (ה) עוּכְלָא. *) כְּלוֹמַר, צָרִיךְ שֶׁיְּהֵא בּוֹ מְעַט גַּאֲוָה, שֶׁלֹּא יְהוּ קַלֵּי הָרֹאשׁ מְסַלְסְלִין בּוֹ, וִיהֵא דְּבָרָיו מִתְקַבְּלִין עֲלֵיהֶן כְּבַעַל כָּרְחָם. וּמְעַטְּרָא לֵיהּ כִּי סָאסָא לְשִׁיבָּלְתָּא. גַּסּוּת מוּעָט נָאֶה וְהוֹגֶנֶת לוֹ לְתַלְמִיד חָכָם, וּמְעַטַּרְתּוֹ כְּסָאסָא הַמְעַטֶּרֶת אֶת הַשִּׁבּוֹלֶת. בְּשַׁמְתָּא דְּאִית בֵּיהּ. גַּסּוּת הָרוּחַ. וּבְשַׁמְתָּא דְּלֵית בֵּיהּ. גַּסּוּת פּוֹרְתָּא, לְפִי שֶׁאֵין בְּנֵי עִירוֹ יְרֵאִים מִמֶּנּוּ וְאֵין בּוֹ כֹּחַ לְהוֹכִיחָם. לֹא מִמֶּנָּה וְלֹא מִמִּקְצָתָהּ. לֹא יַחְפּוֹץ אָדָם לֹא בְּכוּלָּהּ וְלֹא בְּמִקְצָתָהּ. דְּמִי זוּטָר מַאי דְּקָרֵי לֵיהּ קְרָא "תּוֹעֲבַת ה'"? כְּבָשָׂר. שֶׁהוּא רַךְ וְלֹא כְּאֶבֶן שֶׁהוּא קָשֶׁה. לְהִשְׁתַּחֲוֹת. לְהִתְפַּלֵּל. אוֹתָם שֶׁהֵם כְּבָשָׂר יָבוֹאוּ וְיִתְפַּלְּלוּ, כִּי הֵם נִשְׁמָעִים לְפָנַי. אֲבָל גַּסֵּי הָרוּחַ לֹא יָבוֹאוּ. בָּשָׂר כְּתִיב בֵּיהּ וְנִרְפָּא. "וּבָשָׂר כִּי יִהְיֶה בוֹ בְעוֹרוֹ שְׁחִין וְנִרְפָּא". "אָדָם כִּי יִהְיֶה בְעוֹר בְּשָׂרוֹ" "נֶגַע צָרַעַת כִּי תִהְיֶה בְּאָדָם" – לָא כְּתִיב בְּחַד מִינַּיְיהוּ "וְנִרְפָּא". לְפִי דַּרְכְּךָ אַתָּה לָמֵד שֶׁמִּי שֶׁהוּא רַךְ וְעָנָיו כְּבָשָׂר – קָרוֹב לְהִתְרַפְּאוֹת מִיִּסּוּרִין הַבָּאִין עָלָיו, אֲבָל מִי שֶׁהוּא קָשֶׁה כָּאֲדָמָה – אֵין רְפוּאָה לְמַכּוֹתָיו (ו). אָדָם. לָמָּה נִקְרָא שְׁמוֹ אָדָם – שֶׁהוּא אֵפֶר דָּם מָרָה. כְּלוֹמַר, כּוּלּוֹ הֶבֶל, לְכָךְ אַל יִתְגָּאֶה. מָרָה הִיא לִיחְלוּחִית מָרָה הַיּוֹצְאָה מִן הַמְּרִירָה שֶׁבַּכָּבֵד וּמִתְגַּבֶּרֶת בָּאָדָם, הַכֹּל לְפִי הֶחֳדָשִׁים וְשִׁינּוּי הָעִתִּים, וּלְפִי הַמַּאֲכָל שֶׁאוֹכֵל, וְעַל יָדֶיהָ בָּאִין חֳלָיִים וּנְגָעִים וּמַכְאוֹבוֹת. יֵשׁ שֶׁקּוֹרִין בְּדִבְרֵי הָרוֹפְאִים מְרִירָה שְׁחוֹרָה, וְיֵשׁ שֶׁקּוֹרִין מְרִירָה אֲדוּמָּה. שְׁאוֹל. מְקוֹם שֶׁאוֹל בֵּיתוֹ. נִפְחָת. מִתְמַעֵט מֵחֲשִׁיבוּתוֹ וְנַעֲשָׂה פָּחוּת בַּאֲנָשִׁים.

*) [ב"ב פט:]

וְלַשְׂאֵת

מכות יג: שבועות ד. עירובין צו. זבחים קו. מנחות צט: ע"ז נב:
רש"א מ"ז
[כלאית' מגילה כט.]
[שבע תיבות הללו לא נזכרו בע"י]
[גירסת הילקוט שוכני בעפר לא נאמר וכו']
[ג"ל הספל. רש"ל]
[פי' אדם גדול הולך לכבוד למי שהוא גדול כמותו ערוך ערך גב ז]
[שבת לג:]

תוספות שאנץ
אפי' עשה צדקה בסתר שנאמר מתן בסתר יכפה אף א) יד ליד לא ינקה. והכי אמרינן במדרש משלי (פ' י"א) כשאדם בא על אשת איש ונזדמן לו עני אחד ונתן לו פרוטה לצדקה ואומר לא היה הקב"ה מזמין לי אותו עני לעשות צדקה אלא א"כ מחל לי אותו עון על זה נאמר יד ליד לא ינקה: בכל מכל כל אברהם כתיב ביה וה' ברך את אברהם בכל. יצחק כתיב ואוכל מכל. יעקב כתיב וכי יש לי כל וי"א וכל אשר תתן לי: וגבוה ממרחק יידע [רישא דקרא] כי רם ה' ושפל יראה וגבוה ממרחק יידע. פי' הגבוה ממרחק מקודם שתבוא עליו פורענות ימים רבים יידע שכינה מתאוננת עליו כמו וידע אלמנותיו וכן ויודע בהם אנשי סכות: השם אורחותיו. הפסד מצוה כנגד שכרה:

הגהות הב"ח
(א) גמ' דכתיב בה מתן בסתר: (ב) שם אלא רביעית אחת. תז"מ ונ"ב ס"א דם: (ג) רש"י ד"ה דבשלמא בכל מכל כל רבותא: (ד) ד"ה גבוהה וכו' שבולת ימלו כשבולת שראשה נראית: (ה) ד"ה אחד משמונה וכו' עוכלא. נ"ב ול"ע בב"ב דף צ' דמפרש שם מהו עוכלא: (ו) ד"ה בבשר וכו' רפואה למכותיו הס"ד: (ז) תוס' ד"ה כל וכו' ומלוי רבינו מלינו.

גליון הש"ם
תום' ד"ה אדם שאין בו וכו' עד סופו. כי לוג הוא ב' ליטרין וליטרא הוא מאה זוז ביהודה כדאית' בירושלמי הובא בר"ש פ"י דתרומות מ"ח נמצא לוג הוא שני מאות זוז שהם מאה סלעים בגליל ורביעית הלוג הוא כ"ה סלעים. (ברית שלום על התורה פ' כי תשא):

כב א מיי' פ"א מהל' דעות הלכה ז:

כג ב מיי' פ"א מהל' סוטה הלכה ד ה סמג עשין נו טוש"ע אה"ע סי' קעח סעיף ו:

סנהדרין מג: ע"ש

°"וְלַשְׂאֵת וְלַסַּפַּחַת", *וְאֵין שְׂאֵת אֶלָּא לְשׁוֹן גָּבוֹהַּ, שֶׁנֶּא': °"וְעַל [כָּל] הֶהָרִים הָרָמִים וְעַל [כָּל] הַגְּבָעוֹת הַנִּשָּׂאוֹת", וְאֵין סַפַּחַת אֶלָּא טְפֵילָה, שֶׁנֶּאֱמַר °"סְפָחֵנִי נָא אֶל אַחַת הַכְּהוּנּוֹת לֶאֱכֹל פַּת לָחֶם". *א"ר יְהוֹשֻׁעַ בֶּן לֵוִי: בֹּא וּרְאֵה, כַּמָּה גְּדוֹלִים נְמוּכֵי הָרוּחַ לִפְנֵי הקב"ה. שֶׁבְּשָׁעָה שֶׁבֵּית הַמִּקְדָּשׁ קַיָּים אָדָם מַקְרִיב עוֹלָה — שְׂכַר עוֹלָה בְּיָדוֹ, מִנְחָה — שְׂכַר מִנְחָה בְּיָדוֹ. אֲבָל מִי שֶׁדַּעְתּוֹ שְׁפָלָה — מַעֲלֶה עָלָיו הַכָּתוּב כְּאִילּוּ הִקְרִיב כָּל הַקָּרְבָּנוֹת כּוּלָּם, שֶׁנֶּאֱמַר: °"זִבְחֵי אֱלֹהִים רוּחַ נִשְׁבָּרָה", וְלֹא עוֹד אֶלָּא שֶׁאֵין תְּפִלָּתוֹ נִמְאֶסֶת, שֶׁנֶּאֱמַר: °"לֵב נִשְׁבָּר וְנִדְכֶּה אֱלֹהִים לֹא תִבְזֶה". *וְאָמַר ריב"ל: אכָּל הַשָּׂם אוֹרְחוֹתָיו בָּעוֹלָם הַזֶּה — זוֹכֶה וְרוֹאֶה בִּישׁוּעָתוֹ שֶׁל הקב"ה, שֶׁנֶּאֱמַר: °"וְשָׂם דֶּרֶךְ אַרְאֶנּוּ בְּיֵשַׁע אֱלֹהִים", אַל תִּקְרֵי (א) "וְשָׂם" אֶלָּא "וְשָׁם דֶּרֶךְ". § [כֵּיצַד מְקַנֵּא לָהּ כו'.] § הָא גּוּפָא קַשְׁיָא: אָמְרַתְּ: אָמַר לָהּ בִּפְנֵי שְׁנַיִם "אַל תְּדַבְּרִי עִם אִישׁ פְּלוֹנִי זֶה" — אַלְמָא דִּבּוּר סְתִירָה הוּא, וַהֲדַר תָּנֵי: דִּיבְּרָה עִמּוֹ, עֲדַיִין מוּתֶּרֶת לְבֵיתָהּ, וּמוּתֶּרֶת לֶאֱכוֹל בִּתְרוּמָה — אַלְמָא דִּבּוּר לֹא כְּלוּם הוּא! אָמַר אַבָּיֵי, בהָכִי קָאָמַר: "אַל תְּדַבְּרִי" וְדִבְּרָה, "אַל תְּדַבְּרִי" וְנִסְתְּרָה — (וְלֹא כְּלוּם). "אַל תִּסָּתְרִי" וְדִבְּרָה עִמּוֹ — עֲדַיִין מוּתֶּרֶת לְבֵיתָהּ, וּמוּתֶּרֶת לֶאֱכוֹל בִּתְרוּמָה. נִכְנְסָה עִמּוֹ לְבֵית הַסֵּתֶר וְשָׁהֲתָה כְּדֵי טוּמְאָה — אֲסוּרָה לְבֵיתָהּ, וַאֲסוּרָה לֶאֱכוֹל בִּתְרוּמָה. § "וְאִם מֵת חוֹלֶצֶת". § אַמַּאי? תִּתְיַיבֵּם נַמִי יַבּוּמֵי! אָמַר רַב יוֹסֵף: אָמַר קְרָא °"וְיָצְאָה מִבֵּיתוֹ וְהָלְכָה וְהָיְתָה לְאִישׁ אַחֵר", לְאִישׁ אַחֵר — וְלֹא לַיָּבָם. א"ל אַבָּיֵי: אֶלָּא מֵעַתָּה, חֲלִיצָה נַמִי לָא תִּיבָּעֵי! א"ל: אִילּוּ אִיתֵיהּ לְבַעַל מִי לָא בָּעֲיָא גֵּט? הָשְׁתָּא נַמִי תִּיבְּעֵי חֲלִיצָה. וְאִית דְּאָמְרִי, אָמַר רַב יוֹסֵף: רַחֲמָנָא אָמַר "וְיָצְאָה מִבֵּיתוֹ וְהָלְכָה וְהָיְתָה לְאִישׁ אַחֵר" דְּלָא לִיסְתְּרֵיהּ לְבֵיתֵיהּ, וְאַתְּ אָמְרַתְּ תִּתְיַיבֵּם נַמִי יַבּוּמֵי? אֲמַר לֵיהּ אַבָּיֵי: אֶלָּא מֵעַתָּה, לְאַחֵר לֹא תִּינָּשֵׂא, דְּלָא תִּיסְתְּרֵיהּ לְבֵיתֵיהּ! אֲמַר לֵיהּ:
מִי

(ויקרא יד; ישעיה ב; שמואל א ב; תהלים נא; שם; שם נ; ס"א ל"ג; דברים כד)

וְלַשְׂאֵת וְלַסַּפַּחַת. עַל יְדֵי שֶׁמְּנַשֵּׂא עַצְמוֹ בָּא לִידֵי סַפַּחַת, שֶׁאֵינוֹ עִיקָּר כַּאֲנָשִׁים, אֶלָּא נִסְפָּח וְטָפֵל. טְפֵילָה. דָּבָר שֶׁאֵינוֹ חָשׁוּב בְּעַצְמוֹ, אֶלָּא נִטְפָּל בַּאֲחֵרִים. סְפָחֵנִי נָא. אָסְפֵנִי נָא. (ב) בִּנְבוּאַת בֵּית עֵלִי מִשְׁתָּעֵי קְרָא: אַעֲמִיד כֹּהֲנִים גְּדוֹלִים אֲחֵרִים שֶׁיּוֹלִיאוּ אֶת כֹּהֲנֵי זַרְעֲךָ מִגְּדוּלָּתָם, וְיִצְטָרְכוּ לְבַקֵּשׁ מֵהֶם לְאוֹסְפָם וּלְקוֹלְטָם אֶצְלָם. אֶל אַחַת הַכְּהוּנּוֹת. בְּאַחַ' מִן הַמִּשְׁמָרוֹת. שְׂכַר עוֹלָה בְּיָדוֹ. וְלֹא שְׂכַר קָרְבָּן אַחֵר. זִבְחֵי. כָּל הַזְּבָחִים בְּמַשְׁמַע. הַשָּׂם אוֹרְחוֹתָיו. מְחַשֵּׁב הֶפְסֵד מִצְוָה כְּנֶגֶד שְׂכָרָהּ: (*אָמַר לָהּ בִּפְנֵי שְׁנַיִם אַל תְּדַבְּרִי עִם אִישׁ פְּלוֹנִי וְדִבְּרָה עִמּוֹ. שֶׁלֹּא בְּיִחוּד. עֲדַיִין מוּתֶּרֶת לְבֵיתָהּ. לְשַׁמֵּשׁ בֵּיתָהּ. לְשׁוֹן תַּשְׁמִישׁ הוּא. אֲסוּרָה לְבֵיתָהּ וַאֲסוּרָה לֶאֱכוֹל בִּתְרוּמָה. עַד שֶׁתִּשְׁתֶּה. וּלְקַמָּן בְּפֶ' "כְּשֵׁם שֶׁהַמַּיִם בּוֹדְקִין" (דף כח.) יָלֵיף מִ"וְנִטְמָאָה" "וְנִטְמָאָה" שָׁלֹשׁ פְּעָמִים: אֶחָד לַבַּעַל, וְאֶחָד לַבּוֹעֵל, וְאֶחָד לִתְרוּמָה. וְאִם מֵת בְּלֹא בָּנִים. עַד שֶׁלֹּא הִשְׁקָהּ. חוֹלֶצֶת וְלֹא מִתְיַיבֶּמֶת. בַּגְּמָרָא מְפָרֵשׁ טַעְמָא). הָא גּוּפָא קַשְׁיָא אָמְרַתְּ כֵּיצַד מְקַנֵּא לָהּ אָמַר לָהּ בִּפְנֵי שְׁנַיִם כו'. קס"ד: "אָמַר לָהּ" כו' הַיְינוּ פֵּירוּשָׁא דְ"כֵיצַד מְקַנֵּא לָהּ" — אָמַר לָהּ בִּפְנֵי שְׁנַיִם כו', וְאַשְׁמוּעִינַן דְּזֶהוּ הַקִּינּוּי. אַלְמָא דִּיבּוּר סְתִירָה הִיא. אֲפִי' מְדַבֶּרֶת עִמּוֹ בַּשּׁוּק — סְתִירָה חָשִׁיב לָהּ, מִדְּקָאָמַר זֶה הַקִּינּוּי, דְּאִי לָאו דִּסְתִירָה הוּא, וְלָא מִיתַּסְרָא בָּהּ — מַאי קִינּוּי אִיכָּא, וְלָמָּה לִי דְּמַתְרֶה בָּהּ?. וַהֲדַר תָּנֵי. דְּכִי עָבְרָה עַל הַתְרָאָתוֹ וְדִבְּרָה עִמּוֹ — מוּתֶּרֶת לְבֵיתָהּ. אָמַר אַבָּיֵי הָכִי קָאָמַר. "אָמַר לָהּ" לָאו פֵּירוּשָׁא דְ"כֵיצַד מְקַנֵּא לָהּ" הוּא, אֶלָּא תַּרְתֵּי קָתָנֵי. וְה"ק: אָמַר לָהּ "אַל תְּדַבְּרִי" וְנִסְתְּרָה אוֹ דִּבְּרָה, אע"פ שֶׁעָבְרָה עַל קִינּוּיָיו אֵלֶּא דִיבּוּר, אוֹ אִם דִּבְּרָה עִמּוֹ אַחַר קִינּוּי גָּמוּר דְ"אַל תִּסָּתְרִי" — עֲדַיִין בְּאַחַת מִשְׁתֵּי אֵלּוּ מוּתֶּרֶת לְבַעְלָהּ, אֲבָל עָבְרָה עַל קִינּוּיָיו אֵלֶּא סְתִירָה, כְּגוֹן שֶׁאָמַר לָהּ "אַל תִּסָּתְרִי" וְנִכְנְסָה עִמּוֹ לְבֵית הַסֵּתֶר כו'. וְיָצְאָה מִבֵּיתוֹ. לְעֵיל מִינֵּיהּ כְּתִיב: "כִּי מָצָא בָהּ עֶרְוַת דָּבָר" וגו', "וְיָצְאָה מִבֵּיתוֹ" וגו'. "לְאִישׁ אַחֵר" לָמָּה לִי לְמִכְתַּב? אִי לְמִשְׁרְיֵיהּ לְהִנָּסֵבָא עַל יְדֵי גֵּט כְּרִיתוּת — לִכְתּוֹב "וְיָצְאָה מִבֵּיתוֹ וְהָיְתָה לְאִישׁ", לָמָּה לִי לְמִכְתַּב "לְאַחֵר"? אֶלָּא לְמַעוּטֵי יְבָמָה, הֵיכָא דְּלָא גֵּרְשָׁהּ בַּעַל אַחַר שֶׁמָּצָא בָהּ עֶרְוַת דָּבָר. וְהָכִי מִשְׁתַּמְּעֵי קְרָאֵי: "כִּי מָצָא בָהּ עֶרְוַת דָּבָר" — יְגָרְשֶׁנָּה בְּסֵפֶר כְּרִיתוּת. "וְיָצְאָה מִבֵּיתוֹ", כְּלוֹמַר, וּבְכָל צַד שֶׁתֵּצֵא מִבֵּיתוֹ, בֵּין ע"י גֵּירוּשִׁין בֵּין ע"י מִיתָה, אִם בָּאת לִינָּשֵׂא לְאִישׁ אַחֵר — תִּנָּשֵׂא. וְלֹא לַיָּבָם שֶׁאֵינוֹ אַחֵר אֵצֶל נְשׂוּאִין שֶׁל זוֹ, שֶׁמִּכֹּחַ נְשׂוּאֵי רִאשׁוֹן יִבֵּל [?] זְקוּקָה לוֹ. אִי הָכִי חֲלִיצָה נַמִי לָא תִּיבְּעֵי. דְּהָא פְּטָרָהּ רַחֲמָנָא וְשָׁרְיֵיהּ לְאִישׁ אַחֵר בְּכָל עִנְיָן שֶׁתֵּצֵא מִבֵּיתוֹ אַחַר שֶׁנִּמְצָא בָהּ עֶרְוַת דָּבָר. אִילּוּ אִיתֵיהּ לַבַּעַל. מִי מִשְׁתַּרְיָא בְּלֹא גֵט? הָא כְּתִיב "וְכָתַב לָהּ סֵפֶר כְּרִיתוּת", אֲפִי' מָצָא בָהּ עֶרְוַת דָּבָר — כְּרִיתוּת בָּעֲיָא. הָשְׁתָּא נַמִי בָּעֵי' חֲלִיצָה, דְּיָבָם בִּמְקוֹם בַּעַל קָאֵי. אִית דְּאָמְרִי. דְּהָכִי שָׁנֵי רַב יוֹסֵף לְעֵיל: רַחֲמָנָא אָמַר כו' נָוֶה לְבַעְלָהּ לְגָרְשָׁ' מִבֵּיתוֹ כְּשֶׁמָּצָא בָהּ עֶרְוַת דָּבָר כִּי הֵיכִי דְּלָא תִּיסְתְּרֵי' לְבֵיתֵיהּ, כִּדְאָמַר לְעֵיל:* זוֹנָה בְּבֵיתָא כִּי קָרְיָא לְשׁוּמְשְׁמָא. [דף ג:]
מִי

הא גופא קשיא. תימה לרבי: אמאי לא נקט הכא לישנא דריש מס' מכות (דף ב.): "כיצד העדים נעשים זוממין" — "כיצד אין העדים נעשים זוממין" מבעי ליה! הכא נמי הוה ליה למימר הכי: "כיצד מקנא לה" — "כיצד אין מקנא לה" מבעי ליה! והתם מתרץ שפיר. אבל הכא, אפילו לפי התירוץ הוה ליה למיתני: "כיצד אין מקנא לה"! ונראה, דלהכי לא פריך הכא, משום דמצי למימר "אל תדברי" דרישא פירושו סתירה, דהיינו קינוי גמור, ואתי שפיר לישנא ד"כיצד מקנא לה", ולא קשיא מידי אלא רישא לסיפא. וה"פ הכא: אלמא פירוש דמתני' דדיבור — סתירה הוא, מדקתני "כיצד מקנא", ולשון נקי הוא, כדתנן בפרק קמא דכתובות (דף יג.): "ראוה מדברת", ומפרש בגמ': מאי "מדברת" — נסתרה. א"כ תיקשי סיפא, דקתני: דיברה עדיין מותרת לביתה, ואי פירוש דדיבור דמתניתין סתירה — אמאי מותרת? אלא דיבור ממש הוא. ולפי הירושלמי משמע דבעי לתרולי דדיבור דרישא — סתירה, אלא דנקט לשון נקי. והכי איתא התם: סוף דבר שתדבר עמו, הא אם נסתרה עמו ולא דברה — אין סתירתה כלום? פירוש: בתמיה. דבורה אתא מימר לך, אפי' דברה עמו ולא נסתרה — עדיין מותרת לביתה — לשון נקי הוא מתני'. פי': דיבור דרישא לשון נקי. מיהו דסיפא אית לן למימר על כרחך דיבור ממש.

לאחר ולא ליבם. אין להקשות מפרק "האשה שנפלו לה נכסים" (כתובות דף פא.), בשמעתין דשומרת יבם, דפריך התם: והא בעינן "לכשתנשאי לאחר תטלי מה שכתוב ליכי"! אמר רב אשי: יבם כמו אחר דמי. דלענין לשון תנאי ב"ד שוייה כאחר, אבל ב"אחר" דקרא — אין האח בכלל. והכי נמי משמע בפרק "אין מקדישין" (ערכין דף כה:), דקתני: "אם מכר את השדה לאיש אחר" — לאחר ולא לבן. או אינו אלא לאחר ולא לאח? כשהוא אומר "איש" — הרי אח אמור, הא מה אני מקיים "לאחר" — לאחר ולא לבן. דמשמע: טעמא דכתיב "איש", הא לאו הכי — לא הוי אח בכלל "אחר", וכ"ש גבי יבם, דבא מכח נשואי אחיו, דלאו אחר הוא. והכי אמרינן נמי בפ"ק דקידושין (דף יג:): אמר קרא "פן ימות במלחמה ואיש אחר יקחנה". מתקיף לה רב שישא בריה דרב אידי: אימא מאן "אחר" — יבם! ומשני: דיבם לא מקרי "אחר". *אבל קשיא מפרק "האומר" (קדושין דף סז:), דנפקא לן מהכא בפרק "האומר" דלא תפסי קדושין באחות אשה; אימר דאיצטריך קרא דוקא ליבם (ג) *משום דרמיא עליה ליבומי, כדאמרי' בשמעתין, ולכני אחות אשה [?] מנלן? ועוד תקשה, דהכא, אע"ג דכתיב "איש אחר" — ממעטינן יבם, ובערכין מרבינן יבם מ"איש" וממעטינן בן מ"אחר"! וא"ת מ"איש" ממעטינהו בפ' "האומר" (ג"ז שם) — קרובים, ומ"לאחר" — יבם, סוף סוף "ואיש אחר יקחנה" מאי דרשת ביה? **לאחר** ולא ליבם. אי קשיא: והא האי קרא בסוטה ודאי ע"י עדים כתיב, דילפינן "דבר" "דבר" מממון, בסוף מסכת גיטין (דף צ.), וסוטה ודאי אמר בפ"ק דיבמות (דף יא:) דפטורה בלא חליצה, משום דכתיב בה טומאה כעריות! תריץ: ד"לאחר" לא איצטריך למיכתב, אלא ליוצאת משום סתירה, כיון דנפקא לן סוטה ודאית מטומאה דכתיב בה. **אילו** איתיה לבעל מי לא בעיא גט. הקשה רבי בשם ר' אברהם בר מרדכי ז"ל: והא סוטה ודאית, ואיילונית היכא דהכיר בה, ואשת סריס, דבעו גט מבעל היכא דאיתיה — ואפ"ה פטורות מיבם בלא חליצה! ויש לתרץ: סוטה ודאית לא דמיא להכא, (ד) כיון דטומאה סתם הרי היא כערוה גמורה, דגזירת הכתוב הוא דפטורות. ואשת סריס ואיילונית היכא דאיתיה לבעל שרו ליה, ואפ"ה אימעוט בפ"ק דיבמות *מדין יבום, דלא צריך בהו כלל. אבל סוטה ספק לא אימעוט אלא גבי איסורא דבעל. וקמשמע לן קרא: כיון דבא מכח נשואי אחיו — הרי הוא במקום בעל, דאסורה לו ליבם, אבל חליצה בעיא.

דלא ליסתריה לביתיה ואת אמרת תתייבם נמי יבומי. רבינו חננאל הטעים דבריו, ופריש: ורחמנא אמר "אשר לא יבנה" — לבנות ולא לסתור.
מי

[שבועות ו:]

כפול הוא במתני'

מ"ק ה.

[ועיין תוס' קידושין יג: ד"ה תלא ותוס' כתובות פא. ד"ה יבם]

[דף ג:]

[דף יב. וכו']

הגהות הב"ח

(א) גמ' אל תקרי ושם. נ"ב ושם בשי"ן כמו מי שם פה לאדם פירושו ששם דרכו בדרכי השם אל תקרי ושם בשי"ן אלא בשי"ן מענין שומת ב"ד: (ב) רש"י ד"ה ספחני וכו' נא (בנבואת תז"מ ונ"ב ס"א בגזירת: (ג) תום' ד"ה לאחר וכו' דוקא ליבם כדאמרי' בשמעתין כל"ל ותיבות משום דרמיא עליה ליבומי נמחק: (ד) ד"ה אילו וכו' לא דמיא להכא דכיון דטומאה כתיב בה הרי היא כערוה גמורה וגזירת וכו' ואפ"ה אימעוט בפרשת יבמין מדין:

מי קא רמינן לה עליה בעל כרחיה? ואיכא דאמרי, אמר רב יוסף: *הכתוב קראו "אחר", א שאין (א) בן זוגו של ראשון, שזה הוציא רשעה מביתו וזה הכניס רשעה לתוך ביתו. ואת אמרת תתיבם נמי יבומי?! אמר ליה אביי: אלא מעתה, נשאת לאחר ומת בלא בנים לא תתיבם, דהכתוב קראו "אחר"! גביה דהאי מיהא בשם טוב הוה קיימא. רבא אמר: *ק"ו; אם נאסרה במותר לה — באסור לה לא כל שכן? אמר ליה אביי: אלא מעתה, כ"ג שקידש את האלמנה ומת, ויש לו אח כהן הדיוט — לא תתיבם; אם נאסרה במותר לה — באסור לה לא כל שכן? נאסרה?! הא אסירא וקיימא! מותר לה?! אסור לה הוא! אלא, אשת כהן שנאנסה, ומת, ויש לו אח חלל — לא תתיבם; אם נאסרה במותר לה — באסור לה לא כל שכן? ב אונס בישראל מישרא שרי, וגבי דהאי (מיהא) ליכא איסורא.§ **מתני'** ג ואלו אסורות מלאכול בתרומה: האומרת "טמאה אני לך", ושבאו עדים שהיא טמאה, והאומרת "איני שותה", ושבעלה אינו רוצה להשקותה, *ושבעלה בא עליה בדרך.§ **גמ'** ◦אמר רב עמרם: הא מילתא אמר לן רב ששת, ואנהר לן עינין ממתניתין: סוטה שיש לה עדים במדינת הים — אין המים בודקין אותה. מ"ט — דאמר קרא: (במדבר ה) "ונסתרה והיא נטמאה ועד אין בה" — ד דליכא דידע בה, לאפוקי הא, דהא איכא דידע בה. ואנהר לן עינין ממתני', דקתני: ושבאו לה עדים שהיא טמאה. דאתו עדים אימת? אי נימא מקמי דתשתי — *זונה היא! אלא לבתר דשתאי; אי אמרת בשלמא אין המים בודקין אותה — שפיר, אלא אי אמרת מים בודקין אותה — תיגלי מילתא למפרע דסהדי שקרי נינהו! אמר ליה רב יוסף: לעולם אימא לך מים בודקין אותה, והא — אימור זכות תולה לה. במאי קמיפלגי — במתנוונה דרבי. *דתנן, רבי אומר: זכות תולה במים המרים, ואינה יולדת ואינה משבחת, אלא מתנוונה והולכת, לסוף שהיא מתה באותה מיתה. רב ששת סבר: בין לרבי ובין לרבנן הויא מתנוונה, ורב יוסף סבר: לרבי — הויא מתנוונה, לרבנן — לא הויא מתנוונה. מתיב רב שימי בר אשי, *ר' שמעון אומר: אין זכות תולה במים המרים. ואם אתה אומר זכות תולה במים המרים — מדחה אתה את המים בפני כל הנשים השותות, ואתה מוציא שם רע על הטהורות ששתו, והן אומרים: טמאות היו, אלא שתלה להן זכות. ואם איתא, יש לה עדים במדינת הים נמי, אתה מוציא שם רע על הטהורות ששתו, והן אומרים: טמאות היו, אלא שיש להן עדים במדינת הים! לר' שמעון קאמרת? לר' שמעון, מדזכות לא תליא — עדים נמי לא תלו. מתיב *רב: *ואלו שמנחותיהן נשרפות

האומרת

תורה אור

רש"י

מי קא רמינן עליה. למיכנסה בעל כרחיה? דאילו ליבם אמרינן ליה מצות יבום קודמת למצות חליצה, אבל בהא — אסור למימר ליה. ומתמילא אשמועינן קרא דאסור ליבמה, דלא שייך בה יבום, והויא כאשת אח שלא במקום מצוה. **הכתוב קראו אחר.** למי שנושאה, ואת אמרת תתיבם, ותרמי עליה בעל כרחיה?. **נישאת לאחר.** שגרשה ראשון שמצא בה ערות דבר, וניסת כו' — לא תתיבם. דהשתא נמי אחר הוא ואין (ב) בן זוגו של ראשון אם ישאנה, וקרמית *לזה עליה במצות יבום. **גביה דהאי.** אחר, אחיו של זה. **בשם טוב הוה קיימא.** ואיכא למימר הדרה בה. ואין קרוי אחר אלא הנושאה מתוך אלמנות או גירושין על מי שקלקלה תחתיו. **רבא אמר.** האי דקתני מתניתין: ולא מתייבמת — ק"ו: דאם נאסרת בסתירה זו במותר לה — בבעלה שהיה מותר לה, ונתקלקלו עכשיו הנישואין ליאסר עליו. **באסור לה.** דהיינו יבמה, שהוא אסור לה בחיי בעלה — לא כל שכן שנאסרו נשואי הראשון, שלא להתייבם מכח אותן הנישואין. **שקידש את אלמנה.** שהיא אסורה עליו. **לא תתיבם.** מכח ק"ו זה: אם נאסרה כו'! ולקמן מפרש מאי נאסרה ומאי מותר לה, הלא אסור היה מתחילתו. **אלא.** הכי פריך: אשת כהן שנאנסה ונאסרה עליו. דאשת כהן אסורה אפילו באונס. אבל אשת ישראל מותרת, דכתיב (במדבר ה): "והיא לא נתפשה" — הא נתפשה מותרת. ומדכתיב "והיא" — מיעוטא הוא, ומשמע דיש אחרת שאפילו נתפשה אסורה. **ויש לו אחיו.** מאביו. **והוא חלל** — שנולד לאביו מן הגרושה, ונתחלל מן הכהונה, ומותר בנשים הפסולות לכהונה, כדכתיב בכהנים הנושאין פסולות: "ולא יחלל זרעו" (ויקרא כא) — אלמא זרעו חלל. **לא תתיבם.** מק"ו זה: אם נאסרה בבעילה זו לבעלה שהיה מותר לה, ביבמה האסור לה באותה שעה — לא כ"ש שנאסרו עליו נישואי אחיו, שלא ליבמה מכח נשואין?. **ליכא איסורא.** ואילו הוא היתר גמור, ואין זה ק"ו. אבל בזינתה ברצון, שהבעל והיבם שוין באיסור זה אם היתה תחתיו — הוי ק"ו, שהרי מחמת נישואין הראשונים היא נזקקת ליבום, ואם על הבעל נתקלקלה — ק"ו ליבם. **מתני' לאכול בתרומה.** א] אם הוא כהן. **ושבעלה בא עליה בדרך.** דשוב אין המים בודקין אותה. כדלקמן (דף כח.): "ונקה האיש מעון" — בזמן שהאיש מנוקה, שלא בא עליה מאחר שנאסרה עליו — אז האשה ההיא תשא את עונה. אין האיש מנוקה מעון — אין המים בודקין את אשתו. **גמ' ואנהר לן עינין.** הביא לנו ראיה לדבריו ממתניתין. **סוטה שיש לה עדים במדינת הים.** שראו שנטמאה מזה. **ועד אין בה.** אע"ג דדרשינן לעיל לעד אחד נאמן בסוטה, ולסוטה ודאית שלא תשתה עוד — אין מקרא יוצא מידי פשוטו, ודרשינן ליה נמי הכי: "ועד אין בה" — הוא דאמר "והביא האיש את אשתו" וכל הפרשה, הא יש בה עד — אין המים בודקין אותה. **ואנהרינהו לעינין.** משום דקרא לאו ראיה הוא כל כך, דהא דרשינן ליה לסוטה ודאית שיש בה עד אחד לפנינו, וללמד שלא תשתה. **זונה היא.** ופשיטא דאסורה בתרומה, (ג) דהא תנא ליה: האומרת "טמאה אני". **אלא לבתר דשתאי.** ואיצטריך לאשמועינן דלא מחזקינן להו כשקרי על אשר לא בדקוה המים. **שפיר.** ומשום הכי לא מחזקי' להו כשקרי — דמשום דהוו ידעי בה לא בדקי לה מיא. **זכות תליא לה.** דאמר לקמן (דף כ.): זכות תולה במים המרים. **וקמיפלגי.** רב ששת ורב יוסף. **במתנוונה.** דקאמר לקמן (דף כב:) גבי אשה שתלה לה זכות. שלא יצבה בטנה מיד, אבל אינה יולדת לעולם, ואינה משבחת. **אלא מתנוונה והולכת.** מכחשת והולכת. **באותה מיתה.** לצבות בטנה ונפול ירך. **רב ששת סבר.** לא פליגי רבנן עליה דרבי, אלא שסוף שהיא מתה באותה מיתה לחוד. אבל במתנוונה — לא איפלוג, דכל מי שזכות תולה לה — מנוונה היא. וזו, הואיל ולא נתנוונה — לא תלה לה זכות, אלא שאינה ראויה ליבדק כלל, משום עדים. **ורב יוסף סבר.** ראויה ליבדק היא, אלא זכות תולה לה. ואי משום דלא נתנוונה, הא מני — רבנן היא, דאמור לקמן: זכות תולה לה. דקסברי לא הויא מתנוונה כלל. **מדחה אתה** *כח המים בפני הנשים. שלא יהו יראות מהם להודות שהיא טמאה, ולא ימחה שם הקדוש על המים. **ואי איתא.** דיש לה עדים לא מיבדקה, השתא נמי על ידי זו נמי איכא לעז על הטהורות ששתו כו'. **מדזכות לא תליא.** משום האי טעמא, דחייש הוא ללעז על הטהורות — עדים נמי לא תלו. **שמנחותיהן נשרפות.** מנחות קנאות שלה, עשירית האיפה קמח שעורים, נשרפות למטה על בית הדשן. שאינן ראויות ליקרב, ולא לפדות ולצאת לחולין.

האומרת

תוספות

מי קא רמינן עליה בעל כרחיה. הכא הוה מצי למיפרך כדפריך לבסוף, דאמר: אלא מעתה נשאת לאחר ומת בלא בנים לא תתייבם, דלא נסתריה לביתיה! **אשת כהן שנאנסה.** וא"ת: אמאי לא תני לה בפרק "יש מותרות" (יבמות דף פד.), גבי אסורות לבעליהן ומותרות ליבמיהן? יש לומר: הא תני ליה חייבי לאוין, וזו מחייבי לאוין, כדאמר בפרק "הבא על יבמתו" (שם דף נו:): הכל היו בכלל "אחרי אשר הוטמאה" וגו'. והכי מתרץ התם, דפריך מפלוע דכא. ◦אבל יש לתמוה, אמאי לא פריך הכא: ישראל שנשא כשרה ונעשה פלוע דכא, ויש לו אח כשר, דדמי למתני' — מאי הוי ליה לתרולי*?

האומרת טמאה אני לך. אי קשיא: בשלהי מס' נדרים (דף צ:), דפליגי רבה ורב ששת באומרת "טמאה אני לך", דרב ששת אומר: אוכלת בתרומה וכו', תריץ: דהכא מיירי אחר קינוי וסתיר', דרגלים לדבר, אפילו רב ששת מודה. והכי מפרש לה בירושלמי.

ושבאו לה עדים ואמרו שנטמאה. מספקא לרבי אי דוקא נקט עדים שנים, אבל עד אחד לא מהימן. דמוקמינן ליה בגמרא דמיירי לאחר ששתתה, דדוקא קודם ששתתה האמינה תורה לעד אחד, ורב ששת דאמר בגמרא: סוטה שיש לה עדים במדינת הים, דאין המים בודקין אותה — דוקא עדים נקט, ולא עד א'. או דילמא, כיון דהאמינה תורה לעד אחד אחר קינוי וסתירה — ליכא חילוק בין אחד לשנים. מיהו, מסתברא דה"ה לעד אחד, כדעולא דאמר בפרק (ד) "מי *" שאמר" (לקמן דף לא:): כל מקום שהאמינה תורה עד אחד — הרי כאן שנים. **אם** אתה אומר זכות תולה מדחה אתה את המים. וא"ת: לרב ששת, דאמר: בין לרבי בין לרבנן מתנוונה — א"כ, אהיכא קאי ר"ש דאמר מדחה אתה? והלא יראו דמתנוונת, והיאך יוכלו להוציא שם רע על הטהורות ששתו כשלא יתנוונו? יש לומר: הנשים העומדות משום ייסור, ולא יהא ניכר לאחר כשעומדת בעזרה נתנוונה — יוציאו שם רע, (ה) והבועל יגיד להם שקלקל עמה, ולא ידעי שזו מתנוונת. אי נמי: לא יתלו נוונוה במים המרים, וכן היא לא תתלה במים המרים, אלא בחולי אחר.

*) [נ"ל שקינא]

כי

עין משפט נר מצוה

כד א מיי' פ"י מהלכות גירושין הלכה כב סמג עשין נ טוש"ע אה"ע סימן קיט סעיף ה:

כה ב מיי' פי"ח מהל' איסורי ביאה הל' ח סמג לאוין קכא ועשין מח טוש"ע אה"ע סימן ו סעיף יח:

כו ג מיי' פ"ח מהלכות תרומות הלכה טו:

כז ד מיי' פ"ג מהל' סוטה הלכה כג:

[ויעוי' על זה כתבו תוס' יבמות פד: ד"ה שייר]

תוספות שאנץ

מתני' אלו אסורות לאכול בתרומה. פי' אם היא אשת כהן האומרת טמאה אני לך וה"ה דאסורה לבעלה וכדתנן אמרה טמאה אני שוברת כתובתה ויוצאה ולא דמי להההיא דתנן בפ' בתרא דנדרים בראשונה היו אומרים שלשה נשים יוצאות ונוטלות כתובה האומרת טמאה אני לך. השמי' ביני לבינך נטולה אני מן היהודים חזרו לומר האומרת טמאה אני לך תביא ראיה לדבריה ואינה אסורה לבעלה דלמא נתנה עיניה באחר והכא לא חיישינן דשמא עיניה נתנה באחר. וי"ל דהיינו טעמא דהכא איכא רגלים בדבר שהרי קינא לה ונסתרה וליכא למיחש דשמא עיניה נתנה באחר ומ"ה כשאמרה טמאה אני נאמנת אבל התם ליכא רגלים לדבר וכשאומרת טמאה אני היא משקרת ושמא עיניה נתנה באחר ומהאי טעמא ניחא שפיר הא דקאמר התם בתר הכי דאמרה טמאה אני אוכלת בתרומה שלא תוציא לעז על בניה והכא קאמר דאסורה לאכול בתרומה בכל ענין דמשמע בין יש להם בנים בין אין להם אלא לאו משום דכאן שהיא ספק סוטה ואיכא רגלים לדבר שהרי קינא לה ונסתרה ויש בה חששא בכך ולכך היא נאמנת ואינה אוכלת בתרומה אבל התם ליכא רגלים לדבר. וכן נראה מתוך הירושלמי דקאמר התם על הך משנה מתני לא כהך משנה ראשונה דתנינן תמן בראשונה היו אומרים ג' נשים יוצאות ונוטלות כתובה האומרת טמאה אני ומשני א"ר יהודה א"ר בון אפילו תימא כמשנה אחרונה ושאני הכא דאיכא רגלים לדבר. ומשמע דה"פ מתני' דקאמר שוברת כתובתה ויוצאה לא אתיא כמשנה ראשונה דהתם אמר דנוטלת כתובתה ומשני ר' בון אפי' תימא כמשנה אחרונה דקאמר התם דאינה אסורה לאכול בתרומה ואם תיקשי מכלתין דקאמר דאסורה לאכול בתרומה שאני התם דרגלים יש לדבר שהרי קינא לה ונסתרה. עי"ל דהא דקאמר התם דמותרת לאכול בתרומה היינו לרב ששת משום דמיירי באונסין דאשת כהן דלא שכיחי אבל הכא מיירי ברצון דכיון שקינא לה ונסתרה א"כ נבעלת ברצון ומ"ה

מסורת הש"ס

[גיטין צ:]

נ"ל לה יעב"ץ

[יבמות יח:]

לקמן כז.

עיין ביבמות מד: בתוס' ד"ה הכא

לקמן כב:

ג"ז שם וש"נ

ס"א רבא ג"ז שם

נ"א את

הגהות הב"ח

(א) גמ' שאין זה בן זוגו: (ב) רש"י ד"ה נישאת וכו' ואין זה בן זוגו: (ג) ד"ה זונה היא וכו' דהא תנא ליה. נ"ב ע"פ החולץ דף מ"ד במ"ש התוס' בד"ה הכא נמי: (ד) תוס' ד"ה ושבאו וכו' כדעולא דאמר בפ' האשה רבה כל מקום: (ה) ד"ה אם וכו' והבועל יגיד:

גליון הש"ס

גמ' אמר רב עמרם הא מילתא. יבמות דף ו ע"א: **תוס'** ד"ה אשת כהן וכו'. אבל יש לתמוה. עיין יבמות פד ע"ב תוס' ד"ה שייר:

הגהות מהר"ב רנשבורג

א] רש"י ד"ה לאכול בתרומה אם הוא כהן. עי' בפירוש הר"ב ועי' תוי"ט ד"ה טמאה וכו' וכמ"ש עליו הרמ"ז ותבין סוף רש"י ודו"ק:

אמר' דאסורה לאכול בתרומה. ושבעלה בא עליה בדרך פי' רשוב אין המים בודקין אותה כדאמרי' ונקה האיש מעון שלא בא עליה לאחר שנאסרה לו האשה ההיא תשא את עונה אין האיש מנוקה מעון אין המים בודקין את אשתו: גמ' ואנהר לן עינין ממתני' סוטה שיש לה עדים במדינת הים אין המים בודקין אותה דאמר קרא ועד אין בה ואע"ג דדרשי' לעיל דעד א' נאמן בסוטה ולסוטה ודאית שלא תשתה עוד מ"מ אין המקרא יוצא מידי פשוטו. ודרשי' ליה נמי הכי ועד אין בה הוא דאמר והביא האיש את אשתו וכל הפרשה הא יש בה עד אין המים בודקין אותה ואנהר לן עיינין ממתני' הביא לנו ראיה לדבריו ממתני' ואע"ג דהביא מן המקרא מ"מ קרא אינו ראיה כל כך דהא דרשיניה לעיל לסוטה ודאית ויש בה עד אחד לפנינו וללמד שלא תשתה ל"ה. אילימא מקמיה דתשתה זונה היא פ"ה פשיטא דאסורה בתרומה דהא תני לה האומרת טמאה אני ולא נהירא דא"כ הו"ל למפרך הא תנא ליה ברישא. אלא נ"ל זונה היא וקי"ל דזונה אסורה לאכול בתרומה כיון שנבעלה בעילת זנות כדאמרי' בפ' י' יוחסין תנא אלמנה וגרושה וחללה זונה בזמן שהן כסדר חייב על כל אחת ואחת וקאמר דההוא תנא אית ליה איסור מוסיף אבל איפכא כמו זונה וחללה וגרושה ואלמנה אינו חייב אלא אחת דאין כאן איסור מוסיף ואמאי לא כיון דאינה מותרת לאכול בתרומה אלא ש"מ דאסורה. וה"נ אמר' לקמן פ' כשם תרומה נמי לא תיבעי שהרי עשאה ספק וה"נ אמרי' בפרק החולץ: תיגלאי מילתא למפרע דשהדי שקרי נינהו. הק' הר"מ מפונטייזא לר"ת לעולם אימא לך דלאו שהדי שקרי נינהו והאי דלא בדקי לה

עין משפט נר מצוה

כח א מיי' פ"ד מהלכות סוטה הלכה יד:
כט ב מיי' שם הל' טז:

האומרת "טמאה אני", ושבאו לה עדים שהיא טמאה. דאתו עדים אימת? אילימא מקמי דתקדוש – תיפוק לחולין. אלא לבתר דקדוש. אי אמרת בשלמא מים בודקין אותה – אלמא בת מקדש ומקרב היא, וכי קדוש מעיקרא – שפיר קדוש, ומשום הכי מנחתה נשרפת. אלא אי אמרת אין המים בודקין אותה – תיגלי מילתא למפרע, דכי קדוש מעיקרא – בטעות קדוש, ותיפוק לחולין! אמר רב יהודה מדיסקרתא: כגון שזינתה בעזרה, דכי קדוש מעיקרא – שפיר קדוש. מתקיף לה רב משרשיא: והלא פירחי כהונה מלוין אותה! שזינתה מפירחי כהונה עצמן. רב אשי אמר: כגון שנצרכה לנקביה, דאטו פירחי כהונה בכיפה תלי לה? רב פפא אמר: לעולם כדאמרינן מעיקרא. ודקאמרת תיפוק לחולין – מדרבנן, גזירה שמא יאמרו מוציאין מכלי שרת לחול. מתיב רב מרי: *נטמאת מנחתה, עד שלא קדשה בכלי – הרי היא ככל המנחות, ותפדה. משקדשה בכלי – הרי היא ככל המנחות, ותשרף. [א]קדש הקומץ ולא הספיק להקריבו עד שמת הוא או עד שמתה היא – הרי היא ככל המנחות, ותשרף. קרב הקומץ ולא הספיק לאכול שירים עד שמת הוא או עד שמתה היא – הרי היא ככל המנחות, ותאכל. שעל הספק באת מתחילה, כיפרה ספיקה והלכה לה. באו לה עדים שהיא טמאה – מנחתה נשרפת, *[ב]נמצאו עדיה זוממין – מנחתה חולין! עדים זוממין קאמרת?! עדים זוממין קלא אית להו. תניא כוותיה דרב ששת, ולאו מטעמיה: "טהורה" – ולא שיש לה עדים במדינת הים, "וטהורה" – ולא שתלתה לה זכות, "היא" – ולא שישאו ויתנו בה *מוזרות בלבנה. ורבי שמעון, נהי *דוי"ו לא דריש, והא איכא

יש

רש"י

האומרת טמאה אני. שהודתה לבית דין על קלקולה. שהיו מקיימין עליה, כדתני מתני'. מקמי דתקדוש. בכלי שרת. תיפוק לחולין. בפדיון. שלא היה קדושת הגוף אלא קדושת פה, וכל המנחות נפדות כל זמן שלא קדשו בכלי. אלא לבתר דקדוש. דכלי שרת מקדשין את הראוי להם, שלא לצאת עוד לחולין, כדתנן: "כל הנוגע בהם יקדש". וליקרב אינה ראויה, שהרי אינה באה אלא להזכיר עונה של זו שתבדק – והרי היא בדוקה ועומדת. ולנדבה נמי לא חזיא להקריבה, דמנחת שעורים אינה כשירה אלא לסוטה ולעומר. אי אמרת בשלמא מים בודקין אותה. אם שתתה עד שלא באו עדים, אלמא: בשעה שניתנה בכלי ראויה היתה לכלי שרת, דההיא שעתא בת מיקדשא ומיקרב היא מספק, כשאר מנחת סוטה. הלכך, כי קדיש בכלי – שפיר קדיש. ומשום הכי, כי אתו עדים – איפסלא מהקרבה מכאן ולהבא, ולא נפקא לחולין, ונשרפת. אלא אי אמרת אין המים בודקין אותה. הואיל ולא ליבדק עומדת ולא ראויה היא למנחה. תיגלי מילתא למפרע. דלא היתה ראויה לכלי. ואין כלי שרת מקדשין אלא הראוי להם, כדאמר בזבחים (דף פג.). ותיפוק לחולין. בלא פדיון. שקדושת פה שלה וקדושת כלי שלה הכל בטעות, שהיינו סבורים שהיא טעונה מנחה, ואינו כן, והקדש טעות אינו הקדש. שזינתה בעזרה. לאחר שקדשה בכלי. ועל זנות זה באו העדים, ולא על טומאה של סתירה ראשונה. הילכך, כי קדשה בכלי – בת מקדש ומקרב הואי, דלא הוו לה עדים. שנצרכה לנקביה. והניחוה והלכה וזינתה. דאטו פרחי כהונה בכיפה. של ראשה תלויים לה, שלא תשמט מידם? לעולם כדאמרינן מעיקרא. כדהוה סלקא דעתיה ברישא, שעל טומאת סתירה ראשונה באו, ואפילו הכי לא קשיא לרב ששת. דהא דקאמר דכיון דלא חזיא לקידוש תיפוק לחולין – אין הכי נמי, מדאורייתא יצאת לחולין, ומדרבנן היא נשרפת, לפי שאין הכל בקיאין בהלכות לידע שבשביל שהיו לה עדים לא היתה ראויה לקדש, ואתו למימר: מוציאין דבר שקידש בכלי שרת לחולין. הרי היא ככל המנחות. שנטמאו עד שלא קדשו בכלי, ותפדה, ויביא בדמיה את המנחה. קדש הקומץ. שקמצה, ונתן הקומץ בכלי שרת – קדש בקדושת קומץ. שהמנחה טעונה ארבע עבודות כנגד ארבע עבודות של דם זבחים: קמיצה מתוך כלי שרת – כנגד שחיטה, שהסכין של כלי שרת מקדש את הדם. ומתן כלי להקדיש הקומץ בכלי שרת שני – כנגד קבלת דם, הולכה – כנגד הולכה, והקטרת הקומץ – כנגד זריקת הדם. שמת הוא. ושוב אינה שותה, דאמאן בעינן למשרייה? הרי היא ככל המנחות. שאירע בהן פסול בין קמיצה להקטרה, ותישרף למטה. ולא הספיק. כהן לאכול את השירים. כיפרה. מנחה זו את ספיקה. האי כפרה לאו כפרת עון הוא, ולא הזכרת עון, אלא כפרה הראויה לה קאמרינן – שעשתה מנחה זו בשעת הקטרת קומצה כל מה שיש עליה לעשות, שהרי בהכשר קרבה, יבא וישקה אותה ותיבדק. וכיון דבהכשר קרבה – שיריה נאכלין כל זמן שלא אירע בהן פסול בגופן. באו לה עדים שהיא טמאה. שמעיקרא קאי, קודם הקטרה. נמצאו עדיה זוממין. עדי סתירתה, שעל ידיהם באה לכך. מנחתה חולין. לא קדושת פה ולא קדושת כלי, *) ואין מועלין בה, דבטעות הוה. אלמה לא אמרינן תישרף מדרבנן כי נמצאו עדיה זוממין, שמא יאמרו מוציאין מכלי שרת לחול. וש"מ: כי קתני באו לה עדים שהיא טמאה מנחתה נשרפת – מדאורייתא קאמר, דבת מקדש הואי. קלא אית להו. הכל יודעין שהקדישה טעות. כוותיה דרב ששת. דאין המים בודקין סוטה שיש לה עדים. ולא מטעמיה. ד"ועד אין בה". דההוא לאו לספק סוטה מידריש, אלא לסוטה ודאית בעד אחד. אלא מקרא אחרינא נפקא. טהורה. "ואם לא נטמאה האשה וטהורה היא ונקתה ונזרעה זרע", והוה ליה למיכתב: "ואם לא נטמאה ונקתה" וגו'. "וטהורה היא" – לדרשה, למידרש הכי: טהורה – נזרעת זרע, ולא שניצולת מן המים מפני שהיו עדים בטומאתה. וטהורה. וי"ו יתירה, למעוטי שתלתה לה זכות, דההיא לא אמר קרא "ונזרעה זרע". היא. ולא הניצולת מן המים על ידי שהיה קלקולה מפורסם לכל, שכבר היו נושאות ונותנות בה לדבר בה. מוזרות בלבנה. נשים טוות בלבנה: ופרכינן ורבי שמעון. דקאמר אין זכות תולה, נהי דוי"ו לא דריש, מיהו יש לה עדים נפקא מקרא, קשיא; דקפה מוציא שם רע על הטהורות, ואומרו: עדים היו להם.

לא

*) גי' רש"י מועלת בה בטעות כו'

תוספות

כי קדוש מעיקרא שפיר קדוש משום הכי נשרפת. קשיא: כיון דהוה היה מביא מנחתו עליה, אמאי נשרפת? מאי שנא מהא דתנן בפרק ד' (א) במסכת נזיר (דף כד:): האשה שנדרה בנזיר והפרישה את בהמתה בנזיר, והיפר לה בעלה; אם שלו היתה הבהמה – תצא ותרעה בעדר, ואם שלה היתה הבהמה – חטאת תמות. ואע"ג דבשעת הקדש הות בת מקדש, דקי"ל דבעל מיגז גייז, ואפ"ה אמר: כיון דמשלו היתה – תצא ותרעה בעדר, דנפקא לחולין! ותנן נמי התם בפרק "בית שמאי" (שם דף לג.): מי שנדר בנזיר והלך להביא בהמתו; (ב) אם עד שלא נגנבה בהמה נדר – הרי הוא נזיר, ואם משנגנבה בהמה נדר – אינו נזיר. והכי נמי הוו עדים בעולם קודם הקדש, ולאו אדעתא דהכי הקדיש! ועוד: אמאי נשרפת? כיון דקי"ל כבית הלל, דאמרי בפרק "יש נוחלין" (ב"ב דף קכ:) ובפרק "ב"ש" במסכת נזיר (דף לא:) דיש שאלה להקדש – למה אינו נשאל עליה, ותצא לחולין? דכי קדוש מעיקרא בטעות קדוש. ואין להקשות: והא אשם תלוי, אע"ג דכי קדוש מעיקרא – בטעות קדוש, דלא חזי לכפר מידי היכא דלא חטא, ואפ"ה תנן בפרק בתרא דכריתות (דף כג.): המביא אשם תלוי, ונודע שלא חטא – ירעה עד שיסתאב – דהא מפרש התם טעמא: משום דלבו נוקפו – גמר ומקדיש.

גזירה שמא יאמרו מוציאין מכלי שרת לחולין. ואי תקשה: כל הני דתנן "תצא ותרעה בעדר" נגזור שמא יאמרו מוציאין מקדושת הגוף לחולין! תריץ: התם לא מוכחא מילתא, וליכא היכירא בין קדושת פה לקדושת הגוף, ויאמר: קדושת הפה היה. אבל הכא איכא היכירא בין קדושת הפה לקדושת כלי שרת. ול"ע בפרק "שתי מדות" (מנחות דף ל.) ובפרק "התודה" (שם דף עט:).

קרב הקומץ ולא הספיק כו'. נראה דהוא הדין אם קרב הקומץ ובאו עדים שנטמאה, דאמר נמי כיפרה ספיקה. דהכי אמר בפרק בתרא דכריתות (דף כו:), גבי חטאת העוף הבא על הספק: אם (ג) משמילה דמו נודע לה שילדה – אסורה אפילו בהנאה, שעל הספק באת, כיפרה ספיקה.

נמצאו עדים זוממין. נראה (ד) דאקדשה בכלי קאי, וקודם קמילה. דלאחר הקמילה איכא איסורא דרבנן, ונשרפת. דמוקמינן נמי התם הא דתנן: משנמלקה נודע לה, הרי זו תקבר – בנודע לה שלא ילדה, ובדין הוא דמותרת בהנאה, ומאי טעמא תקבר – מדרבנן.

וטהורה ולא שתולה לה זכות. מהכא משמע דבעלה מותר בה לאלתר, ולא אמרי' ימתין עד שלש שנים שמא זכות תלתה לה. דאם היה אסור בה – היכי הוה מלינו למיקרי בה "ונקתה ונזרעה זרע"? וכן הראני רבי בירושלמי: "ונקה האיש מעון" – (ה) אינו חושש שמא תלה זכות, ואתיא כמ"ד הזכות תולה ואינה ניכרת.

[בתוספות לקמן כז. ד"ה דומה וכו' תמצא פירוש על מלה זו]

תוספות שאנץ

לה מיא משום דשמא בעלה בא עליה בדרך דאין המים בודקין אותה. והשיב לו ר"ת תשובתך בצדך דמשני רב יוסף דאימר זכות תלה לה. וה"נ דבא עליה בדרך דתולה ואפילו לרב ששת דפליג עליה ואמר דאין זכות תולה לה ליכא למיחש שמא בא עליה לא מיבעיא לרבנן דאמרי מוסרין לה שני תלמידי חכמים שלא בא עליה דליכא למיחש להכי אלא אפי' לר' יהודה דאמר דאפי' בעלה נאמן עליה בדרך ליכא למיחש דאטו בשופטני עסקי' שאינו מנוקה מעון שבא עליה בדרך ואחר כך משקה אותה אלא לאו ש"מ ליכא למיחש להכי. ותדע דא"כ לר' שמעון אתה מוצא לא שתו המטהרות ששתו שיאמרו

מסורת הש"ס

לקמן כב: [תוספתא פ"ב]

כריתות כב.

[עי' תוספות סנהדרין יד. ד"ה ור"ה]

הגהות הב"ח

(א) תוס' ד"ה כי וכו' דמסכת נזיר וכו' את בהמתה והיפר לה בעלה: (ב) בא"ד להביא בהמתו ומנהגה שנגנבה אם עד שלא וכו' והכא נמי: (ג) ד"ה קרב כו' הבא על הספק אם משמילה נודע לה שלא ילדה אסורה וכו' באת מתחלתה כיפרה ספיקה [illegible]: (ד) ד"ה נמצאו וכו' נראה דקאי אקדשה בכלי וקודם וכו' דתנן אם משנמלקה: (ה) ד"ה וטהורה וכו' אינו חושש:

גליון הש"ס

גמ' קדש הקומץ וכו'. עי' לקמן דף כב ע"ב תד"ה אלו: תוס' ד"ה כי קדוש כו' ועוד כו'. עיין מל"מ פי"א ה"ד מהל' מעה"ק:

טמאות היו אלא שבעליהן באו עליהן בדרך דליכא למימר דר' שמעון סבר דכמו דבזנות לא תלינן עדות נמי לא תלינן דהא כיון (א) דמקרא נפקא לן דאין המים בודקין אשתו כשבא עליה בדרך תלינן דלא פליג ר' שמעון אקרא [illegible] מתנוננה. ואלו שמנחותיהן נשרפות מנחת קנאות עשירית האיפה קמח שעורים נשרפות למטה דבית הדשן:

עדים

א) עי' רש"י לקמן ריש דף ז' ד"ה לא שכיחא. ב) [illegible] ג) [illegible]

יש לה עדים במדינת הים לא שכיחא. וה"ה דלא עליה בעלה בדרך נמי לא שכיח. **כי** היכי דידעי לאתרויי ביה. והכי אמרינן נמי בפ' "אלו הן הגולין" (מכות דף ט:), גבי גולין לעיר מקלט: ומוסרין לו שני תלמידי חכמים שמא יהרגנו בדרך. ודייק בגמרא: מאי לאו דאתרו ביה, דאי קטיל – בר קטלא הוא. אלמא גבי התראה בעינן תלמידי חכמים. **נדה** שהיא בכרת בעלה נאמן עליה. תימה: דמשמע בפרק "אין מעמידין" (ע"ז דף לו:) דיחוד דעריות דאורייתא. אם כן יחוד דנדה מנלן דשרי? ויש לומר: דוקא יחוד דעריות דאין להן היתר, דומיא דבן עם אמו, אסרה תורה. אבל נדה לא*. **היא** הנותנת. האי "היא הנותנת" לא דמי כלל לההוא דפרק קמא דעירובין (דף י.). **אמר** להו ק"ו ופרכוה. יש לומר: דוקא בפירכא "שכן יש היתר (ה) לאיסורה" פרכוהו, אבל ב"היא הנותנת" לא פרכוהו, ולכך הוצרכה לפירכא אחריתי. דאשכחן בדוכתי סגיאין דחמירא להו לאינשי עבירה קלה ומסתפו מינה טפי מעבירה חמורה. כגון בפ"ק דכתובות (דף ד:) דחמירא להו אבילות, דלא הוי אלא מדרבנן, מנדה שהיא בכרת. ובפ' "הנזקין" (גיטין דף נד.): באתריה דרבי יהודה חמירא להו שביעית, דליכא אלא לאו, משבת שהוא בסקילה. וברים פ"ק דבילה (דף ג:) אמר: האי דקיל צריך הרחקה טפי, דאמר: מ"ש גבי שבת דסתם לן תנא כרבי שמעון, וגבי יום טוב כרבי יהודה! שבת דחמיר – סתם לן כר"ש, י"ט דקיל – סתם לן כרבי יהודה. אלמא זימנין בדילי מקילתא טפי מחמירתא, וזימנין איפכא והשתא צריך ליישב הברייתא לפי הירושלמי* והתוספתא. דהכי מיתניא בתוספתא (פ"א): ר' יהודה אומר: נאמן עליה בעלה מקל וחומר, ומה נדה שחייב על ביאתה כרת וכו'. ר' יוסי אומר: הכתוב האמינו, שנא' "והביא האיש את אשתו" וגו'. ובירושלמי מיתניא הכי: רבי יהודה אומר: בעלה נאמן וכו'. אמרו לו: לא, אם אמרת בנדה שיש לה היתר וכו'. אמר להם רבי יהודה: גזירת הכתוב הוא "והביא האיש את אשתו" וגו'. אמרו לו: ובלבד בעדים. והשתא אית לן למימר דבהיא תוספתא פרכוהו, והדר אמר להו קרא, כההיא דירושלמי. אבל (ו) מדרבי יוסי *איכא לתמוה, דמעיקרא אמר להו קרא, והדר אמר להו קל וחומר! *ואומר מים גנובים. נראה דהאי "ואומר" פירושו הכי: כלומר, מאי תלי בהכי שאין היתר לאיסורה – הלא דילרו תוקפו, מאחר שאין היתר לאיסורה אין מתון בדבר, אם לא עכשיו אימתי. וא"ת לא יתקפנו יצרו על אשתו, הואיל ובעלה כבר – מים גנובים ימתקו.

מה

לא שכיחא. ולא מסקי אינשי אדעתייהו למחשדינהו לטהורות בהכי. והא דשני לעיל לר' שמעון: מדזכות לא תלה עדים נמי לא תלו – משום דאכתי לא הוה קיימא לן דרשא דהאי קרא. **מתני'** שמא יבא עליה בדרך. שצריך להשקותה בירושלים בב"ד הגדול, כדלקמן. נאמן עליה. שלא יבא. **גמ'** לא שנו. הא דתנן בקידושין: אבל אשה מתייחדת עם שני אנשים. שמא יצטרך כו'. הכא נמי, הואיל ושניהם אסורין בה – לא סגי בתרי, שמא יצטרך הבעל או שליח ב"ד לנקביו כו'. דליהוי עליה סהדי. אם יבא עליה – יעידו עליו (ד) לב"ד הגדול ולא ישקוה. ל"ש. אשה מתייחדת עם שני אנשים. והוציאוה עשרה. לאשת איש חוץ לעיר במטה, בחזקת מתה, לקלקל עמה. דידעי לאתרויי ביה. ולומר לו: מן התורה, כשאין האיש מנוקה מעון, שבא עליה משנאסרה עליו – אין המים בודקין את אשתו. בעלה נאמן עליה. ואין צריך להעמיד עדים אלו. סוטה שהיא בלאו. ד"לא יוכל בעלה הראשון" וגו', דאמרינן ביבמות בפ"ק (דף יא:): מה אני מקיים "אחרי אשר הוטמאה" – לרבות סוטה שנסתרה. והיא הנותנת. המדה הזאת שהבאת ראיה לדבריך – היא הנותנת את הדין שאנו אומרים שצריך עדים. נדה שהיא בכרת. חמורה עליו ואינו בא עליה. שכן יש לה היתר. כשתטהר, לפיכך אין יצרו תוקפו, שמובטח הוא לאחר זמן. שאין לה היתר. אם תמצא טמאה, ולפיכך לבו רודף אחריה. גנובים. כלומר, דבר האסור לו – יצרו רודף אחריו. ופרכוה. כדאמר: שכן יש לה היתר. היינו ת"ק. דברייתא. אבל אמרו. לר' יהודה לית ליה. **מתני'** ומאיימין עליה. שתהא מודה. על עדי נפשות. כדאמרינן בסנהדרין: הוו יודעין שלא כדיני ממונות דיני נפשות כו', בפרק "אחד דיני ממונות" (דף לז.). הרבה ילדות עושה. וגורם לנערה ילדה שתבא לידי קלקול. ושמא אמת הדבר – אל תביאי עצמך לידי מיתה מנוולת זו. שכנים רעים. יודעים לפתות, ומלויין לה תמיד. שאינה כדאי לשומען. אינה ראויה לה. שאומר לפניה דברי הודאות צדיקים הראשוני', אלא כדי שתודה על קלקולה, כדאמרי' לקמן: יהודה הודה ולא בוש. שוברת כתובתה. כותבת שובר על כתובתה: זניתי והפסדתי כתובתי. ונותנת ביד בעלה – שלא תתבענו לאחר זמן. ואינה נהרגת – שלא התרו בה עדים בשעת מעשה. לשער מזרח. שער החיצון, שבו נכנסין להר הבית. ומשם לשער נקנור, הוא שער העליון שבחומה שבין עזרת ישראל לעזרת נשים. ששם משקין את הסוטות. מפני שלא נתקדש בקדושת עזרה עובי חלל אותו השער, מפני המצורעין שמכניסין ידיהן לבהונות ליתן מדם האשם על בוהן ידו, ומחוסר כפורים שנכנס לעזרה – בכרת, לפיכך לא קדשו', שיוכל לעמוד בחלל השער. שאם היה כהן מוציא את דם האשם חוץ לעזרה – הרי הוא נפסל ביוצא, לפיכך צריך להכניס ידו לתוך חלל העזרה, וביאת מקצת שרא רחמנא. נקנור. אדם גדול היה, והביא דלתות נחושת מאלכסנדריא של מצרים לאותו שער, ונעשו בו נסים, כדתנן בסדר יומא (דף לח.), ונקרא על שמו. ששם משקין סוטות. דבעינן "לפני ה'", כדיליף לקמן. ומטהרין את היולדות. לקמן מפרש מאי היא. אוחז בבגדיה. בבית הצואר שלה. אם נקרעו. אינו חושש. ואם נפרמו. פרימה גדולה מקריעה, שנקרעה לקרעים הרבה, דמינצי"ר בלע"ז. כמו: האי דפריס סילקא (שבת דף עד:). עד שמגלה את לבה. ולקמן יליף לה מקרא. וסותר את שערה. מקליעתו. ולקמן יליף לה.

וקטליאות

תורה אור

יֵשׁ לָהּ עֵדִים בִּמְדִינַת הַיָּם! לָא שְׁכִיחָא.§ **מתני'** [א]כֵּיצַד עוֹשֶׂה לָהּ? מוֹלִיכָהּ לְבֵית דִּין שֶׁבְּאוֹתוֹ מָקוֹם, *[ב]וּמוֹסְרִין לוֹ שְׁנֵי תַלְמִידֵי חֲכָמִים, שֶׁמָּא יָבֹא עָלֶיהָ בַּדֶּרֶךְ. רַבִּי יְהוּדָה אוֹמֵר: בַּעְלָהּ נֶאֱמָן עָלֶיהָ.§ **גמ'** תְּרֵי וְאִיהוּ – הָא תְּלָתָא. לֵימָא מְסַיַּיע לֵיהּ לְרַב. *דְּאָמַר רַב יְהוּדָה אָמַר רַב: [ג]לֹא שָׁנוּ אֶלָּא בָּעִיר, אֲבָל בַּדֶּרֶךְ – עַד דְּאִיכָּא שְׁלֹשָׁה, שֶׁמָּא יִצְטָרֵךְ אֶחָד מֵהֶן לִנְקָבָיו, וְנִמְצָא אֶחָד מֵהֶן מִתְיַיחֵד עִם הָעֶרְוָה. לָא, הָכָא הַיְינוּ טַעְמָא – כִּי הֵיכִי דְּלֶיהֱווּ עֲלֵיהּ סָהֲדֵי. *תַּלְמִידֵי חֲכָמִים – אִין, כּוּלֵּי עָלְמָא – לָא. לֵימָא מְסַיַּיע לֵיהּ לְאִידַּךְ דְּרַב. דְּאָמַר רַב יְהוּדָה אָמַר רַב: *[ד]לֹא שָׁנוּ אֶלָּא כְּשֵׁרִין, אֲבָל פְּרוּצִין – אֲפִילּוּ עֲשָׂרָה נַמִי לָא, מַעֲשֶׂה הָיָה וְהוֹצִיאוּהָ עֲשָׂרָה בְּמִטָּה. לָא, הָכָא הַיְינוּ טַעְמָא – דְּיָדְעִי לְאַתְרוֹיֵי בֵּיהּ.§ "רַבִּי יְהוּדָה אוֹמֵר: בַּעְלָהּ" וכו'.§ תַּנְיָא, *רַבִּי יְהוּדָה אוֹמֵר: בַּעְלָהּ נֶאֱמָן מִקַּל וָחוֹמֶר: וּמַה נִּדָּה שֶׁהִיא בְּכָרֵת – בַּעְלָהּ נֶאֱמָן עָלֶיהָ, סוֹטָה שֶׁהִיא בְּלָאו – לֹא כָּל שֶׁכֵּן? וְרַבָּנַן: הִיא הַנּוֹתֶנֶת, נִדָּה דְּכָרֵת – חֲמִירָא לֵיהּ, וּמְהֵימַן. סוֹטָה דְּלָאו – לָא חֲמִירָא לֵיהּ, וְלָא מְהֵימַן. וְרַבִּי יְהוּדָה מִק"ו מַיְיתֵי לָהּ? וְהָא רַבִּי יְהוּדָה מִקְּרָאֵי מַיְיתֵי לָהּ! דְּתַנְיָא: °"וְהֵבִיא הָאִישׁ אֶת אִשְׁתּוֹ אֶל הַכֹּהֵן" מִן הַתּוֹרָה הָאִישׁ מֵבִיא אֶת אִשְׁתּוֹ. אֲבָל אָמְרוּ חֲכָמִים: מוֹסְרִין לוֹ שְׁנֵי תַלְמִידֵי חֲכָמִים, שֶׁמָּא יָבֹא עָלֶיהָ בַּדֶּרֶךְ. רַבִּי יוֹסֵי אוֹמֵר: *בַּעְלָהּ נֶאֱמָן עָלֶיהָ מִקַּל וָחוֹמֶר: וּמַה נִּדָּה שֶׁהִיא בְּכָרֵת – בַּעְלָהּ נֶאֱמָן עָלֶיהָ, סוֹטָה שֶׁהִיא בְּלָאו – לֹא כ"ש? אָמְרוּ לוֹ: לֹא, אִם אָמַרְתָּ בְּנִדָּה – שֶׁכֵּן יֵשׁ לָהּ הֶיתֵּר, תֹּאמַר בְּסוֹטָה שֶׁאֵין לָהּ הֶיתֵּר, וְאוֹמֵר: °"מַיִם גְּנוּבִים יִמְתָּקוּ" וגו'. ר' יְהוּדָה אוֹמֵר: מִן הַתּוֹרָה הָאִישׁ מֵבִיא אֶת אִשְׁתּוֹ אֶל הַכֹּהֵן, שֶׁנֶּאֱ': "וְהֵבִיא הָאִישׁ אֶת אִשְׁתּוֹ"! אֲמַר לְהוּ: קַל וָחוֹמֶר בְּרֵישָׁא – וּפַרְכוּהָ, וַהֲדַר אֲמַר לְהוּ קְרָא. רַבִּי יְהוּדָה הַיְינוּ תַּנָּא קַמָּא! אִיכָּא בֵּינַיְיהוּ "אֲבָל אָמְרוּ".§ **מתני'** [ה]הָיוּ מַעֲלִין אוֹתָהּ לְבֵית דִּין הַגָּדוֹל שֶׁבִּירוּשָׁלַיִם, וּמְאַיְּימִין עָלֶיהָ כְּדֶרֶךְ שֶׁמְּאַיְּימִין עַל עֵדֵי נְפָשׁוֹת, *וְאוֹמֵר לָהּ: בִּתִּי! הַרְבֵּה יַיִן עוֹשֶׂה, הַרְבֵּה שְׂחוֹק עוֹשֶׂה, הַרְבֵּה יַלְדוּת עוֹשָׂה, הַרְבֵּה שְׁכֵנִים הָרָעִים עוֹשִׂין. (א) עֲשִׂי לִשְׁמוֹ הַגָּדוֹל שֶׁנִּכְתַּב בִּקְדוּשָּׁה שֶׁלֹּא יִמָּחֶה עַל הַמַּיִם. וְאוֹמֵר לְפָנֶיהָ דְּבָרִים (ב) שֶׁאֵינָם כְּדַי לְשׁוֹמְעָן הִיא וְכָל מִשְׁפַּחַת בֵּית אָבִיהָ. אִם אָמְרָה "טְמֵאָה אֲנִי" – שׁוֹבֶרֶת כְּתוּבָּתָהּ וְיוֹצֵאת. [ו]וְאִם אָמְרָה "טְהוֹרָה אֲנִי" – מַעֲלִין אוֹתָהּ לְשַׁעַר הַמִּזְרָח (ג) שֶׁעַל פֶּתַח שַׁעַר נִקָּנוֹר, *[ז]שֶׁשָּׁם מַשְׁקִין אֶת הַסּוֹטוֹת, [ח]וּמְטַהֲרִין אֶת הַיּוֹלְדוֹת, [ט]וּמְטַהֲרִין אֶת הַמְּצוֹרָעִין.* [י]וְכֹהֵן אוֹחֵז בִּבְגָדֶיהָ, אִם נִקְרְעוּ – נִקְרָעוּ, וְאִם נִפְרְמוּ – נִפְרָמוּ, עַד שֶׁהוּא מְגַלֶּה אֶת לִבָּהּ, וְסוֹתֵר אֶת שְׂעָרָהּ. רַבִּי יְהוּדָה אוֹמֵר: *אִם הָיָה לִבָּהּ נָאֶה – לֹא הָיָה מְגַלֵּהוּ, וְאִם הָיָה שְׂעָרָהּ נָאֶה – לֹא הָיָה סוֹתֵר. [כ]הָיְתָה מִתְכַּסָּה בִּלְבָנִים – מְכַסָּהּ בִּשְׁחוֹרִים, הָיָה עָלֶיהָ כְּלֵי זָהָב

וְקַטְלִיאוֹת

הגהות הב"ח

(א) במשנה שכנים הרעים עושין (עשי לשמו וכו' המים) תא"מ ונ"ב ס"א אל תעשי לשמו הגדול שנכתב בקדושה שימחה על המים: (ב) שם דברים שאינה כדאי לשומען: (ג) שם לשער המזרח לשער נקנור כצ"ל ותיבות שעל פתח נמחק: (ד) רש"י ד"ה דליהוו וכו' עליו בב"ד הגדול: (ה) תוס' ד"ה אמר וכו' היתר לאיסורו וכו' ולכך הוצרכו וכו': (ו) בא"ד אבל בדר' יוסי איכא למימר איפכא דמעיקרא:

תוספות שאנץ

עדים במדינת הים לא שכיחא ולא מסקי אינשי אדעתייהו למחשדינהו לטהורות בהכי והאי דשני לעיל לר' שמעון מדזכות לא תלו עדים נמי לא תלו משום דאכתי לא היה קיימא לן דרשא דהאי קרא. וא"ת היאך יוצאו לעז על הטהורות שיש עדים במדינת הים כיון שהיא יולדת והא אמר לקמן דאם היתה יולדת בצער יולדת בריוח ואם היתה יולדת שחורים יולדת לבנים. וי"ל דאינו דבר הניכר כל כך ולא מסקינן אדעתייהו: סוטה שהיא בלאו פי' דלא יוכל בעלה הראשון ואמרינן בפ"ק דיבמות אחרי אשר הוטמאה לרבות סוטה הנסתרת: ואומר מים גנובים ימתקו וגו' תימה מאי ואומר הא כבר נפרך הק"ו וי"ל דה"פ וכי תימא דיש לו לבעל להיות נאמן על אשתו דכיון שהיא שנואה בעיניו לא יבא עליה ומ"ה מייתי ואומר מים גנובים ימתקו וחיישי' שמא יבא עליה: **מתני'** היו מעלין אותה לב"ד הגדול שבירושלים והקשה ה"ר אלחנן דאמאי לא חשיב אותה גבי מילי דבעו ב"ד של ע"א פ"ק דסנהדרין וי"ל דתנא ושייר דהכי נמי לא קתני זקן ממרא דצריך ב"ד של ע"א. ומעלין אותה לשער המזרח ומשם לשער נקנור פ"ה נקנור אדם גדול היה והביא דלתות נחשת מאלכסנדריא של מצרים לאותו שער ונעשו בו נסים כדאמר בסדר יומא ונקראו על שמו הוא שער העליון שבחומה שבין עזרת ישראל לעזרת נשים ששם משקין את הסוטות שלא נתקדש בקדושת העזרה עובי חלל אותו השער מפני המצורעין שמכניסין ידיהן לבהונות ליתן מדם האשם על בוהן ידו ומחוסר כפורים שנכנס לעזרה בכרת. לפי' לא קדשום שיוכל לעמוד בחלל השער שאם היה הכהן מוציא את דם האשם חוץ לעזרה הרי הוא נפסל ביוצא. לפי' צריך להכנים ידו לתוך חלל העזרה וביאה במקצת שריא רחמנא ושם משקים סוטות דבעי לפני ה' ל"ה: ואם נפרמו פרימה גדולה מקריעה שנקרע לקרעים הרבה דמינציי"ר בלע"ז כמו ההוא דפרים סילקא ל"ה.

לבדם

עין משפט נר מצוה

ל א ב מיי' פ"ג מהלכות סוטה הל' א סמג עשין כז:

לא ג טוש"ע אה"ע סי' כב סעיף ה בהגהה:

לב ד מיי' פכ"ב מהל' איסורי ביאה הל' ח טוש"ע שם:

לג ה מיי' פ"ג מהל' סוטה הלכה ב סמג עשין נו:

לד ו מיי' שם הל' ג:

לה ז ח ט מיי' פ"ד מהל' מחוסרי כפרה הלכה ב:

[וע"ע תוס' סנהדרין לז. ד"ה התורה]

לו י מיי' פ"ג מהל' סוטה הלכה יא סמג עשין נז:

לז כ מיי' שם הלכה ז:

עי' רש"א ואולי צ"ל ליישב הברייתא והתוספתא לפי הירושלמי

איכא למימר איפכא גירסת רש"ל ועי' רש"א

ד"ז צ"ל קודם ד"ה אמר להו

[עי' תוספות לקמן ח. ד"ה אם היה]

מסורת הש"ס

קדושין פ: [לקמן כ.]

קדושין פא.

[עיין לקמן כה.]

קדושין פ: ע"ז כה: ע"ש

[תוספתא פ"א ע"ש היטב]

במדבר ה

[לקמן כה.]

משלי ט

[נ"ל ואומרים כ"ה במשנה שבמשניות]

[ועי' תוס' לקמן ח. ד"ה ששם]

סנהדרין מה. [ועי' תוס' לקמן ח. ד"ה וכהן]

עין משפט נר מצוה

לח א מיי' פ"ג מהל' סוטה הלכה ד סמג עשין נו:
לט ב מיי' שם הל' יח:
מ ג מיי' שם הל' ה:
מא ד מיי' שם הל' ו:
מב ה מיי' שם הל' ה:
מג ו ז מיי' שם פ"ד הל' ה סמג שם:
מד ח מיי' שם פ"ג הלכה ב:
מה ט מיי' פ"ב מהל' תשובה הלכה ה וטוש"ע א"ח סי' תרז סעיף ב בהג"ה:

תוספות שאנץ

לבדם נתנה הארץ פ"ה יהודה זכה למלכות בתוספתא דברכות (פ"ד) קאמר דראובן נטל תחלה חלק בעבר הירדן: היו עצמותיו מגולגלין פ"ה איבריו היו מתפרקין בארונו מפני שנדה את עצמו בערבונו של בנימין וחטאתי לך כל הימים אפי' לעולם הבא ומהכא נפקא לן נידוי של תלמיד חכם אפילו על תנאי בא ל"ה: מי גרם שיודה יהוד' פ"ה דאמרי' במדרש ר' תנחומא בשעה שאמר יהודה צדקה ממני אמר ראובן גם אני בלבלתי יצועי אבי ועכשיו יחי ראובן שלדו קיימת כאילו הוא חי וזאת ליהודה בתמיה שעצמותיו מגולגלין: על איברי לשפא למקום שנתקו משם כמו דשף מדוכתיה: מאן דמפרש הטאיה. והתם (יומא פ"ז) רמי כתוב אחד אומר אשרי נשוי פשע כסוי חטאה וכתוב אחר אומר ומודה ועוזב ירוחם. לא קשיא כאן בחטא המפורסם טוב לו להודות לרבים (א) דנראה שאינו נכלם בדבר. ש"מ ממתני' כותבין שובר ופלוגתא היא (בב"ב ק"ע). רבא אמר במקום שאין כותבין. וקשה דהא רבא גופא אמר בגט פשוט דכותבין שובר משום דעבד לוה לאיש מלוה והכא משמע דלית ליה. וי"ל דאית ליה דכותבין והא דקאמר הכא במקום שאין כותבין דיחוי בעלמא הוא כלומר מהא לא תפשוט מידי דאיכא לאוקמא במקום שאין כותבין:

(א) נראה דל"ל כדי שיתביש אבל בחטא שאינו מפורסם טוב לו שלא יגלה חטאו דאם מגלה החטא נראה שאינו נכלם בדבר.

תוספות

מה להלן בשבעים ואחד. תימה: אמאי לא תני להו לסוטה וזקן ממרא בפ"ק דסנהדרין (דף ב.) בהדי הני דהוו בב"ד של שבעים ואחד? וי"ל: משום דגמר של סוטה וזקן ממרא לא היה בבית דין של שבעים ואחד. קשיא: **מה** להלן בבית דין של שבעים ואחד. כיון דילפינן מזקן ממרא, אית לך למימר גבי סוטה שהמקום גורם, כמו גבי זקן ממרא, ולכך היו מעלין אותה ללשכת הגזית – א"כ פסקו המים המרים מיום שגלתה סנהדרין וישבה לה בחנות, כדאמר בפרק "היו בודקין" (סנהדרין דף מא.), לפי שלא רצו לדון דיני נפשות, לפי שהמקום גורם. ובפרק בתרא דמכילתין (לקמן דף מז.) אמרינן דרבן יוחנן בן זכאי הפסיקן. וקודם גלות סנהדרין אומר בפרק "היו בודקין" (שם מא.) דרבן יוחנן בן זכאי תלמיד יושב לפני רבו היה, ולא מקרי "רבן"! ונראה דאיום לא היה מעכב, ואם לא היו מאיימין כלל – אעפ"כ היתה שותה. הילכך היתה נוהגת אפי' לאחר גלות.

לא עבר זר בתוכם. פירש ר"י (ו) בשם רבי שמואל: היינו בחלוקת יחזקאל, שראובן ויהודה שכנים. **שמעת** מינה כותבין שובר. תימה: והא הכא לא אפשר בלא שובר, אם היא אומרת "אבדה כתובתי" – במה יכוף אותה להחזיר כתובתה? בשלמא לוה בעלמא – מעכב הפרעון עד שיחזיר מלוה את השטר, אבל כאן אין פרעון, שהרי כאן אבדה כתובתה, והיכא דלא אפשר דברי הכל כותבין! וי"ל: שהיה יכול לעכב את הגט אלא עד שתחזיר לו הכתובה. אבל תמיה: לפום מאי דמסיק: במקום שאין כותבין כתובה כותבין שובר – למה לי למיכתב שובר? יקרע הגט, ויכתוב עליו "גיטא דנן דקרענוהו לא משום דגיטא פסולא הוא, אלא דלא תהדר ותגבי ביה זימנא אחריתי", כדאמרינן בפ' "הכותב" (כתובות דף פט:) ובפרק קמא דבבא מציעא (דף יח.)! וי"ל: דהכא מיירי מן הסכנה ואילך, דאמר בפרק "הכותב" (כתובות דף פט:) דגובה בעדי גירושין אפילו בלא גט.

אמר רבא במקום שאין כותבין כתובה עסקינן. מקשים: הא במקום שכותבין – אין כותבין שובר. וב"גט פשוט" (ב"ב ד' קעא:) אמר: ה"נ מסתברא דכותבין שובר, דאי אין כותבין – יאכל הלה וחדי! א"ל אביי: אלא מאי – כותבין? אבד שוברו יאכל הלה וחדי! א"ל רבא: אין, עבד לוה לאיש מלוה. אלמא דקיבל אותה סברא דכותבין! ונראה דרבא ס"ל כותבין, אבל הכא – דחייה בעלמא הוא, דליכא למשמע מהכא דכותבין שובר.

ששם

גמרא

תורה אור

וקטליאות נזמים וטבעות – [א]מעבירין ממנה, כדי לנוולה. *ואחר כך [ב]מביא חבל מצרי וקושרו למעלה מדדיה, [ג]וכל הרוצה לראות בא לראות, [ד]חוץ מעבדיה ושפחותיה, מפני שלבה גס בהן. [ה]וכל הנשים מותרות לראותה, שנאמר: °"ונוסרו כל הנשים ולא תעשינה (יחזקאל כג) כזמתכנה".§ **גמ'** מנהני מילי? א"ר חייא בר גמדא א"ר יוסי בר' חנינא: אתיא "תורה", "תורה": כתיב הכא °"ועשה לה הכהן את כל התורה" (במדבר ה) וכתיב התם °"על פי התורה אשר יורוך" (דברים יז), מה להלן בשבעים ואחד – אף כאן בשבעים ואחד.§ "ומאיימין עליה" וכו'.§ °ורמינהו: *כדרך שמאיימין עליה שלא תשתה – [ו]כך מאיימין עליה שתשתה. אומרים לה: בתי, אם ברור לך הדבר שטהורה את – עמדי על בורייך ושתי. לפי שאין מים המרים דומין אלא לסם יבש שמונח על בשר חי, אם יש שם מכה – מחלחל ויורד, אין שם מכה – אינו מועיל כלום! [ז]לא קשיא; כאן – קודם שנמחקה מגילה, כאן – לאחר שנמחקה מגילה.§ "ואומר לפניה" וכו'.§ ת"ר: [ח]אומר לפניה דברים של הגדה ומעשים שאירעו בכתובים הראשונים, כגון: °"אשר (איוב טו) חכמים יגידו ולא כחדו מאבותם". יהודה הודה ולא בוש, מה היה סופו – נחל חיי העולם הבא, ראובן הודה ולא בוש, מה היה סופו – נחל חיי העולם הבא. ומה שכרן? מה שכרן?! כדקא אמרינן! אלא: מה שכרן בעולם הזה – °"להם (שם) לבדם נתנה הארץ ולא עבר זר בתוכם". בשלמא ביהודה אשכחן דאודי, דכתיב: °"ויכר (בראשית לח) יהודה ויאמר צדקה ממני", אלא ראובן מנלן דאודי? *דא"ר שמואל בר נחמני אמר ר' *יוחנן: מאי דכתיב °"יחי ראובן ואל ימות... °וזאת (דברים לג) ליהודה"? כל אותן שנים שהיו ישראל במדבר היו עצמותיו של יהודה מגולגלין בארון, עד שעמד משה ובקש עליו רחמים. אמר לפניו: רבש"ע, מי גרם לראובן שהודה – יהודה, (א) "וזאת ליהודה"?! (ב) מיד °"שמע ה' קול יהודה" (שם) – על איבריה לשפא, ולא הוה קא מעיילין ליה למתיבתא דרקיעא – °"ואל עמו תביאנו" (שם), ולא הוה קא ידע משקל *ומטרח בשמעתא בהדי רבנן – °"ידיו רב לו" (שם), לא הוה קא סלקא ליה שמעתא אליבא דהילכתא – °"ועזר מצריו תהיה" (שם). בשלמא יהודה דאודי – כי היכי דלא תישרף תמר, אלא ראובן למה ליה דאודי? *והאמר רב ששת: [ט]חציף עלי (בר ישראל) דמפריט חטאיה! כי היכי דלא ליחשדו אחוהי (ג).§ "אם אמרה טמאה אני וכו'.§ *שמעת מינה כותבין שובר. אמר אביי: תני: מקרעת. א"ל רבא: והא שוברת קתני! אלא אמר רבא: במקום שאין כותבין כתובה עסקינן.§ "ואם אמרה טהורה אני מעלין אותה לשערי מזרח".§ מעלין אותה?!
התם

רש"י

וקטליאות. תכשיט הוא, כמין חצי עיגול פתוח, וסוגרת בו את חלוקה, ומקיף את גרונה מן הצדדין. חבל המצרי. עשוי מצורי דקל, מסיב הגדל סביב הדקל וכרוך עליו. וקושר למעלה מדדיה. כדי שלא ישמטו בגדיה לארץ. שלבה גס בה. כשאדם רואה בני ביתו דעתו מתגברת עליו, ולא תירא ולא תודה. ואנו מבקשין שתודה, ולא ימחה שם הקדש על המים. וכל הנשים מותרות לראותה. לקמן פריך: והא תנא רישא כל הרוצה לראות בא רואה, ואפילו אנשים! ונוסרו כל הנשים. מקרא הוא ביחזקאל. **גמ'** מנא הני מילי. דבעיא ב"ד הגדול? נהי דבירושלים בעינן להשקותה, כדכתיב: "והעמיד הכהן את האשה לפני ה'", אבל ב"ד הגדול דהיינו שבעים ואחד – מנלן דלא נתכשרו בה אחד משני בתי דינין שהיו שם, של עשרים ושלשה, אחד יושב על פתח הר הבית, ואחד יושב על פתח העזרה, כדאמר בסנהדרין (דף פו:). מה להלן. בזקן ממרא. בשבעים ואחד. דכתיב (דברים יז): "מן המקום ההוא" – מקום מיוחד, דהיינו לשכת הגזית. שאפילו מלאן אבי פגי והמרה עליהן – ילפינן מיניה דאין המראתו המראה (סנהדרין דף יד:). עמדי על בורייך. היסמכי על נקיותיך. קודם שנמחקה מגילה. כדי שלא ימחה השם – מאיימין שלא לשתות, ולאחר שנמחקה – אומרים לה דברי תנחומין לשתות, אם נקיה היא, כדי להתירה לבעלה. שלא תירא מן המים ותאמר "טמאה אני" והיא טהורה, ותוציא לעז על עצמה ועל בניה. בכתובים הראשונים. בדברים הכתובים בתורה, שנעשו בימים הראשונים, כגון הגדה זו דאשר חכמים יגידו ויודו על חטאם, ולא כחדו עונם מאבותיהם, ומי הם – ראובן במעשה בלהה כדלקמן, ויהודה במעשה תמר "צדקה ממני". להם לבדם נתנה הארץ. יהודה זכה למלכות, בתוספתא דברכות (פ"ד). ראובן נטל חלק תחלה בארץ בעבר הירדן. ולא עבר זר בתוכם. דרש רבי תנחומא: אימתי לא עבר זר בתוכם – כשבא משה לברכן. יחי ראובן וזאת ליהודה. אין לך בברכת כל השבטים מתחלת "וזאת" חוץ מזו. עצמותיו של יהודה מתגלגלין בארון. עצמות כל השבטים העלו ממצרים, והוא שאמר יוסף: "והעליתם את עצמותי מזה אתכם" (שמות יג) – עם עצמותיכם. והיו עצמות כל השבטים שלדן קיימת, ויהודה איבריו מתפרקין ומתגלגלין בארונו, מפני שנידה את עצמו בערבונו של בנימין: "וחטאתי לך כל הימים" (בראשית מג) – אפי' לעולם הבא. ומהכא נפקא לן (מכות דף יא:): *נידוי של חכם – אפילו על תנאי הוא בא. מי גרם לראובן שיודה. במעשה יצועי אביו. יהודה. שהודה במעשה תמר. וכן היה מסורת בידיהם. ומדרש אגדה דר' תנחומא: כשאמר יהודה "צדקה ממני" עמד ראובן ואמר: בלבלתי יצועי אבי. ועכשיו יחי ראובן – שלדו קיימת כאילו הוא חי, וזאת ליהודה – שהוא מתגלגל?. לשפא. למקום שנתקו משם, כמו "דשף מדוכתיה" (חולין דף מג:). למתיבתא (ד). לישא וליתן עם שאר החכמים. למשקל ומטרח. לישא וליתן. ידיו רב לו. יהא לו נצחון לריב ריבו. והאי דכתיב "ידיו" – לשון מלחמה הוא, מלחמתה של תורה. אליבא דהילכתא. לא היה זוכה לומר דבר המתקבל. מאן דמפריט חטאיה. לרבים, נראה שאינו (ה) נכלם בדבר. דלא ליחשדו אחוהי. שלא יהו שאר אחיו נחשדין מאביהם. שמע מינה כותבין שובר. ופלוגתא דרבי יהודה ורבי יוסי היא בבבא בתרא (דף קע:). דקאמר רבי יהודה: אין כותבין שובר, אלא יקרעו את השטר, דאם כן צריך זה לשמור שוברו מן העכברים. תני מקרעת. שטר כתובתה. במקום שאין כותבין כתובה. אלא סומכין על תנאי בית דין שתקנו לבתולה מאתים ולאלמנה מנה, וכשמגרשה – מוציאה גיטה וגובה בה, וכשנתאלמנה מביאה עדי מיתה וגובה. והתם כיון דלא אפשר – מודי רבי יהודה שכותבין שובר, דטוב לו שיהא בידו קלף רעה שפרע, כדי שלא תחזור ותביא עדי מיתה אחרים בבית דין אחר, ותתבענו.
התם

מסורת הש"ס

עירובין נח. [ועי' תוספות לקמן ח: ד"ה ואח"כ]

[תוספתא פ"א]

הגהות הב"ח

(א) גמ' מי גרם לראובן שהודה יהודה. נ"ב כתבו התוס' בפ' החובל דף צ"ב ע"א לאמר במדרש וישב ראובן אל הבור מלמד שהיה משקו ומתעניתו על שבלבל יצועי אביו וזה היה קודם מעשה תמר מ"מ לא הודה ברבים עד אחר שהודה יהודה עכ"ל: (ב) שם וזאת ליהודה שמע כצ"ל ותיבת מיד נמחק: (ג) שם דלא ליחשדו אחוהי בהדיה: (ד) רש"י ד"ה למתיבתא לישיבה של מעלה הס"ד ואח"כ מ"ה למשקל וכו' וליתן עם שאר חכמים הס"ד: (ה) ד"ה מאן וכו' שאינו בוש ונכלם: (ו) תוס' ד"ה לא וכו' פירש ר"י. נ"ב וכן פי' רש"י באיוב ט"ו וע"ש:

ב"ק צב: מכות יא: ע"ש [נ"ל יונתן וכ"א בע"י]

גליון הש"ס

גמ' ורמינהו כדרך שמאיימין עליה. עיין לקמן דף יד ע"ב תוד"ה אי משום.

[נ"ל ולמיטרא כך איתא בשאלתות פ' מקץ סי' ל]

ברכות לד: ע"ש
[נ"ל נידוי על תנאי צריך הפרה]
[כתובות פט. עוד שם טז: ע"ש]

הָתָם קָיְימָא! אדְּמַסְקִינַן לָהּ וּמַחְתִּינַן לָהּ, כְּדֵי לְיַיגְּעָהּ. *דְּתַנְיָא, רַבִּי שִׁמְעוֹן בֶּן אֶלְעָזָר אוֹמֵר: בבֵּית דִּין מַסִּיעִין אֶת הָעֵדִים מִמָּקוֹם לְמָקוֹם, כְּדֵי שֶׁתִּטָּרֵף דַּעְתָּן עֲלֵיהֶן, וְיַחְזְרוּ בָּהֶן.§ "שֶׁשָּׁם מַשְׁקִין אֶת הַסּוֹטוֹת" וכו'.§ בִּשְׁלָמָא סוֹטוֹת – דִּכְתִיב: °"וְהֶעֱמִיד הַכֹּהֵן אֶת הָאִשָּׁה לִפְנֵי ה'" (במדבר ה), מְצוֹרָעִין נַמִי – דִּכְתִיב: °"וְהֶעֱמִיד הַכֹּהֵן הַמְטַהֵר" וגו' (ויקרא יד), אֶלָּא יוֹלֶדֶת מַאי טַעְמָא? אִילֵימָא מִשּׁוּם דְּאָתְיָין וְקָיְימִין אַקּוּרְבְּנַיְיהוּ, דְּתַנְיָא: *גאֵין קָרְבָּנוֹ שֶׁל אָדָם קָרֵב אֶלָּא אִם כֵּן עוֹמֵד עַל גַּבָּיו – אִי הָכִי, זָבִין וְזָבוֹת נַמִי! דאה"נ, *וְתַנָּא חֲדָא מִינַּיְיהוּ נָקַט. ת"ר: *האֵין מַשְׁקִין שְׁתֵּי סוֹטוֹת כְּאַחַת, כְּדֵי שֶׁלֹּא יְהֵא לִבָּהּ גַּס בַּחֲבֶירְתָּהּ. רַבִּי יְהוּדָה אוֹמֵר: לֹא מִן הַשֵּׁם הוּא זֶה, אֶלָּא ואָמַר קְרָא °"אוֹתָהּ" (במדבר ה) – לְבַדָּהּ, וְת"ק, הָכְתִיב "אוֹתָהּ"! ת"ק ר"ש הִיא, *דְּדָרֵישׁ טַעְמָא דִּקְרָא. וּמַה טַּעַם קָאָמַר; מַה טַּעַם "אוֹתָהּ" לְבַדָּהּ – כְּדֵי שֶׁלֹּא יְהֵא לִבָּהּ גַּס בַּחֲבֵירְתָּהּ. מַאי בֵּינַיְיהוּ? אִיכָּא בֵּינַיְיהוּ רוֹתֶתֶת. וְרוֹתֶתֶת מִי מַשְׁקִין? וְהָא אֵין עוֹשִׂין מִצְוֹת חֲבִילוֹת. *דִּתְנַן: אֵין מַשְׁקִין שְׁתֵּי סוֹטוֹת כְּאַחַת, זוְאֵין מְטַהֲרִין שְׁנֵי מְצוֹרָעִין כְּאַחַת, חוְאֵין רוֹצְעִין שְׁנֵי עֲבָדִים כְּאַחַת, טוְאֵין עוֹרְפִין שְׁתֵּי עֶגְלוֹת כְּאַחַת, *ילְפִי שֶׁאֵין עוֹשִׂין מִצְוֹת חֲבִילוֹת! אָמַר אַבַּיֵי, וְאִיתֵימָא רַב כָּהֲנָא: לָא קַשְׁיָא; כּכָּאן – בְּכֹהֵן אֶחָד, כָּאן – בִּשְׁנֵי כֹהֲנִים.§ "וְהַכֹּהֵן אוֹחֵז בִּבְגָדֶיהָ".§ תָּנוּ רַבָּנַן: °"וּפָרַע אֶת רֹאשׁ הָאִשָּׁה" (שם), אֵין לִי אֶלָּא רֹאשָׁהּ, גּוּפָהּ מִנַּיִן – ת"ל "הָאִשָּׁה". אִם כֵּן, מַה ת"ל "וּפָרַע אֶת רֹאשָׁהּ" – מְלַמֵּד, שֶׁהַכֹּהֵן סוֹתֵר אֶת שְׂעָרָהּ.§ "ר' יְהוּדָה אוֹמֵר אִם הָיָה לִבָּהּ" וכו'.§ *לְמֵימְרָא, דְּר' יְהוּדָה חָיֵישׁ לְהִרְהוּרָא וְרַבָּנַן לָא חָיְישִׁי? וְהָא אִיפְּכָא שָׁמְעִינַן לְהוּ, דְּתַנְיָא: הָאִישׁ מְכַסִּין אוֹתוֹ פֶּרֶק אֶחָד מִלְּפָנָיו, וְהָאִשָּׁה שְׁנֵי פְּרָקִים, אֶחָד מִלְּפָנֶיהָ וְאֶחָד מִלְּאַחֲרֶיהָ, מִפְּנֵי שֶׁכּוּלָּהּ עֶרְוָה, דִּבְרֵי רַבִּי יְהוּדָה. וַחֲכ"א: להָאִישׁ נִסְקָל עָרוֹם, וְאֵין הָאִשָּׁה נִסְקֶלֶת עֲרוּמָּה! אָמַר רַבָּה: הָכָא טַעְמָא מַאי – שֶׁמָּא תֵּצֵא מִבּ"ד זַכָּאִית, *וְיִתְגָּרוּ בָּהּ פִּרְחֵי כְהוּנָּה, הָתָם – הָא *מִסְתַּלְּקָא. וְכִי תֵימָא, אָתֵי לְאִיגָּרוּיֵי בְּאַחֲרַנְיָיתָא – הָאָמַר *רָבָא: גְּמִירִי דְּאֵין יֵצֶר הָרַע שׁוֹלֵט אֶלָּא בְּמַה שֶּׁעֵינָיו רוֹאוֹת. אָמַר רָבָא: דְּר' יְהוּדָה אַדְּר' יְהוּדָה קַשְׁיָא, דְּרַבָּנַן אַדְּרַבָּנַן ל"ק?! אֶלָּא אָמַר רָבָא: מדְּר' יְהוּדָה אַדְּר' יְהוּדָה ל"ק – כִּדְשַׁנִּין, דְּרַבָּנַן

רש"י

הָתָם קַיְימָא. בְּלִשְׁכַּת הַגָּזִית, כִּדְקָאָמְרַתְּ, שֶׁיְּאַיְּימוּ עָלֶיהָ ב"ד הַגָּדוֹל. וְלִשְׁכַּת הַגָּזִית בָּעֲזָרָה הָיְתָה, חֶצְיָהּ בַּקּוֹדֶשׁ וְחֶצְיָהּ בַּחוֹל, כִּדְאָמַר בְּיוֹמָא פֶּרֶק שֵׁנִי (דף כה.). וּמַחְתִּינַן לָהּ. מִכָּל הַר הַבַּיִת, לְאַחַר שֶׁיְּאַיְּימוּ עָלֶיהָ. כְּדֵי לְיַיגְּעָהּ. וְתִדְלַג מִן הַמַּיִם, וְתוֹדֶה כְּשֶׁתִּרְאֶה בְּצָרָתָהּ. מַסִּיעִין הָיוּ אֶת הָעֵדִים. שֶׁמְּעִידִים עֵדוּת נְפָשׁוֹת, וּכְשֶׁבּוֹדְקִין אוֹתָן הָיוּ מַסִּיעִין אוֹתָן מִפִּינָה לְפִינָה וּמִלִּשְׁכָּה לְלִשְׁכָּה. לִפְנֵי ה'. וְהוּא הַפֶּתַח שֶׁבּוֹ דֶּרֶךְ כְּנִיסָה וִיצִיאָה לְכָל בָּאֵי עֲזָרָה. אַקּוּרְבְּנַיְיהוּ. כְּשֶׁמַּקְרִיבִים אֶת קָרְבַּן קִינֵּיהֶם לְטַהֲרָם בַּאֲכִילַת קָדָשִׁים. וּמִצְוָה עַל הָאָדָם שֶׁיַּעֲמוֹד וְיִשְׁמוֹר עַל קָרְבָּנוֹ, וְנָפְקָא לָן בְּסִפְרֵי מִ"תִּשְׁמְרוּ לְהַקְרִיב לִי בְּמוֹעֲדוֹ" (במדבר כח). וּמִי שֶׁיָּכוֹל לִיכָּנֵס בָּעֲזָרָה – נִכְנָס, וְאֵלּוּ שֶׁלֹּא הָיוּ יְכוֹלוֹת, מִפְּנֵי שֶׁהָיוּ מְחוּסְּרוֹת כַּפָּרָה – עוֹמְדוֹת בַּחֲלַל שַׁעַר נִקָנוֹר שֶׁלֹּא נִתְקַדֵּשׁ. זָבִין וְזָבוֹת נַמִי. כְּשֶׁמַּקְרִיבִין *קָרְבְּנֵיהֶם הֵן מְחוּסְּרֵי כַפָּרָה, וְאֵינָן יְכוֹלִין לִיכָּנֵס. שֶׁלֹּא יְהֵא לִבָּהּ גַּס בַּחֲבֶרְתָּהּ. שֶׁמָּא הָאַחַת עוֹמֶדֶת עַל בּוּרְיָהּ וְאֵינָהּ מוֹדָה לוֹמַר "טְמֵאָה אֲנִי", וַחֲבֶרְתָּהּ שֶׁהִיא טְמֵאָה רוֹאָה אֶת זוֹ שֶׁאֵינָהּ מוֹדָה וְסוֹבֶלֶת אֶת בּוּשְׁתָּהּ, וְלִבָּהּ מִתְגַּבֵּר עָלֶיהָ לַעֲשׂוֹת כָּמוֹ זוֹ, וְאֵינָהּ מוֹדָה. לֹא מִן הַשֵּׁם הוּא זֶה. לֹא זֶהוּ הַטַּעַם שֶׁאָמַרְתָּ, בְּעִיקָּר הַנֶּאֱמָר בַּדָּבָר: אוֹתָהּ. "*וְהִשְׁבִּיעַ אוֹתָהּ הַכֹּהֵן": ר"ש יָהֵיב טַעְמֵי לִקְרָאֵי בְּב"מ (דף קטו.), דְּקָא אָמַר "לֹא תַחֲבֹל בֶּגֶד אַלְמָנָה" – בַּעֲנִיָּה נֶאֱמַר וְלֹא בַּעֲשִׁירָה. דְּטַעַם הַמִּקְרָא, שֶׁאִם אַתָּה מְמַשְׁכְּנָהּ וְאַתָּה חַיָּיב לְהַחֲזִיר לָהּ, וְאַתָּה נִכְנָס שַׁחֲרִית לִיטְּלוֹ וְעַרְבִית לְהַחֲזִירוֹ – מַשִּׂיאָהּ שֵׁם רַע בִּשְׁכֵנוֹתֶיהָ. מַאי בֵּינַיְיהוּ. בֵּין רַבִּי יְהוּדָה לְרַבִּי שִׁמְעוֹן, אִי מִשּׁוּם לִבָּהּ גַּס בָּהּ וְאִי מִשּׁוּם גְּזֵירַת הַכָּתוּב. אִיכָּא בֵּינַיְיהוּ. אִשָּׁה שֶׁאָנוּ רוֹאִים בָּהּ שֶׁהִיא רוֹתֶתֶת מֵאֵימַת הַמַּיִם, וְאֵינָהּ מוֹדָה. לְמ"ד שֶׁלֹּא יְהֵא לִבָּהּ גַּס בָּהּ – זוֹ אָנוּ רוֹאִין שֶׁאֵין לִבָּהּ גַּס בָּהּ. וּלְמַאן דְּלָא דָּרֵישׁ טַעְמָא דִּקְרָא, אֶלָּא גְּזֵירַת הַכָּתוּב – אֵין מַשְׁקִין עִמָּהּ אַחֶרֶת. וְרוֹתֶתֶת מִי מַשְׁקִין. עִמָּהּ אַחֶרֶת? נְהִי דְּאֵין לִבָּהּ גַּס בָּהּ – הָאִיכָּא מִשּׁוּם עֲשִׂיַּית מִצְוֹת חֲבִילוֹת, כִּדְתַנְיָא כו'. חֲבִילוֹת חֲבִילוֹת. שֶׁנִּרְאֶה כְּמִי שֶׁהָיוּ עָלָיו לְמַשָּׂאוֹי, וּמְמַהֵר לִפְרֹק מַשָּׂאוֹ. בְּכֹהֵן אֶחָד. הָוֵי חֲבִילוֹת. וְכֵן לְגַבֵּי עֲבָדִים – בב"ד אֶחָד וּבְאָדוֹן אֶחָד. וּפָרַע. בְּכָל מָקוֹם לְשׁוֹן גִּילּוּי הוּא. גּוּפָהּ מִנַּיִן. כִּדְתְנַן: מְגַלֶּה אֶת לִבָּהּ. סוֹתֵר אֶת שְׂעָרָהּ. מַרְבֶּה בְּגִילּוּיָהּ, שֶׁסּוֹתֵר קְלִיעָתָהּ. חָיֵישׁ לְהִרְהוּרָא. שֶׁלֹּא יִתְּנוּ הָרוֹאִין אֶת לִבָּם בָּהּ. הָאִישׁ מְכַסִּים אוֹתוֹ. כְּשֶׁנִּסְקָל. פֶּרֶק אֶחָד. חֲתִיכַת בֶּגֶד מִלְּפָנָיו וּשְׁאָר כָּל גּוּפוֹ עָרוֹם. שֶׁכּוּלָּהּ עֶרְוָה. אֲחוֹרֶיהָ וּפָנֶיהָ, שֶׁבֵּית הַבֹּשֶׁת נִרְאֶה מִשְּׁנֵי צְדָדִין. הָכָא הַיְינוּ טַעְמָא דר' יְהוּדָה שֶׁמָּא תֵּצֵא מִבּ"ד זַכָּאָה. שֶׁטְּהוֹרָה תִּמָּצֵא וְלֹא יִבְדְּקוּהָ הַמַּיִם, וְיִתְגָּרוּ בָּהּ וְיִהְיוּ רוֹדְפִים אַחֲרֶיהָ כָּל יָמֶיהָ. פִּרְחֵי כְהוּנָּה. נָקַט עַל שֵׁם שֶׁהָיוּ מְלוּוִין בָּעֲזָרָה יוֹתֵר מִשְּׁאָר הָעָם. וְכִי תֵימָא אָתֵי לְאִיגָּרוּיֵי בְּאַחֲרַנְיָיתָא. עַל יְדֵי שֶׁרָאוּ אֶת זוֹ עֲרוּמָּה מִתְגָּרֶה בְּנָשִׁים אֲחֵרוֹת. גְּמִירִי. מָסוֹרֶת בְּיָדֵי מֵרַבּוֹתַי. דְּרַבָּנַן אַדְּרַבָּנַן לָא קַשְׁיָא. בִּתְמִיָּה, דְּשָׁנֵית רַבִּי יְהוּדָה וְלָא חָיְישַׁתְּ לְשִׁנּוּיֵי דְּרַבָּנַן.

הָכָא

תוספות

*ששם משקין את הסוטות. בתוספתא (פ"א) שנא' (מלכים א ח): "את אשר יחטא איש לרעהו ונשא בו אלה להאלותו ובא אלה לפני מזבחך בבית הזה וכו' להרשיע רשע" – "ולבתה בטנה", "ולהצדיק צדיק" – [לתת לו כצדקתו, שנאמר: "ואם לא נטמאה האשה וטהורה היא] ונקתה ונזרעה זרע". היא עומדת מבפנים, והכהן עומד מבחוץ, שנאמר: "והעמיד הכהן את האשה לפני ה'" – האשה לפני ה', ואין כהן לפני ה'.

אין משקין שתי סוטות כאחת. נראה לפרש: שיעמיד שתיהן בעזרה בבת אחת להשקותן, אע"פ שאין שותות כאחת. וכן רליעה. ובתוספתא דפרה (פ"ג) תנא נמי: אין שתי פרות נעשות כאחת, משנעשית אפר מביא אחרת ושורפה על גבה. ותימה: וכי היה אוסר בכה"ג לשחוט שני זבחים כאחד, כגון שני עולות או שני חטאות, שיעמיד שניהן בעזרה וישחוט א' ואחר כך ישחוט השני? והא דאמרי' בפ"ב דשחיטת חולין (דף כט: ושם): "תזבחהו" – שלא יהא א' שוחט שני זבחים, מיירי שיחתוך שני צוארין כאחד, דאיכא איסור דאורייתא, אבל בכה"ג לא מיירי התם. ובפ' "נערה המאורסה" (נדרים עג.) בנדרים, בעי: מהו שיפר אדם לשתי נשיו כאחד – "אותה" דוקא או לאו דווקא? ופשיט להו מהכא.

איכא בינייהו רותתת. נראה דהוה מצי למימר: איכא בינייהו אשה אחרת שאינה סוטה, לר' שמעון מותר, לר' יהודה אסור להעמיד אצלה שום אשה בשער נקנור. (א)דאמר בפרק "טרף בקלפי" (יומא דף מג:) דפליגי נמי הכי רבי ורבי שמעון בקרא ד"והוציא אותה" דכתיב גבי פרה, ואמר: איכא בינייהו חמור, דלרבי דאמר "אותה" לבדה – אסור להוציא עמה חמור. **והא** אין עושין מצות חבילות. תימה: מאי פריך? והלא אין עושין מצות חבילות ליכא אלא איסור מדרבנן, משום דמיחזי עליה כמשא, ואינהו פליגי בקראי.

כאן בשני כהנים. רש"י פירש: וכן גבי עבד – בב"ד אחד ואדון אחד. ותימה: והא טהרת ב' מצורעין דמי לשני עבדים של שני בני אדם!

*והכהן אוחז בבגדיה. בפרק "אלו הן הלוקין" (מכות דף כב:) תניא נמי הכי: חזן הכנסת אוחז בבגדיו כו'. ונראה משום דכתיב בו "ונקלה" – מצוה לנוולו. בתוספתא (פ"א): כהנים מטילים גורלות, וכל מי שיעלה גורלו, אפילו כ"ג – יוצא ועומד בצד סוטה, ואוחז בבגדיה. *אם היה לבה נאה. אע"ג דגזירת הכתוב הוא – שב ואל תעשה לאו מיעקר הוא, כדאיתא פ' "האשה רבה" (יבמות צ.).

האיש נסקל ערום ואין האשה נסקלת ערומה. תימה: מאי קשיא דרבנן אדרבנן? והא מפרש טעמא בפרק "נגמר הדין" (סנהדרין דף מה.) משום דכתיב: "אותו" בלא כסותו, ואין "אותה" בלא כסותה. א"כ למה היה לנו לנוולה מאחר שהכתוב אומר שלא לנוולה? אם היינו מנוולין אותה – א"כ אנו עוקרין הכתוב בידים! וי"ל: בין לר' יהודה בין לרבנן, ד"אותו" לא בא אלא למעט על הכסות שלו. הילכך לרבנן לא שמענו מן התורה מה דינה, והרשות ביד בית דין לעשות כמה שירצו, ובגמרא מפרש במאי פליגי, להכי קשיא דרבנן אדרבנן: כיון דלא חיישינן להרהורים היה לנו לנוולה משום יסור.

ויתגרו בה פרחי כהונה. תימה: כיון דלאו חובה לאנשים לראותה – יתלו סדין של בוץ בינה לבין האנשים, ויסתור שערה, כדאמר קרא. ואי משום כהן המשקה אותה – יהפוך פניו לצד אחר! והכי תני בספרי בהדיא: "ופרע את ראש האשה" – סדין של בוץ פורש בינו לבין העם, כהן פונה לאחוריו ופורעה כדי לקיים בה מצות פריעה. ולרבי יהודה נמי נעשה כך! וי"ל: לר' יהודה, אם היו פורסין סדין בינה לבין האנשים – לא היה ניוול כל כך בפני הנשים כמו באנשים, שאין אשה בושה מפני חברותיה, ולא יוסרו. **גמירי** אין יצר הרע שולט אלא במה שעיניו רואות. מקשי' מפרק "אין דורשין" (חגיגה יא:), דאמר: עריות – בין בפניו בין שלא בפניו נפיש יצרייהו! ולא קשיא מידי, דהתם ה"פ: מאחר שראה הערוה פעם אחת – שוב מהרהר אחריה לעולם, אפי' שלא בפניה. אבל מחמת שראה הנסקלת ערומה – אינו מהרהר אחר אחרת.

ואחר

עין משפט נר מצוה

[שייך לעיל ז. במשנה]

מו א מיי' פ"ג מהל' סוטה הל' ג סמג עשין נז:

מז ב מיי' פ"א מהל' עדות הלכה ז:

מח ג מיי' פ"ה מהלכות כלי המקדש הל' ח:

מט ד מיי' פ"ד מהל' מחוסרי כפרה הל"ב:

נ ה ו מיי' פ"ד מהל' סוטה הלכה ב:

נא ז מיי' פ"א מהל' טומאת צרעת הל"ז:

נב ח מיי' פ"ג מהל' עבדים הלכה ט:

נג ט י מיי' פ"ט מהל' רוצח הלכה ה:

נד כ מיי' פט"ו מהל' סנהדרין הלכה א סמג עשין קב:

[נדרים עג. ע"ש תוספתא דנגעים פ"א ע"ש ותוספת' סוטה פ"א ע"ש]

תוספות שאנץ

אתיין וקיימן אקרבנייהו שמקריבין קיניהן לטהרן באכילת קדשים ומצוה על האדם שיעמוד וישמור על קרבנו ונפקא לן בספרי מתשמרו להקריב לי במועדו ומי שיוכל ליכנס לעזרה נכנס ואלו שלא היו יכולות מפני שהן מחוסרו' כפרה עומדות בחלל שער נקנור שלא נתקדש לה'. מכסין אותו פרק אחד כשנסקל חתיכת בגד מלפניו. ויתגרו בה פרחי כהונה פ"ה פרחי כהונה לאו דוקא אלא נקט אותם על שהן מצויין בעזרה יותר משאר בני אדם:

[שייך לעיל ז. במשנה]

[בסנהדרין איתא רבה]

גליון הש"ס

גמ' אין משקין שתי סוטות. עיין נדרים דף עג ע"א: שם כאן בכהן אחד. עיין מג"א סימן קמז ס"ק יא: שם דר"י אדר"י לא קשיא. פסחים יח ע"א כתובות כד ע"ב: רש"י ד"ה אותה והשביע אותה הכהן. בנדרים דף עג ע"א איתא בהך ברייתא משום שנאמר והשקה אותה לבדה (ובקרא לא כתיב אותה) ופי' הר"ן שם כיון דכתיב והשקה במפיק ה' הוי כאילו כתיב אותה וא"כ הכא נמי כה"ג דאמרינן אמר קרא אותה היינו על ידי מפיק ה' דוהשקה. אבל ברא"ש שם וכן בפי' המפרש בשם רש"י איתא משום שנאמר והשקה לבדה והיינו מדכתיב במפיק ה' וא"כ י"ל דלדחיק לומר דקורא הש"ס לא כלשון אמר קרא אותה מש"ה פי' ובגבורי כנה"ג א"ח בסוף

מסורת הש"ס

סנהדרין לב: [תוספתא סנהדרין פ"ט]

[תענית כז.]

[יבמות מח: וש"נ]

פ"א קינים

[קדושין סח: וש"נ]

נ"ל דתניא

[עי' היטב נדרים עג. ומש"ש על הגליון]

[ברכות מט. פסחים קב:]

[סנהדרין מה.]

[נזיר מה:]

[נ"ל מסתקלא ועי' דבסנהדרין מה. איתא מקטלא]

הגהות הב"ח

(א) תוס' ד"ה איכא וכו' נקנור והכי נמי אמר בפרק טרף וכו' ר' שמעון וכו' דלר' יהודה דאמר אותה:

רש"י הכא דהיינו קרא והשביע אותה והוי הכא ברייתא אחריתא וברמב"ם איתא שנאמר והעמיד אותה הכהן והיינו ע"כ מדכתיב והעמידה במפיק ה"א הוי כאילו כתיב אותה וקשה אמאי נטה ממאי דמפורש בברייתא שנאמר והשקה. ובציור הספר בלשונותו על הרמב"ם כתב דצ"ל ברמב"ם והקריב אותה. וא"כ י"ל דהרמב"ם ס"ל דבברייתא דהכא דנקט אמר קרא אותה היינו קרא דוהקריב אותה:

דְּרַבָּנַן אַדְּרַבָּנַן נַמִּי לָא קַשְׁיָא: הָכָא טַעְמָא מַאי — מִשּׁוּם °"וְנִוַּסְּרוּ כָּל הַנָּשִׁים", הָתָם — אֵין לְךָ יִיסּוּר גָּדוֹל מִזֶּה. וְכִי תֵּימָא, לַעֲבֵיד בָּהּ תַּרְתֵּי — *אָמַר רַב נַחְמָן אָמַר רַבָּה בַּר אֲבוּהּ: אָמַר קְרָא °"וְאָהַבְתָּ לְרֵעֲךָ כָּמוֹךָ" — בְּרוֹר לוֹ מִיתָה יָפָה. לֵימָא, דְּרַב נַחְמָן תַּנָּאֵי הִיא? לָא, דְּכוּלֵּי עָלְמָא אִית לְהוּ דְּרַב נַחְמָן. וְהָכָא בְּהָא קָמִיפַּלְגִי; מָר סָבַר: בִּזְיוֹנֵיהּ עָדִיף לֵיהּ טְפֵי מִצַּעֲרָא דְּגוּפֵיהּ, וּמָר סָבַר: צַעֲרָא דְּגוּפֵיהּ עָדִיף לֵיהּ טְפֵי מִבִּזְיוֹנֵיהּ.§ "הָיְתָה מְכוּסָּה לְבָנִים" וכו'.§ תָּנָא: אאִם הָיוּ שְׁחוֹרִים נָאִים לָהּ — מְכַסִּין אוֹתָהּ בְּגָדִים מְכוֹעָרִים.§ "הָיוּ עָלֶיהָ כְּלֵי זָהָב וכו'.§ פְּשִׁיטָא! הַשְׁתָּא נִוּוּלֵי מְנַוְּולִי לָהּ, הָנֵי מִיבַּעְיָא?! מַהוּ דְּתֵימָא: בְּהָנֵי אִית לָהּ בִּזָּיוֹן טְפֵי, כִּדְאָמְרִי אִינָשֵׁי: *"שְׁלִיחַ עַרְטִיל וְסַיֵּים מְסָאנֵי", קמ"ל.§ "וְאַחַר כָּךְ מֵבִיא חֶבֶל" וכו'.§ בְּעָא מִינֵּיהּ רַבִּי אַבָּא מֵרַב הוּנָא: חֶבֶל הַמִּצְרִי מַהוּ שֶׁיְּעַכֵּב בְּסוֹטָה? מִשּׁוּם שֶׁלֹּא יִשָּׁמְטוּ בְּגָדֶיהָ מֵעָלֶיהָ הוּא — בוּבְצִלְצוּל קָטָן נַמִּי סַגִּי, אוֹ דִּילְמָא מִשּׁוּם דְּאָמַר מָר: *"הִיא חָגְרָה לוֹ בְּצִלְצוּל — לְפִיכָךְ כֹּהֵן מֵבִיא חֶבֶל הַמִּצְרִי וְקוֹשֵׁר לָהּ לְמַעְלָה מִדַּדֶּיהָ" — מְעַכֵּב? א"ל, תְּנֵיתוּהָ: וְאח"כ מֵבִיא חֶבֶל הַמִּצְרִי וְקוֹשְׁרוֹ לָהּ לְמַעְלָה מִדַּדֶּיהָ, גכְּדֵי שֶׁלֹּא יִשָּׁמְטוּ בְּגָדֶיהָ מֵעָלֶיהָ.§ "וְכָל הָרוֹצֶה לִרְאוֹת בָּהּ יִרְאֶה" וכו'.§ הָא גּוּפָא קַשְׁיָא; אָמְרַתְּ: כָּל הָרוֹצֶה לִרְאוֹת בָּהּ רוֹאֶה — אַלְמָא לָא שְׁנָא גַּבְרֵי וְלָא שְׁנָא נָשֵׁי. וַהֲדַר תָּנֵי: כָּל הַנָּשִׁים מוּתָּרוֹת לִרְאוֹתָהּ, נָשִׁים — אִין, אֲנָשִׁים — לָא! אָמַר אַבַּיֵי: תַּרְגְּמָהּ אֲנָשִׁים. אֲמַר לֵיהּ רָבָא: וְהָא כָּל הָרוֹצֶה לִרְאוֹת בָּהּ רוֹאֶה קָתָנֵי! אֶלָּא אָמַר רָבָא: כָּל הָרוֹצֶה לִרְאוֹת בָּהּ — רוֹאֶה, לָא שְׁנָא גַּבְרֵי וְלָא שְׁנָא נָשֵׁי. דוְנָשִׁים חַיָּיבוֹת לִרְאוֹתָהּ, שֶׁנֶּאֱמַר: °"וְנִוַּסְּרוּ כָּל הַנָּשִׁים וְלֹא תַעֲשֶׂינָה כְּזִמַּתְכֶנָה".§

מתני' *בְּמִדָּה שֶׁאָדָם מוֹדֵד — בָּהּ מוֹדְדִין לוֹ; הִיא קִשְּׁטָה אֶת עַצְמָהּ לַעֲבֵירָה — הַמָּקוֹם נִוְּולָהּ, הִיא גִּלְּתָה אֶת עַצְמָהּ לַעֲבֵירָה — הַמָּקוֹם גִּלָּה עָלֶיהָ, בַּיָּרֵךְ הִתְחִילָה בַּעֲבֵירָה תְּחִילָּה, וְאַחַר כָּךְ הַבֶּטֶן — לְפִיכָךְ תִּלְקֶה הַיָּרֵךְ תְּחִילָּה, וְאַחַר כָּךְ הַבֶּטֶן, וּשְׁאָר כָּל הַגּוּף לֹא פָּלֵט.§

גמ' אָמַר רַב יוֹסֵף: אַף עַל גַּב דְּמִדָּה בְּטֵילָה — בְּמִדָּה לָא בָּטֵיל. *דְּאָמַר רַב יוֹסֵף וְכֵן תָּנֵי ר' חִיָּיא: מִיּוֹם שֶׁחָרַב בהמ"ק, אע"פ שֶׁבָּטְלָה סַנְהֶדְרִי — אַרְבַּע מִיתוֹת לֹא בָּטְלוּ. וְהָא בָּטְלוּ! אֶלָּא: דִּין אַרְבַּע מִיתוֹת לֹא בָּטְלוּ; מִי שֶׁנִּתְחַיֵּיב סְקִילָה — אוֹ נוֹפֵל מִן הַגַּג, אוֹ חַיָּה דּוֹרַסְתּוֹ. מִי שֶׁנִּתְחַיֵּיב שְׂרֵיפָה — אוֹ נוֹפֵל בִּדְלֵיקָה, אוֹ נָחָשׁ מַכִּישׁוֹ. מִי שֶׁנִּתְחַיֵּיב הֲרִיגָה — אוֹ נִמְסָר לַמַּלְכוּת, אוֹ לִיסְטִין בָּאִין עָלָיו. מִי שֶׁנִּתְחַיֵּיב חֲנִיקָה — אוֹ טוֹבֵעַ בַּנָּהָר, אוֹ מֵת בִּסְרוֹנְכִי. *תַּנְיָא, הָיָה *רַבִּי אוֹמֵר: מִנַּיִן שֶׁבְּמִדָּה שֶׁאָדָם מוֹדֵד בָּהּ מוֹדְדִין לוֹ — שֶׁנֶּאֱמַר: °"בְּסַאסְּאָה בְּשַׁלְּחָהּ תְּרִיבֶנָּה". אֵין לִי אֶלָּא סְאָה, מִנַּיִן לְרַבּוֹת תַּרְקַב וַחֲצִי תַּרְקַב, קַב וַחֲצִי קַב, רוֹבַע וַחֲצִי רוֹבַע, תּוֹמֶן וְעוּכְלָא מִנַּיִן — תַּלְמוּד לוֹמַר: °"כִּי כָל סְאוֹן סֹאֵן בְּרַעַשׁ". וּמִנַּיִן שֶׁכָּל פְּרוּטָה וּפְרוּטָה מִצְטָרֶפֶת לְחֶשְׁבּוֹן גָּדוֹל — תַּלְמוּד לוֹמַר: °"אַחַת לְאַחַת לִמְצֹא חֶשְׁבּוֹן" וְכֵן מָצִינוּ בְּסוֹטָה, שֶׁבְּמִדָּה שֶׁמָּדְדָה — בָּהּ מָדְדוּ לָהּ: הִיא עָמְדָה עַל פֶּתַח בֵּיתָהּ לֵירָאוֹת לוֹ — לְפִיכָךְ כֹּהֵן מַעֲמִידָהּ עַל שַׁעַר נִקָּנוֹר וּמַרְאֶה קְלוֹנָהּ לַכֹּל, הִיא פָּרְסָה לוֹ סוּדָרִין נָאִין עַל רֹאשָׁהּ — לְפִיכָךְ כֹּהֵן נוֹטֵל כִּפָּה מֵעַל רֹאשָׁהּ וּמַנִּיחוֹ תַּחַת רַגְלֶיהָ, הִיא קִשְּׁטָה לוֹ פָּנֶיהָ — לְפִיכָךְ

פָּנֶיהָ

הָכָא טַעְמָא מַאי. אָמְרִי רַבָּנַן שֶׁמַּלְוֶה לְבַיְישָׁהּ וַאֲפִילּוּ הִיא טְהוֹרָה — מִשּׁוּם "וְנִוַּסְּרוּ כָּל הַנָּשִׁים", שֶׁלֹּא יָבִיאוּ עַצְמָן לִידֵי חֶשֶׁד, וְתִהְיֶינָה צְנוּעוֹת. הָתָם. שֶׁהִיא נִסְקֶלֶת — אֵין לְךָ יִסּוּר גָּדוֹל מִזֶּה לַאֲחֵרוֹת. תַּרְתֵּי. מִיתָה וּבוּשָׁה. מָר סָבַר בִּזְיוֹנָא עָדִיף לֵיהּ. חָשׁוּב עַל הָאָדָם וְשָׁנוּי לוֹ טְפֵי מִצַּעֲרָא דְּגוּפֵיהּ. הִילְכָּךְ מִיתָה יָפָה הִיא לוֹ לִיסָּקֵל לָבוּשׁ, וְאע"פ שֶׁצַּעֲרוֹ נִמְשָׁךְ, שֶׁאֵינוֹ מְמַהֵר לָמוּת, וְלֹא לִיסָּקֵל עָרוֹם וְיִתְבַּזֶּה. *וְרַבִּי יְהוּדָה סָבַר: צַעֲרָא דְּגוּפָא עָדִיף לֵיהּ. וְזוֹ הִיא מִיתָה יָפָה לוֹ — לִיסָּקֵל עָרוֹם, וְאע"פ שֶׁמִּתְבַּזֶּה, וְלֹא יִסָּקֵל בִּלְבוּשׁוֹ וְיִמָּשֵׁךְ צַעֲרוֹ. בְּהָנֵי אִית לָהּ בִּזָּיוֹן טְפֵי. שֶׁהִיא עֲרוּמָּה עַד לִבָּהּ וְרֹאשָׁהּ פָּרוּעַ. וְיִתֵּן עָלֶיהָ תַּכְשִׁיטֵי זָהָב — גְּנַאי הוּא לָהּ. שֶׁדֶּרֶךְ בְּנֵי אָדָם לְהִתְלוֹצֵץ בְּאָדָם עָרוֹם וּמִנְעָלוֹ בְּרַגְלָיו, (א) וְאָמְרִי': שָׁלִיחַ עַרְטִיל וְסַיֵּים מְסָאנֵי. שָׁלִיחַ — מוּפְשָׁט, כִּדְמְתַרְגְּמִינַן "וּפָשַׁט" — וְיַשְׁלַח. עַרְטִיל — עָרוֹם. מִשּׁוּם דְּאָמַר מָר. לְקַמָּן: בְּמִדָּה שֶׁאָדָם מוֹדֵד — בָּהּ מוֹדְדִין לוֹ. הִיא חָגְרָה לוֹ. חָגְרָה אֶת עַצְמָהּ בְּצִלְצוּל נָאֶה לְהִתְנָאוֹת בְּפָנָיו. צִילְצוּל — בנדי"ל בְּלַעַ"ז. תְּנֵיתוּהָ. דְּעִיקַּר הֲבָאָתוֹ אֵינוֹ אֶלָּא כְּדֵי שֶׁלֹּא יִשָּׁמְטוּ. תַּרְגְּמָהּ. לְרֵישָׁא, דְּקָתָנֵי: כָּל הָרוֹצֶה — אֲנָשִׁים. תַּרְגְּמָהּ. פָּרֵשׁ אוֹתָהּ. **מתני'** יָרֵךְ הִתְחִיל בַּעֲבֵירָה תְּחִילָּה. בְּדֶרֶךְ תַּשְׁמִישׁ הַיָּרֵךְ נֶהֱנֶה תְּחִילָּה בְּקֵירוּב בָּשָׂר, לְפִיכָךְ תִּלְקֶה יָרֵךְ תְּחִילָּה לְקַלֵּל אוֹתָהּ, דִּכְתִיב: "בְּתֵת ה' אֶת יְרֵכֵךְ נֹפֶלֶת וְאֶת בִּטְנֵךְ צָבָה" (במדבר ה). **גמ'** וְאע"ג דְּמִדָּה. עַצְמָהּ בְּטֵילָה, שֶׁפָּסְקוּ אַרְבַּע מִיתוֹת בֵּית דִּין. בְּמִדָּה לָא בָּטֵיל. שֶׁמּוֹדְדִין לָהֶם לְעוֹבְרֵי עֲבֵירָה בְּמִדָּה שֶׁמִּתְחַיְּיבִים בָּהּ, וּמֵתִים בְּדוּגְמַת אוֹתָהּ מִיתָה. דְּאָמַר רַב יוֹסֵף. הַגְּמָרָא קָאָמַר, דְּאָמַר רַב יוֹסֵף נַמִּי בְּעָלְמָא, וְכֵן תָּנֵי כו'. דִּין אַרְבַּע מִיתוֹת. דִּין שָׁמַיִם שֶׁהִיא דּוּגְמָתוֹ. נוֹפֵל מִן הַגַּג. דּוּמְיָא דִּסְקִילָה, דִּתְנַן (סנהדרין דף מה.): בֵּית הַסְּקִילָה הָיָה גָּבוֹהַּ שְׁתֵּי קוֹמוֹת, אֶחָד מִן הָעֵדִים דּוֹחֲפוֹ כו'. חַיָּה דּוֹרַסְתּוֹ. אֲרִי דּוֹרְסוֹ בְּצִפָּרְנָיו וּמַפִּילוֹ לָאָרֶץ, וְגַם זֶה דּוֹמֶה לְנִסְקָל. נָחָשׁ מַכִּישׁוֹ. וְהָאֶרֶס שׂוֹרְפוֹ. נִמְסָר לַמַּלְכוּת. וּמִיתַת מַלְכוּת מַתִּיזִין אֶת רֹאשׁוֹ בְּסַיִף. וְהֶרֶג נַמִּי סַיִף הוּא, כִּדְאָמְרִינַן בְּסַנְהֶדְרִין (דף נב:). סְרוֹנְכִי. בומנל"ט, וְהוּא חוֹלִי בִּגְרוֹנוֹ. בְּסַאסְּאָה. בְּתוֹךְ אוֹתָהּ סְאָה עַצְמָהּ, כְּשֶׁחָטָא מְשַׁלְּחָהּ לַאֲבַדּוֹן — תְּרִיבֶנָּה. וְאֵין לִי אֶלָּא סְאָה. עֲבֵירָה גְּדוֹלָה. תַּרְקַב. חֲצִי סְאָה, תְּרֵי וְקַב, דְּהַיְינוּ ג' קַבִּין. תּוֹמֶן וְעוּכְלָא. מִשְׁקָלוֹת קְטַנִּים הֵן, וְשִׁיעוּרָן בְּבָבָא בַּתְרָא בְּ"הַמּוֹכֵר אֶת הַסְּפִינָה" (דף צ.). וּמִנַּיִן שֶׁכָּל פְּרוּטָה וּפְרוּטָה וכו'. וְאע"פ שֶׁלֹּא נִפְרְעוּ מִמֶּנּוּ פַּעַם רִאשׁוֹנָה וּשְׁנִיָּה — לֹא וִיתְּרוּ לוֹ עֲלֵיהֶם, אֶלָּא מִצְטָרְפִין לוֹ אוֹתָן לְחֶשְׁבּוֹן: לֵירָאוֹת לוֹ (ב). פָּרְסָה לוֹ. כְּנֶגְדּוֹ. כִּפָּה. צָעִיף.

---

*וְאַחַר כך מביא חבל המצרי. בירושלמי מפרש: חבל המלרי וכפיפה המלרית בלין משירי הלשכה, כחומת העיר ומגדליה. ולא ידענא אי סודר שנחנק בו וסייף שנהרג בו דאמרינן פרק "נגמר הדין" (סנהדרין דף מג.) דבאין משל לבור, אי פירושו נמי משירי הלשכה, כי הכא.

תנינא ואחר כך מביא חבל המצרי. ולא ידענא מאי פשיט מהכא טפי מהכא, דקתני: היא חגרה לו בצלצול, דמשמע דחבל מלרי בעינן ממש. ועל כרחך לכתחילה למלוה בעינן, אבל לאו דוקא לעכב, דהיכא כתיב חבל המלרי או שום קשירה בתורה, ולמה היה לו לעכב? מיהו, המדקדק בפירוש רש"י לא קשיא מידי. דעיקר הבאתו קמבעיא ליה, אי משום מדה במדה דוקא חבל, או משום שמיטת בגדים, הואיל וצריך לקשור צלצול — לקשור חבל כדי ליפרע ממנה. מיהו, היכא דליכא חבל המלרי ואיכא צלצול — לא מהדרנא יותר מדאי בתר חבל. **מיום** שחרב בהמ"ק וכו'. וה"ה דבזמן הבית נהגו דין ד' מיתות ומי שנתחייב בהן בלא עדים והתראה, שלא (ג) לדונו בסנהדרין, כדאמר בפ' "אחד דיני ממונות" (דף לז:): מעשה ברבי שמעון בן שטח, שהיה בזמן הבית. דתניא, אמר רבי שמעון בן שטח: אראה בנחמה אם לא ראיתי וכו' עד שהכישו נחש. ומקשינן: והאי בר נחש הוא? והתני רבי חייא וכו'! אלא האי דנקט מיום שחרב בית המקדש — מלתא דפסיקא נקט, דבטלו ארבע מיתות לגמרי. **מי** שנתחייב סקילה. מקשי' מפרק "השוכר את הפועלים" (ב"מ דף פג:), דרבי אלעזר ברבי שמעון הוה מפיס גנבי, יומא חד פגע בההוא כובס. אמר להו: תפסוהו, ותפסוהו, (זקפוהו) וזקפוהו. וקא בכי. אמר לו: רבי, אל ירע לך, שהוא ובנו בעלו נערה מאורסה ביוה"כ, וזה שנתלה נחנק. ואמאי לא פריך: והאי בר הכי הוא? בר סקילה הוא! אבל לפרש"י לא קשיא מידי, דפירש התם: משום הכי נתלה — משום דכל הנסקלין נתלין. ויש לומר, דלאו דוקא נקט נופל מן הגג או חיה דורסתו, אלא מעין מיתה שנתחייב בה יהרג. ויש מפרשים: דבנו בעל תחילה, דהויא לה בעולה, דמיתתו הויא בחנק. אבל קשיא לרבי מהא דאמר בפרק "אלו הן הגולין" (מכות י:): דרש ריש לקיש: "והאלהים אנה לידו" — זה שהרג במזיד יושב תחת הסולם, וזה שהרג בשוגג עולה ונופל והורגו. והא לאו בר סקילה הוא?! ותירץ: אע"ג דלאו בר סקילה, מיהו מדה במדה היא, דזורק על חבירו דרך ירידה הוא, כדכתיב (במדבר לה): "ויפל עליו וימות", ואלו מתים דרך ירידה. ואם הרגו בסייף — הקדוש ב"ה נפרע מהם בענין אחר.

מנימין

[שייך לעיל ז: במשנה]

נה א מיי' פ"ג מהל' סוטה הלכה ז:

נו ב ג מיי' שם הל' יא סמג עשין נז:

נז ד מיי' שם הל' ה:

תוספות שאנץ

חבל המצרי מהו שיעכב בסוטה. תימה למה יעכב והלא פריעה דכתיב בקרא אינו מעכב דהא אמר רבי יהודה אם היה לבה נאה אינו מגלה ואם היה שערה נאה אינו פורעו. וי"ל דסבר כרבנן דפליגי עליה דרבי יהודה. עוד (אית בידו) [יש לומר] דקרא לא מיירי אלא היכא שאין לחוש להרהור. דין ד' מיתות לא בטלו מי שנתחייב סקילה או נופל מן הגג. וקשה מדאמרי' (במכות דף י) שנים אחד הרג שוגג ואחד הרג מזיד הקב"ה מזמנן לפונדק אחד זה שהרג בשוגג עולה בסולם ונופל על אותו שהרג מזיד ואמאי והא לא מחייב סקילה שזה שנופל עליו הרי כמו אבן שנסקל בסקילה שנותנין על כריסו. וצ"ל דמיירי שהנופל יש לו בידו סייף או סכין כשנופל על חבירו הוא מתיז ראשו בסייף כמו שעושין במלכות:

יעב"ץ מ"ז

הגהות הב"ח

(א) רש"י ד"ה בהני וכו' ואמרי שליח: (ב) ד"ה לירלות לו פרסה כנגדו כל"ל והד"א: (ג) תוס' ד"ה מיום וכו' והתראה שלא היו יכולין לדונו בסנהדרין:

גליון הש"ם

מתני' במדה שאדם מודד. עיין סנהדרין דף ל ע"א:

[סנהדרין ק. תוספתא פ"ג]

ישעיה כז

שם ט

קהלת ז

תורה אור: יחזקאל כג; ויקרא יט; יחזקאל כג

ס"א ומר סבר

[סנהדרין מה. וש"נ]

כתובות סה:

[לקמן ט:]

[מגילה יב:]

חוהדרין לז: וו"ן רתודו' ל

[בסנהדרין ק. איתא ר' מאיר אומר וכו' וכן מוכרח להיות לפי מאי דמסיק הש"ס לקמן טו: דשמעי' לר' מאיר דקאמר היא האכילתו וכו' ע"ש בפרש"י וכן אי' בתוספתא ריש פרק ג היה ר' מאיר אומר וכו']

[דף כ.]

פָּנֶיהָ מוֹרִיקוֹת. הָכִי תָּנֵי לְקַמָּן:* אֵינָהּ מַסְפֶּקֶת לִשְׁתּוֹת עַד שֶׁפָּנֶיהָ מוֹרִיקוֹת וְעֵינֶיהָ בּוֹלְטוֹת. הֶרְאֲתָה לוֹ בְּאֶצְבְּעוֹתֶיהָ. רָמְזָה לוֹ לָבֹא אֶצְלָהּ. מַאֲכַל בְּהֵמָה. שְׂעוֹרִים. בִּמְקֵידָה שֶׁל חֶרֶשׂ. פְּחוּתָה וּמְגוּנָה שֶׁבַּכּוֹסוֹת. שָׂם בָּהּ פָּנִים. פְּנַאי, לִיפָּרַע מִמֶּנָּה. "וְשַׂמְתִּי אֲנִי אֶת פָּנַי" (ויקרא כ), "וְנָתַתִּי (אֶת) פָּנַי" (שם יז) – כּוּלָּן לְשׁוֹן: פּוֹנֶה אֲנִי מִכָּל עֲסָקַי וְעוֹסְקַנִי בָּהֶן. תִּכַּסֶּה שִׂנְאָה בְּמַשָּׁאוֹן. (שֶׁנֶּאֱמַר בְּמַשָּׁאוֹן), הַמְכַסֶּה דָּבָר הַשָּׂנוּי לַמָּקוֹם בְּמַשָּׁאוֹן – בַּחֹשֶׁךְ, כְּמוֹ "שׁוֹאָה" (איוב ל) – שֶׁעוֹשֶׂה מַעֲשָׂיו בַּחוֹשֶׁךְ. [לעיל ח:] כִּי כָּל סְאוֹן. שֶׁבָּא לְלַמְּדֵנוּ שֶׁאַף עֲבֵירוֹת קְטַנּוֹת נִפְרָעוֹת הֵימֶנּוּ. לָמָּה לִי. מֵ"אַחַת לְאַחַת" נָפְקָא!. לְכַמִּדָּה. [לקמן טו:] (ב) שֶׁבְּמִדָּה שֶׁמּוֹדֵד מוֹדְדִין לוֹ הַפֵּרָעוֹן מֵעֵין הַחֵטְא. שִׁילּוּחָהּ. אִיבּוּדָהּ מִן הָעוֹלָם. ג' כּוֹסוֹת. בַּחֲלוֹמוֹ שֶׁל שַׂר הַמַּשְׁקִים. בִּימֵי פַּרְעֹה נְכֹה. "לָבֹא נְבוּכַדְנֶאצַּר מֶלֶךְ בָּבֶל לְהַכּוֹת אֶת אֶרֶץ מִצְרָיִם". עִם חַבְרוֹתֶיהָ. לִימוֹת הַמָּשִׁיחַ. אַלְמָא: לֹא נִטְרְדָה בְּמַכָּה רִאשׁוֹנָה. וְכִי תֵּימָא הָנָךְ אָזְדוּ. הָרִאשׁוֹנִים כָּלוּ כּוּלָּן, וְאֵלּוּ מֵאוּמּוֹת אֲחֵרוֹת הָיוּ, שֶׁנִּתְיַישְּׁבוּ בְּאֶרֶץ מִצְרַיִם. מִצְרִי רִאשׁוֹן. הוּא עַצְמוֹ נִתְגַּיֵּיר. אַשִּׂיא לִבְנִי מִצְרִית שְׁנִיָּה. בַּת מִצְרִית גִּיּוֹרֶת וְגֵר מִצְרִי. שֶׁתְּהֵא הִיא שְׁנִיָּה לַגֵּירוּת, כְּדֵי שֶׁיְּהֵא בֵּן בְּנִי שְׁלִישִׁי וְרָאוּי לִישָּׂא בַּת יִשְׂרָאֵל, דִּכְתִיב (דברים כג): "בָּנִים אֲשֶׁר יִוָּלְדוּ לָהֶם דּוֹר שְׁלִישִׁי יָבֹא לָהֶם בִּקְהַל ה'". שֶׁאִם הָיִיתִי מַשִּׂיא לִבְנִי מִצְרִית רִאשׁוֹנָה – הָיָה בֵּן בְּנִי שֵׁנִי מִצַּד [חולין לב.] הָאֵם, דְּאָמַר בִּיבָמוֹת (דף עח.) וּבְקִידּוּשִׁין (דף סז.) ["בָּנִים אֲשֶׁר יִוָּלְדוּ] לָהֶם" – הַלֵּךְ אַחַר פְּסוּלָן, אַלְמָא: עֲדַיִין מִצְרִים הֵם, דְּאִילּוּ שְׁאָר אוּמּוֹת מוּתָּרִין לָבֹא בַּקָּהָל מִיָּד. מְנְיָמִין לֵית לֵיהּ הָא דְּאָמַר בִּבְרָכוֹת (דף כח.) שֶׁהָעַמּוֹנִים וְהַמִּצְרִים מוּתָּרִין לָבֹא בַּקָּהָל, שֶׁכְּבָר עָלָה סַנְחֵרִיב וּבִלְבֵּל אֶת כָּל הָאוּמּוֹת. וְהָכִי נַמִי קָתָנֵי בָּתַר דְּהַךְ מִילְּתָא בְּתוֹסֶפְתָּא דְּקִידּוּשִׁין: אָמַר לוֹ ר"ע: מְנְיָמִין טָעִיתָ, שֶׁכְּבָר עָלָה סַנְחֵרִיב וּבִלְבֵּל כו'. אַהָא. מִן הַמִּקְרָא הַזֶּה. חִצַּי כָּלִים. מַכּוֹתַי כָּלוֹת. בִּמְלֹאות סִפְקוֹ. כָּל רְצוֹנוֹ. יֵצֶר לוֹ. תְּבוֹאֶנּוּ צָרָה. אֶלָּא נְוֵה תְּהִלָּה. עַל עִסְקֵי נְוֵה בָתִּים שֶׁבָּנוּ – יְהַלְּלוּהוּ. שֶׁלֹּא שָׁלְטוּ שׂוֹנְאֵיהֶם בְּמַעֲשֵׂה יְדֵיהֶם. לִהְיוֹת נֶהֱנִים מֵהֶם. דָּוִד דִּכְתִיב טָבְעוּ בָאָרֶץ שְׁעָרֶיהָ. לְעֵיל מִינֵּיהּ כְּתִיב: "חָשַׁב ה' לְהַשְׁחִית חוֹמַת בַּת צִיּוֹן", וַעֲלָהּ כְּתִיב: "טָבְעוּ בָאָרֶץ". וּמְצוּדַת צִיּוֹן הִיא עִיר דָּוִד וּבֵיתוֹ, כִּדְכְתִיב בְּסֵפֶר שְׁמוּאֵל (ב ה). וּכְשֶׁבָּאוּ צָרִים בִּימֵי צִדְקִיָּהוּ טָבְעוּ הַשְּׁעָרִים – דַּלְתוֹת הַשְּׁעָרִים שֶׁהָיוּ שֶׁל נְחוֹשֶׁת אוֹ שֶׁל (ג) זָהָב, כְּדֵי שֶׁלֹּא יִשְׁאוּם אוֹיְבִים. וְעֵצִים לֹא נָשְׂאוּ אוֹתָם. מַה שֶּׁבִּקְּשָׁה לֹא נִיתַּן לָהּ. שֶׁאֲסוּרָה לַבּוֹעֵל. וּמַה שֶּׁבְּיָדָהּ נָטְלוּ הֵימֶנָּה. אִם שׁוֹתָה מַיִם – מֵתָה, וְאִם הוֹדְתָה – נֶאֶסְרָה לְבַעְלָהּ, וְהִפְסִידָה כְּתוּבָּתָהּ.

נָחָשׁ

תורה אור

פָּנֶיהָ מוֹרִיקוֹת. הִיא כָּחֲלָה לוֹ עֵינֶיהָ – לְפִיכָךְ עֵינֶיהָ בּוֹלְטוֹת, הִיא קָלְעָה לוֹ אֶת שְׂעָרָהּ – לְפִיכָךְ כֹּהֵן סוֹתֵר אֶת שְׂעָרָהּ, הִיא הֶרְאֲתָה לוֹ בְּאֶצְבַּע – לְפִיכָךְ צִיפּוֹרְנֶיהָ נוֹשְׁרוֹת, *הִיא חָגְרָה לוֹ בְּצִילְצוּל – לְפִיכָךְ כֹּהֵן מֵבִיא חֶבֶל הַמִּצְרִי וְקוֹשֵׁר לָהּ לְמַעְלָה מִדַּדֶּיהָ, הִיא פָּשְׁטָה לוֹ אֶת יְרֵיכָהּ – לְפִיכָךְ יְרֵיכָהּ נוֹפֶלֶת, הִיא קִיבְּלַתּוֹ עַל כְּרֵיסָהּ – לְפִיכָךְ בִּטְנָהּ צָבָה, *הִיא הֶאֱכִילַתּוֹ מַעֲדַנֵּי עוֹלָם – לְפִיכָךְ קָרְבָּנָהּ מַאֲכַל בְּהֵמָה, הִיא הִשְׁקַתְהוּ יַיִן מְשׁוּבָּח בְּכוֹסוֹת מְשׁוּבָּחִים – לְפִיכָךְ כֹּהֵן מַשְׁקָהּ מַיִם הַמָּרִים בִּמְקֵידָה שֶׁל חֶרֶשׂ, הִיא עָשְׂתָה בְּסֵתֶר – (תהלים צא) °"יוֹשֵׁב בְּסֵתֶר עֶלְיוֹן" שָׂם בָּהּ פָּנִים, שֶׁנֶּאֱמַר: (איוב כד) °"וְעֵין נוֹאֵף שָׁמְרָה נֶשֶׁף לֵאמֹר לֹא תְשׁוּרֵנִי עָיִן" (א) וגו'. דָּבָר אַחֵר: הִיא עָשְׂתָה בְּסֵתֶר – הַמָּקוֹם פִּירְסְמָהּ בְּגָלוּי, שֶׁנֶּאֱמַר: (משלי כו) °"תִּכַּסֶּה שִׂנְאָה בְּמַשָּׁאוֹן תִּגָּלֶה רָעָתוֹ בְקָהָל" (וגו'). וּמֵאַחַר דְּנָפְקָא לֵיהּ מֵ"אַחַת לְאַחַת לִמְצֹא חֶשְׁבּוֹן", (ישעיה ט) °"כִּי כָל סְאוֹן סֹאֵן בְּרַעַשׁ" לָמָּה לִי? לְכַמִּדָּה. וּמֵאַחַר דְּנָפְקָא לֵיהּ מִ"כִּי כָל סְאוֹן סֹאֵן בְּרַעַשׁ", (שם כז) °"בְּסַאסְּאָה בְּשַׁלְחָהּ תְּרִיבֶנָּה" לָמָּה לִי? לִכְדְרַב חִינָּנָא בַּר פַּפָּא. דְּא"ר חִינָּנָא בַּר פַּפָּא: אֵין הקב"ה נִפְרָע מִן הָאוּמָּה עַד שְׁעַת שִׁילּוּחָהּ, שֶׁנֶּאֱמַר: "בְּסַאסְּאָה בְּשַׁלְחָהּ" וגו'. *אִינִי? וְהָאָמַר רָבָא: שְׁלֹשָׁה כּוֹסוֹת הָאֲמוּרוֹת בְּמִצְרַיִם לָמָּה? אַחַת – שֶׁשָּׁתַת בִּימֵי מֹשֶׁה, וְאַחַת – שֶׁשָּׁתַת בִּימֵי פַּרְעֹה נְכֹה, וְאַחַת – שֶׁעֲתִידָה לִשְׁתּוֹת עִם חַבְרוֹתֶיהָ! וְכִי תֵּימָא הָנָךְ אָזְדוּ, וְהָנֵי אַחֲרִינֵי נִינְהוּ – *וְהָתַנְיָא, אָמַר רַבִּי יְהוּדָה: מְנְיָמִין גֵּר הַמִּצְרִי הָיָה לִי חָבֵר מִתַּלְמִידֵי ר' עֲקִיבָא. אָמַר מְנְיָמִין גֵּר הַמִּצְרִי: אֲנִי מִצְרִי רִאשׁוֹן, וְנָשָׂאתִי מִצְרִית רִאשׁוֹנָה. אַשִּׂיא לִבְנִי מִצְרִית שְׁנִיָּה, כְּדֵי שֶׁיְּהֵא בֶּן בְּנִי מוּתָּר לָבֹא בַּקָּהָל! אֶלָּא אִי אִיתְּמַר הָכִי אִיתְּמַר, א"ר חִינָּנָא בַּר פַּפָּא: אֵין הקב"ה נִפְרָע מִן הַמֶּלֶךְ עַד שְׁעַת שִׁילּוּחוֹ, שֶׁנֶּאֱמַר: "בְּסַאסְּאָה בְּשַׁלְחָהּ תְּרִיבֶנָּה" וגו'. אַמֵּימָר מַתְנֵי לְהָא דְּרַב חִינָּנָא בַּר פַּפָּא אַהָא: מ"ד: (מלאכי ג) °"כִּי אֲנִי ה' לֹא שָׁנִיתִי וְאַתֶּם בְּנֵי יַעֲקֹב לֹא כְלִיתֶם"? "אֲנִי ה' לֹא שָׁנִיתִי" – לֹא הִכֵּיתִי לְאוּמָּה וְשָׁנִיתִי לָהּ, "וְאַתֶּם בְּנֵי יַעֲקֹב לֹא כְלִיתֶם" – הַיְינוּ דִּכְתִיב: (דברים לב) °"חִצַּי אֲכַלֶּה בָּם" – חִצַּי כָּלִין, וְהֵן אֵינָן כָּלִין. *אָמַר רַב הַמְנוּנָא: אֵין הקב"ה נִפְרָע מִן הָאָדָם עַד שֶׁתִּתְמַלֵּא סְאָתוֹ, שֶׁנֶּאֱמַר (איוב כ) °"בִּמְלֹאות סִפְקוֹ יֵצֶר לוֹ" וגו'. דָּרַשׁ ר' חִינָּנָא בַּר פַּפָּא: מַאי דִּכְתִיב (תהלים לג) °"רַנְּנוּ צַדִּיקִים בַּה' לַיְשָׁרִים נָאוָה תְהִלָּה"? אַל תִּקְרֵי "נָאוָה תְהִלָּה" אֶלָּא נְוֵה תְהִלָּה – זֶה מֹשֶׁה וְדָוִד, שֶׁלֹּא שָׁלְטוּ שׂוֹנְאֵיהֶם בְּמַעֲשֵׂיהֶם; דָּוִד – דִּכְתִיב: (איכה ב) °"טָבְעוּ בָאָרֶץ שְׁעָרֶיהָ", מֹשֶׁה – דְּאָמַר מָר: מִשֶּׁנִּבְנָה מִקְדָּשׁ רִאשׁוֹן נִגְנַז אֹהֶל מוֹעֵד, קְרָשָׁיו קְרָסָיו וּבְרִיחָיו וְעַמּוּדָיו וַאֲדָנָיו. הֵיכָא? אָמַר רַב חִסְדָּא אָמַר אֲבִימִי: תַּחַת מְחִילּוֹת שֶׁל הֵיכָל. [תוספתא ספ"ד] תָּנוּ רַבָּנַן: *סוֹטָה נָתְנָה עֵינֶיהָ בְּמִי שֶׁאֵינוֹ רָאוּי לָהּ. מַה שֶּׁבִּיקְּשָׁה – לֹא נִיתַּן לָהּ, וּמַה שֶּׁבְּיָדָהּ – נְטָלוּהוּ מִמֶּנָּה. שֶׁכָּל הַנּוֹתֵן עֵינָיו בְּמַה שֶּׁאֵינוֹ שֶׁלּוֹ, מַה שֶּׁמְּבַקֵּשׁ – אֵין נוֹתְנִין לוֹ, וּמַה שֶּׁבְּיָדוֹ – נוֹטְלִין הֵימֶנּוּ.

וְכֵן

מנימין גר המצרי וכו'. מקשים מפרק "תפלת השחר" (ברכות דף כח.), דאמר: בו ביום עמד יהודה גר עמוני לפניהם בבית המקדש, ואמר להם: מה אני לבא בקהל? אמר לו ר"ג: אסור אתה. א"ל ר' יהושע: מותר אתה. א"ל ר"ג: והלא כתיב "לא יבא עמוני ומואבי"! אמר לו ר"י: וכי עמון ומואב במקומם הן יושבין? והלא כבר עלה סנחריב מלך אשור ובלבל את כל העולם כולו! א"כ אפילו מנימין היה מותר לבא בקהל! ועוד מקשינן אההיא ד"תפלת השחר" דאמר פ"ק דמגילה (דף יב:): זיל לגבי עמון ומואב דיתבי אדוכתייהו כחמרא *אדורדיא, שנאמר: "שאנן מואב מנעוריו" וגו'. מיהו, הכא בשמעתין לא קשיא מידי, כמו שפרש"י, דמנימין היה טועה, וסבור שלא נתבלבלו, כדקתני סיפא בתוספתא דפ' בתרא דקדושין: אמר לו רבי עקיבא: מנימין, טעית, הלכה: כבר עלה סנחריב ובלבל את האומות, לא מצרים במקומם ולא עמונים ומואבים במקומם. אלא עמון נושא מצרית, ומצרי נושא עמונית, ואחד מן אלו מותר בכל משפחות האדמה, ואחד מכל משפחות האדמה נושא את אלו. (ד) והכא הכי פירושא: עד כאן ל"פ אלא אם נתבלבלו אי לאו, אבל כולי עלמא מודו דישנן בעולם. אבל ההיא דמגילה תיקשה! ופר"ת: דסנחריב, אע"פ שבלבל את כל העולם כולו – ארץ מצרים לא בלבל, כדכתיב (מלכים ב כד) בפרעה נכה: "ולא הוסיף עוד מלך מצרים לצאת מארצו כי לקח מלך בבל מנחל מצרים עד נהר פרת" – אלמא סנחריב לא בלבל. (ה) והכי תנא בסדר עולם: מיום שעלה מלך בבל על ארץ מצרים עוד לא זקפה ראש. אבל עמון (ומואב) בלבל, דכל הנהו (ו) לא אשכחן בהדיא שלא בלבלן, כדכתיב (ישעיה לו): "מי בכל אלהי הארצות" וגו'. ובמצרים אשכחן בהדיא שלא בלבלן אלא שטפן, כדאמרי' בסדר עולם: כשהלך לתרהקה מלך כוש. ועל אותה שעה אמר בתוספתא, אמר לו רבי עקיבא: מנימין טעית וכו'. וגמרא שלנו לא חש להזכיר, לפי שלא היה כיבוש גמור אלא כשטיפת שבנא וסיעתו. וגם מואב שטף, כדאמרינן בסדר עולם: "שלש שנים ונקלה כבוד מואב" (ישעיה טז), שסנחריב שטפן, אבל כיבוש ובלבול לא הוה. ובמואב אשכחן בהדיא דלא בלבל, כדכתיב: "שאנן מואב מנעוריו", וכי אמר ירמיה להאי קרא – הוה שאנן, מכלל דלא בלבל ובמגילה גרסינן "זיל גבי מואב דיתיב אדוכתיה", ול"ג "עמון", דעמון לא יתבי אדוכתייהו. [ובברכות (דף כח.) אמרינן]: וכי עמון ומואב במקומן הן יושבין – ל"ג "ומואב". וחורבן נבוכדנצר לא חשיב בלבול, דכי היה מחריב נבוכדנצר – היה מניח דלת הארץ במקומם, אבל סנחריב היה מעביר לארץ ומבלבלן. והכי אמרינן בפ' בתרא (לקמן מו:) גבי לוז: היא לוז שלא בלבלה סנחריב, ולא החריבה נבוכדנצר, ואף מלאך המות אין לו רשות לעבור שם. ובכ"מ תולה בלבול בסנחריב וחורבן בנבוכדנצר. ולפום רהיטא גרס עמון בהדי מואב, וליתא, כדפרישית, ותו לא מידי. ע"כ פירושו. וקשה לפירושו מן התוספתא, דקתני: לא מצרים במקומם הם יושבין. ויש לנו לשבש כמו כן לפירושו הא דקתני: לא מואבים במקומם. ואי ל"ג מואבים בתוספתא, ועמון במגילה – לא קשיא מידי*. **לא** הכיתי לאומה ושניתי. ה"ה דהאי הוה מצי למיפרך הא דרבא והא דמנימין. ותימה: מאי הוה מצי לתרץ? דלא הוי מצי לתרץ למלך של אומה, מדקאמר "ואתם בני יעקב" – דמשמע אכל בני יעקב קאמר, ובאומה שלימה מיירי!

אין

פי' שמרים

[וע"ע תוס' יבמות עו: ד"ה מנימין ותוס' מגילה יב: ד"ה זיל]

תוספות שאנץ

ג' כוסות האמורות במצרים הוא בחלום שר המשקים של פרעה ובמדרש יש דלעתיד משקה הקב"ה האומות כוס התרעלה וכשיגיעו למצרים ואמר כבר שתיתי פעמים יאמר לה הקב"ה שתה דאין שתיה זו כאחרות אלא א) לא תק עוד והיינו דכתיב אך שמריה ימצו ישתו כל רשעי ארץ: אמר מנימין גר המצרי אני מצרי וכו' כדי שיהא בן בני ראוי לבוא בקהל וא"ת איהו הוי נמי כשר כיון דסנחריב עמד ובלבל כל העולם חוץ ממואב כדאמר בפרק תפלת השחר וכי עמון ומואב במקומן הן יושבין והלא עלה סנחריב ובלבלן. וי"ל דסנחריב לא בלבל אותן של מצרים אלא הביאן בחבלים ובשלשלאות עד לפני ירושלים וכשהצליח חזקיה וראו הנס השלימו עמו וקבלו עול שמים עליהן והחזירן למקומן אי נמי י"ל דההוא דמנימין דהכא היתה אחר מ' שנה שפסקה גלותן וחזרו למקומן וה"נ קאמר התם [בתוספתא דידים] דאמר מנימין כשראה שהתיר ר"י ליהודה גר העמוני ואמר להם אף אני כמו כן אמרו לו לארצך יש קצבה לאחר מ' שנה כדכתיב בקרא גבי מצרים מקץ מ' שנה אשיב ולו אין קצבה: ומיהו פ"ה הכא דלית ליה הא דאמר עמד סנחריב ובלבל כל העולם והכי נמי קתני (בפרק בתרא) [בתר דהך] מילתא [בתוספתא דקידושין אמר לו [ר"ע] מנימין טעית שכבר עלה סנחריב. ל"ה. משנבנה מקדש ראשון נגנז אהל מועד ולית ליה לההוא תנא כמאן דאמר דארון גלה לבבל כדאמר ביומא אלא סבירא ליה כמאן דאמר יאשיהו גנזו:

א) עי' הגירסא בילקוט תהלים רמז תתי"ג.

הגהות הב"ח

(א) גמ' לא תשורני עין וסתר פנים ישים ד"א וכ"ה בע"י: (ב) רש"י ד"ה לכמדה שבמדה: (ג) ד"ה דוד וכו' או של כסף וזהב כלי: (ד) תוס' ד"ה מנימין וכו' נושא את אלו והכי פריך הכא ע"כ ל"פ אלא אם נתבלבלו: (ה) בא"ד לא בלבל מצרים והכי תנא בסדר: (ו) בא"ד דלא אשכחן בהדיא שלא בלבלן ודאי בלבלן כדכתיב:

יבמות עח. ע"ש תוספתא קדושין פ"ה

ערכין טו.

נח א מיי' פ"ג מהל' סוטה הלכה טז סמג עשין כו:

תורה אור

וְכֵן מָצִינוּ *בְּנָחָשׁ הַקַּדְמוֹנִי, שֶׁנָּתַן עֵינָיו בְּמַה שֶּׁאֵינוֹ רָאוּי לוֹ. מַה שֶּׁבִּיקֵּשׁ — לֹא נָתְנוּ לוֹ, וּמַה שֶּׁבְּיָדוֹ — נְטָלוּהוּ מִמֶּנּוּ. אָמַר הקב"ה: אֲנִי אָמַרְתִּי יְהֵא מֶלֶךְ עַל כָּל בְּהֵמָה וְחַיָּה — וְעַכְשָׁיו °אָרוּר הוּא מִכָּל הַבְּהֵמָה וּמִכֹּל חַיַּת הַשָּׂדֶה. אֲנִי אָמַרְתִּי יְהַלֵּךְ בְּקוֹמָה זְקוּפָה — עַכְשָׁיו עַל גְּחוֹנוֹ יֵלֵךְ. אֲנִי אָמַרְתִּי יְהֵא מַאֲכָלוֹ מַאֲכַל אָדָם — עַכְשָׁיו עָפָר יֹאכַל. הוּא אָמַר אֶהֱרוֹג אֶת אָדָם וְאֶשָּׂא אֶת חַוָּה — עַכְשָׁיו "אֵיבָה אָשִׁית בֵּינְךָ וּבֵין הָאִשָּׁה וּבֵין זַרְעֲךָ וּבֵין זַרְעָהּ". וְכֵן מָצִינוּ בְּקַיִן, וְקֹרַח, וּבִלְעָם, וְדוֹאֵג, וַאֲחִיתוֹפֶל, וְגֵחֲזִי, וְאַבְשָׁלוֹם, וַאֲדוֹנִיָּהוּ, וְעוּזִּיָּהוּ, וְהָמָן, שֶׁנָּתְנוּ עֵינֵיהֶם בְּמַה שֶּׁאֵינוֹ רָאוּי לָהֶם. מַה שֶּׁבִּיקְּשׁוּ — לֹא נִיתַּן לָהֶם, וּמַה שֶּׁבְּיָדָם — נְטָלוּהוּ מֵהֶם.§ "בֵּירֵךְ הִתְחִילָּה בַּעֲבֵירָה" וכו'.§ מְנָא הָנֵי מִילֵּי? אִילֵימָא מִשּׁוּם דִּכְתִיב: °"בְּתֵת ה' אֶת יְרֵכֵךְ נֹפֶלֶת וְאֶת בִּטְנֵךְ צָבָה" — וְהָכְתִיב: °"וְצָבְתָה בִטְנָהּ וְנָפְלָה יְרֵכָהּ"! אָמַר אַבָּיֵי: כִּי לָיֵיט — לָיֵיט תְּחִילָּה יָרֵךְ וַהֲדַר בֶּטֶן לָיֵיט, אוּמַיָּא כִּי בָּדְקִי — כִּי אוֹרְחַיְיהוּ בָּדְקִי, בֶּטֶן בְּרֵישָׁא וַהֲדַר יָרֵךְ. בִּקְלָלָה נַמִי כְּתִיב: °"לַצְבּוֹת בֶּטֶן וְלַנְפִּיל יָרֵךְ"! *הַהוּא דְּמוֹדַע לָהּ כֹּהֵן דְּבֶטֶן בְּרֵישָׁא וַהֲדַר יָרֵךְ, שֶׁלֹּא לְהוֹצִיא לַעַז עַל מֵי הַמָּרִים.§ **מתני'** שִׁמְשׁוֹן הָלַךְ אַחַר עֵינָיו — לְפִיכָךְ נִקְּרוּ פְּלִשְׁתִּים אֶת עֵינָיו, שֶׁנֶּאֱמַר °"וַיֹּאחֲזוּהוּ פְלִשְׁתִּים וַיְנַקְּרוּ אֶת עֵינָיו". אַבְשָׁלוֹם נִתְגָּאָה בִּשְׂעָרוֹ — לְפִיכָךְ נִתְלָה בִּשְׂעָרוֹ. וּלְפִי שֶׁבָּא עַל עֶשֶׂר פִּלַגְשֵׁי אָבִיו — לְפִיכָךְ נִתְּנוּ בּוֹ עֶשֶׂר לוֹנְבִיּוֹת, שֶׁנֶּאֱמַר: °"וַיָּסֹבּוּ עֲשָׂרָה (א) אֲנָשִׁים נֹשְׂאֵי כְּלֵי יוֹאָב". וּלְפִי שֶׁגָּנַב ג' *גְּנֵבוֹת: לֵב אָבִיו, וְלֵב ב"ד, וְלֵב יִשְׂרָאֵל, (שֶׁנֶּאֱמַר: °"וַיְגַנֵּב אַבְשָׁלוֹם אֶת לֵב אַנְשֵׁי יִשְׂרָאֵל") — לְפִיכָךְ נִתְקְעוּ בּוֹ ג' שְׁבָטִים, שֶׁנֶּאֱמַר: °"וַיִּקַּח (ב) שְׁלֹשָׁה שְׁבָטִים בְּכַפּוֹ וַיִּתְקָעֵם בְּלֵב אַבְשָׁלוֹם". וְכֵן *לְעִנְיַן הַטּוֹבָה: מִרְיָם הִמְתִּינָה לְמֹשֶׁה שָׁעָה אַחַת, שֶׁנֶּאֱמַר: °"וַתֵּתַצַּב אֲחֹתוֹ מֵרָחֹק" — לְפִיכָךְ נִתְעַכְּבוּ לָהּ יִשְׂרָאֵל ז' יָמִים בַּמִּדְבָּר, שֶׁנֶּאֱמַר: °"וְהָעָם לֹא נָסַע עַד הֵאָסֵף מִרְיָם". יוֹסֵף זָכָה לִקְבּוֹר אֶת אָבִיו, וְאֵין בְּאֶחָיו גָּדוֹל מִמֶּנּוּ, שֶׁנֶּאֱמַר: °"וַיַּעַל יוֹסֵף לִקְבּוֹר אֶת אָבִיו וַיַּעֲלוּ עִמּוֹ גַּם רֶכֶב גַּם פָּרָשִׁים". מִי לָנוּ גָּדוֹל מִיּוֹסֵף שֶׁלֹּא נִתְעַסֵּק בּוֹ אֶלָּא מֹשֶׁה. מֹשֶׁה זָכָה בְּעַצְמוֹת יוֹסֵף, וְאֵין בְּיִשְׂרָאֵל גָּדוֹל מִמֶּנּוּ, שֶׁנֶּאֱמַר: °"וַיִּקַּח מֹשֶׁה אֶת עַצְמוֹת יוֹסֵף עִמּוֹ". מִי גָּדוֹל מִמֹּשֶׁה שֶׁלֹּא נִתְעַסֵּק בּוֹ אֶלָּא הַמָּקוֹם, שֶׁנֶּאֱמַר: °"וַיִּקְבּוֹר אוֹתוֹ בַגַּיְא". לֹא עַל מֹשֶׁה בִּלְבַד אָמְרוּ, אֶלָּא עַל כָּל הַצַּדִּיקִים, שֶׁנֶּאֱמַר: °"וְהָלַךְ לְפָנֶיךָ צִדְקֶךָ כְּבוֹד ה' יַאַסְפֶךָ".§ **גמ'** ת"ר: שִׁמְשׁוֹן בְּעֵינָיו מָרַד, שֶׁנֶּאֱמַר: °"וַיֹּאמֶר שִׁמְשׁוֹן אֶל אָבִיו אוֹתָהּ קַח לִי כִּי הִיא יָשְׁרָה בְעֵינָי" — לְפִיכָךְ נִקְּרוּ פְּלִשְׁתִּים אֶת עֵינָיו, שֶׁנֶּאֱמַר: °"וַיֹּאחֲזוּהוּ פְלִשְׁתִּים וַיְנַקְּרוּ אֶת עֵינָיו". אִינִי? וְהָכְתִיב: °"וְאָבִיו וְאִמּוֹ לֹא יָדְעוּ כִּי מֵה' הִוא"! כִּי אֲזַל מִיהָא — בָּתַר (ג) יַשְׁרוּתֵיהּ אֲזַל. תַּנְיָא, *רַבִּי אוֹמֵר: תְּחִילַּת קִלְקוּלוֹ בְּעַזָּה, לְפִיכָךְ לָקָה בְּעַזָּה. (ד) תְּחִילַּת קִלְקוּלוֹ בְּעַזָּה — דִּכְתִיב: °"וַיֵּלֶךְ שִׁמְשׁוֹן עַזָּתָה וַיַּרְא שָׁם אִשָּׁה זוֹנָה" וגו', לְפִיכָךְ לָקָה בְּעַזָּה — דִּכְתִיב: °"וַיּוֹרִידוּ אוֹתוֹ עַזָּתָה". וְהָכְתִיב: °"וַיֵּרֶד שִׁמְשׁוֹן תִּמְנָתָה"! תְּחִלַּת קִלְקוּלוֹ מִיהָא בְּעַזָּה הָיָה. °"וַיְהִי אַחֲרֵי כֵן וַיֶּאֱהַב אִשָּׁה בְּנַחַל שׂוֹרֵק וּשְׁמָהּ דְּלִילָה". תַּנְיָא, רַבִּי אוֹמֵר: אִילְמָלֵא *(לֹא) נִקְרָא שְׁמָהּ דְּלִילָה — רְאוּיָה הָיְתָה שֶׁתִּקָּרֵא דְּלִילָה; דִּילְדְּלָה אֶת כֹּחוֹ, דִּילְדְּלָה אֶת לִבּוֹ, דִּילְדְּלָה אֶת מַעֲשָׂיו. דִּילְדְּלָה אֶת כֹּחוֹ — דִּכְתִיב °"וַיָּסַר כֹּחוֹ מֵעָלָיו", דִּילְדְּלָה אֶת לִבּוֹ — דִּכְתִיב: °"וַתֵּרֶא דְלִילָה כִּי הִגִּיד לָהּ אֶת כָּל לִבּוֹ", דִּילְדְּלָה אֶת מַעֲשָׂיו — דְּאִיסְתַּלַּק שְׁכִינָה מִינֵּיהּ, דִּכְתִיב: °"וְהוּא לֹא יָדַע כִּי ה' סָר מֵעָלָיו". "וַתֵּרֶא דְלִילָה כִּי הִגִּיד לָהּ אֶת כָּל לִבּוֹ". מְנָא יָדְעָה? א"ר חָנִין א"ר: נִיכָּרִין דִּבְרֵי אֱמֶת. אַבָּיֵי אָמַר: יָדְעָה בּוֹ בְּאוֹתוֹ צַדִּיק דְּלָא מַפֵּיק שֵׁם שָׁמַיִם לְבַטָּלָה. כֵּיוָן דְּאָמַר °"נְזִיר אֱלֹהִים אֲנִי" אָמְרָה: הַשְׁתָּא וַדַּאי קוּשְׁטָא קָאָמַר. °"וַיְהִי כִּי הֵצִיקָה לּוֹ בִדְבָרֶיהָ כָּל הַיָּמִים וַתְּאַלְצֵהוּ". מַאי "וַתְּאַלְצֵהוּ"? אָמַר רַבִּי יִצְחָק דְּבֵי רַבִּי אַמֵּי: בִּשְׁעַת גְּמַר בִּיאָה נִשְׁמְטָה מִתַּחְתָּיו. °"וְעַתָּה הִשָּׁמְרִי נָא וְאַל תִּשְׁתִּי יַיִן וְשֵׁכָר וְאַל תֹּאכְלִי כָּל טָמֵא". מַאי "כָּל טָמֵא"? וְתוּ, עַד הַשְׁתָּא דְּבָרִים טְמֵאִים קָאָכְלָה?! א"ר יִצְחָק דְּבֵי רַבִּי אַמֵּי: דְּבָרִים הָאֲסוּרִים בְּנָזִיר. °"וַיִּבְקַע אֱלֹהִים אֶת הַמַּכְתֵּשׁ אֲשֶׁר בַּלֶּחִי". א"ר יִצְחָק דְּבֵי רַבִּי אַמֵּי: הוּא אִיוָּה לְדָבָר טָמֵא — לְפִיכָךְ נִתְלוּ חַיָּיו בְּדָבָר טָמֵא. °"וַתָּחֶל רוּחַ ה'" וגו'. א"ר חָמָא בַּר' חֲנִינָא: חָלְתָה נְבוּאָתוֹ שֶׁל יַעֲקֹב אָבִינוּ, דִּכְתִיב: °"יְהִי דָן נָחָשׁ עֲלֵי דֶרֶךְ". "לְפַעֲמוֹ בְּמַחֲנֵה דָן". א"ר יִצְחָק דְּבֵי רַבִּי אַמֵּי: מְלַמֵּד, שֶׁהָיְתָה שְׁכִינָה מְקַשְׁקֶשֶׁת לְפָנָיו כְּזוּג, כְּתִיב הָכָא: "לְפַעֲמוֹ בְּמַחֲנֵה דָן", וּכְתִיב הָתָם: °"פַּעֲמוֹן וְרִמּוֹן". "בֵּין צָרְעָה וּבֵין אֶשְׁתָּאוֹל". אָמַר ר' אַסִּי: צָרְעָה וְאֶשְׁתָּאוֹל שְׁנֵי הָרִים גְּדוֹלִים הָיוּ, וַעֲקָרָן שִׁמְשׁוֹן וּטְחָנָן זֶה בָּזֶה. °"וְהוּא יָחֵל לְהוֹשִׁיעַ אֶת יִשְׂרָאֵל". אָמַר רַבִּי חָמָא בְּרַבִּי חֲנִינָא:

(° שופטים ז) הוחל

רש"י

נָחָשׁ הַקַּדְמוֹנִי. נָתַן עֵינָיו בְּחַוָּה וּבָא עָלֶיהָ. וְהַיְינוּ דִּכְתִיב (בראשית ג): "הַנָּחָשׁ הִשִּׁיאַנִי" — לְשׁוֹן תַּשְׁמִישׁ וְנִשּׂוּאִין הוּא. נְטָלוּהוּ מִמֶּנּוּ. קוֹמָה זְקוּפָה. יְהֵא מֶלֶךְ. שֶׁלְּכָךְ עֲשָׂאוֹ עָרוּם מִכֹּל. אֲנִי אָמַרְתִּי יְהַלֵּךְ בְּקוֹמָה זְקוּפָה. מִקְּלָלָתוֹ אַתָּה לָמֵד. וְכֵן כָּל אֵלֶּה אַתָּה לָמֵד מִקִּלְלָתָן. קַיִן. נָתַן עֵינָיו בִּתְאוֹמָה יְתֵירָה שֶׁנּוֹלְדָה עִם הֶבֶל. שֶׁשְּׁתֵּי תְאוֹמוֹת נוֹלְדוּ עִמּוֹ, וְהַיְינוּ דִּכְתִיב (בראשית ד): "אֶת אָחִיו אֶת הָבֶל", שְׁנֵי אֶתִּים — שְׁנֵי רִיבּוּיִים. קֹרַח. עַל הַכְּהוּנָּה, וְנִבְלַע. בִּלְעָם. בְּמָמוֹנוֹ שֶׁל בָּלָק, לְקַלֵּל אֶת יִשְׂרָאֵל. וְנֶהֱרַג בְּמִדְיָן, שֶׁהָלַךְ לִיטּוֹל שְׂכַר עֶשְׂרִים וְאַרְבָּעָה אֶלֶף שֶׁנָּפְלוּ מִיִּשְׂרָאֵל בַּעֲצָתוֹ*. דּוֹאֵג. אַבִּיר הָרוֹעִים וְגָדוֹל שֶׁבַּתַּלְמִידִים הָיָה, וְנִתְקַנֵּא בְּדָוִד שֶׁרְאָהוּ נְבוֹן דָּבָר וְאִישׁ תֹּאַר וּמַרְאֶה פָּנִים בַּהֲלָכָה. כִּדִכְתִיב (שמואל א טז): "הִנֵּה רָאִיתִי בֵּן לְיִשַׁי בֵּית הַלַּחְמִי" וגו', וְאָמַר בְּאַגָּדָה דְּ"חֵלֶק" (דף צג:) דְּכָל הַפָּסוּק הַזֶּה דּוֹאֵג אֲמָרוֹ בְּלָשׁוֹן הָרַע. וַאֲחִיתוֹפֶל. נָתַן עֵינָיו בַּמְּלוּכָה, כִּדְאָמַר בְּ"חֵלֶק" (דף קא:*): רָאָה אֵשׁ יוֹצֵא מֵאַמָּתוֹ, וְכִסָּבוּר שֶׁעָתִיד לִמְלוֹךְ. *וּמַה שֶּׁבְּיָדוֹ נָטְלוּ הֵימֶנּוּ — "לֹא יֶחֱצוּ יְמֵיהֶם". גֵּחֲזִי. בְּמָמוֹנוֹ שֶׁל נַעֲמָן, וְנִצְטָרַע. וַאֲדוֹנִיָּה. בַּאֲבִישַׁג וְנֶהֱרַג. וְעוּזִּיָּה. בִּכְהוּנָּה, "וְהַצָּרַעַת זָרְחָה עַל מִצְחוֹ" (דה"ב כו). כִּי לָיֵיט כו'. וּקְלָלָה הִיא תְּחִלַּת הַפּוּרְעָנוּת. מִיהוּ כִּי בָּדְקִי מַיָּא כִּי אוֹרְחַיְיהוּ בָּדְקִי. שֶׁבַּמֵּעַיִים נִכְנְסוּ תְּחִילָּה וּמְקַלְקְלוֹת אוֹתָן, וְאַחַ"כ נוֹפְלוֹת לַיָּרֵךְ. שֶׁלֹּא לְהוֹצִיא לַעַז. שֶׁיֹּאמְרוּ: לֹא עָשׂוּ כְּסֵדֶר הָאָלָה, וְאֵין פּוּרְעָנוּת זוֹ עַל יָדָן. **מתני'** שִׁמְשׁוֹן הָלַךְ אַחַר עֵינָיו. כִּדְיָלֵיף לְקַמָּן. עַל עֶשֶׂר פִּלַגְשֵׁי אָבִיו. כִּדִכְתִיב בְּסֵפֶר שְׁמוּאֵל (ב טו): "וַיַּעֲזֹב עֶשֶׂר נָשִׁים פִּלַגְשִׁים לִשְׁמוֹר הַבָּיִת". לוֹנְבִיּוֹת. חֲנִיתוֹת. לֵב אָבִיו וְלֵב ב"ד. דִּכְתִיב (שם): "אֵלְכָה נָּא וַאֲשַׁלְּמָה אֶת נִדְרִי" וגו', וּכְתִיב: "אֶת אַבְשָׁלוֹם הָלְכוּ מָאתַיִם אִישׁ קְרוּאִים וְהוֹלְכִים לְתוּמָּם", וְאָמְרִינַן בְּסוֹטָה דִּירוּשַׁלְמִי: קְרוּאִים מִדָּוִד, שֶׁעַל יְדֵי מִצְוַת דָּוִד הָלְכוּ עִמּוֹ. אָמַר לוֹ: כְּתוֹב לִי שֶׁיֵּלְכוּ עִמִּי אוֹתָן שְׁנַיִם שֶׁאֶבְחַר, וְכָתַב לוֹ. וְהָיָה מַרְאֶה חוֹתָמוֹ שֶׁל דָּוִד לִשְׁנַיִם וְהוֹלְכִים אַחֲרָיו, וְכֵן לִשְׁנַיִם אֲחֵרִים, עַד שֶׁכִּינֵּס מָאתַיִם, וְכוּלָּן רָאשֵׁי סַנְהֶדְרָאוֹת. הֲרֵי לֵב אָבִיו וְלֵב ב"ד. וְלֵב אַנְשֵׁי יִשְׂרָאֵל — דִּכְתִיב: "בְּקֶרֶב אִישׁ לְהִשְׁתַּחֲווֹת" וגו', וּכְתִיב: "מִי יְשִׂימֵנִי שׁוֹפֵט בָּאָרֶץ", וּכְתִיב: "וַיְגַנֵּב אַבְשָׁלוֹם אֶת לֵב אַנְשֵׁי יִשְׂרָאֵל". וְאֵין בְּאֶחָיו גָּדוֹל מִמֶּנּוּ. שֶׁהָיָה מֶלֶךְ. הֲרֵי מִדָּה שֶׁמָּדַד — שֶׁנִּקְבַּר אָבִיו בִּגְדוֹלִים, וּבוֹ בַּמִּדָּה מָדְדוּ לוֹ — שֶׁנִּקְבַּר הוּא בִּגְדוֹלִים (ה). מִי לָנוּ. לְעִנְיַן כְּבוֹד קְבוּרָה לִקָּבֵר בִּגְדוֹלִים, גָּדוֹל מִיּוֹסֵף, שֶׁלֹּא נִתְעַסֵּק בּוֹ אֶלָּא מֹשֶׁה, שֶׁהוּא גָּדוֹל מִיִּשְׂרָאֵל, וְאֵין בְּיִשְׂרָאֵל גָּדוֹל מִמֶּנּוּ. הֲרֵי שֶׁבַּמִּדָּה שֶׁמָּדַד לִקְבּוֹר אֶת יוֹסֵף ע"י גָּדוֹל — בָּהּ מָדְדוּ לוֹ, שֶׁאֵין גָּדוֹל בִּכְבוֹדוֹ קָבוּר מִמֶּנּוּ, שֶׁלֹּא נִתְעַסֵּק בּוֹ אֶלָּא הקב"ה. **גמ'** בְּעֵינָיו מָרַד. ע"י עֵינָיו מָרַד בְּבוֹרְאוֹ. כִּי מֵה' הוּא. שֶׁחָשַׁק בְּאוֹתָהּ אִשָּׁה כְּדֵי לְהִתְגָּרוֹת בִּפְלִשְׁתִּים. וְהָכְתִיב וַיֵּרֶד שִׁמְשׁוֹן תִּמְנָתָה. וַיַּרְא שָׁם אִשָּׁה מִבְּנוֹת פְּלִשְׁתִּים וַתִּיטַב בְּעֵינֵי שִׁמְשׁוֹן. וּמַעֲשֶׂה שֶׁל זוֹ שֶׁבְּתִמְנָת קוֹדֵם לְמַעֲשֶׂה שֶׁל זוֹ שֶׁבְּעַזָּה!. תְּחִילַּת קִלְקוּלוֹ מִיהָא בְּעַזָּה הֲוָה. דְּהַהִיא דְּתִמְנָת לָאו קִלְקוּל הוּא כּוּלֵּי הַאי, שֶׁלְּקָחָהּ לוֹ לְאִשָּׁה, וְלֹא בָּא עָלֶיהָ בִּזְנוּת. שֶׁדִּילְדְּלָה. עָקְרָה. כְּמוֹ: אַבְנֵי הַר שֶׁנִּדַּלְדְּלוּ*. מְנָא יָדְעָה. הֲלֹא כַּמָּה כְּזָבִים אָמַר לָהּ קוֹדֶם לָכֵן, וּמְלָאַתּוּ שִׁקְרָן. נִכָּרִין דִּבְרֵי אֱמֶת. מִתְקַבְּלִין וּמְיוּשָּׁבִין וּדְבוּרִים עַל אוֹפַנֵּיהֶם. רָאֲתָה שֶׂעָרוֹ גָּדוֹל וְלֹא הָיָה שׁוֹתֶה יַיִן, וְהֵבִינָה שֶׁהַדְּבָרִים הָאַחֲרוֹנִים שֶׁאָמַר לָהּ שֶׁבַּדָּבָר הַזֶּה הָיָה כֹּחוֹ גָּדוֹל — אֱמֶת הֵן. וַתְּאַלְצֵהוּ. לְשׁוֹן דּוֹחַק וּמְצוּקָה. בִּשְׁעַת גְּמַר בִּיאָה. תַּאֲוַת הָאָדָם מְרוּבָּה. דְּבָרִים הָאֲסוּרִים לְנָזִיר. מִשְׁרַת עֲנָבִים, כְּגוֹן נָזִיר שֶׁשָּׁרָה עֲנָבִים בְּמַיִם וְיֵשׁ בָּהֶם טַעַם יַיִן, דְּלָא נָפְקָא מִ"כֹּל אֲשֶׁר יֵעָשֶׂה מִגֶּפֶן הַיַּיִן" (במדבר ו). מַכְתֵּשׁ. מְקוֹם קְבִיעוּת הַשֵּׁן. אִיוָּה לְדָבָר טָמֵא. לִישָּׂא בַּת אֵל נֵכָר. בְּדָבָר טָמֵא. לְחִי הַחֲמוֹר, שֶׁאִלְמָלֵא הוּא הָיָה מֵת בַּצָּמָא. רוּחַ ה'. רוּחַ נְבוּאָה שֶׁשָּׁרְתָה עַל יַעֲקֹב. מְקַשְׁקֶשֶׁת לְפָנָיו. לְלַוּוֹתוֹ בַּאֲשֶׁר הוֹלֵךְ. הוּחַל

תוספות שאנץ

וכן מצינו בקין נתן עיניו בתאומה יתירה שנולדה עם הבל דשני תאומות נולדו עמו דכתיב את אחיו את הבל שני אתין ב' ריבויין. קרח על כהונה ונבלע. בלעם בממונו של בלק לקלל ישראל ונהרג במדין כשהלך ליטול שכר כ"ד אלף שנפלו מישראל בעצתו. דואג אביר הרועים וגדול שבתלמידים היה ונתקנא בדוד כדכתיב הנה ראיתי בן לישי בית הלחמי ואמר בהגדה בפ' חלק כל הפסוק הזה אמרו דואג בלשון הרע. ואחיתופל נתן עיניו במלוכה כדאמרינן ראה אש יוצאה מאמתו וכסבור שעתיד למלוך. גיחזי בממונו של נעמן ונצטרע אבשלום במלכות ונהרג אדניה באבישג ונהרג ועוזיהו בכהונה והצרעת זרחה במצחו. ל"ה. גנב לב אביו ולב בית דין פ"ה שאמר אלכה ואשלמה את נדרי. וכתיב ואת אבשלום הלכו מאתים איש (וא"ת) [ואמרי' בירושל' דסוטה] שעל ידי מצות דוד אביו הלכו עמו אמר לו כתוב לי שילכו עמי אלו שנים שאבחר וכתב לו והיה מראה חותמו של דוד לשנים והולכין וכן לשנים אחרים עד שכנס מאתים איש וכולן ראשי סנהדראות הרי גנב לב אביו ולב ב"ד. ל"ה: תחלת קלקולו מיהא בעזה היה. פ"ה וההוא דתמנת לאו קלקול הוא כולי האי שלקחה לו לאשה ולא בא עליה בזנות. ל"ה. וכן איכא בירושלמי ואע"ג דגויה היתה שמא בצינעה בא עליה אבל ההיא דעזה לא היה דרך נשואין אלא דרך

[נ"ל לבבות וכ"א במשנה שבמשניות וכן בע"י אבל בתוספתא פ"ג איתא גנבות]

הגהות הב"ח

(א) במשנה ויסבו עשרה נערים נושאי כלי יואב ויכו את אבשלום ולפי שגנב: (ב) שם ויקח יואב שלשה שבטים: (ג) גמרא בתר ישרות עיניו אזל: (ד) שם לקה בעזה תחילה תחילת: (ה) רש"י ד"ה ואין באחיו וכו' בגדולים דמי לנו וכו' שאין לנו גדול בכבוד קבורה כמשה כנ"ל והד"א:

הוּחַל שְׁבוּעָתוֹ שֶׁל אֲבִימֶלֶךְ, דִּכְתִיב: °"אִם תִּשְׁקֹר לִי וּלְנִינִי וּלְנֶכְדִּי". °"וַיִּגְדַּל הַנַּעַר וַיְבָרְכֵהוּ ה'", בַּמֶּה בֵּרְכוֹ? אָמַר רַב יְהוּדָה אָמַר רַב: שֶׁבֵּרְכוֹ בְּאַמָּתוֹ; אַמָּתוֹ כִּבְנֵי אָדָם, וְזַרְעוֹ כְּנַחַל שׁוֹטֵף. °"וַיִּקְרָא שִׁמְשׁוֹן אֶל ה' וַיֹּאמַר ה' אֱלֹהִים זָכְרֵנִי נָא וְחַזְּקֵנִי נָא אַךְ הַפַּעַם הַזֶּה וְאִנָּקְמָה נְקַם אַחַת מִשְּׁתֵי עֵינַי מִפְּלִשְׁתִּים". אָמַר רַב: אָמַר שִׁמְשׁוֹן לִפְנֵי הקב"ה: רבש"ע, זְכוֹר לִי עֶשְׂרִים (*וּשְׁתַּיִם) שָׁנָה שֶׁשָּׁפַטְתִּי אֶת יִשְׂרָאֵל, וְלֹא אָמַרְתִּי לְאֶחָד מֵהֶם הַעֲבֵר לִי מַקֵּל מִמָּקוֹם לְמָקוֹם. °"וַיֵּלֶךְ שִׁמְשׁוֹן וַיִּלְכֹּד שְׁלֹשׁ מֵאוֹת שׁוּעָלִים". מַאי שְׁנָא שׁוּעָלִים? אָמַר רַבִּי אַיְבוּ בַּר נַגְּדִי א"ר חִיָּיא בַּר אַבָּא: אָמַר שִׁמְשׁוֹן: יָבֹא (א)מִי שֶׁחוֹזֵר לַאֲחוֹרָיו, וְיִפָּרַע מִפְּלִשְׁתִּים שֶׁחָזְרוּ בִּשְׁבוּעָתָן. תַּנְיָא, א"ר שִׁמְעוֹן הֶחָסִיד: בֵּין כְּתֵפָיו שֶׁל שִׁמְשׁוֹן שִׁשִּׁים אַמָּה הָיָה, שֶׁנֶּאֱמַר: °"וַיִּשְׁכַּב שִׁמְשׁוֹן עַד חֲצִי הַלַּיְלָה וַיָּקָם בַּחֲצִי הַלַּיְלָה וַיֶּאֱחֹז בְּדַלְתוֹת שַׁעַר הָעִיר וּבִשְׁתֵּי הַמְּזוּזוֹת וַיִּסָּעֵם עִם הַבְּרִיחַ וַיָּשֶׂם עַל כְּתֵפָיו", וּגְמִירִי, דְּאֵין דַּלְתוֹת עַזָּה פְּחוּתוֹת מִשִּׁשִּׁים אַמָּה. °"וַיְהִי טוֹחֵן בְּבֵית הָאֲסוּרִים". א"ר יוֹחָנָן: אֵין טְחִינָה אֶלָּא לְשׁוֹן עֲבֵירָה, וְכֵן הוּא אוֹמֵר: °"תִּטְחַן לְאַחֵר אִשְׁתִּי". מְלַמֵּד שֶׁכָּל אֶחָד וְאֶחָד הֵבִיא לוֹ אֶת אִשְׁתּוֹ לְבֵית הָאֲסוּרִים כְּדֵי שֶׁתִּתְעַבֵּר הֵימֶנּוּ. אָמַר רַב פַּפָּא: הַיְינוּ דְּאָמְרִי אֱינָשֵׁי: קַמֵּי דְּשָׁתֵי חַמְרָא — חַמְרָא, קַמֵּי רְפוֹקָא *גְּרִידַיָּא — דּוּבְלָא. וְא"ר יוֹחָנָן: כָּל הַמְזַנֶּה — אִשְׁתּוֹ מְזַנֶּנֶת עָלָיו, שֶׁנֶּאֱמַר: °"אִם נִפְתָּה לִבִּי עַל אִשָּׁה וְעַל פֶּתַח רֵעִי אָרָבְתִּי", וּכְתִיב: "תִּטְחַן לְאַחֵר אִשְׁתִּי וְעָלֶיהָ יִכְרְעוּן אֲחֵרִין". *וְהַיְינוּ דְּאָמְרִי אֱינָשֵׁי: אִיהוּ בֵּי *קָארֵי וְאִיתְּתֵיהּ בֵּי בּוּצִינֵי. וְא"ר יוֹחָנָן: שִׁמְשׁוֹן דָּן אֶת יִשְׂרָאֵל כַּאֲבִיהֶם שֶׁבַּשָּׁמַיִם, שֶׁנֶּאֱמַר: °"דָּן יָדִין עַמּוֹ כְּאַחַד" וגו'. וְא"ר יוֹחָנָן: שִׁמְשׁוֹן עַל שְׁמוֹ שֶׁל הקב"ה נִקְרָא, שֶׁנֶּאֱמַר °"כִּי שֶׁמֶשׁ וּמָגֵן ה' אֱלֹהִים" וגו'. אֶלָּא מֵעַתָּה לֹא יִמָּחֶה! אֶלָּא, מֵעֵין שְׁמוֹ שֶׁל הקב"ה; מָה הקב"ה מָגֵן עַל כָּל הָעוֹלָם כּוּלּוֹ — אַף שִׁמְשׁוֹן מָגֵן בְּדוֹרוֹ עַל יִשְׂרָאֵל. *וְא"ר יוֹחָנָן: בִּלְעָם חִיגֵּר בְּרַגְלוֹ אַחַת הָיָה, שֶׁנֶּאֱמַר: °"וַיֵּלֶךְ שֶׁפִי". שִׁמְשׁוֹן חִיגֵּר בִּשְׁתֵּי רַגְלָיו הָיָה, שֶׁנֶּאֱמַר: °"שְׁפִיפֹן עֲלֵי אֹרַח".§ ת"ר: חֲמִשָּׁה נִבְרְאוּ מֵעֵין דּוּגְמָא שֶׁל מַעְלָה, וְכוּלָּן לָקוּ בָּהֶן. שִׁמְשׁוֹן בְּכֹחוֹ, שָׁאוּל בְּצַוָּארוֹ, אַבְשָׁלוֹם בִּשְׂעָרוֹ, צִדְקִיָּה בְּעֵינָיו, אָסָא בְּרַגְלָיו. שִׁמְשׁוֹן בְּכֹחוֹ — דִּכְתִיב: °"וַיָּסַר כֹּחוֹ מֵעָלָיו". שָׁאוּל בְּצַוָּארוֹ — דִּכְתִיב: °"וַיִּקַּח שָׁאוּל אֶת הַחֶרֶב וַיִּפֹּל עָלֶיהָ". אַבְשָׁלוֹם בִּשְׂעָרוֹ — כִּדְבָעֵינַן לְמֵימַר קַמָּן. צִדְקִיָּה בְּעֵינָיו — דִּכְתִיב: °"וְאֶת עֵינֵי צִדְקִיָּהוּ עִוֵּר". אָסָא בְּרַגְלָיו — דִּכְתִיב: °"רַק לְעֵת זִקְנָתוֹ חָלָה אֶת רַגְלָיו", *וְאָמַר רַב יְהוּדָה אָמַר רַב: שֶׁאֲחָזַתּוּ פּוֹדַגְרָא. א"ל מָר זוּטְרָא בְּרֵיהּ דְּרַב נַחְמָן לְרַב נַחְמָן: הֵיכִי דָּמֵי פּוֹדַגְרָא? א"ל: *כְּמַחַט בְּבָשָׂר הַחַי. מְנָא יָדַע? אִיכָּא דְּאָמְרִי: מֵיחַשׁ הֲוָה חָשׁ בֵּיהּ, °וְאִיכָּא דְּאָמְרִי: מֵרַבֵּיהּ שְׁמַע לֵיהּ, וְא"ד: °"סוֹד ה' לִירֵאָיו וּבְרִיתוֹ לְהוֹדִיעָם". דָּרַשׁ רָבָא: מִפְּנֵי מָה נֶעֱנַשׁ אָסָא — מִפְּנֵי שֶׁעָשָׂה אַנְגַּרְיָא בְּתַלְמִידֵי חֲכָמִים, שֶׁנֶּאֱמַר: °"וְהַמֶּלֶךְ אָסָא הִשְׁמִיעַ אֶת כָּל יְהוּדָה אֵין נָקִי". מַאי "אֵין נָקִי"? אָמַר רַב יְהוּדָה אָמַר רַב: אֲפִילּוּ חָתָן מֵחַדְרוֹ וְכַלָּה מֵחוּפָּתָהּ.*§ כְּתִיב: °"וַיֵּרֶד שִׁמְשׁוֹן תִּמְנָתָה", וּכְתִיב: °"הִנֵּה חָמִיךְ עֹלֶה תִמְנָתָה"! א"ר אֶלְעָזָר: שִׁמְשׁוֹן שֶׁנִּתְגַּנָּה בָּהּ — כְּתִיב בֵּיהּ יְרִידָה, יְהוּדָה שֶׁנִּתְעַלָּה בָּהּ — כְּתִיב בֵּיהּ עֲלִיָּה. ר' שְׁמוּאֵל בַּר נַחְמָנִי אָמַר: שְׁתֵּי תִמְנָאוֹת הָיוּ, חֲדָא בִּירִידָה וַחֲדָא בַּעֲלִיָּה. רַב פַּפָּא אָמַר: חֲדָא תִּמְנָה הֲוַאי, דְּאָתֵי מֵהַאי גִּיסָּא — יְרִידָה, וּדְאָתֵי מֵהַאי גִּיסָּא — עֲלִיָּה, כְּגוֹן וַרְדּוֹנְיָא וּבֵי בָּארֵי וְשׁוּקָא דְּנֶרֶשׁ. °"וַתֵּשֶׁב בְּפֶתַח עֵינַיִם". א"ר אֲלֶכְּסַנְדְּרִי: מְלַמֵּד שֶׁהָלְכָה וְיָשְׁבָה לָהּ בְּפִתְחוֹ שֶׁל אַבְרָהָם אָבִינוּ, מָקוֹם שֶׁכָּל עֵינַיִם צוֹפוֹת לִרְאוֹתוֹ. ר' חָנִין א"ר: מָקוֹם הוּא שֶׁשְּׁמוֹ עֵינַיִם, וְכֵן הוּא אוֹמֵר: °"תַּפּוּחַ וְהָעֵינָם". ר' שְׁמוּאֵל בַּר נַחְמָנִי אָמַר: שֶׁנָּתְנָה עֵינַיִם לִדְבָרֶיהָ. כְּשֶׁתְּבָעָהּ אָמַר לָהּ: שֶׁמָּא נָכְרִית אַתְּ? אָמְרָה לֵיהּ: גִּיּוֹרֶת אֲנִי. שֶׁמָּא אֵשֶׁת אִישׁ אַתְּ? אָמְרָה לֵיהּ: פְּנוּיָה אֲנִי. שֶׁמָּא קִיבֵּל בָּךְ אָבִיךְ קִידּוּשִׁין? אָמְרָה לֵיהּ: יְתוֹמָה אֲנִי. שֶׁמָּא טְמֵאָה אַתְּ? אָמְרָה לֵיהּ: טְהוֹרָה אֲנִי.§ °"וַיִּטַּע אֵשֶׁל בִּבְאֵר שָׁבַע". אָמַר רֵישׁ לָקִישׁ: מְלַמֵּד שֶׁעָשָׂה פַּרְדֵּס, וְנָטַע בּוֹ כָּל מִינֵי מְגָדִים. רַבִּי יְהוּדָה וְרַבִּי נְחֶמְיָה; חַד אָמַר: פַּרְדֵּס, וְחַד אָמַר: פּוּנְדָּק. בִּשְׁלָמָא לְמ"ד פַּרְדֵּס — הַיְינוּ דִּכְתִיב "וַיִּטַּע", אֶלָּא לְמ"ד פּוּנְדָּק — מַאי "וַיִּטַּע"? כִּדְכְתִיב: °"וַיִּטַּע אָהֳלֵי אַפַּדְנוֹ" וגו'. "וַיִּקְרָא שָׁם בְּשֵׁם ה' אֵל עוֹלָם". אָמַר רֵישׁ לָקִישׁ: אַל תִּיקְרֵי "וַיִּקְרָא" אֶלָּא

רש"י

הוּחַל שְׁבוּעָתוֹ שֶׁל אֲבִימֶלֶךְ. בָּטְלָה, לְשׁוֹן "לֹא יַחֵל דְּבָרוֹ" (במדבר ל). לְפִי שֶׁהֵם עָבְרוּ עַל הַשְּׁבוּעָה תְּחִילָּה. בַּמֶּה בֵּירְכוֹ. כָּל בְּרָכָה שֶׁבַּמִּקְרָא לְשׁוֹן רִיבּוּי הוּא, דָּבָר הַמַּרְבֶּה וּמָלוּי בּוֹ שׁוֹבַע, פויס"ן בְּלַעַ"ז. וּמַה בְּרָכָה נִמְצָא בּוֹ? לֹא מָצִינוּ עוֹשֶׁר בְּשִׁמְשׁוֹן?! שֶׁבֵּרְכוֹ בְּאַמָּתוֹ. לִהְיוֹת זַרְעוֹ כְּנַחַל שׁוֹטֵף. לְמַה שֶּׁנִּתְאַוָּה נִתְבָּרֵךְ. נְקַם אַחַת מִשְּׁתֵי עֵינַי. (ב) שְׂכַר אַחַת מֵעֵינַי תֵּן לִי בִּנְקָמָה זוֹ, וּשְׂכַר הָאַחֶרֶת לָעוֹלָם הַבָּא. שֶׁחוֹזֵר לַאֲחוֹרָיו. כְּשֶׁרָדְפִין אוֹתוֹ אֵינוֹ (מַרְחִיק) לִבְרוֹחַ, אֶלָּא חוֹזֵר עֲקַלְקַלּוֹת. שַׁעַר הָעִיר. (ג) בְּעַזָּה מִשְׁתַּעֵי קְרָא. עַל כְּתֵפָיו. כְּשִׁיעוּר כְּתֵפָיו. קַמֵּי דְּשָׁתֵי חַמְרָא חַמְרָא. לִפְנֵי כָּל אָדָם מְבִיאִין מַה שֶּׁהוּא רָגִיל בּוֹ. לִפְנֵי שׁוֹתֵי יַיִן מְבִיאִין יַיִן. קַמֵּי רְפוֹקָא גְּרִידַיָּא דּוּבְלָא. לִפְנֵי עוֹבֵד אֲדָמָה וְחוֹפֵר בְּגַנּוֹת, שֶׁרָגִיל לֶאֱכוֹל יָרָק — מְבִיאִין סַל מָלֵא יָרָק. דּוּבְלֵי — מִין יָרָק הוּא. קָארֵי וּבוּצִינֵי. מִין אֶחָד הוּא, אֶלָּא שֶׁאֵלּוּ גְּדוֹלִים וְאֵלּוּ קְטַנִּים. כְּלוֹמַר: בַּמֶּה שֶׁהוּא עוֹסֵק הִיא עֲסוּקָה. כְּאֶחָד. כִּיחִידוֹ שֶׁל עוֹלָם בְּמִשְׁפַּט צֶדֶק. שֶׁמֶשׁ. לְשׁוֹן חוֹמָה, כְּמוֹ "וְשַׂמְתִּי כַּדְכֹד שִׁמְשֹׁתַיִךְ" (ישעיה נד). עַל שְׁמוֹ שֶׁל הקב"ה. מַשְׁמַע שֶׁכִּינָהוּ בִּשְׁמוֹ שֶׁל הקב"ה מַמָּשׁ. מֵעֵין שְׁמוֹ. שֶׁאֵין שֶׁמֶשׁ שֵׁם מַמָּשׁ, אֶלָּא מָגֵן וּמַצִּיל. שֶׁפִי. אשלוייש"ש, כְּמוֹ "דְּשַׁף מִדּוּכְתֵּיהּ" (חולין דף מב:). שְׁפִיפוֹן. שְׁפִיָּיה כְּפוּלָה. מֵעֵין דּוּגְמָא כו'. נִשְׁתַּנּוּ מִן הַתַּחְתּוֹנִים לְתִפְאֶרֶת. וַיָּסַר כֹּחוֹ. לָא מַיְיתֵי רְאָיָה אֶלָּא דְּכוּלָּן לָקוּ. שָׁאוּל בְּצַוָּארוֹ. "וַיִּגְבַּהּ מִכָּל הָעָם מִשִּׁכְמוֹ" (שמואל א י). וַיִּפֹּל עָלֶיהָ. מָקוֹם שֶׁהוֹרְגִין בְּחֶרֶב, וְהַיְינוּ צַוָּאר. צִדְקִיָּה בְּעֵינָיו. לָא יָדַעְנָא מְנָלַן דְּנִשְׁתַּנָּה לְשֶׁבַח, וְכֵן אָסָא בְּרַגְלָיו. אֶלָּא כֵּן שָׁמַע מֵרַבּוֹ. פּוֹדַגְרָא. שֵׁם חוֹלִי הוּא שֶׁאוֹחֵז בָּרַגְלַיִם, וְקוֹרֵא לוֹ פּוֹדַגְרָא. נֶעֱנַשׁ אָסָא. לַחֲלוֹת. אַנְגַּרְיָא. עֲבוֹדַת הַמֶּלֶךְ. הִשְׁמִיעַ אֶת כָּל יְהוּדָה. הִזְעִיקָן. "וַיִּשְׂאוּ אֶת אַבְנֵי הָרָמָה", שֶׁהָיָה מֶלֶךְ יִשְׂרָאֵל בּוֹנֶה עָלֶיהָ כְּרַךְ, לְבִלְתִּי תֵּת יוֹצֵא וּבָא לְאָסָא. חָתָן. שֶׁכָּתוּב בּוֹ: "נָקִי יִהְיֶה לְבֵיתוֹ" וגו' (דברים כד). כְּתִיב וַיֵּרֶד שִׁמְשׁוֹן תִּמְנָתָה. אַלְמָא תִּמְנַת בִּירִידָה, וּכְתִיב: "עֹלֶה תִמְנָתָה" — אַלְמָא עֲלִיָּיה הִיא. וְשִׁמְשׁוֹן וִיהוּדָה תַּרְוַיְיהוּ בְּאֶרֶץ יִשְׂרָאֵל הֲווּ. שֶׁנִּתְגַּנָּה בָּהּ. שֶׁנָּשָׂא מִבְּנוֹת פְּלִשְׁתִּים הָאֲסוּרוֹת לוֹ. יְהוּדָה נִתְעַלָּה. שֶׁמִּשָּׁם נוֹלְדוּ פֶּרֶץ וָזֶרַח, שֶׁהֶעֱמִידוּ מְלָכִים וּנְבִיאִים בְּיִשְׂרָאֵל. דְּאָתֵי מֵהַאי גִּיסָּא. שֶׁהָיְתָה מְיוּשֶּׁבֶת בְּאֶמְצַע שִׁיפּוּעַ הָהָר. הַבָּא לָהּ מֵרֹאשׁ הָהָר — יוֹרֵד, הַבָּא לָהּ מֵרַגְלֵי הָהָר — עוֹלֶה. כְּגוֹן וַרְדּוֹנֵי וּבֵי בָּארֵי וְנֶרֶשׁ. עֲיָירוֹת הֵן הַיּוֹשְׁבוֹת בְּשִׁיפּוּעַ הֶהָרִים. מְצַפּוֹת לִרְאוֹתוֹ. שֶׁהָיוּ רְגִילִין לְהִתְקַבֵּל שָׁם וְלָלוּן, וְהָיָה חָבִיב עֲלֵיהֶם. שֶׁנָּתְנָה עֵינַיִם לִדְבָרֶיהָ. דּוּגְמָא וּפֶתַח הֵיתֵר נָתְנָה לְעַצְמָהּ, שֶׁאֵין עֲבֵירָה בַּדָּבָר. גִּיּוֹרֶת אֲנִי. וְאֵינִי גּוֹיָה (ד) וּרְאוּיָה לָךְ. פְּנוּיָה אֲנִי. וּמוּתֶּרֶת לְכָל אָדָם. יְתוֹמָה אֲנִי. (ה) וְהָיִיתִי קְטַנָּה, וְהִשִּׂיאוּנִי אִמִּי וְאַחַיי, וְאֵין נִישּׂוּאִין לְעֵר וְאוֹנָן כְּלוּם לֶאֱסוֹר עָלָיו מִשּׁוּם כַּלָּתוֹ. וְאֵין זְכוּת לָאֵם וְלָאַחִים לְהַשִּׂיא קְטַנָּה, אֶלָּא הָאָב זוֹכֶה בָּהּ, כִּדְכְתִיב: "אֶת בִּתִּי נָתַתִּי לָאִישׁ הַזֶּה" (דברים כב). וְלַהֲךְ סְבָרָא לָאו בִּתּוֹ שֶׁל שֵׁם הָיְתָה, שֶׁמִּשְׁפַּחַת שֵׁשִּׁים לְיַעֲקֹב כָּלוּ שְׁנוֹתָיו שֶׁל שֵׁם, וְיַעֲקֹב כְּבָר הָיָה יוֹתֵר מִבֶּן מֵאָה וָעֶשֶׂר. טְהוֹרָה אֲנִי. מִנִּדָּה. וְנָטַע בּוֹ. לַהֲנָאוֹת עוֹבְרִים וְשָׁבִים. פּוּנְדָּק. לָלוּן שָׁם אוֹרְחִים. וּלְשׁוֹן אש"ל — נוֹטָרִיקוֹן הוּא: אֲכִילָה שְׁתִיָּה לְוָיָה. שֶׁהָיָה מַאֲכִילָן וּמַשְׁקָן, וְאַחַ"כ מְלַוֶּה אוֹתָן. וַיִּטַּע אָהֳלֵי אַפַּדְנוֹ. פָּסוּק הוּא בְּדָנִיֵּאל עַל אֶחָד הַמְּהַלְּכִים. אֶלָּא

תוספות שאנץ

אלא מעתה לא ימחה. תימה לרבי: מאי שנא מ"שלום", דאמר בפ"ק דשבת (דף י:), אמר רב המנונא משמיה דעולא: אסור לאדם שיתן שלום לחבירו בבית המרחץ, משום דשם גופיה איקרי שלום, כדכתיב: "ויקרא לו ה' שלום", ולא קא חשיב ליה במס' סופרים (פ"ד) בהדי שמות שאין נמחקין! ונראה דתנא ושייר. ועדיף מחנון ורחום, דאמר בפרק "שבועת העדות" (שבועות דף לה.) דנמחק, דלא אשכחן שקרא הקב"ה שמו כך חנון. והכא פריך אהא דקאמר: על שמו של הקב"ה נקרא — משמע דשמו נקרא כך. והיינו דקא דחי: אלא מעין שמו, כמו חנון על שם שהוא חונן ומרחם על בריותיו.

נוח

זנות: הוחלה שבועתו של אבימלך וגו' שחולק על מה שפי' רש"י בספר שמואל [ב' ה'] שאותו היבוסי היה מזרעו של אבימלך ולא היו יכולין להורישו מפני השבועה שהיה כתוב על הצלמים כדאמר שם אלא סבירא ליה כמאן דאמר בפרקי דר' אליעזר א) שינתיים היה להם שכרת להם אברהם כשלקח מערת המכפלה ועל שם העיר נקרא יבוסי. אי שמא אע"פ שהוחלה כבר בימי שמשון אעפ"כ לא באו עליהם עד בימי דוד: קמי רפוקא גריוא דובלי. לפני חופר בגנות סל מלא ירק:

א) נ"ל בפרקי דר"א [פרק ל"ו] דשבועה אחרת היתה שכרת אברהם להם כשלקח מערת המכפלה מאת בני חת ועל שם וכו'.

נ"א מחזיק

[וכך העיד הרשב"א בתשובה סי' פ"א שבגמ' שלפניו ליתא מלת ושתים]

הגהות הב"ח

(א) גמ' יבא שועל שחוזר לאחוריו: (ב) רש"י ד"ה נקם אחת משתי עיני דדריש אמר שמשון רבש"ע שכר אחת וכו' זו בעוה"ז ושכר האחרת: (ג) ד"ה שער העיר בשערי עזה: (ד) ד"ה גיורת וכו' ואיני עובדת כוכבים עד שאין אני ראויה לך הס"ד: (ה) ד"ה יתומה אני שהייתי קטנה במיתת אבי והשיאוני וכו' ואין נישואי ער ואונן נשואין כלום וכו' שאין זכות:

(עי' ע"ז כח.)

(עי' בערוך ערך קר ו)

מגילה יג.

סנהדרין קה.

שם מח:

ברכות יח: שבת יג: קנב.

(פי' וכל שכן תלמידי חכמים ערוך ערך אנגריא) ברכות לה

גליון הש"ס

גמ' וא"ד מרביה. לעיל דף ד ע"ב: רש"י ד"ה יתומה אני כו' שמשנת ששים ליעקב. ע"ש וצ"ל חמשים:

אֶלָּא וַיַּקְרִיא, מְלַמֵּד שֶׁהִקְרִיא אַבְרָהָם אָבִינוּ לִשְׁמוֹ שֶׁל הקב"ה בְּפֶה כָּל עוֹבֵר וָשָׁב. כֵּיצַד? לְאַחַר שֶׁאָכְלוּ וְשָׁתוּ עָמְדוּ לְבָרְכוֹ, אָמַר לָהֶם: וְכִי מִשֶּׁלִּי אֲכַלְתֶּם? מִשֶּׁל אֱלֹהֵי עוֹלָם אֲכַלְתֶּם! הוֹדוּ וְשַׁבְּחוּ וּבָרְכוּ לְמִי שֶׁאָמַר וְהָיָה הָעוֹלָם. °"וַיִּרְאֶהָ יְהוּדָה וַיַּחְשְׁבֶהָ לְזוֹנָה כִּי כִסְּתָה פָּנֶיהָ". (בראשית לח) *מִשּׁוּם דְּכִסְּתָה פָּנֶיהָ חֲשָׁבָהּ לְזוֹנָה?! א"ר אֶלְעָזָר: שֶׁכִּסְּתָה פָּנֶיהָ בְּבֵית חָמִיהָ. דְּא"ר שְׁמוּאֵל בַּר נַחְמָנִי א"ר יוֹנָתָן: כָּל כַּלָּה שֶׁהִיא צְנוּעָה בְּבֵית חָמִיהָ – זוֹכָה וְיוֹצְאִין מִמֶּנָּה מְלָכִים וּנְבִיאִים. מְנָלַן – מִתָּמָר, נְבִיאִים – דִּכְתִיב: °"חֲזוֹן יְשַׁעְיָהוּ בֶן אָמוֹץ", (ישעיה א) מְלָכִים – מִדָּוִד, (א) וְאָמַר רַבִּי לֵוִי: דָּבָר זֶה מָסוֹרֶת בְּיָדֵינוּ מֵאֲבוֹתֵינוּ: אָמוֹץ וַאֲמַצְיָה אַחִים הָווּ, °"הִיא מוּצֵאת". (בראשית לח) "הִיא מִתּוֹצֵאת" מִיבְּעֵי לֵיהּ! א"ר אֶלְעָזָר: לְאַחַר שֶׁנִּמְצְאוּ סִימָנֶיהָ בָּא סַמָּאֵל וְרִיחֲקָן, בָּא גַּבְרִיאֵל וְקֵירְבָן. הַיְינוּ דִּכְתִיב °"לַמְנַצֵּחַ עַל יוֹנַת אֵלֶם רְחוֹקִים לְדָוִד מִכְתָּם", (תהלים נו) א"ר יוֹחָנָן: מִשָּׁעָה שֶׁנִּתְרַחֲקוּ סִימָנֶיהָ נַעֲשֵׂית כְּיוֹנָה אִילֶּמֶת. "לְדָוִד מִכְתָּם" – שֶׁיָּצָא מִמֶּנָּה דָּוִד שֶׁהָיָה מָךְ וְתָם לַכֹּל. דָּבָר אַחֵר: "מִכְתָּם" – שֶׁהָיְתָה מַכָּתוֹ תַּמָּה, שֶׁנּוֹלַד כְּשֶׁהוּא מָהוּל. דָּבָר אַחֵר: "מִכְתָּם" – כְּשֵׁם שֶׁבְּקַטְנוּתוֹ הִקְטִין עַצְמוֹ אֵצֶל מִי שֶׁגָּדוֹל מִמֶּנּוּ לִלְמוֹד תּוֹרָה – כָּךְ בְּגְדוּלָּתוֹ. (ב) °"וְהִיא שָׁלְחָה אֶל חָמִיהָ לֵאמֹר לְאִישׁ אֲשֶׁר אֵלֶּה לּוֹ אָנֹכִי הָרָה". (בראשית לח) וְתֵימָא לֵיהּ מֵימַר! *אָמַר רַב זוּטְרָא בַּר טוֹבִיָּה אָמַר רַב, וְאָמְרִי לָהּ אָמַר רַב חָנָא בַּר בִּיזְנָא אָמַר רַבִּי שִׁמְעוֹן חֲסִידָא, וְאָמְרִי לָהּ אָמַר רַבִּי יוֹחָנָן מִשּׁוּם ר' שִׁמְעוֹן בֶּן יוֹחַי: נוֹחַ לוֹ לְאָדָם שֶׁיַּפִּיל עַצְמוֹ לְתוֹךְ כִּבְשַׁן הָאֵשׁ ואַל יַלְבִּין פְּנֵי חֲבֵירוֹ בָּרַבִּים. מְנָלַן – מִתָּמָר. °"הַכֶּר נָא". (שם) א"ר חָמָא בְּרַבִּי חֲנִינָא: בְּ"הַכֶּר" בִּישֵּׂר לְאָבִיו, בְּ"הַכֶּר" בִּישְּׂרוּהוּ. בְּ"הַכֶּר" בִּישֵּׂר – °"הַכֶּר נָא הַכְּתֹנֶת בִּנְךָ הִיא", (שם לז) בְּ"הַכֶּר" בִּישְּׂרוּהוּ – "הַכֶּר נָא לְמִי". "נָא". *אֵין "נָא" אֶלָּא לְשׁוֹן בַּקָּשָׁה, אָמְרָה לֵיהּ: בְּבַקָּשָׁה מִמְּךָ, הַכֶּר פְּנֵי בּוֹרַאֲךָ וְאַל תַּעֲלִים עֵינֶיךָ מִמֶּנִּי. °"וַיַּכֵּר יְהוּדָה וַיֹּאמֶר צָדְקָה מִמֶּנִּי". (שם לח) הַיְינוּ *דְּאָמַר רַב חָנִין בַּר בִּיזְנָא א"ר שִׁמְעוֹן חֲסִידָא: יוֹסֵף שֶׁקִּידֵּשׁ ש"ש בַּסֵּתֶר – זָכָה וְהוֹסִיפוּ לוֹ אוֹת אַחַת מִשְּׁמוֹ שֶׁל הקב"ה, דִּכְתִיב: °"עֵדוּת בִּיהוֹסֵף שָׂמוֹ". (תהלים פא) (ג) יְהוּדָה שֶׁקִּידֵּשׁ ש"ש בְּפַרְהֶסְיָא – זָכָה וְנִקְרָא כּוּלּוֹ עַל שְׁמוֹ שֶׁל הקב"ה. כֵּיוָן שֶׁהוֹדָה וְאָמַר "צָדְקָה מִמֶּנִּי" יָצְתָה בַּת קוֹל וְאָמְרָה: אַתָּה הִצַּלְתָּ תָּמָר וּשְׁנֵי בָנֶיהָ מִן הָאוּר – חַיֶּיךָ שֶׁאֲנִי מַצִּיל בִּזְכוּתְךָ ג' מִבָּנֶיךָ מִן הָאוּר. מַאן נִינְהוּ – חֲנַנְיָה מִישָׁאֵל וַעֲזַרְיָה. "צָדְקָה מִמֶּנִּי". מְנָא יָדַע? יָצְתָה בַּת קוֹל וְאָמְרָה: מִמֶּנִּי יָצְאוּ כְּבוּשִׁים. °"וְלֹא יָסַף עוֹד לְדַעְתָּהּ". (בראשית לח) אָמַר שְׁמוּאֵל סָבָא חֲמוּהּ דְּרַב שְׁמוּאֵל בַּר אַמִּי מִשְּׁמֵיהּ דְּרַב שְׁמוּאֵל בַּר אַמִּי: כֵּיוָן שֶׁיְּדָעָהּ – שׁוּב *לֹא פָּסַק מִמֶּנָּה. כְּתִיב הָכָא "וְלֹא יָסַף עוֹד לְדַעְתָּהּ" וּכְתִיב הָתָם °"קוֹל גָּדוֹל וְלֹא יָסָף". (דברים ה) § "אַבְשָׁלוֹם נִתְגָּאָה בִּשְׂעָרוֹ" וכו'. § ת"ר: אַבְשָׁלוֹם בִּשְׂעָרוֹ מָרַד, שֶׁנֶּאֱמַר: °"וּכְאַבְשָׁלוֹם לֹא הָיָה אִישׁ יָפֶה וגו' וּבְגַלְּחוֹ אֶת רֹאשׁוֹ (וגו') וְהָיָה מִקֵּץ יָמִים לַיָּמִים אֲשֶׁר יְגַלֵּחַ כִּי כָבֵד עָלָיו וְגִלְּחוֹ וְשָׁקַל אֶת שְׂעַר רֹאשׁוֹ מָאתַיִם שְׁקָלִים בְּאֶבֶן הַמֶּלֶךְ". (שמואל ב יד) תָּנָא: אֶבֶן שֶׁאַנְשֵׁי טְבֶרְיָא וְאַנְשֵׁי צִיפּוֹרִי שׁוֹקְלִים בָּהּ – לְפִיכָךְ נִתְלָה בִּשְׂעָרוֹ, שֶׁנֶּאֱמַר: °"וַיִּקָּרֵא אַבְשָׁלוֹם לִפְנֵי עַבְדֵי דָוִד וְאַבְשָׁלוֹם רוֹכֵב עַל הַפֶּרֶד וַיָּבֹא הַפֶּרֶד תַּחַת שׂוֹבֶךְ הָאֵלָה הַגְּדוֹלָה (ד) וַיֶּאֱחַז רֹאשׁוֹ בָאֵלָה וַיֻּתַּן בֵּין הַשָּׁמַיִם וּבֵין הָאָרֶץ וְהַפֶּרֶד אֲשֶׁר תַּחְתָּיו עָבָר". (שם יח) [שְׁקַל סַפְסֵירָא בְּעָא לְמִיפְסְקֵיהּ.] תָּנָא דְּבֵי רַבִּי יִשְׁמָעֵאל: בְּאוֹתָהּ שָׁעָה (ה) נִבְקַע שְׁאוֹל מִתַּחְתָּיו. °"וַיִּרְגַּז הַמֶּלֶךְ וַיַּעַל עַל עֲלִיַּת הַשַּׁעַר וַיֵּבְךְּ וְכֹה אָמַר בְּלֶכְתּוֹ בְּנִי אַבְשָׁלוֹם בְּנִי בְנִי [אַבְשָׁלוֹם] מִי יִתֵּן מוּתִי אֲנִי תַחְתֶּיךָ אַבְשָׁלוֹם בְּנִי בְנִי וְהַמֶּלֶךְ לָאַט אֶת פָּנָיו וַיִּזְעַק הַמֶּלֶךְ קוֹל גָּדוֹל בְּנִי אַבְשָׁלוֹם אַבְשָׁלוֹם בְּנִי בְנִי". (שם יט) הָנֵי תְּמַנְיָא (ו) "בְּנִי" לָמָּה? שִׁבְעָה דְּאַסְּקֵיהּ מִשִּׁבְעָה מְדוֹרֵי גֵיהִנָּם; וְאִידָךְ, אִיכָּא דְּאָמְרִי דְּקָרֵיב רֵישֵׁיהּ לְגַבֵּי גּוּפֵיהּ, וְאִיכָּא דְּאָמְרִי דְּאַיְיתֵיהּ לְעָלְמָא דְּאָתֵי. °"וְאַבְשָׁלוֹם לָקַח וַיַּצֶּב לוֹ בְחַיָּיו". (שם יח) מַאי לָקַח? *אָמַר רֵישׁ לָקִישׁ: שֶׁלָּקַח מִקָּח רַע לְעַצְמוֹ. "אֶת מַצֶּבֶת אֲשֶׁר בְּעֵמֶק הַמֶּלֶךְ" וגו'. א"ר חֲנִינָא בַּר פַּפָּא: בְּעֵצָה עֲמוּקָּה שֶׁל מַלְכּוֹ שֶׁל עוֹלָם, דִּכְתִיב

רש"י

אלא ויקריא. למד לבריות לקרות שם בשם ה' אל עולם. **ביצד לאחר שאכלו ושתו.** משלו, היו עומדין לברכו לאברהם, והוא אומר להם: וכי משלי אכלתם? **שכסתה פניה בבית חמיה.** ולא ראה אותה כל הימים שגדלה בביתו, לפיכך לא הכיר בה (ז). **אמוץ.** אביו של ישעיהו, ואמציה מלך יהודה – אחים הוו. ואמציה מזרע דוד היה, ואמוץ אחיו נביא היה, אלמא נביאים נפיק מינה. **היא מיתוצאת.** הוי משמע לשון הוצאה בעל כרחה, "היא מוצאת" – משמע לשון מאליה. **סימניה.** חותמו ופתילים ומטה. **שבא סמאל,** שהוא שר של אדום, וריחקן, כדי שתשרף ולא יצא דוד ממנה, המכה את אדום בגיא מלח. **יונת אלם רחוקים.** על עסקי הרחקה, שנעשו סימניה רחוקים. **לדוד מכתם.** לאותה (ח) שהיתה ראויה ועומדת לצאת ממנה דוד. **שהוא מך.** עניו. **ותם.** תמים בדרכיו. **מכתו תמה.** מקום מילה, שהוא ראוי למכה – היה תם ושלם, שלא הוצרך לחסרו. **ד"א כשם שבקטנותו.** קודם שמלך. **כך בגדולתו.** לאחר שמלך. **ולשון "מכתם"** – שהיתה תמה מכתו מתחלתו ועד סופו, לא נחסר ענוותנותו ולא נשתנית. **והיא שלחה וגו' לאיש אשר אלה לו.** ולא שלחה לו לאמר: "ממך אני הרה, והרי סימנין שלך". **ותימא ליה מימר.** לשליח: "אמור לו שממנו אני הרה, ואלו סימניו". **ואל ילבין כו'.** אף זו נוח היה לה לישרף ואל תלבין פניו. לפיכך שלחה לו, אם יודה ויגלה הוא עצמו את הדבר – יגלה, ואם לאו – תשרף, ולא תגלה היא את הדבר. **בהכר בישר.** אל אביו דבר שנלטער בו, וב"הכר" בשרוהו. **מנא ידע.** שממנו היא מעוברת? שמא אף אחרים באו עליה. **ויאמר.** בת קול אמרה. **כבושים.** דברים עלומים שנגזרו מלפני, שיצאו מזו מלכים. ואי אפשר לצאת אלא מיהודה, דכתיב (בראשית מט): "גור אריה יהודה". **כבושים** – דברי סתר, גזירת המלך, כמו "בהדי כבשי דקודשא בריך הוא למה לך", בברכות (דף י.) גבי חזקיה. **כיון שידעה.** שידע בה שהיא צדקת, ולשם שמים נתכוונה. **מקץ ימים לימים.** משנה לשנה. שנזיר עולם היה ומגלח אחת לי"ב חודש. **דקריב רישיה לגבי גופיה.** שהיה ראשו מושלך רחוק מגופו, וקירבו. **שלקח מקח רע לעצמו.** והכי קאמר קרא: ואבשלום לקח לו את (ט) המצבה הזאת בחייו, ויצב לו את מצבת אשר בעמק המלך. **עצה עמוקה.** של הקב"ה, שהוא מלך עולם, שגזר על עון מעשה בת שבע. הנני מקים

תוספות

נוח לו לאדם שיפיל את עצמו לתוך כבשן האש. כדאמר בפ' "הזהב" (ב"מ דף נח:): כל היורדין לגיהנם עולין, חוץ משלשה, וחד מינייהו המלבין פני חבירו ברבים. ואומר נמי (שם נט.): נוח לו לאדם שיבעול ספק אשת איש ואל ילבין פני חבירו ברבים, מנלן – מדוד. ונראה האי דלא חשיב ליה (פסחים דף כה.) בהדי ג' עבירות שאין עומדים בפני פקוח נפש: עבודה זרה וגילוי עריות ושפיכות דמים – משום דעבירת הלבנת פנים אינה מפורשת בתורה, ולא נקט אלא עבירות המפורשות.

יצאת בת קול ואמרה ממני יצאו כבושים. בשלהי מסכת מכות (דף כג:) מסיק דהכי גמירי לה.

דקרב רישא לגבי גופיה. תימה: רבי מאיר דאמר ב"חלק" (סנהדרין דף קג:): אבשלום אין לו חלק לעולם הבא, א"כ סבירא ליה דקרב רישיה לגבי גופיה, ולא סבירא ליה דאייתיה לעלמא דאתי – מכל מקום אסקיה משבעה מדורי דגיהנם. ואם כן אמאי לא חשיב ליה בהדי אחז ואחזיה, דאמר (שם קג.): לא חיין ולא נידונין? וי"ל: דלא חשיב אלא מלכים.

דאייתיה לעלמא דאתי. ואי קשיא: הא אמרו ב"חלק" (סנהדרין דף קד.): ברא מזכי אבא, אבא לא מזכי ברא, כדכתיב: "ואין מידי מציל" – אין אברהם מציל את ישמעאל, ולא יצחק את עשו. אבל הבן מציל את האב, כגון יאשיהו, שלא מנו את אמון! וי"ל: משום דאבשלום נטל את שלו בעולם הזה, שנהרג במיתה משונה – הועילה לו תפלת אביו. דומיא דיהויקים, דאמר התם שהיה כתוב על גולגלתו "זאת ועוד אחרת", ונפרע ממנו לאחר מיתה – לא מנו אותו. ועוד: אבשלום לא עבד עבודה זרה. א"נ, מצי למימר: הא דאמר אבא לא מזכי ברא – היינו משום כבוד האב אין מונעין מלמנותו עם רשעים בלא תפלה, אבל תפלה מועלת, ודוד התפלל על אבשלום.

ולעולם

עין משפט נר מצוה

נט א מיי' פ"ו מהלכות דעות הלכה ח:

תוספות שאנץ

וכי משלי אכלתם הודו וברכו למי שאמר והיה העולם. יש במדרש שלא רצו לברך ברצונם עד שאמר להם אברהם פרעו מה שאכלתם ושתיתם והיה אומר להם שהוא עולה למנין גדול כי היו במדבר והיה טורח גדול להביא שם המאכל והמשתה וכשראו כך כי היה רוצה אברהם שיפרעו הכל אז ברכו הקב"ה שלא ברצונם על מנת שלא יפרעו שום דבר: שכסתה פניה בבית חמיה אע"פ שהיה בלבו שהיא תמר טעה בכך לומר אחרת היא שהרי תמר צנועה היתה. א) ל"א שכיסתה פניה בבית חמיה לא ראה אותה כל הימים שגדלה בביתו לפי' לא הכירה: יצאו כבושין דברים עלומים שנגזרו מלפני שיצאו מזו מלכים ואי אפשר לצאת אלא מיהודה כדכתיב גור אריה יהודה כבושין דברי סתר ל"ה.

א) עי' בהגהות הב"ח דגם ברש"י נ"ל ב' הפירושים.

גליון הש"ס

גמ' בהכר בשרוהו. כעין זה לקמן דף יג ע"ב: **שם** יוסף שקדש ש"ש. לקמן דף לו ע"ב: **רש"י** ד"ה מקץ ימים כו' אחת לי"ב חדש. נזיר דף ד ע"א:

מסורת הש"ס

מגילה י:

ב"מ נט. כתובות סז: ברכות מג:

[ברכות ט. סנהדרין מג. פט:] [לקמן לו:]

[סנהדרין יז.]

[סנהדרין קג:]

הגהות הב"ח

(א) גמ' דאמר ר' לוי: (ב) שם כך בגדולתו הקטין עצמו אצל מי שגדול ממנו ללמוד תורה והיא שלחה: (ג) שם יהודה שקדש ש"ש. נ"ב ע"ל פ' אלו נאמרין דף לו ע"ב: (ד) שם הגדולה ויחזק ראשו באלה ויותן: (ה) שם באותה שעה ראה גיהנם נבקע מתחתיו: (ו) שם תמניא זימני בני למה: (ז) רש"י ד"ה שכסתה וכו' לא הכיר בה ל"א שכסתה פניה בבית חמיה וה"ק אע"פ שהיה בלבו שהיא תמר טועה היה בכך לומר אחרת היא שהרי תמר צנועה היא הס"ד: (ח) ד"ה לדוד מכתם לאותה שהיא ראויה: (ט) ד"ה שלקח וכו' לקח לו את המצבה הזאת בחייו:

דִּכְתִיב: "הִנְנִי מֵקִים עָלֶיךָ רָעָה מִבֵּיתֶךָ". כַּיּוֹצֵא בַּדָּבָר אַתָּה אוֹמֵר: "וַיִּשְׁלָחֵהוּ מֵעֵמֶק חֶבְרוֹן", א"ר חֲנִינָא בַּר פָּפָּא: בְּעֵצָה עֲמוּקָּה שֶׁל אוֹתוֹ צַדִּיק שֶׁקָּבוּר בְּחֶבְרוֹן, דִּכְתִיב: "יָדוֹעַ תֵּדַע כִּי גֵר יִהְיֶה זַרְעֲךָ". "כִּי אָמַר אֵין לִי בֵן". וְלָא הָווּ לֵיהּ בְּנֵי? וְהָכְתִיב: "וַיִּוָּלְדוּ לְאַבְשָׁלוֹם שְׁלֹשָׁה בָנִים וּבַת אַחַת"! אָמַר רַב יִצְחָק בַּר אַבְדִּימִי: שֶׁלֹּא הָיָה לוֹ בֵּן הָגוּן לְמַלְכוּת. רַב חִסְדָּא אָמַר: גְּמִירִי, כָּל הַשּׂוֹרֵף תְּבוּאָתוֹ שֶׁל חֲבֵירוֹ — אֵינוֹ מַנִּיחַ בֵּן לְיוֹרְשׁוֹ. וְאִיהוּ קַלְיֵיהּ לְדְיוֹאָב, דִּכְתִיב: "וַיֹּאמֶר אֶל עֲבָדָיו רְאוּ חֶלְקַת יוֹאָב אֶל יָדִי וְלוֹ שָׁם שְׂעוֹרִים לְכוּ וְהַצִּיתוּהָ בָאֵשׁ וַיַּצִּיתוּ עַבְדֵי אַבְשָׁלוֹם אֶת הַחֶלְקָה בָּאֵשׁ". § "וְכֵן לְעִנְיַן הַטּוֹבָה מִרְיָם" וכו'. § מִי דָּמֵי? הָתָם — חֲדָא שַׁעְתָּא, הָכָא — שִׁבְעָה יוֹמֵי! אָמַר אַבַּיֵי: אֵימָא "וּלְעִנְיַן הַטּוֹבָה אֵינוֹ כֵן". א"ל רָבָא: הָא "וְכֵן לְעִנְיַן הַטּוֹבָה" קָתָנֵי! אֶלָּא אָמַר רָבָא, הָכִי קָתָנֵי: וְכֵן לְעִנְיַן הַטּוֹבָה דִּבְאוֹתָהּ מִדָּה. וּלְעוֹלָם *מִדָּה טוֹבָה מְרוּבָּה מִמִּדַּת פּוּרְעָנוּת.

"וַתֵּתַצַּב אֲחוֹתוֹ מֵרָחוֹק". א"ר יִצְחָק: פָּסוּק זֶה כּוּלּוֹ עַל שֵׁם שְׁכִינָה נֶאֱמַר: "וַתֵּתַצַּב" — דִּכְתִיב: "וַיָּבֹא ה' וַיִּתְיַצַּב" וגו', "אֲחוֹתוֹ" — דִּכְתִיב: "אֱמֹר לַחָכְמָה אֲחֹתִי אָתְּ", "מֵרָחוֹק" — דִּכְתִיב: "מֵרָחוֹק ה' נִרְאָה לִי", "לָדַעַת" — דִּכְתִיב: "כִּי אֵל דֵּעוֹת ה'". "מַה" — דִּכְתִיב "מָה ה' אֱלֹהֶיךָ שׁוֹאֵל מֵעִמָּךְ". "יֵעָשֶׂה" — דִּכְתִיב: "כִּי לֹא יַעֲשֶׂה [ה'] אֱלֹהִים דָּבָר", "לוֹ" — דִּכְתִי': "וַיִּקְרָא לוֹ ה' שָׁלוֹם". § "וַיָּקָם מֶלֶךְ חָדָשׁ" וגו'. *רַב וּשְׁמוּאֵל; חַד אָמַר: חָדָשׁ מַמָּשׁ, וְחַד אָמַר: שֶׁנִּתְחַדְּשׁוּ גְּזֵירוֹתָיו. מַאן דְּאָמַר חָדָשׁ מַמָּשׁ — דִּכְתִיב "חָדָשׁ", וּמַאן דְּאָמַר שֶׁנִּתְחַדְּשׁוּ גְּזֵירוֹתָיו — דְּלָא כְּתִיב "וַיָּמָת וַיִּמְלוֹךְ", "אֲשֶׁר לֹא יָדַע אֶת יוֹסֵף" — דַּהֲוָה דָּמֵי כְּמַאן דְּלָא יָדַע לֵיהּ כְּלָל. "וַיֹּאמֶר אֶל עַמּוֹ הִנֵּה עַם בְּנֵי יִשְׂרָאֵל" — תָּנָא: הוּא הִתְחִיל בְּעֵצָה תְּחִילָּה — לְפִיכָךְ לָקָה תְּחִילָּה. הוּא הִתְחִיל בְּעֵצָה תְּחִילָּה — דִּכְתִיב: "וַיֹּאמֶר אֶל עַמּוֹ", לְפִיכָךְ לָקָה תְּחִילָּה — כִּדְכְתִיב: "וּבְכָה וּבְעַמְּךָ וּבְכָל עֲבָדֶיךָ". "הָבָה נִתְחַכְּמָה לוֹ". "לָהֶם" מִיבָּעֵי לֵיהּ! א"ר חָמָא בְּרַבִּי חֲנִינָא: בֹּאוּ וְנֶחְכַּם לְמוֹשִׁיעָן שֶׁל יִשְׂרָאֵל: בַּמֶּה נְדוּנֵם? נְדוּנֵם בָּאֵשׁ — כְּתִיב: "כִּי הִנֵּה ה' בָּאֵשׁ יָבֹא", וּכְתִיב: "כִּי בָאֵשׁ ה' נִשְׁפָּט" וגו', בַּחֶרֶב — כְּתִיב: [*"וּבְחַרְבּוֹ אֶת כָּל בָּשָׂר"]. אֶלָּא בֹּאוּ וּנְדוּנֵם בַּמַּיִם, *שֶׁכְּבָר נִשְׁבַּע הקב"ה שֶׁאֵינוֹ מֵבִיא מַבּוּל לָעוֹלָם, שֶׁנֶּאֱמַר: "כִּי מֵי נֹחַ זֹאת לִי" וגו'. וְהֵן אֵינָן יוֹדְעִין שֶׁעַל כָּל הָעוֹלָם כּוּלּוֹ אֵינוֹ מֵבִיא — אֲבָל עַל אוּמָּה אַחַת הוּא מֵבִיא. אִי נַמִי, הוּא אֵינוֹ מֵבִיא, אֲבָל הֵן בָּאִין וְנוֹפְלִין בְּתוֹכוֹ, וְכֵן הוּא אוֹמֵר: "וּמִצְרַיִם נָסִים לִקְרָאתוֹ". וְהַיְינוּ דְּא"ר אֶלְעָזָר: מַאי דִּכְתִיב "כִּי בַדָּבָר אֲשֶׁר זָדוּ עֲלֵיהֶם" — בַּקְּדֵירָה שֶׁבִּישְּׁלוּ בָּהּ נִתְבַּשְּׁלוּ. *מַאי מַשְׁמַע דְּהַאי "זָדוּ" לִישָּׁנָא דִּקְדֵירָה הוּא — דִּכְתִיב: "וַיָּזֶד יַעֲקֹב נָזִיד". *א"ר חִיָּיא בַּר אַבָּא א"ר סִימַאי: שְׁלֹשָׁה הָיוּ בְּאוֹתָהּ עֵצָה: בִּלְעָם, וְאִיּוֹב, וְיִתְרוֹ. בִּלְעָם שֶׁיָּעַץ — נֶהֱרַג; אִיּוֹב שֶׁשָּׁתַק — נִידּוֹן בְּיִסּוּרִין, יִתְרוֹ שֶׁבָּרַח — *זָכוּ מִבְּנֵי בָנָיו שֶׁיָּשְׁבוּ בְּלִשְׁכַּת הַגָּזִית, שֶׁנֶּאֱמַר: "וּמִשְׁפְּחוֹת סוֹפְרִים יוֹשְׁבֵי יַעְבֵּץ תִּרְעָתִים שִׁמְעָתִים סוּכָתִים הֵמָּה הַקִּינִים הַבָּאִים מֵחַמַּת אֲבִי בֵית רֵכָב", וּכְתִיב: "וּבְנֵי קֵינִי חֹתֵן מֹשֶׁה" וגו'. § "וְנִלְחַם בָּנוּ וְעָלָה מִן הָאָרֶץ". "וְעָלִינוּ" מִיבָּעֵי לֵיהּ! א"ר אַבָּא בַּר כַּהֲנָא: כְּאָדָם שֶׁמְּקַלֵּל אֶת עַצְמוֹ, וְתוֹלֶה קִלְלָתוֹ בַּחֲבֵירוֹ. "וַיָּשִׂימוּ עָלָיו שָׂרֵי מִסִּים". "עֲלֵיהֶם" מִיבָּעֵי לֵיהּ! תָּנָא דְּבֵי ר' אֶלְעָזָר בְּר' שִׁמְעוֹן: מְלַמֵּד שֶׁהֵבִיאוּ מַלְבֵּן וְתָלוּ לוֹ לְפַרְעֹה בְּצַוָּארוֹ, וְכָל אֶחָד וְאֶחָד מִיִּשְׂרָאֵל שֶׁאָמַר לָהֶם: אִיסְטְנִיס אֲנִי, אָמְרוּ לוֹ: כְּלוּם אִיסְטְנִיס אַתָּה יוֹתֵר מִפַּרְעֹה? "שָׂרֵי מִסִּים" — דָּבָר שֶׁמְּשִׂימִים (לְבֵנִים). "לְמַעַן עַנּוֹתוֹ בְּסִבְלוֹתָם". [עַנּוֹתָם מִיבָּעֵי לֵיהּ]! לְמַעַן עַנּוֹתוֹ לְפַרְעֹה, בְּסִבְלוֹתָם דְּיִשְׂרָאֵל. "וַיִּבֶן עָרֵי מִסְכְּנוֹת לְפַרְעֹה". רַב וּשְׁמוּאֵל, חַד אָמַר: שֶׁמְּסַכְּנוֹת אֶת בַּעֲלֵיהֶן, וְח"א: שֶׁמְּמַסְכְּנוֹת אֶת בַּעֲלֵיהֶן. דְּאָמַר מָר: *כָּל הָעוֹסֵק בְּבִנְיָן מִתְמַסְכֵּן. "אֶת פִּיתֹם וְאֶת רַעְמְסֵס". רַב וּשְׁמוּאֵל; חַד אָמַר: פִּיתוֹם שְׁמָהּ, וְלָמָּה נִקְרָא שְׁמָהּ רַעְמְסֵס — שֶׁרִאשׁוֹן רִאשׁוֹן *מִתְרוֹסֵס. וְחַד אָמַר: רַעְמְסֵס שְׁמָהּ, וְלָמָּה נִקְרָא שְׁמָהּ פִּיתוֹם — שֶׁרִאשׁוֹן רִאשׁוֹן פִּי תְהוֹם בּוֹלְעוֹ. "וְכַאֲשֶׁר יְעַנּוּ אוֹתוֹ כֵּן יִרְבֶּה וְכֵן יִפְרֹץ" "כֵּן רַבּוּ וְכֵן פָּרְצוּ" מִיבָּעֵי לֵיהּ! אָמַר ר"ל: רוּחַ הַקֹּדֶשׁ מְבַשַּׂרְתָּן: "כֵּן יִרְבֶּה וְכֵן יִפְרוֹץ". § "וַיָּקֻצוּ מִפְּנֵי בְּנֵי יִשְׂרָאֵל" — מְלַמֵּד שֶׁהָיוּ דּוֹמִין בְּעֵינֵיהֶם כְּקוֹצִים. "וַיַּעֲבִדוּ מִצְרַיִם אֶת בְּנֵי יִשְׂרָאֵל בְּפָרֶךְ"

רש"י

מקים וגו'. הכ"ב אבשלום אותה עלה וקיימה. מגפת – דבריו של הקב"ה, כדכתיב: "לעולם ה' דברך נצב" (תהלים קיט). "ויקרא למצבת על שמו" – גרס לאותה רעה שתקרא על שמו, "ויקרא לה יד אבשלום" – כך היא נקראת. וישלחהו מעמק חברון. דיוסף משתעי קרא, כששלחו יעקב אל אחיו, והוא תחלת סיבת ירידת ישראל למצרים. של אותו צדיק שקבור בחברון. אברהם. אינו בן. דיותר ממה שהוא מודד מודדים לו. דבאותה מדה. דוגמא מעין אותו ענין. ומיהו, יותר ממה שעשה משתלם, דמדה טובה מרובה בתשלומין ממדת פורענות. אמור לחכמה. שהיא אצל הקב"ה, ומפיו, שנאמר: "כי ה' יתן חכמה מפיו דעת ותבונה" (משלי ב). דלא כתיב וימת. מלך מצרים וימלוך תחתיו אחר. ונתחכם למושיען. לבקש לנו חכמה כנגדו. במה נידונם. שלא יוכל לדון אותנו בו. שידענו מדרכיו שמודד מדה כנגד מדה לדור המבול ולאנשי סדום. כי באש ה' נשפט. וכן ישיב לנו גמול (א). שבשלו. לשון "ויזד יעקב נזיד" (בראשית כה). באותה עצה. ד"נתחכמה לו". יושבי יעבץ. תלמידי יעבץ. (ב) אדם גדול בתורה היה, כדכתיב (דה"א ד): "ויקרא יעבץ לאלהי ישראל אם ברך תברכני" – בתורה, "והרבית את גבולי" – בתלמידים וגו', "ויבא אלהים את אשר שאל" (תמורה טז.). תרעתים. מפרש בספרי: ששמעו תרועה בהר סיני. ל"א: תרעתים – על שם שהיו יושבים בשערי ירושלים. שמעתים. ששמעו מצות אביהם. דבבני יונדב בן רכב משתעי קרא, והם היו מבני בניו של יתרו, כדמפרש ואזיל "המה הקינים". סוכתים. על שם שהיו יושבים בסוכות, כדכתיב (ירמיה לה): "ונשב באהלים". וקרי להו "משפחת סופרים" – דהיינו סנהדרין. וכן "תרעתים" – זקני שער. ועלינו מן הארץ מבעי ליה. יגרשונו מן הארץ. מאי "ועלה" – הלואי שיצאו שונאיהם מארצם, הואיל ויראים מפניהם. מלבן. כמין דפוס שבו עושין הלבנים, שממלאין אותו טיט ומחליקין אותו, והיא הלבנה. ותלו לו לפרעה. דעליה קאי קרא, ומיניה סליק: "ויאמר אל עמו וגו' הבה נתחכמה לו וגו' וישימו עליו שרי מסים". אסטנים. מפונק, ואינו יכול לעשות מלאכה. שרי מסים. דבר שמשים רידוי של שומה, שמרגילין ומשימין לעבודה. אותו מלבן שתלו לו, היה לישראל רידוי של השמה. למען ענותו לפרעה. בשביל סבלותם דישראל, שיטו שכם לסבול. שמסכנות את בעליהן. שעל ידי אותן הערים ואותה עבודה נסתכנו מצרים ליטבע בים. שממסכנות. מדלדלות. כדכתיב: "וינצלו את מצרים", ובשביל עבודה זו אירע להן. ולהאי לישנא לא גרסינן: דאמר מר (ג) כל העוסק בבנין מתמסכן. ומאן דגריס לה מתרגמינן להך דרב ושמואל נמי אכל בניינים של כל אדם; מסכנות – פעמים שנופל מהבנין *ומת, ממסכנות – שמביאות את האדם לידי עניות, דאמר מר: כל העוסק בבנין מתמסכן. ראשון ראשון מתרוסס. כשהיו בונין קצת היה מתרוסס ונופל, וחוזרין ובונין והוא נופל. פי התהום בולעו. נבלע בארץ. רוח הקדש מבשרתן. לישראל, ואומר למצרים: אין מועיל לכם, "כן ירבה" תמיד, וכן יפרוץ. ויקוצו. היה דומה להן. כאילו עיניהם וגופן מלאים קוצים, כראותם את ישראל פרים ורבים. בפרך

תוספות

ולעולם מדה טובה מרובה ממדת פורענות. וא"ת: הא מלינו מדת פורענות גדולה ממדת טובה, דכתיב: "איכה ירדוף אחד אלף ושנים יניסו רבבה" (דברים לב) גבי מדת פורענות, וגבי מדה טובה כתיב: "ורדפו מכם חמשה מאה" (ויקרא כו)! וי"ל: דעדיין גבי מדת פורענות איירי (ה) רדיפה ולא הריגה, אבל הכא דכתיב: "ורדפו מכם חמשה" – סיפא דקרא "ונפלו אויביכם לפניכם לחרב". מספר הישר.

*מרים המתינה למשה שעה אחת. לאו דוקא נקט שעה, אלא שליש שעה או רביע. דקתני בתוספתא: מדה טובה מרובה ממדת פורענות על אחת חמש מאות. אבל קשיא לרבי: והא במרגלים נפרע מהם יום לשנה יום לשנה, אם כן היתה מרובה מדת פורענות ממדה טובה של מרים! *ועוד, בפ"ק דחגיגה (דף ה:), דדרש רבי יוחנן: "אותי יום יום ידרושון" שכל העוסק בתורה אפילו יום אחד – כאילו עוסק כל השנה כולה, וכן במדת פורענות כתיב (במדבר יד): "במספר הימים אשר תרתם את הארץ מ' יום" וגו', אלמא דכי הדדי נינהו!

סשיתה

[שייך לעיל ט: במשנה ודע דמלשון תוס' שהעתיק התוי"ט נראה דמיד אחר סוף דיבור דלעיל שסיים מספר הישר כתבו תוספת אבל קשיא לרבי וכו' במרגלים נפרע מהם וכו']

[ויסוד נכון תמצא בתוי"ט]

משלי ז | שמואל א' ב | דברים י | שופטים ו | שמות א | [זבחים קטז. ע"ש]

[יומא עו. סנהדרין ק:] | עירובין נג. | [נ"א וחרבו שלופה בידו (במדבר כב)] | [סנהדרין סט. ע"ש] | שם קו. | [שם וקד. ע"ש] | [יבמות סג.] | [גירסת הערוך בערך פיתום מתמסמם]

תוספות שאנץ

יעבץ אדם גדול היה בתורה. תרעתים מפרש בספרי ששמעו תרועה בהר סיני ל"א תרעתים על שם שהיו יושבין בשערי (ב"ד) [ירושלים] תרעתים זקני שער. שמעתים ששמעו מצות אביהם דבבני יונדב בן רכב משתעי [קרא] והם היו מבני בניו של יתרו. סוכתים על שהיו יושבין בסוכות כדכתיב ונשב באהלים. וקרי משפחות סופרים דהיינו סנהדרין ל"ה: שמסכנות לבעליהן. שעל ידי אותן הערים ואותה עבודה נסתכנו מצרים לטבוע בים: מסכנות מדלדלות כדכתיב וינצלו את מצרים. ובשביל עבודה זו אירע להם. ולהאי לישנא לא גרסינן לה דאמר מר כל העוסק בבנין מתמסכן. ומאן דגרס ליה להך מתרגם להן דרב ושמואל אכל הבניינים של כל אדם מסכנות שנופל מהבנין וממית: ממסכנות שמביאין את האדם לידי עניות דאמר מר כל העוסק וכו'. ל"ה:

הגהות הב"ח

(א) רש"י ד"ה כי באש וכו' גמול הס"ד ואח"כ מ"ה נדונם במים כל הבן הילוד וגו' הס"ד: (ב) ד"ה יושבי וכו' יעבץ אדם גדול וכו' ישראל לאמר אם ברך: (ג) ד"ה שממסכנות וכו' דאמר מר ביבמות כל העוסק: (ד) תוס' ד"ה לעולם וכו' ברדיפה ולא בהריגה:

בְּפָרֶךְ בְּפֶה רַךְ. מְשַׁכּוּס בִּדְבָרִים וּבְשָׂכָר עַד שֶׁהִרְגִּילוּס לַעֲבוֹדָה. בִּפְרִיכָה. בִּשְׁבִרוֹן גּוּף וּמָתְנַיִם וְחָזְקָה: ה"ג בַּעֲבוֹדָה קָשָׁה אָמַר רַבִּי שְׁמוּאֵל בַּר נַחְמָנִי אָמַר ר' יוֹנָתָן שֶׁהָיוּ מַחֲלִיפִין וכו'. וְזוֹ הִיא "קָשָׁה", שֶׁלֹּא הָיוּ רְגִילִים בְּכָךְ. וּלְמַאן דַּאֲמַר. (א) "בְּפָרֶךְ" קַמָּא – בְּפֶה רַךְ, הַאי "בְּפָרֶךְ" בַּתְרָא וַדַּאי פְּרִיכָה הִיא, דְּהָכְתִיב "וַיְמָרְרוּ". וְשׁוֹפְתוֹת. כְּשֶׁמּוֹשִׁיבִין הַסִּיר עַל גַּבֵּי כִּירָה – קָרֵי לָהּ שְׁפִיתָה. אַחַת שֶׁל חַמִּין. לִרְחוֹץ רַגְלֵי בַּעֲלֵיהֶן בַּשָּׂדֶה. בֵּין שְׁפַתָּיִם. בֵּין מַגְרֵי הַשָּׂדוֹת, מְקוֹמוֹת נְמוּכִין. מֵצַר גְּבוּל הַשָּׂדֶה גָּבוֹהַּ מִכָּאן, וַחֲבֵירוֹ מִכָּאן, וְחָרִיץ בָּאֶמְצַע. יוֹנָה. יִשְׂרָאֵל, שֶׁנֶּאֱמַר: "יוֹנָתִי תַמָּתִי" (שיר ו). עוֹרַרְתִּיךָ. לָצֵאת מִמְּעֵי אִמְּךָ. חִבְּלַתְךָ. לְשׁוֹן "חֶבְלֵי יוֹלֵדָה" (הושע יג). מְנַקֵּר. מְנַקֶּה. מְשַׁפֵּר. כְּמוֹ שֶׁעוֹשִׂין לַתִּינוֹקוֹת לְיַישֵּׁב אֶת אֵיבְרֵיהֶם וּלְתַקְּנָן, שֶׁנִּיתָּקִין מִצַּעַר הַלֵּידָה. לֹא כָרַּת שָׁרֵּךְ. לֹא הָיָה לָךְ מְיַלֶּדֶת לַחְתּוֹךְ טִיבּוּר הַוָּלָד. לְמִשְׁעִי. לְהַחֲלִיק בָּשָׂר, כְּמוֹ "חֶלְקַת צַוָּארָיו" (בראשית כז) – שְׁעִיעוּת. עֲגוּלִין. כְּעֵין כִּכָּר עָגוֹל: נַעֲשָׂה לָהֶן נֵס. רְבָבָה כְּצֶמַח הַשָּׂדֶה. גְּדֵלִים מִן הָאָרֶץ כְּצֶמַח הַשָּׂדֶה. וַתָּבֹאִי. לְבֵית אָבִיךְ. הֵם הִכִּירוּהוּ. שֶׁרָאוּ שְׁכִינָתוֹ כְּבָר. זֶה אֵלִי. שֶׁרָאִיתִי כְּבָר. אֱלִישֶׁבַע. בַּת עַמִּינָדָב, אִשְׁתּוֹ שֶׁל אַהֲרֹן. שֶׁהָיְתָה פּוֹעָה לַוָּלָד. מְשַׁעֲשַׁעַת אוֹתוֹ, כְּדֶרֶךְ שֶׁמְּשַׂחֲקִים לַתִּינוֹקוֹת בִּדְבָרִים עֲרֵבִים לְשַׁעְשְׁעוֹ. פּוֹעָה. צוֹעֶקֶת. כְּמוֹ "כַּיּוֹלֵדָה אֶפְעֶה" (ישעיה מב). ה"ג וּרְאִיתֶן עַל הָאָבְנָיִם אָמַר רַבִּי יוֹחָנָן סִימָן גָּדוֹל מָסַר לָהֶן בְּשָׁעָה שֶׁכּוֹרַעַת לֵילֵד יְרֵיכוֹתֶיהָ מִצְטַנְּנוֹת כַּאֲבָנִים ד"א עַל הָאָבְנָיִם כִּדְכְתִיב וָאֵרֵד בֵּית הַיּוֹצֵר וגו' מַה יּוֹצֵר זֶה יָרֵךְ מִכָּאן כו'. סִימָן גָּדוֹל. שֶׁלֹּא תִּטְעֶנּוּ הָאֵם וְתַחְבִּיאֶנּוּ, וְתֹאמַר: "נֵפֶל הָיָה". זֶה לָכֶם הַסִּימָן שֶׁל לֵידָה. וְאָז תִּטְלוּהוּ וְתַהַרְגוּהוּ. ד"א: לְהָכִי קָרֵי לֵיהּ לְמַשְׁבֵּר שֶׁל אִשָּׁה "אָבְנָיִם" כִּדְכְתִיב גַּבֵּי יוֹצֵר כְּלֵי חֶרֶס "אָבְנָיִם", וְאִשָּׁה נַמִּי לְיוֹצֵר דָּמְיָא. סַדָּן. עֵץ עָב שֶׁעָלָיו יוֹשֵׁב וּמְגַלְגֵּל הַכֵּלִים לַעֲשׂוֹתָן כִּדְפוּס הַכְּלִי, לְפִי גָּדְלוֹ וְקָטְנוֹ. סִימָן גָּדוֹל מָסַר לָהֶם. "וּרְאִיתֶן עַל הָאָבְנָיִם אִם בֵּן הוּא" – שֶׁאַתֶּן יְכוֹלוֹת לִרְאוֹת מִיָּד אִם בֵּן הוּא, בְּלֹא שׁוּם הַגְבָּהָה. בֵּן פָּנָיו לְמַטָּה. כְּדֶרֶךְ תַּשְׁמִישׁוֹ. בַּת פָּנֶיהָ לְמַעְלָה. כְּדֶרֶךְ תַּשְׁמִישָׁהּ. וְהָכִי מְפָרֵשׁ בְּמַסֶּכֶת נִדָּה (דף לא.). אֲלֵיהֶן. מַשְׁמַע עַל עִסְקֵי בִּיאָה, לְשׁוֹן "וַיָּבֹא אֵלֶיהָ" (בראשית כט). וַתְּחַיֶּיןָ. הֲוָה לֵיהּ לְמִיכְתַּב: וְלֹא הֵמִיתוּ הַיְלָדִים. "וַתְּחַיֶּיןָ" מַשְׁמַע שֶׁהָיוּ מְסַיְּיעִין לְהַחֲיוֹתָן, שֶׁהָיוּ טוֹמְנוֹת אוֹתָן בְּבָתֵּיהֶן וּמְגַדְּלוֹת אוֹתָם. אִי נֵימָא חַיּוֹת מַמָּשׁ. מְיַלְּדוֹת. כְּחַיָּה נִמְשְׁלָה. וְחַיַּת הַשָּׂדֶה אֵינָהּ צְרִיכָה לִמְיַלֶּדֶת. דִּכְתִיב בֵּיהּ כְּתִיב בֵּיהּ. מִי שֶׁכָּתוּב בּוֹ שֶׁנִּקְרָא בְּשֵׁם בְּהֵמָה וְחַיָּה – הֲרֵי כְּתִיב בּוֹ. וְשֶׁאֵין כְּתִיב בּוֹ – הֲרֵי כְּתִיב בִּכְלָל כְּנֵסִיָּיתָן יַחַד: "מָה אִמְּךָ לְבִיָּא בֵּין אֲרָיוֹת רָבָצָה". אִמְּךָ – כְּנֶסֶת יִשְׂרָאֵל כּוּלָּהּ, נִקְרֵאת לְבִיָּא. אַהֲרֹן וּמֹשֶׁה. שֶׁיָּצְאוּ מִיּוֹכֶבֶד. וַתָּמָת עֲזוּבָה אֵשֶׁת כָּלֵב. וְהִיא מִרְיָם. וּלְקַמָּן מְפָרֵשׁ לָמָּה נִקְרֵאת שְׁמָהּ עֲזוּבָה. וְהַאי "וַתָּמָת" – שֶׁנִּצְטָרְעָה. וַיִּקַּח לוֹ כָלֵב אֶת אֶפְרָת. לְאַחַר שֶׁנִּתְרַפֵּאת חָזַר וּלְקָחָהּ לוֹ. אַלְמָא אֶפְרָת קָרֵי מִרְיָם, וּכְתִיב בְּדָוִד "בֶּן אִישׁ אֶפְרָתִי". וְכָלֵב בֶּן חֶצְרוֹן. פָּסוּק הוּא בְּדִבְרֵי הַיָּמִים. (ב) בֶּן יְפֻנֶּה בֶּן שֶׁנִּפְנָה מֵעֲצַת מְרַגְּלִים. תְּיוּבְתָּא הוּא דְּקָא מְתָרֵץ: לְעוֹלָם בֶּן חֶצְרוֹן הוּא, וְלָמָּה נִקְרָא "בֶּן יְפוּנֶּה" – עַל שֵׁם מַעֲשָׂיו. ה"ג וְאַכַּתִּי בֶּן קְנַז הוּא. חוֹרְגוֹ דִקְנַז. בֶּן אִשְׁתּוֹ שֶׁל קְנַז הָיָה כָּלֵב, וְנִמְצָא עָתְנִיאֵל אָחִיו מֵאִמּוֹ. דַּיְקָא

תורה אור

שהיתה פועה לולד. פירש רבינו חננאל: *לוחשת לחישה ויוצא הולד, כמו שעושים אלו עכשיו באזני האשה. אחרים

[וכ"כ בערוך ערך פע א' ע"ש]

בְּפָרֶךְ". רַבִּי אֶלְעָזָר אָמַר: בְּפֶה רַךְ, רַבִּי שְׁמוּאֵל
בַּר נַחְמָנִי אָמַר: בִּפְרִיכָה. °"וַיְמָרְרוּ אֶת חַיֵּיהֶם (שמות א)
בַּעֲבוֹדָה קָשָׁה בְּחוֹמֶר וּבִלְבֵנִים" וגו'. אָמַר
רָבָא: בַּתְּחִילָּה בְּחוֹמֶר וּבִלְבֵנִים, וּלְבַסּוֹף "וּבְכָל
עֲבוֹדָה בַּשָּׂדֶה". "אֵת כָּל עֲבוֹדָתָם אֲשֶׁר עָבְדוּ
בָהֶם בְּפָרֶךְ". אָמַר רַבִּי שְׁמוּאֵל בַּר נַחְמָנִי אָמַר רַבִּי יוֹנָתָן: שֶׁהָיוּ מַחֲלִיפִין מְלֶאכֶת
אֲנָשִׁים לְנָשִׁים, וּמְלֶאכֶת נָשִׁים לַאֲנָשִׁים. וּלְמ"ד נַמִּי הָתָם בְּפֶה רַךְ – הָכָא וַדַּאי
בִּפְרִיכָה. דָּרַשׁ *רַב עֲוִירָא: בִּשְׂכַר נָשִׁים צִדְקָנִיּוֹת שֶׁהָיוּ בְּאוֹתוֹ הַדּוֹר נִגְאֲלוּ (ס"א רבי עקיבא)
יִשְׂרָאֵל מִמִּצְרַיִם. *בְּשָׁעָה שֶׁהוֹלְכוֹת לִשְׁאוֹב מַיִם, הקב"ה מְזַמֵּן לָהֶם דָּגִים קְטַנִּים (יומא עה.)
בְּכַדֵּיהֶן, וְשׁוֹאֲבוֹת מֶחֱצָה מַיִם וּמֶחֱצָה דָּגִים, וּבָאוֹת וְשׁוֹפְתוֹת שְׁתֵּי קְדֵירוֹת, אַחַת
שֶׁל חַמִּין וְאַחַת שֶׁל דָּגִים, וּמוֹלִיכוֹת אֵצֶל בַּעֲלֵיהֶן לַשָּׂדֶה. וּמַרְחִיצוֹת אוֹתָן, וְסָכוֹת
אוֹתָן, וּמַאֲכִילוֹת אוֹתָן, וּמַשְׁקוֹת אוֹתָן, וְנִזְקָקוֹת לָהֶן בֵּין שְׁפַתַּיִם, שֶׁנֶּאֱמַר: °"אִם (תהלים סח)
תִּשְׁכְּבוּן בֵּין שְׁפַתָּיִם" וגו'. בִּשְׂכַר "תִּשְׁכְּבוּן בֵּין שְׁפַתָּיִם" זָכוּ יִשְׂרָאֵל לְבִיזַּת מִצְרַיִם,
שֶׁנֶּאֱמַר: °"כַּנְפֵי יוֹנָה נֶחְפָּה בַכֶּסֶף וְאֶבְרוֹתֶיהָ בִּירַקְרַק חָרוּץ". וְכֵיוָן שֶׁמִּתְעַבְּרוֹת (שם)
בָּאוֹת לְבָתֵּיהֶם, וְכֵיוָן שֶׁמַּגִּיעַ זְמַן מוֹלְדֵיהֶן, הוֹלְכוֹת וְיוֹלְדוֹת בַּשָּׂדֶה תַּחַת הַתַּפּוּחַ,
שֶׁנֶּאֱמַר: °"תַּחַת הַתַּפּוּחַ עוֹרַרְתִּיךָ" *וגו'. וְהקב"ה שׁוֹלֵחַ מִשְּׁמֵי מָרוֹם מִי שֶׁמְּנַקֵּר (שיר ח) (שמות רבה פ"א)
וּמְשַׁפֵּיר אוֹתָן, כְּחַיָּה זוֹ שֶׁמְּשַׁפֶּרֶת אֶת הַוָּלָד, שֶׁנֶּאֱמַר: °"וּמוֹלְדוֹתַיִךְ בְּיוֹם הוּלֶּדֶת (יחזקאל טז)
אוֹתָךְ לֹא כָרַּת שָׁרֵּךְ וּבְמַיִם לֹא רֻחַצְתְּ לְמִשְׁעִי" וגו'. *וּמְלַקֵּט לָהֶן שְׁנֵי עִגּוּלִין, (ס"א ונותן להם)
אֶחָד שֶׁל שֶׁמֶן וְאֶחָד שֶׁל דְּבַשׁ, שֶׁנֶּאֱמַר: °"וַיֵּנִקֵהוּ דְבַשׁ מִסֶּלַע וְשֶׁמֶן" וגו'. וְכֵיוָן (דברים לב)
שֶׁמַּכִּירִין בָּהֶן מִצְרִים בָּאִין לְהוֹרְגָן, וְנַעֲשָׂה לָהֶם נֵס וְנִבְלָעִין בַּקַּרְקַע, וּמְבִיאִין
שְׁוָורִים וְחוֹרְשִׁין עַל גַּבָּן, שֶׁנֶּאֱמַר: °"עַל גַּבִּי חָרְשׁוּ חוֹרְשִׁים" וגו'. לְאַחַר שֶׁהוֹלְכִין (תהלים קכט)
הָיוּ מְבַצְבְּצִין וְיוֹצְאִין כְּעֵשֶׂב הַשָּׂדֶה, שֶׁנֶּאֱמַר: °"רְבָבָה כְּצֶמַח הַשָּׂדֶה נְתַתִּיךְ". וְכֵיוָן (יחזקאל טז)
שֶׁמִּתְגַּדְּלִין בָּאִין עֲדָרִים עֲדָרִים לְבָתֵּיהֶן, שֶׁנֶּאֱמַר: °"וַתִּרְבִּי וַתִּגְדְּלִי וַתָּבֹאִי בַּעֲדִי (שם)
עֲדָיִים". אַל תִּקְרֵי "בַּעֲדִי עֲדָיִים" אֶלָּא בְּעֶדְרֵי עֲדָרִים. וּכְשֶׁנִּגְלָה הקב"ה עַל הַיָּם – הֵם
הִכִּירוּהוּ תְּחִלָּה, שֶׁנֶּאֱמַר: °"זֶה אֵלִי וְאַנְוֵהוּ". °"וַיֹּאמֶר מֶלֶךְ מִצְרַיִם לַמְיַלְּדוֹת (שמות טו) (שמות א)
הָעִבְרִיּוֹת" וגו'; רַב וּשְׁמוּאֵל; חַד אָמַר: אִשָּׁה וּבִתָּהּ, וְחַד אָמַר: כַּלָּה וַחֲמוֹתָהּ. מ"ד
אִשָּׁה וּבִתָּהּ – יוֹכֶבֶד וּמִרְיָם. וּמ"ד כַּלָּה וַחֲמוֹתָהּ – יוֹכֶבֶד וֶאֱלִישֶׁבַע. תַּנְיָא כְּמ"ד
אִשָּׁה וּבִתָּהּ, דְּתַנְיָא: שִׁפְרָה – זוֹ יוֹכֶבֶד, וְלָמָּה נִקְרָא שְׁמָהּ שִׁפְרָה – שֶׁמְּשַׁפֶּרֶת אֶת
הַוָּלָד. ד"א: שִׁפְרָה – שֶׁפָּרוּ וְרָבוּ יִשְׂרָאֵל בְּיָמֶיהָ. פּוּעָה – זוֹ מִרְיָם, וְלָמָּה נִקְרָא שְׁמָהּ
פּוּעָה – שֶׁהָיְתָה פּוֹעָה (וּמוֹצִיאָה אֶת הַוָּלָד.) ד"א: פּוּעָה – שֶׁהָיְתָה פּוֹעָה בְּרוּחַ הַקּוֹדֶשׁ, (ס"א ל"ג)
וְאוֹמֶרֶת: עֲתִידָה אִמִּי שֶׁתֵּלֵד בֵּן שֶׁמּוֹשִׁיעַ אֶת יִשְׂרָאֵל. °"וַיֹּאמֶר בְּיַלֶּדְכֶן אֶת (שם)
הָעִבְרִיּוֹת" וגו'. מַאי אָבְנָיִם? א"ר חָנָן: סִימָן גָּדוֹל מָסַר לָהֶן. אָמַר לָהֶן: בְּשָׁעָה
שֶׁכּוֹרַעַת לֵילֵד יְרֵיכוֹתֶיהָ מִצְטַנְּנוֹת כַּאֲבָנִים. וְאִית דְּאָמַר: כִּדְכְתִיב °"וָאֵרֵד בֵּית (ירמיה יח)
הַיּוֹצֵר וְהִנֵּה הוּא עוֹשֶׂה מְלָאכָה עַל הָאָבְנָיִם", מַה יּוֹצֵר זֶה – יָרֵךְ מִכָּאן וְיָרֵךְ מִכָּאן
וְסַדָּן בָּאֶמְצַע, אַף אִשָּׁה – יָרֵךְ מִכָּאן וְיָרֵךְ מִכָּאן וְהַוָּלָד בָּאֶמְצַע. °"אִם בֵּן הוּא וַהֲמִתֶּן (שמות א)
אוֹתוֹ". א"ר חֲנִינָא: סִימָן גָּדוֹל מָסַר לָהֶן: בֵּן פָּנָיו לְמַטָּה, בַּת פָּנֶיהָ לְמַעְלָה. °"וַתִּירֶאןָ (שם)
הַמְיַלְּדוֹת אֶת הָאֱלֹהִים וְלֹא עָשׂוּ כַּאֲשֶׁר דִּבֶּר אֲלֵיהֶן" וגו' – "לָהֶן" מִיבְּעֵי לֵיהּ! א"ר
יוֹסֵי בְּר' חֲנִינָא: מְלַמֵּד שֶׁתְּבָעָן לִדְבַר עֲבֵירָה וְלֹא נִתְבְּעוּ. °"וַתְּחַיֶּיןָ אֶת הַיְלָדִים". (שם)
תָּנָא: לֹא דַּיָּין שֶׁלֹּא הֵמִיתוּ אוֹתָן, אֶלָּא שֶׁהָיוּ מְסַפְּקוֹת לָהֶם מַיִם וּמָזוֹן.
°"וַתֹּאמַרְןָ הַמְיַלְּדוֹת אֶל פַּרְעֹה כִּי לֹא כַנָּשִׁים" וגו'. מַאי חָיוֹת? אִילֵימָא חַיּוֹת (שם)
מַמָּשׁ – אַטּוּ חַיָּה מִי לָא צְרִיכָה חַיָּה אַחֲרִיתִי לְאוֹלוּדָהּ? אֶלָּא אָמְרוּ לוֹ: אוּמָּה
זוֹ כְּחַיָּה נִמְשְׁלָה; יְהוּדָה – °"גּוּר אַרְיֵה", דָּן – "יְהִי דָן נָחָשׁ", נַפְתָּלִי – "אַיָּלָה שְׁלוּחָה", (בראשית מט)
יִשָּׂשכָר – "חֲמוֹר גָּרֶם", יוֹסֵף – "בְּכוֹר שׁוֹר", בִּנְיָמִין – "זְאֵב יִטְרָף". דִּכְתִיב בֵּיהּ – כְּתִיב
בֵּיהּ, וּדְלָא כְּתִיב בֵּיהּ – כְּתִיב (בֵּיהּ): °"מָה אִמְּךָ לְבִיָּא בֵּין אֲרָיוֹת רָבָצָה" וגו'. (יחזקאל יט)
°"וַיְהִי כִּי יָרְאוּ הַמְיַלְּדוֹת אֶת הָאֱלֹהִים וַיַּעַשׂ לָהֶם בָּתִּים". רַב וּשְׁמוּאֵל; חַד אָמַר: (שמות א)
בָּתֵּי כְהוּנָּה וּלְוִיָּה, וְחַד אָמַר: בָּתֵּי מַלְכוּת. מ"ד בָּתֵּי כְהוּנָּה וּלְוִיָּה – אַהֲרֹן וּמֹשֶׁה,
וּמ"ד בָּתֵּי מַלְכוּת – דָּוִד נַמִּי מִמִּרְיָם קָאָתֵי, דִּכְתִיב: °"וַתָּמָת עֲזוּבָה (אֵשֶׁת כָּלֵב) (דה"א ב)
וַיִּקַּח לוֹ כָּלֵב אֶת אֶפְרָת וַתֵּלֶד לוֹ אֶת חוּר", וּכְתִיב: °"וְדָוִד בֶּן אִישׁ אֶפְרָתִי" (שמואל א יז)
וגו'. §°"וְכָלֵב בֶּן חֶצְרוֹן הוֹלִיד אֶת עֲזוּבָה אִשָּׁה וְאֶת יְרִיעוֹת וְאֵלֶּה בָנֶיהָ יֵשֶׁר (שם)
וְשׁוֹבָב וְאַרְדּוֹן". בֶּן חֶצְרוֹן? °בֶּן יְפֻנֶּה הוּא! בֶּן שֶׁפָּנָה מֵעֲצַת מְרַגְּלִים. וְאַכַּתִּי בֶּן (במדבר יג)
קְנַז הוּא, דִּכְתִיב: °"וַיִּלְכְּדָהּ עָתְנִיאֵל בֶּן קְנַז אֲחִי כָלֵב"! *אָמַר רָבָא: חוֹרְגוֹ דִקְנַז הֲוָה. (שופטים א) (תמורה טז. ע"ש)
דַּיְקָא

הגהות הב"ח

(א) רש"י ד"ה ולמאן דאמר נמי בפרך: (ב) ד"ה וכלב וכו' הימים הס"ד ואח"כ מ"ה בן שנפנה כצ"ל ותיבות בן יפונה נמחק:

דיקא נמי, דכתיב: "הקנזי", ש"מ. "עזובה" – זו מרים, ולמה נקרא שמה עזובה – שהכל עזבוה מתחילתה. "הוליד"? והלא מינסב הוה נסיב לה! א"ר יוחנן: כל הנושא אשה לשם שמים מעלה עליו הכתוב כאילו ילדה. "יריעות" – שהיו פניה דומין ליריעות. "ואלה בניה" – אל תקרי בניה אלא בוניה; "ישר" – שיישר את עצמו. "שובב" – ששיבב את יצרו, "וארדון" – שרדה את יצרו, ואיכא דאמרי: על שהיו *פניה דומין לורד. "ולאשחור אבי תקוע היו שתי נשים חלאה ונערה". "אשחור" זה כלב, ולמה נקרא שמו אשחור – שהושחרו פניו בתעניות. "אבי" – שנעשה לה כאב, "תקוע" – שתקע את לבו לאביו שבשמים. "היו שתי נשים" – נעשה מרים כשתי נשים; "חלאה ונערה" – לא חלאה ונערה הואי, אלא בתחילה חלאה ולבסוף נערה. "ובני חלאה צרת וצהר ואתנן". "צרת" – שנעשית צרה לחברותיה, "צהר" – שהיו פניה דומין כצהרים, "אתנן" – שכל הרואה אותה מוליך אתנן לאשתו. "ויצו פרעה לכל עמו". א"ר יוסי בר' חנינא: אף על עמו גזר. ואמר ר"י בר' חנינא: שלש גזירות גזר; בתחילה – "אם בן הוא והמתן אותו", *ולבסוף – "כל הבן הילוד היאורה תשליכוהו", ולבסוף – אף על עמו גזר. "וילך איש מבית לוי". להיכן הלך? אמר רב יהודה בר זבינא: שהלך בעצת בתו. תנא: עמרם גדול הדור היה, כיון *(שראה שאמר) פרעה הרשע "כל הבן הילוד היאורה תשליכוהו" אמר: לשוא אנו עמלין, עמד וגירש את אשתו. עמדו כולן וגירשו את נשותיהן. אמרה לו בתו: אבא, קשה גזירתך יותר משל פרעה. שפרעה לא גזר אלא על הזכרים – ואתה גזרת על הזכרים ועל הנקיבות, פרעה לא גזר אלא בעוה"ז – ואתה בעוה"ז ולעוה"ב, פרעה הרשע – ספק מתקיימת גזירתו ספק אינה מתקיימת, אתה צדיק – בודאי שגזירתך מתקיימת, שנאמר: "ותגזר אומר ויקם לך". עמד והחזיר את אשתו, עמדו כולן והחזירו את נשותיהן. "ויקח"? *ויחזור מיבעי ליה! א"ר יהודה בר זבינא: שעשה *לו מעשה ליקוחין. הושיבה באפריון, ואהרן ומרים מרקדין לפניה, ומלאכי השרת אמרו: "אם הבנים שמחה". "את בת לוי". *אפשר, בת מאה ושלשים שנה הויא וקרי לה "בת"? *דא"ר חמא בר' חנינא: זו יוכבד שהורתה בדרך ולידתה בין החומות, שנאמר: "אשר ילדה אותה ללוי במצרים" – לידתה במצרים ואין הורתה במצרים! א"ר יהודה:* שנולדו בה סימני נערות. "ותהר האשה ותלד בן". והא הות מיעברא ביה תלתא ירחי מעיקרא! א"ר יהודה בר זבינא: מקיש לידתה להורתה, מה הורתה שלא בצער – אף לידתה שלא בצער. מכאן לנשים צדקניות שלא היו בפיתקה של חוה. "ותרא אותו כי טוב הוא". תניא, ר"מ אומר: טוב שמו, ר' יהודה אומר: טוביה שמו, רבי נחמיה אומר: הגון לנביאות, אחרים אומרים: נולד כשהוא מהול, וחכמים אומרים: בשעה *שנולד משה נתמלא הבית כולו אור, כתיב הכא: "ותרא אותו כי טוב הוא", וכתיב התם: "וירא אלהים את האור כי טוב". "ותצפנהו שלשה ירחים". דלא מנו מצרים אלא משעה דאהדרה, והיא הות מיעברא ביה תלתא ירחי מעיקרא. "ולא יכלה עוד הצפינו". אמאי? תצפניה ותיזיל! אלא, כל היכא דהוו שמעי מצראי דמתיליד ינוקא ממטו ינוקא התם, כי היכי דלישמעינהו, ומעוי (בהדיהו), דכתיב: "אחזו לנו שועלים שועלים קטנים" וגו'. "ותקח לו תבת גומא". מאי שנא גומא? א"ר אלעזר: *מיכן לצדיקים שממונם חביב עליהן יותר מגופן, וכל כך למה – לפי שאין *פושטין ידיהן בגזל. רבי שמואל בר נחמני אמר: דבר רך, שיכול לעמוד בפני דבר רך ובפני דבר קשה. "ותחמרה בחמר ובזפת". תנא: חמר מבפנים וזפת מבחוץ, כדי שלא יריח אותו צדיק ריח רע. "ותשם בה את הילד ותשם בסוף". רבי אלעזר אומר: ים סוף, רבי שמואל בר נחמני אמר: אגם

תורה אור: יהושע יד; דה"א ד; שם; שמות א; שם ב; איוב כב; תהלים קיג; במדבר כו; שמות ב; בראשית א; שמות ב; שם; שיר ב; שם

רש"י

דיקא נמי דכתיב. קרא אחרינא, כי משתעי בכלב לא קרייה "בן קנז" כדכתיב בעתניאל, אלא "הקנזי" – מאנשי ביתו ומגידוליו של קנז. עזובה שהכל עזבוה. שמתחילה חולנית היתה, כדקרי לה הכא יריעות, ולקמן קרי לה נמי חלאה ועזובה – שעזבוה כל בחורי ישראל מלישא אותה. והא מיסב נסבה. כדכתיב: "ותמת עזובה ויקח לו" וגו' – אלמא איתתיה הואי. לשם שמים. כגון זו, שהיתה חולה ונשאה לשם שמים. שבדק באחיה אהרן ומשה וראה אותם צדיקים, ורוב בנים דומין לאחי האם, בב"ב בי"ש נוחלין" (דף קי.). ליריעות. בלי תואר אדמומית. דמחמת חוליה היתה ירקרקת. בוניה. אלו שמות בעלה, שבנאה ועשאה מבונה כאשר נשים בנישואין ובנים: ישר ושובב וארדון. שיישר את עצמו. מלטעות את טעות המרגלים. ששיבב את עצמו. מעצתן. לשון "הבת השובבה" (ירמיה לא) – יוללנית ומורדת. והכי נמי קרי ליה "מרד" בקרא אחרינא, על שם שמרד בעצת מרגלים. שרדה ביצרו. שהיה מסיתו לטעות עמהן. שהושחרו פניו. שקבל עליו תעניות הרבה שינצל מעצת מרגלים. שנעשה לה כאב. להתעסק בה ברפואות ומזונות הצריכין לחולה. שתקע את לבו לאביו שבשמים. שלא להיות בעצת מרגלים. חלאה. חולי. ולבסוף נערה. שנתרפאה מחליה, וחזרה בתואר פנים כנערה. ובני חלאה. ובנייני חלאה, *שנבנית ונתרפאת, משובחין היו להיות צרת וצהר ואתנן. צרה לחברותיה. מתקנאות ביופיה. מוליך אתנן לאשתו. שהיה מתאוה למשכב נשים. אף על עמו גזר. דרש רבי תנחומא: יום שנולד משה אמרו איצטגניניו: היום נולד מושיען של ישראל, ואין אנו יודעים אם מצרי הוא או יהודי. ועמד וקיבץ כל עמו, ובקש מהן ליתן לו הנולדים בו ביום, וגזר אף על עמו. בתחילה והמתן אותו. לא הושיב שומרים אלא סמך על המילדות. תשליכוהו. שהושיב שומרין וקסדורין לדבר. ולבסוף על עמו. כדפרישית. וכיון שעבר היום ועדיין רואין איצטגניניו שלא לקה – העמיד הגזירה עד יום שהושלך ליאור. גדול הדור היה. והיו הכל נשמעין לדבריו. על הזכרים ועל הנקיבות. שלא יולידו לא זכר ולא נקיבה. אלא בעולם הזה. שנולדים ומתים וחוזרים וחיים הן לעוה"ב. אתה גזרת בעולם הזה ובעולם הבא, שכיון שאינם נולדים – אינן באין לעולם הבא. בת מאה ושלשים. כדמפרש ואזיל, שנולדה בירידתן למצרים. וישראל עמדו שם ר"י שנה, ומשנולד משה לא נתעכבו אלא פ' שנים, כדכתיב: "ומשה בן שמונים שנה וגו' בדברם אל פרעה" (שמות ז), ואותה שנה יצאו. נמצא שעברו מירידתם עד שנולד משה ק"ל שנה, וכשהחזיר עמרם את יוכבד (א) היתה מעוברת ממשה, כדאמרינן לקמן בשמעתין. דאמר רבי חמא. בב"ב בי"ש נוחלין"*. זו יוכבד. בפרטן של יורדי מצרים אתה מוצא שבעים חסר אחת, ובכללן אתה אומר "הבאה מצרימה שבעים" – זו יוכבד שהשלימה מניינן בכניסתן לעיר. סימני נערות. חזרה לימי עלומיה: באורח כנשים, ובתואר פנים, ופשטו הקמטים: *והיא הות מיעברא ביה תלתא ירחי מעיקרא. מקמי דאהדרה כדלקמן. מקיש לידתה וכו'. לא נכתב הריון זה אלא לדרוש כך. בפיתקה של חוה. בגזר דין שלה, ושטר גזירות קללתה דעצבון והריון. הגון לנביאות. ראתה ברוח הקודש שעתיד [להיות הגון] לנבואה. ותצפנהו שלשה ירחים. שלשה חדשים יכלה להצפינו, שלא הלכו המצריים לבדוק אחריה אלא לסוף תשעה חדשים משהחזירה, והיא הוה מיעברא ביה תלתא ירחי מעיקרא. ומהכא נפקא לן. אמאי תצפניה ותיזיל. מאחר שצפון במסתרים היה, כדכתיב: "ותצפנהו", מה יש לה לדאוג? ומעוי התם. וצועק שם. ודרך תינוק לצעוק כששומע קול תינוק חבירו. אחזו לנו שועלים. בת קול אומר למי הים: אחזו לנו שועלים הקטנים (ב) המחבלים את הכרמים בהיותם סמדר, בעוד הפרי קטן. שחביב עליהן ממונן. שדמיו מועטין. ואף על פי שהיה משתמר גופו יותר בשל עלים, שקשים וחזקים. דבר רך. בזה הוא משתמר יפה מן הכל. לפי שהדבר הקשה, כשהמים מוליכין אותו בחוזקה (ג) – הוא נתקל, והוא נישוף ונשבר. אבל דבר רך – נתקל ונזדקר באבן לאחוריו. ריח רע. של זפת.
אגם

תוספות

אחרים אומרים נולד כשהוא מהול. ומקשים: מדקאמר ר"מ טוב שמו – מכלל ד"אחרים" לאו היינו ר"מ. ובשלהי הוריות (דף יג:) אמר: דאסקוה לר"מ אחרים! ובפ"ק דברכות (דף ט:) בגמרא: מאימתי קורין שמע בשחרית (ד) אפליגו ר"מ ואחרים! וא"ר, שראה בקונטרס צרפת: שמועות שקיבל מאלישע בן אבויה – קבעום בשם "אחרים", מפני שהיה שמו "אחר", אבל שאר שמועות – קבעום בשמו ולא מסתברא, דהא לרבי נתן אסקו "יש אומרים", ואית לך שכל שמועותיו קבעו כך, ולר"מ נמי עשו כיוצא בו! אלא נראה דלאחר דאסקוהו אחרים חזר בו ואמר: נולד כשהוא מהול. וכן בפ' קמא דברכות*.

חמר מבחוץ וזפת מבפנים. פירש רבי בשם ר"ש בר קלונימוס: זה וזה בתוך התיבה, והחמר היה מכסה את הזפת. אבל מבחוץ לא זיפפה, שלא ירגישו. כי הגומא דומה לקנה היאור, ולא יבחינו התיבה בתוך קנה היאור.
בשבילי

מסורת הש"ס

נ"ל פניו. יעב"ץ
[ס"א שנבראת]
[וע' תוס' שם ט: ד"ה אחרים וע"ע תוס' ע"ז סד: ותוס' ב"ב טו: ד"ה וי"א]
[נ"ל ואחר כך וכ"א בילקוט ובע"י]
[נ"ל שגזר. כ"א בע"י]
כ"א וישב
[נ"ל לה וכ"א בילקוט ובע"י]
ב"ב קכ.
כס"א בר זבידא
[לקמן יג.]
[ב"ב דף קכג:]
[חולין נא.]
[סנהדרין נט:]
[נ"ל ואח]

הגהות הב"ח

(א) רש"י ד"ה בת מאה וכו' את יוכבד כבר היתה: (ב) ד"ה אחזו וכו' הקטנים שהיו מחבלים: (ג) ד"ה דבר רך וכו' והוא נתקל באבן הוא נישוף ונשבר אבל דבר רך נתקל ונזדקר לאחוריו: (ד) תוס' ד"ה אחרים וכו' אפליגו ר"מ. נ"ב עיין בב"ב דף טו ודף נג בתוס' ד"ה מאן י"א שם תירצו קושיא זו:

גליון הש"ס

רש"י ד"ה ששיבב את עצמו כו' וה"נ קרי ליה מרד. דה"א ד יח:

אֲגַם. שֶׁל עֲצֵי עֲרָבָה וְקָנִים דַּקִּין וְהוּא קָנֶה וְסוּף דִּקְרָא; קָנֶה – קָנִים, סוּף – עֲרָבָה דַּקָּה. לִרְחוֹץ. לִטְבּוֹל שָׁם לְשֵׁם גֵּירוּת. וְכֵן הוּא אוֹמֵר וכו'. שֶׁהַשֵּׁב וּמִתְנַקֶּה מֵעֲוֹנוֹ קָרוּי רָחוּץ. לְשׁוֹן מִיתָה. כִּדְמְפָרֵשׁ וְאָזֵיל, שֶׁהָיוּ מְמַחוֹת בְּיָדָהּ הַצָּלָתוֹ שֶׁל צַדִּיק. דְּאָמַר מָר. גַּבֵּי שַׁרְבִיט הַזָּהָב דַּאֲחַשְׁוֵרוֹשׁ, בְּמַסֶּכֶת מְגִילָּה*. בְּשִׁינֵּי רְשָׁעִים. דְּעוֹג מֶלֶךְ הַבָּשָׁן, בְּמַסֶּכֶת בְּרָכוֹת בִּתְחִלַּת פֶּרֶק "הָרוֹאֶה"*. שֶׁרִיבַּבְתָּה. לְשׁוֹן דְּאִישְׁתַּרְבּוּבֵי. שֶׁרָאֲתָה עִמּוֹ שְׁכִינָה. וְהַאי "אֶת" – לְשׁוֹן עִם, כְּמוֹ "לֹא שָׁלַח יַעֲקֹב אֶת אֶחָיו" (בראשית מב). נַעַר. גָּדוֹל מַשְׁמַע. בַּעַל מוּם. וְהוּא לֵוִי, וְנִפְסָל בְּקוֹל לַעֲבוֹדַת הַשִּׁיר. וְאֵין אַחֵר נוֹפֵל. לַיְאוֹר שֶׁאוֹתוֹ הַיּוֹם בִּטְּלוּ גְּזֵירָתָם. וְכִי יֹאמְרוּ אֲלֵיכֶם. הַגּוֹיִם: דִּרְשׁוּ כְּמוֹתֵינוּ אֶל הָאוֹבוֹת. הַמְצַפְצְפִים וְהַמַּהְגִּים. נָבִיא קָרֵי לְשׁוֹן גְּנַאי, שֶׁהֵם (ב) מְלַפְלְפִין כַּעֲגוּרִים וּמַהְגִּים כַּיּוֹנִים – מוֹצִיאִין קוֹל בִּגְרוֹנָם וְאֵין יוֹדְעִין מָה אוֹמְרִים. כָּךְ דֶּרֶךְ אִיצְטַגְנִינִין – אֵינָן רוֹאִין אֶלָּא סִימָן, אֲבָל לֹא פֵּירוּשׁוֹ שֶׁל כָּל דָּבָר. רָאוּ. אִיצְטַגְנִינֵי פַרְעֹה. שֶׁמּוֹשִׁיעָן שֶׁל יִשְׂרָאֵל כו'. וְהַךְ מִילְּתָא לָאו ר' אֶלְעָזָר קָאָמַר לַהּ, דִּקְרָא לָאו אַמִּצְרִים קָאֵי. אֶלָּא גְּמָרָא קָאָמַר לַהּ, וְקָאֵי אַהָא דְּאָמְרִינַן לְעֵיל: וְאֵין אַחֵר נוֹפֵל, וּכְדְרַבִּי אֶלְעָזָר דְּאָמַר שֶׁאֵין יוֹדְעִים מָה הוֹגִין. הִילְכָּךְ רָאוּ הַמִּצְרִים וְלֹא יָדְעוּ מָה רָאוּ. כֵּיוָן דְּשַׁדְיוּהּ לְמֹשֶׁה בַּמַּיִם. כָּל זְמַן שֶׁהָיָה בַּיְאוֹר אֵין לָקוּת גְּדוֹלָה מִזּוֹ, וּבָטְלָה סִימָן שֶׁל לְקִיָּה. רַגְלִי. בִּשְׁבִילִי. כְּמוֹ "וַיְבָרֶךְ ה' אוֹתְךָ לְרַגְלִי" (בראשית ל). בִּשְׁבִילִי נִצַּלְתֶּם. שֶׁבִּיטְּלוּ מִצְרִים אֶת גְּזֵירָתָם. שִׁירָה עַל הַיָּם. בְּכ"א בְּנִיסָן נֶאֶמְרָה. כִּדְתַנְיָא בְּסֵדֶר עוֹלָם: מֵרַעְמְסֵס לְסוּכּוֹת וּמִסּוּכּוֹת לְאֵיתָם וּמֵאֵיתָם לִפְנֵי פִּי הַחִירוֹת – הֲרֵי ג', בָּרְבִיעִי – "וַיּוּגַּד לְמֶלֶךְ מִצְרַיִם כִּי בָרַח הָעָם", חֲמִישִׁי וְשִׁשִּׁי – רָדְפוּ מִצְרַיִם, (ג) אוֹר שְׁבִיעִי – יָרְדוּ לַיָּם, שֶׁנֶּאֱמַר: "וַיְאֹהֶר אֶת הַלַּיְלָה", לְשַׁחֲרִית אָמְרוּ שִׁירָה. וְיוֹם שְׁבִיעִי הָיָה, וְיוֹ"ט אַחֲרוֹן שֶׁל פֶּסַח הָיָה. דְּאָמַר מָר בְּשִׁבְעָה בַּאֲדָר מֵת מֹשֶׁה. בְּפ"ק דְּקִידּוּשִׁין (דף לח.) יָלְפִינַן לַהּ מִקְּרָאֵי. דִּכְתִיב: "וַיִּבְכּוּ בְנֵי יִשְׂרָאֵל אֶת מֹשֶׁה בְּעַרְבוֹת מוֹאָב שְׁלֹשִׁים יוֹם", וּכְתִיב: "מֹשֶׁה עַבְדִּי מֵת וְעַתָּה קוּם עֲבוֹר", וּכְתִיב: "כִּי בְּעוֹד שְׁלֹשֶׁת יָמִים אַתֶּם עוֹבְרִים אֶת הַיַּרְדֵּן" וגו', וּכְתִיב: "וְהָעָם עָלוּ מִן הַיַּרְדֵּן בֶּעָשׂוֹר לַחֹדֶשׁ הָרִאשׁוֹן". צֵא מֵהֶן ל"ג לְמַפְרֵעַ – תִּמְצָא שֶׁבְּשִׁבְעָה בַּאֲדָר מֵת מֹשֶׁה. וּמִנַּיִן שֶׁבְּשִׁבְעָה בַּאֲדָר נוֹלַד – שֶׁנֶּאֱמַר: "וַיֹּאמֶר אֲלֵיהֶם בֶּן מֵאָה וְעֶשְׂרִים שָׁנָה אָנֹכִי הַיּוֹם" וגו', מַה ת"ל "הַיּוֹם"? – הַיּוֹם מָלְאוּ יָמַי וּשְׁנוֹתַי. שְׁלֹשָׁה יַרְחֵי. הָיוּ, וְהֵן ג' חֳדָשִׁים שֶׁהִצְפִּינַתּוּ. רוּבּוֹ שֶׁל רִאשׁוֹן. לֹא חָסֵר אֶלָּא ז' יָמִים, וְרוּבּוֹ שֶׁל ג' דְּהַיְינוּ נִיסָן, וְאֶמְצָעִי שָׁלֵם – אֲדָר הַשֵּׁנִי שָׁלֵם. מַאי שְׁנָא מִן הָעִבְרִיּוֹת. דְּקָאָמְרָה לַהּ, מִכְּלָל דְּמִצְרִיּוֹת לֹא נִיחָא לַהּ. דָּבָר טָמֵא. זוֹ שֶׁאֲכִילָתָהּ דְּבָרִים טְמֵאִים, וְהַתִּינוֹק טוֹעֵם בַּחֲלָבָהּ כָּל מַה שֶּׁאוֹכֶלֶת, כִּדְאָמְרִי' בְּיוֹמָא (דף עה:) גַּבֵּי לְשַׁד הַשָּׁמֶן. אֶת מִי יוֹרֶה דֵעָה. לְמִי לִימֵּד הקב"ה תּוֹרָה – לְמִי שֶׁגָּמַל וְהִפְרִישׁ עַצְמוֹ מֵחָלָב טָמֵא, וְנֶעְתַּק מִן הַשָּׁדַיִם הַטְּמֵאִים. כְּמוֹ "וַיַּעְתֵּק מִשָּׁם" (בראשית יב). שֶׁהָלְכָה בִּזְרִיזוּת כְּעַלְמָה. שֶׁכָּל כֹּחָהּ עָלֶיהָ כְּמוֹ "חֲזַק וֶאֱמָץ" (דברים לא) – תַּקִּיף וְעַלָּם. שֶׁהֶעֱלִימָה אֶת דְּבָרֶיהָ. שֶׁלֹּא אָמְרָה שֶׁהִיא אֲחוֹתוֹ, וְשֶׁהִיא מְבִיאָה אֶת אִמּוֹ. הֵילִיכִי אֶת הַיֶּלֶד. הֲרֵי לִיךְ שֶׁלִּיךְ. שֶׁהָיְתָה מִתְנַבְּאָה כְּשֶׁהִיא אֲחוֹת אַהֲרֹן. עַד שֶׁלֹּא נוֹלַד מֹשֶׁה, וְהַיְינוּ הַנְּבִיאָה אֲחוֹת אַהֲרֹן.

מַאי

אֲגַם, כִּדְכְתִיב: °"קָנֶה וָסוּף קָמֵלוּ". "וַתֵּרֶד בַּת פַּרְעֹה לִרְחוֹץ עַל הַיְאוֹר". א"ר יוֹחָנָן מִשּׁוּם ר' שִׁמְעוֹן בֶּן יוֹחַי: מְלַמֵּד שֶׁיָּרְדָה לִרְחוֹץ מִגִּלּוּלֵי אָבִיהָ, וְכֵן הוּא אוֹמֵר: °"אִם רָחַץ ה' אֶת צוֹאַת בְּנוֹת צִיּוֹן" וגו'. "וְנַעֲרוֹתֶיהָ הוֹלְכוֹת" וגו'. א"ר יוֹחָנָן: אֵין הֲלִיכָה זוֹ אֶלָּא לְשׁוֹן מִיתָה, וְכֵן הוּא אוֹמֵר: °"הִנֵּה אָנֹכִי הוֹלֵךְ לָמוּת". °"וַתֵּרֶא אֶת הַתֵּיבָה בְּתוֹךְ הַסּוּף", כֵּיוָן דַּחֲזוּ דְּקָא (א) בָּעוּ לְאַצּוֹלֵי לְמֹשֶׁה אָמְרוּ לָהּ: גְּבִירְתֵּנוּ, מִנְהָגוֹ שֶׁל עוֹלָם מֶלֶךְ בָּשָׂר וָדָם גּוֹזֵר גְּזֵירָה, אִם כָּל הָעוֹלָם כּוּלּוֹ אֵין מְקַיְּימִין אוֹתָהּ – בָּנָיו וּבְנֵי בֵיתוֹ מְקַיְּימִין אוֹתָהּ, וְאַתְּ עוֹבֶרֶת עַל גְּזֵירַת אָבִיךְ? בָּא גַּבְרִיאֵל וַחֲבָטָן בַּקַּרְקַע. "וַתִּשְׁלַח אֶת אֲמָתָהּ וַתִּקָּחֶהָ". ר' יְהוּדָה וְר' נְחֶמְיָה; חַד אָמַר: יָדָהּ, וְחַד אָמַר: שִׁפְחָתָהּ. מ"ד יָדָהּ – דִּכְתִיב "אַמָּתָהּ", וּמ"ד שִׁפְחָתָהּ – מִדְּלָא כְּתִיב "יָדָהּ". וּלְמ"ד שִׁפְחָתָהּ, הָא אָמְרַתְּ בָּא גַּבְרִיאֵל וַחֲבָטָן בַּקַּרְקַע! דְּשַׁיֵּיר לָהּ חֲדָא, דְּלָאו אוֹרְחָא דְּבַת מַלְכָּא לְמֵיקַם לְחוּדַהּ. וּלְמַאן דְּאָמַר יָדָהּ – לִיכְתּוֹב "יָדָהּ"! הָא קמ"ל דְּאִישְׁתַּרְבַּב אִישְׁתַּרְבּוּבֵי. *דְּאָמַר מָר: וְכֵן אַתָּה מוֹצֵא בְּאַמָּתָהּ שֶׁל בַּת פַּרְעֹה, וְכֵן אַתָּה מוֹצֵא בְּשִׁינֵּי רְשָׁעִים, דִּכְתִיב: °"שִׁנֵּי רְשָׁעִים שִׁבַּרְתָּ" *וְאָמַר רֵישׁ לָקִישׁ: אַל תִּיקְרֵי "שִׁבַּרְתָּ" אֶלָּא "שֶׁרִיבַּבְתָּה". "וַתִּפְתַּח וַתִּרְאֵהוּ אֶת הַיֶּלֶד". "וַתֵּרֶא" מִיבָּעֵי לֵיהּ! א"ר יוֹסֵי בְּרַבִּי חֲנִינָא: שֶׁרָאֲתָה שְׁכִינָה עִמּוֹ. "וְהִנֵּה נַעַר בֹּכֶה". קָרֵי לֵיהּ יֶלֶד, וְקָרֵי לֵיהּ נַעַר. תָּנָא: הוּא יֶלֶד, וְקוֹלוֹ כְּנַעַר, דִּבְרֵי רַבִּי יְהוּדָה. אָמַר לוֹ רַבִּי נְחֶמְיָה: *א"כ עֲשִׂיתוֹ לְמֹשֶׁה רַבֵּינוּ בַּעַל מוּם. אֶלָּא, מְלַמֵּד שֶׁעָשְׂתָה לוֹ אִמּוֹ חוּפַּת נְעוּרִים בַּתֵּיבָה, אָמְרָה: שֶׁמָּא לֹא אֶזְכֶּה לְחוּפָּתוֹ. "וַתַּחְמוֹל עָלָיו וַתֹּאמֶר מִיַּלְדֵי הָעִבְרִים זֶה". מְנָא יָדְעָה? א"ר יוֹסֵי בְּרַבִּי חֲנִינָא: שֶׁרָאֲתָה אוֹתוֹ מָהוּל. "זֶה" – א"ר יוֹחָנָן: מְלַמֵּד שֶׁנִּתְנַבְּאָה שֶׁלֹּא מִדַּעְתָּהּ: זֶה נוֹפֵל, וְאֵין אַחֵר נוֹפֵל. וְהַיְינוּ דְּאָמַר רַבִּי אֶלְעָזָר: מַאי דִּכְתִיב °"וְכִי יֹאמְרוּ אֲלֵיכֶם דִּרְשׁוּ אֶל הָאוֹבוֹת וְאֶל הַיִּדְּעוֹנִים הַמְצַפְצְפִים וְהַמַּהְגִּים" – צוֹפִין וְאֵינָם יוֹדְעִין מַה צוֹפִין, מַהְגִּים וְאֵינָן יוֹדְעִים מַה מַּהְגִּים. רָאוּ שֶׁמּוֹשִׁיעָן שֶׁל יִשְׂרָאֵל בַּמַּיִם הוּא לוֹקֶה, עָמְדוּ וְגָזְרוּ: "כָּל הַבֵּן הַיִּלּוֹד הַיְאוֹרָה תַּשְׁלִיכוּהוּ". כֵּיוָן דְּשַׁדְיוּהּ לְמֹשֶׁה אָמְרוּ: תּוּ לָא חָזֵינַן כִּי הַהוּא סִימָנָא, בַּטְּלוּ לִגְזֵירָתַיְיהוּ. וְהֵם אֵינָן יוֹדְעִין שֶׁעַל מֵי מְרִיבָה הוּא לוֹקֶה. וְהַיְינוּ דְּאָמַר *רַבִּי חָמָא בְּרַבִּי חֲנִינָא: מַאי דִּכְתִיב °"הֵמָּה מֵי מְרִיבָה אֲשֶׁר רָבוּ" – הֵמָּה שֶׁרָאוּ אִיצְטַגְנִינֵי פַּרְעֹה וְטָעוּ. וְהַיְינוּ דְּקָאָמַר מֹשֶׁה: °"שֵׁשׁ מֵאוֹת אֶלֶף רַגְלִי" וגו'; אָמַר לָהֶן מֹשֶׁה לְיִשְׂרָאֵל: בִּשְׁבִילִי נִצַּלְתֶּם כּוּלְּכֶם. ר' חֲנִינָא בַּר פַּפָּא אָמַר: אוֹתוֹ הַיּוֹם עֶשְׂרִים וְאֶחָד בְּנִיסָן הָיָה, אָמְרוּ מַלְאֲכֵי הַשָּׁרֵת לִפְנֵי הקב"ה: רִבּוֹנוֹ שֶׁל עוֹלָם, מִי שֶׁעָתִיד לוֹמַר שִׁירָה עַל הַיָּם בְּיוֹם זֶה – יִלְקֶה בְּיוֹם זֶה? רַבִּי אַחָא בַּר חֲנִינָא אָמַר: אוֹתוֹ הַיּוֹם שִׁשָּׁה בְּסִיוָן הָיָה, אָמְרוּ מַלְאֲכֵי הַשָּׁרֵת לִפְנֵי הקב"ה: רבש"ע, מִי שֶׁעָתִיד לְקַבֵּל תּוֹרָה מֵהַר סִינַי בְּיוֹם זֶה – יִלְקֶה בְּיוֹם זֶה? בִּשְׁלָמָא לְמ"ד בְּשִׁשָּׁה בְּסִיוָן – מַשְׁכַּחַתְּ לָהּ ג' יַרְחֵי, *דְּאָמַר מָר: בְּשִׁבְעָה בַּאֲדָר מֵת, וּבְשִׁבְעָה בַּאֲדָר נוֹלַד מֹשֶׁה. וּמִשִּׁבְעָה בַּאֲדָר וְעַד שִׁשָּׁה בְּסִיוָן תְּלָתָא יַרְחֵי. אֶלָּא לְמ"ד בְּעֶשְׂרִים וְאֶחָד בְּנִיסָן, הֵיכִי מַשְׁכַּחַתְּ לָהּ? אוֹתָהּ שָׁנָה מְעוּבֶּרֶת הָיְתָה, רוּבּוֹ שֶׁל רִאשׁוֹן וְרוּבּוֹ שֶׁל אַחֲרוֹן וְאֶמְצָעִי שָׁלֵם. "וַתֹּאמֶר אֲחוֹתוֹ אֶל בַּת פַּרְעֹה הַאֵלֵךְ וְקָרָאתִי לָךְ אִשָּׁה מֵינֶקֶת מִן הָעִבְרִיּוֹת". וּמַאי שְׁנָא מֵעִבְרִיּוֹת? מְלַמֵּד, שֶׁהֶחֱזִירוּהוּ לְמֹשֶׁה עַל כָּל הַמִּצְרִיּוֹת כּוּלָּן וְלֹא יָנַק, *אָמַר: פֶּה שֶׁעָתִיד לְדַבֵּר עִם הַשְּׁכִינָה יִינַק דָּבָר טָמֵא?! וְהַיְינוּ דִּכְתִיב °"אֶת מִי יוֹרֶה דֵעָה" וגו'. לְמִי יוֹרֶה דֵעָה וּלְמִי יָבִין שְׁמוּעָה – לִגְמוּלֵי מֵחָלָב וּלְעַתִּיקֵי מִשָּׁדַיִם. "וַתֹּאמֶר לָהּ בַּת פַּרְעֹה לֵכִי"* וגו'. א"ר אֶלְעָזָר: מְלַמֵּד שֶׁהָלְכָה בִּזְרִיזוּת כְּעַלְמָה. ר' שְׁמוּאֵל בַּר נַחְמָנִי אָמַר: "הָעַלְמָה" – שֶׁהֶעֱלִימָה אֶת דְּבָרֶיהָ. "וַתֹּאמֶר לָהּ בַּת פַּרְעֹה הֵילִיכִי אֶת הַיֶּלֶד הַזֶּה". אָמַר רַבִּי חָמָא בְּר' חֲנִינָא: מִתְנַבְּאָה וְאֵינָהּ יוֹדַעַת מַה מִּתְנַבְּאָה, "הֵילִיכִי" – הָא שֶׁלִּיכִי. "וַאֲנִי אֶתֵּן אֶת שְׂכָרֵךְ". א"ר חָמָא בְּר' חֲנִינָא: לֹא דַּיָּין לַצַּדִּיקִים שֶׁמַּחֲזִירִין לָהֶן אֲבֵידָתָן, אֶלָּא שֶׁנּוֹתְנִין לָהֶן שְׂכָרָן. °"וַתִּקַּח מִרְיָם הַנְּבִיאָה אֲחוֹת אַהֲרֹן" וגו'. *אֲחוֹת אַהֲרֹן וְלֹא אֲחוֹת מֹשֶׁה? אָמַר רַב עַמְרָם אָמַר רַב, וְאָמְרִי לָהּ אָמַר רַב נַחְמָן אָמַר רַב: מְלַמֵּד, שֶׁהָיְתָה מִתְנַבְּאָה כְּשֶׁהִיא אֲחוֹת אַהֲרֹן, וְאוֹמֶרֶת

תורה אור: ישעיה יט; שם ז; בראשית כה; שמות ב; תהלים ג; ישעיה ח; במדבר כ; שם יא; ישעיה כח; שמות טו

בשבילי נצלתם כולכם. תימה: אדרבה, בשבילו נגזרו הגזירות – שראו אצטגניני פרעה! יש לומר: הוא היה הראשון המושלך ליאור. וגזירה ראשונה: "אם בן הוא והמתן אותו" – לא בשבילו היתה, אלא משום "ונלחם בנו", ודרך אנשים להלחם.

סרח

[דף טו:] [דף נד:] מגילה טו: מגילה טו: וברכות נד: [בכורות מז.] [סנהדרין קח:] מגילה יג: קדושין לח. מגילה יד:

הגהות הב"ח

(א) גמ' דקא בעת לאצולי: (ב) רש"י ד"ה המצפצפים וכו' שהם אינם אלא מצפצפים כעגורים: (ג) ד"ה שירה וכו' מצרים אחריהם אור:

[נ"ל אמר הקב"ה כ"א בע"י]

[נ"ל ותלך העלמה אר"א וכו']

מאי שנא מעיקרא. דאקדמינהו למצרים מקמי אחי יוסף, ומאי שנא לבסוף דכתיב "הוא ואחיו" והדר "וכל העולים אתו". וכי. דרך לאטדין ולעשות מהן גורן? שמקיפין לו אטד. גדר של קוצים. שלשים וששה כתרים. י"ב נשיאים דישמעאל וכ"ג אלופים נמנו בעשו. וא"ת: כ"ה הן! תימן וקנז נמנו ב' פעמים. וא"ת: קרח נמנה ב' פעמים – שני קרח הן: אחד מבני אליפז ואחד מבני אהליבמה. ומ"מ ל"ה הן, וכתרו של יוסף – הרי ל"ו. קא מעכב. שלא יקברוהו שם. אמר. קרית ארבע שמה, שאינה מחזקת אלא ד' זוגות. הא דא"ר יצחק לאו מלתא דעשו היא, אלא גמרא קאמר ליה, למימר טעמא דקיבורא. דודאי כן הוה כדברי עשו, שאינה מחזקת אלא ח' קברים. איהו. יעקב. קברה ללאה בדידיה. בחלק המגיעו, כדכתיב: "ושמה קברתי את לאה". זבינתיה. כשמכרת הבכורה. נהי דזבינתי לבכורתי. ולא אטול פי שנים אלא כמותו. פשיטותא מי זבינא. חלקי בחלק פשוט לא מכרתי. א"ל אין. פשיטותיך נמי זבנת חלקך במערה זו לגמרי. שכך אמר אבינו בשעת מיתה: "אשר כריתי לי", ואין כירה אלא לשון מכירה, כמו "ואכרה לי בחמשה עשר כסף" (הושע ג). הבו איגרתא. הראו שטר מכירה. יקירן אודניה. כבדו אזניו משמוע. מאי האי. למה אינכם קוברין אותו? שקיל גולפיה. מקל. כמו גולפי טורי בלע מאבימי, בערכין (דף כב.). ואי לא איעסק ביה יוסף אחיו מי לא הוי מיעסקי ביה. כלומר, היאך הניחוהו אחיו ליוסף ליטול לו את השם לבדו של קבורת אביהם? וכי פרקו מעליהן העול ולא חשו לו, ואם לא נתעסק בו הוא, הם לא היו עסוקין בו? והכתיב: "וישאו אותו בניו" – אלמא אף הם היו עסוקין במשאו (ג) וקבורתו. ומסקנא כתיב: "אחרי קברו את אביו" – תלה הכתוב בו, שהוא היה עיקר הדבר. אמרו. אחיו ביניהן: הניחו לו להתעסק בו כנגד כולנו. כבודו. של אבינו במלך יותר מבהדיוטות, שיוסף מלך הוא. נתעסקו בביזה. (ד) של מצרים. כדי שיתברכו מימיו. תמיד. לפי שאין ארץ מצרים שותה ממי גשמים, אלא שכולה עשויה יאורים ותעלים מנילוס עד סוף המדינה כמה פרסאות, ונילוס עולה ומשקה ומתברך וממלא אותן יאורים, ומשקין מהן השדות. והיינו דכתיב (זכריה יד): "והיה *אם לא יעלה מכל משפחות וגו' ולא עליהם יהיה הגשם ואם משפחת מצרים לא תעלה ולא *תבא ולא עליהם", ואין כתיב כאן "הגשם", אלא "ולא עליהם יהיה" – אותו נהר שהן שותין ממנו. ויונתן בן עוזיאל תרגם: ולא עליהם ייסק נילוס. ויהי האחד מפיל הקורה וגו'. בתלמידי אלישע כתיב, במלכים. והוא שאול. השאילוהו לו. תלמידו של משה. ולא שלמד מפיו, אלא תורתו של משה למדו *לאליהו. בקברניט של מלכים. בקברות של מלכים. ולשון יוני הוא. קיים

[לעיל יב.] | ס"א ל"ג | [עירובין נג.] | [ר"ה כו. חולין לב. ע"ש] | [ע' תוס' גיטין נה: ד"ה ביהודה] | [תוספתא פ"ד] | נ"ל אשר לא יעלה מאת המשפחות וגו' ולא | נ"ל באה | ופירוש בבית הקברות של מלכים והיו שם ארונות הרבה ולא היה משה יודע אותו. ערוך ערך קברנט ב | ס"א לאלישע

הגהות הב"ח

(א) גמ' שבאו שם בני עשו: (ב) שם ואי לא איעסק ביה יוסף אחיו מי לא הוו: (ג) רש"י ד"ה ואי לא וכו' ובקבורתו כתיב אחרי כל"ל ותיבת ומסקנא נמחק: (ד) ד"ה נתעסקו בביזה ויגלו את מצרים:

תורה אור

ואומרת: עתידה אמי שתלד בן שמושיע את ישראל. *וכיון שנולד משה נתמלא כל הבית כולה אור, עמד אביה ונשקה על ראשה, אמר לה: בתי, נתקיימה נבואתיך, וכיון שהטילוהו ליאור – עמד אביה וטפחה על ראשה, אמר לה: בתי, היכן נבואתיך? והיינו דכתיב: (שמות ב) "ותתצב אחותו מרחוק לדעה מה יעשה לו" – לידע מה יהא בסוף נבואתה. § "יוסף זכה" וכו'. § מאי שנא מעיקרא, דכתיב: (בראשית נ) "ויעל יוסף לקבור את אביו ויעלו אתו כל עבדי פרעה" וגו' והדר (שם) "וכל בית יוסף ואחיו ובית אביו", ומאי שנא לבסוף דכתיב: (שם) "וישב יוסף מצרימה הוא ואחיו" והדר "וכל העולים אתו לקבור את אביו"? א"ר יוחנן: בתחילה, עד שלא ראו בכבודן של ישראל – לא נהגו בהן כבוד. ולבסוף שראו בכבודן – נהגו בהן כבוד. דכתיב: (שם) "ויבאו עד גורן האטד", וכי גורן יש לו לאטד? א"ר אבהו: מלמד שהקיפוהו כתרים לארונו של יעקב כגורן זה שמקיפים לו אטד, שבאו (א) בני עשו ובני ישמעאל ובני קטורה. תנא: כולם למלחמה באו, כיון שראו כתרו של יוסף תלוי בארונו של יעקב – נטלו כולן כתריהן ותלאום בארונו של יעקב. תנא: שלשים ושישה כתרים נתלו בארונו של יעקב. (שם) "ויספדו שם מספד גדול וכבד מאד". תנא: אפי' סוסים ואפילו חמורים. *(מאילו מאילו) כיון שהגיעו למערת המכפלה אתא עשו קא מעכב, אמר להן: (שם לה) "ממרא קרית הארבע היא חברון", *ואמר רבי יצחק: קרית ארבע – ארבע זוגות היו: אדם וחוה, אברהם ושרה, יצחק ורבקה, יעקב ולאה. איהו קברה ללאה בדידיה, והאי דפייש – דידי הוא. אמרו ליה: זבינתה. אמר להו: נהי דזבינני בכירותא, פשיטותא מי זבני? אמרו ליה: אין, דכתיב: (שם נ) "בקברי אשר כריתי לי", וא"ר יוחנן משום ר"ש בן יהוצדק: *אין כירה אלא לשון מכירה, שכן בכרכי הים קורין למכירה כירה. אמר להו: הבו לי איגרתא. אמרו ליה: איגרתא בארעא דמצרים היא. ומאן ניזיל – ניזיל נפתלי, דקליל כי איילתא, דכתיב: (שם מט) "נפתלי אילה שלוחה הנותן אמרי שפר", א"ר אבהו: אל תקרי "אמרי שפר" אלא "אמרי ספר". חושים בריה דדן תמן הוה, ויקירן ליה אודניה. אמר להו: מאי האי? ואמרו ליה: קא מעכב האי עד דאתי נפתלי מארעא דמצרים. אמר להו: ועד דאתי נפתלי מארעא דמצרים יהא אבי אבא מוטל בבזיון? *שקל קולפא, מחייה ארישיה. נתרן עיניה ונפלו אכרעא דיעקב. פתחינהו יעקב לעיניה ואחיך. והיינו דכתיב: (תהלים נח) "ישמח צדיק כי חזה נקם פעמיו ירחץ בדם הרשע". באותה שעה נתקיימה נבואתה של רבקה, דכתיב: (בראשית כז) "למה אשכל גם שניכם יום אחד". ואע"ג דמיתתן לא ביום אחד הואי – קבורתן מיהא ביום אחד הואי. ואי לא (ב) עסק ביה יוסף אחיו לא הוו מעסקי ביה? והכתיב: (שם נ) "וישאו אותו בניו ארצה כנען"! אמרו: הניחו לו, כבודו במלכים יותר מבהדיוטות. § "מי לנו גדול מיוסף" כו'. § ת"ר: בא וראה כמה חביבות מצות על משה רבינו. שכל ישראל כולן נתעסקו בביזה, והוא נתעסק במצות, שנאמר: (משלי י) "חכם לב יקח מצות" וגו'. *ומנין היה יודע משה רבינו היכן יוסף קבור? אמרו: סרח בת אשר נשתיירה מאותו הדור. הלך משה אצלה, אמר לה: כלום את יודעת היכן יוסף קבור? אמרה לו: ארון של מתכת עשו לו מצרים, וקבעוהו בנילוס הנהר כדי שיתברכו מימיו. הלך משה ועמד על שפת נילוס, אמר לו: יוסף יוסף! הגיע העת שנשבע הקב"ה שאני גואל אתכם, והגיעה השבועה שהשבעת את ישראל. אם אתה מראה עצמך – מוטב, אם לאו – הרי אנו מנוקין משבועתך. מיד צף ארונו של יוסף. ואל תתמה היאך ברזל צף – שהרי כתיב: (מלכים ב ו) "ויהי האחד מפיל הקורה ואת הברזל נפל אל המים" וגו' "אהה אדוני והוא שאול ויאמר איש האלהים אנה נפל ויראהו את המקום ויקצב עץ וישלך שמה ויצף הברזל". והלא דברים ק"ו: ומה אלישע תלמידו של אליהו, ואליהו תלמידו של משה – צף ברזל מפניו, מפני משה רבינו על אחת כמה וכמה. רבי נתן אומר: *בקברניט של מלכים היה קבור. הלך משה ועמד על קברניט של מלכים, אמר: יוסף, הגיע עת שנשבע הקב"ה שאני גואל אתכם, והגיעה שבועה שהשבעת את ישראל. אם אתה מראה עצמך – מוטב, ואם לאו – הרי אנו מנוקין משבועתך. באותה שעה נזדעזע ארונו של יוסף. נטלו משה והביאו אצלו. וכל אותן שנים שהיו ישראל במדבר, היו שני ארונות הללו, אחד של מת ואחד של שכינה מהלכין זה עם זה, והיו עוברין ושבין אומרים: מה טיבן של שני ארונות הללו? אמרו: אחד של מת ואחד של שכינה. וכי מה דרכו של מת להלך עם שכינה? אמרו: קיים

סרח בת אשר נשתיירה מאותו הדור. תימה: והלא מכיר ויאיר בן מנשה נולדו בימי יעקב, והיו מבאי הארץ למה לא שאלם משה, והם היו מבני בניו של יוסף? י"ל: שסוד הגאולה נמסר לסרח, כדאיתא בפרקי ר"א (פרק מח). וכיון שבא משה הלכו זקני ישראל אצלה, לפי שכבר נכשלו על ידי בני אפרים שיצאו שלשים שנה לפני הקץ, ונמלכו עתה בה. ואמרה להם: מה לשון אמר לכם המושיע הזה? אמרו לה: "פקוד פקדתי". אמרה להם: א"כ הוא הוא. לכך הלך גם משה אצלה. מתוספת רבי.

גליון

תאנא ל"ו כתרים נתלו בארונו של יעקב י"ב נשיאים דישמעאל וי"ד דאלופי בני עשו הכתובים בסדר וישלח. ומבני קטורה זמרן ויקשן מדן ומדין ישבק ושוח הרי ששה ויקשן ילד את שבא ואת דדן. ושבא תלה כתרו של אביו. ומדין הוריש כתרו לה' בניו. א) חנוך ועיפה ועפר ואבידע ואלדעה הרי ה' כתרים הרי י' בני קטורה ל"ו כתרים. והשתא אתי שפיר דקתני לעיל אתו בני עשו וישמעאל ובני קטורה ודלא כפ"ה דלא היה לו להזכיר כלל בני קטורה דפ"ה י"ב נשיאים דישמעאל וכ"ג אלופים נמנו בעשו וא"ת כ"ה הם תימן וקנז נמנו ב' פעמים. וא"ת קרח נמנה ב' פעמים [שני קרח הוי] אחד מבני אליפז ואחד מבני אהליבמה מ"מ ל"ה הם וכתרו של יוסף [הרי ל"ו] כפ"ה: שקל קולפא מחייה. תי' דירו' בכתובות אמרי דמסורה היא בידם דיהודה קני ליה לעשו שנא' ידך בעורף אויביך. ב) ויכול להיות שאותו בשעה שהרג לעשו לשניהם והרגו אותו. אמרו סרח בת אשר נשתיירה. וא"ת הרבה נשתיירו מאותו הדור כדתניא בפ' יש נוחלין. יאיר בן מנשה ומכיר בן מנשה נולדו בימי מנשה ולא מתו עד שנכנסו ישראל לארץ. ומכיר ודאי נולד בימי יעקב וגם יוסף גדל את בניו כדכתיב גם בני מכיר בן מנשה יולדו על ברכי יוסף ולא היה הולך אצלה לשאול היכן הוא מכל הגדולים שבדור. וי"ל דאיתא במדרש דאגדה שיגע בו משה ג' ימים עד שפגעה בו סגולה סרח בת אשר אמרה לו מה אתה מבקש אמר לה ארונו של יוסף אמרה לו ארון של מתכת והשתא ניחא שלא הלך אצלה אלא שפגעה בו והגידה לו הדבר. ארון של מתכת יש וקבעוהו בנילוס. וכי דרכו של מת להלך עם השכינה במדרש יש ששמו עצמות יוסף בתוך עור של כבש ונכנסה בו באותו עור רוח חיים והיינו דכתיב נוהג כצאן יוסף: קיים זה מה שכתוב בזה פי' במכילתא מפ' כתיב הכא אנכי וכתיב ביוסף התחת אלהים אנכי. כתיב הכא לא יהיה לך אלהים אחרים וכתיב בזה את האלהים אני ירא. כתיב הכא זכור. וכתיב הכא וטבוח טבח והכן ואין והכן אלא לשבת שנא' והיה ביום הששי והכינו. כל י' הדברים ולא תשנא את אחיך ולא תקום ולא תטור וחי אחיך עמך ל"ה: את מספר ימיך אמלא ואם זכה מוסיפין לו

א) ומה שלא חשב נמי כתרו של דדן נראה משום דיקשן הי' הבכור והירושה חזרה אליו ובזה ניחא נמי דלא חשיב בני דדן. ומיהו בלא"ה ניחא די"ל דמפרש כפי' התרגום אונקלוס ע"ש.
ב) אולי צ"ל ויכול להיות ששניהם הרגו לעשיו באותו שעה.

קַיֵּים זֶה כׇּל מַה שֶּׁכָּתוּב בָּזֶה. וְאִי לָא (א) עָסֵיק בֵּיהּ מֹשֶׁה — יִשְׂרָאֵל לָא הֲווּ מִיעַסְקִי בֵּיהּ? וְהָכְתִיב: °"וְאֶת עַצְמוֹת יוֹסֵף אֲשֶׁר הֶעֱלוּ בְנֵי יִשְׂרָאֵל מִמִּצְרַיִם קָבְרוּ בִשְׁכֶם"! וְתוּ, אִי לָא אִיעַסְקוּ בֵּיהּ יִשְׂרָאֵל — בָּנָיו לָא הֲווּ מִיעַסְקִי בֵּיהּ? וְהָכְתִיב °"וַיִּהְיוּ לִבְנֵי יוֹסֵף לְנַחֲלָה"! אָמְרוּ: הַנִּיחוּ לוֹ, כְּבוֹדוֹ בִּמְרוּבִּים יוֹתֵר מִבִּמְמוּעָטִין. וְתוּ אָמְרוּ: הַנִּיחוּ לוֹ, כְּבוֹדוֹ בִּגְדוֹלִים יוֹתֵר מִבִּקְטַנִּים. "קָבְרוּ בִשְׁכֶם". מַאי שְׁנָא בִּשְׁכֶם? אָמַר ר' חָמָא בְּר' חֲנִינָא: מִשְּׁכֶם גְּנָבוּהוּ וְלִשְׁכֶם נַחֲזִיר אֲבֵידָתוֹ. קָשׁוּ קְרָאֵי אַהֲדָדֵי: כְּתִיב: °"וַיִּקַּח מֹשֶׁה אֶת עַצְמוֹת יוֹסֵף עִמּוֹ", וּכְתִיב: "וְאֶת עַצְמוֹת יוֹסֵף אֲשֶׁר הֶעֱלוּ בְנֵי יִשְׂרָאֵל" וגו'! א"ר חָמָא בְּר' חֲנִינָא: כׇּל הָעוֹשֶׂה דָּבָר וְלֹא גְּמָרוֹ, וּבָא אַחֵר וּגְמָרוֹ — מַעֲלֶה עָלָיו הַכָּתוּב עַל שֶׁגְּמָרוֹ כְּאִילּוּ עֲשָׂאוֹ. רַבִּי אֶלְעָזָר אוֹמֵר: אַף מוֹרִידִין אוֹתוֹ מִגְּדוּלָּתוֹ, דִּכְתִיב: °"וַיְהִי בָּעֵת הַהִיא וַיֵּרֶד יְהוּדָה". רַבִּי שְׁמוּאֵל בַּר נַחְמָנִי אָמַר: אַף קוֹבֵר אִשְׁתּוֹ וּבָנָיו, דִּכְתִיב: °"וַתָּמׇת בַּת שׁוּעַ אֵשֶׁת יְהוּדָה" וגו', וּכְתִיב: "וַיָּמׇת עֵר וְאוֹנָן". אָמַר רַב יְהוּדָה אָמַר רַב: מִפְּנֵי מָה נִקְרָא יוֹסֵף עֲצָמוֹת בְּחַיָּיו — מִפְּנֵי שֶׁלֹּא מִיחָה בִּכְבוֹד אָבִיו, דְּקָאָמְרִי לֵיהּ °"עַבְדְּךָ אָבִינוּ", וְלָא אֲמַר לְהוּ וְלָא מִידֵּי. *וְאָמַר רַב יְהוּדָה אָמַר רַב, וְאִיתֵימָא רַבִּי חָמָא בְּרַבִּי חֲנִינָא: מִפְּנֵי מָה מֵת יוֹסֵף קוֹדֶם לְאֶחָיו — מִפְּנֵי שֶׁהִנְהִיג עַצְמוֹ בְּרַבָּנוּת.§ °"וְיוֹסֵף הוּרַד מִצְרָיְמָה". א"ר אֶלְעָזָר: אַל תִּיקְרֵי "הוּרַד" אֶלָּא "הוֹרִיד" — שֶׁהוֹרִיד אִיצְטַגְנִינֵי פַּרְעֹה מִגְּדוּלָּתָן. "וַיִּקְנֵהוּ פּוֹטִיפַר סְרִיס פַּרְעֹה". אָמַר רַב: שֶׁקְּנָאוֹ לְעַצְמוֹ. (*בָּא גַּבְרִיאֵל וְסֵירְסוֹ,) בָּא גַּבְרִיאֵל וּפֵירְעוֹ. מֵעִיקָּרָא כְּתִיב פּוֹטִיפַר, וּלְבַסּוֹף "פּוֹטִיפֶרַע".§ "מִי לָנוּ גָּדוֹל מִמֹּשֶׁה" וכו'.§ °"וַיֹּאמֶר ה' אֵלַי רַב לָךְ". א"ר לֵוִי: •בְּ"רַב" בִּישֵּׂר, בְּ"רַב" בִּישְּׂרוּהוּ. בְּ"רַב" בִּישֵּׂר — °"רַב לָכֶם", בְּ"רַב" בִּישְּׂרוּהוּ — "רַב לָךְ". דָּבָר אַחֵר: "רַב לָךְ" — רַב יֵשׁ לָךְ, וּמַנּוּ — יְהוֹשֻׁעַ. דָּבָר אַחֵר: "רַב לָךְ" — שֶׁלֹּא יֹאמְרוּ: הָרַב כַּמָּה קָשֶׁה, וְתַלְמִיד כַּמָּה סַרְבָן. וְכׇל כָּךְ לָמָּה? תָּנָא דְּבֵי ר' יִשְׁמָעֵאל: *לְפוּם גַּמְלָא שִׁיחְנָא.§ °"וַיֹּאמֶר אֲלֵיהֶם בֶּן מֵאָה וְעֶשְׂרִים שָׁנָה אָנֹכִי הַיּוֹם". *שֶׁאֵין ת"ל "הַיּוֹם" — הַיּוֹם מָלְאוּ יָמַי וּשְׁנוֹתַי. לְלַמֶּדְךָ שֶׁהקב"ה מַשְׁלִים שְׁנוֹתֵיהֶם שֶׁל צַדִּיקִים מִיּוֹם לְיוֹם וּמֵחֹדֶשׁ לְחֹדֶשׁ, דִּכְתִיב: °"אֶת מִסְפַּר יָמֶיךָ אֲמַלֵּא". "לֹא אוּכַל עוֹד לָצֵאת וְלָבֹא". מַאי "לָצֵאת וְלָבֹא"? אִילֵימָא לָצֵאת וְלָבֹא מַמָּשׁ — וְהָכְתִיב: °"וּמֹשֶׁה בֶּן מֵאָה וְעֶשְׂרִים שָׁנָה בְּמוֹתוֹ לֹא נָס לֵחֹה", וּכְתִיב: °"וַיַּעַל מֹשֶׁה מֵעַרְבוֹת מוֹאָב אֶל הַר נְבוֹ", וְתַנְיָא: שְׁתֵּים עֶשְׂרֵה מַעֲלוֹת הָיוּ שָׁם, וּפְסָעָן מֹשֶׁה בִּפְסִיעָה אַחַת! א"ר שְׁמוּאֵל בַּר נַחְמָנִי א"ר יוֹנָתָן: לָצֵאת וְלָבוֹא בְּדִבְרֵי תוֹרָה, מְלַמֵּד שֶׁנִּסְתַּתְּמוּ מִמֶּנּוּ שַׁעֲרֵי חׇכְמָה. °"וַיֵּלֶךְ מֹשֶׁה וִיהוֹשֻׁעַ וַיִּתְיַצְּבוּ בְּאֹהֶל מוֹעֵד". תָּנָא: אוֹתָהּ שַׁבָּת שֶׁל דְּיוֹ זוּגֵי הָיְתָה, נִיטְּלָה רְשׁוּת מִזֶּה וְנִיתְּנָה לָזֶה. (וְתַנְיָא,) א"ר יְהוּדָה: •אִילְמָלֵא מִקְרָא כָּתוּב אִי אֶפְשָׁר לְאוֹמְרוֹ, הֵיכָן מֹשֶׁה מֵת — בְּחֶלְקוֹ שֶׁל רְאוּבֵן, דִּכְתִיב: °"וַיַּעַל מֹשֶׁה מֵעַרְבוֹת מוֹאָב אֶל הַר נְבוֹ". וּנְבוֹ בְּחֶלְקוֹ שֶׁל רְאוּבֵן קַיְימָא, דִּכְתִיב: °"וּבְנֵי רְאוּבֵן בָּנוּ וגו' וְאֶת נְבוֹ" וגו'. ("נְבוֹ" — שֶׁשָּׁם מֵתוּ ג' נְבִיאִים, מֹשֶׁה וְאַהֲרֹן וּמִרְיָם.) וְהֵיכָן מֹשֶׁה קָבוּר — בְּחֶלְקוֹ שֶׁל גָּד, דִּכְתִיב: °"וַיַּרְא רֵאשִׁית לוֹ" וגו'. וּמֵחֶלְקוֹ שֶׁל רְאוּבֵן עַד חֶלְקוֹ שֶׁל גָּד כַּמָּה הָוֵי — אַרְבָּעָה מִילִין. אוֹתָן אַרְבָּעָה מִילִין מִי הוֹלִיכוֹ? *מְלַמֵּד שֶׁהָיָה מֹשֶׁה מוּטָּל בְּכַנְפֵי שְׁכִינָה, וּמַלְאֲכֵי הַשָּׁרֵת אוֹמְרִים •°"צִדְקַת ה' עָשָׂה וּמִשְׁפָּטָיו עִם יִשְׂרָאֵל", וְהַקָּדוֹשׁ בָּרוּךְ הוּא אוֹמֵר: °"מִי יָקוּם לִי עִם מְרֵעִים מִי יִתְיַצֵּב לִי עִם פֹּעֲלֵי אָוֶן", וּשְׁמוּאֵל אָמַר: °"מִי כְּהֶחָכָם וּמִי יוֹדֵעַ פֵּשֶׁר דָּבָר", וְרַבִּי יוֹחָנָן אָמַר: °"הַחׇכְמָה מֵאַיִן תִּמָּצֵא", וְרַב נַחְמָן אָמַר: °"וַיָּמׇת שָׁם מֹשֶׁה" וגו', סִמְלַיוֹן אָמַר: וַיָּמׇת שָׁם מֹשֶׁה סָפְרָא רַבָּה דְּיִשְׂרָאֵל. תַּנְיָא, רַבִּי אֱלִיעֶזֶר הַגָּדוֹל אוֹמֵר: שְׁנֵים עָשָׂר מִיל עַל שְׁנֵים עָשָׂר מִיל, כְּנֶגֶד מַחֲנֵה יִשְׂרָאֵל, בַּת קוֹל מַשְׁמִיעַ וְאוֹמֵר: וַיָּמׇת מֹשֶׁה סָפְרָא רַבָּה דְּיִשְׂרָאֵל. וְיֵשׁ אוֹמְרִים: לֹא מֵת מֹשֶׁה! כְּתִיב הָכָא: "וַיָּמׇת שָׁם", וּכְתִיב הָתָם: °"וַיְהִי שָׁם עִם ה'"; מַה לְּהַלָּן עוֹמֵד וּמְשַׁמֵּשׁ — אַף כָּאן עוֹמֵד וּמְשַׁמֵּשׁ. °"וַיִּקְבֹּר אֹתוֹ בַגַּיְא בְּאֶרֶץ מוֹאָב מוּל בֵּית פְּעוֹר" א"ר בֶּרֶכְיָה: סִימָן בְּתוֹךְ סִימָן, וַאֲפ"ה — "וְלֹא יָדַע אִישׁ אֶת קְבוּרָתוֹ". וּכְבָר שָׁלְחָה מַלְכוּת הָרְשָׁעָה אֵצֶל גַּסְטְרָא

קַיֵּים זֶה מַה שֶּׁכָּתוּב בָּזֶה. אֲגָדָה זוֹ מְפוֹרֶשֶׁת בִּמְכִילְתָּא בְּפָרָשַׁת "וַיְהִי בְּשַׁלַּח פַּרְעֹה". כְּתִיב בָּזֶה "אָנֹכִי", וּכְתִיב בָּזֶה "הֲתַחַת אֱלֹהִים אָנֹכִי". כְּתִיב בָּזֶה "לֹא יִהְיֶה לְךָ", וּכְתִיב בָּזֶה "הָאֱלֹהִים אֲנִי יָרֵא". "לֹא תִשָּׂא" – "חֵי פַרְעֹה". "זָכוֹר אֶת יוֹם הַשַּׁבָּת" – "וּטְבֹחַ טֶבַח וְהָכֵן", וְאֵין זֶה אֶלָּא יוֹם הַשַּׁבָּת, וְכֵן הוּא אוֹמֵר "וְהֵכִינוּ אֵת אֲשֶׁר יָבִיאוּ". וְכֵן כׇּל עֲשֶׂרֶת הַדִּבְּרוֹת. "לֹא תִשְׂנָא אֶת אָחִיךָ בִּלְבָבֶךָ" "לֹא תִקּוֹם וְלֹא תִטּוֹר" "וְחֵי אָחִיךָ עִמָּךְ". וְאִי לָא אִיעֲסַק בֵּיהּ מֹשֶׁה וְכוּ'. כְּלוֹמַר: הֵיאַךְ הִנִּיחוּ יִשְׂרָאֵל לְמֹשֶׁה לְהִתְעַסֵּק בּוֹ לְבַדּוֹ? וְכִי לֹא חָשׁוּ לִשְׁבוּעָה, וְאִם לֹא נִתְעַסֵּק בּוֹ מֹשֶׁה לֹא הָיוּ הֵם מִתְעַסְּקִין? הָכְתִיב וְכוּ'. אַלְמָא לְאַחַר שֶׁנִּפְטַר מֹשֶׁה בְּעַרְבוֹת מוֹאָב נִתְעַסְּקוּ בָּהֶן יִשְׂרָאֵל, וְהֶעֱבִירוּם אֶת הַיַּרְדֵּן!. וְתוּ אִי לָא הֲווּ מִתְעַסְּקֵי בֵּיהּ יִשְׂרָאֵל. לְאַחַר שֶׁנִּפְטַר מֹשֶׁה, בָּנָיו מִי לָא הֲווּ מִיעַסְקִי בֵּיהּ? וְהֵיאַךְ הִנִּיחוּ בָּנָיו אֶת שְׁאָר הָעָם לְהִתְעַסֵּק בּוֹ? וְהָכְתִיב בִּשְׁכֶם: "וַיִּהְיוּ לִבְנֵי יוֹסֵף לְנַחֲלָה" וגו', אַלְמָא בְּנַחֲלָתָם קְבָרוּהוּ, דְּחָבִיב הָיָה עֲלֵיהֶן!. אָמְרוּ. בָּנָיו בְּעַצְמָם: הַנִּיחוּ לוֹ שֶׁיִּתְעַסְּקוּ בּוֹ כׇּל יִשְׂרָאֵל. כְּבוֹדוֹ בִּמְרוּבִּים יוֹתֵר מִבִּמְמוּעָטִין. וְיִשְׂרָאֵל אָמְרוּ בְּעַצְמָם בְּעוֹד מֹשֶׁה קַיָּים: הַנִּיחוּ שֶׁיִּתְעַסֵּק בּוֹ מֹשֶׁה לְבַדּוֹ, כְּבוֹדוֹ בִּגְדוֹלִים יוֹתֵר מִבִּקְטַנִּים. מִשְּׁכֶם גְּנָבוּהוּ. כִּדְכְתִיב:* "וַיִּשְׁלָחֵהוּ מֵעֵמֶק חֶבְרוֹן וַיָּבֹא שְׁכֶמָה" וְשָׁם הָיוּ רוֹעִין. וְדוֹתָן אֵינָהּ מָקוֹם, וְהַאי דִּכְתִיב (שם): "וַיֹּאמֶר הָאִישׁ נָסְעוּ מִזֶּה" וגו', כָּךְ אָמַר לוֹ: אַתָּה אוֹמֵר "אֶת אַחַי אָנֹכִי מְבַקֵּשׁ" – סָעוּ מִן הָאַחֲוָה הַזֹּאת וְאֵין מַחֲזִיקִין עַצְמָן כְּאַחִין לְךָ, כִּי שָׁמַעְתִּי אוֹמְרִים נֵלְכָה וּנְבַקֵּשׁ דָּתוֹת וְדִינִין הֵיאַךְ לַהֲמִיתוֹ אִם יָבֹא אֶצְלֵנוּ. הָכָא כְּתִיב וַיִּקַּח מֹשֶׁה. וְלֹא שְׁאָר הָעָם. אַף מוֹרִידִין אוֹתוֹ מִגְּדוּלָּתוֹ. מִן הַשָּׁמַיִם, לַמַּתְחִיל וְאֵינוֹ גּוֹמֵר, אֶלָּא אִם כֵּן נֶאֱנַס, כְּמֹשֶׁה שֶׁמֵּת בְּעֵבֶר הַיַּרְדֵּן. [וַיֵּרֶד יְהוּדָה. שֶׁהוּא הִתְחִיל בְּהַצָּלַת יוֹסֵף כְּשֶׁאָמַר "מַה בֶּצַע" וְלֹא גָּמַר]. נִקְרָא יוֹסֵף עֲצָמוֹת בְּחַיָּיו. שֶׁנֶּאֱמַר: "וְהַעֲלִיתֶם אֶת עַצְמוֹתַי מִזֶּה" וְעוֹדֶנּוּ חַי. שֶׁהוֹרִיד אִצְטַגְנִינֵי פַּרְעֹה מִגְּדוּלָּתָן. כְּשֶׁפָּתַר אֶת הַחֲלוֹם וְהֵם לֹא יָדְעוּ לְפוֹתְרוֹ. לְעַצְמוֹ. לְמִשְׁכַּב זָכוּר, מִתּוֹךְ יוֹפְיוֹ. פֵּרְעוֹ. הַיְינוּ סֵירוּס יְתֵירָא. בָּא גַּבְרִיאֵל וְסֵירְסוֹ לָא גָּרַס. בְּרַב בִּישֵּׂר. אֶת בְּנֵי מַחְלְקוּתוֹ "רַב לָכֶם בְּנֵי לֵוִי". וְהקב"ה מְדַקְדֵּק עִם הַצַּדִּיקִים כְּחוּט הַשַּׂעֲרָה, וְנֶעֱנַשׁ בְּאוֹתָהּ מִדָּה. רַב יֵשׁ לָךְ. הִגִּיעַ מַלְכוּתוֹ שֶׁל יְהוֹשֻׁעַ, וְאֵין לְךָ מַלְכוּת נוֹגַעַת בַּחֲבֶירְתָּהּ. ד"א רַב לָךְ. דַּי לְךָ, אַל תַּרְבֶּה בְּבַקָּשָׁה. שֶׁלֹּא יֹאמְרוּ: הָרַב כַּמָּה קָשֶׁה, שֶׁאֵינוֹ שׁוֹמֵעַ לַתַּלְמִיד, וְתַלְמִיד כַּמָּה סַרְבָן, מַפְצִיר. וּלְשׁוֹן חֲכָמִים הוּא כָּךְ: הָיוּ מְסָרְבִין בּוֹ לִישָּׂא אֶת בַּת אֲחוֹתוֹ, בִּנְדָרִים (ד' סג:). הָיוּ מְסָרְבִין בּוֹ שֶׁיֹּאכַל עִמּוֹ, בִּשְׁבוּעוֹת (דף כג:) (ב). לְפוּם גַּמְלָא שִׁיחְנָא. לְפִי כֹּחַ הַגָּמָל מַרְבִּין בְּמַשָּׂאוֹ. אַף כָּאן — לְפִי צִדְקָתוֹ מְדַקְדֵּק אַחֲרָיו. הַיּוֹם מָלְאוּ. בַּיּוֹם זֶה נוֹלַדְתִּי. לֹא נָס לֵיחֹה. לֹא בָּרַח לַחְלוּחִית כֹּחוֹ. דְּיוֹ זוּגֵי. שְׁנֵי זוּגוֹת, שְׁנֵי חֲבֵירִים הָיוּ. בִּתְחִלַּת הַיּוֹם לְמֹשֶׁה, וְסוֹפוֹ לִיהוֹשֻׁעַ. בְּכַנְפֵי הַשְּׁכִינָה. בִּכְנַף לְבוּשׁ הוֹדוֹ. מִי יָקוּם לִי עִם מְרֵעִים. לְהוֹכִיחָם לִשְׁמִי. פֵּשֶׁר דָּבָר. שֶׁהָיָה יוֹדֵעַ לַעֲשׂוֹת פְּשָׁרָה בֵּינִי וּבֵין בָּנַי. סִמְלַיוֹן. שֵׁם חָכָם. סִימָן בְּתוֹךְ סִימָן. כְּלוֹמַר סִימָנִים הַרְבֵּה: בְּאֶרֶץ מוֹאָב, בַּגַּיְא, מוּל בֵּית פְּעוֹר. וְאעפ"כ לֹא יָדַע וגו'. גַּסְטְרָא

סמליון אומר. פי' ר"ת: אית דאמרי מלאך, ואית דאמרי שם חכם. *ערוך. מפני

תוספות שאנץ

לפום גמלא שיחנא. לפי כח הגמל מרבין במשאו. בא גבריאל וסירסו ל"ג. סרבן מסרב מפציר ובלשון משנה מסרבין בו לישא את בת אחותו. וכן במס' שבועות. שמסרב בו חברו לאכול:

גליון הש"ס

גמ' ברב בישר. כעין זה לעיל דף י ע"ב: גמ' אלמלא מקרא כתוב. ר"ה דף יז ע"ב מגילה ד' כ ע"ב: שם צדקת ה' עשה. עיין מנחות ד' ל ע"א תד"ה מכאן ואילך:

הגהות הב"ח

(א) גמ' ואי לא איעסק ביה: (ב) רש"י ד"ה ד"א רב לך וכו' בשבועות הס"ד ואח"כ מ"ה וכל כך למה מה עונש רב בשמעו לא המורים שהרבה בתחנות הרבה ולא נענה הס"ד:

תורה אור: יהושע כד; שם; שמות יג; בראשית לח; שם; שם מד; שם לט; דברים ג; במדבר טז; דברים לא; שמות כג; דברים לד; שם; שם לא; שם לד; במדבר לב; דברים לג; שם; תהלים צד; קהלת ח; איוב כח; דברים לד; שמות לד; דברים לד

[וע' רש"ל ורש"א בח"א]

בראשית לז

ברכות נה. [ע"ש]

ס"א אינו [כן גיר' הערוך ערך פטיפר פי' סירסו לבילים ופירעו לגיד]

כתובות סז. קד. ר"ה יא. קידושין לח. [תוספ' סוטה פי"א]

[תוספתא פ"ד]

ס"א ל"ג

גַּסְטְרָא שֶׁל בֵּית פְּעוֹר: הֶרְאֵנוּ הֵיכָן מֹשֶׁה קָבוּר, עָמְדוּ לְמַעְלָה — נִדְמֶה לָהֶם לְמַטָּה, לְמַטָּה — נִדְמֶה לָהֶם לְמַעְלָה. נֶחְלְקוּ לִשְׁתֵּי כִיתּוֹת, אוֹתָן שֶׁעוֹמְדִים לְמַעְלָה — נִדְמֶה לָהֶן לְמַטָּה, לְמַטָּה — נִדְמֶה לָהֶן לְמַעְלָה, לְקַיֵּים מַה שֶּׁנֶּאֱמַר: °"וְלֹא יָדַע אִישׁ אֶת קְבוּרָתוֹ". ר' חָמָא בְּר' חֲנִינָא אָמַר: אַף מֹשֶׁה רַבֵּינוּ אֵינוֹ יוֹדֵעַ הֵיכָן קָבוּר, כְּתִיב הָכָא: "וְלֹא יָדַע אִישׁ אֶת קְבוּרָתוֹ", וּכְתִיב הָתָם: °"וְזֹאת הַבְּרָכָה אֲשֶׁר בֵּרַךְ מֹשֶׁה אִישׁ הָאֱלֹהִים". וְא"ר חָמָא בְּרַבִּי חֲנִינָא: מִפְּנֵי מָה נִקְבַּר מֹשֶׁה אֵצֶל בֵּית פְּעוֹר — כְּדֵי לְכַפֵּר עַל מַעֲשֵׂה פְּעוֹר. וְאָמַר רַבִּי חָמָא בְּרַבִּי חֲנִינָא: (א) מַאי דִּכְתִיב: °"אַחֲרֵי ה' אֱלֹהֵיכֶם תֵּלֵכוּ", וְכִי אֶפְשָׁר לוֹ לְאָדָם לְהַלֵּךְ אַחַר שְׁכִינָה? וַהֲלֹא כְּבָר נֶאֱמַר: °"כִּי ה' אֱלֹהֶיךָ אֵשׁ אוֹכְלָה הוּא"! אאֶלָּא: לְהַלֵּךְ אַחַר מִדּוֹתָיו שֶׁל הקב"ה: מַה הוּא מַלְבִּישׁ עֲרוּמִּים, דִּכְתִיב: °"וַיַּעַשׂ ה' אֱלֹהִים לְאָדָם וּלְאִשְׁתּוֹ כָּתְנוֹת עוֹר וַיַּלְבִּשֵׁם" — אַף אַתָּה הַלְבֵּשׁ עֲרוּמִּים, הקב"ה בִּיקֵּר חוֹלִים, דִּכְתִיב: °"וַיֵּרָא אֵלָיו ה' בְּאֵלֹנֵי מַמְרֵא" — אַף אַתָּה בַּקֵּר חוֹלִים, הקב"ה נִיחֵם אֲבֵלִים, דִּכְתִיב: °"וַיְהִי אַחֲרֵי מוֹת אַבְרָהָם וַיְבָרֶךְ אֱלֹהִים אֶת יִצְחָק בְּנוֹ" — אַף אַתָּה נַחֵם אֲבֵלִים, הקב"ה קָבַר מֵתִים, דִּכְתִיב: °"וַיִּקְבֹּר אוֹתוֹ בַגַּיְא" — אַף אַתָּה קְבוֹר מֵתִים.§ "כָּתְנוֹת עוֹר". רַב וּשְׁמוּאֵל; חַד אָמַר: דָּבָר הַבָּא מִן הָעוֹר, וְחַד אָמַר: דָּבָר שֶׁהָעוֹר נֶהֱנֶה מִמֶּנּוּ. דָּרַשׁ ר' שַׂמְלַאי: תּוֹרָה תְּחִלָּתָהּ גְּמִילוּת חֲסָדִים וְסוֹפָהּ גְּמִילוּת חֲסָדִים. תְּחִלָּתָהּ גְּמִילוּת חֲסָדִים — דִּכְתִיב: "וַיַּעַשׂ ה' אֱלֹהִים לְאָדָם וּלְאִשְׁתּוֹ כָּתְנוֹת עוֹר וַיַּלְבִּשֵׁם", וְסוֹפָהּ גְּמִילוּת חֲסָדִים — דִּכְתִיב: "וַיִּקְבֹּר אוֹתוֹ בַגַּיְא". דָּרַשׁ רַבִּי שַׂמְלַאי: מִפְּנֵי מָה נִתְאַוָּה מֹשֶׁה רַבֵּינוּ לִיכָּנֵס לְא"י? וְכִי לֶאֱכוֹל מִפִּרְיָהּ הוּא צָרִיךְ אוֹ לִשְׂבּוֹעַ מִטּוּבָהּ הוּא צָרִיךְ? אֶלָּא כָּךְ אָמַר מֹשֶׁה: הַרְבֵּה מִצְוֹת נִצְטַוּוּ יִשְׂרָאֵל, וְאֵין מִתְקַיְּימִין אֶלָּא בְּא"י, אֶכָּנֵס אֲנִי לָאָרֶץ כְּדֵי שֶׁיִּתְקַיְּימוּ כּוּלָּן עַל יָדִי. אָמַר לוֹ הקב"ה: כְּלוּם אַתָּה מְבַקֵּשׁ אֶלָּא לְקַבֵּל שָׂכָר — מַעֲלֶה אֲנִי עָלֶיךָ כְּאִילּוּ עֲשִׂיתָם, שֶׁנֶּאֱמַר: °"לָכֵן אֲחַלֶּק לוֹ בָרַבִּים וְאֶת עֲצוּמִים יְחַלֵּק שָׁלָל תַּחַת אֲשֶׁר הֶעֱרָה לַמָּוֶת נַפְשׁוֹ וְאֶת פֹּשְׁעִים נִמְנָה וְהוּא חֵטְא רַבִּים נָשָׂא וְלַפּוֹשְׁעִים יַפְגִּיעַ". "לָכֵן אֲחַלֶּק לוֹ בָרַבִּים", יָכוֹל כָּאַחֲרוֹנִים וְלֹא כָּרִאשׁוֹנִים — ת"ל: "וְאֶת עֲצוּמִים יְחַלֵּק שָׁלָל", כְּאַבְרָהָם יִצְחָק וְיַעֲקֹב שֶׁהֵן עֲצוּמִים בַּתּוֹרָה וּבַמִּצְוֹת. "תַּחַת אֲשֶׁר הֶעֱרָה לַמָּוֶת נַפְשׁוֹ" — שֶׁמָּסַר עַצְמוֹ לְמִיתָה, שֶׁנֶּאֱמַר: °"וְאִם אַיִן מְחֵנִי נָא" וגו'. "וְאֶת פֹּשְׁעִים נִמְנָה" — שֶׁנִּמְנָה עִם מֵתֵי מִדְבָּר, "וְהוּא חֵטְא רַבִּים נָשָׂא" — שֶׁכִּיפֵּר עַל מַעֲשֵׂה הָעֵגֶל, "וְלַפּוֹשְׁעִים יַפְגִּיעַ" — שֶׁבִּיקֵּשׁ רַחֲמִים עַל פּוֹשְׁעֵי יִשְׂרָאֵל שֶׁיַּחְזְרוּ בִּתְשׁוּבָה. *וְאֵין פְּגִיעָה אֶלָּא תְּפִלָּה, שֶׁנֶּאֱמַר: °"וְאַתָּה אַל תִּתְפַּלֵּל בְּעַד הָעָם הַזֶּה וְאַל תִּשָּׂא בַעֲדָם רִנָּה וּתְפִלָּה וְאַל תִּפְגַּע בִּי".§

הדרן עלך המקנא לאשתו

הָיָה במֵבִיא אֶת מִנְחָתָהּ בְּתוֹךְ כְּפִיפָה מִצְרִית וְנוֹתְנָהּ עַל יָדֶיהָ כְּדֵי לְיַגְּעָהּ. כָּל הַמְּנָחוֹת תְּחִלָּתָן וְסוֹפָן בִּכְלִי שָׁרֵת, וְזוֹ תְּחִלָּתָהּ בִּכְפִיפָה מִצְרִית וְסוֹפָהּ בִּכְלִי שָׁרֵת. גכָּל הַמְּנָחוֹת טְעוּנוֹת שֶׁמֶן וּלְבוֹנָה, דוְזוֹ אֵינָהּ טְעוּנָה לֹא שֶׁמֶן וְלֹא לְבוֹנָה. הכָּל הַמְּנָחוֹת בָּאוֹת מִן הַחִטִּין, וְזוֹ בָּאָה מִן הַשְּׂעוֹרִין. זמִנְחַת הָעוֹמֶר, אע"פ שֶׁבָּאָה מִן הַשְּׂעוֹרִין — הִיא הָיְתָה בָּאָה גֶּרֶשׂ, וְזוֹ בָּאָה קֶמַח. ר"ג אוֹמֵר: כְּשֵׁם שֶׁמַּעֲשֶׂיהָ מַעֲשֵׂה בְהֵמָה — כָּךְ קָרְבָּנָהּ מַאֲכַל בְּהֵמָה.§ **גמ'** תַּנְיָא, אַבָּא חָנִין אוֹמֵר מִשּׁוּם רַבִּי אֱלִיעֶזֶר: (וְכָל כָּךְ לָמָּה) כְּדֵי לְיַגְּעָהּ — כְּדֵי שֶׁתַּחֲזוֹר בָּהּ. אִם כָּכָה חָסָה תּוֹרָה עַל עוֹבְרֵי רְצוֹנוֹ, קַל וָחוֹמֶר עַל עוֹשֵׂי רְצוֹנוֹ. וּמִמַּאי מִשּׁוּם דְּחָסָה הוּא? דִּילְמָא כִּי הֵיכִי דְּלָא תִּימָּחֵק מְגִילָּה! קָסָבַר מַשְׁקָה

רש"י

גַּסְטְרָא. מוֹשֵׁל. כְּמָה שֶׁאָמַר קוֹמוֹס דוּכוּס וְשִׁלְטוֹן. וַחֲבֵירוֹ — רִיהֲטוֹן קוּרְטוֹן גַּסְטְרָא (ברכות דף לג:). וַיְבָרֶךְ אֱלֹהִים אֶת יִצְחָק. נִיחֲמוֹ עַל אָבִיו, וּבֵרְכוֹ בִּרְכַּת אֲבֵלִים. דָּבָר הַבָּא מִן הָעוֹר. שֶׁל צֶמֶר הוּא. שֶׁהָעוֹר נֶהֱנֶה מִמֶּנּוּ. שֶׁל פִּשְׁתָּן, שֶׁאָדָם לוֹבֵשׁ סָמוּךְ לְעוֹרוֹ. תְּחִילָּתוֹ גְּמִילוּת חֲסָדִים. הִלְבִּישׁ עֲרוּמִּים. וְלַפּוֹשְׁעִים יַפְגִּיעַ. בִּשְׁבִיל פּוֹשְׁעִים הִפְגִּיעַ. הֶעֱרָה. הֵרִיק.

הדרן עלך המקנא

הָיָה מֵבִיא אֶת מִנְחָתָהּ. הַבַּעַל, כִּדְכְתִיב: "וְהֵבִיא אֶת קָרְבָּנָהּ עָלֶיהָ" וגו' (במדבר ה). בִּכְפִיפָה מִצְרִית. סַל שֶׁל נְצָרֵי דֶקֶל, זְרָדִים שֶׁגְּדֵילִין סְבִיב הַדֶּקֶל. כְּדֵי לְיַגְּעָהּ. בַּגְּמָרָא מְפָרֵשׁ טַעְמָא. תְּחִילָּתָן וְסוֹפָן. הָשְׁתָּא מַשְׁמַע: כְּשֶׁמְּבִיאָהּ מִבֵּיתוֹ — מְבִיאָהּ בִּכְלִי שָׁרֵת לָעֲזָרָה. וְסוֹפָהּ בִּכְלִי שָׁרֵת. קוֹדֶם קְמִיצָה. כָּל הַמְּנָחוֹת טְעוּנוֹת שֶׁמֶן וּלְבוֹנָה. כִּדְכְתִיב: "וְיָצַק עָלֶיהָ שֶׁמֶן וְנָתַן עָלֶיהָ לְבוֹנָה" (ויקרא ב). וּלְקַמֵּיהּ פָּרֵיךְ: וְהָאִיכָּא מִנְחַת חוֹטֵא!. וְזוֹ אֵינָהּ טְעוּנָה. דִּכְתִיב בָּהּ: "לֹא יִצוֹק עָלֶיהָ שֶׁמֶן" וגו' (במדבר ה). בָּאוֹת מִן הַחִטִּין. דִּכְתִיב: "סֹלֶת חִטִּים תַּעֲשֶׂה אוֹתָם" (שמות כט). מִנְחַת הָעוֹמֶר בָּאָה מִן שְׂעוֹרִים. בְּמַסֶּכֶת מְנָחוֹת (דף סח.) יָלְפִינַן לָהּ מִקְרָאֵי. בָּאָה גֶּרֶשׂ. דִּכְתִיב: "גֶּרֶשׂ כַּרְמֶל תַּקְרִיב אֵת מִנְחַת בִּכּוּרֶיךָ" (ויקרא ב). וּבְמַסֶּכֶת מְנָחוֹת (דף סו.) אָמְרִינַן: בְּמִנְחַת הָעוֹמֶר הַכָּתוּב מְדַבֵּר. גֶּרֶשׂ. בִּשְׂעוֹרִים. מוּבְחָר שֶׁבּוֹ, מְנוּפֶּה בְּי"ג נָפָה, כְּעֵין סוֹלֶת חִטִּים. קֶמַח. הַכֹּל מְעוֹרָב כְּמוֹ שֶׁנִּטְחַן. **גמ'** וְכָל כָּךְ לָמָּה. לָמָּה אָנוּ טוֹרְחִין לְיַגְּעָהּ. עַל עוֹבְרֵי רְצוֹנוֹ. שֶׁאִם זִינְּתָה — עָבְרָה עַל רְצוֹנוֹ שֶׁל מָקוֹם, וְרוֹצָה שֶׁתּוֹדֶה שֶׁלֹּא תִּיבָּדֵק. קָסָבַר. הַאי תַּנָּא, דְּקָאָמַר מִשּׁוּם דְּחָסָה הוּא. מַשְׁקֶה

תוספות

מפני מה נקבר מול בית פעור כדי לכפר על מעשה פעור. ומדרש אגדה: בכל שנה ושנה בעת שחטאו ישראל בבנות מואב, באותו פרק בית פעור עולה למעלה כדי לקטרג ולהזכיר עון, וכשהוא רואה קברו של משה חוזר ושוקע. שמשה רבינו שקעו בקרקע עד חוטמו, וכל שעה שעולה חוזר ונשקע למקום ששקעו משה רבינו. מתוספת רבי.

הדרן עלך המקנא

מביא את מנחתה. אין סדר המשנה וסדר הפרשה מכוונין, שהרי כך סדר הפרשה: קינא לה ונסתרה — מעלה האשה ומביא את מנחתה. הכהן מביא פיילי של חרש, ונותן לתוכו חצי לוג מים מן הכיור, ונותן בו עפר. מעמיד האשה בשער נקנור, ואוחז בבגדיה וסותר את שערה, ונותן את המנחה על ידיה, וביד הכהן מים המרים, ומשביע ומתנה עמה, וכותב את המגילה, ומוחק, ומשקה, ונוטל מנחתה מתוך כפיפה מצרית ונותן לתוך כלי שרת, מניף ומגיש קומץ ומקטיר. ולא ידענו למה שינה התנא הסדר, ואם סדר התנא דוקא או סדר הפרשה.

כדי ליגעה. שהרי היתה נתונה על ידה עד גמר כל הסדר, כדי שתחזור ותודה. ולא שייך למימר דדריש טעמא דקרא, אלא היכא דנפקא לן מינה מידי דמרבי מיניה, וקרא סתמא כתיב וכולל הכל, ואנו דורשין טעמו ואומרים: זהו הטעם של פסוק, הואיל וטעמו בשביל כך — היכא דוקא. כגון: "לא תחבול בגד אלמנה" — משמע בין עניה ועשירה, וקאמר ר"ש טעמא דקרא: שאם אתה ממשכן אותה — אתה משיא לה שם רע בשכינותיה מתוך שאתה משיב לה העבוט, ונאמר: עניה דוקא אין ממשכנין אותה (ב"מ דף קטו.).

אי

תוספות שאנץ

גסטרא דוכוס ושלטון וחבירו בברכות (ד' לג) ריהטון קרטין גיסטרא: **היה** מביא את מנחתה כדכתיב והביא את קרבנה עליה. בתוך כפיפה מצרית וכו'. צורי של דקל זרדין שגדילין סביב הדקל כדי ליגעה ולאו משום תנופה היא. דלא כתיב תנופה בפרשה עד אחר ונתן על כפיה אלא כדי ליגעה ובגמ' מפרש טעמא: היא היתה גרש פ"ה ממובחר שבו מנופה בי"ג נפה כעין סלת חיטים. ל"ה: **גמ'** קסבר משקה

הגהות הב"ח

(א) גמ' על מעשה פעור ואמר ר' חמא בר חנינא מפני מה נסתתר קברו של משה מעיני בשר ודם מפני שגלוי וידוע לפני הקב"ה שעתיד ביהמ"ק ליחרב ולהגלות את ישראל מארצם שמא יבאו לקבורתו של משה באותה שעה ויעמדו בבכיה ויתחננו למשה ויאמרו לו משה רבינו עמוד בתפלה בעדנו ועומד משה ומבטל את הגזירה מפני שחביבים צדיקים במיתתם יותר מבחייהם שכן אתה מוצא בשעה שהיו ישראל במדבר וסרחו במעשיהם ועשו עגל קצף הקב"ה על ישראל ואמר למשה הרף ממני ואשמידם כמה צדיקים היו באותו הדור וכמה חסידים משה ואהרן ויהושע אלדד ומידד וע' זקנים ושאר חכמים ותלמידים ולא עשה בשבילם ולא ביטל הגזירה אלא בשביל משה ואמר ר' חמא בר חנינא מאי דכתיב:

עין משפט נר מצוה

ם א מיי' פ"א מהל' דעות הל"ה סמג עשין ז:
א ב מיי' פ"ג מהל' סוטה הל"ב סמג עשין כ:
ב ג ד מיי' פי"ב מהל' מעשה הקרבנות הל"ז ופ"ג מהל' סוטה הלי"ג:
ג ה ו מיי' פ"ג מהל' סוטה הלי"ב ופי"ב מהל' מעשה הקרבנות הלכה ב:
ד ז מיי' פ"ז מהל' תמידין ומוספין הלי"א:

מסורת הש"ס

דברים לד; שם לג; שם יג; שם ד; בראשית ג; שם יח; שם כה; דברים לד; ישעיה נג; שמות לב; [ברכות לו: תענית ז: ח. סנהדרין לה:] ירמיה ז; בס"י ליתא

[לקמן יט: ועי' בתיו"ט ד"ה כדי ליגעה]

ה א מיי' פי"ג מהל' מעשה הקרבנות הלי"ב:
ו ב מיי' שם פי"ב הלכה ט והל' יג:
ז ג מיי' שם הלי"ד:
ח ד מיי' שם פי"ג הלי"ב:
ט ה מיי' פ"א מהל' בית הבחירה הלי"ח:
י ו מיי' פ"ג מהל' פסולי המוקדשין הל"כ:
יא ז מיי' שם פי"א הל"ג:

אי משום מגילה הא אימחיקא. היה קשה לרבי: והאמרי' לעיל* (דף ז:) דלאחר [שנמחקה] מגילתה מאיימין עליה שתשתה! ונראה, דעל כרחך אית לן למימר דר"א לית ליה איום שתשתה אפי' אחר מחיקת מגילה. ומדלא פריך: נהי דמשקה ואחר מקריבה, אימא דלאחר מחיקה לאלתר היה נוטל המנחה מעל ידיה – ש"מ דפשיטא ליה דעד שעת הקרבה היה מניחה על ידיה. אם כן, למאן דאמר מאיימין עליה שתשתה – אית לן למימר דסבירא ליה מקריב מנחתה ואח"כ שותה, דככר נקרבה.

טעונה

*מַשְׁקָה וְאח"כ מַקְרִיב אֶת מִנְחָתָהּ, דְּאִי מִשּׁוּם מְגִילָּה – הָא אִימְחִיקָא לָהּ. § "כָּל הַמְּנָחוֹת" כו'. § וּרְמִינְהוּ: *אסֵדֶר מְנָחוֹת כֵּיצַד? אָדָם מֵבִיא מִנְחָה מִתּוֹךְ בֵּיתוֹ בִּקְלָתוֹת שֶׁל כֶּסֶף וְשֶׁל זָהָב, וְנוֹתְנָהּ לְתוֹךְ כְּלִי שָׁרֵת, וּמְקַדְּשָׁהּ בִּכְלִי שָׁרֵת, וְנוֹתֵן עָלֶיהָ שַׁמְנָהּ וּלְבוֹנָתָהּ, וּמוֹלִיכָהּ אֵצֶל כֹּהֵן. וְכֹהֵן מוֹלִיכָהּ אֵצֶל מִזְבֵּחַ, וּמַגִּישָׁהּ בְּקֶרֶן דְּרוֹמִית מַעֲרָבִית כְּנֶגֶד חוּדָּהּ שֶׁל קֶרֶן, וְדַיּוֹ. וּמְסַלֵּק אֶת הַלְּבוֹנָה לְצַד אֶחָד, וְקוֹמֵץ מִמָּקוֹם שֶׁנִּתְרַבָּה שַׁמְנָהּ, וְנוֹתְנוֹ לְתוֹךְ כְּלִי שָׁרֵת, וּמְקַדְּשׁוֹ בִּכְלִי שָׁרֵת, וּמְלַקֵּט אֶת לְבוֹנָתָהּ וְנוֹתְנָהּ עַל גַּבָּיו, (וּמַעֲלֶה אוֹתוֹ ס"א ל"ג לְגַבֵּי מִזְבֵּחַ,) וּמַעֲלֵהוּ וּמַקְטִירוֹ בִּכְלִי שָׁרֵת, וּמוֹלְחוֹ וְנוֹתְנוֹ עַל גַּבֵּי הָאִשִּׁים. בקָרַב הַקּוֹמֶץ – שְׁיָרֶיהָ נֶאֱכָלִין. גוְרַשָּׁאִין הַכֹּהֲנִים לִיתֵּן לְתוֹכָהּ יַיִן וְשֶׁמֶן וּדְבַשׁ, וְאֵין אֲסוּרִין אֶלָּא מִלְּהַחְמִיץ. קָתָנֵי מִיהָא: בִּקְלָתוֹת שֶׁל כֶּסֶף וּבִקְלָתוֹת שֶׁל זָהָב! אָמַר רַב פַּפָּא, אֵימָא: דבְּכֵלִים הָרְאוּיִין לִכְלֵי שָׁרֵת. מִכְּלָל דִּכְפִיפָה מִצְרִית לָא חַזְיָא, כְּמַאן – דְּלָא כְּרַבִּי יוֹסֵי בְּרַבִּי יְהוּדָה. *דְּתַנְיָא: כְּלֵי שָׁרֵת שֶׁעֲשָׂאָן שֶׁל עֵץ, רַבִּי הפּוֹסֵל, *וְר' יוֹסֵי בְּר' יְהוּדָה מַכְשִׁיר – אֲפִי' תֵּימָא רַבִּי יוֹסֵי בְּרַבִּי יְהוּדָה, אֵימַר דְּא"ר יוֹסֵי בְּר' יְהוּדָה בַּחֲשׁוּבִין – בִּפְחוּתִין מִי אָמַר? (א) לֵית לֵיהּ לְר' יוֹסֵי בְּר' יְהוּדָה מלאכי א °"הַקְרִיבֵהוּ נָא לְפֶחָתֶךָ"?! § "וְנוֹתְנָהּ לִכְלִי שָׁרֵת וּמְקַדְּשָׁהּ בִּכְלִי שָׁרֵת". שָׁמְעַתְּ מִינָּהּ *וכְּלֵי שָׁרֵת אֵין מְקַדְּשִׁין אֶלָּא מִדַּעַת? אֵימָא: נוֹתְנָהּ בִּכְלֵי שָׁרֵת לְקַדְּשָׁהּ בִּכְלֵי שָׁרֵת. § "וְנוֹתֵן עָלֶיהָ שַׁמְנָהּ וּלְבוֹנָתָהּ" – שֶׁנֶּאֱמַר: ויקרא ב °"וְיָצַק עָלֶיהָ שֶׁמֶן וְנָתַן עָלֶיהָ לְבוֹנָה". § "וּמוֹלִיכָהּ אֵצֶל כֹּהֵן" – דִּכְתִיב: שם °"וֶהֱבִיאָהּ אֶל בְּנֵי אַהֲרֹן" וגו'. § "וְכֹהֵן מוֹלִיכָהּ אֵצֶל מִזְבֵּחַ" – דִּכְתִיב: שם °"וְהִגִּישָׁהּ אֶל הַמִּזְבֵּחַ". § "מַגִּישָׁהּ בְּקֶרֶן דְּרוֹמִית מַעֲרָבִית כְּנֶגֶד חוּדָּהּ שֶׁל קֶרֶן וְדַיּוֹ". מְנָלַן – דִּכְתִיב: שם ו °"וְזֹאת תּוֹרַת הַמִּנְחָה הַקְרֵב אוֹתָהּ בְּנֵי אַהֲרֹן לִפְנֵי ה' אֶל פְּנֵי הַמִּזְבֵּחַ", *וְתַנְיָא: "לִפְנֵי ה'", יָכוֹל בַּמַּעֲרָב – ת"ל: "אֶל פְּנֵי הַמִּזְבֵּחַ", אִי "אֶל פְּנֵי הַמִּזְבֵּחַ" יָכוֹל בַּדָּרוֹם – ת"ל: "לִפְנֵי ה'". הָא כֵּיצַד? מַגִּישָׁהּ בְּקֶרֶן דְּרוֹמִית מַעֲרָבִית כְּנֶגֶד חוּדָּהּ שֶׁל קֶרֶן, וְדַיּוֹ. רַבִּי אֶלְעָזָר אוֹמֵר: יָכוֹל יַגִּישֶׁנָּה בְּמַעֲרָבָהּ שֶׁל קֶרֶן אוֹ לִדְרוֹמָהּ שֶׁל קֶרֶן – אָמַרְתָּ: כָּל מָקוֹם שֶׁאַתָּה מוֹצֵא שְׁנֵי מִקְרָאוֹת, אֶחָד מְקַיֵּים עַצְמוֹ וּמְקַיֵּים דִּבְרֵי חֲבֵירוֹ, וְאֶחָד מְקַיֵּים עַצְמוֹ וּמְבַטֵּל דִּבְרֵי חֲבֵירוֹ – מַנִּיחִין אֶת שֶׁמְּקַיֵּים עַצְמוֹ וּמְבַטֵּל חֲבֵירוֹ, וְתוֹפְסִין אֶת שֶׁמְּקַיֵּים עַצְמוֹ וּמְקַיֵּים חֲבֵירוֹ. כְּשֶׁאַתָּה אוֹמֵר "לִפְנֵי ה'" בַּמַּעֲרָב – בִּיטַּלְתָּה "אֶל פְּנֵי הַמִּזְבֵּחַ" בַּדָּרוֹם, וּכְשֶׁאַתָּה אוֹמֵר "אֶל פְּנֵי הַמִּזְבֵּחַ" בַּדָּרוֹם – קִיַּימְתָּה "לִפְנֵי ה'" בַּמַּעֲרָב. הָא כֵּיצַד? מַגִּישָׁהּ לִדְרוֹמָהּ שֶׁל קֶרֶן. וְהֵיכָן קִיַּימְתָּה? אָמַר רַב אַשִׁי: קָסָבַר הַאי תַּנָּא *כּוּלֵּיהּ מִזְבֵּחַ בַּצָּפוֹן קָאֵי. מַאי וְדַיּוֹ? א"ר אַשִׁי: אִיצְטְרִיךְ, ס"ד אָמִינָא: תִּיבָּעֵי הַגָּשַׁת מִנְחָה גּוּפָהּ, קָמַשְׁמַע לָן. וְאֵימָא הָכִי נַמִי! אָמַר קְרָא: "וְהִקְרִיבָהּ אֶל הַכֹּהֵן וגו' וְהִגִּישָׁהּ אֶל הַמִּזְבֵּחַ", מָה הַקְרָבָה אֵצֶל כֹּהֵן בִּכְלִי – אַף הַגָּשָׁה אֵצֶל מִזְבֵּחַ בִּכְלִי. § "וּמְסַלֵּק אֶת לְבוֹנָתָהּ לְצַד אֶחָד". כִּי הֵיכִי דְּלָא תִּקְמוֹץ בַּהֲדֵי מִנְחָה, כְּדִתְנַן: *יקָמַץ וְעָלָה בְיָדוֹ צְרוֹר, אוֹ גַּרְגֵּר מֶלַח, אוֹ קוֹרֶט לְבוֹנָה – פָּסוּל. § "וְקוֹמֵץ מִמָּקוֹם שֶׁנִּתְרַבָּה שַׁמְנָהּ". מְנָלַן? דִּכְתִיב: שם ב °"מִסָּלְתָּהּ וּמִשַּׁמְנָהּ מִגִּרְשָׂהּ וּמִשַּׁמְנָהּ". § "וְנוֹתְנוֹ לְתוֹךְ כְּלִי שָׁרֵת וּמְקַדְּשׁוֹ בִּכְלִי שָׁרֵת". לָמָּה לִי? הָא קְדָשָׁהּ חֲדָא זִימְנָא! מִידֵּי דַּהֲוָה אַדָּם; דָּם, אע"ג דְּקַדִּישְׁתֵּיהּ סַכִּין בְּצַוַּאר בְּהֵמָה – הֲדַר מַקְדִּישׁ לֵיהּ בִּכְלִי שָׁרֵת, הָכָא נַמִי לָא שְׁנָא. "וּמְלַקֵּט אֶת לְבוֹנָתָהּ וְנוֹתְנָהּ עַל גַּבָּיו" – דִּכְתִיב: שם ו °"וְאֵת כָּל הַלְּבוֹנָה אֲשֶׁר עַל הַמִּנְחָה". § "וּמַעֲלֵהוּ וּמַקְטִירוֹ"

מַשְׁקֶה. הַמַּיִם, וְאח"כ מַקְרִיב מִנְחָתָהּ. וּפְלוּגְתָּא הִיא בְּפֶרֶק "הָיָה נוֹטֵל" (לְקַמָּן דף יט.). וּמִיהוּ, כָּל זְמַן שֶׁלֹּא קָרְבָה מִנְחָתָהּ – אֵינָהּ נִבְדֶּקֶת, דִּכְתִיב: "מַזְכֶּרֶת עָוֹן". וְאע"פ שֶׁשָּׁתְתָה – מַנִּיחִין אוֹתָהּ בְּיָדָהּ כְּדֵי לְיַגְּעָהּ וְתוֹדֶה. וְהָשְׁתָּא וַדַּאי מִשּׁוּם חִסָּיוֹן הוּא, דְּאִי מִשּׁוּם מְגִילָּה – הָא אִימְחִיקָא לָהּ (ב). תורה אור קְלָתוֹת. כְּעֵין סַלִּים. אָדָם מֵבִיא מִנְחָתוֹ לָעֲזָרָה מִתּוֹךְ בֵּיתוֹ בִּקְלָתוֹת וכו'. וְנוֹתְנָהּ. בָּעֲזָרָה בִּכְלִי שָׁרֵת. קס"ד שֶׁצָּרִיךְ לִתְּנָהּ ע"מ כֵּן, שֶׁיְּהֵא דַּעְתּוֹ שֶׁיְּקַדְּשֶׁנָּה הַכְּלִי. וּמַגִּישָׁהּ. מַגִּיעַ אֶת הַכְּלִי לַקֶּרֶן מַעֲרָבִית דְּרוֹמִית. וּלְקַמָּן יָלֵיף לָהּ מִקְרָאֵי. וְדַיּוֹ. לְקַמָּן מְפָרֵשׁ מַאי הִיא, (ג) וּמַאי תֵּיסַק אַדַּעְתִּין דְּנִבְּעֵי טְפֵי. וּמְסַלֵּק הַלְּבוֹנָה לְצַד אֶחָד. בְּתוֹךְ הַכְּלִי עַצְמָהּ. וּלְקַמָּן מְפָרֵשׁ טַעְמָא דְּכוּלָּהּ מַתְנִיתָא. שֶׁנִּתְרַבָּה שַׁמְנָהּ. מִמָּקוֹם שֶׁהִיא נִבְלֶלֶת יָפֶה בַּשֶּׁמֶן. וְנוֹתְנוֹ לִכְלִי שָׁרֵת. שֵׁנִי. וּלְקַמָּן מְפָרֵשׁ טַעְמָא. עַל גַּבֵּי הָאִשִּׁים. עַל הָאֵשׁ. לִיתֵּן לְתוֹכָהּ. לִיתֵּן לְתוֹךְ הַשִּׁירַיִם. בְּכֵלִים הָרְאוּיִין לִכְלֵי שָׁרֵת. אִם הָיָה מַקְדִּישָׁן. רַבִּי פּוֹסֵל. [בִּמְנָחוֹת], וּבְמַסֶּכֶת סוּכָּה יָלֵיף טַעְמָא בְּפֶרֶק "הֶחָלִיל" (דף נ:). בַּחֲשׁוּבִין. בִּכְלֵי עֵץ חֲשׁוּבִין. הַקְרִיבֵהוּ נָא לְפֶחָתֶךָ. סֵיפָא דִּקְרָא: "הֲיִרְצְךָ אוֹ הֲיִשָּׂא פָנֶיךָ". אֵין מְקַדְּשִׁין אֶלָּא מִדַּעַת. שֶׁהַנּוֹתְנוֹ בָּהֶן צָרִיךְ שֶׁיִּתְכַּוֵּין לְשֵׁם כָּךְ. וְא"ת: הֲרֵי מִנְחָה קְדוֹשָׁה וְעוֹמֶדֶת, שֶׁהִקְדִּישָׁהּ בַּפֶּה! קְדוּשַּׁת פֶּה אֵינָהּ אֶלָּא קְדוּשַּׁת דָּמִים, וְאֵינָהּ קְדוּשַּׁת הַגּוּף, וְאֵינָהּ נִפְסֶלֶת בִּטְבוּל יוֹם וּבְלִינָה, וְאִם נִטְמֵאת – נִפְדֵּית. קְדָשָׁהּ בִּכְלִי – קִידְּשָׁהּ קְדוּשַּׁת הַגּוּף, וְנִפְסֶלֶת בִּטְבוּל יוֹם וּבְלִינָה, וְאֵין לָהּ פִּדְיוֹן. נוֹתְנָהּ לְקַדְּשָׁהּ. הַתּוֹרָה הִצְרִיכָתוֹ לִיתְּנוֹ בִּכְלִי שָׁרֵת כְּדֵי שֶׁיְּקַדְּשֶׁנָּה הַכְּלִי, וַאֲפִילּוּ אֵינוֹ מִתְכַּוֵּין לְכָךְ. וְנוֹתֵן עָלֶיהָ. הַזָּר, שֶׁמֶן וּלְבוֹנָה. וְאֵין צָרִיךְ כֹּהֵן לְכָךְ, דִּכְתִיב: "וְיָצַק עָלֶיהָ שֶׁמֶן" וגו' וַהֲדַר "וֶהֱבִיאָהּ אֶל בְּנֵי אַהֲרֹן" וגו'. וְזֹאת תּוֹרַת הַמִּנְחָה. כָּל הַמְּנָחוֹת בְּמַשְׁמַע. הַקְרֵב אוֹתָהּ בְּנֵי אַהֲרֹן וגו' יָכוֹל בַּמַּעֲרָב. יַגִּיעֶנָּה לְדוֹפֶן מַעֲרָבִי שֶׁל מִזְבֵּחַ, דְּהַיְינוּ "לִפְנֵי ה'". שֶׁהַהֵיכָל בַּמַּעֲרָב וְהַמִּזְבֵּחַ בֶּחָצֵר ל"ב אַמָּה רָחְבּוֹ מְמוּצָּע בְּאֶמְצַע הָעֲזָרָה, וְכֵן הַהֵיכָל מְמוּצָּע בְּאֶמְצַע הָעֲזָרָה זֶה מוּל זֶה ל"ב אַמָּה. הֵיכָל וּכְתָלָיו חֲלָלוֹ כ', וּכְתָלָיו ו' אַמָּה עוֹבִי כּוֹתֶל צְפוֹנִי, וְשִׁשָּׁה לְכוֹתֶל דְּרוֹמִי. נִמְצָא מַעֲרָבוֹ שֶׁל מִזְבֵּחַ לִפְנֵי ה', דְּאֵין מַפְסִיק כְּלוּם בֵּינוֹ לְבֵין הַהֵיכָל. דְּאִילּוּ אוּלָם שֶׁלִּפְנֵי הַהֵיכָל – פָּתוּחַ הוּא, וְרָחְבּוֹ עֶשְׂרִים אַמָּה כְּכָל חֲלָלוֹ שֶׁל הֵיכָל. כְּנֶגֶד חוּדָּהּ. כָּל מַה שֶּׁיָּכוֹל לְקָרְבוֹ כְּלַפֵּי מַעֲרָב, וּבִלְבַד שֶׁיְּהֵא שָׁם קְצָת דָּרוֹם, מִשּׁוּם "אֶל פְּנֵי הַמִּזְבֵּחַ". דְּאִי לָאו כְּנֶגֶד חוּדָּהּ – לֵיכָּא לִפְנֵי ה' כְּלָל, שֶׁהֲרֵי זָוִיּוֹת הַהֵיכָל כּוּלָּם כְּנֶגֶד זָוִיּוֹת הַמִּזְבֵּחַ. ר' אֶלְעָזָר אוֹמֵר כו'. דּוֹרְשׁוֹ לַמִּקְרָא בְּעִנְיָן אַחֵר. וְכָךְ דּוֹרְשׁוֹ: מִתּוֹךְ שֶׁנֶּאֱמַר "לִפְנֵי ה' אֶל פְּנֵי הַמִּזְבֵּחַ" יָכוֹל יַגִּישֶׁנָּה לְאֶחָד מֵהֶן, רָצָה – לַמַּעֲרָב, רָצָה – לִדְרוֹמָהּ. וה"ג לָהּ בת"כ. אוֹ לִדְרוֹמָהּ שֶׁל קֶרֶן אָמַרְתָּ. כָּךְ תְּשִׁיבֵנִי. כָּל מָקוֹם שֶׁאַתָּה מוֹצֵא כו'. דַּיְינִן דְּאָתְיָא לְקַיֵּים אֶת שְׁנֵיהֶם – אִי לָא הוּקְמָה רָצָה זֶה רָצָה זֶה, אֶלָּא אֶת הַמְקַיֵּים אֶת שְׁנֵיהֶם קִיַּימְתָּה לִפְנֵי ה' בַּמַּעֲרָב הָא כֵּיצַד מַגִּישָׁהּ לִדְרוֹמָהּ שֶׁל קֶרֶן. ה"ג לָהּ בת"כ: לִדְרוֹמָהּ שֶׁל קֶרֶן, וְלָא בָּעֵי כְּנֶגֶד חוּדָּהּ. וְהֵיכָן קִיַּימְתָּה. הֲלֹא חוּץ לִכְנֶגֶד זָוִיּוֹת הַהֵיכָל הוּא! קָסָבַר הַאי תַּנָּא. ר' אֶלְעָזָר. כּוּלֵּיהּ מִזְבֵּחַ בַּצָּפוֹן קָאֵי. בְּחֵלֶק צְפוֹנִי שֶׁל עֲזָרָה. וְלֵית לֵיהּ דְּמִזְבֵּחַ מְכוּוָּן כְּנֶגֶד הַהֵיכָל וּכְתָלָיו. נִמְצָא דְּרוֹמוֹ שֶׁל מִזְבֵּחַ כְּנֶגֶד אֶמְצַע פֶּתַח הַהֵיכָל. הִלְכָּךְ יַגִּישֶׁנָּה אֶל פְּנֵי הַמִּזְבֵּחַ בַּדָּרוֹם וּבִלְבַד שֶׁיְּהֵא סָמוּךְ לַמַּעֲרָב – נִמְצָא מְקַיֵּים אֶת שְׁנֵיהֶם. וְה"ה נַמִי אִם הָיָה מִזְבֵּחַ מָשׁוּךְ מְעַט מִכְּנֶגֶד זָוִיּוֹת דְּרוֹמִית הַהֵיכָל וְלַצָּפוֹן שֶׁיְּהֵא דְּרוֹמוֹ שֶׁל מִזְבֵּחַ כְּנֶגֶד הַהֵיכָל – הֲוָה מָצֵי לְקַיֵּים אֶת שְׁנֵיהֶם, דִּכְנֶגֶד הַהֵיכָל קָרֵינַן בֵּיהּ "לִפְנֵי ה'", וּבִלְבַד שֶׁיַּגִּישׁ סָמוּךְ לַקֶּרֶן – דְּהַיְינוּ אֵל מַעֲרָב, וְהָא דְּנָקַט לְמִשְׁמַע מִינָּהּ כּוּלֵּיהּ מִזְבֵּחַ בַּצָּפוֹן קָאֵי – מִשּׁוּם דְּג' מַחֲלוֹקוֹת הֵן בְּדָבָר זֶה: ר' יְהוּדָה אִית לֵיהּ מִזְבֵּחַ מְכוּוָּן כְּנֶגֶד הֵיכָל וּכְתָלָיו, בְּפ"ק דְּיוֹמָא (דף טז.), וְר"א בֶּן יַעֲקֹב אִית לֵיהּ כּוּלֵּיהּ מִזְבֵּחַ בַּדָּרוֹם קָאֵי, דְּאָמַר: לְפוֹנִי – שֶׁהוּא לְצַד פָּנוּי מִכְּלוּם, וְר' יוֹסֵי הַגְּלִילִי אִית לֵיהּ כּוּלֵּיהּ מִזְבֵּחַ בַּצָּפוֹן קָאֵי, בִּזְבָחִים בְּפ' "קָדְשֵׁי קָדָשִׁים" (דף נט.). הִלְכָּךְ לְר"א דְּהָכָא, דְּשָׁמְעִי' לֵיהּ ע"כ דְּקָאָמַר: זָוִית דְּרוֹמִית שֶׁל מִזְבֵּחַ לִפְנִים מִכְּנֶגֶד זָוִית שֶׁל הֵיכָל הוּא, וּפָלֵיג אַדְּר"י וְאַדְּר"א בֶּן יַעֲקֹב – מוֹקְמִינַן לֵיהּ כְּר' יוֹסֵי הַגְּלִילִי דְּס"ל דְּכוּלֵּיהּ מִזְבֵּחַ בַּצָּפוֹן, וְלָא מוֹקְמִינַן לֵיהּ בְּמַחֲלוֹקֶת רְבִיעִית. מַאי וְדַיּוֹ. מַאי תֵּיסַק אַדַּעְתֵּיהּ דְּנִבְּעֵי טְפֵי? מִנְחָה גּוּפָהּ. וְלֹא הַכְּלִי שֶׁהִיא בָּהּ. אֶלָּא יָכוֹף הַכְּלִי שֶׁיְּהֵא נוֹגֵעַ סוֹלֶת לַמִּזְבֵּחַ. פָּסוּל. מִשּׁוּם דַּהֲוָה קוֹמֶץ חָסֵר. סַכִּין. הָוֵי כְּלִי שָׁרֵת, דְּתַנְיָא (יוֹמָא דף יב:): כָּל הַכֵּלִים שֶׁעָשָׂה מֹשֶׁה מְשִׁיחָתָן מְקַדַּשְׁתָּן, מִכָּאן וְאֵילָךְ עֲבוֹדָתָן מְחַנַּכְתָּן. הֲדַר מַקְדִּישׁ לֵיהּ בִּכְלִי. שֶׁמְּקַבְּלוֹ בִּכְלִי שָׁרֵת, כְּדִכְתִיב "וַיָּשֶׂם בָּאַגָּנוֹת" (שמות כד). וְאֵת כָּל הַלְּבוֹנָה. גַּבֵּי הַקְטָרָה כְּתִיב, דְּמַקְטֵר קוֹמֶץ וּלְבוֹנָה כִּי הֲדָדֵי.

ה"ג

[לקמן יט.]
תוספתא פ"א דמנחות
סוכה נ: מנחות כח:
[שם וזבחים נו:]
סוכה נ. מנחות ז. [עת: ג.]
מנחות יט: זבחים סג.
[זבחים נז.]
מנחות ו.

הגהות הב"ח

(א) גמ' מי אמר וכי לית ליה לר' יוסי: (ב) רש"י ד"ה משקה וכו' אימחיקא לה הס"ד ואח"כ מ"ה אדם מביא וכו' בקלתות כעין סלים הס"ד ואח"כ מ"ה ונותנה וכו': (ג) ד"ה ודיו וכו' ומאי תיסק.

תוספות שאנץ

ואחר כך מקריב מנחתה ופלוגתא היא בפ' היה נוטל ומיהו כל זמן שלא קירבה מנחתה אינה נבדקת דכתיב מזכרת עון ואע"פ ששתתה משהין אותה בידה כדי ליגעה ותודה. וכהן מוליכה אצל מזבח ומגישה בקרן מערבית דרומית אבל בלילה לא חשיב משום דאין בלילה מעכבת דהא תנן אם לא בלל כשר. וא"ת והא במנחות בפ' הקומץ רבה אמרינן וקמץ הכהן מקמיצה ואילך מצות כהונה (א) ואפי' הכי ממעטי יציקה ובלילה דמקמי הגשה הוו ואמאי נקט מקמיצה ואילך (ב) וי"ל דאיתיה אמ' במסכת ואילך מצות כהונה היה מכשרי קמיצה בזר והא דכתב כהן אצל הגשה היינו שאין זר יכול ליקרב אצל המזבח דכתיב והזר הקרב יומת אבל קמיצה אימר שכשרה בזר לכך נקט מקמיצה ואילך מצות כהונה. וא"ת אמאי לא קאמר מתנופה ואילך מצות כהונה ואפי' הכי ממעטי יציקה דמקמי תנופה היה וי"ל דלאו מילתא היא דהא בשאר מנחות אין תנופה כמו שפירשו בהדיא במנחות (דף ס.) אבל קמיצה דהויא בכל המנחות נקט לה. הקרב אותה בני אהרן לפני המזבח יכול במערב יגיענה לדופן מערבי של מזבח דהיינו לפני ה' שההיכל היה למערב והמזבח לדרומו ל"ב אמה ממוצע באמצע העזרה וכן ההיכל באמצע זה מול זה ל"ב אמה ההיכל וכותליו חללו כ' וכותליו ו' אמה עובי כותל צפוני ושש לכותל דרומי נמצא מערבו של מזבח [לפני ה'] דאין מפסיק בינו לבין ההיכל דאילו אולם שלפני היכל פתוח הוא ורחבו כ' אמה ככל חללו של היכל. ל"ה. אל פני המזבח בדרום פי' משום דכתיב ושחט אותו על ירך המזבח צפונה. וכיון דהוי ירך צפון א"כ הוי פניו לדרום. כנגד חודה כל מה שיכול לקרבו כלפי מערב ובלבד שיהא שם קצת דרום משום אל פני המזבח דאי לאו כנגד חודה ליכא לפני ה'. שהרי זוית ההיכל כולה בעד זוית המזבח. כולי מזבח בצפון קאי בחלק צפוני של עזרה [ולית ליה] דמזבח מכוון כנגד היכל וכותליו. נמצא כותל דרומי של מזבח כנגד אמצעי פתח ההיכל הלכך יגישנה אל פני המזבח בדרום ובלבד שיהא סמוך למערב ונמצא מקיים את שניהם וה"ה נמי אם היה מזבח משוך מעט כנגד זוית ההיכל ולצפון שיהא דרומה של מזבח כנגד ההיכל הוה מצי לקיים את שניהם דכיון דכנגד ההיכל הוה קרי ביה לפני ה'. ובלבד שיהא סמוך לקרן שהוא אצל מערב והאי דנקט (בפ"ק דיומא ר' אליעזר אית ליה) למשמע מיניה דכולי מזבח בצפון קאי משום דג' מחלוקות הן בדבר זה ר' יהודה אית ליה מזבח מכוון כנגד ההיכל וכותליו בפ"ק דיומא ור' אליעזר בר' יעקב אית ליה כולי מזבח בדרום קאי דאמר צפונה שהוא פנוי מכלום. ור' יוסי הגלילי אית ליה כולי מזבח בצפון קאי כדאמר בפ' קדשי הקדשים הילכך לר"א דהכא דשמעי' ליה ע"כ דאמר דרומו של מזבח לפנים מכנגד זוית של היכל הוא ופליג אדר' יהודה ואדר' אליעזר בן יעקב אוקי' ליה כר' יוסי הגלילי דסבי' ליה כולי מזבח בצפון ולא מוקמי ליה במחלוקת רבי' ל"ה. אע"ג דקדשי' סכין חדא זימנא הדר מקדש ליה בכלי שרת משמע מהכא דהסכין הוי קדוש וק' מההוא דפ"ק דחולין דקאמר כגון שבדק קרומית של קנה והכא אמר דצריך שיהא קדוש וקרומית לא הוו קדוש. וי"ל דלא ק' מידי דההיא דהתם אתיא כר' יוסי בר' יהודה דמכשר כלי שרת שעשאן של עץ אבל לעולם בעי' כלי שרת שהסכין הוי קדוש וראיה מיהא דאמרי' חומר בסכין מכלי שרת שהסכין אינו טעון תוך וכלי שרת טעון תוך ואי הוה אמרי' דאין צריך שיהא הסכין קדוש אמאי לא קאמר דסכין אינו קדוש וכלי שרת מקודש אלא אע"פ דלעולם סכין בעי' כלי שרת כדפרש"י ולא כפי' ה"ר [אפרים] דפי' דלגבי שחיטת קדשים לא בעי כלי שרת ומביא ראיה מההיא דחולין דבדק בקרומית של קנה דהוה עץ. ויש לדחות אותה [ראיה] כמו שפירשתי דסבירא ליה כר' יהודה. ועוד היה מביא ה"ר אפרים ראי' מפרק איזהו מקומן שחיטתן בצפון וקיבול דמן בכלי שרת בצפון ומדנקט גבי קבלה כלי שרת ולא נקט גבי שחיטה דלא אמר שחיטתן בכלי שרת בצפון ש"מ דבשחיטה לא בעי כלי שרת. ומיהו אינה ראיה דהא דלא תני שחיטתן בכלי שרת בצפון כמו דתני וקיבול דמן בכלי שרת משום דבקבלה צריך שיהא הכלי בצפון אבל בשחיטה לא צריך. מקטירו ס"ד ה"ג רש"י ז"ל

(א) נראה לנ"ל ואמאי לא אמר נמי מהגשה ואילך מצות כהונה ואפי' הכי. ב) נראה לנ"ל וי"ל דאי לאו קרא דוקמץ הכהן היה מכשיר וכו' אבל קמילה הוה אמינא שכשרה בזר וכו'.

וּמַקְטִירוֹ בִּכְלֵי שָׁרֵת". *בִּכְלֵי שָׁרֵת מַקְטִיר לֵיהּ?! אֶלָּא אֵימָא: מַעֲלֵהוּ בִּכְלֵי שָׁרֵת לְהַקְטִירוֹ.§ "וּמוֹלְחוֹ וְנוֹתְנוֹ עַל גַּבֵּי הָאִשִּׁים". דִּכְתִיב: °"וְכָל קָרְבַּן מִנְחָתְךָ בַּמֶּלַח תִּמְלָח" וגו'.§ "קָרַב הַקּוֹמֶץ שִׁירֶיהָ נֶאֱכָלִין".§ מְנָלַן? דִּכְתִיב °"וְהִקְטִיר הַכֹּהֵן אֶת אַזְכָּרָתָהּ" וגו' וּכְתִיב: °"וְהַנּוֹתֶרֶת מִן הַמִּנְחָה לְאַהֲרֹן וּלְבָנָיו". קָרַב הַקּוֹמֶץ, לְמָר כִּדְאִית לֵיהּ וּלְמָר כִּדְאִית לֵיהּ, דְּאִיתְּמַר: *הַקּוֹמֶץ מֵאֵימָתַי מַתִּיר שִׁירַיִים בַּאֲכִילָה? רַבִּי חֲנִינָא אָמַר: מִשֶּׁתִּשְׁלוֹט בּוֹ הָאוּר, רַבִּי יוֹחָנָן אָמַר: [א]מִשֶּׁתִּיצַּת הָאוּר בְּרוּבּוֹ.§ "וְרַשָּׁאִין הַכֹּהֲנִים לִיתֵּן לְתוֹכוֹ יַיִן וְשֶׁמֶן וּדְבַשׁ". מַאי טַעְמָא? אָמַר קְרָא: "לְמָשְׁחָה" — *לִגְדוּלָּה, כְּדֶרֶךְ שֶׁהַמְּלָכִים אוֹכְלִין.§ "וְאֵין אֲסוּרִין אֶלָּא מִלְּחַמֵּץ" — דִּכְתִיב: °"לֹא תֵאָפֶה חָמֵץ חֶלְקָם", *א"ר שִׁמְעוֹן בֶּן לָקִישׁ: [ב]אֲפִילּוּ חֶלְקָם לֹא תֵאָפֶה חָמֵץ.§ "כָּל הַמְּנָחוֹת" כו'.§ וְכָל הַמְּנָחוֹת טְעוּנוֹת שֶׁמֶן וּלְבוֹנָה?! [ג]וְהָאִיכָּא מִנְחַת חוֹטֵא, דְּרַחֲמָנָא אָמַר: °"לֹא יָשִׂים עָלֶיהָ שֶׁמֶן וְלֹא יִתֵּן עָלֶיהָ לְבוֹנָה"! הָכִי קָאָמַר: כָּל הַמְּנָחוֹת טְעוּנוֹת שֶׁמֶן וּלְבוֹנָה, וּבָאוֹת מִן הַחִיטִּין, וּבָאוֹת סֹלֶת. מִנְחַת חוֹטֵא, אַף עַל פִּי שֶׁאֵינָהּ טְעוּנָה שֶׁמֶן וּלְבוֹנָה — בָּאָה מִן הַחִטִּין וּבָאָה סֹלֶת. מִנְחַת הָעוֹמֶר, אע"פ שֶׁהִיא בָּאָה מִן הַשְּׂעוֹרִין — טְעוּנָה שֶׁמֶן וּלְבוֹנָה, וּבָאָה גֶּרֶשׂ. וְזוֹ אֵינָהּ טְעוּנָה לֹא שֶׁמֶן וְלֹא לְבוֹנָה, וּבָאָה מִן הַשְּׂעוֹרִין, וּבָאָה קֶמַח. *תַּנְיָא, אָמַר ר"ש: בְּדִין הוּא שֶׁתְּהֵא מִנְחַת חוֹטֵא טְעוּנָה שֶׁמֶן וּלְבוֹנָה, שֶׁלֹּא יְהֵא חוֹטֵא נִשְׂכָּר. וּמִפְּנֵי מָה אֵינָהּ טְעוּנָה — שֶׁלֹּא יְהֵא קָרְבָּנוֹ מְהוּדָּר. וּבְדִין הוּא שֶׁתְּהֵא חַטַּאת חֵלֶב טְעוּנָה נְסָכִים, *שֶׁלֹּא יְהֵא חוֹטֵא נִשְׂכָּר. וּמִפְּנֵי מָה [ד]אֵינָהּ טְעוּנָה — שֶׁלֹּא יְהֵא קָרְבָּנוֹ מְהוּדָּר. אֲבָל חַטָּאתוֹ שֶׁל מְצוֹרָע וַאֲשָׁמוֹ — [ה]טְעוּנִין נְסָכִים, לְפִי שֶׁאֵין בָּאִין עַל חֵטְא. אִינִי?! *וְהָאָמַר רַבִּי שְׁמוּאֵל בַּר נַחְמָנִי אָמַר רַבִּי יוֹנָתָן: עַל שִׁבְעָה דְּבָרִים נְגָעִים בָּאִין וכו'! הָתָם מִנִּגְעֵיהּ הוּא דְּאִיכַּפַּר לֵיהּ, כִּי מַיְיתֵי קָרְבָּן — לְאִשְׁתַּרוּיֵי בְּקָדָשִׁים הוּא דְּקָא מַיְיתֵי. אֶלָּא מֵעַתָּה, חַטַּאת נָזִיר תְּהֵא טְעוּנָה נְסָכִים, לְפִי שֶׁאֵינָהּ בָּאָה עַל חֵטְא! סָבַר לָהּ כְּרַבִּי אֶלְעָזָר הַקַּפָּר, *דְּאָמַר: נָזִיר נַמִי חוֹטֵא הוּא.§ "רַבָּן גַּמְלִיאֵל אוֹמֵר כְּשֵׁם" כו'.§ תַּנְיָא, אָמַר לָהֶן רַבָּן גַּמְלִיאֵל לַחֲכָמִים: סוֹפְרִים, הַנִּיחוּ לִי וְאֶדְרְשֶׁנָּה *כְּמִין חוֹמֶר.

(ויקרא ב; שם; שם; שם ו; שם ה — תורה אור)

רש"י

ה"ג: וּמַקְטִירוֹ ס"ד. וְלָא גָּרַס: אַטּוּ בִּכְלֵי שָׁרֵת מַקְטַר לֵיהּ. וְהָכִי קָא קַשְׁיָא לֵיהּ: מַקְטִירוֹ ס"ד? וַהֲרֵי עֲדַיִין לֹא מְלָחוֹ, וְסֵיפָא קָתָנֵי: וּמוֹלְחוֹ וְנוֹתְנוֹ עַל גַּבֵּי הָאִשִּׁים, אַלְמָא הַשְׁתָּא הוּא דְּמַקְטַר לֵיהּ!. **אֶלָּא אֵימָא** מַעֲלֵהוּ לְהַקְטִירוֹ בִּכְלֵי שָׁרֵת. כְּלוֹמַר, מַעֲלֵהוּ בִּכְלֵי שָׁרֵת לְהַקְטִירוֹ לְאַחַר שֶׁיִּמְלָחֶנּוּ. קָרַב הַקּוֹמֶץ לְמָר כִּדְאִית לֵיהּ וכו'. קָרַב הַקּוֹמֶץ דְּקָתָנֵי דְּמַתִּיר שִׁירַיִם בַּאֲכִילָה, מֵאֵימַת חָשִׁיב קְרִיבָה לְהַתִּיר שִׁירַיִם — לְרַבִּי יוֹחָנָן כִּדְאִית לֵיהּ, מִשֶּׁתִּיצַּת הָאוּר בְּרוּבּוֹ, וּלְרַבִּי חֲנִינָא — מִשֶּׁתִּשְׁלוֹט בּוֹ וַאֲפִילּוּ מְעַט. לְמָשְׁחָה. גַּבֵּי מַתְּנוֹת כְּהוּנָּה כְּתִיב (במדבר יח): "לְךָ נְתַתִּים לְמָשְׁחָה". לֹא תֵאָפֶה חָמֵץ חֶלְקָם וגו'. אֲפִילּוּ חֶלְקָם, שִׁירַיִם, לֹא תֵאָפֶה חָמֵץ. דְּדָרְשִׁינַן לֵיהּ הַאי "חֶלְקָם" דִּקְרָא נַמִי לְפָנָיו אַ"לֹא תֵאָפֶה". מִנְחַת חוֹטֵא. הַבָּאָה עַל חֵטְא, דְּמְטַמֵּא מִקְדָּשׁ וּשְׁבוּעַת הָעֵדוּת וּשְׁבוּעַת בִּיטּוּי, דִּכְתִיב הָתָם: "וְאִם לֹא תַשִּׂיג יָדוֹ לִשְׁתֵּי תוֹרִים" וגו' (ויקרא ה). ה"ק וכו'. כְּלוֹמַר, לֹא קָתָנֵי מִילְּתָא בְּאַנְפֵּי נַפְשֵׁיהּ, אֶלָּא כְּרוֹךְ וּתְנֵי הָכִי: כָּל הַמְּנָחוֹת טְעוּנוֹת שֶׁמֶן וּלְבוֹנָה וּבָאוֹת חִטִּין, כְּלוֹמַר: וְשֶׁאֵינָם טְעוּנוֹת — בָּאוֹת מֵיהַת חִטִּין וּבָאוֹת סוֹלֶת. כְּלוֹמַר, חֲדָא מֵהָנֵי מַעַלְיוּתָא אִית בְּהוּ. כֵּיצַד? מִנְחַת חוֹטֵא אע"פ שֶׁאֵינָהּ טְעוּנָה וכו'. **שֶׁלֹּא יְהֵא חוֹטֵא נִשְׂכָּר.** לְהָקֵל בְּמִנְחָתוֹ יוֹתֵר מִשְּׁאָר מְנָחוֹת. **חַטַּאת חֵלֶב.** כָּל חַטָּאת סְתָם קָרֵי חַטַּאת חֵלֶב, דְּבָתַר חֵלֶב כְּתִיב: (א) "כָּל חֵלֶב וְכָל דָּם לֹא תֹאכֵלוּ" (שם ג), וּכְתִיב בַּתְרֵיהּ פָּרָשַׁת חַטָּאת. **נְסָכִים.** סוֹלֶת לְמִנְחָה, וְעִשָּׂרוֹן לַכֶּבֶשׂ יַיִן, וְשֶׁמֶן רְבִיעִית הַהִין, כְּמוֹ שֶׁמַּקְרִיבִין לְעוֹלָה וּשְׁלָמִים. **וּמִפְּנֵי מָה אֵינָם טְעוּנוֹת.** דִּכְתִיב בְּפָרָשַׁת נְסָכִים (במדבר טו): "לְפַלֵּא נֶדֶר אוֹ בִנְדָבָה"; הַבָּא בְּנֶדֶר וּנְדָבָה — טָעוּן נְסָכִים, וְאֵין חַטָּאת וְאָשָׁם טְעוּנִים נְסָכִים. **חַטָּאתוֹ וַאֲשָׁמוֹ שֶׁל מְצוֹרָע.** אִיתְרַבּוּ בְּהֶדְיָא לִנְסָכִים, בְּמַסֶּכֶת מְנָחוֹת בְּפֶרֶק "שְׁתֵּי מִדּוֹת" (דף צא.). **עַל שִׁבְעָה דְּבָרִים נְגָעִים בָּאִין.** וּמְפָרֵשׁ לְהוּ בַּעֲרָכִין בְּפֶרֶק "יֵשׁ בַּעֲרָכִין" (דף טז.). **מִנִּגְעֵיהּ אִיכַּפַּר לֵיהּ.** יִסּוּרִים וּבֹשֶׁת שֶׁל נֶגַע, כִּפְּרוּ לוֹ עַל אוֹתוֹ חֵטְא. **וְכִי קָא מַיְיתֵי קָרְבָּן** לְאִשְׁתַּרוּיֵי בְּקָדָשִׁים הוּא דְּמַיְיתֵי. שֵׁשׁ טוּמְאוֹת שֶׁהִצְרִיכָן הַכָּתוּב כַּפָּרָה לְטָהֳרָתָן: זָב, וְזָבָה, וְיוֹלֶדֶת, וּמְצוֹרָע, וְנָזִיר שֶׁנִּטְמָא. **חַטַּאת נָזִיר.** שֶׁמֵּבִיא בִּמְלֹאת יְמֵי נִזְרוֹ חַטָּאת וְעוֹלָה וּשְׁלָמִים. **נָזִיר חוֹטֵא הוּא.** שֶׁצִּיעֵר עַצְמוֹ מִן הַיַּיִן. **חוֹמֶר.** בוטו"ן בְּלַעַ"ז, וְהוּא שֶׁל זָהָב, וְחוֹתְמִים בּוֹ שְׁנֵי צַוָּארֵי חָלוּק לְנוֹי.

תוספות

טעונה נסכים. א"ל דאינה טעונה נסכים משום דאינה בנדר ונדבה – די"ל ה"פ: בדין הוא, מאחר שהוא חוטא היה צריך לעונשו להביא קרבן גדול, אבל בכור ומעשר אינו בדין. **סבר** לה כרבי אלעזר הקפר. הכא משמע דרבי שמעון ורבי אלעזר הקפר סבירא להו דאפילו נזיר טהור חוטא הוא, דהא נזיר טמא היה מביא חטאת העוף, ועופות אינם טעונים נסכים, כדאיתא בפרק "שתי מדות" (מנחות דף צ:). והכי איתא בהדיא נמי בפרק קמא דנדרים (דף י.) ובפרק ג' דנזיר (דף יט.), דאף על גב דקרא בנזיר טמא כתיב – אנן אפילו נזיר טהור קאמרינן דקסבר רבי אלעזר הקפר חוטא הוא. והיינו טעמא דכתב קרא בנזיר טמא – הואיל ושנה בחטא. וקשה משמעתא קמייתא דנזיר (דף ג:), דתנן: "אהא נאה" – הרי זה נזיר, ודלמא אתנאה לפניו במצות קאמר? אמר שמואל: שתפוס בשערו, ואמר "אתנאה". נזירא עביד מילתא דעבירה ואמרינן ליה נאה? אין, אפילו רבי אלעזר הקפר דאמר נזיר חוטא הוא – הני מילי גבי נזיר טמא, דאיידי דבעי מיסתר דילמא אתי למיעבר על נזירותיה. אבל נזיר טהור – לאו חוטא קרינן ביה! ואם תאמר: שמואל סבירא ליה התם אליבא דרבי אלעזר הקפר דנזיר טהור לאו חוטא, וסתמא דגמרא דהכא ודפ"ג דנזיר (דף יט.) לאו כשמואל, וסתמא דמתניתין דקרי ליה נאה – אליבא דרבנן דאמרי לאו חוטא, לפום סתמא דגמרא. *אם כן, תיקשה דשמואל אדשמואל, דאמר פרק קמא דתענית (דף יא.): כל היושב בתענית נקרא חוטא, סבר לה כרבי אעזר הקפר. ותענית כנזיר טהור הוא, דאמרינן בפ"ק דנדרים (דף י.): רבי אלעזר הקפר אומר וכו' – מכאן שיושב בתענית נקרא חוטא. והתם מיירי בנזיר טהור, כדפרישית, ומדמי ליה יושב בתענית! והשתא אית לן למימר דסתמא דגמ' דנדרים נמי, דמדמי יושב בתענית לנזיר טהור – דלא כשמואל, דאיהו הוה מדמי ליה דוקא לנזיר טמא, לפי שמצער את עצמו מכל דבר, שהרי יושב בתענית ומתחרט, כנזיר טמא שמתחרט משום צער דבעי מיסתר נזירותיה. אבל נזיר טהור אינו צער. מיהו, תיקשה דשמואל אדשמואל, דאמר בפ"ק (לעיל דף יא.) דיושב בתענית נקרא חוטא, ובפרק "החובל" (ב"ק דף צא:) פריך: ואין אדם רשאי לחבול בעצמו? והתניא: יכול נשבע להרע לעצמו וכו' מה הטבה רשות – אף הרעה רשות. ומוקי לה שמואל ביושב בתענית, דהוא רשות! ועוד קשיא מפרק בתרא דכריתות (דף כו.) דאמר: [חטא] שאין אנו מכירין בו אלא המקום – יום הכפורים מכפר. וקא פריך: ספק נזיר שעבר עליו יום הכפורים לא נייתי, דהא כפר עליה יום הכפורים! ומשני: "לכל חטאתם" ולא לכל טומאתם. ולרבי אלעזר הקפר מאי איכא למימר? נזיר כי מייתי קרבן – לאו לכפרה מייתי, אלא לאחולי עליה נזירות טהרה. א"נ, למישרי נפשיה ביין. אלמא דקרבן נזיר לר' אלעזר הקפר לאו לכפרה אתי, והכא משמע משום דבא על חטא אינה טעונה נסכים! והכי אמר נמי בפ"ג דנזיר (דף יט.) דחטאת העוף לר' ישמעאל בא על חטא, דאע"ג דבעל מיעקר עקר, מייתי. ואכתי הוה מצי למיפרך התם לר' שמעון דהכא ולר' ישמעאל מספק נזיר, לר' ישמעאל מספק נזיר טמא, לר' שמעון אפי' מספק נזיר טהור. ובפרק קמא דשבועות (דף ח.) נמי לא מתרך כמו בכריתות דלאו משום כפרה אתי! **סבר** לה כרבי אלעזר הקפר. תימה לי: אמאי תלי מילתיה בר' אלעזר הקפר? והא איהו גופיה אומר נמי בפ"ק דנדרים (דף י.): אבל בנזירות לא התנדבו, שלא יקראו חוטאין, שנאמר: "וכפר עליו מאשר חטא"! וי"ל: אגב שיטפיה, דנקט בכל דוכתא הכי – נקט נמי הכא כי האי לישנא. **כמין** חומר. פי' רבי הילל: מרגלית. ענין אחר: בושם, כמו חומרתא דפילון (שבת דף סב.) – בשמים מעורבין, תרגום "בלולה" – דפילא. ענין אחר פי' רבינו סעדיה גאון: כמין המעשה. דבלשון ארמית אומר אדם לחבירו "מה תמרך" – כלומר: מה מעשיך*.

איכה

תוספות שאנץ

ז"ל ולא גרס אטו בכלי שרת מקטר ליה. והכי קא קשיא ליה והרי עדיין לא מלחן והרי אחרי כן תני ומולחו ונותנו על גבי האשים אלא אימא מעלהו על מנת להקטירו בכלי שרת לאחר שימלחנו ובמנחות (דף כו ע"א) קאמר כי הכא ומקטירו בכלי שרת ולא פריך כי הכא ופי' במסכת יומא פ' שני שעירי (דף סז). נזיר נמי חוטא הוא. פי' שציער עצמו מן היין. וא"ת ליקשי מאשם נזיר דהווה ליה למימר דתהא טעונה נסכים דאינה באה על חטא כדאמר התם בכריתות (דף כז ע"א) אשם נזיר לבטלה אתי. וי"ל דכיון דלבטלה קא אתי אינו טעון נסכים:

הגהות הב"ח

(א) רש"י ד"ה חטאת וכו' כתיב דכתיב כל חלב:

מסורת הש"ס

פסחים סה: יומא סז:

מנחות כו:

[זבחים כח. לה. חולין קלב.]

יבמות מ. שבועות טו: [מנחות נה.]

מנחות ו.

[יבמות לג. וש"נ]

ערכין טז. שבועות ח. [כריתות כו:]

נזיר יט. וש"נ

[קדושין כב:]

גירסת רש"א אכתי

[ע' בערוך ערך המר לרבינו סעדיה גרים כמון חומר שכן בלשון ארמי אומר מאי אסמכת ע"ש]

וע"ע תוס' קדושין כב: ותוס' חולין קלב:]

עין משפט נר מצוה

יב א מיי' פי"ב מהל' מעשה הקרבנות הלכה יג:

יג ב מיי' שם הל' ד:

יד ג מיי' שם הל' ה:

טו ד ה מיי' שם פ"ב הלכה ג סמג עשין קפב:

תורה אור

דשמעיה לר' מאיר דקאמר: *היא האכילתו מעדני עולם – לפיכך קרבנה מאכל בהמה. א"ל: התינח עשירה, ענייה מאי איכא למימר? אלא: כשם שמעשיה מעשה בהמה כך קרבנה מאכל בהמה.§ **מתני'** *אהיה מביא *פילי של חרס ונותן לתוכה חצי לוג מים מן הכיור. ר' יהודה אומר: רביעית. כשם שממעט בכתב, כך ממעט במים. בנכנס להיכל ופנה לימינו, ומקום היה שם אמה על אמה, וטבלא של שיש, וטבעת היתה קבועה בה, כשהוא מגביה, ונוטל עפר מתחתיה, ונותן כדי שיראה על המים, שנאמר: °"ומן העפר אשר יהיה בקרקע (במדבר ה) המשכן יקח הכהן ונתן אל המים".§ **גמ'** תנא: גפילי של חרס חדשה, דברי רבי ישמעאל. מאי טעמא דרבי ישמעאל? גמר "כלי" "כלי" ממצורע, מה להלן דחרס חדשה – אף כאן חרס חדשה. והתם מנלן? דכתיב: °"ושחט את הצפור (ויקרא יד) האחת אל כלי חרש על מים חיים", מה מים חיים שלא נעשתה בהן מלאכה – אף כלי שלא נעשתה בו מלאכה. אי מה להלן מים חיים – אף כאן מים חיים? לרבי ישמעאל הכי נמי. *דאמר ר' יוחנן: מי כיור, רבי ישמעאל אומר: מי מעיין הן, וחכ"א: המשאר מימות הן. איכא למיפרך: מה למצורע – שכן טעון עץ ארז ואזוב ושני תולעת! אמר רבה: אמר קרא "בכלי חרש" – כלי שאמרתי לך כבר. אמר רבא: לא שנו אלא שלא נתאכמו פניו, ואבל נתאכמו פניו – פסולין. מאי טעמא – דומיא דמים, מה מים שלא נשתנו – אף כלי שלא נשתנה. בעי רבא: נתאכמו, והחזירן לתוך כבשן האש ונתלבנו, מהו? מי אמרינן: כיון דאידחו אידחו, או דילמא יכיון דהדור הדור? ת"ש, רבי *אלעזר אומר: עץ ארז ואזוב ושני תולעת שהפשיל בהן קופתו לאחוריו – פסולין. והא התם הדרי ומפשטי! התם חדאיקלוף איקלופי.§ "נכנס להיכל ופנה לימינו" וכו'.§ מ"ט? *דאמר מר: טכל פינות שאתה פונה, לא יהו אלא דרך ימין.§ "מקום היה שם אמה" כו'.§ תנו רבנן: "ומן העפר אשר יהיה". יכול יתקן מבחוץ ויכנים – תלמוד לומר: "בקרקע המשכן". אי "בקרקע המשכן" – יכול יחפור בקרדומות – תלמוד לומר: "אשר יהיה". הא כיצד? כיש שם – הבא, אין שם – תן שם. תניא אידך: "ומן העפר אשר יהיה" וגו' – מלמד שהיה מתקן מבחוץ ומכנים. "בקרקע המשכן". איסי בן יהודה אומר: להביא קרקע
שילה

דשמעיה לרבי מאיר דאמר כו'. בפ"ק (לעיל דף ח:) גבי במדה שאדם מודד. **ענייה.** לא האכילתו מעדנים, למה מביאה מאכל בהמה? **אלא היא עשתה מעשה בהמה.** שהפקירה עצמה לתשמיש למי *שאינה בן זוגה. **מתני' היה מביא.** הכהן. **פילי.** כוס של מים. **מן הכיור.** דכתיב: "מים קדושים" (במדבר ה), ואין קדושים אלא שנתקדשו בכלי. הכי תניא בסיפרי. **כשם שממעט.** רבי יהודה בכתב המגילה, לקמן במתני'* – כך ממעט כאן במים. **ומקום היה שם.** ניכר מתוך שאר רצפת ההיכל. **טבעת קבועה בה.** לאחזה בטבעתה, ולהגביהה מבין הרצפה, שהיא כולה באבני שיש. **כדי שיראה.** צריך ליתן שיעור שיהא נראה וניכר על פני המים. **ונתן אל המים.** מדלא כתיב "ונתן במים", אלא "אל המים", משמע שלא יהא נבלע בתוכן. **גמ' מאי טעמא דרבי ישמעאל.** דבעי חדשה. **גמר ממצורע.** "ושחט את הצפור האחת אל כלי חרש" וגו'. **שלא נעשה בהן מלאכה.** דהא "חיים" כתיב. **לר' ישמעאל.** דפרכת הא אליביה. **הכי נמי.** דבעינן מים חיים לסוטה. דהא מן הכיור הוא נוטל. ושמעינן ליה לר' ישמעאל בעלמא דאמר: מי כיור מי מעיין הן, דהיינו חיים. **משאר מימות הן.** אם רצה ליתן לתוכו מי מקוה – יתן. **איכא למיפרך.** בהא גז"ש דרבי ישמעאל דגמר "כלי" "כלי" ממצורע. **מה למצורע שכן טעון כו'.** לפיכך כלי שלו חדש, תאמר בסוטה שאין בה כל אלו. **אמר רבה וכו' בכלי שאמרתי לך כבר.** הכי משמע ליה לרבה: מדלא כתיב: "ולקח כלי חרש ונתן בו מים", וכתיב: "בכלי חרש" – משמע שכבר הוזכר כלי זה במקום אחר, ואמר רחמנא הכא שבאותו כלי שאמרתי לך במקום אחר – קח אותם, ומאי ניהו – דמצורע. **לא שנו.** רבנן דמתני' דבעו חרס ומכשרי בישן. **אלא שלא נתאכמו.** הושחרו פניו על ידי האור. **דומיא דמים.** אע"ג דלא גמרי ממצורע, מיהו, מינה ובה גמרי כלי דסוטה ממי סוטה. והני דמי סוטה לרבנן לאו חיים נינהו, דמכשרי בשאר מימות – מיהת לא נשתנו, וכלי נמי בעינן דלא נשתנה. **החזירן לכבשן.** של יוצר, שמצרפים בו את הקדרות של חרס חדשות. **שהפשיל קופתו לאחוריו.** מדלא קתני "שנעשה בהן מלאכה" – ש"מ: אמלאכה לא קפיד, אשינויא קפיד. ואלו נתעקמו במשאוי. **והא [התם] דהדרי ומפשטי.** וקתני: פסולין, אלמא: כיון דאידחו – אידחו. **דאיקלופי.** שעל ידי המשוי נתקלפו מקליפתן, דשינויא דלא הדר הוא. **דאמר מר.** בסדר יומא (דף נח:) ובשחיטת קדשים (דף סב:). ויליף לה מ"פונים" "פונים" דשנים עשר בקר דים שעשה שלמה. **ומן העפר אשר יהיה בקרקע המשכן.** אי (א) לא הוה כתיב "בקרקע" *[ה"א בעינן מקרקע המשכן ממש, אבל השתא דכתיב "בקרקע"] משמע דאינו מקפיד אלא שיכנים העפר להיכל. **יכול יתקן.** יזמין עפר מבחוץ ויכנים בהיכל, ודיו בכניסתו. **ת"ל בקרקע.** בקרקעיתו. **אי בקרקע.** קא דרשינן, ולא כתיב "אשר יהיה", יכול לא מצא שם עפר תיחוח נוח ליטול יחפור שם בקרדומות – ת"ל: "אשר יהיה", (ב) ומדלא כתיב "ומקרקע המשכן יקח" – ש"מ: לא הקפיד אלא שיהא מונח בקרקעית המשכן שעה אחת. **הא כיצד?** יש שם עפר תיחוח – הבא משם. **אין שם תן שם.** על הקרקעית, וחוזר ונוטלו ונותנו לתוך המים. **תניא אידך.** פליגא אהך קמייתא. ותנאי היא, כדקתני בה פלוגתא דתנאי. והך דלעיל מיתוקמא כאיסי בן מנחם. (ג) **מן העפר אשר יהיה במשכן.** מדלא כתיב "מקרקע המשכן יקח" – אינו מקפיד אלא שיכנים להיכל, מלמד שמתקן מבחוץ ומכנים מבפנים להיכל, ונותן אל המים, וא"צ להניחו בקרקע ההיכל. **בקרקע המשכן איסי בן יהודה וכו'.** "בקרקע המשכן" למאי אתא, כיון דילפינן מ"אשר יהיה" דא"צ ליטלו מעל גבי קרקעית. **איסי בן יהודה אומר להביא קרקע בית עולמים.** ה"ג לה בסיפרי. ולא גרס: לרבות שילה ונוב וגבעון ובית עולמים. דשילה משכן הוא, ולא צריך לרבויא, דהוא עיקר הכתוב. ונוב וגבעון אין משקין בה סוטות, דהא במה הואי, ולא הוה שם ארון אלא מזבח הנחושת לבדו, ולא קרבה בהן מנחת סוטה ולא שום חובת יחיד שאין לה זמן קבוע, כדאמר בשחיטת קדשים (דף קיז.) ובמגילה (דף ט:). אבל בית עולמים הוצרך לרבות, שלא תאמר: משכן נאמר ולא מקדש. בית המקדש שבירושלים קרי ליה "בית עולמים" לפי שאין אחר קדושתו היתר במקום אחר, ושוב לא שרתה שכינה במקום אחר.
אינו

איכא למיפרך מה למצורע. הא סוגיא כרב אחא בריה דרבא דאמר בפרק "המפלת" (נדה דף כב.): לרבי ישמעאל כל ג"ש שאינה מופנה כל עיקר – למידין ומשיבין. ולפי המסקנא דיליף ליה מ"בכלי" לא תיקשה נמי לרב יהודה דאמר:* אין למידין כל עיקר.

מה מים שלא נעשתה בהם מלאכה. וא"ת: כיון דמי כיור הן, מי לא עסקינן שקדש ממנו כבר? יש לומר: אפי' אם קידש בהן, *שילק מן הדלין שבו – לא היתה מלאכה גבי נטילה. דתנן בפ"ק דידים (מ"ג): עשה בהן מלאכה או ששרה בהן פתו – פסולין, ואפ"ה קתני (שם מ"ה): מים שנחתום מטבל בהן את הגלוסקין – פסולין, ושהוא מדיח בהן ידיו – כשירין. אלמא דלא חשיב מלאכה הדחת ידים, אלא הדחת כלים ומי נחתום, כדקתני התם.

ומה מים שלא נשתנו. תימא: דמאחר דמי כיור הן, ומי כיור כשירין במי מקוה, ומי מקוה שנשתנו מראיהן כשר, כדתנן במסכת מקואות פ"ז (מ"ג) דמי צבע אין פוסלין המקוה בשינוי מראה! ועוד תימה לרבי: מאי שנא דהכא אמר: מה מים שלא נשתנו, ובפרק ב' דמסכת ע"ז (דף לז:) לא מסיק הכי גבי בישולי גוים? ונראה דהכא נמי אסמכתא בעלמא הוא, וליכא אלא פסולא דרבנן.

נתאכמו והחזירן לתוך כבשן האש מהו. תימה: מ"ש דקא מבעיא ליה הכא בנראה וחוזר ונראה? והא בפ' "לולב הגזול" (סוכה דף לג:) קא מבעיא לן ולא אפשיטו! ועוד: מאי שנא מהא דאמר בזבחים פ"ב (דף יח:): בגדי כהונה שהיו מקורעין או מטושטשין ועבד – עבודתו פסולה, ואפי' הכי אם כיבס טשטוש וגיעול שלהן – חזרו להתירן, כדמייתי ברייתא פרק "המזבח מקדש" (שם דף פח.): בגדי כהונה אין עושין אותן מעשה מחט אלא מעשה אורג, נתגעלו – אין מכבסין אותן לא בנתר ולא בחול. ופרכינן: הא במים מכבסין? אמר אביי, ה"ק: הוגעו למים – מכבסין אותן בנתר. אלמא דמכבסין אותן, ולא אמר דנדחו! מ"ר.

והא התם הדרי ומפשטי. פרש"י: מדלא קתני שנעשה בהן מלאכה – ש"מ אמלאכה לא קפיד, אשינוי קפיד. וקשיא לרבי מתוספתא דנגעים פרק "אין מנורע": ר' אליעזר אומר: "עץ ארז ואזוב ושני תולעת" שנאמר בתורה – שלא נעשית בהן מלאכה. אלמא דמלאכה פוסלת בהן לר' אליעזר גופיה!
לרבות

[שם כב:]
שלא ילק מן וכו'. מהרש"א וכ"ה בכ"י

טז א מיי' פ"ג מהל' סוטה הל"ט סמג עשין נז:
יז ב מיי' שם הל"י:
יח ג מיי' שם הל"ט:
יט ד מיי' פי"א מהל' טומאת צרעת הלכה א סמג עשין רלז:
כ ה מיי' פ"ה מהל' ביאת מקדש הלי"ב ועי' בכ"מ בפ"ג מהל' סוטה הל"ט:
כא ו ז מיי' פ"ג מהל' סוטה הל"ט וע"ש בכ"מ:
כב ח מיי' פי"א מהל' טומאת צרעת הל"א סמג עשין רלז:
כג ט מיי' פ"ד מהל' נשיאות כפים הלי"ג:
כד י מיי' פ"ד מהל' סוטה הלי"ג:
כה כ מיי' שם הלי"ב:

תוספות שאנץ

פיילי כוס בספל אדירים מתרגמי' בפיילי: כדי שיראה על פני המים צריך ליתן שיעור כדי שיהיה נראה וניכר על פני המים דכתיב ונתן אל המים מדלא כתיב ונתן במים אלא אל המים משמע שצריך שיבא העפר אל המים שלא יהא נבלע בתוכו ל"ה. לא שנו לרבנן דמתני' דלא בעי חדשים אלא שלא נתאכמו פניו על פני האור. דומיא דמים ואע"ג דלא גמירי ממצורע מיהו מינה ובה גמרי כלי דסוטה ממי דסוטה ונהי דמי סוטה לרבנן לאו חיים נינהו דמכשרי בשאר מימות מיהא לא נשתנו וכלי נמי בעינן דלא נשתנה. תניא אידך פליגא אקמיתא דלעיל ותנאי הוא כדקתני בה פלוגתא דתנאי והך דלעיל מתוקמא כאיסי בן מנחם: מן העפר אשר יהיה במשכן מדלא כתיב ומקרקע המשכן יקח אינו מקפיד אלא שיכנים להיכל מלמד שמתקן מבחוץ ומכנים בפנים ל"ה. איסי בן יהודה אמר לרבות בית עולמים:

[נ"ל שאינו וכן הגיה התוי"ט]
[לעיל ט.]
[ד' יז.]
[נזיר לח.]
[במשנה שבמשניות פיילי וכ"כ הערוך שהוא טס בלשון יון וכ"א בפירוש הרב לברטנורה והתוי"ט]
זבחים כב:
[מתוך מ"ש תוס' ד"ה והא התם וכו' מוכח שהיה גרסתם רבי אליעזר]
זבחים סב: יומא טו: יז: מה. נח:
גי' רש"ל

הגהות הב"ח

(א) רש"י ד"ה ומן וכו' אי הוה כתיב ומן העפר אשר יהיה במשכן ולא הוה כתיב בקרקע משמע דאינו מקפיד אלא שיכנים העפר להיכל כצ"ל ונ"ב נראה שרש"י ז"ל קא מפרש האי יכול כו' דה"ק אילו לא נאמר בקרקע אלא ומן העפר אשר יהיה במשכן יקח הייתי אומר יתקן מבחוץ ויכנים ת"ל בקרקע המשכן ואילו לא נאמר אשר יהיה אלא ומן העפר אשר בקרקע המשכן יקח הייתי אומר דיחפור בקרדומות ת"ל אשר יהיה ופי' רש"י דמדלא כתיב ומקרקע המשכן יקח ולאו דוקא הך לישנא קאמר רש"י אלא ה"ה ומן העפר אשר בקרקע המשכן יקח כמ"ש תחילה דאין חילוק בין מ"ש דומן העפר אשר בקרקע לבין מ"ש דומקרקע אידי ואידי משמעו דיקח מן הקרקע שבמשכן ממש אלא דרש"י הכא לשון קצרה נקט ומהרש"ל בהגהותיו הגיה בלשון רש"י כאן ולאי אפשר לייסבו: (ב) ד"ה אי בקרקע וכו' דמדלא כתיב: (ג) ד"ה ומן העפר אשר יהיה מדלא כתיב ומקרקע כצ"ל ותיבת במשכן נמחק:

שִׁילֹה, נוֹב וְגִבְעוֹן וּבֵית עוֹלָמִים. אִיסִי בֶּן מְנַחֵם אוֹמֵר: אֵינוֹ צָרִיךְ, וּמַה בְּטוּמְאָה קַלָּה לֹא חִלֵּק הַכָּתוּב — בְּטוּמְאַת אֵשֶׁת אִישׁ חֲמוּרָה לֹא כ"ש? א"כ מַה ת"ל "בְּקַרְקַע הַמִּשְׁכָּן" — שֶׁלֹּא יָבִיא מִתּוֹךְ קוּפָּתוֹ. אִיבַּעְיָא לְהוּ: אֵין שָׁם עָפָר, מַהוּ שֶׁיִּתֵּן אֵפֶר? אַלִּיבָּא דְּבֵית שַׁמַּאי לָא תִּיבָּעֵי לָךְ, דְּאָמְרִי: לֹא מָצִינוּ אֵפֶר שֶׁקָּרוּי "עָפָר". כִּי תִּיבָּעֵי לָךְ — אַלִּיבָּא דְּבֵית הִלֵּל, דְּאָמְרִי: *מָצִינוּ אֵפֶר שֶׁקָּרוּי "עָפָר", מַאי? אע"ג דְּאִיקְּרִי "עָפָר" — הָכָא "בְּקַרְקַע הַמִּשְׁכָּן" כְּתִיב, אוֹ דִּילְמָא הַאי "בְּקַרְקַע הַמִּשְׁכָּן" לְכִדְאִיסִי בֶּן יְהוּדָה, וְלְכִדְאִיסִי בֶּן מְנַחֵם הוּא דְּאָתֵי? ת"ש, דְּא"ר יוֹחָנָן מִשּׁוּם ר' יִשְׁמָעֵאל: בִּשְׁלֹשָׁה מְקוֹמוֹת הֲלָכָה עוֹקֶבֶת מִקְרָא; הַתּוֹרָה אָמְרָה °"בֶּעָפָר", וַהֲלָכָה — [א]בְּכָל דָּבָר. הַתּוֹרָה אָמְרָה °בְּתַעַר, וַהֲלָכָה — [ב]בְּכָל דָּבָר. הַתּוֹרָה אָמְרָה °"סֵפֶר", וַהֲלָכָה — [ג]בְּכָל דָּבָר. וְאִם אִיתָא — לִיחְשׁוֹב נַמִי הַאי! *תָּנָא וְשִׁיֵּיר. וּמַאי שִׁיֵּיר דְּהַאי שִׁיֵּיר?! שִׁיֵּיר מְצוֹרָע. דְּתַנְיָא: °"וְהָיָה בַיּוֹם הַשְּׁבִיעִי יְגַלַּח אֶת כָּל שְׂעָרוֹ" — כְּלָל, "אֶת רֹאשׁוֹ וְאֶת זְקָנוֹ וְאֵת גַּבֹּת עֵינָיו" — פְּרָט, "וְאֶת כָּל שְׂעָרוֹ יְגַלֵּחַ" — חָזַר וְכָלַל, כְּלָל וּפְרָט וּכְלָל — אִי אַתָּה דָּן אֶלָּא כְּעֵין הַפְּרָט: מַה פְּרָט מְפוֹרָשׁ — מְקוֹם כִּינּוּס שֵׂעָר וְנִרְאֶה, אַף כָּל מְקוֹם כִּינּוּס שֵׂעָר וְנִרְאֶה. מָה רַבֵּי — רַבֵּי שֵׂעָר הָרַגְלַיִם, מַאי מִיעֵט — מִיעֵט דְּבֵית הַשֶּׁחִי וּדְכוּלֵּיהּ גּוּפֵיהּ. וְהִלְכְתָא: [ד]מְגַלֵּחַ כִּדְלַעַת. דִּתְנַן: *בָּא לוֹ לְהַקִּיף אֶת הַמְּצוֹרָע מַעֲבִיר תַּעַר עַל כָּל בְּשָׂרוֹ, וְקָתָנֵי סֵיפָא: *וּבַיּוֹם הַשְּׁבִיעִי מְגַלְּחוֹ [ה]תִּגְלַחַת שְׁנִיָּה כְּתִגְלַחַת רִאשׁוֹנָה. אָמַר רַב נַחְמָן בַּר יִצְחָק: כִּי קָא חָשֵׁיב — הֲלָכָה עוֹקֶבֶת מִקְרָא, הָא — עוֹקֶבֶת מִדְּרַבָּנַן הִיא. רַב פַּפָּא אָמַר: כִּי קָא חָשֵׁיב — הֲלָכָה עוֹקֶבֶת וְעוֹקֶרֶת, הָא — עוֹקֶבֶת וּמוֹסֶפֶת הִיא. רַב אָשֵׁי אָמַר: הָא מַתְנִיתָא מַנִּי — *רַבִּי יִשְׁמָעֵאל הִיא, דְּדָרֵישׁ כְּלָלֵי וּפְרָטֵי,

כִּדְלַעַת

(ויקרא יז; במדבר ו; דברים כד; ויקרא יד)

רש"י

אֵינוֹ צָרִיךְ. לְרַבּוֹת בֵּית הָעוֹלָמִים. וּמַה טוּמְאָה קַלָּה. לִיכָּנֵס בְּטוּמְאַת הַגּוּף לַמִּקְדָּשׁ, שֶׁאֵינָהּ בְּמִיתַת ב"ד אֶלָּא כָּרֵת — לֹא חִלֵּק הַכָּתוּב בֵּין מִקְדָּשׁ לְמִשְׁכָּן, שֶׁנֶּאֶמְרוּ בְּפָרָשַׁת פָּרָה אֲדוּמָּה שְׁנֵי פְסוּקִים: "כִּי אֶת מִקְדַּשׁ ה' טִמֵּא", (כִּי) "אֶת מִשְׁכַּן ה' טִמֵּא" (במדבר יט). לֹא כָּל שֶׁכֵּן. שֶׁהוּשְׁווּ מִקְדָּשׁ וּמִשְׁכָּן לְבוֹדְקָהּ וּלְבַעֲרָהּ מִתּוֹכָן. א"כ מַה ת"ל בְּקַרְקַע שֶׁלֹּא יָבִיא מִתּוֹךְ קוּפָּתוֹ. לְתוֹךְ כְּלִי וְיַכְנִיס לַהֵיכָל, אֶלָּא מִקַּרְקָעִיתוֹ יִטּוֹל. וְאִם אֵין שָׁם — יָבִיא וְיַנִּיחַ שָׁם, וְאח"כ יִטְּלֶנּוּ. וְנִתְקַיֵּים "אֲשֶׁר יִהְיֶה" וְנִתְקַיֵּים "בְּקַרְקַע" כִּדְדָרְשִׁינַן לְעֵיל. וּבְסִפְרִי לָא תָּנֵי הָכִי לְהַךְ בָּרַיְיתָא, וְאוֹמֵר אֲנִי: מִדְרָשׁ שֵׁנִי הוּא בְּפָנִים אֲחֵרִים: פְּלוּגְתָּא דְּב"ש וּב"ה בִּשְׁחִיטַת חוּלִּין (דף פח:) גַּבֵּי כִּיסּוּי הַדָּם. אַלִּיבָּא דְּב"ה דְּאָמְרֵי אֵפֶר קָרוּי עָפָר, דִּכְתִיב (במדבר יט): "וְלָקְחוּ לַטָּמֵא מֵעֲפַר שְׂרֵפַת הַחַטָּאת", וּב"ש אוֹמְרִים: עֲפַר שְׂרֵיפָה נִקְרָא, עָפָר סְתָמָא לָא אִקְרִי. הָכָא בְּקַרְקַע הַמִּשְׁכָּן כְּתִיב. וּקְרָא יְתֵירָא הוּא, דְּהָא אִתְרַבֵּי מֵ"אֲשֶׁר יִהְיֶה" דְּאֵין צָרִיךְ לְחוֹפְרוֹ מִשָּׁם. הִילְכָּךְ לְמַעוּטֵי אֵפֶר אֲתָא, וּלְמִידְרַשׁ דְּבָעֵינַן דּוּמְיָא דְּקַרְקַע הַמִּשְׁכָּן. עוֹקֶבֶת. מְקַפַּחַת אֶת עֲקֵבוֹ מֵעָמְדוֹ, וְעוֹקֶרֶת. בג' מְקוֹמוֹת הֲלָכָה לְמֹשֶׁה מִסִּינַי בָּאָה וְעוֹקֶרֶת אֶת הַפָּסוּק. הַתּוֹרָה אָמְרָה בֶּעָפָר. לְעִנְיַן כִּסּוּי הַדָּם, וְלֹא הִכְשִׁיר דָּבָר אַחֵר. וַהֲלָכָה בְּכָל דָּבָר. הַמְגַדֵּל צְמָחִים, כְּגוֹן (הַגִּיר) וְהַזַּרְנִיךְ וְהַסִּיד וְחַרְסִית, וּלְבֵינָה שֶׁכְּתָשָׁהּ. הַתּוֹרָה אָמְרָה סֵפֶר. לְעִנְיַן גֵּט כְּרִיתוּת. וַהֲלָכָה בְּכָל דָּבָר. שֶׁכְּתָבוֹ עָלָיו; *עַל עָלֶה שֶׁל זַיִת, עַל הַנְּיָר, וְעַל הַלּוּחַ. (א) הַתּוֹרָה אָמְרָה תַּעַר. לֹא יַעֲבוֹר עַל רֹאשׁוֹ בְּנָזִיר. וַהֲלָכָה בְּכָל דָּבָר. דִּתְנַן (נזיר דף לט.): נָזִיר שֶׁגִּילֵּחַ, בֵּין בְּזוּג בֵּין בְּתַעַר אוֹ שֶׁסִּפְסֵף כָּל שֶׁהוּא — חַיָּיב. וְא"ת: אֵין זוֹ עֲקִירָה אֶלָּא תּוֹסֶפֶת! אִיבְרָא, עֲקִירָה הִיא, שֶׁמַּלְקִין אוֹתוֹ עַל כָּךְ, וְאָסוּר לְהַכּוֹת אֶת יִשְׂרָאֵל בְּחִנָּם, שֶׁהֲרֵי אָמְרָה תּוֹרָה (דברים כה): "לֹא יוֹסִיף" "פֶּן יוֹסִיף". וְאע"ג דִּבְכוּלְּהוּ קְרָאֵי דָּרְשִׁי' בִּשְׁחִיטַת חוּלִּין (דף פח:) וּבְגִיטִּין (דף כא:) וּבְנָזִיר (דף לט:) — לְר' יִשְׁמָעֵאל לָא מַשְׁמַע לֵיהּ קְרָאֵי. ד"וְכָתַב לָהּ" דִּמְרַבִּינַן מִינֵּיהּ לְרַבּוֹת כָּל דָּבָר — דָּרֵישׁ לֵיהּ: בִּכְתִיבָה מִתְגָּרֶשֶׁת וְאֵינָהּ מִתְגָּרֶשֶׁת בְּכֶסֶף, כִּדְדָרְשִׁינַן לָהּ הָתָם, וְכֵן כּוּלָּן. אֶלָּא אַהֲלָכָה לְמֹשֶׁה מִסִּינַי סָמְכִינַן, וּקְרָאֵי אַסְמַכְתָּא בְּעָלְמָא הוּא. הִלְכָּךְ, שְׁאָר מִדְרָשִׁים רִיבּוּיִין דְּכָל הַתּוֹרָה כּוּלָּהּ לָא חָשֵׁיב לְהוּ ר' יִשְׁמָעֵאל כַּהֲלָכָה עוֹקֶבֶת מִקְרָא אֶלָּא הָנֵי תְּלָת. וּבְמַסֶּכֶת קִידּוּשִׁין יְרוּשַׁלְמִי מָצָאתִי מִשְׁנָה זוֹ דְּר' יִשְׁמָעֵאל, וְאֵין תַּעַר מִן הַשְּׁלֹשָׁה, אֶלָּא מַרְצֵעַ. וְהָכִי תַּנְיָא הָתָם: הַתּוֹרָה אָמְרָה סֵפֶר וַהֲלָכָה בְּכָל דָּבָר הַתָּלוּשׁ, הַתּוֹרָה אָמְרָה עָפָר — וַהֲלָכָה בְּכָל דָּבָר הַמְגַדֵּל צְמָחִים, הַתּוֹרָה אָמְרָה מַרְצֵעַ — וַהֲלָכָה אָמְרָה אֲפִי' סוֹל וְסִירָה. וְהוּא נִרְאֶה בְּעֵינַי מְאֹד, דְּהַךְ דְּתַעַר מוֹסֶפֶת הוּא. וְאִם אִיתָא. דְּאֵפֶר נַמִי כָּשֵׁר — לֵיחֲשַׁב נַמִי דְּהָא הֲלָכָה עוֹקֶבֶת מִקְרָא, דְּהַתּוֹרָה אָמְרָה עָפָר וַהֲלָכָה אָמְרָה אַף אֵפֶר! וּמִמַּשְׁמָעוּתֵיהּ לָא מַשְׁמַע לַן, דְּהָא לְרַבִּי יִשְׁמָעֵאל *עָפָר לָאו מִמַּשְׁמָעוּתֵיהּ מַמָּשׁ נָפְקָא לֵיהּ לְעִנְיַן כִּיסּוּי הַדָּם. תָּנָא וְשִׁיֵּיר. לָא חָשְׁבִינְהוּ לְכוּלְּהוּ מְקוֹמוֹת. שִׁיֵּיר מְצוֹרָע. בְּתִגְלַחַת שְׁנִיָּה. שֶׁהוּא צָרִיךְ שְׁנֵי תִּגְלָחוֹת, דִּכְתִיב: "וְכִבֶּס הַמִּטַּהֵר אֶת בְּגָדָיו וגו' וְהָיָה בַּיּוֹם הַשְּׁבִיעִי יְגַלַּח אֶת כָּל שְׂעָרוֹ" וגו'. בְּתִגְלַחַת רִאשׁוֹנָה לֹא כָּתַב כְּלָל וּפְרָט, אֶלָּא "אֶת כָּל שְׂעָרוֹ" סְתָם, דְּמַשְׁמַע כָּל גּוּפוֹ, זְרוֹעוֹתָיו וְשׁוֹקָיו וּבֵית הַשֶּׁחִי, שֶׁיְּהֵא כָּל גּוּפוֹ חָלָק כִּדְלַעַת. וּבְתִגְלַחַת שְׁנִיָּה כָּתוּב בִּכְלָל וּפְרָט, דְּמַשְׁמַע: מְקוֹם כִּינּוּס שֵׂעָר — שֶׁיְּהֵא שָׁם קִיבּוּץ שֵׂעָר הַרְבֵּה, לְמַעוּטֵי זְרוֹעוֹתָיו וְשׁוֹקָיו שֶׁאֵינוֹ מְכוּנָּס. וְנִרְאֶה — לְמַעוּטֵי בֵּית הַשֶּׁחִי. שֵׂעָר הָרַגְלַיִם. דְּאוֹתוֹ מָקוֹם. וְלִישָּׁנָא מְעַלְיָיתָא נָקַט. וַהֲלָכָה מְגַלֵּחַ כּוּלּוֹ כִּדְלַעַת. אַף בְּתִגְלַחַת שְׁנִיָּה קָתָנֵי דִּמְגַלֵּחַ כָּל גּוּפוֹ. כִּדְתְנַן. בְּמַסֶּכֶת נְגָעִים (פי"ד מ"ב). לְהַקִּיף. לְגַלְּחוֹ כּוּלּוֹ, לְשׁוֹן "לֹא תַקִּיפוּ פְּאַת רֹאשְׁכֶם" (ויקרא יט). מַעֲבִיר תַּעַר עַל כָּל בְּשָׂרוֹ. וּבְתִגְלַחַת רִאשׁוֹנָה קָאֵי: ה"ג וְקָתָנֵי סֵיפָא וּבַיּוֹם הַשְּׁבִיעִי מְגַלְּחוֹ תִּגְלַחַת שְׁנִיָּה כְּתִגְלַחַת רִאשׁוֹנָה וְלָא גָּרְסִינַן: יְגַלְּחֶנּוּ שֶׁתְּהֵא תִּגְלַחַת וכו'. דְּלָאו אַקְּרָא קָאֵי, אֶלָּא לְשׁוֹן הַמִּשְׁנָה "וּמְגַלְּחוֹ תִּגְלַחַת שְׁנִיָּה כְּתִגְלַחַת רִאשׁוֹנָה" תְּנַן בָּהּ. אַלְמָא שְׁנִיָּה נַמִי כִּדְלַעַת, דְּהָא תָּנָא לֵיהּ בְּתִגְלַחַת רִאשׁוֹנָה: מַעֲבִיר תַּעַר עַל כָּל בְּשָׂרוֹ. אָמַר רַב נַחְמָן בַּר יִצְחָק. מְצוֹרָע לָא שִׁיּוּרָא הוּא, דְּכִי קָא חָשֵׁיב הֲלָכָה עוֹקֶבֶת מִקְרָא — כְּגוֹן סֵפֶר, תַּעַר, עָפָר, דִּכְתִיב בְּהֶדְיָא, וַהֲלָכָה עוֹקֶבֶת (ב) — מוֹסֶפֶת עַל הַמִּקְרָא. רַב אָשֵׁי אָמַר הָא מַתְנִיתָא. דְּקָתָנֵי: מְקוֹם כִּינּוּס שֵׂעָר וְנִרְאֶה. דְּדָרֵישׁ. כָּל הַתּוֹרָה כּוּלָּהּ בִּכְלָל וּפְרָט, כִּדְאָמְרִינַן בִּשְׁבוּעוֹת בפ"ג (דף כו.): רַבִּי יִשְׁמָעֵאל שִׁימֵּשׁ אֶת רַבִּי נְחוּנְיָא בֶּן הַקָּנָה שֶׁהָיָה דּוֹרֵשׁ אֶת כָּל הַתּוֹרָה בִּכְלָלֵי וּפְרָטֵי, וְר"ע שִׁימֵּשׁ אֶת נַחוּם אִישׁ גַּם זוֹ שֶׁהָיָה דּוֹרֵשׁ כָּל הַתּוֹרָה בְּרִיבּוּיֵי וּמִיעוּטֵי. וּכְבָר פֵּירַשְׁתִּי כָּל מַשְׁמָעוּת כְּלָל וּפְרָט וְרִיבּוּי וּמִיעוּט וְחִילּוּקָן בְּמַסֶּ' סוּכָּה בְּפֶ' "הֶחָלִיל" (דף נ:*).

כִּדְלַעַת

תוספות

לרבות נוב וגבעון שילה ובית עולמים. רש"י גורס: להביא קרקע בית עולמים. ושיבש הגירסא: שילה נוב וגבעון, משום דנוב וגבעון אין משקין בהן סוטות, משום דהויא מנחת יחיד שאין קבוע לה זמן. ותימה ששיבשה משום קושיא זו, דילמא קסבר איסי בן יהודה כרבי יהודה, דאמר בפרק בתרא דשחיטת קדשים (זבחים ד' קיז.): כל שהצבור והיחיד מקריבין באהל מועד שבמדבר – מקריבין באהל מועד שבגלגל, ואין חילוק ביחיד אלא במתו שבראש גגו. והשתא הוצרך לרבות נוב וגבעון, משום דבמה הוו!

ובית העולמים. מקשינן: אמאי איצטריך לרבות בית העולמים? והאמר בפ"ב דשבועות (דף טז:) דמשכן אקרי "מקדש" ומקדש אקרי "משכן", ואי לא הוה כתיב אלא (כי) "את משכן ה' טמא" הוה נמי מקדש בכלל. הכא נמי נימא הכי! וברים מסכת עירובין (דף ב.) דנפקא לן שלמים ששחטן קודם שיפתחו דלתות ההיכל פסולים במקדש, משום דמקדש אקרי "משכן", ואע"ג ד"ושחטו פתח אהל מועד" במשכן כתיב! ולפי גירסת הספר הזה אתי שפיר, דהוי מצי למימר: עיקר ריבויא לא הוה צריך אלא משום נוב וגבעון, ובית עולמים נקט אגב שיטפיה. אבל ר"י פירש: האי דאיצטריך הכא לרבות בית עולמים, משום דכתיב "קרקע" – משמע היכא דאיכא קרקע, לאפוקי בית העולמים דהואי רילפה. ולא מסתברא, משום דמריבויא ד"קרקע" מרבינן בית העולמים, דאי לא הוה כתיב "קרקע" – לא הוה בית העולמים בכלל, ולפירושו לא הוה צריך למיכתב "קרקע" כלל! ועוד קשיא מפ' "טרף בקלפי" (יומא דף מד.), דמייתי ברייתא: "וכל אדם לא יהיה באהל מועד", אין לי אלא אהל מועד שבמדבר, שילה ובית העולמים מנין? אלמא דשילה לא הוה בכלל אהל מועד, וכן בית העולמים. ובפ"ק דעירובין (דף ב.) אמר דבית העולמים הוה בכלל אהל מועד "ושחטו פתח אהל מועד", הואיל ומקדש איקרי "משכן", וכן בפרק "הוציאו לו" (יומא דף נג.), רב ששת אמר: אין לי אלא אהל מועד שבמדבר, שילה ובית עולמים מנין ת"ל – "וכסה"! א).

ואם איתא ליחשב נמי הא. תימה: היכי מצי למיפשט מדר' ישמעאל? והא סבירא ליה כבית שמאי דאפר לא איקרי "עפר", ואליבא דבית שמאי לא קמיבעי' ליה אלא אליביה דב"ה. א"כ ה"נ אפר בכלל משמעותא ד"עפר", משום דהכא "בקרקע" כתיב!

תנא ושייר. ואי קשיא: היכי מצי למימר תנא ושייר? והא "שלשה" קתני, ואמר בפ"ק דקידושין (דף טז:) גבי הענקה: וכי תימא הכא נמי תנא ושייר – והא "ארבעה" קתני! ונראה דהתם דוקא, כיון דנחת למניינא – דוקא הוא, משום דקתני בסיפא: ואי אתה יכול לומר ארבעה באחד מהן כו', ואם איתא דמיתת האב נמי מוציאה – היה יכול לומר ארבעה באשה ב).

מאי

א) [וע"ע תוס' חולין כז. ד"ה יכול] ב) [וע"ע תוס' מנחות יח: ד"ה מניין ותוס' קידושין טז: ד"ה והא ותוס' יבמות ג: ד"ה למעוטי ותוס' כתובות נח: ד"ה חמשה ותוס' גיטין כ: ד"ה אין מוליאין ותוס' ב"ק לה. ד"ה חמשה ועוד שם: ד"ה שלשה]

תוספות שאנץ

ה"ג רש"י ז"ל [ולא גרס] לרבות נוב וגבעון ושילה ובית עולמים משום דשילה משכן הוא ולא צריך לריבויי דהא עיקר הכתוב ביה כתיב ונוב וגבעון אין משקין בהן את הסוטות דהא במת יחיד היא. ולא היה שם ארון אלא מזבח הנחשת לבדו ולא קרבה בהן מנחת סוטה ולא שום חובת יחיד שאין לה זמן קבוע כדאמרי' בשחיט' קדשים ובמסכת מגילה אבל בית עולמים הוצרך לרבות שלא תאמר משכן נאמר ולא מקדש ל"ה. אינו צריך לרבות בית עולמים ומה בטומאה קלה שהיא ליכנס בטומאת הגוף במקדש שאינה מיתת ב"ד אלא כרת לא חלק הכתוב בין משכן למקדש שנ' בפרשה פרה אדומה [שני פסוקים] את (מקדש) [משכן] ה' טמא. וכתיב את מקדש ה' טמא לא כ"ש שהושוו מקדש למשכן לבודקה ולבערה מתוכן ל"ה. אליבא דב"ש לא תיבעי לך דאמרי לא מצינו אפר שקרוי עפר פלוגתייהו גבי כיסוי הדם. ואומר ר"ת דהא דקאמר ב"ש דאפר לא הוי עפר היינו באפר של אוכלין כגון אפר פרה אבל אפר דעצים מודו דהוי עפר ומכסין בו. ומ"ה כתב ר"ת הכי משום דק"ל הא דקאמר פ"ק [דביצה] גבי פלוגתא דב"ש וב"ה הכל מודים בדקר נעוץ מבעוד יום ובאפר כירה שהוא מן המוכן פי' ומותר לכסות בו. ומ"ה פי' דאפר לא הוי [עפר] דקאמר ב"ש. י"ל דמיירי באפר של אוכלין והכי נמי לענין סוטה מיבעיא ליה באפר של אוכלין. ולפי פי' רש"י דפי' התם דהא דקאמר מודים לא קאי אלא אדקר נעוץ ולא אאפר כירה דאפי' באפר כירה פליגי ב"ש ואמרי שאין מכסין בו ולפי זה אתי שפיר הכא דמיבעי ליה לענין סוטה בכל מיני אפר: בג' מקומות התורה עוקבת את המקרא פ"ה עוקבת מקפחת את עקבו והעמדתו ועוקרתו אישטלונ"ר בלע"ז: התורה אמרה בעפר לענין כיסוי ולא הכשר דבר אחר והלכה בכל דבר המגדל צמחים הגיר והגור וסיד וחרם ולבינה שנכתשה. התורה אמרה ספר לענין כריתות ולא ד"א והלכה בכל דבר שאפי' כתבו על העלה של זית ועל הנייר ועל הלוח כשר. התורה אמרה תער לא יעבור על ראשו והלכה בכל דבר כדתניא נזיר שגילח בין בזוג בין בתער או שספסף כל שהוא חייב. וכל הני ג' מקומות הוי עוקרת ועוקבת והקשה בקונטרס גבי נזיר אין זה עקירה איברא עקירה היא שמלקין אותו על כך ואסור להכות ישראל על חנם שהרי אמרה תורה לא יוסיף פן יוסיף. וא"ת מאי קאמר עוקבת אנן דרשי' להו כולהו בכלל ופרט דבכולהו איכא ריבוי דקראי בגיטין ובנזיר ובכסוי הדם ומאי קאמר עוקבת הא מקראי נפקי' להו. וי"ל דסבירא ליה לר' ישמעאל דכולהו הני ריבויי איצטריכו להו כדמפרש התם קרא דוכתב דמרבי' מיניה לרבות כל דבר איצטריכא ליה למדרש בכתיבה מתגרשת ואינה מתגרשת בכסף וכן כולן. אלא הל"מ הם וקרא אסמכתא בעלמא הילכך שאר מדרשים ריבויין דכל התורה כולה לא חשיב להו ר' ישמעאל בהלכה עוקבת מקרא כי אם אלו הג' כפ"ה ופי' באורך. ומה שהביא בירושלמי דמסכת קידושין מייתי משנה דר' ישמעאל [illegible] כדפריך בפ"ק דקידושין גבי ד' מעניקין [illegible] משום דקת' ואי אתה יכול לומר ד' באחד מהם [illegible] למניינא לאפושי לאוין:

מביא

עין משפט נר מצוה

כו א מיי' פי"ד מהל' שחיטה הלכ' יא סמג עשין סד טוש"ע יו"ד סי' כח סעי' כג:

כז ב מיי' פ"ה מהל' נזירות הלכ' יא:

כח ג מיי' פ"ד מהל' גירושין סל' ג ד סמג עשין נ טוש"ע אה"ע סי' קכד סעי' ה:

כט ד מיי' פי"א מהל' טומאת צרעת הל' א סמג עשין רלו רלז:

ל ה מיי' שם הל' ב:

מסורת הש"ס

[חולין פח:]

[סוכה נב. וש"נ]

[גיטין יט.]

נגעים פי"ד מ"ב ע"ש

[שם משנה ג]

[שבועות כו.]

הגהות הב"ח

(א) רש"י ד"ה התורה אמרה תער לא יעבור. נ"ל קודם ד"ה התורה אמרה ספר: (ב) ד"ה הרב"ה וכו' והלכה עוקבת המ' ואח"כ מ"ה הא עוקבת מוספת:

גי' רש"א אפר ע"ש

ד"ה והכא כמיכוף וכו'

כִּדְלַעַת מַנִּי — *ר"ע הִיא, דְּדָרֵישׁ רִיבּוּיֵי וּמִיעוּטֵי. דְּתַנְיָא: °"וְהָיָה בַיּוֹם הַשְּׁבִיעִי יְגַלַּח אֶת כָּל שְׂעָרוֹ" — רִיבָּה, "אֶת רֹאשׁוֹ וְאֶת זְקָנוֹ וְאֵת גַּבֹּת עֵינָיו" — מִיעֵט, "וְאֶת כָּל שְׂעָרוֹ יְגַלֵּחַ" — חָזַר וְרִיבָּה. רִיבָּה וּמִיעֵט וְרִיבָּה — רִיבָּה הַכֹּל. מַאי רִיבָּה — רִיבָּה דְּכוּלֵּיהּ גּוּפֵיהּ, וּמַאי מִיעֵט — אמִיעֵט שֵׂיעָר שֶׁבְּתוֹךְ הַחוֹטֶם. מַאי הָוֵי עֲלָהּ? ת"ש, דְּאָמַר רַב הוּנָא בַּר אַשִׁי אָמַר רַב: אֵין שָׁם עָפָר — במֵבִיא רַקְבּוּבִית יָרָק וּמְקַדֵּשׁ. גוְלָא הִיא, רַקְבּוּבִית יָרָק — הוּא דַּהֲוַאי עָפָר, אֵפֶר — לָא הֲוַאי עָפָר.§ "כְּדֵי שֶׁיֵּרָאֶה עַל הַמַּיִם".§ תָּנוּ רַבָּנַן: *שְׁלֹשָׁה צְרִיכִין שֶׁיֵּרָאוּ: דעֲפַר סוֹטָה, הוְאֵפֶר פָּרָה, ווְרוֹק יְבָמָה. מִשּׁוּם רַבִּי יִשְׁמָעֵאל אָמְרוּ: אַף דַּם צִפּוֹר. מַאי טַעֲמָא דְּרַבִּי יִשְׁמָעֵאל — דִּכְתִיב: °"וְטָבַל אוֹתָם בְּדַם הַצִּפּוֹר" וגו', וְתַנְיָא: "בְּדַם" יָכוֹל בְּדָם וְלֹא בְּמַיִם — ת"ל: (א) "בַּמַּיִם". אִי מַיִם. יָכוֹל בְּמַיִם וְלֹא בְּדָם — ת"ל "בְּדַם". הָא כֵּיצַד — זמֵבִיא מַיִם שֶׁדַּם צִיפּוֹר נִיכָּר בָּהֶן, וְכַמָּה — רְבִיעִית. וְרַבָּנַן: הַהוּא לְגוּפֵיהּ. דְּהָכִי קָאָמַר רַחֲמָנָא: אַטְבֵּיל בְּדָם וּבְמַיִם. וְרַבִּי יִשְׁמָעֵאל: אִם כֵּן, לִכְתּוֹב רַחֲמָנָא "וְטָבַל בָּהֶם", "בְּדַם וּבַמַּיִם" לָמָּה לִי — לְנִיכָּר. וְרַבָּנַן: אִי כָּתַב רַחֲמָנָא "וְטָבַל בָּהֶם" — הֲוָה אָמִינָא הַאי לְחוּדֵיהּ וְהַאי לְחוּדֵיהּ, כָּתַב רַחֲמָנָא "בְּדַם וּבַמַּיִם", לְעָרְבָן. וְר' יִשְׁמָעֵאל: לְעָרְבָן — קְרָא אַחֲרִינָא כְּתִיב: °"וְשָׁחַט אֶת הַצִּפּוֹר הָאֶחָת" וגו'. וְרַבָּנַן: אִי מֵהַהוּא — הֲוָה אָמִינָא: לִישְׁחֲטֵיהּ סָמוּךְ לְמָנָא, וְנִינְקְטִינְהוּ לְוְורִידִין, וּלְקַבְּלֵיהּ לַדָּם בְּמָנָא אַחֲרִינָא, קמ"ל. בְּעָא מִינֵּיהּ ר' יִרְמְיָה מֵר' זֵירָא: גְּדוֹלָה וּמַדְחַת אֶת הַמַּיִם, קְטַנָּה וְנִדְחֵית מִפְּנֵי הַמַּיִם, מַהוּ? א"ל: *לָאו אָמִינָא לָךְ: לָא תַּפֵּיק נַפְשָׁךְ לְבַר מֵהִילְכְתָא?! בְּצִפּוֹר דְּרוֹר שִׁיעֲרוּ רַבָּנַן, אֵין לְךָ גְּדוֹלָה שֶׁמַּדְחַת אֶת הַמַּיִם, וְאֵין לְךָ קְטַנָּה שֶׁנִּדְחֵית מִפְּנֵי הַמַּיִם. ת"ר: *חהִקְדִּים עָפָר לַמַּיִם — פָּסוּל, וְר' שִׁמְעוֹן מַכְשִׁיר. מ"ט דְּרַבִּי שִׁמְעוֹן — דִּכְתִיב: °"וְלָקְחוּ לַטָּמֵא מֵעֲפַר שְׂרֵפַת הַחַטָּאת" וְתַנְיָא, אָמַר ר"ש: וְכִי עָפָר הוּא? וַהֲלֹא אֵפֶר הוּא! שִׁינָּה הַכָּתוּב בְּמַשְׁמָעוֹ לָדוּן הֵימֶנּוּ גְּזֵירָה שָׁוָה; נֶאֱמַר כָּאן "עָפָר" וְנֶאֱמַר לְהַלָּן "עָפָר", מַה לְּהַלָּן עָפָר עַל גַּבֵּי מַיִם — אַף כָּאן עָפָר עַל גַּבֵּי מַיִם, וּמַה כָּאן הִקְדִּים עָפָר לַמַּיִם כָּשֵׁר — אַף לְהַלָּן, הִקְדִּים עָפָר לַמַּיִם כָּשֵׁר. וְהָתָם מְנָלַן? תְּרֵי קְרָאֵי כְּתִיבִי; כְּתִיב "עָלָיו" — אַלְמָא אֵפֶר בְּרֵישָׁא, וּכְתִיב "מַיִם חַיִּים אֶל כֶּלִי" — אַלְמָא מַיִם בְּרֵישָׁא, הָא כֵּיצַד? רָצָה זֶה נוֹתֵן, רָצָה זֶה נוֹתֵן. °וְרַבָּנַן: "אֶל כֶּלִי" — טדַּוְקָא, "עָלָיו" — ילְעָרְבָן. וְאֵימָא "עָלָיו" דַּוְקָא, "אֶל כֶּלִי" — שֶׁתְּהֵא *חִיּוּתָן בִּכְלִי! מַה מָּצִינוּ בְּכָל מָקוֹם מַכְשִׁיר לְמַעְלָה — אַף כָּאן מַכְשִׁיר לְמַעְלָה.§

מתני'

רש"י

בְּדְלַעַת מַנִּי. הָא דְּקָתָנֵי: מְגַלְּחוֹ תִּגְלַחַת שְׁנִיָּה כָּרִאשׁוֹנָה – רַבִּי עֲקִיבָא הִיא. מַאי הָוֵה עֲלָהּ. דְּבָעְיָין דִּלְעֵיל: אִם אֵין שָׁם עָפָר מַהוּ שֶׁיִּתֵּן שָׁם אֵפֶר? ה"ג מֵבִיא רַקְבּוּבִית יָרָק וּמְקַדֵּשׁ רַקְבּוּבִית יָרָק הוּא דַּהֲוֵי עָפָר וכו' וְלָא גָּרַס וְלָא הִיא. וּמְקַדֵּשׁ. נוֹתְנוֹ *בַּמָּקוֹם, וְהַמָּקוֹם מְקַדְּשׁוֹ, וְחוֹזְרוֹ וְנוֹטְלוֹ, וְנוֹתְנוֹ לַמַּיִם. עֲפַר סוֹטָה. דִּכְתִיב (במדבר ה): "אֶל הַמַּיִם" – שֶׁיֵּרָאֶה עֲלֵיהֶן, מִדְּלָא כְּתִיב (ב) "בַּמַּיִם". וְרוֹק יְבָמָה. לְעֵינֵי הַזְּקֵנִים, דִּכְתִיב: "לְעֵינֵי הַזְּקֵנִים וְחָלְצָה וְיָרְקָה" (דברים כה). (ג) וְאֵפֶר פָּרָה. דִּגְזֵירָה שָׁוָה גְּמִירִי מֵהֲדָדֵי עֲפַר סוֹטָה וְאֵפֶר פָּרָה, כִּדְלְקַמָּן. אַף דַּם צִפּוֹר. שֶׁל מְצוֹרָע, שֶׁשּׁוֹחֲטוֹ אֶל כְּלִי חֶרֶס עַל מַיִם חַיִּים. וְצָרִיךְ שֶׁלֹּא יִתֵּן מַיִם אֶלָּא כְּשִׁיעוּר שֶׁיְּהֵא דַּם צִפּוֹר נִיכָּר בָּהֶן. ת"ל מַיִם. גָּרַס. וְלָא גָּרַס "בַּמַּיִם", דְּהָא "עַל הַמַּיִם הַחַיִּים" כְּתִיב בִּקְרָא. וְכַמָּה הֵן רְבִיעִית. כִּדְמְפָרֵשׁ לְקַמָּן. בְּצִפּוֹר דְּרוֹר. שִׁיעֲרוּ חֲכָמִים שֶׁאֵין בְּמִינָהּ גְּדוֹלָה שֶׁמַּדְחָה אֶת הַמַּיִם, וְלֹא קְטַנָּה שֶׁנִּדְחֵת מִפְּנֵי הַמַּיִם שֶׁהֵן רְבִיעִית. אַטְבֵּיל בְּדָם וּבְמַיִם. וַאֲפִי' אֵין נִיכָּר. קְרָא אַחֲרִינָא כְּתִיב. שֶׁשּׁוֹחֵט לְתוֹךְ הַמַּיִם, וַהֲרֵי הֵן מְעוֹרָבִין מֵעִיקָּרָא. וְלִינְקְטִינְהוּ לְוְורִידִים. יֹאחֲזֵם בֵּין אֶצְבְּעוֹתָיו שֶׁלֹּא יֵצֵא מֵהֶן דָּם. גְּדוֹלָה וּמַדְחַת אֶת הַמַּיִם. שֶׁאֵין מַיִם נִיכָּר מִפְּנֵי רוֹב הַדָּם. לָא תַּפֵּיק נַפְשָׁךְ לְבַר מֵהִילְכְתָא. כָּל דִּבְרֵי חֲכָמִים שֶׁנִּקְבְּעוּ, אַל תְּהַרְהֵר אַחֲרֵיהֶן. הִקְדִּים עָפָר לַמַּיִם בְּסוֹטָה פָּסוּל. כִּדְכְתִיב: "וְנָתַן אֶל הַמַּיִם" – אַלְמָא מַיִם בְּרֵישָׁא, וּכְתִיב: "וְעָשָׂה לָהּ הַכֹּהֵן אֶת כָּל הַתּוֹרָה הַזֹּאת" – דְּבָעֵינַן כְּסֵדֶר הַכָּתוּב בַּפָּרָשָׁה. מַה לְּהַלָּן. בְּסוֹטָה, מִצְוָתוֹ לְכַתְּחִילָּה עָפָר אֶל הַמַּיִם, כִּדְכְתִיב בָּהּ – אַף כָּאן בְּפָרָה, עָפָר אֶל הַמַּיִם מִצְוָתוֹ כֵּן לְכַתְּחִילָּה. וְלָא תֵּימָא "וְנָתַן עָלָיו" דַּוְקָא, דְּמַשְׁמַע עָפָר לְכַתְּחִילָּה. וּמַה כָּאן. בְּפָרָה, הִקְדִּים עָפָר לַמַּיִם כָּשֵׁר, כִּדְמְפָרֵשׁ וְאָזֵיל. וְהָתָם מְנָלַן. גַּבֵּי פָרָה, דְּאִם הִקְדִּים עָפָר לַמַּיִם כָּשֵׁר. מַיִם חַיִּים אֶל כְּלִי. מַשְׁמַע מַיִם לְצַד הַכְּלִי, וְלֹא עָפָר חוֹצֵץ בֵּינְתַיִים. וְרַבָּנַן. דְּאָמְרִי לְעֵיל בְּסוֹטָה הִקְדִּים עָפָר לַמַּיִם פָּסוּל, אָמְרִי לָךְ: בְּפָרָה נַמִּי פָּסוּל, ד"אֶל כֶּלִי" דַּוְקָא, דְּמַשְׁמַע מַיִם בְּרֵישָׁא. וְהָא דִּכְתִיב: "וְנָתַן עָלָיו מַיִם" – לְעָרְבָן; לְאַחַר שֶׁנָּתַן אֵפֶר אֶל הַמַּיִם, צָרִיךְ לַהֲפֹךְ הַמַּיִם עָלָיו וּלְעָרְבָן: ה"ג וְאֵימָא עָלָיו דַּוְקָא אֶל כֶּלִי שֶׁתְּהֵא חִיּוּתָן בִּכְלִי. וְאֵימָא "עָלָיו" דַּוְקָא, שֶׁיְּהֵא עָפָר תְּחִילָּה. וְהָא דִּכְתִיב: "מַיִם חַיִּים אֶל כֶּלִי" לָאו לְמֵימְרָא שֶׁיְּהוּ הַמַּיִם לְצַד הַכְּלִי, אֶלָּא לְמֵימַר שֶׁיְּהֵא חִיּוּתָן בַּכְּלִי, שֶׁלֹּא יִטּוֹל מִן הַמַּעְיָן בִּכְלִי אַחֵר וְיִתֵּן לְתוֹךְ זֶה, אֶלָּא בִּכְלִי זֶה יִשְׁאֲבֵם מִן הַמַּעְיָן. מַה מָּצִינוּ בְּכָל מָקוֹם. בְּסוֹטָה. מַכְשִׁיר לְמַעְלָה. עָפָר הוּא הַמַּכְשִׁיר אֶת הַמַּיִם לִבְדּוֹק אוֹתָהּ, וְכֵן דַּם צִפּוֹר שֶׁל מְצוֹרָע שֶׁמַּכְשִׁיר אֶת הַמַּיִם לְהַזָּאָה, אַף כָּאן – עָפָר מַכְשִׁיר אֶת הַמַּיִם.

מתני'

תוספות

מאי הוה עלה. תימה: מאי קא בעי? כיון דלאו שיורא הוא, אם כן תפשוט! וי"ל: דלא איתבריר להו האי דשיירא, אי משום טעמא כדפרי' ולאו שיורא הוא, אי משום דתנא נקט לשיורא. **מביא** מים שדם צפור ניכר בהם וכמה רביעית ורבנן ההוא לגופיה. קשיא לרבי: הכא אמר דרבנן פליגי עלה, ובפ' "ג' מינין" (נזיר דף לח.) קא חשיב ליה בהדי עשר רביעיות מחמש חיוריתא, וקא פריך התם: ותו ליכא? והא איכא, ומייתי מתניתין דהכא: היה מביא פיילי של חרס וכו', ומשני: בפלוגתא לא קא מיירי. והא דמצורע נמי פלוגתא היא, וקא חשיב ליה! ונראה דהא פלוגתא דהכא לא דמיא לפלוגתא דמייתי התם, כגון נוטלין לידים לאחד ואפילו לשנים, ור' יוסי דפליג התם בפ"ק דמסכת ידים (מ"א) ואמר: לא סגי ליה לשנים ברביעית, דבעי לאחרון נמי רביעית. וכן במתניתין היה מביא פיילי של חרס, דת"ק דרבי יהודה לא סגי ליה ברביעית. וכן גבי ביטול מי רגלים, דקאמר תנא קמא כל שהוא. אבל הכא – רבנן מודו בפחות מרביעית לא אפשר, ואי בעי – סגי ברביעית, מיהו, לכתחילה מביא חצי לוג, כדתנן בריש פרק י"ד דמסכת נגעים: כיצד מטהרין את המצורע – היה מביא פיילי של חרס חדשה ונותן לתוכה *חצי לוג מים חיים. והא דתנן בפ' "שתי מדות" (מנחות דף פח.) רביעית מה היתה משמשת, *רביעית מים למצורע – ר' ישמעאל היא. **מביא** מים שדם ניכר בהם וכמה רביעית. וא"ת: וכי אינו ניכר ביותר מרביעית? והא תנן בפ"ז דמסכת מקואות (מ"ה), ומייתי לה בגמרא בכמה דוכתי, בשילהי פ"ק דשחיטת חולין (דף כו.), ובפ"ק דמכות (דף ג:): ג' לוגין מים שנפל לתוכן קורטוב יין ומראיהן כמראה יין. אלמא דאפילו יין ניכר בג' לוגין, וכ"ש דם דסומק טפי! וי"ל: ניכר דקאמר – ממשותו של דם, ולאו בשינוי מראה דעלמא (מ"ר). והשתא לא תיקשה מה שהיה תמיה רבי נמי מהא דקאמרינן ב"הקומץ רבה" (מנחות דף כג.) ופרק "גיד הנשה" (חולין דף צט:): לרבי יהודה דיליף למין במינו דאינו בטל ממאי דכתיב: "ולקח מדם הפר ומדם השעיר", הדבר ידוע שדמו של פר מרובה משל שעיר – אלמא דמין במינו לא בטיל, ורבנן אמרי: עולין אין מבטלין זה את זה. והא הכא דהוה מין שלא במינו, והדבר ידוע שהמים מרובין על הדם, ואפילו הכי כתיב "בדם"! וי"ל: כיון ◉דממשותו ניכר הרי הוא בעין. **קטנה** ונדחית מפני המים מהו. תימה: אליבא דמאן קא מיבעיא להו? אי לרבי ישמעאל – פשיטא דפסול, דהא בעי שיהא דם צפור ניכר. אי לרבנן – הא לא קפדי ◉אהיכר מים! ונראה דהא בעיא לא לשון ספיקא, אלא שהיה תמיה על דברי ר' ישמעאל דאמר: רביעית לעולם דם צפור ניכר בהן – והא פעמים שאינו ניכר, שהמים מדחין אותו כגון קטנה, ופעמים שאין המים ניכרין כגון גדולה, והיכי קים לרבנן לשעוריה בצפור שיהא דמה ניכר לעולם ברביעית? דומיא דפ"ק דר"ה (דף יג.) דאמר ליה רבי ירמיה לרבי זירא: מי קים להו לרבנן בין שליש לפחות משליש? אמר ליה: לאו אמינא לך לא תפיק נפשך לבר מהלכתא וכו'. **שינה** הכתוב במשמעו. תימה לרבי: וכי שינוי הוא שנקרא אפר "עפר"? והכתיב (מלכים ב כג): "וישרוף אותה בנחל קדרון וידק לעפר", וכן "ואכות אותו טחון היטב עד אשר דק לעפר" (דברים ט)! וי"ל: אותן שלא נעשית אפר ע"י שריפה אלא צריכין כתישה נקראין "עפר", אבל פרה – עיקר מצות שריפתה לאפר, אע"פ שאם היו שם אודין היו כותשין אותם, כדאיתא בספרי, וכדתנן בפ"ג דפרה: נשרפה חובטין אותה במקלות משום אודין שלא נעשו אפר. מיהו, עיקר מצות שריפתה – לאפר הוא. **שינה** הכתוב במשמעו. תימה: וכי מפני כך שינה? והאמר בפרק "כיסוי הדם" (חולין דף פח:) דלכך שינה אליבא דב"ה – ללמד שאפר נקרא "עפר"! וי"ל: תרתי שמע מינה.

האלות

עין משפט נר מצוה

לא א מיי' פי"א מהל' טומאת צרעת הל"א סמג עשין רלו רלז:

לב ב ג מיי' פ"ד מהל' סוטה הלי"ב:

לג ד מיי' שם פ"ג הל"י:

לד ה מיי' פ"ט מהל' פרה אדומה הל"א סמג עשין רלג:

לה ו מיי' פ"ד מהל' יבום וחליצה הל' ז סמג עשין נב טוש"ע אה"ע סי' קסט סעי' לא ובסדר חליצה סעי' נג ובפירוש סדר חליצה סעי' עו עז עח:

לו ז מיי' פי"א מהל' טומאת צרעת הל"א סמג עשין רלו רלז:

לז ח מיי' פ"ד מהל' סוטה הלי"ב:

לח ט י מיי' פ"ט מהל' פרה אדומה הל"א סמג עשין רלג:

[עי' בר"ש דאיכא דגרסי הכי במשנה שם אבל לפנינו איתא רביעית ועי' תוס' מנחות פח. ד"ה רביעית]

*רביעית מים למצורע פי' היה מביא מים שדם צפור ניכר בהם וכמה רביעית אתי כר' ישמעאל וא"ת כו' וי"ל כו' וכו"ל. מהרש"ל

תוספות שאנץ

מביא רקבובית ירק ומקדש (דקטנית) [רקבובית] ירק הוא דהוי עפר כו'. ולא גרס ולא היא כפ"ה. נראה הטעם משום דקא בעי מאי הוי עלה ומייתי עלה ת"ש משמע שבא להוכיח האמת מיהו דבכך אין למוחקו דמצינו בכמה מקומות דבעי מאי הוי עלה ומדחי ליה ולא פשיטא ולא מידי: מים שדם צפור ניכר בהם וכמה רביעית. מכאן נראה דל"ג במשניות דמס' נגעים חצי לוג. דקאמר כיצד מטהרין את המצורע מביא פיילי של חרס חדשה ונותן לתוכה חצי לוג של מים חיים ול"ג חצי לוג דהכא משמע דלא בעי אלא רביעית. וי"ל דשפיר גרסי' ליה התם חצי לוג ונעמיד כרבנן כר' ישמעאל דהכא דס"ל דבעי בסוטה חצי לוג וילפי' מצורע מסוטה מג"ש דכלי כלי. ולא נראה דבמנחות פ' ב' מדות סתם לן תנא (א) דר' יהודה דאמר רבי' של מצורע דקאמר כתיב חצי לוג לסוטה ורבי' למצורע אלמא משמע דלא ילפי' להו מהדדי וכן משמע בנזיר פ' ג' מינין דקא חשיב עשר רביעיות הן וקחשיב רביעית דמצורע ופרי' התם והאיכא נמי רבי' דסוטה ומשני בפלוגתא לא קא מיירי אלמא משמע דליכא מאן דפליג גבי רבי' דמצורע מדקא חשיב ליה מן העשר רביעיות ולא ילפי' מצורע מסוטה על כן ל"ג במשניות חצי לוג כדפרישי': וכי עפר היא והלא אפר היא. אע"ג דאמר בפ' כסוי הדם דנפקא להו לב"ה מהכא שמכסין באפר משום דאפר איקרי עפר ולא אמרי' דשינה לר"ש דהכא מ"מ לא משני הקרא לקרות אפר עפר ואין הלשון משמע כן. מה מצינו בכל מקום מכשיר למעלה בתורה עפר הוא המכשיר את

(א) נראה דל"ל סתם לן תנא כת"ק דר"י דקאמר התם חצי לוג מים לסוטה ואעפ"כ תני התם רביעית למצורע אלמא וכו'.

מסורת הש"ס

במקום פי' במסכן. רש"ל

[שבועות כו.]

[תוספתא פ"א ע"ש]

[ר"ה יג.]

תמורה יב: ע"ש [תוספתא דפרה פ"ה]

הגהות הב"ח

(א) גמ' ת"ל מים כנ"ל ואות ב' נמחק: (ב) רש"י ד"ה עפר וכו' כתיב ונתן במים: (ג) ד"ה ואפר נ"ל קודם ד"ה ורוק:

גליון הש"ס

גמ' ורבנן אל כלי וכו'. עיין רש"י פסחים ד' לה ע"א ד"ה מעלה וצ"ע: תוד"ה מביא וכו' דממשותו ניכר. תמוה לי הא לרבנן לא בעי היכר דם. ונהי דדרשא וטבל בדם צריך לגופה מ"מ הא הדם בטל ולא מתקיים בדם וכן לר"י נפיק רק מיתורא והא בלא"ה צריך ממשות ניכר שלא יתבטל. ובעיקר קושיתם י"ל דהא דם במים הוי אינו מינו ובבליר מס' עדיין שם דם עליו דהאוכלו חייב משום דם. ורק בדם הפר דהוי מין במינו דלין ביטולו ברוב כיון דטעמן שוה: ד"ה קטנה כו'. אהיכר מים. אהיכר דם כצ"ל:

מתני' בא לו לכתוב את המגילה, מאיזה מקום הוא כותב (א) – °מ"ואם לא שכב איש" וגו', "ואת כי שטית תחת אישך", ואינו כותב "והשביע הכהן את האשה", וכותב "יתן ה' אותך לאלה ולשבועה ובאו המים המאררים האלה במעיך לצבות בטן ולנפיל ירך", ואינו כותב "ואמרה האשה אמן אמן". רבי יוסי אומר: לא היה מפסיק. *ר' יהודה אומר: כל עצמו אינו כותב אלא "יתן ה' אותך לאלה ולשבועה וגו' ובאו המים המאררים האלה במעיך" וגו'. ואינו כותב "ואמרה האשה אמן אמן".§

גמ' במאי קא מיפלגי? בהאי קרא קמיפלגי: °"וכתב את האלות האלה הכהן בספר". ר"מ סבר: "אלות" – אלות ממש, "האלות" – לרבות קללות הבאות מחמת ברכות, "אלה" – למעוטי קללות שבמשנה תורה, "האלה" – למעוטי צוואות וקבלות אמן. ורבי יוסי: כולהו כדקאמרת, "את" לרבות צוואות וקבלות. ור"מ: *אתים לא דריש. ור' יהודה: כולהו במיעוטי דריש להו: "אלות" – אלות ממש, "האלות" – למעוטי קללות הבאות מחמת ברכות, "אלה" – למעוטי קללות שבמשנה תורה, "האלה" – *למעוטי צוואות וקבלות. ורבי מאיר מ"ש האי ה"י דמרבי ביה, ומאי שנא האי ה"י דממעיט ביה? ה"י דגביה דריבויא – ריבויא היא, ה"י דגביה דמיעוטא – מיעוטא. (ב) והא לית ליה לר"מ מכלל לאו אתה שומע הן! *אמר רבי תנחום: °"הנקי" כתיב. דריש ר"ע: איש ואשה, זכו – שכינה ביניהן, לא זכו – אש אוכלתן. אמר רבא: ודאשה עדיפא מדאיש. (מ"ט) – האי מצרף והאי לא מצרף. אמר רבא: מפני מה אמרה תורה הבא עפר לסוטה? זכתה – יוצא ממנה בן כאברהם אבינו דכתיב ביה °"עפר ואפר", לא זכתה – תחזור לעפרה. *דריש רבא: בשכר שאמר אברהם אבינו, "ואנכי עפר ואפר" זכו בניו לב' מצות, *אפר פרה ועפר סוטה. והאיכא נמי עפר כיסוי הדם! התם הכשר מצוה איכא, הנאה ליכא. *דרש רבא: בשכר שאמר אברהם אבינו: °"אם מחוט ועד שרוך נעל" זכו בניו לב' מצות: חוט של תכלת ורצועה של תפלין. בשלמא רצועה של תפלין, דכתיב: °"וראו כל עמי הארץ כי שם ה' נקרא עליך", *ותניא, ר"א הגדול אומר: אלו תפלין שבראש. אלא חוט של תכלת מאי היא? דתניא, *היה ר"מ אומר: מה נשתנה תכלת מכל מיני צבעונין? מפני שהתכלת דומה לים, וים דומה לרקיע, ורקיע דומה לכסא הכבוד, שנאמר: °"ויראו את אלהי ישראל ותחת רגליו כמעשה לבנת הספיר וכעצם השמים לטהר", וכתיב: °"כמראה אבן ספיר דמות כסא".§

מתני' באינו כותב לא על הלוח, ולא על הנייר, ולא על הדיפתרא

(במדבר ה; שם; בראשית יח; שם יד; דברים כח; שמות כד; יחזקאל א)

רש"י

מתני' (ג) מואם לא שכב איש אותך. "ואם לא שטית טומאה" וגו'. שהן קללות הבאות מחמת ברכות, דמשמע: הא אם שטית לא הנקי. "ואת כי שטית טומאה תחת אישך וכי נטמאת וגו', יתן ה' אותך לאלה ולשבועה בתוך עמך וגו' ובאו המים המאררים" וגו'. וכך הן סדורין בפרשה, אלא ש"והשביע הכהן את האשה בשבועת האלה ואמר הכהן לאשה" מפסיק בראש "יתן ה' אותך" ואינו כותבו, דאינו אלא צוואה שמצוה הכהן להשביע. וגם בסוף "ובאו המים המאררים במעיך לצבות בטן ולנפיל ירך" אינו כותב סוף המקרא "ואמרה האשה", דהיינו קבלה שהאשה תקבל עליה שבועה, ואין זו מן האלות. **לא היה מפסיק.** משהתחיל "אם לא שכב איש אותך" עד "אמן אמן". שהיה כותב צוואה ד"והשביע הכהן את האשה", וקבלה ד"ואמרה האשה אמן אמן". **כל עצמו.** לישנא בעלמא הוא; יזהר בעצמו שלא יהא כותב אלא אלות לבדו. ואפילו "אם לא שכב איש אותך" ו"הנקי" לא היה כותב, וכ"ש "והשביע הכהן". ואינו כותב "ואמרה האשה אמן אמן" שהוא סוף המקרא הזה. **גמ' אלות ממש.** "יתן ה' אותך", "ובאו המים המאררים האלה במעיך" וגו'. **קללות הבאות וכו'.** "הנקי ממי המרים". **אלה.** מיעוטא הוא. **שבמשנה תורה.** דאי כתב קרא "וכתב את האלות בספר" – הוה משמע אלות שבמשנה תורה: "יככה ה' בשחפת", דאלה איקרו, דכתיב: "והיה בשמעו את דברי האלה הזאת" וגו' (דברים כט). **צוואות.** "והשביע הכהן את האשה". דלא תימא לא ידלג, הילכך איצטריך למעטינהו. **וקבלת אמן. ולקמיה פריך:** מ"ש האי ה"י דמרבה ביה, ומ"ש האי ה"י דממעט ביה? **כולהו. ריבויא כדקאמרת,** "אלות" – אלות ממש, *"האלות" – הקללות הבאות מחמת ברכות, "אלה" – למעוטי שבמשנה תורה ושבתורת כהנים. אבל ה"י ד"האלה" לא תדרוש למעוטי צוואות וקבלות, דאתא "את" ורבינהו, וה"י ד"האלה" אורחיה הוא. **ור"י כולהו.** ההי"ן דקרא, מעוטי דריש להו. **דלגבי ריבוי.** ד"האלות", דקאי א"וכתב". **דלגבי מיעוט.** "אלה", דמיעוטא הוא: אלה ולא אחרות. **והא לית ליה לר"מ מכלל לאו אתה שומע הן.** דשמעינן ליה דבעי תנאי כפול, דתנן, *ר"מ אומר: כל תנאי שאינו כתנאי בני גד ובני ראובן – אינו תנאי, דכתיב ביה: "אם יעברו", "ואם לא יעברו". הא לא כפליה – מכלל לאו לא תשמע הן. **א"ר תנחום הנקי כתיב.** בלא יו"ד, דמשמע הנקי אם לא שכב, ותדרוש הכי: טומאה תחת אישך – חנקי. **זכו.** ללכת בדרך ישרה, שלא יהא הוא נואף ולא היא נואפת. **שכינה ביניהם.** שהרי חלק את שמו, ושיכנו ביניהן, יו"ד באיש וה"י באשה. **לא זכו אש אוכלתן.** שהקב"ה מסלק שמו מביניהן, ונמצאו אש ואש. **ודאשה עדיפא מדאיש.** אש של אשה קשה וממהרת לאכול וליפרע משל איש. **מאי טעמא האי מיצרף.** אש של אשה נוחה להדליק מהר, שאין אות של שם מפסיק אלא מחובר הוא, ונקרא אש. אבל של איש – אין אותיות של אש מצטרפות יחד, שהיו"ד של שכינה מפסקת. **הנאה ליכא.** ואין זה קיבול שכר. אבל כאן יש הנאה, בסוטה – לתת שלום, ושלא ירבה ממזרים בישראל אם זונה היא. ואם נקתה – ונזרעה זרע, ומבטלת לעז מעל בניה. ואפר פרה – לטהרן, ולזכות את ישראל ממעשה העגל. **בשכר אם מחוט ועד שרוך נעל.** שהרחיק עצמו מן הגזל. **חוט של תכלת.** כנגד "מחוט", ורצועה של תפילין – כנגד "שרוך", דהיינו רצועה. **בשלמא רצועה של תפילין.** קיבול שכר הוא, דאיכא הנאה, כדכתיב וכו'. אבל חוט של תכלת של ציצית – מאי הנאה איכא? **מה נשתנה תכלת.** שהזקיקו הכתוב לציצית? **שהתכלת דומה לים כו'.** בא ללמדנו שכל המקיים מצות ציצית כאילו הקביל פני שכינה. והכי תניא לה בספרי. (ד) דאיצטריכו כל הני משום דלא אשכחן קראי אלא ברקיע שדומה לכסא הכבוד, הילכך תכלת דומה לים, וים דומה לרקיע. דתכלת לא דמי לרקיע כל כך אלא דומה לדומה, כמו תכלת דומה למראה הים, ואנן קחזינן דים דומה למראה הרקיע. **ורקיע דומה לכסא הכבוד.** קראי קדריש, דכתיב ברקיע: "כמעשה לבנת הספיר", וכתיב בכסא הכבוד: "כמראה אבן ספיר דמות כסא". **מתני'** לוח. של עץ. נייר. של עשבים שכותשין ומדבקין אותן בדבק שקורין גלי"ד, ועושין כמו עור. **דיפתרא**

תוספות

האלות לרבות קללות הבאות מחמת ברכות. תימה לרבי: דהכא דריש ר"מ ה"י ד"האלות", ובפ"ק דהוריות (דף ה.) אמר: ור"מ "קהל" "הקהל" לא דריש! ותו איכא למיתמה: דר"י דריש הכא ה"י דריבויא למעט, והתם דריש "קהל" "הקהל" לרבויא! ותו קשיא דר' יהודה אדרבי יהודה, דהכא משמע דלא דריש "את האלות", ובפ"ק דמנחות (דף יא:) אמר: ר"י סבר "את [כל הלבונה]" לרבות [קורט] אחר!*.

אמר רבי תנחום הנקי כתיב. הכא פרש"י דתדרוש הכי: "טומאה תחת אישך" – "חינקי". אבל בסוף פרק "שבועת העדות" (שבועות דף לו.) פירש: "הנקי" בלא יו"ד, כמו "חנקי", וקאי אקרא דבתריה "ואת כי שטית", דמשמע הכי: חנקי ממים המרים האלה ואת כי שטית. והתם אמר: כי לית ליה לר"מ מכלל לאו אתה שומע הן – בממונא, באיסורא – אית ליה. וסוטה איסורא דאית ביה ממונא הוא. ונשאל רבי: והא בפ"ק דנדרים (דף יא.) אמר בגמרא: מאי "לחולין" – לא חולין ליהוי אלא לקרבן. מני מתני'? אי ר"מ – הא לית ליה מכלל לאו. והכי דייק נמי בסוף הפרק (שם יג:) ובריש פרק שני (דף יד.), אע"ג דאיסורא גרידתא הוא! והשיב רבי: דהתם נמי איסורא דאית ביה ממונא הוא, שאסר ממונו על חבירו.

מפני שהתכלת דומה לים. בירושלמי דפ"ק דברכות: מגיד שהתכלת דומה לים, והים דומה לעשבים, ועשבים לרקיע, ורקיע לכסא, והכסא לספיר, וכתיב: "ואראה והנה (על) [אל] הרקיע וגו'" (יחזקאל י).

אינו כותב וכו' על הנייר אלא על המגילה. תימה: בפ' "המוציא" (שבת דף עח:) דתנן: קלף כדי לכתוב עליו פרשה קטנה שבתפילין "שמע ישראל" – אמאי לא קתני פרשת סוטה, דשיעור זוטא טפי? אור"י: דפרשת סוטה לא שכיח כפרשת תפילין, ואמרינן התם (דף עח.): כל מילתא דשכיח ולא שכיח – אזול רבנן בתר שכיח לקולא.

לא על הלוח ולא על הנייר אלא על המגילה. תימה: אמאי לא מרבינן כל מילי מ"וכתב", כדאמרינן פרק שני דגיטין (דף כא:): "ספר" – אין לי אלא ספר, מנין לרבות כל דבר – ת"ל "וכתב" מ"מ. אם כן מה ת"ל "ספר" – מה ספר שאין בו רוח חיים. ורבנן אי כתב "בספר" – כדאמרת. אלמא: כל היכא דכתיב בספר

תוספות שאנץ

את המים לבדוק אותה וכן דם צפור של מצורע שמכשיר המים להזאה אף כאן בפרה עפר מכשיר את המים. ל"ה: אלא למעוטי קללות של משנה תורה דאי כתב וכתב את האלות האלה בספר ה"א אפי' דמשנה תורה. יככה ה' בשחפת ובקדחת. דאלה איקרו דכתיב והיה בשמעו. ולא תימא דלא דלג להכי איצטריך קרא למעוטינהו אבל לא קאמר למעוטי אותן של תורת כהנים לפי שלא הוצרך למעט לפי שהוא לשון רבים אך אותן של משנה תורה שהן לשון יחיד איצטריך קרא למעוטינהו. צואות וקבלות צוואות וכתב לה קבלות ואמרה האשה אמן אמן. ור' יהודה כולהו במיעוטי דריש להו והקשה ה"ר אלחנן דהכא משמע דלא דרי' ר' יהודה [את] דלא פליג אדר' מאיר אלא מוסיף עליו ובפ"ק דמנחות דרי' את גבי ואת כל הלבונה וצ"ל דאת דהכא לא דרי' אבל בעלמא דרי' להו: והא שמעי' לר' מאיר דאמר מכלל לאו לא תשמע הן דתניא ר' מאיר אומר כל תנאי שאינו כתנאי בני גד ובני ראובן אינו תנאי אם יעברו אם לא יעברו הא לא כפליה מכלל לאו לא תשמע הן. ל"ה. זכו שכינה ביניהם שהרי חלק הקב"ה שמו ושכנו ביניהם יו"ד באיש וה"א באשה לא זכו אש אוכלתן שהקב"ה מסלק שמו מביניהם ונמצאו אש ואש. ודאשה עדיפא אש של אשה נוח לדלוק וממהרת לאכול לפי שאין אות של שם מפסיקתן אלא מחובר הוא אבל אש של איש אינו מחובר יחד לפי שאות של שכינה מפסיקתם. ל"ה. הנאה ליכא ואין זה קיבול שכר אבל כאן יש הנאה בסוטה לתת שלום ושלא ירבו ממזרות בישראל אם זונה היא. ואם נקתה ונזרעה זרע ומבטלת לעז מעל בניה וכן אפר פרה איכא הנאה לטהר ולזכות ישראל ממעשה העגל. ל"ה: מפני שהתכלת דומה לים בא ללמד שכל המקיים מצות ציצית כאילו מקביל פני שכינה והכי תני לה בספרי ואיצטריכו כל הני משום דלא אשכחי' קרא אלא ברקיע הילכך תכלת דומה לים וים דומה לרקיע מפני דתכלת לאו לרקיע כל כך אלא דומה לדומה כמו תכלת קרוב למראה הים ולפי' מזכירין יציאת מצרים בפרשת ציצית לפי שהתכלת דומה לים והקב"ה שיושב על כסא הכבוד עשה לנו נסים בים. ועוד התכלת דומה לים שאנו עושין שליש גדיל ושני שלישי ענף וכן עשה הקב"ה בקע הים בשליש אמצעי ועשה מן הים ג' שלישים שאם יבקענה בשליש התחתון צריך שירדו למטה בתוך הים ואם יבקענה בשליש העליון צריך שיעלו למעלה דק"ל גודשא תילתא והבקיעה בשליש האמצעי לא למעלה ולא למטה על כן ייסד הפייט א) פנו כאן וכאן שליש רום מימות

א) הוא ביוצר ליום אחרון של פסח.

עין משפט נר מצוה

לט א מיי' פ"ג מהל' סוטה הל"ח סמג עשין נו:
מ ב מיי' שם פ"ד הל"ח סמג שם:

רש"ל

[וע' תוספות מנחות יא: ד"ה ורבי שמעון מייתיבים קושיא זו]

מסורת הש"ס

[ברכות טו:]

[פסחים כב: קדושין נז. ב"ק מא: מנחות יא: בכורות ו: נזיר סה: נדה לה.]

[ברכות טו: ע"ש]

שבועות לו. ע"ש קדושין סב.

האלות לרבות הקללות כו'. מהרש"ל

חולין פח:

[בילקוט רמז פ"ג איתא עפר סוטה ואפר פרה]

חולין פט.

[קדושין סא.]

חולין פט. ברכות ו. נז. מנחות לה: [מגילה טו:] [מנחות מג:]

הגהות הב"ח

(א) במשנה מאם לא: (ב) גמ' מיעוטא היא והא לית ליה: (ג) רש"י ד"ה מאם לא וכו' אלא שמה שהשביע וכו' ואינו כותבו וכו' שמצוה לכהן: (ד) ד"ה שהתכלת וכו' ואיצטריכו:

עין משפט
נר מצוה

מא א מיי' פ"ג מהל' סוטה הל"ח ופ"ד הל"ט סמג עשין נו:
מב ב ג ד מיי' שם פ"ד הל"ז:
מג ה מיי' שם הל"ח:

תורה אור

הַדִּיפְתְּרָא אֶלָּא עַל הַמְּגִילָּה, שֶׁנֶּאֱמַר: °"בַּסֵּפֶר". [במדבר ה] אוְאֵינוֹ כּוֹתֵב לֹא בְּקוֹמוֹס וְלֹא בְּקַנְקַנְתּוֹם וְלֹא בְּכָל דָּבָר שֶׁרוֹשֵׁם, אֶלָּא בִּדְיוֹ, שֶׁנֶּאֱמַר: *°"וּמָחָה" [שם] – כְּתָב שֶׁיָּכוֹל (א) לִמָּחוֹת.§ **גמ'** אָמַר רָבָא: במְגִילַּת סוֹטָה שֶׁכְּתָבָהּ בַּלַּיְלָה – פְּסוּלָה, מ"ט – אָתְיָא "תּוֹרָה" "תּוֹרָה"; כְּתִיב הָכָא: °"וְעָשָׂה לָהּ [שם] הַכֹּהֵן אֵת כָּל הַתּוֹרָה הַזֹּאת", וּכְתִיב הָתָם: °"עַל [דברים יז] פִּי הַתּוֹרָה אֲשֶׁר יוֹרוּךָ וְעַל הַמִּשְׁפָּט", מַה מִּשְׁפָּט בַּיּוֹם – אַף מְגִילַּת סוֹטָה בַּיּוֹם. גכְּתָבָהּ לְמַפְרֵעַ פְּסוּלָה, דִּכְתִיב: "וְכָתַב אֶת הָאָלוֹת הָאֵלֶּה" – כִּי דִּכְתִיבָא. * דכְּתָבָהּ קוֹדֶם שֶׁתְּקַבֵּל עָלֶיהָ שְׁבוּעָה – פְּסוּלָה, [שֶׁנֶּא'] "וְהִשְׁבִּיעַ" וְאַחַר כָּךְ "וְכָתַב". [רש"ל] הכְּתָבָהּ אִיגֶּרֶת – פְּסוּלָה, "בַּסֵּפֶר" אָמַר רַחֲמָנָא.

כְּתָבָהּ

דִּיפְתְּרָא. עוֹר שֶׁאֵינָהּ מְעוּבָּד כָּל צָרְכָּהּ, דִּמְלִיחַ וּקְמִיחַ וְלָא עָפִיץ. שֶׁהָיוּ מְעַבְּדִין הַקְּלָפִים בַּעֲפָצִים שֶׁקּוֹרִין גלי"ש. בַּסֵּפֶר. קְלָף. קוֹמוֹס. שְׂרַף הָאִילָן. וּמַתִּיכוֹ בַּמַּיִם, וְכוֹתֵב הֵימֶנּוּ. קַנְקַנְתּוֹם. וויטריאול"ו או אורדימנ"ט קוֹרִין אוֹתוֹ. וְלֹא בְּכָל דָּבָר שֶׁהוּא רוֹשֵׁם. וְנִבְלָע בַּקְּלָף וְאֵינוֹ יָכוֹל לִמְחוֹק, וְקוֹמוֹס וְקַנְקַנְתּוֹס עָבְדֵי רוֹשֶׁם. אֶלָּא בִּדְיוֹ. שֶׁלָּנוּ, שֶׁל שְׂרָף. **גמ'** מִשְׁפָּט בַּיּוֹם. בְּסַנְהֶדְרִין (דף לד:) נָפְקָא לָן מִ"וְהָיָה בְּיוֹם הַנְחִילוֹ". לְמַפְרֵעַ. יָרֵךְ וְלַנְפִּיל בֶּטֶן לַצְבּוֹת בְּמֵעַיִךְ *) וכו' כַּסֵּדֶר הַזֶּה, אוֹ אֶחָד מֵהֶן הֵיפֶךְ, וְהַשְּׁאָר כָּתַב כְּהִילְכָתָן. הָאֵלֶּה. מַשְׁמַע כְּמוֹ שֶׁהֵן סְדוּרִין בַּפָּרָשָׁה. אִגֶּרֶת. בְּלֹא שִׂרְטוּט. בַּסֵּפֶר אָמַר רַחֲמָנָא. וַהֲלָכָה לְמֹשֶׁה מִסִּינַי שֶׁהַסְּפָרִים צְרִיכִין שִׂרְטוּט.

*) נ"ל טולה

עַל

"בספר" כ"ע מודו דמרבינן כל מילי, בר מדבר שיש בו רוח חיים! מיהו, לפי' ר"ת לא קשיא מידי, דפי': התם – בכלל ופרט וכלל דרשינן ליה, *דחזר וכתב "ונתן לה" (ספר כריתות). אבל הכא – כלל ופרט הוא, ואין בכלל אלא מה שבפרט. א"נ, התם קרא יתירא הוא דקא דריש, משום דכתיב תרי זימני "וכתב לה ספר כריתות". ובירושלמי מקשה ליה נמי: הכא כתיב "ספר" והכא כתיב "ספר", הכא את אומר כל דבר שהוא בתלוש, והכא את אומר הכין! שנייא היא הכא, דכתיב "בספר". אבל בגמרא דידן לא אמר התם הכי, דאמר: אי כתיב "בספר" – כדקא אמרת, דהוי מרבינן כל מילי דתלוש בר מדבר שיש בו רוח חיים. ירושלמי: תניא, ר"א בן שמוע אומר: אין כותבין על עורות בהמה טמאה. אמר ר"ש: מכיון דאיתמר למחיקה ניתנה למה אינו כותב? תני ר"א [בר שמעון] אומר: רואה אני את דברי ר"א בן שמוע מדברי אבא, שמא תאמר "איני שותה" ונמצא השם גנוז על עור בהמה טמאה. ותו התם: ר' לוי בר סיסי בעי קמיה רבי: מגילת סוטה מהו שתטמא את הידים? א"ל: הרי זו שאלה. א"ר יוסי: אינה שאלה, כלום גזרו על הספרים שיטמאו את הידים – לא מפני קדושתן? וזו למחיקה נתנה, לא צריכא [דלא], הואיל ונתנה למחיקה.

שנאמר ומחה כתב שיכול למחוק. בירושלמי: אי "מחה", יכול במשקה או במי פירות – ת"ל "וכתב", הא כיצד – כתב שיכול לימחק, ואיזו זו – דיו שאין בו קנקנתוס. והא תני: אם מחק מתוך הספר כשר! תיפתר כהדין תניא, דתנא, אמר ר"מ: כל ימי שהייתי למדין אצל ר' ישמעאל [לא] היינו נותנין קנקנתוס לתוך הדיו.

מה משפט ביום אף מגילת סוטה ביום. כל מעשה סוטה ילפינן מהכא בפ"ב דמגילה (דף כ:) דהשקאה ביום. רש"י פי': מה משפט ביום – בסנהדרין נפקא לן מ"והיה ביום הנחילו את בניו". ולא מסתברא, דהא "ע"פ התורה" כתיב גבי זקן ממרא, דמשתעי בדיני נפשות, והאי קרא ד"ביום הנחילו" משתעי בדיני ממונות. אלא מ"והוקע אותם לה' נגד השמש" נפקא לן התם* דביום. ונראה לי דכל דין סוטה, בין גמר בין תחילה – פסול בלילה, דומיא דדיני נפשות, ולא כדיני ממונות דתחילת דין ביום אבל גמר דין אפילו בלילה. **דכתיב** וכתב את האלות האלה בדכתיבא. תימה לר"י: לקמן בפרק "ואלו נאמרין" (דף לג:), ואיתא נמי בריש פ"ב דמסכת ברכות (דף יג.), ובמסכת מגילה (דף יז:), דק"ש לא יקראנה למפרע, לרבנן מ"והיו" ולרבי מ"דברים" "הדברים". ורבנן – "דברים" "הדברים" לא משמע להו, הילכך איצטריך "והיו" שלא יקראנה למפרע. ואמאי לא נפקא להו מ"האלה" כי הכא, "הדברים האלה" כדכתיבא? וי"ל: כיון דקיבלו וגמירי מרבותינו ד"שמע" אית לן למדרש בכל לשון שאתה שומע – אייתר לך "והיו" שלא יקראנה למפרע, ו"האלה" דרשי להו לדרשא אחריתי. **קודם** שתקבל עליה שבועה פסולה. ירושלמי: ר' קרוספא אמר: איתפלגון ר' יוחנן ור"ל, חד אמר: משביע ואח"כ כותב, וחד אמר: כותב ואח"כ משביע. ומפרש טעמא כדי לסמוך שבועה להשקאה. והתם משמע דבהכי פליגי: מ"ד משביע ואח"כ כותב – אית ליה "חוקה" ו"תורה" מעכב על הסדר, ומאן דאמר כותב ואח"כ משביע – אית ליה אע"ג דמעכב, אינו על הסדר. ותימה: א"כ, כמאן ס"ל? לא כר"י ולא כר' נחמיה בפ' "הוציאו לו" (יומא דף ס.), דמשמע דכ"ע סבירא להו היכא דכתיב "חוקה" מעכב נמי על הסדר! ותמה רבי: דבפרק "ד' מיתות" (סנהדרין דף מט:) אמר רבא אמר רב סחורה אמר רב הונא: כל מקום ששנו חכמים דרך מנין – אין מוקדם ומאוחר, חוץ משבעה סממנין. רב פפא סבא משמיה דרב אמר: אף ד' מיתות. ואידך – בפלוגתא לא קא מיירי. רב פפא אומר: אף סדר יומא. ואידך – ההוא לחומרא בעלמא. דמשמע: הא לאו הכי – הוה חשיב ליה. ואמאי לא חשיב סדר סוטה? דהא איהו אמר הכא: כתבה קודם שתקבל עליה שבועה – פסולה, ומשמע בירושלמי דבעי כל הפרשה על הסדר! ונראה דלא חשיב אלא היכא דשנוין על הסדר. אבל סדר סוטה אינה נשנית על הסדר, שהרי אין סדר המשנה וסדר הפרשה מכוונין, כמו שפירשנו בראש הפרק. וסדר הפרשה עיקר, אבל סדר המשנה אפילו למצוה בעלמא לא. ולהכי לא אמר נמי התם, דאמר "וזהו סדר תמיד" לאפוקי ממצות חליצה, אבל לאפוקי מסדר סוטה ליכא למימר, דאפילו בדיעבד נמי לא. **כתבה** איגרת פסולה. רש"י פירש: אגרת – בלא שרטוט, "בספר" אמר רחמנא, והלכה למשה מסיני שהספרים צריכין שרטוט. ואי קשיא: מאי איריא משום דנקראת "ספר"? תיפוק לי דבלאו הכי אסור לכתוב שום פסוק בלא שרטוט, דאמרי' בפ"ק דגיטין (דף ו:), אמר רב יוסף: מאן לימא לן דר' אביתר בר סמכא הוא, ועוד, הא איהו דשלח ליה לרב יהודה: בני אדם העולים משם לכאן הן קיימו בעצמם "ויתנו הילד בזונה והילדה מכרו ביין וישתו", וכתב ליה בלא שרטוט, וא"ר יצחק: שתים כותבין, שלש אין כותבין! ואמרינן בסוף פרק "מצות חליצה" (יבמות דף קו:) אמר אביי: האי מאן דכתב גיטא דחליצתא – לכתוב הכי: אקריוה לדידה מ"מאן יבמי" עד "יבמי". ופירוש: משום דלא מצי למכתב שלש תיבות רצופין בלא שרטוט, כדמסיק: מר זוטרא שירטט וכתב ליה לכולה פרשתא, מתקיף לה מר בר רב אידי: והא לא ניתן ליכתב! והילכתא כמר זוטרא, אע"ג דלא ניתן ליכתב! תריץ: אי לאו משום דנקראת "ספר" – ה"א: אע"ג דאסור לכתוב בלא שירטוט – המגילה עצמה אינה פסולה, קמ"ל דפסולה, ונראה שלא היו המים בודקין על ידה. מיהו, לא ידענא אם שרטט אותה בין שיטה לשיטה לאחר כתיבה, אע"ג דבשעת כתיבה כתב באיסורא – אי המגילה כשירה בהכי או לא. והא דאמרי' ב"הקומץ רבה" (מנחות דף לב:), ובמגילה (דף יח:), הלכתא: מזוזה צריכה שירטוט, אבל לא תפילין – נראה דהכי הילכתא גמירי לה דאין לו לשרטט תפילין. דאי לא תימא הכי, אלא הא דפסיק: אבל לא תפילין – דלא מיפסלי אי כתבן בלא שרטוט, מיהו צריך לשרטט משום דאסור לכתוב בלא שרטוט – א"כ, הא דמקשה התם מהא דתפילין שבלו אין עושין מהן מזוזה, שאין מורידין אותו מקדושה חמורה לקדושה קלה. טעמא – דאין מורידין, אבל משום שרטוט – לא? ומשני: תנאי היא. אי הוה מצי לשרטט להו – הוה מצי למימר: במשורטטין! אלא ש"מ דהכי גמירי לה, דלא מצי לשרטט להו. אבל ר"ת פירש: הא דאמרי': שלש אין כותבין – היינו אם לא שרטט כלל, אבל אם שרטט בד' פיאות הגליונים, אע"פ דלא שרטט בין שיטה לשיטה – חשוב שירטוט אפי' לענין ס"ת, אלא משום "זה אלי ואנוהו" (שמות טו) צריך לשרטט בין כל שיטה ושיטה. וכן מוכיח בפ"ק דמגילה (דף טז:): "דברי שלום ואמת" – מלמד שצריכה שרטוט כאמיתה של תורה, ופירש ר"ת: דלאו היינו ס"ת, אלא מזוזה. ולישנא ד"אמיתה" – משמע כיחידה של תורה, דהיינו מזוזה דיש בה עול מלכות שמים. וכן עיקר, דאי ס"ת ממש משתעי ההוא קרא ד"ואמת" – א"כ הא דגרסינן בפ"ב דמגילה (דף יט.): מגילה נקראת ספר ונקראת אגרת, נקראת ספר – שאם תפרה בפשתן פסולה, מאי איריא משום ספר? תיפוק ליה משום "ואמת", וניסא צריכה שירטוט ותפירה כאמיתה של תורה! אלא ש"מ לשרטוט דמזוזה איצטריך, דהתם תפירה ליכא, ולענין תפירה נקראת ספר. והשתא לא תקשי הא דפסקינן ב"הקומץ רבה" (מנחות דף לב:) ובמגילה (דף יח:): הילכתא מזוזה צריכה שרטוט, תפילין אין צריכין שרטוט. ומקשה מהא דתפילין שבלו אין עושין מהן מזוזה לפי שאין מורידין, הא משום שרטוט – לא? ומשני: תנאי היא. מדלא משני: במשורטטין – ש"מ דלפי' מנהג ליכא, *הואיל וכן – אין צריך לשרטטן, דגרסינן בירושלמי בפרק *"במה מדליקין": כל הפטור בדבר ועושהו נקרא הדיוט. השתא י"ל: הא דאין צריכין שרטוט – היינו בין השיטין, אבל בד' פיאות – צריכין שרטוט, דלא גריעי מ"שלש אין כותבין". מיהא לפירושו לא תירץ *מאי איצטריך למימר גבי מגילת סוטה דפסולה בלא שרטוט, כיון דאפילו ס"ת הוא – סגי ליה בשרטוט לארבע פיאות. מצאתי בתוספות רבינו יב"א במסכת גיטין, שמעתי מר' אליהו הצרפתי שהיה אומר: מה שאנו כותבים בכתבים בלא שרטוט – ליכא למיחש, דלא כתבינן לשום פסוק אלא לאמירה בעלמא, לפרוס בשלום בלשון עברי, או לדבר בו בלשון לע. אבל כשכותב שמביא אותו לשום פסוק – כי האי גוונא אסור למכתב בלא שרטוט. ולא ידענא מנלן לכתוב בפירושים פסוקים בלא שרטוט, כשמביא לשום פסוק*. **כתבה*** על שני דפין פסולה. מקשים לפירוש רש"י [שפי'] בדפין של ס"ת, מפרק בתרא דגיטין (דף פז:), דתנן: שייר מקצת הגט וכתבו בדף השני, והעדים מלמטה – כשר, ולא חשיב ליה שני ספרים, כיון דמעורה, כדאמרי' בפרק שני דגיטין (דף כ:) אהא: הרי זה גיטך והנייר שלי – אינה מגורשת וכו'. בעי רב פפא: בין שיטה לשיטה בין תיבה לתיבה מהו? וקפריך: ותיפוק ליה משום דספר אחד אמר רחמנא ולא שנים! לא צריכא דמעורה. וב"הקומץ רבה" (מנחות דף לג.) גבי מזוזה אמר רב יהודה אמר נמי, אמר רב יהודה אמר שמואל: כתבה על שני דפין פסולה

תוספות שאנץ

מימות ונפקא ליה מדכתיב בלב ים וק"ל דלבו של אדם הוי בשליש גופו: כתבה אגרת בלא שרטוטין. בספר אמר רחמ' והל"מ הוא דספרים צריכין שרטוט:

מסורת הש"ס

וכתב לה כלל ספר כריתות פרט ונתן חזר וכלל אבל הכא כו'. מהרש"ל

[לקמן כ. עירובין יג.]

[לקמן יט:]

[בסנהדרין לד:]

הגהות הב"ח

(א) גמ' שיכול להמחות:

גליון הש"ס

גמ' כתבה קודם שתקבל. עיין לקמן דף כ ע"א תד"ה א"ר ירמיה:

[נ"ל יציאות השבת]

לא תירץ מאי איכא למימר כו' מהרש"ל

[וע"ע תוס' גיטין ו: ד"ה אמר ותוס' מנחות לב: ד"ה הא]

הואיל ואין צריך לשרטטן מהרש"ל

שייך לדף שאח"ז

מד א מיי' פ"ד מהל' סוטה הל"ח:
מה ב מיי' שם הל"י:
מו ג ד ה ו מיי' שם הלכה יא:
מז ז מיי' שם הל"ז:

תורה אור

[א]כתבה על שני דפין – פסולה, "ספר" – אחד אמר רחמנא, ולא שנים ושלשה ספרים. [ב]כתב אות אחת ומחק אות אחת, וכתב אות אחת ומחק אות אחת – פסולה, דכתיב: °"ועשה לה הכהן את כל התורה הזאת" (במדבר ה). בעי רבא: כתב ב' מגילות לשתי סוטות, ומחקן לתוך כוס אחד, מהו? כתיבה לשמה בעינן – והאיכא, או דילמא בעינן נמי מחיקה לשמה? ואם תמצא לומר: [ג]בעינן נמי מחיקה לשמה, מחקן בב' כוסות וחזר ועירבן, מהו? מחיקה לשמה בעינן – והאיכא, או דילמא הא לאו דידה קא שתיא, והא לאו דידה קא שתיא? ואם תמצא לומר: [ד]הא לאו דידה קא שתיא והא לאו דידה קא שתיא, חזר וחלקן מהו – יש ברירה או אין ברירה? [ה]תיקו. בעי רבא: השקה *בסיב מהו, בשפופרת מהו – דרך שתיה בכך או אין דרך שתיה בכך? תיקו. בעי רב אשי: נשפכו מהן ונשתיירו מהן מהו? [ו]תיקו. א"ר זירא אמר רב: ב' שבועות האמורות בסוטה למה – אחת קודם שנמחקה מגילה, ואחת לאחר שנמחקה. מתקיף לה רבא: תרוייהו קודם שנמחקה מגילה כתיבן! אלא אמר רבא: אחת שבועה שיש עמה אלה, ואחת שבועה שאין עמה אלה. היכי דמי שבועה שיש עמה אלה? אמר רב עמרם אמר רב: משביעני עליך שלא נטמאת, שאם נטמאת – יבואו ביך. אמר רבא: אלה לחודה קיימא, ושבועה לחודה קיימא! אלא אמר רבא: משביעני עליך שאם נטמאת יבואו ביך. אמר רב אשי: אלה – איכא, שבועה – ליכא! אלא אמר רב אשי: משביעני עליך שלא נטמאת, ואם נטמאת – יבואו ביך.§ **מתני'** *[ז]על מה היא אומרת "אמן אמן" – *"אמן על האלה, אמן על השבועה, אמן מאיש זה, אמן מאיש אחר, אמן שלא שטיתי ארוסה, ונשואה, ושומרת

רש"י

על שני דפין. כדפין של ספר תורה, העשויין עמודים. כתב אות אחת ומחקה. על המים, וחזר וכתב אות שלאחריה ומחקה, עד שהשלים את כולה – פסול, דכתיב "את כל התורה" – עד שתהא כולה כאחד. לשמה. בספר לעצמו, דכתיב: "ועשה לה" – לשמה. מחיקה נמי. בכוס. לשמה לעצמה, שיהא ניכר המחיקה שהיא לשמה. השקה בסיב. שהוא חלול, כדרך שהתינוקות שותין. שיש עמה אלה. דכתיב בחדא מינייהו "בשבועת האלה", ולקמיה מפרש היכי דמי. משביעני עליך. בשם, ומזכיר שם. שלא נטמאת. שאת אומר אמת שלא נטמאת – היינו שבועה א] שאין עמה אלה. שאם נטמאת יבואו ביך. המים "לצבות בטן" כו', והיינו אלה. אמר רבא אלה לחודיה קיימא כו'. שבועה ואלה יש כאן, ושניהן על האשה, וקרא כתיב "בשבועת האלה" – שהשבועה של אלה. משביעני עליך שאם נטמאת יבואו ביך. דאיכא השתא* (א) "שבועת האלה", שמשביע את האלה שתחול. שבועה ליכא. על האשה, וקרא כתיב: "והשביע את האשה". משביעני עליך שלא נטמאת ואם נטמאת יבואו ביך. משביעני עליך שיהא אמת מה שאמרת בפנינו שלא נטמאת, ואם נטמאת – יבואו ביך המים, דקיימא שבועה אאשה – שלא נטמאת, ואאלה – שתחול. **מתני'** אמן על האלה וכו'. לכך הוצרכה לכפול. ארוסה ונשואה. על ידי גלגול שבועה הוא מגלגל עליה זנות של אירוסין, אע"פ שלא היה בו קינוי. ומכאן לגלגול שבועה מן התורה.

תוספות

פסולה. מיתיבי: כתבה על שני דפין והניח בשני סיפין – פסולה, הא בסף אחד – כשירה! ראויה לשני סיפין קא אמר. אלמא דשני דפין דקאמר שמואל – בנחתכין זה מזה קאמר, שאין מעורין! להכי מפרש נמי הכא שני דפין שאינן מעורין. ופירש ר"י: הא דאמר נמי בפ' "ראוהו ב"ד" (ר"ה דף כו.): אפי' לרבנן דאמרי קרן פרה פסול, כיון דאית בה גילדי – כשנים ושלש שופרות דמי, ואע"ג דמחברי – התם נמי דרכו להוסיף בכל שנה גלד אחד, והרי הוא כמביאו משופר אחר ומדבקו לזה, כדתנן: דיבק שברי שופרות פסול, מפני שמתחילתו לא היתה ברייתן בבת אחת, וניכר התוספת, ולא מהני חיבורו, ודומה כאילו גט שכתבו על ב' דפין ותפרן יחד דפסול. *דהאי דוקא כשכתב חצי מגילת סוטה על דף זה וחציה על דף אחר אמרינן דחשיב שני ספרים, וה"ה אם כתב לה שתי מגילות ומחקו לתוך כוס אחד. וכן גבי גט, אם נתן לה שני גיטין, אע"ג דכל חד וחד שלם הוא, וספר אחד בפני עצמו – פסולין, ולא מיגרשא בתרוייהו משום שנים או שלשה ספרים, כדאמרינן בפ' "שור שנגח" (ב"ק דף מ.): "כופר" אחד אמר רחמנא, ולא שנים או שלשה כופרין. ובפרק "לולב הגזול" (סוכה דף לה.): לינקוט תרתי תלת – "פרי" אחד אמר רחמנא ולא שנים או שלשה פירות. ואין להקשות: מאי שנא משנתן שופר בתוך שופר, אם קול פנימי שמע – יצא, ולא חשיב ליה כשני שופרות? דהתם בשמיעה תליא מילתא, והוא לא שמע אלא קול הפנימי. **חזר** וחלקן מהו יש ברירה או אין ברירה. האי לא דמי לברירה דמדלה מן הבור, פלוגתא דר' אליעזר ב"י ורבנן ב"שור שנגח" (ב"ק דף נא:), דהתם לא הוכר חלקו של אחד מהן לעולם, אבל הכא – הוכר הכתב ונתערב. וכן ברירה מ"שני לוגין שאני עתיד להפריש", דמייתי בפ' "מרובה" (שם דף סט:) – נמי לא הוכר המעשר מעולם. וכן לכולהו ברירות דמייתי בפ' "כל הגט" (גיטין דף כה.). אבל דמי לברירה דמייתי ב"בכל מערבין" (עירובין דף לז.): שתי נשים שלקחו קיניהן בעירוב, או שנתנו דמי קיניהן לכהן – איזה שירצה יקריב חטאת, ואי זה שירצה יקריב עולה, אע"ג דהוכרו מתחילה דמי כל אחת – לא אמרי' זו מתכפרת במה שנקח מדמי חבירתה, או שתי קינין של אחת יקריב כולן לעולה ושל חבירתה לחטאת, א"נ איפכא, *דאמרי' ברירה. ואע"ג דדחי ליה: התם כשהתנו – מיהו חזינן דקא מייתי לה אשאר ברירות, אלמא דליכא לאיפלוגי בין ברירה שהוכרה מתחילה לשאר ברירות. וכן בפ' "הוציאו לו" (יומא דף נה.) דמייתי מתני', ר' יהודה אומר: לא היו מביאין שופרות לקיני חובה מפני התערובות. ומסיק: משום תערובות דמי חטאת שמתה בעליה. וקא פריך: ונברור ד' זוזי ונשדי במיא והנך לישתרו! ר' יהודה לית ליה ברירה מנלן? ומייתי הסיא דהלוקח יין מבין הכותים, ומסיק: מדתני איו. אלמא דמדמי ברירה ד"אם בא חכם למזרח", אע"ג דליכא היכרא מעיקרא – לברירה דארבעה זוזי, דהוכר מעיקרא. א"כ רבא מאי קא מבעיא ליה דלא פשיט מהני? ומהא נמי דתנן בפ' בתרא דמס' מעילה (דף כא:): פרוטה של הקדש שנפלה לתוך הכיס, או שאמר "פרוטה בכיס זה הקדש", כיון שהוציא הראשונה – מעל, דברי ר"ע. וחכ"א: עד שיוציא את כל הכיס. אלמא לר"ע אית ליה ברירה כי האי גוונא, דאמר: בפרוטה ראשונה הוברר הדבר שפרוטה ראשונה שעלתה בידו היא היתה של הקדש שנפלה. מיהא לא איתברר לן התם במאי פליגי. ומהא נמי ליכא למפשט, דמייתי בבכורות פרק "הלוקח בהמה" (דף כב:): סאה תרומה טמאה שנפלה לק' חולין, ר"א אומר: תירום ותירקב, שאני אומר: היא סאה שעלתה היא סאה שנפלה. ה"נ נימא שהמחק של זאת יגיע לזאת – דהתם מקילינן בדרבנן, דמדאורייתא חד בתרי בטל. וריב"א הקשה בפ' "הוציאו לו" (יומא דף נה:) אהא ונברור ד' זוזי, דתניא בתוספתא דמעילה (פ"א): נזיר שהפריש מעות ואמר "אלו לחטאתי ואלו לעולתי ואלו לשלמי" ונתערבו – הרי לוקח בהן ג' בהמות, בין ממקום אחד בין משלשה מקומות, *מכלל דמי חטאת וכו'. ודוקא בכי האי גוונא שרי, אבל ליקח שליש המעות וליקח בהן בהמה לחטאת ונימא: הוברר הדבר דאלו הוו דמי חטאת – לא אמרי'. מיהו, מכל הני הוה מצי רבא למיפשט! ועוד תימה: אי אית לן למימר ברירה כי האי גוונא – אם כן כל התערובות שבעולם יחזור ויחלק משום ברירה! ועוד: אמאי לא פשיט ליה מפרק קמא דראש השנה (דף יג:), דקיימא לן דיש בילה לשמן ויין – נמצא דאין ברירה בדבר לח, ובפרק "התערובות" (זבחים דף פ.) מייתי ליה פלוגתא דרבי אליעזר ורבנן: כלוחית של חטאת שנפל *לתוך מים וכו'? ונראה, דהכא קא מבעיא ליה: מי אמרינן לא קפיד קרא אלא אמחיקה מן המגילה שתהא נכרת לתוך המים שלה, אבל לתוך כוס אחד – איכא למימר כל חדא שתייא מים דלאו דידה – לאו מחיקה נכרת היא, חזר וחלקן – הרי מים של כל אחת ניכרין, מי אמרינן ברירה, וכו' הרי הוברר מימיה. אי דילמא אין ברירה, כלומר ברירת מים בשעת מחיקה בעינן. אבל על תערובת דיו של כתב המגילה – לא קפדינן, שהרי בשעת מחיקה בטל הכתב, ולא תלי מילתא אלא במחיקה לתוך מים המבוררין לצרכה, וקא מבעיא ליה אי מיא לא בדקי לה משום דלא נמחקה כהלכתה, אי משום דטהורה היא. **בעי** רבא השקה בסיב מהו. ליכא למיפשט מהא דאמר רבא בפרק "ערבי פסחים" (פסחים דף קטו:): כרכן בסיב – אף ידי מצה לא יצא, אלמא אין דרך אכילה בכך. דהתם מפסיק הסיב בין המצה ובין בית הבליעה, אבל הכא דלא מפסיק קא מיבעיא ליה. **על** מה היא אומרת אמן אמן. בפרק שלישי דמסכת שבועות (דף כט:): כל העונה אמן כאילו מוציא שבועה מפיו. ובפרק "שבועת העדות" (שם דף לו.): אמן יש בו קבלה, יש בו שבועה, ויש בו האמנת דברים. *אמן שלא אטמא. ירושלמי: לא שהיה ר"מ אומר המים בודקין אותה מעכשיו, אלא המים פקודים בה, לכשתטמא – המים בודקין אותה למפרע.

שומרת

תוספות שאנץ

על שני דפין פי' כדפין של ספר תורה שקורין קולנייש בלע"ז. פסולה ומיירי שאינן מחוברין יחד אבל אם הן מחוברין השני דפין שפי' קרי' ליה ספר אחד. השקה בסיב שהיא חלולה כדרך שהתינוקות שותין בגבעולי קנבום ל"ה. יש ספרים דגרסי בסיב או בשפופרת מהו כעין קליעה שעושין נקבים כמין סל א) ולאו דומה לשפופרת: **מתני'** אמן שלא שטיתי ארוסה ונשואה על ידי גלגול שבועה הוא מגלגל עליה זנות של אירוסין ואע"ג דלא היה בו קינוי ומכאן מפקי' דגלגול שבועה מן התורה. ומאן דמוקי לה התם ב) למילתא אחריתי מפיק גלגול שבועה מאמן מאיש זה אמן מאיש אחר: ולא מאחר שתתגרש ותסתר לאחר ואחר כך יחזירנה ה"ג ואפי' לר' מאיר דאמר מתנה על העתיד ונטמאת בגירושיה דאינה נאסרת עליו לחזור לו אלא א"כ נשאת על ידי קידושין דכי כתיב לא יוכל בעלה הראשון אשר שלחה וגו' לאחר קידושין ונישואין כתיב כדכתיב והלכה והיתה לאיש אחר ושנאה האיש האחרון ל"ה. ואית דגרסי ולא מאחר שתתגרש ותנשא לאחר ול"נ דכיון דאין האיש מנוקה מעון דלוקה משום לאו דלא יוכל ואין קידושין תופסין בה אין המים בודקין את אשתו. אבל קשה הכא משמע כיון שהיא גרושה לא נאסרה בזנות על בעלה אם יחזירנה. ותימה דפ"ק דמגילה [דף טו] קאמר גבי אסתר וכאשר אבדתי מבית אבא כך אבדתי ממך דעד עכשיו באונס ועכשיו ברצון ואמאי לא גרשה מרדכי כדאיתא הכא. וי"ל משום דגט צריך עדים והיה ירא מרדכי פן יודע הדבר לאחשורוש ומ"ה לא גרשה וכן פי' בפ"ק דמגילה.

א) אולי נ"ל ולאו שפופרת ממש קאמר אלא דומה לשפופרת. ב) ר"ל ביבמות דף נח דמיירי בהשקאה לארוסה ממש ונכנסה לחופה ולא נבעלה ע"ש. ועי' בתוס' קדושין כז ע"ב ד"ה ה"ג.

גירסת רש"א ולאו דוקא.

[גיטין כ:]

שבועה שיש עמו אלה כו'. מהרש"ל

[פי' נתן הסיב במים ובלע הסיב למים כמין ספוג ונתן הסיב בפיה ומוצצת למים. ערוך ערך סב ב]

הגהות הב"ח

(א) רש"י ד"ה משביעני וכו' שבועה של אלה:

קדושין כז: יבמות נח. [פירוש נכון דכולך ילפינן כל אותן דחשיב הכא מן חד אמן יתירה תמצא בתוס' יבמות נח. ד"ה שומרת ותוס' קדושין כז: ד"ה אמן]

ולא אמרינן דשמא אות' שהקריב כולה חטאת שמא עולה או איפכא משום לאמר ברירה כו'. מהרש"ל

הגהות מהר"ב רנשבורג

א] רש"י ד"ה שלא נטמאת וכו' שבועה שאין עמה. מלת שאין נמחק וצ"ב שיש כצ"ל. רש"ל:

נ"ל מחלל

[נ"ל לתוכה]

[שייך לע"ב]

מח א ב ג מיי' פ"ד מהל' סוטה הל' ז:
מט ד מיי' פ"ב מהל' יבום הל"כ סמג עשין נ טוש"ע אה"ע סי' קנט סעי' ג:
נ ה ו ז מיי' פ"ד מהל' סוטה הלכה יז:
נא ח מיי' פ"א מהל' סוטה הל' ב:

תורה אור

וְשׁוֹמֶרֶת יָבָם וּכְנוּסָה. אָמֵן שֶׁלֹּא נִטְמֵאתִי, וְאִם נִטְמֵאתִי — יָבוֹאוּ בִּי. ר"מ אוֹמֵר: [א]אָמֵן שֶׁלֹּא נִטְמֵאתִי, אָמֵן שֶׁלֹּא אֶטָּמֵא. הַכֹּל שָׁוִין [ב]שֶׁאֵין מַתְנֶה עִמָּהּ לֹא עַל קוֹדֶם שֶׁתִּתְאָרֵס (א) וְלֹא עַל אַחַר שֶׁתִּתְגָּרֵשׁ. נִסְתְּרָה לְאֶחָד וְנִטְמֵאת, וְאח"כ הֶחֱזִירָהּ — לֹא הָיָה מַתְנֶה עִמָּהּ. [ג]זֶה הַכְּלָל: כָּל שֶׁתִּבָּעֵל וְלֹא הָיְתָה אֲסוּרָה לוֹ — לֹא הָיָה מַתְנֶה עִמָּהּ.§ גמ' *אָמַר רַב הַמְנוּנָא: שׁוֹמֶרֶת יָבָם שֶׁזִּינְּתָה — אֲסוּרָה לִיבָמָהּ. מִמַּאי — מִדְּקָתָנֵי שׁוֹמֶרֶת יָבָם וּכְנוּסָה; אא"ב אֲסִירָה — מִשּׁוּם הָכִי מַתְנֶה בַּהֲדָהּ, אֶלָּא א"א לָא אֲסִירָה — הֵיכִי מַתְנֶה בַּהֲדָהּ? וְהָתְנַן: זֶה הַכְּלָל: כָּל שֶׁאִילּוּ תִּיבָּעֵל וְלֹא תְּהֵא אֲסוּרָה לוֹ — לֹא הָיָה מַתְנֶה עִמָּהּ! אָמְרִי בְּמַעַרְבָא: [ד]לֵית הִילְכְתָא כְּרַב הַמְנוּנָא. אֶלָּא הָא דְּקָתָנֵי שׁוֹמֶרֶת יָבָם וּכְנוּסָה, הָא מַנִּי — ר"ע הִיא, דְּאָמַר: *אֵין קִידּוּשִׁין תּוֹפְסִין בְּחַיָּיבֵי לָאוִין, וּמְשַׁוֵּי לָהּ כִּי עֶרְוָה. בָּעֵי רַבִּי יִרְמְיָה: מַהוּ שֶׁיַּתְנֶה אָדָם עַל נִישּׂוּאִין הָרִאשׁוֹנִים? עַל נִישּׂוּאֵי אָחִיו מַהוּ? ת"ש: זֶה הַכְּלָל כָּל שֶׁתִּיבָּעֵל וְלֹא תְּהֵא אֲסוּרָה לוֹ — לֹא הָיָה מַתְנֶה עִמָּהּ, [ה]הָא אֲסִירָה — ה"נ דְּמַתְנֶה, ש"מ.§ "ר"מ אוֹמֵר אָמֵן שֶׁלֹּא נִטְמֵאתִי" וכו'.§ תַּנְיָא: *לֹא כְּשֶׁאָמַר ר"מ אָמֵן שֶׁלֹּא אֶטָּמֵא, שֶׁאִם תִּטָּמֵא מַיִם בּוֹדְקִין אוֹתָהּ מֵעַכְשָׁיו. אֶלָּא, [ו]לִכְשֶׁתִּטָּמֵא — מַיִם מְעַרְעֲרִין אוֹתָהּ, וּבוֹדְקִין אוֹתָהּ. בָּעֵי רַב אַשִׁי: מַהוּ שֶׁיַּתְנֶה אָדָם עַל נִישּׂוּאִין הָאַחֲרוֹנִים? הַשְׁתָּא מִיהָא לָא אֲסִירָה לֵיהּ, אוֹ דִּילְמָא זִימְנִין דִּמְגָרֵשׁ לָהּ וַהֲדַר מַהֲדַר לָהּ? ת"ש: הַכֹּל שָׁוִין שֶׁלֹּא הָיָה מַתְנֶה עִמָּהּ לֹא עַל קוֹדֶם שֶׁתִּתְאָרֵס וְלֹא עַל אַחַר שֶׁתִּתְגָּרֵשׁ. (ב) נִסְתְּרָה לְאֶחָד, וְנִטְמֵאת וְאח"כ יַחֲזִירֶנָּה — לֹא הָיָה מַתְנֶה. [ז]הָא יַחֲזִירֶנָּה וְתִיטַּמֵּא — ה"נ דְּמַתְנֵי, ש"מ. ת"ר: "זֹאת תּוֹרַת הַקְּנָאוֹת" — מְלַמֵּד שֶׁהָאִשָּׁה שׁוֹתָה וְשׁוֹנָה, רַבִּי יְהוּדָה אוֹמֵר: "זֹאת" — שֶׁאֵין הָאִשָּׁה שׁוֹתָה וְשׁוֹנָה. אָמַר ר' יְהוּדָה: מַעֲשֶׂה וְהֵעִיד לְפָנֵינוּ נְחוּנְיָא חוֹפֵר שִׁיחִין שֶׁהָאִשָּׁה שׁוֹתָה וְשׁוֹנָה, וְקִיבַּלְנוּ עֵדוּתוֹ בִּשְׁנֵי אֲנָשִׁים אֲבָל לֹא בְּאִישׁ אֶחָד. וַחכ"א: אֵין הָאִשָּׁה שׁוֹתָה וְשׁוֹנָה, בֵּין בְּאִישׁ אֶחָד בֵּין בִּב' אֲנָשִׁים. וְת"ק נַמִי, הָכְתִיב "זֹאת"! וְרַבָּנַן בַּתְרָאֵי נַמִי, הָא כְּתִיב "תּוֹרַת"! אָמַר רָבָא: בְּאִישׁ אֶחָד וּבוֹעֵל אֶחָד — דְּכ"ע לָא פְּלִיגִי [ח]דְּאֵין הָאִשָּׁה שׁוֹתָה וְשׁוֹנָה, דִּכְתִיב

(במדבר ה)

רש"י

שׁוֹמֶרֶת יָבָם וּכְנוּסָה. וְאִם הָיְתָה יְבִמְתּוֹ, וּכְנָסָהּ, וְקִינֵּא לָהּ וְנִסְתְּרָה — מְגַלְגֵּל עָלֶיהָ שְׁבוּעָה שֶׁלֹּא נִטְמֵאת כְּשֶׁהִיא שׁוֹמֶרֶת יָבָם. שׁוֹמֶרֶת יָבָם — מְצַפָּה וּמַמְתֶּנֶת לַיָּבָם שֶׁיְּיַבְּמֶנָּה, כְּמוֹ "וְאָבִיו שָׁמַר אֶת הַדָּבָר" (בראשית לז), "לֹא תִשְׁמוֹר עַל חַטָּאתִי" (איוב יד). אָמֵן שֶׁלֹּא נִטְמֵאתִי. הַיְינוּ קַבָּלַת שְׁבוּעָה, "וְאִם נִטְמֵאתִי יָבֹאוּ בִּי" — הַיְינוּ קַבָּלַת אָלָה, כְּדֶרֶךְ שֶׁהִשְׁבִּיעָהּ, כִּדְאָמַר לְעֵיל בַּגְּמָרָא: מַשְׁבִּיעֲנִי עָלַיִךְ שֶׁלֹּא נִטְמֵאת, וְאִם נִטְמֵאת — יָבֹאוּ בָּךְ. וְהַיְינוּ פֵּירוּשׁוֹ דְּ"אָמֵן עַל הַשְּׁבוּעָה אָמֵן עַל הָאָלָה" דְּתַנְיָא בְּרֵישָׁא. אָמֵן שֶׁלֹּא אֶטָּמֵא. שֶׁאִם תִּטָּמֵא לְאַחַר זְמַן — מַיִם מְעַרְעֲרִין אוֹתָהּ לְאַחַר שֶׁתִּטָּמֵא, כִּדְתַנְיָא בְּבָרַיְיתָא בַּגְּמָרָא. וְלֹא עַל אַחַר שֶׁתִּתְגָּרֵשׁ כו'. וַאֲפִילּוּ לְר"מ, דְּאָמַר: מַתְנֶה עַל הֶעָתִיד. וְנִטְמֵאת. בְּגֵירוּשֶׁיהָ, דְּאֵינָהּ נֶאֱסֶרֶת עָלָיו לַחֲזוֹר לוֹ אֶלָּא א"כ נִישֵּׂאת עַל יְדֵי קִידּוּשִׁין. דְּכִי כְּתִיב (דברים כד): "לֹא יוּכַל בַּעְלָהּ הָרִאשׁוֹן אֲשֶׁר שִׁלְּחָהּ לָשׁוּב לְקַחְתָּהּ" — אַחַר קִידּוּשִׁין וְנִישּׂוּאִין כְּתִיב, כִּדְכְתִיב: "וְהָיְתָה לְאִישׁ אַחֵר וּשְׂנֵאָהּ הָאִישׁ הָאַחֲרוֹן". גמ' שֶׁזִּינְּתָה. כְּשֶׁהִיא שׁוֹמֶרֶת יָבָם. אֲסוּרָה לִיבָמָהּ. כְּאִשָּׁה שֶׁזִּינְּתָה תַּחַת בַּעְלָהּ, שֶׁאֲסוּרָה לְבַעְלָהּ. מִדְּקָתָנֵי שׁוֹמֶרֶת יָבָם. שֶׁמַּשְׁבִּיעָהּ עַל זְנוּת שֶׁזִּינְּתָה כְּשֶׁהִיא שׁוֹמֶרֶת יָבָם. אִי אָמְרַתְּ בִּשְׁלָמָא. זָנְתָה נֶאֱסֶרֶת עָלָיו — מִשּׁוּם הָכִי מַתְנֶה ע"י גִּלְגּוּל אַף עַל אוֹתוֹ זְנוּת, אֶלָּא אִי אָמְרַתְּ כו'. אֵין קִידּוּשִׁין תּוֹפְסִין. לְאִשָּׁה הָאֲסוּרָה עַל הַמְקַדְּשָׁהּ בְּלָאו. וְרַבָּנַן פְּלִיגֵי עֲלֵיהּ, וְאָמְרִי: בְּחַיָּיבֵי כְּרֵיתוֹת הוּא דְּלָא תָּפְסֵי, אֲבָל בְּחַיָּיבֵי לָאוִין — תָּפְסֵי. אַלְמָא לְר"ע מְשַׁוֵּי חַיָּיבֵי לָאוִין חֲמוּרוֹת לְעִנְיַן אִיסּוּרֵיהֶם כְּחַיָּיבֵי כְרֵיתוֹת, שֶׁהַוָּלָד מַמְזֵר. וּלְגַבֵּי לֶאֱסוֹר עַל בַּעְלָהּ נַמִי, כִּי הֵיכִי דְּהַבָּא עַל אֵשֶׁת אִישׁ שֶׁהִיא בְּכָרֵת — אֲסוּרָה עַל בַּעְלָהּ, כֵּן הַבָּא עַל שׁוֹמֶרֶת יָבָם נַמִי, שֶׁהִיא עָלָיו בְּ"לֹא תִהְיֶה אֵשֶׁת הַמֵּת הַחוּצָה לְאִישׁ זָר" (דברים כה) — אוֹסְרָהּ עַל יְבָמָהּ. וּמְשַׁוֵּי לָהּ. לְחַיָּיבֵי לָאוִין. כִּי עֶרְוָה. דְּכָרֵת. נִשּׂוּאִין הָרִאשׁוֹנִים. כְּגוֹן גֵּירְשָׁהּ, וְהֶחֱזִירָהּ וְקִינֵּא לָהּ וְנִסְתְּרָה. [עַל נִשּׂוּאֵי אָחִיו] מַהוּ. לְגַלְגֵּל זְנוּת שֶׁתַּחַת אָחִיו. דְּהָא דִּתְנַן בְּמַתְנִי': אֲרוּסָה וּנְשׂוּאָה שׁוֹמֶרֶת יָבָם וּכְנוּסָה — לָאו בַּחֲדָא אִתְּתָא קָאֵי, שֶׁיַּשְׁקֶנָּה יָבָם וְיַשְׁבִּיעֶנָּה עַל הָאֵירוּסִין וְנִישּׂוּאִין שֶׁל אָחִיו, אֶלָּא מִילֵּי מִילֵּי קָתָנֵי: אִם הַבַּעַל מַשְׁקֶה — מַתְנֶה עִמָּהּ עַל אֲרוּסָה וּנְשׂוּאָה, וְאִם הַיָּבָם שֶׁכְּנָסָהּ מַשְׁקֶה — מַתְנֶה עִמָּהּ שׁוֹמֶרֶת יָבָם וּכְנוּסָה. הָא אֲסִירָה הָכִי נַמִי דְּמַתְנֶה. וְזוֹ נֶאֱסֶרֶת עָלָיו בִּזְנוּת נִישּׂוּאִין הָרִאשׁוֹנִים לְעוֹלָם, וְכֵן בִּזְנוּת נִישּׂוּאֵי אָחִיו, כִּדְאָמַר בְּפ"ק (לעיל דף ג.): וְאִם מֵת חוֹלֶצֶת וְלֹא מִתְיַיבֶּמֶת. לֹא כְּשֶׁאָמַר ר"מ אָמֵן שֶׁלֹּא אֶטָּמֵא. עָלְתָה עַל דַּעְתּוֹ שֶׁתִּבָּדֵק עַכְשָׁיו עַל הֶעָתִיד. מְעַרְעֲרִין אוֹתָהּ. חוֹזְרִין לָהּ לְתוֹךְ גְּרוֹנָהּ, כְּאָדָם הַנֶּחֱנָק ע"י מַשְׁקֶה נִרְאֶה כְּעוֹשֶׂה עַרְעָר, וְהוּא לְשׁוֹן "זַעֲקַת שֶׁבֶר יְעוֹעֵרוּ" (ישעיה טו). עַל נִישּׂוּאִין אַחֲרוֹנִים. לְר"מ, דְּאָמַר מַתְנֶה עַל הֶעָתִיד — מַהוּ שֶׁיַּתְנֶה עִמָּהּ בְּגִלְגּוּל שְׁבוּעָה שֶׁלֹּא תִּטָּמֵא אִם יְגָרְשֶׁנָּה וְיַחֲזִירֶנָּה וְתִטָּמֵא? וְאַחַר כָּךְ יַחֲזִירֶנָּה. טַעְמָא דְּתִטַּמָּא בִּימֵי גֵּירוּשֶׁיהָ דְּלָא מִיתַּסְרָא עֲלֵיהּ, הָא תִּטָּמֵא לְאַחַר חֲזָרָה — הָכִי נַמִי דְּמַתְנֵי עַכְשָׁיו. תּוֹרַת הַקְּנָאוֹת. תּוֹרָה אַחַת לְכָל הַקְּנָאוֹת, שֶׁבְּכוּלָּן יַעֲשֶׂה לָהּ כַּתּוֹרָה הַזֹּאת. רַבִּי יְהוּדָה אוֹמֵר זֹאת. מִיעוּטָא הוּא: זֹאת וְלֹא אַחֶרֶת. חוֹפֵר שִׁיחִין. לְהַכְנִיס מַיִם לְעוֹלֵי רְגָלִים בַּשָּׂדוֹת וּבַדְּרָכִים. בִּשְׁנֵי אֲנָשִׁים. אִם מֵת בַּעְלָהּ זֶה שֶׁהִשְׁקָה, וְנִישֵּׂאת לְאַחֵר וְקִינֵּא לָהּ, וְהִיא נִסְתְּרָה. וְקִבַּלְנוּ עֵדוּתוֹ שֶׁל נְחוּנְיָא שֶׁיַּשְׁקֶנָּה הַשֵּׁנִי. דְּרַבִּי

תוספות

שומרת יבם שזינתה אסורה ליבמה. פי': אפי' לרבנן דאמרי קידושין תופסין בחייבי לאוין, ופליגי אדר"ע – הכא מודו, כדאמר ב"האשה רבה" (יבמות דף צב:) דכתיב בה: "לא תהיה אשת המת החוצה לאיש זר" – לא תהא בה הויה לזר. אלמא דקרא משוי לה כערוה, דלא תפסי בה קידושין משום דאגידא ביה, והויא כארוסתו שזינתה. אמרי במערבא לית הילכתא כרב המנונא. בסוף פ"ק דסנהדרין (דף יז:) מפרש ד"אמרי במערבא" היינו רבי ירמיה. ונראה: אע"ג דפסיק דלית הילכתא כרב המנונא – הילכתא כוותיה, דאמר ב"האשה רבה" (יבמות דף צב:) דרב סבירא ליה דאין קידושין תופסין ביבמה, ושמואל מספקא ליה, ואמר: בעניותינו צריכה גט, ופסיק אמימר כשמואל, ורב גידל אמר רב חייא בר יוסף אמר רב: נישואין יש בה בזנות, כדרב המנונא. וכן ר' יוחנן ור' ינאי סבירא להו התם דאין קידושין תופסין ביבמה. ופשיט לה ר' יוחנן ממתני' ד"לאחר שיחלוץ ליך יבמיך", וא"ל רבי ינאי: אי לאו דדלאי לך חספא מי משכחת מרגניתא תותיה, וא"ל ר"ל לר"י: אי לאו דקלסך גברא רבה – ה"א מתני' ר"ע היא. ומיהו, ר"ל לא פליג אדר' יוחנן, דהא מוקי התם באותו הפרק (דף צה.) הא דקתני: ומה במקום שבא על האיסור קל נאסר האוסר – בשומרת יבם, וכדרב המנונא. ובסוף ההיא גמרא ובשילהי "החולץ" (שם דף מט:) אמרינן נמי: אביי מספקא ליה אי כרב אי כשמואל. ובפ' "הזורק" בגיטין (דף פ:) פליגי לישני דגמרא אי מתני' הוה תיובתא לרב המנונא אי הוה סייעתיה. והתם מצי למידחי סייעתיה כי הכא, לאוקמיה מתניתין כר"ע, אלא דדחי לה מלישנא דמתני' גופיה. בירושלמי מפרש היאך קילס רבי ינאי לרבי יוחנן – שקרא עליו: "הזלים זהב מכיס בני אל יליזו מעיניך", "חכם בני ושמח לבי", "תן לחכם ויחכם עוד", "ישמע חכם ויוסף לקח". א"ל ר"ל: בתר כל אלו פסוקי קילוסיה יכול הוא פתר ליה כר"ע. ותו דחי ליה התם: ויתיבניה, מה איכפת לו ממזר גבי קינוי? התורה אמרה "וקנא את אשתו" – אפילו מקנא אשתו. ולפום מסקנא דהתם משמע דלית הילכתא כרב המנונא. והכי גרס התם: שומרת יבם שזינתה, ר"א אומר: מותרת לביתה, ר' יהושע בן לוי אומר: אסורה לביתה. א"ר ינאי: שומרת יבם שזינתה מותרת לביתה, ותני כן: "ונעלמה מעיני אישה" ולא מעיני יבמה. רבי יעקב בן זבדי בשם ר' אבהו: מעשה היה, וכהנת היתה, והותרה לביתה. א"ר יוסי בר בון: אף לא מכות אין בה. לפי הירושלמי משמע דפליג רבי ינאי ארבי ינאי. הא דאמר ב"האשה רבה" א"ר ינאי: בחבורה נמנו וגמרו אין קידושין תופסין ביבמה – גרסי' הכי בירושלמי: א"ר שמואל לא כן א"ר ינאי נמנו שלשים וכמה זקנים, מנין שאין קדושין תופסין וכו'. מהו שיתנה אדם על נישואין האחרונים. ירושלמי: א"ר ינאי: פשיטא שאדם מוחל על קינוי. גירש – כמי שמחל. היך *עבידא? קינא לה וגירשה החזירה ונסתרה, אי תימא גירש כמי שמחל – צריך לקנאות לה פעם שניה, אי תימא גירש כמי שלא מחל – אין צריך לקנאות לה פעם שניה. אבל אם קינא לה ונסתרה וידע בה, וגירשה והחזירה ונסתרה, שתתה ולא בדקו אותה המים – טהורה היא. או מאחר שאין המים בודקין *את האשה – טמאה היא, ואסורה לביתה. אין האשה שותה ושונה. ירושלמי: כורכמית תוכית, ששתתה ושינתה ושילשה לפני שמעיה ואבטליון. קבלנו עדותו בשני אנשים. ל"ע בפ"ק דקידושין (דף יח.), דמוקמינן התם הא דקתני: "בגניבתו" כיון שנמכר פעם אחת שוב אי אתה רשאי למוכרו – בשני בני אדם, אבל באדם אחד – נמכר ונשנה. [ולפירוש רש"י התם ניחא שפיר, כיון שנמכר פעם אחת וכו']. מתוספת רבי. ורבנן בתראי הכתיב תורת. וא"ת: הא דרשינן ליה בפ"ב דכריתות (דף ט:) שאדם מביא קרבן אחד אפילו אם קינא לאשתו על ידי אנשים הרבה! וי"ל: דהתם מיירי קודם ששתתה קינא לה מפלוני ונסתרה, וקינא לה מפלוני ונסתרה, וכן פעמים הרבה – משקה בפעם אחת על כולן, ומביא מנחה אחת על כולן, ונפקא לן מ"קנאות". אבל הכא דרשינן "תורת" לשותה ושונה, שחזר וקינא לה לאחר שתיה ונסתרה, שחוזרת ושותה שנית. הדרן עלך היה מביא

תוספות שאנץ

גמ' הא מני ר' עקיבא היא דאמר אין קידושין תופסין בחייבי לאוין באשה שהיא על המקדשה בלאו ורבנן פליגי עליה ואמרי בחייבי כריתות הוא דלא תפסי אלמא בחייבי לאוין תפסי. אבל לר' עקיבא משוי חייבי לאוין חמורות לענין איסורידהו כחייבי כריתות שהולד ממזר ולגבי ליאסר על בעלה נמי כי היכי דהבא על אשת איש שהיא בכרת אוסרה על בעלה הבא על שומרת יבם נמי שהיא בלאו דלא תהיה אשת המת אוסרה על יבמה. ל"ה. אבל אליבא דרבנן אע"ג דאיכא מאן דאמר בהאשה רבה דאין א) ביבמה אלא מ"מ לאו משני לאוין בערוה ולא תהא אסורה לו כיון שאין ממזר מיבמה. מהו שיתנה על הנישואין הראשונים פ"ה כגון גירשה והחזירה וקינא לה ונסתרה מהו לגלגל עליה זנות אם זינתה קודם שגירשה שיבדקוה המים הללו. על נישואי אחיו כגון מת אחיו בלא בנים וכנסה היבם וקינא לה ונסתרה מהו לגלגל עליה זנות שתחת אחיו. ואי קשיא דממתני' מצי למפשט דהא תנן במתני' ארוסה ונשואה ושומרת יבם וכנוסה ופ"ה דמתני' לאו בחדא איתתא קאי שישקנה יבם וישביענה על נישואין ואירוסין של אחיו אלא מילי מילי קתני אם הבעל משקה מתנה עמה על ארוסה ואם היבם משקה אותה מתנה עמה שומרת יבם וכנוסה. ל"ה:

א) נראה דצ"ל אפי' למ"ד דאין קדושין תופסין ביבמה מ"מ לא שאני משאר לאוין ולא הוי כערוה ולא תהא וכו'.

יבמות פח. נב: נה. נו. גיטין פ:

[יבמות י: וש"נ]

[תוספתא פ"ב ע"ש]

[כלומר מאי נפקא מיניה]

בירושלמי שלפנינו הגי' כך את האשה שהיא אסורה לביתה טמאה היא ועיין שם בפ"מ

גירסת רש"א

הגהות הב"ח

(א) במשנה קודם שתתארס (ולא על אחר שתתגרש נסתרה לאחד ונטמאת ואח"כ החזירה לא היה מתנה עמה) תא"מ ונ"ב גירסת רש"י ולא על אחר שתתגרש ותסתר לאחד ותיטמא ואח"כ יחזירנה לא היה מתנה עמה ויש גורסין ולא משנתגרשה ונסתרה לאחד ונטמאה ואח"כ החזירה לא היה מתנה עמה פי' אם השביעה אחר שהחזירה לא היה מתנה עמה על מה שזינתה אחר הגירושין קודם שהחזירה והמדפיס עירב שתי הגירסאות יחד ועיין בפי' דר' עובדיה וברמב"ם פ"ד דסנהדרין: (ב) גמ' שתתגרש ותיסתר לאחד ותיטמא ואח"כ יחזירנה הא יחזירנה:

דכתיב: "זאת". בשני אנשים ושני בועלין דכולי עלמא לא פליגי דהאשה שותה ושונה, דכתיב: "תורת". כי פליגי — באיש אחד ושני בועלין, בשני אנשים ובועל אחד; ת"ק סבר: "תורת" — [א]לרבויי כולהי, "זאת" — למעוטי איש אחד ובועל אחד. ורבנן בתראי סברי: "זאת" — למעוטי כולהי, "תורת" לרבויי שני אנשים ושני בועלין. ור' יהודה: "זאת" — למעוטי תרתי, "תורת" — לרבות תרתי; "זאת" למעוטי תרתי — איש אחד ובועל אחד, איש אחד ושני בועלין. "תורת" לרבויי תרתי — שני אנשים ובועל אחד, שני אנשים ושני בועלין.§

הדרן עלך היה מביא

היה [ב*]נוטל את מנחתה מתוך כפיפה מצרית ונותנה לתוך כלי שרת, [ג*]ונותנה על ידה, וכהן מניח (א*) ידו מתחתיה ומניפה. הניף והגיש, קמץ *והקטיר, והשאר נאכל לכהנים. [ד*]היה *משקה ואחר כך מקריב את מנחתה, רבי שמעון אומר: *מקריב את מנחתה ואח"כ היה משקה, שנאמר: °"ואחר ישקה את האשה את המים". אם השקה ואחר כך הקריב את מנחתה — [ה]כשרה.§ **גמ'** *אמר ליה רבי אלעזר לרבי יאשיה דדריה: לא *תיתיב אכרעך עד דמפרשת לה להא מילתא: מנין למנחת סוטה שטעונה תנופה? מנא לן?! "והניף" כתיב בה! בבעלים מנלן? *אתיא "יד" "יד" משלמים; כתיב הכא: °"ולקח הכהן מיד האשה", וכתיב התם: °"ידיו תביאנה", מה כאן כהן — אף להלן כהן, ומה להלן בעלים — אף כאן בעלים. הא כיצד? מניח ידו תחת ידי הבעלים ומניף.§ "הניף והגיש קמץ וכו'. היה משקה ואחר כך מקריב את מנחתה".§ הא אקרבה! הכי קאמר: סדר מנחות כיצד? הניף והגיש, קמץ והקטיר, והשאר נאכל לכהנים. ובהשקאה גופה פליגי רבי שמעון ורבנן, דרבנן סברי: משקה ואח"כ מקריב את מנחתה, ורבי שמעון סבר: מקריב את מנחתה ואחר כך משקה, שנאמר: °"ואחר ישקה".§ "ואם השקה ואחר כך הקריב את מנחתה כשרה".§ ת"ר

[לעיל יד:] [במדבר ה] [ויקרא ז]

רש"י

דרבי יהודה דריש "זאת" — למעוטי שאינה שותה ושונה על ידי בעל א' אם חזר וקינא לה, ודריש "תורת" — לרבות ששותה פעם שניה על ידי בעל שני. ומדקאמר ר' יהודה דע"י בעל שני חוזרת ושותה — מכלל דלתנא קמא אפילו בעל א' משקה שני פעמים. והיינו דפרכינן: ותנא קמא הא כתיב "זאת", ומאי קא ממעט מיניה? דכתיב זאת. ומסתברא דהא מיהת קממעט שלא יקנא לה בעל זה פעם אחרת. שני אנשים ושני בועלים. לאחר שהשקה זה — מת, ונישאת לאחר, וקינא לה מבועל אחר. דכתיב תורת. והא מיהת חדא לרבויי. ור' יהודה. סבירא ליה וכו'. דאחר שריבה הכתוב ומיעט, ולא פירש מה ריבה ומה מיעט, על כרחך לא מסרן הכתוב אלא לחכמים, לפרש לך לפי חכמתם מה ריבה ומה מיעט. ומסתברא דריבויא — אשני אנשים קאי ואפילו בבועל אחד, ולא אשני בועלים ובעל אחד. כיון דקינא לה כבר ונמצאת נקיה, נראה הדבר שאדם קנטרן הוא ומתכוין להקניטה, הילכך לא שנא מחשד ראשון ולא שנא מאחר.

הדרן עלך היה מביא

היה נוטל את מנחתה. הבעל. דהא אמרינן דאין מצות כהונה במנחות אלא מקמיצה ואילך, והגשה נמי תחילת קמיצה היא, שאין זר קרב למזבח. אבל קידוש כלי ויציקה ובלילה שטעונות שמן — כשר בזר. ונותנה על ידה. להניף. וכהן מניח ידו מתחתיה. ובגמרא יליף דתנופה צריכי יד בעלים ויד כהן. ובעלים דמנחת סוטה היא האשה. והגיש. לקרן מערבית דרומית, (ב) כדתניא בפרק ג' בסדר מנחות (דף יט:). וכולהו הנך כתיבי במנחת סוטה: תנופה והקרבה, קמיצה והקטרה. והשאר נאכל. שכל הנקמצות שיריהן נאכלין, דכתיב "תורת" בסתם מנחה (ויקרא ו): "וזאת תורת המנחה" כו' עד "והנותרת ממנה" וגו'. ואח"כ מקריב. בגמרא פריך: הא תנא ליה "והקטיר", ומה יקריב עוד לאחר הקטרה? פלוגתא דרבנן ור' שמעון. בגמרא ילפינן לה מקראי. **גמ'** לר' יאשיה דדריה. אמורא הוא, ובדורו של ר"א בן פדת. (ג) ועוד היה ר' יאשיה שהיה תנא בר פלוגתא דר' יונתן בכוליה גמרא. והיינו דקאמר: לר' יאשיה דדריה, דלא תימא לרבי יאשיה הזקן — דלאו אורח ארעא למימרא ליה הכי, שגדול וזקן ממנו היה. בבעלים מנא לן. שתהא האשה מניפה עם הכהן? דהא קרא בכהן לחודיה כתיב: "ולקח הכהן מיד האשה" וגו'. משלמים. מתנופת חזה ושוק ואימורין דשלמים. ידיו תביאנה. בבעלים כתיב, וגבי תנופה כתיב. מה כאן כהן. בסוטה כתיב כהן בתנופת מנחתה. הא אקרבה. קודם השקאה, דקתני: קמץ והקטיר, והדר תני: היה משקה. הכי קאמר כו'. הא דתנא רישא: הניף והגיש קמץ והקטיר — לאו דווקא קודם השקאה נקט, ולא איירי בהשקאה כלל. אלא איירי בסדר הקרבת מנחת סוטה, שכן הוא: תנופה והגשה קמיצה והקטרה, והכי קאמר: כשבא להקריבה היה נוטלה מתוך כפיפה כו', והדר איירי מי קודם, (ד) או השקאה קודם כל אלה, או אם כל אלה קודמין להשקאה, ופליגי בה רבי שמעון ורבנן.

ה"ג

תוספות

היה נוטל. בירושלמי: כתיב "ולקח הכהן מיד האשה את מנחת הקנאות", וכי על ידו הוא מניף ולא על ידה הוא מניף? אלא מכאן שהוא נוטלה מתוך כלי חול ונותנה בכלי שרת. והיינו משמע דלא כפירוש רש"י, דפירש דבעל היה נוטל. ומצינו למימר דקידוש המנחה כשירה *בזר, מיהו מצוה בכהן ליטול המנחה מידה, ומאחר שהיה נוטלה היה נותנה כמו כן לתוך כלי שרת.

וכהן מניח את ידו תחתיה. האי דאיצטריך תו למיתני: וכהן מניח את ידו תחתיה, ולא קתני בסתם: *ומכניס את ידו — לאשמועינן דתנופה בכהן. ירושלמי: וכהן מניח את ידו תחתיה — ואין הדבר כיעור? מניח מפה. ואינו חולץ? מביא כהן זקן. ואפילו תימא כהן ילד, שאין יצר הרע מצוי לשעה. תני ר' חייא: סוטה גידמת — שני כהנים מניפין על ידיה. אבל בגמרא דידן אמרינן בסוף פרק "ארוסה" (לקמן דף כז.) דגידמת לא היתה שותה. וי"ל דפליגי אי בעינן קרא כדכתיב.

הניף והגיש. בירושלמי יליף הא *דאמר בפרק "כל המנחות" (דף ס:): "והבאת" — לרבות מנחת העומר להגשה, "והקריבה" — לרבות מנחת סוטה להגשה. וכתיב בתריה "והרים", והיכן הוא תנופה? כבר קדמה. ומהתם יליף דשיריה נאכלין, דכתיב בתריה: "והנותרת מן המנחה לאהרן" וגו'.

ואחר ישקה מבעי ליה לשרישומו ניכר. פירוש: ואע"פ שהקריב מנחתה כבר. והוא הדין אי שלא כדין עבוד כהנים, דלא מחקו למגילה כלל עד לאחר הקרבה — דמוחק לה בתר הכי. ונראה דלאו דוקא נקט דקרא אתי לרישומו ניכר, דכיון דכתיב "ומחה" — ממילא שמעינן אי רישומו ניכר — דלאו מחוי הוא, דהא ממעטינהו התם דאין מטילין קנקנתוס לתוך הדיו משום דרישומו ניכר, והוי כתב שאינו יכול למחוק. אלא עיקר קרא לאם הקריב מנחתה ואחר כך השקה כשירה, כדדריש רבי שמעון "והשקה" קמא, והכי אמרינן בירושלמי דלרבנן הקריב מנחתה ואח"כ השקה — כשירה, והתם דריש אלידייהו דרבנן: "ואחר ישקה" למערערין. וה"ג התם: "ואחר ישקה" — על כרחה, שלא בטובתה. מודה ר"ש לחכמים שאם השקה ואחר כך הקריב מנחתה שהיא כשירה, ומודים חכמים לר' שמעון שאם הקריב את מנחתה ואח"כ השקה שהיא כשירה. מה ביניהון — מצוה. רבנן אמרי: מנחת קנאות היא שהיא בודקתה, ור"ש אומר: המים הן בודקין אותה. מאי טעמא דרבנן — "מנחת זכרון מזכרת עון". מאי טעמא דרבי שמעון — "ובאו בה". רבנן אמרי: כותב ומוחק ומשקה ומקריב, ר"ש אומר: כותב ומקריב ומוחק ומשקה. כולי עלמא מודו שמחיקה סמוך להשקאה. ותו גרסינן התם: קרבה מנחתה ואמרה "איני שותה" — מערערין אותה ומשקה אותה בעל כרחה — כרבי שמעון. ברם כרבנן — כבר שתת. השתא אית לך למימרא: אף על גב דלרבנן דרשינן "והשקה" בתרא לאונס — קא סברי דאונס במחיקת מגילה תליא מילתא, וקרא יתירא קא דרשי לאונס.

ורבי

תוספות שאנץ

ור' יהודה סבר תורת לרבויי תרתי פ"ה דאחר שריבה הכתוב ומיעט ולא פירש מה ריבה ומה מיעט ומסתברא טפי דריבויא אשני אנשים קאי ואפי' בבועל אחד ולא בשני בועלין ובעל אחד דכיון דקינא לה כבר ונמצאה נקייה נראה הדבר שאדם קנטרן הוא ומתכוין להקניטה הילכך לא שנא מחשד ראשון ולא שנא מאחר א) הבעל דהא אמרינן דאין מצות כהונה במנחות אלא מקמיצה ואילך והגשה נמי תחלת קמיצה היא ואין זר קרב לגבי מזבח אבל קידוש כלי ויציקה ובלילה כשר בזר. ונותנה על ידה ומניף וכהן מניח ידו תחתיה ובגמ' יליף דתנופה צריכה יד בעלים ויד כהן ובעלים דמנחת סוטה היא האשה ל"ה. ובירושלמי פרי' אמאי לא חיישי' לה להרהורא ומוקי' לה בכהן זקן. אבל ק' דהיכי אמרי' דכהן מניח ידו מתחת יד הבעלים ומניף והא כי האי גונא הויא חציצה דהכי נמי אמרי' במנחות דאין תנופה בחוברין פי' בשותפין וקאמר היכי ליעבוד אי לינפו והדר לינפו כלומר דהשותפין יניפו זה אחר זה תנופה אחת אמר רחמנא ולא שתי תנופות ואי מנח דידיה תחת יד חבריה הויא חציצה. וי"ל דלא דמי דהכא כיון דבעי כהן ובעלים לא הויא חציצה דגזירת הכתוב היא דבעי שניהם אבל התם גבי שני שותפין אם אחד מהם היה מניח ידו תחת יד חבירו הויא חציצה לפי שאינו גזירת הכתוב שיהו שניהן שותפין ועוד י"ל דהכא ה"פ דלא מיירי שהכהן מניח ידו תחת ידה ממש דהוי חציצה אלא ר"ל שכהן תופס אויר הכלי למטה והבעלים אוחזים למעלה וליכא חציצה כלל וה"נ מניח גבי ביכורים שהכהן היה אוחז בשפתיו כלומר בשפת הכלי והבעלים למטה וכמו כן גבי מנחת סוטה דאמרי' איפכא שיד בעלים יהיה למעלה ויד כהן למטה וכמו כן פי' פ"ק דקידושין גבי הסמיכות והתנופות: הניף והגיש קמץ והקטיר אבל מלח לא קתני דהא פשיטא דכתיב על כל קרבנך תקריב מלח. וכן במנחות לא קתני מלח אבל לעי' ר"פ היה מביא קתני לה לפי ששונה שם סדר מנחות באריכות. והניף וקמץ קתני הכא לפי שיש מנחות שאינן טעונות תנופה כדאמרי' בפ' כל המנחות באות מצה. וכן יש הרבה מנחות שאינן טעונות קמיצה כגון מנחת כהן ומנחת נסכים: ב) ומנחתה מתפזרת אבית הדשן. וק' דעל כרח' סבירא ליה להאי תנא דמקריב מנחתה ואחר כך משקה דאז קידשה בבלי שרת דאי סבירא ליה דמשקה ואח"כ מקריב מנחתה א"כ לא קדשה עדיין בכלי שרת וא"כ תיפוק לחולין ג) וא"כ למה הכי ומ"ק המגלה ואחר כך אמרה טמאה אני נשפכין ומנחתה מתפזרת אבית הדשן דמשמע קרא הקטרה היו משקין אותה דהא מאחרין המחיקה בשביל שמא תודה ולא מחקי לה עד לצורך. וי"ל דמיירי דנמחקה שלא כדין דסבור דמחקוה קודם הקטרה ולעולם ההשקאה הוי אחר הקטרה: גמ' אמר ר' אלעזר לר' יאשיה דדריה אמורא היה ובדורו של ר' אלעזר ועוד היה בימי ר' אלעזר בן פדת ר' יאשיה תנא בר פלוגתא דר' יונתן בבולי תלמודא והיינו דקאמר לר' יאשיה דדריה דלא תימא לר' יאשיה הזקן דלאו אורח ארעא למימרא ליה הכי שגדול וזקן ממנו היה. ל"ה: לא תיתיב אכרעיך. פי' אל תשב

אלא

א) נ"ל הדרן עלך היה מביא: פרק היה נוטל פי' הבעל. ב) שייך למשנה לקמן דף כ' ע"א. ג) נראה דל"ל וא"כ היכי קאמר נמחקה המגילה ואח"כ אמרה טמאה אני דהמים נשפכין ומנחתה וכו' דמשמע דקודם הקטרה היו משקין אותה ועוד דהא מאחרין וכו'.

עין משפט נר מצוה

נב א מיי' פ"ג מהל' סוטה הלכ' ט:
א ב מיי' פ"ג מהל' סוטה הלכה יג סמג עשין נז:
ב ג ד מיי' שם הלכ' יו: ס"א כזר
ג ה מיי' פ"ד מהל' סוטה הלכה יז:

ומניח. גירסת רש"ל

הא דאמרינן בכל המנחות שטעונות תנופה שתנופה קודמת להגשה והבאת לרבות כו'. רש"ל

[לקמן כ:]

מסורת הש"ס

[ע' תוספות סנהדרין פב: ד"ה המולח וכו' ותוספות מנחות יח. ד"ה לא וכו' מוכח דגרסתם היה קומץ ומלח והקטיר]

[קדושין לו: וש"נ]

[ועיין מה שפירשו על זה תוס' נזיר כב: ד"ה אמר שמואל וכו']

קדושין לו: מכות יח. מנחות סא. סוכה מז:

הגהות הב"ח

(א) במשנה מניח את ידו מתחתיה ומניף הניף: (ב) רש"י ד"ה והגיש וכו' כדתנן: (ג) ד"ה לר' יאשיה וכו' בן פדת הוה וכו': (ד) ד"ה הכי קאמר וכו' מי קודם זה או זה או השקאה:

ד א מיי' פ"ד מהל' סוטה הל' ד:
ה ב מיי' שם הל' ו ופ"ג שם הלכה י:

ת"ר: "והשקה". מה ת"ל? והלא כבר נאמר "והשקה"! שאם נמחקה מגילה ואומרת "איני שותה" – אמערערין אותה ומשקין אותה בעל כרחה, דברי רבי עקיבא. ר"ש אומר: "ואחר ישקה". מה ת"ל? והלא כבר נאמר "והשקה"! אלא, לאחר כל מעשים כולן האמורין למעלה. מגיד, ג' דברים מעכבין בה: עד שלא קרב הקומץ, ועד שלא נמחקה מגילה, ועד שלא תקבל עליה שבועה. עד שלא קרב הקומץ – ר"ש לטעמיה, דאמר: מקריב את מנחתה ואח"כ משקה. עד שלא נמחקה מגילה – אלא מאי משקה לה? אמר רב אשי: בלא נצרכה לשרישומו ניכר. עד שלא תקבל עליה שבועה. מישתא הוא דלא שתיא, הא מיכתב – כתבי לה? והאמר רבא: *מגילת סוטה שכתבה קודם שתקבל עליה שבועה – לא עשה ולא כלום! *כדי נסבה. במאי קמיפלגי? תלתא קראי כתיבי: "והשקה" קמא, "ואחר ישקה", "והשקה" בתרא. רבנן סברי: "והשקה" קמא – לגופו, שמשקה ואח"כ מקריב את מנחתה. "ואחר ישקה" – מיבעי ליה לשרישומו ניכר. "והשקה" בתרא – שאם *נמחקה מגילה ואומרת "איני שותה" – מערערין אותה ומשקה אותה בעל כרחה. ור"ש סבר: "ואחר ישקה" – לגופו, שמקריב את מנחתה ואח"כ משקה, "והשקה" קמא – שאם השקה ואח"כ הקריב את מנחתה כשרה, "והשקה" בתרא – שאם נמחקה מגילה ואמרה "איני שותה" – מערערין אותה, ומשקין אותה בעל כרחה. ורבנן: בדיעבד לא פתח קרא. וסבר ר"ע משקין אותה בעל כרחה? והתניא, *רבי יהודה אומר: כלבוס של ברזל מטילין לתוך פיה, שאם נמחקה מגילה ואמרה "איני שותה" – מערערין אותה ומשקין אותה בע"כ. אמר רבי עקיבא: כלום אנו צריכין אלא לבודקה – והלא בדוקה ועומדת! אלא, עד שלא קרב הקומץ – יכולה לחזור בה, *משקרב הקומץ – אינה יכולה לחזור בה! ולטעמיך תיקשי לך היא גופה: משקרב הקומץ אינה יכולה לחזור בה? והלא בדוקה ועומדת! לא קשיא; הא – דקהדרא בה מחמת רתיתא, והא – דקהדרא בה מחמת ברויתא. והכי קאמר: כל מחמת ברויתא – כלל כלל לא שתיא. מחמת רתיתא; עד שלא קרב הקומץ, דאכתי לא אמחוק מגילה, אי נמי אמחוק מגילה, דשלא כדין עביד כהנים דמחקי – מצי הדרא בה, משקרב הקומץ, דבדין עביד כהנים דמחקי – לא מצי הדרא בה.

קשיא

ורבי יהודה אומר כלבוס של ברזל מטילין לה לתוך פיה. בפרק "ד' מיתות" (סנהדרין דף נב.) פליגי ר"י ורבנן במצות הנשרפין, דתנן: נותנין סודר קשה לתוך הרכה וכורך על צוארו, זה מושך אילך וזה מושך אילך, עד שפותח את פיו, וזורק את הפתילה לתוך פיו. ר"י אומר: אם מת בידם – לא היו מקיימין בו מצות שריפה, אלא פותח פיו בצבת וכו'. ותימה לר"י: מאי שנא הכא דלרבי יהודה בכלבוס, והתם בצבת? ופי' ר"י: דהכא נמי היו פותחין פיה בצבת, אלא לאחר שפותחין פיה בצבת היו מטילין לתוכה כלבוס שלא תוכל לחזור ולקפוץ פיה. ורבנן מודו נמי [הכא] דאין פותחין פיה על ידי סודרין. דהתם טעם דרבנן משום דשריפה חמורה מחנק, והיו מקרבין מיתתו ע"י חנק וגמר מיתתו בשריפה, משום "ואהבת לרעך כמוך". אבל הכא – אין לקרב מיתתה. *בפי' ר"ח פי' לפי גי' הספרים. וכן פירש: "והשקה" בתרא – מערערין, *"והשקה" קמייתא – לגופו, מה ת"ל – לא שבברייתא נשנית "בתרא" ו"קמא", אלא פירוש של בעל הגמרא הוא ש"והשקה" בתרא בא ללמד שמערערין, "והשקה" קמא לגופיה. ורבי עקיבא סבר ליה כרבנן, שמשקה ואח"כ מקריב מנחתה. ומקשה: היכי. אמר רבי עקיבא מערערין? והא בדוקה ועומדת סבירא ליה! ותו מקשה: ר' עקיבא, בהא מתניתין דפליג עליה רבי שמעון, תני: מחיקה מעכבא, אלמא סבירא ליה שמחיקה והשקאה קודם הקרבת המנחה, כרבנן, וכל זמן שלא נמחקה המגילה מצי הדרא. והכא דפליג בהדי דרבי יהודה תני: קומץ מעכבה – דאלמא הקרבה קודם השקאה, כר' שמעון? ושנינן: תרי תנאי ואליבא דרבי עקיבא. ירושלמי: ולית ליה לרבי עקיבא מערערין? אית ליה בשהתחילה לשתות. וצריך לפרש: דאם נמחקה מגילה קודם שקרב הקומץ, דשלא כדין עבוד כהנים, כיון שהתחילה לשתות – מערערין אותה.

מגילתה

ה"ג ת"ר והשקה מה ת"ל והלא כבר נאמר והשקה שאם נמחקה כו' ולא גרסינן בתרא ברישא וקמא בסיפא *[שאין זה לשון ברייתא], ופי' משובש הוא, וטעה ב"והלא כבר נאמר" דמשמע שזה נאמר מתחילה. והכי פירוש סדר המקראות כך הוא: "וכתב", "ומחה", "והשקה" "והניף (א) המנחה", "והקריב" דהיינו הגשה, "וקמץ", "והקטיר", "ואחר ישקה את האשה את המים" והדר תו כתיב השקאה שלישית: "והשקה את המים והיתה אם נטמאה" וגו'. וקא"ר עקיבא: "והשקה את האשה" דכתיב קודם הקטרת המנחה מה ת"ל? והלא כבר נאמר אחר הקטרת המנחה "והשקה את המים"! והוא דוקא הוא, ואין הראשון דוקא, דמדכתיב "ואחר ישקה את האשה" – ש"מ השקאה אחר הקטרה היא. ומה ת"ל "והשקה את האשה" אחר המחיקה – ללמדך שאם נמחקה המגילה ואמרה "איני שותה", ולא הודית לומר "טמאה אני" – מערערין אותה, כלומר פותחין פיה שלא בטובתה ושופכין את המים לתוך גרונה. ואפי' נמחקה מגילה קודם הקטרה, דשלא כדין עשו הכהנים, דכיון דאינה שותה עד לאחר הקטרה לא היה להם למחוק, דכל מה שיש שהות לאחר את המחיקה מאחרין, שמא תודה. אפילו הכי, הואיל ונמחקה, ואפילו שלא כדין – אין שומעין לה לאמר "איני שותה", אלא או תשתה או תודה. ולכך נאמר "והשקה" אחר המחיקה. *ולא תשתה מיד עד לאחר הקטרה, אלא הא קמשמע לן שהמחיקה גורמת לה לשתות. ר"ש אומר ואחר ישקה מה ת"ל והלא כבר נאמר והשקה. לא פליג אדרבי עקיבא, אלא מר דריש האי קרא ומר דריש האי קרא. (ב) והכי אמר לקמן בשמעתין, דתרוייהו ס"ל מקריב מנחתה ואחר כך משקה. והלא כבר נאמר. פסוק שלישי: "והשקה את המים" לאחר הקטרה, מה ת"ל "ואחר ישקה"?. אחר כל המעשים כולן האמורים למעלה. ומה אמור למעלה – השבעה וקבלה וכתיבה ומחיקה (ג) והקטרת המנחה. מגיד ששלשה דברים. הללו מעכבין: ההקטרה והשבעה ומחיקה. ולקמיה פריך: פשיטא, קודם המחיקה מה תשתה?. לשרישומו ניכר. שאם היה רישומו ניכר – צריך לחזור ולמחוק עד שלא יהא רישומו ניכר. הא מיכתב כתבי לה. כהן למגילה קודם קבלת שבועה? בתמיה. לא עשה כלום. דהכי כתיב "וכתב את האלות" – אחר קבלת שבועה כתיב. כדי נסבה. שלא לצורך, דהא אפילו מיכתב לא קתנינן. במאי קמיפלגי. אמתני' קאי. וברייתא נקט ברישא – לאשמועינן מהיכא יליף ר"ש טעמיה. וקבעי: רבנן השתא היכי דרשי להו לקראי, ור"ש היכי דריש להו לכולהו?. רבנן סברי והשקה קמא. דקודם הקטרה – דוקא הוא. ואע"ג דכתיב "ואחר ישקה" דמשמע: דוקא – על כרחך מקרא האמור ראשון אינו נדרש אלא לגופו, ומקראות יתירות האמורים אחריו ניתנו לדרוש. הילכך, קמא דוקא, לומר שמשקה ואח"כ מקריב את מנחתה. וע"כ "ואחר ישקה", אע"פ שנכתב אחר הקטרה – אקודם הקטרה קאי, ו"אחר" דקאמר – אמחיקה קאי, הכתובה למעלה, (ג) וקאמרי רבנן דאם לא נמחקה יפה לא ישקנה. "והשקה" בתרא לאקודם הקטרה קאי, ולדרשא אתא ע"כ. ור"ש סבר ואחר ישקה. משמע דדוקא הוא, ודוקא כתיבה לאחר הקטרה, לומר שכולן מעכבין בה: הקטרת המנחה, ורושם הניכר. וכולהו מהכא נפקי דקודמין להשקאה. "והשקה" קמא – לאכשורי דאי עביד איפכא. והשקה בתרא שאם נמחקה מגילה. ודוקא אחר הקטרה, דבדין אימחיק – משקין אותה בעל כרחה. והיינו דאיכא בין (ד) לר"ע בין לר"ש, דר"ע לית ליה אם השקה ואח"כ הקריב מנחתה כשרה, הילכך "והשקה" קמא דריש לבעל כרחה, ואע"ג דשלא כדין אימחיק קודם הקטרה. "ואחר ישקה" – לרישומו ניכר, "והשקה" בתרא – לגופיה, לומר שמקריב מנחתה ואח"כ משקה. בדיעבד לא פתח קרא. אין דרך הכתוב לומר בתחילת דבריו שלא כדרך מצותן. אלא בתחילה סדר משפט דבריו, ולבסוף מרבה מקראות לדרוש. כלבוס. שני שינים יש לו, ונותן לתוך פיה זקוף. אלא לבודקה. אם טהורה אם טמאה. והלא בדוקה ועומדת. דכיון דאמרה "איני שותה" – מודה שהיא טמאה. יכולה לחזור בה. ולומר "איני שותה", ואין אונסין אותה, דהא מודה דטמאה היא. משקרב הקומץ וכו'. ולקמיה פריך: היא גופא קשיא, אמאי אינה יכולה לחזור? והלא בדוקה ועומדת היא. דקא הדרא מחמת ברויתא. הא דקתני "בדוקה ועומדת" דקא הדרא בה מחמת ברויתא הוא, שאינה רותחת, וקאמרה "איני שותה" – ודאי טמאה היא. ולכך אינה רותחת – דסמכא מעיקרא, ואמרה: כי מטינא למשתי – לא שתינא. ולא שנא קרב קומץ, ולא שנא לא קרב – לא שתיא, כדמפרש ואזיל: כל מחמת ברויתא כלל כלל לא שתיא, ואפי' קירב הקומץ. והא דמפליג בין קרב ללא קרב – דקא הדרא בה מחמת רתיתא, שאנו רואין אותה רותחת. דאיכא למימר דאינה מאמנת שלא יבדקוה המים ואפילו היא טהורה, ורוצה היתה לסמוך על טהרתה ולשתות, ולפיכך היא רותחת, וכשמגעת לשתות – חוזרת בה. הילכך, עד שלא קרב כו'. וברייתא קמייתא דלעיל דקתני "מערערין אותה" – במחמת ריתותא קאמר.

קשיא

תוספות שאנץ

אלא תעמוד. ה"ג ת"ר והשקה מה ת"ל ול"נ בתרא ברישא וקמא בסיפא שאין זה לשון ברייתא. ועוד בספרי תני לה להך ברייתא. ומפיק להאי דרשא מוהשקה קמא ל"ה. וה"פ והשקה מה ת"ל סדר המקראות כך הוא ומחה והשקה והניף את המנחה והקריב דהיינו הגשה וקמץ והקטיר ואחר ישקה את המים ואח"כ כתיב השקאה שלישית והשקה את המים והיתה אם נטמאה וה"פ והשקה את האשה דכתי' קודם הקטרת מנחה מה תלמוד לומר והלא כבר נאמר אחר הקטרת מנחה והשקה את המים וההוא ודאי דוקא הוא ואין הראשון דוקא דמדכתי' ואחר ישקה את האשה ש"מ השקאה אחר הקטרה ומה ת"ל והשקה אחר המחיקה ללמדך שאם נמחקה המגילה ואמרה איני שותה ולא הודת לומר דטמאה היא מערערין אותה כלומר פותחין את פיה שלא בטובתה ושופכין לתוכה מים ואפי' נמחקה המגלה קודם הקטרה דשלא כדין עשו הכהנים דכיון שאינה שותה עד לאחר הקטרה דכל מה שיש להם לאחר המחיקה מאחרין שמא תודה ואפי' הכי כי נמחקה שלא כדין אין שומעין לה לומר איני שותה אלא או שותה או תודה ולכך כתיב והשקה לאחר המחיקה לומר שהמחיקה גורמת לה שתשתה ר' שמעון אומר ואחר ישקה מה ת"ל והלא כבר נאמר והשקה לא פליג אדר' עקיבא אלא מר דריש האי קרא ומר דריש האי קרא והכי אמרי' לקמן בשמעתין דתרוייהו סבירא להו מקריב את המנחה ואחר כך משקה אבל איכא בינייהו דר' עקיבא לית ליה אם השקה ואחר כך הקריב את המנחה כשרה ור' שמעון אית ליה דכשרה ע"כ ל"ה. וק' לפ"ה חדא שמגיה הספרים דבכל הספרים כתיב בתרא וקמא ועוד ק' אמאי קאמר והלא כבר נאמר והשקה הוה ליה למימר הלא כבר נאמר ואחר כך ישקה דהיינו קרא דלאחר הקטרה. וע"ק למה דאיכא בין ר' עקיבא לר' [שמעון] (ישמעאל) דר' עקיבא לית ליה השקה ואח"כ הקריב המנחה כשרה הילכך והשקה קמא דריש לעיל למשקה בעל כרחה ואע"ג דלא כדין אימחוק ואחר כך ישקה לרישומו ניכר והשקה בתרא לגופו. וא"כ ק' [כיון] דר' עקיבא לא דריש ליה להאי קרא דר' (ישמעאל) [שמעון] אמאי לא מפרש תלמודא היכי דריש ליה ר' עקיבא לקרא. לכ"נ לר"ת שאין למחות ג"ה והשקה בתרא מה ת"ל והלא כבר נאמר והשקה קמא ומהשקה בתרא דריש אם נמחקה מגלה ומן והשקה קמא דריש דמשקה ואחר כך מקריב מנחה ואחר ישקה דריש לרישומו ניכר. ור' עקיבא פליג אדר' (ישמעאל) [שמעון] וקאמר דמשקה ואח"כ מקריב ולכך לא הוצרך כלל לפרש קראי אליבא דר' עקיבא דלגמרי סבירא ליה כרבנן דמשמע הכי לקמן דוהשקה קמא לגופיה לומר דמשקה ואח"כ מקריב מנחתה והא דאמרי' לקמן דר' עקיבא סבירא ליה דמקריב ואח"כ משקה נ"ל דתרי תנאי ואליבא דר' עקיבא כדאמרי' לקמן דפרי' דר' עקיבא אדר' עקיבא. ג' דברים מעכבין עד שלא קירב הקומץ לאו דוקא נקט עיכובא דעד שלא קירב את הקומץ דהא ר' (ישמעאל) [שמעון] גופיה אית ליה דמשקה ואח"כ מקריב כשרה אלא אגב אחרים נקטיה. לא נצרכה לשרישומו ניכר. פי' לא נצרכה לומר אלא שרישומן ניכר. וא"ת מקרא דכתיב ומחה נפקא לן דמשמע דבעי' שאין רישומן ניכר. וי"ל דמקרא דומחה לא ידעי' אלא דצריך שיהא הדיו יכול למחות (ומ"מ א) שלא ימחוהו כיון דראוי למחות קמ"ל האי קרא שצריך למחות לגמרי. במאי קמיפלגי אמתני' קאי ובריתא נקט ברישא לאשמועי' מהיכא יליף ר' שמעון טעמיה וקבעי השתא דרבנן היכי דרשי' להו להאי קרא ור"ש היכי דריש להו לכולהו. ל"ה. והלא בדוקה ועומדת דכיון דאמרה איני שותה מודה

שהיא

א) ומ"מ אינו רלוחה שצריך למחות כ"כ שלא יהא רישומו ניכר קמ"ל.

נ"ל קודם ד"ה ור"י. מהרש"ל

והשקה קמייתא לגופו וא"ל שבברייתא כו' בעל הגמ' הוא שהשקה בתרא כו'. מהרש"ל

מסורת הש"ס

גי' רש"א

לעיל יז:

[ר"ה ה. וש"נ]

לא שתשתה מיד אחר המחיקה אלא הא כו'. מהרש"ל

[תוספתא פ"ב]

[לקמן כ:]

הגהות הב"ח

(א) רש"י ד"ה ה"ג וכו' והניף את המנחה: (ב) ד"ה אחר כל וכו' וכתיבה ומחיקה וקמילה והקטרה מגיד כצ"ל: (ג) ד"ה רבנן סברי וכו' למעלה וקאמר דאם לא כצ"ל ותיבת רבנן נמחק: (ד) ד"ה והשקה בתרא וכו' דאיכא בין ר"ע לר"ש כצ"ל:

גליון הש"ס

רש"י ד"ה ר"ש אומר וכו' והכי אמר לקמן בשמעתין. ד' כ ע"ב:

קַשְׁיָא דְּר' עֲקִיבָא אַדְּרַבִּי עֲקִיבָא: הָתָם אָמַר מְחִיקָה מְעַכְּבָא, וְהָכָא אָמַר קוֹמֶץ מְעַכֵּב! תְּרֵי תַנָּאֵי וְאַלִּיבָּא דר"ע. אִיבַּעְיָא לְהוּ: אָמְרָה "אֵינִי שׁוֹתָה" מֵחֲמַת בְּרִיוּתָא, וְחָזְרָה וְאָמְרָה "שׁוֹתָה אֲנִי", מַהוּ? כֵּיוָן דְּאָמְרָה "אֵינִי שׁוֹתָה" – "טְמֵאָה אֲנִי" קָאָמְרָה, וְכֵיוָן דְּאַחֲזִיק נַפְשָׁהּ בְּטוּמְאָה [א]לָא מָצְיָא הָדְרָה בַּהּ. אוֹ דִּילְמָא, כֵּיוָן דְּאָמְרָה "שׁוֹתָה אֲנִי" – גַּלְיָא דַּעְתָּהּ דְּמֵחֲמַת בִּיעֲתוּתָא הוּא דְּאָמְרָה? תֵּיקוּ. אָמַר אֲבוּהּ דִּשְׁמוּאֵל: [ב]צָרִיךְ שֶׁיִּתֵּן מַר לְתוֹךְ הַמַּיִם. מ"ט – דְּאָמַר קְרָא "מֵי הַמָּרִים" – שֶׁמָּרִים כְּבָר.§ **מתני'** [ג]עַד שֶׁלֹּא נִמְחֲקָה הַמְּגִילָּה אָמְרָה "אֵינִי שׁוֹתָה" – מְגִילָּתָהּ נִגְנֶזֶת, וּמִנְחָתָהּ מִתְפַּזֶּרֶת עַל הַדֶּשֶׁן, וְאֵין מְגִילָּתָהּ כְּשֵׁרָה לְהַשְׁקוֹת בָּהּ סוֹטָה אַחֶרֶת. [ד]נִמְחֲקָה הַמְּגִילָּה וְאָמְרָה "טְמֵאָה אֲנִי" – הַמַּיִם נִשְׁפָּכִין, וּמִנְחָתָהּ מִתְפַּזֶּרֶת עַל בֵּית הַדֶּשֶׁן. *[ה]נִמְחֲקָה הַמְּגִילָּה וְאָמְרָה "אֵינִי שׁוֹתָה" – [ו]מְעַרְעֲרִין אוֹתָהּ, וּמַשְׁקִין אוֹתָהּ בְּעַל כָּרְחָהּ. [ז]אֵינָהּ מַסְפֶּקֶת לִשְׁתּוֹת עַד שֶׁפָּנֶיהָ מוֹרִיקוֹת וְעֵינֶיהָ בּוֹלְטוֹת, וְהִיא מִתְמַלֵּאת גִּידִין. וְהֵם אוֹמְרִים: *הוֹצִיאוּהָ, שֶׁלֹּא תְּטַמֵּא הָעֲזָרָה. [י]אִם יֵשׁ לָהּ זְכוּת – הָיְתָה תּוֹלָה לָהּ. יֵשׁ זְכוּת תּוֹלָה שָׁנָה אַחַת, יֵשׁ זְכוּת תּוֹלָה ב' שָׁנִים, יֵשׁ זְכוּת תּוֹלָה ג' שָׁנִים. [יא]מִכָּאן אוֹמֵר בֶּן עַזַּאי: *חַיָּיב אָדָם לְלַמֵּד אֶת בִּתּוֹ תּוֹרָה, שֶׁאִם תִּשְׁתֶּה – תֵּדַע שֶׁהַזְּכוּת תּוֹלָה לָהּ. ר"א אוֹמֵר: [ח]כָּל הַמְלַמֵּד בִּתּוֹ תּוֹרָה *(כְּאִילּוּ) לוֹמְדָהּ תִּפְלוּת. ר' יְהוֹשֻׁעַ אוֹמֵר: *רוֹצָה אִשָּׁה בְּקַב וְתִפְלוּת מִט' קַבִּין וּפְרִישׁוּת. הוּא הָיָה אוֹמֵר: [ט]חָסִיד שׁוֹטֶה, וְרָשָׁע עָרוּם, וְאִשָּׁה פְּרוּשָׁה, וּמַכּוֹת פְּרוּשִׁין – הֲרֵי אֵלּוּ מְבַלֵּי עוֹלָם.§ **גמ'** *א"ר יְהוּדָה אָמַר שְׁמוּאֵל מִשּׁוּם ר"מ: כְּשֶׁהָיִיתִי לָמֵד תּוֹרָה אֵצֶל ר"ע הָיִיתִי מַטִּיל קַנְקַנְתּוֹם לְתוֹךְ הַדְּיוֹ, וְלֹא אָמַר לִי דָּבָר. כְּשֶׁבָּאתִי אֵצֶל ר' יִשְׁמָעֵאל, א"ל: בְּנִי, מַה מְּלַאכְתְּךָ? אָמַרְתִּי לוֹ: לַבְלָר אֲנִי. אָמַר לִי: בְּנִי, הֱוֵי זָהִיר, שֶׁמְּלַאכְתְּךָ מְלֶאכֶת שָׁמַיִם הִיא. שֶׁמָּא תַּחְסִיר אוֹת אַחַת אוֹ (א) תַּתִּיר אוֹת אַחַת – נִמְצֵאתָ אַתָּה מַחֲרִיב אֶת כָּל הָעוֹלָם כֻּלּוֹ. אָמַרְתִּי לוֹ: דָּבָר אֶחָד יֵשׁ לִי שֶׁאֲנִי מַטִּיל לְתוֹךְ הַדְּיוֹ, וְקַנְקַנְתּוֹם שְׁמוֹ. אָמַר לִי: וְכִי מַטִּילִין קַנְקַנְתּוֹם לְתוֹךְ הַדְּיוֹ? הַתּוֹרָה אָמְרָה "וּמָחָה" – כְּתָב שֶׁיָּכוֹל לִמָּחוֹת! מַאי קָא"ל וּמַאי קָא מַהֲדַר לֵיהּ? הָכִי קָא"ל: לָא מִבַּעְיָא בַּחֲסֵירוֹת וִיתֵירוֹת – דְּבָקִי אֲנָא, אֶלָּא אֲפִילּוּ לְמֵיחַשׁ לִזְבוּב דְּדִילְמָא אָתֵי וְיָתֵיב אַתָּגֵיהּ דְּדָלֵי"ת, וּמָחֵיק לֵיהּ וּמְשַׁוֵּי לֵיהּ רֵי"שׁ – דָּבָר אֶחָד יֵשׁ לִי שֶׁאֲנִי מַטִּיל לְתוֹךְ הַדְּיוֹ וְקַנְקַנְתּוֹם שְׁמוֹ. אִינִי?! וְהָא *תַּנְיָא, אָמַר רַבִּי מֵאִיר: כְּשֶׁהָיִיתִי לָמֵד תּוֹרָה אֵצֶל ר' יִשְׁמָעֵאל הָיִיתִי מַטִּיל קַנְקַנְתּוֹם לְתוֹךְ הַדְּיוֹ, וְלֹא אָמַר לִי דָּבָר. כְּשֶׁבָּאתִי אֵצֶל ר"ע אֲסָרָהּ עָלַי. קַשְׁיָא שִׁמּוּשׁ אַשִּׁמּוּשׁ, קַשְׁיָא אֲסָרָהּ אַאֲסָרָהּ! בִּשְׁלָמָא שִׁמּוּשׁ אַשִּׁמּוּשׁ לָא קַשְׁיָא; מֵעִיקָּרָא אֲתָא לְקַמֵּיהּ דְּר' עֲקִיבָא, כֵּיוָן דְּלָא מָצֵי קָם אַלִּיבֵּיהּ – אֲתָא לְקַמֵּיהּ דר"י וְגָמַר גְּמָרָא, הֲדַר אֲתָא לְקַמֵּיהּ דר"ע סָבַר סְבָרָא. אֶלָּא אֲסָרָהּ אַאֲסָרָהּ קַשְׁיָא! קַשְׁיָא. תַּנְיָא, רַבִּי יְהוּדָה אוֹמֵר: הָיָה ר"מ אוֹמֵר: [יב]לַכֹּל מַטִּילִין קַנְקַנְתּוֹם לְתוֹךְ הַדְּיוֹ חוּץ

חוץ

קַשְׁיָא דר"ע אדר"ע הָתָם קָאָמַר מְחִיקָה מְעַכְּבָא. אֶת הָאוֹנֶס. דְּכָל זְמַן שֶׁלֹּא נִמְחֲקָה, אִם אָמְרָה "אֵינִי שׁוֹתָה" – יְכוֹלָה לַחֲזוֹר בָּהּ. וְלָא אָנְסִינַן לָהּ לְהַשְׁקוֹתָהּ. אֲבָל אִם נִמְחֲקָה הַמְּגִילָּה – מְעַרְעֲרִין אוֹתָהּ עַל כָּרְחָהּ וַאֲפִי' לֹא קָרֵיב הַקּוֹמֶץ, דְּהָא "וְהִשְׁקָה" קַמָּא דְּקוֹדֶם הַקְטָרָה לְהָכִי דָּרְשִׁינַן. וְהָכָא קָאָמַר קוֹמֶץ מְעַכֵּב אֶת הָאוֹנֶס, דְּכָל כַּמָּה דְּלֹא קָרֵב קוֹמֶץ, אִי אָמְרָה "אֵינִי שׁוֹתָה" – לָא אָנְסִינַן לָהּ לְהַשְׁקוֹתָהּ. וְחָזְרָה וְאָמְרָה שׁוֹתָה אֲנִי. לר"ע, מַהוּ לְהַשְׁקוֹתָהּ מֵרְצוֹנָהּ? שֶׁיִּתֵּן מַר. דָּבָר מַר. שֶׁמָּרִים כְּבָר. קוֹדֶם מְחִיקָה. אַלְמָא מֵחֲמַת דָּבָר אַחֵר הֵם מָרִים. וְאֵין מְרִירָה עַל שֵׁם קְלָלַת בְּדִיקָתָם נִקְרָא, דְּהָא מִקַּמֵּי מְחִיקָה לָאו בְּנֵי מִיבְדַּק נִינְהוּ. **מתני'** מְגִילָּתָהּ נִגְנֶזֶת. *בְּצִדֵּי הַהֵיכָל. דְּכָל כִּתְבֵי הַקֹּדֶשׁ שֶׁאֵינָן רְאוּיִין לִקְרוֹת בָּהֶן – נִגְנָזִין, שֶׁלֹּא יִתְבַּזּוּ. עַל בֵּית הַדֶּשֶׁן. שֶׁהָיָה בָּעֲזָרָה, שֶׁשּׂוֹרְפִין שָׁם פְּסוּלֵי קָדָשִׁים וּפְסוּלֵי אֵימוּרִים שֶׁמַּחֲלִיפָן לִפְנִים מִן הַקְּלָעִים, כִּדְאָמְרִינַן בִּשְׁחִיטַת קָדָשִׁים (דף קד:): שְׁלֹשָׁה בֵּית הַדֶּשֶׁן הֵם. דְּהוֹאִיל וְקִדְּשָׁהּ בִּכְלִי נִשְׂרֶפֶת בָּעֲזָרָה. וְהַאי מִתְפַּזֶּרֶת – הַיְינוּ נִשְׂרֶפֶת, כִּדְאָמַר לְקַמָּן (ד' כג.): וְאֵלּוּ שֶׁמִּנְחוֹתֵיהֶם נִשְׂרָפוֹת, וְקָא חָשֵׁיב לְהָא: הָאוֹמֶרֶת "אֵינִי שׁוֹתָה". וְאֵין מְגִילָּתָהּ כְּשֵׁרָה לְהַשְׁקוֹת בָּהּ סוֹטָה אַחֶרֶת. דְּבָעֵינַן כְּתִיבָה לִשְׁמָהּ, דִּכְתִיב: "וְעָשָׂה לָהּ הַכֹּהֵן" – לָהּ לִשְׁמָהּ. הַמַּיִם נִשְׁפָּכִין. כֵּיוָן דְּאָמְרָה "טְמֵאָה אֲנִי" – בְּדוּקָה וְעוֹמֶדֶת הִיא, וּמֵי הַמָּרִים לֹא נִיתְּנוּ אֶלָּא לְבָרֵר אֶת הַסָּפֵק. מְעַרְעֲרִין **אוֹתָהּ**. דִּלְמָא טְהוֹרָה הִיא, וּמֵחֲמַת רְתִיתוּתָהּ קָאָמְרָה. מִתְמַלֵּאת **גִּידִין**. הַגִּידִין שֶׁבְּלֶחָיֶיהָ נוֹפְחִין, וְנִרְאוֹת כִּמְלֵאָה גִּידִין, וְגַם בְּשָׂרָהּ נַעֲשֵׂית שִׁיטָּה שִׁיטָּה שֶׁל נְפִיחָה. וְהָכִי תַּנְיָא בְּסִפְרֵי: כְּמִין שַׂרְבִיטִין מְזוֹרָקִין בָּהּ. **שֶׁלֹּא** תְּטַמֵּא **הָעֲזָרָה**. שַׁעֲרֵי נִקָּנוֹר, אוֹ עֶזְרַת נָשִׁים שֶׁאֵצֶל דֶּרֶךְ שָׁם. וּלְקַמֵּיהּ פָּרֵיךְ: וְהָא אָמְרִינַן בְּעָלְמָא דְּשַׁעֲרֵי נִקָּנוֹר לֹא נִתְקַדְּשׁוּ, וְכ"ש עֶזְרַת נָשִׁים, וּמֵת מוּתָּר לִיכָּנֵס לְמַחֲנֵה לְוִיָּה. תֵּדַע שֶׁזְּכוּת תּוֹלָה לָהּ. תִּרְאֶה וְתִלְמַד בְּפָרָשַׁת סוֹטָה שֶׁהַזְּכוּת תּוֹלָה. דְּיָלְפִינַן מִ"וְנִקְּתָה וְנִזְרְעָה זָרַע" – וְנִקְּתָה ע"י זְכִיּוֹת כְּדֵי זְרִיעַת זֶרַע ט' חֳדָשִׁים, וְי"א יוֹתֵר, כִּדְמְפָרֵשׁ בַּגְּמָ'. מְלַמְּדָהּ תִּיפְלוּת. מְפָרֵשׁ בַּגְּמָ'. רַבִּי יְהוֹשֻׁעַ **אוֹמֵר** רוֹצָה אִשָּׁה בְּקַב וְתִיפְלוּת. גָּרְסִינַן. וּבַגְּמָרָא מְפָרֵשׁ מַאי קָאָמַר. מַכּוֹת פְּרוּשִׁין. מְפָרֵשׁ בַּגְּמָ': שֶׁמַּכֶּה אֶת עַצְמוֹ בַּכְּתָלִים, לְהַרְאוֹת שֶׁהוּא עָנָיו וְצָנוּעַ. **גמ'** לַבְלָר. סוֹפֵר. אִם תְּחַסֵּר אוֹת אַחַת. כְּגוֹן א' "וַה' אֱלֹהִים אֱמֶת" (ירמיה י). אוֹ תְּיַיתֵּר אוֹת אַחַת, כְּגוֹן "בְּרֵאשִׁית בָּרְאוּ אֱלֹהִים". דָּבָר אֶחָד יֵשׁ לִי. לְקַמָּן מְפָרֵשׁ מַאי תְּשׁוּבָה הִיא זוֹ. כְּתָב שֶׁיָּכוֹל לִמָּחוֹת. וְרַבִּי יִשְׁמָעֵאל סָבַר מוּתְקָן לָהּ מִן הַתּוֹרָה, וְלָא בָּעֵי כְּתִיבָה לִשְׁמָהּ. וּפָרָשַׁת סוֹטָה לְחוּדָהּ קָא קָפֵיד. **מַאי** קָאָמַר לֵיהּ וּמַאי מַהֲדַר לֵיהּ. מַאי קָאָמַר לֵיהּ ר' יִשְׁמָעֵאל דְּקָא מַהֲדַר לֵיהּ ר"מ: דָּבָר אֶחָד יֵשׁ לִי שֶׁעוֹשֶׂה רוֹשֶׁם וְאֵינוֹ נִמְחָק. מָה עִנְיַן קַנְקַנְתּוֹס אֵצֶל חִיסּוּר וְיִתּוּר? וּמְשַׁוֵּי לֵיהּ רֵי"שׁ. כְּגוֹן דָּלֶ"ת דְּ"אֶחָד". דָּבָר **אֶחָד** יֵשׁ כו'. וְאֵינוֹ נִמְחָק לְגַמְרֵי. קַשְׁיָא **שִׁימּוּשׁ אַשִּׁימּוּשׁ**. דְּקָאָמַר לְעֵיל שִׁימּוּשׁ דר"ע קוֹדֶם, (ב) וְקָאָמַר הָכָא דר"י קוֹדֶם. לָא מָצֵי לְמֵיקַם אַלִּיבֵּיהּ. עַל עִיקָּרֵי טַעֲמֵיהּ. שֶׁהָיָה אוֹמֵר עַל טָמֵא טָהוֹר וּמַרְאֶה לוֹ פָּנִים, וְעַל טָהוֹר טָמֵא וּמַרְאֶה לוֹ פָּנִים. **אֲתָא** לְקַמֵּיהּ דר"י **וְגָמַר גְּמָרָא**. הַמִּשְׁנָיוֹת סְתוּמוֹת כְּמוֹ שֶׁהֵן, כִּדְגָמִיר לְהוּ מֵרַבּוֹ, וְרַבּוֹ מֵרַבּוֹ. וַהֲדַר **אֲתָא** לְקַמֵּיהּ דר"ע **לְמִיסְבַּר סְבָרָא**. לַעֲמוֹד עַל עִיקַּר טַעֲמֵי הַמִּשְׁנָה, מִפְּנֵי מָה זֶה טָמֵא וְזֶה טָהוֹר, זֶה אָסוּר וְזֶה מוּתָּר, וְעַל מַה כָּל דָּבָר נִסְמָךְ, וְעַל אֵיזֶה מִקְרָא. וְזֶה תַּלְמוּד שֶׁהָיָה בִּימֵי הַתַּנָּאִים. וּלְהָבִין דָּבָר מִתּוֹךְ דָּבָר; כְּשֶׁהָיָה דָּבָר חָדָשׁ נִשְׁאָל בְּבֵית הַמִּדְרָשׁ, מֵהֵיכָן יִלְמְדוּהוּ וּלְאֵיזֶה מִשְׁנָה יְדַמּוּהוּ.

מגילתה נגנזת. ירושלמי: תני, נגנזת תחת צירו של היכל, למה – בשביל לשחקה. לול קטן היה שם, ושם המים נשפכים! תני: אין בהן משום קדושה. מהו לגבל בהן את הטיט? מה בכך, המים נשפכים! תני: יש בהם משום קדושה. נמחקה המגילה ואמרה "איני שותה" מערערין אותה. למה – שגרמה לשם שימחק. כמה ימחק? תני רבי חנין, ב"ש אומרים: אחת, וב"ה אומרים: שתים. א"ר אילעאי: טעמא דב"ה כדי לכתוב י"ה. ***אמר** ר' ירמיה למחוק לה מה"ת **איכא** בינייהו. תימה לרבי: והא בימי ר"מ נפסקו כבר המים המרים כדאמרי' בפ' בתרא (לקמן דף מז.) דר' יוחנן בן זכאי הפסיקן! ועוד, האמר רבא (לעיל ד' יז:): מגילת סוטה שכתבה קודם שתקבל עליה שבועה – לא עשה ולא כלום. א"כ מ"ט דמ"ד מוחקין לה מן התורה? וליכא למימר: מ"ד מוחקין לה מן התורה לית ליה דרבא. א"כ אמאי אמר לר"ש לעיל (ד' יט:) כדי נסבה? לימא: לית ליה דרבא! אלא הכי משמע: דבהא דרבא – כ"ע מודו. ואיכא למימר מ"ד מוחקין לה מה"ת – כגון אם נכתבה אותה פרשה בתורה לאחר שקבלה עליה שבועה, אע"פ שהסופר לא נתכוין לשם סוטה אלא לשם ס"ת. ומה שאין מטילין קנקנתום לתוך הדיו לפרשת סוטה אפי' בזמן הזה – משום דכתיב בה "ומחה", דבעינן כתב שיכול למחות. וכיון דס"ל מוחקין לה מן התורה – ש"מ דקסבר דאאותה פרשה, אפילו כתובה בתורה, קפיד קרא דבעינן שיכול למחוק.

אבל תורה דסתמא כתיב הכי נמי דמחקינן. לפום האי דיחוי ה"מ למיפרך: וכי לית ליה לת"ק הא דתנן: *כל גט שנכתב שלא לשם אשה פסול. כיצד, היה עובר בשוק ושמע קול סופרים מקרין וכו'? וה"מ לתרוצי: דילמא עד כאן לא אמר גבי גט דסתמא פסול – משום דאשה לאו לגירושין עומדת, אבל סוטה אחר שקינא לה ונסתרה – סתמא להשקות עומדת, כדאמרינן בריש מסכת זבחים (דף ב:). א"נ, עד כאן לא פסלינן גבי גט אלא משום דהתם "וכתב לה" אמר רחמנא וכו'. מיהו, היכא דאינתיק לשם רחל – לא הדרא מנתקא ע"י מחיקה לשם לאה. ולרבי אחי בר יאשיה נמי, אע"ג דעשייה דידה מחיקה היא, מיהו מהני קלא דכתב בסתמא "ועשה לה" ולא כתב "ומחה לה" – דרשינן ליה נמי אכתיבה, דבעינן דלכתוב לשם אלות בעולם. מיהו אהני נמי האי דלא כתב

תוספות שאנץ

שהיא טמאה: דאמר קרא מי המרים שמרים כבר קודם מחיקה אלמא מחמת דבר אחר הם מרים ואין מרירותן נקרא על שם בדיקותן דהא מקמי מחיקה לאו בני בדיקה נינהו. ל"ה: **מתני'** מגילתה נגנזת בצדי ההיכל דכל כתבי הקדש שאינן ראוין לקרות בהן נגנזין שלא יתבזו: ומנחתה מתפזרת אבית הדשן דהואיל וקידשה בכלי נשרפת בעזרה והאי מתפזרת בעזרה היינו נשרפת כדא' לקמן ואלו שמנחותיהן נשרפות וקא חשיב לה להא האומרת איני שותה. ל"ה. והיא מתמלאה גידין פ"ה הגידין שבלחייה נופחין ונראית מלאה גידין וגם בבשרה נעשית שיטה שיטה של נפיחה והכי תניא בספרי כמין שרביטין מזורקין בה: שאם תחסר אות אחת כגון אלף וה' אלהים אמת או תתיר אות אחת בראשית בראו אלהים וה"ר מאיר פי' כגון הוה על הוה א) אחרון יו"ד מברך את השם:

א) נראה דצ"ל אם יוסיף יו"ד על הוה אחרון נמצא מברך את השם.

עין משפט נר מצוה

ו א מיי' פ"ד מהל' סוטה הל"ג סמג עשין נו:
ז ב מיי' פ"ג שם הל"י סמג עשין נו:
ח ג מיי' שם פ"ד הלכה ד:
ט ד מיי' שם הל"ו:
י ה מיי' שם הל"ד:
יא ו מיי' שם פ"ג הלכה טז:
יב ז מיי' שם הל"כ:
יג ח מיי' פ"א מהל' ת"ת הלי"ג סמג עשין יב טוש"ע יו"ד סי' רמו סעי' ו:
יד ט מיי' פ"ח מהל' ערכין הלי"ג:
טו י מיי' פ"א מהל' תפלין הל"ד סמג עשין כב טוש"ע יו"ד סימן רעא סעי' ו:

מסורת הש"ס

ס"א בגירי

[לעיל יט:]

[ע' תוספות פסחים לב. ד"ה טבול יבמות ז: ד"ה ורלה ותוס' זבחים לב. ד"ה ובטמאים]

[ע' תוספות לקמן כא: ד"ה בן עזאי]

ס"א אינו [וכ"ה בפיסקא בגמ' לקמן כא: ומוכח שם דלא גרסינן הכי במשנה וכ"כ בתוי"ט]

*[כתובות סב: וע' תוספות לקמן כא: ד"ה רוצה]

עירובין יג.

[לעיל יז:]

עירובין יג.

[גיטין כד.]

הגהות הב"ח

(א) גמ' או תייתר אות א': (ב) רש"י ד"ה קשיא וכו' קודם והכא אמר דר"י:

גליון הש"ס

מתני' מערערין אותה. עיין פרש"י איוב לט כט: **שם** מכאן אומר בן עזאי וכו'. ע' חגיגה ד' ג ע"א תד"ה נשים לשמוע:

תורה אור

חוץ מִפָּרָשַׁת סוֹטָה בִּלְבַד. רַבִּי יַעֲקֹב אוֹמֵר מִשְּׁמוֹ: אחוּץ מִפָּרָשַׁת סוֹטָה שֶׁל מִקְדָּשׁ. מַאי בֵּינַיְיהוּ? אָ"ר יִרְמְיָה: אלִמְחוֹק לָהּ מִן הַתּוֹרָה אִיכָּא בֵּינַיְיהוּ. וְהָנֵי תַּנָּאֵי כִּי הָנֵי תַּנָּאֵי; דְּתַנְיָא: באֵין מְגִילָּתָהּ כְּשֵׁירָה לְהַשְׁקוֹת בָּהּ סוֹטָה אַחֶרֶת, רַבִּי אַחַי בַּר יֹאשִׁיָּה אוֹמֵר: מְגִילָּתָהּ כְּשֵׁירָה לְהַשְׁקוֹת בָּהּ סוֹטָה אַחֶרֶת. אָמַר רַב פַּפָּא: דִּילְמָא לָא הִיא; עַד כָּאן לָא קָאָמַר ת"ק הָתָם, אֶלָּא כֵּיוָן דְּאִינְתִּיק לְשׁוּם רָחֵל — לָא הָדְרָא מִינַּתְקָא לְשׁוּם לֵאָה, אֲבָל תּוֹרָה דִּסְתָמָא כְּתִיבָה — הָכִי נַמִי דְּמָחֲקִינַן. אָמַר רַב נַחְמָן בַּר יִצְחָק: דִּילְמָא לָא הִיא; עַד כָּאן לָא קָאָמַר רַבִּי אַחַי בַּר יֹאשִׁיָּה הָתָם — אֶלָּא בִּמְגִילָּה, דְּאִיכְתּוּב לְשׁוּם אָלוֹת בָּעוֹלָם, אֲבָל תּוֹרָה דִּלְהִתְלַמֵּד כְּתִיבָה — הָכִי נַמִי גדְּלָא מָחֲקִינַן, וְרַבִּי אַחַי בַּר יֹאשִׁיָּה, לֵית לֵיהּ *דכָּתַב לְגָרֵשׁ אֶת אִשְׁתּוֹ וְנִמְלַךְ, מְצָאוֹ בֶּן עִירוֹ וְאָמַר לוֹ: שְׁמִי כְּשִׁמְךָ וְשֵׁם אִשְׁתִּי כְּשֵׁם אִשְׁתְּךָ — פָּסוּל לְגָרֵשׁ בּוֹ? אָמְרִי: הָתָם — °"וְכָתַב לָהּ" אָמַר רַחֲמָנָא, בָּעֵינַן כְּתִיבָה *לִשְׁמָהּ. הָכָא נַמִי °"וְעָשָׂה לָהּ"! מַאי עֲשִׂיָּיה — מְחִיקָה. § "אֵינָהּ מַסְפֶּקֶת לִשְׁתּוֹת עַד שֶׁפָּנְיָה" [כו']. § מַנִּי — ר"ש הִיא, *דְּאָמַר: מַקְרִיב אֶת מִנְחָתָהּ וְאח"כ מַשְׁקָהּ, דְּכַמָּה דְּלָא קָרְבָה מִנְחָתָהּ לָא בָּדְקִי לָהּ מַיָּא, דִּכְתִיב: °"מִנְחַת זִכָּרוֹן מַזְכֶּרֶת עָוֹן". אֵימָא סֵיפָא: יֵשׁ לָהּ זְכוּת — הָיְתָה תּוֹלָה לָהּ, אֲתָאן לְרַבָּנַן. דְּאִי ר"ש — הָאָמַר *אֵין זְכוּת תּוֹלָה בַּמַּיִם הַמָּרִים! אָמַר רַב חִסְדָּא: הָא מַנִּי — ר"ע הִיא, דְּאָמַר: *מַקְרִיב אֶת מִנְחָתָהּ וְאח"כ מַשְׁקָהּ, וּבִזְכוּת — סָבַר לָהּ כְּרַבָּנַן. § "וְהֵם אוֹמְרִים הוֹצִיאוּהָ" וכו'. § מ"ט — דְּדִילְמָא מֵתָה. לְמֵימְרָא דְּמֵת אָסוּר בְּמַחֲנֵה לְוִיָּה? *וְהָתַנְיָא: הטָמֵא מֵת מוּתָּר לִיכָּנֵס לְמַחֲנֵה לְוִיָּה. וְלֹא טְמֵא מֵת בִּלְבַד אָמְרוּ, אֶלָּא ואֲפִילּוּ מֵת עַצְמוֹ, שֶׁנֶּאֱמַר: °"וַיִּקַּח מֹשֶׁה אֶת עַצְמוֹת יוֹסֵף עִמּוֹ", עִמּוֹ בִּמְחִיצָתוֹ! אָמַר אַבַּיֵי: זשֶׁמָּא תִּפְרוֹס נִדָּה. לְמֵימְרָא דִּבְעִיתוּתָא מְרַפְיָא? אִין, דִּכְתִיב: °"וַתִּתְחַלְחַל הַמַּלְכָּה מְאֹד", *וְאָמַר רַב: שֶׁפֵּירְסָה נִדָּה. וְהָא אֲנַן *תְּנַן: חֲרָדָה מְסַלֶּקֶת דָּמִים! פַּחְדָא צָמֵית, בִּיעֲתוּתָא מְרַפְיָא. § "יֵשׁ לָהּ זְכוּת הָיְתָה" וכו'. § מַנִּי מַתְנִי'? לָא אַבָּא יוֹסֵי בֶּן חָנָן, וְלָא ר"א בֶּן יִצְחָק אִישׁ כְּפַר דָּרוֹם, וְלָא רַבִּי יִשְׁמָעֵאל. דְּתַנְיָא: אִם יֵשׁ לָהּ זְכוּת — תּוֹלָה לָהּ שְׁלֹשָׁה חֳדָשִׁים, כְּדֵי הַכָּרַת הָעוּבָּר, דִּבְרֵי אַבָּא יוֹסֵי בֶּן חָנָן. ר"א בֶּן יִצְחָק אִישׁ כְּפַר דָּרוֹם אוֹמֵר: ט' חֳדָשִׁים, שֶׁנֶּאֱמַר: °"וְנִקְּתָה וְנִזְרְעָה זָרַע", וּלְהַלָּן הוּא אוֹמֵר: °"זֶרַע יַעַבְדֶנּוּ יְסוּפַּר" — זֶרַע *הָרָאוּי לְסַפֵּר. רַבִּי יִשְׁמָעֵאל אוֹמֵר: שְׁנֵים עָשָׂר חֹדֶשׁ, וְאע"פ שֶׁאֵין רְאָיָה לַדָּבָר — זֵכֶר לַדָּבָר, *דִּכְתִיב: °"לָהֵן מַלְכָּא מִלְכִּי יִשְׁפַּר עֲלָךְ וַחֲטָיָךְ בְּצִדְקָה פְרוּק וַעֲוָיָתָךְ בְּמִחַן עֲנָיִן

הֵן

(דברים כד; במדבר ה; סס; שמות יג; אסתר ד; במדבר ה; תהלים כב; דניאל ד)

רש"י

חוץ מִפָּרָשַׁת סוֹטָה. וַאֲפִי' בְּס"ת. מִשְּׁמוֹ. שֶׁל ר"מ. שֶׁבַּמִּקְדָּשׁ. שֶׁל כָּל סוֹטָה וְסוֹטָה. מַאי בֵּינַיְיהוּ. כְּלוֹמַר, בְּמַאי קָמִיפַּלְגִי, בְּאֵיזֶה טַעֲמָא? לִמְחוֹק לָהּ. מִפָּרָשַׁת סוֹטָה שֶׁבְּסֵפֶר תּוֹרָה; לְת"ק — מָחֲקִינַן, לְר' יַעֲקֹב — לָא מָחֲקִינַן. כִּי הָנֵי תַּנָּאֵי. דְּאִיפְּלְגוּ נַמִי בִּכְתִיבָה לִשְׁמָהּ. דְּאִינְתִּיק. מִכָּל נָשִׁים לִשְׁמָהּ שֶׁל זוֹ. אָמַר רַב נַחְמָן וכו'. אִיהוּ נַמִי פָּרֵיךְ דְּהָנֵי תַּנָּאֵי לָאו כִּי הָנֵי תַּנָּאֵי, וּפָרֵיךְ לְאִידָךְ גִּיסָא, וְאִית לֵיהּ נַמִי דְּרַב פַּפָּא. וְה"ק: אִיכָּא לְמִיפְרַךְ לְהַאי גִּיסָא, וְאִיכָּא לְמִיפְרַךְ לְהַאי גִּיסָא. כָּתַב. לָהּ גֵּט לְגָרֵשׁ אֶת אִשְׁתּוֹ, וְנִמְלַךְ מִלְּגָרְשָׁהּ. בֶּן עִירוֹ. שֶׁשְּׁמוֹ כִּשְׁמוֹ, וְהוּא מֵאוֹתָהּ הָעִיר. שְׁמִי כְּשִׁמְךָ וכו'. וּבְנֵי עִיר אַחַת אֲנַחְנוּ, וְגֵט זֶה רָאוּי לִי. תְּנֵיהוּ לִי וַאֲגָרֵשׁ בּוֹ אֶת אִשְׁתִּי. פָּסוּל לָזֶה לְגָרֵשׁ בּוֹ. דְּדָרְשִׁינַן "לָהּ" — לִשְׁמָהּ, דִּכְתִיב: "וְכָתַב לָהּ סֵפֶר כְּרִיתוּת". וְהָכָא נַמִי כְּתִיב: "וְעָשָׂה לָהּ הַכֹּהֵן". מַנִּי. הָא דְּקָתָנֵי דְּכֵיוָן שֶׁשָּׁתְתָה נִבְדֶּקֶת — ר"ש הִיא, דְּאָמַר מַקְרִיב מִנְחָתָהּ וְאח"כ מַשְׁקָהּ. דְּאִי לָא אַקְרְבָהּ בְּרֵישָׁא — לָא הֲוָה מִיבַּדְקָה עַד שֶׁתִּקְרַב מִנְחָתָהּ, דִּכְתִיב "מַזְכֶּרֶת עָוֹן". **הָא אָמַר אֵין זְכוּת** תּוֹלָה. בְּמַתְנִי' (לקמן ד' כב:). **ר"ע הִיא.** דְּאָמַר לְעֵיל (ד' יט:): מַשֶּׁקָּרַב הַקּוֹמֶץ אֵינָהּ יְכוֹלָה לַחֲזוֹר בָּהּ. אַלְמָא מַקְרְבֵי לָהּ קוֹדֶם שֶׁתִּשְׁתֶּה. בְּמַחֲנֵה לְוִיָּה. בְּהַר הַבַּיִת. דְּהָא עֶזְרַת נָשִׁים וְגַם שַׁעַר נִקָּנוֹר לֹא נִתְקַדְּשׁוּ בִּקְדוּשַּׁת עֲזָרָה, וַהֲרֵי הֵן כִּשְׁאָר הַר הַבַּיִת. **עִמּוֹ** בִּמְחִיצָתוֹ. וּבַמִּדְבָּר נַמִי הָיוּ ג' מַחֲנוֹת; לִפְנִים מִן הַקְּלָעִים — מַחֲנֵה שְׁכִינָה, "וְהַלְוִיִּם יַחֲנוּ סָבִיב לְמִשְׁכַּן הָעֵדוּת" (במדבר א) — זֶה מַחֲנֵה לְוִיָּה, וְהַדְּגָלִים ג' פַּרְסָאוֹת — זֶה מַחֲנֵה יִשְׂרָאֵל. וּמֹשֶׁה הָיָה לֵוִי וְקָאָמַר "עִמּוֹ". **שֶׁמָּא תִּפְרוֹס** נִדָּה. אַגַּב בִּיעֲתוּתָא דְּמַיִם הַמָּרִים. וְהַנִּדָּה וְהַזָּב וְהַזָּבָה וּבַעַל קֶרִי אֲסוּרִים בְּמַחֲנֵה לְוִיָּה, כְּדְיָלְפִינַן בִּפְסָחִים בְּפֶרֶק "אֵלּוּ דְּבָרִים" (ד' סז.). **פַּחְדָא צָמֵית.** דְּאָגָה שֶׁאֵינָהּ בָּאָה פִּתְאוֹם, אֶלָּא דּוֹאֶגֶת שֶׁמָּא יָבוֹאוּ אוֹיְבִים לְהוֹרְגָהּ — צוֹמֶת אֶת הַמָּקוֹר מִלְּהוֹצִיא דָּם, וַאֲפִי' בִּשְׁעַת וְסְתָּהּ. וְהַהִיא דְּנִדָּה — אַדְּאָגָה אִיתְּמַר, דְּקָתָנֵי: הִגִּיעַ שְׁעַת וְסְתָּהּ וְלֹא בָּדְקָה — טְמֵאָה, מִפְּנֵי שֶׁאוֹרַח בִּזְמַנּוֹ בָּא. ר"מ אוֹמֵר: אִם הָיְתָה בְּמַחְבֵּא וְהִגִּיעַ שְׁעַת וְסְתָּהּ וְלֹא בָּדְקָה — טְהוֹרָה אִם בָּדְקָה אַחֲרֵי כֵן וּמְצָאַתָּהּ טְהוֹרָה, וְלֹא "אָמַר אוֹרַח בִּזְמַנּוֹ בָּא", שֶׁחֲרָדָה מְסַלֶּקֶת אֶת הַדָּמִים. **בִּיעֲתוּתָא.** הַבָּאָה פִּתְאוֹם, כְּגוֹן זוֹ שֶׁלֹּא הָיְתָה חֲרֵידָה עַד עַכְשָׁיו, וּפִתְאוֹם הִיא מַרְגֶּשֶׁת בְּצַעֲרָהּ. וְכֵן בְּאֶסְתֵּר, שֶׁבָּאת לָהּ שְׁמוּעַת מָרְדֳּכַי פִּתְאוֹם. **מְרַפְיָא.** הַדָּמִים, פּוֹתֵחַ אֶת הַמָּקוֹר. מַנִּי מַתְנִי'. דְּקָתָנֵי: יֵשׁ זְכוּת תּוֹלָה ג' שָׁנִים. **כְּדֵי הַכָּרַת** הָעוּבָּר. דְּדָרֵישׁ: "וְנִקְּתָה" ע"י זְכוּת — כְּדֵי "וְנִזְרְעָה זָרַע" — כְּשִׁיעוּר שֶׁהָעוּבָּר נִיכָּר בִּמְעוּבֶּרֶת. **הָרָאוּי** לְסַפֵּר. לִחְיוֹת וְלָבֹא לִידֵי סִיפּוּר שִׁבְחוֹ שֶׁל מָקוֹם. **וְאע"פ** שֶׁאֵין רְאָיָה. גְּמוּרָה לַדָּבָר דִּזְכוּת תּוֹלָה י"ב חוֹדֶשׁ, זֵכֶר לַדָּבָר. וּלְקַמָּן מְפָרֵשׁ אַמַּאי אֵינָהּ רְאָיָה. **לָהֵן מַלְכָּא** מִלְכִּי יִשְׁפַּר עֲלָךְ וגו'. דָּנִיֵּאל אָמַר לִנְבוּכַדְנֶצַּר, כְּשֶׁפָּתַר לוֹ הַחֲלוֹם שֶׁיְּהֵא נִטְרָד מִן הָאֲנָשִׁים וְלִהְיוֹת עִם בְּהֵמָה וְחַיָּה: "לָהֵן מַלְכָּא" — אָמְנָם הַמֶּלֶךְ מַלְכִּי, "יִשְׁפַּר עֲלָךְ" — עֲצָתִי תִּיטַב בְּעֵינֶיךָ, לְהַאֲמִין לַעֲצָתִי. וַחֲטָיָךְ בְּצִדְקָה פְּרוּק. חַטָּאֶךָ ע"י צְדָקָה פְּדֵה. וַעֲוָיָתָךְ בְּמִחַן. וַעֲוֹנוֹתֶיךָ בַּחֲנִינַת הָעֲנִיִּים.

הֵן

תוספות

כתב "וכתב לה", אע"ג דנכתבה לשום אשה אחרת — דכשר. לפום דיחוי דרב נחמן בר יצחק, א"כ הא דקאמר הכא: התם "וכתב לה" אמר רחמנא, אבל הכא לא כתיב אלא "וכתב", "לה" כתיב גבי עשייה — והא בפרק "כל הגט" (גיטין דף כד:) מפרש מ"ט פסלינן לכל הני גיטין, אי כתיב "ונתן ספר כריתות" — ה"א למעוטי האיך קמא שנכתב שלא לשום אשה, כתב רחמנא "וכתב". ואי לא כתיב אלא "וכתב" — ה"א למעוטי האי, דלא איהו כתב לה, אבל יש לו ב' נשים דאיהו קא כתב לה, כשר — כתב רחמנא "וכתב לה", דממעטינן היו לו שתי נשים וכו'. אלמא דממעטי התם מ"וכתב" גרידא היכא דנכתב לשם אשה אחרת! וי"ל: דשאני התם, דלא הוה צריך למיכתב אלא "ונתן לה ספר כריתות", הילכך הוי "וכתב" קרא יתירא, למעוטי נכתב לשם אשה אחרת. אבל הכא לאו יתירא הוא האי "וכתב", הילכך לא ממעטינהו מיניה אלא היכא דלא אכתיב לשם אלות בעולם, כדכתיב: "וכתב את האלות". **הא** מני ר"ע היא ובזכות סבר לה כרבנן. פירש ר"י: דאשכחן הכי בספרי ובירושלמי בהדיא דסבר ר' עקיבא זכות תולה. דגרס בירושלמי: תני, ר' טרפון אומר: כל זכרונות שנאמרו בתורה — לטובה, חוץ מזו שהיא של פורענות. אמר לו ר"ע: אילו נאמר "מזכרת עון" ושתק — הייתי אומר כדבריך, הא אינו אומר "מנחת זכרון" אלא לטובה. אבל אי לא הוי אמר ר"ע בהדיא דזכות תולה — הוה מוקי לה כרבי דמתני' (לקמן ד' כב:) וסבר לה כרבי שמעון. ונראה דלא הוה מצי לאוקמא כרבי, דמדסיפא רבי — רישא לאו רבי. ועוד איכא למאן דאמר בפ"ק (לעיל דף ו.) דבמתנוונה פליגי רבי ורבנן. **לא** טמא מת אלא אפי' מת עצמו. קשיא לר': דהכא משמע דמכניס מת חמור מטמא מת הנכנס. ובפרק בתרא דעירובין בסופו (דף קד:), אמר רב טובי בר קיסנא אמר שמואל: המכניס טמא שרץ במקדש — חייב, שרץ עצמו — פטור, שנאמר: "מזכר ועד נקבה תשלחו" — מי שיש לו טהרה במקוה. ומת נמי אין לו טהרה במקוה! א)ויש לתרץ: דהתם איירי במכניס שרץ שלא נגע בו, ושרץ לא מטמא במשא. ולהכי נקט נמי שרץ ולא נבילה, דאם נטמא המכניס — תיפוק ליה משום גופו שהיה נכנס טמא שרץ במקדש. והכא ה"פ: ולא טמא מת בלבד אמרו, לאחר שפירש מן הטומאה, אלא אפי' מת עצמו, דהויא טומאה בחיבורין במכניסו, דחמירי טפי מטומאה שלא בחיבורין, כדאיתא בפ' שני דמסכת ע"ז (דף לז:). **ביעתותא** מרפיא. תימה לר"י: והא בפרק בתרא דנדה (דף עא.) בגמרא, ב"ש אומרים: כל הנשים מתות נדות, מ"ט דב"ש — אגב ביעתותא [דמלאכא] דמותא חזיא, וב"ה פליגי עליה. וקא מקשה התם: אלא הא דתניא, ב"ש אומרים: °כל הנשים מתים זבין, קרי כאן "מבשרו" ולא מחמת אונסו! אלא טעמא דב"ש וכו'. אלמא דלא אמרי' ביעתותא מרפיא! וי"ל: ביעתותא דמלאך לא מרפיא, דלא חזי אלא בשעת הוצאת הנפש. **יש** זכות תולה שנה אחת. ירושלמי: יש זכות תולה שנה אחת — מנבוכדנצר, "לקצת ירחין תרין עשר". יש זכות תולה שתי שנים — מאמנון, "ויהי לשנתים ימים" (שמואל ב יג). יש זכות תולה שלש שנים — מאחאב, "וישבו שלש שנים אין מלחמה" (מלכים א כב). אמר ר' יוסי: כל *אותן שלש שנים היה עסוק במצות, וכל אותן שתי שנים היה עוסק בתורה. מנחת זכרון — כלל, "מזכרת עון" — פרט. כמדומה הכי פירוש: אימא דמ"מנחת זכרון" ליכא למילף זכרון זכות אלא זכרון עון, ואין בכלל אלא מה שבפרט! אם אומר אתה כן — לא נמצאת מדת הדין מקופחת? מה אם מדת הפורענות מעוטה — הרי מזכרת, מידת הטובה מרובה על אחת כמה וכמה! אלא "מנחת זכרון" — יש לה זכות, "מזכרת עון" — אין לה זכות.

מלוה

א) [ועי' תוספות מנחות נה: ד"ה אין]

תוספות שאנץ

למחוק לה מן התורה פרשת סוטה שבספר תורה לת"ק מחקי' לר' עקיבא לא מחקינן אבל תורה דסתם כתיבא הכי נמי דמחקינן וא"ת מאי שנא מהא דאמרינן בגיטין ההוא גברא דעל לבי כנישתא ויהב ספר תורה לדביתהו אמר רב יוסף למאי ניחוש לה אי משום כריתות הא בעי' וכתב לה לשמה אלמא אמרי' דאע"ג דסתם כתיבא לא אמרי' דהוי לשמה ודוחק הוא לומר דרב יוסף פליג ארב פפא דהכא ואומר דשאני גט דאפי' כתב הסופר שם אשה ושם האיש לא מהני אם לא אמר ליה הבעל שיכתוב הגט אבל הכא גבי סוטה מגלת סוטה שנכתבה בלא אמירת האשה כשרה ומשו"ה אמרינן דבין כתיבא לשמה דמחק. אבל ק' דהכא משמע דלהתלמד עדיף יותר ופי' בריש פ' כל הגט. אבל ק' מאי הא דקאמר בתר הכי דר' אחא לית ליה כתב לגרש את אשתו ונמלך כו'. והא לא דמי גט לסוטה כדפי'. וי"ל דמ"מ פריך הכי דכיון דלית ליה לשמה א"כ לא לדרוש לשמה נמי גבי גט וכתב לה לשמה כי היכי דלא דריש לשמה ליה גבי סוטה: למימר דמת אסור במחנה לויה בתמיה דהא עזרת נשים ושער נקנור לא נתקדשו בקדושת העזרה והרי הן כשאר הבית. ל"ה: וא"ת מאי מקשי' מדרבנן מיהא אסור דהכי אמרי' התם חצר חדשה שנחדשו בה דברים הרבה שאין טבול יום וטמא מת נכנס במחנה לויה וגם תנן במס' כלים מקודש ממנו החיל שאין גוים וטמאי מתים נכנסין היכא דאירע וי"ל דיש חילוק בין קודם שנכנס לשם לטמא אז דאסור ליכנס במחנה לויה אבל היכא דאירע לו תוך המחנה אז מותר להיות שם דה"נ אמרי' במס' תמיד אירע קרי באחד מהם היה הולך במסיבה לבית הטבילה וכשחוזר בא לו אצל אחיו הכהנים: אלא אפי' מת עצמו וק' מאי אפי' אדרבה מת קיל טפי כדאמר (בעירובין ק"ד) טמא שרץ שנכנס לעזרה חייב והמכניס שרץ למקדש פטור משום דכתיב מזכר עד נקבה תשלחו מי שיש לו טהרה במקוה מת נמי אין לו טהרה במקוה וי"ל דפלוגתא דתנאי היא התם. (א"ת יש במינו טהרה במקוה דשרץ כדאמר בפ' דר' עקיבא דיש במינו טהרה במקוה בעי גבי מפץ דהתם איצטריך קרא במפץ לומר דבעי במינו ה"נ כתיב מזכר לד' דבעי במינו). עמו במחיצתו ובמדבר נמי היו ג' מחנות לפנים מן הקלעים מחנה שכינה והלוים יחנו סביב למשכן העדות זה מחנה לויה ומשה לוי היה וקאמר (עמי) [עמו] ל"ה: ואשכח קרא דאמר ותני פי' בהארכת זמן כלומר דקרא כתיב כשהב"ה מאריך זמן עד ג' פעמים הלכך הו"ל ג' שנים:

דלמא

עין משפט נר מצוה

טז א מיי' פ"ג מהל' סוטה הל"ח ופ"ד הלכה ט:

יז ב מיי' שם פ"ג הל"ח ופ"ד הל"ד והל' יא סמג עשין נו:

יח ג מיי' פ"ג שם ופ"ד הל"א:

יט ד מיי' פ"ג מהל' גירושין הל"א סמג עשין נ טוש"ע אה"ע סי' קלא סעי' ב:

כ ה מיי' פ"ג מהל' בית הבחירה הל"ט ופ"ג מהל' ביאת מקדש הלכה ד סמג לאוין רעג ועשין קעד:

כא ו מיי' פ"ג מהל' סוטה הל"ב:

מסורת הש"ס

גיטין כד. ערכין יג.

[גיטין כ. וש"נ]

[לעיל יט:]

[לעיל ו. לקמן כב:]

[לעיל יט:]

תוספתא דכלים פ"א ע"ש פסחים סז. נזיר מה.

מגילה טו.

נדה לט. עא.

[ע' סנהדרין קז:]

ב"ב ד.

בס"י ובירושלמי איתא כל אותן י"ב חודש

גליון הש"ס

גמ' והתניא טמא מת. ע' זבחים ל' ע"א תד"ה ובטומאות: תוס' ד"ה ביעתותא כו' כל הנשים צ"ל האנשים:

הֵן תֶּהֱוֵי אַרְכָא לִשְׁלֵוְתָךְ", וּכְתִיב: °"כֹּלָּא מְטָא עַל נְבוּכַדְנֶצַּר מַלְכָּא", וּכְתִיב: °"לִקְצָת יַרְחִין תְּרֵי עֲשַׂר"! לְעוֹלָם רַבִּי יִשְׁמָעֵאל, וְאַשְׁכַּח קְרָא דְּאָמַר וְתָנֵי, דִּכְתִיב: °"כֹּה אָמַר ה' עַל שְׁלֹשָׁה פִּשְׁעֵי אֱדוֹם". וּמַאי אע"פ שֶׁאֵין רְאָיָה לַדָּבָר זֵכֶר לַדָּבָר? דִּלְמָא שָׁאנֵי גּוֹיִם דְּלָא מַפְקִיד דִּינָא עֲלַיְיהוּ. § "וְיֵשׁ זְכוּת תּוֹלָה ג' שָׁנִים" כו'. § זְכוּת דְּמַאי? אִילֵימָא זְכוּת דְּתוֹרָה — הָא [א] אֵינָהּ מְצֻוָּוה וְעוֹשָׂה הִיא! אֶלָּא זְכוּת דְּמִצְוָה — זְכוּת דְּמִצְוָה מִי מַגְנָא כּוּלֵּי הַאי? וְהָתַנְיָא: אֶת זוֹ דָּרַשׁ רַבִּי מְנַחֵם בַּר יוֹסֵי: °"כִּי נֵר מִצְוָה וְתוֹרָה אוֹר", תָּלָה הַכָּתוּב אֶת הַמִּצְוָה בְּנֵר, וְאֶת הַתּוֹרָה בְּאוֹר; אֶת הַמִּצְוָה בְּנֵר — לוֹמַר לְךָ: מַה נֵּר אֵינָהּ *מְגִינָּה אֶלָּא לְפִי שָׁעָה — אַף מִצְוָה אֵינָהּ מְגִינָּה אֶלָּא לְפִי שָׁעָה. וְאֶת הַתּוֹרָה בְּאוֹר, לוֹמַר לְךָ: מָה אוֹר *מֵגֵין לְעוֹלָם — אַף תּוֹרָה מְגִינָּה לְעוֹלָם, וְאוֹמֵר: °"בְּהִתְהַלֶּכְךָ תַּנְחֶה אוֹתָךְ" וגו'; "בְּהִתְהַלֶּכְךָ תַּנְחֶה אוֹתָךְ" — זֶה הָעוה"ז, "בְּשָׁכְבְּךָ תִּשְׁמוֹר עָלֶיךָ" — זוֹ מִיתָה, "וַהֲקִיצוֹתָ הִיא תְשִׂיחֶךָ" — לֶעָתִיד לָבֹא. מָשָׁל לְאָדָם שֶׁהָיָה מְהַלֵּךְ בְּאִישׁוֹן לַיְלָה וַאֲפֵלָה, וּמִתְיָירֵא מִן הַקּוֹצִים וּמִן הַפְּחָתִים וּמִן הַבַּרְקָנִים, וּמֵחַיָּה רָעָה וּמִן (א) הַלִּיסְטִין, וְאֵינוֹ יוֹדֵעַ בְּאֵיזֶה דֶּרֶךְ מְהַלֵּךְ. נִזְדַּמְּנָה לוֹ אֲבוּקָה שֶׁל אוּר — נִיצַּל מִן הַקּוֹצִים וּמִן הַפְּחָתִים וּמִן הַבַּרְקָנִים, וַעֲדַיִין מִתְיָירֵא מֵחַיָּה רָעָה וּמִן הַלִּיסְטִין, וְאֵינוֹ יוֹדֵעַ בְּאֵיזֶה דֶּרֶךְ מְהַלֵּךְ. *כֵּיוָן שֶׁעָלָה עַמּוּד הַשַּׁחַר — נִיצַּל מֵחַיָּה רָעָה וּמִן הַלִּיסְטִין, וַעֲדַיִין אֵינוֹ יוֹדֵעַ בְּאֵיזֶה דֶּרֶךְ מְהַלֵּךְ. הִגִּיעַ לְפָרָשַׁת דְּרָכִים — נִיצַּל מִכּוּלָּם. ד"א: עֲבֵירָה מְכַבָּה מִצְוָה, וְאֵין עֲבֵירָה מְכַבָּה תּוֹרָה, שֶׁנֶּאֱמַר: °"מַיִם רַבִּים לֹא יוּכְלוּ לְכַבּוֹת אֶת הָאַהֲבָה"! א"ר יוֹסֵף: מִצְוָה, בְּעִידָּנָא דְּעָסֵיק בָּהּ — מַגְנָא וּמַצְלָא, בְּעִידָּנָא דְּלָא עָסֵיק בָּהּ — אַגּוֹנֵי מַגְנָא, אַצּוֹלֵי לָא מַצְלָא. תּוֹרָה, בֵּין בְּעִידָּנָא דְּעָסֵיק בָּהּ וּבֵין בְּעִידָּנָא דְּלָא עָסֵיק בָּהּ — מַגְנָא וּמַצְלָא. מַתְקִיף לָהּ *רַבָּה: אֶלָּא מֵעַתָּה, דּוֹאֵג וַאֲחִיתוֹפֶל מִי לָא עָסְקֵי בַּתּוֹרָה? אַמַּאי לָא הֵגִינָּה עֲלַיְיהוּ? אֶלָּא אָמַר רָבָא: תּוֹרָה, בְּעִידָּנָא דְּעָסֵיק בָּהּ — מַגְנָא וּמַצְלָא, בְּעִידָּנָא דְּלָא עָסֵיק בָּהּ — אַגּוֹנֵי מַגְנָא, אַצּוֹלֵי לָא מַצְלָא. מִצְוָה, בֵּין בְּעִידָּנָא דְּעָסֵיק בָּהּ בֵּין בְּעִידָּנָא דְּלָא עָסֵיק בָּהּ — אַגּוֹנֵי מַגְנָא, אַצּוֹלֵי לָא מַצְלָא. רָבִינָא אָמַר: לְעוֹלָם זְכוּת תּוֹרָה. וּדְקָאָמְרַתְּ אֵינָהּ מְצֻוָּוה וְעוֹשָׂה, נְהִי [ב] דְּפִקּוּדֵי לָא מִפַּקְּדָא — בְּאַגְרָא *דְּמַקְרְיָין וּמַתְנְיָין בְּנַיְיהוּ, וְנָטְרָן לְהוּ לְגַבְרַיְיהוּ עַד דְּאָתוּ מִבֵּי מִדְרְשָׁא — מִי לָא פַּלְגָאן בַּהֲדַיְיהוּ? מַאי פָּרָשַׁת דְּרָכִים? א"ר חִסְדָּא: זֶה ת"ח וְיוֹם מִיתָה. רַב נַחְמָן בַּר יִצְחָק אָמַר: זֶה ת"ח וְיִרְאַת חֵטְא. מָר זוּטְרָא אָמַר: זֶה ת"ח דְּסַלְקָא לֵיהּ שְׁמַעְתְּתָא אַלִּיבָּא דְּהִלְכְתָא. "ד"א עֲבֵירָה מְכַבָּה מִצְוָה וְאֵין עֲבֵירָה מְכַבָּה תּוֹרָה". א"ר יוֹסֵף: דַּרְשַׁהּ רַבִּי מְנַחֵם בַּר יוֹסֵי לְהַאי קְרָא כִּי סִינַי, *וְאִילְמָלֵא דַּרְשׁוּהּ דּוֹאֵג וַאֲחִיתוֹפֶל הָכִי לָא רָדְפוּ בָּתַר דָּוִד, דִּכְתִיב: °"לֵאמֹר אֱלֹהִים עֲזָבוֹ" וגו'. מַאי דְּרוּשׁ — °"וְלֹא יִרְאֶה בְךָ עֶרְוַת דָּבָר" וגו', וְהֵן אֵינָן יוֹדְעִין שֶׁעֲבֵירָה מְכַבָּה מִצְוָה וְאֵין עֲבֵירָה מְכַבָּה תּוֹרָה. מַאי °"בּוֹז יָבוּזוּ לוֹ"? אָמַר עוּלָּא: לֹא כְּשִׁמְעוֹן אֲחִי עֲזַרְיָה, וְלֹא כְּר' יוֹחָנָן דְּבֵי נְשִׂיאָה, אֶלָּא כְּהִלֵּל וְשֶׁבְנָא. דְּכִי אֲתָא רַב דִּימִי אֲמַר: הִלֵּל וְשֶׁבְנָא אַחֵי הֲווֹ, הִלֵּל עָסַק בַּתּוֹרָה, שֶׁבְנָא עֲבַד עִיסְקָא. לְסוֹף א"ל: תָּא נֶעֱרוֹב וְלִיפְלוֹג! יָצְתָה בַּת קוֹל וְאָמְרָה: °"אִם יִתֵּן אִישׁ אֶת כָּל הוֹן בֵּיתוֹ" וגו'. § אוֹמֵר

(Margin references: דניאל ד; שם; עמוס א; משלי ו; שם; שיר ח; תהלים עא; דברים כג; שיר ח; שם)

רש"י

הֵן תֶּהֱוֵי אַרְכָא לִשְׁלֵוְתָךְ. וְאָז תְּהֵא אוֹרֶךְ זְמַן לְשַׁלְוָתְךָ, שֶׁלֹּא יָבֹאוּ עָלֶיךָ הַפּוּרְעָנוּת. וְכֵן עָשָׂה נְבוּכַדְנֶצַּר, הָיָה מְקַבֵּץ בְּכָל יוֹם עֲנִיֵּי יִשְׂרָאֵל שֶׁהֵבִיא בַּגּוֹלָה וְהָיוּ צְרִיכִין מְזוֹנוֹת, וּמְפַרְנְסָם. וְאַף דָּנִיֵּאל כְּשֶׁהֵשִׂיאוֹ עֵצָה זוֹ — לְכָךְ נִתְכַּוֵּין, שֶׁרָאָה אֶת יִשְׂרָאֵל בַּגּוֹלָה מְחַזְּרִין עַל הַפְּתָחִים. וּכְתִיב כּוֹלָּא מְטָא. כָּל הַפּוּרְעָנוּת הִגִּיעַ עַל נְבוּכַדְנֶצַּר. לִקְצָת יַרְחִין תְּרֵי עֲשַׂר. אַלְמָא תָּלָה לוֹ הַזְּכוּת י"ב חֹדֶשׁ. לְעוֹלָם. מַתְנִי' דְּקָתָנֵי ג' שָׁנִים — ר' יִשְׁמָעֵאל הִיא. וְאַשְׁכַּח קְרָא דְּאָמַר וְתָנֵי. שׁוֹנֶה בְּהַאֲרָכַת זְמַן. כְּלוֹמַר, מִקְרָא כָּתוּב שֶׁהקב"ה מַאֲרִיךְ זְמַן עַד ג' פְּעָמִים, הִלְכָּךְ הָווּ לְהוּ ג' שָׁנִים. דְּלָא מְפַקֵּיד דִּינָא עֲלַיְיהוּ. אֵין מְמַהֲרִין מִן הַשָּׁמַיִם לִפְקוֹד עֲוֹנוֹתָם עֲלֵיהֶם בָּעוֹלָם הַזֶּה. אֲבָל מִיִּשְׂרָאֵל מְמַהֲרִין לִיפָּרַע בָּעוה"ז וּמְדַקְדְּקִין אַחֲרֵיהֶם. זְכוּת דְּמַאי. מְגִינָּה כָּל כָּךְ. זְכוּת דְּתוֹרָה. שֶׁהָיְתָה עוֹסֶקֶת בַּתּוֹרָה. הָא לָא מִפַּקְדָא. דִּכְתִיב: "וְלִמַּדְתֶּם אוֹתָם אֶת בְּנֵיכֶם" (דברים יא) — וְלֹא אֶת בְּנוֹתֵיכֶם. וְכֵיוָן דְּאֵינָהּ מְצוּוָּה — אֵין שְׂכָרָהּ גָּדוֹל כִּמְצוּוֶּה וְעוֹשֶׂה. הִיא תְשִׂיחֶךָ. תָּלִין בַּעַדְךָ אֶת זְכוּתְךָ. פְּחָתִים. גּוּמּוֹת. נִזְדַּמְּנָה לוֹ אֲבוּקָה שֶׁל אוּר. כָּךְ, זָכָה לְקַיֵּים מִצְוָה — נִיצַּל מִמִּקְצָת פּוּרְעָנִיּוֹת. וַעֲדַיִין מִתְיָירֵא מֵחַיָּה רָעָה וּמִן הַלִּיסְטִין. שֶׁדַּרְכָּן לֵילֵךְ בַּלַּיְלָה, פֶּן יִפְגְּעוּ בּוֹ, דִּכְתִיב: "תָּשֶׁת חוֹשֶׁךְ וִיהִי לָיְלָה בּוֹ תִרְמוֹשׂ כָּל חַיְתוֹ יָעַר" (תהלים קד). הִגִּיעַ עַמּוּד הַשַּׁחַר. וְאַף כָּאן, זָכָה לַתּוֹרָה — נִיצַּל מִן הַחֵטְא וּמִן הַיִּסּוּרִין. וַעֲדַיִין אֵינוֹ יוֹדֵעַ כו'. שֶׁמָּא יִכְפֶּנּוּ יִצְרוֹ לִיבָּטֵל, וְיָשִׁיב עָלָיו יצה"ר וּפוּרְעָנוּת. הִגִּיעַ לְפָרָשַׁת דְּרָכִים. וְשָׁם הִכִּיר אֶת דַּרְכּוֹ. וְאַף כָּאן, הִגִּיעַ לְיוֹם הַמִּיתָה וְלֹא פֵּירַשׁ מִן הַתּוֹרָה עַד יוֹם מוֹתוֹ — נִיצַּל מִכּוּלָּן. וְהָכִי מְפָרֵשׁ לָהּ לְקַמֵּיהּ. עֲבֵירָה מְכַבָּה. שְׂכַר מִצְוָה. וְאֵין עֲבֵירָה מְכַבָּה. שְׂכַר מִי שֶׁעָסַק בַּתּוֹרָה קוֹדֶם לָכֵן. אַלְמָא, מִצְוָה לָא מַגְנָא כּוּלֵּי הַאי. לְכַבּוֹת אֶת הָאַהֲבָה. זוֹ תּוֹרָה, דִּכְתִיב (שיר ב): "הֱבִיאַנִי אֶל בֵּית הַיָּיִן וְדִגְלוֹ עָלַי אַהֲבָה". יַיִן — סוֹד. אָמַר רַב יוֹסֵף. לְעוֹלָם מְגִינָּה עַל הַיִּסּוּרִין הַרְבֵּה, וּמַאי "אֵינָהּ מְגִינָּה" דְּקָאָמַר (ב) ת"ק — מִן הַחֵטְא, שֶׁלֹּא יִתְקְפֶנּוּ יצה"ר קָאָמַר. מִצְוָה בְּעִידָּנָא דְּעָסֵיק בָּהּ. וְהַיְינוּ "לְפִי שָׁעָה" דְּקָאָמַר — מַגְנָא מִן הַיִּסּוּרִין, וּמַצְלָא מִיצה"ר, שֶׁלֹּא יַכְשִׁילֶנּוּ לַחֵטְא. בְּעִידָּנָא דְּלָא עָסֵיק בָּהּ. מִשֶּׁנִּגְמַר הַמִּצְוָה וְאֵינוֹ עָסוּק בָּהּ — אַגּוֹנֵי מַגְנָא מִן הַפּוּרְעָנוּת, אַצּוֹלֵי לָא מַצְלָא. וּדְקָתָנֵי בַּבָּרַיְיתָא: עֲבֵירָה מְכַבָּה מִצְוָה — לָאו מִלְּהָגֵן מִן הַיִּסּוּרִין קָאָמַר, אֶלָּא מִלִּיטּוֹל שָׂכָר לֶעָתִיד. אַמַּאי לָא תָּגֵין עֲלֵיהֶן. מִיֵּצֶר הָרַע, שֶׁהֶחֱטִיאָם וַעֲשָׂאָם רְשָׁעִים גְּמוּרִים. כְּלוֹמַר, אַמַּאי לֹא תַּצִּילֵהוּ מִן הָעֲבֵירוֹת? לְעוֹלָם זְכוּת דְּתוֹרָה. וְלֹא שֶׁעוֹסֶקֶת בַּתּוֹרָה, אֶלָּא שֶׁטּוֹרַחַת בִּבְנָהּ וּבְבַעְלָהּ שֶׁיַּעַסְקוּ. דְּמַקְרְיָאן וּמַתְנְיָאן. שֶׁטּוֹרְחוֹת עַל בְּנֵיהֶן לַהֲבִיאָן לְבֵית הַסֵּפֶר לִקְרוֹא מִקְרָא וְלִשְׁנוֹת מִשְׁנָה. וְנָטְרָן לְגַבְרַיְיהוּ. וּמַמְתִּינוֹת לְבַעֲלֵיהֶן שֶׁיּוֹצְאִין לְעִיר אַחֶרֶת לִלְמוֹד תּוֹרָה. מַאי פָּרָשַׁת דְּרָכִים. מַהוּ מְדַמֶּה לְ"הִגִּיעַ לְפָרָשַׁת דְּרָכִים"? דְּהָא, אֲבוּקָה — הַיְינוּ מִצְוָה, עַמּוּד הַשַּׁחַר — הַיְינוּ תּוֹרָה, אֶלָּא פָּרָשַׁת דְּרָכִים מַאי הִיא? וְיוֹם הַמִּיתָה. וְהוּא תַּלְמִיד חָכָם בְּיוֹם מוֹתוֹ, וְיָדַע שֶׁלֹּא פֵּירַשׁ לִפְרוֹק מֵעָלָיו עוֹל תּוֹרָה. וְיִרְאַת חֵטְא. זָכָה לְיִרְאַת חֵטְא אַחַר שֶׁזָּכָה לַתּוֹרָה — נִיצַּל מִכּוּלָּן. שֶׁהַתּוֹרָה מְלַמַּדְתּוֹ דִּבְרֵי מִצְוָה וְדִבְרֵי אִיסּוּר, וּמַה שֶּׁהוּא צָרִיךְ לִפְרוֹשׁ, וְיִרְאַת חֵטְא מוֹנְעוֹ מִלִּרְדּוֹף אַחֲרֵי יִצְרוֹ. דְּסַלְקָא לֵיהּ שְׁמַעְתְּתָא אַלִּיבָּא דְּהִלְכְתָא. וה"ק: עָלָה עַמּוּד הַשַּׁחַר נִיצּוֹל מִן הַחַיָּה כו', זָכָה לַתּוֹרָה — נִיצּוֹל מיצה"ר וּמִן הַחֵטְא. וַעֲדַיִין אֵינוֹ יוֹדֵעַ בְּאֵיזוֹ דֶּרֶךְ מְהַלֵּךְ — אִם יִזְכֶּה שֶׁיְּסַיְּיעוּהוּ מִן הַשָּׁמַיִם לְהִתְקַבֵּל דְּבָרָיו בֵּין חֲבֵירָיו, לְהוֹרוֹת כַּהֲלָכָה וְכַמִּשְׁפָּט. הִגִּיעַ לְפָרָשַׁת דְּרָכִים — כְּלוֹמַר, זָכָה לְכָךְ — נִיצּוֹל מִכּוּלָּם. לֵאמֹר אֱלֹהִים עֲזָבוֹ. כָּךְ הָיוּ אוֹמְרִים עָלָיו: אֱלֹהִים עֲזָבוֹ שֶׁבָּא עַל אֵשֶׁת אִישׁ, וְאֵין אָנוּ נֶעֱנָשִׁין עָלָיו. "רִדְפוּ וְתִפְשׂוּהוּ כִּי אֵין מַצִּיל" — אֵין לוֹ זְכוּת שֶׁיַּצִּילֶנּוּ, שֶׁהָעֲבֵירָה כִּבְּתָה זְכֻיּוֹתָיו. לֹא יִרְאֶה בְךָ. עֲבֵירָה, וְאִם יִרְאֶה — וְשָׁב מֵאַחֲרֶיךָ. שִׁמְעוֹן אֲחִי עֲזַרְיָה. תַּנָּא הוּא, בְּמִשְׁנָה קַמַּיְיתָא דִּזְבָחִים, וְלָמַד תּוֹרָה עַל יְדֵי אָחִיו שֶׁהָיָה עוֹסֵק בִּפְרַקְמַטְיָא, כְּדֵי שֶׁיַּחֲלוֹק בִּזְכוּת לִמּוּדוֹ שֶׁל שִׁמְעוֹן — לְכָךְ הוּא נִקְרָא עַל שֵׁם עֲזַרְיָה אָחִיו. וְכֵן ר' יוֹחָנָן לָמַד ע"י הַנָּשִׂיא שֶׁהָיָה מְפַרְנְסוֹ. הִלֵּל עָסַק בַּתּוֹרָה. מִתּוֹךְ עוֹנִי רַב, כִּדְמְפָרֵשׁ בְּמַסֶּ' יוֹמָא (דף לה:). לִימְדָהּ

תוספות

מצוה בין בעידנא דעסיק בה בין בעידנא דלא עסיק בה אגוני מגנא אצולי לא מצלא. ותימה: מאי האי דקתני בברייתא: תלה את המצוה בנר, מה נר אינה מגינה אלא לפי שעה — אף מצוה אינה מגינה אלא לפי שעה? אי מיצר הרע — אינה מגינה כלל, אי מן הפורענות — מגינה לעולם! ותורה נמי, למה תלאה הכתוב באור משום דמגינה לעולם? אי מן הפורענות — מצוה נמי מגנא לעולם, ואי (ג) מיצר הרע דמצלא — הא לא מצלא אלא לפי שעה!

זה תלמיד חכם דסלקא ליה שמעתתא אליבא דהלכתא. תימה: והיאך ניצול מכולן? והלא לא ניצול מיצר הרע בעידנא דלא עסיק בתורה! וי"ל: סתם תלמיד חכם תורתו אומנתו, ועוסק בה ומהרהר כל שעה, ואינו הולך ד' אמות בלא תורה.

והן אינן יודעין שעבירה מכבה מצוה. תימה: והא אמר לעיל, בין לרב יוסף בין לרבא: מצוה אגוני מגנא מן הפורענות אפילו בעידנא דלא עסיק בה, ועבירה מכבה מצוה — לאו מלהגין מן היסורין קאמר, אלא מליטול שכר לעתיד לבא, כמו שפרש"י!

תוספות שאנץ

דלא מפקד דינא עליהו ואין ממהרין מן השמים לפקוד עונותיהם עליהם בעולם הזה אבל בישראל ממהרין ליפרע בעולם הזה ומדקדקין אחריהם. אלא מעתה דואג ואחיתופל כו' אמאי לא מגין עלייהו מגין לאו דוקא אלא ר"ל אמאי לא מציל עליהו: אלמלי דרשו דואג ואחיתופל הכי לא רדפו בתר דוד מאי דרוש וכו'. נראה דל"ג דואג שהרי על מעשה בת שבע קיימין הכא ודואג מת כבר ועברו ימים רבים כדאמר בחלק דואג ואחיתופל לא ראו זה את זה שדואג היה בימי שאול ואחיתופל בימי דוד ובת שבע היתה בת אליעם והוא היה בן אחיתופל כדכתיב בפסוק וכן מוכח (כרי' בן מומי) ולא מצינו שעשה דוד רק בדבר אוריה החתי וקרא דלא יהיה בך ערות דבר איירי בערוה ממש. והיינו במעשה בת שבע לפי' ל"ג דואג ואע"ג שכתוב בכל הספרים אלא (בי) אחיתופל לבד. לא כשמעון אחי עזריה תנא הוא ולמד תורה על ידי אחיו שהיה עוסק בפרקמטיא ומפרנסו כדי שיחלוק בזכות למודו של שמעון לכך נקרא על שם עזריה אחיו. וכן ר' יוחנן למד על ידי נשיא שהיה מפרנסו: הלל עסק בתורה מתוך עוני כדאמר ביומא (א) בשמיהו שנאמר ושם רשעים ירקב ואומר פי' ר"ג שפי' ושבנא דתרי שבנא הוו שבנא הסופר צדיק היה כדכתיב לך בא אל הסוכן הזה ואל שבנא אשר על הבית. וכתיב ויצא אל אליקים אשר על הבית ושבנא הסופר כשיצאו אל רבשקא. אלמא אחר היה שבימי שבנא הראשון לא היה אליקים על הבית. ומיהו אומר הר' אלחנן דשבנא הראשון ושבנא אשר על הבית אחד הוה והא דכתיב אליקים אשר על הבית היינו שסופו היה על הבית.

א) נ"ל ושבנא וא"ת והא שבנא רשע היה ולא מסקינן בשמיה וכו' ואומר ר"י דתרי שבנא הוו וכו'.

עין משפט נר מצוה

כב א מיי' פ"א מהל' ת"ת הלכ' א ופ"ג מהל' סוטה הלכה כ סמג עשין יב טוש"ע י"ד סימן רמו סעיף ו:

כג ב מיי' פ"ג מהל' סוטה הלכה כ:

מסורת הש"ס

[נ"ל מאירה קן גירסת הילקוט]

[נ"ל מאיר כ"א בע"י]

[נ"ל רבא]

[ברכות יז.]

[נ"ל ואילמלי ע' תוספות מגילה כח.]

הגהות הב"ח

(א) גמ' הליסטים כנ"ל וכן בכל הענין: (ב) רש"י ד"ה אמר רב יוסף וכו' דקאמר בלישנא קמא: (ג) תוס' ד"ה מצוה וכו' ואי דמצלא מיצר הרע לא מגלא:

גליון הש"ס

גמ' כיון שעלה עמוד השחר. עיין פסחים ב ע"א ברש"י ד"ה בכי טוב:

[שייך במשנה דלעיל כ.]

כד א מיי' פכ"א מהל' סנהדרין הלכה ז סמג לאוין רח טוש"ע ח"מ סימן יז סעיף ה:

כה ב מיי' פ"ט מהל' מתנות עניים הלכה יג סמג עשין קסה טוש"ע י"ד סי' רנג סעיף א:

כו ג מיי' פי"ט מהלכות אישות הלכה יט סמג עשין מח נו טוש"ע אה"ע סימן קיב סעיף יד:

[ג"ז שייך שם]

כז ד ה מיי' פי"ב מהל' זכייה ומתנה הלכה ט טוש"ע אה"ע סי' לא סעיף ב וטוש"ע ח"מ סי' רמח סעיף א וסעיף ג:

תורה אור

"אוֹמֵר בֶּן עַזַּאי חַיָּיב אָדָם לְלַמֵּד אֶת וכו'. ר' אֱלִיעֶזֶר אוֹמֵר כָּל הַמְלַמֵּד אֶת בִּתּוֹ תּוֹרָה מְלַמְּדָהּ תִּיפְלוּת". § תִּיפְלוּת ס"ד?! אֶלָּא אֵימָא: כְּאִילּוּ לִמְּדָהּ תִּיפְלוּת. א"ר אֲבָהוּ: מ"ט דְּר"א — דִּכְתִיב: °"אֲנִי חָכְמָה שָׁכַנְתִּי עָרְמָה", כֵּיוָן שֶׁנִּכְנְסָה חָכְמָה בְּאָדָם — נִכְנְסָה עִמּוֹ עַרְמוּמִית. וְרַבָּנַן, הַאי "אֲנִי חָכְמָה" מַאי עָבְדִי לֵיהּ? מִיבָּעֵי לֵיהּ לְכִדְרַבִּי יוֹסֵי בְּר' חֲנִינָא. דְּא"ר יוֹסֵי בְּר' חֲנִינָא: אֵין דִּבְרֵי תוֹרָה מִתְקַיְּימִין אֶלָּא בְּמִי שֶׁמַּעֲמִיד עַצְמוֹ עָרוֹם עֲלֵיהֶן, שֶׁנֶּאֱמַר: "אֲנִי חָכְמָה שָׁכַנְתִּי עָרְמָה". א"ר יוֹחָנָן: אֵין דִּבְרֵי תוֹרָה מִתְקַיְּימִין אֶלָּא בְּמִי שֶׁמֵּשִׂים עַצְמוֹ כְּמִי שֶׁאֵינוֹ, שֶׁנֶּאֱמַר: °"וְהַחָכְמָה מֵאַיִן תִּמָּצֵא". § "רַבִּי יְהוֹשֻׁעַ אוֹמֵר: רוֹצָה אִשָּׁה" וכו'. § מַאי קָאָמַר? הָכִי קָאָמַר: *רוֹצָה אִשָּׁה בְּקַב וְתִיפְלוּת עִמּוֹ, מִתִּשְׁעַת קַבִּין וּפְרִישׁוּת. § "הוּא הָיָה אוֹמֵר: חָסִיד שׁוֹטֶה" כו'. § הֵיכִי דָּמֵי חָסִיד שׁוֹטֶה? כְּגוֹן דְּקָא טָבְעָה אִיתְּתָא בְּנַהֲרָא, וְאָמַר: לָאו אוֹרַח אַרְעָא לְאִיסְתַּכּוּלֵי בָּהּ וְאַצּוֹלַהּ. הֵיכִי דָּמֵי רָשָׁע עָרוּם? אָמַר רַבִּי *יוֹחָנָן: אזֶה הַמַּטְעִים דְּבָרָיו לַדַּיָּין קוֹדֶם שֶׁיָּבֹא בַּעַל דִּין חֲבֵירוֹ. ר' אֲבָהוּ אוֹמֵר: זֶה הַנּוֹתֵן דִּינָר לְעָנִי לְהַשְׁלִים לוֹ מָאתַיִם זוּז. דִּתְנַן: *במִי שֶׁיֵּשׁ לוֹ מָאתַיִם זוּז — לֹא יִטּוֹל לֶקֶט שִׁכְחָה וּפֵאָה וּמַעֲשַׂר עָנִי. הָיָה לוֹ מָאתַיִם חָסֵר דִּינָר, אֲפִילּוּ אֶלֶף נוֹתְנִין לוֹ כְּאַחַת — הֲרֵי זֶה יִטּוֹל. רַבִּי אַסִּי אָמַר רַבִּי יוֹחָנָן: זֶה הַמַּשִּׂיא עֵצָה לִמְכּוֹר בִּנְכָסִים מוּעָטִין. דְּאָמַר רַבִּי אַסִּי א"ר יוֹחָנָן: *גיְתוֹמִים שֶׁקָּדְמוּ וּמָכְרוּ בִּנְכָסִים מוּעָטִין, מַה שֶּׁמָּכְרוּ — מָכְרוּ. אַבַּיֵי אָמַר: *דזֶה הַמַּשִּׂיא עֵצָה לִמְכּוֹר בִּנְכָסִים כְּרַבָּן שִׁמְעוֹן בֶּן גַּמְלִיאֵל. דְּתַנְיָא: "נְכָסַי לְךָ וְאַחֲרֶיךָ לִפְלוֹנִי", וְיָרַד הָרִאשׁוֹן וּמָכַר וְאָכַל — הַשֵּׁנִי מוֹצִיא מִיַּד הַלָּקוֹחוֹת, דִּבְרֵי רַבִּי. רשב"ג אוֹמֵר: האֵין לַשֵּׁנִי אֶלָּא מַה שֶּׁשִּׁיֵּיר רִאשׁוֹן. רַב יוֹסֵף בַּר חָמָא אָמַר רַב שֵׁשֶׁת: זֶה הַמַּכְרִיעַ אֲחֵרִים בְּאוֹרְחוֹתָיו. רַבִּי זְרִיקָא אָמַר רַב הוּנָא: זֶה הַמֵּיקֵל לְעַצְמוֹ וּמַחְמִיר לַאֲחֵרִים. עוּלָּא אָמַר: זֶה

שֶׁקָּרָא

לִימְּדָהּ תִּיפְלוּת ס"ד. וְכִי תּוֹרָה תִּיפְלוּת קָרָא לָהּ?!. **כְּאִילּוּ.** שֶׁמִּתּוֹכָהּ הִיא מְבִינָה עַרְמוּמִית, וְעוֹשָׂה דְּבָרֶיהָ בְּהֶלְנֵעַ. **חָכְמָה.** תּוֹרָה. **שֶׁמַּעֲמִיד עַצְמוֹ עָרוֹם עָלֶיהָ.** שֶׁפֵּירַשׁ מִכָּל עֲסָקִים וְנַעֲשָׂה עָלֶיהָ עָנִי וַחֲסַר כֹּל. [ל"א: שֶׁמֵּשִׂים עַצְמוֹ עָרוֹם עָלֶיהָ גָּרְסִי'], שֶׁמַּעֲרִים שֶׁיִּתְקַיֵּים תּוֹרָתוֹ, לִקְבּוֹץ עַל יָד וְלִלְמוֹד מִכָּל אָדָם. **מֵאַיִן תִּמָּצֵא.** מִן הֶעָשׂוּי כְּאַיִן. **רוֹצָה אִשָּׁה בְּקַב וְתִיפְלוּת.** חֲפֵיצָה לִיזּוֹן בִּמְזוֹנוֹת מוּעָטִין וִיהֵא תִּיפְלוּתָהּ מָצוּי לָהּ בְּתַשְׁמִישׁ, מִט' קַבִּין וּפְרִישׁוּת — לִפְרוֹשׁ מִן הַתִּיפְלוּת. לְפִיכָךְ אֵין טוֹב שֶׁתִּלְמוֹד תּוֹרָה. **שֶׁמַּטְעִים דְּבָרָיו לַדַּיָּין.** דְּמִשֶּׁנִּקְבְּעוּ בְּלֵב הַדַּיָּין שַׁעֲרֵי זְכִיּוֹתָיו לִדְבָרָיו שֶׁל זֶה — קָשֶׁה לְסַלְּקָן, וַהֲרֵי עַרְמוּתוֹ. וְרָשָׁע הוּא, שֶׁעוֹבֵר עַל "לֹא תִשָּׂא שֵׁמַע שָׁוְא" (שמות כג). **לְהַשְׁלִים מָאתַיִם זוּז.** וּמֵעַתָּה לֹא יִטּוֹל לֶקֶט, וְיֵשׁ לוֹ קְרוֹבִים שֶׁיִּטְּלוּם. **בִּנְכָסִים מוּעָטִין.** דִּתְנַן (ב"ב דף קלט:): מִי שֶׁמֵּת וְהִנִּיחַ בָּנִים וּבָנוֹת, בִּזְמַן שֶׁהַנְּכָסִים מְרוּבִּין — הַבָּנִים יִרְשׁוּ וְהַבָּנוֹת יִזּוֹנוּ, נְכָסִים מוּעָטִין — הַבָּנוֹת יִזּוֹנוּ וְהַבָּנִים יִשְׁאֲלוּ עַל הַפְּתָחִים. **שֶׁקָּדְמוּ וּמָכְרוּ.** קוֹדֶם שֶׁבָּאוּ הַבָּנוֹת לְב"ד וְהֶעֱמִידוּם ב"ד לַנְּכָסִים בְּחֶזְקַת בָּנוֹת. **הַמַּכְרִיעַ אֲחֵרִים בְּאוֹרְחוֹתָיו.** "רְאוּ וַעֲשׂוּ כָּמוֹנִי וּלְכוּ בִּדְרָכַי". לֹא נִתְכַּוֵּין זֶה אֶלָּא לְהַרְאוֹת עַצְמוֹ כְּחָסִיד בְּעֵינֵי הַבְּרִיּוֹת, וְאֵין תּוֹכוֹ כְּבָרוֹ, אֶלָּא שֶׁלֹּא יְדַקְדְּקוּ אַחֲרָיו לִבְדּוֹק בְּתוֹעֲבוֹתָיו.

שֶׁקָּרָא

*בן עזאי אומר חייב אדם וכו'. ירושלמי: דבן עזאי דלא כר"א בן עזריה, דדריש (חגיגה דף ג.): "הקהל את העם האנשים והנשים והטף", אנשים באו ללמוד, נשים לשמוע. ונראה דפי' דמלוה לשמוע הנשים כדי שידעו לקיים מלוה, ולא משום שידעו שזכות תולה[א]. מטרונה שאלה את ר' אלעזר: מפני מה [ב] חטא אחת במעשה העגל והן מתין בה ג' מיתות? אמר לה: אין אשה חכמה אלא בפלך. אמר לו הורקנוס בנו: בשביל שלא להשיבה דבר אחד מן התורה אבדת ממני ג' מאות כור מעשר בכל שנה! [ג] א"ל: ישרפו ד"ת ולא ימסרו דברי תורה לנשים.

*רוצה אשה בקב ותיפלות. פר"ח: רוצה אשה שיהא בעלה חמר ויהא מצוי אצלה בכל שבת לתת לה עונתה, ולא יביא לה אלא קב חטים בלבד. ולא יהא גמל שהולך בדרך רחוקה, ואינו נותן לה עונה אלא אחת לשלשים יום. ואע"פ שמביא לה לשכרו ט' קבין — חביבה עליה העונה בכל שבת וקב אחד, מט' קבין ופרישות ל' יום. ורבי פירש בשם רב האי: המשרה אשתו ע"י שליש לא יפחות לה מקביים חיטין מן שבת לשבת, כדמוכח בגמרא בפרק "אע"פ" (כתובות דף סד:), ועונתה מצוי לה. ואילו המורד על אשתו (שם סג.) מוסיפין על כתובתה ג' דינרים בשבת, ושער בינוני הוא ד' סאין בסלע, *וסלע ד' דינרים, נמצאת סאה בדינר, וג' סאין בג' דינרים שהן י"ח קבין. הרי שחכמים עמדו על סוף דעתה שהיא רוצה בתיפלות ועמו שני קביים, מי"ח קביים שיפרוש ממנה, דקביים אחד מט' בי"ח קבין. **היכי** דמי חסיד שוטה. ירושלמי: ראה תינוק מבעבע בנהר, אמר: לכשאחלוץ תפילין אצילנו, עד כשהוא חולץ תפילין — הוציא זה את נפשו. **זה** הנותן דינר לעני להשלים לו מאתים זוז. הא דרבי אבהו, והא דרבי יוחנן, ומבריח מזונות מן האלמנה, קרי ירושלמי מכות פרושים. ותו גרס התם: חד תלמיד מדר' בון הוו לו מאתים זוז חסר דינר, והוה רבי יליף למזכי עמיה חד לתלת שנים מעשר מסכני. חד זמן עבדין ביה תלמידיו עין בישא ומלוון ליה. אתא בעי מזכי עמיה היך דהוה יליף. א"ל: רבי, אית לי שיעורא. אמר: זה — מכת פרושים נגעו ביה. רמז לתלמידיו ואעלוניה לקפילין וחסרוניה חד קרט, וזכה עמיה היך דהוה יליף. שנינו בפרק בתרא דמסכת פאה (מ"ט): מי שיש לו חמשים זוז והוא נושא ונותן בהן — ה"ז לא יטול. ובגמרא, *הדא אמר: חמשין דעבדין טבין מן מאתן דלא עבדין. **יתומים** שקדמו ומכרו בנכסים מועטין. ונראה דוקא לענין מזון הבנות אמרינן מה שמכרו מכרו. אבל לענין מזון האשה, כיון דמשועבד לה בעל למזונות בחייו — הנכסים בחזקתם, שאינם יכולין למכור, כדאמרי' בפ' "הנושא" (כתובות קג.): יתומים שמכרו מדור אלמנה — לא עשו ולא כלום. ומ"ש מדר' אסי א"ר יוחנן: יתומים שקדמו ומכרו בנכסים מועטים וכו'? התם לא משתעבדי לה מחיים. אי נמי: בית זה עצמו דרה בו בחיי הבעל, אבל מזונות — בכל יום צריכה למזונות, ולא דמו מזונות אשה למדור. והוא הדין אם מכרו בנכסים מרובין — מה שמכרו מכרו, דמטלטלי לא משתעבדי למזונות. ואמרי' בפ' "מציאת האשה" (שם סט.): בין מכרו בין משכנו — אין מוציאין למזונות. והאי דנקט נכסים מועטין — אורחא דמילתא נקט, דלא מזבין אינש נכסים משום הפסד מזונות היכא דאיכא נכסים מרובים. רבי פי' בתוספותיו דר' יוחנן פליג אההיא דמסקינן בפרק "ב' דייני גזירות" (שם דף קט.), אמר רבי יצחק בן אילעאי משמיה דחזקיה: כל מקום שאמר ר"ג "רואה אני את דברי אדמון" — הלכה כמותו. וגבי נכסים מועטין תנינא התם (דף קח:) ובפרק "מי שמת" (ב"ב קלט:), אמר אדמון וכי בשביל שאני זכר הפסדתי? ואמר ר"ג: רואה אני את דברי אדמון. לא ידענא מאי דוקקיה לפרש כך *אליבא דאדמון טפי מאליבא דרבנן. **אביי** אמר זה המשיא עצה למכור בנכסים כרשב"ג. רשב"ם פי' ב"יש נוחלין" (ב"ב דף קלז.): משום דגרם לעבור על דברי הנותן, וערום — דאהנו מעשיו, והרי הוא חוטא ולא לו. ומיהו, המוכר עצמו, דהיינו ראשון, לא מיקרי רשע, ואף על גב דלכתחילה אסור לעשות כך — דלא חמיר איסוריה, שהרי השליטו הנותן בגוף ופירות לעשות כרצונו. וקשיא לפירושו: בסוף פרק "מי שהיה נשוי" (כתובות דף נה:) דאמר אביי: "נכסי לך ואחריך לפלוני", ועמדה וניסת, בעל לוקח הוי ואין "לאחריך" במקום בעל כלום. ומי אמר אביי הכי? והאמר אביי: איזהו רשע ערום — זה המשיא כו'. מי קאמר תינשא? ניסת קאמר. אלמא דמדמי מוכר עצמו למשיא! ומיהו, יש לפרש: כיון דמשיא נקרא רשע — מכלל דלמוכר אסור לעשות לכתחילה, אע"ג דלא נקרא רשע, כדקתני התם: אין לו לראשון אלא אכילת פירות בלבד. ואי קשיא: מדקאמר אביי: זה המשיא עלה וכו' כרשב"ג — מכלל דאביי ס"ל כרשב"ג, והכי אמר אביי נמי בהדיא בפרק "מי שהיה נשוי" (ג"ש שם): בעל לוקח הוי, ואין "לאחריך" במקום לוקח כלום, וב"יש נוחלין" (ב"ב דף קלז.) מפרש טעמא משום דקסבר קנין פירות כקנין הגוף דמי. ובסוף פרק "השולח" (גיטין דף מח:) אמר אביי: נקטינן, בעל בנכסי אשתו — צריך הרשאה, אע"ג דפירות דידיה הוי — הגוף צריך הרשאה. דמשמע דס"ל דלאו כקנין הגוף דמי! יש לתרץ: דוקא גבי "אחריך" ס"ל לאביי דכקנין הגוף דמי, דאפי' ר"ל דאמר לאו כקנין הגוף דמי — מתרלינן אליביה: "אחריך" שאני, ופי' רשב"ם ד"אחריך" משמע גוף ופירות נתן לראשון, דהא בהדיא פי': אחריך ירש פלוני. ואף הוא פסק שם כרשב"ג, וז"ל: בעלמא סבירא לן דלאו כקנין הגוף דמי, כדפסקי' בפרק "החולץ" (יבמות דף לו:), הכא — "אחריך" שאני. וכן עיקר, דלא תקשי הלכתא אהלכתא, דפסקינן כר"ל פרק "החולץ", והא ד"אחריך" קיימא לן כרשב"ג דפסקי' הלכתא לקמיה, ולא פליג ר"ל. ומדאביי נמי איכא למשמע דהכי קיימא לן, כדאמר אביי: איזהו רשע וכו'. ולקמן נמי, ההיא אתתא דהוה לה דיקלא בארעא דרב ביבי כו', אזל איהו אקנייה לבנו קטן כרשב"ג, עד "אפילו רשב"ג לא קאמר" — מהתם שמעינן דהלכה כרשב"ג, הלכך בעינן לפרושי דרשב"ג ס"ל כר"ל, דלאו כקנין הגוף דמי, והכא היינו טעמא ד"אחריך" שאני, ולא תקשה הלכתא אהלכתא. תימה לר': אמאי לא קא חשיב נמי ההיא ד"אלו הן הנשרפין" (סנהדרין דף עו:), אמר רב כהנא משום ר"ע: איזו עני ורשע ערום — זה המשהה בתו בוגרת? ויש לומר: דעני ורשע לא קא חשיב.

רבי

תוספות שאנץ

מתני' רוצה אשה בקב ותפלות מט' קבין ופרישות חולק היה אבן עזאי דאמר חייב אדם ללמד בתו תורה. ואומר ר' יהושע חפיצה היא בקב במזונות מועטין ויהא תפלותיה מצוי לה שתהא עם בעלה מט' קבין ופרישות לפרוש מן התפלות לפי' אין טוב שתלמוד תורה (ותפלות) פי' הערוך דזה החשבון מצינו במורד על אשתו מתשמיש המטה דמוסיף לה ג' דינרין בשבוע והיינו י"ח קבין דשער בינוני ד' סאין בסלע וסלע ד' דינרין והסאה ששת קבין א"כ הוה להו כ"ד קבין בד' דינרין וי"ח קבין בג' דינרין והמשרה אשתו על ידי שליש שאינו מורד בתשמיש אינו נותן לה אלא ב' קבין וזהו קב לתשעה: **גמ'** למכור בנכסים מועטין. דתנן מי שמת והניח בנים ובנות בזמן שהנכסים מועטים הבנות יזונו והבנים ישאלו על הפתחים. וכשקדמו ומכרו קודם שיבואו הבנות לב"ד מה שמכרו מכרו. וא"כ הוי רשע במשיא עצה לבנים שימכרו בנכסים מועטין ל"ה: זה המכריע אחרים באורחותיו פ"ה שאומ' להם ראו עשו כמוני באורחותי ולא נתכוון זה אלא להראות עצמו כחסיד בעיני הבריות ואין תוכו כברו אלא שלא ידקדקו אחריו לבדוק תועבותיו. ל"ה: זה שקרא ושנה שקרא ושנה משנה ולא שמש תלמידי חכמים ללמוד תלמוד וסברת טעמי המשנה מה הם ורשע הוא שאין תורתו על בורייה ואין למידין הימנו שעל ידי הטעמים יש חילוק באיסור והיתר ובדיני ממונות לזכות ולחייב לטמא ולטהר כדאמר בבמה דוכתין מ"ט אמר מר הכי ומ"ט אמר מר הכי ואמרי מאי בינייהו איכא בינייהו כך וכך ולפי' הוה רשע וערום שהשומע קולו כששונה משניותיו כסבור שבקי בטעמיהם ונוהגין בו כבוד כתלמידי חכמים ל"ה. וי"מ ולא שמש תלמידי חכמים שמוש ממש הרי

ס"א

כתובות סב:

[ברב אלפס איתא רבי חנינא וכן איתא בתנחומא פ' משפטים]

פאה פ"ח מ"ח

כתובות קג. יבמות סז: ב"ב קמ.

כתובות נה: ב"ב קלז. קעד: ערכין כג.

[ר"ל ירושלמי]

אליבא דרבנן טפי מאליבא דאדמון. מהרש"ל.

משלי ח

איוב כח

שמות כג

הגהות מהר"ב רנשבורג

א] תוס' ד"ה בן עזאי אומר חייב אדם וכו' ולא משום שידעו זכות תולה. נ"ב בירושלמי דפרקין בהלכה ד: ב] בא"ד מפני מה חטא אחת במעשה העגל. נ"ב ר"ל החטא היה שזה באותן אחד לבנו והן מתים בסייף ובמגפה ובמיתת הדרוקן: ג] בא"ד אבדת ממני ג' מאות כור מעשר בכל שנה. נ"ב שהאשה חשובה הזאת נתנה מעשרותיה שהיה ג' מאות כור בכל שנה להורקנוס בנו של ר"א ועתה אחרי שלחאה ר"א פסקה מליתן לו:

שֶׁקָּרָא וְשָׁנָה וְלֹא שִׁימֵּשׁ תַּלְמִידֵי חֲכָמִים.§ אִתְּמַר, קָרָא וְשָׁנָה וְלֹא שִׁימֵּשׁ ת"ח, ר' אֶלְעָזָר אוֹמֵר: הֲרֵי זֶה עַם הָאָרֶץ, ר' שְׁמוּאֵל בַּר נַחְמָנִי אָמַר: הֲרֵי זֶה בּוּר, ר' יַנַּאי אוֹמֵר: ה"ז כּוּתִי, רַב אַחָא בַּר יַעֲקֹב אוֹמֵר: הֲרֵי זֶה מָגוֹשׁ. אֲמַר רַב נַחְמָן בַּר יִצְחָק: מִסְתַּבְּרָא כְּרַב אַחָא בַּר יַעֲקֹב, דְּאָמְרִי אֱינָשֵׁי: רָטֵין מָגוֹשָׁא וְלָא יָדַע מַאי אָמַר, תָּנֵי תַנָּא וְלָא יָדַע מַאי אָמַר. ת"ר: *אֵיזֶהוּ ע"ה? כָּל שֶׁאֵינוֹ קוֹרֵא ק"ש שַׁחֲרִית וְעַרְבִית בְּבִרְכוֹתֶיהָ, דִּבְרֵי ר' מֵאִיר. וַחכ"א: כָּל שֶׁאֵינוֹ מַנִּיחַ תְּפִילִּין. בֶּן עַזַּאי אוֹמֵר: כָּל שֶׁאֵין לוֹ צִיצִית בְּבִגְדוֹ. ר' יוֹנָתָן בֶּן יוֹסֵף אָמַר: כָּל שֶׁיֵּשׁ לוֹ בָּנִים וְאֵינוֹ מְגַדְּלָן לְתַלְמוּד תּוֹרָה. *אֲחֵרִים אוֹמְרִים: אֲפִילּוּ קוֹרֵא וְשׁוֹנֶה וְלֹא שִׁימֵּשׁ ת"ח — זֶהוּ ע"ה. קָרָא וְלֹא שָׁנָה — הֲרֵי זֶה בּוּר, לֹא קָרָא וְלֹא שָׁנָה — עָלָיו הַכָּתוּב אוֹמֵר: °"וְזָרַעְתִּי אֶת בֵּית יִשְׂרָאֵל וְאֶת בֵּית יְהוּדָה זֶרַע אָדָם וְזֶרַע בְּהֵמָה".§ °"יְרָא אֶת ה' בְּנִי וָמֶלֶךְ וְעִם שׁוֹנִים אַל תִּתְעָרָב" אָמַר רַבִּי יִצְחָק: אֵלּוּ שֶׁשּׁוֹנִים הֲלָכוֹת. פְּשִׁיטָא! מַהוּ דְּתֵימָא שׁוֹנִין בְּחֵטְא, וְכִדְרַב הוּנָא. *דְּאָמַר רַב הוּנָא: כֵּיוָן שֶׁעָבַר אָדָם עֲבֵירָה וְשָׁנָה בָּהּ — הוּתְּרָה לוֹ, קמ"ל. תָּנָא: הַתַּנָּאִים מְבַלֵּי עוֹלָם. מְבַלֵּי עוֹלָם ס"ד?! אָמַר רָבִינָא: שֶׁמּוֹרִין הֲלָכָה מִתּוֹךְ מִשְׁנָתָן. תַּנְיָא נַמִי הָכִי, א"ר יְהוֹשֻׁעַ: וְכִי מְבַלֵּי עוֹלָם הֵן? וַהֲלֹא מְיַשְּׁבֵי עוֹלָם הֵן, שֶׁנֶּאֱמַר: °"הֲלִיכוֹת עוֹלָם לוֹ"! אֶלָּא שֶׁמּוֹרִין הֲלָכָה מִתּוֹךְ מִשְׁנָתָן.§ "אִשָּׁה פְּרוּשָׁה" וכו'.§ ת"ר: בְּתוּלָה צַלְיָינִית, וְאַלְמָנָה שׁוֹבָבִית, וְקָטָן שֶׁלֹּא כָּלוּ לוֹ חֳדָשָׁיו — הֲרֵי אֵלּוּ מְבַלֵּי עוֹלָם. אִינִי? וְהָאָמַר רַבִּי יוֹחָנָן: לָמַדְנוּ יִרְאַת חֵטְא מִבְּתוּלָה, וְקִיבּוּל שָׂכָר מֵאַלְמָנָה. יִרְאַת חֵטְא מִבְּתוּלָה, דְּר' יוֹחָנָן שְׁמַעָהּ לְהַהִיא בְּתוּלָה דְּנָפְלָה אַאַפַּהּ, וְקָאָמְרָה: רבש"ע, בָּרָאתָ גַּן עֵדֶן וּבָרָאתָ גֵּיהִנָּם, בָּרָאתָ צַדִּיקִים וּבָרָאתָ רְשָׁעִים, יְהִי רָצוֹן מִלְּפָנֶיךָ שֶׁלֹּא יִכָּשְׁלוּ בִּי בְּנֵי אָדָם. קִיבּוּל שָׂכָר מֵאַלְמָנָה — דְּהַהִיא אַלְמָנָה דַּהֲוַאי בֵּי כְנִישְׁתָּא בְּשִׁיבָבוּתָהּ, כָּל יוֹמָא הֲוַת אָתְיָא וּמַצְלָה בֵּי מִדְרָשֵׁיהּ דְּר' יוֹחָנָן. אָמַר לָהּ: בִּתִּי, לֹא בֵּית הַכְּנֶסֶת בְּשִׁיבָבוּתֵךְ? אָמְרָה לֵיהּ: רַבִּי, וְלֹא *שְׂכַר פְּסִיעוֹת יֵשׁ לִי? כִּי קָאָמַר — כְּגוֹן יוֹחָנִי בַּת רְטִיבִי. מַאי "קָטָן שֶׁלֹּא כָּלוּ לוֹ חֳדָשָׁיו"? הָכָא תַּרְגִּימוּ: זֶה ת"ח הַמְבַעֵט בְּרַבּוֹתָיו, רַבִּי אַבָּא אָמַר: זֶה תַּלְמִיד שֶׁלֹּא הִגִּיעַ לְהוֹרָאָה וּמוֹרֶה. *דְּא"ר אַבָּהוּ אָמַר רַב הוּנָא אָמַר רַב: מַאי דִּכְתִיב °"כִּי רַבִּים חֲלָלִים הִפִּילָה וַעֲצוּמִים כָּל הֲרוּגֶיהָ"; "כִּי רַבִּים חֲלָלִים הִפִּילָה" — אזֶה ת"ח שֶׁלֹּא הִגִּיעַ לְהוֹרָאָה וּמוֹרֶה, "וַעֲצוּמִים כָּל הֲרוּגֶיהָ" — בזֶה ת"ח שֶׁהִגִּיעַ לְהוֹרָאָה וְאֵינוֹ מוֹרֶה. וְעַד

שֶׁקָּרָא. מִקְרָא. וְשָׁנָה. מִשְׁנָה. וְלֹא שִׁימֵּשׁ תַּלְמִידֵי חֲכָמִים. לִלְמוֹד סְבָרַת הַגְּמָרָא בְּטַעֲמֵי הַמִּשְׁנָה מַה הֵם רָשָׁע הוּא, שֶׁאֵין תּוֹרָתוֹ עַל בּוּרְיָהּ, וְאֵין לִלְמוֹד הֵימֶנּוּ. שֶׁע"י הַטְּעָמִים יֵשׁ חִילּוּק בְּאִיסּוּר וְהֶיתֵּר, וּבְדִינֵי מָמוֹנוֹת לִזְכּוֹת וּלְחַיֵּיב, וּבְטָהֳרוֹת לְטַמֵּא וּלְטַהֵר, כִּדְאָמַר בְּכַמָּה דּוּכְתֵּי: מ"ט אָמַר מָר הָכִי וּמָר הָכִי, וְאָמַר: מַאי בֵּינַיְיהוּ? אִיכָּא בֵּינַיְיהוּ כָּךְ וְכָךְ. וְעָרוּם הוּא — שֶׁהַשּׁוֹמֵעַ אֶת קוֹלוֹ שׁוֹנֶה מִשְׁנִיּוֹתָיו כְּסָבוּר הוּא שֶׁבָּקִי בְּטַעֲמֵיהֶם, וְנוֹהֲגִין בּוֹ כָּבוֹד כְּתַלְמִידֵי חֲכָמִים: אִתְּמַר גְּרַס. ה"ז ע"ה. שֶׁחָשׁוּד עַל הַמַּעַשְׂרוֹת וְעַל הַטָּהֳרוֹת. בּוּר. גָּרוּעַ מֵעַם הָאָרֶץ. כּוּתִי. וְאָסוּר לֶאֱכוֹל פִּיתּוֹ וְיֵינוֹ. דְּכֵיוָן שֶׁלֹּא שִׁימֵּשׁ חֲכָמִים אֵינוֹ מַקְפִּיד עַל דִּבְרֵי חֲכָמִים לְדַעְתָּם וְלֹא שָׁנָה אֶלָּא לְהַרְאוֹת עַצְמוֹ כְּת"ח. מָגוֹשׁ. מְכַשֵּׁף הָאוֹחֵז אֶת הָעֵינַיִם וְגוֹנֵב אֶת הַלְּבָבוֹת, וְאַף זֶה כֵּן. רָטֵין. תַּרְגּוּם "חוֹבֵר חָבֶר" (דברים יח) הוּא — מָגוֹשׁ. לוֹחֵשׁ הַמְכַשֵּׁף אֶת לְחָשָׁיו וְאֵינוֹ מֵבִין מָה הֵם וּמַה פֵּירוּשָׁם, אֶלָּא כָּךְ מַעֲשֵׂיהֶם — שֶׁהַמְכַשֵּׁפוּת בָּא ע"י אוֹתָם הַלְּחָשִׁים. תָּנֵי תַּנָּא. וְאַף זֶה תַּנָּא שֶׁלֹּא שִׁימֵּשׁ בַּתַּלְמוּד — שׁוֹנֶה מִשְׁנָתוֹ וְאֵינוֹ יוֹדֵעַ מַה הִיא. אֵיזֶהוּ עַם הָאָרֶץ. שֶׁנֶּחֱשָׁד עַל הַטָּהֳרוֹת וְעַל הַמַּעַשְׂרוֹת, וּמוּחְזָק מַגָּעוֹ טָמֵא. כָּל שֶׁאֵינוֹ קוֹרֵא ק"ש. דְּהָא וַדַּאי אֵינוֹ יוֹדֵעַ כְּלוּם. אֲבָל יוֹדֵעַ לִקְרוֹת וְקוֹרֵא — לָא ע"ה הוּא. שֶׁשּׁוֹנִין הֲלָכוֹת. שֶׁלֹּא שִׁימְּשׁוּ לְתַלְמִידֵי חֲכָמִים, וְלֹא הִקְפִּידוּ עַל טַעֲמֵי הַמִּשְׁנִיּוֹת. הֲלָכוֹת. מִשְׁנָיוֹת. פְּשִׁיטָא. דְּהָכִי הוּא, אֶלָּא בְּמַאי נִדְרְשֵׁיהּ אִי לָאו בְּהָכִי?. הוּתְּרָה לוֹ. דּוֹמֶה בְּעֵינָיו הֶיתֵּר. מְבַלֵּי עוֹלָם ס"ד. וּמָה הֵם גּוֹרְמִין לַאֲחֵרִים?. שֶׁמּוֹרִין הֲלָכָה מִתּוֹךְ מִשְׁנָתָן. קָאָמַר, שֶׁמְּבַלִּין עוֹלָם בְּהוֹרָאוֹת טָעוּת. דְּכֵיוָן דְּאֵין יוֹדְעִין טַעֲמֵי הַמִּשְׁנָה — פְּעָמִים גּוֹרְמִין שֶׁמְּדַמִּין לָהּ דָּבָר שֶׁאֵינוֹ דּוֹמֶה. וְעוֹד, יֵשׁ מִשְׁנָיוֹת הַרְבֵּה (בְּמִשְׁנָיוֹת) דְּאָמְרִינַן: הָא מַנִּי פְּלוֹנִי הוּא, וִיחִידָאָה הִיא, וְלֵית הִלְכְתָא כְּוָותֵיהּ. וְעוֹד, שֶׁאֵינָן יוֹדְעִים בְּמַחֲלוֹקֶת תַּנָּאִים הָרִאשׁוֹנִים הֲלָכָה כְּדִבְרֵי מִי. הִלְכָּךְ מוֹרִין הוֹרָאוֹת טָעוּת. הֲלִיכוֹת עוֹלָם לוֹ. הַשּׁוֹנֶה הֲלָכוֹת — עוֹלָם שֶׁלּוֹ בִּזְכוּתוֹ. צַיְילָנִית. בַּעֲלַת תְּפִלָּה. וְאַלְמָנָה שׁוֹבָבִית. בַּעֲלַת שְׁכֵינוּת, הוֹלֶכֶת וּמְבַקֶּרֶת שְׁכֵינוֹתֶיהָ תָּמִיד. הֲרֵי אֵלּוּ מְבַלֵּי עוֹלָם. שֶׁאֵינָן אֶלָּא נוֹאֲפוֹת וּמְכַשֵּׁפוֹת, וּמַרְאוֹת עַצְמָן כְּלִדְקָנִיּוֹת שֶׁלֹּא יִבְדְּקוּ אַחֲרֵיהֶן. קָטָן שֶׁלֹּא כָּלוּ לוֹ חֳדָשָׁיו. לְקַמָּן מְפָרֵשׁ. וְקִיבּוּל שָׂכָר מֵאַלְמָנָה. שֶׁהָיְתָה טוֹרַחַת עַצְמָהּ יוֹתֵר מִן הַצּוֹרֶךְ כְּדֵי לְקַבֵּל שָׂכָר, כִּדְמְפָרֵשׁ וְאָזֵיל — לָמַדְנוּ שֶׁיַּטְרִיחַ אָדָם עַצְמוֹ בַּמִּצְוָה לְקַבֵּל שָׂכָר יוֹתֵר. בָּרָאתָ צַדִּיקִים. לִנְחוֹל ג"ע. בָּרָאתָ רְשָׁעִים. לִירַשׁ גֵּיהִנָּם. שֶׁלֹּא יִכָּשְׁלוּ בִּי בְּנֵי אָדָם. לְהַפְסִיד חֶלְקָם עַל יְדֵי מִגַּן עֵדֶן, וְלִירַשׁ גֵּיהִנָּם. כִּי קָאָמַר. מְבַלֵּי עוֹלָם. כְּגוֹן יוֹחָנִי בַּת רְטִיבִי. אַלְמָנָה מְכַשֵּׁפָה הָיְתָה, וּכְשֶׁמַּגִּיעַ עֵת לֵידַת אִשָּׁה הָיְתָה עוֹצֶרֶת רַחְמָהּ בְּמַכְשֵׁפוֹת, וּלְאַחַר שֶׁמִּצְטַעֶרֶת הַרְבֵּה הָיְתָה אוֹמֶרֶת: אֵלֵךְ וַאֲבַקֵּשׁ רַחֲמִים, אוּלַי תִּשָּׁמַע תְּפִלָּתִי, וְהוֹלֶכֶת וְסוֹתֶרֶת כְּשָׁפֶיהָ, וְהַוָּלָד יוֹצֵא. פַּעַם אַחַת הָיָה לָהּ שָׂכִיר יוֹם בְּבֵיתָהּ, וְהִיא הָלְכָה לְבֵית הָאִשָּׁה הַיּוֹלֶדֶת, וְשָׁמַע הַשָּׂכִיר קוֹל הַכְּשָׁפִים מִתְקַשְׁקְשִׁין בִּכְלִי כְּמוֹ שֶׁהַוָּלָד מְקַשְׁקֵשׁ בִּמְעֵי הָאֵם, וּבָא וּפָתַח אֶת מְגוּפַת הַכְּלִי וְהַכְּשָׁפִים יָצְאוּ, וְהַוָּלָד נוֹלַד, וְיָדְעוּ כִּי בַּעֲלַת כְּשָׁפִים הִיא. הַמְבַעֵט בְּרַבּוֹתָיו. וְקָרֵי לֵיהּ קָטָן שֶׁלֹּא כָּלוּ לוֹ חֳדָשָׁיו עַל יְדֵי שֶׁיָּמָיו מִתְקַצְּרִין, כִּדְאָמְרִינַן בְּפֶרֶק קַמָּא דַּחֲגִיגָה (דף ה.). כִּי רַבִּים חֲלָלִים הִפִּילָה. בְּאִשָּׁה זָרָה מִשְׁתָּעֵי. וְתַלְמִיד שֶׁאֵינוֹ נוֹהֵג עַצְמוֹ כַּשּׁוּרָה קָרֵי לֵיהּ נַמִי הָכִי. זֶה תַּלְמִיד שֶׁלֹּא הִגִּיעַ כו'. "הִפִּילָה" לְשׁוֹן נֵפֶל, שֶׁלֹּא כָּלוּ לוֹ חֳדָשָׁיו. וַעֲצוּמִים. לְשׁוֹן "עוֹצֵם עֵינָיו" (ישעיה לג) — שֶׁסּוֹגְרִים פִּיהֶם וְאֵינָם מוֹרִים לְצוֹרְכֵי הוֹרָאָה. וְעַד

רבי שמואל בר נחמני אמר ה"ז בור. תימה: כמאן ס"ל לא כאחרים ולא כר' יהודה דאחרים לא קרו בור *אלא לשנה ולא קרא, ור' יהודה אפי' עם הארץ לא משוי ליה, דאמר בסוף פרק "אלו מציאות" (ב"מ דף לג:) דדרש ר' יהודה בר אילעאי: "שמעו דבר ה' החרדים אל דברו" וגו', "החרדים אל דברו" – אלו תלמידי חכמים, "אחיכם" – אלו בעלי מקרא, "שנאיכם" – אלו בעלי משנה, "מנדיכם" – אלו עם הארץ. אלמא דבעלי משנה או בעלי מקרא לאו בכלל ע"ה נינהו! **כל** שאינו קורא ק"ש שחרית וערבית דברי ר"מ. תימה לר"י: דאמר בפ' "הניזקין" (גיטין דף סא.) ובפ' "ג' שאכלו" (ברכות דף מז:): איזהו עם הארץ – כל שאינו אוכל חולין בטהרה, דברי ר"מ! ופירש: דהרבה ענייני עם הארץ הן; ויש שאין מקבלין ממנו עדות, כדאמרינן בפ' "אלו עוברין" (פסחים דף מט:): ששה דברים נאמרו בעם הארץ: אין מקבלין מהן עדות וכו', ובפ' "חומר בקודש" (חגיגה דף כב.): כמאן מקבלין סהדותא מעם הארץ – כר' יוסי. ויש כשר לענין עדות ונחשד על הטהרות ועל המעשרות, או לענין זימון, או לענין שביעית, א"נ לענין דברים שאינן נקחין אלא מן המומחה, כדאיתא בפ' שני דמסכת ע"ז (דף לט:). בירושלמי: אשה פרושה – זו היא שיושבת ומלעבת בדברי תורה, "ותאמר אלי תבא וישכב עמה בלילה הוא", א"ר אבהו: כביכול היה במחשבה, הוא לבדו יודע שלא עלתה על דעתה אלא בשביל להעמיד שבטים. הוסיפו עליהם בתולתא ליימנית* ואלמנה שובבית, [*מי חגלה נסבת שם ביש], ותינוק שהוא עולה לחדשיו. (בתולה ליימנית – מליימה, אובדת בתוליה. ותינוק שהוא עולה לחדשיו) – ר' חלקיה בשם ר' סימון: זה שהוא גדול בתורה שלא בפירקו, ומבזה את הגדולים ממנו. א"ר יוסי: זהו שבן תשע ואבריו נראה כבן י"ב, והוא בא על אחת מכל העריות האמורות בתורה, והן מתות על ידו והוא פטור. רבי פירש: מליימה אובדת בתוליה – מחמת לומות בתוליה נושרות. אבל מורי אחי הרב ר"מ פי': עושה חסידה ומתפללת, כדגרסינן בגמ' דידן: צליינית, וכאילו למה ועושה תעניות שתהא נענת בתפלתה – ואינה עושה אלא לגנב את העין, שלא יבדקו אחריה, ומזנה ואובדת בתוליה.

ועד

תוספות שאנץ

הרי זה בור. בור גרוע מעם הארץ: רטין מגושא לוחש המכשף את לוחשיו ואינו יודע מה הם ומה פירושם אלא כך מעשיהם שמכשפות בא על ידי לחשים: תני תנא אף תנא זה שלא שמש תלמידי חכמים בתלמוד שונה משנתו ואינו יודע מה הוא. ל"ה: איזהו עם הארץ פ"ה שנחשד על הטהרות ועל המעשרות ומוחזק מגעו טמא: כל שאינו קורא ק"ש דהא ודאי לא ידע מידי אבל ידע לקרות וקורא לאו עם הארץ הוא דברי ר' מאיר. וי"מ דהך ברייתא מתניא לענין זימון שאין מזמנין על עם הארץ. עוד מצי למימר דמיתניא לענין דאמרי' פרק ואלו עוברין שעם הארץ פסול לעדות ואין מכריזין על אבדתו אבל ק' מההיא דפ' הנזקין [דף ס"א] דקאמר איזהו עם הארץ כל שאינו אוכל חוליו בטהרה דברי ר' מאיר וחכמים אומרים כל שאינו מעשר פירותיו ולענין מאי מיתניא אי לענין זימון ליתא דאמרי' בפרק שלשה שאכלו דעם הארץ שאינו מעשר פירותיו דהיינו עם הארץ דרבנן. ואי לענין דמאי ליתא דהא מי שחשוד על טהרות אינו חשוד על הדמאי כדמוכח בפ"ק דיבמות ועוד ק' דר"מ אדר' מאיר דהכא קאמר דהוי עם הארץ כל שאינו אוכל חוליו בטהרה ויש לומר דהתם לענין דההיא אלו עוברין מיתניא. ואור"י דההיא דהניזקין א) דההיא דנותנין לעם הארץ בנות חברים גדולות ופוסקין להם על מנת שלא תעשה על גביו טהרות ר'ש'ב'ג'א' אין צריך לפסוק שאפי' לא פסק עמו כן הדין שלא תעשה על גביו טהרות אלא בפרישות אחר תינהוג גם כשהיא תחתיו. ואחר כך שונה רשב"ג איזהו עם הארץ כל שאינו אוכל חוליו בטהרה דברי ר' מאיר וחכמים אומרים כל שאינו מעשר פירותיו וה"ק איזהו עם הארץ שישיאנו לו חבר בתו בזה הענין שתנהוג טהרה תחתיו כל שאינו אוכל כו'. וחכמים אומרים אפי' למי שאינו מעשר פירותיו משיאין לו בת חבר: אחרים אומרים אפי' קרא ושנה משמע מהכא דאחרים לא הוי ר' מאיר ואע"ג דבבוליה תלמודא אמרי' מאן אחרים ר' מאיר נ"ל דברוב מקומות הוו אחרים ר' מאיר כדאמרינן מאן יש אומרים ר' נתן ובפ"ק דגיטין גר' ב) יש אומרים לא היינו ר' מאיר אלא ר' נתן דברוב המקומות יש אומרים היינו ר' נתן: המורים הלכה מתוך משנתם שמבלים עולם בהוראת טעות דכיון דאינם יודעים טעם המשנה מדמים להם דבר שאינו דומה. ויש אומר' משניות הרבה דאמר הא מני פלוני היא ויחידא היא ולית הלכתא כותיה ומורים בטעות ל"ה: בתולה צליינית בעלת תפלות ואלמנה שבבית בעלת שכנית הולכת ומבקרת שכינותיה תמיד שאינן אלא מנאפות ומכשפות ומראות עצמן כצדקניות שלא יבדקו אחריהן ל"ה. כגון יוחני בת רטבי פ"ה אלמנה מכשפנית היתה וכשמגיע עת לדת האשה עוצרת האשה במכשפות ולאחר שמצטערת האשה הרבה היתה אומרת יוחני אלך ואבקש אולי תשמע תפלתי והולכת ופותחת הכלי שהיו הכשפים בתוכו וסותרת הכשפים ואז הולד יוצא. פעם אחת היה לה שכיר יום בביתה והיא הלכה לבית האשה היולדת ושמע השכיר קול הכשפים מקשקש' בתוך הכלי כמו שהולד מקשקש במעי האם ובא השכיר וסתר את מגופת הכלי והכשפים יצאו והולד נולד וידעו כל העולם כי בעלת כשפים היא ל"ה: המבעט ברבותיו וקרי ליה קטן שלא כלו חדשיו על ידי שימיו מתקצרין כדאמ' פ"ק דחגיגה

בשוין

א) נ"ל דהכוונה להניזקין מתניה לענין שנותנין לע"ה בנות חברים וכו' והוא כתוספתא דע"ז פ"ג ועי' בתוס'. ב) נ"ל יש אומרים אחר דברי ר' נתן וכו' ע"כ דר"מ לא אתי אלא כרבוב המקומות וכו'.

אלא לקרא ולא שנה כו' מהרש"א

כח א מיי' פ"ה מהלכות ת"ת הלכה ד טוש"ע י"ד סימן רמו סעיף יג:

כט ב מיי' שם טוש"ע שם סעיף יז:

ברכות מז: [ע"ש דזהו דעת ר' אליעזר אבל ר' מאיר ס"ל שם דכל שאינו אוכל חולין בטהרה וכן איתא בגיטין סא. וכן תנאה אחר סיומים ועי' בתוס' ד"ה כל ובתוס' גיטין סא.]

[לפמ"ש תוס' לעיל יב. ד"ה אחרים וע"ש מ"ש על הגליון יתיישב גם הכא]

קדושין כ. מ. ע"ש יומא פו. ערכין ל: מ"ק כז:

[מגלה כח: ושם איתא אל תקרי הליכות אלא הלכות]

[מליימה אובדת בתוליה] כ"ה בירושלמי

[ב"מ קז.]

ע' יע: [ע"ש]

ירמיה לא | משלי כד | חבקוק ג | משלי ז

גליון הש"ס

גמ' דאמר ר' אבהו. נ"ל אבא:

עין משפט
נר מצוה

ל א מיי' פ"ג מהל' ת"ת הלכה ה ופ"י מהל' תשובה הלכה ה סמג עשין יב טוש"ע י"ד סימן רמו סעיף כ:

לא ב מיי' פ"ג מהל' סוטה הלכה כ:

לב ג ד ה מיי' שם פ"ד הלכה יד:

וְעַד כַּמָּה — עַד אַרְבְּעִין שְׁנִין. אִינִי?! וְהָא *רַבָּה אוֹרֵי! בְּשָׁוִין.§ "וּמַכּוֹת פְּרוּשִׁין" וכו'.§ ת"ר: שִׁבְעָה פְּרוּשִׁין הֵן: פָּרוּשׁ שִׁיכְמִי, פָּרוּשׁ נִקְפִּי, פָּרוּשׁ קִיזָאִי, פָּרוּשׁ מְדוּכְיָא, פָּרוּשׁ "מֶה חוֹבָתִי וְאֶעֱשֶׂנָּה", פָּרוּשׁ מֵאַהֲבָה, פָּרוּשׁ מִיִּרְאָה. פָּרוּשׁ שִׁיכְמִי — זֶה הָעוֹשֶׂה מַעֲשֵׂה שְׁכֶם, פָּרוּשׁ נִקְפִּי — זֶה הַמְנַקֵּיף אֶת רַגְלָיו. פָּרוּשׁ קִיזָאִי — א"ר נַחְמָן בַּר יִצְחָק: זֶה הַמַּקִּיז דָּם לַכְּתָלִים. פָּרוּשׁ מְדוּכְיָא — אָמַר רַבָּה בַּר שֵׁילָא: דְּמִשְׁפַּע כִּי מְדוּכְיָא. פָּרוּשׁ "מֶה חוֹבָתִי וְאֶעֱשֶׂנָּה". הָא מַעַלְיוּתָא הִיא! אֶלָּא דְּאָמַר "מֶה חוֹבָתִי תּוּ וְאֶעֱשֶׂנָּה". פָּרוּשׁ מֵאַהֲבָה פָּרוּשׁ מִיִּרְאָה. אֲמַרוּ לֵיהּ אַבָּיֵי וְרָבָא לְתַנָּא: לָא תִּיתְנֵי פָּרוּשׁ מֵאַהֲבָה פָּרוּשׁ מִיִּרְאָה. *דְּאָמַר רַב יְהוּדָה אָמַר רַב: אלְעוֹלָם יַעֲסוֹק אָדָם בַּתּוֹרָה וּבַמִּצְוֹת אֲפִי' שֶׁלֹּא לִשְׁמָהּ, שֶׁמִּתּוֹךְ שֶׁלֹּא לִשְׁמָהּ בָּא לִשְׁמָהּ. אָמַר רַב נַחְמָן בַּר יִצְחָק: דִּמְטַמְּרָא מְטַמְּרָא, וּדְמִגַּלְיָא מִגַּלְיָא, בֵּי דִינָא רַבָּה לִיתְפָּרַע מֵהָנֵי דְּחָפוּ גּוּנְדֵי. אֲמַר לָהּ יַנַּאי מַלְכָּא לִדְבֵיתֵיהּ: אַל תִּתְיָרְאִי מִן הַפְּרוּשִׁין, וְלֹא מִמִּי שֶׁאֵינָן פְּרוּשִׁין, אֶלָּא מִן הַצְּבוּעִין שֶׁדּוֹמִין לִפְרוּשִׁין, שֶׁמַּעֲשֵׂיהֶן כְּמַעֲשֵׂה זִמְרִי, וּמְבַקְשִׁין שָׂכָר כְּפִנְחָס.§ **מתני'** *ר"ש אוֹמֵר: אֵין זְכוּת תּוֹלָה בַּמַּיִם הַמָּרִים, וְאִם אַתָּה אוֹמֵר הַזְּכוּת תּוֹלָה בַּמַּיִם הַמְאָרְרִין — *מְדַהֶה אַתָּה אֶת הַמַּיִם בִּפְנֵי כָּל הַנָּשִׁים הַשּׁוֹתוֹת, וּמוֹצִיא אַתָּה שֵׁם רַע עַל הַטְּהוֹרוֹת שֶׁשָּׁתוּ, שֶׁאוֹמְרִים: טְמֵאוֹת הֵן, אֶלָּא שֶׁתָּלְתָה לָהֶן זְכוּת. *רַבִּי אוֹמֵר: הַזְּכוּת תּוֹלָה בַּמַּיִם הַמְאָרְרִים, וְאֵינָהּ יוֹלֶדֶת וְאֵינָהּ מִשְׁבַּחַת, באֶלָּא מִתְנַוּוֹנָה וְהוֹלֶכֶת, לְסוֹף הִיא מֵתָה בְּאוֹתָהּ מִיתָה. *גנִטְמֵאת מִנְחָתָהּ עַד שֶׁלֹּא קָדְשָׁה בַּכְּלִי — הֲרֵי הִיא כְּכָל הַמְּנָחוֹת, וְתִפָּדֶה. דוְאִם מִשֶּׁקָּדְשָׁה בַּכְּלִי — הֲרֵי הִיא כְּכָל הַמְּנָחוֹת, וְתִשָּׂרֵף. *הוְאֵלּוּ שֶׁמִּנְחוֹתֵיהֶן נִשְׂרָפוֹת: הָאוֹמֶרֶת

רש"י

וְעַד כַּמָּה. הֲוֵי רָאוּי לְהוֹרָאָה?. וְהָא רַבָּה אוֹרֵי. וְכָל שְׁנוֹתָיו אֵינָן אֶלָּא מ', כִּדְאָמְרִי' בְּר"ה (דף יח.): רַבָּה וְאַבַּיֵּי מִדְּבֵית עֵלִי קָאָתוּ כו'. בְּשָׁוִין. אִם שָׁוֶה לִגְדוֹל הָעִיר בְּחָכְמָה — מוּתָּר לְהוֹרוֹת. אוֹ שֶׁאֵין זָקֵן מִמֶּנּוּ בָּעִיר. פָּרוּשׁ שִׁיכְמִי פָּרוּשׁ נִקְפִּי פָּרוּשׁ קִיזָאִי פָּרוּשׁ מְדוּכְיָא. כּוּלְּהוּ מְפָרֵשׁ לְהוּ. מַעֲשֵׂה שְׁכֶם. שֶׁמָּלוּ שֶׁלֹּא לְשֵׁם שָׁמַיִם. אַף זֶה — מַעֲשָׂיו לַהֲנָאָתוֹ, שֶׁיְּכַבְּדוּהוּ בְּנֵי אָדָם, וְלֹא לְשֵׁם שָׁמַיִם. הַמְנַקֵּיף רַגְלָיו. מְהַלֵּךְ בִּשְׁפָלוּת, עָקֵב בְּצַד גּוּדָל וְאֵינוֹ מֵרִים רַגְלָיו מִן הָאָרֶץ, וּמִתּוֹךְ כָּךְ מְנַקֵּף אֶצְבְּעוֹתָיו בָּאֲבָנִים. מַקִּיז דָּם לַכְּתָלִים. עוֹשֶׂה עַצְמוֹ כְּעוֹצֵם עֵינָיו שֶׁלֹּא יִסְתַּכֵּל בַּנָּשִׁים, וּמִתּוֹךְ כָּךְ מַכֶּה רֹאשׁוֹ בַּכּוֹתֶל וְהַדָּם יוֹצֵא. דְּמִשְׁפַּע. הוֹלֵךְ כָּפוּף. כִּי מְדוּכְיָא. בּוּכְנָא, עָשׂוּי כְּמַקֶּבֶת וְרֹאשׁוֹ כָּפוּף. פָּרוּשׁ מַה חוֹבָתִי וְאֶעֱשֶׂנָּה. לִמְדוּנִי מֶה עָלַי לַעֲשׂוֹת וְאֶעֱשֶׂה. הָא מַעַלְיוּתָא הִיא. אִם אֵינוֹ בָּקִי בָּאִיסּוּרִין וְדִקְדּוּקֵי מִצְוֹת וּבָא לִלְמוֹד. מַה חוֹבָתִי תּוּ וְאֶעֱשֶׂנָּה. מַה לַּעֲשׂוֹת עוֹד וְלֹא עָשִׂיתִי. וּמַרְאֶה עַצְמוֹ כְּאִילּוּ קִיֵּים אֶת הַכֹּל. פָּרוּשׁ מֵאַהֲבָה. מֵאַהֲבַת שְׂכַר הַמִּצְוֹת, (א) וְלֹא לְאַהֲבַת מִצְוֹת הַבּוֹרֵא. מִיִּרְאָה. שֶׁל עוֹנָשִׁין. אֶלָּא מָה עַל הָאָדָם לַעֲשׂוֹת — מֵאַהֲבַת הַשֵּׁ"י, כַּאֲשֶׁר צִוָּנוּ ה' אֱלֹהֵינוּ, וְסוֹף הַשָּׂכָר לָבֹא. דִּמְטַמְּרָא מְטַמְּרָא כו'. הַנִּסְתָּרוֹת נִסְתָּרוֹת מִבְּנֵי אָדָם וְהַגְּלוּיוֹת גְּלוּיוֹת, וּמ"מ לְב"ד הַגָּדוֹל כּוּלָּם גְּלוּיוֹת, וְהוּא יִפָּרַע מִן הַמִּתְכַּסִּים בְּטַלִּיתוֹת וּמַרְאִין עַצְמָן כִּפְרוּשִׁין, וְאֵינָן פְּרוּשִׁין. אַל תִּתְיָרְאִי מִן הַפְּרוּשִׁין. שֶׁהַפְּרוּשִׁין הָיוּ שׂוֹנְאִין אוֹתוֹ, לְפִי שֶׁהָרַג מִן הַחֲכָמִים הַרְבֵּה, וְנֶהְפַּךְ לִהְיוֹת צְדוֹקִי, כִּדְאָמַר בְּקִידּוּשִׁין (דף סו.). וּכְשֶׁמֵּת הָיְתָה אִשְׁתּוֹ יְרֵאָה מֵהֶן שֶׁלֹּא יַעֲבִירוּ הַמְּלוּכָה מִבָּנֶיהָ, וְהָיְתָה אוֹמֶרֶת לוֹ לְבַקֵּשׁ מִלִּפְנֵיהֶם עָלֶיהָ. וְאָמַר לָהּ: אַל תִּתְיָרְאִי מִן הַפְּרוּשִׁין, שֶׁצַּדִּיקִים הֵן וְלֹא יִגְמְלוּךְ רָעָה, וְלֹא לְבָנַיִךְ שֶׁלֹּא חָטְאוּ לָהֶם. וְלֹא מִמִּי שֶׁאֵינָן פְּרוּשִׁין. שֶׁהֵם אוֹהֲבַיי. אֶלָּא מִן הַצְּבוּעִים. כְּלוֹמַר, שֶׁאֵין מַרְאִיתָם כְּתוֹלְדוֹתָם, אֶלָּא צְבוּעִין מִבַּחוּץ וְאֵין תּוֹכָן כְּבָרָם. שֶׁמַּעֲשֵׂיהֶם כְּמַעֲשֵׂה זִמְרִי. שֶׁהֵן רְשָׁעִים, וּמְבַקְשִׁים שָׂכָר כְּפִנְחָס — אוֹמְרִים לַבְּרִיּוֹת לְכַבְּדָן כְּפִנְחָס. וְאִיכָּא דִּמְפָרֵשׁ לָהּ לְעִנְיַן צְנִיעוּתָא. **מתני'** הֲרֵי הִיא כְּכָל הַמְּנָחוֹת. שֶׁנִּטְמְאוּ עַד שֶׁלֹּא קָדְשָׁה בַּכְּלִי. וְתִפָּדֶה. וְתֵצֵא לְחוּלִּין, וּמֵהַמָּעוֹת יִקְנֶה אַחֶרֶת. וְתִשָּׂרֵף. שֶׁקָּדְשָׁה קְדוּשַּׁת הַגּוּף, וְאֵינָהּ יוֹצְאָה עוֹד לְחוּלִּין. וְכָל

תוספות

ועד כמה עד ארבעין שנין. פי': משנה שהתחיל ללמוד עד ארבעים שנה, ולא משנה שנולד. כדאמרינן בפ"ק דמסכת ע"ז (דף ה:): "ולא נתן ה' לכם לב לדעת עד היום הזה" — ש"מ לא קאים איניש אדעתיה דרביה עד ארבעין שנין. וזה היה ממתן תורה עד מ' שנה, שאז התחילו ללמוד. **בשוין** · רש"י פי': אם שוה לגדול העיר בחכמה מותר להורות. קשה לר"י מפרק "הרואה" (ברכות דף סג.) דאמר אביי: באתרא דאית גבר — תמן לא תיהוי גבר. פשיטא! לא צריכא דשוין. אלמא היכא דשוין אין לו לקפוץ להוראה! להכי מסתברא הכא לפרש: והא רבה דאורי והוא לא הגיע להוראה, שכל ימיו לא היה אלא מ' שנה! בשוין; הא דאמר שאין לו להורות עד ארבעין שנין — היינו כששוה לגדול העיר בחכמה, וגדול העיר הגיע להוראה, הלכך כיון שיש שם חכם כמותו הגיע להוראה בשנים והוא לא הגיע לשני הוראה — אין לו להורות לפניו. אבל אם גדול העיר הוא בחכמה, אע"ג שלא הגיע לכלל שנים — מורה. ורבה — גדול העיר בחכמה היה. אבל ר"י פי' ההוא דפרק "הרואה", דמיירי באדם שנכנס לעיר שיש שם חכם מורה — תמן לא תהוי גבר, אפי' בשוין. אבל אם הוא קבוע בעיר כמותו, ושוה לו בחכמה — מותר לו להורות, כמו שפי' רש"י. ור"ת פי' התם: באתר דאית גבר — ממונה, משתדל בצרכי ציבור — לא תקפוץ לתוך שררות אפי' בשוין. ולפי' לא מיירי בהוראה.

פרוש מאהבה פרוש מיראה. בירושל' פרק "הרואה": עשה מאהבה ועשה מיראה; עשה מאהבה, שאם באת לשנוא — דע שאתה אוהבו, ואין אוהב שונא. עשה מיראה, שאם באת לבעוט — דע שאתה ירא, ואין ירא מבעט. שבעה פרושין הן: פרוש שכמי וכו' פרוש מן הנכייה כו'. פרוש שכמי — טעון מצותיה על כתפיה, פרוש נקפי — אקיף לי ואני עבד מצוה. פרוש קיזאי — עבד חדא חובה וחדא מצוה, ומקיז חדא בחדא. פרוש מן הנכייה — מאי דאית לי אנא מנכה ועבד מצות. פרוש "אדע חובתי ואעשנה" — הי דא חובתי עבדית דאעביד מצות דכותה. פרוש יראה — כאיוב, פרוש אהבה — כאברהם, דכתיב (ישעיה מא): "זרע אברהם אוהבי". אין לך חביב מכולם אלא פרוש אהבה כאברהם.

לעולם יעסוק אדם בתורה ובמצות אע"פ שלא לשמה. ואי קשיא: הא אמרינן בפ"ק דתענית (דף ז.): כל העוסק בתורה שלא לשמה נעשית לו סם המות, ובשלהי פרק "היה קורא" במסכת ברכות (דף יז.): כל העוסק בתורה שלא לשמה נוח לו שלא נברא! נראה לתרץ: עוסק שלא לשמה — כגון מיראת היסורין כי הכא, ומאהבת קיבול פרס, שאינו מתכוין להשלים רצון יוצרו שציוהו על כך, אלא להנאתו, כדאמרינן בפ"ק דמסכת ע"ז (דף יט.): "במצותיו חפץ מאד" — ולא בשכר מצותיו. והיינו דתנן (אבות פ"א מ"ג): אל תהיו כעבדים המשמשין את הרב ע"מ לקבל פרס, וכי הא דאמר בפ' "עגלה ערופה" (לקמן מז.), ואיתא בנזיר פרק "מי שאמר הריני נזיר" (דף כג:), ובפרק בתרא דהוריות (דף י:): לעולם יעסוק אדם וכו' — שבשכר מ"ב קרבנות שהקריב בלק זכה ויצאה ממנו רות. גם הוא נתכוין להנאתו, שהעלה קרבן לשם להשלים חפציו בשכרו ולא לשם שמים. וכדאמרי' פ"ק דר"ה (דף ד.): האומר "סלע זו לצדקה ע"מ שיחיה בני" — ה"ז צדיק גמור. אבל ההיא שלא לשמה דתענית ומס' ברכות — אינו עוסק בתורה כדי לקיים, לא מאהבה ולא מיראה, אלא להוסיף על חטאתו פשע, שעתה שגגות נעשו לו זדונות, שאע"פ שידע שעובר — לא מנע מכל תאות לבו, כדמפרש התם (ברכות יז.): תכלית חכמה תשובה ומעשים טובים, שלא יהא אדם קורא ושונה ומשמש תלמידי חכמים ובועט באביו ובאמו וברבו או במי שגדול הימנו, שנאמר: "ראשית חכמה יראת ה' שכל טוב לכל עושיהם", ללומדיהם לא נאמר, אלא לעושיהם — לעושים לשמה*. **אלו** שמנחותיהם נשרפות. תימה: אמאי לא חשיב נמי מת הוא או שמתה היא, דאמרי' בפ"ק (לעיל דף ו:) דנשרפת! וליכא למימר דוקא היינו לאחר שקידש הקומץ, כדתני' לעיל, אבל הכא לא חשיב אלא הנשרפת משקדשה בכלי. דה"ה אם משקדשה בכלי דנשרפת, ואיידי דקתני סיפא קירב הקומץ דנאכלת — נקט רישא קידש הקומץ. ורבותא נקט: אע"פ דכבר קדוש וקרוב להקרבה טפי מקידשה בכלי — אפ"ה נשרפת. *ושבעלה **בא** עליה בדרך. תימה לר"י: אמאי נשרפת? כיון דבדרך בא עליה — היינו קודם שתקדוש, וכיון דאין המים בודקין אותה, כדאמר: *"ונקה האיש מעון" בזמן שהאיש מנוקה מעון וכו' — תיגלי מילתא למפרע דכי קדוש — בטעות קדוש. כדאמרינן גבי "ושבאו לה עדים שהיא טמאה", דהואיל ולא לבדוק עומדת, ולא ראויה למנחה — לא היתה ראויה לכלי, ואין כלי שרת מקדשין אלא בראוי להן! ונראה, דדוקא לגבי שבאו לה עדים שייך למימר הכי, משום דמנחה לברר עון, וכשיש שם עדים — הרי העון מבורר וא"צ בירור. אבל הכא, שבא עליה בדרך, שצריך לברר, אע"ג דאין המים בודקין, כי קדוש מעיקרא — שפיר קדוש, מאחר שלא נתברר העון, ולא הוי אלא כמו שנשאו ונתנו בה מוזרות בלבנה קודם לכן, דאין המים בודקין, ואפ"ה מנחה שפיר קדוש. והאי דלא חשיב במתני' מנחת ארוסה ושומרת יבם אלמנה לכ"ג — מפני שידוע פסול שלהן, שאינן נבדקות ואין מביאין אותם לשתות.
האומרת

תוספות שאנץ

בשוין אם שוה לגדול שבעיר בחכמה מותר לו להורות אע"ג דאינו בר מ' שנה או שאין בעיר זקן הימנו ל"ה. מעשה שכם שמלו שלא לשום שמים אף זה עושה מעשיו להנאתו כדי שיכבדוהו בני אדם ולא לשום שמים ל"ה: המנקף את רגליו מהלך בשפלות עקב בצד גודל ואינו מניף רגליו מן הארץ ומתוך כך מנקף אצבעותיו באבנים. דמשפע כי מדוכא בוכנא שהיא עשויה כמקבת וראשו כפוף: פרוש מה חובתי ואעשנה. למדיני מה לעשות ואעשה. פרוש מאהבה פרוש מיראה וקשה דמשמע דלא הוי למעליותא. ולקמן בס"פ כשם משמע דהוי מעליותא דאמר הנהו תרי תלמידי דהוי יתבי קמיה דרבא חד אמר אקריון בחלמי וישמחו בך אוהבי שמך וחד אמר אקריון בחלמי מה רב טובך אשר צפנת ליראיך. אמר להו רבא תרוייכו רבנן אתן אלא מר מאהבה ומר מיראה אלמא משמע דמעליותא הוא. וצ"ל דתרי עניני מאהבה ומיראה הוי והכא ה"פ פרוש מאהבת שכר שמתחרט אם לא תתמלא תאותו ופרוש מיראה כאדם שירא מרבו ודואג לכבודו שלא יקפיד עליו אבל פרוש מאהבת יוצרו כאשר צוהו ה' אלהיו וסוף השכר לבא וכן מיראת יוצרו הוי מעליותא ביותר עוד יש פרוש מאהבה ומיראה דהוי מעליא כגון נותן צדקה בשביל שיחיו בניו ובנותיו ואינו מתחרט כשלא באו תאותו והיינו פרוש מאהבה ופרוש מיראת עונשין שלא יהיו בניו ובנותיו וג"כ הוי מעליותא כיון שאינו מתחרט ופירושא דהכא מאהבה ומיראה מיירי כשמתחרטין אם לא תמלא תאותן דהשתא הוי תרתי גוונא דמאהבה ומיראה למעליותא זה למעלה מזה כדפי' והשלישי דהכא אינו טוב אבל מכל מקום יעסוק כו'. והא דאמר בירושלמי פירושא פרוש מאהבה כאברהם פרוש מיראה כאיוב צ"ל דחולק על תלמוד שלנו אך ק' מההיא דאמר בפ' החולץ מפני מה גרים מעונים בזמן הזה ר' יוסי אומר לפי שאינן עושין מאהבת המקום אלא מיראת עונשין ולא היו חוששין לעשות אם לא (דוואגים) [דואגים] מן העונשין כי ביותר קשה להם להכנס בעול המצות א) ולפי' הוי גרעותא כיון דאין מקבלין עליהן עול מלכות שמים מאהבה ועל ידי יסורין באין עליהן. לעולם יעסוק אדם בתורה שלא לשמה פי' כדפי' בפ' מקום שנהגו: א"ל ינאי מלכא לדביתהו אל תתיראי מן הפרושין פ"ה שהיתה אשתו יראה מן הפרושין ב) שלא יגמלו עליך רעה ולא לבניך שלא חטאו להם ולא ממי שאינן פרושין לפי שהן אוהבי אלא מן הצבועין כלומר שאין מראיתם כתולדותם אלא צבועין מבחוץ ואית דפרשי לענין צניעותא

א) אולי צ"ל וי"ל דמ"מ הוי גריעותא. ב) וא"ל שאל תתיראי מהם שלא יגמלוך רעה.

מסורת הש"ס

[בע"ז יט: איתא רבא ע"ש פרש"י]

סנהדרין קז: פסחים נ: ערכין טז: לקמן מז. הוריות י: נזיר כג:

לעיל ו. כ:

פי' מתחיך גווני

[לעיל ו.]

שם:

[לעיל ו.]

[ועי' תוספות ברכות יז. ד"ה העוסק וכו' ומה שנ"ב בנידון]

[שייך לדף שאח"ז]

[לקמן כח.]

הגהות הב"ח

(א) רש"י ד"ה פרוש וכו' שכר המצות. נ"ב עיין ס"פ כסס דף לה:

גליון הש"ס

גמ' ת"ר שבעה פרושים הן. עיין בירושלמי פ"ט דברכות ה"ה ועיין עלה למתני' חייב אדם לברך על הרעה.

האומרת "טְמֵאָה אֲנִי לָךְ", וְשֶׁבָּאוּ לָהּ עֵדִים שֶׁהִיא טְמֵאָה, וְהָאוֹמֶרֶת "אֵינִי שׁוֹתָה", וְשֶׁבַּעְלָהּ אֵינוֹ רוֹצֶה לְהַשְׁקוֹתָהּ, וְשֶׁבַּעְלָהּ בָּא עָלֶיהָ בַּדֶּרֶךְ. וְכָל הַנְּשׂוּאוֹת לְכֹהֲנִים — מִנְחוֹתֵיהֶן נִשְׂרָפוֹת. בַּת יִשְׂרָאֵל שֶׁנִּשֵּׂאת לְכֹהֵן — מִנְחָתָהּ נִשְׂרֶפֶת, וְכֹהֶנֶת שֶׁנִּשֵּׂאת לְיִשְׂרָאֵל — מִנְחָתָהּ נֶאֱכֶלֶת. מַה בֵּין כֹּהֵן לְכֹהֶנֶת: *מִנְחַת כֹּהֶנֶת נֶאֱכֶלֶת, וּמִנְחַת כֹּהֵן אֵינָהּ נֶאֱכֶלֶת, כֹּהֶנֶת מִתְחַלֶּלֶת וְכֹהֵן אֵין מִתְחַלֵּל, כֹּהֶנֶת מִטַּמְּאָה לַמֵּתִים וְאֵין כֹּהֵן מִטַּמֵּא לַמֵּתִים, כֹּהֵן אוֹכֵל בְּקָדְשֵׁי קָדָשִׁים וְאֵין כֹּהֶנֶת אוֹכֶלֶת בְּקָדְשֵׁי קָדָשִׁים. מַה בֵּין אִישׁ לְאִשָּׁה: הָאִישׁ פּוֹרֵעַ וּפוֹרֵם וְאֵין הָאִשָּׁה פּוֹרַעַת וּפוֹרֶמֶת, *הָאִישׁ מַדִּיר אֶת בְּנוֹ בְּנָזִיר וְאֵין הָאִשָּׁה מַדֶּרֶת בְּנָהּ בְּנָזִיר, *הָאִישׁ מְגַלֵּחַ עַל נְזִירוּת אָבִיו וְאֵין הָאִשָּׁה מְגַלַּחַת עַל נְזִירוּת אָבִיהָ, הָאִישׁ מְקַדֵּשׁ אֶת בִּתּוֹ וְאֵין הָאִשָּׁה מְקַדֶּשֶׁת אֶת בִּתָּהּ, הָאִישׁ מוֹכֵר אֶת בִּתּוֹ וְאֵין הָאִשָּׁה מוֹכֶרֶת אֶת בִּתָּהּ, *הָאִישׁ נִסְקָל עָרוֹם וְאֵין הָאִשָּׁה נִסְקֶלֶת עֲרוּמָּה, הָאִישׁ נִתְלֶה וְאֵין הָאִשָּׁה נִתְלֵית, הָאִישׁ נִמְכָּר בִּגְנֵיבָתוֹ וְאֵין הָאִשָּׁה נִמְכֶּרֶת בִּגְנֵיבָתָהּ.§

גמ' ת"ר: *כָּל הַנְּשׂוּאוֹת לִכְהוּנָּה מִנְחוֹתֵיהֶן נִשְׂרָפוֹת. כֵּיצַד? כֹּהֶנֶת לְוִיָּה וְיִשְׂרְאֵלִית שֶׁנִּשֵּׂאת לְכֹהֵן — אֵין מִנְחָתָהּ נֶאֱכֶלֶת, מִפְּנֵי שֶׁיֵּשׁ לוֹ חֵלֶק בָּהּ. וְאֵינָהּ עוֹלָה כָּלִיל — מִפְּנֵי שֶׁיֵּשׁ לָהּ חֵלֶק בָּהּ. אֶלָּא, הַקּוֹמֶץ קָרֵב בְּעַצְמוֹ וְהַשִּׁירַיִם קְרֵיבִין בְּעַצְמָן. אִיקְּרֵי כָּאן *כָּל שֶׁהוּא מִמֶּנּוּ לָאִשִּׁים הֲרֵי הוּא בְּבַל תַּקְטִירוּ! אָמַר יְהוּדָה בְּרֵיהּ דְּרַ"שׁ בֶּן פָּזִי: דְּמַסִּיק לְהוּ לְשׁוּם עֵצִים, כְּר"א. *דְּתַנְיָא, ר"א אוֹמֵר: לְרֵיחַ נִיחוֹחַ אִי אַתָּה מַעֲלֶה, אֲבָל אַתָּה מַעֲלֵיהוּ לְשׁוּם עֵצִים. הָנִיחָא לְר"א, דְּאִית לֵיהּ הַאי סְבָרָא, אֶלָּא לְרַבָּנַן דְּלֵית לְהוּ הַאי סְבָרָא, מַאי אִיכָּא לְמֵימַר? דְּעָבְדִי לְהוּ כְּר"א בְּרַ"שׁ. *דְּתַנְיָא, רַבִּי אֶלְעָזָר בְּרַ"שׁ אוֹמֵר: הַקּוֹמֶץ קָרֵב בְּעַצְמוֹ, וְהַשִּׁירַיִם מִתְפַּזְּרִים עַל בֵּית הַדֶּשֶׁן. וַאֲפִילּוּ

רש"י

וְכָל הַנְּשׂוּאוֹת [לְכֹהֲנִים] מִנְחוֹתֵיהֶן נִשְׂרָפוֹת. וַאֲפִילּוּ קָרַב הַקּוֹמֶץ כְּהִלְכָתוֹ וְלֹא נִטְמְאוּ — נִשְׂרָפִין שִׁירַיִם בְּבֵית הַדֶּשֶׁן, כִּדְמְפָרֵשׁ בַּגְּמָרָא. כֹּהֶנֶת. בַּת כֹּהֵן. מִנְחָתָהּ נֶאֱכֶלֶת. ד"כָל מִנְחַת כֹּהֵן כָּלִיל תִּהְיֶה לֹא תֵאָכֵל" כְּתִיב (ויקרא ו). אֲבָל (א) כֹּהֶנֶת הַנְּשׂוּאָה לְיִשְׂרָאֵל — נֶאֱכֶלֶת, וְכֵן כֹּהֶנֶת אַלְמָנָה וּגְרוּשָׁה שֶׁהֵבִיאָה מִנְחָתָהּ — נֶאֱכֶלֶת. כֹּהֶנֶת מִתְחַלֶּלֶת. מִן הַתְּרוּמָה וּמִן הַכְּהוּנָּה אִם נִבְעֲלָה לְפָסוּל. וְכֹהֵן אֵין מִתְחַלֵּל. אִם נָשָׂא גְּרוּשָׁה זוֹנָה וַחֲלָלָה. וְטַעַם דְּכוּלָּהּ מַתְנִי' מְפָרֵשׁ בַּגְּמָ'. בְּקָדְשֵׁי קָדָשִׁים. חַטָּאת וְאָשָׁם וּמִנְחָה, דִּבְכוּלָּם כְּתִיב: "כָּל זָכָר בַּכֹּהֲנִים [יֹאכְלֶנּוּ]". מַה בֵּין אִישׁ לְאִשָּׁה. בְּיִשְׂרָאֵל נַמִי קָמַיְירֵי. אִישׁ פּוֹרֵעַ וּפוֹרֵם. כְּשֶׁהוּא מְנוּגָּע, פּוֹרֵעַ רֹאשׁוֹ וּפוֹרֵם בְּגָדָיו. הָאִישׁ מַדִּיר אֶת בְּנוֹ. קָטָן בְּנָזִיר. וְחָלָה הַנְּזִירוּת עָלָיו אֲפִילּוּ לִכְשֶׁיִּגְדַּל. מְגַלֵּחַ עַל נְזִירוּת אָבִיו. אִם נָדַר אָבִיו בִּנְזִירוּת, וְהִפְרִישׁ קָרְבְּנוֹתָיו וּמֵת, וְהָיָה בְּנוֹ נָזִיר — הַבֵּן מְגַלֵּחַ בְּיוֹם מְלֹאת, וּמֵבִיא קָרְבָּנוֹת שֶׁהִפְרִישׁ אָבִיו. מְקַדֵּשׁ אֶת בִּתּוֹ. מְקַבֵּל קִידּוּשֵׁי בִּתּוֹ קְטַנָּה שֶׁלֹּא מִדַּעְתָּהּ. מוֹכֵר אֶת בִּתּוֹ. לְאָמָה כְּשֶׁהִיא קְטַנָּה.

גמ' מִנְחוֹתֵיהֶן נִשְׂרָפוֹת. אַחַת מִנְחַת סוֹטָה וְאַחַת מִנְחַת נְדָבָה. מִפְּנֵי שֶׁיֵּשׁ לוֹ חֵלֶק בָּהּ. שֶׁהוּא מַקְרִיבָהּ מִשֶּׁלּוֹ, וּכְתִיב "כָּל מִנְחַת כֹּהֵן" וגו'. וְאֵינָהּ עוֹלָה כָּלִיל (ב) שֶׁיֵּשׁ לָהּ חֵלֶק בָּהּ. שֶׁלְּכַפָּרָתָהּ הִיא בָּאָה, וְאֵין מִנְחַת זָר וּבַת כֹּהֵן קְרֵבִין כָּלִיל בְּלֹא קְמִיצָה. הַשִּׁירַיִם קְרֵיבִין לְעַצְמָן. לְאַחַר שֶׁקָּרַב הַקּוֹמֶץ. קְרֵי כָּאן כָּל שֶׁמִּמֶּנּוּ כו'. "כִּי כָל שְׂאוֹר וְכָל דְּבַשׁ לֹא *תַקְרִיבוּ לַה'" (ויקרא ב) הֲוָה לֵיהּ לְמִכְתַּב. לָמָּה לֵיהּ לְמִכְתַּב "מִמֶּנּוּ"? אֶלָּא לְמִדְרְשֵׁיהּ נַמִי בְּאַנְפֵּי נַפְשֵׁיהּ; לֹא תַקְטִירוּ כָּל שֶׁמִּמֶּנּוּ עוֹלֶה כְּבָר אִשֶּׁה לַה'. וְיֵשׁ בִּכְלָל לָאו זֶה בְּשַׂר כָּל קָרְבָּנוֹת חוּץ מֵעוֹלָה, וְיֵשׁ בִּכְלָל זֶה שְׁיָרֵי מְנָחוֹת. וְהָכָא נַמִי, דִּלְמָא בָּתַר חֵלֶק שֶׁלָּהּ אִית לָן לְמֵיזַל, וְהָוְיָא הַקְטָרַת קוֹמֶץ כְּהִלְכָתוֹ, וְאֵלּוּ שִׁירַיִם גְּמוּרִין הֵם, וְיֶשְׁנָן בְּ"בַל תַּקְטִירוּ". דְּמַסִּיק לְהוּ לְשֵׁם עֵצִים. דְּנֵימָא הָכִי: אִם רְאוּיִם הֵן לְהַקְטִיר וְלֹא הָיְתָה רְאוּיָה לִיקָּמֵץ, כְּדִין מִנְחַת כֹּהֵן — הֲרֵי זוֹ הַקְטָרָה לִשְׁמָהּ, וּקְמִיצָה לֹא מַעֲלָה וְלֹא מוֹרֶדֶת. וְאִם רְאוּיָה הָיְתָה לִיקָּמֵץ וְאֵלּוּ שְׁיָרֶיהָ — הֲרֵי הֵן כִּשְׁאָר עֲצֵי הַמַּעֲרָכָה. כְּר"א. פְּלוּגְתַּיְיהוּ בִּזְבָחִים:* אֵבְרֵי חַטָּאת שֶׁנִּתְעָרְבוּ בְּאֵבְרֵי עוֹלָה, ר"א אוֹמֵר: יִתֵּן לְמַעְלָה, וְרוֹאֶה אֲנִי אֶת בְּשַׂר חַטָּאת עַל הַמִּזְבֵּחַ כְּאִילּוּ הֵן עֵצִים. וַחֲכ"א: תְּעוּבַּר צוּרָתָן וְיֵצְאוּ לְבֵית הַשְּׂרֵיפָה, שֶׁאָסוּר לְהַקְטִיר אֵבְרֵי חַטָּאת, מִשּׁוּם לָאו ד"כָל שֶׁמִּמֶּנּוּ לָאִשִּׁים". וְר"א סָבַר: בַּתְרֵיהּ דְּהַהוּא קְרָא כְּתִיב: "קָרְבַּן רֵאשִׁית תַּקְרִיבוּ אוֹתָם לַה'" — שְׂאוֹר וּדְבַשׁ בִּכּוּרִים אַתָּה מֵבִיא מִן הַתְּמָרִים, וּמִנְחַת שְׁתֵּי הַלֶּחֶם שֶׁהוּא רֵאשִׁית מִן הַשְּׂאוֹר. "וְאֶל הַמִּזְבֵּחַ לֹא יַעֲלוּ לְרֵיחַ נִיחוֹחַ" קָאֵי נַמִי אַ"מִּמֶּנּוּ אִשֶּׁה לַה'" דְּאוֹקְמֵיהּ בְּ"בַל תַּקְטִירוּ", וְאַשְׁמְעִינַן דְּלֹא אָסַר הַקְטָרָתוֹ אֶלָּא כְּשֶׁמִּתְכַּוֵּין לְרֵיחַ נִיחוֹחַ. כְּר"א בְּרַ"שׁ. בִּמְנָחוֹת בְּפֶ' "אֵלּוּ מְנָחוֹת" (דף עג:) גַּבֵּי מִנְחַת חוֹטֵא כֹּהֵן, שֶׁמֵּבִיא עַל שְׁמִיעַת קוֹל, אוֹ עַל בִּיטּוּי שְׂפָתַיִם, אוֹ עַל טוּמְאַת מִקְדָּשׁ וְקָדָשָׁיו בְּדַלֵּי דַלּוּת. וּפְלִיגִי רַבָּנַן עֲלֵיהּ דְּרַבִּי שִׁמְעוֹן וְאָמְרִי: "וְהָיְתָה לַכֹּהֵן כַּמִּנְחָה" — מִנְחַת חוֹבָתוֹ שֶׁל כֹּהֵן כָּלִיל כְּמִנְחַת נִדְבָתוֹ, וְאֵינָהּ נִקְמֶצֶת. (ג) [וְר"ש דָּרֵישׁ לֵיהּ לִקְרָא הָתָם הָכִי: וְכִי נֶאֱמַר וְהָיְתָה לַכֹּהֵן כְּמִנְחָתוֹ? לֹא נֶאֱמַר אֶלָּא] כְּמִנְחַת חוֹטֵא שֶׁל יִשְׂרָאֵל, מַה שֶּׁל יִשְׂרָאֵל נִקְמֶצֶת — אַף מִנְחַת חוֹטֵא שֶׁל כֹּהֵן נִקְמֶצֶת. אִי מַה מִּנְחַת יִשְׂרָאֵל שְׁיָרֶיהָ נֶאֱכָלִין, אַף זוֹ שְׁיָרֶיהָ נֶאֱכָלִין — ת"ל: "וְהָיְתָה לַכֹּהֵן כַּמִּנְחָה"; לַכֹּהֵן כַּמִּנְחָה לְעִנְיַן עֲבוֹדַת כֹּהֵן שֶׁטְּעוּנָה קְמִיצָה, וְלֹא לָאִשִּׁים כַּמִּנְחָה. הָא כֵּיצַד? הַקּוֹמֶץ קָרֵב לְעַצְמוֹ וְהַשִּׁירַיִם קְרֵיבִין לְעַצְמָם. וְלֵית לֵיהּ "כָּל שֶׁמִּמֶּנּוּ לָאִשִּׁים" כְּלָל. ר"א בְּרַ"שׁ פָּלֵיג עֲלֵיהּ, וְאָמַר: קוֹמֶץ קָרֵב לְעַצְמוֹ וְשִׁירַיִם מִתְפַּזְּרִין לְאִיבּוּד.

ה"ג

תוספות

האומרת טמאה אני. ירושלמי: האומרת "טמאה אני" לא כחטאת שמתה בעליה היא? וחטאת שמתה בעליה ילכו המעות לים המלח! דמיא לאשם תלוי. אם לאשם תלוי — אפי' מקדשה בכלי! א"ר: מתני' דמיא לאשם תלוי שנשחט, דתנינן תמן: אם משנשחט נודע לו — הדם ישפך והבשר יצא לבית השריפה.

כל הנשואות לכהנים מנחותיהן נשרפות. פרש"י: אחד מנחת סוטה ואחד מנחת נדבה. ותימה: מנחת נדבה מה חלק יש לו בה? והא אפילו רבי יהודה דאומר בפ' "אין בין המודר" (נדרים דף לה:): אדם מביא על אשתו כל קרבנות שהיא חייבת — דווקא שהיא חייבת, כדמפרש בספרי, כגון אם [הקיפה] נזירות בראשה וחיללה את השבת, דומיא דמנחת סוטה שהיא חובה, דיליף לה מ"והביא את קרבנה עליה" — כל קרבן שעליה. אבל מנחת נדבה — מודה רבי יהודה שאינו מביא! וי"ל: משום הכי יש לו חלק, משום דקי"ל: מה שקנתה אשה קנה בעלה. כדתנן בפ"ד דנזיר (דף כד.): אם שלה היתה בהמה — החטאת תמות, וקא דייק בגמ': מנא להו? מה שקנתה אשה קנה בעלה! הלכך יש לו חלק בה, אפילו לרבנן, דפליגי אדר' יהודה ואמרי דווקא קרבן שמכשירה לו מביא עליה, דמה שקנת' קנה בעלה. מיהו, בירושלמי דפרק "היה מביא" משמע דבמנחת סוטה איירי. והכי איתא התם: "מנחתה" — מלמד שהיא קדשה לשמה. כשם שהיא קדשה לשמה — כך היא קדשה לשמו. ותני רבי חייא ופליג; ליקרב כליל אינה יכולה מפני שותפתה של אשה, לאכול אינה יכולה — מפני שותפתו של איש, [אלא] הקומץ* לעצמו והשירים קריבין לעצמן. ואת אומר "מנחתה"? אלא מה דאישתעי קרא אישתעי מתני'. ותו התם: "והביא את קרבנה עליה" — בעלה מהו שיפריש עליה חוץ מדעתה? מכיון שיש לו שותפות במנחה — מפריש עליה חוץ מדעתה. וא"ת: מאחר שיש לו חלק בה, א"כ הויא לה מנחת שותפות, ואומר בפ"ק דזבחים (דף ה:): הניח מנחה לשני בניו ומת — קריבה, ואין בה משום שותפות. הא יש בה משום שותפות — אינה קריבה, משום דכתיב בה "נפש", והכי קתני בסיפרי בהדיא! וי"ל: כיון דעיקר כפרה משום דידה — "נפש" קרינן בה, דהא הניח מנחתו לשני בניו, דמסיק התם (דף ו.) דקניא להו — אלמא משום דמכפרי קרינא ביה "נפש".

הקומץ קרב בעצמו. וא"ת: אמאי לא שדינן לכולה מנחה בתר דידה, ויהו שיריה נאכלין, כדאמר בפ' "אין בין המודר" (נדרים דף לו:), ואיתא בפ"ק דזבחים (דף ו.) ובפ"ק דתמורה (דף ג:): מתכפר עושה תמורה, והכא היא מתכפרת במנחה זו! י"ל: התם מיקני למתכפר כולי זבח, ואין לו למקדיש חלק בו. אבל הכא — יש לו לבעל חלק במנחה.

דמסיק להו לשום עצים. רש"י פי', דנימא הכי: אם ראוין הן להקטיר ולא היתה ראויה לקמוץ וכו'. ותימה: מאי תנאי שייך? הא ודאי כאילו מעורבין שיריים, והוי כאברי עולה ואברי חטאת שנתערבו דפליגי בה ר"א ורבנן (זבחים עז.), דלא שייך בה תנאי, דליכא שום ספק, אלא ודאי מקצתן ראויה להקטיר *ומקצתן לאכול ולהקטיר, ואותן מה שבתוכן אין ראוי להקטיר לשם עצים בכל מקום שהוא, ולא שייך שום תנאי! וכמדומה דרש"י נקט לי' אגב שטפיה דההיא דפרק "נושאין על האנוסה" (יבמות ק.), דתנן: כהנת שנתערב ולדה בולד שפחתה — נותנין עליהם חומרי ישראל וחומרי כהנים. ומפרש בגמרא דמנחתם נקמצת כמנחת ישראל ואינה נאכלת כמנחת כהנים, וכולה סוגיא כי הכא. והתם ודאי שייך תנאי, כשהאחד מקריב מנחה אינו יודע אם כהן הוא או ישראל וצריך להתנות כמו שפירש רש"י כאן. והא דתנן ב"הקומץ רבה" (מנחות דף כג.): נתערב קומצה בשיריה או בשיריים של חבירתה, לא יקטיר — אית לן למימר דסתמא כרבנן דפליגי אדרבי אליעזר.

הקומץ קרב לעצמו והשיריים לעצמן. בירושל' בעי אליביה דר"ש: אלין שיריים משום מה הם באים, משום קומץ או משום שיריים? אי תימר משום קומץ — אינו נותנו בלילה, ואינו נותנו לאחר מיתה, ואינו מחשב להן. ואי תימר משום שיריים — נותנו בלילה, ונותנו לאחר מיתה. מהו שיחשב להן? ופשיט לה מדר"א בר"ש, דאמר דמתפזרין על גבי הדשן שלמטה, כדמפרש בפ' "ואלו הן מנחות". הדא אמרו: נותנו בלילה, ונותנו לאחר מיתה, ומחשב להן. א"ר יוסי בר בון: אינו מחשב להן, שלא הוכשרו לא לאכילת אדם ולא לאכילת מזבח.

כהן

תוספות שאנץ

צניעותא ל"ה: כהנת מתחללת מן התרומה ומן הכהונה אם נבעלה לפסול לה ולאו דוקא נקט כהנת דה"ה דאלמנת בת ישראל שנשאת לכהן גדול אלא רבותא נקט דאפילו כהנת מתחללת מכהונה: מגלח

על נזירות אביו אם נדר בנזירות והפריש קרבנותיו ומת והיה בנו נזיר הבן מגלח ביום מלאת ימי נזרו ומביא קרבנות שהפריש אביו: איקרי כאן כל שממנו לאישים הרי הוא בבל תקטירו פ"ה דהוה ליה למכתב כי כל שאור וכל דבש לא תקטירו לה' ולמה כתב ממנו אלא למדרשי' באפי נפשיה לא תקטירו כל שממנו עולה כבר אשה לה' ויש בכלל לאו זה בשר כל הקרבנות חוץ מעולה ויש בכלל זה שירי מנחות והכא נמי אמר' דלמא בתר חלק שלה אית לן למיזל והויא ליה הקטרה דקומץ כהלכתה ואלו שירים גמורין הן והרי הן בבל תקטירו. דמסיק להו לשם עצים וכר' אליעזר ופלוגתיהו בזבחים אברי חטאת שנתערבו באברים של עולה רבי אליעזר אומר יתנם למעלה ורואין בשר החטאת כאילו הן עצים וחכמים אומרים תעובר צורתו ויצאו לבית השריפה שאסור להקטיר אברי חטאת משום לאו דכל שממנו לאישים ור' אליעזר סבר בתריה דההוא קרא כתיב קרבן ראשית תקריבו אותם לה' ואל המזבח לא יעלו לריח ניחוח וקאי נמי אממנו לה' דאוקמה בבל תקטירו ואשמעינן דלא אסרה הקטרה אלא כשמכוין להם לריח ניחוח ל"ה: דתניא ר' אליעזר אומר הקומץ קרב בעצמו והשירים מתפזרין גבי מנחת כהן חוטא שהביא מנחה על שמיעת קול או על ביטוי שפתים או על טומאת מקדש וקדשיו בדלי דלות ופליגי רבנן עליה ואמרי מנחת חובתו של כהן כליל כמנחת נדבתו ואינה נקמצת ור' שמעון דריש לקרא התם וכי נאמר והיתה לכהן כמנחתו והלא לא נאמר אלא כמנחה והאי קרא במנחת חוטא כתיב ודריש לה הכי ואם כהן הוא תהיה לו כמנחת חוטא של ישראל מה מנחת חוטא של ישראל נקמצת אף מנחת כהן חוטא נקמצת אי מה מנחת חוטא ישראל שיריה נאכלין אף זו שיריה נאכלין ת"ל והיתה לכהן כמנחה לענין עבודת כהן שטעונה קמיצה ולא לאישים כמנחה הא כיצד הקומץ קרב בעצמו והשירים קרבין לעצמן. ור' אליעזר סבר ליה כאבוה דבעי קמיצה ומיהו שירים קרבין לעצמן לית ליה דכל שממנו לאישים כו' אלא קומץ קרב לעצמו והשירים מתפזרין לאיבוד ל"ה:

ה"ג

נה א מיי' פ"ה מהל' טומאת צרעת הלכה א:
נו ב מיי' פ"ב מהל' נזירות הלכה יג:
נז ג מיי' שם פ"ח הלכה טו:
א ד מיי' פ"ב מהלכות סוטה הלכה ב:
ב ה מיי' שם הלכה ח והלכה ט:

ואפי' רבנן לא פליגי עליה דר' אלעזר בר' שמעון אלא במנחת חוטא של כהנים, דבת הקרבה היא, אבל בהא — אפי' רבנן מודו.§ "בת ישראל הנשואה" וכו'.§ מ"ט? דאמר קרא "וכל מנחת כהן כליל תהיה לא תאכל" (ויקרא ו) — כהן ולא כהנת.§ "כהנת מתחללת כהן אין מתחלל".§ מנלן? דאמר קרא: "ולא יחלל זרעו בעמיו" (שם כא) — זרעו מתחלל, והוא אינו מתחלל.§ "כהנת מטמאה" כו'.§ מ"ט? אמר קרא: "אמור אל הכהנים בני אהרן" (שם) — *בני אהרן ולא בנות אהרן.§ "כהן אוכל בקדשי קדשים"§ דכתיב: "כל זכר בבני אהרן יאכלנה".§ "ומה בין איש" (שם ו) כו'.§ ת"ר: "איש", אין לי *אלא איש, אשה מנין? כשהוא אומר: "והצרוע אשר בו" (שם יג) — אהרי כאן שנים, א"כ מה ת"ל "איש" — לענין שלמטה, איש פורע וכו'.§ "האיש מדיר את בנו בנזיר ואין האשה מדרת בנה בנזיר".§ *אמר ר' יוחנן: בהלכה היא בנזיר.§ "האיש מגלח על נזירות אביו ואין האשה מגלחת על נזירות אביה".§ *אמר ר' יוחנן: גהלכה היא בנזיר.§ "האיש מקדש את בתו ואין האשה מקדשת את בתה"§ דכתיב: "את בתי נתתי לאיש הזה" (דברים כב).§ "האיש מוכר את בתו ואין האשה מוכרת את בתה".§ דכתיב "וכי ימכור איש את בתו" (שמות כא).§ "האיש נסקל ערום" כו'.§ *מ"ט? "ורגמו אותו" (ויקרא כד), מאי אותו? אילימא אותו ולא אותה — והכתיב: "והוצאת את האיש ההוא או את האשה ההיא" (דברים יז)! אלא: אותו בלא כסותו, ולא אותה בלא כסותה.§ "האיש נתלה ואין" כו'.§ *מ"ט? אמר קרא: "ותלית אותו על עץ" (שם כא) — אותו ולא אותה.§ "האיש נמכר בגניבתו ואין האשה נמכרת בגניבתה".§ מ"ט? אמר קרא: "ונמכר בגניבתו" (שמות כב) — בגניבתו ולא בגניבתה.§

הדרן עלך היה נוטל

ארוסה *ושומרת יבם — דלא שותות ולא נוטלות כתובה, שנאמר: "אשר תשטה אשה תחת אישה" (במדבר ה) — פרט לארוסה ושומרת יבם. האלמנה לכהן גדול, גרושה וחלוצה לכהן הדיוט, ממזרת ונתינה

רש"י

ה"ג **ואפי' רבנן לא פליגי עליה אלא במנחת חוטא של כהנים דבת הקרבה היא.** דמקשי חובתו לנדבתו, דלא בעי קמיצה. אבל הא — דלאו בת הקרבה היא, דדלמא בתרה דידה אזלינן, ושיריים גמורים נינהו, ואפילו רבנן מודו דמתפזרין. **מאי טעמא.** קאמר מתני' מנחת כהנת נאכלת כשאינה נשואה לכהן, וכשהיא נשואה לכהן — אינה נאכלת, כליל מיהא לא הויא. **לא יחלל זרעו.** בכהן הנושא פסולה לכהונה כתיב, ודרשינן בקידושין (דף עז.): "לא יחלל" שני חילולין; אחד לה ואחד לזרעו, שהכהן מחלל את שתיהן. אבל הוא אין מתחלל. **בני אהרן.** "לנפש לא יטמא", ולא בנות אהרן באזהרה זו. **כל זכר בבני אהרן יאכלנה.** במנחה כתיב. **איש.** צרוע הוא. **אין לי.** שנחלט בטומאת נתקים אלא איש, אשה מנין? כשהוא אומר סמוך לו: "והצרוע אשר בו הנגע", ולא איבעי ליה למכתב אלא "בגדיו יהיו פרומים וראשו יהיה פרוע", דהא כתיב לעיל, דבמצורע קמיירי. אלא לרבות צרוע שני, כגון אשה. ה"ג: **א"כ מה ת"ל איש לענין שלמטה איש פורע ופורם וכו'** (א). מה ת"ל איש, מאחר שסופינו לרבות את האשה? לענין שלמטה. לאו למעוטי מטומאה האמורה בפסוק זה בא למעוטי, אלא מענין האמור בפסוק שלאחריו, דכתיב ביה פריעה ופרימה, לומר לך: איש פורע ופורם ולא אשה. **הלכה היא בנזיר.** הלכה למשה מסיני הוא בהלכות נזיר. **נתתי לאיש.** באביה נתלית נתינתה. **ורגמו אותו.** אי נימא (ב) אותו ולא אותה — והכתיב גבי נערה המאורסה "והוצאתם את שניהם וסקלתם אותם"! אלא הא דממעט אשה — לענין ערום. דנפיק מהאי קרא מיעוטא, ד"אותו" משמע ולא כסותו, ולהכי נקט ליה להאי משמעותא דערום בלשון זכר גבי איש, למימרא: הא אותה — בכסותה. **נמכר בגניבתו.** אם אין לו מה לשלם.

הדרן עלך היה נוטל

ארוסה. שקינא לה ארוס. **ושומרת יבם.** שקינא לה יבם. **לא שותות.** דממעטינהו קרא. **ולא נוטלות כתובה.** שהיא גרמה לאסור עצמה עליו, שנסתרה אחר קינוי. דמקינוי ואיסור לא אימעיט, כדמפרש בגמרא. ואפילו לית לן דרב המנונא* (ג) דשומרת יבם שזינתה מותרת ליבמה, נהי דמותרת — מיהו לא בעי למינסב אשה זונה, והיא הפסידה כתובתה. **תחת אישה.** ביושבת תחתיו הכתוב מדבר. **נתינה**

תוספות

כהן ולא כהנת. ירושלמי: ר' אבהו בעי קמיה ר"ל: והכתיב (ויקרא כב): "וכהן כי יקנה נפש קנין כספו", מעתה כהן ולא כהנת! א"ל: "והכהן המשיח תחתיו מבניו" — את שבנו עומד תחתיו, יצתה זו שאין בנה עומד תחתיה. ה"ה דבפרק "הזרוע" (חולין דף קלב.) הוה מצי לשנויי נמי הכי: "ונתן לכהן הזרוע", דלא אמר לכהן ולא לכהנת, אלא אפילו לכהנת — דהכא טעמא משום דכתיב: "והכהן המשיח תחתיו מבניו". אבל התם דחי ליה משום ד"אהרן ובניו" כתיב בפרשת מנחה. אי נמי, משום דהתם הוי מיעוט אחר מיעוט.

*מה **בין איש לאשה.** [שייך לעמוד א' במשנה] בתוספתא (פ"ב) קא חשיב: עובר על מצות עשה שהזמן גרמא, מה שאין כן באשה. האיש עובר על "בל תקיף" ועל "בל תשחית" ועל "בל תטמא למתים", מה שאין כן באשה. האיש נדון בבן סורר ומורה, ונעטף ומספר, ואין האשה נעטפת ומספרת. האיש נמכר ונשנה ואין האשה נמכרת ונשנית. האיש נרצע ונמכר לעבד עברי, וקונה לעבד עברי, ואין האשה נרצעת ונמכרת וקונה. ולא קתני התם כל הני דמתני' אלא דזכאי בבתו, משום דמפרש התם בכסף ובשטר ובביאה. ותימה: אמאי לא חשיב נמי סמיכות תנופות הגשות וקמיצות דבין כהן לכהנת, וכל הני דתנן בפ"ק דקידושין (דף לו.), ולא קתני נמי שהעברי יוצא בשנים וביובל ובמיתת האדון משא"כ בעבריה, הזב מטמא בראיות ולא הזבה, מצורע אסור בתשמיש המטה ולא מצורעת, כדמפרש בריש פרק "מחוסרי כפרה" (כריתות דף ח:): "מחוץ לאהלו" ולא מחוץ לאהלה.

*[נ"ז שייך לע"א במשנה] **האיש** מגלח על נזירות. בפ"ד דנזיר (דף ל.) ובפרק בתרא דכריתות (דף כז:) מפ' דדוקא על מעות סתומין, ולא על מעות מפורשין.

שנאמר את בתי. מרישא דקרא יליף ליה: "ואמר אבי הנערה אל הזקנים" — משמע: למעט אמה, דאינה זכאה בבתה לתת.

ותלית אותו ולא אותה. בפרק "נגמר הדין" (סנהדרין דף מו.) נפקא לן מ"וכי יהיה באיש" — ולא באשה.

בגניבתו ולא בגניבתה. תימה: כיון דאי גנבה אינה נמכרת בגניבתה, א"כ אין ב"ד רשאין למוכרה, דבית דין אין מוכרין אלא בגניבתו. ובפ"ק דקידושין (דף יד:) ממעטי רבנן מ"ורצע את אזנו" — אזנו שלו ולא אזן של מוכר עצמו, דדוקא מכרוהו בית דין נרצע. ואשה, הואיל ואין בית דין מוכרין אותה — אנא ידענא דאינה נרצעת, ואמאי איצטריך לרבנן *למילף מ"העבד" ולא אמה העבריה דאינה נרצעת? וי"ל: כיון דאינה נמכרת אלא ע"י אביה, סד"א תיהוי מכירה דאב במקום מכירת בית דין, ותרצע — להכי איצטריך קרא.

הדרן עלך היה נוטל

ושומרת יבם לא שותות ולא נוטלות כתובה. ירושלמי: יודעת היתה שאין ארוסה שותה, ולמה הכניסה עצמה *למספר הזה המרובה — בשביל לפוסלה מכתובתה. פר"ח: ארוסה אע"פ שאין לה כתובה יש לה מנה ומאתים, ועל מנה ומאתים קתני הכא: לא נוטלת כתובתה. רש"י פי': דליכא למיפשט ממתני' הא דאמר רב המנונא *שומרת יבם שזינתה אסורה ליבמה, דאפילו אי לית לן דרב המנונא, מיהו אי לא בעי יבם למינסב אשה זונה — אינה נוטלת כתובתה. מיהו, תימה: אי לית לן דרב המנונא, קרא מאי איצטריך למעוטי? והא תנן בפרק "היה מביא" (לעיל דף יח:): כל שתיבעל ולא תהא אסורה לו — לא היה מתנה, דמה קינוי שייך היכא דלא מיתסרא בסתירותיה? אלא מדאיצטריך למעוטי — ש"מ דמיתסרא! מיהו, ליכא למיפשט מהכא, משום דמוקי לה בגמרא כגון שבא עליה יבם בבית אחיו, דקנאה לפוטרה בגט בלא חליצה אפילו אליבא דשמואל, הלכך שייכא נמי אשתו ליאסר עליו בזנות כדברי הכל. **אלמנה** לכ"ג וכו'. האי דלא עריב ותני להו: אלו לא שותות ולא נוטלות כתובתן, ולתני ארוסה ושומרת יבם אלמנה לכ"ג וכו' מעוברת חבירו ומניקת חבירו ואיילונית זקינה וכו' — י"ל: משום הכי פלגינהו — משום דחלוקין בטעמם. מיהו, תימה: אמאי לא תנא מעוברת בתר בבא דאלמנה לכ"ג, דדמי בטעמא? וה"ל למיתני בתחלת הפרק: אלו לא שותות, ובתר ליחשב וליזל כולהו כל הני דדמיין להדדי כל חד. וטפי הוה שייך למיתני אלו בראש כולן, ממאי דתני קצת דלא שותות, והדר תני אלו! שאינה

[ויקרא כב]
[קדושין לה.]
[כריתות ח: ערכין ג.]
נזיר כח:
[שם ל.]
סנהדרין מה.
שם מו.
יבמות נח. קדושין כז:
[לעיל יח.]
[קדושין טו.]
נ"ל למספק

תוספות שאנץ

ה"ג ואפי' רבנן לא פליגי עליה אלא במנחת חוטא דבת הקרבה היא דמקשינן חובתו לנדבתו דלא בעיא קמיצה אבל הא דלאו בת הקרבה היא דלמא בתר דידה אזלי' ושירים גמורין נינהו אפי' רבנן מודו דמתפזרין אבית הדשן לה"ה. ה"ג א"כ מה ת"ל איש לענין שלמטה לא למעוטי מטומאה האמורה בפסוק זה בא למעוטי אלא מענין האמור בפסוק של אחריו דכתיב ביה פריעה ופרימה דליכא למימר דלענין שלמעלה קאמר דדוקא איש נחלט ואין האשה נחלטת א) דהא אינה פורעת ופורמת. אותו בלא כסותו ולא אותה בלא כסותה. וא"ת לרבנן דר' יהודה דלעיל דאמרי אין האשה נסקלת ערומה משום דחיישינן להרהור ובעי נמי ברור לה מיתה יפה ב) ותיפוק לי מהאי קרא. וי"ל דאי מהאי הוה אמינא דאשה בין בכסותה בין שלא בכסותה קמ"ל רב נחמן דאמר קרא ואהבת לרעך כמוך. אבל ר' יהודה דאמר לעיל דאין מכסין אותה אלא שני פרקים משום דצערא דגופה עדיף טפי (ולית ליה) [וא"ת אטו לית ליה] הך דרשא דהכא הא אותה בכסותה. וי"ל דאה"נ דלית ליה א"נ איתא ליה וסבירא ליה דקרא לא אתא אלא שיכסו אותה שני פרקים אבל יותר לא משום צערא דגופה עדיף טפי ורוצה לומר הא אותה בכסותה בשני פרקים שמכסין אותה: בגנבתו ולא בגנבתה כו'. ואע"ג דדרשי' מהאי קרא בגנבתו ולא בכפלו בגנבתו ולא בזוממו (שאם הודה לא ישלם פי' שנים ממה שהוזם) בגנבתו גנבה אחת ולא ב' גנבות י"ל דכולהו הני דרשות ש"מ: **סליק פירקא**

פרק שלישי ארוסה ושומרת יבם לא שותות ולא נוטלות כתובה שהיא גרמה לאסור עצמה שנסתרה אחר קנוי פרשב"ם. ואפי' למאן דלית ליה דרב המנונא דאמר שומרת יבם שזינתה אסורה ליבמה מ"מ נהי דהוי מותרת לו. אי לא בעי לאינסובי משום שהיא זונה תפסיד כתובתה כיון שזינתה. מיהו אומר ר"י דהלכה ג) דארוסה זו שזינתה דנאסרה בביאה זו על בעלה והך כר' עקיבא דמשוי חייבי לאוין [...] גדול לא שותות ולא נוטלות כתובה ואע"ג דשאר אלמנה לכהן גדול לא קנסוה רבנן ואית לה כתובה כדאיתא בפ' אלמנה ניזונת זו אין לה כתובה שסתירתה גרמה לה ליאסר עליו ואפי' ראויה לו הלכך לאו [...] עדיפא מכשרה ל"ה ולא שותות דלא נאמרו בפרשה אלא בראויה לקיימה והכי תני בספרי כי תשטה אשתו בראויה לאישות הכתוב מדבר פרט לאלמנה לכהן גדול וא"ת אמאי לא תאני כולהו בחד בבא וי"ל [...] נפקא לן [מקרא אחרינא דכתיב] תחת אישה ביושבת תחתיו הכתוב מדבר וא"ת תיפוק לי שאינה שותה משום דכתיב ונקה האיש מעון וזה אינו מנוקה מעון כיון שנשא אשה שאינה ראויה לו. וי"ל דחשבי' ליה [...] העון בא אחר הקינוי והוו המים בודקין אשתו אי לאו טעמא דלעיל וא"ת אמאי לא פליגי ב"ש וב"ה גבי ארוסה ושומרת יבם כמו דפליגי בסמוך גבי מתו בעליהן עד שלא שתו והוו להו לב"ש לומר דנוטלות כתובה [...] שומרת יבם דכ"ע מודו דאין להם כתובה דהיא יודעת שאין בעלה יכול לבודקה משנסתרה ולא תיזהר מליסתור והיא נתנה אצבעה בין שיניה ולכך אין לה כתובה אבל מתו בעליהן אין יודעות שלא יהיו בעליהן [...] לא סמכי אדעתיהו שימותו בעליהן והן נזהרות ביותר מליסתר לפי' קאמר ב"ש דנוטלות כתובה ועוד י"ל דשאני התם גבי מתו בעליהן שאינן חשובות עוברות על דת כיון שיכולין בעליהן לבדקן אבל ארוסה

א) [...]דיק אמרינן דנפ"ל מקרא דאשה נמי נחלטת ואולי דט"ס הוא וצ"ל דהא והצרוע כתיב. ב) ר"ל כמו דאיתא בסנהדרין דף מה וע"ש ברש"י ד"ה להרהורא ובתוס' שם ד"ה הא. ג) נראה דצ"ל דהלכה דשומרת יבם שזינתה דנאסרת על היבם והך כר"ע וכו'.

הגהות הב"ח

(א) רש"י ד"ה ה"ג וכו' ופורם כו' פי' מה ת"ל: (ב) ד"ה ורגמו אותו מאי אותו אילימא וכו' ולא בכסות: (ג) רש"י ד"ה ולא נוטלות וכו' ושומרת יבם:

ונתינה לישראל, ובת ישראל לממזר ולנתין – לא שותות ולא נוטלות כתובה. ואלו לא שותות ולא נוטלות כתובה: א האומרת "טמאה אני", ב ושבאו לה עדים שהיא טמאה, ג והאומרת "איני שותה". אמר בעלה "איני משקה", ושבעלה בא עליה בדרך – נוטלות כתובה ולא שותות. *מתו בעליהן עד שלא שתו, *בש"א: נוטלות כתובה ולא שותות, *וב"ה א': ד או שותות או לא נוטלות כתובתן. מעוברת חבירו ומניקת חבירו – לא שותות ולא נוטלות כתובה, דברי ר"מ. וחכ"א: ה יכול הוא *להפרישה ולהחזירה לאחר זמן. ו איילונית, וזקינה, ושאינה ראויה לילד – לא נוטלות כתובה ולא שותות, ר"א אומר: יכול הוא לישא אשה אחרת ולפרות ולרבות הימנה. ושאר כל הנשים – או שותות או לא נוטלות כתובה. ז אשת כהן – שותה ומותרת לבעלה. ח אשת סריס – שותה. ט ע"י כל עריות מקנין, י חוץ מן הקטן וממי שאינו איש. כ ואלו שב"ד מקנין להן: מי שנתחרש בעלה, או נשתטה, או שהיה חבוש בבית האסורין. ל לא להשקותה אמרו, אלא לפוסלה מכתובתה. ר' יוסי אומר: אף להשקותה, לכשיצא בעלה מבית האסורין – ישקנה.§ **גמ'** *מישתא הוא דלא שתייא, הא קנויי – מקני לה, מה"מ? דת"ר: "דבר אל בני ישראל ואמרת" (א) – לרבות ארוסה ושומרת יבם לקינוי. ומתני' מני – רבי יונתן היא, דתניא: "תחת אישך" – פרט לארוסה, יכול שאני מוציא אף שומרת יבם – ת"ל: "איש איש", דברי רבי יאשיה. ר' יונתן אומר: "תחת אישך" – פרט לשומרת יבם, אוציא שומרת יבם ולא אוציא את ארוסה – תלמוד לומר: "אשר תשטה אשה תחת אישה" – פרט לארוסה. מר אלימא ליה ארוסה, דקידושי דידיה, וסוקלין על ידו, ומר אלימא ליה שומרת יבם, דלא מיחסרא מסירה לחופה. ורבי יונתן, האי "איש איש" מאי עביד ליה? מיבעי ליה *לרבות אשת חרש, ואשת שוטה, ואשת

שעמום

תורה אור: במדבר ה

רש"י

נתינה. מן הגבעונים, ואסורין לבא בישראל, כדאמרינן ביבמות (דף עח:): דוד גזר עליהן. לא שותות. דלא נאמרה פרשה אלא בראויה לקיימה. והכי תניא בספרי: "כי תשטה אשתו" – בראויה לאישות הכתוב מדבר, פרט לאלמנה לכ"ג וכו'. ולא נוטלת כתובתה. ואע"ג דשאר אלמנה לכ"ג לא קנסוה רבנן כתובה, כדאמרינן בכתובות בפרק "אלמנה ניזונית" (דף ק:) – זו אין לה, דסתירתה גרמה לה ליאסר עליו ואפי' היא ראויה לו, הלכך – לאו בת כתובה היא, דלא עדיפא מכשרה. אמר בעלה איני משקה ושבעלה בא עליה בדרך. שהוא גרם לה שלא תשתה – נוטלת כתובתה. מתו בעליהן. של כל סוטות הנסתרות וראויות לשתות, ולא הספיקו להשקותן כו'. ולא שותות. דבעינן: "והביא האיש את אשתו" וגו'. וב"ה אומרים או שותות או לא נוטלות כתובה. כלומר, מתוך שלא שותות – לא נוטלות כתובה. ובגמ' מפרש פלוגתייהו. מעוברת חבירו. שמת, והניחה מעוברת ומניקה, או שגירשה והיא מעוברת או מניקה. ואסרוה חכמים לינשא עד שיהא הולד בן ב' שנים, שכך זמן יניקתו. והלך זה ונשאה, וקינא לה – לא שותה, שהרי אינה ראויה לו לקיימה. יכול הוא להפרישה. עד כ"ד חדש, ולהחזירה. הלכך ראויה לאישות קרינא ביה. איילונית. דוכרניתא, דלא ילדה. שממעי אמה נבראת כך, ואין לה סימני אשה, לא דדים ולא שערות וקולה עבה. ושאינה ראויה לילד. ששתת כוס עיקרין. ואסורות לקיימה למי שאין לו בנים, שהרי נצטוו ישראל על פריה ורביה. אשת כהן שותה ומותרת לבעלה. אם נמצאת נקיה. ובגמ' פריך: פשיטא! אשת סריס. כגון *שנסתרס לאחר שנשאה, דקדמה שכיבת בעל לבועל. שותה. ובגמ' פריך: פשיטא!. ע"י כל העריות מקנין. אם קינא לה מאביה ומאחיה ומאחד מכל העריות שבתורה, ונסתרה – הוי קינויו קנוי, ונאסרת עליו, ושותה. ובגמ' פריך: פשיטא!. חוץ מן הקטן. דכתיב: "ושכב איש אותה". וממי שאינו איש. ובגמ' מפרש לה. ואלו שב"ד מקנין להן. אם רואין אותם מתנהגות בפריצות. לא להשקותה אמרו. הם לא ישקוה, דבעינן "והביא האיש את אשתו". ובעלה נמי לא ישקנה בקינוי זה *לכשיצא, דבעינן "וקינא והביא". ורבי יוסי לא בעי "וקינא והביא". גמ' הא קנוי מקני לה. ליאסר עליו, מדקתני: לא נוטלות כתובה: ה"ג דבר אל בני ישראל ואמרת אליהם לרבות ארוסה ושומרת יבם לקינוי ולא גרס "איש איש", דלדרשא אחרינא דרשינן ליה לקמן (דף כו.). אלא ריבויא מ"ואמרת אליהם". וה"נ אמר לקמן בפירקין:* "ואמרת" רבויא הוא. יכול שאני מוציא כו'. דממשמעות קרא משמע לן ארוסה למעוטי, דלא קרינן בה "תחת אישך". אבל שומרת יבם קרינן בה "תחת אישך" כדמפרש לקמי' דלא מיחסרא מסירה לחופה. ורבי יונתן. משמע ליה מיעוטא קמא לשומרת יבם. אבל ארוסה – קרינא בה אישות, אי לאו דהדר מעטיה קרא אחרינא, כדמפרש לקמן: משום דהוא קידשה, ואינה באה לו מכח קדושי אחרים, ועוד שנסקלת על ידו, מה שאין כן בשומרת יבם. מר אלימא ליה ארוסה. רבי יונתן חשיבא ליה ארוסה אשה גמורה טפי משומרת יבם. דקדושי דידיה. שע"י קידושי עצמו באה לו. וסוקלין על ידו. אם זינתה נסקלת בשבילו. דלא מחסרא מסירה לחופה. דנקנית ליבם בביאה גרידתא, ואפי' בזנות, להיות כאשתו לכל דבר, כדתנן ביבמות (דף נג:) ומייתי' לה לקמן בפירקא. לרבות אשת חרש (ב) שוטה. שב"ד מקנין להן. וברייתא היא בשילהי פירקין.

שעמום

תוספות

שאינה ראויה לילד. רש"י פי': ששתת כוס עיקרין. אבל בפ' "אע"פ" (כתובות דף ס:) לא משמע הכי, דמייתי התם ברייתא ותני בה: או שהיתה היא עקרה זקינה ואיילונית ושאינה ראויה לילד, אלמא דשאינה ראויה לילד לאו עקרה. ולפרש"י ששתת כוס עיקרין היינו עקרה! וזה לשון ר"ח התם: איכא למישאל: היינו איילונית היינו עקרה היינו שאינה ראויה לילד! ותשובה: שאמרנו בפרק "יש נוחלין" (ב"ב דף קיט:): ניסת לכ' – יולדת עד מ', ניסת למ' – שוב אינה יולדת. וה"ה שנוכל לפרש שאינה ראויה לילד – ששהתה אחר בעלה עשר שנים ולא היה דעתה לינשא. דאמר בסוף פרק "ד' אחים" (יבמות דף לד:): אמר רב נחמן אמר שמואל: כל ששהתה אחר בעלה י' שנים – שוב אינה מתעברת. כי אתא רבין אר"י: ל"ש אלא שאין דעתה לינשא. ואע"ג דאמר בגמ' בעקרה וזקינה, ולפי' ר"ח לא הזכיר עקרה במשנה – י"ל דלא דק בלישנא. מיהו, תימה: אמאי לא תנא נמי במתני' עקרה? **ושאר** כל הנשים או שותות. תימה: הא משנה יתירא מאי קמ"ל? הא שמעינן ליה מרישא: והאומרת איני שותה – אינה נוטלת כתובתה! ואומר רבי: דווקא מעוברת אינה שותה, משום דאיכא סכנת נפשות, כדאמר בפרק "החולץ" (יבמות דף מב:). אבל ניסת בתוך ג' חדשים – מאי דהוה הוה, ותו לא קנסינן ליה להוציא, וקרינן בה אשתו הראויה לו. ובכהן אפילו לרבנן אינה שותה, דמסקינן בפ' "החולץ" (שם לז.): אפילו לרבנן יוציא בגט.

ורבי יונתן האי איש איש מאי עביד ליה מיבעי ליה וכו'. תימה: והא איהו דאמר בפ' "אלו הנחנקין" (סנהדרין דף פה:) גבי "איש איש" ד"כי יקלל את אביו ואת אמו" קאמר: דברה תורה כלשון בנ"א, ולא דריש ליה לדרשה אחריתי! וכ"ת: היכא דאיכא למדרש, אפי' מאן דאית ליה ד"ת מודה הוא דדרשינן – א"כ מאי פריך בריש פרק "השואל" (ב"מ דף לד:) אהא דקא בעי אבידה מנלן דשומר שכר חייב – דתני': "אם גנוב יגנב". אין לי אלא גניבה, אבידה מנין – ת"ל "גנוב יגנב" מ"מ. הניחא למ"ד לא ד"ת, אלא למ"ד אמרי', מא"ל? והא התם איכא למדרש, ולא דרשינן, אלא אמר ד"ת, והכא אמאי דריש להו? ואמרי' בפ' "השוחט והמעלה" (זבחים קח:) נמי: ורבי יוסי, מדההוא "איש איש" דברה – האי "איש איש" נמי דברה, אלא השוחט להדיוט דחייב מנא ליה? ולא אמרת: כיון דמצי למדרש, מודה הוא דלא אמר דברה! וקשה לייבב שמועות דד"ת, דקשי' דר"מ אדר"מ, ודר' יהודה אדר' יהודה, ודרבי יוסי אדר' יוסי, ודר"ש אדר"ש. דר"מ – דאמר בפ' "ד' מיתות" (סנהדרין דף נו.), לרבנן גבי "איש איש" דכתיב גבי ברכת השם: ד"ת, ור"מ דריש ליה: לרבות כינויים. ובפ"ב דמסכת ע"ז (דף כז.) נמי פליג ר' יהודה ור' יוסי. דא"ר יהודה: כותי לא ימול ישראל מפני שהוא מל לשם הר גריזים. אמר לו ר' יוסי: וכי היכן מצינו מילה בתורה לשמה? ומפרש טעמא דר' יהודה משום דכתיב "לה' המול". ורבי יוסי – "המול ימול" כתיב. ואידך נמי, הכתיב "המול ימול" – ד"ת כלשון בני אדם. [אלמא דרבי יוסי לית ליה דברה תורה כו']. והתם בההוא שמעתא גופיה פלוגתא ר"מ ור' יהודה, ואמרינן: ימול כותי ולא ימול ארמאי, דברי ר"מ. והיינו כר' יוסי, דאמר: כותי שפיר דמי, דלא אמר ד"ת. ובפ' "ד' מחוסרי כפרה" (כריתות דף יא.) אמרינן לאחרים: בשלמא "והפדה לא נפדתה" – דקסבר ד"ת, ואחרים היינו ר"מ, כדאיתא בסוף מס' הוריות (דף יג:). דר' יהודה – מהא ד"המול ימול" דקא אמר ד"ת, ובפ' "מציאת האשה" (כתובות דף סז:) מייתי ברייתא: "העבט תעביטנו" – זה שאין לו ואין רוצה להתפרנס נותנין לו לשם מתנה וכו', דברי רבי יהודה, וחכ"א: יש לו ואינו רוצה להתפרנס – אין נזקקין לו. אלא מה אני מקיים "תעביטנו" – ד"ת. אבל ר' יהודה דריש ליה. וכן בפ' "בנות כותים" (נדה לג:) ובפ' "יוצא דופן" (שם דף מד:): "איש איש", מה ת"ל "איש איש" – לרבות תינוק בן יום א' שמטמא בזיבה, דברי רבי יהודה, ר' ישמעאל בנו של ר' יוחנן בן ברוקה אומר: א"צ, הרי הוא אומר "והזב את זובו וגו'". א"כ מה ת"ל "איש איש" – ד"ת. דר' יוסי – מההיא ד"השוחט והמעלה" (זבחים דף קח:) דאייתינן לעיל, דקאמר "איש איש" – ד"ת, וההיא ד"המול ימול" דאיהו דדריש לה ופליג אדר' יהודה דאמר ד"ת. דר"ש – ההוא "איש איש" דקא"ר יוסי בפ' "השוחט" (גם זה שם) ד"ת, פליג עליה ר"ש ואמר ודריש: לרבות שנים שאחזו באבר והעלו, שחייבין. ובפ' "אלו מציאות" (ב"מ לא:) אמר: יש לו ואינו רוצה להתפרנס – אין נזקקין לו. א"כ מה ת"ל "תעביטנו" – ד"ת! ונראה: דמאן דס"ל דאמר ד"ת – מודה כל היכא דאיכא למדרש דרשינן לי'. וכל הני תנאי סברי להו

ד"ת

תוספות שאנץ

ארוסה ושומרת יבם כיון שאין בעליהן יכולין לבדקן חשובות כעוברות על דת ואפי' בלא קינוי אמרי' בגמ' דעוברת על דת יש לה להפסיד כתובתה אפי' בלא התראה: מתו בעליהן כו' ובה"א או שותות או לא נוטלות כתובה ובכתובות פ' האשה שנפלו פריך או שותות והביא האיש את אשתו אמר רחמנא וליכא אלא מתוך שלא שותות לא נוטלות כתובה: מעוברת חברו ומינקת חבירו פ"ה אם מת והניח מעוברת או מינקת או שגרשה בעלה והיא מעוברת ומניקה ואסרוה חכמים לינשא עד שיהא הולד בן ב' שנים שכך זמן יניקתו והלך זה ונשאה וקנא לה לא שותה שהרי אינה ראויה לקיימה משמע מתוך פ"ה דאפי' מגורשת צריכה להמתין כ"ד חדש ודלא כפי' ה"ר שמשון מפלאירא בפרק אע"פ דדוקא באלמנה אמרי' דצריכה להמתין כ"ד חדש משום דמשעבדא ליה להניק בנו אבל בגרושה שאינה משעבדא להניקו אינה צריכה להמתין והכ' משמע דצריכה גרושה להמתין וכן פר"ת דבין גרושה ובין אלמנ' צריכה להמתין כ"ד חדש ומביא ראיה לדבריו דאף לב"ש דאמרי שומטת דד מפיו ולא משעבדא ליה אפי' הכי קאמרי שלא תנשא עד לאחר כ"ד חדש וכן משמע דאין חילוק בין גרושה לאלמנה מהני טעמי דמייתי ביבמות וכן פי' פ' אע"פ והא דלא תני להו בהדי אלמנה לכהן גדול משום דליכא בהני כי אם איסור דרבנן אבל בהני דלעיל איכא איסורא דאורייתא. ואע"ג דתני לעיל חלוצה דאין בה אלא איסורא דרבנן משום דאגב דנקט גרושה נקט חלוצה ומחד קרא מסמיך להו ביבמות. יכול הוא להפרישה עד כ"ד חדש ולהחזירה הלכך ראויה לאישות קרי' ביה: וק' דמשמע דלהפרישה ר"ל בלא גט וה"נ דייקא תלמודא בפ' החולץ דיקא נמי דקתני יוציא ולא קתני יפריש משמע דאי הוה קתני יפריש הוה ר"ל בלא גט והכא נמי להפריש ר"ל בלא גט. וק' דאמרי' בפ' החולץ לא ישא אדם מעוברת חברו ומניקת חברו ואם נשא יוציא ולא יחזיר עולמית דבר' ר' מאיר וחכ"א יוציא וכשיגיע זמנו לכנוס יכנוס וקאמר רבא לדברי חכמים יוציא בגט והכא אמר דאין צריכה גט וי"ל דלעולם צריכה גט והאי דקאמר התם דיקא נמי דקתני יוציא ולא קתני יפריש ה"פ דיקא נמי דקתני יוציא משמע בגט ולא קתני יפריש דמשמע בין בגט בין בלא גט ולהפריש דהכא ר"ל בגט. עוד אומר רב יוסף בכור שור דלעולם ר"ל להפרישה בלא גט ולא ק' דהתם אמרי' דצריכה גט לפי דליכא אלא חד איסורא דרבנן וחכמים עשו חיזוק לדבריהם כשל תורה ולכך צריכה גט אבל הכא חמיר עליה משום דאיכא תרי איסורי משום דהיא מעוברת חברו ועוד דקינא לה ונסתרה לכך אינה צריכה גט וכן עשה במעשה שאירע בנו מאדם אחד שקידש

עין משפט נר מצוה

ג א מיי' פ"ב מהל' סוטה הלכה א סמג עשין כח:
ד ב מיי' שם פ"א הלכה יד:
ה ג מיי' שם פ"ב הלכה א סמג שם:
ו ד מיי' שם הלכה ז:
ז ה מיי' שם הלכה ט:
ח ו מיי' שם הלכה י:
ט ז מיי' שם פ"ג הל' כא:
י ח מיי' שם פ"ב הלכ' ו:
יא ט י מיי' שם פ"א הלכה א סמג עשין ט טוש"ע אה"ע סימן קעח סעיף ב:
יב כ מיי' שם הלכה י טוש"ע שם סעיף יג:
יג ל מיי' שם הלכה יח:

[עי' תוס' לקמן כה. ד"ה ב"ש]

מסורת הש"ס

יבמות לח: כתובות פא.
[עי' תוספות לקמן כה: ד"ה ב"ה]
[עי' תוס' יבמות לו: ד"ה ולא קתני]
[לקמן כה.]
[עי' היטב ברש"י לקמן כו. ד"ה קמ"ל וכו']
[לקמן כז.]
[ס"א לכשיצא]
[דף כו.]

הגהות הב"ח

(א) גמ' ואמרת אליהם לרבות: (ב) רש"י ד"ה לרבות אשת חרש ואשת שוטה:

גליון הש"ס

גמ' ואמרת לרבות ארוסה. עיין לקמן דף כו ע"א תד"ה ואמרת:

יד א מיי' פ"ב מהל' סוטה הלכה ה:
טו ב מיי' פ"ח מהל' תרומות הלכה ו טוש"ע אה"ע סימן קסו סעיף ט:

גי' רש"ל ר' יונתן נמי מצי

תורה אור

שִׁעֲמוּם. וְרַבִּי יֹאשִׁיָּה: הַאי "תַּחַת אִישָׁהּ" מַאי עָבֵיד לֵיהּ? מִיבָּעֵי לֵיהּ *לְהַקִּישׁ אִישׁ לְאִשָּׁה וְאִשָּׁה לְאִישׁ. אֶלָּא טַעְמָא דִּכְתִיבִי הָנֵי קְרָאֵי, הָא לָאו הָכִי – הֲוָה אָמֵינָא אֲרוּסָה שָׁתְיָא? *וְהָא כִּי אֲתָא רַבִּי אַחָא בַּר חֲנִינָא מִדָּרוֹמָא, אֲתָא וְאַיְיתֵי מַתְנִיתָא בִּידֵיהּ: °"מִבַּלְעֲדֵי אִישֵׁךְ" – *אמִשֶּׁקָּדְמָה שְׁכִיבַת בַּעַל לְבוֹעֵל, וְלֹא שֶׁקָּדְמָה שְׁכִיבַת בּוֹעֵל לְבַעַל! אָמַר רָמִי בַּר חָמָא: מַשְׁכַּחַתְּ לָהּ כְּגוֹן שֶׁבָּא עָלֶיהָ אָרוּס בְּבֵית אָבִיהָ. דִּכְוָותָהּ גַּבֵּי שׁוֹמֶרֶת יָבָם – כְּגוֹן שֶׁבָּא עָלֶיהָ יָבָם בְּבֵית חָמִיהָ, הָא שׁוֹמֶרֶת יָבָם קָרֵית לָהּ?! אִשְׁתּוֹ מַעַלְיְיתָא הִיא! *דְּהָאָמַר רַב: קָנָה לַכֹּל! כִּשְׁמוּאֵל, דְּאָמַר: בלֹא קָנָה אֶלָּא לַדְּבָרִים הָאֲמוּרִים בַּפָּרָשָׁה. אִי הָכִי, לֵימָא רַב דְּאָמַר כְּרַבִּי יֹאשִׁיָּה וּשְׁמוּאֵל דְּאָמַר כְּרַבִּי יוֹנָתָן? אָמַר לָךְ רַב: אֲנָא דַּאֲמַרִי אֲפִילּוּ לְרַבִּי יוֹנָתָן, מִדְּאִיצְטְרִיךְ קְרָא לְמַעוּטָהּ – מִכְּלָל דְּאִשְׁתּוֹ מַעַלְיְיתָא הִיא.

וּשְׁמוּאֵל

במדבר ה

[לקמן כז.]

יבמות נח.

[מי שקדמה]

יבמות נו. נח.

שִׁעֲמוּם. לָקוּי בְּתִמָּהוֹן לֵב. הַאי תַּחַת אִישָׁהּ. בַּתְרָלָה הָאָמוּר בְּסוֹף הַפָּרָשָׁה: "זֹאת תּוֹרַת הַקְּנָאוֹת" וגו'. לְהַקִּישׁ אִשָּׁה לְאִישׁ. בָּרַיְיתָא הִיא בְּשִׁילְהֵי פִּרְקִין. וְהָתָם מְפָרֵשׁ לְמַאי הִלְכְתָא. הָנֵי קְרָאֵי. דִּמְמַעֲטֵי אֲרוּסָה. מִבַּלְעֲדֵי אִישֵׁךְ. מַשְׁמַע שֶׁבַּעְלָהּ נָתַן בָּהּ אֶת שְׁכָבְתּוֹ קוֹדֶם לִסְתִירָה זוֹ. מַשְׁכַּחַתְּ לָהּ. דְּאִילְטְרִיךְ לְמַעוּטֵי אֲרוּסָה מִקְּרָא אַחֲרִינָא, וְלָא מְמַעֲטָא מֵהָתָם. כְּגוֹן שֶׁבָּא עָלֶיהָ אָרוּס בְּבֵית אָבִיהָ. בִּזְנוּת. בְּבֵית חָמִיהָ. לְאַחַר שֶׁמֵּת אָחִיו. שׁוֹמֶרֶת יָבָם קָרֵית לָהּ. דְּקָאָמְרַתְּ דְּלָא תִּשְׁתֶּה? הָא אִשְׁתּוֹ מַעַלְיְיתָא הִיא בְּבִיאַת זְנוּת!. דְּהָא אָמַר רַב. בִּיבָמוֹת: קָנָה לַכֹּל. דִּתְנַן: הַבָּא עַל יְבִמְתּוֹ בֵּין בְּשׁוֹגֵג בֵּין בְּמֵזִיד, דְּהַיְינוּ בִּזְנוּת – קָנָה. וְאָמַר רַב: "קָנָה" דְּקָתָנֵי מַתְנִי' – קָנָה לַכֹּל; אִם כֹּהֵן הוּא – מַאֲכִילָהּ בִּתְרוּמָה, וְיוֹרְשָׁהּ, וּמִיטַּמֵּא לָהּ, וּמַשְׁקָהּ, וּפוֹטְרָהּ בְּגֵט בְּלֹא חֲלִיצָה. כִּשְׁמוּאֵל. הָא דַּאֲתָא קְרָא לְמַעוּטֵי – כִּשְׁמוּאֵל, דְּאָמַר: לֹא קָנָה אֶלָּא לִדְבָרִים הָאֲמוּרִים בְּפָרָשַׁת יְבָמָה: לָקוּם עַל שֵׁם אָחִיו בְּנַחֲלָתוֹ, וּלְפוֹטְרָהּ בְּגֵט. דְּהָא דְּקָנֵי לָהּ יָבָם בְּבִיאָה כָּל דְּהוּ מִ"יְּבָמָהּ יָבֹא עָלֶיהָ" נָפְקָא לָן, דְּלָא כְּתִיב: יְבָמָהּ יִקָּחֶנָּה לוֹ לְאִשָּׁה, אֶלָּא "יָבֹא עָלֶיהָ וּלְקָחָהּ לוֹ לְאִשָּׁה", וְאַשְׁמְעִינַן דְּבִיאָתוֹ עָלֶיהָ הֵן הֵן לִיקּוּחֵי הָאִישׁוּת שֶׁלּוֹ. הִלְכָּךְ, לְמִידֵי דְּאִיתְּמַר בְּהַךְ פָּרָשָׁתָא – רַבִּינְהוּ קְרָא נִישּׂוּאִין הַלָּלוּ, אֲבָל לְמִידֵי אַחֲרִינָא – לָאו נִישּׂוּאִין נִינְהוּ. וּמָה אָמוּר בַּפָּרָשָׁה – פְּטוּר חֲלִיצָה ע"י יִבּוּם, וְ"יָקוּם עַל שֵׁם אָחִיו" – שֶׁיּוֹרֵשׁ אֶת נִכְסֵי אָחִיו וְאֵין אֶחָיו חוֹלְקִין עִמּוֹ. לֵימָא רַב. דְּאָמַר קָנָה לַכֹּל – כְּרַבִּי יֹאשִׁיָּה, דְּאָמַר שׁוֹמֶרֶת יָבָם שׁוֹתָה, וְאוֹקִימְנָא דְּבָא עָלֶיהָ. אֲנָא דַּאֲמַרִי אֲפִילּוּ כְּרַבִּי יוֹנָתָן כו'. וְכָל שֶׁכֵּן כְּרַבִּי יֹאשִׁיָּה. וְהָא דְּאִילְטְרִיךְ לְרַבִּי יֹאשִׁיָּה לְרַבּוּיֵי מֵ"אִישׁ אִישׁ" – לָאו דַּוְקָא, אֶלָּא אַסְמַכְתָּא בְּעָלְמָא, וְעִיקַּר קְרָא לְאֵשֶׁת חֵרֵשׁ וְשׁוֹטָה.

וּשְׁמוּאֵל

ד"ת. מיהו, היכא דמצי למידרשיה להעמיד קבלתא או סברתא – דרשינן ליה. ובהא פליגי, מאן דאית ליה דאמר דברה ומאן דלית ליה דברה: מאן דאית ליה דברה – אין לו כח להוציא יתור הלשון ממשמעות ואם אינו ענין לגופו, אלא כיון דמצינו למימר דברה תורה – אמר: ד"ת, ולא נוציאנו ממשמעותו, דלאו קרא יתירא הוה. להכי פריך בפ' "השואל" (ב"מ דף לד:): הניחא למ"ד לא ד"ת – אם כן "יגנב" קרא יתירא הוא, ואם אינו ענין לגניבה – תנהו ענין לאבידה, ד"יגנב" גניבה משמע ולא אבידה. אלא למ"ד דברה תורה – א"כ לאו קרא יתירא הוא, מאי איכא למימר? ובפרק "השוחט והמעלה" (זבחים דף קח:) אע"ג דאמרינן: מדא"ר יוסי האי "איש איש" דברה תורה, ההוא "איש איש" נמי דברה תורה – הוה מצי למידרשיה שפיר, חדא לדברה תורה ואידך לרבויא, ד"איש איש" משמע שפיר כל ריבויי, כרבי יונתן דהכא דדריש האי "איש איש" ד"כי תשטה" לרבויא, ו"איש איש כי יקלל" לדברה תורה – הוה *רבי יוסי מצי למידרשיה "איש איש" דשחוטי חוץ – לרבות שוחט. אלא משום דכתיב "איש איש" דשחוטי חוץ ו"איש איש" דמעלה בחוץ בחד ענינא – מהדר למדרשינהו בחד ענינא. וסוגיא דריש נדרים (דף ג.) צריך לפרושי הכי: דמרבינן מ"נזיר להזיר" לעשות כינויי נזירות כנזירות, וידות נדרים כנדרים. ומקיש נדרים לנזירות, דכתיב "לנדור נדר נזיר להזיר". וקא דייק: מ"ש גבי נזירות דכתיב "נזיר להזיר" – נדרים נמי "לנדור נדר", היקשא למה לי? אי כתב "נדר לנדור" כדכתיב "נזיר להזיר" – כדקאמרת, ולא צריך היקשא, השתא דכתיב "לנדור נדר" – ד"ת. ופי': כיון דלא שינה קרא בדיבוריה – א"כ דברה כלשון בני אדם, ולאו קרא יתירא הוא למדרש מיניה לרבות כינוין וידות. דמשמעות דקרא לא נפקא אלא מריבוי דקרא, ובלא קרא יתירא לא מסתבר לרבוייהו, ולמימר דליחייב "קונס" ו"קונם" כמו שיאמר "קרבן", וכן אם יאמר "הריני" או "אהא" כמו שיאמר "הריני נזיר", הלכך צריך קרא יתירא. ולא דמי לכינוי השם דמרבינן "איש איש" אפילו למ"ד ד"ת, דאותן כינויין אשכחן דכתיבי בקרא, כמו: אל, צבאות, אהיה, שדי, כל הני דקתני בשבועות (דף לה.). ועוד, דכינוי כתיב בההוא קרא דמברך השם "איש איש כי יקלל אלהיו" (ויקרא כד). והיינו דאמרי' התם בריש נדרים: הניחא למ"ד ד"ת – דאליביה לא צריך למידרשיה וכו'. והכי אמר בפ' "ד' מחוסרי כפרה" (כריתות דף יא.) דאמר ליה ר"א ב"ע לרבי ישמעאל: בעלמא כוותיך סבירא לי' דדברה תורה, והכא שאני; מכדי כתיב ליה קרא: "כי לא חופשה", "והפדה לא נפדתה" למה לי? ש"מ לחציה שפחה וחציה בת חורין. אלמא, אפילו למאן דאית ליה ד"ת – דרשינן ליה משום עניינא דקרא, הואיל וניתן לידרש. ה"ה דדרשינן ליה נמי להעמיד קבלתן או סברתן היכא דלא עקר ליה ממשמעותיה, כגון "יגנב" דכתיב בהדיא גניבה ודרשינן מיניה אבידה משום כפל הלשון. הלכך, כל הני דפרק "אלו מציאות" (ב"מ דף לא.) ד"השב תשיבם" "שלח תשלח" "הוכח תוכיח" "עזוב תעזוב" "הקים תקים" "מות יומת" "השב תשיב" "חבל תחבול" "פתח תפתח" "נתון תתן" – כולי עלמא מודו בהו, דדרשא דידהו לא עקר להו ממשמעותיה. והא דאמרינן: הניחא למ"ד לא אמרי' ד"ת – היינו ר"ע, דלא אשכחיניה דקאמר ד"ת, דדריש בפ' "ד' מחוסרי כפרה" (כריתות דף יא.): "והפדה לא נפדתה" – לפדויה ואינה פדויה. ובפרק "הערל" (יבמות דף ע.) בשמעתתא קמייתא דא"ר אליעזר "איש איש" ד"ת, ודריש ליה רבי עקיבא לרבות הערל. וכן בריש "חלק" (סנהדרין דף נ:) ובפ' "ד' מיתות" (שם דף סד:), "הכרת תכרת", דא"ר עקיבא: "הכרת" – בעוה"ז, "תכרת" – לעוה"ב. והכי משמע נמי סוגיין בפ' "אין עומדין" (ברכות דף לא*:) "אם ראה תראה", דלרבי ישמעאל דאמר ד"ת, ולרבי עקיבא: "אם ראה" – מוטב, ואם לאו – "תראה". אבל ר' ישמעאל אומר בכל דוכתי ד"ת, כגון הני דפליג אדר"ע, ובפ' "ד' מחוסרי כפרה" (כריתות דף יא.) נמי. וכן ר' אלעזר ב"ע בפרק קמא דקידושין (דף יז:) ובפרק "אלו מציאות" (ב"מ דף לא:) גבי "הענק תעניק". לבד מההיא דכריתות, כדמפרש התם טעמא, ור' אלעזר בר' יוסי בריש "חלק" (סנהדרין דף נ:). והא דאמר בפ' "אלו הן הגולין" (מכות דף יב.) בקרא "אם יצא יצא": הא כמ"ד ד"ת, הא כמ"ד לא דברה – מ"ד התם דברה מסברא קאמר לה, כדמפרש אביי התם: מסתברא כמאן דאמר דברה וכו'*. **ורבי** יונתן האי איש מאי עביד ליה וכו'. תימה: האי ריבוי לרבי יאשיה מנליה, והיקשא דאיש לאשה לר' יונתן מנא ליה? וכי אית לן למימר דפליגי בהא נמי, דר' יאשיה לית ליה דאשת חרש שותה ור' יונתן לית ליה דסומא אינה שותה! **דהאמר** רב קנה לכל. הני לישני דפליגי ב"הבא על יבמתו" (יבמות דף נח.) בשומרת יבם שנפלה מן הנשואין או מן האירוסין – לא שייכא דוקא אלא לענין תרומה, משום דכבר אכלה, אבל לענין להשקותה וליורשה ולטמא לה – לא*. **בספרים** גרס: אי הכי לימא רב דאמר כרבי יאשיה, ולא א"ש "אי הכי". ובפרש"י לא גרס. והוא לא שבש הגירסא, אלא בפתס פי': לימא רב דאמר וכו'. ושמא בספרו לא היה כתוב "אי הכי". **כשמואל** דאמר לא קנה אלא לדברים כו'. תימה: כיון דקנה מיהת לדברים האמורים בפרשה לפוטרה בגט, דכיון שבא עליה – הרי היא כאשתו לאותן דברים, א"כ מ"ט דרבי יונתן דאלימא ליה ארוסה משומרת יבם? אי משום דארוסה קידושין דידיה – שומרת יבם נמי ביאה דידיה היא, ונתנקה על ידו. וכ"ש דתקשה לרב, דאמר: אנא דאמינא אפילו לרבי יונתן! ותו: מאי דוחקיה למימר כשמואל? והא מסיק דאפילו רב הוה אתי מלתייהו אליביה, ולענין השקאה קפיד רחמנא דבעינן ביאה לשם אישות! וביבמות בפרק "הבא על יבמתו" (דף נח.) מוקי לה נמי הא דתנן: [אמן שלא סטיתי ארוסה ונשואה] שומרת יבם ונשואה – כגון דבא עליה יבם בבית אחיו וכו', כי הכא. ומקשה: מידי הוא טעמא אלא לרב – האמר רב: קנה לכל. ולא מתרץ: גבי השקאה – גזירת הכתוב דבעינן ביאה לשם אישות! **אמר** לך אנא דאמרי אפי' לרבי יונתן. נראה דהכי פירושו: לא מיבעיא לרבי יאשיה דמרבה שומרת יבם, דאמינא כוותיה. והאי דאיצטריך לרבויי משום דכתיב הכא "תחת אישך", דמשמע שבא עליה לשם אישות וכו' – לא צריכא למימר, דקרא אסמכתא בעלמא הוא, כמו שפירש רש"י. ואף מה שפירש לשמואל ההיא דאיצטריך רבי יונתן למעוטי שומרת יבם – אסמכתא בעלמא הוא, תימה: נהי דלאו אשתו היא, אי לאו מעטיה קרא – מהיכא תיתי דבעינן אשתו טפי לענין השקאה מלענין קינוי? אי משום דכתיב: "והביא האיש את אשתו" – (אלא) ה"נ גבי קינוי כתיב: "וקינא את אשתו"! ירושלמי: ארוסה לא שותה. וישקנה! גזירת הכתוב הוא: "והביא האיש את אשתו". ולא יקנא לה! התורה אמרה "וקינא את אשתו" "וקינא את אשתו" – אפי' מקצת אשתו. ר' יודן בעי: כמה דתימר תמן "וקינא את אשתו" – אפילו מקצת אשתו, דכוותה "תחת אישך" "תחת אישך" – אפי' מקצת אישך. היך עבידה? קינא לה ועודה ארוסה, וכנסה ונסתרה – משקה אותה על קינויו. קינא לה עודה שומרת יבם, וכנסה ונסתרה – משקה אותה על קינויו. קינא לה ועודה ארוסה, וכנסה ונסתרה וידע בה – תצא בכתובתה, ואם לאו – תצא שלא בכתובתה. *(קינא לה ועודה שומרת יבם, וכנסה ונסתרה וידע בה – תצא בכתובתה, ואם לאו – תצא שלא בכתובתה). לא קינא לה בעלה ומת, ונפלה לפני היבם וקינא לה, ולא הספיק לכונסה עד שמת, ונפלה לפני אחיו – אינו משקה אותה, שלא נפלה לו אלא מחמת אחיו הראשון. אבל אם קינא לה היבם, וכנסה ומת, ונפלה לפני היבם, וכנסה ונסתרה – משקה אותה על קינויו. *) **שאני** התם דלית לה אימתא דבעל. וא"ת: הני דבעי למפסט מארוסה ושומרת יבם לית להו נמי אימתא דבעלה, דהא בעלייהו לאו גבייהו נינהו! וי"ל: אפ"ה אית ליה אימתא, פן ירגישו בעליהן בפריצותן.

שמע

*) שייך לדף כה ע"א

[ועמ"ש על הגליון]

[וע"ע תוס' כריתות יא. ד"ה מאי טעמא, במנחות יז: ד"ה מאי האלכל וכו']

[ועי' היטב תוס' יבמות נז. ד"ה מן הנישואין]

ל"ג בס"א ובירושלמי שלפנינו איתא קינא לה בעלה ומת ונפלה לפני היבם וכנסה ונסתרה משקה אותה על קינויו

תוספות שאנץ

שקידש מעוברת חברו ולא נשאה והורה דיכול הוא להפרישה בלא גט משום דחמיר עליה דאיכא תרי איסורי חדא דמעוברת חברו ועוד דכלה בלא ברכה אסורה לבעלה כנדה ה"נ כיון דאיכא תרי איסורי חמיר עליה ויכול להפרישה בלא גט אבל גם מההיא דאמר בפ' החולץ קידש תוך ג' חדשים וברח פליגי בה רב אחא ורפרם חד אמר שמותי משמתי' ליה וחד אמר ערוקי מסתיה משמע דוקא משום דברח הא אם לא ברח תרווייהו מודו דמשמתי' ליה ואמאי והא אמרינן הכא דיכול להפרישה בלא גט. וי"ל דשאני התם משום דשמא יבוא הדבר לידי קלקולא כדמפ' ביבמו' גזירה שמא יקח אחותו מאביו ויבם אשת אביו מאמו ויוציא את אמו לשוק ויפטר את יבמתו לשוק אבל הכא דליכא למיחש דאיירי שנשאה לאחר ג' חדשים להכי אמרי' דיכול להפריש בלא גט: האילונית פ"ה דוכרנית שממעי אמה נכרת שלא היו לה סימני אשה לא דדין ולא שערות וקולה עבה: ושאינה ראויה לילד פ"ה כגון ששתת כוס עיקרין, ור"ח פי' שנישאת לאיש בת מ' שנה ושוב אינה יולדת לעולם כדאיתא [נב"ב דף קיט] לא שותות לפי שאסור לקיימה למי שאין לו בנים לפי שהרי נצטוו ישראל על פריה ורביה ל"ה ואשת סרים שותה פ"ה דמיירי בשנסתרם לאחר שנשאה דאי מקודם שנשאה א"כ קדמה שכיבת בועל לבעל ואנן בעי' שקדמה שכיבת בעל לבועל ובגמ' פרי' פשיטא דשותה: על ידי כל העריות מקנין אם קינא לה מאביה ומאחיה ומאחר מכל העריות ונסתרה הוי קינויו קינוי: ואלו שב"ד מקנין להם אם רואין אותם שמתנהגות בפריצות ולא להשקותן אמרו דהם לא ישקוה והביא האיש את אשתו כתיב ובעלה נמי לכשיצא לא ישקנה בקינוי זה דבעי' וקינא את אשתו והביא ור' יוסי לית ליה וקינא את אשתו והביא: גמ' דבר אל בני ישראל ואמרת אליהם לרבות ארוסה ושומרת יבם לקינוי ויש ספרים דגרסי איש איש ול"ג ליה דלדרשא אחריני דרשי' ליה לקמן אלא ריבויא הוי מואמרת וה"נ אמרי' לקמן בפי' ואמרת ריבויא הוא ל"ה: למר אלימא ליה שומרת יבם דלא מחסרא מסירה לחופה דנקנית ליבם בביאה גרידתא ואפי' בזנות להיות כאשתו לכל דבר כדתניא ביבמות ומייתי לה לק' בפרקי' א) ואפי' למאן דאמר ביבמות דביאה אירוסין עושה ואינה עושה נישואין הינו היכא דלא נתכוון לקנות בביאה זו אפי' הוי ביאה זנות הויא כאשתו לכל דבר ואפי' לשמואל דאמר דלא קנה אלא לדברים האמורים בפרשת יבם מ"מ קונה בביאה זו לדברים האמורים בפרשה ב) שאינו כשאר נישואין. וא"ת והיכי אוקימנא למתני' כר' יונתן והא מתני' מפיק ארוסה ושומרת יבם שאינן שותות ולא נוטלות כתובה ג) אתיא כר' יונתן ולא כר' יאשיה. ועוד שמא מתני' לא היתה חוששת להביא תרי קראי אלא מסמיך אתרויהו מחד קרא. [ע"כ שייך לע"א] ואשת שעמום פ"ה לקוי בתמהון לבב והאמר רב קנה לכל דהבא על יבמתו בין בשוגג בין במזיד דהינו בזנות קנה לכל דאם הוא כהן מאכילה בתרומה ויורשה ומטמא [לה] ומשקה ופוטרה בגט בלא חליצה ל"ה. כשמואל דאמר לא קנה אלא לדברים האמורים בפרשה בפרשת יבמה פי' בפרשת יבמה לקום על שם אחיו ולפוטרה בגט דהא דקני להיבם בביאה כל דהו מיבמה יבא עליה נפקא דלא כתב יבמה יקח לה לאשה אלא כתיב יבמה יבא עליה ולקחה לו לאשה אשמועי' דביאתו עליה הן הן ליקוחין ואישות שלו הלכך למידי דאתמר בפרשה רבינהו ומה אמור בפרשה פטור חליצה על ידי יבום ויקום על שם אחיו שיורש נכסי אביו ואין שאר

א) נראה דצ"ל מצא"כ בארוסה דאפי' למ"ד וכו' דביאה שאחר קדושין נשואין עושה היינו היכא דנתכוון לקנות בביאה זו אבל בשומרת יבם אפי' הוי ביאת וכו'. ב) או"ל מצא"כ בשאר נשואין. ג) לכאורה נראה דצ"ל ולא אתיא לא כר' יונתן ולא כר' יאשיה וכו' וחסר בהעתקה התירוץ ע"ז.

ושמואל אמר: אנא דאמרי אפילו לרבי יאשיה, מדאיצטריך קרא לרבוייה — מכלל דלאו אשתו היא כלל. איבעיא להו: עוברת על דת, צריכה התראה להפסידה כתובתה או אינה צריכה? מי אמרינן: כיון דעוברת על דת היא — לא בעיא התראה, או דלמא תיבעי התראה, דאי הדרה בה — תיהדר בה? ת"ש: *ארוסה ושומרת יבם — לא שותות ולא נוטלות כתובה. *מישתא הוא דלא שתיא — הא קנויי מקני לה. למאי — לאו להפסידה כתובתה? אמר אביי: לא, לאוסרה עליו. רב פפא אמר: להשקותה כשהיא נשואה. *כדתניא: אין מקנין לארוסה להשקותה כשהיא ארוסה, [א]אבל מקנין לארוסה להשקותה כשהיא נשואה. אמר רבא, ת"ש: אלמנה לכהן גדול, גרושה וחלוצה לכהן הדיוט, ממזרת ונתינה לישראל, בת ישראל לממזר ולנתין — לא שותות ולא נוטלות כתובה. מישתא הוא דלא שתיא, הא קנויי — מקני להו. ולמאי? אי לאוסרן עליו — הא אסירן וקיימן, אלא לאו להפסידן כתובתן? אמר רב יהודה מדיסקרתא: לא, לאוסרה (א) לבועל כבעל. דתנן: *כשם שאסורה לבעל כך אסורה לבועל. א"ר חנינא מסורא, ת"ש: ואלו שבית דין מקנין להן: מי שנתחרש בעלה, או נשתטה, או שהיה חבוש בבית האסורין. ולא להשקותה אמרו, אלא לפוסלה מכתובתה. ש"מ: [ב]בעי התראה, ש"מ. וכולהו מאי טעמא לא אמרי מהא? דלמא שאני התם, דלית לה אימתא דבעל כלל. איבעיא להו: עוברת על דת ורצה בעל לקיימה, [ג]מקיימה או אינו מקיימה? מי אמרינן בקפידא דבעל תלא רחמנא — והא לא קפיד, או דלמא כיון דקפיד — קפיד? ת"ש: ואלו שבית דין מקנין להן: מי שנתחרש בעלה, או נשתטה, או שהיה חבוש בבית האסורין. ואי אמרת רצה בעל לקיימה מקיימה — עבדי ב"ד מידי דדלמא לא ניחא ליה לבעל? סתמא דמילתא, כיון דעוברת על דת היא — מינח ניחא ליה. איבעיא להו: בעל שמחל על קינויו, קינויו מחול או אינו מחול? מי אמרינן בקינוי דבעל תלא רחמנא — ובעל הא מחיל ליה לקינויו, או דלמא כיון דקני ליה מעיקרא — לא מצי מחיל ליה? ת"ש: ואלו שב"ד מקנין להן: מי שנתחרש בעלה, או נשתטה, או שהיה חבוש בבית האסורין. ואי אמרת בעל שמחל על קינויו, קינויו מחול — עבדינן מידי דאתי בעל מחיל ליה? סתמא דמלתא אדם מסכים על דעת ב"ד. ת"ש: *ומוסרין לו שני ת"ח שמא יבא עליה בדרך. ואי אמרת בעל שמחל על קינויו קינויו מחול — לחלייה לקינויה, ולבעול! מ"ש תלמידי חכמים — דגמירי, דאי בעי למיבעל אמרי ליה: אחליה לקינוייך ובעלה. ת"ש, *דאמר ר' יאשיה: שלשה דברים סח לי זעירא מאנשי ירושלים: [ד]בעל שמחל על קינויו — קינויו מחול, וזקן ממרא שרצו בית דין למחול לו — מוחלין לו, [ה]ובן סורר ומורה שרצו אביו ואמו למחול לו — מוחלין לו. וכשבאתי אצל חבירי שבדרום, על שנים הודו לי, ועל זקן ממרא [ו]לא הודו לי, שלא ירבו מחלוקת בישראל. ש"מ: בעל שמחל על קינויו קינויו מחול, ש"מ. פליגי בה רב אחא ורבינא; חד אמר: [ז]קודם סתירה — מחול, לאחר סתירה — אינו מחול. וחד אמר: לאחר סתירה נמי מחול. ומסתברא כמאן דאמר אינו מחול, ממאי — מדקא מהדרי רבנן לרבי יוסי. דתניא, *רבי יוסי אומר: בעלה נאמן עליה מקל וחומר; ומה נדה שהיא בכרת — בעלה נאמן עליה, סוטה שהיא בלאו — לא כל שכן? אמרו לו: לא, אם אמרת בנדה — שכן יש לה היתר, תאמר בסוטה — שאין לה היתר. ואי אמרת לאחר סתירה מחול לה — משכחת לה דיש לה היתר, דאי בעי — מחיל ליה לקינויה ובעיל. אלא ש"מ לאחר סתירה אינו מחול, שמע מינה. § "מתו בעליהן עד שלא שתו ב"ש" כו'. § במאי קמיפלגי? בית שמאי סברי: *שטר העומד לגבות — כגבוי דמי, וב"ה

ושמואל דאמר אנא דאמרי אפי' לרבי יאשיה. דאמר: שוטה. דמדאצטריך לרבויי לשתיה — ש"מ לאו אשתו היא ליורשה וליטמא לה ולהאכילה תרומה. וכ"ש לרבי יונתן דאמר אינה שותה — משום דלאו אשתו היא. והא דאיצטריך למעוטי — אסמכתא בעלמא היא, ולאו דקרא להכי אתא, אלא להקיש אשה לאיש, כדשני לעיל. עוברת על דת. יהודית, שאינה צנועה; יוצאה וראשה פרועה, וטווה בשוק, ומדברת עם כל אדם. דאמר בכתובות בפרק "המדיר" (דף עב.) דיוצאה שלא בכתובה. צריכה התראה. שמא תחזור, ואם תחזור — לא תפסיד כתובתה. או אינה צריכה התראה, דבלאו התראה מפסדא. למאי. כיון דלא שתיא, קינוי למאי אהני? לאפסודי כתובתה. ואי לאו דקני — לא מפסדא. אלמא צריכה התראה. וזו עוברת על דת היא, שנסתרה עם אנשים. להשקותה כשהיא נשואה. (ב) ואם תסתר לאחר נישואין שותה על ידי קינוי של אירוסין. שאינו יכול להשקותה כשהיא ארוסה, דבעינן "תחת אישה". לאוסרה אבועל. קינוי לא מהני אלא לאוסרה על בועלה, אם ימות זה או יגרשנה, ולא שתת (ג). אלא לפוסלה מכתובתה. מכלל דאי לא אתרו בה — לא מפסדא. דתנן. לקמן בפרק "כשם שהמים בודקין" (דף כז:). שאני התם. הא דבעי התראה. דלית לה אימתא דבעל. ואי לאו דאתרו בה בי דינא, לא הוה לן למקנסה. דכיון דלית לה אימתא אין תימה בדבר אם עוברת על דת, ואין זה פריצותא יתירתא. אבל מי שבעלה אצלה, ואינה יראה ממנו ועוברת על דת — פריצותא יתירתא אית בה, ואיכא למימר דבלאו התראה נמי מפסדא כתובתה. תלא רחמנא. דכתיב: "וקנא את אשתו". או דלמא כיון דקפיד קפיד. כלומר, כיון דאורחיה דבעל למיקפד בהכי — על כרחיה דהאי נמי הויא קפידא לגביה. עבדינן מילתא דדלמא לא ניחא ליה. והילך אנו נעשים שלוחים לו בדבר שהוא חוב לו, שאינו חפץ בו, וקיימא לן (כתובות דף יא.): דאין חבין לאדם שלא בפניו. שמחל על קנויו. והשתא ס"ד דקבעי בין שמחל קודם סתירה בין שמחל לאחר הסתירה: ואם תימצי לומר עוברת על דת שרצה לקיימה מקיימה — הני מילי בלא קינוי, אבל היכא דאיכא קינוי וסתירה ורצה למחול, מהו? מי עקר קינוי ושריא ליה, או לאו? עבדינן מידי דאתי בעל ומחיל. ואיכא זילותא דבי דינא. סתמא דמילתא אדם מסכים כו'. וסמכינן אסתם דעתיה דאינשי, ומקנינן לה, ואי אתי ומחיל — מחיל. מאי שנא תלמידי חכמים. אירולא הוא, והכי קאמר: לעולם מחיל. ודיקא ליה מתני'; מאי שנא דבעינן תלמידי חכמים — משום דגמירי דאסורה ליה בדלא מחיל קינוי, ואי אתי למיבעל — אמרין ליה: אחלי לקינויך. סח לי זעירא. שהיה מאנשי ירושלים. זקן ממרא. שהמרה על ב"ד של לשכת הגזית, ומיתתו בחנק. שהיא בלאו. "אחרי אשר הוטמאה" לרבות סוטה שנסתרה, בפ"ק דיבמות (דף יא:). במאי קמיפלגי. איזה טעם נותנין לדבריהם. ב"ש סברי שטר העומד לגבות כגבוי דמי. מי שיש לו שטר חוב על חבירו ושיעבד לו בו נכסיו — מוחזק בעל השטר בנכסים יותר מן הלוה. והלכך, כיון דנכסי ברשותיה קיימי — הוו להו יורשי הבעל תובעין, והמוציא מחבירו עליו הראיה, ועליהן להביא ראיה שזינתה בסתירה זו, ואבדה כתובתה. וב"ית

שמע מינה בעל שמחל על קינויו קינויו מחול. ותפשוט נמי עוברת על דת: אם רצה בעלה לקיימה — מקיימה, אפילו התרה בה (ד).

*בית שמאי אומרים נוטלת כתובתה. ואם תאמר: מ"ש דאמרי ב"ש נוטלת כתובתה, ובפרק "מי שמת" (ב"ב דף קנח.) גבי נפל הבית עליו ועל אשתו, *נפל הבית עליו ועל אביו, והיתה עליו כתובת אשה וכו', דאמרי ב"ש: יחלוקו, הואיל וספק הוא מי מת ראשון. וכן בפרק "החולץ" (יבמות דף לח:) ובכתובות בפרק "האשה שנפלו לה נכסים" (דף פ:) גבי שומרת יבם שמתה: מה יעשו בנכסים הנכנסין והיוצאין עמה, בית שמאי אומרים: יחלוקו, ומפרש בגמרא בפ' "החולץ" (יבמות דף לח:) משום

תוספות שאנץ

שאר אחיו חולקין עמו ל"ה: אמר לך רב אנא דאמרי אפי' לר' יונתן וכ"ש לר' יאשיה וא"ת כיון דאשתו מעלייתא היא אמאי איצטריך ליה לר' יאשיה איש איש לרבות. וי"ל דלאו דוקא הוא אלא אסמכתא בעלמא הוא ועיקר קראי לאשת חרש ושוטה ושמואל אמר אנא דאמרי אפי' לר' יאשיה פי' וכ"ש לר' יונתן דאינה שותה משום דלאו אשתו היא. וא"ת כיון דלאו אשתו היא אמאי איצטריך לר' יונתן קרא למעוטי וי"ל דאינו אלא אסמכתא בעלמ' וקרא לאו להכי אתי אלא לאקושי אשה לאיש כדשני' לעיל ל"ה: אמר אביי לא לאוסרה עליו. וא"ת למ"ד דאוסרין על הייחוד למה לי למתני' למימר דמהני קנוי לאסרה עליו פשיטא וי"ל דאצטריך מתני' אפי' היכא דאינה אסורה משום ייחוד כגון בפתח פתוח לרשו' הרבים דאין שם משום ייחוד ואפי הכי לענין סוטה הוי רשות היחיד וה"נ אמרי' חצר שרבים נכנסין לה בזו ויוצאין לה בזו רשות היחיד לשבת ורשות הרבים לטומאה. משמע דוקא היכא דאיכא תרתי פתחא אבל היכא דליכא אלא פתח אחד הוי רשות היחיד לטומאה אי נמי כגון שבעלה בעיר דאמר בשלהי קידושין בעלה בעיר אין חוששין לה משום ייחוד ואפי' הכי לענין תורת סוטה אשמעינן מתני' דחשבי' ליה לסתירה ואפי' בעלה בעיר כיון דלא משתמיט תנא בשום מקום לומר שלא תחשב סתירה לענין סוטה כשבעלה בעיר: ש"מ בעי התראה ש"מ ובפתח פתוח לרשות הרבים ליכא לאוקמיה ואינה עוברת על דת דהא מסתמא כיון דאינה עוברת על דת לא היו ב"ד מקנין אותה כדי להפקיע כתובתה בכדי אבל ק' דאיתא בתוספ' דכתובות בהדיא נשים שאמרו שעוברות על דת צריכות התראה ויוצאות בלא כתובה ואם לא התרו בהן יוציא ויתן כתובה ולמה לא הביאה כאן התלמוד ושמא דלא הוה ידע לה: זקן ממרא שהמרה על ב"ד של לשכת הגזית ומיתתו בחנק: ב"ש סברי שטר העומד לגבות כגבוי דמי מי שיש לו שטר חוב על חברו ושעבד לו כל נכסיו מוחזק בעל השטר יותר מן הלוה והלכך כיון דנכסי ברשותיה קיימי הוו להו יורשי הבעל תובעין והמוציא מחבירו עליו הראיה ועליהן להביא ראיה שזינתה ואבדה כתובתה וב"ה

הגהות הב"ח

(א) גמ' אבועל כבעל: (ב) רש"י ד"ה להשקותה וכו' דאם תסתר: (ג) ד"ה לאוסרה וכו' ולא שתת הס"ד ואח"כ מ"ה דתנן לקמן בפ' כשם הס"ד ואח"כ מ"ה אלא לפוסלה מכתובתה: (ד) תום' ד"ה שמע וכו' התרה בה. נ"ב עיין פירושו בטו"ת שלי סי' קמ"ג:

מסורת הש"ס: יבמות נח. | [לעיל כד.] | [יבמות נח:] | לקמן כז: | לעיל ז. | סנהדרין פח. | [לעיל ז.] | יבמות לח: כתובות פא. גיטין לז. שבועות מח: [ב"ב קנ.]

עין משפט נר מצוה:

טז א מיי' פ"ב מהל' סוטה הל' ה:

יז ב ג מיי' פכ"ד מהל' אישות הל' יד טז סמג עשין מח טוש"ע אה"ע סימן קטו סעיף ד:

יח ד מיי' פ"א מהל' סוטה הלכה ז טוש"ע אה"ע סי' קעח סעי' יב:

[שייך לעיל כד. במשנה]

יט ה מיי' פ"ז מהל' ממרים הלכ' ח סמג לאוין רכ:

[שם קנז.]

כ ו מיי' שם פ"ג הלכה ד סמג לאוין נג:

כא ז מיי' פ"א מהל' סוטה הלכה ז סמג עשין נו טוש"ע אה"ע סימן קעח סעיף יב:

כב א מיי' פ"ב מהל' סוטה הלכה ב:

תורה אור

וב"ה סברי: שטר העומד לגבות – לאו כגבוי דמי. § "מעוברת חבירו" כו'. § אמר רב נחמן אמר רבה בר אבוה: מחלוקת בעקרה וזקינה, אבל איילונית – דברי הכל לא שותה ולא נוטלת כתובתה, שנאמר: °"ונקתה ונזרעה זרע" (במדבר ה) – מי שדרכה להזריע, יצאה זו שאין דרכה להזריע. מיתיבי: *א המקנא לארוסתו ולשומרת יבם שלו, אם עד שלא כנסה נסתרה – לא שותה ולא נוטלת כתובתה. (תוספ' פ"ה)

מעוברת

ובית הלל סברי לאו כגבוי דמי. והויא לה היא תובעת מספק, דדלמא זנאי. הלכך איניהו ודאי והיא ספק, ואין ספק מוציא מידי ודאי, ועליה להביא ראיה שלא זינתה. מחלוקת. דפליג ר"א ואמר: יכול לישא אחרת כו'. בעקרה וזקינה. דליכא למימר אינה שותה. אלא טעמא משום דלא חזיא לקיימא – עלה פליג ר"א ואמר: ראויה לקיימא היא, דיכול לישא אשה אחרת. אבל איילונית. נהי נמי דראויה לקיימא, מיהו לא שתיא מהאי טעמא דראויה להריון בעינן. ועקרה – על ידי מכה, וזקינה – מינא דבת הריון היא קודם לכן, אבל איילונית מבטן אמה לקויה היא ולא חזיא.

לא

משום דזיקת נשואה עושה ספק נשואה. אלמא דמספיקא אמרי ב"ש יחלוקו, ולא מוקמי לכולהו נכסי בחזקת יורשי האשה מטעם שטר העומד לגבות כגבוי דמי! וי"ל: גבי נפל הבית עליו ועל אביו לא היו לבן נכסים, אלא שהיא אומרת: האב ראשון מת, וירש הבן, ונשתעבדו לכתובתה. התם ודאי נכסי האב לא עמדו מעולם בכח האשה, ואעפ"כ, כיון דאמר כגבוי דמי – הרי הוא ספק אם האב מת ראשון דעמדו הנכסים בחזקתה, או הבן מת ראשון ואין לה באותם נכסים כלום ובחזקת היורשין הן. הלכך ספק הוא אם עמד שטר שלה לגבות מאותן נכסים כלל, הלכך חולקין. וכן נפל הבית עליו ועל אשתו, ספק אם היא מתה ראשונה וירשה הבעל, שלא ניתנה לגבות מחיים, אי נמי איפכא, ויורשיה באין מכחה. וכן גבי שומרת יבם שמתה, אמר: הואיל והללו באין לירש והללו באין לירש – יחלוקו. אבל הכא, שהיא בחיים והכתובה ניתן לגבות לאחר מיתת הבעל, דכיון דדמיא כגבויה – על היורשין להביא ראיה שזינתה. וכה"ג אומר בפרק "החולץ" (יבמות דף לח:): רישא דאיתא לדידה – הויא לה איהי ודאי ואינהו ספק, ואין ספק מוציא מידי ודאי סיפא מתה – הללו באין לירש והללו באין לירש. *בית הלל אומרים או שותות או לא נוטלות כתובתן. [שייך לעיל במשנה] בפ' "החולץ" (גז"ש) מפרש: מתוך שלא שותות לא נוטלות כתובתן. ולא ידענא בנכסי צאן ברזל מאי קא סבר ב"ה. דבפ' "מי שמת" (ב"ב דף קנח.), גבי נפל הבית עליו ועל אשתו, אמרי ב"ה: הנכסים בחזקתן עומדות. ופי': נכסי צאן ברזל. ופליגי אמוראי בגמרא בחזקת מי, בחזקת יורשי הבעל או בחזקת יורשי האשה, ובר קפרא תני: הללו באין לירש והללו באין לירש – יחלוקו. אבל הכא שהיא בחיים – בחזקתה הן עומדים. או דלמא כיון דאחריותם היו על הבעל – היו בחזקתו, ול"ש, ושייכא בפלוגתא דהתם. ובנכסי מלוג לא פליג ב"ה, דאפי' גבי ספק מוקי להו בחזקת יורשי האשה, וכ"ש הכא דאפי' ודאי זינתה לא הפסידתה, כדאמר בפרק "אלמנה ניזונית" (כתובות דף קא.): היוצאת משום שם רע – נוטלת מה שבפניה ויוצאה. ופי': נכסי מלוג. ואם תאמר: מ"ש מתניתין מפלוגתא דרב הונא ורב יהודה ורב נחמן ור' יוחנן, דפליגי בפ"ק דכתובות (דף יב:): "מנה לי בידך", והלה אמר "איני יודע", רב הונא ורב יהודה אמרי: חייב, רב נחמן ורבי יוחנן אמרי: פטור. ה"נ: היא טוענת ברי, אבל הוא אינו יכול לטעון טענת ברי, ותהוי תיובתא דרב הונא! וי"ל: מאחר שהתורה עשאה ספק עד שתשתה – אינה יכולה לטעון טענת ברי. ופלוגתא דמתני' התם "הנושא את האשה ולא מצא לה בתולים" – לא שייכא להכא, דהתם אפילו ב"ש מודו, דשמא אותו שטר מעולם לא עמד לגבות, שהרי הבעל טוען מקחו מקח טעות. והכא לא שייך למימר אליבא דב"ה: העמד אשה על חזקתה ואימור לא זינתה – שהרי רגלים [לדבר], שקינא לה ונסתרה, והכתוב הוציאה מאותה חזקה ועשאה ספק. **בית** הלל סברי שטר העומד לגבות לאו כגבוי דמי. אי קשיא מהא דאמר בפ' "המקבל" (ב"מ דף קי.): יתומים אמרו "אנו השבחנו", וב"ח אומר "אביכם השביח", על מי להביא ראיה? סבר רב הונא למימר: ארעא בחזקת יתמי קיימא, ועל ב"ח להביא ראיה. אמר ליה ההוא סבא, הכי אמר ר' יוחנן: על היתומים להביא ראיה. מאי טעמא? ארעא, כיון דלגוביינא קיימא – כמאן דגבי דמי, ויתמי נייתי ראיה ונשקול. וכי ר' יוחנן שבק בית הלל ועביד כב"ש? יש לתרץ: הכא, דהשיעבוד עצמו של כתובה עומד בספק – לא קיימא ארעא לגוביינא, אמרי ב"ה דלאו כגבוי דמי. אבל התם – היתומים מודו לב"ח בקרקע עצמו שהוא משועבד לו, ואינם מעכבין לפניו הקרקע. הלכך, אפילו בית הלל מודו דבכה"ג כגבוי דמי, ולא קיימא ארעא בחזקת יתמי. וכיון דלא קיימא בחזקת יתמי – על היתומים להביא ראיה מן השבח. דומיא דעיר ואילן דמייתי עלה: ספק זה קודם ספק זה קודם – קוצץ ונותן דמים. אלמא, כיון דלמיקץ קאי, דבין אם קדם האילן בין אם קדם העיר – קוצץ, אלא שאם קדם האילן קוצץ ונותן דמים, אמרי ליה: זיל קוץ, ודמי – אייתי ראיה ושקול. גבי הא ארעא נמי, אמרי ליתמי: הבו ליה ארעא לב"ח, דהא לגוביינא קיימא, ושבח אייתו ראיה ושקילו. מפי מורי"ה. **לאו** כגבוי דמי. הכא לא שייכא כל הני פלוגתא דרבי מאיר ורבנן דפליגי בפרק "השואל" (ב"מ דף ק:) דכל העומד לבצור (א) כבצור דמי, ופלוגתא דר' שמעון בן גמליאל ורבי פרק קמא דסנהדרין (דף טו.), ובפרק "השולח" (גיטין דף לט.) בכל העומד לגזוז, ופלוגתא דרבי שמעון ורבנן בפרק "המנחות והנסכים" (מנחות דף קב:): כל העומד לזרוק כזרוק דמי, וכן לפדות ולשרוף. דלאו בחדא מחיתא נחות להו, דהכא כ"ע מודו דאמרי' לאו כגבוי דמי, והעמד ממון בחזקת בעליו, שהרי צריך דיינין, ולאו בידו הוא, כדאמר *גבי גר: מי יימר דמזדקקין ליה בי דינא. [קדושין סג:] וטעמא דר' מאיר כבצורות דמיין – משום דבידו, ואין צריכין לגופן, הלכך לא חשיב להו כקרקע. והכי אמר בפרק "בהמה המקשה" (חולין דף עג.) גבי ידות הכלים דאין מטבילין אלא עד מקום מדה – משום דעומדין ליקצץ. וגבי שערו העומד לגזוז אמר בפרק קמא דסנהדרין (דף טו.) דמודה רבי מאיר דלאו כגזוז דמי, משום דאשבוחי אשבח כל מה דקאי. ומיהו רבן שמעון בן גמליאל פליג ואמר כגזוז דמי, דלא עביד איניש דשביק ליה. והני דרבי שמעון – טעמא אחרינא אית בהו, ולא אמר אלא במקום מצוה, כגון זריקת דם ופדיית פרה כשמצא אחרת נאה ממנה, ושריפתה. אבל בהני דרבי מאיר ורשב"ג – לא שייך האי טעמא. והא דאמר גבי שופר של עבודה זרה בפרק "ראוהו בית דין" (ר"ה דף כח.), וגבי לולב של אשירה (סוכה דף לא:), ומנעל בפרק "מצות חליצה" (יבמות דף קג:): כתותי מכתת שיעוריה – אפי' רבנן מודו, משום דאיסור הנאה הוא ולא הוי אלא כעפרא דארעא בעלמא, וליכא שיעורא. ופרה – חיבת הקדש מהני. וצריך עיון: כלאי הכרם אמאי מטמאין טומאת אוכלים ולא אמר כתותי מכתת שיעוריה? הלכך ליכא לדמויי להדדי. והא דאמר בפרק "נערה" (כתובות דף נא.): כל העומד לקצור כקצור דמי – התם טעמא דלא תקנו לב"ח לגבות אלא דבר הצריך לקרקע קצת, וכן פירש רש"י (ב"מ טו:): שבח המגיע לכתפים – שעומד בקרוב לקצור וצריך עדיין קצת לקרקע*. [ועי' היטב תוס' ב"ק לה: ד"ה שבח ותוס' ב"ב מב: ד"ה ...] **מיתיבי** המקנא לארוסתו. כך ברייתא זו שנויה בתוספתא (פ"ה): המקנא לארוסתו ולשומרת יבם שלו, אם משכנסה נסתרה – או שותה או לא נוטלת כתובה. הרוצה שנשא עקרה או זקינה, ויש לו אשה ובנים – או שותה או לא נוטלת כתובתה. [מעוברת עצמו או מניקת עצמו – או שותה או לא נוטלת כתובתה]. (רש"ל) כהנת לויה וישראלית שנשאו לכהן ללוי וישראל, ממזרת לממזר, נתינה לנתין, ואשת גר לגר ועבד משוחרר, והאיילונית – או שותה או לא נוטלת כתובתה. רבי שמעון בן אלעזר אמר: איילונית לא שותה ולא נוטלת כתובתה, שנא': "ונקתה ונזרעה זרע" – שראוי ליזרע, פרט לאיילונית שאינה ראויה להזרע. אבל המקנא לארוסתו ולשומרת יבמתו שלו, עד שלא כנסה נסתרה – לא שותות ולא נוטלות כתובתה. הרוצה [שנשא עקרה וזקינה ואין לו אשה ובנים – לא שותות ולא נוטלת כתובה. מעוברת חבירו ומניקת חבירו – לא שותות ולא נוטלות כתובה]. רבי אליעזר אומר: יכול הוא להפרישה ולהחזירה לאחר זמן.

שנשא

תוספות שאנץ

וב"ה סברי לאו כגבוי דמי והויא לה היא תובעת כתובתה מספק דדילמא זנאי הלכך אינהו ודאי והיא ספק ואין ספק מוציא מידי ודאי ועליה להביא ראיה שלא זינתה ל"ה. מחלוקת בעקרה וזקנה פ"ה מחלוקת דפליג רבי אליעזר ואמר א) ראויה לקיימה היא דיכול לישא אשה אחרת אבל אילונית כי נמי ראויה לקיימה היא מיהו לא שתיא מהאי טעמא דראויה להריון בעינן ועקרה ע"י מכה ב)

א) נ"ל ואמר דיכול לישא אשה אחרת כו' בעקרה וזקינה דליכא למימר אינה שותה אלא טעמא משום דלא חזיא לקיימה עלה פליג ר"א ואמר וכו'.

ב) וזקינה מינא דבת הריון היא קודם לכן אבל איילונית מבטן אמה לקוייה היא ולא חזיא.

הגהות הב"ח

(א) תוס' ד"ה לאו וכו' דכבצורות דמיין:

מְעוּבֶּרֶת חֲבֵירוֹ וּמֵינֶקֶת חֲבֵירוֹ — לֹא שׁוֹתוֹת וְלֹא נוֹטְלוֹת כְּתוּבָּה, דִּבְרֵי ר' מֵאִיר. שֶׁהָיָה רַבִּי מֵאִיר אוֹמֵר: *אלֹא יִשָּׂא אָדָם מְעוּבֶּרֶת חֲבֵירוֹ וּמֵינֶקֶת חֲבֵירוֹ, וְאִם נָשָׂא — יוֹצִיא וְלֹא יַחֲזִיר עוֹלָמִית. וַחֲכָמִים אוֹמְרִים: ביוֹצִיא, וּכְשֶׁיַּגִּיעַ זְמַנּוֹ לִכְנוֹס — יִכְנוֹס. גוְהָרוֹבֶא שֶׁנָּשָׂא עֲקָרָה וּזְקֵינָה, וְאֵין לוֹ אִשָּׁה וּבָנִים מֵעִיקָּרָא — לֹא שׁוֹתָה וְלֹא נוֹטֶלֶת כְּתוּבָּה. ר' אֶלְעָזָר אוֹמֵר: יָכוֹל הוּא לִישָּׂא אַחֶרֶת וְלִפְרוֹת וְלִרְבּוֹת הֵימֶנָּה. דאֲבָל *הַמְקַנֵּא לַאֲרוּסָתוֹ וּלְשׁוֹמֶרֶת יָבָם שֶׁלּוֹ, וּמִשֶּׁנִּכְנְסָה נִסְתְּרָה — אוֹ שׁוֹתָה אוֹ לֹא נוֹטֶלֶת כְּתוּבָּה. המְעוּבֶּרֶת וּמֵינֶקֶת עַצְמוֹ — אוֹ שׁוֹתָה אוֹ לֹא נוֹטֶלֶת כְּתוּבָּתָהּ. והָרוֹבֶא שֶׁנָּשָׂא עֲקָרָה וּזְקֵינָה וְיֵשׁ לוֹ אִשָּׁה וּבָנִים — אוֹ שׁוֹתָה אוֹ לֹא נוֹטֶלֶת כְּתוּבָּה. זאֵשֶׁת מַמְזֵר לְמַמְזֵר, וְאֵשֶׁת נָתִין לְנָתִין, וְאֵשֶׁת גֵּר וְעֶבֶד מְשׁוּחְרָר, וְאַיְילוֹנִית — אוֹ שׁוֹתָה אוֹ לֹא נוֹטֶלֶת כְּתוּבָּה.

קָתָנֵי מִיהָא אַיְילוֹנִית, תְּיוּבְתֵּיהּ דְּרַב נַחְמָן! אָמַר לָךְ רַב נַחְמָן: תַּנָּאֵי הִיא, וַאֲנָא דַּאֲמַרִי כִּי הַאי תַּנָּא. דְּתַנְיָא, *ר' שִׁמְעוֹן בֶּן אֶלְעָזָר אוֹמֵר: אַיְילוֹנִית לֹא שׁוֹתָה וְלֹא נוֹטֶלֶת כְּתוּבָּה, שֶׁנֶּאֱמַר: °"וְנִקְּתָה וְנִזְרְעָה זָרַע" (במדבר ה) — מִי שֶׁדַּרְכָּהּ לְהַזְרִיעַ, יָצְאתָה זוֹ שֶׁאֵין דַּרְכָּהּ לְהַזְרִיעַ. וְרַבָּנַן, הַאי "וְנִקְּתָה וְנִזְרְעָה זָרַע" מַאי עָבְדִי לֵיהּ? מִיבָּעֵי לְהוּ לִכְדְתַנְיָא: "וְנִקְּתָה וְנִזְרְעָה [זָרַע]" שֶׁאִם הָיְתָה עֲקָרָה — נִפְקֶדֶת, דִּבְרֵי ר' עֲקִיבָא. אָמַר לוֹ ר' יִשְׁמָעֵאל: אִם כֵּן יִסָּתְרוּ כָּל הָעֲקָרוֹת וְיִפָּקְדוּ, וְזוֹ הוֹאִיל וְלֹא נִסְתְּרָה — הִפְסִידָה?! אִם כֵּן מַה תַּלְמוּד לוֹמַר "וְנִקְּתָה וְנִזְרְעָה זָרַע"? חשֶׁאִם הָיְתָה יוֹלֶדֶת בְּצַעַר — יוֹלֶדֶת בְּרֶיוַח, נְקֵבוֹת — יוֹלֶדֶת זְכָרִים, קְצָרִים — יוֹלֶדֶת אֲרוּכִּים, שְׁחוֹרִים — יוֹלֶדֶת לְבָנִים. § "אֵשֶׁת מַמְזֵר לְמַמְזֵר". פְּשִׁיטָא! מַהוּ דְּתֵימָא: אַפּוּשֵׁי פְּסוּלִין לָא לֵיפּוּשׁ, קָא מַשְׁמַע לָן. § "אֵשֶׁת גֵּר וְעֶבֶד מְשׁוּחְרָר (א) וְאַיְילוֹנִית". § פְּשִׁיטָא! מַהוּ דְּתֵימָא: °"דַּבֵּר אֶל בְּנֵי יִשְׂרָאֵל" (שם) — וְלֹא גֵּרִים, קמ"ל. וְאֵימָא הָכִי נַמִּי! "וְאָמַרְתָּ" רִבּוּיָא הוּא. § "אֵשֶׁת כֹּהֵן שׁוֹתָה" כו'. § (אֵשֶׁת כֹּהֵן שׁוֹתָה,) פְּשִׁיטָא! מַהוּ דְּתֵימָא: °"וְהִיא לֹא נִתְפָּשָׂה" (שם) — אֲסוּרָה, הָא נִתְפְּשָׂה — מוּתֶּרֶת, וְזוֹ הוֹאִיל וְנִתְפְּשָׂה אֲסוּרָה אֵימָא לֹא תִּשְׁתֶּה, קָא מַשְׁמַע לָן. § "וּמוּתֶּרֶת לְבַעְלָהּ". § פְּשִׁיטָא! אָמַר רַב הוּנָא: בְּמִתְנַוְּונָה. מִתְנַוְּונָה — הָא בְּדָקוּהָ מַיָּא! טבְּמִתְנַוְּונָה דֶּרֶךְ אֵבָרִים. מַהוּ דְּתֵימָא: הָא זַנּוּיֵי זַנַּאי, וְהָא דְּלָא בְּדָקוּהָ מַיָּא כִּי אוֹרְחֵיהּ — מִשּׁוּם דְּבְאוֹנֶס זַנַּאי, וּלְגַבֵּי כֹּהֵן אֲסִירָא, קָא מַשְׁמַע לָן. § "אֵשֶׁת סָרִיס שׁוֹתָה". § פְּשִׁיטָא! מַהוּ דְּתֵימָא: "מִבַּלְעֲדֵי אִישֵׁךְ" אָמַר רַחֲמָנָא, וְהַאי לָאו בַּר הָכִי הוּא, קָא מַשְׁמַע לָן. § "עַל יְדֵי כָּל עֲרָיוֹת מְקַנִּין". § פְּשִׁיטָא! מַהוּ

תורה אור

רש"י

לֹא שׁוֹתוֹת. דִּכְתִיב: "תַּחַת אִישֵׁךְ". וְלֹא יַחֲזִיר עוֹלָמִית. קְנָסָא קַנְסוּהוּ רַבָּנַן. לִכְשֶׁיַּגִּיעַ זְמַנּוֹ. לְאַחַר כ"ד חֹדֶשׁ לְלֵידַת הַוָּלָד. וְהָרוֹבֶא. בָּחוּר כְּמוֹ "יֶלֶד" (בראשית כא) – רַבְיָא. מְעוּבֶּרֶת עַצְמוֹ. שֶׁהָיְתָה אִשְׁתּוֹ מְעוּבֶּרֶת וְקִינֵּא לָהּ. אוֹ שׁוֹתוֹת. וְלָא אָמְרִינַן: לָא לִיקְטְלֵיהּ לַוָּלָד. אֵשֶׁת מַמְזֵר לְמַמְזֵר. כְּלוֹמַר, אִשָּׁה הָרְאוּיָה לְמַמְזֵר וְנִישֵּׂאת לְמַמְזֵר, וְקִינֵּא לָהּ וְנִסְתְּרָה. אוֹ שׁוֹתָה כו'. וּלְקַמָּן פָּרֵיךְ: פְּשִׁיטָא!. אֲנָא דַּאֲמַרִי כִּי הַאי תַּנָּא. דְּאִית לֵיהּ עֲקָרָה וּזְקֵנָה שׁוֹתוֹת. מִדְּלָא נָקַט אֶלָּא אַיְילוֹנִית, וְנָסֵיב תַּלְמוּדָא מִ"וְנִקְּתָה וְנִזְרְעָה זָרַע" וְלָא מִשּׁוּם דְּאֵינָהּ רְאוּיָה לְקַיְּימָהּ – אַלְמָא כְּרַבִּי אֶלְעָזָר ס"ל, דְּיָכוֹל לִישָּׂא אַחֶרֶת וְלִפְרוֹת וְלִרְבּוֹת, וְאַפ"ה אַיְילוֹנִית לָא. וְזוֹ. כָּל אִשָּׁה נְגוּעָה עֲקָרָה, מִשּׁוּם דְּלָא נִסְתְּרָה הִפְסִידָה?. לָא לֵיפּוּשׁ פְּסוּלִין. לֹא נַעֲשֶׂה שָׁלוֹם בֵּינֵיהֶם, הַלְוַאי לֹא יִפְרֶה וְלֹא יִרְבֶּה, הוֹאִיל וְכָל דּוֹרוֹתָיו מַמְזֵרִין. וְהִיא לֹא נִתְפָּשָׂה כו'. כְּלוֹמַר, מַהוּ דְּתֵימָא: פָּרָשַׁת סוֹטָה עַל כָּרְחֵךְ בְּאֵשֶׁת יִשְׂרָאֵל קַיְימָא, מִדִּכְתִיב "וְהִיא" מִיעוּטָא, מַשְׁמַע: זוֹ הִיא דְּכִי לֹא נִתְפְּשָׂה אֲסוּרָה הָא נִתְפְּשָׂה כו', וַעֲלָהּ קָאֵי קְרָא דְּבַתְרֵיהּ: "וְעָבַר עָלָיו רוּחַ" וגו'. דְּהֵיכָא דְּמִסְתַּפְקָא לָן בְּהַךְ אִם נִטְמְאָה וְאִם לֹא נִטְמְאָה – שׁוֹתָה, אֲבָל אֵשֶׁת כֹּהֵן, דְּלֵיתָהּ בִּכְלַל "וְהִיא לֹא נִתְפָּשָׂה" – לֵיתָהּ נַמִּי בִּכְלַל הַשְׁקָאָה, קמ"ל. בְּמִתְנַוְּונָה. לְאַחַר שֶׁשָּׁתְתָה אִיצְטְרִיךְ לְאַשְׁמוּעִינַן דְּמוּתֶּרֶת לְבַעְלָהּ. דְּלָא תֵּימָא: זוֹנָה הִיא, שֶׁהֲרֵי בְּדָקוּהָ הַמַּיִם. מִתְנַוְּונָה. הָא וַדַּאי בְּדָקוּהָ הַמַּיִם, וְזוֹנָה הִיא, אֶלָּא שֶׁתָּלָה לָהּ זְכוּת. וְאַמַּאי מוּתֶּרֶת לְבַעְלָהּ?. בְּמִתְנַוְּונָה דֶּרֶךְ אֵבָרִים. שֶׁאֵינָהּ מִתְנַוְּונָה בַּמֵּעַיִם וּבַיְּרֵכַיִם, אֶלָּא רֹאשָׁהּ וּשְׁאָר אֵבָרֶיהָ כְּבֵדִים עָלֶיהָ. מַהוּ דְּתֵימָא: הָא לָאו זְכוּת תָּלָה לָהּ, דְּאִם כֵּן – הֲוָה לָהּ לְהִתְנַוְּונָה דֶּרֶךְ בְּדִיקַת הַמַּיִם, אֶלָּא בְּאוֹנֶס זִינְּתָה, לְפִיכָךְ מִתְנַוְּונָה שֶׁלֹּא כְּדַרְכָּהּ, וּלְכֹהֵן מִיהָא תִּיתְסַר. מִבַּלְעֲדֵי אִישֵׁךְ. מַשְׁמַע דְּאִישָׁהּ בַּר הָכִי הוּא. קָא מַשְׁמַע לָן. דְּלְמִיקְדַּם שְׁכִיבַת בַּעַל לַבּוֹעֵל הוּא דַּאֲתָא, וְסָרִיס בַּר שְׁכִיבָה הוּא, וְאַף עַל גַּב דְּלָאו בַּר זְרִיעָה הוּא. *וּבְסָרִיס חַמָּה קָאָמַר דְּמוּתָּר לְקַיְּימָהּ, וְלָא בִּסְרִיס אָדָם, שֶׁאָסוּר לְקַיְּימָהּ מִשּׁוּם "לֹא יָבֹא פְּצוּעַ דַּכָּא" (דברים כג).

תוספות

[*שנשא עקרה וזקינה וכו']. ותימה: אמאי לא תנא איילונית בהדי עקרה וזקינה? **לא** ישא אדם מעוברת חבירו. בירושלמי: עליו הכתוב אומר (משלי כג): "אל תסיג גבול עולם ובשדה יתומים אל תבא". *ומודים חכמים לרבי אלעזר שאם היו לו בנים ואשה [שהיא שותה או לא נוטלת כתובה. היו לו אשה ובנים] ומתו בין קינוי לסתירה – כבר נראית לשתות. **מעוברת** עצמו או שותה וכו'. רש"י פי': ולא אמרינן דלא לקטליה לולד. ותימה: אמאי אית לן למקטליה? מה איכפת לן נמתין עד שתלד. הא תנן בפ"ק דערכין (דף ז.): האשה היוצאה ליהרג – אין ממתינין לה עד שתלד, והתם גזירת הכתוב הוא: "ומתו גם שניהם" – לרבות את הולד. והתם משמע טעמא דרבי קרא, הא לא רבי קרא – לא קטליניה ליה, משום דממונא דבעל הוא, כדכתיב (שמות כא): "כאשר ישית עליו בעל האשה"! והכא הכי פירושא: מעוברת עצמו, אע"ג דקינא לה כשהיא מעוברת – שותה לאחר שתלד, ולא אמרינן כמו גבי מעוברת חבירו, דאי קינא לה כשהיא מעוברת וילדה, ומת הולד או הפילה – אפ"ה אינה שותה, דלאו בת קינוי היתה, דממעט לה בספרי מ"כי תשטה אשתו", וכדאמרינן בירושלמי: לא היו [לו] אשה ובנים וכו' כבר [נראית] שלא לשתות. **אמר** לו רבי ישמעאל א"כ יסתרו כל עקרות ויפקדו. תימה: ור' ישמעאל לימא ליה לנפשיה: יסתרו כל יולדות בצער, וילדו בריות, וזו הואיל ולא נסתרה הפסידה! **ואמרת** ריבויא הוא. תימה: והא אפיקתיה לעיל (דף כד.): לרבות הארוסה ושומרת יבם לקינוי! **וזו** הואיל ונתפשה אסורה אימא לא תשתה בלל קמ"ל. תימה לר"י: אמאי לא פריך הכא: ואימא הכי נמי, כדפריך לעיל? ונראה: כל היכא דקרא דמסיק אדעתיה מתוכו למדרש הכי ומדריש לדרשא אחריתי – לא פריך: ואימא ה"נ, דקמ"ל דכך ניתן למדרש למשה בסיני ולא בע"א. כגון "והיא נתפשה" – לאסור אשת כהן, "מבלעדי אישך" – מי שקדמה שכיבת בעל. אבל לעיל, "בני ישראל" משמע בהדיא למעוטי גרים. וכן בפרק שני דיבמות (דף כב.) בגמרא דמי שיש לו אח מ"מ זוקק את אשת אחיו ליבום, דקא פריך: פשיטא, אחיו הוא! מהו דתימא לילף אחוה אחוה מבני יעקב, קמ"ל – התם פריך: ואימא הכי נמי, משום דאין גזרה שוה למחצה, וצריך טעמא להוציא מאותה סברא או קרא. וכן לענין ליורשו (שם:) וליטמא לו, פשיטא אחיו הוא! סד"א: "לא יטמא בעל בעמיו", יש בעל שמטמא ויש שאינו מטמא, הא כיצד? מטמא לאשתו כשרה ואינו מטמא לאשתו פסולה – ה"נ, קמ"ל. ואימא הכי נמי – דהא קרא ממעט פסולין, והאי פסול הוא. וכן בפ"ק דערכין (דף ז.) גבי האשה שיוצאת ליהרג אין ממתינים לה עד שתלד, פשיטא, גופה היא! מהו דתימא (כי) "כאשר ישית עליו בעל האשה" כתיב, והאי ממונא דבעל הוא – קמ"ל. ואימא ה"נ – *דמאי נפקא לן מהתם דממונא דבעל הוא. אבל הכא, כיון דאשמועינן דעיקר קרא לדרשא אחריתי – תו לא סלקי דעתא למעוטי מיניה מידי. וכן פר"י. **אשת** סרים. רש"י פי': בסריס חמה, ולא בסריס אדם, שאסור לקיימה. ולא ידעינן מנלן דסריס אדם, כגון ששתה כוס עיקרין, דאסור לקיימה? אי משום האי ברייתא דמייתי בפרק שני דיבמות (דף כ:) ובפרק "הערל" (שם דף פט:): פלוע דכא וכרות שפכה, סריס אדם והזקן וכו' עד אסור לקיימה – הא קתני נמי זקן, וכי זקן אסור לקיים? אלא על כרחיך אפלוע דכא וכרות שפכה קאי, כדקתני טעמא: משום שנאמר "לא יבא פלוע דכא וכרות שפכה", אבל אסריס דקתני בברייתא – לא ידענא מנליה דקאי נמי עלה. אבל

תוספות שאנץ

ואיילונית במעי אמה לקייה ולא חזיא ל"ה: ואשת ממזר לממזר כלומר אשה הראויה לממזר ונשאת לממזר וקינא לה ונסתרה ל"ה אילונית או שותה או לא נוטלת כתובה ומיירי בשיש לו אשה ובנים דומיא דעקרה וזקנה: ולא ליפוש בפסולין פ"ה לא נעשה שלום ביניהם לא יפרה ולא ירבה הואיל וכל דורותיו ממזרים: מ"ד והיא לא נתפשה כו' כלומר מהו דתימא פרשה סוטה על כרחך באשת ישראל קיימא מדכתיב והיא משמע זו היא דכי לא נתפשה אסורה הא נתפשה כו' ועלה קאי קרא דבתריה ועבר עליו דהיכ' דמספקא לן בהך אם נטמאה אי לא [נטמאה] שותה אבל אשת כהן דליתא בכלל והיא לא נתפשה ליתא נמי בכלל השקאה קמ"ל ל"ה. במתנונה דרך אברים שאין מתנוונה במעים אלא ראשה ושאר אברים כבדים עליה מ"ד א). מ"ד מבלעדי אישך כו' משמע דאישה בר הכי הוא קא משמע לן דלמי שקדמה שכיבתו לבועל הוא דאתא וסרים בר הכי הוא ואע"ג דלאו בר איזרועי הוא ובסרים חמה קאמר דמותר לקיימה ולא בסרים אדם שאסור לקיימה משום לא יבא פצוע דכה ל"ה. שחוף

עין משפט נר מצוה

כן גירסת רש"א אבל גירסת רש"ל הד"א עם דיבור דלעיל

עי' בירושלמי דקאי אאיילונית רש"ל

כג א מיי' פי"א מהל' גירושין הלכה כה סמג עשין נ טוש"ע אה"ע סימן יג סעיף יא:

כד ב מיי' שם הלכה כח טוש"ע שם סעיף יב:

כה ג מיי' פ"ב מהל' סוטה הלכה י:

כו ד מיי' שם הלכה ה:

כז ה מיי' שם הלכה ז:

כח ו מיי' שם הלכה י:

כט ז מיי' שם הלכה ו:

ל ח מיי' שם הלכה י ופ"ג שם הלכה כב סמג עשין נו:

לא ט מיי' שם פ"ג הלכה כא:

מסורת הש"ס

יבמות לו:

[תוספתא ריש פ"ה ע"ש]

[שם בתוספתא]

ברכות לא: [ושם מוחלפת השיטה ועי' תוס' לעיל כב. ד"ה ור' יונתן וכו' ועי' תוס' מנחות יז: ד"ה מאי האכל וכו' ול"ע]

[ועי' היטב ברש"י דמשנה לעיל כד. ד"ה אשת סרים ועי' רש"א]

רש"ל מ"ז

נ"ל דהא

הגהות הב"ח

(א) גמ' משוחרר פשיטא כל"ל ותיבת ואיילונית נמחק:

א) נראה דל"ל מ"ד הא לאו זכות תלה לה וכו' ולכהן מיהא ליתסר ועי' ברש"י.

מהו דתימא: °"נטמאה" "נטמאה" שני פעמים, במדבר ה *אחד לבעל ואחד לבועל – היכא דקא מיתסרא בהא זנות, אבל הא, הואיל ואסורה וקיימא אימא לא, קא משמע לן.§ "חוץ מן הקטן" [וכו'].§ "איש" אמר רחמנא ולא קטן. "ושאינו איש" למעוטי מאי? אילימא למעוטי שחוף – והאמר שמואל: שחוף אמקנין על ידו, בופוסל בתרומה. מקנין על ידו, פשיטא! מהו דתימא: °"ושכב איש אותה שכבת זרע" אמר רחמנא, שם והא לאו בר הכי הוא, קמ"ל. "ופוסל בתרומה" פשיטא! מהו דתימא: °"לא יחלל זרעו" אמר ויקרא כא רחמנא, דאית ליה זרע – ליחלל, דלית ליה זרע – לא ליחלל, קמ"ל! ואלא למעוטי גוי – והאמר רב המנונא: גגוי מקנין על ידו, דופוסל בתרומה. "מקנין על ידו" פשיטא! מהו דתימא "נטמאה" "נטמאה" שתי פעמים, אחד לבעל ואחד לבועל – היכא דקמיתסרא בהא זנות, אבל הא – הואיל ואסורה וקיימא אימא לא, קמשמע לן. "ופוסל בתרומה" פשיטא! מהו דתימא: °"ובת כהן כי תהיה שם כב לאיש זר" אמר רחמנא, דבר הויה – אין, דלאו בר הויה – לא, קמשמע לן דפסיל מדרבי יוחנן. *דאמר רבי יוחנן משום רבי ישמעאל: המנין לגוי ועבד שבאו על הכהנת ועל הלויה ועל בת ישראל שפסלוה – שנאמר: °"ובת כהן כי תהיה שם אלמנה וגרושה" – מי שיש לו אלמנות וגירושין בה, יצאו גוי ועבד שאין לו אלמנות וגירושין בה! ואלא למעוטי מאי? א"ר פפא: ולמעוטי בהמה, דאין זנות בבהמה. *אמר ליה רבא מפרזקיא לרב אשי: מנא הא מילתא דאמור רבנן: זאין זנות בבהמה – דכתיב: °"לא תביא אתנן זונה ומחיר כלב" וגו', *ותניא: דברים כג חאתנן כלב ומחיר זונה מותרין, שנאמר: "גם שניהם" שנים ולא ארבעה. ואלא "שכבת זרע" ל"ל? מיבעי ליה *לכדתניא: "ש"ז" – פרט לדבר אחר. מאי דבר אחר? אמר רב ששת: פרט לשקינא לה שלא כדרכה. אמר ליה רבא: שלא כדרכה – °"משכבי אשה" כתיב! אלא אמר ויקרא יח רבא: טפרט לשקינא לה דרך אברים. א"ל אביי: פריצותא בעלמא היא, ופריצותא מי אסר רחמנא?! אלא אמר אביי: פרט לשקינא לה בנשיקה. הניחא למ"ד *העראה יזו הכנסת עטרה, אבל נשיקה ולא כלום היא – היינו דאתי קרא למעוטי נשיקה. אלא למאן דאמר העראה זו נשיקה, מאי איכא למימר? לעולם לשקינא לה דרך אברים. ומהו דתימא: בקפידא דבעל תליא רחמנא, ובעל הא קא קפיד, קמשמע לן. אמר שמואל: ישא אדם

דומה

רש"י

מהו דתימא נטמאה נטמאה שני פעמים. אמורים בפרשה, ודרשינן ליה לקמן (דף כז:): אחד לבעל ואחד לבועל. היכא דמיתסרא אבועל בהא סתירה – משתעי קרא דנוהג בה דין סוטה, אבל הא דאסורה כו'. קמ"ל. דכי אתא קרא – לגופיה אתא, דהיכא דאינו קרוב לה – נאסר עליה על ידי קינוי זה, ולאו למעוטי קרובים אתא. איש אמר רחמנא. "ושכב איש אותה". שחוף. שבשרו נשחף וכלה ויבש, ואין בו כח. ובתורת כהנים בקללות שנינו דוגמתו: יש לך אדם שהוא חולה ומוטל במטה אבל בשרו שמור עליו – תלמוד לומר "את השחפת", מלמד שבשרו נשחף. מקנין על ידו כו'. כמו: והוינן בה: מקנין על ידו, פשיטא!. ופוסל בתרומה פשיטא. אם הוא אחד מן הפסולים המחללין את האשה, כגון נכרי עבד חלל נתין וממזר, דקיימא לן בקדושין* וביבמות* (א) דפסולין האשה בביאתן מ"ובת כהן כי תהיה לאיש זר", כיון שנבעלה למי שזר אצלה – פסלה. לא יחלל זרעו. מדלא כתיב "לא יחל" – דרשינן שני חילולין, אחד לה ואחד לזרעה. דאית ליה זרע מחלל. את האשה בביאתו, דלית ליה זרע – לא יחלל. קא משמע לן. שמואל, דפוסל. שמעינן ליה מהא, דקאמר מקנין על ידי שחוף!. ובת כהן כי תהיה לאיש זר וגו'. ומיניה נפקא לן דפסולין פסלי לאשה בביאתן. ומדאפקיה בלשון הויה נדרוש: דאית ליה הויה – מי שקידושין תופסין בה. כגון ממזר נתין וחלל – פסלי. אבל נכרי ועבד – הרי הן כבהמה, וכיון דלית להו הויה – לא נפסלו. נכרי אין לו קידושין בישראל, דכתיב (ויקרא כ): "איש אשר ינאף את אשת רעהו" ותניא בסנהדרין (דף נב:): פרט לאשת (ב) אחרים. אלמא לית להו אישות. עבד – "עם החמור" כתיב בהו, עם הדומה לחמור. מי שיש לו אלמנות וגירושין בה. הוא דכי אין לה זרע ממנו "ושבה אל בית אביה מלחם אביה תאכל", דלא פסלה בביאתו. יצא נכרי ועבד שאין לו אלמנות וגירושין בה, שלא תפסו לו בה קידושין, וכשמת, אין שם אלמנות עליה, וביבמות פריך: אימא לקולא, דמי שיש לו אלמנות וגירושין הוא דכי אית לה זרע לא תיכול, אבל נכרי ועבד, אפי' אית לה זרע מיניה – תיכול! והתם מסקי לה *ב"הבא על יבמתו". ומיהו, שמעינן [ליה מהא] דמקנין ע"י נכרי!. ואלא. "מי שאינו איש" דמתני' – למעוטי (ג) בהמה. דאין זנות לבהמה. אינה נעשית זונה בבעילת בהמה, ואינה נאסרת על בעלה. אתנן זונה. נתן טלה באתננה. מחיר כלב. החליף כלב בטלה. אתנן כלב. שאם אדם אומר לזונה: "הילך טלה והבעלי לכלבי". מחיר זונה. היתה לו שפחה זונה, והחליפה בטלה. ומדקאמר אתנן כלב מותר – מכלל דלאו זנות הוא. דאי זנות הוא – הוה חייל עלה שם אתנן. ואלא שכבת זרע למה לי. כיון דאמרת מקנין ע"י שחוף. לשקינא לה שלא כדרכה. "אל תסתרי עמו להבעל שלא כדרכה". משכבי אשה כתיב. הוקשו שני משכבותיה לכל דברים. וכיון דנאסרת עליו – אמאי לא הוי קינוי?. דרך אברים פריצותא בעלמא הוא. שוכב עמה בקירוב בשר. פריצותא מי קאסר רחמנא. אשה על בעלה בהכי? וכיון דלא מתסרא עליה בהכי – פשיטא דלאו קינוי הוא!. בנשיקה. משיק השמש באותו מקום. היינו דאתא קרא למעוטיה. דלא תימא הערה היא. אלא למאן דאמר. ביבמות (דף נה:): הערה האמורה בתורה שהיא כגמר ביאה בכל העריות, כדכתיב (ויקרא כ): "את מקורה הערה" "את שארו הערה" – זו נשיקה, מאי איכא למימר – היכי מצית למימר דאתא קרא למעוטה? הלא כגמר ביאה היא לכל דבר חוץ משפחה חרופה!. בקפידא דבעל תליא. דכתיב: "וקינא". ובעל – הא חזינן ליה דקפיד, שהרי קינא לה על כך.

דומה

תוספות

אבל הא הואיל ואסורה וקיימא אימא לא קא משמע לן. תימה: הא שמעינן לה מאלמנה לכהן גדול דאסורה וקיימא לבעל, ואפי' הכי איצטריך קרא ד"כי תשטה אשתו" למעוטי, הא לאו הכי – הוה סוטה! וכן על מי שאמר: "איש" אמר רחמנא ולא קטן, נראה דדוקא משתיה ממעט לה קרא, אבל נאסרה על ידי בן תשע שנים ויום אחד אע"פ שאינו איש, שהרי ביאתו פוסלת בתרומה, כדאיתא בפרק "אלמנה" (יבמות דף סח.), ונסקלת הערוה על ידו, כדאיתא בפ' "ד' מיתות" (סנהדרין דף נה:), ומקומו בפרק "יוצא דופן" (נדה דף מה.). דומיא דכל עריות מקנא על ידן, דלא איצטריך לאשמועינן אלא דשותות, אבל דנאסרו – פשיטא, וכי משום דעריות נינהו גריעי?

שחוף. פירש רבינו חננאל: שאינו בועל כדרכו ואינו מזריע. דתניא:* איזהו מרוח אשך – זה הקליטים שנכנס רוח באשכיו, דברי ר"ע. רבי ישמעאל אומר: זה השחוף. תימה: אמאי נקט שמואל שחוף ולא נקט סריס? ושמא שחוף הוי רבותא טפי.

אבל הא הואיל ואסירא וקיימא. תימא: מאי קמ"ל רב הונא? והא מתני' היא: ע"י כל עריות מקנין! וי"ל דהכי פירושו: מי שנאסר בכל בת ישראל ע"י בעילת זנות, אפילו אינה קרובתו. יצא גוי, דבלאו הכי כל בת ישראל מתסרא וקיימא לגביה. יצא גוי שאין לו אלמנות וגירושין בה. פירש רש"י: דנפקא לן מדכתיב: "אשר ינאף את אשת רעהו" – פרט לאשת אחרים. תימה: והא נפקא לן בקידושין בפרק "האומר" *מ"לא תתחתן בם"! וכמדומה דלא אתי קרא פרט לאשת אחרים אלא למעוטי ישראל הבא על הגויה אשת גוי, וקמ"ל אע"ג דבעולת בעל יש להן – ישראל בגויה פטור*.

למעוטי בהמה. תימה: דהכא משמע דבזנות תליא מילתא. אם כן רבא דאמר בפ' "הבא על יבמתו" (יבמות דף נד.) דיש זנות לבהמה – מתני' למעוטי מאי? וכי אית לן למימר דל"ל דשמואל או דרב *הונא?!:

מנא הא מילתא דאמרי רבנן אין זנות לבהמה. ה"ג בפ' "כל האסורין" (תמורה ל:): מנא הא מילתא *דאין זנות לבהמה? אמר ליה: לא נישתמיט קרא ונכתוב אתנן זונה וכלב, א"נ הכי: אתנן כלב וכו'. אלא למאן דאמר העראה זו נשיקה מאי איכא למימר. והיינו שמואל בפ' "הבא על יבמתו" (יבמות דף נה:), והכא אליביה דשמואל נמי מסקינן. ותימה: אדרבה, איפכא מסתברא; למאן דאמר העראה זו נשיקה, וחשיבה ביאה גבי שאר עריות, היינו דאיצטריך קרא הכא למעוטי. אלא למ"ד העראה זו הכנסת עטרה ולא חשיבה נשיקה גבי שאר עריות, הכא מאי איצטריך למעוטה?

דומה

תוספות שאנץ

שחוף שבשרו נשחף וכלה ויבש ואין בו כח ובת"כ בקללות שנינו דוגמתו יש לך אדם שהוא חולה ומוטל במטה אבל בשרו שמור עליו ת"ל את השחפת מלמד שבשרו נשחף ל"ה. מקנין על ידו פשיטא הוי כמו והוינן בה מקנין על ידו [פשיטא]. ופוסל בתרומה אם הוא אחד מן הפסולין המחללין את האשה כגון גוי ועבד וחלל ונתין וממזר דקיימא לן בקידושין וביבמות דפסלי: מקנין על ידי גוי מכאן מביא ר"ת ראיה באשה שנשתמדה לעבודה זרה ונשאה גוי ונתגיירו היא ובעלה ואומר ר"ת דאסורה ליה כשם שאסורה לבעל כך אסורה לבועל ויש ר"ל דאין אסורה ליה דרחמנא אפקריה לזרעי דגוי דכתיב וזרמת סוסים זרמתם ומביאין ראיה מדאמרי' והא אסתר פרהסיא הואי ואמאי לא פריך אסתר ערוה היא אם איתא דגוי עושה ערוה ופוסלה בביאתו אלא ש"מ מדלא כתיב הכי דאין גוי עושה ערוה ואינו פוסל בביאתו ועוד מביאין ראיה מדפריך פ"ק דכתובות ולדרוש להו דאונס שרי משמע שאין גוי פוסל בביאתו ומיהו אומר ר"ת דליתא דהא אמרי' הכא מקנין על ידי גוי ואמרי' נמי כאשר אבדתי מבית אבי כך אבדתי ממך [אלמא] דגוי פוסל בביאתו והא דפריך התם ולידרוש להו דאונס שרי התם משום דקרקע עולם היא ואינה עושה שום דבר ואז שרי והשתא ניחא ומיהא דלא פרי' והא אסתר ערוה הואי משום דידע דלענין זה מהני מה שהיתה קרקע עולם אבל פריך והא פרהסיא הואי דלענין חלול השם אינו סבור דמהני ולכך מתרץ אהא נמי קרקע עולם היתה ואינה חייבת למסור עצמה דהיכא דהויא קרקע עולם יעבור ואל יהרג וכן נמי לענין שפיכת דמים אם יאמרו לישראל נשליך אותך על תינוק זה או נהרוג אותך יעבור ואל יהרג דהוי כמו קרקע עולם דהם זורקין אותו על התינוק ואינו עושה שום דבר ומהאי טעמא ניחא הא דאמר ביבמות אין אונס בערוה לפי שאין קישוי אלא לדעת פי' אין אונס כלומר דיהרג ואל יעבור למה לי טעמא לפי שאין קישוי אלא לדעת בלא האי טעמא אין אונס דאמרי' בכל [התורה כולה] יעבור ואל יהרג חוץ מע"ז וג"ע וש"ד אלא לפי מה דפרישית ניחא דהיכא דהוי קרקע עולם שרי להכי איצטריך האי טעמא לפי שאין קישוי אלא לדעת ואסור: מנין לגוי ועבד שבאו על כהנת ועל הישראלית שפסלוה. וא"ת מאי קבעי מנין והא אית ליה לר' יוחנן דגוי ועבד הבא על בת ישראל הולד ממזר כדאמר בפרק עשרה יוחסין והשתא ממזר הוי מיפסל בביאתו מיבעיא דה"נ פריך תלמודא התם וצ"ל הא דידיה הא דרביה אי נמי אמוראי נינהו ואליבא דרבי יוחנן.

דומה

עין משפט נר מצוה

לב א מיי' פ"א מהל' סוטה הלכה א סמג עשין נו טוש"ע אה"ע סי' קעח סעיף ב:

לג ב מיי' פ"א מהל' איסורי ביאה הלכה יא סמג לאוין כ טור אה"ע סימן כ:

לד ג מיי' פ"א מהל' סוטה הלכה א סמג עשין נו טוש"ע אה"ע סי' קעח סעיף ב:

לה ד ה מיי' פי"ח מהל' איסורי ביאה הלכה ב ופ"ו מהל' תרומות הלכה ז סמג לאוין קיא טוש"ע אה"ע סימן ו סעיף ח:

לו ו מיי' פ"א מהל' סוטה הלכה ו טוש"ע אה"ע סימן קעח סעיף כב:

לז ז מיי' פי"ח מהלכות איסורי ביאה הלכה א סמג לאוין קכא טוש"ע אה"ע סי' ו סעיף ח:

לח ח מיי' פ"ד מהל' איסורי מזבח הלכ' יח:

לט ט מיי' פ"ג מהל' סוטה הלכה כב:

מ י מיי' פ"א מהלכות איסורי ביאה הלכ' י סמג לאוין קכו טוש"ע אה"ע סימן כ סעיף א בהג"ה:

מסורת הש"ס

[לקמן כח.] [דף עה:] [דף סח:] יבמות מה. ע"ש סח: קדושין עה: [דף סח:] [תוספתא בכורות פ"ה] [ועי' היטב תוס' סנהדרין נב: ד"ה פרט לאשת אחרים ותוס' קדושין כא: ד"ה אשת] יבמות נט: תמורה ל. שם [וביבמות איתא ותנן ע"ש וצ"ע] יבמות נה. [צ"ל המנונא] [ובש"ס שלפנינו וכן בתוס' שם בתמורה איתא דאמרי רבנן] [נ"ל באלמנה לכ"ג דף סט.] ג"ז שם

הגהות הב"ח

(א) רש"י ד"ה ופוסל וכו' וביבמות דפסלי האשה: (ב) ד"ה ובת כהן וכו' פרט לאשת נכרי אלמא: (ג) ד"ה ואלא מי וכו' למעוטי בהמה:

תורה אור

דוּמָה, וְאַל יִשָּׂא בַּת דוּמָה, שֶׁזּוֹ בָּאָה מִטִּיפָּה כְּשֵׁרָה, וְזוֹ בָּאָה מִטִּיפָּה פְּסוּלָה. וְר' יוֹחָנָן אָמַר: יִשָּׂא אָדָם בַּת דוּמָה וְאַל יִשָּׂא דוּמָה, שֶׁזּוֹ עוֹמֶדֶת בְּחֶזְקַת כַּשְׁרוּת, וְזוֹ אֵינָהּ עוֹמֶדֶת בְּחֶזְקַת כַּשְׁרוּת. מֵיתִיבֵי: נוֹשֵׂא אָדָם דוּמָה? אָמַר רָבָא: וְתִסְבְּרָא נוֹשֵׂא לְכַתְּחִלָּה?! אֶלָּא, אִם נָשָׂא. תְּנֵי נַמִי: בַּת דוּמָה. אוְהִלְכְתָא: יִשָּׂא אָדָם בַּת דוּמָה, וְאַל יִשָּׂא דוּמָה. דְּתָנֵי רַב תַּחֲלִיפָא בַּר מַעַרְבָא קַמֵּיהּ דְּר' אַבָּהוּ: *באִשָּׁה מְזַנָּה – בָּנֶיהָ כְּשֵׁרִין, ברוֹב בְּעִילוֹת אַחַר הַבַּעַל. בָּעֵי רַב עַמְרָם: הָיְתָה פְּרוּצָה בְּיוֹתֵר מַהוּ? אַלִּיבָּא דְּמ"ד *אֵין אִשָּׁה מִתְעַבֶּרֶת אֶלָּא סָמוּךְ לְוִוסְתָּהּ – לָא תִּיבָּעֵי לָךְ, דְּלָא יָדַע בָּהּ וְלָא מַנְטַר לָהּ. כִּי תִּיבָּעֵי לָךְ – אַלִּיבָּא דְּמ"ד אֵין אִשָּׁה מִתְעַבֶּרֶת אֶלָּא סָמוּךְ לִטְבִילָתָהּ, מַאי? כֵּיוָן דְּיָדַע בָּהּ – נָטוּרֵי מַנְטַר לָהּ, אוֹ דִּלְמָא גכֵּיוָן דִּפְרוּצָה בְּיוֹתֵר – לָא? תֵּיקוּ. § "וְאֵלּוּ שֶׁבֵּ"ד" כו'. § ת"ר: "אִישׁ", מַה ת"ל "אִישׁ אִישׁ" – לְרַבּוֹת *אֵשֶׁת חֵרֵשׁ, וְאֵשֶׁת שׁוֹטֶה, וְאֵשֶׁת שִׁעֲמוּם, וְשֶׁהָלַךְ בַּעְלָהּ לִמְדִינַת הַיָּם, וְשֶׁהָיָה חָבוּשׁ בְּבֵית הָאֲסוּרִין, שֶׁבֵּ"ד מְקַנִּין לָהֶן לְפוֹסְלָן מִכְּתוּבָּתָן. יָכוֹל אַף לְהַשְׁקוֹתָן – ת"ל: (במדבר ה) "וְהֵבִיא הָאִישׁ אֶת אִשְׁתּוֹ". ר' יוֹסֵי אוֹמֵר: אַף לְהַשְׁקוֹתָהּ, וְלִכְשֶׁיֵּצֵא בַּעְלָהּ מִבֵּית הָאֲסוּרִין יַשְׁקֶנָּה. בְּמַאי קָא מִיפַּלְגִי? רַבָּנַן סָבְרִי: בָּעֵינַן "וְקִינֵּא וְהֵבִיא", וְר' יוֹסֵי סָבַר: לָא בָּעֵינַן "וְקִינֵּא וְהֵבִיא". ת"ר: (שם) "אֲשֶׁר תִּשְׂטֶה אִשָּׁה תַּחַת אִישָׁהּ" – *דלְהַקִּישׁ אִישׁ לְאִשָּׁה וְאִשָּׁה לְאִישׁ. לְמַאי הִלְכְתָא? אָמַר רַב שֵׁשֶׁת: כְּשֵׁם השֶׁאִם הוּא סוּמָא לֹא הָיָה מַשְׁקֶה, דִּכְתִיב: (שם) "וְנֶעְלַם מֵעֵינֵי אִישָׁהּ" – כָּךְ הִיא, אִם הָיְתָה סוּמָא לֹא הָיְתָה שׁוֹתָה. רַב אַשִׁי אָמַר: וכְּשֵׁם שֶׁחִיגֶּרֶת וְגִידֶּמֶת לֹא הָיְתָה שׁוֹתָה, דִּכְתִיב: וְהֶעֱמִיד

רש"י

דוּמָה. נִטְעֶנֶת וְנִדְבֶּרֶת בְּפִי כֹּל עַל נִיאוּפֶיהָ. דוּמָה – לְשׁוֹן קִלְּסָה וְדִיבּוּר, כִּדְאָמְרִי' בְּנִדָּה (דף סו.): דּוּמַת עִירֵךְ עָלְתָה בֵּיךְ. וְהַהוּא לָאו חֲשַׁד הוּא, אֶלָּא דִּיבּוּר יָתֵר שֶׁהָיוּ נִדְבָּרִים בָּהּ עַל חֲבִיבוּתָהּ שֶׁל בַּעְלָהּ. וְאַף קִלְּסָה לְשׁוֹן דִּיבּוּר יָתֵר הוּא, לְפִיכָךְ הוּא נֶהְפָּךְ לִלְשׁוֹן שֶׁבַח וְלִלְשׁוֹן גְּנַאי, כִּדְאָמַר: (שֶׁמְּקַלְּסִין אוֹתוֹ). וְזוֹ בָּאָה מִבִּיאָה פְּסוּלָה. שֶׁמָּא מִנָּכְרִי אוֹ מַמְזֵר: [שֶׁזּוֹ]. הַבַּת עוֹמֶדֶת בְּחֶזְקַת כַּשְׁרוּת וּמוּתֶּרֶת לְבַעְלָהּ, וּלְטִיפָּה פְּסוּלָה לָא חָיְישִׁינַן, דְּרוֹב בְּעִילוֹת אַחַר הַבַּעַל וּמִבַּעְלָהּ נִתְעַבְּרָה. וְזוֹ אֵינָהּ עוֹמֶדֶת בְּחֶזְקַת כַּשְׁרוּת. שֶׁמְּזַנָּה תַּחְתָּיו וְנֶאֱסֶרֶת עָלָיו, וְהוּא אֵינוֹ רוֹאֶה וְאֵינוֹ מְגָרְשָׁהּ, וּבָא עָלֶיהָ בְּאִיסּוּר. וְתִסְבְּרָא נוֹשֵׂא לְכַתְּחִילָּה. הָא וַדַּאי מְקַלְקְלָה לֵיהּ! אֶלָּא עַל כָּרְחָךְ מִשְׁתַּבְּשָׁא הִיא, וּבָעֵית לְתָרוּצָהּ וּלְמִתְנֵי: אִם נָשָׂא אָדָם דּוּמָה – מוּתָּר. וְכֵיוָן דְּבָעֵית לְתָרוּצָהּ – אַלְמָא תַּנָּא לָאו דַּוְקָא, וְלָא מוֹתְבִינַן מִינָּהּ, דְּאִיכָּא לְמֵימַר בְּהָא נַמִי טָעָה, וְתָנֵי נַמִי: בַּת דוּמָה. וְאַנַן נַמִי כִּי אָמְרִינַן יִשָּׂא אָדָם זוֹ וְלֹא יִשָּׂא זוֹ – לָאו לְכַתְּחִילָּה אִם יִמְצָא אַחֶרֶת, (א) אֲבָל מִי שֶׁאֵינוֹ מוֹצֵא אֶלָּא שְׁתַּיִם אֵלּוּ – יִשָּׂא זוֹ וְאַל יִשָּׂא זוֹ. דְּתָנֵי רַב תַּחֲלִיפָא כו'. הִלְכָּךְ בַּת דוּמָה, כֵּיוָן דִּכְשֵׁרָה הִיא – טוֹב לוֹ שֶׁיִּשָּׂאֶנָּה, שֶׁתְּהֵא תַּחְתָּיו בְּחֶזְקַת הֵיתֵּר, וְאַל יִשָּׂא דוּמָה שֶׁמְּקַלְקַלְתּוֹ לְשַׁמֵּשׁ עִמָּהּ מִשֶּׁנֶּאֶסְרָה לוֹ. הָיְתָה פְּרוּצָה בְּיוֹתֵר. דְּאִיכָּא לְמֵיחַשׁ דְּרוֹב בְּעִילוֹתֶיהָ מִשֶּׁל אֲחֵרִים. מַהוּ. שֶׁיְּהוּ בָּנֶיהָ כְּשֵׁרִים. אֵין אִשָּׁה מִתְעַבֶּרֶת אֶלָּא סָמוּךְ לְוִוסְתָּהּ. לִפְנֵי וֶסֶת נִדּוּתָהּ יוֹם אֶחָד. דְּלָא יָדַע הַבַּעַל אֶת וֶסֶת נִדָּתָהּ, דְּלִנְטְרָהּ אוֹתוֹ הַיּוֹם מִלְּזְנוּת, שֶׁלֹּא תִּתְעַבֵּר בִּזְנוּת. כִּי תִּיבָּעֵי לָךְ כו'. פְּלוּגְתָּא בְּמַסֶּ' נִדָּה (דף לא:). סָמוּךְ לִטְבִילָתָהּ. לְאַחַר שֶׁטָּבְלָה, בְּיוֹם טְבִילָתָהּ אוֹ לְיוֹם מָחָר. אוֹ דִּלְמָא כֵּיוָן דִּפְרוּצָה הִיא בְּיוֹתֵר. לָא מָצֵי מִינְטַר לָהּ, שֶׁנִּשְׁמֶטֶת מֵאֶצְלוֹ פִּתְאוֹם. וְקִינֵּא וְהֵבִיא. הַמְקַנֵּא לָהּ יַשְׁקֶנָּה. וְאִי קַשְׁיָא: בְּקִינּוּי נַמִי הָא כְּתִיב "אֶת אִשְׁתּוֹ", דְּמַשְׁמַע דְּבַעְלָהּ מְקַנֵּא לָהּ וְלֹא אַחֵר! הָא מִתְרַבֵּי מֵ"אִישׁ אִישׁ". אֲשֶׁר תִּשְׂטֶה אִשָּׁה תַּחַת אִישָׁהּ. קְרָא יְתֵירָא הוּא לִדְרָשָׁה בְּסוֹף הַפָּרָשָׁה: "זֹאת תּוֹרַת הַקְּנָאוֹת" וגו'. לְהַקִּישׁ אִישׁ לְאִשָּׁה. כִּדְמְפָרֵשׁ וְאָזֵיל לְמַאי הִלְכְתָא. רַב אַשִׁי אָמַר כו'. מָר מְפָרֵשׁ הֶיקֵּישָׁא דְּאִישׁ לְאִשָּׁה, וּמָר מְפָרֵשׁ הֶיקֵּישָׁא דְּאִשָּׁה לְאִישׁ, וְלָא פְּלִיגִי.

תוספות

דומה. פירש ר"ח: שמלעיזין עליה בני אדם שהיא מזנה, כדגרסינן (יבמות דף כה.) [אמר אביי, אמרה לי אם]: דומי דמתא יומא ופלגא, והוא *עד שישאו ויתנו בה מוזרות בלבנה. פי' מוזרות – נשים שטוות פשתן משזר, כך מפרש בגמרא א"י. מה שהביא רבינו חננאל דומי דמתא יומא ופלגא – לא הביא אלא לראיה דלשון "דומה" – לזות שפתים הוא. ומיהו, הכא לא איירי בדומה כה"ג, דא"כ – אפי' כנס יוציא, דהא פסקינן התם בפ"ב דיבמות (דף כה.) כרבי בקלא דלא פסיק היכא דדומי מתא יומא ופלגא, דקאמר: הואיל ומכוער הדבר – תצא. ואפילו רבי יוחנן מודי הכא אם כנס דלא יוציא*. רוב בעילות אחר הבעל. לא איירי אלא בקלא דפסק, דפסקינן כרב (יבמות כה.) דלא תצא, דרוב בעילות אחר הבעל. ואע"ג דרב דאמר בסוף פרק "אלמנה" דיבמות (דף סט:): הבא על ארוסתו בבית חמיו – הולד ממזר, ומוקי בגמרא בדדיימא מיניה ומעלמא, ולא שדינן לה בתר דידיה – דוקא ארוס, שאין מצוי אצלה, אבל בבעל שכנסה – מודי. ולשמואל נ"ש, דלעולם הולד שתוקי. וכגון דליתא לדומה גופא קמן דלישיילה, אבל איתא קמן, ואמרה: לכשר נבעלתי – נאמנת. דאמרינן בפרק "עשרה יוחסין" (קדושין דף עה.) גבי ארוסה שעיברה, אע"ג דמוקמינן לה בפרק "אלמנה לכ"ג" (יבמות סט:) כגון דדיימא מעלמא: מאי שתוקי דאמר שמואל – בדוקי, שבודקין את אמו ואומרת: לכשר נבעלתי, דאמר רב יהודה אמר שמואל: הלכה כרבן גמליאל דאמר היא נאמנת, דאפילו ברוב פסולין אצלה. והוא הדין האי דקאמר הכא: אל ישא בת דומה – כגון דליתא לדומה קמן דנישיילה. אבל איכא למתמה, ללישנא בתרא דאמר בפרק "אלמנה": בנא עליה, דכ"ע לא פליגי דבתר דידיה שדינן. והא הכא דבעלה קבוע אצלה כל שעה לא שדי ליה שמואל בתריה דבעל, בתר ארוס לא כל שכן! ואפי' אם תמצא לומר דשאני התם, דידעינן בברור דבא עליה ארוס, אבל הכא גבי בעל לא ידעינן ביאה ודאית דבא עליה, מ"מ לרבא תקשה, דאמר: אפי' בארוסה שעיברה אמר מסתברא דלא דיימא מיניה – בהא קאמר רב הולד ממזר ושמואל אמר הולד שתוקי, אבל דיימא מיניה – בתר דידיה שדינן ליה ואפי' לרב וכ"ש לשמואל. והא הכא אע"ג דאית לה בעל קבוע, והוה לן למימר רוב בעילות אחר הבעל ולא שדי ליה בדידיה, כ"ש התם! אליבא דמ"ד אין אשה מתעברת אלא סמוך לווסתה וכו'. י"ל כגון שלא קבעה ווסת. וה"ה דהמ"ל: וכגון דלא קבעה ווסת לא תבעי לך, כי תבעי לך – היכא דקבעה ווסת. אלא מילתא דפסיקא נקט. תימה לרבי: והא אמרי' התם בפ' "המפלת" (נדה דף כה:): ההוא שפירא דאתא לקמיה דמר שמואל, אמר: האי בר מ"א יומא הוא, ותשיב מיום דאזלה לטבילה עד ההוא יומא ולא הוה אלא מ' יומא, אמר: האי בנדותה בעל, וכפתיה ואודי. ותקשה למ"ד סמוך לווסתה! ונראה דמ"ד סמוך לווסתה – רוב עיבורין קאמר, מיהו מודי דזימנין מיקרי דמיעברה נמי סמוך לטבילתה, או באחד מאותן הימים שבין טבילתה לווסתה. וכן למ"ד סמוך לטבילתה. איש איש לרבות אשת חרש וכו'. נראה דעיקר קרא לא איצטריך אלא לאוסרה לבעל ולבועל ע"י קינוי זה, אבל משום לפוסלה מכתובתה – לא צריך קרא, דהא אפילו רבן שמעון בן גמליאל דאמר בפרק בתרא דכתובות (דף קי:): כתובת אשה דאורייתא – לאו ממש דאורייתא, אלא אית ליה סמך מדאורייתא, כדאמרינן התם בפ"ק (דף י.): מכאן סמכו חכמים לכתובת אשה מן התורה. אלא תנא דנקט כתובה – מילתא אגב אורחיה קמ"ל, דעוברת על דת צריכה התראה להפסיד כתובתה. רב אשי אמר כשם שחיגרת וגידמת אינה שותה דכתיב והעמיד הכהן את האשה. תימה לר"י: מאי שנא הכא דממעט מ"והעמיד" חיגרת, וגבי ערכין דכתיב "והעמיד והעריך" לא ממעט אלא גוסס, בפ"ק דערכין (דף ד.). וכן העמדה דכתיב בקדשים בעלי מומין, דאמרי' בפרק "השוחט" (חולין ל.): שחטה ועדיין מפרכסת, דבת העמדה והערכה היא. וגבי יבם כתיב (דברים כה): "ועמד ואמר", ואפ"ה חליץ נחתכו רגליו [למטה] מן הארכובה! מיהו, מחלילה לא תקשי, דהתם *מפרש טעמא משום דכתיב בה "מעל רגלו", ועיקר קרא ד"ועמד ואמר" – כדדריש ליה בספרי: מלמד שאינו אומר דבריו אלא בעמידה. ותירץ: מדרבי רחמנא בן חדש לערכין – ש"מ דלהעמדה ממש לא קפיד רחמנא. וכן בהמה בעלת מום – עיקרה לפדיון עומדת, ולא חילק בה הכתוב בין בעלת מום אפי' נשברו או נחתכו רגליה, דלא עדיפא מאדם דלא קפיד קרא אעמידתו*. דכתיב והעמיד הכהן את האשה ונתן על כפיה. אי קשיא: דהכא משמע דרב אשי בעי קרא כדכתיב ובפרק "נגמר הדין" (סנהדרין מה:) אמרי': אמר ליה מר קשישא בריה דרב חסדא לרב אשי: ומי לא בעינן קרא כדכתיב? והתנן: היה אחד מהם גידם או חיגר וכו', מאי טעמא, לאו משום דבעינן קרא כדכתיב? לא, משום דכוליה קרא יתירא הוא. דמשמע: אי לאו דהוי יתירא דלא בעינן קרא כדכתיב! בשלמא דרב ששת דממעט סומא מ"עיני" – איכא למימר קרא יתירא, דהוה מצי למימר "ונעלם מאישה" וכן "והעמיד" דאמר רב אשי – איכא למימר קרא יתירא הוא, דהא כתיב "והעמידה לפני

עין משפט נר מצוה

[עי' לעיל ו:]

מא א ב ג מיי' פט"ו מהל' איסורי ביאה הלכה כ טוש"ע אה"ע סימן ד סעיף טו:

מב ד ה ו מיי' פ"ב מהל' סוטה הלכה ב והלכה ג:

לאיירי בקלא דפסיק דפסקינן כרב דלא תצא הס"ד ואח"כ מה"ד דרוב בעילות אחר הבעל ואע"ג דרב כו'. רש"א

תוספות שאנץ

דומה לשון קלסה ולשון חשד הוא כדאמרינן בנדה דומת עירך עלתה ביך וכן מידם הוה דיימא חמותיה מיניה: שזו עומדת בחזקת כשרות. הבת עומדת בחזקת כשרות ולטיפה פסולה לא חיישינן דרוב בעילות אחר הבעל ומבעלה נתעברה: וקינא והביא אמר רחמנא המקנא לה ישקנה. ואי קשיא בקינוי נמי כתיב וקנא (והביא) את אשתו דמשמע בעלה יקנא לה ולא אחר. הא איתרבי מאיש איש (אשר תשטה אשה תחת אישה) ל"ה: רב אשי אמר כו'. מר מפרש היקשא דאיש לאשה ומר מפרש הקישא דאשה לאיש ולא פליגי:

הדרן עלך ארוסה

גליון הש"ם

תום' ד"ה אליבא דמ"ד וכו' ונראה דמ"ד וכו'. עי' נדה דף י ע"ב תד"ה דהוית: ד"ה רב אשי אמר וכו' ותירץ מדרבי רחמנא בן חדש. וי"ל כנ"ל. וכ"ה בתי"ט פ"א דערכין מ"ג:

מסורת הש"ם

רש"ל מ"ז

[תוספתא יבמות פי"ב]

[נדה לא:]

[לעיל כז.]

[לעיל כז:]

[יבמות קג.]

[ועיין היטב תוס' ערכין ז: ד"ה ולא אוליא]

הגהות הב"ח

(א) רש"י ד"ה ותסברא וכו' אחרת אלא דמי שאינו:

°"וְהֶעֱמִיד הַכֹּהֵן אֶת הָאִשָּׁה לִפְנֵי ה' וְנָתַן עַל כַּפֶּיהָ" — כָּךְ הוּא, אִם הָיָה חִיגֵּר אוֹ גִידֵּם לֹא הָיָה מַשְׁקֶה. מָר בַּר רַב אַשִׁי אָמַר: אכְּשֵׁם שֶׁאִילֶּמֶת לֹא הָיְתָה שׁוֹתָה, דִּכְתִיב: °"וְאָמְרָה הָאִשָּׁה אָמֵן אָמֵן" — כָּךְ הוּא, אִם הָיָה אִילֵּם לֹא הָיָה מַשְׁקֶה.§

הדרן עלך ארוסה

כְּשֵׁם בשֶׁהַמַּיִם בּוֹדְקִין אוֹתָהּ — כָּךְ הַמַּיִם בּוֹדְקִין אוֹתוֹ, שֶׁנֶּאֱמַר: °"וּבָאוּ" "וּבָאוּ". כְּשֵׁם *גשֶׁאֲסוּרָה לַבַּעַל — כָּךְ אֲסוּרָה לַבּוֹעֵל, שֶׁנֶּאֱמַר: °"נִטְמָאָה" "וְנִטְמָאָה", דִּבְרֵי ר' עֲקִיבָא. א"ר יְהוֹשֻׁעַ: כָּךְ הָיָה דּוֹרֵשׁ זְכַרְיָה בֶּן הַקַּצָּב. רַבִּי אוֹמֵר: שְׁנֵי פְּעָמִים הָאֲמוּרִים בַּפָּרָשָׁה "נִטְמָאָה" "וְנִטְמָאָה" — אֶחָד לַבַּעַל וְאֶחָד לַבּוֹעֵל.§ *בּוֹ בַּיּוֹם דָּרַשׁ ר' עֲקִיבָא:* °"וְכָלִי חֶרֶשׂ אֲשֶׁר יִפּוֹל מֵהֶם אֶל תּוֹכוֹ כֹּל אֲשֶׁר בְּתוֹכוֹ יִטְמָא". אֵינוֹ אוֹמֵר "טָמֵא" אֶלָּא "יִטְמָא" — לְטַמֵּא אֲחֵרִים, לִמֵּד עַל כִּכָּר שֵׁנִי שֶׁמְּטַמֵּא אֶת הַשְּׁלִישִׁי, א"ר יְהוֹשֻׁעַ: מִי יְגַלֶּה עָפָר מֵעֵינֶיךָ רַבָּן יוֹחָנָן בֶּן זַכַּאי, שֶׁהָיִיתָ אוֹמֵר: עָתִיד דּוֹר אַחֵר לְטַהֵר כִּכָּר שְׁלִישִׁי, שֶׁאֵין לוֹ מִקְרָא מִן הַתּוֹרָה שֶׁהוּא טָמֵא. וַהֲלֹא ר' עֲקִיבָא תַּלְמִידְךָ מֵבִיא לוֹ מִקְרָא מִן הַתּוֹרָה שֶׁהוּא טָמֵא, שֶׁנֶּאֱמַר: "כֹּל אֲשֶׁר בְּתוֹכוֹ יִטְמָא".§ בּוֹ בַּיּוֹם דָּרַשׁ ר' עֲקִיבָא: °"וּמַדּוֹתֶם מִחוּץ לָעִיר אֶת פְּאַת קֵדְמָה אַלְפַּיִם בָּאַמָּה" וגו', וּמִקְרָא אַחֵר אָמַר: °"מִקִּיר הָעִיר וָחוּצָה אֶלֶף אַמָּה סָבִיב". אִי אֶפְשָׁר לוֹמַר אֶלֶף אַמָּה — שֶׁכְּבָר נֶאֱמַר אַלְפַּיִם אַמָּה, וְאִי אֶפְשָׁר לוֹמַר אַלְפַּיִם אַמָּה — שֶׁכְּבָר נֶאֱמַר אֶלֶף אַמָּה, הָא כֵּיצַד? אֶלֶף אַמָּה מִגְרָשׁ, וְאַלְפַּיִם אַמָּה *תְּחוּם הַשַּׁבָּת. ר' אֱלִיעֶזֶר בְּנוֹ שֶׁל ר' יוֹסֵי הַגְּלִילִי אוֹמֵר: *דאֶלֶף אַמָּה מִגְרָשׁ, וְאַלְפַּיִם אַמָּה שָׂדוֹת וּכְרָמִים.§ בּוֹ בַּיּוֹם דָּרַשׁ רַבִּי עֲקִיבָא: °"אָז יָשִׁיר מֹשֶׁה וּבְנֵי יִשְׂרָאֵל אֶת הַשִּׁירָה הַזֹּאת לַה' וַיֹּאמְרוּ לֵאמֹר". שֶׁאֵין ת"ל "לֵאמֹר", וּמַה ת"ל "לֵאמֹר" — מְלַמֵּד שֶׁהָיוּ יִשְׂרָאֵל עוֹנִין שִׁירָה אַחֲרָיו שֶׁל מֹשֶׁה עַל כָּל דָּבָר וְדָבָר כְּקוֹרִאין אֶת הַלֵּל. ("אָשִׁירָה לַה' כִּי גָאֹה גָּאָה"), לְכָךְ נֶאֱמַר "לֵאמֹר". רַבִּי נְחֶמְיָה אוֹמֵר: כְּקוֹרִין אֶת שְׁמַע, וְלֹא כְּקוֹרִין אֶת הַלֵּל.§ בּוֹ בַּיּוֹם דָּרַשׁ ר' יְהוֹשֻׁעַ בֶּן הוּרְקָנוֹס: לֹא עָבַד אִיּוֹב אֶת הקב"ה אֶלָּא מֵאַהֲבָה, שֶׁנֶּא': °"הֵן יִקְטְלֵנִי לוֹ אֲיַחֵל". וַעֲדַיִין הַדָּבָר שָׁקוּל, לוֹ אֲנִי מְצַפֶּה אוֹ אֵינִי מְצַפֶּה? ת"ל: °"עַד אֶגְוָע לֹא אָסִיר תֻּמָּתִי מִמֶּנִּי" — מְלַמֵּד שֶׁמֵּאַהֲבָה עָשָׂה. אָמַר רַבִּי יְהוֹשֻׁעַ: מִי יְגַלֶּה עָפָר מֵעֵינֶיךָ רַבָּן יוֹחָנָן בֶּן זַכַּאי, שֶׁהָיִיתָ דּוֹרֵשׁ כָּל יָמֶיךָ שֶׁלֹּא עָבַד אִיּוֹב אֶת הַמָּקוֹם אֶלָּא מִיִּרְאָה, שֶׁנֶּאֱמַר °"אִישׁ תָּם וְיָשָׁר יְרֵא אֱלֹהִים וְסָר מֵרָע", וַהֲלֹא יְהוֹשֻׁעַ תַּלְמִיד תַּלְמִידְךָ לִמֵּד שֶׁמֵּאַהֲבָה עָשָׂה.§ **גמ'** "אוֹתוֹ" — לְמַאן? אִילֵימָא לַבַּעַל, בַּעַל מַאי עֲבִיד? וְכִי תֵּימָא, דְּאִי

(מראי מקומות בשולי הגמרא: במדבר ה; שם; שם; ויקרא יא; במדבר לה; שם; שמות טו; רש"ל מ"ז; איוב יג; שם כז; שם א)

[רש"י]

וְהֶעֱמִיד. וְלֹא חִגֶּרֶת. וְנָתַן עַל כַּפֶּיהָ. וְלֹא גִידֶּמֶת קְטוּעַת יָדַיִם.

הדרן עלך ארוסה

כְּשֵׁם. כָּךְ בּוֹדְקִין אוֹתוֹ. בַּגְּמָ' מְפָרֵשׁ לָהּ. שֶׁנֶּאֱמַר וּבָאוּ וּבָאוּ. בַּגְּמָ' מְפָרֵשׁ אִי וָי"ו יְתֵירָא דָּרֵישׁ, אוֹ "וּבָאוּ" "וּבָאוּ" יְתֵירֵי דִּכְתִיבֵי בְּעִנְיָנָא. נִטְמָאָה וְנִטְמָאָה. וָי"ו יְתֵירָא דָּרֵישׁ: "אֲשֶׁר תִּשְׂטֶה אִשָּׁה תַּחַת אִישָׁהּ וְנִטְמָאָה". וְכָךְ הָיָה ר' זְכַרְיָה דּוֹרֵשׁ. וָי"ו יְתֵירָא. שְׁתֵּי פְּעָמִים. "וְנִסְתְּרָה וְהִיא נִטְמָאָה" לָא מִמִּנְיָינָא הוּא, דְּאוֹקִימְנָא לְטוּמְאָה וְדָאִית בְּעֵד אֶחָד בְּפ"ק (לעיל ג:). אֶלָּא "וְקִנֵּא אֶת אִשְׁתּוֹ וְהִיא נִטְמָאָה", "וְהָיְתָה אִם נִטְמְאָה". וְעוֹד כְּתִיב: "אֲשֶׁר תִּשְׂטֶה אִשָּׁה תַּחַת אִישָׁהּ וְנִטְמָאָה", *וּבַגְּמָרָא דָּרֵישׁ לָהּ ר"ע לִתְרוּמָה, וְרַבִּי נַמִי מוֹדֵי. וְהַאי דְּנָקַט הָכָא תְּרֵי מִינַּיְיהוּ וְתוּ לָא — מִשּׁוּם (א) דְּשָׁמְעִינַן לְר"ע דְּדָרֵישׁ בַּעַל וּבוֹעֵל מֵרִיבּוּיָא דְּוָי"ו יְתֵירָא, וְקָא"ל רַבִּי: בַּעַל וּבוֹעֵל מִ"נִּטְמְאָה" "וְנִטְמָאָה" נָפְקִי, וְלָא דָּרְשִׁי וָי"ו. בּוֹ בַּיּוֹם דָּרַשׁ. בְּמַסֶּ' בְּרָכוֹת (דף כח.) אָמְרִינַן דְּכָל הֵיכָא דְּתָנֵי "בּוֹ בַּיּוֹם" — הוּא יוֹם שֶׁהוֹשִׁיבוּ אֶת ר"א בֶּן עֲזַרְיָה לִנְשִׂיאוּת, שֶׁנִּתְרַבּוּ תַּלְמִידִים, שֶׁנָּתְנוּ רְשׁוּת לִיכָּנֵס לַכֹּל. שֶׁהָיָה רַבָּן גַּמְלִיאֵל אוֹמֵר: כָּל ת"ח שֶׁאֵין תּוֹכוֹ כְּבָרוֹ אַל יִכָּנֵס לְבֵהמ"ד. וְרָבְתָה תּוֹרָה בּוֹ בַּיּוֹם, וְלֹא הָיְתָה הֲלָכָה תְּלוּיָה בְּבֵית הַמִּדְרָשׁ שֶׁלֹּא פֵּירְשׁוּהָ. וְהָא דְּקָתָנֵי לָהּ הָכָא — נִרְאֶה בְּעֵינַי דְּהַךְ דְּרָשָׁה דְּ"נִטְמְאָה" "וְנִטְמָאָה" דִּלְעֵיל, נַמִי בּוֹ בַּיּוֹם הֲוַאי: כְּלִי חֶרֶשׂ הוּא רִאשׁוֹן, שֶׁנִּטְמָא מִן הַשֶּׁרֶץ. וְהָאוֹכֶל שֶׁבְּתוֹכוֹ שֵׁנִי, שֶׁנִּטְמָא בִּכְלִי. אֵינוֹ אוֹמֵר טָמֵא. "כֹּל אֲשֶׁר בְּתוֹכוֹ טָמֵא", אֶלָּא "יִטְמָא", לְמִדְרַשׁ נַמִי: "יְטַמֵּא" — שֶׁמְּטַמֵּא אֲחֵרִים. לִימֵּד עַל כִּכָּר שֵׁנִי. לְהָכִי נָקַט כִּכָּר, לְפִי שֶׁהוּא מָצוּי בְּתַנּוּר שֶׁהוּא כְּלִי חֶרֶשׂ. שֶׁמְּטַמֵּא אֶת הַשְּׁלִישִׁי. בִּתְרוּמָה. וַאֲפִי' בְּחוּלִּין, דִּקְרָא סְתָמָא כְּתִיב. עָתִיד דּוֹר אַחֵר. מִן הָעֲתִידִין לָבֹא, שֶׁיְּטַהֵר אֶת הַשְּׁלִישִׁי אַף בִּתְרוּמָה. שֶׁאֵין לוֹ מִקְרָא מִן הַתּוֹרָה, וַאֲנַן הוּא דִּמְטַמְּאִינַן לֵיהּ בִּתְרוּמָה מִק"ו, כִּדְמְפָרֵשׁ בַּגְּמָרָא. וְדוֹר אַחֵר פָּרֵיךְ לֵיהּ לְק"ו, כִּדְלְקַמָּן בַּגְּמָרָא. וְר"ע תַּלְמִידְךָ מֵבִיא מִקְרָא שֶׁהוּא טָמֵא. אַף בְּחוּלִּין. מִגְרָשׁ. רְחָבָה פְּנוּיָה מִזְּרִיעָה וּמִבָּתִּים וּמֵאִילָנוֹת לְנוֹי הָעִיר, לִהְיוֹת לָהּ לַאֲוִיר. וְאַלְפַּיִם לֹא הוּזְכְּרוּ לִתֵּן לַלְוִיִּם, וְלֹא נֶאֶמְרוּ אֶלָּא לְיִיאַת תְּחוּם שַׁבָּת. שָׂדוֹת וּכְרָמִים. וְאַלְפַּיִם סָבִיב נִתְּנוּ לַלְוִיִּם, מֵהֶם הִנִּיחוּ אֶלֶף סָבִיב הָעִיר לְמִגְרָשׁ, וְהַשְּׁאָר שָׂדוֹת וּכְרָמִים. שֶׁאֵין ת"ל לֵאמֹר. שֶׁאֵינוֹ דּוֹמֶה לִשְׁאָר "לֵאמֹר" שֶׁבַּתּוֹרָה, שֶׁהַשְּׁכִינָה מְדַבֵּר הַדִּבּוּר לְמֹשֶׁה לַחֲזוֹר הוּא וְלְאָמְרוֹ לְיִשְׂרָאֵל, אֲבָל כָּאן אֵין לוֹמַר כֵּן. כְּקוֹרֵא אֶת הַהַלֵּל. בַּגְּמָ' מְפָרֵשׁ. כְּקוֹרִין אֶת שְׁמַע. בַּגְּמָרָא מְפָרֵשׁ. מֵאַהֲבָה. שֶׁאוֹהֵב אֶת הַמָּקוֹם. שָׁקוּל. מִשְׁקָלוֹ שָׁוֶה, מַכְרִיעַ לְכָאן וּלְכָאן. לוֹ אֲנִי מְיַיחֵל אוֹ אֵינִי מְיַיחֵל. וְה"ק: "הֵן יִקְטְלֵנִי" — הֲלֹא הוּא הוֹרְגֵנִי — לֹא אֲיַיחֵל לוֹ עוֹד. דְּיֵשׁ "לֹא" שֶׁהוּא נִדְרָשׁ כְּמוֹ "לוֹ" בְּלָמֶ"ד וָי"ו, כִּדְמְפָרֵשׁ בַּגְּמָרָא. מִיִּרְאָה. מִדַּאֲגַת הַפּוּרְעָנוּת שֶׁלֹּא תָּבֹא עָלָיו. יְרֵא אֱלֹהִים. וְלֹא אוֹהֵב אֱלֹהִים. תַּלְמִיד תַּלְמִידְךָ. תַּלְמִידוֹ שֶׁל ר"ע הָיָה. **גמ'** דְּאִי

[תוספות]

לפני ה'". וכן הא דאמר מר בר רב אשי דאילמת אינה שותה משום דכתיב "ואמרה". ואפי' למ"ד (סנהדרין דף מה:): לא בעינן קרא כדכתיב — מודה דאילמת אינה שותה, משום דלא מיא לקבולי שבועה. ואפי' גבי חליצה, דקרייה לא מעכבא — אילם ואילמת שחלצו חליצתן פסולה משום דר' זירא כל הראוי לבילה. אלא "ונתן על כפיה", אע"ג דלאו קרא יתירא הוא — בעי קרא כדכתיב. והכי משמע בפרק "שלשה מינין בנזיר" (דף מו:) דמאן דבעי קרא כדכתיב, דנזיר ממורט או אין לו כפים אין לו תקנה משום דכתיב "ונתן על כפי הנזיר", וכן אין לו בהן יד משום דכתיב "על בהן ידו" — תריץ דרב אשי מהדר למר קשישא לפום סברתו, דבעי למידק ממתני' דבעינן קרא כדכתיב, וא"ל רב אשי: מהכא ליכא למידק מידי, דהתם קרא יתירא. מיהו רב אשי ס"ל דבעינן קרא כדכתיב.

הדרן עלך ארוסה

כשם שהמים בודקין אותה כך בודקין אותו. ירושלמי: "המאררים", אמר רבי תנחומא: מנין "המאררים" נגד רמ"ח אברים שיש בה ונגד רמ"ח אברים שיש בו. כשם שהמים בודקין אותה על כל ביאה וביאה שהיא מקבלת מבעלה לאחר הבועל — כך הן בודקין אותו. וכשם שהיא אסורה לאחיו של בעל — כך היא אסורה לאחיו של בועל. היא, על ידי שדרכה ליאסר — בין לו בין לאחר היא נבדקת, אבל הוא — לכשתשתה הוא נבדק. בדקו אותו ולא אותה — אני אומר הזכות תולה. ניחא כמאן דאמר הזכות תולה לה ואינו ניכרת, ברם כמאן דאמר הזכות תולה וניכרת — הרי לא הוכרה אלא אני אומר: מים מגולים שתה ונלבה! הכין לא הוון בעייא מבדקוניה אלא כדין?! אלא אני אומר: ⊕עם אחרים נסתרה. ולא כן סברינן מימר: לכשתשתה הוא נבדק? תיפתר שהיה הוא מזיד והיא שוגגת, ובדקו אותו ולא בדקו אותה. בדקו אותה ולא בדקו אותו — אני אומר הזכות תלה ליה. ניחא כמ"ד הזכות תולה ואינו ניכרת, ברם כמ"ד הזכות תולה וניכרת — הרי הוא לא הוכר, אלא אני אומר מים מגולים שתת ונלבת! הכין לא הוה בעי מבדקונה אלא כדין?! אלא אני אומר: עם אחרים נסתרה. מעתה גרש יהא מותר בה! תיפתר שהיה הוא שוגג והיא מזידה, ובדקו אותה ולא אותו. הוא מזיד והיא שוגגת פשיטא שהיא מותרת לביתה. גירש מהו שיהא מותר בה? ⊕אפשר לומר מזיד בה ואת אמרת הכין? הוא שוגג והיא מזידה פשיטא שהיא אסורה לביתה. גירש מהו שיהא מותר בה? אפשר לומר יצאה מתחת ידו ואת אמר הכין? ומנין שהדבר תלוי בה? שמעון ב"ר אבא בשם ר' יוחנן אמר: "ואל אשת עמיתך לא תתן שכבתך לזרע לטמאה בה" — בה הדבר תלוי, אם היתה מזידה — אסורה, שוגגת — מותרת.

ההוא

תוספות שאנץ

כשם שהמים בודקין אותה כך בודקין אותו בגמרא מפרש לה. שנאמר ובאו ובאו הא נמי מפרש בגמ' אי וא"ו יתירה [דריש] או ובאו יתירה דריש. כך היה ר' זכריה בן הקצב דורש וא"ו יתירה. ונטמאה ב' פעמים פ"ה אבל ונסתרה והיא נטמאה לאו ממניינא הוא דהא אוקימנא לעיל בפ"ק לטומאה ודאית בעד אחד. ולא נהירא דהא כבר שמעינן בריש מכילתין טומאה דעד אחד מוהיא לא נתפשה. וכי תימא דאיצטריך לומר דבעי' סתירה כעין טומאה דאמר התם דאיתקש סתירה לטומאה ומשום [דכתיב] ונסתרה והיא נטמאה. הא ממילא שמעי' ליה. ולכן צ"ל דגמ' דקאמר (לקמן כח) ומה תלמוד לומר והיא נטמאה דטומאה יתירה קדריש ודלא כפ"ה בגמ' דלא קרא יתירא קדריש דמישמע ישהוא סובר שאין כאן אלא ב' ונטמאה וקנא את אשתו והיא נטמאה ועוד כתיב אשר תשטה אשה תחת אישה ונטמאה א) ובגמ' צ"ל דכדי' ונסתרה והיא נטמאה יתירה כדפרי'. בו ביום דרש ר' עקיבא פ"ה דאמר בברכות דכל היכא דתני בו ביום הוי ביום שהשיבו את רבי אלעזר בן עזריה בנשיאות [שנתרבו] תלמידים שנתנו רשות לכל ליכנס שהיה ר"ג אומר כל תלמיד שאין תוכו כברו אל יכנס לבית המדרש ורבתה תורה בו ביום ולא היתה הלכה תלויה בבית המדרש שלא פירושה והא דתני לה הכא נראה בעיני דהך דרשא דונטמאה ונטמאה דלעיל נמי בו ביום הואי ל"ה: וכל כלי חרש שהוא ראשון שנטמא מן השרץ והאוכל שבתוכו שני שנטמא מן הכלי אינו אומר טמא אלא יטמא כל אשר בתוכו יטמא למדרשיה ביה נמי יטמא לאחרים לימד על ככר שני להכי נקט ככר לפי שמצוי בתנור שהוא כלי חרס: שמטמא את השלישי ואפי' בחולין דקרא סתמא כתיב ל"ה. וליכא למימר דליהוי אויר התנור כמאן דמלי טומאה וליהוי האוכל ראשון דא"כ אף כלים שבאוירו יטמא וליתא דאמרי' בפ"ק דפסחים מכל האוכל אשר יאכל אוכלין ומשקין מטמאין מאויר כלי חרס ואין כל הכלים מטמאין מאויר כלי חרס: גמ' חד

(א) אולי צ"ל אבל תלמוד נלמד קדרים ונסתרה וכו'

[עין משפט נר מצוה]

מג א מיי' פ"ב מהל' סוטה הלכה ב והלכה ג:

א ב מיי' פ"ג מהל' סוטה הלכה יז סמג עשין נו:

ב ג מיי' שם פ"ב הלכ' יב טוש"ע אה"ע סי' יא סעיף א וסימן קעח סעיף יז:

ג ד מיי' פי"ג מהל' שמיטה ויובל הלכה ב וע"ש בכ"מ סמג עשין קנה:

[מסורת הש"ס]

לעיל כה.

[נ"ל וכל כלי]

[ועוד כתיב והיא לא נטמאה ובגמ' דריש לה ר"ע חד לתרומה כו' רש"ל]

פסחים יח. חולין לג:

[שבת סט: עי' ענ: קנג: עירובין עט: קנ: סנהדרין סו:]

[ד"ה פירש עי' תוס' מנחות צח: ד"ה מגרש]

הגהות הב"ח

(א) רש"י ד"ה שתי וכו' דשמעיה לר"ע:

גליון הש"ס

תוס' ד"ה כשם כו' אלא אני אומר עם אחרים נסתרה. נ"ל עם אחרות נסתר:

בא"ד אפשר לומר מזיד בה. עי' יבמות דף לה ע"א תד"ה אע"פ:

דְּאִי אִית בֵּיהּ עָוֹן בָּדְקִי לֵיהּ מַיָּא. כִּי אִית בֵּיהּ עָוֹן בְּדִידֵיהּ מִי בָּדְקִי לָהּ מַיָּא לְדִידָהּ?! וְהָא *תַּנְיָא: °"וְנִקָּה הָאִישׁ מֵעָוֹן וְהָאִשָּׁה הַהִיא תִּשָּׂא אֶת עֲוֹנָהּ"; אבִּזְמַן שֶׁהָאִישׁ מְנוּקֶּה מֵעָוֹן — הַמַּיִם בּוֹדְקִין אֶת אִשְׁתּוֹ, אֵין הָאִישׁ מְנוּקֶּה מֵעָוֹן — אֵין הַמַּיִם בּוֹדְקִין אֶת אִשְׁתּוֹ! וְאֶלָּא לַבּוֹעֵל — לִיתְנֵי כִּדְקָתָנֵי סֵיפָא: כְּשֵׁם שֶׁאֲסוּרָה לַבַּעַל, כָּךְ אֲסוּרָה לַבּוֹעֵל! לְעוֹלָם לַבּוֹעֵל. וְרֵישָׁא, אַיְּידֵי דְּתָנָא "אוֹתָהּ" — תָּנֵי "אוֹתוֹ", סֵיפָא, אַיְּידֵי דְּתָנָא "בַּעַל" — תָּנָא "בּוֹעֵל". § "שֶׁנֶּאֱמַר וּבָאוּ וּבָאוּ". אִיבַּעְיָא לְהוּ: "בָּאוּ" "וּבָאוּ" קָאָמַר, אוֹ "וּבָאוּ" "וּבָאוּ" קָאָמַר? ת"ש: כְּשֵׁם שֶׁאֲסוּרָה לַבַּעַל — כָּךְ אֲסוּרָה לַבּוֹעֵל, שֶׁנֶּאֱמַר: "נִטְמָאָה" "וְנִטְמָאָה". וַעֲדַיִין תִּיבָּעֵי: "נִטְמָאָה" (א) "נִטְמְאָה" קָאָמַר אוֹ "נִטְמָאָה" "וְנִטְמָאָה" קָאָמַר? ת"ש, מִדְּקָתָנֵי סֵיפָא, רַבִּי אוֹמֵר: שְׁנֵי פְּעָמִים הָאֲמוּרִין בַּפָּרָשָׁה "וְנִטְמָאָה" "וְנִטְמְאָה" — אֶחָד לַבַּעַל וְאֶחָד לַבּוֹעֵל, מִכְּלָל דְּרַבִּי עֲקִיבָא *וָוי קָדָרֵישׁ. הִלְכָּךְ, לְרַבִּי עֲקִיבָא שִׁיתָּא קְרָאֵי כְּתִיבִי: חַד לְצַוָּאָה דִּידָהּ, וְחַד לְצַוָּאָה דִּידֵיהּ, חַד לַעֲשִׂיָּה דִּידָהּ, וְחַד לַעֲשִׂיָּה דִּידֵיהּ, חַד לִידִיעָה דִּידָהּ, וְחַד לִידִיעָה דִּידֵיהּ. וְרַבִּי: תְּלָתָא קְרָאֵי כְּתִיבִי; חַד לְצַוָּאָה, וְחַד לַעֲשִׂיָּה, וְחַד לִידִיעָה. וְרַבִּי, כְּשֵׁם שֶׁהַמַּיִם בּוֹדְקִין אוֹתָהּ — כָּךְ בּוֹדְקִין אוֹתוֹ מְנָא לֵיהּ? נָפְקָא לֵיהּ מִדְּתַנְיָא: °"לַצְבּוֹת בֶּטֶן וְלַנְפִּל יָרֵךְ" — בִּטְנוֹ וִירֵיכוֹ שֶׁל בּוֹעֵל. אַתָּה אוֹמֵר בִּטְנוֹ וִירֵיכוֹ שֶׁל בּוֹעֵל, אוֹ אֵינוֹ אֶלָּא בִּטְנָהּ וִירֵיכָהּ שֶׁל נִבְעֶלֶת? כְּשֶׁהוּא אוֹמֵר "וְצָבְתָה בִטְנָהּ וְנָפְלָה יְרֵיכָהּ" — הֲרֵי בִּטְנָהּ וִירֵיכָהּ שֶׁל נִבְעֶלֶת אָמוּר, וּמָה אֲנִי מְקַיֵּים "לַצְבּוֹת בֶּטֶן וְלַנְפִּל יָרֵךְ" — בִּטְנוֹ וִירֵיכוֹ שֶׁל בּוֹעֵל. וְאִידָךְ: הַהוּא, *בדְּמוֹדַע לָהּ כֹּהֵן דְּבֶטֶן בְּרֵישָׁא וַהֲדַר יָרֵךְ, שֶׁלֹּא לְהוֹצִיא לַעַז עַל הַמַּיִם הַמָּרִים. וְאִידָךְ: א"כ לִכְתּוֹב קְרָא בִּטְנָהּ וִירֵיכָהּ, מַאי בֶּטֶן וְיָרֵךְ — ש"מ לַבּוֹעֵל. וְאֵימָא כּוּלֵּי לְהָכִי הוּא דַּאֲתָא! אִם כֵּן לִכְתּוֹב בִּטְנוֹ וִירֵיכוֹ, מַאי בֶּטֶן וְיָרֵךְ — ש"מ תַּרְתֵּי. § "א"ר יְהוֹשֻׁעַ: כָּךְ הָיָה דּוֹרֵשׁ זְכַרְיָה" כו'. § ת"ר: שָׁלֹשׁ פְּעָמִים הָאֲמוּרִין בַּפָּרָשָׁה "אִם נִטְמְאָה" "נִטְמָאָה" "וְנִטְמָאָה" לָמָּה? *אֶחָד לַבַּעַל, וְאֶחָד לַבּוֹעֵל, וְאֶחָד לִתְרוּמָה, דִּבְרֵי רַבִּי עֲקִיבָא. אָמַר רַבִּי יִשְׁמָעֵאל: קַל וָחוֹמֶר; וּמַה גְּרוּשָׁה שֶׁמּוּתֶּרֶת לִתְרוּמָה — אֲסוּרָה לִכְהוּנָּה, זוֹ שֶׁאֲסוּרָה בִּתְרוּמָה — אֵינוֹ דִּין שֶׁאֲסוּרָה לִכְהוּנָּה? מַה ת"ל "וְהִיא נִטְמָאָה" "וְהִיא לֹא נִטְמָאָה", אִם נִטְמְאָה — לָמָּה שׁוֹתָה, אִם לֹא נִטְמְאָה — לָמָּה מַשְׁקָהּ? גמַגִּיד לְךָ הַכָּתוּב שֶׁהַסָּפֵק אֲסוּרָה. דמִכָּאן אַתָּה דָּן לְשֶׁרֶץ; וּמַה סוֹטָה השֶׁלֹּא עָשָׂה בָּהּ שׁוֹגֵג כְּמֵזִיד וְאוֹנֶס כְּרָצוֹן — עָשָׂה בָּהּ סָפֵק כְּוַדַּאי, שֶׁרֶץ שֶׁעָשָׂה בּוֹ שׁוֹגֵג כְּמֵזִיד וְאוֹנֶס כְּרָצוֹן — אֵינוֹ דִּין שֶׁיַּעֲשֶׂה בּוֹ סָפֵק כְּוַדַּאי

תורה אור: במדבר ה | שם

רש"י

דְּאִי אִית בֵּיהּ עָוֹן. שֶׁבָּא עָלֶיהָ לְאַחַר שֶׁנִּסְתְּרָה. בִּזְמַן שֶׁהָאִישׁ מְנוּקֶּה מֵעָוֹן. שֶׁלֹּא בָּא עָלֶיהָ מִשֶּׁנֶּאֶסְרָה עָלָיו – "הָאִשָּׁה הַהִיא תִּשָּׂא עֲוֹנָהּ" שֶׁיִּבְדְּקוּהָ הַמַּיִם. אֶלָּא לַבּוֹעֵל לִיתְנֵי. "כָּךְ בּוֹדְקִין אֶת הַבּוֹעֵל" בְּהֶדְיָא, כִּדְתָנֵי סֵיפָא בְּהֶדְיָא "כָּךְ אֲסוּרָה לַבּוֹעֵל", וְלָא תָנָא "כָּךְ אֲסוּרָה לוֹ". בָּאוּ וּבָאוּ קָאָמַר. מֵרִבּוּיָא דְּוָי"ו, אוֹ "וּבָאוּ" "וּבָאוּ" הַכְּפוּלִים בַּפָּרָשָׁה דָּרֵישׁ?. שֶׁנֶּאֱמַר נִטְמָאָה וְנִטְמָאָה. ש"מ רַבִּי עֲקִיבָא וָי"ו דָּרֵישׁ. וַעֲדַיִין. בְּהָא גּוּפָא מִיבַּעְיָא לִי: "נִטְמְאָה וְנִטְמָאָה" דָּרֵישׁ, מֵרִבּוּיָא וָי"ו, אוֹ חַד "נִטְמָאָה" וְחַד "וְנִטְמָאָה" קָדָרֵישׁ?. שִׁיתָּא קְרָאֵי. תְּלָתָא "וּבָאוּ" כְּתוּבִים שָׁם: "וּבָאוּ הַמַּיִם הַמְאָרְרִים הָאֵלֶּה בְּמֵעַיִךְ לַצְבּוֹת בֶּטֶן" – לְהוֹדִיעַ לָנוּ דְּבֶטֶן וַהֲדַר יָרֵךְ, שֶׁלֹּא לְהוֹצִיא לַעַז, כִּדְאָמְרִי' בְּפ"ק (לעיל ט:). וְחַד "וְהִשְׁקָה אֶת הָאִשָּׁה אֶת מֵי הַמָּרִים הַמְאָרְרִים וּבָאוּ בָהּ הַמַּיִם" וגו' – לְצַוָּאָה, שֶׁהַקָּבָּ"ה גּוֹזֵר שֶׁיָּבוֹאוּ בָּהּ הַמַּיִם לְמָרִים. וְחַד (ב) לַעֲשִׂיָּה – "וְהִשְׁקָהּ אֶת הַמַּיִם וְהָיְתָה אִם נִטְמְאָה" וגו' – לַעֲשִׂיָּה, כָּאן הוֹדִיעַ הַכָּתוּב אֶת יִשְׂרָאֵל דְּמַבְטִיחַ לָהֶן שֶׁיִּבְדְּקוּהָ הַמַּיִם. וּבְכוּלָּם כְּתִיב וָי"ו יְתֵירֵי, הֲרֵי שִׁית. דִּידֵיהּ. דְּבוֹעֵל. דִּידָהּ. דְּאִשָּׁה, יְדִיעָה וְצַוָּאָה וַעֲשִׂיָּה, כִּדְפָרִישִׁית. וְרַבִּי. דְּלָא דָּרֵישׁ וָי"ו, תְּלָתָא קְרָאֵי הוּא דִּכְתִיבִי, וְכוּלְּהוּ לְדִידָהּ – יְדִיעָה וַעֲשִׂיָּה וְצַוָּאָה. שֶׁלֹּא לְהוֹצִיא לַעַז. מִשּׁוּם דְּהוּא אָמַר לָהּ בִּקְלָלָה בְּרֵישָׁא: "אֶת יְרֵכֵךְ נוֹפֶלֶת" וגו', וְסוֹף הַמַּיִם לִבְדּוֹק כְּדֶרֶךְ כְּנִיסָתָן, דִּכְתִיב: "וְצָבְתָה בִטְנָהּ" וַהֲדַר "וְנָפְלָה יְרֵכָהּ". לְכָךְ הוּצְרַךְ לְהוֹדִיעַ תְּחִילָּה שֶׁהַמַּיִם כְּדֶרֶךְ כְּנִיסָתָן יִבְדְּקוּהָ. וְאֵימָא כּוּלֵּיהּ לְהָכִי הוּא דַּאֲתָא. לַבּוֹעֵל, לְהוֹדִיעַ דְּבֶטֶן לָקֵי בְּרֵישָׁא מְנָלַן?. מַאי בֶּטֶן וְיָרֵךְ. סְתָם? הָכָא וְהָכָא דָּרֵישׁ לֵיהּ. שְׁלֹשָׁה פְּעָמִים. "וְקִינֵּא אֶת אִשְׁתּוֹ וְהִיא נִטְמָאָה", "וְהָיְתָה אִם נִטְמְאָה", "תַּחַת אִישָׁהּ וְנִטְמָאָה". וְאֶחָד לִתְרוּמָה. שֶׁאֲפִילּוּ הִיא בַּת כֹּהֵן, וּבַעֲלָהּ כֹּהֵן – נִפְסֶלֶת מִן הַתְּרוּמָה. קַל וָחוֹמֶר. אֵינוֹ צָרִיךְ לְהָבִיא מִן הַמִּקְרָא לְפוֹסְלָהּ מִן הַכְּהוּנָּה מִלִּינָּשֵׂא לְכֹהֵן, דְּמִקַּל וָחוֹמֶר אָתֵי. מַה גְּרוּשָׁה. בַּת כֹּהֵן שֶׁנִּתְגָּרְשָׁה מִיִּשְׂרָאֵל וְזֶרַע אֵין לָהּ, שֶׁמּוּתֶּרֶת בִּתְרוּמָה, כִּדְכְתִיב: "מִלֶּחֶם אָבִיהָ תֹּאכֵל" (ויקרא כב) – פְּסוּלָה לִכְהוּנָּה. זוֹ שֶׁפְּסוּלָה מִתְּרוּמָה. מֵרִבּוּיָא דְּ"נִטְמָאָה" כִּדְקָאָמְרַתְּ, אֵינוֹ דִּין שֶׁפְּסוּלָה לִכְהוּנָּה? וּלְקַמָּן פָּרֵיךְ: וְהָא לָא אַיְירֵי רַבִּי עֲקִיבָא בִּפְסוּל כְּהוּנָּה כְּלָל, דְּלָא אִצְטְרִיכָא קְרָא, וּמַאי קָאָמַר לֵיהּ רַבִּי יִשְׁמָעֵאל?. מַה ת"ל וְהִיא נִטְמָאָה כו'. גָּרְסִינַן, וְלָא גָּרַס: א"כ. דְּמִילְּתָא בְּאַנְפֵּי נַפְשָׁהּ הִיא, וְלָא "נִטְמָאָה" יְתֵירָא קָמִיבַּעְיָא לֵיהּ, דְּהָא דָּרְשִׁינַן. וְלָאו רַבִּי יִשְׁמָעֵאל לְחוּדֵיהּ קָאָמַר לָהּ, אֶלָּא סְתָמָא הִיא, וּקְרָאֵי דְּעִנְיָינָא קָדָרֵישׁ וְאָזֵיל. מַה תַּלְמוּד לוֹמַר וְקִנֵּא אֶת אִשְׁתּוֹ וְהִיא נִטְמָאָה. דְּמַשְׁמַע דְּוַדַּאי נִטְמְאָה, וּמַה תַּלְמוּד לוֹמַר "אוֹ עָבַר עָלָיו וגו' וְהִיא לֹא נִטְמָאָה". אִי פְּשִׁיטָא לֵיהּ דְּנִטְמְאָה – לָמָּה שׁוֹתָה, וְאִי פְּשִׁיטָא דְּלָא נִטְמְאָה – לָמָּה מַשְׁקָהּ?. מַגִּיד לְךָ הַכָּתוּב שֶׁעַל הַסָּפֵק אֲסוּרָה. וְהָכִי קָאָמַר קְרָא: אִשָּׁה זוֹ, שֶׁמָּא נִטְמְאָה וְשֶׁמָּא לֹא נִטְמְאָה, וְקָאָמַר לָךְ דְּיַשְׁקֶנָּה לְבָרֵר הַסְּפֵיקָא, וְאִי לָא מַשְׁקֶה לָהּ – אֲסוּרָה. וּמִכָּאן אַתָּה. לָמֵד ק"ו לְשֶׁרֶץ, סָפֵק נָגַע בִּטְהָרוֹת סָפֵק לֹא נָגַע, דְּמַחְזְקִינַן לָהּ בְּטוּמְאָה מִסָּפֵק. סוֹטָה לֹא עָשָׂה בָּהּ כו'. דִּכְתִיב: "וְהִיא לֹא נִתְפָּשָׂה" – אֲסוּרָה, הָא נִתְפְּשָׂה – מוּתֶּרֶת. וְהוּא הַדִּין לְשׁוֹגֵג; אִשְׁתּוֹ וְאֵשֶׁת אִישׁ עִמּוֹ בַּבַּיִת, וְנִתְכַּוֵּון לְאִשְׁתּוֹ וְנִזְדַּמְּנָה לוֹ זוֹ, וְאַף הִיא שׁוֹגֶגֶת, כִּסְבוּרָה שֶׁהוּא בַּעְלָהּ.

וּמִמָּקוֹם

תוספות

ההוא דמודע לה כהן. פירוש: הכהן צריך להודיע שלא להוציא *לעז. וכיון דגלי לן קרא דהוא נבדק כמותה, וכתיב בה צואה ידיעה ועשייה – לא צריך למכתב תו ביה. **זו שאסורה בתרומה** אינה דין שאסורה לכהונה. וליכא למימר: בת ישראל יוכיח, שאסורה בתרומה ומותרת לכהונה. דה"פ: ומה גרושה שמותרת לתרומה אסורה לכהונה ע"י מעשה שנעשה בה, דהיינו גירושין, זו וכו' אינו דין שאסורה לכהונה ע"י זנות שנעשה בה? אבל בת ישראל מה שפסולה בתרומה אינו ע"י מעשה. ועוד, אם תנשא בת ישראל לכהן תהא מותרת לתרומה, מה שאין כן באלו שאין להם היתר לעולם. בספרי מתני הכי: ומה גרושה קלה שמותרת לחזור למגרשה בישראל – פסולה מן הכהונה, סוטה חמורה דין הוא שפסולה מן הכהונה.

מה ת"ל היא נטמאה וכו'. כגירסת רש"י. וכן סיומא: ללמדך שלעולם אין משקין אלא על הספק. וא"ת: וכי איצטריך קרא למיסר ספיקא? יש לומר: הכתוב אוסרה קודם שתיה כאילו היא ודאי. ואע"ג דליכא מלקות, כדמוכח בפ"ק דיבמות (דף יא:*), מיהו לאו הבא מכלל עשה איכא, ואפי' אם היא טהורה – נענש בב"ד של מעלה אם בא עליה, כמו על חייבי עשה. ולא כשאר ספיקות כגון ספק חלב ספק שומן ואכלו, ונודע שהוא שומן, אע"ג דצריך כפרה וסליחה – מיהו לא חמיר כחייבי עשה.

אינו דין שעשה בו ספק כודאי. ליכא למיפרך: נזיר ועושה פסח יוכיחו, שעשה בהן אונס כרצון, דנפקא לן מ"כי ימות מת עליו בפתע פתאום" בספרי, ובפרק ב' דכריתות (דף ט.), ואפ"ה לא עשה בהן ספק טומאת התהום כודאי! לפי שטומאת התהום הלכה הוא, *ולא סתרינן ק"ו מהלכה. וה"ה דאין להוכיח משם, דהכי אמר בהוכחה: אף אני אביא זה, והלא אין ללמוד הימנו. אבל הא איכא למתמה: אמאי לא פרכינן: מה לסוטה שכן רגלים לדבר שהרי קינא לה ונסתרה, כדפרכינן לעיל בריש פ"ק (דף ג:)! ואין לומר: משום דלעיל מיירי בטומאה דבתר קינוי וסתירה, דמהימן עד א' – התם ודאי איכא רגלים, אבל הכא ילפינן מסתירה דבתר קנויא גרידא, דליכא למיפרך שכן קינא לה – דקנויא לא חשיב רגלים בלא סתירה, דהא בריש מסכת נדה (דף ג:) דמייתי התם: מקוה שנמדד ונמצא חסר – כל הטהרות שנעשו על גביו, בין ברה"ר בין ברה"י – טמא. ר"ש אומר: ברה"ר טהור, ברה"י תולין. ושניהם לא למדוה אלא מסוטה; רבנן סברי: כסוטה, מה סוטה ספק הוא ועשאוה כודאי – אף כו'. ופריך: אי מסוטה, נימא: מה סוטה ברה"י טמא ודאי, הכא נמי טמא ודאי! הכי השתא?! התם יש רגלים לדבר, שהרי קנא לה ונסתרה, הכא מאי רגלים לדבר איכא? אלמא: אע"ג דמסתירה דבתר קנויא יליף כי הכא, פריך. והכא אמאי לא פריך הכי? ויש לומר: דסתירה על ידי קנויא בסוטה הוי כספק מגע שרץ, שהרי בלא קנויא לא היה שום ספק בסתירה גרידא – דלא נחשדו על העריות, הלכך הקנויא גורם הספק. וה"פ במס' נדה: התם גבי סוטה וספק שרץ הרי ריעותא, דהיינו השרץ והבועל קמן אצל הטהרות והאשה. אבל גבי מקוה – קודם טבילה לא ראינו שום ריעותא דאיכא לספוקי על ידה. ולעיל בפ"ק, קודם העדאת עדים – לא הואי שום ריעותא.

מכאן

עין משפט נר מצוה

[לעז וקאמר לה הס"ד ואח"כ מה"ד ש"מ תרתי וכיון דגלי לן כו' רש"א]

ד א מיי' פ"ב מהלכות סוטה הלכה ח ופ"ג הלכה יז יח:

ה ב מיי' שם פ"ב הלכ' ו:

ו ג ד מיי' פט"ז מהל' אבות הטומאה הלכה א ב:

ז ה מיי' פ"ג מהלכות סוטה הלכה כד:

[ועי' היטב תוס' שם ד"ה מאי]

ואין דנין ק"ו כו' רש"א

מסורת הש"ס

[לקמן מז: שבועות ה. יבמות נח. קידושין כז:]

[יומא מה. וש"נ]

לעיל ט:

[לעיל כו:]

הגהות הב"ח

(א) גמ' ועדיין תיבעי נטמאה ונטמאה קאמר או אם נטמאה ונטמאה: (ב) רש"י ד"ה שיתא וכו' וחד והשקה כצ"ל ותיבת לעשייה נמחק:

תוספות שאנץ

חד לצואה דידה שהקדוש ברוך הוא גוזר שיבואו בה המים וחד לידיעה דידה להודיעה דבטן ואחר כך ירך שלא להוציא לעז כדאמר פ"ק. וחד לעשייה והשקה את המים והיתה אם נטמאה ותמעול מעל באישה. ובאו בה המים המאררים למרים ל"ה. וגר' דידה בריסא תחלה לפי שעיקר המעשה באשה הוא. א"ר ישמעאל ק"ו אינו צריך להביא מקרא לפסלה מלהנשא לכהן דמק"ו אתיא ומה גרושה בת כהן שנתגרשה מישראל וזרע אין לה שמותרת בתרומה כדכתיב מלחם אביה תאכל פסלה מן הכהונה זו שפסולה לתרומה מריבויא (בעלמא) [דונטמאה] כדקאמרת אינו דין שפסולה לכהן ל"ה. מה ת"ל והיא נטמאה ה"ג ול"ג אם כן מה ת"ל ונסתרה והיא נטמאה א) והיא נטמאה יתירה לא דרי' דהא דרשי' לעיל בפ"ק ול"נ כמש"כ במתני'. ועוד פ"ה דלאו ר' ישמעאל לחודיה קאמר לה אלא סתמא היא וקראי דעניינא קא דריש ואזיל ל"ה: ומכאן אתה דן לשרץ פ"ה מכאן אתה למד בק"ו דשרץ ספק נגע ספק לא נגע בטהרות דמחזקי' ליה בטומאה מספק. ומה סוטה שלא עשה בה שוגג כמזיד פ"ה סוטה שלא עשה בה כו' דכתיב והיא לא נתפשה אסורה הא נתפשה מותרת וה"ה לשוגג אשתו ואשת איש עמו ונתכוין לאשתו ונזדמנה לו זאת ואף היא שוגגת כסבורה שהוא בעלה עשה בה ספק כודאי ל"ה. ונראה דאין ק"ו גמור אלא גלוי מלתא בעלמא הוא דאי ק"ו גמור הוא א"כ נילף כל איסורין שעשה בה שוגג כמזיד שיעשה בהם ספק כודאי מהאי ק"ו (עם) [וגם] נחלוק בין רשות היחיד לרשות הרבים כמו בטומאה: ועוד דאיכא למיפרך מה לסוטה שכן נסתרה ויש רגלים לדבר תאמר בשרץ שאין בו כן אלא ש"מ דאין זה ק"ו גמור אלא גלוי מלתא בעלמא הוא ובכולי תלמודא גמרי' ספק טומאה ברה"י מסוטה כדאמר הלכתא גמירי לה מסוטה והוי כמו הלכה למשה מסיני. א"נ מדכתיב ונסתרה והיא נטמאה בסוטה ילפינן טומאה והלכתא גמירי לה מסוטה לאו דוקא אלא כלומר דמסוטה גמרינן לה והא דילפינן מסוטה היינו ספק טומאה ברה"י דכל ספק טומאה ברה"ר דספקו טהור לא גמרי מינה.

תרומה

א) נ"ל דלא נטמאה יתירה קדריש דהא דרשינן לעיל וכו'.

ח א מיי' פט"ו מהל' אבות הטומאה הלכה ח ופט"ז הלכה ב:

ט ב מיי' שם פט"ז הלכה ב:

י ג מיי' שם ופט"ו הלכה ח:

כְּוַדַּאי. וּמִמָּקוֹם שֶׁבָּאתָ: אמַה סוֹטָה רְשׁוּת הַיָּחִיד — אַף שֶׁרֶץ רְשׁוּת הַיָּחִיד, וּמַה סוֹטָה בדָּבָר שֶׁיֵּשׁ בּוֹ דַּעַת לִישָּׁאֵל — אַף שֶׁרֶץ דָּבָר שֶׁיֵּשׁ בּוֹ דַּעַת לִישָּׁאֵל. גוּמִכָּאן אָמְרוּ: גדָּבָר שֶׁיֵּשׁ בּוֹ דַּעַת לִישָּׁאֵל, בִּרְשׁוּת הַיָּחִיד — סְפֵיקוֹ טָמֵא, בִּרה"ר — סְפֵיקוֹ טָהוֹר. *וְשֶׁאֵין בּוֹ דַּעַת לִישָּׁאֵל, בֵּין בִּרה"י בֵּין בִּרה"ר — סְפֵיקוֹ טָהוֹר. וְרַבִּי יִשְׁמָעֵאל, א"ר עֲקִיבָא תְּרוּמָה וּמְהַדֵּר לֵיהּ אִיהוּ כְּהוּנָּה? וְתוּ: לְרַבִּי עֲקִיבָא כְּהוּנָּה מְנָא לֵיהּ? וְכִי תֵּימָא: כְּהוּנָּה לָא צְרִיכָא קְרָא, שֶׁהֲרֵי

וּמִמָּקוֹם שֶׁבָּאתָ. הוֹאִיל וְלֹא לָמַדְתָּ דִּמְטַמְּאִינַן מִסָּפֵק אֶלָּא מִסּוֹטָה, חֲזוֹר וְדוֹן: דְּמַה סוֹטָה הָא דִּטְמֵאָה מִסָּפֵק, בִּרה"י הוּא, מָקוֹם הָרָאוּי לִיסָּתֵר — אַף טוּמְאָה בִּרְשׁוּת הַיָּחִיד סְפֵיקוֹ טָמֵא, אֲבָל בִּרה"ר טָהוֹר. וּמַה סוֹטָה דָּבָר שֶׁיֵּשׁ בּוֹ דַּעַת לִישָּׁאֵל הִיא. אִם נִטְמֵאת אִם לָאו. אַף סְפֵק טוּמְאָה — דָּבָר שֶׁיֵּשׁ בּוֹ בְּנוֹגֵעַ זֶה דַּעַת לִישָּׁאֵל אִם נָגַע אִם לָאו, וְהוּא אוֹמֵר "אֵינִי יוֹדֵעַ". כְּגוֹן אָדָם, אוֹ טְהָרוֹת שֶׁהָיָה אָדָם עָסוּק בָּהֶם בְּשָׁעָה שֶׁנּוֹלַד הַסָּפֵק: וּפָרְכִינַן לְרַבִּי יִשְׁמָעֵאל א"ר עֲקִיבָא. "וְאֶחָד לִתְרוּמָה", וְקָמַהֲדַר לֵיהּ אִיהוּ: א"ל מִקְרָא לְהָבִיא בִּכְהוּנָּה?. וְתוּ. מִבַּעְיָא לָן: לְרַבִּי עֲקִיבָא דְּלָא אַיְירֵי בִּכְהוּנָּה. מְנָא לֵיהּ. דַּאֲסוּרָה לִכְהוּנָּה אִם מֵת זֶה? וְהָא לֵיכָּא לְמֵימַר דִּשְׁרָיָא, דְּהַשְׁתָּא לִתְרוּמָה אָסַר לָהּ — לִכְהוּנָּה מִבַּעְיָא? וּמִק"ו הוּא לֹא יָלֵיף, דְּא"כ הַיְינוּ ר' יִשְׁמָעֵאל. וְכ"ת כְּהוּנָּה לֹא צָרִיךְ קְרָא. דְּמִמֵּילָא אֲסוּרָה, שֶׁהֲרֵי עָשָׂה בָּהּ הַכָּתוּב בְּסוֹטָה סְפֵק זוֹנָה כְּוַדַּאי זוֹנָה לְאוֹסְרָהּ עַל בַּעְלָהּ, הִלְכָּךְ לְגַבֵּי כְּהוּנָּה נַמִי אֲסִירָא, דִּכְתִיב: "זוֹנָה לֹא יִקָּחוּ", וְזוֹ בְּחֶזְקַת זוֹנָה הִיא. אִי

[פסחים יט: נדה ד: ה:]

מכאן אמרו וכו' ברשות הרבים ספיקו טהור. בפ"ק דשחיטת חולין (דף ט:) ובפרק "אין מעמידין" (ע"ז דף לז:) אמר דספק טומאה ברשות הרבים הלכתא גמירי לה מסוטה, דמשמע דדוקא במקום סתירה טמא, אבל שלא במקום סתירה גמירי דטהור ודאי הוא. ותימה: למאי אילטריך הלכתא? לימא העמד טהור על חזקתו, ואימור לא נטמא? והכי אמר בהדיא נמי בריש מסכת נדה (דף ג.) דרבי שמעון גמר לה מספק טומאה ברה"ר. ואמר, ורבנן — הכי השתא?! התם גברא בחזקת טהרה קאי, מספיקא לא מחתינא ליה טומאה! וי"ל: אי לאו הלכתא דגמרינן דברה"ר טהור — הוה אמינא: סתירה דנקט קרא — לא דבר הכתוב אלא בהווה, וה"ה לכל ספק טומאה בכל מקום שנולדה, דמסברא אין לטהר זו יותר מזו, וסד"א דגזירת מלך כך היא בכל ספק טומאה. הלכך אילטריך הלכתא להעמיד ספק טומאה ברשות הרבים אחזקתה, דלא מחתינן ליה טומאה מספק. ירושלמי דפירקין קמא: מ"מ יש רגלים לדבר לפלטיא בלילה, לחורבה ביום, למבואות אפילות ביום. שאלו את בן זומא: מפני מה ספק רה"י טמא? אמר לון: סוטה מה היא לבעלה, ודאי או ספק? אמרו ליה: ספק. אמר להו: מצינו שהיא אסורה לבעלה, ומכאן אתה דן לשרץ: מה כאן רשות היחיד — אף להלן, ומה כאן דבר שיש בו דעת לישאל — אף וכו'. מכאן אמרו: דבר שיש בו דעת לישאל וכו'. מיליהון דרבנן פליגין, דמר רבי זעירא ור' יוסי בשם ר' יוחנן: (א) קטנה שזינתה — אין לה רצון להאסר על בעלה, והא תנינן: כל דבר שיש בו דעת לישאל ספיקו טמא, ברם הכא אע"פ שיש בו דעת לישאל ספיקו טהור. ומפני מה ספק רה"ר טהור? אמר להו: מצינו שהציבור עושין את הפסח בטומאה בזמן שרובו של ציבור טמאים. אם טומאה ודאית הותרה לצבור — ק"ו לספק טומאה. וסיום הברייתא בתוספתא דמסכת טהרות פרק "הנבילות השחוטות":* רשב"ג אומר: מפני מה ספק רה"י טמא וספק רה"ר טהור — מפני שאפשר לישאל ליחיד, ואי אפשר לישאל לרבים. ברשות הרבים ספיקו טהור. מקשי' מפרק "שני נזירין" (נזיר דף נז.), דתנן: שני נזירין שאמר להן אחד: ראיתי אחד מכם שנטמא, ואיני יודע איזה מכם הוא — שניהן מביאין קרבן טומאה. וקדייק בגמרא: ואמאי? כל ספק טומאה מהיכא גמירי — מסוטה, מה סוטה בועל ונבעלת — אף כל ספק טומאה ברה"י כגון דאיכא בי תרי. אבל הכא שני נזירין והאי דקאים גביהון — הא תלתא, הוי ליה ספק טומאה ברה"ר! אלמא כל היכא דאיכא תלת חשיב ליה כרה"ר, א"כ הא דתנן בפרק "האשה שהיא עושה צרכיה" (נדה ס:): שלש נשים שהיו ישינות במטה אחת, ונמצא דם תחת אחת מהן — כולן טמאות, אמאי? כיון דאיכא שלש הוה ליה כרה"ר! מיהו, מהתם לא קשיא מידי, דלא דמי לשרץ. דשרץ אפשר שלא נגע וטהור, אבל התם — אחת מהן ודאי טמאה, שילא הדם מגופה, והיאך נטהר כולם. ולא דמי אלא לשני שבילין (טהרות פ"ה מ"ה). אבל מפרק קמא דנדה (דף ב.) מקשינן, דתנן: כילד דיה שעתה? היתה יושבת במטה ועסוקה בטהרות, ופירשה וראתה — היא טמאה, וכולן טהורות. ודייק בגמרא (דף ה:): טעמא דדיה שעתה, הא מעת לעת — מטה נמי מטמא. מכדי דבר שאין בו דעת לישאל ספיקו טהור! תרגמא כשחברותיה נושאות אותה במטה, דהויא לה יד חברותיה. סוף סוף חברותיה והיא הויא שלש, והוה ליה ספק טומאה ברה"ר, ואמאי מטמינן לה? ונראה דלא חשבינן טומאה ברה"ר אלא היכא דספיקא היתה יכולה להיות גלויה לכל, כגון ההיא דנזיר, ותשעה לפרדעים ושרץ אחד ביניהם (כתובות דף טו.). אבל ההיא דנדה — המגע ודאי הוא, שנגעה במטה, ואין שום ספק אלא אם ראתה או לאו. ומקום המקור מקום סתר הוא ולא שייך למימר ביה רה"ר, אפילו אם נולד ספק ראייתה ברשות הרבים. אבל בהא איכא למתמה: אמאי משוינן מטה כספק טומאה ברשות היחיד? והא לא דמיא לסוטה, דסוטה — ודאי שרץ וספק מגע, כגון בועל הוא השרץ וספק אם בעל, אבל התם — ודאי מגע וספק מעת לעת הוא שרץ, דשמא לא ראתה. ואנן לא ילפינן מסוטה אלא דדמי לסוטה, דהא דבר שאין בו דעת לישאל ממעטינן הואיל ולא דמי לסוטה! ועוד, תניא בהדיא בתוספתא דטהרות פרק [הנבילות] השחוטות (פ"ו): נגע באחד בלילה, ואינו יודע אם חי אם מת, למחר עומד ונמצא מת, רבי מאיר מטהר, שספק רשות הרבים טהור. אלמא דמסוטה גמירי, אע"ג דהוי ודאי מגע וספק שרץ, ותימה: מאי שנא דמטהרינן דבר שאין בו דעת לישאל, הואיל ולא דמי לסוטה, ובכי האי גוונא *לא מטהרינן? וי"ל: דהכי הלכתא גמירי לה. א"נ: עיקר הדבר שאין בו דעת לישאל נפקא לן מ"והבשר אשר יגע בכל טמא לא יאכל" כדלקמן בשמעתין. וכיון דגלי לן קרא דאיכא לפלוגי בין דבר שיש בו דעת לישאל לשאין בו דעת. דדבר שיש בו דעת ספיקו טמא, ולא פירש טומאתו היכן — נלמוד סתום מן המפורש מסוטה, דמפרש בו: דוקא מקום סתירה. ואע"ג דמסיק: אי מסוטה הוה אמינא דעת נוגע ומגיע — אגב שיטפיה נקט ליה. אי נמי, הכי פירושו: ואי הוה גלי לן קרא בסוטה דבעינן דבר שיש בו דעת לישאל — הוה אמינא דעת נוגע ומגיע. סיום הברייתא דנגע באחד בלילה: וחכמים מטמאין, שכל הטומאות כשעת מציאתן. ומודים חכמים לרבי מאיר שאם ראוהו חי מבערב, אע"פ שבא שחרית ומצאו מת — טהור, מפני שזה ספק רה"ר. אלמא דבין לרבנן בין לרבי מאיר אפילו בלילה חשבינן ליה רשות הרבים. וקשיא מהא דתנן במסכת טהרות פרק שמיני (מ"ג): המאבד ביום ומצא ביום — טהור, ביום ומצא בלילה, בלילה ומצא ביום של אחריו — ספיקו טמא. זה הכלל: כל שעבר עליו הלילה או מקלתו — ספיקו טמא. אלמא דלילה חשיב לעולם כרשות היחיד. ולעיל איתינן נמי מירושלמי: מ"מ, יש רגלים לדבר לפלטיא בלילה, לחורבה ביום, למבואות אפילים ביום. אלמא דפלטיא בלילה חשיב רה"י! בתוספתא דטהרות פרק ז': יש דברים ברה"ר ועשאום כרה"י: קופה *ברה"י גבוה י' טפחים והטומאה בתוכו, ספק נגע ספק לא נגע — ספיקו טהור. הכניס ידו לתוכה, ספק נגע ספק לא נגע — ספיקו טמא. היתה כפושה על כתיפו וככר תרומה כרוך בסיב או בנייר ונתן בתוכו, ספק נגע ספק לא נגע — טהור. הכניס ידו לתוכה, ספק נגע ספק לא נגע — ספיקו טמא. חמור ברה"ר גבוה י' טפחים וטומאה נתונה על גביו, ספק נגע ספק לא נגע — ספיקו טהור. פשט ידו על גביו, ספק נגע ספק לא נגע — ספיקו טמא. סלע ברה"ר גבוה י' טפחים וטומאה עליו, ספק נגע ספק לא נגע — ספיקו טהור. עלה לראשו, ספק נגע ספק לא נגע — ספיקו טמא. היה זה רוכב על חמורו וזה רוכב על חמורו, אחד טמא ואחד טהור, ספק נגעו זה בזה ספק לא נגעו, ר' יעקב מטמא ורבי יוסי מטהר. בנו של זה רוכב על כתיפיו ובנו של זה רוכב על *כתף, אחד טהור ואחד טמא, ספק נגעו זה בזה ספק לא נגעו — ר' יעקב מטמא ורבי יוסי מטהר. היתה חבילה על כתיפיו והרוק מדובק בכותל למעלה מי' טפחים, ספק הסיט ספק לא הסיט, ר' יעקב מטמא ורבי יוסי מטהר. שהיה ר' יעקב אומר: כל שהוא למעלה מעשרה טפחים ברה"ר — הרי הוא כרה"י. ורבי יוסי אומר: כל שדרך הילוכו ברה"ר טהור. ועוד מפרש התם דין בקעה בימות החמה ובימות הגשמים: אלו הן ימות החמה — משתעקר תבואה, ואלו הן ימות הגשמים — משתרד רביעה שניה. ובפרק "מי שמת" (ב"ב דף קנג:) מפרש: הא דאמרינן בימות החמה רה"ר לטומאה — לא שנו אלא שלא עברו עליו ימות הגשמים, אבל עברו עליו ימות הגשמים — רשות היחיד לכאן ולכאן.

(פרק ו)

לא מדמינן לסוטה וי"ל כו' רש"ל

נ"ל כתפיו

ותו לרבי עקיבא כהונה מנא ליה. רש"י פי': דמקל וחומר לא יליף, דאם כן היינו רבי ישמעאל. ותימה: אי לית ליה קל וחומר דרבי ישמעאל, א"כ כיון שנבעלה לפסול לה בעילה ודאית מנא ליה דפסולה לכהונה? והא ביבמות בפרק "אלמנה" (דף סח:) ילפינן ליה מהאי קל וחומר! ועוד: הא ליכא למיפרך עליה מידי! יש לומר: הכא לית ליה קל וחומר, משום דאי לא הוו כתיבי אלא תלתא קראי, הוה אמינא: חד לבועל וחד לבעל וחד לכהונה, דחמיר טפי, כדפריך לרבי ישמעאל. אבל גבי בעילת פסולין — כתיבה תרומה בהדיא.

שכן

הגהות הב"ח

(א) תוס' ד"ה מכאן וכו' בשם ר"י קטנה. נ"ב עי' ביבמות סוף דף לג:

שֶׁהֲרֵי עָשָׂה בָּהּ סְפֵק זוֹנָה כְּזוֹנָה. תְּרוּמָה נַמִי לָא תִּיבָּעֵי קְרָא, שֶׁהֲרֵי עָשָׂה בָּהּ סְפֵק זוֹנָה כְּזוֹנָה! אֶלָּא, לְר׳ עֲקִיבָא אַרְבָּעָה קְרָאֵי כְּתִיבִי: חַד לַבַּעַל, וְחַד לַבּוֹעֵל, וְחַד לִכְהוּנָּה, וְחַד לִתְרוּמָה. וְרַבִּי יִשְׁמָעֵאל: תְּלָתָא קְרָאֵי כְּתִיבִי; חַד לַבַּעַל, וְחַד לַבּוֹעֵל, וְחַד לִתְרוּמָה, וּכְהוּנָּה אָתְיָא בְּקַל וָחוֹמֶר. וְרַבִּי יִשְׁמָעֵאל, מִמַּאי דְּאִיצְטְרִיךְ קְרָא לִתְרוּמָה, וּכְהוּנָּה אָתְיָא בְּקַל וָחוֹמֶר? דִּילְמָא כִּי אִצְטְרִיךְ – לִכְהוּנָּה, וּתְרוּמָה שַׁרְיָא! אָמַר לָךְ: מִסְתַּבְּרָא, דּוּמְיָא דְּבַעַל וּבוֹעֵל, מַה בַּעַל וּבוֹעֵל – מֵחַיִּים, אַף תְּרוּמָה נַמִי – מֵחַיִּים, לְאַפּוּקֵי כְּהוּנָּה דִּלְאַחַר מִיתָה. וְר״ע: דּוּמְיָא דְּבַעַל וּבוֹעֵל לֵית לֵיהּ. וְאִי נַמִי אִית לֵיהּ – *מִילְּתָא דְּאָתְיָא בְּקַל וָחוֹמֶר טָרַח וְכָתַב לָהּ קְרָא. [פסחים יח: ב״ק כה.] אָמַר רַב גִּידֵּל אָמַר רַב: דָּבָר שֶׁיֵּשׁ בּוֹ דַּעַת לִישָּׁאֵל וְאֵין בּוֹ דַּעַת לִישָּׁאֵל מֵהַאי קְרָא נָפְקָא: °"וְהַבָּשָׂר (ויקרא ז) אֲשֶׁר יִגַּע בְּכָל טָמֵא לֹא יֵאָכֵל", וַדַּאי טָמֵא הוּא דְּלָא יֵאָכֵל, הָא סָפֵק טָמֵא וְסָפֵק טָהוֹר – יֵאָכֵל. אֵימָא סֵיפָא: °"וְהַבָּשָׂר כָּל טָהוֹר יֹאכַל בָּשָׂר", (שם) וַדַּאי טָהוֹר הוּא דְּיֹאכַל בָּשָׂר, הָא סָפֵק טָמֵא וְסָפֵק טָהוֹר – לֹא יֹאכַל. אֶלָּא לָאו שְׁמַע מִינָּהּ: כָּאן – שֶׁיֵּשׁ בּוֹ דַּעַת לִישָּׁאֵל, כָּאן – שֶׁאֵין בּוֹ דַּעַת לִישָּׁאֵל. וְאִיצְטְרִיךְ דְּרַב גִּידֵּל אָמַר רַב, וְאִיצְטְרִיךְ לְמִיגְמַר מִסּוֹטָה; דְּאִי מִדְּרַב – הֲוָה אָמִינָא בֵּין בִּרְשׁוּת הַיָּחִיד וּבֵין בִּרְשׁוּת הָרַבִּים – אִיצְטְרִיךְ לְמִיגְמַר מִסּוֹטָה, וְאִי מִסּוֹטָה – הֲוָה אָמִינָא עַד דְּאִיכָּא דַּעַת נוֹגֵעַ וּמַגִּיעַ, צְרִיכָא. § "בּוֹ בַּיּוֹם דָּרַשׁ רַבִּי עֲקִיבָא וְכָל כְּלִי חֶרֶשׂ" כו׳. § וּמֵאַחַר דְּאֵין לוֹ לָמָּה טָמֵא? אָמַר רַב יְהוּדָה אָמַר רַב: מִן הַתּוֹרָה אֵין לוֹ, מִדִּין קַל וָחוֹמֶר יֵשׁ לוֹ: וּמַה טְבוּל יוֹם שֶׁמּוּתָּר בְּחוּלִּין – פּוֹסֵל בִּתְרוּמָה, כִּכָּר שֵׁנִי שֶׁפָּסוּל בְּחוּלִּין – אֵינוֹ דִּין א שֶׁיַּעֲשֶׂה שְׁלִישִׁי בִּתְרוּמָה? אִיכָּא לְמִיפְרַךְ: מַה לִּטְבוּל יוֹם שֶׁכֵּן אַב הַטּוּמְאָה! תֵּיתֵי

מִטְּבוּל

רש״י

אי הכי לתרומה נמי לא תיבעי קרא. ונילף מההוא טעמא גופיה – שהרי עשה הכתוב בסוטה ספק זונה כודאי זונה, ובתרומה הא ידעינן דזונה אסורה, דכתיב (ויקרא כב): "כי תהיה לאיש זר" – כי תבעל לזר אלמה, "היא בתרומת הקדשים לא תאכל" ואין לך פסול גדול מזה כשהיא אשת איש ונבעלה לאחר. ולר׳ עקיבא מהאי קרא נפקא לן ביבמות (ד׳ סח.) כל הפסולים דפסלי, והנך נמי דלא תפסי בהו קידושין, דכיון דלר׳ עקיבא אין קידושין תופסין בשום פסול – לא משמע ליה "כי תהיה" לשון הויה, אלא כי תבעל. **אלא לרבי עקיבא ארבעה קראי כתיבי.** יתירי, ב׳ "נטמאה", וחד "ונטמאה", ורבי עקיבא דריש וי״ו – הרי ארבעה. **וכהונה אתיא מקל וחומר.** ולא דריש וי״ו. ופרכינן: לר׳ ישמעאל, כיון דלא דריש וי״ו, ממאי דקרא לתרומה מדריש, וכהונה אתיא בקל וחומר, ואתו כולהו? דילמא קרא לכהונה אתא, דכיון דלא כתיב תרומה בהדיא – הנא אמינא: תרומה לא אתרבאי לאיסורא, אלא כהונה הוא דאתרבאי, דחמירא מיניה, ותרומה שריא. **אמר לך מסתברא.** דקרא – תרומה רבי, דומיא דתרין "נטמאה" דרבי בהן בעל ובועל, דמחיים דבעל קמיתסרא להו, כגון, אם יגרשנה אסורה לבועל. הילכך, מקרא שלישי נמי – למידי דמיתסר ביה מחיים (א) דבעל אתי, והיינו תרומה, א) ולמעוטי כהונה. שאין פסוק זה בא לאוסרה אלא לאחר מיתה, דמחיים – הא אסירא וקיימא, דהא מגרש לה, והויא לה גרושה, ואסורה לכהונה. **ורבי עקיבא.** דמצריך קרא לכהונה – דומיא דבעל ובועל לית ליה. ואי לא כתיב קרא יתירא – לא הוה מרבינן אלא כהונה דחמירא. דכל חד וחד קרא באנפי נפשיה הוא, ולא אמרינן הא לא מרבי אלא דומיא דהנך. **ואי נמי אית ליה.** ומיתוקם קרא לתרומה, אפילו הכי אתא וי״ו יתירא לכהונה. ואע״ג דאיכא למילפה בקל וחומר – טרח וכתב לה קרא. **אלא לאו שמע מינה.** "הבשר אשר יגע", דדבר שאין בו דעת לישאל הוא, דבשר הוי נוגע – הילכך ספיקו טהור. "וכל טהור יאכל בשר", דאיירי בטומאת הגוף, דיש בו דעת לישאל – בההוא קאמר לך: ספיקו טמא. **דעת נוגע ומגיע.** במטמא ונטמא, כי סוטה דיש בה דעת ויש דעת בבועל המטמאה, קמשמע לן דרב גידל דנפקא מ"כל טהור" – הא ספק לא יאכל, כיון דיש בו דעת בזה שנטמא. אבל במטמא לא בעינן דעת. **ומאחר דאין לו.** מקרא מן התורה, למה הוא טמא בתרומה לרבי יוחנן, (ב) דקאמר: עתיד דור אחר לטהרו, אבל הוא היה מטמאו? **ומה טבול יום.** שלא העריב שמשו. **שמותר בחולין.** כדאמרינן ביבמות ב"הערל" (דף עד:): תלתא קראי כתיבי, טבל ועלה – (ג) מותר לחולין ולמעשר, העריב שמשו – אוכל בתרומה, הביא כפרתו בטומאה שהיא בת קרבן – מותר בקדשים. **ככר שני שפסול בחולין.** דכתיב (ויקרא יא): "כל אשר בתוכו יטמא", חולין ותרומה וקדשים במשמע – דין הוא שיעשה שלישי בתרומה – ו"דיו" ליכא למימר, דאם כן בטל ליה קל וחומר, דהא שני בתרומה מקרא משמע כי חולין, וקיימא לן (ב״ק דף כה.): דהיכא דמיפרך קל וחומר – לא אמרינן "דיו". **שכן אב הטומאה.** כגון טמא מת, או זב או מצורע, שהן בטומאתן אבות.

מִטְּבוּל

א) ולא למעוטי כהונה שאין פסול זה כו׳. רש״ל

תוספות

שכן עשה בה ספק זונה כזונה. תימה: אמאי לא אמר: כיון דטמאה הכתוב מספק – מהיכא תיתי דמותרת בתרומה ולכהונה? ויש לומר: אי לאו קראי – איכא למימר דלא טמאה אלא לענין בעלה, דאיכא ספק חייבי מיתות בית דין על ידו. אבל לענין תרומה וכהונה – הוה אמינא: אוקי איתתא אחזקה. אבל בירושלמי דפרק קמא, מתוך קושיא זו דריש חד מהני תלתא קראי ליבם. והכי איתא התם: תני, ר׳ מאיר אומר: שלש טומאות אמורות בפרשה, אחד לבעל ואחד לבועל ואחד לתרומה. מלינו אשה שהיא אסורה לביתה ומותרת לאכול בתרומה? למה לא, אילו בת כהן שניסאת לישראל ונאנסה, שמא אינה מותרת לביתה ואסורה לאכול בתרומה, לא מלינו אשה שהיא אסורה לביתה ומותרת לאכול בתרומה? אמר ר׳ אבין, הכין איתאמרת: אחת לבעל ואחת לבועל ואחת ליבם. אמר ר׳ יוסי, מתניתא אמרה כן: ואם מת חולצת ולא מתייבמת. **חד** לתרומה וחד לכהונה. אין להקשות: וכי ספק חמור מן ודאי? דאילו ודאי זינתה – מותרת בתרומה ולכהונה, דהא בפ׳ "אלמנה" ביבמות (דף סח.) מרבינן מ"ובת כהן כי תהיה לאיש זר" כיון שנבעלה לפסול לה, שזר אצלה – פסלה, ומרבינן גר עמוני ומואבי וכו׳. וקא פריך התם: אימא חייבי כריתות נמי. פירוש: אינהו נמי הוו בכלל נבעלה לפסול לה, ומאי שנא דלא תני להו לעיל? ומשני: "כי תהיה" כתיב, דוקא בני הויה, לאפוקי חייבי כריתות דלאו בני הויה נינהו. אלמא דחייבי כריתות לא מפסלי בביאתן. ואשת איש איהי נמי מחייבי כריתות, ואם כן מספקא אמאי מיפסלי? ורש״י שיבש שם אותה הגירסא, וזה לשונו: אימר נבעלה לפסול לה חייבי כריתות. אבל חייבי לאוין כיון דתפסי להו בה קידושין – לא פסלי לה, וכותי ונתין וממזר דפסלי מנלן? הנך דלית בהו הויה. מדאפקה להך ביאה בלשון הויה – שמע מינה בהנך דתפסי בה קדושין משתעי קרא, ואפ״ה פסלי. ולאפוקי חייבי כריתות לא גרסינן. אי הכי כותי ועבד וכו׳. והוא הדין דהוה מצי למימר חייבי כריתות לא מפסלי, אלא משום דאיירי בהו לעיל, דקתני כותי והיינו גוי, ובמתניתין תנן: העבד פוסל משום ביאה. ומשני: פסלי מדרבי יוחנן כו׳. ואית דמפרשי: ואימא נבעלה לפסול לה חייבי כריתות נמי וכו׳. וקשיא לי בגוה טובא; חדא, דתנן בפרק "ארבעה אחין" (שם דף לג:): אם היו כהנות – נפסלו מן התרומה בבעילת אשת איש. ועוד, קל וחומר: חייבי לאוין פסלי, חייבי כריתות לא פסלי? ועוד: הא אמר ב"עשרה יוחסין" (קדושין דף עז:): כהן הבא על אחותו – זונה משוי לה, וכיון דזונה משוי לה – בעילתה פוסלתה. דתניא: לויה שנשבית או שנבעלה בעילת זנות – נותנין לה מעשר ואוכלת. לויה – אין, אבל תרומה לכהנת – לא*)!

*) [וע״ש ברש״י שהאריך עוד בזה]

שלישי

עין משפט נר מצוה

יא א מיי׳ פ״א מהל׳ אבות הטומאה הל״ג:

תוספות שאנץ

תרומה נמי לא תיבעי לך שהרי עשה בה ספק זונה כזונה. משמע מהכ׳ דזונה אסורה בתרומה וה״נ משמע ביבמות פ׳ ד׳ אחין גבי שני אחין שקידשו ב׳ נשים ובשעת כניסה לחופה החליפו נשותיהן זה לזה וקאמר בגמ׳ אם היו כהנות נשואות לישראל נפסלות בתרומ׳ דבי נשא אלמא משמע דזונה אסורה לאכול בתרומה וכן משמע בפ׳ החולין גבי הכל מודים הבא על חייבי כריתות שבנה פגום וקאמר בסמוך וכי תימא איכא למפרך מה לאלמנה שכן היא עצמה מתחללת ה״נ (לימא) [כלומר] גבי בא על חייבי כריתות דמתחללת דכיון דנבעלה עשאה זונה משמע דהויא דומיא דאלמנה שמתחללת ואסורה לכהונה ה״נ זונה אסורה בתרומה וה״נ משמע בפ׳ האשה רבה דאמר התם לויה שנשבית או שנבעלה בעילת זנות נותנין לה מעשר ואוכלת משמע הא לתרומה לא. וא״ת ומהיכא נפקא לן דזונה אסורה בתרומה דלא אשכחן (בתרומ׳) [בקרא] אלא איסור כהונה. וי״ל דנפקא לן מדכתיב ובת כהן כי תהיה לאיש זר ודרשי׳ פ׳ אלמנה לכהן גדול כיון שנבעלה לפסול בה פסולה מן התרומה כיון שנבעלה לזר אצלה ואין לך פסול גדול מזה כשהיא אשת איש ונבעלה לאחר (ל״ה. אלא) ולר״ע דס״ל דאין קידו׳ תופסין בחייבי לאוין בשום פסול לא משמע ליה כי תהיה לשון הויה אלא כי תבעל. [ל״ה] (ג׳ קראי כתיבי): מה בעל ובועל מחיים. פ״ה דמחיים דבעל קא מתסר להו כגון שאם יגרשנה אסורה לבועל. הלכך מקרא ג׳ [נמי] למידי דמתסר ביה מחיים דבעל אתי והיינו תרומה למעוטי כהונ׳ שאין פסוק זה בא לאסרה אלא לאחר מיתה דמחיים הוה ליה אסירא וקיימא דאי מגרשה הויא גרושה ואסורה לכהונה. ל״ה: ודאי טמא הוא דלא יאכל הא ספק טמא ספק טהור יאכל. וליכא למימר ודאי טמא הוא דאיכא לאו הא ספק טמא ליכא לאו כי אם עשה דהא יש לנו לומר דכיון דמפקי׳ ליה מאיסורא אוקימנא אהיתירא: ה״א עד דאיכא דעת נוגע ומגיע. במיטמא ומטמא כסוטה דיש בה דעת ויש נמי דעת בבועל המטמא קמ״ל דרב גידל: ומאחר דאין לו. מקרא מן התורה למה הוא טמא בתרומה לרבי יוחנן דאמר עתיד דור אחר לטהרו אבל הוא היה מטמא. ל״ה: ומה טבול יום שמותר בחולין. כדאמר בהערל ג׳ קראי כתיבי טבל ועלה א) לחולין דכתיב כל אשר בתוכו יטמא חולין ותרומה וקדשים [במשמע] דין הוא שיעשה ג׳ בתרומה ודיו ליכא למימר דאין ג׳ פוסל בו דא״כ מפרי׳ ק״ו והיכא דמפרי׳ ק״ו ל״א דיו. כל״ה. וא״ת תינח לרבנן אבל לר׳ טרפון דאית ליה דיו אפי׳ מפרי׳ ק״ו מאי איכא למימר. וי״ל דר׳ טרפון סבירא ליה כר׳ עקיבא דאמר ג׳ לחולין מן התורה וה״ה לתרומה ורביעי לקדש מדכתיב והבשר אשר יגע בכל טמא. ע״ל היכא א״ר טרפון דאמרי׳ דיו [אף] דמפרי׳ ק״ו היכא דאשמעי׳ הק״ו חידוש אבל האי ק״ו דלא [אתי] אלא לגלויי מדרש הפסוק דאשמעי׳ מה שידעי׳ מקרא לא אמרי׳ דיו. תיתי מטבול יום דשרץ. אדם שנגע [בשרץ] ראשון לטומאה הוא ולא אב [הטומאה] וכי טבל הותר לחולין ואסור לתרומה ואפי׳ לנגיעה דכתיב נמי הערב שמש בכלים במים יובא וטהר והאי לנגיעה הוא להשתמש בו תרומה ואשמעי׳ דכלי טבול יום פסיל ליה. ל״ה. מה לטבול יום דשרץ שכן נעשה במינו אב הטומאה אם היה נוגע כלי זה או אדם זה במת נעשה אב הטומאה ב) אפי׳ על ידי מת דכתיב כל אשר יגע בו (הזב) [הטמא] יטמא ומהכא נ״ל טמא מת דמטמא אדם וכלים וע״כ בט״מ שי״ל טהרה במקוה [כתיב] דהא כתיב לעיל מיניה והזה הטהור על הטמא וחטאו ורחץ במים דבר שיש לו טהרה נעשה אב הטומאה על ידי מגע המת יצאו אוכלין ומשקין וכלי חרס דאין להם טהרה במקוה ואין נעשה במינם אב הטומאה וא״ת בהאי כבר נמי מצינו במינו אב הטומאה בכופת שאור כדאמר בפ׳ העור והרוטב כופת שאור שיחדה לישיבה טמא טומאת אוכלין אלמא יש במינו של ככר אב הטומאה דהא י״ל טומאת מדרס. וי״ל דשאני [התם] דכששימש [מעשה] עץ שימש אבל מ״מ לא מצינו במינו של ככר אב הטומאה. אבל ק׳ דאמרי׳ בפ׳ א״ר עקיבא דכלי חרס שאין לו טהרה במקוה אינו מטמא מדרס כדאיתא במסקנא התם וא״כ בכופת שאור שיחדו לישיבה למה מטמא מדרס כיון ג) שאינו במינו טהרה במקוה אין במינו אב הטומאה דכל דבר שאין לו טהרה במקוה אינו נעשה אב הטומאה וא״כ היכי מטמא מדרס א״כ צ״ל ע״כ שכלי עץ מינו הוא לפי ששניהן גידולי קרקע וא״כ למה [לא] יחשוב [נמי] מין ככר כיון שיש במינו של גידולי קרקע וא״כ מצינו בככר דעושה אב הטומאה. וי״ל דמ״מ כיון שלא מצינו מין ככר שהוא אוכל שיש במינו אב הטומאה לא חשיב ליה מינו. א״נ י״ל דיכול לומר דכופת שאור וכלי עץ שניהם דומין זה לזה שאינם ראויין לאכול ועוד דשניהם גידולי קרקע אבל ככר נהי דהוי גידולי קרקע מ״מ ראוי הוא לאכול משא״כ בכופת שאור א״כ לא מצינו שמינו של ככר [יהיה] אב הטומאה: טבול יום יוכיח שאין כלי שטף הראוי לטבילה מטמא מאוירו וקא פסיל תרומה. ל״ה. הצד השוה שבהן שמטמאין ופוסלין בתרומה כ״ש ככר שני שפוסל בחולין שיפסול. ה״ג רש״י ופי׳ הצד השוה צריך למצוא חומרא שוה לתלות בו טעם פסול תרומה ומהו הצד השוה שבהן טבול יום איקרי טמא דכתיב ובא השמש וטהר מכלל דעד השתא טמא ורח״ם [כתב] דילפי׳ ליה דאיקרי טמא מחילול חלול. כדאמר פ׳ הנשרפין. ופ״ה וכלי חרס איקרי טמא דכתיב תנור וכירים יותץ טמאים הם וכ״ש דככר שני ד) שפוסל בחולין שהוא טמא ואסור בחולין שיפסול בתרומה. פ״ה דה״ג

דה״ג אבל בכל הספרים כתיב הצד השוה שבהן שמותרין בחולין ופוסלין בתרומה ולהאי לישנא אין אדם יכול לפ׳ איזהו כלי חרס שמותר בחולין ופוסל בתרומה. ובדוחק גדול י״ל כלי חרס המוקף צמיד פתיל שמציל על החולין שבתוכו ואינו מציל בתרומה. והרבה געגועין ותשובות ובטול שיטת התלמוד יש בדבר. חדא דלא אשכחן דכלי חרס המוקף צמיד פתיל דאינו מציל בתרומה דבמסכת חגיגה אמרי׳ אין חטאת ניצלת בצמיד פתיל אבל תרומה לא תני בה. ועוד אפי׳ אמרי׳ דאינו מציל אין זה פסול בתרומה דהא לא פסיל מידי אלא דאינו מגין ומאליה היא נטמאת מאהל המת ומאי קאמר ופוסלין בתרומה. ועוד כל הצד השוה שבתלמוד שבא ללמוד חומר צריך שיהא הצד השוה חמור וזה הוי קל דקאמר הצד השוה שבהן שמותרין בחולין ואין שיטה זו בכל התלמוד לכ״נ דגרסי׳ הצד השוה שבהן שטמאין. וללשון שפי׳ דגרס שמטמאין אל תשיבנו מהא דאמרי׳ כלי חרס יוכיח שאין זה הוכחה דכלי חרס אינו טהור בחולין והיה לו להביא הוכחה מדבר הדומה לטבול יום שאע״פ שטהור בחולין פסול בתרומה שאין זו תשובה דאין צריך הוכחה אלא לסתור תשובתו שתולה טעם החמור דפסול תרומה מפני שהוא אב הטומאה וקא מהדר ליה כלי חרס יוכיח שאין בו חומר זה ופוסל וכן שיטת רוב הדינין כי ההיא דפ׳ כל הבשר דאמר מנין לבשר בחלב שאסור בהנאה אמרת ק״ו ומה ערלה שלא נעבדה בה עברה אסור בהנאה בשר בחלב שנעבדה בה עברה בבישול אינו דין שאסור בהנאה מה לערלה שכן לא היתה לה שעת הכושר חמץ בפסח יוכיחו מה לחמץ בפסח שכן כרת כלאי הכרם יוכיחו והא כלאי הכרם דנעבדה בהן עבירה בזריעה וחמץ בפסח נמי עבר בבל יראה ולא דמי לערלה בקולא דידה וקא הויא הוכחה ע״כ ל״ה. ורבינו משולם ה) רוצה לישב גרס׳ הספרים מה להצד השוה שבהן שמותרין בחולין אפי׳ קודם הערב השמש ופסולין בתרומה עד הערב השמש ומיירי שנשברו ולא שנשברו לגמרי לפירורין דקין שאינן ראויין לשום כלי בעולם דחשובין כעפר ואין צריכין הערב שמש אלא שנשברו ועדיין ראוין הם לכלי אחר כדי שיעורו כגון בגד שנקרע רובו ושייר בו כדי מעפורת או כלי חרס שניקב כדי מוציא משקה שטהור מלטמא ו) ומ״מ צריך הערב שמש לתרומה וסייעתא לזה מברייתא [דתו״כ] דתניא ואותו תשבורו יכול ישברנו ודיו ת״ל וכל כלי חרס. וה״פ נאמר בפ׳ של מעלה הערב שמש וסמיך ליה וכל כלי חרס וא״ו מוסיף על ענין ראשון ז) (וה״ק) וכל כלי חרס אשר יגע בו הזב ישבר יכול ישברנו ודיו בכך ת״ל וכל כלי חרס ולמעלה כתיב הערב השמש לימד על כלי חרס שטעון הערב השמש והוא שנשבר כמו שפירשנו ומותב׳ אשמעתין מההיא דאמר במסכת שבת בחזרת כלי מתכות לטומאתן רבא אמר גזירה שמא יאמרו טבילה בת יומא עולה. אלמא כשנטמאו ונשברו מיד טהרו בלא הערב השמש אי לאו גזירה והכא אמרי׳ דטעון הערב שמש. וי״ל דהתם יש סברא לומר דכשנשברו וחזר וריתכן דודאי טהורין [מיד] לפי שעשוין כלים חדשים ופנים חדשות באו לכאן כדאמר בסנדל שנפסקה אחת מאזניו ח). וה״נ הוי בכלי שנוצר עתה מחדש ולכך יש לנו לומר דטהורין אי לאו טעמא דשמא יאמרו אבל ודאי אם נשברה ולא חזר וריתכן [הרי הם עדיין בתורת ברייתו] דצריך הערב השמש ואי קשיא לך מההיא דחולין טלית טבולת יום שהתחיל לקורעה כיון שנקרעה רובה טהורה דכיון דלא חס עלה ואטבלה אלמא לקריעה לא בעי הערב השמש. וי״ל דהתם כיון דאטבליה ולא היה שם אלא טומאה דטבול יום צריך הערב שמש וכשקרעה בטלה מתורת כלי וטהורה לגמרי כי כל קריעה ושבירה כך הוא דינה שהוא טמא לגמרי ושברו השבירה מוציאתו מטומאת כלי ונטהר מטומאתו אבל בעי׳ הערב השמש כדפרי׳ וכשהכלי טבולת יום ושוברו נטהר מטומאת טבול יום ולא בעי הערב השמש והא דאמרי׳ בפ׳ דם חטאת כלי חרס שבישל בו חטאת ויצאו חוץ לקלעים ונטמאו ונקבו ונשברו במקום קדוש. אלמא דכלי לאחר שבירתו מותר להכניסו למקום קדוש בלא הערב השמש וכן בגד שיצא חוץ לקלעים ונטמא קורעו ומכניסו במקום קדוש. צ״ל דכל הכנסות דקאמר לאחר הערב השמש. והשיב לו ר״ת לרבי׳ משולם על שהביא ראיה מת״כ כדי לקיים הגרסא שמותק רש״י מי לא יראך ופנים לא ישיאך הרב העומד במליאתך אנהגך אביאך להודיעך ולהראך פן יודע בחשך פלאך כי עמדת אחרי סוף הוראה לחדש דבר מעתה לעשות מדות בכלים הנשברים כשבר נבל יוצרים וראייתך חסורי מחסרא שהגהת הג״ה בת״כ כדי להביא ראיה לשיבותך. ואפי׳ לשיבותך אם תשלח לי קלף אשיב לך תשובות אלף כי העולם סומכים על הגהתך וטועים הם ובריתא זו של ת״כ משובשת היא בכל הספרים שלכם וזו היא הצעה של ברייתא. ואותו תשבורו יכול ישברנו ודאי (ת״ל ואותו) והרי הוא אומר וכלי חרס אשר יגע בו הזב ישבר וה״פ יכול ישברנו ודאי כלומר האי דכתב בזב ישבר יכול ישברנו ממש כדין כלי חרס שמצוה לשוברו והרי הוא אומר בזב ישבר ת״ל אותו אותו אתה שובר ואי אתה שובר כלי חרס של זב אמרת ק״ו ומה כלי חרס של זב דחמור אינו טעון שבירה

הנוגע

א) נ״ל לאכול בחולין ובמעשר. ככר שני שפסול לחולין דכתיב כו׳. ב) נ״ל תאמר באוכל שאינו נעשה אב הטומאה אפי׳ כו׳. ג) נ״ל שאין לו טהרה במקוה אינו מטמא טומאת מדרס וע״כ נ״ל משום דכלי עץ מינו הוא לפי שכלים גידולי קרקע [וכל שיש במינו טהרה במקוה מטמא מדרס וכמו דאמרינן שם גבי מפץ ע״ש] וא״כ למה לא יחשוב נמי מין ככר כיון דשניהם גידולי קרקע כו׳. ד) נ״ל דפסיל טפי מטבול יום שהוא כו׳. ה) כ״ה הובא בשלטי הגבורים על הגהות מרדכי שבת פ׳ כירה עש״ה. ו) גסערלת ממה שהיה הואיל וכלי הוא לענין אחר כדאמר חמץ מדות בכלי חרס. ואע״פ כשנקב טהור למפרע מ״מ כו׳. כל״ל וכ״ה שם. ז) לימד על הנשבר שטעון הערב שמש והרי הוא אומר בזב וכל כו׳ כל״ל וכ״ה שם. ח) ומתרסיותיו ותקנה טמאה נפסקה שניה ותקנה טהורה פנים חדשות באו לכאן כל״ל וכ״ה שם וע״ש.

הגהות הב״ח (א) רש״י ד״ה אמר לך וכו׳ מחיים דבעל אתי: (ב) ד״ה ומאחר וכו׳ לר׳ יוחנן פריך דקאמר: (ג) ד״ה שמותר בחולין וכו׳ ועלה אוכל בחולין ובמעשר:

מִטְּבוּל יוֹם דְּשֶׁרֶץ. מַה לִּטְבוּל יוֹם דְּשֶׁרֶץ — שֶׁכֵּן בְּמִינוֹ אַב הַטּוּמְאָה! כְּלִי חֶרֶס יוֹכִיחַ. מַה לִּכְלִי חֶרֶס — שֶׁכֵּן מְטַמֵּא מֵאֲוִירוֹ! טְבוּל יוֹם יוֹכִיחַ. וְחוֹזֵר הַדִּין; לֹא רְאִי זֶה כִּרְאִי זֶה, וְלֹא רְאִי זֶה כִּרְאִי זֶה, הַצַּד הַשָּׁוֶה שֶׁבָּהֶן — שֶׁמּוּתָּרִין בְּחוּלִּין וּפוֹסְלִין בִּתְרוּמָה, כׇּל שֶׁכֵּן כִּכָּר שֵׁנִי שֶׁפּוֹסֵל בְּחוּלִּין דְּפוֹסֵל בִּתְרוּמָה. וְדוֹר אַחֵר פָּרֵיךְ: מַה לְּהַצַּד הַשָּׁוֶה שֶׁבָּהֶן (א) — שֶׁכֵּן *יֵשׁ בָּהֶן צַד חָמוּר! וְרַבָּן יוֹחָנָן בֶּן זַכַּאי: צַד חָמוּר לָא פָּרֵיךְ. תַּנְיָא, אָמַר רַבִּי יוֹסֵי: *מִנַּיִן לָרְבִיעִי בַּקּוֹדֶשׁ שֶׁפָּסוּל? וְדִין הוּא: מַה מְּחוּסַּר כִּיפּוּרִים, שֶׁמּוּתָּר בִּתְרוּמָה — פָּסוּל בַּקּוֹדֶשׁ, שְׁלִישִׁי שֶׁפָּסוּל בִּתְרוּמָה — אֵינוֹ דִּין הוּא שֶׁיֵּעָשֶׂה רְבִיעִי בַּקּוֹדֶשׁ? וְלָמַדְנוּ שְׁלִישִׁי לַקּוֹדֶשׁ אמִן הַתּוֹרָה, וּרְבִיעִי במִקַּל וָחוֹמֶר. שְׁלִישִׁי לַקּוֹדֶשׁ מִן הַתּוֹרָה מְנָלַן? דִּכְתִיב: °"וְהַבָּשָׂר אֲשֶׁר יִגַּע בְּכׇל טָמֵא לֹא יֵאָכֵל", מִי לָא עָסְקִינַן דְּנָגַע בְּשֵׁנִי, וְאָמַר רַחֲמָנָא "לֹא יֵאָכֵל". רְבִיעִי מִקַּל וָחוֹמֶר — כְּדַאֲמָרַן. אָמַר ר' יוֹחָנָן: טַעַם בְּרִיבִּי אֵינִי יוֹדֵעַ מַה הוּא, שֶׁהֲרֵי תְּשׁוּבָתוֹ בְּצִדּוֹ: אוֹכֶל הַבָּא מֵחֲמַת טְבוּל יוֹם יוֹכִיחַ, שֶׁפָּסוּל בִּתְרוּמָה וְאֵינוֹ עוֹשֶׂה רְבִיעִי בַּקּוֹדֶשׁ. *דְּתַנְיָא, אַבָּא שָׁאוּל אוֹמֵר: טְבוּל יוֹם תְּחִילָּה לַקּוֹדֶשׁ לְטַמֵּא שְׁנַיִם וְלִפְסוֹל אֶחָד, ר' מֵאִיר אוֹמֵר: מְטַמֵּא אֶחָד וּפוֹסֵל אֶחָד, וַחֲכָמִים אוֹמְרִים: גכְּשֵׁם שֶׁפּוֹסֵל אוֹכְלֵי תְרוּמָה וּמַשְׁקֵי תְרוּמָה — כָּךְ פּוֹסֵל אוֹכְלֵי קוֹדֶשׁ וּמַשְׁקֵי קוֹדֶשׁ. מַתְקִיף לָהּ רַב פַּפָּא: מִמַּאי דְּר' יוֹסֵי כְּרַבָּנַן סְבִירָא לֵיהּ? דִּילְמָא כְּאַבָּא שָׁאוּל ס"ל, דְּאָמַר: לְטַמֵּא שְׁנַיִם וְלִפְסוֹל אֶחָד? אִי סָלְקָא דַּעְתָּךְ כְּאַבָּא שָׁאוּל ס"ל — לַיְיתֵיהּ לָרְבִיעִי בַּקּוֹדֶשׁ מֵאוֹכֶל שֶׁבָּא מֵחֲמַת טְבוּל יוֹם: וּמָה אוֹכֶל הַבָּא מֵחֲמַת טְבוּל יוֹם, דִּטְבוּל יוֹם גּוּפֵיהּ מוּתָּר בְּחוּלִּין — אָמַרְתָּ עוֹשֶׂה רְבִיעִי בַּקּוֹדֶשׁ, אוֹכֶל שְׁלִישִׁי

רש"י

מִטְּבוּל יוֹם דְּשֶׁרֶץ. אָדָם שֶׁנָּגַע בְּשֶׁרֶץ רִאשׁוֹן לְטוּמְאָה (ב) הָיָה, וְלֹא אַב הַטּוּמְאָה, וְכִי טָבַל — הוּתַּר לְחוּלִּין וְאָסוּר לִתְרוּמָה וַאֲפִי' לִנְגִיעָה. דִּכְתִיב נַמִי הַעֲרֵב שֶׁמֶשׁ בְּכֵלִים "בַּמַּיִם יוּבָא וְטָמֵא עַד הָעֶרֶב וְטָהֵר" (ויקרא יא), וְהָא לִנְגִיעָה הוּא, לְהִשְׁתַּמֵּשׁ בּוֹ תְּרוּמָה, וַאֲשְׁמְעִינַן דִּכְלִי טְבוּל יוֹם פָּסַל לֵיהּ. שֶׁכֵּן יֵשׁ בְּמִינוֹ אַב הַטּוּמְאָה. אִם הָיָה נוֹגֵעַ כְּלִי זֶה אוֹ אָדָם זֶה בְּמֵת, נַעֲשָׂה אַב הַטּוּמְאָה לְטַמֵּא אָדָם וְכֵלִים — תֹּאמַר בְּאוֹכֶל שֶׁאֵינוֹ נַעֲשֶׂה אַב הַטּוּמְאָה אֲפִי' ע"י מֵת. דִּכְתִיב (במדבר יט): "וְכֹל אֲשֶׁר יִגַּע בּוֹ הַטָּמֵא יִטְמָא", וּמֵהָכָא נָפְקָא לָן טְמֵא מֵת דִּמְטַמֵּא אָדָם וְכֵלִים. וְעַל כׇּרְחָךְ בִּטְמֵא מֵת שֶׁיֵּשׁ לוֹ טׇהֳרָה בְּמִקְוֶה כְּתִיב, דְּהָא כְּתִיב לְעֵיל מִינֵּיהּ: "וְהִזָּה הַטָּהוֹר עַל הַטָּמֵא וְרָחַץ בַּמַּיִם" — דָּבָר שֶׁיֵּשׁ לוֹ טׇהֳרָה (ג) נַעֲשֶׂה אַב הַטּוּמְאָה בְּמַגַּע טְמֵא מֵת עַל יְדֵי מַגַּע הַמֵּת, יָצְאוּ אוֹכָלִים וּמַשְׁקִין, וּכְלִי חֶרֶס שֶׁאֵין לוֹ טׇהֳרָה. כְּלִי חֶרֶשׂ יוֹכִיחַ. שֶׁאֵין בְּמִינוֹ אַב הַטּוּמְאָה, וּמְטַמֵּא אֶת הַתְּרוּמָה כְּשֶׁהוּא רִאשׁוֹן, וְכ"ש שֶׁפּוֹסְלָהּ. אַף אַתָּה אַל תִּתְמַהּ עַל כִּכָּר שֵׁנִי, שֶׁאע"פ שֶׁאֵין בְּמִינוֹ אַב הַטּוּמְאָה — יִפְסוֹל. דְּטַעְמָא לָאו בְּאַב הַטּוּמְאָה תָּלֵי. מַה לִּכְלִי חֶרֶס כו' טְבוּל יוֹם יוֹכִיחַ. שֶׁאֵין כְּלִי שֶׁטֶף הָרָאוּי לִטְבִילָה מְטַמֵּא מֵאֲוִירוֹ — וּפָסֵיל תְּרוּמָה. לֹא רְאִי. טְבוּל יוֹם כִּרְאִי כְּלִי חֶרֶשׂ, לוֹמַר שֶׁטַּעַם פְּסוּל הַתְּרוּמָה תָּלוּי מִשּׁוּם שֶׁמְּטַמֵּא מֵאֲוִירוֹ — דְּהָא טְבוּל יוֹם אֵינוֹ מְטַמֵּא מֵאֲוִירוֹ וּפָסֵיל. וְלֹא רְאִי כְּלִי חֶרֶשׂ לִהְיוֹת אַב הַטּוּמְאָה בְּמִינוֹ כִּרְאִי טְבוּל יוֹם, דְּלֵיכָּא לְמֵימַר טַעְמָא דִּטְבוּל יוֹם דְּפָסֵיל בִּתְרוּמָה מִשּׁוּם דְּמִין אַב הַטּוּמְאָה הוּא — דְּהָא לֵיתָא לְהָא חוּמְרָא בִּכְלִי חֶרֶשׂ, וּפָסֵיל. הַצַּד הַשָּׁוֶה שֶׁבָּהֶן. צָרִיךְ אַתָּה לִמְצוֹא חוֹמֶר שָׁוֶה בִּשְׁנֵיהֶם לִתְלוֹת בּוֹ טַעַם פְּסוּל תְּרוּמָה, וּמַהוּ צַד הַשָּׁוֶה שֶׁבָּהֶן — שֶׁמְּטַמְּאִין; טְבוּל יוֹם אִיקְרֵי טָמֵא, דִּכְתִיב (ויקרא כב): "וּבָא הַשֶּׁמֶשׁ וְטָהֵר" מִכְּלָל דְּעַד הַשְׁתָּא טָמֵא, וּכְלִי חֶרֶשׂ כְּתִיב (שם יא): "תַּנּוּר וְכִירַיִם יוּתָּץ טְמֵאִים הֵם", וּפוֹסְלִין בִּתְרוּמָה. וְכ"ש כִּכָּר שֵׁנִי דְּפָסֵיל טְפֵי מִטְּבוּל יוֹם, שֶׁהוּא טָמֵא וְאָסוּר בְּחוּלִּין, שֶׁיִּפְסוֹל בִּתְרוּמָה: וּבְכׇל הַסְּפָרִים כְּתִיב: הַצַּד הַשָּׁוֶה שֶׁבָּהֶן שֶׁמּוּתָּר בְּחוּלִּין וּפוֹסֵל בִּתְרוּמָה. וּלְהַךְ לִישָּׁנָא אֵין אָדָם יָכוֹל לְפָרֵשׁ אֵיזֶהוּ כְּלִי חֶרֶשׂ שֶׁמּוּתָּר בְּחוּלִּין (ד) וּפְסוּלִין בִּתְרוּמָה. וּבְדוֹחַק גָּדוֹל יֵשׁ לְפָרֵשׁ: כְּלִי חֶרֶשׂ הַמּוּקָּף צָמִיד פָּתִיל, שֶׁמַּצִּיל עַל חוּלִּין שֶׁבְּתוֹכוֹ וְאֵין מַצִּיל עַל הַתְּרוּמָה שֶׁבְּתוֹכוֹ. וְהַרְבֵּה גִּמְגּוּמִין וּתְשׁוּבוֹת וּבִיטּוּל שִׁיטַת הַגְּמָרָא יֵשׁ בַּדָּבָר; חֲדָא — דְּלָא אַשְׁכְּחַן דְּאֵינוֹ מַצִּיל בִּתְרוּמָה, דְּבַחֲגִיגָה (דף כה.) אָמַר: אֵין חַטָּאת נִיצֶּלֶת בְּצָמִיד פָּתִיל, אֲבָל תְּרוּמָה — לָא תְּנַן בָּהּ. וְעוֹד: אֵין זֶה פּוֹסֵל בִּתְרוּמָה, דְּהָא לָא פָּסֵיל מִידֵי, אֶלָּא אֵינוֹ מָגֵן, וּמֵאֵלֶיהָ הִיא נִטְמֵאת מֵאֹהֶל הַמֵּת. וְעוֹד: כׇּל "הַצַּד הַשָּׁוֶה" שֶׁבַּגְּמָרָא שֶׁבָּא לִלְמוֹד חוֹמֶר — צָרִיךְ שֶׁיְּהֵא חָמוּר, וְזֶה קַל, דְּקָאָמַר: הַצַּד הַשָּׁוֶה שֶׁבָּהֶן — שֶׁמּוּתָּרִין בְּחוּלִּין, וְאֵין זוֹ שִׁיטָה בְּכׇל הַגְּמָרָא. וְלָלָשׁוֹן שֶׁפֵּירַשְׁתִּי אַל תְּשִׁיבֵנִי: מַה שֶּׁאוֹמֵר כְּלִי חֶרֶשׂ יוֹכִיחַ — שֶׁהָיָה לוֹ לְהָבִיא הוֹכָחָה בַּדָּבָר הַדּוֹמֶה לִטְבוּל יוֹם, שֶׁאע"פ שֶׁטָּהוֹר לְחוּלִּין פָּסוּל לִתְרוּמָה. שֶׁאֵין זוֹ תְּשׁוּבָה, דְּאֵין צָרִיךְ הוֹכָחָה אֶלָּא לִסְתּוֹר תְּשׁוּבָתוֹ שֶׁתּוֹלֶה טַעַם הַחוּמְרָא דִּפְסוּל תְּרוּמָה מִפְּנֵי שֶׁהוּא אַב הַטּוּמְאָה, וְקָא מַהֲדַר לֵיהּ: כְּלִי חֶרֶשׂ יוֹכִיחַ שֶׁאֵין בּוֹ חוֹמֶר זֶה, וּפוֹסֵל. וְכֵן שִׁיטַת רוֹב הַדִּינִין, כִּי הַהוּא דְּ"כׇל הַבָּשָׂר" (חולין דף קטו:): מִנַּיִן לְבָשָׂר בְּחָלָב שֶׁאָסוּר בַּהֲנָאָה — קַל וָחוֹמֶר: וּמָה עׇרְלָה שֶׁלֹּא נֶעֶבְדָה בָּהּ עֲבֵירָה — אֲסוּרָה בַּהֲנָאָה, בָּשָׂר בְּחָלָב שֶׁנֶּעֶבְדָה בּוֹ עֲבֵירָה בְּבִישּׁוּלוֹ — אֵינוֹ דִּין שֶׁאָסוּר בַּהֲנָאָה? מַה לְּעׇרְלָה שֶׁכֵּן לֹא הָיְתָה לָהּ שְׁעַת הַכּוֹשֶׁר — חָמֵץ בְּפֶסַח יוֹכִיחַ. מַה לְּחָמֵץ שֶׁבּוֹ כָּרֵת — כִּלְאֵי הַכֶּרֶם יוֹכִיחַ. וְהָא כִּלְאֵי הַכֶּרֶם נֶעֶבְדָה בּוֹ עֲבֵירָה בִּזְרִיעָתָ', וְחָמֵץ בְּפֶסַח נַמִי עָבַר בְּ"בַל יֵרָאֶה" וְלָא דָּמוּ לְעׇרְלָה בְּקוּלָּא דִּידַהּ, וְקָא הָוְיָא הוֹכָחָה. צַד חָמוּר. טְבוּל יוֹם יֵשׁ בְּמִינוֹ אַב הַטּוּמְאָה, כְּלִי חֶרֶשׂ מְטַמֵּא מֵאֲוִירוֹ. וְרַבִּי יוֹחָנָן צַד חָמוּר לָא פָּרֵיךְ. לָא חָשֵׁיב לֵיהּ פִּירְכָא, הוֹאִיל וְאֵין חוֹמֶר שֶׁבִּשְׁנֵיהֶם שָׁוֶה. מִנַּיִן לָרְבִיעִי בַּקּוֹדֶשׁ שֶׁהוּא פָּסוּל. וְלָא אָמְרִינַן טָהוֹר הוּא כִּבִתְרוּמָה. מְחוּסַּר כִּפּוּרִים. בְּטוּמְאוֹת הַצְּרִיכוֹת קׇרְבָּן, כְּגוֹן זָב וְזָבָה וְיוֹלֶדֶת וּמְצוֹרָע. שֶׁמּוּתָּר בִּתְרוּמָה פָּסוּל בַּקּוֹדֶשׁ. בִּיבָמוֹת יָלְפִינַן לָהּ בְּפֶרֶק "הֶעָרֵל" (דף עד:). שְׁלִישִׁי שֶׁפָּסוּל בִּתְרוּמָה. כִּדְיָלְפִינַן לְעֵיל מִטְּבוּל יוֹם. דִּין הוּא שֶׁיֵּעָשֶׂה רְבִיעִי בַּקּוֹדֶשׁ. וְלָא תֵּימָא: דַּיּוֹ לַבָּא מִן הַדִּין לִהְיוֹת כַּנִּדּוֹן, וְנֵימָא הָכִי: שְׁלִישִׁי שֶׁפָּסוּל בִּתְרוּמָה דַּיּוֹ הוּא שֶׁיְּהֵא פָּסוּל לְקוֹדֶשׁ — דְּאִם כֵּן בָּטֵיל לֵיהּ הַאי קַל וָחוֹמֶר, דִּשְׁלִישִׁי בַּקּוֹדֶשׁ לָא אִיצְטְרִיךְ. דְּלָא מִיבַּעְיָא, דְּכִי הֵיכִי דְּבִתְרוּמָה אַיְיתִינֵיהּ בְּקַל וָחוֹמֶר מִטְּבוּל יוֹם — הָכִי נַמִי אָתֵי קוֹדֶשׁ בְּהַהוּא קַל וָחוֹמֶר, אֶלָּא אֲפִילּוּ מִן הַתּוֹרָה לְמַדְנוּהוּ. וְהַיְינוּ דְּקָאָמַר: לָמַדְנוּ שְׁלִישִׁי לְקוֹדֶשׁ מִן הַתּוֹרָה. הִילְכָּךְ אִי אָמְרִינַן "דַּיּוֹ" — אִיפְרַךְ לֵיהּ ק"ו כו'. מִי לָא עָסְקִינַן. מִי לָא מָצֵינַן לְמִישְׁמַע מִינַּהּ דַּאֲפִי' נָגַע בַּשֵּׁנִי נַמִי קָאָמַר "לֹא יֵאָכֵל". דְּהָא "בְּכׇל טָמֵא" כְּתִיב, וְשֵׁנִי אִיקְרֵי טָמֵא, דִּכְתִיב: "כֹּל אֲשֶׁר בְּתוֹכוֹ יִטְמָא" וְהַאי בִּבְשַׂר שְׁלָמִים כְּתִיב, דְּקֹדֶשׁ נִינְהוּ. טַעַם בְּרִיבִּי. טַעֲמוֹ שֶׁל ר' יוֹסֵי, שֶׁהוּא חָכָם וּגְדוֹל הַדּוֹר, אֵינִי יוֹדֵעַ מַהוּ, שֶׁלָּמַד רְבִיעִי בַּקּוֹדֶשׁ. שֶׁהֲרֵי מִקַּל וָחוֹמֶר זֶה תְּשׁוּבָתוֹ בְּצִדּוֹ. אוֹכֶל הַבָּא מֵחֲמַת טְבוּל יוֹם. שֶׁנָּגַע בִּטְבוּל יוֹם, וְהוּא שֶׁל קֹדֶשׁ אוֹ שֶׁל תְּרוּמָה — יוֹכִיחַ, שֶׁפָּסוּל בִּתְרוּמָה מִן הַתּוֹרָה, כִּדְפְרִישִׁית לְעֵיל, דִּבְכֵלִים נַמִי כְּתִיב "הָעֶרֶב שֶׁמֶשׁ" לְגַבֵּי תְרוּמָה, וְאֵינוֹ אֶלָּא לִנְגִיעָה. וְאֵינוֹ עוֹשֶׂה רְבִיעִי בַּקּוֹדֶשׁ, לְרַבָּנַן דִּפְלִיגִי עֲלֵיהּ דְּאַבָּא שָׁאוּל, וְאָמְרוּ: טְבוּל יוֹם פּוֹסֵל בַּקּוֹדֶשׁ וְאֵינוֹ מְטַמֵּא לִפְסוֹל אֶת מִי שֶׁיַּחֲזוֹר וְיִגַּע בּוֹ. וְקָא סָלְקָא דַּעְתָּא דְּר' יוֹסֵי כְּרַבָּנַן סְבִירָא לֵיהּ. הִילְכָּךְ תְּשׁוּבָתוֹ בְּצִדּוֹ: דְּאִ"כ הָכִי נַמִי נִדְרַשׁ לְהַאי ק"ו שֶׁיִּפְסוֹל אוֹכֶל הַבָּא מֵחֲמַת טְבוּל יוֹם אֶת הַקּוֹדֶשׁ: וּמַה מְּחוּסַּר כִּפּוּרִים שֶׁמּוּתָּר בִּתְרוּמָה פָּסוּל בַּקּוֹדֶשׁ, אוֹכֶל הַנּוֹגֵעַ בִּטְבוּל יוֹם, שֶׁפָּסוּל בִּתְרוּמָה — (ה) דִּין הוּא שֶׁיֵּעָשֶׂה רְבִיעִי בַּקּוֹדֶשׁ. טְבוּל יוֹם תְּחִילָּה לְקוֹדֶשׁ. מַעֲלָה עָשׂוּ בַּקּוֹדֶשׁ לִהְיוֹת טְבוּל יוֹם אֶצְלוֹ כָּרִאשׁוֹן לְטוּמְאָה, וִיטַמֵּא שְׁנַיִ' בַּקּוֹדֶשׁ זֶה מִזֶּה, שֶׁאוֹכֶל שֶׁנּוֹגֵעַ בִּטְבוּל יוֹם נַעֲשֶׂה שֵׁנִי, וְעוֹשֶׂה אֶת חֲבֵירוֹ שְׁלִישִׁי, וּשְׁנֵיהֶם קְרוּיִין טְמֵאִין — שֶׁמְּקַלְקְלִין אֶת אֲחֵרִים. וְהַשְּׁלִישִׁי פּוֹסֵל אֶת הָרְבִיעִי לִהְיוֹת הוּא עַצְמוֹ פָּסוּל, אֲבָל לֹא יִפְסוֹל אֶת אֲחֵרִים בְּמַגָּעוֹ. רַבִּי מֵאִיר אוֹמֵר מְטַמֵּא אֶחָד וּפוֹסֵל אֶחָד. הֲרֵי הוּא כִּשְׁאָר שֵׁנִי שֶׁפּוֹסֵל אֶת הַתְּרוּמָה וְהַנּוֹגֵעַ בּוֹ פּוֹסֵל אֶת הַקּוֹדֶשׁ. כָּךְ טְבוּל יוֹם הַפּוֹסֵל אֶת הַתְּרוּמָה — הַנּוֹגֵעַ בּוֹ טָמֵא לְקוֹדֶשׁ, וְלִפְסוֹל עוֹד אֶחָד. כָּךְ פּוֹסֵל כו'. וְאֵין הַנּוֹגֵעַ בִּטְבוּל יוֹם פּוֹסֵל אֶת הַקּוֹדֶשׁ, אֶלָּא הוּא עַצְמוֹ פָּסוּל. מִמַּאי דְּרַבִּי יוֹסֵי כְּרַבָּנַן סְבִירָא לֵיהּ. דְּתֶהֱוֵי תְּשׁוּבָה בְּצִדּוֹ, דִּילְמָא כְּאַבָּא שָׁאוּל סְבִירָא לֵיהּ? וְהוּא הַדִּין דַּהֲוָה מָצֵי רַב פַּפָּא לְמֵימַר: דִּילְמָא כְּר' מֵאִיר סְבִירָא לֵיהּ, וְאֵין כָּאן עוֹד תְּשׁוּבָה, דְּהָא עָבֵיד רְבִיעִי. אֶלָּא רְבוּתָא נָקַט, כְּלוֹמַר: מַאן לֵימָא לָן דְּלָא מַחְמִיר כְּאַבָּא שָׁאוּל? דִּילְמָא כְּוָותֵיהּ סְבִירָא לֵיהּ, דְּאוֹכֶל הַבָּא מֵחֲמַת טְבוּל יוֹם, אִם שֶׁל קוֹדֶשׁ הוּא — מְטַמֵּא אֶחָד וּפוֹסֵל אֶחָד, דְּהַהוּא דְּנָגַע בֵּיהּ פָּסֵיל לֵיהּ דְּאוֹרַיְיתָא. וַאֲפִילּוּ הָוֵי קַמָּא תְּרוּמָה — פָּחוּל לְקוֹדֶשׁ מִקַּל וָחוֹמֶר מִמְּחוּסַּר כִּפּוּרִים, כִּדְדָרֵישׁ רַבִּי יוֹסֵי לְעֵיל, וְדָרֵישׁ לֵיהּ נַמִי הָכָא: וּמַה מְּחוּסַּר כִּפּוּרִים שֶׁמּוּתָּר בִּתְרוּמָה פָּסוּל לְקוֹדֶשׁ, אוֹכֶל תְּרוּמָה הַבָּא מֵחֲמַת טְבוּל יוֹם שֶׁפָּסוּל בִּתְרוּמָה — אֵינוֹ דִּין הוּא שֶׁיֵּעָשֶׂה רְבִיעִי בַּקֹּדֶשׁ. (ו) וְהֵיכָא דַּהֲוָה לֵיהּ דְּקוֹדֶשׁ עֲבוּד רַבָּנַן מַעֲלָה שֶׁיְּטַמֵּא אֶחָד וְיִפְסוֹל אֶחָד. דְּאִי סָלְקָא דַּעְתָּךְ כְּאַבָּא שָׁאוּל סְבִירָא לֵיהּ. (ז) מִקַּל וָחוֹמֶר דִּמְחוּסַּר כִּפּוּרִים פָּסֵיל לְקַמָּא, וּמִמַּעֲלָה דְּרַבָּנַן מְטַמֵּא לֵיהּ. כֵּיוָן דְּמִדְּאוֹרַיְיתָא פָּסֵיל לֵיהּ לְהַהוּא דְּנָגַע בֵּיהּ — לַיְיתֵיהּ לָרְבִיעִי בַּקּוֹדֶשׁ מֵאוֹכֶל הַבָּא מֵחֲמַת טְבוּל יוֹם. וּמָה אוֹכֶל הַבָּא מֵחֲמַת טְבוּל יוֹם דִּטְבוּל יוֹם. שֶׁבָּא מִכֹּחוֹ שָׁרֵי בְּחוּלִּין — עוֹשֶׂה רְבִיעִי בַּקּוֹדֶשׁ, כְּלוֹמַר: פּוֹסֵל אֶת הַקּוֹדֶשׁ מִקַּל וָחוֹמֶר מִמְּחוּסַּר כִּפּוּרִים. שְׁלִישִׁי

ויקרא ז

תוספות שאנץ

הנוגע בשרץ הקל אינו דין שלא יטעון שבירה ת"ל אותו א"כ למה נאמר ואותו תשבורו מלמד שאין לו טהרה במקוה אלא שוברו. ד"א אותו תשבורו אותו אתה שובר לטהרתו [וכו']. ואל תתמה על זה דדרשי' דאינו טעון שבירה מק"ו אע"ג דאיכא מיעוט חוזר ודורש ק"ו ומוקי למיעוט בדרשא אחריתי וגם בכמה מקומות בתלמוד מצינו כמו כן וצא ולמד מברייתא שבצדה בתו"כ תנור וכירים יותץ יכול יתצם בודאי ת"ל וטמאים יהיו לכם דמקיימין אותן בטומאה: מה להצד השוה שבהן שכן יש בהן צד חמור. טבול יום יש במינו אב הטומאה. כלי חרס שמטמא מאוירו. וק' ומה פירכא היא זו הלא אין לך דין שבתלמוד שלא נוכל להקשות בו שיש בו צד חמור. וכי האי גונא אמרי' באלו נערות אלמא קסבר עולא כל היכא דאיכא ממון ומלקות ממונא משלם מילקא לא לקיא וקאמר דגמרי' מחובל בחברו ומעדים זוממים דעושה שם הצד השוה ופריך מה להצד השוה שכן יש בהן צד חמור וכן במכות [ד:] פרי' [הכי] ומאי פירכא היא זו. ואו' ר"י דלא פרי' ליה אלא במקום שהצד [חמור] הן משונין א). כמו הכא שהטבול יום הוי במינו אב הטומאה וכן כלי חרס אין לך שום דבר שמטמא מאוירו אלא כלי חרס. וכן בכתובות בעדים זוממים דאינם צריכין [התראה] מה שאין כן בשאר [דברים] וכן בחובל בחבירו דחייב בה' דברים מה שאין כן בשאר מזיקין וכן במכות וכי האי גונא בשילהי פ' ד' מיתות דפרי' מה להצד השוה שבהן שכן משונין: מנין לרביעי בקדש שהוא פסול. ולא אמרי' טהור [הוא] כבתרומה. ומה מחוסר הצריכות קרבן כגון זב וזבה ויולדת ומצורע שמותר בתרומה ופסול בקדשים. פ' הערל. ג' כדילפי' לעיל מק"ו דטבול יום דין הוא שיעשה רביעי בקדש וליכא למימר דיו לבא מן הדין להיות כנדון והכי ג' דפסול בתרומה דיו הוא שיהא פסול בקדש דא"כ בטל ק"ו דלג' בקדש לא איצטריך דכי היכי דאייתניה בתרומה בק"ו דטבול יום אתי נמי קדש בההיא ק"ו אלא אפי' מן התורה קאמר למדנו ג' לקדש מן התורה הילכך אי אמרי' דיו מפרי' הק"ו. ל"ה. ומקשי התוספות לקדש מק"ו דטבול יום ומה טבול יום שמותר בחולין פוסל בקדש שני שפוסל בחולין אינו דין בקדש וכי תימא דדייקי' מן הק"ו (הג') [דשני] לג' אם אינו ענין לג' דהא ידעינן ליה

תוספות שאנץ

מקרא דוהבשר אשר יגע בכל טמא מי לא עסקי' (דרביעי) [דנגע] בשני תנהו ענין לרביעי בקדש. ונראה דאין זה קושיא דלעולם הוה מוקמי' הק"ו אג'. וכי תימא הא ידעי' ליה מקרא דוהבשר [י"ל] דמילתא דאתיא בק"ו טרח וכתב לה קרא. ומהאי טעמא ניחא דליכא להקשות [ל"ל] קרא דוהבשר ונילף ג' בקדש מק"ו דטבול יום ומה טבול יום שמותר בחולין פסול בקדש שני שפסול בחולין דין הוא שיעשה ג' בקדש וד' בקדש מק"ו דמחוסר כפורים כדאמר ולאו מילתא היא כדפרי' דמלתא דאתי בק"ו טרח וכתב לה קרא. וג' דלפ"ה ניחא הכל: מי לא עסקי' דנגע בשני. פ"ה דנפקא לן מדכתיב בכל טמא ושני איקרי טמא דכתיב כל אשר בתוכו יטמא: טעם בריבי. טעמו של ר' יוסי שהיה חכם וגדול הדור. איני יודע מה הוא שלמד רביעי בקדש מק"ו זה שהרי אוכל הבא מחמת טבול יום והוא דקדש או דתרומה יוכיחו שפסול בתרומה מן התורה כדפי' לעיל דבכלים נמי בעי הערב השמש ואינה אלא לנגיעה ואינו עושה רביעי בקדש לרבנן דפליגי עליה דאבא שאול ואמרו טבול יום פוסל את הקדש ואינו מטמאו לפסול את מי שיחזור ויגע. וס"ד דר' יוסי כרבנן סבירא ליה הילכך תשובתו בצדו דא"כ ה"נ נדרשי' להאי ק"ו שיפסול אוכל הבא מחמת טבול יום את הקדש ומה מחוסר כפורים שמותר בתרומה פוסל הקדש אוכל הנוגע בטבול יום שפסול שיעשה רביעי בקדש. כל"ה. טבול יום תחלה לקדש מעלה עשו בקדש להיות טבול יום אצלו כראשון שנים בקדש זה מזה האוכל שנגע בטבול יום יטמא חברו הנוגע בו ושניהם קרויין טמאים שמקלקלים את אחרים והג' פוסל את הד' להיות הוא עצמו פסול אבל לא יפסול אחרים במגעו. ר' מאיר אומר מטמא אחד ופוסל אחד הרי הוא כשאר שני שפוסל התרומה והנוגע בו פוסל הקדש כך טבול יום הפוסל בתרומה לקדש לפסול עוד אחד: כך פוסל. ואין הנוגע בטבול יום פוסל הקדש אלא הוא עצמו פסול. ממאי דר' יוסי כרבנן סבירא ליה דתתהוי תשובתו בצדו דילמא כאבא שאול סבירא ליה וה"ה דהוה מצי לרב פפא למימר סבירא ליה ואין כאן עוד תשובה דהא עביד רביעי אלא רבותא נקט כלומר מאן לימ' לן שאול דילמא כותיה סבירא ליה דאוכל הבא מחמת טבול יום אם של קדש הוא מטמא אחד ופוסל אחד דההוא דנגע ביה הוה פסיל ליה דאורייתא ואפי' הוי קמא תרומה פסול לקדש מק"ו ממחוסר

יב א ב מיי' פי"א מהל' אבות הטומאה הל"ד:
יג ג מיי' שם פ"ו הל"ג סמג עשין רמז:
פסחים יח. חגיגה כד. [תוספתא חגיגה פ"ג]
[פסחים עז. כתובות לב. מכות ד: ע' תוס' כתובות לב. ד"ה שכן וכו' שהאריכו בסוגיא דהכא]
מעילה ח. ע"ש [נדה עח:]

א) וכ"ה התוס' כתובות לב. ד"ה שכן בשם ר"י.

הגהות הב"ח (א) גמ' שכן יש בהם לג. נ"ב עיין בתוספות פרק אלו נערות דף לב ד"ה שכן יש: (ב) רש"י ד"ה מטבול וכו' לטומאה הוא ולא אב: (ג) ד"ה שכן וכו' טהרה במקוה נעשה אב וכו' שאין להן טהרה במקוה הס"ד: (ד) ד"ה ובכלל הספרים וכו' ופסול בתרומה ובדוחק וכו' מה לחמץ בפסח שכן יש בו כרת: (ה) ד"ה אוכל הבא וכו' קודש הטבול הוא: (ו) ד"ה ממאי וכו' בתרומה לא יהא הוא: (ז) ד"ה דאי סלקא וכו' דמק"ו דמחוסר:

שְׁלִישִׁי הַבָּא מֵחֲמַת שֵׁנִי, דְּשֵׁנִי גּוּפֵיהּ אָסוּר בְּחוּלִּין – אֵינוֹ דִּין שֶׁעוֹשֶׂה רְבִיעִי בַּקּוֹדֶשׁ? וְכִי תֵּימָא, מִשּׁוּם דְּאִיכָּא לְמִיפְרַךְ: מַה לִּטְבוּל יוֹם שֶׁכֵּן אַב הַטּוּמְאָה – הָא אַיְיתִינָהּ מִמְּחוּסַּר כִּיפּוּרִים, וְלָא פַּרְכֵיהּ. אָמַר רַב אַסִי אָמַר רַב, וְאָמְרִי לָהּ אָמַר רַבָּה בֶּן אִיסִי אָמַר רַב: ר"מ וְר' יוֹסֵי וְר' יְהוֹשֻׁעַ וְר' אֶלְעָזָר וְר' אֱלִיעֶזֶר כּוּלְּהוּ סְבִירָא לְהוּ [א]דְּאֵין שֵׁנִי עוֹשֶׂה שְׁלִישִׁי בְּחוּלִּין. ר"מ – *דִּתְנַן: [ב]כָּל הַטָּעוּן בִּיאַת מַיִם מִדִּבְרֵי סוֹפְרִים – מְטַמֵּא אֶת הַקּוֹדֶשׁ, וּפוֹסֵל אֶת הַתְּרוּמָה, וּמוּתָּר בְּחוּלִּין וּבְמַעֲשֵׂר, דִּבְרֵי ר"מ, וַחֲכָמִים [ג]אוֹסְרִין בְּמַעֲשֵׂר. ר' יוֹסֵי – הָא דַּאֲמָרַן, דְּאִם אִיתֵיהּ – לַיְיתֵיהּ לָרְבִיעִי בִּתְרוּמָה וַחֲמִישִׁי בַּקּוֹדֶשׁ. רַבִּי יְהוֹשֻׁעַ – דִּתְנַן, *ר"א אוֹמֵר: הָאוֹכֵל אוֹכֶל רִאשׁוֹן – רִאשׁוֹן, שֵׁנִי – שֵׁנִי, שְׁלִישִׁי – שְׁלִישִׁי. רַבִּי יְהוֹשֻׁעַ אוֹמֵר: [ד]הָאוֹכֵל אוֹכֶל רִאשׁוֹן וְאוֹכֶל שֵׁנִי – שֵׁנִי, [ה]שְׁלִישִׁי – שֵׁנִי בַּקּוֹדֶשׁ וְאֵין שֵׁנִי בִּתְרוּמָה, [ו]בְּחוּלִּין שֶׁנַּעֲשׂוּ עַל טָהֳרַת תְּרוּמָה. עַל טָהֳרַת הַתְּרוּמָה – אִין, עַל טָהֳרַת הַקּוֹדֶשׁ – [ז]לָא. אַלְמָא קָסָבַר: אֵין שֵׁנִי עוֹשֶׂה שְׁלִישִׁי בְּחוּלִּין. ר"א (א) – דְּתַנְיָא, ר' אֶלְעָזָר אוֹמֵר: שְׁלָשְׁתָּן שָׁוִין, הָרִאשׁוֹן שֶׁבַּקּוֹדֶשׁ וְשֶׁבַּחוּלִּין וְשֶׁבַּתְּרוּמָה – מְטַמֵּא שְׁנַיִם וּפוֹסֵל אֶחָד בַּקּוֹדֶשׁ, מְטַמֵּא אֶחָד וּפוֹסֵל אֶחָד בִּתְרוּמָה, וּפוֹסֵל אֶחָד בְּחוּלִּין. ר' אֱלִיעֶזֶר – דִּתְנַן, *ר"א אוֹמֵר: חַלָּה נִיטֶּלֶת מִן הַטְּהוֹרָה עַל הַטְּמֵאָה. [ח]כֵּיצַד? שְׁתֵּי עִיסּוֹת אַחַת טְהוֹרָה וְאַחַת טְמֵאָה, נוֹטֵל כְּדֵי חַלָּה מֵעִיסָּה שֶׁלֹּא הוּרְמָה חַלָּתָהּ, וְנוֹתֵן פָּחוֹת מִכַּבֵּיצָה בְּאֶמְצַע, כְּדֵי לִיטּוֹל מִן הַמּוּקָּף. וַחֲכָמִים

רש"י

שְׁלִישִׁי הַבָּא מֵחֲמַת שֵׁנִי כו'. דְּשָׁמְעִינַן מִינֵּיהּ תַּרְתֵּי; ש"מ: אוֹכֶל הַבָּא מֵחֲמַת טְבוּל יוֹם דִּסְבִירָא לֵיהּ כְּאַבָּא שָׁאוּל, וש"מ: שְׁלִישִׁי הַבָּא מֵחֲמַת שֵׁנִי נִהְיֵי דַּחֲמִישִׁי בַּקֹּדֶשׁ לֹא אָמַר דְּנַיְיתֵי מִינָּהּ, כִּדְקָעָבֵיד בִּטְבוּל יוֹם, דְּהָתָם מַעֲלָה דְּרַבָּנַן הִיא, וּבְקוֹדֶשׁ מִקּוֹדֶשׁ מַיְירֵי, וְרַבִּי יוֹסֵי מִדְּאוֹרַיְיתָא קָאָמַר, אֲבָל רְבִיעִי מִיהָא מַיְיתֵי מִינָּהּ. וְכ"ת כו' הָא אַיְיתִינָהּ. ר' יוֹסֵי מִק"ו מִמְּחוּסַּר כִּיפּוּרִים, דְּאִיכָּא לְמִיפְרַךְ נַמִי: מַה לִּמְחוּסַּר כִּיפּוּרִים – שֶׁכֵּן אַב הַטּוּמְאָה, וְלָא פָּרֵיךְ. דְּלָא חֲשִׁיב לֵיהּ ר' יוֹסֵי פִּירְכָא, דְּהַשְׁתָּא דְּטָבַל לָהּ אָזְלָה לָהּ הַהִיא טוּמְאָה. כָּל הַטָּעוּן בִּיאַת מַיִם מִדִּבְרֵי סוֹפְרִים. כָּל שֶׁהוּא טָהוֹר מִן הַתּוֹרָה, וַחֲכָמִים הִזְקִיקוּהוּ לָבֹא בַּמַּיִם וְלִיטָּהֵר, כְּגוֹן הַבָּא רֹאשׁוֹ וְרוּבּוֹ בַּמַּיִם שְׁאוּבִין, וְהָאוֹכֵל חֲצִי פְּרָס אוֹכָלִין טְמֵאִין, וְהַיָּדַיִם שֶׁהִצְרִיכוּם טְבִילָה – כּוּלָּם בְּתוֹרַת שְׁנַיִם הַטְּעִינוּם. מְטַמְּאִין אֶת הַקֹּדֶשׁ. לִהְיוֹת שְׁלִישִׁי וְיַעֲשֶׂה רְבִיעִי, וּפוֹסְלִין אֶת הַתְּרוּמָה. וַחֲכָמִים אוֹסְרִין בְּמַעֲשֵׂר. בַּאֲכִילָה, אֲבָל נְגִיעָה שָׁרֵי. וְחוּלִּין אַף לֶאֱכוֹל. וְהָכִי אָמַר בַּחֲגִיגָה (דף יח:). וְהוּא הַדִּין נַמִי דְּלְרַבָּנַן אֵין שֵׁנִי עוֹשֶׂה שְׁלִישִׁי בְּחוּלִּין, וְהַאי דְּלָא חֲשִׁיב לְהוּ – לְפִי שֶׁלֹּא נִתְפָּרְשׁוּ שְׁמוֹתָן, וְר"מ וּמַחֲלוֹקְתּוֹ קָאָמַר. דְּאִם אִיתָא. דִּשְׁלִישִׁי בְּחוּלִּין מִן הַתּוֹרָה – לַיְיתֵיהּ רְבִיעִי בִּתְרוּמָה מִק"ו מִטְּבוּל יוֹם, כִּדְאַיְיתֵי לִשְׁלִישִׁי לְעֵיל מִשֵּׁנִי בְּחוּלִּין. וַחֲמִישִׁי בַּקֹּדֶשׁ. מֵרְבִיעִי בִּתְרוּמָה, מִק"ו מִמְּחוּסַּר כִּיפּוּרִים, כִּדְאַיְיתֵי לָרְבִיעִי לְעֵיל מִשְּׁלִישִׁי בִּתְרוּמָה. הָאוֹכֵל אוֹכֶל רִאשׁוֹן. חֲצִי פְּרָס מֵאוֹכֶל רִאשׁוֹן – נַעֲשֶׂה גּוּפוֹ רִאשׁוֹן לְטוּמְאָה מִדְּרַבָּנַן, וְהָאוֹכֵל אוֹכֶל שֵׁנִי – נַעֲשֶׂה גּוּפוֹ שֵׁנִי. וּבִשְׁחִיטַת חוּלִּין מְפָרֵשׁ טַעְמָא שֶׁעוֹשֶׂה אֶת הָאוֹכֵל חָמוּר כַּמַּאֲכָל, בְּ"הַשּׁוֹחֵט" (חולין ד' לג.). רַבִּי יְהוֹשֻׁעַ אוֹמֵר הָאוֹכֵל אוֹכֶל רִאשׁוֹן אוֹ אוֹכֶל אוֹכֶל שֵׁנִי שֵׁנִי. מַאֲכָל רִאשׁוֹן לָא עָבֵיד לֵיהּ רִאשׁוֹן אֶלָּא שֵׁנִי, שֶׁאֵין הָאוֹכֵל חָמוּר כַּמַּאֲכָל. אֲבָל מַאֲכָל שֵׁנִי עוֹשֶׂה אוֹתוֹ שֵׁנִי. וְהָתָם מְפָרֵשׁ טַעְמָא: מָצִינוּ שֶׁהַשֵּׁנִי עוֹשֶׂה שֵׁנִי עַל יְדֵי מַשְׁקִין. שְׁלִישִׁי שֵׁנִי לַקֹּדֶשׁ. הָאוֹכֵל אוֹכֶל שְׁלִישִׁי נַעֲשֶׂה גּוּפוֹ שֵׁנִי לַקֹּדֶשׁ, שֶׁאִם יִגַּע בַּקֹּדֶשׁ – יְטַמְּאֶנּוּ לִפְסוֹל עוֹד אֶחָד. וְהָתָם מְפָרֵשׁ טַעְמָא. וְכָל הָנָךְ טוּמְאוֹת מִדְּרַבָּנַן נִינְהוּ. בְּחוּלִּין שֶׁנַּעֲשׂוּ עַל טָהֳרַת תְּרוּמָה. בְּאֵיזוֹ חוּלִּין אָמְרוּ שֶׁהָאוֹכֵל שְׁלִישִׁי שֶׁלָּהֶן נַעֲשֶׂה שֵׁנִי לַקֹּדֶשׁ – בְּחוּלִּין שֶׁנַּעֲשׂוּ עַל טָהֳרַת תְּרוּמָה. שֶׁבַּעֲלֵיהֶם כֹּהֵן וְרָגִיל בִּתְרוּמָה, וְקִיבֵּל עָלָיו לֶאֱכוֹל חוּלִּין שֶׁלּוֹ בְּטָהֳרַת תְּרוּמָה. כְּדֵי שֶׁיְּהֵא רָגִיל לִתְרוּמוֹתָיו בְּטָהֳרָה (ב) הַזְּקוּקָה לָהֶן. הִילְכָּךְ מַשְׁכַּחַתְּ בְּהוּ שְׁלִישִׁי, דִּבְחוּלִּין אֲחֵרִים לָא מַשְׁכַּחַתְּ שְׁלִישִׁי: ה"ג עַל טָהֳרַת תְּרוּמָה אִין חוּלִּין גְּרֵידֵי לָא. וּמַאן דְּגָרֵיס "עַל טָהֳרַת הַקֹּדֶשׁ לָא", הָכִי מְפָרֵשׁ לָהּ: עַל טָהֳרַת הַקֹּדֶשׁ – לָא, דְּהָווּ לְהוּ חוּלִּין גְּרֵידֵי. שֶׁהַמַּתְפִּיס חוּלִּין לְטָהֳרַת הֶקְדֵּשׁ – בָּטְלָה דַּעְתּוֹ, וְאֵין בִּדְבָרָיו כְּלוּם: שְׁלָשְׁתָּן שָׁוִין. הָנָךְ דִּמְפָרֵשׁ לְהוּ רִאשׁוֹן שֶׁל חוּלִּין וְרִאשׁוֹן שֶׁל תְּרוּמָה וְרִאשׁוֹן שֶׁל קוֹדֶשׁ. מְטַמֵּא שְׁנַיִם וּפוֹסֵל אֶחָד בַּקֹּדֶשׁ. דְּהַיְינוּ רְבִיעִי. מְטַמֵּא אֶחָד וּפוֹסֵל אֶחָד בִּתְרוּמָה. דַּהֲוָה לֵיהּ שְׁלִישִׁי. וּפוֹסֵל אֶחָד בְּחוּלִּין. דַּהֲוָה לֵיהּ שֵׁנִי. וְתַנָּא דִּפְלִיג עֲלֵיהּ סָבַר: רִאשׁוֹן שֶׁל חוּלִּין לָא אָזֵיל בַּקֹּדֶשׁ עַד רְבִיעִי, שֶׁאֵין קֹדֶשׁ בָּא לִידֵי רְבִיעִי אֶלָּא אִם כֵּן הָיָה רִאשׁוֹן שֶׁל קוֹדֶשׁ. וּמִיהוּ, שָׁמְעִינַן מִינָּהּ דְּאֵין שְׁלִישִׁי בְּחוּלִּין. ר"א אוֹמֵר חַלָּה נִיטֶּלֶת מִן הַטְּהוֹרָה עַל הַטְּמֵאָה. רֵישָׁא דְּמַתְנִי' בְּמַסֶּכֶת חַלָּה (פ"ב מ"ז) הָכִי: שִׁיעוּר חַלָּה אֶחָד מִכ"ד. נִטְמְאָה עִיסָּתָהּ, שׁוֹגֶגֶת אוֹ אֲנוּסָה – אֶחָד מִמ"ח, נִטְמֵאת בְּמֵזִיד – אֶחָד מִכ"ד, שֶׁלֹּא יְהֵא חוֹטֵא נִשְׂכָּר. ר"א אוֹמֵר: הֵיכָא דְּנִטְמֵאת מְזִידָה – תָּלוּשׁ אַחֶרֶת בְּטָהֳרָה, וְתִטּוֹל מִן הַטְּהוֹרָה עַל הַטְּמֵאָה. מִשּׁוּם דְּמִצְוָה לִתְרוֹם מִן הַמּוּקָּף, כֵּיצַד תַּעֲשֶׂה שֶׁיְּהֵא מִן הַמּוּקָּף וּטְהוֹרָה? נוֹטֶלֶת כְּדֵי חַלַּת הַטְּמֵאָה מֵעִיסָּה הַטְּהוֹרָה עַד שֶׁלֹּא הוּרְמָה חַלָּתָהּ. דְּאִי הוּרְמָה חַלָּתָהּ דִּטְהוֹרָה – תּוּ לָא מָצֵי לְאַפְרוּשֵׁי מִן הַפָּטוּר עַל הַחִיּוּב, וְלָא חָיֵיל עֲלֵיהּ תּוּ שֵׁם חַלָּה. וְנוֹתֶנֶת פָּחוֹת מִכַּבֵּיצָה בָּאֶמְצַע כְּדֵי לִתְרוֹם מִן הַמּוּקָּף. מוּקָּף לְשׁוֹן מְחוּבָּר וּמְקוֹרָב, כְּמוֹ "אֵין מַקִּיפִין שְׁתֵּי חָבִיּוֹת" בְּמַסֶּכֶת בֵּיצָה (דף לב:). וּמִקְּרָא נָפְקָא לָן: "וַהֲרֵמוֹתֶם מִמֶּנּוּ" – מִן הַמּוּקָּף לוֹ, בְּסִפְרֵי. הִילְכָּךְ צְרִיכָה לְהַקִּיף

תוספות

שלישי הבא מחמת שני וכו'. פירש רש"י: דשמעינן מיניה תרתי; שמעינן מיניה אוכל הבא מחמת טבול יום דסבירא ליה כאבא שאול, ושמעינן מיניה דשלישי הבא מחמת שני וכו'. תימה: כיון דיליף ק"ו לשלישי ממחוסר כיפורים – לאו ממילא שמעינן מיניה דאית ליה כאבא שאול? דבהאי קל וחומר גופיה דמחוסר כיפורים נפקא לן אוכל הבא מחמת טבול יום דעביד רביעי. א"כ אמאי הוי ליה למיתניה לרביעי בקודש מאוכל הבא מחמת טבול יום? וכי לא מייתי ליה שפיר טפי ממחוסר כיפורים גופיה מדהוי מייתי ליה מאוכל הבא מחמת טבול יום דאוכל הבא מחמת טבול יום גופיה לא שמעינן ליה אלא מק"ו דמחוסר כיפורים! ונראה: דאפי' הכי הוי ניחא ליה טפי לעשות שלישי מק"ו ראשון, כגון שלישי הבא מחמת שני, דאלים טפי למיעד רביעי – ממאי דמייתי ליה ממחוסר כיפורים, שצריך למייתי שלישי גופיה (למייתי) מק"ו דטבול יום דפסול בתרומה. אע"ג דבין כך ובין כך הוי ק"ו בן ק"ו – מיהו לאלומי כח שלישי עדיף ליה טפי.

הא אייתינה ממחוסר כיפורים ולא פרכינן. רש"י פי': משום דכיון דטבל אזלה ליה ההיא טומאה. ולא ידענא אמאי פי' הכי, הא ע"כ אית לן למימר דר' יוסי סבירא ליה כרבן יוחנן בן זכאי, דמייתי שלישי בתרומה ב"מה הלד". דאי לא תימא הכי – שלישי מנא ליה? ובאותו "מה הלד" גופיה מייתי רבי יוסי רביעי ממחוסר כיפורים ומכלי חרס, ומשום הכי לא פריך. ספר הישר: מסיק בפ"ק דשבת (דף יד.): זימנין דאכיל אוכלין טמאין וכו'. הקשה ריב"א הלוי ז"ל: אלמא דאוכלין טמאין פוסלין את הגויה בכבילה, דאפי' כבילה מטמאין למשקין דתרומה דשדי לפומיה. והתנן בפרק "כיצד משתתפין" (עירובין דף פג:): חציה לבית המנוגע, וחצי חציה לפסול את הגויה – דהיינו שני בילים! ותירץ מורי: אין דרך בני אדם לשתות אלא לאחר אכילת שני בילים, וקודם לכן מילתא דלא שכיחא היא. ואין נראה לר"י תירוץ זה; חדא – שאפילו בלשון לא דקדק, שבכאן הוא אמר "לפסול את הגויה", ולשם הוא אומר "אלו פוסלין בתרומה", משמע אפילו במגע, ובכאן לא גזרו אלא טומאת פנים אטו טומאת חוץ. ועוד: היאך אנו אומרים ביומא פרק אחרון (דף פ:), אמר רב פפא: הנח לטומאת גויה דלאו דאורייתא. ומותיב: מי אמר רב פפא הכי? והכתיב: "לא תטמאו בהם" ואמר רב פפא: מכאן לטומאת גויה דאורייתא! ומתרץ: מדרבנן, וקרא אסמכתא בעלמא. ואם היה מגזרת י"ח דבר, וכי בזה היה טועה בעל הגמרא שהם דאורייתא? והלא פשט איסורם בכל העולם! אלא ודאי נראה דתרי גזירות הוו, חדא גזירת טומאת פנים אטו טומאת חוץ, דהיינו פסול גויה. דהרואה סבר דמותר להגיע טומאה למשקין, דהא זה כשאכל תרומה ואח"כ שותה משקין טמאים, נוגעין זה בזה בתוך מעיו ולא חיישינן – להכי נמי לא נחוש אפי' בחוץ – להכי גזרו. ודוקא בשני בילים, אבל בכבילה – לא. שהרי האוכל כבילה מתעכל בתוך מעיו ונשאר בין שיניו, ולכשיהיה בבני מעיו יפחת הרבה מכבילה. ואין אדם טועה, שאפילו אוכל אוכלין טמאין בכבילה ושותה משקין דתרומה לא יאמר: א"כ, טהורין הן בכבילה אפי' בחוץ – דהא בפנים לא היה כבילה, שהרי נתעכל האוכל ולא היה כשיעור לטמא. ודוקא באוכלין מצריך יותר מכשיעור משום דמתעכל, אבל משקין פסלי גויה בכדי רביעית, דאין דרך משקה להתעכל בתוך מעיו. וא"ת: היה להן להוסיף יותר מעט! מ"מ, כיון דנחית לשיעוריה – העמיד אותה על שני בילים שהוא שיעור ידוע. וגזירה אחרת אותה של שבת, שגזרו בכבילה אף על מגע. ואותה של שחיטת חולין (דף לד.) דאמר עולא: האוכל אוכל שלישי של חולין שנעשו על טהרת תרומה נפסל גופו מלאכול בתרומה, איני יודע לפרש אם היה מאותה גזירה ראשונה – מ"מ למה גזרו? אי משום טומאת חוץ – הלא אפילו אם היה נוגע בשלישי שבתרומה לא היה נפסל, שאין שלישי עושה רביעי בתרומה, כדמוכח התם.* דתניא: חולין שנעשו על טהרת הקדש – הרי הוא כחולין, רבי אלעזר ברבי צדוק אומר: הרי הן כטומאה לתרומה, לטמא שנים ולפסול אחד. א"כ אינו רביעי! וא"ת מגזרה שניה, ומשום משקין, דאכיל אוכלין טמאין ושתה משקין דתרומה – אם כן למה נפסל גופו? יהי' טמא אפי' במגע! וא"ת גזרה שלישית היא – מ"מ הטעם לא נודע, אלא א"כ נאמר רבו בגזרות וגזרו גזירה לגזרה. ולפי פירוש הקונטרס שפירש בשחיטת חולין – אינו נראה ואינו מיושב יפה, שמפרש: האוכל אוכל ראשון – זהו חצי פרס. שהרי אנו אומרים: מאי טעמא? דילמא אכיל אוכלין טמאין ושתי משקין דתרומה – וזהו אפילו בכבילה. ע"כ לשון ספר הישר.

מר

עין משפט נר מצוה

יד א מיי' פי"א מהל' אבות הטומאה הלכה ב:

טו ב מיי' שם פט"ז הל' ב ופ"ט הל' א ופ"י הל' ב ועי' בכ"מ ופי"א הל' ב ג ד:

טז ג מיי' פט"ז מהל' טומאת אוכלין הל' ח:

יז ד מיי' פ"ח מהל' שאר אבות הטומאות הלכה י:

יח ה ו ז מיי' שם פי"א הלכה יב:

יט ח מיי' פ"ה מהל' בכורים הל' יד ופ"ז שם הל' יב ועי' בכ"מ טוש"ע י"ד סימן שכג:

מסורת הש"ס

חגיגה יח: חולין לג: פרה פי"א מ"ה

טהרות פ"ב מ"ב שבת יד. חולין לג:

חלה פ"ב מ"ח

[חגיגה דף כ. וחולין דף לה:]

הגהות הב"ח

(א) גמ' דתניא ר' אלעזר. נ"ב עיין פ"ב דטהרות משנה ז': (ב) רש"י ד"ה בחולין וכו' בטהרה (הזקוקה). תז"מ ונ"ב ס"א שהזקוקה:

תוספות שאנץ

יוסי לעיל דריש ליה נמי הכא הכי ל"ה. אמר רב ר' מאיר ור' יוסי כו'. כל הטעון ביאת מים כו'. וחכמים אוסרים במעשר באכילה אבל בנגיעה שרי וחולין אף לאכילה והכי קאמר בחגיגה וה"ה דלרבנן אין שני עושה שלישי בחולין והא דלא חשיב להו (לעיל) עם האחרים לפי שלא נתפרשו [שמותן] ור' מאיר ומחלוקתו קאמר ל"ה. ותימה דמשמע דרבנן דפליגי עליה דר' עקיבא דאמרי אין שני עושה ג' בחולין מיירי (אפי') [בטומאה] בדרבנן ור' עקיבא אמר למילתיה אפי' בדרבנן. וק' דאמרי' בפ' השוחט גבי השוחט חיה ועוף ולוקמ' כר' עקיבא דאמר ידים תחלות נינהו גבי מכנים ידיו לבית המנוגע ומשני דלמ' ה"מ בדאורייתא אבל בטומאה דרבנן לא פי' דבטומאה דרבנן לא הי' אומר ר' עקיבא דשני עושה ג' בחולין. ואומר ה"ר אלחנן דההיא דהכא לא תיקשי דאיכא למימר דהכא לא מיתי [אלא דאיכא] תנאין שסוברים דאין שני עושה ג' בחולין ובאין בזה להוציא מדר' עקיבא והא דמייתי הכא ר' מאיר איכא למימר דמייתי ראיה מדשקל ר' מאיר במלתיה ומותר בחולין ובמעשר א"כ קיל שני דאוריי' להתירו בחולין ובמעשר יש מי שאומר בשם רב האיי גאון ז"ל דכל היכא דאיכא פלוני ופלוני ופלוני כולהו סבירא להו דאין הלכה כמותן תנאים דכולהו שיטה אחת אמור ורבנן דידהו פליגי עלייהו. והשתא ק' מהכא דק"ל דאין שני עושה ג' בחולין וכן פוסק הר' אלחנן מירושל' וגם לא אשכחן רבנן דפליגי על אלו תנאים דהא רבנן דר' מאיר מודי דאין ב' [עושה ג'] כשפ"ה וגם על ר' יהושע ליכא מאן דפליג עליה: ר' יהושע אומר האוכל אוכל ראשון ואוכל שני שני בפ' השוחט מפ' טעמא שני שני למה לפי שמצינו ששני עושה שני על ידי משקין וכל הנך טומאות דרבנן נינהו. ה"ג על טהרת תרומה אבל חולין גרידי לא ומאן דגרי' על טהרת הקדש לא ה"פ על טהרת הקדש לא דהוה ליה חולין גרידי שהמתפים חולין על טהרת הקדש בטלה דעתו אצל כל אדם ואין בדבריו כלום ל"ה. ר' אליעזר אומר ניטלת מן הטהורה על הטמאה פ"ה רישא דמתני' במס' חלה הכי איתא [שיעור] חלה אחד מכ"ד נטמאת עיסתה שוגגת או אנוסה אחד ממ"ח נטמאת במזיד אחד מכ"ד שלא יהא חוטא נשכר. ר' אליעזר אומר נטמאת מזידה תלוש אחרת בטהרה ותטול מן הטהורה על הטמאה וכיצד יעשה שיהא מן המוקף ובטהרה נוטלת כדי חלת הטמאה מעיסה הטהורה עד שלא הורמה חלתה דאי הורמה חלתה דטהורה תו לא מצי לאפרושי מן הפטור על החיוב דלא חייל עליה תו שם חלה: כדי לתרום מן המוקף. מקרא נפקא לן בספרי והרמותם ממנו מן המוקף לו הלכך צריך להקיף את העיסה קודם שתקרא לה שם והכי מקיפה לה נותנת בעריבה לצד אחד ונותנת מן העיסה הטהורה פחות מכביצה בין הטמאה לטהורה והאמצעית נוגעת בשתיהן ומצרפתן וקורא שם על החלה ומסלקה עם קריאת שם ופחות מכביצה אינו מטמא אחרים אע"פ שהוא עצמו מקבל טומאה כדתניא בת"כ מכל האוכל מלמד שהוא מטמא בכל שהוא יכול יטמא אחרים בכל שהוא ת"ל אשר יאכל ודרשי' אוכל הנאכל בבת אחת ושיערו חכמים זהו כביצת תרנגולת. ומה שפ"ה קורא לה שם לחלה ומסלקה עם קריאת שם למה הוצרך לפר' כן נר' משום דקשי' ליה אפי' אין שני עושה ג' בחולין מ"מ כיון שקרא לה שם הויא לה העיסה תרומה ושני עושה ג' בתרומה לכך הוצרך לפ' שמסלק תחלה ועם הסלוק קורא לה שם. והק' הר' אלחנן והלא אין זה מוקף ובעי' מוקף ממש ויש רוצים לומר דקרינן כי האי גונא מוקף. ול"נ דאמרי' פ"ק דנדה אשה והיא טבולת יום לשה את העיסה וקוצה הימנה חלתה

וחכמים אוסרין. ותניא: כביצה. סברוה, אידי ואידי בעיסה ראשונה, *וחולין הטבולין לחלה לא כחלה דמו. מאי לאו בהא קמיפלגי; דמר סבר: אין שני עושה שלישי בחולין, ומר סבר: שני עושה שלישי בחולין? אמר רב מרי בריה דרב כהנא: דכולי עלמא אין שני עושה שלישי בחולין, והכא – בחולין הטבולין לחלה קמיפלגי; מר סבר: כחלה דמו, ומר סבר: לא כחלה דמו. ואיבעית אימא: דכולי עלמא חולין הטבולין לחלה לא כחלה דמו, ואין שני עושה שלישי בחולין, והכא – במותר לגרום טומאה לחולין שבארץ ישראל קמיפלגי; מ"ס: *מותר לגרום טומאה לחולין שבארץ ישראל, ומר סבר: *אסור לגרום טומאה לחולין שבארץ ישראל. § "בו ביום דרש רבי עקיבא" וכו'. § במאי קא מיפלגי? מר סבר: *תחומין דאורייתא, ומר סבר: *דרבנן. § ת"ר: *בו ביום דרש רבי עקיבא: בשעה שעלו ישראל מן הים נתנו עיניהם לומר שירה, וכיצד אמרו שירה – כגדול המקרא את הלל, והן עונין אחריו ראשי פרקים; משה אמר "אשירה לה'" והן אומרים "אשירה לה'", משה אמר "כי גאה גאה" והן אומרים "אשירה לה'". רבי אליעזר בנו של רבי יוסי הגלילי אומר: כקטן המקרא את הלל, והן עונין אחריו כל מה שהוא אומר; משה אמר "אשירה לה'" והן אומרים "אשירה לה'", משה אמר "כי גאה גאה" והן אומרים "כי גאה גאה". רבי נחמיה אומר: כסופר הפורס על שמע בבית הכנסת, שהוא פותח תחילה והן עונין אחריו. במאי קמיפלגי? רבי עקיבא סבר: "לאמר" – אמילתא קמייתא, ורבי אליעזר בנו של ר"י הגלילי סבר: "לאמר" – אכל מילתא ומילתא, ור' נחמיה סבר: "ויאמרו" – דאמור כולהו בהדי הדדי, "לאמר" – דפתח משה ברישא. תנו רבנן, דרש רבי יוסי הגלילי: בשעה שעלו ישראל מן הים נתנו עיניהם לומר שירה, וכיצד אמרו שירה? עולל מוטל על ברכי אמו, ותינוק יונק משדי אמו, כיון שראו את השכינה – עולל הגביה צוארו, ותינוק שמט דד מפיו, ואמרו "זה אלי ואנוהו", שנאמר: "מפי עוללים ויונקים יסדת עוז". היה רבי מאיר אומר: מנין *שאפי' עוברים שבמעי אמן אמרו שירה – שנאמר:

במקהלות

(שמות טו) (תהלים ח)

רש"י

להקיף החלה אלא העיסה קודם שתקרא לה שם. והכי מקיפה לה: נותנת בעריבה לצד אחד, (א) ונותנת מן העיסה הטהורה פחות מכביצה בין החלה הטהורה ובין העיסה הטמאה, והאמצעית נוגעת בשתיהן, ומצרפתן, וקורא שם על החלה, ומסלקת עם קריאת השם. ופחות מכביצה אינו מטמא את החלה, ואע"פ שהוא עצמו מקבל טומאה. כדתניא בתורת כהנים: "מכל האוכל אשר יאכל" – מלמד שהוא מיטמא בכל שהוא, יכול יטמא לאחרים בכל שהוא – ת"ל: "אשר יאכל" ודרשינן ליה בפרק בתרא דיומא (דף פ.): אוכל הנאכל בבת אחת, ושיערו חכמים: אין בית הבליעה מחזיק יותר מביצת תרנגולת. וחכמים אוסרין. כדבעינן לפרושי טעמא. ותניא כביצה. ותניא בברייתא דאליבא דר' אליעזר: ונותנת אף כביצה באמצע. ואפ"ה לא מטמא לה לחלה עד שלא נקרא עליה שם. סברוה רבנן. הני דבי מדרשא דבעו למשמע מינה דר' אליעזר *אין שני עושה שלישי בחולין, ס"ל: אידי ואידי, הך ברייתא נמי אליבא דרבי אליעזר דשרי כביצה, ומתני' דאמר פחות – תרווייהו בעיסה ראשונה, העיסה הטמאה – ראשונה לטומאה היא, ואפ"ה קאמר ר' אליעזר בברייתא כביצה. ואע"ג דמיטמאה אמצעית מחמת ראשונה, והויא לה שניה – לא הדרא ועבדא לה לחלה, עד שלא קרא עליה שם, שלישי. ואע"ג דמעיסת חולין הטבולין לחלה הוא, דכ"ע, בין לר' אליעזר בין לרבנן – לאו כחלה דמיא, למיהוי עלה תורת תרומה. מאי לאו בהא קמיפלגי. רבי אליעזר ורבנן. דר' אליעזר דשרי, סבר: אין שני עושה שלישי בחולין, ורבנן דאסרי סברי: שני עושה שלישי בחולין, ואיטמא לה חלה לפני קריאת השם, ואע"ג דחולין הוא, ואשתכח דספינן לכהן חלה טמאה בחזקת שהיא טהורה. ותנא דמתני' דאמר לר' אליעזר פחות מכביצה – לאו משום דאית ליה שני עושה שלישי, אלא משום דכמה דאפשר למעוטי טומאה דאמצעית ממעטינן, דאסור לגרום טומאה לחולין, אלא משום תקנת תרומה הוא דשרי, והא אפשר בהכי. אי נמי, משום דילמא לא מיזדהר בה שלא תגע חלה באמצעית זו אחר קריאת השם. וחכמים אוסרין, דילמא אתי למיעבד כביצה ומטמא אמצעית, והדרא ומטמיא לחלה. לא דכ"ע. ואפילו לרבנן אין שני עושה שלישי בחולין. והאי דקאסרי רבנן – משום דקסברי: חולין הטבולין לחלה כחלה דמו, ומיפסלי משום שם שלישי. ואיבעית אימא דכ"ע לאו כחלה דמי ודכ"ע אין שני עושה שלישי בחולין והכא במותר לגרום טומאה לחולין כו'. טעמא דרבנן דאסרי – משום אמצעית הוא, דמיטמאה מחמת העיסה שהיא ראשונה, וקסברי: אסור לגרום טומאה לחולין, משום תקנת תרומה. ור' אליעזר סבר: מותר לגרום טומאה לאמצעית כדי לתקן חלה בטהרה. ותנא דמתניתין ותנא דברייתא אליבא דר' אליעזר נמי בהא פליגי, דתנא דמתניתין סבר: אע"ג דמותר לגרום לה טומאה, מיהו כל כמה דאפשר למעוטי – לא מפשינן להו, לגרום להן טומאה בחנם, והא אפשר בהכי, הלכך, כביצה – לא, דחשיב. ותנא דברייתא סבר: כיון דמותר לגרום – לא שנא שיעורא רבה ולא שנא שיעורא זוטרא, דאפילו בכדי ביצה נמי מותר לגרום. אי נמי, תנא דמתני' סבר דילמא נגע חלה באמצעית אחר קריאת השם, ותנא ברא לא חייש. במאי קמיפלגי. ר"ע ור' אליעזר בנו של ר' יוסי הגלילי. כגדול המקרא את ההלל. מקריהו לציבור להוציאן ידי חובתן. והן עונין אחריו ראשי פרקים הללויה. שהוא ראש הפרשה; על כל דבר שהוא אומר עונין אחריו הללויה. דתנן במסכת סוכה (דף לח.): מי שהיה עבד או אשה או קטן מקרין אותו – הוא עונה אחריהן מה שהם אומרים, ואם היה גדול מקרא אותו – עונה אחריו הללויה. כסופר. מלמד תינוקות. והוא תדיר בבית הכנסת ופורס על שמע לעשרה הנועדים. פורס – לשון פרוס החג, לפני החג (שקלים דף ה); מתחיל בברכות שלפני קריאת שמע, והן עונין אחריו וקורין כולן יחד. וכך שרתה רוח הקודש על כולם, וכוונו יחד את השירה ככתבה. לאמר אמילתא קמייתא קאי. שעונין תמיד "אשירה לה'". ורבי נחמיה סבר ויאמרו. אמשה ובני ישראל קאי, ומשמע דאמור כולהו בהדי הדדי. לאמר דפתח משה ברישא. הכי קאמר: "ויאמרו" כולם, אחר שפירשו "לאמר", דהיינו אחר שפתח חכם. עולל. גדול מיונק, כדכתיב (שמואל א טו): "מעולל ועד יונק". ודרך המקרא לומר כן, כלומר: כלה הכל מן החשוב עד הגרוע, כמו "משור ועד שה" (שם).

במקהלות

תוספות

מר סבר תחומין דאורייתא ומר סבר תחומין דרבנן. תימה: דהכא משמע דאי הוה משתעי קרא דאלפים אמה בלוים – דהוה סבר דתחומין דרבנן, אלא טעמא משום דמשתעי בשבת. והא יליף לתחומין בפרק "מי שהוציאוהו" (עירובין דף נא.) מג"ש מקום ממקום ומקום מניסה וכו', א"כ אפי' הוה משתעי בשדות וכרמים הוי מצי למילף בהו ג"ש, דמקום דכתיב גבי שבת היינו אלפים. דהא פריך התם: ונילף "מקיר העיר וחוצה", אע"ג דההוא קרא משתעי לדברי הכל בלוים! ובספ"ק דעירובין (דף יז:) משמע: מאן דסבר דתחומין דאורייתא נפקא לן מ"אל יצא איש ממקומו". **רבי** נחמיה אומר כסופר הפורס על שמע בבית הכנסת. בתוספתא (פ"ו), ר' נחמיה אומר: כבני אדם שקורין את שמע, שנאמר "ויאמרו לאמר" – מלמד שהיה משה פותח תחילה, וישראל עונין אחריו וגומרין. משה אמר "אז ישיר משה" וישראל אומרים "אשירה לה'", משה אמר "עזי וזמרת יה" וישראל אומרים "זה אלי ואנוהו", משה אמר "ה' איש מלחמה" וישראל אומרים "ה' שמו". **רבי** מאיר אומר מנין שאפי' עוברין שבמעי אמן. אין לומר דרבי יוסי הגלילי ורבי מאיר פליגי, דרבי יוסי אית ליה דוקא עוללים ויונקים ולא עוברים. אלא מקרא ד"מפי עוללים ויונקים" נפקא ליה דתינוק שמט דד מפיו, דמשמע: יונקים – בשעה שהוא יונק, ולכך איצטריך קרא ד"מפי עוללים". דאי לאו הכי, כיון דנפקא לן מקרא (ב) "ממקור ישראל במקהלות ברכו אלקים" אפילו עוברים – לא הוה צריך למימר תו עוללים ויונקים. דבפ' "שלשה שאכלו" (ברכות דף מט:) תנינן: בעשרה אומרים "נברך אלהינו" וכו'. רבי יוסי הגלילי אומר: לפי רוב הקהל מברכין, שנאמר: "במקהלות ברכו אלקים". א"ר עקיבא: מה מצינו בבית הכנסת אחד מרובין ואחד מועטין אומר "ברכו את ה'". וקדייק עליה בגמ' (שם דף נ.): ורבי עקיבא, האי קרא דר"י הגלילי מאי עביד ליה – מבעי ליה לכדר' מאיר וכו'.

ואידך

עין משפט נר מצוה

כ א מיי' פ"ז מהל' ביכורים הל' יב:

כא ב מיי' שם ופי"א מהל' אבות הטומאות הלכה טו:

כב ג מיי' פ"ז מהל' ביכורים הל' יב ופט"ז מהל' טומאת אוכלין הל' ט:

כג ד מיי' פכ"ז מה' שבת הלכה א סמג לאוין סה [טור או"ח סי' שצז]:

מסורת הש"ס

[נדה ו:]

עי' רש"א

[גיטין נג. נדה שם]

[עירובין לה: ביצה לו:]

[תוספתא פ"ו]

[נדה ו:]

[עירובין לו. נט.]

[צ"ל עזי וזמרת יה והן כו'. כך איתא בתוספתא]

[צ"ל עזי וזמרת יה והן אומרים עזי וזמרת יה רבי נחמיה וכו' כך איתא בתוספתא]

ברכות נ. כתובות ז:

הגהות הב"ח

(א) רש"י ד"ה (בע"א) ונותנת וכו' ונותנת מן העיסה הטהורה. נ"ב לאו דוקא אלא אף מן הטהורה ולמ"ד מותר לגרום טומאה אפי' היכא דאפשר אבל אי נותנת מן הטמאה כ"ש דניחא טפי וכ"כ הרמב"ם: (ב) תוספות ד"ה ר' מאיר וכו' מקרא במקהלות ברכו אלקים ממקור ישראל אפילו כנ"ל:

תוספות שאנץ

חלתה ומניחתה בכפיפה או באנחותא [ומקפת] וקורא לה שם אלמא משמע דבעי' מן המוקף ממש. (ואומר ר"י דשאני התם הילכך תקנו בכפיפה או באנחותא שאם אתה אומר שתקרא לה שם בעודה בידה א"כ תטמא החלה שהיא טבולת יום לכך תקנו להניחה בכפיפה להבחין שהיא טבולת יום ודכוותיה קאמר בהניזקין שתקנו בכפיפה ואנחותא א) משו' היכירא) ב) וא"ת המטמא העיסה טמאו אותו כביצה שבנתים ומאי אוני קריאת חשם ואומר הר' אלחנן שמפרי' החלה מן העיסה ומקיפו לצד העיסה הטהורה והשתא הוי ליה רביעי דתרומ' א"נ שאוחז בידו תחלה אמצעית. אידי ואידי בעיסה ראשונה ה"ג רש"י. וקאי אעיסה הטמאה ראשונה [ואע"ג דמיטמאה אמצעית מחמת ראשונה] והויא לה שניה לא [הדרא] ועבדא לה לחלה עד שלא קרא שם שלישי ואית דגרסי אידי ואידי בעיסה שניה וקאי (אביצה) [אאמצעית] ואפחות מכביצה. ג) וכר' יונתן דגר' ראשונה

מאי לאו בהא קמיפלגי פ"ה ר' אליעזר ורבנן דר' אליעזר דשרי סבר אין שני עושה ג' בחולין ורבנן סברי [שני] עושה שלישי בחולין. ואיטמי לה לחלה לפני קריאת השם ואע"ג דחולין הוא ואשתכח דספי' לכהן חלה טמאה בחזקת טהורה. ותנא דמתני' דאמר לר' אליעזר פחות מכביצה לאו משום דאית ליה ב' עושה ג' אלא משום דכמה דאפשר למעוטי טומאה דאמצעי' ממעטי' דאסור לגרום טומאה לחולין אלא משום תקנת תרומה הוא דשרי' והא אפשר בהכי א"נ משום דילמא לא מיזדהר שלא תגע חל' באמצעית [זו] לאחר קריאת שם וחכמים אוסר' דלמא אתי למעבד [כביצה] ומטמיא אמצעי' והדרא ומטמיא לחלה כל"ה. מר סבר מותר לגרום טומאה לחולין פ"ה היינו דר' אליעזר סבר דמותר לגרום טומאה לאמצעית כדי לתקן חלה בטהרה ותנא דברייתא אליבא דר' אליעזר נמי בהא פליגי דתנא דמתני' סבר דמותר לגרום טומאה משום תקנת חלה מיהו כל כמה דאפשר למעוטי טומאה לא מפשי' לגרום להם טומאה בחנם והא אפשר בהכי הלכך כביצה לא (דריש) [דחשיב] בו ותנא דברייתא סבר כיון דמותר לגרום לא שנא שיעורא רבה ולא שנא שיעורא זוטא דאפי' לכביצה נמי מותר לגרום. א"נ תנא דמתני' סבר דלמא נגע חלה לאמצעי' אחר קריאת שם ותנא ברא לא חייש כל"ה. ומר סבר תחומין דרבנן דאמר בירו' דאפי' מאן דאית ליה דתחום אלפים לא הוי אלא מדרבנן מ"מ תחום דג' פרסאות הוי דאורייתא. **מתני'** שאין ת"ל לאמר פ"ה דלא הוי כמו שאר לאמר שבתורה דהתם השכינה מדברת עם משה דיבורו וחוזר הוא ואומרו לישראל אבל כאן אין שייך לאמר כן: **גמ'** מפי עוללים ויונקים עולל גדול מיונק כדכתיב מעולל

ועד

א) וכ"כ רש"י בנדה דף ו' ע"ש. ב) נראה דצ"ל ולכן פירש ר' אלחנן דקורא לה שם כשהיא מחוברת לעיסה וא"ת הא העיסה הטמאה מטמאה את החלה ע"י אותו כביצה וכו'. ג) אולי צ"ל ויותר נראה דגרסי' ראשונה כפ"ה.

תורה אור

תהלים סח "בְּמַקְהֵלוֹת בָּרְכוּ אֱלֹהִים ה' מִמְּקוֹר יִשְׂרָאֵל". (*וְהָא לָא חָזוּ! אָמַר רַבִּי תַּנְחוּם: כֶּרֶס נַעֲשָׂה לָהֶן כְּאַסְפַּקְלַרְיָא הַמְּאִירָה, וְרָאוּ.) § "בּוֹ בַּיּוֹם דָּרַשׁ רַבִּי יְהוֹשֻׁעַ בֶּן הוּרְקָנוֹס שֶׁלֹּא עָבַד אִיּוֹב" כו'. § וְלֶיחֱזֵי הַאי "לֹא" אִי בְּלָמֶ"ד אָלֶ"ף כְּתִיב – לֹא הוּא, אִי בְּלָמֶ"ד וָי"ו כְּתִיב – לוֹ הוּא! *וְכָל הֵיכָא דִּכְתִיב בְּלָמֶ"ד אָלֶ"ף "לֹא" הוּא? *אֶלָּא מֵעַתָּה

ישעיה סג °"בְּכָל צָרָתָם לֹא צָר" דִּכְתִיב בְּלָמֶ"ד אָלֶ"ף, הָכִי נַמִי דְּלָא הוּא?! וְכ"ת ה"נ – וְהָכְתִיב "וּמַלְאַךְ פָּנָיו הוֹשִׁיעָם"! אֶלָּא *(לָאו,) מַשְׁמַע הָכִי וּמַשְׁמַע הָכִי. תַּנְיָא, רַבִּי מֵאִיר אוֹמֵר: נֶאֱמַר "יְרֵא אֱלֹהִים" בְּאִיּוֹב וְנֶאֱמַר "יְרֵא אֱלֹהִים" בְּאַבְרָהָם, מַה יְּרֵא אֱלֹהִים הָאָמוּר בְּאַבְרָהָם – מֵאַהֲבָה, אַף יְרֵא אֱלֹהִים הָאָמוּר בְּאִיּוֹב – מֵאַהֲבָה. וְאַבְרָהָם גּוּפֵיהּ

שם מא מְנָלַן – דִּכְתִיב: °"זֶרַע אַבְרָהָם אוֹהֲבִי". מַאי אִיכָּא בֵּין עוֹשֶׂה מֵאַהֲבָה לְעוֹשֶׂה מִיִּרְאָה? אִיכָּא הָא דְּתַנְיָא, רַבִּי שִׁמְעוֹן בֶּן אֶלְעָזָר אוֹמֵר: [א]גָּדוֹל הָעוֹשֶׂה מֵאַהֲבָה יוֹתֵר מִן הָעוֹשֶׂה מִיִּרְאָה, שֶׁזֶּה תָּלוּי לְאֶלֶף דּוֹר, וְזֶה תָּלוּי לְאַלְפַּיִם דּוֹר;

שמות כ הָכָא כְּתִיב: °"לַאֲלָפִים לְאֹהֲבַי וּלְשֹׁמְרֵי מִצְוֹתָי",

דברים ז וְהָתָם כְּתִיב: °"וּלְשֹׁמְרֵי מִצְוֹתָיו לְאֶלֶף דּוֹר". הָתָם נַמִי כְּתִיב: "לְאֹהֲבָיו וּלְשֹׁמְרֵי מִצְוֹתָיו לְאֶלֶף דּוֹר"! הַאי לְדִסְמִיךְ לֵיהּ, וְהַאי לְדִסְמִיךְ לֵיהּ. הָנְהוּ תְּרֵי תַּלְמִידֵי דַּהֲווּ יָתְבִי קַמֵּיהּ דְּרָבָא,

תהלים לא חַד אֲמַר לֵיהּ: אַקְרְיוּן בְּחֶלְמַאי °"מָה רַב טוּבְךָ אֲשֶׁר צָפַנְתָּ לִּירֵאֶיךָ", וְחַד אֲמַר לֵיהּ: אַקְרְיוּן

שם ה בְּחֶלְמַאי °"וְיִשְׂמְחוּ כָל חוֹסֵי בָךְ לְעוֹלָם יְרַנֵּנוּ וְיַעְלְצוּ בְךָ אֹהֲבֵי שְׁמֶךָ". אֲמַר לְהוּ: תַּרְוַיְיכוּ רַבָּנַן צַדִּיקֵי גְּמוּרֵי אַתּוּן, מָר – מֵאַהֲבָה, וּמָר – מִיִּרְאָה. §

הדרן עלך כשם שהמים

מִי שֶׁקִּינֵּא לְאִשְׁתּוֹ וְנִסְתְּרָה, אֲפִילּוּ שָׁמַע מֵעוֹף הַפּוֹרֵחַ – יוֹצִיא וְיִתֵּן כְּתוּבָּה, דִּבְרֵי רַבִּי אֱלִיעֶזֶר. רַבִּי יְהוֹשֻׁעַ אוֹמֵר: [ב]עַד שֶׁיִּשְׂאוּ וְיִתְּנוּ בָּהּ מוֹזְרוֹת בַּלְּבָנָה. אָמַר *עֵד אֶחָד "אֲנִי רְאִיתִיהָ שֶׁנִּטְמֵאת" – לֹא הָיְתָה שׁוֹתָה. וְלֹא עוֹד, אֶלָּא [ג]אֲפִילּוּ עֶבֶד אֲפִילּוּ שִׁפְחָה – הֲרֵי אֵלּוּ נֶאֱמָנִין, אַף לְפוֹסְלָהּ מִכְּתוּבָּתָהּ. [ד]חֲמוֹתָהּ, וּבַת חֲמוֹתָהּ, וְצָרָתָהּ, וִיבִמְתָּהּ, וּבַת בַּעְלָהּ – הֲרֵי אֵלּוּ נֶאֱמָנוֹת. וְלֹא לְפוֹסְלָהּ מִכְּתוּבָּתָהּ, אֶלָּא שֶׁלֹּא תִּשְׁתֶּה. *שֶׁהָיָה בַּדִּין: וּמָה אִם עֵדוּת רִאשׁוֹנָה שֶׁאֵין אוֹסַרְתָּהּ אִיסּוּר עוֹלָם – אֵינָהּ מִתְקַיֶּימֶת בְּפָחוֹת מִשְּׁנַיִם, עֵדוּת אַחֲרוֹנָה שֶׁאוֹסַרְתָּהּ אִיסּוּר עוֹלָם – אֵינוֹ דִּין שֶׁלֹּא תִּתְקַיֵּים "בְּפָחוֹת מִשְּׁנַיִם"? תַּלְמוּד לוֹמַר

במדבר ה °"וְעֵד אֵין בָּהּ" – *כָּל עֵדוּת שֶׁיֵּשׁ בָּהּ. קַל וָחוֹמֶר לְעֵדוּת הָרִאשׁוֹנָה מֵעַתָּה: וּמָה אִם עֵדוּת

רש"י

בְּמַקְהֵלוֹת. כְּשֶׁנִּקְהֲלוּ עַל הַיָּם. מִמְּקוֹר. אַף אוֹתָם שֶׁבַּמָּקוֹר. וְלֶיחֱזֵי הַאי לֹא כו'. וְאַמַּאי אָמַר: הַדָּבָר עֲדַיִין שָׁקוּל? ה"נ דְּלָא הוּא. וְה"ק קְרָא: אֵינוֹ חוֹשֵׁשׁ לְצָרָתָם וְלֹא צָר בָּהּ?!. בְּאַבְרָהָם. "כִּי יְרֵא אֱלֹהִים אַתָּה" (בראשית כב). תָּלוּי. זְכוּתוֹ לְדוֹרוֹתָיו לְהָגֵן עֲלֵיהֶם עַד אַלְפַּיִם דּוֹר. לַאֲלָפִים לְאוֹהֲבַי. סָמַךְ אוֹהֲבָיו לַאֲלָפִים, וְאִידָךְ קְרָא סָמַךְ לְאֶלֶף דּוֹר אֶל שׁוֹמְרֵי מִצְוֹתָיו, דְּהַיְינוּ מִיִּרְאָה. וְאֵין אֵלּוּ דּוֹמִין (א) לְפָרוּשׁ מֵאַהֲבָה לְפָרוּשׁ מִיִּרְאָה (לעיל דף כב:), דְּהָנְהוּ מֵאַהֲבַת שָׂכָר וּמִיִּרְאַת פּוּרְעָנוּת הַקְּלָלוֹת וְהָעוֹנָשִׁין, (ב) וְהָכָא מֵאַהֲבַת הַמָּקוֹם וּמִיִּרְאָתוֹ, שֶׁמּוֹרָאוֹ גָּדוֹל וּמוּטָל עַל הַבְּרִיּוֹת. וְיִשְׂמְחוּ כָל חוֹסֵי בָךְ וגו'. סֵיפֵיהּ דִּקְרָא: "וְיַעְלְצוּ בְךָ אוֹהֲבֵי שְׁמֶךָ".

הדרן עלך כשם שהמים

מִי שֶׁקִּינֵּא לָהּ וְנִסְתְּרָה. אִם לְאַחַר שֶׁקִּינֵּא לָהּ נִסְתְּרָה. אֲפִי' שָׁמַע מֵעוֹף הַפּוֹרֵחַ. שֶׁנִּסְתְּרָה, יוֹצִיא וְיִתֵּן כְּתוּבָּה. וְרַבִּי אֱלִיעֶזֶר לְטַעְמֵיהּ, דְּאָמַר בְּפ"ק (לעיל דף ב:): סְתִירָה לֹא בָּעֵיָא עֵדוּת, וַאֲפִילּוּ עֶבֶד וַאֲפִילּוּ שִׁפְחָה נֶאֱמָנִין – דְּהַיְינוּ נַמִי כְּעוֹף הַפּוֹרֵחַ. דְּאִיתְקַשׁ לְטוּמְאָה, דְּכוּלְּהוּ מְהֵימְנֵי בָּהּ. הִילְכָּךְ נֶאֶסְרָה עָלָיו, וְאִם אֵינוֹ רוֹצֶה לְהַשְׁקוֹתָהּ – יוֹצִיא וְיִתֵּן כְּתוּבָּה. רַבִּי יְהוֹשֻׁעַ אוֹמֵר עַד שֶׁיִּשְׂאוּ וְיִתְּנוּ בָּהּ מוֹזְרוֹת בַּלְּבָנָה. כְּלוֹמַר, מִשּׁוּם סְתִירָה שֶׁאֵין בָּהּ ב' עֵדִים – אֵינָהּ נֶאֱסֶרֶת עָלָיו. וְר' יְהוֹשֻׁעַ לְטַעְמֵיהּ, דְּאָמַר: מַשְׁקֶה עַל פִּי שְׁנַיִם. מִיהוּ, כְּשֶׁיִּשְׂאוּ וְיִתְּנוּ מוֹזְרוֹת בַּלְּבָנָה בִּפְרִיצוּתָהּ – מְכוֹעָר הַדָּבָר, וְתֵצֵא, דְּהָא אֲפִילּוּ מַיָּא תּוּ לָא בָּדְקֵי לָהּ, כִּדְתַנְיָא בְּפ"ק (לעיל דף ו:): "וְטְהוֹרָה הִיא" – וְלֹא שֶׁיִּשְׂאוּ וְיִתְּנוּ בָּהּ מוֹזְרוֹת בַּלְּבָנָה. אֲנִי רְאִיתִיהָ שֶׁנִּטְמֵאת. בְּאוֹתָהּ סְתִירָה, שֶׁהִיא עַל פִּי שְׁנַיִם עֵדִים לְרַבִּי יְהוֹשֻׁעַ, וּלְרַבִּי אֱלִיעֶזֶר ע"פ עוֹף הַפּוֹרֵחַ. לֹא הָיְתָה שׁוֹתָה. דְּעֵד אֶחָד נֶאֱמָן בָּהּ אַף לְהַפְסִידָהּ כְּתוּבָּתָהּ, שֶׁרַגְלַיִם לַדָּבָר. וּמִקְּרָאֵי יָלְפִינַן לָהּ לְקַמָּן בְּמַתְנִי'. הֲרֵי אֵלּוּ נֶאֱמָנִים אַף לְפוֹסְלָהּ מִכְּתוּבָּתָהּ. שֶׁלֹּא תִּשְׁתֶּה וְלֹא תִּטּוֹל כְּתוּבָּתָהּ. חֲמוֹתָהּ וּבַת חֲמוֹתָהּ וְצָרָתָהּ וִיבִמְתָּהּ. אֵשֶׁת אֲחִי בַּעְלָהּ, אַף הִיא כְּצָרָתָהּ וְשׂוֹנְאָתָהּ, שֶׁדּוֹאֶגֶת הֵימֶנָּה שֶׁסּוֹפָהּ לִהְיוֹת צָרָתָהּ; אִם יָמוּת בַּעְלָהּ בְּלֹא בָנִים – תִּתְיַבֵּם לְבַעְלִי. וּבַת בַּעְלָהּ – מֵאִשָּׁה אַחֶרֶת. אֵלּוּ חָמֵשׁ נָשִׁים שׂוֹנְאוֹת אוֹתָהּ. וּבִיבָמוֹת (דף קיז:) מְפָרֵשׁ טַעְמָא אַמַּאי סָנוּ לָהּ, וְאֵינָן נֶאֱמָנוֹת לָהּ לָשׂוּם עֵדוּת שֶׁהִיא לְרָעָתָהּ. הֲרֵי אֵלּוּ נֶאֱמָנוֹת. לָהּ לְעֵדוּת זוֹ, שֶׁהַתּוֹרָה הֶאֱמִינָה כָּל עֵדוּת שֶׁיֵּשׁ בָּהּ. וּמִיהוּ, לֹא לְפוֹסְלָהּ מִכְּתוּבָּתָהּ, הוֹאִיל וְשׂוֹנְאוֹת אוֹתָהּ, אֶלָּא שֶׁלֹּא תִּשְׁתֶּה. שֶׁהָיָה בַּדִּין. שֶׁלֹּא יְהֵא נֶאֱמָן בָּהּ עֵד אֶחָד, אִם לֹא מִגְּזֵירַת הַכָּתוּב. הָרִאשׁוֹנָה. סְתִירָה, שֶׁאֵין אוֹסַרְתָּהּ אִיסּוּר עוֹלָם אֶלָּא עַד שֶׁתִּשְׁתֶּה. אֵינָהּ מִתְקַיֶּימֶת בְּפָחוֹת מִשְּׁנַיִם. כִּדְבָעֵינַן לְמֵימַר מִגְּזֵירָה שָׁוָה, וְרַבִּי יְהוֹשֻׁעַ הִיא. עֵדוּת הָאַחֲרוֹנָה. טוּמְאָה. כָּל עֵדוּת שֶׁיֵּשׁ בָּהּ. נֶאֱמָן בָּהּ. וּבַגְּמָרָא יָלְפִינַן לָהּ דְּהָכִי קָאָמַר: תְּרֵי לֵית בָּהּ אֶלָּא חַד, וְקָאָמַר "וְהִיא לֹא נִתְפָּשָׂה" לְמֵיסְרָהּ, אַלְמָא מְהֵימַן. שֶׁאוֹסַרְתָּהּ

תוספות

ואידך, דהיינו רבי יוסי הגלילי – מ"מקור ישראל" נפקא. אלמא דלר' יוסי הגלילי נמי עוברים אומרים שירה. ובפ"ק דכתובות (דף ז:) דריש לה דברכת חתנים בעשרה, מדהוי מצי למיכתב "מבטן ישראל", וכתיב "ממקור" – על עיסקי מקור. בתוספתא מסיים הכי: ואותן המלאכים שאמרו "מה אנוש כי תזכרנו" אמר להן הקב"ה: באו וראו את השירה. כיון שראו את ישראל פתחו אף הן ואמרו שירה, שנאמר: "ה' אדונינו מה אדיר שמך בכל הארץ" וגו'. ור"ש בן *אלעזר אומר: לא נאמרה פרשה זו אלא לענין עקידה. **גדול** העושה מאהבה. בירושלמי (ברכות פ"ט): ר"ע הוה מתדין קמיה טורנוסרופוס הרשע, אתת עונתא דקרית שמע, שרי קרי וגחך. א"ל: סבא סבא! או חרש אתה או מבעט ביסורין את? א"ל: תיפח רוחיה דההוא רשיעא, לא חרש אנא ולא מבעט ביסורין אנא, אלא כל ימי הייתי קורא הפסוק הזה: "ואהבת את ה' אלהיך בכל לבבך ובכל נפשך ובכל מאודך", רחמתיה בכל לבי, רחמתיה בכל נפשי, רחמתיה בכל ממוני. לא הות (ג) בדיק ליה. וכיון דמטי ליה בכל נפשיה, ואתיא עונתיה דקרית שמע ולא איפליג עליה – בגין כן אנא קרי וגחיך.

הדרן עלך כשם שהמים

מי שקינא לה. פרק זה היה הגון שיהא שנוי ומעורב בפרק ראשון לאחר אותה בבא ד"אלו אסורות לאכול בתרומה", ואח"כ היה לו לשנות כילד עושה לה וכל הסדר. אבל תימה דלאחר שנה שבדקוה המים הוא חוזר לקינוי. ה"ג בסדר המשנה: משקינא לה, אפילו שמע מעוף הפורח. והכי מסתברא. ונראה דה"פ: מאחר שקינא לה, אפילו קודם סתירה שמע פריצותא, שהרי עכשיו קצת רגלים לדבר – מכוער הדבר, ומוציאה בכתובתה, מאחר שלא נסתרה ולא נאסרה עליו. ובענין זה מצוה לגרשה. דאפילו לב"ה *[דאמר אפילו אם] הקדיחה תבשילו – היינו רשות, מיהו מצוה ליכא אלא בכה"ג, ואם מקיימה – דומה לאדם שנפל זבוב לתוך תמחוי, שמוללו ואוכלו. ולבית שמאי חובה, הואיל וקינא לה – רגלים לדבר. מיהו, כתובתה גובה, הואיל ולא נסתרה. והשתא אתי שפיר דרבי יהושע. אבל לפירוש רבינו שלמה דפירש משקינא לה – אפי' שמע מעוף הפורח שנסתרה, דעוף פורח היינו עבד ושפחה שנאמנין בעידי סתירה, ואם אינו רוצה להשקותה, יוציא ויתן כתובתה – וכי היה רבי יהושע מחייב כתובה לאחר שישאו ויתנו בה מוזרות בלבנה? והלא אין המים בודקין אותה, כדאמרינן בפרק קמא (לעיל דף ו:). ומאחר שהיא גרמה שתיאסר עליו, ואין יכולה לשתות – הויא כארוסה ושומרת יבם, שלא שותות ולא נוטלות כתובה! מיהו, מצי למימר: הא דאמרינן אין המים בודקין אותה לאחר שישאו ויתנו בה מוזרות בלבנה – דוקא לאחר קינוי ועידי סתירה לרבי יהושע, אבל כאן אין עידי סתירה, אלא שמוזרות בלבנה נושאות ונותנות בפריצותה. כאן

עין משפט נר מצוה

כד א מיי' פ"י מהל' תשובה הלכה ג ג:

א ב מיי' פ"א מהל' סוטה הלכה ח סמג עשין נו טוש"ע אה"ע סימן קעח סעיף יא:

ב ג מיי' שם הלכה טו טוש"ע שם סעיף יד:

ג ד מיי' שם וטוש"ע שם סעיף טו:

[כל זה ליתא בילקוט ובע"י]

[ע' נדרים לב.]

[בע"י ליתא]

לעיל ב.

שם ג:

[שבועות לב.]

[נ"ל מנסיא]

[עמ"ש תוס' בחולין סה. ד"ה אע"פ כו' מוכח דגירסתם הכא כך הוא דפריך וכל היכא דכתיב לא באל"ף ממש הוא והא כתיב בכל צרתם לא צר ומלאך פניו הושיעם הכי נמי דלא הוא וכ"ת ה"נ והכתיב עמו אנכי בצרה תהלים צ"א]

הגהות הב"ח

(א) רש"י ד"ה לאלפים וכו' לפרוש מאהבה. נ"ב ע"ל בדף כב ע"ב: (ב) בא"ד והעונשים והנך מאהבת: (ג) תוספות ד"ה גדול וכו' לא הות כדין לי וכיון דמטיה לי בכל נפשי ואתית עניתה:

תוספות שאנץ

ועד יונק ודרך המקרא לומר כן כולל הכל מן החשוב עד הגרוע כמו משור ועד שה. ל"ה: אלא מעתה בכל צרתם (לו) [לא] צר ה"נ. תימה אמאי לא בעי ה"נ מכמה פסוקים כמו אשר (לו) [לא] כרעים כדדרשי' אע"פ שאין לו עכשיו ועתיד לגדל אחר זמן וכן אשר (לו) [לא] חומה אע"פ שאין לו עכשיו. וי"ל דלא בעי משום דפשי' ליה דלא בעי' למימר אשר (לו) [לא] כרעים ממש שהרי ארבה וסלעם וחרגול ידועים הם בסימניהון וא"כ פשיטא ליה שלא היו כשרים וכן אשר (לו) [לא] חומה פשיטא ליה דאינו ר"ל לא ממש דהא בעיר שיש לו חומה משתעי קרא ולהכי משתעי הכי אבל בכל צרתם (לו) [לא] צר אינו פשוט לו כל כך כמו שהבאתי שיש לתלות ולפרש כמו ולא היתה צרתם צרה כי אם להם. פרעה לקה ואבד. סיסרא לקה ואבד. סנחריב לקה ואבד. וכן נבוכדנצר לקה ואחר כן יאבדו כל אויביך ה' במהרה בימינו אמן:

סליק פירקא

מי שקינא לאשתו ונסתרה ר' אליעזר אומר אפי' שמע מעוף הפורח כו'. פ"ה אפי' עד אחד היינו כמו עוף הפורח ואפי' עבד ואפי' שפחה נאמנין ונאסרה עליו. ואם אינו רוצה להשקותה יוציא ויתן כתובה ור"א לטעמי' (דאמר דלא בעי עדות) דאמר לעיל בפ"ק דמשקה לה על פי עד אחד [דסתירה לא בעי עדות]. ור' יהושע אומר עד שישאו ויתנו בה מוזרות בלבנה. פי' נשים הטוות בלבנה (והוי) פריצותה ומכוער הדבר ותצא דאפי' מיא תו לא בדקי לה כלומר דסבירא ליה דבעי ב' עדים. וק' חדא דהא אמרינן יוציא ויתן כתובה. א) וי"ל אם [אינו] רוצה להשקותה דהוה ליה למתני ישקנה כיון דסבי' ליה דמשקה על פי עד אחד. ועוד ק' מאי דאמר דעוף הפורח ר"ל עד אחד דאטו מי סניא ליה למתני' אפי' שמע מעד אחד כדקתני בסמוך בתר הכי. לכך פרשב"ם אפי' שמע מעוף הפורח ר"ל על ידי קול בעלמא שמע שנסתרה יוציא ויתן כתובה דנהי דלא משקה על ידי קול מ"מ רבנן אסרוה לו וצריך שיוציא ויתן כתובה דהרי נמצא רגלים לדבר שהרי קינא לה (ונסתרה מקודם לכן. ויוציא ויתן כתובה) הואיל והחמיר בה הכתוב לאוסרה בעד אחד או על פי עצמו. (וה"נ לר') [אבל ר'] יהושע דסבירא ליה דמשקה על פי שנים הואיל והקל בה הכתוב שלא אסרה בעד אחד אלא על פי שנים אף חכמים לא חייבוהו להוציא וליתן כתובה עד שישאו ויתנו בה מוזרות בלבנה. ולא דמי להני דאמרינן לעיל מתו בעליהן עד שלא שתו דאמרי' מתוך שלא שתו לא נוטלות כתובה והכא אמרי' דיוציא ויתן כתובה דשאני התם לפי שראויות היו לשתות קודם שמתו וכשמתו בעליהן דין הוא דכיון דנדחות מלשתות שאין להם כתובה אבל הכא דזאת האשה [לא הייתה] ראויה מעולם [לשתות] אין לה להפסיד כתובה בחנם. ור"ח ז"ל פי' אפי' שמע מעוף הפורח שנטמאת יוציא ויתן כתובה כיון שיש לה קול על טומאה. ר' יהושע אומר עד שישאו ויתנו. אך קשה דהוה ליה למתני בפי' שמע מעוף הפורח שנטמאת כמו דאמר בסמוך עד אחד אומר אני ראיתיה שנטמאת וע"ק דאמר בירוש' בסוף פירקין בעי ר' יוסי שמע מעוף הפורח באויר שאמר אני ראיתיה שנטמאת על זה בא להעיד אם להשקותה כבר נדחית שלא לשתות אלא בא כדי להפסידה כתובתה הרי אין מפסידין ממון על פי עד אחד וא"כ מאי קא מיבעיא ליה התם בזה הא מתני' מיירי בכי

א) נראה דל"ל והוה ליה למתני ישקנה וכו' עד אחד [ומיהו י"ל דס"ל אם אינו רוצה להשקותה]. ועוד קשה וכו'.

ד א מיי' פ"א מהל' סוטה הלכה טז והל' יז ופי"ב מהל' גירושין הל' יח סמג עשין נ טוש"ע אה"ע סימן יז סעיף לז:
ה ב מיי' פ"א מהל' סוטה הל' טז והל' יז:
ו ג מיי' שם הלכה יח ופי"ב מהל' גרושין הלכה כ ופ"ט מהל' רוצח ושמירת נפש הל' טו טז יז סמג עשין עח נ טוש"ע אה"ע סי' יז סעי' לז:

עֵדוּת אַחֲרוֹנָה שֶׁאוֹסַרְתָּהּ אִיסּוּר עוֹלָם — הֲרֵי הִיא מִתְקַיֶּימֶת בְּעֵד אֶחָד, עֵדוּת הָרִאשׁוֹנָה שֶׁאֵין אוֹסַרְתָּהּ אִיסּוּר עוֹלָם — אֵינוֹ דִּין שֶׁתִּתְקַיֵּים בְּעֵד אֶחָד? תַּלְמוּד לוֹמַר: °"כִּי מָצָא בָהּ עֶרְוַת דָּבָר" וּלְהַלָּן הוּא אוֹמֵר °"עַל פִּי שְׁנַיִם עֵדִים יָקוּם דָּבָר", מַה לְּהַלָּן עַל פִּי שְׁנַיִם — אַף כָּאן (א) פִּי שְׁנַיִם. *עֵד אוֹמֵר "נִטְמֵאת" וְעֵד אוֹמֵר "לֹא נִטְמֵאת", אִשָּׁה אוֹמֶרֶת "נִטְמֵאת" וְאִשָּׁה אוֹמֶרֶת "לֹא נִטְמֵאת" — הָיְתָה שׁוֹתָה. אֶחָד אוֹמֵר "נִטְמֵאת" וּשְׁנַיִם אוֹמְרִים "לֹא נִטְמֵאת" — הָיְתָה שׁוֹתָה. שְׁנַיִם אוֹמְרִים "נִטְמֵאת" וְאֶחָד אוֹמֵר "לֹא נִטְמֵאת" — לֹא הָיְתָה שׁוֹתָה.§ **גמ'** הַאי תַּלְמוּד לוֹמַר "כִּי מָצָא בָהּ עֶרְוַת דָּבָר", *ת"ל "בָּהּ" — בָּהּ וְלֹא בְּקִינּוּי, "בָּהּ" וְלֹא בִּסְתִירָה, מִיבְּעֵי לֵיהּ! הָכִי נַמִּי קָאָמַר: תַּלְמוּד לוֹמַר "בָּהּ" — "בָּהּ" וְלֹא בְּקִינּוּי, בָּהּ וְלֹא בִּסְתִירָה. וְטוּמְאָה בְּעָלְמָא, בְּלֹא קִינּוּי וּבְלֹא סְתִירָה, דְּלָא מְהֵימַן עֵד אֶחָד מְנָלַן? נֶאֱמַר כָּאן "דָּבָר" וְנֶאֱמַר לְהַלָּן "דָּבָר", מַה לְּהַלָּן בִּשְׁנֵי עֵדִים — אַף כָּאן בִּשְׁנֵי עֵדִים.§ "עֵד אוֹמֵר נִטְמֵאת".§ טַעְמָא — דְּקָא מַכְחִישׁ לֵיהּ, הָא לָא קָא מַכְחִישׁ לֵיהּ — עֵד אֶחָד מְהֵימַן, מְנָהָנֵי מִילֵּי? דְּתָנוּ *רַבָּנַן: °"וְעֵד אֵין בָּהּ" — בִּשְׁנַיִם הַכָּתוּב מְדַבֵּר. אַתָּה אוֹמֵר בִּשְׁנַיִם אוֹ אֵינוֹ אֶלָּא בְּאֶחָד? תַּלְמוּד לוֹמַר: °"לֹא יָקוּם עֵד אֶחָד בְּאִישׁ" וגו'; מִמַּשְׁמַע שֶׁנֶּאֱמַר "לֹא יָקוּם עֵד" אֵינִי יוֹדֵעַ שֶׁהוּא אֶחָד? מַה תַּלְמוּד לוֹמַר "אֶחָד" — זֶה בָּנָה אָב: *כָּל מָקוֹם שֶׁנֶּאֱמַר "עֵד" — הֲרֵי כָּאן שְׁנַיִם, עַד שֶׁיִּפְרוֹט לְךָ הַכָּתוּב "אֶחָד". וְאָמַר רַחֲמָנָא: תְּרֵי לֵית בָּהּ, אֶלָּא חַד, "וְהִיא לֹא נִתְפָּשָׂה" — אֲסוּרָה. וְכֵיוָן דְּמִדְּאוֹרַיְיתָא עֵד אֶחָד מְהֵימַן — אִידָךְ הֵיכִי מָצֵי מַכְחִישׁ לֵיהּ? וְהָא אָמַר עוּלָּא: *[א]כָּל מָקוֹם שֶׁהֶאֱמִינָה תּוֹרָה עֵד אֶחָד — הֲרֵי כָּאן שְׁנַיִם, וְאֵין דְּבָרָיו שֶׁל אֶחָד בִּמְקוֹם שְׁנַיִם! אֶלָּא אָמַר עוּלָּא: תְּנֵי: לֹא הָיְתָה שׁוֹתָה. וְכֵן אָמַר רַבִּי יִצְחָק: לֹא הָיְתָה שׁוֹתָה. וְרַבִּי חִיָּיא אָמַר: הָיְתָה שׁוֹתָה. לְרַבִּי חִיָּיא קַשְׁיָא דְּעוּלָּא! לָא קַשְׁיָא; [ב]כָּאן — בְּבַת אַחַת, כָּאן — בְּזֶה אַחַר זֶה. תְּנַן: עֵד אוֹמֵר "נִטְמֵאת" וּשְׁנַיִם אוֹמְרִים "לֹא נִטְמֵאת" — הָיְתָה שׁוֹתָה. הָא חַד וְחַד — לֹא הָיְתָה שׁוֹתָה, תְּיוּבְתָּא דְּרַבִּי חִיָּיא! אָמַר לָךְ רַבִּי חִיָּיא: וְלִיטַעֲמִיךְ, אֵימָא סֵיפָא: שְׁנַיִם אוֹמְרִים "נִטְמֵאת" וְאֶחָד אוֹמֵר "לֹא נִטְמֵאת" — לֹא הָיְתָה שׁוֹתָה. הָא חַד וְחַד הָיְתָה שׁוֹתָה! אֶלָּא, כּוּלָּהּ בִּפְסוּלֵי עֵדוּת, וְר' נְחֶמְיָה הִיא. *דְּתַנְיָא, רַבִּי נְחֶמְיָה אוֹמֵר: כָּל מָקוֹם שֶׁהֶאֱמִינָה תּוֹרָה עֵד אֶחָד — הַלֵּךְ אַחַר רוֹב דֵּעוֹת, וְעָשׂוּ שְׁתֵּי נָשִׁים בְּאִישׁ אֶחָד, כִּשְׁנֵי אֲנָשִׁים בְּאִישׁ אֶחָד. [ג]וְאִיכָּא דְּאָמְרִי: כָּל הֵיכָא דַּאֲתָא עֵד אֶחָד כָּשֵׁר מֵעִיקָּרָא — אֲפִי' *מֵאָה נָשִׁים נַמִּי כְּעֵד אֶחָד דָּמְיָין. וְהָכָא

שֶׁאוֹסַרְתָּהּ אִיסּוּר עוֹלָם. כִּדְאָמַר (לעיל דף כח.) בְּסוֹטָה סָפֵק מִ"נִּטְמְאָה" "וְנִטְמְאָה", וְכ"ש וַדָּאִית. עֵד אוֹמֵר נִטְמֵאת וְעֵד אוֹמֵר לֹא נִטְמֵאת. אוֹקֵי חַד בַּהֲדֵי חַד, וַהֲרֵי הִיא כִּסְפֵיקָא, וְשׁוֹתָה. וּשְׁנַיִם אוֹמְרִים לֹא נִטְמֵאת. כְּלוֹמַר: לֹא נִטְמֵאת בְּפָנֶיךָ. שֶׁכְּשֶׁבָּאתָ וּמָצָאתָ שֶׁנִּסְתְּרוּ יַחַד — גַּם אָנוּ הָיִינוּ עִמְּךָ, וּבְפָנֵינוּ לֹא נִטְמֵאת. הֲרֵי נִסְתַּלֵּק הָעֵד הַזֶּה וּבָטְלוּ דְּבָרָיו מִפְּנֵי הַשְּׁנַיִם, וַהֲרֵי הִיא בִּסְפֵיקָא אִם נִטְמֵאת קוֹדֶם שֶׁבָּאוּ אֵלּוּ וּמְצָאוּם, וְהָיְתָה שׁוֹתָה. וּבַגְּמָ' מְפָרֵשׁ לְמַאי אִיצְטְרִיכוּ כָּל הָנָךְ בָּבֵי. **גמ'** בָּהּ וְלֹא בְּקִינּוּי כו'. לְמַאי אִיצְטְרִיךְ גְּזֵירָה שָׁוָה? הָא כְּתִיב גַּבֵּי טוּמְאָה: "וְעֵד אֵין בָּהּ", וּמִיעוּטָא הוּא. בָּהּ עֵד אֶחָד נֶאֱמָן, וְלֹא בְּעֵדוּת אַחֶרֶת. וְהָוְיָא לָהּ עֵדוּת סְתִירָה כִּשְׁאָר כָּל עֵדְיוֹת שֶׁבַּתּוֹרָה! וְטוּמְאָה בְּעָלְמָא. עֵד א' שֶׁהֵעִיד עַל אִשָּׁה שֶׁלֹּא קִינֵּא לָהּ בַּעְלָהּ, וְאָמַר "נִטְמֵאת", מְנַיִין דְּלָא מְהֵימַן, וְלָא אָמְרִינַן אַטּוּמְאַת אִשָּׁה הֵימְנֵיהּ רַחֲמָנָא, לָא שְׁנָא לְאַחַר קִינּוּי וְלָא שְׁנָא בְּלֹא קִינּוּי, תַּלְמוּד לוֹמַר כו'. וְכִי הֵימְנֵיהּ רַחֲמָנָא בְּטוּמְאָה שֶׁאַחַר קִינּוּי וְיֵשׁ עֵדֵי סְתִירָה שְׁנַיִם, וְעֵד מֵעִיד שֶׁנִּטְמֵאת, שֶׁרַגְלַיִם לַדָּבָר. וּבְפֶרֶק קַמָּא (לעיל דף ג.) פָּרְכִינַן: וְהָא כִּי כְּתִיב קִינּוּי בָּתַר הָכִי כְּתִיב! וּמְשַׁנִּינַן: "וְעָבַר" כְּתִיב — שֶׁכְּבָר עָבַר. הָא לָא מַכְחִישׁ לֵיהּ כו'. הוּא הַדִּין דַּהֲוָה לֵיהּ לְמִבְּעֵי אֲרֵישָׁא, דְּקָתָנֵי בְּהֶדְיָא: אֶחָד אוֹמֵר "אֲנִי רְאִיתִיהָ שֶׁנִּטְמֵאת" לֹא הָיְתָה שׁוֹתָה, אַלְמָא מְהֵימַן. אֶלָּא מִשּׁוּם דְּבָעֵי לְאַקְשׁוּיֵי עֲלָהּ: כִּי מַכְחִישׁ לֵיהּ מַאי הָוֵי? הָא הֵימְנֵיהּ רַחֲמָנָא לְהַאי דְּאָמַר "נִטְמֵאת" כְּבֵי תְּרֵי, וַהֲוֵי לֵיהּ הַאי דְּמַכְחִישׁ לֵיהּ חַד, וְאֵין דְּבָרָיו שֶׁל אֶחָד בִּמְקוֹם שְׁנַיִם. הֲרֵי כָּאן שְׁנַיִם. הֲרֵי הוּא כִּשְׁנַיִם. קַשְׁיָא דְּעוּלָּא. דְּכֵיוָן דְּהֶאֱמִינָהּ תּוֹרָה — הֲרֵי הֶעֱמִידָתוֹ בִּמְקוֹם שְׁנַיִם. כָּאן בְּבַת אַחַת. מַתְנִי' — כְּשֶׁהֵעִידוּ שְׁנֵיהֶם בְּתוֹךְ כְּדֵי דִיבּוּר, דְּבָטְלוּ דְּבָרָיו מִיָּד, דְּלֹא נִתְקַיְּימָה עֵדוּתָן בְּבֵ"ד. וְהֵיכָא דְּהֶאֱמִינְהוֹ תּוֹרָה כִּשְׁנַיִם — כְּגוֹן אִם הֵעִיד עֵדוּתוֹ וְיָצָא, דְּתוּ לָא מָצֵי חַד לְאַכְחוּשֵׁיהּ. הָא חַד וְחַד. עַל כָּרְחֵךְ "לֹא הָיְתָה שׁוֹתָה" תְּנָא בְּרֵישָׁא, דְּאִי "הָיְתָה שׁוֹתָה" קָתָנֵי — הָא תּוּ לָמָּה לִי? הַשְׁתָּא בְּחַד הָוֵי הַכְחָשָׁה, תְּרֵי מִבַּעְיָא?! פְּשִׁיטָא דְּאֵין אֶחָד בִּמְקוֹם שְׁנַיִם! וּמַתְנִי' לְדִיּוּקָא דִּידֵיהּ תְּנָא לֵיהּ, דְּאִי לְאַשְׁמוּעִינַן הִיא גּוּפָהּ — פְּשִׁיטָא, דְּלָא אִיצְטְרִיךְ. **אָמַר לָךְ ר' חִיָּיא** וּלְטַעְמִיךְ. דִּסְבִירָא לָךְ דְּמַתְנִי' לְגוּפֵיהּ לָא אִיצְטְרִיךְ, דְּהָא פְּשִׁיטָא דְּאֵין א' בִּמְקוֹם שְׁנַיִם, וּלְדִיּוּקָא אָתָא, סֵיפָא — מַאי תִּידּוֹק מִינָּהּ? אֶלָּא מַתְנִי' לָא לְדִיּוּקָא אָתָא, אֶלָּא לְאַשְׁמוּעִינַן הִיא גּוּפָהּ אִיצְטְרִיךְ, דִּשְׁנַיִם דְּקָא תָּנָא — בִּפְסוּלֵי עֵדוּת קָאָמַר, כְּגוֹן נָשִׁים אוֹ עֲבָדִים, וְאַשְׁמוּעִינַן דִּשְׁתֵּי נָשִׁים מְבַטְּלוֹת דִּבְרֵי עֵד א', בֵּין בְּרֵישָׁא בֵּין בְּסֵיפָא. וּלְקַמָּן פָּרֵיךְ: תַּרְתֵּי לָמָּה לִי? וְהַאי דְּלָא שָׁנֵי ר' חִיָּיא מְצִיעֲתָא בְּזֶה אַחַר זֶה (ג) — מִשּׁוּם דְּקָא דָּיֵיק מַתְנִי' בְּבַת אַחַת, דְּקָתָנֵי: וּשְׁנַיִם אוֹמְרִים לֹא א) *רְאִינוּהָ — אַלְמָא בַּהֲדֵי הֲדָדֵי קָאָתוּ, דִּלְעוֹלָם בִּמְקוֹם שְׁנַיִם לֹא הֶאֱמִינָה תּוֹרָה עֵד אֶחָד. כָּל מָקוֹם שֶׁהֶאֱמִינָה תּוֹרָה כו'. הוֹצִיאַתּוּ לְעֵדוּת זֶה מִכְּלַל כָּל עֵדְיוֹת שֶׁבַּתּוֹרָה, לְפִיכָךְ פְּסוּלִין וּכְשֵׁרִין שָׁוִין בָּהּ, וְהַלֵּךְ אַחַר רוֹב דֵּעוֹת הַמְּעִידִין בַּדָּבָר. וְאִיכָּא דְּאָמְרִי כָּל הֵיכָא דַּאֲתָא עֵד כָּשֵׁר מֵעִיקָּרָא. וְאָמַר "נִטְמֵאת", וְנִתְקַבְּלָה עֵדוּתוֹ, וְאַחַר כָּךְ בָּאוּ מֵאָה נָשִׁים — כְּעֵד א' דָּמְיָין, וַהֲוָה לֵיהּ קַמָּא שְׁנַיִם, וְאֵין דְּבָרָיו שֶׁל אֶחָד בִּמְקוֹם שְׁנַיִם, וְאֵינָהּ שׁוֹתָה. וְהָכָא

א) נ"ל ראית ועי' רש"א

כאן בבת אחת כאן בזה אחר זה. קשיא: דהכא משמע כיון שנתקבל עדותו של ראשון, ואע"פ שלא עשו ע"י עדותו שום מעשה ולא שום הוראה, רק שלא העיד השני בתוך כדי דיבורו של ראשון — הוי דבריו של שני במקום ראשון כדבריו של אחד במקום שנים, הכי משמע לפירוש רש"י. והא בפרק "האשה שהלכה" (יבמות דף קיז:) תנן: עד אומר מת, וניסת, ובא אחר ואמר לא מת — לא תצא. וקא דייק בגמ': טעמא — דניסת, הא לכתחילה — לא תנשא, והאמר עולא וכו'! ומשני, הכי קאמר: עד אומר מת והתירוה לינשא, ובא אחר ואמר לא מת — לא תצא מהתירה הראשון. והא התם, דבזה אחר זה מיירי, דהא ניסת בנתיים — ואפ"ה, בכה"ג בזה אחר זה, אם לא ניסת — לא תנשא אא"כ התירוה לינשא, דאמר: "לא תצא מהתירה הראשון". ופירש נמי רש"י התם: דדוקא שהתירוה קודם שיבא עד השני המכחישו, אבל אם קודם שהתירוה — מודה עולא דלא סמכינן אקמא, דהכתי לא אחשביניה כתרי! להכי נראה לפרש הכא: בזה אחר זה — שקיבלו עדות הראשון, והורו ע"פ עדותו. מיהו, תימה: עולא גופיה, דאמר הכי אליביה: תני לא היתה שותה — מה דוחקיה למימר הכי? והא מתניתין לא משמע ששהה השני אחר הראשון עד שהורו ואסרוה עליו, ואמרו: אינה שותה! וי"ל: דמתניתין בסתם קתני. אי נמי: רבי יצחק ועולא הוה מתרצי להכיא ד"האשה זוטא" כדמתרצי אליבא דר' יוחנן בפ' שני דכתובות (דף כב:): משום לזות שפתים. והכיא ד"האשה רבה" (יבמות דף פח:) לא דמיא לתרוייהו, משום דגברא אתי וקאי. **הא** חד וחד לא היתה שותה תיובתא דרבי חייא. נראה: האי דלא דחי ליה בזה אחר זה — משום דסוף סוף תיקשי דיוקא דסיפא, דשנים אומרים נטמאת וא' אומר לא נטמאת לא היתה שותה, הא חד וחד — היתה שותה, במאי מוקמת לה? ע"כ בבת אחת, מאי קמ"ל — היינו רישא! הילכך צריך לתרולי כר' נחמיה, בין לר' יצחק בין לר' חייא, הני תרתי בבי דסיפא. תימה: היכי הוה מתרץ ר' יצחק מתני' דפרק "אמרו לו" (כריתות דף יא:) דתנן: עד אמר אכל ועד אמר לא אכל, אשה אומרת אכל ואשה אומרת לא אכל — מביא אשם תלוי. כיון דהאמינה תורה עד אחד, דנפקא לן מ"או הודע אליו חטאתו" (ויקרא ד) — חטאת הוי ליה לאיתויי! בשלמא רבי חייא הוה מוקי לה בבת אחת. ירושלמי: גידל בר בנימן בשם רב אמר: בכל מקום *) שהכשירו עד אחד — עדות האשה כאיש, האיש מכחיש את האשה והאשה מכחשת את האיש. דתנן: עד א' אמר נטמאת ואשה אומרת לא נטמאת, אשה אומרת נטמאת ועד א' אמר לא נטמאת. תנא דבי רבי אומר כן. ותו בירושלמי: עד אחד אמר נטמאת ועד אחד אמר לא נטמאת, שמעון ב"ר אבא בשם ר' יוחנן: כאן לא היתה שותה, ובעגלה ערופה היו עורפין. וטעמא — מפני שכאן רגלים לדבר. ומסיק נמי התם דבעידי טומאה לא אמרינן עדות שבטלה מקצתה בטלה כולה, מפני שרגלים לדבר.

*) שהכשירו עדות האשה כאיש האיש כו' את האיש ניתני עד אחד כו'. רש"ל

תוספות שאנץ

בכי האי גונא לכ"נ כפרשב"ם דקאי אסתירה ולא קאי אטומאה: **גמ'** טעמא דקא מכחיש ליה הא לא מכחיש ליה עד אחד נאמן וה"ה דהוה ליה למבעי ארישא מה"מ דעד אחד נאמן דקתני בהדיא עד אחד אומר אני ראיתיה שנטמאת לא היתה שותה אלמא נאמן. אלא משום הכי מייתי מסיפא משום דבעי אקשויי עלה כי מכחיש ליה מאי הוי הא הימניה רחמנא להאי דאמר נטמאת כבי תרי והוי ליה האי דמכחיש חד ואין דבריו של אחד במקום שנים ל"ה. לא קשיא כאן בבת אחת הא דאמרינן דשותה מיירי כשבאו בבת אחת והעידו שנים ביחד ולא נתקיימה עדותן בב"ד והיכא התורה האמינתו כשנים בהעידו זה אחר זה: א) ועולא מי לא מפליג כי בבת אחת בין בזה אחר זה דשני תני רבה שותה דלא משני כמו ר' חייא והא אמרינן בפרק האשה שלום על הא דתנן עד אחד אומר מת ונשאת ובא עד ואמר לא מת הרי זו לא תצא ודייק בגמ' טעמא דנשאת הא לא נשאת לא תנשא והאמר עולא כו'. ומשני ה"ק התירוה להנשא אע"ג דלא נשאת אלמא משמע דמפליג עולא בין בת אחת לזה אחר זה. וי"ל דאין הכי נמי הוה מצי מפליג עולא הכא אלא שינויי דר' חייא לא סבירא ליה משום דמקשי תלמודא על מילתיה. א"נ י"ל דגבי אשה בעלמא שהיא ב) דרבנן מפליג בין בבת אחת בין בזה אחר זה דיש להקל עליה אבל גבי סוטה שהיא דאורייתא בין בבת אחת לזה אחר זה: הא חד וחד לא היתה שותה ותיובתא דר' חייא ופ"ה דה"ה דהוה מצי לשנויי מתני' בזה אחר זה המציעתא ולא ק' ליה לר' חייא אלא לא בעי לאוקומי רישא בחד טעמא וסיפא בחד טעמא ועוד דסוף סוף דמדיוקא ג) דמציעתא הלך מוכח רישא בבת אחת ומציעתא וסיפא בין בבת אחת בין בזה אחר זה דלעולם במקום שנים לא האמינה תורה עד אחד כפ"ה. ורשב"ם פי' דלא מצי לשנויי דמיירי בזה אחר זה ודיוקא דמתני' בבת אחת משום דקתני ושנים אומרים שנטמאת משמע דבהדדי אתו: ד) ואיכא דאמרי כל היכא דאתא עד אחד כשר מעיקרא והכא במ"ע דקתני עד אחד אומר נטמאת ושנים אומרים לא נטמאת היתה שותה ואוקמ' בפסולי עדות ובין בבת אחת בין בזה אחר זה. (וע"כ) ר' נחמיה וע"כ בזה אחר זה איצטריך עיקר לאשמועי' דאי לבת אחת מאי רוב דעות איכא בחד וחד נמי היתה שותה והב"ע

[תוספתא פ"ה]
לעיל ג.
שם ב.
גם זה שם: סנהדרין ל.
יבמות פח: קיז: כתובות כב: לקמן מז:
לקמן מז: יבמות פח: קיז: [תוספתא יבמות פי"ד ע"ש]
[לקמן מז: יבמות פח: קטו. קיז:]
[נ"ל נטמאת]

א) אולי נ"ל וקשה דמשמע דעולא לא מפליג בין בבת אחת וכו' דשני דקתני דלא היתה שותה ולא משני כמו ר' חייא וא"ת הא אמרינן: ב) אולי נ"ל דגבי אשה משום חומר דא"א החמירו מדרבנן להפליג בין בת אחת וכו' אבל בסוטה לענין דאורייתא אינו מפליג בין וכו'. ג) אולי נ"ל דמדיוקא דמציעתא גופיה מוכח דמיירי בבת אחת מדקתני ושנים אומרים וכו' וכן בסיפא בודאי מיירי אפילו בבת אחת דלעולם וכו'. ד) נראה דל"ל אלא כולה בפסולי עדות והא דקתני וכו' שותה אוקמינן וכו' ור' נחמיה היא.

הגהות הב"ח (א) במשנה אף כאן על פי: (ב) רש"י ד"ה אמר לך וכו' רבי חייא מציעתא בזה אחר זה דלעולם במקום שנים לא האמינה תורה עד אחד משום דקא דייק וכו' לא ראית אלמא בהדי הדדי קאתו הס"ד ונ"ב כלומר לא הוה ניחא ליה לאוקמי מתני' דלא מיירי אלא בזה אחר זה דמסתמא ודאי כיון דלאו העדות ביחד באו בבת אחת לב"ד אבל בסמוך קא מפרש רש"י דבזא"ז נמי מוקמינן לה ובין בבת אחת ובין בזא"ז קמיירי:

וְהָכָא בְּמַאי עָסְקִינַן — כְּגוֹן דַּאֲתַאי אִשָּׁה
מֵעִיקָּרָא. וְתַרְצַהּ לְדְרַבִּי נְחֶמְיָה הָכִי: ר' נְחֶמְיָה
אוֹמֵר: כָּל מָקוֹם שֶׁהֶאֱמִינָה תּוֹרָה עֵד אֶחָד —
הַלֵּךְ אַחַר רוֹב דֵּיעוֹת, וְעָשׂוּ שְׁתֵּי נָשִׁים בְּאִשָּׁה
אַחַת כִּשְׁנֵי אֲנָשִׁים בְּאִישׁ אֶחָד, אֲבָל שְׁתֵּי
נָשִׁים בְּאִישׁ אֶחָד — כִּי פַּלְגָּא וּפַלְגָּא דָּמֵי. וְתַרְתֵּי
בִּפְסוּלֵי עֵדוּת לָמָּה לִי? מַהוּ דְּתֵימָא: כִּי
אָזְלִינַן בָּתַר רוֹב דֵּיעוֹת — לְחוּמְרָא, אֲבָל לְקוּלָּא
— לָא אָזְלִינַן, קמ"ל.§

הדרן עלך מי שקינא

אֵלּוּ *נֶאֱמָרִין בְּכָל לָשׁוֹן: [א]פָּרָשַׁת סוֹטָה,
[ב]וִידּוּי מַעֲשֵׂר, [ג]קְרִיַּת שְׁמַע, [ד]וּתְפִלָּה,
[ה]וּבִרְכַּת הַמָּזוֹן, [ו]וּשְׁבוּעַת הָעֵדוּת, [ז]וּשְׁבוּעַת
הַפִּקָּדוֹן. וְאֵלּוּ נֶאֱמָרִין בִּלְשׁוֹן הַקּוֹדֶשׁ: [ח]מִקְרָא
בִּיכּוּרִים, [ט]וַחֲלִיצָה, בְּרָכוֹת וּקְלָלוֹת, [י]בִּרְכַּת
כֹּהֲנִים, וּבִרְכַּת כֹּהֵן גָּדוֹל, [כ]וּפָרָשַׁת הַמֶּלֶךְ,
[ל]וּפָרָשַׁת עֶגְלָה עֲרוּפָה, [מ]וּמְשׁוּחַ מִלְחָמָה בְּשָׁעָה
דברים כו שֶׁמְּדַבֵּר אֶל הָעָם. מִקְרָא בִּיכּוּרִים כֵּיצַד? °"וְעָנִיתָ
וְאָמַרְתָּ לִפְנֵי ה' אֱלֹהֶיךָ", וּלְהַלָּן הוּא אוֹמֵר
שם כז °"וְעָנוּ הַלְוִיִּם וְאָמְרוּ", מַה לְהַלָּן בִּלְשׁוֹן הַקּוֹדֶשׁ
שם כה — אַף כָּאן בִּלְשׁוֹן הַקּוֹדֶשׁ. חֲלִיצָה כֵּיצַד? °"וְעָנְתָה
וְאָמְרָה", וּלְהַלָּן הוּא אוֹמֵר "וְעָנוּ הַלְוִיִּם וְאָמְרוּ", מַה לְהַלָּן בִּלְשׁוֹן הַקּוֹדֶשׁ — אַף כָּאן
בִּלְשׁוֹן הַקּוֹדֶשׁ. ר' יְהוּדָה אוֹמֵר: "וְעָנְתָה וְאָמְרָה כָּכָה" — עַד שֶׁתֹּאמַר בַּלָּשׁוֹן הַזֶּה.
בְּרָכוֹת וּקְלָלוֹת כֵּיצַד? כֵּיוָן שֶׁעָבְרוּ יִשְׂרָאֵל אֶת הַיַּרְדֵּן וּבָאוּ אֶל הַר גְּרִיזִים וְאֶל
שם יא הַר עֵיבָל שֶׁבְּשׁוֹמְרוֹן, שֶׁבְּצַד שְׁכֶם, שֶׁבְּאֵצֶל אֵלוֹנֵי מוֹרֶה, שֶׁנֶּאֱמַר: °"הֲלֹא הֵמָּה
בראשית יב בְּעֵבֶר הַיַּרְדֵּן" וגו', וּלְהַלָּן הוּא אוֹמֵר: °"וַיַּעֲבֹר אַבְרָם בָּאָרֶץ עַד מְקוֹם שְׁכֶם עַד
אֵלוֹן מוֹרֶה", מָה אֵלוֹן מוֹרֶה הָאָמוּר לְהַלָּן — שְׁכֶם, אַף אֵלוֹן מוֹרֶה הָאָמוּר כָּאן — שְׁכֶם.
שִׁשָּׁה שְׁבָטִים עָלוּ לְרֹאשׁ הַר גְּרִיזִים וְשִׁשָּׁה שְׁבָטִים עָלוּ לְרֹאשׁ הַר עֵיבָל,
וְהַכֹּהֲנִים וְהַלְוִיִּם וְהָאָרוֹן עוֹמְדִים לְמַטָּה בָּאֶמְצַע. הַכֹּהֲנִים מַקִּיפִין אֶת הָאָרוֹן,
יהושע ח וְהַלְוִיִּם אֶת הַכֹּהֲנִים, וְכָל יִשְׂרָאֵל מִכָּאן וּמִכָּאן, שֶׁנֶּאֱמַר: °"וְכָל יִשְׂרָאֵל וּזְקֵנָיו
וְשׁוֹטְרָיו וְשׁוֹפְטָיו עוֹמְדִים מִזֶּה וּמִזֶּה לָאָרוֹן" וגו'. הָפְכוּ פְּנֵיהֶם כְּלַפֵּי הַר
גְּרִיזִים וּפָתְחוּ בִּבְרָכָה: "בָּרוּךְ הָאִישׁ אֲשֶׁר לֹא יַעֲשֶׂה פֶּסֶל וּמַסֵּכָה", וְאֵלּוּ
דברים כז וָאֵלּוּ עוֹנִין אָמֵן. הָפְכוּ פְּנֵיהֶם כְּלַפֵּי הַר עֵיבָל וּפָתְחוּ בִּקְלָלָה: °"אָרוּר הָאִישׁ אֲשֶׁר
יַעֲשֶׂה פֶסֶל וּמַסֵּכָה", וְאֵלּוּ וָאֵלּוּ עוֹנִין אָמֵן, עַד שֶׁגּוֹמְרִין בְּרָכוֹת וּקְלָלוֹת. וְאַחַר
כָּךְ הֵבִיאוּ אֶת הָאֲבָנִים, וּבָנוּ אֶת הַמִּזְבֵּחַ, וְסָדוּהוּ בְּסִיד, וְכָתְבוּ עָלָיו אֶת כָּל
שם דִּבְרֵי הַתּוֹרָה בְּשִׁבְעִים לָשׁוֹן, שֶׁנֶּאֱמַר: °"בַּאֵר הֵיטֵב". וְנָטְלוּ אֶת הָאֲבָנִים וּבָאוּ
וְלָנוּ

וְהָכָא בְּמַאי עָסְקִינַן. דְּקָתָנֵי: עֵד אֶחָד אוֹמֵר "נִטְמֵאת" וּשְׁנַיִם אוֹמְרִים
"לֹא נִטְמֵאת" הָיְתָה שׁוֹתָה, וְאוֹקִימְנָא בִּפְסוּלֵי עֵדוּת וּבֵין בְּבַת אַחַת בֵּין
בְּזֶה אַחַר זֶה, כְּר' נְחֶמְיָה. וְעַל כָּרְחֵיךְ דִּבְזֶה אַחַר זֶה אִיצְטְרִיךְ עִיקָּר
לְאַשְׁמוּעִינַן, דְּאִי בְּבַת אַחַת — מַאי הַלֵּךְ אַחַר רוֹב דֵּיעוֹת אִיכָּא? כְּחַד
וְחַד נַמִי הָיְתָה שׁוֹתָה! [אֶלָּא] בְּהָכִי תורה אור
עָסְקִינַן; דְּהַהוּא דַּאֲתָא מֵעִיקָּרָא וְאָמַר
"נִטְמֵאת" — אִשָּׁה הֲוָיָא. הִילְכָּךְ אֲפִי'
בְּזֶה אַחַר זֶה — אָתוּ תַּרְתֵּי וּמְבַטְּלִי לָהּ.
וְתַרְצַהּ לְדְרַבִּי נְחֶמְיָה הָכִי כו'. דְּהָא
דַּאֲמָרַן לְעֵיל: וְעָשׂוּ שְׁתֵּי נָשִׁים בְּאִישׁ
אֶחָד כו' — לָאו סֵיפָא דְּמִילְּתֵיהּ דְּרַבִּי
נְחֶמְיָה הוּא, אֶלָּא פֵּירוּשָׁא דְּמִילְּתֵיהּ
הוּא, דְּתָנוּ פָּרְשִׁין לָהּ הָכִי. **כִּי פַּלְגָּא
וּפַלְגָּא** דָּמֵי. כְּלוֹמַר, כִּי חַד וְחַד. וְאִי
בְּבַת אַחַת אָתוּ — אוֹקֵי תְּרֵי לְגַבֵּי חַד,
וְאוֹקְמֵיהּ אַסְפֵיקָא. וְאִי בְּזֶה אַחַר זֶה,
וְהַהוּא דְּהֶאֱמִינָהּ תּוֹרָה קָדֵם וַאֲתָא
בְּרֵישָׁא — הֲוָה לֵיהּ כִּשְׁנַיִם, וְהָנָךְ כְּחַד,
וְאֵין דִּבְרֵיהֶם בִּמְקוֹמוֹ. וְהֵיכָא דִּשְׁתַּיִם
אוֹמְרוֹת "נִטְמֵאת" וְעֵד אֶחָד כָּשֵׁר אוֹמֵר
"לֹא נִטְמֵאת" — הָיְתָה שׁוֹתָה, דְּכִי חַד
וְחַד נִינְהוּ. וּמַתְנִיתִין דְּקָתָנֵי: לֹא הָיְתָה
שׁוֹתָה — כְּגוֹן דְּהַהוּא חַד הֲוָה פָּסוּל.
וְתַרְתֵּי **בִּפְסוּלֵי** עֵדוּת לָמָּה לִי. לְמִתְנֵי
מַתְנִי' הַלֵּךְ אַחַר רוֹב דֵּיעוֹת? **לְחוּמְרָא**.
שֶׁתִּשְׁתֶּה. **לְקוּלָּא**. לְהָקֵל מֵעָלֶיהָ, שֶׁלֹּא
תִּשְׁתֶּה. **לָא אָזְלִינַן**. בָּתַר רוֹב דֵּיעוֹת
בִּפְסוּלֵי עֵדוּת, וְהֵיכָא דִּשְׁתַּיִם אוֹמְרוֹת
"נִטְמֵאת" וְאֶחָד אוֹמֵר "לֹא נִטְמֵאת",
כֵּיוָן דְּאִיכָּא הַכְחָשָׁה כָּל דְּהוּ — נֵימָא:
אוֹקֵי הַאי לְגַבֵּי הָנָךְ, וְאוֹקֵי מִילְּתָא
אַסְפֵיקָא וְתִשְׁתֶּה, קָא מַשְׁמַע לָן.

הדרן עלך מי שקינא

אֵלּוּ נֶאֱמָרִין *(בְּכָל לָשׁוֹן) גָּרְסִינַן. **פָּרָשַׁת סוֹטָה**. מַה שֶּׁהַכֹּהֵן
אוֹמֵר לָהּ, וְלָא אָמְרִי' צָרִיךְ לְאוֹמְרָהּ
בִּלְשׁוֹן הַקּוֹדֶשׁ כְּדֶרֶךְ שֶׁנִּכְתַּב. וּבְסִפְרִי
אָמְרִי' דְּאִי לָא כְּתִיב קְרָא לְהַתִּיר בְּכָל
לָשׁוֹן כִּדְלְקַמָּן — ה"א נִיגְמַר מִיבָּמָה בְּקַל
וָחוֹמֶר; וּמַה יְבָמָה קַלָּה לֹא עָשָׂה בָּהּ
כָּל הַלְּשׁוֹנוֹת כִּלְשׁוֹן הַקּוֹדֶשׁ — סוֹטָה
חֲמוּרָה לֹא כָּל שֶׁכֵּן. **וִידּוּי מַעֲשֵׂר**.
בַּשָּׁנָה הַשְּׁלִישִׁית: "בִּעַרְתִּי הַקּוֹדֶשׁ מִן
הַבַּיִת" (דברים כו). שֶׁהוּא מוֹצִיא כָּל
מַעַשְׂרוֹתָיו וּמְבַעֲרָן מִבֵּיתוֹ, וְאֵין יָכוֹל
עוֹד לְהַשְׁהוֹתָם, וְנוֹתֵן מַעֲשֵׂר רִאשׁוֹן
לַלֵּוִי, וּמַעֲשַׂר עָנִי לָעֲנִיִּים, וּמַעֲשֵׂר שֵׁנִי
שֶׁל שְׁתֵּי שָׁנִים שֶׁעָבְרוּ — מַעֲלֵיהוּ לִירוּשָׁלַיִם עַכְשָׁיו אִם לֹא הֶעֱלָהוּ, וּמִתְוַדֶּה: "בִּעַרְתִּי הַקֹּדֶשׁ" — זֶה מַעֲשֵׂר שֵׁנִי, "וְגַם נְתַתִּיו לַלֵּוִי" — זֶה מַעֲשֵׂר רִאשׁוֹן, "לַגֵּר
לַיָּתוֹם וְלָאַלְמָנָה" — זֶה מַעֲשַׂר עָנִי. וְאוֹמְרוֹ בְּכָל לָשׁוֹן, כִּדְיָלֵיף לְקַמָּן, וְלָא אָמְרִינַן: בְּלָשׁוֹן זֶה הִזְקִיקוֹ הַכָּתוּב לְאוֹמְרָהּ בִּלה"ק. **וּשְׁבוּעַת הָעֵדוּת וּשְׁבוּעַת
הַפִּקָּדוֹן**. בְּכָל לָשׁוֹן שֶׁהִשְׁבִּיעוּהוּ וְכָפַר וְלֹא הוֹדָה — חַיָּיב קָרְבַּן עוֹלֶה וְיוֹרֵד הָאָמוּר בִּשְׁבוּעַת הָעֵדוּת, וְאָשָׁם גְּזֵילוֹת בִּשְׁבוּעַת הַפִּקָּדוֹן. **וְאֵלּוּ נֶאֱמָרִין
בִּלה"ק**. וְלָא אָמְרִינַן: נִגְמַר מֵהָנָךְ דִּלְעֵיל שֶׁנִּכְתַּב וְנִסְדַּר עֲלֵיהֶן כָּל מִצְוַת דִּיבּוּרָם וְאֵין צָרִיךְ לְאוֹמְרָן בִּלה"ק, כִּדְכְתִיב בְּכוּלְּהוּ. מִשּׁוּם דְּבְהָנֵי כְּתִיב
עֲנִיָּיה. **מִקְרָא בִּיכּוּרִים**. שֶׁהָיָה קוֹרֵא מֵ"אֲרַמִּי אוֹבֵד אָבִי" עַד סוֹף כָּל הַפָּרָשָׁה. **וַחֲלִיצַת יְבָמָה**. הִיא אוֹמֶרֶת "מֵאֵן יְבָמִי" וגו', וְהוּא אוֹמֵר "לֹא
חָפַצְתִּי לְקַחְתָּהּ", וְאַחַר הַחֲלִיצָה הִיא אוֹמֶרֶת "כָּכָה יֵעָשֶׂה לָאִישׁ" וגו'. **בְּרָכוֹת וּקְלָלוֹת**. שֶׁאָמְרָן יְהוֹשֻׁעַ וְיִשְׂרָאֵל בְּהַר גְּרִיזִים וְהַר עֵיבָל. **בִּרְכַּת
כֹּהֲנִים**. נְשִׂיאוּת כַּפַּיִם. **בִּרְכַּת כֹּהֵן גָּדוֹל**. בְּיוֹם הַכִּפּוּרִים, אַחַר עֲבוֹדַת הַיּוֹם, שֶׁלְּפָנַי וְלִפְנִים הָיָה קוֹרֵא בַּתּוֹרָה אֶת הַפָּרָשָׁה, וּמְבָרֵךְ שְׁמֹנֶה
[א] בְּרָכוֹת, כִּדְמְפָרֵשׁ בְּמַתְנִיתִין. **וּפָרָשַׁת הַמֶּלֶךְ**. מְפָרֵשׁ בְּסוֹף פִּירְקָא, וְהִיא פָּרָשַׁת הַקְהֵל*. **וּפָרָשַׁת עֶגְלָה עֲרוּפָה**. "יָדֵינוּ לֹא שָׁפְכוּ" וגו', "כַּפֵּר
לְעַמְּךָ יִשְׂרָאֵל" וגו' (דברים כא). **פָּרָשַׁת מְשׁוּחַ מִלְחָמָה**. (שם כ) "וְהָיָה כְּקָרָבְכֶם אֶל" וגו', "שְׁמַע יִשְׂרָאֵל אַתֶּם קְרֵבִים הַיּוֹם" וגו', "כִּי ה' אֱלֹהֵיכֶם" וגו'.
[דף לג.] **כֵּיצַד**. כְּמוֹ תְּנַן. וּלְהַלָּן הוּא **אוֹמֵר**. בִּבְרָכוֹת וּקְלָלוֹת שֶׁל הַר גְּרִיזִים. וּלְקַמָּן *מְפָרֵשׁ הָתָם גּוּפֵיהּ מְנָא לָן (א). *) **אֵינוֹ צָרִיךְ**. לְלַמְּדָהּ בִּגְזֵרָה
שָׁוָה, שֶׁמֵּעַצְמָהּ הִיא לְמֵידָה. **וְעָנְתָה וְאָמְרָה כָּכָה**. *דְּמַשְׁמַע: כְּלָשׁוֹן זֶה תֹּאמַר. **שֶׁבְּשׁוֹמְרוֹן**. אֵצֶל שׁוֹמְרוֹן. **לְמַטָּה בָּאֶמְצַע**. בֵּין שְׁנֵי הֶהָרִים.
מִכָּאן וּמִכָּאן. עַל הֶהָרִים. **הָפְכוּ**. הַלְוִיִּם פְּנֵיהֶם כְּלַפֵּי הַר גְּרִיזִים, וּפָתְחוּ בִּבְרָכָה; כָּל הָאֲרוּרִים הָיוּ אוֹמְרִים תְּחִלָּה בִּלְשׁוֹן בְּרָכָה. **אֵלּוּ
וָאֵלּוּ**. שֶׁבְּהַר גְּרִיזִים וְשֶׁבְּהַר עֵיבָל. וְהָא דִּכְתִיב: "וְאֵלֶּה יַעַמְדוּ לְבָרֵךְ" — לֹא שֶׁהָיוּ הַשְּׁבָטִים מְבָרְכִין וּמְקַלְּלִין, אֶלָּא הַלְוִיִּם הָעוֹמְדִים בֵּין שְׁנֵי הֶהָרִים,
הוֹפְכִין פְּנֵיהֶם לְהַר גְּרִיזִים בִּבְרָכָה וּלְהַר עֵיבָל בִּקְלָלָה. **הֵבִיאוּ אֶת הָאֲבָנִים**. כִּדְכְתִיב: "וּבָנִיתָ שָּׁם מִזְבֵּחַ וגו' וְכָתַבְתָּ עֲלֵיהֶן אֶת כָּל דִּבְרֵי הַתּוֹרָה
הַזֹּאת בַּאֵר הֵיטֵב". **וְנָטְלוּ אֶת הָאֲבָנִים**. סָתְרוּ אֶת הַמִּזְבֵּחַ לְאַחַר שֶׁהֶעֱלוּ הָעוֹלוֹת וְהַשְּׁלָמִים, כִּדְכְתִיב: "וְהַעֲלִיתָ עָלָיו עוֹלוֹת" (שם כז).
וְלָנוּ
*) עיין רש"א

מהו דתימא כי אזלינן בתר רוב דיעות לחומרא **אבל** לקולא **לא** קמ"ל. ואם תאמר: הא ממתני' בפרק "האשה שהלכה" (יבמות ד' קיז:) וממתני' דפרק "עגלה ערופה" (לקמן דף מז.) שמעינן להו! י"ל: דהכא איצטריך, דאפילו לקולא, אע"ג דרגלים לדבר. ועוד: דלא תנא פסולי העדות בהדיא במתני', להכי תנא גבי כל חד וחד.

הדרן עלך מי שקנא

ה"ג בסדר המשנה
אלו נאמרין בלשונם. ופירוש: כל אדם בלשונו שהוא שומע. לאפוקי למדי שאינו אומר בלשון פרסי, אם אינו שומעו. אבל בכל לשון — משמע בין שומע בין אינו שומע. ובגמרא לא משמע הכי. **קרית** שמע ותפלה. תימה: אמאי שייר הלל, וקידוש של שבת, וברכת הפירות, וברכת המצות? וליכא למימר דלא נקט אלא דאורייתא, דהא בפרק "מי שמתו" (ברכות דף כא.) משמע דתפלה וקרית שמע דרבנן! ועוד: דהתם (דף כ:) משמע דקידוש דאורייתא, והכי משמע נמי בריש מסכת נזיר (דף ג:) בשלמא מקרא מגילה איכא למימר: להכי שייר, דתנא בפ"ב דמגילה (דף יז.): הלועז ששמע אשורית — יצא. אלא הני אמאי שייר?! ונראה דהני נאמרים בכל לשון אפי' אינו שומע, הלכך לא דמו להני דמתני', דנאמרין דוקא בלשונם*.
איהו

א א מיי' פ"ג מהל' סוטה הל"ז סמג עשין נו:

ב ב מיי' פי"א מהל' מעשר שני הל"ה סמג עשין קלח:

ג ג מיי' פ"ב מהל' ק"ש הל"י סמג עשין יח טוש"ע או"ח סי' סב סעי' ב [וברב אלפס ברכות ר"פ שני דף ט. וברא"ש שם סי' כ]:

ד ד טוש"ע א"ח סי' קא סעי' ד:

ה ה מיי' פ"א מהל' ברכות הל"ו סמג עשין כו טוש"ע או"ח סי' קפה סעי' א:

ו ו מיי' פ"ט מהל' שבועות הלי"ב סמג לאוין רמח:

ז ז מיי' שם פ"ז הל' ז סמג שם:

ח ח מיי' פ"ג מהל' ביכורים הל"י סמג עשין קא:

ט ט מיי' פ"ד מהל' יבום וחליצה הל"ח סמג עשין נב טוש"ע אה"ע סי' קסט סעי' כט ובסדר חליצה סעי' מח ובפי' סדר חליצה סעי' סז:

י י מיי' פי"ד מהל' נשיאות כפים הלכה יא סמג עשין כ טוש"ע או"ח סי' קכח סעי' יד:

יא כ מיי' פ"ג מהל' חגיגה הל"ה סמג עשין רל:

[והא דלא תני במתני' שבועת הדיינין ושבועת ביטוי ע' תוס' שבועות לט. ד"ה ואלו נאמרין וכו' וע' תוי"ט ד"ה ושבועת הפקדון]

יב ל מיי' פ"ט מהל' רוצח ושמירת נפש הל"ג סמג עשין עח:

יג מ מיי' פ"ז מהל' מלכים הל"ג סמג עשין קכ:

תוספות שאנץ

והב"ע כגון דההיא דאתא מעיקרא אשה הואי. הילכך בזה אחר זה אתו תרתי ומבטלי ליה: ותרצה לדר' נחמיה. דאמר עשו שתי נשים כאיש אחד לאו סיפיה דמלתיה דר' נחמיה הוא אלא פירוש דמלתא היא דאנן פרשי לה הכי: כי פלגא ופלגא כחד וחד ואי בבת אחת אתו אוקי חד להדי חד ואוקמי' אספיקא ואי בזה אחר זה וההוא דהאמינה תורה קדם ברישא הוה ליה איהו כשנים והנך כחד ואין דבריהם במקומו. והיכא דשנים אומרים שנטמאת ועד אחד כשר אומר שלא נטמאת היתה שותה דכי חד וחד נינהו ומתני' דקתני לא היתה שותה כגון דההוא חד הוי פסול:

סליק פירקא

אלו נאמרין בכל לשון פרשת סוטה מה שהכהן אומר לה. ולא אמרינן שצריך לאומרם בלשון הקדש כדרך שנכתב נצטווה לאומרו ובספרי אמרי' דאי לא כתב קרא להתיר בכל לשון ה"א דנגמר מיבמה מק"ו ומה יבמה קלה לא עשה בה כל הלשונות כלשון הקדש סוטה שהיא חמורה לא כל שכן ל"ה. וא"ת אמאי לא חשיב שבועת הדיינין דאמר בפ' שבועת הדיינין דאף היא בכל לשון נאמרה. וי"ל דתנא ושייר ומה שייר דהא שייר שבועת הביטוי דאף היא בכל לשון נאמרה. וא"ת תנא תאני אלו ואת אמרת תנא ושייר דה"נ פריך פ"ק דקידושין. וי"ל דכל היכא דליכא אלא חד אלו איכא למימר בדוקא תני אבל היכא דתני אלו ואלו שונה ומשייר דהא (א) אלו לאו דוקא. והא דנקט אלו בריש

ברכות מ: שבועות לט.

רש"א מ"ז

הגהות הב"ח

(א) רש"י ד"ה ולהלן וכו' מנא לן הס"ד ואח"כ מ"ה וענתה ואמרה ככה אינו צריך וכו' היא למידה וענתה כצ"ל והד"א:

[דברים לא]

[דף לג.]

דרוש ככה כלשון זה רש"א

(א) נראה דצ"ל דהא ע"כ חד אלו לאו דוקא.

גמ' ולנו במקומן. § **גמ'** פרשת סוטה מנלן? דכתיב: °"ואמר הכהן לאשה" (במדבר ה) – בכל לשון שהוא אומר. תנו רבנן: משמיעין אותה, בכל לשון שהיא שומעת, על מה היא שותה, ובמה היא שותה, על מה נטמאת, ובמה היא נטמאת. על מה היא שותה – על עסקי קינוי וסתירה, ובמה היא שותה – במקידה של חרש, על מה נטמאת – על עסקי שחוק וילדות, ובמה היא נטמאת – בשוגג או במזיד, באונס [או] ברצון. וכל כך למה – שלא להוציא לעז על מים המרים. § "וידוי מעשר". מנלן? דכתיב: °"ואמרת לפני ה' אלהיך בערתי הקודש מן הבית" (דברים כו), ויליף אמירה מסוטה, בכל לשון שהוא אומר. א"ל רב זביד לאביי: ולילף אמירה מלוים, מה להלן בלשון הקודש – אף כאן בלשון הקודש! דנין *אמירה גרידתא מאמירה גרידתא, ואין דנין אמירה גרידתא מעניה ואמירה. תניא, רשב"י אומר: אדם אומר שבחו בקול נמוך וגנותו בקול רם. שבחו בקול נמוך – מן וידוי המעשר, גנותו בקול רם – ממקרא ביכורים. וגנותו בקול רם?! והאמר רבי יוחנן משום רבי שמעון בן יוחי: מפני מה תקנו [א]תפלה בלחש? כדי שלא לבייש את עוברי עבירה, שהרי לא חלק הכתוב מקום בין חטאת לעולה! לא תימא גנותו, אלא אימא צערו. *כדתניא: °"וטמא טמא יקרא" (ויקרא יג) – [ב]צריך להודיע צערו לרבים, ורבים מבקשים עליו רחמים. וכל מי שאירע בו דבר – צריך להודיע לרבים, ורבים מבקשים עליו רחמים. גופא, א"ר יוחנן משום רבי שמעון בן יוחי: מפני מה תיקנו תפלה בלחש – שלא לבייש את עוברי עבירה, שהרי [ג]לא חלק הכתוב מקום בין חטאת לעולה. ולא? והא איכא דמים, *[ד]דם חטאת למעלה [ה]ודם עולה למטה! התם כהן הוא דידע. והאיכא [ו]חטאת נקבה, [ז]עולה זכר! התם מיכסיא באליה. תינח כבשה, שעירה מאי איכא למימר? התם איהו דקא מיכסיף נפשיה, דאיבעי ליה לאיתויי כבשה וקא מייתי שעירה. חטאת דעבודה זרה, דלא סגי דלאו שעירה מאי איכא למימר! התם ניכסיף וניזיל, כי היכי דנכפר ליה. § "קריאת שמע". מנלן? דכתיב: °"שמע ישראל" (דברים ו) – בכל לשון שאתה שומע. תנו רבנן: *קריאת שמע ככתבה, דברי רבי. וחכמים אומרים: [ח]בכל לשון. מאי טעמא דרבי? אמר קרא: °"והיו" (שם) – בהווייתן יהו. ורבנן: אמר קרא "שמע" – בכל לשון שאתה שומע. ורבנן נמי, הא כתיב "והיו"! ההוא, [ט]שלא יקראנה למפרע. ורבי, שלא יקראנה למפרע מנליה? נפקא ליה מ"דברים", "הדברים" – [י]ורבנן? "דברים" "הדברים" לא משמע להו. ורבי נמי, הכתיב "שמע"! ההוא מיבעי ליה [כ]להשמיע לאזניך מה שאתה מוציא מפיך. ורבנן סברי לה כמאן דאמר: [ל]הקורא את שמע ולא השמיע לאזנו – יצא. לימא קסבר רבי: כל

רש"י

ולנו במקומן. בבית מלונם בגלגל, ושם הקימו את האבנים. **גמ'** ה"ג: ואמר אל האשה בכל לשון שהיא שומעת. ומהאי קרא יליף לה בספרי. ול"ג: ואמר הכהן לאשה. **אל האשה.** משמע דברים הנכנסין בלבה, שתהא מכרת בלשון. **על מה היא שותה.** כדמפרש ואזיל, שאומר לה: פריצות גרם ליך שתשתה. **ובמה היא שותה.** בכלי מאוס, במקידה של חרש. **ועל מה נטמאת.** מי הביאה לידי טומאה – שחוק וקלות ראש. כדי לייסר את הנשים שלא יקלו ראשן עם האנשים, שעל ידי כך באות לידי "וצבתה בטנה". **ובמה היא נטמאה.** משמיעין אותה הלכות המים המאררים על איזו טומאה הן בודקין אותה; שאם נטמאה והיא מזידה וברצון – בדקוה, ואם שוגגת, כגון אמרו לה "מת בעליך" או אנוסה – לא יבדקוה. **וכל כך למה.** לנו להודיע בהלכות המים? בשלמא הנך קמייתא – משום "ונוסרו כל הנשים" (יחזקאל כג) אלא הך, למה. **שלא להוציא לעז.** שאם נטמאת באונס או שוגגת, ולא נבדקת – שלא תהא סבורה: אילו נטמאתי מזידה גם כן לא היו בודקים אותי. ה"ג: **וידוי מעשר** מנלן? דכתיב: "ואמרת" וגו', ויליף אמירה אמירה מסוטה: א"ל רב זביד לאביי: ונילף אמירה אמירה מלוים? א"ל: דנין אמירה גרידתא מאמירה גרידתא, ואין דנין אמירה גרידתא מעניה ואמירה. **שבחו.** "לא עברתי ממצותיך ולא שכחתי" (דברים כו), היינו שבח עצמו. **בקול נמוך.** מדלא כתיב ביה עניה. **וגנותו.** כגון "ארמי אובד אבי" – היינו גנותו, שמתודין שאביהן לבן הארמי היה רשע. **מפני מה תקנו.** שיהא אדם אומר תפלתו בלחש, כדאשכחנא בחנה "וקולה לא ישמע" (שמואל א א). **שלא לבייש את עוברי עבירה.** המתודים בתפלתם על עבירות שבידם. **צערו.** צרות שעברו עליו. דהיינו צרות שעברו על ישראל: צרת לבן הארמי, צרת מצרים. **שהרי לא חלק הכתוב מקום בין חטאת לעולה.** לא קבע לשחיטת חטאת מקום בפני עצמו, שלא ידעו שהיא חטאת, ומתבייש. **טמא טמא יקרא.** כלומר: סורו מעליו שטמא הוא. **והאיכא** כו'. כלומר, והרי יש סימנים אחרים להכירה!. **למעלה מחוט הסיקרא.** דכתיב (ויקרא ד): "על קרנות", ובעולה לא כתב קרנות, והוא נותן דמים למטה מחוט הסיקרא, וכן שאר כל הדמים. **התם כהן.** לחודיה הוא דידע, ולא שאר כל העולם, ואין בושת בכך. **מכסיא.** הנקבות של נקבה. **באליה.** בזנב, ולא ניכר. **שעירה מאי איכא למימר.** שאין לה זנב, וניכר הנקבות. **דאיבעיא ליה לאתויי כשבה.** אם היה לו בשת. שהרי כל החטאות של יחיד, רצה – כשבה, רצה – שעירה, חוץ מחטאת עבודה זרה שכתיב בה "עז בת שנתה" בפרשת "שלח לך אנשים". **התם נייתי וניכסיף.** הטיל עליו הכתוב שיתבייש, שתהא לו כפרה מעונש גדול כזה. **ככתבה.** בלשון הקודש. **הקורא את שמע צריך שישמיע לאזנו.** פלוגתא היא במסכת ברכות (דף טו.).

לימא

תוספות

איהו הוא דקא מכסיף נפשיה. תימה: והא אמר בשמעתא קמייתא דמנחות (דף ג.) דבין זכרים לנקיבות לאו דעתייהו דאינשי! ואמר רבי: התם דווקא אמרי [הכי] דאין מעשיו מוכיחים, מפני שסומכין השומעין על דבורו שהוא שוחט חטאת לשם עולה, אבל נסתמא, כי הכא – ודאי מרגישים בדבר.

ליכסיף וליזיל כי היכי דליכפר ליה. וא"ת: יחלוק כמו כן בקביעות מקום שחיטתה, כי היכי דליהוי ליה כפרה גמורה! י"ל: כיון שחלק הכתוב בדבר אחד, שיש היכר בדבר, מה צריך יותר. מ"ר.

ורבי שלא יקראנה למפרע מנליה. תימה: דהכא משמע דבין רבי ובין רבנן אית להו דקריאת שמע דאורייתא. וכן תנאי דפליגי התם* [ברכות טו.] בקורא את שמע ולא השמיע לאזנו. וכן ב"ש וב"ה התם בפרק קמא דברכות (דף י:) דתנן: בית שמאי אומרים בערב כל אדם יטה ויקרא ובבקר יעמוד, שנאמר: "בשכבך ובקומך", וב"ה אומרים: בשעה שבני אדם שוכבין. אלמא דתרווייהו סבירא להו דקרא משתעי בק"ש. וסתמא דגמרא נמי התם *[דף כ.] פריך: תנא היכא קאי דקתני מאימתי – תנא אקרא קאי, דכתיב: "בשכבך ובקומך". ותו בפ"ב (שם דף יג:) בפלוגתא דרבי זוטרא ורבי יאשיה, דתניא: "והיו" – שלא יקראם למפרע, "הדברים על לבבך" רבי זוטרא אמר: עד כאן מצות כוונה, מכאן ואילך מצות קריאה. רבי יאשיה אומר: עד כאן מצות קריאה, מכאן ואילך מצות כוונה. אמר מר רבי זוטרא וכו'. מ"ש מכאן ואילך מצות קריאה – דכתיב "לדבר בם", ה"נ הא כתיב "ודברת בם" וכו'. אמר מר רבי יאשיה וכו'. מ"ש מכאן ואילך מצות כוונה – דכתיב "על לבבכם", ה"נ כתיב "על לבבך"! אלא עד כאן מצות כוונה וקריאה, מכאן ואילך כוונה בלא קריאה. מ"ש עד כאן מצות כוונה וקריאה – דכתיב "ודברת בם", ה"נ כתיב "לדבר בם"! ההוא בדברי תורה כתיב. מדקאמר: ההוא בדברי תורה – מכלל "ודברת בם" – דוקא בק"ש. ותו התם:* [דף טז.] הפועלים שעשו מלאכה עם בעל הבית – קורין ק"ש ומברכין לפניה ולאחריה, ואוכלים ומברכין לאחריה שתים. כילד? ברכה ראשונה כתיקנה, שניה כולל בונה ירושלים בברכת הארץ, ולא מברך "הטוב והמטיב" משום דמדרבנן היא, דביבנה תקנוה מכלל דק"ש דחייב לקרות – דאורייתא. ובפרק "מי שמתו" (ברכות ד' כא.*) [וע"ש ברש"י ותוס' ד"ה הכי גרסינן] בגמרא בעל קרי, פריך סתמא דגמרא: קריאת שמע דרבנן! – אהא דקאמר דק"ש וברכת המזון דאורייתא. ותו, אמרינן התם (דף כא. ע"ש): אמר שמואל: ספק קרא ק"ש ספק לא קרא – אינו חוזר וקורא, ספק אמר אמת ויציב ספק לא אמר – חוזר ואומר. מאי טעמא – ק"ש מדרבנן! ודוחק לומר דכל הני דמשמע מינייהו דמדאורייתא הוי אסמכתא בעלמא, דאין שיטת הגמרא א) לדייק כל כך על אסמכתא רבי ורבנן. ועוד, דאמר: לימא קסבר כל התורה בכל לשון נאמרה, ואי הוי אסמכתא בעלמא – לא הוה צריך למידק מיניה ב).

ורבנן סברי לה כמ"ד הקורא את שמע ולא השמיע לאזנו יצא. תימה: מאי דוחקיה למימר הכי? הוה מצי למימר: ורבנן תרתי שמעינן מיניה, כדאמר בפרק "היה קורא" (ברכות דף טו.), דתנן: הקורא את שמע ולא השמיע לאזנו יצא, רבי יוסי אומר: לא יצא. ומפרש בגמרא: מ"ט דר' יוסי – משום דכתיב: "שמע" – השמיע לאזניך, ות"ק: "שמע" – בכל לשון שאתה שומע. ואידך – תרתי ש"מ.

כל

א) [וע' היטב תוס' עירובין כג: ד"ה פשטיה וב"ב קמז. ד"ה מנין]: ב) [וע' תוס' ברכות כח. ד"ה ה"ג ובד"ה ההוא וכתו' מנחות מג: ד"ה ואיזו]

עין משפט נר מצוה

יד א מיי' פ"ט מהל' תפלה הל"ט סמג עשין יט טוש"ע או"ח סי' קא סעי' ב:
טו ב מיי' פ"ו מהל' טומאת צרעת הל"ח:
טז ג מיי' פ"ו מהל' מעשה הקרבנות הל' כ סמג עשין קסב:
יז ד מיי' שם הל"ז:
יח ה מיי' שם הל"ו:
יט ו מיי' שם הל"ט:
כ ז מיי' שם הל"ח:
כא ח מיי' פ"ב מהל' ק"ש הל"י סמג עשין יח טוש"ע או"ח סי' סב סעי' א:
כב ט מיי' שם הל"ח וסמג שם טוש"ע או"ח סי' סד סעי' א:
כג י כ מיי' שם הל"ח וסמג שם טוש"ע או"ח סי' סב סעי' ג:

מסורת הש"ס

[נ"א ענייה ואמירה מעניה ואמירה]
שבת סז. מו"ק ה. חולין עח. נדה סו.
[קנים ריש פ"א]
ברכות יג. מגילה יז.

גליון הש"ס

גמ' ורבנן דברים הדברים לא משמע להו. עיין לעיל דף יז ע"ב תד"ה דכתיב:

תוספות שאנץ

בריש אגב דנקטיה בסיפא גמ' ה"ג ואמר הכהן אל האשה בכל לשון שהיא שומע' ומהאי קרא יליף לה בספרי ול"ג ואמר הכהן לאשה: אל האשה משמע דברים הנכנסין בלבה כדמפרש ואזיל ומיהו מה שפ"ה דמהאי קרא יליף לה בספרי אינה ראיה ואין בכך למחוק גירסת הספרים דמצינו בכמה מקומות שחולק על תלמוד שלנו כגון גבי האי דאמר בגמ' לק' בפ' בתרא שאם נמצא ההורג אחר שנתערפה העגלה הורגין אותו ונפקא לן מן ולארץ לא יכופר ובספרי מפיק לה מן ואתה תבער הדם הנקי. אבל ק' מאי סביר' ליה להאי תנא דמתני' אי סבירא ליה דכל התורה כלה בכל לשון נאמרה א"כ למה לי קרא לאיתויי בגמ' למימר להכשירה בכל לשון. ואי סבירא נאמרה למה לי קרא במתני' בהני דנאמרין בלשון הקדש. לכ"נ א) דמהני סביר' ליה דכל התורה בכל לשון נאמרה מדמייתי קרא במתני' שנ' בכל לשון אבל התלמוד מפרש כן אליבא דמ"ד בלשון הקדש נאמרה. וכל כך למה. למה לנו להודיעה הלכות המים בשלמא הנך קמייתא משום ונוסרו כל הנשים. אלא הך למאי: ומשני שלא להוציא לעז שאם נטמאת באונס או שוגגת ולא נבדקה שלא תהי סבורה אילו נטמאת מזידה אף הם לא היו בודקין אותה ל"ה: וגנותו בקול רם ממקרא בכורים [illegible]

כל התורה בכל לשון נאמרה. דאי סלקא דעתך בלשון הקודש נאמרה – "והיו" דכתב רחמנא למה לי? איצטריך, משום דכתיב "שמע". לימא קסברי רבנן כל התורה כולה בלשון קודש נאמרה, דאי סלקא דעתך בכל לשון – "שמע" דכתב רחמנא למה לי? איצטריך, משום דכתיב "והיו".§ "תפלה".§ רחמי היא, כל היכי דבעי מצלי. ותפלה בכל לשון? *והאמר רב יהודה: אלעולם אל ישאל אדם צרכיו בלשון ארמית, דאמר רבי יוחנן: כל השואל צרכיו בלשון ארמי – אין מלאכי השרת נזקקין לו, לפי שאין מלאכי השרת מכירין בלשון ארמי! לא קשיא; בהא – ביחיד, הא – בצבור. ואין מלאכי השרת מכירין בלשון ארמי? והתניא: *יוחנן כהן גדול שמע ב"ק מבית קדש הקדשים שהוא אומר: נצחו טליא דאזלו לאגחא קרבא לאנטוכיא. ושוב מעשה בשמעון הצדיק ששמע בת קול מבית קדש הקדשים, שהוא אומר: בטילת עבידתא דאמר שנאה לאייתאה על היכלא, ונהרג גסקלגס, ובטלו גזירותיו. וכתבו אותה שעה וכיוונו. ובלשון ארמי היה אומר! אי בעית אימא: בת קול שאני, דלאשמועי עבידא. ואי בעית אימא: גבריאל הוה, דאמר מר: *בא גבריאל ולימדו שבעים לשון.§ "ברכת המזון".§ דכתיב: (דברים ח) "ואכלת ושבעת וברכת את ה' אלהיך" – בכל לשון שאתה מברך.§ "שבועת העדות".§ דכתיב: (ויקרא ה) "ונפש כי תחטא ושמעה קול אלה" – בכל לשון שהיא שומעת.§ "שבועת הפקדון".§ אתיא "תחטא" "תחטא" משבועת העדות.§ "ואלו נאמרין בלשון הקודש: מקרא ביכורים וחליצה" כו', עד "מקרא ביכורים" כיצד? (דברים כו) "וענית ואמרת לפני ה' אלהיך" ולהלן הוא אומר (שם כז) "וענו הלוים ואמרו אל כל איש ישראל", מה עניה האמורה להלן בלשון הקודש – אף כאן בלה"ק. ולוים גופייהו מנלן? אתיא, "קול" "קול" ממשה, כתיב הכא "קול רם" וכתיב התם (שמות יט) "משה ידבר והאלהים יעננו בקול", מה להלן בלשון הקודש – אף כאן בלשון הקודש.§ "חליצה כיצד" וכו'.§ ורבנן, האי "ככה" מאי עבדי ליה? מיבעי להו [יבמות קה:] *לדבר שהוא מעשה מעכב. ור' יהודה: מ"כה" "ככה". גורבנן: "כה" "ככה" לא משמע להו. ורבי

רש"י

לימא קסבר רבי. מדאיצטריך קרא שתהא קריאת שמע ככתבה. כל התורה בכל לשון נאמרה. לקרות בבית הכנסת. משום דכתיב שמע. איצטריך "והיו". דלא תדרשיה לקריאת שמע בכל לשון, אלא להשמיע לאזניו. תפלה. דקתני מתני': בכל לשון – לא צריך קרא, דהא רחמי נינהו, והשתא לישנא דידע לכוין לבו תורה אור לילי. יחיד. צריך שיסייעוהו מלאכי השרת, דציבור לא צריכי להו, דכתיב (איוב לו): "הן אל כביר לא ימאס" – אינו מואס בתפלתן של רבים. נצחו טליא דאזלו לאגחא קרבא באנטוכיא. שהלכו פרחי כהונה בני בית חשמונאי להלחם עם יוונים לפני יום הכפורים, ונלחמו ביום הכפורים, ושמע יוחנן בת קול כשהיה עובד עבודת יום הכפורים. [שבת יב:] עבידתא. חיל, לשון "העביד את חילו עבודה גדולה" (יחזקאל כט). גסקלגס. שם מלך יון. שאני בבת קול. אותה מידה הממונה על כך יודעת בשבעים לשונות, מפני שעשויה להשמיע, והיא משתלחת לכל הלשונות, פעמים לזה ופעמים לזה. [תוספתא פי"ג] דאמר מר. לקמן בפרקא (דף לו:). ולימדו. ליוסף, שבעים לשונות: ה"ג ברכת המזון דכתיב וברכת ולא גרסינן "מנלן". דלא בעיא קרא, דמהיכא תיתי דבעינן לשון קודש? בכל לשון שהיה מברך. לא קבע לו הכתוב לשון. שבועת העדות מנלן. דאי לא כתב קרא, איכא למימר דבעינן דומיא דשבועת הר גריזים והר עיבל, שהוא בלשון הקודש. ושמעה. מדלא כתיב "והשביעוה באלה". [לקמן לו:] יעננו בקול. במתן תורה, ובלשון הקודש ניתנה. לדבר שהוא מעשה מעכב. בפ', כגון חליצה ורקיקה. ד"ככה" משמע עיכובא, דאסור לשנות. וסמכו ל"יעשה", לומר שהמעשה מעכב. [שבועות לד. כריתות ט.] ורבי

תוספות

כל התורה כולה בכל לשון נאמרה. פי' ר"ת: הא פשיטא דבשעת מ"ת ניתנו למשה בלשון קודש. והאי דקאמר הכא – (א) היינו אם ניתנה להעתיקה בלשון אחר או לא. ומפירושו נשמע דלמ"ד לא ניתנה להעתיקה בלשון אחר – לא ניתנה לקרות כמו כן בלשון אחר. דמי שהיה קורא אותה בלשון פרסי והיא כתובה לשון עברי – כאילו היה קורא בעל פה. כדאמרינן בפ' שני דמגילה (דף יח.): קראה תרגום לא יצא. היכי דמי? אילימא דכתיבא מקרא וקא קרי תרגום – היינו על פה הוא. לא צריכא דכתיבא תרגום וקא קרי תרגום. ולא ידענא לפירושו היכי סלקא דעתיה למימר אליבא דרבי דבכל לשון ניתנה ליכתב. אם כן, הא דאמר רבי ק"ש ככתבה – היינו בכל לשון, שהרי בכל לשון ניתנה ליכתב – אם כן היינו רבנן! ועו, תפשוט מיהא התם דאליבא דרבי בלשון הקודש נאמרה. ועו, מאי קמבעיא ליה? והא פלוגתא היא בפ"ק דמגילה (דף ח:), תנן: אין בין ספרים למזוזות ותפילין אלא שהספרים נכתבין בכל לשון ותפילין ומזוזות אינן נכתבין אלא אשורית בלבד, רשב"ג אומר: אף ספרים לא התירו שיכתבו אלא יוונית בלבד! וי"ל: מהא דאמר רבי קרית שמע ככתבה – ליכא למידק מיניה, דאיכא למימר: ככתבה המיוחד לה כשנכתבה יחידי, כגון במזוזות ותפילין, דכ"ע מודו דבלשון הקודש. והא דקאמר: לימא קסבר רבי כל התורה בכל לשון נאמרה – ה"פ: ולית ליה דרשב"ג דאמר דוקא יוונית. ולרבנן דאמרי בלשון הקודש – לית להו דרבנן דאמרי ספרים נכתבים בכל לשון. כך צריך לפרש לפי פירוש ר"ת. **ברכת** המזון דכתיב ואכלת ושבעת. רש"י שיבש הגירסא, דלא גרס "מנלן". ופי': משום דלא בעי קרא, דמהיכא תיתי דליבעי לשון הקודש? ומיהו, נראה עיקר כגירסת הספרים דגרסי בהו "מנלן". דסד"א נילף ברכה מברכות הר גריזים, דכתיב בהו: "אלה יעמדו לברך" (דברים כז), מה להלן בלשון קודש – אף כאן, דהא בהאי ג"ש ילפינן בפירקין (לקמן דף לח.) ברכת כהנים דבלשון הקודש – להכי כתיב: "וברכת את ה'". כלומר, מאחר שהברכה והשבח כלפי השכינה – תוכל לברך בכל לשון שתרצה, ומסתמא בלשון שאתה מכיר, שתתן שבח להקב"ה בלבב שלם להנאתך. והכי נמי איתא בירושלמי [דפרקין, דאמר התם]: "וברכת" – כדי שיהא יודע למי מברך. [ומשמע בפרק "כיצד מברכין"] (ברכות דף מ:): אפילו אמרה בלשון חול שלא כתיקונה – יצא, דומיא דבנימין רעיא כרך ריפתא, בתר דכרך אמר "בריך רחמנא מריה דהאי פיתא" ואמר רב דיצא ידי ברכה ראשונה. ומ"ואמרת לפני ה' אלהיך" דכתיב גבי וידוי [מעשר – לא יליף, דלא] דמי להאי, דהכא כתיב "את ה'", אבל התם "לפני ה'", דלהכי כתיב "לפני ה'" דמשמע דבעזרה היה מתודה, ולהכי איצטריך גזירה שוה דאמירה אמירה. **שבועת** העדות מנא לן. נראה לפרש: אי לאו קרא הוה אמינא נילף "קול" "קול" ממשה, להכי כתיב "ושמעה" דמשמע בכל לשון שהיא שומעת, מדלא כתיב "והשביעה בשבועת האלה". אבל לפירוש רש"י, דפי': אי לאו קרא הוה אמינא דומיא דשבועת הר גריזים והר עיבל שהיו בלשון הקודש – אדרבה, נילף משבועת סוטה שהיא בלשון חול! ועוד, נילף "אלה" "אלה" מסוטה דכתיב בה "בשבועת האלה"! להכי אית לך למימר: אי לאו דכתיב "ושמעה" – לא הוה ידענא אי הוה לן למילף "קול" "קול" או "אלה" "אלה". **אתיא** תחטא תחטא. נראה דהא גזירה שוה לאו דוקא נקט לה הכא, דהא מהיכא תיתי דנבעי בלשון קודש? אדרבה, בלא גזירה שוה ד"תחטא" "תחטא" הוה משמע טפי דבכל לשון, דהוה ילפינן מעילה מעילה מסוטה, אלא אגב דילפינן בשבועות (דף לד.) בהא גזירה שוה, דבתביעת ממון הכתוב מדבר – נקט לה נמי הכא. **וענית** ואמרת ולהלן הוא אומר וענו הלוים ואמרו. תימה: אדרבה, נילף "ואמרת לפני ה' אלהיך" מ"ואמרת לפני ה' אלהיך" מוידוי מעשר, דהא מדדמי ליה ילפינן! ואם תאמר: הכא עניה עניה גמיר – הא לעיל פריך: ונילף אמירה מלוים, *ומהדר: דנין עניה ואמירה מעניה ואמירה, ואין דנין עניה גרידתא מעניה גרידתא (נ"א: ואין דנין אמירה גרידתא מעניה ואמירה)! **אתיא** קול קול. אין לומר: אדרבה, נילף "קול" "קול" משבועת הפקדון! דעניה וקול מעניה וקול גמיר, ואין דנין עניה וקול מקול גרידא. **ורבי** יהודה מכה ככה. לא ידענא אי דריש ר' יהודה מ"כה" "ככה" דכל האמור בפרשה אפילו קריאה מעכבא, דאין לשנות מכל האמור, דלהכי אהני "כה" "ככה", וממילא הוי לשון קודש נמי עיכובא, דפרשה נאמרה בלשון קודש. ותימה לומר כן: דא"כ כמאן מרבותיו ס"ל? לא כרבי אליעזר ולא כר' עקיבא, דתרוייהו מודו דקריאה לא מעכבא, ולא פליגי אלא ברקיקה (יבמות דף קד:), דלר' אליעזר מעכבא כיון דהוי מעשה, ולרבי עקיבא לא מעכבא, מעשה באיש בעי'. *ואם אית לך למימר דרבי יהודה סבר דדוקא בלשון קודש מעכב, אבל אם לא קראה כלל אינו מעכב – גם הוא סברא תמוה. שאם לא קראה כלל – אינו מעכב ואם קראה בלשון חול – מעכב? ומסתברא טפי למימר דסבירא ליה דקריאה מעכב, ופליג אתנא דמתניתין בפרק "מצות חליצה" (שם דף קד:), דקא סבר רבי יהודה לא נחלקו רבי עקיבא ורבי אליעזר בדבר זה. והכי אמר בעלמא, כגון בפרק "רבי אליעזר דמילה" (שבת דף קלה:) גבי פלוגתא

דב"ש

עין משפט נר מצוה

כד א ב טוש"ע א"ח סי' קא סעיף ד וע"ש:

תוספות שאנץ

כל התורה בכל לשון נאמרה פ"ה כגון קריאת התורה ול"נ דמקריאה אי אפשר להיות דאין חיובא אלא מדרבנן ותקנת עזרא. לכ"נ לפ' כל הפרשיות שצריכות לקרות כגון פרשת זכור א) ופרשת עגלה ערופה והני דמפרש במתני' דצריכין לקרותן בלשון הקדש אי ליכא קרא ב) דמרבי להו לקרותה בכל לשון גם זה פי' פרק הקורא [במגילה דף יז]. שאין מלאכי השרת מכירין בלשון ארמי. י"מ פ"ק דשבת דמכירין בו אבל אינן חוששין בו ואין נראה מכאן דמשמע בסמוך דאין מכירין בו כלל. ברכת המזון דכתיב ואכלת ושבעת וברכת ה"ג ול"ג מנא לן דלא בעי קרא דמהיכא תיתי דניבעי לשון הקדש אבל גבי שבועת העדות גר' מנא לן דאי לא כתיב קרא איכא למימר דבעי דומיא דשבועת הר גריזים והר עיבל שהיא בלשון הקדש. ל"ה. יש אומר בפשט שצריך לברך בעל הבית דכתיב וברכת את ואת ריבויא הוא לרבות את בעל הבית:

א) אולי צ"ל ופרשת פרה אדומה ועי' ברא"ש בברכות בר"פ היה קורא.
ב) אולי צ"ל אי ליכא קרא דמרבי להו היה מותר לקרותן בכל לשון.

הגהות הב"ח

(א) תום' ד"ה כל וכו' דקאמר הכא בכל לשון היינו אם:

גליון הש"ס

גמ' ורבנן כה ככה לא משמע להו. עיין לקמן דף לח ע"א תד"ה ורי"א: רש"י ד"ה יחיד וכו' צבור לא צריכי להו. עיין בספר בתי כהונה ח"ב בית אבות דף ל ע"א: ד"ה שאני בת קול. ע' סנהדרין דף יא ע"א תד"ה בת קול ובתוי"ט פט"ז מ"ו דיבמות:

גי' רש"א וי"ל דנין וכו' ע"ש

נ"א ואין לומר

גמרא

ורבי יהודה, האי "וענתה ואמרה" מאי עביד ליה? מיבעי ליה לאגמורי ללוים דבלשון הקודש. וליליף "קול" ממשה! ענייה עניה – גמיר, "קול", "קול" – לא גמיר. תניא נמי הכי, רבי יהודה אומר: כל מקום שנאמר "כה" "ככה", ענייה ואמירה – אינו אלא לשון הקודש; "כה" – "כה תברכו", "ככה" – דחליצה, עניה ואמירה – דלוים.§ "ברכות וקללות כיצד? כיון שעברו ישראל את הירדן" כו'.§ תנו רבנן: "הלא המה בעבר הירדן" – מעבר לירדן ואילך, דברי רבי יהודה. "אחרי דרך מבוא השמש" – מקום שחמה זורחת. "בארץ הכנעני היושב בערבה" – אלו הר גריזים והר עיבל שיושבין בהם כותיים, "מול הגלגל" – סמוך לגלגל. "אצל אלוני מורה" – שכם, ולהלן הוא אומר: "ויעבר אברם בארץ עד מקום שכם עד אלון מורה", מה אלון מורה האמור להלן שכם – אף כאן שכם. (א) תניא, אמר רבי אלעזר ברבי יוסי: בדבר זה זייפתי ספרי כותיים. אמרתי להם: זייפתם תורתכם ולא העליתם בידכם כלום. שאתם אומרים אלוני מורה שכם – אף אנו מודים שאלוני מורה שכם. אנו למדנוה בגזרה שוה, אתם במה למדתום? רבי אלעזר אמר: "הלא המה בעבר הירדן" – סמוך לירדן, (ב) דאי מעבר הירדן ואילך – הלא כתיב: "והיה בעברכם את הירדן". "אחרי דרך מבוא השמש" – מקום שהחמה שוקעת. "בארץ הכנעני" – ארץ חוי היא! "היושב בערבה" – והלא בין הרים וגבעות הן יושבין! "מול הגלגל" – והלא לא ראו את הגלגל! רבי אליעזר ב"י אומר: לא בא הכתוב אלא להראות להן דרך בשניה כדרך שהראה להן בראשונה: "דרך" – בדרך לכו, ולא בשדות וכרמים, "היושב" – בישוב לכו, ולא במדברות, "בערבה" – בערבה לכו, ולא בהרים וגבעות. תנו רבנן: *כיצד עברו ישראל את הירדן? בכל יום ארון נוסע אחר שני דגלים, והיום נסע תחילה, שנאמר: "הנה ארון הברית אדון כל הארץ עובר לפניכם". בכל יום ויום לוים נושאין את הארון, והיום נשאוהו כהנים, שנאמר: "והיה כנוח כפות רגלי הכהנים נושאי ארון ה'" וגו'. תניא: *רבי יוסי אומר: בשלשה מקומות נשאו כהנים את הארון; כשעברו את הירדן, וכשהסיבו את יריחו, וכשהחזירוהו למקומו.

וכיון

רש"י

ור' יהודה האי. גזירה שוה דעניה ואמירה מאי עביד ליה?. עניה עניה גמר. גזירה שוה דעניה עניה למד מרבו, ג"ש ד"קול" "קול" – לא שמע, ואין האדם דן גז"ש אא"כ קבלה. כל מקום שנאמר כה ככה עניה ואמירה. כדבר התלוי בדיבור – אינו אלא לשון קודש: ה"ג כה כה תברכו. כלומר, לענין נשיאות כפים איתמר, דילפי לה רבנן לקמן (דף לח.) בגזירה שוה, ואתא ר' יהודה למימר: בגופה כתיב. ה"ג: ככה דחליצה עניה ואמירה דלוים ולא גרסינן "מלוים". כלומר: לענין לוים אמר דילפי לה רבנן ב"קול" "קול", ואתא איהו למימר דמעניה עניה ילפה מיבמה, דכתיב בה "ככה". הלא המה בעבר הירדן. כשהיו ישראל במדבר נאמר להם סימני הר גריזים ועיבל ומקומם שהם בעבר השני של ירדן. ישראל היו למזרח הירדן, כדכתיב: בני גד ובני ראובן לקחו נחלתן "מעבר לירדן יריחו קדמה מזרחה" (יהושע יג), ונאמר להם שהרים האלה במערב הירדן (ג) ואילך הרבה להלן מן הירדן לצד מערב, ולא סמוך לירדן. אחרי דרך מבוא השמש. ומהו "מבוא השמש" – זהו מזרח, שהשמש באה משם. כלומר, רחוק ממזרחו של ירדן. ומצינו בבראשית רבה: כל מקום שנאמר "אחרי" – מופלג. שיושבים בהם כותיים. עכשיו הן יושבין בהן. שהושיבן בהם סנחריב כשהגלה עשרת השבטים, דכתיב: "ויבא מלך אשור (ד) אנשים מבבל ומכותה ומעוא וגו' ויושיבם בערי שמרון" (מלכים ב יז). והנך ערי שומרון נינהו, כדתניא במתניתין "שבשומרון": תניא לא גרס, דכולה חדא מתניתא היא בספרי. ספרי כותיים. שיש להם תורה שבכתב, ואינן מאמינים בתורה שבעל פה. בעברכם. משמע: בו ביום תקימו את האבנים בהר עיבל. אחרי דרך. מופלג מן המערב ד"אחרי" לשון הפלגה, והאי "מבוא השמש" – מערב הוא, לשון "כי בא השמש" (בראשית כח), מקום שחמה שוקעת, מופלג משקיעתה. והיינו לצד מזרח, סמוך לירדן מיד. בארץ הכנעני ארץ החוי היא. בניחותא; אינה ארץ הכנעני אלא ארץ החוי, דהא שכם חוי היא, דכתיב (שם לג): "ויבא יעקב שלם" וגו', וכתיב (שם לד): "שכם בן חמור החוי נשיא הארץ". היושב בערבה. אינו, אלא הרים. מול הגלגל. רחוקים מן הגלגל הם. והסימנים הללו לא עליהם נאמרו, ולמה נאמרו?. ר"א בן יעקב אומר לא בא הכתוב כו'. ורבי אלעזר נמי אדרבי אליעזר בן יעקב סמך, וכוותיה מפרש לקרא. כדרך שהראה להם בראשונה. בצאתם ממצרים, בעמוד ענן לנחותם הדרך – כך בא עכשיו ליישר דרכיהם ולהורותם הדרך. לפי שגלוי לפניו שעתיד הענן לפסוק במיתת משה ולא ילך עם יהושע, הורה להם: לאחר שיעברו את הירדן לכבוש את הארץ ילכו דרך כבושה, ודרך *יישוב, ודרך ארץ הכנעני שהיא ערבה, ואל יקיפו סמוך לשפת הירדן דרך ארץ החוי שהיא הרים וגבעות, אלא יכנסו לתוכה מצד מערב רחוק מן הירדן, ויקיפו ויכבשו. אחר שני דגלים. כדכתיב בפרשת "נשא" גבי מסעות דגלים. לפניכם. משמע: לפני כולכם. בכל יום היו הלוים נושאים. בני קהת, כדכתיב: "ומשמרתם הארון והשלחן" וגו' (במדבר ג). וכשסיבבו את יריחו. כדכתיב: "ויקרא יהושע בן נון אל הכהנים ויאמר אליהם שאו את ארון ברית ה'" וגו': וכשהחזירוהו למקומו. בימי שלמה לבית קדשי הקדשים, דכתיב: "ויבאו כל זקני ישראל וישאו הכהנים את הארון" (מלכים א ח) והיינו החזירוהו למקומו, שכשהגלה בימי עלי מתוך בית קדשי הקדשים של משכן שעשה משה – משם נוטל. שהמשכן נקבע בשילה, וכשהחזירוהו פלשתים לא היה לו מקום קבוע, שהרי חרב משכן שילה. ונשתהא בבית אבינדב, ומשם הביאו דוד לסוף עשרים שנה לבית עובד אדום, ומשם לעיר דוד, עד שבנה שלמה את בית המקדש, ובנה לו הדביר לפנים מן ההיכל, ואמה טרקסין חוצצת במקום הפרוכת, והוא קרוי מקומו המיוחד, כדכתיב: "ויביאו הכהנים את ארון ברית ה' אל מקומו אל דביר הבית" וגו' (שם).

וכיון

[תוספתא פ"ח] [שם] ס"א מישור

תוספות

דב"ש וב"ה. תמיה לרבי: כיון דהטיל הכתוב "ככה" בין קריאה למעשה, [נימא] דלעכבו תרוייהו! ותו איכא למיתמה: אדרבה, הוה לן למימר אליבא דרבי יהודה: אפילו אי לא הוה כתיב אלא "כה" – דקריאה מעכבא ולא מעשה. דהא שמעינן ליה בפ"ק דר"ה (דף ט:) דמקרא נדרש לפניו ולא לאחריו, דאמר: "יובל" – אע"פ שלא שמטו, אע"פ שלא תקעו. יכול אע"פ שלא שילחו – ת"ל "היא", דברי רבי יהודה. ומפרש טעמא: מקרא נדרש לפניו ולא לאחריו, ולא לפני פניו. כלומר, עיכובא ד"היא" נדרש דוקא א"וקראתם דרור" שלפניו, ולא א"ושבתם איש אל אחוזתו" של אחריו, ולא אתקיעה שלפני פניו! וי"ל דה"פ: ורבי יהודה האי דמעשה מעכב – מ"כה" "ככה". דאי לא הוי כתיב אלא "כה" ה"א דדרשינן ליה דוקא אקריאה שלפניו – להכי כתיב "ככה" יתירא, למדרשיה נמי אמעשה שלאחריו.

מול הגלגל סמוך לגלגל. משמע: מקום הרואה את הגלגל, כדאמר (חולין דף יט:): "ממול ערפו" – מול הרואה את העורף. ולהכי אמר רבי אלעזר: מול הגלגל – והלא לא ראו את הגלגל. ירושלמי: מה מקיים ר"א הר גריזים והר עיבל – שתי גבשושית היו עשוי, וקראו זה הר גריזים וזה הר עיבל. על דעתיה דרבי יהודה – מאה ועשרים מיל הלכו באותו היום, על דעת ר"א – לא זזו ממקומם. ותו בירושלמי: דר' ישמעאל אומר: כל ביאות שנאמרו בתורה לאחר י"ד שנים נאמרו, ז' שנים שכיבשו ושבע שנים שחילקו. ודכוותיה לא נאמר ברכות וקללות אלא לאחר י"ד שנים. היתיב ר' חנינא קמיה ר' מנא: והכתיב "והיה בעברכם את הירדן תקימו את האבנים האלה"! א"ל: אבנים הקימו אותם מיד, ברכות וקללות – לאחר י"ד שנים נאמרות.

וכשהחזירוהו למקומו. ואי קשה: והא בדברי הימים (ב ה) כתיב "וישאו הלוים את הארון"! תריץ: דהאי אחד מכ"ד מקומות שנקראו הכהנים לוים. דהא כתיב התם: "ויעלו את הארון ואת אהל מועד" וגו', וכתיב: "העלו אותם הכהנים הלוים", ופירוש: הכהנים – הארון, והלוים – אהל מועד וכליו. וכתיב: "ויביאו הכהנים את ארון ברית ה' אל מקומו", וכתיב במלכים: "וישאו הכהנים את הארון", וכתיב: "ויעלו את ארון ה' ואת אהל מועד" וגו', וכתיב: "ויעלו אותם הכהנים והלוים". אי נמי: הכהנים נטלוהו ממקומו אשר נטה לו דוד ומסרוהו ללוים, והלוים נשאו עד ההיכל, והכניסוהו הכהנים לדביר. הרי כל המקראות מקויימים, ועל זה אמר רבי יוסי "כשהחזירוהו למקומו".

יותר

הגהות הב"ח

(א) גמ' אף כאן שכם (תניא) תז"מ ונ"ב רש"י ל"ג ליה ובילקוט פ' ראה נמי ליתיה: (ב) שם סמוך לירדן דכתיב והיה בעברכם כצ"ל ותיבות דאי מעבר הירדן ואילך הלא נמחק ונ"ב כך הוא בילקוט: (ג) רש"י ד"ה הלא המה וכו' במערב הירדן מעבר הירדן ואילך הרבה: (ד) ד"ה שיושבין וכו' מלך אשור מבבל ומכותא ומעוא וגו' וישב בערי כצ"ל ותיבת אנשים נמחק:

גליון הש"ס

גמ' רבי אלעזר אמר וכו'. עיין בבכור שור ריש ברכות: **רש"י** ד"ה וכשהחזירוהו למקומו. ומצינו עוד שנשאוהו הכהנים כשהיה דוד בורח מפני אבשלום דכתיב בשמואל ב' ט"ו ויצב לדוק ואביתר את ארון אלהים ירושלים וצ"ל כיון דנכלל בכלל החזרת מקומו מקרי חד. ועיין רד"ק ביהושע ג' בפסוק והכהנים הלוים נושאים אותו:

וְכֵיוָן שֶׁנִּיטְבְּלוּ רַגְלֵי כֹהֲנִים בַּמַּיִם חָזְרוּ הַמַּיִם לַאֲחוֹרֵיהֶם, שֶׁנֶּאֱמַר: °"וּכְבוֹא נוֹשְׂאֵי הָאָרוֹן עַד הַיַּרְדֵּן וגו' וַיַּעַמְדוּ הַמַּיִם הַיּוֹרְדִים מִלְמַעְלָה קָמוּ נֵד אֶחָד". וְכַמָּה גּוֹבְהָן שֶׁל מַיִם – שְׁנֵים עָשָׂר מִיל עַל שְׁנֵים עָשָׂר מִיל, כְּנֶגֶד מַחֲנֵה יִשְׂרָאֵל, דִּבְרֵי ר' יְהוּדָה. אָמַר לוֹ ר' אֶלְעָזָר בְּר' שִׁמְעוֹן: לִדְבָרֶיךָ, אָדָם קַל אוֹ מַיִם קַלִּים? הֱוֵי אוֹמֵר מַיִם קַלִּים, אִם כֵּן בָּאִין מַיִם וְשׁוֹטְפִין אוֹתָן! אֶלָּא מְלַמֵּד, שֶׁהָיוּ מַיִם נִגְדָּשִׁין וְעוֹלִין כֵּיפִּין עַל גַּבֵּי כֵּיפִּין, יָתֵר מִשְּׁלֹשׁ מֵאוֹת מִיל, עַד שֶׁרָאוּ אוֹתָן כָּל מַלְכֵי מִזְרָח וּמַעֲרָב, שֶׁנֶּאֱמַר: °"וַיְהִי כִשְׁמוֹעַ כָּל מַלְכֵי הָאֱמוֹרִי אֲשֶׁר בְּעֵבֶר הַיַּרְדֵּן יָמָּה וְכָל מַלְכֵי הַכְּנַעֲנִי אֲשֶׁר עַל הַיָּם אֵת אֲשֶׁר הוֹבִישׁ ה' אֶת מֵי הַיַּרְדֵּן מִפְּנֵי בְנֵי יִשְׂרָאֵל עַד עָבְרָם וַיִּמַּס לְבָבָם וְלֹא הָיָה בָם עוֹד רוּחַ מִפְּנֵי בְּנֵי יִשְׂרָאֵל". וְאַף רָחָב הַזּוֹנָה אָמְרָה לִשְׁלוּחֵי יְהוֹשֻׁעַ: °"כִּי שָׁמַעְנוּ אֵת אֲשֶׁר הוֹבִישׁ ה' אֶת מֵי יַם סוּף" וגו', וּכְתִיב: °"וַנִּשְׁמַע וַיִּמַּס לְבָבֵנוּ וְלֹא קָמָה עוֹד" וגו'. *עוֹדָם בַּיַּרְדֵּן אָמַר לָהֶם יְהוֹשֻׁעַ: דְּעוּ עַל מָה אַתֶּם עוֹבְרִים אֶת הַיַּרְדֵּן – עַל מְנָת שֶׁתּוֹרִישׁוּ אֶת יוֹשְׁבֵי הָאָרֶץ מִפְּנֵיכֶם, שֶׁנֶּאֱמַר: °"וְהוֹרַשְׁתֶּם אֶת כָּל יוֹשְׁבֵי הָאָרֶץ מִפְּנֵיכֶם" וגו'. אִם אַתֶּם עוֹשִׂין כֵּן – מוּטָב, וְאִם לָאו – בָּאִין מַיִם וְשׁוֹטְפִין אוֹתִיכֶם. מַאי "אוֹתִיכֶם" – אוֹתִי וְאֶתְכֶם. עוֹדָם בַּיַּרְדֵּן אָמַר לָהֶן יְהוֹשֻׁעַ: "הָרִימוּ לָכֶם אִישׁ אֶבֶן אַחַת עַל שִׁכְמוֹ לְמִסְפַּר שִׁבְטֵי יִשְׂרָאֵל" וגו', וּכְתִיב: °"לְמַעַן תִּהְיֶה זֹאת אוֹת בְּקִרְבְּכֶם כִּי יִשְׁאָלוּן בְּנֵיכֶם מָחָר לֵאמֹר מָה הָאֲבָנִים הָאֵלֶּה לָכֶם" וגו' – סִימָן לְבָנִים שֶׁעָבְרוּ אָבוֹת אֶת הַיַּרְדֵּן. עוֹדָם בַּיַּרְדֵּן אָמַר לָהֶן יְהוֹשֻׁעַ: °"שְׂאוּ לָכֶם מִזֶּה מִתּוֹךְ הַיַּרְדֵּן מִמַּצַּב רַגְלֵי הַכֹּהֲנִים הָכִין שְׁתֵּים עֶשְׂרֵה אֲבָנִים וְהַעֲבַרְתֶּם אוֹתָם עִמָּכֶם וְהִנַּחְתֶּם אוֹתָם בַּמָּלוֹן אֲשֶׁר תָּלִינוּ בוֹ הַלָּיְלָה" וגו'. יָכוֹל בְּכָל מָלוֹן וּמָלוֹן – ת"ל: "אֲשֶׁר תָּלִינוּ בוֹ הַלָּיְלָה". אָמַר רַבִּי *יְהוּדָה: אַבָּא חֲלַפְתָּא, וְרַבִּי אֱלִיעֶזֶר בֶּן מַתְיָא, וַחֲנַנְיָא בֶּן חֲכִינַאי, עָמְדוּ עַל אוֹתָן אֲבָנִים וְשִׁיעֲרוּם, כָּל אַחַת וְאַחַת שְׁקוּלָה כְּאַרְבָּעִים סְאָה, וּגְמִירִי דְּטְעוּנָא דְּמִדְלֵי אִינִישׁ לְכַתְפֵיהּ תִּילְתָּא דְּטְעוּנֵיהּ הָוֵי, מִכָּאן אַתָּה מְחַשֵּׁב לְאֶשְׁכּוֹל, שֶׁנֶּאֱמַר: °"וַיִּשָּׂאֻהוּ בַמּוֹט בִּשְׁנָיִם". מִמַּשְׁמַע שֶׁנֶּאֱמַר "בַּמּוֹט" אֵינִי יוֹדֵעַ שֶׁבִּשְׁנַיִם? מַה תַּלְמוּד לוֹמַר "בִּשְׁנָיִם" – בִּשְׁנֵי מוֹטוֹת. אָמַר רַבִּי יִצְחָק: טוּרְטָנֵי וְטוּרְטָנֵי דְּטוּרְטָנֵי. הָא כֵּיצַד? שְׁמֹנָה נָשְׂאוּ אֶשְׁכָּל, אֶחָד נָשָׂא רִימּוֹן, וְאֶחָד נָשָׂא תְּאֵינָה. יְהוֹשֻׁעַ וְכָלֵב לֹא נָשְׂאוּ כְּלוּם, אִי בָּעֵית אֵימָא – מִשּׁוּם דַּחֲשִׁיבֵי, וְאִי בָּעֵית אֵימָא – שֶׁלֹּא הָיוּ בְּאוֹתָהּ עֵצָה. פְּלִיגִי בָּהּ רַבִּי אַמִּי וְרַבִּי יִצְחָק נַפָּחָא; חַד אָמַר: לְדִבְרֵי רַבִּי יְהוּדָה כַּחֲנָיָיתָן

רש"י

וְכֵיוָן שֶׁנִּיטְבְּלוּ כו'. בִּשְׂפַת מִזְרָחִית בִּכְנִיסָתָן לְתוֹכוֹ – חָזְרוּ הַמַּיִם לַאֲחוֹרֵיהֶם, שֶׁלֹּא הָיוּ יוֹרְדִין מִן הַכֹּהֲנִים וּלְמַטָּן, אֶלָּא שָׁם עוֹמְדִים, וְהַמַּיִם הַבָּאִים תָּמִיד נִגְבָּהִים וְעוֹלִין לְמַעְלָה, כִּדְכְתִיב: "קָמוּ נֵד אֶחָד". וְהַכֹּהֲנִים עָמְדוּ שָׁם עַד שֶׁעָבְרוּ כּוּלָּם: כַּמָּה גּוֹבְהָן שֶׁל מַיִם גָּרַס. י"ב מִיל כְּנֶגֶד מַחֲנֵה יִשְׂרָאֵל. שֶׁהָיוּ שְׁנֵים עָשָׂר מִיל עַל שְׁנֵים עָשָׂר מִיל, וְהֵם עָבְרוּ כַּחֲנִיָּיתָם – רוֹחַב מַחֲנֵיהֶם עָבְרוּ יַחַד כְּמוֹת שֶׁהוּא, רוֹחַב שְׁנֵים עָשָׂר מִיל. נִמְצְאוּ שֶׁלֹּא שָׁהוּ בְּעָבְרָן אֶלָּא מַהֲלַךְ שְׁנֵים עָשָׂר מִיל שֶׁל אוֹרֶךְ מַחֲנֵיהֶם, עַד שֶׁעָלוּ אַחֲרוֹנִים שֶׁל סוֹף הַמַּחֲנֶה, וּכְנֶגְדָּן גָּבְהוּ הַמַּיִם. הֱוֵי אוֹמֵר מַיִם קַלִּים. לָרוּץ מִן הָאָדָם. וְא"כ שֶׁהַמַּיִם לֹא גָּבְהוּ אֶלָּא שְׁנֵים עָשָׂר מִיל וְחָזְרוּ לִמְקוֹמָם – נִמְצָא שֶׁעֲדַיִין לֹא הִסְפִּיקוּ לַעֲבוֹר, וּבָאִין מַיִם וְשׁוֹטְפִין אוֹתָן. כֵּיפִּין. אוֹלָמוֹת, אַרוּקוולו"ד. וְאַף רָחָב אָמְרָה לִשְׁלוּחֵי יְהוֹשֻׁעַ. קוֹדֶם שֶׁעָבְרוּ אֶת הַיַּרְדֵּן, שֶׁעַל קְרִיעַת יַם סוּף הָיוּ מִתְפַּחֲדִין עֲדַיִין. עוֹדָם בַּיַּרְדֵּן אָמַר לָהֶן יְהוֹשֻׁעַ כו'. כִּדְכְתִיב: "וְהַכֹּהֲנִים נוֹשְׂאֵי הָאָרוֹן עוֹמְדִים בְּתוֹךְ הַיַּרְדֵּן עַד תֹּם כָּל הַדְּבָרִים אֲשֶׁר צִוָּה ה' אֶת יְהוֹשֻׁעַ לְדַבֵּר אֶל הָעָם". וְזֶהוּ הַדָּבָר, דְּהָכִי כְּתִיב בְּמֹשֶׁה: "כִּי אַתֶּם עוֹבְרִים אֶת הַיַּרְדֵּן אֶל אֶרֶץ כְּנָעַן וְהוֹרַשְׁתֶּם" וגו'. כְּלוֹמַר, כְּשֶׁיַּעַבְרוּ אֶת הַיַּרְדֵּן הִתְנָה עִמָּהֶם עַל מְנָת לְהוֹרִישָׁם: וְשׁוֹטְפִין אוֹתִיכֶם גָּרְסִינַן בַּבָּרַיְיתָא. הָרִימוּ לָכֶם וגו'. הֵם הָאֲבָנִים שֶׁהֵקִימוּ תַּחַת מַצַּב רַגְלֵי הַכֹּהֲנִים לְזִכָּרוֹן, לִהְיוֹת סִימָן לַבָּנִים שֶׁעָבְרוּ אָבוֹת אֶת הַיַּרְדֵּן. שְׂאוּ מִזֶּה מִתּוֹךְ הַיַּרְדֵּן מִמַּצַּב וכו'. הֵם שֶׁהֵקִימוּ בְּהַר עֵיבָל וּבָנוּ הַמִּזְבֵּחַ, וְקִפְּלוּם וּקְבָעוּם בַּגִּלְגָּל. דְּמַדְלֵי אִינִישׁ אַכַּתְפֵיהּ. שֶׁהָאָדָם עַצְמוֹ מַגְבִּיהוֹ עַל כְּתֵיפוֹ וְאֵין אַחֵר מְסַיְּיעוֹ. תִּילְתָּא דְּטְעוּנֵיהּ הוּא. אֵינוֹ אֶלָּא שְׁלִישׁ מַשּׂאוֹי שֶׁנּוֹשֵׂא כְּשֶׁמַּטְעִינוֹ אַחֵר. נִמְצָא שֶׁהָיָה כָּל אֶחָד מֵהֶן נוֹשֵׂא מַשָּׂא ק"ך סְאִין. וּמִכָּאן אַתָּה מְחַשֵּׁב. כַּמָּה הָיָה בָּאֶשְׁכּוֹל שֶׁנְּשָׂאוּהוּ שְׁמֹנָה אֲנָשִׁים, וְהָיוּ מְסַיְּיעִין זֶה אֶת זֶה כְּשֶׁמְּרִימִין אוֹתוֹ עַל כְּתֵיפָן: מִמַּשְׁמַע שֶׁנֶּאֱמַר *"וַיִּשָּׂאֻהוּ" אֵינִי יוֹדֵעַ שֶׁבִּשְׁנַיִם. אָמַר רַבִּי יִצְחָק טוּרְטָנֵי וְטוּרְטָנֵי דְּטוּרְטָנֵי. מַשּׂאוֹי וּמַשּׂאוֹי תַּחַת מַשּׂאוֹי. שֶׁהַתַּחְתּוֹנִים מְסַיְּיעִין אֶת הָעֶלְיוֹנִים, וּבְכָל אֶחָד הָיוּ שְׁנֵי מוֹטוֹת. כֵּיצַד? שְׁנֵי מוֹטוֹת הוֹלְכִין זֶה אֵצֶל זֶה וְאַרְבָּעָה נוֹשְׂאִין אוֹתָם, וּשְׁנֵי מוֹטוֹת אֲחֵרִים וְאַרְבָּעָה בְּנֵי אָדָם נוֹשְׂאִין אוֹתָם, וְהֵם בַּאֲלַכְסוֹן מִתַּחַת שְׁנַיִם הָעֶלְיוֹנִים, מוֹט אֶחָד לְרֹאשׁ הָאֶחָד וּמוֹט אֶחָד לְרֹאשׁ הַשֵּׁנִי, וְהוֹלְכִין בַּאֲלַכְסוֹן. וְרַבִּי יִצְחָק לָאו מִקְּרָא שְׁמִיעַ לֵיהּ, אֶלָּא דִּפְשִׁיטָא לֵיהּ דְּרִימּוֹן וּתְאֵינָה סַגֵּי בִּשְׁנַיִם, וִיהוֹשֻׁעַ וְכָלֵב לֹא נָשְׂאוּ כְּלוּם – פָּשׁוּ לְהוּ תַּמְנְיָא לְאֶשְׁכּוֹל, וְאִם לָאו מִדְרָשׁ הָרִאשׁוֹן הַמְלַמְּדֵנוּ דְּלָאו מוֹט אֶחָד קָאָמַר קְרָא – לֹא הָיִינוּ יוֹדְעִים לְכַוֵּין שְׁמֹנָה בְּנֵי אָדָם לְמַשָּׂאוֹ, אֶלָּא דְּשָׁמְעִינַן מִינֵּיהּ דִּשְׁנֵי מוֹטוֹת הָיוּ, וַאֲתָא רַבִּי יִצְחָק לְאַשְׁמוּעִינַן דִּשְׁנֵי מַשָּׂאוֹת הָיוּ שָׁם, וְכָל אֶחָד שְׁנֵי מוֹטוֹת. שֶׁלֹּא הָיוּ בְּאוֹתָהּ עֵצָה. לְהָבִיא אֶשְׁכּוֹל מְשׁוּנֶּה כָּזֶה. שֶׁהַמְרַגְּלִים לְרָעָה נִתְכַּוְּונוּ, לוֹמַר: כְּשֵׁם שֶׁפֵּירוֹתֶיהָ מְשׁוּנִּים כָּךְ יוֹשְׁבֶיהָ מְשׁוּנִּים, וְגִבּוֹרִים וּגְבוֹהִים. לְדִבְרֵי רַבִּי יְהוּדָה. שֶׁאָמַר: לֹא גָּבְהוּ הַמַּיִם אֶלָּא שְׁנֵים עָשָׂר מִילִין כְּאוֹרֶךְ מַחֲנֵיהֶם – דֶּרֶךְ חֲנִיָּיתָם עָבְרוּ בַּיַּרְדֵּן, כָּל רוֹחַב מַחֲנֵיהֶם עָבְרוּ יַחַד. הִילְכָּךְ לֹא הָיָה אוֹרֶךְ הַעֲבָרָה אֶלָּא שְׁנֵים עָשָׂר מִילִין. וּלְדִבְרֵי

תוספות

יותר משלש מאות מיל. תימה לר"י: והא ליכא מעיבא לארעא אלא תלתא פרסי!* וי"ל: שהיו נגדשין והולכין למעלה מן העננים. ירושלמי, רבי לוי אומר: עד לבו של רקיע. תמן אמרינן: עד בבל, נאמר כאן "הרחק" ונאמר להלן "מארץ רחוקה מבבל".

עודם בירדן אמר להם יהושע. [ירושלמי], אמר ריש לקיש: בירדן קיבלו עליהן את הנסתרות. אמר להן יהושע: אם אין אתם מקבלין את הנסתרות – המים באין ושוטפין אתכם. אמר רבי סימון ב"ר זביד: ויאות, תדע לך שהוא כן, שהרי עכן חטא ורובם של סנהדרין נפלה בעי. אמר ר' לוי: בינה הותרה הרצועה, יצתה בת קול ואמרה: אין לכם עסק בנסתרות. **גמירי** כל טונא. ירושלמי: לא דמי ההוא דטעין מן ארעא אל ארכבותיה, ומן ארכבותיה לכתיפיה, לההוא דתלי ליה [מן ארעא על כתיפיה], ולא דמי ההוא דתלי ליה לההוא [דאוחרן טעין ליה].

טורטני וטורטני דטורטני. פירש ר"ח: דטורטני בלשון יון קנה של מאזנים. וכילד נשאוהו? הביאו שני עמודים וסירגום בחבלים, ונתנו האשכול על גבי חבלים, ונתנו מוטות בחבלים בקצה העמודים המסורגים והאשכול. נתן מוט א' מן הקצה מזה הראש, וכיוצא בה בראש מקצה האחר. נמצאו שתי מוטות בראש העמודים המסורגים בחבלים, והאשכול נתון בחבלים. *ועל כל מוט מאלו המוטות שתי מוטות פחותין מהן, מוט בראש זה ומוט בראש זה, נמצאו ארבע מוטות בראשי שני מוטות הנתונים בראשי העמודים. וכל מוט ומוט מאלו ד' מוטות היו טוענים אותן שני אנשים, נמצא שמנה סובלין את האשכול. וזה פירוש טורטני וכו' – כלומר, מוטות ומוטות על מוטות. ירושלמי: כתיב "איש אחד איש אחד למטה", על דעתיה דרבי ישמעאל דו אומר לשונות ריבוי הן – שנים עשר היו; שמנה באשכול, ארבעה בתאנים ורימונים ובנושאי כלים. על דעתיה דרבי עקיבא דו אומר ⊕לשונות כפולים – עשרים וארבעה היו; ט"ז באשכול, שמנה בתאנים ורימונים ונושאי כלים. על דעתיה דרבי ישמעאל טורטרין, על דעתיה דרבי עקיבא טורטרין וטורטרי טורטרין.

תוספות שאנץ

ממשמע שנאמר במוט איני יודע שבשנים אמר ר' יצחק טורטני וטרטוני דטורטני משוי ומשוי תחת משוי שהתחתונים מסייעים את העליונים ובכל מוט אחד היה מוטות קטנים אחד לראש האחד ואחד לראש השני והולכין באלכסון (כזה). וד' בני אדם נושאים מוט אחד וד' אחרים נושאים מוט האחר ור' יצחק לא מקרא שמיע ליה. וא"ת מנא לן דבעי ח' בני אדם דלמא ה"פ איני יודע שבשנים א) דצריך בני אדם למוט אחד ולשני מוטות ד' בני אדם ופר"ח הכי ומה ת"ל בשני מוטו' דצריך לכל מוט ומוט ב' מוטות לב' ראשי המוט ולא היו המוטות באלכסון כדי שלא יפול האשכול לארץ אלא האשכול היתה מונחת על המוטות כמין דף שהולכת מזה לזה (כזה). וצריך שני בני אדם לד' ראשי המוטות ואם כן הוו ח' בני אדם. ור"ת פי' דנפקא לן במוט ר"ל שנים דשני בדין היו למזבח הזהב אחד מימין ואחד משמאל וידעינן ליה מדכתיב ועל מזבח הזהב יפרשו בגד תכלת ושמו את בדיו ואחר כך כתיב ונתנו על המוט משמע דהמוט זהו מה שאמור למעלה ושמו את בדיו אם כן מצינו מוט דקרא ר"ל שנים:
שלח

א) נראה דצ"ל דצריך ב' בני אדם למוט אחד אלא בשנים בב' מוטות והיינו ד' בני אדם ופר"ח.

מסורת הש"ס / תורה אור

[כדאיתא ב"ב עה:]
יהושע ג; שם ה; שם ב; שם; במדבר לג; יהושע ד; שם; במדבר יג
[תוספתא פ"ח]
ס"א כמוט
[נ"ל רבי יוסי]
ושוב נתנו מוט אחד מן הקלה כו'. רש"ל

גליון הש"ס

תום' ד"ה טורטני וכו' לשונות כפולים כ"ד היו. עי' במתני' ריש סנהדרין ומנין לעדה כו':

כה א מיי' פ"ז מהל' איסורי מזבח הל' ב סמג עשין קעט:

כַּחֲנָיָיתָן עָבְרוּ, לְדִבְרֵי רַבִּי אֶלְעָזָר בְּר' שִׁמְעוֹן בְּזֶה אַחַר זֶה עָבְרוּ. וְחַד אָמַר: בֵּין מָר וּבֵין מָר כַּחֲנָיָיתָן עָבְרוּ. מָר סָבַר: אָדָם קַל, וּמָר סָבַר: מַיִם קַלִּים. °"שְׁלַח לְךָ אֲנָשִׁים" [במדבר יג], אָמַר רֵישׁ לָקִישׁ: שְׁלַח לְךָ — מִדַּעְתְּךָ, וְכִי אָדָם זֶה בּוֹרֵר חֵלֶק רַע לְעַצְמוֹ? וְהַיְינוּ דִּכְתִיב: °"וַיִּיטַב בְּעֵינַי הַדָּבָר" [דברים א], (א) אָמַר רֵישׁ לָקִישׁ: בְּעֵינַי, וְלֹא בְּעֵינָיו שֶׁל מָקוֹם. °"וְיַחְפְּרוּ לָנוּ אֶת הָאָרֶץ" [שם], אָמַר ר' חִיָּיא בַּר אַבָּא: מְרַגְּלִים לֹא נִתְכַּוְּונוּ אֶלָּא לְבוּשְׁתָּהּ שֶׁל אֶרֶץ יִשְׂרָאֵל, כְּתִיב הָכָא: "וְיַחְפְּרוּ לָנוּ אֶת הָאָרֶץ", וּכְתִיב הָתָם: °"וְחָפְרָה הַלְּבָנָה וּבוֹשָׁה הַחַמָּה" [ישעיה כד] וגו'. °"וְאֵלֶּה שְׁמוֹתָם לְמַטֵּה רְאוּבֵן שַׁמּוּעַ בֶּן זַכּוּר" [במדבר יג]. אָמַר רַבִּי יִצְחָק: דָּבָר זֶה מָסוֹרֶת בְּיָדֵינוּ מֵאֲבוֹתֵינוּ: מְרַגְּלִים עַל שֵׁם מַעֲשֵׂיהֶם נִקְרְאוּ, וְאָנוּ לֹא עָלְתָה בְּיָדֵינוּ אֶלָּא אֶחָד: °"סְתוּר בֶּן מִיכָאֵל" [שם], סְתוּר — שֶׁסָּתַר מַעֲשָׂיו שֶׁל הקב"ה, מִיכָאֵל — שֶׁעָשָׂה עַצְמוֹ מָךְ, אָמַר רַבִּי יוֹחָנָן: אַף אָנוּ נֹאמַר: "נַחְבִּי בֶּן וָפְסִי", נַחְבִּי — שֶׁהֶחְבִּיא דְּבָרָיו שֶׁל הקב"ה, וָפְסִי — שֶׁפִּיסַּע עַל מִדּוֹתָיו שֶׁל הקב"ה. °"וַיַּעֲלוּ בַנֶּגֶב וַיָּבֹא עַד חֶבְרוֹן" [שם]. "וַיָּבֹאוּ" מִבָּעֵי לֵיהּ! אָמַר רָבָא: מְלַמֵּד שֶׁפֵּירַשׁ כָּלֵב מֵעֲצַת מְרַגְּלִים, וְהָלַךְ וְנִשְׁתַּטֵּחַ עַל קִבְרֵי אָבוֹת. אָמַר לָהֶן: אֲבוֹתַי! בַּקְּשׁוּ עָלַי רַחֲמִים שֶׁאֶנָּצֵל מֵעֲצַת מְרַגְּלִים. יְהוֹשֻׁעַ, כְּבָר בִּקֵּשׁ מֹשֶׁה עָלָיו רַחֲמִים, שֶׁנֶּאֱמַר: °"וַיִּקְרָא מֹשֶׁה לְהוֹשֵׁעַ בִּן נוּן יְהוֹשֻׁעַ" [שם] — יָהּ יוֹשִׁיעֲךָ מֵעֲצַת מְרַגְּלִים. וְהַיְינוּ דִּכְתִיב: °"וְעַבְדִּי כָלֵב עֵקֶב הָיְתָה רוּחַ אַחֶרֶת עִמּוֹ" [שם יד] וגו'. "וְשָׁם אֲחִימָן שֵׁשַׁי וְתַלְמַי" וגו'. *אֲחִימָן — מְיוּמָּן שֶׁבְּאֶחָיו, שֵׁשַׁי — שֶׁמֵּשִׂים אֶת הָאָרֶץ כִּשְׁחָתוֹת, תַּלְמַי — שֶׁמֵּשִׂים אֶת הָאָרֶץ תְּלָמִים תְּלָמִים. ד"א: אֲחִימָן בָּנָה עֲנָת, שֵׁשַׁי בָּנָה אָלֵשׁ, תַּלְמַי בָּנָה תַּלְבּוּשׁ. "יְלִידֵי הָעֲנָק" — שֶׁמַּעֲנִיקִין חַמָּה בְּקוֹמָתָן. *°"וְחֶבְרוֹן שֶׁבַע שָׁנִים נִבְנְתָה" [שם יג]. [מַאי נִבְנְתָה?] אִילֵימָא נִבְנְתָה מַמָּשׁ — אֶפְשָׁר אָדָם בּוֹנֶה בַּיִת לִבְנוֹ קָטָן קוֹדֶם לִבְנוֹ גָּדוֹל?! דִּכְתִיב: °"וּבְנֵי חָם כּוּשׁ וּמִצְרַיִם" [בראשית י] וגו', אֶלָּא שֶׁהָיְתָה מְבוּנָּה עַל אֶחָד מִשִּׁבְעָה בְּצוֹעַן. וְאֵין לְךָ טְרָשִׁים בְּכָל א"י יָתֵר מֵחֶבְרוֹן, (מִשּׁוּם) [ס"א ל"ג] דְּקָבְרִי בָּהּ שִׁכְבֵי. וְאֵין לְךָ מְעוּלָּה בְּכָל הָאֲרָצוֹת יָתֵר מֵאֶרֶץ מִצְרַיִם, שֶׁנֶּאֱמַר: °"כְּגַן ה' כְּאֶרֶץ מִצְרַיִם" [שם יג], וְאֵין לְךָ מְעוּלָּה בְּכָל אֶרֶץ מִצְרַיִם יָתֵר מִצּוֹעַן, דִּכְתִיב: °"כִּי הָיוּ בְצֹעַן שָׂרָיו" [ישעיה ל] — וַאֲפִילּוּ הָכִי חֶבְרוֹן מְבוּנָּה אֶחָד מִשִּׁבְעָה בְּצוֹעַן. וְחֶבְרוֹן טְרָשִׁים הָוְיָא?! וְהָא כְּתִיב: °"וַיְהִי [ש"ב טו] מִקֵּץ אַרְבָּעִים שָׁנָה וַיֹּאמֶר אַבְשָׁלוֹם אֶל הַמֶּלֶךְ אֵלְכָה נָּא" וגו', וְאָמַר *רַב אַוְיָא וְאִיתֵּימָא רַבָּה בַּר בַּר חָנָה: שֶׁהָלַךְ לְהָבִיא כְּבָשִׂים מֵחֶבְרוֹן. *וְתַנְיָא: [א]אֵילִים מִמּוֹאָב, כְּבָשִׂים מֵחֶבְרוֹן! מִינָּהּ, אַיְּדֵי דִּקְלִישָׁא אַרְעָא — עָבְדָה רַעְיָא, וְשָׁמֵן קִנְיָינָא. °"וַיָּשֻׁבוּ מִתּוּר הָאָרֶץ [במדבר יג] וַיֵּלְכוּ

רש"י

וּלְדִבְרֵי ר"א בַּר שִׁמְעוֹן. דְּקָאָמַר יוֹתֵר מִשָּׁלֹשׁ מֵאוֹת מִיל, בְּזֶה אַחַר זֶה עָבְרוּ אִישׁ אַחַר אִישׁ, נִמְלְאוּ שֶׁשָּׁהוּ הַרְבֵּה לַעֲבוֹר. דְּאִי כַּחֲנָיָיתָן עָבְרוּ — מִשּׁוּם קוּלָּא דְּמַיִם מֵאָדָם לֹא נִגְבָּהִין כָּל כָּךְ. מַיִם קַלִּים. הַרְבֵּה הֵם קַלִּים מִן הָאָדָם. וּמָר סָבַר: אָדָם קַל לָרוּץ כְּמוֹ הַמַּיִם. מִדַּעְתְּךָ. אֲנִי אֵינִי מְצַוֶּה אוֹתְךָ, אֲבָל יִשְׂרָאֵל הֵם אוֹמְרִים לְךָ. כִּדְכְתִיב (דברים א): "וַתִּקְרְבוּן אֵלַי כּוּלְּכֶם" וגו' — אֲנִי אֵינִי מְעַכֵּב עַל יָדְךָ. כְּלוּם יֵשׁ אָדָם. כְּלוֹמַר, אִם הקב"ה נָוֶה — כְּלוּם הָיָה אוֹמֵר לוֹ לַעֲשׂוֹת דָּבָר שֶׁסּוֹפוֹ לָבֹא לִידֵי תַּקָּלָה?. לְבוּשְׁתָּהּ שֶׁל אֶרֶץ יִשְׂרָאֵל. (ב) אוֹתָהּ שְׁאֵילָה שֶׁשָּׁאֲלוּ תְּחִילָּה, שִׁלּוּחַ הַמְרַגְּלִים. [לֹא עָלָה בְּיָדֵינוּ. אֵין אָנוּ יוֹדְעִין לִדְרוֹשׁ]. סָתַר דְּבָרָיו. הִכְחִישׁ וְעָשָׂה שׂוֹנְאוֹ [שֶׁל הקב"ה] בַּדַּאי. שֶׁעָשָׂה שׂוֹנְאוֹ שֶׁל הקב"ה מָךְ. חַלָּשׁ, כִּדְאָמְרִי' לְקַמָּן: אֲפִילּוּ בַּעַל הַבַּיִת אֵינוֹ יָכוֹל לְהוֹצִיא כֵּלָיו מִשָּׁם. שֶׁהֶחְבִּיא דְּבָרָיו. וְלֹא אֲמָרָן כְּמוֹת שֶׁהֵן. שֶׁפִּיסֵּעַ. דִּילֵּג, שֶׁלֹּא אֲמָרָן כַּאֲשֶׁר הֵם. יְהוֹשֻׁעַ. לֹא הוּצְרַךְ לֵילֵךְ, שֶׁכְּבָר בִּיקֵּשׁ עָלָיו מֹשֶׁה רַחֲמִים. וְהַיְינוּ דִּכְתִיב וְעַבְדִּי כָלֵב וגו'. "וַהֲבִיאוֹתִיו אֶל הָאָרֶץ אֲשֶׁר בָּא שָׁמָּה", וְהִיא חֶבְרוֹן, כִּדְכְתִיב (יהושע יד): "וַיִּתֵּן אֶת חֶבְרוֹן לְכָלֵב", ש"מ כָּלֵב הוּא דְּאָזֵיל לְחֶבְרוֹן. מְיוּמָּן. גִּבּוֹר שֶׁבָּהֶם, כְּמוֹ שֶׁיַּד הַיָּמִין חֲשׁוּבָה מִן הַשְּׂמֹאל. שֶׁעוֹשֶׂה אֶת הָאָרֶץ כִּשְׁחִיתוֹת. שֶׁמְּקוֹם רַגְלָיו מַעֲמִיק בָּאָרֶץ מֵרוֹב כּוֹבְדוֹ וְנִיכָּר שָׁם כְּגוּמָא וּכְשַׁחַת. וְלָשׁוֹן שֵׁשִׁי לֹא פּוֹרַשׁ לָנוּ מַאי דָּמֵי לִשְׁחִיתוּת. וְנִרְאֶה: לְשׁוֹן "עַמּוּדֵי *שֵׁשׁ", שֶׁהֵם כְּבֵדִים, וּמְקוֹם מַעֲמָדָם נִיכָּר. תְּלָמִים. כְּתֶלֶם הַמַּחֲרֵישָׁה שֶׁמַּעֲלֶה הֶעָפָר וּמַעֲמִיק בָּאָרֶץ. שֶׁהָיוּ מַעֲנִיקִים אֶת הַחַמָּה בְּקוֹמָתָן. מֵרוֹב גּוֹבַהּ קוֹמָתָן דּוֹמִין כְּאִילּוּ צַוָּארָם נוֹקֵב וְעוֹנֵק בַּנֶּקֶב שֶׁהַחַמָּה יוֹצְאָה בּוֹ. לִבְנוֹ קָטָן. כְּנַעַן קָטָן הַבָּנִים שֶׁל חָם הָיָה, וּמִצְרַיִם שֵׁנִי לַבָּנִים. מְבוּנָּה. לְשׁוֹן "אִבָּנֶה מִמֶּנָּה" (בראשית טז), כְּלוֹמַר מְיוּשֶּׁבֶת בְּפֵירוֹת. טְרָשִׁים. סְלָעִים, שֶׁאֵין עוֹשִׂין פֵּירוֹת כְּאֶרֶץ לַחָה. דְּקָבְרִי בָּהּ שִׁכְבֵי. לָא גָּרְסִינַן: מ"ט. אֶלָּא ה"ק: וְתֵדַע דִּטְרָשִׁין הִיא וְאֵינָהּ רְאוּיָה לְפֵירוֹת כְּכָל שְׁאָר הָאָרֶץ, לְפִיכָךְ יִחֲדוּהָ לִקְבוּרַת מֵתִים. כִּי הָיוּ בְצוֹעַן שָׂרָיו. שֶׁל מֶלֶךְ יִשְׂרָאֵל, שֶׁשּׁוֹלְחִים אֶל פַּרְעֹה לַעֲזוֹר לוֹ עַל מֶלֶךְ אַשּׁוּר. אַלְמָא פַּרְעֹה בְּצוֹעַן יָתֵיב, וְשָׁם הוֹלְכִין לְבַקְּשׁוֹ. אֵלְכָה נָּא וַאֲשַׁלֵּם אֶת נְדָרַי (ג). אֵלְכָה נָא בְּחֶבְרוֹן וַאֲשַׁלֵּם הַנֶּדֶר שֶׁנָּדַרְתִּי בִּגְשׁוּר, כִּדְכְתִיב בַּתְרֵיהּ: "כִּי נֵדֶר נָדַר עַבְדְּךָ בְּשִׁבְתִּי בִגְשׁוּר". וּבְחֶבְרוֹן מַאי בָּעֵי? וַהֲלֹא לֹא הָיָה שָׁם הַמִּזְבֵּחַ, כִּי אִם בְּגִבְעוֹן. לְהָבִיא כְּבָשִׂים לְעוֹלָה. דְּאָמַר מָר דְּמַס' מְנָחוֹת: כְּבָשִׂים מֵחֶבְרוֹן. אַלְמָא אֶרֶץ מִרְעֶה הָיְתָה. מִינָּהּ. כְּלוֹמַר, מֵחֲשׁוּבָתְךָ אַתָּה מְסַיְּיעֵנִי, שֶׁלֹּא הָיְתָה חֲשׁוּבָה לִיזָּרַע כִּשְׁאָר הָאָרֶץ מֵאַחַר שֶׁהִיא בַּת טְרָשִׁים, כִּדְאָמְרִי' בְּבָבָא מְצִיעָא בְּ"הַשּׂוֹכֵר" (דף פ.): וְאִי אַרְעָא דְּמַחְזְקָא בְּגָרוֹנְדֵּי [הִיא — שְׁנֵיהֶם מְשַׁלְּמִין]. דִּקְלִישָׁא אַרְעָא. עָפָר שֶׁל טְרָשִׁים דַּק וְקָלוּשׁ וּמוּעָט הוּא, וּמִתּוֹךְ כָּךְ לֹא הָיוּ חוֹרְשִׁים וְזוֹרְעִים אוֹתָהּ תְּבוּאָה מַאֲכַל אָדָם. וְעָבְדָה רַעְיָא. מַצְמַחַת וּמַעֲלָה עֲשָׂבִים, וְאוֹכְלִים הַצֹּאן. וְשָׁמֵן קִנְיָינָא. הַמִּקְנֶה, הַצֹּאן. שֶׁכֵּן דֶּרֶךְ הַצֹּאן לְהַשְׁבִּיחַ בְּאֶרֶץ יְבֵשָׁה וּטְרָשִׁים יוֹתֵר מֵאֶרֶץ לַחָה. וַיֵּלְכוּ

תוספות

כחנייתן עברו. י"ל: הראשונים לעולם כשהיו מגיעין לשפת עבר השני לצד מערב, היו הולכין למטה בירדן ועושין מקום מעמד לבאין אחריהם, שהרי רוחב מחנה ישראל היה שנים עשר מיל, ורוחב הירדן לא היה כ"א חמשים אמה, ומיל הוא אלפים אמה! וי"ל, דדוקא באורך ורוחב חנייתן נכנסו בירדן, אבל לאחר שנכנסו בירדן — נמשכו זה אצל זה וצמצמו עצמן. שאם לא תאמר כן, אלא כדרך חנייתן עמדו בירדן — אם כן לא עמדו כולם בירדן בשעה שהתנה יהושע עמהן, שהרי אתה מוצא ברוחב שנים עשר מיל ת"פ רצועות רחבות חמשים אמה כרוחב הירדן, ואורך כל רצועה י"ב מיל על רוחב נ' אמה. ואם היה לך להקיף אותן ת"פ רצועות מדת ארכן זו אצל זו — היה אורכו קרוב לאלף ות' (ומ') [רש"ל מ"ז] פרסאות כאורך הירדן, והירדן לא נכרת כי אם עד ים הערבה ויוצא הוא ממערת פמייס שהוא בחלק דן, כדאיתא בפ' "מעשר בהמה" (בכורות דף נה.), ואורך כל ארץ ישראל לא היה כ"א ת' פרסאות. ועוד: דהיאך היו יכולין לשמוע התנאים מפי יהושע? אלא ע"כ בירדן לא היו עומדים כדרך חנייתן אלא מצומצמין. ותימה לר"י: נהי דדרך חנייתן עברו, מ"מ הלא עמדו בירדן עד שגמר יהושע התנאים, ונטלו האבנים, ולא חזר לאיתנו עד שעברו כולן — א"כ אותם נ' אמה של ירדן ששהות זה שעברו היו המים נגדשין ועולין יותר על י"ב מיל! וי"ל: אותו גודש שהיה מיותר על י"ב מיל לא הגיע לכלל גובה מיל, ולהכי לא חשיב ליה. **בזה** אחר זה עברו. תימה: א"כ אמאי תלי ליה ר' אלעזר בקלות המים? והלא אינו תלויה אלא בעיכוב העברתם! וי"ל: דבתרתי פליגי, על מה שמשוה קלות האדם לקלות המים — אמר: זה אינו, שאפילו אם היו עוברין דרך חנייתן היו המים נגדשין יותר *מי"ג [נ"א מי"ב] מיל, והוא לא אמר אלא י"ב. ועוד: שבזה אחר זה עברו. ועל זה תמיה רבי: אם בזה אחר זה עברו — מה קצבה שייך, דקאמר שלש מאות? שלפי חשבון גודל המים היו עוברים ברוחב חצי מיל שהוא אורך ג' מאות חסר י"ב. כילד? שתעשה י"ב רצועות מי"ב מיל על י"ב מיל, וכל רצועה ברוחב מיל ואורך י"ב מיל, וכשתצרפם זו אצל זו באורך — יהיה אורך קמ"ד מיל על רוחב מיל. תחלוק רוחב הרצועות ותצרפנה לאורך — יהיה אורך רפ"ח מיל על רוחב חצי מיל. והא מנא ליה שכך וזהו! ונראה דלר"א בר שמעון לא עברו כלל דרך חנייתן, שהרי בשעת חנייתן היו מפוזרים, מפני שהיו נוטים אהליהם זה רחוק מזה כדרך חניית שיירות. אבל כשעברו — נמשכין כולן זה אצל זה, ושמא לא היה כל ישראל כי אם ברוחב חצי מיל על חצי מיל, וכשעברו זה אחר זה כדרך בני אדם העוברין דרך שביל אחד, בעשרה בני אדם זה אצל זה — יכול להיות כשיעור ס' ריבוא ששוהין בהעברתן כל כך. **מר** סבר אדם קל. נראה דה"פ: אע"פ שהדבר ידוע שמים קלים — היינו דוקא כשהן יורדין כדי דרך מרוצתן, אבל כאן נגדשין ועולין — שיעור קלות מים ושיעור קלות אדם שוה. **אבותי** בקשו עלי רחמים. וא"ת: והאמר בפרק "מי שמתו" (ברכות דף יח.) דמיתי לא ידעין מידי, ומשמע במסקנא* ואפילו אבות העולם! יש לומר: דעל ידי תפלה שזה מתפלל — מודיעין להן שכך נתפלל. והכי אמר בפרק שני דתענית (דף טז.): למה יוצאין לבית הקברות — כדי שיבקשו עליהם מתים רחמים. וכן בפרקי דחסידים,* בעובדא דרבי מנא דאשתטח אמערתא דאבוה. **ואמר** רב אויא ואיתימא רבה בר בר חנן שהלך להביא כבשים מחברון. אע"ג דמסיק בפרק שני דתמורה (דף יד:) דלאקרובי אזל, מיהו שמעינן מיהת דשמן קניינא, מדסלקא דעתך למימר שהלך להביא כבשים. מלמד

מסורת הש"ס

וכ"ה במ"ר הכא שבריא כשיש

יומא י.

כתובות קיב.

[תמורה יד: ע"ש]

מנחות פז.

[ד' יט: ע"ש היטב ותוס' לייסב]

[תענית כג.]

הגהות הב"ח

(א) גמ' וייטב בעיני הדבר ואמר ר"ל: (ב) רש"י ד"ה לבושתה וכו' אותן שאלו כצ"ל ותיבת שאילה נמחק: (ג) ד"ה אלכה נא ואשלם את נדרי אשר נדרתי לה' בחברון אלכה נא:

תוספות שאנץ

שלח לך אנשים לדעתך איני מצוה לך אבל ישר' הם אומר' שתשלחם כדכתיב ותקרבון אלי כלכם: וכי יש אדם כו' כלומר אם צוה הקב"ה [היה מצוה] לעשות לי דבר שסופו לבא לידי תקלה. וייטב בעיני הדבר ולא בעיני המקום ובמדרש רבה מפרש שאף בעיני משה לא היטיב אלא משל לאדם האומר לחבירו מכור לי חמורך ואנסנו ונאות לו להוליכו בהר ובבקעה ואמר כיון שאין אתה מעכב על ידי שלא אעשה ממנו מה שארצה לנסותו לא אנסנו וכן היה משה סבור שיאמרו לו ישר' כיון שאתה מודה לשלוח מרגלים לא תשלח עוד וה"ק הכא וייטב בעיני הדבר שהייתי סבור שתניחו מלשלוח כי היה לכם להאמין במקום ב"ה. אבל לא בעיני המקום שהיה גלוי לפניו שתשלחו ותבאו לידי תקלה. א"נ י"ל דהמד"ר חולק עם תלמוד שלנו. מרגלים לא נתכונו בו. אינו רוצה לומר מרגלים ממש אלא אותן ששאלו תחלה שילוח מרגלים: שעשה עצמו מך משונאו של הקב"ה כביכול כדאמר לקמן אפילו בעל הבית אינו יכול להוציא כליו משם: שעושה הארץ כשחיתות שמקום רגליו מעמיק הארץ מרוב כובדו. ופ"ה לשון ששי לא פורש לי מאי דמי לשחיתות וצ"ל לשון עמודי שיש שהם כבדים ומקום מעמדם ניכר ל"ה. אלימא נבנתה ממש. וחולק התלמוד על המדרש דאיתא התם מפני מה זכו הכנענים לישב בארצם מ"ז שנים יותר ממצרים בשכר שכבדו הזקן אברהם אבינו שאמרו לו

תורה אור

וילכו ויבאו". א"ר יוחנן משום רבי שמעון בן יוחי: מקיש הליכה לביאה, מה ביאה בעצה רעה – אף הליכה בעצה רעה. °"ויספרו לו ויאמרו באנו" וגו', וכתיב: "אפס כי עז העם". אמר רבי יוחנן (סימן: אמ"ת לבד"ו לוי"ה) משום ר"מ: כל לשון הרע שאין בו דבר אמת בתחילתו – אין מתקיים בסופו. °"ויהס כלב את העם אל משה". אמר רבה: שהסיתן בדברים. *פתח יהושע, דקא משתעי אמרי ליה: דין *ראש קטיעה ימלל! אמר: אי משתעינא – אמרי בי מילתא וחסמין לי. אמר להן: וכי זו בלבד עשה לנו בן עמרם?! סברי בגנותיה קא משתעי, אישתיקו. אמר להו: הוציאנו ממצרים, וקרע לנו את הים, והאכילנו את המן. אם יאמר: עשו סולמות ועלו לרקיע, לא נשמע לו? °"עלה נעלה וירשנו אותה" וגו'! "והאנשים אשר עלו עמו אמרו: לא נוכל" וגו'. אמר *רבי חנינא בר פפא: דבר גדול דברו מרגלים באותה שעה; "כי חזק הוא ממנו" – *אל תקרי "ממנו" אלא "ממנו", כביכול, אפילו בעל הבית אינו יכול להוציא כליו משם. °"ארץ אוכלת יושביה היא" דרש רבא: אמר הקב"ה אני חשבתיה לטובה, והם חשבו לרעה. אני חשבתיה לטובה – דכל היכא דמטו – מת חשיבא דידהו, כי היכי דניטרדו ולא לישאלו אבתרייהו. ואיכא דאמרי: *איוב נח נפשיה, ואטרידו כולי עלמא בהספידא. הם חשבו לרעה – "ארץ אוכלת יושביה היא". °"ונהי בעינינו כחגבים וכן היינו" וגו'. אמר רב משרשיא: מרגלים שקרי הוו; בשלמא "ונהי בעינינו כחגבים" – לחיי, אלא "וכן היינו בעיניהם" – מנא הוו ידעי? ולא היא, כי הוו מברי אבילי – תותי ארזי הוו מברי, וכי חזינהו – סלקו יתבי באילני, שמעי דקאמרי: קחזינן אינשי דדמו לקמצי באילני. °"ותשא כל העדה ויתנו את קולם ויבכו" *אמר רבה אמר רבי יוחנן: אותו *היום [ערב] תשעה באב היה. אמר הקב"ה: הן בכו בכיה של חנם – ואני אקבע להם בכיה לדורות. "ויאמרו כל העדה לרגום אותם באבנים", וכתיב: °"וכבוד ה' נראה באהל מועד". אמר רבי חייא בר אבא: מלמד שנטלו אבנים וזרקום כלפי מעלה. °"וימותו האנשים מוציאי דבת הארץ רעה במגפה", אמר רבי שמעון בן לקיש: שמתו מיתה משונה. אמר רבי חנינא בר פפא, דרש ר' שילא איש כפר תמרתא: מלמד שנשתרבב לשונם ונפל על טיבורם, והיו תולעים יוצאות מלשונם ונכנסות בטיבורם, ומטיבורם ונכנסות בלשונם. ורב נחמן בר יצחק אמר: באסכרה מתו.§ וכיון שעלה האחרון שבישראל מן הירדן חזרו מים למקומן, שנאמר: °"ויהי בעלות הכהנים נושאי ארון ברית ה' מתוך הירדן נתקו כפות רגלי הכהנים אל החרבה וישובו מי הירדן למקומם וילכו כתמול שלשום על כל גדותיו", נמצא ארון ונושאיו וכהנים מצד אחד וישראל מצד אחד. נשא ארון את נושאיו ועבר, שנאמר: °"ויהי כאשר תם כל העם לעבור ויעבור ארון ה' והכהנים לפני העם". ועל דבר זה נענש עוזא, שנאמר: °"ויבאו עד גורן כידון וישלח עוזא את ידו לאחוז את הארון", אמר לו הקב"ה: עוזא! נושאיו נשא, עצמו לא כל שכן?! °"ויחר אף ה' בעוזא, ויכהו שם על השל" וגו'. רבי יוחנן ור"א; חד אמר: על עסקי שלו, וחד אמר: שעשה צרכיו בפניו. °"וימת שם עם ארון האלהים" א"ר יוחנן: עוזא בא לעוה"ב, שנאמר: "עם ארון האלהים", מה ארון לעולם קיים – אף עוזא בא לעוה"ב. °"ויחר לדוד על אשר פרץ ה' פרץ בעוזא"? א"ר אלעזר: שנשתנו פניו כחררה. אלא מעתה, כל היכא דכתיב "ויחר" ה"נ? התם כתיב "אף", הכא לא כתיב "אף". דרש רבא: מפני מה נענש דוד – מפני שקרא לדברי תורה ◦זמירות, שנאמר: °"זמירות היו לי חוקיך בבית מגורי". אמר לו הקב"ה: ד"ת שכתוב בהן °"התעיף עיניך בו ואיננו" אתה קורא אותן "זמירות"?! הריני מכשילך בדבר שאפילו תינוקות של בית רבן יודעין אותו, אדכתיב: °"ולבני קהת לא נתן כי עבודת הקודש" וגו', ואיהו אתייה בעגלתא. °"ויך באנשי בית שמש כי ראו בארון". משום דראו – "ויך" (אלהים)?! רבי אבהו ורבי אלעזר; חד אמר: קוצרין ומשתחוים היו, וחד אמר: מילי נמי אמור:

מאן

וילכו ויבאו. לא גרסינן "וכתיב", *[אלא] "וילכו" – יתירא הוא. כיון דכתיב [לעיל] "וישובו" – לא הוה ליה למימר אלא "ויבאו אל משה" וגו'. מקיש הליכתן. שהלכו לתור, לביאתן. אף הליכתן להוציא דבה נתכוונו. אינו מתקיים. שמחזיקין אותן השומעין כבדאין, לפיכך אומר דבר אמת תחילה כדי שיאמינו. ואף מרגלים לכך פתחו בשבח הארץ תחילה. ויהס. שיתקן. אל משה. בדברים. שהתחיל לדבר במשה, והיו סבורים שבגנותו רוצה לספר. שהסיתם בדברים. כדמפרש ואזיל. דחזייה. כלב ליהושע שרצה לדבר, ושיתקוהו בנזיפה, ואמרו לו: ראש הקטוע ידבר?! מי שראשו קטוע, שאין לו בנים ליטול חלק בארץ, הוא ידבר בפנינו?. וחסמין לי. משתקין אותי. עלה נעלה. אף לשמים אם יאמר עלינו. ממנו. מן הקב"ה. אל תקרי. לא גרס, שאין הפרש קרייה בין "ממנו" הנאמר על יחיד שמדברים עליו, ל"ממנו" של רבים שאומרים על עצמן. אינו יכול להוציא כליו. אם הפקידם שם. בעל הבית. אדון העולם. אני חשבתיה לטובה. שהראיתיה להם כאוכלת יושביה, שמתים בה תדיר. שכיב איוב. שלא תגין זכותו עליהם. והיינו דקאמר כלב: "סר צלם מעליהם". ה"ג ולא היא כי הוו מברי אבילי תותי ארזי הוו מברי. ולא היו שקרנים בזאת, (ולא היו נראים בהן שקרנים), דאינהו שמעינהו לאמוריים שקורין אותן חגבים. דכי הוו אמוריים מברין את אביליהם כשחוזרין מן הקבר, כדאמר לעיל דכל היכא דמטו שכיב חשיבא מנייהו, ומברין לאבל סעודה לנחמו, תותי ארזי הוו מברי להו. וכדחזינהו. והם יראים לעמוד לפניהם, סלקי ויתבי באילני. וזרקום כלפי מעלה. (שדי) לרגום אותם, [וקאי] נמי אכבוד ה'. במגפה. מדלא קרינן במגפה – משמע במיוחדת וראויה להם, במדה כנגד מדה. באסכרה מתו. שהיא באה על לשון הרע, כדאמרינן ב"במה מדליקין" (שבת דף לג:). וכיון שעלה כו'. סיפא דברייתא דלעיל היא. אלא איידי דתנא בה: ומכאן אתה מחשב לאשכול נקט לה לפרשת מרגלים הכא. שבו המים למקומם. שהכהנים עמדו במקומם עד שעברו כל העם, וכשעברו – נתקו כפות רגלי הכהנים אל החרבה, ונמשכו לאחוריהם פסיעה אחת, נמצאו כהנים מצד זה כו'. ואע"ג דההוא קרא ד"ויהי כאשר תם כל העם לעבור" קדים, דמשמע דהאי "נתקו רגלי הכהנים" בעבר השני כתיב – לא הוי הכי, אלא אין מוקדם ומאוחר. דאי כסדרן כתיב – הא נפקי להו מן הירדן, דכתיב: "ויעבור ארון ה' והכהנים לפני העם" והעם עלו, וכיון דארון והכהנים עלו ועברו אחריהם עד שבאו לפניהם – הרי יצאו מן הירדן, ומאי תו דקאמר: "ויצו יהושע את הכהנים לאמר עלו מן הירדן"? אלא אין מוקדם ומאוחר, והאי "עלו מן הירדן" דקאמר להו – הכי קאמר להו: סלקו רגליכם לאחוריכם, ועודם בעבר המזרחית, וכתיב בתריה: "נתקו כפות רגלי הכהנים אל החרבה, וישובו מי הירדן אל מקומם". נשא ארון את נושאיו ועבר. והיינו קרא קמא דכתיב: "ויהי כאשר תם כל העם לעבור [ויעבור] ארון ה'" וגו'. על עסקי שלו. שגגה, ששגג לאחוז בו. שעשה צרכיו. ו"של" – לשון "כי ישל זיתך" (דברים כח) "ובשלייתה" (שם) – דבר המוטל מלמעלה למטה. הארון קיים לעולם. שהרי נגנז, כדאמר ביומא (דף נג:) שגנזו יאשיהו. חררה. עוגה שאופין על פני הגחלים. נענש דוד. שמת עוזא על ידו. זמירות היו לי חוקיך בבית מגורי. כשהייתי בורח מפני אויבי ואגור מפניהם – הייתי משתעשע בחוקיך, והיו לי לזמירות לשעשעני. התעיף. לשון [כפול]. "וכפלת" מתרגמינן ותיעוף (שמות כו). שאם תכפיל עיניך לסתום עין בהפסק הדעת מהסתכל בהן – מיד "ואיננו". לא נתן. עגלות. משה לבני קהת, לפי שיש עליהם לשאת בכתף, כי לא היו ממונים אלא על דבר קדושת הארון והשלחן [והמנורה ומזבח הזהב]. ויך באנשי בית שמש. לא בתוך הכאה דדוד כתיב, אלא כשהביאוהו הפרות מפלשתים. ואיידי דאיירי בארון נקט לה. משום דראו. ונסתכלו בו – ויך? בתמיה. קוצרין ומשתחוים היו. לא בטלו ממלאכתן לכבודו, והאי "ראו" – לשון בזיון, כמו "אל תראוני שאני שחרחורת" (שיר א).

מאן

מלמד שמתו מיתה משונה. נראה ד"רעה במגפה" דרש.

שלשה

רש"ל נ"א אלא כתיב

במדבר יג

שם

ס"א דחזייה ליהושע

[פי' להכי קרי ליה ריש קטיעה לפי שקראו משה יהושע כלומר ראש שמו קטוע לפי שהיו"ד אות קטיעה היא. ערוך ערך רש ב]

שם

[מנחות נג: ערכין טו.]

שם

[ע' ב"ב טו:]

שם

נ"י שראו

שם יד

[תענית כט. סנהדרין קד:]

ס"א הלילה ליל

יהושע ד

שם

דה"א יג

שמואל ב ו

שם

שם

תהלים קיט

משלי כג

במדבר ז

שמואל א ו

גליון הש"ס

גמ' זמירות שנאמר וכו'. עי' עירובין יח ע"ב ובמהרש"א בח"א שם:

כו א מיי' פ"ב מהל' כלי המקדש הלכה יב סמג עשין קסח:

[ע' פרש"י דהכא ותוס' ערכין טו: ד"ה אל תקרי וכו' וכן בשאלתות ליתא]

תוספות שאנץ

לו נשיא אלהים אתה בתוכנו: וילכו ויבאו. ל"ג וכתיב [אלא] וילכו יתירא הוא כיון דכתיב וישובו לא הוה ליה למימ' אלא ויבאו אל משה: ראש קטיעא מי שאין לו בנים ליטול חלק בארץ הוא ידבר בפנינו: אל תקרי ממנו ל"ג שאין הפרש ממנו דיחיד לממנו דרבים ל"ה. וא"ד איוב נח נפשיה שלא תגין זכותו עליהם. והיינו דאמר איוב בימי משה היה והיינו דכתיב היש בה עץ (אם) [עין] זה איוב כלומר העודנו חי ולמה נקרא עץ שהיה מגין עליהם בזכותו כעץ: ה"ג ולא היא כי הוו מברי ואבלי. כי הוו אמוריים מברין מלאכל סעודת אבלים כשחוזרין מן הקבר דאמר לעיל בכל דוכתא דמטו שכיב חשיבא מיניהו: כד חזנהו. מרגלים והיו יראים לעמוד בפניהם סלקי ויתבי באילנות. לקומצי איתא במדרש מעשה בבתו של ענה שהלכה לפרדס אביה ולקטה רמון מן האילן וזרקה הקליפה והיה שם אחד מן המרגלים ונכנס בתוכה והיתה יראה פן יבוא אביה בפרדס ויראה הקליפה ונטלה הקליפה וזרקה חוץ מן הפרדס ויצא המרגל משם והלך לו: במגפה. מדלא כתיב במגפה משמע במיתה מיוחדת ומשונה: באסכרה. שהיא באה על לשון הרע. וכיון שעלה אחרון שבישראל כו'. סיפיה דברייתא דלעיל היא אלא איידי דתנא בה ומכאן אתה מחשב לאשכול נקט לפרשת מרגלי' הכא ואחר כך חוזר לדיבורו: נמצא ארון ונושאיו וכהנים מצד אחד כו'. דאע"ג דההוא קרא דויהי כאשר תמו כל העוברים לעבור קדים דמשמע דהאי נתקו רגלי הכהנים בעבר השני א) הא נפקי להו מן הירדן דכתיב ויעבור ארון ה' והכהנים לפני העם והעם כבר עלו וכיון דארון וכהנים עברו אחריהם עד שבא לפניהם הרי יצאו להם מן הירדן ומאי תו דקאמר ויצו יהושע את הכהנים לומר עלו מן הירדן אלא אין מוקדם ומאוחר בתורה והאי עלו מן הירדן דקאמר להו ה"ק להו סלקו רגליכם לאחוריכם ועודם בעבר המזרחי וכתיב בתריה נתקו כפות רגלי הכהנים אל החרבה ויצאו מי הירדן למקומם: נשא ארון את נושאיו ועבר והיינו קרא קמא דכתיב ויהי כאשר תמו כל העוברים לעבור ל"ה. ויך באנשי בית שמש לא בתוך הכאה דדוד כתיב אלא כשהביאו הפרות מפלשתים ואיידי דאיירי בארון נקט לה: משום דראו בו ונסתכלו [ויך בתמי']. קוצרים ומשתחוים היו ולא בטלו מן המלאכה לכבודו

א) נראה דל"ל כתיב לא הוי הכי אלא אין מוקדם ומאוחר בתורה דאי כסדרן כתיב הא נפקי וכו'.

מאן אמריך (להא) דאימריית, ומאן אתא עלך דאיפייסת. "ויך בעם שבעים איש וחמשים אלף איש" (ש"א ו) רבי אבהו ורבי אלעזר, חד אמר: שבעים איש היו, וכל אחד ואחד שקול כחמשים אלף, וחד אמר: חמשים אלף היו, וכל אחד ואחד שקול כשבעים סנהדרין. "ויהי כי צעדו נושאי ארון ה' ששה צעדים ויזבח שור ומריא" (ש"ב ו), וכתיב: "שבעה פרים ושבעה אילים" (דה"א טו). אמר רב פפא בר שמואל: על כל פסיעה ופסיעה – שור ומריא, על כל שש ושש פסיעות – שבעה פרים ושבעה אילים. אמר ליה רב חסדא: אם כן, מילאת את כל ארץ ישראל במות! אלא אמר רב חסדא: על כל שש ושש פסיעות – שור ומריא, על כל ששה סדרים של שש פסיעות – שבעה פרים ושבעה אילים. כתיב: "כידון" (דה"א יג) וכתיב "נכון" (ש"ב ו). אמר רבי יוחנן: בתחלה כידון, ולבסוף נכון. § *נמצאת אתה אומר שלשה מיני אבנים היו; אחד שהקים משה (א) בארץ מואב, שנאמר: "בעבר הירדן בארץ מואב הואיל משה באר" (דברים א) וגו', ולהלן הוא אומר: "וכתבת עליהן את כל דברי התורה הזאת" (שם כז) וגו', ואתיא "באר" "באר". ואחד שהקים יהושע בתוך הירדן, שנאמר: "ושתים עשרה אבנים הקים יהושע בתוך הירדן" (יהושע ד). ואחד שהקים בגלגל, שנאמר: "ואת שתים עשרה האבנים האלה אשר לקחו" (שם) וגו'. ת"ר: כיצד כתבו ישראל את התורה? *רבי יהודה אומר: על גבי אבנים כתבוה, שנאמר: "וכתבת על האבנים את כל דברי התורה הזאת" (דברים כז) וגו', ואחר כך סדו אותן בסיד. אמר לו רבי שמעון: לדבריך, היאך למדו אומות של אותו הזמן? תורה? אמר לו: בינה יתירה נתן בהם הקב"ה, ושיגרו נוטירין שלהן, וקילפו את הסיד והשיאוה. ועל דבר זה נתחתם גזר דינם לבאר שחת, שהיה להן ללמוד ולא למדו. ר' שמעון אומר: על גבי סיד כתבוה, וכתבו להן למטה: "למען אשר לא ילמדו אתכם לעשות ככל" (שם כ) וגו'. הא למדת שאם היו חוזרין בתשובה – היו מקבלין אותן. אמר רבא בר שילא: מ"ט דרבי שמעון – דכתיב: "והיו עמים משרפות סיד" (ישעיה לג) – על עסקי סיד. ור' יהודה: כי סיד; מה סיד אין לו תקנה אלא שריפה – אף אותם אומות העולם אין להם תקנה אלא שריפה. כמאן אזלא הא דתניא "ושבית שביו" (דברים כא) – לרבות כנענים שבחוצה לארץ, שאם חוזרין בתשובה – מקבלין אותן? כמאן

מאן אמריך דאימריית. מי הכעיסך כשכעסת ולא הצלת את עצמך מן השביה, ועתה מי מפייסך כשנתפייסת לבא אליך? **וכתיב שבעה פרים ושבעה אילים.** בדברי הימים. והכי רישיה דקרא: "ויהי בעזור האלהים את הלוים נושאי ארון ברית ה' ויזבחו שבעה פרים ושבעה אילים". **מילאת כל ארץ ישראל במות.** מזבחות, דעל כל פסיעה מזבח. **כתיב כידון.** בדברי הימים כתיב: "ויבאו עד גורן כידון וישלח עוזא" וגו' ובשמואל כתיב: "גורן נכון". **בתחלה.** כשבא הארון שם – נעשה להם ככידון ההורג, שהרג עוזא. **ולבסוף.** לאחר שנשתהה שם ששה חדשים בבית עובד אדום – נעשה נכון, שהכין את ביתו, דכתיב (שמואל ב ו): "ויברך ה' את עובד אדום" (אשתו ושמנה כלותיה). אשתו של עובד אדום ושמנה כלותיה ילדו *ששה ששה בכרס אחד, והיינו דכתיב: "פעלתי השמיני כי ברכו אלהי" (דה"א כו), וכתיב בתריה: "ששים ושנים לעובד אדום". ושמעתי בשם ר' מנחם בר' חלבו: גורן נכון הוא גורן ארונה היבוסי. וא"כ הוא ה"ג: בתחלה נכון ולבסוף כידון. על שם המזבח שמתחלתו בנוי וסופו חרב. וכידון – לשון שבר וחורבן הוא, כמו "יראו עיניו כידו" (איוב כא). **נמצאת.** סיפא דברייתא דלעיל הוא, אלא משום דקתני בה: ועל דבר זה נענש עוזא – אפסקיה בכל הני. שהעמיד משה בעבר הירדן בערבות מואב. ותנא דברייתא, כי קרי לארץ כנען קרי עבר המזרח עבר הירדן, וכי קרי בערבות מואב או בשאר המסעות קרי ארץ כנען עבר הירדן, והוא עבר המערבי. **בגלגל.** לאחר שבנו מהן המזבח בהר עיבל, קיפלום והביאום לגלגל, וקבעום שם. **כיצד כתבו.** על המזבח בהר עיבל. **היאך למדו אומות העולם.** בעתיקות תורה? הלא לא נצטוו לכותבה בשבעים לשון אלא לבא וללמדה כל הרוצה, שלא יהא פתחון פה לאומות העולם לומר: לא היה לנו מהיכן ללומדה. **נוטירין שלהן.** סופרים שלהם, והם קורין אותן נוטירין. **והשיאוה.** והעתיקוה. כלומר, נטלוה משם ע"י העתקה. **וכתבו מלמטה.** בסוף הדף: "למען אשר לא ילמדו עוד" וגו'. לעיל מיניה כתיב: "כי החרם תחרימם". ודבר זה כתבו למטה להודיע לשבעה אומות היושבים חוץ מגבולי ישראל, שלא נצטוו להחרימם, אלא אותן שבתוך גבולים נצטוו להחרים, כדי שלא ילמדו אותנו מעשיהם המקולקלים. אבל אתם היושבים חוצה לה, אם אתם חוזרין בתשובה – נקבל אתכם. ושבתוכה אין מקבלין, שמלחמת ירשה עושין. וה"ג לה בהדיא בתוספתא (פ"ח): אם אתם חוזרין בכם – אנו מקבלים אתכם. **מ"ט דר"ש.** דקאמר: על גבי סיד כתבוה. **על עסקי סיד.** שהתורה נכתבה עליו, והיתה מגולה לפניהם, ולא למדוה. **אלא שריפה.** גיהנם. שכל זמן שאין מתגיירין והם קרויין עמים אין תקנה להם אלא משרפות הסיד: ה"ג **ושבית שביו לרבות כנענים שבחו"ל.** דקרא בחו"ל כתיב: "כי תצא למלחמה" – מארץ לחוצה לארץ. והכי תניא בספרי: "כי תצא למלחמה" – במלחמת הרשות הכתוב מדבר. ד"כי תצא" משמע: כשעלה על דעתך לצאת. "ושבית שביו" – לרבות כנענים שבתוכה. בא הכתוב להתיר כנענים שבחוצה לארץ ולקיים מהם יפת תואר, שלא יהיו בכלל "לא תחיה כל נשמה". דהאי "ושבית" קרא יתירא הוא. כמאן

שלשה מיני אבנים היו. ירושלמי: ג' מיני אבנים הן; אבני המלון, ואבנים שהניחום יהושע תחת כפות רגלי הכהני', ואיסטליות שנתן להם משה. אמר רבי יצחק: פשוט לן, ארבעה מיני אבנים הוה. אמר ר' סימון בר זבידא: ויאות, אין תימר אבני המלון – לשעה היו ונגנזו, אין תימר אבנים שהקים יהושע תחת כפות רגלי הכהנים – משוקעות הן במים, אין תימר איסטליות שנתן להן משה – כבר נכנסו עמהן לארץ. אלא אם כן במה אנו קיימין – באבנים שהקים יהושע להן על גב הירדן. **כיצד כתבו ישראל את התורה.** בתוספתא, רבי יהודה אומר: על גבי המזבח כתבוה. אבל בירושלמי תני: על אבני המלון נכתבו, דברי ר' יהודה, ר' יוסי אמר: על אבני מזבח נכתבו. מאן דאמר על אבני המלון – בכל יום ויום אומות העולם היו משלחין נוטירין ומשיאין את התורה, שהיתה כתובה בשבעים לשון. מ"ד על אבני המזבח לא לשעה היו ונגנזו? [עוד הוא מעשה נסים, נתן הקב"ה בינה בלב כל אומה ואומה והשיאו את התורה שהיתה כתובה בע' לשון. מ"ד על אבני המלון נכתבו – ניחא "ושדת אותם בסיד", אלא] מאן דאמר על אבני המזבח [נכתבו, מאי] ושדת בסיד? בין כל אבן ואבן. **ועל דבר זה נתחתם גזר דינם לבאר שחת.** ואם תאמר: תיפוק ליה דבשעת מתן תורה החזירה הקב"ה על כל אומה ולשון ולא קבלוה! וי"ל: דעונש זה גדול הוא, שלאחר שהיתה כתובה בידם ולא רצו ללמוד. ומיהו, תימה: והאמר בפ"ק דמסכת ע"ז (דף ג:) דעדיין יש להן פתחון פה, שיאמרו: כלום כפית עלינו הר כגיגית כישראל? וכל זמן שיש להן פתחון פה – איך נתחתם גזר דינם? **לרבות כנענים שבחוצה לארץ.** תימה: היאך קבלוה לרחב, שהרי היא היתה מכנענים שבתוכה, כדאיתא בספרי בפרשת "בהעלותך": ומה אם מי שהיתה מעם שנאמר בו: "לא תחיה כל נשמה" [על שקירבה עצמה – כך קירבה המקום] ולהכי קא'. ואמרינן נמי במס' מגילה (דף יד:*) שנתגיירה ונסבה יהושע. והכא משמע דכנענים שבתוכה לדברי הכל שאין מקבלין אותן! ושמא על פי הדיבור היה. *ואמר לו שקודם שהתחילו המלחמה היו מקבלין – שהרי כתיבת התורה על גבי האבנים היה קודם שהתחילו במלחמה, ואפילו הכי לא היו מקבלין (אלא) היושבים חוץ לגבול ישראל, כמו שפרש"י. *ואי הוה מצינו למימר דאם היו חוזרין אז בתשובה בשעה שכתבו את התורה, אפילו כנענים שבתוכה היו מקבלין, ואפילו לר' יהודה, ו"למען אשר לא ילמדו אתכם לעשות" קאי נמי אשבעה אומות. והכי משמע נמי לשון הספרי בפרשת "שופטים ושוטרים": "למען אשר לא ילמדו אתכם לעשות" – [מלמד] שאם עושין תשובה אין נהרגין. אין מקבלין אותן לא קתני, אלא אין נהרגין. משמע, אותם שלוה הקב"ה "לא תחיה כל נשמה" – אין נהרגין. ולא נאמר "לא תחיה כל נשמה" אלא לאחר שהתחיל יהושע במלחמה, שהרי יהושע *שלח שלש פרוזטגמאות: הרוצה להשלים – ישלים, להלחם – ילחם. אלמא אותן שהיו רוצין להשלים לא היה הורגן. [וצריך לומר] אותן שהיו רוצין להשלים קודם שהתחיל במלחמה ראשונה, ואף רחב קיבלה עליה קודם שהתחילו במלחמה. ולא נחלקו רבי יהודה ורבי שמעון אלא באותן כנענים שחוץ לגבולים, אם מקבלים אותם לאחר מכאן; דרבי שמעון לא איצטריך למימר: הא למדת שאם חוזרים בתשובה מקבלין אותן, אלא אכנענים שבתוכה לארץ, ולאחר שהתחילו במלחמה, שדינם כדין [שאר] אומות, שמקבלין מהן לעולם. כמאן

לכבודו: מאן אמריך דאמרת. מי הכעיסך שהכעסת ולא הצלת את עמך מן השביה. ועוד מי פייסך שנתפייסת. ל"ה. כתיב כידון בדברי הימים ויבאו עד גורן כידון ובשמואל כתיב גורן נכון. בתחלה כשבא הארון שם נעשה להם ככידון ההורג שהרג את עוזה ולאחר שנשתהה שם ג' חדשים בבית עובד אדום נעשה להם נכון שהכין את ביתו כדכתיב ויברך ה' את עובד אדום. ושמעתי בשם רבי מנחם בר' חלבו גרן נכון הוא גרן ארונה היבוסי. וא"כ הוא (גרן) [ה"ג] בתחלה נכון ולבסוף כידון על שם המזבח שתחלתו בנוי ולבסוף חרוב וכידון לשון שבר וחורבן הוא כמו יראו עיניו כידו. כפ"ה: וכתבו להם למטה למען אשר לא ילמדו אתכם וגו'. לעיל מיניה [כתיב] כי החרם תחרימם ודבר זה כתבו למטה להודיע לז' אומות היושבין חוץ מגבולי ארץ ישראל שלא נצטוינו להחרימם אלא על אותם שבתוך הגבולים נצטוינו להחרימם כדי שלא ילמדו אותנו מעשיהם המקולקלין אבל אותן היושבין בחוצה לארץ אם חוזרין בתשובה נקבל אותם ושבתוכה אין מקבלין דמלחמת ירשה הם עושים וה"ג בתוס' אם אתם חוזרין בכם אנו מקבלין אתכם. ל"ה: ה"ג ושבית שביו לרבות כנענים שבחוצה לארץ. [דקרא בחו"ל כתיב] כי תצא למלחמה מארץ לחוצה לארץ והכי תני בספרי כי תצא למלחמה במלחמת הרשות הכתוב מדבר משמע כשתעלה על דעתך [לצאת]. ושבית

[כדאיתא ברכות סד.]

[תוספתא פ"ח]

[תוספתא שם]

[וע"ש תוס' ד"ה דאגיירה]

גירסת רש"א ואין לומר

גירסת רש"א ומיהו הוה מצינו

[וע' תוס' גיטין מו. ד"ה כיון] רש"ל

הגהות הב"ח

(א) גמ' שהקים משה בעבר הירדן בארץ מואב:

כמאן? כר' שמעון. *בא וראה כמה נסים נעשו באותו היום: עברו ישראל את הירדן, ובאו להר גריזים ולהר עיבל יותר משששים מיל, ואין כל בריה יכולה לעמוד בפניהם, וכל העומד בפניהם מיד נתרז. שנאמר: °"את אימתי אשלח לפניך והמותי את כל העם אשר תבא בהם" וגו'. ואומר: °"תפול עליהם אימתה ופחד עד יעבר עמך ה'" — זו *ביאה ראשונה. "עד יעבר עם זו קנית" — זו ביאה שניה. אמור מעתה: ראויין היו ישראל לעשות להם נס בביאה שניה כביאה ראשונה, אלא שגרם החטא. ואחר כך הביאו את האבנים, ובנו את המזבח, וסדוהו בסיד, וכתבו עליהם את כל דברי התורה בשבעים לשון, שנאמר: °"באר היטב". והעלו עולות ושלמים, ואכלו ושתו ושמחו, וברכו וקללו, °וקיפלו את האבנים ובאו ולנו בגלגל, שנאמר: °"והעברתם אותם עמכם והנחתם אותם במלון". יכול בכל מלון ומלון — ת"ל: "אשר תלינו בו הלילה", וכתיב: °"ואת שתים עשרה האבנים האלה אשר לקחו" וגו'. תנא: צרעה לא עברה עמהם. ולא? והא כתיב: °"ושלחתי את הצרעה לפניך"! אמר ר' שמעון בן לקיש: על שפת ירדן עמדה וזרקה בהן מרה. וסימתה עיניהן מלמעלה, וסירסתן מלמטה, שנאמר: °"ואנכי השמדתי את האמורי מפניהם אשר כגובה ארזים גבהו וחסון הוא כאלונים ואשמיד פריו ממעל ושרשיו מתחת" וגו'. רב פפא אמר: שתי צרעות הואי, חדא דמשה וחדא דיהושע, דמשה לא עבר, דיהושע עבר.§

"ששה שבטים עלו לראש הר גריזים" כו'.§ מאי °"והחציו"? אמר רב כהנא: כדרך שחלוקין כאן כך חלוקין באבני אפוד. מיתיבי: [א]שתי אבנים טובות היו לו לכהן גדול על כתיפיו, אחת מכאן ואחת מכאן, ושמות שנים עשר שבטים כתוב עליהם, ששה על אבן זו וששה על אבן זו, שנאמר: °"ששה משמותם על האבן האחת" וגו'. שניה כתולדותם ולא ראשונה כתולדותם, מפני שיהודה מוקדם. וחמשים אותיות היו, עשרים וחמש על אבן זו ועשרים וחמש על אבן זו. רבי חנינא בן גמליאל אומר: לא

(שמות כג) (שם טו) (דברים כז) (יהושע ד) (שם) (שמות כג) (עמוס ב) (יהושע ח) (שמות כח) — תורה אור

רש"י

כמאן כר' שמעון. דאמר שכתב להם שיחזרו בתשובה ויקבלום. אלמא לא היו העומדין חוץ לגבולין בכלל "לא תחיה כל נשמה". אבל לר' יהודה כולן בכלל "לא תחיה". נתרז. מתקלקל מרעי. והמותי. לשון מהומה ועירבוב הגוף ומה שבתוכו. ביאה ראשונה. בימי יהושע. ביאה שניה. בימי עזרא. ליעשות להם נס. לעלות בזרוע, ולא יהיו משתעבדים למלכות. אלא שגרם חטאם של ישראל בימי בית ראשון, ונגזר עליהם שלא יעלו אלא ברשות, כדכתיב: "מי בכם מכל עמו" (עזרא א). פריו ממעל. עיניו. ושרשיו מתחת. סירוס. (א) והעלו עולות ושלמים. שכך נצטוו באותה פרשה: "אבנים שלמות תבנה וגו' וזבחת שלמים" וגו'. מאי והחציו. ביהושע הכי כתיב בהאי קרא דמתני': "וכל ישראל וגו' חציו אל מול הר גריזים והחציו אל מול הר עיבל". למה לי למיכתב "והחציו" דמשמע או חציו המיוחד, או חציו הנזכר במקום אחר? כדרך שחלוקין. השבטים בהר גריזים והר עיבל, כדכתיב (דברים כז) (ו): "אלה יעמדו לברך את העם" וגו' "ואלה יעמדו על הקללה" — כך חלוקים באבני אפוד שאמור בהן "ששה משמותם" וגו', הנך ששה דהר גריזים כתובים על האחת וששה דהר עיבל כתובין על השנית. והיינו דכתיב "והחציו" — אותו חציו החקוק באחת מן האבנים. כתולדותם. כסדר לידתן. ששה האחרונים כסדרן: גד ואשר יששכר וזבולן יוסף ובנימין, זהו סדר לידתן. וששה ראשונים נכתבו כך: יהודה ראובן שמעון ולוי דן ונפתלי, כסדר לידתן חוץ מיהודה. ועשרים וחמשה על אבן זו. לקמן פריך: ששה אחרונים עשרים וארבע הוא דהוו!

לא

תוספות

כמאן כר"ש. וא"ת: דלמא ביפת תואר אפילו ר' יהודה מודה? דהא לא דברה תורה אלא כנגד היצר, והואיל והותרו שאר נכריות, דהלכה למשה מסיני דקנאין פוגעין בו, כדאיתא בפרק שני דע"ז (דף לו:) — הותרו אפילו כנענים שבחוצה לארץ במקום שהותרה יפת תואר! דאמר בפ"ק דקידושין (דף כא:): איבעיא להו, כהן מהו ביפת תואר? רב אמר: מותר, ושמואל אמר: אסור. בביאה ראשונה — כ"ע לא פליגי דשרי, שלא דברה תורה אלא כנגד היצר הרע! ועוד: אפילו ר"ש מה הוצרך להתירה? מאי שנא מכהן, אע"ג דזונה היא — לא איצטריך קרא למשרייה, הואיל ולא דברה תורה אלא כנגד היצר הרע! וי"ל: כיון דלא התיר יפת תואר אלא במלחמות הרשות שבו הכתוב מדבר — שמע מינה דגבי כנענים לא אמרינן: לא דברה תורה אלא כנגד היצה"ר. דאע"ג דאיכא יצר — אמר "לא תחיה" אפילו במקום יפת תואר. הלכך, לרבי יהודה דאית ליה כנענים שבחוצה לה נמי בכלל "לא תחיה" ואין מקבלין אותן — לא היה מתיר במקום יפת תואר. מיהו, איכא למיתמה: לר"ש, דאמר מקבלים אותם ואינם בכלל "לא תחיה", למה לי קרא "ושבית שביו" לרבות יפת תואר? ואכתי *נימא איפכא: דדוקא לרבי יהודה איצטריך, וגזירת הכתוב הוא גבי יפת תואר שבחוצה לה, אע"פ שכנענים אחרים שבחוצה לה הם בכלל "לא תחיה"! וי"ל: דעיקר טעמא דר"ש — אקרא "ושבית שביו" סמיך. דאי מההיא קרא "למען אשר לא ילמדו" — איכא למימר כר' יהודה דאתא למשרייה, או שאר אומות, או כנענים קודם שהתחילו במלחמה. **ואחר** כך הביאו את האבנים. ה"ג בתוספתא (פ"ח): והביאו את האבנים שהעלו מן הירדן, ובנו את המזבח, והעלו עולות ושלמים. ולא גרסינן: וכתבו עליו את התורה.

***מאי** והחציו חציו של מול הר גריזים מרובה מחציו של הר עיבל. לשון הירושלמי מיושב יותר, דגרסינן התם: מה תלמוד לומר "והחציו" — מלמד שמעוטין בהר גריזים ומרובין בהר עיבל. למה — שאין שבטו של לוי כולו שם, שאם היה כל שבט לוי שם — היו שוין. ר' שמואל בר נחמני בשם ר' יונתן אמר: אילו היה כל שבטו של לוי שם — לא היו שוין, למה — שכבר נפלו משבטו של שמעון עשרים וארבעה אלף בשטים. א"ר יוסי בר בון: אילו היה שם כל שבטו של לוי היו שוין, למה — שלא בא משבט ראובן וגד אלא מ' אלף חלוצי צבא. והשתא אתי שפיר "והחציו אל מול הר עיבל" — חציו המבורר שהוא הרוב, דהוי חציו בשבטים ורובא בגברי. ומיהו, כשתדקדק במנין אחרון שנאמר בו "לאלה תחלק הארץ" (במדבר כו) לאחר שמתו מרגלים, כדכתיב "ובאלה לא היה איש" וגו', והיה בשנת הארבעים, לאחר פטירת אהרן דכתיב ביה "ויעל אהרן הכהן וגו' וימת שם בשנת הארבעים לצאת בני ישראל מארץ מצרים בחדש החמישי" (שם לג), והכי מוכח בסדר עולם — תמצא במנין שבטים שעמדו על הר גריזים עודף על אותן שעמדו בהר עיבל תשע אלף חסר ק"ל. ואפילו אם עמדו לוים למטה שמנה אלף — עדיין היו מרובין של הר גריזים קרוב לאלף, שהרי אתה מוצא בפרטן של אותן שבטים שעמדו על הר עיבל שלש מאות ושבעת אלפים ותתק"ל, ובפרטן של הר גריזים ג' מאות וששה עשר אלף ות"ת! וי"ל: הא דאמרינן בירושלמי שאם היה שם כל שבט לוי היו שוין — לאו דוקא שוין, שהרי מרובין היו, אלא כלומר, לא היו של הר גריזים פחותין. [והשתא שלא היו כל שבט לוי שם — צריך לומר] שעמדו לוים למטה תשע אלף או יותר. אבל הא דאמר רבי שמואל בר נחמני בשם ר' יונתן: אילו היה שם כל שבטו של לוי לא היו שוין, למה שכבר נפלו משבטו של שמעון עשרים וארבעה אלף — קשיא, שהרי המנין היה אחרי כן, כדכתיב: "ויהי אחרי המגפה" וגו' (שם כה). ומה שחלק עליו ר' יוסי בר בון לפי שלא בא משבט ראובן וגד אלא מ' אלף חלוצי צבא — א"כ לא נשארו משבט ראובן אלא ג' אלף ותש"ל, שהרי כל פקודי שבט [ראובן] לא היו כי אם מ"ג אלף ותש"ל, והיאך היו אותן ג' אלף ותש"ל של ראובן שנשארו מעבר לירדן ממלאין לכ"ד אלף שנפלו משמעון שהיה בשנת הארבעים? מיהו, הא לא קשיא, דאיכא למימר דהכי קאמר: מחמת חסרון משבט שמעון שנפלו במגפה, אפילו היה שם שבטו של לוי לא היו שוין, דמתוך כך היו של הר גריזים מועטין. ולא שיחסרו מהן עשרים וארבעה אלף משמעון [אלא ג' אלפים או פחות]. ועלה קאי רבי יוסי בר בון: אפילו לדבריך, כשאתה מחסר כנגדו ג' אלף ותש"ל משבט ראובן שנשארו מעבר לירדן, והיו שוין, שמחמת חסרון משבט שמעון אין חסר יותר מג' אלף ותש"ל. אבל ההיא דר' שמואל בר נחמני תיקשי, כדפרישית, שהמגפה היתה קודם למנין. **עשרים** וחמש על אבן זו ועשרים וחמש על אבן זו. ירושלמי: והלא אינן אלא כ"ג מכאן וכ"ז מכאן! פי': לתנא דתני התם כשם שחלוקים כאן כך חלוקין באבני אפוד, מקשה: א"כ על אותה אבן שהיו עליה של הר גריזים *היו כ"ג ועל השניה כ"ז, וזבולון מלא! ומשני, א"ר יוחנן: בנימין היה חציו מכאן, וצ"ל דעל השניה שכתובין עליה אותו של הר עיבל היה כתוב "ב"נ" ועל הראשונה "ימ"ן". א"ר זבידא: ויאות, מי כתיב "ששה שמותם"? לא כתיב אלא "ששה משמותם", משמותם ולא כל שמותם.

לעשות

תוספות שאנץ

שביו לרבות כנענים שבתוכם. בא הכתוב להתיר כנענים שבחוצה לארץ ולקיים מהם יפת תואר שלא יהא בכלל לא תחיה כל נשמה: כמאן כר' שמעון שכתב להם שיחזרו בתשובה ודוקא אותם העומדין בגבולין אבל העומדין חוץ לגבולין לא היו בכלל לא תחיה כל נשמה. שאם היו רוצים לפנות את ארצם והולכין להם לא נצטוו להחרימם כמו שפינה הגרגשי והלך לו. (אלא) [אבל] לר' יהודה כולם בכלל דלא תחיה וא"ת לר' יהודה דאמר דנצטוו להחרימם כל הכנענים שבחוצה לארץ למה לי קרא דלא תתחתן בם תיפוק לי' מלא תחיה כל נשמה. וי"ל דאיצטריך כגון אותן שלא יוכלו להחרימם כדאי' בספר שופטים וכגון הגרגשי שפינה והלך לו: דמשה לא עבר דיהושע עבר. תי' פשיטא דשל משה לא עבר דלמה היתה עוברת הירדן והלא לא כבשו אז אלא ארץ סיחון ועוג ושמא אותן שנמלטו מארץ סיחון ועוג לעבר הירדן של ארץ כנען לא הזיקה הצרעה עד יהושע:

ואין

עין משפט נר מצוה

כז א מיי' פ"ט מהל' כלי המקדש הל' ט וע"ש בכ"מ:

מסורת הש"ס

(תוספתא פ"ח)

סנהדרין לח: ברכות ז.

אימא דר' יהודה איצטריך דוקא וגזה"כ גבי יפ"ת כו' כ"ה בס"י

שייך לע"ב

הגהות הב"ח

(א) רש"י ד"ה והעלו נ"ל קודם ד"ה פריו:

גליון הש"ס

גמ' וקיפלו את האבנים. כמו וקלפו רש"י חולין מד ע"א ד"ה דאקפל:

רש"ל

רש"ל ועי' רש"א

היו כ"ג ועל הראשונה רש"ל ובמהרש"א הגיה של הר גריזים היו כ"ז ועל השניה כ"ג וזבולן כו'

כח א ב מיי' פ"ט מהל' כלי המקדש הל' ט וע"ש בכ"מ:

אלא כדרך שחלוקין בחומש הפקודים חלוקין באבני אפוד, אלא כדרך שחלוקין בחומש שני. כיצד? בני לאה כסידרן, בני רחל אחד מכאן ואחד מכאן, ובני שפחות באמצע. ואלא מאי אני מקיים "כתולדותם" — כשמותן שקרא להן אביהן, ולא כשמות שקרא להן משה: ראובן ולא ראובני, שמעון ולא שמעוני, דן ולא הדני, גד ולא הגדי, תיובתא דרב כהנא! תיובתא. ואלא מאי "והחציו"? תנא: חציו של מול הר גריזים מרובה מחציו של הר עיבל, מפני שלוי למטה. אדרבה, מפני שלוי למטה בצרי להו! הכי קאמר: אף על פי שלוי למטה — בני יוסף עמהם, שנאמר: °"וידברו בני יוסף את יהושע לאמר מדוע נתתה לי נחלה גורל אחד וחבל אחד ואני עם רב ויאמר אליהם יהושע אם עם רב אתה עלה לך היערה", אמר להן: לכו והחבאו עצמכם ביערים, שלא תשלוט בכם עין הרע. אמרו ליה: *זרעיה דיוסף לא שלטא ביה עינא בישא, דכתיב: °"בן פורת יוסף בן פורת עלי עין" ואמר ר' אבהו: אל תהי קורא "עלי עין" אלא עולי עין. רבי יוסי בר' חנינא אמר: מהכא, °"וידגו לרוב בקרב הארץ" — מה דגים שבים מים מכסין עליהן ואין העין שולטת בהן, אף זרעו של יוסף אין העין שולטת בהן. הני חמשים אותיות? חמשים נכי חדא הויין! א"ר יצחק: יוסף הוסיפו לו אות אחת, שנאמר: °"עדות ביהוסף שמו בצאתו על ארץ מצרים". מתקיף לה רב נחמן בר יצחק: "כתולדותם" בעינן! אלא, כל התורה כולה בנימן כתיב, והכא בנימין שלם, כדכתיב: °"ואביו קרא לו בנימין". *אמר רב חנא בר ביזנא א"ר שמעון חסידא: יוסף שקידש שם שמים בסתר — הוסיפו עליו אות אחת משמו של הקב"ה, (א) יהודה שקידש שם שמים בפרהסיא — נקרא כולו על שמו של הקב"ה. יוסף מאי היא — דכתיב: °"ויהי כהיום הזה ויבא הביתה לעשות מלאכתו" א"ר יוחנן: מלמד ששניהם לדבר עבירה נתכוונו. "ויבא הביתה לעשות מלאכתו", *רב ושמואל; חד אמר: לעשות מלאכתו ממש, וחד אמר: לעשות צרכיו נכנס. "ואין איש מאנשי הבית" וגו'. אפשר בית גדול כביתו של אותו רשע לא היה בו איש?! תנא דבי ר' ישמעאל: אותו היום יום חגם היה, והלכו כולן לבית עבודה זרה שלהם, והיא אמרה להן חולה היא, אמרה: אין לי יום שניזקק לי יוסף כיום הזה. °"ותתפשהו בבגדו לאמר" וגו'. באותה שעה באתה דיוקנו של אביו ונראתה לו בחלון, אמר לו: יוסף! עתידין אחיך שיכתבו על אבני אפוד ואתה ביניהם, רצונך שימחה שמך מביניהם ותקרא רועה זונות? *דכתיב: °"ורועה זונות יאבד הון". מיד — °"ותשב באיתן קשתו", א"ר יוחנן משום ר' מאיר: ששבה קשתו לאיתנו. "ויפוזו זרועי ידיו" — נעץ ידיו בקרקע ויצאה שכבת זרעו מבין ציפורני ידיו. "מידי אביר יעקב", מי גרם לו שיחקק על אבני אפוד — אלא אביר יעקב. "משם רועה אבן ישראל" — משם זכה ונעשה רועה, שנאמר: °"רועה ישראל האזינה נוהג כצאן יוסף". תניא, היה ראוי יוסף לצאת ממנו י"ב שבטים כדרך שיצאו מיעקב אביו, שנאמר: °"אלה תולדות יעקב יוסף", אלא שיצא שכבת זרעו מבין ציפורני ידיו. ואעפ"כ יצאו מבנימין אחיו, וכולן נקראו על שמו, שנאמר: °"ובני בנימין בלע ובכר ואשבל" וגו'. "בלע" — שנבלע בין האומות, "ובכר" — בכור לאמו היה, "ואשבל" — ששבאו אל, "גרא" — שגר באכסניות, "ונעמן" — שנעים ביותר, "אחי וראש" — אחי הוא וראשי הוא, "מופים וחופים" — הוא לא ראה בחופתי ואני לא ראיתי בחופתו, "וארד" — שירד לבין אומות העולם. א"ד: "וארד" — *שפניו דומין לוורד. א"ר חייא בר אבא אמר רבי יוחנן: בשעה שאמר לו פרעה ליוסף: °"ובלעדיך לא ירים איש את ידו" וגו', אמרו איצטגניני פרעה: עבד שלקחו רבו בעשרים כסף תמשילהו עלינו? אמר להן: גנוני מלכות אני רואה בו. אמרו לו: א"כ, יהא יודע בשבעים לשון! בא גבריאל ולימדו שבעים לשון. לא הוה קגמר, הוסיף לו אות אחת משמו של הקב"ה, ולמד, שנאמר: °"עדות ביהוסף שמו בצאתו על ארץ מצרים, (שפת לא ידעתי אשמע".) ולמחר, כל לישנא דאישתעי פרעה בהדיה — אהדר ליה. אישתעי איהו בלשון הקדש — לא הוה קא ידע מאי הוה אמר. א"ל: אגמרי. אגמריה ולא גמר. אמר ליה: אישתבע לי דלא מגלית. אישתבע לו. כי א"ל °"אבי השביעני לאמור" — א"ל: זיל איתשיל אשבועתך. אמר ליה: ואיתשלי נמי אדידך? ואע"ג דלא ניחא ליה א"ל: "עלה וקבור את אביך כאשר השביעך". יהודה מאי היא — דתניא, היה ר"מ אומר: כשעמדו ישראל על הים היו שבטים מנצחים זה עם זה, זה אומר: אני יורד תחלה לים, וזה אומר: אני יורד תחלה לים, קפץ שבטו

רש"י

לא כדרך שחלוקין בחומש הפקודים. כלומר, לא כדרך שסדורים בחומש הפקודים, הוא ספר "וידבר" שנסדרו בראשו "אלה שמות האנשים אשר יעמדו" וגו' (במדבר א). בחומש שני. בתחילת "ואלה שמות": ראובן שמעון לוי ויהודה ויששכר וזבולון באחד מהן, בשני: בנימין דן ונפתלי גד ואשר ויוסף. א"כ מה ת"ל כתולדותם. הואיל ולא כדרך לידתן נסדרו. תיובתא דרב כהנא. דלכולי עלמא אין זה סדר הר גריזים והר עיבל. דאילו סדר הר גריזים — שמעון ולוי ויהודה יששכר ויוסף ובנימין, ודהר עיבל — ראובן גד ואשר וזבולון דן ונפתלי. מרובה מחציו כו'. והיינו דקאמר "והחציו אל מול הר עיבל"; החציו — ממועט שבחציו*. מפני שלוי למטה. זקני כהונה ולויה היו עם הארון בין שני ההרים, כדלקמן. בל שכן דבצרי להו. חציו של הר גריזים, שהרי שבט לוי מהן היה. אלא הכי קאמר אע"פ ששבט לוי למטה. אפ"ה חציו של הר גריזים מרובה, מפני שיוסף עמהן, ומרובין היו. וידברו בני יוסף וגו'. סופו דקרא "ואני עם רב אשר עד כה ברכני ה'". עולי עין. עולין על העין, ואין העין עולה עליהם. וידגו לרוב. כן ברכן יעקב למנשה ואפרים. בציר חדא הוו. אבנן השניה קאי. כתולדותם בעינן. כשמות אשר קרא להם אביהם. בסתר. שנתייחד עם הערוה, והעמיד על עצמו, וכבש את יצרו. יהודה שקידש שם שמים בפרהסיא. על הים כדלקמן. נקרא כולו. שם בן ארבעה אותיות כלול בשמו של יהודה. לדבר עבירה. והאי "מלאכתו" — תשמיש. מלאכתו ממש. מלאכה. צרכיו. תשמיש. יאבד הון. שם טוב, שהוא יקר מכל הון. קשתו. שכבת זרעו, על שם שיורה כחץ. ויפוזו. לשון ויפוזו שהזיי"ן והפד"י מתחלפין, כמו "זעקת" — צעקת. שנעץ אצבעותיו בקרקע. ונסמך עליהן, כדי שיתייסר ויטרד בצערו, ויעבור תוקף יצרו. מידי אבירותיו של יעקב. משם זכה להיות רועה, ומשם זכה להיות באבן מאבני ישראל. רועה ישראל האזינה. כלפי שכינה נאמר. נוהג כצאן יוסף. קרי "כצאן יוסף" — המנהיגים כצאנו של יוסף. אלמא מיקרו ישראל צאנו של יוסף, והוא הרועה. אלה תולדות יעקב יוסף. תולדות שיצאו מיעקב, כנגדן ראוי לצאת מיוסף. ואף על פי כן יצאו מבנימין אחיו. אותן עשרה שפיחתו מיוסף בעשר אצבעותיו. שגר באכסניא. בארץ נכריה. מופים. מפורש במדרש רבי תנחומא: שהיה פיו כפי יעקב אביו בהלכות שקיבל משם ועבר. אצטגנינות. חכמים וחוזים בכוכבים, ויודעים בחכמת המזלות. גנוני מלכות. גווני מלכות, בחכמה גבורה ויופי. עדות ביהוסף שמו. סיפיה דקרא "שפת לא ידעתי אשמע". איתשיל אשבועתך. השאל לחכמים שיתירוה לך. אושפיזכן

תוספות

לעשות צרכיו. נראה, משום דהוליאו בלשון ביאה "ויבא הביתה" — קא דייק נמי דלעשות צרכיו נכנס. באותה שעה באתה דיוקנו של אביו. כתב רבינו משה הדרשן: "ואין איש מאנשי הבית [שם בבית" — דמשמע דוקא מאנשי הבית] לא היה שם, מכלל דאיש אחר שלא מאנשי הבית, כלומר חלוק ומופלג מתורת אנשי הבית — היה שם. וזהו דמות דיוקנו של אביו. ותימה קצת: מנלן דנראית לו בחלון? ושמא מדכתיב "בבית", דמשמע: בבית לא*. איתשיל נמי אדידך ואע"ג דלא ניחא ליה. ותימה: הלא לא היה יכול לישאל על נדרו כי אם מדעתו של פרעה, כמו ההוא מעשה דלדקיהו ונבוכדנלר דמייתי התם! *מיהו, מהכא משמע *דהוה בפניו, דאמר בפ' "ר' אליעזר" בנדרים (דף סה.): המודר הנאה מחברו אין מתירין לו אלא בפניו, פי': בפניו — ואפילו בעל כרחו. ומיהו, תימה לומר דהנודר על דעת חבירו מתירים לו שלא מדעת חבירו! ושמא אוקמיה במלתא דגיזום בעלמא, שגיזמו כך. מיהו, לא היה יכול לישאל עליו אי לא ניחא ליה לפרעה.

והיו

הגהות הב"ח

(א) גמ' יהודה שקידש. נ"ב ע"ל בפ"ק דף י ע"ב:

תוספות שאנץ

ואין איש מאנשי הבית יש במדרש שבדק יוסף עצמו ולא מצא מעשה של איש שלא היה לו מילה שמצא עצמו טומטום: שגר באכסניות בארץ נכריה: מופים מפרש בתנחומא שהיה פיו כשל אביו בהלכות שקבל משם ועבר: אשתעי איהו בלשון הקדש. צ"ע אי הוו ע' לשון חוץ מלשון הקדש דהא הכא לא הוה ידע ליה ואמר בסוכה שע' פרים שמקריבין בחג הסוכות כנגד ע' אומות חוץ מישראל ואמר נמי בסדר פנחס דמונה ס"ה משפחות בישראל וע' באומות היינו דכתיב כי אתם המעט ה' משפחות מעט מכל העמים:

תורה אור

שִׁבְטוֹ שֶׁל בִּנְיָמִין וְיָרַד לַיָּם תְּחִילָּה, שֶׁנֶּאֱמַר:
תהלים סח °"שָׁם בִּנְיָמִן צָעִיר רוֹדֵם", אַל תִּקְרֵי "רוֹדֵם" אֶלָּא
רֵד יָם. וְהָיוּ שָׂרֵי יְהוּדָה רוֹגְמִים אוֹתָם, שֶׁנֶּאֱמַר:
שם °"שָׂרֵי יְהוּדָה רִגְמָתָם". לְפִיכָךְ *זָכָה בִּנְיָמִין
הַצַּדִּיק וְנַעֲשָׂה אוּשְׁפִּיזְכָן לַגְּבוּרָה, שֶׁנֶּאֱמַר:
דברים לג °"וּבֵין כְּתֵפָיו שָׁכֵן". אָמַר לוֹ רַבִּי יְהוּדָה: לֹא כָּךְ
הָיָה מַעֲשֶׂה, אֶלָּא זֶה אוֹמֵר: אֵין אֲנִי יוֹרֵד
תְּחִילָּה לַיָּם, וְזֶה אוֹמֵר: אֵין אֲנִי יוֹרֵד תְּחִילָּה לַיָּם,
קָפַץ נַחְשׁוֹן בֶּן עַמִּינָדָב וְיָרַד לַיָּם תְּחִילָּה,
הושע יב שֶׁנֶּאֱמַר: °"סְבָבוּנִי בְכַחַשׁ אֶפְרַיִם וּבְמִרְמָה
בֵּית יִשְׂרָאֵל וִיהוּדָה עוֹד רָד עִם אֵל". וְעָלָיו
תהלים סט מְפָרֵשׁ בְּקַבָּלָה: °"הוֹשִׁיעֵנִי אֱלֹהִים כִּי בָאוּ מַיִם
עַד נָפֶשׁ טָבַעְתִּי בִּיוֵן מְצוּלָה וְאֵין מָעֳמָד וגו'
שם °אַל תִּשְׁטְפֵנִי שִׁבּוֹלֶת מַיִם וְאַל תִּבְלָעֵנִי
מְצוּלָה" וגו'. בְּאוֹתָהּ שָׁעָה הָיָה מֹשֶׁה מַאֲרִיךְ
בִּתְפִלָּה, אָמַר לוֹ הקב"ה: יְדִידַיי טוֹבְעִים בַּיָּם,
וְאַתָּה מַאֲרִיךְ בִּתְפִלָּה לְפָנַי?! אָמַר לְפָנָיו: רִבּוֹנוֹ
שמות יד שֶׁל עוֹלָם! וּמַה בְּיָדִי לַעֲשׂוֹת? אָמַר לוֹ: °"דַּבֵּר
אֶל בְּנֵי יִשְׂרָאֵל וְיִסָּעוּ וְאַתָּה הָרֵם אֶת מַטְּךָ
וּנְטֵה אֶת יָדְךָ" וגו'. לְפִיכָךְ זָכָה יְהוּדָה לַעֲשׂוֹת
תהלים קיד מֶמְשָׁלָה בְּיִשְׂרָאֵל, שֶׁנֶּאֱמַר: °"הָיְתָה יְהוּדָה
לְקָדְשׁוֹ יִשְׂרָאֵל מַמְשְׁלוֹתָיו"; מַה טַּעַם הָיְתָה
יְהוּדָה לְקָדְשׁוֹ וְיִשְׂרָאֵל מַמְשְׁלוֹתָיו — מִשּׁוּם
דְּ"הַיָּם רָאָה וַיָּנֹס". תַּנְיָא, *רַבִּי אֱלִיעֶזֶר בֶּן יַעֲקֹב
אוֹמֵר: אִי אֶפְשָׁר לוֹמַר לֵוִי לְמַטָּה — שֶׁכְּבָר נֶאֱמַר
לְמַעְלָה, וְאִי אֶפְשָׁר לוֹמַר לְמַעְלָה — שֶׁכְּבָר
נֶאֱמַר לְמַטָּה. הָא כֵּיצַד? זִקְנֵי כְהוּנָּה וּלְוִיָּה
לְמַטָּה, וְהַשְּׁאָר לְמַעְלָה. רַבִּי יֹאשִׁיָּה אוֹמֵר: כָּל
הָרָאוּי לְשָׁרֵת — לְמַטָּה. וְהַשְּׁאָר לְמַעְלָה. רַבִּי אוֹמֵר:
אֵלּוּ וְאֵלּוּ לְמַטָּה הֵן עוֹמְדִים, הָפְכוּ פְּנֵיהֶם כְּלַפֵּי
הַר גְּרִיזִים וּפָתְחוּ בִּבְרָכָה, כְּלַפֵּי הַר עֵיבָל
דברים כז וּפָתְחוּ בִּקְלָלָה. מַאי °"עַל" — עַל בְּסָמוּךְ. *כִּדְתַנְיָא:
ויקרא כד °"וְנָתַתָּ עַל הַמַּעֲרֶכֶת לְבוֹנָה זַכָּה", רַבִּי אוֹמֵר: *עַל
— בְּסָמוּךְ. אַתָּה אוֹמֵר עַל בְּסָמוּךְ, אוֹ אֵינוֹ אֶלָּא
שמות מ עַל מַמָּשׁ? כְּשֶׁהוּא אוֹמֵר °"וְסַכּוֹתָ עַל הָאָרֹן"*
הֱוֵי אוֹמֵר עַל — בְּסָמוּךְ.§ "הָפְכוּ פְּנֵיהֶם כְּלַפֵּי
הַר גְּרִיזִים וּפָתְחוּ בִּבְרָכָה" כו'.§ תָּנוּ רַבָּנַן: בָּרוּךְ
בִּכְלָל בָּרוּךְ בִּפְרָט, *אָרוּר בִּכְלָל אָרוּר
בִּפְרָט, לִלְמוֹד וּלְלַמֵּד לִשְׁמוֹר וְלַעֲשׂוֹת — הֲרֵי
אַרְבַּע

אוּשְׁפִּיזְכָן לַגְּבוּרָה. שֶׁבֵּית קָדְשֵׁי הַקֳּדָשִׁים בָּנוּי בְּחֶלְקוֹ. בְּכַחַשׁ אֶפְרַיִם. שֶׁיָּרְאוּ לִסְמוֹךְ עָלָיו, וְכִחֲשׁוּ בֶּאֱמוּנָתָם. רָד עִם אֵל. יָרַד בַּיָּם עַל שֶׁבָּטַח בְּהקב"ה. יִשְׂרָאֵל מַמְשְׁלוֹתָיו. דִּיהוּדָה, שֶׁנִּתְקַדֵּשׁ לִמְשׁוֹל בָּהֶן. שֶׁכְּבָר נֶאֱמַר לֵוִי לְמַעְלָה. מֹשֶׁה כָּתַב בַּתּוֹרָה: "אֵלֶּה יַעַמְדוּ לְבָרֵךְ וגו' שִׁמְעוֹן לֵוִי וִיהוּדָה". שֶׁכְּבָר נֶאֱמַר לֵוִי לְמַטָּה. בְּסֵפֶר יְהוֹשֻׁעַ, (ח) כִּדְכְתִיב: "וְכָל יִשְׂרָאֵל וּזְקֵנָיו עוֹמְדִים מִזֶּה וּמִזֶּה לָאָרוֹן נֶגֶד הַכֹּהֲנִים וְהַלְוִיִּם". אַלְמָא: כֹּהֲנִים וּלְוִיִּם לְמַטָּה הָיוּ. הָרָאוּי לְשָׁרֵת. לָשֵׂאת אֶת הָאָרוֹן, דְּהַיְינוּ מִבֶּן שְׁלֹשִׁים וְעַד בֶּן חֲמִשִּׁים. לְמַטָּה. אֵצֶל הָאָרוֹן. אֵלּוּ וְאֵלּוּ. יִשְׂרָאֵל וּלְוִיִּם, לְמַטָּה הָיוּ, כִּדְכְתִיב בְּסֵפֶר יְהוֹשֻׁעַ. עַל הַר גְּרִיזִים וְעַל הַר עֵיבָל. שֶׁכָּתַב מֹשֶׁה בַּתּוֹרָה, עַל — בְּסָמוּךְ, כִּדְמְפָרֵשׁ וְאָזֵיל. עַל בְּסָמוּךְ. שֶׁהָיָה מוֹשִׁיב שְׁנֵי בָּזִיכֵי לְבוֹנָה בֵּין שְׁנֵי הַסְּדָרִים. וְסַכּוֹתָ עַל הָאָרוֹן. עַל כָּרְחָךְ לָאו עַל מַמָּשׁ, דְּהָאִי מְחִיצָּה הֲוַאי פָּרוֹכֶת וְלָא הָיָה סָכָךְ. בָּרוּךְ בִּכְלָל בָּרוּךְ בִּפְרָט. כָּל הַבְּרָכוֹת וְהַקְּלָלוֹת נֶאֶמְרוּ בְּהַר גְּרִיזִים וּבְהַר עֵיבָל בִּכְלָל וּפְרָט: בָּרוּךְ אֲשֶׁר יָקִים אֶת דִּבְרֵי הַתּוֹרָה הַזֹּאת, אָרוּר אֲשֶׁר לֹא יָקִים — הֲרֵי בִּכְלָל. וְכָל אַחַת וְאַחַת בִּפְרָט, בָּרוּךְ וְאָרוּר. בָּרוּךְ אֲשֶׁר לֹא יַעֲשֶׂה פֶסֶל וּמַסֵּכָה, אָרוּר אֲשֶׁר יַעֲשֶׂה פֶסֶל וּמַסֵּכָה, וְכֵן כּוּלָּן. לִלְמוֹד וּלְלַמֵּד לִשְׁמוֹר וְלַעֲשׂוֹת. כָּל הַמִּצְוֹת כּוּלָּן טְעוּנוֹת אַרְבָּעָה אֵלֶּה: "וּלְמַדְתֶּם אוֹתָם וּשְׁמַרְתֶּם לַעֲשׂוֹתָם", וּכְתִיב: "וְלִמַּדְתֶּם אוֹתָם אֶת בְּנֵיכֶם" וגו' — הֲרֵי כָּאן אַרְבַּע מִצְוֹת לְכָל מִצְוָה. וְעַל אַרְבַּעְתָּן נִמְסְרוּ אָרוּר וּבָרוּךְ בִּכְלָל וּפְרָט: בָּרוּךְ אֲשֶׁר יִלְמְדוּ, אָרוּר אֲשֶׁר לֹא יִלְמְדוּ. וְכֵן לְלַמֵּד, וְכֵן לִשְׁמוֹר, וְכֵן לַעֲשׂוֹת. בְּכָל אֶחָד אַרְבַּע בְּרִיתוֹת; בְּרִית לְבָרוּךְ בִּכְלָל, בְּרִית לְבָרוּךְ בִּפְרָט, בְּרִית לְאָרוּר בִּכְלָל, בְּרִית לְאָרוּר בִּפְרָט. (זה הפירוש שייך לע"ב) אַרְבַּע וְאַרְבַּע. אַרְבַּע בְּרִיתוֹת לִלְמוֹד, וְאַרְבַּע לְלַמֵּד — הֲרֵי שְׁמֹנֶה. שְׁמֹנֶה וּשְׁמֹנֶה. הָא אִיכָּא עוֹד שְׁמֹנֶה, לִשְׁמוֹר וְלַעֲשׂוֹת. וְכֵן בְּסִינַי. כְּשֶׁנֶּאֶמְרוּ כָּל הַמִּצְוֹת לְמֹשֶׁה, נִתְּנוּ כּוּלָּן בְּאָרוּר וּבָרוּךְ, בִּכְלָל וּפְרָט. וְכֵן בְּעַרְבוֹת מוֹאָב. כְּשֶׁאֲמָרָהּ לְיִשְׂרָאֵל, כִּדְכְתִיב (דברים א): "בְּעֵבֶר הַיַּרְדֵּן בְּאֶרֶץ מוֹאָב הוֹאִיל מֹשֶׁה" וגו'. שֶׁנֶּאֱמַר אֵלֶּה דִּבְרֵי הַבְּרִית וגו'. בָּתַר קְלָלוֹת וּבְרָכוֹת כְּתִיב "מִלְּבַד הַבְּרִית" וגו'. אַלְמָא, כִּבְרִית עַרְבוֹת מוֹאָב בִּבְרָכוֹת וּקְלָלוֹת כָּךְ בְּרִית בְּחוֹרֵב. דְּהַר גְּרִיזִים וּדְהַר עֵיבָל לָא אִיצְטְרִיךְ לְאַתּוּיֵי קְרָא, דְּעֲלָהּ קָאֵי, וּבָהּ אַיְירֵי. "וּשְׁמַרְתֶּם אֶת דִּבְרֵי הַבְּרִית הַזֹּאת" לָא גָּרֵס לֵיהּ הָכָא. אַרְבָּעִים

[עי' יומא יב. וזבחים נב.]

[תוספתא פ"ח ע"ש]

מנחות סב. לח.

[תוספתא פ"ח]

והיו שרי יהודה רגמתם רוגמין אותן. כך שנויה ברייתא במכילתין: משל למה הדבר דומה למלך בשר ודם שהיו לו שני בנים, אחד גדול ואחד קטן. אמר לקטן: העמידני עם הנץ החמה, אמר לגדול: העמידני בג' שעות. בא הקטן להעמידו עם הנץ החמה, ולא הניחו גדול, אמר לו: לא אמר לי אלא עד ג' שעות. והקטן אמר: לא אמר לי אלא עד הנץ החמה. מתוך שהיו עומדים להודין ננער אביהן, אמר להן: בניי, מכל מקום שניכם לא כיוונתם אלא לכבודי — אף אני לא אקפח את שכרכם. מה שכר נטלו שבטו של בנימין שירד תחילה לים — ששרתה שכינה בחלקו, שנאמר וכו'. ומה שכר נטלו שבטו של יהודה — זכה למלכות, שנאמר: "שרי יהודה רגמתם" — אין רגמתם אלא מלכות, שנאמר" "באדין אמר בלשצר והלבישו לדניאל ארגוונא" (דניאל ה).

אי אפשר לומר לוי למטה וכו'. ירושלמי, ר"ש אומר: שמעון ולוי, מה שמעון כולו למעלה — אף לוי כולו למעלה. מה אני מקיים הדין תנייה "נגד הכהנים והלוים" — כדאמר ר' יהושע בן לוי: בעשרים וארבעה מקומות הכהנים נקראו לוים, וזה אחד מהן "והכהנים הלוים בני צדוק" (יבמות פו:).

מאי על על בסמוך כדתניא רבי אומר וכו'. האי דלא מייתי מתניתין בפרק "שתי הלחם" (מנחות נו.): אבא שאול אומר: שם היו נותנין בזיכי לבונה של לחם הפנים. ואטפחיים ריוח באמצע קאי, שהיו נותנין בזיכי לבונה של לחם הפנים. אמרו לו: והלא כבר נאמר "ונתת על המערכת לבונה זכה". אמר להם: והלא כבר נאמר "ועליו מטה מנשה". יש לומר: משום דברייתא מפרש בהדיא: "על" — בסמוך. ונראה, אפי' רבי מאיר ור' יהודה דפליגי התם אאבא שאול, ואמרי "על" ממש, והכי משמע נמי ב"הקומץ רבה" (שם כז.) כל היכא דאיכא למימר "על" ממש — דאמרי' ["על" ממש]. דבעי שם רבי יצחק: איברים שסדרן בצידי מערכה מהו? אליבא דמאן דאמר "על" ממש — לא תיבעי לך, ד"על העצים" כתיב. [מ"מ] הכא כולי עלמא מודו ד"על" בסמוך, ולא אמרי' המברכין על הר גריזים ממש והמקללים על הר עיבל. כדאמרינן בירושלמי: יכול אלו שבהר גריזים היו אומרים ברכות ואלו שבהר עיבל היו אומרים קללות — תלמוד לומר: "הברכות והקללות" — אלו ואלו היו אומרים ברכות, ואלו ואלו אומרים קללות. יכול אלו שבהר גריזים היו עונין אחר הברכות אמן, ואלו שבהר עיבל היו עונין אחר הקללות אמן — ת"ל: "וענו כל העם ואמרו אמן" — אלו ואלו היו עונין אחר הברכות והקללות אמן. הא כילד? בשעה שהיו אומרים ברכות — היו הופכין פניהם וכו'. ופלוגתא דרבי יוחנן וריש לקיש דפליגי בפרק "התודה" (שם דף עח.): השוחט את התודה לפנים ולחמה חוץ לחומה, וכן בפרק "תמיד נשחט" (פסחים דף סג.): השוחט הפסח על החמץ — לא שייכא להכא. ונראה לר"י: דרבי מודה נמי דכל "על" — לכתחלה ולמצוה "על" ממש, ושאני הכא דגזירת הכתוב היא, וכדפרישית, ובדיעבד מכשר "על" בסמוך. דומיא דההיא דפרק "שתי הלחם" (מנחות דף נב.) דאם סידר מערכת לחם הפנים שתים של שבע שבע — [אמר רבי]: רואין את העליונות כאילו אינן. [והא בעינן "ונתת על המערכת לבונה"! מאי "על" — בסמוך. ורבי לטעמיה, דאמר: "על" בסמוך]. וגבי בזיכי לבונה טעמא נמי, כיון דמשמע "על" בסמוך — אמרינן דהאי "על" נמי לכתחילה בסמוך קאמר; חדא שלא יפרוס הלחם, ועוד, [דכי יהיב] בסמוך [הוי] דרך כבוד טפי לפני מלך מלכי המלכים הקדוש ברוך הוא, כדאמרינן ב"כל המנחות באות מצה" (שם סב.) גבי כבשי עצרת, דכתיב: "והניף הכהן אותם על לחם הביכורים", יכול יניח כבשים על גבי לחם — תלמוד לומר: "על שני כבשים". אי על שני כבשים, יכול לחם על גבי כבשים — תלמוד לומר: "על לחם הביכורים" וכו'. ר' חנינאי אומר: מניח הלחם בין שתי ירכותיהם של כבשים ומניף, ונמצא מקיים שני מקראות הללו. אמר רבי: לפני מלך ב"ו אין עושין [כן], לפני ממ"ה עושין כן? אלא מניח זה בצד זה ומניף. והא בעינן "על"? אמר רב חסדא לרב המנונא, ואמרי לה רב המנונא לרב חסדא: רבי לטעמיה, דתניא וכו'.

רבי

[מנחות כז. עח: פסחים סג: סנהדרין יג:]

[נ"ל את הפרוכת הוי אומר וכו']

רש"ל

כט א מיי' פי"ד מהל' תפלה הל' ג סמג עשין כ טוש"ע א"ח סי' קכח סעיף יג:
ל ב מיי' שם הל' ט:
לא ג מיי' שם הלכה י:

רבי שמעון מוציא הר גריזים. הכי מסיים לה בירושלמי: וכן היה ר"ש אומר: אין לך כל דבר ודבר מן התורה שאין כרות עליה תקע"ו בריתות: שתים עשרה בברוך. ולא ידענא אמאי י"ב, ושמא ברית כנגד כל שבט ושבט. וי"ב בארור. י"ב בכלל וי"ב בפרט – הרי מ"ח בריתות. ללמוד וללמד לשמור ולעשות – הרי קצ"ב בריתות. וכן בהר סיני, וכן בערבות מואב – הרי תקע"ו בריתות.

ונשתלשו בערבות מואב. וא"ת: מאי איצטריך למימר שלישי דערבות מואב? והא לא איירי ר' ישמעאל בערבות מואב כלל! יש לומר: משום סיפא נקט לה, דבעי למימר: אין לך כל דבר מצוה ומצוה.

רבי שמעון בן יהודה אומר. ירושלמי: עד כדון דברים שנכללו ונפרטו, דברים שנכללו ולא נפרטו? [אמר ליה] כן אמר ר' יוחנן משום ר' ישמעאל: דבר שהיה בכלל ויצא מן הכלל ללמד – לא ללמד על עצמו יצא, אלא ללמד על הכלל כולו יצא. אמר לו: לא בדבר אחד, דילמא בשני דברים?! בתמיה, והכא בשני דברים אנן קיימין! אמר ר' תנחומא: מכיון דכתיב בסוף "אמן" – כמו שכולו דבר אחד. כתיב: "אשר לא יקים את דברי התורה", וכי יש תורה נופלת? רבי שמעון בן אליקים אומר: זה החזן שהוא עומד, רבי שמעון בן חלפתא אמר: זה *הבית שלמטה. דאמר רב הונא בר יהודה בשם שמואל דעל הדבר הזה קרע יאשיה, ואמר: עלי להקים, ר' אחא בשם ר' תנחום בר' חייא: למד ולימד, שמר ועשה, והיתה סיפקו בידו להחזיק ולא החזיק – הרי זה בכלל ארור. ר' ירמיה בשם רבי חייא בר' אבא: לא למד ולא לימד, לא שמר ולא עשה, ולא היתה סיפקו בידו להחזיק, והחזיק – הרי זה בכלל ברוך. דאמר רבי חנא א"ר ירמיה: עתיד הקב"ה לעשות צל לבעלי מצות בצילן של בעלי תורה, שנא' (קהלת ז): "כי בצל החכמה בצל הכסף", ואומר: "עץ חיים היא למחזיקים בה" (משלי ג).

אמר רב משרשיא ערבא וערבא דערבא. כמדומה דהכי בעי למימר: דלר"ש בן יהודה קבל עליו כל אחד מישראל לתרי"ג מצות *קנ"ח ריבוא ריבואות וח' אלפים ריבואות ותי"ג ריבואות ושבע אלפים ומאתים בריתות, לשש מאות אלף ושלשת אלפים וחמשים וחמש מאות בשביל ערבותן, אם יעברו עליהן. ולרבי אליבא דרבי שמעון – ששים ריבוא פעמים ושלשת אלפים ותקנ"ה פעמים, חשבון זה בריתות קיבלו עליהן.

ברכה אחת קודמת לקללה. ירושלמי: יכול משהיו אומרים ברכות היו אומרים קללות – תלמוד לומר "הברכה" ו"הקללה", קללה באחת וברכה באחת.

ונאמר

אַרְבַּע, אַרְבַּע וְאַרְבַּע – הֲרֵי שְׁמוֹנֶה, שְׁמוֹנֶה וּשְׁמוֹנֶה הֲרֵי שֵׁשׁ עֶשְׂרֵה. וְכֵן בְּסִינַי, וְכֵן בְּעַרְבוֹת מוֹאָב, שֶׁנֶּאֱ': °"אֵלֶּה דִבְרֵי הַבְּרִית אֲשֶׁר צִוָּה ה' אֶת מֹשֶׁה" וגו', וּכְתִיב: °"וּשְׁמַרְתֶּם אֶת דִּבְרֵי הַבְּרִית הַזֹּאת" וגו'. נִמְצָא מ"ח בְּרִיתוֹת עַל כָּל מִצְוָה וּמִצְוָה. ר"ש מוֹצִיא הַר גְּרִיזִים וְהַר עֵיבָל, וּמַכְנִיס אֹהֶל מוֹעֵד שֶׁבַּמִּדְבָּר. וּבִפְלוּגְתָּא דְּהָנֵי תַּנָּאֵי. דְּתַנְיָא, רַבִּי יִשְׁמָעֵאל אוֹמֵר: *כְּלָלוֹת נֶאֶמְרוּ בְּסִינַי, וּפְרָטוֹת בְּאֹהֶל מוֹעֵד. ר' עֲקִיבָא אוֹמֵר: כְּלָלוֹת וּפְרָטוֹת נֶאֶמְרוּ בְּסִינַי, וְנִשְׁנוּ בְּאֹהֶל מוֹעֵד, וְנִשְׁתַּלְּשׁוּ בְּעַרְבוֹת מוֹאָב. *וְאֵין לְךָ כָּל דְּבַר מִצְוָה וּמִצְוָה שֶׁכְּתוּבָה בַּתּוֹרָה שֶׁלֹּא נִכְרְתוּ עָלֶיהָ אַרְבָּעִים וּשְׁמֹנֶה בְּרִיתוֹת. ר' שִׁמְעוֹן בֶּן יְהוּדָה אִישׁ כְּפַר עַכּוֹ אָמַר מִשּׁוּם רַבִּי שִׁמְעוֹן: אֵין לְךָ מִצְוָה וּמִצְוָה שֶׁכְּתוּבָה בַּתּוֹרָה, שֶׁלֹּא נִכְרְתוּ עָלֶיהָ אַרְבָּעִים וּשְׁמֹנֶה בְּרִיתוֹת שֶׁל שֵׁשׁ מֵאוֹת אֶלֶף וּשְׁלֹשֶׁת אֲלָפִים וַחֲמֵשׁ מֵאוֹת וַחֲמִשִּׁים. אָמַר רַבִּי: לְדִבְרֵי רַבִּי שִׁמְעוֹן בֶּן יְהוּדָה אִישׁ כְּפַר עַכּוֹ שֶׁאָמַר מִשּׁוּם רַבִּי שִׁמְעוֹן – אֵין לְךָ כָּל מִצְוָה וּמִצְוָה שֶׁבַּתּוֹרָה שֶׁלֹּא נִכְרְתוּ עָלֶיהָ אַרְבָּעִים וּשְׁמֹנֶה בְּרִיתוֹת שֶׁל שֵׁשׁ מֵאוֹת אֶלֶף וּשְׁלֹשֶׁת אֲלָפִים וַחֲמֵשׁ מֵאוֹת וַחֲמִשִּׁים, נִמְצָא לְכָל אֶחָד וְאֶחָד מִיִּשְׂרָאֵל שֵׁשׁ מֵאוֹת אֶלֶף וּשְׁלֹשֶׁת אֲלָפִים וַחֲמֵשׁ מֵאוֹת וַחֲמִשִּׁים. מַאי בֵּינַיְיהוּ? אָמַר רַב מְשַׁרְשְׁיָא: עָרְבָא וְעָרְבָא דְּעָרְבָא אִיכָּא בֵּינַיְיהוּ. דָּרַשׁ רַבִּי יְהוּדָה בֶּן נַחְמָנִי מְתוּרְגְּמָנֵיהּ דְּרַבִּי שִׁמְעוֹן בֶּן לָקִישׁ: כָּל הַפָּרָשָׁה כּוּלָּהּ לֹא נֶאֶמְרָה אֶלָּא בְּנוֹאֵף וְנוֹאֶפֶת. °"אָרוּר הָאִישׁ אֲשֶׁר יַעֲשֶׂה פֶסֶל וּמַסֵּכָה" וגו', בְּ"אָרוּר" סַגִּי לֵיהּ?! אֶלָּא: זֶה הַבָּא עַל הָעֶרְוָה וְהוֹלִיד בֵּן, וְהָלַךְ לְבֵין אוּמּוֹת הָעוֹלָם, וְעָבַד עֲבוֹדָה זָרָה – אֲרוּרִין אָבִיו וְאִמּוֹ שֶׁל זֶה שֶׁכָּךְ גָּרְמוּ לוֹ. ת"ר: °"וְנָתַתָּה אֶת הַבְּרָכָה עַל הַר גְּרִיזִים וְאֶת הַקְּלָלָה" וגו'. מַה תַּלְמוּד לוֹמַר? אִם לְלַמֵּד שֶׁתְּהֵא בְּרָכָה עַל הַר גְּרִיזִים וּקְלָלָה עַל הַר עֵיבָל – הֲרֵי כְּבָר נֶאֱמַר: °"אֵלֶּה יַעַמְדוּ לְבָרֵךְ אֶת הָעָם עַל הַר גְּרִיזִים", וּכְתִיב: °"וְאֵלֶּה יַעַמְדוּ עַל הַקְּלָלָה בְּהַר עֵיבָל". אֶלָּא, לְהַקְדִּים בְּרָכָה לִקְלָלָה. יָכוֹל יִהְיוּ כָּל הַבְּרָכוֹת קוֹדְמוֹת לַקְּלָלוֹת – תַּלְמוּד לוֹמַר: "בְּרָכָה" וּ"קְלָלָה", בְּרָכָה אַחַת קוֹדֶמֶת לִקְלָלָה, וְאֵין כָּל הַבְּרָכוֹת קוֹדְמוֹת לַקְּלָלוֹת. וּלְהַקִּישׁ בְּרָכָה לִקְלָלָה, לוֹמַר לְךָ: מַה קְּלָלָה בַּלְוִיִּם – אַף בְּרָכָה בַּלְוִיִּם, וּמַה קְּלָלָה בְּקוֹל רָם – אַף בְּרָכָה בְּקוֹל רָם, וּמַה קְּלָלָה בִּלְשׁוֹן הַקּוֹדֶשׁ – אַף בְּרָכָה בִּלה"ק, וּמַה קְּלָלָה בִּכְלָל וּפְרָט – אַף בְּרָכָה בִּכְלָל וּפְרָט, וּמַה קְּלָלָה אֵלּוּ וְאֵלּוּ עוֹנִין וְאוֹמְרִים אָמֵן – אַף בְּרָכָה אֵלּוּ וְאֵלּוּ עוֹנִין וְאוֹמְרִים אָמֵן.§

מתני' בִּרְכַּת כֹּהֲנִים כֵּיצַד? *אבַּמְּדִינָה אוֹמֵר אוֹתָהּ שָׁלֹשׁ בְּרָכוֹת, בוּבַמִּקְדָּשׁ בְּרָכָה אַחַת. גבַּמִּקְדָּשׁ אוֹמֵר אֶת הַשֵּׁם כִּכְתָבוֹ

אַרְבָּעִים וּשְׁמֹנֶה בְּרִיתוֹת. לְכָל אֶחָד מִיִּשְׂרָאֵל. שֵׁשׁ עֶשְׂרֵה תְּלָתָא זִימְנֵי מ"ח הָוֵי. מוֹצִיא הַר גְּרִיזִים. לְפִי שֶׁלֹּא אָמַר יְהוֹשֻׁעַ עֲלֵיהֶן כָּל הַתּוֹרָה, אֶלָּא מִצְוֹת שֶׁבַּפָּרָשָׁה. וּמַכְנִיס אֹהֶל מוֹעֵד. שֶׁלְּאַחַר שֶׁהוּקַם הַמִּשְׁכָּן נִדְבַּר הקב"ה עִם מֹשֶׁה בְּיִשּׁוּב וְלִמְּדוֹ כָּל הַתּוֹרָה, כִּדְכְתִיב: "וַיְדַבֵּר ה' אֵלָיו מֵאֹהֶל מוֹעֵד לֵאמֹר" (ויקרא א). כְּלָלוֹת נֶאֶמְרוּ בְּסִינַי. בִּסְתָם נֶאֶמְרָה תּוֹרָה בְּסִינַי וְלֹא נִתְפָּרְשָׁה לוֹ. כְּגוֹן בְּסִינַי נֶאֱמַר (שמות כ): "וְזָבַחְתָּ עָלָיו אֶת עוֹלֹתֶיךָ וְאֶת שְׁלָמֶיךָ", וְלֹא פֵּירֵשׁ מַתַּן דָּמִים כֵּיצַד, הַקְטָרַת אֵימוּרִים וְהֶפְשֵׁט וְנִתּוּחַ וְכָלִיל שֶׁל עוֹלָה, וּבְסֵפֶר וַיִּקְרָא בְּאֹהֶל מוֹעֵד פֵּירְשָׁהּ. וְנִשְׁתַּלְּשׁוּ בְּעַרְבוֹת מוֹאָב. מִפִּי מֹשֶׁה לְיִשְׂרָאֵל. ת"ק סְבִירָא לֵיהּ כְּר' יִשְׁמָעֵאל, הִלְכָּךְ הַר סִינַי וְאֹהֶל מוֹעֵד חֲדָא הִיא, וְר' שִׁמְעוֹן ס"ל כְּר"ע, הִלְכָּךְ תְּרֵי נִינְהוּ. ר"ש בְּרַבִּי יְהוּדָה אוֹמֵר אַרְבָּעִים וּשְׁמֹנֶה בְּרִיתוֹת. לְכָל אֶחָד שֶׁל שֵׁשׁ מֵאוֹת אֶלֶף וּשְׁלֹשֶׁת אֲלָפִים וַחֲמֵשׁ מֵאוֹת וַחֲמִשִּׁים, כְּמִנְיַן שֶׁהָיוּ (בְּסִינַי) [בַּמִּדְבָּר], שֶׁכָּל אֶחָד נַעֲשָׂה עָרֵב עַל כָּל אֶחָיו. ה"ג בַּתּוֹסֶפְתָּא (פ"ח, ע"ש), א"ר: לְדִבְרֵי ר"ש בֶּן יְהוּדָה אֵין לָנוּ כָּל מִצְוָה וּמִצְוָה שֶׁלֹּא נִכְרְתוּ עָלֶיהָ מ"ח בְּרִיתוֹת שֶׁל שֵׁשׁ מֵאוֹת אֶלֶף וּשְׁלֹשֶׁת אֲלָפִים וַחֲמֵשׁ מֵאוֹת וַחֲמִשִּׁים, וְיֵשׁ בְּכָל אַחַת שֵׁשׁ מֵאוֹת אֶלֶף וּשְׁלֹשֶׁת אֲלָפִים חֲמֵשׁ מֵאוֹת וַחֲמִשִּׁים. מַאי בֵּינַיְיהוּ. מַאי מוֹסִיף רַבִּי, וּבְמַאי פְּלִיגִי?. אָמַר רַב מְשַׁרְשְׁיָא עָרְבָא וְעָרְבָא דְּעָרְבָא. אִם נַעֲשָׂה כָּל אֶחָד עָרֵב עַל עַרְבוּתוֹ שֶׁל חֲבֵירוֹ אוֹ לֹא. רַבִּי שִׁמְעוֹן בֶּן יְהוּדָה סָבַר: לֹא נַעֲשָׂה כָּל אֶחָד עָרֵב עַל חֲבֵירוֹ אֶלָּא שֶׁיִּשְׁמְרוּ אֶת הַמִּצְוֹת. נִמְצָא כָּל אֶחָד וְאֶחָד עָרֵב עַל מ"ח בְּרִיתוֹת שֶׁל כָּל אֶחָד וְאֶחָד, אֲבָל לֹא נַעֲשָׂה כָּל אֶחָד וְאֶחָד עָרֵב עַל עֲרֵבוּת שֶׁל חֲבֵירוֹ, אֶלָּא עַל חוֹבָתוֹ שֶׁל חֲבֵירוֹ. וַאֲתָא רַבִּי לְמֵימַר: לְדִבְרֵי ר' שִׁמְעוֹן שֶׁבָּא לִמְנוֹת אֶת בְּרִיתוֹת הָעֲרֵבוּת – יֵשׁ לוֹ לִמְנוֹת אַרְבָּעִים וּשְׁמֹנֶה בְּרִיתוֹת שֶׁל שִׁשִּׁים רִיבּוֹא לְכָל אֶחָד, וּבְכָל אֶחָד הָאֵלֶּה יֵשׁ שִׁשִּׁים רִיבּוֹא, שֶׁכּוּלָּם נִתְעָרְבוּ זֶה בָּזֶה עַל חוֹבוֹתָם וְעַל עַרְבוּתָם. נִמְצָא כָּל אֶחָד מְקַבֵּל עָלָיו עֲרֵבוּת שֶׁל שִׁשִּׁים רִיבּוֹא בִּשְׁבִיל חוֹבוֹת שֶׁל חֲבֵירוֹ, וְכָל אֶחָד מִשִּׁשִּׁים רִיבּוֹא הַלָּלוּ קִבֵּל עָלָיו בְּרִיתוֹת שִׁשִּׁים רִיבּוֹא בִּשְׁבִיל עֲרֵבוּת שֶׁנִּתְעָרְבוּ אֶחָיו עַל חֲבֵירֵיהֶם, וְזֶה קִבֵּל עָלָיו אַף עֲרֵבוּת שֶׁל עֲרֵבִים. כָּל הַפָּרָשָׁה. שֶׁל הַר גְּרִיזִים, לֹא נֶאֶמְרָה אֶלָּא בְּנוֹאֵף וְנוֹאֶפֶת. בְּאָרוּר סַגִּי לֵיהּ. בִּתְמִיָּה: כּוֹפֵר בָּעִיקָּר הוּא, וְסַגִּי לֵיהּ בְּאָרוּר?!. אֶלָּא זֶה הַבָּא עַל הָעֶרְוָה. אֵשֶׁת אִישׁ, וְהוֹלִיד מַמְזֵר. וּמִתּוֹךְ בּוֹשְׁתּוֹ שֶׁאָסוּר לָבֹא בַּקָּהָל וְאֵינוֹ מוֹצֵא אִשָּׁה – הוּא הוֹלֵךְ לְבֵין הַגּוֹיִים וְעוֹבֵד עֲבוֹדָה זָרָה. אֲרוּרִים אֵלֶּה שֶׁעֲשָׂאוּהוּ לַעֲבוֹד פֶּסֶל וּמַסֵּכָה. וְכֵן דּוֹרֵשׁ אֶת כּוּלָּן כָּל אַחַת לְפִי פְּשָׁטָהּ: אוֹתוֹ שֶׁל עֲרָיוֹת כְּגוֹן שׁוֹכֵב עִם חוֹתַנְתּוֹ וְאֵשֶׁת אָבִיו וְעִם אֲחוֹתוֹ – כּוּלָּם בְּאֵשֶׁת אִישׁ, וּלְמֵיקַם בִּתְרֵי אֲרוּרֵי. שׁוֹכֵב עִם כָּל בְּהֵמָה – אֵשֶׁת אִישׁ שֶׁעָשְׂתָה מַעֲשֵׂה בְּהֵמָה, שֶׁמְּנָאֶפֶת. מְקַלֵּל אָבִיו וְאִמּוֹ – הַבָּא עַל אֵשֶׁת אִישׁ מְזַלְזֵל בְּאָבִיו וּבְאִמּוֹ שֶׁגִּידְּלוּ גִּידּוּלִין רָעִים בְּבֵיתָם. מַשְׁגֶּה עִוֵּר – מְפַתֶּה אֵשֶׁת אִישׁ שֶׁהִיא סוּמָא בַּדָּבָר וְאֵינָהּ יוֹדַעַת עוֹנְשׁוֹ כָּמוֹהוּ. מַשִּׂיג גְּבוּל רֵעֵהוּ – בָּא עַל אִשְׁתּוֹ, הֲרֵי הוּא הִשִּׂיג גְּבוּל. מַכֵּה רֵעֵהוּ בַּסֵּתֶר – גּוֹרֵם לוֹ בְּלַחַשׁ סְתָרָיו שֶׁתָּמוּת בִּבְדִיקַת מַיִם הַמָּרִים. לוֹקֵחַ שׁוֹחַד לְהַכּוֹת נֶפֶשׁ – לוֹקֵחַ שׁוֹחַד לִהְיוֹת עוֹקֵב אַחַר הַמְנָאֵף וּלְפַתּוֹת לוֹ אֵשֶׁת אִישׁ, וְגוֹרֵם לוֹ מִיתָה. מַטֵּה מִשְׁפַּט גֵּר יָתוֹם – אֵינִי יוֹדֵעַ לְדוֹרְשׁוֹ. יָכוֹל כָּל הַבְּרָכוֹת כּוּלָּן קוֹדְמוֹת לִקְלָלוֹת. שֶׁיִּגְמְרוּ כָּל הַבְּרָכוֹת תְּחִילָּה עַד "בָּרוּךְ אֲשֶׁר יָקִים" וגו', וְאח"כ יִפְתְּחוּ בִּקְלָלָה. בִּלְשׁוֹן הַקּוֹדֶשׁ. כִּדְיָלְפִינַן "קוֹל" "קוֹל" מִמֹּשֶׁה. **מתני'** הָכִי גָּרְסִינַן בְּמַתְנִי': בִּרְכַּת כֹּהֲנִים כֵּיצַד כו' בַּמְּדִינָה אוֹמֵר אוֹתָהּ שָׁלֹשׁ בְּרָכוֹת. שֶׁמַּפְסִיקִין הַכֹּהֲנִים בֵּין פָּסוּק לְפָסוּק, וְעוֹנִין הַצִּיבּוּר אָמֵן. בַּמִּקְדָּשׁ בְּרָכָה אַחַת. לְפִי שֶׁאֵין עוֹנִין אָמֵן בַּמִּקְדָּשׁ, וְאֵין צָרִיךְ כָּאן שׁוּם הֶפְסֵק, וְהָכִי מְפָרֵשׁ בַּגְּמָרָא.

כִּכְתָבוֹ

תורה אור: דברים כח; שם כט; דברים כז; שם יא; שם כז; שם

חגיגה ו. זבחים קטו:

[תוספתא פ"ח ע"ש]

רש"ל

נ"א הכ"ד שלמטה. רש"א

קנ"ג ריבוא ריבואות וה' אלפים ריבואות ות"ת ריבואות ועוד שלשים ושבעה ריבואות אלפים וה' אלפים ומאתים בריתות כו'. רש"ל

תמיד פ"ז מ"ב

תוספות שאנץ

אלא זה הבא על הערוה אשת איש והוליד ממזר ומתוך בושתו שאסור לבא בקהל ואינו מוצא אשה הולך לבין העמים ועובד עבודת כוכבים. וארורים אלו שעשאוהו לעבוד פסל ומסכה וכן דורש כלם כל אחת לפי פשטה אותן של עריות כגון שוכב עם חותנתו ואשת אביו ועם אחותו כלם באשת איש ולמיקם בתרי ארורי שוכב עם כל בהמה זו אשת איש שעשתה מעשה בהמה שמנאפת. מקלל אביו ואמו בא על אשת איש מזלזל באביו ואמו שגידלו למעשה רעים. משגה עור מפתה אשת רעהו שהיא סומא בדבר ואינה יודעת העונש כמוהו. משיג גבול רעהו בא על אשת רעהו הרי הוא מסיג גבול רעהו שנאסרה אשתו לו. מכה רעהו בסתר א) לוקח שוחד להרוג נפש להיות עוקבת אחר המנאף ולפתות לו אשת איש וגורם לו מיתה. מטה משפט גר יתום פ"ה איני יודע לדרשו. ורבינו שמשון מקוצי מפרש זה הבא על אשת איש והוליד ממנה בן ממזר הולך לדור בעיר אחרת בארץ מרחק באשר ימצא. ונמצא שהוא גר ויתום שהוא כגר שאין לו אב שזה שהולידו אינו מודה שהוא בנו וגם אמו אלמנה שנאסרה על בעלה ויושבת עגונה באלמנות חיות:

מה

א) נ"ל מכה רעהו בסתר גורס לו בלחש סתריו שתמות בבדיקת מים המרים לוקח שוחד להכות נפש לוקח שוחד להיות עוקב אחר המנאף וכו'.

כְּכְתָבוֹ, וּבַמְּדִינָה בְּכִינּוּיוֹ. [א]בַּמְּדִינָה — כֹּהֲנִים נוֹשְׂאִים אֶת יְדֵיהֶן כְּנֶגֶד כִּתְפֵיהֶן, [ב]וּבַמִּקְדָּשׁ עַל גַּבֵּי רָאשֵׁיהֶן, [ג]חוּץ מִכֹּהֵן גָּדוֹל שֶׁאֵינוֹ מַגְבִּיהַּ אֶת יָדָיו לְמַעְלָה מִן הַצִּיץ. ר' יְהוּדָה אוֹמֵר: אַף כֹּהֵן גָּדוֹל מַגְבִּיהַּ יָדָיו לְמַעְלָה מִן הַצִּיץ, שֶׁנֶּאֱמַר: °"וַיִּשָּׂא אַהֲרֹן אֶת יָדָיו אֶל הָעָם וַיְבָרְכֵם". (ויקרא ט)

§ **גמ'** תָּנוּ רַבָּנַן: °"כֹּה תְבָרְכוּ" (במדבר ו) — [ד]בִּלְשׁוֹן הַקּוֹדֶשׁ. אַתָּה אוֹמֵר בִּלְשׁוֹן הַקּוֹדֶשׁ, אוֹ אֵינוֹ אֶלָּא בְּכָל לָשׁוֹן? נֶאֱמַר כָּאן "כֹּה תְבָרְכוּ" וְנֶאֱמַר לְהַלָּן °"אֵלֶּה יַעַמְדוּ לְבָרֵךְ אֶת הָעָם" (דברים כז), מַה לְּהַלָּן בִּלְשׁוֹן הַקּוֹדֶשׁ — אַף כָּאן בִּלְשׁוֹן הַקּוֹדֶשׁ. רַבִּי יְהוּדָה אוֹמֵר: אֵינוֹ צָרִיךְ, הֲרֵי הוּא אוֹמֵר "כֹּה" — עַד שֶׁיֹּאמְרוּ בַּלָּשׁוֹן הַזֶּה. תַּנְיָא אִידָךְ: "כֹּה תְבָרְכוּ" — [ה]בַּעֲמִידָה. אַתָּה אוֹמֵר בַּעֲמִידָה אוֹ אֵינוֹ אֶלָּא אֲפִי' בִּישִׁיבָה? נֶאֱמַר כָּאן "כֹּה תְבָרְכוּ" וְנֶאֱמַר לְהַלָּן "אֵלֶּה יַעַמְדוּ לְבָרֵךְ", מַה לְּהַלָּן בַּעֲמִידָה — אַף כָּאן בַּעֲמִידָה. ר' נָתָן אוֹמֵר: אֵינוֹ צָרִיךְ, הֲרֵי הוּא אוֹמֵר °"לְשָׁרְתוֹ וּלְבָרֵךְ בִּשְׁמוֹ" (שם י), מַה [ו]מְשָׁרֵת בַּעֲמִידָה — אַף מְבָרֵךְ בַּעֲמִידָה. וּמְשָׁרֵת גּוּפֵיהּ מְנָלַן? [ז]דִּכְתִיב: °"לַעֲמוֹד לְשָׁרֵת" (שם יח). תַּנְיָא אִידָךְ: "כֹּה תְבָרְכוּ" — בִּנְשִׂיאוּת כַּפַּיִם. אַתָּה אוֹמֵר בִּנְשִׂיאוּת כַּפַּיִם, אוֹ אֵינוֹ אֶלָּא שֶׁלֹּא בִּנְשִׂיאוּת כַּפַּיִם? נֶאֱמַר כָּאן "כֹּה תְבָרְכוּ" וְנֶאֱמַר לְהַלָּן °"וַיִּשָּׂא אַהֲרֹן אֶת יָדָיו אֶל הָעָם וַיְבָרְכֵם" (ויקרא ט), מַה לְּהַלָּן בִּנְשִׂיאוּת כַּפַּיִם — אַף כָּאן [ז]בִּנְשִׂיאוּת כַּפַּיִם. קַשְׁיָא לֵיהּ לְר' יוֹנָתָן: אִי מַה לְּהַלָּן כֹּהֵן גָּדוֹל וְרֹאשׁ חוֹדֶשׁ וַעֲבוֹדַת צִבּוּר — אַף כָּאן כֹּהֵן גָּדוֹל וְרֹאשׁ חוֹדֶשׁ וַעֲבוֹדַת צִיבּוּר! ר' נָתָן אוֹמֵר: אֵינוֹ צָרִיךְ, הֲרֵי הוּא אוֹמֵר °"הוּא וּבָנָיו כָּל הַיָּמִים" (דברים יח) — מַקִּישׁ בָּנָיו לוֹ, מַה הוּא בִּנְשִׂיאוּת כַּפַּיִם — אַף בָּנָיו בִּנְשִׂיאוּת כַּפַּיִם, וּכְתִיב "כָּל הַיָּמִים", וְאִיתְקַשׁ בְּרָכָה לְשֵׁירוּת. וְתַנְיָא אִידָךְ: "כֹּה תְבָרְכוּ אֶת בְּנֵי יִשְׂרָאֵל" — [ח]בַּשֵּׁם הַמְּפוֹרָשׁ. אַתָּה אוֹמֵר בַּשֵּׁם הַמְּפוֹרָשׁ, אוֹ אֵינוֹ אֶלָּא בְּכִינּוּי? ת"ל: °"וְשָׂמוּ אֶת שְׁמִי" (במדבר ו) — שְׁמִי הַמְיוּחָד לִי. יָכוֹל אַף בַּגְּבוּלִין כֵּן — נֶאֱמַר כָּאן "וְשָׂמוּ אֶת שְׁמִי" וְנֶאֱמַר לְהַלָּן °"לָשׂוּם אֶת שְׁמוֹ שָׁם" (דברים יב), מַה לְּהַלָּן בֵּית הַבְּחִירָה — אַף כָּאן בְּבֵית הַבְּחִירָה. רַבִּי יֹאשִׁיָּה אוֹמֵר: אֵינוֹ צָרִיךְ, הֲרֵי הוּא אוֹמֵר °"בְּכָל הַמָּקוֹם אֲשֶׁר אַזְכִּיר אֶת שְׁמִי אָבוֹא אֵלֶיךָ" (שמות כ), בְּכָל מָקוֹם ס"ד?! אֶלָּא מִקְרָא זֶה מְסוֹרָס הוּא; בְּכָל מָקוֹם אֲשֶׁר אָבוֹא אֵלֶיךָ וּבֵרַכְתִּיךָ — שָׁם אַזְכִּיר אֶת שְׁמִי. וְהֵיכָן אָבוֹא אֵלֶיךָ וּבֵרַכְתִּיךָ — בְּבֵית הַבְּחִירָה, שָׁם אַזְכִּיר אֶת שְׁמִי — בְּבֵית הַבְּחִירָה. תַּנְיָא אִידָךְ: "כֹּה תְבָרְכוּ אֶת בְּנֵי יִשְׂרָאֵל", אֵין לִי אֶלָּא בְּנֵי יִשְׂרָאֵל, גֵּרִים נָשִׁים וַעֲבָדִים מְשׁוּחְרָרִים מִנַּיִן? ת"ל: °"אָמוֹר לָהֶם" (במדבר ו) — לְכוּלְּהוּ. תַּנְיָא אִידָךְ: "כֹּה תְבָרְכוּ" — [ט]פָּנִים כְּנֶגֶד פָּנִים. אַתָּה אוֹמֵר פָּנִים כְּנֶגֶד פָּנִים, אוֹ אֵינוֹ אֶלָּא פָּנִים כְּנֶגֶד עוֹרֶף? ת"ל: "אָמוֹר לָהֶם" — כְּאָדָם הָאוֹמֵר לַחֲבֵירוֹ. תַּנְיָא אִידָךְ: "כֹּה תְבָרְכוּ" — [י]בְּקוֹל רָם. אוֹ אֵינוֹ אֶלָּא בְּלַחַשׁ? ת"ל: "אָמוֹר לָהֶם" — כְּאָדָם שֶׁאוֹמֵר לַחֲבֵירוֹ. אָמַר אַבָּיֵי: *[כ]נְקִטִינַן, לִשְׁנַיִם קוֹרֵא "כֹּהֲנִים" וּלְא' אֵינוֹ קוֹרֵא "כֹּהֵן", שֶׁנֶּא': "אָמוֹר לָהֶם" — לִשְׁנַיִם. וְאָמַר רַב חִסְדָּא: נְקִטִינַן, כֹּהֵן קוֹרֵא "כֹּהֲנִים" וְאֵין יִשְׂרָאֵל קוֹרֵא "כֹּהֲנִים", שֶׁנֶּאֱמַר "אָמוֹר לָהֶם" — אֲמִירָה מִשֶּׁלָּהֶם

[פירושו תמצא ברש"י עירובין ה. ד"ה והאמר]

רש"י

בִּכְתָבוֹ. בְּיוּ"ד הֵ"י. בְּכִינּוּיוֹ. בְּאָלֶ"ף דָּלֶ"ת. כְּנֶגֶד כִּתְפוֹתֵיהֶם. מִפְּנֵי שֶׁצָּרִיךְ נְשִׂיאוּת כַּפַּיִם, כִּדְאָמְרִי' בַּבָּרַיְיתָא בַּגְּמָרָא. וּבַמִּקְדָּשׁ. לְמַעְלָה מֵרָאשֵׁיהֶם, מִפְּנֵי שֶׁמְּבָרְכִין אֶת הָעָם בַּשֵּׁם הַמְּפוֹרָשׁ, וּשְׁכִינָה לְמַעְלָה מִקִּשְׁרֵי אֶצְבְּעוֹתֵיהֶם. שֶׁאֵין מַגְבִּיהַּ לְמַעְלָה מִן הַצִּיץ אֶת יָדָיו. מִפְּנֵי שֶׁהַשֵּׁם כָּתוּב עָלָיו.

גמ' בִּנְשִׂיאוּת כַּפַּיִם. שֶׁיַּגְבִּיהוּ אֶת יְדֵיהֶם. קַשְׁיָא לֵיהּ לְרַבִּי יוֹנָתָן. אַהַךְ גְּזֵירָה שָׁוָה; אִי בִּגְז"שׁ יָלְפַתְּ לָהּ — אִיכָּא לְמִיפְרַךְ: מַה לְּמִלּוּאִים — שֶׁכֵּן קָרְבַּן צִיבּוּר, כִּדְכְתִיב (ויקרא ט): "וַיֵּרֶד מֵעֲשׂוֹת הַחַטָּאת וְהָעוֹלָה וְהַשְּׁלָמִים", וְכוּלָּן שֶׁל צִיבּוּר, כִּדְכְתִיב: "קְחוּ שְׂעִיר עִזִּים" וגו'. וְרֹאשׁ חֹדֶשׁ הֲוָה, כִּדְכְתִיב: "בְּיוֹם הַחֹדֶשׁ הָרִאשׁוֹן בְּאֶחָד לַחֹדֶשׁ תָּקִים" וגו' (שמות מ), וְהוּא הָיָה יוֹם שְׁמִינִי לַמִּלּוּאִים, כִּדְתַנְיָא בְּסֵדֶר עוֹלָם: אוֹתוֹ הַיּוֹם נָטַל עֶשֶׂר עֲטָרוֹת. ר' נָתָן אוֹמֵר אֵינוֹ צָרִיךְ. מִשּׁוּם דְּפָרְכָא לֵיהּ גז"ש, מַיְיתֵי לֵיהּ בְּהֶקֵּישָׁא. אַף בָּנָיו בִּנְשִׂיאוּת כַּפַּיִם. וְלָא תִּיקְשֵׁי תּוּ "שֶׁכֵּן כ"ג", דְּאֵין מְשִׁיבִין עַל הַהֶיקֵּשׁ. וּכְתִיב כָּל הַיָּמִים. וְלָא תִּיקְשֵׁי לָךְ תּוּ רֹאשׁ חֹדֶשׁ וַעֲבוֹדַת צִבּוּר. וְאִיתְקַשׁ בְּרָכָה לְשֵׁירוּת. כְּלוֹמַר, וְאַע"ג דִּבְהַאי קְרָאֵי לָאו בְּרָכָה כְּתִיבָא אֶלָּא שֵׁירוּת "לַעֲמוֹד לְשָׁרֵת בְּשֵׁם ה' הוּא וּבָנָיו כָּל הַיָּמִים" — אִיתְקוּשׁ בְּרָכָה וְשֵׁירוּת בִּקְרָא אַחֲרִינָא, כִּדְאָמְרִי' לְעֵיל: "לְשָׁרְתוֹ וּלְבָרֵךְ בִּשְׁמוֹ". (א) בַּשֵּׁם הַמְיוּחָד. כִּכְתָבוֹ. בְּכָל הַמָּקוֹם ס"ד. וְכִי בְּכָל מָקוֹם שֵׁם הַמְיוּחָד נִזְכָּר? הָכְתִיב (שמות ג): "זֶה שְׁמִי" "וְזֶה זִכְרִי" — לֹא כְּשֶׁאֲנִי נִכְתָּב אֲנִי נִקְרָא (פסחים דף נ.)! וְעוֹד: וְכִי בְּכָל מָקוֹם שְׁכִינָה בָּאָה וְשׁוֹרָה, דִּכְתִיב: "אָבֹא אֵלֶיךָ"? וְהוּא לֹא יִחֵד מָקוֹם לְהַזְכָּרַת הַשֵּׁם!. מְסוֹרָס הוּא. מְהוּפָּךְ; "בְּכָל הַמָּקוֹם אֲשֶׁר אָבֹא אֵלֶיךָ" — בְּאֹהֶל מוֹעֵד שֶׁבַּמִּדְבָּר, וּבְשִׁילֹה וּבְבֵית עוֹלָמִים. אוֹ אֵינוֹ אֶלָּא אֲפִילוּ פָּנִים כְּנֶגֶד עוֹרֶף. שֶׁאֵין הַצִּיבּוּר צְרִיכִין לְהָסֵב פְּנֵיהֶם לְצַד הַכֹּהֲנִים. לִשְׁנַיִם קוֹרֵא כֹּהֲנִים. כְּשֶׁיֵּשׁ שָׁם שְׁנֵי כֹּהֲנִים לְבָרֵךְ, שְׁלִיחַ צִבּוּר כְּשֶׁגָּמַר בִּרְכַּת הוֹדָאָה קוֹרֵא אוֹתָן "כֹּהֲנִים", וְהֵן הוֹפְכִין פְּנֵיהֶן שֶׁהָיוּ הֲפוּכִין לְצַד הַתֵּיבָה לְהִתְפַּלֵּל. (ב) דְּהָא אָמְרִינַן לְקַמָּן: יְהִי רָצוֹן מִלְּפָנֶיךָ שֶׁתְּהֵא בְּרָכָה זוֹ כו'. אָמוֹר לָהֶם. מִקְּרָא דִּ"לָהֶם" נָפְקָא לָן, שֶׁשְּׁלִיחַ צִבּוּר מַזְהִיר אוֹתָן לְבָרֵךְ. כֹּהֵן קוֹרֵא כֹּהֲנִים. אִם שְׁלִיחַ צִבּוּר כֹּהֵן הוּא — קוֹרֵא וּמַזְהִיר אֶת חֲבֵירָיו הָעוֹמְדִים לְפָנָיו לְהַחֲזִיר פְּנֵיהֶם וּלְבָרֵךְ אֶת יִשְׂרָאֵל, וְאִם יִשְׂרָאֵל הוּא — אֵינוֹ קוֹרֵא "כֹּהֲנִים". מִשֶּׁלָּהֶם

תוספות

ונאמר להלן אלה יעמדו לברך. תימה: אדרבה, אימא: ונאמר להלן "ואכלת ושבעת וברכת", מה להלן בכל לשון, כדאמר לעיל (דף לג.)! וי"ל: דמסתברא ליה טפי למילף ברכת כהנים מברכת הר גריזים, דשתיהן מפורש בתורה, דהברכות עצמן נמי מפורשות, שהיה היפך הקללות המפורשות "ארור האיש" – לברכה. אבל לשון ברכת המזון אינה מפורשת בתורה. **ורבי** יהודה אומר הרי הוא אומר כה. אבל לרבנן לא משמע להו עיכובא "כה", אלא "ככה".

קשיא ליה לר' יונתן. אינו לשון הברייתא, אלא לשון פי' הגמרא. וה"ג לה בסיפרי: ר' יונתן אומר אי מה להלן וכו'. **וכתיב** כל הימים. תימה: אכתי עבודת יחיד מהיכא לן דאיתרבי דאיכא נשיאות כפים? והא בכל הימים איכא נמי עבודת צבור, כגון תמיד! ונראה, דודאי לדברי הכל אימעיט עבודת יחיד מנשיאות כפים, ור' יונתן נמי, אגב שיטפיה נקט ליה. ולא הוה נשיאות כפים בכל יום אלא בעבודת תמיד, כדתנן בפ"ה דסדר תמיד (דף לב:) דלאחר שנתנו איברים על גבי כבש ומלחום ירדו ובאו להן ללשכת הגזית. אמר להן הממונה "ברכו ברכה אחת" והם ברכו. קראו עשרת הדברות, שמע, והיה אם שמוע, ויאמר. וברכו את העם ג' ברכות: אמת ויציב, ועבודה, וברכת כהנים. והוא הדין במוספין ובתמיד של בין הערבים.

ואיתקש ברכה לשירות. לעיל קאי, דקאמר מקיש בניו לו – אימא לענין שירות דוקא איתקוש! להכי קאמר: כיון דאיתקוש לשירות – הוא הדין לברכה, דהא איתקוש ברכה לשירות. **או** אינו אלא בכינוי. רבינו הלל פי' בספרי: בכינוי – כגון אל, אלהים, צבאות, ולא מסתבר, דהיכי תיסק אדעתא לשבושי קרא למימר "יברכך אלהים" במקום שם בן ארבע אותיות? אלא בכינוי יש לומר: כקריאתו באל"ף דל"ת. **הרי** הוא אומר בכל המקום אשר אבא אליך וברכתיך. הכי תני בספרי: בכל מקום אשר אני נגלה – שם תהא מזכיר את שמי. והיינו דקמתמה הכא: בכל מקום ס"ד? וכי בכל מקום אשר אני מצוה שמי להזכיר, דהיינו אפילו בגבולין, תברכו? ד"בכל מקום אשר אבא אליך" – משמע: אני בעצמי, שיהא שם גילוי שכינה! אלא מקרא מסורס הוא: בכל מקום אשר אבא אליך, שאני נגלה שם – שם אני מצוך להזכיר שמי המיוחד לי, והיינו דוקא בבית הבחירה. והיינו דקתני בספרי: בכל מקום אשר אני נגלה – שם תהא מזכיר את שמי. ונראה דמזה הטעם נמנעו כהנים לברך בשם המיוחד משמת שמעון הצדיק, כדאמרי' בפרק "טרף בקלפי" (יומא דף לט:) – לפי שלא זכו שוב לגילוי שכינה. ונראה לר"י: כהן שבירך ברכת כהנים בישיבה – לא עשה ולא כלום, הואיל ואיתקוש ברכה לשירות, וגבי שירות אמר בפ"ב דזבחים (דף כג:) דיושב מחלל עבודה, הילכך אף כאן צריך לחזור ולברך מעומד. **או** אינו אלא בלחש. תימה לר"י: אמאי לא נפקא לן מיניה מג"ש ד"ברכה" "ברכה" מהר גריזים: מה להלן בקול רם – אף כאן בקול רם? ומצינו למימר דלא איצטריך אלא לר"י, דלא יליף ליה מגזירה שוה אלא מ"כה". **לשנים** קורא כהנים. בירושלמי פרק "אין עומדין", אמר רב חסדא: צריך שיהא החזן ישראל. רב נחמן בר יצחק אומר: אם היה כהן א' – אומר "כהן", שנים אומר "כהנים". אמר רב חסדא: אפי' כהן קורא "כהנים", שאין קורא "כהנים" אלא לאותו השבט.

כל

הגהות הב"ח

(א) רש"י ד"ה ואיתקש וכו' בשמו הס"ד ואח"כ מ"ה בשם המפורש בשם המיוחד: (ב) ד"ה לשנים וכו' להתפלל הא דאמרי' וכו' זו כו'. נ"ב ס"א ואינו בכלל ברכה הא דאמרינן כה תברכו פנים בפנים:

עין משפט נר מצוה

לב א מיי' פי"ד מהל' תפלה הלכה ג סמג עשין כ טוש"ע א"ח סי' קכח סעיף יב [וברב אלפס פרק הקורא את המגילה דף רעד. וברא"ש שם סימן י"ח]:

לג ב ג מיי' שם הל' ט:

לד ד ה מיי' שם הלכה יא וסמג שם טוש"ע שם סעיף יד [וברב אלפס שם וברא"ש שם]:

לה ו מיי' פ"ה מהל' ביאת מקדש הלכה טז יז:

לו ז ח מיי' פי"ד מהל' נשיאות כפים הלכה י יא:

לז ט מיי' שם הל' ג יב סמג עשין כ טוש"ע א"ח סי' קכח סעיף י:

לח י מיי' שם הלכה יא טור ש"ע שם סעיף יד:

לט כ מיי' שם הלכה ח טוש"ע שם סעיף י:

תוספות שאנץ

מה משרת בעמידה אף מברך בעמידה י"מ דכהן בעל תשובה ראוי הוא לדוכן ולא מקשי' ליה לפסול עבודה דכהן שנשתמד דכתיב לא יקרב אלי לשרתני ותנן בפ' בתרא דמנחו' כהנים ששימשו בבית חוניו לא ישמשו בירושלם הא בנוב וגבעון מותרין וכ"ש בזמן הזה לדוכן ואמרי' נמי התם הרי אלו כבעלי מומין ולא מצינו בשום מקום שבעל מום שפסול לדוכן אלא א"כ היו מומין שבגלוי שהעולם מסתכלין בו. אף בניו בנשיאות כפים ולא תקשי תו שכן כהן גדול דאין משיבין על ההיקש וכתיב כל הימים ואל תקשי לך תו ראש חדש ועבודת צבור ל"ה: לשנים קורא כהנים פ"ה כשיש שם שני כהנים לברך שליח צבור כשגמר ברכת הודאה (עד חוץ מבית הכנסת) ל"ה:

גליון הש"ס

גמ' דכתיב לעמוד לשרת. מה דקשה הא באותו קרא עצמו בפ' עקב כתיב לעמוד לפני ה' לשרתו ולברך בשמו. עי' בספר זית רענן פ' עקב ובתשובת שבות יעקב ח"ב סי' א'. ובסמ"ג מ"ע מצוה כ' כתב להיתר ור' נתן נפקא ליה עמידה מדכתי' לעמוד לשרתו ולברך בשמו עכ"ל ול"ע ועי' תוספות מנחות דף קט ע"א ד"ה לא:

מִשֶּׁלָּהֶם תְּהֵא. וְהִילְכְתָא כְּווֹתֵיהּ דְּאַבַּיֵי, אִוְלֵית הִילְכְתָא כְּווֹתֵיהּ דְּרַב חִסְדָּא.§ (סִימָן: מתאו"ה לברכ"ה דוכ"ן בעבוד"ה כו"ם מכי"ר נהנ"ה בעגל"ה).§ אָמַר ר' יְהוֹשֻׁעַ בֶּן לֵוִי: מִנַּיִן שֶׁהקב"ה מִתְאַוֶּה לְבִרְכַּת כֹּהֲנִים — שֶׁנֶּאֱמַר: °"וְשָׂמוּ אֶת שְׁמִי עַל בְּנֵי יִשְׂרָאֵל וַאֲנִי אֲבָרְכֵם". (במדבר ו) וְאָמַר רַבִּי יְהוֹשֻׁעַ בֶּן לֵוִי: בכָּל כֹּהֵן שֶׁמְּבָרֵךְ — מִתְבָּרֵךְ, וְשֶׁאֵינוֹ מְבָרֵךְ — אֵין מִתְבָּרֵךְ, שֶׁנֶּאֱמַר: °"וַאֲבָרְכָה מְבָרְכֶיךָ". (בראשית יב) וְאָמַר ר' יְהוֹשֻׁעַ בֶּן לֵוִי: *גכָּל כֹּהֵן שֶׁאֵינוֹ עוֹלֶה לַדּוּכָן — עוֹבֵר בִּשְׁלֹשָׁה עֲשֵׂה: "כֹּה תְבָרְכוּ", "אָמוֹר לָהֶם", "וְשָׂמוּ אֶת שְׁמִי". רַב אָמַר: חוֹשְׁשִׁין שֶׁמָּא בֶּן גְּרוּשָׁה אוֹ בֶּן חֲלוּצָה הוּא. וְלָא פְּלִיגִי; הָא — דְּסָלֵיק לִפְרָקִים, הָא — דְּלָא סָלֵיק לִפְרָקִים. וְאָמַר ר' יְהוֹשֻׁעַ בֶּן לֵוִי: דכָּל כֹּהֵן שֶׁאֵינוֹ עוֹלֶה בַּעֲבוֹדָה שׁוּב אֵינוֹ עוֹלֶה, שֶׁנֶּאֱמַר: °"וַיִּשָּׂא אַהֲרֹן אֶת יָדָיו אֶל הָעָם וַיְבָרְכֵם וַיֵּרֶד מֵעֲשֹׂת הַחַטָּאת וְהָעֹלָה וְהַשְּׁלָמִים". (ויקרא ט) מַה לְּהַלָּן בַּעֲבוֹדָה — אַף כָּאן בַּעֲבוֹדָה. אִינִי? וְהָא ר' אַמִי וְרַבִּי אַסִי סָלְקִי! רַבִּי אַמִי וְרַבִּי אַסִי מֵעִיקָּרָא הֲווּ עָקְרִי כַּרְעַיְיהוּ, מִמְּטָא לָא הֲוָה מָטוּ הָתָם. וְכִדְתָנֵי ר' אוֹשַׁעְיָא: הלֹא שָׁנוּ אֶלָּא שֶׁלֹּא עָקַר אֶת רַגְלָיו, אֲבָל עָקַר אֶת רַגְלָיו — עוֹלֶה. *וּתְנַן נַמִי: אִם הַבְטָחָתוֹ שֶׁנּוֹשֵׂא אֶת כַּפָּיו וְחוֹזֵר לִתְפִלָּתוֹ — רַשַּׁאי, וְהָוֵינַן בָּהּ: הָא לָא עָקַר? אֶלָּא דְּנָד פּוּרְתָּא, הָכָא נַמִי — דְּעָקַר פּוּרְתָּא. וְאָמַר ריב"ל: אֵין נוֹתְנִין כּוֹס שֶׁל בְּרָכָה לְבָרֵךְ אֶלָּא לְטוֹב עַיִן, שֶׁנֶּאֱמַר: °"טוֹב עַיִן הוּא יְבֹרָךְ כִּי נָתַן מִלַּחְמוֹ לַדָּל" אַל תִּיקְרֵי "יְבוֹרָךְ" אֶלָּא "יְבָרֵךְ". (משלי כב) וְאָמַר ר' יְהוֹשֻׁעַ בֶּן לֵוִי: מִנַּיִן שֶׁאֲפִי' עוֹפוֹת מַכִּירִין בְּצָרֵי הָעַיִן — שֶׁנֶּאֱמַר: °"כִּי חִנָּם מְזֹרָה הָרָשֶׁת בְּעֵינֵי כָּל בַּעַל כָּנָף". (שם א) וְאָמַר רַבִּי יְהוֹשֻׁעַ בֶּן לֵוִי: כָּל הַנֶּהֱנֶה מִצָּרֵי הָעַיִן עוֹבֵר בְּלָאו, שֶׁנֶּאֱמַר °"אַל תִּלְחַם אֶת לֶחֶם רַע עָיִן וגו', כִּי כְּמוֹ שָׁעַר בְּנַפְשׁוֹ כֵּן הוּא אֱכוֹל וּשְׁתֵה יֹאמַר לָךְ" וגו'. (שם כג) רַב נַחְמָן בַּר יִצְחָק אָמַר: עוֹבֵר בִּשְׁנֵי לָאוִין, "אַל תִּלְחַם" וְ"אַל תִּתְאָו". וְא"ר יְהוֹשֻׁעַ בֶּן לֵוִי: אֵין עֶגְלָה עֲרוּפָה בָּאָה אֶלָּא בִּשְׁבִיל צָרֵי הָעַיִן, שֶׁנֶּאֱמַר: °"וְעָנוּ וְאָמְרוּ יָדֵינוּ לֹא שָׁפְכוּ אֶת הַדָּם הַזֶּה". (דברים כא) וְכִי *עַל לִבֵּנוּ עָלְתָה שֶׁזִּקְנֵי ב"ד שׁוֹפְכֵי דָמִים הֵם? אֶלָּא, לֹא בָּא לְיָדֵינוּ וּפְטַרְנוּהוּ, וְלֹא רְאִינוּהוּ וְהִנַּחְנוּהוּ; לֹא בָּא לְיָדֵינוּ וּפְטַרְנוּהוּ בְּלֹא מְזוֹנוֹת. לֹא רְאִינוּהוּ וְהִנַּחְנוּהוּ בְּלֹא לְוָיָה. אָמַר אַדָּא א"ר שַׂמְלַאי: יבֵּית הַכְּנֶסֶת שֶׁכּוּלָּהּ כֹּהֲנִים — כּוּלָּן עוֹלִין לַדּוּכָן. לְמִי מְבָרְכִין? אָמַר ר' זֵירָא: לַאֲחֵיהֶם שֶׁבַּשָּׂדוֹת. אִינִי?! *וְהָתָנֵי אַבָּא בְּרֵיהּ דְּרַב מְנְיָמִין בַּר חִיָּיא: חעַם שֶׁאֲחוֹרֵי כֹּהֲנִים אֵינָן בִּכְלַל בְּרָכָה! לָא קַשְׁיָא; טהָא — דַּאֲנִיסֵי, הָא — דְּלָא אֲנִיסֵי. וְהָתָנֵי רַב שִׁימִי מִבִּירְתָא דְּשִׁיחוֹרֵי: בֵּית הַכְּנֶסֶת שֶׁכּוּלָּהּ כֹּהֲנִים — מִקְצָתָן עוֹלִין וּמִקְצָתָן עוֹנִין אָמֵן! לָא קַשְׁיָא; יהָא — דְּאִישְׁתַּיֵּיר בֵּי עֲשָׂרָה, הָא — דְּלָא אִישְׁתַּיֵּיר בֵּי עֲשָׂרָה. גּוּפָא, תָּנָא אַבָּא בְּרֵיהּ דְּרַב מְנְיָמִין בַּר חִיָּיא: עַם שֶׁאֲחוֹרֵי כֹּהֲנִים אֵינָן בִּכְלַל בְּרָכָה. פְּשִׁיטָא; אֲרִיכֵי בְּאַפֵּי גּוּצֵי — לָא מַפְסְקִי, תֵּיבָה — לָא מַפְסְקָא, מְחִיצָה מַאי? ת"ש, *דְּאָמַר רַבִּי יְהוֹשֻׁעַ בֶּן לֵוִי: כאֲפִילּוּ מְחִיצָה שֶׁל בַּרְזֶל אֵינָהּ מַפְסֶקֶת בֵּין יִשְׂרָאֵל לַאֲבִיהֶם שֶׁבַּשָּׁמַיִם. אִיבַּעְיָא לְהוּ: צְדָדִין מַהוּ? אָמַר אַבָּא מָר בַּר רַב אַשִׁי: ת"ש, דִּתְנַן: לנִתְכַּוֵּון *לְהַזּוֹת לְפָנָיו

וְהִזָּה

תורה אור

מִשֶּׁלָּהֶם תְּהֵא. אַזְהָרָה זוֹ הַכֹּהֲנִים יַזְהִירוּ. וְשָׂמוּ אֶת שְׁמִי. תָּלָה הַכָּתוּב הַדָּבָר בָּהֶן, לִהְיוֹת בְּרָכָה זוֹ שִׂימַת שְׁמוֹ עַל עַמּוֹ, וְלֹא עֲשָׂאָהּ צוֹרֶךְ יִשְׂרָאֵל אֶלָּא צוֹרֶךְ מָקוֹם. וַאֲבָרְכָה מְבָרֲכֶיךָ. דְּאִילּוּ "וַאֲנִי אֲבָרֲכֵם" אַיִּשְׂרָאֵל קָאֵי, כְּר"ע דְּאָמַר בְּ"אֵלּוּ טְרֵיפוֹת" (חולין דף מט.): לָמַדְנוּ בְּרָכָה לְיִשְׂרָאֵל מִפִּי כֹּהֲנִים, מִפִּי הַגְּבוּרָה לֹא לָמַדְנוּ, כְּשֶׁהוּא אוֹמֵר "וַאֲנִי אֲבָרֲכֵם" הֱוֵי אוֹמֵר הַכֹּהֲנִים מְבָרְכִים אֶת יִשְׂרָאֵל, וְהקב"ה מַסְכִּים עַל יָדָם. לִפְרָקִים. בְּחַגִּים וּבְמוֹעֲדִים. שֶׁאֵינוֹ עוֹלֶה בַּעֲבוֹדָה. קוֹדֶם שֶׁיְּסַיֵּים שְׁלִיחַ צִבּוּר "רְצֵה" צָרִיךְ לַעֲלוֹת עַל הַדּוּכָן. וַיֵּרֶד מֵעֲשׂוֹת. אַלְמָא בְּעוֹד עֲבוֹדָה בְּיָדוֹ בֵּירֵךְ, וְאַח"כ "וַיֵּרֶד מֵעֲשׂוֹת". אַלְמָא הַשְׁתָּא הוּא דְּגָמַר. מֵעִיקָּרָא הֲווּ עָקְרִי כַּרְעַיְיהוּ. מִמְּקוֹמָן בַּעֲבוֹדָה, אֲבָל רָחוֹק הָיָה מְקוֹמָן מִן הַדּוּכָן, וְלָא מָטוּ עַד דְּגָמְרָה בִּרְכַּת הָעֲבוֹדָה. וּתְנַן נַמִי. בִּבְרָכוֹת: אִם הַבְטָחָתוֹ כו'. רֵישָׁא הָכִי אִיתָא: הָעוֹבֵר לִפְנֵי הַתֵּיבָה לֹא יַעֲנֶה אָמֵן אַחַר הַכֹּהֲנִים מִפְּנֵי הַטֵּירוּף. וְאִם אֵין שָׁם כֹּהֵן אֶלָּא הוּא — לֹא יִשָּׂא אֶת כַּפָּיו, שֶׁלֹּא תִּיטָּרֵף דַּעְתּוֹ בְּשׁוּבוֹ לִתְפִלָּתוֹ וְלֹא יֵדַע לְהַתְחִיל מִיָּד בְּ"שִׂים שָׁלוֹם". וְאִם הַבְטָחָתוֹ, שֶׁהוּא מְלוּמָּד בַּדָּבָר וְלֹא תִּטָּרֵף דַּעְתּוֹ — נוֹשֵׂא אֶת כַּפָּיו וְחוֹזֵר לִתְפִלָּתוֹ. רַשַּׁאי. לִישָּׂא אֶת כַּפָּיו. וְהָא לֹא עָלָה בַּעֲבוֹדָה. אֶלָּא דְּעָקַר פּוּרְתָּא, וְש"מ סַגֵּי בְּהָכִי שֶׁעוֹקֵר מְעַט רַגְלָיו לֵילֵךְ לְצַד הַדּוּכָן בַּעֲבוֹדָה. לְבָרֵךְ. בהמ"ז. לְטוֹב עַיִן. שׂוֹנְאֵי בֶצַע וְגוֹמְלֵי חֶסֶד בְּמָמוֹנָן. מַכִּירִין בְּצָרֵי עַיִן. וְאֵין אוֹכְלִים מִשֶּׁלָּהֶם. כִּי חִנָּם מְזוֹרָה הָרֶשֶׁת. לְעֵיל מִינֵּיהּ מִשְׁתָּעֵי בְּצָרֵי עַיִן: "נֶאֶרְבָה לְדָם" וגו' "כָּל הוֹן יָקָר נִמְצָא" וגו' "כִּי חִנָּם מְזוֹרָה הָרֶשֶׁת" — לְשׁוֹן "יְזוֹרֶה עַל נָוֵהוּ גָּפְרִית", כָּךְ דַּרְכָּם שֶׁל צַיָּידִים לִזְרוֹת חִטִּים וּשְׂעוֹרִים בְּרִשְׁתָּם כְּדֵי שֶׁיָּבוֹאוּ הָעוֹפוֹת לֶאֱכוֹל, וְאֵלּוּ צָרֵי הָעַיִן חִנָּם מְאַבְּדִין מְזוֹנוֹת שֶׁזּוֹרִין בְּרִשְׁתָּם בְּעֵינֵי כָּל בַּעַל כָּנָף, שֶׁאַף הֵן מַכִּירִין בָּהֶן וְאֵין נֶהֱנִין מִמְּזוֹנוֹתֵיהֶן. כִּי כְּמוֹ שָׁעַר בְּנַפְשׁוֹ. "שָׁעַר" זֶה עַל כָּרְחֵנוּ לְשׁוֹן פָּעַל הוּא, וּנְקוּדָּתוֹ מוֹכַחַת עָלָיו, שֶׁחֶלְיוֹ קָמַץ וְחֶלְיוֹ פַּתָּח וְטַעְמוֹ לְמַטָּה, כְּאִילּוּ זֶה הָאוֹכֵל מֵירֵר וְהִשְׂעִיר בְּנַפְשׁוֹ שֶׁל צַר עַיִן, וְכָךְ הוּא לְשׁוֹן "כַּתְּאֵנִים הַשּׁוֹעָרִים" (ירמיה כט). וּמְנַחֵם בֶּן סָרוּק פֵּירְשׁוֹ לְשׁוֹן שִׁיעוּר — תָּמִיד הוּא מְשַׁעֵר כַּמָּה יֹאכַל זֶה וְעַד מָתַי. וּפְטַרְנוּהוּ בְּלֹא מְזוֹנוֹת. כְּלוֹמַר, לִמְזוֹנוֹת הוּצְרַךְ וְלֹא הָיָה לוֹ, וְרָאָה אֶחָד נוֹשֵׂא מְזוֹנוֹת וּבָא לַחוֹטְפָם מִמֶּנּוּ לְאוֹנֶס רְעָבוֹן, וְעָמַד זֶה עָלָיו וַהֲרָגוֹ. בְּלֹא לְוָיָה. חֲבוּרָה שֶׁיֵּלֵךְ עִמָּהֶם. שֶׁבַּשָּׂדוֹת. דַּאֲנִיסֵי בִּמְלַאכְתָּן, וְאֵין יְכוֹלִין לָבֹא. דְּלָא אֲנִיסֵי. הָעוֹמְדִין בְּבהכ"נ אֲחוֹרֵי הַכֹּהֲנִים לָא אֲנִיסֵי, אֶלָּא שֶׁאֵין הַבְּרָכָה חֲשׁוּבָה עֲלֵיהֶם לַעֲקוֹר רַגְלֵיהֶם וְלָבֹא לִפְנֵי הַכֹּהֲנִים לִהְיוֹת מִתְבָּרְכִים פָּנִים כְּנֶגֶד פָּנִים כַּדָּת. הִלְכָּךְ אֵינָם בִּכְלַל בְּרָכָה, כִּדְאָמְרִי': "כֹּה תְבָרְכוּ" — פָּנִים כְּנֶגֶד פָּנִים. מִבִּירְתָא דְשִׁחוֹרֵי. לְשׁוֹן בִּירָה. שִׁחוֹרֵי — מָקוֹם. אִישְׁתַּיֵּיר בֵּי עֲשָׂרָה. מִקְצָתָן עוֹלִין לַדּוּכָן, וְהָעֲשָׂרָה עוֹנִין אָמֵן. לֹא אִישְׁתַּיֵּיר בֵּי עֲשָׂרָה — לָא חָשִׁיב לִבְרָכָה לְחוּדַיְיהוּ, הִילְכָּךְ כּוּלָּן עוֹלִין וּמְבָרְכִין לַאֲחֵיהֶם שֶׁבַּשָּׂדוֹת. אֲרִיכֵי בְּאַפֵּי גּוּצֵי לָא מַפְסְקֵי. בֵּין כֹּהֲנִים, מִהְיוֹת בִּכְלַל בְּרָכָה, דְּאִם כֵּן אֵין לַדָּבָר סוֹף.

וְהִזָּה

כל כהן שאינו עולה לדוכן עובר בשלשה עשה. ירושלמי במסכת נזיר פרק "כהן גדול": מהו שיטמא אדם לנשיאת כפיס? אחוי דר' אבא בר כהן אמר קמיה ר' יוסי בשם ר' אחא: מטמא כהן לנשיאת כפיס. שמע ר' אחא ואמר: אנא לא אמרי ליה כלוס. חזר ואמר או דילמא לא שמע מיניה, אלא כיון דאמר ר' יהודה בר פזי בשם ר"א: כל כהן שעמד בבהכ"נ ואינו נושא את כפיו – עובר בעשה, וסבר למימר שמצות עשה דוחה למצות ל"ת, אמר אנא לא אמרית ליה, אייתוניה ואנא מלקי ליה. [ר' אבוה הוי יתיב ומתני (רש"ל) בבי כנישתא דקיסרין והוי תמן מיתנא, ואתא עונתא דנשיאת כפיס ולא שאלון ליה], אתא עונתא דמיכליא ושאלון ליה. אמר להון: על נשיאות כפיס לא שאילתון לי, ועל מיכלא אתון שאלון? כד שמעון כן הוה כל חד וחד מנהון משמט גרמיה וערק.

הא דסליק לפרקים. ה"ה אי לא סליק אלא דמחזיק נפשיה ע"י מתנות כהונה, כמו שאמר בפרק "הזרוע" (חולין דף קלג.): אמר אביי: מריש הוה חטיפנא מתנתא וכו', עד משקל נמי לא שקילנא לבר ממעלי יומא דכיפורי, לאחזוקי נפשי בכהני. ולפרוס ידיה? אנסי ליה עידניה. הא דאניסי הא דלא אניסי. בסוף מסכת ר"ה (דף לה.) אמרי' דדוקא הני שבשדות אניסי, אבל הני דקיימי במתא – לא אניסי.

מחיצה מאי. י"ל דדוקא בדלא אניסי קמבעיא ליה, אבל בדאניסי – פשיטא, דמי גרע מאחיהם שבשדות? וא"ת: אי לא אניסי אמאי עדיפי מעם שאחורי הכהנים בלא הפסק מחיצה? י"ל: עם שאחורי הכהנים מראין בעצמן כאילו אין הברכה חשובה בעיניהם, דכתיב: "אמור להם" – פנים כנגד פנים, והן עומדים אחורי עורף. אבל בהפסק מחיצה, כיון דלא קיימי אחורי עורף – לאו מילתא היא, דלא חזינן דקפיד קרא בהכי. מההיא דסוף מס' ר"ה (דף לה.) משמע דה"ה לתפלה, והכי משמע נמי בפרק "כילד צולין" (פסחים דף פה:), דתנן: אבר שיצא מקצתו לחוץ; מן האגף ולפנים – כלפנים, מן האגף ולחוץ – כלחוץ. אמר רב: וכן לתפלה. ופליגא דר' יהושע בן לוי, דאמר רבי יהושע בן לוי אפי' מחיצה וכו'. מדקא פשיט סתמא דגמ' ממילת' דריב"ל – ש"מ דקיימא

מ א מיי' פי"ד מהל' נשיאות כפים הל' ח סמג עשין כ טוש"ע א"ח סי' קכח סעיף י:

מא ב מיי' שם פט"ו הל' יב [וברב אלפס פרק הקורא את המגילה דף רעד. וברא"ש שם סימן כב]:

מב ג מיי' שם סמג שם טוש"ע א"ח סי' קכח סעיף ב:

מג ד ה מיי' שם הל' יא טוש"ע שם סעיף ח:

מד ו מיי' שם הל' י סמג שם טוש"ע שם סעיף כ:

מה ז מיי' שם פט"ו הל' ט סמג שם טוש"ע שם סעיף כה:

מו ח ט מיי' שם הל' ח טוש"ע שם סעי' כד:

מז י מיי' שם הלכה ט טוש"ע שם סעי' כה:

מח כ ל מיי' שם הל' ח טוש"ע שם סעיף כד וסימן נה סעיף כ:

תוספות שאנץ

ת"ש דא"ר יהושע בן לוי אפי' מחיצה של ברזל אינה מפסקת בין ישראל לאביהם שבשמי' וקשה דלענין מה מיירי אי לענין צירוף קשה מדאמרי' פרק כל גגות ציבור בקטנה ויחיד בגדולה אין מצטרפין וא"כ פליג עליה דר' יהושע בן לוי ואי לענין לצאת בו ידי חובתו א"ר יהושע בן לוי דאפי' מחיצה ברזל וכו' אבל לעולם אינו מצטרף וא"כ הכי קאמר רב התם וכן בתפלה פרק אין צולין גבי פסח הנאכל בחבורה מן האגף ולפנים כלפנים מן האגף ולחוץ כלחוץ אגף היינו משקוף ואמר רב עלה וכן לתפלה והיכי קאמר רב שלא יצא ידי חובתו והתנן היה עובר אחורי בית הכנסת ושמע קול שופר או קול מגילה אם כוון לבו יצא ופר"י דהתם עובר אחורי בית הכנסת ושמע קול א) מודה דיצא ידי חובתו אבל לענין דבר שבקדושה צריך כגון קדיש וברכו וקדושה לדין זה אמר רב דמפסקת:

א) נ"ל דלא בעי עשרה שפיר יצא יד"ח אבל לענין דבר שבקדושה דצריך עשרה כגון וכו'.

(מנחות מד.)

ברכות לה.

לקמן מה:

ר"ה לה.

פסחים פה:

פרה פרק יב מ"ב

תורה אור

אוְהִזָּה לְאַחֲרָיו, לְאַחֲרָיו וְהִזָּה לְפָנָיו — הַזָּאָתוֹ פְּסוּלָה. לְפָנָיו וְהִזָּה עַל צְדָדִין שֶׁבְּפָנָיו — הַזָּאָתוֹ כְּשֵׁרָה. אָמַר רָבָא בַּר רַב הוּנָא: בכֵּיוָן שֶׁנִּפְתַּח סֵפֶר תּוֹרָה — אָסוּר לְסַפֵּר אֲפִילּוּ בִּדְבַר הֲלָכָה, שֶׁנֶּאֱמַר: °"וּבְפִתְחוֹ עָמְדוּ כָל הָעָם", וְאֵין עֲמִידָה אֶלָּא שְׁתִיקָה, שֶׁנֶּאֱ': °"וְהוֹחַלְתִּי כִּי לֹא יְדַבֵּרוּ כִּי עָמְדוּ לֹא עָנוּ עוֹד". ר' זֵירָא אָמַר רַב חִסְדָּא: מֵהָכָא °"וְאָזְנֵי כָל הָעָם אֶל סֵפֶר הַתּוֹרָה". וְאָמַר ר' יְהוֹשֻׁעַ בֶּן לֵוִי: גכָּל כֹּהֵן שֶׁלֹּא נָטַל יָדָיו — לֹא יִשָּׂא אֶת כַּפָּיו, שֶׁנֶּאֱמַר: °"שְׂאוּ יְדֵיכֶם קֹדֶשׁ וּבָרְכוּ אֶת ה'". *שָׁאֲלוּ תַּלְמִידָיו אֶת ר' אֶלְעָזָר בֶּן שַׁמּוּעַ: בַּמֶּה הֶאֱרַכְתָּ יָמִים? אָמַר לָהֶן: מִיָּמַי לֹא עָשִׂיתִי בֵּית הַכְּנֶסֶת קַפֶּנְדַּרְיָא, וְלֹא פָּסַעְתִּי עַל רָאשֵׁי עַם קוֹדֶשׁ, וְלֹא נָשָׂאתִי כַּפַּי בְּלֹא בְּרָכָה. מַאי מְבָרֵךְ? אָמַר רַבִּי זֵירָא אָמַר רַב חִסְדָּא: ד"אֲשֶׁר קִדְּשָׁנוּ בִּקְדוּשָּׁתוֹ שֶׁל אַהֲרֹן וְצִוָּנוּ לְבָרֵךְ אֶת עַמּוֹ יִשְׂרָאֵל בְּאַהֲבָה". כִּי עָקַר כַּרְעֵיהּ מַאי אָמַר? ה"יְהִי רָצוֹן מִלְּפָנֶיךָ ה' אֱלֹהֵינוּ שֶׁתְּהֵא בְּרָכָה זוֹ שֶׁצִּוִּיתָנוּ לְבָרֵךְ אֶת עַמְּךָ יִשְׂרָאֵל, לֹא יְהֵא בָּהּ מִכְשׁוֹל וְעָוֹן". וְכִי מַהֲדַר אַפֵּיהּ מִצִּיבּוּרָא מַאי אָמַר? אַדְבְּרֵיהּ רַב חִסְדָּא לְרַב עוּקְבָא, וְדָרַשׁ: ו"רִבּוֹנוֹ שֶׁל עוֹלָם, עָשִׂינוּ מַה שֶּׁגָּזַרְתָּ עָלֵינוּ, עֲשֵׂה עִמָּנוּ

מַה

נחמיה ח | איוב לב | נחמיה ח | תהלים קלד

רש"י

וְהִזָּה לְאַחֲרָיו. וְאַף שָׁם הָיוּ כֵּלִים הַצְּרִיכִין הַזָּאָה. הַזָּאָתוֹ פְּסוּלָה. דְּבָעֵינַן כַּוָּונָה לְטָהֳרָה, כִּדְכְתִיב (במדבר יט): "וְהִזָּה הַטָּהוֹר עַל הַטָּמֵא" – שֶׁיְּהֵא מִתְכַּוֵּין לוֹ. עַל הַצְּדָדִין שֶׁבְּפָנָיו. לַצְּדָדִין שֶׁיֵּשׁ מִמֶּנּוּ וּלְהַלָּן, וְלֹא לַצְּדָדִין שֶׁיֶּשְׁנוֹ מִמֶּנּוּ וּלְאָחוֹר. וְהָכִי נַמִי, הָעוֹמְדִין בִּצְדָדִין שֶׁל כֹּהֵן הֵימֶנּוּ וּלְהַלָּן – בִּכְלַל בְּרָכָה הֵן, דִּכְלְפָנָיו דָּמֵי. אֲבָל שֶׁל אַחַר הֵימֶנּוּ, אע"פ שֶׁאֵינָן אֲחוֹרֵיהֶן מַמָּשׁ – כִּלְאַחֲרָיו דָּמֵי. וּבְפִתְחוֹ. וּכְשֶׁהִתְחִיל, וּבְעֶזְרָא כְּתִיב. עָמְדוּ. שָׁתְקוּ. שֶׁלֹּא נָטַל יָדָיו. לִפְנֵי עֲלוֹתוֹ לַדּוּכָן. בַּמֶּה הֶאֱרַכְתָּ יָמִים. אֵיזֶה זְכוּת בְּיָדְךָ שֶׁהֶאֱרַכְתָּ יָמִים. קַפֶּנְדַּרְיָא. לְקַצֵּר דַּרְכּוֹ דֶּרֶךְ בהכ"נ לִיכָּנֵס בְּפֶתַח זֶה וְלָצֵאת כְּנֶגְדּוֹ. וּלְשׁוֹן קַפֶּנְדַּרְיָא מְפָרֵשׁ בִּבְרָכוֹת (דף סג:): אַדְּמַקִּיפְנָא אַדָּרֵי אֵיעוּל בְּהָא – עַד שֶׁאֲנִי מַקִּיף סְבִיב הַשּׁוּרוֹת הַלָּלוּ – אֶכָּנֵס בָּזֶה וַאֲקַצֵּר דַּרְכִּי. וְדָרֵי – שׁוּרוֹת בָּתִּים. וְלֹא פָּסַעְתִּי עַל רָאשֵׁי עַם קוֹדֶשׁ. שֶׁהָיוּ יוֹשְׁבִים הַתַּלְמִידִין בְּבֵית הַמִּדְרָשׁ עַל גַּבֵּי קַרְקַע, וְהַמְהַלֵּךְ בֵּינֵיהֶם כְּשֶׁהֵן יוֹשְׁבִין וְנִכְנָס לֵישֵׁב בִּמְקוֹמוֹ מַרְחִיב פְּסִיעוֹתָיו בְּעַל כָּרְחוֹ, וְהוּא לְשׁוֹן מְפַסֵּעַ, (א) וְנִרְאֶה כִּמְפַסֵּעַ עַל רָאשֵׁיהֶם. לְפִיכָךְ צָרִיךְ לְהַקְדִּים, אוֹ יֵשֵׁב לוֹ מִבַּחוּץ. וְלֹא נָשָׂאתִי כַּפַּי לְבָרֵךְ. שֶׁכֹּהֵן הָיָה. בְּלֹא בְּרָכָה. בְּרָכָה דִּמְפָרֵשׁ וְאָזֵיל מַאי מְבָרֵךְ. וְכִי עָקַר כַּרְעֵיהּ. בַּעֲבוֹדָה לְמֵיסַק, וְהוּא מַחֲזִיר פָּנָיו כְּלַפֵּי תֵּיבָה, מַאי אָמַר?. וְכִי מַהֲדַר אַפֵּיהּ מִצִּיבּוּרָא. כְּשֶׁגּוֹמֵר בִּרְכוֹתָיו מַחֲזִיר פָּנָיו לְצַד הַתֵּיבָה עַד שֶׁיִּגְמוֹר שְׁלִיחַ צִבּוּר "הַמְבָרֵךְ אֶת עַמּוֹ יִשְׂרָאֵל בַּשָּׁלוֹם".

מַה

מגילה כז:

תוספות

דקיימא לן כוותיה. וכמדומה דהכי פסק רבינו חננאל, דבכל דוכתא קי"ל כר' יהושע בן לוי. ומקשה מפ' "כל גגות" (עירובין דף צב.), דיתיב ר' זירא ורבה בר רב חנן, ויתיב אביי גבייהו, ויתבי וקאמרי: שמע מינה ממתני' דיורי גדולה בקטנה ואין דיורי קטנה בגדולה וכו' עד לבור בגדולה ושליח צבור בקטנה – יוצאין ידי חובתן, צבור בקטנה וש"צ בגדולה – אין יוצאין ידי חובתן. תשעה בגדולה וא' בקטנה – מצטרפין, תשעה בקטנה וא' בגדולה – אין מצטרפין. וה"ה גדולה בגדולה, דליכא למימר דיורי גדולה בגדולה. אלמא לענין תפלה לא אמר אפילו מחיצה של ברזל אין מפסקת! ונראה דלא דמי, דהיכא דאיכא עשרה בגדולה ושליח צבור עמהן, ואחד בגדולה כיוצא בה, מתוך שמוציא בני הגדולה – יוצא גם זה שבאחרת, כה"ג אמרינן דוקא אפילו מחיצה וכו', שהרי מוציא אפילו אחיו שבשדות, כדאיתא במסכת ראש השנה (דף לה.). אבל היכא דצריך לצרופינהו – ודאי לא מצטרפי. וההיא דפ' "אין עומדין" (ברכות דף לב:) דא"ר אלעזר: מיום שחרב בית המקדש נפסקה חומת ברזל בין ישראל לאביהן שבשמים – לא שייכא להכא. דההיא אמר לגבי הא שאין תפלתן מקובלת כמו בזמן שבהמ"ק קיים. מיהו, לענין זה אין מפסקת, אם יתברכו הצבור ע"י ברכת כהנים שעמהן בבית הכנסת, או יוציא ש"צ ידי חובתן – גם זה יתברך ויוצא ידי חובתו עמהן, דכלפי אבינו שבשמים לא תלי בהפסק מחיצה.

והזה על הצדדין שבפניו הזאתו כשרה. בירושלמי בפרק "אין עומדין" אמרי': הדא אמרה העומדין מן הצדדין – בכלל ברכה. **כיון** שנפתח ספר תורה **אסור** לספר **אפי'** בדבר הלכה. מקשינן מפרק קמא דברכות (דף ח.), דאמר: רב ששת הוה מהדר אפיה וגריס, אמר: אינהו בדידהו ואנן בדידן. ומצינו למימר דמהדר אפיה שאני. אי נמי רב ששת שאני, משום דהוה מאור עינים, והוה פטור מקריאה משום דהוה דברים שבכתב אי אתה רשאי לאומרן על פה, וכיון דפטור מקריאה – אפילו בשעת שמיעה היה יכול לעסוק בדבר הלכה. והיינו דקאמר: אנן בדידן, כגון דברי הלכה – (כגון) דברים דעל פה, ואינהו בדידהו – דברים שבכתב. מיהו, מסתברא כפירוש ר"ת, דפי' התם: דוקא רב ששת וכיוצא בו דתורתו אומנתו. אבל האידנא כרבא סבירא לן, דאמר רבא: כיון שנפתח ס"ת וכו'. והאי דהוה מהדר אפי' – י"ל דלא הויא אורחא דמילתא לאיעסוקי בדבר הלכה באנפי ציבורא בעוד שהן עסוקין בשמיעת התורה*.

כל כהן שלא נטל ידיו. פירש רש"י, אמר לי רבי: אם נטל ידיו שחרית ונטהר – כהן אינו צריך ליטול ידיו כשעולה לדוכן. וכמדומה שהועתק מהגהת תלמיד, שהרי אין לשונו משמע כך, דפירש שלא נטל ידיו – לפני עלותו לדוכן, משמע ממש סמוך. ועוד: דמייתי גמרא קרא: "שאו ידיכם קדש וברכו" – משמע תיכף לנטילת ידים ברכת כהנים, דמשמע ליה השתא דבברכת כהנים משתעי קרא, דהיא בנשיאות ידים. ומשמע בירושלמי פ"ח דברכות דבברכה דמשתעי קרא בעינן נטילת ידים סמוך לה, דמייתי לה התם אברכת המזון. והכי איתא: שלשה תכיפות הן; תיכף לסמיכה שחיטה, שנאמר: "וסמך ושחט". תיכף לנטילת ידים ברכה, שנא': "שאו ידיכם וברכו". תיכף לגאולה תפלה, שנא': "יהיו לרצון אמרי פי" וגו', וכתיב בתריה: "יענך ה' ביום צרה". ובפ' "כילד מברכין" (ברכות מב.) משמע דההיא ברכה איירי בברכת המזון, מיהו, שמעינן מינה דבעינן תיכף נטילת ידים בברכה דמשתעי ביה קרא, והכא מייתי לה אברכת כהנים. ועוד: אי איירי הכא בשלא נטל ידיו בשחרית – אמאי נקט כהן לנשיאות כפים? תיפוק ליה משום דברי תורה, שצריך ליטול ידיו, כדאמרי' בפ"ק דברכות (דף יא:) ובפ"ב (שם יד:), אמר רבי חייא בר רב אשי: זימנין סגיאין הוה קאימנן קמיה דרב לתנויי לן פירקא בסיפרא דבי רב, ומקדים וקאי ומשי ידיה ומברך ומנח תפילין, והדר אמר לן! ואמר נמי התם *דבעי לאהדורי בתר מיא לנט"י לק"ש מיל, ומה לי ק"ש ומה לי ברכת כהנים? אי משום דצריך ברכה לפניה – הכא נמי צריך ברכה לפניה, כדאמר לקמן! להכי מסתבר דהכא בנטילת ידים תיכף לברכה מיירי. ושיעור תכיפה איכא למישמע מתכיפת סמיכה לשחיטה, דאמרי' בפ' "כל הפסולין" (זבחים לג.): כל הסמיכות שהיו שם קורא אני בהם תיכף לסמיכה שחיטה, חוץ מזו שהיתה בשער נקנור, שאין מצורע יכול ליכנס שם. אלמא כדי מהלך משער נקנור עד בית המטבחים לא חשיבה תכיפה, ובמסכת מדות (פ"ה מ"א) משמע דלא הוי טפי מעשרים ושתים אמה, מקום דריסת רגלי ישראל ומקום דריסת רגלי הכהנים שכל אחד היו י"א אמה.

וכי מהדר **אפיה מצבורא מאי אמר.** סדר נשיאת כפים מפי' רבינו שלמה: עוקר רגליו בעבודה ממקומו, ובא לפני התיבה, ומתפלל "יהי רצון שתהא ברכה זו" וכו', ומאריך בה עד שיאמרו אמן של הודאה מפי הצבור. וקורא "כהנים" אם שנים הם, ואם אחד אינו קורא ש"ל, והוא מחזיר פניו מאליו, כדאביי, דאמר לעיל: לאחד אינו קורא. וכשכלה דבור מהקורא מברכין "אשר קדשנו" כו'. ואחר כך מתחילין בברכה. וכשכלה אמן אחרון מפי צבור הן מחזירין, וכופפין קשרי אצבעותיהן אם רוצין. ושליח צבור מתחיל "שים שלום", והכהנים יתפללו "רבונו של עולם עשינו מה שגזרת" וכו', ומאריכין בה עד שתכלה ברכה מפי שליח צבור, עוקרין רגליהן והולכין להן. בשאלתות פרשת "ויקח קרח": כהן שהשתמד – לא ישא את כפיו, דגרע מהורג את הנפש, דאמרינן בפ' "אין עומדין" (ברכות לב:): כהן שהרג את הנפש – לא ישא את כפיו. ורבינו גרשום מאור הגולה השיב בתשובותיו דנושא כפיו, וקורא ראשון בתורה. דכיון דחזר בתשובה – חוזר לקדושתו. דתנן בסוף מסכת מנחות (דף קט.): "אך לא יעלו כהני הבמות אל מזבח ה' בירושלים כי אם אכלו מצות בתוך אחיהם" – והרי הן כבעלי מומין שחולקין ואוכלין. וכשם שבעלי מומין נושאין את כפיהם וקורא ראשון בתורה – ואף זה. שאם לא תאמר כן – נמצאת מרפה ידיהן של בעלי תשובה, שיאמרו בשמדותן: אוי לאותה בושה אוי לאותה כלימה, וימנעו מעשות תשובה. ואמר ר' יוחנן:* כל האומר מנשה אין לו חלק לעולם הבא – מרפה ידיהן של בעלי תשובה, ותנא דבי רבי ישמעאל:* הואיל והלך זה ונעשה כומר לעבודה זרה, אדחה אבן אחר הנופל וכו'. [וע"ע תוס' מנחות קט. ד"ה לא ישמשו ותוס' תענית כז. ד"ה אי מה].

עד

[ועי' תוס' ברכות ח. ד"ה רב ששת]

[דף טו.]

[סנהדרין קג.]

[קדושין כ:]

עין משפט נר מצוה

מט א מיי' פ"י מהל' פרה אדומה הל' ז:

נ ב מיי' פי"ב מהל' תפלה הל' ט סמג עשין כה טוש"ע א"ח סימן קמו סעיף ב:

נא ג מיי' פט"ו מהל' נ"כ הל' ה סמג עשין כ טוש"ע א"ח סימן קכח סעיף ו:

נב ד מיי' שם פי"ד הלכה יב סמג שם טוש"ע שם סעיף יא:

נג ה מיי' שם טוש"ע שם סעיף ט:

נד ו מיי' שם טוש"ע שם סעיף טו:

הגהות הב"ח

(א) רש"י ד"ה ולא פסעתי וכו' לשון מפסע ואזיל ונראה. נ"ב עי' פ' מצות חליצה דף קה ע"ב:

תוספות שאנץ

כיון דנפתח ספר תורה אסור לדבר אפי' בדברי תורה. פי' רשב"ם אבל אי מהדר אפיה לית לן בה דאמר פ"ק דברכות רב ששת מהדר אפיה וגריס. ואינו נראה לר"ת דא"כ היה ליה לתלמודא לאיתויי הא דרב ששת ולומר שמותר בזה הענין. על כן נראה לי דרב ששת א) לא פליג דבדבר הלכה שרי:

א) נ"ל דרב ששת פליג וס"ל דלדבר הלכה שרי.

עין משפט נר מצוה

נה א מיי' פי"ד מהל' נשיאות כפים הל' ו סמג עשין כ טוש"ע א"ח סימן קכח סעיף טז:
נו ב ג ד ה מיי' שם הלכה ה טוש"ע שם סעיף יח:
נז ו ז מיי' שם הלכה ו טוש"ע שם סעיף טז:
נח ח ט מיי' פי"ב מהל' תפלה הלכה ו סמג עשין כה טוש"ע א"ח סימן קמא סעיף ה:
נט י כ מיי' שם הלכה יא סמג שם טוש"ע א"ח סי' קמה סעיף א:
ס ל מיי' שם הל' יג סמג שם טוש"ע א"ח סימן רפב סעיף ה:
סא מיי' שם סמג שם טוש"ע א"ח סימן קמז סעיף ז וסי' רפד סעיף ו:
סב נ טוש"ע א"ח סימן קמח:
סג ס ע מיי' פי"ב מהל' תפלה הלכה כד סמג עשין כה טוש"ע א"ח סי' קמט:

גמרא

תורה אור

מה שהבטחתנו. "השקיפה ממעון קדשך מן השמים" וגו'. (דברים כו) אמר רב חסדא: אאין הכהנים רשאים לכוף קישרי אצבעותיהן עד שיחזרו פניהם מן הצבור. א"ר זירא א"ר חסדא: באין הקורא רשאי לקרות "כהנים" עד שיכלה "אמן" מפי הצבור, גואין הכהנים רשאין להתחיל בברכה עד שיכלה דיבור מפי הקורא, דואין הצבור רשאין לענות אמן עד שתכלה ברכה מפי הכהנים, הואין הכהנים רשאין להתחיל בברכה אחרת עד שיכלה אמן מפי הצבור. ואמר רבי זירא אמר רב חסדא: ואין הכהנים רשאין להחזיר פניהם מן הצבור עד שיתחיל שליח צבור ב"שים שלום", זואינן רשאין לעקור רגליהם ולילך עד שיגמור שליח צבור "שים שלום". וא"ר זירא אמר רב חסדא: חאין הצבור רשאין לענות אמן עד שתכלה ברכה מפי הקורא, טואין הקורא רשאי לקרות בתורה עד שיכלה אמן מפי הצבור, יואין המתרגם רשאי להתחיל בתרגום עד שיכלה פסוק מפי הקורא, כואין הקורא רשאי להתחיל בפסוק אחר עד שיכלה תרגום מפי המתרגם. אמר רבי תנחום א"ר יהושע בן לוי: להמפטיר בנביא צריך שיקרא בתורה תחילה. ואמר רבי תנחום אמר רבי יהושע בן לוי: אין מהמפטיר רשאי להפטיר בנביא עד שיגלל ס"ת. ואמר רבי תנחום אמר רבי יהושע בן לוי: נאין שליח צבור רשאי להפשיט את התיבה בצבור, מפני כבוד צבור. ואמר רבי תנחום אמר רבי יהושע בן לוי: סאין הצבור רשאין לצאת עד שינטל ספר תורה *ויניח במקומו, ושמואל אמר: עד שיצא. ולא פליגי; עהא — דאיכא פיתחא אחרינא, הא — דליכא פיתחא אחרינא. אמר רבא: בר אהינא אסברה לי: "אחרי ה' אלהיכם תלכו". (שם יג) בזמן שהכהנים מברכים את העם מה הן אומרים? אמר ר' זירא אמר רב חסדא: "ברכו ה' מלאכיו גבורי כח" וגו', (תהלים קג) "ברכו ה' כל צבאיו משרתיו עושי רצונו", "ברכו ה' כל מעשיו בכל מקומות ממשלתו ברכי נפשי את ה'". במוספי דשבתא מה הן אומרים? אמר רבי אסי: "שיר המעלות (שם קלד) הנה ברכו את ה' כל עבדי ה'" וגו', "שאו ידיכם קדש וברכו את ה'", "ברוך ה' מציון (שם קלה) שוכן ירושלים הללויה". ולימא נמי: "יברכך ה' (שם קלד) מציון" דכתיב בההוא עניינא! אמר יהודה בריה דר"ש בן פזי: מתוך שהתחיל בברכותיו של הקב"ה מסיים בברכותיו של הקב"ה. במנחתא דתעניתא מאי אמרי? אמר רב אחא בר יעקב: "אם עונינו ענו בנו ה' עשה למען (ירמיה יד) שמך", "מקוה ישראל מושיעו בעת צרה (שם) למה תהיה כגר בארץ" וגו', "למה תהיה כאיש נדהם כגבור לא יוכל להושיע" וגו'. בנעילה

רש"י

מה שהבטחתנו. שמספים על ידינו, כדכתיב: "ואני אברכם" (במדבר ו). לכוף קשרי אצבעותיהם. שפושטין אצבעותיהם כשמברכין, ולאחר שגמרו סוגרין אגרוף שלהם כשאר בני אדם. קשרי אצבע הם החליות שכופפין ופושטין בהם. אין הקורא. שליח צבור שקורא "כהנים" שיחזירו פניהם לברך. אמן. של ברכת הודאה. דיבור. "כהנים". לעקור רגליהם. מן הדוכן, אלא עומדין כפופין לפני התיבה. יש ללמוד מכאן סדר נשיאות כפים כך הוא: עוקר רגליו בעבודה ממקומו, ובא לפני התיבה, ומתפלל "יהי רצון שתהא ברכה" כו' כדלעיל, ומאריך בה עד שתכלה אמן של הודאה מפי צבור. ושליח צבור קורא "כהנים" אם שנים הם, ואם יחיד הוא — אינו קורא, והוא מחזיר פניו מאיליו, כדאביי דאמר לעיל (דף לח.): לא' אין קורא "כהנים". (א) וכשכלה דיבור מפי קורא מברך "אשר קדשנו" כו', ואח"כ מתחילין בברכה, וכשכלה אמן אחרון מפי צבור, הן מחזירין פניהם, וכופפין קשריהם אם רוצים, ושליח צבור מתחיל "שים שלום", והכהנים מתפללין "רבש"ע עשינו מה שגזרת עלינו" כו', ומאריכין בה עד שתכלה ברכה מפי שליח צבור, ועוקרין רגליהם והולכין להם. עד שיכלה אמן. של ברכת התורה. וכל הני — משום דתרי קלי לא משתמעי. עד שתגלל ס"ת. במטפחותיו, כדי שלא יהו הגוללים טרודים מלשמוע הפטרה מפי המפטיר. להפשיט את התיבה בצבור. כל זמן שהצבור בהכ"נ. שהיה דרכם להביא ס"ת מבית אחר שמשתמר בו לבית הכנסת, ופורסין בגדים נאים סביב התיבה ומניחין אותה בתוכה. וכשיוצאין משם ונוטלין ס"ת להוליכו לבית המשתמר בו — לא יפשיטו הבגדים מן התיבה בפני הצבור, שטורח לצבור לעכב שם עם ס"ת, אלא מוליך ס"ת לביתו ומניחו, והעם יוצאים אחריו, ואח"כ הוא בא ומפשיט את התיבה. איכא פיתחא אחרינא. משנטל ס"ת לצאת דרך פתחו, הרוצה לצאת בפתח אחר — יוצא, ואפי' לא יצא ס"ת. ליכא פיתחא אחרינא — נכון שיצא ס"ת תחילה, ולא יצא האדם בפתח לפני ס"ת. בר אהינא אסברה לי. חכם ששמו בר אהינא אסברה לי — הבינני טעמו של דבר. העם מה הם אומרים. שיראו מסבירי פנים, ומודים לפניו על ברכותיו, להראות שהן נוחות להן. ברכו ה' מלאכיו ברכו ה' כל צבאיו ברכו ה' כל מעשיו. שלש מקראות הן, כנגד ג' ברכות. במוספי דשבתא. שהוא נשיאת כפים חדש, שאינו בחול — צריך לחדש את דברי העם. ברוך ה' מציון. אינו באותו מזמור, והיינו דקא פריך: וניימא "יברכך ה' מציון" דכתיב בההוא עניינא!. במנחתא דתעניתא. שנושאין בו כפים. מה שאין כן בשאר מנחות — משום שכרות, כדאמרינן במסכת תענית בפ' בתרא (דף כו:). בהזכרת

תוספות

עד שיכלה אמן מפי הצבור. פירש ר"י: אע"ג דאמרינן בפרק "שלשה שאכלו" (ברכות דף מז.): אין הבוצע רשאי לבצוע עד שיכלה אמן מפי העונין, ואמר רב חסדא: מפי רוב העונין, דכל העונה אמן יותר מדאי אינו אלא טועה. מיהו, לענין ברכת כהנים כיון דמשום לשמוע הוא — לא משתמע כל זמן שעונין, דהוו להו תרי קלי — קולות העונין וקול כהנים המברכים, ולא משתמעי. ואי תקשי לדברי הרב: א"כ לא ישאו שנים כפיהם, דהא אמרינן בפ"ג דמגילה (דף כא:): בתורה אחד קורא ואחד מתרגם, וקתני סיפא דאפי' שנים בנביא אין קורין, וטעמא מפרש בירושלמי דפרק "אין עומדין" משום שאין שני קולות נכנסין באוזן אחד. ואנן אומרים לעיל: לשנים קורא כהנים! אלא מאי אית לך למימר — ברכות, איידי דחביבי להו — יהבו דעתייהו ומשתמעי תרי קלי, כדאמר גבי מגילה: קראוה שנים — יצא. גבי אמן נמי — יהבי דעתייהו, ולישתמע תרי קלי! תריץ: דלא דמו תרי קלי וקורין דבר אחד, לתרי קלי שקורין שני דברים כגון אמן והני ברכות. כדתנן בפרק "ראוהו ב"ד" (ר"ה כו:): שופר של ר"ה של יעל פשוט ופיו מצופה זהב וב' חצוצרות משתי צדדיו, שמצות היום בשופר. ופריך בגמ' (שם כז.): ותרי קלי מי משתמעי? והתניא: "זכור" ו"שמור" בדיבור אחד נאמרו, מה שאין הפה יכול לדבר ומה שאין האוזן יכול לשמוע! ע"כ היכא דהקולות משונות כגון קול אחד "זכור" והשני "שמור" — אין האוזן יכולה לשמוע כלל. וקול שופר וקול חצוצרות י"ל דאין משונין, להכי מסיק התם דמשתמעי איידי דחביבי. אי נמי: בעי דלישמעי נמי הברכה הני דמאריכין באמן, אע"פ שטועין, וכל שעה שהן בעצמן עונין — אין שומעין קול חבריהם. ותפוס לשון אחרון, דהא מסיק התם: תרי קלי מחד גברא לא משתמעי, כגון "זכור" ו"שמור" מפי הגבורה, מתרי גברי משתמעי. משמע, אפי' דומיא ד"זכור" ו"שמור", איידי דחביבי. וקול שופר וקול חצוצרות תרי קלין משונין זה מזה, דומיא ד"זכור" ו"שמור", ומשתמעי איידי דחביב.

במנחתא דתעניתא מאי אמרי. אע"ג דפסקינן בפ' "בשלשה פרקים" (תענית ד' כו:) כר' יוסי דאמר: ליכא נשיאות כפים במנחתא דתעניתא, משום דשכיח שכרות, ואתי לאחלופי בשאר יומי — י"ל: הכא אליבא סתמא דמתני' דהתם בעי, דקתני ד' פעמים ביום. אי נמי אפי' לר' יוסי, כדאמר התם: מאחר דקי"ל כר' יוסי האידנא — מ"ט פרסי כהני ידייהו במנחתא דתעניתא? כיון דסמוך לשקיעת החמה קפרסי בתפלה — כתפלת נעילה דמי. אם עונינו ענו בנו. א"ת: הני פסוקים דמנחתא מאי הסברת פנים איכא בהו? י"ל: משום דהיו מתענין על הצרה שלא תבא על הצבור. ואמר בפ"ק דתענית (דף יב:) ובפ' בתרא דמגילה (דף ל:) דבריבעא בתרא דיומא בעי רחמי, דהיינו ממנחה ואילך, כדכתיב (עזרא ט): "ואני יושב משומם עד מנחת הערב ובמנחת הערב קמתי מתעניתי ובקרעי בגדי ומעילי ואכרע על ברכי ואפרוש כפי אל ה' אלקים". הלכך התירו למבעי רחמי בעידנא דפרסי ידייהו, דעת רצון הוא, וענו ליבורא אמן, כדמשמע בפ' "הרואה" (ברכות נה:): האי מאן דחזי חלמא ולא ידע מאי חזי — ליקו קמי כהני בעידנא דפרסי ידייהו, ולימא: רבון העולמים, חלום חלמתי וכו'. בנעילה

תוספות שאנץ

אין הכהנים רשאין לכוף קשרי אצבעותיהם. פ"ה שכופפין אותן וכו'. עד שיכלה אמן מפי הצבור: אין שליח צבור רשאי להפשיט את התיבה בצבור. פ"ה שהיה דרכם להביא ספר תורה מבית אחר שמשתמר לבית הכנסת ופורסין בגדים נאים סביב התיבה ומניחין אותה בתוכה וכשיוצאין משם ונוטלין ספר תורה להוליכו לבית המשתמר לא יפשיטו הבגדים בפני הצבור שטורח הצבור לעכב שם עם ספר תורה אלא מוליך ספר תורה והעם יוצאין אחריו ואחר כך בא ומפשיט התיבה:

הגהות הב"ח

(א) רש"י ד"ה לעקור וכו' וכשיכלה הדיבור מפי הקורא מברכים אשר:

גליון הש"ס

גמ' מפני כבוד צבור. מגילה דף כב ע"ב יומא ע ע"א גיטין דף ס ע"ב:

[בר"ף וברא"ש בפרק הקורא את המגילה עומד וכן בטור א"ח סי' קמט ליתא להנך שתי תיבות ויניח במקומו וכן נראה מפרש"י דהכא ד"ה איכא פיתחא וכו' שלא היה גרסתם הכי ועיין בב"י ותמצא פרש"י מבואר על דרך זה]

בנעילה דְיוֹמָא דְכִיפּוּרֵי מַאי אָמַר? אָמַר מָר זוּטְרָא, וְאָמְרִי לָהּ בְּמַתְנִיתָא: (א) °"הִנֵּה כִי כֵן יְבֹרַךְ גָּבֶר יְרֵא ה'", "יְבָרֶכְךָ ה' מִצִּיּוֹן וּרְאֵה בְּטוּב יְרוּשָׁלָיִם כֹּל יְמֵי חַיֶּיךָ", "וּרְאֵה בָנִים לְבָנֶיךָ שָׁלוֹם עַל יִשְׂרָאֵל". הֵיכָן אוֹמְרָן? רַב יוֹסֵף אָמַר: בֵּין כָּל בְּרָכָה וּבְרָכָה, וְרַב שֵׁשֶׁת אָמַר: בְּהַזְכָּרַת הַשֵּׁם. פְּלִיגִי בָּהּ רַב מָרִי וְרַב זְבִיד; חַד אָמַר: פְּסוּקָא לְקָבֵל פְּסוּקָא, וְחַד אָמַר: אַכָּל פְּסוּקָא אָמַר לְהוּ לְכוּלְּהוּ. א"ר חִיָּיא בַּר אַבָּא: כָּל הָאוֹמְרָן בַּגְּבוּלִין — אֵינוֹ אֶלָּא טוֹעֶה. אָמַר רַבִּי חֲנִינָא בַּר פַּפָּא: תֵּדַע דְּבַמִּקְדָּשׁ נַמִּי לָא מִיבָּעֵי לְמֵימְרִינְהוּ, אכְּלוּם יֵשׁ לְךָ עֶבֶד שֶׁמְּבָרְכִין אוֹתוֹ וְאֵינוֹ מַאֲזִין? א"ר אַחָא בַּר חֲנִינָא: תֵּדַע דְּבַגְּבוּלִין נַמִּי מִיבָּעֵי לְמֵימְרִינְהוּ, כְּלוּם יֵשׁ עֶבֶד שֶׁמְּבָרְכִין אוֹתוֹ וְאֵין מַסְבִּיר פָּנִים? א"ר אֲבָהוּ: מֵרֵישׁ הֲוָה אָמִינָא לְהוּ, כֵּיוָן דַּחֲזֵינָא לֵיהּ לְרַבִּי אַבָּא דְּמִן עַכּוֹ דְּלָא אָמַר לְהוּ — אֲנָא נַמִּי לָא אָמִינָא לְהוּ. וְאָמַר רַבִּי אֲבָהוּ: מֵרֵישׁ הֲוָה אָמִינָא עִינְוְתָנָא אֲנָא, כֵּיוָן דַּחֲזֵינָא לֵיהּ לְרַבִּי אַבָּא דְּמִן עַכּוֹ דַּאֲמַר אִיהוּ חַד טַעְמָא וַאֲמַר אָמוֹרֵיהּ חַד טַעְמָא, וְלָא קָפֵיד — אָמִינָא לָאו עִינְוְתָנָא אֲנָא. וּמַאי עִינְוְתָנוּתֵיהּ דְּרַבִּי אֲבָהוּ? דְּאָמְרָה לָהּ דְּבֵיתְהוּ דְּאָמוֹרֵיהּ דְּרַבִּי אֲבָהוּ לִדְבֵיתְהוּ דְּרַבִּי אֲבָהוּ: הָא דִּידַן לָא צָרִיךְ לֵיהּ לְדִידָךְ, וְהַאי דְּגָחֵין וְזָקֵיף עֲלֵיהּ — יְקָרָא בְּעָלְמָא הוּא דְּעָבֵיד לֵיהּ. אָזְלָא דְּבֵיתְהוּ וְאָמְרָה לֵיהּ לְרַבִּי אֲבָהוּ. אֲמַר לָהּ: וּמַאי נָפְקָא לִיךְ מִינָּהּ? מִינַּי וּמִינֵּיהּ יִתְקַלֵּס עִילָּאָה. וְתוּ, רַבִּי אֲבָהוּ אִימְנוּ רַבָּנַן עֲלֵיהּ לְמַמְנְיֵיהּ בְּרֵישָׁא. כֵּיוָן דַּחֲזְיֵיהּ לר' אַבָּא דְּמִן עַכּוֹ (ב) דִּנְפִישֵׁי לֵיהּ בַּעֲלֵי חוֹבוֹת, אֲמַר לְהוּ: *אִיכָּא רַבָּה. ר' אֲבָהוּ וְר' חִיָּיא בַּר אַבָּא אִיקְּלְעוּ לְהַהוּא אַתְרָא, רַבִּי אֲבָהוּ דָּרֵשׁ בְּאַגַּדְתָּא, רַבִּי חִיָּיא בַּר אַבָּא דָּרֵשׁ בִּשְׁמַעְתָּא. שַׁבְקוּהּ כּוּלֵּי עָלְמָא לְרַבִּי חִיָּיא בַּר אַבָּא, וַאֲזוּל לְגַבֵּיהּ דר' אֲבָהוּ. חֲלַשׁ דַּעְתֵּיהּ. אָמַר לֵיהּ: אֶמְשׁוֹל לְךָ מָשָׁל לְמָה הַדָּבָר דּוֹמֶה — לִשְׁנֵי בְּנֵי אָדָם, אֶחָד מוֹכֵר אֲבָנִים טוֹבוֹת וְאֶחָד מוֹכֵר מִינֵי סִידְקִית, עַל מִי קוֹפְצִין — לֹא עַל זֶה שֶׁמּוֹכֵר מִינֵי סִידְקִית? כָּל יוֹמָא הֲוָה מְלַוֵּה רַבִּי חִיָּיא בַּר אַבָּא לְרַבִּי אֲבָהוּ עַד אוּשְׁפִּיזֵיהּ מִשּׁוּם יְקָרָא דְּבֵי קֵיסָר. הַהוּא יוֹמָא אַלְוְיֵיהּ רַבִּי אֲבָהוּ לְרַבִּי חִיָּיא בַּר אַבָּא עַד אוּשְׁפִּיזֵיהּ, וַאֲפִילּוּ הָכִי לָא אִיתוֹתַב דַּעְתֵּיהּ מִינֵּיהּ. בִּזְמַן שֶׁשְּׁלִיחַ צִבּוּר אוֹמֵר מוֹדִים, הָעָם מָה הֵם אוֹמְרִים? אָמַר רַב: מוֹדִים אֲנַחְנוּ לָךְ ה' אֱלֹהֵינוּ עַל שֶׁאָנוּ מוֹדִים לָךְ. וּשְׁמוּאֵל אָמַר: אֱלֹהֵי כָל בָּשָׂר עַל שֶׁאָנוּ מוֹדִים לָךְ. רַבִּי סִימַאי אוֹמֵר: יוֹצְרֵנוּ יוֹצֵר בְּרֵאשִׁית עַל שֶׁאָנוּ מוֹדִים לָךְ. נְהַרְדְּעֵי אָמְרִי מִשְּׁמֵיהּ דְּרַבִּי סִימַאי: בְּרָכוֹת וְהוֹדָאוֹת לְשִׁמְךָ הַגָּדוֹל עַל שֶׁהֶחֱיִיתָנוּ וְקִיַּמְתָּנוּ עַל שֶׁאָנוּ מוֹדִים לָךְ. רַב אַחָא בַּר יַעֲקֹב מְסַיֵּים בָּהּ הָכִי: כֵּן תְּחַיֵּינוּ וּתְחָנֵּנוּ וּתְקַבְּצֵנוּ וְתֶאֱסוֹף גָּלֻיּוֹתֵינוּ לְחַצְרוֹת קָדְשֶׁךָ, לִשְׁמוֹר חוּקֶּיךָ וְלַעֲשׂוֹת רְצוֹנְךָ בְּלֵבָב שָׁלֵם, עַל שֶׁאָנוּ מוֹדִים לָךְ. אָמַר רַב פַּפָּא: בהִילְכָּךְ נֵימְרִינְהוּ לְכוּלְּהוּ. אָמַר ר' יִצְחָק: לְעוֹלָם תְּהֵא אֵימַת צִבּוּר עָלֶיךָ, שֶׁהֲרֵי כֹּהֲנִים פְּנֵיהֶם כְּלַפֵּי הָעָם וַאֲחוֹרֵיהֶם כְּלַפֵּי שְׁכִינָה. רַב נַחְמָן אָמַר מֵהָכָא: °"וַיָּקָם *הַמֶּלֶךְ דָּוִד עַל רַגְלָיו וַיֹּאמֶר שְׁמָעוּנִי אַחַי וְעַמִּי", אִם אַחַי לָמָּה עַמִּי, וְאִם עַמִּי לָמָּה אַחַי? אָמַר רַבִּי אֶלְעָזָר: אָמַר לָהֶם דָּוִד לְיִשְׂרָאֵל: אִם אַתֶּם שׁוֹמְעִין לִי — אַחַי אַתֶּם, וְאִם לָאו — עַמִּי אַתֶּם, וַאֲנִי רוֹדֶה אֶתְכֶם בְּמַקֵּל. רַבָּנַן אָמְרִי מֵהָכָא:* (ג) גדְּאֵין הַכֹּהֲנִים רַשָּׁאִין לַעֲלוֹת בְּסַנְדְּלֵיהֶן לַדּוּכָן, דוְזֶהוּ אַחַת מִתֵּשַׁע תַּקָּנוֹת שֶׁהִתְקִין רַבָּן יוֹחָנָן בֶּן זַכַּאי. מַאי טַעְמָא — לָאו מִשּׁוּם כְּבוֹד צִבּוּר? אָמַר רַב אַשִׁי: לָא, הָתָם שֶׁמָּא נִפְסְקָה לוֹ רְצוּעָה בְּסַנְדָּלוֹ וַהֲדַר אָזֵיל לְמִקְטְרֵיהּ, וְאָמְרִי: בֶּן גְּרוּשָׁה אוֹ בֶּן חֲלוּצָה הוּא. § "וּבַמִּקְדָּשׁ בְּרָכָה אַחַת" כו'. §
וְכָל

תהלים קכח (beside the verse הנה כי כן)

דה"א כח (beside ויקם המלך דוד); בקרא כתיב דויד המלך

ר"ה לא: (beside דאין הכהנים)

רש"י

בְּהַזְכָּרַת הַשֵּׁם. כְּשֶׁהַכֹּהֲנִים מַזְכִּירִין אֶת הַשֵּׁם. פְּסוּקָא לְקָבֵל פְּסוּקָא. שֶׁהַכֹּהֲנִים אוֹמְרִים פָּסוּק רִאשׁוֹן וְהֵם אוֹמְרִים אֶחָד מֵאֵלּוּ. וּבַשֵּׁנִי הָיוּ אוֹמְרִים אֶת הַשֵּׁנִי, וּבַשְּׁלִישִׁי אֶת הַשְּׁלִישִׁי. וְכֵן בְּמוּסָף וְכֵן בְּמִנְחָה, שֶׁהֲרֵי כּוּלָּן שְׁלֹשָׁה שְׁלֹשָׁה הֵם. אֵינוֹ אֶלָּא טוֹעֶה. שֶׁלֹּא נִתְקְנוּ לוֹמַר אֶלָּא לִכְבוֹד שֵׁם הַמְיוּחָד הַנִּזְכָּר בַּמִּקְדָּשׁ. וְאֵינוֹ מַסְבִּיר פָּנִים. לְהַרְאוֹת שֶׁבִּרְכַּת רַבּוֹ חֲשׁוּבָה לוֹ וַעֲרֵיבָה עָלָיו, וְתִגָּמֵל לְרַבּוֹ עָלָיו בְּכָךְ. אָמוֹרֵיהּ. הַמְתַרְגֵּם לָרַבִּים מַה שֶּׁהוּא לוֹחֵשׁ לוֹ בִּשְׁעַת הַדְּרָשָׁה. לָא צָרִיךְ לְדִידָךְ. חָכָם הוּא כְּמוֹ בַּעֲלֵיךְ. יְקָרָא דְּמַלְכוּתָא. (ד) שֶׁהֲרֵי רַבִּי אֲבָהוּ נְשׂוּא פָנִים בְּבֵית הַמֶּלֶךְ, כִּדְאָמְרִי' בַּחֲגִיגָה (דף יד.): "נְשׂוּא פָנִים" — כְּגוֹן ר' אֲבָהוּ בֵּי קֵיסָר. וּבְסַנְהֶדְרִין (דף יד.) אָמַר דַּהֲווּ נָפְקִי אֲמְהָתָא דְּבֵי קֵיסָר לְאַפֵּיהּ, וּמְשָׁרְיָן קַמֵּיהּ "רַבָּה דְּעַמֵּיהּ מַדְבְּרָנָא דְאוּמָּתֵיהּ". וְתוּ רַבָּנַן אִימְנוּ עֲלֵיהּ. וְעוֹד זוֹ מֵעַנְוְותָנוּתוֹ. דִּנְפִישֵׁי עֲלֵיהּ חוֹבוֹת. שֶׁהָיָה צָרִיךְ לִלְווֹת. אָמַר ר' אֲבָהוּ אִית לָן רַבָּה. חָכָם גָּדוֹל, וְרָאוּי לֵישֵׁב בָּרֹאשׁ יוֹתֵר מִמֶּנִּי — כְּדֵי שֶׁיּוֹשִׁיבוּהוּ בָּרֹאשׁ. וְנוֹתְנִין לוֹ מָנוֹת. וּמַעֲשִׁירִין אוֹתוֹ כְּדֵי שֶׁיְּהֵא חָשׁוּב וְיִשְׁמְעוּ דְּבָרָיו, כִּדְתַנְיָא: "וְהַכֹּהֵן הַגָּדוֹל מֵאֶחָיו" — גַּדְּלוּהוּ מִשֶּׁל אֶחָיו (יומא דף יח.). ה"ג רַבִּי אֲבָהוּ דָּרֵשׁ בְּאַגַּדְתָּא שְׁמַעְתָּא. הֲלָכוֹת; דִּינִין, וְאִיסּוּר, וּטְהָרוֹת. סִידְקִית. כְּלֵי מְלָאכוֹת נָשִׁים וַעֲנִיִּים, כְּגוֹן פְּלָכִים מְחָטִין וְצִינּוֹרוֹת. לֹא עַל מוֹכֵר סִידְקִית. בִּתְמִיָּה. מִתּוֹךְ שֶׁדְּמֵיהֶם קַלִּים יֵשׁ לָהֶם קוֹנִים הַרְבֵּה. וּלְהָפִיס דַּעְתּוֹ הוּא אוֹמֵר. עַל שֶׁאָנוּ מוֹדִים לָךְ. עַל שֶׁנָּתַתָּ בְּלִבֵּנוּ לִהְיוֹת (מוֹדִים לָךְ) דְּבוּקִים בְּךָ וּמוֹדִים לָךְ. רַבִּי סִימַאי. מוֹסִיף הוּא. וְכֵן כּוּלָּם מוֹסִיפִין הֵן עַל הָרִאשׁוֹנִים. שְׁמָעוּנִי אַחַי וְעַמִּי. מַזְהִירָם הָיָה לְהִתְנַדֵּב לְבֶדֶק הַבַּיִת לְבִנְיַן הַמִּקְדָּשׁ. אִם אַתֶּם שׁוֹמְעִים לִי. לִהְיוֹת שְׁלֵמִים לַמָּקוֹם — אַחַיי וַחֲבֵרַיי אַתֶּם. אַלְמָא, הַמֶּלֶךְ אֵימַת צִבּוּר עָלָיו אִם כְּשֵׁרִים הֵם. עַמִּי אַתֶּם. כְּבוּשִׁים תַּחְתַּי. לָאו מִשּׁוּם אֵימְתָא דְּצִיבּוּרָא. מִפְּנֵי שֶׁמִּסְתַּלְּקִין בְּגָדָיו הָעֲשׂוּיִין לְמִדָּתוֹ בַּהַגְבָּהַת יָדָיו, וְנִרְאִין סַנְדָּלָיו לַצִּבּוּר, וְהֵן אֵין רְאוּיִן לֵרָאוֹת, מִפְּנֵי טִיט שֶׁעֲלֵיהֶן. דִּילְמָא מִפְּסְקָא רְצוּעָה. וּגְנַאי הוּא לְעַצְמוֹ, וּמִתְלוֹצְצִים עָלָיו כְּשֶׁסַּנְדָּלוֹ מוּתֶּרֶת וְיָתֵיב לְמִקְטְרֵיהּ, וַחֲבֵירָיו מְבָרְכִין, וְאָתֵי לְמֵימַר: אֵינוֹ רָאוּי לִנְשִׂיאוּת כַּפַּיִם, וְהָלַךְ וְיָשַׁב לוֹ.
וְכָל

ס"א ל"ג (beside מודים לך)

ס"א אית לכו נ"א א"ל עד דמצלנא ליה לרבי אבא לא אתא עד דאציל ליה

תוספות

בנעילה דיומא דכיפורי מאי אמר. לא ידענא אמאי לא אמר בנעילה דתענית כי היכא דאמר במנחתא דתעניתא, דהא משמע בגמרא בפ' "בשלשה פרקים" (תענית כו:) דבתענית הוה נמי נעילה, אבל מוסף לא הוה בהו!

כל האומרם בגבולין אינו אלא טועה. פירש ר"י: אע"ג דאמרי' בפרק "הרואה" (ברכות נה:): האי מאן דחזי חלמא וכו' — דהתם משום סכנה התירו, שמא חלום מסוכן הוא שצריך רפואה, דהא אפילו בשבת התירו להתענות תענית חלום. פירש ר"ח: הני כולהו, רבי חייא בר אבא ודרבי חיננא בר פפא ודרבי אבהו — הילכתא נינהו.

על שאנחנו מודים לך. בערוך בערך הודאה פירש רב משה ראש ישיבה בן מרנא יעקב: דקא מודו צבור — על שליח צבור אינון סומכין, ומאי "על שאנו מודים לך" — על ההודאה דקאמר שליח צבור, וקא ענו אינון אמן. בירושלמי פ"ק דברכות איתא נמי: רבי אבא ב"ר זבדא בשם רב: מודים אנחנו לך שאנו חייבין להודות לך שמך, תרננה שפתי כי אזמרה לך וגו', בא"י האל ההודאות. ר' שמואל ב"ר אויא בשם רבי אחא: הודייה ושבח לשמך הגדול, לך גבורה לך תפארת, יהי רצון מלפניך ה' אלהינו ואלהי אבותינו שתסמכנו בתפלתנו, ותזקפנו מכפיפתנו, כי אתה הוא סומך נופלים וזוקף כפופים מלא רחמים ואין עוד מלבדך, בא"י האל ההודאות. בר קפרא אומר: לך כריעה לך ברכה לך כפופה לך השתחויה, כי לך תכרע כל ברך, וכל לשון לך תשבע, לך ה' הגדולה והגבורה וגו' והעושר והכבוד מלפניך וגו', ועתה ה' אלהינו בכל לב ובכל נפש לך משתחוים, כל עצמותי תאמרנה ה' מי כמוך, בא"י האל ההודאות. אמר רבי יודן: נהגין אמרי רבנן כולהון. ואית דאמר: או *אדה או אדה או אדה.

[נ"ל הדא או הדא]

שמא תפסוק רצועה בסנדלו. פירש ר"ח: שמע מינה דמותר ליכנס בבית הכנסת בסנדל ובמנעל, דלא אסרו אלא שלא לעלות לדוכן בסנדל. ורבי הביא כמו כן מפרק שלישי דמגילה (דף כד:): האומר איני עובר לפני התיבה בסנדל — אף יחף לא יעבור. אלמא דאפילו לפני התיבה מותר לעבור בסנדל. והכי מסיק בהדיא בפרק "הרואה" (ברכות דף סג.), אמר רבא: מה ביתו — אקפנדריא קפיד איניש, ארקיקה ואמנעל לא קפיד איניש, אף בית הכנסת — קפנדריא אסור, ורקיקה ומנעל שרי.
וכל

עין משפט נר מצוה

סד א מיי' פי"ד מהל' נשיאות כפים הלכה ז סמג עשין כ טוש"ע א"ח סימן קכח סעיף כו:

סה ב מיי' פ"ט מהל' תפלה הלכה ד סמג עשין יט טוש"ע א"ח סי' קכז סעיף א [וברב אלפס ברכות פ"ג דף טו: וברא"ש שם סי' כ]:

סו ג מיי' פי"ד מהל' נשיאות כפים הל' ו סמג עשין כ טוש"ע א"ח סי' קכח סעיף ה:

סז ד מיי' שם הלכה ו וע"ש בכ"מ:

הגהות הב"ח

(א) גמ' במתניתא תנא הנה: (ב) שם דמן עכו (דנפישי) תז"מ ונ"ב ס"א דתפישי: (ג) שם מהכא דת"ר אין הכהנים: (ד) רש"י ד"ה יקרא דמלכות שהיה ר' אבהו:

גליון הש"ס

גמ' אמר רב פפא הילכך נימרינהו לכולהו. כעין זה שבת דף כ ע"א חולין דף סה ע"א ובדף עו ע"ב:

וְכָל כָּךְ לָמָּה — *לְפִי שֶׁאֵין עוֹנִין אָמֵן בַּמִּקְדָּשׁ. תָּנוּ רַבָּנַן: מִנַּיִן שֶׁאֵין עוֹנִין אָמֵן בַּמִּקְדָּשׁ — שֶׁנֶּאֱ': °"קוּמוּ וּבָרְכוּ אֶת ה' אֱלֹהֵיכֶם מִן הָעוֹלָם וְעַד הָעוֹלָם". וּמִנַּיִן שֶׁעַל כָּל בְּרָכָה וּבְרָכָה תְּהִלָּה — שֶׁנֶּאֱמַר: °["וִיבָרְכוּ שֵׁם כְּבוֹדֶךָ] וּמְרוֹמַם עַל כָּל בְּרָכָה וּתְהִלָּה", עַל כָּל בְּרָכָה וּבְרָכָה תֵּן לוֹ תְּהִלָּה.§ **מתני'** בִּרְכוֹת כֹּהֵן גָּדוֹל כֵּיצַד? *[א]חַזַּן הַכְּנֶסֶת נוֹטֵל סֵפֶר תּוֹרָה וְנוֹתְנָהּ לוֹ לְרֹאשׁ הַכְּנֶסֶת, וְרֹאשׁ הַכְּנֶסֶת נוֹתְנָהּ לַסְּגָן, וְהַסְּגָן נוֹתְנָהּ לְכֹהֵן גָּדוֹל, וְכ"ג עוֹמֵד וּמְקַבֵּל, וְקוֹרֵא °"אַחֲרֵי מוֹת" °וְ"אַךְ בֶּעָשׂוֹר", וְגוֹלֵל אֶת הַתּוֹרָה וּמַנִּיחָהּ בְּחֵיקוֹ, וְאוֹמֵר: יָתֵר מִמַּה שֶׁקָּרִיתִי לִפְנֵיכֶם כָּתוּב כָּאן. °"וּבֶעָשׂוֹר" שֶׁבְּחוּמַּשׁ הַפְּקוּדִים קוֹרֵא עַל פֶּה. וּמְבָרֵךְ עָלֶיהָ שְׁמֹנֶה בְּרָכוֹת: עַל הַתּוֹרָה, וְעַל הָעֲבוֹדָה, וְעַל הַהוֹדָיָה, וְעַל מְחִילַת הֶעָוֹן, וְעַל הַמִּקְדָּשׁ, וְעַל יִשְׂרָאֵל, וְעַל הַכֹּהֲנִים, וְעַל יְרוּשָׁלַיִם, *וְהַשְּׁאָר תְּפִלָּה.§ **גמ'** *שָׁמְעַתְּ מִינָּהּ חוֹלְקִין כָּבוֹד לְתַלְמִיד בִּמְקוֹם הָרַב. אָמַר אַבַּיֵי: כּוּלָּהּ מִשּׁוּם כְּבוֹדוֹ דְּכ"ג הוּא.§ "וְכ"ג עוֹמֵד וּמְקַבֵּל וְקוֹרֵא" וכו'.§ עוֹמֵד — מִכְּלָל דְּיוֹשֵׁב הוּא? וְהָאָמַר מָר: *[ב]אֵין יְשִׁיבָה בָּעֲזָרָה אֶלָּא לְמַלְכֵי בֵית דָּוִד בִּלְבַד, שֶׁנֶּאֱמַר: °"וַיָּבֹא הַמֶּלֶךְ דָּוִד וַיֵּשֶׁב לִפְנֵי ה' וַיֹּאמֶר מִי אָנֹכִי" וגו'! כְּדְאָמַר רַב חִסְדָּא: בְּעֶזְרַת נָשִׁים, [ג]הָכָא נַמִי — בְּעֶזְרַת נָשִׁים.[א] מֵיתִיבֵי: וְהֵיכָן קוֹרִין בּוֹ — *בָּעֲזָרָה, רַבִּי אֱלִיעֶזֶר בֶּן יַעֲקֹב אוֹמֵר: בְּהַר הַבַּיִת, שֶׁנֶּאֱ': וַיִּקְרָא

נחמיה ט | שם | ויקרא טז | ויקרא כג | במדבר כט | ש"ב ז

תורה אור

וְכָל כָּךְ לָמָּה. שֶׁבַּמִּקְדָּשׁ אוֹמֵר אֶת שְׁלָשְׁתָּן בְּרָכָה אַחַת? שֶׁאֵין עוֹנִין אָמֵן בַּמִּקְדָּשׁ. וְאֵין כָּאן בַּמֶּה לְהַפְסִיק. קוּמוּ וּבָרְכוּ אֶת ה' אֱלֹהֵיכֶם מִן הָעוֹלָם וְעַד הָעוֹלָם. בְּסֵפֶר עֶזְרָא כְּתִיב, שֶׁכָּל בְּרָכָה שֶׁהָיוּ מְבָרְכִין בַּמִּקְדָּשׁ כָּךְ הָיוּ מְבָרְכִין: "בָּרוּךְ ה' אֱלֹהֵי יִשְׂרָאֵל מִן הָעוֹלָם וְעַד הָעוֹלָם" לְמָגֵן אַבְרָהָם, וְכֵן לִמְחַיֵּה הַמֵּתִים. **וִיבָרְכוּ שֵׁם כְּבוֹדֶךָ.** וּשְׁאָר הָעָם יַעֲנוּ: בשכמל"ו, שֶׁהָעָם עוֹנִין לְהַלֵּל וּלְהוֹדוֹת. **מתני'** בִּרְכוֹת כ"ג. בְּיוֹם הַכִּפּוּרִים, לְאַחַר שֶׁכָּלְתָה עֲבוֹדַת הַיּוֹם קוֹרֵא בַּתּוֹרָה, כִּדְמְפָרֵשׁ וְאָזֵיל, וּמְבָרֵךְ שְׁמֹנֶה בְּרָכוֹת, כִּדְבָעֵינַן לְמֵימַר לְקַמָּן. **חַזַּן הַכְּנֶסֶת.** שַׁמָּשׁ הַכְּנֶסֶת, שֶׁטּוֹרַח עִיסְקֵי הַכְּנֶסֶת עָלָיו: לְהַכְנִיס וּלְהוֹצִיא, וּלְהַפְשִׁיט אֶת הַתֵּיבָה, וּלְהָכִין הַכֹּל. **רֹאשׁ הַכְּנֶסֶת.** עַל פִּיו נֶחְתָּכִין דִּבְרֵי הַכְּנֶסֶת: מִי יַפְטִיר בְּנָבִיא, מִי יִפְרוֹס עַל שְׁמַע, מִי יֵרֵד לִפְנֵי הַתֵּיבָה. **סְגָן.** הַמּוּכָן תַּחַת כ"ג, שֶׁאִם יֶאֱרַע בּוֹ פְּסוּל — יְשַׁמֵּשׁ תַּחְתָּיו. **וְקוֹרֵא אַחֲרֵי מוֹת.** שֶׁהוּא סֵדֶר יוֹם הַכִּפּוּרִים. וּפָרָשָׁה רִאשׁוֹנָה לְחוּדָהּ קָאָמַר. **וְאַךְ בֶּעָשׂוֹר.** פָּרָשַׁת "שׁוֹר אוֹ כֶשֶׂב" הַסְּמוּכָה הִיא לְ"אַחֲרֵי מוֹת", וְיָכוֹל לִגְלוֹל ס"ת לְשָׁם בְּעוֹד שֶׁהַתּוּרְגְּמָן מְתַרְגֵּם מִקְרָא אַחֲרוֹן שֶׁל פָּרָשַׁת "אַחֲרֵי מוֹת" וְאֵין כָּאן שְׁהוּת כְּדֵי שֶׁיַּפְסִיק מְתַרְגֵּם, וְאֵין כָּאן גְּנַאי לַצִּבּוּר. **וְגוֹלֵל אֶת הַתּוֹרָה.** וְאַעַ"פ שֶׁעֲדַיִין יִקְרָא "בֶּעָשׂוֹר" שֶׁל חוּמַּשׁ הַפְּקוּדִים — עַל פֶּה יִקְרָא אוֹתָהּ, וְלֹא יִגְלוֹל ס"ת לְשָׁם, מִפְּנֵי שֶׁהוּא רָחוֹק, וְיֵשׁ שְׁהוּת שֶׁיַּפְסִיק מְתַרְגֵּם וְיִשְׁתּוֹק לִפְנֵיהֶם וְאֵין מַתְחִיל בְּפָסוּק אַחֵר, וְאִיכָּא גְּנַאי. **וְאוֹמֵר יָתֵר מִמַּה שֶּׁקָּרִיתִי לִפְנֵיכֶם כָּתוּב כָּאן.** אַעַ"פ שֶׁאֲנִי עָתִיד לִקְרוֹת עוֹד פָּרָשָׁה שְׁלִישִׁית, אַל תְּדַמּוּ לוֹמַר שֶׁחֲסֵירָה הִיא מִן הַסֵּפֶר הַזֶּה וּלְכָךְ אֲנִי גּוֹלְלוֹ, דְּיוֹתֵר מִמַּה שֶׁקָּרִיתִי לִפְנֵיכֶם בְּעִנְיַן הַיּוֹם כָּתוּב בּוֹ. וּבַגְּמָרָא בָּעֵי: כָּל כָּךְ לָמָּה? וּמְשַׁנִּינַן: שֶׁלֹּא לְהוֹצִיא לַעַז עַל סֵפֶר תּוֹרָה. **עַל הַתּוֹרָה.** בְּרָכָה שֶׁל אַחֲרֶיהָ, **וְעַל הָעֲבוֹדָה** — רְצֵה. **וְעַל הַהוֹדָאָה** — מוֹדִים. לְפִי שֶׁנִּגְמְרָה הָעֲבוֹדָה, וְאֵין עֲבוֹדָה בְּלֹא הוֹדָאָה, כִּדְאָמְרִי' בְּמַסֶּכֶת מְגִילָּה (דף יח.): "זוֹבֵחַ תּוֹדָה יְכַבְּדָנְנִי" — אַחַר זְבִיחָה הוֹדָאָה. **וְעַל מְחִילַת הֶעָוֹן.** "אַתָּה בְחַרְתָּנוּ", שֶׁחוֹתֵם "מֶלֶךְ מוֹחֵל וְסוֹלֵחַ לַעֲוֹנוֹתֵינוּ וְלַעֲוֹנוֹת עַמּוֹ" וגו'. **וְעַל הַמִּקְדָּשׁ.** מִתְפַּלֵּל עַל הַמִּקְדָּשׁ, וְחוֹתֵם בְּ"בָרוּךְ אֲשֶׁר בָּחַר בַּמִּקְדָּשׁ". **וְעַל יִשְׂרָאֵל.** מִתְפַּלֵּל עַל יִשְׂרָאֵל, וְחוֹתֵם "בָּרוּךְ הַבּוֹחֵר בְּעַמּוֹ יִשְׂרָאֵל". וְכֵן עַל יְרוּשָׁלַיִם. וּבְמַסֶּכֶת סוֹטָה יְרוּשַׁלְמִית מְפָרֵשׁ לָהּ. **וְעַל שְׁאָר הַתְּפִלָּה.** בַּגְּמָרָא מְפָרֵשׁ לָהּ. **גמ'** **שְׁמַע מִינָּהּ.** מִדְּקָתָנֵי: חַזַּן הַכְּנֶסֶת נוֹטֵל סֵפֶר תּוֹרָה וְנוֹתְנוֹ לְרֹאשׁ הַכְּנֶסֶת כו', וְאֵין חַזַּן הַכְּנֶסֶת נוֹתְנָהּ לְכ"ג, אֶלָּא מְכַבֵּד אֶת רֹאשׁ הַכְּנֶסֶת בִּפְנֵי הַסְּגָן וּבִפְנֵי כֹּהֵן גָּדוֹל, וְרֹאשׁ הַכְּנֶסֶת מְכַבֵּד הַסְּגָן בִּפְנֵי כ"ג — ש"מ חוֹלְקִין כָּבוֹד לְתַלְמִיד; תַּלְמִיד קָטָן חוֹלֵק כָּבוֹד לְתַלְמִיד גָּדוֹל מִמֶּנּוּ, וְאַעַ"פ שֶׁהָרַב שָׁם, וְאֵין גְּנַאי לָרַב. וּסְתָמָא כְּמ"ד חוֹלְקִין, דִּפְלוּגְתָּא הִיא בְּ"יֵשׁ נוֹחֲלִין" גַּבֵּי בְּנוֹת צְלָפְחָד (ב"ב קיט:). **כּוּלָּהּ מִשּׁוּם כְּבוֹדוֹ דְּכ"ג.** וּלְעוֹלָם אֵין חוֹלְקִין. וְהָכָא כּוּלָּהּ מִשּׁוּם יְקָרָא דְּכ"ג הוּא, שֶׁמַּרְאִין אֶת חֲוָלוֹתָיו, מַעֲלָה לְמַעְלָה מִמַּעֲלָה. **אֵין יְשִׁיבָה בָּעֲזָרָה.** דְּאֵין כָּבוֹד שָׁמַיִם בְּכָךְ, וַאֲפִי' מַלְאֲכֵי הַשָּׁרֵת אֵין לָהֶם שָׁם יְשִׁיבָה, דִּכְתִיב (ישעיה ו): "עוֹמְדִים מִמַּעַל לוֹ", ["קִרְבֵת] עַל חַד מִן קָאֲמַיָּא" (דניאל ז). **אֶלָּא לְמַלְכֵי בֵית דָּוִד.** שֶׁחָלַק לָהֶם הַמָּקוֹם כָּבוֹד, לְהַרְאוֹת שֶׁמַּלְכוּתוֹ שְׁלֵימָה. **כִּדְאָמַר רַב חִסְדָּא.** לְקַמָּן. **בְּעֶזְרַת נָשִׁים.** הָיוּ קוֹרִין בּוֹ. וְהִיא הָיְתָה חוֹל כִּשְׁאָר הַר הַבַּיִת, שֶׁלֹּא נִתְקַדֵּשׁ אֶלָּא מִן הַחוֹמָה וְלִפְנִים. וַאֲפִילוּ חֲלַל שַׁעַר נִקָּנוֹר הָעוֹלֶה מֵעֶזְרַת נָשִׁים לְעֶזְרַת יִשְׂרָאֵל לֹא נִתְקַדֵּשׁ. וַיִּקְרָא

וכל כך למה לפי שאין עונין אמן במקדש. תימה: והלא היו עונין "ברוך שכמל"ו" כשהיו שומעים שם הקדוש, כדתנן בפרק "אמר להן הממונה" (יומא דף לה:) ובפרק "טרף בקלפי" (שם דף לט.), וזה היה הפסק גדול מעניית אמן! ועוד: שהיו נופלין על פניהם. שהרי כשהיו שומעין את השם מפי כהן גדול בשעת הגרלה היו נופלין על פניהם, כדאיתא בירושלמי: הקרובים היו נופלין על פניהם, והרחוקים היו אומרים "ברוך שם כבוד מלכותו לעולם ועד", ואלו ואלו לא היו זזין משם עד שהיה מתעלם מהן! ונראה דהתם ה"פ: הקרובים היו נופלים, וכ"ש שהיו אומרים "בשכמל"ו", אבל הרחוקים לא היו נופלין, אלא בלא נפילה היו אומרים, והיה שם הקדוש מתעלם ומשכח מן השומעים קודם שהיו זזין משם. מ"מ קרא חזינן שהיו מפסיקין בענייתן "בשכמל"ו"! ושמא היו עונין "בשכמל"ו" לאלתר, כשהיו שומעין שם הנכבד והנורא, ולא היו ממתינין עד סוף הפסוק. ולפי שלא היו מפסיקין בין פסוק לפסוק — חשוב להו כמו ברכה אחת. **ומנין** שעל כל ברכה תהלה שנא' ומרומם על כל ברכה ותהלה. ואותה תהלה מפרש בפ"ב דמסכת תענית (דף טז:), שהיא "בשכמל"ו".

שמעת מינה חולקין כבוד לתלמיד במקום הרב. פי' הרב ר' יצחק בר מרדכי בפרק "בא לו" (יומא סט:): נראה דאסגן קאי, שמקבל ס"ת מראש הכנסת ואינה מקבלה מחזן בית הכנסת, נמצא שזה חלק לו לסגן כבוד, שראש הכנסת צריך לקבל מיד חזן הכנסת וליתן לסגן. ומשני אביי: כולה משום כבודו דכ"ג, דסופו לקבלה מיד הסגן, אע"פ שסגן חשוב ומכובד — עדיין כהן גדול מעולה ממנו. **שמעת** מינה. וא"ת: אמאי לא משני: כגון דפליג ליה כ"ג יקרא לסגן, וסגן לראש הכנסת, כדפסיק התם ב"יש נוחלין" (ב"ב דף קיט:): והילכתא חולקין והילכתא אין חולקין. קשיא הילכתא אהילכתא. ל"ק; הא — דפליג ליה רביה יקרא, הא — דלא פליג ליה? י"ל: הכא בסתמא קתני, דלעולם היה המנהג כך, בין פליג בין לא פליג. ופלוגתייהו התם נמי בין פליג בין לא פליג. דאי פלוגתייהו בדפליג — לפסוק בהדיא כמ"ד חולקין, ואי בדלא פליג — לפסוק כמ"ד אין חולקין. **והאמר** מר אין ישיבה בעזרה. לא ידעתי מקומו. ומייתי לה בפ"ק דתמיד (דף כז.). ובפ' "עשרה יוחסין" (קדושין עח:), ובפ' ב' דיומא (דף כה.). ובתוספות רבי הראני דב"חלק" (סנהדרין קא:) בגמ' דג' מלכים מקומו. ומורי הרב רבי מאיר בר קלונימוס הראני מקומו בתוספתא דסנהדרין* בפרק "כהן גדול". ונראה דבתוספתא דר' חייא מקומה. דהא מקשה בירושלמי: לא כן תני רבי חייא: לא היתה ישיבה בעזרה אלא למלכי בית דוד. ואמר ר' אמי בשם ר"ל: אף למלכי בית דוד לא היתה ישיבה בעזרה. תיפתר שסמך לו בכותל וישב לו. והכתיב: "ויבא המלך דוד וישב לפני ה'"! אמר ר' אייבו ב"ר נגרי: שישב עצמו בתפלה. תמן תנינן: יצאת כת הראשונה וישבה לה בהר הבית, השניה בחיל, השלישית במקומה. רבי נחמיה בשם ר' מנא: מי תנינן ישבה לה *(לא) במקומה, עמדה לה במקומה. והא דרבי אמי דמייתי בירושלמי דאף למלכי בית דוד לא היתה ישיבה במקומה — בתחילת מדרש שוחר טוב, והתם משמע דלבית דוד היה מתוקן כסא ושם היתה ישיבה. וי"ל שאותו כסא היה חוץ לעזרה. והכי איתא התם: "אשרי האיש" זש"ה "ויבא המלך דוד וישב לפני ה'", וכן תני רבי חייא: אין ישיבה בעזרה אלא למלכות בית דוד. רבי אמי בשם ריש לקיש אמר: אין ישיבה בעזרה אלא במקום מלכות בית דוד בלבד. משמע דבאותו מקום היתה ישיבה לכל אדם, ומינה דייק דכסאו היה נתון חוץ לעזרה, מכלל דאף לעצמו אין ישיבה בעזרה. ותו התם: וכן הוא אומר: "וישב לפני ה'". ולא כן א"ר הונא בשם רבי שמעון: אין ישיבה למעלה, שאין להם קפילת רגל, שנאמר: "ורגליהם רגל ישרה", וכתיב: "שרפים עומדים ממעל לו", וכתיב: "וכל צבא השמים עומדים מימינו ומשמאלו". למעלה אין ישיבה ודוד יושב?! אמר רבי אמי: אף למלכי בית דוד אין להן ישיבה בעזרה. מהו "וישב לפני ה'" — שסמך עצמו לכותל. ולמי היתה ישיבה בעזרה ובהיכל — הוי אומר לכ"ג, שנאמר: "ועלי הכהן יושב על הכסא", אם כן מהו "וישב" — שישב עצמו בתפלה. וקשה לר"י: אם לכ"ג היתה ישיבה, א"כ מאי מקשה הכא? והא אנן בכ"ג קיימינן! ותו *קשיא מפ' שני דזבחים (דף יט:), דאמר התם: כילד קידש — מניח ידו הימנית על גבי רגלו הימנית ומקדש. אמר לו: הפלגת, אי אפשר לעשות כן. שפיר קאמר ליה. אמר רב יוסף: חבירו מסייעו. מאי בינייהו? עמידה מן הצד איכא בינייהו*. כתב

סח א מיי' פ"ג מהל' עבודת יוה"כ הל' י סמג עשין רט:

סט ב מיי' פ"ז מהלכות בית הבחירה הל' ו ופי"ד מהל' סנהדרין הל' יב ופ"ב מהל' מלכים הלכה ד:

ע ג מיי' פ"ג מהלכות עבודת יוה"כ הל' י:

תענית טז: ברכות סג.

רש"א

יומא סח:

[יומא סט. לקמן מא: ב"ב קיט:]

[סנהדרין קא: ע"ש תמיד כז. ע"ש קדושין עח: יומא כה. ע"ש סט:]

[שם ביומא סט: ע"ש תוספתא פ"ז]

נ"א ועל שאר

[פ"ד]

ס"א איתא

[עי' מהרש"א]

הגהות מהר"ב רנשבורג

א] גמ' הכא נמי בעזרת נשים מיתיבי. מלת מיתיבי נמחק ונ"ב דתניא כצ"ל לענ"ד ועי' מה שכתבתי ביומא דף סט ע"ב ועי' שו"ת כנה"ג לא"ח בכללי הגמרא אות פ"א ומ"ש על סוגיין ל"ע:

ופריך וליתב מיתב ומשני אמר קרא לשרת. כצ"ל רש"א

"ויקרא בו לפני הרחוב אשר לפני שער המים"! אמר רב חסדא: בעזרת נשים.§ וקורא "אחרי מות" ו"אך בעשור".§ ורמינהי: *מדלגין בנביא ואין מדלגין בתורה! אמר אביי: לא קשיא, כאן — בכדי שיפסוק התורגמן, כאן — בכדי שלא יפסוק התורגמן. והא עלה קתני: מדלגין בנביא ואין מדלגין בתורה, ועד כמה מדלגין — עד כדי שלא יפסוק התורגמן. מכלל דבתורה כלל כלל לא! אלא אמר אביי: לא קשיא; כאן — בענין אחד, כאן — בשני ענינין, והתניא: מדלגין בתורה בענין אחד, ובנביא בשני ענינין, וכאן וכאן בכדי שלא יפסוק התורגמן. ואין מדלגין מנביא לנביא. ובנביא של שנים עשר — מדלגין, ובלבד שלא ידלג מסוף הספר לתחילתו.§ "וגולל את התורה ומניחה בחיקו" כו'.§ וכל כך למה — שלא להוציא לעז על ס"ת.§ "ובעשור שבחומש הפקודים קורא על פה".§ *וליכרכיה לספר וליקרי! א"ר הונא בר יהודה א"ר ששת: לפי שאין גוללין ס"ת בצבור. וליתי ס"ת אחרינא וליקרי! רב הונא בר יהודה אמר: משום פגמו של ראשון, ר"ש בן לקיש אמר: לפי *שאין מברכין ברכה שאינה צריכה. ומי חיישינן לפגמא? *והאמר רבי יצחק נפחא: ר"ח טבת שחל להיות בשבת מביא שלש תורות, וקורא אחת מעניינו של יום, ואחת של ר"ח, ואחת בשל חנוכה! תלתא גברי בתלתא סיפרי ליכא פגמא, חד גברא בתרי סיפרי — איכא פגמא.§ "ומברך עליה שמנה ברכות" כו'.§ *ת"ר: [מברכין] על התורה כדרך שמברכין בבהכ"נ, ועל העבודה, ועל ההודאה, ועל מחילת עון כתיקנן. על המקדש בפני עצמו, ועל הכהנים בפני עצמן, על ישראל בפני עצמן, ועל ירושלים בפני עצמה.§ "והשאר תפלה".§ *ת"ר: השאר תפלה "תחנה רנה ובקשה שעמך ישראל צריכין ליושע", וחותם ב"שומע תפלה". מכאן ואילך, כל אחד ואחד מביא ספר תורה מתוך ביתו וקורא בו, וכל כך למה — כדי להראות חזותו לרבים.§

מתני' פרשת המלך כיצד? מוצאי יו"ט הראשון של חג, בשמיני, במוצאי שביעית, עושין לו בימה של עץ בעזרה, והוא יושב עליה, שנאמר: "מקץ שבע שנים במועד" וגו'. חזן הכנסת נוטל ס"ת ונותנה לראש הכנסת, וראש הכנסת נותנה לסגן, והסגן נותנה לכהן גדול, וכ"ג נותנה למלך. והמלך עומד ומקבל, וקורא יושב. אגריפס המלך עמד וקבל, וקרא עומד, ושבחוהו חכמים. וכשהגיע "לא תוכל לתת עליך איש נכרי" — זלגו עיניו דמעות. אמרו לו: "אל תתירא אגריפס, אחינו אתה, אחינו אתה"! וקורא מתחילת "אלה הדברים" עד "שמע", ו"שמע", "והיה אם שמוע", "עשר תעשר", "כי תכלה לעשר", ופרשת המלך, וברכות וקללות, עד שגומר כל הפרשה. ברכות שכהן גדול מברך אותן — המלך מברך אותן, אלא שנותן של רגלים תחת מחילת העון.§

גמ' בשמיני סלקא דעתך? אימא: בשמינית. וכל הני למה לי? צריכי, דאי כתב רחמנא "מקץ" — הוה אמינא נימנו מהשתא, ואע"ג דלא מתרמי בשמיטה, כתב רחמנא "שמיטה". ואי כתב רחמנא "שמיטה" — ה"א בסוף שמיטה, כתב רחמנא "במועד". ואי כתב "במועד" — ה"א מריש שתא, כתב רחמנא "בחג הסוכות". ואי כתב רחמנא "בחג הסוכות" — הוה אמינא אפי' יו"ט אחרון, כתב רחמנא "בבוא כל ישראל" — מאתחלתא

רש"י

ויקרא כו'. בספר עזרא כתיב. קתני מיהא לרבנן: בעזרה היו קוראים. מתני' בכדי שלא יפסוק התורגמן הוא. שפרשת "שור או כשב" קרובה לפרשת "אחרי מות", ולא גמר התורגמן לתרגם עד שזה רואה "אך בעשור", ומתחיל כשמפסיק זה. ועד כמה מדלגין. בנביא. כאן בענין אחד. מדלגין בתורה. כגון מתני', דתרווייהו בעניינא דיה"כ נינהו, הילכך מדלגין בכדי שלא יפסוק. וברייתא דקתני דאפי' בכדי שלא יפסוק תורגמן אין מדלגין — בשני עניינין, שזה בענין יום הכפורים וזה ב"צו את אהרן" או בפרשה אחרת. שאין הלב שהוא נמשך אחר ענין אחד ממהר לצאת ממנו, לשמוע ולהבין דברי ענין אחר, הילכך תורה שהמצות תלויות בה ומשמיעין אותה לצבור, ופסוק אחד שלא יבין בו הוא שוכחו ועובר עליו ואינו מקיימו, ובאה חורבה על כך — לכן אין מדלגין מענין לענין, ואפילו אין התורגמן מפסיק. אבל בנביא — שפיר דמי. והתניא. בניחותא. ובנביא בשני ענינין. וכל שכן בענין אחד. ובנביא של שנים עשר מדלגין. מנבואה לחברתה, דכוליה חד ספרא הוא. מסוף הספר לתחלתו. למפרע. וכל כך למה. לו לומר להם? שלא להוציא לעז. שלא יאמרו: פרשה שהוא קורא על פה אינה כתובה בו, וספר משובש הוא. משום פגמו. של ספר תורה ראשון, שלא יאמרו: מצא בו פסול. בעניינו של יום. פרשה של אותה שבת לפי סדר פרשיות התורה. ת"ר השאר תפלה. זו היא, שיש ברכה אחת ובו תפלה תחנה רנה ובקשה שעמך כו'. מכאן ואילך. לאחר שגמר כהן גדול לקרות פרשה בברכותיה, כל אחד מן הצבור מביא ספר תורה מביתו לעזרה. דקסבר: *אין עירוב והוצאה ליום הכפורים. אי נמי, *ירושלים דלתותיה נעולות בלילה ומערבין את כולה. להראות חזותו. של ס"ת, ונויו. דאמר מר (נזיר דף ב:): "זה אלי ואנוהו" — התנאה לפניו במצות, בס"ת נאה, בציצית נאה. מתני' בשמיני. בגמרא פריך: בשמיני ס"ד? הא אמרת: במוצאי יו"ט הראשון! ומשנינן, אימא: בשמינית, במוצאי שביעית, בסוכות שבתחילת שנה שמינית. בימה. אלמבר"א. שנאמר מקץ שבע שנים. בסוף שבע שנים. ואותה קרייה על ידי מלך היא. כדתניא בספרי בפרשת המלך: "את משנה התורה הזאת" — אין קורין ביום הקהל אלא במשנה תורה. וקורא יושב. וקורא בישיבה. אגריפס המלך. מלך ישראל היה, מזרעו של הורדוס, והוא שנחרב בהמ"ק בימיו. זלגו עיניו דמעות. שהמקרא הזה פוסלו מן המלכות. אחינו אתה. *שאמו מישראל. וקורא מתחילת אלה הדברים עד שמע. שב"ואתחנן". ושמע והיה אם שמוע. ע"י דילוג, ומשם מדלג ל"עשר תעשר", ומשם מדלג וקורא "כי תכלה לעשר" וברכות וקללות, ומשם חוזר למפרע וקורא "אשימה עלי מלך". "שמע" — קבלת מלכות שמים, "והיה אם שמוע" — קבלת עול מצות, כדאמר בפ' שני דברכות (דף יג.), וכן ברכות וקללות — קבלת בריתות של תורה. ומשמיע לרבים "עשר תעשר" "כי תכלה לעשר" — מפני שהוא זמן אסיף ומתנות עניים והפרשת תרומות ומעשרות. ואע"פ שפרשת המלך מפסקת בין "עשר" ל"כי תכלה" — קורא את אלה יחד, שלא להפסיק במעשרות, ואח"כ קורא פרשת המלך. ואי משום דיש כאן דילוג בתורה *בכדי (שלא) יפסיק התורגמן — אין למלך תורגמן, ואין מתרגמין אחריו*. ברכות שכ"ג מברך. ביוה"כ אחר מקרא פרשה, כדאמרן (יומא סח.): מברך עליה שמונה ברכות. המלך מברך. אחר קריאתו. של רגלים. "מקדש ישראל והזמנים" מברך תחת (א) ברכות של מחילת העון שביוה"כ. גמ' צריכי. כל הסימנין הללו: מקץ שנת השמיטה, ובחג הסוכות, ובמועד. שבערבות מואב נאמרה פרשה זו. משנת ארבעים והלאה. נימנוהו מהשתא. ואע"ג דלא מתרמי בשמיטה, שלא מנו שמיטין עד לאחר שבע שכיבשו ושבע שחילקו, כדאמרי' (בקידושין) (דף מ:) [בערכין] (דף יב:). בסוף שמיטה. קודם ר"ה של שמינית, דהא "מקץ שבע" — בסוף שנה משמע. מריש שתא. שכולן נקראו מועד, כדכתיב (ויקרא כג): "אלה מועדי ה'", וקחשיב נמי ר"ה. מאימת

תוספות

כתב רחמנא בחג הסוכות. תימה: השתא דכתיב "בחג הסוכות" — "במועד" למה ליה? ועוד: לא ליכתוב אלא "מקץ שבע שנים שנת השמיטה בבא כל ישראל לראות", ואנא ידענא דלאו היינו מר"ה, דאז אינם באים לראות! וי"ל: אם כן הוה אמינא בחג המצות, להכי איצטריך בחג הסוכות. מיהו "במועד" לא הוה לריך. ונראה דלהכי איצטריך: משום ד"בבא כל ישראל לראות" משמע: מאתחלתא דמועד ביום ראשון — קמ"ל "במועד", דמשמע: בתוך המועד. ואהני "בבא כל ישראל" דמשמע: מאתחלתא דמועד — לא ביום ב' או ביום ג', אלא במוצאי יו"ט הראשון. אבל פי' רש"י תמוה, דפי' דמהאי טעמא ביום טוב ראשון לא — דתיקון בימה אינה דוחה יו"ט. כיון דגזירת הכתוב לקרות מאתחלתא דמועד — יקראו בלא בימה, מנלן דבימה מעכבת? להכי מסתבר כדפי'. ונראה דהיו בונין הבימה מעי"ט בנין של פרקים, ובחולו של מועד לא היו עושין שום בנין אלא מקימין אותה ומחברין הפרקים יחד. ואם לא בנו אותה מערב יו"ט — נראה דבניינה לא היה דוחה אפילו חולו של מועד. מלוה

עין משפט נר מצוה

עא א מיי' פי"ב מהל' תפלה הלכה ח יג סמג עשין יט טוש"ע א"ח סימן קמד סעיף א:
עב ב מיי' שם הל' יג:
עג ג ד ה ו מיי' וסמג שם טוש"ע שם:
עד ז מיי' שם הל"ג ופ"ג מהל' עבודת יוה"כ הלכה י סמג שם טוש"ע א"ח שם סעיף ג:
עה ח מיי' פ"ג מהל' עבודת יוה"כ שם:
עו ט מיי' פי"ג מהל' תפלה הלכה כד סמג עשין יט טוש"ע א"ח סימן תרפד סעיף ג:
עז י מיי' שם פי"ב הל' כג סמג שם טור ש"ע א"ח סימן קמד סעיף ד:
עח כ מיי' שם ופ"ג מהל' עבודת יוה"כ הלכה י סמג וטוש"ע שם:
עט ל מיי' פ"ג מהל' עבודת יוה"כ הל' יא סמג עשין רט:
פ מ מיי' פ"ג מהלכות חגיגה הלכה ג סמג עשין רל:
פא ס מיי' שם הל' ד:
פב ע מיי' שם הל' ג:

רש"ל

הגהות הב"ח

(א) רש"י ד"ה של רגלים וכו' תחת ברכת מחילת כצ"ל ותיבת של נמחק:

גליון הש"ם

רש"י ד"ה אחינו אתה שאמו מישראל. עי' ב"ק דף פח ע"א ועי' מהרש"א בח"א ריש ב"ב:

מסורת הש"ס

נחמיה ח
יומא סט: מגילה כג.
יומא ע.
שם ע"ש
[ברכות לג.]
מגילה כט: יומא ע.
יומא ע.
שם
יומא סו: כריתות יד.
עירובין ו: כב. קא.
דברים לא
שם יז
שם א
שם ו
[עי' תוספות ב"ב ג: ד"ה כל לאמר וכו' השיגו על זה]
ס"א בכדי שיפסיק
[עי' תוי"ט ד"ה עשר]

עין משפט נר מצוה

פג א מיי' פ"ג מהלכות חגיגה הלכה ד סמג עשין רל:

פד ב מיי' שם הל' ג:

פה ג מיי' פ"ו מהל' ת"ת הל' יב טוש"ע י"ד סימן רמד סעיף יד:

פו ד מיי' פ"ב מהל' מלכים הלכה ג:

פז ה עיין בס' יראים סימן נה שמנה אותו במנין תרי"ג מצות:

גמרא

מֵאַתְחַלְתָּא דְּמוֹעֵד.§ "וְחַזַּן הַכְּנֶסֶת נוֹטֵל ס"ת וְנוֹתְנוֹ לְרֹאשׁ הַכְּנֶסֶת".§ *שָׁמְעַתְּ מִינָּהּ חוֹלְקִין כָּבוֹד לְתַלְמִיד בִּמְקוֹם הָרַב — אָמַר אַבַּיֵי: אכּוּלָּהּ מִשּׁוּם כְּבוֹדוֹ דְּמֶלֶךְ.§ "וְהַמֶּלֶךְ עוֹמֵד וּמְקַבֵּל וְקוֹרֵא יוֹשֵׁב. אַגְרִיפַּס הַמֶּלֶךְ עָמַד וְקִיבֵּל וְקָרָא עוֹמֵד".§ עוֹמֵד — מִכְּלָל דְּיוֹשֵׁב? וְהָאָמַר מָר: *אֵין יְשִׁיבָה בָּעֲזָרָה אֶלָּא לְמַלְכֵי בֵית דָּוִד בִּלְבַד, שֶׁנֶּאֱ': °"וַיָּבֹא הַמֶּלֶךְ דָּוִד וַיֵּשֶׁב לִפְנֵי ה' וַיֹּאמֶר" וגו'! [שמואל ב ז] כִּדְאָמַר רַב חִסְדָּא: בְּעֶזְרַת נָשִׁים, בהָכָא נַמִי — בְּעֶזְרַת נָשִׁים.§ "וְשִׁבְּחוּהוּ חֲכָמִים".§ שִׁבְּחוּהוּ — מִכְּלָל דְּשַׁפִּיר עֲבַד? הָאָמַר רַב אָשֵׁי: אֲפִי' לְמ"ד *גנָשִׂיא שֶׁמָּחַל עַל כְּבוֹדוֹ כְּבוֹדוֹ מָחוּל, דמֶלֶךְ שֶׁמָּחַל עַל כְּבוֹדוֹ — אֵין כְּבוֹדוֹ מָחוּל, שֶׁנֶּאֱ': °"שׂוֹם תָּשִׂים עָלֶיךָ מֶלֶךְ" [דברים יז] — שֶׁתְּהֵא אֵימָתוֹ עָלֶיךָ! מִצְוָה שָׁאנֵי.§ "וּכְשֶׁהִגִּיעַ לְלֹא תוּכַל לָתֵת".§ תָּנָא *מִשְּׁמֵיהּ דְּרַבִּי נָתָן: בְּאוֹתָהּ שָׁעָה נִתְחַיְּיבוּ שׂוֹנְאֵי יִשְׂרָאֵל כְּלָיָיה, השֶׁהֶחֱנִיפוּ לוֹ לְאַגְרִיפַּס. אָמַר ר' שִׁמְעוֹן בֶּן חֲלַפְתָּא: מִיּוֹם שֶׁגָּבַר אֶגְרוֹפָהּ שֶׁל חֲנוּפָּה נִתְעַוְּותוּ (א) הַדִּינִין, וְנִתְקַלְקְלוּ הַמַּעֲשִׂים, וְאֵין אָדָם יָכוֹל לוֹמַר לַחֲבֵירוֹ "מַעֲשַׂי גְּדוֹלִים מִמַּעֲשֶׂיךָ". דָּרַשׁ ר' יְהוּדָה בַּר מַעֲרָבָא, וְאִיתֵּימָא ר' שִׁמְעוֹן בֶּן פָּזִי: מוּתָּר לְהַחֲנִיף לָרְשָׁעִים בָּעוֹלָם הַזֶּה, שֶׁנֶּאֱמַר: °"לֹא יִקָּרֵא עוֹד לְנָבָל נָדִיב וּלְכִילַי לֹא יֵאָמֵר שׁוֹעַ" [ישעיה לב], מִכְּלָל דְּבָעוֹלָם הַזֶּה שָׁרֵי. ר' שִׁמְעוֹן בֶּן לָקִישׁ אָמַר, מֵהָכָא: °"כִּרְאוֹת פְּנֵי אֱלֹהִים וַתִּרְצֵנִי" [בראשית לג]. וּפְלִיגָא דְּרַבִּי לֵוִי, דְּאָמַר רַבִּי לֵוִי: מָשָׁל שֶׁל יַעֲקֹב וְעֵשָׂו לְמָה הַדָּבָר דּוֹמֶה? לְאָדָם שֶׁזִּימֵּן אֶת חֲבֵירוֹ וְהִכִּיר בּוֹ שֶׁמְּבַקֵּשׁ לְהוֹרְגוֹ, אָמַר לוֹ: טַעַם תַּבְשִׁיל זֶה שֶׁאֲנִי טוֹעֵם — כְּתַבְשִׁיל שֶׁטָּעַמְתִּי בְּבֵית הַמֶּלֶךְ. אָמַר: יָדַע לֵיהּ מַלְכָּא. מִיסְתַּפֵי וְלָא קָטֵיל לֵיהּ. אָמַר רַבִּי אֶלְעָזָר: כָּל אָדָם שֶׁיֵּשׁ בּוֹ חֲנוּפָּה מֵבִיא אַף לָעוֹלָם, שֶׁנֶּאֱ': °"וְחַנְפֵי לֵב יָשִׂימוּ אָף" [איוב לו], וְלֹא עוֹד, אֶלָּא שֶׁאֵין תְּפִלָּתוֹ נִשְׁמַעַת, שֶׁנֶּאֱמַר: °"לֹא יְשַׁוְּעוּ כִּי אֲסָרָם" [שם].§ סִימָן: א"ף עוב"ר גיהנ"ם ביד"ו ניד"ה גול"ה§ וְאָמַר רַבִּי אֶלְעָזָר: כָּל אָדָם שֶׁיֵּשׁ בּוֹ חֲנוּפָּה — אֲפִילּוּ עוּבָּרִין שֶׁבִּמְעֵי אִמָּן מְקַלְּלִין אוֹתוֹ, שֶׁנֶּאֱ': °"אוֹמֵר לְרָשָׁע צַדִּיק אָתָּה יִקְּבוּהוּ עַמִּים יִזְעָמוּהוּ לְאוּמִּים" [משלי כד]. *וְאֵין קוֹב אֶלָּא קְלָלָה שֶׁנֶּאֱ': °"לֹא קַבֹּה אֵל" [במדבר כג], וְאֵין לְאוֹם אֶלָּא עוּבָּרִין, שֶׁנֶּאֱ': °"וּלְאוֹם מִלְאוֹם יֶאֱמָץ" [בראשית כה]. וְאָמַר רַבִּי אֶלְעָזָר: כָּל אָדָם שֶׁיֵּשׁ בּוֹ חֲנוּפָּה נוֹפֵל בַּגֵּיהִנָּם, שֶׁנֶּאֱ': °"הוֹי הָאוֹמְרִים לָרַע טוֹב וְלַטּוֹב רָע" וגו' [ישעיה ה], מַה כְּתִיב אַחֲרָיו — "לָכֵן כֶּאֱכֹל קַשׁ לְשׁוֹן אֵשׁ וַחֲשַׁשׁ לֶהָבָה יִרְפֶּה" וגו'. וְאָמַר רַבִּי אֶלְעָזָר: כָּל הַמַּחֲנִיף *לַחֲבֵירוֹ [בע"י איתא לרשעו] — סוֹף נוֹפֵל בְּיָדוֹ, וְאִם אֵינוֹ נוֹפֵל בְּיָדוֹ — נוֹפֵל בְּיַד בָּנָיו, וְאִם אֵינוֹ נוֹפֵל בְּיַד בָּנָיו — נוֹפֵל בְּיַד בֶּן בְּנוֹ, שֶׁנֶּאֱ': °"וַיֹּאמֶר יִרְמְיָה לַחֲנַנְיָה אָמֵן כֵּן יַעֲשֶׂה ה', יָקֵם ה' אֶת דְּבָרֶיךָ" [ירמיה כח], וּכְתִי': וַיְהִי

רש"י

מֵאֵימַת דְּמַתְחִיל מוֹעֵד. וּמִיהוּ בְּיו"ט לָא. שֶׁאֵין תִּיקּוּן הַבִּימָה דּוֹחֶה לָא אֶת הַשַּׁבָּת וְלָא יו"ט. וּמֵאֶתְמוֹל נַמִי לָא עָבְדִינַן לַהּ, דְּדַחֲקָא לַהּ עֲזָרָה. וְהַאי טַעְמָא מְפָרֵשׁ בַּגְּמָ' יְרוּשַׁלְמִי (פ"א) בְּמַסֶּ' מְגִילָּה, דְּקָתָנֵי: הַקָּהֵל מְאַחֲרִין כְּשֶׁחָל לִהְיוֹת בְּשַׁבָּת, וְקָאָמַר: מִפְּנֵי הַבִּימָה. וְנַעְבְּדַהּ מֵאֶתְמוֹל! דְּדַחֲקָא לַהּ עֲזָרָה, אנקוברי"ר בְּלַעַ"ז. לְמַלְכֵי בֵּית דָּוִד. אֲבָל לֹא לְמַלְכֵי בֵּית חַשְׁמוֹנַאי. אֲפִי' לְמַאן דְּאָמַר. בְּקִידּוּשִׁין בְּפ"ק (דף לב:). אֶגְרוֹפָהּ. כֹּחָהּ שֶׁל חֲנוּפָּה. דְּאַע"ג דְּאִמּוֹ מִיִּשְׂרָאֵל — אֵין רָאוּי לַמַּלְכוּת, דְּעֶבֶד הָיָה, וְזִילָא מִילְּתָא. נִתְעַוְּותוּ הַדִּינִין. שֶׁהֶחֱנִיפוּ הַדַּיָּינִין אֶת בַּעֲלֵי הַדִּין. וְנִתְקַלְקְלוּ הַמַּעֲשִׂים. שֶׁהַגְּדוֹלִים רָאוּ עוֹבְרֵי עֲבֵירָה וְלֹא מִיחוּ בְּיָדָם, מִפְּנֵי חֲנוּפָּה. וְאֵין אָדָם שֶׁיָּכוֹל לוֹמַר לַחֲבֵירוֹ מַעֲשַׂי גְּדוֹלִים מִמַּעֲשֶׂיךָ. שֶׁמִּתּוֹךְ שֶׁלֹּא מִיחוּ בְּעוֹבְרֵי עֲבֵירָה לָמְדוּ הַדּוֹרוֹת אֶת מַעֲשֵׂיהֶם, וְנִמְצָא כּוּלָּן עוֹבְרִין. לְכִילַי. לְשׁוֹן "כָּלְתָה נַפְשִׁי" (תהלים קיט), שֶׁמִּתְאַוֶּה לִשְׁתּוֹת יַיִן תָּדִיר. וּפְלִיגָא. הָא דְּרֵישׁ לָקִישׁ, דְּאָמַר: לְהַחֲנִיפוֹ לְעֵשָׂו נִתְכַּוֵּון, לוֹמַר לוֹ: "רָאִיתִי פָנֶיךָ כִּרְאוֹת פְּנֵי" וגו' — פְּלִיגָא אַדְּרַבִּי לֵוִי, דְּאָמַר: לֹא לְהַחֲנִיפוֹ נִתְכַּוֵּין, אֶלָּא לְאַיֵּים עָלָיו, וּלְהוֹדִיעוֹ שֶׁהוּא רָגִיל לִרְאוֹת מַלְאָכִים. לֹא יְשַׁוְּעוּ כִּי אֲסָרָם. כְּשֶׁיָּבוֹאוּ עֲלֵיהֶם יִסּוּרִין לֹא יוֹעִילָם שַׁוְעָה. וַיֹּאמֶר יִרְמְיָהוּ לַחֲנַנְיָה הַנָּבִיא. שֶׁאָמַר נְבוּאַת שֶׁקֶר עַל גָּלוּת יְכָנְיָה וּכְלֵי הַקּוֹדֶשׁ שֶׁגָּלוּ עִמּוֹ: בְּעוֹד שְׁנָתַיִם יָמִים אֲנִי מְשִׁיבָם אֶל הַמָּקוֹם הַזֶּה, "אָמֵן כֵּן יַעֲשֶׂה ה'" — חֲנוּפָּה הִיא זוֹ, שֶׁהָיָה לוֹ לוֹמַר בְּהֶדְיָא: שֶׁקֶר אַתָּה נִיבָּא: *וַיְהִי הוּא בְּשַׁעַר בִּנְיָמִן. לְאַחַר כַּמָּה יָמִים הָיָה יִרְמְיָה יוֹצֵא מִירוּשָׁלַיִם לָלֶכֶת אֶרֶץ בִּנְיָמִין לַחֲלוֹק נַחֲלָה שֶׁנָּפְלָה לוֹ, וּתְפָסוֹ יִרְאִיָּיה וַיֹּאמֶר לוֹ: אֶל הַכַּשְׂדִּים אַתָּה נוֹפֵל. גְּמוּלָה

תורה אור

מסורת הש"ס

[לעיל מ: וש"נ]

[שם וש"נ]

סנהדרין יט: כתובות יז. קדושין לב:

[תוספתא פ"ז]

שייך לדף שאח"ז

תוספות

מצוה שאני. והכי פרכינן נמי בפרק "כ"ג" בסנהדרין (דף יט:) גבי מלך, דתנן: לא חולץ ולא חולצין לאשתו, רבי יהודה אומר: אם רצה לחלוץ וליבם — זכור לטוב. איני? והאמר רב אשי וכו'! ומשני: מצוה שאני. וקשיא לר"י: אמאי לא משני הכי בפרק שני דכתובות (דף יז.): מעבירין את המת מלפני כלה, וזה וזה לפני מלך ישראל. אמרו עליו על אגריפס המלך שעבר לפני הכלה ושבחוהו חכמים. וקא פריך: מכלל דשפיר עבד? והאמר רב אשי וכו'! ומשני: פרשת דרכים הוה. ואמאי לא משני: מצוה שאני? ותו איכא למיתמה: והא ההיא גופיה דרב אשי איירי במקום מצוה. דמעיקרא אמרי':* אפי' למ"ד הרב שמחל על כבודו כבודו מחול — נשיא שמחל על כבודו אין כבודו מחול. ומותיב ליה: מעשה ברבי אליעזר ורבי יהושע ורבי צדוק שהיו מסובין בבית המשתה בנו של ר"ג ברבי, והיה ר"ג עומד ומשקה עליהן וכו'! אלא אי אתמר — הכי אתמר, אמר רב אשי: אפי' למ"ד נשיא שמחל על כבודו, דהיינו רבי יהושע שקבל הכוס מרבן גמליאל, וכן רבי (אלעזר בר) צדוק — מלך שמחל על כבודו אין כבודו מחול. משמע אפילו במקום מצוה, דומיא דנשיא, כההוא מעשה דרבן גמליאל שהיה סעודת מצוה ומחל על כבודו בשביל כבוד חכמים אורחין שהיו מסובין בסעודתו, דמייתי עליה דאברהם אבינו "והוא עומד עליהם". אלמא דאפי' במקום מצוה אמר רב אשי אין כבודו מחול! ונראה לתרץ: דדוקא הכא שייך למימר מצוה שאני, דמוחל על כבודו משום כבוד התורה, שהוא כבוד השכינה, וכן ההיא דפרק "כהן גדול" (סנהדרין יט:) דחולץ או מיבם — מוחל על כבודו כדי לקיים מצות מלך עולמים, ומראה בעצמו שאימת שכינה עליו. אבל ההיא דכתובות (דף יז.) ופ"ק דקידושין (דף לב:) שמוחל על כבודו כדי לחלוק כבוד לבשר ודם, כגון לכלה ות"ח — בזה גזירת הכתוב הוא שאינו מוחל, אפי' במקום מצוה. שהרי מצות כיבוד עצמו, שהן צריכין לעשות בו למלך כבוד — גדולה ממצות כיבוד שחייב המלך לנהוג בהו, שהרי גם עליהן אמרה תורה "שום תשים עליך מלך" שתהא אימתו עליך, ולא אימתך עליו. נמצא דמה שהמלך מכבדו — ליכא מצוה. **אותו** היום נתחייבו שונאי ישראל כלייה. ירושלמי: תני, רבי חנינא ברבי גמליאל אומר: הרבה חללים נפלו באותו יום שהחניפו לו. ודבר תמוה לומר, אם היה ראוי *מפני התורה כיון דאמו היתה מישראל, אלא משום דזילא מילתא, כמו שפירש"י — שיתחייבו על חנופה מועטת כזאת עונש גדול! (ב) ופירש ר"י: אע"ג דאמר בפרק "מצות חליצה" (יבמות קב.) ובפרק "החולץ" (שם מה:) גבי רב מרי דמנייה רבא אפורסי דבבל, וגבי אושפיזכניה דרב אדא בר אהבה: אם היתה אמו מישראל, "מקרב אחיך" קרינן ביה (קדושין דף עו:) — היינו דוקא גבי נשיאות ושררות בעלמא, דלינהג שררות במתא, דדרשינן: "שום תשים עליך מלך מקרב אחיך", מדסמך משימות ל"מקרב אחיך" — ש"מ דבעינן בהו מקרב אחיך קצת, כגון אמו מישראל. אבל מלך — חזר ושנה עליו: "מקרב אחיך תשים עליך מלך", דקפיד קרא גבי מלך עד שיהא ממש מקרב, ממוצע מאביו ואמו מישראל. וזו היתה החנופה, שמלך בזרוע שלא כדין תורה, והודו לו והחזיקו בכך. נהי שלא יוכלו למחות — היה להן לשתוק ולא להחזיקו. וזהו עונש החנופה בדבר עבירה, שמחניף לחבירו מחמת יראתו מפניו ואינו חושש על יראת הקב"ה, ועושה עין שלמעלה כאילו אינה רואה. בירושלמי ד"עשרה יוחסין" בגמרא "אין בודקין מן המזבח": כתיב "שום תשים עליך מלך". אין לי אלא מלך, מנין לרבות שוטרי הרבים וגבאי צדקה וסופרי דיינין ומכין ברצועות — ת"ל: "מקרב אחיך תשים עליך מלך", כל שתשימוהו עליך — לא יהא אלא מן הברורין שבאחיך.

[קדושין לב:]

[סנהדרין לב.]

נ"א מדין

כל המחניף לחבירו. יש לפרש: שלא במקום סכנה. אבל במקום סכנה — מותר. כי ההיא דפרק "ארבעה נדרים" (דף כב.): *עולא אזל לארעא דישראל, לוו בהדיה תרי בני חוזאי, קם חד שחטיה לחבריה. אמר ליה לעולא: יאות עבדי? אמר ליה: אין, ופרע לו בית השחיטה. כי אתא לקמיה דרבי יוחנן, אמר ליה: דלמא ח"ו אחזקית ידי עוברי עבירה? א"ל רבי יוחנן: נפשך הצלתה.

עי' במסורת המאור כלל ג פ"ב מד ע"א

הגהות הב"ח

(א) גמ' נתעוותו (הדינין) תז"מ. ונ"ב גי' רש"י הדיינין: (ב) תום' ד"ה אותו וכו' ופי' ר"י. נ"ב עיין בתוס' פרק החולץ דף מה פירשו בע"א בשם ר"ש:

גליון הש"ס

תום' ד"ה אותו היום וכו' אלא מן הברורים שבאחיך. ועי' ב"ב דף ג ע"ב תד"ה כל: **ד"ה** כל המחניף וכו' במקום סכנה מותר. מג"א סימן קנ:

הדרן עלך אלו נאמרין

תורה אור

°"וַיְהִי הוּא בְּשַׁעַר בִּנְיָמִן וְשָׁם בַּעַל פְּקִידוּת וּשְׁמוֹ יִרְאִיָּה בֶּן שֶׁלֶמְיָה בֶּן חֲנַנְיָה וַיִּתְפֹּשׂ אֶת יִרְמְיָהוּ הַנָּבִיא לֵאמֹר אֶל הַכַּשְׂדִּים אַתָּה נֹפֵל. וַיֹּאמֶר (לו) יִרְמְיָהוּ שֶׁקֶר אֵינֶנִּי נֹפֵל *אֶל הַכַּשְׂדִּים" וגו', וּכְתִי' "וַיִּתְפֹּשׂ* (א) יִרְמְיָהוּ וַיְבִיאֵהוּ אֶל הַשָּׂרִים". אוְא"ר אֶלְעָזָר: כָּל עֵדָה שֶׁיֵּשׁ בָּהּ חֲנוּפָּה — מְאוּסָה כְּנִדָּה, שֶׁנֶּאֱמַר: °"כִּי עֲדַת חָנֵף גַּלְמוּד", *שֶׁכֵּן בִּכְרַכֵּי הַיָּם קוֹרִין לְנִדָּה גַּלְמוּדָה. מַאי גַּלְמוּדָה — גְּמוּלָה (ב) מִבַּעְלָהּ. וְאָמַר ר' אֶלְעָזָר: כָּל עֵדָה שֶׁיֵּשׁ בָּהּ חֲנוּפָּה — לְסוֹף גּוֹלָה, כְּתִיב הָכָא: "כִּי עֲדַת חָנֵף גַּלְמוּד", וּכְתִי' הָתָם: °"וְאָמַרְתְּ בִּלְבָבֵךְ מִי יָלַד לִי אֶת אֵלֶּה וַאֲנִי שְׁכוּלָה וְגַלְמוּדָה גֹּלָה וְסוּרָה" וגו'. א"ר יִרְמְיָה בַּר אַבָּא: *אַרְבַּע כִּיתּוֹת אֵין מְקַבְּלוֹת פְּנֵי שְׁכִינָה: כַּת לֵיצִים, וְכַת חֲנֵיפִים, וְכַת *שַׁקָּרִים, וְכַת מְסַפְּרֵי לָשׁוֹן הָרַע. כַּת לֵיצִים — דִּכְתִיב: °"מָשַׁךְ יָדוֹ אֶת לוֹצְצִים", כַּת חֲנֵיפִים — דִּכְתִיב: °"כִּי לֹא לְפָנָיו חָנֵף יָבֹא", כַּת שַׁקָּרִים — דִּכְתִי': °"דּוֹבֵר שְׁקָרִים לֹא יִכּוֹן לְנֶגֶד עֵינָי", כַּת מְסַפְּרֵי לָשׁוֹן הָרַע — דִּכְתִיב: °"כִּי לֹא אֵל חָפֵץ רֶשַׁע אָתָּה לֹא יְגֻרְךָ רָע", *צַדִּיק אַתָּה ה', לֹא יָגוּר בִּמְגוּרְךָ רָע.§

הדרן עלך אלו נאמרין

מְשׁוּחַ מִלְחָמָה אבְּשָׁעָה שֶׁמְּדַבֵּר אֶל הָעָם — בִּלְשׁוֹן הַקּוֹדֶשׁ הָיָה מְדַבֵּר, שֶׁנֶּאֱמַר: °"וְהָיָה כְּקָרָבְכֶם אֶל הַמִּלְחָמָה וְנִגַּשׁ הַכֹּהֵן" — זֶה כֹּהֵן מְשׁוּחַ מִלְחָמָה, °"וְדִבֶּר אֶל הָעָם" — בִּלְשׁוֹן הַקּוֹדֶשׁ. °"וְאָמַר אֲלֵיהֶם שְׁמַע יִשְׂרָאֵל" וגו'. "עַל אוֹיְבֵיכֶם" — וְלֹא עַל אֲחֵיכֶם. לֹא יְהוּדָה עַל שִׁמְעוֹן, וְלֹא שִׁמְעוֹן עַל בִּנְיָמִין, שֶׁאִם תִּפְּלוּ בְּיָדָם — יְרַחֲמוּ עֲלֵיכֶם, כְּמָה שֶׁנֶּאֱמַר: °"וַיָּקוּמוּ הָאֲנָשִׁים אֲשֶׁר נִקְּבוּ בְשֵׁמוֹת וַיַּחֲזִיקוּ בַשִּׁבְיָה וְכָל מַעֲרוּמֵּיהֶם הִלְבִּישׁוּ מִן הַשָּׁלָל וַיַּלְבִּישׁוּם וַיַּנְעִילוּם וַיַּאֲכִילוּם וַיַּשְׁקוּם וַיְסֻכוּם וַיְנַהֲלוּם בַּחֲמֹרִים לְכָל כּוֹשֵׁל וַיְבִיאוּם יְרֵחוֹ עִיר הַתְּמָרִים אֵצֶל אֲחֵיהֶם וַיָּשׁוּבוּ שֹׁמְרוֹן" וגו'. עַל אוֹיְבֵיכֶם אַתֶּם הוֹלְכִים, שֶׁאִם תִּפְּלוּ בְּיָדָם — אֵין מְרַחֲמִין עֲלֵיכֶם. °"אַל יֵרַךְ לְבַבְכֶם אַל תִּירְאוּ וְאַל תַּחְפְּזוּ" וגו'. "אַל יֵרַךְ לְבַבְכֶם" — מִפְּנֵי צַהֲלַת סוּסִים וְצִיחְצוּחַ חֲרָבוֹת, "אַל תִּירְאוּ" — מִפְּנֵי הֲגָפַת תְּרִיסִין וְשִׁפְעַת הַקַּלְגַּסִּין, "אַל תַּחְפְּזוּ" — מִקּוֹל קַרְנוֹת, "אַל תַּעַרְצוּ" — מִפְּנֵי קוֹל צְוָוחוֹת, °"כִּי ה' אֱלֹהֵיכֶם הַהוֹלֵךְ עִמָּכֶם" — הֵם בָּאִין בְּנִצְחוֹנוֹ שֶׁל בָּשָׂר וָדָם, וְאַתֶּם בָּאִים בְּנִצְחוֹנוֹ שֶׁל מָקוֹם. פְּלִשְׁתִּים בָּאוּ בְּנִצְחוֹנוֹ שֶׁל גָּלְיָת, מֶה הָיָה סוֹפוֹ — לַסּוֹף נָפַל בַּחֶרֶב וְנָפְלוּ עִמּוֹ. בְּנֵי עַמּוֹן בָּאוּ בְּנִצְחוֹנוֹ שֶׁל שׁוֹבַךְ, מֶה הָיָה סוֹפוֹ — לַסּוֹף נָפַל בַּחֶרֶב וְנָפְלוּ עִמּוֹ. וְאַתֶּם אִי אַתֶּם כֵּן, "כִּי ה' אֱלֹהֵיכֶם הַהוֹלֵךְ עִמָּכֶם לְהִלָּחֵם לָכֶם" וגו' — זֶה מַחֲנֵה הָאָרוֹן.§ **גמ'** מַאי קָאָמַר? הָכִי קָאָמַר: שֶׁנֶּאֱמַר "וְדִבֶּר" וּלְהַלָּן אוֹמֵר °"מֹשֶׁה יְדַבֵּר וְהָאֱלֹהִים יַעֲנֶנּוּ בְקוֹל", מַה לְּהַלָּן בִּלְשׁוֹן הַקּוֹדֶשׁ — אַף כָּאן בִּלְשׁוֹן הַקּוֹדֶשׁ. תָּנוּ רַבָּנַן: "וְנִגַּשׁ הַכֹּהֵן וְדִבֶּר אֶל הָעָם". יָכוֹל כָּל כֹּהֵן שֶׁיִּרְצֶה — ת"ל: °"וְדִבְּרוּ הַשּׁוֹטְרִים", מַה שּׁוֹטְרִים בִּמְמוּנֶּה — אַף כֹּהֵן בִּמְמוּנֶּה. וְאֵימָא כֹּהֵן גָּדוֹל! דּוּמְיָא דְּשׁוֹטֵר, מַה שּׁוֹטֵר שֶׁיֵּשׁ מְמוּנֶּה עַל גַּבָּיו — אַף כֹּהֵן שֶׁיֵּשׁ מְמוּנֶּה עַל גַּבָּיו. כֹּהֵן גָּדוֹל נַמִי, הָאִיכָּא מֶלֶךְ עַל גַּבָּיו! בַּעֲבוֹדָתוֹ קָאָמַר. וְאֵימָא סְגַן! סְגַן לָאו מְמוּנֶּה הוּא. דְּתַנְיָא, *אָמַר רַבִּי חֲנִינָא סְגַן הַכֹּהֲנִים: לָמָּה סְגַן מְמוּנֶּה — שֶׁאִם אֵירַע בּוֹ פְּסוּל בְּכֹהֵן גָּדוֹל נִכְנָס וּמְשַׁמֵּשׁ תַּחְתָּיו.§ "וְאָמַר אֲלֵיהֶם שְׁמַע יִשְׂרָאֵל".§ מַאי שְׁנָא "שְׁמַע יִשְׂרָאֵל"? אָמַר רַבִּי יוֹחָנָן מִשּׁוּם רַבִּי שִׁמְעוֹן בֶּן יוֹחַי, אָמַר לָהֶן הַקָּדוֹשׁ בָּרוּךְ הוּא לְיִשְׂרָאֵל: אֲפִילּוּ לֹא קִיַּימְתֶּם אֶלָּא קְרִיאַת שְׁמַע שַׁחֲרִית וְעַרְבִית — אִי אַתֶּם נִמְסָרִין בְּיָדָם.§ "אַל יֵרַךְ לְבַבְכֶם אַל תִּירְאוּ" כו'.§ תָּנוּ רַבָּנַן: בפַּעֲמַיִם מְדַבֵּר עִמָּם, אַחַת בַּסְּפָר וְאַחַת בַּמִּלְחָמָה. בַּסְּפָר מַה הוּא אוֹמֵר — שִׁמְעוּ

רש"י

גְּמוּלָה. גְּדוֹלָה, כְּמוֹ "וַיִּגָּמַל" (בראשית כא). מָשַׁךְ יָדוֹ. הקב"ה מִהְיוֹת אֶת לוֹצְצִים. לֹא יְגוּרְךָ רָע. לֹא יָגוּר עִמְּךָ רַע. וְגַבֵּי מְסַפְּרֵי לָשׁוֹן הָרַע כְּתִיב, דִּכְתִיב בְּהַהוּא פָּרָשָׁתָא: "כִּי אֵין בְּפִיהוּ נְכוֹנָה" וגו'.

הדרן עלך אלו נאמרין

מְשׁוּחַ מִלְחָמָה. כֹּהֵן *שֶׁנִּתְרַבָּה לְכָךְ, שֶׁנֶּאֱמַר: "וְנִגַּשׁ הַכֹּהֵן" וגו'. וּבַגְּמָרָא פָּרֵיךְ: מַאי קָאָמַר?. וַיָּקוּמוּ הָאֲנָשִׁים. כְּתִיב גַּבֵּי פֶּקַח בֶּן רְמַלְיָהוּ שֶׁנִּלְחַם עִם אָחָז, בְּדִבְרֵי הַיָּמִים, שֶׁשָּׁבוּ מִבְּנֵי יְהוּדָה הַרְבֵּה, וְשָׁם הָיָה נָבִיא עוֹדֵד שְׁמוֹ, וְהוֹכִיחָם לִבְנֵי יִשְׂרָאֵל וְאָמַר לָהֶם: בַּחֲמַת ה' עַל בְּנֵי יְהוּדָה נְתָנָם בְּיֶדְכֶם וְהִכִּיתֶם בָּהֶם לְאֵין מַרְפֵּא וְעַתָּה אַתֶּם אוֹמְרִים לִכְבּוֹשׁ אוֹתָם לַעֲבָדִים שִׁמְעוּנִי וְהָשִׁיבוּ אֶת הַשִּׁבְיָה וגו'. לְכָל כּוֹשֵׁל. כָּל הַכּוֹשְׁלִים שֶׁבָּהֶם, שֶׁאֵינָן יְכוֹלִין לֵילֵךְ בְּרַגְלֵיהֶם. צַהֲלַת סוּסִים. נְגַף סוּסִים קָרוּי צָהֳלָה בִּלְשׁוֹן הַמִּקְרָא. קַלְגַּסִּין. חַיָּילוֹת. הֲגָפַת תְּרִיסִין. מַגִּיפִין וְסוֹגְרִין וּמְדַבְּקִין הַתְּרִיסִין זֶה סָמוּךְ לָזֶה, כְּדֵי שֶׁיִּתְקַשְּׁקוּ זֶה עַל זֶה. וְהַקּוֹל נִשְׁמָע כְּקוֹל הָמוֹן, לְחַיֵּיס עַל שֶׁכְּנֶגְדָּם. שׁוֹבַךְ. שַׂר צְבָא הֲדַדְעֶזֶר. **גמ'** מַאי קָאָמַר. הֵיכִי יָלֵיף לְשׁוֹן הַקּוֹדֶשׁ מֵהָכָא?. דּוּמְיָא דְּשׁוֹטֵר. תֵּירוּצָא הִיא: הַשּׁוֹפֵט מְמוּנֶּה עַל הַשּׁוֹטֵר, שֶׁשּׁוֹטֵר עָשׂוּי לִנְגּוֹשׂ אֶת מִי שֶׁיְּצַוֶּה הַשּׁוֹפֵט לָכוֹף. וְאֵימָא סְגַן. מְדַבֵּר דְּבָרִים הַלָּלוּ, דְּהָא מְמוּנֶּה הוּא, וְיֵשׁ מְמוּנֶּה עַל גַּבָּיו. לָמָּה סְגַן מְמוּנֶּה. לְאֵיזֶה דָּבָר הוּא מְמוּנֶּה וּמוּכָן. שֶׁאִם אֵירַע בּוֹ'. אֲבָל בְּעוֹד שֶׁלֹּא אֵירַע פְּסוּל לְכֹהֵן גָּדוֹל — אֵין לַסְּגָן גְּדוּלָּה שֶׁל כְּלוּם. מַאי שְׁנָא שְׁמַע יִשְׂרָאֵל. לָמָּה מַתְחִיל בְּלָשׁוֹן זֶה?. פַּעֲמַיִם מְדַבֵּר עִמָּהֶם אַחַת בַּסְּפָר. כְּשֶׁיָּצְאוּ מֵאַרְצָם.

תוספות

משוח מלחמה. נראה, האי דלא תנא הכי "משוח מלחמה בשעה שמדבר אל העם כילד", כדקתני בפרק "אלו נאמרין" (לעיל דף לב.) "מקרא בכורים כילד" – משום דהתם סליק מיניה, דתני לעיל מיניה "ואלו נאמרין בלשון קודש". אבל תימה: למה הקדים פרק זה קודם פרק "עגלה ערופה"? והלא שנה משוח מלחמה בבבא אחרונה אחרי כולן! ויש לומר: דהתם הקדים פרשת עגלה ערופה, משום דאיירי בפרשת המלך – נקט בתריה פרשת עגלה ערופה. אבל הכא, שבא לפרשה – מקדים משוח מלחמה משום דזוטרי מיליה, ופסיק ושדי להו. וא"ת: וליתני לעיל "פרשת משוח מלחמה" כדתני "פרשת עגלה ערופה"! יש לומר: דלא שייך למימר "פרשת משוח מלחמה", שהרי לא נתנה משום מלות קריאה אלא משום התראה. **הכי** קאמר שנאמר ודבר. ירושלמי: למה? בגין דכתי' "ודבר". הרי ק"ש, דכתי' בה "ודברת בם", והיא נאמרת בכל לשון! אלא בגין דכתיב בה אמירה. הרי פרשת ודוי מעשר, הרי כתיב בה אמירה והיא נאמרת בכל לשון! אמר רבי חגי: נאמר כאן הגשה ונאמר להלן הגשה: "ונגשו הכהנים בני לוי", מה נגישה שנא' להלן בלשון קודש – אף כאן בלשון קודש. עד כדון כרבי עקיבא, דאמר לשונות רידויין הן, כרבי ישמעאל דאמר לשונות כפולין הן, ברם מאי? אמר ר' חייא בר אבא: נאמר כאן נגישה ונאמר להלן נגישה: "ונגש משה אל הערפל", מה לשם לשון הקודש – אף כאן לשון הקודש. *מסתברא דלא, "ופקדו שרי צבאות בראש העם" ואחרי כן "ונגש הכהן ודבר אל העם", בתר דמתקן להון הוא משמע לון.

סגן לאו ממונה הוא. ואם תאמר: הא אמרינן בסנהדרין, פרק "כהן גדול" (דף יט.): כשהוא מנחם אחרים – כל העם עוברין זה אחר זה, והממונה ממצעו. ותניא: כשהוא עומד בשורה לנחם את האחרים – סגן ומשוח מלחמה עומד בימינו. ואמר רב פפא, ש"מ מהא מתניתין תלת: שמע מינה – היינו סגן היינו ממונה! יש לומר: ודאי ממונה היה לדברים שמינוהו אחיו הכהנים, כדתנן (יומא דף כח.): "אמר להם הממונה", אבל מן התורה אין לו שום מנוי ושררה יותר על אחיו הכהנים, ואינו אלא עין מינוי אמרכל וגיזבר, שגידלוהו אחיו הכהנים*. מאה

עין משפט נר מצוה

א א מיי' פ"ז מהלכות מלכים הלכה ג סמג עשין קכ:

ב ב מיי' שם הלכה ב:

הגהות הב"ח

(א) גמ' וכתיב ויתפש יראיה בן שלמיה בירמיהו ויביאהו: (ב) שם גמולה דא מבעלה:

[נ"ל לא]

[נ"ל שקרנים. כ"ה בסנהדרין]

[וע"ע תוס' יומא עו: ד"ה אמר להם ותוס' מנחות ק. ד"ה אמר]

מסורת הש"ס

נ"ל על

נ"ל יראיה בירמיהו

ס"א שנתברר [ר"ה כו.]

סנהדרין קג. ע"ש

[שבת קמט: חגיגה יב: סנהדרין קג.] [יומא לט. ע"ש נזיר מז: ע"ש]

שמעו דברי מערכי המלחמה וחזרו. במלחמה מה הוא אומר — "אל ירך לבבכם אל תיראו ואל תחפזו ואל תערצו", כנגד ארבעה דברים שאומות העולם עושין: מגיפין, ומריעין, צווחין ורומסין.§ "פלשתים באו בנצחונו של גלית" כו'.§ גלית, אמר רבי יוחנן: שעמד בגילוי פנים לפני הקב"ה, שנאמר: °"ברו לכם איש וירד אלי", *ואין "איש" אלא הקב"ה, שנא': °"ה' איש מלחמה". אמר הקב"ה: הריני מפילו על יד בן איש, שנא': °"ודוד בן איש אפרתי הזה". א"ר יוחנן משום רבי מאיר: בשלשה מקומות לכדו פיו לאותו רשע: אחד — "ברו לכם איש וירד אלי"; ואידך — "אם יוכל להלחם אתי והכני" וגו', ואידך, דקאמר ליה לדוד °"הכלב אנכי כי אתה בא אלי במקלות". דוד נמי אמר ליה °"אתה בא אלי בחרב בחנית ובכידון"! (א) הדר אמר ליה "ואנכי בא אליך בשם ה' צבאות אלהי (ישראל) מערכות ישראל אשר חרפת". °"ויגש הפלשתי השכם והערב", אמר ר' יוחנן: כדי לבטלן מק"ש שחרית וערבית. °"ויתיצב ארבעים יום", א"ר יוחנן: כנגד ארבעים יום שנתנה בהן תורה. °"ויצא איש הבינים ממחנות פלשתים" וגו'. מאי בינים? אמר רב: שמבונה מכל מום, ושמואל אמר: בינוני שבאחיו, דבי רבי שילא אמר: שהוא עשוי כבנין, רבי יוחנן אמר: בר מאה פפי וחדא נאנאי. "וגלית שמו מגת", תני רב יוסף: שהכל דשין את אמו כגת. כתיב: "מערות" וקרינן: "מערכות", תני רב יוסף: שהכל הערו באמו. כתיב: °"הרפה" וכתיב: "ערפה", רב ושמואל; חד אמר: הרפה שמה, ולמה נקרא שמה ערפה — שהכל עורפין אותה מאחריה. וחד אמר: ערפה שמה, ולמה נקרא שמה הרפה — שהכל דשין אותה כהריפות, וכן הוא אומר: °"ותקח האשה ותפרוש המסך על פני הבאר ותשטח עליה הריפות". ואי בעית אימא מהכא: °"אם תכתוש את האויל במכתש בתוך הריפות בעלי". °"את ארבעת אלה יולדו להרפה בגת ויפלו ביד דוד וביד עבדיו". מאי נינהו? אמר רב חסדא: סף ומדון גלית וישבי בנוב. "ויפלו ביד דוד וביד עבדיו" — דכתיב: °"ותשק ערפה לחמותה ורות דבקה בה", אמר רבי יצחק: אמר הקדוש ברוך הוא: יבואו בני הנשוקה ויפלו ביד בני הדבוקה. דרש רבא: בשכר ארבע דמעות שהורידה ערפה על חמותה זכתה ויצאו ממנה ארבעה גבורים, שנאמר: °"ותשאנה קולן ותבכינה עוד". כתיב: "חץ חניתו" וקרינן: "עץ חניתו". אמר רבי אלעזר: עדיין לא הגיענו לחצי שבחו של אותו רשע. מכאן שאסור לספר בשבחן של רשעים. ולא לפתח ביה כלל! לאודועי שבחיה דדוד.§ "בני עמון באו בנצחונו של שובך" כו'.§ כתיב "שובך" וכתיב "שופך", רב ושמואל; חד אמר: שופך שמו, ולמה נקרא שמו שובך — שעשוי כשובך. וחד אמר: שובך שמו, ולמה נקרא שמו שופך — שכל הרואה אותו, נשפך לפניו כקיתון. °"אשפתו כקבר פתוח כולם גבורים". רב ושמואל, ואמרי לה רבי אמי ורבי אסי; חד אמר: בשעה שזורקין חץ — עושין אשפתות של חללים, ושמא תאמר שאומנין בקרב — ת"ל: "כולם גבורים". וחד אמר: בשעה שעושין צורכיהן — עושין אשפתות אשפתות של זבל, ושמא תאמר מפני שחולי מעיים הם — תלמוד לומר: "כולם גבורים". אמר רב מרי: שמע מינה, האי מאן דנפיש זיבליה — חולי מעיים הוא, למאי נפקא מינה — ליטרח בנפשיה. °"דאגה בלב איש ישחנה". *ר' אמי ורבי אסי; חד אמר: ישחנה מדעתו, וחד אמר: ישיחנה לאחרים.§ "ואתם אי אתם כן" כו'.§ וכל כך למה? מפני *שהשם וכל כינויו מונחין

מאה פפי וחד נאנאי. בירושלמי בפרק "החולץ" אגמרא וחיינן אשם תלוי: את ש"מ [שהאשה] מתעברת וחוזרת ומתעברת, את ש"מ שאין האשה מתעברת משני בני אדם כאחת. ופליגי על רבנן דאגדתא, דרבנן דאגדתא אומרים: "ויצא איש הבינים ממערכות פלשתים" — ממאה ערלות פלשתים, שהערו בה מאה ערלות פלשתים. אמר רבי מתניא: ולא פליגין, עד שלא נסרחה הזרע — האשה מתעברת משני בני אדם כאחת, ומשנסרחה הזרע – אין האשה מתעברת משני בני אדם כאחת. זה משמע שכולן מאה היו אבותיו, שהרי מכולן נתעברה אמו. ולא כפי' רש"י שפירש וחד נאנאי – שאחד מהן אביו. ופי' הערוך:* נאנאי – כלב, שבאו עליה מאה אנשים וכלב אחד. וכן מפורש בויקרא רבה ובאגדה דשמואל, אמר ר' יצחק: אותה הלילה שפירשה ערפה מחמותה נתערבו בה גיים של מאה בני אדם, הדא דכתיב: "והוא מדבר עמם והנה איש הבינים וגו' ממערכות פלשתים", "ממערות" כתיב – ממאה ערלות פלשתים. רבי תנחומא אמר: אף כלב אחד, שנאמר: "ויאמר הפלשתי אל דוד הכלב אנכי" וגו'. ותו התם: "ויתיצב ארבעים יום", אמר רבי ברכיה ב"ר יצחק: בשכר ארבעים פסיעות שהלכה ערפה עם חמותה, נתלה לבנה ארבעים יום. **מפני** שהשם וכל כנויו מונחים בארון. תוספתא (פ"ז ע"ש): "כי ה' אלהיכם ההולך עמכם" – זה השם הנתון בארון, שנאמר: "וישלח אותם משה" וגו' – מלמד שהיה פנחס משוח מלחמה, "וכלי הקודש" – זה הארון, ויש אומרים: אלו בגדי כהונה, שנא': "ובגדי הקודש אשר לאהרן". [רבי יהודה בן לקיש] אומר: ב' ארונות היו עמהם, זה שיוצא עמהן למלחמה היו בו שברי לוחות, שנאמר: "ויסעו מהר ה'" וגו', זה שהיה עמהן היה בו ס"ת, שנאמר: "ויעפילו לעלות" וגו'. ובירושלמי אמרי': ארון אחד היה.

מאלו התוס' לא מצאתי יותר

שמעו דברי מערכי מלחמה. מי ראוי לחזור ומי ראוי לילך. וחזרו הראוים לחזור, כגון בנה בית ונטע כרם ואירש אשה וירא ורך הלבב. ואע"ג דכתיב בהן: "ודברו השוטרים" – לקמן אמרינן דכהן קאמר להו, אלא שהשוטרים משמיעין דבריו לעם. **אל ירך לבבכם אל תיראו ואל תחפזו ואל תערצו.** ארבעה אזהרות כנגד ארבעה דברים שאומות העולם היו עושין לאיים: מגיפין בתריסין, ומריעין בקרנות, וצווחין בקולם, ורומסין בנהלת סוסיהן ודהרותם. אבל נצוח חרבות ושפעת קלגסים הן עיקר המלחמה, ואינן לאיים. **בגילוי פנים.** בחוצפה. **ברו.** בחרו. **לכדו פיו.** אמר פיו את כשלונו. **וירד אלי.** משמע: עלי – שהוא יגבר, דהוה ליה למימר "וילחם אתי". **ואידך והכני.** ואע"ג דהדר אמר "ואם אני אוכל לו והכיתיו", מכל מקום פתיחת פיו לרעתו (ב). **דוד הדר קאמר ליה ואני בא.** ואין זו פתיחת פה לרעה, דאמר ליה: אתה בא למשול בי על ידי דבר שאין בו ממש, ואני בא למשול בך בשם שהנצחונות שלו. **כנגד ארבעים יום.** שאיחרה תורה להתקבל, ניתן לו כח להתייצב. **מכל מום.** מתוקן ומנוקה מכל מום של כיעור. **שבאחיו.** ארבעה (ג) היו (לו), כדלקמן. **בר מאה פאפי וחד נאנאי.** בן התערובת. שבאו הרבה אנשים על אמו בלילה אחת ונתעברה מן אחד, נמצא האחד אביו וכולן מנאפים. **נאנאי.** זהו אב בלשון פרסי. **פאפי.** פרשטר"א. ולשון "איש הבינים" – שיצא מבין אנשים הרבה. **כתיב מערות.** ממערות פלשתים. **כתיב ערפה.** "שם האחת ערפה" (רות א), וכתיב "הרפה" – "אשר בילידי הרפה". והיא ערפה, כדאמרי' לקמן שנגזר עליה שיפלו בניה בחרב ביד בני רות שדבקה בשכינה. **עורפין אותה.** הפקירה עצמה כבהמה, (ד) פנים כנגד עורף. **כהריפות.** חטין כתושין. **סף ומדון וגלית וישבי.** כולם בספר שמואל*. **בני הנשוקה.** שנשקה לחמותה להפרד מעמה, שלא נתגיירה. **ותבכינה עוד.** פעם שניה, דלעיל מיני' כתי': "ותשאנה קולן ותבכינה". **ארבע דמעות.** שתי בכיות משתי עינים. **חץ.** לשון חצי, הודיעך הכתוב שלא סיפר בחצי גבורתו. **לאודועי שבחיה דדוד.** שנלחם עם גבור כמוהו. **כתיב שובך.** בספר שמואל (ב' י), וכתיב שופך בדברי הימים (א' יט). **אשפתו כקבר פתוח.** בחיילות של נבוכדנצר כתיב. ואיידי דנקט פלוגתא דרב ושמואל בדרשות דקראי, נקט לה. **מפני שאומנים.** אבל אינם גבורים. **של זבל.** מחמת שאוכלין הרבה בגבורה. **שמע מינה.** מדקאמר: שמא תאמר חולי מעיים הם. **ליטרח בנפשיה.** לבקש לו רפואות, טרם יכבד חוליו עליו. **דאגה בלב איש ישחנה.** יסחנה מדעתו. **ישיחנה לאחרים.** **וכל כך למה.** אומר להם, ומה היא הבטחה הזו שהבטיחן "כי ה' אלהיכם ההולך", ולא אמר "כי ה' אלהיכם עמכם", ומה היא הליכה זו דמשמע הולך ממש? **שהשם וכל כינויו** עומדין **בארון.** היוצא עמהם במלחמה. שפיטפט

הגהות הב"ח

(א) גמ' ובכידון דוד הדר אמר וכו' צבאות אלהי מערכות כצ"ל ותיבת ישראל נמחק: (ב) רש"י ד"ה ואידך וכו' לרעתו הוא הס"ד: (ג) ד"ה שבאחיו ארבעה אחים היו: (ד) ד"ה עורפין וכו' כבהמה אף פנים:

מסורת הש"ס

[ערך בן ד']

[לקמן מח. סנהדרין צג: עו:]

[וכ' כח]

יומא עג. [סנהדרין ק:]

[ב"ב יד:]

מוּנָּחִין בָּאָרוֹן, וְכֵן הוּא אוֹמֵר: "וַיִּשְׁלַח אוֹתָם מֹשֶׁה אֶלֶף לַמַּטֶּה לַצָּבָא אוֹתָם וְאֶת פִּינְחָס". "אוֹתָם" – אֵלּוּ סַנְהֶדְרִין, "פִּינְחָס" – זֶה מְשׁוּחַ מִלְחָמָה, "וּכְלֵי הַקּוֹדֶשׁ" – זֶה אָרוֹן וְלוּחוֹת שֶׁבּוֹ, "וַחֲצוֹצְרוֹת הַתְּרוּעָה" – אֵלּוּ הַשּׁוֹפָרוֹת. תָּנָא: לֹא לְחִנָּם הָלַךְ פִּינְחָס לַמִּלְחָמָה, אֶלָּא לִיפָּרַע דִּין אֲבִי אִמּוֹ, שֶׁנֶּאֱמַר: "וְהַמְּדָנִים מָכְרוּ אוֹתוֹ אֶל מִצְרָיִם" וגו'. לְמֵימְרָא דְּפִינְחָס מִיּוֹסֵף אָתֵי? וְהָא כְּתִיב: "וְאֶלְעָזָר בֶּן אַהֲרֹן לָקַח לוֹ מִבְּנוֹת פּוּטִיאֵל לוֹ לְאִשָּׁה", *מַאי לָאו – דְּאָתֵי מִיִּתְרוֹ שֶׁפִּיטֵּם עֲגָלִים לַעֲבוֹדָה זָרָה? לָא, מִיּוֹסֵף שֶׁפִּטְפֵּט בְּיִצְרוֹ. וַהֲלֹא שְׁבָטִים מְבַזִּין אוֹתוֹ: רְאִיתֶם בֶּן פּוּטִי זֶה, בֶּן שֶׁפִּיטֵּם אֲבִי אִמּוֹ עֲגָלִים לַעֲבוֹדָה זָרָה יַהֲרוֹג נָשִׂיא מִיִּשְׂרָאֵל! אֶלָּא, אִי אֲבוּהּ דְּאִימֵּיהּ מִיּוֹסֵף – אִימֵּיהּ דְּאִימֵּיהּ מִיִּתְרוֹ, וְאִי אִימֵּיהּ דְּאִימֵּיהּ מִיּוֹסֵף – אֲבוּהּ דְּאִימֵּיהּ מִיִּתְרוֹ. דַּיְקָא נַמִי, דִּכְתִיב: "מִבְּנוֹת פּוּטִיאֵל" – תְּרֵי מַשְׁמַע, שְׁמַע מִינָּהּ. §

מתני' "וְדִבְּרוּ הַשּׁוֹטְרִים אֶל הָעָם לֵאמֹר מִי הָאִישׁ אֲשֶׁר בָּנָה בַיִת חָדָשׁ וְלֹא חֲנָכוֹ יֵלֵךְ וְיָשֹׁב לְבֵיתוֹ" וגו'. [א]אֶחָד הַבּוֹנֶה בֵּית הַתֶּבֶן, בֵּית הַבָּקָר, בֵּית הָעֵצִים, בֵּית הָאוֹצָרוֹת. אֶחָד הַבּוֹנֶה, וְאֶחָד הַלּוֹקֵחַ, וְאֶחָד הַיּוֹרֵשׁ, וְאֶחָד שֶׁנִּתַּן לוֹ מַתָּנָה. "וּמִי הָאִישׁ אֲשֶׁר נָטַע כֶּרֶם וְלֹא חִלְּלוֹ" וגו' – [ב]אֶחָד הַנּוֹטֵעַ כֶּרֶם, וְאֶחָד הַנּוֹטֵעַ חֲמִשָּׁה אִילָנֵי מַאֲכָל, וַאֲפִילּוּ מֵחֲמֵשֶׁת הַמִּינִין. אֶחָד הַנּוֹטֵעַ, וְאֶחָד הַמַּבְרִיךְ, וְאֶחָד הַמַּרְכִּיב, וְאֶחָד הַלּוֹקֵחַ, וְאֶחָד הַיּוֹרֵשׁ, וְאֶחָד שֶׁנִּתַּן לוֹ מַתָּנָה. "וּמִי הָאִישׁ אֲשֶׁר אֵרַשׂ אִשָּׁה" וגו' – [ג]אֶחָד הַמְאָרֵס אֶת הַבְּתוּלָה וְאֶחָד הַמְאָרֵס אֶת הָאַלְמָנָה. אֲפִי' שׁוֹמֶרֶת יָבָם, וַאֲפִי' שָׁמַע שֶׁמֵּת אָחִיו בַּמִּלְחָמָה – חוֹזֵר וּבָא לוֹ. כָּל אֵלּוּ (א) וְאֵלּוּ שׁוֹמְעִין דִּבְרֵי כֹהֵן מַעַרְכֵי מִלְחָמָה, וְחוֹזְרִין, וּמְסַפְּקִין מַיִם וּמָזוֹן, וּמְתַקְּנִין אֶת הַדְּרָכִים. וְאֵלּוּ שֶׁאֵינָן חוֹזְרִין: [ד]הַבּוֹנֶה בֵּית שַׁעַר, אַכְסַדְרָה וּמִרְפֶּסֶת, [ה]הַנּוֹטֵעַ אַרְבַּע אִילָנֵי מַאֲכָל, וַחֲמִשָּׁה אִילָנֵי סְרָק, [ו]הַמַּחֲזִיר אֶת גְּרוּשָׁתוֹ, אַלְמָנָה לְכֹהֵן גָּדוֹל, גְּרוּשָׁה וַחֲלוּצָה לְכֹהֵן הֶדְיוֹט, מַמְזֶרֶת וּנְתִינָה לְיִשְׂרָאֵל, בַּת יִשְׂרָאֵל לְמַמְזֵר וּלְנָתִין – לֹא הָיָה חוֹזֵר. רַבִּי יְהוּדָה אוֹמֵר: אַף הַבּוֹנֶה בַּיִת עַל מְכוֹנוֹ לֹא הָיָה חוֹזֵר. ר' אֱלִיעֶזֶר אוֹמֵר: אַף הַבּוֹנֶה בֵּית לְבֵנִים בַּשָּׁרוֹן לֹא הָיָה חוֹזֵר. [ז]אֵלּוּ שֶׁאֵין זָזִין מִמְּקוֹמָן: בָּנָה בַיִת וַחֲנָכוֹ, נָטַע כֶּרֶם וְחִלְּלוֹ, הַנּוֹשֵׂא אֶת אֲרוּסָתוֹ, הַכּוֹנֵס אֶת יְבִמְתּוֹ. שֶׁנֶּאֱ': "נָקִי יִהְיֶה לְבֵיתוֹ שָׁנָה אֶחָת". "לְבֵיתוֹ" – זֶה בֵּיתוֹ, "יִהְיֶה" – זֶה כַּרְמוֹ, "וְשִׂמַּח אֶת אִשְׁתּוֹ" – זוֹ אִשְׁתּוֹ, "אֲשֶׁר לָקָח" – לְהָבִיא אֶת יְבִמְתּוֹ. [ח]אֵין מְסַפְּקִין *(לָהֶם) מַיִם וּמָזוֹן וְאֵין מְתַקְּנִין אֶת הַדְּרָכִים. §

גמ' תָּנוּ רַבָּנַן: "וְדִבְּרוּ הַשּׁוֹטְרִים". יָכוֹל דְּבָרִים שֶׁל עַצְמָן? כְּשֶׁהוּא אוֹמֵר: "וְיָסְפוּ הַשּׁוֹטְרִים" – הֲרֵי דְּבָרִים שֶׁל עַצְמָן אָמוּר, הָא מָה אֲנִי מְקַיֵּים "וְדִבְּרוּ הַשּׁוֹטְרִים" – בְּדִבְרֵי מְשׁוּחַ מִלְחָמָה הַכָּתוּב מְדַבֵּר. הָא כֵּיצַד? [ט]כֹּהֵן מְדַבֵּר, וְשׁוֹטֵר מַשְׁמִיעַ. תָּנֵי חֲדָא: כֹּהֵן מְדַבֵּר וְשׁוֹטֵר מַשְׁמִיעַ. וְתַנְיָא אִידָךְ: כֹּהֵן מְדַבֵּר וְכֹהֵן מַשְׁמִיעַ. וְתַנְיָא אִידָךְ: שׁוֹטֵר מְדַבֵּר וְשׁוֹטֵר מַשְׁמִיעַ. אָמַר אַבַּיֵי: הָא כֵּיצַד? [י]מִ"וְנִגַּשׁ" וְעַד "וְדִבְּרוּ" – כֹּהֵן מְדַבֵּר וְכֹהֵן מַשְׁמִיעַ. מִ"וְדִבְּרוּ" עַד "וְיָסְפוּ" – כֹּהֵן מְדַבֵּר וְשׁוֹטֵר מַשְׁמִיעַ, מִ"וְיָסְפוּ" וְאֵילָךְ – שׁוֹטֵר מְדַבֵּר וְשׁוֹטֵר מַשְׁמִיעַ. § "מִי הָאִישׁ אֲשֶׁר בָּנָה בַיִת חָדָשׁ" כו'. § תָּנוּ רַבָּנַן: "אֲשֶׁר בָּנָה". אֵין לִי אֶלָּא אֲשֶׁר בָּנָה, לָקַח וְיָרַשׁ וְנִיתַּן לוֹ בְּמַתָּנָה מִנַּיִן – ת"ל: "מִי הָאִישׁ אֲשֶׁר בָּנָה בַיִת". אֵין לִי אֶלָּא בַּיִת, מִנַּיִן לְרַבּוֹת בֵּית הַתֶּבֶן וּבֵית הַבָּקָר וּבֵית הָעֵצִים וּבֵית הָאוֹצָרוֹת – ת"ל: "אֲשֶׁר בָּנָה", מִכָּל מָקוֹם. יָכוֹל שֶׁאֲנִי מְרַבֶּה אַף הַבּוֹנֶה בֵּית שַׁעַר אַכְסַדְרָה וּמִרְפֶּסֶת – תַּלְמוּד לוֹמַר: "בַּיִת", מָה בַּיִת הָרָאוּי לְדִירָה – אַף כֹּל הָרָאוּי לְדִירָה. ר' אֱלִיעֶזֶר בֶּן יַעֲקֹב אוֹמֵר: "בַּיִת" – כְּמַשְׁמָעוֹ. "לֹא חָנַךְ" "וְלֹא חֲנָכוֹ" – [כ]פְּרָט לְגַזְלָן. לֵימָא, דְּלָא כְּרַבִּי יוֹסֵי הַגְּלִילִי, דְּאִי *רַבִּי יוֹסֵי הַגְּלִילִי – הָא אָמַר: "וְרַךְ הַלֵּבָב" – זֶה הַמִּתְיָירֵא מֵעֲבֵירוֹת

מעבירות

שֶׁפִּטְפֵּט. זִילְזֵל וְכָבַשׁ אוֹתוֹ, וְלֹא *חֲטָאוֹ. וַהֲלֹא שְׁבָטִים מְבַזִּים אוֹתוֹ. כִּדְאָמְרִינַן בְּ"אֵלּוּ הֵן הַנִּשְׂרָפִין" (סנהדרין דף פב:), לְפִיכָךְ הוּצְרַךְ לְיַחֲסוֹ שָׁם: "פִּינְחָס בֶּן אֶלְעָזָר בֶּן אַהֲרֹן הַכֹּהֵן". תְּרֵי פּוּטִי. מִדְּלָא כְּתִיב פּוּטְאֵל. **מתני'** בֵּית הָאוֹצָרוֹת. לְאוֹצַר יַיִן שֶׁמֶן וּתְבוּאָה. וְאֶחָד הַלּוֹקֵחַ. בַּיִת בָּנוּי, שֶׁהֲרֵי אֶצְלוֹ הוּא חָדָשׁ. וּבַגְּמָרָא מְרַבִּינַן לֵיהּ מִקְּרָא. חֲמִשָּׁה אִילָנֵי מַאֲכָל. דְּהָכִי הָוֵי כֶּרֶם, שְׁתַּיִם כְּנֶגֶד שְׁתַּיִם וְאַחַת יוֹצְאָה זָנָב. כָּזֶה

* *

* *

*

וַאֲפִילּוּ מֵה' מִינִין. מִצְטָרְפִין. (ב) חִילְּלוֹ. בִּשְׁנַת הָרְבִיעִית לִנְטִיעָתוֹ, שֶׁחִלֵּל אֶת הַפֵּירוֹת בְּמָעוֹת כְּדֶרֶךְ מַעֲשֵׂר שֵׁנִי, וּמַעֲלֶה אֶת הַמָּעוֹת לִירוּשָׁלַיִם וְאוֹכְלָן, כִּדְכְתִיב (ויקרא יט): "קֹדֶשׁ הִלּוּלִים" וְגָמַר קֹדֶשׁ קֹדֶשׁ מִמַּעֲשֵׂר. ה"ג כָּל אֵלּוּ שׁוֹמְעִין דִּבְרֵי כֹּהֵן מַעַרְכֵי מִלְחָמָה וְחוֹזְרִין. כְּמוֹ: שׁוֹמְעִין דִּבְרֵי מַעַרְכֵי מִלְחָמָה שֶׁל כֹּהֵן. כְּלוֹמַר, שֶׁהַכֹּהֵן אוֹמֵר לָהֶן. סְרָק. כְּגוֹן אֲרָזִים וְשִׁקְמִים, שֶׁאֵינָן עֵץ פְּרִי. וְהַמַּחֲזִיר גְּרוּשָׁתוֹ. וְאֵירְסָהּ – אֵינוֹ חוֹזֵר, שֶׁאֵינָהּ חֲדָשָׁה לוֹ, וּקְרָא אַ"אִשָּׁה חֲדָשָׁה" קְפִיד, כִּדְכְתִיב: "כִּי יִקַּח אִישׁ אִשָּׁה חֲדָשָׁה" (דברים כד). אַלְמָנָה. וְאֵירְסָהּ כֹּהֵן גָּדוֹל – אֵינוֹ חוֹזֵר בִּשְׁבִילָהּ, דְּאִימְעוּט מִ"וְלֹא לְקָחָהּ", מִדְּלָא כְּתִיב "וְלֹא לָקַח". עַל מְכוֹנוֹ. סְתָרוֹ וּבְנָאוֹ בְּמִדָּה רִאשׁוֹנָה – אֵינוֹ חוֹזֵר, דְּלָאו חָדָשׁ הוּא, הוֹאִיל וְלֹא חִידֵּשׁ לְהוֹסִיף עָלָיו, וַאֲפִילּוּ אֶצְלוֹ אֵינוֹ חָדָשׁ, וְגָרַע מֵהַלּוֹקֵחַ וְהַיּוֹרֵשׁ. אַף הַבּוֹנֶה בֵּית לְבֵנִים בַּשָּׁרוֹן. מָקוֹם הוּא שֶׁשְּׁמוֹ שָׁרוֹן, וְאֵין הַקַּרְקַע יָפָה לִלְבֵנִים, וְלֹא הָוֵי דָּבָר קַיָּימָא, שֶׁפַּעֲמַיִם צָרִיךְ לְחַדְּשָׁהּ בְּשֶׁבַע שָׁנִים. וְאֵלּוּ שֶׁאֵין זָזִין מִמְּקוֹמָן. דְּהָנָךְ דִּלְעֵיל הוֹלְכִין עַד לַסְּפָר, וְשָׁם שׁוֹמְעִין דִּבְרֵי כֹּהֵן וְחוֹזְרִין מִן הַמַּעֲרָכָה לְאֶרֶץ יִשְׂרָאֵל, וְאֵינָם חוֹזְרִין לְבָתֵּיהֶם, אֶלָּא עוֹסְקִין בְּסִיפּוּק מַיִם וּמָזוֹן לְהוֹלְכֵי מִלְחָמָה. וְאֵלּוּ אֵין זָזִין מִמְּקוֹמָן אֲפִילּוּ לָלֶכֶת עַד הַסְּפָר וְלָשׁוּב ע"פ כֹּהֵן. הַבּוֹנֶה בַּיִת וַחֲנָכוֹ. וְלֹא דָּר בּוֹ עֲדַיִין שָׁנָה. וְכֵן הַנּוֹטֵעַ כֶּרֶם וְחִילְּלוֹ. וַעֲדַיִין לֹא עָבְרָה שְׁנַת רְבִיעִית עָלָיו שְׁלֵימָה. נָקִי יִהְיֶה לְבֵיתוֹ. בִּשְׁבִיל בֵּיתוֹ. יִהְיֶה. רִבּוּיָא הוּא, הוֹסִיף לְךָ הֲוָיָה אַחֶרֶת לִהְיוֹת כָּזוֹ. **גמ'** יָכוֹל דְּבָרִים שֶׁל עַצְמָן. יָכוֹל שֶׁהַדְּבָרִים הַלָּלוּ שֶׁהֵם אוֹמְרִים "מִי הָאִישׁ אֲשֶׁר בָּנָה" וגו' – שֶׁל עַצְמָן הֵן, וְלֹא הָיָה כֹּהֵן אוֹמְרָן אֶלָּא הַשּׁוֹטְרִים? ת"ל וְיָסְפוּ הַשּׁוֹטְרִים. "לְדַבֵּר אֶל הָעָם וְאָמְרוּ מִי הָאִישׁ" וגו'. וְיָסְפוּ – מַשְׁמַע שֶׁדָּבָר זֶה הֵם מוֹסִיפִים מִשֶּׁלָּהֶם. הֲרֵי דְּבָרִים שֶׁל עַצְמָן אָמוּר. שֶׁהַדָּבָר זֶה לְבַדּוֹ הֵן מוֹסִיפִין עַל שֶׁל כֹּהֵן. מִדְּעַד הָשְׁתָּא גַּבֵּי נָטַע וְגַבֵּי אֵירֵס אִשָּׁה לֹא כְּתִיב "וְיָסְפוּ", וְהָכָא כְּתִיב "וְיָסְפוּ" – ש"מ עַד הֵנָּה דִּבְרֵי כֹהֵן, וְאֶת זוֹ הֵן מוֹסִיפִין. הָא מָה אֲנִי מְקַיֵּים וְדִבְּרוּ הַשּׁוֹטְרִים. בְּבָנָה וְנָטַע וְאֵירַס. בְּדִבְרֵי מְשׁוּחַ מִלְחָמָה הַכָּתוּב מְדַבֵּר. שֶׁהַכֹּהֵן אוֹמֵר וְהַשּׁוֹטְרִים מַשְׁמִיעִין אוֹתָן. מִוְנִגַּשׁ עַד וְדִבְּרוּ. דְּהַיְינוּ "שְׁמַע יִשְׂרָאֵל אַתֶּם קְרֵבִים" וגו' עַד "לְהוֹשִׁיעַ אֶתְכֶם". מִי הָאִישׁ. רִיבּוּיָא הוּא, דְּמָצֵי לְמִיכְתַּב "מִי אֲשֶׁר בָּנָה", וּמִדְּלָא כְּתִיב "אֲשֶׁר בַּיִת בָּנָה" – דְּרוֹשׁ בֵּיהּ: בָּנָה מ"מ. וְהַאי דִּכְתִיב "בַּיִת" – לְמַעוּטֵי בֵּית שַׁעַר אַכְסַדְרָה וּמִרְפֶּסֶת, שֶׁהֵם עֲשׂוּיִם לִדְרִיסַת רֶגֶל, וְלֹא רְאוּיִם לָדוּר בָּהֶם. בֵּית שַׁעַר. בֵּית כְּנִיסַת שַׁעַר הֶחָצֵר, לְהִסְתּוֹפֵף שָׁם שׁוֹמֵר הַפֶּתַח. וְלֹא חֲנָכוֹ. מִדְּלָא כְּתִיב (ג) "חָנַךְ" – הָוֵי מִיעוּטָא: חֲנָכוֹ לָזֶה וְלֹא לְאַחֵר, פְּרָט לְגוֹזֵל בַּיִת. כְּרַבִּי יוֹסֵי הַגְּלִילִי. דְּמַתְנִי'.

מעבירות

תורה אור
במדבר לא — "וַיִּשְׁלַח אוֹתָם"
בראשית לז — "וְהַמְּדָנִים"
שמות ו — "וְאֶלְעָזָר"
דברים כ — "וְדִבְּרוּ"
שם — "וּמִי הָאִישׁ אֲשֶׁר נָטַע"
שם — "וּמִי הָאִישׁ אֲשֶׁר אֵרַשׂ"
שם כד — "נָקִי יִהְיֶה"
שם כ — "וְיָסְפוּ"

מסורת הש"ס:
ס"א חס בו
כ"כ קט: [סנהדרין פב:]
[טעות הדפוס וכן במשנה ליתא]
[לקמן מז.]

עין משפט נר מצוה:
ג א מיי' פ"ז מהל' מלכים הל"ה סמג עשין קכ:
ד ב מיי' שם הל"ו:
ה ג מיי' שם הל"ז:
ו ד מיי' שם הל"ה:
ז ה מיי' שם הל"ו:
ח ו מיי' שם הל"ח:
ט ז מיי' שם הל"י:
י ח מיי' שם הלי"א:
יא ט י מיי' שם הל"ג:
יב כ מיי' שם הל' ה ו:

הגהות הב"ח
(א) במשנה כל אלו שומעין כצ"ל ותיבת ואלו נמחק: (ב) רש"י ד"ה ואפילו וכו' מצטרפין הס"ד ואח"כ מ"ה ולא חיללו וכו' שמחלל את הפירות: (ג) ד"ה ולא וכו' כתיב ולא חנך:

מֵעֲבֵירוֹת שֶׁבְּיָדוֹ! אֲפִילּוּ תֵּימָא רַבִּי יוֹסֵי הַגְּלִילִי, כְּגוֹן דַּעֲבַד תְּשׁוּבָה וִיהַב דְּמֵי. אִי הָכִי הֲוָה לֵיהּ לוֹקֵחַ, וְלִיהֲדַר! כֵּיוָן דְּמֵעִיקָּרָא בְּתוֹרַת גְּזֵילָה אֲתָא לְיָדֵיהּ — לָא.§ °"וּמִי הָאִישׁ אֲשֶׁר נָטַע כֶּרֶם" כו'.§ תָּנוּ רַבָּנַן: "אֲשֶׁר נָטַע". אֵין לִי אֶלָּא נָטַע, לָקַח וְיָרַשׁ וְנִיתַּן לוֹ בְּמַתָּנָה מִנַּיִן — תַּלְמוּד לוֹמַר: "וּמִי הָאִישׁ אֲשֶׁר נָטַע כֶּרֶם". אֵין לִי אֶלָּא כֶּרֶם, מִנַּיִן לְרַבּוֹת חֲמִשָּׁה אִילָנֵי מַאֲכָל וַאֲפִילּוּ מִשְּׁאָר מִינִין — תַּלְמוּד לוֹמַר: "אֲשֶׁר נָטַע". יָכוֹל שֶׁאֲנִי מַרְבֶּה הַנּוֹטֵעַ אַרְבָּעָה אִילָנֵי מַאֲכָל, וַחֲמִשָּׁה אִילָנֵי סְרָק — תַּלְמוּד לוֹמַר: "כֶּרֶם". רַבִּי אֱלִיעֶזֶר בֶּן יַעֲקֹב אוֹמֵר: "כֶּרֶם" — כְּמַשְׁמָעוֹ. "לֹא חִילֵּל" "וְלֹא חִילְּלוֹ" — פְּרָט לְמַבְרִיךְ וּלְמַרְכִּיב. וְהָא אֲנַן תְּנַן: אֶחָד הַנּוֹטֵעַ וְאֶחָד הַמַּבְרִיךְ וְאֶחָד הַמַּרְכִּיב! אָמַר רַבִּי זֵירָא אָמַר רַב חִסְדָּא: לָא קַשְׁיָא; אכָּאן — *בְּהַרְכָּבַת אִיסּוּר, כָּאן — בְּהַרְכָּבַת הֶיתֵּר. הַאי הַרְכָּבַת הֶיתֵּר הֵיכִי דָּמֵי? אִילֵימָא יַלְדָּה בְּיַלְדָּה — תֵּיפּוֹק לֵיהּ דְּבָעֵי מִיהֲדַר מִשּׁוּם יַלְדָּה רִאשׁוֹנָה! אֶלָּא יַלְדָּה בִּזְקֵינָה — *וְהָאָמַר רַבִּי אַבָּהוּ: ביַלְדָּה שֶׁסִּיבְּכָהּ בִּזְקֵינָה — *בָּטְלָה יַלְדָּה בִּזְקֵינָה וְאֵין בָּהּ דִּין עָרְלָה! אָמַר רַבִּי יִרְמְיָה: לְעוֹלָם יַלְדָּה בְּיַלְדָּה, וּכְגוֹן דְּנָטַע לְהָךְ קַמַּיְיתָא לְסְיָיג וּלְקוֹרוֹת. *דִּתְנַן: גהַנּוֹטֵעַ לְסְיָיג וּלְקוֹרוֹת — פָּטוּר מִן הָעָרְלָה. וּמַאי שְׁנָא יַלְדָּה בִּזְקֵינָה דְּבָטְלָה, וּמַאי שְׁנָא יַלְדָּה בְּיַלְדָּה דְּלָא בָּטְלָה? הָתָם, אִי מִימְלִיךְ עֲלָהּ — לָאו בַּת מִיהֲדַר הִיא. הָכָא, אִי מִימְלִיךְ עֲלָהּ — בַּת מִיהֲדַר הִיא, [דְּהָא מֵעִיקָּרָא לְפֵירֵי קַיְימָא], מִידֵי דַּהֲוָה אַעָלוּ מֵאֵילֵיהֶן. *דִּתְנַן: דעָלוּ מֵאֵילֵיהֶן — חַיָּיבִין בְּעָרְלָה. וְלוֹקְמַהּ בְּכֶרֶם שֶׁל שְׁנֵי שׁוּתָּפִין דְּהַאי הָדַר אַדִּידֵיהּ וְהַאי הָדַר אַדִּידֵיהּ? אָמַר רַב פָּפָּא, זֹאת אוֹמֶרֶת: הכֶּרֶם שֶׁל שְׁנֵי שׁוּתָּפִין — אֵין חוֹזְרִין עָלָיו מֵעַרְכֵי הַמִּלְחָמָה. וּמַאי שְׁנָא *מֵחֲמִשָּׁה אַחִין וּמֵת אֶחָד מֵהֶן בַּמִּלְחָמָה דְּכוּלָּן חוֹזְרִין? הָתָם — כָּל חַד וְחַד קָרֵינָא בֵּיהּ "אִשְׁתּוֹ", הָכָא — כָּל חַד וְחַד לָא קָרֵינָא בֵּיהּ "כַּרְמוֹ". רַב נַחְמָן בַּר יִצְחָק אָמַר: בְּמַבְרִיךְ אִילָן בְּיָרָק. וְהַאי תַּנָּא הוּא, *דְּתַנְיָא: הַמַּבְרִיךְ אִילָן בְּיָרָק, רַבָּן שִׁמְעוֹן בֶּן גַּמְלִיאֵל מַתִּיר מִשּׁוּם רַבִּי יְהוּדָה בֶּן גַּמְדָּא אִישׁ כְּפַר עַכּוֹ, וַחֲכָמִים אוֹסְרִין. כִּי אֲתָא רַב דִּימִי אָמַר רַבִּי יוֹחָנָן: הָא מַנִּי — רַבִּי אֱלִיעֶזֶר בֶּן יַעֲקֹב הִיא; לָא אָמַר רַבִּי אֱלִיעֶזֶר בֶּן יַעֲקֹב הָתָם "כֶּרֶם" כְּמַשְׁמָעוֹ? הָכָא נַמִי "נָטַע" כְּמַשְׁמָעוֹ, נוֹטֵעַ — אִין, מַבְרִיךְ וּמַרְכִּיב — לָא. כִּי אֲתָא רַב דִּימִי אָמַר רַבִּי יוֹחָנָן מִשּׁוּם רַבִּי אֱלִיעֶזֶר בֶּן יַעֲקֹב: חיַלְדָּה פְּחוּתָה מִטֶּפַח — חַיֶּיבֶת בְּעָרְלָה כָּל שְׁנוֹתֶיהָ, דְּמִתְחַזְיָא כְּבַת שַׁתָּא. טוְהָנֵי מִילֵּי — שְׁתַּיִם כְּנֶגֶד שְׁתַּיִם וְאַחַת יוֹצְאָה זָנָב, אֲבָל כּוּלֵּיהּ כֶּרֶם — קָלָא אִית לֵיהּ. כִּי אֲתָא רַב דִּימִי אָמַר רַבִּי יוֹחָנָן מִשּׁוּם רַבִּי אֱלִיעֶזֶר בֶּן יַעֲקֹב: *מֵת יתּוֹפֵס אַרְבַּע אַמּוֹת לְקְ"שׁ, דִּכְתִיב: °"לוֹעֵג לָרָשׁ חֵרֵף עוֹשֵׂהוּ". אָמַר רַבִּי יִצְחָק אָמַר רַבִּי יוֹחָנָן מִשּׁוּם רַבִּי אֱלִיעֶזֶר בֶּן יַעֲקֹב: חוֹרַגְתָּא הַגְּדֵילָה בֵּין הָאַחִין — אֲסוּרָה לִינָּשֵׂא לָאַחִין, דְּמִתְחַזְיָא כִּי אַחְתַּיְיהוּ. כוְלָא הִיא, קָלָא אִית לֵיהּ לְמִילְּתָא. וְאָמַר *רַבִּי יִצְחָק אָמַר ר' יוֹחָנָן מִשּׁוּם ר' אֱלִיעֶזֶר בֶּן יַעֲקֹב: ללֶקֶט שִׁכְחָה וּפֵאָה שֶׁעֲשָׂאָן בַּגּוֹרֶן — הוּקְבְּעוּ לְמַעֲשֵׂר. אָמַר עוּלָּא: לָא אֲמָרַן מאֶלָּא בַּשָּׂדֶה, אֲבָל בָּעִיר — קָלָא אִית לֵיהּ לְמִילְּתָא. וְאָמַר רַבִּי יִצְחָק אָמַר רַבִּי יוֹחָנָן מִשּׁוּם ר' אֱלִיעֶזֶר בֶּן יַעֲקֹב: ניַלְדָּה הַפְּחוּתָה מִטֶּפַח — אֵינָהּ מְקַדֶּשֶׁת אֶת הַזְּרָעִים. סוְהָנֵי מִילֵּי — שְׁתַּיִם כְּנֶגֶד שְׁתַּיִם וְאַחַת יוֹצְאָה זָנָב, אֲבָל כּוּלֵּי כֶּרֶם — מַקְדִּישׁ. וְאָמַר רַבִּי יִצְחָק אָמַר רַבִּי יוֹחָנָן מִשּׁוּם רַבִּי אֱלִיעֶזֶר בֶּן יַעֲקֹב:

מֵת

תורה אור: דברים כ | משלי יז

מסורת הש"ס: ברכות יח. | [ברכות מ:] | [ועיין תוס' ר"ה ט: ד"ה מרכיב] | מנחות סט: ע"ש נדרים נז: ע"ש [ועיין תוספות ע"ז מט. ד"ה שאם] | ערלה פ"א מ"ח | שם מ"ב | [לקמן מד.] | תוספתא דכלאים פ"א | רש"ל | (רש"ל מ"ז)

מֵעֲבֵירוֹת שֶׁבְּיָדוֹ. וְהָאִי אִית לֵיהּ לְמִיהֲדַר מִשּׁוּם "הַיָּרֵא וְרַךְ הַלֵּבָב". תַּלְמוּד לוֹמַר אֲשֶׁר נָטַע. מִדְּלָא כְּתִיב "אֲשֶׁר כֶּרֶם נָטַע" — דְּרוֹשׁ בֵּיהּ נַמִי נָטַע מִכָּל מָקוֹם, וַאֲפִי' אֵינוֹ כֶּרֶם, שֶׁהֲרֵי לֹא הִזְכִּיר כֶּרֶם עֲדַיִין. תַּלְמוּד לוֹמַר כֶּרֶם. דְּדָמֵי לְכֶרֶם. וּפָחוֹת שֶׁבַּכְּרָמִים חֲמִשָּׁה גְּפָנִים הֵם. כֶּרֶם כְּמַשְׁמָעוֹ. וְלֹא שְׁאָר אִילָנוֹת. חִילְּלוֹ. מַשְׁמַע מִיעוּטָא: לָזֶה וְלֹא לְאַחֵר. כָּאן בְּהַרְכָּבַת אִיסּוּר. בְּרַיְיתָא בְּהַרְכָּבַת אִיסּוּר, מִין בְּשֶׁאֵינוֹ מִינוֹ וּמַעֲטֵיהּ קְרָא כְּדְמַעֵיט "וְלֹא חֲנָכוֹ" גַּבֵּי בַּיִת — פְּרָט לְגַזְלָן. מַבְרִיךְ. שֶׁכּוֹפֵף [הַזְּמוֹרָה אוֹ הָאִיחוּר] בָּאָרֶץ. מַרְכִּיב. שֶׁנּוֹקֵב הָאִילָן וְנוֹטֵל מִן הָרַךְ שֶׁבְּעַנְפֵי הָאִילָן וְתוֹחֵב לְתוֹכוֹ, וְעוֹשֶׂה עָנָף בְּתוֹךְ הַנֶּקֶב, וְנוֹשֵׂא מִמִּין אוֹתוֹ אִילָן שֶׁנּוֹטֵל מִמֶּנּוּ. וְיִשְׂרָאֵל מוּתָּר לְהַרְכִּיב מִשְּׁנֵי אִילָנוֹת שֶׁזֶּה פֵּירוֹתָיו גַּסִּין וְזֶה פֵּירוֹתָיו דַּקִּין דְּהָווּ מִמִּין אֶחָד, זֶה בָּזֶה. הַאי הַרְכָּבַת הֶיתֵּר. דְּאוֹקַמְתְּ מַתְנִי' בָּהּ, הֵיכִי דָּמֵי דְּחוֹזֵר מִפְּנֵי חִילּוּל הַהַרְכָּבָה?. אִי נֵימָא יַלְדָּה בְּיַלְדָּה. שֶׁאַף זוֹ שֶׁבַּקַּרְקַע שֶׁהִרְכִּיב אֶת הֶעָנָף בָּהּ נְטִיעָה הִיא, וַעֲדַיִין לֹא הִגִּיעָה לְשָׁנָה רְבִיעִית לְחַלְּלָהּ — הָא לָאו מִשּׁוּם הַרְכָּבָה הָדַר, דְּבְלָאו הַרְכָּבָה נַמִי בָּעֵי לְמִיהֲדַר מִן הַמִּלְחָמָה, מִשּׁוּם יַלְדָּה רִאשׁוֹנָה!. בִּזְקֵינָה. שֶׁכְּבָר נִתְחַלְּלָה. שֶׁסִּיבְּכָהּ. לְשׁוֹן "נֶאֱחַז בַּסְּבַךְ" (בראשית כב), שֶׁעֲשָׂאָהּ עָנָף בִּזְקֵינָה. בָּטְלָה לְגַבֵּי זְקֵינָה. וְאֵינָהּ חַיֶּיבֶת בְּעָרְלָה. וְאֵין בָּהּ דִּין רְבָעִי. וְכִי תְּנַן בְּמַסֶּכֶת עָרְלָה דְּמַרְכִּיב חַיָּיב בְּעָרְלָה — [זְקֵינָה] בְּיַלְדָּה תְּנַן, שֶׁאַף אוֹתוֹ עָנָף חַיָּיב בְּעָרְלָה, וְאַע"ג שֶׁקְּלָטוֹ מִזְּקֵינָה — נַעֲשָׂה עַכְשָׁיו יַלְדָּה שֶׁזּוּ הִיא נְטִיעָתוֹ. לְעוֹלָם יַלְדָּה בְּיַלְדָּה. וּדְקַשְׁיָא לָךְ: בְּלֹא הַרְכָּבָה נַמִי בָּעֵי לְמִיהֲדַר מִמַּעַרְכֵי הַמִּלְחָמָה אַקַּמַּיְיתָא. כְּגוֹן דְּנַטְעָהּ לְקַמַּיְיתָא לִסְיָיג. כְּגוֹן שֶׁהָיְתָה פִּרְצָה בְּגֶדֶר שָׂדֵהוּ וּנְטָעָהּ בַּפִּרְצָה לְסָתְמוֹ, לְשׁוֹן "סוּגָה בַּשּׁוֹשַׁנִּים" (שיר ז) — גְּדוּרָה בַּשּׁוֹשַׁנִּים. וּלְקוֹרוֹת. לָקוֹץ מִמֶּנָּה קוֹרוֹת לִכְשֶׁתִּגְדַּל. וּמַאי שְׁנָא יַלְדָּה בְּיַלְדָּה. כִּי הַךְ יַלְדָּה קַמַּיְיתָא, דִּכְזְקֵינָה הִיא לְעִנְיַן עָרְלָה, (דְּלֹא) בָּטְלָה הַרְכָּבָה בָּהּ לְהִפָּטֵר מִן הָעָרְלָה כְּמוֹתָהּ?. הָתָם. גַּבֵּי זְקֵנָה, לָאו בַּת אִימְלוֹכֵי הִיא, לַחֲזוֹר וְלִהְיוֹת יַלְדָּה עַל שׁוּם מַחֲשָׁבָה. אֲבָל נָטַע לִסְיָיג, אִי מַמְלִיךְ עֲלָהּ בְּתוֹךְ שְׁנֵי עָרְלָה לְקַיְּימָהּ לְפֵירוֹת — חַיֶּיבֶת בְּעָרְלָה. הִילְכָּךְ, יַלְדָּה דְּקָא מַרְכִּיב בְּגַוָּהּ לַאֲכִילָה — חַיֶּיבֶת בְּעָרְלָה. וְאַע"ג דְּלָא אִימְלִיךְ אַקַּמַּיְיתָא, הָא מִיהָא לַאֲכִילָה הוּא, וּמֵהַנְיָא נַחֲשָׁבָה. דְּעִיקָּר דִּידָהּ נַמִי, אִי הֲוָה חָשֵׁיב עֲלָהּ — הֲוָה מֵהַנֵּי מַחֲשָׁבָה, וְאַע"ג דִּבְשַׁעַת נְטִיעָה לָאו לְהָכִי נְטָעָהּ. מִידֵי דַּהֲוָה אָעָלוּ מֵאֵילֵיהֶן. דִּבְשַׁעַת נְטִיעָה לֵיכָּא כַּוָּונָה. וְלוֹקְמָהּ בְּכֶרֶם שֶׁל שְׁנֵי שׁוּתָּפִין. לָמָּה לִי לְאַהֲדוּרֵי אַשִּׁינּוּיָא דְּחִיקָא, בְּנוֹטֵעַ לִסְיָיג וּלְקוֹרוֹת? לוֹקְמָהּ בְּנוֹטֵעַ לַאֲכִילָה!

וּדְקַשְׁיָא לָךְ: תֵּיפּוֹק לֵיהּ מִשּׁוּם דְּבָעֵי לְמֶהְדַּר מִשּׁוּם רִאשׁוֹנָה — לִישַׁנֵּי: כְּגוֹן שֶׁהַנְּטִיעָה שֶׁל רְאוּבֵן וּבָא שִׁמְעוֹן וְהִרְכִּיב בָּהּ לִהְיוֹת פֵּירוֹת הַרְכָּבָה שֶׁלּוֹ!. וּמַאי שְׁנָא מֵחֲמִשָּׁה אַחִין. בָּרַיְיתָא הִיא לְקַמָּן בְּפִרְקִין (דף מד.). כּוּלָּן חוֹזְרִין. מִפְּנֵי שֶׁהִיא שׁוֹמֶרֶת יָבָם לְכוּלָּם. קָרֵינָא בֵּיהּ אִשְׁתּוֹ. שֶׁמָּא לָזֶה תִּתְיַיבֵּם. כָּל חַד וְחַד לָא קָרֵינָא בֵּיהּ כַּרְמוֹ. הַמְיוּחָד לוֹ, שֶׁאֵין לְךָ בָּהּ גֶּפֶן שֶׁאֵין לִשְׁנֵיהֶם חֵלֶק בָּהּ. רַב נַחְמָן אָמַר. הָא דְּקָתָנֵי מַתְנִי': מַרְכִּיב חוֹזֵר — בְּמַרְכִּיב אִילָן בְּיָרָק, דְּלָא בָּעֵי לְמִיהֲדַר מִשּׁוּם קַמָּא. וְאִם תֹּאמַר: מִין בְּשֶׁאֵינוֹ מִינוֹ הוּא, וְאִימַעִיטָא לָהּ הַרְכָּבַת אִיסּוּר מִ"וְלֹא חִילְּלוֹ" פְּרָט לְמַבְרִיךְ וּמַרְכִּיב — הַאי תַּנָּא הוּא דְּאָמַר מוּתָּר. כְּפַר עַכּוֹ. כֵּן שְׁמָהּ. הָא מַנִּי. דְּקָתָנֵי פְּרָט לְמַבְרִיךְ וּמַרְכִּיב לָאו סְתָמָא הִיא אֶלָּא סֵיפָא דְּמִילְּתָא דְּרַבִּי אֱלִיעֶזֶר בֶּן יַעֲקֹב הִיא וַאֲפִי' הַרְכָּבַת הֶיתֵּר לֹא הָדַר עֲלָהּ. פְּחוּתָה מִטֶּפַח. שֶׁהִיא שְׁפַל קוֹמָה, וְלֹא תִּגְבַּהּ לְעוֹלָם עַד טֶפַח. כָּל שְׁנוֹתֶיהָ. מִדְּרַבָּנַן כָּל הַיָּמִים עָרְלָה נוֹהֶגֶת בָּהּ. דְּמִתְחַזְיָא כְּבַת שַׁתָּא, וְהָרוֹאֶה שֶׁאוֹכְלִין פֵּירוֹתֶיהָ אוֹמֵר שֶׁפֵּירוֹת עָרְלָה מוּתָּרִין. קָלָא אִית לֵיהּ. הַכֹּל אוֹמְרִים כֶּרֶם יֵשׁ לִפְלוֹנִי מְשׁוּנֶּה מִכָּל הַכְּרָמִים, וְיוֹדְעִין שֶׁהִיא זְקֵינָה. לְהָכִי נָקַט שְׁתַּיִם כו' — דְּסָבַר לָהּ כְּמַאן דְּאָמַר בְּמַסֶּכֶת בְּרָכוֹת (דף לה.): כֶּרֶם רְבָעִי תְּנַן, שֶׁאֵין עָרְלָה נוֹהֶגֶת בִּנְטִיעָה אַחַת אֶלָּא בְּכֶרֶם שָׁלֵם. לִקְרִיאַת שְׁמַע. שֶׁאָסוּר לִקְרוֹת בְּאַרְבַּע אַמּוֹתָיו, מִשּׁוּם לוֹעֵג לָרָשׁ, שֶׁזֶּה קוֹרֵא וְזֶה אֵינוֹ יָכוֹל לִקְרוֹת. חוֹרַגְתָּא. בַּת אִשְׁתּוֹ. שֶׁגְּדֵלָה בֵּין הָאַחִין. בְּנֵי הַבַּעַל מֵאִשָּׁה אַחֶרֶת. דְּמִתְחַזְיָא כִּי אַחְתַּיְיהוּ. מִי שֶׁאֵינוֹ מַכִּיר בָּהּ, וְרוֹאֶה אוֹתָהּ שֶׁגְּדֵלָה אֶצְלוֹ, כִּסָבוּר שֶׁהִיא אֲחוֹתוֹ, וְאוֹמֵר שֶׁנּוֹשֵׂא אֲחוֹתוֹ. לֶקֶט שִׁכְחָה וּפֵאָה שֶׁעֲשָׂאָן. הֶעָנִי גּוֹרֶן, שֶׁכִּינֵּס הַרְבֵּה כְּאֶחָד וְעָשָׂה מֵהֶן כְּרִי. הוּקְבְּעוּ לְמַעֲשֵׂר. מִדְּרַבָּנַן, דְּמַאן דְּחָזֵי סָבוּר שֶׁגָּדַל בְּשָׂדֵהוּ. וְה"מ בַּשָּׂדֶה. שֶׁלֹּא יָדְעוּ הַכֹּל, (א) שֶׁנִּכְנְסוּ מְעַט מְעַט, וּסְבוּרִין שֶׁגָּדַל שָׁם. אֲבָל בָּעִיר — כָּל שְׁכֵנָיו רָאוּ שֶׁכִּינֵּס עַל יַד עַל יַד, וְיוֹדְעִין שֶׁהֵן שֶׁל לֶקֶט שִׁכְחָה וּפֵאָה, וּפָטוּר מִן הַמַּעֲשֵׂר. כִּדְתַנְיָא בְּסִפְרֵי: "וּבָא הַלֵּוִי כִּי אֵין לוֹ חֵלֶק וְנַחֲלָה עִמָּךְ" — בְּדָבָר שֶׁאֵין לוֹ בּוֹ חֵלֶק וְנַחֲלָה עִמָּךְ הוּא בָּא וְנוֹטֵל מַעֲשֵׂר רִאשׁוֹן שֶׁלּוֹ, יָצָא לֶקֶט שִׁכְחָה וּפֵאָה שֶׁיֵּשׁ לוֹ חֵלֶק וְנַחֲלָה עִמָּךְ, שֶׁאַף לַעֲנִיֵּי לְוִיִּם הֵם מוּפְקָרִים כִּשְׁאָר עֲנִיֵּי יִשְׂרָאֵל. אֵינָהּ מְקַדֶּשֶׁת אֶת הַזְּרָעִים. מִשּׁוּם כִּלְאֵי הַכֶּרֶם, דִּכְתִיב בֵּהוּ: "תִּקְדַּשׁ הַמְלֵאָה הַזֶּרַע". וְנִרְאֶה לִי דְּקָסָבַר כִּדְאָמְרִינַן בִּמְנָחוֹת (דף טו:): קַנְבּוֹס וְלוּף אָסְרָה תּוֹרָה, שְׁאָר זְרָעִים מִדְּרַבָּנַן נִינְהוּ, וּבְכִי הַאי כֶּרֶם לֹא גְּזוּר רַבָּנַן אִשְּׁאָר זְרָעִים. אֲבָל כּוּלֵּיהּ כֶּרֶם. (ב) גָּדוֹל, שֶׁהִיא שְׁפַלַּת קוֹמָה, הוֹאִיל וַחֲשׁוּבָה גְּזוּר עֲלֵיהּ.

מֵת

עין משפט נר מצוה

יג א מיי' פ"ז מהל' מלכים הל"ו:
יד ב מיי' פ"י מהל' מ"ש הל' טז סמג עשין קלז טוש"ע יו"ד סי' רלד סעי' כב:
טו ג מיי' שם הל"ב טוש"ע שם סעי' כג:
טז ד מיי' שם הל"ה טוש"ע שם סעי' כז:
יז ה מיי' פ"ז מהל' מלכים הל"ו:
יח ו מיי' שם הל"ז:
יט ז מיי' פ"א מהל' כלאים הל"ה סמג לאוין רפא טוש"ע יו"ד סי' רנה סעי' א וסעי' ג:
כ ח ט מיי' פ"י מהל' מ"ש הלי"ט סמג עשין קלז טוש"ע יו"ד סי' רלד סעי' כא:
כא י מיי' פ"ג מהל' ק"ש הל"ב סמג עשין יח טוש"ע או"ח סי' עא סעי' ז וטוש"ע יו"ד סימן שסז סעיף ב ג ו:
כב כ טוש"ע אה"ע סי' טו סעי' יא וסעי' כג:
כג ל מ מיי' פ"ב מהל' תרומות הל"ט:
כד נ ס מיי' פ"ו מהל' כלאים הל"ד סמג לאוין רפ טוש"ע יו"ד סי' רצו סעי' כב:

תוספות שאנץ

זאת אומרת כרם של ב' שותפין לאו דוקא נקט זאת אומרת דאמתני' לא קאי אלא הני אמוראי דבי מדרשא דלא בעו לשנויי הכי סבירא להו הכי: וה"מ שתים כנגד שתים ואחת יוצאה זנב כזה. ולהכי נקט שתים כנגד שתים דסבי' ליה כמ"ד בברכות כרם רבעי שאין ערלה נוהגת בנטיעה אחת אלא בכרם שלם: חורגתא הגדילה בין האחין אסורה להנשא לאחין פ"ה בת אשתו הגדילה בין בני הבעל שיש לו מאשה אחרת דאיתחזיא כי אחתיהו מי שאינו מכיר בה סבור שנשא אחותו. ולא היא דחורגתא קלא אית לה ומותרת. ותי' לר"י דאמר בירושלמי אשת (חורגו) [חמיו] אסורה מפני מראית העין וכמאן אתיא וצ"ל דאתיא כר' אליעזר בן יעקב. ור"י אומר דאפי' למסקנא דהכא אתי שפיר דהאי חורגתא כשהיא גדילה בין האחין יודעין העולם שאינה אחותם אבל אשת (חורגו) [חמיו] שאינה עומדת אצלו אין נותנין העולם לב להבחין א"כ (איכא לאו כיון) [אתו למימר] שאשתו של זה אמו של זו. אבל אמרי' בירושלמי החורג והחורגת שגדלין זה עם זה אסורין לינשא ר' חנינא בן יודן או' יתנסבון באתרא דלא חכמין להון פי' ינשאו עצמן במקום שאין מכירים אותן וחולק על תלמוד שלנו שמתירן בלאו הכי: לקט שכחה ופיאה שעשאן בגורן הוקבעו. פ"ה עני שכנס הרבה ביחד ועשה מהן כרי הוקבעו למעשר מדרבנן דמאן דחזי סבר שגדל בשדהו. וה"מ בשדה שכינסן בשדה ולא ידעו הכל שנתכנס מעט מעט וסבורין שגדל שם אבל בעיר כל שכניו ראו שכינס על יד על יד ויודעין שהם של לקט שכחה ופאה ופטור מן המעשר כדאמרי' בספרי ובא הלוי כי אין לו חלק ונחלה עמך מי שאין לו חלק ונחלה הוא בא ונוטל מעשר ראשון שלו יצאו לקט שכחה ופאה שיש לו חלק ונחלה עמך שאף לעניי לוים הם מופקרין כלשאר עניי ישראל ל"ה:

סח

הגהות הב"ח

(א) רש"י ד"ה וה"מ וכו' הכל שנכנסו מעט: (ב) ד"ה אבל כוליה כרם כרם גדול:

גליון הש"ס

גמ' ולא היא קלא אית ליה. עיין יבמות דף כא ע"א תד"ה ומותר:

אמֵת תּוֹפֵס אַרְבַּע אַמּוֹת לְטוּמְאָה. א*וְתָנָא תּוּנָא: חֲצַר הַקֶּבֶר — הָעוֹמֵד בְּתוֹכָהּ טָהוֹר, וְהוּא — שֶׁיְּהוּ בָּהּ אַרְבַּע אַמּוֹת, דִּבְרֵי בֵּית שַׁמַּאי. ב"ה אוֹמְרִים: באַרְבָּעָה טְפָחִים. בַּמֶּה דְּבָרִים אֲמוּרִים — שֶׁפִּתְחָהּ מִלְמַעְלָה, אֲבָל פִּתְחָהּ מִן הַצַּד — דִּבְרֵי הַכֹּל אַרְבַּע אַמּוֹת. כְּלַפֵּי לַיָּיא?! אַדְּרַבָּה, מִן הַצַּד — מִידְרִיד וְנָפֵיק, מִלְמַעְלָה — אִי אֶפְשָׁר דְּלָא מַאֲהִיל! אֶלָּא, בַּמֶּה דְּבָרִים אֲמוּרִים — שֶׁפִּתְחָהּ מִן הַצַּד, אֲבָל פִּתְחָהּ מִלְמַעְלָה — אַרְבַּע אַמּוֹת. וְהָנֵי מִילֵּי חֲצַר הַקֶּבֶר, דִּמְסַיְּימָא מְחִיצָתָא, אֲבָל מֵת בְּעָלְמָא — תָּפֵיס.§ °"מִי הָאִישׁ אֲשֶׁר אֵרַשׂ אִשָּׁה" כו'.§ ת"ר: אֲשֶׁר אֵרַשׂ[ב] — אֶחָד הַמְאָרֵס אֶת הַבְּתוּלָה, וְאֶחָד הַמְאָרֵס אֶת הָאַלְמָנָה, וְאֶחָד שׁוֹמֶרֶת יָבָם. וַאֲפִילּוּ *חֲמִשָּׁה אַחִין וּמֵת אֶחָד מֵהֶם בַּמִּלְחָמָה — כּוּלָּן חוֹזְרִין. °"לֹא לָקַח" "וְלֹא לְקָחָהּ" — פְּרָט לְאַלְמָנָה לְכֹהֵן גָּדוֹל, גְּרוּשָׁה וַחֲלוּצָה לְכֹהֵן הֶדְיוֹט, מַמְזֶרֶת וּנְתִינָה לְיִשְׂרָאֵל, בַּת יִשְׂרָאֵל לְמַמְזֵר וּלְנָתִין. לֵימָא דְּלָא כְּרַבִּי יוֹסֵי הַגְּלִילִי, דְּאִי רַבִּי יוֹסֵי הַגְּלִילִי הָא אָמַר: °"הַיָּרֵא וְרַךְ הַלֵּבָב" — זֶה הַמִּתְיָירֵא מֵעֲבֵירוֹת שֶׁבְּיָדוֹ? אֲפִילּוּ תֵּימָא ר' יוֹסֵי הַגְּלִילִי, כִּדְרַבָּה, *דְּאָמַר רַבָּה: גלְעוֹלָם אֵינוֹ חַיָּיב עַד שֶׁיִּבְעוֹל. מַה טַּעַם "לֹא יִקָּח" — מִשּׁוּם "לֹא יְחַלֵּל", מִשּׁוּם הָכִי אֵינוֹ לוֹקֶה עַד שֶׁיִּבְעוֹל. תָּנוּ רַבָּנַן: "אֲשֶׁר בָּנָה", "אֲשֶׁר נָטַע", "אֲשֶׁר אֵרַשׂ" — *דלִימְּדָה תּוֹרָה דֶּרֶךְ אֶרֶץ: שֶׁיִּבְנֶה אָדָם בַּיִת, וְיִטַּע כֶּרֶם, וְאח"כ יִשָּׂא אִשָּׁה. וְאַף שְׁלֹמֹה אָמַר בְּחָכְמָתוֹ: °"הָכֵן בַּחוּץ מְלַאכְתֶּךָ וְעַתְּדָהּ בַּשָּׂדֶה לָךְ אַחַר וּבָנִיתָ בֵיתֶךָ". "הָכֵן בַּחוּץ מְלַאכְתֶּךָ" — זֶה בַּיִת, "וְעַתְּדָהּ בַּשָּׂדֶה לָךְ" — זֶה כֶּרֶם, "אַחַר וּבָנִיתָ בֵיתֶךָ" — זוֹ אִשָּׁה. ד"א: "הָכֵן בַּחוּץ מְלַאכְתֶּךָ" — זֶה מִקְרָא, "וְעַתְּדָהּ בַּשָּׂדֶה לָךְ" — זֶה מִשְׁנָה, "אַחַר וּבָנִיתָ בֵיתֶךָ" — זֶה גְּמָ'. ד"א: "הָכֵן בַּחוּץ מְלַאכְתֶּךָ" — זֶה מִקְרָא וּמִשְׁנָה, "וְעַתְּדָהּ בַּשָּׂדֶה לָךְ" — זֶה גְּמָרָא, "אַחַר וּבָנִיתָ בֵיתֶךָ" — אֵלּוּ מַעֲשִׂים טוֹבִים. ר' אֱלִיעֶזֶר בְּנוֹ שֶׁל ר"י הַגְּלִילִי אוֹמֵר: "הָכֵן בַּחוּץ מְלַאכְתֶּךָ" — זֶה מִקְרָא וּמִשְׁנָה וּגְמָרָא, "וְעַתְּדָהּ בַּשָּׂדֶה לָךְ" — אֵלּוּ מַעֲשִׂים טוֹבִים, "אַחַר וּבָנִיתָ בֵיתֶךָ" — *דְּרוֹשׁ וְקַבֵּל שָׂכָר.§ "וְאֵלּוּ שֶׁאֵינָן חוֹזְרִין הַבּוֹנֶה בֵּית שַׁעַר" כו'.§ תָּנָא: אִם הוֹסִיף בּוֹ דִּימוֹס אֶחָד — חוֹזֵר.§ "ר' אֱלִיעֶזֶר אוֹמֵר אַף הַבּוֹנֶה בֵּית לְבֵנִים בַּשָּׁרוֹן לֹא הָיָה חוֹזֵר".§ תָּנָא: מִפְּנֵי שֶׁמְּחַדְּשִׁין אוֹתוֹ פַּעֲמַיִם בַּשָּׁבוּעַ.§ "וְאֵלּוּ שֶׁאֵין זָזִין מִמְּקוֹמָן בָּנָה בַּיִת חָדָשׁ וַחֲנָכוֹ" וכו'.§ תָּנוּ רַבָּנַן: °"אִשָּׁה חֲדָשָׁה". אֵין לִי אֶלָּא אִשָּׁה חֲדָשָׁה, אַלְמָנָה וּגְרוּשָׁה מִנַּיִן — תַּלְמוּד לוֹמַר: "אִשָּׁה", מִכָּל מָקוֹם. אִם כֵּן מַה ת"ל "אִשָּׁה חֲדָשָׁה" — מִי שֶׁחֲדָשָׁה לוֹ, יָצָא מַחֲזִיר גְּרוּשָׁתוֹ שֶׁאֵין חֲדָשָׁה לוֹ. ת"ר: °"לֹא יֵצֵא בַּצָּבָא". יָכוֹל בַּצָּבָא הוּא דְּלָא יָצָא, אֲבָל יְסַפֵּק מַיִם וּמָזוֹן וִיתַקֵּן הַדְּרָכִים — תַּלְמוּד לוֹמַר: °"וְלֹא יַעֲבוֹר עָלָיו לְכָל דָּבָר". יָכוֹל שֶׁאֲנִי מַרְבֶּה אַף הַבּוֹנֶה בַּיִת וְלֹא חֲנָכוֹ, נָטַע כֶּרֶם וְלֹא חִלְּלוֹ, אֵרַס אִשָּׁה וְלֹא לְקָחָהּ — ת"ל: "עָלָיו" — עָלָיו אִי אַתָּה מַעֲבִיר, אֲבָל אַתָּה מַעֲבִיר עַל אֲחֵרִים. וּמֵאַחַר דִּכְתַב "לֹא יַעֲבוֹר", "לֹא יֵצֵא בַּצָּבָא" לָמָּה לִי? הלַעֲבוֹר עָלָיו בִּשְׁנֵי לָאוִין.§

מתני' °"וְיָסְפוּ הַשּׁוֹטְרִים לְדַבֵּר אֶל הָעָם" וגו'. ר' עֲקִיבָא אוֹמֵר: הַיָּרֵא וְרַךְ הַלֵּבָב — וכְּמַשְׁמָעוֹ, שֶׁאֵינוֹ יָכוֹל לַעֲמוֹד בְּקִשְׁרֵי הַמִּלְחָמָה וְלִרְאוֹת חֶרֶב שְׁלוּפָה. *רַבִּי יוֹסֵי הַגְּלִילִי אוֹמֵר: הַיָּרֵא וְרַךְ הַלֵּבָב — זֶהוּ הַמִּתְיָירֵא מִן הָעֲבֵירוֹת שֶׁבְּיָדוֹ, לְפִיכָךְ תָּלְתָה לוֹ הַתּוֹרָה אֶת כָּל אֵלּוּ, שֶׁיַּחֲזוֹר בִּגְלָלָן. רַבִּי יוֹסֵי אוֹמֵר: אַלְמָנָה לְכֹהֵן גָּדוֹל, גְּרוּשָׁה וַחֲלוּצָה לְכֹהֵן הֶדְיוֹט, מַמְזֶרֶת וּנְתִינָה לְיִשְׂרָאֵל, בַּת יִשְׂרָאֵל לְמַמְזֵר וּלְנָתִין — הֲרֵי הוּא הַיָּרֵא וְרַךְ הַלֵּבָב. °"וְהָיָה כְּכַלֹּת הַשּׁוֹטְרִים לְדַבֵּר אֶל הָעָם וּפָקְדוּ שָׂרֵי צְבָאוֹת בְּרֹאשׁ הָעָם", וּבַעֲקֵיבוֹ שֶׁל עָם; זמַעֲמִידִין זְקִיפִין לִפְנֵיהֶם, וַאֲחֵרִים מֵאֲחוֹרֵיהֶם, וְכַשִּׁילִין שֶׁל בַּרְזֶל בִּידֵיהֶן, וְכָל הַמְבַקֵּשׁ לַחֲזוֹר — הָרְשׁוּת בְּיָדוֹ לְקַפֵּחַ אֶת שׁוֹקָיו, שֶׁתְּחִלַּת

מֵת תּוֹפֵס אַרְבַּע אַמּוֹת לְטוּמְאָה. חֲכָמִים גָּזְרוּ שֶׁיְּהֵא הַמֵּת מְטַמֵּא כָּל הַנִּכְנָס בְּאַרְבַּע אַמּוֹתָיו, כְּדֵי שֶׁלֹּא יַרְגִּילוּ אוֹכְלֵי טְהָרוֹת לִיקָּרֵב לוֹ, וִיהֵא סָבוּר שֶׁלֹּא הֶאֱהִיל. וְיֵשׁ לָחוּשׁ שֶׁמָּא יִפְשׁוֹט יָדוֹ וְיַאֲהִיל וְלָאו אַדַּעְתֵּיהּ. וְתָנָא תּוּנָא. וְכֵן תָּנֵי תַּנָּא דִּידָן בַּמִּשְׁנָה הַשְּׁנוּיָה בֵּינֵינוּ בְּבֵית הַמִּדְרָשׁ בְּסֵדֶר טְהָרוֹת (אהלות פט"ו מ"ח). חֲצַר הַקֶּבֶר. שֶׁלִּפְנֵי הַמְּעָרָה. כִּדְאָמַר סֵדֶר בִּנְיַן הַקְּבָרוֹת בְּבָבָא בַּתְרָא (דף ק:) שֶׁעוֹשִׂין מְעָרוֹת גְּדוֹלוֹת שֶׁל *שֵׁשׁ עַל שֵׁשׁ, וְחוֹפֵר בְּכוֹתְלֶיהָ סָבִיב כּוּכִין אֲרוּכּוֹת כְּמִדַּת הַמֵּת וְתוֹחֲבוֹ לְתוֹכָן. וְהַמְּעָרָה מְקוֹרָה בְּתִקְרָה וְכִיסּוּי. וְעוֹשֶׂה גּוּמָא רְחָבָה בְּצַד הַמְּעָרָה, וּפוֹתֵחַ פִּי הַמְּעָרָה לְתוֹךְ הַגּוּמָא בְּכוֹתֶל הַמְּעָרָה כְּמִין פֶּתַח, וְאוֹתָהּ גּוּמָא הִיא חֲצַר הַקֶּבֶר. הָעוֹמֵד בְּתוֹכוֹ טָהוֹר. כָּל מָקוֹם שֶׁהוּא עוֹמֵד בָּהּ טָהוֹר. דְּכֵיוָן דִּמְעָרָה חֲלוּקָה הֵימֶנָּה וּמְחִיצוֹתֶיהָ נִיכָּרוֹת — לָא גְּזוּר רַבָּנַן בַּמֵּתִים שֶׁבְּתוֹכָהּ שֶׁיִּתְפְּסוּ ד' אַמּוֹת סְבִיבוֹתֶיהָ לְצַד הַמְּעָרָה. דְּכִי גְּזוּר רַבָּנַן אַרְבַּע אַמּוֹת — בְּמֵת הַמּוּטָּל בָּאֲוִיר, וּכְגוֹן לְמַעְלָה אֵצֶל גַּג הַמְּעָרָה, כְּדֵי לְהַרְחִיק אֶת הָאָדָם מִלְּהַאֲהִיל עַל הַטּוּמְאָה. אֲבָל כָּאן יֵשׁ הֶיכֵּר. וְהוּא שֶׁיֵּשׁ בָּהּ אַרְבַּע אַמּוֹת. הוּא דַּחֲשִׁיבָא מָקוֹם לְעַצְמָהּ. אֲבָל פָּחוֹת מִכָּאן — בְּטֵלָה אֵצֶל הַמְּעָרָה, וְלָא חֲשִׁיבָא לְמֶיהֱוֵי מָקוֹם לְעַצְמָהּ. וּב"ה אוֹמְרִים אַרְבָּעָה טְפָחִים. הָוֵי מָקוֹם חָשׁוּב בְּכָל דּוּכְתָּא. בַּמֶּה דְּבָרִים אֲמוּרִים. ב"ה אָמְרוּ לֵיהּ. כְּשֶׁפִּתְחָהּ שֶׁל חָצֵר לְמַעְלָה. שֶׁאֵין לָהּ כְּנִיסַת מִדְרוֹן בְּמַעֲלוֹת מִן הַצַּד, אֶלָּא כְּשֶׁיּוֹרְדִין לָהּ — קוֹפְצִין לָהּ, וּכְשֶׁעוֹלִין מִתּוֹכָהּ — מְטַפֵּס וְעוֹלֶה. וּלְקַמָּן פָּרֵיךְ: אִיפְכָא מִיסְתַּבְּרָא. כְּלַפֵּי לַיָּיא. כְּנֶגֶד אֵיפוֹא הָפַכְתָּ דְּבָרֶיךָ?! לַיָּיא — אֵיפוֹא, כִּדְאָמַר בִּבְרָכוֹת (דף נח.): כְּגַנֵּי לַיָּיא — כַּדִּים שְׁבוּרִים לְהֵיכָן הוֹלְכִים. אִיפְכָא מִסְתַּבְּרָא; מִן הַצַּד, כְּשֶׁעָשׂוּי לֶחָצֵר מִדְרוֹן לָצֵאת דֶּרֶךְ רְגָלִים — אִיכָּא לְמֵימַר: כֵּיוָן דְּלָא גְּזוּר רַבָּנַן אַרְבַּע אַמּוֹת בִּמְחִיצוֹת נִיכָּרוֹת — סַגִּי לְהַאי חָצֵר בְּאַרְבָּעָה טְפָחִים, וְהָעוֹמֵד בָּהּ הֲרֵי זֶה טָהוֹר, שֶׁאֵין לָנוּ בַּמֶּה לְטַמְּאוֹ, דְּאֵינוֹ צָרִיךְ לְטַפֵּס וְלַעֲלוֹת שֶׁיִּפְשׁוֹט זְרוֹעוֹתָיו וְיַאֲהִיל וּכְנָפָיו עַל חֲלַל הַפֶּתַח. דְּכִי נָפֵיק — מִידַּדֵּי וְנָפֵיק, נִשְׁמָט וְנִמְשָׁךְ לוֹ מִן הַפֶּתַח שֶׁל מְעָרָה לְצַד פֶּתַח שֶׁל חָצֵר וְיוֹצֵא לוֹ. מִלְמַעְלָה אִי אֶפְשָׁר דְּלָא מַאֲהִיל. כֵּיוָן דְּאֵינוֹ אֶלָּא אַרְבָּעָה טְפָחִים — אִי אֶפְשָׁר לוֹ לִפְרוֹשׂ כְּנָפָיו וּלְטַפֵּס וְלַעֲלוֹת אֶלָּא אִם כֵּן מַאֲהִיל עַל חֲלַל הַפֶּתַח! וְהָנֵי מִילֵּי כו'. הַשְׁתָּא מְהַדֵּר לְפָרוּשֵׁי סִיַּיעְתֵּיהּ מֵהָכָא; מִדְּאִיצְטְרִיךְ לְמִיתְנֵי: הָעוֹמֵד לְתוֹכוֹ טָהוֹר — ש"מ הָנֵי מִילֵּי חֲצַר הַקֶּבֶר דִּמְסַיְּימָא מְחִיצָתָא, דִּמְעָרָה לְחוּדֵיהּ, וְדֶחָצֵר לְחוּדֵיהּ, וְיֵשׁ הֶיכֵּר בַּדָּבָר. אֲבָל מֵת בְּעָלְמָא, הַמּוּטָּל בָּאֲוִיר — מוֹדוּ בֵּית הִלֵּל דְּתָפֵיס אַרְבַּע אַמּוֹת, מִדְּאִיצְטְרִיךְ לְמִיתְנֵי: הָעוֹמֵד לְתוֹכוֹ טָהוֹר. דְּאִי בְּעָלְמָא לָא גְּזוּר — לָמָּה לִי לְאַשְׁמוּעִינַן הָכָא דְּטָהוֹר?. וַאֲפִי' הִיא לוֹ שׁוֹמֶרֶת יָבָם. שֶׁלֹּא קִדְּשָׁהּ הוּא, אֶלָּא מִכֹּחַ אָחִיו בָּאָה לוֹ. לְקָחָהּ. מִדְּלָא כְּתִיב "לָקַח" — מִיעוּטָא הוּא לְמַעוּטֵי לְקִיחַת אִיסּוּר. כִּדְרַבָּה. דְּאָמַר: אֵין עֲבֵירָה בְּקִידּוּשִׁין עַד שֶׁיִּבְעוֹל, שֶׁיָּבִיא זַרְעוֹ אוֹ אֶת הָאִשָּׁה לִידֵי חִילּוּל. וּמַמְזֶרֶת וּנְתִינָה אֵין עֲבֵירָה בְּקִידּוּשִׁין, דְּלָא כְּתִיב בֵּיהּ "לֹא יִקַּח", אֶלָּא "לֹא יָבֹא" וְ"לֹא תִתְחַתֵּן". אֲבָל אַלְמָנָה כְּתִיב בָּהּ "לֹא יִקַּח", וּקְקִיחָה הַיְינוּ קִידּוּשִׁין. וְאִיצְטְרִיךְ דְּרַבָּה, דְּלָא תֵּימָא מִקִּידּוּשִׁין עָבֵד לֵיהּ אִיסּוּר. וּנְתִינָה. מִן הַגִּבְעוֹנִים דִּכְתִיב בְּהוּ: "וַיִּתְּנֵם יְהוֹשֻׁעַ לְחוֹטְבֵי עֵצִים" (יהושע ט) וְהֵן מִשִּׁבְעָה אוּמּוֹת. וְעַתְּדָהּ בַּשָּׂדֶה לָךְ. וְנִגְּבָּה בַּשָּׂדֶה מְלַאכְתֶּךָ לָךְ. גְּמָרָא. לָתֵת סְבָרָא לְהָבִין בְּטַעֲמֵי הַמִּשְׁנָה, וַהֲלָכָה כְּדִבְרֵי מִי. אִם הוֹסִיף בּוֹ דִּימוֹס אֶחָד. שׁוּרָה שֶׁל אֲבָנִים, אוֹ בְּגוֹבַהּ אוֹ בְּעוֹבִי — תּוּ לָא הָוֵי עַל מְכוֹנוֹ, וְקָרֵינָא בֵּיהּ חָדָשׁ. שֶׁמְּחַדְּשִׁין אוֹתוֹ. שֶׁאֵינוֹ מִתְקַיֵּים. בַּשָּׁבוּעַ. בַּשְּׁמִיטָּה. אֵין לִי אֶלָּא חֲדָשָׁה. בְּתוּלָה. אַלְמָנָה וּגְרוּשָׁה. מֵאַחֵר, וּנְשָׂאָהּ זֶה. יָכוֹל אַף בָּנָה בַּיִת. חָדָשׁ וְלֹא חֲנָכוֹ יְהֵא כָּזֶה, שֶׁיְּהֵא נָקִי מִן הַכֹּל. **מתני'** וְיָסְפוּ הַשּׁוֹטְרִים. עַל דִּבְרֵי כֹּהֵן. בְּקִשְׁרֵי. כְּשֶׁמִּתְקַשְּׁרִים לַעֲמוֹד לְפוּפִים שֶׁלֹּא יַפְרִידוּם אוֹיְבִים. לְפִיכָךְ. שֶׁהַיָּרֵא זֶהוּ הַיָּרֵא מֵעֲבֵירוֹת — תָּלָה הַתּוֹרָה בָּנָה וְנָטַע וְאֵירַס לַחֲזוֹר בִּגְלָלָן, כְּדֵי שֶׁיִּתְלֶה בְּכָךְ הַחֲזָרָה, וְלֹא יִתְבַּיֵּישׁ לוֹמַר מֵעֲבֵירוֹת שֶׁבְּיָדוֹ הוּא יָרֵא וְחוֹזֵר. ר' יוֹסֵי אוֹמֵר כו'. בַּגְּמָרָא מְפָרֵשׁ בְּמַאי פָּלֵיג אַדְּרַבִּי יוֹסֵי הַגְּלִילִי. וּבַעֲקֵבוֹ שֶׁל עָם. בְּסוֹפוֹ שֶׁל עַם, שֶׁעוֹמְדִים שֶׁלֹּא יַחְזְרוּ אַחֲרוֹנִים לַאֲחוֹרֵיהֶם לָנוּס. מַעֲמִידִין זְקִיפִין מִלִּפְנֵיהֶם. בְּרֹאשָׁהּ שֶׁל צַד הַמִּלְחָמָה מַעֲמִידִין בְּנֵי אָדָם גִּבּוֹרִים מְמוּנִים לְכָךְ, וְיַזְקִיפוּהוּ, וְיַגְבִּירוּ אֶת אַנְשֵׁי הַכַּת בְּדִבְרֵיהֶם: [וַאֲחֵרִים]. וַאֲנָשִׁים אֲחֵרִים מֵאֲחוֹרֵיהֶם. וְכַשִּׁילִין שֶׁל בַּרְזֶל בִּידֵיהֶם. לִשְׁמוֹר שֶׁלֹּא יָנוּסוּ. וְכַשִּׁילִין כְּעֵין אֵלִין, שֶׁקּוֹרִין ווריי"ש. שֶׁתְּחִילַּת

כה א מיי' פ"ג מהל' אבל הלי"ג סמג לאוין רלה טוש"ע יו"ד סי' שעא סעי' ה:
כו ב מיי' פ"ו מהל' טומאת מת הל"ט וע"ש בכ"מ:
[ב] מיי' פ"ז מהל' מלכים דין ז:
כז ג מיי' פט"ו מהל' איסורי ביאה הל"ב ופי"ז הל"ב:
כח ד מיי' פ"ה מהל' דעות הלי"א:
כט ה מיי' פ"ז מהל' מלכים הל' י"א:
ל ו מיי' שם הלט"ו:
לא ז מיי' שם הל"ד:

ב"ב קא. אהלות פט"ו מ"ח; נ"ל ד'; [לעיל מג:]; [קדושין עח. ע"ש]; [תוספתא פ"ז]; [סנהדרין נח. זבחים מה.]; [לעיל מג.]

תורה אור: דברים כ; שם; שם; משלי כד; דברים כד; שם; שם; שם כ; שם

לב א מיי' פ"ז מהל' מלכים הל"ד:
לג ב מיי' פ"ד מהל' תפילין הל"ו וע"ש בכ"מ סמג עשין כב טוש"ע או"ח סי' כה סעי' ט:
לד ג מיי' פ"ה מהל' מלכים הל"א וע"ש בכ"מ סמג עשין קיז:
א ד מיי' פ"ט מהל' רוצח הל"ג סמג עשין עח:
ב ה מיי' שם הל"א:
ג ו מיי' שם הלי"א:
ד ז מיי' שם הל"ה:
ה ח מיי' שם הל"ד:
ו ט מיי' שם הל"א:

תורה אור

שתחילת ניסה נפילה, שנאמר: °"נס ישראל לפני פלשתים וגם מגפה גדולה היתה בעם", (שמואל א ד) ולהלן הוא אומר: °"וינוסו [אנשי] ישראל מפני פלשתים ויפלו חללים" וגו'. (שם לא) אבד"א – במלחמות הרשות, אבל במלחמות מצוה – הכל יוצאין, אפילו חתן מחדרו וכלה מחופתה. אמר רבי יהודה: במה דברים אמורים – במלחמות מצוה, אבל במלחמות חובה – הכל יוצאין, אפי' חתן מחדרו וכלה מחופתה.§ **גמ'** מאי איכא בין רבי יוסי לר"י הגלילי? איכא בינייהו עבירה דרבנן. כמאן אזלא הא דתניא: *שח בין תפילה לתפילה – בעבירה היא בידו, וחוזר עליה מעורכי המלחמה. כמאן – כר"י הגלילי. מאן תנא להא דתנו רבנן: שמע קול קרנות והריע, הגפת תריסין והרתיע, צחצוח חרבות ומים שותתין לו על ברכיו – חוזר. כמאן – לימא, רבי עקיבא היא ולא רבי יוסי הגלילי? בהא אפי' ר' יוסי הגלילי מודה, משום דכתיב: °"ולא ימס את לבב אחיו כלבבו".§ "והיה (דברים כ) ככלות השוטרים" כו'.§ האי מפני שתחילת ניסה נפילה – מפני שתחילת נפילה ניסה מבעי ליה! אימא: מפני שתחילת נפילה ניסה.§ "בד"א במלחמות הרשות" כו'.§ א"ר יוחנן: רשות דרבנן – זו היא מצוה דרבי יהודה, מצוה דרבנן – זו היא חובה דרבי יהודה. אמר רבא: גמלחמות יהושע לכבש – דברי הכל חובה, מלחמות בית דוד לרווחה – דברי הכל רשות. כי פליגי – למעוטי גוים דלא ליתי עלייהו; מר קרי לה מצוה ומר קרי רשות. נפקא מינה *לעוסק במצוה, שפטור מן המצוה.§

הדרן עלך משוח מלחמה

עגלה ערופה יבלשון הקודש, שנאמר: °"כי (שם כא) ימצא חלל באדמה ויצאו זקניך ושופטיך". שלשה מבית דין הגדול שבירושלים היו יוצאין, רבי יהודה אומר: החמשה, שנאמר: "זקניך" – שנים, "ושופטיך" – שנים, ואין בית דין שקול – מוסיפין עליהן עוד אחד. ונמצא טמון בגל, או תלוי באילן, או צף על פני המים – לא היו עורפין, שנאמר: "באדמה" – ולא טמון בגל, "נופל" – ולא תלוי באילן, "בשדה" – ולא צף על פני המים. זנמצא סמוך לספר או לעיר שרובה גוים, או לעיר שאין בה ב"ד – לא היו (א) עורפין. חאין מודדין אלא לעיר שיש בה ב"ד.§ **גמ'** מאי קאמר? אמר ר' אבהו, ה"ק: שנאמר: "וענו ואמרו", ולהלן הוא אומר: °"וענו הלוים ואמרו" וגו', (שם כז) מה ענייה האמורה להלן בלשון הקודש – אף כאן בלשון הקודש. וסדר עגלה ערופה כיצד – "כי ימצא חלל באדמה ויצאו זקניך ושופטיך", שלשה מב"ד הגדול שבירושלים היו יוצאין.§ "רבי יהודה אומר חמשה" וכו'.§ *ת"ר: "ויצאו זקניך ושופטיך", (סנהדרין יד.) "זקניך" – שנים, "ושופטיך" – שנים, ואין בית דין שקול – מוסיפין עליהן עוד אחד, הרי כאן חמשה, דברי ר' יהודה. ר' שמעון אומר: "זקניך" – שנים, ואין ב"ד שקול – מוסיפין עליהן עוד אחד, הרי כאן שלשה. ור' שמעון נמי, הא כתיב "ושופטיך"! ההוא מיבעי ליה: למיוחדין שבשופטיך. ורבי יהודה: מ"זקני" "זקניך" נפקא. ור' שמעון? אי כתב רחמנא "זקני" – הוה אמינא אפי' זקני השוק, כתב רחמנא "זקניך". ואי כתב רחמנא "זקניך" – הוה אמינא אפי' סנהדרי קטנה, כתב רחמנא "ושופטיך" – טלמיוחדין שבשופטיך. ור' יהודה: גמר "זקני" "זקני" °מזקני העדה, מה להלן מיוחדין שבעדה אף כאן מיוחדין שבעדה. (ויקרא ד) אי גמר – לגמרה לכולה מילתא מהתם, "זקניך ושופטיך" למה לי? אלא (ב) וי"ו "ושופטיך" למנינא. *ורבי שמעון? [עמ"ש תוס' סנהדרין יד. ד"ה ורבי שמעון]

שתחילת ניסה נפילה. בגמ' פריך: איפכא מבעי ליה, שהניסה היא תחילת הנפילה. בד"א. דחוזרין מן המערכה, ויש שאינן זזין ממקומן – במלחמות הרשות. אבל במלחמות מצוה. כגון כיבוש ארץ ישראל בימי יהושע – הכל יוצאין. רבי יהודה אומר כו'. מפרש בגמ'. **גמ'** עבירה דרבנן. לר"י הגלילי אפי' עבר על דברי סופרים חוזר, ולרבי יוסי עד שיעבור על דבר תורה, דומיא דאלמנה לכהן גדול. וכגון שנשאה, דאיכא איסור. שח בין תפילה לתפילה. בין הנחת תפילין של יד לתפילין של ראש. שח. סיפר. עבירה היא בידו. אם לא חזר ובירך. דהכי אמרי' במנחות (דף לו.): שח – מברך שתים, לא שח – מברך אחת. ומים שותתין על ברכיו. מי רגלים, מחמת יראה. מפני שתחילת נפילה ניסה מבעי ליה. "תחילת" משמע הגרמת הדבר, והכי איבעי ליה למימר: כשהן נסין – זו היא תחילת הגרמת הנפילה. ובניסה לא שייך למימר "תחילה", דהא ממש קא עקרי. רשות דרבנן זו היא מצוה דר' יהודה. ובאותה מלחמה שאמרו חכמים שהיא רשות, ואין חתן יוצא לה – אמר נמי ר' יהודה דאין חתן יוצא לה, אלא שרבי יהודה קורא אותה מצוה. ונפקא מינה לפוטרו משאר מצות בעודו עסוק בה, כדמפרש רבא ואזיל. מצוה דרבנן. דאמרו בה הכל יוצאין – אמר נמי ר' יהודה הכל יוצאין, אלא דקרי לה חובה. ולאו מידי אשמעינן בהא, אלא כולה משום מצוה ורשות נקטו פלוגתייהו, אלא משום דקרו רבנן להא רשות – די להם אם קראו את זו מצוה, ואפילו היא חובה, שהרי אין הדבר אלא להעלותם מעלה אחת ולומר: אבל בזו הכל יוצאין. וגבי רשות דיים לקרות את שלמעלה ממנה מצוה. ורבי יהודה דקרי לקמייתא מצוה – לאשמועי' דהעוסק בה פטור מן המצוה. והוצרך להעלות את זו מעלה אחת לומר: אבל בזו הכל יוצאין – הילכך קרייה חובה, כדאיתא. אמר רבא כו'. מילתיה דרבי יוחנן מפרש ואזיל. וקאמר: דהא דאמר רבי יוחנן דאיפליגו רבנן ורבי יהודה באחת המלחמות בקריאת השם – נפקא לן מיניה לענין עוסק במצוה, דלמר חובה ולמר רשות. ופריש לן נמי רבא בהי מינייהו איפליגו. מלחמות יהושע דלכבש. בהא ליכא למאן דקרי רשות, דאפילו חובה נמי איתא, והעוסק בה פטור מן המצוה. ורבנן הוא דלא איכפת להו לקרותה חובה, דדיים לקרותה מצוה אצל הרשות, שהרי אין אנו צריכין אלא למצוא בה מעלה אחת, ומצוה לגבי רשות מעלה היא. ומלחמת בית דוד. שנלחם בארם צובה להוסיפה על ארץ ישראל, ובשאר סביבותיה להעלות לו מנחה ומס עובד. דברי הכל רשות. ואפילו רבי יהודה להא לאו מצוה קרי לה, והעוסק בה אינו פטור מן המצוה. כי פליגי. ר' יהודה ורבנן במצוה ורשות, דלמר פטור מן המצוה ולמר חייב – במלחמה שהיא למעוטי נכרים דלא ליתו עלייהו. (מנחות לו.)

הדרן עלך משוח מלחמה

עגלה ערופה בלשון הקודש. נאמרת. מה שהזקנים אומרים "ידינו לא שפכו" והכהנים אומרים "כפר לעמך ישראל" – בלשון הקודש הוזקקו מן התורה לאמרה. שנאמר כי ימצא חלל. ובגמרא פריך: היכי יליף מהכא? היו יוצאין. ובאין שם, ומודדין מן החלל לצד העיירות שסביבותיו, לידע איזו קרובה. בגל. גל של אבנים. נמצא סמוך לספר כו'. מפרש טעמא בגמ'. **גמ'** מאי קאמר. היכי יליף לשון הקודש מהכא? ואין ב"ד שקול. אין עושין ב"ד שיהא יכול ליחלק שוה בשוה, אלא שיהא הרוב לצד אחד, לקיים "אחרי רבים להטות" (שמות כג). למיוחדין. הנך דלשכת הגזית. מזקני זקניך. מדמצי למיכתב "זקני" וכתב "זקניך" – מיוחדין שבזקניך. זקני השוק. אע"פ שאינן סנהדרין. שופטיך. זקנים שהם שופטים את ישראל. מזקני העדה. דסמיכת פר העלם דבר, ואייתר ליה "שופטיך" להביא עוד שנים. לגמרה לכולה מילתא מהתם. דהא רבי יהודה התם נמי חמשה קאמר, ויליף לה מקראי בפ"ק דסנהדרין. אלא [וי"ו] ושופטיך למניינא. כלומר, לא גמיר גז"ש, ואילטרי' "שופטיך" לסנהדרי גדולה כר"ש, וי"ו [(סוכה כה.) (סנהדרין יד.)]

תוספות שאנץ

סח בין תפלה לתפלה עבירה היא בידו. פ"ה סח בין הנחת תפלין של יד להנחת תפלין של ראש עבירה היא בידו אם לא חזר וברך דהכי אמרי' במנחו' סח מברך שתים לא סח מברך אחת פ"ה במנחות בפ' הקומץ דמברכין להניח תפלין לשל יד [ועל של ראש] לא מברך כלל אם לא סח בנתים אבל אם סח מברך על של ראש על מצות תפלין. ול"נ לר"ת דבפ' הרואה דקא חשיב מאה ברכות דחייב אדם לברך בכל יום קא חשיב להניח תפלין ועל מצות תפלין וכי ס"ד דלא נתקן אלא היכא דסח בנתים. ומיהו י"ל דמיירי בשני בני אדם אחד יש לו תפלין של יד ואחד יש לו תפלין של ראש. ור"ת אומר דמברכין להניח תפלין לשל יד ועל מצות תפלין לשל ראש היכא דלא סח ואם סח בנתים מברך לשל ראש להניח תפלין ועל מצות תפלין. ולפי זה היכא דאין לו תפלין של יד מברך על של ראש שתים דהא הוי כאילו סח בנתים:

סליק

הגהות הב"ח

(א) במשנה לא היו (עורפין). תז"מ ונ"ב ס"א מודדין: (ב) גמ' למה לי אלא ושופטיך כו' שמעון ו' למניינא כצ"ל וכן ברש"י:

גליון הש"ס

מתני' אין מודדין. עיין מכות י ע"ב תד"ה אד אמר:

וי"ו לא משמע ליה (מאי קאמר רחמנא — המיוחדין שבשופטיך). אלא מעתה "ויצאו" שנים "ומדדו" שנים — לר' יהודה הרי כאן תשעה, לרבי שמעון הרי כאן שבעה! ההוא מיבעי ליה לכדתניא: °"ויצאו" — [א]הן ולא שלוחיהן, "ומדדו" — [ב]שאפי' נמצא בעליל לעיר היו מודדין, שמצוה לעסוק במדידה. מתניתין דלא כר"א בן יעקב. דתניא, *ר' אליעזר בן יעקב אומר: "זקניך" — זו סנהדרין, "שופטיך" — זה מלך וכהן גדול; מלך — דכתיב: °"מלך במשפט יעמיד ארץ", כהן גדול — דכתיב: °"ובאת אל הכהנים הלוים ואל השופט אשר יהיה" וגו'. איבעיא להו: רבי אליעזר בן יעקב במלך וכהן גדול הוא דפליג, אבל בסנהדרי — אי כרבי יהודה אי כרבי שמעון סבירא ליה, או דלמא בסנהדרי נמי פליג — עד דאיכא כולה סנהדרי? אמר רב יוסף: ת"ש, *מצאן זקן ממרא אבי פגי והמרה עליהן, יכול תהא המראתו המראה — תלמוד לומר: °"וקמת ועלית אל המקום", [ג]מלמד שהמקום גורם. דנפוק כמה? אילימא דנפוק מקצתן — דלמא הנך דאיכא גואי כוותיה סבירא להו! אלא פשיטא — דנפוק כולהו, ולמאי? אי לדבר הרשות — מי מצו נפקי? והכתיב: °"שררך אגן הסהר אל יחסר המזג", [ד]שאם נצרך אחד מהם לצאת, אם יש שם עשרים ושלשה כנגד סנהדרי קטנה — יוצא, ואם לאו — אינו יוצא! אלא פשיטא — לדבר מצוה, למאי — לאו למדידת עגלה, ורבי אליעזר בן יעקב היא? א"ל אביי: לא, דלמא להוסיף על העיר ועל העזרות. *כדתנן: [ה]אין מוסיפין על העיר ועל העזרות אלא בבית דין של שבעים ואחד. תניא כוותיה דרב יוסף: מצאן אבית פגי והמרה עליהן, כגון שיצאו למדידת עגלה או להוסיף על העיר ועל העזרות, יכול תהא המראתו המראה — ת"ל: "וקמת ועלית", מלמד שהמקום גורם.§ "נמצא טמון בגל או תלוי באילן".§ לימא מתניתין ר' יהודה היא ולא רבנן. דתניא: °"ושכחת עומר בשדה" — פרט לטמון, דברי רבי יהודה. וחכ"א: "בשדה" — [ו]לרבות את הטמון? אמר רב: אפי' תימא רבנן, °הכא מענייניה דקרא, התם מענייניה דקרא. (א) דכתיב: °"כי ימצא חלל" — היכא דמשתכח, "באדמה" — פרט לטמון. והתם מענייניה דקרא, דכתיב: °"כי תקצור קצירך בשדך ושכחת עומר", שכחה דומיא דקציר, מה קציר בגלוי — אף שכחה בגלוי, כתב רחמנא "בשדה" — לרבות את הטמון. לרבי יהודה נמי תיפוק ליה משכחה דומיא דקציר! אין הכי נמי. ואלא "בשדה" למה לי? מיבעי ליה [ז]לרבות שכחת קמה. ורבנן, שכחת קמה מנא להו? נפקא להו מ"כי תקצור קצירך בשדך". (ב) ור' יהודה — מיבעי ליה לכדרבי אבהו. דאמר רבי אבהו אמר ר' אלעזר. דאמר ר"א: [ח]פרט לשצפו עומרין לתוך שדה חבירו. ורבנן — מ"בשדה" "בשדך". ור' יהודה — "בשדה" "בשדך" לא משמע ליה. בעי ר' ירמיה: *צפו עומרין לתוך שדהו מהו? אויר שדה כשדה דמי, או לאו כשדה דמי? א"ל רב כהנא לרב פפי, ואמרי לה רב כהנא לרב זביד: תפשוט ליה מדרבי אבהו א"ר אלעזר, דאמר: פרט לשצפו עומרין לתוך שדה חבירו, דחבירו — אין, [ט]לתוך שדהו — לא. וליטעמיך, לתוך שדה חבירו, צפו — אין, מונחין — [י]לא? והא בעינן "בשדך" וליכא! אלא, לתוך שדה חבירו — ואפילו מונחין, והאי דקאמר צפו — דלא משכחת לה אלא בצפו. תא שמע: *עומר שהחזיק בו להוליכו לעיר, והניחו על גבי חבירו, ושכחו — התחתון שכחה, והעליון אינו שכחה. רבי שמעון בן יהודה אומר משום רבי שמעון: שניהם אינן שכחה, התחתון מפני שהוא טמון, והעליון מפני שהוא צף. עד כאן לא פליגי אלא בתחתון, אבל בעליון — דברי הכל לא הואי שכחה! שאני התם, כיון דאחזיק ביה — זכה ביה. אי הכי, מאי איריא על גבי חבירו? אפילו בשדה נמי! אין הכי נמי, והאי דקתני על גבי חבירו — משום תחתון. והא מפני שהוא צף קאמר! אימא: מפני שהוא כצף. אמר אביי: *הריני כבן עזאי בשוקי טבריא. אמר ליה ההוא מדרבנן לאביי: שני חללים זה על גבי זה, מהיכן הוא מודד? מין במינו הוי טמון, ומין במינו לא הוי צף, [כ]ומעליון מודד. או דלמא מין במינו הוי צף, ומין במינו לא הוי טמון, ומתחתון מודד. או דלמא מין במינו הוי צף, ומין במינו הוי טמון, ולא מתחתון מודד ולא מעליון מודד? א"ל:

תניתוה

רש"י

וי"ו ד"ושופטיך" דריש ר' יהודה למניינא, להביא עוד שנים. בעליל לעיר. במגולה ופשוט שאין עיר קרובה כזו. מתני'. דלא קתני מלך וכהן גדול – דלא כר' אליעזר בן יעקב. אי כרבי יהודה. חמשה, אי כרבי שמעון שלשה, ולא בעי כולה סנהדרין. מצאן זקן ממרא. לב"ד הגדול, שאינו נעשה ממרא אלא בב"ד של שבעים ואחד, כדיליף בפרק קמא דסנהדרין. אבי פאגי. כל שהוא בתוך היקף החיצון של ירושלים קרוי בי פאגי. ולי נראה שהוא לשון חבישה, כמו שקורין ליגל"א של עיר, כמו חמור ובית פאגי (ב"מ דף ט.) – בשטידור"א, בית ראש של חפסר קורין כן. והמרה עליהן. כלומר, על מה ששאל מהם שם ואמרו לו ההלכה – הלך לעירו והורה לעשות כדרך שהיה מורה בתחילה, דהוה ליה ממרא על פיהם. המקום. המיוחד למשפט, והוא לשכת הגזית. דנפיק מינייהו כמה. לבי פאגי דאיצטריך לאשמועינן דפטור משום טעמא דחוץ לב"ד?. דלמא הנך דאיכא גוואי כוותיה סבירא להו. ומהיכא תיתי לן חיובא, דאיצטריך קרא למיפטריה?. שררך. זה סנהדרין, שיושבת בטיבורה של א"י. אגן הסהר. שעשויין כחצי לבנה עגולה בשורת ישיבתן, כדי שיהו כולן רואין זה את זה. המזג. כשיעור מזג, שני חלקים מים ואחד יין. ואף כאן צריך שישתייר שליש. על עיר. על ירושלים. תניא כרב יוסף. דאמר: רבי אליעזר בן יעקב כולהו סנהדרי בעי. מתני'. דיליף פרט לטמון – רבי יהודה היא. בשדה. "ושכחת עומר בשדה" – לרבי יהודה משמע "בשדה" – על פני השדה, ולרבנן משמע בתוך השדה. התם מענייניה דקרא. צריכין למידרשיה, והכא מענייניה דקרא תדרוש ליה. גבי חלל כתיב: "כי ימצא חלל" – כל היכא דמשתכח, ואפי' טמון, הלכך על כרחך כי אתא "באדמה" – למעוטי טמון בא, דתדרוש ביה: על פני האדמה. דאי לרבויי – לא איצטריך. אף שכחה בגלוי. והוה ממעט טמון ממשמעותא אי לאו דהדר רביה. לשכחת קמה. שאם שכח זוית אחת לקצור – קאי עלה ב"לא תשוב לקחתו". והכי משמע: ושכחת עומר, או ושכחת בשדה. נפקא להו. מ"בשדך ושכחת", קרי ביה ששכח את קצת שדהו. שצפו עומרין לתוך שדה חבירו. שנשבה הרוח והרימה את העומרין מן הארץ והציפתן לתוך שדה חבירו ושכחן, כסבור שאינן שלו – נפקא מ"בשדך" ולא בשדה חבירך, דלא הוו שכחה. ורבנן. מיעוטא דשדה חבירו נפקא להו מדהוה ליה למכתב "כי תקצור קצירך בשדה ושכחת" וכתיב "בשדך". צפו עומרין לתוך שדהו. (ג) שהיו מוטלים על גבי אבן או עמוד, או זו על זו. פרט לשצפו. וקא סלקא דעתך צפו ממש, על גבי אבן או על גבי עמוד. וליטעמיך לתוך שדה חבירו. צפו על גבי אבן הוא דמעיט, אבל מונחים – לא מיעט? והא "בשדך" כתיב! אלא הא דקאמר צפו – לאו דוקא צפו על שום דבר קאמר, דאפי' מונחים על גבי קרקע נמי קאמר אינו שכחה. והאי דקאמר צפו – דלא משכחת עומרין לתוך שדה חבירו אלא בצפו, שהרוח מצפפתן על הארץ ומדיחתן לשם. שהחזיק בו להוליכו לעיר. ס"ד השתא דאורחא דמילתא נקט, ולאו דוקא. זכה ביה. ותו לא הוי שכחה, דבעינן שכוח מעיקרו, כדאמר בב"מ בפרק קמא (דף יא.). מפני שהוא כצף. שהוא פטור על שהחזיק בו כאילו היה עודנו צף מעל הקרקע ומונח בידו. הריני כבן עזאי בשוקי טבריא. יום אחד היה דעתו צלולה, אמר: הריני כאן בפומבדיתא מוכן להשיב דבר לשואל בעומק ובחריפות, כבן עזאי שהיה חריף ודורש בשוקי טבריא. שני חללים זה על גב זה. והאחד משוך להלן מחבירו מעט, ואם תמדוד מזה – יקרב לעיר אחת, ואם תמדוד מחבירו – יקרב לעיר אחרת. ולא מזה מודד כו'. וה"ה דמיבעיא ליה נמי: או דלמא מין במינו לא הוי טמון, מין במינו לא הוי צף, ומשניהם מודד. אלא שהוא בכלל אלו.

מסורת הש"ס

ס"א ל"ג | [סנהדרין יד: כל הענין] | תורה אור: משלי כט, דברים יז, שם, שיר ז | שם | שבועות יד. סנהדרין ב: יד: | דברים כד | שם כא, שם כד | [גי' ערוך עפו וכו' וכ"ה בכ"מ הל' מ"ע הל"ה] | [תוספתא פאה פ"ג ע"ש] | [עירובין כט: קידושין כ. ערכין ל:]

עין משפט נר מצוה

ז א ב מיי' פ"ט מהל' רוצח הלכה א סמג עשין עח:
ח ג מיי' פ"ג מהלכות ממרים הלכה ה והל' ז סמג לאוין קסג:
ט ד מיי' פ"ג מהלכות סנהדרין הלכה ב:
י ה מיי' פ"ו מהל' בית הבחירה הלכה יא:
יא ו מיי' פ"ה מהלכות מתנות עניים הל' א:
יב ז מיי' שם פ"א הל' ו:
יג ח ט מיי' שם הלכה ה:
יד י מיי' שם הלכה ד וע"ש:
טו כ מיי' פ"ט מהלכות רוצח הלכה י:

הגהות הב"ח

(א) גמ' הכא מענייניה דקרא דכתיב כי ימצא חלל כל היכא וכו' עומר בשדה שכחה דומיא דקציר: (ב) שם קצירך בשדך ושכחת ור' יהודה: (ג) רש"י ד"ה צפו וכו' שדהו שמוטלין כצ"ל ותיבת שהיו נמחק:

גליון הש"ס

גמ' ויצאו הן ולא שלוחיהן. עיין יבמות דף קא ע"ב תד"ה וקראו לו ובערכין דף ב ע"א תד"ה קרבנו: שם הכא מענייני' דקרא. מכות דף ח ע"ב ערכין דף ל ע"ב:

טז א מיי' פ"ט מה' רוצח הלכה יח:
יז ב מיי' שם הלכה ה:
יח ג מיי' שם הלכה ח:
יט ד מיי' שם הלכה ז ח ופ"ז מהל' בית הבחירה הלכה יד:
כ ה ו מיי' פ"ט מהל' רוצח הלכה ט:
כא ז מיי' שם הלכה ד ופ"ד מהל' עבודת כוכבים הל' ד ופ"ז מהל' בית הבחירה הל' יד ופי"ד מהל' טומאת צרעת הלכה יא:
כב ח מיי' פ"ה מהל' נזקי ממון הל' ג ופ"ח מה' טומאת מת הלכה ז טור ח"מ סימן רעד:
כג ט מיי' פ"ט מהל' רוצח הלכה ט י:
כד י מיי' שם הלכה ב סמג עשין עח:
כה כ מיי' שם פ"י הל' ג:
כו ל מיי' שם הלכה ב:
כז מ נ מיי' שם פ"ט הלכה ב ג סמג שם:
כח ס מיי' שם פ"י הלכה ט:
כט ע פ מיי' שם פ"ט הלכה ג:

תְּנִיתוּהָ: אעוֹמֶר שֶׁהֶחֱזִיק בּוֹ לְהוֹלִיכוֹ לָעִיר, וְהִנִּיחוֹ עַל גַּבֵּי חֲבֵירוֹ, וּשְׁכָחוֹ – הַתַּחְתּוֹן שִׁכְחָה, וְהָעֶלְיוֹן אֵינוֹ שִׁכְחָה. ר' שִׁמְעוֹן בֶּן יְהוּדָה אוֹמֵר מִשּׁוּם ר' שִׁמְעוֹן: שְׁנֵיהֶן אֵינָן שִׁכְחָה, הַתַּחְתּוֹן מִפְּנֵי שֶׁהוּא טָמוּן, וְהָעֶלְיוֹן מִפְּנֵי שֶׁהוּא צָף. סַבְרוּהָ דְּהָנֵי תַּנָּאֵי כְּר' יְהוּדָה סְבִירָא לְהוּ, דְּאָמַר: "בַּשָּׂדֶה" – פְּרָט לְטָמוּן. מַאי לָאו – בְּהָא קָא מִיפַּלְגִי, דְּמָר סָבַר: מִין בְּמִינוֹ הָוֵי טָמוּן, וּמָר סָבַר: לָא הָוֵי טָמוּן? לָא, אִי כְּר' יְהוּדָה סְבִירָא לְהוּ – דְּכ"ע מִין בְּמִינוֹ הָוֵי טָמוּן. וְהָכָא בִּפְלוּגְתָּא דְּרַבִּי יְהוּדָה וְרַבָּנַן קָמִיפַּלְגִי, דְּרַבָּנַן – כְּרַבָּנַן, וְר' שִׁמְעוֹן בֶּן יְהוּדָה – כְּרַבִּי יְהוּדָה. אִי הָכִי, מַאי אִירְיָא עַל גַּבֵּי חֲבֵירוֹ? אֲפִי' בְּעָפָר וּבִצְרוֹר נַמִי! אִין הָכִי נַמִי, וּלְהוֹדִיעֲךָ כֹּחוֹ דְּר' יְהוּדָה, דְּאָמַר: אֲפִי' מִין בְּמִינוֹ הָוֵי טָמוּן. תָּנוּ רַבָּנַן: א"חָלָל" – וְלֹא חָנוּק, "חָלָל" – וְלֹא מְפַרְפֵּר, "בָּאֲדָמָה" – וְלֹא טָמוּן בְּגַל, "נוֹפֵל" – וְלֹא תָּלוּי בְּאִילָן, "בַּשָּׂדֶה" – וְלֹא צָף עַל פְּנֵי הַמַּיִם. ר' אֶלְעָזָר אוֹמֵר: בְּכוּלָּן, אִם הָיָה חָלָל – עוֹרְפִין. תַּנְיָא, אָמַר רַבִּי יוֹסֵי בַּר יְהוּדָה: אָמְרוּ לוֹ לְר"א: אִי אַתָּה מוֹדֶה שֶׁאִם הָיָה חָנוּק וּמוּטָל בָּאַשְׁפָּה שֶׁאֵין עוֹרְפִין? אַלְמָא: "חָלָל" – וְלֹא חָנוּק. הָכָא נַמִי "בָּאֲדָמָה" – וְלֹא טָמוּן בְּגַל, "נוֹפֵל" – וְלֹא תָּלוּי בְּאִילָן, "בַּשָּׂדֶה" – וְלֹא צָף עַל גַּבֵּי מַיִם. וְר"א: "חָלָל" יְתֵירָא כְּתִיב.§ "נִמְצָא סָמוּךְ לַסְּפָר אוֹ לְעִיר שֶׁרוּבָּהּ גּוֹיִם כו'.§ ◦דִּכְתִיב: "כִּי יִמָּצֵא" – *פְּרָט לְמָצוּי.§ "אוֹ לְעִיר שֶׁאֵין בָּהּ ב"ד".§ דְּבָעֵינָא "זִקְנֵי הָעִיר", וְלֵיכָּא.§ "אֵין מוֹדְדִין אֶלָּא לְעִיר" כו'.§ פְּשִׁיטָא, כֵּיוָן דְּתָנָא "לְעִיר שֶׁאֵין בָּהּ ב"ד" – אֲנָא יָדַעְנָא דְּאֵין מוֹדְדִין אֶלָּא לְעִיר שֶׁיֵּשׁ בָּהּ בֵּית דִּין! הָא קָא מַשְׁמַע לָן כִּדְתַנְיָא: במִנַּיִן שֶׁאִם נִמְצָא סָמוּךְ לְעִיר שֶׁאֵין בָּהּ ב"ד, שֶׁמַּנִּיחִין אוֹתָהּ ◦וּמוֹדְדִין לְעִיר שֶׁיֵּשׁ בָּהּ בֵּית דִּין – ת"ל: °"וְלָקְחוּ זִקְנֵי הָעִיר הַהִיא" – מִכָּל מָקוֹם.§ **מתני'** גנִמְצָא *מְכוּוָּן בֵּין שְׁתֵּי עֲיָירוֹת – שְׁתֵּיהֶן מְבִיאוֹת שְׁתֵּי עֲגָלוֹת, דִּבְרֵי רַבִּי אֱלִיעֶזֶר. *דוְאֵין יְרוּשָׁלַיִם מְבִיאָה עֶגְלָה עֲרוּפָה. נִמְצָא רֹאשׁוֹ בְּמָקוֹם אֶחָד וְגוּפוֹ בְּמָקוֹם אַחֵר – מוֹלִיכִין הָרֹאשׁ אֵצֶל הַגּוּף, דִּבְרֵי רַבִּי אֱלִיעֶזֶר. רַבִּי עֲקִיבָא אוֹמֵר: ההַגּוּף אֵצֶל הָרֹאשׁ. *מֵאַיִן הָיוּ מוֹדְדִין? רַבִּי אֱלִיעֶזֶר אוֹמֵר: מִטִּיבּוּרוֹ, רַבִּי עֲקִיבָא אוֹמֵר: ומֵחוֹטְמוֹ, רַבִּי אֱלִיעֶזֶר בֶּן יַעֲקֹב אוֹמֵר: מִמָּקוֹם שֶׁנַּעֲשָׂה חָלָל – מִצַּוָּארוֹ.§ **גמ'** מַאי טַעְמָא דְּרַבִּי אֱלִיעֶזֶר – קָסָבַר: אֶפְשָׁר לְצַמְצֵם, וּ"קְרוֹבָה" – וַאֲפִילּוּ קְרוֹבוֹת.§ "וְאֵין יְרוּשָׁלַיִם מְבִיאָה עֶגְלָה עֲרוּפָה".§ דְּאָמַר קְרָא: °"לְרִשְׁתָּהּ", וְקָסָבַר: *זיְרוּשָׁלַיִם לֹא נִתְחַלְּקָה לִשְׁבָטִים.§ "נִמְצָא רֹאשׁוֹ בְּמָקוֹם" כו'.§ בְּמַאי קָמִיפַּלְגִי? אִילֵימָא לְעִנְיַן מְדִידָה קָמִיפַּלְגִי, הָא מִדְּקָתָנֵי סֵיפָא "מֵאַיִן הָיוּ מוֹדְדִין" – מִכְּלָל דְּרֵישָׁא לָא בִּמְדִידָה עָסְקִינַן! אָמַר ר' יִצְחָק: *בְּמֵת מִצְוָה קָנָה מְקוֹמוֹ קָמִיפַּלְגִי, וְהָכִי קָאָמַר: לְקוֹבְרוֹ חקָנָה מְקוֹמוֹ, וְהֵיכָא דְּנִמְצָא רֹאשׁוֹ בְּמָקוֹם אֶחָד וְגוּפוֹ בְּמָקוֹם אַחֵר – מוֹלִיכִין הָרֹאשׁ אֵצֶל הַגּוּף, דִּבְרֵי ר' אֱלִיעֶזֶר. ר' עֲקִיבָא אוֹמֵר: טהַגּוּף אֵצֶל הָרֹאשׁ. בְּמַאי קָמִיפַּלְגִי – מָר סָבַר: גּוּפֵיהּ בְּדוּכְתֵּיהּ נָפֵיל, רֵישָׁא דְּנָאדֵי וְנָפֵיל. וּמָר סָבַר: רֵישָׁא הֵיכָא דְּנָפֵיל נָפֵיל, גּוּפָא הוּא דִּרְהִיט אָזֵיל.§ "מֵאַיִן הָיוּ מוֹדְדִין".§ בְּמַאי קָמִיפַּלְגִי? מָר סָבַר: עִיקַּר חִיּוּתָא בְּאַפֵּיהּ, וּמָר סָבַר: עִיקַּר חִיּוּתָא בְּטִיבּוּרֵיהּ. לֵימָא כִּי הָנֵי תַּנָּאֵי: *מֵהֵיכָן הַוָּלָד נוֹצָר – מֵרֹאשׁוֹ, וְכֵן הוּא אוֹמֵר: °"מִמְּעֵי אִמִּי אַתָּה גוֹזִי", וְאוֹמֵר: °"גָּזִּי נִזְרֵךְ וְהַשְׁלִיכִי" וגו'. ◦אַבָּא שָׁאוּל אוֹמֵר: מִטִּיבּוּרוֹ, וּמְשַׁלֵּחַ שָׁרָשָׁיו אֵילָךְ וְאֵילָךְ. אֲפִילּוּ תֵּימָא אַבָּא שָׁאוּל, ע"כ לָא קָאָמַר אַבָּא שָׁאוּל אֶלָּא לְעִנְיַן יְצִירָה, דְּכִי מִיתְצַר וָלָד – מִמְּצִיעָתֵיהּ מִיתְצַר, אֲבָל לְעִנְיַן חִיּוּתָא – דְּכוּלֵּי עָלְמָא בְּאַפֵּיהּ הוּא, דִּכְתִיב: °"כֹּל אֲשֶׁר נִשְׁמַת רוּחַ חַיִּים בְּאַפָּיו" וגו'.§ "רַבִּי אֱלִיעֶזֶר בֶּן יַעֲקֹב אוֹמֵר: מִמָּקוֹם שֶׁנַּעֲשָׂה חָלָל – מִצַּוָּארוֹ".§ מַאי טַעְמָא דְּרַבִּי אֱלִיעֶזֶר בֶּן יַעֲקֹב – כִּדְכְתִיב: °"לָתֵת אוֹתָךְ אֶל צַוְּארֵי חַלְלֵי רְשָׁעִים".§ **מתני'** ינִפְטְרוּ זִקְנֵי יְרוּשָׁלַיִם וְהָלְכוּ לָהֶן, ◦זִקְנֵי אוֹתָהּ הָעִיר מְבִיאִין עֶגְלַת בָּקָר אֲשֶׁר כלֹא מָשְׁכָה בְּעוֹל, לוְאֵין הַמּוּם פּוֹסֵל בָּהּ, מוּמוֹרִידִין אוֹתָהּ לְנַחַל אֵיתָן. אֵיתָן – כְּמַשְׁמָעוֹ, קָשֶׁה. אע"פ שֶׁאֵינוֹ אֵיתָן – כָּשֵׁר. נוְעוֹרְפִין אוֹתָהּ בְּקוֹפִיץ מֵאֲחוֹרֶיהָ. סוּמְקוֹמָהּ אָסוּר מִלִּזְרוֹעַ וּמִלַּעֲבוֹד, וּמוּתָּר לִסְרוֹק שָׁם פִּשְׁתָּן וּלְנַקֵּר שָׁם אֲבָנִים. עזִקְנֵי אוֹתָהּ הָעִיר רוֹחֲצִין אֶת יְדֵיהֶן בְּמַיִם בִּמְקוֹם עֲרִיפָה שֶׁל עֶגְלָה, וְאוֹמְרִים °"יָדֵינוּ לֹא שָׁפְכָה אֶת הַדָּם הַזֶּה וְעֵינֵינוּ לֹא רָאוּ". *וְכִי עַל דַּעְתֵּינוּ עָלְתָה שֶׁזִּקְנֵי ב"ד שׁוֹפְכֵי דָמִים הֵן? פאֶלָּא, שֶׁלֹּא בָא (א) עַל יָדֵינוּ וּפְטַרְנוּהוּ (בְּלֹא מָזוֹן), וְלֹא רְאִינוּהוּ וְהִנַּחְנוּהוּ (בְּלֹא לְוָיָה.)

וְהַכֹּהֲנִים

תניתוה. לחדא מינייהו, דפלוגתא היא בטמון. אבל לף לא פשט לה מינה, דהא אוקימנא טעמא דעליון משום דאחזיק ביה הוא, ולף לא ידעינן מאי הוי עלה. סברוה. רבנן דבי מדרשא, דבעו למיפשט מינה דפלוגתא בטמון דמין במינו הוא, דהני תנאי, אפילו תנא קמא דאמר תחתון שכחה – כר' יהודה סבירא ליה, דאמר "בשדה" – פרט לטמון, וטעמא משום דמין במינו לא הוי טמון. חלל. לא מקרי אלא בכלי ברזל, כעין חרב. בבולן. ואפי' מפרפר, לף וטמון, ותלוי. ומוטל באשפה. דלא הוי לף ולא טמון, ולא תלוי ואפי' הכי אין עורפין, דחלל קבעי. אלמא קרא כדכתיב בעית. חלל יתירא כתיב. "הקרובים אל החלל", ועוד חללים טובא, למדרש: חלל דוקא ולא חנוק. פרט למצוי. תדיר, כגון ספר, או עיר שרובה נכרים. קמ"ל כדתניא כו'. והכי קאמר: נמצא סמוך לעיר שאין בה ב"ד – אין מודדין לה, אלא לעיר שיש בה ב"ד מודדין, איזו היא עיר שיש בה ב"ד קרובה לו. ואי לא הדר תניא – הוה אמינא אין מודדין כלל. ת"ל ולקחו זקני העיר מכל מקום. דהאי "העיר" קרא יתירא הוא, דמצי למכתב (ב) "והיתה העיר הקרובה אל החלל ולקחו זקניה עגלת בקר". מתני' מכוון. מלומצם, שאין זו קרובה לו מזו אפי' כמלא חוט. ואין ירושלים כו'. מפרש טעמא בגמ'. מוליכין הראש אצל הגוף. בגמ' מפרש למאי הלכתא מוליכין. גמ' אפשר לצמצם. אפשר לכוין המדה, ואמת מדדו – שאין זו קרובה לו מזו כלל, והוו להו שתיהן קרובות. וקסבר. נמי: "קרובה" דכתיב בקרא – אפילו קרובות במשמע, ◦כמו "ובהמה רבה" (יונה ד). דאם"ד אי אפשר לצמצם – אין כאן קרובה אלא אחת, ואנן הוא דלא ידעינן הי מינייהו, והוה ליה למימר: (ג) יביאו עגלה בשותפות ויתנו: אם שלנו קרובה – חלקכם יהא קנוי לנו, ואם עירכם קרובה – חלקנו יהא קנוי לכם. אילימא לענין מדידה. קאמר: יביאו הראש אצל הגוף, תורה אור דממקום שנמצא הגוף שם צריך למדוד, ויביאו הראש לכאן – והא מדקתני כו'. קנה מקומו. לקוברו שם. דזה אחד מי' תנאים שהתנה יהושע, בפרק "מרובה" (ב"ק דף פא.). עיקר חיותא כו'. הלכך עיקר חלל מיקרי, ומודדין מיניה, כדכתיב: "אל הערים אשר סביבות החלל". אתה גוזי. אתה מראשי, יצרת ראשי תחילה. דגוזי לישנא דרישא, כמו "גזי נזרך" – שער ראשך תלשי וגלי ראשך. אפילו תימא אבא שאול. כר' עקיבא סבירא ליה. מ"ט דרבי אליעזר בן יעקב. דאמר: מן הצואר הוא קרוי חלל. דכתיב אל צוארי חללי רשעים. והלכך ממנו מודדין, כדכתיב "אל החלל". מתני' נפטרו זקני ירושלים כו'. שאין עליהם אלא למדוד, כדכתיב: "ויצאו זקניך ושופטיך ומדדו". ואע"פ שאינו איתן כשר. דלא כתיב ביה עיכובא, ולא נאמר אלא למצוה. בקופיץ. כמין סכין גדול. מאחוריה. ממול עורפה. מקומה אסור. לעולם. ומותר לסרוק שם פשתן. דוקא נקט עבודה שאינה בגופה של קרקע, כדמפרש בגמרא. לא בא לידינו ופטרנוהו. בגמ' מפרש: "בלא מזונות". והיינו "ידינו לא שפכו" – לא נהרג על ידינו שפטרנוהו בלא מזונות והולך ללסטם את הבריות, ועל (ד) כך נהרג. לא ראינוהו והנחנוהו. יחידי בלא חבורה, והיינו "ועינינו לא ראו".

והכהנים

הגהות הב"ח

(א) גמ' שלא בא לידינו כצ"ל ותיבת על נמחק: (ב) רש"י ד"ה ת"ל וכו' למכתב והיה העיר: (ג) ד"ה וקסבר וכו' והוה (והוה) ליה למימר יביאו נ"ב הכי איתא בפ' שני דבכורות דף יח: (ד) ד"ה לא בא וכו' ועל ידי כך נהרג:

[יומא כג: ב"ק פב:]

דברים כא

גליון הש"ס

גמ' דכתיב כי ימצא פרט למצוי. עיין סנהדרין דף פ"ו ע"א תד"ה מונמא: שם ומודדין לעיר שיש בה ב"ד. עיין ב"ב דף כג ע"ב תד"ה בדליכא: שם אבא שאול אומר מטבורו. עיין נדה דף כה ע"א תד"ה תחלת: שם זקני אותה העיר. עיין באר שבע הוריות דף ג ע"ב ד"ה ה"נ מסתברא: רש"י ד"ה וקסבר כו' כמו ובהמה רבה. עיין קידושין דף יח ע"א ברש"י ד"ה טובא משמע ועיין תמורה דף ט ע"א:

[סנהדרין פו. ועי' תוס' שם ד"ה מונמא ערכין ל:]
דברים כא
בכורות יז: תוספתא דנגעים פ"א
סנהדרין פח. ובכמה דוכתי
[יומא יב. מגילה כו.]
ב"ק פא. [עירובין יז. סנהדרין מז:]
[יומא פה.]
תהלים עא
ירמיה ז
בראשית ז
יחזקאל כא
דברים כא
לעיל לח:
[בירושלמי ובע"י לא גרסי' וכ"ה ברש"י כאן ועי' תוי"ט]

א וְהַכֹּהֲנִים *אוֹמְרִים: °"כַּפֵּר לְעַמְּךָ יִשְׂרָאֵל אֲשֶׁר פָּדִיתָ [ה'] וְאַל תִּתֵּן דָּם נָקִי בְּקֶרֶב עַמְּךָ יִשְׂרָאֵל". לֹא הָיוּ צְרִיכִין לוֹמַר "וְנִכַּפֵּר לָהֶם הַדָּם", ב אֶלָּא רוּחַ הַקּוֹדֶשׁ מְבַשַּׂרְתָּן: אֵימָתַי שֶׁתַּעֲשׂוּ כָּכָה — הַדָּם מִתְכַּפֵּר לָהֶם.§ **גמ'** וִיהֵא מוּם פּוֹסֵל בְּעֶגְלָה מִקַּל וָחוֹמֶר: וּמָה פָּרָה ג שֶׁאֵין הַשָּׁנִים פּוֹסְלוֹת בָּהּ — ד מוּם פּוֹסֵל בָּהּ, עֶגְלָה ה שֶׁהַשָּׁנִים פּוֹסְלוֹת בָּהּ — אֵינוֹ דִּין שֶׁיְּהֵא מוּם פּוֹסֵל בָּהּ! שָׁאנֵי הָתָם, דְּאָמַר קְרָא: "אֲשֶׁר אֵין בָּהּ מוּם", בָּהּ — מוּם פּוֹסֵל, וְאֵין מוּם פּוֹסֵל בְּעֶגְלָה. אֶלָּא מֵעַתָּה, לֹא יְהוּ שְׁאָר עֲבוֹדוֹת פּוֹסְלוֹת בָּהּ, אַלְמָה א"ר יְהוּדָה אָמַר רַב: * ו הִנִּיחַ עָלֶיהָ עוּדָה שֶׁל שַׂקִּין — פְּסוּלָה, וּבְעֶגְלָה עַד שֶׁתִּמְשׁוֹךְ! שָׁאנֵי פָּרָה, ז דְּיָלְפִינַן °"עוֹל" °"עוֹל" מֵעֶגְלָה. עֶגְלָה נַמִי, תֵּיתֵי "עוֹל" "עוֹל" מִפָּרָה! הָא מִיעֵט רַחֲמָנָא "בָּהּ". בְּעֶגְלָה נַמִי כְּתִיב "בָּהּ"! הַהוּא מִיבָּעֵי לֵיהּ לְמַעוּטֵי קֳדָשִׁים, ח דְּלָא פָּסְלָה בְּהוּ עֲבוֹדָה. סָלְקָא דַּעְתָּךְ אָמִינָא לֵיתֵי בְּק"ו מֵעֶגְלָה: וּמָה עֶגְלָה שֶׁאֵין מוּם פּוֹסֵל בָּהּ — עֲבוֹדָה פּוֹסֶלֶת בָּהּ, קֳדָשִׁים ט שֶׁמּוּם פּוֹסֶלֶת בָּהֶן — אֵינוֹ דִּין שֶׁעֲבוֹדָה פּוֹסֶלֶת בָּהֶן? אִיכָּא לְמִיפְרַךְ: מַה לְּעֶגְלָה — שֶׁכֵּן שָׁנִים פּוֹסְלוֹת בָּהּ. אַטּוּ קֳדָשִׁים מִי לֵיכָּא דְּפָסְלֵי בְּהוּ שָׁנִים? כִּי אִיצְטְרִיךְ קְרָא — לְהָנָךְ קֳדָשִׁים דְּפָסְלָה בְּהוּ שָׁנִים. וְקֳדָשִׁים דְּלָא פָּסְלָה בְּהוּ עֲבוֹדָה מֵהָכָא נָפְקָא? מֵהָתָם נָפְקָא: °"עַוֶּרֶת אוֹ שָׁבוּר אוֹ חָרוּץ אוֹ יַבֶּלֶת אוֹ גָרָב אוֹ יַלֶּפֶת לֹא תַקְרִיבוּ אֵלֶּה לַה'", אֵלֶּה אִי אַתָּה מַקְרִיב, אֲבָל אַתָּה מַקְרִיב קֳדָשִׁים שֶׁנֶּעֶבְדָה בָּהֶן עֲבוֹדָה! אִיצְטְרִיךְ, סד"א: ה"מ — הֵיכָא דְּעָבַד בָּהֶן עֲבוֹדַת הֶיתֵּר, אֲבָל עֲבוֹדַת אִיסּוּר — אֵימָא לִיתַּסְרוּ, צְרִיכָא. וְהָא נַמִי מֵהָכָא נָפְקָא: °"וּמִיַּד בֶּן נֵכָר לֹא תַקְרִיבוּ אֶת לֶחֶם אֱלֹהֵיכֶם מִכָּל אֵלֶּה", אֵלֶּה אִי אַתָּה מַקְרִיב, אֲבָל אַתָּה מַקְרִיב קֳדָשִׁים שֶׁנֶּעֶבְדָה בָּהֶן עֲבוֹדָה! אִיצְטְרִיךְ, ס"ד אָמִינָא: הָנֵי מִילֵּי — הֵיכָא דְּעָבַד בָּהֶן כְּשֶׁהֵן חוּלִּין, אֲבָל עָבַד בָּהֶן כְּשֶׁהֵן קֳדָשִׁים — אֵימָא לִיתַּסְרוּ, צְרִיכָא. גּוּפָא, אָמַר רַב יְהוּדָה אָמַר רַב: הִנִּיחַ עָלֶיהָ עוּדָה שֶׁל שַׂקִּין — פְּסוּלָה, וּבְעֶגְלָה — עַד שֶׁתִּמְשׁוֹךְ. מֵיתִיבֵי: "עוֹל" — אֵין לִי אֶלָּא עוֹל, שְׁאָר עֲבוֹדוֹת מִנַּיִן? אָמַרְתָּ, ק"ו: וּמָה עֶגְלָה שֶׁאֵין מוּם פּוֹסֵל בָּהּ — שְׁאָר עֲבוֹדוֹת פּוֹסְלוֹת בָּהּ, פָּרָה שֶׁמּוּם פּוֹסֵל בָּהּ — אֵינוֹ דִּין שֶׁשְּׁאָר עֲבוֹדוֹת פּוֹסְלִין בָּהּ? וְאִם נַפְשָׁךְ לוֹמַר: נֶאֱמַר כָּאן "עוֹל" וְנֶאֱמַר לְהַלָּן "עוֹל", מַה לְּהַלָּן שְׁאָר עֲבוֹדוֹת פּוֹסְלוֹת בָּהּ — י אַף כָּאן שְׁאָר עֲבוֹדוֹת פּוֹסְלוֹת. מַאי "אִם נַפְשָׁךְ לוֹמַר"? וְכִי תֵּימָא: אִיכָּא לְמִיפְרַךְ; מַה לְּעֶגְלָה שֶׁכֵּן שָׁנִים פּוֹסְלוֹת בָּהּ, אִי נַמִי קֳדָשִׁים יוֹכִיחוּ, שֶׁמּוּם פּוֹסֵל בָּהֶן וְאֵין עֲבוֹדָה פּוֹסֶלֶת בָּהֶן — נֶאֱמַר כָּאן "עוֹל" וְנֶאֱמַר לְהַלָּן "עוֹל", מַה לְּהַלָּן שְׁאָר עֲבוֹדוֹת — אַף כָּאן שְׁאָר עֲבוֹדוֹת. וּמִמָּקוֹם שֶׁבָּאתָה; מַה לְּהַלָּן עַד שֶׁתִּמְשׁוֹךְ — אַף כָּאן עַד שֶׁתִּמְשׁוֹךְ! תַּנָּאֵי הִיא, דְּאִיכָּא דְּמַיְיתִי לָהּ מֵעֶגְלָה, אִיכָּא דְּמַיְיתִי לָהּ מִגּוּפַהּ דְּפָרָה. דְּתַנְיָא: "עוֹל" — אֵין לִי אֶלָּא עוֹל, שְׁאָר עֲבוֹדוֹת מִנַּיִן — ת"ל: °"אֲשֶׁר לֹא עָלָה עָלֶיהָ עוֹל" מִכָּל מָקוֹם. אִם כֵּן מַה ת"ל "עוֹל" — כ עוֹל פּוֹסֵל בֵּין בִּשְׁעַת עֲבוֹדָה בֵּין שֶׁלֹּא בִּשְׁעַת עֲבוֹדָה, שְׁאָר עֲבוֹדוֹת אֵין פּוֹסְלוֹת אֶלָּא בִּשְׁעַת עֲבוֹדָה. וְאֵימָא: "אֲשֶׁר לֹא עָלָה עָלֶיהָ" — כְּלָל, "עוֹל" — פְּרָט, כְּלָל וּפְרָט אֵין בַּכְּלָל אֶלָּא מַה שֶּׁבַּפְּרָט, עוֹל — אִין, מִידֵּי אַחֲרִינָא — לָא! "אֲשֶׁר" — רִבּוּיָא הוּא. וְתַנְיָא נַמִי גַּבֵּי עֶגְלָה כִּי הַאי גַּוְונָא: "עוֹל" — אֵין לִי אֶלָּא עוֹל, שְׁאָר עֲבוֹדוֹת מִנַּיִן — ת"ל: °"אֲשֶׁר לֹא עוּבַּד בָּהּ" ל מ"מ. א"כ מַה ת"ל "עוֹל" — מ עוֹל פּוֹסֵל בֵּין בִּשְׁעַת עֲבוֹדָה בֵּין שֶׁלֹּא בִּשְׁעַת עֲבוֹדָה, שְׁאָר עֲבוֹדוֹת אֵין פּוֹסְלוֹת אֶלָּא בִּשְׁעַת עֲבוֹדָה. וְאֵימָא "אֲשֶׁר לֹא עוּבַּד בָּהּ" — כְּלָל, "עוֹל" — פְּרָט, כְּלָל וּפְרָט אֵין בַּכְּלָל אֶלָּא מַה שֶּׁבַּפְּרָט, עוֹל — אִין, מִידֵּי אַחֲרִינָא — לָא! "אֲשֶׁר" — רִבּוּיָא הוּא. א"ר אַבָּהוּ, בְּעֵי מִינֵּיהּ מֵר' יוֹחָנָן: מְשִׁיכַת עוֹל בְּכַמָּה? א"ל: כִּמְלֹא עוֹל. אִיבַּעְיָא לְהוּ: לְאָרְכּוֹ אוֹ לְרָחְבּוֹ? אָמַר לְהוּ הַהוּא מֵרַבָּנַן, וְר' יַעֲקֹב שְׁמֵיהּ: לְדִידִי מְפָרְשָׁא לִי מִינֵּיהּ דְּרַבִּי יוֹחָנָן: נ מְשִׁיכַת עוֹל לְרָחְבּוֹ, טֶפַח. וְלֵימָא טֶפַח! הָא קמ"ל: שִׁיעוּרָא דְּעוֹל — טֶפַח הָוֵי. לְמַאי נָפְקָא מִינַּהּ — לְמִקָּח וּמִמְכָּר. א"ר יוֹחָנָן בֶּן שָׁאוּל: מִפְּנֵי מָה אָמְרָה תּוֹרָה: הָבִיא עֶגְלָה בְּנַחַל? אָמַר הקב"ה: יָבֹא דָּבָר שֶׁלֹּא עָשָׂה פֵּירוֹת, וְיֵעָרֵף בְּמָקוֹם שֶׁאֵין עוֹשֶׂה פֵּירוֹת, וִיכַפֵּר עַל מִי שֶׁלֹּא הִנִּיחוּהוּ לַעֲשׂוֹת פֵּירוֹת. מַאי פֵּירוֹת? אִילֵימָא פְּרִיָּה וּרְבִיָּה — אֶלָּא מֵעַתָּה אַזָּקֵן וְאַסָּרִיס ה"נ דְּלָא עָרְפִינַן?! אֶלָּא מִצְוֹת.§ "וּמוֹרִידִין אוֹתָהּ אֶל נַחַל אֵיתָן". אֵיתָן כְּמַשְׁמָעוֹ, קָשֶׁה".§ תָּנוּ רַבָּנַן: מִנַּיִן *לְאֵיתָן שֶׁהוּא קָשֶׁה — שֶׁנֶּאֱמַר: אֵיתָן

תורה אור: דברים כא | במדבר יט | ויקרא כב | שם | במדבר יט | דברים כא

רש"י

וְהַכֹּהֲנִים אוֹמְרִים. כִּדְכְתִיב לְעֵיל: "וְנִגְּשׁוּ הַכֹּהֲנִים בְּנֵי לֵוִי", וְלֹא פֵּירֵשׁ עַל (א) מִי הֵם נִגָּשִׁים. וְלֹא הָיוּ צְרִיכִים לוֹמַר וְנִכַּפֵּר לָהֶם הַדָּם. כְּלוֹמַר: "וְנִכַּפֵּר" דִּכְתִיב בִּקְרָא — לָאו אַ"וְעָנוּ וְאָמְרוּ" קָאֵי, שֶׁיְּהֵא אַף זֶה בִּכְלַל אֲמִירָה, אֶלָּא מִילְּתָא בְּאַנְפֵּי נַפְשָׁהּ הִיא, שֶׁרוּחַ הַקּוֹדֶשׁ בִּישֵּׂר אֶת יִשְׂרָאֵל ע"י מֹשֶׁה רַבֵּינוּ: לִכְשֶׁיַּעֲשׂוּ כֵּן — "וְנִכַּפֵּר לָהֶם הַדָּם". **גמ'** עֶגְלָה. בַּת שְׁנָתָהּ הִיא, וְאִם עָבְרָה שְׁנָתָהּ — פְּסוּלָה. דְּכָל מָקוֹם שֶׁנֶּאֱמַר בַּתּוֹרָה עֵגֶל סְתָם — בֶּן שָׁנָה הוּא, *דְּיָלֵיף מִ"וְעֵגֶל וָכֶבֶשׂ (ב) בְּנֵי שָׁנָה". פָּרָה אֲדוּמָּה. אֵין שִׁיעוּר לִשְׁנוֹתֶיהָ. מוּם פּוֹסֵל בָּהּ. דִּכְתִיב בְּפָרָה אֲדוּמָּה: "אֵין בָּהּ מוּם" (במדבר יט). בָּהּ. מִיעוּט. אֶלָּא מֵעַתָּה. דְּכָל הֵיכָא דִּכְתַב "בָּהּ" — מִיעוּטָא הוּא, וְלָא גָּמְרִינַן מִינֵּיהּ בְּקַל וָחוֹמֶר. לֹא יְהוּ שְׁאָר עֲבוֹדוֹת פּוֹסְלוֹת. בְּפָרָה, דְּהָא "עוֹל" בִּלְבַד כְּתִיב בָּהּ. אֶלָּא דְּגָמַר לָהּ בְּק"ו מֵעֶגְלָה, דִּכְתִיב (דברים כא): "אֲשֶׁר לֹא עוּבַּד בָּהּ" — כָּל עֲבוֹדוֹת בְּמַשְׁמַע. וְאִי "בָּהּ" מִיעוּטָא — לָא נִגְמַר מִינֵּיהּ! אַלְמָה אָמַר רַב יְהוּדָה הִנִּיחַ. עַל פָּרָה: עוּדָה שֶׁל שַׂקִּין — אֲגוּדָה שֶׁל שַׂקִּין, פְּסוּלָה, וְאַעַ"ג דְּלָאו עוֹל הוּא, וּבַעֲלִיָּיה לְחוּדֵיהּ מִיפַּסְלָא, כִּדְכְתִיב בְּפָרָה בִּמְלֶאכֶת עוֹל הָאֲמוּרָה בָּהּ "אֲשֶׁר לֹא עָלָה" — בַּעֲלִיָּיה לְחוּדָהּ, וַאֲפִילּוּ שֶׁלֹּא מְשָׁכָהּ. וּבְעֶגְלָה עַד שֶׁתִּמְשׁוֹךְ. שֶׁתִּטַּלְטֵל הַמַּשָּׂא מְעַט, דִּבְעֶגְלָה כְּתִיב "אֲשֶׁר לֹא מָשְׁכָה", וּלְקַמָּן פָּרֵיךְ: כֵּיוָן דִּשְׁאָר עֲבוֹדוֹת בְּפָרָה לָא כְּתִיבִי, וּמֵעֶגְלָה יָלְפִינַן — אַמַּאי מִיפְסַל בַּעֲלִיָּיה לְחוּדָהּ דִּשְׁאָר מַשְּׂאוֹי שֶׁאֵינוֹ עוֹל מַמָּשׁ? מ"מ שְׁמַע מִינָּהּ דְּגָמַר פָּרָה מֵעֶגְלָה בְּק"ו בִּשְׁאָר עֲבוֹדוֹת, וְאַעַ"ג דִּכְתִיב בָּהּ מִיעוּטָא. שָׁאנֵי פָּרָה דְּיָלְפִינַן עוֹל עוֹל. וְכֵיוָן דִּגְזֵירָה שָׁוָה מוּפְנָה הִיא — הֲוָה לֵיהּ כְּמַאן דִּכְתִיב בְּגוּפָהּ. וּמִיעוּטָא דְ"בָּהּ" דָּרֵישׁ לֵיהּ לִדְרָשָׁא אַחֲרִינָא כִּדְלְקַמָּן. עֶגְלָה נַמִי תֵּיתֵי עוֹל עוֹל מִפָּרָה. לְמוּם. לְמַעוּטֵי קֳדָשִׁים דְּלָא פָּסְלָה בְּהוּ עֲבוֹדָה. מֵהַקְרָבָה. אֲבָל פָּרָה לָא מְמַעֲטָא דְּאָתְיָא מִג"שׁ. מִי לֵיכָּא דְּפָסְלֵי בְּהוּ שָׁנִים. וַהֲרֵי פֶּסַח וְחַטָּאת דִּכְתִיב בְּהוּ "בְּנֵי שְׁנָתָן", וְכִי אִיצְטְרִיךְ "בָּהּ" לְמַעֲטִינְהוּ מִפְּסוּל עֲבוֹדָה — לְהָכִי אִיצְטְרִיךְ, דְּאִי לָא מַעֲטִינְהוּ — הֲווּ גָּמְרֵי בְּקַל וָחוֹמֶר מֵעֶגְלָה. שֶׁנֶּעֶבְדָה בָּהֶן עֲבוֹדָה גָּרְסִי'. עֲבוֹדַת אִיסּוּר. כְּגוֹן בְּשַׁבָּת, אוֹ כִּלְאַיִם בְּשׁוֹר וַחֲמוֹר. עֲבוֹדַת אִיסּוּר נַמִי מֵהַאי קְרָא נָפְקָא. דְּכֵיוָן דִּתְרֵי קְרָאֵי כְּתִיבִי — עַל כָּרְחָךְ חַד מִינַּיְיהוּ לַעֲבוֹדַת אִיסּוּר! עוֹל. גַּבֵּי פָּרָה תַּנְיָא. שְׁאָר עֲבוֹדוֹת פּוֹסְלוֹת בָּהּ. דִּכְתִיב: "אֲשֶׁר לֹא עוּבַּד בָּהּ". וְאִם נַפְשָׁךְ לוֹמַר. וְאִם יֵשׁ לְךָ לְהָשִׁיב עַל ק"ו זֶה — לֵךְ וּלְמַד בְּג"ש: נֶאֱמַר כָּאן "עוֹל" כו'. מַאי אִם נַפְשָׁךְ לוֹמַר. מַאי הֲוָה לָךְ לְמִיפְרַךְ, דִּשְׁבַקְתֵּהּ תַּנָּא לְאוֹרְחֵיהּ וְיָלֵיף בִּגְזֵירָה שָׁוָה?. נֶאֱמַר כָּאן כו'. וְהַאי "עוֹל" יְתֵירָא הוּא, דְּהָא בִּכְלַל שְׁאָר עֲבוֹדוֹת הוּא. וּמִמָּקוֹם שֶׁבָּאתָ. לָאו תַּנָּא קָתָנֵי לָהּ, אֶלָּא תְּיוּבְתֵּיהּ קָא מְפָרֵשׁ וְאָזֵיל גְּמָרָא דְּקָא מוֹתִיב לְרַב יְהוּדָה, דְּאָמַר לְעֵיל שְׁאָר מַשָּׂאוֹת פּוֹסֵל בְּפָרָה בַּעֲלִיָּיה בְּעָלְמָא: וְהָא כֵּיוָן דִּשְׁאָר מַשָּׂאוֹי בְּפָרָה לָא כְּתִיב, וּמֵעֶגְלָה יָלֵיף לָהּ בִּגְזֵירָה שָׁוָה — וּמִמָּקוֹם שֶׁבָּאתָ מִשָּׁם יֵשׁ לְךָ לִלְמוֹד נַמִי, דְּמָה עֶגְלָה עַד שֶׁתִּמְשׁוֹךְ — אַף פָּרָה בִּשְׁאָר מַשָּׂאוֹת, דְּיָלְפִינַן מֵעֶגְלָה — עַד שֶׁתִּמְשׁוֹךְ!. ת"ל אֲשֶׁר לֹא עָלָה עָלֶיהָ עוֹל מ"מ. דָּרֵישׁ לֵיהּ: בְּלֹא עוֹל, מִדְּלָא כְּתִיב "אֲשֶׁר לֹא עָלָה עוֹל עָלֶיהָ". וְתוּ הֲדַר כְּתִיב "עוֹל" לִדְרָשָׁא, כִּדְדָרְשִׁינָא וְאָזֵיל. א"כ כו' שֶׁלֹּא בִּשְׁעַת עֲבוֹדָה. וַאֲפִילּוּ הִנִּיחוֹ עָלֶיהָ לְהָקֵל מַשָּׂא מִיָּדוֹ, וְלֹא לִמְשׁוֹךְ. אֶלָּא בִּשְׁעַת עֲבוֹדָה. כְּלוֹמַר שֶׁעֲבוֹדָה זוֹ לְצוֹרֶךְ הִיא. אֲבָל אַקְרַאי בְּעָלְמָא, שֶׁהִנִּיחַ שַׂק עָלֶיהָ וְלֹא לְהוֹלִיכוֹ, אֶלָּא אַקְּרַי וְאוֹתֵיב — לֹא פְּסָלָהּ. מְשִׁיכַת עוֹל. לִפְסוֹל בְּעֶגְלָה. שֶׁאֵינוֹ עוֹשֶׂה פֵּירוֹת. עֶגְלָה בַּת שְׁנָתָהּ לֹא יָלְדָה. בְּמָקוֹם שֶׁאֵין עוֹשֶׂה פֵּירוֹת. נַחַל אֵיתָן קָשֶׁה. שֶׁלֹּא הִנִּיחוּהוּ. שֶׁהֲרָגוּהוּ. אֵיתָן

מסורת הש"ס: יומא לז. | [ר"ה י.] | ע"ז כג. | [ר"ה יח. וש"נ]

עין משפט נר מצוה

ל א ב מיי' פ"ט מהל' רוצח הלכה ג סמג עשין סח:
לא ג מיי' פ"א מהל' פרה אדומה הלכה א סמג עשין רלב רלג:
לב ד מיי' שם הלכה ז:
לג ה מיי' פ"י מהלכות רוצח הלכה ב:
לד ו ז ח מיי' פ"א מהל' פרה אדומה הלכה ז:
לה ט מיי' פ"א מהל' איסורי מזבח הלכ' א:
לו י כ מיי' פ"א מהל' פרה אדומה הלכ' ז:
לז ל נ מיי' פ"י מהל' רוצח הלכה ג:

הגהות הב"ח

(א) רש"י ד"ה והכהנים וכו' על מה הם: (ב) ד"ה עגלה וכו' וכבש בני שנה:

°"איתן מושבך ושים בסלע קנך" ואומר: °"שמעו הרים את ריב ה' והאיתנים מוסדי ארץ". אחרים אומרים: מנין לאיתן שהוא ישן – שנאמר: °"גוי איתן הוא גוי מעולם הוא".§ "ועורפין אותה בקופיץ מאחוריה".§ מ"ט – גמר "עריפה" "עריפה" מחטאת העוף.§ "ומקומה אסור מלזרוע ומליעבד".§ ת"ר: °"אשר לא יעבד בו ולא יזרע" – לשעבר, דברי רבי יאשיה. רבי יונתן אומר: להבא. *רבא אמר: להבא – דכ"ע לא פליגי, דכתיב "ולא יזרע". כי פליגי – לשעבר; רבי יאשיה סבר: מי כתיב "ולא (א) יעובד"? ורבי יונתן: מי כתיב "אשר לא נעבד"? ורבי יאשיה: "אשר" – לשעבר משמע, ור' יונתן: "אשר" רבויא הוא.§ "ומותר לסרוק שם פשתן ולנקר שם אבנים".§ ת"ר: "אשר לא יעבד בו ולא יזרע". אין לי אלא זריעה, שאר עבודות מנין – תלמוד לומר: "אשר לא יעבד בו" – מכל מקום. אם כן מה ת"ל "ולא יזרע" – לומר לך: מה זריעה מיוחדת שהיא בגופה של קרקע – אף כל שהיא בגופה של קרקע, יצא סריקת פשתן וניקור אבנים שאינן בגופה של קרקע. ואימא: "אשר לא יעבד בו" – כלל, "ולא יזרע" – פרט, כלל ופרט – אין בכלל אלא מה שבפרט, זריעה – אין, מידי אחרינא – לא! "אשר" רבויא הוא.§ "זקני העיר רוחצין ידיהן" כו'.§ ת"ר: °"וכל זקני העיר ההיא הקרובים אל החלל ירחצו את ידיהם על העגלה הערופה בנחל". שאין ת"ל "הערופה", ומה ת"ל "הערופה" – על מקום עריפתה של עגלה. "ואמרו ידינו לא שפכו את הדם הזה ועינינו לא ראו". וכי על לבנו עלתה שב"ד שופכין דמים? אלא, לא בא לידינו ופטרנוהו – בלא מזונות, ולא ראינוהו והנחנוהו – בלא לויה. תניא, היה ר"מ אומר: אכופין ללויה, ששכר הלויה אין לה שיעור, שנאמר: °"ויראו השומרים איש יוצא מן העיר ויאמרו לו הראנו נא את מבוא העיר ועשינו עמך חסד", וכתיב: "ויראם את מבוא העיר", ומה חסד עשו עמו – שכל אותה העיר הרגו לפי חרב, ואותו האיש ומשפחתו שלחו. °"וילך האיש ארץ החתים ויבן עיר ויקרא שמה לוז היא שמה עד היום הזה", תניא: היא לוז שצובעין בה תכלת, היא לוז שבא סנחריב ולא בלבלה, נבוכדנצר ולא החריבה, ואף מלאך המות אין לו רשות לעבור בה. אלא זקנים שבה, בזמן שדעתן קצה עליהן – יוצאין חוץ לחומה והן מתים. והלא דברים ק"ו: ומה כנעני זה שלא דיבר בפיו, ולא הלך ברגליו – גרם הצלה לו ולזרעו עד סוף כל הדורות, מי שעושה לויה ברגליו – על אחת כמה וכמה. במה הראה להם? חזקיה אמר: בפיו עקם להם, ר' יוחנן אמר: באצבעו הראה להם. תניא כוותיה דר' יוחנן: בשביל שכנעני זה הראה באצבעו – גרם הצלה לו ולזרעו עד סוף כל הדורות. *אמר רבי יהושע בן לוי: המהלך בדרך ואין לו לויה – יעסוק בתורה, שנאמר: °"כי לוית חן הם לראשך וענקים לגרגרותיך". ואמר ר' יהושע בן לוי: בשביל ארבעה פסיעות שליוה פרעה לאברהם, שנאמר: °"ויצו עליו פרעה אנשים" וגו' – נשתעבד בבניו ארבע מאות שנה, שנאמר: °"ועבדום וענו אותם ארבע מאות שנה". אמר רב יהודה אמר רב: כל המלוה את חבירו ארבע אמות בעיר – אינו ניזוק. רבינא אלויה לרבא בר יצחק ד' אמות בעיר, מטא לידיה היזיקא ואיתציל. ת"ר: בהרב לתלמיד – עד עיבורה של עיר, חבר לחבר – עד תחום שבת, תלמיד לרב – אין לו שיעור. וכמה? א"ר ששת: געד פרסה. ולא אמרן אלא רבו שאינו מובהק, דאבל רבו מובהק – שלשה פרסאות. *רב כהנא אלויה לרב שימי בר אשי מפום נהרא עד בי ציניתא דבבל. כי מטו התם אמר ליה: ודאי דאמריתו הני ציניתא דבבל משני אדם הראשון איתנהו? א"ל: אדכרתן מלתא דאמר רבי יוסי בר' חנינא: מאי דכתיב: °"בארץ לא עבר בה איש ולא ישב אדם שם", וכי מאחר שלא עבר – היכן ישב, (ומאחר שלא ישב – היכן עבר)? אלא, ארץ שגזר עליה אדם הראשון לישוב – נתישבה, ארץ שלא גזר עליה אדם הראשון – לא נתישבה. *רב מרדכי אלויה לרב אשי מהגרוניא ועד בי כיפי, ואמרי לה עד בי דורא. אמר רבי יוחנן משום רבי מאיר: הכל שאינו מלוה ומתלוה – כאילו שופך דמים. שאילמלי ליווהו אנשי יריחו לאלישע לא גירה דובים לתינוקות, שנאמר: °"ויעל משם בית אל והוא עלה בדרך ונערים קטנים יצאו מן העיר ויתקלסו בו ויאמרו לו עלה קרח עלה קרח", אמרו לו: עלה, שהקרחת עלינו את המקום. מאי "ונערים קטנים"? אמר ר' אלעזר: *שמנוערים מן המצות, קטנים – שהיו מקטני אמנה. תנא: נערים היו ובזבזו עצמן כקטנים. מתקיף לה רב יוסף: *ודלמא על שם מקומן? מי לא כתיב: °"וארם יצאו גדודים וישבו מארץ ישראל נערה קטנה", וקשיא לן: נערה וקטנה? ואמר ר' פדת: קטנה דמן נעורן! התם לא מפרש מקומה, הכא – מפורש מקומן. °"ויפן אחריו ויראם ויקללם בשם ה'". מה ראה? אמר רב: ראה ממש, כדתניא, רבן שמעון בן גמליאל אומר: *כל מקום שנתנו חכמים עיניהם – או מיתה או עוני. ושמואל אמר: ראה שכולן נתעברה בהן אמן ביום הכיפורים, ורבי יצחק נפחא אמר: בלורית ראה להן כגוים, ורבי יוחנן אמר: ראה שלא היתה בהן לחלוחית של מצוה. ודלמא בזרעייהו ניהוה הוה! אמר רבי אלעזר: לא בם ולא בזרעם, עד סוף כל הדורות.§ °"ותצאנה שתים דובים מן היער ותבקענה מהם ארבעים ושני ילדים". רב

רש"י

איתן מושבך ושים בסלע קנך. אלמא איתן הוא סלע. מוסדי ארץ. הם הרים, וכל הר – של אבנים הוא. שהוא ישן. ולא שהוצאה קרקעיתו מחדש מקרקע אחריתי. גוי מעולם הוא. היינו ישן. מחטאת עוף. דכתיב בה "ממול ערפו" (ויקרא ה). כולי עלמא לא פליגי. דהא כתיב "ולא יזרע" – משמע להבא, מדלא כתיב "ואשר לא יזרע", דלהוי משמע לשעבר: *מי כתיב ולא יעבד. אי הוה כתיב "אל נחל איתן ולא יעבד בו" – הוה משמע להבא, אבל השתא דכתיב (ב) "לא יעבד" – משמע לשעבר, ד"אשר" לאו לשון נוחה הוא. אשר לשעבר משמע. אע"ג ד"לא יעבד" להבא משמע – הני מילי בלאו "אשר", אבל השתא דכתיב "אשר" – על כרחיך מוכח עליה דלשעבר הוא. רבויא הוא. לא בא אלא לרבות כל עבודות כדלקמן, דלא תדרשיה בכלל ופרט. כופין ללויה. כופין את מי שאינו רוצה ללוות את חבירו לדרך, שילוהו. ויקרא שמה לוז. סיפיה דקרא "היא שמה עד היום הזה", ומיניה יליף דלא נתבלבלה ולא חרבה, כדאמרינן: *כל מקום שנאמר "עד היום הזה" – לעולם ולעולמי עולמים הוא. שלא דבר בפיו. דלא כתיב אלא "ויראם" – באצבעו או בעקמימות שפתים, כדלקמן. ולזרעו. כדאמרינן שאין מלאך המות שולט בהם. שליוהו פרעה. כדכתיב: "ויצו עליו פרעה אנשים וישלחו אותו". אינו ניזוק. אותו היוצא לדרך. עד עיבורה של עיר. שהוא יוצא ממנה, והוא כבית החיצון שבתוך שבעים אמה ושירים לבתי העיר. בי ציניתא דבבל. מקום הוא ובו דקלים הרבה. כמו ליני הר הברזל (סוכה דף כט:). לא נתיישב. והיינו "לא ישב אדם שם" – לא גזר אדם הראשון יישוב שם. והיינו דאמרי אינשי: איתנהו משני אדם הראשון, שגזר עליו אדם הראשון, יישוב דקלים ולא יישוב אחר. שהקרחת עלינו את המקום. שכשהיו המים הרעים היתה פרנסתינו להביא מים ולמכור. מקטני אמנה. שהיו דואגים שפסקה פרנסתם בשביל שנתרפאו המים. ודלמא. קטנים ממש הוו, ועל שם מקומם נקראו נערים – שהיו מן נעורן? הכא מפרש מקומן. יריחו. ליהוו

עין משפט נר מצוה

לח א ב ג ד מיי' פי"ד מהל' אבל הלכה ג סמג עשין ב:
לט ה מיי' שם הלכה ב:

הגהות הב"ח

(א) גמ' ר' יאשיה סבר מי כתיב ולא יעבד אשר לא יעבד כתיב ור' יונתן סבר מי כתיב אשר לא נעבד אשר לא יעבד כתיב ור' יאשיה אשר לשעבר: (ב) רש"י ד"ה מי כתיב וכו' השתא דכתיב אשר לא יעבד:

מסורת הש"ס

במדבר כד | מיכה ו | ירמיה ה | דברים כא | עי' במהרש"א | [וג"ל אמר רבא כ"א בילקוט] | [יומא נג. ע"ש ובע"ג] | שם | שופטים א | שם | עירובין נד. | משלי א | בראשית יב | שם טו | ברכות לא. | ירמיה ב | נ"א נ"ג | [ברכות לא. ע"ש] | מלכים ב ב | [חגיגה יז.] | מלכים ב ה | חולין ה. | שם ב | חגיגה ה: מ"ק יז: נדרים ז: | מלכים ב ב

רב ושמואל; חד אמר: נס, וחד אמר: נס בתוך נס. מאן דאמר נס — יער הוה, דובים לא הוו. מ"ד נס בתוך נס — לא יער הוה ולא דובים הוו. וליהוי דובים ולא ליהוי יער? דבעיתי. אמר רבי חנינא: בשביל ארבעים ושנים קרבנות שהקריב בלק מלך מואב הובקעו מישראל ארבעים ושנים ילדים. איני? והאמר רב יהודה אמר רב:* לעולם יעסוק אדם בתורה ובמצות, ואע"פ שלא לשמה, שמתוך שלא לשמה — בא לשמה. שבשכר ארבעים ושנים קרבנות שהקריב בלק מלך מואב זכה ויצתה ממנו רות *שיצא ממנו שלמה, שכתוב ביה: °"אלף עולות יעלה שלמה". *ואמר רבי יוסי בן חוני: רות בתו של עגלון בנו של בלק היתה! תאותו מיהא לקללה הוי. °"ויאמרו אנשי העיר אל אלישע הנה נא מושב העיר טוב כאשר אדוני רואה" וגו'. וכי מאחר דמים רעים וארץ משכלת, אלא מה טובתה? אמר רבי חנין: חן מקום על יושביו. אמר רבי *יוחנן: שלשה חינות הן: חן מקום על יושביו, חן אשה על בעלה, חן מקח על *מקחו. *תנו רבנן: שלשה חלאין חלה אלישע: אחד שגירה דובים בתינוקות, ואחד שדחפו לגחזי בשתי ידים, ואחד שמת בו, שנאמר: °"ואלישע חלה את חליו אשר ימות בו". תנו רבנן: *לעולם תהא שמאל דוחה וימין מקרבת. לא כאלישע שדחפו לגחזי בשתי ידיו, ולא כיהושע בן פרחיה שדחפו לישו הנוצרי בשתי ידיו. אלישע מאי היא — דכתיב: °"ויאמר נעמן הואל קח ככרים", וכתיב: "ויאמר אליו לא לבי הלך כאשר הפך איש מעל מרכבתו לקראתך העת לקחת את הכסף ולקחת בגדים וזיתים וכרמים וצאן ובקר ועבדים ושפחות?" ומי שקיל כולי האי? כסף ובגדים הוא דשקיל! אמר ר' יצחק: באותה שעה היה אלישע עוסק בשמנה שרצים, אמר לו: רשע, הגיע עת ליטול שכר שמנה שרצים °"וצרעת נעמן תדבק בך ובזרעך לעולם". °"וארבעה אנשים היו מצורעים", אמר רבי יוחנן: זה גחזי ושלשת בניו. *°"וילך אלישע דמשק". למה הלך? אמר ר' יוחנן: שהלך להחזירו לגחזי בתשובה ולא חזר. אמר לו: חזור בך. אמר לו: כך מקובלני ממך: *כל מי שחטא והחטיא את הרבים — אין מספיקין בידו לעשות תשובה. מאי עבד? איכא דאמרי: אבן שואבת תלה לו לחטאת ירבעם והעמידו בין שמים לארץ, ואיכא דאמרי: שם חקק לה אפומה, והיתה אומרת "אנכי" ו"לא יהיה לך", ואיכא דאמרי: רבנן דחה מקמיה, דכתיב: °"ויאמרו בני הנביאים אל אלישע הנה נא המקום אשר אנחנו יושבים שם לפניך צר ממנו", מכלל דעד האידנא לא הוה דחיק. יהושע בן פרחיה מאי היא — כדהוה קא קטיל ינאי מלכא לרבנן, שמעון בן שטח אטמינהו אחתיה, ר' יהושע בן פרחיה אזל ערק לאלכסנדריא של מצרים. כי הוה שלמא שלח ליה שמעון בן שטח: מני ירושלים עיר הקודש לך אלכסנדריא של מצרים: אחותי! בעלי שרוי בתוכך ואני יושבת שוממה. אמר: ש"מ הוה ליה שלמא. כי אתא אקלע להההוא אושפיזא, קם קמייהו ביקרא שפיר, עבדי ליה יקרא טובא. יתיב וקא משתבח: כמה נאה אכסניא זו! א"ל ישו הנוצרי: רבי, עיניה טרוטות. א"ל: רשע, בכך אתה עוסק? אפיק ארבע מאה שיפורי ושמתיה. כל יומא אתא לקמיה ולא קבליה. יומא חד הוה קרי קרית שמע, אתא לקמיה. הוה בדעתיה לקבוליה, אחוי ליה בידיה. סבר מדחא דחי ליה, אזל זקף לבינתא פלחא. אמר ליה: חזור בך! א"ל: כך מקובלני ממך: כל החוטא ומחטיא את הרבים — אין מספיקין בידו לעשות תשובה. דאמר מר: ישו הנוצרי כישף והסית והדיח והחטיא את ישראל. תניא, רבי שמעון בן אלעזר אומר: יצר, תינוק, ואשה — תהא שמאל דוחה וימין מקרבת.§

מתני' [א]נמצא ההורג עד שלא *נערפה העגלה — תצא ותרעה בעדר. [ב]משנערפה העגלה — תקבר במקומה, שעל ספק באתה מתחילתה, כיפרה ספיקה והלכה לה. [ג]נערפה העגלה ואחר כך נמצא ההורג — הרי זה יהרג. [ד]עד אחד אומר "ראיתי את ההורג" ועד אחד אומר "לא ראית", אשה אומרת "ראיתי" ואשה אומרת "לא ראית" — היו עורפין. [ה]עד אחד אומר "ראיתי" ושנים אומרים "לא ראית" — היו עורפין. [ו]שנים אומרים "ראינו", ואחד אומר להן "לא ראיתם" — לא היו עורפין. [ז]משרבו הרוצחנין בטלה עגלה ערופה. משבא אליעזר בן דינאי, ותחינה בן פרישה *היה נקרא, חזרו לקרותו בן הרצחן. [ח]משרבו המנאפים פסקו המים המרים. ורבי יוחנן בן זכאי הפסיקן, שנאמר: °"לא אפקוד על בנותיכם כי תזנינה ועל כלותיכם כי תנאפנה כי הם" וגו'. משמת יוסי *בן יועזר איש צרידה ויוסי בן (א) יהודה איש ירושלים בטלו האשכלות, שנאמר: °"אין אשכול לאכול בכורה אותה נפשי". *יוחנן כהן גדול העביר הודיית המעשר. אף הוא בטל את המעוררין ואת הנוקפין.

עד

ליהוו דובים ולא ליהוו יער. מאי עבד ליה יער דקרית ליה נס?. דבעיתי. הדובים להתגרות בהם כשאין מקום קרוב להם לנוס ולהתחבאות, וכשהן קרובים ליער — יוצאין בהבטחה. זכה ויצתה ממנו רות. שיצאו ממנה דוד ושלמה שהרבו להקריב קרבנות. אלמא: זה היה שכרו. לקללה הוה. למעט את ישראל, ואותה כוונה כאן נתקיימה. ואלא מאי טיבותיה. דמקום, הואיל והמים רעים והארץ משכלת?. חן מקום על יושביו. ואפילו הוא רע — נראה להם טוב. חן האשה. תמיד על בעלה, ואפי' היא מכוערת — נושאת חן בעיניו. אחד שגירה דובים. בעון שגירה דובים בתינוקות. חלה. חד, "את חליו" — תרי, וחד — "אשר ימות בו". מי שקיל כולי האי. בהאי קרא כתיב שמנה דברים: כסף ובגדים וזאן ובקר ועבדים ושפחות וזיתים וכרמים. כסף ובגדים הוא דשקל. דכתיב: "ויצר ככרים כסף בשני חריטים ושתי חליפות בגדים". בשמנה שרצים. בפרק "שמנה שרצים" (שבת קז.). הגיע עת ליטול שכר. תורתך בעולם הזה. אבן שואבת. שמגבהת את המתכת מן הארץ ומעמידתו באויר. [וע"י אותו אבן העמיד העגלים של ירבעם באויר]. רבנן דחה. דוחה היה את התלמידים מפני אלישע כשהיה משמש לפניו. דכתיב לאחר שפירש ממנו: "המקום אשר אנחנו יושבין" בית המדרש של רבנן — "צר ממנו", שנתוספו התלמידים שהיה גחזי דוחה. ינאי מלכא קטליה לרבנן. כדאמרינן בקידושין ב"האומר לשלוחו" (דף סו.). בעלי שרוי בתוכך. נשיא היה, כדאמרינן בחגיגה (דף טז:). קם קמייהו שפיר. כיבדתו. אכסניא זו יפה. במעשיה. טרוטות. עגולות. בכך אתה עוסק. מסתכל באשת איש. אחוי ליה בידיה. שיקבלנו. יצר. של תשמיש, תקרבנו בימין — שלא יקוץ בפריה ורביה, וכן תינוק — פן יברח ויאבד את עצמו, ואשה — אף היא דעתה קלה, ואם ירדפוה אלא לתרבות רעה. **מתני'** תצא ותרעה בעדר. כשאר חולין. והאי תנא לית ליה הא דאמרינן בכמה דוכתי: עגלה ערופה נאסרה מחיים, וירידתה לנחל איתן אוסרתה. ובמסכת כריתות מוקמינן לה למילתא בפלוגתא דתנאי בפרק בתרא (דף כה.). כיפרה ספיקה. היא עשתה את שלה, ואם לא נמצא ההורג — נתכפר הספק. ולכשנמצא — נעשה ודאי, ויהרג. ומיהו היא באיסור הנאה דידה קיימא, דכפרה כתיב בה כקדשים. שנים אומרים ראינו לא היו עורפין. דהא נודע מי הכהו, ואע"פ שאינו עכשיו בפנינו לדונו. בטלה עגלה ערופה. שהרי מכירין (הן) בהן מי הרגיל בהן להרוג. לא אפקוד. על ניאוף נשותיכם לבודקן. ומפני מה — "על בנותיכם כי תזנינה", ועוד "כי הם עם הזונות יפרדו" — הם עצמן נואפין כפרדים הללו. האשכולות. מפרש בגמרא: שהכל בהן. עד ימיהן לא היה מחלוקת בחכמי ישראל, כולן היו אומרים דברים כנתינתן למשה מסיני, והן הראשונים שנחלקו בסמיכת קרבנות ביו"ט, כדאמרינן בחגיגה (דף טז.), והוא היה מחלוקת ראשון שהיה בישראל בדברי תורה. העביר הודיית המעשר. שלא יהיו מתוודין "בערתי הקדש" כו'. ובגמרא מפרש טעמא. עוררין ונוקפין. בגמרא מפרש טעמא.

מ א ב ג מיי' פ"י מהל' רוצח הלכה ח:
מא ד מיי' שם פ"ט הלכה יג:
מב ה ו מיי' שם הלכ' יד:
מג ז מיי' שם הלכ' יב:
מד ח מיי' פ"ג מהל' סוטה הלכה יט:

[נזיר כג: ע"ש סנהדרין קה: ע"ש הוריות י: ע"ש]
גי' הערוך חנינא
סנהדרין קז: [ב"מ פז.]

הגהות הב"ח
(א) גמ' ויוסי בן (יהודה) תז"מ. ונ"ב ס"א יוחנן:

תורה אור
סנהדרין קה: פסחים נ: ערכין טז. לעיל כב: הוריות י: נזיר כג:
מלכים א ג
[הך מילתא שיצא ממנו וכו' יעלה שלמה ליתא בכל אותן מקומות הנרשמים בליוני לעיל כב: פסחים נ: וכו']
שם ב ב
[נ"ל לוקחו ערוך ערך חנא א]
שם יג
[סנהדרין קז: ע"ש]
מלכים ב ה
שם ז
שם ח
[נ"ל ויבא]
[יומא פז. וש"נ]
שם ו
כריתות כה. חולין פב.
נ"א בן פרישה עי' בתי"ט
הושע ד
מיכה ז
תמורה טו: [ע"ש]
מעשר שני פ"ה מט"ו

מה א מיי' פ"ט מהל' רוצח הלכה יא יב:
מו ב מיי' שם הלכ' יג:
מז ג מיי' שם הלכ' יד טו:
מח ד מיי' פי"א מהל' מעשר שני הלכ' יג:

*עַד יָמָיו הָיָה פַּטִּישׁ מַכֶּה בִּירוּשָׁלַיִם, וּבְיָמָיו א"צ לִשְׁאוֹל עַל הַדְּמַאי.§ **גמ'** ת"ר: מִנַּיִן שֶׁאִם *נֶעֶרְפָה הָעֶגְלָה וְאח"כ נִמְצָא הַהוֹרֵג, שֶׁאֵין פּוֹטֶרֶת אוֹתוֹ — ת"ל: °"וְלָאָרֶץ לֹא יְכוּפַּר לַדָּם אֲשֶׁר שֻׁפַּךְ בָּהּ כִּי אִם בְּדַם שֹׁפְכוֹ".§ "עֵד אֶחָד אוֹמֵר רָאִיתִי אֶת הַהוֹרֵג" כו'.§ טַעְמָא — דְּמַכְחִישׁ לֵיהּ, הָא לָא מַכְחִישׁ לֵיהּ — עֵד אֶחָד מְהֵימַן. מְנָהָנֵי מִילֵּי? דְּת"ר: °"לֹא *נוֹדַע מִי הִכָּהוּ", [א]הָא נוֹדַע מִי הִכָּהוּ, אֲפִילּוּ אֶחָד בְּסוֹף הָעוֹלָם — לֹא הָיוּ עוֹרְפִין. רַבִּי עֲקִיבָא אוֹמֵר: מִנַּיִן לְסַנְהֶדְרִין שֶׁרָאוּ אֶחָד שֶׁהָרַג אֶת הַנֶּפֶשׁ וְאֵין מַכִּירִין אוֹתוֹ, שֶׁלֹּא הָיוּ עוֹרְפִין — ת"ל: °"וְעֵינֵינוּ לֹא רָאוּ", וַהֲלֹא רָאוּ. הַשְׁתָּא דְּאָמְרַתְּ עֵד אֶחָד מְהֵימַן, אִידָךְ חַד הֵיכִי מָצֵי מַכְחִישׁ לֵיהּ? וְהָאָמַר עוּלָּא: כָּל מָקוֹם *שֶׁהֶאֱמִינָה תּוֹרָה עֵד אֶחָד — הֲרֵי כָּאן שְׁנַיִם, וְאֵין דְּבָרָיו שֶׁל אֶחָד בִּמְקוֹם שְׁנַיִם! אָמַר לָךְ עוּלָּא: תְּנֵי: לֹא הָיוּ עוֹרְפִין. וְכֵן א"ר יִצְחָק: תְּנֵי: לֹא הָיוּ עוֹרְפִין. וְר' חִיָּיא אָמַר: תְּנֵי: הָיוּ עוֹרְפִין. וּלְרַבִּי חִיָּיא קַשְׁיָא דְּעוּלָּא! לָא קַשְׁיָא; [ב]כָּאן — בְּבַת אַחַת, כָּאן — בְּזֶה אַחַר זֶה. תְּנַן: עֵד אֶחָד אוֹמֵר "רָאִיתִי אֶת הַהוֹרֵג" וּשְׁנַיִם אוֹמְרִים "לֹא רָאִיתָ" — הָיוּ עוֹרְפִין. הָא חַד וְחַד — לֹא הָיוּ עוֹרְפִין, תְּיוּבְתָּא דְּרַבִּי חִיָּיא. וְלִיטַעֲמִיךְ אֵימָא סֵיפָא: שְׁנַיִם אוֹמְרִים "רָאִינוּ" וְעֵד אֶחָד אוֹמֵר "לֹא רְאִיתֶם" — לֹא הָיוּ עוֹרְפִין, הָא חַד וְחַד — הָיוּ עוֹרְפִין! אֶלָּא, מַתְנִי' כּוּלָּהּ בִּפְסוּלֵי עֵדוּת, וְכִדְרַבִּי נְחֶמְיָה דְּאָמַר: *כָּל מָקוֹם שֶׁהֶאֱמִינָה תּוֹרָה עֵד אֶחָד — הַלֵּךְ אַחַר רוֹב דֵּעוֹת, וְעָשׂוּ שְׁתֵּי נָשִׁים בְּאִישׁ אֶחָד כִּשְׁנֵי אֲנָשִׁים בְּאִישׁ אֶחָד. וְאִיכָּא דְּאָמְרִי: [ג]כָּל הֵיכָא דַּאֲתָא עֵד אֶחָד כָּשֵׁר מֵעִיקָּרָא — אֲפִילּוּ *מֵאָה נָשִׁים כִּי אֶחָד דָּמְיָין, וְהָכָא בְּמַאי עָסְקִינַן — כְּגוֹן דַּאֲתַאי אִשָּׁה מֵעִיקָּרָא. וְתַרְצָהּ לִדְרַבִּי נְחֶמְיָה הָכִי; רַבִּי נְחֶמְיָה אוֹמֵר: כָּל מָקוֹם שֶׁהֶאֱמִינָה תּוֹרָה עֵד אֶחָד — הַלֵּךְ אַחַר רוֹב דֵּעוֹת, וְעָשׂוּ שְׁתֵּי נָשִׁים בְּאִשָּׁה אַחַת כִּשְׁנֵי אֲנָשִׁים בְּאִישׁ אֶחָד. אֲבָל שְׁתֵּי נָשִׁים בְּאִישׁ אֶחָד — כִּי פַּלְגָּא וּפַלְגָּא דָּמֵי. וְתַרְתֵּי פְּסוּלֵי עֵדוּת לָמָּה לִי? מַהוּ דְּתֵימָא: כִּי אָזְלִינַן בָּתַר רוֹב דֵּעוֹת — לְחוּמְרָא, אֲבָל לְקוּלָּא — לָא, קמ"ל.§ "מִשֶּׁרַבּוּ הָרוֹצְחִין" כו'.§ ת"ר: *מִשֶּׁרַבּוּ הָרוֹצְחָנִין בָּטְלָה עֶגְלָה עֲרוּפָה לְפִי שֶׁאֵינָהּ בָּאָה אֶלָּא עַל הַסָּפֵק; מִשֶּׁרַבּוּ הָרוֹצְחָנִין בְּגָלוּי בָּטְלָה עֶגְלָה עֲרוּפָה.§ "מִשֶּׁרַבּוּ הַנּוֹאֲפִין" כו'.§ *ת"ר: °"וְנִקָּה הָאִישׁ מֵעָוֹן", בִּזְמַן שֶׁהָאִישׁ מְנוּקֶּה מֵעָוֹן — הַמַּיִם בּוֹדְקִין אֶת אִשְׁתּוֹ, אֵין הָאִישׁ מְנוּקֶּה מֵעָוֹן — אֵין הַמַּיִם בּוֹדְקִין אֶת אִשְׁתּוֹ. וְאוֹמֵר °"לֹא אֶפְקוֹד עַל בְּנוֹתֵיכֶם כִּי תִזְנֶינָה" כו'. מַאי "וְאוֹמֵר"? וְכִי תֵּימָא: עֲוֹן דִּידֵיהּ — אִין, דִּבְנֵיהּ וּדִבְנָתֵיהּ — לָא, תָּא שְׁמַע: "לֹא אֶפְקוֹד עַל בְּנוֹתֵיכֶם כִּי תִזְנֶינָה וְעַל כַּלּוֹתֵיכֶם כִּי תְנָאַפְנָה". וְכִי תֵּימָא: עֲוֹן אֵשֶׁת אִישׁ — אִין, עֲוֹן דִּפְנוּיָה — לָא, ת"ש: "כִּי הֵם עִם הַזּוֹנוֹת יְפָרֵדוּ וְעִם הַקְּדֵשׁוֹת יְזַבֵּחוּ" וגו'. מַאי "וְעָם לֹא יָבִין *יִלָּבֵט"? אָמַר רַבִּי אֶלְעָזָר: אָמַר לָהֶם נָבִיא לְיִשְׂרָאֵל: אִם אַתֶּם מַקְפִּידִין עַל עַצְמְכֶם — מַיִם בּוֹדְקִין נְשׁוֹתֵיכֶם, וְאִם לָאו — אֵין הַמַּיִם בּוֹדְקִין נְשׁוֹתֵיכֶם. "מִשֶּׁרַבּוּ בַּעֲלֵי הֲנָאָה — נִתְעַוְּותוּ הַדִּינִין, וְנִתְקַלְקְלוּ הַמַּעֲשִׂים, וְאֵין נוֹחַ בָּעוֹלָם. מִשֶּׁרַבּוּ רוֹאֵי פָּנִים בַּדִּין — בָּטֵל °"לֹא תָגוּרוּ", וּפָסַק "לֹא תַכִּירוּ", וּפָרְקוּ עוֹל שָׁמַיִם וְנָתְנוּ עֲלֵיהֶם עוֹל בָּשָׂר וָדָם. מִשֶּׁרַבּוּ לוֹחֲשֵׁי לְחִישׁוֹת בַּדִּין — רַבָּה חֲרוֹן אַף בְּיִשְׂרָאֵל, וְנִסְתַּלְּקָה הַשְּׁכִינָה, מִשּׁוּם שֶׁנֶּאֱמַר: *°"בְּקֶרֶב אֱלֹהִים יִשְׁפּוֹט". מִשֶּׁרַבּוּ °"אַחֲרֵי בִצְעָם לִבָּם הוֹלֵךְ" — רַבּוּ °"הָאוֹמְרִים לָרַע טוֹב וְלַטּוֹב רָע", מִשֶּׁרַבּוּ הָאוֹמְרִים לָרַע טוֹב וְלַטּוֹב רָע — רַבּוּ "הוֹי הוֹי" בָּעוֹלָם. מִשֶּׁרַבּוּ מוֹשְׁכֵי הָרוֹק — רַבּוּ הַיְּהִירִים, וְנִתְמַעֲטוּ הַתַּלְמִידִים, וְהַתּוֹרָה חוֹזֶרֶת עַל לוֹמְדֶיהָ. מִשֶּׁרַבּוּ הַיְּהִירִים — הִתְחִילוּ בְּנוֹת יִשְׂרָאֵל לְהִנָּשֵׂא לַיְּהִירִים, שֶׁאֵין דּוֹרֵינוּ רוֹאֶה אֶלָּא לְפָנִים. אִינִי?! וְהָאָמַר מָר: הַאי מַאן דִּמְיַהֵר — *אֲפִילּוּ אַאִינְשֵׁי בֵּיתֵיהּ לָא מִיקַּבַּל, שֶׁנֶּאֱמַר: °"גֶּבֶר יָהִיר וְלֹא יִנְוֶה", לֹא יִנְוֶה — אֲפִי' בְּנָוֶה שֶׁלּוֹ! מֵעִיקָּרָא קָפְצָה עֲלֵיהּ, לְסוֹף מִיתְזִיל עֲלַיְיהוּ. מִשֶּׁרַבּוּ מְטִילֵי מְלַאי עַל בַּעֲלֵי בָתִּים — רַבָּה הַשּׁוֹחַד וְהַטָּיַית מִשְׁפָּט, וּפָסְקָה טוֹבָה. מִשֶּׁרַבּוּ "מְקַבְּלֵנִי טוֹבָתְךָ" וּ"מַחֲזִקְנִי טוֹבוֹתֶיךָ" — רַבּוּ °"אִישׁ הַיָּשָׁר בְּעֵינָיו יַעֲשֶׂה", שְׁפָלִים הוּגְבְּהוּ וְהַגְּבוֹהִים הוּשְׁפָּלוּ, וּמַלְכוּתָא אָזְלָא וְנָוְלָא. מִשֶּׁרַבּוּ צָרֵי עַיִן וְטוֹרְפֵי טֶרֶף — רַבּוּ מְאַמְּצֵי הַלֵּב וְקוֹפְצֵי יָדַיִם מִלְּהַלְווֹת, וְעָבְרוּ עַל מַה שֶּׁכָּתוּב בַּתּוֹרָה °"הִשָּׁמֶר לְךָ פֶּן" וגו'. מִשֶּׁרַבּוּ °"נְטוּיוֹת גָּרוֹן וּמְשַׂקְּרוֹת עֵינָיִם" — רַבּוּ מֵי הַמָּרִים, אֶלָּא שֶׁפָּסְקוּ. מִשֶּׁרַבּוּ מְקַבְּלֵי מַתָּנוֹת — נִתְמַעֲטוּ הַיָּמִים וְנִתְקַצְּרוּ הַשָּׁנִים, דִּכְתִיב: °"וְשׂוֹנֵא מַתָּנֹת יִחְיֶה". *מִשֶּׁרַבּוּ זְחוּחֵי הַלֵּב — רַבּוּ מַחֲלוֹקֶת בְּיִשְׂרָאֵל. *מִשֶּׁרַבּוּ תַּלְמִידֵי שַׁמַּאי וְהִלֵּל שֶׁלֹּא שִׁמְּשׁוּ כָּל צוֹרְכָּן — רַבּוּ מַחֲלוֹקֶת בְּיִשְׂרָאֵל, וְנַעֲשֵׂית תּוֹרָה כִּשְׁתֵּי תוֹרוֹת. מִשֶּׁרַבּוּ מְקַבְּלֵי צְדָקָה מִן הַגּוֹיִם — הָיוּ יִשְׂרָאֵל לְמַעְלָה וְהֵם לְמַטָּה, יִשְׂרָאֵל לְפָנִים וְהֵם לְאָחוֹר.§ "מִשֶּׁמֵּת יוֹסֵי בֶּן יוֹעֶזֶר" כו'.§ מַאי אֶשְׁכּוֹלוֹת? *אָמַר רַב יְהוּדָה אָמַר שְׁמוּאֵל: אִישׁ שֶׁהַכֹּל בּוֹ.§ "יוֹחָנָן כֹּהֵן גָּדוֹל הֶעֱבִיר הוֹדָיַית הַמַּעֲשֵׂר" כו'.§ מ"ט? אָמַר רַבִּי יוֹסֵי בַּר' חֲנִינָא: [ד]לְפִי שֶׁאֵין נוֹתְנִין אוֹתוֹ כְּתִיקּוּנוֹ, דְּרַחֲמָנָא אָמַר דְּיָהֲבִי לַלְוִיִּם, וְאָנַן

תורה אור: במדבר לה; דברים כא; שם; במדבר ה; הושע ד; דברים א; תהלים פב; יחזקאל לג; ישעיה ה; חבקוק ב; שופטים יז; דברים טו; ישעיה ג; משלי טו

עד ימיו היה פטיש מכה בירושלים. בְּבֵית הַנַּפָּחִים בְּחוּלּוֹ שֶׁל מוֹעֵד, לַעֲשׂוֹת מְלָאכֶת דָּבָר הָאָבֵד שֶׁמּוּתֶּרֶת בַּמּוֹעֵד. וְעָמַד הוּא וְגָזַר עַל הַנַּפָּחִים אֲפִילּוּ בְּדָבָר הָאָבֵד, מִפְּנֵי שֶׁקּוֹלָן נִשְׁמָע לְמֵרָחוֹק, וְאֵין הַכֹּל יוֹדְעִין שֶׁהִיא לְדָבָר הָאָבֵד. וְהָכִי אָמְרִינַן לָהּ בְּמוֹעֵד קָטָן (יא.). כָּל יָמָיו לֹא הוּצְרַךְ אָדָם לִשְׁאֹל לַחֲבֵירוֹ עַל הַדְּמַאי. אִם מְעוּשָּׂר אִם לָאו, שֶׁהוּא הִתְקִין שֶׁיְּהוּ כָּל הַלּוֹקְחִין מֵעַם הָאָרֶץ מְעַשְּׂרִין. גמ' אפילו אחד בסוף העולם. הִכִּיר בּוֹ. והא אמר עולא כו'. סוּגְיָא זוֹ כּוּלָּהּ פֵּירַשְׁתִּיהָ בְּפֶרֶק "מִי שֶׁקִּינֵּא" (לעיל לא:), וְאֵינָהּ חֲלוּקָה כָּאן כְּלוּם. אלא על הספק. וְעַכְשָׁיו יוֹדְעִים אֶת הַהוֹרְגִים מִי הֵם. מנוקה מעון. נִיאוּף בְּאִשָּׁה הָאֲסוּרָה לוֹ, בֵּין מִזּוֹ שֶׁנִּסְתְּרָה בֵּין מֵאַחֶרֶת. עון דבניה ודבנתיה. שֶׁהֵם נוֹאֲפִין. לא. אֵינוֹ מוֹנֵעַ אֶת אִשְׁתּוֹ מִלִּיבָּדֵק. תא שמע לא אפקוד. לִבְדּוֹק אֶת הַנָּשִׁים, וּמַה טַּעַם — "עַל בְּנוֹתֵיכֶם כִּי תִזְנֶינָה". נתעוותו הדינין. דְּמִתּוֹךְ שֶׁהֵם בַּעֲלֵי הֲנָאָה אֵין מַטְרִיחִין עַצְמָן לְעַיֵּין בַּדִּין, וּבְאִיסּוּר וְהֶיתֵּר לְהוֹרוֹת לַצִּיבּוּר, וּמִתּוֹךְ כָּךְ נִתְקַלְקְלוּ מַעֲשֵׂיהֶם. וְכֵיוָן שֶׁכֵּן — אֵין לְהקב"ה נַחַת רוּחַ בְּעוֹלָמוֹ, וְאֵין עוֹלָמוֹ נוֹחַ לוֹ. לוחשי לחישות. עוֹרְכֵי הַדַּיָּינִין, וּמִתְלַחֲשִׁים עִם הַדַּיָּינִין לִפְתּוֹחַ לָהֶם פֶּתַח בִּזְכוּתוֹ שֶׁל זֶה וּבְחוֹבָתוֹ שֶׁל זֶה. רבה חרון אף. שֶׁעַל הַטָּיַית הַמִּשְׁפָּט חֲרוֹן אַף בָּא, שֶׁנֶּאֱמַר (שמות כב): "אִם עַנֵּה תְעַנֶּה אוֹתוֹ וגו' וְחָרָה אַפִּי". נצב בעדת אל. בִּזְמַן שֶׁ"בְּקֶרֶב אֱלֹהִים יִשְׁפּוֹט". הולכי אחר בצעם. לַהֲנָאָתָם. האומרים לרע טוב. שֶׁמְּשַׁבְּחִין אֶת הָרְשָׁעִים. רבו הוי הוי. דִּכְתִיב "הוֹי" "הוֹי" בְּהַהִיא פָּרָשָׁתָא טוּבָא. מושכי הרוק. מַאֲרִיכִין הָרוֹק, וּמִדַּת גַּאֲוָה הוּא. ונתמעטו התלמידים. כִּדְקי"ל (קידושין דף מט:): סִימָן לְגַסּוּת הָרוּחַ — עֲנִיּוּת שֶׁל תּוֹרָה. חוזרת על לומדיה. מְחַזֶּרֶת, אוּלַי תִּמְצָא לוֹמְדֶיהָ. ולבסוף מתזיל עלייהו. נִמְאָס בְּעֵינֵיהֶם. מטילי מלאי. הַדַּיָּינִים מַטִּילִין מְלַאי פְּרַקְמַטְיָא שֶׁלָּהֶם עַל בַּעֲלֵי בָּתִּים הַיּוֹדְעִים בְּטִיב סְחוֹרָה, שֶׁיִּשְׂתַּכְּרוּ הַדַּיָּינִין עַל יָדוֹ. רבו איש הישר בעיניו יעשה. שֶׁרוֹאֶה שֶׁהַדַּיָּינִין מַסְבִּירִים לוֹ פָּנִים מִפְּנֵי טוֹבָה שֶׁעָשָׂה לוֹ, וְאֵינוֹ מִתְיָירֵא מֵהֶם. שפלים הוגבהו. שֶׁאֵין אֵימַת הַגְּדוֹלִים עַל הַקְּטַנִּים, וְאֵין נִיכָּר בֵּין גָּבוֹהַּ לְשָׁפֵל. ומלכותא. מַלְכוּתָם שֶׁל יִשְׂרָאֵל, אָזְלָא וְנָוְלָא — הוֹלֶכֶת וּמִתְנַוְּולֶת. צרי עין. מְלַהֲטוֹת אַחֵרִים בְּמָמוֹנָם. טורפי טרף. גַּזְלָנִים וּמַחְמְלֵי הַלֵּב מִן הָעֲנִיִּים לָתֵת לָהֶם. רבו מים המרים. רַבּוּ הַמְקַנְּאִים לִנְשׁוֹתֵיהֶם, וְהָיָה לַמַּיִם הַמָּרִים לְהַרְבּוֹת. אלא שפסקו מלהשקותם. כִּדְאָמְרִינַן, שֶׁאֵין הַמַּיִם בּוֹדְקִין מִשֶּׁרַבּוּ הַמְנָאֲפִים. זחוחי הלב. שֶׁאֵין מַטִּין אֶת אָזְנָם לִשְׁמוֹעַ יָפֶה מִפִּי רַבָּם, וְסוֹמְכִים עַל בִּינָתָם לְדַקְדֵּק שְׁמוּעָתָם. ישראל לפנים. כִּינּוּי הוּא. שהכל בו. תּוֹרָה בַּאֲמִתָּהּ, וְאֵין דּוֹפִי וְשִׁכְחָה וּמַחֲלוֹקֶת.

ואנן

מ"ק יח.
[תוספתא כריתות פ"ד] כתובות לו:
יומא כג:
יבמות פח: קיז: כתובות כב: לעיל לא:
יבמות פח: לעיל לא: [תוספתא יבמות פי"ד ע"ש]
[לעיל לא: וש"נ]
[תוס' פי"ד ע"ש כמה וכמה שינויים נכונים] לעיל כח. שבועות ה. קדושין כז: יבמות נח.
[פי' לשון טורח וליאות]
מפרש"י נראה דל"ל ג"כ רישא דקרא אלקים נצב בעדת אל
כ"ב נח.
[חולין ז.]
[סנהדרין פח.]
[תמורה טו: ע"ש]

תורה אור

וַאֲנַן אִקָא יָהֲבִינַן לַכֹּהֲנִים. וְלוֹדֵי אַשְּׁאָר מַעַשְׂרוֹת! אָמַר רֵישׁ לָקִישׁ: בּכָּל בַּיִת שֶׁאֵין מִתְוַדֶּה עַל מַעֲשֵׂר רִאשׁוֹן — שׁוּב אֵין מִתְוַדֶּה עַל שְׁאָר מַעַשְׂרוֹת. מַאי טַעֲמָא? אָמַר אַבַּיֵי: הוֹאִיל וּפָתַח בּוֹ הַכָּתוּב תְּחִילָּה. מִכְּלָל דְּאַפְרוּשֵׁי הָווּ מַפְרְשֵׁי? וְהָא תַּנְיָא: אַף הוּא בִּיטֵּל *אֶת הַוִּידּוּי, וְגָזַר עַל הַדְּמַאי. גלְפִי שֶׁשָּׁלַח בְּכָל גְּבוּל יִשְׂרָאֵל וְרָאָה שֶׁאֵין מַפְרִישִׁין אֶלָּא תְּרוּמָה גְּדוֹלָה בִּלְבַד, וּמַעֲשֵׂר רִאשׁוֹן וּמַעֲשֵׂר שֵׁנִי — *מִקְצָתָן מְעַשְּׂרִין וּמִקְצָתָן אֵין מְעַשְּׂרִין, אָמַר לָהֶם: בָּנַי, בּוֹאוּ וְאוֹמַר לָכֶם: כְּשֵׁם שֶׁתְּרוּמָה גְּדוֹלָה יֵשׁ בָּהּ עֲוֹן מִיתָה — כָּךְ תְּרוּמַת מַעֲשֵׂר וְטֶבֶל יֵשׁ בָּהֶן עֲוֹן מִיתָה. דעָמַד וְהִתְקִין לָהֶם: הַלּוֹקֵחַ פֵּירוֹת מֵע"ה מַפְרִישׁ מֵהֶן מַעֲשֵׂר רִאשׁוֹן וּמַעֲשֵׂר שֵׁנִי; מַעֲשֵׂר רִאשׁוֹן — מַפְרִישׁ מִמֶּנָּה תְּרוּמַת מַעֲשֵׂר *וְנוֹתְנָהּ לְכֹהֵן. וּמַעֲשֵׂר שֵׁנִי — עוֹלֶה וְאוֹכְלוֹ בִּירוּשָׁלַיִם. מַעֲשֵׂר רִאשׁוֹן וּמַעֲשֵׂר עָנִי — הַמּוֹצִיא מֵחֲבֵירוֹ עָלָיו הָרְאָיָה! תַּרְתֵּי תִּקֵּן: בִּיטֵּל וִידּוּי דַּחֲבֵירִים, וְגָזַר עַל דְּמַאי שֶׁל עַמֵּי הָאָרֶץ.§ "וְאַף הוּא בִּיטֵּל אֶת הַמְעוֹרְרִים".§ מַאי מְעוֹרְרִים? אָמַר רַחֲבָה: *בְּכָל יוֹם וָיוֹם שֶׁהָיוּ עוֹמְדִים לְוִיִּם עַל דּוּכָן וְאוֹמְרִים: °"עוּרָה לָמָּה תִישַׁן ה'", (תהלים מד) אָמַר לָהֶן: וְכִי יֵשׁ שֵׁינָה לִפְנֵי הַמָּקוֹם? וַהֲלֹא כְּבָר נֶאֱמַר: °"הִנֵּה לֹא יָנוּם וְלֹא יִישָׁן שׁוֹמֵר יִשְׂרָאֵל"! (שם קכא) אֶלָּא, בִּזְמַן שֶׁיִּשְׂרָאֵל שְׁרוּיִין בְּצַעַר וְגוֹיִם בְּנַחַת וְשַׁלְוָה — לְכָךְ נֶאֱמַר: "עוּרָה לָמָּה תִישַׁן ה'".§ "וְאֶת הַנּוֹקְפִים".§ מַאי נוֹקְפִים? אָמַר רַב יְהוּדָה אָמַר שְׁמוּאֵל: *שֶׁהָיוּ מְסָרְטִין לָעֵגֶל בֵּין קַרְנָיו כְּדֵי שֶׁיִּפּוֹל דָּם בְּעֵינָיו. אֲתָא אִיהוּ בַּטֵּיל, מִשּׁוּם דְּמִיחֲזֵי כִּי מוּמָא. בְּמַתְנִיתָא תָּנָא: שֶׁהָיוּ חוֹבְטִין אוֹתוֹ בְּמַקְלוֹת, כְּדֶרֶךְ שֶׁעוֹשִׂין אוֹתוֹ לִפְנֵי עֲבוֹדָה זָרָה. אָמַר לָהֶם: עַד מָתַי אַתֶּם מַאֲכִילִין נְבֵילוֹת לַמִּזְבֵּחַ! נְבֵילוֹת?! הָא שָׁחֵיט לְהוּ! אֶלָּא טְרֵיפוֹת, שֶׁמָּא נִיקַּב קְרוּם שֶׁל מוֹחַ. עָמַד וְהִתְקִין לָהֶם טַבָּעוֹת בַּקַּרְקַע.§ "עַד יָמָיו הָיָה פַּטִּישׁ מַכֶּה בִּירוּשָׁלַיִם".§ בְּחוּלּוֹ שֶׁל מוֹעֵד.§ "כָּל יָמָיו לֹא הָיָה אָדָם צָרִיךְ לִשְׁאוֹל עַל הַדְּמַאי".§ כִּדְאָמְרָן.§

(ישעיה כד) **מתני'** מִשֶּׁבָּטְלָה סַנְהֶדְרִין הבָּטֵל הַשִּׁיר מִבֵּית הַמִּשְׁתָּאוֹת, שֶׁנֶּאֱמַר: °"בַּשִּׁיר לֹא יִשְׁתּוּ יָיִן" וגו'. מִשֶּׁמֵּתוּ נְבִיאִים הָרִאשׁוֹנִים — בָּטְלוּ אוּרִים וְתוּמִּים. מִשֶּׁחָרַב בהמ"ק — בָּטֵל הַשָּׁמִיר, וְנוֹפֶת צוּפִים, וּפָסְקוּ אַנְשֵׁי אֲמָנָה מִיִּשְׂרָאֵל, שֶׁנֶּאֱמַר: °"הוֹשִׁיעָה ה' כִּי גָמַר חָסִיד" וגו'. (תהלים יב) רשב"ג אוֹמֵר, *הֵעִיד ר' יְהוֹשֻׁעַ: מִיּוֹם שֶׁחָרַב בהמ"ק אֵין יוֹם שֶׁאֵין בּוֹ קְלָלָה, וְלֹא יָרַד הַטַּל לִבְרָכָה, וְנִיטַּל טַעַם הַפֵּירוֹת. ר' יוֹסֵי אוֹמֵר: אַף נִיטַּל שׁוּמַּן הַפֵּירוֹת. ר' שִׁמְעוֹן בֶּן אֶלְעָזָר אוֹמֵר: הַטָּהֳרָה נָטְלָה אֶת (*הַטַּעַם וְאֶת) הָרֵיחַ, הַמַּעַשְׂרוֹת נָטְלוּ אֶת שׁוּמַּן הַדָּגָן. (א) וַחֲכָמִים אוֹמְרִים: הַזְּנוּת וְהַכְּשָׁפִים כִּילּוּ אֶת הַכֹּל.§ **גמ'** וּמִמַּאי דְּמִשֶּׁבָּטְלָה סַנְהֶדְרִי כְּתִיב? אָמַר רַב הוּנָא בְּרֵיהּ דְּרַב יְהוֹשֻׁעַ: דְּאָמַר קְרָא °"זְקֵנִים מִשַּׁעַר שָׁבָתוּ בַּחוּרִים מִנְּגִינָתָם". (איכה ה) אָמַר רַב: *אוּדְנָא דְּשָׁמְעָא זִמְרָא תֵּיעָקַר. אָמַר רָבָא: זִמְרָא בְּבֵיתָא — חוּרְבָּא בְּסִיפָּא, שֶׁנֶּאֱמַר: °"קוֹל יְשׁוֹרֵר בַּחַלּוֹן חֹרֶב בַּסַּף כִּי אַרְזָה עֵרָה". (צפניה ב) מַאי "כִּי אַרְזָה עֵרָה"? אָמַר ר' יִצְחָק: (ב) *בַּיִת *הַמְסוּבָּךְ בָּאֲרָזִים עִיר הוּא?! אֶלָּא, אֲפִי' בַּיִת *הַמְסוּבָּךְ בָּאֲרָזִים מִתְרוֹעֵעַ. אָמַר רַב אַשִׁי: שְׁמַע מִינַּהּ, כִּי מַתְחִיל חוּרְבָּא — בְּסִיפָּא מַתְחִיל, שֶׁנֶּאֱמַר: "חֹרֶב בַּסַּף", וְאִיבָּעֵית אֵימָא, מֵהָכָא — °"וּשְׁאִיָּה יֻכַּת שָׁעַר". (ישעיה כד) אָמַר מָר בַּר רַב אַשִׁי: לְדִידִי *חֲזִי לִיהּ, וּמְנַגַּח כִּי תּוֹרָא. אָמַר רַב הוּנָא: זִמְרָא דְּנַגָּדֵי וּדְבַקָּרֵי — שָׁרֵי, *דְּגַרְדָּאֵי — אֲסִיר. רַב הוּנָא בַּטֵּיל זִמְרָא, קָם מֵאָה אַוְּזֵי בְּזוּזָא, וּמֵאָה סְאָה חִיטֵּי בְּזוּזָא וְלָא אִיבְּעֵי. אֲתָא רַב חִסְדָּא זַלְזֵיל בֵּיהּ, אִיבָּעֵאי אַוְּזָא בְּזוּזָא וְלָא מִשְׁתַּכַּח. אָמַר רַב יוֹסֵף: זָמְרֵי גַּבְרֵי וְעָנֵי נָשֵׁי — פְּרִיצוּתָא, זָמְרֵי נָשֵׁי וְעָנֵי גַּבְרֵי — כְּאֵשׁ בִּנְעוֹרֶת. לְמַאי נַפְקָא מִינַּהּ — לְבַטּוּלֵי הָא מִקַּמֵּי הָא. אָמַר ר' יוֹחָנָן: כָּל הַשּׁוֹתֶה בְּאַרְבָּעָה מִינֵי זֶמֶר — מֵבִיא חָמֵשׁ פּוּרְעָנִיּוֹת לָעוֹלָם, שֶׁנֶּאֱמַר: °"הוֹי מַשְׁכִּימֵי בַבֹּקֶר שֵׁכָר יִרְדֹּפוּ מְאַחֲרֵי בַנֶּשֶׁף יַיִן יַדְלִיקֵם, (שם ה) וְהָיָה כִנּוֹר וָנֶבֶל תֹּף וְחָלִיל וָיַיִן מִשְׁתֵּיהֶם וְאֵת פֹּעַל ה' לֹא יַבִּיטוּ", מַה כְּתִיב אַחֲרָיו: °"לָכֵן גָּלָה עַמִּי מִבְּלִי (שם) דָעַת" — שֶׁגּוֹרְמִין גָּלוּת לָעוֹלָם, "וּכְבוֹדוֹ מְתֵי רָעָב" — שֶׁמְּבִיאִין רָעָב לָעוֹלָם, "וַהֲמוֹנוֹ צִחֵה צָמָא" — שֶׁגּוֹרְמִין לַתּוֹרָה שֶׁתִּשְׁתַּכַּח מִלּוֹמְדֶיהָ, °"וַיִּשַּׁח אָדָם וַיִּשְׁפַּל אִישׁ" — (שם) שֶׁגּוֹרְמִין שִׁפְלוּת לְשׂוֹנְאוֹ שֶׁל הקב"ה, *וְאֵין "אִישׁ" אֶלָּא הַקָּדוֹשׁ ב"ה, שֶׁנֶּאֱמַר: °"ה' אִישׁ מִלְחָמָה". (שמות טו) "וְעֵינֵי גְבֹהִים תִּשְׁפַּלְנָה" — שֶׁגּוֹרְמִין שִׁפְלוּת שֶׁל יִשְׂרָאֵל. וּמַה כְּתִיב אַחֲרָיו — "לָכֵן הִרְחִיבָה

וַאֲנַן יָהֲבֵי לֵיהּ לַכֹּהֲנִים. דְּקָנְסִינְהוּ עֶזְרָא, כִּדְאָמְרִי' בִּיבָמוֹת (דף פו:). וְכֵיוָן דְּאֵינָן נוֹתְנִין כְּתִקְנָן אֵין יְכוֹלִין לוֹמַר "וְגַם נְתַתִּיו לַלֵּוִי כְּכָל מִצְוָתְךָ". תְּחִילָּה. "וְנָתַתָּה לַלֵּוִי" — זֶה מַעֲשֵׂר רִאשׁוֹן, "לַגֵּר" — זֶה מַעֲשֵׂר עָנִי, "בִּשְׁעָרֶיךָ" — זֶה מַעֲשֵׂר שֵׁנִי, דִּכְתִיב: "לֹא תוּכַל לֶאֱכוֹל בִּשְׁעָרֶיךָ" (דברים יב). אַף הוּא. יוֹחָנָן כֹּהֵן גָּדוֹל. טֶבֶל וּתְרוּמַת מַעֲשֵׂר עֲוֹן מִיתָה. בְּ"אֵלּוּ הֵן הַנִּשְׂרָפִין" (סנהדרין פג.) יָלְפִי' לָהּ. וּכְשֶׁהֵם לוֹקְחִין מֵעַם הָאָרֶץ, וְהֵם לֹא הִפְרִישׁוּ אֶלָּא תְּרוּמָה — עוֹדֵהוּ טֶבֶל לְמַעַשְׂרוֹת, וְהֵם נֶעֱנָשִׁים מִיתָה. מַפְרִישׁ תְּרוּמַת מַעֲשֵׂר וְנוֹתְנָהּ לַכֹּהֵן. מַפְרִישׁ כָּל הַמַּעַשְׂרוֹת מִמֶּנָּה לְהוֹצִיא מִידֵי טֶבֶל, וְאַחַר כָּךְ מַפְרִישׁ מִתּוֹךְ מַעֲשֵׂר רִאשׁוֹן תְּרוּמַת מַעֲשֵׂר, מַה שֶּׁעַל הַלֵּוִי לְהַפְרִישׁ — וְנוֹתְנוֹ לַכֹּהֵן. מִשּׁוּם דְּאִית בֵּיהּ עֲוֹן מִיתָה הֶחְמִיר עֲלַיְיהוּ שֶׁלֹּא לְעַכְּבוֹ אֶצְלוֹ וְלִמְכּוֹר לַכֹּהֵן כְּשֵׁם שֶׁהוּא מְעַכֵּב אֶצְלוֹ מַעֲשֵׂר רִאשׁוֹן וּמַעֲשֵׂר עָנִי, וְאוֹמֵר: הַמּוֹצִיא מֵחֲבֵירוֹ עָלָיו הָרְאָיָה, גְּזֵירָה דִּלְמָא כִּי מַשְׁהֵי לֵיהּ גַּבֵּיהּ — אָכֵיל לֵיהּ. אֲבָל מַעֲשֵׂר רִאשׁוֹן וּמַעֲשֵׂר עָנִי מוּתָּרִים לְזָרִים, וְאֵין בָּהֶן אֶלָּא גֶּזֶל כֹּהֵן, הִלְכָּךְ — הַמּוֹצִיא מֵחֲבֵירוֹ עָלָיו הָרְאָיָה. אַלְמָא אַפְרוּשֵׁי נַמִי לָא הָווּ מַפְרְשֵׁי, וְאַתְּ אָמְרַתְּ לְפִי שֶׁאֵין נוֹתְנִין אוֹתוֹ כְּתִקְנָן, הָא אַפְרוּשֵׁי מַפְרְשֵׁי לֵיהּ. תַּרְתֵּי תִּקּוּן. לְעוֹלָם הַעֲבָרַת הוֹדָאוֹת מַעֲשֵׂר מִשּׁוּם שֶׁאֵינָם נוֹתְנִין אוֹתוֹ לַלְוִיִּם הוּא, וְהָא דְּתַנְיָא לְפִי שֶׁשָּׁלַח כו' — לָאו אַבִּיטֵּל אֶת הַוִּידּוּי קָאֵי, אֶלָּא אַגָּזַר עַל הַדְּמַאי קָאֵי. וְתַרְתֵּי תַּקָּנוֹת תִּקֵּן: בִּיטֵּל וִידּוּי שֶׁל חֲבֵרִים, אע"פ שֶׁמַּפְרִישִׁין אוֹתוֹ — לְפִי שֶׁאֵין נוֹתְנִין אוֹתוֹ כְּתִקּוּנוֹ. וְגָזַר עַל הַדְּמַאי עַל לוֹקֵחַ מֵעַם הָאָרֶץ, לְפִי שֶׁשָּׁלַח כו'. מְסָרְטִין. כְּשֶׁהָיוּ רוֹצִין לְהַפִּילוֹ לָאָרֶץ לְשׁוֹחֲטוֹ. שֶׁיִּפּוֹל דָּם בְּעֵינָיו. וְאֵינוֹ רוֹאֶה, וְאֵינוֹ מִתְחַזֵּק כָּל כָּךְ עַל רַגְלָיו. וְנוֹקְפִין — לְשׁוֹן "וְנִקַּף סִבְכֵי הַיַּעַר" (ישעיה י). חוֹבְטִין. לְהַפִּילוֹ לָאָרֶץ. וְנוֹקְפִין — לְשׁוֹן חֲבָטָה וּמַכָּה, כִּדְאָמְרִי':

אֵין אָדָם מְנַקֵּף אֶצְבָּעוֹ, דָּם נִיקּוּף מְרַצֶּה כְּדַם עוֹלָה (חולין דף ז:). טַבָּעוֹת. לְהַכְנִיס צַוַּאר בְּהֵמָה לְתוֹכוֹ. כִּדְאָמְרִינַן. שֶׁתִּיקֵּן שֶׁיְּהוּ כָּל הַלּוֹקְחִין מַפְרִישִׁין, וְלֹא הָיָה אָדָם צָרִיךְ לִשְׁאוֹל לַחֲבֵירוֹ, חָבֵר שֶׁלָּקַח מֵעַם הָאָרֶץ: הִפְרַשְׁתָּ דְּמַאי? **מתני'** בַּשִּׁיר לֹא יִשְׁתּוּ יַיִן. וּבַגְּמָ' מְפָרֵשׁ מְנָא לָן דְּמִשֶּׁבָּטְלָה סַנְהֶדְרִין הוּא. נְבִיאִים הָרִאשׁוֹנִים. בַּגְּמָרָא מְפָרֵשׁ. נוֹפֶת צוּפִים. מְפָרֵשׁ בַּגְּמָ'. אַנְשֵׁי אֲמָנָה. בּוֹטְחִים בְּהקב"ה וְסוֹמְכִין עָלָיו לַעֲשׂוֹת טוֹב, וְאֵין דּוֹאֲגִין לְחֶסְרוֹן. **גמ'** אָמַר רַב יוֹסֵף. הָכִי קָאָמַר: וְכִי בַּיִת הַמְסוּבָּךְ בַּאֲרָזִים עִיר הוּא שֶׁלֹּא יְהֵא נוֹחַ לֵיחָרֵב? מִתְרוֹעֵעַ. לְשׁוֹן עֵרָה, כְּמוֹ "עָרוּ עָרוּ" (תהלים קלז). בְּסִיפָּא מַתְחִיל. מֵאִיסְקוּפַּת הַבַּיִת וּפְתָחָיו מַתְחִיל. וּשְׁאִיָּה. לְשׁוֹן בַּיִת הַשָּׁמֵם מֵאֵין יוֹשֵׁב. וּמִתּוֹךְ כָּךְ שְׂעִירִים מְרַקְּדִים שָׁם, וּמְנַגְּחִין וְכוֹתְתִין אֶת שְׁעָרָיו. זִמְרֵי דְּנַגָּדֵי. מוֹשְׁכֵי סְפִינוֹת בְּחֶבֶל — שָׁרֵי, שֶׁאֵינוֹ אֶלָּא לְזָרְזָם בִּמְלַאכְתָּם. וּדְבַקָּרֵי. שֶׁמְּזַמְּרִין בְּשָׁעָה שֶׁחוֹרְשִׁין, וְאֵינוֹ אֶלָּא לְכַוֵּין אֶת הַשְּׁוָורִים לְתַלְמֵיהֶם, שֶׁהוֹלְכִין לְקוֹל הַשִּׁיר, דְּעָרֵב עֲלֵיהֶם. דְּגַרְדָּאֵי. אֵינוֹ אֶלָּא לִשְׂחוֹק. בָּטֵל זִמְרָא. גָּזַר עַל דּוֹרוֹ שֶׁלֹּא יְזַמְּרוּ בְּבָתֵּיהֶם וּבְבֵית מִשְׁתָּאוֹת. וְלָא אִיבְּעֵי. וְלֹא הָיוּ רוֹצִים לִקְנוֹתָם בְּכָךְ. זַלְזֵיל בֵּהּ. וְלֹא הִקְפִּיד לִמְחוֹת בְּיָדָם. כְּאֵשׁ בִּנְעוֹרֶת. לְפִי שֶׁהָעוֹנֶה מַטֶּה אָזְנוֹ לִשְׁמוֹעַ אֶת הַמְזַמֵּר לַעֲנוֹת אַחֲרָיו, וְנִמְצְאוּ הָאֲנָשִׁים נוֹתְנִים לִבָּם לְקוֹל הַנָּשִׁים. וְקוֹל בְּאִשָּׁה עֶרְוָה, כִּדְכְתִיב: "הַשְׁמִיעִנִי אֶת קוֹלֵךְ" (שיר ב), וּמַבְעִיר אֶת יִצְרוֹ כְּאֵשׁ בִּנְעוֹרֶת. אֲבָל זָמְרֵי גַּבְרֵי וְעָנְיָין נָשֵׁי — קְצָת פְּרִיצוּת יֵשׁ, דְּקוֹל בְּאִשָּׁה עֶרְוָה, אֲבָל אֵינוֹ מַבְעִיר יִצְרוֹ כָּל כָּךְ, שֶׁאֵין הַמְזַמְּרִים מַטִּים אָזְנָם לְקוֹל הָעוֹנִים. לְבַטּוּלֵי הַאי מִקַּמֵּי הַאי. אִם אֵין שׁוֹמְעִין לָנוּ לְבַטֵּל אֶת שְׁנֵיהֶם, נַקְדִּים לְבַטֵּל אֶת זֶה שֶׁהוּא כְּאֵשׁ בִּנְעוֹרֶת. צִחֵה צָמָא. "לָמָּה" (שמות יז) מְתַרְגֵּם לְחוּתָא.

הִרְחִיבָה

מסורת הש"ס:
[תוספ' פי"ג] ב"מ ל. יומא ט.
[עי' תוס' שבת יג. ד"ה רבא]
[עי' תוס' יומא ט. ד"ה מעשר]
[תוספתא פי"ג]
[תוס' פי"ג ע"ש]
[בירושלמי ל"ג]
[עי' הגי' בע"י]
ב"ק כח.

עין משפט נר מצוה:
מט א מיי' פ"א מהל' מעשר הלכה ד:
נ ב מיי' פי"א מהלכות מעשר שני הלכה ז יב:
נא ג מיי' פ"ט מהלכ' מעשר הלכה א סמג עשין קלח:
נב ד מיי' שם הלכה ב:
נג ה מיי' פ"ה מהלכות תענית הלכה יד סמג עשין מד"ס ג טור ש"ע א"ח סי' תקס סעיף ג:

הגהות הב"ח
(א) במשנה שומן הדגן (וחכמים אומרים) תא"מ ונ"ב ס"א ל"ג ליה [וכן בירושלמי ליתא]: (ב) גמ' אמר רב יצחק וכי בית:

גליון הש"ס
גמ' אודנא דשמעא. רי"ף פ"ה דברכות:

[במשנה שבמשניות איתא משום ר' יהושע וכ"ה לקמן בפיסקא]
נ"ל המסוכך וכ"ה ברש"א
[גיר' הערוך בערך בקר ג' דגלדאי שהן עבדנין מפני שיש בזמר שלהן גדופין אסרן רב הונא]
[לעיל מב: סנהדרין לג. לו:]

עין משפט נר מצוה | מסורת הש"ס

הרחיבה שאול נפשה ופערה פיה לבלי חק וירד הדרה והמונה ושאונה ועלז בה".§ "משמתו נביאים הראשונים".§ מאן נביאים הראשונים? אמר רב הונא: זה *דוד ושמואל ושלמה. רב נחמן אמר: בימי דוד, זימנין סליק וזימנין לא סליק, *שהרי שאל צדוק – ועלתה לו, שאל אביתר – ולא עלתה לו, שנאמר: °"ויעל אביתר". מתיב רבה בר שמואל: °"ויהי לדרוש אלהים (א) כל ימי זכריה המבין בראות אלהים". מאי לאו באורים ותומים? לא, בנביאים. ת"ש: משחרב בהמ"ק ראשון בטלו ערי מגרש, ופסקו אורים ותומים, ופסק מלך מבית דוד. ואם לחשך אדם לומר: °"ויאמר התרשתא להם אשר לא יאכלו מקדש הקדשים עד עמוד כהן לאורים ותומים" – [אמור לו:] כאדם שאומר לחבירו "עד שיחיו מתים ויבא משיח בן דוד"! אלא אמר רב נחמן בר יצחק: מאן נביאים הראשונים – לאפוקי מחגי זכריה ומלאכי, דאחרונים נינהו. דת"ר: *משמתו חגי זכריה ומלאכי נסתלקה רוח הקודש מישראל, ואע"פ כן היו משתמשים בבת קול. שפעם אחת היו מסובין בעליית בית גוריא ביריחו, נתנה עליהן בת קול מן השמים ואמרה: יש בכם אדם אחד שראוי שתשרה שכינה עליו, אלא שאין דורו ראוי לכך, נתנו עיניהם בהלל הזקן. וכשמת, הספידוהו: הי חסיד, הי עניו, תלמידו של עזרא! ושוב פעם אחרת היו מסובין בעלייה ביבנה, נתנה להן בת קול מן השמים ואמרה להן: יש בכם אדם א' שראוי שתשרה שכינה עליו, אלא שאין דורו זכאין לכך, נתנו עיניהם בשמואל הקטן. וכשמת, הספידוהו: הי עניו, הי חסיד, תלמידו של הלל! ואף הוא אמר בשעת מיתתו: שמעון וישמעאל לחרבא, וחברוהי לקטלא, ושאר עמא לביזא, ועקן סגיאין עתידין למיתי על עמא. ואף על ר' יהודה בן בבא בקשו לומר "הי חסיד, הי עניו", אלא שנטרפה שעה, שאין מספידין על הרוגי מלכות.§ "משחרב בהמ"ק בטל השמיר" כו'.§ ת"ר: *שמיר שבו בנה שלמה את בהמ"ק, שנא': °"והבית בהבנותו אבן שלמה מסע נבנה" – הדברים ככתבן, דברי ר' יהודה. אמר לו ר' נחמיה: וכי אפשר לומר כן? והלא כבר נאמר: °"כל אלה אבנים יקרות וגו' מגוררות במגרה"! אם כן מה ת"ל: "לא נשמע בבית בהבנותו" – אשהיה מתקין מבחוץ ומכניס מבפנים. אמר רבי: נראין דברי רבי יהודה •באבני מקדש, ודברי ר' נחמיה באבני ביתו. ור' נחמיה, שמיר למאי אתא? מיבעי ליה לכדתניא: [ב] אבנים הללו אין כותבין אותן בדיו, משום שנאמר: °"פתוחי חותם", ואין מסרטין עליהם באיזמל, משום שנאמר: "במלואותם". אלא כותב עליהם בדיו ומראה להן שמיר מבחוץ, והן נבקעות מאליהן, כתאינה זו שנבקעת בימות החמה ואינה חסירה כלום, וכבקעה זו שנבקעת בימות הגשמים ואינה חסירה כלום. ת"ר: *שמיר זה – ברייתו כשעורה, ומששת ימי בראשית נברא, ואין כל דבר קשה יכול לעמוד בפניו. במה משמרין אותו – כורכין אותו בספוגין של צמר, ומניחין אותו *באיטני של אבר מליאה סובי שעורין. אמר רבי אמי: •משחרב מקדש ראשון בטלה שירא פרנדא וזכוכית לבנה. תניא נמי הכי: משחרב מקדש ראשון *בטלה שירא פרנדא וזכוכית לבנה ורכב ברזל, וי"א: אף יין קרוש הבא משניר, הדומה כעיגולי דבילה.§ "ונופת צופים".§ מאי נופת צופים? אמר רב: סולת שצפה על גבי נפה, ודומה לעיסה שנילושה בדבש ושמן. ולוי אמר: שתי כברות הנדבקות בתנור, ותופחות ובאות עד שמגיעות זו לזו. ורבי יהושע בן לוי אמר: זה דבש הבא מן *הציפיא. מאי משמע? כדמתרגם *רב ששת: כמא דנתזן דבריאתה ושייטן ברומי עלמא ומתיין דובשא מעישבי טורא. תנן התם: *כל הנצוק טהור – חוץ מדבש זיפים והצפיחים. מאי זיפים? אמר רבי יוחנן: דבש שמזייפין בו, ור"ל אמר: על שם מקומו, כדכתיב: °"זיף וטלם ובעלות". כיוצא בדבר אתה אומר: °"בבא הזיפים ויאמרו לשאול הלא דוד" וגו'. מאי זיפים? אמר רבי יוחנן: בני אדם המזייפין דבריהם, ורבי אלעזר אומר: על שם מקומן, כדכתיב: "זיף וטלם ובעלות".§ "ופסקו אנשי אמנה".§ אמר רבי יצחק: אלו בני אדם שהן מאמינין בהקב"ה. דתניא, רבי אליעזר הגדול אומר: כל מי שיש לו פת בסלו ואומר "מה אוכל למחר" – אינו אלא מקטני אמנה. *והיינו דאמר ר' אלעזר: מאי דכתיב: °"כי מי בז ליום קטנות", מי גרם לצדיקים שיתבזבז שולחנן לעתיד לבא – קטנות שהיה בהן, שלא האמינו בהקב"ה. רבא אמר: אלו קטני בני רשעי ישראל, שמבזבזין

רש"י

הרחיבה שאול נפשה. לאחר שהביאו חמש פורעניות הללו לעולם – סופן נופלין בגיהנם. זימנין סליק. פעמים (ב) עולים בידם – שנענים, ופעמים שלא עלה בידם. שהרי כשברח דוד מפני אבשלום יצא מירושלים, שאל צדוק באורים ותומים – ועלתה לו, שהשיבוהו, ושאל אביתר – ולא עלתה לו, שנאמר: "ויעל אביתר" – שנסתלק מן הכהונה מפני שלא נענה באורים ותומים. והכי תניא בסדר עולם גבי ארון: וכברחו מפני אבשלום יצא עמו, עד שעלה במעלה הזיתים ונשאל באורים ותומים, ונסתלק אביתר מן הכהונה גדולה. נכנס צדוק תחתיו, כדכתיב (שמואל ב טו): "ויאמר המלך לצדוק השב את הארון" וגו'. בימי זכריהו. והוא בנו של יהוידע, שהיה בימי יואש. ערי מגרש. ערי לוים שהטעינן הכתוב מגרשות. עד עמוד כהן וגו'. אלמא הוו אורים בבית שני. אמור לו. לא שהיו אורים ותומים, אלא כאדם שאומר לחבירו כו'. אלמא כל ימי המקדש ראשון הוו!. דתניא. חגי זכריה ומלאכי נקראו אחרונים. שמעון וישמעאל. רבן שמעון שהיה נשיא, ורבי ישמעאל בן אלישע (ג) כהן גדול, שהרגתם מלכות יון. לחרבא. שעתידין ליהרג בחרב. לקטלא. לשאר מיתות, כגון רבי עקיבא שסרקו בשרו במסריקות פיפיות של ברזל, כדאמר בברכות (דף סא:), •ור' חנניה בן תרדיון שנשרף, ורבי יהודה בן בבא בלונביאות של ברזל, כדאמר בסנהדרין (דף יד.). שאין מספידין על הרוגי מלכות. מאימת המלך, לפיכך מיתו בידם. דברים ככתבן. כמשמען: אבן שלמה מסע – כמה שהסיעה מן ההר, ולא סיתתוה שום בכלי ברזל. והלא כבר נאמר מגוררות במגירה וגו'. שמיר למאי אתא. דאמרי' במס' גיטין (דף סח.) שהביאו שמיר ע"י אשמדאי מלכא דשדאי. אבנים הללו. שבאפוד וחשן. פתוחי חותם. חקק משמע. במלואותם. שיהיו שלמות, שלא יחסרו מהם כלום. ומראה להם שמיר. על פני הדיו *כחריץ האות. איטני של אבר. גוכתא – מש"א בלע"ז. שירא פרנדא. מין משי הוא. סלת צפה על גבי נפה. מרוב שומנה מדבקת בדופני נפה, ודומים לעיסה חיה שנילושה ביין כו'. נופת – דבק הנפה, נופים – שנפה. שתי כברות הנדבקות כו'. שהיתה ברכה מלויה בעיסה, וכשמדבקין ככרות בדופני התנור אחת בדופן זה ואחת בדופן זה שכנגדו, והן תפוחות – אנפליי"ר בלע"ז, עד שמגעת פני זו לזו. כלומר זה שגדל ומתפשט והולך ותולה באויר, כן אלו נפות ותפוחות באויר. מן הצופים. ההרים הגבוהים, שמשם צופה למרחוק. מאי משמע. מהיכא ילפת שדבש בא מן ההרים?. כדמתרגם רב יוסף. "כאשר תעשינה הדבורים"*. כל הנצוק. המערה מכלי טהור לכלי טמא – אין הקילוח מצרפן להיות חיבור, לטמא את מה שבתוך הכלי שהוא מערה ממנו. חוץ מדבש זיפין. שהוא עב מאד. והרי הוא כמחובר, שכשהקילוח פוסק הוא הולך מלמטה למעלה. והכי אמרינן *במדות. הצפחת. ברסק"א בלע"ז, שהן עבות (ד) ונכנסת השעוה עם הדבש. שמזייפין בו. מתוך שהוא טוב ועב – מערבין בו מים ויין, ואין נכרות בו. שמזייפין. שקרנים והולכי רכיל. שמאמינים בהקדוש ברוך הוא. לוותר ממונם לנוי הדור מצוה, ולצדקה, ולהוצאת שבתות וימים טובים. שיתבזו שולחנם לעתיד לבא. שאין מקבלין שכר שלם, והכי משמע: כי מי בז ליום הבא את הצדיקים. קטנות. קטנות אמנה. קטני רשעי בני ישראל. שמתו כשהן קטנים. שמבזבזין

עין משפט נר מצוה

נד א מיי' פ"א מהל' בית הבחירה הלכה ח סמג לאוין רל:

נה [ב השמיט הרמב"ם ומצאתי שהמ"ל פ"ט מהל' כלי המקדש דין ז' תמה על זה]:

הגהות הב"ח

(א) גמ' לדרוש אלהים בימי זכריהו המבין בראות האלהים כצ"ל ותיבת כל נמחק: (ב) רש"י ד"ה זימנין סליק פעמים עולה בידם: (ג) ד"ה שמעון וכו' בן אלישע שהיה כ"ג: (ד) ד"ה הצפחת וכו' עבות ונכנסת השעוה:

גליון הש"ס

גמ' באבני מקדש. עי' במסכת תמיד פ"א ובדברי המפרש שם ד"ה אמר אביי דמתקנן ומייתי מעיקרא: שם משחרב מקדש ראשון וכו'. עי' שבת כ ע"ב תד"ה אנן חולין פד ע"ב ד"ה בזוגיתא: רש"י ד"ה (ד"ה) לקטלא ור"ח בן תרדיון וכו'. כדאיתא בע"ז דף ח ע"א:

[גיר' הערוך בטבי פי' מן ושמת בטנא ערך טן ו']

[נ"ל הצופים וכ"מ בפרש"י וכ"ה בכתי"ע]

[נ"ל שנאמר למען אנסנו הילך בתורתי כך איתא בילקוט רמז רנ"ח]

מסורת הש"ס

[ברש"י שבע"י בחריץ]

תורה אור

[נ"ל שמואל ודוד כ"א בע"י]

[יומא עג: עי' שם ונ"ע]

ש"ב טו

דה"ב כו

עזרא ב

דברים א

[נ"ל במכשירין פ"ה מ"ט]

סנהדרין יא. יומא ט: [תוספתא פי"ג]

[תוספתא פט"ו]

מלכים א ו

שם ז

שמות כח

[תוספתא פט"ו ע"ש]

[עי' תוס' שבת כ: ד"ה אנן ותוס' ב"מ כט: ד"ה בזכוכית וחולין פד: ד"ה בזוגיתא]

ס"א רב יוסף

מכשירין פ"ה מ"ט נזיר נ.

יהושע טו

תהלים נד

זכריה ד

תורה אור

שֶׁמְּבַזְבְּזִין דִּין אֲבִיהֶם לֶעָתִיד לָבוֹא. אוֹמְרִים לְפָנָיו: רִבּוֹנוֹ שֶׁל עוֹלָם, מֵאַחַר שֶׁאַתָּה עָתִיד לִיפָּרַע מֵהֶן – לָמָּה הִקְהִיתָה שִׁינֵּיהֶם בָּם? אָמַר ר' אִילְעָא בַּר יְבֶרֶכְיָה: אִלְמָלֵא תְּפִלָּתוֹ שֶׁל דָּוִד הָיוּ כָּל יִשְׂרָאֵל מוֹכְרֵי רְבָב, שֶׁנֶּאֱמַר: תהלים ט °"שִׁיתָה ה' מוֹרָה לָהֶם". וְא"ר אִילְעָא בַּר יְבֶרֶכְיָה: אִלְמָלֵא תְּפִלָּתוֹ שֶׁל חֲבַקּוּק הָיוּ ב' תַּלְמִידֵי חֲכָמִים מִתְכַּסִּים בְּטַלִּית אַחַת וְעוֹסְקִין בַּתּוֹרָה, שֶׁנֶּאֱמַר: חבקוק ג °"ה' שָׁמַעְתִּי שִׁמְעֲךָ יָרֵאתִי ה' פָּעָלְךָ בְּקֶרֶב שָׁנִים חַיֵּיהוּ", אַל תִּקְרָא "בְּקֶרֶב שָׁנִים" אֶלָּא "בְּקָרוֹב שְׁנַיִם". וְאָמַר ר' אִילְעָא בַּר יְבֶרֶכְיָה: *שְׁנֵי תַּלְמִידֵי חֲכָמִים הַמְהַלְּכִין בַּדֶּרֶךְ וְאֵין בֵּינֵיהֶן דִּבְרֵי תוֹרָה – רְאוּיִן לִישָּׂרֵף בָּאֵשׁ, שֶׁנֶּאֱמַר: מלכים ב ב °"וַיְהִי הֵמָּה הוֹלְכִים הָלוֹךְ וְדַבֵּר וְהִנֵּה רֶכֶב אֵשׁ" וגו'. טַעֲמָא – דְּאִיכָּא דִּיבּוּר, הָא לֵיכָּא דִּיבּוּר – רְאוּיִן לִישָּׂרֵף. וְא"ר אִילְעָא בַּר יְבֶרֶכְיָה: שְׁנֵי ת"ח הַדָּרִין בְּעִיר אַחַת וְאֵין נוֹחִין זֶה לָזֶה בַּהֲלָכָה – אֶחָד מֵת וְאֶחָד גּוֹלֶה, שֶׁנֶּאֱמַר: דברים ד °"לָנוּס שָׁמָּה רוֹצֵחַ אֲשֶׁר יִרְצַח אֶת רֵעֵהוּ בִּבְלִי דַעַת", וְאֵין דַּעַת אֶלָּא תּוֹרָה, שֶׁנֶּאֱמַר: הושע ד °"נִדְמוּ עַמִּי מִבְּלִי הַדָּעַת". אָמַר ר' יְהוּדָה בְּרֵיהּ דְּר' חִיָּיא: כָּל ת"ח הָעוֹסֵק בַּתּוֹרָה מִתּוֹךְ הַדְּחָק – תְּפִלָּתוֹ נִשְׁמַעַת, שֶׁנֶּאֱמַר ישעיה ל °"כִּי עַם בְּצִיּוֹן יֵשֵׁב בִּירוּשָׁלַיִם בָּכוֹ לֹא תִבְכֶּה חָנוֹן יָחְנְךָ לְקוֹל זַעֲקֶךָ כְּשָׁמְעָתוֹ עָנָךְ", וּכְתִיב בַּתְרֵיהּ: שם °"וְנָתַן (א) ה' לָכֶם לֶחֶם צַר וּמַיִם לָחַץ". ר' אֲבָהוּ אוֹמֵר: מַשְׂבִּיעִין אוֹתוֹ מִזִּיו שְׁכִינָה, שֶׁנֶּאֱמַר: שם °"וְהָיוּ עֵינֶיךָ רוֹאוֹת אֶת מוֹרֶיךָ". ר' אַחָא בַּר חֲנִינָא אָמַר: אַף אֵין הַפַּרְגּוֹד נִנְעָל בְּפָנָיו, שֶׁנֶּאֱמַר: שם °"וְלֹא יִכָּנֵף עוֹד מוֹרֶיךָ".§ "רשב"ג אוֹמֵר מִשּׁוּם ר' יְהוֹשֻׁעַ מִיּוֹם שֶׁחָרַב בהמ"ק אֵין" וכו'.§ אָמַר רָבָא: בְּכָל יוֹם וָיוֹם מְרוּבָּה קִלְלָתוֹ מִשֶּׁל חֲבֵירוֹ, שֶׁנֶּאֱמַר: דברים כח °"בַּבֹּקֶר תֹּאמַר מִי יִתֵּן עֶרֶב וּבָעֶרֶב תֹּאמַר מִי יִתֵּן בֹּקֶר". הֵי בֹּקֶר? אִילֵימָא בֹּקֶר דִּלְמָחָר – מִי יָדַע מַאי הָוֵי? אֶלָּא דְּחָלֵיף. וְאֶלָּא עָלְמָא אַמַּאי קָא מְקַיֵּים? אַקְּדוּשָּׁה דְּסִידְרָא, וְאַ"יְּהֵא שְׁמֵיהּ רַבָּא" דְּאַגַּדְתָּא, שֶׁנֶּאֱ': איוב י °"אֶרֶץ עֵפָתָה כְּמוֹ אוֹפֶל צַלְמָוֶת וְלֹא סְדָרִים", הָא יֵשׁ סְדָרִים – תּוֹפִיעַ מֵאוֹפֶל.§ "וְלֹא יָרַד טַל לִבְרָכָה וְנִיטַּל טַעַם פֵּירוֹת" וכו'.§ תַּנְיָא, *ר"ש בֶּן אֶלְעָזָר אוֹמֵר: טָהֳרָה בִּטְּלָה טַעַם וָרֵיחַ, מַעֲשֵׂר בִּיטֵּל שׁוּמַּן דָּגָן. רַב הוּנָא [תוספתא פט"ו ע"ש] אַשְׁכַּח תּוּמַרְתָּא דְּחִינּוּנִיתָא, שְׁקָלָהּ כְּרָכָהּ בְּסוּדָרֵיהּ, אֲתָא רַבָּה בְּרֵיהּ, א"ל: מוֹרְחִינָא רֵיחָא דְּחִינּוּנִיתָא. א"ל: בְּנִי, טָהֳרָה יֵשׁ בְּךָ. יַהֲבָהּ נִיהֲלֵיהּ. אַדְּהָכִי אֲתָא אַבָּא בְּרֵיהּ, שְׁקָלָהּ יַהֲבָהּ נִיהֲלֵיהּ. א"ל: בְּנִי, שִׂמַּחְתָּ אֶת לִבִּי וְהִקְהִיתָה אֶת שִׁינַּי. הַיְינוּ דְּאָמְרֵי אֱנָשֵׁי: רַחֲמֵי דְּאַבָּא אַבְּנֵי, רַחֲמֵי דִּבְנֵי – אַבְּנֵי דְּהָווּ לֵיהּ. רַב אַחָא בַּר יַעֲקֹב אִיטַּפַּל בֵּיהּ בְּרַב יַעֲקֹב בַּר בְּרָתֵיהּ. כִּי גְּדַל א"ל: אַשְׁקְיַין מַיָּא. אֲמַר לוֹ: לָאו בְּרִיךְ אֲנָא. וְהַיְינוּ דְּאָמְרֵי אֱנָשֵׁי: רְבִי רְבִי, בַּר בְּרָתָךְ אֲנָא.§

גיטין ז. נדה סח: **מתני'** *אבַּפּוֹלְמוֹס שֶׁל אַסְפַּסְיָינוּס גָּזְרוּ עַל עַטְרוֹת חֲתָנִים וְעַל הָאֵירוּס. בַּפּוֹלְמוֹס שֶׁל טִיטוּס גָּזְרוּ עַל עַטְרוֹת כַּלּוֹת, וְשֶׁלֹּא יְלַמֵּד אָדָם אֶת בְּנוֹ °יְוָונִית. בַּפּוֹלְמוֹס הָאַחֲרוֹן גָּזְרוּ שֶׁלֹּא תֵּצֵא הַכַּלָּה בְּאַפִּרְיוֹן בְּתוֹךְ הָעִיר, וְרַבּוֹתֵינוּ הִתִּירוּ שֶׁתֵּצֵא הַכַּלָּה בְּאַפִּרְיוֹן בְּתוֹךְ הָעִיר. מִשֶּׁמֵּת ר"מ בָּטְלוּ מוֹשְׁלֵי מְשָׁלִים, מִשֶּׁמֵּת בֶּן עַזַּאי בָּטְלוּ הַשַּׁקְדָּנִים, מִשֶּׁמֵּת בֶּן זוֹמָא בָּטְלוּ הַדַּרְשָׁנִים, מִשֶּׁמֵּת ר"ע בָּטַל כְּבוֹד הַתּוֹרָה, מִשֶּׁמֵּת ר' חֲנִינָא בֶּן דּוֹסָא בָּטְלוּ אַנְשֵׁי מַעֲשֶׂה, מִשֶּׁמֵּת ר' יוֹסֵי קַטְנוּתָא פָּסְקוּ חֲסִידִים. וְלָמָּה נִקְרָא שְׁמוֹ קַטְנוּתָא – שֶׁהָיָה קַטְנוּתָא שֶׁל חֲסִידִים. מגילה כח. מִשֶּׁמֵּת רַבִּי יוֹחָנָן בֶּן זַכַּאי בָּטַל זִיו הַחָכְמָה, מִשֶּׁמֵּת ר"ג הַזָּקֵן *בָּטַל כְּבוֹד הַתּוֹרָה וּמֵתָה טָהֳרָה וּפְרִישׁוּת, מִשֶּׁמֵּת רש"א רַבִּי יִשְׁמָעֵאל בֶּן פָּאבִי בָּטְלָה זִיו הַכְּהוּנָּה, °מִשֶּׁמֵּת רַבִּי בָּטַל עֲנָוָה וְיִרְאַת חֵטְא.§ [גמ' ת"ר,] *ר' פִּנְחָס בֶּן יָאִיר [גירסת ע"י רבי יהושע] אוֹמֵר: מִשֶּׁחָרַב בהמ"ק בּוֹשׁוּ חֲבֵרִים וּבְנֵי חוֹרִין, וְחָפוּ רֹאשָׁם, וְנִדַּלְדְּלוּ אַנְשֵׁי מַעֲשֶׂה, וְגָבְרוּ בַּעֲלֵי זְרוֹעַ וּבַעֲלֵי לָשׁוֹן, וְאֵין דּוֹרֵשׁ וְאֵין מְבַקֵּשׁ וְאֵין שׁוֹאֵל, עַל מִי לָנוּ לְהִשָּׁעֵן – עַל אָבִינוּ שֶׁבַּשָּׁמַיִם. ר"א הַגָּדוֹל אוֹמֵר: מִיּוֹם שֶׁחָרַב בֵּית הַמִּקְדָּשׁ שָׁרוּ חַכִּימַיָּא לְמֶהֱוֵי כְּסָפְרַיָּא, וְסָפְרַיָּא כְּחַזָּנַיָּא, וְחַזָּנַיָּא כְּעַמָּא דְּאַרְעָא, וְעַמָּא דְאַרְעָא אָזְלָא

שֶׁמְּבַזְבְּזִין דִּין אֲבִיהֶם. קוֹרְעִים דִּין אֲבִיהֶם. שֶׁכְּשֶׁבָּאִין לְדוּנָם אוֹמְרִים לְפָנָיו וכו'. הִקְהִיתָה שִׁינֵּיהֶם. לָמָּה הֶאֱכַלְתָּם וְלַעַרְתָּם עָלֵינוּ בְּמוֹתֵינוּ, וְנִפְרַעְתָּ מֵהֶם בְּחַיֵּיהֶם. מוֹכְרֵי רְבָב. רְבָב הוּא דָּבָר מָאוּס, כְּגוֹן חֵלֶב וְשׁוּמָּן, וְנִדְבָּק בַּבְּגָדִים וְנִמְאָסִין, וְאֵין לְךָ אָדָם מִתְעַסֵּק בָּהֶם אֶלָּא עָנִי. שִׁיתָה ה' מוֹרָה לָהֶם. לְעֵיל מִינֵּיהּ כְּתִיב: "כִּי לֹא לָנֶצַח יִשָּׁכַח אֶבְיוֹן תִּקְוַת עֲנָוִים תֹּאבַד לָעַד שִׁיתָה ה' מוֹרָה לָהֶם" – תֵּן לָהֶם מָרוּת לְאוֹתָן עֲנִיִּים, עוֹשֶׁר, שֶׁיְּהוּ הַגּוֹיִם נוֹהֲגִין בָּהֶם כָּבוֹד, וְיֵדְעוּ הַגּוֹיִם שֶׁהֵן אֱנוֹשׁ וְאֵינָם אֱלוֹהוּת, שֶׁאֵין כָּל הַכָּבוֹד וְהַגְּדוּלָּה שֶׁלָּהֶם. מִתְכַּסִּין בְּטַלִּית אַחַת. מִשּׁוּם עוֹנִי. בְּקֶרֶב שָׁנִים. אוֹתָהּ פְּעוּלָּה שֶׁלְּךָ, דְּהַיְינוּ דְּבַר תּוֹרָה, שֶׁהִיא בְּקֵירוּב שְׁנַיִם – שֶׁשְּׁנַיִם צְרִיכִין לְהִתְקָרֵב יַחַד בְּכִיסּוּי אֶחָד. חַיֵּיהוּ. רַפְּאֵהוּ, וְהַרְוַוח לָהֶם וְתֵן לָהֶם חַיּוּתָם. הֵמָּה הוֹלְכִים הָלוֹךְ וְדַבֵּר. בְּדִבְרֵי תוֹרָה. בְּאֵלִיָּהוּ וֶאֱלִישָׁע תענית י: כְּתִיב. רְאוּיִן לִישָּׂרֵף. שֶׁעַל מְנָת כֵּן בָּא הָרֶכֶב אֵשׁ עֲלֵיהֶם. אֶחָד מֵת. ע"י חֲבֵירוֹ שֶׁהֲרָגוֹ בְּשׁוֹגֵג, וְזֶה גּוֹלֶה לְעָרֵי מִקְלָט. *וְאִם אֵין כָּאן מִיתָה – סִימָן נ"א ואם כן לְמִיתָה, (ב) וְגָלוּת סִימָן לְגָלוּת, שֶׁאֶחָד מֵת וְאֶחָד גּוֹלֶה. בִּבְלִי דַעַת. עַל שֶׁלֹּא הָיָה לָהֶם דַּעַת לִהְיוֹת מְלַמְּדִין זֶה אֶת זֶה וְלוֹמְדִין זֶה מִזֶּה. נִדְמוּ עַמִּי. וְסֵיפֵיהּ דִּקְרָא "וַתִּשְׁכַּח תּוֹרַת אֱלֹהֶיךָ". כִּי עַם בְּצִיּוֹן יֵשֵׁב. אֵלּוּ יוֹשְׁבֵי יְשִׁיבַת תּוֹרָה, וְסֵיפָא דִּקְרָא "חָנוֹן יָחְנְךָ לְקוֹל זַעֲקֶךָ". לֶחֶם צַר. בְּמִי הַכָּתוּב מְדַבֵּר – בְּמִי שֶׁמְּזוֹנוֹתָיו קָשִׁין עָלָיו, וְאעפ"כ יוֹשֵׁב וְעוֹסֵק בַּתּוֹרָה. וְהָיוּ עֵינֶיךָ וגו'. וְכֵן בַּתְרֵיהּ כְּתִיב: "וְלֹא יִכָּנֵף". פַּרְגּוֹד. מְחִיצָּה. לֹא יִכָּנֵף. לֹא יִתְכַּסֶּה מִמְּךָ בִּכְנַף בִּגְדוֹ וּמְחִיצָּתוֹ. דִּלְמָחָר. מִי יִתֵּן שֶׁיָּבֹא יוֹם. מִי יָדַע. אִם יֵיטַב מִן הַלַּיְלָה. אֶלָּא דְּחָלֵיף. מִי יִתֵּן וְהָיָה זֶה, יוֹם הַבָּא כָּזֶה שֶׁעָבַר. אֶלָּא עָלְמָא אַמַּאי מְקַיֵּים. מֵאַחַר שֶׁהַקְּלָלָה הוֹלֶכֶת תָּמִיד וְרַבָּה. אַקְּדוּשָּׁה דְּסִידְרָא. סֵדֶר קְדוּשָּׁה. שֶׁלֹּא תִּקְּנוּהָ אֶלָּא שֶׁיְּהוּ כָּל יִשְׂרָאֵל עוֹסְקִין בַּתּוֹרָה בְּכָל יוֹם דָּבָר מוּעָט, שֶׁאוֹמֵר קְרִיָּאתוֹ וְתַרְגּוּמוֹ, וַהֲרֵי הֵן כְּעוֹסְקִין בַּתּוֹרָה. וְכֵיוָן שֶׁנּוֹהֵג בְּכָל יִשְׂרָאֵל, בְּתַלְמִידִים וּבְעַמֵּי הָאָרֶץ, וְיֵשׁ כָּאן שְׁתַּיִם: קְדוּשַּׁת הַשֵּׁם וְתַלְמוּד הַתּוֹרָה – חָבִיב הוּא. וְכֵן "יְהֵא שְׁמֵיהּ רַבָּה מְבָרַךְ" שֶׁעוֹנִין אַחַר הַגָּדָה שֶׁהַדַּרְשָׁן דּוֹרֵשׁ בָּרַבִּים – בְּכָל שַׁבָּת הָיוּ נוֹהֲגִין כָּךְ, וְשָׁם הָיוּ נִקְבָּצִין כָּל הָעָם לִשְׁמוֹעַ, לְפִי שֶׁאֵינוֹ יוֹם שֶׁל מְלָאכָה, וְיֵשׁ כָּאן תּוֹרָה וְקִידּוּשׁ הַשֵּׁם. סְדָרִים. סִדְרֵי פָּרָשִׁיּוֹת דְּתוֹרָה. טָהֳרָה. שֶׁפָּסְקָה מִיִּשְׂרָאֵל. בִּיטְּלָה טַעַם. הַפֵּירוֹת, וְרֵיחָם. שֶׁמִּתּוֹךְ שֶׁהָיוּ טְהוֹרִים וְנוֹהֲגִין בְּטָהֳרָה – אַף הקב"ה מְטַהֵר פֵּירוֹתֵיהֶן מֵרֵיחַ רַע וּמִטַּעַם רַע. מַעֲשֵׂר בִּיטֵּל שׁוּמַּן דָּגָן. בַּעֲוֹן פִּיסּוּק מַעַשְׂרוֹת פָּסַק שׁוּמַּן הַדָּגָן, כִּשְׁמוֹ שֶׁל מַעֲשֵׂר דְּאִיקְּרֵי חֵלֶב, כִּדְכְתִיב: "כָּל חֵלֶב יִצְהָר" וגו' (במדבר יח). דְּחִינּוּנִיתָא. שְׁמֵינָה, וְיֵשׁ בָּהּ רֵיחַ טוֹב, וּמִין תְּמָרִים הוּא לְעַצְמָן. טָהֳרָה יֵשׁ בְּךָ. לְפִיכָךְ מְרִיחָה לְךָ, וְלֹא בָּטֵל הָרֵיחַ מֵאֶצְלְךָ. אֲתָא בְּרֵיהּ. דְּרַבָּה בַּר רַב הוּנָא. א"ל. רַב הוּנָא לִבְרֵיהּ. שִׂמַּחְתָּ אֶת לִבִּי. בְּטָהֳרָתְךָ. וְהִקְהִיתָה אֶת שִׁינַּי. שֶׁהֶרְאֵיתַנִי שֶׁאַהֲבָתְךָ עַל בִּנְךָ יוֹתֵר מֵעָלַי, שֶׁנָּטַלְתָּ מִמֶּנִּי וְנָתַתָּ לוֹ. רַחֲמֵי. אַהֲבָה. אִיטַּפַּל בֵּיהּ. גִּידְּלוֹ בְּבֵיתוֹ. רְבִי רְבִי. גַּדֵּל גַּדֵּל אוֹתִי, וְאַעֲ"פ כֵּן אֵינִי בִּנְךָ. בַּר בְּרָתָךְ אֲנָא. וְאֵין עָלַי לְכַבֶּדְךָ כְּבֵן. **מתני'** בַּפּוֹלְמוֹס. חַיִל שֶׁהֵבִיא אַסְפַּסְיָינוּס עַל יְרוּשָׁלַיִם. עַטְרוֹת חֲתָנִים וְאֵירוּס. מְפָרֵשׁ בַּגְּמָרָא. בַּפּוֹלְמוֹס שֶׁל טִיטוּס. שֶׁהֵבִיא הוּרְקָנוּס אַחֲרִיסְתּוֹבְּלוּס אָחִיו. וּבֵין זֶה לָזֶה הָיוּ חֲמִשִּׁים וּשְׁתַּיִם שָׁנָה, כִּדְאָמַר בְּסֵדֶר עוֹלָם. עַטְרוֹת כַּלּוֹת. מְפָרֵשׁ בַּגְּמָרָא. בַּפּוֹלְמוֹס הָאַחֲרוֹן. הוּא שֶׁל חוּרְבַּן הַבַּיִת, וְשֶׁל טִיטוּס נַמִּי הֲוָה. בְּאַפִּרְיוֹן בְּתוֹךְ הָעִיר. שֶׁהָיוּ מוֹלִיכִין אוֹתָהּ מִבֵּית אָבִיהָ לְבֵית בַּעְלָהּ, וְאַפִּרְיוֹן שֶׁל מְעִילִים וְטַלִּיתּוֹת מוּזְהָבוֹת מוּקָּפוֹת לָהּ. מוֹשְׁלֵי מְשָׁלוֹת. לָתֵת אוֹת אַמַּתְלָא וְטַעַם לַחָכְמָה לִיכָּנֵס בָּהּ בְּשַׁעֲרֵי בִינָה. כְּגוֹן מִמְּשָׁלוֹת שׁוּעָלִים, דְּאָמַר בְּסַנְהֶדְרִין (דף לח:): כִּי הֲוָה דָּרֵישׁ ר"מ בְּפִירְקָא הֲוָה דָּרֵישׁ תִּילְתָּא שְׁמַעְתָּא, וְתִילְתָּא אַגַּדְתָּא, וְתִילְתָּא מַתְלֵי. שַׁקְדָנִים. שׁוֹקְדִין עַל דַּלְתוֹת בֵּית הַמִּדְרָשׁ לַיְלָה וָיוֹם, כִּדְאָמַר בִּיבָמוֹת (דף סג:): אֲבָל מָה אֶעֱשֶׂה שֶׁנַּפְשִׁי חָשְׁקָה בַּתּוֹרָה. הַדַּרְשָׁנִים. שֶׁהָיָה בָּקִי בְּטַעֲמֵי הַמִּקְרָאוֹת, כִּדְאָמַר: לֹא זָכִיתִי שֶׁתֵּאָמֵר יְצִיאַת מִצְרַיִם בַּלֵּילוֹת עַד שֶׁדְּרָשָׁהּ בֶּן זוֹמָא (ברכות דף יב:). בָּטַל כְּבוֹד תּוֹרָה. שֶׁהָיָה נוֹתֵן לִבּוֹ לִדְרוֹשׁ כָּל קוֹץ וְקוֹץ שֶׁל כָּל אוֹת, וְכ"ש תֵּיבוֹת יְתֵירוֹת וְאוֹתִיּוֹת יְתֵירוֹת, כְּגוֹן "בַּת" "וּבַת" אֲנִי דּוֹרֵשׁ (סנהדרין דף נא:). וְזֶהוּ כְּבוֹד תּוֹרָה גָּדוֹל, שֶׁאֵין בָּהּ דָּבָר לְבַטָּלָה. אַנְשֵׁי מַעֲשֶׂה. בָּטוּחַ בַּחֲשִׁיבוּתוֹ וְעוֹשֶׂה מַעֲשִׂים מוּפְלָאִים. כִּדְאָמַר בְּתַעֲנִית (דף כה.): נִמְטֵי כְּשׁוּרַיִךְ, יֹאמַר לַחוֹמֶץ וְיִדְלוֹק, וְלָעִזִּים לְהָבִיא זְאֵבִים בְּקַרְנֵיהֶם. קַטְנוּתָם שֶׁל חֲסִידִים. שֶׁהָיוּ הַחֲסִידִים הוֹלְכִים וְכָלִים, וְהוּא הָיָה מִקְטַנֵּיהֶם וְסוֹפָן. זִיו הַחָכְמָה. זֶה לֹא יָדַעְנָא מַאי הִיא. מִשֶּׁמֵּת ר"ג הַזָּקֵן בָּטַל כְּבוֹד הַתּוֹרָה. בְּמַסֶּכֶת מְגִילָּה (דף כא.) אָמַר: שֶׁעַד שֶׁמֵּת הוּא הָיָה בְּרִיאוּת בָּעוֹלָם, וְלֹא הָיוּ לְמֵידִין תּוֹרָה אֶלָּא מְעוּמָּד. מִשֶּׁמֵּת הוּא – יָרַד חוֹלִי לָעוֹלָם, וְהוּצְרְכוּ לִלְמוֹד תּוֹרָה מְיוּשָּׁב. בָּטַל זִיו הַכְּהוּנָּה. שֶׁהָיָה חָכָם וְעָשִׁיר, וְכֹהֲנִים רַבִּים אוֹכְלִין עַל שׁוּלְחָנוֹ. וּבְנֵי חוֹרִין. מְיוּחָסִין. חָפוּ רֹאשָׁם. שֶׁגָּבְרָה יַד עַזֵּי פָנִים מַמְזֵרִים, שֶׁהֵם עֲשִׁירִים וְאֵלּוּ עֲנִיִּים. נִדַּלְדְּלוּ אַנְשֵׁי מַעֲשֶׂה. אֵין חָשׁ לָהֶם. וְאֵין דּוֹרֵשׁ. לְיִשְׂרָאֵל. וְאֵין מְבַקֵּשׁ. עֲלֵיהֶם רַחֲמִים. שָׁרוּ חַכִּימַיָּא. הִתְחִילוּ הַחֲכָמִים. סָפְרַיָּא. מְלַמְּדֵי תִינוֹקוֹת, שֶׁהֵם קְטַנִּים מִן הַחֲכָמִים. כְּעַמָּא דְּאַרְעָא. כְּעַמֵּי הָאָרֶץ.

נה א מיי' פ"ה מהל' תענית הלכה טו סמג עשין מד"ס ג טוש"ע א"ח סימן תקס סעיף ז:

הגהות הב"ח
(א) גמ' ונתן לכם אדני לחם צר: (ב) רש"י ד"ה אחד וכו' סימן למיתה איכא וגלות:

גליון הש"ס
מתני' יוונית. עיין תוספות מנחות דף סד ע"ב ד"ה ארור וכר"ש פ"א מ"א דפאה: **שם** משמת רבי בטל ענוה. עיין תוספות כתובות דף קג ע"ב ד"ה אותו יום:

אָזְלָא *וְדַלְדְּלָה, וְאֵין שׁוֹאֵל וְאֵין מְבַקֵּשׁ, עַל מִי יֵשׁ לְהִשָּׁעֵן – עַל אָבִינוּ שֶׁבַּשָּׁמַיִם. *בְּעִקְבוֹת מְשִׁיחָא חוּצְפָּא יִסְגֵּא, *וְיוֹקֶר יַאֲמִיר, הַגֶּפֶן תִּתֵּן פִּרְיָהּ, וְהַיַּיִן בְּיוֹקֶר, וּמַלְכוּת תֵּהָפֵךְ לְמִינוּת, וְאֵין תּוֹכַחַת. בֵּית וַעַד יִהְיֶה לִזְנוּת, וְהַגָּלִיל יֶחֱרַב, וְהַגַּבְלָן יִשּׁוֹם, וְאַנְשֵׁי הַגְּבוּל יְסוֹבְבוּ מֵעִיר לְעִיר וְלֹא יְחוֹנָּנוּ, וְחָכְמוֹת סוֹפְרִים תִּסְרַח, וְיִרְאֵי חֵטְא יִמָּאֲסוּ, וְהָאֱמֶת תְּהֵא נֶעְדֶּרֶת. *נְעָרִים פְּנֵי זְקֵנִים יַלְבִּינוּ, *זְקֵנִים יַעַמְדוּ מִפְּנֵי קְטַנִּים, בֵּן מְנַוֵּל אָב, בַּת קָמָה בְּאִמָּהּ, כַּלָּה בַּחֲמוֹתָהּ, אוֹיְבֵי אִישׁ אַנְשֵׁי בֵיתוֹ, פְּנֵי הַדּוֹר כִּפְנֵי הַכֶּלֶב, הַבֵּן אֵינוֹ מִתְבַּיֵּישׁ מֵאָבִיו, וְעַל מָה יֵשׁ לָנוּ לְהִשָּׁעֵן – עַל אָבִינוּ שֶׁבַּשָּׁמַיִם.§

(גמ') אָמַר רַב: לֹא שָׁנוּ אֶלָּא שֶׁל מֶלַח וְגָפְרִית, אֲבָל שֶׁל הֲדַס וְשֶׁל וֶרֶד – מוּתָּר. וּשְׁמוּאֵל אוֹמֵר: אַף שֶׁל הֲדַס וְשֶׁל וֶרֶד אָסוּר, שֶׁל קָנִים וְשֶׁל חֵילֶת מוּתָּר. וְלֵוִי אָמַר: [א]אַף שֶׁל קָנִים וְשֶׁל חֵילֶת אָסוּר. וְכֵן תָּנֵי לֵוִי בְּמַתְנִיתֵיהּ: אַף שֶׁל קָנִים וְשֶׁל חֵילֶת אָסוּר.§ "וְעַל הָאִירוּס".§ מַאי אִירוּס? א"ר אֶלְעָזָר: טַבְלָא דְּחַד פּוּמָא. רַבָּה בַּר רַב הוּנָא עֲבַד לֵיהּ לִבְרֵיהּ טַנְבּוּרָא. אֲתָא אֲבוּהּ תַּבְרֵיהּ, אֲמַר לֵיהּ: מִיחֲלַף בְּטַבְלָא דְּחַד פּוּמָא. זִיל עֲבִיד לֵיהּ אַפּוּמָא דְּחַצְבָא, אוֹ אַפּוּמָא דְּקַפִּיזָא.§ "בַּפּוּלְמוּס שֶׁל טִיטוּס גָּזְרוּ עַל עַטְרוֹת כַּלּוֹת" וכו'.§ מַאי עַטְרוֹת כַּלּוֹת? אָמַר רַבָּה בַּר בַּר חָנָה אָמַר ר' יוֹחָנָן: עִיר שֶׁל זָהָב. תַּנְיָא נַמִי הָכִי: [ב]אֵיזֶהוּ עַטְרוֹת כַּלּוֹת – עִיר שֶׁל זָהָב. אֲבָל עוֹשֶׂה אוֹתָהּ כִּיפָּה שֶׁל מֵילָת. תָּנָא: אַף עַל חוּפַּת חֲתָנִים גָּזְרוּ. מַאי חוּפַּת חֲתָנִים? זְהוֹרִית הַמּוּזְהֶבוֹת. תַּנְיָא נַמִי הָכִי: *אֵלּוּ הֵן חוּפַּת חֲתָנִים – זְהוֹרִית הַמּוּזְהָבוֹת, אֲבָל עוֹשֶׂה פַּפִּירִית וְתוֹלֶה בָּהּ כָּל מַה שֶּׁיִּרְצֶה.§ "וְשֶׁלֹּא יְלַמֵּד אֶת בְּנוֹ יְוָנִית".§ *ת"ר: כְּשֶׁצָּרוּ מַלְכֵי בֵית חַשְׁמוֹנַאי זֶה עַל זֶה הָיָה הוֹרְקָנוֹס מִבַּחוּץ וְאַרִיסְטוֹבְלוֹס מִבִּפְנִים. בְּכָל יוֹם וָיוֹם הָיוּ מְשַׁלְשְׁלִין דִּינָרִים בְּקוּפָּה וּמַעֲלִין לָהֶן תְּמִידִים. הָיָה שָׁם זָקֵן אֶחָד שֶׁהָיָה מַכִּיר בְּחָכְמַת יְוָנִית. לָעַז לָהֶם בְּחָכְמַת יְוָנִית, אָמַר לָהֶן: כׇּל זְמַן שֶׁעוֹסְקִים בַּעֲבוֹדָה – אֵין נִמְסָרִין בְּיֶדְכֶם. לְמָחָר שִׁלְשְׁלוּ לָהֶם דִּינָרִים בְּקוּפָּה וְהֶעֱלוּ לָהֶם חֲזִיר. כֵּיוָן שֶׁהִגִּיעַ לַחֲצִי חוֹמָה נָעַץ צִפָּרְנָיו (א) – נִזְדַּעְזְעָה א"י אַרְבַּע מֵאוֹת פַּרְסָה. אוֹתָהּ שָׁעָה [ג]אָמְרוּ: אָרוּר אָדָם שֶׁיְּגַדֵּל חֲזִירִים, וְאָרוּר אָדָם שֶׁיְּלַמֵּד לִבְנוֹ חָכְמַת יְוָנִית. וְעַל אוֹתָהּ שָׁנָה שָׁנִינוּ: מַעֲשֶׂה וּבָא עוֹמֶר מִגַּגּוֹת צְרִיפִים, וּשְׁתֵּי הַלֶּחֶם מִבִּקְעַת עֵין סוֹכֵר. אִינִי?! וְהָאָמַר רַבִּי: בְּא"י לָשׁוֹן סוּרְסִי לָמָּה? אֶלָּא אִי לְשׁוֹן הַקֹּדֶשׁ אִי לָשׁוֹן יְוָנִית. וְאָמַר *רַב יוֹסֵף: בְּבָבֶל לָשׁוֹן אֲרַמִּי לָמָּה? אֶלָּא אוֹ לְשׁוֹן הַקֹּדֶשׁ אוֹ לְשׁוֹן פַּרְסִי! לְשׁוֹן יְוָנִית לְחוּד וְחָכְמַת יְוָנִית לְחוּד. וְחָכְמַת יְוָנִית מִי אֲסִירָא? *וְהָאָמַר רַב יְהוּדָה אָמַר שְׁמוּאֵל מִשּׁוּם *רשב"ג: מַאי דִּכְתִיב: °"עֵינִי עוֹלְלָה לְנַפְשִׁי מִכֹּל בְּנוֹת עִירִי" – אֶלֶף יְלָדִים הָיוּ בְּבֵית אַבָּא, חֲמֵשׁ מֵאוֹת לָמְדוּ תּוֹרָה, וַחֲמֵשׁ מֵאוֹת לָמְדוּ חָכְמַת יְוָנִית, וְלֹא נִשְׁתַּיֵּיר מֵהֶן אֶלָּא אֲנִי כָּאן, וּבֶן אֲחִי אַבָּא בְּעַסְיָא. שָׁאנֵי שֶׁל בֵּית ר"ג, דִּקְרוֹבִין לַמַּלְכוּת הֲווּ. דְּתַנְיָא: [ד]הַמְסַפֵּר קוֹמֵי – הֲרֵי זֶה מִדַּרְכֵי הָאֱמוֹרִי. אַבְטוּלְמוֹס בֶּן רְאוּבֵן [ה]הִתִּירוּ (ב) לְסַפֵּר קוֹמֵי, שֶׁהוּא קָרוֹב לַמַּלְכוּת. שֶׁל בֵּית רַבָּן גַּמְלִיאֵל הִתִּירוּ לָהֶן חָכְמַת יְוָנִית מִפְּנֵי שֶׁקְּרוֹבִין לַמַּלְכוּת.§ "בַּפּוּלְמוּס הָאַחֲרוֹן גָּזְרוּ שֶׁלֹּא תֵּצֵא כַּלָּה בָּאַפִּרְיוֹן" וכו'.§ מ"ט – מִשּׁוּם צְנִיעוּתָא.§ "מִשֶּׁמֵּת רַבָּן יוֹחָנָן בָּטְלָה הַחָכְמָה".§ ת"ר: *מִשֶּׁמֵּת רַבִּי אֱלִיעֶזֶר נִגְנַז ס"ת, מִשֶּׁמֵּת רַבִּי יְהוֹשֻׁעַ בָּטְלָה עֵצָה וּמַחֲשָׁבָה, מִשֶּׁמֵּת ר"ע בָּטְלוּ זְרוֹעֵי תוֹרָה וְנִסְתַּתְּמוּ מַעַיְינוֹת הַחָכְמָה, מִשֶּׁמֵּת רַבִּי אֶלְעָזָר בֶּן עֲזַרְיָה בָּטְלוּ עַטְרוֹת חָכְמָה, °שֶׁ"עֲטֶרֶת חֲכָמִים עָשְׁרָם". מִשֶּׁמֵּת רַבִּי חֲנִינָא בֶּן דּוֹסָא בָּטְלוּ אַנְשֵׁי מַעֲשֶׂה, מִשֶּׁמֵּת אַבָּא יוֹסֵי בֶּן קְטוּנְתָּא בָּטְלוּ חֲסִידִים, וְלָמָּה נִקְרָא שְׁמוֹ אַבָּא יוֹסֵי בֶּן קְטוּנְתָּא – שֶׁהָיָה מִקְּטַנֵּי חֲסִידִים. מִשֶּׁמֵּת בֶּן עַזַּאי בָּטְלוּ הַשַּׁקְדָנִין, מִשֶּׁמֵּת בֶּן זוֹמָא בָּטְלוּ הַדַּרְשָׁנִין, מִשֶּׁמֵּת רשב"ג עָלָה גּוֹבַאי וְרַבּוּ צָרוֹת, מִשֶּׁמֵּת רַבִּי הוּכְפְּלוּ צָרוֹת.§ "מִשֶּׁמֵּת רַבִּי בָּטְלָה עֲנָוָה וְיִרְאַת חֵטְא".§ אֲמַר לֵיהּ רַב יוֹסֵף לְתַנָּא: לָא תִּיתְנֵי עֲנָוָה, דְּאִיכָּא אֲנָא. [ו]אֲמַר לֵיהּ רַב נַחְמָן לְתַנָּא: לָא תִּיתְנֵי יִרְאַת חֵטְא, דְּאִיכָּא אֲנָא.§

הדרן עלך עגלה ערופה וסליקא לה מסכת סוטה

יש נוסחאות כתוב במשנה מאמר זה (אכן התי"ט האריך להוכיח דליתא במשנה אלא בברייתא בע"ז דף כ:)

*רבי פנחס בן יאיר אומר (ס"א זהירות מביא לידי זריזות) וזריזות מביא לידי נקיות ונקיות מביאה לידי טהרה וטהרה מביאה לידי פרישות ופרישות מביאה לידי קדושה וקדושה מביאה לידי ענוה וענוה מביאה לידי יראת חטא ויראת חטא מביאה לידי חסידות וחסידות מביאה לידי רוח הקודש ורוח הקודש מביאה לידי תחיית המתים ותחיית המתים בא ע"י אליהו הנביא ז"ל במהרה בימינו יבא ויגאלנו כיר"א.§

[עמ"ש בס"ד על גליון ע"ז כ: עיקר הנוסחא ועיין עוד בירושלמי שקלים פרק ג דף ו עמוד א' דדריש לכל הנהו מקרא ואז תבין יסוד מאמר הלזה]

רש"י

אָזְלָא וְנַוְולָא. הוֹלְכִים וְדָלִים וּמִתְנַוְּולִים. בְּעִקְבוֹת הַמָּשִׁיחַ. בְּסוֹף הַגָּלוּת, לִפְנֵי בִּיאַת מָשִׁיחַ. וְהַיַּיִן בְּיוֹקֶר. שֶׁהַכֹּל עוֹסְקִין בְּמִשְׁתָּאוֹת. *וְאֵין תּוֹכָחָה. אֵין לְךָ אָדָם שֶׁיּוּכַל לְהוֹכִיחַ, שֶׁכּוּלָּם נִכְשָׁלִים בַּחֲטָאוֹת, וּכְשֶׁמּוֹכִיחִין אוֹמֵר לוֹ: אַתָּה כָּמוֹנִי. וּבֵית הַוַּעַד. שֶׁל חֲכָמִים יִהְיוּ לְבֵית זְנוּת, שֶׁכָּלוּ הַחֲכָמִים וְאֵין לוֹמֵד תּוֹרָה, וִיהֵא חָרֵב מֵאֵין אִישׁ, וּבַעֲלֵי זִימָּה מִתְגּוֹדְדִים שָׁם. מִפְּנֵי שֶׁחוּץ לָעִיר הָיוּ בָּתֵּי מִדְרָשׁוֹת שֶׁלָּהֶם.

גמ' שֶׁל מֶלַח וְשֶׁל גָּפְרִית. עִנְיַן עֲטָרָה: עוֹשִׂין מֵאֶבֶן שֶׁל מֶלַח שֶׁהוּא צָלוּל כְּאֶבֶן הַבְּדוֹלַח, וְקוֹרִין שלייממי"א, וְצוֹבְעִין אוֹתָהּ כְּמִין צִיּוּרִין בְּגָפְרִית, כְּשֵׁם שֶׁעוֹשִׂין בִּכְלֵי זָהָב וָכֶסֶף, וְקוֹרִין נאול"א. חֵילֶת. ליסק"א, כְּמִין גּוֹמֶא הַגָּדֵל בַּמַּיִם. טַבְלָא דְּחַד פּוּמָא. זוּג שֶׁל עִינְבָּל אֶחָד, שֶׁמְּקַשְׁקְשִׁין בּוֹ לְשִׁיר בְּבֵית הַמִּשְׁתָּאוֹת. טַנְבּוּרָא. כָּךְ קוֹרִין אוֹתוֹ בִּלְשׁוֹן לַעַז – טַנְבּוּר. וְהוּא עָשׂוּי דָּפְנוֹתָיו עֲגוּלוֹת כְּעֵין נָפָה, וְקוֹשְׁרִין בְּדָפְנוֹתָיו חוּטִין שֶׁל בַּרְזֶל, וְשׁוֹטְחִין עַל פִּיו עוֹר כְּשֶׁהוּא לַח, וּמוֹתֵחַ, וְהוּא מִתְיַיבֵּשׁ שָׁם מֵאֵלָיו. וּכְשֶׁמַּכִּין עָלָיו בְּמַקֵּל דַּק הוּא מוֹצִיא קוֹל צָלוּל. וְיֵשׁ אוּמָּנִין שֶׁיּוֹדְעִין לְהַכּוֹת עָלָיו מַכָּה אַחַר מַכָּה כַּסֵּדֶר, עַד שֶׁנִּשְׁמַע כְּמִין שִׁיר. מִיחֲלַף בְּטַבְלָא דְּחַד פּוּמָא. זוּג שֶׁל עִינְבָּל שֶׁעוֹשִׂים בְּבֵית מִשְׁתָּאוֹת. דּוֹמֶה לוֹ בְּקוֹל, וְאָתֵי לְמֶעֱבַד הַהוּא דִּגְזוּר עֲלֵיהּ. קַפִּיזָא. כְּלִי מַחֲזִיק ג' לוּגִּין. עִיר שֶׁל זָהָב. עֲטָרָה שֶׁל זָהָב וְעִיר שֶׁל זָהָב מְצוּיֶּרֶת עָלֶיהָ. כִּיפָּה. כְּמוֹ כּוֹבַע שֶׁל צֶמֶר לָבָן שֶׁקּוֹרִין פילטר"א. זְהוֹרִית הַמּוּזְהָבוֹת. טַלִּית צְבוּעָה שָׁנִי, וּבוֹ קְבוּעִין טַסֵּי זָהָב עַד שֶׁמַּעֲמִידִין אוֹתָהּ כְּמִין כִּיפָּה. אֲבָל עוֹשֶׂה הוּא פַּפִּירִית. כְּמִין כִּיפָּה שֶׁל מַעְגְּלֵי עֵץ כְּמוֹ שֶׁאָנוּ עוֹשִׂין, וְתוֹלִין בָּהּ צְנִיפִין וּרְדִידֵי זָהָב, כְּמוֹ שֶׁאָנוּ עוֹשִׂין. חָכְמַת יְוָנִית. לָשׁוֹן חָכְמָה שֶׁמְּדַבְּרִים בּוֹ בְּנֵי פַּלָּטִין, וְאֵין שְׁאָר הָעָם מַכִּירִין בּוֹ. מַלְכֵי בֵּית חַשְׁמוֹנַאי. שְׁנֵי אַחִים שֶׁהָיוּ מִתְקוֹטְטִין עַל הַמְּלוּכָה, הוֹרְקָנוֹס וַאֲרִיסְטוֹבְּלוֹס. הָיָה הוֹרְקָנוֹס מִבַּחוּץ. צָר עַל יְרוּשָׁלַיִם, וְהֵבִיא עִמּוֹ חֵיל רוֹמִיִּים. מְשַׁלְשְׁלִים לָהֶם דִּינָרֵי כֶסֶף בְּקוּפָּה. מִתְּרוּמַת הַלִּשְׁכָּה לִתְמִידִים.

הָיָה שָׁם זָקֵן אֶחָד. מִבִּפְנִים. לָעַז לָהֶם. לְאוֹתָן שֶׁבַּחוּץ. נָעַץ צִפָּרְנָיו נִזְדַּעְזְעָה. מֵחֲמַת הַמֶּלֶךְ, שֶׁנִּצְטַעֲרָה עַל חִילּוּל שְׁמוֹ. וְעַל אוֹתָהּ שָׁנָה שָׁנִינוּ כו'. שֶׁאוֹתָהּ שָׁנָה הֶחֱרִיבוּ הַחַיָּילוֹת אֶת הַזְּרָעִים שֶׁסְּבִיבוֹת מְדִינַת יְרוּשָׁלַיִם, וְהוּצְרַךְ לְהָבִיא אוֹתָהּ שָׁנָה אֶת הָעוֹמֶר מִגַּגּוֹת צְרִיפִים. וּבִשְׁאָר הַשָּׁנִים מִצְוַת הָעוֹמֶר לְהָבִיא מִן הַקָּרוֹב לִירוּשָׁלַיִם, כִּדִכְתִיב (ויקרא כג): "כַּרְמֶל (ג) תַּקְרִיבוּ" – שֶׁיְּהֵא הַזֶּרַע לַח וְהַכַּר מָלֵא מִמֶּנּוּ. וּכְשֶׁהוּא בָּא מֵרָחוֹק מִתְיַיבֵּשׁ וּמִתְמָעֵךְ, וְאֵין כַּר הַשִּׁבֹּלֶת מָלֵא מִן הַגַּרְעִין. לָשׁוֹן סוּרְסִי. קָרוֹב הוּא לִלְשׁוֹן אֲרַמִּי. וְאוֹמֵר אֲנִי שֶׁזֶּה לְשׁוֹן גְּמָרַת יְרוּשַׁלְמִי, וְאוּמּוֹת הָעוֹלָם קוֹרִין אוֹתוֹ לינג"א סוריי"א. אוֹ לְשׁוֹן יְוָנִי. שֶׁהָיוּ קְרוֹבִין לְאֶרֶץ יָוָן, וּלְשׁוֹן יָוָן יָפֶה מִזֶּה, וְהָיָה לוֹ לְסַפֵּר בּוֹ: מַאי דִּכְתִיב – לֹא גָּרַס, אֶלָּא ר"ש קָרָא מִקְרָא זֶה עַל עַצְמוֹ וְאָמַר שֶׁעָלָיו לְעוֹלֵל אֶת עֵינָיו בִּבְכִי יוֹתֵר מִן הַכֹּל. עוֹלְלָה. מְנַוֶּולֶת אֶת (ד) עֵינַי. לְנַפְשִׁי. עַל נַפְשִׁי, מִפְּנֵי קוֹרוֹתַי. מְסַפֵּר קוֹמֵי. שְׂעָרוֹ שֶׁלְּפָנָיו, וּמַנִּיחַ בְּלוֹרִית מֵאֲחוֹרָיו. מִדַּרְכֵי הָאֱמוֹרִי. שֶׁהֵן מַנִּיחִין בְּלוֹרִית לְשֵׁם עֲבוֹדָה זָרָה. נִגְנַז סֵפֶר תּוֹרָה. שֶׁהָיָה בַּעַל הֲלָכוֹת מִפִּי שְׁמוּעָה הַרְבֵּה, וּסְדוּרוֹת בְּפִיו כְּאִילּוּ כָּתוּב בְּסֵפֶר. כִּדְאָמַר בְּסַנְהֶדְרִין (דף סח.): הַרְבֵּה תּוֹרָה לָמַדְתִּי מֵרַבּוֹתַי, וְלֹא עוֹד, אֶלָּא שֶׁאֲנִי שׁוֹנֶה שְׁלֹשֶׁת אֲלָפִים הֲלָכוֹת בִּנְטִיעוֹת קִישּׁוּאִין, וּשְׁלֹשׁ מֵאוֹת בְּבַהֶרֶת עַזָּה. עֵצָה וּמַחֲשָׁבָה. שֶׁהָיָה זָהִיר בִּדְרָשׁוֹת, וּבָקִי בַּהֲלָכוֹת וּבִתְשׁוּבַת הָאֶפִּיקוֹרְסִים וּלְהָבִין בִּרְמִיזוֹתָם, כִּדְאָמְרִי' בְּפ"ק דַּחֲגִיגָה (דף ה:): כִּי נָח נַפְשֵׁיהּ אָמְרוּ לֵיהּ רַבָּנַן: מַאי תֶּהֱוֵי עֲלָן מִמִּינִים? אָמַר לָהֶן: אָבְדָה עֵצָה מִבְּנֵי יִשְׂרָאֵל – נִסְרְחָה חָכְמָה שֶׁל אוּמּוֹת הָעוֹלָם. זְרוֹעֵי תוֹרָה. עוֹמֶק סְבָרָא וְלִסְמוֹךְ טַעֲמֵי תוֹרָה שֶׁבְּעַל פֶּה עַל מִדְרְשֵׁי הַמִּקְרָאוֹת וְאוֹתִיּוֹת הַיְתֵרִים וּלְשׁוֹנוֹת הַמִּשְׁתַּנִּים בַּמִּקְרָא. רַבִּי אֶלְעָזָר בֶּן עֲזַרְיָה. עָשִׁיר הוּא כִּדְאָמְרִי' (שבת דף נד:): תְּרֵיסַר אַלְפֵי עֶגְלֵי הֲוָה מְעַשֵּׂר מֵעֶדְרֵיהּ כׇּל שַׁתָּא. דְּאִיכָּא אֲנָא. שֶׁאֲנִי עַנְוְתָן.

הדרן עלך עגלה ערופה וסליקא לה מסכת סוטה

עין משפט נר מצוה

(והמלכות. השולטת על רוב העולם תהא למינות נמשכים אחר טעות שלו ותלמידיו נקראו מינים העתק מדפוס אמשטרדם ישן)

נו א ב מיי' פ"ה מהלכ' תענית הלכה טו סמג עשין מד"ס ג טוש"ע א"ח סימן תקס סעיף ד:

נז ג מיי' פ"ה מהל' כ"מ הלכה ט סמג עשין סו טוש"ע ח"מ סי' תט סעיף ב:

נח ד מיי' פי"א מהל' ע"ז הלכה א סמג לאוין נ טוש"ע יו"ד סי' קעח סעיף א:

נט ה מיי' שם הלכה ג טוש"ע שם סעיף ב:

רש"א מ"ז

הגהות הב"ח

(א) גמ' נעץ צפרניו בחומה נזדעזעה א"י ד' מאות פרסה על ד' מאות פרסה אותה שעה כצ"ל וכן ברש"י: (ב) שם התירו לו לספר קומי: (ג) רש"י ד"ה ועל אותה וכו' לירושלים כדכתיב כרמל תקריב נ"ב עיין במנחות דף ס"ד: (ד) ד"ה עוללה מנוולת את עיני לנפשי:

גליון הש"ס

גמ' א"ל רב נחמן לתנא לא תיתני. עיין מגילה דף כח ע"ב רש"י ד"ה רנב"י:

[עי' תוס' ע"ז לב. ד"ה (ונ"ל)]

[תוס' פט"ו]

מסורת הש"ס

[גי' ע"י ומנוולה וכ"ה ברש"י שלפנינו]

סנהדרין לז.

ס"א והיוקר יעוות [עי' סנהדרין לז: ובפרש"י שם]

[בע"י הגירסא גדולים]

[תוס' פט"ו ע"ש]

ב"ק פב: מנחות סד:

[נ"ל רבי יוסי]

ב"ק פג. [גיטין נח. ע"ש ונ"ע ולפי גירסת רש"י ניחא]

איכה ג

משלי יד

The following קדיש requires the presence of a מנין.

יִתְגַּדַּל וְיִתְקַדַּשׁ שְׁמֵהּ רַבָּא
בְּעָלְמָא דְּהוּא עָתִיד לְאִתְחַדָּתָא
וּלְאַחְיָאָה מֵתַיָּא, וּלְאַסָּקָא יָתְהוֹן לְחַיֵּי עָלְמָא
וּלְמִבְנֵא קַרְתָּא דִירוּשְׁלֵם, וּלְשַׁכְלָלָא הֵיכְלֵהּ בְּגַוַּהּ
וּלְמֶעְקַר פָּלְחָנָא נֻכְרָאָה מֵאַרְעָא
וְלַאֲתָבָא פָּלְחָנָא דִשְׁמַיָּא לְאַתְרֵהּ
וְיַמְלִיךְ קֻדְשָׁא בְּרִיךְ הוּא בְּמַלְכוּתֵהּ וִיקָרֵהּ
(נוסח ספרד: וְיַצְמַח פֻּרְקָנֵהּ וִיקָרֵב מְשִׁיחֵהּ)
בְּחַיֵּיכוֹן וּבְיוֹמֵיכוֹן וּבְחַיֵּי דְכָל בֵּית יִשְׂרָאֵל
בַּעֲגָלָא וּבִזְמַן קָרִיב, וְאִמְרוּ אָמֵן.

יְהֵא שְׁמֵהּ רַבָּא מְבָרַךְ לְעָלַם וּלְעָלְמֵי עָלְמַיָּא.

יִתְבָּרַךְ וְיִשְׁתַּבַּח וְיִתְפָּאַר וְיִתְרוֹמַם וְיִתְנַשֵּׂא
וְיִתְהַדָּר וְיִתְעַלֶּה וְיִתְהַלָּל
שְׁמֵהּ דְּקֻדְשָׁא בְּרִיךְ הוּא
לְעֵלָּא מִן כָּל בִּרְכָתָא
/ בעשרת ימי תשובה: לְעֵלָּא לְעֵלָּא מִכָּל בִּרְכָתָא/
וְשִׁירָתָא, תֻּשְׁבְּחָתָא וְנֶחֱמָתָא, דַּאֲמִירָן בְּעָלְמָא
וְאִמְרוּ אָמֵן. (קהל: אָמֵן)

עַל יִשְׂרָאֵל וְעַל רַבָּנָן
וְעַל תַּלְמִידֵיהוֹן וְעַל כָּל תַּלְמִידֵי תַלְמִידֵיהוֹן
וְעַל כָּל מָאן דְּעָסְקִין בְּאוֹרַיְתָא
דִּי בְּאַתְרָא (בארץ ישראל: קַדִּישָׁא) הָדֵין, וְדִי בְּכָל אֲתַר וַאֲתַר
יְהֵא לְהוֹן וּלְכוֹן שְׁלָמָא רַבָּא
חִנָּא וְחִסְדָּא, וְרַחֲמֵי, וְחַיֵּי אֲרִיכֵי, וּמְזוֹנֵי רְוִיחֵי
וּפֻרְקָנָא מִן קֳדָם אֲבוּהוֹן דִּי בִשְׁמַיָּא
וְאִמְרוּ אָמֵן.

יְהֵא שְׁלָמָא רַבָּא מִן שְׁמַיָּא
וְחַיִּים (טוֹבִים) עָלֵינוּ וְעַל כָּל יִשְׂרָאֵל
וְאִמְרוּ אָמֵן.

Bow, take three steps back, as if taking leave of the Divine Presence, then bow, first left, then right, then center, while saying:

עֹשֶׂה שָׁלוֹם/ בעשרת ימי תשובה: הַשָּׁלוֹם/ בִּמְרוֹמָיו
הוּא יַעֲשֶׂה בְרַחֲמָיו שָׁלוֹם, עָלֵינוּ וְעַל כָּל יִשְׂרָאֵל
וְאִמְרוּ אָמֵן.

The following Kaddish requires the presence of a minyan.

Magnified and sanctified may His great name be,
in the world that will in future be renewed,
reviving the dead and raising them up to eternal life.
He will rebuild the city of Jerusalem
and in it re-establish His Temple.
He will remove alien worship from the earth
and restore to its place the worship of Heaven.
Then the Holy One, blessed be He,
will reign in His sovereignty and splendor.
May it be in your lifetime and in your days,
(*Nusaḥ Sepharad:* make His salvation flourish,
and hasten His messiah,)
and in the lifetime of all the House of Israel,
swiftly and soon – and say: Amen.

May His great name be blessed for ever and all time.

Blessed and praised,
glorified and exalted,
raised and honored,
uplifted and lauded
be the name of the Holy One,
blessed be He,
beyond any blessing,
song, praise and consolation uttered in the world –
and say: Amen.

To Israel, to the teachers,
their disciples and their disciples' disciples,
and to all who engage in the study of Torah,
in this (*in Israel add:* holy) place or elsewhere,
may there come to them and you great peace,
grace, kindness and compassion,
long life, ample sustenance and deliverance,
from their Father in Heaven –
and say: Amen.

May there be great peace from heaven,
and (good) life for us and all Israel –
and say: Amen.

Bow, take three steps back, as if taking leave of the Divine Presence, then bow, first left, then right, then center, while saying:

May He who makes peace in His high places,
in His compassion make peace for us and all Israel –
and say: Amen.

The following paragraph is recited three times:

הַדְרָן עֲלָךְ מַסֶּכֶת סוֹטָה וְהַדְרָךְ עֲלָן, דַּעְתָּן עֲלָךְ מַסֶּכֶת סוֹטָה וְדַעְתָּךְ עֲלָן, לָא נִתְנְשֵׁי מִנָּךְ מַסֶּכֶת סוֹטָה וְלָא תִתְנְשֵׁי מִנָּן, לָא בְּעָלְמָא הָדֵין וְלָא בְּעָלְמָא דְאָתֵי.

יְהִי רָצוֹן מִלְּפָנֶיךָ יהוה אֱלֹהֵינוּ וֵאלֹהֵי אֲבוֹתֵינוּ, שֶׁתְּהֵא תּוֹרָתְךָ אֻמָּנוּתֵנוּ בָּעוֹלָם הַזֶּה, וּתְהֵא עִמָּנוּ לָעוֹלָם הַבָּא. חֲנִינָא בַּר פַּפָּא, רָמֵי בַּר פַּפָּא, נַחְמָן בַּר פַּפָּא, אֲחַאי בַּר פַּפָּא, אַבָּא מָרִי בַּר פַּפָּא, רַפְרָם בַּר פַּפָּא, רָכִישׁ בַּר פַּפָּא, סוּרְחַב בַּר פַּפָּא, אַדָּא בַּר פַּפָּא, דָּרוּ בַּר פַּפָּא.

הַעֲרֶב נָא יהוה אֱלֹהֵינוּ אֶת דִּבְרֵי תוֹרָתְךָ בְּפִינוּ וּבְפִי עַמְּךָ בֵּית יִשְׂרָאֵל, וְנִהְיֶה אֲנַחְנוּ וְצֶאֱצָאֵינוּ (וְצֶאֱצָאֵי צֶאֱצָאֵינוּ) וְצֶאֱצָאֵי עַמְּךָ בֵּית יִשְׂרָאֵל, כֻּלָּנוּ יוֹדְעֵי
שְׁמֶךָ וְלוֹמְדֵי תוֹרָתְךָ לִשְׁמָהּ. מֵאֹיְבַי תְּחַכְּמֵנִי מִצְוֹתֶךָ תהלים קיט
כִּי לְעוֹלָם הִיא־לִי: יְהִי־לִבִּי תָמִים בְּחֻקֶּיךָ לְמַעַן לֹא אֵבוֹשׁ: לְעוֹלָם לֹא־אֶשְׁכַּח פִּקּוּדֶיךָ כִּי־בָם חִיִּיתָנִי: בָּרוּךְ אַתָּה יהוה לַמְּדֵנִי חֻקֶּיךָ: אָמֵן אָמֵן אָמֵן סֶלָה וָעֶד.

מוֹדִים אֲנַחְנוּ לְפָנֶיךָ יהוה אֱלֹהֵינוּ וֵאלֹהֵי אֲבוֹתֵינוּ שֶׁשַּׂמְתָּ חֶלְקֵנוּ מִיּוֹשְׁבֵי בֵּית הַמִּדְרָשׁ, וְלֹא שַׂמְתָּ חֶלְקֵנוּ מִיּוֹשְׁבֵי קְרָנוֹת. שֶׁאָנוּ מַשְׁכִּימִים וְהֵם מַשְׁכִּימִים, אָנוּ מַשְׁכִּימִים לְדִבְרֵי תוֹרָה, וְהֵם מַשְׁכִּימִים לִדְבָרִים בְּטֵלִים. אָנוּ עֲמֵלִים וְהֵם עֲמֵלִים, אָנוּ עֲמֵלִים וּמְקַבְּלִים שָׂכָר, וְהֵם עֲמֵלִים וְאֵינָם מְקַבְּלִים שָׂכָר. אָנוּ רָצִים וְהֵם רָצִים, אָנוּ רָצִים לְחַיֵּי הָעוֹלָם הַבָּא, וְהֵם רָצִים לִבְאֵר
שָׁחַת, שֶׁנֶּאֱמַר: וְאַתָּה אֱלֹהִים תּוֹרִדֵם לִבְאֵר שַׁחַת תהלים נה
אַנְשֵׁי דָמִים וּמִרְמָה לֹא־יֶחֱצוּ יְמֵיהֶם וַאֲנִי אֶבְטַח־בָּךְ:

יְהִי רָצוֹן מִלְּפָנֶיךָ יהוה אֱלֹהַי, כְּשֵׁם שֶׁעֲזַרְתַּנִי לְסַיֵּם מַסֶּכֶת סוֹטָה כֵּן תְּעַזְּרֵנִי לְהַתְחִיל מַסֶּכְתּוֹת וּסְפָרִים אֲחֵרִים וּלְסַיְּמָם, לִלְמֹד וּלְלַמֵּד לִשְׁמֹר וְלַעֲשׂוֹת וּלְקַיֵּם אֶת כָּל דִּבְרֵי תַלְמוּד תּוֹרָתְךָ בְּאַהֲבָה, וּזְכוּת כָּל הַתַּנָּאִים וְאָמוֹרָאִים וְתַלְמִידֵי חֲכָמִים יַעֲמֹד לִי וּלְזַרְעִי שֶׁלֹּא תָמוּשׁ הַתּוֹרָה מִפִּי וּמִפִּי זַרְעִי וְזֶרַע זַרְעִי
עַד עוֹלָם, וְיִתְקַיֵּם בִּי: בְּהִתְהַלֶּכְךָ תַּנְחֶה אֹתָךְ בְּשָׁכְבְּךָ משלי ו
תִּשְׁמֹר עָלֶיךָ וַהֲקִיצוֹתָ הִיא תְשִׂיחֶךָ: כִּי־בִי יִרְבּוּ יָמֶיךָ משלי ט
וְיוֹסִיפוּ לְךָ שְׁנוֹת חַיִּים: אֹרֶךְ יָמִים בִּימִינָהּ בִּשְׂמֹאולָהּ משלי ג
עֹשֶׁר וְכָבוֹד: יהוה עֹז לְעַמּוֹ יִתֵּן יהוה יְבָרֵךְ אֶת־עַמּוֹ תהלים כט
בַשָּׁלוֹם:

The following paragraph is recited three times:

הַדְרָן We shall return to you, tractate *Sota,* and your glory is upon us. Our thoughts are upon you, tractate *Sota,* and your thoughts are upon us. We will not be forgotten from you, tractate *Sota,* and you will not be forgotten from us; neither in this world nor in the World-to-Come.

יְהִי רָצוֹן May it be Your will, Lord our God and God of our ancestors, that Your Torah will be our avocation in this world and will accompany us to the World-to-Come. Ḥanina bar Pappa, Ramei bar Pappa, Naḥman bar Pappa, Aḥai bar Pappa, Abba Mari bar Pappa, Rafram bar Pappa, Rakhish bar Pappa, Surḥav bar Pappa, Adda bar Pappa, Daru bar Pappa.

הַעֲרֶב נָא Please, Lord our God, make the words of Your Torah sweet in our mouths and in the mouths of Your people, the house of Israel, so that we, our descendants (and their descendants), and the descendants of Your people, the house of Israel, may all know Your name and
study Your Torah for its own sake. Your commandments *Psalms 119*
make me wiser than my enemies, for they are ever with me. Let my heart be undivided in Your statutes, in order that I may not be put to shame. I will never forget Your precepts, for with them You have quickened me. Blessed are You, O Lord; teach me Your statutes. Amen, Amen, Amen, Selah, Forever.

מוֹדִים We give thanks before You, Lord Our God and God of our ancestors, that You have placed our lot among those who sit in the study hall and that you have not given us our portion among those who sit idly on street corners. We rise early and they rise early. We rise early to pursue matters of Torah and they rise early to pursue frivolous matters. We toil and they toil. We toil and receive a reward and they toil and do not receive a reward. We run and they run. We run to the life of the World-to-Come and they run to the pit of destruction,
as it is stated: But You, God, will bring them down into *Psalms 55*
the pit of destruction; men of blood and deceit shall not live out half their days; but as for me, I will trust in You.

יְהִי רָצוֹן May it be Your will, Lord my God, just as you have assisted me in completing tractate *Sota* so assist me to begin other tractates and books and conclude them to learn and to teach, to observe and to perform, and to fulfill all the teachings of Your Torah with love. And may the merit of all the *tanna'im* and *amora'im* and Torah scholars stand for me and my descendants so that the Torah will not move from my mouth and from the mouths of my descendants and the descendants of my
descendants forever. And may the verse: When you *Proverbs 6*
walk, it shall lead you, when you lie down, it shall watch over you; and when you awaken, it shall talk with you
be fulfilled in me. For in the Torah your days shall be *Proverbs 9*
multiplied, and the years of your life shall be increased.
Length of days is in her right hand; in her left hand are *Proverbs 3*
riches and honor. May the Lord give strength to His *Psalms 29*
people; the Lord will bless His people with peace.